Small Business Sourcebook

ISSN 0883-3397

Small Business Sourcebook

The Entrepreneur's Resource

TWENTY-NINTH EDITION

Volume 2

Specific Small Business Profiles

(Entries 7781-17564)

Sonya D. Hill
Project Editor

GALE
CENGAGE Learning

Detroit • New York • San Francisco • New Haven, Conn • Waterville, Maine • London

Small Business Sourcebook, 29th edition

Project Editor: Sonya D. Hill

Editorial Support Services: Charles Beaumont

Composition and Electronic Prepress: Gary Leach

Manufacturing: Rita Wimberley

For product information and technology assistance, contact us at
Gale Customer Support, 1-800-877-4253.
For permission to use material from this text or product,
submit all requests online at **www.cengage.com/permissions.**
Further permissions questions can be emailed to
permissionrequest@cengage.com

While every effort has been made to ensure the reliability of the information presented in this publication, Gale, a part of Cengage Learning, does not guarantee the accuracy of the data contained herein. Gale accepts no payment for listing; and inclusion in the publication of any organization, agency, institution, publication, service, or individual does not imply endorsement of the editors or publisher. Errors brought to the attention of the publisher and verified to the satisfaction of the publisher will be corrected in future editions.

EDITORIAL DATA PRIVACY POLICY. Does this publication contain information about you as an individual? If so, for more information about our data privacy policies, please see our Privacy Statement at www.gale.cengage.com.

Gale
27500 Drake Rd.
Farmington Hills, MI, 48331-3535

ISBN-13: 978-1-4144-6919-5 (set)
ISBN-10: 1-4144-6919-5 (set)
ISBN-13: 978-1-4144-6920-1 (vol. 1)
ISBN-10: 1-4144-6920-9 (vol. 1)
ISBN-13: 978-1-4144-6921-8 (vol. 2)
ISBN-10: 1-4144-6921-7 (vol. 2)
ISBN-13: 978-1-4144-6986-7 (vol. 3)
ISBN-10: 1-4144-6986-1 (vol . 3)
ISBN-13: 978-1-4144-6987-4 (vol . 4)
ISBN-10: 1-4144-6987-X (vol . 4)
ISBN-13: 978-1-4144-6988-1 (vol . 5)
ISBN-10: 1-4144-6988-8 (vol . 5)
ISBN-13: 978-1-4144-7694-0 (vol . 6)
ISBN-10: 1-4144-7694-9 (vol . 6)

ISSN 0883-3397

Printed in the United States of America
1 2 3 4 5   16 15 14 13 12

FD184

Contents

Volume 1

Introduction vii

User's Guide ix

Acknowledgments xv

List of Small Business Profiles xvii

Standard Industrial Classification (SIC) Codes for
Profiled Small Businesses xxi

Licensing Assistance Programs xxxv

Guide to Publishers. xxxix

Glossary cxxv

Small Business Profiles .1

> Provides start-up information, associations and other organiza-
> tions, educational programs, directories of educational programs,
> reference works, sources of supply, statistical sources, trade
> periodicals, videocassettes/ audiocassettes, trade shows and
> conventions, consultants, franchises and business opportunities,
> computerized databases, computer systems/software, libraries,
> and research centers.

Volume 2

Introduction. vii

User's Guide ix

Acknowledgments xv

List of Small Business Profiles xvii

Standard Industrial Classification (SIC) Codes for
Profiled Small Businesses xxi

Small Business Profiles 519

Volume 3

Introduction. vii

User's Guide ix

Acknowledgments xv

List of Small Business Profiles xvii

Standard Industrial Classification (SIC) Codes for
Profiled Small Businesses xxi

List of General Small Business Topics xxxv

Small Business Profiles 1119

General Small Business Topics 1356

> Includes associations and other organizations, educational
> programs, directories of educational programs, reference works,
> sources of supply, statistical sources, trade periodicals,
> videocassettes/audiocassettes, trade shows and conventions,
> consultants, computerized databases, computer systems/
> software, libraries, and research centers.

Volume 4

Introduction. vii

User's Guide ix

Acknowledgments xv

List of General Small Business Topics xvii

General Small Business Topics 1737

Volume 5

Introduction. vii

User's Guide ix

Acknowledgments xv

List of General Small Business Topics xvii

General Small Business Topics 2333

State Listings 2645

> Offers sources of small business assistance by state, territory,
> and Canadian province, including small business development
> centers, small business assistance programs, SCORE offices,
> better business bureaus, chambers of commerce, minority busi-
> ness assistance programs, financing and loan programs, procure-
> ment assistance programs, incubators/research and technol ogy
> parks, educational programs, legislative assistance, small busi-
> ness development consultants, and publications

Volume 6

Introduction. vii

User's Guide ix

Acknowledgments xv

State Listings 2925

Federal Government Assistance 3071

> Lists U.S. federal government agencies and offices,including
> regional, branch, and district offices, which focus on small busi-
> ness issues, programs, assistance, and policy

Master Index 3163

The appeal of small business ownership remains perpetually entrenched in American culture as one of the most viable avenues for achieving the American Dream. To many entrepreneurs going into business for themselves represents financial independence, an increased sense of identity and self-worth, and the fulfillment of personal goals. Small business owners strive to make their mark in today's competitive marketplace by establishing healthy businesses that can, over time, become legacies handed down from one generation to the next. Entrepreneurs from each generation tackle the obstacles and adversities of the current business and economic climate to test their business savvy and generate opportunities. Today's entrepreneurs face many of the problems of their predecessors, as well as some distinctly new challenges.

With the rightsizing, downsizing, and reorganization of corporate America, many individuals have decided to confront the risks of developing and operating their own businesses. Small business ownership is rapidly becoming a viable alternative to what is perceived as an equally unstable corporate environment. These entrepreneurs, many of whom have firsthand experience with the problems and inefficiencies inherent in today's large corporations, seek to improve upon an archaic business model and to capitalize on their own ingenuity and strengths. Led by their zeal, many would-be entrepreneurs let their desire, drive, and determination overshadow the need for business knowledge and skill. Ironically, aids in obtaining these components of entrepreneurial success are widely available, easily accessible, and often free of charge.

Small Business Sourcebook (*SBS*) is a six-volume annotated guide to more than 21,199 listings of live and print sources of information designed to facilitate the start-up, development, and growth of specific small businesses, as well as over 26,073 similar listings on general small business topics. An additional 8,679 state-specific listings and over 1,997 U.S. federal government agencies and offices specializing in small business issues, programs, and assistance are also included. *SBS* covers 340 specific small business profiles and 99 general small business topics.

Features of This Edition

This edition of *Small Business Sourcebook* has been revised and updated, incorporating thousand of changes to names, addresses, contacts, and descriptions of listings from the previous edition.

Contents and Arrangement

The geographical scope of *SBS* encompasses the United States and Canada, with expanded coverage for resources pertaining to international trade and for resources that have a U.S. or Canadian distributor or contact. Internet sites that are maintained outside of the U.S. and Canada are also included if they contain relevant information for North American small businesses. Resources that do not relate specifically to small businesses are generally not included.

The information presented in *SBS* is grouped within four sections: Specific Small Business Profiles, General Small Business Topics, State Listings, and Federal Government Assistance. Detailed outlines of these sections may be found in the Users' Guide following this Introduction. Also included is a Master Index to Volumes 1 through 6.

Specific Small Business Profiles This section includes the following types of resources: start-up information, associations and other organizations, educational programs, directories of educational programs, reference works, sources of supply, statistical sources, trade periodicals, videocassettes/audiocassettes, trade shows and conventions, consultants, franchises and business opportunities, computerized databases, computer systems/software, Internet databases, libraries, and research centers-all arranged by business type. Entries range from Accounting Service to Word Processing Service, and include such businesses as Airbag Replacement Service Centers, Computer Consulting, Damage Restoration Service, and Web Site Design.

General Small Business Topics This section offers such resources as associations, books, periodicals, articles, pamphlets, educational programs, directories of educational programs, videocassettes/audiocassettes, trade shows and conventions, consultants, computerized databases, Internet databases, software,libraries, and research centers, arranged alphabetically by business topic.

State Listings Entries include government, academic, and commercial agencies and organizations, as well as select coverage of relevant state-specific publications; listings are arranged alphabetically by state, territory, and Canadian province. Some examples include small business development consultants, educational programs, financing and loan programs, better business bureaus, and chambers of commerce.

Federal Government Assistance Listings specializing in small business issues, programs, assistance, and policyare arranged alphabetically by U.S. government agency or office; regional or branch offices are listed alphabetically by state.

Master Index All entries in Volumes 1 through 6 are arranged in one alphabetic index for convenience.

Entries in *SBS* include (as appropriate andavailable):

- Organization, institution, or product name

- Contact information, including contact name, address and phone, toll-free, and fax numbers

- Author/editor, date(s), and frequency

- Availability, including price

- Brief description of purpose, services, or content

- Company and/or personal E-mail addresses

- Web site addresses

SBS also features the following:

Guide to Publishers—An alphabetic listing of 2,425 companies, associations, institutions, and individuals that publish the periodicals, directories, guidebooks, and other publications noted in the Small Business Profiles and General Topics sections. Users are provided with full contact information, including address, phone, fax,and e-mail and URL when available. The Guide to Publishers facilitates contact with publishers and provides a one- stop resource for valuable information.

Method of Compilation

SBS was compiled by consulting small business experts and entrepreneurs, as well as a variety of resources, including direct contact with the associations, organizations, and agencies through telephone surveys, Internet research, or through materials provided by those listees; government resources; and data obtained from other relevant Gale directories. *SBS* was reviewed by a team of small business advisors, all of whom have numerous years of expertise in small business counseling and identification of small business information resources. The last and perhaps most important resource we utilize is direct contact with our readers, who provide valuable comments and suggestions to improve our publication. *SBS* relies on these comprehensive market contacts to provide today's entrepreneurs with relevant, current, and accurate informationon all aspects of small business.

Available in Electronic Formats

Licensing. Small Business Sourcebook is available for licensing. The complete database is provided in a fielded format and is deliverable on such media as disk or CD-ROM. For more information, contact Gale's Business Development Group at1-800-877-GALE, or visit our website at www.gale.com/bizdev.

Comments and Suggestions Welcome

Associations, agencies, business firms, publishers, and other organizations that provide assistance and information to the small business community are encouraged to submit material about their programs, activities, services, or products. Comments and suggestions from users of this directory are also welcomed and appreciated. Please contact:

Project Editor
Small Business Sourcebook
Gale, Cengage Learning
27500 Drake Rd.
Farmington Hills, MI 48331-3535
Phone: (248) 699-4253
Fax: (248) 699-8070
E-mail: BusinessProductsgale.com
URL: www.gale.com

Small Business Sourcebook (*SBS*) provides information in a variety of forms and presentations for comprehensive coverage and ease of use. The directory contains four parts within two volumes:

- Specific Small Business Profiles
- General Small Business Topics
- State Listings
- Federal Government Assistance

Information on specific businesses is arranged by type of business; the many general topics that are of interest to the owners, operators, or managers of all small businesses are grouped in a separate section for added convenience. Users should consult the various sections to benefit fully from the information *SBS* offers. For example, an entrepreneur with a talent or interest in the culinary arts could peruse a number of specific small business profiles, such as Restaurant, Catering, Cooking School, Specialty Food/Wine Shop, Bakery/Doughnut Shop, Healthy Restaurant, or Candy/Chocolate Store. Secondly, the General Small Business Topics section could be consulted for any applicable subjects, such as Service Industry, Retailing, Franchising, and other relevant topics. Then, the appropriate state within the State Listings section would offer area programs and offices providing information and support to small businesses, including venture capital firms and small business development consultants. Finally, the Federal Government Assistance section could supply relevant government offices, such as procurement contacts.

Features Included in Volumes 1 through 3

List of Small Business Profiles. This list provides an alphabetic outline of the small businesses profiled, with cross-references for related profiles and for alternate names by which businesses may be identified. The page number for each profile is indicated.

Standard Industrial Classification (SIC) Codes for Profiled Small Businesses. This section lists four-digit SIC codes and corresponding classification descriptions for the small businesses profiled in this edition. The SIC system,

which organizes businesses by type, is a product of the Statistical Policy Division of the U.S. Office of Management and Budget. Statistical data produced by government, public, and private organizations is usually categorized according to SIC codes, thereby facilitating the collection, comparison, and analysis of data as well as providing a uniform method for presenting statistical information. Hence, knowing the SIC code for a particular small business increases access and the use of a variety of statistical data from many sources.

Guide to Publishers. This resource lists alphabetically the companies, associations, institutions, and individuals that publish the periodicals, directories, guidebooks, and other publications noted in the "Small Business Profiles" and "General Topics" sections. Users are provided with full contact information, including address, phone, fax, and e-mail and URL when available. The "Guide" facilitates contact with publishers and provides a one-stop resource for valuable information.

Glossary of Small Business Terms. This glossary defines nearly 400 small business terms, including financial, governmental, insurance, procurement, technical, and general business definitions. Cross-references and acronyms are also provided.

Small Business Profiles A-Z. A total of 340 small businesses is represented in volumes 1 through 3. Profiles are listed alphabetically by business name. Entries within each profile are arranged alphabetically by resource type, within up to 17 subheadings.These subheadings are detailed below:

- *Start-up Information*—Includes periodical articles, books, manuals, book excerpts, kits, and other sources of information. Entries offer title; publisher; address; phone, fax, toll-free numbers; company e-mail and URL addresses; and a description. Bibliographic data is provided for cited periodical articles whenever possible.

- *Associations and Other Oganizations*—Includes trade and professional associations whose members gather and disseminate information of interest to small business owners. Entries offer the association's name; address; phone, toll-free and fax numbers; company e-mail address; contact name; purpose and objective; a description of membership; telecommunication services; and a listing of its publications, including publishing frequency.

- **Educational Programs**—Includes university and college programs, schools, training opportunities, association seminars, correspondence courses, and other educational programs.Entries offer name of program or institution, sponsor name, address, phone, toll-free and fax numbers, e-mail and URL addresses; and description of program.

- **Directories of Educational Programs**—Includes directories and other publications that list educational programs. Entries offer name of publication; publisher name, address, and phone, toll-free and fax numbers; editor; frequency or date of publication; price; and description of contents, including directory arrangement and indexes.

- **Reference Works**—Includes handbooks, manuals, textbooks, guides, directories, dictionaries, encyclopedias, and other published reference materials. Entries offer name of publication; publisher name, address, and phone, toll-free and fax numbers; e-mail and URL addresses; and, when available, name of author or editor, publication year or frequency, and price. A brief description is often featured.

- **Sources of Supply**—Includes buyer's guides,directories, special issues of periodicals, and other publications that list sources of equipment, supplies, and services related to the operation of the profiled small business. Entries offer publication name; publisher name, address, and phone, toll-free and fax numbers; e-mail and URL addresses; and, when available, editor's name, frequency or publication year, and price. A brief description of the publication, including directory arrangement and indexes, is often provided.

- **Statistical Sources**—Includes books, reports, pamphlets, and other sources of statistical data of interest to an owner, operator or manager of the profiled small business, such as wage, salary, and compensation data; financial and operating ratios; prices and costs; demographics; and other statistical information. Entries offer publication/data source name; publisher (if applicable); address; phone, toll-free and fax numbers of data source; publication date or frequency; and price. A brief description of the publication/data source is often provided.

- **Trade Periodicals**—Includes trade journals, newsletters, magazines, and other serials that offer information about the management and operation of the profiled small business. Such periodicals often contain industry news; trends and developments; reviews; articles about new equipment and supplies;

and other information related to business operations. Entries offer publication name; publisher name, address, phone, toll-free and fax numbers, and e-mail and URL addresses; editor name; publication frequency; andprice. A brief description of the publication's content is also included, when known.

- **Videocassettes/Audiocassettes**—Includes videocassettes, audiocassettes, and other audiovisual media offering information on the profiled small business. Entries offer program title; distributor name, address, phone, toll-free and fax numbers, and e-mail and URL addresses; description of program; release date; price; and format(s).

- **Trade Shows and Conventions**—Includes tradeshows, exhibitions, expositions, conventions, and other industry meetings that provide prospective and existing business owners with the opportunity to meet and exchange information with their peers, review commercial exhibits, establish business or sales contacts, and attend educational programs. Entries offer event name; sponsor or management company name, address, phone, toll-free and fax numbers, and e-mail and URL addresses; a description of the event, including audience, frequency, principal exhibits, and dates and locations of event for as many years ahead as provided by the event's sponsor.

- **Consultants**—Includes consultants and consulting organizations that provide services specifically related to the profiled small business. Entries offer individual consultant or consulting organization name, address, and phone, toll-free and fax numbers; company and individual e-mail addresses; and a brief description of consulting services. (For e-mail and URL addresses, see the Small Business Development Consultants subheadings in the State Listings section in Volume 2.)

- **Franchises and Business Opportunities**—Includes companies granting franchise licenses for enterprises falling within the scope of the profiled small business, as well as other non-franchised business opportunities that operate within a given network or system. Entries offer franchise name, address, phone, toll-free and fax numbers, and e-mail and URL addresses, as well as a description of the franchise or business opportunity, which has been expanded whenever possible to include the number of existing franchises, the founding date of the franchise, franchise fees, equity capital requirements, royalty fees, any managerial assistance offered, and available training.

- **Computerized Databases**—Includes diskettes, magnetic tapes, CD-ROMs, online systems, and other computer-readable databases. Entries offer database name; producer name, address, phone, toll-free and fax numbers, e-mail and URL addresses; description; and available format(s), including vendor name.

(Many university and public libraries offer online information retrieval services that provide searches of databases, including those listed in this category.)

- **Computer Systems/Software**—Includes software-eand computerized business systems designed to assist in the operation of the profiled small business. Entries offer name of the software or system; publisher name, address, phone, toll-free and fax-numbers; price; and description.

- **Libraries**—Includes libraries and special collections that contain material especially applicable to the profiled small business. Entries offer library or collection name; parent organization (where applicable); address; phone, toll-free and fax numbers; e-mail and URL addresses; contact name and title; scope of collection; and description of holdings, subscriptions, and services.

- **Research Centers**—Includes university-related and independently operated research institutes and information centers that generate, through their research programs, data related to the operation of the profiled small business. Also listed are associations and other business-related organizations that conduct research programs. Entries offer name of organization; address; phone, toll-free and fax numbers; company web site address; contact name and personale-mail; a description of principal fields of research or services; publications, including title and frequency; and related conferences.

Features Included in Volumes 2 through 6

General Small Business Topics. This section offers chapters on different topics in the operation of any small business, for example, venture capital and other funding, or compensation. Chapters are listed alphabetically by small business topic; entries within each chapter are arranged alphabetically, within up to 14 subheadings, by resource type:

- **Associations and OtherOrganizations**—Includes trade and professional associations that gather and disseminate information of interest to small business owners. Entries offer the association's name; address; phone, toll-free and fax numbers; organization e-mail and URL addresses; contact name;purpose and objectives; a description of membership; telecommunication services; and a listing of its publications, including publishing frequency.

- **Educational Programs**—Includes university and college programs, schools, training opportunities, association seminars, correspondence courses, and other educational programs. Entries offer name of program or institution, sponsor name, address, phone, toll-free and fax numbers, e-mail and URL addresses, and description of program.

- **Directories of Educational Programs**—Includes directories and other publications that list educational programs. Entries offer name of publication; publisher name, address, phone, toll-free and fax numbers, and e-mail and URL addresses; editor; frequency or date of publication; price; and description of contents, including arrangement and indexes.

- **Reference Works**—Includes articles, handbooks, manuals, textbooks, guides, directories, dictionaries, encyclopedias, and other published reference materials. Entries offertitle of article, including bibliographic information; name of publication; publisher name, address, phone, toll-free and fax numbers, and e-mail and URL addresses; and, when available, name of author oreditor, publication year or frequency, and price. A brief descriptionis often featured.

- **Sources of Supply**—Includes buyer's guides,directories, special issues of periodicals, and other publications that list sources of equipment, supplies, and services. Entries offer publication name; publisher name, address, phone, toll-free and fax numbers, and e-mail and URL addresses; editor's name, frequency or publication year, price, and a brief description of the publication, when available.

- **Statistical Sources**—Includes books, reports, pamphlets, and other sources of statistical data of interest to an owner, operator, or manager of a small business, such as wage, salary, and compensation data; financial and operating ratios; prices and costs; demographics; and other statistical information. Entries offer publication/data source name; publisher (if applicable); address; phone, toll-free and fax numbers of data source; publication date or frequency; and price. A brief description is often provided.

- **Trade Periodicals**—Includes journals, newsletters, magazines, and other serials. Entries offer name of publication; publisher name, address, phone, toll-free and fax numbers, and e-mail and URL addresses; and name of editor, frequency, and price.A brief description of the periodical's content is included when known.

- **Videocassettes/Audiocassettes**—Includes videocassettes, audiocassettes, and other audiovisual media. Entries offer program title; distributor name, address, phone, toll-free and fax numbers, and e-mail and URL addresses; price; description of program; release date; and format(s).

- **Trade Shows and Conventions**—Includes tradeshows, exhibitions, expositions, seminars, and conventions. Entries offer event name; sponsor or management company name, address, phone, toll-free and fax numbers, and e-mail and URL addresses; frequency of event; and dates and locations of the event for as many years ahead as known.

- **Consultants**—Includes consultants and consulting organizations. Entries offer individual consultant or-consulting organization name, address, and phone, toll-free and fax numbers; company and individual e-mail addresses; and a brief description of consulting services. (See also Consultants in the State Listings section.)

- **Computerized Databases**—Includes diskettes, CD-ROMs, magnetic tape, online systems and other computer-readable databases. Entries offer database name; producer, address, phone, toll-free and fax numbers, and e-mail and URL addresses; description; and available format(s), including vendor name. (Many university and public libraries offer online information retrieval services that provide searches of databases, including those listed in this category.)

- **Computer Systems/Software**—Includes software and computerized business systems. Entries offer name of the software or system; publisher name, address, phone, toll-free and fax numbers, and e-mail and URL addresses; price; and description.

- **Libraries**—Includes libraries and special collections that contain material applicable to the small business topic. Entries offer library or collection name, parent organization (where applicable), address, phone and fax numbers, e-mail and URL addresses, scope of collection, and description of holdings and services.

- **Research Centers**— Includes university-related and independently operated research institutes and information centers that generate, through their research programs, data related to specific small business topics. Entries offer name of organization, address, phone, toll-free and fax numbers, e-mail and URL addresses, a description of principal fields of research or services, and related conferences.

State Listings. This section lists various sources of information and assistance available within given states, territories, and Canadian provinces; entries include governmental, academic, and commercial agencies, and are arranged alphabetically within up to 15 subheadings by resource type:

- **Small Business Development Center Lead Office**— Includes the lead small business development center (SBDC) for each state.

- **Small Business Development Centers**—Includes any additional small business development centers (SBDC) in the state, territory, or province. SBDCs provide support services to small businesses, including individual counseling, seminars, conferences, and learning center activities.

- **Small Business Assistance Programs**—Includes state small business development offices and other programs offering assistance to small businesses.

- **SCORE Offices**—Includes SCORE office(s) for each state. The Service Corps of Retired Executives Association (SCORE), a volunteer program sponsored by the Small Business Administration, offers counseling, workshops, and seminars across the U.S. for small business entrepreneurs.

- **Better Business Bureaus**—Includes various better business bureaus within each state. By becoming a member of the local Better Business Bureau, a small business owner can increase the prestige and credibility of his or her business within the community, as well as make valuable business contacts.

- **Chambers of Commerce**—Includes various chambers of commerce within each state. Chambers of Commerce are valuable sources of small business advice and information; often, local chambers sponsor SCORE counseling several times per month for a small fee, seminars, conferences, and other workshops to its members. Also, by becoming a member of the local Chamber of Commerce, a small business owner can increase the prestige and credibility of his or herbusiness within the community, as well as make valuable business contacts.

- **Minority Business Assistance Programs**—Includes minority business development centers and other sources of assistance for minority-owned business.

- **Financing and Loan Programs**—Includes venture capital firms, small business investment companies (SBIC), minority enterprise small business investment companies (MESBIC), and other programs that provide funding to qualified small businesses.

- **Procurement Assistance Programs**—Includes state services such as counseling, set-asides, and sheltered-market bidding, which are designed to aid small businesses in bidding on government contracts.

- **Incubators/Research and Technology Parks**— Includes small business incubators, which provide newly established small business owners with work sites, business services, training, and consultation; also includes research and technology parks, which sponsor research and facilitate commercialization of new technologies.

- **Educational Programs**—Includes university and college programs, as well as those sponsored by other organizations that offer degree, nondegree, certificate, and correspondence programs in entrepreneurship and in small business development.

- **Legislative Assistance**—Includes committees, subcommittees, and joint committees of each state's senate and house of representatives that are concerned with small business issues and regulations.

- *Consultants*—Includes consultants and consulting firms offering expertise in small business development.

- *Publications*—Includes publications related to small business operations within the profiled state.

- *Publishers*—Includes publishers operating in or for the small business arena within the profiled state.

Federal Government Assistance. This section lists federal government agencies and offices, many with additional listings for specific offices, as well as regional or district branches. Main agencies or offices are listed alphabetically; regional, branch, ordistrict offices are listed after each main office or agency.

Master Index. This index provides an alphabetic listing of all entries contained in Volumes 1 throgh 6. Citations are referenced by their entry numbers. Publication titles are rendered in italics.

The editors would like to extend sincere thanks to the following members of the Small Business Sourcebook advisory board for their expert guidance, recommendations, and suggestions for the ongoing development of this title:

Susan C. Awe
Assistant Director,
William J. Parish Memorial Business Library

Jill Clever
Business Technology Specialist,
Toledo-Lucas County Public Library

Jules Matsoff
District Manager,
Service Corps of Retired Executives (SCORE) Milwaukee
Chapter

Ken MacKenzie
President,
Southeast Business Appraisal

The editors would also like to thank the individuals from associations and other organizations who provided information for the compilation of this directory.

List of Small Business Profiles

This list is an outline of the 341 small businesses profiled in this edition of Small Business Sourcebook. The beginning page number of each profile is provided. For convenience, this index also provides cross-references to small businesses known by alternate names, businesses contained within other small business profiles, and synonymous or related businesses.

Abstracting and Indexing Service 1
Accounting Service 2
Adult Day Care Center 18
Advertising Service 22
Airbag Replacement/Service Centers . .39
Air Charter Service 41
Air-conditioning/Heating and Cooling
 Contractor. 45
Air Purification/Cleaning Service 53
Ambulance Service 55
Amusement Arcade 56
Amusement/Water Park 58
Animal Breeder. 60
Animal Clinic 64
Antique Shop 68
Apartment Locating Service 71
Appliance Store 73
Appraisal Service 75
Aquarium Maintenance/Leasing
 Service 77
Archery/Target/Shooting Range 78
Architectural Restoration/Conservation .80
Art Gallery. 86
Art Supplies Store 91
Assisted Living Facilities 92
Association Management Service 95
Auctioneer/Broker 97
Auto Supply Store 100
Automobile Detailing/Painting Service .104
Automobile/Truck Leasing Service . . .106
Baby Store 109
Bagel Shop 111
Bait and Tackle Shop. 113
Bakery/Doughnut Shop 116
Bar/Cocktail Lounge 122
Beauty Supply Center 126
Bed and Breakfast Operation. 128
Beekeeping 130
Beeper/Paging Service 132
Bicycle Shop 133
Billiards Hall. 135
Blacktop Surfacing Business 137
Blind Cleaning/Installation. 140
Body Care Shop 141
Book Publishing. 144
Bookbinder 153

Bookkeeping 155
Bookstore 160
Bottled Water Service 164
Bowling Alley 166
Brewery Operation 167
Bridal Shop/Bridal Consultant. 170
Building/Home Inspection Service . . .174
Building Maintenance/Custodial Service-
 177
Bulletin Board Service 183
Business Broker Service 184
Business Consulting Service 188
Business Services Operation 210
Butcher Shop 216
Cable Network 218
Calligraphy Service. 222
Camera Shop 224
Campground Management 226
Candy/Chocolate Shop 229
Car Alarm and Stereo Store 232
Car Inspection Service. 233
Car Towing Service. 234
Car Wash 235
Career Counseling 236
Carpentry Service 241
Catering Service 244
CD-ROM Developer/Producer 247
Cellular Phone/Telephone Business . .256
Charter Boat Service 266
Check Cashing Service 267
Children's Apparel Shop 268
Children's Day Care Center. 271
Chimney Sweeping Business 279
Christmas Decoration Store 280
Christmas Tree Farm 281
Clipping Service 283
Clothing Designer 285
Clothing Store. 291
Coffee Service 297
Coin/Stamp Dealer 299
Comedy Club 303
Comic Book/Collectibles Store 304
Commercial/Graphic Art Business . . .306
Commercial Mail Receiving Agency . .315
Compact Disc/Record Store 317
Computer Consulting. 318

Computer Data Storage Company . . .322
Computer Learning/Training Center . .326
Computer Maintenance and Repair
 Service. 330
Computer Programming and Data
 Processing Service. 333
Computer Store. 340
Computer System Integrators. 345
Computerized Billing Service 349
Computerized Matching Service 351
Concession Stand Business 352
Concierge/Virtual Assistant Service . .354
Consignment Shop. 355
Construction Company. 357
Consumer Electronics Store 386
Convenience Store 390
Cooking School. 393
Copy Shop 396
Cosmetics Business 398
Costume Shop 401
Craft Artisan. 403
Craft/Hobby Business 410
"Create-Your-Own..." Store 416
Credit Card Issuing Service. 417
Credit Repair Service 419
Credit Reporting and Collection
 Service. 421
Damage Restoration Service 426
Dance School. 427
Delicatessen/Sandwich Shop 432
Desktop Publishing Company. 437
Dial-It Services 441
Disc Jockey Service 442
Domestic Help/Maid Service 443
Driving School. 446
Drug Store/Pharmacy 448
Dry Cleaning Service/Coin-Operated
 Laundry 455
Editorial/Freelance Writing Business. .458
Electrical Contractor 464
Electrical Lighting Supply Store 468
Electronic/Online Publishing 470
Employee Leasing Service 471
Employment Agency 472
Engraving/Monogramming Service. . .477
Environmental Consultant 478

Environmental Store 498
Estate Planning. 512
Estate Sales Business. 514
Executive Recruiting Agency 515
Fashion Accessories Business . . .519
Fax Service 523
Film and Video Production Operation .524
Financial Planning Service 532
Fish and Seafood Store 574
Fish Farm 576
Floor Covering/Restoration Business .580
Florist. 583
Food Delivery Service 586
Freight Forwarding Service 590
Fund-Raising Consultant 593
Funeral Service 598
Fur Farm. 601
Fur Store. 602
Furniture Restoration Service. 603
Gambling Organization/Service. 605
Genealogy Service. 608
Gift Basket Service. 617
Gift/Card Shop 618
Glass Repair and Replacement
    Service. 621
Golf Shop 623
Gourmet Coffee/Tea House 626
Greenhouse/Garden Center/Nursery Busi-
    ness 630
Greeting Card Publishing 638
Grocery Store 639
Gunsmith/Gun Shop 646
Hair Replacement/Electrolysis Clinic. .648
Hair Salon/Barber Shop 649
Handwriting Analysis Consultant 653
Hardware Store 655
Hat Store 658
Hazardous Waste Disposal Business .659
Health Food Store 663
Healthy Restaurant. 667
Hearing Aid Testing and Fitting
    Service. 671
Herb Farm 674
Home Accessory Store 677
Home Furnishings Store. 681
Home Health Care Service 685
Horse Riding Academy 690
Hotel/Motel/Resort Operations 694
Ice Cream/Frozen Yogurt Shop. 705
Image Consultant. 712
Import/Export Service 714
Incubator. 724
Information Broker 725
Insulation Contractor. 728
Insurance Agency 729
Interior Design Service. 743
Internet/Online Service Provider 748
Investment/Securities Broker 765
Jewelry Store 820
Job Training/Retraining 823
Kiosk/Pushcart/Vendor Business 825
Landscape Equipment and Supplies. .827
Landscaping Service 828

Lawn Maintenance Service 834
Limousine Service 838
Lingerie Shop 840
Liquor Store 841
Literary Agency 844
Locksmith 845
Luggage and Leather Goods Busi-
    ness 846
Lumberyard 847
Machine Shop/Metalworking Shop . . .851
Mail Order Business 854
Management Consulting Service. . . .856
Manufacturer's Representative 868
Marine Shop. 870
Market Research and Analysis 874
Martial Arts Studio 880
Masonry, Stonework, and Plastering
    Contractors 882
Massage Therapist. 885
Mediation Service 887
Medical and Dental Instrument
    Manufacturing. 889
Medical Claims Service 893
Medical Laboratory Service 894
Medical Supplies Store 898
Medical Transcription Service. 901
Messenger/Delivery/Subpoena
    Service. 902
Miniature Golf Course Operation. . . .903
Modeling School/Agency 904
Mortgage Broker 905
Motorcycle/Moped Store. 914
Movie Theatre Operation 916
Moving Service 919
Music School 920
Music Shop 928
Musical Instrument Repair/Piano Tuning
    Service. 932
Nail Salon 933
Nanny Service 934
New Age Services and Supplies 935
New and Used Car Dealer 937
Newsletter Publishing 946
Novelty Items Business 948
Nursing Home/Long-Term Care
    Center 949
Nutritional Consultant/Diet Planner. . .957
Office Design Service 964
Office Supply/Equipment Store 967
Online Store 969
Paint/Wall Covering Center 973
Painting Contractor. 975
Party Entertainment Service 977
Party/Reunion Planning Service 979
Pawnbroker 981
Payroll Preparation Service 982
Periodical/Newspaper Publishing. . . .984
Personal Shopping Service 991
Pest Control Service 992
Pet Boarding/Grooming Service 996
Pet Cemetery 998
Pet Obedience School 999
Pet Shop 1001

Pet Sitting Service 1006
Photo Finishing Center. 1008
Photographer, Commercial 1009
Photographic Studio 1013
Physical Fitness Center 1016
Physical Therapy Clinic/Practice . . .1024
Pizzeria. 1029
Plant Leasing Service 1034
Plumbing Service 1035
Porcelain Refinishing Service 1040
Power Washing Service 1041
Prepaid Phone Card Business 1042
Print/Frame Shop 1043
Printing Business 1045
Private Investigation/Personal Security
    Service 1052
Private Label Product Manufacturer/
    Retailer. 1054
Professional Organizer 1055
Property Management 1057
Public Relations Consultant 1062
Public Warehousing/Ministorage Opera-
    tion 1066
Quick Oil Change Service 1069
Radio Station 1071
Radon Testing Service 1077
Real Estate Agency. 1078
Real Estate Investment Service. . . .1096
Recording Studio 1119
Recreational Vehicle Dealer 1122
Recycling Business 1124
Rental Service 1128
Restaurant 1133
Resume Service 1158
Roofing Contractor 1159
Satellite Dish Service 1161
Screen Printing Business 1163
Security Systems Service 1165
Seminar Planner/Lecturer 1173
Service Station/Auto Repair and Service
    Shop 1175
Sewer and Drain Cleaning Business .1182
Sewing Center. 1185
Shoe Repair Shop 1187
Shoe Store 1188
Sign Shop 1191
Silk Plant Shop 1193
Skating Rink Operation. 1194
Ski Shop 1195
Software Publishing. 1197
Solar Energy Design/Contracting Busi-
    ness. 1208
Specialized Staffing. 1213
Specialty Foods/Wine Shop 1217
Sporting Goods Store 1223
Sports Promotional Service 1229
Surveying Service. 1235
Swimming Pool/Hot Tub Business . .1238
Tailor Shop. 1240
Talent Agency 1241
Tanning Parlor/Sauna. 1242
Tattoo Parlor. 1243
Tax Preparation Business 1244

Taxicab/Van Shuttle Service 1256
Taxidermy Service 1259
Teacher Supply Store. 1260
Telemarketing Service 1261
Telephone Answering Service 1263
Television/Radio Repair Service . . .1264
Television Station 1265
Temporary Employment Agency . . .1274
Tennis Court/Racquet Club Opera-
    tion 1276
Tire Dealer 1278
Tobacco Shop 1280

Tour Guide Operation/Adventure
    Service 1282
Toy Business 1288
Trade Show/Conference Management
    Service 1292
Translating/Interpreting Service 1300
Travel Agency 1303
Trucking Business. 1311
Tutoring Service. 1316
Typesetting Business. 1318
Typing/Stenographic Service 1321
Upholstery/Carpet Services 1322

Vending Machine Merchandising and
    Service Business 1325
Videocassette Rental Store 1327
Vision Center 1329
Voice Mail Service 1333
Water Conditioning Service 1335
Web Site Design 1339
Weight Reduction/Control Center . . .1351
Welcome Service 1353
Window Dressing Business 1354
Word Processing Service 1355

Standard Industrial Classification (SIC) Codes for Profiled Small Businesses

Included here are the four-digit SIC codes and corresponding classification descriptions for the businesses profiled in this edition. The SIC system, which organizes businesses by type, is a product of the Statistical Policy Division of the U.S. Office of Management and Budget. Statistical data produced by government, public, and private organizations usually are categorized according to SIC codes, thereby facilitating the collection, comparison, and analysis of data as well as providing a uniform method for presenting statistical information. Hence, knowing the SIC code for a particular small business increases the access to, and the use of, a variety of statistical data from many sources. The following SIC codes were obtained from the 1987 edition of the Standard Industrial Classification Manual, the most recent version available. (The term "nec" stands for "not elsewhere classified.")

Accounting Service

7291   Tax return preparation services

8721   Accounting, auditing, and bookkeeping services

Adult Day Care Center

8322   Individual and family social services (includes adult day carecenters)

Advertising Service

7311   Advertising agencies (includes advertising consultants)

7312   Outdoor advertising agencies

7313   Radio, television, and publishers' advertising representatives

7319   Advertising, nec

7331   Direct mail advertising services

8999   Services, nec (includes advertising copywriters)

Airbag Replacement Service Centers

7538   General automotive repair shops

7539   Automotive repair shops, nec

Air Charter Service

4512   Air transportation, scheduled (includes air cargo and passenger carriers)

4513   Air courier services

4522   Air transportation, nonscheduled (includes charter service)

Air-conditioning/Heating and Cooling Contractor

1711   Plumbing, heating, and air-conditioning contractors

Air Purification/Cleaning Service

7699   Repair shops and related services, nec (includes furnace cleaning service)

Ambulance Service

4119   Local passenger transportation, nec (includes ambulance service, road)

4522   Air transportation, nonscheduled (includes ambulance service, air)

Amusement Arcade

7993   Coin-operated amusement devices

Amusement/Water Park

7996   Amusement parks

7999   Amusement and recreation services, nec (includes waterslides and wave pools)

Animal Breeder

0279   Animal specialties, nec (includes kennels, breeding and raising own stock)

0752   Animal specialty services, except veterinary (includes breeding of animals other than farm animals)

Animal Clinic

0742   Veterinary service for animal specialties (includes animal hospitals for pets and other animals)

Antique Shop

5932   Used merchandise stores (includes retail antique stores)

Reupholstery and Furniture Repair

7641   Reupholstery and furniture repair (includes antique furniture repair and restoration)

7699   Repair shops and related services, nec (includes antique repair and restoration, except furniture)

Apartment Locating Service

6531   Real Estate Agents and Managers

Appliance Store

5722   Household appliance stores

Appraisal Service

7389   Business services, nec (includes appraisers, except real estate)

6531   Real estate agents and managers (includes appraisers, realestate)

Aquarium Maintenance/Leasing Service

7359   Equipment rental and leasing, nec

8999   Services, nec

Archery/Target/Shooting Range

7999   Amusement and recreation services, nec (includes archery ranges, shooting galleries, shooting ranges, and trap-shooting facilities, except membership)

Architectural Restoration/Conservation

8712   Architectural Services

Art Gallery

5932   Used merchandise stores (includes retailers of art objects)

5999   Miscellaneous retail stores, nec (includes art dealers)

8412   Museums and art galleries (includes noncommercial art galleries)

Art Supplies Store

5999   Miscellaneous retail stores, nec (includes retail artists' supplies and materials stores)

Assisted Living Facilities

8051   Skilled nursing care facilities (includes extended care facilities and skilled nursing homes)

8052   Intermediate care facilities (includes intermediate care nursing homes)

8059   Nursing and personal care facilities, nec (includes rest homeswith health care)

Association Management Service

8611   Business associations

8621   Professional membership organizations

8631   Labor unions and similar labor organizations

8641   Civic, social, and fraternal associations

8699   Membership organizations, nec

8741   Management services (does not include operating staff)

Auctioneer

5154   Livestock (includes wholesale livestock auctioning)

5999   Miscellaneous retail stores, nec (includes retail general merchandise auction rooms)

7389   Business services, nec (includes auctioneering services)

Auto Supply Store

5531   Auto and home supply stores

Automobile Detailing/Painting Service

7532   Automotive paint shops

7542   Carwashes (includes detailing, cleaning and polishing, new autos on a contract or fee basis; washing and polishing, automotive; waxing and polishing, automotive)

Automobile/Truck Leasing Service

7513   Truck rental and leasing, without drivers

7514   Passenger car rental, without drivers

7515   Passenger car leasing, without drivers

Baby Store

5999   Miscellaneous retail stores, nec (includes retail baby)

Bagel Shop

2051   Bread and other bakery products, except cookies and crackers (includes bagels)

5461   Retail bakeries (includes retail bagel stores)

Bait and Tackle Shop

5941   Sporting goods stores and bicycle shops (includes bait and tackle shops and fishing equipment, retail)

Bakery/Doughnut Shop

5461   Retail bakeries

Bar/Cocktail Lounge

5813   Drinking places alcoholic beverages (includes bars, cocktail lounges, saloons, tap rooms, taverns, and like establishments)

Beauty Supply Center

5087   Service establishment equipment and supplies (includes wholesale barber shop and beauty parlor equipment and supplies)

Bed and Breakfast Operation

7011   Hotels and motels (includes bed and breakfast inns)

Beekeeping

0279   Animal specialties, nec (includes apiaries and bee farms)

Beeper/Paging Service

4812   Radiotelephone communications (includes beeper and paging services)

Bicycle Shop

5941   Sporting goods stores and bicycle shops

7699   Repair shops and related services, nec (includes bicycle repair shops)

Billiards Hall

7999   Amusement and recreation services, nec (includes billiard parlors)

Blacktop Surfacing Business

1771   Concrete work (includes blacktop work: private driveways and private parking areas contractors)

Blind Cleaning/Installation

2431   Millwork (includes wood blinds and shutters)

2591   Drapery hardware and window blinds and shades

Body Care Shop

5999   Miscellaneous retail stores, nec (includes cosmetics stores)

Book Publishing

2731   Books; publishing or publishing and printing

Bookbinder

2789   Bookbinding and related work

Bookkeeping

8721   Accounting, auditing, and bookkeeping services

Bookstore

5932   Used merchandise stores (includes used book retailers)

5942   Bookstores

Bottled Water Service

5149   Groceries and related products, nec (includes natural spring and mineral water bottling and distribution services)

5499   Miscellaneous food stores (includes mineral water, retail)

Bowling Alley

7933   Bowling centers

Brewery Operation

2082   Malt beverages

Bridal Shop/Bridal Consultant

5621   Women's clothing stores (includes retail bridal shops, exceptcustom designers)

Building/Home Inspection

7389   Business services, nec (includes safety inspection, except automotive)

Building Maintenance/Custodial Service

7349   Building cleaning and maintenance services, nec (includes interior building cleaning services, contract janitorial services, and like enterprises)

Bulletin Board Service

4822   Telegraph and other message communications (includes electronic mail services)

7379   Computer related services, nec

Business Broker Service

7389   Business services, nec (includes business brokers buying andselling business enterprises)

Business Consulting Service

8748   Business consulting services, nec

Business Services Operation

8744   Facilities support management services (includesbasemaintenance, providing personnel on continuing basis)

Butcher Shop

5423   Meat and fish (seafood) markets, including freezer provisioners

5499   Miscellaneous food stores (includes retail poultry dealers)

Cable Network

1623   Water, Sewer, Pipeline, and Communications and Power Line Construction (includes cable television line construction-contractors)

1731   Electrical Work (includes cable television hookup-contractors)

4841   Cable and Other Pay Television Services

Calligraphy Service

7389   Business services, nec (includes lettering services)

Camera Shop

5946   Camera and photographic supply stores

7699   Repair shops and related services, nec (includes camera repair shops)

Campground Management

7033   Recreational vehicle parks and campsites

Candy/Chocolate Shop

5441   Candy, nut, and confectionery stores

Car Alarm and Stereo Store

5531   Auto and home supply stores (includes automobile accessorydealers, retail)

5731   Radio, television, and consumer electronics stores (includesautomotive stereo equipment, retail)

Car Inspection Service

7549   Automotive services, except repair services and car washes(includes inspection service, automotive)

Car Towing Service

7549   Automotive services, except repair services and car washes(includes automotive towing and wrecker services)

Car Wash

7542   Car washes

Career Counseling

7389   Business services, nec (includes career counseling service)

Carpentry Service

1751   Carpentry work

Catering Service

5812   Eating places (includes caterers)

CD-ROM Developer/Producer

7372   Prepackaged software (includes pre-packaged computer software publishers)

7379   Computer related services, nec (includes database developers)

Cellular Phone/Telephone Business

4812   Radiotelephone communications

5999   Miscellaneous retail stores, nec (includes telephone stores, retail)

Charter Boat Service

4499   Water transportation service, nec (includes boat rental, commercial)

Check Cashing Service

6099   Functions related to depository banking, nec (includes check cashing agencies)

Children's Apparel Shop

5611   Men's and boys' clothing stores

5641   Children's and infants' wear stores

5651   Family clothing stores

5699   Miscellaneous apparel and accessory stores (includes children's wear)

5932   Used merchandise stores (includes retail second hand clothing stores)

Children's Day Care Center

8351   Child day care services

Chimney Sweeping Business

7349   Building cleaning and maintenance services, nec (includeschimney cleaning service)

Christmas Decoration Store

5999   Miscellaneous retail stores, nec

Christmas Tree Farm

0811   Timber tracts (includes Christmas tree growing)

Clipping Service

7389   Business services, nec (includes press clipping service)

Clothing Designer

2311   Men's and boys' suits, coats, and overcoats

2325   Men's and boys' separate trousers and slacks

2329   Men's and boys' clothing, nec

2331   Women's, misses', and juniors' blouses and shirts

2335   Women's, misses', and juniors' dresses

2337   Women's, misses', and juniors' suits, skirts, and coats

2361   Girls', children's, and infants' dresses, blouses, and shirts

Clothing Store

5611   Men's and boys' clothing and accessory stores

5621   Women's clothing stores

5632   Women's accessory and specialty stores

5641   Children's and infants' wear stores

5651   Family clothing stores

5699   Miscellaneous apparel and accessory stores

5932   Used merchandise stores (includes retail secondhand clothing stores)

Coffee Service

5149   Groceries and related products, nec (includes coffee, wholesale)

Coin/Stamp Dealer

5961   Catalog and mail order houses (includes retail mail order coinand stamp businesses)

5999   Miscellaneous retail stores, nec

Comedy Club

5813   Drinking placesMalcoholic beverages (includes nightclubs)

Comic Book/Collectibles Store

5999   Miscellaneous retail stores, nec

Commercial/Graphic Art Business

7336   Commercial art and graphic design

Commercial Mail Receiving Agency

7389   Business services, nec (includes post office contract stations)

Compact Disc/Record Store

5735   Recorded and prerecorded tape stores

Computer Consulting

7379   Computer related services, nec (includes computer consultants

Computer Data Storage Company

3572   Computer storage devices

Computer Learning/Training Center

8243   Data processing schools

Computer Maintenance and Repair Service

7378   Computer maintenance and repair

Computer Programming and Data Processing Service

7374   Computer processing and data preparation services

Computer Store

5734   Computer and computer software stores

Computer System Integrators

7371   Computer programming services

7373   Computer integrated systems design

7379   Computer related services, nec (includes computer consultants and database developers)

Computerized Billing Service

7374   Computer processing and data preparation and processing services

Computerized Matching Service

7299   Miscellaneous personal services, nec (includes dating services)

7375   Information retrieval services

Concession Stand Business

5812   Eating places (includes concession stands in airports and sports arenas, and refreshment stands)

7999   Amusement and recreation services, nec (concession operators andamusement concessions)

Consignment Shop

5932   Used merchandise stores (includes clothing stores, secondhand retail; furniture stores, secondhand retail; home furnishing stores, secondhand retail)

Construction Company

1521   General contractors—single family houses

1522   General contractors—residential buildings other than single-family

Consumer Electronics Store

5731   Radio, television, and consumer electronics stores

Convenience Store

5411   Grocery stores (includes retail convenience food stores)

Cooking School

8299   Schools and educational services, nec (includes cooking schools)

Copy Shop

7334   Photocopying and duplicating services

Cosmetics Business

2844   Perfumes, cosmetics, and other toilet preparations

5122   Drugs, drug proprietaries, and druggists' sundries (includes cosmetics—wholesale)

5963   Direct selling establishments (includes canvassers, headquarters for retail sale of merchandise, and direct selling organizations—retail)

5999   Miscellaneous retail stores, nec (includes cosmeticsstores—retail)

Costume Shop

7299   Miscellaneous personal services, nec (includes costume rental)

7922   Theatrical producers and miscellaneous theatrical services(includes theatrical costume design)

Craft Artisan

3269   Pottery products, nec (includes art and ornamental ware; pottery; ceramic articles for craft shops; cookware; crockery; china, earthenware and stoneware figures; kitchen articles; coarse earthenware; lamp bases; and vases)

Craft/Hobby Shop

5945   Hobby, toy, and game shops (includes retail hobby stores and craft kit and supply retailers)

5947   Gift, novelty, and souvenir shops pottery; ceramic articles for craft shops; cookware; crockery; china, earthenware and stoneware figures; kitchen articles; coarse earthenware; lamp bases; and vases)

Create Your Own...Store

3269   Pottery Products, nec

5947   Gift, Novelty, and Souvenir Shops

5999   Micellaneous Retail Stores, nec

Credit Card Issuing Service

6153   Short-Term Business Credit Institutions, Except Agricultural (includes credit card service, collection by central agency)

7389   Business Services, nec (includes credit card service collection by individual firms)

Credit Repair Service

7299   Miscellaneous personal services, nec (includes debt counseling and adjustment services)

Credit Reporting and Collection Service

7322   Adjustment and collection services

7323   Credit reporting services

Damage Restoration Service

1790   Special trade contractors, nec (includes cleaning building exteriors, dampproofing buildings, dewatering, fireproofing buildings, steam cleaning of building exteriors, and waterproofing)

Dance School

7911   Dance studios, schools, and halls

Delicatessen/Sandwich Shop

5812   Eating places (includes sandwich bars or shops and submarine sandwich shops)

Desktop Publishing Company

2711   Publishing, or publishing and printing newspapers

2721   Publishing, or publishing and printing periodicals

2731   Publishing, or publishing and printing books

2741   Miscellaneous publishing

Dial-it Services

4813   Telephone communications, except radio-telephone

Diaper Service

7219   Laundry and garment services, nec

Disc Jockey Service

8999   Services, nec

Domestic Help/Maid Service

7349   Building cleaning and maintenance services, nec (includes housekeeping and office cleaning services)

8811   Private households (includes private households employing cooks, maids, and other domestic help)

Driving School

8249   Vocational schools, nec (includes truck driving schools)

8299   Schools and educational services, nec (includes automobile driving instruction)

Drug Store/Pharmacy

5912   Drug stores and proprietary stores

Dry Cleaning Service/Coin-Operated Laundry

7215   Coin-operated laundries and dry cleaning services

7216   Dry cleaning plants, except rug cleaning

Editorial/Freelance Writing Business

8999   Services, nec (includes writing and ghostwriting services)

Electrical Contractor

1731   Electrical work (includes trade contractors engaged in on-site electrical work)

Electrical Lighting Supply Store

5719   Miscellaneous home furnishings stores (includes retail lamp and shade shops)

Employee Leasing Service

7363   Help supply services

Employment Agency

361   Employment agencies

Engraving/Monogramming Service

3479   Coating, engraving, and allied services, nec (includes jewelryand silverware engraving)

7389   Business services, nec (includes advertising embroidery services, embossing services, and identification engraving services)

Environmental Consultant

8748   Business consulting services, nec

Environmental Store

5999   Miscellaneous retail stores, nec

Estate Planning

8811   Private Households

Estate Sales Business

6530   Real estate agents and managers

Executive Recruiting Agency

7361   Employment agencies (includes executive placement)

Fashion Accessories Business

3961   Costume jewelry and costume novelties, except precious metal

5137   Women's, children's, and infants' clothing and accessories

5632   Women's accessory and specialty stores

Fax Service

4822   Telegraph and other message communications (includes facsimile transmission services)

Film and Video Production Operation

7812   Motion picture and videotape production services

Financial Planning Service

282   Investment Advice

Fish and Seafood Store

5421   Meat and fish (seafood) markets, including freezer provisioners

Fish Farm

0273   Animal aquaculture (includes fish farms except hatcheries)

Floor Covering/Restoration Business

5713   Floor covering stores—retail

Florist

5992   Florists

Food Delivery Service

5812   Eating places

5963   Direct selling establishments (includes door-to-door selling organizations and mobile lunch wagons)

5999   Miscellaneous retail stores, nec

Formalwear Rental Business

7299   Miscellaneous personal services, nec (includes tuxedo rental)

Freight Forwarding Service

4731   Arrangement of transportation of freight and cargo (includes freight forwarding services)

Fund Raising Consultant

7389   Business services, nec (includes fund raising on a contract or fee basis)

Funeral Service

7261   Funeral services and crematories

Fur Farm

0271   Fur-bearing animals and rabbits

Fur Store

5632   Women's accessory and specialty stores (includes fur shops and furriers)

Furniture Restoration Service

7641   Reupholstery and furniture repair

Gambling Organizations/Service

7011   Hotels and Motels (includes casino hotels)

7993   Coin-Operated Amusement Devices

7999   Amusement and Recreation Services, nec (includes gambling establishments not primarily operating coin-operated machines and lotteries, operation of)

9311   Public Finance Taxation, and Monetary Policy (includes gambling control boards-government and lottery control boards-government)

Genealogy Service

7299   Miscellaneous personal services, nec (includes genealogical investigation service)

Gift Basket Service

5961   Catalog and mail-order houses

Gift/Card Shop

5943   Stationery stores

5947   Gift, novelty, and souvenir shops (includes card shops)

Glass Repair and Replacement Service

1751   Carpentry work (includes prefabricated window and door installation)

7536   Automotive glass replacement shops

Golf Shop

5941   Sporting goods stores and bicycle shops (includes retail golf goods and equipment stores)

Gourmet Coffee/Tea House

5499   Miscellaneous food stores (includes coffee stores, retail)

5812   Eating places (includes coffee shops)

Greenhouse/Garden Center/Nursery Business

0181   Ornamental floricultural and nursery products (includes greenhouses for floral products, growing of nursery stock, growing of potted plants)

5261   Retail nurseries, lawn and garden supply stores (includes nursery stock, seeds, and bulbs, retail)

Greeting Card Publishing

2771   Greeting card publishing and printing

8999   Services, nec (includes hand painting of greeting cards)

Grocery Store

5411   Grocery stores

Gunsmith/Gun Shop

5941   Sporting good stores and bicycle shops (includes firearms, retail)

7699   Repair shops and related services, nec (includes gunsmith shops)

Hair Replacement/Electrolysis Clinic

7299   Miscellaneous personal services, nec (includes depilatory salons, electrolysis, and hair weaving or replacement services)

Hair Salon/Barber Shop

7231   Beauty shops (includes beauty and barber shops combined)

7241   Barber shops

Handwriting Analysis Consultant

7389   Business services, nec (includes handwriting analysis)

Hardware Store

5251   Hardware stores

Hat Store

5611   Men's and boys' clothing and accessory stores (includes retail hat stores)

5621   Women's accessory and specialty stores (includes retail millinery stores)

Hazardous Waste Disposal Business

4953   Refuse systems (includes hazardous waste material disposal sites)

Healthy Restaurants

5812   Eating Places

Health Food Store

5499   Miscellaneous food stores (includes health food stores)

Hearing Aid Testing and Fitting Service

5999   Miscellaneous retail stores, nec (includes hearing aids, retail)

8099   Health and allied services, nec (includes hearing testing service)

Herb Farm

0191   General farms, primarily crop

2833   Medical chemicals and botanical products (includes herb grinding, grading, and milling)

5499   Miscellaneous food stores (includes spice and herb stores)

Home Accessory Store

5714   Drapery, curtain, and upholstery stores

5719   Miscellaneous home furnishings stores

Home Furnishings Store

5712   Furniture stores

5719   Miscellaneous home furnishings stores

5932   Used merchandise stores (including antique and secondhand retail furniture stores)

Home Health Care Service

8082   Home health care services

Horse Riding Academy

752   Animal specialty services, except veterinary (includes boarding and training horses)

Hotel/Motel/Resort Operation

7011   Hotels and motels (includes resort hotels)

Housesitting Service

8999   Services, nec

Ice Cream/Frozen Yogurt Shop

5451   Dairy products stores (includes retail packaged ice cream stores)

5812   Eating places (includes retail dairy bars)

563   Direct selling establishments (includes ice cream wagons)

Image Consultant

8299   Schools and educational services, nec (includes personal development schools)

8743   Public relations services

Import/Export Service

4731   Arrangement of the transportation of freight and cargo

Incubator

7389   Business services, nec

8748   Business consulting services, nec

Information Broker

7375   Information retrieval services

Insulation Contractor

1742   Plastering, dry wall, acoustical, and insulation work (includes insulation installation contractors)

Insurance Agency

6411   Insurance agents, brokers, and services

Interior Design Service

7389   Business services, nec (includes interior decoration consulting services and interior design services)

Internet/Online Service Provider

4822   Telegraph and other message communications (includes electronicmail services)

7379   Computer related services, nec

Investment/Securities Broker

6211   Security brokers, dealers, and flotation companies

Jewelry Store

5632   Women's accessory and specialty stores (includes costume jewelry stores)

5944	Jewelry stores
7631	Watch, clock, and jewelry repair

Job Training/Retraining

8331	Job training and vocational rehabilitation services (includesjob training)

Kiosk/Pushcart/Vendor Business

5812	Eating places (includes box lunch stands, concession stands,food bars, hamburger and hot dog stands, ice cream stands, refreshment stands, and soft drink stands)

Landscaping Service

0781	Landscape counseling and planning services
0782	Lawn and garden services
0783	Ornamental shrub and tree services

Lawn Maintenance Service

0782	Lawn and garden services
0783	Ornamental shrub and tree services

Limousine Service

4119	Local passenger transportation, nec (includes hearse and limousine rental, with drivers)
7514	Passenger car rental (includes limo rental, w/o drivers)

Lingerie Shop

5632	Lingerie storesMretail

Liquor Store

5921	Liquor stores

Literary Agency

7389	Business services, nec (includes agents and brokers for authors and non-performing artists)

Locksmith

7699	Repair shops and related services, nec (includes locksmith shops and made-to order lock parts)

Luggage and Leather Goods Business

5948	Luggage and leather goods stores

Lumberyard

5211	Lumber and other building materials dealers

Machine Shop/Metalorking Shop

3541	Machine tools, metal cutting types
3542	Machine tools, metal forming types
3544	Special dies and tools, die sets, jigs and fixtures, and industrial molds
3545	Cutting tools, machine tool accessories, and machinists' precision measuring devices
3549	Metalworking machinery, nec

Mail Order Business

5961	Catalog and mail order houses

Management Consulting Service

8742	Management consulting services

Manufacturer's Representative

7389	Business services, nec

Marine Shop

5551	Boat dealers (includes retail marine supply dealers)

Market Research and Analysis

8732	Commercial, economic, sociological, and educational research
8742	Management consulting services

Martial Arts Studio

7999	Amusement and recreation services, nec (includes Judo and Karate instruction)

Masonry, Stonework, and Plastering Contractors

1741	Masonry, stone setting, and other stonework
1742	Plastering, dry wall, acoustical, and insulation work

Massage Therapist

7299	Massage parlor 8049 Offices and clinics of health practitioners,nec

Mediation Service

7389	Business services, nec (includes arbitration and conciliationservices)

Medical and Dental Instrument Manufacturing

3841	Surgical and medical instruments and apparatus
3843	Dental equipment and supplies

Medical Claims Service

6411	Insurance agents, brokers, and service (includes processing ofmedical claims on a contract or fee basis)

Medical Laboratory Service

8071	Medical laboratories

Medical Supplies Store

5047	Medical, dental, and hospital equipment and supplies

Medical Transcription Service

7374	Computer processing and data preparation and processing services

Messenger/Delivery/Subpoena Service

4215	Courier services, except by air (includes letter, mail, package,and parcel delivery services)
4822	Telegraph and other message communication (includes cablegrams, mailgrams, electronic mail, and other message services)
7389	Business services, nec (includes process serving services)

Miniature Golf Course Operation

7999	Amusement and recreation services, nec (includes miniature golf course operations)

Modeling School/Agency

7363	Help supply services (includes modeling services)

8299   Schools and educational services, nec (includes modeling schools)

Mortgage Broker

6162   Mortgage bankers and loan correspondents (includes mortgage brokers using own money)

6163   Loan brokers (includes mortgage brokers arranging for loans but using money of others)

6211   Security brokers, dealers, and flotation companies (includes buying and selling mortgages)

Motorcycle/Moped Store

5571   Motorcycle dealers

Movie Theatre Operation

7832   Motion picture theatres, except drive-ins

7833   Drive-in motion picture theatres

Moving Service

4212   Local trucking, without storage (includes furniture and other moving services)

4214   Local trucking, with storage (includes furniture and household goods moving services)

Music School

8299   Schools and educational services, nec (includes music schools)

Music Shop

5736   Musical instrument stores

5932   Used merchandise stores (includes retailers of secondhand musical instruments)

7699   Repair shops and related services, nec (includes musical instrument repair shops)

Musical Instrument Repair/Piano Tuning Service

7699   Repair shops and related services, nec (includes musical instrument repair shops and piano tuning and repair)

Nail Salon

7231   Beauty shops (includes manicure and pedicure salons)

Nanny Service

7299   Miscellaneous personal services, nec (includes babysitting bureaus)

New Age Services and Supplies

5999   Miscellaneous retail stores, nec

8999   Services, nec

New and Used Car Dealer

5511   Motor vehicle dealers (new and used)

5521   Motor vehicle dealers (used only)

Newsletter Publishing

2721   Periodicals; publishing or publishing and printing

2741   Miscellaneous publishing (includes business service newsletterspublishing and/or printing)

Novelty Items Business

2499   Wood products, nec (includes wood and wood fiber novelties)

2514   Metal household furniture (includes metal novelty furniture)

2679   Converted paper and paperboard products, nec (includes papernovelties)

3199   Leather goods, nec (includes leather novelties)

3229   Pressed and blown glass and glassware, nec (includes novelty glassware made in glassmaking plants)

3231   Glass products, made of purchased glass (includes glassnovelties)

3499   Fabricated metal products, nec (includes metal novelties and specialties, except advertising novelties)

3961   Costume jewelry and costume novelties, except precious metal andgems

3999   Manufacturing industries, nec (includes bone, beaded and shell novelties)

Nursing Home/Long-Term Care Center

8051   Skilled nursing care facilities

8052   Intermediate care facilities (includes intermediate care nursing homes)

8059   Nursing and personal care facilities, nec (includes convalescent homes, rest homes, and like facilities)

Nutritional Consultant/Diet Planner

7299   Miscellaneous personal services, nec (includes diet workshops)

8049   Offices and clinics of health practitioners, nec (includes offices of nutritionists and offices of dietitians)

Office Design Service

7389   Business services, nec (includes interior decorating and design services)

Office Supply/Equipment Store

5943   Stationery stores (includes retail office forms and supplies stores)

Online Store

5734   Computer and computer software stores

7375   Information retrieval services

Paint/Wall Covering Center

5231   Paint, glass, and wallpaper stores

Painting Contractors

1721   Painting and paperhanging contractors

Party Entertainment Services

7929   Bands, orchestras, actors, and other entertainers and entertainment groups

Party/Reunion Planning Service

7359   Equipment rental and leasing, nec (includes party supplies rental and leasing)

8999   Services, nec

Pawnbroker

5932   Used merchandise stores (includes pawnshops)

Payroll Preparation Service

8721   Accounting, auditing, and bookkeeping services (includes payrollaccounting service)

Periodical/Newspaper Publishing

2721   Periodicals; publishing or publishing and printing

Personal Shopping Service

7299   Miscellaneous personal services, nec (includes shopping servicesfor individuals)

Pest Control Service

0851   Forestry services (includes forest pest control)

7342   Disinfecting and pest control services

Pet Boarding/Grooming Service

0279   Animal specialties, nec (includes breeding kennels)

0752   Animal specialty services (includes boarding kennels, doggrooming services, and related services)

Pet Cemetery

0782   Lawn and garden services (includes independent cemetery upkeep services)

6531   Real estate agents and managers (includes cemetery management services)

6553   Cemetery subdividers and developers (includes animal cemetery operations)

Pet Obedience School

0752   Animal specialty services, except veterinary (includes training of pets and other animal specialties)

Pet Shop

5999   Miscellaneous retail stores, nec (includes pet shops)

Pet Sitting Service

0752   Animal specialty services, except veterinary

Photo Finishing Center

7384   Photo finishing laboratories

7819   Services allied to motion picture production (includes motion picture film processing)

Photographer, Commercial

7335   Commercial photography

Photographic Studio

7221   Photographic studios, portrait

Physical Fitness Center

7991   Physical fitness facilities

Physical Therapy Clinic/Practice

8049   Offices and clinics of health practitioners, nec (includes offices of physical therapists)

Pizzeria

5812   Eating places (includes pizza parlors and pizzerias)

Plant Leasing Service

7359   Equipment rental and leasing, nec (includes plants)

Plumbing Service

1711   Plumbing, heating, and air-conditioning contractors

Porcelain Refinishing Service

1799   Special trade contractors, nec

Power Washing Service

1799   Special trade contractors, nec (includes cleaning of building exteriors)

7349   Building cleaning and maintenance services, nec (includes cleaning of building interiors)

7542   Car washes (includes automotive washing and polishing)

Prepaid Phone Card Business

4812   Radiotelephone communications

4813   Telephone communications, except radiotelephone

Print/Frame Shop

7699   Repair shops and related services, nec (includes custom picture framing services)

Printing Business

2752   Commercial printing, lithographic

2754   Commercial printing, gravure

2759   Commercial printing, nec

2761   Manifold business form printers

Private Investigation/Personal Security Service

7381   Detective, guard, and armored car services

Private Label Product Manufacturer/Retailer

3999   Manufacturing industries, nec

5399   Miscellaneous general merchandise stores

5499   Miscellaneous food stores 5699 Miscellaneous apparel and accessory stores

5999   Miscellaneous retail stores, nec

Professional Organizer

7299   Miscellaneous personal services, nec

7389   Business services, nec

Property Management

6531   Real estate agents and managers

Public Relations Consultant

8743   Public relations services

Public Warehousing/Ministorage Operation

4221   Farm product warehousing and storage

4222   Refrigerated warehousing and storage

4225   General warehousing and storage

4226   Special warehousing and storage, nec (includes fur storage, household goods warehousing and storage, whiskey warehousing, and like enterprises)

Quick Oil Change Service

5541   Gasoline service stations (includes automobile servicestations—retail)

7538   General automotive repair shops

Radio Station

4832   Radio broadcasting stations

Radon Testing Service

1799   Special trade contractors, nec

8734   Testing laboratories

Real Estate Agency

6531   Real estate agents and managers

Real Estate Investment Service

6798   Real estate investment trusts

Recording Studio

7399   Business services, nec (includes recording studios operating on a contract or fee basis)

Recreational Vehicle Dealer

5561   Recreational vehicle dealers

Recycling Business

5093   Scrap and waste materials

Rental Service

7299   Miscellaneous personal services, nec (includes clothing rental)

7352   Medical equipment rental and leasing

7353   Heavy construction equipment and leasing

7359   Equipment rental and leasing, nec

7377   Computer rental and leasing

7999   Amusement and recreation services, nec (includes pleasure boat rental, canoe and rowboat rental, bicycle, motorcycle and moped rental, and sporting goods rental)

Restaurant

5812   Eating places (includes sit-down, carry-out, and fast food)

Resume Service

7338   Secretarial anc court reporting services (includes resumewriting services)

Roofing Contractor

1761   Roofing, siding, and sheet metal work

Satellite Dish Service

4841   Cable and other pay television services (includes directbroadcast satellite services and satellite master antenna systems services)

Screen Printing Business

2261   Finishers of broadwoven fabrics of cotton (includes printing andfinishing of cotton broadwoven fabrics)

2262   Finishers of broadwoven fabrics of manmade fiber and silk(includes printing manmade fiber and silk broadwoven fabrics)

2759   Commercial printing, nec (includes screen printing on glass, plastics, paper, and metal, including highway signs)

Security Systems Service

7382   Security systems services

Seminar Planner/Lecturer

8999   Services, nec (including lecturers)

Service Station/Auto Repair and Service Shop

5541   Gasoline service stations

7532   Top, body, and upholstery repair shops and paint shops

7533   Automotive exhaust system repair shops

7534   Tire retreading and repair shops

7536   Automotive glass replacement shops

7537   Automotive transmission repair shops

7538   General automotive repair shops

7539   Automotive repair shops, nec

Sewer and Drain Cleaning Business

7699   Repair shops and related services, nec (includes sewer cleaning and rodding and septic tank cleaning) Sewing Center 5722 Household appliance stores (includes retail sewing machine stores)

5949   Sewing, needlework, and piece goods stores

7699   Repair shops and related services, nec (includes sewing machine repair shops)

Shoe Repair Shop

7251   Shoe repair shops and shoeshine parlors

Shoe Store

5661   Shoe stores

Sign Shop

3993   Signs and advertising specialties

7389   Business services, nec (includes sign painting shops)

Silk Plant Shop

5999   Miscellaneous retail stores, nec (includes artificial flowers—retail)

Skating Rink Operation

7999   Amusement and recreation services, nec (includes ice and rollerskating rink operations)

Ski Shop

5941   Sporting goods stores and bicycle shops

Software Publishing

7372   Packaged software

Solar Energy Design/Contracting Business

1711   Plumbing, heating, and air-conditioning contractors (includes solar heating apparatus contractors)

1742   Plastering, dry wall, acoustical, and insulation work (includes solar reflecting insulation film contractors)

Specialized Staffing

7361   Employment Agencies

7363   Help Supply Services

Specialty Foods/Wine Shop

5499   Miscellaneous food stores

5921   Liquor stores (includes packaged wine—retail)

Sports Promotional Services

7941   Professional Sports Clubs and Promoters

Sporting Goods Store

5941   Sporting goods stores and bicycle shops

Surveying Service

8713   Surveying services (includes surveying: land, water, and aerial)

Swimming Pool/Hot Tub Business

1799   Special trade contractors, nec (includes swimming pool construction contractors)

5999   Miscellaneous retail stores, nec (includes hot tubs, retail)

7389   Business services, nec (includes swimming pool cleaning and maintenance services)

7999   Amusement and recreation services, nec (includes swimming pool operations)

Tailor Shop

5699   Miscellaneous apparel and accessory stores (includes custom tailor shops) 7219 Laundry and garment services, nec (includes tailor shops, except custom or merchant tailors)

Talent Agency

7922   Theatrical producers and miscellaneous theatrical services (includes agents)

Tanning Parlor/Sauna

7299   Miscellaneous personal services (includes steam baths and tanning salons)

Tattoo Parlor

7299   Miscellaneous personal services, nec (includes tattoo parlors)

Tax Preparation Business

7291   Tax return preparation services

8721   Accounting, auditing, and bookkeeping services

Taxicab/Van Shuttle Service

4121   Taxicabs

Taxidermy Service

7699   Repair shops and related services, nec (includes taxidermy)

Teacher Supply Store

5999   Miscellaneous retail stores, nec

Telemarketing Service

7389   Business services, nec (includes telemarketing services operating on a contract or fee basis)

Telephone Answering Service

7389   Business services, nec (includes answering services)

Television/Radio Repair Service

7622   Radio and television repair shops

Television Station

4833   Television broadcasting stations

Temporary Employment Agency

7363   Help supply services (includes temporary help services)

Tennis Court/Racquet Club Operation

7997   Membership sports and recreation clubs (includes racquetball and tennis clubs)

7999   Amusement and recreation services, nec (includes nonmembership racquetball and tennis court operations)

Tire Dealer

5531   Auto and home supply stores (includes retail tire dealers) 7534 Tire retreading and repair shops

Tobacco Shop

5993   Tobacco stores and stands

Tour Guide Operation/Adventure Service

4725   Tour operations

7999   Amusement and recreation services, nec (includes tour guides)

Toy Business

5945   Hobby, toy, and game shops

Trade Show/Conference Management Service

7389   Business services, nec (includes trade show arrangement)

Translating/Interpreting Service

7389   Business services, nec (includes translation service)

Travel Agency

4724   Travel agencies

Trucking Business

4212   Local trucking, without storage services

4213   Trucking, except local

4214   Local trucking, with storage services

Tutoring Service

8299   Schools and educational services, nec (includes tutoring services)

Typesetting Business

2791   Typesetting

Typing/Stenographic Service

7338   Secretarial and court reporting services (includes stenographic and typing services)

Upholstery/Carpet Services

1752   Floor laying and other floor work, nec (includes carpet laying and removing services)

5714 Drapery, curtain, and upholstery stores (includes upholstery materials stores)

7217 Carpet and upholstery cleaning

Vending Machine Merchandising and Service Business

5962 Automatic merchandising machine operators (includes retail sale of products through vending machines)

7359 Equipment rental and leasing services, nec (includes vending machine rental businesses)

Videocassette Rental Store

5735 Recorded and prerecorded tape stores (includes retail videotape stores)

7841 Videotape rental establishments

Vision Center

5995 Optical goods stores

Voice Mail Service

4813 Telephone communications, except radiotelephone (includes voice telephone communications)

Water Conditioning Service

7389 Business services, nec (includes water softener services)

Web Site Design

7371 Computer programming services (includes custom computer programsor systems software development and computer software systems analysis and design)

Weight Reduction/Control Center

7991 Physical fitness facilities (includes reducing facilities and slenderizing salons)

Welcome Service

7389 Business service, nec (includes welcoming service)

Window Dressing Business

3993 Signs and advertising specialties (includes advertising displays, except printed, and window and lobby cutouts and displays)

7319 Advertising, nec (includes display advertising services, exceptoutdoor)

Word Processing Service

7338 Secretarial and court reporting services (includes wordprocessing services)

START-UP INFORMATION

7781 ▪ Design and Launch Your Online Boutique in a Week
Pub: Entrepreneur Press
Ed: Melissa Campanelli. Released: June 2008. Price: $17.95. Description: Guide to start an online boutique includes information on business planning, Website design and funding.

7782 ▪ In Fashion: From Runway to Retail, Everything You Need to Know to Break Into the Fashion Industry
Pub: Crown Business Books
Ed: Annemarie Iverson. Released: August 10, 2010. Price: $16.99. Description: Whether your dream is to photograph models, outfit celebrities, design fashions, this book provides details into every aspect for working in the fashion industry.

7783 ▪ "Money Matters: Using Sound Resources, You Can Find Capital For Your Business" in Black Enterprise (Vol. 38, November 2007, No. 4)
Pub: Earl G. Graves Publishing Co. Inc.
Ed: Carolyn M. Brown. Description: Profile of fashion designer Kara Saun who inspired an angel investor from Connecticut to help launch her Fall 2006 clothing line.

7784 ▪ Start Your Own Fashion Accessories Business
Pub: Entrepreneur Press
Released: March 1, 2009. Price: $17.95. Description: Entrepreneurs wishing to start a fashion accessories business will find important information for setting up a home workshop and office, exploring the market, managing finances, publicizing and advertising the business and more.

ASSOCIATIONS AND OTHER ORGANIZATIONS

7785 ▪ Fashion Group International
8 W 40th St., 7th Fl.
New York, NY 10018
Ph:(212)302-5511
Fax:(212)302-5533
Co. E-mail: cheryl@fgi.org
URL: http://www.fgi.org
Contact: Cheryl Ingersoll, Regional Dir.
Description: Fashion, apparel, accessories, beauty and home industries. Works to advance professionalism in fashion and its related lifestyle industries with a particular emphasis on the role and development of women. Provides a public forum for examination of important contemporary issues in fashion and the business of fashion. Works to present timely information regarding national and global trends and to attain greater recognition of women's achievements in business and to promote career opportunities in fashion.

REFERENCE WORKS

7786 ▪ "Apparel" in Retail Merchandiser (Vol. 51, July-August 2011, No. 4, pp. 14)
Pub: Phoenix Media Corporation
Description: NPD Group Inc. released current sales statistics for the women's apparel market along with men's apparel. It also reported annual shoes sales for 2010. Statistical data included.

7787 ▪ "As Seen On TV" in Canadian Business (Vol. 80, November 5, 2007, No. 22, pp. 93)
Pub: Rogers Media
Ed: Zena Olijnyk. Description: StarBrand Media Inc. is one of the companies providing fans with information on how and where to purchase the items that television characters are using. StarBrand created the style section found on different television shows' Websites, such as that of the Gossip Girl and Smallville. The benefits of using sites like StarBrand are evaluated.

7788 ▪ "Better Than New" in Bellingham Business Journal (Vol. February 2010, pp. 16)
Pub: Sound Publishing Inc.
Ed: Ashley Mitchell. Description: Profile of family owned Better Than New clothing store that sells overstock items from department stores and clothing manufacturers. The stores location makes it easy to miss and its only advertising is a large sign posted outside. This is the sixth store owned by the couple, Keijeo and Sirba Halmekanqas.

7789 ▪ "The Bottom Line" in Retail Merchandiser (Vol. 51, July-August 2011, No. 4, pp. 60)
Pub: Phoenix Media Corporation
Description: Hanky Panky believes that comfort and style don't have to be mutually exclusive when designing their line of intimate apparel for women. The lingerie retailer was launched in 1977.

7790 ▪ "Buying Chanel (All Of It)" in Conde Nast Portfolio (Vol. 2, June 2008, No. 6, pp. 34)
Pub: Conde Nast Publications, Inc.
Ed: Willow Duttge. Description: Overview of the luxury company Chanel and an estimated guess as to what the company is worth.

7791 ▪ "A Change Would Do You Good" in Canadian Business (Vol. 80, November 19, 2007, No. 23, pp. 15)
Pub: Rogers Media
Ed: Geoff Kirbyson. Description: Western Glove Works will be manufacturing clothing offshore, including Sheryl Crow's jeans collection, in countries such as China and the Philippines. The company decided to operate offshore after 86 years of existence due to the high price of manufacturing jeans in Canada. Western Glove's focus on producing celebrity-endorsed goods is discussed.

7792 ▪ "Common Thread" in Entrepreneur (Vol. 36, March 2008, No. 3, pp. 144)
Pub: Entrepreneur Media Inc.
Ed: Sara Wilson. Description: Profile of Stacey Benet and her business, Alice and Olivia, and how she jumpstarted her career in the clothing industry after she wore a self-designed pair of pants that caught the attention of a Barney's New York representative is presented.

7793 ▪ "Consignment Shop Closes Without Warning to Customers, Landlord" in Sun Journal (June 30, 2010)
Pub: Freedom Communications Inc.
Ed: Laura Oleniacz. Description: Off The Racks consignment shop located on Glenburnie Road in New Bern, North Carolina closed without warning to customers or its landlord. The consignors who donated clothing to the store were left unpaid.

7794 ▪ "Consignment Shop Offers Children's Clothes, Products" in Frederick News-Post (August 19, 2010)
Pub: Federick News-Post
Ed: Ed Waters Jr. Description: Sweet Pea Consignments for Children offers used items for newborns to pre-teens. The shop carries name brand clothing as well as toys, books and baby products.

7795 ▪ "Crowdsourcing their Way into One Big Mess" in Brandweek (Vol. 51, October 25, 2010, No. 38, pp. 26)
Pub: Nielsen Business Media, Inc.
Ed: Gregg S. Lipman. Description: The Gap, was counting on crowdsourcing to provide feedback for its new logo, but it did not prove positive for the retailer. However, a massive outcry of negative opinion, via crowdsourcing, may not always equal valid, constructive criticism.

7796 ▪ "Designers' Hats Foretell a Big Comeback Next Fall" in Charlotte Observer (February 8, 2007)
Pub: Knight-Ridder/Tribune Business News
Ed: Crystal Dempsey. Description: According to designer experts, hats are making a comeback and will make a big fashion statement, fall 2007.

7797 ▪ "Doing Good: Fair Fashion" in Entrepreneur (Vol. 35, October 2007, No. 10, pp. 36)
Pub: Entrepreneur Media Inc.
Ed: J.J. Ramberg. Description: Indigenous Designs was launched in 1993, when organic clothing was not yet popular. However, the company has become successful in the industry, with $4 million dollars in revenue, owing to the growing environment awareness of consumers. A history of how the company was formed and an overview of their production process are provided.

7798 ▪ "Fall Fever" in Canadian Business (Vol. 81, October 13, 2008, No. 17, pp. S12)
Pub: Rogers Media Ltd.
Description: Buyer's guide of men's suits and jackets for fall are presented, including a suit by Boss

Hugo Boss recommended for fun in the city after finishing work. Designers Ermenegildo, Michael Kors, and Arnold Brant are also highlighted.

7799 ■ "Finishing Touches: the Fashion Statement is in the Detail" in *Black Enterprise* **(Vol. 37, January 2007, No. 6, pp. 106)**
Pub: Earl G. Graves Publishing Co. Inc.
Ed: Sonia Alleyne. **Description:** Men are discovering the importance of dressing for success. Paying attention to the details such as shoes, socks, cuffs, and collars are just as important as finding the right suit.

7800 ■ "Former Apprentice Candidate Launches Jewelry Line" in *Black Enterprise* **(Vol. 37, October 2006, No. 3, pp. 36)**
Pub: Earl G. Graves Publishing Co. Inc.
Ed: Philana Patterson. **Description:** Star of the second season of NBC's The Apprentice, Stacie J, has launched a line of jewelry and accessories which will be sold at Claire's stores nationwide.

7801 ■ *Fugitive Denim: A Moving Story of People and Pants in the Borderless World of Global Trade*
Pub: W.W. Norton & Company
Ed: Rachel Snyder. **Released:** April 2009. **Price:** $16.95. **Description:** In-depth study of the global production and processes of how jeans are designed, sewn, and transported as well as how the cotton for denim is grown, regulated, purchased and processed.

7802 ■ "Going Western with a Touch of Style" in *Women In Business* **(Vol. 63, Summer 2011, No. 2, pp. 8)**
Pub: American Business Women's Association
Ed: Maureen Sullivan. **Description:** Tips on ways women should dress up in Western style are presented. The wearing of Western-style denims is recommended. Use of accessories such as belt buckles, boots and hats is also encouraged.

7803 ■ "H&M Offers a Dress for Less" in *Canadian Business* **(Vol. 83, September 14, 2010, No. 15, pp. 20)**
Pub: Rogers Media Ltd.
Ed: Laura Cameron. **Description:** Swedish clothing company H&M has implemented loss leader strategy by pricing some dresses at extremely low prices. The economy has forced retailers to keep prices down despite the increasing cost of manufacturing, partly due to Chinese labor becoming more expensive. How the trend will affect apparel companies is discussed.

7804 ■ "Haute Flyers" in *Canadian Business* **(Vol. 80, November 19, 2007, No. 23, pp. 68)**
Pub: Rogers Media
Ed: Rachel Pulfer. **Description:** Duckie Brown has been nominated by the Council of Fashion Designers of America as best menswear designer in the U.S. for 2007, along with leaders Calvin Klein and Ralph Lauren. The New York-based company was formed the day after September 11, 2001, but the timing did not hamper its growth. The works and plans of owners Steven Cox and Daniel Silver are described.

7805 ■ "Hot Kicks, Cool Price" in *Black Enterprise* **(Vol. 37, December 2006, No. 5, pp. 34)**
Pub: Earl G. Graves Publishing Co. Inc.
Ed: Topher Sanders. **Description:** Stephon Marbury of the New York Nicks introduced a new basketball shoe, the Starbury One, costing $14.98. The shoes are an addition to the Starbury clothing line and although the privately owned company would not disclose figures; stores sold out of a month's worth of inventory in merely three days.

7806 ■ "How to Keep Your Cool and Your Friends in a Heat Wave" in *Canadian Business* **(Vol. 83, August 17, 2010, No. 13-14, pp. 79)**
Pub: Rogers Media Ltd.
Ed: Angelina Chapin. **Description:** A buyer's guide of menswear clothing for businessmen is presented. The products include an antiperspirant and deodorant, men's dress shorts, shoes and bamboo fabric undershirt.

7807 ■ *Hug Your Customers*
Pub: Hyperion Books
Ed: Jack Mitchell. **Price:** $19.95. **Description:** The CEO of Mitchells/Roberts, two very successful clothing stores, professes his belief in showering customers with attention. His secrets for long-term business success include advice about attracting a good staff, lowering marketing costs, and maintaining higher gross margins and revenues.

7808 ■ "Insider" in *Canadian Business* **(Vol. 80, Winter 2007, No. 24, pp.)**
Pub: Rogers Media
Ed: Zena Olijnyk. **Description:** Luluemon Athletica started in 1998 after Dennis Wilson takes a yoga class and notices a demand from women for breathable clothes. The company opened their first outlet in Vancouver in November 2000 then opened their first U.S. store in 2003 until finally going public July 27, 2007 where its stocks doubled in value within days of trading.

7809 ■ "Island Co.: Isle Style" in *Entrepreneur* **(Vol. 35, October 2007, No. 10, pp. 172)**
Pub: Entrepreneur Media Inc.
Ed: Sara Wilson. **Description:** Island Co., producer of travel clothing and swimsuits was formed by Spencer Antle in 2002. Its office projects the Caribbean atmosphere, a strategy Antle used to promote the company's theme to its clients. Future plans for the company are also indicated.

7810 ■ "It's In the Bag" in *Entrepreneur* **(Vol. 36, April 2008, No. 4, pp. 122)**
Pub: Entrepreneur Media, Inc.
Ed: Celeste Hoang. **Description:** Sandy Stein launched Alexx Inc in 2004, which markets keychains, called Finders Key Purse, with unique designs to help find keys easier inside the purse. Some of the key ring designs are hearts, sandals, and crowns. The company has approximately $6 million worth of sales in 2007.

7811 ■ "It's So You! Consignment Chop Owner Thrilled to See Vision Come to Fruition" in *News-Herald* **(August 27, 2010)**
Pub: News-Herald
Ed: Brandon C. Baker. **Description:** Profile of Laurel Howes and her It's So You! Boutique. The consignment shop is located in Willoughby's Pine Ride Plaza in Ohio. The shop targets all women, but particularly those who are not that comfortable with shopping consignment.

7812 ■ "Izod, Loft Outlets Coming To Tanger" in *New Hampshire Business Review* **(Vol. 33, March 25, 2011, No. 6, pp. 30)**
Pub: Business Publications Inc.
Description: Izod and Lots stores will open at the Tanger Outlet Center in Tilton, New Hampshire. Both stores will feature fashions and accessories.

7813 ■ "Let It Shine: Organization Helps Disadvantaged Girls See Their Worth" in *Black Enterprise* **(Vol. 38, February 2008, No. 7, pp. 142)**
Pub: Earl G. Graves Publishing Co. Inc.
Ed: George Alexander. **Description:** Wilson Mourning, founder of the clothing label Honey Child, attributes her success to her mother and other positive women who helped her through her adolescence. Mourning created a mentoring organization that helps young girls in the Miami, Florida area to develop life skills.

7814 ■ "Life's Work: Manolo Blahnik" in *Harvard Business Review* **(Vol. 88, December 2010, No. 12, pp. 144)**
Pub: Harvard Business School Publishing
Ed: Alison Beard. **Description:** Shoe designer Manolo Blahnik recounts his beginnings in the shoe industry and the influence art has had on his work, as well as balancing art and commerce. He also discusses the importance of quality materials and craftsmanship and the benefits of managing an independent, family-owned business.

7815 ■ "Making It Work" in *Retail Merchandiser* **(Vol. 51, July-August 2011, No. 4, pp. 43)**
Pub: Phoenix Media Corporation
Ed: Anthony DiPaolo. **Description:** Profile of Anthony DiPaolo and his purchase of the Work 'N Gear retail store in 2002. The brick and mortar shop sells work wear and healthcare apparel and DiPaolo believes customer respect is essential to his success.

7816 ■ *Mass Merchandisers & Off-Price Apparel Buyers*
Pub: Briefings Media Group
Contact: Alan M. Douglas, President
E-mail: psnyder@douglaspublications.com
Released: Annual, latest edition 2011-2012. **Price:** $329, individuals directory price; $659, individuals directory/CD combo price. **Covers:** 7,900 buyers and 3,400 companies in mass merchandise and off-price apparel industry. **Entries Include:** Company name, address, phone, fax, e-mail, URL, names and titles of key personnel, geographical area served, branch office or subsidiary names and addresses, products and/or services provided, sales volume, parent company name. **Arrangement:** Geographical. **Indexes:** Store/company name, new listings, jobbers, online retailers.

7817 ■ "Midas Touch" in *Entrepreneur* **(Vol. 36, April 2008, No. 4, pp. 160)**
Pub: Entrepreneur Media, Inc.
Ed: Sara Wilson. **Description:** Lana Fertelmeister is a model-turned-jewelry designer. Her company, Lana Jewelry, designs fine jewelry for women. Her jewelry line is available in more than 100 stores worldwide and has been worn by celebrities like Cameron Diaz and Sandra Bullock.

7818 ■ "Research and Markets Adds: 2011 U.S. Women's & Children's Clothing Wholesale Report" in *Health & Beauty Close-Up* **(October 16, 2010)**
Pub: Close-Up Media Inc.
Description: The Women's & Children's Clothing Wholesale Report is an annual report containing timely and accurate industry statistics, forecasts and demographics.

7819 ■ "Retail News: Children's Boutique Relocates to Conway" in *Sun News* **(June 4, 2010)**
Pub: The Sun News
Description: Little Angel's Children's Boutique and Big Oak Frame Shop have moved to downtown locations in Conway, South Carolina. Little Angel's will sell children's clothing and accessories, shoes and gifts, while the frame shop will offer custom framing along with the sale of stationary, invitations and local prints.

7820 ■ "Rule of the Masses: Reinventing Fashion Via Crowdsourcing" in *WWD* **(Vol. 200, July 26, 2010, No. 17, pp. 1)**
Pub: Conde Nast Publications Inc.
Ed: Cate T. Corcoran. **Description:** Large apparel brands and retailers are crowdsourcing as a way to increase customer loyalty and to build their businesses.

7821 ■ "Spell It Out" in *Entrepreneur* **(Vol. 36, April 2008, No. 4, pp. 123)**
Pub: Entrepreneur Media, Inc.
Ed: Emily Weisberg. **Description:** IM:It is an apparel and accessories company that markets products with instant messaging (IM) acronyms and emoticons. Examples of these are "LOL" and "GTG". Other details on IM:It products are discussed.

7822 ■ *They Made America*
Pub: Little Brown Company/Time Warner Book Group
Ed: Harold Evans, Gail Buckland, David Lefer. **Released:** 2006. **Price:** $18.95. **Description:** Coffee table book highlighting entrepreneurship; this book is filled with interesting illustrated portraits of entrepreneurs and innovators like Thomas Edison, George Doriot (a venture capital pioneer), and Ida Rosenthal (inventor of the Maidenform bra).

7823 ■ **"The Ultimate Home Shopping Network"** in *Austin Business JournalInc.* (Vol. 28, October 17, 2008, No. 31, pp. A1)
Pub: American City Business Journals
Ed: Sandra Zaragoza. Description: New York-based Etcetera sells their clothing through more than 850 fashion consultants in the U.S. Central Texas is one of the company's top markets and the company is looking to increase its fashion consultants in the area from five to about 20 since they believe there is plenty of room to expand their customer base in the area.

7824 ■ **"Web Sight: Do You See What I See?"** in *Entrepreneur* (Vol. 35, October 2007, No. 10, pp. 58)
Pub: Entrepreneur Media Inc.
Ed: Heather Clancy. Description: Owners of Trunkt, a boutique in New York that showcases independent designs, have created a new style of Website called Trunkt.org. The Website allows buyers to select the products they want to see and designers can choose anytime which of their items will be displayed on the site. An explanation of the strategy that helped bring Trunkt closer to its clients is presented.

7825 ■ **"Well-Heeled Startup"** in *Business Journal Portland* (Vol. 27, November 12, 2010, No. 37, pp. 1)
Pub: Portland Business Journal
Ed: Erik Siemers. Description: Oh! Shoes LLC expects to receive about $1.5 million in funding from angel investors, while marketing a new line of high heel shoes that are comfortable, healthy, and attractive. The new line of shoes will use the technology of athletic footwear while having the look of an Italian designer. Oh! Shoes hopes to generate $35 million in sales by 2014.

7826 ■ **"Women Prioritize Luxury Spending"** in *Marketing to Women* (Vol. 22, July 2009, No. 7, pp. 8)
Pub: EPM Communications, Inc.
Description: In 2008, women spent 7 percent less on luxury items than in the previous year, according to Unity Marketing. Some luxury items, such as facial care products, are faring better than others. Statistical data included.

VIDEOCASSETTES/AUDIOCASSETTES

7827 ■ *Accessories*
Meridian Education Corp.
132 West 31st Street, 17th Floor
New York, NY 10001
Ph:(609)671-0266
Free: 800-257-5126
Co. E-mail: custmserv@films.com
URL: http://meridian.films.com
Released: 1990. Price: $45.00. Description: Describes all sorts of accessories and how they can be used to stretch any wardrobe. Also details the differences between fad pieces and the timeless classics which can be used over and over again. Availability: VHS.

7828 ■ *Accessory Allure*
Cambridge Educational
c/o Films Media Group
132 West 31st Street, 17th Floor
Ste. 124
New York, NY 10001
Free: 800-257-5126
Fax:(609)671-0266
Co. E-mail: custserve@films.com
URL: http://www.cambridgeol.com
Released: 1987. Price: $29.95. Description: This video shows viewers how to make the most of their wardrobe by using scarves, earrings, hats, and other accessories. Availability: VHS.

TRADE SHOWS AND CONVENTIONS

7829 ■ **Baltimore Women's Show**
S & L Productions, Inc.
1916 Crain Hwy., Ste. 16
Glen Burnie, MD 21061

Ph:(410)863-1180
Fax:(410)863-1187
URL: http://www.mdhomeandgarden.com
Released: Annual. Audience: Women 25-65 yrs. Principal Exhibits: Products and services for women.

7830 ■ **Beauty Fair**
The Finnish Fair Corp.
Messuaukio 1
PO Box 21
FIN-00521 Helsinki, Finland
Ph:358 9 15091
Fax:358 9 1509218
Co. E-mail: info@finnexpo.fi
Released: Annual. Audience: General public. Principal Exhibits: Beauty and fashion, cosmetics and services; hair products and services; clothing, showes, bags, accessories, jewelry, education, and publications.

7831 ■ **Florida Fashion Focus Show**
Southern Apparel Exhibitors, Inc.
1856 Sheridan St.
Evanston, IL 60201
Ph:(847)475-1856
Free: 888-249-1377
Co. E-mail: info@saemiami.com
URL: http://www.saemiami.com
Released: 5/yr. Audience: Trade buyers. Principal Exhibits: Ladies ready-to-wear clothing; handbags, jewelry, and accessories. Order-writing for future delivery.

7832 ■ **Mitteldeutsche Handwerksmesse: Central German Handicrafts Fair**
Leipziger-Messe GmbH
PO Box 100720
D-04007 Leipzig, Germany
Ph:49 341 67 80
Fax:49 341 678 87 62
Co. E-mail: info@leipziger-messe.de
URL: http://www.leipziger-messe.de
Released: Annual. Audience: General public. Principal Exhibits: Building and conversion, home, arts and crafts, health, lifestyle, food crafts, vehicles, rare handicrafts.

7833 ■ **Mode Accessories International Exposition**
Two Plus One Group Inc.
220 Duncan Mill Rd., Ste. 618
Toronto, ON, Canada M3B 3J5
Ph:(416)510-0114
Fax:(416)510-0165
Co. E-mail: twoplusone@mode-accessories.com
URL: http://www.mode-accessories.com
Released: Semiannual. Audience: Fashion accessory retailers, women's wear boutiques, gift shops. Principal Exhibits: Fashion accessories, fashion apparel.

7834 ■ **Pittsburgh Women's Show**
Trigger Agency
3539 Clipper Mill Rd.
Baltimore, MD 21211
Free: 800-830-3976
Fax:(410)878-9911
Co. E-mail: info@triggeragency.com
URL: http://www.triggeragency.com
Released: Annual. Audience: Trade and public. Principal Exhibits: Products and services for women relating to health, fitness, business, careers, and finance.

7835 ■ **Women's and Children's Apparel and Accessories Mart**
Dallas Market Center Co.
Attn: SG Marketing Mgr.
2100 Stemmons Fwy.
Dallas, TX 75207
Ph:(214)655-6100
Free: 800-325-6587
Fax:(214)655-6238
Co. E-mail: info@dmcmail.com
Audience: Apparel and accessories and home furnishings retailers. Principal Exhibits: Regional Merchandising Mart servicing department and specialty store buyers nationwide.

FRANCHISES AND BUSINESS OPPORTUNITIES

7836 ■ **Apricot Lane**
Country Visions, Inc.
3333 Vaca Valley Pky., Ste. 900
Vacaville, CA 95688
Free: 800-425-8883
Co. E-mail: franchiseinfo@apricotlanefranchise.com
URL: http://www.apricotlanefranchise.com
No. of Franchise Units: 50. Founded: 1991. Franchised: 1992. Description: Specialty retail franchise that combines opportunities from the gift and fashion accessory industries to other affordable fashion jewelry, handbags, accessories and gifts in the styles and trends customers are looking for Equity Capital Needed: $30,000. Franchise Fee: $25,000. Financial Assistance: Third party referral. Training: Site selection and lease negotiation assistance; turnkey store design and construction; sales point system; home training program and onsite training; initial inventory orders; grand opening marketing kit; and onsite merchandising.

7837 ■ **Clothes Mentor**
14200 Wayzata Blvd.
Minnetonka, MN 55305
Free: (866)261-2030
Fax:(614)467-2093
No. of Franchise Units: 45. No. of Company-Owned Units: 1. Founded: 2001. Franchised: 2007. Description: New/used women's clothing & accessories. Equity Capital Needed: $140,000-$229,000. Franchise Fee: $20,000. Royalty Fee: 4%. Financial Assistance: Limited third party financing available. Training: Includes 2 weeks training at headquarters and ongoing support.

LIBRARIES

7838 ■ **Conde Nast Publications Library and Information Services**
4 Times Sq., 17th Fl.
New York, NY 10036
Ph:(212)286-2860
URL: http://www.condenastdigital.com
Contact: Sarah Chubb, Pres.
Scope: Fashion, houses, gardens, home furnishings, interior design, health, personalities, photographs. Holdings: 7000 volumes. Subscriptions: 200 journals and other serials; 4 newspapers.

7839 ■ **Fashion Institute of Technology–Gladys Marcus Library**
7th Ave. at 27th St.
E-Bldg. E502
New York, NY 10001-5992
Ph:(212)217-4340
Fax:(212)217-4371
Co. E-mail: greta_earnest@fitnyc.edu
URL: http://fitnyc.edu/library
Contact: Prof. N.J. Wolfe, Lib.Dir.
Scope: Costume, fashion, interior design, management engineering technology, fashion buying and merchandising, textiles, toy design, packaging design, advertising. Services: Interlibrary loan; copying; Library open to the public for reference use only by appointment. Holdings: 130,260 books; 113,265 nonprint units; 20,637 bound periodical volumes; 125,000 fashion slides; 4712 reels of microfilm; 438 CD-ROM serials and digital monographs. Subscriptions: 4000 journals and other serials.

7840 ■ **George Brown College of Applied Arts & Technology Archives**
500 Macpherson Ave., Rm. F-103
PO Box 1015, Sta. B
Toronto, ON, Canada M5T 2T9

Ph:(416)415-5000, x4771
Fax:(416)415-4772
Co. E-mail: rmacaula@georgebrown.ca
URL: http://llc.georgebrown.ca/llc/er_dept/archives/
    gb_er_archives.aspx

Contact: Robert Macaulay, Coll.Archv.
Scope: College history, labor relations, fashion industry, post-secondary education, nursing schools, collegiate sports. **Services:** Copying; archives open to the public with restrictions and by appointment

only. **Holdings:** 190 cubic meters of records and manuscripts; 2700 linear meters publications, clippings, photographs, filsm, audio and video recordings.

REFERENCE WORKS

7841 ■ *National E-mail and Fax Directory*
Pub: Gale
Released: Annual, Latest edition 26th; April, 2011.
Price: $265, individuals. **Covers:** Approximately 130,000 fax numbers and nearly 85,000 e-mail addresses for businesses, government agencies, and other institutions and organizations. **Entries Include:** Company or organization name, address, phone, fax, and e-mail addresses. **Arrangement:** Same information provided alphabetically and classified by subject. **Indexes:** Subject.

FRANCHISES AND BUSINESS OPPORTUNITIES

7842 ■ Pak Mail
7173 S Havan St., Ste. 600
Centennial, CO 80112
Free: 800-833-2821
Fax:800-336-7363
Co. E-mail: sales@pakmail.org
URL: http://www.pakmail.com
No. of Franchise Units: 500. **Founded:** 1983. **Franchised:** 1984. **Description:** One-stop shop offers the customer a convenient location to send packages, make copies, send or receive a fax or rent a private mailbox. **Equity Capital Needed:** $130,000-$164,300. **Franchise Fee:** $29,950. **Financial Assistance:** Third party finance packages. **Managerial Assistance:** Offers assistance with site selection, lease negotiation, build-out & merchandising, operations processes, & marketing programs and ongoing networking. **Training:** Provides training, education & ongoing support to build your business.

START-UP INFORMATION

7843 ■ "Fast-Forward Fortune" in *Small Business Opportunities* **(July 2010)**
Pub: Harris Publications Inc.
Description: Profile of Steve Dalbec and his home-based Home Video Studio where he earns income by offering a wide variety of video services to clients from duplicating CDs, video to DVD transfer, sports videos and more. Dalbec believes this is the perfect home-based business.

7844 ■ "Fun And Easy Gold Mines" in *Small Business Opportunities* **(Fall 2008)**
Pub: Entrepreneur Media Inc.
Description: Twenty-five businesses that cater to the booming children's market are profiled; day care services, party planning, special events video-making, tutoring, personalized children's toys and products and other services geared toward the kids market are included.

ASSOCIATIONS AND OTHER ORGANIZATIONS

7845 ■ Association for Information Media and Equipment
PO Box 9844
Cedar Rapids, IA 52409-9844
Ph:(319)654-0608
Fax:(319)654-0609
URL: http://www.aime.org
Contact: Betty Gorsegner Ehlinger, Exec. Dir.
Description: Producers and distributors of nontheatrical film/video and video related-technologies; organizations that use film and video-related technologies; manufacturer/vendors of related equipment and services; interested others. Promotes the use of motion media in the instructional and informational fields; works to educate schools and libraries regarding copyright laws as applied to film and video; offers networking opportunities among members and the sharing of information; lobbies for increased funds for school media materials; compiles statistics; sponsors market research. **Publications:** *AIME News* (quarterly); *Copyright Law: What Every School, College and Public School Library Should Know* and *Copyright: New Issues* .

7846 ■ Association of Moving Image Archivists
1313 N Vine St.
Hollywood, CA 90028
Ph:(323)463-1500
Fax:(323)463-1506
Co. E-mail: amia@amianet.org
URL: http://www.amianet.org
Contact: Wendy Shay, Pres./Dir.
Description: Works to advance the field of moving image archiving by fostering cooperation among individuals and institutions concerned with the collection, description, preservation, exhibition, and use of moving image materials (film and video). Seeks to

improve public awareness of preservation needs through educational programs. **Publications:** *The Moving Image* (semiannual).

7847 ■ Canadian Media Production Association
151 Slater St., Ste. 902
Ottawa, ON, Canada K1P 5H3
Ph:(613)233-1444
Free: 800-656-7440
Fax:(613)233-0073
Co. E-mail: angela.tupper@cmpa.ca
URL: http://www.cftpa.ca
Contact: Norm Bolen, Pres./CEO
Description: Represents film, television and interactive media companies across the country. Promotes and stimulates the Canadian production industry. Seeks to negotiate and manage labour agreements, and actively lobby the federal and provincial governments on various policy areas including taxation, trade, copyright, broadcasting and film. **Publications:** *Action Newsletter* (quarterly); *Guide* (annual).

7848 ■ Canadian Motion Picture Distribution Association–Association Canadienne des Distributeurs de Films
55 St. Clair Ave. W, Ste. 210
Toronto, ON, Canada M4T 2S4
Ph:(416)961-1888
Fax:(416)968-1016
Co. E-mail: info@cmpda.ca
URL: http://www.cmpda.ca
Description: Film studios and distributors; marketers and distributors of television programming. Promotes increased distribution of American films in Canada. Conducts marketing and promotional activities.

7849 ■ Content Delivery and Storage Association
39 N Bayles Ave.
Port Washington, NY 11050
Ph:(516)767-6720
Fax:(516)883-5793
Co. E-mail: mporter@contentdeliveryandstorage.org
URL: http://www.cdsaonline.org
Contact: Martin Porter, Exec. Dir.
Description: Serves as the advocate for the growth and development of all recording media and as a forum for the exchange of information regarding global trends and innovations. Provides members an opportunity to join forces and be a strong industry voice allowing them to grow and expand their business. Encompasses all facets of the recording media. **Publications:** *Mediaware* (9/year).

7850 ■ Directors Guild of Canada–La Guilde Canadienne des Realisateurs
111 Peter St., Ste. 402
Toronto, ON, Canada M5V 2H1
Ph:(416)482-6640
Free: 888-972-0098

Fax:(416)482-6639
Co. E-mail: mail@dgc.ca
URL: http://www.dgc.ca
Contact: Sturla Gunnarsson, Pres.
Description: Creative and logistical personnel in the film and television industries. Facilitates professional and economic advancement of members. Promotes and seeks to advance the quality and vitality of Canadian feature film and television production. Develops and maintains standards of training and practice; negotiates and enforces contracts and other collective agreements with employers on behalf of members; maintains dispute settlement and arbitration mechanisms. Facilitates communication among members; makes available member benefit and insurance programs; conducts lobbying activities. **Publications:** *Montage* (quarterly).

7851 ■ Documentary Organisation of Canada–Documentaristes du Canada
215 Spadina Ave., Ste. 126
Toronto, ON, Canada M5T 2C7
Ph:(416)599-3844
Free: 877-467-4485
Fax:(416)979-3936
Co. E-mail: info@docorg.ca
URL: http://www.docorg.ca
Contact: John Christou, Chm.
Description: Independent filmmakers. Promotes excellence in filmmaking; seeks to advance the economic interests of independent filmmakers. Provides professional development opportunities. Represents members' interests before government, industry organizations and the public; sponsors promotional programs. **Publications:** *POV* (quarterly).

7852 ■ Film Studies Association of Canada–Association Canadienne D'etudes Cinematographiques
University of Lethbridge
Centre for the Arts W864
4401 University Dr.
Lethbridge, AB, Canada T1K 3M4
Ph:(403)394-3922
Co. E-mail: aaron.taylor2@uleth.ca
URL: http://www.filmstudies.ca
Contact: Philippa Gates, Pres.
Description: Film studies institutes, educators, and students. Promotes the study and appreciation of the history and art of film and related media. Conducts research and educational programs. **Publications:** *Canadian Journal of Film Studies* (semiannual); *Continuity* (quarterly).

7853 ■ Independent Media Arts Alliance–Alliance Des Arts Mediatiques Independants
4067, Boul. Saint-Laurent, Ste. 200-A
Montreal, QC, Canada H2W 1Y7
Ph:(514)522-8240
Fax:(514)866-4725
Co. E-mail: info@imaa.ca
URL: http://www.imaa.ca
Contact: Amanda Dawn Christie, Pres.
Description: Regroups over 85 artist-run centres across Canada including production, distribution and

exhibition. Represents and advocates for independent media artists. **Publications:** *Annual Review* (annual).

7854 ■ InfoComm International

11242 Waples Mill Rd., Ste. 200
Fairfax, VA 22030
Ph:(703)273-7200
Free: 800-659-7469
Co. E-mail: customerservice@infocomm.org
URL: http://www.infocomm.org
Contact: Randal A. Lemke PhD, Exec. Dir.
Purpose: Represents for-profit individuals and organizations that derive revenue from the commercialization or utilization of communications technology. Ensures the credibility and desirability of its members' products and services by representing the communications industry to the public, business, education, and governments. **Publications:** *ICIA Membership Directory* (annual); *InfoCommunity News* (quarterly).

7855 ■ International Animated Film Association - Canada–Association Internationale du Film d'Animation

CP 5226
St. Laurent, QC, Canada H4L 4Z8
Co. E-mail: asifacanada@mail.com
URL: http://www.awn.com/asifa-canada
Description: Producers of animated films. Promotes excellence in film animation. Promotes and publicizes members' productions; serves as a clearinghouse on film animation; represents members' interests.

7856 ■ International Association of Audio Visual Communicators

PO Box 270779
Flower Mound, TX 75027
Ph:(469)464-4180
Fax:(469)464-4170
Co. E-mail: sheemonw@cindys.com
URL: http://www.cindys.com
Description: Media producers, managers, and creative and technical people in industry, government, education, and technical, promotional, and enrichment fields. .

7857 ■ International Documentary Association

1201 W 5th St., Ste. M270
Los Angeles, CA 90017
Ph:(213)534-3600
Fax:(213)534-3610
Co. E-mail: michael@documentary.org
URL: http://www.documentary.org
Contact: Michael Lumpkin, Exec. Dir.
Description: Individuals and organizations involved in nonfiction film and video. Objectives are: to promote nonfiction film and video; to encourage the progress of the documentary arts and sciences; to support the efforts of nonfiction film and videomakers throughout the world. Provides a forum for documentaries and allied members of the film and video industries to meet and discuss areas of mutual interest related to all aspects of nonfiction film and video arts, sciences, production, financing, and distribution. Holds screenings of all Oscar-nominated documentaries. .

7858 ■ Media Communications Association International

PO Box 5135
Madison, WI 53705-0135
Free: 888-899-6224
Fax:888-862-8150
Co. E-mail: loiswei@aol.com
URL: http://www.mca-i.org
Contact: Don Glass, Pres.-Elect
Description: Individuals engaged in multimedia communications needs analysis, scriptwriting, producing, directing, consulting and operations management in the video, multimedia and film fields. Seeks to advance the benefits and image of media communications professionals. **Publications:** *Media Communications International Association* (annual).

7859 ■ University Film and Video Association

3800 Barham Blvd., Ste. 103
Los Angeles, CA 90068
Free: (866)647-8382
Co. E-mail: ufvahome@aol.com
URL: http://www.ufva.org
Contact: Peter J. Bukalski, Treas.
Description: Professors and video/filmmakers concerned with the production and study of film and video in colleges and universities. Conducts research programs; operates placement service; presents annual grants. .

7860 ■ Wedding and Event Videographers Association International

8499 S Tamiami Trail
PMB 208
Sarasota, FL 34238
Ph:(941)923-5334
Fax:(941)921-3836
Co. E-mail: info@weva.com
URL: http://www.weva.com
Contact: Roy Chapman, Founder/Chm.
Description: Professional wedding and event videographers. Serves as a trade organization representing members' commercial interests. Provides educational programs and resources to wedding and event videographers. **Publications:** *The Business of Wedding and Special Event Videography*; *Wedding and Event Videography Resource Guide* .

DIRECTORIES OF EDUCATIONAL PROGRAMS

7861 ■ *Directory of Private Accredited Career Schools and Colleges of Technology*

Pub: Accrediting Commission of Career Schools and Colleges of Technology
Contact: Michale S. McComis, Exec. Dir.
Released: On web page. **Price:** Free. **Description:** Covers 3900 accredited post-secondary programs that provide training programs in business, trade, and technical fields, including various small business endeavors. Entries offer school name, address, phone, description of courses, job placement assistance, and requirements for admission. Arrangement is alphabetical.

7862 ■ *Film & Television Directory*

Pub: Peter Glenn Publications
Contact: Chip L. Brill, Director
Released: Biennial. **Price:** $30, individuals. **Covers:** More than 11,000 producers/production companies, crews, support services, and film commissions in the film, music, and video industries in the United States and parts of Canada. **Entries Include:** Company name, address, phone, fax, E-mail and URL addresses, name and title of contact. **Arrangement:** Classified by line of business. **Indexes:** Product/service; advertisers by name.

7863 ■ *The Ultimate Directory of Film Technicians*

Pub: Scarecrow Press Inc.
Contact: Billy H. Doyle, Author
Price: $70, individuals Hardback; $44.95, individuals Hardback. **Covers:** Film technicians from the beginning of the film industry to the present, including executives, producers, directors, screenwriters, cinematographers, set and costume designers, composers, art directors, choreographers, publicists, and editors. **Entries Include:** Birth and death dates and career information.

REFERENCE WORKS

7864 ■ "A&E Networks" in *Brandweek* (Vol. 49, April 21, 2008, No. 16, pp. SR9)

Pub: VNU Business Media, Inc.
Ed: Anthony Crupi. **Description:** Provides contact information for sales and marketing personnel for the A&E Networks as well as a listing of the station's top programming and an analysis of the current season and the target audience for those programs running in the current season. A&E has reinvented itself as a premium entertainment brand over the last five years and with its $2.5 million per episode acquisition of

The Sopranos, the station signaled that it was serious about getting back into the scripted programming business. The acquisition also helped the network compete against other cable networks and led to a 20 percent increase in prime-time viewers.

7865 ■ "ABC" in *Brandweek* (Vol. 49, April 21, 2008, No. 16, pp. SR6)

Pub: VNU Business Media, Inc.
Ed: John Consoli. **Description:** Provides contact information for sales and marketing personnel for the ABC network as well as a listing of the station's top programming and an analysis of the current season and the target audience for those programs running in the current season.

7866 ■ "ACTRA Phones It In" in *Canadian Business* (Vol. 80, January 15, 2007, No. 2, pp. 8)

Pub: Rogers Media
Ed: Denis Seguin. **Description:** The strike held by the members of the ACTRA or Canadian Cinema, Television and Radio Artists from January 8 2007, due to the contract dispute with the trade association representing Canadian producers, is discussed.

7867 ■ "Alliance Unit Signs Movie Distribution Deal" in *Globe & Mail* (January 24, 2006, pp. B6)

Pub: CTVglobemedia Publishing Inc.
Ed: Grant Robertson. **Description:** The details on the distribution agreement between Movie Distribution Income Fund and Weinstein Co. are presented. Movie Distribution Income Fund is a unit of Alliance Atlantis Communication Inc.

7868 ■ "Autoline Goes West" in *Michigan Vue* (Vol. 13, July-August 2008, No. 4, pp. 6)

Pub: Entrepreneur Media Inc.
Ed: Dave Gibbons. **Description:** Profile of Blue Sky Productions, a Detroit-based production company that produces the nationally syndicated television series "Autoline", which traditionally probes inside the Detroit auto industry; the company recently decided to shoot in Southern California, an area that now has an immense auto industry but has been virtually ignored by the media. Blue Sky originally slated four shows but ended up producing eleven due to the immense amount of material they discovered concerning the state of California's auto market.

7869 ■ "Beyond YouTube: New Uses for Video, Online and Off" in *Inc.* (October 2007, pp. 53-54)

Pub: Gruner & Jahr USA Publishing
Ed: Leah Hoffmann. **Description:** Small companies are using video technology for embedding messages into email, broadcasting live interactive sales and training seminars, as well as marketing campaigns. Experts offer insight into producing and broadcasting business videos.

7870 ■ "Boxing, Tech Giants Team to Help Teens" in *Hispanic Business* (January-February 2009, pp. 44)

Pub: Hispanic Business
Ed: Daniel Soussa. **Description:** Microsoft and Oscar de la Hoya are providing teens a head start for careers in the sciences by offering a competition in the categories of photography, short films or Web-based games.

7871 ■ "Business Through Hollywood's Lens" in *Harvard Business Review* (Vol. 88, October 2010, No. 10, pp. 146)

Pub: Harvard Business School Publishing
Ed: Batia Wiesnefeld, Gino Cattani. **Description:** The authors contend that businesses are likely to be portrayed as villains in movies because corruption has higher entertainment draw. However, movies also depict popular opinion, which encourages businesses to be accountable and to help build communities.

7872 ■ "Buzz Marketing for Movies" in *Business Horizons* (September-October 2007, pp. 395)

Pub: Elsevier Technology Publications
Ed: Iris Mohr. **Description:** Application of buzz marketing through the context of movie differentiation strategies such as cosmetic movie features, dif-

ferentiation to reach market segments, growing a movie segment, positioning to support the movie image, positioning to extend the movie image, and differentiation via non-traditional channels are all discussed.

7873 ■ *Canadian Society of Cinematographers—Directory*
Pub: Canadian Society of Cinematographers
Contact: Joan Hutton, President
Released: Biennial. **Covers:** Over 400 directors of photography, videographers, operators, assistants, and focus pullers in Canada. **Entries Include:** Name, address, phone, fax, biographical data, description of activities. **Arrangement:** Alphabetical. **Indexes:** Geographical.

7874 ■ "CBS" in *Brandweek* (Vol. 49, April 21, 2008, No. 16, pp. SR6)
Pub: VNU Business Media, Inc.
Ed: John Consoli. **Description:** Provides contact information for sales and marketing personnel for the CBS network as well as a listing of the station's top programming and an analysis of the current season and the target audience for those programs running in the current season.

7875 ■ "CBS Television Distribution" in *Brandweek* (Vol. 49, April 21, 2008, No. 16, pp. SR13)
Pub: VNU Business Media, Inc.
Ed: Marc Berman. **Description:** Provides contact information for sales and marketing personnel for CBS Television Distribution as well as a listing of the station's top programming and an analysis of the current season and the target audience for those programs running in the current season. Due to the unprecedented, decade-plus advantage of first-run leaders such as Wheel of Fortune, Oprah, Judge Judy and Entertainment Tonight, CBS is poised to remain a leader among the syndicates.

7876 ■ "Cineplex Sees Past the Big Picture" in *Globe & Mail* (February 8, 2007, pp. B9)
Pub: CTVglobemedia Publishing Inc.
Ed: Shirley Won. **Description:** Cineplex Entertainment LP reported $4.6 million profit in the final quarter of 2006. The movie chain is introducing video-game tournaments and live rock concerts to improve sales.

7877 ■ "Comcast Networks" in *Brandweek* (Vol. 49, April 21, 2008, No. 16, pp. SR9)
Pub: VNU Business Media, Inc.
Ed: Anthony Crupi. **Description:** Provides contact information for sales and marketing personnel for the Comcast networks as well as a listing of the station's top programming and an analysis of the current season and the target audience for those programs running in the current season. Experts believe Comcast will continue to acquire stations into their portfolio.

7878 ■ "Commotion Pictures; Bill C-10: Is It Censorship or Merely Inept?" in *Canadian Business* (Vol. 81, March 31, 2008, No. 5, pp. 10)
Pub: Rogers Media
Ed: Denis Seguin. **Description:** Filmmakers are claiming that Bill C-10 amounts to censorship as it could retract a production's eligibility for a tax credit if it is deemed offensive. However, the bill's backers say that the bill protects against tax dollars being directed at productions that run contrary to public policy.

7879 ■ "The CW" in *Brandweek* (Vol. 49, April 21, 2008, No. 16, pp. SR8)
Pub: VNU Business Media, Inc.
Ed: John Consoli. **Description:** Provides contact information for sales and marketing personnel for the CW network as well as a listing of the station's top programming and an analysis of the current season and the target audience for those programs running in the current season. Purchases of advertising feel that Warner Bros. and CBS made a mistake merging The WB and UPN into the new CW rather than folding UPN into the more-established WB; compared to last season ratings are down more than 20 percent across the board.

7880 ■ "Deal Made for Pontiac Home of Film Studio" in *Crain's Detroit Business* (Vol. 25, June 1, 2009, No. 22, pp. 3)
Pub: Crain Communications Inc. - Detroit
Ed: Daniel Duggan. **Description:** Details of the $75 million movie production and training facility in Pontiac, Michigan are revealed.

7881 ■ *Directors Guild of America—Directory of Members*
Pub: Directors Guild of America Inc.
Contact: Michael Apted, President
Ed: Darrell L. Hope, Editor, darrellh@dga.org. **Released:** Annual, February; Latest edition 2009. **Price:** $25 plus $6 shipping. **Covers:** Over 11,000 motion picture and television directors and their assistants providing films and tapes for entertainment, commercial, industrial, and other non-entertainment fields; international coverage. **Entries Include:** DGA member name; contact or representative address, phone; specialty; brief description of experience and credits. **Arrangement:** Alphabetical. **Indexes:** Geographical, women and minority members, agents.

7882 ■ "Discovery Networks" in *Brandweek* (Vol. 49, April 21, 2008, No. 16, pp. SR9)
Pub: VNU Business Media, Inc.
Ed: Anthony Crupi. **Description:** Provides contact information for sales and marketing personnel for the Discovery networks as well as a listing of the station's top programming and an analysis of the current season and the target audience for those programs running in the current season. The networks flagship station returned to the top 10 in 2007, averaging 1.28 million viewers.

7883 ■ "Disney-ABC Domestic Television Distribution" in *Brandweek* (Vol. 49, April 21, 2008, No. 16, pp. SR13)
Pub: VNU Business Media, Inc.
Ed: Marc Berman. **Description:** Provides contact information for sales and marketing personnel for Disney-ABC Domestic Television Distribution as well as a listing of the station's top programming and an analysis of the current season and the target audience for those programs running in the current season.

7884 ■ "The Display Group Is Super-Sized" in *Michigan Vue* (Vol. 13, July-August 2008, No. 4, pp. 34)
Pub: Entrepreneur Media Inc.
Description: Profile of the Display Group, located in downtown Detroit, this company provides custom designed mobile marketing displays as well as special event production services for trade show displays. The rental house and design service is also beginning to see more business due to the film initiative, which provides incentives for films that are shooting in Michigan.

7885 ■ "Elemental Nabs $5.5 Million" in *The Business Journal-Portland* (Vol. 25, July 18, 2008, No. 19, pp. 1)
Pub: American City Business Journals, Inc.
Ed: Aliza Earnshaw. **Description:** Elemental Technologies Inc., a Portland, Oregon-based software company got $5.5 million in new funding, bringing its total invested capital to $7.1 million in nine months since October 2008. The company plans to launch Badaboom, software for converting video into various formats, later in 2008.

7886 ■ "Ex-MP? Ex-con? Exactly!" in *Canadian Business* (Vol. 83, October 12, 2010, No. 17, pp. 16)
Pub: Rogers Media Ltd.
Ed: James Cowan. **Description:** British author Jeffrey Archer's novels could be made into movies. Archer sold 250 million books in 63 countries, which include political thrillers, spy novels, and crime capers.

7887 ■ "Exiting Stage Left" in *Baltimore Business Journal* (Vol. 28, June 18, 2010, No. 6, pp. 1)
Pub: Baltimore Business Journal
Ed: Scott Dance. **Description:** Film professionals including crew members and actors have been leaving Maryland to find work in other states such as

Michigan, Louisiana, and Georgia where bigger budgets and film production incentives are given. Other consequences of this trend in local TV and film production are discussed.

7888 ■ "Film Giants Disney, Pixar Talk Marriage" in *Globe & Mail* (January 19, 2006, pp. B1)
Pub: CTVglobemedia Publishing Inc.
Ed: Merissa Marr; Nick Wingfield. **Description:** The plans of Walt Disney Co. to acquire Pixar Animation Studios are presented.

7889 ■ "Film Incentives: A Hit or a Flop?" in *Michigan Vue* (Vol. 13, July-August 2008, No. 4, pp. 10)
Pub: Entrepreneur Media Inc.
Description: Michigan's new film incentive legislation is fulfilling its core purpose, according to Lisa Dancsok of the Michigan Economic Development Corp. (MEDC), by kickstarting the state's entry into the multi-billion dollar industry; the initiative is considered to be very competitive with other states and countries and is thought to be a way in which to help revitalize Michigan's struggling economy.

7890 ■ "For DVD Company, No Extra Innings: Capturing a Season Takes Fast Work" in *Boston Business Journal* (Vol. 27, December 7, 2007)
Pub: American City Business Journals Inc.
Ed: Terry Lefton. **Description:** Details of the development of MLB's annual World Series film by MLB Productions are discussed. The company is compelled to produce the film in a short period of time due to a promised November 27, 2007 delivery date. According to Elizabeth Scott, MLB vice president of programming and business affairs, she was concerned about the things that could directly affect sales.

7891 ■ "Fox" in *Brandweek* (Vol. 49, April 21, 2008, No. 16, pp. SR3)
Pub: VNU Business Media, Inc.
Ed: John Consoli. **Description:** Provides contact information for sales and marketing personnel for the Fox network as well as a listing of the station's top programming and an analysis of the current season and the target audience for those programs running in the current season. In terms of upfront advertising dollars, it looks as if Fox will be competing against NBC for third place due to its success at courting the 18-49-year-old male demographic.

7892 ■ "Fox Cable Entertainment Networks" in *Brandweek* (Vol. 49, April 21, 2008, No. 16, pp. SR10)
Pub: VNU Business Media, Inc.
Ed: Anthony Crupi. **Description:** Provides contact information for sales and marketing personnel for the Fox Cable Entertainment networks as well as a listing of the station's top programming and an analysis of the current season and the target audience for those programs running in the current season.

7893 ■ "Free Fall" in *Canadian Business* (Vol. 79, September 11, 2006, No. 18, pp. 28)
Pub: Rogers Media
Ed: Zena Olijnyk. **Description:** Second quarter results of Imax Corp are reviewed. The company's performance and its future prospects are also presented.

7894 ■ "Frost and Sullivan" in *Investment Weekly News* (December 19, 2009, pp. 150)
Pub: Investment Weekly News
Description: Demand for video analytics solutions concerning security and business intelligence is growing, especially in such regions as the Middle East, Europe and Africa. Significant advancements in the field of intelligent analysis of video hold promising opportunities in security applications.

7895 ■ "How Pixar Fosters Collective Creativity" in *Harvard Business Review* (Vol. 86, September 2008, No. 9, pp. 64)
Pub: Harvard Business School Press
Ed: Ed Catmull. **Description:** Pixar Animation Studios illustrates peer-culture methods for fostering product development. These include allowing any

employee to communicate with any other employee, providing a safe environment for new ideas, and watching the academic community closely for innovations.

7896 ■ "Imax Becomes Toast of Movie Industry" in *Globe & Mail* **(January 10, 2006, pp. B2)**
Pub: CTVglobemedia Publishing Inc.
Ed: Grant Robertson. **Description:** The United States-based mainstream theatres company Imax Corp., has reported a 35 percent rise in its ticket sales, showing the growing interest of the American audience in the Imax formatted films. A complete focus on this trend is presented.

7897 ■ "Imax in Play as It Explores Options" in *Globe & Mail* **(March 10, 2006, pp. B3)**
Pub: CTVglobemedia Publishing Inc.
Ed: Shirley Won. **Description:** Imax Corp. has put up itself for sale, and has also confirmed that it has received unsolicited offers for purchase.

7898 ■ "It's a New Game: Killerspin Pushes Table Tennis to Extreme Heights" in *Black Enterprise* **(Vol. 37, October 2006, No. 3, pp. 73)**
Pub: Earl G. Graves Publishing Co. Inc.
Ed: Bridget McCrea. **Description:** Profile of Robert Blackwell and his company Killerspin L.L.C., which is popularizing the sport of table tennis. Killerspin has hit $1 million in revenues due to product sales primarily generated through the company's website, magazines, DVDs, and event ticket sales.

7899 ■ "Johnny Royal of Luthier Society Unveils Archimedes 1.0 Trailer" in *Internet Wire* **(October 22, 2009)**
Pub: Comtex News Network, Inc.
Description: Luthier Society, a social media and viral branding agency, has released the first viral video for the company's ROI weighted-value software platform named Archimedes 1.0; users of the software will be able to determine the depth of their outreach efforts, saturation rate, value of their Internet presence and the geo-spatial location of their audience; this will give a true, monetized value for ROI (Return on Investment) in social media marketing.

7900 ■ "Johnson's Taps Online Animation" in *Marketing to Women* **(Vol. 21, April 2008, No. 4, pp. 3)**
Pub: EPM Communications, Inc.
Description: Johnson's has launched a new integrated campaign for its baby lotion in an effort to appeal to the growing number of moms online.

7901 ■ "Kawasaki's New Top Gun" in *Brandweek* **(Vol. 49, April 21, 2008, No. 16, pp. 18)**
Pub: VNU Business Media, Inc.
Description: Discusses Kawasaki's marketing plan which included designing an online brochure in which visitors could create a video by building their own test track on a grid and then selecting visual special effects and musical overlay. This engaging and innovative marketing technique generated more than 166,000 unique users within the first three months of being launched.

7902 ■ "The Last Ingredient?" in *Canadian Business* **(Vol. 81, October 13, 2008, No. 17, pp. 88)**
Pub: Rogers Media Ltd.
Ed: Rachel Pulfer. **Description:** Views and information on Cookie Jar Group's plan to acquire rights for Strawberry Shortcake and the Care Bears are discussed. The move would make Cookie Jar a major player in the global children's entertainment market. Cookie Jar chief executive, Michael Hirsh is believed to be securing funds for the planned $195 million acquisition.

7903 ■ "The Life Changers" in *Canadian Business* **(Vol. 81, October 27, 2008, No. 18, pp. 86)**
Pub: Rogers Media Ltd.
Description: The first season of 'The Life Changers' was produced in September 2007 to feature stories about research and development (R&D) efforts by

universities in Atlantic Canada. The program addresses the need to inform the public about university R&D and its outcomes.

7904 ■ "Lifetime Networks" in *Brandweek* **(Vol. 49, April 21, 2008, No. 16, pp. SR10)**
Pub: VNU Business Media, Inc.
Ed: Anthony Crupi. **Description:** Provides contact information for sales and marketing personnel for the ABC network as well as a listing of the station's top programming and an analysis of the current season and the target audience for those programs running in the current season. Lifetime will still produce its original signature movies but will now focus its emphasis more clearly on series development in order to appeal to a younger, hipper female demographic.

7905 ■ "Lights, Camera, Action: Tools for Creating Video Blogs" in *Inc.* **(Volume 32, December 2010, No. 10, pp. 57)**
Pub: Inc. Magazine
Ed: John Brandon. **Description:** A video blog is a good way to spread company news, talk about products, and stand out among traditional company blogs. New editing software can create two- to four-minute blogs using a webcam and either Windows Live Essentials, Apple iLife 2011, Powerdirector 9 Ultra, or Adobe Visual Communicator 3.

7906 ■ "Lights, Camera...Incentive" in *Austin Business JournalInc.* **(Vol. 28, October 10, 2008, No. 30, pp. 1)**
Pub: American City Business Journals
Ed: Sandra Zaragoza. **Description:** Film industry insiders are saying that state level tax breaks are needed to boost the sector, together with the help of the $700 billion bailout bill, which is expected to provide $470 million in tax incentives to the movie industry. Other details on filmmakers' call for more tax incentives for Texas' film industry are discussed.

7907 ■ "Like Being There" in *Canadian Business* **(Vol. 79, August 14, 2006, No. 16-17, pp. 77)**
Pub: Rogers Media
Ed: Gerry Blackwell. **Description:** Latest video conferencing facilities at the Halo Collaboration Studio, are discussed.

7908 ■ "Looking Like a Million Bucks" in *Entrepreneur* **(Vol. 37, August 2009, No. 8, pp. 102)**
Pub: Entrepreneur Media, Inc.
Ed: Jason Daley. **Description:** Sunset Tan's Jeff Bozz says he and Devin Haman are executive producers of the show and that they want to stretch the truth a bit and make fun of it. Haman says the business is all about VIP service for everyone and that they want all their clients to feel like celebrities.

7909 ■ "Making Sense of Ambiguous Evidence" in *Harvard Business Review* **(Vol. 86, September 2008, No. 9, pp. 53)**
Pub: Harvard Business School Press
Ed: Lisa Burrell. **Description:** Documentary filmmaker Errol Morris emphasizes the role of perception in portraying objective reality, and how investigation and analysis enhance the accuracy of that portrayal.

7910 ■ *Media Review Digest*
Pub: Pierian Press
Ed: C. Edward Wall, Editor. **Released:** Annual. **Price:** $295, individuals. **Publication Includes:** List of producers and suppliers of entertainment and educational media, including film, video, audio, and miscellaneous resources. **Entries Include:** Name, address. Principal content of publication is a list of citations and cross-references to reviews found in non-print entertainment and educational media. **Arrangement:** Classified by type of media, then by company name.

7911 ■ "Moosylvania Releases Latest XL Marketing Trends Report" in *Wireless News* **(October 6, 2009)**
Pub: Close-Up Media
Description: Moosylvania, a digital promotion and branding agency that also has an on-site research facility, has released its 2nd XL Marketing Trends Report which focuses on digital video; the study

defines the top digital video trends marketers must focus on now and well into the future and notes that in 2010, Mobile Web Devices, such as smart phones will outnumber computers in this country. Statistical data included.

7912 ■ "Moving Pitchers" in *Entrepreneur* **(Vol. 37, December 2009, No. 12, pp. 46)**
Pub: Entrepreneur Media, Inc.
Ed: Gwen Moran. **Description:** Online videos have become accessible for business development and marketing due to the decline in production costs and the growth in viewership. Research company comScore reveals that 153 million Internet users in the U.S. watched an online video in August 2009. The benefits of using online videos to further market one's company are explained.

7913 ■ "MTV Networks" in *Brandweek* **(Vol. 49, April 21, 2008, No. 16, pp. SR10)**
Pub: VNU Business Media, Inc.
Ed: Anthony Crupi. **Description:** Provides contact information for sales and marketing personnel for the MTV networks as well as a listing of the station's top programming and an analysis of the current season and the target audience for those programs running in the current season. MTV networks include MTV, VH1, Nickelodeon and Comedy Central.

7914 ■ *My Life From Scratch: A Sweet Journey of Starting Over, One Cake at a Time*
Pub: Broadway Books
Released: June 8, 2010. **Price:** $14.00. **Description:** Lively account of Old World recipes, Bullock-Prado, a former Hollywood film developer and sister to actress Sandra Bullock, recounts the joys and heartbreak of running her own patisserie in Montpelier, Vermont. Having fled Los Angeles with her husband, Ray for the simpler pleasures of a small town near the Green Mountains, she opened her own bake shop, Gesine Confectionary in 2004, mostly on the fame of the macaroons she refashioned from her German mother's favorite almond treat, mandelhoernchen (and the casual mention of her sister in an interview). Her memoir follows one day in a busy baker's life, from waking at 3 a.m. to prepare the batter and bake her croissants, scones, and sticky buns, before opening her shop at 7 a.m., through the hectic lunch, and 3 p.m. tea time.

7915 ■ "NBC" in *Brandweek* **(Vol. 49, April 21, 2008, No. 16, pp. SR6)**
Pub: VNU Business Media, Inc.
Ed: John Consoli. **Description:** Provides contact information for sales and marketing personnel for the NBC network as well as a listing of the station's top programming and an analysis of the current season and the target audience for those programs running in the current season. NBC also devised a new strategy of announcing its prime-time schedule 52 weeks in advance which was a hit for advertisers who felt this gave them a better opportunity to plan for product placement. Even with the station's creative sales programs, they could face a challenge from Fox in terms of upfront advertisement purchases.

7916 ■ "NBC Universal Cable" in *Brandweek* **(Vol. 49, April 21, 2008, No. 16, pp. SR11)**
Pub: VNU Business Media, Inc.
Ed: Anthony Crupi. **Description:** Provides contact information for sales and marketing personnel for the NBC Universal Cable networks as well as a listing of the station's top programming and an analysis of the current season and the target audience for those programs running in the current season. The network's stations include USA, Sci Fi and Bravo. Ad revenue for the network grew 30 percent in the first quarter.

7917 ■ "NBC Universal Domestic Television Distribution" in *Brandweek* **(Vol. 49, April 21, 2008, No. 16, pp. SR13)**
Pub: VNU Business Media, Inc.
Ed: Marc Berman. **Description:** Provides contact information for sales and marketing personnel for NBC Universal Domestic Television Distribution as

well as a listing of the station's top programming and an analysis of the current season and the target audience for those programs running in the current season.

7918 ■ "A Network of One: Local Writer Adds Web Interviews to Creative Output" in *La Crosse Tribune* (September 14, 2009)
Pub: La Crosse Tribune
Ed: Geri Parlin. **Description:** Profile of Andrew Revels, a freelance and aspiring writer, who has created a website in order to help gain attention for his own writing as well as for other local artists, musicians and comedians. His latest endeavor includes interviewing local talent and broadcasting the interviews on his site each week.

7919 ■ "New Recession-Proof Internet Marketing Package Allows Businesses to Ramp Up Web Traffic and Profits" in *PR Newswire* (Jan. 25, 2010)
Pub: PR Newswire Association, LLC
Description: Profile of Reel Web Design, a leading marketing firm in New York City that caters to small to medium sized businesses with smaller budgets that need substantial return on investment; Reel Web Design offers video production and submission, web design and maintenance and press release writing among additional services.

7920 ■ "New TurnHere Survey Reveals Online Video Trends" in *Internet Wire* (October 22, 2009)
Pub: Comtex News Network, Inc.
Description: TurnHere, Inc., the leading online video marketing services company, released the findings of its recent survey regarding current and future trends in online video among marketing agencies and brand recognition; the report found that online video has and will continue to play a prominent role in the realm of marketing edging out both search and email marketing campaigns. Additional highlights and statistical data included.

7921 ■ "No Risk? No Reward" in *Canadian Business* (Vol. 79, September 11, 2006, No. 18, pp. 93)
Pub: Rogers Media
Ed: Dennis Seguin. **Description:** Box office performances of the Canadian films are presented. Strategies to revitalize the film businesses in Canada are suggested.

7922 ■ "No Straight Lines: How Video Visionary Julien 'Little X' Lutz Creates His Images" in *Black Enterprise* (Vol. 38, January 2008)
Pub: Earl G. Graves Publishing Co. Inc.
Ed: Sonia Alleyne. **Description:** Profile of Julien Lutz, who turned his passion for drawing into a successful career.

7923 ■ "Northern Overexposure" in *Canadian Business* (Vol. 79, August 14, 2006, No. 16-17, pp. 36)
Pub: Rogers Media
Description: Fall in revenue from foreign film productions in Canada due to its overexposure, and incentives offered by other nations to foreign film productions, are discussed.

7924 ■ "Note to Marketers: A Viral Video Has a Life of Its Own" in *Advertising Age* (Vol. 80, October 5, 2009, No. 33, pp. 29)
Pub: Crain's Communications
Ed: Ken Wheaton. **Description:** Internet marketers do not decide whether or not an online video goes viral. It is the audience that decides what online videos to spread and such fare is usually passed around due to its content being downright witty or creative or so laughably bad that the audience wants to share it.

7925 ■ "Online Marketing and Promotion of Canadian Films via Social Media Tools" in *CNW Group* (January 27, 2010)
Pub: Comtex News Network, Inc.
Description: Telefilm Canada announced the launch of a pilot initiative aimed at encouraging the integration of online marketing and the use of social media

tools into means of distribution ahead of a films' theatrical release. During this pilot phase Web-Cine 360 will target French-language feature films.

7926 ■ "Out to Draw Work, Talent" in *Crain's Detroit Business* (Vol. 24, April 14, 2008, No. 15, pp. 3)
Pub: Crain Communications, Inc.
Ed: Bill Shea. **Description:** Profile of Southfield-based Kinetic Post Inc., a growing post-production house that offers video, audio, animation, print, online and related services to corporations and advertising agencies.

7927 ■ "People; E-Commerce, Online Games, Mobile Apps" in *Advertising Age* (Vol. 80, October 19, 2009, No. 35, pp. 14)
Pub: Crain's Communications
Ed: Nat Ives. **Description:** Profile of People Magazine and the ways in which the publisher is moving its magazine forward by exploring new concepts in a time of declining newsstand sales and advertising pages; among the strategies is e-commerce such as the brand People Style Watch in which consumers are able highlight clothing and jewelry and then connect to retailers' sites and a channel on Taxi TV, the network of video-touch screens in New Your City taxis.

7928 ■ "People; E-Commerce, Online Games, Mobile Apps: This Isn't Your Mom's People" in *Advertising Age* (Vol. 80, October 19, 2009, No. 35)
Pub: Crain's Communications
Ed: Nat Ives. **Description:** Profile of People Magazine and the ways in which the publisher is moving its magazine forward by exploring new concepts in a time of declining newsstand sales and advertising pages; among the strategies are e-commerce such as the brand People Style Watch in which consumers are able highlight clothing and jewelry and then connect to retailers' sites and a channel on Taxi TV, the network of video-touch screens in New Your City taxis.

7929 ■ "Picture of Success" in *Black Enterprise* (Vol. 38, December 2007, No. 5, pp. 71)
Pub: Earl G. Graves Publishing Co. Inc.
Ed: Sheiresa McRae. **Description:** Profile of Kenya Cagle, president and CEO of Caglevision Inc., an independent motion picture production company. Cagle, former off-Broadway child actor, kept his company afloat with financial backing and support from friends, employees, and business colleagues.

7930 ■ *The Pixar Touch: The Making of a Company*
Pub: Pantheon Books
Ed: David A. Price. **Released:** 2009. **Price:** $27.95. **Description:** Profile of how Pixar's founders turned their computer-animated films into a successful movie studio.

7931 ■ "Port in the Storm" in *Canadian Business* (Vol. 81, October 13, 2008, No. 17, pp. 101)
Pub: Rogers Media Ltd.
Ed: Calvin Leung. **Description:** Interport Inc.'s state-of-the-art studio complex in Toronto is discussed. The strong Canadian dollar, along with disputes within the movie industry, are creating challenges for the studio to secure Hollywood projects. Interport plans to compete for Hollywood projects based on quality.

7932 ■ "Pretentious and Loving It" in *Entrepreneur* (Vol. 37, August 2009, No. 8, pp. 34)
Pub: Entrepreneur Media, Inc.
Ed: Eric Mahoney. **Description:** Pitchfork.com features reviews of albums from independent artists. Their most innovative section is Pitchfork.tv, featuring videos of bands, and Forkcast along with their Features section that contains articles about bands and their histories.

7933 ■ "Promoting Academic Programs Using Online Videos" in *Business Communication Quarterly* (December 2007, pp. 478)
Pub: Sage Publications USA
Ed: Thomas Clark, Julie Stewart. **Description:** Xavier Entrepreneurial Center successfully used online videos to promote the effectiveness of its academic programs. Online videos are a cost-effective way of publicizing academic programs.

7934 ■ "Push Is On To Build Region's Prospects In Film Industry" in *Crain's Cleveland Business* (Vol. 28, November 19, 2007, No. 46, pp. 1)
Pub: Crain Communications, Inc.
Ed: Jay Miller. **Description:** Overview of a bill that has been introduced by state Representative Thomas Patton that would grant a 25 percent state income tax credit on investments of $300,000 or more in motion picture or television productions filmed in Ohio.

7935 ■ "The Rage Offstage at Marvel" in *Barron's* (Vol. 88, June 30, 2008, No. 26, pp. 19)
Pub: Dow Jones & Co., Inc.
Ed: Bill Alpert. **Description:** Lawsuits against Marvel Entertainment and Stan Lee are pushing the claims from Peter F. Paul that Stan Lee Media was undone by the actions of the accused. Paul's associates argue that Stan Lee Media owns rights to Marvel characters and that they want half the profits that Marvel is making.

7936 ■ "Ready, Aim, (Cool) Fire" in *Saint Louis Business Journal* (Vol. 32, September 2, 2011, No. 1, pp. 1)
Pub: Saint Louis Business Journal
Ed: E.B. Solomont. **Description:** Coolfire Originals' CEO Jeff Keane is co-producing 'Welcome Sweetie Pie's' with Los Angeles, California-based Pilgrims Films and Television Films for the Oprah Winfrey Network. The reality show focuses on restaurant owner Robbie Montgomery of Sweetie Pie's in St. Louis, Missouri.

7937 ■ "Recovery on Tap for 2010?" in *Orlando Business Journal* (Vol. 26, January 1, 2010, No. 31, pp. 1)
Pub: American City Business Journals
Ed: Melanie Stawicki Azam, Richard Bilbao, Christopher Boyd, Anjali Fluker. **Description:** Economic forecasts for Central Florida's leading business sectors in 2010 are presented. These sectors include housing, film and TV, sports business, law, restaurants, aviation, tourism and hospitality, banking and finance, commercial real estate, retail, health care, insurance, higher education, and manufacturing. According to some local executives, Central Florida's economy will slowly recover in 2010.

7938 ■ "Red One and The Rain Chronicles" in *Michigan Vue* (Vol. 13, July-August 2008, No. 4, pp. 30)
Pub: Entrepreneur Media Inc.
Ed: Evan Cornish. **Description:** Troy-based film school the Motion Picture Institute (MPI) implemented the latest technology by shooting the second of their trilogy, "The Rain Chronicles", on the Red One camera. This is the first feature film in Michigan to utilize this exciting new camera, which includes proprietary software for rendering and color correction. Brian K. Johnson heads up the visual effects team as visual effects supervisor and lead CG artist. His company, Dream Conduit Studios, had to tackle the task of employing the new work flow through a post-production pipeline that would allow him to attack complex visual effects shots, many of which were shot with a moving camera, a technique rarely seen in films at this budgetary level where the camera is traditionally locked off.

7939 ■ "Regal Venture Puts Imax Back in the Spotlight" in *Globe & Mail* (March 13, 2007, pp. B5)
Pub: CTVglobemedia Publishing Inc.
Ed: Shirley Won. **Description:** Imax Corp. has signed new contract with cinema hall operating giant Regal Entertainment Corp. for constructing two more giant screen theaters. Share prices of Imax Corp. have increased sharply after this announcement.

7940 ■ **"ROIonline Announces Streaming Video Products"** in *Marketing Weekly News* (December 5, 2009, pp. 155)
Pub: Investment Weekly News
Description: ROIonline LLC, an Internet marketing firm serving business-to-business and the industrial marketplace, has added streaming video options to the Internet solutions it offers its clients; due to the huge increase of broadband connections, videos are now commonplace on the Internet and can often convey a company's message in a must more efficient, concise and effective way that will engage a website's visitor thus delivering a high return on a company's investment.

7941 ■ **"S3 Entertainment Group Partners with WFW International for Film Services in Michigan"** in *Michigan Vue* (July-August 2008)
Pub: Entrepreneur Media Inc.
Description: William F. White (WFW), one of North America's largest production equipment providers has partnered with S3 Entertainment Group (S3EG), a Michigan-based full-service film production services company due to the new incentives package which currently offers the highest incentives in the United States, up to 42 percent. S3EG will actively store, lease, manage, distribute and sell WFW's equipment to the growing number of production teams that are filming in the state.

7942 ■ **"Screen Time"** in *Canadian Business* (Vol. 81, October 13, 2008, No. 17, pp. 93)
Pub: Rogers Media Ltd.
Ed: Calvin Leung. **Description:** Young Canadian entertainment business up-and-comers like Ari Lantos and Brian Mossof plan to produce movies that cold earn and entertain audiences rather than focusing on winning awards. English movies continue to struggle in Canada, while French-language films continue to thrive. Details on Canada's movie industry are furnished.

7943 ■ **"Scripps Networks"** in *Brandweek* (Vol. 49, April 21, 2008, No. 16, pp. SR12)
Pub: VNU Business Media, Inc.
Ed: Anthony Crupi. **Description:** Provides contact information for sales and marketing personnel for the Scripps networks as well as a listing of the station's top programming and an analysis of the current season and the target audience for those programs running in the current season. Scripps networks include HGTV and the Food Network. HGTV boasts on of the industry's best commercial-retention averages, keeping nearly 97 percent of its viewers during advertising breaks.

7944 ■ **"Several Studio Projects in Production"** in *Crain's Detroit Business* (Vol. 26, January 18, 2010, No. 3, pp. 21)
Pub: Crain Communications, Inc.
Ed: Bill Shea. **Description:** Overview of several projects in development in the metro Detroit area due to Michigan's film industry incentives which include a 25 percent tax credit for infrastructure projects.

7945 ■ *The SHOOT Directory for Commercial Production and Postproduction*
Pub: Nielsen Business Media
Contact: Roberta Griefer, Publisher
E-mail: rgriefer@shootonline.com
Ed: Robert Goldrich, Editor, rgoldrich@shootonline.com. **Released:** Annual, latest edition June 2004. **Price:** $99 plus shipping and handling charges. **Covers:** Companies that provide television commercial production and postproduction services, including film video and audio production, duplication, editing, animation, film-to-tape transfer, and standards conversion in the U.S. and Canada. **Entries Include:** Company name, address, phone, fax, names and titles of key personnel. **Arrangement:** Classified by type of company. **Indexes:** Geographical.

7946 ■ **"Show and Tell"** in *Entrepreneur* (Vol. 36, May 2008, No. 5, pp. 54)
Pub: Entrepreneur Media, Inc.
Ed: Heather Clancy. **Description:** FreshStart Telephone uses recorded video testimonials of customers, by using Pure Digital Flip Video that downloads

content directly to the computer, and uploads it in the company's website to promote their wireless phone service.

7947 ■ **"Small Businesses Benefiting from Movie-Struck Hub"** in *Boston Business Journal* (Vol. 27, October 12, 2007, No. 37, pp. 1)
Pub: American City Business Journals Inc.
Ed: Naomi R. Kooker. **Description:** Revision of the Massachusetts' film tax credits has attracted filming of major motion pictures in the state and local businesses have benefited. A list of businesses that saw boosts from the movie-making industry's presence is presented.

7948 ■ **"Sony Pictures Television"** in *Brandweek* (Vol. 49, April 21, 2008, No. 16, pp. SR13)
Pub: VNU Business Media, Inc.
Ed: Marc Berman. **Description:** Provides contact information for sales and marketing personnel for Sony Pictures Television Distribution as well as a listing of the station's top programming and an analysis of the current season and the target audience for those programs running in the current season.

7949 ■ **"State Expects Increase of $50 Million from Film Bills; Come Back, Al Roker"** in *Crain's Detroit Business* (March 24, 2008)
Pub: Crain Communications, Inc.
Ed: Bill Shea. **Description:** Overview of the new film initiative and its incentives designed to entice more film work to Michigan; the measures could bring $50 million to $100 million in movie production work for the rest of this year compared to the $4 million total the state saw last year. Also discusses the show "DEA" which was filmed in Detroit and stars Al Roker.

7950 ■ **"State Film Business Tops $1.3 Billion"** in *The Business Journal-Portland* (Vol. 25, August 22, 2008, No. 24, pp. 1)
Pub: American City Business Journals, Inc.
Ed: Andy Giegerich. **Description:** Oregon's film industry has generated $1.39 billion in direct and indirect economic impact in 2007, a 55 percent rise from 2005 levels. The growth of the industry is attributed to tax incentives issued in 2007, which attracted film production companies from other states.

7951 ■ **"Sticking to Stories; Havey Ovshinksy Changes Method, Keeps the Mission"** in *Crain's Detroit Business* (Vol. 24, March 31, 2008)
Pub: Crain Communications, Inc.
Ed: Daniel Duggan. **Description:** Profile of Harvey Ovshinsky, an award-winning documentary filmmaker who has reinvented his work with corporations who want to market themselves with the transition to digital media. His company, HKO Media, takes Ovshinsky's art of storytelling and enhances it through multimedia operations on the Internet through a joint venture with a man he once mentored, Bob Kernen.

7952 ■ **"Summit, Lions Gate are in Talks to Merge Studios"** in *Wall Street Journal Eastern Edition* (November 29, 2011, pp. B2)
Pub: Dow Jones & Company Inc.
Ed: Erica Orden, Michelle Kung. **Description:** Movie studio Summit Entertainment LLC is in talks with television producer Lions Gate Entertainment Corporation about a possible merger. Previous talks have taken place, but no deal was ever reached. Such a deal would create a large, independent studio able to compete in the market with the big Hollywood giants.

7953 ■ **"Suspense Hangs Over Fledging Film Industry"** in *Crain's Detroit Business* (Vol. 26, January 18, 2010, No. 3, pp. 3)
Pub: Crain Communications, Inc.
Ed: Bill Shea. **Description:** Overview of the film incentive package which has fostered a growth in the industry with 52 productions completed in 2009, bringing in $223.6 million in gross in-state production expenditures of which the state will refund $87.2 million. Opposition to the incentives has been growing among legislatures who believe that the initiatives cost more than they ultimately bring into the state.

Experts believe that the initiatives will remain since they have already fostered economic growth and are good for the state's image.

7954 ■ **"Telemundo"** in *Brandweek* (Vol. 49, April 21, 2008, No. 16, pp. SR8)
Pub: VNU Business Media, Inc.
Ed: John Consoli. **Description:** Provides contact information for sales and marketing personnel for the Telemundo network as well as a listing of the station's top programming and an analysis of the current season and the target audience for those programs running in the current season.

7955 ■ **"This Just In. State House Introduces Film-Industry Stimulus Bills"** in *Crain's Detroit Business* (Vol. 24, March 3, 2008, No. 9)
Pub: Crain Communications Inc. - Detroit
Description: House Bills 5841-5856 would give Michigan the most competitive incentives in the U.S. to encourage projects by film industry. Provisions of the bill are outlined.

7956 ■ **"Ticket Tiff Erupts Over Fund Ads"** in *Globe & Mail* (January 31, 2007, pp. B1)
Pub: CTVglobemedia Publishing Inc.
Description: The opposition of Cineplex Entertainment LP to Mackenzie Financial Corp.'s advertisement about high cost of movie ticket is discussed.

7957 ■ **"Turner Broadcasting System"** in *Brandweek* (Vol. 49, April 21, 2008, No. 16, pp. SR13)
Pub: VNU Business Media, Inc.
Ed: Anthony Crupi. **Description:** Provides contact information for sales and marketing personnel for the Turner Broadcasting System networks as well as a listing of the station's top programming and an analysis of the current season and the target audience for those programs running in the current season. Recent acquisitions are also discussed.

7958 ■ **"Twentieth Television"** in *Brandweek* (Vol. 49, April 21, 2008, No. 16, pp. SR16)
Pub: VNU Business Media, Inc.
Ed: Marc Berman. **Description:** Provides contact information for sales and marketing personnel for Twentieth Television as well as a listing of the station's top programming and an analysis of the current season and the target audience for those programs running in the current season.

7959 ■ *University Film and Video Association—Membership Directory*
Pub: University Film and Video Association
Released: Annual. **Covers:** about 800 persons concerned with the production and study of motion pictures and video in colleges and universities. **Entries Include:** Name, affiliation, address, phone. **Arrangement:** Alphabetical. **Indexes:** Affiliation, geographical.

7960 ■ **"Univision"** in *Brandweek* (Vol. 49, April 21, 2008, No. 16, pp. SR8)
Pub: VNU Business Media, Inc.
Ed: John Consoli. **Description:** Provides contact information for sales and marketing personnel for the Univision network as well as a listing of the station's top programming and an analysis of the current season and the target audience for those programs running in the current season. Univision is the No. 1 network on Friday nights in the 18-34 demographic, beating all English-language networks.

7961 ■ **"Video Surveillance Enters Digital Era, Makes Giant Strides"** in *Arkansas Business* (Vol. 26, September 28, 2009, No. 39, pp. 1)
Pub: Journal Publishing Inc.
Ed: Jamie Walden. **Description:** Arkansas business owners are finding that the newest technology in video surveillance is leading to swift apprehension of thieves due to the high-quality digital imagery now being captured on surveillance equipment. Motion detection software for these systems is enhancing the capabilities of these systems and providing opportunities for businesses that would normally have problems integrating these systems.

7962 ■ "A View to a Killer Business Model" in *Black Enterprise* (Vol. 40, December 2009, No. 5, pp. 50)
Pub: Earl G. Graves Publishing Co., Inc.
Ed: Sonya A. Donaldson. **Description:** Profile of Gen2Media Corp., a production, technology and Internet marketing firm based in Florida with offices in New York; Gen2Media is utilizing the advances in technology to now include video in its online marketing offerings.

7963 ■ "Warner Bros. Domestic Television Distribution" in *Brandweek* (Vol. 49, April 21, 2008, No. 16, pp. SR16)
Pub: VNU Business Media, Inc.
Ed: Marc Berman. **Description:** Provides contact information for sales and marketing personnel for Warner Bros. Domestic Television Distribution as well as a listing of the station's top programming and an analysis of the current season and the target audience for those programs running in the current season.

7964 ■ "We May Finally Find the Silver Lining" in *Crain's Detroit Business* (Vol. 24, April 7, 2008, No. 14, pp. 8)
Pub: Crain Communications, Inc.
Ed: Description: Discusses a possible economic turnaround for Michigan which could be brought forth with such things as the new film initiative incentives which may make filming in the state more appealing than filming in Canada due to the weakened state of the dollar and more exportation from Michigan companies.

7965 ■ "Why Some Get Shaften By Google Pricing" in *Advertising Age* (Vol. 79, July 14, 2008, No. 7, pp. 3)
Pub: Crain Communications, Inc.
Ed: Abbey Klaassen. **Description:** Google's search advertising is discussed as well as the company's pricing structure for these ads.

SOURCES OF SUPPLY

7966 ■ *DVD Replication Directory*
Pub: Corbell Publishing Co.
Contact: Maureen Healy, Publisher
Released: Annual, Latest edition 5th, 2007. **Price:** $457, individuals plus 40 shipping. **Covers:** Over 100 video duplicators in the U.S. and Canada. **Entries Include:** Name, address, phone, fax, url, e-mail address, names and titles of key personnel, financial data, types of accounts, geographical area served, number of employees, formats duplicated, other services offered. **Arrangement:** Alphabetical. **Indexes:** Company name.

STATISTICAL SOURCES

7967 ■ *RMA Annual Statement Studies*
Pub: Robert Morris Associates (RMA)
Released: Annual. **Price:** $175.00 2006-07 edition, $105.00. **Description:** Contains composite balance sheets and income statements for more than 360 industries, including the accounting, auditing, and bookkeeping industries. Also contains five years of comparative historical data for discerning trends. Includes 16 commonly used ratios, computed for most of the size groupings for nearly every industry.

TRADE PERIODICALS

7968 ■ *AV Video & Multimedia Producer*
Pub: Access Intelligence L.L.C.
Released: Monthly. **Description:** Magazine covering audio-visual, video and multimedia production, presentation, people, technology and techniques.

7969 ■ *ICG Magazine*
Pub: International Cinematographers Guild
Contact: David Geffner, Exec. Ed.
E-mail: davidgeffner@icgmagazine.com
Released: Monthly. **Description:** Trade magazine covering cinematography lighting techniques in film and video.

7970 ■ *Journal of Film and Video*
Pub: University of Illinois Press
Ed: Stephen Tropiano, Editor. **Released:** Quarterly. **Price:** $45 print; $75 print with UFVA membership; $45 institutions print; $125 institutions print with UFVA membership; $30 students print with UFVA membership. **Description:** Film and video journal.

7971 ■ *Video Systems*
Pub: Penton Media Inc.
Contact: Michael Goldman, Sen. Ed.
E-mail: mgoldman@prismb2b.com
Released: Monthly. **Description:** Magazine for users of professional video equipment.

7972 ■ *Videography*
Pub: New Bay Media, LLC
Contact: Eric Trabb, Grp. Publisher
Released: Monthly. **Description:** Magazine for film, video, and audio professionals.

7973 ■ *Videomaker Magazine*
Pub: York Publishing Inc.
Released: Monthly. **Price:** $19.97. **Description:** Videomaker covers camcorders, video editing, desktop video and audio production for video. Includes a buyer's guide to a relevant product type in every issue.

VIDEOCASSETTES/ AUDIOCASSETTES

7974 ■ *Basic Shooting*
Videomaker
PO Box 4591
Chico, CA 95927
Ph:(530)891-8410
Free: 800-284-3226
Fax:(530)891-8443
Co. E-mail: customerservice@videomaker.com
URL: http://www.videomaker.com
Released: 1994. **Price:** $12.95. **Description:** Discusses lighting, reflector power, microphone techniques, lens filters, and more. **Availability:** VHS.

7975 ■ *Hollywood Directors and Their Craft*
First Light Video Publishing
2321 Abbot Kinney Blvd., Top Fl.
Venice, CA 90291
Ph:(310)577-8581
Free: 800-262-8862
Fax:(310)574-0886
Co. E-mail: sales@firstlightvideo.com
URL: http://www.firstlightvideo.com
Released: 1994. **Description:** Seven directors (Clint Eastwood, John Badham, Robert Wise, Delbert Mann, Abraham Polonsky, Michael Schultz, and John Flynn) analyze their working methods. Covers career preparation, choosing a project, the writer, casting, pre-production, the cinematographer, on the set, working with actors, the editor, previews and premieres, the development of personal style, and social responsibility. **Availability:** VHS.

7976 ■ *Making a Video Program*
Stagestep
4701 Bath St., 46B
Philadelphia, PA 19137
Ph:(215)636-9000
Free: 800-523-0960
Fax:(267)672-2912
Co. E-mail: stagestep@stagestep.com
URL: http://stagestep.com
Price: $148.95. **Description:** An overview of the video production process, from scriptwriting and pre-production planning to editing, titling, and preview screening. **Availability:** VHS.

7977 ■ *Sound Success*
Videomaker
PO Box 4591
Chico, CA 95927
Ph:(530)891-8410
Free: 800-284-3226
Fax:(530)891-8443
Co. E-mail: customerservice@videomaker.com
URL: http://www.videomaker.com
Released: 1997. **Price:** $12.95. **Description:** Discusses types of mics, overcoming audio problems indoors and out, and how music can enhance your videos. **Availability:** VHS.

TRADE SHOWS AND CONVENTIONS

7978 ■ Home Media Expo
Home Entertainment Events
201 Sandpointe Ave., Ste. 500
Santa Ana, CA 92707
Free: 800-854-3112
Fax:(714)513-8848
URL: http://www.homemediaexpo.com
Released: Annual. **Audience:** Video/DVD store owners, employees, and distributors (trade only). **Principal Exhibits:** Mainstream and adult products; interactive media; Internet; studios; novelty products; adult toys; service providers; Internet service providers; video and DVD equipment, supplies, and services; Blu-ray discs.

CONSULTANTS

7979 ■ Creative Resource Publishing
W2974 Butternut Ln.
Green Lake, WI 54941-9614
Ph:(920)295-3824
Fax:(920)424-3133
Co. E-mail: info@workplacetrauma.com
Contact: Alfred A. Folker, Owner
E-mail: folker@charter.net
Scope: Provides video production consulting including studio planning, video publishing, scripting, cable television franchising and sales, corporate television and insurance sales training. Serves all industries and public agencies. **Publications:** "Targeting Workplace Trauma". **Seminars:** How to Deal With Aggressive News Reporters; Opportunities in Video Publishing. **Special Services:** Web Design and Site Management.

7980 ■ Full Voice
3217 Broadway Ave., Ste. 300
Kansas City, MO 64111
Ph:(816)941-0011
Free: 800-684-8764
Fax:(816)931-8887
Co. E-mail: info@infullvoice.com
URL: http://www.fullvoice.us
Contact: Michienne Dixon, Principle
E-mail: garrett@infullvoice.com
Scope: Vocal performance training firm offering consulting services and personal training sessions in the implementation of effective vocal communication techniques for the development of business relationships and career enhancement. Formalizes a program of proven techniques into a practical method of helping individuals improve their ability to better present themselves when speaking in a professional situation. Industries served: All. **Publications:** "You Can Sound Like You Know What You're Saying". **Seminars:** You Can Sound Like You Know What You're Saying; The Psychology of Vocal Performance; Security. . .the Ability to Accept Change; Knowing. . .the Key to Relaxed Public Communication; The Effective Voice for Customer Service Enhancement; You Can Speak With Conviction; How To Make Yours a Championship Team; Functional English For Foreign Trade. **Special Services:** FULL VOICE™.

FRANCHISES AND BUSINESS OPPORTUNITIES

7981 ■ Home Video Studio
8148 Raven Rock Dr.
Indianapolis, IN 46256
Ph:(317)964-8048
Free: 800-464-8220

Fax:(317)577-1522
No. of Franchise Units: 68. **Founded:** 1991. **Franchised:** 2006. **Description:** Home based video studio. **Equity Capital Needed:** $69,050-$97,300. **Franchise Fee:** $25,000. **Financial Assistance:** Yes. **Training:** Yes.

7982 ■ Videomasters Inc.
2200 Dunbarton Dr., Ste. D
Chesapeake, VA 23325
Free: 800-836-9461
Fax:(757)424-8693
No. of Franchise Units: 80. **Founded:** 1980. **Franchised:** 1982. **Description:** Video and audio products are available. **Equity Capital Needed:** $36,950. **Franchise Fee:** $950 annually. **Financial Assistance:** No. **Training:** Yes.

COMPUTERIZED DATABASES

7983 ■ BaselineFT's In Production Database
New York Times Media Group
3415 S Sepulveda Blvd., Ste. 200
Los Angeles, CA 90034
Ph:(310)482-3400
Free: 800-858-3669
Fax:(310)393-7799
URL: http://www.baselineresearch.com
Description: Lists more than 5000 film and television projects that are either announced, in pre-production, production, post-production, or awaiting release. Monitors activity in the entertainment industry through press releases, local film commissions, industry sources, and phone calls to producers. **Availability:** Online: New York Times Media Group. **Type:** Full text.

COMPUTER SYSTEMS/ SOFTWARE

7984 ■ Authorware 7–Macro Media
MACRO-Media
345 Park Ave.
San Jose, CA 95110
Ph:(408)536-6000
Free: 800-288-4797
Fax:(408)537-6000
URL: http://www.adobe.com
Price: Contact Adobe. **Description:** Available for Apple Macintosh Plus, SE, or II computers. System provides post production, storyboarding, and special effects functions.

LIBRARIES

7985 ■ California Film Commission–Location Resource Center Library
7080 Hollywood Blvd., Ste. 900
Los Angeles, CA 90028-6906
Ph:(213)736-2465
Fax:(213)860-2970
Co. E-mail: lmosher@film.ca.gov
Contact: Lisa Mosher, Lib.Mgr.
Scope: Motion pictures. **Services:** Library open to the public. **Holdings:** 200 books; 300,000 photographs. **Subscriptions:** 6 journals and other serials.

7986 ■ University of North Carolina School of the Arts–Semans Library
UNC School of the Arts
1533 S. Main St.
Winston-Salem, NC 27127
Ph:(336)770-3270
Fax:(336)770-3271
Co. E-mail: rebeccab@uncsa.edu
URL: http://www.uncsa.edu/library
Contact: Rebecca Brown, Hd. of Access Svcs.
Scope: Music, art and design, theater, film, dance, humanities. **Services:** Interlibrary loan; Library open to the public. **Holdings:** 111,000 books; 9000 bound periodical volumes; 50,000 music scores; 45,000 sound recordings; 5200 DVDs and videos. **Subscriptions:** 470 journals and other serials; 25 newspapers.

7987 ■ Watkins College of Art, Design, & Film Library
2298 Rosa L. Parks Blvd.
Nashville, TN 37228
Ph:(615)277-7427
Fax:(615)383-4849
Co. E-mail: library@watkins.edu
URL: http://www.watkins.edu/library
Contact: Lisa Williams, Libn.
Scope: Film, fine arts, interior design, graphic design, photography. **Services:** Library open to the public for reference use only. **Holdings:** 11,600 books; 1200 videotapes and films. **Subscriptions:** 50 journals and other serials; 11 newspapers.

START-UP INFORMATION

7988 ■ "On Their Own: Bronx High School Students Open a Bank Branch" in *Black Enterprise* **(Vol. 38, February 2008, No. 7, pp. 42)**
Pub: Earl G. Graves Publishing Co. Inc.
Ed: Jessica Jones. **Description:** Students at Fordham Leadership Academy for Business and Technology in New York City opened a student-run bank branch at their high school. The business paid high school seniors $11 per hour to work as tellers. Students were also taught interviewing basics.

ASSOCIATIONS AND OTHER ORGANIZATIONS

7989 ■ Accounting and Finance Benchmarking Consortium
4606 FM 1960 W, Ste. 250
Houston, TX 77069-9949
Free: 800-324-4685
URL: http://www.afbc.org
Description: Accounting and finance managers of corporations with an interest in benchmarking. Promotes the use of benchmarking, wherein businesses compare their processes with those of their competitors, as a means of improving corporate efficiency and profitability. Facilitates exchange of information among members; conducts target operations, procurement, development, and maintenance studies; identifies model business practices. .

7990 ■ ADVOCIS
390 Queens Quay W, Ste. 209
Toronto, ON, Canada M5V 3A2
Ph:(416)444-5251
Free: 800-563-5822
Fax:(416)444-8031
Co. E-mail: info@advocis.ca
URL: http://www.advocis.ca
Contact: Greg Pollock, Pres./CEO
Description: Professional association for Canadian insurance and financial advisors with members representing most cities and towns across the country. Founding member of the Financial Planners Standards Council (FPSC), the body that grants the CFP designation. Members provide financial advice, and market and sell financial products to over 9 million Canadians. **Publications:** *Advisor Voice* (monthly); *FORUM* (monthly).

7991 ■ Canadian Association of Insolvency and Restructuring Professionals–Association Canadienne des Professionnels de l'Insolvabilite et de la reorganisation
277 Wellington St. W
Toronto, ON, Canada M5V 3H2
Ph:(416)204-3242
Fax:(416)204-3410
Co. E-mail: info@cairp.ca
URL: http://www.cairp.ca
Contact: Mark Yakabuski, Pres.
Description: Promotes excellence in the field of insolvency and business recovery services. Lobbies for reform of bankruptcy laws; sponsors continuing professional development courses; delivers qualification program for bankruptcy transfers in conjunction with the federal government. **Publications:** *Rebuilding Success* (semiannual). **Telecommunication Services:** electronic mail, norm.kondo@cairp.ca.

7992 ■ Canadian Credit Institute Educational Foundation–Fondation Scolaire de l'Institut Canadien du Credit
219 Dufferin St., Ste. 216C
Toronto, ON, Canada M6L 3J1
Ph:(416)572-2615
Free: 888-447-3324
Fax:(416)572-2619
Co. E-mail: geninfo@creditedu.org
URL: http://www.creditedu.org
Contact: Reggie Delovtich, Gen. Mgr.
Description: Financial institutions and providers of financial planning services. Promotes adherence to high standards of ethics and practice by members. Provides financial support to credit initiatives.

7993 ■ Canadian Institute of Financial Planning–Institut Canadien de Planification Finaniere
3660 Hurontario St., Ste. 600
Mississauga, ON, Canada L5B 3C4
Free: (866)635-5526
Co. E-mail: cifp@cifps.ca
URL: http://www.cifp.ca/Desktop/English/Index.asp
Contact: Keith Costello, Pres./CEO
Description: Works to promote excellence in the field of financial planning. Facilitates communication and cooperation among members, which includes financial planning professionals. Sponsors continuing professional education courses.

7994 ■ Canadian Investor Relations Institute–Institut Canadien de Relations avec les Investisseurs
560, 20 Toronto St.
Toronto, ON, Canada M5C 2B8
Ph:(416)364-8200
Fax:(416)364-2805
Co. E-mail: enquiries@ciri.org
URL: http://www.ciri.org
Contact: Tom Enright, Pres./CEO
Description: Executives responsible for communication between public corporations, investors and the financial community; dedicated to advancing the stature and credibility of the investor relations profession and the competency of members. **Publications:** *Newsline* (bimonthly).

7995 ■ Financial Managers Society
100 W Monroe St., Ste. 1700
Chicago, IL 60603-1907
Ph:(312)578-1300
Free: 800-275-4367
Fax:(312)578-1308
Co. E-mail: info@fmsinc.org
URL: http://www.fmsinc.org
Contact: Dick Yingst, Pres./CEO
Description: Works for the needs of finance and accounting professionals from banks, thrifts and credit unions. Offers career-enhancing education, specialized publications, national leadership opportunities and worldwide connections with other industry professionals. **Publications:** *Financial Managers Society—Membership and Peer Consulting Directory* (annual); *Record Retention Manual* .

7996 ■ Financial Planning Association
7535 E Hampden Ave., Ste. 600
Denver, CO 80231
Ph:(303)759-4900
Free: 800-322-4237
Fax:(303)759-0749
Co. E-mail: webfeedback@fpanet.org
URL: http://www.fpanet.org
Contact: Marvin W. Tuttle Jr., Exec. Dir.
Description: Works to support the financial planning process in order to help people achieve their goals and dreams. Believes that everyone needs objective advice to make smart financial decisions and that when seeking the advice of a financial planner, the planner should be a CFP professional. **Publications:** *FPA This Week* (weekly); *Journal of Financial Planning* (monthly).

7997 ■ Financial Women International
200 N Glebe Rd., Ste. 820
Arlington, VA 22203
Free: (866)236-2007
Fax:(866)807-6081
Co. E-mail: info@fwi.org
URL: http://www.fwifoundation.org
Contact: Nancy Kinder, Pres.
Description: Individuals working in or with the financial services industry. Maintains FWI Educational Foundation. **Publications:** *Today's Financial Women* .

7998 ■ Financial Women's Association of New York
215 Park Ave. S, Ste. 1712
New York, NY 10003
Ph:(212)533-2141
Fax:(212)982-3008
Co. E-mail: fwaoffice@fwa.org
URL: http://www.fwa.org
Contact: Nancy Sellar, Exec. Dir.
Description: Persons of professional status in the field of finance in the New York metropolitan area. Works to promote and maintain high professional standards in the financial and business communities; provide an opportunity for members to enhance one another's professional contacts; achieve recognition of the contribution of women to the financial and business communities; encourage other women to seek professional positions within the financial and business communities. Activities include educational trips to foreign countries; college internship program including foreign student exchange; high school mentorship program; Washington and international briefings; placement service for members. Maintains speakers' bureau. **Publications:** *FWA Connections* (11/year).

7999 ■ LIMRA International
300 Day Hill Rd.
Windsor, CT 06095
Ph:(860)688-3358
Free: 800-235-4672
Fax:(860)298-9555
Co. E-mail: customer.service@limra.com
URL: http://www.limra.com
Contact: Robert A. Kerzner CLU, Pres./CEO
Description: Life insurance and financial services companies. Conducts market, consumer, economic, financial, and human resources research; monitors industry distribution systems and product and service developments. Provides executive and field management development schools and seminars. Offers human resource development consulting services, including needs analysis and program design, evaluation, and implementation. .

8000 ■ National Association of Personal Financial Advisors
3250 N Arlington Heights Rd., Ste. 109
Arlington Heights, IL 60004
Ph:(847)483-5400
Fax:(847)483-5415
Co. E-mail: info@napfa.org
URL: http://www.napfa.org
Contact: Ellen Turf, CEO
Description: Full-time, fee-only financial planners. Serves as a network for fee-only planners to discuss issues relating to practice management, client services, and investments selection. Works to encourage and advance the practice of fee-only financial planning by developing the skills of members and increasing the awareness of fee-only financial planning of consumers. **Publications:** *NAPFA Advisor* (monthly); *NAPFA Membership Directory* (annual); *NAPFA NewsLink* (bimonthly).

DIRECTORIES OF EDUCATIONAL PROGRAMS

8001 ■ *The Canadian Book of Charities*
Pub: Mavora Publications Inc.
Contact: Yvonne Trapman, Dir. of Communications
Released: Annual, Latest edition 2008. Price: $24.95, single issue including taxes and shipping. **Covers:** Charitable organizations throughout Canada; information on giving charitable gifts; tax treatment of charitable donations; and more. **Entries Include:** Contact information. **Arrangement:** Alphabetical, regional.

REFERENCE WORKS

8002 ■ "3Par: Storing Up Value" in *Barron's* (Vol. 90, August 30, 2010, No. 35, pp. 30)
Pub: Barron's Editorial & Corporate Headquarters
Ed: Mark Veverka. **Description:** Dell and Hewlett Packard are both bidding for data storage company 3Par. The acquisition would help Dell and Hewlett Packard provide customers with a one-stop shop as customers move to a private cloud in the Internet.

8003 ■ "13D Filings" in *Barron's* (Vol. 88, March 24, 2008, No. 12, pp. M13)
Pub: Dow Jones & Company, Inc.
Description: HealthCor Management called as problematic the plan of Magellan Health Services to use its high cash balances for acquisitions. Carlson Capital discussed with Energy Partners possible changes in the latter's board. Investor Carl Icahn suggested that Enzon Pharmaceuticals consider selling itself or divest some of its assets.

8004 ■ "13D Filings: Investors Report to the SEC" in *Barron's* (Vol. 88, March 17, 2008, No. 11, pp. M11)
Pub: Dow Jones & Company, Inc.
Description: Nanes Delorme wants Vaalco Energy to keep an investment bank on an open-bid process to sell the company. West Creek Capital plans to nominate two directors at the 2008 annual meeting of the Capital Senior Living just as ValueVest Management wants to nominate the same number of people at Ampex's annual meeting.

8005 ■ "A 16-Year Housing Slump? It Could Happen" in *Barron's* (Vol. 88, March 17, 2008, No. 11, pp. 27)
Pub: Dow Jones & Company, Inc.
Ed: Gene Epstein. **Description:** Housing remains a good protection against inflation but over very long periods. Inflation-adjusted stock prices did even better but have greater volatility. Commodities, on the other hand, underperformed both housing and stocks as inflation hedges. House prices tend to rise faster than the consumer price index is because land is inherently limited.

8006 ■ "75 Most Powerful Blacks on Wall Street" in *Black Enterprise* (Vol. 37, October 2006, No. 3, pp. 136)
Pub: Earl G. Graves Publishing Co. Inc.
Ed: Carolyn M. Brown. **Description:** Profiles of seventy-five African American top executives. The listing is a compilation of the brightest and best venture capitalists, asset managers, CEOs, traders, and investment bankers.

8007 ■ "The 100 Most Bullish Stocks" in *Canadian Business* (Vol. 81, Summer 2008, No. 9, pp. 81)
Pub: Rogers Media Ltd.
Ed: Megan Harman; Lauren McKeon. **Description:** 100 of the most bullish stocks are taken from the list of the 500 best-performing stocks. The idea is to narrow the list help investors in their investment decisions since it is difficult to choose from a large list. Analysts rate the companies with 5 being the most bullish and 1 the least. Other details of the roster are presented.

8008 ■ "401(k) Keys to Stable Value" in *Barron's* (Vol. 88, March 10, 2008, No. 10, pp. 40)
Pub: Dow Jones & Company, Inc.
Ed: Tom Sullivan. **Description:** Stable-value funds offer investors stability in a period of volatility in financial markets, attracting $888 million in funds. The Securities and Exchange Commission approved the launch of actively managed exchange-traded funds.

8009 ■ "2008: Year of the Rat Race" in *Mergers & Acquisitions: The Dealmaker's Journal* (March 1, 2008)
Pub: SourceMedia, Inc.
Ed: Danelle Fugazy. **Description:** Although China still presents opportunities to Western investors, many are discovering that much more research needs to be done concerning doing business in that country before investing there becomes truly mainstream. According to one source, there are at least 300,000 small state-owned enterprises in China and millions of middle-market privately owned companies; the Chinese stock market can only handle about 50 to 70 IPOs a year and lists about 1,500 companies at a time.

8010 ■ "A Conversation With; Ron Gatner, Jones Lang LaSalle" in *Crain's Detroit Business* (Vol. 24, October 6, 2008, No. 40, pp. 9)
Pub: Crain Communications, Inc.
Description: Interview with Ron Gatner who is a corporate real estate adviser with the real estate company Jones Lang LaSalle as well as the company's executive vice president and part of the tenant advisory team; Gatner speaks about the impact that the Wall Street crisis is having on the commercial real estate market in Detroit.

8011 ■ "A Good Step, But There's a Long Way to Go" in *Business Week* (September 22, 2008, No. 4100, pp. 10)
Pub: McGraw-Hill Companies, Inc.
Ed: James C. Cooper. **Description:** Despite the historic action by the U.S. government to nationalize the mortgage giants Freddie Mac and Fannie Mae, rising unemployment rates may prove to be an even bigger roadblock to bringing back the economy from its downward spiral. The takeover is meant to restore confidence in the credit markets and help with the mortgage crisis but the rising rate in unemployment

may make many households unable to take advantage of any benefits which arise from the bailout. Statistical data included.

8012 ■ *Access to Finance*
Pub: Brookings Institution Press
Ed: Barr. Released: December 2006. Price: $39.95. **Description:** Challenges to help make financial systems more inclusive to promote successful venture in new markets while utilizing new technologies and government policies to expand financial access to smaller companies.

8013 ■ "ACE Agrees to Pay Out $266 Million to Investors" in *Globe & Mail* (February 17, 2006, pp. B1)
Pub: CTVglobemedia Publishing Inc.
Ed: Brent Jang. **Description:** Canada-based commercial aviation firm ACE Aviation Holdings has agreed to pay 266 million dollars to its investors after filing a bankruptcy one year ago. Complete details of this pay off are discussed.

8014 ■ "ACE Back in Unfriendly Skies" in *Globe & Mail* (February 14, 2006, pp. B17)
Pub: CTVglobemedia Publishing Inc.
Ed: Brent Jang. **Description:** ACE Aviation Holdings Inc. reported $258 million profit for 2005. The opinions of analysts on the share price of the company for 2006 are presented.

8015 ■ "Advance America Closing All Pa. Stores" in *American Banker* (Vol. 172, December 20, 2007, No. 244, pp. 11)
Pub: SourceMedia Inc.
Ed: William Launder. **Description:** Advance America Cash Advance Centers Inc. is closing its 66 locations in Pennsylvania while it awaits a state Supreme Court ruling about the excessively high fees it carries for loan products.

8016 ■ "Advertising May Take a Big Hit in Southwest/AirTran Merger" in *Baltimore Business Journal* (Vol. 28, October 1, 2010, No. 21, pp. 1)
Pub: Baltimore Business Journal
Ed: Gary Haber. **Description:** Advertising on television stations and the publishing industry in Baltimore could drop as a result of the merger between rival discount airlines Southwest Airlines and AirTran Airways. Southwest is among the top advertisers in the U.S., spending $126 million in 2009. No local jobs are expected to be affected because neither airline uses a local advertising firm.

8017 ■ "After Price Cuts, Competition GPS Makers Lose Direction" in *Brandweek* (Vol. 49, April 21, 2008, No. 16, pp. 16)
Pub: VNU Business Media, Inc.
Ed: Steve Miller. **Description:** Garmin and TomTom, two of the leaders in portable navigation devices, have seen lowering revenues due to dramatic price cuts and unexpected competition from the broadening availability of personal navigation on mobile phones. TomTom has trimmed its sales outlook for its first quarter while Garmin's stock dropped 40 percent since February.

8018 ■ "Ag Firms Harvest Revenue Growth" in *The Business Journal-Serving Metropolitan Kansas City* (Vol. 26, July 18, 2008, No. 45, pp. 1)
Pub: American City Business Journals, Inc.
Ed: Steve Vockrodt. **Description:** Five of the biggest agricultural companies in the Kansas City area, except one, reported multibillion-dollar revenue increases in 2007. The companies, which include Lansing Trade Group, posted a combined $9.5 billion growth. The factors that affected the revenue increase in the area's agricultural companies, such as prices and high demand, are also examined.

8019 ■ "AIG Fixed; Is Michigan Next?" in *Crain's Detroit Business* (Vol. 24, September 22, 2008, No. 38, pp. 1)
Pub: Crain Communications, Inc.
Ed: Jay Greene. **Description:** Michigan's economic future is examined as is the mortgage buyout plan and American International Group Inc.'s takeover by the U.S. government.

8020 ■ "Air Canada Boss Gains $3.5 Million in Options" in *Globe & Mail* (January 19, 2007, pp. B5)

Pub: CTVglobemedia Publishing Inc.

Ed: Brent Jang. **Description:** Air Canada chairman Robert Milton's sale of 200,000 shares in stock options is discussed.

8021 ■ "Algoma Resolves Hedge Fund Fight" in *Globe & Mail* (March 8, 2006, pp. B1)

Pub: CTVglobemedia Publishing Inc.

Ed: Greg Keenan. **Description:** Algoma Steel Inc. has ended a dispute with Paulson and Co., a New York hedge fund, by offering to pay $200 million special dividend, appointing new directors, and continue to go for a sale.

8022 ■ "Algoma Shares Soar on Growing Sale Rumors" in *Globe & Mail* (February 13, 2007, pp. B1)

Pub: CTVglobemedia Publishing Inc.

Ed: Andrew Willis; Greg Keenan. **Description:** The stock prices of Algoma Steel Inc. have touched record high of $40 on the Toronto Stock Exchange. The growing rumors about the possible takeover bid is the major reason for the stock price growth.

8023 ■ "All Eyes On Iris" in *Canadian Business* (Vol. 81, July 22, 2008, No. 12-13, pp. 20)

Pub: Rogers Media Ltd.

Ed: Jack Mintz. **Description:** Provincial governments in Alberta are believed to be awaiting Alberta Finance Minister Iris Evans' financial and investment policies as well as Evans' development of a new saving strategy. Alberta is the only Canadian province that is in position to invest in sovereign wealth funds after it eliminated its debt in 2005.

8024 ■ "All Revved Up" in *Barron's* (Vol. 90, September 13, 2010, No. 37, pp. 18)

Pub: Barron's Editorial & Corporate Headquarters

Ed: Christopher C. Williams. **Description:** Shares of Advance Auto Parts has returned 55 percent in a span of three years and the stock could still reach the mid-60s by 2011 from its price of 46.07 in the second week of September 2010. The shares are trading at just 13 times the 2011 earnings.

8025 ■ "All-Star Advice 2010" in *Black Enterprise* (Vol. 41, October 2010, No. 3, pp. 97)

Pub: Earl G. Graves Publishing Co. Inc.

Ed: Renita Burns, Sheiresa Ngo, Marcia Wade Talbert. **Description:** Financial experts share tips on real estate, investing, taxes, insurance and debt management.

8026 ■ "Amit Wadhwaney" in *Canadian Business* (Vol. 80, March 12, 2007, No. 6, pp. 22)

Pub: Rogers Media

Ed: Rachel Pulfer. **Description:** Manager of Third Avenue International Value Fund, Amit Wadhwaney, shares his views on buying Canadian agricultural and forestry stocks.

8027 ■ "Analysts Not Fazed By Constellation's Halt to New Nuclear Plants" in *Baltimore Business Journal* (Vol. 28, October 22, 2010, No. 24)

Pub: Baltimore Business Journal

Ed: Scott Dance. **Description:** Wall Street analysts believe that Constellation Energy Group Inc.'s decision to pull out of the nuclear construction business would not change their outlook on the company. New nuclear power had been one of Constellation's long-term goals, but the company pulled the plug on the project. It is believed that most investors were not expecting any payoff from the venture.

8028 ■ "And In This Briefcase" in *Mergers & Acquisitions: The Dealmaker's Journal* (March 1, 2008)

Pub: SourceMedia, Inc.

Description: ACG San Diego decided to address the impact the changes in the economy will have on potential private equity transactions as well as what criteria private equity firms are looking for when assessing a company. At the opening of the chapter's 2008 breakfast meeting, real-world case studies were utilized with the audiences' participation in order to assess pre-deal risk scenarios.

8029 ■ "The Annual Entitlement Lecture: Trustees of Medicare and Social Security Issue Another Dismal Report" in *Barron's* (March 31, 2008)

Pub: Dow Jones & Company, Inc.

Ed: Thomas G. Donlan. **Description:** Expenditures on Medicare hospital insurance and the revenues available to pay for it have led to a gap of capital valued at $38.6 trillion. Slashing the benefits or raising taxes will not solve the gap which exists unless the government saves the money and invests it in private markets.

8030 ■ "Apartment Tower in River North Fetches More Than $90 Million" in *Crain's Chicago Business* (Vol. 34, October 24, 2011, No. 42, pp. 17)

Pub: Crain Communications Inc.

Ed: Alby Gallun. **Description:** Apartment tower in River North was sold for over $90 million to a Texas pension fund adviser. Details are included.

8031 ■ "Are You Ready for Dow 20,000?" in *Barron's* (Vol. 88, March 24, 2008, No. 12, pp. 26)

Pub: Dow Jones & Company, Inc.

Ed: Jonathan R. Laing. **Description:** Stock strategist James Finucane forecasts that the Dow Jones Industrial Average will rise from its 12,361 level to as high as 20,000 from 2008 to 2009. He believes that stock liquidation and a buildup of cash provide the perfect conditions for a huge rally.

8032 ■ "As Capital Gains Tax Hike Looms, Merger Activity Percolates" in *Baltimore Business Journal* (Vol. 28, August 27, 2010, No. 16, pp. 1)

Pub: Baltimore Business Journal

Ed: Scott Dance. **Description:** Concerns for higher capital gains taxes in 2011 have been provoking buyers and sellers to engage in mergers and acquisitions activity, which is expected to gain momentum before the end of 2010. Companies that had saved cash during the recession have been taking advantage of the buyer's market. Other trends in local and national mergers and acquisitions activity are presented.

8033 ■ "Asia Breathes a Sigh of Relief" in *Business Week* (September 22, 2008, No. 4100, pp. 32)

Pub: McGraw-Hill Companies, Inc.

Ed: Bruce Einhorn; Theo Francis; Chi-Chu Tschang; Moon Ihlwan; Hiroko Tashiro. **Description:** Foreign bankers, such as those in Asia, that had been investing heavily in the United States began to worry as the housing crisis deepened and the impact on Freddie Mac and Fannie Mae became increasingly clear. Due to the government bailout, however, central banks will most likely continue to buy American debt.

8034 ■ "ATS Secures Investment From Goldman Sachs" in *The Business Journal - Serving Phoenix and the Valley of the Sun* (Vol. 29, September 26, 2008, No. 4, pp. 1)

Pub: American City Business Journals, Inc.

Ed: Patrick O'Grady. **Description:** Goldman Sachs made an investment to American Traffic Solutions Inc. (ATS) which will allow it to gain two seats on the board of the red-light and speed cameras maker. The investment will help ATS maintain its rapid growth which is at 83 percent over the past 18 months leading up to September 2008.

8035 ■ "Attend To Your Corporate Housekeeping" in *Women Entrepreneur* (December 4, 2008)

Pub: Entrepreneur Media Inc.

Ed: Nina Kaufman. **Description:** Business owners can lose all the benefits and privileges of the corporate form if they do not follow proper corporate formalities such as holding an annual meeting, electing officers and directors and adopting or passing corporate resolutions. Creditors are able to take from one's personal assets if such formalities have not been followed.

8036 ■ "Au Revoir Or Goodbye?" in *Barron's* (Vol. 88, July 14, 2008, No. 28, pp. 5)

Pub: Dow Jones & Co., Inc.

Ed: Alan Abelson. **Description:** Former Senator Phil Gramm's opinion that the U.S. is a "nation of whiners" as they moan about recession is another example of the disconnection between Washington and Wall Street on one hand and the real world on the other. It would be a catastrophe for most of the world if Fannie Mae and Freddie Mac were to go under and take their trillions of mortgage debt with them.

8037 ■ "Auction-Rate Cash Frees Up" in *The Business Journal-Portland* (Vol. 25, August 15, 2008, No. 23, pp. 1)

Pub: American City Business Journals, Inc.

Ed: Aliza Earnshaw. **Description:** FEI Co. and Radi-Sys Corp. have received notices that UBS AG will buy back the auction-rate securities that were sold to them in around two years from 2008. FEI had $110.1 million invested in auction-rate securities while Radi-Sys holds $62.8 million of these securities.

8038 ■ "Auto Supplier Stock Battered In Wake Of Wall Street Woes" in *Crain's Detroit Business* (Vol. 24, September 29, 2008, No. 39, pp. 4)

Pub: Crain Communications, Inc.

Ed: Ryan Beene. **Description:** Due to the volatility of the stock market and public perception of the $700 billion banking bailout, auto suppliers are now facing a dramatic drop in their shares. Statistical data included.

8039 ■ "BABs in Bond Land" in *Barron's* (Vol. 89, July 6, 2009, No. 27, pp. 14)

Pub: Dow Jones & Co., Inc.

Ed: Jim McTague. **Description:** American Recovery and Reinvestment Act has created taxable Build America Bonds (BAB) to finance new construction projects. The issuance of the two varieties of taxable BABs is expected to benefit the municipal bond market.

8040 ■ "Back in the Race" in *Barron's* (Vol. 88, March 17, 2008, No. 11, pp. 43)

Pub: Dow Jones & Company, Inc.

Ed: Leslie P. Norton. **Description:** Katherine Schapiro was able to get Sentinel International Equity's Morningstar classification to blended fund from a value fund rating after joining Sentinel from her former jobs at Strong Overseas Fund. Schapiro aims to benefit from the global rebalancing as the U.S.'s share of the world economy shrinks.

8041 ■ "Back on Track-Or Off the Rails?" in *Business Week* (September 22, 2008, No. 4100, pp. 22)

Pub: McGraw-Hill Companies, Inc.

Ed: Peter Coy; Tara Kalwarski. **Description:** Discusses the possible scenarios the American economy may undergo due to the takeover of Fannie Mae and Freddie Mac. Statistical data included.

8042 ■ "Bad-Loan Bug Bites Mid-Tier Banks; More Pain, Tighter Lending Standards Ahead, CEOs Say" in *Crain's Chicago Business* (May 5, 2008)

Pub: Crain Communications, Inc.

Ed: Steve Daniels. **Description:** Mid-sized commercial banks form the bedrock of Chicago's financial-services industry and they are now feeling the results of the credit crisis that has engulfed the nation's largest banks and brokerages. Commercial borrowers are seeing tighter terms on loans and higher interest rates while bank investors are unable to forecast lenders' earnings performance from quarter to quarter. Statistical data included.

8043 ■ "Bad Loans Start Piling Up" in *Crain's New York Business* (Vol. 24, January 7, 2008, No. 1, pp. 2)

Pub: Crain Communications, Inc.

Ed: Tom Fredrickson. **Description:** Problems in the subprime mortgage industry have extended to other lending activities as evidenced by bank charge-offs on bad commercial and industrial loans which have more than doubled in the third quarter.

8044 ▪ *Bad Money*
Pub: Viking Press/Penguin Group
Ed: Kevin Phillips. **Released:** April 15, 2008. **Description:** How the financial sector has hijacked the American economy, aided by Washington's ruinous faith in the efficiency of markets.

8045 ▪ "Bad Paper" in *Canadian Business* (Vol. 80, November 19, 2007, No. 23, pp. 34)
Pub: Rogers Media
Ed: Al Rosen. **Description:** The Canadian government froze the market for non-bank asset-backed commercial paper (ABCP) August 2007, which means holders will be unable to withdraw investments. The crisis and value of ABCP are discussed.

8046 ▪ "Bailout Forgets the 'Little Guys'" in *The Business Journal-Milwaukee* (Vol. 25, September 26, 2008, No. 53, pp. A1)
Pub: American City Business Journals, Inc.
Ed: Rich Kirchen. **Description:** Community Bankers of Wisconsin and the Wisconsin Bankers Association are urging members to approach congressional representatives and remind them to include local banks in building the $700 billion bailout plan. WBA president and CEO Kurt Bauer thinks that it is only fair to include smaller institutions in the bailout. The initial bailout plan and its benefit for the smaller banks are examined.

8047 ▪ "Bailout May Force Cutbacks, Job Losses" in *The Business Journal - Serving Phoenix and the Valley of the Sun* (Vol. 29, September 26, 2008, No. 4, pp. 1)
Pub: American City Business Journals, Inc.
Ed: Mike Sunnucks. **Description:** Economists say the proposed $700 billion bank bailout could affect Arizona businesses as banks could be forced to reduce the amount and number of loans it has thereby forcing businesses to shrink capital expenditures and then jobs. However, the plan could also stimulate the economy by taking bad loans off banks balance sheets according to another economist.

8048 ▪ "BancVue to Expand" in *Austin Business JournalInc.* (Vol. 29, November 27, 2009, No. 38, pp. 1)
Pub: American City Business Journals
Ed: Kate Harrington. **Description:** Significant growth of BancVue in the past six years has prompted the company to look for a site that could increase its office space from 25,000 square feet to 65,000 square feet. BancVue offers bank and credit union software solutions and is planning to lease or buy a property in Austin, Texas.

8049 ▪ "Bank Bullish on Austin" in *Austin Business JournalInc.* (Vol. 29, November 13, 2009, No. 36, pp. A1)
Pub: American City Business Journals
Ed: Kate Harrington. **Description:** American Bank's presence in Austin, Texas has been dominated by new management and a new 20,000 square foot building. This community bank intends to focus on building relationship with commercial banking customers. American Bank also plans to extend investment banking, treasury management, and commercial lending services.

8050 ▪ "Bank Forces Brooke Founder To Sell His Holdings" in *The Business Journal-Serving Metropolitan Kansas City* (October 10, 2008)
Pub: American City Business Journals, Inc.
Ed: James Dornbrook. **Description:** Robert Orr who is the founder of Brooke Corp., a franchise of insurance agencies, says that he was forced to sell virtually all of his stocks in the company by creditors. First United Bank held the founder's stock as collateral for two loans worth $5 million and $7.9 million, which were declared in default in September 2008. Details of the selling of the company's stocks are provided.

8051 ▪ "Bank on It" in *Hawaii Business* (Vol. 53, November 2007, No. 5, pp. 60)
Pub: Hawaii Business Publishing
Ed: Kathleen Bryan. **Description:** Many Baby Boomers that are preparing to retire would like to give back and make a difference. One way to make

gifts of Individual Retirement Assets (IRA). During 2007 people over 70 years can make withdrawals from an IRA and donate it without realizing the income as taxable.

8052 ▪ "Bank Sticks to Rate Rise Script but 'Modest' is the Salient Word" in *Globe & Mail* (January 25, 2006, pp. B5)
Pub: CTVglobemedia Publishing Inc.
Ed: Heather Scoffield. **Description:** The reasons behind the decision of Bank of Canada to increase interest rate, which is posted at 3.5 percent, are presented.

8053 ▪ "Banking Bailout: Boost or Bust?" in *Crain's Detroit Business* (Vol. 24, September 29, 2008, No. 39, pp. 1)
Pub: Crain Communications, Inc.
Ed: Amy Lane. **Description:** Economic insiders discuss the banking bailout and how it might impact the state of Michigan.

8054 ▪ "Banking Crisis Rattles Local Businesses" in *Puget Sound Business Journal* (Vol. 29, October 10, 2008, No. 25, pp. 1)
Pub: American City Business Journals
Ed: Kirsten Grind. **Description:** Customers of Washington Mutual in the Puget Sound region started withdrawing large sums of cash due to fears of the banks unstable condition.

8055 ▪ "A Banking Play Without Banking Plagues" in *Barron's* (Vol. 88, March 31, 2008, No. 13, pp. 26)
Pub: Dow Jones & Company, Inc.
Ed: Jack Willoughby. **Description:** Fiserv's shares have been dragged down by about 20 percent which presents an appealing entry point since the shares could rise by 30 percent or more by 2009. The company enables banks to post and open new checks and keeps track of loans which are not discretionary processes of banks.

8056 ▪ "Banking on Twitter" in *Baltimore Business Journal* (Vol. 27, February 6, 2010, No. 40, pp. 1)
Pub: American City Business Journals
Ed: Gary Haber. **Description:** Ways that banks are using Twitter, Facebook and other social networking sites to provide customer services is discussed. First Mariner Bank is one of those banks that are finding the social media platform as a great way to reach customers. Privacy issues regarding this marketing trend are examined.

8057 ▪ "The Bankrate Double Pay" in *Barron's* (Vol. 88, March 24, 2008, No. 12, pp. 27)
Pub: Dow Jones & Company, Inc.
Ed: Neil A. Martin. **Description:** Shares of Bankrate may rise as much as 25 percent from their level of $45.08 a share due to a strong cash flow and balance sheet. The company's Internet business remains strong despite weakness in the online advertising industry and is a potential takeover target.

8058 ▪ "Bankruptcies Shoot Up 68 Percent" in *Sacramento Business Journal* (Vol. 25, July 18, 2008, No. 20, pp. 1)
Pub: American City Business Journals, Inc.
Ed: Kathy Robertson. **Description:** Personal bankruptcy in the Sacramento area rose by 88 percent for the first half of 2008 while business bankruptcies rose by 50 percent for the same period. The numbers of consumer bankruptcy reflects the effect of high debt, rising mortgage costs, and declining home values on U.S. households.

8059 ▪ "Bankruptcy Blowback" in *Business Week* (September 22, 2008, No. 4100, pp. 36)
Pub: McGraw-Hill Companies, Inc.
Ed: Jessica Silver-Greenberg. **Description:** Changes to bankruptcy laws which were enacted in 2005 after banks and other financial institutions lobbied hard for them are now suffering the consequences of the laws which force more troubled borrowers to let their homes go into foreclosure; lenders suffer financially every time they have to take on a foreclosure and the laws in which they lobbied so hard to see enacted

are now becoming a problem for these lending institutions. Details of the changes in the laws are outlined as are the affects on the consumer, the economy and the lenders.

8060 ▪ "Banks Fall Short in Online Services for Savvy Traders" in *Barron's* (Vol. 88, March 17, 2008, No. 11, pp. 35)
Pub: Dow Jones & Company, Inc.
Ed: Theresa W. Carey. **Description:** Banc of America Investment Services, WellsTrade, and ShareBuilder are at the bottom of the list of online brokerages because they offer less trading technologies and product range. Financial shoppers miss out on a lot of customized tools and analytics when using these services.

8061 ▪ "Banks Fret About Gist Of Bailout" in *The Business Journal-Serving Metropolitan Kansas City* (Vol. 27, September 26, 2008, No. 2)
Pub: American City Business Journals, Inc.
Ed: James Dornbrook. **Description:** Banks from the Kansas City area hope that the proposed $700 billion bailout will not send the wrong message. UMB Financial Corp. chairman says that he hopes that the bailout would benefit companies that were more risk restrained and punish those that took outsized risk. Other bank executives' perceptions on the planned bailout are given.

8062 ▪ "Banks Seeing Demand for Home Equity Loans Slowing" in *Crain's Cleveland Business* (Vol. 28, December 3, 2007, No. 48, pp. 1)
Pub: Crain Communications, Inc.
Ed: Shawn A. Turner. **Description:** Discusses the reasons for the decline in demand for home equity loans and lines of credit. Statistical data included.

8063 ▪ "Barbarians Set Bar Low With Lowly Canadian Telco" in *Globe & Mail* (March 31, 2007, pp. B1)
Pub: CTVglobemedia Publishing Inc.
Ed: Derek DeCloet. **Description:** The efforts of the private equity fund Kohlberg, Kravis, Roberts and Co. to acquire the Canadian telecommunications firm BCE are described.

8064 ▪ "Bargain Hunting In Vietnam" in *Barron's* (Vol. 88, July 14, 2008, No. 28, pp. M6)
Pub: Dow Jones & Co., Inc.
Ed: Elliot Wilson. **Description:** Vietnam's economy grew by just 6.5 percent for the first half of 2008 and its balance of payments ballooned to $14.4 billion. The falling stock prices in the country is a boon for bargain hunters and investing in the numerous domestic funds is one way of investing in the country. Some shares that investors are taking an interest in are also discussed.

8065 ▪ "Barron's Lipper Fund Listings" in *Barron's* (Vol. 89, July 13, 2009, No. 28, pp. 19)
Pub: Dow Jones & Co., Inc.
Description: Statistical tables are presented which show the assets and return of mutual funds up to a ten year period. The listing covers funds with at least $200 million in assets.

8066 ▪ "BASF Launches $4.9 Billion Bid for Rival Engelhard" in *Globe & Mail* (January 4, 2006, pp. B7)
Pub: CTVglobemedia Publishing Inc.
Ed: Mike Esterl; Steve Levine. **Description:** The plans of BASF AG, to acquire Engelhard Corp. for $4.9 billion, are presented.

8067 ▪ "Battered U.S. Auto Makers in Grip of Deeper Sales Slump" in *Globe & Mail* (April 4, 2007, pp. B1)
Pub: CTVglobemedia Publishing Inc.
Ed: Greg Keenan. **Description:** The fall in Canadian sales and market share of Ford Motor Co., General Motors Corp. and Chrysler Group is discussed.

8068 ■ "Battle of the Titans" in *Canadian Business* **(Vol. 81, March 17, 2008, No. 4, pp. 15)**
Pub: Rogers Media
Ed: Rachel Pulfer. **Description:** Regulatory authorities in Canada gave Thomson Corp and Reuters Group PLC the permission to go ahead with their merger. The merged companies could eclipse Bloomberg LP's market share of 33 percent. Authorities also required Thomson and Reuters to sell some of their databases to competitors.

8069 ■ "BCE's Aliant Trust Spinoff Valued at About $8.5 Billion" in *Globe & Mail* **(March 8, 2006, pp. B1)**
Pub: CTVglobemedia Publishing Inc.
Ed: Catherine McLean. **Description:** The details pertaining to the spinoff of Aliant Inc.'s landline business into an income trust by BCE Inc. are presented. The trust is valued at $8.5 billion.

8070 ■ "BDC Launches New Online Business Advice Centre" in *Internet Wire* **(July 13, 2010)**
Pub: Comtex
Description: The Business Development Bank of Canada (BDC) offers entrepreneurs the chance to use their new online BDC Advice Centre in order to seek advice regarding the challenges of entrepreneurship. Free online business tools and information to help both startups and established firms are also provided.

8071 ■ "The Bear Arrives - With Bargain Hunters" in *Barron's* **(Vol. 88, July 7, 2008, No. 27, pp. M3)**
Pub: Dow Jones & Co., Inc.
Ed: Kopin Tan. **Description:** US stock markets have dropped 20 percent below their highs, entering the bear market at the end of June 2008. It was also the worst performance of the stock markets during June. Wine maker Constellation Brands, however, reported a 50 percent rise in net income for the first quarter of 2008.

8072 ■ "Bear Market Tough On Investors" in *The Business Journal-Milwaukee* **(Vol. 25, July 4, 2008, No. 41, pp. A1)**
Pub: American City Business Journals, Inc.
Ed: Rich Kirchen. **Description:** Public companies and their investors in the Milwaukee area suffered as the bear market took hold of the Wisconsin stock market. There were 18 stocks out of the 36 publicly traded stocks that have fallen into the bear market, meaning a 20 percent decline from the market peak in the fall of 2007. The impacts of the bear market on investors are evaluated.

8073 ■ "The Bear's Back" in *Barron's* **(Vol. 88, July 7, 2008, No. 27, pp. 17)**
Pub: Dow Jones & Co., Inc.
Ed: Randall W. Forsyth; Vito Racanelli. **Description:** US stock markets have formally entered the bear market after the Dow Jones Industrial Average dropped 20 percent from its high as of June 2008. Investors remain uncertain as to how long the bear market will persist, especially with the US economy on the edge of recession.

8074 ■ "The Beauty of Banking's Big Ugly" in *Barron's* **(Vol. 89, July 27, 2009, No. 30, pp. 31)**
Pub: Dow Jones & Co., Inc.
Ed: Andrew Bary. **Description:** Appeal of the shares of Citigroup comes from its sharp discount to its tangible book value and the company's positive attributes include a strong capital position, high loan-loss reserves, and their appealing global-consumer. The shares have the potential to generate nice profits and decent stock gains as the economy turns.

8075 ■ "Behind the Numbers: When It Comes to Earnings, Look for Quality, Not Just Quantity" in *Black Enterprise* **(July 2008, pp. 35)**
Pub: Earl G. Graves Publishing Co. Inc.
Ed: Chris Keenan. **Description:** It is important for investors to examine the quality of a company's earnings rather than fixate on the quantity of those earnings. Advice is given regarding issues investors can look at when trying to determine the potential growth of a firm.

8076 ■ "Bertha's Birth Stirs Juice" in *Barron's* **(Vol. 88, July 14, 2008, No. 28, pp. M11)**
Pub: Dow Jones & Co., Inc.
Ed: Tom Sellen. **Description:** Price of frozen concentrated orange juice, which has risen to four-month highs of $1.3620 in July 2008 is due, in part, to the hurricane season that has come earlier than normal in the far eastern Atlantic thereby possibly harming the 2008-2009 Florida orange crop. Future tropical-storm development will affect the prices of this commodity.

8077 ■ "Best Cash Flow Generators" in *Canadian Business* **(Vol. 81, Summer 2008, No. 9, pp. 73)**
Pub: Rogers Media Ltd.
Ed: Calvin Leung. **Description:** Table showing the five-year annualized growth rate and one-year stock performance of companies that have grown their cash flow per share at an annualized rate of 15 percent or more over the past five years. Analysts project that the cash flow trend will continue. Other details of the stock performance index are presented.

8078 ■ "Best Defensive Stocks" in *Canadian Business* **(Vol. 81, Summer 2008, No. 9, pp. 67)**
Pub: Rogers Media Ltd.
Ed: Calvin Leung. **Description:** Stocks of the companies presented have market capitalization of greater than $1 billion and dividend gains of at least 2 percent. A table showing the average one-year total return of the stocks is provided.

8079 ■ "The Best Five-Month Run Since 1938" in *Barron's* **(Vol. 89, August 3, 2009, No. 31, pp. M3)**
Pub: Dow Jones & Co., Inc.
Ed: Kopin Tan. **Description:** US stock markets ended July 2009 registering the highest five-month rise since 1938. The shares of Cablevision could rise as the company simplifies its structure and spins off its Madison Square Garden unit. The shares of Potash Corp. could fall as the company faces lower earnings due to falling potash purchases.

8080 ■ "Best Growth Stocks" in *Canadian Business* **(Vol. 82, Summer 2009, No. 8, pp. 28)**
Pub: Rogers Media
Ed: Calvin Leung. **Description:** Canadian stocks that are considered as the best growth stocks, and whose price-earnings ratio is less than their earnings growth rate, are suggested. Suggestions include pharmaceutical firm Paladin Labs, which was found to have 13 consecutive years of revenue growth. Paladin Labs acquires or licenses niche drugs and markets them in Canada.

8081 ■ "Best Income Trust" in *Canadian Business* **(Vol. 81, Summer 2008, No. 9, pp. 69)**
Pub: Rogers Media Ltd.
Ed: Calvin Leung. **Description:** Table showing five-year annualized growth rate and one-year stock performance of real estate investment trusts firms in Canada is presented. Calgary-based Boardwalk REIT is projected to grow the fastest among North American REITs over the next two years. Other details on the stock performance analysis are presented.

8082 ■ "Best Managed Companies" in *Canadian Business* **(Vol. 81, Summer 2008, No. 9, pp. 71)**
Pub: Rogers Media Ltd.
Ed: Calvin Leung. **Description:** Table showing the five-year annualized growth rate and one-year stock performance of companies that have grown their cash flow per share at an annualized rate of 15 percent or more over the past five years. Analysts project that the cash flow trend will continue. Other details of the stock performance index are presented.

8083 ■ "Best Turnaround Stocks" in *Canadian Business* **(Vol. 81, Summer 2008, No. 9, pp. 65)**
Pub: Rogers Media Ltd.
Ed: Calvin Leung. **Description:** Share prices of Sierra Wireless Inc. and EXFO Electro Optical Engineering Inc. have fallen over the past year but

have good chance at a rebound considering that the companies have free cash flow and no long-term debt. One-year stock performance analysis of the two companies is presented.

8084 ■ "Best Value Stocks" in *Canadian Business* **(Vol. 82, Summer 2009, No. 8, pp. 30)**
Pub: Rogers Media
Ed: Calvin Leung. **Description:** Canadian companies that are believed to have the best value stocks are suggested. Suggestions include publishing firm Glacier Media, which has reported a four-fold growth in sales in the last three years. While publishers like Glacier Media face challenges such as declining circulation, the firm's industry diversification is expected to help it weather the economic downturn.

8085 ■ "Bet on the Subcontinent" in *Canadian Business* **(Vol. 81, April 14, 2008, No. 6, pp. 27)**
Pub: Rogers Media
Ed: Calvin Leung. **Description:** Morgan Stanley Capital International India Index is down 28 percent for the first half of 2008 but this index rebounded 6 percent in 2002 then skyrocketed 65 percent in 2003. The economic reforms in the 1990's have created a growing middle class and households that can afford discretionary items will grow from eight million to 94 million by 2025. India's equity market could outperform developed markets if its economy grows at its current rate.

8086 ■ "Betting Big, Winning Big" in *Barron's* **(Vol. 88, March 17, 2008, No. 11, pp. 49)**
Pub: Dow Jones & Company, Inc.
Ed: Lawrence C. Strauss. **Description:** Bruce Berkowitz explains that the reason that his portfolio is concentrated is because getting more positions makes the portfolio more average compared to putting the money into your 10th or 20th-best idea. Berkowitz' picks include Berkshire Hathaway, Well-Care Health Plus, Sears Holdings, and Mohawk Industries.

8087 ■ "Betting on a Happy Ending" in *Barron's* **(Vol. 88, July 7, 2008, No. 27, pp. 14)**
Pub: Dow Jones & Co., Inc.
Ed: Dimitra DeFotis. **Description:** Shares of Time Warner, priced at $14.69 each, appear under-priced as financial analysts discount the value of the company. The company should be worth more than $20 a share as the company is spinning off Time Warner Cable.

8088 ■ "Betting On Volatile Materials" in *Barron's* **(Vol. 88, July 14, 2008, No. 28, pp. M11)**
Pub: Dow Jones & Co., Inc.
Ed: John Marshall. **Description:** Economic slowdowns in the U.S., Europe and China could cause sharp short-term declines in the materials sector. The S&P Materials sector is vulnerable to shifts in the flow of funds. Statistical data included.

8089 ■ "Beware this Chinese Export" in *Barron's* **(Vol. 90, August 30, 2010, No. 35, pp. 21)**
Pub: Barron's Editorial & Corporate Headquarters
Ed: Bill Alpert, Leslie P. Norton. **Description:** A look at 158 China reverse-merger stocks in the U.S. reveal that the median underperformed the index of U.S. listed Chinese companies by 75 percent in their first three years. These reverse merger stocks also lagged the Russell 2000 index of small cap stocks by 66 percent.

8090 ■ "Beware the Ides of March" in *Canadian Business* **(Vol. 81, April 14, 2008, No. 6, pp. 13)**
Pub: Rogers Media
Ed: Jeff Sanford. **Description:** Financial troubles of Bear Stearns in March, 2008 was part of the credit crunch that started in the summer of 2007 in the U.S. when subprime mortgages that were written for people who could barely afford the payments started defaulting. The bankruptcy protection given to 20 as-

set backed commercial paper trusts is being fought by the investors in these securities who could stand to lose 40 percent of their money under the agreement.

8091 ■ "Beware of Rotting Money" in Barron's (Vol. 89, July 13, 2009, No. 28, pp. 31)

Pub: Dow Jones & Co., Inc.

Ed: Thomas G. Donlan. **Description:** Inflation can take hold of a country and do it great harm; it is caused by people, most particularly central bankers in charge of the world's reserve currency. Arrogant economists pushed the belief that the government can engineer the economy and it is argued that there is trouble ahead when the government tries to control the economy.

8092 ■ "Beyond Microsoft and Yahoo!: Some M&A Prospects" in Barron's (Vol. 88, March 17, 2008, No. 11, pp. 39)

Pub: Dow Jones & Company, Inc.

Ed: Eric J. Savitz. **Description:** Weak quarterly earnings report for Yahoo! could pressure the company's board to cut a deal with Microsoft. Electronic Arts is expected to win its hostile $26-a-share bid for Take-Two Interactive Software. Potential targets and buyers for mergers and acquisitions are mentioned.

8093 ■ "The Big 50" in Canadian Business (Vol. 81, Summer 2008, No. 9, pp. 125)

Pub: Rogers Media Ltd.

Description: Large publicly held corporations are ranked based on market capitalization and stock performance. Potash Corp. of Saskatchewan topped the roster with 169.3 percent of return and even surpassing its 2007 result of 107 percent. A table showing the 2008 rankings of the companies is presented.

8094 ■ "Big Gains Brewing at Anheuser-Busch InBev" in Barron's (Vol. 90, August 30, 2010, No. 35, pp. 34)

Pub: Barron's Editorial & Corporate Headquarters

Ed: Christopher C. Williams. **Description:** Anheuser-Busch InBev is realizing cost synergies and it posted better than expected returns two years after the merger that formed the company. One analyst believes its American depositary receipt could be worth as much as 72 in a year.

8095 ■ "Big Trouble at Sony Ericsson" in Barron's (Vol. 88, March 24, 2008, No. 12, pp. M9)

Pub: Dow Jones & Company, Inc.

Ed: Angelo Franchini. **Description:** Sony Ericsson is facing trouble as it warned that its sales and net income before taxes will fall by nearly half for the first quarter of 2008. The joint venture of Sony and Ericsson has a global mobile phone market share of nine percent as of 2007, fourth largest in the world.

8096 ■ "Blackstone Set to Sell Stake" in Globe & Mail (March 17, 2007, pp. B6)

Pub: CTVglobemedia Publishing Inc.

Ed: Tennille Tracy. **Description:** The plan of Blackstone Group to sell 10 percent of its stake to raise $4 billion and its proposal to go for initial public offering is discussed.

8097 ■ "Blackstone's Outlook Still Tough" in Barron's (Vol. 88, March 17, 2008, No. 11, pp. 19)

Pub: Dow Jones & Company, Inc.

Ed: Andrew Bary. **Description:** Earnings for the Blackstone Group may not recover soon since the company's specialty in big leveraged buyouts is floundering and may not recover until 2009. The company earns lucrative incentive fees on its funds but those fees went negative in the fourth quarter of 2007 and there could be more fee reversals in the future.

8098 ■ "A Bleak Earnings View" in Barron's (Vol. 88, March 10, 2008, No. 10, pp. 15)

Pub: Dow Jones & Company, Inc.

Description: Analysts expect consumer discretionary profits in the S&P 500 to drop 8.4 percent in the first quarter of 2008. A less confident consumer is expected to pull profits down, putting forecasts of earnings growth in the S&P 500 at risk. Statistical data included.

8099 ■ "Bloody Monday for Bear?" in Barron's (Vol. 88, March 17, 2008, No. 11, pp. M14)

Pub: Dow Jones & Company, Inc.

Ed: Steven M. Sears. **Description:** Shares of Bear Stearns could slip further at the start of the trading week unless the company is bought out or bolstered by some other development over the weekend. Prices of the company's shares in the options market suggests about a 30 percent chance that the stock falls below $20 before March expirations expire.

8100 ■ "Blue-Collar Broker" in Boston Business Journal (Vol. 31, July 15, 2011, No. 25, pp. 1)

Pub: Boston Business Journal

Ed: Tim McLaughlin. **Description:** Richard F. Connolly Jr. was ranked 91st in Barron's latest annual ranking of top financial advisers and his team at Morgan Stanley Smith Barney oversee an estimated $3.7 billion in assets. However, anyone who knew him knows that he's just a blue-collar broker from Woburn who loves golf.

8101 ■ "BMW Revs Up for a Rebound" in Barron's (Vol. 89, July 13, 2009, No. 28, pp. M7)

Pub: Dow Jones & Co., Inc.

Ed: Jonathan Buck. **Description:** Investors may like BMW's stocks because the company has maintained its balance sheet strength and has an impressive production line of new models that should boost sales in the next few years. The company's sales are also gaining traction, although their vehicle delivery was down 1.7 percent year on year on June 2009, this was still the best monthly sales figure for 2009.

8102 ■ "Boar Market: Penny-Wise Consumers Favoring Pork" in Crain's Chicago Business (Vol. 31, April 14, 2008, No. 15, pp. 4)

Pub: Crain Communications, Inc.

Ed: Bruce Blythe. **Description:** Interview with Alan Cole who is the president of Cedar Hill Associates Inc. and who discusses ways in which his company is taking advantage of the record highs of oil and natural gas as well as his overall outlook on the market.

8103 ■ "Board This Powertrain" in Barron's (Vol. 89, July 27, 2009, No. 30, pp. 30)

Pub: Dow Jones & Co., Inc.

Ed: Naureen S. Malik. **Description:** Siemens' American Depositary Receipts have risen 60 percent from their March 2009 low and they should continue heading higher. The company has solid earnings and revenue growth since they lead in growing markets such as alternative energy and health-care infrastructure. Their shares also look cheap at 1.9 times book value.

8104 ■ "Boeing Earns Its Wings With Strong Quarter" in Crain's Chicago Business (Vol. 31, April 28, 2008, No. 17, pp. 4)

Pub: Crain Communications, Inc.

Ed: Daniel Rome Levine. **Description:** Interview with Michael A. Crowe, the senior managing director at Mesirow Financial Investment Management, who discusses highlights from the earnings season so far, his outlook for the economy and the stock market as well as what his company is purchasing. Mr. Crowe also recommends shares of five companies.

8105 ■ "BofA Cutting 70 Charlotte Tech Jobs" in Charlotte Observer (January 31, 2007)

Pub: Knight-Ridder/Tribune Business News

Ed: Rick Rothacker. **Description:** Bank of America announced the elimination of 70 technology positions at their Charlotte, North Carolina facility. The move is part of the company's effort to increase efficiency.

8106 ■ "BofA May Part With U.S. Trust" in Boston Business Journal (Vol. 31, May 20, 2011, No. 17, pp. 1)

Pub: Boston Business Journal

Ed: Tim McLaughlin. **Description:** Bank of America Corporation is willing to sell its U.S. Trust private banking division to improve its capital ratio. The unit remains to be the corporation's core asset and posted $696 million revenue in the first quarter 2010 in contract with Merrill Lynch Global Wealth Management's $3.5 billion. Analysts say that U.S. Trust would fetch more than $3 billion.

8107 ■ "BofA Will Reach the Top with Countrywide Deal" in Business North Carolina (Vol. 28, March 2008, No. 3, pp. 36)

Pub: Business North Carolina

Description: Bank of America, headquartered in Charlotte, North Carolina, will add Countrywide to its let of credits. Countrywide is the largest U.S. mortgage lender. Statistical data included.

8108 ■ "Bonds v. Stocks: Who's Right About Recession?" in Barron's (Vol. 90, August 23, 2010, No. 34, pp. M3)

Pub: Barron's Editorial & Corporate Headquarters

Ed: Kopin Tan. **Description:** The future of treasury securities and stocks should the U.S. enter or avoid a recession are discussed. The back to school business climate and BHP Billiton's bid for Potash Corporation of Saskatchewan are also discussed.

8109 ■ "The Book On Indigo" in Canadian Business (Vol. 81, July 22, 2008, No. 12-13, pp. 29)

Pub: Rogers Media Ltd.

Ed: Thomas Watson. **Description:** Indigo Books & Music Inc. reported record sales of $922 million resulting in a record net profit of $52.8 million for the 2008 fiscal year ended March 29, 2008. Earnings per share were $2.13, greater than Standard & Poor's expected $1.70 per share. Additional information concerning Indigo Books is presented.

8110 ■ "Boring Bonds Gain Pizzazz as Investors Flock to Debt Issues" in Baltimore Business Journal (Vol. 28, June 11, 2010, No. 5, pp. 1)

Pub: Baltimore Business Journal

Ed: Gary Haber. **Description:** Companies and nonprofit organizations have increased the pace of bond offerings in order to take advantage of the bonds' appeal among willing investors. Companies mostly issued corporate bonds to replace existing debt at lower interest rates and save them money from interest payments.

8111 ■ "Boston Hedge Fund Pours Money Into Real Estate Projects" in Charlotte Business Journal (Vol. 25, December 3, 2010, No. 37, pp. 1)

Pub: Charlotte Business Journal

Ed: Will Boye. **Description:** Boston-based hedge fund Baupost Group has been financing real estate project in Charlotte, North Carolina including more than 80 acres just north of uptown. Aside from purchasing the $23.8 million note for the Rosewood Condominiums from Regions Financial Corporation, the Baupost Group is also negotiating with Regions to buy the $93.9 million debt of the EipCentre real estate project.

8112 ■ "Bottler Will Regain Its Pop" in Barron's (Vol. 88, March 17, 2008, No. 11, pp. 56)

Pub: Dow Jones & Company, Inc.

Ed: Alexander Eule. **Description:** Discusses he 30 percent drop in the share price of PepsiAmericas Inc. from their 2007 high which presents an opportunity to buy into the company's dependable U.S. market and fast growing Eastern European business. The bottler's Eastern European operating profits in 2007 grew to $101 million from $21 million in 2006.

8113 ■ "Bottom-Fishing and Speed-Dating in India" in Barron's (Vol. 88, March 24, 2008, No. 12, pp. M12)

Pub: Dow Jones & Company, Inc.

Ed: Elliot Wilson. **Description:** Indian stocks have fallen hard in 2008, with Mumbai's Sensex 30 down 30 percent from its January 2008 peak of 21,000 to 14,995 in March. The India Private Equity Fair 2008 attracted 140 of the world's largest private equity firms and about 24 of India's fastest-growing corporations. Statistical data included.

8114 ■ **"Bountiful Barrels: Where to Find $140 Trillion"** in *Barron's* (Vol. 88, July 14, 2008, No. 28, pp. 40)

Pub: Dow Jones & Co., Inc.

Ed: Andrew Bary. **Description:** Surge in oil prices has caused a large transfer of wealth to oil-producing countries thereby reshaping the global economy. Oil reserves of oil exporting countries are now valued at $140 trillion. Economist Stephen Jen believes that this wealth will be transformed into paper assets as these countries invest in global stocks and bonds.

8115 ■ **"Bracing for a Bear of a Week"** in *Barron's* (Vol. 88, March 17, 2008, No. 11, pp. 24)

Pub: Dow Jones & Company, Inc.

Ed: Jacqueline Doherty. **Description:** JPMorgan Chase and the Federal Reserve Bank of New York's opening of a line of credit to Bear Stearns cut the stock price of Bear Stearns by 47 percent to 30 followed by speculation of an imminent sale. JP Morgan may be the only potential buyer for the firm and some investors say Bears could be sold at $20 to $30. Bears prime assets include its enormous asset base worth $395 billion.

8116 ■ **"Briefly"** in *Crain's Detroit Business* (Vol. 25, June 15, 2009, No. 24, pp. 18)

Pub: Crain Communications Inc. - Detroit

Ed: Tom Henderson, Jay Greene. **Description:** Details of the merger between Pl= anning Alternatives Ltd. and Oakland Wealth Management are highlighted. The two investment advisory firms will have a combined staff of 12 and will maintain two offices.

8117 ■ **"Bristol-Myers Close to Settling Lawsuit"** in *Globe & Mail* (January 23, 2006, pp. B6)

Pub: CTVglobemedia Publishing Inc.

Ed: Barbara Martinez. **Description:** The details of shareholder case against Bristol-Myers Squibb Co. are presented. The dispute is over the company's claim on the efficiency of Vanlev drug.

8118 ■ **"Brooke Agents Claim Mistreatment"** in *The Business Journal-Serving Metropolitan Kansas City* (Vol. 27, October 24, 2008, No. 7, pp. 1)

Pub: American City Business Journals, Inc.

Ed: James Dornbrook. **Description:** Franchisees of Brooke Corp., an insurance franchise, face uncertainty as their bills remain unpaid and banks threaten to destroy their credit. The company bundled and sold franchisee loans to different banks, but the credit crunch left the company with massive debts and legal disputes.

8119 ■ **"Building Portfolios for a World of 2.5 Percent Gains"** in *Barron's* (Vol. 88, July 7, 2008, No. 27, pp. L9)

Pub: Dow Jones & Co., Inc.

Ed: Karen Hube. **Description:** Interview with Harold Evenski whom is a financial planner running a fee-only planning practice; he continues to caution investors against pursuing short-term gains and focusing on long-term trends. He advises investors against investing in commodity and real estate stocks and is concerned about the possible effects of high inflation.

8120 ■ *Business Black Belt: Develop the Strength, Flexibility and Agility to Run Your Company*

Pub: Career Press, Inc.

Ed: Burke Franklin. **Released:** November 1, 2010. **Price:** $15.99. **Description:** Manual offering insights that will enable anyone to become successful in small business. Seventy short chapters included topics such as attitude, management, marketing, selling, employees, money, MBAs, lawyers, consultants, and investors.

8121 ■ **"The Business End of Staying in Business"** in *Contractor* (Vol. 56, September 2009, No. 9, pp. 51)

Pub: Penton Media, Inc.

Ed: Al Schwartz. **Description:** Advice on how to manage a new plumbing business in the United States are offered. The transition from being a work-

man to an employer is seen as one that accompanies a steep learning curve. The importance of managing cash flow is also highlighted.

8122 ■ **"Business Still Expected to Take Hit in 2008"** in *Business Journal-Serving Phoenix and the Valley of the Sun* (December 28, 2007)

Pub: American City Business Journals, Inc.

Ed: Chris Casacchia. **Description:** Community banks in 2008 are still projected to suffer from the repercussions of the subprime mortgage and credit crises. Meanwhile, the asset devaluation of big banks and global investment companies are higher than that of smaller banks. The third quarter and fourth quarter losses of banks such as Bear Stearns are discussed as well.

8123 ■ **"Business Still Expected To Take Hit In 2008"** in *Business Journal-Serving Phoenix and the Valley of the Sun* (December 28, 2007)

Pub: American City Business Journals, Inc.

Ed: Chris Casacchia. **Description:** Community banks are expected to suffer through 2008 due to the subprime mortgage and credit crisis. Meanwhile, the asset devaluation of big banks and global investment companies are higher than that of smaller banks. Third and fourth quarter losses of banks, including Bear Sterns, are discussed.

8124 ■ **"Business Through Hollywood's Lens"** in *Harvard Business Review* (Vol. 88, October 2010, No. 10, pp. 146)

Pub: Harvard Business School Publishing

Ed: Batia Wiesnefeld, Gino Cattani. **Description:** The authors contend that businesses are likely to be portrayed as villains in movies because corruption has higher entertainment draw. However, movies also depict popular opinion, which encourages businesses to be accountable and to help build communities.

8125 ■ **"C.A. Bancorp Inc. (TSX:BKP) Announces First Quarter 2007 Financial Results"** in *Canadian Corporate News* (May 16, 2007)

Pub: Comtex News Network Inc.

Ed: Description: Financial report for the first quarter of 2007 for C.A. Bancorp Inc., a publicly traded Canadian merchant bank and asset manager providing investors access to a range of private equity and alternative asset class investment opportunities. Statistical data and highlights included.

8126 ■ **"Calming Customers"** in *The Business Journal-Portland* (Vol. 25, August 29, 2008, No. 25, pp. 1)

Pub: American City Business Journals, Inc.

Ed: Kirsten Grind; Rob Smith. **Description:** Credit unions and banks in the Portland area are reaching out to clients in an effort to reassure them on the security of their money and the firms' financial stability. Roy Whitehead of Washington Federal Savings, for instance, wrote 41,000 customers of the bank to reassure them. The strategies of different banks and credit unions to answer their client's worries are discussed

8127 ■ **"Cambodia Calls"** in *Barron's* (Vol. 89, July 27, 2009, No. 30, pp. M7)

Pub: Dow Jones & Co., Inc.

Ed: Leslie P. Norton. **Description:** Interest in frontier markets could jump if enthusiasm about growth in the developed world gathers steam. Cambodia is the latest market to get attention where a handful of investors are trying to set up funds. One investor believes that Cambodia is back open for business but others are still cautious about investing in the country.

8128 ■ **"Canadian Banks Too Timid in China, Beijing Tells Flaherty"** in *Globe & Mail* (January 22, 2007, pp. B1)

Pub: CTVglobemedia Publishing Inc.

Ed: Steven Chase. **Description:** The article discusses Canadian banks' investments on China according to the views of federal Finance Minister Jim Flaherty.

8129 ■ **"The Canadians Are Coming!"** in *Canadian Business* (Vol. 80, October 22, 2007, No. 21, pp. 15)

Pub: Rogers Media

Ed: Rachel Pulfer. **Description:** Toronto-Dominion Bank declared its acquisition of the New Jersey-based Commerce Bancorp for C$8.5 billion. Royal Bank of Canada has scooped up Trinidad-based Financial Group for C$2.2 billion. Details of the foreign acquisitions, as well as the impact of high Canadian dollars on the mergers are discussed.

8130 ■ **"Candidates Won't Bash Fed; Rate Cuts Bash Savers"** in *Barron's* (Vol. 88, March 24, 2008, No. 12, pp. 31)

Pub: Dow Jones & Company, Inc.

Ed: Jim McTague. **Description:** Candidates in the 2008 US presidential election, like the current administration, do not and will not bash the Federal Reserve. The Federal Reserve's aggressive interest rate cuts hurt the incomes of people depending on their savings accounts.

8131 ■ **"Capturing Generation Y: Ready, Set, Transform"** in *Credit Union Times* (Vol. 21, July 14, 2010, No. 27, pp. 20)

Pub: Summit Business Media

Ed: Senthil Kumar. **Description:** The financial services sector recognizes that Generation Y will have a definite impact on the way business is conducted in the future. The mindset of Generation Y is social and companies need to use networking tools such as Facebook in order to reach this demographic.

8132 ■ **"The Case of the Deflated IPO"** in *Boston Business Journal* (Vol. 29, June 24, 2011, No. 7, pp. 1)

Pub: American City Business Journals Inc.

Ed: Scott Dance. **Description:** IPO market is on the rebound from the recession but for some companies in Maryland, the time is not yet ripe to go public. One of the companies that chooses to wait for better timing is SafeNet Inc. and it is eyeing some possible acquisitions while doing so.

8133 ■ **"Cash Flow Myths"** in *Canadian Business* (Vol. 80, March 12, 2007, No. 6, pp. 25)

Pub: Rogers Media

Ed: Al Rosen. **Description:** Expert advice to Canadian investors about understanding the cash flow statements of companies before investing money is presented.

8134 ■ **"Cemex Paves a Global Road to Solid Growth"** in *Barron's* (Vol. 88, March 10, 2008, No. 10, pp. 24)

Pub: Dow Jones & Company, Inc.

Ed: Sandra Ward. **Description:** Shares of Cemex are expected to perform well with the company's expected strong performance despite fears of a US recession. The company has a diverse geographical reach and benefits from a strong worldwide demand for cement.

8135 ■ **"Centrue Sets Down New Roots in St. Louis; Bank Looks to Expand in Exurbs of Chicago"** in *Crain's Chicago Business* (May 5, 2008)

Pub: Crain Communications, Inc.

Ed: H. Lee Murphy. **Description:** Centrue Financial Corp. has moved its headquarters from Ottawa to suburban St. Louis in search of higher-growth markets. The banks acquisitions and expansion plans are also discussed.

8136 ■ **"Certified Financial Planner Board of Standards Reacts to Jobs Program"** in *Professional Services Close-Up* (September 14, 2011)

Pub: Close-Up Media Inc.

Description: Certified Financial Planner Board of Standards Consumer Advocate, Eleanor Blayney, believe that people should be looking inward at their own ability to change their employment future. She shares tips for the job market to help out.

8137 ■ *The Changing Geography of Banking and Finance*
Pub: Springer Publishing Company
Ed: Pietro Alessandrini, Michele Fratianni, Alberto Zazzaro. **Released:** May 1, 2009. **Price:** $139.00. **Description:** The two contrasting trends that have emerged from the integration and consolidation processes of the banking industry in both Europe and the United States in the 1990s is examined.

8138 ■ **"Check Provider Says It Plans to Close Call Center in Charlotte" in** *Charlotte Observer* **(February 6, 2007)**
Pub: Knight-Ridder/Tribune Business News
Ed: Rick Rothacker. **Description:** Clarke American Checks Inc. is closing its call center located in Charlotte, North Carolina. Clarke provides checks and other services to financial institutions and customers.

8139 ■ **"Chuck's Big Chance" in** *Barron's* **(Vol. 89, July 13, 2009, No. 28, pp. L3)**
Pub: Dow Jones & Co., Inc.
Ed: Leslie P. Norton. **Description:** Charles Schwab is cutting prices and rolling out new products to lure customers and the company is well positioned to benefit from Wall Street's misery. Their shares are trading at just 17 times earnings, which should be at least at a multiple of 20.

8140 ■ **"CIBC Spends $1.1 Billion on Caribbean Expansion" in** *Globe & Mail* **(March 14, 2006, pp. B1)**
Pub: CTVglobemedia Publishing Inc.
Ed: Sinclair Stewart. **Description:** Canadian Imperial Bank of Commerce (CIBC), the fifth-largest bank of Canada, is planning to spend $1.1billion to buy major share of Barbados-based First Caribbean International Bank. The details of the acquisition plan are presented.

8141 ■ **"Citadel Hires Three Lehman Execs" in** *Chicago Tribune* **(October 2, 2008)**
Pub: McClatchy-Tribune Information Services
Ed: James P. Miller. **Description:** Citadel Investment Group LLC, Chicago hedge-fund operator, has hired three former senior executives of bankrupt investment banker Lehman Brothers Holding Inc. Citadel believes that the company's hiring spree will help them to further expand the firm's capabilities in the global fixed income business.

8142 ■ **"Citi Ruling Could Chill SEC, Street Legal Pacts" in** *Wall Street Journal Eastern Edition* **(November 29, 2011, pp. C1)**
Pub: Dow Jones & Company, Inc.
Ed: Jean Eaglesham, Chad Bray. **Description:** A $285 million settlement was reached between the Securities and Exchange Commission and Citigroup Inc. over allegations the bank misled investors over a mortgage-bond deal. Now, Judge Jed S. Rakoff has ruled against the settlement, a decision that will affect the future of such attempts to prosecute Wall Street fraud. Rakoff said that the settlement was "neither fair, nor reasonable, nor adequate, nor in the public interest."

8143 ■ **"Citigroup Moves to Buy Japan's Nikko" in** *Globe & Mail* **(March 7, 2007, pp. B12)**
Pub: CTVglobemedia Publishing Inc.
Ed: Jonathan Soble; Dan Wilchins. **Description:** Citigroup Inc. offered $10.8 billion to acquire troubled Nikko Cordial Corp., Japan's largest securities firm.

8144 ■ **"Citizens Unveils Mobile App for Business Customers" in** *New Hampshire Business Review* **(Vol. 33, March 25, 2011, No. 6, pp. 27)**
Pub: Business Publications Inc.
Description: Citizens Financial Group offers a new mobile banking application that allows business customers to manage cash and payments from a mobile device.

8145 ■ **"Clash of the Titans" in** *Canadian Business* **(Vol. 80, March 12, 2007, No. 6, pp. 27)**
Pub: Rogers Media
Ed: Andrew Wahl. **Description:** The frequent allegations of Google Inc. and Microsoft Corp. against each

other over copyright and other legal issues, with a view to taking away other's market share, is discussed.

8146 ■ **"Climbing the Wall of Worry, Two Steps at a Time" in** *Barron's* **(Vol. 89, July 13, 2009, No. 28, pp. L16)**
Pub: Dow Jones & Co., Inc.
Ed: Brian Blackstone. **Description:** Statistical table that shows the performance of different mutual funds for the second quarter of 2009 is presented. The data shows that on average, the 8,272 diversified equity funds gained 17 percent for this quarter.

8147 ■ **"CNinsure Offers Safety in Numbers" in** *Barron's* **(Vol. 90, September 13, 2010, No. 37, pp. 29)**
Pub: Barron's Editorial & Corporate Headquarters
Ed: Teresa Rivas. **Description:** China's insurance holding company CNinsure has a long growth future due to the nascent insurance market in the country. It has also been diversifying its offerings and it has a broad network in the nation. The shares of the company are trading cheaply at nearly 14 times its 2011 earnings, and is considered a good point for investors.

8148 ■ **"Coca-Cola Looks Ready to Pause" in** *Barron's* **(Vol. 88, March 10, 2008, No. 10, pp. 18)**
Pub: Dow Jones & Company, Inc.
Ed: Michael Santoli. **Description:** Shares of Coca-Cola are expected to turn sideways or experience a slight drop from $59.50 each to the mid-50 level. The company has seen its shares jump 40 percent since 2006, when it was in a series of measures to improve profitability.

8149 ■ **"Cogeco Profit Jumps 47 Percent in First Quarter" in** *Globe & Mail* **(January 13, 2006, pp. B3)**
Pub: CTVglobemedia Publishing Inc.
Ed: Catherine McLean. **Description:** The reasons behind 47 percent increase in first quarter 2006 profits for Cogeco Inc. are presented.

8150 ■ *A Colossal Failure of Common Sense: The Inside Story of the Collapse of Lehman Brothers*
Pub: Crown Business
Ed: Lawrence G. McDonald, Patrick Robinson. **Released:** 2009. **Price:** $27.00. **Description:** Former employee of Lehman Brothers details the failure of leadership that led to the demise of the company.

8151 ■ **"Coming: Cheaper Oil and a Stronger Buck" in** *Barron's* **(Vol. 88, March 24, 2008, No. 12, pp. 53)**
Pub: Dow Jones & Company, Inc.
Ed: Lawrence C. Strauss. **Description:** Carl C. Weinberg, the chief economist of High Frequency Economics, forecasts that Chinese economic growth will slow down and that oil prices will drop to $80 a barrel in 2008. He also believes that the US dollar will start rising the moment the Federal Reserve stops cutting interest rates.

8152 ■ **"Coming Soon: Bailouts of Fannie and Freddie" in** *Barron's* **(Vol. 88, July 14, 2008, No. 28, pp. 14)**
Pub: Dow Jones & Co., Inc.
Ed: Jonathan R. Laing. **Description:** Assurances from the government that Fannie Mae and Freddie Mac are adequately capitalized and able to carry on their duties as guarantors or owners of over $5 trillion of U.S. home mortgages are designed to keep both entities afloat until they attempt to raise $10 billion in new equity. The government would assume any losses in a bailout and owners of the banks' papers would profit as yields drop.

8153 ■ **"Commentary. On Federal Reserve's Cut of Interest Rates" in** *Small Business Economic Trends* **(January 2008, pp. 3)**
Pub: National Federation of Independent Business
Description: Federal Reserve cut interest rates and announced its economic outlook on September 18, 2007 to stimulate spending. The cut in interest rates, however, may not help in supporting consumer

spending because savers may lose interest income. The expected economic impact of the interest rate cuts and the U.S. economic outlook are also discussed.

8154 ■ **"Commentary. Small Business Economic Trends" in** *Small Business Economic Trends* **(February 2008, pp. 3)**
Pub: National Federation of Independent Business
Ed: William C. Dunkelberg, Holly Wade. **Description:** Commentary on the economic trends for small businesses in the U.S. is presented. Analysis of the U.S. Federal Reserve Board's efforts to prevent a recession is given. Reduction in business inventories is also discussed.

8155 ■ **"Commodities: Who's Behind the Boom?" in** *Barron's* **(Vol. 88, March 31, 2008, No. 13, pp. 3)**
Pub: Dow Jones & Company, Inc.
Ed: Gene Epstein. **Description:** Proliferation of mutual funds and exchange traded funds tied to commodities indexes has helped speculative buying reach unusual levels. Index funds are estimated to account for 40 percent of all bullish bets on commodities. Commodities could drop by 30 percent as speculators retreat. Statistical data included.

8156 ■ **"Commodity Speculation: Over the Top?" in** *Barron's* **(Vol. 89, July 13, 2009, No. 28, pp. 22)**
Pub: Dow Jones & Co., Inc.
Ed: Gene Epstein. **Description:** Commodity Futures Trading Commission is planning to impose position limits on speculators of oil and other commodities as energy costs rebound from their lows. These regulations make much sense and these position limits would greatly diminish the cash commitment of the commodity index traders if these were imposed on speculators and swaps dealers properly.

8157 ■ **"Compelling Opportunities" in** *Barron's* **(Vol. 88, March 10, 2008, No. 10, pp. 39)**
Pub: Dow Jones & Company, Inc.
Ed: Neil A. Martin. **Description:** Michael L. Reynal, portfolio manager of Principal International Emerging Markets Fund, is bullish on the growth prospects of stocks in emerging markets. He is investing big on energy, steel, and transportation companies.

8158 ■ **"Competitors Line Up to Save Failing Banks" in** *The Business Journal - Serving Phoenix and the Valley of the Sun* **(Vol. 28, July 25, 2008, No. 47, pp. 1)**
Pub: American City Business Journals, Inc.
Ed: Chris Casacchia. **Description:** Financial institutions in Arizona are positioning themselves as possible buyers in the event of failure of one of their competitors. These banks have already approached the Federal Deposit Insurance Corp. about their ability to take over their more troubled competitors.

8159 ■ **"Compounding Opportunity" in** *Hispanic Business* **(October 2007, pp. 72, 74-75)**
Pub: Hispanic Business
Ed: Hildy Medina. **Description:** New banks are targeting Hispanic entrepreneurs.

8160 ■ **"Comtech's Winning Streak" in** *Crain's New York Business* **(Vol. 24, January 7, 2008, No. 1, pp. 3)**
Pub: Crain Communications, Inc.
Description: Comtech Telecommunications Corp., a designer and manufacturer of equipment that helps military track troops and vehicles on the field, has been one of the stock market's biggest winners over the past decade. Statistical data included.

8161 ■ **"Connect the Thoughts" in** *Canadian Business* **(Vol. 81, October 27, 2008, No. 18, pp. 8)**
Pub: Rogers Media Ltd.
Ed: Jeff Sanford. **Description:** Thomas Homer-Dixon believes the financial crisis that hit Wall Street is a systemic crisis and may result in the reconfiguration

of financial markets in ways that people may never understand. He also thinks the U.S. may borrow against its assets, making it a weaker nation.

8162 ▪ "Conquering Your Fear of Fees" in *Entrepreneur* **(Vol. 37, October 2009, No. 10, pp. 86)**
Pub: Entrepreneur Media, Inc.
Ed: Rosalind Resnick. **Description:** Entrepreneurs should study money management charges carefully before investing. They should understand how different forms of investments work and how much money managers and mutual funds charge for their services.

8163 ▪ "Consumers Finding It Harder to Get and Keep Credit" in *Chicago Tribune* **(January 10, 2009)**
Pub: McClatchy-Tribune Information Services
Ed: Susan Chandler. **Description:** Five tips to maintain a good credit rating in these economic times are outlined and discussed.

8164 ▪ "Conversation Starters for the Holiday" in *Barron's* **(Vol. 89, July 6, 2009, No. 27, pp. 7)**
Pub: Dow Jones & Co., Inc.
Ed: Michael Santoli. **Description:** Investors are concerned that the US will experience high inflation due to low interest rates and improved money supply. US consumer spending has increased to 70 percent of gross domestic product, brought by health-care spending increases, while savings rates have risen to 6.9 percent.

8165 ▪ "A Conversation With Money Manager William Vellon" in *Crain's Chicago Business* **(Vol. 31, November 17, 2008, No. 46, pp. 4)**
Pub: Crain Communications, Inc.
Ed: Mike Colias. **Description:** Interview with William Vellon, the executive vice-president of Kingsbury Capital Investment Advisors; Vellon discusses ways in which the government can help the financial sector, his client base and bargains that investors should consider.

8166 ▪ "Cool on Chicago Office Properties" in *Crain's Chicago Business* **(Vol. 31, March 31, 2008, No. 13, pp. 16)**
Pub: Crain Communications, Inc.
Ed: Eddie Baeb. **Description:** Investors predict values on Chicago office buildings to drop 1.3 percent over the next year.

8167 ▪ "Copper Giant to Spin Off Silver Assets" in *Globe & Mail* **(February 27, 2006, pp. B1)**
Pub: CTVglobemedia Publishing Inc.
Ed: Sinclair Stewart; Andrew Willis. **Description:** The reasons behind the sale of silver mining assets by Codelco are presented.

8168 ▪ "Copper, Zinc Prices Hammered" in *Globe & Mail* **(February 3, 2007, pp. B7)**
Pub: CTVglobemedia Publishing Inc.
Ed: John Partridge. **Description:** The decline in the global prices of copper and zinc metals in January 2007 is discussed. Copper prices fell by 12 percent while zinc prices dropped by 6.3 percent.

8169 ▪ "Copy Karachi?" in *Barron's* **(Vol. 88, June 30, 2008, No. 26, pp. 5)**
Pub: Dow Jones & Co., Inc.
Ed: Randall W. Forsyth. **Description:** Karachi bourse had a historic 8.6 percent one-day gain because the bourse banned short-selling for a month and announced a 30 billion rupee fund to stabilize the market. The shares of General Motors are trading within the same values that it had in 1974. The reasons for this decline are discussed.

8170 ▪ "Corn May Get Shucked By Soy" in *Barron's* **(Vol. 88, March 31, 2008, No. 13, pp. M12)**
Pub: Dow Jones & Company, Inc.
Ed: Angie Pointer. **Description:** Acreage allotted to soybeans could jump by 12 percent from 2007's 63.6 million as the price for soybeans reaches record highs. Corn acreage could drop by 6.7 percent as other crops expand and higher fertilizer prices shift farmers away from corn.

8171 ▪ "Corporate Elite Show Resilience" in *The Business Journal-Serving Greater Tampa Bay* **(Vol. 28, August 1, 2008, No. 32, pp. 1)**
Pub: American City Business Journals, Inc.
Ed: Margie Manning; Alexis Muellner. **Description:** Stocks of the largest public companies in Tampa Bay, Florida, outperformed the S&P 500 index by 28 percent in the first half of 2008. The escalation is attributed to the growth orientation of the companies in the area and the lack of exposure to the real estate and financial services sectors.

8172 ▪ "Corus Eases Off Ailing Condo Market; Office Developers Get Majority of 1Q Loans" in *Crain's Chicago Business* **(April 28, 2008)**
Pub: Crain Communications, Inc.
Ed: H. Lee Murphy. **Description:** Corus Bankshares Inc., a specialist in lending for the condominium high-rise construction market, is diversifying its portfolio by making loans to office developers and expects to be investing in hotels through the rest of the year. Corus' $7.57 billion loan portfolio is also discussed in detail as well as the company's earnings and share price. Statistical data included.

8173 ▪ "Cost Cuts Lead Dealers to Record Profits" in *Globe & Mail* **(March 24, 2006, pp. B3)**
Pub: CTVglobemedia Publishing Inc.
Ed: Omar El Akkad. **Description:** The reasons behind posting of $4.3 billion profit by Canadian securities sector, for 2005, are presented.

8174 ▪ "Countdown" in *Canadian Business* **(Vol. 81, March 3, 2008, No. 3, pp. 27)**
Pub: Rogers Media
Ed: Al Rosen. **Description:** According to a recent poll only 42 percent of portfolio managers in Canada are aware that the country is planning to adopt the International Financial Reporting Standards beginning 2011. The shift to the new standards will have significant impacts on investment values and will be the biggest revolution in Canadian financial reporting. The effects of the transition on portfolio managers and investors are analyzed.

8175 ▪ "CPI, Coal Lead Local Stock Decline" in *Saint Louis Business Journal* **(Vol. 32, October 14, 2011, No. 7, pp. 1)**
Pub: Saint Louis Business Journal
Ed: Greg Edwards. **Description:** Coal companies and CPI Corporation were among those whose stocks have declined in St. Louis, Missouri. The stocks of local firms have plunged by 28 percent during the first nine months of 2011.

8176 ▪ "Crain's Picks Top '08 Stocks" in *Crain's New York Business* **(Vol. 24, January 7, 2008, No. 1, pp. 3)**
Pub: Crain Communications, Inc.
Ed: Aaron Elstein. **Description:** Listing of five stocks that Crain's believes can deliver solid gains for shareholders.

8177 ▪ *Crash Proof 2.0: How to Profit From the Economic Collapse*
Pub: John Wiley & Sons, Inc.
Ed: Peter D. Schiff. **Released:** September 22, 2009. **Price:** $27.95. **Description:** Factors that will affect financial stability in the coming years are explained. A three step plan to battle the current economic downturn is also included.

8178 ▪ "The Credit Crisis Continues" in *Barron's* **(Vol. 88, March 10, 2008, No. 10, pp. M12)**
Pub: Dow Jones & Company, Inc.
Ed: Randall W. Forsyth. **Description:** Short-term Treasury yields dropped to new cyclical lows in early March 2008, with the yield for the two-year Treasury note falling to 1.532 percent. Spreads of the mortgage-backed securities of Fannie Mae and Freddie Mac rose on suspicion of collapses in financing.

8179 ▪ "Credit Crisis Puts Market in Unprecedented Territory" in *Crain's New York Business* **(Vol. 24, January 7, 2008, No. 1, pp. 14)**
Pub: Crain Communications, Inc.
Ed: Aaron Elstein. **Description:** Banks are being forced to take enormous losses due to investors who

are refusing to buy anything linked to subprime mortgages and associated securities.

8180 ▪ "Credit Unions Cast Wary Eye at Paulson Plan, But Not Panicking Yet" in *The Business Review Albany* **(Vol. 35, April 11, 2008, No. 1)**
Pub: The Business Review
Ed: Barbara Pinckney. **Description:** Credit unions are suspicious of US Treasury Secretary Henry Paulson's plan to establish a single federally insured depository institution charter for all institutions covered by federal deposit insurance. The charter would replace national banks, federal savings associations, and federal credit union charters.

8181 ▪ "Credit Unions Gain: New Members Sign Up, Fleeing Banks" in *Puget Sound Business Journal* **(Vol. 29, October 10, 2008, No. 25, pp. 1)**
Pub: American City Business Journals
Ed: Kirsten Grind. **Description:** Credit unions are gaining new members due to customers' lack of confidence in federal banks.

8182 ▪ "Critics: Efforts to Fix Loans Won't Stop Foreclosure Wave" in *Business First Columbus* **(Vol. 25, November 14, 2008, No. 12, pp. A1)**
Pub: American City Business Journals
Ed: Adrian Burns. **Description:** Efforts by U.S. banks to help homeowners pay mortgages are seen to have little if any impact on foreclosures. Banks have announced plans to identify and aid troubled borrowers. Statistical data included.

8183 ▪ *Currency Internationalization: Global Experiences and Implications for the Renminbi*
Pub: Palgrave Macmillan
Ed: Wensheng Peng, Chang Shu. **Released:** January 5, 2010. **Price:** $100.00. **Description:** A collection of academic studies relating to the potential internationalization of China's remninbi. It also discusses the increasing use of China's remninbi currency in international trade and finance.

8184 ▪ "Customers Turned Off? Not at Best Buy" in *Barron's* **(Vol. 88, March 24, 2008, No. 12, pp. 29)**
Pub: Dow Jones & Company, Inc.
Ed: Sandra Ward. **Description:** Shares of Best Buy, trading at $42.41 each, are expected to rise to an average of $52 a share due to the company's solid fundamentals. The company's shares have fallen 20 percent from their 52-week high and are attractive given the company's bright prospects in the video game sector and high-definition video.

8185 ▪ "CVRD Inco Strike Shuts Sudbury Mines" in *Globe & Mail* **(April 2, 2007, pp. B1)**
Pub: CTVglobemedia Publishing Inc.
Ed: Andy Hoffman. **Description:** The closure of nickel mining operations at the Sudbury mines due to the strike by employees of CVRD Inco Ltd. is described. The prospects of a rise in the prices of nickel are discussed, besides the production of metals in Canada.

8186 ▪ "Cyclicals, Your Day Is Coming" in *Barron's* **(Vol. 89, July 27, 2009, No. 30, pp. 24)**
Pub: Dow Jones & Co., Inc.
Ed: Dimitra DeFotis. **Description:** Cyclical stocks are likely to be big winners when the economy improves and 13 stocks that have improving earnings, decent balance sheets, and dividends are presented. These candidates include U.S. Steel, Alcoa, Allegheny Tech, Dow Chemical, and Nucor.

8187 ▪ "Darkness Falling..." in *Barron's* **(Vol. 89, July 20, 2009, No. 29, pp. 13)**
Pub: Dow Jones & Co., Inc.
Description: Newsletter writer Arch Crawford believes that market indicators signal a possible downturn in US stock markets. High risk areas also include China and Japan .

8188 ■ "Data Dispel Some Notions About Value of Stock Buybacks" in *Crain's Cleveland Business* (Vol. 28, November 19, 2007, No. 46, pp. 9)
Pub: Crain Communications, Inc.
Ed: Megan Johnston. **Description:** According to new research on buybacks and their benefits, companies engaged in stock buybacks frequently do not enjoy a nice boost in their share prices despite the conventional wisdom that states that investors like stock buybacks.

8189 ■ "Dating Games" in *Canadian Business* (Vol. 79, September 25, 2006, No. 19, pp. 23)
Pub: Rogers Media
Ed: John Gray. **Description:** Increasing stock option scandals in Canada and American companies is discussed.

8190 ■ "Deal Braces Cramer for Growth Run" in *The Business Journal-Serving Metropolitan Kansas City* (Vol. 26, July 4, 2008, No. 43, pp. 1)
Pub: American City Business Journals, Inc.
Ed: James Dornbook. **Description:** Gardner, Kansas-based Cramer Products Inc. bought 100 percent of the stocks of Louisville, Kentucky-based Active Ankle Inc. from 26 private investors increasing its revenue by 20 percent. The latter is the second largest vendor of Cramer. Other details of the merger are presented.

8191 ■ "Deal or No Deal?" in *Canadian Business* (Vol. 80, January 15, 2007, No. 2, pp. 38)
Pub: Rogers Media
Ed: Andrew Wahl; Zena Olijnkyk; Jeff Sanford; Erin Pooley. **Description:** The trends in the stock prices of companies like Loblaw Companies Ltd., Domtar Inc. and Biovail Corp., from January 2006 to January 2007, are analyzed.

8192 ■ "The Deal - Rhymes With Steal - Of A Lifetime" in *Barron's* (Vol. 88, March 24, 2008, No. 12, pp. 24)
Pub: Dow Jones & Company, Inc.
Ed: Andrew Bary. **Description:** JPMorgan Chase's impending acquisition of Bear Stearns for $2.50 a share is a huge steal for the former. JPMorgan is set to acquire a company with a potential annual earnings of $1 billion while the Federal Reserve funds Bear's illiquid assets by providing $30 billion in non-recourse loans.

8193 ■ "Dean Foods" in *Ice Cream Reporter* (Vol. 23, November 20, 2010, No. 12, pp. 8)
Pub: Ice Cream Reporter
Description: The impact of higher commodity prices can be seen in the recent news from Dean Foods, the largest U.S. dairy company, which reported that rising butterfat and other dairy commodity costs have led to lower-than-expected quarterly profits after it cut prices to compete with private-label brands.

8194 ■ "Debutante NYSE Soars 20 Percent" in *Globe & Mail* (March 9, 2006, pp. B1)
Pub: CTVglobemedia Publishing Inc.
Ed: John Partridge. **Description:** The debutant share trading of NYSE Group Inc. is discussed. The prices rose by 20 percent before closing.

8195 ■ "Decision CEO Cool to Acquisitions" in *Globe & Mail* (April 19, 2007, pp. B6)
Pub: CTVglobemedia Publishing Inc.
Ed: Andy Hoffman. **Description:** The increase in the shares of Denison Mines Corp. due to hike in Uranium prices is discussed.

8196 ■ "Decline in Assets Is Costly for Advisers" in *The Business Journal-Serving Metropolitan Kansas City* (Vol. 27, October 24, 2008)
Pub: American City Business Journals, Inc.
Ed: James Dornbrook. **Description:** Financial advisers in the Kansas City, Missouri area are forced to cut costs as their assets have decreased sharply due to the huge drop in stock prices. American Century Investments are forced to diversify into foreign as-

sets and cut 90 jobs as its assets dropped to $84 billion. Diversification has softened the impact of the steep decline in stock prices for Waddell & Reed Financial Inc.

8197 ■ *A Demon of Our Own Design: Markets, Hedge Funds, and the Perils of Financial Innovation*
Pub: John Wiley and Sons, Inc.
Ed: Richard Bookstaber. **Released:** December 2008. **Price:** $16.95 paperback. **Description:** Longtime hedge-fund manager offers his take on a market and investment system that he believes is needlessly complex owing to investment banks, hedge funds, innovation, regulation, and safeguards and further compounded by investor and market instabilities. These complexities could create a large-scale disaster.

8198 ■ "Detecting Crookery" in *Canadian Business* (Vol. 80, February 12, 2007, No. 4, pp. 23)
Pub: Rogers Media
Ed: Al Rosen. **Description:** Expert advice to Canadian investors on proper financial reporting is presented and ways to protect their investments are discussed.

8199 ■ "Detroit Hosts Conferences on Green Building, IT, Finance" in *Crain's Detroit Business* (Vol. 25, June 1, 2009, No. 22, pp. 9)
Pub: Crain Communications Inc. - Detroit
Ed: Tom Henderson. **Description:** Detroit will host three conferences in June 2009, one features green technology, one information technology and the third will gather black bankers and financial experts from across the nation.

8200 ■ "Deutsche Bank Joins the Club" in *Barron's* (Vol. 88, March 31, 2008, No. 13, pp. M6)
Pub: Dow Jones & Company, Inc.
Ed: Arindam Nag. **Description:** Deutsche Bank's tangible leverage has worsened sharply in the past year from 2.1 percent to 2.3 percent during 2002-2006 to only 1.6 percent. The bank has also been accumulating a lot of illiquid assets and its Level-3 assets are three times its tangible equity.

8201 ■ "Diana Sands; Vice-President of Investor Relations, Boeing Co." in *Crain's Chicago Business* (Vol. 31, May 5, 2008, No. 18, pp. 32)
Pub: Crain Communications, Inc.
Ed: John Rosenthal. **Description:** Profile of Diana Sands who is the vice-president of investor relations at Boeing Co. which entails explaining the company's performance to securities analysts and institutional investors.

8202 ■ "Diary of a Short-Seller" in *Conde Nast Portfolio* (Vol. 2, June 2008, No. 6, pp. 44)
Pub: Conde Nast Publications, Inc.
Ed: Jesse Eisinger. **Description:** Profile of David Einhorn who is a fund manager that spoke out against finance company Allied Capital whose stock fell nearly 20 percent the day after Einhorn's critique; Einhorn subsequently had to contend with attacks against his credibility as well as investigations by the S.E.C.; Einhorn's experience illuminates our current economic crisis.

8203 ■ "Diaz Announces Financial and Operating Results for the First Three Months of 2007" in *Canadian Corporate News* (May 16, 2007)
Pub: Comtex News Network Inc.
Description: Diaz Resources Ltd., an oil and gas exploration and production company, announced its financial results during the first quarter of 2007 which were hampered by lower gas prices and declining production volumes but anticipates the financial results should steadily improve in the second quarter of 2007.

8204 ■ "Dick Haskayne" in *Canadian Business* (Vol. 81, March 31, 2008, No. 5, pp. 72)
Pub: Rogers Media
Ed: Andy Holloway. **Description:** Dick Haskayne says that he learned a lot about business from his

dad who ran a butcher shop where they had to make a decision on buying cattle and getting credit. Haskayne says that family, friends, finances, career, health, and infrastructure are benchmarks that have to be balanced.

8205 ■ *Dictionary of Finance, Investment and Banking*
Pub: Palgrave Macmillan
Ed: Erik Banks. **Released:** 2010. **Price:** $42.95. **Description:** Comprehensive dictionary covering terms used in finance, investment and banking sectors.

8206 ■ *Dictionary of Real Estate Terms*
Pub: Barron's Educational Series, Incorporated
Ed: Jack P. Friedman, Jack C. Harris, J. Bruce Lindeman. **Released:** October 2008. **Price:** $13.99. **Description:** More than 2,500 real estate terms relating to mortgages and financing, brokerage law, architecture, rentals and leases, property insurance, and more.

8207 ■ "Different This Time?" in *Canadian Business* (Vol. 81, April 14, 2008, No. 6, pp. 38)
Pub: Rogers Media
Ed: Matthew McClearn. **Description:** Irving Fisher believed that the low interest rates of the 1920's spurred investors to borrow and use the money to speculate with the proceeds thereby increasing the debt to unmanageable levels prior to the stock market crash in Oct. 29, 1929. The U.S. economic conditions in 1929 and U.S. economic conditions in 2008 are discussed.

8208 ■ "Digging Deep for Gold" in *Barron's* (Vol. 88, March 24, 2008, No. 12, pp. 49)
Pub: Dow Jones & Company, Inc.
Ed: Suzanne McGee. **Description:** David Iben, manager of the Nuveen Tradewinds Value Opportunities Fund, looks for value in companies and industries where the consensus of analysts is negative. He started investing in gold stocks well before gold prices started to rise.

8209 ■ *The Directory of Venture Capital and Private Equity Firms: 2009*
Pub: Grey House Publishing
Ed: Laura Mars-Proietti. **Released:** April 1, 2009. **Price:** $450.00. **Description:** Updated and expanded edition that includes new entries offering access to more than 3,500 domestic and international venture capital and private equity firms; detailed contact information and extensive data on investments and funds is included.

8210 ■ "Disappearing Act" in *Globe & Mail* (April 21, 2007, pp. B1)
Pub: CTVglobemedia Publishing Inc.
Ed: David Parkinson. **Description:** The effects of the buyout of BCE Inc. on the trends of stock prices at the Toronto Stock Exchange are described.

8211 ■ "Discount Beers Take Fizz Out Of Molson" in *Globe & Mail* (February 10, 2006, pp. B3)
Pub: CTVglobemedia Publishing Inc.
Ed: Omar El Akkad. **Description:** The reasons behind the decline in profits by 60 percent for Molson Coors Brewing Co., during fourth quarter 2005, are presented.

8212 ■ "Dividing to Conquer" in *Barron's* (Vol. 88, March 31, 2008, No. 13, pp. 22)
Pub: Dow Jones & Company, Inc.
Ed: Andrew Bary. **Description:** Altria's spin off of Philip Morris International could unlock substantial value for both domestic and international cigarette concerns. The strong brands and ample payouts from both companies will most likely impress investors.

8213 ■ "Do-It-Yourself Portfolio Management" in *Barron's* (Vol. 89, July 13, 2009, No. 28, pp. 25)
Pub: Dow Jones & Co., Inc.
Ed: Mike Hogan. **Description:** Services of several portfolio management web sites are presented. These web sites include MarketRiders E.Adviser, TD Ameritrade and E*Trade.

8214 ■ "Do the Math" in *Canadian Business*
(Vol. 79, October 9, 2006, No. 20, pp. 17)
Pub: Rogers Media
Ed: Al Rosen. **Description:** Faulty practices followed by regulators in Canadian stock market are discussed. The need for authorities to protect investors against these frauds are emphasized.

8215 ■ "Dr. Mark Holder" in *Crain's*
Cleveland Business **(Vol. 30, June 29, 2009, No. 25, pp. 14)**
Pub: Crain Communications, Inc.
Ed: Kathy Ames Carr. **Description:** Dr. Mark Holder is the director of the financial engineering program at Kent State University. Dr. Holder discusses his role to help teach his students how to market themselves for finance jobs in a down economy.

8216 ■ "Doctor's Orders" in *Canadian*
Business **(Vol. 79, November 20, 2006, No. 23, pp. 73)**
Pub: Rogers Media
Ed: Jeff Sanford. **Description:** George Cohon, the founder of McDonald's in Canada and Russia, speaks about the Canadian market and the experience of starting McDonald's in Canada.

8217 ■ "DoEs and DonEts" in *Canadian*
Business **(Vol. 79, July 17, 2006, No. 14-15, pp. 29)**
Pub: Rogers Media
Ed: Andy Holloway; Erin Pooley; Thomas Watson. **Description:** Strategic tips for planning systematic investments, in order to make life more enjoyable after retirement, are elucidated.

8218 ■ "Dofasco Quarterly Profit Plunges on Lower Steel Prices, Rising Costs" in *Globe &*
Mail **(February 4, 2006, pp. B3)**
Pub: CTVglobemedia Publishing Inc.
Ed: Shirley Won. **Description:** Dofasco Inc. posted 71% decline in profits for fourth quarter 2005. The revenue drop is attributed to fall in steel prices.

8219 ■ "Dofasco Warms to New Thyssen Bid" in *Globe & Mail* **(January 4, 2006, pp. B1)**
Pub: CTVglobemedia Publishing Inc.
Ed: Greg Keenan. **Description:** The details on ThyssenKrupp AG's bid for Dofasco Inc., at $63 a share, are presented.

8220 ■ "The Dogs of TSX" in *Canadian*
Business **(Vol. 81, Summer 2008, No. 9, pp. 77)**
Pub: Rogers Media Ltd.
Ed: Calvin Leung. **Description:** Table showing the one-year stock performance of the ten highest dividend-yielding stocks on the S&P/TSX 60 Composite Index is presented. This technique is similar to the 'Dogs of the Dow' approach. The idea in this investment strategy is to buy equal amounts of stocks from these companies and selling them a year later, and then repeat the process.

8221 ■ "The Dominance of Doubt" in *Barron's* **(Vol. 89, July 13, 2009, No. 28, pp. M3)**
Pub: Dow Jones & Co., Inc.
Ed: Description: Five straight down days leading up to July 10, 2009 in the U.S. stock market reminds one strategist of 1982 when there was a feeling that things could never be the same again. One analyst is bullish on the stocks of Apple Inc. and sees the stocks rising to at least 180 in 12 months. The prospects of the shares of GM and Ford are also discussed.

8222 ■ "Don't Bet Against The House" in *Barron's* **(Vol. 88, July 14, 2008, No. 28, pp. 20)**
Pub: Dow Jones & Co., Inc.
Ed: Sandra Ward. **Description:** Shares of Nasdaq OMX have lost more than 50 percent of their value from November 2007 to July 2008 but the value of these shares could climb 50 percent on the strength of world security exchanges. Only 15 percent of the company's revenues come from the U.S. and the shares are trading at 12.5 times the amount expected for 2008.

8223 ■ "Don't Expect Quick Fix" in *The*
Business Journal-Serving Metropolitan
Kansas City **(Vol. 27, October 3, 2008, No. 3, pp. 1)**
Pub: American City Business Journals, Inc.
Ed: James Dornbrook. **Description:** United States governmental entities cannot provide a quick fix solution to the current financial crisis. The economy requires a systemic change in the way people think about credit. The financial services industry should also focus on core lending principles.

8224 ■ "Don't Get Lulled by the Calm" in *Barron's* **(Vol. 89, July 27, 2009, No. 30, pp. M13)**
Pub: Dow Jones & Co., Inc.
Ed: Steven M. Sears. **Description:** Options traders expect volatility to return in the fall of 2009 and to bring correlation with it. September and October are typically the most volatile months and the trick is to survive earnings season.

8225 ■ "Don't' Hang Up On FairPoint" in *Barron's* **(Vol. 88, July 7, 2008, No. 27, pp. M5)**
Pub: Dow Jones & Co., Inc.
Ed: Fleming Meeks. **Description:** Shares of FairPoint Communications, priced at $6.63 each, are undervalued and should be worth over $12 each. The company increased its size by more than five times by acquiring Verizon's local telephone operations in Vermont, New Hampshire, and Maine, but must switch customers in those areas into their system by the end of September 2007.

8226 ■ "Dow Jones Gives Apple-Loving Sales Professionals a Boost" in *Information*
Today **(Vol. 26, February 2009, No. 2, pp. 30)**
Pub: Information Today, Inc.
Description: Dow Jones Sales Triggers for iPhone and iPod program helps sales professionals stay current to prospects and customers in their fields by providing real-time news on business changes, including management moves, mergers, and new investments. The application presents events that trigger best opportunities and allows users to look up companies and executives to retrieve information.

8227 ■ "Downtown Bank Got High Marks for Irwin Purchase, Is Looking For More" in *Business Courier* **(Vol. 27, September 3, 2010, No. 18, pp. 1)**
Pub: Business Courier
Ed: Steve Watkins. **Description:** First Financial Bancorp is looking to acquire more troubled banks following its purchase of Irwin Union Bank. The bank has reported a $383 million bargain purchase gain during the third quarter of 2009.

8228 ■ "Drilling Deep and Flying High" in *Barron's* **(Vol. 88, June 30, 2008, No. 26, pp. 34)**
Pub: Dow Jones & Co., Inc.
Ed: Kenneth Rapoza. **Description:** Shares of Petrobras could rise another 25 percent if the three deepwater wells that the company has found proves as lucrative as some expect. Petrobras will become an oil giant if the reserves are proven.

8229 ■ "Drug-Maker Plans IPO" in *Business*
Courier **(Vol. 24, November 23, 2008, No. 32, pp. 1)**
Pub: American City Business Journals, Inc.
Ed: James Ritchie; Steve Watkins. **Description:** Xanodyne Pharmaceuticals Inc. filed plans with the Securities and Exchange Commission on November 9, 2007 for an initial public offering. The company, with annual sales of $75 million, had lost $222 million since it was founded in 2001.

8230 ■ "Drug, Seed Firms Offer Antidote For Inflation" in *Crain's Chicago Business* **(Vol. 31, April 21, 2008, No. 16, pp. 4)**
Pub: Crain Communications, Inc.
Ed: Daniel Rome Levine. **Description:** Interview with Jerrold Senser, the CEO of Institutional Capital LLC in Chicago, in which he discusses the ways that the company is adjusting to the economic slowdown and

rising inflation, his favorite firms for investment and his prediction of an economic turnaround; he also recommends five companies he feels are worth investing in.

8231 ■ "Drug Trial Halt at YM Sets Stage for Selloff" in *Globe & Mail* **(January 31, 2007, pp. B3)**
Pub: CTVglobemedia Publishing Inc.
Ed: Leonard Zehr. **Description:** The decision of YM Biosciences Inc. to stop its trial of cancer drug tesmilifene and stocks following government concern over the safety of the drug is discussed.

8232 ■ "Dueling Visions" in *Barron's* **(Vol. 89, July 27, 2009, No. 30, pp. 13)**
Pub: Dow Jones & Co., Inc.
Ed: Michael Santoli. **Description:** Goldman Sachs' market strategists believe the stock market has entered a "sustained-rally" mode while Morgan Stanley's strategist believes this is a "rally to sell into". What is not known in the stock market is how much of a "V"-shaped recovery in earning the market rebound has already priced in.

8233 ■ "Dynamic Duo" in *Barron's* **(Vol. 88, March 10, 2008, No. 10, pp. 45)**
Pub: Dow Jones & Company, Inc.
Ed: Shirley A. Lazo. **Description:** General Dynamics, the world's sixth-largest military contractor, raised its dividend payout by 20.7 percent from 29 cents to 35 cents a share. Steel Dynamics, producer of structural steel and steel bar products, declared a 2-for-1 stock split and raised its quarterly dividend by 33 percent to a split-adjusted 10 cents a share.

8234 ■ "easyhome Ltd. Discovers Employee Fraud at an Easyfinancial Kiosk Company" in *Internet Wire* **(October 14, 2010)**
Pub: Comtex
Description: Canada's leading merchandise leasing company and provider of financial services, easyhome Ltd., reported employee fraud totaling $3.4 million that was perpetrated against the firm's easyfinancial services business.

8235 ■ "Economic Prognosis" in *Barron's*
(Vol. 89, July 13, 2009, No. 28, pp. 11)
Pub: Dow Jones & Co., Inc.
Ed: Karen Hube. **Description:** Loomis Sayles Bond Fund manager Dan Fuss believes that the economy is bottoming and that recovery will be long and drawn out. Fuss guesses that the next peak in 10-year Treasury yields will be about 6.25%in around 4 and a half or five years ahead of 2009.

8236 ■ "An Educated Play on China" in *Barron's* **(Vol. 88, June 30, 2008, No. 26, pp. M6)**
Pub: Dow Jones & Co., Inc.
Ed: Mohammed Hadi. **Description:** New Oriental Education & Technology Group sells English-language courses to an increasingly competitive Chinese workforce that values education. The shares in this company have been weighed down by worries on the impact of the Beijing Olympics on enrollment and the Sichuan earthquake. These shares could be a great way to get exposure to the long-term growth in China.

8237 ■ "Effect of Oil Prices on the Economy" in *Canadian Business* **(Vol. 81, September 15, 2008, No. 14-15, pp. 5)**
Pub: Rogers Media Ltd.
Ed: Joe Chidley. **Description:** Rise of oil prices above $100 in February 2008 and $140 in July signals the birth of a "new economy" according to commentators; this shift is causing uneasiness from oil industry professionals who are unsure of how this trend could be sustained. Oil dropped below $120 in August, which could slow down global economic growth followed by oil demand, then oil prices.

8238 ■ "Egg Fight: The Yolk's on the Short" in *Barron's* **(Vol. 88, July 7, 2008, No. 27, pp. 20)**
Pub: Dow Jones & Co., Inc.
Ed: Christopher C. Williams. **Description:** Shares of Cal-Maine Foods, the largest egg producer and distributor in the US, are due for a huge rise because

of the increase in egg prices. Short sellers, however, continue betting that the stock, priced at $31.84 each, will eventually go down.

8239 ■ "The Emerging Capital Market for Nonprofits" in *Harvard Business Review* **(Vol. 88, October 2010, No. 10, pp. 110)**
Pub: Harvard Business School Publishing
Ed: Robert S. Kaplan, Allen S. Grossman. **Description:** Demonstration of how nonprofits can use intermediaries to grow their organizational structures, giving them improved scale and impact is offered. Some intermediaries play a mutual-fund role and conduct due diligence, while others act as venture capital funds and implement strategy.

8240 ■ "The Emperor Strikes Back" in *Canadian Business* **(Vol. 80, March 26, 2007, No. 7, pp. 48)**
Pub: Rogers Media
Ed: Rachel Pulfer. **Description:** The financial performance of Fairfax Financial Holdings Ltd. in 2006 is presented. The efforts of chief executive Prem Watsa to lead the company towards growth track are also presented.

8241 ■ "EnCana Axes Spending on Gas Wells" in *Globe & Mail* **(February 16, 2006, pp. B1)**
Pub: CTVglobemedia Publishing Inc.
Ed: Dave Ebner. **Description:** The reasons behind EnCana Corp.'s cost spending measures by $300 million on natural gas wells are presented. The company projects 2 percent cut in gas and oil sales for 2006.

8242 ■ "End of the Beginning" in *Canadian Business* **(Vol. 81, November 10, 2008, No. 19, pp. 17)**
Pub: Rogers Media Ltd.
Ed: David Wolf. **Description:** The freeze in the money markets and historic decline in equity markets around the world finally forced governments into aggressive coordinated action. The asset price inflation brought on by cheap credit will now work in reverse and the tightening of credit will be difficult economically. Canada is exposed to the fallout everywhere, given that the U.S, the U.K. and Japan buy 30 percent of Canada's output.

8243 ■ "End of an Era" in *Barron's* **(Vol. 88, July 7, 2008, No. 27, pp. 3)**
Pub: Dow Jones & Co., Inc.
Ed: Alan Abelson. **Description:** June 2008 was a very bad month for US stocks, with investors losing as much as 41.9 percent in the first half of 2008 signaling an end to the financial environment that prevailed around the world since the 1980's. The US job market lost 62,000 jobs in June 2008.

8244 ■ "Energy Firms Face Stricter Definitions" in *Globe & Mail* **(March 26, 2007, pp. B3)**
Pub: CTVglobemedia Publishing Inc.
Ed: David Ebner. **Description:** The Alberta Securities Commission has imposed strict securities regulations on oil and gas industries. Energy industries will have to submit revenue details to stake holders.

8245 ■ "Energy, MLPs: Pipeline to Profits" in *Barron's* **(Vol. 89, July 27, 2009, No. 30, pp. 9)**
Pub: Dow Jones & Co., Inc.
Ed: Dimitra DeFotis. **Description:** Energy master limited partnership stocks are range-bound in the next few months from July 2009 but there are there are some opportunities that remain. These include Energy Transfer Equity, Enterprise GP holdings, NuStar GP Holdings, and Plains All American Pipeline.

8246 ■ "Engine of Growth: U.S. Industry Funk hasn't Hurt Cummins or Its Investors" in *Barron's* **(Vol. 88, July 14, 2008, No. 28, pp. 43)**
Pub: Dow Jones & Co., Inc.
Ed: Shirley A. Lazo. **Description:** Engine maker Cummins increased its quarterly common dividend by 40 percent to 17.5 cents per share from 12.5 cents. CVS Caremark's dividend saw a hike of 18.4 percent from 9.5 cents to 11.25 cents per share while

its competitor Walgreen is continuing its 75th straight year of dividend distribution and its 33rd straight year of dividend hikes.

8247 ■ "Essential Releases Record First Quarter Results" in *Canadian Corporate News* **(May 14, 2007)**
Pub: Comtex News Network Inc.
Description: The first quarter of 2007 saw record financial performance despite numerous challenges for Essential Energy Services Trust. Statistical data included.

8248 ■ "ETF Score Card" in *Barron's* **(Vol. 89, July 13, 2009, No. 28, pp. 51)**
Pub: Dow Jones & Co., Inc.
Description: Statistical table is presented which shows the net assets of various exchange-traded funds is presented. The table also shows the total return of these funds up to a three-year time period.

8249 ■ "European Stocks on Deck" in *Barron's* **(Vol. 89, July 27, 2009, No. 30, pp. M7)**
Pub: Dow Jones & Co., Inc.
Ed: Vito J. Racanelli. **Description:** European stocks are cheap and these trade at a discount to U.S. equities rarely seen in the past 40 years. This represents an opportunity for Americans and trends show that Europe's stocks outperform when there is a discrepancy between the price to earnings ratio in European stocks versus U.S. stocks and when sentiment on European equities are downbeat.

8250 ■ "Europe's Meltdown" in *Canadian Business* **(Vol. 83, June 15, 2010, No. 10, pp. 76)**
Pub: Rogers Media Ltd.
Ed: Bryan Borzykowski. **Description:** As European countries such as Greece, Spain, and Portugal struggle with debt problems, it is worth noting that its equities trade at a 30 percent discount to the U.S. and that a 10 percent drop in the Euro translates to a 10 percent rise in profitability for exporters. Investors may also want to focus on business-to-business operations rather than consumer-focused ones.

8251 ■ "Everyone Out of the Pool" in *Barron's* **(Vol. 89, July 20, 2009, No. 29, pp. 18)**
Pub: Dow Jones & Co., Inc.
Ed: Sandra Ward. **Description:** Shares of Pool Corp. could drop as continued weakness in the housing market weakens the market for swimming pool equipment. The company's shares are trading at $18.29, about 20 times projected 2009 earnings of $0.91 a share.

8252 ■ "Expect a Rally as Waders Dive In" in *Barron's* **(Vol. 89, July 20, 2009, No. 29, pp. 11)**
Pub: Dow Jones & Co., Inc.
Ed: Vito J. Racanelli. **Description:** US stock markets may experience a rally in the autumn of 2009 as skeptical investors start to return to the market. The Standard & Poor's Index may jump to the 1025-1050 point levels during this rally.

8253 ■ "Experts: Market Shaky But Resilient" in *The Business Journal-Serving Metropolitan Kansas City* **(Vol. 27, September 19, 2008, No. 1)**
Pub: American City Business Journals, Inc.
Ed: Steve Vockrodt. **Description:** Investment advisers believe that the local investors in Kansas City who have a long-term approach towards their portfolios may come out even or even experience gains despite the Wall Street financial crisis. The impacts of the crisis are expected to take time to reach the area of Kansas City. The potential impacts of the Wall Street meltdown are examined further.

8254 ■ "Falling Markets' Nastiest Habits" in *Barron's* **(Vol. 88, July 7, 2008, No. 27, pp. 7)**
Pub: Dow Jones & Co., Inc.
Ed: Michael Santoli. **Description:** US market conditions reflect a bear market, with the S&P 500 index falling 20 percent below its recent high as of June

2008. The bear market is expected to persist in the immediate future, although bear market rallies are likely to occur.

8255 ■ "Falling Share Prices Will Convince Big Oil Producers to Pay Up to Drill" in *Globe & Mail* **(April 21, 2007, pp. B1)**
Pub: CTVglobemedia Publishing Inc.
Ed: Boyd Erman. **Description:** The effect of the increase in operational costs and the decline in share prices, on the exploration of petroleum deposits in Canada, is described.

8256 ■ "Fannie and Freddie: How They'll Change" in *Business Week* **(September 22, 2008, No. 4100, pp. 30)**
Pub: McGraw-Hill Companies, Inc.
Ed: Jane Sasseen. **Description:** Three possible outcomes of the fate of struggling mortgage giants Freddie Mac and Fannie Mae after the government bailout are outlined.

8257 ■ "Fast Revival Unlikely For Indian 'Net Stocks" in *Barron's* **(Vol. 88, July 7, 2008, No. 27, pp. 12)**
Pub: Dow Jones & Co., Inc.
Ed: Leslie P. Norton. **Description:** Shares of Indian Internet companies Rediff.com and Sify are not likely to stage a rebound due to weak financial results. Rediff.com shares have declined 39.2 percent in 2008, while Sify shares are down 35.8 percent.

8258 ■ "February Hot for Mutual Fund Sales" in *Globe & Mail* **(March 3, 2006, pp. B10)**
Pub: CTVglobemedia Publishing Inc.
Ed: Keith Damsell. **Description:** The details on Canadian mutual fund sector, which posted $4.7 billion for February 2005, are presented.

8259 ■ "The Fed Still Has Ammunition" in *Barron's* **(Vol. 90, August 30, 2010, No. 35, pp. M9)**
Pub: Barron's Editorial & Corporate Headquarters
Ed: Randall W. Forsyth. **Description:** Federal Reserve chairman Ben Bernanke said the agency still has tools to combat deflation and a second downturn but these strategies are not needed at this time. The prospects of the Federal Open Market Committee's purchasing of treasuries are also discussed.

8260 ■ "Fed Tackles Bear of a Crisis" in *Barron's* **(Vol. 88, March 17, 2008, No. 11, pp. M10)**
Pub: Dow Jones & Company, Inc.
Ed: Randall W. Forsyth. **Description:** Emergency funding package for Bear Stearns from the Federal Reserve Bank of New York through JPMorgan Chase is one of the steps taken by the central bank shore up bank liquidity. Prior to the emergency funding, the central bank announced the Term Securities Lending Facility to allow dealers to borrow easily saleable Treasuries in exchange for less-liquid issues.

8261 ■ "Federal Bailout, Three Years Later" in *Business Owner* **(Vol. 35, September-October 2011, No. 5, pp. 6)**
Pub: DL Perkins Company
Description: State of the economy and small business sector three years after the government stimulus and bailout programs were instituted.

8262 ■ "Feeling the Heat: Effects of Stress, Commitment, and Job Experience On Job Performance" in *Academy of Management Journal* **(Aug. 2007)**
Pub: Academy of Management
Ed: Larry W. Hunter, Sherry M.B. Thatcher. **Description:** Links between bank branch employees' felt job stress, organizational commitment, job experience, and performance is analyzed. Results found are uniform with the attention view of stress.

8263 ■ "Fees Come Down; Markets Come Down More" in *Barron's* **(Vol. 89, July 13, 2009, No. 28, pp. L8)**
Pub: Dow Jones & Co., Inc.
Ed: J.R. Brandstrader. **Description:** Investors spent less on mutual fund fees in 2009 than they did in the last 25 years. These fees include administration, ac-

counting, and legal expense. Despite the popularity of money market funds which has contributed to this decline, the short-term yields of these funds fell in the last year.

8264 ■ "A Few Points of Contention" in Barron's (Vol. 88, July 14, 2008, No. 28, pp. 3)
Pub: Dow Jones & Co., Inc.
Ed: Michael Santoli. **Description:** Headline inflation tends to revert to the lower core inflation, which excludes food and energy in its calculation over long periods. Prominent private equity figures believe that regulators should allow more than the de facto 10 percent to 25 percent limit of commercial banks to hasten the refunding of the financial sector.

8265 ■ "Fewer Banks Offer Big Gifts to Lure Clients" in Globe & Mail (March 14, 2006, pp. D1)
Pub: CTVglobemedia Publishing Inc.
Ed: Chris Reidy. **Description:** Fewer banks are offering gifts to lure the customers in this year in the wake of less favorable interest rates in the spring season. The market climate is analyzed.

8266 ■ "Fifth Third CEO Kabat: A World of Difference" in Business Courier (Vol. 26, January 1, 2010, No. 37, pp. 1)
Pub: American City Business Journals, Inc.
Ed: Steve Watkins. **Description:** CEO Kevin Kabat of Cincinnati-based Fifth Third Bancorp believes that the bank's assets of $111 billion and stock value of more than $10 indicate the recovery from the low stock prices posted in February 2009. He attributes the recovery from the federal government's stress test finding in May 2009 that Fifth Third needs to generate $1.1 billion.

8267 ■ "Finalist: BlackEagle Partners L.L.C." in Crain's Detroit Business (Vol. 24, March 24, 2008, No. 12, pp. 12)
Pub: Crain Communications, Inc.
Ed: Brent Snavely. **Description:** Overview of private-equity firm, BlackEagle Partners L.L.C., an upstart that acquired Rockford Products Corp. in order to improve the performance of the company who does business with several major tier-one automotive suppliers; Rockford manufactures highly engineered chassis and suspension components for automakers and the automotive aftermarket.

8268 ■ "The Finance Function In A Global Corporation" in Harvard Business Review (Vol. 86, July-August 2008, No. 8, pp. 108)
Pub: Harvard Business School Press
Ed: Mihir A. Desai. **Description:** Designing and implementing a successful finance function in a global setting is discussed. Additional topics include the internal capital market, managing risk and budgeting capital internationally.

8269 ■ "Financial Education: Boomer's Spending Hurts Retirement" in Employee Benefit News (Vol. 25, November 1, 2011, No. 14, pp. 18)
Pub: SourceMedia Inc.
Ed: Ann Marsh. **Description:** Financial planners and employers need to educate clients and employees about retirement planning. Boomers are spending money that should be saved for their retirement.

8270 ■ Financing Your Small Business
Pub: Barron's Educational Series, Incorporated
Ed: Robert Walter. **Released:** December 2003. **Description:** Tips for raising venture capital, dealing with bank officials, and initiating public offerings of stock shares for small business.

8271 ■ "Finding Good Bets Down on the Farm" in Crain's Chicago Business (Vol. 31, March 24, 2008, No. 12, pp. 4)
Pub: Crain Communications, Inc.
Ed: Daniel Rome Levine. **Description:** Interview with money manager Jeff James, the portfolio manager for Driehaus Capital Management LLC, who discusses the Federal Reserve and recommends several companies in which to make investments.

8272 ■ "Finger-Pointing Time" in Barron's (Vol. 88, March 10, 2008, No. 10, pp. 9)
Pub: Dow Jones & Company, Inc.
Ed: Michael Santoli. **Description:** Discusses who is to blame for the financial crisis brought about by the credit crunch in the United States; the country's financial markets will eventually digest this crisis but will bottom out first before the situation improves.

8273 ■ "First Financial Aiming for Banking Big Leagues" in Business Courier (Vol. 26, December 4, 2009, No. 32, pp. 1)
Pub: American City Business Journals, Inc.
Ed: Steve Watkins. **Description:** First Financial Bancorp could dominate the community banking market of Greater Cincinnati after buying failed banks with the supervision of the FDIC. Details of the transactions are presented.

8274 ■ "FirstMerit's Top Executive Turns Around Credit Quality" in Crain's Cleveland Business (Vol. 28, October 15, 2007, No. 41, pp. 3)
Pub: Crain Communications, Inc.
Ed: Shawn A. Turner. **Description:** Discusses the ways in which chairman and CEO Paul Greig has been able to improve FirstMerit Corp.'s credit quality and profit margin. Strategies included selling more than $70 million in bad loans, hiring a new chief credit officer and redirecting its focus on cross-selling its wealth and investment services to its commercial customers. Statistical data included.

8275 ■ "FIS-Metavante Deal Paying Off for Many" in Business Journal-Milwaukee (Vol. 28, December 17, 2010, No. 11, pp. A1)
Pub: Milwaukee Business Journal
Ed: Rich Kirchen. **Description:** Jacksonville, Florida-based Fidelity National Information Services Inc., also known as FIS, has remained committed to Milwaukee, Wisconsin more than a year after purchasing Metavante Technologies Inc. FIS has transferred several operations into Metropolitan Milwaukee and has continued its contribution to charitable organizations in the area.

8276 ■ "A Flawed Yardstick for Banks" in Barron's (Vol. 88, July 14, 2008, No. 28, pp. M6)
Pub: Dow Jones & Co., Inc.
Ed: Arindam Nag. **Description:** Return on equity is no longer the best measure for investors to judge banks by in a post-subprime-crises world. Investors should consider the proportion of a bank's total assets that are considered risky and look out for any write-downs of goodwill when judging a bank's financial health.

8277 ■ "Florida's Housing Gloom May Add To Woes of National City" in Crain's Cleveland Business (Vol. 28, October 29, 2007, No. 43, pp. 1)
Pub: Crain Communications, Inc.
Ed: Shawn A. Turner. **Description:** Already suffering by bad loans in the troubled mortgage market, National City Corp. is attempting to diversify its geographic presence beyond the slow-growth industrial Midwest by acquiring two Florida firms. Analysts worry that the acquisitions may end up making National City vulnerable to a takeover if the housing slump continues and credit quality becomes more of an issue for the bank.

8278 ■ "Flying High?" in Canadian Business (Vol. 80, April 9, 2007, No. 8, pp. 42)
Pub: Rogers Media
Ed: Thomas Watson. **Description:** The increase in Bombardier Inc.'s income by 30 percent to $112 million and increase in its share prices are discussed. The caution of analysts about its accounting methods that may adversely hit the company in future, too is discussed.

8279 ■ Fooling Some of the People All of the Time
Pub: John Wiley & Sons, Inc.
Ed: David Einhorn. **Released:** March 10, 2010. **Price:** $29.95. **Description:** A chronicle of the ongoing saga between author, David Einhorn's hedge fund, Greenlight Capital, and Allied Capital, a leader in the private finance industry.

8280 ■ Fool's Gold: How the Bold Dream of a Small Tribe at J.P. Morgan Was Corrupted by Wall Street Greed
Pub: Free Press
Ed: Gillian Tett. **Released:** 2009. **Price:** $26.00. **Description:** An explanation of how swaps and CDOs, which were invented by J.P. Morgan, ended up creating more risk not controlling it.

8281 ■ "For Baxter, A Lingering PR Problem; Ongoing Focus On Heparin Deaths Ups Heat On CEO" in Crain's Chicago Business (April 21, 2008)
Pub: Crain Communications, Inc.
Ed: Mike Colias. **Description:** Baxter International Inc.'s recall of the blood-thinning medication heparin has exposed the company to costly litigation and put the perils of overseas drug manufacturing in the spotlight. Wall Street investors predict that an indefinite halt in production of the drug should not hurt the company's bottom line since heparin represents a tiny sliver of the business. Since Baxter began recalling the drug in January its shares have continued to outpace most other medical stocks.

8282 ■ "For Buffet Fans, the Price Is Right" in Barron's (Vol. 89, July 13, 2009, No. 28, pp. 17)
Pub: Dow Jones & Co., Inc.
Ed: Andrew Bary. **Description:** Shares of Warren Buffett's Berkshire Hathaway have fallen to $85,000 and these are cheap since they are trading at just 1.2 times estimated book value and are well below its peak of $149,000. One fan of the stock expects it to top $110,000 in the next year from June 2009.

8283 ■ "For Gilead, Growth Beyond AIDS" in Barron's (Vol. 88, June 30, 2008, No. 26, pp. 18)
Pub: Dow Jones & Co., Inc.
Ed: Jay Palmer. **Description:** First-quarter 2008 revenue for Gilead Sciences grew by 22 percent and an earnings gain of 19 percent thanks to their HIV-treatment drugs that comprised over two-thirds of the company's sales in 2007. An analyst has a 12-month target from June, 2008 of 65 per share. The factors behind the company's prospects are also discussed.

8284 ■ "Ford Canada's Edsel of a Year: Revenue Plummets 24 Percent in '05" in Globe & Mail (February 2, 2006, pp. B1)
Pub: CTVglobemedia Publishing Inc.
Ed: Greg Keenan. **Description:** Ford Motor Company of Canada Ltd. posted 24% decline in revenues for 2005. The drop in earnings is attributed to plant shutdown in Oaksville, Canada.

8285 ■ "Former Mayor Driving $500 Million Real Estate Equity Fund" in The Business Journal - Serving Phoenix and the Valley of the Sun (Vol. 28, August 15, 2008, No. 50, pp. 1)
Pub: American City Business Journals, Inc.
Ed: Jan Buchholz. **Description:** Paul John, the former mayor of Phoenix, is establishing a $500 million real estate asset management fund. The fund is dubbed Southwest Next Capital Management and has attracted three local partners, namely Joseph Meyer, Jay Michalowski, and James Mullany, who all have background in finance and construction.

8286 ■ "The Four Cheapest Plays in Emerging Markets" in Barron's (Vol. 89, July 27, 2009, No. 30, pp. 34)
Pub: Dow Jones & Co., Inc.
Ed: Lawrence C. Strauss. **Description:** Portfolio manager Arjun Divecha of the GMO Emerging Markets III Fund says that the main thing in investing in emerging markets is getting the country right since getting it wrong makes it harder to add value. Divecha says that the four countries that they are positive on are Turkey, Russia, South Korea, and Thailand.

8287 ■ "Fraud Alleged at Norshield; Investors Out $215 Million" in Globe & Mail (March 8, 2007, pp. B1)
Pub: CTVglobemedia Publishing Inc.
Ed: Paul Waldie. **Description:** The investigation of the diversion of $215 million in investors' money by

the management of Norshield Asset Management (Canada) Ltd. is described.

8288 ■ **"Freak Weather Dampens Intrawest Forecast"** in *Globe & Mail* (February 8, 2006, pp. B3)

Pub: CTVglobemedia Publishing Inc.

Ed: Peter Kennedy. **Description:** Intrawest Corp. dropped its earnings forecast by 7 percent. The impact of weather on earnings is discussed.

8289 ■ **"Friends With Money"** in *Canadian Business* (Vol. 81, Summer 2008, No. 9, pp. 22)

Pub: Rogers Media Ltd.

Description: Two of the most well connected managers in Canadian capital markets Rob Farquharson and Brian Gibson will launch Panoply Capital Asset Management in June. The investment management company aims to raise a billion dollars from institutions and high-net worth individuals.

8290 ■ **"From Buyout to Busted"** in *Business Week* (September 22, 2008, No. 4100, pp. 18)

Pub: McGraw-Hill Companies, Inc.

Ed: Emily Thornton; Deborah Stead. **Description:** Bankruptcy filings by private equity-backed companies are at a record high with 134 American firms taken private (or invested in) by buyout firms that have filed for protection this year under Chapter 11; this is 91 percent higher than the previous year, which had set a record when 70 of such companies filed for protection under Chapter 11.

8291 ■ **"From Fastenal, a Boost"** in *Barron's* (Vol. 89, July 20, 2009, No. 29, pp. M13)

Pub: Dow Jones & Co., Inc.

Ed: Shirley A. Lazo. **Description:** Fastenal increased its semi-annual common payout from $0.35 to $0.37 a share. Core Laboratories declared a special dividend of $0.75 a share along with its quarterly payout of $0.10. Ryder System and Landstar System raised their payouts to $0.23 and $0.045 a share respectively.

8292 ■ **"The Frugal Billionaire"** in *Canadian Business* (Vol. 79, Winter 2006, No. 24, pp. 63)

Pub: Rogers Media

Ed: Joe Castaldo. **Description:** The achievements of David Cheriton are described, along with his investments in various firms, including Google Inc.

8293 ■ **"Full-Court Press for Apple"** in *Barron's* (Vol. 88, March 24, 2008, No. 12, pp. 47)

Pub: Dow Jones & Company, Inc.

Ed: Mark Veverka. **Description:** Apple Inc. is facing more intellectual property lawsuits in 2008, with 30 patent lawsuits filed compared to 15 in 2007 and nine in 2006. The lawsuits, which involve products such as the iPod and the iPhone, present some concern for Apple's shareholders.

8294 ■ **"Function Over Forms?"** in *Barron's* (Vol. 88, June 30, 2008, No. 26, pp. 17)

Pub: Dow Jones & Co., Inc.

Ed: Eric Savitz. **Description:** Securities and Exchange Commission (SEC) chairman Christopher Cox wants the SEC to consider an overhaul of the forms used to meet the agency's disclosure requirements. Cox also said that the U.S. Generally Accepted Accounting Standards has too many rules with exceptions and alternative interpretations.

8295 ■ **"Funds "Friend" Facebook"** in *Barron's* (Vol. 89, July 27, 2009, No. 30, pp. 30)

Pub: Dow Jones & Co., Inc.

Ed: Leslie P. Norton. **Description:** Mutual-fund companies are the latest entrants to the "social media" space and several companies have already set up Facebook and Twitter pages. The use of this technology pose special challenges for compliance and regulators especially since the Financial Industry Regulatory Authority reminds companies that advertising, sales and literature are governed by regula-

8296 ■ **"The Future of Private Equity"** in *Canadian Business* (Vol. 80, March 26, 2007, No. 7, pp. 19)

Pub: Rogers Media

Ed: Jack Mintz. **Description:** The impact growing Canadian economy and competition in global business on the performance of private equity funds is analyzed.

8297 ■ **"Future's Brighter for Financial Stocks"** in *Barron's* (Vol. 89, July 20, 2009, No. 29, pp. 14)

Pub: Dow Jones & Co., Inc.

Ed: Jacqueline Doherty. **Description:** Shares of US financial companies are projected to rise as their earnings start to normalize. Earnings of these companies have been hurt by credit losses but have been bolstered by one-time gains.

8298 ■ **"Futures Shock for the CME"** in *Crain's Chicago Business* (Vol. 31, November 10, 2008, No. 45, pp. 8)

Pub: Crain Communications, Inc.

Ed: Ann Saphir. **Description:** Chicago-based CME Group Inc., the largest futures exchange operator in the U.S., is facing a potentially radically altered regulatory landscape as Congress weighs sweeping reform of financial oversight. The possible merger of the CFTC and the Securities and Exchange Commission are among CME's concerns. Other details of possible regulatory measures are provided.

8299 ■ **"Futures of the Street"** in *Barron's* (Vol. 88, June 30, 2008, No. 26, pp. 27)

Pub: Dow Jones & Co., Inc.

Ed: Michael Santoli. **Description:** Prospects of the securities industry in terms of jobs and profit sources are discussed. Suggestions on what the industry needs with regards to its use of capital are also discussed.

8300 ■ **"Gas Glut Pummels Prices"** in *Barron's* (Vol. 89, July 27, 2009, No. 30, pp. M8)

Pub: Dow Jones & Co., Inc.

Ed: Christine Buurma. **Description:** Natural gas-futures prices have fallen 73 percent and the glut of output from onshore gas fields and the weak demand signals that a rebound is not near. An analyst expects U.S. production to show increasingly steep declines but the oversupply situation is not good for prices.

8301 ■ **"Gateway Delays Start"** in *The Business Journal-Serving Metropolitan Kansas City* (Vol. 27, October 31, 2008, No. 8, pp. 1)

Pub: American City Business Journals, Inc.

Ed: Rob Roberts. **Description:** Economic problems caused, in part, by the Wall Street crisis has resulted in the setback of a proposed mixed-use redevelopment project, The Gateway. The $307 million project, which includes the Kansas Aquarium, will be delayed due to financing problems. Details of the project are given.

8302 ■ **"GE Looking to Extend Hot Streak"** in *Business Courier* (Vol. 24, January 25, 2008, No. 42, pp. 1)

Pub: American City Business Journals, Inc.

Ed: John Newberry. **Description:** GE Aviation has enjoyed strong revenues and sales due to increase aircraft engine orders. It has an engine backlog order of $19 million as of the end of 2007. Data on the aviation company's revenues, operating profit and total engine orders for the year 2004 to 2007 are presented.

8303 ■ **"General Motors Can't Kick Incentives-But They Work"** in *Advertising Age* (Vol. 79, July 7, 2008, No. 26, pp. 3)

Pub: Crain Communications, Inc.

Ed: Jean Halliday. **Description:** General Motors Corp. was able to maintain their market share just as Toyota Motor Corp. was beginning to pass the manufacturer; GM lured in customers with a sales incentive that they heavily advertised and subsequently helped build demand; investors, however,

were not impressed and GM shares were hammered to their lowest point in 50 years after analysts speculated the company might go bankrupt.

8304 ■ **"Generation Y - An Opportunity for a Fresh Financial Start"** in (September 11, 2010, pp. 241)

Pub: VerticalNews

Description: Eleanor Blayney, the consumer advocate for the Certified Financial Planner Board of Standards, offers a financial strategy for Generation Y individuals starting their financial planning. The first segment of the non-profit's Lifelong Financial Strategies initiative is called 'Starting Out', and focuses on ways Generation Y people can avoid pitfalls of earlier generations by making smart financial decisions.

8305 ■ **"Genzyme: Underrated Oversold"** in *Barron's* (Vol. 88, March 24, 2008, No. 12, pp. 58)

Pub: Dow Jones & Company, Inc.

Ed: Johanna Bennett. **Description:** Shares of biotechnology company Genzyme appear oversold and underrated at their $71.86 level. The company's finances are on a solid foundation, with revenues over $3.8 billion in 2007 and forecasts of $4.5-4.7 billion in revenue for 2008.

8306 ■ **"Get It While Its Hot"** in *Canadian Business* (Vol. 80, January 15, 2007, No. 2, pp. 49)

Pub: Rogers Media

Ed: John Gray. **Description:** The rise in the demand for processed uranium and increase in the number of investors interested to invest in metal industries is discussed.

8307 ■ **"Get Off The Rollercoaster"** in *Michigan Vue* (Vol. 13, July-August 2008, No. 4, pp. 19)

Pub: Entrepreneur Media Inc.

Ed: Donald N. Hobley Jr. **Description:** Benefits of creating and implementing a solid financial plan during these rocky economic times are examined. Things to keep in mind before meeting with a financial planner include risk assessment, investment goals, the length of time required to meet those goals and the amount of money one has available to invest.

8308 ■ **"Getting In on the Ground Floor"** in *Barron's* (Vol. 89, July 27, 2009, No. 30, pp. 32)

Pub: Dow Jones & Co., Inc.

Ed: Jacqueline Doherty. **Description:** Shares of AvalonBay Communities have fallen 61 percent in the past two and a half years to July 2009 but at $56, the stock is trading near the asset value. The shares could rise as the economy improves and if the recovery takes longer, investors will be rewarded with a yield of 3.5 percent.

8309 ■ **"Getting More Out of Retirement"** in *Agency Sales Magazine* (Vol. 39, November 2009, No. 10, pp. 48)

Pub: MANA

Ed: Joshua D. Mosshart. **Description:** Overview of the Tax Increase Prevention and Reconciliation Act, which lets employees convert to a Roth IRA in 2010. The benefits of conversion depend on age and wealth and it is best to consult a tax advisor to determine the best strategy for retirement planners.

8310 ■ **"Getting Out of an IRS Mess"** in *Black Enterprise* (Vol. 37, December 2006, No. 5, pp. 53)

Pub: Earl G. Graves Publishing Co. Inc.

Ed: Carolyn M. Brown. **Description:** Owing back taxes to the IRS can lead to huge penalties and interest. Here are some tips on how to handle paying the IRS what you owe them.

8311 ■ **"Giants Now Admit They Roam Planet Earth; Time To Buy?"** in *Barron's* (Vol. 88, March 31, 2008, No. 13, pp. 39)

Pub: Dow Jones & Company, Inc.

Ed: Eric J. Savitz. **Description:** Oracle's third-quarter results showed that top-line growth fell short of expectations but the company is expected to fare better than most applications companies in the downturn. Google had a flat growth in the number of people who click their online ads. The time for investors in the tech sector with a long-term horizon has arrived.

8312 ■ "Give a Little Back" in *Canadian Business* (Vol. 79, November 20, 2006, No. 23, pp. 17)

Pub: Rogers Media

Ed: Jack Mintz. **Description:** The plans of Jim Flaherty, Canada's minister of finance, to remove the corporate tax bias on income paid to pension plans are discussed.

8313 ■ "Give Me Liberty With DirecTV" in *Barron's* (Vol. 89, July 13, 2009, No. 28, pp. M5)

Pub: Dow Jones & Co., Inc.

Ed: Fleming Meeks. **Description:** Shares of Liberty Entertainment look cheap at $25.14 and the same goes for DirecTV at $23.19. A merger between the two companies was announced and the deal will likely close by September 2009. Barclays Capital has a target of $30 for Liberty Media and $32 for DirecTV.

8314 ■ "Global Good Time" in *Canadian Business* (Vol. 80, January 15, 2007, No. 2, pp. 53)

Pub: Rogers Media

Ed: Thomas Watson. **Description:** Speculations on the stock prices of global emerging markets for 2007 are presented.

8315 ■ "Global Steel Makers Circle Stelco" in *Globe & Mail* (April 19, 2007, pp. B3)

Pub: CTVglobemedia Publishing Inc.

Ed: Greg Keenan. **Description:** The details of the take over bids offered to Stelco Inc. are presented. Due to these bids the shares of Stelco Inc rose up to 70 percent.

8316 ■ "Gold Handshake" in *Canadian Business* (Vol. 79, September 11, 2006, No. 18, pp. 25)

Pub: Rogers Media

Ed: John Gray. **Description:** Goldcorp Inc.'s company's planned takeover of Glamis Gold Ltd. is discussed. Implications of the merger on its investors are presented.

8317 ■ "Gold Still Has That Glitter" in *Barron's* (Vol. 89, July 20, 2009, No. 29, pp. M8)

Pub: Dow Jones & Co., Inc.

Ed: Allen Sykora. **Description:** Gold prices appear to be ready for an increase starting in the fall of 2009 due to an increase in demand. The price of the August 2009 gold contract fell to as low as $904.08 an ounce before recovering to $937.50.

8318 ■ "A Good Book Is Worth a Thousand Blogs" in *Barron's* (Vol. 88, July 14, 2008, No. 28, pp. 42)

Pub: Dow Jones & Co., Inc.

Ed: Gene Epstein. **Description:** Nine summer book suggestions on economics are presented. The list includes 'The Revolution' by Ron Paul, 'The Forgotten Man' by Amity Shales, 'The Commitments of Traders Bible' by Stephen Briese, and 'Economic Facts and Fallacies' by Thomas Sowell.

8319 ■ "Good Going, Partners: Energy-Asset Firms Do Their Parents Proud" in *Barron's* (Vol. 89, July 27, 2009, No. 30, pp. M8)

Pub: Dow Jones & Co., Inc.

Ed: Shirley A. Lazo. **Description:** Four master limited partnerships boosted their dividends. Sunoco Logistics raised theirs by 11.2 percent, El Paso Pipeline by 12 percent, Holly Energy upped their dividends by a penny, and Western Gas hiked their dividend to 31 cents per unit.

8320 ■ "Good Things Happen When We Buy Local" in *Crain's Detroit Business* (Vol. 24, October 6, 2008, No. 40, pp. 7)

Pub: Crain Communications, Inc.

Description: Michigan is facing incredibly difficult economic times. One way in which each one of us can help the state and the businesses located here is by purchasing our goods and services from local

vendors. The state Agriculture Department projected that if Michigan households earmarked $10 per week in their grocery purchases to made-in-Michigan products, this would generate $30 million a week in economic impact.

8321 ■ "Google's Next Stop: Below 350?" in *Barron's* (Vol. 88, March 10, 2008, No. 10, pp. 17)

Pub: Dow Jones & Company, Inc.

Ed: Jacqueline Doherty. **Description:** Share prices of Google Inc. are expected to drop from their level of $433 each to below $350 per share. The company is expected to miss its earnings forecast for the first quarter of 2008, and its continued aggressive spending on non-core areas will eventually bring down earnings.

8322 ■ "Gordon Nixon" in *Canadian Business* (Vol. 80, November 5, 2007, No. 22, pp. 9)

Pub: Rogers Media

Ed: Rachel Pulfer. **Description:** Royal Bank of Canada (RBC) CEO, Gordon Nixon, believes the Canadian financial services segment is heavily regulated. Nixon also feels that it has become difficult for local banks to enter the market since foreign banks can easily come in and compete with them. His views on RBC's success are provided.

8323 ■ "Gordon Nixon Q&A" in *Canadian Business* (Vol. 80, November 5, 2007, No. 22, pp. 9)

Pub: Rogers Media

Ed: Rachel Pulfer. **Description:** Royal Bank of Canada (RBC) chief executive officer Gordon Nixon believes that the Canadian financial services segment is heavily regulated. Nixon also feels that it has become difficult for local banks to enter the market since foreign banks can easily come in and compete with Canadian banks. His views on RBC's success are provided.

8324 ■ "Graduates to the TSX in 2008" in *Canadian Business* (Vol. 81, Summer 2008, No. 9, pp. 79)

Pub: Rogers Media Ltd.

Ed: Calvin Leung. **Description:** Table showing the market capitalization and stock performance of the companies that jumped to the TSX Venture Exchange is presented. The 17 companies that made the leap to the list will have an easier time raising capital, although leeway must be made in investing since they are still new businesses.

8325 ■ "The Great Deleveraging" in *Canadian Business* (Vol. 81, October 13, 2008, No. 17, pp. 45)

Pub: Rogers Media Ltd.

Ed: Jeff Sanford. **Description:** 'Hell Week' of financial crisis on Wall Street is believed to have started with the downgrade of AIG Inc.'s credit rating. AIG is a major player in the credit derivatives market, and its bankruptcy would have affected firms on Wall Street.

8326 ■ "The Great Fall" in *Barron's* (Vol. 88, March 10, 2008, No. 10, pp. 5)

Pub: Dow Jones & Company, Inc.

Ed: Alan Abelson. **Description:** Discusses the US economy is considered to be in a recession, with the effects of the credit crisis expected to intensify as a result. Inflation is estimated at 4.3 percent in January 2008, while 63,000 jobs were lost in February 2008.

8327 ■ "The Great Moderation" in *Canadian Business* (Vol. 80, February 12, 2007, No. 4, pp. 25)

Pub: Rogers Media

Ed: David Wolf. **Description:** Caution over the changes to stock inventory levels and their adverse impact on the Canadian economy is discussed.

8328 ■ "Great Stocks Cheap" in *Canadian Business* (Vol. 80, January 15, 2007, No. 2, pp. 31)

Pub: Rogers Media

Ed: Calvin Leung. **Description:** The stock performance of top 10 international companies like Furgo, Moody's Investor Service, Adidas Group and Nestle is analyzed.

8329 ■ "Green Assets Powering Boralex Shares" in *Globe & Mail* (March 30, 2007, pp. B10)

Pub: CTVglobemedia Publishing Inc.

Ed: Richard Blackwell. **Description:** The impact of econ-friendly power plant portfolio on the stock performance of Kingsey Falls-based Boralex Inc. is analyzed.

8330 ■ "The Green Trap" in *Canadian Business* (Vol. 80, April 9, 2007, No. 8, pp. 19)

Pub: Rogers Media

Ed: Al Rosen. **Description:** Expert advice to companies on investing in environmental-friendly measures is presented.

8331 ■ "Greenberg Sues U.S. Over AIG Rescue" in *Wall Street Journal Eastern Edition* (November 22 , 2011, pp. C3)

Pub: Dow Jones & Company, Inc.

Ed: Liam Pleven, Serena Ng. **Description:** Former Chief Executive Officer of American International Group Inc., Maurice R. 'Hank' Greenberg, has filed a lawsuit against the United States and the Federal Reserve Bank of New York on behalf of shareholders and his company, Starr International Company Inc., claiming that the government was wrong in taking control of the insurance giant and used it to move tens of millions of dollars to the trading partners of AIG.

8332 ■ "A Greenish Light for Financial-Sector Funds" in *Barron's* (Vol. 88, March 24, 2008, No. 12, pp. 52)

Pub: Dow Jones & Company, Inc.

Ed: Tom Sullivan. **Description:** Financial sector funds have lost value in 2008 through 17 March, and investors are advised to reduce investments in the financial sector. Exchange-traded funds present a good way to own financial stocks.

8333 ■ "Greg Stringham" in *Canadian Business* (Vol. 81, March 3, 2008, No. 3, pp. 8)

Pub: Rogers Media

Ed: Michelle Magnan. **Description:** Canadian Association of Petroleum Producers' Greg Stringham thinks that the new royalty plan will result in companies pulling out their investments for Alberta's conventional oil and gas sector. Stringham adds that Alberta is losing its competitive advantage and companies must study their cost profiles to retrieve that advantage. The effects of the royalty system on Alberta's economy are examined further.

8334 ■ "A Gripping Read: Bargains & Noble" in *Barron's* (Vol. 88, March 17, 2008, No. 11, pp. 20)

Pub: Dow Jones & Company, Inc.

Ed: Jonathan R. Laing. **Description:** Barnes & Noble's earnings forecast for the fiscal year ending in January, 2008 to be $1.70 to $1.90 per share which is way lower than the $2.12 analyst consensus. The company also said that sales at stores one-year old or older dropped 0.5 percent in the fourth quarter. However, the shares are now cheap at 4.9 times enterprise value with some analysts putting a price target of 41 per share.

8335 ■ *Grow Your Money: 101 Easy Tips to Plan, Save and Invest*

Pub: HarperBusiness

Ed: Jonathan D. Pond. **Released:** December 2007. **Price:** $26.95. **Description:** In what should be required reading for anyone entering the work world, the author offers helpful investment and financial definitions, debt-management strategies, retirement and home ownerships considerations and more.

8336 ■ "Growth Back on CIBC's Agenda" in *Globe & Mail* (March 3, 2006, pp. B1)

Pub: CTVglobemedia Publishing Inc.

Ed: Sinclair Stewart. **Description:** The details on business growth of Canadian Imperial Bank of Commerce, which posted $547 million profit for first quarter 2006, are presented.

8337 ■ "Handleman Liquidation Leaves Questions For Shareholders" in *Crain's Detroit Business* (Vol. 24, October 6, 2008, No. 40, pp. 4)

Pub: Crain Communications, Inc.

Ed: Nancy Kaffer. **Description:** Discusses Handleman Co., a Troy-based music distribution company, and their plan of liquidation and dissolution as well as how shareholders will be affected by the company's plan. Handleman filed its plan to liquidate and dissolve assets with the Securities and Exchange Commission in mid-August, following several quarters of dismal earnings.

8338 ■ "Hank and Ben: Hedgies' BFFs" in *Barron's* (Vol. 88, March 31, 2008, No. 13, pp. 50)

Pub: Dow Jones & Company, Inc.

Ed: Tom Sullivan. **Description:** David Ballin of Alternative Investment Solutions says that everything in the financial markets is tainted and beaten-up which presents an extraordinary opportunity for hedge funds as long as they back up their decisions with sharp and intensive research. He adds that money managers should short suspect stocks and go long on undeservedly battered stocks in the same sector.

8339 ■ "Hank Paulson On the Housing Bailout and What's Ahead" in *Business Week* (September 22, 2008, No. 4100, pp. 19)

Pub: McGraw-Hill Companies, Inc.

Ed: Maria Bartiromo. **Description:** Interview with Treasury Secretary Henry Paulson in which he discusses the bailout of Fannie Mae and Freddie Mac as well as the potential impact on the American economy and foreign interests and investments in the country. Paulson has faith that the government's actions will help to stabilize the housing market.

8340 ■ "A Harbinger?" in *The Business Journal-Milwaukee* (Vol. 25, August 29, 2008, No. 49, pp. A1)

Pub: American City Business Journals, Inc.

Ed: Rich Kirchen. **Description:** Stock prices of Marshall & Ilsley Corp. (M&I) and MGIC Investment Corp. are expected to rebound after insiders were reported to have bought stocks of the companies. M&I director David Lubar bought $4.3 million, while MGIC CEO and chairman Curt Culver bought 20,000 stocks of MGIC. Other views and information on the insiders' purchase of stocks are presented.

8341 ■ "Hartco Income Fund Announces the Completion of the CompuSmart Strategic Review" in *Canadian Corporate News* (May 14, 2007)

Pub: Comtex News Network Inc.

Description: Hartco Income Fund announced that it has completed the process of exploring strategic options for CompuSmart and found that it should implement a plan to sell select stores and assets while consolidating remaining CompuSmart locations over the next sixty days.

8342 ■ "Has Microsoft Found a Way to Get at Yahoo?" in *Advertising Age* (Vol. 79, July 7, 2008, No. 26, pp. 4)

Pub: Crain Communications, Inc.

Ed: Abbey Klaassen. **Description:** Microsoft's attempt to acquire Yahoo's search business is discussed as is Yahoo's plans for the future at a time when the company's shares have fallen dangerously low.

8343 ■ "Hastily Enacted Regulation Will Not Cure Economic Crisis" in *Crain's Chicago Business* (Vol. 31, May 5, 2008, No. 18, pp. 18)

Pub: Crain Communications, Inc.

Ed: Stephen P. D'Arcy. **Description:** Policymakers are looking for ways to respond to what is possibly the greatest financial crisis of a generation due to the collapse of the housing market, the credit crisis and the volatility of Wall Street.

8344 ■ "Hawaii's Identity Crisis" in *Hawaii Business* (Vol. 53, November 2007, No. 5, pp. 10)

Pub: Hawaii Business Publishing

Ed: Kelli Abe Trifonovitch. **Description:** Some Hawaiians have shown that the Superferry controversy makes it seem to the rest of the world as if they do not know what they are doing, and intensifies several issues regarding the stability of investing in Hawaii. With or without the Superferry, there is still no evidence that investors are afraid to put their money in Hawaii.

8345 ■ "Hawaii's Top Twenty Financial Advisors" in *Hawaii Business* (Vol. 53, February 2008, No. 8, pp. 32)

Pub: Hawaii Business Publishing

Description: Listing of Hawaii's top 20 financial advisors is presented. Details on the methodology used to create the rankings are discussed.

8346 ■ "HBDiversityStockIndex" in *Hispanic Business* (October 2009, pp. 1)

Pub: Hispanic Business

Description: Data covering the Hispanic Business Diversity Stock Index is highlighted. The HBDSI was up 0.12 percent through September 3, 2009. Statistical data included.

8347 ■ "Headwinds From the New Sod Slow Aer Lingus" in *Barron's* (Vol. 88, March 10, 2008, No. 10, pp. M6)

Pub: Dow Jones & Company, Inc.

Ed: Sean Walters; Arindam Nag. **Description:** Aer Lingus faces a drop in its share prices with a falling US market, higher jet fuel prices, and lower long-haul passenger load factors. British media companies Johnston Press and Yell Group are suffering from weaker ad revenue and heavier debt payments due to the credit crunch.

8348 ■ "The Heat Is On" in *Crain's Chicago Business* (Vol. 31, April 28, 2008, No. 17, pp. 4)

Pub: Crain Communications, Inc.

Ed: Steve Daniels. **Description:** Discusses Nicor Inc., a natural-gas utility serving 2 million customers in Chicago's suburbs, and its potential acquirers; shares of the company have dropped 17 percent this year making Nicor the second-worst among 31 utilities in an index tracked by Standrd & Poor's. Statistical data included.

8349 ■ "Heat's On, but Glacier Not Retreating" in *Globe & Mail* (January 26, 2006, pp. B3)

Pub: CTVglobemedia Publishing Inc.

Ed: Grant Robertson. **Description:** The details on Glacier Ventures International Corp., which acquired Hollinger International Inc.'s assets, are presented.

8350 ■ "Hello, 9000! The Dow's Run Is Far From Over" in *Barron's* (Vol. 89, July 27, 2009, No. 30, pp. 20)

Pub: Dow Jones & Co., Inc.

Ed: Andrew Bary. **Description:** Another 10 percent gain is possible for the rest of 2009 as the Dow Jones Industrial Average moved above 9000 level for the week ending July 24, 2009. Blue chip stocks could do well in the next 10 years.

8351 ■ "Here are the Stocks of the Decade" in *Business Courier* (Vol. 26, December 18, 2009, No. 34, pp. 1)

Pub: American City Business Journals, Inc.

Ed: Steve Watkins. **Description:** Listing of companies with stocks that made big gains since December 1999 to November 30, 2009 is presented.

8352 ■ "Here's How Buffett Spent 2007" in *Barron's* (Vol. 88, March 10, 2008, No. 10, pp. 48)

Pub: Dow Jones & Company, Inc.

Ed: Andrew Bary. **Description:** Earnings of Berkshire Hathaway may decline in 2008 due to a tighter insurance market, but its portfolio is expected to continue growing. Warren Buffett purchased $19.1 billion worth of stocks in 2007.

8353 ■ "The Hidden Tax" in *Canadian Business* (Vol. 81, April 14, 2008, No. 6, pp. 28)

Pub: Rogers Media

Ed: Al Rosen. **Description:** Accounting fraud could take out a sizable sum from one's retirement fund when computed over a long period of time. The much bigger tax on savings is the collective impact of the smaller losses that do not attract the attention they deserve. Ensuring that investors are not unnecessarily taxed 2 percent of their total investments every year outweighs the benefit of a 2 percent reduction in personal tax rates.

8354 ■ "H.I.G. Capital Announces Acquisition of Next Generation Vending" in *Benzinga.com* (October 29, 2011)

Pub: Benzinga.com

Ed: Benzinga Staff. **Description:** H.I.G. Capital LLC, a leader in global private investments, acquired Next Generation Vending and Food Service Inc.. Next Generation is a provider of vending services for corporate and institutional clients in Northeastern United States.

8355 ■ "High-Yield Turns Into Road Kill" in *Barron's* (Vol. 88, July 7, 2008, No. 27, pp. M7)

Pub: Dow Jones & Co., Inc.

Ed: Emily Barrett. **Description:** High-yield bonds have returned to the brink of collapse after profits have recovered from the shock brought about by the collapse of Bear Stearns. The high-yield bond market could decline again due to weakness in the automotive sector, particularly in Ford and General Motors.

8356 ■ "Higher Freight Rates Keep CPR Rolling in Profit" in *Globe & Mail* (February 1, 2006, pp. B3)

Pub: CTVglobemedia Publishing Inc.

Ed: Brent Jang. **Description:** Canadian Pacific Railway Ltd. posted $135.4 million in revenues for fourth quarter 2005. The company's earnings projections for 2006 and workforce reduction plans are presented.

8357 ■ "His Banking Industry Software Never Caught On, so Bill Randle is Now Targeting the Health Care Market" in *Inc.* (March 2008)

Pub: Gruner & Jahr USA Publishing

Ed: Alex Salkever. **Description:** Profile of Bill Randle, bank executive turned entrepreneur; Randle tells how he changed his focus for his company from banking software to healthcare software. The firm employs ten people who secure online billing and recordkeeping systems for hospitals and insurers. Randle discusses critical decisions that will impact his firm in the coming year. Three experts offer advice.

8358 ■ "Hispantelligence Report" in *Hispanic Business* (July-August 2009, pp. 8)

Pub: Hispanic Business

Description: After forty years, Hispanic-owned businesses have grown to more than three million, according to a U.S. Census report. The Hispanic business stock index is also presented. Statistical data included.

8359 ■ "Hit the Books" in *Black Enterprise* (Vol. 38, July 2008, No. 12, pp. 42)

Pub: Earl G. Graves Publishing Co. Inc.

Ed: Mellody Hobson. **Description:** Four books that deal with investing are discussed as is the idea that reading even 15 minutes a day from one of these books will give you tools that far exceed what you can learn from magazines and the business section of your daily newspaper.

8360 ■ "Hits and Misses" in *Canadian Business* (Vol. 80, December 25, 2006, No. 1, pp. 69)

Pub: Rogers Media

Ed: Calvin Leung. **Description:** The performance of stocks of several Canadian companies is discussed.

8361 ■ "Hitting Bottom?" in *Barron's* (Vol. 88, March 24, 2008, No. 12, pp. 21)

Pub: Dow Jones & Company, Inc.

Ed: Jacqueline Doherty. **Description:** Brokerage houses and banks may stabilize in 2008 as a result of regulatory responses brought about by the near-collapse of Bear Stearns. Some of their shares may rise by as much as 20 percent from 2008 to 2009.

8362 ■ "Hold Your Nose, Say 'Da'" in *Canadian Business* (Vol. 79, September 11, 2006, No. 18, pp. 151)
Pub: Rogers Media
Ed: Thomas Watson. **Description:** The changing business environment and investment opportunities in Russia despite its instable democracy are discussed. Russia's potential and its ability to attract productive investment are presented.

8363 ■ "Hollinger Shares Plummet on Reports" in *Globe & Mail* (March 10, 2007, pp. B5)
Pub: CTVglobemedia Publishing Inc.
Ed: Richard Blackwell. **Description:** The fall in the share prices of Hollinger Inc. to 49 percent soon after the company filed its annual statements is discussed.

8364 ■ "The Home Game" in *Canadian Business* (Vol. 80, October 8, 2007, No. 20, pp. 68)
Pub: Rogers Media
Ed: Rachel Pulfer. **Description:** Analysis of Canada's banking industry is presented. Trends show that Canadian banks avoid risks in their investments, and usually choose to take safer paths. Experts believe these trends affect the country's economy and that Canadian banks do not play a significant role in economic development.

8365 ■ "A Home of Her Own" in *Hawaii Business* (Vol. 53, October 2007, No. 4, pp. 51)
Pub: Hawaii Business Publishing
Ed: Maria Torres-Kitamura. **Description:** It was observed that the number of single women in Hawaii purchasing their own home has increased, as that in the whole United States where the percentage has increased from 14 percent in 1995 to 22 percent in 2006. However, First Hawaiian Bank's Wendy Lum thinks that the trend will not continue in Hawaii due to lending restrictions. The factors that women consider in buying a home of their own are presented.

8366 ■ "Home Sweet Home?" in *Canadian Business* (Vol. 79, September 11, 2006, No. 18, pp. 17)
Pub: Rogers Media
Ed: David Wolf. **Description:** Fading attractiveness of the Canadian stock market for its domestic investors is discussed. Changing investor's trends toward cross-border investments are presented.

8367 ■ "Homebuilders Continue to be Our Nemesis" in *Contractor* (Vol. 56, July 2009, No. 7, pp. 50)
Pub: Penton Media, Inc.
Ed: Bob Mader. **Description:** Homebuilders rank high on the greed scale along with Wall Street brokers. There is this one instance when a builder gave copies of another contractor's quotes that have just been blackened out and another instance when one builder let other bidders visit a site while the current mechanical contractor is working.

8368 ■ "Honesty Doesn't Pay" in *Canadian Business* (Vol. 79, Winter 2006, No. 24, pp. 28)
Pub: Rogers Media
Ed: Al Rosen. **Description:** The effects of the outlook of financial analysts and investment bankers, on their career prospects, are described.

8369 ■ "Hong Kong's Boom in IPO" in *Barron's* (Vol. 89, July 13, 2009, No. 28, pp. M7)
Pub: Dow Jones & Co., Inc.
Ed: Nick Lord. **Description:** Hong Kong's IPO (initial public offering) market is booming with 13 Chinese IPOs already on the market for the year as July 2009. One of them is Bawang International which raised $214 million after generating $9 billion in order which makes it 42 times oversubscribed.

8370 ■ *House of Cards*
Pub: Doubleday, a Division of Random House
Ed: William D. Cohan. **Released:** March 10, 2009. **Price:** $27.95. **Description:** The fall of Bear Stearns and the beginning of the Wall Street Collapse.

8371 ■ *House of Cards: A Tale of Hubris and Wretched Excess on Wall Street*
Pub: Anchor Press
Ed: William D. Cohan. **Released:** February 9, 2010. **Price:** $16.95. **Description:** A historical account of the events leading up to the Bear Stearns implosion.

8372 ■ "Housing Hedge" in *Canadian Business* (Vol. 79, July 17, 2006, No. 14-15, pp. 66)
Pub: Rogers Media
Ed: Jeff Sanford. **Description:** The idea of starting a hedge scheme for housing is presented using the advent of pension schemes as an example to follow.

8373 ■ "How to Avoid the Three Big Mistakes" in *Barron's* (Vol. 88, March 10, 2008, No. 10, pp. 30)
Pub: Dow Jones & Company, Inc.
Ed: Karen Hube. **Description:** Investors, particularly those having retirement investments, are advised to diversify their investments, refrain from market timing, and minimize payments to maximize investment gains. An investor committing these mistakes could lose as much as $375,000 dollars over ten years.

8374 ■ "How to Beat the Pros" in *Canadian Business* (Vol. 81, Summer 2008, No. 9, pp. 59)
Pub: Rogers Media Ltd.
Ed: Calvin Leung. **Description:** Table showing the results of the Investor 500 beat the S&P/TSX composite index is presented. The average total return, best performing stocks and total return of the 2007 stock screen are provided.

8375 ■ "How CoolBrand's Thrills Turned to Chills" in *Globe & Mail* (January 25, 2007, pp. B1)
Pub: CTVglobemedia Publishing Inc.
Ed: Keith McArthur. **Description:** The key reasons behind the sudden share price fall of ice cream giant CoolBrands International Inc. are discussed.

8376 ■ "How to Deal" in *Canadian Business* (Vol. 81, November 10, 2008, No. 19, pp. 36)
Pub: Rogers Media Ltd.
Ed: Calvin Leung. **Description:** The Great Depression, Japan's Lost Decade, and the Swedish Banking Crisis is compared to the 2008 financial crisis in the U.S. The chances for recession in the U.S. are discussed along with investment strategies to survive.

8377 ■ "How Foreigners Could Disrupt U.S. Markets" in *Barron's* (Vol. 90, September 13, 2010, No. 37, pp. 30)
Pub: Barron's Editorial & Corporate Headquarters
Ed: Jim McTague. **Description:** An informal meeting by the House Homeland Security Panel concluded that U.S. stock exchanges and related trading routes can be the subject of attacks from rogue overseas traders. A drop in funding for the U.S. Department of Defense is discussed.

8378 ■ "How to Handle a Bank Error: Act Quickly When You See a Mistake on Your Statement" in *Black Enterprise* (Vol. 41, December 2010, No. 5)
Pub: Earl G. Graves Publishing Co. Inc.
Ed: Sheiresa Ngo. **Description:** Contact your bank or financial institution immediately after discovering an error in your account.

8379 ■ "How High Can Soybeans Fly?" in *Barron's* (Vol. 88, March 10, 2008, No. 10, pp. M14)
Pub: Dow Jones & Company, Inc.
Ed: Kenneth Rapoza. **Description:** Prices of soybeans have risen to $14.0875 a bushel, up 8.3 percent for the week. Increased demand, such as in China and in other developing economies, and the investment-driven commodities boom are boosting prices.

8380 ■ "How Interest Rate Changes Affect You" in *Agency Sales Magazine* (Vol. 39, September-October 2009, No. 9, pp. 50)
Pub: MANA
Ed: Lee Eisinberg. **Description:** Falling interest rates make the prices of previously issued bonds rise and new issues are offered at lower rates. For stock investors, rising interest rates can have a positive or negative effect. Terminologies related to investing are explained.

8381 ■ *How to Make Money in Stocks: A Winning System in Good Times and Bad*
Pub: The McGraw-Hill Companies
Ed: William J. O'Neil. **Released:** June 12. 2009. **Price:** $16.95. **Description:** The bestselling guide to buying stocks, from the founder of Investor's Business Daily. The technique is based on a study of the greatest stock market winners dating back to 1953 and includes a seven-step process for minimizing risk, maximizing return, and finding stocks that are ready to perform.

8382 ■ "How Not to Raise Bank Capital" in *Barron's* (Vol. 88, June 30, 2008, No. 26, pp. M6)
Pub: Dow Jones & Co., Inc.
Ed: Sean Walters. **Description:** French bank Natixis wants to raise 1 billion euros from cash provided by their two major owners. Natixis will reimburse Banque Populaire and Caisses d'Epargne with hybrid securities so this move will not benefit Natixis' core Tier 1 ratio. This has also given the impression that the company is afraid of a full rights issue which could shake investors' faith in the bank.

8383 ■ "How Our Picks Beat The Bear" in *Barron's* (Vol. 88, July 14, 2008, No. 28, pp. 18)
Pub: Dow Jones & Co., Inc.
Ed: Andrew Bary. **Description:** Performance of the stocks that Barron's covered in the first half of 2008 is discussed; some of the worst picks and most rewarding pans have been in the financial sector while the best plays were in the energy, materials, and the transportation sectors.

8384 ■ "How Sweet It Will Be" in *Barron's* (Vol. 89, July 13, 2009, No. 28, pp. M13)
Pub: Dow Jones & Co., Inc.
Ed: Debbie Carlson. **Description:** Raw sugar experienced a rally in the first half of 2009 and the long term outlook for sugar prices is still good. However, there is a likely near-term correction due to the onset of Brazilian harvest that could be 20.7 percent higher for 2009 as compared to the previous year and October contracts could fall to 15.61 cents per pound.

8385 ■ "HSBC Canada Posts 8.8 Percent Profit Gain in 2006" in *Globe & Mail* (February 20, 2007, pp. B14)
Pub: CTVglobemedia Publishing Inc.
Ed: Andrew Willis. **Description:** HSBC Bank Canada reported profits of $497 million in 2006. The financial results of the company for 2006 are presented.

8386 ■ "Ian Gordon" in *Canadian Business* (Vol. 81, Summer 2008, No. 9, pp. 10)
Pub: Rogers Media Ltd.
Ed: Matthew McClearn. **Description:** Bolder Investment Partners' Ian Gordon discussed the economic theory promulgated by Russian economist Nikolai Kondratieff. The cycle begins with a rising economy then followed by deflationary depression. Details of his views on the Kondratieff cycle and its application to the current economy are presented.

8387 ■ "Identity Crisis: The Battle For Your Data" in *Canadian Business* (Vol. 81, March 17, 2008, No. 4, pp. 12)
Pub: Rogers Media
Description: Nigel Brown explains that businesses must protect their data through encryption and tightening up access to data. Brown also points out that banks and merchants bear most of the costs for identity fraud and leaves individuals with a lot of pain and heartache in clearing their name.

8388 ■ **"If You Go Into the Market Today..." in** *Canadian Business* **(Vol. 82, Summer 2009, No. 8, pp. 18)**

Pub: Rogers Media

Ed: Jeff Sanford. **Description:** Opinions of experts and personalities who are known to have bear attitudes towards the economy were presented in the event 'A Night with the Bears' in Toronto in April 2009. Known bears that served as resource persons in the event were Nouriel Roubini, Eric Sprott, Ian Gordon, and Meredith Whitney. The bears were observed to have differences regarding consumer debt.

8389 ■ **"An Ill Wind: Icelandic Bank Failures Chill Atlantic Canada" in** *Canadian Business* **(Vol. 81, November 10, 2008, No. 19, pp. 10)**

Pub: Rogers Media Ltd.

Ed: Charles Mandel. **Description:** Bank failures in Iceland have put a stop to flights ferrying Icelanders to Newfoundland to purchase Christmas gifts, thereby threatening Newfoundland's tourism industry. The credit of Newfoundland's fisheries is also being squeezed since most of Atlantic Canadian seafood processors hold lines of credit from Icelandic banks.

8390 ■ **"Immigration Issues Frustrate Owners From Overseas" in** *The Business Journal-Serving Greater Tampa Bay* **(Vol. 28, August 15, 2008)**

Pub: American City Business Journals, Inc.

Ed: Margie Manning. **Description:** Investors who availed the E-2 visa program believe that the tightened restrictions on the visa program has trapped them in the United States. The E-2 investor visa program was designed to attract investors into the U.S., but restrictions were tightened after the September 11, 2001 attacks. Other views and information on E-2 and its impact on investors are presented.

8391 ■ **"The Impact of Brand Quality on Shareholder Wealth" in** *Journal of Marketing* **(Vol. 75, September 2011, No. 5, pp. 88)**

Pub: American Marketing Association

Ed: Sundar G. Bharardwaj, Kapil R. Tuli, Andre Bonfrer. **Description:** The effects of brand quality on idiosyncratic risk, systematic risk, and stock returns are investigated. Findings reveal that unexpected changes in brand quality negatively associated with idiosyncratic risk changes and positively related to stock returns. However, unexpected changes in brand quality will reduce shareholder wealth due to positive relationship with changes n systematic risk.

8392 ■ **"Imports Frothing Up Beer Market" in** *Globe & Mail* **(February 16, 2006, pp. B4)**

Pub: CTVglobemedia Publishing Inc.

Ed: Andy Hoffman. **Description:** The reasons behind the rise in market share of beer imports, in Canada, are presented.

8393 ■ **"In the Bag?" in** *Canadian Business* **(Vol. 81, March 3, 2008, No. 3, pp. 57)**

Pub: Rogers Media

Ed: Calvin Leung. **Description:** American stocks are beginning to appear cheap amidst the threat of a worldwide economic slowdown, United States economic crisis and declining stock portfolios. Investors looking for bargain stocks should study the shares of Apple and Oshkosh Corp. Evaluation of other cheap-looking stocks such as the shares of Coach and 3M is also given.

8394 ■ **"In China, Railways to Riches" in** *Barron's* **(Vol. 88, July 7, 2008, No. 27, pp. M9)**

Pub: Dow Jones & Co., Inc.

Ed: Assif Shameen. **Description:** Shares of Chinese railway companies look to benefit from multimillion-dollar investments aimed at upgrading the Chinese railway network. Investment in the sector is expected to reach $210 billion for the 2006-2010 period.

8395 ■ **"In India, A Gold-Price Threat?" in** *Barron's* **(Vol. 88, June 30, 2008, No. 26, pp. M12)**

Pub: Dow Jones & Co., Inc.

Ed: Melanie Burton. **Description:** Gold purchases in India are falling as record prices take its toll on demand. Gold imports to India fell by 52 percent in May 2008 from the previous year and local prices are higher by one-third from the previous year to 12,540 rupees for 10 grams.

8396 ■ **"In Praise of How Not to Invest" in** *Barron's* **(Vol. 89, July 13, 2009, No. 28, pp. 11)**

Pub: Dow Jones & Co., Inc.

Ed: Vito J. Racanelli. **Description:** One research study found that the shares of companies that have growing market shares and expanding asset bases underperform. This is contrary to the widely held premise that stock prices for these companies rise. It is argued that this result is caused by these companies' tendency to sacrifice profitability to grab market share and this is reflected in their stock prices.

8397 ■ **"In Sickness and In Wealth Management" in** *Hispanic Business* **(Vol. 30, March 2008, No. 3, pp. 28)**

Pub: Hispanic Business

Ed: Rick Munarriz. **Description:** Discusses the investment and wealth management firms owned and operated by Hispanics. There are only a handful of these firms owned by Hispanics, as most of them prefer capital preservation by investing in hard assets like cash and real estate than in capital appreciation.

8398 ■ **"In Surging Oil Industry, Good Fortune Comes In Stages" in** *Barron's* **(Vol. 88, July 7, 2008, No. 27, pp. 12)**

Pub: Dow Jones & Co., Inc.

Ed: Sandra Ward. **Description:** Shares of US land oil and gas driller Helmerich and Payne, priced at $69 each, are estimated to be at peak levels. The shares are trading at 17 times 2008 earnings and could be in for some profit taking.

8399 ■ **"In the Wake of Pet-Food Crisis, Iams Sales Plummet Nearly 17 Percent" in** *Advertising Age* **(Vol. 78, May 14, 2007, No. 18, pp. 3)**

Pub: Crain Communications, Inc.

Ed: Jack Neff. **Description:** Although the massive U.S. pet-food recall impacted more than 100 brands, Procter & Gamble Co.'s Iams lost more sales and market share than any other industry player. According to Information Resources data, the brand's sales dropped 16.5 percent in the eight-week period ended April 22. Many analysts feel that the company could have handled the crisis in a better manner.

8400 ■ **"Inflation Woes: Secure Your Portfolio Against Rising Prices" in** *Black Enterprise* **(Vol. 37, January 2007, No. 6, pp. 40)**

Pub: Earl G. Graves Publishing Co. Inc.

Ed: Donald Jay Korn. **Description:** Inflation has a huge impact on investing and it is important to take the steady increase on cost into account when looking at your financial goals and investing in your future. Statistical data included.

8401 ■ **"Inland Snaps Up Rival REITs" in** *Crain's Chicago Business* **(Vol. 31, November 17, 2008, No. 46, pp. 3)**

Pub: Crain Communications, Inc.

Ed: Alby Gallun. **Description:** Discusses Inland American Real Estate Trust Inc., a real estate investment trust that is napping up depressed shares of publicly traded competitors, a possible first step toward taking over these companies; however, with hotel and retail properties accounting for approximately 70 percent of its portfolio, the company could soon face its own difficulties.

8402 ■ **"Inmet Selling Nunavut Mining Properties" in** *Globe & Mail* **(February 15, 2006, pp. B6)**

Pub: CTVglobemedia Publishing Inc.

Ed: Allan Robinson. **Description:** The details on Wolfden Resources Inc.'s acquisition of mining assets of Inmet Mining Corp. are presented.

8403 ■ **"Insider" in** *Canadian Business* **(Vol. 81, March 3, 2008, No. 3, pp. 96)**

Pub: Rogers Media

Description: History of gold usage and gold trading is presented in a timeline. Gold was a symbol of power and wealth in 2500 B.C., and in 1500 B.C., it became the first currency to be recognized internationally. Other remarkable events in the gold industry and laws that covered gold are discussed.

8404 ■ **"An Insurance Roll-Up In Danger of Unraveling" in** *Barron's* **(Vol. 88, March 17, 2008, No. 11, pp. 51)**

Pub: Dow Jones & Company, Inc.

Ed: Bill Alpert. **Description:** Shares of National Financial Partners have fallen below their initial offering price as sputtering sales and management turnover leave many investors wondering. One of the company's star brokers is being sued for their "life settlement" contracts while another broker is being pursued by the IRS for unpaid taxes.

8405 ■ **"Intangible Assets" in** *Canadian Business* **(Vol. 79, July 17, 2006, No. 14-15, pp. 17)**

Pub: Rogers Media

Ed: Al Rosen. **Description:** Need for investors to check the actual worth of a company and not to get carried away by the inflated claims made by the company is emphasized.

8406 ■ **"International ETFs: Your Passport to the World" in** *Barron's* **(Vol. 89, July 13, 2009, No. 28, pp. L10)**

Pub: Dow Jones & Co., Inc.

Ed: John Hintze. **Description:** International exchange traded funds give investors more choices in terms of investment plays and there are 174 U.S. ETF listings worth $141 billion as of July 2009. Suggestions on how to invest in these funds based on one's conviction on how the global economy will unfold are presented.

8407 ■ **"International Nickel Ventures Corporation Reports Results for the First Quarter 2007" in** *Canadian Corporate News* **(May 16, 2007)**

Pub: Comtex News Network Inc.

Description: Profile of International Nickel Ventures Corporation (INV) including its financial report for the first quarter of fiscal 2007, its partnership and possible acquisition of Teck Cominco Limited, and its plans for the future. Statistical data included.

8408 ■ *The Internationalization of Asset Ownership in Europe*

Pub: Cambridge University Press

Ed: Harry Huizinga, Lars Jonung. **Released:** November 2005. **Price:** $112.00. **Description:** Ten financial experts provide analysis of the growth and the implications of foreign ownership in Europe's financial markets.

8409 ■ **"Investment Manager Disciplined" in** *Sacramento Business Journal* **(Vol. 25, July 4, 2008, No. 18, pp. 1)**

Pub: American City Business Journals, Inc.

Ed: Mark Anderson. **Description:** Community Capital Management's David A. Zwick is permanently barred by the Securities and Exchange Commission (SEC) from associating with any broker or dealer, after investigations revealed that he took part in paying kickbacks to a bond trader. Other views and information on Community Capital, and on the SEC investigation on Zwick, are presented.

8410 ■ **"Investors Lost Patience A Long Time Ago" in** *Globe & Mail* **(January 21, 2006, pp. B5)**

Pub: CTVglobemedia Publishing Inc.

Ed: Konrad Yakabuski. **Description:** The financial impasse at Quebecor World Inc., under chief executive officer Pierre Karl Peladeau, is discussed.

8411 ■ **"Investors Shrug Off the Turmoil" in** *Globe & Mail* **(March 1, 2007, pp. B1)**

Pub: CTVglobemedia Publishing Inc.

Ed: Geoffrey York. **Description:** The decision of Chinese investors to continue to buy stocks despite the decade's biggest market crash is discussed. The rise in the stock price indexes of China is described.

8412 ■ "Is the VIX in Denial?" in *Barron's*
(Vol. 88, July 7, 2008, No. 27, pp. M12)
Pub: Dow Jones & Co., Inc.
Ed: Lawrence McMillan. **Description:** Volatility Index
(VIX) of the Chicago Board Options Exchange did
not rise significantly despite the drop in the US stock
markets, rising to near 25. This market decline,
however, will eventually result in investor panic and
the rise of the VIX.

**8413 ■ "Islamic Banks Get a 'Libor' of Their
Own" in** *Wall Street Journal Eastern Edition*
(November 25 , 2011, pp. C4)
Pub: Dow Jones & Company Inc.
Ed: Katy Burne. **Description:** The London interbank
offered rate, or Libor, has been used by banks
internationally for years. It is the rate at which banks
lend money to each other. The rate has not been
used by Islamic banks, but now sixteen banks have
come up with the Islamic Interbank Benchmark Rate.

8414 ■ "It Could Be Worse" in *Barron's* **(Vol.
89, July 27, 2009, No. 30, pp. 5)**
Pub: Dow Jones & Co., Inc.
Ed: Alan Abelson. **Description:** Media sources are
being fooled by corporate America who is peddling
an economic recovery rather than reality as shown
by the report of a rise in existing home sales which
boosted the stock market even if it was a seasonal
phenomenon. The phrase "things could be worse"
sums up the reigning investment philosophy in the
U.S. and this has been stirring up the market.

8415 ■ "It Takes More Than One" in *Black
Enterprise* **(Vol. 38, July 2008, No. 12, pp. 38)**
Pub: Earl G. Graves Publishing Co. Inc.
Ed: James A. Anderson. **Description:** Interview with
Eric Small, the CEO of SBK-Brooks Investment
Corp., whom discusses the importance of versatility
when trying to find the best investment choices; the
primary factors investors should be mindful of; his
current stock picks; and recommendations for invest-
ing in an uncertain and volatile market.

**8416 ■ "Itochu Joins KKR in Samson
Buyout" in** *Wall Street Journal Eastern
Edition* **(November 25 , 2011, pp. B7)**
Pub: Dow Jones & Company Inc.
Description: Samson Investment Company is the
target of a $7.2 billion leveraged buyout by a consor-
tium led by US investment firm Kohlberg Kravis
Roberts & Company and Tokyo-based Itochu Corporation, part of the consortium is coming in on the deal
for a 25 percent holding, for which it will pay $1.04
billion.

8417 ■ "It's Good to be Goldman" in
Barron's **(Vol. 89, July 20, 2009, No. 29, pp. 5)**
Pub: Dow Jones & Co., Inc.
Ed: Randall W. Forsyth. **Description:** Profits of Gold-
man Sachs rose to $3.44 billion in the second quarter
of 2009, aided by federal financial stimulus programs.
CIT Group is facing bankruptcy and may need up to
$6 billion to survive. The federal economic stimulus
programs are benefiting Wall Street more than the
US economy itself.

**8418 ■ "It's Time to Wise Up: Income Trusts"
in** *Canadian Business* **(Vol. 79, November 6,
2006, No. 22, pp. 24)**
Pub: Rogers Media
Ed: Mark Rosen. **Description:** The effects bogus
financial reporting of income trusts on investors are
analyzed.

**8419 ■ "Ivernia Mine Closing Could Boost
Lead" in** *Globe & Mail* **(April 4, 2007, pp. B5)**
Pub: CTVglobemedia Publishing Inc.
Ed: Andy Hoffman. **Description:** The closing of Ivernia Inc.'s mine in view of government investigation
into alleged lead contamination at the port of Esperance is discussed. The likely increase in the price of
lead is also discussed.

**8420 ■ "Jamieson Eyes $175 Million Trust
IPO" in** *Globe & Mail* **(March 7, 2006, pp. B1)**
Pub: CTVglobemedia Publishing Inc.
Ed: Sinclair Stewart; Leonard Zehr. **Description:** The
reasons behind $175 million initial public offering
plans of Jamieson Laboratories Ltd. are presented.

**8421 ■ "Jean Coutu Resuscitates Bottom
Line" in** *Globe & Mail* **(January 11, 2006, pp.
B5)**
Pub: CTVglobemedia Publishing Inc.
Ed: Bertrand Marotte. **Description:** The details on
Jean Coutu Group (PJC) Inc., which posted $30.8
million profits for second quarter 2005, are presented.

**8422 ■ "Judge Gives RIM One Last Chance"
in** *Globe & Mail* **(February 25, 2006, pp. B5)**
Pub: CTVglobemedia Publishing Inc.
Ed: Barrie McKenna; Paul Waldie. **Description:**
United States District Court Judge James Spencer
offers more time for Research In Motion Ltd. (RIM) to
settle the patent infringement dispute with NTP Inc.
RIM's shares increase by 6.2 percent following the
decision.

8423 ■ "The Judgment Deficit" in *Harvard
Business Review* **(Vol. 88, September 2010,
No. 9, pp. 44)**
Pub: Harvard Business School Publishing
Ed: Amar Bhide. **Description:** The importance of
individual, decentralized initiative and judgment in the
capitalist system is outlined. While financial models
have their use, they cannot always account appropriately for the inherent uncertainty in economic
decision making.

8424 ■ "Juiced on Energy" in *Barron's* **(Vol.
88, July 14, 2008, No. 28, pp. 33)**
Pub: Dow Jones & Co., Inc.
Ed: Leslie P. Norton. **Description:** Brad Evans and
his team at Heartland Value Plus were able to
outperform their peers by significantly under-
committing to financials and overexposing themselves
with energy stocks. Brad Evans believes that there is
a lot of value left in energy stocks such as natural
gas.

**8425 ■ "Julie Holzrichter; Managing Director
of Operations, CME Group Inc." in** *Crain's
Chicago Business* **(Vol. 31, May 5, 2008, No.
18)**
Pub: Crain Communications, Inc.
Ed: Ann Saphir. **Description:** Profile of Julie Holzrichter who works as the managing director of operations
for CME Group Inc. and is known as a decisive leader
able to intercept and solve problems.

8426 ■ "Just Hang Up" in *Barron's* **(Vol. 88,
March 10, 2008, No. 10, pp. 45)**
Pub: Dow Jones & Company, Inc.
Ed: Tiernan Ray. **Description:** Sprint's shares are
expected to continue falling while the company attempts to attract subscribers by cutting prices, cutting
earnings in the process. The company faces tougher
competition from better-financed AT&T and Verizon
Communications.

8427 ■ "Keeping the Faith in Fuel-Tech" in
Barron's **(Vol. 88, March 24, 2008, No. 12, pp.
20)**
Pub: Dow Jones & Company, Inc.
Ed: Christopher C. Williams. **Description:** Shares of
air pollution control company Fuel-Tech remain on
track to reach $40 each from their $19 level due to a
continued influx of contracts. The stock has suffered
from lower-than-expected quarterly earnings and
tougher competition but stand to benefit from increased orders.

8428 ■ "Kid Rock" in *Canadian Business*
(Vol. 81, Summer 2008, No. 9, pp. 54)
Pub: Rogers Media Ltd.
Ed: John Gray. **Description:** Damien Reynolds is
the founder, chairman and chief executive officer of
Vancouver-based Longview Capital Partners. The
investment bank, founded in 2005, is one of the
fastest-growing companies in British Columbia. The
recent economic downturn has battered the stocks of
the company and its portfolio of junior miners.

8429 ■ *King of Capital*
Pub: John Wiley and Sons, Inc.
Ed: Amey Stone; Mike Brewster. **Released:** 2004.
Price: $16.95. **Description:** Biography of Sandy
Weill describes how he became a billionaire business
giant by creating successful companies from smaller,
sometimes failing firms; creating successful new

products where none previously existed; and making
deals no one thought possible. He is also responsible
for changing the landscape of the banking industry
and insurance business when he created Citigroup in
1998, the world's largest financial services firm.

8430 ■ "The Latin Beat Goes On" in *Barron's*
(Vol. 88, July 7, 2008, No. 27, pp. L5)
Pub: Dow Jones & Co., Inc.
Ed: Tom Sullivan. **Description:** Latin American
stocks have outperformed other regional markets due
to rising commodities prices and favorable economic
climate. Countries such as Brazil, Mexico, Chile, and
Peru provide investment opportunities, while Argentina and Venezuela are tougher places to invest.

8431 ■ "Laugh or Cry?" in *Barron's* **(Vol. 88,
March 24, 2008, No. 12, pp. 7)**
Pub: Dow Jones & Company, Inc.
Ed: Alan Abelson. **Description:** Discusses the
American economy which is just starting to feel the
effect of the credit and housing crises. JPMorgan
Chase purchased Bear Stearns for $2 a share, much
lower than its share price of $60, while quasi-
government entities Fannie Mae and Freddie Mac
are starting to run into trouble.

8432 ■ "Leaders and Lagards" in *Barron's*
(Vol. 89, July 13, 2009, No. 28, pp. 14)
Pub: Dow Jones & Co., Inc.
Ed: J.R. Brandstrader. **Description:** Statistical table
that shows the returns of different mutual funds in different categories that include U.S. stock funds, sector funds, world equity funds, and mixed equity funds
is presented. The data presented is for the second
quarter of 2009.

**8433 ■ "Leaders Weigh In On Fannie Mae,
Freddie Mac Failure, Fed Bailout" in** *The
Business Journal - Serving Phoenix and the
Valley of the Sun* **(Vol. 28, September 12,
2008, No. 53, pp. 1)**
Pub: American City Business Journals, Inc.
Ed: Chris Casacchia; Mike Sunnucks; Jan Buchholz.
Description: Fannie Mae and Freddie Mac's federal
takeover was a move to help stabilize the financial
market and it helped bring down interest rates in the
past week. Local executives from Arizona's Phoenix
area share their thoughts on the immediate effect of
the takeover and its upside and downside.

**8434 ■ "Legg's Compensation Committee
Chair Defends CEO Fetting's Pay" in** *Boston
Business Journal* **(Vol. 29, July 22, 2011, No.
11, pp. 1)**
Pub: American City Business Journals Inc.
Ed: Gary Haber. **Description:** Legg Mason Inc. CEO
Mark R. Fetting has been awarded $5.9 million pay
package and he expects to receive questions regarding it in the coming shareholders meeting. However,
Baltimore, Maryland-based RKTL Associates chairman emeritus Harold R. Adams believes Fetting has
done a tremendous job in bringing Legg's through a
tough market.

8435 ■ "Lehman's Hail Mary Pass" in
Business Week **(September 22, 2008, No.
4100, pp. 28)**
Pub: McGraw-Hill Companies, Inc.
Ed: Matthew Goldstein; David Henry; Ben Levison.
Description: Overview of Lehman Brothers' CEO
Richard Fuld's plan to keep the firm afloat and end
the stock's plunge downward; Fuld's strategy calls for
selling off a piece of the firm's investment manage-
ment business.

**8436 ■ "Lenders Capitalize on a Thinning
Bulge Bracket" in** *Mergers & Acquisitions:
The Dealmaker's Journal* **(March 1, 2008)**
Pub: SourceMedia, Inc.
Description: Regardless of what the economic
markets look like, private equity firms will continue to
invest capital and mid-market finance firms are
becoming very attractive acquisition opportunities
since not as much capital is needed to buy them.

8437 ■ "Lenders" in *The Business Journal -
Serving Phoenix and the Valley of the Sun*
(Vol. 28, July 25, 2008, No. 47, pp. 1)
Pub: American City Business Journals, Inc.
Ed: Jan Buchholz. **Description:** Private equity lender
Investor Mortgage Holdings Inc. has continued grow-

ing despite the crisis surrounding the real estate and financial industries and has accumulated a $700 million loan portfolio. Private lending has become increasingly important in financing real estate deals as commercial credit has dried up.

8438 ■ "Lending Door Slams" in *Puget Sound Business Journal* **(Vol. 29, October 24, 2008, No. 27, pp. 1)**
Pub: American City Business Journals
Ed: Jeanne Lang Jones, Kirsten Grind. **Description:** KeyBank's closure of its Puget Sound unit that services single-family homebuilders is part of a nationwide shutdown that includes similar closures in other cities. Bank of America is adopting more conservative terms for homebuilding loans while Union Bank of California is still offering credit for market rate housing.

8439 ■ "Lending Idea Gets Mixed Review" in *Tampa Bay Business Journal* **(Vol. 29, October 30, 2009, No. 45, pp. 1)**
Pub: American City Business Journals
Ed: Kent Hoover, Margie Manning. **Description:** Tampa Bay area, Florida's community banks have expressed disapproval to the proposal of President Obama to increase lending to small business, wherein the government will provide cheap capital through US Treasury Troubled Asset Relief Program (TARP). The banks were hesitant on the plan because of the strings attached to TARP.

8440 ■ "Less Malaise in Malaysia" in *Barron's* **(Vol. 88, March 17, 2008, No. 11, pp. M12)**
Pub: Dow Jones & Company, Inc.
Ed: Assif Shameen. **Description:** Shares of Malaysia's Bursa have been in freefall while the Malaysia government prolongs its pitch to sell a 10 percent stake of the exchange to NYSE Euronext. Asian bourses had produced very good returns for five years and charge some of the highest fees for exchanges. A key growth driver for Asian bourses could be the derivatives markets and exchange-traded funds.

8441 ■ "Let Us Count the Ways" in *Barron's* **(Vol. 88, July 7, 2008, No. 27, pp. M10)**
Pub: Dow Jones & Co., Inc.
Ed: Bennet Sedacca. **Description:** Investors are advised to remain cautious after the drop in stock prices in June 2008. The stock markets remain in the downtrend after reaching a peak in October 2007 and are on the verge of a collapse.

8442 ■ "A Lifetime of Making Deals" in *Crain's Detroit Business* **(Vol. 24, March 24, 2008, No. 12, pp. 11)**
Pub: Crain Communications, Inc.
Ed: Tom Henderson. **Description:** Profile of Walter "Bud" Aspatore who received Crain's Lifetime Achievement Award for mergers and acquisitions; Aspatore is chairman and co-founder of Amherst Partners L.L.C., an investment banking firm that does evaluations and financings, specializes in turnarounds and advises private and public companies on mergers and acquisitions.

8443 ■ "Lifetime Planning with a Twist" in *Contractor* **(Vol. 56, July 2009, No. 7, pp. 40)**
Pub: Penton Media, Inc.
Ed: Irv Blackman. **Description:** Private Placement Life Insurance lets wealthy investors make their investment gains tax-free and can be set up so investors can make tax-free loans from the policy. This can be used on a younger member of the family as a wealth-building strategy if the investor is uninsurable.

8444 ■ "A Limited Sphere of Influence" in *Mergers & Acquisitions: The Dealmaker's Journal* **(March 1, 2008)**
Pub: SourceMedia, Inc.
Ed: Ken MacFadyen. **Description:** Changes to the interest rate has had little impact on the mergers and acquisitions market since the federal funds rate does not link directly to the liquidity available to the M&A market; lenders are looking at cash flows and are likely to remain cautious due to other factors impacting the market.

8445 ■ "Listen to Bond Market on Tembec" in *Globe & Mail* **(January 25, 2006, pp. B1)**
Pub: CTVglobemedia Publishing Inc.
Ed: Derek DeCloet. **Description:** The feasibility of Tembec Inc.'s restructuring efforts is discussed.

8446 ■ "Listen Up: There's a Revolution in the Cubicle" in *Barron's* **(Vol. 89, July 27, 2009, No. 30, pp. 18)**
Pub: Dow Jones & Co., Inc.
Ed: Jay Palmer. **Description:** Plantronics will be among the first beneficiaries when the unified communications revolution arrives in the office. Plantronics' shares could rise to around 30 in 2009 from the 20s as of July 2009. Unified communications could create a huge new multimillion-dollar market for Plantronics.

8447 ■ "The Little Biotech that Could" in *Barron's* **(Vol. 89, July 27, 2009, No. 30, pp. 19)**
Pub: Dow Jones & Co., Inc.
Ed: Christopher C. Williams. **Description:** OSI Pharmaceuticals' shares is a compelling investment bet among small biotech firms due to its Tarceva anticancer drug which has a 23 percent market share as well as their strong balance sheet. OSI is planning to expand the use of Tarceva which could re-ignite sales and one analyst expects the shares to trade in the 40s one year from July 2009.

8448 ■ "Loblaw Posts 40 Percent Profit Drop as it Scrambles to Lower Costs" in *Globe & Mail* **(February 9, 2006, pp. B1)**
Pub: CTVglobemedia Publishing Inc.
Ed: Marina Strauss. **Description:** The reasons behind 40 percent decline in profits for Lobalaw Companies Ltd., for fourth quarter 2005, are presented.

8449 ■ "Local Firms Will Feel Impact Of Wall St. Woes" in *The Business Journal-Milwaukee* **(Vol. 25, September 19, 2008, No. 52, pp. A1)**
Pub: American City Business Journals, Inc.
Ed: Rich Kirchen. **Description:** Wall Street's crisis is expected to affect businesses in Wisconsin, in terms of decreased demand for services and products and increased financing costs. Businesses in Milwaukee area may face higher interest rates and tougher loan standards. The potential impacts of the Wall Street crisis on local businesses are examined further.

8450 ■ "Locally Based Stocks Escape Worst of Market's Turmoil" in *Crain's Detroit Business* **(Vol. 24, September 22, 2008, No. 38, pp. 4)**
Pub: Crain Communications, Inc.
Ed: Daniel Duggan. **Description:** Locally-based companies did not take as big a hit as might be expected with the shock to the financial markets last week; this is due mainly to the fact that the region does not have heavy exposure to energy or capital markets.

8451 ■ "Long - And Leery" in *Barron's* **(Vol. 88, March 31, 2008, No. 13, pp. 47)**
Pub: Dow Jones & Company, Inc.
Ed: Jack Willoughby. **Description:** Tom Claugus' Bay Resource Partners hedge fund has returned 20 percent annually since it started in 1993. Claugus says that he is as aggressively long as he has ever been despite the dangers of the U.S. market. Claugus' stock picks include Canadian Natural Resources, NII Holdings, and Discover Financial.

8452 ■ "Loop 360 Offices Planned" in *Austin Business JournalInc.* **(Vol. 28, December 5, 2008, No. 38, pp. A1)**
Pub: American City Business Journals
Ed: Kate Harrington. **Description:** Nearly 356,000 square feet of office space is planned in the South Capital of Texas Highway Corridor, also known as Loop 360 in Austin. Riverside Developers plans to wait until the economy improves before starting construction.

8453 ■ "Lotus Starts Slowly, Dodges Subprime Woes" in *Crain's Detroit Business* **(Vol. 24, April 14, 2008, No. 15, pp. 3)**
Pub: Crain Communications, Inc.
Ed: Tom Henderson. **Description:** Discusses Lotus Bancorp Inc. and their business plan, which although is not right on target due to the subprime mortgage meltdown, is in a much better position than its competitors due to the quality of their loans.

8454 ■ "Lower Prices No Shoo-In as Telcos Near Deregulation" in *Globe & Mail* **(March 28, 2007, pp. B1)**
Pub: CTVglobemedia Publishing Inc.
Ed: Catherine McLean. **Description:** The fall in market share and low quality of service among other issues that may disallow telecommunication industries in Canada from setting their phone rates is discussed.

8455 ■ "Lundin Deal Leaves Nickel Market Thin" in *Globe & Mail* **(April 5, 2007, pp. B4)**
Pub: CTVglobemedia Publishing Inc.
Ed: Andy Hoffman. **Description:** The likely acquisition of Rio Narcea Gold Mines Ltd. by Lundin Mining Corp. and the decreasing number of nickel mining companies on the list of Toronto Stock Exchange are discussed.

8456 ■ "Luster Lost" in *Saint Louis Business Journal* **(Vol. 32, September 16, 2011, No. 3, pp. 1)**
Pub: Saint Louis Business Journal
Ed: E.B. Solomont. **Description:** Express Cripts shares have plunged 22.71 percent since late July amid regulatory concerns, as the luster of the second-largest deal announced for 2011 wore off. Express Scripts has become the largest pharmacy benefit manager in the country after the $29 billion deal to take rival Medco Health Solutions.

8457 ■ "Magna Banks on Big Cash Hoard" in *Globe & Mail* **(March 1, 2006, pp. B3)**
Pub: CTVglobemedia Publishing Inc.
Ed: Greg Keenan. **Description:** The details on Magna International Inc., which posted decline in profits at $639 million for 2005, are presented.

8458 ■ "Magna Shares Sink on Tepid Outlook" in *Globe & Mail* **(January 13, 2006, pp. B1)**
Pub: CTVglobemedia Publishing Inc.
Ed: Greg Keenan. **Description:** The impact of Magna International Inc.'s sales projection for 2006, on its shares, is discussed.

8459 ■ *Major Financial Institutions of the World*
Pub: Graham & Whiteside
Ed: Victoria Bentley, Editor. **Released:** Latest edition 16th; Published May, 2012. **Price:** $1,460, individuals. **Covers:** More than 10,000 worldwide financial corporations, including banks, insurance companies, investment companies, and leasing companies. Also includes contact information for senior executives. **Entries Include:** Most listings include name, address, phone, telex, names of executives, principal activities, names of principal shareholders; subsidiary companies and financial summary where available.

8460 ■ "Making It Click" in *Barron's* **(Vol. 88, March 17, 2008, No. 11, pp. 31)**
Pub: Dow Jones & Company, Inc.
Ed: Theresa W. Carey. **Description:** Listing of 23 online brokers that are evaluated based on their trade experience, usability, range of offerings, research amenities, customer service and access, and costs. TradeStation Securities takes the top spot followed by thinkorswim by just a fraction.

8461 ■ "M&I Execs May Get Golden Parachutes" in *Business Journal-Milwaukee* **(Vol. 28, December 31, 2010, No. 14, pp. A3)**
Pub: Milwaukee Business Journal
Ed: Rich Kirchen. **Description:** Marshall and Isley Corporation's top executives have a chance to receive golden-parachute payments it its buyer, BMO Financial Group, repays the Troubled Asset Relief Program (TARP) loan on behalf of the company. One

TARP rule prevents golden-parachute payments to them and the next five most highly paid employees of TARP recipients.

8462 ■ "M&T On the March?" in *Baltimore Business Journal* (Vol. 28, November 12, 2010, No. 27, pp. 1)
Pub: Baltimore Business Journal

Ed: Gary Haber. **Description:** Information on the growth of M&T Bank, as well as its expansion plans are presented. M&T recently acquired Wilmington Trust and took over $500 million in deposits from the failed K Bank. Analysts believe that M&T would continue its expansion through Washington DC and Richmond, Virginia, especially after a bank executive acknowledged that the markets in those areas are attractive.

8463 ■ "Many Roads Lead to Value" in *Barron's* (Vol. 88, March 10, 2008, No. 10, pp. 46)
Pub: Dow Jones & Company, Inc.

Ed: Lawrence C. Strauss. **Description:** David J. Williams, lead manager of Excelsior Value & Restructuring Fund, invests in struggling companies and those companies whose turnarounds show promise. Morgan Stanley, Lehman Brothers, and Petroleo Brasileiro are some of the companies he holds shares in, while he has unloaded shares of Citigroup, Freddie Mac, and Sallie Mae.

8464 ■ "Market Recoups Its Losses - And Its Optimism" in *Barron's* (Vol. 89, July 20, 2009, No. 29, pp. M3)
Pub: Dow Jones & Co., Inc.

Ed: Kopin Tan. **Description:** US stock markets gained heavily in the third week of July 2009, rising by about 7 percent during the week. The shares of human resource management companies could be overpriced as they are trading at very high price-earnings multiples. Baxter International faces a class-action suit due to its alleged conspiracy with CSL to fix blood-plasma product prices.

8465 ■ "Market Swings Intensify Yearning for Bonds" in *Globe & Mail* (March 9, 2007, pp. B9)
Pub: CTVglobemedia Publishing Inc.

Ed: Keith Damsell. **Description:** The rise in demand for proper fixed-income bonds in Canada as a result of uncertainties in the equity market is discussed. Some big Canadian fixed-income funds are presented.

8466 ■ "Market Volatility and Your Retirement" in *Agency Sales Magazine* (Vol. 39, August 2009, No. 8, pp. 48)
Pub: MANA

Ed: Joshua D. Mosshart. **Description:** Strategies for retirees in managing investments amid market volatility are presented. Retirees should keep their withdrawal assumptions conservative, maintain sensible asset allocation, review and rebalance their portfolio and allow a financial professional to guide them. Insights on market volatility are also given.

8467 ■ "Market Watch: A Sampling of Advisory Opinion" in *Barron's* (Vol. 88, March 17, 2008, No. 11, pp. M10)
Pub: Dow Jones & Company, Inc.

Ed: Paul Schatz; William Gibson; Michael Darda. **Description:** S&P 500 bank stocks were down 46 percent from their 2007 peak while the peak to through fall in 1989-1990 was just over 50 percent. This suggests that the bottom on the bank stocks could be near. The Federal Reserve Board announced they will lend up to $200 billion to primary lenders in exchange other securities.

8468 ■ "Market Watch" in *Barron's* (Vol. 88, March 24, 2008, No. 12, pp. M18)
Pub: Dow Jones & Company, Inc.

Ed: Ashraf Laidi; Marc Pado; David Kotok. **Description:** Latest measures implemented by the Federal Reserve to address the credit crisis did not benefit the US dollar, with the Japanese yen and the euro recouping earlier losses against the dollar. Goldman

Sachs reported earnings of $3.23 per share, claiming a stronger liquidity position. The US markets bottomed early on 22 January 2007, according to evidence.

8469 ■ "Markets Defy the Doomsayers" in *Barron's* (Vol. 88, March 24, 2008, No. 12, pp. M5)
Pub: Dow Jones & Company, Inc.

Ed: Leslie P. Norton. **Description:** US stock markets registered strong gains, with the Dow Jones Industrial Average rising 3.43 percent on the week to close at 12,361.32, in a rally that may be seen as short-covering. Shares of Hansen Natural are poised for further drops with a slowdown in the energy drink market.

8470 ■ "The Market's (Very) Tender Spring Shoots" in *Barron's* (Vol. 88, March 31, 2008, No. 13, pp. M3)
Pub: Dow Jones & Company, Inc.

Ed: Kopin Tan. **Description:** Expansion in price-earnings multiples and a lower credit-default risk index has encouraged fans of the spring-awakening theory. Shares of industrial truckers have gone up 32 percent in 2008 and some shares are pushing five-year highs brought on by higher efficiency and earnings from more load carried. The prospects of the shares of Foot Locker are also discussed.

8471 ■ *The Match King: Ivar Kreuger, the Financial Genius Behind a Century of Wall Street Scandals*
Pub: Basic Books

Ed: Frank Portnoy. **Released:** 2009. **Price:** $26.95. **Description:** Ivar Kreuger, the so-called Match King, used a pyramid scheme to become the financier to European leaders.

8472 ■ "The Medium 150" in *Canadian Business* (Vol. 81, Summer 2008, No. 9, pp. 129)
Pub: Rogers Media Ltd.

Description: Medium-sized companies are ranked based on market capitalization and stock performance. Timminico Ltd. topped the roster with 1,294.2 percent returns, while Petrominerales Ltd. ranked second with 325.4 percent. A table showing the 2008 rankings of the companies is presented.

8473 ■ "Merchant Cash-Advance Company Enters Canada" in *Cardline* (Vol. 8, February 29, 2008, No. 9, pp. 1)
Pub: SourceMedia Inc.

Description: Merchant cash-advance company is expanding operations into Canada.

8474 ■ "Merrill Lynch in Talks to Buy BlackRock Stake" in *Globe & Mail* (February 13, 2006, pp. B4)
Pub: CTVglobemedia Publishing Inc.

Ed: Dennis K. Breman; Randall Smith. **Description:** Financial services firm Merrill Lynch and Co. Inc. is planning to acquire money managing company BlackRock Inc. for 8 million dollars. Sources report that this deal would create 1-trillion dollar huge fund management venture.

8475 ■ "Mettle Detector" in *Canadian Business* (Vol. 79, July 17, 2006, No. 14-15, pp. 63)
Pub: Rogers Media

Ed: Calvin Leung. **Description:** The difficulties faced in completing the Certified Financial Analyst course, and the rewards one can expect after its completion, are discussed.

8476 ■ "MF Global Moved Clients' Funds to BNY Mellon" in *Wall Street Journal Eastern Edition* (November 19 , 2011, pp. B2)
Pub: Dow Jones & Company Inc.

Ed: Aaron Lucchetti. **Description:** Since the collapse of securities brokerage MF Global Holdings Ltd., one question has remained: where did the hundreds of millions of dollars in customers' accounts go? It has been revealed that MF Global moved those millions from its own brokerage unit to Bank of New York Mellon Corporation in August of this year, just two months before filing for bankruptcy protection.

8477 ■ "MFS Survey: Generation X/Y Perplexed and Conservative about Future Investing" in *Wireless News* (November 16, 2010)
Pub: Close-Up Media Inc.

Description: Generation X and Y tend to have a conservative approach to investing according to a survey conducted by MFS Investment Management. Statistical data included.

8478 ■ "Micro-Cap Companies" in *Canadian Business* (Vol. 81, Summer 2008, No. 9, pp. 157)
Pub: Rogers Media Ltd.

Description: Micro-cap companies have lower than $221 million in terms of market capitalization. Burnaby, British Columbia-based Fancamp Exploration Ltd. topped the roster with 1,116.7 percent in return. A table showing the 2008 rankings of the companies is presented.

8479 ■ "Microsoft's Big Gamble" in *Canadian Business* (Vol. 81, March 3, 2008, No. 3, pp. 13)
Pub: Rogers Media

Ed: Andrew Wahl. **Description:** Microsoft Corp. is taking a big risk in buying Yahoo, as it is expected to pay more than $31 a share to finalize the acquisition. The deal would be seven and a half times bigger than any other that Microsoft has entered before, an execution of such deal is also anticipated to become a challenge for Microsoft. Recommendations on how Microsoft should handle the integration of the two businesses are given.

8480 ■ "Mine Woes Could Rouse Zinc" in *Barron's* (Vol. 88, July 7, 2008, No. 27, pp. M12)
Pub: Dow Jones & Co., Inc.

Ed: Andrea Hotter. **Description:** Prices of zinc could increase due to supply problems in producing countries such as Australia and China. London Metal Exchange prices for the metal have dropped about 36 percent in 2008.

8481 ■ "Mining Executive Telfer Pocketed Millions" in *Globe & Mail* (April 5, 2007, pp. B4)
Pub: CTVglobemedia Publishing Inc.

Ed: Andy Hoffman. **Description:** The issue of huge compensation for former executive of both Goldcorp Inc. and UrAsia Energy Ltd., Ian Telfer, for his efficient management of stock options is discussed.

8482 ■ "Mining Goldman for Insight" in *Barron's* (Vol. 89, July 20, 2009, No. 29, pp. M8)
Pub: Dow Jones & Co., Inc.

Ed: Steven M. Sears. **Description:** Methods of investing in options for companies with earnings estimates from Goldman Sachs are discussed. These methods take advantage of increased volatility generated by earnings revisions.

8483 ■ "Misguided" in *Canadian Business* (Vol. 81, July 22, 2008, No. 12-13, pp. 30)
Pub: Rogers Media Ltd.

Ed: Al Rosen. **Description:** Canada's securities regulations are discussed; differing views on using principles-based and rules-based securities regulations are also presented.

8484 ■ "Misplaced Trust" in *Canadian Business* (Vol. 79, October 23, 2006, No. 21, pp. 65)
Pub: Rogers Media

Ed: John Gray. **Description:** The reasons for the drop in the share prices of the income trusts of Retrocom Investment Management Inc. are analyzed.

8485 ■ "Missing MF Global Funds Could Top $1.2 Billion" in *Wall Street Journal Eastern Edition* (November 22 , 2011, pp. A1)
Pub: Dow Jones & Company Inc.

Ed: Aaron Lucchetti, Dan Strumpf. **Description:** As the investigation into the collapse of securities brokerage MF Global Holdings Ltd. continues, the question of what happened to customers' funds has to be answered. Now, it is believed that the actual amount of missing funds is much more than the $600 million originally thought, and could be well over $1.2 billion.

8486 ■ "A Mixed-Bag Quarter" in *Barron's* **(Vol. 88, July 7, 2008, No. 27, pp. 19)**
Pub: Dow Jones & Co., Inc.

Ed: Shirley A. Lazo. **Description:** Seven component companies of the Dow Jones Industrial Average increased their dividend payouts in the second quarter of 2008 despite the weak performance of the index. Five companies in the Dow Jones Transportation index and three in the Dow Jones Utilities also increased their dividends.

8487 ■ "Modern-Day Midas Hasn't Lost Touch" in *Globe & Mail* **(January 19, 2006, pp. B4)**
Pub: CTVglobemedia Publishing Inc.

Ed: Shirley Won. **Description:** The investment plans of chief executive officer Rob McEwen of U.S. Gold Corp. are presented.

8488 ■ "Molson Coors Ends Ill-Fated Foray Into Brazil" in *Globe & Mail* **(January 17, 2006, pp. B1)**
Pub: CTVglobemedia Publishing Inc.

Ed: Andy Hoffman. **Description:** The details of loss incurred by Molson Coors Brewing Co., from the sale of Cervejarias Kaiser SA to Fomento Economico Mexicano S.A. de C.V., are presented.

8489 ■ "Moms Mull Money" in *Marketing to Women* **(Vol. 21, February 2008, No. 2, pp. 6)**
Pub: EPM Communications, Inc.

Description: According to a survey by Countrywide Bank, women, especially mothers, are more concerned about their financial fitness than men.

8490 ■ "MoneyGram In Pact With Payday Lender" in *American Banker* **(Vol. 173, March 7, 2008, No. 46, pp. 6)**
Pub: SourceMedia Inc.

Ed: William Launder. **Description:** Details of pact between MoneyGram International Inc. and Advance America Cash Advance Centers are examined.

8491 ■ "Montreal Exchange Buoyed by U.S. Takeover Moves" in *Globe & Mail* **(March 16, 2007, pp. B1)**
Pub: CTVglobemedia Publishing Inc.

Ed: Sinclair Stewart. **Description:** The rise in the share prices of Montreal Exchange due to the derivatives exchange's bid to acquire the Chicago Board of Trade is discussed. The trends pertaining to the consolidation of global stock markets are described.

8492 ■ "Moody and Paranoid" in *Barron's* **(Vol. 88, March 10, 2008, No. 10, pp. M14)**
Pub: Dow Jones & Company, Inc.

Ed: Steven M. Sears. **Description:** Discusses the options market which remains liquid but is cautious of possible failures, especially for financial companies. Investors are in absolute fear when trading with options involving the financial sector.

8493 ■ "More Gains in the Pipeline" in *Barron's* **(Vol. 89, August 3, 2009, No. 31, pp. M5)**
Pub: Dow Jones & Co., Inc.

Ed: Fleming Meeks. **Description:** Shares of El Paso Corp. could recover as the company concludes a deal with a private-equity group to fund pipeline construction. The company's shares are trading at $10.06 and could move up to $12 as bad news has already been priced into the stock.

8494 ■ "More Jobs Moving Out of City" in *Business Courier* **(Vol. 24, March 14, 2008, No. 49, pp. 1)**
Pub: American City Business Journals, Inc.

Ed: Steve Watkins; Laura Baverman. **Description:** UBS Financial Services Inc. is moving Gradison to Kenwood Town Place in Sycamore Township a year after UBS acquired Gradison. The township does not have a tax on earnings so the move will save Gradison's employees the 2.1 percent Cincinnati tax.

8495 ■ "Mortgage Securities Drop Hits Home" in *The Business Journal-Serving Metropolitan Kansas City* **(Vol. 27, October 17, 2008, No. 5)**
Pub: American City Business Journals, Inc.

Ed: Rob Roberts. **Description:** Sale of commercial mortgage-backed securities (CMBS) in Kansas City, Missouri have declined. The area may avoid layoffs if the United States government succeeds in stabilizing the economy. Major CMBS players in the area include Midland Loan Services Inc. and KeyBank Real Estate Capital.

8496 ■ "Mortgages Going Under" in *Black Enterprise* **(Vol. 41, December 2010, No. 5, pp. 20)**
Pub: Earl G. Graves Publishing Co. Inc.

Description: Nearly one-fifth of the country's homeowners are underwater in their mortgages, which means they owe more on their home than the home's worth. Statistical data included.

8497 ■ "Move Over - Or Out" in *Puget Sound Business Journal* **(Vol. 29, November 28, 2008, No. 32, pp. 1)**
Pub: American City Business Journals

Ed: Kirsten Grind. **Description:** Real estate agents in the state of Washington are either moving to smaller real estate firms or quitting the industry due to the weak housing market. Lesser-known firms are experiencing an influx of experienced real estate agents, while 2,800 agents in the state have left the industry.

8498 ■ "Mover and Sheika" in *Conde Nast Portfolio* **(Vol. 2, June 2008, No. 6, pp. 104)**
Pub: Conde Nast Publications, Inc.

Ed: John Arlidge. **Description:** Profile of Princess Sheika Lubna who is the first female foreign trade minister in the Middle East, the United Arab Emirates biggest business envoy, paving the way for billions in new investment, and also a manufacturer of her own perfume line.

8499 ■ "'Mr. CEO, Please Do Elaborate On Your Firm's Metrics'" in *Business Courier* **(Vol. 24, February 29, 2008, No. 47, pp. 1)**
Pub: American City Business Journals, Inc.

Ed: Jon Newberry. **Description:** Discusses a rogue caller who goes by the name of Joe Herrick, Steven Nissan and Joe Harris has joined in over a dozen conference calls, asking chief executive officers on their plans and commenting on the companies' operations. The mystery caller attempts to pass himself off as a financial analyst. Transcripts of some conference calls, in which the rogue caller is involved, are provided.

8500 ■ "Mr. Deeds" in *Canadian Business* **(Vol. 81, March 31, 2008, No. 5, pp. 24)**
Pub: Rogers Media

Ed: Thomas Watson. **Description:** Ron Sandler has the right experience to save Northern Rock PLC get through its liquidity problems. Sandler is known for saving Lloyd's of London in the mid-90's and he is not afraid to make enemies. Ron Sandler's assignment to help Northern Rock comes at a time when the health of the U.K. housing is not great.

8501 ■ "MTI Faces Touch Choices" in *The Business Review Albany* **(Vol. 35, April 4, 2008, No. 53, pp. 1)**
Pub: The Business Review

Ed: Richard A. D'Errico. **Description:** Mechanical Technology Inc.'s auditor, PricewaterhouseCoopers LLP is concerned about the company's limited current cash and its $105 million accumulated deficit. MTI has already sold 1.45 million of its PlugPower Inc. shares, but still considers to sell more of the Plug stock. The problems at MTI and the difficult decisions it has to face to solve them are examined.

8502 ■ "Muddy Portfolio Raises a Question: Just What Is National City Worth?" in *Crain's Detroit Business* **(Vol. 24, April 7, 2008, No. 14)**
Pub: Crain Communications, Inc.

Ed: Jay Miller. **Description:** National City Bank is looking at strategies to help it deal with its credit and loan problems which are reflected in its falling stock price. One possible solution is a merger with another bank, however most national banks are facing their own home-loan portfolio issues and may be unable to tackle another company's unresolved problems. Statistical data included.

8503 ■ "Mutual Fund Sales of $23.4 Billion Best Since 2001" in *Globe & Mail* **(January 5, 2006, pp. B3)**
Pub: CTVglobemedia Publishing Inc.

Ed: Omar El Akkad. **Description:** The details on $23.4 billion net sales of mutual fund sector, in Canada, are presented.

8504 ■ "Naked Investing" in *Canadian Business* **(Vol. 80, January 15, 2007, No. 2, pp. 27)**
Pub: Rogers Media

Ed: Al Rosen. **Description:** The need for Canadian investors to learn important facts about income trusts before investing in them is discussed.

8505 ■ "Nancy Hughes Anthony" in *Canadian Business* **(Vol. 81, October 13, 2008, No. 17, pp. 104)**
Pub: Rogers Media Ltd.

Ed: Andy Holloway. **Description:** Profile of Nancy Hughes Anthony, who believes her experience operating large enterprises as a public servant helped her earn positions that ultimately brought her to her current position as chief executive and president of the Canadian Bankers Association. She also thinks there should be more public-private sector coordination within industries.

8506 ■ "Nanoready?" in *Entrepreneur* **(Vol. 36, May 2008, No. 5, pp. 20)**
Pub: Entrepreneur Media, Inc.

Ed: Andrea Cooper. **Description:** Experts predict that the medicine and energy sectors are among those that will see nanotechnology innovations in the coming years, and that nanotechnology will produce significant commercial value in new products. Some entrepreneurs are investing in nanotech and are partnering with universities. Details on nanotech funding concerns are discussed.

8507 ■ "Nationwide Bank Ready for December Conversion" in *Business First-Columbus* **(October 12, 2007, pp. A1)**
Pub: American City Business Journals, Inc.

Ed: Adrian Burns. **Description:** Nationwide Bank will increase marketing to its customers, including the 45,000 that came from the acquisition of Nationwide Federal Credit Union in December 2006. Upgrading its online banking system and Website will bring the company and its services closer to clients. The influence of the insurance industry on the bank's marketing strategy is also examined.

8508 ■ "Need Grub? Start Texting at Kroger" in *Business Courier* **(Vol. 24, December 21, 2008, No. 36, pp. 1)**
Pub: American City Business Journals, Inc.

Ed: Laura Baverman. **Description:** Discusses the University of Cincinnati which is teaming up to release a technology platform called Macopay that would link a cell phone to a bank account and allow a person to make payments at participating retailers by sending a text message. Details with regard to the new service and its growth potential are discussed.

8509 ■ "Needed: A Strategy; Banking In China" in *The Economist* **(Vol. 390, January 3, 2009, No. 8612, pp. 54)**
Pub: The Economist Newspaper Inc.

Description: International banks are competing for a role in China but are finding obstacles in their paths such as a reduction in the credit their operations may receive from Chinese banks and the role they can play in the public capital markets which remain limited.

8510 ■ *Nerds on Wall Street: Math, Machines and Wired Markets*
Pub: John Wiley & Sons, Inc.

Ed: David J. Leinweber. **Released:** May 27, 2009. **Price:** $39.95. **Description:** The history of technology and how it will transform investing and trading on Wall Street is outlined.

8511 ■ "Netflix Gets No Respect" in *Barron's* **(Vol. 89, July 27, 2009, No. 30, pp. 26)**
Pub: Dow Jones & Co., Inc.
Ed: Tiernan Ray. **Description:** Netflix met expectations when they announced their second quarter sales but their shares still fell by almost 10 percent. Analysts say their entry into the "streaming video" business is a mixed bag since customers are increasingly buying the cheaper monthly plan and this is dragging the economics of the business.

8512 ■ "NetSpend, Payday Firm in Pact" in *American Banker* **(Vol. 173, February 22, 2008, No. 7, pp. 7)**
Pub: SourceMedia Inc.
Ed: Daniel Wolfe. **Description:** NetSpend Corporation of Austin, Texas is providing its prepaid cards to Advance America Cash Advance Centers Inc., a Spartanburg, South Carolina payday lender.

8513 ■ "The New Arsenal of Risk Management" in *Harvard Business Review* **(Vol. 86, September 2008, No. 9, pp. 92)**
Pub: Harvard Business School Press
Ed: Kevin Bueler; Andrew Freeman; Ron Hulme. **Description:** Goldman Sachs Group Inc. is used to illustrate methods for successful risk management. The investment bank's business principles, partnerships, and oversight practices are discussed.

8514 ■ "New Century's Fall Has a New Culprit" in *Barron's* **(Vol. 88, March 31, 2008, No. 13, pp. 20)**
Pub: Dow Jones & Company, Inc.
Ed: Jonathan R. Laing. **Description:** Court examiner Michael Missal reports that New Century Financial's auditor contributed to New Century's demise by its negligence in permitting improper and imprudent practices related to New Century's accounting processes. New Century's bankruptcy filing is considered the start of the subprime-mortgage crisis.

8515 ■ "New Drug Could Revitalize Amgen" in *Barron's* **(Vol. 88, July 7, 2008, No. 27, pp. 23)**
Pub: Dow Jones & Co., Inc.
Ed: Johanna Bennett. **Description:** Shares of the biotechnology company Amgen could receive a boost from the release of the anti-osteoporosis drug denosumab. The shares, priced at $48.84 each, are trading at 11 times expected earnings for 2008 and could also be boosted by cost cutting measures.

8516 ■ "A New Kid on the Block" in *Barron's* **(Vol. 88, March 17, 2008, No. 11, pp. 58)**
Pub: Dow Jones & Company, Inc.
Ed: Thomas G. Donlan. **Description:** Discusses the Federal Reserve which has offered to lend $100 billion in cash to banks and $200 billion in Treasuries to Wall Street investment banks that have problems with liquidity. The reluctance of the banks to lend money to meet a margin call on securities that could still depreciate is the reason why the agency is going into the direct loan business.

8517 ■ "New Law Lets Shareholders Play Hardball With Firms" in *Globe & Mail* **(January 2, 2006, pp. B1)**
Pub: CTVglobemedia Publishing Inc.
Ed: Janet McFarland. **Description:** Business lawyer Wes Voorheis discusses about the launching of Bill 198 by plaintiffs' lawyers on behalf of ordinary retail investors.

8518 ■ "New Money" in *Entrepreneur* **(Vol. 36, February 2008, No. 2, pp. 62)**
Pub: Entrepreneur Media Inc.
Ed: C.J. Prince. **Description:** Tips on how to handle business finance, with regard to the tightened credit standards imposed by leading institutions, are provided. These include: selling receivables, margining blue chips, and selling purchase orders.

8519 ■ "The New Nimble" in *Barron's* **(Vol. 90, August 30, 2010, No. 35, pp. S12)**
Pub: Barron's Editorial & Corporate Headquarters
Ed: Suzanne McGee. **Description:** Financial advisors are making investments based on short-lived market trends due to the uncertainty in the long-term

market. This strategy can be demanding and advisors should only try it if they are confident about their skill in spotting short-term trends.

8520 ■ "The New Risk Tolerance" in *Entrepreneur* **(Vol. 37, September 2009, No. 9, pp. 66)**
Pub: Entrepreneur Media, Inc.
Ed: Rosalind Resnick. **Description:** Offers advice on where to invest personal money in the United States. One could lose money from investing in gold and treasuries. High-quality corporate bonds and Treasury Inflation-Protected Securities are seen as ideal investments.

8521 ■ "New Thinking for a New Financial Order" in *Harvard Business Review* **(Vol. 86, September 2008, No. 9, pp. 26)**
Pub: Harvard Business School Press
Ed: Diana Farell. **Description:** Factors driving the current global economy are analyzed with a focus on the influence of new public and private sectors and the impact of unregulated markets.

8522 ■ "A New Way to Tell When to Fold" in *Barron's* **(Vol. 88, July 7, 2008, No. 27, pp. 27)**
Pub: Dow Jones & Co., Inc.
Ed: Theresa W. Carey. **Description:** Overview of the Online trading company SmartStops, a firm that aims to tell investors when to sell the shares of a particular company. The company's Web site categorizes stocks as moving up, down, or sideways, and calculates exit points for individual stocks based on an overall market trend.

8523 ■ "New Ways to Catch a Thief" in *Barron's* **(Vol. 88, March 10, 2008, No. 10, pp. 37)**
Pub: Dow Jones & Company, Inc.
Ed: Theresa W. Carey. **Description:** Online brokerage firms employ different methods to protect the accounts of their customers from theft. These methods include secure Internet connections, momentary passwords, and proprietary algorithms.

8524 ■ "New Year, New Estate Plan" in *Hawaii Business* **(Vol. 53, February 2008, No. 8, pp. 54)**
Pub: Hawaii Business Publishing
Ed: Antony M. Orme. **Description:** Discusses the start of the new year which can be a time to revise wills and estate plans as failure to do so may create problems of unequal inheritance and increase in estate tax exemption, which could disinherit beneficiaries. Other circumstances that can prompt changes in wills and estate plans are presented.

8525 ■ "The Next Government Bailout?" in *Barron's* **(Vol. 88, March 10, 2008, No. 10, pp. 21)**
Pub: Dow Jones & Company, Inc.
Ed: Jonathan Laing. **Description:** Fannie Mae may need a government bailout as it faces huge hits brought about by the effects of the housing crisis. The shares of the government-sponsored enterprise have dropped 65 percent since the housing crisis began.

8526 ■ "Nightmare on Wall Street" in *Canadian Business* **(Vol. 81, October 13, 2008, No. 17, pp. 9)**
Pub: Rogers Media Ltd.
Ed: Rachel Pulfer. **Description:** Information on events that happened on Wall Street on the week that started September 15, 2008, as well on its effect on financial markets around the world, are presented. Lehman Brothers filed for bankruptcy on September 15, 2008 after negotiations with Barclays Group and Bank of America failed. Details on AIG and Morgan Stanley are also presented.

8527 ■ "No Fast Cash Class" in *Black Enterprise* **(Vol. 37, December 2006, No. 5, pp. 72)**
Pub: Earl G. Graves Publishing Co. Inc.
Ed: Earl G. Graves. **Description:** There are no shortcuts to a obtaining a career as a financial planner. Certified Financial Planner Board of Standards has specific requirements for certification which include having a bach-

elor's degree from an accredited U.S. school before candidates are even eligible for taking the certification exam. Other criteria and requirements are discussed.

8528 ■ "No Surprises" in *Canadian Business* **(Vol. 79, September 25, 2006, No. 19, pp. 49)**
Pub: Rogers Media
Ed: Jeff Sanford. **Description:** The increasing income trust sector in Canada is discussed.

8529 ■ "Nortel Plays Big to Settle Lawsuits" in *Globe & Mail* **(February 9, 2006, pp. B1)**
Pub: CTVglobemedia Publishing Inc.
Ed: Catherine McLean. **Description:** The details on Nortel Networks Corp.'s settlement of cases with shareholders are presented.

8530 ■ "Not In My Backyard" in *Entrepreneur* **(Vol. 36, May 2008, No. 5, pp. 42)**
Pub: Entrepreneur Media, Inc.
Ed: Farnoosh Torabi. **Description:** More investors are turning to overseas real estate investments as the U.S. market sees a slowdown. Analysts say that risk-averse investors opt for funds with record of strong returns and U.S. real estate investment trusts that partner with foreign businesses for transparency purposes. Other details about foreign real estate investments are discussed.

8531 ■ "A Novel Fix for the Credit Mess" in *Barron's* **(Vol. 88, March 31, 2008, No. 13, pp. 10)**
Pub: Dow Jones & Company, Inc.
Ed: Michael Santoli. **Description:** Due to the common bank-leverage factor of 10, the $250 billion of lost bank capital would have supported $2.5 trillion in lending capacity. Jeffrey Lewis suggests onerous regulations on bank-holding companies that own 10 to 25 percent, as they are partly to blame. Statistical data included.

8532 ■ "Now in Play, Score Keeps Head Up and Stick on Ice" in *Globe & Mail* **(January 20, 2007, pp. B5)**
Pub: CTVglobemedia Publishing Inc.
Ed: Grant Robertson. **Description:** The hike in the shares of Score Media Inc. due to its new services is presented.

8533 ■ "Now That's Rich" in *Canadian Business* **(Vol. 80, February 12, 2007, No. 4, pp. 92)**
Pub: Rogers Media
Ed: Thomas Watson. **Description:** The effort of chief executive officer of Stelco Inc. Rodney Mott in resolving the issue of financial loss of the company by taking up backdating options for share price is discussed.

8534 ■ "Now You See It..." in *Canadian Business* **(Vol. 81, November 10, 2008, No. 19, pp. 20)**
Pub: Rogers Media Ltd.
Ed: Sharda Prashad. **Description:** Total return swaps were offered by Deutsche Bank AG and UBS AG to foreign investors for them to avoid paying taxes on the proceeds of their shares of Fording Canadian Coal Trust when Teck Cominco offered to buy the company. This means that the Canadian government is losing tax revenue from foreigners and it is argued that a simpler tax system would avoid this practice.

8535 ■ "Number of Mechanic's Liens Triple Since 2005" in *The Business Journal - Serving Phoenix and the Valley of the Sun* **(Vol. 28, August 22, 2008, No. 51, pp. 1)**
Pub: American City Business Journals, Inc.
Ed: Jan Buchholtz. **Description:** Experts are blaming the mortgage and banking industries for the tripling of mechanic's liens that were filed in Arizona from 2005 through August 6, 2008. The rise in mechanic's liens is believed to indicate stress in the real estate community. Other views and information on the rise of mechanic's liens filed in Arizona are presented.

8536 ■ "The Numbers Speak For Themselves" in *Barron's* **(Vol. 88, July 14, 2008, No. 28, pp. 16)**
Pub: Dow Jones & Co., Inc.
Ed: Bill Alpert. **Description:** Discusses quant fund managers versus traditional long-short equity funds after quants outperformed traditional funds in the year 2000. Causes for the underperformance are outlined and statistical data is included.

8537 ■ "Nvidia Shares Clobbered After Gloomy Warning" in *Barron's* **(Vol. 88, July 7, 2008, No. 27, pp. 25)**
Pub: Dow Jones & Co., Inc.
Ed: Eric J. Savitz. **Description:** Shares of graphics chip manufacturer Nvidia suffered a 30 percent drop in its share price after the company warned that revenue and gross margin forecasts for the quarter ending July 27, 2008 will be below expectations. Stan Glasgow, chief operating officer of Sony Electronics, believes the US economic slowdown will not affect demand for the company's products. Statistical data included.

8538 ■ "Nvidia's Picture Brighter Than Stock Price Indicates" in *Barron's* **(Vol. 88, March 24, 2008, No. 12, pp. 46)**
Pub: Dow Jones & Company, Inc.
Ed: Eric J. Savitz. **Description:** Shares of graphics chip maker Nvidia, priced at $18.52 each, do not indicate the company's strong position in the graphics chip market. The company's shares have dropped due to fears of slower demand for PCs, but the company is not as exposed to broader economic forces.

8539 ■ "N.Y. Investors Reject AnorMed Board Proposal" in *Globe & Mail* **(February 21, 2006, pp. B11)**
Pub: CTVglobemedia Publishing Inc.
Ed: Leonard Zehr. **Description:** The reasons behind the denial of investors over the restructuring plans of AnorMed are presented.

8540 ■ "Nymex Dissidents Rattle Sabers" in *Crain's Chicago Business* **(Vol. 31, April 21, 2008, No. 16, pp. 2)**
Pub: Crain Communications, Inc.
Ed: Ann Saphir. **Description:** Two groups of New York Mercantile Exchange members say they have more than enough votes to stop CME Group Inc.'s $10 billion deal to acquire the oil and metals exchange and they are threatening a proxy fight if the Chicago exchange doesn't raise its offer.

8541 ■ "OccuLogix Shares Plummet 65 Percent" in *Globe & Mail* **(February 4, 2006, pp. B5)**
Pub: CTVglobemedia Publishing Inc.
Ed: Leonard Zehr. **Description:** The shares of OccuLogix drop by 65%in Canada. The decline in share price is attributed to failure of blood filtering system.

8542 ■ "October 2009: Recovery Plods Along" in *Hispanic Business* **(October 2009, pp. 10-11)**
Pub: Hispanic Business
Ed: Dr. Juan Solana. **Description:** Economist reports on a possible economic recovery which will not be allowed to rely on a strong domestic demand in order to sustain it. Consumers, looking to counterbalance years of leverage financing based on unrealistic, ever-increasing home and portfolio valuations, are saving rather than spending money.

8543 ■ "Office Market May Turn Down" in *Crain's New York Business* **(Vol. 24, January 14, 2008, No. 2, pp. 26)**
Pub: Crain Communications, Inc.
Description: Although still dominated by Wall Street, the downturn in the economy is raising fears that the continuing fallout from the subprime mortgage crisis could result in layoffs that will derail the office market.

8544 ■ "Ohio Commerce Draws Closer to Profitability" in *Crain's Cleveland Business* **(Vol. 28, October 29, 2007, No. 43, pp. 14)**
Pub: Crain Communications, Inc.
Ed: Shawn A. Turner. **Description:** Overview of the business plan of Ohio Commerce Bank, a de novo, or startup bank that is close to turning the corner to

profitability. The bank opened in November 2006 and focuses on dealing with small businesses totaling $5 million or less in annual revenues.

8545 ■ "Oil Patch Expects Richer Shell Offer" in *Globe & Mail* **(January 3, 2006, pp. B1)**
Pub: CTVglobemedia Publishing Inc.
Ed: Andrew Willis; Patrick Brethour. **Description:** The concerns investors over the feasibility of Royal Dutch Shell PLC's acquisition of Shell Canada Ltd., for $7.6 billion, are presented. Shell Canada Ltd. reports rise in shares by ten percent.

8546 ■ "Oil Picks and Pans" in *Canadian Business* **(Vol. 79, August 14, 2006, No. 16-17, pp. 67)**
Pub: Rogers Media
Ed: Graham Scott. **Description:** A survey on investments in Canadian energy companies and the inflation caused by oil price hike, are discussed.

8547 ■ "Oil's Going Down, Down, Down" in *Canadian Business* **(Vol. 79, October 9, 2006, No. 20, pp. 148)**
Pub: Rogers Media
Ed: Ian McGugan. **Description:** Strategies for investors to benefit from the fall in global crude oil prices are discussed.

8548 ■ "Ok, So Now What?" in *Canadian Business* **(Vol. 79, November 6, 2006, No. 22, pp. 113)**
Pub: Rogers Media
Ed: Calvin Leung. **Description:** Details of healthy income-generating corporations, such as Cedar Fair L.P., are presented.

8549 ■ "The Old Railway is on a Roll" in *Globe & Mail* **(January 26, 2006, pp. B1)**
Pub: CTVglobemedia Publishing Inc.
Description: The reasons behind 5 percent rise in shares for Canadian National Railway Co. are presented.

8550 ■ "On the Trail of the Bear" in *Canadian Business* **(Vol. 81, March 17, 2008, No. 4, pp. 28)**
Pub: Rogers Media
Ed: Thomas Watson. **Description:** Discusses the conservative rule of thumb which is to invest in equity markets when a five to ten percent market rally is sustained for more than a few months. Bear markets on the S&P 500 bear markets in the 20th century only lasts over a year based on average. It is also good to remember that bear markets are followed by bulls that exceed the previous market highs.

8551 ■ "One-Time Area Trust Executive Finds Trouble in N.H." in *The Business Journal-Serving Metropolitan Kansas City* **(September 12, 2008)**
Pub: American City Business Journals, Inc.
Ed: Steve Vockrodt. **Description:** About 200 investors, some from Missouri's Kansas City area, claim that they had conducted business with Noble Trust Co.. The trust company was placed under New Hampshire Banking Department's conservatorship after $15 million was discovered to be missing from its account. It is alleged that the money was lost in a Colorado Ponzi scheme.

8552 ■ "Opportunity Now Lies at Short End of the Market" in *Barron's* **(Vol. 88, June 30, 2008, No. 26, pp. M9)**
Pub: Dow Jones & Co., Inc.
Ed: Michael S. Derby. **Description:** Renewed credit concerns and the lesser chance of a Federal Reserve interest rate hike boosted the bond market. Some portfolio managers are more bullish on short-dated securities as they expect the market to adjust to a more appropriate outlook.

8553 ■ "An Opportunity for Patience" in *Barron's* **(Vol. 88, June 30, 2008, No. 26, pp. M5)**
Pub: Dow Jones & Co., Inc.
Ed: Fleming Meeks. **Description:** Shares of Louisiana-Pacific are near their 52-week low at $8.95 per share making them look like a better buy than

they were at $11.51 in May, 2008. The company is a player in a cyclical business and its balance sheet is sound compared to its peers with net debt at just $84 million or 20 percent of total capital.

8554 ■ "Optimize.ca Supplies Free Online Financial Advice" in *Entertainment Close-Up* **(October 9, 2010)**
Pub: Close-Up Media Inc.
Description: Optimize.ca provides free online financial advice, focusing on instant savings for their mutual funds and other banking products while improving rates of return and overall financial health.

8555 ■ "Oracle: No Profit of Doom" in *Barron's* **(Vol. 88, March 31, 2008, No. 13, pp. 40)**
Pub: Dow Jones & Company, Inc.
Ed: Mark Veverka. **Description:** Oracle's revenues grew by 21 percent but fell short of expectation and their profits came in at the low-end of expectations. The company's shares dropped 8 percent but investors are advised to pay more attention to the company's earnings expansion rather than revenue growth in a slow economy. Nokia's Rick Simonson points out that their markets in Asia and particularly India is growing so they are not as affected by the U.S. economic conditions.

8556 ■ "The Oracle's Endgame; Wrigley Investment Isn't What Many Call a Classic Buffett Play" in *Crain's Chicago Business* **(May 5, 2008)**
Pub: Crain Communications, Inc.
Ed: Ann Saphir. **Description:** Discusses Warren Buffett's deal with Mars Inc. to buy Wm. Wrigley Jr. Co., a move which would make Mr. Buffett a minority shareholder in a privately held company, a departure from his typical investment strategy. Mr. Buffett's Berkshire Hathaway Inc. agreed to provide $4.4 billion to help finance the $23 billion deal to pay another $2.1 billion for an equity stake in the company once it became a subsidiary of Mars.

8557 ■ "Out of Fashion" in *Barron's* **(Vol. 88, March 17, 2008, No. 11, pp. 48)**
Pub: Dow Jones & Company, Inc.
Ed: Robin Goldwyn Blumenthal. **Description:** Shares of Perry Ellis International and G-III Apparel Group have taken some beating in the market despite good growth earnings prospects. Perry Ellis sees earnings growth of 8 to 11 percent for fiscal 2009, while G-III Apparel expects earnings growth of 25 percent.

8558 ■ "Over A Barrel" in *Canadian Business* **(Vol. 81, July 21, 2008, No. 11, pp. 13)**
Pub: Rogers Media Ltd.
Ed: Thomas Watson. **Description:** Analysts predict that the skyrocketing price of fuel will cause a crackdown in the market as purported in the peak oil theory. It is forecasted that the price of oil will reach $200 per barrel. Details of the effect of the increasing oil prices on the market are presented.

8559 ■ "Over a Barrel" in *Canadian Business* **(Vol. 80, February 12, 2007, No. 4, pp. 52)**
Pub: Rogers Media
Ed: Andrew Nikoforuk. **Description:** The potential of tar sands of Alberta in becoming the largest source of oil in the world and huge investments of Canadian companies to mine for the oil there are discussed.

8560 ■ "Packaging Firm Wraps Up Remake; Overseas Plants Help Firm Fatten Margins" in *Crain's New York Business* **(January 7, 2008)**
Pub: Crain Communications, Inc.
Description: Sealed Air Corp., a packaging manufacturer, has seen its share price fall nearly 20 percent over the past two years, making it one of the worst performers in the packaging sector.

8561 ■ "Pain Ahead as Profit Pressure Increases" in *Crain's Chicago Business* **(Vol. 31, May 5, 2008, No. 18, pp. 4)**
Pub: Crain Communications, Inc.
Ed: Daniel Rome Levine. **Description:** Interview with David Klaskin, the chairman and chief investment officer at Oak Ridge Investments LLC, who discusses the outlook for the economy and corporate earnings, particularly in the housing and auto industries, the

impact of economic stimulus checks, the weakness of the dollar and recommendations of stocks that individual investors may find helpful.

8562 ■ *Paper Fortunes: Modern Wall Street: Where It's Been and Where It's Going*
Pub: St. Martin's Press LLC
Ed: Roy C. Smith. **Released:** 2010. **Price:** $35.00. **Description:** Comprehensive history of Wall Street and lessons learned with insight into ways Wall Street will reinvent itself in this new economy.

8563 ■ "Patchy Oil Profits" in *Canadian Business* (Vol. 80, February 12, 2007, No. 4, pp. 89)
Pub: Rogers Media
Ed: Michelle Magnan. **Description:** The fall in fourth-quarter earnings of several oil and gas companies in Canada, in view of rise in their expenditure, is discussed.

8564 ■ "Paterson Plots Comeback With Internet IPO" in *Globe & Mail* (February 20, 2006, pp. B1)
Pub: CTVglobemedia Publishing Inc.
Ed: Grant Robertson. **Description:** The initial public offering plans of chief executive officer Scott Paterson of JumpTV.com are presented.

8565 ■ "Peak Performer" in *Canadian Business* (Vol. 81, October 13, 2008, No. 17, pp. 30)
Pub: Rogers Media Ltd.
Ed: Andrea Jezovit. **Description:** Jerry Del Missier's promotion as president of Barclays Capital (BarCap) has made him the likely successor to BarCap chief executive Bob Diamond. Diamond believes the technology Jerry Del Missier built on BarCap is producing record performance for the company. Public opinion on Jerry Del Missier, as well as his views, is discussed.

8566 ■ "Penny Chief Shops For Shares" in *Barron's* (Vol. 88, July 7, 2008, No. 27, pp. 29)
Pub: Dow Jones & Co., Inc.
Ed: Teresa Rivas. **Description:** Myron Ullman III, chairman and chief executive officer of J.C. Penney, purchased $1 million worth of shares of the company. He now owns 393,140 shares of the company and an additional 1,282 on his 401(k) plan.

8567 ■ "Peter Bynoe Trades Up" in *Black Enterprise* (Vol. 38, July 2008, No. 12, pp. 30)
Pub: Earl G. Graves Publishing Co. Inc.
Ed: Alexis McCombs. **Description:** Chicago-based Loop Capital Markets L.L.C. has named Peter Bynoe managing director of corporate finance. Bynoe was previously a senior partner at the law firm DLA Piper U.S. L.L.P., where he worked on stadium deals.

8568 ■ "Pioneer Bank Ready to Expand" in *Austin Business JournalInc.* (Vol. 28, December 19, 2008, No. 40, pp. 1)
Pub: American City Business Journals
Ed: Christopher Calnan. **Description:** Pioneer Bank, an 18-month old community bank based in Dripping Springs, Texas is planning to raise $6 million to open branches in the Austin area, including Hays County locations such as San Marcos, Buda, and Kyle. Pioneer's deposits have growing from $2.2 million to $54 million in 18 months.

8569 ■ "Place Restrictions on Your Stock Shares" in *Business Owner* (Vol. 35, July-August 2011, No. 4, pp. 14)
Pub: DL Perkins Company
Description: It is critical for any small business owner to be certain that the buyer or recipient of any part of the company represents that the stock is being acquired or given for investment purposes only.

8570 ■ "A Place in the Sun" in *Canadian Business* (Vol. 81, July 22, 2008, No. 12-13, pp. 56)
Pub: Rogers Media Ltd.
Description: Experts believe that it is the best time for Canadians to own a retirement home in the U.S., where real estate prices are up to 50 percent below their peak. Other views concerning the economic

conditions occurring in the United States, as well as on the implications for Canadians planning to invest in the country are presented.

8571 ■ "Planning Ahead: Steven Taylor Mulls a Second Career After Retirement" in *Black Enterprise* (Vol. 37, November 2006, No. 4, pp. 82)
Pub: Earl G. Graves Publishing Co. Inc.
Ed: Sheryl Nance Nash. **Description:** Many workers are unprepared for retirement. Profile of Steven Taylor, a soon to retire dietary correctional officer who looked to Walt Clark, president of Clark Capital Financial in Maryland, to assess his retirement goals. Detailed advice and statistical data included.

8572 ■ "Playing Citigroup's Woes" in *Barron's* (Vol. 88, March 31, 2008, No. 13, pp. M7)
Pub: Dow Jones & Company, Inc.
Ed: Steven M. Sears. **Description:** Citigroup's first-quarter earnings estimate was slashed to a $1.15-per-share-loss from 28 cents. A strategist recommends buying the company's shares at Sept. 20, 2008 put and selling a Sept. 17.50 put with a maximum profit of $166 if the shares is at or below $17.50 at expiration.

8573 ■ "Playing Defense" in *Crain's Chicago Business* (Vol. 31, November 10, 2008, No. 45, pp. 4)
Pub: Crain Communications, Inc.
Ed: Monee Fields-White. **Description:** Chicago's money managers are increasingly investing in local companies such as Caterpillar Inc., a maker of construction and mining equipment, Kraft Foods Inc. and Baxter International Inc., a manufacturer of medical products, in an attempt to bolster their portfolios. These companies have a history of surviving tough economic times.

8574 ■ "PNC Begins Search for New Local HQ" in *Baltimore Business Journal* (Vol. 28, June 4, 2010, No. 4, pp. 1)
Pub: Baltimore Business Journal
Ed: Daniel J. Sernovitz. **Description:** PNC Financial Services Group Inc. is searching for a new headquarters building in Greater Baltimore, Maryland. The company is seeking about 150,000 square feet for its regional operations. However, PNC could also end up moving out of Baltimore for space in the surrounding suburbs.

8575 ■ "Polite Conversation" in *Mergers & Acquisitions: The Dealmaker's Journal* (March 1, 2008)
Pub: SourceMedia, Inc.
Description: In January, industry leaders and deal-makers met at Davos to discuss topics ranging from the possibility of a recession to what lies ahead in the deal market.

8576 ■ "The Power of Alumni Networks" in *Harvard Business Review* (Vol. 88, October 2010, No. 10, pp. 34)
Pub: Harvard Business School Publishing
Ed: Lauren H. Cohen, Christopher J. Malloy. **Description:** Research indicates that members of alumni associations tend to invest in similar ways; implications for the mutual funds sector are discussed.

8577 ■ "Private Equity Firms Focus on Failing Banks" in *Baltimore Business Journal* (Vol. 28, July 16, 2010, No. 10, pp. 1)
Pub: Baltimore Business Journal
Ed: Gary Haber. **Description:** Four deals in which assets of failed banks were acquired by private equity firms have been approved by the Federal Deposit Insurance Corporation in the past couple of years. Bay Bank FSK, for example, purchased Bay National Bank's assets in July 2010. Forecasts on more private equity acquisitions in the community banking industry are given.

8578 ■ "Private Equity Firms Shopping Valley For Deals" in *The Business Journal - Serving Phoenix and the Valley of the Sun* (Vol. 29, September 19, 2008, No. 3, pp. 1)
Pub: American City Business Journals, Inc.
Ed: Mike Sunnucks. **Description:** Private equity firms from California, Boston, New York, and overseas are expected to invest in growth-oriented real estate

markets that include Phoenix. Real estate experts revealed that privately held investment and acquisition firms are looking to invest in real estate markets hit by the housing crisis. Views and information on private equity firms' real estate investments are presented.

8579 ■ "Private TV Industry's Profit Climbs Four Percent" in *Globe & Mail* (March 29, 2006, pp. B6)
Pub: CTVglobemedia Publishing Inc.
Ed: Simon Tuck. **Description:** The private television industry in Canada is experiencing 4 percent increase in its profits, i.e. $242.2 millions. The revenues of CTV contributed more to this increase in profits.

8580 ■ "Profico Takes Itself Off the Market" in *Globe & Mail* (March 14, 2006, pp. B1)
Pub: CTVglobemedia Publishing Inc.
Ed: Deborah Yedlin; Dave Ebner. **Description:** Profico Energy Management Ltd., Canada's largest junior energy explorer, has backed off its potential acquisition plans. The decreased prices of the natural gas are the main reasons that caused Profico to back off from the acquisition plan.

8581 ■ "Profit Predictions Look Too Plump" in *Barron's* (Vol. 88, March 31, 2008, No. 13, pp. 37)
Pub: Dow Jones & Company, Inc.
Ed: Johanna Bennett. **Description:** Full-year forecast points to a 14 percent gain for 2008 but the second-half profit increases would have to grow at a fast rate and peak at 61 percent in the fourth quarter to achieve this. Trends in the U.S. economic conditions are also discussed.

8582 ■ "Public Opinion" in *Entrepreneur* (Vol. 36, April 2008, No. 4, pp. 28)
Pub: Entrepreneur Media, Inc.
Ed: Aliza Sherman. **Description:** According to a 2007 report from Group and Organization Management, women in top positions can lead publicly traded companies to stock price and earnings growth. Some women business owners say that going public has provided them with the capital to grow. Details on the potential of women-managed publicly traded companies are discussed.

8583 ■ "Put It on MasterCard" in *Barron's* (Vol. 89, July 27, 2009, No. 30, pp. 16)
Pub: Dow Jones & Co., Inc.
Ed: Bill Alpert. **Description:** Shares of MasterCard trade at a discount at just 15 times its anticipated earnings and some believe that these shares may be a better play in an economic recovery. The prospects of these shares are compared with those of Visa.

8584 ■ "Putting SogoTrade Through Its Paces" in *Barron's* (Vol. 89, July 27, 2009, No. 30, pp. 27)
Pub: Dow Jones & Co., Inc.
Ed: Theresa W. Carey. **Description:** SogoTrade options platform streams options quotes in real time and lets users place a trade in several ways. The site also features notable security tactics and is a reasonable choice for bargain-seekers. OptionsXpress' Xtend platform lets users place trades and get real time quotes.

8585 ■ "Putting the World at Your Fingertips" in *Barron's* (Vol. 88, July 7, 2008, No. 27, pp. L13)
Pub: Dow Jones & Co., Inc.
Ed: Neil A. Martin. **Description:** Currency-traded exchange funds allow investors to diversify their assets and take advantage of investment opportunities such as speculation and hedging. Investors can use these funds to build positions in favor of or against the US dollar.

8586 ■ "Q&A: David Labistour" in *Canadian Business* (Vol. 81, March 17, 2008, No. 4, pp. 10)
Pub: Rogers Media
Ed: Lauren McKeon. **Description:** David Labistour says that the difference between being a co-op retailer and a corporate-owned retailer in the case of Mountain Equipment Co-op (MEC) is that the company is owned by their customers and not by share-

holders. Labistour also says that MEC works with their factories to ensure that these maintain ethical standards in the manufacturing process.

8587 ■ "Qualcomm Could Win Big as the IPhone 3G Calls" in *Barron's* **(Vol. 88, July 4, 2008, No. 28, pp. 30)**
Pub: Dow Jones & Co., Inc.
Ed: Eric J. Savitz. **Description:** Apple iPhone 3G's introduction could widen the smartphone market thereby benefiting handset chipmaker Qualcomm in the process. Qualcomm Senior V.P., Bill Davidson sees huge potential for his company's future beyond phones with their Snapdragon processor. The prospects of Sun Microsystems' shares are also discussed.

8588 ■ "Quality at Bargain Prices" in *Black Enterprise* **(Vol. 41, December 2010, No. 5, pp. 30)**
Pub: Earl G. Graves Publishing Co. Inc.
Ed: James A. Anderson. **Description:** Monica L. Walker, CEO of Holland Capital Management, suggests investors to watch prevailing trends in the financial market and to focus on using bottom-up analysis to identify companies meeting their investment criteria.

8589 ■ *The Quants*
Pub: Crown Business Books
Ed: Scott Patterson. **Released:** January 25, 2011. **Price:** $16.00. **Description:** The story of four rich and powerful men, along with Jim Simons, the founder of the most successful hedge fund in history and how they felt and what they thought in the days and weeks during the crash of Wall Street.

8590 ■ "Quarreling Parties Keep Schenectady Redevelopment Plan In Limbo" in *The Business Review Albany* **(Vol. 35, April 4, 2008, No. 53)**
Pub: The Business Review
Ed: Michael DeMasi. **Description:** First National Bank of Scotia chairman Louis H. Buhrmaster opposes the Erie Boulevard design project. as it could negatively affect access to the bank. Buhrmaster, aslo a vice president for Schenectady Industrial Corp, prohibits environmental assessment at the former American Locomotive property. The issues affecting the progress of the planned redevelopment at Schenectady are analyzed

8591 ■ "Quebecor World Cuts Dividend" in *Globe & Mail* **(January 20, 2006, pp. B1)**
Pub: CTVglobemedia Publishing Inc.
Description: The reasons behind the decrease in dividend by Quebecor World Inc., and its impact on investors, are discussed.

8592 ■ "A Questionable Chemical Romance" in *Barron's* **(Vol. 88, July 14, 2008, No. 28, pp. 28)**
Pub: Dow Jones & Co., Inc.
Ed: Andrew Bary. **Description:** Dow Chemical paid $78-a-share for the surprise takeover of Rohm & Haas. The acquisition is reducing Dow Chemical's financial flexibility at a time when chemical companies are being affected by high costs and a weak U.S. economy.

8593 ■ "Quick Earnings Revival Unlikely" in *Barron's* **(Vol. 88, June 30, 2008, No. 26, pp. 31)**
Pub: Dow Jones & Co., Inc.
Ed: Johanna Bennett. **Description:** Analysts are pushing back their prediction of a U.S. economy turnaround to 2009. A recession in the first half of 2008 may not have happened but unemployment is rising and house prices continue to fall.

8594 ■ *Raising Capital*
Pub: Greenwood Publishing Group, Inc.
Ed: David Nour. **Released:** March 1, 2009. **Price:** $39.95. **Description:** An overview to help entrepreneurs find capital for starting and maintaining a small business is presented. The author shows how to develop long-term relationships with financial partners and ways to attract financing to fund the startup and

growth phases of any business. Entrepreneurs tell how they raised money from friends, family, angel investors, banks and venture capitalists and private equity firms.

8595 ■ "Raptor Opens Consultancy" in *Austin Business Journal* **(Vol. 31, July 8, 2011, No. 18, pp. 1)**
Pub: American City Business Journals Inc.
Ed: Christopher Calnan. **Description:** Boston hedge fund operator Raptor Group launched Raptor Accelerator, a consulting business providing sales and advisory services to early-stage companies in Central Texas. Aside from getting involved with the startups in which the Raptor Group invests, Raptor Accelerator will target firms operating in the sports, media, entertainment, and content technology sectors.

8596 ■ "Ratio-Cination" in *Canadian Business* **(Vol. 79, October 23, 2006, No. 21, pp. 164)**
Pub: Rogers Media
Ed: Ian McGugan. **Description:** Tips for investors, on how to make market observations before selecting companies for purchasing stocks, are presented.

8597 ■ "The RBC Dynasty Continues" in *Globe & Mail* **(January 30, 2006, pp. B1)**
Pub: CTVglobemedia Publishing Inc.
Ed: Gordon Pitts. **Description:** The details on business growth of Royal Bank of Canada, under chief executive officer Gordon Nixon, are presented.

8598 ■ "Ready for the Back Burner" in *Barron's* **(Vol. 88, March 17, 2008, No. 11, pp. 47)**
Pub: Dow Jones & Company, Inc.
Ed: Vito J. Racanelli. **Description:** McDonald's has promised to return $15 billion to $17 billion to shareholders in 2007-2009 but headwinds are rising for the company. December, 2007 same-store sales were flat and the company's traffic growth in the U.S. is slowing. Its shares are likely to trade in tandem with the market until recession fears recede.

8599 ■ "Ready for a Rally?" in *The Economist* **(Vol. 390, January 3, 2009, No. 8612, pp. 54)**
Pub: The Economist Newspaper Inc.
Description: Analysts predict that the recession could end by 2010. The current economic crisis is presented in detail.

8600 ■ "Real Estate Woes Mount for State's Smaller Banks" in *Boston Business Journal* **(Vol. 27, November 30, 2007, No. 44, pp. 1)**
Pub: American City Business Journals Inc.
Ed: Craig M. Douglas. **Description:** Massachusetts banking industry is facing a steep increase on loan defaults such as in home mortgages and condominium projects, contrary to public belief that the local industry is safe from the real estate meltdown. The dollar value of local banks' nonperforming loans doubled in 2007, and is rising statewide. Other banking issues in the state are discussed.

8601 ■ "Recession Fears Power Gold" in *Barron's* **(Vol. 88, March 17, 2008, No. 11, pp. M14)**
Pub: Dow Jones & Company, Inc.
Ed: Melanie Burton. **Description:** Gold prices have been more attractive as the U.S. dollar weakens and the Dow Jones Industrial Average has slipped almost 10 percent in 2008. The rate cuts from the Federal Reserve Board has also spurred inflation fears adding upward pressure to the price of the metal.

8602 ■ "Recession Management" in *Canadian Business* **(Vol. 81, March 3, 2008, No. 3, pp. 62)**
Pub: Rogers Media
Ed: Joe Castaldo. **Description:** Some companies such as Capital One Financial Corp. are managing their finances as if a recession has already taken place to prepare themselves for the looming economic downturn. Intel Corp., meanwhile shows how increasing its investments during a recession could be advantageous. Tips on how companies can survive a recession are provided.

8603 ■ "Reduce the Risk of Failed Financial Judgments" in *Harvard Business Review* **(Vol. 86, July-August 2008, No. 8, pp. 24)**
Pub: Harvard Business School Press
Ed: Robert G. Eccles; Edward J. Fiedl. **Description:** Utilization of business consultants, evaluators, appraisers, and actuaries to decrease financial management risks is discussed.

8604 ■ "REIT's Decry Foreign Limits on Investment" in *Globe & Mail* **(March 29, 2007, pp. B4)**
Pub: CTVglobemedia Publishing Inc.
Ed: Elizabeth Church. **Description:** The planned legislation by Canadian government for regulation foreign investments by real estate investment trusts is discussed.

8605 ■ "Reports of Banks' Revival were Greatly Exaggerated" in *Barron's* **(Vol. 88, July 7, 2008, No. 27, pp. L14)**
Pub: Dow Jones & Co., Inc.
Ed: Jack Willoughby. **Description:** Performance of mutual funds improved for the second quarter of 2008 compared to the previous quarter, registering an average gain of 0.13 percent; funds focusing on natural resources rose the highest, their value rising by an average of 24.50 percent.

8606 ■ "Research Reports" in *Barron's* **(Vol. 89, July 20, 2009, No. 29, pp. M12)**
Pub: Dow Jones & Co., Inc.
Description: Shares of Bank of the Ozarks, Broadpoint Gleacher Securities Group, Halozyme Therapeutics, and Take Two Interactive are rated as Buy. The shares of Fluor and PetMed Express are rated as Outperform, while those of Humana and Janus Capital Group are rated as Hold and Underweight respectively.

8607 ■ "Research Reports: How Analysts Size Up Companies" in *Barron's* **(Vol. 88, March 31, 2008, No. 13, pp. M13)**
Pub: Dow Jones & Company, Inc.
Ed: Anita Peltonen. **Description:** Sirius Satellite's shares are ranked Outperform as it awaits approval from the Federal Communications Commission in its merger with XM. TiVo's shares are ranked Avoid as the company is in a sector that's being commoditized. Verizon Communications' rising dividend yield earns it a Focus List ranking. The shares of Bear Stearns, Churchill Downs, Corning, and Deerfield Triarc Capital are also reviewed. Statistical data included.

8608 ■ "Retail Woes: The Shoe Doesn't Fit for Gerald Loftin's Stock Picks" in *Black Enterprise* **(Vol. 38, July 2008, No. 12, pp. 40)**
Pub: Earl G. Graves Publishing Co. Inc.
Ed: Steve Garmhausen. **Description:** Each of the three stocks that Gerald Loftin picked in May 2007 have lost money; DSW, the designer shoe retailer, fell by 63.7 percent; paint and coatings retailer Sherwin-Williams Co. fell by 7.2 percent; and Verizon Communications Inc. fell by 1.4 percent. Statistical data included.

8609 ■ "Return to Wealth; Bank Strategy" in *The Economist* **(Vol. 390, January 3, 2009, No. 8612, pp. 56)**
Pub: The Economist Newspaper Inc.
Description: UBS' strategy to survive these trying economic times is presented. Statistical data included. UBS has a stronger balance-sheet than most of its investment-banking peers and has reduced its portfolio.

8610 ■ "The Right Time for REITs" in *Barron's* **(Vol. 88, July 14, 2008, No. 28, pp. 32)**
Pub: Dow Jones & Co., Inc.
Ed: Mike Hogan. **Description:** Discusses the downturn in U.S. real estate investment trusts so these are worth considering for investment. Several Websites that are useful for learning about real estate investment trusts for investment purposes are presented.

8611 ■ **"Risk Management Starts at the Top"** in *Business Strategy Review* (Vol. 21, Spring 2010, No. 1, pp. 18)
Pub: Wiley-Blackwell

Ed: Paul Strebel, Hongze Lu. **Description:** Authors question why, at the end of 2008, Citigroup, Merrill Lynch and UBS had well over $40 billion in sub-prime write-downs and credit losses, while some of their competitors were much less exposed. Their research into the situation revealed correlations of great import to today's firms.

8612 ■ **"Risk and Reward"** in *Canadian Business* (Vol. 81, October 13, 2008, No. 17, pp. 21)
Pub: Rogers Media Ltd.

Ed: Calvin Leung. **Description:** Macro-economist and currency analyst Mark Venezia believes that stable financial institutions, free-market reforms, and the role of central banks in keeping inflation and exchange rates stable could make emerging-market bonds strong performers for better future returns. Venezia's other views on emerging-market bonds are discussed.

8613 ■ **"Rock Festival: High Spirited Conventioneers Celebrate Their Good Fortune"** in *Canadian Business* (Vol. 81, March 31, 2008, No. 5)
Pub: Rogers Media

Ed: Jeff Sanford. **Description:** Soaring prices of commodities in the mining industry have been very good for the attendees of the 76th annual conference of the Prospectors & Developers Association of Canada. A speaker at the conference expects commodity prices to come off a bit but not fall dramatically as it did in the 1980's.

8614 ■ **"Rogue's Gallery"** in *Canadian Business* (Vol. 81, November 10, 2008, No. 19, pp. 44)
Pub: Rogers Media Ltd.

Ed: Rachel Pulfer. **Description:** Laissez-faire capitalism or poor oversight of Fannie Mae and Freddie Mac are causes for the financial crisis in the U.S., depending or Democrat or Republican viewpoint. Events leading up to the 2008 financial crisis are covered.

8615 ■ **"Roundtable - The Auto Sector Shifts Gears"** in *Mergers & Acquisitions: The Dealmaker's Journal* (March 1, 2008)
Pub: SourceMedia, Inc.

Description: Industry professionals discuss the current state of the automotive sector as well as what they predict for the future of the industry; also provides information for investors about opportunities in the sector.

8616 ■ **"Rules Will Tighten, Bankers are Told: House Panel Chairman Expects More Regulation"** in *Charlotte Observer* (February 6, 2007)
Pub: Knight-Ridder/Tribune Business News

Ed: Binyamin Appelbaum. **Description:** House Financial Services Committee will impose more federal regulation on banks offering mortgages.

8617 ■ **"Ryder's Shock Absorbers Are In Place"** in *Barron's* (Vol. 88, March 24, 2008, No. 12, pp. 19)
Pub: Dow Jones & Company, Inc.

Ed: Christopher C. Williams. **Description:** Shares of Ryder System Inc. are expected to continue rising on the back of rising earnings, forecast at $5.20 a share for 2009. The shares of the truck freight company hit a 52-week high of $62.27 each and may reach $70 a share.

8618 ■ *Safety Net*
Pub: Crown Business Books

Ed: James Glassman. **Released:** February 22, 2011. **Price:** $23.00. **Description:** Ways to build a financial investment strategy that protects you, while ensuring growth in a strong financial future are presented.

8619 ■ **"St. Elizabeth Fights for Share at St. Lukes"** in *Business Courier* (Vol. 27, November 12, 2010, No. 28, pp. 1)
Pub: Business Courier

Ed: James Ritchie. **Description:** Key information on how St. Elizabeth Healthcare helps partner St. Luke's Hospitals increase market share in the healthcare industry are presented. Some of St. Luke's hospitals, such as the St. Elizabeth Fort Thomas in Kentucky, are struggling with low occupancy rates, prompting St. Elizabeth to invest about $24 million to help St. Luke's increase its market share.

8620 ■ **"Sales Gave W&S Record '07"** in *Business Courier* (Vol. 24, March 14, 2008, No. 49, pp. 1)
Pub: American City Business Journals, Inc.

Ed: Jon Newberry. **Description:** Western & Southern Financial Group was able to achieve a record $365 million in net income thanks in large part to the double-digit increases in profits by its W&S Agency Group field offices and non-insurance businesses. The sale of their Integrated Investment Services Subsidiary and shares in several Marriot hotels also added to the record profit.

8621 ■ **"Samll Fortunes"** in *Business Courier* (Vol. 27, July 23, 2010, No. 12, pp. 1)
Pub: Business Courier

Ed: Steve Watkins. **Description:** Small banks in Cincinnati, Ohio have been faring well despite the economic crisis, a survey has revealed. Sixty percent of local small banks have capital levels above 15.8 percent median. But regulators are seen to close more banks in 2010 than since the financial crises began.

8622 ■ **"Satellite Down, Stock Up: Raytheon Is On Target With Ten Percent Dividend Increase"** in *Barron's* (Vol. 88, March 31, 2008, No. 13)
Pub: Dow Jones & Company, Inc.

Ed: Shirley A. Lazo. **Description:** Raytheon hiked their quarterly dividend to 28 cents per share from 25.5 cents. Aircastle slashed their quarterly common dividend by 64 percent for them to retain additional capital that can be used to increase their liquidity position.

8623 ■ **"Schwab: Lower Returns Ahead"** in *Barron's* (Vol. 89, July 13, 2009, No. 28, pp. L4)
Pub: Dow Jones & Co., Inc.

Ed: Leslie P. Norton. **Description:** Charles Schwab says that 8 percent to 10 percent equity-market returns are not realistic these days and that 4 percent to 5 percent are more realistic in the next four to five years from 2009. Schwab expects inflation to be close to 10 percent per annum in a couple of years.

8624 ■ **"Score One for 'Barron's'"** in *Barron's* (Vol. 89, July 13, 2009, No. 28, pp. 14)
Pub: Dow Jones & Co., Inc.

Ed: Andrew Bary. **Description:** 57 companies that were bullishly covered on 'Barron's' for the first half of 2009 were up an average of 20.4 percent compared to the 10.2 percent gain in the relevant market indexes. The bearish stock picks by 'Barron's' were down 3.4 percent compared to a 6.4 percent for the benchmarks.

8625 ■ **"Scotiabank Targets More Baby Boomers"** in *Globe & Mail* (March 4, 2006, pp. B5)
Pub: CTVglobemedia Publishing Inc.

Ed: Elizabeth Church. **Description:** Bank of Nova Scotia posted $844 million profit for first quarter 2006. The plans of the bank to achieve baby boomer client base are presented.

8626 ■ **"Scottsdale Bank Plans 4Q Opening"** in *The Business Journal - Serving Phoenix and the Valley of the Sun* (Vol. 28, August 15, 2008, No. 50)
Pub: American City Business Journals, Inc.

Ed: Chris Casacchia. **Description:** Arizona's Department of Financial Institutions has approved Scottsdale Business Bank, a community bank which plans

to open in the fourth quarter of 2008. The bank, which is to be located near McCormick Ranch in Scottsdale, Arizona, will cater to small business owners in the professional sector, such as accountants and doctors.

8627 ■ **"Screening for the Best Stock Screens"** in *Barron's* (Vol. 90, September 13, 2010, No. 37, pp. 36)
Pub: Barron's Editorial & Corporate Headquarters

Ed: Mike Hogan. **Description:** Pros and cons of the new and revised stock screening tools from Zack, Finviz.com, and GuruFocus are discussed. FinVix. com is more capable for screening through stocks and the service is free.

8628 ■ **"Sears' Lampert Solid in Game of Valuation Chicken"** in *Globe & Mail* (February 25, 2006, pp. B2)
Pub: CTVglobemedia Publishing Inc.

Ed: Eric Reguly. **Description:** The feasibility of share value of Sears Canada Inc., following Sears Holdings Corp.'s acquisition, is discussed.

8629 ■ **"SEC Doesn't Buy Biovail's Claims"** in *Barron's* (Vol. 88, March 31, 2008, No. 13, pp. 20)
Pub: Dow Jones & Company, Inc.

Ed: Bill Alpert. **Description:** Overstatement of earnings and chronic fraudulent conduct has led the SEC to file a stock fraud suit against Biovail, Eugene Melnyk and three others present or former employees of Biovail. Melnyk had the firm file suit in 2006 that blames short-sellers and stock researchers for the company's drop in share price.

8630 ■ **"SEC Report On Rating Agencies Falls Short"** in *Barron's* (Vol. 88, July 14, 2008, No. 28, pp. 35)
Pub: Dow Jones & Co., Inc.

Ed: Jack Willoughby. **Description:** The Securities and Exchange Commissions report on credit-rating firms should have drawn attention to the slipshod practices in the offerings of collateralized debt obligations. The report fell short of prescribing correctives for the flawed system of these agencies' relationship with their clients.

8631 ■ **"Selling Pressures Rise in China"** in *Barron's* (Vol. 88, March 10, 2008, No. 10, pp. M9)
Pub: Dow Jones & Company, Inc.

Ed: Mohammed Hadi. **Description:** There are about 1.6 trillion yuan worth of shares up for sale in Chinese stock markets in 2008, adding to the selling pressures in these markets. The Chinese government has imposed restrictions to prevent a rapid rise in selling stocks.

8632 ■ **"Sense of Discovery"** in *Business Journal Portland* (Vol. 27, November 19, 2010, No. 38, pp. 1)
Pub: Portland Business Journal

Ed: Erik Siemers. **Description:** Tigard, Oregon-based Exterro Inc. CEO Bobby Balachandran announced plans to go public without the help of an institutional investor. Balachandran believes Exterro could grow to a $100 million legal compliance software company in the span of three years. Insights on Exterro's growth as market leader in the $1 billion legal governance software market are also given.

8633 ■ **"Sentiment Split on Financials"** in *Barron's* (Vol. 88, March 24, 2008, No. 12, pp. M14)
Pub: Dow Jones & Company, Inc.

Ed: Steven M. Sears. **Description:** Experts in the financial sector are split as to whether or not the worst of the financial crisis brought on by the credit crunch is over. Some options traders are trading on are defensive puts, expecting the worst, while investors buying calls are considered as bullish.

8634 ■ **"Serious Signal Flashing?"** in *Barron's* (Vol. 88, July 7, 2008, No. 27, pp. 11)
Pub: Dow Jones & Co., Inc.

Description: Discusses the Hindenburg Omen, named after the airship disaster of May 1937, which is considered a predictor of market crashes and has appeared twice in June 2008. There is a 25 percent probability that the US stock market will suffer a crash in the July-October 2008 period.

8635 ■ "A Shallow Pool" in *Canadian Business* **(Vol. 81, Summer 2008, No. 9, pp. 44)**
Pub: Rogers Media Ltd.
Ed: Joe Castaldo. **Description:** Bank of Canada projected in its 'Monetary Policy Report' a growth rate of 1.4 percent in 2008 and does not expect the economy to fully recover until mid-2010. The Canadian stock market has been recovering although slowly with just a 1.6 percent gain by April 30. Other details on the Canadian equity market are presented.

8636 ■ "Shanghai Butterfly" in *Canadian Business* **(Vol. 80, March 12, 2007, No. 6, pp. 69)**
Pub: Rogers Media
Ed: Thomas Watson. **Description:** The volatile nature of Shanghai stock markets and its impact on investors and the economy is discussed.

8637 ■ "Shipwreck Floats Nickel's Boat" in *Globe & Mail* **(January 24, 2007, pp. B1)**
Pub: CTVglobemedia Publishing Inc.
Ed: John Partridge. **Description:** The rise in the price of nickel to $38,300 a tonne following a shipwreck in which 1,000 tonnes of the metal was lost is discussed.

8638 ■ "Shorts Story" in *Barron's* **(Vol. 89, July 6, 2009, No. 27, pp. 16)**
Pub: Dow Jones & Co., Inc.
Ed: Gene Epstein. **Description:** Shares of Compass Minerals, J2 Global Communications, K12, Middleby, and Pactiv should be shorted by investors. These companies suffer from weaknesses in their business models, making them vulnerable to a share price decline.

8639 ■ "Should the Fed Regulate Wall Street?" in *Barron's* **(Vol. 88, March 24, 2008, No. 12, pp. M15)**
Pub: Dow Jones & Company, Inc.
Ed: Randall W. Forsyth. **Description:** Greater regulation of the financial sector by the Federal Reserve is essential for it to survive the crisis it is experiencing. The resulting regulation could be in complete contrast with the deregulation the sector previously experienced.

8640 ■ "Silver Standard Reports First Quarter 2007 Results" in *Canadian Corporate News* **(May 14, 2007)**
Pub: Comtex News Network Inc.
Description: Silver Standard Resources Inc. reports a first quarter loss of $1.6 million compared with the first quarter of 2006 in which the loss was $1.1 million. Statistical data included.

8641 ■ "Six Great Stock Funds for the Long Haul" in *Barron's* **(Vol. 89, July 13, 2009, No. 28, pp. L5)**
Pub: Dow Jones & Co., Inc.
Ed: Lawrence C. Strauss; Tom Sullivan. **Description:** Six mutual funds that have solid long-term performance, transparency, savvy stock picking, and discipline are presented. The managers of these funds are also evaluated. These funds include the T. Rowe Price Emerging Market Stock Fund, Fairholme, and Dodge & Cox Stock.

8642 ■ "Six Things You Can Do To Ride Out A Turbulent Market" in *Hispanic Business* **(Vol. 30, March 2008, No. 3, pp. 20)**
Pub: Hispanic Business
Ed: Hildy Medina; Michael Bowker. **Description:** Top financial experts' views on managing investment portfolios during turbulent periods in the stock market are reported. Experts prefer investing in health care, short term investments, international bonds and preferred stocks or just maintain cash until such times as the market settles.

8643 ■ "A Slice of Danish; Fixing Finance" in *The Economist* **(Vol. 390, January 3, 2009, No. 8612, pp. 55)**
Pub: The Economist Newspaper Inc.
Description: Denmark's mortgage-holders and the county's lending system is presented.

8644 ■ "The Small 300" in *Canadian Business* **(Vol. 81, Summer 2008, No. 9, pp. 137)**
Pub: Rogers Media Ltd.
Description: Small cap-companies are ranked based on market capitalization and stock performance. Calgary-based Grande Cache Coal Corp. topped the roster with 1,000 percent of return resulting from strong sales. A table showing the 2008 rankings of the companies is presented.

8645 ■ *The Small Business Owner's Manual: Everything You Need to Know to Start Up and Run Your Business*
Pub: Career Press, Incorporated
Ed: Joe Kennedy. **Released:** June 2005. **Price:** $19.99 (US), $26.95 (Canadian). **Description:** Comprehensive guide for starting a small business, focusing on twelve ways to obtain financing, business plans, selling and advertising products and services, hiring and firing employees, setting up a Web site, business law, accounting issues, insurance, equipment, computers, banks, financing, customer credit and collection, leasing, and more.

8646 ■ "Smaller Banks Could Face Tough 2008" in *Austin Business JournalInc.* **(Vol. 28, January 2, 2009, No. 1, pp. 3)**
Pub: American City Business Journals
Ed: Christopher Calnan. **Description:** The turbulence in the banking industry is expected to reach Texas in 2009 and industry insiders believe there will be a shift in deposits from small, regional banks to larger banks due to low consumer confidence. One economist says that a large number of banks are going to go out of business in 2009.

8647 ■ "Smart Investor's Shopping List: Coke, Walgreen, Drill Bits; A Conversation with Money Manager Paula Dorion-Gray" in *Crain's Chicago Business*
Pub: Crain Communications, Inc.
Ed: Bruce Blythe. **Description:** Interview with Paula Dorion-Gray, president of Dorion-Gray Retirement Planning Inc., discusses the state of the investing environment, favored industries, industries to avoid, and her approach towards investing.

8648 ■ "Smart Medicine" in *Canadian Business* **(Vol. 80, February 26, 2007, No. 5, pp. 73)**
Pub: Rogers Media
Ed: Zena Olijnyk. **Description:** The stock price stability and future earnings prospects of Canadian biotechnology firm YM Biosciences are analyzed.

8649 ■ "The Smell of Fear: Is a Bottom Near?" in *Barron's* **(Vol. 88, March 17, 2008, No. 11, pp. M3)**
Pub: Dow Jones & Company, Inc.
Ed: Kopin Tan. **Description:** Liquidity problems at Bear Stearns frightened investors in markets around the world due to the fear of the prospects of a big bank's failure. Shares of health maintenance organizations got battered led by WellPoint, and Humana but longer-term investors who could weather short-term volatility may find value here. The value of J. Crew shares is also discussed.

8650 ■ "A Socko Payout Menu: Rural Phone Carrier Plots to Supercharge Its Shares" in *Barron's* **(Vol. 88, June 30, 2008, No. 26, pp. M5)**
Pub: Dow Jones & Co., Inc.
Ed: Shirley A. Lazo. **Description:** CenturyTel boosted its quarterly common payout to 70 cents from 6.75 cents per share die to its strong cash flows and solid balance sheet. Eastman Kodak's plan for a buyback will be partially funded by its $581 million tax refund. CME Group will buyback stocks through 2009 worth $1.1 billion.

8651 ■ "Solace for the Freshly Flaherty'd" in *Canadian Business* **(Vol. 79, November 6, 2006, No. 22, pp. 114)**
Pub: Rogers Media
Ed: Ian McGugan. **Description:** Tips to manage investments with relation to cash distribution tax on income trusts are presented.

8652 ■ "Some Big Biotechs Buying Own Stock" in *Boston Business Journal* **(Vol. 30, November 5, 2010, No. 41, pp. 1)**
Pub: Boston Business Journal
Ed: Julie M. Donnelly. **Description:** Biotechnology companies such as Biogen Idec and Genzyme Corporation are conducting stock buybacks as they look to invest their cash holdings. Other analysts see the buybacks as reluctance in committing to longer-term investments.

8653 ■ "Some Relief Possible Following Painful Week" in *Barron's* **(Vol. 88, July 14, 2008, No. 28, pp. M3)**
Pub: Dow Jones & Co., Inc.
Ed: Kopin Tan. **Description:** Dow Chemical is offering a 74 percent premium to acquire Rohm & Haas' coatings and electronics materials operations. Frontline amassed a 5.6 percent stake in rival Overseas Shipholding Group and a merger between the two would create a giant global fleet with pricing power. Highlights of the U.S. stock market during the week that ended in July 11, 2008 are discussed. Statistical data included.

8654 ■ "Something to Like" in *Canadian Business* **(Vol. 81, April 14, 2008, No. 6, pp. 22)**
Pub: Rogers Media
Ed: Jack Mintz. **Description:** Jim Flaherty's policy on tax-free savings account (TFSA) will allow Canadians to accumulate wealth at a much faster rate and these accounts could be especially good for people who are subject to high effective taxes on savings. Investors should put their money into a Registered Retirement Savings Plan (RRSP) when it comes to risky investments but the TFSA is better than an RRSP if investors expect very high taxes on withdrawals from their RRSP.

8655 ■ "The Spark's Back in Sanyo" in *Barron's* **(Vol. 88, March 31, 2008, No. 13, pp. M9)**
Pub: Dow Jones & Company, Inc.
Ed: Jay Alabaster. **Description:** Things are looking up for Sanyo Electric after its string of calamities that range from major losses brought on by earthquake damage to its semiconductor operations and its near collapse and bailout. The company looks poised for a rebound as they are on track for their first net profit since 2003 and could beat its earnings forecast for 2008.

8656 ■ "Spectre of Iran War Spooks Oil Markets" in *Globe & Mail* **(March 28, 2007, pp. B1)**
Pub: CTVglobemedia Publishing Inc.
Ed: Shawn McCarthy. **Description:** The increase in the price of crude oil by $5 a barrel to reach $68 in the United States following speculation over war against Iran, is discussed.

8657 ■ "Spread Your Wings" in *Canadian Business* **(Vol. 81, March 17, 2008, No. 4, pp. 31)**
Pub: Rogers Media
Ed: Megan Harman. **Description:** Financing from angel investors is one avenue that should be explored by startups. Angel investors are typically affluent individuals who invest their own money. Angel investors usually want at least 10 times their initial investment within eight years but they benefit the businesses through their help in decision-making and the industry expertise they provide.

8658 ■ "Sprint Tries to Wring Out Positives" in *The Business Journal-Serving Metropolitan Kansas City* **(Vol. 26, August 8, 2008, No. 48)**
Pub: American City Business Journals, Inc.
Ed: Suzanna Stagemeyer. **Description:** Sprint Nextel Corp. reported that 901,000 subscribers left the company in the quarter ending June 30, 2008; fewer than the nearly 1.1 million it lost in the previous quarter. Customer turnover also dropped to just less than 2 percent, compared to 2.45 percent in the first quarter of 2008.

8659 ■ "Staffing Firm Grows by Following Own Advice-Hire a Headhunter" in *Crain's Detroit Business* (Vol. 24, October 6, 2008, No. 40, pp. 1)

Pub: Crain Communications, Inc.

Ed: Sherri Begin. **Description:** Profile of Venator Holdings L.L.C., a staffing firm that provides searches for companies in need of financial-accounting and technical employees; the firm's revenue has increased from $1.1 million in 2003 to a projected $11.5 million this year due to a climate in which more people are exiting the workforce than are coming in with those particular specialized skills and the need for a temporary, flexible workforce for contract placements at companies that do not want to take on the legacy costs associated with permanent employees. The hiring of an external headhunter to find the right out-of-state manager for Venator is also discussed.

8660 ■ "Stand-Up Guy" in *Barron's* (Vol. 88, July 7, 2008, No. 27, pp. L11)

Pub: Dow Jones & Co., Inc.

Ed: Suzanne McGee. **Description:** James O'Shaughnessy, a mutual fund manager with O'Shaughnessy Asset Management, is bullish on both financial and energy stocks. He was formerly involved with Bear Stearns until he left the firm in March 2008.

8661 ■ *Start Your Own Blogging Business, Second Edition*

Pub: Entrepreneur Press

Released: July 1, 2010. **Price:** $17.95. **Description:** Interviews with professional bloggers from some of the most popular blogs on the Internet will help anyone interested in starting their own blogging business.

8662 ■ "State of Play" in *Canadian Business* (Vol. 79, June 19, 2006, No. 13, pp. 25)

Pub: Rogers Media

Ed: Andrew Wahl; Zena Olijnyk; Jeff Sanford. **Description:** Top 100 information technology companies in Canada are ranked by their market capitalization as of June 1. The statistics that show the revenues of these companies are also presented.

8663 ■ "State Shock Prices Take Large Tumble" in *The Business Journal-Milwaukee* (Vol. 25, September 12, 2008, No. 51, pp. A1)

Pub: American City Business Journals, Inc.

Ed: Rich Rovito. **Description:** Weak economic times have caused the stocks of most publicly traded companies in Wisconsin to dip in 2008. Companies that appeared on the worst performing stocks list also experienced drops in share price to as much as 70 percent. Information about the companies that experienced increases in stock prices is also presented. Statistical data included.

8664 ■ "Stay Calm, Bernanke Urges Markets" in *Globe & Mail* (March 1, 2007, pp. B1)

Pub: CTVglobemedia Publishing Inc.

Ed: Brian McKenna. **Description:** The views of Ben Bernanke, the chief of the United States Federal Reserve Board, on the future trends of the United States' economy are presented. The effect of the global stock market trends on the American stock markets is discussed.

8665 ■ "Stelco Investors Told Their Stock Now Worthless" in *Globe & Mail* (January 23, 2006, pp. B4)

Pub: CTVglobemedia Publishing Inc.

Ed: Greg Keenan. **Description:** The reasons behind Ontario Superior Court's approval of Stelco Inc.'s restructuring proposal are presented.

8666 ■ "Stock Analysts' Pans" in *Canadian Business* (Vol. 81, Summer 2008, No. 9, pp. 75)

Pub: Rogers Media Ltd.

Ed: Calvin Leung. **Description:** Table showing the one-year stock performance of companies that are least loved by analysts and are rated either to be a Hold or Sell. These companies should not be included in the investment portfolio, at least in the short term.

8667 ■ "Stock Car Racing" in *Canadian Business* (Vol. 81, September 15, 2008, No. 14-15, pp. 29)

Pub: Rogers Media Ltd.

Ed: Thomas Watson. **Description:** Some analysts predict a Chapter 11-style tune-up making GM and Ford a speculative turnaround stock. However, the price of oil could make or break the shares of the Big Three U.S. automobile manufacturers and if oil goes up too high then a speculative stock to watch is an electric car company called Zenn Motor Co.

8668 ■ "Stock Delisting Could Hamper First Mariner" in *Boston Business Journal* (Vol. 29, July 29, 2011, No. 12, pp. 1)

Pub: American City Business Journals Inc.

Ed: Gary Haber. **Description:** Possible delisting of First Mariner Bancorp from the Nasdaq stock exchange could adversely impact the bank's ability to attract institutional investors. Some institutions limit their investments to companies trading on the Nasdaq.

8669 ■ "Stockgroup Completes US $4.5 Million Financing" in *Canadian Corporate News* (May 16, 2007)

Pub: Comtex News Network Inc.

Description: Stockgroup, a financial media company focused on collaborative technologies and user-generated content, will use the proceeds of the private placement for acquisitions and general working capital.

8670 ■ *Street Fighters: The Last 72 Hours of Bears Stearns, the Toughest Firm on Wall Street*

Pub: Portfolio

Ed: Kate Kelly. **Released:** 2009. **Price:** $25.95. **Description:** An account of the investment bank, Bears Stearns fight for survival is documented.

8671 ■ "Stressed Out: 7 Banks Rated 'At Riks'" in *Saint Louis Business Journal* (Vol. 32, September 16, 2011, No. 3, pp. 1)

Pub: Saint Louis Business Journal

Ed: Greg Edwards. **Description:** St. Louis, Missouri has seven banks that are well above the 100 percent level that is considered 'at risk' based on a risk measurement called the Texas ratio. The banks are the Sun Security bank, 1st Advantage Bank, Superior Bank, Truman Bank, Reliance Bank, St. Louis Bank and Meramec Valley Bank.

8672 ■ "Struggling Community Banks Find Little Help In Wall Street Bailout" in *Crain's Detroit Business* (Vol. 24, September 29, 2008)

Pub: Crain Communications, Inc.

Ed: Tom Henderson. **Description:** Both public and private Michigan bands have been hit hard by poorly performing loan portfolios and although their problems were not caused by high-risk securities but by a longtime statewide recession and a housing slump, these community banks have little hope of seeing any of the bailout money that has been allotted for the larger institutions.

8673 ■ "Stymiest's RBC Compensation Triggers Shareholder Outrage" in *Globe & Mail* (January 28, 2006, pp. B3)

Pub: CTVglobemedia Publishing Inc.

Ed: Sinclair Stewart. **Description:** The concerns of shareholders over the issue of Royal Bank of Canada's $6.6 million pay package for chief executive officer Barbara Stymiest, in 2004, are presented.

8674 ■ "Subprime Hits Huntington" in *Business First-Columbus* (November 23, 2007, pp. A1)

Pub: American City Business Journals, Inc.

Ed: Adrian Burns. **Description:** Huntington Bancshares Inc. picked up a $1.5 billion exposure to the country's subprime mortgage mess. It caused the bank to set aside $450 million to cover increases in loan losses. When Huntington acquired Sky Financial, it absorbed a 17-year relationship Sky had with Franklin Credit Corporation, which is a subprime lender and servicer.

8675 ■ "The Suits Look Better Than the Shares" in *Barron's* (Vol. 88, March 31, 2008, No. 13, pp. 25)

Pub: Dow Jones & Company, Inc.

Ed: Bill Alpert. **Description:** Jos. A. Bank's inventory has increased sharply raising questions about the company's growth prospects. The company's shares have already dropped significantly from 46 to 23 and could still continue its slide. The company is also battling a class action suit where plaintiffs allege that the Bank inventories were bloated.

8676 ■ "SunBank Plans Expansion Via Wall-Mart" in *Business Journal-Serving Phoenix and the Valley of the Sun* (Vol. 10, November 9, 2007)

Pub: American City Business Journals, Inc.

Ed: Chris Casacchia. **Description:** SunBank plans to install 12 to 14 branches in Wal-Mart stores in Arizona and hire 100 bankers by the end of 2008. Wal-Mart also offers financial products at other stores through partnerships with other banks.

8677 ■ "Surprise Package" in *Business Courier* (Vol. 27, June 25, 2010, No. 8, pp. 1)

Pub: Business Courier

Ed: Dan Monk, Jon Newberry, Steve Watkins. **Description:** More than 60 percent of the chief executive officers (CEOs) in Greater Cincinnati's 35 public companies took a salary cut in 2009, but stock grants resulted in large paper gains for the CEOs. The salary cuts show efforts of boards of directors to observe austerity. Statistics on increased values of stock awards for CEOs, median pay for CEOs, and median shareholder return are also presented.

8678 ■ "A Survival Guide for Crazy Times" in *Canadian Business* (Vol. 81, March 3, 2008, No. 3, pp. 61)

Pub: Rogers Media

Ed: David Wolf. **Description:** Investors should ensure that their portfolios are positioned defensively more than the average as the U.S. and Canadian markets face turbulent times. They should not assume that U.S. residential property is a good place to invest only because prices have dropped and the Canadian dollar is showing strength. Other tips that investors can use during unstable periods are supplied.

8679 ■ "Surviving the Storm" in *Canadian Business* (Vol. 81, July 22, 2008, No. 12-13, pp. 50)

Pub: Rogers Media Ltd.

Ed: Jeff Sanford. **Description:** Investment adviser Harry Dent and finance professor Paul Marsh discuss their views and forecasts on the United States' economic condition. Dent believes advisors should concentrate on wealth preservation rather than on returns. Other views regarding U.S. economic conditions are also presented.

8680 ■ "A Swifter, Better Marketplace" in *Barron's* (Vol. 89, July 13, 2009, No. 28, pp. M13)

Pub: Dow Jones & Co., Inc.

Ed: Eric W. Noll. **Description:** Listed-derivatives market is moving towards greater trading through computerized systems with an emphasis on speed and innovation. The market for listed options is also being changed by new techniques from other markets such as algorithmic trading, dark pools, and new-order priority systems.

8681 ■ "Sykes Group Targets GunnAllen" in *The Business Journal-Serving Greater Tampa Bay* (Vol. 28, September 5, 2008, No. 37, pp. 1)

Pub: American City Business Journals, Inc.

Ed: Margie Manning. **Description:** GAH Holdings LLC. a newly formed investment company by John H. Sykes of Sykes Enterprises Inc., will add capital to Tampa Bay Area investment banking firm GunnAllen Holdings Inc. The capital infusion is to aid GunnAllen Holdings in expanding and diversifying as GAH becomes its largest shareholder.

8682 ■ **"Take a Flyer on Choice"** in *Canadian Business* (Vol. 79, October 23, 2006, No. 21, pp. 163)

Pub: Rogers Media

Description: The variations in the stock market prices of companies like Nike Inc. and Black & Decker Corp. from October 2005-06 are discussed.

8683 ■ **"Take It to the Bank"** in *Barron's* (Vol. 89, July 13, 2009, No. 28, pp. 20)

Pub: Dow Jones & Co., Inc.

Ed: Jim McTague. **Description:** Banks are one of the safest place to put one's principal due to the temporary increase in the Federal Deposit Insurance Corp.'s insurance of bank accounts up to $250,000 and also because of the Cdars (Certificates of Deposit Registry Service) program which spreads the deposit to several banks thereby making the account covered as if it the money was deposited at multiple banks.

8684 ■ **"Takeover Frenzy Stokes Steel Stocks"** in *Globe & Mail* (February 7, 2006, pp. B1)

Pub: CTVglobemedia Publishing Inc.

Description: The impact of merger speculations, on shares of steel companies such as Ipsco Inc., is discussed.

8685 ■ **"Taking Collections"** in *Investment Dealers' Digest* (Vol. 75, October 9, 2009, No. 38, pp. 19)

Pub: SourceMedia, Inc.

Ed: Aleksandrs Rozens. **Description:** Although the nation's debt-collection industry has grown with increased reliance by consumers on credit, valuations of these firms have lessened due to the economy which has hurt some of the success of these firms in obtaining the debt back from consumers who are experiencing trying economic times.

8686 ■ **"Taking the Over-the-Counter Route to US"** in *Barron's* (Vol. 88, July 7, 2008, No. 27, pp. 24)

Pub: Dow Jones & Co., Inc.

Ed: Eric Uhlfelder. **Description:** Many multinational companies have left the New York Stock Exchange and allowed their shares to trade over-the-counter. The companies have taken advantage of a 2007 SEC rule allowing publicly listed foreign companies to change trading venues if less than 5 percent of global trading volume in the past 12 months occurred in the US.

8687 ■ **"Tamara Vrooman"** in *Canadian Business* (Vol. 80, November 19, 2007, No. 23, pp. 9)

Pub: Rogers Media

Ed: Regan Ray. **Description:** Profile of Tamara Vrooman, newly appointed CEO of Canada's largest credit union, Vancity. Vrooman believes that Vancity has an advantage over big bank when it comes to the flexibility of products the company offers. The role of Vancity and credit unions in the banking sector of Canada is discussed.

8688 ■ **"Tanganyika Announces First Quarter 2007 Results"** in *Canadian Corporate News* (May 14, 2007)

Pub: Comtex News Network Inc.

Description: Tanganyika Oil Company Ltd., announced the interim operating and financial results for the first quarter ending March 31, 2007. Statistical data included.

8689 ■ **"Tao of Downfall"** in *International Journal of Entrepreneurship and Small Business* (Vol. 11, August 31, 2010, No. 2, pp. 121)

Pub: Publishers Communication Group

Ed: Wenxian Zhang, Ilan Alon. **Description:** Through historical reviews and case studies, this research seeks to understand why some initially successful entrepreneurs failed in the economic boom of past decades. Among various factors contributing to their downfall are a unique political and business environment, fragile financial systems, traditional cultural influences and personal characteristics.

8690 ■ **"Tech's Payout Problem"** in *Barron's* (Vol. 90, September 13, 2010, No. 37, pp. 19)

Pub: Barron's Editorial & Corporate Headquarters

Ed: Andrew Bary. **Description:** Big tech companies have the potential to be good dividend payers, but instead just hoard their cash for acquisitions and share buybacks. If these companies offered more dividends, they could boost their shares and attract more income-oriented investors.

8691 ■ *The Ten Laws of Enduring Success*

Pub: Crown Business Books

Ed: Maria Bartiromo, Catherine Whitney. **Released:** March 1, 2011. **Price:** $15.00. **Description:** A new meaning for success is described by financial expert, Maria Bartiromo, with advice on how to adapt with the changing times.

8692 ■ **"TerraVest Income Fund Releases 2007 First Quarter Financial Results"** in *Canadian Corporate News* (May 14, 2007)

Pub: Comtex News Network Inc.

Description: Overview of TerraVest Income Fund's financial results for the quarter ended March 31, 2007 in which the net earnings increased 36.7 percent to $3.7 million from the 2006 first quarter. Statistical data included.

8693 ■ **"That's About It for Quantitative Easing"** in *Barron's* (Vol. 89, July 20, 2009, No. 29, pp. M11)

Pub: Dow Jones & Co., Inc.

Ed: Brian Blackstone. **Description:** US Federal Reserve appears to have decided to halt quantitative easing, causing bond prices to drop and yields to rise. The yield for the 1-year Treasury bond rose more than 0.3 percentage point to about 3.65 percent.

8694 ■ **"The End of the Line for Line Extensions?"** in *Advertising Age* (Vol. 79, July 7, 2008, No. 26, pp. 3)

Pub: Crain Communications, Inc.

Ed: Description: After years of double-digit growth, some of the most heavily extended personal-care products have slowed substantially or even declined in the U.S. Unilever's Dove and P&G's Pantene and Olay are two such brands that have been affected. Statistical data included.

8695 ■ **"The File On...Skoda Minotti"** in *Crain's Cleveland Business* (Vol. 28, October 8, 2007, No. 40, pp. 26)

Pub: Crain Communications, Inc.

Ed: Kimberly Bonvissuto. **Description:** Overview of Skoda Minotti, the accounting and financial services firm located in Mayfield Village; the company has 140 employees and an expanded slate of services.

8696 ■ **"The REIT Stuff"** in *Canadian Business* (Vol. 80, March 26, 2007, No. 7, pp. 72)

Pub: Rogers Media

Description: The stock performance of various real estate investment trusts in Canada is analyzed.

8697 ■ **"There's More Upside in Germany"** in *Barron's* (Vol. 90, September 6, 2010, No. 36, pp. M7)

Pub: Barron's Editorial & Corporate Headquarters

Ed: Jonathan Buck. **Description:** Germany's stocks have gone up since the beginning of 2010, and investors can still benefit. These stocks will benefit from Germany's stellar economic performance and the relative weakness of the Euro. The prospects of the shares of Daimler and Hochtief are discussed.

8698 ■ **"They Have Issues: New Black-Owned Investment Bank Nets $90 Million In Managed Issues"** in *Black Enterprise* (Vol. 38, March 2008)

Pub: Earl G. Graves Publishing Co. Inc.

Ed: Marcia A. Wade. **Description:** Castle Oak Securities LP has co-managed multiple deals for more than 35 blue-chip clients. Their first deal earned $300 million for General Electric Capital Corporation and Castle Oak has since co-managed nine more deals with GE Capital, seven for Citigroup, six for American Express, and three for Goldman Sachs.

8699 ■ **"They've Fallen, But They Can Get Up"** in *Barron's* (Vol. 88, March 10, 2008, No. 10, pp. 43)

Pub: Dow Jones & Company, Inc.

Ed: Kopin Tan. **Description:** Shares of senior housing companies present buying opportunities to investors because of their low prices. Companies such as Brookdale Senior Living are not as dependent on housing prices but have suffered declines in share prices.

8700 ■ **"Time to Change Direction"** in *Canadian Business* (Vol. 79, October 23, 2006, No. 21, pp. 21)

Pub: Rogers Media

Ed: Jack Mintz. **Description:** The decision of BCE Inc. to get converted into an income trust is discussed. The economic factors responsible for the conversion of firms to income trusts are analyzed.

8701 ■ **"Time to Leave the Party?"** in *Barron's* (Vol. 88, March 24, 2008, No. 12, pp. M16)

Pub: Dow Jones & Company, Inc.

Ed: Andrea Hotter. **Description:** Prices of commodities such as gold, copper, crude oil, sugar, cocoa, and wheat have fallen from their all-time highs set in the middle of March 2008. Analysts, however, caution that this decline in prices may be temporary, and that a banking crisis may trigger new price rises in commodities.

8702 ■ **"Time for a Little Pruning"** in *Barron's* (Vol. 89, July 6, 2009, No. 27, pp. 13)

Pub: Dow Jones & Company, Inc.

Ed: Dimitra DeFotis. **Description:** Investors are advised to avoid the shares of Whole Foods, American Tower, T. Rowe Price, Iron Mountain, Intuitive Surgical, Salesforce.com, and Juniper Networks due to their high price to earnings ratios. The shares of Amazon.com, Broadcom, and Expeditors International of Washington remain attractive to investors despite their high price to earnings ratios due to their strong growth.

8703 ■ **"A Timely Boon for Small Investors"** in *Barron's* (Vol. 88, March 24, 2008, No. 12, pp. 48)

Pub: Dow Jones & Company, Inc.

Ed: Theresa W. Carey. **Description:** Nasdaq Data Store's new program called Market Replay allows investors to accurately track stock price movements. The replay can be as long as a day of market time and allows investors to determine whether they executed stock trades at the best possible price.

8704 ■ **"Tiptoeing Beyond Treasuries"** in *Barron's* (Vol. 88, March 31, 2008, No. 13, pp. M6)

Pub: Dow Jones & Company, Inc.

Ed: Michael S. Derby. **Description:** Risk-free assets like treasuries are still a good place for cash even if market conditions have calmed down and Treasury yields are low. Investors looking for yield and safety might want to consider Treasury inflation-indexed securities that are attractive given new inflation pressures.

8705 ■ **"Tofutti Brands"** in *Ice Cream Reporter* (Vol. 23, September 20, 2010, No. 10, pp. 6)

Pub: Ice Cream Reporter

Description: Tofutti Brands announced net sales at $4.5 million for second quarter 2010.

8706 ■ **"A Tonic for Irrationality"** in *Barron's* (Vol. 89, July 13, 2009, No. 28, pp. 12)

Pub: Dow Jones & Company, Inc.

Description: Financial-personality assessment being introduced by Barclays Wealth, measures six personality aspects related to financial behavior through a profile that measures such traits including risk tolerance, composure and perceived financial expertise. The profile helps the company create a portfolio that are structured to meet their client's personality needs.

8707 ■ "Too Much Information?" in *Black Enterprise* **(Vol. 37, December 2006, No. 5, pp. 59)**
Pub: Earl G. Graves Publishing Co. Inc.
Ed: James C. Johnson. **Description:** African American business owners often face the dilemma of whether or not to divulge their minority status when soliciting new customers and financial institutions. The quality of the products or services is always the key factor and race should never define one's business; however, it is appropriate to market oneself as a minority or women-owned business, especially if the company is in an industry where those clients are offered top-tier contracts.

8708 ■ "Too Much Precaution About Biotech Corn" in *Barron's* **(Vol. 88, March 17, 2008, No. 11, pp. 54)**
Pub: Dow Jones & Company, Inc.
Ed: Mark I. Schwartz. **Description:** In the U.S., 90 percent of cultivated soybeans are biotech varietals as well as 60 percent of the corn. Farmers have significantly reduced their reliance on pesticides in the growing of biotech corn. Biotech cotton cultivation has brought hundreds of millions of dollars in net financial gains to farmers. The European Union has precluded the cultivation or sale of biotech crops within its border.

8709 ■ "Too Much too Soon" in *Barron's* **(Vol. 89, July 27, 2009, No. 30, pp. 33)**
Pub: Dow Jones & Co., Inc.
Ed: Leslie P. Norton. **Description:** Shares of hhgregg have risen 85 percent in the year leading up to July 2009 and analysts believe the stock could hit 25. However, their 113 outlets are concentrated in states where unemployment is above 10 percent and expanding into areas already overstored. Competition is also rife and credit availability is still tight.

8710 ■ "Tool-o-Rama" in *Barron's* **(Vol. 90, September 6, 2010, No. 36)**
Pub: Barron's Editorial & Corporate Headquarters
Description: New trading tool features from several online brokers are discussed. The new features from Fidelity, ChoiceTrade, JunoTrade and TradeKing are examined. Investors can now screen exchanged traded funds in the same way as stocks with Fidelity, while ChoiceTrade can run in any browser without the need to install additional plug-ins.

8711 ■ "Top 10 Retirement Mistakes and How to Avoid Them" in *Canadian Business* **(Vol. 83, July 20, 2010, No. 11-12, pp. 39)**
Pub: Rogers Media Ltd.
Ed: Jacqueline Nelson, Angelina Chapin. **Description:** Some of the top retirement mistakes is relying on selling one's house to find a retirement. Other mistakes are paying too much for investments and planning to work in retirement since no one can be sure that they will be healthy enough to accomplish this. Suggestions to avoid these pitfalls are discussed.

8712 ■ "Top 50 By 1-Year Return" in *Canadian Business* **(Vol. 81, Summer 2008, No. 9, pp. 121)**
Pub: Rogers Media Ltd.
Description: Table showing the top 50 Canadian companies ranked in terms of one-year return is presented. Toronto, Canada-based Timminco Ltd. topped the roster with a 1,294.2 percent in one-year return. However, the share prices of the company were affected by the recent controversy in its silicon purification process.

8713 ■ "Top 50 By 5-Year Return" in *Canadian Business* **(Vol. 81, Summer 2008, No. 9, pp. 123)**
Pub: Rogers Media Ltd.
Description: Table showing the rankings of the top 50 Canadian companies in terms of five-year return is presented. Silver Wheaton Corp. topped the roster with a 178.5 percent in five-year return. The company's share prices have skyrocketed despite increasing silver prices.

8714 ■ "Top 50 in the Capital Market" in *Canadian Business* **(Vol. 81, Summer 2008, No. 9, pp. 117)**
Pub: Rogers Media Ltd.
Description: Research in Motion Ltd. topped the list of companies in Canada in terms of market capitaliza-

tion. The company's share prices surge to 119.8 percent in the year ended April 4. A table showing the top 50 Canadian companies in terms of market capitalization is presented.

8715 ■ "Top 50 In Profits" in *Canadian Business* **(Vol. 81, Summer 2008, No. 9, pp. 116)**
Pub: Rogers Media Ltd.
Description: Royal Bank of Canada topped the Investor 500 by profits list despite the slower economic growth in Canada and the U.S. The bank was in the runner-up position in the 2007. RBC's growth strategy is through hefty acquisitions in the U.S. A table ranking the top 50 companies in Canada in terms of profits is presented.

8716 ■ "Top 50 In Total Revenue" in *Canadian Business* **(Vol. 81, Summer 2008, No. 9, pp. 119)**
Pub: Rogers Media Ltd.
Description: Table showing the top 50 Canadian companies in terms of total revenue is presented. Manulife Financial Corp. topped the list with revenue of 34.5 billion. The financial services firm is the 6th largest provider of life insurance in the world and the second largest in North America.

8717 ■ "Top Law Firms Join Forces" in *Business Journal Portland* **(Vol. 27, December 3, 2010, No. 40, pp. 1)**
Pub: Portland Business Journal
Ed: Andy Giegerich. **Description:** Law Firms Powell PC and Roberts Kaplan LLP will forge a collaboration, whereby 17 Roberts Kaplan attorneys will join the Portland, Oregon-based office of Lane Powell. The partnership is expected to strengthen the law firms' grip on Portland's banking clients.

8718 ■ "Tory or Liberal, Blue or Red, the Impact of the Election is All in Your Head" in *Globe & Mail* **(January 14, 2006, pp. B19)**
Pub: CTVglobemedia Publishing Inc.
Ed: Derek DeCloet. **Description:** The effect of the outcome of 2006 Canadian federal elections on stock markets is discussed.

8719 ■ "The Trader's Edge" in *Barron's* **(Vol. 88, March 31, 2008, No. 13, pp. 56)**
Pub: Dow Jones & Company, Inc.
Ed: Dan McGuire. **Description:** There is a $3,000 a year annual limit to deducting investor's losses and normal investment expenses are purportedly deductible as miscellaneous expenses on Schedule A only to the extent that they exceed two percent of adjusted gross income. Professional gamblers who can use Schedule C are unable deduct a net gaming loss against income from any other sources.

8720 ■ "Traditional VS. Roth IRA" in *Black Enterprise* **(Vol. 37, October 2006, No. 3, pp. 58)**
Pub: Earl G. Graves Publishing Co. Inc.
Ed: K. Parker; Carolyn M. Brown. **Description:** Government taxes the traditional IRAs different than it taxes Roth IRAs.

8721 ■ "Treasuries Buffeted by Stocks" in *Barron's* **(Vol. 89, July 27, 2009, No. 30, pp. M9)**
Pub: Dow Jones & Co., Inc.
Ed: Randall W. Forsyth. **Description:** Warren Buffett favors equities over long-term government bonds or stocks even with the Dow index at an eight-month high. The 10-year Treasury was up two basis points to 3.67 percent as of July 24, 2009. Corporate bond issuance hit a record $1.79 trillion for the first half of 2009.

8722 ■ "Treasuries Rally Despite Huge Supply" in *Barron's* **(Vol. 89, July 13, 2009, No. 28, pp. M10)**
Pub: Dow Jones & Co., Inc.
Ed: Randall W. Forsyth. **Description:** Prices of U.S. Treasuries were sent higher and their yields lower despite four auctions of coupon securities because of the strong appetite for government securities around the world. The reopening of the 10-year note in the week ending July 10, 2009 drew the strongest bidding since 1995.

8723 ■ "A Trend Is His Friend" in *Barron's* **(Vol. 89, July 27, 2009, No. 30, pp. 28)**
Pub: Dow Jones & Co., Inc.
Ed: Eric Uhlfelder. **Description:** Global Diversified Program fund under Quality Capital Management is managed through a trading system called the Advanced Resource Allocator which rebalances short-term tactical moves to gather quick profits. CEO Aref Karim's allocations are based on risk and he says their sentiments toward the market conditions are agnostic.

8724 ■ "The Trials of Brian Hunter" in *Canadian Business* **(Vol. 81, March 3, 2008, No. 3, pp. 64)**
Pub: Rogers Media
Ed: Thomas Watson. **Description:** Brian Hunter was a considered a brilliant trader in Wall Street before he was blamed for the fall of the Amaranth hedge fund. Some people blame Hunter for placing bets based on unpredictable weather when he was a trader for Amaranth Advisors LLC. The accusation against Hunter that he conspired to manipulate natural gas prices is also discussed.

8725 ■ "Trilogy Metals Inc.: Private Placement" in *Canadian Corporate News* **(May 16, 2007)**
Pub: Comtex News Network Inc.
Description: Trilogy Metals Inc. announces a private placement of 10,000,000 units at $0.08 per unit in an effort to raise total gross proceeds of $800,000 which will be allocated to working capital, new acquisitions, and to service existing debt.

8726 ■ "Trust Buyouts Not My Fault, Flaherty Says" in *Globe & Mail* **(April 3, 2007, pp. B1)**
Pub: CTVglobemedia Publishing Inc.
Ed: Tara Perkins; Doug Saunders; Steven Chase. **Description:** The causes of the acquisition of Canadian firms by foreign investors are discussed by the Canadian Finance Minister Jim Flaherty.

8727 ■ "Trust Distrust" in *Canadian Business* **(Vol. 79, July 17, 2006, No. 14-15, pp. 61)**
Pub: Rogers Media
Ed: John Gray. **Description:** The need to frame better trust deeds in order to protect the investor's money as well as their returns is examined.

8728 ■ "TUSK Announces 2007 First Quarter Results" in *Canadian Corporate News* **(May 14, 2007)**
Pub: Comtex News Network Inc.
Description: TUSK Energy Corp. announced its financial and operating results for the first quarter ending March 31, 2007.

8729 ■ "TV Revenue Slide Hits CanWest Profit" in *Globe & Mail* **(January 13, 2006, pp. B3)**
Pub: CTVglobemedia Publishing Inc.
Ed: Grant Robertson. **Description:** CanWest Global Communications Corp. posted drop in profits by 14 percent for first quarter 2006. The downward trend in profits is attributed to low television revenues.

8730 ■ "UBS Buys Out Canadian Partner" in *Globe & Mail* **(January 20, 2006, pp. B1)**
Pub: CTVglobemedia Publishing Inc.
Ed: Andrew Willis. **Description:** The details on UBS AG's acquisition of UBS Securities Canada Inc. are presented.

8731 ■ "An Unfair Knock on Nokia" in *Barron's* **(Vol. 88, March 10, 2008, No. 10, pp. 36)**
Pub: Dow Jones & Company, Inc.
Ed: Mark Veverka. **Description:** Discusses the decision by the brokerage house Exane to recommend a Sell on Nokia shares, presumably due to higher inventories, which is unfounded. The news that the company's inventories are rising is not an indicator of falling demand for its products. The company is also benefiting from solid management and rising market share.

8732 ■ **"Unify Corp. Back in the Black, Poised to Grow" in** *Sacramento Business Journal* **(Vol. 25, August 29, 2008, No. 26, pp. 1)**
Pub: American City Business Journals, Inc.
Ed: Melanie Turner. **Description:** It was reported that Unify Corp. returned to profitability in the fiscal year ended April 30, 2008 with a net income of $1.6 million, under the guidance of Todd Wille. Wille, who took over as the company's chief executive officer in October 2000, was named as Turnaround CEO of the Year in June 2008 for his efforts.

8733 ■ **"Universal Energy Group Releases March 31, 2007 Financial Statements" in** *Canadian Corporate News* **(May 14, 2007)**
Pub: Comtex News Network Inc.
Description: Universal Energy Group Ltd., a company that sells electricity and natural gas to small to mid-size commercial and small industrial customers as well as residential customers, announced the release of its March 31, 2007 financial statements. Management's analysis and discussion of the company's financial condition and results of operations are listed. Statistical data included.

8734 ■ **"Unpleasant Surprise" in** *Barron's* **(Vol. 88, March 24, 2008, No. 12, pp. 60)**
Pub: Dow Jones & Company, Inc.
Ed: Shirley A. Lazo. **Description:** Discusses the $175 million that footwear company Genesco received in a settlement with Finish Line and UBS is considered as a stock distribution and is taxable as dividend income. Railroad company CSX raised its quarterly common payout from 15 cents to 18 cents.

8735 ■ **"The Upside of Fear and Loathing" in** *Barron's* **(Vol. 88, March 24, 2008, No. 12, pp. 11)**
Pub: Dow Jones & Company, Inc.
Ed: Michael Santoli. **Description:** Fear and risk aversion prevalent among investors may actually serve to cushion the decline and spark a rally in US stock prices. Surveys of investors indicate rising levels of anxiety and bearishness, indicating a possible positive turnaround.

8736 ■ **"USAmeriBank Deals for Growth" in** *The Business Journal-Serving Greater Tampa Bay* **(Vol. 28, September 26, 2008, No. 40, pp. 1)**
Pub: American City Business Journals, Inc.
Ed: Margie Manning. **Description:** It is believed that the pending $14.9 million purchase of Liberty Bank by USAmeriBank could be at the forefront of a trend. Executives of both companies expect the deal to close by the end of 2008. USAmeriBank will have $430 million in assets and five offices in Pinellas, Florida once the deal is completed.

8737 ■ **"Valener Announces that Gaz Metro has Achieved a Key Step in Acquiring CVPS" in** *CNW Group* **(September 30, 2011)**
Pub: CNW Group
Description: Valener Inc., which owns about 29 percent of Gaz Metro Ltd. Partnership, announced that Gaz Metro welcomes the sale of Central Vermont Public Service Corporation (CVPS). Valener owns an indirect interest of 24.5 percent in the wind power projects jointly developed by Beaupre Eole General Partnership and Boralex Inc. on private lands in Quebec. Details of the deal are included.

8738 ■ **"Valenti: Roots of Financial Crisis Go Back to 1998" in** *Crain's Detroit Business* **(Vol. 24, October 6, 2008, No. 40, pp. 25)**
Pub: Crain Communications, Inc.
Ed: Tom Henderson; Nathan Skid. **Description:** Interview with Sam Valenti III who is the chairman and CEO of Valenti Capital L.L.C., a wealth-management firm; Valenti discusses in detail the history that led up to the current economic crisis as well as his prediction for the future of the country.

8739 ■ **"Virtus.com Wins 'Best of Industry' WebAward for Excellence in Financial Services" in** *Investment Weekly News* **(October 24, 2009)**
Pub: Investment Weekly News
Description: Web Marketing Association honored Virtus.com, the Website of Virtus Investment Part-

ners, Inc., for Outstanding Achievement in Web Development and Acsys Interactive was awarded the Financial Services Standard of Excellence Award for developing the site. The site was part of a rebranding effort and is a one-stop portal for both financial advisors and their investors.

8740 ■ **"Vital Signs: The Big Picture" in** *Canadian Business* **(Vol. 81, Summer 2008, No. 9, pp. 153)**
Pub: Rogers Media Ltd.
Description: Results of the Investor 500 showing percentage of companies with positive returns, most actively traded companies over the past six months and market capitalization by industry are presented. Stock performance and revenues of publicly held corporations in Canada are also provided.

8741 ■ **"Vive La Resistance: Competing Logics and the Consolidation of U.S. Community Banking" in** *Academy of Management Journal* **(August 2007)**
Pub: Academy of Management
Ed: Christopher Marquis, Michael Lounsbury. **Description:** Ways in which competing logics facilitate resistance to institutional change is presented, highlighting on banking professionals' resistance to large, national banks acquisitions of smaller, local banks.

8742 ■ **"Voice: Rebuilding Trust" in** *Business Strategy Review* **(Vol. 21, Summer 2010, No. 2, pp. 79)**
Pub: Wiley-Blackwell
Ed: David De Cremer. **Description:** The financial world's attempts to rebuild trust are charted. Three steps to jump-start that process are outlined.

8743 ■ **"Wachovia Gears Up for Major Arizona Expansion" in** *Business Journal-Serving Phoenix and the Valley of the Sun* **(Vol. 5, Oct. 5, 2007)**
Pub: American City Business Journals, Inc.
Ed: Chris Casacchia. **Description:** Wachovia, America's fourth-largest bank is finalizing a deal to build its Arizona headquarters in downtown Phoenix. The bank plans to add an additional 100 employees by June 2008 and double its financial network to 30 offices in four years. Wachovia will also convert fifteen World Savings Bank branches it acquired in 2006 through Golden West Financial Corporation.

8744 ■ **"Wait for the Call" in** *Canadian Business* **(Vol. 80, April 9, 2007, No. 8, pp. 74)**
Pub: Rogers Media
Ed: Andrew Wahl. **Description:** The effort of chief executive of BCE Inc. Michael Sabia to deal with rumors about the company's private equity deal with Kohlberg Kravis Roberts & Co. is discussed.

8745 ■ **"Wall Street Is No Friend to Radical Innovation" in** *Harvard Business Review* **(Vol. 88, July-August 2010, No. 7-8, pp. 28)**
Pub: Harvard Business School Publishing
Ed: Julia Kirby. **Description:** Research indicates that investors are skittish about backing a business that proposes significant changes to its product or service status quo.

8746 ■ **"W&S to Trim Rich Retirement Plan" in** *Business Courier* **(Vol. 27, October 15, 2010, No. 24, pp. 1)**
Pub: Business Courier
Ed: Dan Monk. **Description:** Insurance firm Western & Southern Financial Group announced that it will reduce the pension benefits of its 4,000 associates by more than 30 percent starting January 1, 2011. The move is expected to reduce annual retirement payments by several thousand dollars per associate. Western is a Fortune 500 company and has $34 billion in total assets.

8747 ■ **"Want People to Save? Force Them" in** *Harvard Business Review* **(Vol. 88, September 2010, No. 9, pp. 36)**
Pub: Harvard Business School Publishing
Ed: Dan Ariely. **Description:** Contrasts in U.S. attitudes towards savings and government regulation with those of Chile, where all employees are required to save 11 percent of their salary in a retirement account, are highlighted.

8748 ■ **"Want Some of This?" in** *Canadian Business* **(Vol. 80, April 9, 2007, No. 8, pp. 71)**
Pub: Rogers Media
Ed: Jeff Sanford. **Description:** The economic impact of growing private equity in Canada is discussed.

8749 ■ **"The Way to the Market's Heart?" in** *Canadian Business* **(Vol. 80, March 26, 2007, No. 7, pp. 74)**
Pub: Rogers Media
Ed: Erin Pooley. **Description:** The financial and stock performance of Canadian biotechnology companies Medicure Inc. and Angiotech Pharmaceuticals Inc. are analyzed.

8750 ■ **"The Wealth Portfolio" in** *Canadian Business* **(Vol. 79, Winter 2006, No. 24, pp. 146)**
Pub: Rogers Media
Ed: Jeff Sanford. **Description:** The trends pertaining to the pricing of shares of public enterprises, at the Montreal stock exchange, are described.

8751 ■ **"Website for Women 50+ Launches" in** *Marketing to Women* **(Vol. 21, April 2008, No. 4, pp. 5)**
Pub: EPM Communications, Inc.
Description: Vibrantnation.com is an online community targeting women over age 50; members can share recommendations on a variety of topics such as vacation spots, retailers and financial issues.

8752 ■ **"A Week of the Worst Kind of Selling" in** *Barron's* **(Vol. 88, June 30, 2008, No. 26, pp. M3)**
Pub: Dow Jones & Co., Inc.
Ed: Kopin Tan. **Description:** In the week that ended on June 27, 2008 the selloff in the U.S. stock market was brought on by mounting bank losses and the spread of economic slowdown on top of high oil prices. The 31 percent decrease in the share price of Ingersoll-Rand since October 2007 may have factored in most of its risks. The company has completed its acquisition of Trane to morph into a refrigeration-equipment company.

8753 ■ **"Welcome to the Neighborhood" in** *Hawaii Business* **(Vol. 53, October 2007, No. 4, pp. 48)**
Pub: Hawaii Business Publishing
Ed: Jolyn Okimoto Rosa. **Description:** Finance Factors is planning to build branches in Manoa, and Liliha, as part of its strategy to position itself in high-yield areas. The company chose Manoa and Liliha due to thee sites' rich deposits. Its strategy with regards to the branches' location and to the building design is discussed.

8754 ■ **"Wells Fargo Will Soon Lead Local Banks in Deposits" in** *Austin Business JournalInc.* **(Vol. 28, December 5, 2008, No. 38, pp. A1)**
Pub: American City Business Journals
Ed: Christopher Calnan. **Description:** Acquisition of Wachovia Corporation by Wells Fargo and Company will leave the latter as the top bank for deposits in Austin, Texas. The merged bank will have deposits of more than $ billion, more than the $3.9 billion deposits Bank of America maintains in the area.

8755 ■ **"Wenzel Downhole Tools Ltd. Announces First Quarter Results for 2007" in** *Canadian Corporate News* **(May 14, 2007)**
Pub: Comtex News Network Inc.
Description: Wenzel Downhole Tools Ltd., a manufacturer, renter, and seller of drilling tools used in gas and oil exploration, announced its financial results for the first quarter ended March 31, 2007 which includes achieved revenues of $14.5 million. Statistical data included.

8756 ■ **"Weyerhaeuser's REIT Decision Shouldn't Scare Investors Away" in** *Barron's* **(Vol. 88, June 30, 2008, No. 26, pp. 18)**
Pub: Dow Jones & Co., Inc.
Ed: Christopher Williams. **Description:** Weyerhaeuser Co.'s management said that a conversion to a real estate investment trust was not likely in 2009 since the move is not tax-efficient as of the moment

and would overload its non-timber assets with debt. The company's shares have fallen by 19.5 percent. However, the company remains an asset-rich outfit and its activist shareholder is pushing for change.

8757 ■ "What Ever Happened to TGIF?" in
Barron's **(Vol. 88, March 10, 2008, No. 10, pp. M3)**
Pub: Dow Jones & Company, Inc.

Ed: Kopin Tan. **Description:** US stock markets fell in early March 2008 to their lowest level in 18 months, venturing close to entering a bear market phase. The S&P 500 has dropped an average of 0.78 percent on Fridays for 2008.

8758 ■ *What Has EX-IM Bank Done for Small Business Lately?: Congressional Hearing*
Pub: DIANE Publishing Company

Ed: Donald A. Manzullo. **Description:** Covers Congressional hearing: Witnesses: Philip Merrill, President and CEO, Export Import Bank of the U.S.; Victoria Hadfield, President, Semiconductor Equipment and Materials International (SEMI), North America; and Michael Vaden, President and CEO, Rutland Plastic Technologies, Inc. Attachments: April 1, 2005, letter to Chairman Philip Merrill from Semiconductor Manufacturing International Corporation (SMIC); Attachment A - Chronology of SMIC Transaction; Attachment B-Appendices; Appendix A: March 21, 2005, letter from EX-IM Chairman Philip Merrill to Congressman Donald A. Manzullo from the State of Illinois; and Appendix B: Congressional letter written on SMIC and equipment suppliers behest. Includes charts and tables.

8759 ■ "What Has Sergey Wrought?" in
Barron's **(Vol. 89, July 13, 2009, No. 28, pp. 8)**
Pub: Dow Jones & Co., Inc.

Ed: Alan Abelson. **Description:** Sergey Aleynikov is a computer expert that once worked for Goldman Sachs but he was arrested after he left the company and charged with theft for bringing with him the code for the company's proprietary software for high-frequency trading. The stock market has been down for four straight weeks as of July 13, 2009 which reflects the reality of how the economy is still struggling.

8760 ■ "What You Should Know If Your Bank Fails" in *Black Enterprise* **(Vol. 41, December 2010, No. 5, pp. 29)**
Pub: Earl G. Graves Publishing Co. Inc.

Ed: John Simons. **Description:** The Federal Deposit Insurance Corporation announced that the number of banks in trouble has reached the highest level since March 1993. Advice from the FDIC is cited. Statistical data included.

8761 ■ "What'll You Have Tonight?" in
Barron's **(Vol. 88, July 4, 2008, No. 28, pp. 22)**
Pub: Dow Jones & Co., Inc.

Ed: Neil A. Martin. **Description:** Shares of Diageo could rise by 30 percent a year from June 2008 after it slipped due to U.S. sales worries. The company also benefits from the trend toward more premium alcoholic beverage brands worldwide especially in emerging markets.

8762 ■ "What's In a Name?" in *Barron's* **(Vol. 88, March 17, 2008, No. 11, pp. 7)**
Pub: Dow Jones & Company, Inc.

Ed: Alan Abelson. **Description:** Eliot Spitzer's resignation incidentally caused the stock market to go up by 400 points. The Federal Reserve Board's new Term Securities Lending Facility provides liquidity to the big lenders by funneling $200 billion in the form of 28-day loans of Treasuries. The analysis of Paul Brodsky and Lee Quaintance of QB Partners on the demand for commodities is also discussed.

8763 ■ "What's In a Relationship? The Case of Commercial Lending" in *Business Horizons* **(Vol. 51, March-April 2008, No. 2, pp. 93)**
Pub: Elsevier Advanced Technology Publications

Description: Academic literature on relationship lending and banking to small and medium enterprises is analyzed. This practice is best suited to some SME

types but creates special challenges for bank managers. Relationship lending may also be better delivered by community banks.

8764 ■ "What's More Important: Stag or Inflation?" in *Barron's* **(Vol. 88, July 14, 2008, No. 28, pp. M8)**
Pub: Dow Jones & Co., Inc.

Ed: Randall W. Forsyth. **Description:** Economists are divided on which part of stagflation, an economic situation in which inflation and economic stagnation occur simultaneously and remain unchecked for a period of time, is more important. Some economists say that the Federal government is focusing on controlling inflation while others see the central bank as extending its liquidity facilities to the financial sector.

8765 ■ "When to Roll Over" in *Black Enterprise* **(Vol. 37, November 2006, No. 4, pp. 50)**
Pub: Earl G. Graves Publishing Co. Inc.

Ed: Carolyn M. Brown. **Description:** Being proactive and rolling over your funds if you own stock of your former employee will give you more control over your money, especially if the company merges or is sold.

8766 ■ "Where Are the Vultures?" in *Mergers & Acquisitions: The Dealmaker's Journal* **(March 1, 2008)**
Pub: SourceMedia, Inc.

Ed: Ken MacFadyen. **Description:** Although the real estate market is distressed, not many acquisitions are being made by distress private equity investors; this is due, in part, to the difficulty in assessing real estate industry firms since it is a sector which is so localized.

8767 ■ "Where the Money Is" in *Conde Nast Portfolio* **(Vol. 2, June 2008, No. 6, pp. 113)**
Pub: Conde Nast Publications, Inc.

Description: Revenue generated from treatments for common brain disorders that are currently on the market are listed.

8768 ■ "Where Next?" in *Business Strategy Review* **(Vol. 21, Summer 2010, No. 2, pp. 20)**
Pub: Blackwell Publishers Ltd.

Description: The emergence of large, vibrant and seemingly unstoppable new markets has been the good news story for the past decade. Brazil, Russia, India and China (BRIC) are among those emerging into the economic light. Amid the turbulence and rapid growth, new and various markets will continue to emerge. For investors and business leaders, the critical question is simple: where next?

8769 ■ "Where Oil-Rich Nations Are Placing Their Bets" in *Harvard Business Review* **(Vol. 86, September 2008, No. 9, pp. 119)**
Pub: Harvard Business School Press

Ed: Rawi Abdelal; Ayesha Khan; Tarun Khanna. **Description:** Investment strategies of the Gulf Cooperation Council nations are examined in addition to how these have impacted the global economy and capitalism.

8770 ■ "Where to Stash Your Cash" in *Barron's* **(Vol. 88, March 17, 2008, No. 11, pp. 41)**
Pub: Dow Jones & Company, Inc.

Ed: Mike Hogan. **Description:** Investors are putting their money in money-market mutual funds seeking fractionally better yields and a safe haven from the uncertainties that was brought about by subprime lending. These funds, however, are hovering near 3.20 percent which is less than the 4 percent inflation rate.

8771 ■ "Where To Look for Income" in *Women In Business* **(Vol. 63, Summer 2011, No. 2, pp. 50)**
Pub: American Business Women's Association

Ed: William J. Lynott. **Description:** Advice on ways to invest in the US market are presented, with information on Certificates of Deposit and Money Markets included.

8772 ■ "Whiplashed? That's a Bullish Sign" in *Barron's* **(Vol. 88, March 31, 2008, No. 13, pp. 34)**
Pub: Dow Jones & Company, Inc.

Ed: Richard W. Arms. **Description:** Huge volatility often occurs just ahead of a substantial rally, according to an analysis of the volatility in the Dow Jones Index since 2000. The Average Percentage Change based on a 10-day moving average of volatility is a way to measure the level of fear in the market and reveals when buying or selling have been overdone.

8773 ■ "Whistling Past the Graveyard?" in *Barron's* **(Vol. 88, March 17, 2008, No. 11, pp. 15)**
Pub: Dow Jones & Company, Inc.

Ed: Michael Santoli. **Description:** Discusses the Federal Reserve's move to provide $200 billion to the system which can be seen as an effort to avoid the liquidity problems that Bear Stearns suffered. The Federal Reserve's move seems to frighten investors rather than reassure them.

8774 ■ "Who Gets the Last Laugh?" in *Barron's* **(Vol. 88, March 31, 2008, No. 13, pp. 17)**
Pub: Dow Jones & Company, Inc.

Ed: Leslie P. Norton. **Description:** Nord/LB will take a charge of 82.5 million euros to cover potential losses apparently related to Vatas' refusal to take the shares of Remote MDx Inc. after buying the shares. Remote MDx's main product is an ankle bracelet to monitor criminals; the firm has lost over half of its market cap due to the Nord/LB troubles and questions about its revenues.

8775 ■ "Why Intel Should Dump Its Flash-Memory Business" in *Barron's* **(Vol. 88, March 10, 2008, No. 10, pp. 35)**
Pub: Dow Jones & Company, Inc.

Ed: Eric J. Savitz. **Description:** Intel Corp. must sell its NAND flash-memory business as soon as it possibly can to the highest bidder to focus on its PC processor business and take advantage of other business opportunities. Apple should consider a buyback of 10 percent of the company's shares to lift its stock.

8776 ■ "Why It Pays to be in the Boardroom" in *Globe & Mail* **(January 16, 2006, pp. B1)**
Pub: CTVglobemedia Publishing Inc.

Ed: Janet McFarland. **Description:** The reasons behind higher stock compensation for board directors, in Canada, are presented. The survey is conducted by Patrick O'Callaghan & Associates and Korn/Ferry International.

8777 ■ "Why the Rally Should Keep Rolling...for Now" in *Barron's* **(Vol. 89, July 27, 2009, No. 30, pp. M3)**
Pub: Dow Jones & Co., Inc.

Ed: Kopin Tan. **Description:** Stocks rallied for the second straight week as of July 24, 2009 and more companies reported better than expected earnings but the caveat is that companies are beating estimates chiefly by slashing expenses and firing workers. The regulatory risks faced by CME Group and the IntercontinentalExchange are discussed as well as the shares of KKR Private Equity Investors LP.

8778 ■ "Why the Rout in Financials Isn't Over" in *Barron's* **(Vol. 88, June 30, 2008, No. 26, pp. 23)**
Pub: Dow Jones & Co., Inc.

Ed: Robin Goldwyn Blumenthal. **Description:** Top market technician Louise Yamada warns that the retreat in the shares of financial services is not yet over based on her analysis of stock charts. Yamada's analysis of the charts of Citigroup, Fifth Third Bancorp and Merrill Lynch are discussed together with the graphs for these shares. Statistical data included.

8779 ■ "Why WestJet's Culture Guru Chooses to Fly Under the Radar" in *Globe & Mail* **(January 22, 2007, pp. B1)**
Pub: CTVglobemedia Publishing Inc.

Ed: Brent Jang. **Description:** The views of co-founder Donald Bell of WestJet Airlines Ltd. on company's shares and services are presented.

8780 ■ "Wielding a Big Ax" in *Barron's* (Vol. 89, July 13, 2009, No. 28, pp. 26)

Pub: Dow Jones & Co., Inc.

Ed: Shirley A. Lazo. **Description:** Weyerhaeuser cut their quarterly common payout by 80 percent from 25 cents to a nickel a share which they say will help them preserve their long-term value and improve their performance. Paccar also cut their quarterly dividend by half to nine cents a share. Walgreen however, boosted their quarterly dividend by 22.2 percent to 13.75 cents a share.

8781 ■ "Will the Force Be With Salesforce?" in *Barron's* (Vol. 88, March 24, 2008, No. 12, pp. 20)

Pub: Dow Jones & Company, Inc.

Ed: Mark Veverka. **Description:** Shares of Salesforce.com are likely to drop from the $44.83-a-share level in the face of a deteriorating economy and financial sector and thus lower demand for business software. The company is unlikely to deliver on its ambitious earnings forecasts for 2008 especially with strengthening competition from Oracle.

8782 ■ "Wind Point Partners Closes Southfield HQ" in *Crain's Detroit Business* (Vol. 26, January 18, 2010, No. 3, pp. 18)

Pub: Crain Communications, Inc.

Ed: Tom Henderson. **Description:** Wind Point Partners, a private-equity firm that expanded its headquarters to Southfield in 1997, has closed down its Michigan operations opting to move its headquarters back to Illinois.

8783 ■ "With Mine Approval, Crystallex's Value as Target Seen on Rise" in *Globe & Mail* (March 28, 2006, pp. B3)

Pub: CTVglobemedia Publishing Inc.

Ed: Wendy Stueck. **Description:** Crystallex International Corp. obtains Venezuelan Ministry of Basic Industry and Mining's authorization on Las Cristinas mining project. The impact of the approval, which posted rise in shares by 21 percent for the company, is discussed.

8784 ■ "Wobbling Economy" in *The Business Journal-Serving Metropolitan Kansas City* (Vol. 27, September 26, 2008, No. 2, pp. 1)

Pub: American City Business Journals, Inc.

Ed: Rob Roberts. **Description:** Real estate developers in Kansas City Metropolitan Area are worried of the possible impacts of the crisis at Wall Street. They expect tightening of the credit market, which will result in difficulty of financing their projects. The potential effects of the Wall Street crisis are examined further.

8785 ■ "Woes Portend Consumer Shift" in *The Business Journal-Serving Metropolitan Kansas City* (Vol. 27, September 26, 2008, No. 2, pp. 1)

Pub: American City Business Journals, Inc.

Ed: Suzanna Stagemeyer. **Description:** Black Bamboo owner Tim Butt believes that prolonged tightening of the credit market will result in consumer spending becoming more cash-driven that credit card driven. The financial crisis has already constricted spending among consumers. Forecasts for the US economy are provided.

8786 ■ "A World of Opportunity: Foreign Markets Offer Diversity to Keen Investors" in *Canadian Business* (Vol. 81, Summer 2008, No. 9)

Pub: Rogers Media Ltd.

Ed: Andrew Wahl. **Description:** International Monetary Fund projected in its 'World Economy Outlook' that there is a 25 percent chance that a global recession will occur in 2008 and 2009. Global growth rate is forecasted at 3.7 percent in 2008. Inflation in Asia emerging markets and forecasts on stock price indexes are presented.

8787 ■ "World's Best CEOs" in *Barron's* (Vol. 88, March 24, 2008, No. 12, pp. 33)

Pub: Dow Jones & Company, Inc.

Ed: Andrew Bary. **Description:** Listing of the 30 best chief executive officers worldwide which was compiled through interviews with investors and analysts, analysis of financial and stock market performance, and leadership and industry stature.

8788 ■ "The Worst Lies Ahead for Wall Street; More Losses Certain" in *Crain's New York Business* (Vol. 24, January 21, 2008, No. 3, pp. 1)

Pub: Crain Communications, Inc.

Ed: Aaron Elstein. **Description:** Due to the weakening economy, many financial institutions will face further massive losses forcing them to borrow more at higher interest rates and dragging down their earnings for years to come. The effects on commercial real estate and credit card loans are also discussed as well as the trend to investing in Asia and the Middle East.

8789 ■ "Xstrata's Takeover Bid Comes Up Short in Shareholder's Eyes" in *Globe & Mail* (March 27, 2007, pp. B16)

Pub: CTVglobemedia Publishing Inc.

Ed: Andy Hoffman. **Description:** The share holders of LionOre Mining International have expressed dissatisfaction over $4.6 billion take over by Xstrata PLC. Share holders are demanding more prices for share value.

8790 ■ "Yahoo! - Microsoft Pact: Alive Again?" in *Barron's* (Vol. 89, July 27, 2009, No. 30, pp. 8)

Pub: Dow Jones & Co., Inc.

Ed: Mark Veverka. **Description:** Yahoo! reported higher than expected earnings in the second quarter of 2009 under CEO Carol Bartz who has yet to articulate her long-term vision and strategy for turning around the company. The media reported that Yahoo! and Microsoft are discussing an advertising-search partnership which should benefit both companies.

8791 ■ "YoCream" in *Ice Cream Reporter* (Vol. 23, September 20, 2010, No. 10, pp. 6)

Pub: Ice Cream Reporter

Description: YoCream reported a sales increase for third quarter 2010 at 15.6 percent and net income increasing 25 percent to $2,141,000 for that quarter.

8792 ■ "You Won't Go Broke Filling Up On These Stocks" in *Barron's* (Vol. 88, July 14, 2008, No. 28, pp. 38)

Pub: Dow Jones & Co., Inc.

Ed: Assif Shameen. **Description:** Due to high economic growth, pro-business policies and a consumption boom, the Middle East is a good place to look for equities. The best ways in which to gain exposure to this market include investing in the real estate industry and telecommunications markets as well as large banks that serve corporations and consumers.

8793 ■ "Young People Speak Out On Credit Union Board Involvement" in *Credit Union Times* (Vol. 21, July 14, 2010, No. 27, pp. 20)

Pub: Summit Business Media

Ed: Myriam Di Giovanni. **Description:** Results of a Credit Union Times survey of Generation Y individuals about serving on Credit Union boards across the country are examined.

8794 ■ "Your 2010 Windfall" in *Small Business Opportunities* (July 2010)

Pub: Harris Publications Inc.

Description: Make this a year of fiscal health and wealth. A survey says most will strive to save this year.

8795 ■ "Your Exposure to Bear Stearns" in *Barron's* (Vol. 88, March 17, 2008, No. 11, pp. 45)

Pub: Dow Jones & Company, Inc.

Ed: Tom Sullivan; Jack Willoughby. **Description:** Bear Stearns makes up 5.5 percent of Pioneer Independence's portfolio, 1.4 percent of Vanguard Windsor II's portfolio, 1.2 percent of Legg Mason Value Trust, about 1 percent of Van Kampen Equity & Income, and 0.79 percent of Putnam Fund for Growth & Income. Ginnie Mae securities are now trading at 1.78 percentage points over treasuries due to the mortgage crises.

8796 ■ *Your Guide to Arranging Bank and Debt Financing for Your Own Business in Canada*

Pub: Productive Publications

Ed: Iain Williamson. **Released:** December 31, 2000. **Description:** Bank financing for small businesses in Canada is discussed.

8797 ■ "Zell Takes a Gamble on Tribune" in *Globe & Mail* (April 3, 2007, pp. B1)

Pub: CTVglobemedia Publishing Inc.

Ed: Sinclair Stewart. **Description:** The purchase of the majority share in Tribune Co. by Samuel Zell is described. Samuel Zell's plans to keep the company's assets intact are discussed.

8798 ■ "Zucker Closes Deal on HBC With Sweeter Takeover Offer" in *Globe & Mail* (January 27, 2006, pp. B1)

Pub: CTVglobemedia Publishing Inc.

Ed: Marina Strauss; Sinclair Stewart; Jacquie McNish. **Description:** Jerry Zucker, vice-president of InterTech Group Inc., has finalized a deal to buy retail store Hudson Bay Co, for 1.1 billion dollars. The shares will be purchased at a rate of 15.25 dollars per share in an all cash transaction. Complete details of the buyout are discussed.

TRADE PERIODICALS

8799 ■ *Bacard's Global Investor*

Pub: Ferney Scribes Inc.

Ed: Andre Bacard, Editor. **Released:** Monthly. **Price:** $129, U.S.. **Description:** Provides monthly updates of select no-load global and international funds, model portfolios, foreign market graphs, monthly analysis and current recommendations. Recurring features include news of research and a column titled Mutual Fund in the Spotlight.

8800 ■ *Banking & Financial Services Policy Report*

Pub: Aspen Publishers

Contact: Shulte Roth

Released: 12/yr. **Price:** $689 with free standard shipping on U.S prepaid orders. **Description:** Journal covering topics related to the converging banking and financial services industries.

8801 ■ *Deposit Growth Strategies*

Pub: Siefer Consultants Inc.

Ed: Joe Sheller, Editor. **Released:** Monthly. **Price:** $329, U.S.; $259 charter rate. **Description:** Cover methods to increase deposits at financial institutions, as well as marketing strategies for deposit growth. Both personal accounts and commercial accounts are covered.

8802 ■ *Fidelity Investor*

Pub: FundWorks, Inc.

Contact: Karen Frost, Assistant Editor

Ed: James H. Lowell, III, Editor. **Released:** Monthly. **Price:** $199. **Description:** Contains investment advice covering Fidelity mutual funds. Recurring features include interviews, model portfolios, performance reviews, and best buys.

8803 ■ *Financial and Estate Planning*

Pub: CCH Inc.

Released: Monthly. **Price:** $1,479 CD-ROM; $1,465 print. **Description:** Monthly plus the monthly Estate Planning Review; financial planning to build and preserve wealth; forms and planning aids; will and trust forms and clauses; investment plans; insurance and annuity forms; tax planning and administration for estates and trusts; in-depth articles offering new planning ideas; analysis of court decisions; new rulings and legislative developments; year begins first of any month.

8804 ■ *Financial Services Review*

Pub: Cadmus Journal Services

Contact: Vickie Bajtelsmit, Editorial Board Member

Released: Quarterly. **Description:** Journal that covers personal finance.

8805 ■ Global Custodian
Pub: Asset International Inc.
Contact: Giles Turner, News Ed.
E-mail: gturner@globalcustodian.com
Released: 5/yr. **Price:** $440 online only; $560 print and online; $390 print only. **Description:** Business journal for global investment and operations professionals.

8806 ■ International Tax and Public Finance
Pub: Springer Netherlands
Contact: John D. Wilson, Editor-in-Chief
Released: Bimonthly. **Price:** $1,013 institutions print or online; $1,215.60 institutions print & enchanced access. **Description:** Journal covering tax and public finance worldwide.

8807 ■ Journal of Entrepreneurial and Small Firm Finance
Pub: University of California Press
Released: 3/yr. **Description:** Journal that focuses on small business and financial issues.

8808 ■ Journal of Financial Planning
Pub: Financial Planning Association
Ed: Marv Tuttle, Editor, marv.tuttle@fpanet.org. **Released:** 12/year. **Price:** Included in membership; $119, nonmembers; $144, Canada; $154, elsewhere. **Description:** Provides coverage of industry events and developments as well as happenings within the association. Carries articles on regulatory, ethical, and public relations aspects of the industry. Recurring features include letters to the editor, news of members, a calendar of events, feature articles, and original contributions.

8809 ■ Journal of IT Financial Management
Pub: IT Financial Management Association
Released: Triennial. **Description:** Journal covering financial management of information technology organizations.

8810 ■ NACOMEX Insider
Pub: NACOMEX USA Inc.
Contact: Robert Zises
Ed: Robert Zises, Editor, zises@nacomex.com. **Released:** Quarterly. **Price:** $199, U.S.. **Description:** Provides information on historical values, current tactics, and residual value forecasting for ad valorem tax, bankruptcy, loss compensation, and related purposes. Recurring features include news of research and a column titled Industry Round-up.

8811 ■ National Financing Law Digest
Pub: Strafford Publications Inc.
Ed: Jennifer Vaughan, Editor. **Released:** Monthly. **Price:** $687. **Description:** Digest offers complete coverage of workouts, bankruptcy, lender's liability, and the growing number of court decisions related to the changing economic climate. Reports on state and federal cases of national significance.

8812 ■ The Neatest Little FundLetter
Pub: Jason Kelly
Ed: Jason Kelly, Editor. **Released:** Monthly. **Price:** $75, U.S.; $100, elsewhere. **Description:** Aims to help readers use the various tools to create and manage their own mutual fund portfolio better than professional managers. Also includes how-to articles and model portfolios. Columns titled Kelly's Quicklist, FundFolio, and FundFilter.

8813 ■ Plan Sponsor
Pub: Asset International Inc.
Contact: Robert Jones, Publisher
Released: Monthly. **Price:** $229; $259 Canada; $390 other countries. **Description:** Trade magazine for pension fund and endowment executives.

8814 ■ Quarterly Journal of Business & Economics
Pub: University of Nebraska
Contact: Margo Young, Managing Editor
E-mail: myoung1@unl.edu
Ed: Gordon V. Karels, Editor. **Released:** Quarterly. **Price:** $24; $45 institutions; $37 out of country; $55 institutions, other countries. **Description:** Journal reporting on finance and economics.

VIDEOCASSETTES/ AUDIOCASSETTES

8815 ■ Ask for the Order. . .and Get It!
Dartnell Corp.
2222 Sedwick Drive, Ste. 101
Durham, NC 27713
Free: 800-233-8720
Fax:800-508-2592
Co. E-mail: customerservice@dartnellcorp.com
URL: http://www.dartnellcorp.com
Released: 1972. **Description:** Hammers home a key principle of salesmanship—to get an order you must ask for it; from the "Tough-Minded Salesmanship" series. **Availability:** VHS; 3/4U; Special order formats.

8816 ■ Basics of Successful Investing
Tapeworm Video Distributors
25876 The Old Road 141
Stevenson Ranch, CA 91381
Ph:(661)257-4904
Fax:(661)257-4820
Co. E-mail: sales@tapeworm.com
URL: http://www.tapeworm.com
Price: $29.95. **Description:** Guides viewers through the basics of money management and financial planning. **Availability:** VHS.

8817 ■ The Charles J. Givens Financial Library
Nightingale-Conant Corp.
6245 W. Howard St.
Niles, IL 60714
Ph:(847)647-0300
Free: 800-560-6081
URL: http://www.nightingale.com
Released: 1990. **Price:** $399.00. **Description:** Givens shares advice on practical ways to manage money and build wealth. Comes with six 90-minute audio cassettes and a reference manual. **Availability:** VHS.

8818 ■ The Cold Call
Video Arts, Inc.
c/o Aim Learning Group
8238-40 Lehigh
Morton Grove, IL 60053-2615
Free: 877-444-2230
Fax:(416)252-2155
Co. E-mail: service@aimlearninggroup.com
URL: http://www.aimlearninggroup.com
Released: 1976. **Price:** $695.00. **Description:** This program demonstrates the specific skills and disciplines of telephone selling, and the dangers of ignoring them. **Availability:** VHS; 8mm; 3/4U; Special order formats.

8819 ■ The Competitive Edge
Film Library/National Safety Council California Chapter
4553 Glencoe Ave., Ste. 150
Marina Del Rey, CA 90292
Ph:(310)827-9781
Free: 800-421-9585
Fax:(310)827-9861
Co. E-mail: California@nsc.org
URL: http://www.nsc.org/nsc_near_you/FindYourLocalChapter/Pages/California.aspx
Released: 1989. **Description:** This program emphasizes finding out your customer's most immediate concern, and selling to that concern. **Availability:** VHS; 3/4U.

8820 ■ Corporate Financial Management: Emerging Trends and Recent Developments
Bisk Education
9417 Princess Palm Ave.
Tampa, FL 33619
Free: 800-874-7877
Co. E-mail: info@bisk.com
URL: http://www.bisk.com
Price: $179.00. **Description:** Discusses financial management techniques and recent developments in corporate finance. Furnishes information on Activity-Based Cost Management (ABC), Total Quality Man-

agement (TQM), and Internal Controls and Management Accounting. Includes workbook and quizzer. **Availability:** VHS.

8821 ■ Financial Management Workshops
Bullfrog Films, Inc.
PO Box 149
Oley, PA 19547
Ph:(610)779-8226
Free: 800-543-3764
Fax:(610)370-1978
Co. E-mail: video@bullfrogfilms.com
URL: http://bullfrogfilms.com
Released: 1985. **Description:** This complete personal financial instructional program is available on separate tapes or as a package. **Availability:** VHS; 3/4U.

8822 ■ Financial Planning and Management
RMI Media
1365 N. Winchester St.
Olathe, KS 66061-5880
Ph:(913)768-1696
Free: 800-745-5480
Fax:800-755-6910
Co. E-mail: actmedia@act.org
URL: http://www.actmedia.com
Released: 1978. **Description:** A series of programs which offer ideas on cost cutting and controlling the family budget. Programs are available individually. **Availability:** VHS; 3/4U.

8823 ■ Good Money Management
Cambridge Educational
c/o Films Media Group
132 West 31st Street, 17th Floor
Ste. 124
New York, NY 10001
Free: 800-257-5126
Fax:(609)671-0266
Co. E-mail: custserve@films.com
URL: http://www.cambridgeol.com
Released: 1986. **Description:** This tape demonstrates how to personally manage and properly distribute your income. **Availability:** VHS.

8824 ■ A Happy Beginning
Resources for Education & Management, Inc.
1804 Montreal Ct., Ste. A
Tucker, GA 30084
Released: 1971. **Description:** An examination of closing the sale, asking for the order, and answering the customer's objections. How to become a confident sale closer. **Availability:** VHS; 3/4U.

8825 ■ How to Close the Sale
Dartnell Corp.
2222 Sedwick Drive, Ste. 101
Durham, NC 27713
Free: 800-233-8720
Fax:800-508-2592
Co. E-mail: customerservice@dartnellcorp.com
URL: http://www.dartnellcorp.com
Released: 1981. **Description:** This program shows salespeople how to ask for the order, and how to get it. **Availability:** VHS; 3/4U; Special order formats.

8826 ■ How to Manage Your Money
RMI Media
1365 N. Winchester St.
Olathe, KS 66061-5880
Ph:(913)768-1696
Free: 800-745-5480
Fax:800-755-6910
Co. E-mail: actmedia@act.org
URL: http://www.actmedia.com
Released: 1981. **Description:** A panel of certified public accountants show how the viewer can beat inflation, create a flexible budget, how to improve financial stability, and how to add to one's buying power. **Availability:** VHS; EJ; 3/4U.

8827 ■ How to Take the Butt Out of a Sales Rebuttal
Dartnell Corp.
2222 Sedwick Drive, Ste. 101
Durham, NC 27713
Free: 800-233-8720

Fax:800-508-2592
Co. E-mail: customerservice@dartnellcorp.com
URL: http://www.dartnellcorp.com
Released: 1967. **Description:** A look at how to cope with the difficult problem of rebutting a customer's objection-without being objectionable. **Availability:** VHS; 3/4U; Special order formats.

8828 ■ *Investing for Women by Women*
Tapeworm Video Distributors
25876 The Old Road 141
Stevenson Ranch, CA 91381
Ph:(661)257-4904
Fax:(661)257-4820
Co. E-mail: sales@tapeworm.com
URL: http://www.tapeworm.com
Released: 1996. **Price:** $34.95. **Description:** Discusses stock market investing and retirement planning options for women. **Availability:** VHS.

8829 ■ *Knowing the Prospect*
Resources for Education & Management, Inc.
1804 Montreal Ct., Ste. A
Tucker, GA 30084
Released: 1971. **Description:** Shows the relationship of product or service benefits to the sales prospect's personal goals, and illustrates the value of knowing a prospect's needs. Ignores the fast-talking sales pitch. **Availability:** VHS; 3/4U.

8830 ■ *Making It Live*
Resources for Education & Management, Inc.
1804 Montreal Ct., Ste. A
Tucker, GA 30084
Released: 1971. **Description:** This tape demonstrates a key to sales success-knowing your product or service and telling your story with enthusiasm and conviction. **Availability:** VHS; 3/4U.

8831 ■ *The Making of a Salesman*
Exec-U-Service Associates
4326 US Highway 1
Princeton, NJ 08540
Released: 1984. **Description:** Provides basic material to enhance a sales training program. All programs are available individually. **Availability:** VHS; 3/4U; Special order formats.

8832 ■ *Managing Your Personal Finances*
RMI Media
1365 N. Winchester St.
Olathe, KS 66061-5880
Ph:(913)768-1696
Free: 800-745-5480
Fax:800-755-6910
Co. E-mail: actmedia@act.org
URL: http://www.actmedia.com
Released: 1989. **Price:** $89.00. **Description:** The ability to handle personal expenses and finance accounts is a must for any adult in today's society. **Availability:** VHS; 3/4U.

8833 ■ *More Awkward Customers*
Video Arts, Inc.
c/o Aim Learning Group
8238-40 Lehigh
Morton Grove, IL 60053-2615
Free: 877-444-2230
Fax:(416)252-2155
Co. E-mail: service@aimlearninggroup.com
URL: http://www.aimlearninggroup.com
Released: 1973. **Description:** This program shows the importance of knowing your stock and services so that you can deal professionally with awkward customers. **Availability:** 3/4U.

8834 ■ *Networking for Your Personal & Financial Growth*
Chesney Communications
2302 Martin St., Ste. 125
Irvine, CA 92612
Ph:(949)263-5500
Free: 800-223-8878

Fax:(949)263-5506
Co. E-mail: videocc@aol.com
URL: http://www.videocc.com
Released: 1989. **Price:** $49.95. **Description:** Anne Boe talks about the importance of networking to financial success, and points out that 80 percent of all millionaires are networkers. **Availability:** VHS; 3/4U.

8835 ■ *Overcoming Objections*
Film Library/National Safety Council California Chapter
4553 Glencoe Ave., Ste. 150
Marina Del Rey, CA 90292
Ph:(310)827-9781
Free: 800-421-9585
Fax:(310)827-9861
Co. E-mail: California@nsc.org
URL: http://www.nsc.org/nsc_near_you/FindYourLocalChapter/Pages/California.aspx
Released: 198?. **Description:** This film emphasizes the importance of understanding the customer's point of view. **Availability:** VHS; 3/4U.

8836 ■ *The Perfect Sale*
Skillsoft
107 Northeastern Blvd.
Nashua, NH 03062
Free: 877-545-5763
Co. E-mail: info@netg.com
URL: http://www.skillsoft.com/
Released: 1984. **Description:** This program emphasizes the art of selling from approach to close. **Availability:** VHS; 3/4U.

8837 ■ *Prescription for Complaints*
Video Arts, Inc.
c/o Aim Learning Group
8238-40 Lehigh
Morton Grove, IL 60053-2615
Free: 877-444-2230
Fax:(416)252-2155
Co. E-mail: service@aimlearninggroup.com
URL: http://www.aimlearninggroup.com
Released: 1975. **Price:** $695.00. **Description:** This program shows a six-step, objective method for dealing with customer complaints. **Availability:** VHS; 8mm; 3/4U; Special order formats.

8838 ■ *Presenting the Story*
Resources for Education & Management, Inc.
1804 Montreal Ct., Ste. A
Tucker, GA 30084
Released: 1971. **Description:** How a salesman can best communicate benefits to a customer. Emphasis is on preparation of the story and practice. **Availability:** VHS; 3/4U.

8839 ■ *The Road to Wise Money Management: Planning, Credit, and Your First Paycheck*
Cambridge Educational
c/o Films Media Group
132 West 31st Street, 17th Floor
Ste. 124
New York, NY 10001
Free: 800-257-5126
Fax:(609)671-0266
Co. E-mail: custserve@films.com
URL: http://www.cambridgeol.com
Released: 1989. **Price:** $79.00. **Description:** A comprehensive guide to managing personal finances, including checkbook maintenance, credit, savings, short- and long-term goals, and details of a paycheck. Includes a study guide. **Availability:** VHS.

8840 ■ *Self-Motivation in Selling*
Learning Communications LLC
5520 Trabuco Rd.
Irvine, CA 92620
Free: 800-622-3610
Fax:(949)727-4323
Co. E-mail: sales@learncom.com
URL: http://www.learncomhr.com
Released: 1979. **Description:** A look at how to avoid sales slumps and maintain peak performances. Four untitled programs cover frustrations and turndowns,

seeking feedback, how to keep personal problems from affecting performance, and how sales managers can keep their people motivated. **Availability:** VHS; 3/4U.

8841 ■ *So You Want to Be a Success at Selling?*
Video Arts, Inc.
c/o Aim Learning Group
8238-40 Lehigh
Morton Grove, IL 60053-2615
Free: 877-444-2230
Fax:(416)252-2155
Co. E-mail: service@aimlearninggroup.com
URL: http://www.aimlearninggroup.com
Released: 1982. **Price:** $790.00. **Description:** Four videos that describe the fundamental skills of selling, from the initial research to the close. Part 1 focuses on the preparation, including client research and product knowledge. Part 2 looks at the skills and techniques of sales presentation. Part 3 shows how to deal with problem clients. Part 4 demonstrates the tactics for successfully closing a sale. Also available as a complete seminar kit. **Availability:** VHS; 8mm; 3/4U; Special order formats.

8842 ■ *U.S. News & World Report: Building Your Fortune*
Anchor Bay Entertainment
1699 Stutz Dr.
Troy, MI 48084
Ph:(248)816-0909
Free: 800-786-8777
Fax:(248)816-3335
URL: http://www.anchorbayentertainment.com
Released: 1990. **Price:** $14.95. **Description:** Guidance and information on securing your future via financial planning and tax strategies. **Availability:** VHS.

8843 ■ *When You're Turned Down—Turn On!*
Dartnell Corp.
2222 Sedwick Drive, Ste. 101
Durham, NC 27713
Free: 800-233-8720
Fax:800-508-2592
Co. E-mail: customerservice@dartnellcorp.com
URL: http://www.dartnellcorp.com
Released: 1977. **Description:** Examines the question: When is a turndown a true rejection and when is it just a disguised objection?; from the "Tough—Minded Salesmanship" series. **Availability:** VHS; 3/4U; Special order formats.

TRADE SHOWS AND CONVENTIONS

8844 ■ *ABA/BMA National Conference for Community Bankers*
American Bankers Association
1120 Connecticut Ave. NW
Washington, DC 20036
Free: 800-BAN-KERS
Co. E-mail: custserv@aba.com
URL: http://www.aba.com
Released: Annual. **Audience:** Chairmen and presidents, mainly of banks with less than $500 million in assets, community bank CEOs, bank directors, and other community bank executives. **Principal Exhibits:** Products and services related to investment management, customer service improvements, advertising, asset/liability management, bank management, electronic data interchange, employee recruitment/training, insurance, strategic planning models, including preparation for the 21st century, new revenue sources, cost control techniques, mainframe computers, market research, MCIF technology, minicomputers in community banking applications, software: platform, optical disk, and loan pricing, sweep accounts, and relationship banking for community bankers. **Dates and Locations:** 2011 Feb 20-23, San Diego, CA.

8845 ■ *ABA Sales Management Workshop*
American Bankers Association
1120 Connecticut Ave. NW
Washington, DC 20036

Free: 800-BAN-KERS
Co. E-mail: custserv@aba.com
URL: http://www.aba.com
Released: Annual. **Audience:** Senior community bank executives, marketing directors, mid-level bank retail managers, sales managers. **Principal Exhibits:** Services related to creating and maintaining customers.

8846 ■ BMA Annual Marketing Forum
American Bankers Association
1120 Connecticut Ave. NW
Washington, DC 20036
Free: 800-BAN-KERS
Co. E-mail: custserv@aba.com
URL: http://www.aba.com
Released: Annual. **Audience:** Bankers including community bank CEO's, marketing directors, sales managers, advertising directors, public relations managers. **Principal Exhibits:** Financial services marketing offering banking solutions in advertising services, bank equipment/systems, computer software, database marketing, direct marketing/sales, incentive/premium programs, insurance services, investment services, marketing consulting, merchandising, publishing, research, retail delivery, sales training, service quality, signage, and telemarketing.

8847 ■ BMA Private Wealth Sales Management Workshop, an ABA Program
American Bankers Association
1120 Connecticut Ave. NW
Washington, DC 20036
Free: 800-BAN-KERS
Co. E-mail: custserv@aba.com
URL: http://www.aba.com
Released: Annual. **Audience:** Trust, private banking and asset management officers, bank brokerage managers, sales managers, business development managers, and regional department managers. **Principal Exhibits:** Provides marketing education and information, professional growth and networking resources to marketing professionals in the financial services industry. **Dates and Locations:** 2011 Mar 06-08, Miami, FL.

8848 ■ The Bond Market Association - Fixed Income Summit Expo on E-Commerce & Technology
Flagg Management, Inc.
353 Lexington Ave.
New York, NY 10016
Ph:(212)286-0333
Fax:(212)286-0086
Co. E-mail: flaggmgmt@msn.com
URL: http://www.flaggmgmt.com
Released: Annual. **Audience:** Bond Market Association members, government bond officers, fixed income brokers and dealers. **Principal Exhibits:** Online services, Internet systems, fixed-income trading and executions systems, real-time systems, Internet and other new products and solutions; online trading and execution systems; bond market services; online research and global markets information.

8849 ■ Financial Managers Society Annual Conference
Financial Managers Society
100 W. Monroe St., Ste. 810
Chicago, IL 60603-1959
Ph:(312)578-1300
Free: 800-ASK-4FMS
Fax:(312)578-1308
URL: http://www.fmsinc.org
Released: Annual. **Audience:** CEOs, CFOs, treasurers, controllers, investment officers, internal auditors of banks, thrift and credit unions. **Principal Exhibits:** Companies offering products/services to CEOs, CFOs, treasurers, controllers, investment officers, and internal auditors of banks, thrifts, and credit unions.

8850 ■ Futures and Options Expo
Futures Industry Association
2001 Pennsylvania Ave. NW, Ste. 600
Washington, DC 20006
Ph:(202)466-5460

Fax:(202)296-3184
Co. E-mail: msaunders@futuresindustry.org
URL: http://www.futuresindustry.org
Released: Annual. **Audience:** Futures commission merchants, futures exchanges, clearing houses, brokers, commodity trading advisors, banks, and money managers. **Principal Exhibits:** Equipment, supplies, and services for the futures, options and derivatives industries.

8851 ■ National Agricultural Bankers Conference
American Bankers Association
1120 Connecticut Ave. NW
Washington, DC 20036
Free: 800-BAN-KERS
Co. E-mail: custserv@aba.com
URL: http://www.aba.com
Released: Annual. **Audience:** Bank CEOs, mainly from community banks in rural areas, executive vice presidents, senior vice presidents, economists, analysts. **Principal Exhibits:** The latest developments in the agricultural lending business, as well as strategies for better market share, profitability and customer service.

CONSULTANTS

8852 ■ Alan Biller and Associates
535 Middlefield Rd., Ste. 230
Menlo Park, CA 94025
Ph:(650)328-7283
Fax:(650)323-4417
Co. E-mail: support@adbiller.com
URL: http://www.adbiller.com
Contact: Michael Ashman, Principle
E-mail: adbiller@adbiller.com
Scope: Offers services from investment advising to pension planning, especially Taft Hartley Planning. Serves as expert witness in cases related to Investments and Fiduciary Standards. **Publications:** "Fourteen Things to Expect From Your Investment Consultant"; "First Principles of Performance Evaluation"; "Organization and Structure of a Fund"; "Hedge Fund Hoopla: As Taft-Hartley Funds Get Interested, What Should Trustees Ask?"; "Does Private Equity Have a Role in Your Portfolio?"; "Soft-Dollars Harm to Pension Funds, Markets"; "Baubles, Bangles and Bright Shiny Things"; "Equity Style Benchmarks for Fund Analysis"; "A Plan Sponsor's Guide to Commissions".

8853 ■ Arnold S. Goldin & Associates Inc.
5030 Champion Blvd., Ste. G-6231
Boca Raton, FL 33496
Ph:(561)994-5810
Fax:(561)994-5860
Co. E-mail: arnold@goldin.com
URL: http://www.goldin.com
Contact: Arnold S. Goldin, Principle
E-mail: arnold@goldin.com
Scope: An accounting and management consulting firm. Serves clients worldwide. Provides management services. Handles monthly write-ups and tax returns.

8854 ■ Automated Accounting
23325 Gerbera St.
Moreno Valley, CA 92553
Ph:(951)653-5053
Co. E-mail: autoacc@earthlink.net
Contact: Gary Capolino, Owner
Scope: A business management consulting firm that caters to small businesses. Offers software installation services, tax preparation services and business plan advisory services. **Publications:** "Inflated Real Estate Prices. . .How Did This Happen," Moreno Valley Magazine, Aug, 2005.

8855 ■ Bedford Associates Inc.
211 Greenwood Ave., Ste. 2-2
PO Box 221
Bethel, CT 06801
Ph:(203)846-0230

Fax:(203)846-1487
Co. E-mail: nick.kroot@bedford.com
URL: http://www.bedford.com
Contact: Stacy Luce, Mgr
E-mail: jose.badia@atsbedford.com
Scope: Offers expertise in the areas of computer information systems design and management. Services include airline systems consulting; transaction processing facility (TPF) and airline control system (ALCS) services; system development and maintenance; step by step (SST) and C-view sales, support and maintenance; supplemental staffing (either on site or remotely); web development services.

8856 ■ DST International
27 Melcher St., 1st Fl.
Boston, MA 02210-1516
Ph:(617)482-8800
Fax:(617)482-8878
Co. E-mail: boston@dstintl.com
URL: http://www.dstinternational.com
Contact: Robert Evans, Principle
E-mail: rhonda.lepsch@atsdstintl.com
Scope: Firm specializing in asset management systems and work management systems. Asset management systems designed to satisfy the solution requirements needed by fund managers, dealers, settlement staff, custodians and record keepers operating as international asset managers, from front office simulation, opinion management and modeling functions, through data management, dealing and settlement to custody and corporate actions.

8857 ■ Everett & Co.
3126 S Franklin St.
Englewood, CO 80113
Ph:(303)761-7999
Fax:(303)781-8296
Contact: Wayne Everett, Principle
Scope: Provides strategic real estate solutions and project management.

8858 ■ Financial Computer Support Inc.
16 Commerce Dr.
Oakland, MD 21550-3940
Ph:(301)334-1800
Free: 877-432-2267
Fax:(301)334-1896
Co. E-mail: fcsitechsupport@morningstar.com
Contact: David Huxford, Principal
Scope: Independent user group which provides computer and administrative support for financial planners, money managers, and insurance agents. Serves finance and insurance industries. **Publications:** "Check Out Carmen Petote," Jul, 2006; "Control the Information Flow with Rep Level Access," Feb, 2005.

8859 ■ InfoSource Management Services Inc.
PO Box 590
Sicamous, BC, Canada V0E 2V0
Ph:(250)804-6113
Free: 888-804-4700
Fax:(250)836-3667
Contact: Sherry Leggett, President
Scope: Firm provides customized financial reports that highlight the areas where change will improve the bottom line.

8860 ■ Integrated Business Information Systems Ltd.
22 Colonial Pl.
New Haven, CT 06515
Ph:(203)397-1523
Fax:(203)397-1523
Contact: Dr. Michael L. Schneider, Principle
E-mail: mischni@idt.net
Scope: Provides financial and marketing software applications, design and development for PC LAN, Wang VS and IBM AS or 400 computers. Offers sales and support for several software products from other vendors, including Tele-magic, Real world, Lotus Notes and Power Builder. Industries served: Finance, marketing, investment, airlines, insurance and reinsurance worldwide. **Publications:** "Future Scope".

8861 ■ M. S. Franks & Company Inc.
11 La Cuesta Rd.
Orinda, CA 94563-2303
Ph:(925)254-1469
Fax:(925)254-7783
Co. E-mail: msf@msfranksco.com
URL: http://www.msfranksco.com
Contact: Michael Franks, Owner
E-mail: msf@msfranksco.com
Scope: Offers services in cash management, check processing, general ledger, financial reporting, loan processing, international, branch operations and merger integrations. Specializes in operations design to financial service companies with a focus on impact analysis, user requirements, work flow analysis and design, project communications, development of training programs and material, project management. **Seminars:** Facilitating Great Meetings; Creating Great Project Documentation; Producing Great Meeting Notes.

8862 ■ Nikmal Financial Services
23 Victoria Heights Rd.
Hyde Park, MA 02136
Ph:(617)361-2101
Fax:(617)249-2093
Contact: Selma H. Lamkin, President
E-mail: selma@nikmal.com
Scope: Services provided include seminars and workshops on personal finance, small business management, economic awareness courses; preparation of personal and business tax returns; training of financial personnel; and financial management services including accounting and auditing, tax reports, record-keeping, and all payroll taxes. Serves private industries as well as government agencies. **Publications:** "What is Wrong with Our Legal System and How to Fix It," American Training Institute, 2002. **Seminars:** Preparing Your Business Plan; Financial Planning for the Not-So-Wealthy.

8863 ■ Olson Research Associates Inc.
10290 Old Columbia Rd.
Columbia, MD 21046-2379
Ph:(410)290-6999
Free: 888-657-6680
Fax:(410)290-6726
Co. E-mail: info@olsonresearch.com
URL: http://www.olsonresearch.com
Contact: Brad Olson, President
E-mail: sregan@atsolsonresearch.com
Scope: A firm of consultants, educators and publishers providing consulting services, simulation models, financial risk management reporting, educational programs and books for financial institutions. **Publications:** "Risk Management Digest"; "Strategic Financial Management," Ivy Press Inc; "The Double Whammy," Oct, 2000. **Seminars:** Policy Development Workshops; Seminars for Bank Directors; Financial Risk Management and Interest Rate Risk; Getting the Maximum Benefit From A/L Benchmarks; Revising Your ALCO Policies.

8864 ■ Rose & Crangle Ltd.
117 N 4th St.
PO Box 285
Lincoln, KS 67455
Ph:(785)524-5050
Fax:(785)524-3130
Co. E-mail: rcltd@nckcn.com
URL: http://www.roseandcrangle.com
Contact: Jeanne Crangle, Principle
E-mail: rcltd@nckcn.com
Scope: Firm provides evaluation, planning and policy analyzes for universities, associations, foundations, governmental agencies and private companies engaged in scientific, technological or educational activities. Special expertise in the development of new institutions. Special skills in providing planning and related group facilitation workshops. **Publications:** "Preface to Bulgarian Integration Into Europe and NATO: Issues of Science Policy And research Evaluation Practice," Ios Press, 2006; "Allocating Limited National Resources for Fundamental Research," 2005.

8865 ■ Samuel E. Bodily Associates
Office:172, 100 Darden Blvd.
PO Box 6550
Charlottesville, VA 22903
Ph:(434)924-4813
Fax:(434)243-7677
Co. E-mail: bodilys@virginia.edu
Contact: Samuel E. Bodily, Principle
E-mail: bodilys@virginia.edu
Scope: Consultant specializes in financial analysis, capital investment, business/product/market planners, financial risk analysis and decision sciences. **Publications:** "I Can't Get No Satisfaction: How Bundling and Multi-Part Pricing Can Satisfy Consumers and Suppliers," Feb, 2006; "Organizational Use of Decision Analysis," Oct, 2004; "Real Options," Oct, 2004.

8866 ■ SS & C Technologies
33 W Monroe, Ste. 420
Chicago, IL 60603-2401
Ph:(312)443-7501
Free: 800-234-0556
Fax:(312)443-7509
Co. E-mail: solution@sscinc.com
URL: http://www.ssctech.com
Contact: Stephen V. R. Whitman, Senior VP
E-mail: swhitman@atssscinc.com
Scope: Software development, consulting service, and turnkey systems provides servicing the investment/private wealth management, the financial/accounting services, and other markets requiring technical systems integration solutions. **Special Services:** Sun Solaris/MS NT Server Platforms. Software partners with Lotus Notes; Microsoft; Sybase; Ardent (Universe); and others.

8867 ■ Thornton Financial FNIC
1024 Centre Ave., Bldg. E
Fort Collins, CO 80526-1849
Ph:(970)221-2089
Fax:(970)484-5206
Contact: Jo-Ellen M. Thornton, President
Scope: Offers personal financial planning and small business planning which focuses on written plans, capitalization, strategic planning, and marketing. Also offers career and life planning. **Seminars:** Capitalizing the Small Business; Financial Independence at Any Income Level; Small Business Management.

8868 ■ Weich & Bilotti Inc.
600 Worcester Rd., 4th Fl.
Framingham, MA 01702
Ph:(508)663-1600
Fax:(508)663-1682
Co. E-mail: info@weich-bilotti.com
URL: http://www.weich-bilotti.com
Contact: Mervyn D. Weich, President
E-mail: mweich@weich-bilotti.com
Scope: Specializes in business plans, venture capital, computer information systems, turnaround/interim management, retail consulting, start-up process, college recruiting and IS and IT personnel.

FRANCHISES AND BUSINESS OPPORTUNITIES

8869 ■ The Comprehensive Financial Planning System
T&M Financial, Inc.
3706 SW Topeka Blvd., Ste. 400
Topeka, KS 66609
Ph:(785)266-8333
Free: 800-550-CFPS
Fax:(785)266-7819
No. of Franchise Units: 5. **No. of Company-Owned Units:** 1. **Founded:** 1962. **Franchised:** 2004. **Description:** Client-based financial planning. **Equity Capital Needed:** $11,400. **Financial Assistance:** Yes. **Training:** Yes.

8870 ■ 4Pillars Consulting Group Inc.
Franchise Development
2300-2850 Shaughnessy St.
Port Coquitlam, BC, Canada V3C 6K5
Ph:(250)384-7112
Free: (866)600-2364
Fax:(866)591-2941
Co. E-mail: franchise@4pillars.ca
URL: http://www.4pillars.ca
No. of Franchise Units: 42. **No. of Company-Owned Units:** 1. **Founded:** 2002. **Franchised:** 2002. **Description:** Independent debt restructuring firm providing Financial Restructuring Solutions to individuals and families who suffer from debt and cash flow difficulties. The 4 Pillars system allows our consultants to successfully help thousands of Canadians avoid bankruptcy and eliminate debt. **Equity Capital Needed:** $74,000. **Franchise Fee:** $39,500. **Financial Assistance:** Assistance financing up to $15,000 of franchise fee is available. **Training:** Provides 2 weeks training and ongoing support.

8871 ■ The Interface Financial Group
2182 DuPont Dr., Ste. 221
Irvine, CA 92612-1320
Ph:(905)475-5701
Free: 800-387-0860
Fax:(866)475-8688
Co. E-mail: dtbanf@interfacefinancial.biz
URL: http://www.interfacefinancial.com
No. of Franchise Units: 166. **Founded:** 1971. **Franchised:** 1991. **Description:** Franchise buys quality accounts receivables from client companies at a discount to provide short-term working capital to expanding businesses. **Equity Capital Needed:** $100,000+. cash investment; $88,300-$139,300 total investment **Franchise Fee:** $36,000. **Royalty Fee:** 8%. **Financial Assistance:** No. **Training:** Offers 6 days onsite training and ongoing support.

8872 ■ Weigh House Investors Services
4141 Yonge St., Ste. 304
Toronto, ON, Canada M2P 2A8
Ph:(416)640-0550
Free: (866)918-0550
Fax:(416)640-0552
Co. E-mail: info@weighhouse.com
URL: http://www.secondopinions.ca
No. of Franchise Units: 2. **No. of Company-Owned Units:** 1. **Founded:** 2004. **Franchised:** 2007. **Description:** Second Opinion offices offer financial consulting services to retail and corporate clients. We remain completely independent and unbiased and do not sell products of any kind. Our only fee is an hourly fee paid directly by our clients which gives us a major competitive advantage. Our main services include: PerformanceCHECKa, PortfolioCHECKa, and Manager SEARCH. **Equity Capital Needed:** $50.00. **Franchise Fee:** $30,000. **Training:** Yes.

COMPUTERIZED DATABASES

8873 ■ ABA Banking Journal
Simmons-Boardman Publishing Corp.
345 Hudson St., 12th Fl.
New York, NY 10014
Ph:(212)620-7200
Free: 800-895-4389
URL: http://www.simmonsboardman.com
Description: Contains the complete text of ABA Banking Journal, a magazine on commercial bank operation and management. Covers employee relations, recruiting, and training; installment, mortgage, commercial, and industrial lending; correspondent, foreign, and retail banking; deposit gathering; bank cards; asset and liability management; data processing and telecommunications; security; government relations; and legal and regulatory developments. Also provides a calendar of ABA-sponsored courses, seminars, and workshops. **Availability:** Online: LexisNexis Group, Intuit Inc., Simmons-Boardman Publishing Corp. **Type:** Full text.

8874 ■ ABI/INFORM
ProQuest LLC
789 E Eisenhower Pky.
PO Box 1346
Ann Arbor, MI 48106-1346
Ph:(734)761-4700
Free: 800-521-0600

Fax:(734)761-6450
Co. E-mail: info@proquest.com
URL: http://www.proquest.com
Description: Contains approximately 6 million full text or bibliographic citations to articles from more than 800 business and management publications worldwide. **Availability:** Online: Wolters Kluwer Health, ProQuest LLC, ProQuest LLC, Questel SA, STN International, Colorado Alliance of Research Libraries, Financial Times Ltd., LexisNexis Group, ProQuest LLC. **Type:** Full text; Bibliographic; Image.

8875 ■ *American Banker Financial Publications*
SourceMedia Inc.
1 State St. Plz., 27th Fl.
New York, NY 10004
Ph:(212)803-8200
Free: 800-221-1809
Fax:(212)843-9600
Co. E-mail: custserv@AmericanBanker.com
URL: http://www.americanbanker.com
Description: Provides full text of the daily financial services newspaper and other financial newsletters which follow trends, developments, and news in banking and related financial areas. Includes topics such as capital markets, bank regulation, insurance letters, and public finance letters. **Availability:** Online: ProQuest LLC. **Type:** Full text.

8876 ■ *Banking Information Source*
ProQuest LLC
789 E Eisenhower Pky.
PO Box 1346
Ann Arbor, MI 48106-1346
Ph:(734)761-4700
Free: 800-521-0600
Fax:(734)761-6450
Co. E-mail: info@proquest.com
URL: http://www.proquest.com
Description: Contains more than 575,000 citations with abstracts, and full text articles, to articles and other published materials dealing with the management and marketing of financial services by banks, credit unions, insurance companies, investment and real estate firms, thrift institutions, and government agencies. Covers advertising, pricing, sales, marketing, pricing, personnel development and compensation, facilities planning, and product innovations. Pulled from more than 500 industry sources, including journals, newspapers, newsletters, reports, Bank Marketing Association's Golden Coin Awards competition entries, Stonier Theses, and School of Bank Marketing papers. Citations also provided for banking-related articles from *American Banker*, *The Wall Street Journal*, and *The New York Times*. **Availability:** Online: ProQuest LLC, ProQuest LLC, LexisNexis Group, ProQuest LLC. **Type:** Bibliographic; Full text.

8877 ■ *BANKSCOPE*
Bureau van Dijk Electronic Publishing
Rivierstaete
Amsteldijk 166
NL-1079 LH Amsterdam, Netherlands
Ph:31 20 5400 100
Fax:31 20 5400 111
Co. E-mail: info@bvdinfo.com
URL: http://www.bvdinfo.com
Description: Contains financial information on more than 30,000 banks worldwide, including data on approximately 13,760 U.S. banks. Includes up to 16 years of spreadsheet information on the top 6500 European banks, the top 1400 North American banks, the 200 Japanese commercial and sogo banks, more than 2900 other major banks, and the leading 38 supranational banking and financial organizations. Provides details on ownership (shareholders and banking subsidiaries) for 4000 major banks worldwide. Also includes 2 years of Reuters full-text articles related to banks and financial organizations and Fitch IBCA, Sovereign, Moody's, and S&P ratings, Capital Intelligence Ratings and Bank Reports, E.I.U. Country Finance Reports and EIU Country Risk Ratings and Reports. Includes software for conducting in-depth financial analysis of company data. Also enables the user to prepare customized company or group reports, conduct peer and statistical analyses, perform comprehensive searches, and download data

in various formats such as Excel, Lotus, ASCII, and RTF. **Availability:** Online: Bureau van Dijk Electronic Publishing. **Type:** Directory; Numeric; Statistical; Image.

8878 ■ *Barron's Online*
Dow Jones & Company Inc.
1 World Financial Ctr.
200 Liberty St.
New York, NY 10281
Ph:(212)416-2000
Fax:(212)416-4348
Co. E-mail: info@dowjones.com
URL: http://www.dowjones.com
Description: Provides the complete text of *Barron's*, providing articles and reports covering worldwide financial markets. Includes market data, news and market commentary, interviews, statistics, tools and resources (including specific analysis of online investing). Available as a stand-alone subscription product. **Availability:** Online: Dow Jones & Company Inc. **Type:** Full text; Numeric; Statistical.

8879 ■ *BlockDATA*
Thomson Reuters
3 Times Sq.
New York, NY 10036
Ph:(646)223-4000
Co. E-mail: salesinquires@thomsonreuters.com
URL: http://thomsonreuters.com/products_services/financial
Description: Provides information on the 400 most active listed, over-the-counter (OTC), and foreign securities traded on the AutEx Trading Information System (described in a separate entry). Includes industry profiles and trends as well as three months of trades data for comparative analysis. **Availability:** Online: Thomson Reuters, Thomson Reuters. **Type:** Full text; Numeric.

8880 ■ *The Bond Buyer Online*
Investcorp International Inc.
1 State St. Plaza, 27th Fl.
New York, NY 10004
Ph:(212)803-8200
Free: 800-221-1809
Co. E-mail: custserv@sourcemedia.com
URL: http://www.sourcemedia.com
Description: Contains more than 259,000 articles reporting news and information on the fixed-income securities markets. Provides information on municipal bond issues available for negotiated and competitive bidding in each state, including name of borrowing entity, purpose of issue, issue and maturity dates, amount, interest cost to borrower, and underwriter. Also covers bond sales by state, results of bond elections, proposed bond issues, federal laws and regulations affecting the taxable and tax-exempt bond markets and U.S. Treasury bonds and securities, as well as news and commentary on events, economic trends, and government policies affecting the municipal bond market. Corresponds to *The Bond Buyer*. NOTE: On DIALOG, includes the complete text of *MUNIWEEK*, from 1986 to date. **Availability:** Online: Investcorp International Inc., ProQuest LLC, ProQuest LLC, ProQuest LLC. **Type:** Directory; Full text.

8881 ■ *BondWatch*
Thomson Reuters
3 Times Sq.
New York, NY 10036
Ph:(646)223-4000
Co. E-mail: salesinquires@thomsonreuters.com
URL: http://thomsonreuters.com/products_services/financial
Description: Contains real-time data as well as graphs and analyses of prices and yields for U.S. government bonds, bills, and notes. Includes MOR 2600 hedge fund managers; more than 14,000 managers of fixed income assets with 41,000 contacts; more than 7900 North American mutual funds, variable annuities, and pension funds with fixed income holdings representing over $1.9 trillion; and more than 13,200 non-U.S. mutual funds and pension funds with fixed income holdings representing over $617 billion. **Availability:** Online: Thomson Reuters. **Type:** Numeric; Full text.

8882 ■ *Business Wire*
Berkshire Hathaway Inc.
44 Montgomery St., 39th Fl.
San Francisco, CA 94104
Ph:(415)986-4422
Free: 800-227-0845
Fax:(415)788-5335
Co. E-mail: SF_sales_group@bizwire.com
URL: http://www.businesswire.com
Description: Contains more than 1.4 million records that make up the complete text of press releases from public and private companies and other organizations, such as hospitals and universities. Covers new products, stock offerings, mergers, legal actions, financial information, personnel changes, and company announcements of general interest. Includes headline recaps hourly plus recaps of high tech headlines in some systems. Records include company name, headline, publication date, ticker symbol, byline; dateline, time, word count (usually less than 500), and text, including contact information. Covers industries such as banking, computers, telecommunications, entertainment, aviation, biotechnology, and mining; general news and features; some international events; and sports. **Availability:** Online: Thomson Reuters, Mzinga Inc., ProQuest LLC, Dow Jones & Company Inc., LexisNexis Group, Bloomberg LP. **Type:** Full text.

8883 ■ *CANNEX*
CANNEX Financial Exchanges Ltd.
1200 Bay St., Ste. 1001
Toronto, ON, Canada M5R 2A5
Ph:(416)926-0882
Free: 800-387-1269
Fax:(416)926-0706
Co. E-mail: cannex@cannex.com
URL: http://www.cannex.com
Description: Contains current interest and product information for Term Deposits/GICs (Certificates of Deposit), mortgages, RRSPs (IRAs), annuities, RRIFs (similar to annuities), and savings and checking account products offered by banks, trust companies, savings and loans, and life insurance companies in Australia, New Zealand, the U.S. and Canada. **Availability:** Online: CANNEX Financial Exchanges Ltd. **Type:** Numeric.

8884 ■ *Capital Stock*
Haver Analytics
60 E 42nd St.
New York, NY 10165
Ph:(212)986-9300
Fax:(212)986-5857
Co. E-mail: data@haver.com
URL: http://www.haver.com
Description: Contains more than 2000 annual time series covering all of the information contained in *Fixed Reproducible Tangible Wealth in the United States* by The Bureau of Economic Analysis. Detailed estimates by industry and by type of equipment or structure. **Availability:** Online: Haver Analytics. **Type:** Time series.

8885 ■ *CNQ Market Data Feed*
TMX Group Inc.
Exchange Tower, 3rd Fl.
130 King St. W
Toronto, ON, Canada M5X 1J2
Ph:(416)947-4670
Free: 888-873-8392
Fax:(416)947-4662
Co. E-mail: info@tsx.com
URL: http://www.tmx.com
Description: Provides each trade and bid/ask quote for all stocks, options, and futures listed on the Toronto Stock Exchange, Montreal Exchange, Vancouver Stock Exchange, and Alberta Stock Exchange. **Availability:** Online: TMX Group Inc. **Type:** Numeric.

8886 ■ *Dial-Data*
Track Data Corp.
95 Rockwell Pl.
Brooklyn, NY 11217
Ph:(718)522-7373

Free: 800-367-5968
Co. E-mail: info@trackdata.com
URL: http://www.trackdata.com
Description: A database system that contains current and historical data on securities, options, and commodities. Comprises the following three files. Securities—contains data from 1970 to date on more than 12,000 stocks, warrants, rights, bonds, and government issues. Includes both fundamental (e.g., earnings, shares outstanding) and technical data for all issues from the New York Stock Exchange (NYSE), American Stock Exchange (AMEX), NASDAQ Over-The-Counter market, International Stock Exchange (London), Montreal Exchange, Toronto Exchange, and government issues. Data items available include daily price and volume for NYSE and AMEX bonds; daily bid, ask, and yield for government issues; coupon and maturity data for both; and open, high, low, close, and volume interest data for all exchanges. Splits and dividends are reported on the evening of the day they occur. Options—contains data on all options listed on NYSE; Chicago Board Options Exchange (CBOE); AMEX; Philadelphia Exchange; and Pacific Stock Exchange (PSE). Daily price, volume, high, low, open, and close interest data as well as fundamental and technical data are available on all underlying securities from 1973 to date. Commodities—contains daily price, volume, high, low, open, and close interest data by contract on all commodities from the following exchanges: CBOE; Chicago Board of Trade (CBOT); Chicago Mercantile Exchange (CME); Commodity Exchange, Inc.; International Monetary Exchange; Kansas City Board of Trade; Mid America Exchange; Minneapolis Grain Exchange; New York Coffee, Sugar, and Cocoa Exchange; New York Cotton Exchange; New York Futures Exchange; New York Mercantile Exchange; and Winnipeg Grain Exchange. Covers commodities from 1963 to date, with selected cash series data from 1959 to date. Also includes 200 indexes and statistics on the daily or weekly performance of the securities market. Primary sources include NYSE, Dow Jones, Standard & Poor's, Value Line, and daily market summaries compiled from MERLIN data. Indexes and statistics date from 1972, with some data from 1970. **Availability:** Online: Track Data Corp. **Type:** Numeric.

8887 ■ *Dividend Record*
Standard & Poor's
55 Water St.
New York, NY 10041
Ph:(212)438-2000
Free: 800-523-4534
Fax:(212)438-7375
Co. E-mail: questions@standardandpoors.com
URL: http://www.standardandpoors.com
Description: Contains dividend disbursement data for more than 22,000 equity securities listed on the New York Stock Exchange (NYSE) and American Stock Exchange (AMEX), the NASDAQ market and the Toronto and Montreal stock exchanges. Also contains data on American Depository Receipts, mutual funds, closed-end investment companies, limited partnerships, and real-estate investment trusts. Comprised of and stock and cash dividend announcements, including initial dividends, dividends resumed, increase or decrease in dividends, omitted or suspended dividends, and additional, extra, special, or optional dividends. Also includes announcements of stock splits, stock redemptions, tender offers, rights offerings, spin-offs, stock exchange rulings, and due bill information. Provides, for each dividend, its declaration date, ex-dividend date, stock-of-record date, and payment date, as well as the amount of the dividend. Sources include the stock exchanges, National Association of Securities Dealers (NASD), and company information. Corresponds to Standard & Poor's printed *Dividend Record* services. **Availability:** Online: Standard & Poor's. **Type:** Numeric.

8888 ■ *e-JEP*
American Economic Association
2014 Broadway, Ste. 305
Nashville, TN 37203
Ph:(615)322-2595

Fax:(615)343-7590
Co. E-mail: aeainfo@vanderbilt.edu
URL: http://www.vanderbilt.edu/AEA
Description: Contains the full text of the *Journal of Economic Perspectives*. Includes articles, reports, and other material for economists and economics professionals. Features analysis and critiques of recent research findings and developments in public policy. Includes coverage of global economics issues and developments. Features articles on education in economics, employment issues for economists, and other issues of concern to professional economists. **Availability:** Online: American Economic Association, Thomson Reuters; CD-ROM: American Economic Association. **Type:** Full text.

8889 ■ *EDR Sanborn Maps*
Environmental Data Resources Inc.
440 Wheelers Farms Rd.
Milford, CT 06461
Ph:(203)783-0300
Free: 800-352-0050
Fax:(203)231-6802
Co. E-mail: jhan@edrnet.com
URL: http://www.edrnet.com
Description: Contains more than 1.2 million Sanborn fire insurance maps covering the history of some 12,000 cities and towns in the United States from 1866 to the present. Enables users to search by latitude and longitude. **Availability:** Online: Environmental Data Resources Inc. **Type:** Image.

8890 ■ *Ford Equity Research Databases*
Ford Equity Research Inc.
11722 Sorrento Valley Rd., Ste. I
San Diego, CA 92121
Ph:(858)755-1327
Free: 800-842-0207
Fax:(858)455-6316
Co. E-mail: info@fordequity.com
URL: http://www.fordequity.com
Description: Contains more than 200 financial data items for each of 4000 leading common stocks. Primary data include company name, CUSIP number, ticker symbol, quality rating, growth persistence rating, 12-month earnings per share, normal earnings per share, dividend rate, projected earnings growth rate, standard deviation of annual earnings, book value, debt/equity ratio, end-of-month share price, previous month share price, shares outstanding, percent of shares held by institutions, beta, quarterly earnings series for the past 4 quarters, an estimate for the coming quarter, an industry classification, and company annual revenues. Derived data include the past month price gain, market capitalization, total assets, cash flow per share, price/earnings ratio, current/normal earnings ratio, dividend payout ratio, dividend yield, total return, price/book value ratio, preferred equity, return on equity, plowback on equity, and the results of intrinsic value and earnings trend analysis performed by Ford. Includes the U.S. Daily Current Database, U.S. Historical Database, International Database, and International Historical Database. **Availability:** Online: Thomson Reuters; Diskette: Ford Equity Research Inc;Magnetic Tape: Ford Equity Research Inc. **Type:** Numeric.

8891 ■ *IGM CorporateWatch*
informa global markets
Graybar Bldg., Ste. 615
420 Lexington Ave.
New York, NY 10170
Ph:(212)509-5802
Fax:(212)949-4189
Co. E-mail: sales@informagm.com
URL: http://www.informagm.com/gml
Description: Contains news and analyses of developments in the US new issue market, Eurobonds, and private placements. Provides information from the United States, Europe, and the Asia-Pacific region. Covers corporate securities, equities, emerging markets, and international debt. Provides commentary and analysis, summary tables of recent deals, reporting of market developments and deal launches, bond and loan news, bond and credit news, and more. **Availability:** Online: Thomson Reuters, informa global markets. **Type:** Full text; Numeric.

8892 ■ *InvestmentNews*
Crain Communications Inc.
1155 Gratiot Ave.
Detroit, MI 48207
Ph:(313)446-6000
Free: 800-678-2427
Fax:(313)446-1616
Co. E-mail: info@crain.com
URL: http://www.crain.com
Description: Contains investment news, articles, and features from the print version of *InvestmentNews*. Includes material for investors, financial planners, investment advisors, and other players in the stock market. Includes interviews, company profiles, investment analysis, calendars of upcoming events, and more. Includes classified advertisements for jobs, services, products, and other resources. Includes news archives, company reports, and a financial services stock index. **Availability:** Online: Crain Communications Inc. **Type:** Full text; Numeric.

8893 ■ *MarketScope*
Standard & Poor's
55 Water St.
New York, NY 10041
Ph:(212)438-2000
Free: 800-523-4534
Fax:(212)438-7375
Co. E-mail: questions@standardandpoors.com
URL: http://www.standardandpoors.com
Description: A financial information service that contains descriptive and financial data on more than 9500 companies, reports and analysis of the stock and bond markets, and financial investment news. Comprised of the following 2 section: Reference Section—contains descriptive information for each company, including background information, commentaries on future prospects, earnings and dividend projections (for 1100 major companies), and sales and earnings data by lines of business. Also contains current and historical statistical data (updated daily), including price range, price/earnings ratio, earnings per share, dividends, yield, and book value. Corporate and market developments are incorporated throughout the day. Also provides Stock Appreciation Ranking System (STARS), using 1 to 5 stars to rank the investment status of approximately 1100 stocks. Action Section—includes commentaries on current market activity (updated 7 times a day); economic analysis and projections, including EconomyWatch and MoneyWatch, by Standard & Poor's chief economist; analyses of developments that influence a company or industry group (updated continuously, throughout the day); MarketMovers, identification of 2000 active and volatile stock issues and rationale for their movements (updated continuously, throughout the day); interest rates for Federal funds, Treasury Bills, Treasury Notes, Treasury Bonds, and broker loan rates (updated at least 5 times a day); technical indicators; and high-yielding investment-grade municipal bonds. Data updated daily include stock allocation model, takeover candidates, and dollar, treasury, and international commentaries (provided by MMS International); a calendar of expected initial public stock offerings, indicating lead underwriter, business description, number of shares in offering, and expected price; performance data on new stocks for a 3-month period following initial public offering, including gain or loss percentage, recent bid, initial offering price, date of public offering, and stock symbol; an economic calendar, with forecasts of selected indicators; changes in key economic indicators, including comments by Standard & Poor's chief economist on key economic events and their impact; recommendations on specific stocks to buy for achieving 4 investment goals: long-term growth, emerging growth, income/total return, and speculative/cyclical; a master list of recommended stocks; *Fair Value*, Standard & Poor's proprietary quantitative stock valuation system; and Platinum Portfolio, which combines top rated stocks from *Fair Value* and STARS. **Availability:** Online: Dow Jones & Company Inc., Track Data Corp., TD AMERITRADE Holding Corp., Bloomberg LP, Thomson Reuters, Standard & Poor's. **Type:** Numeric; Full text.

8894 ■ *Municipal Futures Data-Line*
Thomson Reuters
22 Thomson Pl.
Boston, MA 02210

Ph:(617)856-2900
Free: 800-367-8215
Fax:(617)856-5610
Co. E-mail: clientservice@tm3.com
URL: http://www.tm3.com
Description: Contains charts, graphs, and commentary on the municipal and Treasury cash and derivative markets. Provides data to analyze hedge and arbitrage strategies and municipal futures contract options. Includes a bond buyer index estimate, valuation of the municipal futures contract, and technical indicators. **Availability:** Online: Thomson Reuters. **Type:** Full text; Numeric.

8895 ■ *Municipal Market Data-Line*
Thomson Reuters
22 Thomson Pl.
Boston, MA 02210
Ph:(617)856-2900
Free: 800-367-8215
Fax:(617)856-5610
Co. E-mail: clientservice@tm3.com
URL: http://www.tm3.com
Description: Contains charts, graphs, and commentary on the municipal and Treasury markets. Provides analyses of municipal values, yields, and supply. Includes a daily municipal market index, daily commentary, technical indicators, and details of new issues. **Availability:** Online: Thomson Reuters. **Type:** Full text; Numeric.

8896 ■ *opTrack Service*
Track Data Corp.
95 Rockwell Pl.
Brooklyn, NY 11217
Ph:(718)522-7373
Free: 800-367-5968
Co. E-mail: info@trackdata.com
URL: http://www.trackdata.com
Description: Provides real-time strategies and analyses for index and equity options as well as daily, weekly, and monthly graphs of the underlying securities price movement. Includes a directory of ticker symbols for the 6000 securities covered. **Availability:** Online: Track Data Corp. **Type:** Full text.

8897 ■ *Pink Sheets*
OTC Markets Group Inc.
304 Hudson St., 2nd Fl.
New York, NY 10013
Ph:(212)896-4400
Fax:(212)868-3848
Co. E-mail: info@otcmarkets.com
URL: http://www.otcmarkets.com
Description: Contains information on current prices of NASDAZ and non-NASDAQ over-the-counter securities. Covers new and updated issues of more than 15,000 U.S. and foreign companies. Provides listings for NYSE and AMEX securities for off the board trading. Includes a list of market makers for these issues. **Availability:** Online: Solera Holdings Inc., Bloomberg LP, OTC Markets Group Inc. **Type:** Full text; Numeric.

8898 ■ *Securities Law Daily*
The Bureau of National Affairs Inc.
1801 S Bell St.
Arlington, VA 22202
Free: 800-372-1033
Co. E-mail: customercare@bna.com
URL: http://www.bna.com
Description: Contains reports the latest developments in securities and futures law. Covers state and federal legislative, regulatory, and judicial actions affecting securities, commodities, and corporate activities. Includes coverage of U.S. Congress, state and federal courts, the Commodities Futures Trading Commission, and the Securities and Exchange Commission (SEC). Addresses such topics as insider trading, mutual funds, SEC regulation, investment advisors, global markets, and more. **Availability:** Online: Thomson Reuters, The Bureau of National Affairs Inc. **Type:** Full text.

8899 ■ *Securities Regulation & Law Report*
The Bureau of National Affairs Inc.
1801 S Bell St.
Arlington, VA 22202

Free: 800-372-1033
Co. E-mail: customercare@bna.com
URL: http://www.bna.com
Description: Contains the complete text of *Securities Regulation & Law Report*, covering federal and state regulations and laws on securities and futures trading and accounting. Includes corporate governance and attorney responsibility, enforcement activities, commodity futures regulation, and accounting standards and practices. Provides information on the most recent court cases, legal precedents, administrative opinions, and legislative and regulatory proposals and actions. Provides authoritative information on preparing, reviewing, and auditing financial statements filed with the SEC. Sources include Securities and Exchange Commission, Commodities Futures Trading Commission, industry, courts, and Congress. **Availability:** Online: Thomson Reuters, LexisNexis Group, The Bureau of National Affairs Inc. **Type:** Full text.

8900 ■ *Trendvest Ratings*
Trendvest Management Inc.
923 First Colonial Rd., No. 1805
Virginia Beach, VA 23454
Ph:(757)412-4301
Fax:(757)412-4302
Co. E-mail: editor@trendvest.com
URL: http://www.trendvest.com
Description: Contains investment ratings for common stocks and aggregate indicators for the stock, bond, and gold markets. For each stock or market, provides a single numeric rating (e.g., 234 or -28) based on such factors as market values and market price momentum. High positive ratings indicate opportunities for buying; low negative ratings, for selling. Database service enables the user to download up to 50 data items for some 6000 common stocks for analysis and portfolio management. **Availability:** Online: Trendvest Management Inc. **Type:** Full text; Numeric.

8901 ■ *U.S. Weekly Statistics*
Haver Analytics
60 E 42nd St.
New York, NY 10165
Ph:(212)986-9300
Fax:(212)986-5857
Co. E-mail: data@haver.com
URL: http://www.haver.com
Description: Contains weekly financial and economic series aggregated from DAILY plus aggregate reserves, official reserve assets, bank assets and liabilities, commercial paper outstanding, money supply, bank credit, unemployment claims, car and truck production by firm, and production of raw steel, coal, and lumber. Also includes complete commitment of traders' data from the Commodity Futures Trading Commission. **Availability:** Online: Haver Analytics. **Type:** Statistical; Numeric.

8902 ■ *Value Line DataFile*
Value Line Inc.
220 E 42nd St., 6th Fl.
New York, NY 10017
Ph:(212)907-1500
Free: 800-531-1425
Fax:(212)907-1992
Co. E-mail: vlcr@valueline.com
URL: http://www.valueline.com
Description: Provides annual and quarterly financial histories and projections in the U.S., Canada, Europe, and Asia. Includes more than 80 industry composites. Includes stock market information and other financial business data. Covers more than 7500 securities listed on the major North American stock exchanges, NASDAQ, and OTC markets. The following time series are available: annual data since 1955; quarterly data from 1963 to date; full 10-Q data from 1985. Also features a composite of financial data for industrial companies. Information is obtained from company quarterly and annual financial statements. Also available as Datafile II, for Microsoft Access and Borland Paradox formats, offering a more limited data set. **Availability:** Online: Thomson Reuters, FactSet Research Systems Inc., Citigroup Inc., GIT Satellite LLC. **Type:** Time series; Numeric.

8903 ■ *Value Line Electronic Convertibles*
Value Line Inc.
220 E 42nd St., 6th Fl.
New York, NY 10017
Ph:(212)907-1500
Free: 800-531-1425
Fax:(212)907-1992
Co. E-mail: vlcr@valueline.com
URL: http://www.valueline.com
Description: Contains evaluation data for approximately 600 convertible securities. Includes price, yield, premium, issue size, liquidity, and maturity. Enables the user to perform calculations to evaluate the effects of changes in prices, common dividends, quality ratings, and interest rates. **Availability:** Online: Value Line Inc. **Type:** Numeric.

8904 ■ *Value Line Estimates and Projections File*
Value Line Inc.
220 E 42nd St., 6th Fl.
New York, NY 10017
Ph:(212)907-1500
Free: 800-531-1425
Fax:(212)907-1992
Co. E-mail: vlcr@valueline.com
URL: http://www.valueline.com
Description: Contains projected performance ratings and estimates of earnings-per-share, dividends-per-share, sales/revenue ratios, and 3-to-5 year growth in dividends per share for the 1700 common stocks that appear in the Value Line Investment Survey. Includes analysis of more than 70 variables, including investment measures (e.g., timeliness, safety, financial strength), price performance indicators (e.g., beta, stability, growth), estimates of price growth persistence and earnings predictability, quarterly estimates of sales and earnings-per-share, and projected growth rates and annual estimates. **Availability:** Online: Thomson Reuters, FactSet Research Systems Inc., GIT Satellite LLC. **Type:** Numeric.

LIBRARIES

8905 ■ Bank of Nova Scotia Archives
44 King St. W., 19th Fl.
Toronto, ON, Canada M5H 1H1
Co. E-mail: archives@scotiabank.com
URL: http://www.scotiabank.com
Contact: Jane Nokes, Dir./Corp.Archv.
Scope: Banking, finance, economics, business. **Services:** Archives open to the public. **Holdings:** Records; art; antiques; photographs.

8906 ■ Compass Lexecon Library
332 S. Michigan Ave., Ste. 1300
Chicago, IL 60604
Ph:(312)322-0845
Fax:(312)322-0881
Co. E-mail: cgriffin@lexecon.com
Contact: Christine Griffin, Rec./Off.Svcs.Mgr.
Scope: Economics, securities, finance, government, business, reference. **Services:** Library not open to the public. **Subscriptions:** 54 journals and other serials; 5 newspapers.

8907 ■ Fiscal Agents–Financial Information Service–Research Department - Library (PO Box)
PO Box 5000
Oakville, ON, Canada L6J 5C7
Ph:(905)842-2790
Fax:(905)844-8552
Co. E-mail: library@fiscalagents.com
URL: http://www.fiscalagents.com/fiscalreports
Scope: Industry, trust services, investment products, insurance. **Services:** Copying; Library open to the public at librarian's discretion. **Holdings:** 12 reports. **Subscriptions:** 3 newspapers.

8908 ■ Huddleston, Bolen LLP Law Library
611 3rd Ave.
PO Box 2185
Huntington, WV 25701
Ph:(304)529-6181

Fax:(304)522-4312
Co. E-mail: laldridge@huddlestonbolen.com
URL: http://www.huddlestonbolen.com/
Contact: Lauren Aldridge, Law Libn.

Scope: Taxation/estate, corporate/securities/banking, federal litigation, labor. **Services:** Library not open to the public. **Holdings:** 35,000 books.

8909 ■ Independent Community Bankers of America Information Center
1615 L St. NW, 9th Fl.
Washington, DC 20036
Ph:(202)659-8111
Free: 800-422-8439
Fax:(202)659-3604
Co. E-mail: library@icba.org
URL: http://www.icba.org
Contact: Susan R. Fournier, Dir.

Scope: Banking and finance, legislative and regulatory documents, small bank operations, bank structure. **Services:** Interlibrary loan; Library not open to the public. **Holdings:** 3500 books, periodicals, and clippings; 300 audio/visual items. **Subscriptions:** 240 journals and other serials.

8910 ■ Ontario Teachers' Pension Plan Board–Knowledge Centre
5650 Yonge St., Ste. 800
North York, ON, Canada M2M 4H5
Ph:(416)730-3770
Fax:(416)730-3773
Co. E-mail: inquiry@otpp.com
URL: http://www.otpp.com/wps/wcm/connect/otpp_en/home
Contact: Laurie Alberico, Mgr.

Scope: Pension management, investment, economics, finance. **Services:** Library not open to the public. **Holdings:** 900 books. **Subscriptions:** 30 journals and other serials.

8911 ■ Principal Financial Group–Online Library
711 High St.
Des Moines, IA 50392-0510
Ph:(515)246-7163
Free: 800-986-3343
Fax:(866)496-6515
Co. E-mail: kelly.kay@principal.com
URL: http://www.principal.com
Contact: Kay Kelly, Online Info.Cons.

Scope: Human Resources research. **Services:** Library not open to the public. **Holdings:** Figures not available.

8912 ■ Russell Reynolds Associates, Inc. Library
200 S. Wacker Dr., Ste. 2900
Chicago, IL 60606-5896
Ph:(312)993-9696
Fax:(312)876-1919
Co. E-mail: bradford.mclane@russellreynolds.com
URL: http://www.russellreynolds.com/
Contact: Bradford McLane

Scope: Business, financial services, banking. **Services:** Interlibrary loan; copying; Library open to the public by appointment. **Holdings:** 1000 books; company Annual reports; subject files. **Subscriptions:** 50 journals and other serials.

8913 ■ Willamette Management Associates Library
8600 W. Bryn Mawr Ave., Ste. 950
Chicago, IL 60631
Ph:(773)399-4300
Fax:(773)399-4310
Co. E-mail: vaplatt@willamette.com
URL: http://www.willamette.com
Contact: Victoria A. Platt, Info.Spec.

Scope: Business valuation, tax, gift and estate, finance. **Services:** Interlibrary loan; copying. Library not open to the public.

RESEARCH CENTERS

8914 ■ Boston University–Morin Center for Banking and Financial Law
School of Law, Rm. 1524
765 Commonwealth Ave.
Boston, MA 02215
Ph:(617)353-3023
Free: 888—285-7003
Fax:(617)353-2444
Co. E-mail: ckhurley@bu.edu
URL: http://www.bu.edu/law/morincenter
Contact: Prof. Cornelius K. Hurley, Dir.
E-mail: ckhurley@bu.edu

Scope: Banking and financial institutions, particularly law and regulation of the financial services industry, pension and trust fund administration, law and regulation of depository institutions, securities activities of banks, deposit insurance funds, international banking, asset management, and financing. **Publications:** Annual Review of Banking Law; Review of banking and financial law (semiannually); Review of Financial Law (semiannually). **Educational Activities:** Edward Lane-Retiker Speaker Series, on current issues in banking and financial institutions law and policy, once per semester, open to the public; Lectures, on current issues in banking and financial institutions law for financial institution executives and legal counsel or other interested parties.

8915 ■ Filene Research Institute
PO Box 2998
Madison, WI 53701-2998
Ph:(608)231-8550
Fax:(608)238-4709
Co. E-mail: markm@filene.org
URL: http://filene.org
Contact: Mark Meyer, CEO
E-mail: markm@filene.org

Scope: Research on the economic, social and technological environment affecting the financial services sector, particularly credit unions; consumer finance issues; public policy and educational issues of credit unions, cooperatives and financial service providers. **Publications:** Investigative reports; Research reports; Special reports. **Educational Activities:** Research colloquia workshops.

8916 ■ McGill University–Desmarais Global Finance Centre
Desautels Faculty of Management
1001 Sherbrooke St. W
Montreal, QC, Canada H3A 1G5
Ph:(514)398-8144
Fax:(514)398-3876
Co. E-mail: vihang.errunza@mcgill.ca
URL: http://www.mcgill.ca/desautels/dgfc
Contact: Prof. Vihang R. Errunza, Dir.
E-mail: vihang.errunza@mcgill.ca

Scope: Modern finance, focusing on international financial markets, asset pricing and risk management,

and corporate finance and governance. **Educational Activities:** Seminars, conferences.

8917 ■ Princeton University–Bendheim Center for Finance
Department of Economics
26 Prospect Ave.
Princeton, NJ 08540-5296
Ph:(609)258-0770
Fax:(609)258-0771
Co. E-mail: jessicab@princeton.edu
URL: http://www.princeton.edu/bcf
Contact: Jessica O'Leary, Mgr.
E-mail: jessicab@princeton.edu

Scope: Securities markets, credit markets, corporate finance, capital budgeting, and portfolio analysis. **Educational Activities:** Conferences (annually); Seminars (weekly), for university students and staff, as well as invited guests, held every Wednesday.

8918 ■ Research Foundation of CFA Institute
PO Box 3668
Charlottesville, VA 22903-0668
Ph:(434)951-5499
Free: 800—247-8132
Fax:(434)951-5370
Co. E-mail: rf@cfainstitute.org
URL: http://www.cfainstitute.org/about/foundation/Pages/index.aspx
Contact: John D. Rogers, Pres./CEO
E-mail: rf@cfainstitute.org

Scope: Financial analysis and portfolio management. **Publications:** Monographs.

8919 ■ Stetson University–Roland and Sara George Investments Institute
421 N Woodland Blvd., Unit 8398
DeLand, FL 32723
Ph:(386)822-7100
Free: 800—688-0101
Fax:(386)822-7491
Co. E-mail: lbelcher@stetson.edu
URL: http://business.stetson.edu/george/
Contact: Prof. Lawrence J. Belcher, Dir.
E-mail: lbelcher@stetson.edu

Scope: Investments. **Educational Activities:** Investment Seminars for academics and practitioners (annually); Public forums, on investing.

8920 ■ University of Chicago–Center for Research in Security Prices
105 W Adams St., Ste. 1700
Chicago, IL 60603
Ph:(312)263-6400
Fax:(312)263-6430
Co. E-mail: subscriptions@crsp.chicagobooth.edu
URL: http://www.crsp.chicagogsb.edu
Contact: David Barclay, COO
E-mail: subscriptions@crsp.chicagobooth.edu

Scope: Historical financial data.

8921 ■ University of Pennsylvania–Rodney L. White Center for Financial Research
3254 Steinberg Hall-Dietrich Hall
Philadelphia, PA 19104-6367
Ph:(215)898-7616
Fax:(215)573-8084
Co. E-mail: rlwctr@finance.wharton.upenn.edu
URL: http://finance.wharton.upenn.edu/lAtrlwctr
Contact: Dr. Donald B. Keim, Dir.
E-mail: rlwctr@finance.wharton.upenn.edu

Scope: Finance, including financial management, money and capital markets, urban and real estate finance, and international finance and financial institutions, designed to accelerate the flow of applied and theoretical research to business and academic communities. **Educational Activities:** Seminars (annually).

Fish and Seafood Store

ASSOCIATIONS AND OTHER ORGANIZATIONS

8922 ■ International Institute of Fisheries Economics and Trade
Oregon State University
Dept. of Agricultural and Resource Economics
Corvallis, OR 97331-3601
Ph:(541)737-1439
Fax:(541)737-2563
Co. E-mail: iifet@oregonstate.edu
URL: http://oregonstate.edu/Dept/IIFET
Contact: Kara Keenan, Asst.
Description: Individuals from the fisheries industry, government, and universities. Objectives are to: promote discussion on factors affecting seafood trade and fisheries management; facilitate cooperative research projects and data exchange. **Publications:** *Conference Proceedings* (biennial); *IIFET Newsletter* (semiannual);Membership Directory (annual).

8923 ■ Maine Lobstermen's Association
21 Western Ave., Ste. 1
Kennebunk, ME 04043
Ph:(207)967-4555
Fax:(866)407-3770
Co. E-mail: info@mainelobstermen.org
URL: http://www.mainelobstermen.org
Contact: Patrice McCarron, Exec. Dir.
Description: Licensed lobstermen and supporting business. Gives Maine's lobstermen a voice and influence at the highest levels of government. .

8924 ■ Northwest Fisheries Association
2208 NW Market St., Ste. 318
Seattle, WA 98107
Ph:(206)789-6197
Fax:(206)789-8147
Co. E-mail: info@northwestfisheries.org
URL: http://www.northwestfisheries.org
Contact: Chris Adams, Pres.
Description: Primary and secondary seafood processors, seafood brokers, distributors, and direct support industries. Provides a positive business climate for members and enhances the flow of information throughout the Pacific fishing and seafood industry. .

8925 ■ Southeastern Association of Fish and Wildlife Agencies
8005 Freshwater Farms Rd.
Tallahassee, FL 32308
Ph:(850)893-0084
URL: http://www.seafwa.org
Contact: Robert M. Brantly, Exec. Sec.
Description: Directors of state game and fish commissions in 16 southern states, and the Commonwealth of Puerto Rico, and the Virgin Islands. Aims to: protect the right of jurisdiction of southeastern states over their wildlife resources on public and private lands; study state and federal wildlife legislation and regulations as they affect the area; consult with and make recommendations to federal wildlife and public land agencies on federal management programs and programs involving federal aid to southeastern states; serve as a clearinghouse for exchange of ideas on wildlife management and research techniques. Sponsors: Cooperative Fish Disease Study at Auburn University in Alabama; Cooperative Wildlife Disease Study at the University of Georgia in Athens. **Publications:** *Southeastern Association of Fish and Wildlife Agencies Proceedings* (annual).

REFERENCE WORKS

8926 ■ "Convictions Under the Fisheries Act" in *Canadian Corporate News* (May 16, 2007)
Pub: Comtex News Network Inc.
Description: Fisheries and Oceans Canada is mandated to protect and conserve marine resources and thus released a list of fishers fined for various offences under the Fisheries Act in March and April.

8927 ■ "Counting Crabs: Supply Dips, Putting Crimp on Memorial Day Feast" in *Boston Business Journal* (Vol. 29, June 3, 2011, No. 4, pp. 1)
Pub: American City Business Journals Inc.
Ed: Scott Dance. **Description:** Restaurateurs in Baltimore City experienced low supply of crabs this Memorial Day 2011 owing to the early season and the fact that many small crabbers took time off during the weekend. Sales were cut in half compared with previous Memorial Day weekends and prices rose to as much as $185 to $200 per box of crabs. Normal supply is expected, though, as summer pushes on.

8928 ■ "An Ill Wind: Icelandic Bank Failures Chill Atlantic Canada" in *Canadian Business* (Vol. 81, November 10, 2008, No. 19, pp. 10)
Pub: Rogers Media Ltd.
Ed: Charles Mandel. **Description:** Bank failures in Iceland have put a stop to flights ferrying Icelanders to Newfoundland to purchase Christmas gifts, thereby threatening Newfoundland's tourism industry. The credit of Newfoundland's fisheries is also being squeezed since most of Atlantic Canadian seafood processors hold lines of credit from Icelandic banks.

8929 ■ "Life After Cod" in *Globe & Mail* (March 18, 2006, pp. B1)
Pub: CTVglobemedia Publishing Inc.
Ed: Gordon Pitts. **Description:** Canadian fishing industry is under threat because of Chinese processing competition, high energy costs, rise of powerful retailers and the rise of Canadian dollar value. Fishing industry of Canada is analyzed.

8930 ■ "The Mood of a Nation" in *Canadian Business* (Vol. 81, April 14, 2008, No. 6, pp. 56)
Pub: Rogers Media
Ed: Joe Castaldo. **Description:** Independent Fish Harvesters Inc. processes more kilograms a year and has had to hire more workers but its managers worry about how a slowdown in the U.S. economy will affect his business. A planned shopping complex in Mirabel Quebec, the manufacturing industry in Kitchener, Ontario, and a cattle farming business in Sarnia, Ontario are discussed to provide a snapshot of the challenges that business in Canada are facing as recession looms.

8931 ■ "Oil Rich" in *Canadian Business* (Vol. 79, Winter 2006, No. 24, pp. 57)
Pub: Rogers Media
Ed: Calvin Leung. **Description:** The efforts of John Risley, the Chairman of the Candaian firm Clearwater Fine Foods Inc., to educate consumers about the health aspects of seafood, are described.

8932 ■ "Paying the Price" in *Baltimore Business Journal* (Vol. 28, July 9, 2010, No. 9, pp. 1)
Pub: Baltimore Business Journal
Ed: Emily Mullin. **Description:** Crab prices have never been higher in Baltimore, Maryland and businesses have been led to count on strengthening demand for seafood. For instance, the average price for a dozen large crabs has increased by 5 percent to $58.90. How restaurants have responded to the increase in prices is discussed, along with factors that might have caused the harvest of smaller crabs.

8933 ■ "Something's Fishy" in *Canadian Business* (Vol. 83, September 14, 2010, No. 15, pp. 71)
Pub: Rogers Media Ltd.
Ed: Matthew McClearn. **Description:** The Marine Stewardship Council (MSC) is offering a widely recognized blue check mark to certify that the seafood being sold has not been overfished, nor harvested in a way that harms the ecosystems. However, the MSC certification of Fraser sockeye salmon has put into question its credibility.

TRADE PERIODICALS

8934 ■ *Seafood Price-Current*
Pub: Urner Barry Publications Inc.
Ed: Paul B. Brown, Jr., Editor. **Released:** Semiweekly. **Price:** $383. **Description:** Provides seafood market price quotations for fresh and frozen fin and shell fish throughout the United States.

8935 ■ *Shrimp Notes*
Pub: Shrimp World Inc.
Ed: William D. Chauvin, Editor, chauvin@shrimpcom.com. **Released:** Monthly. **Description:** Analyzes factors determining the shrimp market status, including U.S. shrimp imports, domestic production, and economic factors.

LIBRARIES

8936 ■ Oregon State University–Seafoods Research Laboratory Library
2001 Marine Dr., Rm. 253
Astoria, OR 97103
Ph:(503)325-4531
Fax:(503)325-2753
Co. E-mail: michael.morrissey@oregonstate.edu
URL: http://osuseafoodlab.oregonstate.edu/
Contact: Dr. Michael T. Morrissey, Dir.
Scope: Fisheries, marine food science and technology, fish processing, seafood safety. **Holdings:** 380 volumes.

RESEARCH CENTERS

8937 ■ North Central Regional Aquaculture Center
13 Natural Resources Bldg.
Michigan State University
East Lansing, MI 48824-1222
Ph:(517)353-1962
Fax:(517)353-7181
Co. E-mail: batters2@msu.edu
URL: http://www.ncrac.org
Contact: Dr. Ted R. Batterson, Dir.
E-mail: batters2@msu.edu

Scope: Aquaculture products, focusing on increasing production of fish; improving breeding and culture technology for walleye, yellow perch, hybrid striped bass; and sunfish; developing techniques to preserve and transport gametes for year-round production; improving fish strains; enhancing development of domestic commercial aquaculture industry; and reducing foreign product dependency for the benefit of producers, consumers, and the economy. **Services:** Information exchange between industry and researchers. **Educational Activities:** Cooperative research projects; Extension educational programs.

8938 ■ Northeastern Regional Aquaculture Center
2113 Animal Sciences Bldg.
University of Maryland
College Park, MD 20742-2317
Ph:(301)405-6085
Fax:(301)314-9412
Co. E-mail: rharrell@umd.edu
URL: http://www.nrac.umd.edu
Contact: Dr. Reginal Harrell, Dir.
E-mail: rharrell@umd.edu

Scope: Aquaculture in the Northeastern United States. **Services:** Offers information exchange between industry and researchers. **Publications:** Northeastern Aquaculture. **Educational Activities:** Cooperative research projects; Extension educational programs.

8939 ■ Southern Regional Aquaculture Center
127 Experiment Station Rd.
PO Box 197
Stoneville, MS 38776-0197
Ph:(662)686-3285
Fax:(662)686-3320
Co. E-mail: ctucker@drec.msstate.edu
URL: http://www.msstate.edu/dept/srac
Contact: Dr. Craig S. Tucker, Dir.
E-mail: ctucker@drec.msstate.edu

Scope: Aquaculture and seafood products, focusing on increasing production of fish and shellfish, enhancing development of domestic commercial aquaculture industry, and reducing foreign product dependency for the benefit of producers, consumers, and the economy. **Services:** Information exchange between industry and researchers. **Educational Activities:** Cooperative research projects; Extension educational programs.

ASSOCIATIONS AND OTHER ORGANIZATIONS

8940 ■ American Fisheries Society
5410 Grosvenor Ln., Ste. 110
Bethesda, MD 20814-2199
Ph:(301)897-8616
Fax:(301)897-8096
Co. E-mail: grassam@fisheries.org
URL: http://www.fisheries.org
Contact: Ghassan N. Rassam, Exec. Dir.

Description: International scientific organization of fisheries and aquatic science professionals, including fish culturists, fish biologists, water quality scientists, fish health professionals, fish technologists, educators, limnologists, and oceanographers. Promotes the development of all branches of fishery science and practice, and the conservation, development, and wise utilization of fisheries, both recreational and commercial. Strengthens professional standards by certifying fisheries scientists, stressing professional ethics, and providing forums for the exchange of scientific and management information. Represents members through written and verbal testimony before legislative and administrative bodies concerning aquatic environmental issues. Maintains over 30 committees. **Publications:** *AFS Membership Directory and Handbook* (annual); *Fisheries* (monthly); *Journal of Aquatic Animal Health* (quarterly); *North American Journal of Aquaculture* (quarterly); *North American Journal of Fisheries Management* (bimonthly); *Transactions of the American Fisheries Society* (bimonthly).

8941 ■ American Institute of Fishery Research Biologists
7909 Sleaford Pl.
Bethesda, MD 20814
Co. E-mail: allen.shimada@noaa.gov
URL: http://www.aifrb.org
Contact: Richard Beamish, Pres.

Description: Professional scientific and educational organization formed to: advance the theory and practice of fishery science in pursuit of greater scientific understanding of living marine and freshwater natural resources, their habitat, their biological and physical environment, and their fisheries; support the education of students and the general public, and the professional development and recognition of researchers, practitioners, and institutions in fishery science and related areas of natural resource management public policy, and public affairs; and foster the application of scientific knowledge to the sustainable use, conservation and sound management of living aquatic resources and their allied human applications (having commercial, recreational, subsistence, and aesthetic or intrinsic value to society). **Publications:** *BRIEFS* (bimonthly);Membership Directory (periodic).

8942 ■ Atlantic Salmon Federation
PO Box 5200
St. Andrews, NB, Canada E5B 3S8
Ph:(506)529-1033
Fax:(506)529-4438
Co. E-mail: savesalmon@asf.ca
URL: http://www.asf.ca
Contact: Bill Taylor, Pres./CEO

Description: Represents the interest of conservationists, scientists, government personnel, and salmon anglers. Promotes the preservation and better management of Atlantic salmon stocks. Encourages international cooperation; coordinates education and research in the field. Maintains aquarium exhibits. **Publications:** *Atlantic Salmon* (quarterly). **Telecommunication Services:** electronic mail, btaylor@asf.ca.

8943 ■ Florida Tropical Fish Farms Association
PO Box 1519
Winter Haven, FL 33882
Ph:(863)293-5710
Fax:(863)299-5154
Co. E-mail: flassn@aol.com
URL: http://www.ftffa.com
Contact: David Boozer, Exec. Dir.

Description: Growers of tropical fish and aquatic plants; associate members are manufacturers and suppliers of allied products in Florida and elsewhere in the U.S. Seeks to elevate trade standards and promote the industry. Sponsors quarterly meeting to hear speakers on the care of tropical fish, applicable laws, and other aspects of the trade. Resources include an organization-owned co-op. .

8944 ■ International Association of Astacology
Auburn University
Dept. of Fisheries and Allied Aquaculture
203 Swingle Hall
Auburn University, AL 36849-5419
Ph:(334)844-4786
Fax:(334)844-9208
Co. E-mail: garzaan@auburn.edu
URL: http://iz.carnegiemnh.org/crayfish/iaa/index.htm
Contact: James Fetzner, Pres.

Description: Individuals from industry, academia, and state and federal government wildlife agencies. Promotes the scientific study and cultivation of freshwater crayfish. Sponsors 8 working groups in areas such as biology, ecology, and zoogeography. .

8945 ■ International Institute of Fisheries Economics and Trade
Oregon State University
Dept. of Agricultural and Resource Economics
Corvallis, OR 97331-3601
Ph:(541)737-1439
Fax:(541)737-2563
Co. E-mail: iifet@oregonstate.edu
URL: http://oregonstate.edu/Dept/IIFET
Contact: Kara Keenan, Asst.

Description: Individuals from the fisheries industry, government, and universities. Objectives are to: promote discussion on factors affecting seafood trade and fisheries management; facilitate cooperative research projects and data exchange. **Publications:** *Conference Proceedings* (biennial); *IIFET Newsletter* (semiannual);Membership Directory (annual).

8946 ■ National Shellfisheries Association
University of Connecticut
Dept. of Marine Sciences
1080 Shennecossett Rd.
Groton, CT 06340
Ph:(860)405-9282
Fax:(860)405-9153
Co. E-mail: creswell@ufl.edu
URL: http://shellfish.org
Contact: Mr. R. Leroy Creswell, Pres.

Description: Biologists, hydrographers, public health workers, shellfish producers, and fishery administrators. Encourages research on mollusks and crustaceans, with emphasis on those forms of economic importance known as shellfish. .

8947 ■ North Pacific Anadromous Fish Commission
889 W Pender St., Ste. 502
Vancouver, BC, Canada V6C 3B2
Ph:(604)775-5550
Fax:(604)775-5577
Co. E-mail: secretariat@npafc.org
URL: http://www.npafc.org
Contact: Mr. Vladimir Fedorenko, Exec. Dir.

Description: Represents administrators and scientists devoted to the conservation of salmon in the North Pacific Ocean. Seeks to prohibits commercial salmon fishing in the high seas of the Pacific, between the United States, Canada, Japan, Republic of Korea and Russian Federation. Coordinates fisheries enforcement and scientific researches on the high seas of the North Pacific. **Publications:** *NPAFC Annual Report* (annual); *NPAFC Bulletin*; *NPAFC Technical Report*; *Statistical Yearbook* (annual).

8948 ■ Northwest Atlantic Fisheries Organization–Organisation des Peches de l'Atlantique Nord-Ouest
PO Box 638
Dartmouth, NS, Canada B2Y 3Y9
Ph:(902)468-5590
Fax:(902)468-5538
Co. E-mail: info@nafo.int
URL: http://www.nafo.int
Contact: Dr. Vladimir Shibanov, Exec. Sec.

Description: Contracting parties working to investigate, protect, and conserve the fishery resources of the Northwest Atlantic Ocean. Provides resource management. Compiles statistics; maintains research programs. **Publications:** *Journal of Northwest Atlantic Fishery Science*; *Meeting Proceedings* (annual); *Scientific Council Reports* (annual).

8949 ■ Pacific Coast Shellfish Growers Association
120 State Ave. NE
PMB No. 142
Olympia, WA 98501
Ph:(360)754-2744

Fax:(360)754-2743
Co. E-mail: pcsga@pcsga.org
URL: http://www.pcsga.org
Contact: Margaret Pilaro Barrette, Exec. Dir.
Description: Oyster, clam, mussel, scallop, geoduck growers, openers, packers and shippers in Alaska, California, Oregon, Washington, Hawaii and Mexico.
.

8950 ■ Pacific Salmon Commission
600-1155 Robson St.
Vancouver, BC, Canada V6E 1B5
Ph:(604)684-8081
Fax:(604)666-8707
Co. E-mail: info@psc.org
URL: http://www.psc.org
Contact: Don Kowal, Exec. Sec.
Description: Formed by treaty between Canada and the United States for the conservation, management and optimum production of Pacific Salmon. **Publications:** *Fraser River Panel Annual Report*; *Pacific Salmon Commission Annual Report* .

8951 ■ Southeastern Fisheries Association
1118-B Thomasville Rd.
Tallahassee, FL 32303
Ph:(850)224-0612
Fax:(850)222-3663
Co. E-mail: bobfish@aol.com
URL: http://www.southeasternfish.org/index.html
Contact: Bob Jones, Exec. Dir.
Description: Producers, distributors and suppliers of seafood in the South Atlantic and Gulf of Mexico areas. Disseminates information on legislation, both proposed and implemented, that affects fishermen in that area. Promotes and represents commercial fishermen's interests in legislative, industrial and environmental matters. Provides HAACP training onsite. **Publications:** *Importing Seafood - A Buyer's Guide*; *International Conference on Shrimp Bycatch* .

8952 ■ U.S. Trout Farmers Association
PO Box 1647
Pine Bluff, AR 71613
Ph:(870)850-7900
Fax:(870)850-7902
Co. E-mail: ustfa@thenaa.net
URL: http://www.ustfa.org
Contact: Charlie Conklin, Pres.
Description: Trout farmers, suppliers, academics, students, and individuals interested in the trout farming industry. Promotes the trout farming industry and recreational trout fishing. Establishes Trout Farmers Quality Assurance Program; monitors legislation related to the aquaculture industry. **Publications:** *Trout Talk* (quarterly).

REFERENCE WORKS

8953 ■ "Counting Crabs: Supply Dips, Putting Crimp on Memorial Day Feast" in *Boston Business Journal* **(Vol. 29, June 3, 2011, No. 4, pp. 1)**
Pub: American City Business Journals Inc.
Ed: Scott Dance. **Description:** Restaurateurs in Baltimore City experienced low supply of crabs this Memorial Day 2011 owing to the early season and the fact that many small crabbers took time off during the weekend. Sales were cut in half compared with previous Memorial Day weekends and prices rose to as much as $185 to $200 per box of crabs. Normal supply is expected, though, as summer pushes on.

8954 ■ *Fisheries of the United States*
Pub: National Marine Fisheries Service
Contact: Deborah Hogans, Member
Ed: Barbara K. O'Bannon, Editor. **Released:** Annual, Latest edition 2009. **Price:** $20, individuals s/n 003-020-00178-5. **Covers:** fisheries throughout the country as compiled in government statistical reports.

8955 ■ "An Ill Wind: Icelandic Bank Failures Chill Atlantic Canada" in *Canadian Business* **(Vol. 81, November 10, 2008, No. 19, pp. 10)**
Pub: Rogers Media Ltd.
Ed: Charles Mandel. **Description:** Bank failures in Iceland have put a stop to flights ferrying Icelanders to Newfoundland to purchase Christmas gifts, thereby

threatening Newfoundland's tourism industry. The credit of Newfoundland's fisheries is also being squeezed since most of Atlantic Canadian seafood processors hold lines of credit from Icelandic banks.

8956 ■ "Life After Cod" in *Globe & Mail* **(March 18, 2006, pp. B1)**
Pub: CTVglobemedia Publishing Inc.
Ed: Gordon Pitts. **Description:** Canadian fishing industry is under threat because of Chinese processing competition, high energy costs, rise of powerful retailers and the rise of Canadian dollar value. Fishing industry of Canada is analyzed.

8957 ■ "The Mood of a Nation" in *Canadian Business* **(Vol. 81, April 14, 2008, No. 6, pp. 56)**
Pub: Rogers Media
Ed: Joe Castaldo. **Description:** Independent Fish Harvesters Inc. processes more kilograms a year and has had to hire more workers but its managers worry about how a slowdown in the U.S. economy will affect his business. A planned shopping complex in Mirabel Quebec, the manufacturing industry in Kitchener, Ontario, and a cattle farming business in Sarnia, Ontario are discussed to provide a snapshot of the challenges that business in Canada are facing as recession looms.

8958 ■ "Oil Rich" in *Canadian Business* **(Vol. 79, Winter 2006, No. 24, pp. 57)**
Pub: Rogers Media
Ed: Calvin Leung. **Description:** The efforts of John Risley, the Chairman of the Canadian firm Clearwater Fine Foods Inc., to educate consumers about the health aspects of seafood, are described.

8959 ■ "Paying the Price" in *Baltimore Business Journal* **(Vol. 28, July 9, 2010, No. 9, pp. 1)**
Pub: Baltimore Business Journal
Ed: Emily Mullin. **Description:** Crab prices have never been higher in Baltimore, Maryland and businesses have been led to count on strengthening demand for seafood. For instance, the average price for a dozen large crabs has increased by 5 percent to $58.90. How restaurants have responded to the increase in prices is discussed, along with factors that might have caused the harvest of smaller crabs.

8960 ■ "Small Fish, Big Box Stores" in *Hawaii Business* **(Vol. 53, November 2007, No. 5, pp. 55)**
Pub: Hawaii Business Publishing
Ed: Jolyn Okimoto Rosa. **Description:** Ohana Seafoods can be found at big-box stores such as Costco, Marukai and Don Quijote. Owner Jeffrey Yee spends his weekend at a farmers market to have direct contact with his customers and get feedback right away. Ohana offers ready-to cook fish products, sauces and fish.

8961 ■ "Something's Fishy" in *Canadian Business* **(Vol. 83, September 14, 2010, No. 15, pp. 71)**
Pub: Rogers Media Ltd.
Ed: Matthew McClearn. **Description:** The Marine Stewardship Council (MSC) is offering a widely recognized blue check mark to certify that the seafood being sold has not been overfished, nor harvested in a way that harms the ecosystems. However, the MSC certification of Fraser sockeye salmon has put into question its credibility.

TRADE PERIODICALS

8962 ■ *Alternative Aquaculture Network*
Pub: Alternative Aquaculture Association
Ed: Steven Van Gorder, Editor. **Released:** Quarterly. **Description:** Provides research and practical information on the application of low-energy/high-productivity methods for small and medium scale aquaculture. Covers developments in integrated and recirculating methods of aquaculture, emphasizing energy efficiency and resource conservation. Recurring features include editorials, letters to the editor, book reviews, and a calendar of events.

8963 ■ *Aquaculture Magazine*
Pub: Achill River Corp.
Contact: Greg Gallagher, Editor & Publisher
Released: Bimonthly. **Price:** $24; $30 Canada and Mexico; $44 two years; $50 Canada and Mexico 2 years; $60 other countries. **Description:** Magazine serving aqua culturists engaged in the production, processing, and marketing of finfish, shellfish, crustaceans, and aquatic plants.

8964 ■ *Fishery Bulletin*
Pub: U.S. Government Printing Office and Superintendent of Documents
Contact: Richard D. Brodeur PhD, Sci. Ed.
E-mail: rick.brodeur@noaa.gov
Released: Quarterly. **Price:** $36; $50.40 other countries international. **Description:** Bulletin publishing original research on all aspects of fishery science.

8965 ■ *National Fisherman*
Pub: National Fisherman
Contact: Jerry Fraser, Editor-in-Chief
E-mail: jfraser@divcom.com
Released: Monthly. **Price:** $14.95; $24.95 Canada; $39.95 other countries; $26.95 two years; $46.95 two years Canada; $76.95 two years and other countries. **Description:** Magazine covering commercial fishing and boat building.

8966 ■ *North American Journal of Aquaculture*
Pub: American Fisheries Society
Ed: Christopher C. Kohler, Editor. **Released:** Quarterly. **Price:** $45 print, North America; $25 online, North America; $70 print and online, North America; $54 out of country print; $25 out of country online; $79 out of country print and online. **Description:** Aquaculture journal.

TRADE SHOWS AND CONVENTIONS

8967 ■ American Fisheries Society Annual Meeting
American Fisheries Society
5410 Grosvenor Ln., Ste. 110
Bethesda, MD 20814-2199
Ph:(301)897-8616
Fax:(301)897-8096
Co. E-mail: main@fisheries.org
URL: http://www.fisheries.org
Released: Annual. **Audience:** Fisheries biologists, administrators, and related professionals. **Principal Exhibits:** Equipment, supplies, and services related to fishery and marine biology. **Dates and Locations:** 2011 Sep 04-08, Seattle, WA; 2012 Aug 19-23.

CONSULTANTS

8968 ■ Aquatic Control Inc.
3001 Cascade Dr.
PO Box 100
Valparaiso, IN 46383
Ph:(812)497-2410
Free: 800-753-5253
Fax:(812)497-2460
Co. E-mail: sales@aquaticcontrol.com
URL: http://www.aquaticcontrol.com
Contact: Scott Shuler, Treas & Sec
E-mail: scotts@aquaticcontrol.com
Scope: Provides consulting services in aquatic and terrestrial ecology, including fish and wildlife population management, industrial fish and wild life enhancement programs, aquatic weed control, fish stocking, management of cooling reservoirs, and lake aeration equipment, consultation installation and maintenance.

8969 ■ Canadian Fishery Consultants Ltd.
199/187 Obeysekara Cres., Rajagiriya Rd.
PO Box 606
Colombo B3J 2R7, Sri Lanka
Ph:(902)422-4698

Fax:(902)422-8147
Co. E-mail: cfcl@canfish.com
URL: http://www.canfish.com
Contact: Wayne Lewis, Vice President
Scope: Natural resources management consultants specialize in supplying professional expertise to sectors within the fishing/aquaculture industry. Offers a range of expertise dealing with the culturing, harvesting, processing, and marketing of fish species. Projects executed have involved financial and technical feasibility studies; design, evaluation, and retrofitting of fish processing facilities; resource analysis; site selection; design of fish culturing facilities; and increasing commercial use of fish processing wastes and by-catch. Industries served: fisheries, resource sector, processing/fish handling industry, government departments, environmental sectors, port authorities, international financing institutions. **Seminars:** Care of Live Shellfish During Shipping; Use of Fish Offal in Aquaculture Feed; Hold Live Fish and Shellfish; Exporting Goods and Services to the Caribbean.

8970 ■ Southern Fish Culturists Inc.
7608 US Hwy. 441 S
PO Box 490251
Leesburg, FL 34749
Ph:(352)787-1360
Contact: Jack DeQuine, President
Scope: Provides counseling services in problems of aquatic ecology: Effects of pollution on aquatic organisms, fish kill evaluations, environmental assessments, fish and bait culture, fisheries management and aquatic weed control. Serves private industries as well as government agencies.

LIBRARIES

8971 ■ Auburn University–International Center for Aquaculture and Aquatic Environments Library
Dept. of Fisheries and Allied Aquacultures
203 Swingle Hall
Auburn University, AL 36849
Ph:(334)844-4786
Fax:(334)844-9208
Co. E-mail: fish@auburn.edu
URL: http://www.ag.auburn.edu/fish/international
Contact: Bryan L. Duncan, Dir.
Scope: Aquaculture in fresh, brackish, and marine water; aquatic plants management; nutrition and feeds; parasites and disease; limnology; water quality and management for aquaculture; International development for fisheries and aquaculture. **Holdings:** 2500 books; Annual reports of the Fisheries Resources Unit, 1936 to present; 10,000 slides and pictures; 250 dissertations; 550 theses.

8972 ■ Columbia River Inter-Tribal Fish Commission–StreamNet Library
Columbia River Inter-Tribal Fish Commission
729 NE Oregon St., Ste. 190
Portland, OR 97232-2107
Ph:(503)238-0667
Fax:(503)235-4228
Co. E-mail: oftl@critfc.org
URL: http://www.fishlib.org
Contact: Lenora Oftedahl, StreamNet Reg.Libn.
Scope: Fisheries science, habitat and watersheds, fisheries management, Columbia River Basin. **Services:** Interlibrary loan; copying; Library open to the public. **Holdings:** 60,000 volumes. **Subscriptions:** 20 journals and other serials.

8973 ■ Desmond-Fish Library
472 Rte. 403
PO Box 265
Garrison, NY 10524
Ph:(845)424-3020
Fax:(845)424-4061
Co. E-mail: donick@highlands.com
URL: http://dfl.highlands.com
Contact: Carol Donick, Lib.Dir.
Scope: Hudson River art and history, Hamilton Fish. **Services:** Interlibrary loan; copying; Library open to the public. **Holdings:** 27,000 books. **Subscriptions:** 100 journals and other serials.

8974 ■ Fisheries Museum of the Atlantic Library
68 Bluenose Dr.
PO Box 1363
Lunenburg, NS, Canada B0J 2C0
Ph:(902)634-4794
Free: (866)579-4909
Fax:(902)634-8990
Co. E-mail: fma@gov.ns.ca
URL: http://museum.gov.ns.ca/fma/
Contact: Heather-Anne Getson, Hist.
Scope: Fisheries history, history, naval architecture, natural history of fish. **Services:** Library open to the public for reference use only. **Holdings:** 2000 books; reports; archival material; 134 reels of microfilm; audio/visual materials. **Subscriptions:** 24 journals and other serials; 2 newspapers.

8975 ■ Ocean Resource Conservation Alliance Library
PO Box 1189
Sechelt, BC, Canada V0N 3A0
Ph:(604)885-7518
Fax:(604)885-2518
Contact: Mr. Teri Dawe, Dir.
Scope: Environmental and socioeconomic effects of fish farming. **Services:** Copying; Library open to the public by appointment. **Holdings:** 37 books; 63 bound periodical volumes; 5 files. **Subscriptions:** 3 newspapers.

8976 ■ Oklahoma Fisheries Research Laboratory Library
500 E. Constellation St.
Norman, OK 73072-7900
Ph:(405)325-7288
Fax:(405)325-7631
Co. E-mail: gregsumm@aol.com
URL: http://www.biosurvey.ou.edu/fishlab.html
Contact: Greg L. Summers, Dir.
Scope: Freshwater fisheries, aquatic ecology, fish, limnology, fishery management, animal genetics. **Services:** Copying; Library open to the public for reference use only. **Holdings:** 68,000 volumes.

8977 ■ U.S. National Oceanic & Atmospheric Administration–Library and Information Services Division–Central Library (1315)
1315 East-West Hwy.
SSMC 3, 2nd Fl.
Silver Spring, MD 20910
Ph:(301)713-2600
Fax:(301)713-4598
Co. E-mail: library.reference@noaa.gov
URL: http://www.lib.noaa.gov
Contact: Janice Beattie, Div.Dir.
Scope: Geodesy, surveying, oceanography, geophysics, geodetic and hydrographic surveying, photogrammetry, nautical and aeronautical cartography, fisheries, geodetic astronomy, meteorology, climatology, hydrology, atmospheric physics, ocean engineering, mathematics, computer science. **Services:** Interlibrary loan; copying; SDI; Library open to the public for reference use only. **Holdings:** 800,000 volumes; 100,100 bound periodical volumes; 100,400 bound documents; 19,500 microfiche; 34,000 reports, maps, charts, data publications. **Subscriptions:** 9040 journals and other serials.

RESEARCH CENTERS

8978 ■ Aquatic Research Institute
2242 Davis Ct.
Hayward, CA 94545
Ph:(510)782-4058
Fax:(510)784-0945
Co. E-mail: rofen@novalek.com
Contact: Dr. Robert R. Rofen, Dir.
E-mail: rofen@novalek.com
Scope: Aquaculture, fisheries, aquatic sciences, and technology. **Services:** Consulting, in aquatic sciences and technology.

8979 ■ Auburn University–Alabama Agricultural Experiment Station–Department of Fisheries and Allied Aquacultures
203 Swingle Hall
Auburn, AL 36849
Ph:(334)844-4786
Fax:(334)844-9208
Co. E-mail: goodmrk@auburn.edu
URL: http://www.ag.auburn.edu/fish
Contact: Randall K. Goodman, Dir.
E-mail: goodmrk@auburn.edu
Scope: Aquaculture in fresh, brackish, and marine water; fisheries management in large and small impoundments, and rivers; aquatic plants management; nutrition and feeds; parasites and disease; limnology; water quality and management for aquaculture; international development for fisheries and aquaculture; aquatic ecology and environmental assessment; environmental education. **Publications:** Newsletter Quarterly (quarterly). **Educational Activities:** Aquaculture Training Program, from mid-March to mid-July; Master of Aquaculture Program; Philosophy Degree Programs, in aquaculture and fisheries; Short courses, for fisheries biologists and aquaculturists.

8980 ■ Canadian Centre for Fisheries Innovation–Le Centre Canadien pour l'Innovation dans les Pecheries
PO Box 4920
St. John's, NL, Canada A1C 5R3
Ph:(709)778-0517
Fax:(709)778-0516
Co. E-mail: robert.verge@mi.mun.ca
URL: http://www.ccfi.ca
Contact: Robert Verge, Mng.Dir.
E-mail: robert.verge@mi.mun.ca
Scope: Marine and freshwater fisheries, including aquaculture, harvesting and processing, and fisheries equipment development. Projects include design and development of harvesting technologies and vessels; fish product development; aquaculture issues; development of new fisheries; and fish genetics. **Services:** Research and development, technology transfer, workshops, and information dissemination, to the Canadian fishery and aquaculture industry. **Publications:** Annual report; Project Reports.

8981 ■ Maine Aquaculture Innovation Center
5717 Corbett Hall, Rm. 436
Orono, ME 04469-5717
Ph:(207)581-2263
Fax:(207)581-1479
Co. E-mail: maic@maineaquaculture.org
URL: http://www.maineaquaculture.org
Contact: Christopher V. Davis, Exec.Dir.
E-mail: maic@maineaquaculture.org
Scope: Aquaculture, including identification of suitable aquaculture sites, toxic phytoplankton monitoring lease sites, shellfish poisoning by toxic phytoplankton, shellfish genetics, public aquaculture of soft-shell clams, finfish health management, new and novel species, product quality control, aquaculture equipment, recycling fish processing wastes, and finfish feed technology, new species research, and environmental monitoring.

8982 ■ Memorial University of Newfoundland–Centre for Aquaculture and Seafood Development
Fisheries & Marine Institute
PO Box 4920
St. John's, NL, Canada A1C 5R3
Ph:(709)778-0532
Free: 800—563-5799
Fax:(709)778-0670
Co. E-mail: heather.manuel@mi.mun.ca
URL: http://www.mi.mun.ca/casd
Contact: Heather Manuel, Dir.
E-mail: heather.manuel@mi.mun.ca
Scope: Development of new seafood products, added value products, equipment and process material development, and market base enhancement, techniques in food science and technology, food engineering, food safety, and marketing and management. Aquaculture research in areas of fish nutrition, shellfish culture, site evaluations, land based systems, and technical advisory services. **Services:** Of-

fers analytical services, such as nutritional, microbial, and quality assessments; Provides assistance, to companies in selecting equipment, processing, and quality control and productivity concerns. **Educational Activities:** Educational services and technical workshops, in harvesting, aquaculture, processing and industrial engineering.

8983 ■ Oceanic Institute

41-202 Kalanianaole Hwy.
Waimanalo, HI 96795
Ph:(808)259-7951
Fax:(808)259-5971
Co. E-mail: hr@oceanicinstitute.org
URL: http://www.oceanicinstitute.org
Contact: Anthony C. Ostrowski PhD, Pres.
E-mail: hr@oceanicinstitute.org
Scope: Marine aquaculture focusing on technological development for commercial feasibility domestically and abroad, of finfish, ornamentals, and marine shrimp of all species; hatchery technologies, including maturation, spawning, larval rearing, and juvenile production; growout systems, including facility design, feeds, health management, and production capability development; marine shrimp work, focusing on the development of populations of high-health, genetically improved species for the global broodstock market; specialized work in nutrition, including feeds science and technology, aquatic nutrition, aquatic food processing, aquatic nutraceuticals, analytical biochemistry, and aquatic microbiology; applied environmental science, focusing on aquaculture development systems with design monitoring and analytical capabilities for water quality, tissues, and soils; technologies and training, including aquaculture, information transfer, local, domestic, and international training programs; technology commercialization in Egypt, Indonesia, Ecuador, and Peru; and stock enhancement strategies, including the exchange of aquaculture technology between Asia, South Pacific, and the West. **Services:** Technical services. **Publications:** Annual report (annually); Research papers (periodically). **Educational Activities:** Training courses, in marine aquaculture practices; Workshops, in marine aquaculture practices.

8984 ■ State University of New York at Stony Brook–Living Marine Resources Institute

School of Marine & Atmospheric Sciences
Stony Brook, NY 11794-5000
Ph:(631)632-8700
Fax:(631)632-8820
Co. E-mail: wwise@notes.cc.sunysb.edu
URL: http://www.somas.stonybrook.edu/institutes/lmri.html
Contact: William Wise, Dir.
E-mail: wwise@notes.cc.sunysb.edu
Scope: Commercial fisheries, sport fisheries, and aquaculture. Activities focus on shellfish biology, population dynamics, finfish biology, algal blooms (commonly known as brown tides), seaweed physiology and mariculture, and bay scallop population dynamics. Conducts studies on the economic structure of living marine resource industries, the effects of development on fisheries habitat, and marine fisheries policy and management. **Services:** Public lectures.

8985 ■ University of British Columbia–Fisheries Centre

Aquatic Ecosystems Research Laboratory
2202 Main Mall
Vancouver, BC, Canada V6T 1Z4
Ph:(604)822-2731
Fax:(604)822-8934
Co. E-mail: r.sumaila@fisheries.ubc.ca
URL: http://www.fisheries.ubc.ca
Contact: Dr. Ussif Rashid Sumaila, Dir.
E-mail: r.sumaila@fisheries.ubc.ca
Scope: Assessment and management of artisanal and commercial fisheries, impact of fisheries on aquatic ecosystems, recreational fisheries, coastal and watershed management, co-management of shared fishery resources and conflict resolution, and the conservation of endangered species and exploited aquatic animal resources. **Publications:** Research reports (bimonthly). **Educational Activities:** Seminars (weekly), during spring and fall, open to all; Workshops (biennially).

8986 ■ University of Idaho–Aquaculture Research Institute

Bldg. 2260, Poultry Hill
PO Box 442260
Moscow, ID 83844-2260
Ph:(208)837-9096
Fax:(208)837-6047
Co. E-mail: rhardy@uidaho.edu
URL: http://www.webs.uidaho.edu/aquaculture
Contact: Prof. Ronald W. Hardy PhD, Dir.
E-mail: rhardy@uidaho.edu
Scope: Commercial and conservation aquaculture, including fish culture and production efficiency; fish nutrition and growth physiology; fish genetics and breeding; fish health and pathology; fish waste management and water quality assurance; aquaculture marketing and economics; aquaculture facility design; and fish behavior and life histories. Focus is on salmonids and endangered species of the Pacific Northwest. **Services:** Aquaculture industry assistance. **Publications:** Idaho Aquaculture News (quarterly). **Educational Activities:** K-12 outreach activities; Workshops, short courses.

8987 ■ University of Maryland–Crane Aquaculture Facility

1413 Animal Sciences Center
Department of Animal & Avian Sciences
College Park, MD 20742-2311
Ph:(301)405-1366
Fax:(301)405-7980
Co. E-mail: curry@umd.edu
URL: http://ansc.umd.edu/facilities/index.cfm?directory=MERC_aqua_unit.cfm
Contact: Dr. Curry Woods, Supvr.
E-mail: curry@umd.edu
Scope: Domestic and genetic selection of striped bass or rockfish for accelerated growth and earlier maturation. Other activities include striped bass reproduction, nutrition, disease prevention, stress physiology and cryobiology. **Services:** Provides juvenile to mature striped bass for outside research, demonstrations, and donations; Technology transfer for aquaculture industry.

8988 ■ University of Memphis–Ecological Research Center

Park Ave. Campus
Memphis, TN 38152
Ph:(901)678-2594
Fax:(901)327-8001
Co. E-mail: bsimco@memphis.edu
URL: http://www.memphis.edu/erc
Contact: Dr. Bill A. Simco, Co-Dir.
E-mail: bsimco@memphis.edu
Scope: Wildlife and fisheries studies and environmental assessments, including investigations of endangered species, wildlife management, and studies of migratory birds and wetlands. Also conducts aquaculture studies on channel catfish reproduction, factors limiting production, and stress responses to aquaculture practices. Research and graduate training in Urban Ecology.

8989 ■ University of New Hampshire–New Hampshire Sea Grant College Program

Chase Ocean Engineering Lab
24 Colovos Rd.
Durham, NH 03824-3505
Ph:(603)862-7007
Fax:(603)862-0241
Co. E-mail: jonathan.pennock@unh.edu
URL: http://www.seagrant.unh.edu
Contact: Jonathan R. Pennock PhD, Dir.
E-mail: jonathan.pennock@unh.edu
Scope: Marine and estuarine sciences, including lobster resources and the lobster industry; social and scientific issues relating to fisheries management; fisheries development, marketing, harvesting, and processing; aquaculture; construction in the coastal zone; marine pollution; cumulative impacts of the coastal environment; coastal law and policy; marine biotechnology; and marine recreation and tourism, including environmental impact and use conflict, sport fishing, and economic development. **Educational Activities:** Coastal Floating Lab Program; Great Bay Coast Watch Program; Great Bay Living Lab Program; Sea Grant Extension Program; Sea Trek Program; UNH Marine Docent Program.

8990 ■ Western Regional Aquaculture Center

School of Aquatic & Fishery Sciences, Box 355020
University of Washington
Seattle, WA 98195-5020
Ph:(206)543-4291
Fax:(206)685-4674
Co. E-mail: grahamy@u.washington.edu
URL: http://www.fish.washington.edu/wrac
Contact: Dr. Graham Young, Exec.Dir.
E-mail: grahamy@u.washington.edu
Scope: Aquaculture and seafood products, focusing on increasing production of fish and shellfish, developing and testing vaccines for the IHN virus which affects commercial trout and salmon stocks, enhancing development of domestic commercial aquaculture industry, and reducing foreign product dependency for the benefit of producers, consumers, and the economy. **Services:** Information exchange between industry and researchers. **Publications:** Waterlines (semiannually). **Educational Activities:** Cooperative research projects; Extension educational programs.

Floor Covering/Restoration Business

ASSOCIATIONS AND OTHER ORGANIZATIONS

8991 ■ American Floorcovering Alliance
210 W Cuyler St.
Dalton, GA 30720
Ph:(706)278-4101
Free: 800-288-4101
Fax:(706)278-5323
Co. E-mail: afa@americanfloor.org
URL: http://www.americanfloor.org
Contact: Wanda J. Ellis, Exec. Dir.

Description: Floorcovering manufacturers and companies providing services or supplies to the floor covering industry. Promotes the floor covering industry. Provides insurance programs for members. **Publications:** *Floor Covering Weekly* (weekly); *Floor Focus* (monthly); *Floor Tek Source Guide* (biennial); *Industry Profile* (quarterly).

8992 ■ Carpet and Rug Institute
PO Box 2048
Dalton, GA 30722-2048
Ph:(706)278-3176
Fax:(706)278-8835
Co. E-mail: snewberry@carpet-rug.org
URL: http://www.carpet-rug.org
Contact: Werner Braun, Pres.

Description: Represents the carpet and rug industry; sources of extensive carpet information for consumers, writers, interior designers, specifiers, facility managers, architects, builders and building owners and managers. **Publications:** *Carpet and Rug Manufacturing Plants and Corporate Locations in the U.S. and Canada* (annual).

8993 ■ Floor Covering Installation Contractors Association
7439 Millwood Dr.
West Bloomfield, MI 48322
Ph:(248)661-5015
Fax:(248)661-5018
Co. E-mail: keo@fcica.com
URL: http://www.fcica.com
Contact: Kimberly Oderkirk, Exec. VP

Description: Installation contractors, carpet manufacturers, and suppliers to the installation trade. Aims to establish acceptable levels of performance for the carpet installation industry; to promote standards of business ethics; to encourage quality installations. Acts as liaison with retailers, manufacturers, and suppliers; represents the industry before government agencies regarding proposed or enacted regulation and legislation. Fosters the sale and use of the industry's products and services. Serves as clearinghouse for resolving problems of mutual interest inside and outside the industry. Assists local installation workrooms/ contractors' groups. Sponsors training programs. **Publications:** *Bottom Line E-News* (biweekly); *The Flooring Contractor* (quarterly);Membership Directory (annual).

8994 ■ North American Association of Floor Covering Distributors
401 N Michigan Ave., Ste. 2200
Chicago, IL 60611
Ph:(312)321-6836
Fax:(312)673-6962
Co. E-mail: info@nafcd.org
URL: http://www.nafcd.org
Contact: Maurice A. Desmarais CAE, Exec. VP

Description: Floor covering distributors and firms selling to them. Aims to promote, protect, and advance the best interests of wholesale floor covering distribution; to foster sound business principles in all phases of floor covering wholesaling; to increase the use of wholesale floor covering products by the retailer; to improve understanding between manufacturers and wholesalers of floor covering products, and increase distribution of floor covering and related products through wholesale distribution channels; to improve the conditions under which the industry must operate; to collect and disseminate pertinent industry data; to assist its members through education, research, and training. **Publications:** *National Association of Floor Covering Distributors—Membership* (annual); *News and Views* (bimonthly);Book (semiannual).

8995 ■ Resilient Floor Covering Institute
115 Broad St., Ste. 201
LaGrange, GA 30240
Ph:(706)882-3833
Fax:(706)882-3880
Co. E-mail: info@rfci.com
URL: http://www.rfci.com

Description: Supports the manufacturers of vinyl composition tile, solid vinyl tile, or sheet vinyl and rubber tile and people who use its products. Provides technical information and data regarding the resilient flooring industry. .

8996 ■ Terrazzo Tile and Marble Association of Canada
163 Buttermill Ave., Unit 8
Concord, ON, Canada L4K 3X8
Ph:(905)660-9640
Free: 800-201-8599
Fax:(905)660-0513
Co. E-mail: association@ttmac.com
URL: http://www.ttmac.com
Contact: Doug Bordt, Pres.

Description: Aims to develop a method of standardizing terrazzo, tile and marble installation techniques. Works as a technical resource and liaison for architects, designers and engineers.

8997 ■ World Floor Covering Association
2211 E Howell Ave.
Anaheim, CA 92806
Ph:(714)978-6440
Free: 800-624-6880
Fax:(714)978-6066
Co. E-mail: wfca@wfca.org
URL: http://www.wfca.org
Contact: D. Christopher Davis, Pres./CEO

Description: Retail floorcovering store owners and managers; floorcovering distributors and manufacturers. Provides liaison, through a Washington, DC lobbyist, between the membership and government organizations that affect the business. Conducts seminars promoting professional development and increased profits; compiles business activity statistics; sponsors research. **Publications:** *World Floor Covering Association—Annual Management Report* .

REFERENCE WORKS

8998 ■ "Behind the Scenes: Companies At the Heart of Everyday Life" in *Inc.* (February 2008, pp. 26-27)
Pub: Gruner & Jahr USA Publishing

Ed: Athena Schindelheim. **Description:** Profiles of companies providing services to airports, making the environment safer and more efficient, as well as more comfortable for passengers and workers. Centerpoint Manufacturing provides garbage bins that can safely contain explosions producing thousands of pounds of pressure; Infax, whose software displays arrival and departure information on 19-foot-wide screens; Lavi Industries, whose products include security barricades, hostess stands, and salad-bar sneeze guards; and SATech maker of rubber flooring that helps ease discomfort for workers having to stand for long periods of time.

8999 ■ *Floor Covering Weekly—Annual Product Source Guide*
Pub: FCW

Contact: Santiago Montero, Editor & Publisher
E-mail: smontero@hearst.com

Released: Annual, Latest edition 2011. **Price:** $66, Canada; $61, individuals; $101, two years; $184, out of country. **Publication Includes:** Lists of manufacturers and importers of carpet, rugs, carpet cushion, fiber, resilient wood, and ceramic floor coverings; separate listing of distributors by state, retail groups and associations. **Entries Include:** For manufacturers—Company name, address, phone, regional sales offices, names and titles of key personnel, local distributors, products. For distributors—Company name, address, phone, manufacturers represented. **Arrangement:** Alphabetical. **Indexes:** Geographical by distributor.

9000 ■ "Ground Floor Opportunity" in *Small Business Opportunities* (July 2008)
Pub: Entrepreneur Media Inc.

Description: Profile of Doug Disney, the founder of the booming franchise Tile Outlet Always in Stock, which sells ceramic and porcelain tile and stone products at wholesale prices; Disney found inspiration in a book he read in two days and that motivated him to expand his venture into a huge franchise opportunity.

9001 ■ "Info Junkie" in *Crain's Chicago Business* (Vol. 34, October 24, 2011, No. 42, pp. 35)
Pub: Crain Communications Inc.

Ed: Christina Le Beau. **Description:** Greg Colando, president of Flor Inc., an eco-friendly carpet company located l Chicago discusses his marketing program to increase sales.

9002 ■ *North American Association of Floor Covering Distributors—Membership Directory*
Pub: North American Association of Floor Covering Distributors
Released: Annual. **Covers:** Association happenings and approximately 300 member distributors and suppliers of floor coverings. **Entries Include:** Company name, location (code indicates if a branch location), products, contacts.

9003 ■ "Take the Right Approach to Concrete Polishing Rentals" in *Rental Product News* (Vol. 33, June 2011)
Pub: Cygnus Business Media
Ed: Jenny Lescohier. **Description:** A recent trend in flooring is concrete polishing for a practical, beautiful and sustainable way to decorate homes and businesses. Things to keep in mind when assessing the value of adding concrete polishing equipment to an existing rental store are evaluated.

STATISTICAL SOURCES

9004 ■ *Carpets and Rugs Market U.S.A.*
Pub: Rector Press, Ltd.
Contact: Lewis Skolnick, Pres
Released: 2009. **Price:** Contact Rector Press.

9005 ■ *RMA Annual Statement Studies*
Pub: Robert Morris Associates (RMA)
Released: Annual. **Price:** $175.00 2006-07 edition, $105.00. **Description:** Contains composite balance sheets and income statements for more than 360 industries, including the accounting, auditing, and bookkeeping industries. Also contains five years of comparative historical data for discerning trends. Includes 16 commonly used ratios, computed for most of the size groupings for nearly every industry.

9006 ■ *Standard & Poor's Industry Surveys*
Pub: Standard & Poor's Corp.
Released: Annual. **Price:** $3633.00. **Description:** Two-volume book that examines the prospects for specific industries, including trucking. Also provides analyses of trends and problems, statistical tables and charts, and comparative company analyses.

TRADE PERIODICALS

9007 ■ *FCICA Update*
Pub: Floor Covering Installation Contractors Association (FCICA)
Released: Bi-Weekly **Description:** Features articles on members and conferences in the floor covering installation industry. Recurring features include interviews, news of research, and a calendar of events.

9008 ■ *Floor Covering News*
Pub: RO-EL Productions Inc.
Contact: Louis Iannaco, Sen. Ed.
Released: Biweekly. **Description:** Magazine featuring articles of interest to floor covering retailers, distributors, and manufacturers.

9009 ■ *Floor Covering Weekly*
Pub: FCW
Contact: Kimberly Gavin, Exec. Ed.
E-mail: kimgavin@aol.com
Released: Weekly. **Price:** $60 U.S. and Canada; $110 U.S. and Canada two years. **Description:** Business newspaper of the floor covering industry.

9010 ■ *Floor Focus*
Pub: Floor Focus Inc.
Contact: Kemp Harr, Publisher
Ed: Darius Helm, Editor, dhfloorfocus@optonline.net. **Released:** Monthly. **Price:** $49.95; $59.95 out of country; $99.95 other countries. **Description:** Trade magazine for retailers, manufacturers, contract dealers, and commercial users of floor coverings.

9011 ■ *ICS Cleaning Specialist*
Pub: Business News Publishing Company II L.L.C.
Contact: Phil Johnson, Gp. Publisher
E-mail: johnsonp@bnpmedia.com
Released: Monthly. **Description:** Trade magazine for the floor care and service industry.

9012 ■ *National Floor Trends Magazine*
Pub: Business News Publishing Company II L.L.C.
Contact: Michael Chmielecki, Assoc. Ed.
E-mail: chmieleckim@bnpmedia.com
Released: Monthly. **Description:** Trade magazine for the floor covering industry.

9013 ■ *Rug News*
Pub: Rug News Magazine
Contact: Leslie Stroh, Publisher
E-mail: lstroh@museumbooks.com
Ed: Dasha Morgan, Editor, dmorgan@museumbooks.com. **Released:** Monthly. **Price:** $78; $100 Canada; $162 other countries; $442 other countries to India by air; $120 delivered via first class mail. **Description:** Trade magazine covering the area rug industry.

9014 ■ *Strategy*
Pub: National Association of Floor Covering Distributors
Ed: Dennis Coyle, Editor. **Released:** BIM. **Price:** Included in membership. **Description:** Provides news of the Association and the floor covering industry. Recurring features include news of members, notices of publications available, news of educational opportunities, reports of meetings, and a calendar of events.

TRADE SHOWS AND CONVENTIONS

9015 ■ **Chicago Design Show**
Merchandise Mart Properties Inc.
222 Merchandise Mart, Ste. 470
Chicago, IL 60654
Free: 800-677-6278
URL: http://www.merchandisemart.com
Released: Annual. **Audience:** Interior design trade professionals and consumers. **Principal Exhibits:** Contemporary design in furniture, fashion, food.

CONSULTANTS

9016 ■ **Surface Technologies Inc.**
18 Willotta Dr.
Suisun City, CA 94534-1446
Ph:(707)864-6313
Free: 800-241-2982
Fax:(707)864-6313
Contact: Richard E. Larson, President
Scope: Specializes in carpet, tile, wood, stone, and vinyl floor covering inspection and testing. Evaluates floor covering samples for durability, clean ability, and longevity of appearance. Trains hotel and other institutional personnel to maintain, clean, and repair floor coverings. Industries served include floor and wall covering and upholstery fabric manufacturers, as well as producers of all types of architectural surfaces. **Seminars:** Complaint Reduction Program; Selling Floor Covering Defensively; Turn Complaints into More Business; Presented to department stores and floor covering specialty stores.

FRANCHISES AND BUSINESS OPPORTUNITIES

9017 ■ **Carpet Network**
109 Gaither Dr., No. 302
Mt. Laurel, NJ 08054
Ph:(856)273-9393
Free: 800-428-1067
Co. E-mail: franchise@carpetnetwork.com
URL: http://www.carpetnetwork.com
No. of Franchise Units: 27. **Founded:** 1992. **Franchised:** 1992. **Description:** Mobile carpet and window treatment business. **Equity Capital Needed:** $68,485-$92,705. **Franchise Fee:** $39,500. **Financial Assistance:** Yes. **Training:** 2 week training program consisting of 1 week home study course including video aids; 1 week at Carpet Network College, located in Mt. Laurel, NJ. Ongoing personalized support by the home office, 24-hr. toll-free help-Line, newsletters, workshops, marketing and operational support, global website and intranet system.

9018 ■ **Floor Coverings International**
Floor Coverings International, Ltd.
5250 Triangle Pky., Ste. 100
Norcross, GA 30082-5201
Ph:800-955-4324
Free: 800-342-5324
Fax:(404)366-4606
No. of Franchise Units: 110. **Founded:** 1988. **Franchised:** 1988. **Description:** Mobile floor covering retailer. **Equity Capital Needed:** $90,000-$100,000. **Franchise Fee:** $30,000. **Financial Assistance:** Yes. **Training:** Yes.

9019 ■ **The Mad Matter**
The Mad Matter Franchise Corp.
PO Box 128
Cumming, GA 30028
Ph:(770)887-9150
Free: 800-685-1144
Fax:(770)887-9240
No. of Company-Owned Units: 2. **Founded:** 1992. **Franchised:** 2003. **Description:** Sale and installation of specialty flooring. **Equity Capital Needed:** Estimated $69,000-$121,000, includes franchise fee. **Franchise Fee:** $30,000-$50,000. **Financial Assistance:** No. **Training:** Yes.

9020 ■ **MarbleLife**
MarbleLife, Inc.
300 Northstar Ct.
Sandord, FL 32771
Ph:(407)302-4171
Fax:(407)302-9311
No. of Franchise Units: 55. **Founded:** 1989. **Franchised:** 1990. **Description:** Stone restoration and preservation. **Equity Capital Needed:** $25,000 liquid; net worth $150,000+. **Franchise Fee:** $15,000-$75,000. **Financial Assistance:** Yes. **Training:** Yes.

9021 ■ **Mr. Sandless Inc.**
2970 Concord Rd.
Aston, PA 19014
Ph:(610)364-2080
Fax:(610)364-2081
No. of Franchise Units: 212. **No. of Company-Owned Units:** 9. **Founded:** 2004. **Franchised:** 2005. **Description:** Sandless wood floor refinishing. **Equity Capital Needed:** $28,400-$56,650. **Franchise Fee:** $15,000. **Royalty Fee:** 5%. **Financial Assistance:** Third party financing available. **Training:** Provides 1 week at headquarters and ongoing support.

9022 ■ **N-Hance**
1530 N 1000 West
Logan, UT 84321
Ph:(435)890-1010
Free: (866)642-6231
Fax:(435)604-8452
No. of Franchise Units: 192. **Founded:** 2001. **Franchised:** 2003. **Description:** Wood floor & cabinet renewal systems. **Equity Capital Needed:** $35,600-$118,450. **Franchise Fee:** $27,000-$44,500. **Royalty Fee:** $220-$660/month. **Financial Assistance:** Assistance with franchise fee. **Training:** Offers 1 week on training at headquarters and ongoing support.

9023 ■ **Prosource Wholesale Floorcoverings**
CCA Global Partners
4301 Earth City Expy.
Earth City, MO 63045
Free: 800-466-6984
Fax:(314)506-0953
Co. E-mail: mjameson@pswwholesale.com
URL: http://www.prosourcefloors.com
No. of Franchise Units: 138. **No. of Company-Owned Units:** 3. **Founded:** 1990. **Franchised:** 1991. **Description:** Members-only wholesale flooring showroom. **Equity Capital Needed:** $750,000 net worth; $375,000 minimum investment. **Franchise Fee:** $46,450. **Financial Assistance:** Yes. **Training:** Initial training provided at headquarters in St. Louis and ongoing support.

9024 ■ **Re-Bath, LLC**
421 W Alameda Dr.
Tempe, AZ 85282
Ph:(480)844-1575

Free: 800-426-4573
Fax:(480)833-7199
No. of Franchise Units: 225. **Founded:** 1979. **Franchised:** 1991. **Description:** Custom-manufactured, high-impact acrylic bathtub liners, wall systems and shower liners designed to go over existing bathtubs, ceramic tile walls and shower bases. **Equity Capital Needed:** $3,500-$89,000. **Franchise Fee:** $6,000-$40,000. **Financial Assistance:** Yes. **Training:**

Phases of installation, operations, sales and marketing. Both classroom and hands-on training.

LIBRARIES

9025 ■ Congoleum Corporation Technical Research Library
PO Box 3127
Mercerville, NJ 08619-0127

Ph:(609)584-3601
URL: http://www.congoleum.com
Contact: Joanne L. Stout

Scope: Plastics, chemistry, paper, floor coverings, coatings. **Services:** Library not open to the public. **Holdings:** 1500 books; official patent gazettes (current year). **Subscriptions:** 35 journals and other serials.

ASSOCIATIONS AND OTHER ORGANIZATIONS

9026 ■ American Institute of Floral Designers
720 Light St.
Baltimore, MD 21230
Ph:(410)752-3318
Fax:(410)752-8295
Co. E-mail: aifd@assnhqtrs.com
URL: http://www.aifd.org
Contact: Sharon McGukin AIFD, Pres.
Description: Active floral designers, associates, retired floral designers and other individuals. Works to promote the profession and art of floral design. Maintains student chapter. .

9027 ■ Canadian Ornamental Plant Foundation
975 McKeown Ave., 5A - No. 218
North Bay, ON, Canada P1B 8H5
Ph:(705)495-2563
Free: 800-265-1629
Fax:(705)495-1449
Co. E-mail: info@copf.org
URL: http://www.copf.org
Contact: Peggy Walsh Craig, Managing Dir.
Description: Growers and breeders of ornamental plants. Encourages development of new plant strains. Strengthens relations between growers and breeders; provides support to research projects. **Publications:** COPF News (quarterly).

9028 ■ Canadian Rose Society
No. 100 Chancellor Ave.
Victoria, BC, Canada V8Z 1R4
Co. E-mail: info@canadianrosesociety.org
URL: http://www.canadianrosesociety.org
Contact: Shari-Lyn Safir, Pres.
Description: Noncommercial rose growers and rose enthusiasts. Promotes the hobby of rose breeding and growing. Conducts educational programs; sponsors competitions; maintains speakers' bureau. **Publications:** The Annual (annual); Canadian Rosarian (annual); The CRS CommPoster (5/year).

9029 ■ Flowers Canada
99 5th Ave., Ste. 305
Ottawa, ON, Canada K1S 5P5
Free: 800-447-5147
Fax:(866)671-8091
Co. E-mail: flowers@flowerscanada.org
URL: http://flowerscanada.ca
Contact: Jeff Waters, Pres.
Description: Retail florists, distributors, and greenhouse operators. Promotes growth and development in the domestic floriculture industry. Provides technical and promotional services to floral retailers, producers, and distributors; sponsors continuing professional development and educational programs for members. Represents members' interests before government agencies; serves as a liaison between members and related trade organizations. Makes available discount credit card, insurance, automotive fleet, lodging, and other business services to members. **Publications:** News Vine (bimonthly); Membership Directory (annual).

9030 ■ Heritage Rose Foundation
PO Box 831414
Richardson, TX 75083
Co. E-mail: steprose@mac.com
URL: http://www.heritagerosefoundation.org
Contact: Stephen Scanniello, Pres.
Description: Individuals interested in old-fashioned roses. Collects, preserves, studies, and promotes old-fashioned roses. Locates commercial sources of specific old-fashioned roses and identifies "mystery" roses; provides information on growing roses from cuttings and photographing them to facilitate identification. Conducts educational programs. **Publications:** Heritage Rose Foundation News (quarterly); Rosa Mundi (semiannual).

9031 ■ Society of American Florists
1601 Duke St.
Alexandria, VA 22314-3406
Ph:(703)836-8700
Free: 800-336-4743
Fax:(703)836-8705
Co. E-mail: info@safnow.org
URL: http://www.safnow.org
Contact: Peter J. Moran, Exec. VP/CEO
Description: Growers, wholesalers, retailers, and allied tradesmen in the floral industry. Lobbies Congress on behalf of the industry; sponsors educational programs; promotes the floral industry; prepares materials for consumers and for high school and college students; provides business resources. Sponsors Floricultural Hall of Fame, American Academy of Floriculture, and Professional Floral Commentators International. Compiles statistics; sponsors competitions. **Publications:** Dateline: Washington; Floral Management (monthly).

9032 ■ Wholesale Florist and Florist Supplier Association
147 Old Solomons Island Rd., Ste. 302
Annapolis, MD 21401
Ph:(410)573-0400
Free: 888-289-3372
Fax:(410)573-5001
Co. E-mail: info@wffsa.org
URL: http://www.wffsa.org
Contact: Jim Wanko, Exec. VP
Description: Proprietorships, partnerships or corporations conducting wholesale businesses in fresh flowers, greens, or plants, or engaged in the manufacture and/or wholesaling of florist supplies; others actively engaged in the floral industry are associate members. Preserves and strengthens the wholesale florists' position in the floral industry. Provides a unified voice to promote the wholesalers' contributions to the industry. .

DIRECTORIES OF EDUCATIONAL PROGRAMS

9033 ■ Directory of Private Accredited Career Schools and Colleges of Technology
Pub: Accrediting Commission of Career Schools and Colleges of Technology
Contact: Michale S. McComis, Exec. Dir.
Released: On web page. **Price:** Free. **Description:** Covers 3900 accredited post-secondary programs that provide training programs in business, trade, and technical fields, including various small business endeavors. Entries offer school name, address, phone, description of courses, job placement assistance, and requirements for admission. Arrangement is alphabetical.

REFERENCE WORKS

9034 ■ "Cold-Storage Cargo Facility a Late Bloomer" in Houston Business Journal (Vol. 40, August 28, 2009, No. 16, pp. 1A)
Pub: American City Business Journals
Ed: Jennifer Dawson. **Description:** Trammell Crow Company leased half of the 61,000 square foot IAH International Air Cargo Centre II to Tradewinds Cargo Handling. The facility, located at George Bush Intercontinental Airport, is intended to be a destination of fresh flowers and food from Latin America.

9035 ■ "Floral-Design Kiosk Business in Colorado Springs Blossoming" in Colorado Springs Business Journal (September 24, 2010)
Pub: Dolan Media Newswires
Ed: Monica Mendoza. **Description:** Profile of Shellie Greto and her mother Jackie Martin who started a wholesale flower business in their garage. The do-it-yourself floral arrangement firm started a kiosk business in supermarkets called Complete Design.

9036 ■ "Flower Confidential" in Business Horizons (Vol. 51, January-February 2008, No. 1, pp. 73)
Pub: Elsevier Advanced Technology Publications
Ed: Mimi Dollinger. **Description:** Review of the book, "Flower Confidential: The Good, the Bad, and the Beautiful Business of Flowers", which offers insight for anyone starting or running a successful flower shop.

9037 ■ Flower Confidential: The Good, the Bad, and the Beautiful in the Business of Flowers
Pub: Algonquin Publishing
Ed: Amy Stewart. **Released:** January 4, 2007. **Price:** $23.95. **Description:** Author mixes botany, history and commerce for small business owners running a florist shop.

9038 ■ "Holiday Bloom: Event Designer Collin Abraham Heightens Glamour With Florals" in Black Enterprise (Vol. 41, November 2010, No. 4)
Pub: Earl G. Graves Publishing Co. Inc.
Ed: Sean Drakes. **Description:** Profile of Collin Abraham, who works out of his Harlem boutique to ar-

range unique floral pieces to complement the social gatherings and main events he plans for his clients.

9039 ■ "Verizon Small Business Awards Give Companies a Technology Edge" in *Hispanic Business* **(July-August 2009, pp. 32)**
Pub: Hispanic Business
Ed: Patricia Marroquin. **Description:** Verizon Wireless awards grants to twenty-four companies in California. The winning businesses ranged from barbershop to coffee shop, tattoo parlor to florist.

9040 ■ "VISA: Canadians Spend $97 Million on Mom This Mother's Day" in *Canadian Corporate News* **(May 16, 2007)**
Pub: Comtex News Network Inc.
Description: Visa Canada finds that Canadians are spending more on Mother's Day in recent years. Since 2002, sales of jewelry, flowers, and cards have climbed steadily in the week before Mother's Day weekend.

9041 ■ *Wholesale Florist & Florist Supplier Association—Membership Directory*
Pub: Wholesale Florists & Florist Supplier Association
Contact: Trish Lilly, Exec. VP
E-mail: plilly@wffsa.org
Released: Biennial, summer/winter. **Entries Include:** Company name, address, phone, names of executives, list of products or services. **Arrangement:** Geographical. **Indexes:** Alphabetical.

STATISTICAL SOURCES

9042 ■ *RMA Annual Statement Studies*
Pub: Robert Morris Associates (RMA)
Released: Annual. **Price:** $175.00 2006-07 edition, $105.00. **Description:** Contains composite balance sheets and income statements for more than 360 industries, including the accounting, auditing, and bookkeeping industries. Also contains five years of comparative historical data for discerning trends. Includes 16 commonly used ratios, computed for most of the size groupings for nearly every industry.

TRADE PERIODICALS

9043 ■ *California Garden*
Pub: San Diego Floral Association
Released: Bimonthly. **Description:** Magazine on floriculture and horticulture.

9044 ■ *Flora Magazine*
Pub: Cenflo Inc.
Contact: Kenneth M. Benjamin, Publisher
Released: Bimonthly. **Price:** $32.95; $54 two years; $16.95 students; $52.95 Canada; $92 Canada 2 years. **Description:** Magazine for volume buyers of floral products.

9045 ■ *Florists' Review Magazine*
Pub: Florist's Review Enterprises Inc.
Released: Monthly. **Price:** $42; $72 two years; $82 three years; $55 Canada; $85 Canada 2 years; $60 other countries; $90 other countries 2 years. **Description:** Retail florist and wholesalers trade magazine.

9046 ■ *Flowers&*
Pub: Teleflora
Contact: Richard Salvaggio, Publisher
Released: Monthly. **Price:** $54; $60 Canada; $22.50 students one time; $70 out of area. **Description:** Trade magazine for retail florists.

9047 ■ *Fresh Facts*
Pub: Fresh Produce & Floral Council
Contact: Linda Stine
Ed: Linda Stine, Editor. **Released:** Weekly. **Price:** Free. **Description:** Discusses trends and issues in fresh fruit, vegetable, and floral supply.

9048 ■ *Green Profit Magazine*
Pub: Ball Publishing
Released: 9/yr. **Description:** Trade magazine for flower and plant retailers.

9049 ■ *Greenhouse Management and Production*
Pub: GIE Media, Inc.
Contact: Chris Foster, Publisher
E-mail: chris.foster@gie.net
Released: Monthly. **Description:** Commercial greenhouse growers magazine.

9050 ■ *Michigan Florist*
Pub: Michigan Floral Association
Ed: Heidi Anderson, Editor, mrsheidianderson@hotmail.com. **Released:** Bimonthly. **Price:** $50 members; $5 single issue. **Description:** Magazine for retail florists, wholesalers and growers; covering products, industry services, floral arrangements, floral business, and related concerns.

VIDEOCASSETTES/ AUDIOCASSETTES

9051 ■ *Floral Design*
Silver Mine Video Inc.
31316 Via Colinas, Ste. 104
Westlake Village, CA 91362-3905
Ph:(818)707-0300
URL: http://www.quicksilverrecords.zoomshare.com
Price: $29.95. **Description:** Presents easy to make flower arrangements. **Availability:** VHS.

9052 ■ *Floral Fundamentals*
Nancy's Notions Ltd.
333 Beichl Ave.
P.O. Box 683
Beaver Dam, WI 53916-0683
Ph:(920)887-7321
Free: 800-725-0361
Fax:800-255-8119
Co. E-mail: customerservice@nancysnotions.com
URL: http://www.nancysnotions.com
Released: 1989. **Description:** Kathy demonstrates how to arrange flowers in three different styles: the mound, the triangle, and the centerpiece. **Availability:** VHS.

9053 ■ *Flower Arrangements Made Easy*
Tapeworm Video Distributors
25876 The Old Road 141
Stevenson Ranch, CA 91381
Ph:(661)257-4904
Fax:(661)257-4820
Co. E-mail: sales@tapeworm.com
URL: http://www.tapeworm.com
Price: $14.95. **Description:** Expert floral designer Kim Alexander demonstrates how to create three fresh flower arrangements. **Availability:** VHS.

9054 ■ *The Flower Shop Series*
RMI Media
1365 N. Winchester St.
Olathe, KS 66061-5880
Ph:(913)768-1696
Free: 800-745-5480
Fax:800-755-6910
Co. E-mail: actmedia@act.org
URL: http://www.actmedia.org
Released: 1987. **Description:** Flower expert Phil Easter demonstrates the art of floral design using various themes. **Availability:** VHS; 3/4U.

9055 ■ *Holiday Centerpieces*
Videomaker
PO Box 4591
Chico, CA 95927
Ph:(530)891-8410
Free: 800-284-3226
Fax:(530)891-8443
Co. E-mail: customerservice@videomaker.com
URL: http://www.videomaker.com
Price: $14.95. **Description:** Provides instruction for creating flower arrangements for Fall and Christmas. **Availability:** VHS.

9056 ■ *Silk Arrangements*
Videomaker
PO Box 4591
Chico, CA 95927
Ph:(530)891-8410
Free: 800-284-3226

Fax:(530)891-8443
Co. E-mail: customerservice@videomaker.com
URL: http://www.videomaker.com
Price: $14.95. **Description:** Provides instruction for creating four attractive flower arrangements for all seasons. **Availability:** VHS.

9057 ■ *Table Centerpieces*
Videomaker
PO Box 4591
Chico, CA 95927
Ph:(530)891-8410
Free: 800-284-3226
Fax:(530)891-8443
Co. E-mail: customerservice@videomaker.com
URL: http://www.videomaker.com
Price: $14.95. **Description:** Provides instruction for creating two fresh Spring flower arrangements and how to make a florists bow. **Availability:** VHS.

TRADE SHOWS AND CONVENTIONS

9058 ■ Great Lakes Floral Expo
Michigan Floral Association
1152 Haslett Rd.
PO Box 67
Haslett, MI 48840
Ph:(517)575-0110
Fax:(517)575-0115
Co. E-mail: rcrittenden@michiganfloral.org
URL: http://www.michiganfloral.org
Released: Annual. **Principal Exhibits:** Floral equipment, supplies, and services.

9059 ■ Northeast Floral Expo
Connecticut Florists Association
590 Main St., Bart Ctr.
Monroe, CT 06468
Free: 800-352-6946
Fax:(203)261-5429
Co. E-mail: CTFLORISTS@aol.com
URL: http://www.flowersplantsinct.com/cfaindex.htm
Released: Annual. **Audience:** Florists and related trade professionals. **Principal Exhibits:** Florist supplies, cut flowers, potted plants, wire services, and dried and artificial flowers and plants. **Dates and Locations:** 2011 Mar 12-13, Sturbridge, MA.

9060 ■ Nursery/Landscape Expo
Texas Nursery & Landscape Association
7730 S. IH-35
Austin, TX 78745-6698
Ph:(512)280-5182
Free: 800-880-0343
Fax:(512)280-3012
Co. E-mail: info@tnlaonline.org
URL: http://www.txnla.org
Released: Annual. **Audience:** Nursery, landscape and related trades professionals. **Principal Exhibits:** Plant materials including foliage, bedding plants, trees, palms; allied products including machinery, equipment and supplies for horticulture and landscape industry.

9061 ■ OFA Short Course
Ohio Florists Association
2130 Stella Ct., Ste. 200
Columbus, OH 43215-1033
Ph:(614)487-1117
Fax:(614)487-1216
Co. E-mail: ofa@ofa.org
URL: http://www.ofa.org
Released: Annual. **Audience:** Growers, retailers, garden centers, and other trade professionals. **Principal Exhibits:** Exhibits for the greenhouse grower and related industries. **Dates and Locations:** 2011 Jul 09-12, Columbus, OH.

9062 ■ Tropical Plant Industry Exhibition
Florida Nursery Growers and Landscape
1533 Park Ctr. Dr.
Orlando, FL 32835-5705
Ph:(407)295-7994
Free: 800-375-3642

Fax:(407)295-1619
Co. E-mail: info@fngla.org
URL: http://www.fngla.org
Released: Annual. **Audience:** Trade. **Principal Exhibits:** Large foliage plants; horticultural, interiorscape, florist, and interior foliage industry products.

CONSULTANTS

9063 ■ The Landplan Collaborative Ltd.
319 Woolwich St.
Guelph, ON, Canada N1H 3W4
Ph:(519)824-8664
Fax:(519)824-6776
Co. E-mail: landplan@thelandplan.com
URL: http://www.thelandplan.com
Contact: Sherry Mennen, Principle
E-mail: oscott@thelandplan.com
Scope: Offers consulting services in landscape architecture, environmental planning, heritage research and planning and resource planning. Also plan and design rural, urban, regional and heritage landscapes; manage projects and procure government approvals; provide expert testimony to boards and tribunals and teaching skills to universities and colleges.

FRANCHISES AND BUSINESS OPPORTUNITIES

9064 ■ Flowerama of America
3165 W Airline Hwy.
Waterloo, IA 50703
Free: 800-728-6004
Fax:(319)291-8676
Co. E-mail: info@flowerama.com
URL: http://www.flowerama.com
No. of Franchise Units: 71. **No. of Company-Owned Units:** 8. **Founded:** 1971. **Franchised:** 1972. **Description:** Franchise program operates under the concepts of mass-merchandising and cash-and-carry floral sales. **Equity Capital Needed:** $50,000-$100,000 (cash). **Franchise Fee:** $35,000. **Financial Assistance:** Financing assistance available. **Training:** 4-6 week training program (held at the corporate offices in Waterloo, Iowa). Store layouts and design, assistance during construction, store set-up and product merchandising are provided.

9065 ■ Grower Direct Fresh Cut Flowers Inc.
9613-41 Ave., Ste. 201
Edmonton, AB, Canada T6E 5X7
Ph:(780)436-7774
Fax:(780)436-3336
Co. E-mail: franchises@grower.com
URL: http://www.grower.com
No. of Franchise Units: 41. **No. of Company-Owned Units:** 1. **Founded:** 1991. **Description:** Supplies top quality, fresh cut flowers and marketing

expertise to its retail outlets. **Equity Capital Needed:** $55,000-$75,000. **Franchise Fee:** $15,000. **Training:** Provides 10 days training.

9066 ■ KaBloom
2000 East Winston Rd.
Anaheim, CA 92806-5546
Ph:(781)935-6500
Free: 800-KaB-loom
Fax:(781)935-9410
Co. E-mail: support@kabloom.com
URL: http://www.kabloom.com
No. of Franchise Units: 116. **No. of Company-Owned Units:** 7. **Founded:** 1998. **Franchised:** 2001. **Description:** Flower shops. **Equity Capital Needed:** $176,000-$302,000. **Franchise Fee:** $30,000. **Royalty Fee:** 4.5-5.5%. **Financial Assistance:** Third party financing available. **Training:** 3 weeks at corporate headquarters and ongoing support provided.

9067 ■ Suspended In Time, Inc.
122 S Mountainway Dr.
Orem, UT 84058
Ph:(801)227-0075
Free: (866)756-0059
Fax:(801)221-1003
Co. E-mail: info@suspendedintime.com
URL: http://www.suspendedintime.com
No. of Franchise Units: 47. **Founded:** 1997. **Description:** With the remarkable discovery of Suspended in Time's technology in floral preservation over the last 10 years, we are expanding our business opportunities. This is not a Freeze Dry Method. We offer an excellent dealership package with low start-up fees. This preservation process only takes an average of 3-5 days to complete. **Equity Capital Needed:** $4,886. **Financial Assistance:** No. **Training:** Training provided at the corporate location 3, 10 hour days, which includes lunch - large discount on room accommodations and ongoing support as long as needed.

LIBRARIES

9068 ■ American Floral Art School–Floral Library
634 S. Wabash Ave., Ste. 210
Chicago, IL 60605
Ph:(312)922-9328
Co. E-mail: americanfl@americanfloralartschool.com
URL: http://www.americanfloralartschool.com
Contact: James Moretz, Owner/Dir.
Scope: Flower arrangement and symbolism, floral design, language of flowers. **Services:** Library is accessible on a restricted basis. **Holdings:** 6000 books; 500 uncataloged items; periodicals; photographs; video tapes. **Subscriptions:** 60 journals and other serials; 2 newspapers.

9069 ■ American Horticultural Society Library
7931 E. Boulevard Dr.
Alexandria, VA 22308
Ph:(703)768-5700
Free: 800-777-7931
Fax:(703)768-8700
Co. E-mail: tunderwood@ahs.org
URL: http://www.ahs.org/
Contact: Tom Underwood, Exec.Off.
Scope: Horticulture. **Services:** Library open to the public by appointment. **Holdings:** 5000 books.

9070 ■ Chicago Park District–Garfield Park Conservatory
300 N. Central Park Ave.
Chicago, IL 60624-1945
Ph:(312)746-5100
Fax:(773)638-1777
URL: http://www.garfield-conservatory.org/
Contact: Mary Eysenbach, Dir.
Scope: Horticulture. **Services:** Library not open to the public. **Holdings:** 600 books. **Subscriptions:** 2 journals and other serials.

9071 ■ Georgia State Botanical Garden of Georgia Library
Callaway Bldg.
University of Georgia
2450 S. Milledge Ave.
Athens, GA 30605
Ph:(706)542-1244
Fax:(706)542-3091
Co. E-mail: garden@uga.edu
URL: http://www.uga.edu/botgarden/faccallaway.html
Contact: Karen Kulp, Libn.
Scope: Plants, gardening, horticulture, botany, conservation, ethnobotany, landscape design, floral crafts. **Services:** Library open to the public for reference use only. **Holdings:** 2000 books; 85 videotapes; CD-ROMs; archives; manuscripts. **Subscriptions:** 14 journals and other serials.

9072 ■ U.S. National Arboretum Library
3501 New York Ave., NE
Washington, DC 20002-1958
Ph:(202)245-2726
Fax:(202)245-4575
Co. E-mail: everlyr@ars.usda.gov
URL: http://www.usna.usda.gov/
Contact: Robin Everly, Lib.
Scope: Botany, taxonomy, floristics, horticulture, gardening, plant genetics and breeding. **Services:** Interlibrary loan (through National Agricultural Library only); Library open to the public by appointment for onsite research only. **Holdings:** 10,000 books; 500 periodical titles. **Subscriptions:** 165 journals and other serials.

Food Delivery Service

START-UP INFORMATION

9073 ▪ The 100 Best Businesses to Start When You Don't Want To Work Hard Anymore
Pub: Career Press Inc.
Ed: Lisa Rogak. **Price:** $16.99. **Description:** Author helps burned-out workers envision a new future as a small business owner. Systems analysis, adventure travel outfitting, bookkeeping, food delivery, furniture making, and software development are among the industries examined.

ASSOCIATIONS AND OTHER ORGANIZATIONS

9074 ▪ Canadian Restaurant and Foodservices Association–Association Canadienne des Restaurateurs et des Services Alimentaires
316 Bloor St. W
Toronto, ON, Canada M5S 1W5
Ph:(416)923-8416
Free: 800-387-5649
Fax:(416)923-1450
Co. E-mail: info@crfa.ca
URL: http://www.crfa.ca
Contact: Garth Whyte, Pres./CEO
Description: Restaurant and food service corporations, hotels, caterers, and food service suppliers and educators. Seeks to create a favorable business environment for members. Represents members' interests before government; conducts trade research. Makes available group buying programs and other services to members; owns and operates three industry trade shows. **Publications:** Canadian Foodservice Industry Operations Report (biennial); Foodservice Facts (annual); Legislation Guide (quarterly).

9075 ▪ Foodservice and Packaging Institute
201 Park Washington Ct.
Falls Church, VA 22046
Ph:(703)538-3552
Fax:(703)241-5603
Co. E-mail: fpi@fpi.org
URL: http://www.fpi.org
Contact: Lynn Dyer, Pres.
Description: Manufacturers of raw material and machinery; suppliers and distributors of: single-use cups, plates and related items for service of food and/or beverages; nestable containers for food packaging and containers for oven usage, placemats and doilies, egg cartons and trays for prepackaging meat and produce. Promotes sanitation and the environmentally-responsible use of food and beverage packaging. Compiles market data. **Publications:** Executive Briefs (biweekly); Single Service News (semiannual).

9076 ▪ International Flight Services Association
1100 Johnson Ferry Rd., Ste. 300
Atlanta, GA 30342
Ph:(404)252-3663
Fax:(404)252-0774
Co. E-mail: ifsa@kellencompany.com
URL: http://www.ifsanet.com
Contact: Pam Chumley, Exec. Admin.
Description: Works to serve the needs and interests of the airline and railway personnel, in-flight and railway caterers and suppliers responsible for providing passenger foodservice on regularly scheduled travel routes. .

9077 ▪ International Foodservice Manufacturers Association
2 Prudential Plz.
180 N Stetson Ave., Ste. 4400
Chicago, IL 60601
Ph:(312)540-4400
Fax:(312)540-4401
Co. E-mail: ifma@ifmaworld.com
URL: http://www.ifmaworld.com
Contact: Larry Oberkfell, Pres./CEO
Description: National and international manufacturers and processors of food, food equipment, and related products for the away-from-home food market. Associate and allied members provide support services to the industry through marketing, publishing, distribution, consulting, promotion, research, advertising, public relations, and brokering. Activities are aimed at marketing, merchandising, sales training, and market research. Compiles statistics. **Publications:** IFMA World (9/year); Membership Directory (annual).

9078 ▪ National Council of Chain Restaurants
325 7th St. NW, Ste. 1100
Washington, DC 20004
Ph:(202)783-7971
Free: 800-673-4692
Fax:(202)737-2849
Co. E-mail: info@nrf.com
URL: http://www.nccr.net
Contact: Rob Green, Exec. Dir.
Description: Represents major multi-unit, multi-state foodservice, restaurant and lodging companies in the U.S. Activities are directed to legislative and regulatory matters affecting members. .

9079 ▪ National Restaurant Association Educational Foundation
175 W Jackson Blvd., Ste. 1500
Chicago, IL 60604-2702
Ph:(312)715-1010
Free: 800-765-2122
Co. E-mail: info@restaurant.org
URL: http://www.nraef.org
Contact: Linda Bacin, Interim Exec. Dir.
Description: Serves as an educational foundation supported by the National Restaurant Association and all segments of the foodservice industry including restaurateurs, foodservice companies, food and equipment manufacturers, distributors and trade associations. Advances the professional standards of the industry through education and research. Offers video training programs, management courses and careers information. Conducts research and maintains hall of fame. .

REFERENCE WORKS

9080 ▪ "Alliance to End Hunger to Hold Press Conference on Fasting, Prayer and Budget Cuts" in Food & Beverage Close-Up (March 28, 2011)
Pub: Close-Up Media
Description: A coalition of religious and other leaders are launching a new campaign to protect programs for vulnerable people. Partners include: Alliance to End Hunger, American Jewish World Service, Bread for the World, Congressional Hunger Center, Feeding America, Food for the Hungry, Islamic Relief USA, Meals on Wheels Association of America, New Manna Inc., ONE, Society of Saint Andrews, Sojourners, and World Food Program USA.

9081 ▪ "Aramark Rolls Out Ballpark Food Truck" in Nation's Restaurant News (Vol. 45, August 8, 2011, No. 16, pp. 4)
Pub: Penton Media Inc.
Ed: Ron Ruggless. **Description:** Aramark installed its first ballpark food truck serving Asian-inspired noodle bowls at the outfield concourse at Coors Field in Colorado.

9082 ▪ "Cluster Truck Events Updates on Curbside Dining Sweeps in Las Vegas" in Food & Beverage Close-Up (November 4, 2011)
Pub: Close-Up Media
Description: Gourmet food trucks will provide mobile dining for attendees of the South Point Gourmet Food Truck Fest held in Las Vegas, Nevada November 5, 2011.

9083 ▪ "Coastal Luxury Management Reports Los Angeles Food and Wine Tickets On Sale" in Food & Beverage Close-Up (August 24, 2011)
Pub: Close-Up Media
Description: Wolfgang Puck's Sunday Brunch and Charity Auction will raise money for Saint Vincent Meals on Wheels program.

9084 ▪ "Consumers Who Saw a Food Truck This Summer" in Nation's Restaurant News (Vol. 45, September 26, 2011, No. 20, pp. 8)
Pub: Penton Media Inc.
Description: A guide to the number of customers encountering food trucks during summer 2011 is presented by region.

9085 ▪ "Counter Service" in Nation's Restaurant News (Vol. 45, September 26, 2011, No. 20, pp. 8)
Pub: Penton Media Inc.
Description: As food trucks continue their momentum, a study was conducted showing how many consumer would visit a food truck. Nearly two thirds of 18-44 year olds would likely visit a food truck, while individuals over the age of 65 only 38 percent would eat from a food truck.

9086 ■ "Counter Service: We Gear Up Some Food Truck Stats" in *Nation's Restaurant News* (Vol. 45, August 8, 2011, No. 16, pp. 6)
Pub: Penton Media Inc.
Description: According to a recent survey, people do not see food truck service as a trend and 84 percent of social media users said they would visit food trucks at least once a week.

9087 ■ "Food-Truck Learnings Travel Indoors" in *Nation's Restaurant News* (Vol. 45, June 27, 2011, No. 13, pp. 3)
Pub: Penton Media Inc.
Ed: Lisa Jennings. **Description:** Challenges faced by owners of food truck businesses are discussed. Ways a food truck can be used to promote a restaurant's menu are covered.

9088 ■ "Gallo Family Vineyards to Raise Funds for Meals On Wheels" in *Food & Beverage Close-Up* (November 4, 2011)
Pub: Close-Up Media
Description: Gallo family is committed to raising funds for Meals On Wheels Association of America and hosts a fundraiser annually.

9089 ■ "Having Words with Matt Maroni: Chef-Owner, Gaztro-Wagon, Chicago" in *Nation's Restaurant News* (Vol. 45, April 4, 2011, No. 7, pp. 62)
Pub: Penton Media Inc.
Ed: Mike Dempsey. **Description:** Profile of Matt Maroni, chef and owner of Gaztro-Wagon in Chicago, Illinois is presented. Maroni tells how he found his niche in the food truck industry.

9090 ■ "Howl-o-ween" in *Decatur Daily* (October 25, 2011)
Pub: Decatur Daily
Ed: Catherine Godbey. **Description:** Animal Friends Humane Society provides free pet food and cat litter to Meals on Wheels clients.

9091 ■ "Keep On Truckin'" in *Boston Business Journal* (Vol. 31, August 5, 2011, No. 28, pp. 3)
Pub: Boston Business Journal
Ed: Lisa van der Pool. **Description:** Food truck business is booming in Boston with more than 25 trucks dotting the area including 15 new truck locations approved by the city in July 2011. The business is rather costly to start because it requires more than $100,000 capital and the food truck can run between $50,000 to $100,000.

9092 ■ "Learn New Ideas from Experienced Menu Makers" in *Nation's Restaurant News* (Vol. 45, June 27, 2011, No. 13, pp. 82)
Pub: Penton Media Inc.
Ed: Nancy Kruse. **Description:** National Restaurant Association Restaurant, Hotel-Motel Show featured the Food Truck Spot, a firm committed to all aspects of mobile catering, foodtruck manufacturers, leasers of fully equipped truck and a food-truck franchising group.

9093 ■ "Meals on Wheels Filling 'Blizzard Bags'" in *Tulsa World* (November 5, 2011)
Pub: Tulsa World
Ed: Sara Plummer. **Description:** Cathy Perlingiere, director of volunteer services for Meals on Wheels of Metro Tulsa, Oklahoma reports that they do not deliver meals when the Tulsa Public Schools close because of weather so they try to prepare 'blizzard bags' with nonperishable food items to cover about three meals for when drivers cannot deliver.

9094 ■ "More Volunteers Needed to Make a Difference" in *Times-News* (October 18, 2011)
Pub: Times-News
Ed: Roselee Papandrea. **Description:** Meals on Wheels program in the Burlington, North Carolina area is seeking volunteers to deliver meals to senior citizens.

9095 ■ "New Technology, Growing Fan Base Fuel Truck Trend" in *Nation's Restaurant News* (Vol. 45, June 13, 2001, No. 12, pp. 16)
Pub: Penton Media Inc.
Ed: Ron Ruggless. **Description:** Food trucks drove more interest at this year's National Restaurant Association Restaurant Hotel-Motel Show in Chicago. The trend continues to show long-term growth.

9096 ■ "Oberweis Tests Home Ice Cream Delivery" in *Ice Cream Reporter* (Vol. 21, November 20, 2008, No. 12, pp. 1)
Pub: Ice Cream Reporter
Description: Oberweis Dairy launched its Treat Delivery Program in the Saint Louis area. The program allows customers to order milkshakes, ice cream cones, sundaes and scoops of ice cream and they are delivered to their home or office. Oberweis is a fourth generation family run business.

9097 ■ "Silver Key Seeks Volunteer Drivers in Colorado Springs" in *Colorado Springs Business Journal* (October 21, 2011)
Pub: Dolan Media
Ed: Amy Gillentine. **Description:** Silver Keyis look for drivers to use their own vehicles to deliver Meals on Wheels to area seniors. For many of these senior citizens, it is the only outside contact they have an entire day.

9098 ■ "Speakers Address Authenticity, R&D Evolution" in *Nation's Restaurant News* (Vol. 45, October 24, 2011, No. 32, pp. 32)
Pub: Penton Media Inc.
Ed: Bret Thorn. **Description:** Culinary trends are discussed, along with an examination of the food truck trend and how this small sector is creating a great influence on food and communication with customers and delivery expectations.

9099 ■ "Substantial Deal Expected to Create Jobs, Help Industrial Market" in *Tampa Bay Business Journal* (Vol. 30, January 8, 2010, No. 3)
Pub: American City Business Journals
Ed: Janet Leiser. **Description:** Food distribution firm Gordon Food Service (GFS) is on the brink of purchasing Albertson's million-square-foot warehouse along with 158 acres of space. The deal between GFS and Albertson's could expand GFS' presence in west Central Florida. A history of GFS' growth is included

9100 ■ "Tap Into Food Truck Trend to Rev Up Sales, Build Buzz" in *Nation's Restaurant News* (Vol. 45, February 7, 2011, No. 3, pp. 18)
Pub: Penton Media Inc.
Ed: Brian Sacks. **Description:** Food truck trend is growing, particularly in New York City, Philadelphia, Washington DC, and Los Angeles, California. Man entrepreneurs are using a mobile food component to market their food before opening a restaurant.

9101 ■ "Tualatin Senior Center Under Construction" in *Daily Journal of Commerce* (October 21, 2011)
Pub: Dolan Media
Ed: Angela Webber. **Description:** Juanita Pohl Center in Tualatin Community Park is the home to TualatinAEs Meals on Wheels program that delivers meals to seniors in the area.

9102 ■ "Working the Streets" in *Baltimore Business Journal* (Vol. 28, July 30, 2010, No. 12, pp. 1)
Pub: Baltimore Business Journal
Ed: Amanda Pino. **Description:** Reports show that street vendors are popping up on new corners in Baltimore, Maryland, with city-inspected stainless steel food carts in tow. Applications for street vending licenses shot up at the end of 2009 and into this summer. It is believed that pinning down the exact number of vendors operating at any one point is difficult.

TRADE PERIODICALS

9103 ■ *Canadian Pizza Magazine*
Pub: Annex Publishing & Printing Inc.
Contact: Martin McAnulty, Gp. Publisher
E-mail: fire@annexweb.com
Ed: Laura Aiken, Editor, laiken@annexweb.com. **Released:** 8/yr. **Price:** $18 Canada. **Description:** Trade magazine for the pizza industry.

9104 ■ *IDDBA Legis-Letter*
Pub: International Dairy-Deli-Bakery Association
Contact: Roberta Rush
Ed: Carol L. Christison, Editor, cchristison@iddba.org. **Price:** Included in membership. **Description:** Reports on legislative activity concerning the supermarket dairy-deli-bakery industry.

9105 ■ *WrapUp*
Pub: International Dairy-Deli-Bakery Association
Ed: Carol L Christison, Editor, cchristison@iddba.org.
Released: Quarterly. **Price:** Included in membership. **Description:** Reports on news, activities, and topics of interest to the Association.

VIDEOCASSETTES/ AUDIOCASSETTES

9106 ■ *Food Service Industry Video Series: Career Opportunities*
Meridian Education Corp.
132 West 31st Street, 17th Floor
New York, NY 10001
Ph:(609)671-0266
Free: 800-257-5126
Co. E-mail: custmserv@films.com
URL: http://meridian.films.com
Released: 1991. **Price:** $45.00. **Description:** Presents information on education and training for a variety of careers in the food service industry: cook, chef, waiter/waitress, counter attendant, short-order cook, dishwasher, hostess, bookkeeper, maintenance, purchasing, management, cashier, dietitian, busperson, baker and more. **Availability:** VHS.

9107 ■ *Food Service Industry Video Series: Employee Skills*
Meridian Education Corp.
132 West 31st Street, 17th Floor
New York, NY 10001
Ph:(609)671-0266
Free: 800-257-5126
Co. E-mail: custmserv@films.com
URL: http://meridian.films.com
Released: 1991. **Price:** $45.00. **Description:** Presents information on preparing for a job interview in the food service industry and the skills necessary to be successful in that field. **Availability:** VHS.

9108 ■ *Food Service Industry Video Series: Food Preparation*
Meridian Education Corp.
132 West 31st Street, 17th Floor
New York, NY 10001
Ph:(609)671-0266
Free: 800-257-5126
Co. E-mail: custmserv@films.com
URL: http://meridian.films.com
Released: 1991. **Price:** $45.00. **Description:** Overviews food preparation techniques in all areas of food service including entrees, salads, and bakery. Also includes information on food service presentation. **Availability:** VHS.

9109 ■ *Food Service Industry Video Series: Management Skills*
Meridian Education Corp.
132 West 31st Street, 17th Floor
New York, NY 10001
Ph:(609)671-0266
Free: 800-257-5126
Co. E-mail: custmserv@films.com
URL: http://meridian.films.com
Released: 1991. **Price:** $45.00. **Description:** Overviews the skills necessary for success as a manager in the food service industry, including math skills, adaptability, costs, record keeping and more. **Availability:** VHS.

9110 ■ *Food Service Industry Video Series: Safety and Sanitation*
Meridian Education Corp.
132 West 31st Street, 17th Floor
New York, NY 10001
Ph:(609)671-0266

Free: 800-257-5126
Co. E-mail: custmserv@films.com
URL: http://meridian.films.com
Released: 1991. **Price:** $45.00. **Description:** Presents viewers with information on sanitation in a food service environment. **Availability:** VHS.

9111 ■ *Food Services*
RMI Media
1365 N. Winchester St.
Olathe, KS 66061-5880
Ph:(913)768-1696
Free: 800-745-5480
Fax:800-755-6910
Co. E-mail: actmedia@act.org
URL: http://www.actmedia.com
Released: 1987. **Description:** Methods of food preparation and equipment maintenance used in the food industry are discussed. **Availability:** VHS; 3/4U.

TRADE SHOWS AND CONVENTIONS

9112 ■ ApEx
Canadian Restaurant and Food Services Association
316 Bloor St. W.
Toronto, ON, Canada M5S 1W5
Ph:(416)923-8416
Free: 800-387-5649
Fax:(416)923-1450
Co. E-mail: info@crfa.ca
URL: http://www.crfa.ca
Audience: Trade. **Principal Exhibits:** Products and services for the restaurant and hospitality industry, as well as institutions, convenience stores, delis and bakeries. **Dates and Locations:** 2011 Apr 03-04, Moncton, NB.

FRANCHISES AND BUSINESS OPPORTUNITIES

9113 ■ Cena
12501 N Hwy. 395, Ste. 3
Spokane, WA 99218
Ph:(509)448-1725
Free: 888-667-2362
Fax:(509)448-9380
No. of Franchise Units: 10. **No. of Company-Owned Units:** 1. **Founded:** 2004. **Franchised:** 2005. **Description:** Meal preparation/assembly center and wine shop. **Equity Capital Needed:** $148,400-$205,500; express/kiosk option available. **Franchise Fee:** $30,000. **Royalty Fee:** 5%. **Financial Assistance:** No. **Training:** Provides 4 days training at headquarters, 3 days onsite and ongoing support.

9114 ■ Coffee Perks
2985 Mercury Rd.
Jacksonville, FL 32207
Free: (866)473-7571
Fax:(904)737-7946
No. of Franchise Units: 3. **No. of Company-Owned Units:** 1. **Founded:** 1993. **Franchised:** 2004. **Description:** Office coffee & food-service distribution. **Equity Capital Needed:** $116,100. **Franchise Fee:** $18,000. **Royalty Fee:** 6%. **Financial Assistance:** Limited in-house and third party equipment financing available. **Training:** Offers 2 weeks training at headquarters, 1 week at franchisees location with ongoing support.

9115 ■ Farmer Boys
Farmer Boys Food, Inc.
3452 University Ave.
Riverside, CA 92501
Ph:(909)275-9900
Fax:(909)275-9930
No. of Franchise Units: 48. **No. of Company-Owned Units:** 17. **Founded:** 1981. **Franchised:** 1997. **Description:** Restaurants and food delivery services. **Equity Capital Needed:** $515,375-$795,505. **Franchise Fee:** $40,000. **Royalty Fee:** 5%. **Financial Assistance:** Third party financing available. **Training:** Yes.

9116 ■ The Firkin Group of Pubs
Firkin Pub International, Inc.
20 Steelcase Rd. W, No. 1C
Markham, ON, Canada L3R 1B2
Ph:(905)305-9792
Fax:(905)305-9719
Co. E-mail: larry@firkinpubs.com
URL: http://www.firkinpubs.com
No. of Franchise Units: 15. **No. of Company-Owned Units:** 15. **Founded:** 1987. **Franchised:** 1987. **Description:** Restaurants and food delivery services. **Equity Capital Needed:** $350,000. **Franchise Fee:** $30,000. **Royalty Fee:** 5%. **Financial Assistance:** Third party financing available. **Training:** Training provided at headquarters and ongoing support.

9117 ■ Hooters of America, Inc.
1815 The Exchange
Atlanta, GA 30339
Ph:(770)951-2040
Fax:(770)933-9464
No. of Franchise Units: 210. **No. of Company-Owned Units:** 90. **Founded:** 1985. **Franchised:** 1988. **Description:** Business of restaurant and food delivery services. **Equity Capital Needed:** $800,000. **Franchise Fee:** $75,000. **Financial Assistance:** No. **Training:** Yes.

9118 ■ Insomnia Cookies Franchising LLC
650 5th Ave., 31st Fl.
New York, NY 10019
Ph:(212)286-2403
Fax:(866)422-8402
No. of Company-Owned Units: 14. **Founded:** 2002. **Franchised:** 2006. **Description:** Cookies & baked goods stores/late-night delivery. **Equity Capital Needed:** $65,600-$111,400. **Franchise Fee:** $25,000. **Royalty Fee:** 6%. **Financial Assistance:** No. **Training:** Offer 2-3 weeks training at headquarters, 2-3 weeks onsite and ongoing support.

9119 ■ Let's Eat
2202 North Westshore Blvd., Suite 200
Tampa, FL 33607
Ph:(813)258-0555
Fax:(813)258-9100
No. of Franchise Units: 5. **No. of Company-Owned Units:** 3. **Founded:** 2004. **Franchised:** 2005. **Description:** Meal preparation service. **Equity Capital Needed:** $99,000-$193,500. **Franchise Fee:** $25,500-$26,500. **Royalty Fee:** 6%. **Financial Assistance:** No.

9120 ■ The Lunch Lady Group Inc.
151 Spinnaker Way, Unit 11
Concord, ON, Canada L4K 4C3
Ph:(905)660-5994
Free: 800-603-6656
Fax:(905)660-0972
Co. E-mail: franchise@thelunchlady.ca
URL: http://www.thelunchlady.ca
No. of Franchise Units: 38. **No. of Company-Owned Units:** 3. **Founded:** 1995. **Franchised:** 1999. **Description:** Offering HOT lunches delivered to Public School children. **Equity Capital Needed:** $80,000-$100,000. **Franchise Fee:** $25,000. **Training:** Offers 2 week training program and ongoing support.

9121 ■ Mancino's, Samuel Italian Eatery
Nu-Ventures Inc.
1324 W Milham
Portage, MI 49024
Ph:(269)226-4400
Free: 888-432-8379
Fax:(269)226-4466
No. of Franchise Units: 38. **Founded:** 1959. **Franchised:** 1994. **Description:** Franchise of restaurants and food delivery services of food. **Equity Capital Needed:** $200,000-$250,000. **Franchise Fee:** $30,000. **Financial Assistance:** No. **Training:** Yes.

9122 ■ Off the Grill Franchising, LLC
1728 General George Patton Dr., Ste. 200
Brentwood, TN 37027
Ph:(615)370-0700
Free: 877-OTG-2100

Fax:(615)371-1405
No. of Franchise Units: 13. **No. of Company-Owned Units:** 2. **Founded:** 1999. **Franchised:** 1999. **Description:** Carry out and delivery; steaks, burgers, and chicken. **Equity Capital Needed:** $250,000. **Franchise Fee:** $25,000. **Financial Assistance:** No. **Training:** Yes.

9123 ■ Padows's Hams & Deli
Padow's Deli Inc.
9864 W Broad St.
Glen Allen, VA 23060
Ph:(804)965-6262
No. of Franchise Units: 10. **No. of Company-Owned Units:** 2. **Founded:** 1936. **Franchised:** 1995. **Description:** Retail and mail order food. **Equity Capital Needed:** $250,000-$400,000. **Franchise Fee:** $25,000-$35,000. **Financial Assistance:** No. **Training:** Yes.

9124 ■ Sarpino's Pizzeria Canada Ltd.
Sarpino's World LTD
1133 Regent St., Ste. 203
Fredericton, NB, Canada E3B 3Z2
Ph:(506)462-9270
Fax:(506)451-8692
Co. E-mail: rbuckingham@nb.aibn.com
URL: http://www.sarpinos.com
No. of Franchise Units: 9. **No. of Company-Owned Units:** 1. **Founded:** 2001. **Franchised:** 2002. **Description:** Pizzeria. **Equity Capital Needed:** $195,000-$235,000. **Franchise Fee:** $25,000. **Training:** Provides 2 weeks training.

LIBRARIES

9125 ■ American Institute of Food Distribution, Inc.–Information and Research Center
1 Broadway Plaza, 2nd Fl.
Elmwood Park, NJ 07407
Ph:(201)791-5570
Fax:(201)791-5222
Co. E-mail: jkastrinsky@foodinstitute.com
URL: http://www.foodinstitute.com/
Contact: Brian Todd, Pres./CEO
Scope: Food industry. **Services:** Center open to the public on fee basis. **Subscriptions:** 400 journals and other serials.

9126 ■ Coca-Cola Company–The INFOSOURCE
PO Box 1734
Atlanta, GA 30301
Ph:(404)515-4636
Fax:(404)253-4575
Co. E-mail: koinfo@na.ko.com
URL: http://www.coca-cola.com
Contact: Heather Turnbull, Sr.Res.Anl.
Scope: Business, Legal, Marketing, Technical - including beverages, soft drinks, fruit juices, food technology, nutrition, chemistry, engineering.

9127 ■ ConAgra Grocery Products R&D Technical Library
3353 Michelson Dr.
Irvine, CA 92612-0650
Ph:(949)437-2859
Fax:(949)437-3372
Co. E-mail: gilbertson@yahoo.com
URL: http://www.conagrafoods.com
Contact: Christopher L. Gilbertson
Scope: Food science, technology, and packaging. **Services:** Library not open to the public. **Holdings:** 4500 books; 1000 bound periodical volumes; 98 VF drawers of patents; 1300 government documents; 4 VF drawers of Annual reports.

9128 ■ Food Marketing Institute Information Service
2345 Crystal Dr., Ste. 800
Arlington, VA 22202

Ph:(202)452-8444
Fax:(202)429-4519
Co. E-mail: fmi@fmi.org
URL: http://www.fmi.org
Contact: Ms. Leslie G. Sarasin, Pres./CEO
Scope: Food distribution. **Services:** Interlibrary loan; copying; service open to the public by appointment. **Holdings:** 7000 volumes. **Subscriptions:** 100 journals and other serials.

9129 ■ Noble and Associates Library
2155 W. Chesterfield Blvd.
Springfield, MO 65807
Ph:(417)875-5000
Co. E-mail: julie.tumy@noble.net
URL: http://www.noble.net
Contact: Julie Tumy, Pres.

Scope: Food, food service, advertising, construction, agriculture. **Services:** Interlibrary loan; copying; SDI; Library not open to the public. **Holdings:** 500 books; 1000 reports. **Subscriptions:** 300 journals and other serials; 5 newspapers.

9130 ■ Technomic, Inc.–Knowledge Center
300 S. Riverside Plaza, Ste. 1200
Chicago, IL 60606
Ph:(312)876-0004
Fax:(312)876-1158
Co. E-mail: curban@technomic.com
URL: http://www.technomic.com
Contact: Chris Urban, Dir., Knowledge Ctr.
Scope: Management, food/food service, restaurants. **Holdings:** 250 books. **Subscriptions:** 70 journals and other serials.

RESEARCH CENTERS

9131 ■ National Restaurant Association–Quality Assurance Executive Study Group
1200 17th St. NW
Washington, DC 20036
Ph:(202)331-5900
Free: 800—424-5156
Fax:(202)331-2429
Co. E-mail: nmadison@restaurant.org
URL: http://www.restaurant.org/education/study-groups/qa
Contact: Dawn Sweeney, Pres./CEO
E-mail: nmadison@restaurant.org
Scope: Quality assurance and quality control in food service facilities.

ASSOCIATIONS AND OTHER ORGANIZATIONS

9132 ■ Express Delivery and Logistics Association
400 Admiral Blvd.
Kansas City, MO 64106
Ph:(816)221-0254
Free: 888-838-0761
Fax:(816)472-7765
Co. E-mail: jim@expressassociation.org
URL: http://www.expressassociation.org
Contact: Jim Conway, Pres.
Description: Represents air couriers, small package express delivery companies, airlines and associated industry members (75); supports companies and facilities such as airlines and airports. Seeks to: provide industry forum for ideas, educate members about new technologies within the industry; represent air couriers before governmental bodies; inform members of legislation affecting the industry; develop and maintain relationships among members. Conducts seminars and workshops. **Publications:** *XLA Alert* (periodic); *XLA Express* (quarterly); *XLA Extra* (biweekly).

9133 ■ National Customs Brokers and Forwarders Association of America
1200 18th St. NW, No. 901
Washington, DC 20036
Ph:(202)466-0222
Fax:(202)466-0226
Co. E-mail: staff@ncbfaa.org
URL: http://www.ncbfaa.org
Contact: Jeffrey C. Coppersmith, Pres.
Description: Treasury-licensed customs brokers, FMC-licensed independent ocean freight forwarders, and CNS-registered air cargo agents; associate members in 25 foreign countries. Seeks to maintain high standards of business practice throughout the industry. Monitors legislative and regulatory issues affecting customs brokers and forwarders; conducts seminars on new developments and techniques in the industry; provides forum for exchange among brokers and forwarders. Conducts educational programs. **Publications:** *NCBFAA Membership Directory: The Who's Who of American Customs Brokers and International Freight Forwarders* (annual).

9134 ■ National Industrial Transportation League
1700 N Moore St., Ste. 1900
Arlington, VA 22209
Ph:(703)524-5011
Fax:(703)524-5017
Co. E-mail: info@nitl.org
URL: http://www.nitl.org
Contact: Bruce Carlton, Pres./CEO
Description: Seeks to promote adequate national and international transportation; encourages the exchange of ideas and information concerning traffic and transportation; and cooperates with regulatory agencies and other transportation companies in developing an understanding of legislation. **Publications:** *The Notice* (weekly); *Reference Manual* (quarterly).

9135 ■ Overseas Automotive Council
PO Box 13966
Research Triangle Park, NC 27709-3966
Ph:(919)406-8846
Fax:(919)549-4824
Co. E-mail: jdenton@mema.org
URL: http://www.aftermarketsuppliers.org/Councils/OAC
Contact: John Brunke, Chm.
Description: Multi-faceted resource for individuals involved in the international marketing and sales of automotive products manufactured in the United States. Provides a forum, which enhances the prestige of the American automotive industry, promoting friendly trade relationships with understanding of the various cultures involved. **Publications:** *Overseas Automotive Council—Membership Roster* (annual).

REFERENCE WORKS

9136 ■ *American Motor Carrier Directory*
Pub: UBM Global Trade
Contact: Amy Middlebrook, Gp. Publisher
E-mail: amiddlebrook@cbizmedia.com
Released: Annual, December. **Publication Includes:** Lists of all licensed Less Than Truckload (LTL) general commodity carriers in the United States; includes specialized motor carriers and related services; includes refrigerated carriers, heavy haulers, bulk haulers, riggers, and specified commodity carriers; state and federal regulatory bodies governing the trucking industry; tariff publishing bureaus; freight claim councils; industry associations, etc. **Entries Include:** For carriers and services—Company name, address of headquarters and terminals, phones, tariffs followed, names of executives, insurance, and equipment information, services or commodities handled. Principal content of publication is listing of direct point-to-point services of LTL general commodity carriers throughout the United States and to Canada and Mexico. **Arrangement:** Alphabetical.

9137 ■ "Cold-Storage Cargo Facility a Late Bloomer" in *Houston Business Journal* (Vol. 40, August 28, 2009, No. 16, pp. 1A)
Pub: American City Business Journals
Ed: Jennifer Dawson. **Description:** Trammell Crow Company leased half of the 61,000 square foot IAH International Air Cargo Centre II to Tradewinds Cargo Handling. The facility, located at George Bush Intercontinental Airport, is intended to be a destination of fresh flowers and food from Latin America.

9138 ■ "Con-Way Project Back in High Gear" in *Business Journal Portland* (Vol. 27, November 5, 2010, No. 36, pp. 1)
Pub: Portland Business Journal
Ed: Wendy Culverwell. **Description:** Trucking firm Con-Way Inc. intends to sell parcels of land from a property comprising 16 blocks and 20 prime acres west of the Pearl District in Portland, Oregon. In 2009, Con-Way abandoned plans to sell the property. As Con-Way reclaims control over design and usage of the property, it also expressed willingness to cooperate with a master developer on a related real estate project.

9139 ■ "Could This Be Your Next Office Building?" in *Austin Business Journal* (Vol. 31, May 13, 2011, No. 10, pp. A1)
Pub: American City Business Journals Inc.
Ed: Cody Lyon. **Description:** Falcon Containers moved to a 51-acre site in Far East Austin, Texas and started construction of a 2,500-square-foot headquarters made from eight 40-foot shipping containers. Falcon's CEO Stephen Shang plans to use his headquarters building as a showroom to attract upscale, urban hipsters. Insights on the construction's environmental and social impact are shared.

9140 ■ *Directory of Freight Forwarders and Custom House Brokers*
Pub: International Wealth Success, Inc. IWS
Released: Annual, January. **Price:** $20, individuals. **Covers:** Several hundred freight forwarders and custom house brokers involved in international trade. **Entries Include:** Company or firm name, address, phone. **Arrangement:** Geographical.

9141 ■ "Freeing the Wheels of Commerce" in *Hispanic Business* (July-August 2007, pp. 50, 52, 54)
Pub: Hispanic Business
Ed: Keith Rosenblum. **Description:** SecureOrigins, a border-based partnership with high-tech innovators is working to move goods faster, more efficiently, and securely.

9142 ■ "Is 'Tsunami' of Freight in our Future?" in *Business Courier* (Vol. 26, November 27, 2009, No. 31, pp. 1)
Pub: American City Business Journals, Inc.
Ed: Dan Monk. **Description:** Freight companies are planning for cargo-container shipping facilities on the riverfront of Cincinnati in light of the completion of the $5 billion Panama Canal expansion in 2015. The city's capability to utilize the growth in freight has been under investigation by authorities.

9143 ■ "Martin Marietta Expands Rock Solid Port Manatee Presence" in *Tampa Bay Business Journal* (Vol. 30, January 8, 2010, No. 3, pp. 1)
Pub: American City Business Journals
Ed: Jane Meinhardt. **Description:** Raleigh, North Carolina-based Martin Marietta Materials Inc. has been granted by Florida's Manatee County Port Authority with a 30-year, $42 million contract. Through the contract, an aggregate terminal will be built by Martin Marietta at the port. Construction work is anticipated to start in earl 2010 with terminal operations commencing by late summer 2010.

9144 ■ *Messenger Courier Association of America—Network Guide and Membership Directory*
Pub: Messenger Courier Association of America
Contact: Bob Decaprio, Exec. Dir.
Released: Annual, January. **Price:** $235. **Covers:** Approximately 500 member air courier companies.

Entries Include: Company name, office personnel, warehouse facilities area served. **Arrangement:** Geographical by airport city.

9145 ■ National Customs Brokers & Forwarders Association of America—Membership Directory
Pub: National Customs Brokers & Forwarders Association of America
Contact: Barbara Reilly CAE, Exec. VP
Released: Annual, Latest edition 2011 New edition expected 2012. **Price:** $30, individuals per copy. **Covers:** About 600 customs brokers, international air cargo agents, and freight forwarders in the United States. **Entries Include:** Company name, address, phone, telex, fax, cable address, year established, FMC license number, contact, branch or affiliate cities, and line of business. **Arrangement:** Classified by membership class, then alphabetical. **Indexes:** Geographical.

9146 ■ Official Export Guide
Pub: UBM Global Trade
Contact: Alan Glass, Chm./Pres./CEO
Released: Annual, January; inter-edition supplements. **Price:** $449.50 sale price; $899 regular price. **Covers:** Customs officials, port authorities, embassies and consulates, chambers of commerce, foreign trade zones, and other organizations and agencies involved in international trade; prospective foreign buyers; related trade services. **Entries Include:** Generally, organization or company name, address, phone, phone, telex, fax, names and titles of key personnel. **Arrangement:** Geographical, then classified by service.

9147 ■ Quick Caller Area Air Cargo Directory QC
Pub: Fourth Seacoast Publishing Company Inc.
Contact: Tom Buysse
Released: Annual, Latest edition 2010. **Price:** $21.95, individuals each, plus shipping charges; payment must accompany order; $19.95, individuals 2-12 copies. **Covers:** firms in the east (New York/New Jersey metro area edition); midwest (Detroit and Chicago editions); New England (Boston edition); the south (Miami/Orlando/Florida and Atlanta editions); and the west (San Francisco/Oakland Bay area and Los Angeles editions) and Pacific Northwest (Seattle/Portland/Vancouver edition); includes airlines, charter services, air freight forwarders, and related air freight services, including trucking, warehousing, and packaging. **Entries Include:** Firm name, location, description of services. **Arrangement:** By line of business/service.

9148 ■ Smart Mail
Pub: Pitney-Bowes
Released: Quarterly. **Covers:** Courier companies that provide same day, overnight and second-day delivery service of small packages throughout the United States. **Entries Include:** Courier name, rates, phone, destinations, delivery times, types of service, hours of operation, company profile. **Arrangement:** Geographical.

9149 ■ "StorageByMail Lets Customers Ship Away Their Clutter" in Inc. (Vol. 33, April 2011, No. 3, pp. 92)
Pub: Inc. Magazine
Ed: Issie Lapowsky. **Description:** StorageByMail allows people to put items into storage by mailing them to the company. The firm charges a monthly fee, customers describe contents of each box, and ship to the Jersey City facility using a preprinted label. StorageByMail pays the $25 shipment charge.

9150 ■ "Truckers Walk Strike Line" in Puget Sound Business Journal (Vol. 29, October 24, 2008, No. 27, pp. 1)
Pub: American City Business Journals
Ed: Steve Wilhelm. **Description:** Teamsters Local 174 went on strike against Oak Harbor Freight Lines Inc. over alleged company violations of federal labor laws. The union also accuses the company of engaging directly with employees and holding mandatory meetings about contract negotiations.

9151 ■ "Virginia Albanese: President and CEO" in Inside Business (Vol. 13, September-October 2011, No. 5, pp. NC4)
Pub: Great Lakes Publishing Company
Ed: Jeannie Roberts. **Description:** Profile of Virginia Albanese, CEO of FedEx's Custom Critical Division in Akron, Ohio. Albanese discusses her philosophy on business leadership.

STATISTICAL SOURCES

9152 ■ RMA Annual Statement Studies
Pub: Robert Morris Associates (RMA)
Released: Annual. **Price:** $175.00 2006-07 edition, $105.00. **Description:** Contains composite balance sheets and income statements for more than 360 industries, including the accounting, auditing, and bookkeeping industries. Also contains five years of comparative historical data for discerning trends. Includes 16 commonly used ratios, computed for most of the size groupings for nearly every industry.

TRADE PERIODICALS

9153 ■ Fastline—Bluegrass Truck Edition
Pub: Fastline
Released: 13/yr. **Price:** $18; $30 two years; $45 Canada and Mexico; $95 other countries. **Description:** Illustrated buying guide for the trucking industry.

9154 ■ Fastline—Florida Truck Edition
Pub: Fastline
Released: 13/yr. **Price:** $18; $30 two years; $45 Canada and Mexico; $95 other countries. **Description:** Illustrated buying guide for the trucking industry.

9155 ■ Fastline—Georgia Truck Edition
Pub: Fastline
Released: 13/yr. **Price:** $18; $30 two years; $45 Canada and Mexico; $95 other countries. **Description:** Illustrated buying guide for the trucking industry.

9156 ■ Fastline—Tennessee Truck Edition
Pub: Fastline
Released: Monthly. **Price:** $18; $30 two years; $45 Canada and Mexico; $95 other countries; $35 3 years. **Description:** Illustrated buying guide for the trucking industry.

9157 ■ Fastline—Tri-State Truck Edition
Pub: Fastline
Released: 13/yr. **Price:** $18; $30 two years; $45 Canada and Mexico; $95 other countries. **Description:** Illustrated buying guide for the trucking industry.

9158 ■ Mailing Systems Technology MAST
Pub: RB Publishing Co.
Contact: John E. Thompson, Managing Editor
E-mail: john.t@rbpub.com
Ed: Dan O'Rourke, Editor, dan.o@rbpub.com. **Description:** Trade magazine covering mailing and office practices.

9159 ■ Trans Digest
Pub: Transportation Consumer Protection Council Inc.
Contact: William J. Augello
Ed: Stephen W. Beyer, Editor. **Released:** Monthly. **Price:** Included in membership. **Description:** Provides the shipping community with news relating to the transportation of goods, including agency actions and decisions, legislative developments, and court decisions. Recurring features include recent court decisions; questions & answers; tariff watch; notices of seminars and educational materials.

TRADE SHOWS AND CONVENTIONS

9160 ■ TransComp
National Industrial Transportation League
1700 N. Moore St., Ste. 1900
Arlington, VA 22209-1904
Ph:(703)524-5011

Fax:(703)524-5017
Co. E-mail: info@nitl.org
URL: http://www.nitl.org
Released: Annual. **Audience:** Transportation professionals. **Principal Exhibits:** Computer services, software, and innovations for transportation operations. Motor, rail, air, water and International modal carriers, freight payment services, EDI, custom brokers, bar coding, tariff watch services and other products and services for enhancing domestic and international freight transportation management. **Dates and Locations:** 2011 Nov 11-16, Atlanta, GA.

FRANCHISES AND BUSINESS OPPORTUNITIES

9161 ■ eShipping
173 English Landing Dr., Ste. 210
Parkville, MD 64152
Ph:(816)505-0198
Fax:(816)880-0047
No. of Franchise Units: 13. **No. of Company-Owned Units:** 4. **Founded:** 2001. **Franchised:** 2006. **Description:** Freight and shipping services. **Equity Capital Needed:** $30,755-$64,150. **Franchise Fee:** $22,500-$23,700. **Royalty Fee:** 35%. **Financial Assistance:** Limited third party and in-house financing available. **Training:** Provides 3-4 days training and ongoing support.

9162 ■ United Shipping Solutions
6985 Union Park Ctr., Ste. 565
Midvale, UT 84047
Ph:(801)352-0012
Free: (866)744-7486
Fax:(801)352-0339
No. of Franchise Units: 126. **Founded:** 2002. **Franchised:** 2002. **Description:** Transportation services. **Equity Capital Needed:** $53,700-$103,500. **Franchise Fee:** $50,000-$53,000. **Royalty Fee:** 6%. **Financial Assistance:** No. **Training:** Offers 7 days at headquarters, 7 days at franchisees location and ongoing training as needed (recurrent and/or advanced).

COMPUTERIZED DATABASES

9163 ■ MileMaker
Rand McNally & Co.
8255 N Central Park Ave.
Skokie, IL 60076
Ph:(847)329-8100
Free: 800-777-6277
Co. E-mail: info@randmcnally.com
URL: http://www.randmcnally.com
Description: Contains highway mileage and route information used by the transportation industry for motor freight rating and motor fuel tax reporting, based on the Motor Carrier's Road Atlas. Covers more than 160,000 geographic points and roadway in the United States, Canada, and Mexico for a potential 14.2 billion mileage/kilometer combinations. Enables users to retrieve mileages and routing by city and state names, Standard Point Location Codes, and 5-digit ZIP codes. Includes Practical Miles, a calculation of the shortest time route between two points, which allow for estimation of arrival time. Also offers a module for HazMat (Hazardous Materials). **Availability:** Online: Rand McNally & Co. **Type:** Directory; Numeric.

LIBRARIES

9164 ■ Air Transport Association of America Library
1301 Pennsylvania Ave. NW, Ste. 1100
Washington, DC 20004-7017
Ph:(202)626-4000
Fax:(202)626-4181
Co. E-mail: ata@airlines.org
URL: http://www.airlines.org

Contact: Mrs. Marion Mistrik, Libn.
Scope: Scheduled air carrier financial and traffic statistics, air transportation, law, aviation law, aeronautics. **Services:** Interlibrary loan; copying; Library open to the public by appointment. **Holdings:** 12,000 volumes; 12 VF drawers of pamphlets and Annual reports; 350 reels of microfilm; 3 drawers of microfiche; 500 report files. **Subscriptions:** 120 journals and other serials; 10 newspapers.

ASSOCIATIONS AND OTHER ORGANIZATIONS

9165 ■ Association of Fund-Raising Distributors and Suppliers
1100 Johnson Ferry Rd., Ste. 300
Atlanta, GA 30342
Ph:(404)252-3663
Fax:(404)252-0774
Co. E-mail: afrds@kellencompany.com
URL: http://www.afrds.org
Contact: Jon Krueger, Exec. Dir.
Description: Distributors, suppliers, and manufacturers of products sold to fundraising organizations. Seeks to enhance the image of the product fundraising industry. Works to establish a code of ethics; conducts public relations activities and seminars. .

9166 ■ Association of Fundraising Professionals
4300 Wilson Blvd., Ste. 300
Arlington, VA 22203
Ph:(703)684-0410
Free: 800-666-FUND
Fax:(703)684-0540
Co. E-mail: afp@afpnet.org
URL: http://www.afpnet.org
Contact: Andrew Watt, Pres./CEO
Description: Fundraising executives who work for non-profit and philanthropic organizations. Purposes are: to foster the development and growth of professional fundraising executives committed to the philanthropic process; to establish professional ethical standards and to require its members to adhere to those standards; to provide guidance and assistance to philanthropic institutions and agencies with fundraising programs; to offer continuing professional education and career enhancement services for philanthropic fundraising professionals. Maintains speakers' bureau. .

9167 ■ Association of Professional Researchers for Advancement
401 N Michigan Ave., Ste. 2200
Chicago, IL 60611
Ph:(312)321-5196
Fax:(312)673-6966
Co. E-mail: info@aprahome.org
URL: http://www.aprahome.org
Contact: Michael Quevli, Pres.-Elect
Description: Individuals involved in educational, medical, cultural, and religious organizations; fundraising consultants. Facilitates education and dissemination of information about prospect research; encourages professional development and cooperative relationships among members. Prospect research is aimed at securing gifts, grants, and charitable donations for nonprofit organizations. **Publications:** *APRA Member Directory* (annual); *Connections* (quarterly); *Quarterly* (quarterly);Annual Report (annual). .

9168 ■ Giving Institute
303 W Madison St., Ste. 2650
Chicago, IL 60606
Ph:(312)981-6794
Fax:(312)265-2908
Co. E-mail: info@givinginstitute.org
URL: http://www.givinginstitute.org
Contact: Mr. Thomas W. Mesaros, Chm.
Purpose: Represents fund-raising counseling firms engaged in consulting on the management and planning of campaigns for hospitals, universities, religious groups, community funds, arts organizations, social service groups and other nonprofit institutions. Conducts research in philanthropy. .

9169 ■ Partnership for Philanthropic Planning
233 McCrea St., Ste. 400
Indianapolis, IN 46225
Ph:(317)269-6274
Fax:(317)269-6276
Co. E-mail: info@pppnet.org
URL: http://www.pppnet.org
Contact: Tanya Howe Johnson, Pres./CEO
Description: Professional association of individuals from the fundraising, accounting, estate planning, insurance, and related fields. Members specialize in developing charitable gifts through bequests, trusts, annuities, life insurance, and real property. Provides education and networking opportunities. Conducts research. **Publications:** *The Journal of Gift Planning* (quarterly); *Proceedings of the National Conference on Planned Giving* (annual).

REFERENCE WORKS

9170 ■ "3CDC's Biggest Year" in *Business Courier* (Vol. 26, December 18, 2009, No. 34, pp. 1)
Pub: American City Business Journals, Inc.
Ed: Lucy May. **Description:** Cincinnati Center City Development Corporation (3CDC) will make 2010 its biggest year with nearly $164 million projects in the works. Historic tax credits and continued help from the city have allowed the private nonprofit organization to finance mega projects such as the $43 million renovation and expansion of Washington Park. Other projects that 3CDC will start or complete in 2010 are presented.

9171 ■ "$40M Fund Created for Big Energy Project" in *Austin Business JournalInc.* (Vol. 29, November 27, 2009, No. 38, pp. 1)
Pub: American City Business Journals
Ed: Christopher Calnan. **Description:** A group of Texas businessmen, called Republic Power Partners LP, is planning to raise $40 million in order to launch an alternative energy project. The 6,000-megawatt initiative would generate solar, biomass and wind power in West Texas and could cost as much as $10 billion.

9172 ■ "Alliance to End Hunger to Hold Press Conference on Fasting, Prayer and Budget Cuts" in *Food & Beverage Close-Up* (March 28, 2011)
Pub: Close-Up Media
Description: A coalition of religious and other leaders are launching a new campaign to protect programs for vulnerable people. Partners include: Alliance to End Hunger, American Jewish World Service, Bread for the World, Congressional Hunger Center, Feeding America, Food for the Hungry, Islamic Relief USA, Meals on Wheels Association of America, New Manna Inc., ONE, Society of Saint Andrews, Sojourners, and World Food Program USA.

9173 ■ *American Association of Fund-Raising Counsel Membership Directory*
Pub: American Association of Fund-Raising Counsel Inc.
Contact: Michael F. Ward, Exec. Dir.
Released: Annual. **Covers:** Member fund-raising consulting firms. **Entries Include:** Company name, address, phone, fax, geographical area served, types of clients, description of services. **Arrangement:** Alphabetical.

9174 ■ *Annual Register of Grant Support*
Pub: Information Today Inc.
Released: Annual, Latest edition 2011. **Price:** $269, individuals hardbound (plus $20 S&H); $242.10, individuals first time standing order (plus $20 S&H). **Covers:** More than 3,100 current grant programs offered by government agencies, private foundations, educational and professional associations, corporations, unions, religious groups and other organizations; covers programs offering grants to individuals for study, travel, etc., as well as to nonprofit organizations. **Entries Include:** Organization name, address, phone; major interests; program names and purposes; nature and amounts of support; eligibility requirements; application instructions; names of persons to whom inquiries are to be submitted. **Arrangement:** Classified by subject area or grant purpose (e.g., special populations, humanities, international affairs, etc.). **Indexes:** Subject, organization and program, geographical, and individual name.

9175 ■ "Bethesda Stepping Out" in *Business Courier* (Vol. 27, October 15, 2010, No. 24, pp. 1)
Pub: Business Courier
Ed: James Ritchie. **Description:** Nonprofit organization Bethesda Inc. is planning to donate $5 million a year for the next three years to Greater Cincinnati health care reforms. Bethesda revealed that it announced its donations to pressure other organizations to help.

9176 ■ "Big Shoes to Fill for New United Way Chairman" in *Business Courier* (Vol. 27, June 25, 2010, No. 8, pp. 4)
Pub: Business Courier
Ed: Lucy May. **Description:** David Dougherty, chairman of the nonprofit United Way of Greater Cincinnati, explains how he can surpass the nonprofit's 2009 campaign kickoff that raised $62 million. For 2010, Dougherty has prepared a $2 million matching grant from a group of local individuals, corporations, and foundations. Dougherty also discusses what he learned from participating in the 2009 campaign.

9177 ■ "Boring Bonds Gain Pizzazz as Investors Flock to Debt Issues" in *Baltimore Business Journal* (Vol. 28, June 11, 2010, No. 5, pp. 1)
Pub: Baltimore Business Journal
Ed: Gary Haber. **Description:** Companies and nonprofit organizations have increased the pace of

bond offerings in order to take advantage of the bonds' appeal among willing investors. Companies mostly issued corporate bonds to replace existing debt at lower interest rates and save them money from interest payments.

9178 ■ "Bringing Charities More Bang for Their Buck" in *Crain's Chicago Business* **(Vol. 34, May 23, 2011, No. 21, pp. 31)**
Pub: Crain Communications Inc.
Ed: Lisa Bertagnoli. **Description:** Marcy-Newberry Association connects charities with manufacturers in order to use excess items such as clothing, janitorial and office supplies.

9179 ■ "Business Put Cash Behind Bernstein" in *Baltimore Business Journal* **(Vol. 28, August 20, 2010, No. 15, pp. 1)**
Pub: Baltimore Business Journal
Ed: Scott Dance. **Description:** Baltimore, Maryland-based businesses have invested $40,000 to support lawyer Gregg L. Bernstein in the 2010 State Attorney election. The election campaign is being fueled by fear of a crime surge. Many businesses have been dealing with crimes such as muggings, shootings, and car break-ins.

9180 ■ "Chemed's Vitas Aims to Acquire" in *Business Courier* **(Vol. 27, July 9, 2010, No. 10, pp. 1)**
Pub: Business Courier
Ed: James Ritchie. **Description:** Chemed Corporation's Vitas Healthcare Corporation is looking for smaller nonprofit hospices as it looks to become more streamlined in a tougher reimbursement environment. CFO David Williams syas they want to acquire these hospices as fast as they can integrate them.

9181 ■ "Coastal Luxury Management Reports Los Angeles Food and Wine Tickets On Sale" in *Food & Beverage Close-Up* **(August 24, 2011)**
Pub: Close-Up Media
Description: Wolfgang Puck's Sunday Brunch and Charity Auction will raise money for Saint Vincent Meals on Wheels program.

9182 ■ "Coming Up Short" in *Boston Business Journal* **(Vol. 30, October 15, 2010, No. 36, pp. 1)**
Pub: Boston Business Journal
Ed: Tim McLaughlin, Mary Moore. **Description:** Boston, Massachusetts-based nonprofits have been profiting less from charity golf tournaments. Nonprofits have been collecting less than 50 cents on the dollar from such events. But nonprofits have been restructuring golf tournaments in order to boost profits.

9183 ■ "Corporate Responsibility" in *Professional Services Close-Up* **(July 2, 2010)**
Pub: Close-Up Media
Description: List of firms awarded the inaugural Best Corporate Citizens in Government Contracting by the Corporate Responsibility Magazine is presented. The list is based on the methodology of the Magazine's Best Corporate Citizen's List, with 324 data points of publicly-available information in seven categories which include: environment, climate change, human rights, philanthropy, employee relations, financial performance, and governance.

9184 ■ "Courier 250 Companies Hope to Rebound From 2009" in *Business Courier* **(Vol. 27, July 16, 2010, No. 11, pp. 1)**
Pub: Business Courier
Ed: Dan Monk, Jon Newberry. **Description:** Private companies that are featured in the Courier 250 publication have lost almost $4 billion in revenue, while combined sales dropped by 11 percent to 32 billion in 2009. Courier 250 is a guide to public companies, large nonprofits, private firms, and other related entities in Ohio's Cincinnati region.

9185 ■ "Don't Cry For Me?" in *Canadian Business* **(Vol. 83, July 20, 2010, No. 11-12, pp. 47)**
Pub: Rogers Media Ltd.
Ed: Joe Castaldo. **Description:** Canada's theaters are faced with low ticket sales, donations and endowments. The industry is producing popular works as a response to the situation.

9186 ■ "Echo Vintage Clothing Fundraiser Set July 24" in *Tri-City Herald* **(July 22, 2010)**
Pub: McClatchy-Tribune
Description: Bicentennial Echo Vintage Clothing Show and Tea was held July 24, 2010 at the Echo City Hall Ballroom in Echo, Oregon. The event is held every two years to fund project in Echo and to maintain the vintage clothing collection.

9187 ■ "The Emerging Capital Market for Nonprofits" in *Harvard Business Review* **(Vol. 88, October 2010, No. 10, pp. 110)**
Pub: Harvard Business School Publishing
Ed: Robert S. Kaplan, Allen S. Grossman. **Description:** Demonstration of how nonprofits can use intermediaries to grow their organizational structures, giving them improved scale and impact is offered. Some intermediaries play a mutual-fund role and conduct due diligence, while others act as venture capital funds and implement strategy.

9188 ■ "Endowments for Colleges Hit Hard in '09" in *Milwaukee Business Journal* **(Vol. 27, February 12, 2010, No. 20, pp. A1)**
Pub: American City Business Journals
Ed: Corrinne Hess. **Description:** Southeast Wisconsin college endowments declined by as much as 35 percent in 2009 due to the economic downturn. A list of 2009 endowments to colleges in southeast Wisconsin and their percent change from 2008 is presented.

9189 ■ "Fight Ensues Over Irreplaceable Gowns" in *Tampa Bay Business Journal* **(Vol. 30, January 15, 2010, No. 4, pp. 1)**
Pub: American City Business Journals
Ed: Janet Leiser. **Description:** People's Princess Charitable Foundation Inc. founder Maureen Rorech Dunkel has sought Chapter 11 bankruptcy protection before a state court decides on the fate of the five of 13 Princess Diana Gowns. Dunkel and the nonprofit were sued by Patricia Sullivan of HRH Venture LLC who claimed they defaulted on $1.5 million in loans.

9190 ■ "FIS-Metavante Deal Paying Off for Many" in *Business Journal-Milwaukee* **(Vol. 28, December 17, 2010, No. 11, pp. A1)**
Pub: Milwaukee Business Journal
Ed: Rich Kirchen. **Description:** Jacksonville, Florida-based Fidelity National Information Services Inc., also known as FIS, has remained committed to Milwaukee, Wisconsin more than a year after purchasing Metavante Technologies Inc. FIS has transferred several operations into Metropolitan Milwaukee and has continued its contribution to charitable organizations in the area.

9191 ■ "For Putting Down Roots in Business: Amy Norquist: Greensulate, New York City" in *Inc.* **(Volume 32, December 2010, No. 10, pp. 106)**
Pub: Inc. Magazine
Ed: Christine Lagorio. **Description:** Profile of Amy Norquist who left her position at an environmental nonprofit organization to found Greensulate. Her firm insulates rooftops with lavender, native grasses and succulents called sedum in order to eliminate carbon from the atmosphere.

9192 ■ "Freedom Center May have New Path" in *Business Courier* **(Vol. 26, October 30, 2009, No. 27, pp. 1)**
Pub: American City Business Journals, Inc.
Ed: Dan Monk, Lucy May. **Description:** National Underground Railroad Freedom Center in Price Hill, Cincinnati is in negotiations with US Rep. John Conyers for its possible classification as an independent establishment within the US federal government. If this happens, funding for the museum might be possibly augmented and the rights to use national archives might be furnished.

9193 ■ "Gallo Family Vineyards to Raise Funds for Meals On Wheels" in *Food & Beverage Close-Up* **(November 4, 2011)**
Pub: Close-Up Media
Description: Gallo family is committed to raising funds for Meals On Wheels Association of America and hosts a fundraiser annually.

9194 ■ "Generous Donations Fund Repairs for Benton Trail Kiosk" in *Morning Sentinel* **(December 22, 2010)**
Pub: Morning Sentinel
Ed: Scott Monroe. **Description:** The new kiosk at the entrance to a trail off Benton Avenue was paid for through donations and community contributions after the original was destroyed by vandals. The new kiosk's material was donated by the Huhtamaki manufacturing firm.

9195 ■ "GoodNews.com and the Little Cupcake Shoppe Support Calgary Food Bank With Unique $1.00 Deal" in *Marketwire Canada* **(March 9, 2011)**
Pub: Marketwire Canada
Description: Socially-conscious group-buying Website, GoodNews.com has partnered with The Little Cupcake Shoppe in Calgary, to raise funds for the Inter-Faith Food Bank. The fundraiser will feature a half dozen, pre-packaged assorted miniature cupcakes for $1.00. The entire amount is donated to the Calgary Food Bank.

9196 ■ "Katie's Cupcakes to Celebrate One-Year Anniversary" in *Bellingham Business Journal* **(Vol. March 2010, pp. 3)**
Pub: Sound Publishing Inc.
Description: Katie Swanson, owner of Katie's Cupcakes, celebrated her firm's one-year anniversary with a fundraiser for the Whatcom Humane Society by offering free specialty cupcakes and other special events to the public. The specialty cupcakes will feature either a paw or bone and will be available throughout the month of March.

9197 ■ "A Lifetime of Giving: Food Bank CEO Fights Hunger One Mouth At a Time" in *Black Enterprise* **(Vol. 41, November 2010, No. 4, pp. 86)**
Pub: Earl G. Graves Publishing Co. Inc.
Ed: Tamara E. Holmes. **Description:** Profile of Valerie Traore, CEO of Food Bank of South Jersey. Traore stresses the importance of volunteerism that she learned from her grandparents. Hunger relief became her passion when she served as a temp office worker for the Maryland Food Bank in Baltimore. She earned her Bachelor's of Science in management and has dedicated herself to a career in nonprofit service.

9198 ■ "Meals on Wheels Filling 'Blizzard Bags'" in *Tulsa World* **(November 5, 2011)**
Pub: Tulsa World
Ed: Sara Plummer. **Description:** Cathy Perlingiere, director of volunteer services for Meals on Wheels of Metro Tulsa, Oklahoma reports that they do not deliver meals when the Tulsa Public Schools close because of weather so they try to prepare 'blizzard bags' with nonperishable food items to cover about three meals for when drivers cannot deliver.

9199 ■ "Mercy Parent Nets Almost $1B in 2011" in *Sacramento Business Journal* **(Vol. 28, September 30, 2011, No. 31, pp. 1)**
Pub: Sacramento Business Journal
Ed: Kathy Robertson. **Description:** Catholic Healthcare West has reported almost $1 billion in profits for 2010. The company has reported a profit margin of 8.7 percent. It also absorbed more than $1 billion in costs from charity care and government programs.

9200 ■ *National Guide to Funding in Arts and Culture*
Pub: Foundation Center
Released: Biennial, latest edition 8th; May, 2004. **Price:** $75, individuals. **Covers:** over 5,200 foundations and corporate direct giving programs in the U.S. that fund arts and culture-related projects and organizations in the U.S. **Entries Include:** Company or organization name, address, phone, names and titles of key personnel, geographical area served, financial data, requirements for eligibility. **Arrangement:** Geographical by state, then alphabetical. **Indexes:** Organization or company name, subject, geographical, type of support, donor/officer/trustee name.

9201 ■ *National Guide to Funding for the Environment and Animal Welfare*
Pub: Foundation Center
Released: Biennial, latest edition 7th; June, 2004. **Price:** $75, individuals. **Covers:** Over 3,500 foundations and corporate direct giving programs that fund programs in conservation, ecological research, litigation, waste reduction, animal welfare, advocacy, and related projects; limited international coverage. **Entries Include:** Organization or company name, address, phone, financial data, giving priorities, name and title of contact, names and titles of key personnel. **Arrangement:** Geographical. **Indexes:** Grantmaker name, subject, geographical, type of support given, donor/officer/trustee.

9202 ■ *National Guide to Funding in Health*
Pub: Foundation Center
Released: Irregular, latest edition 9th; Published April, 2005. **Price:** $175, individuals. **Covers:** Over 11,500 foundations and corporations in the U.S. That fund health-related projects and institutions. **Entries Include:** Organization or company name, address, phone, financial data, giving priorities, applications procedures, name and title of contact, names and titles of key personnel. **Arrangement:** Geographical by state. **Indexes:** Grantmaker name, subject, geographical, donor/officer/trustee, type of support.

9203 ■ "A New Alliance For Global Change" in *Harvard Business Review* (Vol. 88, September 2010, No. 9, pp. 56)
Pub: Harvard Business School Publishing
Ed: Bill Drayton, Valeria Budinich. **Description:** Collaboration between social organizations and for-profit firms through the development of hybrid value chains to target complex global issues is promoted. While social organizations offer links to communities and consumers, firms provide financing and scale expertise.

9204 ■ "Nonprofit to Grow" in *Austin Business JournalInc.* (Vol. 29, January 22, 2010, No. 46, pp. 1)
Pub: American City Business Journals
Ed: Sandra Zaragoza. **Description:** Southwest Key Programs Inc. received a $2.1 million grant from the U.S. Economic Development Administration to help finance the building of a $3.6 million 'Social Enterprise Complex'. The complex is expected to create at least 100 jobs in East Austin, Texas. Details of the plan for the complex are presented.

9205 ■ "Nonprofit Ready to Get More Girls into 'STEM' Jobs" in *Austin Business JournalInc.* (Vol. 29, December 25, 2009, No. 42, pp. 1)
Pub: American City Business Journals
Ed: Sandra Zaragoza. **Description:** Girlstart has completed its $1.5 million capital campaign to buy the building it will care the Girlstart Tech Center. Girlstart is a nonprofit organization that prepares girls for science, technology, engineering and mathematics or STEM careers. Details of the program are highlighted.

9206 ■ "Nonprofits Find Plenty of Optimism for the Future" in *Business Courier* (Vol. 26, January 1, 2010, No. 37, pp. 1)
Pub: American City Business Journals, Inc.
Ed: Lucy May. **Description:** Forecasts of various nonprofits in Cincinnati, Ohio such as the United Way of Greater Cincinnati, the Greater Cincinnati Foundation and The Fine Arts Fund for 2010 are presented.

9207 ■ "Nonprofits May Lose MBE Status in MD" in *Boston Business Journal* (Vol. 29, September 2, 2011, No. 17, pp. 1)
Pub: American City Business Journals Inc.
Ed: Scott Dance. **Description:** A business group has been pushing to bar nonprofits from Maryland's Minority Business program. Nonprofits have been found to take a large portion of state contracts intended for women- and minority-owned businesses. The group is also crafting proposed legislation to remove nonprofits from the program.

9208 ■ "One Laptop Per Child Weighs Going For-Profit" in *Boston Business Journal* (Vol. 31, May 20, 2011, No. 17, pp. 1)
Pub: Boston Business Journal
Ed: Mary Moore. **Description:** Nonprofit organization One Laptop Per Child is thinking of shifting into a for-profit structure in order to raise as much as $10 million in capital to achieve its goal of distributing more XO laptops to poor children worldwide. The organization has distributed 2 million computers since 2008 with Uruguay, Peru and Rwanda as its biggest markets.

9209 ■ "Paralysis Foundation has Big Plans" in *Austin Business JournalInc.* (Vol. 29, December 11, 2009, No. 40, pp. 1)
Pub: American City Business Journals
Ed: Sandra Zaragoza. **Description:** Lone Star Paralysis Foundation revealed plans to launch a fundraising effort for the advancement of cures for spinal cord injuries via adult stem cells and also fund a new spinal injury rehabilitation center. Efforts to raise about $3 million will begin as soon as the adult stem cell research study by Dr. Wise Young receives Food and Drug Administration approval.

9210 ■ "Pet Food Bank 'Shares the Love'" in *Pet Product News* (Vol. 64, December 2010, No. 12, pp. 6)
Pub: BowTie Inc.
Description: Winston-Salem, North Carolina-based nonprofit Share the Love Pet Food Bank has donated 60,000 pounds of pet food since its establishment in 2009. It has been linking pet food manufacturers and rescue groups to supply unsold pet food to needy animals. The nonprofit intends to reach out to more animal welfare groups by building more warehouses.

9211 ■ "Points of Light Sells MissionFish to eBay" in *Non-Profit Times* (Vol. 25, May 15, 2011, No. 7, pp. May 15, 2011)
Pub: NPT Publishing Group Inc.
Description: eBay purchased MissionFish, a subsidiary of Points of Light Institute for $4.5 million. MissionFish allows eBay sellers to give proceeds from sales to their favorite nonprofit organization and helps nonprofits raise funds by selling on eBay.

9212 ■ "Preserving a Nonprofit's Mission" in *Boston Business Journal* (Vol. 31, June 17, 2011, No. 21, pp. 3)
Pub: Boston Business Journal
Ed: Mary Moore. **Description:** Young Women's Christian Association Boston (YWCA) agreed to absorb the LeadBoston social issues and youth programs operated by the Boston Center for Community Justice. The BCCJ is scheduled to close after failing to stabilize its finances.

9213 ■ *Profits for Non-Profits: Running a Successful Gift Shop*
Pub: Lulu.com
Ed: Nancy Kirk. **Released:** January 2005. **Price:** $19.95. **Description:** Guide for managing a non-profit gift shop in a hospital, zoo, museum or any other non-profit entity.

9214 ■ "Race-Week Schedule Filling Up With Galas, Nonprofit Fundraisers" in *Boston Business Journal* (Vol. 29, July 22, 2011, No. 11, pp. 1)
Pub: American City Business Journals Inc.
Ed: Alexander Jackson. **Description:** Baltimore, Maryland-based businesses and nonprofit groups have been planning their own events to coincide with the Baltimore Grand Prix during the Labor Day weekend. They also plan to partner with others in hopes of drumming up new business, raising money or to peddle their brands.

9215 ■ "Rebels' Cause: Adult Stem Cell" in *Austin Business Journal* (Vol. 31, June 3, 2011, No. 13, pp. 1)
Pub: American City Business Journals Inc.
Ed: Sandra Zaragoza. **Description:** MedRebels Foundation was launched in February 2011 with the goal of providing millions of dollars for research funding, education and advocacy for adult stem cell-focused medicine. The foundation, whose major contributor is SpineSmith LP, is a collaboration of other adult stem cell-related companies and nonprofit partners. It hopes to raise $200,000 by the end of 2011.

9216 ■ "Speak Better: Five Tips for Polished Presentations" in *Women Entrepreneur* (September 19, 2008)
Pub: Entrepreneur Media Inc.
Ed: Suzannah Baum. **Description:** Successful entrepreneurs agree that exemplary public speaking skills are among the core techniques needed to propel their business forward. A well-delivered presentation can result in securing a new distribution channel, gaining new customers, locking into a new referral stream or receiving extra funding.

9217 ■ "Staples Advantage Receives NJPA National Contract for Janitorial Supplies" in *Professional Services Close-Up* (April 22, 2011)
Pub: Close-Up Media
Description: Staples Advantage, the business-to-business division of Staples Inc. was awarded a contract for janitorial supplies to members of the National Joint Powers Alliance (NJPA). NJPA is a member-owned buying cooperative serving public and private schools, state and local governments, and nonprofit organizations.

9218 ■ "Tech Giving 2.0" in *Boston Business Journal* (Vol. 31, August 5, 2011, No. 28, pp. 1)
Pub: Boston Business Journal
Ed: Mary Moore. **Description:** Entrepreneurs and venture capitalists in Boston have launched Technology Underwriting Greater Good, the tech industry's answer to the criticism that they are not charitable. The foundation finances nonprofits that aid young people through entrepreneurship, education and life experience. Other tech firms in Boston doing charitable works are discussed.

9219 ■ "Tech Tax Heroes Go from Political Neophytes to Savvy Fundraisers" in *Baltimore Business Journal* (Vol. 27, November 20, 2009, No. 28)
Pub: American City Business Journals
Ed: Scott Dance. **Description:** A group of computer services and information technology executives in Maryland have arranged a private dinner that will function as a fundraiser for Governor Martin O'Malley and Lieutenant Governor Anthony Brown. The event is seen as an effort to ensure the industry's involvement in the state after fighting for the repeal of the tech tax in 2007.

9220 ■ "Tim Tebow Foundation to Hold Pink 'Cleats for a Cure' Auction" in *Travel & Leisure Close-Up* (October 20, 2011)
Pub: Close-Up Media
Description: Tim Tebow Foundation partnered with XV Enterprises to hold the 'Cleats for a Cure' auction on eBay. Tebow is auctioning off a pair of pink cleans he wore during the Denver Broncos vs. Tennessee Titans game October 3, 2010. All funds will go toward finding a cure for breast cancer.

TRADE PERIODICALS

9221 ■ *The Chronicle of Philanthropy*
Pub: The Chronicle of Philanthropy
Contact: Gwen Gaiser, Dir. of Production
Released: 24/yr. **Price:** $72; $125 two years; $72 online access only; $99.75 Canada; $72 Canada online access only; $135 other countries; $72 other countries online access only. **Description:** Magazine covering fundraising, philanthropy, and non-profit organizations. Includes information on tax rulings, new grants, and statistics, reports on grant makers, and profiles of foundations.

9222 ■ *Communication Briefings*
Pub: Briefings Publishing Group
Contact: Joe McGavin, Exec. Editor
E-mail: jmcgavin@briefings.com
Ed: Nicole Behrens, Editor, nbehrens@briefings.com. **Released:** Monthly. **Price:** $169, individual. **Description:** Provides communication ideas and techniques for a wide variety of areas, including public relations, advertising, fund raising, speeches, media relations, human resources, and employee/manager relations. Carries interviews with top communicators, business

leaders, university experts, and research specialists. Recurring features include news of research, book reviews, and abstracts of articles from national publications.

9223 ■ *Foundation News & Commentary*
Pub: Council on Foundations
Contact: Paula Kelly, Contributing and Web Ed.
E-mail: kellp@cof.org
Released: Bimonthly. **Description:** Magazine for foundations and grantseekers.

9224 ■ *The NonProfit Times*
Pub: NPT Publishing Group Inc.
Contact: Paul Clolery, VP/Editorial Dir.
Released: 24/yr. **Price:** $65; $32 digital only; $69 digital & print; $30 students; $99 Canada and Mexico. **Description:** Trade journal serving nonprofit organizations.

TRADE SHOWS AND CONVENTIONS

9225 ■ International Conference on Fundraising
Association of Fundraising Professionals
4300 Wilson Blvd., Ste. 300
Arlington, VA 22203-4168
Ph:(703)684-0410
Fax:(703)684-0540
URL: http://www.afpnet.org
Released: Annual. **Audience:** Decision makers for development offices for nonprofits. **Principal Exhibits:** Fund raising tools.

CONSULTANTS

9226 ■ Ashland Group L.P.
11550 Fuqua St., Ste. 560
Houston, TX 77034
Ph:(281)484-1700
Free: 800-684-2246
Fax:(281)484-1822
Co. E-mail: info@ashlandgroup.com
URL: http://www.ashlandgroup.com
Contact: Randy Casey, Managing Partner
E-mail: rcasey@ashlandgroup.com
Scope: Government and political affairs agency that specializes in government relations, advocacy communications, media relations, campaign management and government contract lobbying. Offers creative and innovative tax issues. **Publications:** "State Tax Guide," Jan, 2009; "State Tax Guide," Jan, 2007.

9227 ■ Capitol City Services Inc.
1865 Lamplight Dr.
PO Box 25038
Woodbury, MN 55125-0038
Ph:(651)702-2533
Fax:(651)204-1668
Contact: Billy Watkins, Principle
Scope: Information gathering, document retrieval, monitoring, research and reporting service.

9228 ■ Democracy Data & Communications L.L.C.
44 Canal Center Plz., Ste. 200
Alexandria, VA 22314-1542
Ph:(703)684-9690
Fax:(703)683-9626
Co. E-mail: info@democracydata.com
Contact: Gary Pruce, VP of Operations
E-mail: wmb@atsdemocracydata.com
Scope: Provides grassroots technology solutions and online database management.

9229 ■ Essex & Drake Fund Raising Counsel
1202 University Ave.
San Jose, CA 95126
Ph:(408)294-7779

Fax:(408)297-2722
Co. E-mail: contact@essexdrake.com
URL: http://www.essexdrake.com
Contact: Sharon Trenson Svensson, President
E-mail: sharon@atsessexdrake.com
Scope: Specializes in board development including governance issues, finding and putting new board members to work and moving the board to relevant action. Organizes fund raising campaigns including feasibility studies, major gift campaigns and strategy development. Offers training in board excellence and all areas of fund raising. **Publications:** "Fund raising for Non-Profits," Harper Collins. **Seminars:** Launching and Sustaining a Planned Giving Program in a Small Development Department, May, 2009; Web 2.0 for Nonprofits, San Francisco, Mar, 2009; Building and Sustaining a Board Driven Major Gifts Program, San Francisco; Marketing Your Organization for Fund raising Success; Strategies for a Successful Capital Campaign; Achieving Successful Online Fund raising; Identifying and Building Relationships with Major Donors; Best Practices in Managing a Capital, Endowment or Combination Campaign.

9230 ■ Guy Rodgers & Associates Inc.
748 Montebello Cir.
PO Box 9123
Chesapeake, VA 23322-7257
Ph:(757)686-0088
Free: 800-636-8683
Fax:(757)382-9095
Co. E-mail: graa@acninc.net
Contact: Guy Rodgers, Owner
E-mail: graa@pinn.net
Scope: Legislative and campaign consulting, grassroots and coalition development, fund raising, and political training.

9231 ■ The Hathaway Group Inc.
1010 Pendleton St.
Alexandria, VA 22314-1837
Ph:(703)837-1818
Fax:(703)837-1822
Contact: Timothy Hathaway, President
E-mail: trh@thehathawaygroup.com
Scope: Political consultant whose services includes voter and databases, network design and administration, web site creation, maintenance and hosting, and fax broadcasting.

9232 ■ Jeffrey Lant Associates Inc.
50 Follen St., Ste. 507
PO Box 38
Cambridge, MA 02138
Ph:(617)547-6372
Fax:(617)547-0061
Co. E-mail: drjlant@worldprofit.com
URL: http://www.jeffreylant.com
Contact: Sandy Hunter, Director of Information Technology
E-mail: sandi@atsworldprofit.com
Scope: Firm sets up businesses online, design websites and assists with marketing. **Publications:** "E-mail El Dorado," JLA Publications, 1998; "Web Wealth: How to Turn the World Wide Web Into a Cash Hose for Your Business. Whatever You're Selling," 1997; "Multi-Level Money," JLA Publications, 1994; "No More Cold Calls," JLA Publications, 1997; "Cash Copy"; "How to make at least $100000 a year"; "E-Money". **Seminars:** Business and personal development, including Establishing and Operating Your Successful Consulting Business; Successfully Promoting Your Small Business and Professional Practice; Succeeding in Your Mail Order Business; Successfully Raising Money for Your Nonprofit Organization from Foundations, Corporations and Individuals; Money Making Marketing: Finding the People Who Need What You're Selling and Making Sure They Buy It; Getting Corporations, Foundations, and Individuals to Give You the Money Your Nonprofit Organization Needs.

9233 ■ Matson & Associates
7831 Western Ct. SE
Olympia, WA 98501-6839
Ph:(360)956-9694

Fax:(360)754-8114
Co. E-mail: matsonassoc@olywa.net
URL: http://www.matsonassociates.com
Contact: Linda W. Matson, Principle
E-mail: lmatson@matsonassociates.com
Scope: Consulting in the areas of: strategic planning, issue management, needs analysis, political action, campaign consulting, campaign management, fund raising and custom-designed education and recruitment programs. **Seminars:** Politics. . .A Cost of Doing Business; Political Action Committee Development; Coalition Building; Keystone Conference; Activist/Advocate Training.

9234 ■ Maximum Response Marketing
PO Box 505, Sta. Central
Halifax, NS, Canada B3J 2R7
Ph:(902)444-9457
Fax:(902)444-9457
Co. E-mail: maxresponse@hotmail.com
Contact: Charles Salmon, President
E-mail: maxresponse@hotmail.com
Scope: Specialists in designing effective, results-driven, direct marketing programs that generate inquiries, orders or donations for business, consumer and not-for-profit. Services include campaign planning and implementation; project management; creative direction and package design; direct mail copywriting and copy editing; database analysis and segmentation; mailing list procurement and evaluation; developing privacy policies; print procurement and supplier liaison; email marketing strategy, copy and list; telemarketing, scripting and training. **Seminars:** Direct Mail Fundraising Communications and Fundraising, Mount Saint Vincent University, 2004; Federal Privacy Legislation, Atlantic Regional Meeting, United Way of Canada, 2003; DM Campaign Basics, United Way of Canada National Conference, 2002; Bayers Lake Business Seminar Service, 2002; Using DM to Group Your Business, Atlantic Regional Meeting, United Way of Canada, 2002; Tips, Tools and Techniques: DM Fundraising 101, Atlantic Philanthropy Conference, 1999; Direct Marketing Tips Tools and Techniques and A Strategic Approach to Direct Mail Creative, Dalhousie University; How to Use Direct Marketing to Build Your Business in the Export Marketplace, ACOA (Atlantic Canada Opportunities Agency)-Trade Outreach Sessions; How to Cultivate Your Customers Using Direct Marketing Tools, NS Dept. of Agriculture-Bi-Annual Conference.

9235 ■ Stevens, Reed, Curcio and Potholm
201 N Union St., Ste. 200
Alexandria, VA 22314
Ph:(703)683-8326
Fax:(703)683-8826
Co. E-mail: pcurcio@srcpmedia.com
URL: http://www.srcpmedia.com
Contact: Jay Payne, Vice President
E-mail: epotholm@atssrcpmedia.com
Scope: Republican media consulting firm that specializes in media production, public opinion research, direct mail design, opposition research and political strategy.

9236 ■ Triad Strategies
116 Pine St.
Harrisburg, PA 17101
Ph:(717)238-2970
Fax:(717)238-2390
Co. E-mail: jconnovitch@triadstrategies.com
URL: http://www.triadstrategies.com
Contact: Michael J. Acker, Senior VP
E-mail: macker@atstriadstrategies.com
Scope: Government relations firm. Services include legislative and regulatory monitoring, legislative and executive branch lobbying, independent and quasi-public agency lobbying, issue research, issue management, grassroots organizing, public relations, strategic planning, and network marketing.

FRANCHISES AND BUSINESS OPPORTUNITIES

9237 ■ Heavenly Gold Card
Nova Media Inc.
1724 N State
Big Rapids, MI 49307-9073

Ph:(231)796-4637
No. of Franchise Units: 1. **Founded:** 1981. **Franchised:** 1992. **Description:** Fund raising for non profit organizations. **Equity Capital Needed:** $100. **Franchise Fee:** $100. **Financial Assistance:** Yes. **Training:** Yes.

9238 ■ Magis Fund Raising Specialists Services For Non-Profits
Magis Fund Raising Specialists
845 Heathermoor Ln.
Perrysburg, OH 43551
Ph:(419)874-4459
Fax:(419)874-4459
No. of Franchise Units: 2. **No. of Company-Owned Units:** 2. **Founded:** 1989. **Franchised:** 1991. **Description:** Provides full-service fund raising, financial development, marketing and public relations services to non-profit organizations. Conducts major pledge campaigns for new facilities, increases annual giving by 20%or more, builds endowments of $1 million or more, conducts feasibility studies, fundraising audits, personnel searches, writes grant proposals, trains leadership, conducts seminars and workshops, strategic planning, video presentations and newsletters. is needed; business can be conducted from your home or added to an existing, already established office. **Equity Capital Needed:** $100,000. **Franchise Fee:** $25,000. **Financial Assistance:** Yes. **Managerial Assistance:** Daily back-up and support. Sales and marketing system. Expertise in all areas of fundraising and development. New products and services are constantly tested and offered. **Training:** 1 week of preliminary materials provided for at-home study. Second week at Magis' headquarters, where all systems are taught. Third week at your location. Ongoing contact by phone, fax and regular seminars.

COMPUTERIZED DATABASES

9239 ■ *Foundation Directory Online*
The Foundation Center
79 5th Ave.
New York, NY 10003
Ph:(212)620-4230
Free: 800-424-9836
Fax:(212)807-3677
Co. E-mail: order@foundationcenter.org
URL: http://foundationcenter.org
Description: Contains descriptions of thousands of currently active grantmaking foundations and the grants they sponsor. Offers five subscription levels with various access to the top 20,000 U.S. foundations, descriptions of more than 1.9 million recent grants, profiles of more than 98,000 grantmakers, profiles of approximately 12,000 grantmaking public charities and more than 1300 corporate giving programs. Also offers daily philanthropy news and RFPs, interactive maps and charts, IRS 990s database, funder portfolios, and more. Corresponds to *The Foundation Directory Part 1* (print), *The Foundation Directory Part 2* (print), and *The Foundation Directory Supplement* (print). **Availability:** Online: ProQuest LLC, ProQuest LLC, The Foundation Center. **Type:** Directory; Numeric.

LIBRARIES

9240 ■ Brakeley Inc. Library
86 Prospect St.
Stamford, CT 06901
Ph:(203)348-8100
Fax:(203)978-0114
Co. E-mail: info@brakeley.com
URL: http://www.brakeley.com/
Scope: Fundraising, philanthropy. **Services:** Library open to the public with special permission. **Holdings:** 300 books; 30 VF drawers of clippings, pamphlets,

foundation Annual reports; reports. **Subscriptions:** 10 journals and other serials.

9241 ■ Council for Advancement and Support of Education Information Center
1307 New York Ave. NW, Ste. 1000
Washington, DC 20005-4701
Ph:(202)328-2273
Fax:(202)387-4973
Co. E-mail: infocenter@case.org
URL: http://www.case.org
Contact: Megan Galaida, Dir.
Scope: Alumni administration, educational fundraising, communications, marketing, institutional advancement. **Services:** Center not open to the public (open to CASE members by appointment). **Holdings:** Books; periodicals; reports; studies; speeches; surveys; college, university, and independent school publications and literature; CD-ROMs. **Subscriptions:** 40 journals and other serials.

9242 ■ Council on Foundations Resource Center
2121 Crystal Dr., Ste. 700
Arlington, VA 22202
Ph:(703)879-0688
Free: 800-673-9036
URL: http://www.cof.org
Contact: Luis Maldonado, Dir.
Scope: Philanthropy, grantmaking, foundations, management. **Services:** Library not open to the public. **Holdings:** 5000 books; reports; articles; periodicals; archives; videotapes. **Subscriptions:** 10 journals and other serials; 3 newspapers.

9243 ■ Foundation Center Cleveland Library
1422 Euclid Ave., Ste. 1600
Cleveland, OH 44115-2001
Ph:(216)861-1933
Fax:(216)861-1936
Co. E-mail: cgb@foundationcenter.org
URL: http://foundationcenter.org/cleveland
Contact: Cynthia Glunt Bailie, Dir.
Scope: Reports by and of foundations; government grants; corporate philanthropy; grantsmanship; proposal writing. **Services:** Interlibrary loan; copying; instructional sessions in the use of specialized materials on grants; Library open to the public. **Holdings:** 1400 volumes; 500 pamphlets; 1000 current Annual reports of foundations; clippings on philanthropic foundations. **Subscriptions:** 25 journals and other serials.

9244 ■ Foundation Center, Washington, DC Library
1627 K St. NW, 3rd Fl.
Washington, DC 20006
Ph:(202)331-1400
Fax:(202)331-1739
Co. E-mail: library@foundationcenter.org
URL: http://foundationcenter.org/washington/
Contact: Patricia Pasqual, Dir.
Scope: Private philanthropic giving, corporations, foundations. **Services:** Copying; Library open to the public. **Holdings:** 2500 volumes. **Subscriptions:** 50 journals and other serials.

9245 ■ Imagine Canada–John Hodgson Library
2 Carlton St., Ste. 600
Toronto, ON, Canada M5B 1J3
Ph:(416)597-2293, x-255
Free: 800-263-1176
Fax:(416)597-1169
Co. E-mail: library@imaginecanada.ca
URL: http://library.imaginecanada.ca/services
Contact: Kimberley Turner, Mgr., Lib.Svcs.
Scope: Philanthropy, fundraising, marketing, voluntarism, management, government legislation. **Services:**

Library not open to the public. **Holdings:** 7000 titles. **Subscriptions:** 5 journals and other serials; 1 newspaper.

9246 ■ State University of New York at Buffalo–University Development Library
3435 Main St.
Buffalo, NY 14214-3010
Ph:(716)829-2630
Fax:(716)829-2636
Co. E-mail: alkutner@buffalo.edu
URL: http://ublib.buffalo.edu/libraries/
Contact: Ann L. Kutner, Res.Anl.
Scope: Fund raising, fund raising management. **Services:** Copying; Library open to the public. **Holdings:** 100 volumes. **Subscriptions:** 15 journals and other serials; 3 newspapers.

9247 ■ Tucson Pima Public Library–Grants and Nonprofit Information Collection
101 N. Stone Ave.
PO Box 27470
Tucson, AZ 85701
Ph:(520)791-4010
Fax:(520)594-5621
Co. E-mail: prickly@ci.tucson.az.us
URL: http://www.library.pima.gov
Contact: Nancy Ledeboer, Lib.Dir.
Scope: Grants, foundations, corporate philanthropy, fundraising, nonprofit management, charities, government grants. **Services:** Copying; regular orientations to the Grants Collection; Library open to the public. **Holdings:** 200 books; 50 reports. **Subscriptions:** 9 journals and other serials; 3 newspapers.

RESEARCH CENTERS

9248 ■ Indiana University-Purdue University at Indianapolis–Center on Philanthropy
550 W North St., Ste. 301
Indianapolis, IN 46202-3491
Ph:(317)274-4200
Fax:(317)684-8900
Co. E-mail: rooney@iupui.edu
URL: http://www.philanthropy.iupui.edu
Contact: Patrick M. Rooney PhD, Exec.Dir.
E-mail: rooney@iupui.edu
Scope: Theoretical, ethical, historical, practical, and applied aspects of philanthropy and non-profit management. **Services:** Research, surveys, project evaluation, etc.. **Publications:** Indiana Gives (quadrennially); Million Dollar List (quarterly); Occasional papers; Philanthropic Giving Index (semiannually); Philanthropy Matters (semiannually). **Educational Activities:** Conferences (weekly), in cooperation with other academic institutions and nonprofit organizations; Fund Raising School (weekly), providing training in ethical fund raising and management principles and practices to staff, board members, and other volunteers of the independent sector; Professional training, in grantmaking, nonprofit organizations, working with trustees and volunteers, and fundraising communications; Seminars; Symposium on fundraising (annually).

9249 ■ New York University–National Center on Philanthropy and the Law
School of Law
139 MacDougal St., 1st Fl.
New York, NY 10012
Ph:(212)998-6168
Fax:(212)995-3149
Co. E-mail: ncpl.info@nyu.edu
URL: http://www1.law.nyu.edu/ncpl
Contact: Prof. Harvey P. Dale, Dir.
E-mail: ncpl.info@nyu.edu
Scope: Philanthropy and the law. **Educational Activities:** Conferences and seminars; Courses on nonprofit law, tax aspects of charitable giving, and tax-exempt organizations.

ASSOCIATIONS AND OTHER ORGANIZATIONS

9250 ■ American Board of Funeral Service Education
3414 Ashland Ave., Ste. G
St. Joseph, MO 64506
Ph:(816)233-3747
Fax:(816)233-3793
Co. E-mail: exdir@abfse.org
URL: http://www.abfse.org
Contact: Dr. Gretchen L. Warner, Exec. Dir.
Description: Representatives from National Funeral Directors Association, International Conference of Funeral Service Examining Boards of the United States, the National Funeral Directors and Mortuaries Association and college program representatives and public members. Seeks to: formulate and enforce rules and regulations setting up standards concerning the schools and colleges teaching mortuary science; accredit schools and colleges of mortuary science. Sponsors the National Scholarship for Funeral Service program to provide capable young men and women studying in the field with financial assistance. Compiles statistics. .

9251 ■ American Institute of Commemorative Art
8015 Van Ness Way
Indianapolis, IN 46240
Ph:(317)731-6556
Fax:(317)731-6556
Co. E-mail: lelandb@monuments-aica.com
URL: http://www.monuments-aica.com
Contact: Mr. Leland B. Longstreth, Exec. Dir.
Description: Retailers of memorials and cemetery monuments with strong interest in commemorative design. **Publications:** *Milestone* (quarterly).

9252 ■ Casket and Funeral Supply Association of America
49 Sherwood Terr., Ste. Y
Lake Bluff, IL 60044-2231
Ph:(847)295-6630
Fax:(847)295-6647
Co. E-mail: brussell@cfsaa.org
URL: http://www.cfsaa.org
Contact: Mark B. Allen, Exec. Dir.
Description: Manufacturers and distributors of burial caskets and other funeral supplies. .

9253 ■ Catholic Cemetery Conference
1400 S Wolf Rd., Bldg. No. 3
Hillside, IL 60162-2197
Ph:(708)202-1242
Free: 888-850-8131
Fax:(708)202-1255
Co. E-mail: info@catholiccemeteryconference.org
URL: http://www.ntriplec.com
Contact: Dennis Fairbank, Exec. Dir.
Description: Archdiocesan and diocesan directors of Catholic cemeteries; associate members are administrators of Catholic cemeteries. **Publications:** *The Catholic Cemetery: A Vision for the Millennium; Design and Construction Manual; Field Operation Manual; Mausoleum Maintenance Manual; National Catholic Cemetery Conference—Membership and Resource Directory* (annual).

9254 ■ Cremation Association of North America
401 N Michigan Ave.
Chicago, IL 60611
Ph:(312)245-1077
Fax:(312)321-4098
Co. E-mail: info@cremationassociation.org
URL: http://www.cremationassociation.org
Contact: Kathy Bell, Exec. Dir.
Description: Cemeteries, crematories, funeral directors, and manufacturers. Seeks to increase public awareness and knowledge of cremation and memorialization. Conducts research; compiles statistics. Holds certification programs and trade show. **Publications:** *Cremationist* (quarterly); *Newsletter Update* (bimonthly).

9255 ■ Funeral Consumers Alliance
33 Patchen Rd.
South Burlington, VT 05403
Ph:(802)865-8300
Free: 800-765-0107
Fax:(802)865-2626
Co. E-mail: fca@funerals.org
URL: http://www.funerals.org
Contact: Joshua Slocum, Exec. Dir.
Description: Promotes a consumer's right to choose a dignified, meaningful, affordable funeral. Provides educational material to the public and affiliates. Monitors the funeral and cemetery industry for consumers nationwide. Responds to consumer complaints. Maintains speakers' bureau. **Publications:** *The FCA Newsletter* (quarterly);*Membership Directory* (periodic).

9256 ■ International Cemetery, Cremation and Funeral Association
107 Carpenter Dr., Ste. 100
Sterling, VA 20164
Ph:(703)391-8400
Free: 800-645-7700
Fax:(703)391-8416
Co. E-mail: hq@iccfa.com
URL: http://www.iccfa.com
Contact: Robert M. Fells, Exec. Dir./Gen. Counsel
Description: Owners and managers of cemeteries and funeral homes; related suppliers and professional service firms. **Publications:** *ICFA Buyer's Guide and Membership Directory* (annual); *International Cemetery and Funeral Management* (10/year).

9257 ■ Jewish Funeral Directors of America
385 Craig Ct.
Deerfield, IL 60015
Ph:(847)607-9156
Free: 888-477-5567
Fax:(847)607-9159
Co. E-mail: jfdamer@aol.com
URL: http://www.jfda.org
Contact: Danielle Hornick, Exec. Dir.
Description: Predominantly serves members of the Jewish faith. Assists people of the Jewish faith arrange meaningful and affordable funerals in the Jewish tradition. **Publications:** *How to Explain Death to Children* (3/year); *Jewish Funeral Director* (annual).

9258 ■ Monument Builders of North America
136 S Keowee St.
Dayton, OH 45402
Free: 800-233-4472
Fax:(937)222-5794
Co. E-mail: info@monumentbuilders.org
URL: http://www.monumentbuilders.org
Contact: James P. Bell, Pres.
Description: Monument retailers, manufacturers, and wholesalers; bronze manufacturers and suppliers. Provides sales, advertising, and management materials to members. Develops modern and religious memorial designs. Provides Affinity Programs such as discounts and low-cost credit card processing. Opposes "restrictive business practices and unfair competition". Compiles statistics; conducts specialized education and certification programs; maintains speakers' bureau. **Publications:** *Monument Builders News* (monthly).

9259 ■ National Concrete Burial Vault Association
PO Box 917525
Longwood, FL 32791-7525
Ph:(407)788-1996
Free: 888-88N-CBVA
Fax:(407)774-6751
Co. E-mail: ncbva@ncbva.org
URL: http://ncbva.org
Contact: Mr. Thomas A. Monahan CAE, Exec. Dir.
Description: Manufacturers of concrete burial vaults. Provides a unified voice for the concrete burial vault industry regardless of product affiliation, brand recognition or location. .

9260 ■ National Funeral Directors Association
13625 Bishop's Dr.
Brookfield, WI 53005-6607
Ph:(262)789-1880
Free: 800-228-6332
Fax:(262)789-6977
Co. E-mail: nfda@nfda.org
URL: http://www.nfda.org
Contact: Christine Pepper CAE, CEO
Description: Federation of state funeral directors' associations with individual membership of funeral directors. Seeks to enhance the funeral service profession and promote quality services to the consumers. Conducts professional education seminars and home study courses. Compiles statistics. **Publications:** *National Funeral Directors Association—Directory of Members* (annual).

9261 ■ National Funeral Directors and Morticians Association
6290 Shannon Pkwy.
Union City, GA 30291
Ph:(404)286-6740
Free: 800-434-0958

Fax:(404)286-6573
Co. E-mail: info@nfdma.com
URL: http://www.nfdma.com
Contact: Dr. Carol T. Williams, Interim Exec. Dir.

Description: State, district and local funeral directors and embalmers associations and their members. Promotes ethical practices; encourages just and uniform laws pertaining to funeral directing and embalming industry. .

9262 ■ Selected Independent Funeral Homes
500 Lake Cook Rd., Ste. 205
Deerfield, IL 60015
Ph:(847)236-9401
Free: 800-323-4219
Fax:(847)236-9968
Co. E-mail: info@selectedfuneralhomes.org
URL: http://www.selectedfuneralhomes.org
Contact: Mr. Robert Paterkiewicz, Exec. Dir.

Description: Funeral directors. Aims to study, develop, and establish a standard of service for the benefit of its consumers. Provides a continuing forum for the exchange, development and dissemination of knowledge and information beneficial to members and the public. **Publications:** *Membership Roster* (quarterly).

REFERENCE WORKS

9263 ■ "Balancing Freedom of Speech with the Right To Privacy" in *Pace Law Review* **(Fall 2007)**
Pub: American Society on Aging

Ed: Anna Zwierz Messa. **Description:** Information is offered to help authorities and funeral directors cope with protests occurring during a funeral.

9264 ■ "Cremation: Desecration, purification, or convenience?" in (Vol. 28, Summer 2004, No. 2, pp. 15-20)
Pub: American Society on Aging

Ed: Michael C. Kearl. **Description:** The methods of disposing of the remains of the deceased is a problem all societies face. Different aspects of funeral burials, including dropping into sea or converting to ashes by fire as well as new immortality-enhancing technologies are discussed.

9265 ■ *Funeral Consumers Alliance*
Pub: Funeral Consumers Alliance
Contact: Joshua Slocum, Exec. Dir.
E-mail: joshua@funerals.org

Released: Quarterly. **Price:** Free. **Covers:** over 120 nonprofit funeral consumer groups that educate the public about affordable funeral options. Monitors funeral industry practices for consumers. **Entries Include:** Name, address, phone, email address. **Arrangement:** Geographical.

9266 ■ "Funeral Directors Get Creative As Boomers Near Great Beyond" in *Advertising Age* **(Vol. 79, October 13, 2008, No. 38, pp. 30)**
Pub: Crain Communications, Inc.

Ed: Lenore Skenazy. **Description:** Despite the downturn in the economy, the funeral business is thriving due to the number of baby boomers who realize the importance of making preparations for their death. Marketers are getting creative in their approach and many companies have taken into consideration the need for a more environmental friendly way to dispose of bodies and thus have created innovative businesses that reflect this need.

9267 ■ *Funeral Home & Cemetery Directory—Buyer's Guide*
Pub: Nomis Publications Inc.
Contact: Peggy Rouzzo, Advertising Sales Mgr.
E-mail: peggy@nomispublications.com

Released: Annual, Latest edition 2011. **Price:** $30, individuals. **Covers:** Over 2,000 suppliers to the funeral and cemetery industry. **Entries Include:** Company name, address, phone, fax. **Arrangement:** Classified by product/service. **Indexes:** Product/service.

9268 ■ "Funeral Picketing Laws and Free Speech" in *Kansas Law Review* **(Vol. 55, April 2007, No. 3, pp. 575-627)**
Pub: American Society on Aging

Ed: Stephen R. McAllister. **Description:** In-depth information covering laws governing protests and freedom of speech during funerals is presented.

9269 ■ "Funerals-R-Us: From Funeral Home to Mega-Industry" in (Vol. 28, Summer 2004, No. 2, pp. 11-14)
Pub: American Society on Aging

Ed: Thomas Lynch. **Description:** Viewpoint from a funeral director as he looks at funerals and the sacred, secular, private, emotional, social and practical duties and practices associated with funerals.

9270 ■ "A Grave Situation" in *Chronicle of Higher Education* **(Vol. 54, November 30, 2007, No. 14)**
Pub: Pace Law School

Ed: Don Troop. **Description:** W. Scott Walston has been selling funeral caskets with the University of Georgia's logo on them to graduates who pass away; however the University System of Georgia has a rule that forbids college logos on burial items.

9271 ■ *NFDA Directory of Members and Transportation Guide*
Pub: National Funeral Directors Association NFDA
Contact: Kellie Schilling, Dir. of Bus. Devel.

Released: Annual, Latest edition 2008-2009. **Price:** $35, members print; $125, nonmembers. **Covers:** 19,000 members of state funeral director associations affiliated with the National Funeral Directors Association. **Entries Include:** Company name, address, phone, and principal executive. **Arrangement:** Geographical.

9272 ■ *Purple Directory*
Pub: Shugar's Publishing
Contact: Miriam E. Pipes, Publisher/Ed. in Ch.

Released: Annual, Latest edition 10th, 2012-2013. **Price:** $40, individuals inclusive of shipping and handling. **Covers:** Approximately 2,700 African-American funeral firms in the U.S. **Entries Include:** Firm name, address, phone; some listings include fax and name and title of contact. **Arrangement:** Geographical by state.

STATISTICAL SOURCES

9273 ■ *RMA Annual Statement Studies*
Pub: Robert Morris Associates (RMA)

Released: Annual. **Price:** $175.00 2006-07 edition, $105.00. **Description:** Contains composite balance sheets and income statements for more than 360 industries, including the accounting, auditing, and bookkeeping industries. Also contains five years of comparative historical data for discerning trends. Includes 16 commonly used ratios, computed for most of the size groupings for nearly every industry.

TRADE PERIODICALS

9274 ■ *Casket & Funeral Supply Association of America Newsletter*
Pub: Casket & Funeral Supply Association of America

Ed: George W. Lemke, Editor, lemke@cfsaa.org. **Released:** Monthly. **Description:** Carries news items of interest to the funeral supply industry, including information on annual conventions, Federal Trade Commission regulations and other court rulings, and cost and pricing issues.

9275 ■ *The Director*
Pub: National Funeral Directors Association
Contact: Chris Raymond, Editor-in-Chief

Released: Monthly. **Price:** $50; $65 other countries including Canada. **Description:** Magazine for the funeral service profession. Includes medical updates, business trends, federal regulations, and bereavement issues.

9276 ■ *The FCA Newsletter*
Pub: Funeral Consumers Alliance
Contact: Lisa Carlson

Ed: Lisa Carlson, Editor. **Released:** Quarterly. **Price:** $35, members. **Description:** Concerned with the funeral industry, activities of affiliates, and legislation related to consumer rights in making funeral arrangements. Includes articles and bibliographies pertaining to funerals, death, and dying.

9277 ■ *NFDA Bulletin*
Pub: National Funeral Directors Association
Ed: Renee L. Gryzkewicz, Editor, rgryzkewicz@nfda.org. **Released:** Monthly. **Price:** Included in membership. **Description:** Covers association activities and funeral business management topics. Reports on association news, government regulation, public relations issues, and local developments.

FRANCHISES AND BUSINESS OPPORTUNITIES

9278 ■ Select Community Funeral Homes Inc.
Select Management Partnerships
111 Paradise Row
Saint John, NB, Canada E2K 3H6
Ph:(506)632-1135
Free: 877-473-5328
Fax:(506)652-3251
Co. E-mail: information@selectfunerals.com
URL: http://www.selectfunerals.com
No. of Company-Owned Units: 6. **Founded:** 1872. **Description:** Offers management system for independent funeral homes. **Equity Capital Needed:** Varies, depending upon size of business. **Franchise Fee:** Varies. **Training:** Yes.

COMPUTER SYSTEMS/ SOFTWARE

9279 ■ Funeral Directors Management System
Davidson Software Systems Inc.
860 F Ave., Ste. 104
Plano, TX 75074
Ph:(866)230-0800
Free: 800-678-3367
Fax:(972)398-6454
Co. E-mail: info@aldorsolutions.com
URL: http://www.aldorsolutions.com
Price: Contact for pricing. **Description:** Available for IBM computers and compatibles. System stores funeral home information.

LIBRARIES

9280 ■ Center for Thanatology Research & Education, Inc. Library
391 Atlantic Ave.
Brooklyn, NY 11217-1701
Ph:(718)858-3026
Fax:(718)852-1846
Co. E-mail: thanatology@pipeline.com
URL: http://thanatology.org
Contact: Roberta Halporn, Dir.
Scope: Aging, dying, death, bereavement, gravestone studies. **Services:** Copying; Library open to the public by appointment. **Holdings:** 2945 books; 40 bound periodical volumes; 20 online databases; 1 CD-ROM; videotapes; audiocassettes; photographs; rubbings; archives. **Subscriptions:** 6 journals and other serials.

9281 ■ Funeral Consumers Alliance Library
33 Patchen Rd.
South Burlington, VT 05403
Ph:(802)865-8300
Free: 800-765-0107
Fax:(802)865-2626
Co. E-mail: info@funerals.org
URL: http://www.funerals.org/
Contact: Joshua Slocum, Exec.Dir.
Scope: Death, dying, grief, burials, cremation, funeral law. **Services:** Library open to the public for reference use only. **Holdings:** 150 books.

9282 ■ National Funeral Directors Association–Howard C. Raether Library
13625 Bishop's Dr.
Brookfield, WI 53005-6607

Ph:(262)789-1880
Free: 800-228-6332
Fax:(262)789-6977
Co. E-mail: kwalczak@nfda.org
URL: http://www.nfda.org/about-nfda-/research-a-
information/208.html
Contact: Kathie Walczak, Res. & Info.Spec.
Scope: Funeral service, mortuary management,
death customs, burial, bereavement, embalming,
mortuary science, restorative art. **Services:** Copying;

Performs searches on fee basis; Library open to
researchers by appointment. **Holdings:** 3100 books;
300 bound periodical volumes; 300 prints and
pamphlets; reports; manuscripts; archives; microfilm.
Subscriptions: 48 journals and other serials.

**9283 ■ Northampton Community
College–Paul and Harriett Mack Library**
3835 Green Pond Rd.
Bethlehem, PA 18020

Ph:(610)861-5358
Fax:(610)861-5373
Co. E-mail: ssander@northampton.edu
URL: http://www.northampton.edu/Library.htm
Contact: Sandra Sander, Lib.Dir.
Scope: Nursing, dental auxiliaries, funeral service,
veterinary technology. **Services:** Interlibrary loan;
copying; Center open to the public. **Holdings:** 65,341
books; periodicals; and AV titles. **Subscriptions:** 429
journals and other serials; 6 newspapers.

ASSOCIATIONS AND OTHER ORGANIZATIONS

9284 ■ Empress Chinchilla Breeders Cooperative
43188 Cottonwood Creek Rd.
Crawford, CO 81415
Ph:(970)921-7231
Co. E-mail: empresschinchilla@gmail.com
URL: http://www.empresschinchilla.org
Contact: Mr. Gene Adcock, Pres.
Description: Breeders of chinchillas for fur. Conducts research; supervises live animal and pelt shows. .

9285 ■ Fur Council of Canada–Conseil Canadien de la Fourrure
1435 St. Alexandre, Ste. 1270
Montreal, QC, Canada H3A 2G4
Ph:(514)844-1945
Fax:(514)844-8593
Co. E-mail: info@furcouncil.com
URL: http://www.furcouncil.com/home.aspx
Contact: Paula Lishman
Description: Fur trappers and processors and distributors of fur and fur apparel. Promotes increased demand for fur and fur clothing. Represents members' commercial interests; conducts promotional activities.

9286 ■ Fur Information Council of America
8424 A Santa Monica Blvd., No. 860
West Hollywood, CA 90069
Ph:(323)782-1700
Fax:(323)651-1417
Co. E-mail: info@fur.org
URL: http://www.fur.org
Contact: Keith Kaplan, Exec. Dir.
Description: Fur retailers, manufacturers, and others involved in the fur industry. Aims to promote the fur industry and foster high standards, quality, and craftsmanship. Conducts public relations and advertising work. Committed to the wise use and humane care of animals; develops programs to ensure high standards for animal welfare in the fur industry; works with wildlife biologists to promote sound wildlife management. **Publications:** *American Fur Industry Fashion-Newsletter* (annual); *Furs Naturally* .

TRADE PERIODICALS

9287 ■ *Canadian Cooperative Wool Growers Magazine*
Pub: Canadian Co-Operative Wool Growers Ltd.
Contact: Eric Bjergso, Gen Mgr

Released: Annual. **Description:** Company magazine covering wool marketing and livestock supplies.

ASSOCIATIONS AND OTHER ORGANIZATIONS

9288 ■ Empress Chinchilla Breeders Cooperative
43188 Cottonwood Creek Rd.
Crawford, CO 81415
Ph:(970)921-7231
Co. E-mail: empresschinchilla@gmail.com
URL: http://www.empresschinchilla.org
Contact: Mr. Gene Adcock, Pres.
Description: Breeders of chinchillas for fur. Conducts research; supervises live animal and pelt shows. .

9289 ■ Fur Council of Canada–Conseil Canadien de la Fourrure
1435 St. Alexandre, Ste. 1270
Montreal, QC, Canada H3A 2G4
Ph:(514)844-1945
Fax:(514)844-8593
Co. E-mail: info@furcouncil.com
URL: http://www.furcouncil.com/home.aspx
Contact: Paula Lishman
Description: Fur trappers and processors and distributors of fur and fur apparel. Promotes increased demand for fur and fur clothing. Represents members' commercial interests; conducts promotional activities.

9290 ■ Fur Information Council of America
8424 A Santa Monica Blvd., No. 860
West Hollywood, CA 90069
Ph:(323)782-1700
Fax:(323)651-1417
Co. E-mail: info@fur.org
URL: http://www.fur.org
Contact: Keith Kaplan, Exec. Dir.
Description: Fur retailers, manufacturers, and others involved in the fur industry. Aims to promote the fur industry and foster high standards, quality, and craftsmanship. Conducts public relations and advertising work. Committed to the wise use and humane care of animals; develops programs to ensure high standards for animal welfare in the fur industry; works with wildlife biologists to promote sound wildlife management. **Publications:** *American Fur Industry Fashion-Newsletter* (annual); *Furs Naturally* .

START-UP INFORMATION

9291 ■ *The 100 Best Businesses to Start When You Don't Want To Work Hard Anymore*
Pub: Career Press Inc.
Ed: Lisa Rogak. **Price:** $16.99. **Description:** Author helps burned-out workers envision a new future as a small business owner. Systems analysis, adventure travel outfitting, bookkeeping, food delivery, furniture making, and software development are among the industries examined.

ASSOCIATIONS AND OTHER ORGANIZATIONS

9292 ■ **American Society of Furniture Designers**
144 Woodland Dr.
New London, NC 28127
Ph:(910)576-1273
Fax:(910)576-1573
Co. E-mail: info@asfd.com
URL: http://www.asfd.com
Contact: Christine Evans, Exec. Dir.
Description: Represents professional furniture designers, teachers, students, corporate suppliers of products and services; others who supply products and services related to furniture design. Seeks to promote the profession of furniture design. Conducts and cooperates in educational courses and seminars for furniture designers and persons planning to enter the field. Maintains placement service. **Publications:** *ASFD Official Directory* (biennial).

REFERENCE WORKS

9293 ■ *American Society of Furniture Designers—Membership Directory*
Pub: American Society of Furniture Designers
Contact: Christine Evans, Exec. Dir.
Released: Annual, January. **Price:** $75 Corporate membership representative; $225 Professional/International Professional membership; $140 Affiliate/Associate membership; $600 Corporate/International Corporate membership. **Covers:** Over 160 member furniture designers.

TRADE PERIODICALS

9294 ■ *Casual Living*
Pub: Reed Business Information
Contact: Cinde W. Ingram, Editor-in-Chief
E-mail: cingram@casualliving.com
Released: Monthly. **Price:** $20; $4 single issue. **Description:** Trade magazine for the casual furnishings industry.

9295 ■ *Laminating Design and Technology*
Pub: Cygnus Business Media
Ed: Tim Fixmer, Editor. **Released:** Bimonthly. **Price:** $48; $68; $99 Canada and Mexico; $99 other countries. **Description:** Trade magazine covering decorative surface fashion and functionality.

VIDEOCASSETTES/AUDIOCASSETTES

9296 ■ *Refinishing Furniture with Bob Flexner*
Taunton Press
63 S. Main St.
PO Box 5506
Newtown, CT 06470-5506
Ph:(203)426-8171
Free: 800-888-8286
Fax:(203)426-3434
URL: http://www.taunton.com
Released: 1989. **Price:** $29.95. **Description:** Viewers can make old furniture look like new with Bob's handy instructions. **Availability:** VHS.

9297 ■ *Repairing Furniture with Bob Flexner*
Taunton Press
63 S. Main St.
PO Box 5506
Newtown, CT 06470-5506
Ph:(203)426-8171
Free: 800-888-8286
Fax:(203)426-3434
URL: http://www.taunton.com
Released: 1989. **Price:** $29.95. **Description:** Bob saves viewers money by showing them how to fix furniture instead of buying new stuff. **Availability:** VHS.

FRANCHISES AND BUSINESS OPPORTUNITIES

9298 ■ *Certirestore Certified Furniture Restoration*
310 Northern Pacific Ave.
Fargo, ND 58102
Ph:(701)277-1005
Free: 888-50C-ERTI
Fax:(701)277-0534
URL: http://www.certirestore.com
No. of Franchise Units: 28. **Founded:** 1989. **Franchised:** 2004. **Description:** Shop based, full service furniture restoration and repair franchise opportunity. We focus on providing professional furniture restoration to commercial clients, moving and insurance companies, restaurants, offices, churches, government and schools. Our staff has over 20 years of combined hands-on experience in the furniture restoration and repair industry. **Equity Capital Needed:** $29,500-$89,250. **Franchise Fee:** $49,500. **Financial Assistance:** Registered with the SBA and can be viewed at www.franchiseregistry.com **Training:** Provides the tools, supplies, equipment, support and hands-on training. In their 12 day in-shop training class you will restore and repair several pieces of furniture, as well as marketing and business training.

9299 ■ *Furniture Medic of Canada*
ServiceMaster
5462 Timberlea Blvd.
Mississauga, ON, Canada L4W 2T7
Ph:(905)670-0000
Free: 800-263-5928
Fax:(905)670-0077
Co. E-mail: thould@smclean.com
URL: http://www.furnituremedic.com
No. of Franchise Units: 50. **No. of Company-Owned Units:** 8. **Founded:** 1993. **Franchised:** 1993. **Description:** Provides furniture repair services and complete refinishing. **Equity Capital Needed:** $20,000-$50,000. **Franchise Fee:** $25,000 + $17,200 + equipment packaging. **Training:** Yes.

9300 ■ **Furniture Medic, L.P.**
3839 Forest Hill-Irene Rd.
Memphis, TN 38125
Ph:(901)597-8600
Free: 800-255-9687
Fax:(901)597-8663
Co. E-mail: brwilliams@smclean.com
URL: http://www.furnituremedicfranchise.com
No. of Franchise Units: 500. **Founded:** 1992. **Franchised:** 1993. **Description:** Onsite furniture repair and restoration of furniture, antiques, cabinetry, paneled walls etc. **Equity Capital Needed:** $42,900, includes products and equipment. **Franchise Fee:** $29,900. **Financial Assistance:** SMAC can finance up to 80% of license, tools, and supplies. W/A/C and adequate working capital, fixed rate, simple interest and attractive terms. **Training:** 5 week program, seminars, regional meetings, 24/7 technical assistance with key support in marketing, financial, customer acquisition and retention.

9301 ■ **Guardsman Furniturepro**
The Valspar Corp.
4999 36th St., SE
Grand Rapids, MI 49512
Free: 800-496-6377
Fax:(616)285-7882
Co. E-mail: furniturepro@valspar.com
URL: http://www.guardsmanfurniturepro.com
No. of Franchise Units: 123. **Founded:** 1806. **Franchised:** 1994. **Description:** Onsite, mobile, wood touch-up, repair service & refinishing industry. **Equity Capital Needed:** $7,000-$10,000. **Franchise Fee:** $7,000. **Royalty Fee:** Varies. **Financial Assistance:** No. **Managerial Assistance:** Ongoing support, such as initial promotional assistance programs, continuing education courses, research and development of new products and financial management assistance. **Training:** All franchisees receive complete technical and business training and provides quality onsite support.

9302 ■ **Leather Medic**
5565 Lee St., Ste. 1
Lehigh Acres, FL 33971
Free: 888-561-0423
Fax:(239)561-5715
Co. E-mail: klife@leathermedic.com
URL: http://www.leathermedic.com
No. of Franchise Units: 35. **No. of Company-Owned Units:** 1. **Founded:** 1988. **Description:** Repairing and refinishing leather furniture. **Equity**

Capital Needed: $47,500. **Franchise Fee:** $47,500. **Financial Assistance:** In-house financing available. **Training:** Offers 2 weeks of one-on-one training.

9303 ■ Weathersby Guild
PO Box 746
Lilburn, GA 30048-0746
Ph:(678)481-7518
Free: (866)523-9929
Fax:(770)923-6044
Co. E-mail: kent@weathersbyguild.com
URL: http://www.weathersbyguild.com
No. of Franchise Units: 11. **No. of Company-Owned Units:** 1. **Founded:** 1972. **Franchised:** 2002. **Description:** On location mobile furniture repair service oriented to serving the household goods moving industry. The operation can be easily scaled to full-service. Store-front capability to include complete refinishing, upholstery and interior decorating. **Equity Capital Needed:** $22,000-$25,000, total minimum investment $29,000. **Franchise Fee:** $16,500. **Financial Assistance:** No. **Training:** The guild concept reflects our focus on skill level. Our twenty-one day training course is intensive and includes on-the-job training with a specialty in service to the moving van industry. Provides ongoing training and support.

COMPUTERIZED DATABASES

9304 ■ *Avery Index to Architectural Periodicals*
Columbia University
300 Avery
1172 Amsterdam Ave.
MC 0301
New York, NY 10027
Ph:(212)854-3501
Co. E-mail: avery@libraries.cul.columbia.edu
URL: http://library.columbia.edu/indiv/avery
Description: Contains more than 675,000 citations to articles from more than 2500 current architecture and related periodicals, emphasizing the fields of architectural design and history. Sources include more than 2500 periodical titles in all Western languages, including all major architectural magazines published in the United States, Great Britain, and the British Commonwealth, as well as most South American, European, and Japanese periodicals

with English summaries. **Availability:** Online: ProQuest LLC, EBSCO Publishing, EBSCO Publishing. **Type:** Bibliographic.

LIBRARIES

9305 ■ Art Institute of Portland Library
1122 NW Davis St.
Portland, OR 97209-2911
Ph:(503)382-4759
Free: (88)
Fax:(503)228-4227
Co. E-mail: nthurston@aii.edu
URL: http://www.artinstitute.edu/portland/
Contact: Nancy Thurston, LRC Dir.
Scope: Fashion and costume history, interior decoration, furniture history, world history, textiles, clothing and fashion industry, graphic design, multimedia, digital media production, media arts and animation, game art, advertising. **Services:** Copying; color copying; A/V viewing; Library open to professionals in the field. **Holdings:** 21,933 books; 900 videocassettes. **Subscriptions:** 204 journals and other serials; 3 newspapers.

9306 ■ Edward-Dean Museum & Gardens Art Reference Library
9401 Oak Glen Rd.
Cherry Valley, CA 92223
Ph:(951)845-2626
Fax:(951)845-2628
Co. E-mail: lreisner@rivcoeda.org
URL: http://www.edward-deanmuseum.org
Contact: Terri Bowen, Asst.Musm.Mgr.
Scope: Furniture, decorative arts, sculpture, architecture, costume design, history. **Services:** Library open to the public by special permission. **Holdings:** 1200 books.

9307 ■ Furniture Library Association Library
1009 N. Main St.
High Point, NC 27262
Ph:(336)883-4011
Fax:(336)883-6579
Co. E-mail: info@furniturelibrary.com
URL: http://www.furniturelibrary.com
Contact: Carl Vuncannon, Cur.
Scope: Early architecture; design - interior, furniture, fabric; furniture styles, 1600 to present. **Services:** Photographing; Library open to the public. **Holdings:**

7000 books; bound periodical volumes, including over 100 years of furniture catalogs; Furniture World; trade journals. **Subscriptions:** 10 journals and other serials.

9308 ■ Grand Rapids Public Library–Furniture Design Collection
111 Library St., NE
Grand Rapids, MI 49503-3268
Ph:(616)988-5400
Fax:(616)988-5402
Co. E-mail: mwarner@grpl.org
URL: http://www.grpl.org
Contact: Marcia Warner, Dir.
Scope: Furniture history and design - all periods and styles. **Services:** Copying; collection open to furniture designers and scholars by appointment only. **Holdings:** 4000 items. **Subscriptions:** 4 journals and other serials.

9309 ■ Harrington College of Design–Design Library
200 W. Madison St., 2nd Fl.
Chicago, IL 60606-3433
Ph:(312)939-4975
Free: (866)590-4423
Co. E-mail: elaine@interiordesign.edu
URL: http://www.interiordesign.edu
Contact: Elaine Lowenthal, Lib.Dir.
Scope: Architecture, design, building materials, furniture, decorative arts, modern design. **Services:** Interlibrary loan; copying; Library open to the public by appointment for reference use only with referral from another Library. **Holdings:** 22,000 books; 900 bound periodical volumes; 23,000 slides; 450 videotapes; 35,000 digital images. **Subscriptions:** 125 journals and other serials.

9310 ■ Kendall College of Art & Design Library
17 Fountain St. NW, 2nd Fl.
Grand Rapids, MI 49503-3002
Ph:(616)451-1868
Free: 800-676-2787
Fax:(616)831-9689
Co. E-mail: kcadlibrary@ferris.edu
URL: http://www.kcad.edu/facilities/library/
Contact: Michael J. Kruzich, Lib.Dir.
Scope: Fine arts, applied arts, design. **Services:** Library open to the public. **Holdings:** 13,000 books; 1695 bound periodical volumes; 50,000 slides; 71 online databases. **Subscriptions:** 95 journals; 1 newspaper.

ASSOCIATIONS AND OTHER ORGANIZATIONS

9311 ■ American Gaming Association
1299 Pennsylvania Ave. NW, Ste. 1175
Washington, DC 20004
Ph:(202)552-2675
Fax:(202)552-2676
Co. E-mail: info@americangaming.org
URL: http://www.americangaming.org
Contact: Frank J. Fahrenkopf Jr., Pres./CEO
Description: Represents the commercial casino entertainment industry by addressing federal legislative and regulatory issues affecting its members and their employees and customers; provides leadership in addressing newly emerging national issues and in developing industrywide programs on critical issues; serves as the industry's national information clearinghouse which provides the media, elected officials, other decision makers and the public with timely and accurate gaming industry data. **Publications:** *Inside the AGA* (bimonthly); *Responsible Gaming Quarterly* (quarterly).

9312 ■ Casino Chip and Gaming Token Collectors Club
PO Box 691085
Houston, TX 77269-1085
Co. E-mail: membership@ccgtcc.com
URL: http://www.ccgtcc.com
Contact: Doug Smith, Pres.
Description: Member club of the American Numismatic Association. Collectors of casino gaming chips and tokens. Coordinates the exchange of information regarding gaming chips and tokens and the casinos where they are used. Conducts educational programs and competitions. **Publications:** *Casino Collectibles News* (quarterly); *Club Directory* (periodic).

9313 ■ Gamblers Anonymous
PO Box 17173
Los Angeles, CA 90017
Ph:(213)386-8789
Free: 888-424-3577
Fax:(213)386-0030
Co. E-mail: isomain@gamblersanonymous.org
URL: http://www.gamblersanonymous.org
Description: Men and women who have joined together in order to stop gambling and to help other compulsive gamblers do the same; is self-supporting, declines outside contributions, and neither opposes nor endorses outside causes. .

9314 ■ National Association of Casino Party Operators
PO Box 5626
South San Francisco, CA 94083
Free: 888-922-0777
Co. E-mail: info@casinoparties.com
URL: http://www.nactpo.com
Contact: Mike Miller, Dir.
Description: Casino party operators, party planners, party rental shop owners, theme party and special events operators, and others involved in casino party rental business. Strives to strengthen the casino and theme party industry and advance the industry into more geographical markets. Promotes members' interests. .

9315 ■ National Council on Problem Gambling
730 11th St. NW, Ste. 601
Washington, DC 20001
Ph:(202)547-9204
Free: 800-522-4700
Fax:(202)547-9206
Co. E-mail: ncpg@ncpgambling.org
URL: http://www.ncpgambling.org
Contact: Keith S. Whyte, Exec. Dir.
Description: Professionals in health, education, and law; recovering gamblers; supportive citizens. Advocates for programs and services to assist problem gamblers and their families. Makes referrals for compulsive gamblers and their families; seeks to stimulate the concern of the medical profession, educators, legislators, and the criminal justice system. Conducts training programs for professionals and information programs to encourage business management, educators, and the public to become aware of and to understand compulsive gambling. Compiles statistics; maintains speakers' bureau. Administers national 24 hour toll-free helpline for individuals with gambling problems. .

9316 ■ National Indian Gaming Association
224 2nd St. SE
Washington, DC 20003
Ph:(202)546-7711
Fax:(202)546-1755
Co. E-mail: estevens@indiangaming.org
URL: http://www.indiangaming.org
Contact: Ernest L. Stevens, Chm.
Description: Indian nations operating gambling establishments are members; tribes, organizations, and businesses supporting Indian gaming establishments are associate members. Works to protect and preserve the welfare of tribes seeking to achieve economic self-sufficiency through the operation of gaming establishments. Seeks to expand political self-determination of Indian nations. Cooperates with government agencies in the formulation and application of laws and regulations applicable to Indian gaming. Provides technical assistance and other support to tribal gaming establishments. Conducts educational programs. **Publications:** *Handbook for Tribal Leaders*; *Indian Gaming Integrity*; *2005 Indian Gaming Resource Directory*;Annual Report (annual).

9317 ■ North American Gaming Regulators Association
1000 Westgate Dr., Ste. 252
St. Paul, MN 55114
Ph:(651)203-7244
Fax:(651)290-2266
Co. E-mail: phil.sanderson@lottery.state.tx.us
URL: http://www.nagra.org
Contact: Phil Sanderson, Pres.
Description: Domestic and foreign governmental agencies, bureaus, commissions, and Native American tribes and First Nations charged with the regulation and enforcement of any type of gambling. Works for the mutual exchange of regulatory techniques for training enforcement personnel; provides a medium for communication of common problems; offers resources to states enacting legislation; speaks on matters concerning non-profit and related gambling. **Publications:** *NAGRA News*; *Standards on Bingo*; *Standards on Pull-Tabs* .

REFERENCE WORKS

9318 ■ "AG Warns Slots MBE Plan Risky" in *Boston Business Journal* (Vol. 29, May 27, 2011, No. 3, pp. 1)
Pub: American City Business Journals Inc.
Ed: Scott Dance. **Description:** Attorney General Doug Gansler states that the law extending the minority business program on slots parlors contracting through 2018 could be open to lawsuits. He recommended that the state should conduct a study proving that minority- and women-owned businesses do not get a fair share in the gaming industry before it signs the bill to avoid lawsuits from majority-owned firms.

9319 ■ "Betting On Slots" in *Baltimore Business Journal* (Vol. 28, November 19, 2010, No. 28, pp. 1)
Pub: Baltimore Business Journal
Ed: Rachel Bernstein. **Description:** Penn National Gaming Company's Hollywood Casino in Perryville, Maryland has been betting on the slot machines to lure slot players to the region to boost the town's growth. The success of Maryland's first casino is expected to lead to the development of land in the area.

9320 ■ "Broadway Casino Climbing Hills to Get to Gambling" in *Business Courier* (Vol. 26, January 1, 2010, No. 37, pp. 1)
Pub: American City Business Journals, Inc.
Ed: Dan Monk. **Description:** Rock Ventures LLC, operators of the Broadway Commons Casino, needs approval from the Ohio General Assembly and the to-be-created Ohio Casino Control Commission to commence operations.

9321 ■ "Can Turfway Park Stay in the Race?" in *Business Courier* (Vol. 26, January 8, 2010, No. 38, pp. 1)
Pub: American City Business Journals, Inc.
Ed: Jon Newberry. **Description:** Legalization of slot machine gambling in Kentucky could affect raceway Turfway Park and the state's thoroughbred industry. Thousands of farms and jobs in the industry could be lost if slot machine gambling is approved.

9322 ■ *Casino Gaming in the United States*
Pub: Scarecrow Press Inc.
Contact: Thomas R. Mirkovich, Author
Price: $95, individuals Hardback; $59.95, individuals Hardback. **Covers:** Bibliography of nearly 900 books, articles, periodicals, Internet sites and government publications from 1985-94 on casino gambling. Also includes state gambling agencies, associations, Indian gaming locations, consultants, and public gam-

ing companies. **Entries Include:** For publications—Publication title, subject, author, web site address where applicable. For organizations—Name, address, phone.

9323 ■ "Casino Minority Spend: $80 Million" in *Business Courier* (Vol. 27, August 20, 2010, No. 16, pp. 1)
Pub: Business Courier
Ed: Lucy May. **Description:** Real estate developers are planning to invest $80 million to build the Harrah's casino project in Cincinnati, Ohio. Rock Ventures LLC is seeking a 20 percent inclusion rate in the project.

9324 ■ "Casinos See College as Job Jackpot" in *The Business Journal-Serving Metropolitan Kansas City* (Vol. 26, August 1, 2008, No. 47)
Pub: American City Business Journals, Inc.
Ed: Suzanna Stagemeyer. **Description:** Wyandotte County casino managers revealed plans to develop partnerships with Kansas City Kansas Community College. The planned partnership is expected to include curriculum development and degree programs that would help train employees for the planned casinos. Other views and information on the project are presented.

9325 ■ "City Hopes Casino Will Be $333M Jackpot" in *Business First Buffalo* (October 5, 2007, pp. 1)
Pub: American City Business Journals, Inc.
Ed: James Fink. **Description:** Construction of the $333 million Seneca Buffalo Creek Casino, which includes a hotel, spa and restaurants, is schedule to begin in October 2007. The 5,000 square-foot casino is expected to generate revenue and provide 1,000 jobs for the City of Buffalo, New York.

9326 ■ "Contractors: Slots MBE Goal a Test" in *Baltimore Business Journal* (Vol. 27, November 20, 2009, No. 28, pp. 1)
Pub: American City Business Journals
Ed: Scott Dance. **Description:** Slot machine manufacturers in Maryland have been searching minority business enterprises (MBEs) that will provide maintenance and delivery services to the machines. MBEs will also build the stands where the machines will be mounted.

9327 ■ "Deal With Tribes Revives Revenue Stream" in *Crain's Detroit Business* (Vol. 24, March 24, 2008, No. 12, pp. 6)
Pub: Crain Communications, Inc.
Ed: Amy Lane. **Description:** Michigan Bureau of State Lottery's 2003 launch of its Club Keno game caused the Little River Band of Ottawa Indians and the Little Traverse Bay Bands of Odawa Indians to halt payments of shared casino revenue with the state. The federal lawsuit that resulted has now been settled and tribal revenue-sharing will resume as well as $26 million in previous payments to the state of Michigan that the tribes had put into escrow.

9328 ■ *Double or Nothing: How Two Friends Risked It All to Buy One of Las Vegas' Legendary Casinos*
Pub: HarperBusiness
Ed: Tom Breitling, with Cal Fussman. **Released:** March 2008. **Price:** $24.95. **Description:** Founders of a successful Internet travel agency share their experience from startup to selling the company.

9329 ■ "Fight Over Casino Funds Limits Kitty for MEDC" in *Crain's Detroit Business* (Vol. 24, January 21, 2008, No. 3, pp. 3)
Pub: Crain Communications Inc. - Detroit
Ed: Amy Lane. **Description:** Michigan Economic Development Corporation is facing uncertainty due to a Michigan American Indian tribe from the southwestern portion of the state withholding its 8 percent casino revenue share.

9330 ■ "For Yung, Lady Luck a Fickle Mistress" in *Business Courier* (Vol. 24, November 30, 2008, No. 33, pp. 1)
Pub: American City Business Journals, Inc.
Ed: Dan Monk. **Description:** Bill Yung's Columbia Sussex Corp. won the bid for the parent company of

Tropicana casinos in November 2006, and a year after, the company is facing regulatory and labor issues.

9331 ■ "Giant Garages Could Rise Up Downtown" in *Business Courier* (Vol. 27, October 22, 2010, No. 25, pp. 1)
Pub: Business Courier
Ed: Dan Monk. **Description:** More than 2,500 new parking spaces could rise up to the eastern edge of downtown Cincinnati, Ohio as public and private investors collect resources for new garage projects. These projects are expected to accommodate almost 1,500 monthly parkers who will lose access at Broadway Commons due to the construction of Harrah's casino.

9332 ■ "Internet Cafe Logging in to Chardon Plaza?" in *News-Herald* (July 16, 2011)
Pub: Journal Register Ohio
Ed: Betsy Scott. **Description:** Pearl's High Rollers Inc. applied for an Internet sweepstakes café license that would reside in a vacant space in Chardon Plaza. City officials have created regulations for such businesses and Pearl's applied for a license and is awaiting approval.

9333 ■ "Internet Café Regulations Head to City Council Vote" in *Vindicator* (April 13, 2011)
Pub: Vindicator
Ed: David Skolnick. **Description:** Youngstown City Council's safety committee agrees with proposed changes to the policy regulating Internet gaming cafes and sweepstakes businesses. The new amendments allow Internet café customers to buy Internet time and go to Websites and play sweepstakes games of change.

9334 ■ "Internet Café 'Sweepstakes' Expanding in Arkansas" in *Arkansas Business* (Vol. 28, September 5, 2011, No. 36, pp. 1)
Pub: Arkansas Business Publishing Group
Ed: Mark Friedman. **Description:** Despite the fact that video games resembling casino games in Lucky's Business Center in Little Rock, representatives of the Internet café insist they are not offering gambling but a type of sweepstakes promotion and that business model is thriving. Lucky's, Cancun Cyber Café & Business Center Inc., and Wild Rides Business Center & Internet Café has opened in the area in the last few weeks.

9335 ■ "Lotteries Scratch Their Way to Billions" in *Saint Louis Business Journal* (Vol. 31, August 19, 2011, No. 52, pp. 1)
Pub: Saint Louis Business Journal
Ed: Kelsey Volkmann. **Description:** Missouri Lottery reported $1 billion in sales in 2011. A six-fold increase in the lottery's advertising budget is seen to drive the revenue increase; a 4.5 percent rise in its scratch-off tickets and new sponsorships has also contributed to the development.

9336 ■ "Maryland Ready to Defend Slots Minority Policy" in *Boston Business Journal* (Vol. 29, July 8, 2011, No. 9, pp. 3)
Pub: American City Business Journals Inc.
Ed: Scott Dance. **Description:** The legality of Maryland's minority inclusion policy may be put under scrutiny once the lawsuit filed by rejected slots developer Baltimore City Entertainment Group on July 5, 2011 is heard in court. The lawsuit aims to stop the bidding process on a proposed casino in Baltimore because the minority policy amounts to reverse discrimination.

9337 ■ "Power Partnerships" in *Business Courier* (Vol. 27, October 22, 2010, No. 25, pp. 1)
Pub: Business Courier
Ed: Lucy May. **Description:** The $400 million Harrah's casino and the $47 million redevelopment and expansion of Washington Park are project aimed at boosting the economy in downtown Cincinnati, Ohio. These projects will be done in cooperation with the

National Association for the Advancement of Colored People. Insights into the role of minority-owned businesses in regional economic development are explored.

9338 ■ "Silverdome Bidders Bring New Proposals" in *Crain's Detroit Business* (Vol. 24, March 17, 2008, No. 11, pp. 23)
Pub: Crain Communications, Inc.
Ed: Daniel Duggan. **Description:** Discusses the seven plans which have been proposed as part of the third round of bidding for the Pontiac Silverdome; proposals range from Global Baseball Inc., a baseball league that would pit a team from every country against one another, to an Indian casino, a musical "hall of fame", a convention center, a horse track, a hotel and an indoor water park.

9339 ■ "Table Games Get a Leg Up" in *Philadelphia Business Journal* (Vol. 28, January 15, 2010, No. 48, pp. 1)
Pub: American City Business Journals
Ed: Athena Merritt, Peter Van Allen. **Description:** Casino operators expect the addition of live table games such as poker and blackjack at existing and planned casinos in Philadelphia will generate 1,000 new jobs. Most of the jobs will be dealers and floor supervisors.

9340 ■ "The Trader's Edge" in *Barron's* (Vol. 88, March 31, 2008, No. 13, pp. 56)
Pub: Dow Jones & Company, Inc.
Ed: Dan McGuire. **Description:** There is a $3,000 a year annual limit to deducting investor's losses and normal investment expenses are purportedly deductible as miscellaneous expenses on Schedule A only to the extent that they exceed two percent of adjusted gross income. Professional gamblers who can use Schedule C are unable deduct a net gaming loss against income from any other sources.

9341 ■ "Turfway Slowing its Gait" in *Business Courier* (Vol. 26, November 6, 2009, No. 28, pp. 1)
Pub: American City Business Journals, Inc.
Ed: Jon Newberry. **Description:** Kentucky's Turfway Park will be decreasing its weekly race schedule from five days to three days in the first two months of 2010, and to four days in March 2010. The decision to make reductions in the schedule is attributed to the relocation of thoroughbred racing to states that allow casino gambling. As a result, Turfway Park's resources and purse money would be focused on less days.

9342 ■ "Vegas in the D; Local Architects Collaborate On MGM Grand" in *Crain's Detroit Business* (Vol. 23, October 1, 2007, No. 40, pp. 1)
Pub: Crain Communications Inc. - Detroit
Ed: Daniel Duggan. **Description:** Local Detroit architects, Smith Group and Hamilton Anderson Associates are among the contractors vying for subcontracted architecture, construction and consulting contracts for the new MGM Grand Detroit casino and hotel.

9343 ■ "What Happens in Vegas Could Happen in Baltimore, Too" in *Boston Business Journal* (Vol. 29, June 17, 2011, No. 6, pp. 1)
Pub: American City Business Journals Inc.
Ed: Daniel J. Sernovitz. **Description:** At least 36 companies expressed their interest in developing a casino in South Baltimore following the state commission's announcement for bids. Developers have until July 28, 2011 to submit their proposals. Baltimore's strong economy is the major factor for the interest, yet the fact that blackjack and poker are outlawed in Maryland could be a drawback.

9344 ■ *Winner Takes All: Steve Wynn, Kirk Kerkorian, Gary Loveman, and the Race to Own Vegas*
Pub: Hyperion
Ed: Christina Binkley. **Released:** 2009. **Price:** $25.95. **Description:** The story of three men, Steve Wynn, Kirk Kerkorian, and Gary Loveman, each with different backgrounds are reinventing Las Vegas.

SOURCES OF SUPPLY

9345 ■ *American Casino Guide*
Pub: Casino Vacations
Ed: Steve Bourie, Editor. **Released:** Annual, Latest edition 2011. **Price:** $18.95, individuals plus shipping charges; $11.75, individuals discounted price. **Covers:** more than 700 casino/resorts, riverboat casinos, and Indian casinos in the U.S. **Entries Include:** Casino name, address, phone, toll-free number, room rates, dining information, games offered, features, web site addresses. **Arrangement:** Geographical. **Indexes:** Name.

TRADE PERIODICALS

9346 ■ *Anthony Curtis' Las Vegas Advisor*
Pub: Huntington Press
Contact: Anthony Curtis, Editor & Publisher
Released: Monthly. **Price:** $50, U.S.; $60, Canada; $70, elsewhere. **Description:** Acts as a consumer's information source for Las Vegas visitors. Recurring features include letters to the editor, a calendar of events, book reviews, notices of publications available, and columns titled Couponomy, Top Ten Las Vegas Values, Dining, Entertainment News, Advance Planner, Letters & Tips, Gambling, Fast Track, Last Second Flash, Accommodations, Comp City, and Extra Stuff.

9347 ■ *Current Blackjack News*
Pub: Pi Yee Press
Contact: Stanford Wong
Ed: Stanford Wong, Editor, stanfwong@aol.com. **Released:** Monthly. **Price:** $129, individuals regular mail; $89 through email. **Description:** Features reviews of rule changes for the game of blackjack and reports on casinos in Nevada, Mississippi, Louisiana, Illinois, Iowa, New Jersey, New York, Connecticut, Minnesota, and other areas with legalized casino gambling. Announces new casino openings, as well as highlighting profitable opportunities to win at casinos.

9348 ■ *Las Vegas Insider*
Pub: Las Vegas Insider
Ed: Donald Currier, Editor. **Released:** Monthly. **Price:** $45, U.S.. **Description:** Offers advice on low cost hotels, room bargains, food, gaming tips, and tourist information in Las Vegas, Reno, and Atlantic City. Recurring features include news of research, a calendar of events, job listings, book reviews, and notices of publications available.

9349 ■ *Lottery, Parimutuel & Casino Regulation*
Pub: Wakeman/Walworth Inc.
Ed: Keyes Walworth, Editor. **Released:** Weekly, 48/year. **Price:** $345, U.S. and Canada; $365, elsewhere; $620, two years U.S. and Canada; $680, two years elsewhere. **Description:** Covers state lottery regulations, prize structures, distribution of revenue, taxation and regulation of casinos, pari-mutuel gaming, horse racing, and other forms of gambling.

9350 ■ *Winning!*
Pub: NewsLinc
Contact: Steven M. Brown, Managing Editor
E-mail: sbrown@natcom.publications.com
Released: Monthly. **Price:** $21, individuals in the U.S.. **Description:** Covers contests, sweepstakes, gambling, lotteries, and bingo.

TRADE SHOWS AND CONVENTIONS

9351 ■ North American Association of State and Provincial Lotteries Conference and Trade Show
North American Association of State and Provincial Lotteries
6 N. Broadway
Geneva, OH 44041

Ph:(440)466-5630
Fax:(440)466-5649
Co. E-mail: info@nasplhq.org
URL: http://www.naspl.org
Released: Annual. **Audience:** Lottery industry professionals. **Principal Exhibits:** Lottery equipment, supplies, and services.

CONSULTANTS

9352 ■ Casino, Hotel & Resort Consultants L.L.C.
8100 Via Del Cerro Ct.
Las Vegas, NV 89117
Ph:(702)646-7200
Fax:(702)646-6680
Co. E-mail: info@hraba.com
URL: http://www.hraba.com
Contact: John S. Hraba, President
E-mail: jshraba@aol.com
Scope: Casino and hospitality industry consultants. Firm specializes in developing and implementing customized forecast and labor management control systems that deliver immediate, positive impact to the company's bottom line. Involved in production planning, employ surveys and communication, inventory management, business process reviews, audits, development and implementation of key management reports. **Seminars:** Payroll Cost Control; Effective Staff Scheduling.

LIBRARIES

9353 ■ Atlantic City Free Public Library–Alfred M. Heston Collection
1 N. Tennessee Ave.
Atlantic City, NJ 08401
Ph:(609)345-2269
Fax:(609)345-5570
Co. E-mail: reflib@acfpl.org
URL: http://www.acfpl.org
Contact: Heather Halpin Perez, Archv.
Scope: Local history, genealogy, Atlantic City government records. **Services:** Copying; collection open to the public two days a week (Wednesdays and Thursdays) and by appointment; limited remote reference help. **Holdings:** 5000 books; 200 bound periodical volumes; 30 online subscriptions; photographs; scrapbooks; oral histories. **Subscriptions:** 15 journals and other serials; 5 newspapers.

9354 ■ Loto-Quebec–Centre de Documentation
500 Sherbrooke St. W., Ste. 2000
Montreal, QC, Canada H3A 3G6
Ph:(514)282-8000
Free: (866)611-5686
Fax:(514)873-8999
Co. E-mail: centred@loto-quebec.com
Scope: Lotteries, casinos, horse racing, video games, sports betting. **Services:** Interlibrary loan; copying; Center open to the public. **Holdings:** 5000 books; 215 Annual reports; 2900 monographs; 27,000 bibiliographic records. **Subscriptions:** 180 journals and other serials.

9355 ■ University of Nevada, Las Vegas–Special Collections–Gaming Studies Collection (4505)
4505 Maryland Pkwy.
Box 457010
Las Vegas, NV 89154-7010
Ph:(702)895-2234

Fax:(702)895-2253
Co. E-mail: peter.michel@unlv.edu
URL: http://www.library.unlv.edu/speccol/
Contact: David G. Schwartz, GSRC Coord.
Scope: History and statistical basis of games and gambling; economics and regulation of the gaming industry; psychological, social, and political effects of gambling; history of specific hotel and casinos throughout the world; fiscal history of gaming; social and cultural realities of gaming. **Services:** Copying; collection open to the public. **Holdings:** Figures not available.

9356 ■ Washoe County Law Library
Court House
75 Court St., Rm. 101
Box 30083
Reno, NV 89520-3083
Ph:(775)328-3250
Fax:(775)328-3441
Co. E-mail: lawlib@washoecounty.us
URL: http://www.washoecounty.us/lawlib
Contact: Howard Conyers, Law Lib.Dir.
Scope: Nevada, California and Federal Law. **Services:** Interlibrary loan; copying; Library open to the public. **Holdings:** 54,605 books; 4931 bound periodical volumes; 9214 volumes in microform; 52,000 microfiche. **Subscriptions:** 393 periodicals.

RESEARCH CENTERS

9357 ■ McGill University–International Centre for Youth Gambling Problems and High-Risk Behaviors–Centre international d'étude sur le je et les comportements àrisque chez les jeunes
Duggan House
3724 McTavish St.
Montreal, QC, Canada H3A 1Y2
Ph:(514)398-1391
Fax:(514)398-3401
Co. E-mail: jeffrey.derevensky@mcgill.ca
URL: http://www.youthgambling.com
Contact: Prof. Jeffrey L. Derevensky PhD, Co-Dir.
E-mail: jeffrey.derevensky@mcgill.ca
Scope: Youth gambling and risk-taking behaviors. **Publications:** Journal of Gambling Studies (monthly); YGI Newsletter (quarterly). **Educational Activities:** Conferences (5/year); Training programs (5/year), for researchers, treatment providers and educators; Workshops (monthly). **Awards:** Award for graduate paper on gambling (annually).

9358 ■ Pennsylvania Family Institute
23 N Front St.
Harrisburg, PA 17101-1606
Ph:(717)545-0600
Fax:(717)545-8107
Co. E-mail: mgeer@pafamily.org
URL: http://www.pafamily.org
Contact: Michael Geer, Pres.
E-mail: mgeer@pafamily.org
Scope: Family issues as they relate to government policy, including divorce, day-care, parenting, drug abuse, abortion, welfare, gambling, youth culture, and education. **Services:** Assists advocacy groups in planning seminars and conferences. **Publications:** Pennsylvania Citizen Magazine Newsletter (monthly); Pennsylvania Families & Schools (bimonthly); Research Reports. **Educational Activities:** CME seminars in Pennsylvania on life issues; sex education and other topics.

ASSOCIATIONS AND OTHER ORGANIZATIONS

9359 ■ Board for Certification of Genealogists
PO Box 14291
Washington, DC 20044
Co. E-mail: office@bcgcertification.org
URL: http://www.bcgcertification.org
Contact: Ms. Laura DeGrazia CG, Pres.
Description: Works to formulate and administer standards of professional genealogical research. Grants certification in classifications of Certified Genealogists, Certified Genealogical Lecturers, and Certified Genealogical Instructors. Maintains free online roster of persons who have been certified. Investigates and offers resolutions for complaints against the work of certificants. **Publications:** *BCG Application Guide*; *BCG Genealogical Standards Manual*; *Onboard* (3/year).

9360 ■ Czechoslovak Genealogical Society International
PO Box 16225
St. Paul, MN 55116-0225
Ph:(651)450-2322
Co. E-mail: info@cgsi.org
URL: http://www.cgsi.org
Contact: Ginger Simek, Pres.
Description: Individuals of Bohemian, Moravian, Silesian, Carpatho-Rusyn, Slovakian, German, or Jewish descent. Promotes awareness and interest in Czechoslovakian culture and genealogy. Provides a forum for information exchange; collects and disseminates research materials. **Publications:** *Czechoslovak Surname Index* (annual); *Nase Rodina* (quarterly).

9361 ■ Federation of Genealogical Societies
PO Box 200940
Austin, TX 78720-0940
Free: 888-FGS-1500
Fax:888-347-1350
Co. E-mail: office@fgs.org
URL: http://www.fgs.org
Contact: Patricia Farmer Oxley, Pres.
Description: Genealogical societies, genealogical libraries, historical societies, family associations, and other organizations dealing with genealogy and family history. Aims to: stimulate the activities of state and local organizations interested in genealogy and family history; collect, preserve, and disseminate information with reference to genealogical and historical data; promote careful documentation and scholarly genealogical writing and publication; avoid duplication of effort; promote interest in genealogy and family history. Supports state organizations' efforts to promote legislation to open and protect the integrity of birth, death, and marriage records. Provides educational programs to further genealogical knowledge. Acts as collection agent for National Archives Gift Fund. **Publications:** *FGS Forum* (quarterly).

9362 ■ Gottscheer Heritage and Genealogy Association
PO Box 725
Louisville, CO 80027-0725
Co. E-mail: anthro@privatei.com
URL: http://www.gottschee.org
Contact: Elizabeth Nick, Pres.
Description: Descendants of the Gottschee Region of Slovenia, which was inhabited by German-speaking people from the 14th century until 1941, when they were relocated to Untersteiermark (lower Syria) and the Gottschee Region was transferred to Italian rule. Gottschee is now a part of Slovenia. Seeks to preserve the history of the Gottschee region and its German-speaking inhabitants. Conducts historical and genealogical research on the Gottschee Region and its German-speaking inhabitants; assists family historians and genealogists. Provides support to agencies maintaining historic properties in the Gottschee Region; organizes tours to view Gottschee historic sites. **Publications:** *The Gottschee Tree* (quarterly); *The Gottscheer Connection* (3/year).

9363 ■ Groberg - Holbrook Genealogical Organization
1605 S Woodruff Ave.
Idaho Falls, ID 83404
Co. E-mail: mmpowell9@msn.com
URL: http://www.dvgroberg.com
Contact: Joseph Groberg
Description: Members of the Groberg and Holbrook families; other interested individuals. Seeks to strengthen family ties and foster and encourage family genealogical research. Serves as a clearinghouse on the Groberg and Holbrook families and their histories; assists family historians and genealogists. **.Telecommunication Services:** electronic mail, tom@govirtuoso.com.

9364 ■ Italian Genealogical Group
PO Box 626
Bethpage, NY 11714-0626
Co. E-mail: info@italiangen.org
URL: http://www.italiangen.org
Contact: Mike Genovese
Description: Individuals of Italian descent. Promotes study of Italian family history and genealogy. Serves as a clearinghouse on Italian history, culture, and genealogy; sponsors educational and social programs. **Publications:** *Italian Genealogical Newsletter* (monthly).

9365 ■ Lancaster Mennonite Historical Society
2215 Millstream Rd.
Lancaster, PA 17602-1499
Ph:(717)393-9745
Fax:(717)393-8751
Co. E-mail: lmhs@lmhs.org
URL: http://www.lmhs.org
Contact: Charles G. Bauman, Chm.
Description: Individuals interested in the historical background, religious thought and expression, culture, and genealogy of Mennonite- and Amish-related groups originating in Pennsylvania. Sponsors field trips and exhibits. Maintains speakers' bureau,

library, archives and museum. Conducts historical and genealogical seminars, research publications, and children's programs. Compiles statistics. **Publications:** *Pennsylvania Mennonite Heritage* (quarterly).

9366 ■ National Genealogical Society
3108 Columbia Pike, Ste. 300
Arlington, VA 22204-4370
Ph:(703)525-0050
Free: 800-473-0060
Fax:(703)525-0052
Co. E-mail: ngs@ngsgenealogy.org
URL: http://www.ngsgenealogy.org
Contact: Janet A. Alpert, Pres.
Description: Individuals, families, societies and organizations. Promotes genealogical research and education; stimulates and fosters preservation and publication of records of genealogical interest including national, state, county, township, city, town, church, cemetery, Bible, and family records. **Publications:** *National Genealogical Society—Newsletter* (bimonthly); *National Genealogical Society Quarterly* (quarterly); *UPfront with NGS* (semimonthly).

9367 ■ National Public Records Research Association
2501 Aerial Center Pkwy., Ste. 103
Morrisville, NC 27560
Ph:(919)459-2078
Fax:(919)459-2075
Co. E-mail: info@nprra.org
URL: http://www.nprra.org
Contact: Kelly McKown, Pres.
Description: Companies that provide research and information from public records. .

9368 ■ New Canaan Historical Society
13 Oenoke Ridge
New Canaan, CT 06840
Ph:(203)966-1776
Fax:(203)972-5917
Co. E-mail: newcanaan.historical@snet.net
URL: http://www.nchistory.org
Contact: Janet Lindstrom, Exec. Dir.
Description: Individuals interested in the history of New Canaan, CT. Seeks to "bring together and arrange the historical events of the town of New Canaan and the genealogies of the families who have lived in town". Sponsors research and educational programs; serves as a clearinghouse on the history of New Canaan, CT; maintains six historical structures; operates museums within these structures. **Publications:** *Tydings* (quarterly).

REFERENCE WORKS

9369 ■ *Address Book for Germanic Genealogy*
Pub: Genealogical Publishing Company Inc.
Ed: Ernest Thode, Editor. **Released:** Irregular, Latest edition 6th. **Price:** $24.95, individuals paperback. **Covers:** Over 2,700 sources useful for genealogical researchers with interest in Germany, Austria, Switzerland, and other German-speaking areas;

includes about 275 European genealogical societies, 282 European governmental archives, 194 American societies, 380 European religious archives, 175 American religious archives, 770 European municipal archives, 254 genealogists, and numerous libraries, publishers, museums, organizations, etc. **Entries Include:** Name of source, address, brief description. **Arrangement:** By type of resource.

9370 ■ Biography and Genealogy Master Index

Pub: Gale
Released: Annual, Latest edition 2011. **Price:** $611, individuals volume 2. **Description:** BGMI and its updates provide consolidated indexes that indicate whether a biographical sketch being sought is contained in one or more of about 5,000 volumes and editions of more than 1,700 biographical dictionaries and who's who listing contemporary and historical personalities; the indexes contain more than 15 million citations. Publications indexed include "Who's Who in America," "American Men and Women of Science," "Standard & Poor's Register of Corporations, Directors, and Executives," and other standard biographical reference works. **Entries Include:** Name, year of birth (and death, where applicable), code indicating publication in which biographical sketch appears, code indicating when a portrait is included. Available in an abridged version titled "Abridged Biography and Genealogy Master Index." **Arrangement:** Alphabetical.

9371 ■ Directory of Family Associations

Pub: Genealogical Publishing Company Inc.
Ed: Elizabeth Petty Bentley, Editor. **Released:** Irregular, Latest edition 4th. **Price:** $21, individuals paperback. **Covers:** Over 6,000 organizations, each devoted to the study of a family name. **Entries Include:** Family name, related family names, organization name, address, phone, contact name, publications. **Arrangement:** Alphabetical.

9372 ■ Directory of Professional Genealogists

Pub: Association of Professional Genealogists
Ed: Kathleen W. Hinckley, Editor. **Released:** Biennial, latest edition 2004-2005. **Covers:** Member genealogists and related research services. **Entries Include:** Genealogist's name or company name, address; telephone, fax, e-mail biography. **Arrangement:** Geographical. **Indexes:** Institutional members, geographical speciality, research speciality, related service, member residence by state.

9373 ■ Dutch Genealogical Research

Pub: Ye Olde Genealogie Shoppe
Contact: Charles M. Franklin, Author
Released: Irregular. **Price:** $14, individuals softbound. **Publication Includes:** Lists of United States and Dutch vital statistics offices, periodical publishers, libraries, and genealogical societies of assistance in Dutch genealogical research. **Entries Include:** Generally, listings show organization, agency, or other name, address.

9374 ■ French and French-Canadian Family Research

Pub: Ye Olde Genealogie Shoppe
Contact: J. Konrad, Author
Released: Irregular. **Price:** $10, individuals softbound. **Publication Includes:** List of French and French Canadian genealogical societies and provincial archives in French and French Canadian provinces. **Entries Include:** Institution name, and address. **Arrangement:** Alphabetical. **Indexes:** Organization name.

9375 ■ Genealogical Helper—Bureau of Missing Ancestors Section

Pub: Everton Publishers Inc.
Price: $12, individuals online edition; $29, individuals includes online edition; $53, two years includes online edition. **Covers:** About 1,000 amateur and professional genealogists who are researching family names; listings are paid. **Entries Include:** Researcher's name, address, status (whether amateur, family genealogist, or professional), county of residence of researcher, and information on families and surnames being researched. **Arrangement:** Alphabetical by researcher name. **Indexes:** Surname.

9376 ■ Genealogical and Local History Books in Print

Pub: Genealogical Publishing Company Inc.
Ed: Marian Hoffman, Editor. **Released:** Latest edition 5th. **Publication Includes:** List of over 4,600 suppliers of genealogical books, microform, and computer software in four volumes. **Entries Include:** Organization or personal name, address, name and title of contact, product. Principal content is a description of genealogical and local history books, reprints, microform collections, and specific surname publications, with ordering information. Titles of five separate volumes are: Family History Volume; General Reference Volume; World Resources Volume; U.S. Sources & Resources Volume: Alabama-New York; U.S. Sources & Resources Volume: North Carolina-Wyoming. **Arrangement:** Alphabetical, by publisher name.

9377 ■ Genealogical Periodical Annual Index

Pub: Heritage Books Inc.
Contact: Karen T. Ackermann, Author
Released: Annual, Latest edition Volume 40. **Price:** $36, individuals Cloth. **Publication Includes:** Contact information for about 330 periodicals published by genealogical societies and genealogists and used in indexing surnames, place names, and related topics for this book. **Entries Include:** Name of publication, name of publisher, address, issues indexed, title abbreviation used in book. Publication mainly consists of an index containing 14,000 genealogical citations (surnames, place names, etc.). **Arrangement:** Alphabetical by title abbreviation.

9378 ■ The Genealogist's Address Book

Pub: Genealogical Publishing Company Inc.
Ed: Elizabeth Petty Bentley, Editor. **Released:** Biennial, latest edition 6th; Published 2009. **Price:** $69. 95, individuals Paperback. **Covers:** 27,000 archives, historical societies, libraries, and genealogical societies; religious and ethnic organizations, research centers, surname registries, hereditary societies, and other groups useful to persons doing genealogical research. **Entries Include:** Name, address, phone, name and title of contact. **Arrangement:** Geographical.

9379 ■ German Family Research Made Simple

Pub: Ye Olde Genealogie Shoppe
Contact: John Konrad, Author
Price: $15, individuals softbound. **Publication Includes:** Lists with addresses of archives, periodicals, professional researchers, and publishers of maps likely to be helpful to genealogists; covers each state within Germany. **Entries Include:** Name, address. **Arrangement:** Classified by type of source.

9380 ■ Handbook of Genealogical Sources

Pub: George K. Schweitzer
Contact: Dr. George K. Schweitzer, Author
Released: Irregular. **Price:** $12, individuals plus shipping and handling. **Covers:** About 750 libraries, repositories, archives, court houses, etc., with detailed instructions for obtaining genealogical information from them. **Entries Include:** Source name, address, types of data available. **Arrangement:** Alphabetical.

9381 ■ Handy Book for Genealogists

Pub: Everton Publishers Inc.
Contact: Bob Arbon, VP
Released: Irregular, latest edition 11th; published 2005. **Price:** $50, individuals; $60, individuals with CD. **Publication Includes:** List of associations, societies, libraries, archives, and other organizations and institutions that provide genealogical information.

9382 ■ In Search of Your German Roots

Pub: Genealogical Publishing Company Inc.
Ed: Angus Baxter, Editor. **Released:** Irregular, latest edition 4th; 2008. **Price:** $16.95, individuals paperback. **Publication Includes:** Lists of genealogical associations in Germany and German genealogical societies in the United States. **Entries Include:** Association name and address, names and titles of key personnel, and description of services provided. Principal content of publication is researching techniques for genealogists. **Arrangement:** Alphabetical.

9383 ■ "Interactive Stores a Big Part of Borders' Turnaround Plan" in Crain's Detroit Business (Vol. 24, February 18, 2008, No. 7, pp. 4)

Pub: Crain Communications Inc. - Detroit
Description: Borders Group Inc. is using digital technology and interactive media as a part of the firm's turnaround plan. The digital store will allow shoppers to create CDs, download audio books, publish their own works, print photos and search family genealogy.

9384 ■ International Vital Records Handbook

Pub: Genealogical Publishing Company Inc.
Ed: Thomas Jay Kemp, Editor. **Released:** Triennial, latest edition 5th; 2009. **Price:** $49.95, individuals paperback. **Covers:** vital records offices for 67 countries and territories in North America, the British Isles and other English-speaking countries, and Europe. **Entries Include:** Office name, address, phone, application fees, method of payment, description of holdings, actual application forms to use in obtaining copies of records, and alternative record locations. **Arrangement:** Geographical.

9385 ■ The Source

Pub: The Generations Network
Ed: Lou Szucs, Editor. **Released:** Irregular. **Publication Includes:** Lists of federal archives, record centers, state archives, and historical societies, research libraries, heraldry and lineage societies, genealogy publications and publishers, sources of business records, and fraternal organizations. **Entries Include:** Name of the genealogical source, location, contents of the record, means of access, use in research or family history. Main content of the publication is discussion of records useful for research in American genealogy, including Native Americans, Jewish Americans, and African Americans. **Arrangement:** Classified by type of source. **Indexes:** Subject.

9386 ■ "Underworld Acquires Yukon Gold Property" in Canadian Corporate News (May 16, 2007)

Pub: Comtex News Network Inc.
Description: Underworld Resources Inc., a well-structured junior exploration company, announced that it has secured an option to earn a 100 percent right, title, and interest in the 11,850 acre White and Black Fox gold Properties in Yukon Territory, Canada. The company will be exploring both vein hosted and sedimentary hosted gold targets.

TRADE PERIODICALS

9387 ■ Ancestry

Pub: Palm Beach County Genealogical Society Inc.
Contact: Majorie W. Nelson, Circulation
E-mail: mwnelson69@aol.com
Released: Quarterly. **Price:** $20 volume. **Description:** Genealogical magazine.

9388 ■ Everton's Genealogical Helper & Genealogy Online

Pub: Everton Publishers Inc.
Contact: Walter Fuller, Publisher
Released: Bimonthly. **Price:** $27. **Description:** Genealogy magazine.

9389 ■ Family Findings

Pub: White Publishing Co.
Ed: Richard Cochrane, Editor. **Released:** Quarterly. **Price:** $15, individuals; $4, single issue. **Description:** Consists of genealogical news.

9390 ■ Genealogical Computing

Pub: MyFamily.com Inc.
Ed: Elizabeth Kelley Kerstens, Editor. **Released:** Quarterly. **Price:** $25, U.S.; $30, Canada; $35, elsewhere. **Description:** Focuses on the uses of personal computers for genealogical records management. Reviews and discusses the applications of various computer software and offers how-to articles and tips from users. Recurring features include program directories, survey results, letters to the editor, and interest group directories.

9391 ■ Genealogical Journal of Jefferson County, New York
Pub: NewYorkAncestry.com
Ed: Patricia R. James, Editor. **Released:** Quarterly. **Price:** $20 plus postage. **Description:** Journal of genealogical information.

9392 ■ Heartlines
Pub: Heart of America Genealogical Society
Contact: Marilyn R. Finke, President
Released: 4/year. **Description:** Supplies information on genealogical research resources, news of the Society and its library, news of other genealogical societies, and a list of library acquisitions.

9393 ■ The Hoosier Genealogist
Pub: Indiana Historical Society Press
Contact: M. Teresa Baer
Ed: M. Teresa Baer, Editor, tbaer@indianahistory.org. **Released:** Quarterly. **Price:** $40, members; $4, single issue. **Description:** Contains state and local historical and genealogical information.

9394 ■ Hunterdon Historical Newsletter
Pub: Hunterdon County Historical Society
Contact: Roxanne K. Carkhuff, Editorial Chair
Price: $15, individuals; $25, institutions. **Description:** Publishes local history and genealogy articles, as well as Society news. Recurring features include a collection, book reviews, and Notes and Queries, Acquisitions, and Family Associations.

9395 ■ Immigration Digest
Pub: Family History World
Ed: Arlene H. Eakle, PhD, Editor, eakle@xmission.com. **Released:** 3/year. **Price:** $13.50, single issue plus $3 shipping. **Description:** Reports on new resources to link immigrant ancestors with their origins. Includes analytical reviews of source books and passenger lists.

9396 ■ Irish Families
Pub: Irish Genealogical Foundation
Contact: Michael C. O'Laughline, Owner
Released: 12/year. **Price:** $54 6/year; $104 12/year; Included in membership. **Description:** Promotes research on Irish heritage and genealogy. Recurring features include letters to the editor, news of members, a calendar of events, news of research, and notices of publications available.

9397 ■ ISGS Newsletter
Pub: Illinois State Genealogical Society
Ed: Karl Moore, Editor. **Released:** Bimonthly. **Price:** Included in membership. **Description:** Keeps members abreast of what is going on in Illinois and surrounding areas in genealogy. Recurring features include a question and answer column.

9398 ■ Loyalist Gazette
Pub: United Empire Loyalists' Association of Canada
Ed: Robert McBride, Editour. **Released:** Semiannual. **Price:** $16; $30 two years; $43 three years; $23 other countries. **Description:** Scholarly journal covering history and genealogy related to the United Empire Loyalists and The Revolutionary War period.

9399 ■ The Maple Leaflet
Pub: French-Canadian Genealogical Society of Connecticut Inc.
Contact: Ivan N. Robinson, President
Ed: Ivan Robinson, Editor. **Released:** Quarterly, 2/year. **Price:** $20, members. **Description:** Contains articles on French-Canadian Genealogical Society of Connecticut's library events and new acquisitions.

9400 ■ Missouri State Genealogical Association Journal
Pub: Missouri State Genealogical Association
Contact: Jerry R. Ennis, Treas.
E-mail: jennis@charter.net
Ed: Robert M. Doerr, Editor, bdoerr@rollanet.org. **Released:** Quarterly. **Description:** Journal covering genealogy in Missouri.

9401 ■ National Genealogical Society Quarterly
Pub: National Genealogical Society
Ed: Thomas W. Jones, PhD, Editor. **Released:** Quarterly. **Price:** $12 printing. **Description:** Genealogy journal.

9402 ■ New England Connexion
Pub: New England Connexion
Contact: Nancy H. Smit
Ed: Nancy H. Smit, Editor. **Released:** Quarterly. **Price:** $10, individuals. **Description:** Covers New England genealogy.

9403 ■ New England Historical and Genealogical Register
Pub: New England Historic Genealogical Society
Ed: Henry B. Hoff, Editor, nehgreditor@aol.org. **Released:** Quarterly. **Description:** Scholarly journal focusing on genealogy and history.

9404 ■ NGS Newsmagazine
Pub: National Genealogical Society
Contact: R. Henderson
Ed: Elizabeth Kelley Kerstens, Editor, henderson@ngsgenealogical.org. **Released:** 4/year. **Price:** Included in membership. **Description:** Features news of the Society and the genealogical community, articles on genealogical methods, sources, repositories, and members' queries. Recurring features include a calendar of events.

9405 ■ Northern Arizona Genealogical Society Bulletin
Pub: Northern Arizona Genealogical Society
Ed: Virginia Grundvig, Editor, chichicoivig@juno.com. **Released:** Quarterly. **Price:** $15. **Description:** Focuses on the Society's activities and provides genealogical information.

9406 ■ Oklahoma Genealogical Society Quarterly
Pub: Oklahoma Genealogical Society
Released: Quarterly. **Price:** $15, single issue; $18 family. **Description:** Features information pertaining to local genealogy and history.

9407 ■ Oregon Genealogical Society Quarterly
Pub: Oregon Genealogical Society Inc.
Ed: Nancy Hodgkinson, Editor, nlh43@aol.com. **Released:** Quarterly. **Price:** $25, individuals; $3, single issue. **Description:** Contains information on the Society's activities, Oregon history, and genealogical research.

9408 ■ Polish Genealogical Society—Journal
Pub: Polish Genealogical Society of America Inc.
Ed: William F. Hoffman, Editor, wfhoffman@aol.com. **Released:** Quarterly. **Description:** Promotes research in Polish genealogies and heraldry. Carries information on research methodology, geographic locations, bibliographies, and selected histories. Recurring features include original material by professional genealogists and personal accounts by amateurs, letters to the editor, book reviews, news of research, an information-exchange section, and a question-and-answer column.

9409 ■ Presidential Families Gazette
Pub: Presidential Families of America
Contact: Dr. Lawrence Kent, Founder
Released: 3/year. **Price:** Included in membership. **Description:** Publishes general Society news and on subjects relating to Presidents of the U.S. and to their kin who are PFA members.

9410 ■ Research News
Pub: Family History World
Ed: Arlene H. Eakle, PhD, Editor, eakle@xmission.com. **Released:** Monthly. **Price:** $5.50, single issue; $25 one volume. **Description:** Carries practical information on genealogical research. Identifies new research methods, tools, and publications. Recurring features include statistics, book reviews, and news of research. Recurring features include Back issues available.

9411 ■ The Searcher
Pub: Southern California Genealogical Society & Family Research Library
Ed: Released: Bimonthly. **Price:** Included in membership; $2.50, individuals. **Description:** Contains articles and news pertaining to genealogy and family research. Recurring features include feature articles, genealogical records; listings of the Society's library acquisitions; news of members; editorials; book reviews; a calendar of events; letters to the editor; notices of seminars, workshops, and conferences; and columns titled Periodical News and Queries.

9412 ■ Voyageur Magazine
Pub: Voyageur Magazine
Contact: Bill Meindl, Publisher
Ed: Victoria Goff, Editor. **Released:** Semiannual, (June & Dec.). **Price:** $16. **Description:** Magazine on the history of a 26-county region of northeast Wisconsin.

FRANCHISES AND BUSINESS OPPORTUNITIES

9413 ■ Swyrich Corporation
Hall of Names Marketing
830 Development Dr.
Kingston, ON, Canada K7M 5V7
Ph:(613)384-2257
Free: 800-265-7099
Fax:(613)384-0606
No. of Franchise Units: 350. **No. of Company-Owned Units:** 2. **Founded:** 1968. **Franchised:** 1970. **Description:** offers history of names software. **Equity Capital Needed:** $7,500. **Franchise Fee:** $5,000. **Financial Assistance:** No. **Training:** Yes.

COMPUTERIZED DATABASES

9414 ■ American Journey: The African-American Experience
Cengage Learning Inc.
27500 Drake Rd.
Farmington Hills, MI 48331-3535
Ph:(248)699-4253
Free: 800-877-4253
Fax:(248)699-8069
Co. E-mail: galeord@gale.com
URL: http://gale.cengage.com
Description: Contains primary source letters and other documents providing an insight into the African-American experience. Includes African-Americans during the colonial period, African-Americans and the Civil War, African-Americans on the frontier, the history of African-American music, and the civil rights struggle. Corresponds to the online database of the same name. **Availability:** CD-ROM: Cengage Learning Inc. **Type:** Full text; Audio; Image.

9415 ■ Anthropological Literature Database
Harvard University
21 Divinity Ave.
Cambridge, MA 02138
Ph:(617)495-2253
Fax:(617)496-2741
Co. E-mail: tozref@fas.harvard.edu
URL: http://hcl.harvard.edu/libraries/tozzer
Description: Contains more than 570,000 records from approximately 4370 journals and monographic titles dealing with anthropology and other related disciplines, including archaeology, art history, biological/physical anthropology, cultural/social anthropology, economics, history, linguistics, music, religious studies, and sociology. Includes articles, reports, commentaries, review essays, and obituaries. Also includes the complete contents of Anthropological Literature: An Index to Periodical Articles and Essays (published in book form since 1979). **Availability:** Online: Harvard University. **Type:** Bibliographic.

9416 ■ Current Biography: 1940 to Present
EBSCO Publishing
10 Estes St.
Ipswich, MA 01938
Ph:(978)356-6500
Free: 800-653-2726
Fax:(978)356-6565
Co. E-mail: information@ebscohost.com
URL: http://www.ebscohost.com/wilson
Description: Contains more than 25,000 articles and obituaries for prominent people from 1940 to date. Users may conduct searches by keyword, name, profession, place of origin, race/ethnicity, birth date, and gender. Corresponds to the print Current Biography Yearbook. **Availability:** Online: EBSCO Publishing. **Type:** Full text.

9417 ■ *Family Tree Maker*
Ancestry.com Inc.
360 West 4800 North
Provo, UT 84604
Ph:(801)705-7000
Fax:(801)705-7001
Co. E-mail: support@ancestry.com
URL: http://corporate.ancestry.com
Description: Contains information on family genealogies researched and compiled by a variety of sources. Offers a selection of 26 CD-ROM titles, each available separately. **Availability:** CD-ROM: Ancestry.com Inc. **Type:** Directory.

9418 ■ *International Genealogical Index*
Church of Jesus Christ of Latter-Day Saints
35 NW Temple St., Ste. 344
Salt Lake City, UT 84150
Ph:(801)240-2584
Free: (866)406-1830
Fax:(801)240-1794
Co. E-mail: fhl@familysearch.org
URL: http://www.familysearch.org
Description: Indexes more than 280 million birth, christening, and marriage records. Available as part of the FamilySearch series. **Availability:** Online: Church of Jesus Christ of Latter-Day Saints. **Type:** Directory.

LIBRARIES

9419 ■ Adams County Genealogical Society Library
PO Box 231
West Union, OH 45693-0231
Ph:(937)386-2309
Co. E-mail: acgs@bright.net
URL: http://www.bright.net/lAtacgs
Contact: Ethel Chambers, Pres.
Scope: Genealogy, family histories, Adams County. **Services:** Copying; Library open to the public on a limited schedule. **Holdings:** 1200 books; 200 bound periodical volumes; 30 manuscripts; 50 archives; 100 reels of microfilm; 60 exchange newsletters.

9420 ■ American-Canadian Genealogical Society Library
4 Elm St.
PO Box 6478
Manchester, NH 03103-7242
Ph:(603)622-1554
Co. E-mail: acgs@acgs.org
URL: http://www.acgs.org/library/
Contact: Gerard Savard, Pres.
Scope: French-Canadian, American materials, genealogy, history. **Services:** Copying; Library open to the public (fee). **Holdings:** 4500 books; 3000 bound periodical volumes; family histories; town histories; marriage repertories, Quebec and some U.S. - New England; archival resources; maps. **Subscriptions:** 41 journals and other serials.

9421 ■ American-French Genealogical Society Library
PO Box 830
Woonsocket, RI 02895-0870
Ph:(401)765-6141
Fax:(401)597-6290
Co. E-mail: database@afgs.org
URL: http://www.afgs.org
Contact: Janice Burkhart, Pres./Libn.
Scope: French-American genealogy, vital records from Quebec and United States, family history and biography. **Services:** Library open to the public ($5 fee per visit for non-members). **Holdings:** 10,000 books; 1000 bound periodical volumes; microfilm; microfiche. **Subscriptions:** 114 journals and other serials.

9422 ■ Annie Halenbake Ross Library Special Collections
232 W. Main St.
Lock Haven, PA 17745
Ph:(570)748-3321

Fax:(570)748-1050
Co. E-mail: ross1@rosslibrary.org
URL: http://www.rosslibrary.org/
Contact: Diane L. Whitaker, Exec.Dir.
Scope: Pennsylvania, genealogy. **Services:** Interlibrary loan; copying; Library open to the public. **Holdings:** 133,608 books; 85 bound periodical volumes; 833 reels of microfilm. **Subscriptions:** 115 journals and other serials; 10 newspapers.

9423 ■ Atchison County Kansas Genealogical Society–Collection
Atchison Public Library
401 Kansas
Atchison, KS 66002-0303
Ph:(913)367-1902
Fax:(913)367-2717
Co. E-mail: ackgs2@yahoo.com
URL: http://skyways.lib.ks.us/genweb/society/atchison/ackgs.htm
Contact: Ollie Winzer, Libn.
Scope: Atchison County, Kansas, surrounding counties, Missouri, genealogy. **Services:** Library open to the public for reference use only. **Holdings:** 300 books; 10 bound periodical volumes; 34 reports; 30 microfiche; 400 reels of microfilm.

9424 ■ Barton County Historical Society
85 S. Hwy. 281
PO Box 1091
Great Bend, KS 67530-1091
Ph:(620)793-5125
Fax:(620)793-5125
Co. E-mail: director@bartoncountymuseum.org
URL: http://bartoncountymuseum.org/
Contact: Beverly Komarek, Exec.Dir.
Scope: Barton County, Kansas. **Services:** Copying; Library open to the public with restrictions. **Holdings:** Reports; manuscripts; archives. **Subscriptions:** 1 journal; 1 newspaper.

9425 ■ Branches and Twigs Genealogical Society–Collection
Kingman Carnegie Library
455 N. Main
Kingman, KS 67068-1395
Ph:(316)532-3061
Fax:(316)532-2528
Co. E-mail: kingc1lb@websurf.net
URL: http://skyways.lib.ks.us/library/kingman/
Contact: Grace G. Helm, Lib.Dir.
Scope: Genealogy. **Services:** Interlibrary loan; copying; SDI; Library open to the public. **Holdings:** 312 books; 8000 microfiche; 210 reels of microfilm; manuscripts. **Subscriptions:** 3 journals and other serials; 2 newspapers.

9426 ■ Brigham Young University–Family History Library
2250 Harold B. Lee Library
Provo, UT 84602
Ph:(801)422-6200
Fax:(801)422-0466
Co. E-mail: howard_bybee@byu.edu
URL: http://www.lib.byu.edu/sites/familyhistory
Contact: Howard Bybee, Family Hist.Libn.
Scope: Genealogy. **Services:** Scanning; copying; Center open to the public. **Holdings:** 35,000 journals, serials, and newspapers on microfilm; maps; online databases; primary and secondary source material in microform. **Subscriptions:** 50 journals and other serials; 400 newspapers.

9427 ■ British Columbia Genealogical Society Resource Centre
PO Box 88054
Richmond, BC, Canada V6X 3T6
Ph:(604)502-9119
Fax:(604)502-9119
Co. E-mail: bcgs@bcgs.ca
URL: http://www.bcgs.ca
Contact: Mrs. Betty Allen, Lib.Adm.
Scope: Genealogy, history. **Services:** Library open to the public on fee basis for non-members. **Holdings:** 6500 books; 250 bound periodical volumes; 200 reels of microfilm; 12,000 microfiche; Canadian census films; maps; 13,000 publication titles. **Subscriptions:** 275 journals and other serials.

9428 ■ Brooklyn Historical Society Library
4442 Ridge Rd.
PO Box 44422
Brooklyn, OH 44144-0422
Ph:(216)749-2804
Co. E-mail: groundhogsgarden@wowway.com
Contact: Edward Koschmann, VP
Scope: Brooklyn history, area history. **Services:** Library open to the public with restrictions. **Holdings:** Reports; area yearbooks; photographs; records; newspaper clippings, 1930-1964; maps; local newspapers.

9429 ■ Brown County Genealogy Society Library
PO Box 83
Georgetown, OH 45121
Ph:(937)378-2582
Contact: Ann Kenney
Scope: Local history, genealogy. **Services:** Copying; Library open to the public. **Holdings:** 300 books; microfilm; reports; archives; microfiche. **Subscriptions:** 350 journals and other serials.

9430 ■ Chase County Historical Society–Museum and Library
301 Broadway
PO Box 375
Cottonwood Falls, KS 66845
Ph:(316)273-8500
URL: http://skyways.lib.ks.us/genweb/society/cottonwd/
Contact: Pat Donelson, Cur.
Scope: Chase County history, genealogy. **Services:** Copying; Library open to the public. **Holdings:** 200 books; 85 reels of microfilm; Collectibles; pictures. **Subscriptions:** 1 newspaper.

9431 ■ Cherokee County Genealogical-Historical Society Library
100 S. Tennessee
PO Box 33
Columbus, KS 66725-0033
Ph:(620)429-2992
Co. E-mail: cckghs@columbus-ks.com
URL: http://skyways.lib.ks.us/genweb/cherokee/society/cckghs.html
Contact: Helen Kelley, Libn.
Scope: Genealogy - Cherokee County, Kansas. **Services:** Interlibrary loan; copying; research and copies for donation to society; Library open to the public. **Holdings:** 1100 books; 1000 reels of microfilm. **Subscriptions:** 22 journals and other serials.

9432 ■ Cherry County Historical Society
PO Box 1380
Valentine, NE 69201-0284
Ph:(402)376-2105
Co. E-mail: dtorg@threeriver.net
URL: http://www.rootsweb.com/lAtnecherry/
Contact: Jan Howell, Cur.
Scope: Genealogy. **Services:** Copying. **Holdings:** 300 books; 200 bound periodical volumes; 500 archival materials; 150 reels of microfilm; photographs; newspapers, 1887 to present.

9433 ■ Church of Jesus Christ of Latter-Day Saints–Cleveland, Ohio Stake Family History Center
c/o Philip Franklin
25000 Westwood Rd.
PO Box 45263
Westlake, OH 44145
Ph:(440)777-1518
URL: http://www.familysearch.org
Contact: Phil Franklin, Hd.Libn.
Scope: Genealogy. **Services:** Access to the microfilm collection of the main Center in Salt Lake City; Center open to the public. **Holdings:** 265 reels of microfilm of U.S., British, Canadian collections; 112 reels of microfilm of non-English speaking countries (continental European, Afro-Asian, Latin American, Iberian Peninsula, Scandinavian Collections).

9434 ■ Church of Jesus Christ of Latter-day Saints–Valley Forge, Pennsylvania Stake–Family History Center (721 P)
721 Paxon Hollow Rd.
Broomall, PA 19008
Ph:(610)356-8507
Contact: John Lee, Dir.
Scope: Genealogy. **Services:** Access to microfilm and microfiche records of the main Library in Salt Lake City; Center open to the public. **Holdings:** 1500 books; 42,000 microfiche; 1000 reels of microfilm.

9435 ■ Clarkesville-Habersham County Library
PO Box 2020
178 E. Green St.
Clarkesville, GA 30523
Ph:(706)754-4413
Fax:(706)754-3479
URL: http://www.habershamga.com/libraries.cfm
Scope: Genealogy, history. **Services:** Library open to the public; copying. **Holdings:** 45,000 books; 150 bound periodical volumes; 1000 CD-ROMs; 1000 videotapes; 300 audiocassettes. **Subscriptions:** 80 journals and other serials; 4 newspapers.

9436 ■ Collegiate Reformed Dutch Church Library
45 John St., Rm. 1000
New York, NY 10038-3706
Ph:(212)233-1960
Fax:(212)406-1856
Co. E-mail: rhollenga@collegiatechurch.org
URL: http://www.collegiatechurch.org
Contact: Maria Hollenga, Libn.
Scope: Genealogical data, 1633 to present. **Services:** Library not open to the public. **Holdings:** 45 books; archival materials; documents. **Subscriptions:** 20 journals and other serials.

9437 ■ Collin County Genealogical Society Library
PO Box 865052
Plano, TX 75086-5052
Ph:(972)769-4240
Co. E-mail: ccgs_nl_editor@hotmail.com
URL: http://www.rootsweb.com/lAttxcolcgs
Scope: Collin County, Texas history and genealogy. **Services:** Library open to the public with restrictions. **Holdings:** Figures not available.

9438 ■ Connecticut Society of Genealogist Library
175 Maple St.
East Hartford, CT 06118-2634
Ph:(860)569-0002
Fax:(860)569-0339
Co. E-mail: csginc@csginc.org
URL: http://www.csginc.org
Contact: Stephanie Hyland, Off.Mgr.
Scope: Genealogy. **Services:** Copying; Library open to the public. **Holdings:** Books; manuscripts; microfiche; CD-ROM.

9439 ■ Connecticut State Library–History and Genealogy Unit
231 Capitol Ave.
Hartford, CT 06106-1537
Ph:(860)757-6580
Fax:(860)757-6677
Co. E-mail: isref@cslib.org
URL: http://www.cslib.org/handg.htm
Contact: Richard C. Roberts, Unit Hd.
Scope: Genealogy, state history. **Services:** Library open to the public. **Holdings:** Books; bound periodical volumes; manuscripts; archives; microfiche; microfilms; patents; reports. **Subscriptions:** 75 journals and other serials; 75 newspapers.

9440 ■ Croatian Genealogical & Heraldic Society Library
2527 San Carlos Ave.
San Carlos, CA 94070
Ph:(415)592-1190

Fax:(415)592-1526
Co. E-mail: croatians@aol.com
URL: http://www.croatians.com
Contact: Adam S. Eterovich, Dir.
Scope: Genealogy, heraldry, census, Croatian history prior to 1900. **Services:** Library open to the public by appointment. **Holdings:** 2000 books; 20 bound periodical volumes; 20 drawers of index cards; 30 manuscripts. **Subscriptions:** 10 journals and other serials; 5 newspapers.

9441 ■ Darke County Historical Society Library
205 N. Broadway St.
PO Box 908
Greenville, OH 45331-0908
Co. E-mail: ahuffman@wesnet.com
URL: http://dcgs.dcoweb.org
Contact: Alice Huffman, Pres.
Scope: Genealogy, Darke County history. **Services:** Library open to the public for reference use only. **Holdings:** 1200 books; 20,000 microfiche; 5000 surname folders.

9442 ■ Decatur Genealogical Society Library
PO Box 1548
1255 W. South Side Dr.
Decatur, IL 62525-1548
Ph:(217)429-0135
Co. E-mail: decaturgensoc@att.net
URL: http://www.rootsweb.ancestry.com/lAtildecgs/library.htm
Contact: Cheri Hunter, Libn.
Scope: Genealogy; Macon County history. **Services:** Copying; Library open to the public for a nonimal fee. **Holdings:** 60,000 books; 16,000 bound periodical volumes; 5000 microfiche; census on microfilm; birth, marriage, court, and death and cemetery records; family histories; microfiche, microfilm. **Subscriptions:** 180 journals and other serials (some exchanges) and other serials.

9443 ■ Finney County Genealogical Society Library
403 S. 4th St.
PO Box 592
Garden City, KS 67846-0592
Co. E-mail: myravgormley@yahoo.com
URL: http://www.rootsweb.ancestry.com/lAtksfinney
Scope: Genealogy. **Services:** Copying; Library open to the public. **Holdings:** 1025 books; 427 periodical volumes; 500 reports; 1500 microfiche; 85 microfilm. **Subscriptions:** 14 journals and other serials.

9444 ■ Firelands Historical Society Library
9 Case Ave.
PO Box 572
Norwalk, OH 44857-0572
Ph:(419)663-0392
Contact: Henry Timman, Libn.
Scope: Genealogy, local history. **Services:** Copying; Library open to the public. **Holdings:** 5000 books; 10,000 archival materials; 50 reels of microfilm; photographs; manuscripts.

9445 ■ Franklin Area Historical Society Library
302 Park Ave.
Franklin, OH 45005-3549
Ph:(937)746-8295
Contact: Harriet Foley, Libn.
Scope: Franklin history, Warren County history, military history. **Services:** Library open to the public by appointment (and Sunday afternoon, April to November). **Holdings:** 940 books; 24 bound periodical volumes; vertical files. **Subscriptions:** 1 newspapers.

9446 ■ Frederic Remington Area Historical Society Library
PO Box 133
Whitewater, KS 67154
Ph:(316)799-2913
URL: http://skyways.lib.ks.us/towns/Brainerd
Contact: Melvin Epp, Pres.
Scope: Local history, local family history. **Services:** Library open to the public with restrictions. **Holdings:** 75 books; 100 manuscripts; 15 archive volumes; 600 slides on CD; 101 reels of microfilm; 36 videotapes.

9447 ■ French-Canadian Genealogical Society of Connecticut, Inc.–French-Canadian Genealogical Library
53 Tolland Green
PO Box 928
Tolland, CT 06084-0928
Ph:(860)872-2597
Co. E-mail: hoffman@fcgsc.org
URL: http://www.fcgsc.org/library.htm
Contact: Germaine Hoffman, Lib.Dir.
Scope: French-Canadian genealogy and history. **Services:** Copying; Library open to the public with restrictions. **Holdings:** 3000 books; 500 bound periodical volumes; 550 other cataloged items; 10,000 index cards on Acadians; index to 10,000 births, deaths, and marriages of Franco-Americans in Connecticut; 5000 index cards on Worcester County, Massachusetts, area; maps; periodicals.

9448 ■ German-Texan Heritage Society–Charles G. Trenckmann Memorial Library
PO Box 684171
507 E. 10th St.
Austin, TX 78768-4171
Ph:(512)482-0927
Free: (866)482-4847
Fax:(512)482-0636
Co. E-mail: info@germantexans.org
URL: http://germantexans.org/
Contact: Jean Warneke, Exec.Dir.
Scope: German cultural heritage of Texas, German Texana, genealogy, Texas history, German history, German literature, travel to Germany. **Services:** Library open to the public for reference use only. **Holdings:** 472 pioneer books; 1150 research books; 50 manuscripts; 163 multimedia materials; 400 archival materials; microfiche. **Subscriptions:** 10 journals and other serials.

9449 ■ Godfrey Memorial Library
134 Newfield St.
Middletown, CT 06457-2534
Ph:(860)346-4375
Fax:(860)347-9874
Co. E-mail: library@godfrey.org
URL: http://www.godfrey.org
Contact: James Benn, Dir.
Scope: Genealogy, local history, biography. **Services:** Genealogical research; copying; Library open to the public. **Holdings:** 18,000 books; microfiche; microfilm. **Subscriptions:** 3 journals and other serials.

9450 ■ Greeley County Historical Society Library
PO Box 231
Tribune, KS 67879
Ph:(620)376-4996
Co. E-mail: greeley@pld.com
Contact: Nadine Cheney, Cur.
Scope: Kansas history, genealogy, agriculture, poetry, diaries. **Services:** Copying; email; Library open to the public. **Holdings:** 500 books, maps, newspapers, telephone directories, soldier's enrollments, Civil War and obituaries; reports; manuscripts; patents; archives; microfilm. **Subscriptions:** 4 journals and other serials.

9451 ■ Guysborough Historical Society Archives
PO Box 232
Guysborough, NS, Canada B0H 1N0
Ph:(902)533-4008
Fax:(902)533-2258
Co. E-mail: guysborough.historical@ns.sympatico.ca
URL: http://www.guysboroughcountyheritage.ca
Contact: Judy Webber Hayne, Cur.
Scope: Local history, genealogy, historical research. **Services:** Copying; Library open to members only. **Holdings:** Books; reports.

9452 ■ Hamilton City Library–Bluestem Genealogical Society Collection
21 E. Main St.
Hamilton, KS 66853
Ph:(770)678-3646

Fax:(770)678-3646
Co. E-mail: hclibrary66853@yahoo.com
URL: http://hamiltoncity.mykansaslibrary.org
Contact: Janice Ashley, Dir./Libn.
Scope: Genealogy - Greenwood County, Kansas, U.S. **Services:** Interlibrary loan; Library open to the public with restrictions. **Holdings:** 100 books; 100 bound periodical volumes; 21 reels of microfilm. **Subscriptions:** 50 journals and other serials.

9453 ■ Harper County Genealogical Society Library
c/o Harper Public Library
1002 Oak St.
Harper, KS 67058
Ph:(620)896-2959
Co. E-mail: harperlib@cyberlodge.com
URL: http://skyways.lib.ks.us/genweb/society/harper/
Contact: Tina Welch, Libn.
Scope: Harper County (Kansas) history; Kansas history; genealogy. **Services:** Library open to the public for reference use only. **Holdings:** 400 books; 1 microfiche; 11 reels of microfilm.

9454 ■ Haskell County Historical Society
Fairgrounds
PO Box 101
Sublette, KS 67877
Ph:(316)675-8344
Co. E-mail: museum@pld.com
Scope: Local history. **Services:** Library open to the public for reference use only. **Holdings:** 59 reels of microfilm; 60 yearbooks. **Subscriptions:** 2 journals and other serials; 1 newspaper.

9455 ■ Heritage Commission Corporation Library
147 W. Mound St.
PO Box 457
South Charleston, OH 45368
Ph:(937)462-7277
Contact: Janice Brubaker, Sec.
Scope: Local history, genealogy, D.T&I Railroad. **Services:** Interlibrary loan; Library open to the public. **Holdings:** 100 books; 25 feet of archival material. **Subscriptions:** 10 journals and other serials.

9456 ■ HeritageQuest Library
500 N. Marketplace Dr., Ste. 222
PO Box 549
Centerville, UT 84014
Ph:(801)298-5358
Fax:(801)298-5468
Co. E-mail: custserv@heritagequest.com
URL: http://www.heritagequestonline.com
Contact: Chris Cowan, Lib.Dir.
Scope: Genealogy. **Services:** Microfilming. **Holdings:** 250,000 reels of microfilm including census records, mortality schedules, ship passenger lists, military records, vital records, deeds, wills, tax lists, county and family histories; 250 CD-ROMs; books; indexes; digital CDs.

9457 ■ Houston Public Library–Clayton Library–Center for Genealogical Research (5300)
5300 Caroline St.
Houston, TX 77004-6896
Ph:(832)393-2600
URL: http://www.hpl.lib.tx.us/clayton
Contact: Susan Kaufman, Mgr.
Scope: Genealogy. **Services:** Copying; Center open to the public. **Holdings:** 75,000 books; 3000 bound periodical volumes; 80,000 reels of microfilm; 60,000 microfiche; VF material. **Subscriptions:** 285 journals and other serials.

9458 ■ Huguenot Society of America Library
General Society of Mechanics and Tradesmen Bldg., Ste. 510
20 W 44th St.
New York, NY 10036
Ph:(212)755-0592

Fax:(212)317-0676
Co. E-mail: hugsoc@verizon.net
URL: http://www.huguenotsocietyofamerica.org
Scope: French Huguenot migration to America, Huguenot history in France and elsewhere, biography, genealogy. **Services:** Copying; Library open on a limited schedule and by appointment. **Holdings:** 10,000 items; 30 manuscripts; 20 autograph letters.

9459 ■ Huguenot Society of South Carolina Library
138 Logan St.
Charleston, SC 29401
Ph:(843)723-3235
Fax:(843)853-8476
Co. E-mail: archivist@huguenotsociety.org
URL: http://www.huguenotsociety.org/library.htm
Contact: Harriott Cheves Leland, Archv./Res.
Scope: Genealogical data on Huguenots and allied families. **Services:** Library open to the public. **Holdings:** 4500 volumes; 16 VF drawers of genealogical data; microfilm; microfiche; CDs; 2200 vertical files. **Subscriptions:** 19 journals and other serials.

9460 ■ Huxford Genealogical Society, Inc.–Huxford Library
PO Box 595
Homerville, GA 31634
Ph:(912)487-2310
Fax:(912)487-3881
Co. E-mail: huxford@windstream.net
URL: http://www.huxford.com/library.htm
Contact: Sharon James Keith, Libn.
Scope: Genealogy. **Services:** Copying; research Library open to nonmembers on a fee basis. **Holdings:** 4000 volumes; 1300 family surname files; 79 boxes of magazines; 600 boxes of microfilm; reports; manuscripts; archives; Georgia Death Index; Florida Death Index. **Subscriptions:** 2000 journals and other serials.

9461 ■ Jackson County Public Library–Indiana & Jackson County History and Genealogy Collection
303 W. 2nd St.
Seymour, IN 47274
Ph:(812)522-3412
Fax:(812)522-5456
Co. E-mail: csellers@myjclibrary.org
URL: http://www.myjclibrary.org/services/information/localhistory
Contact: Charlotte Sellers, Local Hist.Spec.
Scope: Indiana and Jackson County genealogy and history. **Services:** Library open to the public. **Holdings:** Books; maps; microfiche; microfilm; records; papers; pictures. **Subscriptions:** 2 journals and other serials.

9462 ■ James A. Garfield Historical Society Library
8107 Main St.
Garrettsville, OH 44231
Co. E-mail: garfieldhistoricalsociety@yahoo.com
URL: http://garfield.sparcc.org/history/about.htm
Contact: Gary Twardzik, Chm.
Scope: Garrettsville history. **Services:** Library open to the public with restrictions.

9463 ■ Jewish Historical Society of New York, Inc. Library
8 W. 70th St.
New York, NY 10023
Ph:(212)415-5544
Co. E-mail: swsiegel@pipeline.com
Contact: Steven W. Siegel, Pres.
Scope: American and New York Jewish history, Jewish genealogy. **Services:** Provides telephone and email reference service only. **Holdings:** Figures not available.

9464 ■ Judah L. Magnes Museum–Western Jewish History Center
2911 Russell St.
Berkeley, CA 94705
Ph:(510)549-6950, x356

Fax:(510)849-3673
Co. E-mail: wjhc@magnes.org
URL: http://www.magnes.org/collections/archives/western-jewish-americana
Contact: Aaron T. Kornblum, Archv.
Scope: The history and experiences of the Jewish community in the thirteen western United States, particularly relating to the San Francisco Bay Area. **Services:** Copying; Center open by appointment only. **Holdings:** 336 rolls of microfilm; 677 archival collections; 288 audio tapes (89 oral histories); books; vertical subject file; photographs.

9465 ■ Kings County Museum Library
37 Cornwallis St.
Kentville, NS, Canada B4N 2E2
Ph:(902)678-6237
Fax:(902)678-2764
Co. E-mail: museum@okcm.ca
URL: http://www.okcm.ca
Contact: Bria Stokesbury, Cur.
Scope: Genealogy, local history. **Services:** Copying; Library open to the public for a fee. **Holdings:** 300 books; 2000 archival materials; 100 microfiche; 200 reels of microfilm. **Subscriptions:** 4 journals and other serials.

9466 ■ Kittochtinny Historical Society Library
175 E. King St.
Chambersburg, PA 17201
Ph:(717)264-1667
Co. E-mail: history@pa.net
URL: http://www.rootsweb.com/lAtpakhs/
Contact: Lillian F. Colletta
Scope: History, genealogy. **Services:** Library open to the public on a limited schedule. **Holdings:** Books; manuscripts; newspapers (microfilm, hard copy); cemetery records; funeral directors' records; abstracts of wills; family files; historical files; historical photographs. **Subscriptions:** 3 journals and other serials.

9467 ■ Lake Erie Islands Historical Society Library
PO Box 25
25 Town Hall Pl.
Put-in-Bay, OH 43456
Ph:(419)285-2804
Fax:(419)285-3814
Co. E-mail: director@leihs.org
URL: http://www.leihs.org
Scope: Battle of Lake Erie, early trimotor aviation, Lake Erie western basin history, John Brown Jr., Put-in-Bay and Lake Erie steamships. **Services:** Copying; Library open to the public at librarian's discretion. **Holdings:** 800 books; reports; 3500 archival materials; genealogical files; manuscripts; microfilm. **Subscriptions:** 6 journals and other serials.

9468 ■ Leavenworth County Historical Society and Museum Library
1128 5th Ave.
Leavenworth, KS 66048
Ph:(913)682-7759
Fax:(913)682-7759
Co. E-mail: leavenworthhistory@sbcglobal.net
URL: http://www.leavenworthhistory.org/default.aspx
Contact: Mark Bureman, Musm.Adm.
Scope: Leavenworth County history, genealogy. **Services:** Copying; Library open to the public. **Holdings:** 1000 books; 10,000 archival materials; microfilm. **Subscriptions:** 3 journals and other serials.

9469 ■ Library of Congress–Humanities and Social Sciences Division–Local History & Genealogy Reading Room (101 I)
101 Independence Ave., SE
Thomas Jefferson Bldg., LJ G42
Washington, DC 20540-4660
Ph:(202)707-5537
Fax:(202)707-1957
URL: http://www.loc.gov/rr/genealogy
Contact: Judith P. Roach, Team Hd.
Scope: U.S. local history; genealogy - International in scope. **Services:** Copying; section open to adults only. **Holdings:** Books; vertical files; manuscripts; microfilms; newspapers; photographs; maps.

9470 ■ Madison County Historical Society Library
260 E. High St.
PO Box 124
London, OH 43140
Ph:(740)852-2977
Co. E-mail: lplgen@oplin.org
URL: http://hometown.aol.com/payne3467/mchs.html
Contact: Dorthy Richmond, Musm.Dir.
Scope: Madison County history. **Services:** Library open to the public. **Holdings:** 2000 books.

9471 ■ Manitoba Genealogical Society Inc.–MGS Reosurce Center and Library
E-1045 St. James St.
Winnipeg, MB, Canada R3H 1B1
Ph:(204)783-9139
Fax:(204)783-0190
Co. E-mail: library@mbgenealogy.com
URL: http://www.mbgenealogy.com/index.php?page=library-resources
Contact: Mary Bole, Libn.
Scope: Large collection of Manitoba local history books; 1279 transcripts of Manitoba cemeteries; Anglican, Roman Catholic and United Church BMD indexes; all Manitoba census returns; a good collections of Ontario, Saskatchewan and Great Britain material. **Services:** Library open to the public on Tuesday to Thursday (free to members but $5 per day for visitors). **Holdings:** 8000 volumes; genealogical resource periodicals; microfilm; microfiche; CD-ROMs, directories, telephone books. **Subscriptions:** 120 journals and other serials.

9472 ■ Marion Area Genealogical Society Library
169 E. Church St.
PO Box 844
Marion, OH 43301-0844
Ph:(740)387-4255
Fax:(740)387-0117
Co. E-mail: mchist@gte.net
URL: http://www.rootsweb.com/lAtohmags/
Contact: Maxine Marshall, Geneal.
Scope: Marion County history, Ohio history, genealogy, Marion city history. **Services:** Copying; Library open to the public. **Holdings:** 250 books; 100 bound periodical volumes; 50 reports.

9473 ■ McAllen Memorial Library–McAllen Genealogical Society Collection
Main Library, 1st Fl.
601 N. Main St.
McAllen, TX 78501
Ph:(956)688-3300
Co. E-mail: genref@mcallen.net
URL: http://www.mcallenlibrary.net/research/genealogy.aspx
Contact: Jose A. Gamez, Lib.Dir.
Scope: Genealogy. **Services:** Copying; Library open to the public. **Holdings:** 6500 books; 640 bound periodical volumes. **Subscriptions:** 20 journals and other serials.

9474 ■ Mennonite Historians of Eastern Pennsylvania MHEP–Mennonite Historical Library & Archives
Mennonite Heritage Center
565 Yoder Rd.
Harleysville, PA 19438-1020
Ph:(215)256-3020
Fax:(215)256-3023
Co. E-mail: alderferjoel@mhep.org
URL: http://www.mhep.org/index.php?id_pag=4
Contact: Joel D. Alderfer, Libn./Cur.
Scope: History - Mennonite church, Anabaptist, local; genealogy; folklore; church music; Pennsylvania Germans; peace and non-resistance. **Services:** Copying; microfilm reader and printer; Library open to the public. **Holdings:** 12,000 books; 786 bound periodical volumes; 393 manuscript collections; 592 bound church bulletins; 236 reels of microfilm; 2075 audiocassettes; 3500 photographs; archival collections (668 linear shelf ft.); 61 videotapes; 650 flat file items (broadsides, posters, prints, and maps); 480

vertical and genealogical files; 130 transcripts (church and cemetery records, diaries, account books). **Subscriptions:** 130 journals and other serials; 30 newspapers.

9475 ■ Milford Area Historical Society Library
906 Main St.
Milford, OH 45150
Ph:(513)248-0324
Contact: Maxine Van Aken, Libn.
Scope: Local history, genealogy. **Services:** Copying; Library open to the public. **Holdings:** 250 books; 30 bound periodical volumes; 150 archival items; 200 photographs.

9476 ■ The Montgomery County KS Genealogy Society Library
PO Box 444
Coffeyville, KS 67337-0444
Ph:(620)251-1370
Fax:(316)251-1512
Co. E-mail: royd@hit.net
URL: http://www.rootsweb.com/lAtksmontgo/
Contact: Karyl Buffington
Scope: Genealogy. **Services:** Interlibrary loan; copying; Library open to the public. **Holdings:** Archival materials; newspapers and censuses; microfiche; reels of microfilm; obits (1975-1995). **Subscriptions:** 12 journals and other serials.

9477 ■ Montgomery's Inn Museum–Heritage Resource Centre
4709 Dundas St. W
Etobicoke, ON, Canada M9A 1A8
Ph:(416)394-8113
Fax:(416)394-6027
Co. E-mail: montinn@toronto.ca
URL: http://www.toronto.ca/culture/museums/montgomery.htm
Contact: Randall Reid, Sr.Prog.Off.
Scope: Decorative arts, local history, genealogy. **Services:** Library open to the public for reference use only. **Holdings:** 1000 books.

9478 ■ Napa Valley Genealogical & Biographical Society Library
1701 Menlo Ave.
Napa, CA 94558
Ph:(707)252-2252
Co. E-mail: nvgbs@earthlink.net
URL: http://www.napavalleygenealogy.org
Contact: Sandra Hoover, Libn.
Scope: Genealogy. **Services:** Copying; Library open to the public on fee basis. **Holdings:** 6000 books; Hartford Times; family and surname files, census microfilm.

9479 ■ National Society of the Sons of the American Revolution–Genealogy Library
804 W. Main St.
Louisville, KY 40202
Ph:(502)589-1776
Fax:(502)589-1671
Co. E-mail: library@sar.org
URL: http://www.sar.org/library/library.html
Contact: Michael A. Christian, Lib.Dir.
Scope: American history and genealogy, Revolutionary War, Colonial America. **Services:** Copying; Library open to the public on a fee basis. **Holdings:** 40,000 books; 2800 volumes periodicals; 15,000 microforms. **Subscriptions:** 20 journals and other serials.

9480 ■ National Society of the Sons of Utah Pioneers Library
3301 E. 2920 S.
Salt Lake City, UT 84109
Ph:(801)484-4441
Free: (866)724-1847
Fax:(801)484-2067
Co. E-mail: sup1847@comcast.com
URL: http://www.sonsofutahpioneers.org/about/suplibrary/
Contact: Marilyn Johnson, Lib.Dir.
Scope: Genealogy, pioneer history. **Services:** Library open to the public for reference use only. **Holdings:** 5000 books; 5000 personal pioneer histories; articles;

family histories; old photographs; genealogical histories; magazines; microfiche; films; manuscripts; archives; microfiche. **Subscriptions:** 10 journals and other serials.

9481 ■ Ness County Historical Society Library
113 S. Iowa St.
Ness City, KS 67560-1992
Ph:(785)798-3415
Fax:(785)798-2313
Co. E-mail: director@nesscitylibrary.org
URL: http://skyways.lib.ks.us/towns/NessCity/museum.html
Contact: Jean Schlegel, Dir.
Scope: History of Ness County, Kansas; antiques; cemetery information. **Services:** Interlibrary loan; copying; Library open to the public. **Holdings:** 17,000 books; 100 bound periodical volumes; microfilm; artifacts. **Subscriptions:** 4 journals and other serials.

9482 ■ New York Genealogical and Biographical Society Library
36 W. 44th St., 7th Fl.
New York, NY 10036-8105
Ph:(212)626-6850
Fax:(212)626-6857
Co. E-mail: library@nygbs.org
URL: http://www.newyorkfamilyhistory.org
Contact: Edward Smith, Dir.
Scope: Genealogy, biography, U.S. and local history. **Services:** Copying by mail; Library search services by mail; Library open to the public with limitations (membership available to all). **Holdings:** 80,000 volumes; 4800 bound periodical volumes; 33,000 manuscripts; 14,000 reels of microfilm; 9000 microfiche; 250 CDs; 80 audiocassettes. **Subscriptions:** 1320 journals and other serials.

9483 ■ Norfolk Historical Society Archives
Norfolk Heritage Centre
109 Norfolk St., S.
Simcoe, ON, Canada N3Y 2W3
Ph:(519)426-1583
Fax:(519)426-1584
Co. E-mail: office@norfolklore.com
URL: http://www.norfolklore.com
Contact: Scott Gillies, Mgr./Cur.
Scope: History - local, Ontario, United States, Europe; census; vital statistics; cemeteries; churches. **Services:** Microfilm loan services; copying; Library open to non-members for a fee. **Holdings:** 4000 books; 3000 bound periodical volumes; 1000 microfiche; 2000 reels of microfilm; archives.

9484 ■ North York Central Library–Canadiana Department
5120 Yonge St.
Toronto, ON, Canada M2N 5N9
Ph:(416)395-5535
Fax:(416)395-5668
Co. E-mail: khuntley@torontopubliclibrary.ca
URL: http://www.torontopubliclibrary.ca/detail.jsp?R=LIB01
Contact: Kim Huntley, Mgr.
Scope: North York history, genealogy, local history of Ontario and historical Canadiana. **Services:** Copying; collection open to the public for reference use only. **Holdings:** Over 125,000 monographs; microfilm. **Subscriptions:** 100 journals and other serials and newspapers.

9485 ■ Norwegian American Genealogical Center and Naeseth Library
415 W. Main St.
Madison, WI 53703-3116
Ph:(608)255-2224
Fax:(608)255-6842
Co. E-mail: genealogy@nagcnl.org
URL: http://www.nagcnl.org
Contact: Blaine Hedberg, Exec.Dir.
Scope: Norwegian-American genealogy and history. **Services:** Copying; Library open to the public by appointment. **Holdings:** 3100 books; 3800 reels of microfilm; 60 notebooks. **Subscriptions:** 45 journals and other serials.

9486 ■ Norwegian-American Historical Association Archives
1510 St. Olaf Ave.
Rolvaag Library
St. Olaf College
Northfield, MN 55057-1097
Ph:(507)786-3229
Fax:(507)786-3734
Co. E-mail: naha-archivists@stolaf.edu
URL: http://www.naha.stolaf.edu/archives/index.htm
Contact: Gary DeKrey, Archv.
Scope: Norwegian-American history, genealogy, and culture. **Services:** Interlibrary loan (through St. Olaf College Library; PALS); archives open to the public by appointment. **Holdings:** 8000 books; 1500 bound periodical volumes; newspapers; correspondence; diaries, scrapbooks; obituaries; photographs. **Subscriptions:** 15 journals and other serials.

9487 ■ Ohio Genealogical Society–Coshocton County Chapter Library
PO Box 128
Coshocton, OH 43812-0128
Ph:(740)622-4706
Fax:(740)622-4706
Co. E-mail: bjoans@tusco.net
URL: http://www.coshoctongenealogy.org/
Contact: Joan Sheets, Pres.
Scope: Genealogy. **Holdings:** Figures not available.

9488 ■ Ohio Genealogical Society–Perry County, Ohio Chapter (OGS) Library
PO Box 275
Junction City, OH 43748-0275
Ph:(740)342-4194
Co. E-mail: susays@columbus.rr.com
URL: http://perrycountychapterogs.org
Contact: Sue Saylor, Treas.
Scope: Genealogy. **Services:** Copying; genealogical searches. **Holdings:** 2000 books; 100 bound periodical volumes; 100 manuscripts; 100 microfiche; 43 microfilm.

9489 ■ Perry Historians Library
763 Dix Hill Rd.
New Bloomfield, PA 17068
Ph:(717)582-4896
Co. E-mail: djzinn@pa.net
URL: http://www.ThePerryHistorians.org
Contact: Donna Zinn
Scope: Genealogy, local history. **Services:** Copying; Library open to the public on a limited schedule; provides genealogical and historical research services. **Holdings:** 5000 books; 500 reels of microfilm; 1000 land drafts; 4500 family surname files; 1 million index cards. **Subscriptions:** 9 journals and other serials.

9490 ■ Rawlins County Genealogical Society Library
PO Box 405
Atwood, KS 67730-0405
Ph:(785)626-3805
Fax:(785)626-3805
Co. E-mail: atwoodli@ruraltel.net
URL: http://skyways.lib.ks.us/genweb/rawlins/rawgenesoc.html
Contact: Delores Luedke, Res.
Scope: Genealogy. **Services:** Library open to the public for reference use only. **Holdings:** Figures not available.

9491 ■ Rock Island County Illinois Genealogical Society Library
822 11th Ave.
Moline, IL 61265-1221
Ph:(309)764-8590
Co. E-mail: ricigs@frontiernet.net
URL: http://www.rootsweb.ancestry.com/lAtilbgsrim/index.html
Contact: Deb Van Sant, Libn.
Scope: Genealogy. **Services:** Library open to the public. **Holdings:** 12,000 books; 800 bound periodical volumes; 100 microfiche; 50 CD-ROMs. **Subscriptions:** 20 journals and other serials.

9492 ■ Ross County Genealogical Society Library
PO Box 6352
Chillicothe, OH 45601
Ph:(740)773-2715
Co. E-mail: rcgs@bright.net
URL: http://www.rootsweb.com/lAtohrcgs
Contact: Kathy Wright, Libn.
Scope: Genealogy. **Services:** Copying; Library open to the public. **Holdings:** Books; microfiche; reels of microfilm.

9493 ■ Russell County Historical Society Library
331 Kansas St.
PO Box 245
Russell, KS 67665
Ph:(785)483-3637
Co. E-mail: rchs@russellks.net
URL: http://www.rwisp.com/lAtrchs/
Contact: Pauline Bender
Scope: Genealogy; history - county and general. **Services:** Copying; Library open to the public. **Holdings:** 300 books; 750 archival items; 3000 microfiche. **Subscriptions:** 2 journals and other serials.

9494 ■ St. Clair Shores Public Library–Local History Center
22500 E. 11 Mile Rd.
St. Clair Shores, MI 48081
Ph:(586)771-9020
Fax:(586)771-8935
Co. E-mail: orlandor@libcoop.net
URL: http://www.libcoop.net/stclairshores/
Contact: Rosemary Orlando, Lib.Dir.
Scope: Michigan history and genealogy. **Services:** Library open to the public. **Holdings:** Books and periodicals; photographs.

9495 ■ St. Louis Genealogical Society Library
1640 S. Lindbergh Blvd.
St. Louis, MO 63143-0010
Ph:(314)647-8547
Fax:(314)647-8548
Co. E-mail: library@stlgs.org
URL: http://www.stlgs.org
Contact: Barbara McLean, Libn.
Scope: Genealogy, family histories. **Services:** Copying; limited genealogical research (fee based); Library open to the public. **Holdings:** 20,000 items including books, journals, maps, and CDs. **Subscriptions:** 275 journals and other serials.

9496 ■ Scarborough Historical Society–Scarborough Archives
6282 Kingston Rd.
Scarborough, ON, Canada M1K 5C4
Ph:(416)396-6930
Co. E-mail: info@scarboroughhistorical.com
URL: http://www.scarboroughhistorical.com/archives/
Scope: History, genealogy. **Services:** Copying; microfilm/microfiche reading; archives open to the public by appointment. **Holdings:** 800 published volumes.

9497 ■ Shenandoah County Library–Local History and Genealogy Collection
514 Stoney Creek Blvd.
Edinburg, VA 22824
Ph:(540)984-8200
Fax:(540)984-8207
URL: http://www.shenandoah.co.lib.va.us
Contact: Ed Hoole, Chm.
Scope: Shenandoah County and the Shenandoah Valley history and genealogy; Civil War; Pennsylvania; Maryland; West Virginia; Virginia. **Services:** Copying; Library open to the public. **Holdings:** Books; microforms; microfilm; records; photographs; letters; archival materials; Civil War materials. **Subscriptions:** 30 journals and other serials; 6 newspapers.

9498 ■ Societe de Genealogie de Quebec Library
C.P. 9066
Ste. Foy, QC, Canada G1V 4A8
Ph:(418)651-9127

Fax:(418)651-2643
Co. E-mail: sgq@total.net
URL: http://www.sgq.qc.ca
Contact: Mariette Parent, Libn.
Scope: Genealogy. **Services:** Copying; Library open to the public ($5 fee for non-members). **Holdings:** 10,000 books; microfiche; microfilm; archives. **Subscriptions:** 120 journals and other serials.

9499 ■ Southern Ohio Genealogical Society Reference Library
PO Box 414
Hillsboro, OH 45133
URL: http://www.sogs.info
Contact: Pat Young, Libn.
Scope: Genealogy, local history. **Services:** Library open to the public. **Holdings:** 1200 books; 250 bound periodical volumes; 100 family files; 85 family history files; 3700 burial records of veterans buried in Highland County, OH; 83 volumes of published family histories; 75 family history manuscripts; census maps; passenger and immigration records.

9500 ■ Stafford County Historical & Genealogical Society Library
100 N. Main St.
Stafford, KS 67578
Ph:(620)234-5664
Co. E-mail: mjhathaway61@earthlink.net
URL: http://home.earthlink.net/lAtmjhathaway61
Contact: Michael Hathaway, Exec.Sec.
Scope: Stafford County and Kansas history. **Services:** Library open to the public. **Holdings:** 5000 books; 23 reels of microfilm; 20 manuscripts; 10 patents; 1000 archives folders; 29,000 Gray Studio glass plate negatives. **Subscriptions:** Stafford Courier and St. John News.

9501 ■ Thomas Raddall Research Centre Archives
PO Box 1078
Liverpool, NS, Canada B0T 1K0
Ph:(902)354-4058
Co. E-mail: rafusela@gov.ns.ca
URL: http://www.queensmuseum.netfirms.com/archives.html
Contact: Linda Rafuse, Dir.
Scope: Genealogy, local history, businesses, shipping. **Services:** Copying; Library open to the public. **Holdings:** 100 books; 100 bound periodical volumes; 600 archival files; 2500 microfiche; 300 reels of microfilm. **Subscriptions:** 2 journals and other serials.

9502 ■ W.A. Rankin Memorial Library
502 Indiana St.
Neodesha, KS 66757
Ph:(620)325-3275
Co. E-mail: rankin.library@neodesha.net
URL: http://www.rootsweb.ancestry.com/lAtkswarml
Contact: Mary Meckley, Dir.
Scope: Local history, family genealogies. **Services:** Interlibrary loan; copying; Library open to the public. **Holdings:** 20,000 books; 200 reels of microfilm. **Subscriptions:** 50 magazines; 5 newspapers.

9503 ■ Warren County Genealogical Society Library
406 Justice Dr.
Lebanon, OH 45036-0296
Ph:(513)695-1144
Co. E-mail: wcgs@co.warren.oh.us
URL: http://www.co.warren.oh.us/genealogy/index.htm
Contact: Dana Palmer, Pres.
Scope: Genealogy. **Services:** Copying; research on Warren families for small fee; Library open to the public. **Holdings:** 3000 volumes; microfiche; microfilm. **Subscriptions:** 70 journals and other serials.

9504 ■ Washington County Historical & Genealogical Society Library
PO Box 31
216 Ballard St.
Washington, KS 66968
Ph:(785)325-2198

Fax:(785)325-2198
Co. E-mail: wchgs31@hotmail.com
URL: http://skyways.lib.ks.us/genweb/washingt/wchs.
htm
Contact: Jack Barley, Pres.
Scope: Washington County history, Washington County genealogy. **Services:** Copying; Library open to the public. **Holdings:** Microfilm newspapers.

9505 ■ West Hants Historical Society–Genealogies Collections
281 King St.
PO Box 2335
Windsor, NS, Canada B0N 2T0
Ph:(902)798-4706
Fax:(902)798-8535
Co. E-mail: whhs@ns.aliantzinc.ca
URL: http://www.westhantshistoricalsociety.ca
Contact: Lilla Siderius, Geneal.
Scope: Genealogy, local history. **Services:** Copying; Library open to the public on a limited schedule and by appointment. **Holdings:** 400 books; 12 reels of microfilm; maps. **Subscriptions:** 2 journals and other serials.

9506 ■ Wichita Genealogical Society Library
PO Box 3705
Wichita, KS 67201-3705
URL: http://www.wichitagensoc.org
Contact: Sage Joyner, Lib. Liaison
Scope: Genealogy, local history. **Services:** Library open to the public. **Holdings:** Figures not available.

9507 ■ World Jewish Genealogy Organization Library
1605 48th St.
Brooklyn, NY 11219-0009
Ph:(718)435-4400
Fax:(718)633-7050
Contact: Rabbi N. Halberstam, Libn.
Scope: Judaica. **Services:** Library not open to the public. **Holdings:** 12,000 books.

RESEARCH CENTERS

9508 ■ College of Southern Maryland–Southern Maryland Studies Center
8730 Mitchell Rd.
PO Box 910
La Plata, MD 20646-0910
Ph:(301)934-7626
Fax:(301)934-7699
Co. E-mail: smsc@csmd.edu
URL: http://www.csmd.edu/library/SMSC
Contact: Bradley Gottfried PhD, Pres.
E-mail: smsc@csmd.edu
Scope: Southern Maryland region, including culture and development of Calvert, Charles, St. Mary's and the southern areas of Anne Arundel and Prince George's counties.

9509 ■ Historic Annapolis Foundation–Research Center
Shiplap House
18 Pinkney St.
Annapolis, MD 21401

Ph:(410)267-7619
Free: 800—603-4020
Fax:(410)267-1030
Co. E-mail: john.guild@annapolis.org
URL: http://www.annapolis.org
Contact: John Guild, Pres./CEO
E-mail: john.guild@annapolis.org
Scope: State and local history, historic preservation, urban planning, and decorative arts. **Publications:** Historic Annapolis Foundation Journal (semiannually). **Awards:** Preservation Awards (annually), given to individuals and organizations who have demonstrated best practices in preservation in the Greater Annapolis Community.

9510 ■ Samford University–Institute of Genealogy and Historical Research
Samford University Library
800 Lakeshore Dr.
Birmingham, AL 35229
Ph:(205)726-4447
Fax:(205)726-4009
Co. E-mail: ighr@samford.edu
URL: http://www4.samford.edu/schools/ighr
Contact: Della Holland Darby, Dir.
E-mail: ighr@samford.edu
Scope: Genealogy studies.

9511 ■ Southwest Minnesota State University–Southwest Minnesota Historical Center
Social Science, Rm. 141
1501 State St.
Marshall, MN 56258
Ph:(507)537-7373
Fax:(507)537-6147
Co. E-mail: jlouwagie@southwestmsu.edu
URL: http://www.southwestmsu.edu/history_center/
Contact: Jan Louwagie, Coord.
E-mail: jlouwagie@southwestmsu.edu
Scope: Local history, church histories, Iceland, agricultural history, and genealogy. **Educational Activities:** Conferences; Speakers series.

9512 ■ Starsmore Center for Local History
Colorado Springs Pioneers Museum
215 S Tejon St.
Colorado Springs, CO 80903
Ph:(719)385-5990
Fax:(719)385-5645
Co. E-mail: lwitherow@springsgov.com
URL: http://www.springsgov.com/Page.aspx-
?NavID=2547
Contact: Leah Davis Witherow, Archv.
E-mail: lwitherow@springsgov.com
Scope: Colorado history, local history, and genealogy. **Services:** Consultation, for paper and photograph preservation.

9513 ■ Stearns History Museum
235 33rd Ave. S
St. Cloud, MN 56301-3752
Ph:(320)253-8424
Free: (866)-253-8424

Fax:(320)253-2172
Co. E-mail: jdecker@stearns.history.museum
URL: http://www.stearns.history.museum
Contact: John W. Decker
E-mail: jdecker@stearns.history.museum
Scope: Genealogy, county history, architecture, agriculture, Luxembourg immigration, local sports, and granite industry. **Publications:** Crossings Magazine (bimonthly). **Educational Activities:** Annual genealogical conference/workshop; Century Farms, first week in June; Spring bus tour, third Friday in May.

9514 ■ University of Moncton–Centre for Acadians Studies–Centre d'Études Acadiennes
Moncton, NB, Canada E1A 3E9
Ph:(506)858-4085
Fax:(506)858-4530
Co. E-mail: isabelle.cormier@umoncton.ca
URL: http://www.umoncton.ca/etudeacadiennes/cen-
tre/cea.html
Contact: Isabelle Cormier, Dir.
E-mail: isabelle.cormier@umoncton.ca
Scope: Acadian history, genealogy, and folklore. **Publications:** Contact-Acadie (annually).

9515 ■ University of Wisconsin—Eau Claire–Eau Claire Area Research Center
McIntyre Library
105 Garfield Ave.
Eau Claire, WI 54702
Ph:(715)836-2739
Fax:(715)836-2949
Co. E-mail: mcfarlcd@uwec.edu
URL: http://www.uwec.edu/library/archives/arc.htm
Contact: Colleen McFarland
E-mail: mcfarlcd@uwec.edu
Scope: History of western Wisconsin, lumbering history, genealogy, and university history.

9516 ■ University of Wisconsin—Green Bay–Area Research Center
2420 Nicolet Dr.
Green Bay, WI 54311-7001
Ph:(920)465-2539
Fax:(920)465-2388
Co. E-mail: andersod@uwgb.edu
URL: http://www.uwgb.edu/library/spc/arc.asp
Contact: Debra Anderson
E-mail: andersod@uwgb.edu
Scope: Local history and genealogy, Northeastern Wisconsin, Belgian Americans, and University records.

9517 ■ University of Wisconsin—Parkside–Archives and Area Research Center
900 Wood Rd.
PO Box 2000
Kenosha, WI 53141-2000
Ph:(262)595-2411
Fax:(262)595-2545
Co. E-mail: webern@uwp.edu
URL: http://www.uwp.edu/departments/library/
archives
Contact: Nicholas Weber, Dir.
E-mail: webern@uwp.edu
Scope: State and local history and genealogy.

TRADE PERIODICALS

9518 ■ Gifts & Decorative Accessories
Pub: Sandow Media Corp.
Contact: Caroline Kennedy, Editor-in-Chief
E-mail: ckennedy@giftsanddec.com
Released: Monthly. **Price:** $36; $39 Canada; $135 other countries. **Description:** International magazine for retailers of gifts, greeting cards, decorative accessories, and stationery-related merchandise.

TRADE SHOWS AND CONVENTIONS

9519 ■ Accent on Design - A Division of the New York International Gift Fair
George Little Management, LLC (New York, New York)
1133 Westchester Ave., Ste. N136
White Plains, NY 10606
Ph:(914)421-3200
Free: 800-272-SHOW
Co. E-mail: cathy_steel@glmshows.com
URL: http://www.glmshows.com
Released: Annual. **Audience:** Buyers from specialty, department, and jewelry stores and; gift shops; interior designers; home products importers and distributors; mail order catalogs. **Principal Exhibits:** General giftware, tabletop and housewares, decorative and personal accessories, museum gifts, ethnic, traditional, country and contemporary design products, juvenile products, floral products and pet products.

9520 ■ Boston Gift Show
Urban Expositions
1395 S. Marietta Pkwy., Bldg. 400, Ste. 210
Marietta, GA 30067
Ph:(678)285-3976
Free: 800-318-2238
Released: Annual. **Audience:** Specialty and department store retailers, importer/export firms, distributors, gift shops, mail-order/catalog, houses and boutique. **Principal Exhibits:** Stationery, gourmet products and foods, toys, general gifts, floral items, decorative and personal accessories, souvenirs, jewelry, traditional and contemporary crafts, and tabletop items. Features Handmade and Made in New England sections.

9521 ■ California Gift Show
George Little Management, LLC (on behalf of dmg world media)
888 S. Figueroa St., Ste. 700
Los Angeles, CA 90017
Ph:(213)362-5640
Fax:(213)362-5660
Co. E-mail: customerservice@glmshows.com
URL: http://www.californiagiftshow.com/
Released: Semiannual, and July. **Audience:** Retailers from qualified specialty, gallery, gift and department stores from 50 U.S. and 60 foreign countries.

Principal Exhibits: The product categories are: child's play, fashion jewelry/accessories, fine gift, gardens, general gift, gourmet and housewares, high design/contemporary handcrafted, home accents, international/multicultural, stationery, resort/souvenirs/novelty, pampered pets, body and soul, aromatherapy/personal care.

9522 ■ Home Entertainment Show
Trigger Agency
3539 Clipper Mill Rd.
Baltimore, MD 21211
Free: 800-830-3976
Fax:(410)878-9911
Co. E-mail: info@triggeragency.com
URL: http://www.triggeragency.com/
Released: Biennial. **Audience:** Consumers, trade and press. **Principal Exhibits:** Home theater and high-fidelity audio equipment, supplies, and services.

9523 ■ Memphis Gift and Jewelry Show Fall
Helen Brett Enterprises, Inc.
5111 Academy Dr.
Lisle, IL 60532-2171
Ph:(630)241-9865
Free: 800-541-8171
Fax:(630)241-9870
URL: http://www.gift2jewelry.com
Released: Semiannual. **Audience:** Wholesale buyers. **Principal Exhibits:** Giftware and jewelry, apparel, home decor, novelties, silk flowers, fine/costume jewelry and accessories. **Dates and Locations:** 2011 Aug 27-29, Memphis, TN.

9524 ■ New Orleans Gift and Jewelry Show Spring
Helen Brett Enterprises, Inc.
5111 Academy Dr.
Lisle, IL 60532-2171
Ph:(630)241-9865
Free: 800-541-8171
Fax:(630)241-9870
URL: http://www.gift2jewelry.com
Released: Semiannual. **Audience:** Wholesale buyers. **Principal Exhibits:** Giftware and jewelry, apparel, home decor, rugs, silk plants, fine jewelry, costume jewelry, loose gemstones.

9525 ■ Pittsburgh Gift Show
Pittsburgh & Western New York Gift Shows
100 Bickford St.
Rochester, NY 14606-2298
Ph:(585)254-2580
Free: 800-997-GIFT
Fax:(585)458-1511
Co. E-mail: giftshows@coralproductions.com
URL: http://www.pittsburghgiftshow.com
Released: Semiannual, Twice a year. **Audience:** Gift retailers. **Principal Exhibits:** Gifts, decorative accessories, jewelry, florals, stationery, crafts, and general and unique merchandise, collectibles. **Dates and Locations:** 2011 Mar 04-06, Monroeville, PA.

9526 ■ Washington Gift Show
George Little Management, LLC (New York, New York)
1133 Westchester Ave., Ste. N136
White Plains, NY 10606
Ph:(914)421-3200
Free: 800-272-SHOW
Co. E-mail: cathy_steel@glmshows.com
URL: http://www.glmshows.com
Released: Semiannual. **Audience:** Specialty and department store retailers, importers, and distributors. **Principal Exhibits:** Gifts, stationery, gourmet products, floral industry products and services, decorative accessories, souvenirs, crafts, jewelry, personal accessories, china, glass, fine and fashion jewelry, collectibles, and related tabletop items.

9527 ■ Western New York Gift Show
Pittsburgh & Western New York Gift Shows
100 Bickford St.
Rochester, NY 14606-2298
Ph:(585)254-2580
Free: 800-997-GIFT
Fax:(585)458-1511
Co. E-mail: giftshows@coralproductions.com
URL: http://www.pittsburghgiftshow.com
Released: Semiannual. **Audience:** Gift retailers. **Principal Exhibits:** Gifts, decorative accessories, jewelry, floral, stationery, crafts, and general merchandise.

FRANCHISES AND BUSINESS OPPORTUNITIES

9528 ■ Cookies in Bloom
7208 La Cosa Dr.
Dallas, TX 75248
Ph:(972)490-8644
Free: 800-222-3104
Fax:(972)490-8846
No. of Franchise Units: 15. **Founded:** 1988. **Franchised:** 1992. **Description:** Cookie gift business. **Equity Capital Needed:** $85,000-$140,000. **Franchise Fee:** $19,500. **Royalty Fee:** 5%. **Financial Assistance:** No. **Training:** 10 days at headquarters, 5 days at franchisee's location, on-the-job training at corporate approved shop and ongoing support.

9529 ■ FruitFlowers/Incredibly Edible Delites
Incredible Franchise Corp.
3720 W Chester Pike
Newtown Sq., PA 19073
Ph:(610)353-8702
Fax:(610)353-8760
No. of Franchise Units: 25. **No. of Company-Owned Units:** 2. **Founded:** 1984. **Franchised:** 1993. **Description:** Floral fruit and vegetable bouquets. **Equity Capital Needed:** $250,000. **Franchise Fee:** $30,000. **Financial Assistance:** Yes. **Training:** Yes.

START-UP INFORMATION

9530 ■ *The Specialty Shop: How to Create Your Own Unique and Profitable Retail Business*
Pub: AMACOM
Ed: Dorothy Finell. **Released:** February 27, 2007. **Price:** $21.95. **Description:** Advise to start retail businesses, including bakeries, gift shops, toy stores, book shops, tea houses, clothing boutiques, and other unique stores.

ASSOCIATIONS AND OTHER ORGANIZATIONS

9531 ■ **Gift Associates Interchange Network**
1100 Main St.
Buffalo, NY 14209-2356
Ph:(716)887-9504
Free: 800-746-9428
Fax:(716)878-0479
Co. E-mail: rosanne.battaglia@abc-amega.com
URL: http://www.gaingroup.com
Contact: Rosanne Battaglia, Member Development Rep.
Description: Represents manufacturers and importers of giftware, tabletop accessories, china, greeting cards, silk and floral products, book publishers, desk and wall calendar manufacturers. Collects, computes, and exchanges factual ledger information on mutual customers. Conducts seminars. .

9532 ■ **Souvenir Wholesale Distributors Association**
2105 Laurel Bush Rd., Ste. 200
Bel Air, MD 21015
Ph:(443)640-1055
Fax:(443)640-1031
Co. E-mail: marci@ksgroup.org
URL: http://www.postcardcentral.org
Contact: Marci L. Hickey CMP, Exec. VP
Description: Represents distributors and manufacturers of post cards, souvenirs, and novelty items. .

REFERENCE WORKS

9533 ■ **"Award Win Highlights Slingsby's Green Credentials" in** *Ecology,Environment & Conservation Business* **(August 20, 2011, pp. 3)**
Pub: HighBeam Research
Description: Slingsby, an industrial and commercial equipment supplier, was joint winner with Hallmark Cards of the Baildon Business in the Community's Yorkshire and Humber Long Term Environmental Improvement Award. The firm cites its commitment to reducing environmental impact.

9534 ■ **"Doing Good: Cause and Effect" in** *Entrepreneur* **(Vol. 36, February 2008, No. 2, pp. 23)**
Pub: Entrepreneur Media Inc.
Description: Lisa Knoppe established Art for a Cause LLC that employs people with mental and

physical disabilities. The company makes hand-painted tools and furniture to be sold at gift retailers and hardware stores.

9535 ■ **Gift and Decorative Accessories Center Association—Directory**
Pub: Gift and Decorative Accessories Center Association
Contact: Diane Carnevale Jones, Exec. Dir.
Released: Continuous. **Price:** Free. **Covers:** About 60 individuals who are giftware manufacturers' representatives in New England; also lists their manufacturers and suppliers. **Entries Include:** For representatives—Name, address, phone, e-mail, manufacturers and products represented. **Arrangement:** Alphabetical.

9536 ■ **Gift, Housewares & Home Textiles Buyers**
Pub: Briefings Media Group
Contact: Alan M. Douglas, President
E-mail: chart@douglaspublications.com
Released: Annual, latest edition 2011-2012. **Price:** $329, individuals directory price; $659, individuals directory/CD combo. **Covers:** 12,700 buyers in the gift, housewares, and textiles industry throughout the United States, Puerto Rico, the Virgin Islands, and Canada. **Entries Include:** Company name, address, phone, fax; e-mail; URL; names and titles of key personnel; financial data; branch/subsidiary names and addresses; products and/or services provided; price points; sales volume; type of stores; number of stores; divisions of parent companies; corporate buying offices. **Arrangement:** Geographical. **Indexes:** Store name, new listings, mail order, online retailer.

9537 ■ **Greeting Card Industry Directory**
Pub: Greeting Card Association
Contact: Susan January, President
Released: Biennial, Latest edition 13th. **Price:** $75, members; $150, nonmembers plus shipping & handling charges. **Covers:** Over 3,000 greeting card publishers and suppliers in the United State and many foreign countries. **Entries Include:** Company name, address, phone, e-mail, Internet, toll-free, fax numbers, key personnel, licensed properties, plant locations, description of products & services, distribution outlets and methods, geographic area covered, industry background, and related information. **Arrangement:** Alphabetical. **Indexes:** Product, geographical, brand name.

9538 ■ **"Halls Give Hospital Drive $11 Million Infusion" in** *The Business Journal-Serving Metropolitan Kansas City* **(Vol. 26, July 18, 2008)**
Pub: American City Business Journals, Inc.
Ed: Rob Roberts. **Description:** Don Hall, chairman of Hallmark Cards Inc., and eight family members have announced that they will give $11 million to Children's Mercy Hospitals and Clinics for its $800 million expansion plan. Hall Family Foundation president Bill Hall that contributions such as that for Children's Mercy reflect the charitable interests of the foundation's board and founders. The possible impacts of the Hall's donation are analyzed.

9539 ■ **Profits for Non-Profits: Running a Successful Gift Shop**
Pub: Lulu.com
Ed: Nancy Kirk. **Released:** January 2005. **Price:** $19.95. **Description:** Guide for managing a non-profit gift shop in a hospital, zoo, museum or any other non-profit entity.

9540 ■ **Publishers Weekly—Calendar Roundup Issue**
Pub: Reed Business Information
Released: Annual, Latest edition 2010. **Publication Includes:** Listing of more than 100 publishers of calendars and engagement books. **Entries Include:** Publisher name, address, phone, brief descriptions of calendars being planned for the next year, with prices, discounts, etc. **Arrangement:** Alphabetical.

9541 ■ **"Retail Briefs - Dollar Store Opens in Long Leaf Mall" in** *Star-News* **(November 5, 2010)**
Pub: Star-News Media
Ed: Judy Royal. **Description:** Dollar Delight$ opened a new shop in Long Leaf Mall in Wilmington, North Carolina. The store will carry gift bags, balloons, party supplies, greeting cards, school supplies, health and beauty products, hardware, baby items, toys, Christmas goods, crafts, housewares and jewelry in its inventory.

9542 ■ **"Retail News: Children's Boutique Relocates to Conway" in** *Sun News* **(June 4, 2010)**
Pub: The Sun News
Description: Little Angel's Children's Boutique and Big Oak Frame Shop have moved to downtown locations in Conway, South Carolina. Little Angel's will sell children's clothing and accessories, shoes and gifts, while the frame shop will offer custom framing along with the sale of stationary, invitations and local prints.

9543 ■ **"Use Common Sense in Office Gift-Giving" in** *Women In Business* **(Vol. 61, October-November 2009, No. 5, pp. 32)**
Pub: American Business Women's Association
Ed: Maureen Sullivan. **Description:** Tips on office gift-giving during the Christmas season are discussed. Aside from ensuring appropriateness of the gift with respect to the recipient, a fixed giving budget must be adhered to. Gifts that can be used by anyone may be selected and those with religious overtones must be avoided.

9544 ■ **"VISA: Canadians Spend $97 Million on Mom This Mother's Day" in** *Canadian Corporate News* **(May 16, 2007)**
Pub: Comtex News Network Inc.
Description: Visa Canada finds that Canadians are spending more on Mother's Day in recent years. Since 2002, sales of jewelry, flowers, and cards have climbed steadily in the week before Mother's Day weekend.

9545 ▪ "Worldwide Food Services (EREI) Tests Mini Dollar Store Program" in *Internet Wire* **(August 6, 2009)**
Pub: Comtex News Network, Inc.
Description: Mini Dollar Stores and Eagle View LLC, wholly-owned subsidiaries of Worldwide Food Services, Inc., recently met with government officials and purchasing agents to lay out a test program which would distribute Mini Dollar Store items into VA hospital gift shops.

STATISTICAL SOURCES

9546 ▪ *Greeting Cards - US*
Pub: MarketResearch.com
Released: 2008. **Price:** $3995.00. **Description:** The U.S. greeting card industry remains a mature and stable market with sales growth of 8.7% between 1999 and 2004.

9547 ▪ *RMA Annual Statement Studies*
Pub: Robert Morris Associates (RMA)
Released: Annual. **Price:** $175.00 2006-07 edition, $105.00. **Description:** Contains composite balance sheets and income statements for more than 360 industries, including the accounting, auditing, and bookkeeping industries. Also contains five years of comparative historical data for discerning trends. Includes 16 commonly used ratios, computed for most of the size groupings for nearly every industry.

TRADE PERIODICALS

9548 ▪ *Country Business*
Pub: Country Sampler Group
Released: Bimonthly. **Description:** Trade magazine covering issues for independent gift retailers.

9549 ▪ *Gifts & Decorative Accessories*
Pub: Sandow Media Corp.
Contact: Caroline Kennedy, Editor-in-Chief
E-mail: ckennedy@giftsanddec.com
Released: Monthly. **Price:** $36; $39 Canada; $135 other countries. **Description:** International magazine for retailers of gifts, greeting cards, decorative accessories, and stationery-related merchandise.

9550 ▪ *Gifts & Tablewares*
Pub: Business Information Group
Contact: Brenda Bishop, Publisher
E-mail: bbishop@gifts-and-tableware.com
Released: 7/yr. **Price:** $43.95 Canada plus taxes; $49.95 in U.S.; $54.95 other countries. **Description:** Magazine featuring gifts, tableware, social stationery, housewares, and home accessories.

9551 ▪ *Giftware News*
Pub: Talcott Communication Corp.
Contact: Daniel Von Rabenau, Publisher
E-mail: dvr@talcott.com
Released: Monthly. **Price:** $43; $59 two years; $82 3 years; $55 Canada; $196 other countries. **Description:** Magazine serving professionals in the gift, stationery, collectibles, tabletop, and home accessories industries.

9552 ▪ *Party & Paper Retailer*
Pub: Great American Publishing Co.
Contact: Gavin Cribbs, Advertising Mgr
Released: Monthly. **Price:** $25; $56 Canada; $100 other countries. **Description:** Trade magazine for retailers of paper tableware, decorations, stationery, greeting cards, balloons, and other party-related items.

TRADE SHOWS AND CONVENTIONS

9553 ▪ Accent on Design - A Division of the New York International Gift Fair
George Little Management, LLC (New York, New York)
1133 Westchester Ave., Ste. N136
White Plains, NY 10606
Ph:(914)421-3200

Free: 800-272-SHOW
Co. E-mail: cathy_steel@glmshows.com
URL: http://www.glmshows.com
Released: Annual. **Audience:** Buyers from specialty, department, and jewelry stores and; gift shops; interior designers; home products importers and distributors; mail order catalogs. **Principal Exhibits:** General giftware, tabletop and housewares, decorative and personal accessories, museum gifts, ethnic, traditional, country and contemporary design products, juvenile products, floral products and pet products.

9554 ▪ Boston Gift Show
Urban Expositions
1395 S. Marietta Pkwy., Bldg. 400, Ste. 210
Marietta, GA 30067
Ph:(678)285-3976
Free: 800-318-2238
Released: Annual. **Audience:** Specialty and department store retailers, importer/export firms, distributors, gift shops, mail-order/catalog, houses and boutique. **Principal Exhibits:** Stationery, gourmet products and foods, toys, general gifts, floral items, decorative and personal accessories, souvenirs, jewelry, traditional and contemporary crafts, and tabletop items. Features Handmade and Made in New England sections.

9555 ▪ California Gift Show
George Little Management, LLC (on behalf of dmg world media)
888 S. Figueroa St., Ste. 700
Los Angeles, CA 90017
Ph:(213)362-5640
Fax:(213)362-5660
Co. E-mail: customerservice@glmshows.com
URL: http://www.californiagiftshow.com/
Released: Semiannual, and July. **Audience:** Retailers from qualified specialty, gallery, gift and department stores from 50 U.S. and 60 foreign countries. **Principal Exhibits:** The product categories are: child's play, fashion jewelry/accessories, fine gift, gardens, general gift, gourmet and housewares, high design/contemporary handcrafted, home accents, international/multicultural, stationery, resort/souvenirs/novelty, pampered pets, body and soul, aromatherapy/personal care.

9556 ▪ Charlotte Gift and Jewelry Show
Charlotte Gift and Jewelry Show
3710 Latrobe Dr., Ste. 110
Charlotte, NC 28211
Ph:(704)365-4150
Fax:(704)365-4154
Co. E-mail: michael@charlottegiftshow.com
URL: http://www.charlottegiftshow.com
Released: Quarterly. **Audience:** Trade buyers. **Principal Exhibits:** Gifts, housewares, jewelry, crafts, silk plants and flowers, tabletop, glassware, collectibles, accessories, home decorating accessories, basketry, and other related products.

9557 ▪ Home Entertainment Show
Trigger Agency
3539 Clipper Mill Rd.
Baltimore, MD 21211
Free: 800-830-3976
Fax:(410)878-9911
Co. E-mail: info@triggeragency.com
URL: http://www.triggeragency.com/
Released: Biennial. **Audience:** Consumers, trade and press. **Principal Exhibits:** Home theater and high-fidelity audio equipment, supplies, and services.

9558 ▪ Memphis Gift and Jewelry Show Fall
Helen Brett Enterprises, Inc.
5111 Academy Dr.
Lisle, IL 60532-2171
Ph:(630)241-9865
Free: 800-541-8171
Fax:(630)241-9870
URL: http://www.gift2jewelry.com
Released: Semiannual. **Audience:** Wholesale buyers. **Principal Exhibits:** Giftware and jewelry, apparel, home decor, novelties, silk flowers, fine/costume jewelry and accessories. **Dates and Locations:** 2011 Aug 27-29, Memphis, TN.

9559 ▪ Montreal Spring Gift Show
dmg world media
180 Duncan Mill Rd., Ste. 400
4th Fl.
Toronto, ON, Canada M3B 1Z6
Ph:(416)385-1880
Free: 888-823-7469
Fax:(416)385-1855
Co. E-mail: corpinfo@ca.dmgworldmedia.com
URL: http://www.dmgworldmedia.com
Released: Annual. **Principal Exhibits:** Giftware and related items.

9560 ▪ New Orleans Gift and Jewelry Show Spring
Helen Brett Enterprises, Inc.
5111 Academy Dr.
Lisle, IL 60532-2171
Ph:(630)241-9865
Free: 800-541-8171
Fax:(630)241-9870
URL: http://www.gift2jewelry.com
Released: Semiannual. **Audience:** Wholesale buyers. **Principal Exhibits:** Giftware and jewelry, apparel, home decor, rugs, silk plants, fine jewelry, costume jewelry, loose gemstones.

9561 ▪ Offinger's Handcrafted Marketplace
Offinger Management Co.
1100-H Brandywine Blvd.
PO Box 3388
Zanesville, OH 43702-3388
Ph:(740)452-4541
Free: 888-878-6334
Fax:(740)452-2552
Co. E-mail: OMC.Info@Offinger.com
URL: http://www.offinger.com
Released: Quarterly. **Audience:** Trade professionals. **Principal Exhibits:** Gift decor and gift-related items, such as candles, gourmet food, framed prints, country, primitive, folk art products, floral, crafts, and jewelry. **Dates and Locations:** 2011 Mar 19-19, Columbus, OH; 2011 Aug 20-20, Columbus, OH; 2011 Nov 05-05, Columbus, OH.

9562 ▪ Pittsburgh Gift Show
Pittsburgh & Western New York Gift Shows
100 Bickford St.
Rochester, NY 14606-2298
Ph:(585)254-2580
Free: 800-997-GIFT
Fax:(585)458-1511
Co. E-mail: giftshows@coralproductions.com
URL: http://www.pittsburghgiftshow.com
Released: Semiannual, Twice a year. **Audience:** Gift retailers. **Principal Exhibits:** Gifts, decorative accessories, jewelry, florals, stationery, crafts, and general and unique merchandise, collectibles. **Dates and Locations:** 2011 Mar 04-06, Monroeville, PA.

9563 ▪ Vancouver Fall Gift Show
dmg world media inc. (Vancouver, British Columbia)
4601 CanadaWay, Ste. 402
Burnaby, BC, Canada V5G 4X7
Ph:(604)433-5121
Fax:(604)434-6853
URL: http://www.dmgworldmedia.com
Released: Annual. **Audience:** Retail buyers from gift shops; drugstores; hardware and general stores; bed, bath and linen stores; and department stores. **Principal Exhibits:** Giftware, housewares, jewelry, leather goods, toys, and games.

9564 ▪ Vancouver Spring Gift Show
dmg world media inc. (Vancouver, British Columbia)
4601 CanadaWay, Ste. 402
Burnaby, BC, Canada V5G 4X7
Ph:(604)433-5121
Fax:(604)434-6853
URL: http://www.dmgworldmedia.com
Released: Annual. **Audience:** Retail buyers from gift shops; drugstores; hardware and general stores; bed, bath, and linen stores; and department stores. **Principal Exhibits:** Bed, bath, and linen supplies; interior design supplies; jewelry and accessories; souvenirs, stationery, store fixtures, tabletop gourmet items, and toys and games.

9565 ■ Washington Gift Show
George Little Management, LLC (New York, New York)
1133 Westchester Ave., Ste. N136
White Plains, NY 10606
Ph:(914)421-3200
Free: 800-272-SHOW
Co. E-mail: cathy_steel@glmshows.com
URL: http://www.glmshows.com
Released: Semiannual. **Audience:** Specialty and department store retailers, importers, and distributors. **Principal Exhibits:** Gifts, stationery, gourmet products, floral industry products and services, decorative accessories, souvenirs, crafts, jewelry, personal accessories, china, glass, fine and fashion jewelry, collectibles, and related tabletop items.

9566 ■ Western New York Gift Show
Pittsburgh & Western New York Gift Shows
100 Bickford St.
Rochester, NY 14606-2298
Ph:(585)254-2580
Free: 800-997-GIFT
Fax:(585)458-1511
Co. E-mail: giftshows@coralproductions.com
URL: http://www.pittsburghgiftshow.com
Released: Semiannual. **Audience:** Gift retailers. **Principal Exhibits:** Gifts, decorative accessories, jewelry, floral, stationery, crafts, and general merchandise.

FRANCHISES AND BUSINESS OPPORTUNITIES

9567 ■ Hometown Threads
209 Hudson Trace
Augusta, GA 30907

Ph:(706)737-7687
Fax:(706)737-7690
URL: http://www.hometownthreads.com
No. of Franchise Units: 44. **No. of Company-Owned Units:** 4. **Founded:** 1998. **Franchised:** 2001. **Description:** Retail embroidery store located within Wal-Mart encourage shoppers to create and buy custom designed gifts and products. **Equity Capital Needed:** Total investment $165,000. **Franchise Fee:** $29,000. **Royalty Fee:** 6%. **Financial Assistance:** Third party financing options available. **Training:** Offers 3 weeks training at headquarters, 2 weeks at franchisees location with ongoing support.

9568 ■ The Panhandler
Liv Canada Gift Group Inc.
294 Walker Dr., Unit 2
Brampton, ON, Canada L6T 4Z2
Ph:(905)790-9023
Free: (866)463-4124
Fax:(905)790-7059
Co. E-mail: franchises@franchisebancorp.com
URL: http://www.livcan.com
No. of Franchise Units: 25. **Founded:** 1970. **Franchised:** 1970. **Description:** Boutiques specializing in gift, home decor, and kitchen items. **Equity Capital Needed:** $140,000-$180,000. **Franchise Fee:** $25,000. **Financial Assistance:** No. **Training:** Yes. s.

9569 ■ Party Land
5215 Militia Hill Rd.
Plymouth Meeting, PA 19462
Ph:(610)941-6200
Free: 800-778-9563
Fax:(610)941-6301
Co. E-mail: jbarry@partyland.com
URL: http://www.partyland.com
No. of Franchise Units: 43. **Founded:** 1986. **Franchised:** 1988. **Description:** Retail party supply

stores. **Equity Capital Needed:** $280,000. **Franchise Fee:** $35,000. **Royalty Fee:** 5%. **Financial Assistance:** Third party financing available. **Training:** 1 week training.

LIBRARIES

9570 ■ Hallmark Cards, Inc.–Business Research Library
PO Box 419034
Mail Drop 216
Kansas City, MO 64141
Ph:(816)274-5111
Free: 800-425-5627
Fax:(816)274-5061
URL: http://www.hallmark.com
Contact: Isidro de la Herran, Bus.Res.Lib.Mgr.
Scope: Marketing, business forecasting, demographics, operations research. **Services:** Library not open to the public. **Holdings:** 800 books. **Subscriptions:** 100 journals and other serials.

9571 ■ Hallmark Cards, Inc.–Creative Research Library
2501 McGee, No. 146
Kansas City, MO 64108
Ph:(816)274-5525
Fax:(816)274-7245
Co. E-mail: hallmarkplus@hallmark.com
URL: http://www.hallmark.com
Contact: Mark Spencer, Mgr., Creative Rsrc.Ctr.
Scope: Fine art, lettering, advertising, graphic art, design, illustration, photography. **Services:** Library open to Hallmark employees only. **Holdings:** 18,000 books; 60 bound periodical volumes. **Subscriptions:** 150 journals and other serials; 3 newspapers.

ASSOCIATIONS AND OTHER ORGANIZATIONS

9572 ■ Independent Glass Association
354 Westlind Rd.
Syracuse, NY 13219
Ph:(315)706-9172
Fax:(810)227-0443
Co. E-mail: info@iga.org
URL: http://www.iga.org
Contact: Dave Zoldowski, Pres.
Description: Helps automotive and architectural glass retailers compete with the national chains. Unites the efforts, interests and ideas of its members. Offers marketing, billing, and purchasing programs and promotes a high standard for consumer safety, quality, service and fair trade principles. Encourages a competitive, free market environment and the independence of each member. **Publications:** *Beacon Bulletin* (weekly).

9573 ■ International Window Film Association
PO Box 3871
Martinsville, VA 24115-3871
Ph:(276)666-4932
Fax:(276)666-4933
Co. E-mail: admin@iwfa.com
URL: http://www.iwfa.com/industry.htm
Contact: Darrell L. Smith, Exec. Dir.
Description: Manufacturers, distributors, suppliers, and installers of solar control, safety and security film for windows in automobiles, houses, and commercial buildings. Acts as a forum for communication and works to increase professionalism in the window film industry. Maintains educational programs and speakers' bureau. **Publications:** *Flat Glass Training Manual* (annual).

9574 ■ National Glass Association
1945 Old Gallows Rd., Ste. 750
Vienna, VA 22182
Ph:(703)442-4890
Free: (866)DIAL-NGA
Fax:(703)442-0630
Co. E-mail: pjames@glass.org
URL: http://www.glass.org
Contact: Steven R. Burnett, Chm.
Description: Manufacturers, installers, retailers, distributors and fabricators of flat, architectural, automotive and specialty glass and metal products, mirrors, shower and patio doors, windows and tabletops. Provides informational, educational and technical services. **Publications:** *AutoGlass Installation Guide* (annual); *Glass Magazine* (monthly); *Window & Door Magazine* (bimonthly).

REFERENCE WORKS

9575 ■ "On the Cutting Edge" in *Inc.*
(November 2007, pp. 28)
Pub: Gruner & Jahr USA Publishing
Ed: Elaine Appleton Grant. **Description:** Information is provided about a Nashville-area glass and glazing company that is on the market for $8.2 million. The

owner started the company from the back of his truck in 2990 with $2,200. The firm has $9 million worth of contracts signed through 2008. Statistical data included.

TRADE PERIODICALS

9576 ■ *Architects' Guide to Glass, Metal & Glazing*
Pub: Key Communications Inc.
Released: 6/yr. **Price:** $19 one day; $39 one month; $259; Free to qualified subscribers. **Description:** Trade annual covering glass for architects.

9577 ■ *Glass Canada*
Pub: Annex Publishing & Printing Inc.
Contact: Martin McAnulty, Gp. Publisher
E-mail: fire@annexweb.com
Ed: Mike Davey, Editor, mdavey@annexweb.com.
Released: 6/yr. **Price:** $39. **Description:** Magazine covering business and technical developments and concerns in the Canadian glass industry.

9578 ■ *Glass Magazine*
Pub: National Glass Association
Released: 11/yr. **Price:** $34.95 U.S., Canada, and Mexico; $44.95 other countries; Free to qualified subscribers. **Description:** Architectural glass magazine.

FRANCHISES AND BUSINESS OPPORTUNITIES

9579 ■ Apple Auto Glass Limited
7111 Kennedy Rd., Unit 4
Mississauga, ON, Canada L5S 0A4
Ph:(289)562-5633
Free: 800-267-6175
Fax:(289)562-5642
Co. E-mail: franchiseingappleautoglass@belron-canada.ca
URL: http://www.appleautoglass.com
No. of Franchise Units: 118. **No. of Company-Owned Units:** 4. **Founded:** 1983. **Description:** The franchise system specializes in auto glass repair and replacement, sunroofs, auto upholstery and vehicle accessories. **Equity Capital Needed:** $100,000-$300,000. **Franchise Fee:** $25,000. **Training:** Training provided as required.

9580 ■ Atlantic Windshield Repair, Inc.
PO Box 361153
Birmingham, AL 35236
Free: 877-230-4487
Co. E-mail: atlanticwindshieldrepair@hotmail.com
URL: http://www.atlanticwindshieldrepair.com
No. of Franchise Units: 7. **No. of Company-Owned Units:** 2. **Founded:** 1997. **Franchised:** 2003. **Description:** Complete package, including art equipment, training and electronic filing with over 200 insurance companies. Check status of jobs and print reports directly from the website. Set-up multiple shops and multiple installers and have the ability to check their progress with just a click of the mouse.

See instantly what jobs you have been paid for and any that are waiting to be paid, and reorder supplies using only your dealership number. **Equity Capital Needed:** $25,000-$45,000. **Franchise Fee:** $19,000. **Royalty Fee:** 6%. **Training:** An initial 3 day training course covering windshield repair, insurance filing, customer service and advanced techniques and procedures. Ongoing video training and call in support available.

9581 ■ Belron Canada Inc.
8288 Boul, PIE-IX
Montreal, QC, Canada H1Z 3T6
Ph:(514)593-3824
Fax:(514)593-6404
Co. E-mail: palessi@belroncanada.com
URL: http://www.belroncanada.com
No. of Franchise Units: 204. **No. of Company-Owned Units:** 190. **Founded:** 1965. **Franchised:** 1982. **Description:** Provides services and solutions for auto glass repair and replacement. Operates under four retail banners - Apple Auto Glass, Speedy Glass, Lebeau Vitres d'autos, DURO vitres d'autos - and conducts its wholesale activities under the Vanfax and Technicentre Plus trade names. It also offers claims management services. **Equity Capital Needed:** $40,000-$90,000. **Franchise Fee:** $10,000.

9582 ■ DURO vitres d'autos
9061 Boul Pie IX
Montreal, QC, Canada H1Z 3V6
Ph:(514)593-3876
Fax:(514)326-8118
Co. E-mail: mmelancon@belroncanada.com
URL: http://www.durovitresdautos.com
No. of Franchise Units: 53. **No. of Company-Owned Units:** 9. **Founded:** 1954. **Franchised:** 1990. **Description:** Part of Belron Canada providing glass repair/replacement service that is fast and accessible. **Equity Capital Needed:** $30,000-$80,000. **Franchise Fee:** $10,000. **Training:** Yes.

9583 ■ Glass Doctor
The Dwyer Group
1020 N University Parks Dr.
Waco, TX 76707
Free: 800-298-9858
Fax:800-378-9480
No. of Franchise Units: 136. **Founded:** 2004. **Description:** Auto, commercial, and residential glass replacement. **Equity Capital Needed:** $109,681-$261-681. **Franchise Fee:** $22,000/$100,000 population. **Financial Assistance:** Yes. **Training:** Yes. s.

9584 ■ Novus Glass / Novus Franchising Inc.
TCC International, Inc.
12800 Hwy. 13 S, Ste. 500
Savage, MN 55378
Free: 800-944-6811
Fax:(952)946-0481
Co. E-mail: jimo@novusglass.com
URL: http://www.novusglass.com
No. of Franchise Units: 2,000. **No. of Company-Owned Units:** 11. **Founded:** 1972. **Franchised:** 1985. **Description:** The franchisees offer customers a convenient, economical alternative to windshield

replacement by repairing stone-damaged wind-shields. **Equity Capital Needed:** $22,800-$206,800. **Franchise Fee:** $10,000. **Financial Assistance:** Yes. **Managerial Assistance:** franchisees receive a monthly newsletter filled with information on technical procedures, sales tips, motivational profiles and product news. **Training:** Gives franchisees the ongoing training and support needed to from their first day of training and throughout their career as a franchise owner. Offers complete technical and business training at the Minneapolis, MN headquarters. Offers one-

on-one consultation with an 8-day program and teaches how to offer a full-service windshield repair franchise.

RESEARCH CENTERS

9585 ■ Alfred University–Center for Glass Research
Binns-Merrill Hall
New York State College of Ceramics
Alfred, NY 14802

Ph:(607)871-2662
Fax:(607)871-2383
Co. E-mail: stevenshj@alfred.edu
URL: http://cgr.alfred.edu
Contact: Dr. Harrie J. Stevens, Dir.
E-mail: stevenshj@alfred.edu

Scope: Manufacture, characterization, and properties of glass. **Services:** Glass information and research.

ASSOCIATIONS AND OTHER ORGANIZATIONS

9586 ■ American Junior Golf Association
1980 Sports Club Dr.
Braselton, GA 30517
Ph:(770)868-4200
Free: 877-373-2542
Fax:(770)868-4211
Co. E-mail: ajga@ajga.org
URL: http://www.ajga.org
Contact: Stephen A. Hamblin, Exec. Dir.
Description: Works for the overall growth and development of young men and women through competitive junior golf. Provides exposure vehicle for college scholarships. **Publications:** *Golfweek* .

9587 ■ Association of Golf Merchandisers
PO Box 7247
Phoenix, AZ 85011-7247
Ph:(602)604-8250
Fax:(602)604-8251
Co. E-mail: info@agmgolf.org
URL: http://www.agmgolf.org
Contact: Desane Blaney, Exec. Dir.
Description: Golf buyers and vendors. Dedicated to maximizing members' learning and earning capabilities. Conducts continuing educational programs; provides networking opportunities, scholarships and a forum for communication; compiles statistics. **Publications:** *AGM Merchandise Manual* .

9588 ■ Golf Range Association of America
PO Box 240
Georgetown, CT 06829
Ph:(203)938-2720
Fax:(203)938-2721
Co. E-mail: steve@golfrange.org
URL: http://www.golfrange.org
Contact: Mr. Steve J. di Costanzo, Founder/Pres.
Description: Owners of golf driving ranges and other practice facilities; suppliers to the golf practice industry. Promotes growth and development of the golf industry. Gathers and disseminates information on economic and social trends affecting the golf industries; conducts educational programs. **Publications:** *Golf Range Development and Operations*; *Golf Range Magazine* (bimonthly); *Profile of Golf Practice Facility Operations 2003* .

9589 ■ International Golf Federation
PO Box 708
Far Hills, NJ 07931-0708
Ph:(908)234-2300
Fax:(908)234-2178
Co. E-mail: igfinfo@usga.org
URL: http://www.internationalgolffederation.org
Contact: Stephanie Parel, Joint Deputy Sec.
Description: Strives to encourage the international development of golf, and to foster friendship and sportsmanship among the peoples of the world through the conduct of the biennial Amateur Team Championships for the Eisenhower Trophy and the Espirito Santo Trophy. Promotes golf as an Olympic sport and acts as the Federation for golf in the Olympic games. **Publications:** *International Golf Federation—Record Book: World Amateur Team Championships* (biennial).

9590 ■ Ladies Professional Golf Association
100 International Golf Dr.
Daytona Beach, FL 32124-1092
Ph:(386)274-6200
Fax:(386)274-1099
Co. E-mail: feedback@lpga.com
URL: http://www.lpga.com
Contact: Sherri Steinhauer, Pres.
Description: Represents and promotes women golfers, teachers and competitors. Compiles statistics on tournaments, money winnings, and scoring. **Publications:** *Ladies Professional Golf Association— Schedule Directory* (annual); *Player Guide* (annual).

9591 ■ National Golf Foundation
1150 S U.S. Hwy. 1, Ste. 401
Jupiter, FL 33477
Ph:(561)744-6006
Free: 888-275-4643
Fax:(561)744-6107
Co. E-mail: general@ngf.org
URL: http://www.ngf.org
Contact: Dr. Joseph F. Beditz, Pres./CEO
Description: Golf-oriented businesses including: equipment and apparel companies; golf facilities; golf publications; golf course architects, developers and builders; companies offering specialized services to the golf industry; golf associations; teachers, coaches and instructors and other interested individuals. Serves as a market research and strategic planning organization for the golf industry and promotes public golf course development in the U.S. Provides information and consulting services for golf course planning, construction, and operation. Conducts golf course development and operations seminars including the National Institute of Golf Management. **Publications:** *Golf Facilities in the U.S.* (annual); *Golf Industry Report* (bimonthly).

9592 ■ Professional Golfers' Association of America
100 Ave. of the Champions
Palm Beach Gardens, FL 33418
Ph:(561)624-8400
Co. E-mail: webmaster.pga@turner.com
URL: http://www.pga.com
Contact: Allen Wronowski, Pres.
Description: Recruits and trains men and women to manage a variety of golf businesses, including golf clubs, courses, and tournaments. Sponsors PGA Championship, PGA Seniors' Championship, Ryder Cup Matches, PGA Grand Slam of Golf, Club Professional Championship, PGA Foundation, and Senior Club Professional Championship; PGA Junior Championship; PGA Assistants Championship. Conducts Professional Golf Management; certifies college programs in golf management at 14 universities. Sponsors winter tournament program for club professionals including tournaments held in south Florida. Offers complimentary employment services for PGA members and employers, owns and operates PGA Golf Club and PGA Learning Center. .

9593 ■ United States Golf Association
PO Box 708
Far Hills, NJ 07931
Ph:(908)234-2300
Free: 800-223-0041
Fax:(908)234-9687
Co. E-mail: membership@usga.org
URL: http://www.usga.org
Contact: James B. Hyler Jr., Pres.
Description: Regularly organized golf clubs and golf courses. Serves as governing body for golf in the United States. Turfgrass Visiting Service promotes scientific work in turf management. Provides data on rules, handicapping, amateur status, tournament procedure, turf maintenance, and golf balls and implements. Administers Golf House Museum, a collection of memorabilia including clubs of champions, the Moon Club, and paintings, insignia, and portraits of USGA champions. Sponsors USGA Research and Educational Fund. Conducts 13 annual national championships and research programs; sponsors teams for international competitions. **Publications:** *Golf Journal* (9/year).

REFERENCE WORKS

9594 ■ "Coming Up Short" in *Boston Business Journal* (Vol. 30, October 15, 2010, No. 36, pp. 1)
Pub: Boston Business Journal
Ed: Tim McLaughlin, Mary Moore. **Description:** Boston, Massachusetts-based nonprofits have been profiting less from charity golf tournaments. Nonprofits have been collecting less than 50 cents on the dollar from such events. But nonprofits have been restructuring golf tournaments in order to boost profits.

9595 ■ "Driving Passion" in *Small Business Opportunities* (Spring 2008)
Pub: Harris Publications Inc.
Ed: Chuck Green. **Description:** Profile of Joe Assell, founder of Golftec, a company offering golf instruction that uses the latest technology with professional teachers.

9596 ■ "Get on the Green" in *Entrepreneur* (Vol. 35, November 2007, No. 11, pp. 44)
Pub: Entrepreneur Media Inc.
Ed: James Park. **Description:** Golf is a sport where business people are provided with a casual atmosphere where they can open a conversation regarding business topics. Details on how spending time on the course provides a good environment for business discussions.

9597 ■ *Golf Magazine—Golf Club Buyers' Guide Issue*
Pub: Time4 Media Inc.
Ed: Rob Sauerhaft, Editor. **Released:** Annual, May. **Publication Includes:** List of golf club manufacturers. **Entries Include:** Company name, address, phone, description of product line, whether women's or left-handed models are available, type of shaft and club head, prices. Principal content of publication is

feature articles on golf equipment, tips on improving readers' golf scores, and interviews with golfing personalities. **Arrangement:** Alphabetical.

9598 ■ "Here's the Deal" in *Crain's Cleveland Business* **(Vol. 30, June 15, 2009, No. 23, pp. 14)**
Pub: Crain Communications, Inc.
Description: Incentives being offered by hotels, restaurants, golf courses and major chains in order to promote bookings for meetings or conferences in the Cleveland area are listed.

9599 ■ "Hit the Green" in *Canadian Business* **(Vol. 79, August 14, 2006, No. 16-17, pp. 73)**
Pub: Rogers Media
Ed: Andrew Wahl. **Description:** Reorganization of the bankrupt 4everSports golf company in the United States is discussed.

9600 ■ "Hitting the Green" in *Canadian Business* **(Vol. 81, July 22, 2008, No. 12-13, pp. 34)**
Pub: Rogers Media Ltd.
Ed: Andy Holloway. **Description:** RBC is sponsoring the Canadian Open golf tournament, which is the second-oldest event in the PGA Tour. RBC is expected to receive television exposure on CBS and the Golf Channel. Additional information relating to the sponsorship is presented.

9601 ■ "How Has City Golf Privatization Played?" in *Business Courier* **(Vol. 27, September 10, 2010, No. 19, pp. 1)**
Pub: Business Courier
Ed: Dan Monk. **Description:** It was reported that private contractors are getting more revenue from fewer golfers on city-owned courses in Cincinnati, Ohio. In 1998, the city handed over seven municipal courses to private management. However, some believe that the city has escalated a price war among the region's golf courses.

9602 ■ "Internal Auditor Wants Ethics Review of City's Casper Golf Contract" in *Business Courier* **(Vol. 27, September 10, 2010, No. 19, pp. 1)**
Pub: Business Courier
Ed: Dan Monk. **Description:** Mark Ashworth, an internal auditor for Cincinnati, Ohio is pushing for an ethics review of management contract for seven city-owned golf courses. Ashworth wants the Ohio Ethics Commission to investigate family ties between a superintendent for the Cincinnati Recreation Commission and Billy Casper Golf.

9603 ■ "Major Golf Retail Show in the Rough for 2010" in *Orlando Business Journal* **(Vol. 26, January 15, 2010, No. 33, pp. 1)**
Pub: American City Business Journals
Ed: Anjali Fluker. **Description:** The 57th Annual PGA Merchandise Show in Orlando, Florida is projected to attract 39,000 attendees in 2010, compared with 41,000 in 2009. According to the Orange County Convention Center, economic benefits that could be obtained from the 2010 edition of the golf retail show might reach only $77 million, compared with $78 million generated last year.

9604 ■ "Making the Cut; Osprey Takes Undervalued Courses to the Leader Board" in *Crain's Detroit Business* **(Vol. 24, April 7, 2008, No. 14)**
Pub: Crain Communications, Inc.
Ed: Jason Deegan. **Description:** Profile of Osprey Management Co., a diverse real estate company that continues to expand its golf portfolio through the company's recreation division; although many developers are getting out of the field due to Michigan's sluggish golf industry, Osprey has found success by purchasing properties in turmoil for more affordable prices.

9605 ■ "Members Make Sacrifices for a World-Class Course" in *Crain's Detroit Business* **(Vol. 24, April 7, 2008, No. 14, pp. 21)**
Pub: Crain Communications, Inc.
Ed: Jason Deegan. **Description:** Rees Jones Inc. completed a $1.8 million redesign of the Oakland Hills Country Club golf course last year. By all indica-

tions, the redesign has been a success since it is among the handful of courses good enough to host future majors which is beneficial for the local economy.

9606 ■ "Mixing Business and Pleasure On the Green" in *Black Enterprise* **(Vol. 41, October 2010, No. 3, pp. 65)**
Pub: Earl G. Graves Publishing Co. Inc.
Ed: Annya M. Lott. **Description:** Glow Golf, sponsored by Glow Sports, will offer instruction to 150 female corporate executives and entrepreneurs to learn the fundamentals of the game of golf.

9607 ■ "A New Way to Swing" in *Canadian Business* **(Vol. 81, December 8, 2008, No. 21, pp. S8)**
Pub: Rogers Media Ltd.
Ed: Robert Thompson. **Description:** Golf developer Mike Keiser believes that remote is the new luxury, and finances golf projects in out-of-the-way locales in various countries. Keiser is currently developing Cabot Links in Canada, which is expected to open by 2011.

9608 ■ "On the Green: Sheila Johnson Adds $35 Million Golf Resort To Her Expanding Portfolio" in *Black Enterprise* **(January 2008)**
Pub: Earl G. Graves Publishing Co. Inc.
Ed: Donna M. Owens. **Description:** Profile of Sheila Johnson, CEO of Salamander Hospitality LLC, made history when she purchased the Innisbrook Resort and Golf Club, making her the first African American woman to own this type of property. The resort includes four championship golf courses, six swimming pools, four restaurants, eleven tennis courts, three conference halls, and a nature preserve.

9609 ■ "PGA Tour: Course Management" in *Retail Merchandiser* **(Vol. 51, September-October 2011, No. 5, pp. 38)**
Pub: Phoenix Media Corporation
Ed: Eric Slack. **Description:** PGA Tour must reach new customers and solidify relationships with its traditional base in order to continue its success. The PGA brand equity has translated into one of the largest retail licensing operations worldwide.

9610 ■ "PGA Tourney Drives Area Economy, Image" in *Crain's Detroit Business* **(Vol. 24, April 7, 2008, No. 14, pp. 22)**
Pub: Crain Communications, Inc.
Ed: Jason Deegan. **Description:** Discusses the major economic impact the 2008 PGA Championship will have when it visits the south course at Oakland Hills Country Club August 4-10.

9611 ■ "Wild-Goose Chaser" in *Entrepreneur* **(Vol. 37, September 2009, No. 9, pp. 96)**
Pub: Entrepreneur Media, Inc.
Ed: Jason Daley. **Description:** Geese Police owner David Marcks says he discovered that trained collies could chase geese off golf courses, which started his business. He gives new franchises two dogs to start their business. The company has fared well even during the economic crisis.

TRADE PERIODICALS

9612 ■ *Golf Digest*
Pub: Conde Nast Publications Inc.
Contact: Jerry Tarde, Editor-in-Chief
Released: 12/yr. **Price:** $14.97; $27.94 two years.
Description: International magazine for golfers.

9613 ■ *Golf Magazine*
Pub: Time4 Media Inc.
Contact: Charlie Kammerer, Publisher
E-mail: charlie_kammerer@golf.com
Released: Monthly. **Price:** $20 Canada; $30 two years. **Description:** Magazine devoted to golf.

9614 ■ *Mountainwest Golf*
Pub: Harris Publishing Inc.
Contact: Magdalene Mercado, Gp. Sec.
Released: Quarterly. **Price:** $8.95; $15.95 two years; $21.95 3 years; $28.95 other countries; $55.95 other countries 2 years; $81.95 other countries 3 years; $23.95 Canada; $45.95 Canada 2 years; $66.95 Canada 3 years. **Description:** Magazine covering local golfing.

9615 ■ *Sporting Goods Dealer*
Pub: Bill Communications Inc.
Contact: Mark Sullivan, Publisher
E-mail: msullivan@sgdealer.com
Ed: Mike Jacobsen, Editor, mjacobsen@sgdealer.com. **Released:** Bimonthly. **Description:** Magazine which offers expert reporting on trends affecting team dealers and retailers who service schools, colleges, pro and local teams.

TRADE SHOWS AND CONVENTIONS

9616 ■ Cincinnati Golf Show
Hart Productions, Inc.
2234 Bauer Rd., Ste. B
Batavia, OH 45103
Ph:(513)797-7900
Free: 877-704-8190
Fax:(513)797-1013
URL: http://www.hartproductions.com
Released: Annual. **Audience:** General public. **Principal Exhibits:** Golf equipment, apparel, and travel destinations. **Dates and Locations:** 2011 Jan 14-16, Cincinnati, OH.

9617 ■ FUN Expo
Reed Exhibitions North American Headquarters
383 Main Ave.
Norwalk, CT 06851
Ph:(203)840-4800
Fax:(203)840-5805
Co. E-mail: export@reedexpo.com
URL: http://www.reedexpo.com
Released: Annual. **Principal Exhibits:** Amusement and recreation products for family and location based entertainment centers, small amusement parks and family oriented businesses such as bowling centers, skating rinks, sports parks, miniature golf courses, golf driving ranges, family restaurants, resorts and other entertainment/recreation businesses. **Dates and Locations:** 2011 Mar 01-03, Las Vegas, NV.

9618 ■ International Golf Course Conference and Show
Golf Course Superintendents Association of America
1421 Research Pk. Dr.
Lawrence, KS 66049-3859
Ph:(785)841-2240
Free: 800-472-7878
Fax:(785)832-4420
Co. E-mail: infobox@gcsaa.org
URL: http://www.gcsaa.org
Released: Annual. **Audience:** Golf course superintendents owners, builders, architects, club managers and related turf professionals. **Principal Exhibits:** Equipment, supplies, and services for golf course and facility maintenance.

9619 ■ PGA Merchandise Show
Professional Golfers Association of America PGA
100 Ave. of the Champions
Palm Beach Gardens, FL 33410
Ph:(203)840-5628
Fax:(203)840-9628
URL: http://www.pga.com
Released: Annual. **Audience:** Golf professionals, retail buyers, club managers and superintendents.
Principal Exhibits: Golf apparel, clubs, bags, balls, range equipment, club components, golf cars, golf shoes, and related equipment, supplies, and services.

CONSULTANTS

9620 ■ Charles F. Ankrom Inc.
1831 SW Crane Creek Ave.
PO Box 898
Palm City, FL 34990-2215
Ph:(772)283-1440
Fax:(561)220-4998
Contact: Charles F. Ankrom, President
Scope: Offers services in golf course architecture, land use planning, recreation facilities, market and financial studies, all related to golf courses and golf course communities, and public or municipal courses and resorts.

9621 ■ Jim Castello Marketing Communications Consultants
711 Red Wing Dr.
Lake Mary, FL 32746
Ph:(407)321-6322
Contact: James E. Castello Jr., President
Scope: Consultant develops creative ideas and marketing strategies, including collateral programs, public relations, advertising, and brochures. Industries served: All golf related industry/business, golf manufacturers, golf resorts, golf residential developments, golf professionals, golf clothing, golf accessories, golf associations, and golf travel. **Seminars:** How To Seminar for Family Fun Center Entrepreneurs; How To Seminar for Creativity in Golf Marketing; The Golf Business on the Internet.

FRANCHISES AND BUSINESS OPPORTUNITIES

9622 ■ Golf USA, Inc.
7608 N Harvey Ave.
Oklahoma City, OK 73116
Ph:(405)751-0015
Free: 800-488-1107
Fax:(405)755-0065
No. of Franchise Units: 100. **No. of Company-Owned Units:** 2. **Founded:** 1987. **Franchised:** 1989. **Description:** Retail golf stores. **Equity Capital Needed:** $154,050-$449,200. **Franchise Fee:** $34,000-$44,000. **Financial Assistance:** No. **Training:** Yes.

COMPUTER SYSTEMS/ SOFTWARE

9623 ■ Proshop Retail
Handicomp, Inc.
PO Box 87
Jenison, MI 49428-0087
Ph:(616)457-9581
Free: 800-833-0033
Fax:(616)457-6833
Co. E-mail: handisales@handicomp.com
URL: http://www.handicomp.com/
Contact: Ken Kapcia
Price: Contact Handicomp for pricing. **Description:** Available for IBM and NCR Tower computers. System geared for the golf pro shop. Assists with inventory and accounting needs.

LIBRARIES

9624 ■ Canadian Golf Hall of Fame Library and Archives
1333 Dorval Dr.
Oakville, ON, Canada L6M 4X7
Ph:(905)849-9700
Fax:(905)845-7040
Co. E-mail: khewson@rcga.org
URL: http://www.rcga.org/
Contact: Karen Hewson, Dir.
Scope: Golf. **Services:** Copying; photograph printing. **Holdings:** 3500 books; 200 bound periodical volumes; 10 manuscripts; 1000 lin.ft. archival materi-

als; 100 microfiche; 50,000 images. **Subscriptions:** 10 journals and other serials.

9625 ■ Ralph W. Miller Golf Library/Museum Library
One Industry Hills Pkwy.
City of Industry, CA 91744
Ph:(626)854-2354
Fax:(626)854-2425
Co. E-mail: golflore@earthlink.net
Contact: Saundra Sheffer, Libn.
Scope: Golf - history, instruction; Scottish history; biographies; records and statistics; humor; golf course achitecture. **Services:** Copying; Library open to the public for reference use only. **Holdings:** 5200 books; 1620 bound periodical volumes; 9000 photographs; 4300 VF articles; 2500 bound articles on golf, 1890 to present; 1 VF drawer of archival materials; 350 16mm films; 250 videotapes; 220 framed artworks. **Subscriptions:** 20 journals and other serials.

9626 ■ United States Golf Association Library
PO Box 708
Far Hills, NJ 07931
Ph:(908)234-2300, x1107
Fax:(908)470-5013
Co. E-mail: nstulack@usga.org
URL: http://www.usgamuseum.com/
Contact: Nancy Stulack, Libn.
Scope: Golf. **Services:** Library open to the public by appointment. **Holdings:** 25,000 books; 800 bound periodical volumes; 125 scrapbooks of newspaper clippings; archives; microfilm. **Subscriptions:** 20 journals and other serials.

START-UP INFORMATION

9627 ■ *How to Open a Financially Successful Coffee, Espresso and Tea Shop*
Pub: Atlantic Publishing Company

Ed: Lora Arduser, Elizabeth Godsmark, Douglas R. Brown. **Released:** July 23, 2009. **Price:** $39.95. **Description:** Coffee is currently the largest food import in the U.S. Comprehensive and detailed information is offered for anyone interested in opening a coffee, espresso or tea shop.

9628 ■ *"It's Tea-Riffic! Natural Bottled Tea Satisfies Void In Beverage Market" in Small Business Opportunities* (November 2007)
Pub: Harris Publications Inc.

Description: Profile of Skae Beverage International LLC, offering franchise opportunities for its New Leaf all-natural tea beverage, available in eight flavors of green, white and blue tea.

9629 ■ *"Proven Success Pays Off" in Small Business Opportunities* (January 2011)
Pub: Harris Publications Inc.

Ed: Description: Industry pioneers of the fast-casual restaurant launch new venture with sales of $43 million. Profile of Newk's Express Cafe and its founders is included.

9630 ■ *The Specialty Shop: How to Create Your Own Unique and Profitable Retail Business*
Pub: AMACOM

Ed: Dorothy Finell. **Released:** February 27, 2007. **Price:** $21.95. **Description:** Advise to start retail businesses, including bakeries, gift shops, toy stores, book shops, tea houses, clothing boutiques, and other unique stores.

ASSOCIATIONS AND OTHER ORGANIZATIONS

9631 ■ Coffee Association of Canada
885 Don Mills Rd., Ste. 301
Toronto, ON, Canada M3C 1V9
Ph:(416)510-8032
Fax:(416)510-8044
Co. E-mail: info@coffeeassoc.com
URL: http://www.coffeeassoc.com
Contact: Sandy McAlpine, Pres.

Description: Coffee importers and processors. Seeks to make "the coffee beverage experience a more integral and meaningful part of Canadian lives." Serves as a clearinghouse on the coffee industry; represents members' interests in publicly addressing industry issues.

9632 ■ National Coffee Association of U.S.A.
45 Broadway, Ste. 1140
New York, NY 10006
Ph:(212)766-4007

Fax:(212)766-5815
Co. E-mail: info@ncausa.org
URL: http://www.ncausa.org
Contact: Robert F. Nelson, Pres./CEO

Description: Green coffee importers, jobbers, brokers, and agents; instant coffee and liquid extract processors; roasters and allied coffee industries; exporters; retailers. Promotes sound business relations and mutual understanding among members of the trade, and to increase coffee consumption. Collects and publishes consumer, market and technical information on the coffee industry. **Publications:** *CoffeeTrax* (quarterly); *National Coffee Drinking Trends* (annual); *US Coffee Industry Review 2005* .

9633 ■ Specialty Coffee Association of America
330 Golden Shore, Ste. 50
Long Beach, CA 90802
Ph:(562)624-4100
Fax:(562)624-4101
Co. E-mail: info@scaa.org
URL: http://www.scaa.org
Contact: Tim O'Connor, Pres.

Description: Coffee roasters, green coffee brokers, retailers, distributors, and others involved in the gourmet coffee industry. Provides business, professional, promotional, and educational assistance in the areas of cultivation, processing, preparation, and marketing of specialty coffee; increase consumer awareness, understanding, and consumption of specialty coffee. Provides a forum for discussion of the purpose and unified character of the industry and represents members in national and regional coffee concerns. Distributes posters, surveys, articles, and other promotional information; develops coffee education curricula for culinary school programs. Maintains reference materials. Sponsors tastings of specialty coffees. **Publications:** Membership Directory (annual).

9634 ■ Tea Association of the U.S.A.
362 5th Ave., Ste. 801
New York, NY 10001
Ph:(212)986-9415
Fax:(212)697-8658
Co. E-mail: info@teausa.com
URL: http://teausa.org
Contact: Joseph P. Simrany, Pres.

Description: Packers, importers, brokers, agents, and other firms dedicated to the interests and growth of the U.S. tea industry. .

9635 ■ Tea Council of the United States of America
362 5th Ave., Ste. 801
New York, NY 10001
Ph:(212)986-9415
Fax:(212)697-8658
Co. E-mail: info@teausa.com
URL: http://www.teausa.com
Contact: Joseph P. Simrany, Pres.

Description: Represents companies and countries trading tea in the U.S. Works to increase tea consumption. **Publications:** *Tea World* (annual); *TeaBits* (quarterly).

REFERENCE WORKS

9636 ■ *Beans: Four Principles for Running a Business in Good Times or Bad*
Pub: John Wiley & Sons, Incorporated

Ed: Leslie Yerkes, Charles Decker, Bob Nelson **Released:** June 2003. **Price:** $19.95. **Description:** Profile of Monorail Espresso, the popular Seattle coffee company that has become prosperous by intentionally staying small and building a strong customer service program.

9637 ■ *"Blue Tractor Barbeque and Brewery, Cafe Havana" in Crain's Detroit Business* (Vol. 23, October 1, 2007, No. 40, pp. 15)
Pub: Crain Communications Inc. - Detroit

Ed: Daniel Duggan. **Description:** Two restaurants are converted from a Buddhist Temple to become the most unique spaces in Ann Arbor, Michigan.

9638 ■ *"Brewed to Succeed; Mokarbia Perks Up Sales for King Coffee" in Crain's Detroit Business* (Vol. 24, March 17, 2008, No. 11, pp. 3)
Pub: Crain Communications, Inc.

Ed: Brent Snavely. **Description:** Profile of King Coffee Tea Services, Royal Oak-based company, whose distributing deal with Mokarabia coffee has generated an increase in sales.

9639 ■ *"Brewing a Love-Haiti Relationship" in The Business Journal - Serving Phoenix and the Valley of the Sun* (Vol. 28, July 4, 2008, No. 44)
Pub: American City Business Journals, Inc.

Ed: Yvonne Zusel. **Description:** Jean and Alicia Marseille have ventured into a coffee distribution company called Ka Bel LLC which markets Marabou brand of coffee imported from Haiti. Part of the proceeds of the business is donated to entrepreneurs from Jean's country, Haiti. Details of the Marseille's startup business and personal mission to help are discussed.

9640 ■ *"City Board Tweaks Internet Cafe Ordinance" in Ocala Star-Banner* (July 19, 2011)
Pub: Ocala Star-Banner

Ed: Susan Latham Carr. **Description:** Ocala Planning and Zoning Commission revised the proposed draft of the Internet Café ordinance by eliminating the cap on the number of locations allowed, but keeping fees and number of devices the same.

9641 ■ *"Dunnellon Welcomes Internet Cafe Jobs" in Ocala Star-Banner* (August 18, 2011)
Pub: Ocala Star-Banner

Ed: Fred Hiers. **Description:** Despite the fact that a few Internet cafes offering patrons to win cash and are facing legal challenges, the city's planning commission would welcome the cafes in order to provide more jobs for its residents.

9642 ■ *"Fair Exchange" in Food and Drink* (Winter 2010, pp. 84)
Pub: Schofield Media Group

Ed: Don Mardak. **Description:** Bartering can assist firms in the food and beverage industry to attract new customers, maximize resources, and reduce cash expenses.

9643 ■ **"Internet Cafe Logging in to Chardon Plaza?"** in *News-Herald* **(July 16, 2011)**
Pub: Journal Register Ohio
Ed: Betsy Scott. **Description:** Pearl's High Rollers Inc. applied for an Internet sweepstakes café license that would reside in a vacant space in Chardon Plaza. City officials have created regulations for such businesses and Pearl's applied for a license and is awaiting approval.

9644 ■ **"Internet Café 'Sweepstakes' Expanding in Arkansas"** in *Arkansas Business* **(Vol. 28, September 5, 2011, No. 36, pp. 1)**
Pub: Arkansas Business Publishing Group
Ed: Mark Friedman. **Description:** Despite the fact that video games resembling casino games in Lucky's Business Center in Little Rock, representatives of the Internet café insist they are not offering gambling but a type of sweepstakes promotion and that business model is thriving. Lucky's, Cancun Cyber Café & Business Center Inc., and Wild Rides Business Center & Internet Café has opened in the area in the last few weeks.

9645 ■ **"Lombard Leaves Starbucks"** in *Black Enterprise* **(Vol. 38, July 2008, No. 12, pp. 28)**
Pub: Earl G. Graves Publishing Co. Inc.
Ed: Tamara E. Holmes. **Description:** Ken Lombard stepped down from his position as head of Starbuck's entertainment division; the company is restructuring its entertainment unit in an attempt to revitalize sales and reduce costs.

9646 ■ **"Lux Coffees, Breads Push Chains to React"** in *Advertising Age* **(Vol. 77, June 26, 2006, No. 26, pp. S14)**
Pub: Crain Communications, Inc.
Ed: Kate MacArthur. **Description:** Fast-food giants such as McDonald's, Burger King, Dunkin' Donuts and Subway have adjusted their menus in order to become more competitive with gourmet coffee shops and bakeries like Panera Bread and Starbucks which have taken a large share in the market. Statistical data included.

9647 ■ *Nirvana in a Cup: The Founding of Oregon Chai*
Pub: Moby Press
Ed: Tedde McMillen; Heather Hale. **Released:** July 2006. **Price:** $12.99. **Description:** Profile of a mother-daughter team who founded Oregon Chai, a tea company.

9648 ■ **"Show Me the Love"** in *Canadian Business* **(Vol. 79, November 6, 2006, No. 22, pp. 77)**
Pub: Rogers Media
Ed: Jeannette Hanna. **Description:** The strategies to improve brand image with relation to success of Tim Horton's brand are presented.

9649 ■ **"South Park Draws Brewers, Vintners"** in *Puget Sound Business Journal* **(Vol. 29, August 29, 2008, No. 19, pp. 1)**
Pub: American City Business Journals
Ed: Heidi Dietrich. **Description:** Craft breweries and wineries are moving into Seattle, Washington's South Park neighborhood due to the area's low rents, convenience, and ample equipment space. These industries bring a more upscale flavor to the heavily industrial area and the tastings and festivals draw people from throughout the Seattle region.

9650 ■ **"Starbucks Drive-Throughs: Can the Cafe Keep Its Cool?"** in *Globe & Mail* **(January 6, 2006, pp. B7)**
Pub: CTVglobemedia Publishing Inc.
Ed: Steven Gray. **Description:** The feasibility of Starbucks Corp.'s plans to introduce drive-through cafes is discussed.

9651 ■ *The Starbucks Experience*
Pub: McGraw-Hill
Ed: Joseph A. Michelli. **Released:** September 14, 2006. **Price:** $24.95. **Description:** Boardroom strategies, employee motivation tips, community involvement, and customer satisfaction are issues addressed, using Starbucks as a model.

9652 ■ *The Starbucks Experience: 5 Principles for Turing Ordinary into Extraordinary*
Pub: McGraw-Hill
Ed: Joseph A. Michelli. **Released:** November 2006.

9653 ■ **"Starbucks' Wheel Strategy"** in *Puget Sound Business Journal* **(Vol. 29, October 3, 2008, No. 24, pp. 1)**
Pub: American City Business Journals
Ed: Greg Lamm. **Description:** Starbuck Corporation has placed drive-through windows in nearly 50 percent of its locations. Dorothy Kim, executive vice president of global strategy, revealed that the firm's transformation strategy includes the addition of even more drive-through windows since people want the car-friendly conveniences.

9654 ■ **"Sun Capital Partners Affiliate Acquires Timothy's Coffees"** in *Miami Daily Business Review* **(March 26, 2008)**
Pub: ALM Media Inc.
Description: An affiliate of Sun Capital Partners acquired Timothy's Coffees of the World. Timothy's operates and franchises 166 stores offering coffees, muffins, and Michel's Baguette products.

9655 ■ **"This CEO's Mom Taught Him Everything He Needs to Know"** in *Globe & Mail* **(February 19, 2007, pp. B9)**
Pub: CTVglobemedia Publishing Inc.
Ed: Gordon Pitts. **Description:** Interview with Paul House, chairman and chief executive officer of Tim Hortons Inc., who shares a few things about his entrepreneurial life and career.

9656 ■ **"Top Coffee Has Concord Ties"** in *Charlotte Observer* **(February 7, 2007)**
Pub: Knight-Ridder/Tribune Business News
Ed: Adam Bell. **Description:** McDonald's highly rated premium coffee is supplied by Concord's S&D Coffee, one of three McDonald's coffee suppliers. The blend outranked Starbucks and Dunkin' Donuts coffee by Consumer Reports.

9657 ■ **"Verizon Small Business Awards Give Companies a Technology Edge"** in *Hispanic Business* **(July-August 2009, pp. 32)**
Pub: Hispanic Business
Ed: Patricia Marroquin. **Description:** Verizon Wireless awards grants to twenty-four companies in California. The winning businesses ranged from barbershop to coffee shop, tattoo parlor to florist.

9658 ■ **"Waste Not"** in *Entrepreneur* **(Vol. 36, April 2008, No. 4, pp. 21)**
Pub: Entrepreneur Media, Inc.
Ed: JJ Ramberg. **Description:** RecycleBank is a company that provides homes with carts in which recyclables are thrown. An identification chip measures the amount of recyclables and converts them into points, which can be redeemed in stores, such as Starbucks and Whole Foods. RecycleBank earns revenue from cities that save landfill waste spending with the use of the program.

9659 ■ **"'We Had to Won the Mistakes'"** in *Harvard Business Review* **(Vol. 88, July-August 2010, No. 7-8, pp. 108)**
Pub: Harvard Business School Publishing
Ed: Adi Ignatius. **Description:** Interview with Howard Schultz, CEO of Starbucks, covers topics that include investment in retraining, the impact of competition, premium quality, authenticity, customer services, strategy development, work-and-life issues, and international presence.

9660 ■ **"While Competitors Shut Doors, Subway Is Still Growing"** in *Advertising Age* **(Vol. 79, July 21, 2008, No. 28, pp. 4)**
Pub: Crain Communications, Inc.
Ed: Emily Bryson York. **Description:** Subway, the largest fast-food chain, with 22,000 U.S. locations, is adding 800 this year, despite the economic downturn that has caused competitors such as Starbucks to close stores and McDonald's to focus its expansion abroad.

STATISTICAL SOURCES

9661 ■ *Standard & Poor's Industry Surveys*
Pub: Standard & Poor's Corp.
Released: Annual. **Price:** $3633.00. **Description:** Two-volume book that examines the prospects for specific industries, including trucking. Also provides analyses of trends and problems, statistical tables and charts, and comparative company analyses.

TRADE PERIODICALS

9662 ■ *Fresh from the Roaster*
Pub: Green Mountain Coffee
Contact: Rick Peyser
Ed: Released: Quarterly. **Price:** Free. **Description:** Offers information about coffee roasting, brewing, and drinking. Recurring features include a letter from the president, financial update, and a recipe.

9663 ■ *Tea and Coffee Trade Journal*
Pub: Lockwood Trade Publications Inc.
Released: Monthly. **Price:** $49; $83 two years; $152 other countries airmail; $68 other countries surface mail; $258 two years airmail; $116 two years surface mail. **Description:** Magazine on coffee and tea roasters and packers.

FRANCHISES AND BUSINESS OPPORTUNITIES

9664 ■ **Barnie's Coffee & Tea Co., Inc.**
2126 W Landstreet Rd., Ste. 300
Orlando, FL 32809-7902
Ph:(407)854-6600
Free: 800-456-1416
Fax:(407)854-6666
No. of Franchise Units: 23. **No. of Company-Owned Units:** 14. **Founded:** 1980. **Franchised:** 1981. **Description:** Gourmet coffee and tea. **Equity Capital Needed:** $222,000-$414,000 total investment. **Franchise Fee:** $25,000. **Royalty Fee:** 7%. **Financial Assistance:** No. **Training:** Yes.

9665 ■ **The Bearclaw Coffee Company**
780 Taylor St.
Chelsea, MI 48118
Ph:(734)395-3864
Fax:(734)433-0009
No. of Franchise Units: 20. **No. of Company-Owned Units:** 5. **Founded:** 2002. **Franchised:** 2003. **Description:** Coffee and espresso drinks. **Equity Capital Needed:** $73,700-$293,000. **Franchise Fee:** $24,500. **Royalty Fee:** 6%. **Financial Assistance:** Third party financing available. **Training:** Provides 1 week at headquarters, at franchisee's location with ongoing support.

9666 ■ **Cafe Ala Carte**
Cafe Ala Carte Corp.
19512 S Coquina Way
Weston, FL 33332
Ph:(949)349-1030
Fax:(954)349-3100
No. of Franchise Units: 2. **No. of Company-Owned Units:** 13. **Founded:** 1996. **Franchised:** 2000. **Description:** Carts serving coffee and espresso drinks. **Equity Capital Needed:** $56,200-$80,800 total investment. **Franchise Fee:** $25,000. **Royalty Fee:** 8-5%. **Financial Assistance:** Third party financing available. **Training:** Provides 1 week at headquarters, 1 week in Fort Lauderdale, FL with ongoing support.

9667 ■ **Cafe Depot/Coffee Depot**
2464 Jean-Talon E
Montreal, QC, Canada H2E 1W2
Ph:(514)281-2067
Fax:(514)281-6405
Co. E-mail: info@cafedepot.ca
URL: http://www.cafedepot.ca
No. of Franchise Units: 62. **No. of Company-Owned Units:** 5. **Founded:** 1994. **Franchised:** 2003. **Description:** We specialize in coffees from all over the world serving delicious sandwiches and des-

serts in a warm friendly atmosphere. **Equity Capital Needed:** $100,000 start-up capital required; $250,000 investment required. **Franchise Fee:** $25,000. **Training:** Yes.

9668 ■ Caffino
4070 Nelson Ave., Ste. G
Concord, CA 94520
Ph:(925)363-3200
Fax:(925)246-9985
No. of Franchise Units: 19. **No. of Company-Owned Units:** 8. **Founded:** 1993. **Franchised:** 2002. **Description:** Coffee. **Equity Capital Needed:** $212,900-$373,000. **Franchise Fee:** $10,000. **Royalty Fee:** 8%. **Financial Assistance:** No. **Training:** Provides 3 weeks training at headquarters. ers.

9669 ■ Coffee Beanery
Coffee Beanery, Ltd.
3429 Pierson Pl.
Flushing, MI 48433
Ph:(810)733-1020
Free: 888-385-2326
Fax:(810)733-1536
Co. E-mail: stacyp@beanerysupport.com
URL: http://www.coffeebeanery.com
No. of Franchise Units: 93. **No. of Company-Owned Units:** 2. **Founded:** 1976. **Franchised:** 1985. **Description:** The Coffee Beanery retails whole bean coffees and beverages, espresso and cappuccino in a variety of styles in carts, kiosks, in-line mall stores and street front cafes. **Equity Capital Needed:** $74,250-$545,000. **Franchise Fee:** $27,500. **Financial Assistance:** No. **Training:** 4 weeks training at corporate headquarters plus 1 week orientation including customer service, merchandising, marketing & daily operations. Additional onsite training, site selection assistance, lease negotiation, layout & construction supervision, and on-going support via 800 line, Internet, fax, enewsletter, & field support.

9670 ■ Coffee News
Coffee News USA, Inc.
120 Linden St.
Bangor, ME 04402-8444
Ph:(207)941-0860
Fax:(207)941-1050
Co. E-mail: bill@coffeenews.com
URL: http://www.coffeenewsusa.com
No. of Franchise Units: 802. **Founded:** 1988. **Franchised:** 1995. **Description:** Weekly publication for distribution in coffee shops and restaurants. **Equity Capital Needed:** $6,000 per franchise, plus a one-time training fee of $2,500 for first franchise. **Franchise Fee:** $8,500. **Financial Assistance:** Visa/MasterCard. **Managerial Assistance:** Newsletter published every two months and full line of products available for purchase. **Training:** Quarterly training sessions, open to all franchisees and personal mentor program.

9671 ■ Coffee Time Donuts Inc.
77 Progress Ave.
Toronto, ON, Canada M1P 2Y7
Ph:(416)288-8515
Fax:(416)288-8895
Co. E-mail: franchising@coffeetime.ca
URL: http://www.coffeetime.ca
No. of Franchise Units: 184. **No. of Company-Owned Units:** 18. **Founded:** 1982. **Franchised:** 1989. **Description:** The menu includes donuts, muffins, croissants, pastries and gourmet blend coffee, soups, chili, salads, sandwiches and various hot and cold beverages. store, serving customers in a warm and efficient manner and fostering good employee relationships. **Equity Capital Needed:** $100,000-$360,000. **Financial Assistance:** No. **Training:** Yes.

9672 ■ Country Style
2 E Beaver Creek Rd., Bldg. 1
Richmond Hill, ON, Canada L4B 2N3
Ph:(905)762-4670
Free: 800-563-6688
Fax:(905)764-1601
Co. E-mail: bill@mtygroup.com
URL: http://www.countrystyle.com
No. of Franchise Units: 473. **No. of Company-Owned Units:** 3. **Founded:** 1962. **Franchised:** 1963. **Description:** The franchise is a pioneer in

country style coffee. **Equity Capital Needed:** $100,000. **Franchise Fee:** $35,000. **Training:** Provides 4 weeks initial training.

9673 ■ Coyote Canyon - A Steak Buffet
Stockade Franchising, LP
2908 N Plum St.
Hutchinson, KS 67502-8400
Ph:(620)669-9372
Fax:(620)669-0531
No. of Franchise Units: 7. **Founded:** 1999. **Franchised:** 1999. **Description:** One low price all you can eat steak buffet. **Equity Capital Needed:** $1,000,000 net worth; $250,000 liquid assets. **Franchise Fee:** $20,000. **Financial Assistance:** No. **Training:** Yes.

9674 ■ Dazbog Coffee
1090 Yuma St.
Denver, CO 80204
Ph:(303)892-9999
Fax:(303)893-9999
No. of Franchise Units: 5. **No. of Company-Owned Units:** 4. **Founded:** 1996. **Franchised:** 2006. **Description:** Coffee. **Equity Capital Needed:** $187,300-$376,800. **Franchise Fee:** $25,000. **Royalty Fee:** 6%. **Financial Assistance:** Third party financing available.

9675 ■ Dunn Bros Coffee
111 3rd Ave. S, Ste. 220
Minneapolis, MN 55401-2552
Ph:(612)334-9746
Fax:(612)334-9749
No. of Franchise Units: 83. **No. of Company-Owned Units:** 3. **Founded:** 1987. **Franchised:** 1994. **Description:** Coffeehouse. **Equity Capital Needed:** $125,750-$453,600. **Franchise Fee:** $24,000-$32,000. **Royalty Fee:** 5%. **Financial Assistance:** Third party financing available. **Training:** Offers 2 1/2 weeks at headquarters and ongoing support.

9676 ■ Ellianos Coffee Co.
426 SW Commerce Dr., Ste. 105
Lake City, FL 32055
Ph:(386)755-5828
Fax:(386)758-2999
No. of Franchise Units: 7. **Founded:** 2002. **Franchised:** 2003. **Description:** Drive-thru coffee shop. **Equity Capital Needed:** $169,300-$292,500. **Franchise Fee:** $20,000. **Royalty Fee:** 5%. **Financial Assistance:** Third party financing available. **Training:** Offers 1-2 weeks at headquarters, 3 days onsite with ongoing support.

9677 ■ Gloria Jean's Gourmet Coffees
Diedrich Coffee
17691 Mitchell N, Ste. A
Irvine, CA 92614
Ph:(949)260-6757
Fax:(949)260-6745
Co. E-mail: nromero@gloriajeans.com
URL: http://www.gloriajeans.com
No. of Franchise Units: 110. **No. of Company-Owned Units:** 8. **Founded:** 1979. **Franchised:** 1986. **Description:** Retail gourmet coffee franchisor offering coffee, teas, and accessories. **Equity Capital Needed:** $350,000 net worth; $125,000 liquidity. **Franchise Fee:** $32,500. **Financial Assistance:** No. **Training:** Yes.

9678 ■ Good Earth Coffee House & Bakery
4020 7 St., SE
Calgary, AB, Canada T2G 2Y8
Ph:(403)294-9330
Free: 888-294-9330
Fax:(403)294-9329
Co. E-mail: franchise@goodearthcafes.com
URL: http://www.goodearthcafes.com
No. of Franchise Units: 35. **Founded:** 1991. **Franchised:** 2005. **Description:** An innovative coffeehouse and fresh food concept, with 15 years of success. We began with a passion for excellent coffee and wholesome, healthful food. While our company has grown, we have stayed true to our original purpose... to be a coffeehouse with good food. Join

our team and prosper with purpose. **Equity Capital Needed:** $125,000-$250,000. **Franchise Fee:** $35,000. **Training:** Provides 4-6 weeks training.

9679 ■ A Grande Finale Franchise LLC
995 Ash St.
Broomfield, CO 80020
Ph:(720)849-2432
Fax:(303)410-9568
No. of Company-Owned Units: 2. **Founded:** 1999. **Franchised:** 2007. **Description:** Desserts, coffee, and tea. **Equity Capital Needed:** $125,900-$237,800. **Franchise Fee:** $35,000-$60,000. **Royalty Fee:** 5-6%. **Financial Assistance:** No.

9680 ■ The Human Bean Drive Thru
545 Rossanley Dr., Ste. A
Medford, OR 97501
Ph:(541)608-0564
Fax:(541)608-3757
No. of Franchise Units: 35. **No. of Company-Owned Units:** 12. **Founded:** 1998. **Franchised:** 2002. **Description:** Specialty coffee. **Equity Capital Needed:** $154,050-$618,000. **Franchise Fee:** $20,000. **Royalty Fee:** None. **Financial Assistance:** Third party financing available. **Training:** Offers 3 weeks training at headquarters and at franchisee's location at time of opening and ongoing support.

9681 ■ It's A Grind Coffee House
It's a Grind Franchise LLC
6272 E Pacific Coast Hwy., Ste. E
Long Beach, CA 90803
Ph:(562)594-5600
Free: (866)424-5282
Fax:(562)594-4100
URL: http://www.itsagrind.com
No. of Franchise Units: 83. **No. of Company-Owned Units:** 6. **Founded:** 1995. **Franchised:** 2001. **Description:** Provides help in establishing and running a coffee house. **Equity Capital Needed:** $400,000 net worth; $125,000 cash available. **Franchise Fee:** $36,000. **Financial Assistance:** Third party financing. **Training:** Yes.

9682 ■ Kelly's Coffee & Fudge Factory
PO Box 21538
Bakersfield, CA 93390
Ph:(661)663-8416
Fax:(661)664-4785
No. of Franchise Units: 42. **Founded:** 1983. **Franchised:** 1983. **Description:** Coffee and fudge retail store. **Equity Capital Needed:** $350,000. **Franchise Fee:** $20,000. **Financial Assistance:** No. **Training:** Yes.

9683 ■ Lox of Bagels
11801 Prestwick Rd., Ste. 301
Potomac, MD 20854
Ph:(301)299-8523
Free: 800-879-6927
No. of Franchise Units: 12. **Founded:** 1983. **Franchised:** 1996. **Description:** Bagels and gourmet coffee. **Equity Capital Needed:** $50,000 in equity with typical cost of $150,000-$200,000 per unit. **Franchise Fee:** $9,500. **Financial Assistance:** Yes. **Training:** Yes.

9684 ■ Melt Inc.
31556 Loma Linda Rd.
Temecula, CA 92592
Ph:(949)707-0456
Fax:(949)707-0457
No. of Franchise Units: 8. **No. of Company-Owned Units:** 2. **Founded:** 2003. **Franchised:** 2005. **Description:** Gelato, Italian coffee, and crepes. **Equity Capital Needed:** $200,000-$400,000 (Express/kiosk option available). **Franchise Fee:** $25,000. **Royalty Fee:** 6%. **Financial Assistance:** Third party financing available. **Training:** Includes 6 days training at headquarters, 4 days at franchisee's location and ongoing support.

9685 ■ Mocha Delites Inc.
PO Box 674228
Marietta, GA 30006-0071
Free: 800-539-9532

Fax:888-453-1172
URL: http://www.mochadelites.com
No. of Franchise Units: 41. **No. of Company-Owned Units:** 3. **Founded:** 2000. **Franchised:** 2001. **Description:** Coffeehouse. **Equity Capital Needed:** $53,500-$232,500. **Franchise Fee:** $22,500. **Royalty Fee:** 5%. **Financial Assistance:** Limited third party financing available. **Training:** 1 week at corporate headquarters, 1 week of onsite, and ongoing support included. ded.

9686 ■ Mountain Mudd Espresso
2120 3rd Ave., N
Billings, MT 59101
Free: 800-218-6833
Fax:(406)256-6070
No. of Franchise Units: 5. NCU 12. **Founded:** 1994. **Franchised:** 2007. **Description:** Specialty coffee. **Equity Capital Needed:** $22,500-$266,000. **Franchise Fee:** $5,000-$10,000. **Royalty Fee:** 4%. **Financial Assistance:** Third party financing available. **Training:** Provides 5 days training at headquarters and ongoing at franchisee's location.

9687 ■ PJ's Coffee of New Orleans
Raving Brands
109 New Camellia Blvd., Ste. 201
Covington, LA 70433
Ph:(404)351-3500
URL: http://www.pjscoffee.com
No. of Franchise Units: 107. **No. of Company-Owned Units:** 1. **Founded:** 1978. **Franchised:** 1989. **Description:** Founded in New Orleans, PJ's has been brewing its distinguished brand of signature roasts for over 25 years. Our beans are hand-selected, hand-roasted and brewed to perfection. PJ's also offers a variety of gourmet pastries and deserts. **Equity Capital Needed:** $400,000 net worth; $100,000 liquid assets. **Franchise Fee:** $25,000. **Financial Assistance:** Relationships with multiple financial institutions with experience in assisting franchisees. **Training:** Raving Brands University classroom and onsite training provided. From register operation to food preparation, from hiring staff to accounting procedures, you'll improve your management skills, setup your back office and develop an airtight sales and marketing plan.

9688 ■ The Second Cup Ltd.
6303 Airport Rd.
Mississauga, ON, Canada L4V 1R8
Ph:(905)362-1818
Free: 800-569-6318
Fax:(905)362-1121
Co. E-mail: franchising@secondcup.com
URL: http://www.secondcup.com
No. of Franchise Units: 350. **No. of Company-Owned Units:** 7. **Founded:** 1975. **Franchised:** 1975. **Description:** Retails specialty coffee. **Equity Capital Needed:** Equity of approximately $350,000 (cash & assets). **Franchise Fee:** $40,000. **Training:** Provides 6 weeks training.

9689 ■ Tapioca Express Inc.
1908 Central Ave.
South El Monte, CA 91733
Ph:(626)453-0777
Free: 888-887-1616
Fax:(626)453-0778
Co. E-mail: franchise@tapiocaexpress.com
URL: http://www.tapiocaexpress.com
No. of Franchise Units: 50. **Founded:** 1999. **Franchised:** 2000. **Description:** Tapioca & milk tea beverages **Equity Capital Needed:** $136,000-$402,000. **Franchise Fee:** $15,000. **Royalty Fee:** $2.5%. **Financial Assistance:** No. **Training:** Offers 8 days at company store and ongoing support.

9690 ■ Tealuxe, A Tea Bar & Cafe
Tealuxe, Inc.
201 Newtown Rd.
Plainview, NY 11803
Free: 888-TEA-LUXE
URL: http://www.tealuxe.com
No. of Company-Owned Units: 3. **Founded:** 1996. **Franchised:** 2003. **Description:** A tea bar and cafe. **Equity Capital Needed:** $150,000-$250,000. **Franchise Fee:** $25,000. **Financial Assistance:** No. **Training:** Yes.

9691 ■ Tim Hortons
874 Sinclair Rd.
Oakville, ON, Canada L6K 2Y1
Ph:(905)845-6511
Fax:(905)845-0265
Co. E-mail: franchise_requests@timhortons.com
URL: http://www.timhortons.com
No. of Franchise Units: 3,000. **No. of Company-Owned Units:** 18. **Founded:** 1964. **Franchised:** 1964. **Description:** Offers the highest quality fresh baked goods to enjoy with our famous premium blend Tim Hortons Coffee. **Equity Capital Needed:** $194,000. **Franchise Fee:** $50,000. **Training:** Yes.

9692 ■ Timothy's World Coffee
Threecaf Brands Canada Inc.
7880 Keele St., Ste. 101
Vaughan, ON, Canada L4K 4G7
Ph:(905)482-7300
Free: 877-434-3223
Fax:(905)482-7330
Co. E-mail: franchise@timothys.com
URL: http://www.timothys.com
No. of Franchise Units: 81. **No. of Company-Owned Units:** 8. **Founded:** 1975. **Franchised:** 1979. **Description:** Specializes in a variety of whole bean and freshly brewed specialty coffees, pastries, light sandwiches and coffee accessories. Offers good quality control in the selection, capping and roasting of coffee beans. **Equity Capital Needed:** $300,000-$450,000. **Franchise Fee:** $25,000 + GST. **Training:** Offers 3 week training program.

9693 ■ Van Houtte L.P.
8300 19th Ave.
Montreal, QC, Canada H1Z 4J8
Ph:(514)789-4611
Free: 877-593-7722
Fax:(514)593-9582
Co. E-mail: clmonette@vanhoutte.com
URL: http://www.vanhoutte.com
No. of Franchise Units: 70. **Founded:** 1919. **Franchised:** 1983. **Description:** Cafe offering coffee and espresso drinks, tea, soups and sandwiches. **Equity Capital Needed:** $150,000 minimum investment required; $150,000 minimum start-up capital required. **Franchise Fee:** $40,000 Canadian.

LIBRARIES

9694 ■ Unilever Bestfoods–Library/Information Center
800 Sylvan Ave.
Englewood Cliffs, NJ 07632
Ph:(201)894-7532
Fax:(201)894-7532
Contact: Beth Currie, Mgr.
Scope: Tea, food technology. **Services:** Interlibrary loan; Library not open to the public. **Holdings:** 10,000 books; 300 bound periodical volumes; U.S. chemical patents (1970 to 1993, on microfilm; 1994 to present, on CD-ROM). **Subscriptions:** 250 journals and other serials.

START-UP INFORMATION

9695 ■ *How to Open and Operate a Financially Successful Landscaping, Nursery or Lawn Service Business: With Companion CD-ROM*
Pub: Atlantic Publishing Company
Ed: Lynn Wasnak. **Released:** June 1, 2009. **Price:** $39.95. **Description:** Guide provides understanding of the basic concepts of starting and running a service business, focusing on the operation of a small nursery, landscaping, or lawn service or combining the three operations. It also offers tips for running the business from the home.

ASSOCIATIONS AND OTHER ORGANIZATIONS

9696 ■ American Horticultural Society
7931 E Boulevard Dr.
Alexandria, VA 22308-1300
Ph:(703)768-5700
Free: 800-777-7931
Fax:(703)768-8700
Co. E-mail: membership@ahs.org
URL: http://www.ahs.org
Contact: Tom Underwood, Exec. Dir.
Description: Represents amateur and professional gardeners. Aims to educate and inspire people of all ages to become successful and environmentally responsible gardeners by advancing the art and science of horticulture. Operates free seed exchange and gardeners' information service for members. Offers internships and children's services. **Publications:** *AHS A-Z Encyclopedia of Garden Plants*; *AHS Encyclopedia of Plants and Flowers*; *AHS Great Plant Guide*; *The American Gardener* (bimonthly).

9697 ■ American Hydrangea Society
PO Box 53234
Atlanta, GA 30355
Co. E-mail: pearlworks@hotmail.com
URL: http://www.americanhydrangeasociety.org
Contact: Sandy Jones, Pres.
Description: Represents growers and other individuals with an interest in the genus Hydrangea. Promotes the study of the cultivation of Hydrangea and related plant species. Conducts educational programs and serves as a clearinghouse on Hydrangea. Hosts members only garden tour each June. .

9698 ■ American Nursery and Landscape Association
1200 G St., NW
Ste. 800
Washington, DC 20005
Ph:(202)789-2900
Fax:(202)789-1893
Co. E-mail: cbeirne@anla.org
URL: http://www.anla.org
Contact: Robert J. Dolibois CAE, Exec. VP
Description: Vertical organization of wholesale growers; landscape firms; garden centers; mail order nurseries; suppliers. Promotes the industry and its

products. Offers management and consulting services and public relations programs. Provides government representation and bank card plan for members. Maintains hall of fame. .

9699 ■ American Seed Trade Association
1701 Duke St., Ste. 675
Alexandria, VA 22314
Ph:(703)837-8140
Fax:(703)837-9365
Co. E-mail: info@amseed.org
URL: http://www.amseed.com
Contact: Kelly Keithly, Chm.
Description: Breeders, growers, assemblers, conditioners, wholesalers, and retailers of grain, grass, vegetable, flower, and other seed for planting purposes. **Publications:** *Corn and Sorghum Proceedings* (annual); *Soybean Seed Proceedings* (annual).

9700 ■ Canadian Nursery Landscape Association–Association Candienne des Pepinieristes et des Paysagistes
RR No. 4, Sta. Main
7856 5th Line S
Milton, ON, Canada L9T 2X8
Ph:(905)875-1399
Free: 888-446-3499
Fax:(905)875-1840
Co. E-mail: info@canadanursery.com
URL: http://www.canadanursery.com
Contact: Victor Santacruz CAE, Exec. Dir.
Description: Growers, retail garden centers, lawn care and gardening services, sod growers, landscape, construction, and maintenance contractors, and other horticultural industries. Promotes expansion of the nursery and related industries. Devises standards and develops and administers tests to ensure competence in nursery production, garden supply retailing, landscape contracting, and construction and maintenance. Makes available support and services to members including discount insurance policies and merchant credit cards, educational programs, and representation before government agencies. Sponsors research; compiles statistics. **Publications:** *CNLA Newsbrief* (bimonthly); Directory (annual).

9701 ■ Flowers Canada
99 5th Ave., Ste. 305
Ottawa, ON, Canada K1S 5P5
Free: 800-447-5147
Fax:(866)671-8091
Co. E-mail: flowers@flowerscanada.org
URL: http://flowerscanada.ca
Contact: Jeff Waters, Pres.
Description: Retail florists, distributors, and greenhouse operators. Promotes growth and development in the domestic floriculture industry. Provides technical and promotional services to floral retailers, producers, and distributors; sponsors continuing professional development and educational programs for members. Represents members' interests before government agencies; serves as a liaison between members and related trade organizations. Makes available discount credit card, insurance, automotive

fleet, lodging, and other business services to members. **Publications:** *News Vine* (bimonthly); Membership Directory (annual).

9702 ■ Hobby Greenhouse Association
8858 Possum Rd.
Worden, IL 62097-1020
Co. E-mail: tomsherron@msn.com
URL: http://www.hobbygreenhouse.org
Contact: Tom Karasek, Pres.
Description: Greenhouse owners and those who grow plants indoors with lights; windowsill and porch gardeners. Promotes the hobby of greenhouse and indoor gardening. Provides information on plants and diseases, propagation of seeds, insect control, and greenhouse building and maintenance. **Publications:** *Directory of Manufacturers of Residential Greenhouses and Distributors of Imported Greenhouses* (annual); *HGA News* (quarterly); *Hobby Greenhouse* (quarterly).

9703 ■ National Gardening Association
1100 Dorset St.
South Burlington, VT 05403
Ph:(802)863-5251
Free: 800-538-7476
Fax:(802)864-6889
URL: http://www.garden.org
Contact: Michael Metallo, Pres./CEO
Description: Serves as a clearinghouse for home, community and educational gardening information. Conduct programs providing technical assistance, materials, and grants to children's gardens nationwide. Sponsor events forums and programs to raise the awareness for the benefits of gardening. Constituents include home gardeners, community garden groups, nursing and rehabilitation homes, schools, youth clubs, camps, educators and parents. Aims to promote home, school and community gardening as a means to renew and sustain the essential connection between people, plants and the environment. Promotes environmental responsibility, advance multi-disciplinary learning and scientific literacy, and create partnerships that restore and enhance communities. **Publications:** *Environmental Survey* (triennial); *Gardening with Kids* (3/year); *Growing Ideas* (quarterly); *Growing Ventures*; *Math in the Garden*; *National Gardening Survey* (annual); *What Gardeners Think* (triennial).

9704 ■ North American Flowerbulb Wholesalers Association
2424 Hwy. 72/221 E
Greenwood, SC 29649
Ph:(864)229-1618
Fax:(864)229-5719
Co. E-mail: nafwa1@aol.com
URL: http://www.nafwa.com
Contact: Jack C. De Vroomen, Sec.-Treas.
Description: Wholesalers and dealers of flower bulbs and related floricultural commodities. .

9705 ■ Nursery and Landscape Association Executives of North America
2130 Stella Ct.
Columbus, OH 43215
Ph:(614)487-1117

Fax:(614)487-1216
Co. E-mail: nlae@ofa.org
URL: http://www.nlae.org
Contact: Amy Graham, Pres.
Description: Professional society of executives of state, national, regional, and provincial nursery trade associations. .

9706 ■ Ornamental Concrete Producers Association
759 Phelps Johnson Rd.
Leitchfield, KY 42754
Ph:(270)879-6319
Fax:(270)879-0399
Co. E-mail: ocpa@windstream.net
URL: http://www.ocpainfo.com
Contact: Donna Dunkelberger, Exec. Dir.
Description: Producers of ornamental concrete products. Seeks to advance the ornamental concrete and related industries. Conducts educational programs; sponsors competitions; holds mold auctions. .

DIRECTORIES OF EDUCATIONAL PROGRAMS

9707 ■ *Directory of Private Accredited Career Schools and Colleges of Technology*
Pub: Accrediting Commission of Career Schools and Colleges of Technology
Contact: Michale S. McComis, Exec. Dir.
Released: On web page. **Price:** Free. **Description:** Covers 3900 accredited post-secondary programs that provide training programs in business, trade, and technical fields, including various small business endeavors. Entries offer school name, address, phone, description of courses, job placement assistance, and requirements for admission. Arrangement is alphabetical.

REFERENCE WORKS

9708 ■ "Active Sales" in *Green Industry Pro* (Vol. 23, September 2011)
Pub: Cygnus Business Media
Ed: Gregg Wartgow. **Description:** Craig den Hartog, owner of Emerald Magic Lawn Care located in Holtsville, New York, describes the various marketing tactics he has developed to increase sales in the current economic environment. Statistical data included.

9709 ■ "All the Trimmings" in *Green Industry Pro* (Vol. 23, March 2011, No. 3, pp. 29)
Pub: Cygnus Business Media
Ed: Gregg Wartgow. **Description:** When choosing lawn mowing equipment, it is advised to purchase commercial-grade 21-inch walk mowers rather than less expensive consumer-grade mowers. John Deere is reentering the commercial 21-inch walk behind mower market after a five-year hiatus.

9710 ■ *Andersen Horticultural Library's Source List of Plants and Seeds*
Pub: Andersen Horticultural Library
Ed: Richard T. Isaacson, Editor. **Released:** Irregular, latest edition 6th, 2004. **Price:** $39.95, individuals postpaid. **Covers:** More than 600 nurseries that offer over 70,000 different plants. **Entries Include:** Company name, address, phone. **Arrangement:** Alphabetical. **Indexes:** Product code, geographical.

9711 ■ "Be Innovative In Other Ways" in *Green Industry Pro* (Vol. 23, March 2011, No. 3, pp. 4)
Pub: Cygnus Business Media
Ed: Rod Dickens. **Description:** Emphasis is put on the importance of putting the customer first in order to successfully market any product or service. Six marketing ideas are presented to promote a landscaping business.

9712 ■ "Customer Retention is Proportionate to Employee Retention" in *Green Industry Pro* (Vol. 23, September 2011)
Pub: Cygnus Business Media
Description: Presented in a question-answer format, information is provided to help retain customers as well as keeping workers happy.

9713 ■ "Customized Before Custom Was Cool" in *Green Industry Pro* (July 2011)
Pub: Cygnus Business Media
Ed: Gregg Wartgow. **Description:** Profile of Turf Care Enterprises and owner Kevin Vogeler, who discusses his desire to use more natural programs using little or no chemicals in 1986. At that time, that sector represented 20 percent of his business, today it shares 80 percent.

9714 ■ "Deep in the Heart of Drought" in *Green Industry Pro* (Vol. 23, October 2011)
Pub: Cygnus Business Media
Ed: Gregg Wartgow. **Description:** Challenges faced by landscape contractors during the recent drought in Texas are explored. Despite these challenges, opportunity for contractors providing irrigation services has risen.

9715 ■ "Dozens 'Come Alive' in Downtown Chicago" in *Green Industry Pro* (July 2011)
Pub: Cygnus Business Media
Ed: Gregg Wartgow. **Description:** Highlights from the Come Alive Outside training event held in Chicago, Illinois July 14-15, 2011 are shared. Nearly 80 people representing 38 landscape companies attended the event that helps contractors review their services and find ways to sell them in new and various ways.

9716 ■ "Finding a Way to Continue Growing" in *Green Industry Pro* (Vol. 23, March 2011, No. 3, pp. 31)
Pub: Cygnus Business Media
Description: Profile of Brett Lemcke, VP of R.M. Landscape located in Rochester, New York. Lemcke tells how his Landscape Industry Certified credentials helped him to grow his business and beat out his competition.

9717 ■ "Five Distinct Divisions, One Collective Focus" in *Green Industry Pro* (Vol. 23, October 2011)
Pub: Cygnus Business Media
Ed: Gregg Wartgow. **Description:** Profile of ACLS Inc., an amalgamation of All Commercial Landscape Service (commercial maintenance), All Custom Landscape Service (design/build), Fresno Tree Service, Certified Water Consulting (irrigation), and Tractor Service (disking and flailing services on everything from one-acre lots to hundreds of acres of open land). The firm discusses its rebranding effort in order to increase sales.

9718 ■ "Forward Motion" in *Green Industry Pro* (July 2011)
Pub: Cygnus Business Media
Ed: Gregg Wartgow. **Description:** Several landscape contractors have joined this publication's Working Smarter Training Challenge over the last year. This process is helping them develop ways to improve work processes, boost morale, drive out waste, reduce costs, improve customer service, and be more competitive.

9719 ■ "Gain the 'Come Alive Outside' Selling Edge" in *Green Industry Pro* (July 2011)
Pub: Cygnus Business Media
Ed: Jim Paluch. **Description:** Marketing the 'Come Alive Outside' slogan can help landscapers to increase their market share by identifying and applying these elements to each customer as well as their workers.

9720 ■ *Garden Seed Inventory*
Pub: Seed Savers Exchange
Ed: Arllys Adelmann, Editor. **Released:** Irregular, latest edition 2005. **Price:** $26, individuals softcover (current edition). **Publication Includes:** List of 255 mail-order companies supplying non-hybrid vegetable seeds; coverage includes the U.S. and Canada. **Entries Include:** Company name, address, and description, type of seeds offered. Principal content is an inventory of 255 mail-order seed catalogs and descriptions of the 8,494 non-hybrid seed varieties they offer. Detailed descriptions are compiled from the catalogs. **Arrangement:** Classified by varieties of seeds offered.

9721 ■ "The Green Industry Jobs Gap" in *Green Industry Pro* (Vol. 23, October 2011)
Pub: Cygnus Business Media
Ed: Gregg Wartgow. **Description:** According to the U.S. Bureau of Labor Statistics, the landscaping industry employs over 829,000 workers. According to another private study, the industry would employ more if they were able to find more people interested in performing the required work.

9722 ■ "Hey, You Can't Do That" in *Green Industry Pro* (Vol. 23, September 2011)
Pub: Cygnus Business Media
Ed: Rod Dickens. **Description:** Manufacturers of landscape equipment are making better use of energy resources, such as the use of fuel-injection systems instead of carburetors, lightweight materials, better lubricants, advanced battery technology, and innovative engine designs.

9723 ■ "How to Dominate in Residential Maintenance" in *Green Industry Pro* (Vol. 23, October 2011)
Pub: Cygnus Business Media
Ed: Gregg Wartgow. **Description:** Lawn care services were ranked among the most expendable consumer expenditures, according to the National Retail Federation data accumulated in early 2011. This makes it critical for any landscape firm to target sales efforts toward higher-income households and higher-value homes.

9724 ■ "How To Turn Your Efforts Into Results" in *Green Industry Pro* (Vol. 23, September 2011)
Pub: Cygnus Business Media
Ed: Bob Coulter. **Description:** Working Smarter Training Challenge teaches that leaders are able to carry out solutions directly into their organization, develop skills and drive business results in key areas by creating a culture of energized workers who are able to take ownership of their performance as well as the performance of the company as a whole.

9725 ■ "KC Sewer Solutions May Overflow With Green Ideas" in *The Business Journal-Serving Metropolitan Kansas City* (August 22, 2008)
Pub: American City Business Journals, Inc.
Ed: Suzanna Stagemeyer. **Description:** Adding green solutions such as small, dispersed basins to catch runoffs and the use of deep rooted natural plants to fix the sewer system of Kansas could probably justify the $2.3 billion worth of funds needed for the project. The city has been ordered by the EPA and the Missouri Department of Natural Resources to fix their sewer systems that are overwhelmed by significant rains.

9726 ■ "Labor of Love" in *Green Industry Pro* (Vol. 23, March 2011, No. 3, pp. 14)
Pub: Cygnus Business Media
Ed: Gregg Wartgow. **Description:** Profile of CLS Landscape Management in Chino, California and its owner who started the company when he was 21 years old. Kevin Davis built his landscape firm into a $20 million a year business without using any dedicated salesperson.

9727 ■ "The Price of Profitability" in *Green Industry Pro* (Vol. 23, March 2011, No. 3, pp. 18)
Pub: Cygnus Business Media
Ed: Tony Bass. **Description:** Profit Builder Process is used to help landscaping companies be more competitive. Landscape contractors report pricing among their largest challenges and although the economy is improving, homeowners are paying closer attention to quality and service.

9728 ■ "Rediscovering the Land of Opportunity" in *Green Industry Pro* (July 2011)
Pub: Cygnus Business Media
Ed: Gregg Wartgow. **Description:** Landscape contractors need to discover new strategies that will generate leads and convert those leads into sales.

9729 ■ "Take Control of Your Company's Finances" in *Green Industry Pro* (Vol. 23, March 2011, No. 3, pp. 24)
Pub: Cygnus Business Media
Ed: Gregg Wartgow. **Description:** Understanding that when certain leading indicators that affect the outcome of certain lagging indicators are aligned, companies will be able to take control of their firm's finances. Ways to improve the processes that drive financial performance for landscape firms are outlined.

9730 ■ "Take This Job and Love It" in *Green Industry Pro* (Vol. 23, October 2011)
Pub: Cygnus Business Media
Ed: Gregg Wartgow. **Description:** Details of the lawsuit filed by the Professional Landcare Network (PLANET) against the U.S. Department of Labor are explained. Challenges faced by landscape firms because of employment costs are outlined. Statistical data included.

9731 ■ "Time to Fight Back" in *Green Industry Pro* (Vol. 23, March 2011, No. 3, pp. 8)
Pub: Cygnus Business Media
Ed: Rod Dickens. **Description:** Lawn care operators in the United States must learn from Canada that a shift to socialism will impact their industry in a negative way. Government regulation over the application of control products regarding environmental health in Canada has been a death sentence for small lawn care businesses.

9732 ■ "Tough Climate for Nurseries" in *Crain's Cleveland Business* (Vol. 30, June 29, 2009, No. 25, pp. 1)
Pub: Crain Communications, Inc.
Ed: Stan Bullard. **Description:** After 81 years in the business, Sunnybrook Farms & Nursery is closing its doors. The owner sites the bad economy along with cold weather the reason for lack of sales. Other nursery owners discuss the bad economy and weather conditions and how they are affecting their business.

9733 ■ "Way More Than Mowing" in *Green Industry Pro* (Vol. 23, September 2011)
Pub: Cygnus Business Media
Ed: Rod Dickens. **Description:** Shipp Shape Lawn Services located in Sylvester, Georgia now offers aeration, fertilizing and weed control, mulching, yard renovation, flowerbed maintenance, landscaping, as well as irrigation repairs and installation in order to diversify the business and stay competitive.

STATISTICAL SOURCES

9734 ■ *The Market for Lawn, Garden, & Snow Equipment*
Pub: Business Trend Analysts, Inc.
Released: 2004-2005 **Price:** $2195.00. **Description:** An in-depth industry report tracking market size and growth for residential and commercial mowers, edgers and trimmers, shredders and grinders, yard vacs and blowers, garden tractors, snowthrowers, chain saws, commercial grounds care equipment, lawn and more.

9735 ■ *RMA Annual Statement Studies*
Pub: Robert Morris Associates (RMA)
Released: Annual. **Price:** $175.00 2006-07 edition, $105.00. **Description:** Contains composite balance sheets and income statements for more than 360 industries, including the accounting, auditing, and bookkeeping industries. Also contains five years of comparative historical data for discerning trends. Includes 16 commonly used ratios, computed for most of the size groupings for nearly every industry.

9736 ■ *The U.S. Lawn and Garden Market, 5th Edition*
Pub: MarketResearch.com
Released: 2003. **Price:** $2250.00. **Description:** The information in The U.S. Lawn and Garden Market is based on both primary and secondary research. Primary research involved on-site examination of the retail milieu, interviews with marketing, public relations and industry analysts within the lawn and garden market and consultants to the industry.

TRADE PERIODICALS

9737 ■ *The American Gardener*
Pub: American Horticultural Society
Contact: Viveka Neveln
E-mail: advertising@ahs.org
Ed: David J. Ellis, Editor, dellis@ahs.org. **Released:** Bimonthly. **Price:** $10. **Description:** The official publication of the American Horticultural Society, The American Gardener is written primarily for avid and experienced amateur North American gardeners. In-depth articles focus on ornamental plant groups, garden design, prominent horticulturists or plant breeders, and innovative horticultural research programs. By advancing the art and science of horticulture, we seek to educate and inspire readers to become successful and environmentally responsible gardeners.

9738 ■ *American Nurseryman*
Pub: American Nurseryman Publishing Co.
Released: Semimonthly. **Price:** $48; $80 other countries; $84 Canada; $135 other countries air mail; $141.75 Canada air mail. **Description:** Trade magazine containing information on commercial horticulture: nursery, landscape and garden center management.

9739 ■ *The Avant Gardener*
Pub: Horticultural Data Processors
Ed: Thomas Powell, Editor. **Released:** Monthly. **Price:** $24 year. **Description:** Contains information on such subjects as indoor and outdoor plants, edible plants, new products, methods of cultivation, breeding and growing techniques, pest control, fertilizers, and landscaping. Recurring features include several special issues per year on specific topics.

9740 ■ *Baer's Garden Newsletter*
Pub: John Baer's Sons
Ed: Gerald S. Lestz, Editor. **Released:** Quarterly. **Price:** Free. **Description:** Presents news for gardeners—new developments in flowers and gardens, information on where to send for gardening catalogs, and articles on such topics as public gardens and gardening with children. Includes news of research, book reviews, and notices of publications available.

9741 ■ *California Garden*
Pub: San Diego Floral Association
Released: Bimonthly. **Description:** Magazine on floriculture and horticulture.

9742 ■ *Chicago Home and Garden*
Pub: Chicago Home & Garden
Ed: Jan Parr, Editor, jparr@chicagomag.com. **Released:** Quarterly. **Price:** $9.95; $25; $35 other countries. **Description:** Magazine covering home and garden style in the Chicago, IL, area.

9743 ■ *Country Home*
Pub: Meredith Corp.
Released: Monthly, 10/yr. **Price:** $4.95 newstand; $21.97 two years. **Description:** Magazine furnishing information on American interior design, architecture, antiques and collectibles, gardening, art, and culinary endeavor.

9744 ■ *FloraCulture International Magazine*
Pub: Ball Publishing
Contact: Jaap Kras, Publisher
E-mail: jaap@floracultureinternational.com
Ed: Ron van del Ploeg, Editor, ron@floracultureinternational.com. **Released:** Bimonthly. **Price:** $75; $142.50 other countries. **Description:** Trade magazine for professional growers of cut flowers and flowering plants worldwide.

9745 ■ *Garden Center Products & Supplies*
Pub: GIE Media, Inc.
Contact: Tiffany O'Kelley, Assoc. Publisher
E-mail: tokelley@gie.net
Released: Monthly. **Description:** Catalog focusing on nursery and floral products and services.

9746 ■ *Green Profit Magazine*
Pub: Ball Publishing
Released: 9/yr. **Description:** Trade magazine for flower and plant retailers.

9747 ■ *Greenhouse Business*
Pub: Perkins Communications L.L.C.
Contact: Lynn Perkins, Circulation Mgr
Released: Monthly. **Price:** $50 U.S. and Canada; $100 other countries. **Description:** Trade magazine for commercial greenhouse growers.

9748 ■ *Greenhouse Management and Production*
Pub: GIE Media, Inc.
Contact: Chris Foster, Publisher
E-mail: chris.foster@gie.net
Released: Monthly. **Description:** Commercial greenhouse growers magazine.

9749 ■ *Horticulture*
Pub: FW Media Inc.
Contact: Patty Craft, Publisher & Editorial Dir.
Released: 8/yr. **Price:** $19.95; $39.95 Canada; $39.95 other countries. **Description:** Magazine for the amateur gardener.

9750 ■ *HortIdeas*
Pub: Greg and Pat Williams
Ed: Greg Williams, Editor, gwill@mis.net. **Released:** Monthly. **Price:** $25, individuals; $32, Canada and Mexico; $30, elsewhere by surface mail; $42, elsewhere by air mail. **Description:** Reviews the latest research on vegetable, fruit, and flower gardening. Provides practical information and tips on growing techniques, tools, plant varieties, and resources in abstract form with full references to original sources. Recurring features include book reviews. Remarks: Also available via e-mail.

9751 ■ *Landscape Trades*
Pub: Landscape Ontario Horticultural Trades Association
Contact: Lee Ann Knudsen, Publisher
E-mail: lak@landscapeontario.com
Released: 9/yr (not published Feb., Aug., and Dec.). **Price:** $43.58; $78.74 two years; $110.24 3 years. **Description:** Landscape/nursery magazine.

9752 ■ *Missouri Botanical Garden Annals*
Pub: Missouri Botanical Garden Press
Contact: Allison Brock, Assoc. Ed.
E-mail: allison.brock@mobot.org
Released: Quarterly, March, June, September, December. **Price:** $180; $190 Canada and Mexico; $215 other countries. **Description:** Trade magazine covering original research in botany.

9753 ■ *New Horizons*
Pub: Horticultural Research Institute
Ed: Released: 2/year. **Price:** Included in membership. **Description:** Explores research of the science and art of nursery, retail garden center, and landscape plant production, marketing, and care.

9754 ■ *Nursery News*
Pub: Cenflo Inc.
Contact: Tom Benjamin, Sales Mgr
E-mail: tom@cenflo.com
Released: Monthly. **Price:** $20; $36 two years; $125 other countries. **Description:** Trade newspaper (tabloid) for nursery industry.

9755 ■ *Organic Gardening*
Pub: Rodale Inc.
Contact: Scott Meyer, Exec. Ed.
Released: Bimonthly. **Price:** $23.94 two years plus free delivery. **Description:** Horticulture and gardening magazine.

9756 ■ *Ornamental Outlook*
Pub: Meister Publishing Co.
Contact: Joe W. Monahan, Publisher
Released: Monthly. **Description:** Trade magazine for the environmental horticulture industry.

9757 ■ *Pacific Coast Nurseryman and Garden Supply Dealer*
Pub: Cox Publishing Company Inc.
Contact: Kathleen Pyle, Managing Editor
Released: Monthly. **Price:** $30; $50 two years; $45 Canada; $45 other countries surface mail. **Description:** Business management magazine for professionals in the environmental horticulture industry.

9758 ■ *Plants & Gardens News*
Pub: Brooklyn Botanic Garden
Ed: Niall Dunne, Editor, nialldunne@bbg.org. **Released:** Quarterly. **Price:** Included in membership. **Description:** Discusses gardening, planting tips, news of gardening products, sources for new seeds and plants, and book reviews. Recurring features include plant profile, news of research, and fun for kids.

9759 ■ *Tree City USA Bulletin*
Pub: National Arbor Day Foundation
Contact: John E. Rosenow, Publisher
Ed: James R. Fazio, Editor. **Released:** Bimonthly. **Price:** $3, single issue; $15 membership subscription. **Description:** Provides tree planting and care instructions and information.

9760 ■ *Tri-Ology*
Pub: Florida Department of Agriculture and Consumer Services
Contact: Dr. Greg Hodges, Bureau Ch.
E-mail: hodgesg@doacs.state.fl.us
Released: Monthly. **Description:** Government scientific publication covering plant pests and disease. Online only.

9761 ■ *Yard and Garden*
Pub: Cygnus Business Media
Released: 8/yr. **Description:** Yard and garden magazine featuring product news and retailer success stories.

VIDEOCASSETTES/AUDIOCASSETTES

9762 ■ *Foliage Plant Production*
CEV Multimedia
1020 SE Loop 289
Lubbock, TX 79404
Ph:(806)745-8820
Free: 877-610-5017
Fax:800-243-6398
Co. E-mail: cev@cevmultimedia.com
URL: http://www.cevmultimedia.com
Price: $95.00. **Description:** Presents techniques for producing foliage plants in the greenhouse, covering propagation, equipment, facilities, tip cuttings, leaf-stem bud cuttings, seed, direct stick usage, light intensity, watering, and fertilization. Part of the "Greenhouse Production Series." **Availability:** VHS.

9763 ■ *Training Greenhouse Workers to Handle Pesticides Safely*
CEV Multimedia
1020 SE Loop 289
Lubbock, TX 79404
Ph:(806)745-8820
Free: 877-610-5017
Fax:800-243-6398
Co. E-mail: cev@cevmultimedia.com
URL: http://www.cevmultimedia.com
Released: 1986. **Price:** $95.00. **Description:** Features the key points of applicator training such as pesticide types, toxicology, pesticide regulation, safety equipment, protective clothing, and first-aid procedures. **Availability:** VHS.

TRADE SHOWS AND CONVENTIONS

9764 ■ Birmingham Home and Garden Show
Home And Garden Show TV
PO Box 430
Pinson, AL 35126-0430
Ph:(205)680-0234
Free: 800-226-3976
Fax:(205)680-0615
Co. E-mail: sales@homeandgardenshow.tv
Released: Annual. **Audience:** General public. **Principal Exhibits:** Home and garden products and services.

9765 ■ Buffalo Home and Garden Show
dmg world media inc. (Buffalo, New York)
325 Essjay Rd. Ste. 100
Williamsville, NY 14221
Ph:(716)631-2266
Fax:(716)631-2425
URL: http://www.dmgworldmedia.com
Released: Annual. **Audience:** General public. **Principal Exhibits:** Everything for your home and garden. Windows, doors, siding, sheds, gazebo's, lawn equipment, swimming pools, spas, mirrors, kitchen cabinets, bathroom products, closet organizers, security, playground equipment, electronics, furniture, fireplaces and any other product related to building, remodeling, decorating and landscaping.

9766 ■ Builders St. Charles Home Show
Home Builders Association of Greater St. Louis
10104 Old Olive St. Rd.
St. Louis, MO 63141
Ph:(314)994-7700
Fax:(314)432-7185
URL: http://www.stlhba.com
Released: Annual. **Audience:** General public and construction industry. **Principal Exhibits:** Home remodeling equipment and supplies, lawn and garden equipment, swimming pools, home furnishings, model homes and kitchen and bath. **Dates and Locations:** 2011 Apr 08-10, St. Charles, MO.

9767 ■ Cincinnati Home and Garden Show
Hart Productions, Inc.
2234 Bauer Rd., Ste. B
Batavia, OH 45103
Ph:(513)797-7900
Free: 877-704-8190
Fax:(513)797-1013
URL: http://www.hartproductions.com
Released: Annual. **Audience:** General public. **Principal Exhibits:** Home and garden products and services.

9768 ■ Farwest Nursery Show
Oregon Association of Nurseries
29751 SW Town Center Loop W
Wilsonville, OR 97070
Ph:(503)682-5089
Free: 800-342-6401
Fax:(503)682-5099
Co. E-mail: info@oan.org
URL: http://www.oan.org
Released: Annual. **Audience:** Wholesale nursery growers, garden centers, and landscapers. **Principal Exhibits:** Nursery stock, equipment, machinery, chemicals, and miscellaneous supplies and services for the wholesale and retail green industry.

9769 ■ Minneapolis Home & Garden Show
dmg world media
Northcliffe House
2 Derry St.
London W8 5TT, United Kingdom
Ph:44 20 79386000
URL: http://www.dmgevents.com
Released: Annual. **Audience:** General public. **Principal Exhibits:** Home and garden products and services.

9770 ■ Nursery/Landscape Expo
Texas Nursery & Landscape Association
7730 S. IH-35
Austin, TX 78745-6698
Ph:(512)280-5182
Free: 800-880-0343
Fax:(512)280-3012
Co. E-mail: info@tnlaonline.org
URL: http://www.txnla.org
Released: Annual. **Audience:** Nursery, landscape and related trades professionals. **Principal Exhibits:** Plant materials including foliage, bedding plants, trees, palms; allied products including machinery, equipment and supplies for horticulture and landscape industry.

9771 ■ Spokane Home and Garden Show
Creighton and Associates, Inc.
611 E. Broward Blvd., Ste. 207
Fort Lauderdale, FL 33301
Released: Annual. **Audience:** General public. **Principal Exhibits:** Products and services for the home and garden. Broad spectrum home improvement show. **Dates and Locations:** 2011 Apr 01-03, Spokane, WA.

9772 ■ Spring Home & Patio Show
Industrial Expositions, Inc.
1675 Larimer St., No.700
PO Box 480084
Denver, CO 80248-0084
Ph:(303)892-6800
Free: 800-457-2434
Fax:(303)892-6322
Co. E-mail: info@iei-expos.com
URL: http://www.iei-expos.com/
Released: Annual. **Audience:** General public. **Principal Exhibits:** Garden and home improvement equipment, interior designs, landscaping techniques and supplies, and patios and patio furniture and supplies.

9773 ■ Tacoma Home and Garden Show
O'Loughlin Trade Shows (Tacoma, Washington)
PO Box 110849
Tacoma, WA 98411-0849
Ph:(253)756-2121
Fax:(253)756-6898
URL: http://www.otsusa.com
Released: Annual. **Audience:** General public. **Principal Exhibits:** Home and garden equipment, supplies, and services; related products.

9774 ■ The World's Showcase of Horticulture
Southern Nursery Association
1827 Powers Ferry Rd. SE, Ste. 4-100
Atlanta, GA 30339-8422
Ph:(770)953-3311
Fax:(770)953-4411
URL: http://www.sna.org
Released: Annual. **Audience:** Wholesale and retail nursery professionals and landscapers. **Principal Exhibits:** Nursery products, including plants, chemicals, machinery and equipment, soil and soil supplements, and plant containers.

CONSULTANTS

9775 ■ Jobs In Horticulture Inc.
57 Rosedown Blvd.
PO Box 521731
Debary, FL 32713-4115
Ph:(386)753-0996
Free: 800-428-2474
Fax:(386)753-0997
Co. E-mail: info@hortjobs.com
URL: http://www.hortjobs.com
Contact: Joan Ferrell, Principal
E-mail: joan@hortjobs.com
Scope: Career consulting and career services with emphasis on horticulture.

FRANCHISES AND BUSINESS OPPORTUNITIES

9776 ■ Grower Direct Fresh Cut Flowers Inc.
9613-41 Ave., Ste. 201
Edmonton, AB, Canada T6E 5X7
Ph:(780)436-7774
Fax:(780)436-3336
Co. E-mail: franchises@grower.com
URL: http://www.grower.com
No. of Franchise Units: 41. **No. of Company-Owned Units:** 1. **Founded:** 1991. **Description:** Supplies top quality, fresh cut flowers and marketing expertise to its retail outlets. **Equity Capital Needed:** $55,000-$75,000. **Franchise Fee:** $15,000. **Training:** Provides 10 days training.

COMPUTERIZED DATABASES

9777 ■ *Alaska AVHRR Data*
U.S. Geological Survey
47914 252nd St.
Sioux Falls, SD 57198-0001
Ph:(605)594-6151
Free: 800-252-4547
Fax:(605)594-6589
Co. E-mail: custserv@usgs.gov
URL: http://edc.usgs.gov
Description: Contains AVHRR satellite data orga-
nized in two-month periods for the Alaska growing
season, consisting of composited mosaics (images
pieced together from different acquisition dates to
provide maximum greenness). One year of data typi-
cally fills two discs. **Availability:** CD-ROM: U.S.
Geological Survey. **Type:** Image.

9778 ■ *Southwest Exotic Plant Mapping Program*
United States Geological Survey
2255 N Gemini Dr.
Flagstaff, AZ 86001
Ph:(928)556-7000
Co. E-mail: webmaster@flagmail.wr.usgs.gov
URL: http://arizona.usgs.gov/Flagstaff
Description: Contains regional maps displaying
exotic plant species distributions based on the field
data contributions of collaborators. A project of the
USGS Colorado Plateau Research Station. Covers
Arizona, New Mexico and adjacent areas of adjoining
states. Enables users to search by plant species.
Availability: Online: United States Geological
Survey. **Type:** Image; Time series.

COMPUTER SYSTEMS/ SOFTWARE

9779 ■ Advance Grower Solutions–Nursery/ Greenhouse Accounting Software
Doane Agricultural Services Co.
4900 SW Griffith Dr., Ste. 248
Beaverton, OR 97005
Ph:(503)646-5581
Free: 800-367-7082
Fax:(503)646-0622
Co. E-mail: rickg@adgrower.com
URL: http://www.advgrower.com/
Price: Prices vary depending on modules needed.
Description: Available for IBM computers and
compatibles. System provides accounting and report
capabilities for nursery and landscaping businesses.

LIBRARIES

9780 ■ American Horticultural Society Library
7931 E. Boulevard Dr.
Alexandria, VA 22308
Ph:(703)768-5700
Free: 800-777-7931
Fax:(703)768-8700
Co. E-mail: tunderwood@ahs.org
URL: http://www.ahs.org/
Contact: Tom Underwood, Exec.Off.
Scope: Horticulture. **Services:** Library open to the
public by appointment. **Holdings:** 5000 books.

9781 ■ Atlanta Botanical Garden–Sheffield Botanical Library
1345 Piedmont Ave., NE
Atlanta, GA 30309
Ph:(404)591-1546
Fax:(404)876-7472
Co. E-mail: lschwarz@atlantabotanicalgarden.org
URL: http://www.atlantabotanicalgarden.org
Contact: LuAnne Schwarz, Libn.
Scope: Botany, horticulture, gardening. **Services:**
Library open to the public for reference use only.
Holdings: 8000 books; 125 unbound periodical titles;
society newsletters. **Subscriptions:** 125 journals and
other serials.

9782 ■ Bartlett Arboretum and Gardens–Horticulture Resource Library
151 Brookdale Rd.
Stamford, CT 06903-4199
Ph:(203)322-6971
Fax:(203)595-9168
Co. E-mail: horticulture@bartlettarboretum.org
URL: http://www.bartlettarboretum.org
Contact: Eric Morgan, Cur./Interim Dir. of Educ.
Scope: Horticulture, plant science, botany, arboricul-
ture. **Services:** Library open to the public. **Holdings:**
2500 books; 1000 bound periodical volumes; 30 VF
drawers. **Subscriptions:** 25 journals and other seri-
als.

9783 ■ Berkshire Botanical Garden Horticulture Library
PO Box 826
5 W. Stockbridge Rd.
Stockbridge, MA 01262
Ph:(413)298-3926
Fax:(413)298-4897
Co. E-mail: info@berkshirebotanical.org
URL: http://www.berkshirebotanical.org
Contact: Molly Boxer, Exec.Dir.
Scope: Horticulture. **Services:** Library open to the
public by appointment. **Holdings:** 900 books. **Sub-
scriptions:** 20 journals and other serials.

9784 ■ Birmingham Botanical Gardens Library
2612 Lane Park Rd.
Birmingham, AL 35223
Ph:(205)414-3920
Fax:(205)414-3922
Co. E-mail: hopel@bham.lib.al.us
URL: http://www.bbgardens.org/library.php
Contact: Hope Long, Lib.Dir.
Scope: Horticulture, botany, floriculture, gardens and
gardening, landscaping, flower arranging and children's books, organic gardening, insects, animals,
nature crafts. **Services:** Copying; printing (black and
white, color); faxing; Library open to the public. **Holdings:** 7000 circulating books; 850 reference books;
450 children's books; 100 CD-ROMs; DVDs. **Subscriptions:** 60 journals and other serials.

9785 ■ Brookgreen Gardens Library
PO Box 3368
Pawleys Island, SC 29585-3368
Ph:(843)235-6000
Free: 800-849-1931
Fax:(843)235-6003
Co. E-mail: info@brookgreen.org
URL: http://www.brookgreen.org
Contact: Robin Salmon, VP & Cur.
Scope: Sculpture, South Carolina history. **Services:**
Library not open to the public. **Holdings:** 2000 books;
2000 newspaper clippings; 15,000 slides; 2000
photographs.

9786 ■ Brooklyn Botanic Garden Library
1000 Washington Ave.
Brooklyn, NY 11225-1099
Ph:(718)623-7200
Co. E-mail: library@bbg.org
URL: http://www.bbg.org/lib/
Contact: Pat Jonas, Dir. of Lib.Svcs.
Scope: Horticulture, botany. **Services:** Interlibrary
loan; copying. **Holdings:** 60,000 volumes; 28,000
(3500 titles) bound periodical volumes; 5120 pam-
phlets; manuscripts; archives. **Subscriptions:** 500
journals and other serials.

9787 ■ Cheekwood Botanical Gardens Library
1200 Forrest Park Dr.
Nashville, TN 37205
Ph:(615)353-2148
Co. E-mail: info@cheekwood.org
URL: http://www.cheekwood.org
Scope: Horticulture, landscape architecture, plant
science, ecology, wildflowers, garden design, botani-
cal art, orchids, herbs, natural history. **Services:**
Interlibrary loan; copying; Library open to the public
with restrictions. **Holdings:** 4750 books; 260 bound

periodical volumes; 72 slide programs; 147 videocassettes; flower and seed catalogs. **Subscriptions:**
108 journals and other serials.

9788 ■ Chicago Park District–Garfield Park Conservatory
300 N. Central Park Ave.
Chicago, IL 60624-1945
Ph:(312)746-5100
Fax:(773)638-1777
URL: http://www.garfield-conservatory.org/
Contact: Mary Eysenbach, Dir.
Scope: Horticulture. **Services:** Library not open to
the public. **Holdings:** 600 books. **Subscriptions:** 2
journals and other serials.

9789 ■ Cleveland Botanical Garden–Eleanor Squire Library
11030 East Blvd.
Cleveland, OH 44106
Ph:(216)707-2812
Fax:(216)721-2056
Co. E-mail: info@cbgarden.org
URL: http://www.cbgarden.org/Learn/Library.html
Contact: Gary Esmonde, Libn.
Scope: Gardening, horticulture, landscape architec-
ture, herbs, flower arranging, botany. **Services:**
Library open to the public with paid admission
(members may borrow); rare books open to the public
by appointment for review, research, and study. **Hold-
ings:** 17,000 books; seed and nursery catalogs;
slides; botanical prints; 1000 rare books. **Subscriptions:** 50 journals and other serials.

9790 ■ Cornell University–Bailey Hortorium Library
430 Mann Library Bldg.
Ithaca, NY 14853
Ph:(607)255-0455
Fax:(607)256-5407
Co. E-mail: pf13@cornell.edu
URL: http://www.plantbio.cornell.edu/hortorium/
   bhortlibr.cfm
Contact: Dr. William Crepet, Dept. Chairperson
Scope: Taxonomic botany and horticulture. **Services:**
Interlibrary loan; Library open to the public. **Hold-
ings:** 30,000 books; 20,000 reprints on taxonomic
botany and allied subjects; 1500 reprints on paleo-
botany; 8000 photographs of type specimens and
other important specimens in European herbaria.
Subscriptions: 260 journals and other serials.

9791 ■ Cylburn Arboretum Association Library
4915 Greenspring Ave.
Baltimore, MD 21209
Ph:(410)367-2217
Fax:(410)367-7112
Co. E-mail: info@cylburnassociation.org
URL: http://www.cylburnassociation.org/
Scope: Horticulture, gardening, wild flowers, trees,
shrubs. **Services:** Library open to the public on a
limited schedule. **Holdings:** 1600 books; 2 VF draw-
ers of clippings and pamphlets; seed catalogs. **Sub-
scriptions:** 2 journals and other serials.

9792 ■ Dawes Arboretum Library
7770 Jacksontown Rd., SE
Newark, OH 43056
Ph:(740)323-2355
Free: 800-44-DAWES
Fax:(740)323-4058
Co. E-mail: information@dawesarb.org
URL: http://www.dawesarb.org
Contact: Beth Spieles, Interpretive Educ.
Scope: Horticulture, botany, ecology, nature, forestry,
gardening. **Services:** Copying; printing; Internet ac-
cess; Library open to the public for reference use
only. **Holdings:** 1400 books. **Subscriptions:** 50
journals and other serials.

9793 ■ Denver Botanic Gardens–Helen Fowler Library
909 York St.
Denver, CO 80206-3799
Ph:(720)865-3570

Fax:(720)865-3723
Co. E-mail: library@botanicgardens.org
URL: http://www.botanicgardens.org/content/helen-fowler-library
Contact: Colleen Nunn, Hd.Libn.
Scope: Horticulture, botany. **Services:** Interlibrary loan; copying; Library open to the public (only members may borrow). **Holdings:** 30,000 books; 400 bound periodical volumes; 8000 pamphlets; 300 brochures describing botanic gardens; 1000 slides; 150 index seminum lists. **Subscriptions:** 431 journals and other serials.

9794 ■ Detroit Garden Center Library
Moross House, 2nd Fl.
1900 E. Jefferson, Ste. 227
Detroit, MI 48207
Ph:(313)259-6363
Fax:(313)259-0107
Co. E-mail: information@detroitgardencenter.org
URL: http://www.detroitgardencenter.org
Contact: Beverly Donaldson, Libn.
Scope: Horticulture, floral culture. **Services:** Library open to the public for research. **Holdings:** 5000 books. **Subscriptions:** 10 journals and other serials.

9795 ■ Georgia State Botanical Garden of Georgia Library
Callaway Bldg.
University of Georgia
2450 S. Milledge Ave.
Athens, GA 30605
Ph:(706)542-1244
Fax:(706)542-3091
Co. E-mail: garden@uga.edu
URL: http://www.uga.edu/botgarden/faccallaway.html
Contact: Karen Kulp, Libn.
Scope: Plants, gardening, horticulture, botany, conservation, ethnobotany, landscape design, floral crafts. **Services:** Library open to the public for reference use only. **Holdings:** 2000 books; 85 videotapes; CD-ROMs; archives; manuscripts. **Subscriptions:** 14 journals and other serials.

9796 ■ Harvard University–Botany Libraries
22 Divinity Ave.
Cambridge, MA 02138
Ph:(617)495-2366
Fax:(617)495-8654
Co. E-mail: botref@oeb.harvard.edu
URL: http://www.huh.harvard.edu/libraries/
Contact: Judith A. Warnement, Dir.
Scope: Systematic botany and horticulture. **Services:** Copying; Library open to the public for reference use only. **Holdings:** 286,000 volumes and pamphlets; archives; manuscripts; microfiche; portraits; photographs. **Subscriptions:** 1500 journals and other serials.

9797 ■ Holden Arboretum–Warren H. Corning Library
9500 Sperry Rd.
Kirtland, OH 44094
Ph:(440)946-4400
Fax:(440)256-5836
Co. E-mail: holden@holdenarb.org
URL: http://www.holdenarb.org/resources/Libraryat-TheHoldenArboretum.asp
Contact: Susan Swisher, Libn.
Scope: Horticulture, botany, environmental education, natural history, conservation. **Services:** Library open to the public for reference use only. **Holdings:** 9500 books and pamphlets; 10 VF drawers; 10,000 slides; 100 videocassettes. **Subscriptions:** 125 journals and other serials.

9798 ■ L.A. County Arboretum and Botanic Garden–Plant Science Library
301 N. Baldwin Ave.
Arcadia, CA 91007-2697
Ph:(626)821-3213
Fax:(626)445-1217
Co. E-mail: susan.eubank@arboretum.org
URL: http://www.arboretum.org
Contact: Susan Eubank, Plant Sci.Libn.
Scope: Botany, horticulture. **Services:** Interlibrary loan; copying; Library open to the public. **Holdings:** 28,000 volumes; microfiche; maps. **Subscriptions:** 300 journals and other serials.

9799 ■ Lenhardt Library of the Chicago Botanic Garden
1000 Lake Cook Rd.
Glencoe, IL 60022
Ph:(847)835-8201
Co. E-mail: library@chicagobotanic.org
URL: http://www.chicagobotanic.org/library/index.html
Contact: Leora Siegel, Dir.
Scope: Horticulture, botany, gardening, plant conservation, landscape design, garden design, Midwest ecology, botanical illustration, phytopathology, horticultural therapy. **Services:** Interlibrary loan; copying; Library open to the public. **Holdings:** 28,000 books; 600 videos and DVDs; 10,000 slides; 1000 nursery catalogs. **Subscriptions:** 1000 journals and other serials.

9800 ■ Longwood Gardens, Inc. Library
PO Box 501
Kennett Square, PA 19348-0501
Ph:(610)388-1000
Fax:(610)388-2078
Co. E-mail: library@longwoodgardens.org
URL: http://www.longwoodgardens.org/LibraryandArchives.html
Scope: Botany, horticulture, allied sciences. **Services:** Interlibrary loan; copying; Library open to the public with restrictions. **Holdings:** 31,000 volumes; 57 lin.ft. hanging shelves; 36 lin.ft. plant materials; 18 lin.ft. Foundations organizations, bibliographies; 9 lin. ft. of high school, university, and colleges records; 15 botanical gardens; 12 geographical; 1751 volumes of microforms; archives. **Subscriptions:** 300 journals and other serials.

9801 ■ Massachusetts Horticultural Society Library
Elm Bank Horticulture Ctr.
900 Washington St.
Wellesley, MA 02482-5725
Ph:(617)933-4910
Fax:(617)933-4901
Co. E-mail: library@masshort.org
URL: http://www.masshort.org
Contact: Maureen Horn, Libn.
Scope: Ornamental horticulture, garden history, landscape design, pomology, early agriculture, floras of the world. **Services:** Interlibrary loan; copying; Library open to the public for reference use only. **Holdings:** 31,000 books; 24 VF drawers of pamphlets and clippings; 4000 documents; archives. **Subscriptions:** 50 journals and other serials.

9802 ■ Memphis Botanic Garden Foundation, Inc.–Goldsmith Civic Garden Center | Sybile Malloy Memorial Library
750 Cherry Rd.
Memphis, TN 38117
Ph:(901)685-1566
Fax:(901)682-1561
Co. E-mail: jim.duncan@memphistn.gov
URL: http://www.memphisbotanicgarden.com
Contact: Jim Duncan, Exec.Dir.
Scope: Horticulture, gardening, landscape design, flower arranging, environmental science, botany, agriculture. **Services:** Copying; Library open to the public for reference use only. **Holdings:** 2150 books; 10 bound periodical volumes; 200 horticultural magazines and pamphlets. **Subscriptions:** 15 journals and other serials.

9803 ■ Missouri Botanical Garden Library
4500 Shaw Blvd.
St. Louis, MO 63110
Ph:(314)577-5155
Free: 800-642-8842
Fax:(314)577-0840
Co. E-mail: doug.holland@mobot.org
URL: http://www.mobot.org
Contact: Douglas Holland, Lib.Dir.
Scope: Plant taxonomy and floristic, horticulture, botanical history and exploration. **Services:** Interlibrary loan; copying; Library open to the public by appointment. **Holdings:** 62,300 monographs; 66,000 bound periodical volumes; 100,000 pamphlets; 35,000 slides; 7000 vegetation and topographic

maps; 220,000 archival items; 3059 historic manuscripts; 40,000 microfiche of herbaria; 7000 art works; 1300 vertical files. **Subscriptions:** 2000 journals and other serials.

9804 ■ Morton Arboretum–Sterling Morton Library
4100 Illinois Rte. 53
Lisle, IL 60532-1293
Ph:(630)968-0074
Fax:(630)719-7950
Co. E-mail: library@mortonarb.org
URL: http://www.mortonarb.org/sterling-morton-library.html
Contact: Michael Stieber, Lib.Adm.
Scope: Botany, horticulture, dendrology, botanical art and illustration, arboriculture, landscape architecture, natural history, ecology and the environment. **Services:** Interlibrary loan; copying; SDI; Library open to the public. **Holdings:** 28,000 volumes; 1000 nursery and seed catalogs. **Subscriptions:** 800 journals and other serials.

9805 ■ National Gardening Association Library
1100 Dorset St.
South Burlington, VT 05403-8000
Ph:(802)863-5251
Fax:(802)864-6889
Co. E-mail: sarahp@garden.org
URL: http://www.garden.org
Scope: Gardening - vegetable, fruit, ornamental; plant and soil science, flowers, herbs. **Services:** Library not open to the public. **Holdings:** 7500 books. **Subscriptions:** 40 journals and other serials.

9806 ■ New York Botanical Garden–LuEsther T. Mertz Library
200th St. & Kazimiroff Blvd.
Bronx, NY 10458-5126
Ph:(718)817-8728
Fax:(718)817-8956
Co. E-mail: libref@nybg.org
URL: http://library.nybg.org/
Contact: Susan Fraser, Dir.
Scope: Systematic and Floristic botany, gardening, horticulture, plant ecology, landscape design. **Services:** Interlibrary loan; copying; Library open to the public. **Holdings:** 260,000 volumes; 12,000 serial titles; 371 lin.ft. of nursery catalogs and seed lists; 675 lin.ft. of scientific reprints and pamphlets; 184 lin. ft. microforms; 100,000 photographs and slides; 3000 artifacts; 4800 lin.ft. of archival materials. **Subscriptions:** 711 journals and other serials.

9807 ■ Norfolk Botanical Garden Society–Frederic Heutte Memorial Library
6700 Azalea Garden Rd.
Norfolk, VA 23518-5337
Ph:(757)441-5830
Fax:(757)441-5828
Co. E-mail: library@nbgs.org
URL: http://www.norfolkbotanicalgarden.org
Contact: Marcia Oubre, Libn.
Scope: Horticulture and allied subjects. **Services:** Library open to the public for reference use only. **Holdings:** 3500 books.

9808 ■ Pennsylvania Horticultural Society–McLean Library
100 N. 20th St., 5th Fl.
Philadelphia, PA 19103-1455
Ph:(215)988-8800
Fax:(215)988-8810
Co. E-mail: wiredgardener@pennhort.org
URL: http://www.pennsylvaniahorticulturalsociety.org
Contact: Janet Evans, Lib.Mgr.
Scope: Ornamental horticulture, botany, landscape design, garden history. **Services:** Interlibrary loan; photocopying; Garden Q&A (telephone plant information service); Library open to the public for reference use only (borrowing privileges for members and PHS staff). **Holdings:** 16,500 books; 4000 bound periodical volumes; 1000 slides; 250 videotapes on gardening. **Subscriptions:** 100 journals and other serials.

9809 ■ Planting Fields Arboretum–The Garden Library
PO Box 58
Oyster Bay, NY 11771
Ph:(516)922-8647
Fax:(516)922-8610
URL: http://www.plantingfields.org
Contact: Rosemarie Papayanopulos, Horticulture Libn.

Scope: Horticulture, botany. **Services:** Library open to the public for browsing and reference use only (members of Planting Fields Foundation and Arboretum staff, as well as members of garden societies that meet on the grounds, have borrowing privileges). **Holdings:** 8000 books. **Subscriptions:** 150 journals and other serials.

9810 ■ Rancho Santa Ana Botanic Garden Library
1500 N. College Ave.
Claremont, CA 91711-3157
Ph:(909)625-8767
Fax:(909)626-7670
URL: http://www.rsabg.org
Contact: Harvey Brenneise, Hd.Libn.

Scope: Botany, horticulture, drought tolerant plants, ethnobotany of California Indians, evolutionary biology. **Services:** Copying; Library open to qualified users. **Holdings:** 50,000 volumes; 28,360 reprints; 2000 maps; nursery catalogs. **Subscriptions:** 1000 serials.

9811 ■ Rochester Civic Garden Center Horticultural Library
5 Castle Park
Rochester, NY 14620
Ph:(585)473-5130
Fax:(585)473-8136
Co. E-mail: gardencenter@frontiernet.net
URL: http://rcgc.org/rcgc-library
Contact: Carolyn W. Van Ness, Lib.Dir.

Scope: Horticulture, landscaping, plant identification, garden history, nature study, flower arrangement. **Services:** Interlibrary loan; Library open to the public for reference use only. **Holdings:** 4000 books; 875 bound periodical volumes; 12 VF drawers of clippings; pamphlets. **Subscriptions:** 34 journals and other serials.

9812 ■ Rodale Inc. Library
33 E. Minor St.
Emmaus, PA 18098
Ph:(610)967-8729
Fax:(610)967-7708
Co. E-mail: lynn.donches@rodale.com
Contact: Lynn Donches, Chf.Libn.

Scope: Health, gardening, sports. **Services:** Library open to the public by appointment. **Holdings:** 40,000 books. **Subscriptions:** 1500 journals and other serials.

9813 ■ San Francisco Botanical Garden at Strybing Arboretum–Helen Crocker Russell Library of Horticulture
Golden Gate Park
1199 9th Ave.
San Francisco, CA 94122-2370
Ph:(415)661-1316
Fax:(415)661-3539
Co. E-mail: bpitschel@sfbotanicalgarden.org
URL: http://www.sfbotanicalgarden.org/library/index.html
Contact: Brandy Kuhl, Hd.Libn.

Scope: Horticulture, plant propagation, landscape gardening, flora of Mediterranean climates, plant hunting, history of gardening, children and gardens, ethnobotany, botanical illustration, garden design, biology. **Services:** Copying; slide duplication; Library open to the public. **Holdings:** 27,000 books, including 300 rare volumes; 2500 bound periodical volumes; 1 shelf of William Hammond Hall Archives; 3000 slide transparencies of plants (accessible through online catalog); 26 VF drawers of brochures and pamphlets; 3000 old and current nursery catalogs. **Subscriptions:** 450 journals and other serials.

9814 ■ Santa Barbara Botanic Garden–Blaksley Library
1212 Mission Canyon Rd.
Santa Barbara, CA 93105
Ph:(805)682-4726, x-107
Fax:(805)563-0352
Co. E-mail: jariel@sbbg.org
URL: http://www.sbbg.org/index.cfm?fuseaction=collections.library
Contact: Joan Ariel, Lib.Dir.

Scope: Botany; floras of Western North America and Mediterranean climates; California horticulture; California offshore islands; cactus and succulents. **Services:** Copying; Library open to the public by appointment. **Holdings:** 15,000 books; 2800 bound volumes; 700 maps; 20,000 plant images. **Subscriptions:** 200 journals and other serials.

9815 ■ Texas Discovery Gardens Horticulture Library
PO Box 152537
Dallas, TX 75315
Ph:(214)428-7476
Fax:(214)428-5338
Co. E-mail: tdg@texasdiscoverygardens.org
URL: http://texasdiscoverygardens.org
Contact: Melissa Martin, Exec.Dir.

Scope: General horticulture. **Services:** Library accessible on a restricted basis only. **Holdings:** 1000 bound periodical volumes. **Subscriptions:** 4 journals and other serials.

9816 ■ U.S. National Arboretum Library
3501 New York Ave., NE
Washington, DC 20002-1958
Ph:(202)245-2726
Fax:(202)245-4575
Co. E-mail: everlyr@ars.usda.gov
URL: http://www.usna.usda.gov/
Contact: Robin Everly, Lib.

Scope: Botany, taxonomy, floristics, horticulture, gardening, plant genetics and breeding. **Services:** Interlibrary loan (through National Agricultural Library only); Library open to the public by appointment for onsite research only. **Holdings:** 10,000 books; 500 periodical titles. **Subscriptions:** 165 journals and other serials.

9817 ■ University of Alberta–Devonian Botanic Garden Library
Edmonton, AB, Canada T6G 2E1
Ph:(770)987-3054, x2240
Fax:(780)987-4141
Co. E-mail: rbelland@ualberta.ca
URL: http://www.devonian.ualberta.ca
Contact: Rene Belland, Cur.

Scope: Horticulture, botany, gardening, landscape design, natural history, plant diversity, conservation. **Services:** Library open to the public with restrictions. **Holdings:** 1000 books; reports; manuscripts; archives. **Subscriptions:** 6 journals and other serials.

9818 ■ University of California, Berkeley–Botanical Garden–Myrtle R. Wolf Botanical & Horticultural Library (200 C)
200 Centennial Dr., No. 5045
Berkeley, CA 94720-5045
Ph:(510)643-8040
Fax:(510)642-5045
Co. E-mail: hforbes@berkeley.edu
URL: http://botanicalgarden.berkeley.edu/
Contact: Holly Forbes, Cur.

Scope: Horticulture, floras, plant taxonomy, botanical gardens. **Services:** Library open to the public for reference use only. **Holdings:** 3000 books; 30 feet of other cataloged items. **Subscriptions:** 20 journals and other serials.

9819 ■ University of California, Davis–Arboretum Library
1 Shield Ave.
Davis, CA 95616
Ph:(530)752-4880

Fax:(530)752-5796
Co. E-mail: arboretum@ucdavis.edu
URL: http://arboretum.ucdavis.edu
Contact: Mia Ingolia, Cur.

Scope: Botany, horticulture, gardening, ecology. **Services:** Library open to the public for reference use only. **Holdings:** 1543 books; 86 bound periodical volumes; unbound periodicals; vertical files. **Subscriptions:** 14 journals and other serials.

9820 ■ University of Michigan–Matthaei Botanical Gardens Library
1800 N. Dixboro Rd.
Ann Arbor, MI 48105-9406
Ph:(734)763-0645
Fax:(734)998-6205
Co. E-mail: bgrese@umich.edu
URL: http://www.lsa.umich.edu/mbg
Contact: Robert Grese, Dir.

Scope: Botany, horticulture, natural history of plants, ecology of plants. **Services:** Library not open to the public. **Holdings:** 3200 volumes. **Subscriptions:** 7 journals and other serials.

9821 ■ University of Minnesota–Minnesota Landscape Arboretum–Andersen Horticultural Library (3675)
3675 Arboretum Dr.
Chaska, MN 55318-9613
Ph:(952)443-1405
Fax:(952)443-2521
Co. E-mail: hortlib@umn.edu
URL: http://www.arboretum.umn.edu/library.aspx
Contact: Katherine Allen, Libn.

Scope: Horticulture, botany, natural sciences, landscape architecture. **Services:** Collection is non-circulating; Library open to the public. **Holdings:** 100,000 volumes; 12 AV programs; 9 feet of manuscripts; 1388 microforms; 350 periodicals. **Subscriptions:** 350 journals and other serials.

9822 ■ University of Pennsylvania–Morris Arboretum Library
100 E. Northwestern Ave.
Philadelphia, PA 19118-3620
Ph:(215)247-5777
Fax:(215)248-4439
Co. E-mail: info@morrisarboretum.org
URL: http://www.business-services.upenn.edu/arboretum/
Contact: Joan Markham, Libn.

Scope: Ornamental horticulture, garden history (especially Victorian period), floristic botany, urban forestry and silviculture, plant exploration. **Services:** Interlibrary loan; Library open to the public for reference use only. **Holdings:** 4000 books; 2000 bound periodical volumes. **Subscriptions:** 100 journals and other serials.

9823 ■ University of Washington Botanic Gardens–Elisabeth C. Miller Horticulture Library
3501 NE 41 St.
Box 354115
Seattle, WA 98105-5699
Ph:(206)543-0415
Fax:(206)897-1435
URL: http://www.millerlibrary.org
Contact: Martha Ferguson, Lib.Spec.

Scope: Horticulture, gardening, urban forestry, botanical gardens. **Services:** Copying; Library open to the public. **Holdings:** 15000 books; 1000 bound periodical volumes; archives. **Subscriptions:** 300 serials.

9824 ■ Worcester County Horticultural Society Library
11 French Dr.
PO Box 598
Boylston, MA 01505-0598
Ph:(508)869-6111, x-116
Fax:(508)869-0314
Co. E-mail: librarian@towerhillbg.org
URL: http://www.towerhillbg.org
Contact: Kathy Bell

Scope: Agriculture, botany, conservation, gardening, fruit culture, general horticulture, landscape design. **Services:** Library open to the public for reference use only. **Holdings:** 8500 books; 1000 bound periodical volumes; 200 seed, tool, plant, and equipment catalogs; 14,500 slides. **Subscriptions:** 35 journals and other serials; 40 newsletters.

RESEARCH CENTERS

9825 ■ Auburn University–Alabama Agricultural Experiment Station–Ornamental Horticulture Research Center
411 N McGregor Ave.
PO Box 8276
Mobile, AL 36689
Ph:(251)342-2366
Fax:(251)342-1022
Co. E-mail: olivejw@auburn.edu
URL: http://www.aaes.auburn.edu/researchcenters/ ohrc
Contact: John W. Olive, Dir.
E-mail: olivejw@auburn.edu
Scope: Pest control, including insects, diseases, and weeds; culture of container-grown woody ornamentals and greenhouse crops, including propagation, fertilization, growing media, and environmental effects; and growth regulators. Applied research conducted in support of commercial nursery industry. **Educational Activities:** Horticulture Field Day (semiannually).

9826 ■ Horticultural Research Institute
1000 Vermont Ave. NW, Ste. 300
Washington, DC 20005-4914
Ph:(202)789-2900
Fax:(202)789-1893
Co. E-mail: mteffeau@anla.org
URL: http://www.hriresearch.org
Contact: Marc Teffeau, Res.Dir.
E-mail: mteffeau@anla.org
Scope: Problems and opportunities in the nursery and landscape industry. **Publications:** Peer-Reviewed Journal of Environmental Horticulture (quarterly). **Awards:** Research Grants (annually).

9827 ■ Ohio State University–Agricultural Technical Institute
1328 Dover Rd.
Wooster, OH 44691-4000
Ph:(330)287-1331
Free: 800—647-8283
Fax:(330)262-7634
Co. E-mail: nameth.2@osu.edu
URL: http://ati.osu.edu
Contact: Prof. Stephen Nameth, Dir.
E-mail: nameth.2@osu.edu
Scope: Floriculture, landscape science, nursery, turf, crops, greenhouse production, agricultural engineering and mechanics, agronomic industries, soil and water management, dairy and livestock science, and construction. **Services:** Telephone reference service. **Educational Activities:** Continuous education and distance learning.

ASSOCIATIONS AND OTHER ORGANIZATIONS

9828 ■ Souvenir Wholesale Distributors Association
2105 Laurel Bush Rd., Ste. 200
Bel Air, MD 21015
Ph:(443)640-1055
Fax:(443)640-1031
Co. E-mail: marci@ksgroup.org
URL: http://www.postcardcentral.org
Contact: Marci L. Hickey CMP, Exec. VP
Description: Represents distributors and manufacturers of post cards, souvenirs, and novelty items. .

REFERENCE WORKS

9829 ■ "Award Win Highlights Slingsby's Green Credentials" in *Ecology,Environment & Conservation Business* **(August 20, 2011, pp. 3)**
Pub: HighBeam Research
Description: Slingsby, an industrial and commercial equipment supplier, was joint winner with Hallmark Cards of the Baildon Business in the Community's Yorkshire and Humber Long Term Environmental Improvement Award. The firm cites its commitment to reducing environmental impact.

9830 ■ *Greeting Card Industry Directory*
Pub: Greeting Card Association
Contact: Susan January, President
Released: Biennial, Latest edition 13th. **Price:** $75, members; $150, nonmembers plus shipping & handling charges. **Covers:** Over 3,000 greeting card publishers and suppliers in the United State and many foreign countries. **Entries Include:** Company name, address, phone, e-mail, Internet, toll-free, fax numbers, key personnel, licensed properties, plant locations, description of products & services, distribution outlets and methods, geographic area covered, industry background, and related information. **Arrangement:** Alphabetical. **Indexes:** Product, geographical, brand name.

9831 ■ "Halls Give Hospital Drive $11 Million Infusion" in *The Business Journal-Serving Metropolitan Kansas City* **(Vol. 26, July 18, 2008)**
Pub: American City Business Journals, Inc.
Ed: Rob Roberts. **Description:** Don Hall, chairman of Hallmark Cards Inc., and eight family members have announced that they will give $11 million to Children's Mercy Hospitals and Clinics for its $800 million expansion plan. Hall Family Foundation president Bill Hall that contributions such as that for Children's Mercy reflect the charitable interests of the foundation's board and founders. The possible impacts of the Hall's donation are analyzed.

9832 ■ "Search and Discover New Opportunities" in *DM News* **(Vol. 31, December 14, 2009, No. 29, pp. 13)**
Pub: Haymarket Media, Inc.
Ed: Chantal Tode. **Description:** Although other digital strategies are gaining traction in Internet marketing, search marketing continues to dominate this advertising forum. Companies like American Greetings, which markets e-card brands online, are utilizing social networking sites and affiliates to generate a higher demand for their products.

STATISTICAL SOURCES

9833 ■ *Greeting Cards - US*
Pub: MarketResearch.com
Released: 2008. **Price:** $3995.00. **Description:** The U.S. greeting card industry remains a mature and stable market with sales growth of 8.7% between 1999 and 2004.

TRADE SHOWS AND CONVENTIONS

9834 ■ National Stationery Show
George Little Management, LLC (New York, New York)
1133 Westchester Ave., Ste. N136
White Plains, NY 10606

Ph:(914)421-3200
Free: 800-272-SHOW
Co. E-mail: cathy_steel@glmshows.com
URL: http://www.glmshows.com
Released: Annual. **Audience:** Retail buyers, including: representatives from specialty, department, chain, independent retail, catalog publishers, card and gift shops. **Principal Exhibits:** Greeting cards, social stationery, and related products such as calendars, desk accessories, small leather goods, photo frames, party goods, home office products, prints and posters, postcards, note paper, games, toys, balloons, and wedding, back-to-school, and holiday supplies. **Dates and Locations:** 2011 May 15-18, New York, NY.

LIBRARIES

9835 ■ American Life Foundation–Prang-Mark Society Library
1601 Sheridan Ln.
Norristown, PA 19403-3336
Ph:(610)539-3010
Contact: John Crosby Freeman, Coord.
Scope: Printing, early greeting cards, tradecards. **Services:** Library open to the public by appointment only (June 1 through September 1). **Holdings:** 7000 books.

9836 ■ Hallmark Cards, Inc.–Creative Research Library
2501 McGee, No. 146
Kansas City, MO 64108
Ph:(816)274-5525
Fax:(816)274-7245
Co. E-mail: hallmarkplus@hallmark.com
URL: http://www.hallmark.com
Contact: Mark Spencer, Mgr., Creative Rsrc.Ctr.
Scope: Fine art, lettering, advertising, graphic art, design, illustration, photography. **Services:** Library open to Hallmark employees only. **Holdings:** 18,000 books; 60 bound periodical volumes. **Subscriptions:** 150 journals and other serials; 3 newspapers.

START-UP INFORMATION

9837 ■ "Local Flavor" in *Entrepreneur* **(Vol. 35, November 2007, No. 11, pp. 110)**
Pub: Entrepreneur Media Inc.
Ed: Nichole L. Torres. **Description:** Local food products are growing in the market today as consumers are becoming interested in where their food comes; you can start a business by investigating the kinds of foods popular in your region.

ASSOCIATIONS AND OTHER ORGANIZATIONS

9838 ■ American Institute of Food Distribution
10 Mountainview Rd., Ste. S125
Upper Saddle River, NJ 07458
Ph:(201)791-5570
Fax:(201)791-5222
Co. E-mail: memberservices@foodinstitute.com
URL: http://www.foodinstitute.com
Contact: Mr. Brian Todd, Pres./CEO
Description: Canners, packers, freezers, manufacturers, brokers, wholesalers, retailer-cooperatives, chains, independent retailers, growers, trade associations, banks, advertising and government agencies, supply houses, and others working for or with the food trades. Serves as central information service for the food trades. Issues statistical and analytical digests on food distribution and related topics. **Publications:** *Food Institute Report* (weekly); *OSHA Manual*; *Regulatory Directory* (periodic).

9839 ■ Canadian Federation of Independent Grocers–Federation Canadienne des Epiciers Independants
2235 Sheppard Ave. E, Ste. 902
Willowdale, ON, Canada M2J 5B5
Ph:(416)492-2311
Free: 800-661-2344
Fax:(416)492-2347
Co. E-mail: info@cfig.ca
URL: http://www.cfig.ca
Contact: John F.T. Scott, Pres./CEO
Description: Independent retail grocers. Promotes growth and development of members' businesses. Represents the commercial and regulatory interests of independent grocers; conducts promotional activities.

9840 ■ Food Industry Association Executives
5657 W 10770 N
Highland, UT 84003
Ph:(801)599-1095
Fax:(815)550-1731
Co. E-mail: jolsen@fiae.net
URL: http://www.fiae.net
Contact: Jim Olsen, Pres.
Description: Professional executives of local, state, and national retail grocers associations. **Publications:** Membership Directory (annual).

9841 ■ Food Marketing Institute
2345 Crystal Dr., Ste. 800
Arlington, VA 22202-4801
Ph:(202)452-8444
Fax:(202)429-4519
Co. E-mail: fmi@fmi.org
URL: http://www.fmi.org
Contact: Leslie G. Sarasin, Pres./CEO
Description: Grocery retailers and wholesalers. Maintains liaison with government and consumers. Conducts 30 educational conferences and seminars per year. Conducts research programs; compiles statistics. **Publications:** *Facts About Supermarket Development* (annual); *Food Marketing Industry Speaks* (annual).

9842 ■ Grocery Manufacturers Association
1305 I St. NW, Ste. 300
Washington, DC 20005
Ph:(202)639-5900
Fax:(202)639-5932
Co. E-mail: info@gmaonline.org
URL: http://www.gmaonline.org
Contact: Pamela G. Bailey, Pres./CEO
Description: Global manufacturers of food and nonfood products sold in the United States. **Publications:** *GMA Executive Update* (weekly); *State Legislative Report* (weekly); *Washington Report* (monthly).

9843 ■ International Council of Grocery Manufacturer Associations
1350 I St. NW, Ste. 300
Washington, DC 20005
Ph:(202)337-9400
Fax:(202)337-4508
Co. E-mail: info@icgma.com
URL: http://www.icgma.com
Contact: Cal Dooley, Pres./CEO
Description: Grocery manufacturers' associations of Australia, Austria, Belgium, Brazil, Canada, Denmark, France, Germany, Italy, Japan, Mexico, New Zealand, South Africa, Switzerland, the United Kingdom, the United States, and Venezuela. Promotes high standards in the manufacture and distribution of grocery products. Coordinates activities of grocery manufacturers worldwide. .

9844 ■ National Frozen and Refrigerated Foods Association
PO Box 6069
Harrisburg, PA 17112
Ph:(717)657-8601
Fax:(717)657-9862
Co. E-mail: info@nfraweb.org
URL: http://www.nfraweb.org
Contact: H.V. Shaw Jr., Pres./CEO
Description: Comprised of over 400 member companies representing all segments of the frozen and refrigerated dairy foods industry. Promotes the sales and consumption of frozen and refrigerated foods through education, training, research, sales planning and menu development and provides a forum for industry dialogue. Sponsors National Frozen Food Month, in March; June Dairy Month; June and July Ice Cream and Novelties Promotion; Frozen and

Refrigerated Foods Festival, in October; and Bring Us To Your Table! Freezer Favorites. **Publications:** *Frozen Food Book of Knowledge*; *NFRA Update* (monthly); *Year End Report* (annual).

9845 ■ National Grocers Association
1005 N Glebe Rd., Ste. 250
Arlington, VA 22201-5758
Ph:(703)516-0700
Fax:(703)812-1821
Co. E-mail: feedback@nationalgrocers.org
URL: http://www.nationalgrocers.org
Contact: Peter J. Larkin, Pres./CEO
Description: Independent food retailers; wholesale food distributors servicing 29,000 food stores. Promotes industry interests and works to advance understanding, trade and cooperation among all sectors of the food industry. Represents members' interests before the government. Aids in the development of programs designed to improve the productivity and efficiency of the food distribution industry. Offers services in areas such as store planning and engineering, personnel selection and training, operations and advertising. Sponsors seminars and in-house training. Maintains liaison with Women Grocers of America, which serves as an advisory arm. **Publications:** *Congressional or Regulatory Update* (periodic).

9846 ■ Women Grocers of America
1005 N Glebe Rd., Ste. 250
Arlington, VA 22201-5758
Ph:(703)516-0700
Fax:(703)516-0115
Co. E-mail: kcomley@nationalgrocers.org
URL: http://www.nationalgrocers.org/WGA/WGA.html
Contact: Kristen Comley, Liaison
Description: Serves as an information and advisory arm to the National Grocers Association . Supports and encourages the education of students pursuing grocery industry-related careers in the independent segment of the industry through its scholarship program. Encourages all segments of the food industry to promote breast cancer awareness and prevention. Participates in and supports the programs offered by the National Grocers Association. .

DIRECTORIES OF EDUCATIONAL PROGRAMS

9847 ■ *Major Food & Drink Companies of the World*
Pub: Graham & Whiteside
Ed: Heather Brewin, Editor. **Released:** Annual, Latest edition 16th; Published May, 2012. **Price:** $1,460, individuals. **Covers:** Over 9,200 worldwide companies involved in the food and drink industry. **Entries Include:** Company name, address, phone and names and titles of key personnel.

REFERENCE WORKS

9848 ■ "AdvacePierre Heats Up" in *Business Courier* **(Vol. 27, October 29, 2010, No. 26, pp. 1)**
Pub: Business Courier
Ed: John Newberry. **Description:** Bill Toler, chief executive officer of AdvancePierre Foods, is aiming

for more growth and more jobs. The company was formed after the merger of Pierre Foods with two Oklahoma-based food processing companies. Toler wants to expand production and is set to start adding employees in the next 6-12 months.

9849 ■ "Bagging Profits; High-End Grocers Expand Despite Stale Economy" in *Crain's Detroit Business* **(Vol. 24, March 24, 2008, No. 12, pp. 1)**
Pub: Crain Communications, Inc.
Ed: Nancy Kaffer. **Description:** Discusses the expansion plans of several high-end grocery stores in the Detroit area and the reasons why, despite the poor economy, these gourmet grocers are doing well. Statistical data included.

9850 ■ "Baking Up Bigger Lance" in *Charlotte Business Journal* **(Vol. 25, December 3, 2010, No. 37, pp. 1)**
Pub: Charlotte Business Journal
Ed: Ken Elkins. **Description:** Events that led to the merger between Charlotte, North Carolina-based snack food manufacturer Lance Inc. and Pennsylvania-based pretzel maker Snyder's of Hanover Inc. are discussed. The merger is expected to help Lance in posting a 70 percent increase in revenue, which reached $900 million in 2009. How the merger would affect Snyder's of Hanover is also described.

9851 ■ "Bankruptcies" in *Crain's Detroit Business* **(Vol. 24, October 6, 2008, No. 40, pp. 26)**
Pub: Crain Communications, Inc.
Description: Current businesses that have filed for Chapter 7 or 11 protection in U.S. Bankruptcy Court include an auto dealership, a gun range and a grocery service.

9852 ■ "Battered Loblaw Makes Deep Job Cuts" in *Globe & Mail* **(January 23, 2007)**
Pub: CTVglobemedia Publishing Inc.
Description: Loblaw Companies Ltd., supermarket giant, is eliminating up to 1,000 administrative jobs and shifting more buying responsibilities to its suppliers. The grocer will also introduce a national inventory strategy called "category management".

9853 ■ "Beer Sales 'Foament' a Dispute" in *Philadelphia Business Journal* **(Vol. 28, October 9, 2009, No. 34, pp. 1)**
Pub: American City Business Journals
Ed: Peter van Allen. **Description:** Malt Beverages Distributors Association of Pennsylvania filed a case against the Liquor Control Board (LCB) at the Pennsylvania Supreme Court in order to further restrict store sales. The dispute stems from the supermarket chains circumventing the liquor law with the blessings of LCB.

9854 ■ "Bertha's Birth Stirs Juice" in *Barron's* **(Vol. 88, July 14, 2008, No. 28, pp. M11)**
Pub: Dow Jones & Co., Inc.
Ed: Tom Sellen. **Description:** Price of frozen concentrated orange juice, which has risen to four-month highs of $1.3620 in July 2008 is due, in part, to the hurricane season that has come earlier than normal in the far eastern Atlantic thereby possibly harming the 2008-2009 Florida orange crop. Future tropical-storm development will affect the prices of this commodity.

9855 ■ "Better Made's Better Idea: Diversify Despite Rising Costs" in *Crain's Detroit Business* **(Vol. 24, September 22, 2008, No. 38, pp. 18)**
Pub: Crain Communications, Inc.
Ed: Nathan Skid. **Description:** Better Made Snack Foods Inc. is planning to expand its product lines and market reach as well as boost manufacturing capability during a time in which the company is being buffeted by rising commodity and fuel costs. The company feels that diversification is the key to maintain sales and growth.

9856 ■ "Businessman Legend Passes: Charles H. James II Credited With Transforming Family Business" in *Black Enterprise* **(December 2007)**
Pub: Earl G. Graves Publishing Co. Inc.
Ed: Tara C. Walker. **Description:** Profile of Charles H. James II, president and chairman of The James Corporation, a family-owned multigenerational food distribution company that started as a produce firm.

9857 ■ "Cheese Spread Whips Up a Brand New Bowl" in *Brandweek* **(Vol. 49, April 21, 2008, No. 16, pp. 17)**
Pub: VNU Business Media, Inc.
Ed: Mike Beirne. **Description:** Mrs. Kinser's Pimento Cheese Spread is launching a new container for its product in order to attempt stronger brand marketing with a better bowl in order to win over the heads of households as young as in their 30s. The company also intends to begin distribution in Texas and the West Coast. Mrs. Kinser's is hoping that the new packaging will provide a more distinct branding and will help consumers distinguish what flavor they are buying.

9858 ■ "Coca-Cola Bottler Up for Sale: CEO J. Bruce Llewellyn Seeks Retirement" in *Black Enterprise* **(Vol. 37, December 2006, No. 5, pp. 31)**
Pub: Earl G. Graves Publishing Co. Inc.
Ed: Marcia A. Wade. **Description:** J. Bruce Llewellyn of Brucephil Inc., the parent company of the Philadelphia Coca-Cola Bottling Co. has agreed to sell its remaining shares to Coca-Cola Co., which previously owned 31 percent of Philly Coke. Analysts believe that Coca-Cola will eventually sell its shares to another bottler.

9859 ■ "Condensed Capitalism" in *Human Resource Management* **(Vol. 49, September-October 2010, No. 5, pp. 965-968)**
Pub: John Wiley
Ed: Matthew M. Bodah. **Description:** Review of the book, 'Condensed Capitalism: Campbell Soup and the Pursuit of Cheap Production in the Twentieth Century'.

9860 ■ *Directory of Foodservice Distributors*
Pub: Chain Store Guide
Released: Annual, Latest edition 2011. **Price:** $425, individuals Directory; $495, individuals online lite; $1,175, individuals online pro. **Covers:** About 4,700 companies in the United States and Canada with at least $500,000 in sales to foodservice companies. Included companies must distribute more than one product line and obtain no more than 95% of its total sales volume from self-manufactured merchandise. **Entries Include:** Company name, address, phone and fax numbers, e-mail and web addresses; Internet order processing indicator and sales percentage; total sales; foodservice and wholesale sales; product lines; total units served; foodservice accounts served; trading areas; distribution center locations; markets served; buying/marketing group name and location; subsidiaries names and locations; divisional, regional and branch office locations; year founded; public company indicator; key personnel with titles; 20,500 foodservice distribution contacts; 9,642 Name, address, phone, fax. **Arrangement:** Geographical. **Indexes:** Product lines, alphabetical, exclusions.

9861 ■ *Directory of Supermarket, Grocery & Convenience Store Chains*
Pub: Chain Store Guide
Released: Annual, Latest edition 2011. **Price:** $425, individuals Directory; $495, individuals Online lite; $1,175, individuals Online pro. **Covers:** Over 3,269 supermarket, grocery, and convenience store chains operating 71,000 stores in the United States and Canada. **Entries Include:** For supermarkets/groceries—company name, address, phone, fax, e-mail and web address; total annual sales; grocery sales; Internet order processing indicator; total units; number of units by type; number of units by trade name; number of units franchised to and from; total selling square feet; prototype sizes; average number of checkouts; projected number of units by specialty department; primary wholesaler type, name and location; parent company name and location; subsidiary name and

location; divisional and branch office locations; warehouse locations; year founded; public company indicator; key personnel with titles. For convenience stores—company name, address, phone and fax numbers, web and e-mail addresses; total annual sales; convenience store sales; gasoline sales percentage; Internet order processing indicator; total units; number of units by trade name; number of units franchised to and from; total selling square footage; prototype sizes; average number of checkouts; projected number of openings and remodeling; packaged liquor indicators; trading areas; distribution center locations; number of units by specialty department; primary wholesaler type, name and location; parent company, subsidiary, warehouse, divisional and branch office names and locations; year founded; public company indicator; key personnel with titles. **Arrangement:** Geographical with sections for supermarkets and convenience stores. **Indexes:** Top 200 chains, trading area, alphabetical, exclusions.

9862 ■ "Eagle's Wine Kiosk Is Area's 1st" in *Pittsburgh Post-Gazette* **(October 28, 2010)**
Pub: Pittsburgh-Post Gazette
Ed: Bob Batz Jr. **Description:** Giant Eagle Market District store at Settlers Ridge opened the first self-serve wine kiosk in Western Pennsylvania. The kiosk will have a built-in breathalyzer panel to ensure safety.

9863 ■ "Egg Fight: The Yolk's on the Short" in *Barron's* **(Vol. 88, July 7, 2008, No. 27, pp. 20)**
Pub: Dow Jones & Co., Inc.
Ed: Christopher C. Williams. **Description:** Shares of Cal-Maine Foods, the largest egg producer and distributor in the US, are due for a huge rise because of the increase in egg prices. Short sellers, however, continue betting that the stock, priced at $31.84 each, will eventually go down.

9864 ■ *Ethnic Solidarity for Economic Survival: Korean Greengrocers in New York City*
Pub: Russell Sage Foundation Publications
Ed: Pyong Gap Min. **Released:** August 2008. **Price:** $32.50. **Description:** Investigations into the entrepreneurial traditions of Korean immigrant families in New York City running ethnic businesses, particularly small grocery stores and produce markets. Social, cultural and economic issues facing these retailers are discussed.

9865 ■ "Fast Fact: Quality of Foods, Cost Top Factors in Determining Where to Grocery Shop" in *Marketing to Women* **(Vol. 22, August 2009)**
Pub: EPM Communications, Inc.
Description: Efficient check-outs, customer service and a wide variety of products were all less important to female shoppers than the quality of food and value, which were seen as the ultimate factors in a woman's decision as to which grocery store they decide to frequent.

9866 ■ "Floral-Design Kiosk Business in Colorado Springs Blossoming" in *Colorado Springs Business Journal* **(September 24, 2010)**
Pub: Dolan Media Newswires
Ed: Monica Mendoza. **Description:** Profile of Shellie Greto and her mother Jackie Martin who started a wholesale flower business in their garage. The do-it-yourself floral arrangement firm started a kiosk business in supermarkets called Complete Design.

9867 ■ "Food Fight" in *Canadian Business* **(Vol. 79, November 6, 2006, No. 22, pp. 18)**
Pub: Rogers Media
Ed: Zena Olijnyk. **Description:** The war between Canadian grocers and Wal-Mart due to its plans for opening new stores is analyzed.

9868 ■ "Fresh Direct's Crisis" in *Crain's New York Business* **(Vol. 24, January 14, 2008, No. 2, pp. 3)**
Pub: Crain Communications, Inc.
Ed: Lisa Fickenscher. **Description:** Freshdirect, an Internet grocery delivery service, finds itself under siege from federal immigration authorities, customers

and labor organizations due to its employment practice of hiring illegals. At stake is the grocer's reputation as well as its ambitious growth plans, including an initial public offering of its stock.

9869 ■ "Frosted Flakes Goes For Gold" in *Marketing to Women* **(Vol. 21, April 2008, No. 4, pp. 3)**
Pub: EPM Communications, Inc.
Description: Kellogg is appealing to health-conscious moms with its new product Frosted Flakes Gold.

9870 ■ "GM's Decision to Boot Dealer Prompts Sale" in *Baltimore Business Journal* **(Vol. 27, November 6, 2009, No. 26, pp. 1)**
Pub: American City Business Journals
Ed: Daniel J. Sernovitz. **Description:** General Motors Corporation's (GM) decision to strip Baltimore's Anderson Automotive Group Inc. of its GM franchise has prompted the owner, Bruce Mortimer, to close the automotive dealership and sell the land to a developer. The new project could make way for new homes, a shopping center and supermarket.

9871 ■ "Good Things Happen When We Buy Local" in *Crain's Detroit Business* **(Vol. 24, October 6, 2008, No. 40, pp. 7)**
Pub: Crain Communications, Inc.
Description: Michigan is facing incredibly difficult economic times. One way in which each one of us can help the state and the businesses located here is by purchasing our goods and services from local vendors. The state Agriculture Department projected that if Michigan households earmarked $10 per week in their grocery purchases to made-in-Michigan products, this would generate $30 million a week in economic impact.

9872 ■ "Green and Clean" in *Retail Merchandiser* **(Vol. 51, July-August 2011, No. 4, pp. 56)**
Pub: Phoenix Media Corporation
Description: Green Valley Grocery partnered with Paragon Solutions consulting firm to make their stores environmentally green.

9873 ■ "The Harris Teeter Grocery Chain Has Started a New Ice Cream Club for Shoppers" in *Ice Cream Reporter* **(Vol. 21, July 20, 2008)**
Pub: Ice Cream Reporter
Description: Store loyalty cards are being issued to Harris Teeter customers to purchase any variety of Ben & Jerry's, Haagen-Dazs, Dove, Starbucks, Ciao Bella, Clemmy's, Purely Decadent, So Delicious, Harris Teeter Naturals, HT Traders, Hunter Farms or Denali Ice Cream. One point is earned for every dollar spent, 30 total points earns a $5 electronic coupon towards the next purchase.

9874 ■ "Health Care Leads Sectors Attracting Capital" in *Hispanic Business* **(Vol. 30, March 2008, No. 3, pp. 14)**
Pub: Hispanic Business
Ed: Scott Williams. **Description:** Discusses the capital gains of Hispanic-owned companies and other Hispanic leaders in the investment and retail fields in the year 2007. Sectors like health care, media, food and technology saw a healthy flow of capital due to successful mergers, acquisitions and increased private equity investments.

9875 ■ "High Growth Reported for the Natural Supermarket Pet Department Close-Up" in *Canadian Corporate News* **(October 20, 2008)**
Pub: Comtex News Network Inc.
Description: Leading natural supermarket chains have been outperforming mainstream grocers by carrying natural and organic pet products. Statistical data included.

9876 ■ "Hometown Value" in *Retail Merchandiser* **(Vol. 51, July-August 2011, No. 4, pp. 50)**
Pub: Phoenix Media Corporation
Ed: Todd Vowell. **Description:** Profile of family-owned Vowell's Marketplace located in Noxapater, Mississippi. The 10-store chain caters to its Southern roots and is run by the third generation of the Vowell family.

9877 ■ "Hopes Grow for Milk Price Increase From Tesco" in *Farmer's Weekly* **(March 28, 2008, No. 320)**
Pub: Reed Business Information
Description: Farmers will see an increase in the price supermarket Tesco will pay for their milk.

9878 ■ "Impulse Buys Find Their Way Into Grocery Cart" in *Marketing to Women* **(Vol. 23, November 2010, No. 11, pp. 6)**
Pub: EPM Communications, Inc.
Description: Impulse purchases are made by 90 percent of grocery shoppers according to a recent study. The number of items shoppers buy impulsively during a typical trip to the grocery store in 2010 are outlined.

9879 ■ "In the Wake of Pet-Food Crisis, Iams Sales Plummet Nearly 17 Percent" in *Advertising Age* **(Vol. 78, May 14, 2007, No. 18, pp. 3)**
Pub: Crain Communications, Inc.
Ed: Jack Neff. **Description:** Although the massive U.S. pet-food recall impacted more than 100 brands, Procter & Gamble Co.'s Iams lost more sales and market share than any other industry player. According to Information Resources Inc. data, the brand's sales dropped 16.5 percent in the eight-week period ended April 22. Many analysts feel that the company could have handled the crisis in a better manner.

9880 ■ "Industry Vet To Spread Glory's Word" in *Business First-Columbus* **(November 9, 2007, pp. A1)**
Pub: American City Business Journals, Inc.
Ed: Dan Eaton. **Description:** Glory Foods, Inc. chose Jacqueline Neal as its new president in October 2007. Neal has eleven years experience in brand management and has worked with food industry leaders such as Mars Inc., Kraft Foods Inc., and Nabisco Holdings Corporation. Neil's plans for the company are presented.

9881 ■ "J&J Snack Rakes in Sales" in *Philadelphia Business Journal* **(Vol. 28, September 25, 2009, No. 32, pp. 1)**
Pub: American City Business Journals
Ed: Peter van Allen. **Description:** Analysts expect J&J Snack Foods Corporation to boost earnings by 48 percent for fiscal year ending September 2009. Stable commodity prices have benefited the company.

9882 ■ "Kroger Forges Ahead with Fuel Centers" in *Business Courier* **(Vol. 26, December 25, 2009, No. 35, pp. 1)**
Pub: American City Business Journals, Inc.
Ed: Jon Newberry. **Description:** Cincinnati-based grocery chain Kroger Company plans to construct more fuel centers near supermarkets and food stores despite declining profit margins in gasoline sales. Statistical data included.

9883 ■ "Kroger Girds for Invasion of U.K. Chain" in *Business Courier* **(Vol. 24, November 2, 2008, No. 29, pp. 1)**
Pub: American City Business Journals, Inc.
Ed: Jon Newberry. **Description:** Tesco PLC will be opening its first Fresh & Easy Neighborhood Markets in Southern California. The company has committed $500 million per year to get a share of the $500 billion US food retailing market and will be opening more stores in quick succession. Tesco's arrival can be difficult for Kroger because Kroger had obtained much of its success by using Tesco's UK model.

9884 ■ "Lafley Gives Look At His Game Plan" in *Business Courier* **(Vol. 24, March 21, 2008, No. 50, pp. 1)**
Pub: American City Business Journals, Inc.
Ed: Lisa Biank Fasig. **Description:** Overview of A.G. Lafley's book entitled 'The Game-Changer', is presented. Lafley, Procter & Gamble Co.'s chief executive officer, documented his philosophy and strategy in his book. His work also includes Procter & Gamble's hands-on initiatives such as mock-up grocery stores and personal interviews with homeowners.

9885 ■ "Landlord Puts 7 Tops Locations On Market" in *Business First Buffalo* **(November 16, 2007, pp. 1)**
Pub: American City Business Journals, Inc.
Ed: James Fink. **Description:** New York-based Benesen Capital Partners LLC has put its 388,000-square-foot property up for sale. Seven Tops Grocery Markets have two to nine years remaining on their lease contracts.

9886 ■ "LCB Puts a Cork in Kiosk Wine Sales" in *Times Leader* **(December 22, 2010)**
Pub: Wilkes-Barre Publishing Company
Ed: Andrew M. Seder. **Description:** The Pennsylvania Liquor Control Board closed down thirty Pronto Wine Kiosks located in supermarkets throughout the state. The Board cited mechanical and technological issues such as products not dispensing.

9887 ■ "Li'l Guy Rolls Up Into Bigger Company" in *The Business Journal-Serving Metropolitan Kansas City* **(Vol. 26, September 12, 2008)**
Pub: American City Business Journals, Inc.
Ed: Suzanna Stagemeyer. **Description:** Li'l Guy Foods, a Mexican food company in Kansas City, Missouri, has merged with Tortilla King Inc. Li'l Guy's revenue in 2007 was $3.3 million, while a newspaper report said that Tortilla King's revenue in 2001 was $7.5 million. Growth opportunities for the combined companies and Li'l Guy's testing of the Wichita market are discussed.

9888 ■ "A Local Affair: Decisions for Tops Again Being Made at Amherst HQ" in *Business First Buffalo* **(December 7, 2007, pp. 3)**
Pub: American City Business Journals, Inc.
Ed: James Fink. **Description:** Tops Market LLC merged with Morgan Stanley Private Equity and names its new CEO, Frank Curci. The company headquarters moved to its new location in Amherst, New York.

9889 ■ "Lords Should Get Real About Food" in *Farmer's Weekly* **(March 28, 2008, No. 320)**
Pub: Reed Business Information
Description: Discusses the reasons why farming needs subsidies and suggests that the House of Lords should look at the way that grocery stores are operating.

9890 ■ "Market Share" in *Business Journal-Milwaukee* **(Vol. 28, December 3, 2010, No. 9, pp. A1)**
Pub: Milwaukee Business Journal
Ed: Stacy Vogel Davis. **Description:** Roundy's Supermarkets' market share has decreased with the expansion of low-price grocery chains in Milwaukee, Wisconsin. Wal-Mart stores Inc., Aldi Inc., and Target Corporation have all opened new stores in the area.

9891 ■ "Marketer Bets Big on U.S.'s Growing Canine Obsession" in *Advertising Age* **(Vol. 79, April 14, 2008, No. 15, pp. 14)**
Pub: Crain Communications, Inc.
Ed: Emily Bryson York. **Description:** Overview of FreshPet, a New Jersey company that began marketing two brands of refrigerated dog food-Deli Fresh and FreshPet Select-which are made from fresh ingredients such as beef, rice and carrots. The company projects continued success due to the amount of money consumers spend on their pets as well as fears derived from the 2007 recalls that inspired consumers to look for smaller, independent manufacturers that are less likely to source ingredients from China.

9892 ■ "Moms Give More Thought to Nutrition" in *Marketing to Women* **(Vol. 21, February 2008, No. 2, pp. 8)**
Pub: EPM Communications, Inc.
Description: Moms are thinking more about nutritional issues than they did in the past and spending more time reading labels in the grocery store. 74 percent of moms consider the nutritional content of foods purchased for their children more now than they did two years ago.

9893 ■ **"Moms Rely on Coupons, Specials to Lower Grocery Bills"** in *Marketing to Women* (Vol. 23, November 2010, No. 11, pp. 8)
Pub: EPM Communications, Inc.
Description: Eighty-four percent of moms surveyed reported using coupons when grocery shopping in order to lower costs. They are also purchasing less snack foods, fewer brand name items, alcoholic beverages, organic items, meat and fresh fruits and vegetables.

9894 ■ *National Frozen and Refrigerated Foods Association—Membership Directory*
Pub: National Frozen & Refrigerated Foods Association Inc.
Contact: Nevin B. Montgomery, Pres./CEO
E-mail: nevin@nfraweb.org
Released: Annual, Latest edition 2009. **Price:** $25. **Covers:** 800 member companies worldwide, including distributors, manufacturers, sales agents, logistics providers, suppliers, retailers, and food service operators. **Entries Include:** Company name, address, phone, names of executives, products or services, trade and brand names. **Arrangement:** Geographical within membership category; supplier members and manufacturer members listed in product classifications. **Indexes:** Company name.

9895 ■ **"Need Fiber in Your Diet? Pour Some Milk"** in *Globe & Mail* (April 10, 2007, pp. B7)
Pub: CTVglobemedia Publishing Inc.
Ed: William Illsey Atkinson. **Description:** The growing market and demand for functional foods and neutraceuticals in Canada is discussed. The research being conducted by University of Manitoba's Richardson Centre for Functional Foods and Nutraceuticals to explore new health compounds in food is highlighted.

9896 ■ **"Need Grub? Start Texting at Kroger"** in *Business Courier* (Vol. 24, December 21, 2008, No. 36, pp. 1)
Pub: American City Business Journals, Inc.
Ed: Laura Baverman. **Description:** Discusses the University of Cincinnati which is teaming up to release a technology platform called Macopay that would link a cell phone to a bank account and allow a person to make payments at participating retailers by sending a text message. Details with regard to the new service and its growth potential are discussed.

9897 ■ **"Neighbors Rally for Dollar Store"** in *Chattanooga Times/Free Press* (August 4, 2010)
Pub: Chattanooga Times/Free Press
Description: Neighbors are rallying to keep the Family Dollar Store in their city open. The proposed new store would expand the grocery portion of its retail discount shop.

9898 ■ **"New Stores, New Headquarters in Schenectady for Golub Corporation"** in *Business Review, Albany New York* (November 23, 2007)
Pub: American City Business Journals, Inc.
Ed: Michael DeMasi. **Description:** Details of Golub Corporation's expansion plan are presented. The supermarket chain, which has 116 stores in six northeastern states, plans to open thirty more stores within the next three or four years. The company will also build 524,000 square feet of warehouse space which will help in supplying new stores. Its corporate headquarters will also move to a vacant lot in Schenectady, New York.

9899 ■ **"A Nice Consistency"** in *Inc.* (Vol. 31, January-February 2009, No. 1, pp. 94)
Pub: Mansueto Ventures LLC
Ed: Jason Del Rey. **Description:** PJ Madison spent almost a quarter of its revenue promoting its latest product, organic ice cream. The Texas-based firm saw sales increase dramatically.

9900 ■ **"P&G's Iams Finds Itself in a Pet-Food Dogfight"** in *Advertising Age* (Vol. 78, March 5, 2007, No. 10, pp. 6)
Pub: Crain Communications, Inc.
Ed: Jack Neff. **Description:** Proctor & Gamble Co.'s Iams has been slow to embrace the trend toward foods for pets that appear fit for human consumption.

Competitors such as Nestle Purina have made big gains with its colorful premium Beneful brand and dry nuggets that look like chunks of vegetables and meat. Statistical data included.

9901 ■ **"Patience May Pay Off"** in *Barron's* (Vol. 89, July 13, 2009, No. 28, pp. 30)
Pub: Dow Jones & Co., Inc.
Ed: Johanna Bennett. **Description:** New CEO Craig Herkert can turn around Supervalu and their shares could double to $30 in three years from June 2009 according to one investment officer. Herkert knows how to run a lean and tight operation since he has worked for Albertsons and Wal-Mart in the past.

9902 ■ **"Phillips Edison Launches $1.8B Retail REIT"** in *Business Courier* (Vol. 27, October 15, 2010, No. 24, pp. 1)
Pub: Business Courier
Ed: Dan Monk. **Description:** Retail center operator Phillips Edison & Company is organizing a real estate investment trust (REIT) to raise $1.8 billion to finance the planned purchase of 150 grocery-centered shopping centers around the U.S. The offering would be Phillips largest. Phillips Edison employesss 174 workers and operates 250 shopping centers nationwide.

9903 ■ **"Procter & Gamble Boosts Bet on Exclusive Brands"** in *Business Courier* (Vol. 27, July 9, 2010, No. 10, pp. 1)
Pub: Business Courier
Ed: Jon Newberry. **Description:** Procter & Gamble is creating more special versions of its brands such as Pringles and Pampers exclusively for retail partners such as Tesco in the U.K. The greater push towards this direction is seen as a way to regain market share.

9904 ■ *Progressive Grocer's Marketing Guidebook*
Pub: Trade Dimensions
Released: Annual, Latest edition 2011. **Covers:** Over 1,000 U.S. and Canadian supermarket chains, large independents and wholesalers; also includes 350 specialty distributors include smaller food wholesalers, food brokers, non-food distributors, and candy/tobacco/media distributors and over 15,000 key executives and buyers. **Entries Include:** For retailers and wholesalers—Company name, address, phone, email and websites, number of stores operated or served, areas of operation, major grocery supplier, three-year financial summary, buying policies, private label information, lists of executives, buyers, and merchandisers. For specialty distributors—Name, address, phone, list of key personnel including buyers' categories, list of items handled, URL. **Arrangement:** Alphabetical by hierarchy, geographical by eight regions and 50 market areas. **Indexes:** Grocery related organizations, chain and wholesalers, state index, store operating name/parent company reference.

9905 ■ **"Putting 'Great' Back Into A&P"** in *Crain's New York Business* (Vol. 24, January 7, 2008, No. 1, pp. 3)
Pub: Crain Communications, Inc.
Description: After five straight years ending in 2005, A&P Grocery lost revenue; due to a sweeping plan to freshen up its supermarkets the company returned to growth mode and was able to acquire longtime competitor Pathmark Stores.

9906 ■ **"Ralcorp Investigated for Rejecting ConAgra Bid"** in *Saint Louis Business Journal* (Vol. 32, September 16, 2011, No. 3, pp. 1)
Pub: Saint Louis Business Journal
Ed: Evan Binns. **Description:** New York-based Levi & Korsinsky started investigating Ralcorp Holidngs Inc. after it rejected ConAgra Foods Inc.'s third and latest takeover bid of $5.17 billion. The investigation would determine whether Ralcorp's directors had acted on behalf of shareholders' best interest.

9907 ■ **"Restaurants Slammed by Economy"** in *Business Courier* (Vol. 24, April 4, 2008, No. 52, pp. 1)
Pub: American City Business Journals, Inc.
Ed: Lisa Biank Fasig. **Description:** Restaurants in Cincinnati are closing some of their stores due to growing costs of fuel, eggs and meat. The establish-

ments are also affected by lower consumer spending that was brought on by unemployment, higher grocery prices and foreclosures. The economic problems in Cincinnati are also compared to those in other cities.

9908 ■ **"Roundy' Pushing Chicago Expansion"** in *Milwaukee Business Journal* (Vol. 27, February 12, 2010, No. 20, pp. A1)
Pub: American City Business Journals
Ed: Rich Kirchen. **Description:** Roundy Supermarkets Inc. is expanding in Chicago, Illinois as the Milwaukee-based company is set to open one store in downtown Chicago and another in the Arlington suburb. The store openings have been pushed back to spring and early summer in 2010 due to the economic downturn.

9909 ■ **"Safeway"** in *Ice Cream Reporter* (Vol. 23, September 20, 2010, No. 10, pp. 8)
Pub: Ice Cream Reporter
Description: Safeway supermarkets have upsized their private label ice cream to a full half gallon, thus reversing the trend where most brands were shrinking their containers.

9910 ■ **"Silver Springs Creamery Opens Retail"** in *Bellingham Business Journal* (Vol. March 2010, pp. 3)
Pub: Sound Publishing Inc.
Description: Eric Sundstrom, owner of Silver Springs Creamery, announced the opening of its on-site retail store that will sell the farm's goat and cow cheese, yogurt, ice cream and flesh milk.

9911 ■ **"Similac Introduces New Packaging"** in *Marketing to Women* (Vol. 21, February 2008, No. 2, pp. 3)
Pub: EPM Communications, Inc.
Description: Baby formula brand Similac introduces a new ready to feed packaging which requires no mixing, measuring or preparation.

9912 ■ **"Small Fish, Big Box Stores"** in *Hawaii Business* (Vol. 53, November 2007, No. 5, pp. 55)
Pub: Hawaii Business Publishing
Ed: Jolyn Okimoto Rosa. **Description:** Ohana Seafoods can be found at big-box stores such as Costco, Marukai and Don Quijote. Owner Jeffrey Yee spends his weekend at a farmers market to have direct contact with his customers and get feedback right away. Ohana offers ready-to cook fish products, sauces and fish.

9913 ■ **"Still Stretching"** in *Business Courier* (Vol. 24, December 28, 2008, No. 37, pp. 1)
Pub: American City Business Journals, Inc.
Ed: Lucy May. **Description:** Minority-owned businesses have experienced growth in 2007 as Cincinnati and Hamilton County used a workforce development and economic inclusion policy. Kroger Co., for example, has been inducted to the Billion Dollar Roundtable in 2007 for attaining $1 billion in annual spending with suppliers that are minority- owned. The need for more progress within the minority-owned enterprises is discussed.

9914 ■ **"Stone to Run Hickory Farmer's Market"** in *Charlotte Observer* (January 31, 2007)
Pub: Knight-Ridder/Tribune Business News
Ed: Jen Aronoff. **Description:** Betty Stone has been hired to manage the Downtown Hickory Farmers Market. The market will run from May 5 through October 6, 2007.

9915 ■ **"Substantial Deal Expected to Create Jobs, Help Industrial Market"** in *Tampa Bay Business Journal* (Vol. 30, January 8, 2010, No. 3)
Pub: American City Business Journals
Ed: Janet Leiser. **Description:** Food distribution firm Gordon Food Service (GFS) is on the brink of purchasing Albertson's million-square-foot warehouse along with 158 acres of space. The deal between GFS and Albertson's could expand GFS' presence in west Central Florida. A history of GFS' growth is included

9916 ▪ **"Super Success" in** *Small Business Opportunities* **(November 2008)**
Pub: Entrepreneur Media Inc.

Description: Profile of PromoWorks LLC, a company founded by Michael Kent, that distributes samples of food at grocery stores for clients like Kraft Foods, Inc. and Kellogg Co. and also handles the logistics, provides the employees and tracks the products' sales.

9917 ▪ **"A Switch in the Kitchen" in** *Barron's* **(Vol. 88, March 24, 2008, No. 12, pp. 17)**
Pub: Dow Jones & Company, Inc.

Description: Men are doing more kitchen duties, with 18 percent of meals at home being made by men in 2007 compared to 11 percent four years previously. Young wives, however, choose to forgo work and stay at home.

9918 ▪ **"The End of the Line for Line Extensions?" in** *Advertising Age* **(Vol. 79, July 7, 2008, No. 26, pp. 3)**
Pub: Crain Communications, Inc.

Ed: Description: After years of double-digit growth, some of the most heavily extended personal-care products have slowed substantially or even declined in the U.S. Unilever's Dove and P&G's Pantene and Olay are two such brands that have been affected. Statistical data included.

9919 ▪ **"They Like It Cold" in** *Business Journal Portland* **(Vol. 27, October 15, 2010, No. 33, pp. 1)**
Pub: Portland Business Journal

Ed: Erik Siemers. **Description:** Ajinomoto Frozen Foods USA Inc. has been investing in its Portland, Oregon facility. The company has completed a new rice production line. It has also spent $1.2 million on a new packaging technology.

9920 ▪ **"Top 50 Exporters" in** *Hispanic Business* **(Vol. 30, July-August 2008, No. 7-8, pp. 42)**
Pub: Hispanic Business, Inc.

Ed: Hildy Medina. **Description:** Increases in exports revenues reported by food exporters and green companies in a time of economic slowdown in the U.S are described. Food exporters have benefited from the growth of high-volume grocery stores in underdeveloped countries and the German governments' promotion of solar energy has benefited the U.S. solar heating equipment and solar panel manufactures.

9921 ▪ **"Trading Down at the Supermarket" in** *Barron's* **(Vol. 88, July 14, 2008, No. 28, pp. 36)**
Pub: Dow Jones & Co., Inc.

Ed: Alexander Eule. **Description:** Shares of Ralcorp Holdings are cheap at around $49.95 after slipping 20 percent prior to their acquisition of Post cereals from Kraft. Some analysts believe its shares could climb over 60 percent to $80 as value-seeking consumers buy more private label products.

9922 ▪ **"V&J Scores Partnership with Shaq" in** *Business Journal-Milwaukee* **(Vol. 25, October 12, 2007, No. 2, pp. A1)**
Pub: American City Business Journals, Inc.

Ed: Rich Kirchen. **Description:** O'Neal Franchise Group has agreed to a partnership with V&J Foods of Milwaukee to handle Auntie Anne's shops in New York, South Africa, Michigan, and the Caribbean. V&J O'Neal Enterprises will open six Auntie Anne's soft pretzel shops in Detroit towards the end of 2007. Planned international ventures of the partnership are presented.

9923 ▪ **"'Wal-Mart Effect' Feeds Grocer Price Wars" in** *Globe & Mail* **(March 15, 2007, pp. B14)**
Pub: CTVglobemedia Publishing Inc.

Ed: Marina Strauss. **Description:** The decrease in profit reports by Canadian grocery giants amidst high expansion plans by Wal-Mart Stores Inc. are discussed. This industry is witnessing the most severe pricing competitions in recent times.

9924 ▪ **"Wary Investors Turn to a Different Market for Strong Returns" in** *Boston Business Journal* **(Vol. 29, September 2, 2011, No. 17, pp. 1)**
Pub: American City Business Journals Inc.

Ed: Daniel J. Sernovitz. **Description:** Maryland-based investors have been choosing to put their money in the supermarket business. Retail property sales have increased during the second quarter of 2011.

9925 ▪ **"Waugh Chapel to Expand" in** *Baltimore Business Journal* **(Vol. 28, August 27, 2010, No. 16, pp. 1)**
Pub: Baltimore Business Journal

Ed: Daniel J. Sernovitz. **Description:** Developer Greenberg Gibbons Corporation has broken ground on a $275 million, 1.2 million-square-foot addition to its Village at the Waugh Chapel mixed-use complex. Aside from creating 2,600 permanent jobs, the addition, named Village South, is expected to lure Target and Wegmans Food Markets to Crofton, Maryland. Funding for this project is discussed.

9926 ▪ **"Wegmans Uses Database for Recall" in** *Supermarket News* **(Vol. 56, September 22, 2008, No. 38)**
Pub: Penton Business Media, Inc.

Ed: Carol Angrisani. **Description:** Wegmans used data obtained through its loyalty card that, in turn, sent automated telephone calls to every customer who had purchased tainted pet food when Mars Petcare recalled dog food products.

9927 ▪ **"Welch's Uses Taste Strips in Ads" in** *Marketing to Women* **(Vol. 21, April 2008, No. 4, pp. 3)**
Pub: EPM Communications, Inc.

Description: Welch's is positioning its 139-year-old brand in a new and inventive way with a new marketing campaign in which print ads will feature a tamper-evident flavor pouch that contains a dissolving taste strip flavored with Welch's grape juice.

9928 ▪ **"What's New" in** *Crain's Cleveland Business* **(Vol. 30, June 29, 2009, No. 25, pp. 19)**
Pub: Crain Communications, Inc.

Description: More Than Gourmet, located in Akron, Ohio has introduced a new line of ready-to-use sauces, packed in 11-ounce containers that hold three-five servings.

STATISTICAL SOURCES

9929 ▪ *Grocery Industry Market Share Report*
Pub: Chain Store Guide Information Services

Ed: Compiled by Chain Store Guide staff. **Released:** 2008. **Price:** $195.00 (PDF or Excel File). The Grocery Industry Market Share Report is a three-year historical market profile of all government-mandated statistical areas. The report includes market share information on chain and independent supermarkets, mass merchandisers selling grocery products, wholesale clubs as well as dollar stores.

9930 ▪ *The Market for Value-Added Fresh Produce*
Pub: MarketResearch.com

Released: 1999. **Price:** $2750.00. **Description:** This Packaged Facts report discusses how precuts (those popular bags of shredded lettuce), as well as organics, have rocketed at double-digit rates to the $9.7 billion mark at retail.

9931 ▪ *RMA Annual Statement Studies*
Pub: Robert Morris Associates (RMA)

Released: Annual. **Price:** $175.00 2006-07 edition, $105.00. **Description:** Contains composite balance sheets and income statements for more than 360 industries, including the accounting, auditing, and bookkeeping industries. Also contains five years of comparative historical data for discerning trends. Includes 16 commonly used ratios, computed for most of the size groupings for nearly every industry.

9932 ▪ *Standard & Poor's Industry Surveys*
Pub: Standard & Poor's Corp.

Released: Annual. **Price:** $3633.00. **Description:** Two-volume book that examines the prospects for specific industries, including trucking. Also provides analyses of trends and problems, statistical tables and charts, and comparative company analyses.

9933 ▪ *The U.S. Kids' Foods Market*
Pub: MarketResearch.com

Released: 1999. **Price:** $2750.00. **Description:** Analyzes the market for children's prepared foods, concentrating on cereals, lunch foods and snacks, beverages, meals and entrees, and ice cream and frozen novelties. Offers sales data; gives insight into marketing; highlights the demographic forces driving the market; profiles major players; and provides market forecasts.

TRADE PERIODICALS

9934 ▪ *Canadian Grocer*
Pub: Rogers Media Publishing
Contact: Nancy Kwon, Managing Editor

Released: 10/yr. **Price:** $89 plus applicable taxes. **Description:** Magazine serving the grocery trade, food distribution industry, and supermarkets.

9935 ▪ *The Food & Beverage International*
Pub: Journal Publications Inc.
Contact: Rodney Ruppert, Web Asst.

Released: Bimonthly. **Description:** Trade magazine covering the food and beverage industry.

9936 ▪ *The Food & Beverage Journal*
Pub: Journal Publications Inc.
Contact: Michael Walsh, Publisher

Ed: Ellen Walsh, Editor, ewalsh@fbworld.com. **Released:** Bimonthly. **Price:** $30; $40 two years. **Description:** Trade magazine for the food and beverage industry in the western U.S.

9937 ▪ *The Food Industry Advisor*
Pub: GC Publishing Company Inc.
Contact: Tom Cirino, Account Exec.

Released: Monthly. **Price:** $48. **Description:** Trade newspaper (tabloid) covering retail and wholesale activities in the Pennsylvania/Tri-state food industry. Official publication of the Pennsylvania Food Merchants Association.

9938 ▪ *The Food Institute Report*
Pub: American Institute of Food Distribution Inc.
Contact: Brian Todd, Sr. VP
E-mail: bTodd@foodinstitute.com

Released: Weekly. **Description:** Reports on developments in the food industry, including new products, the food service industry, mergers and acquisitions, current legislation and regulations, judicial decisions, and financial and marketing information.

9939 ▪ *Food Trade News*
Pub: Best-Met Publishing Company Inc.
Contact: Richard J. Bestany, Advertising Dir
E-mail: rbestany@best-met.com

Released: Monthly. **Price:** $69. **Description:** Newspaper for the retail supermarket industry.

9940 ▪ *Grocery Headquarters*
Pub: Macfadden Communications Group L.L.C.
Contact: Seth Mendelson, Publisher/Editorial Dir./VP
E-mail: smendelson@groceryheadquarters.com

Released: Monthly. **Price:** Free to qualified subscribers. **Description:** Magazine (tabloid) serving the supermarket industry.

9941 ▪ *IGA Grocergram*
Pub: Pace Communications Inc.

Released: Monthly. **Description:** Retail grocery magazine.

9942 ▪ *Iowa Grocer*
Pub: Iowa Grocery Industry Association
Contact: Jerry Fleagle, President

Released: Bimonthly. **Description:** Magazine for grocery industry - retail and supply.

9943 ■ *The Packer*
Pub: Vance Publishing Corp.
Released: Weekly. **Price:** $65; $114 two years; $96 out of country. **Description:** Newspaper on produce marketing.

9944 ■ *Progressive Grocer*
Pub: Nielsen Business Media
Contact: Meg Major, Editor-in-Chief
E-mail: mmajor@progressivegrocer.com
Released: 13/yr. **Description:** Magazine for chain and independent supermarkets and wholesale grocers.

9945 ■ *Shelby Report of the Southeast*
Pub: Shelby Publishing Company Inc.
Contact: Ron Johnston, Pres./Publisher
Released: Monthly. **Price:** $36; $60 two years; $75 3 years. **Description:** Retail and wholesale food trade newspaper.

9946 ■ *Shelby Report of the Southwest*
Pub: Shelby Publishing Company Inc.
Contact: Penny Smith, Account managing editorager
E-mail: pennys@shelbypublishing.com
Ed: Lorrie Griffith, Editor, editor@shelbypublishing.com. **Released:** Monthly. **Price:** $36; $60 two years. **Description:** Retail and wholesale food trade newspaper.

VIDEOCASSETTES/ AUDIOCASSETTES

9947 ■ *Successful Food Demonstration & Sampling*
International Dairy-Deli-Bakery Association (IDDBA)
636 Science Dr.
PO Box 5528
Madison, WI 53705-0528
Ph:(608)310-5000
Fax:(608)238-6330
Co. E-mail: iddba@iddba.org
URL: http://www.iddba.org
Price: $100.00. **Description:** Presents ways supermarket dairy, deli, bakery and food-service employees can sell more through food demonstrations and sampling. **Availability:** VHS.

TRADE SHOWS AND CONVENTIONS

9948 ■ Connecticut Food Association Convention
Connecticut Food Association
195 Farmington Ave., Ste. 200
Farmington, CT 06032
Ph:(860)677-8097
Fax:(860)677-8418
Co. E-mail: ctfood@ctfoodassociation.org
URL: http://www.ctfoodassociation.org/
Released: Annual. **Audience:** Trade professionals. **Principal Exhibits:** Wholesale and retail food industry equipment, supplies, and services.

9949 ■ Food & Fuel Expo
Tennessee Grocers Association
1838 Elm Hill Pike., Ste. 136
Nashville, TN 37210-3726
Ph:(615)889-0136
Free: 800-238-8742
Fax:(615)889-2877
URL: http://www.tngrocer.org
Released: Annual. **Audience:** Food wholesalers, retail grocers, and retail industry personnel. **Principal Exhibits:** Food products and equipment, supplies, and services.

9950 ■ Michigan Grocers Association Annual Convention and Trade Show
Michigan Grocers Association
221 N. Walnut St.
Lansing, MI 48933
Ph:(517)372-6800
Free: 800-947-6237
Fax:(517)372-3002
Co. E-mail: contact@michigangrocers.org
URL: http://www.michigangrocers.org
Released: Annual. **Principal Exhibits:** Equipment, supplies, and services for wholesale and retail grocers and suppliers.

9951 ■ Missouri Grocers Association Annual Convention and Trade Show
Missouri Grocers Association
315 N. Ken Ave.
Springfield, MO 65802
Ph:(417)831-6667
Free: 800-260-4642
Fax:(417)831-3907
URL: http://www.missourigrocers.com
Released: Annual. **Audience:** Owner and operators; independent retailers. **Principal Exhibits:** Grocery equipment, supplies, and services.

9952 ■ NFRA Convention
National Frozen Food Association
4755 Linglestown Rd., Ste. 300
PO Box 6069
Harrisburg, PA 17112
Ph:(717)657-8601
Fax:(717)657-9862
Co. E-mail: info@nfraweb.org
URL: http://www.nfraweb.org
Audience: Frozen food buyers, brokers, manufacturers, suppliers, distributors, and warehouse personnel. **Principal Exhibits:** Manufacturers showcasing and sampling their products; a reception. **Dates and Locations:** 2011 Oct 22-25, Orlando, FL.

9953 ■ Western Food Industry Expo
Arizona Food Marketing Alliance
120 E. Pierce St.
Phoenix, AZ 85004
Ph:(602)252-9761
Fax:(602)252-9021
Co. E-mail: droth@afmaaz.org
URL: http://www.afmaaz.org
Released: Annual. **Audience:** Trade buyers, retail operators, convenience store franchises, independent store owners, wholesalers, distributors, manufacturers, and marketing agencies. **Principal Exhibits:** Grocery store equipment, supplies, and services, including frozen foods, meats, poultry, store supplies, health and beauty aids, bakery products, beer, and wine.

CONSULTANTS

9954 ■ Maine Coalition For Safe Kids Inc.
304 Hancock Pl., Ste. 3G
PO Box 404
Bangor, ME 04402
Ph:(207)973-5788
Free: 800-706-7233
Fax:(207)778-5097
Co. E-mail: safekids@somtel.com
Contact: Robert L. Bull, Mgr
E-mail: mainesafekids@msn.com
Scope: Consultants to management in food marketing, offering market development services, consumer research, trade research, preparation of training manuals, training workshops for sales supervisors and store supervisors, and sales promotion services. Serves government also. Provides injury safety solutions to the children. **Seminars:** Supermarket Supervision; Home Health Care Product Retailing; Marketing to Aging Americans; Childhood Injury Prevention.

9955 ■ R.D. Network Inc.
PO Box 375
Lafayette Hill, PA 19444
Ph:(215)482-4461
Free: 877-482-4991
Fax:(215)836-0378
Co. E-mail: info@rdnetwork.com
URL: http://www.rdnetwork.com
Contact: Melissa Altman, Principle
E-mail: info@rdnetwork.com
Scope: Dietitians, diet technicians, and certified dietary managers available nationwide and worldwide through an international registry for consulting positions to wellness and employee education programs, drug or alcohol rehabilitation, hospital, LTC, nutrition and labeling communications, nutrition consultation, weight control classes, healthcare staff supplementation, media and program development, and all nutrition and food-related needs. Expert witness and speakers bureau also available. Industries served: healthcare, food industry, food service, restaurateurs, supermarkets, pharmaceutical companies, home health agencies, insurance companies, HMOs, and government agencies. **Seminars:** Healthy Dining Etiquette for Executives and Sales Staff Diet and Wellness; Cardiovascular Nutrition; Starting a Nutrition Consulting Practice; AIDS and Diet Therapy; Nutrition Care for Your Parents in Their Elder Years; Increase Your Energy-Increase Your Sales.

9956 ■ Thole Associates
1400 Shadwell Cir.
Lake Mary, FL 32746-4344
Ph:(407)333-2174
Fax:(407)333-2174
Contact: Jerome L. Thole, President
Scope: Consulting organization specializing in food and drug store merchandising and operations. In addition to serving retailers, the firm provides consulting service to wholesalers and manufacturers as well. Areas of expertise include store operations, store conditions, operating cost control, customer service training, research, and budget control and scheduling. Industries served: retail food supermarket and drug companies. **Seminars:** How to Improve Customer Service-Without Sacrificing Productivity; Customer Satisfaction-Develop a Strategy for Success; How to Control Expense in Tough Economic Times.

FRANCHISES AND BUSINESS OPPORTUNITIES

9957 ■ The Honeybaked Ham Co. and Cafe
The HBH Franchise Co. LLC
3875 Mansell Rd.
Alpharetta, GA 30022
Ph:(678)966-3254
Free: (866)968-7424
Fax:(678)966-3134
URL: http://www.honeybakedonline.com
No. of Franchise Units: 183. **No. of Company-Owned Units:** 280. **Founded:** 1957. **Franchised:** 1998. **Description:** Specialty retailer of high quality spiral-sliced hams and turkeys. **Equity Capital Needed:** $350,000 net worth with $100,000 available as equity contribution. **Franchise Fee:** $30,000. **Financial Assistance:** No. **Training:** Comprehensive 14 day program at corporate training store.

COMPUTERIZED DATABASES

9958 ■ *Consumer Buying Power*
The Nielsen Co.
770 Broadway
New York, NY 10003-9595
URL: http://www.claritas.com/sitereports/default.jsp
Description: Contains current-year estimates and 5-year projections of total household expenditures for more than 350 product categories, including goods and services, and 73 summary categories. Provides estimated potential consumer expenditures by store types for 41 retail store types, such as eating places; furniture; grocery; shoes; and sporting goods; as well as a breakdown of average household expenditures, such as apparel; education; electronic devices; food at home; furniture; major appliances; medical expenses; and personal care. Also includes average household expenditures for 53 Yellow Page headings. **Availability:** Online: The Nielsen Co. **Type:** Statistical.

LIBRARIES

9959 ■ American Institute of Food Distribution, Inc.–Information and Research Center
1 Broadway Plaza, 2nd Fl.
Elmwood Park, NJ 07407

Ph:(201)791-5570
Fax:(201)791-5222
Co. E-mail: jkastrinsky@foodinstitute.com
URL: http://www.foodinstitute.com/
Contact: Brian Todd, Pres./CEO

Scope: Food industry. **Services:** Center open to the public on fee basis. **Subscriptions:** 400 journals and other serials.

9960 ■ National Grocers Co. Ltd.–ISD Technical Library
6 Monogram Pl.
Weston, ON, Canada M9R 4C4
Ph:(416)246-7665
Fax:(416)246-7875

Contact: Fran Markland, Libn.
Scope: Grocery business. **Services:** Library not open to the public. **Holdings:** Figures not available.

RESEARCH CENTERS

9961 ■ St. Joseph's University–Academy of Food Marketing
150 Mandeville Hall
5600 City Ave.
Philadelphia, PA 19131
Ph:(610)660-1600
Fax:(610)660-1604
Co. E-mail: rhiggins@sju.edu
URL: http://www.sju.edu/academics/hsb/foodmarketing/academy

Contact: Robert R. Higgins, Exec.Dir.
E-mail: rhiggins@sju.edu

Scope: Food marketing from farm gate to table, including analysis and evaluation of concepts, precepts, and practices of the food industry in America and elsewhere. Conducts special studies on problems of food marketing in urban low-income areas, in-home electronic shopping, household buying behavior, national and international food consumption, and nutrient intake. Also seeks to improve efficiency in retail and wholesale operations, evaluates procedures for development of new products, examines aspects of consumer research, analyzes the effectiveness of coupons and in-store promotions, and investigates bulk foods and warehouse productivity. **Educational Activities:** Industry seminars.

ASSOCIATIONS AND OTHER ORGANIZATIONS

9962 ■ **American Custom Gunmakers Guild**
22 Vista View Ln.
Cody, WY 82414-9606
Ph:(307)587-4297
Fax:(307)587-4297
Co. E-mail: acgg@acgg.org
URL: http://www.acgg.org
Contact: Jan Billeb, Exec. Dir.

Description: Seeks to preserve and promote the art of fine custom gun making. **Publications:** *Directory of Custom Gun making Services* (biennial); *Directory of Regular Members* (biennial); *Gunmaker* (quarterly); *Realizing Your Dream: A Client's Guide to Building a Custom Gun* .

9963 ■ **Sporting Arms and Ammunitions Manufacturers Institute**
11 Mile Hill Rd.
Newtown, CT 06470-2359
Ph:(203)426-4358
Fax:(203)426-3592
Co. E-mail: rpatterson@saami.org
URL: http://www.saami.org
Contact: Mr. Rick Patterson

Description: Producers of firearms, ammunition, and propellants. Promotes and facilitates voluntary compliance with industry performance standards for sporting ammunitions. .

DIRECTORIES OF EDUCATIONAL PROGRAMS

9964 ■ *Directory of Private Accredited Career Schools and Colleges of Technology*
Pub: Accrediting Commission of Career Schools and Colleges of Technology
Contact: Michale S. McComis, Exec. Dir.

Released: On web page. **Price:** Free. **Description:** Covers 3900 accredited post-secondary programs that provide training programs in business, trade, and technical fields, including various small business endeavors. Entries offer school name, address, phone, description of courses, job placement assistance, and requirements for admission. Arrangement is alphabetical.

REFERENCE WORKS

9965 ■ "Bankruptcies" in *Crain's Detroit Business* (Vol. 24, October 6, 2008, No. 40, pp. 26)
Pub: Crain Communications, Inc.

Description: Current businesses that have filed for Chapter 7 or 11 protection in U.S. Bankruptcy Court include an auto dealership, a gun range and a grocery service.

9966 ■ "EOTech Product Improves Holographic Gun Sights" in *Crain's Detroit Business* (Vol. 24, February 4, 2008, No. 5, pp. 9)
Pub: Crain Communications Inc. - Detroit

Description: L-3 Communications EOTech Inc. procured new business contracts to fulfill military and law enforcement's demand for improved holographic sites used on handheld weapons.

9967 ■ "Fire Destroys Surplus Store, Sets Off Live Rounds Near Jacksonville NAS" in *Florida Times-Union* (December 5, 2010)
Pub: Florida Times-Union

Ed: John Leacock. **Description:** Fire which caused numerous explosions at a military surplus store near Jacksonville Naval Air Station is under investigation. Heat and flames ignited lighter fluid and set off live rounds of ammunition sold in the store.

9968 ■ *Lethal Logic: Exploding the Myths that Paralyze American Gun Policy*
Pub: Potomac Books

Ed: Dennis A. Henigen. **Released:** 2009. **Price:** $29.95. **Description:** Marketing tactics being used by gun manufacturers regarding possible new gun control laws are examined.

9969 ■ *The World Directory of Custom Bullet Makers*
Pub: Corbin Manufacturing & Supply Inc.

Released: Annual, August. **Price:** $24.50 print; $9.50 e-book. **Covers:** 300 manufacturers of custom projectiles for small arms (to 20 mm). **Entries Include:** Company name, address, phone, telex, names and titles of key personnel, subsidiary and branch names and locations, description of products and services provided, including specific calibers of bullets produced. **Arrangement:** Alphabetical. **Indexes:** Product/service, geographical.

TRADE PERIODICALS

9970 ■ *Gun Digest*
Pub: Krause Publications Inc.
Contact: Bruce Wolberg, Advertising Contact

Ed: Andy Belmas, Editor, andy.belmas@fwmedia.com. **Released:** 26/yr. **Price:** $20 13 issues; $37.98; $113.98; $171.98 other countries. **Description:** Newspaper (tabloid) serving as marketplace for buying and selling collectible firearms.

9971 ■ *Gun & Knife Show Calendar*
Pub: Krause Publications Inc.

Released: Quarterly. **Price:** $15.95; $31.90 two years; $47.85 3 years. **Description:** Magazine containing listing of gun and knife shows in the U.S. and Canada.

9972 ■ *The Gun Report*
Pub: World Wide Gun Report Inc.

Released: Monthly. **Price:** $35; $45 other countries. **Description:** Magazine on antique gun collecting.

9973 ■ *Rifle*
Pub: Wolfe Publishing Co.
Contact: Mark Harris, Assoc. Publisher

Released: Bimonthly. **Price:** $19.97; $51 combo; $11.99 military; $19.95 online. **Description:** Covers all types of rifles-centerfires, rimfires, air rifles and muzzle loaders.

9974 ■ *Shooting Industry*
Pub: Publishers Development Corp.
Contact: Anita Carson, Sales Mgr
E-mail: anita@shootingindustry.com

Ed: Russ Thurman, Editor, russ@shootingindustry.com. **Released:** Monthly. **Price:** $45 other countries. **Description:** Magazine serving the firearms industry.

9975 ■ *Shotgun News*
Pub: PRIMEDIA Los Angeles

Ed: Robert W. Hunnicutt, Editor. **Released:** 3/month. **Price:** $16; $29.95 36 issues; $56.95 72 issues; $22.50 Canada; $42.95 Canada 36 issues; $82.95 Canada 72 issues; $23.50 other countries; $44.95 other countries 36 issues; $86.95 Canada 72 issues. **Description:** Gun sales magazine for collectors, dealers and hunters.

VIDEOCASSETTES/ AUDIOCASSETTES

9976 ■ *Choose Your Weapon*
Gun Video
4585 Murphy Canyon Rd.
San Diego, CA 92123
Ph:(858)569-4000
Free: 800-942-8273
Fax:(858)569-0505
Co. E-mail: info2@gunvideo.com
URL: http://www.gunvideo.com

Released: 1991. **Price:** $49.95. **Description:** A comprehensive look at gun types, operation, safety and usage. **Availability:** VHS.

9977 ■ *Gun Safety*
Tapeworm Video Distributors
25876 The Old Road 141
Stevenson Ranch, CA 91381
Ph:(661)257-4904
Fax:(661)257-4820
Co. E-mail: sales@tapeworm.com
URL: http://www.tapeworm.com

Price: $14.95. **Description:** Professional firearms instructor Dan West presents the five basic safety rules of gun safety. **Availability:** VHS.

9978 ■ *Handgun Fundamentals*
RMI Media
1365 N. Winchester St.
Olathe, KS 66061-5880
Ph:(913)768-1696
Free: 800-745-5480

Fax:800-755-6910
Co. E-mail: actmedia@act.org
URL: http://www.actmedia.com
Released: 1987. **Description:** Expert Jeff Cooper presents a guide to handgun use and safety, including grip and stance, sighting, target shooting, rapid fire, and gun care. **Availability:** VHS; 3/4U.

TRADE SHOWS AND CONVENTIONS

9979 ■ The Shooting, Hunting, and Outdoor Trade Show
Reed Exhibitions Contemporary Forums
11900 Silvergate Dr.
Dublin, CA 94568
Ph:(925)828-7100
Fax:800-329-9923
Co. E-mail: info@cforums.com
URL: http://www.contemporaryforums.com
Audience: Federally licensed firearms dealers and legitimate sporting goods dealers. **Principal Exhibits:** Shooting and hunting equipment and products; sports accessories, clothing, and supplies.

LIBRARIES

9980 ■ Brady Center to Prevent Gun Violence Library
1225 Eye St. NW, Ste. 1100
Washington, DC 20005
Ph:(202)289-7319
Fax:(202)898-1851
URL: http://www.bradycenter.org
Scope: Handgun violence, firearms litigation, accidental shootings, Second Amendment, gun control, children and guns, violence prevention. **Services:** Copying; SDI; Library open to the public by appointment. **Holdings:** 1000 articles; 8 VF; books; videotapes. **Subscriptions:** 10 journals and other serials.

9981 ■ Francis Marion University–James A. Rogers Library I Special Collections
Francis Marion University
Florence, SC 29502
Ph:(843)661-1310
Co. E-mail: jdurant@fmarion.edu
URL: http://www.fmarion.edu/rogerslibrary
Contact: Joyce M. Durant, Lib. Dean
Scope: Firearms; Americana. **Services:** Interlibrary loan; copying; Library open to the public with restrictions on borrowing. **Holdings:** 10,000 books; 30 manuscripts. **Subscriptions:** 978 journals and other serials; 28 newspapers.

9982 ■ J.M. Davis Arms & Historical Museum–Charles R. Suydam Library
333 N. Lynn Riggs Blvd.
Claremore, OK 74017
Ph:(918)341-5707

Fax:(918)341-5771
Co. E-mail: info@thegunmuseum.com
URL: http://www.thegunmuseum.com
Contact: Duane Kyler
Scope: Firearms, edged weapons, American Indian artifacts, steins, musical instruments. **Services:** Library open to the public. **Holdings:** 3300 volumes; 30 bound periodical volumes; old gun catalogs; pins, buttons, and badges. **Subscriptions:** 15 journals and other serials.

9983 ■ National Rifle Association of America–National Firearms Museum Library
11250 Waples Mill Rd.
Fairfax, VA 22030-7400
Ph:(703)267-1603
Fax:(703)267-3913
Co. E-mail: kjohnston@nrahq.org
URL: http://nra.nationalfirearms.museum
Contact: Karin Johnston, Asst.Cur.
Scope: Firearms, arms technology, cartridges/reloading, military history. **Services:** Library open to the public by appointment. **Holdings:** 3500 books; 300 video tapes. **Subscriptions:** 125 journals and other serials.

9984 ■ National Rifle Association of America–NRA-ILA Library
11250 Waples Mill Rd.
Fairfax, VA 22030-7400
Free: 800-672-3888
Fax:(703)267-3957
URL: http://home.nra.org/
Scope: Firearms and hunting; criminal justice; natural resources; legislative issues. **Services:** Library not open to the public. **Holdings:** 2300 books; 750 lin.ft. of vertical file materials. **Subscriptions:** 70 journals and other serials; 7 newspapers.

9985 ■ Ontario Ministry of Community and Correctional Services–Centre of Forensic Sciences
25 Grosvenor St., 2nd Fl.
Toronto, ON, Canada M7A 2G8
Ph:(416)314-3200
URL: http://www.mcscs.jus.gov.on.ca/english/default. html
Contact: Eva Gulbinowicz, Libn.
Scope: Forensic science, toxicology, biology, chemistry, engineering, firearms, photography, questioned documents. **Services:** Interlibrary loan; copying (limited); Library open to criminal justice and medical professionals by telephone appointment. **Holdings:** 20,000 books; 4000 bound periodical volumes; 1000 reports; 13,000 reprints; 2500 government documents and pamphlets; 15,000 slides. **Subscriptions:** 300 journals and other serials; 2 newspapers.

9986 ■ Royal Canadian Artillery Museum Library
Canadian Forces Base Shilo
PO Box 5000, Sta. Main
Shilo, MB, Canada R0K 2A0

Ph:(204)765-3000
Fax:(204)765-5289
Co. E-mail: stag@mts.net
URL: http://www.rcamuseum.com/
Contact: Clive C. Prothero, Cur.
Scope: Military history; artillery - ordnance, carriages, ammunition, technical data, small arms, vehicles. **Services:** Copying; scanning; Library open to the public by appointment for research. **Holdings:** 13,000 books; 13,000 bound periodical volumes; 428 maps; 81 boxes of documents; 118 videotapes; pamphlets. **Subscriptions:** 14 journals and other serials; 5 newspapers.

9987 ■ Second Amendment Foundation Library
James Madison Bldg.
12500 NE 10th Pl.
Bellevue, WA 98005
Ph:(425)454-7012
Free: 800-426-4302
Fax:(425)451-3959
Co. E-mail: adminforweb@saf.org
URL: http://www.saf.org
Scope: Second amendment, gun rights. **Services:** Library not open to the public. **Holdings:** 200 books; 30 reports. **Subscriptions:** 2 journals and other serials; 2 newspapers.

9988 ■ Shooting Federation of Prince Edward Island Library
PO Box 1900
Charlottetown, PE, Canada C1A 7N9
Ph:(902)892-2938
Fax:(902)628-1714
Co. E-mail: deighanj@isn.net
Contact: James Deighan, Ed.
Scope: Fire arms - rules, regulations. **Services:** Library not open to the public. **Holdings:** 100 books; 200 bound periodical volumes. **Subscriptions:** 9 journals and other serials; 11 newspapers.

9989 ■ U.S. Bureau of Alcohol, Tobacco and Firearms–National Laboratory Center Library
6000 Ammendale Rd.
Beltsville, MD 20705-1250
Ph:(240)264-3770
Fax:(240)264-1493
Co. E-mail: susan.barned@atf.gov
Contact: Sue Barned, MLS, Libn.
Scope: Alcohol, analytical techniques, forensic sciences, firearms, tobacco, explosives. **Services:** Library not open to the public. **Holdings:** 4700 books; 4000 bound periodical volumes; 200 total journal titles; government documents; archives. **Subscriptions:** 42 journals and other serials.

ASSOCIATIONS AND OTHER ORGANIZATIONS

9990 ■ American Electrology Association
6 Market Pl., Ste. 1
Essex Junction, VT 05452
Ph:(802)879-1898
Co. E-mail: infoaea@electrology.com
URL: http://www.electrology.com
Contact: Leslie Quinn Cody CPE

Description: Electrologists united for education, professional advancement, and protection of public welfare. Promotes uniform legislative standards throughout the states. Coordinates efforts of affiliated associations in dealing with problems of national scope. Sponsors the International Board of Electrologist Certification and Council on Accreditation of Electrology Schools/Programs. Maintains referral, reference, advisory, and consulting services. **Publications:** *Journal of the American Electrology Association* (semiannual).

9991 ■ American Hair Loss Council
30 S Main St.
Shenandoah, PA 17976-2331
Ph:(570)462-1101
Co. E-mail: info@ahlc.org
URL: http://www.ahlc.org
Contact: Betty Budgen, Membership Dir.

Description: Dermatologists, plastic surgeons, cosmetologists, barbers, and interested others. Provides nonbiased information regarding treatments for hair loss in both men and women. Facilitates communication and information exchange between professionals in different areas of specialization. Conducts educational programs; compiles statistics. **Publications:** *AHLC News* (quarterly).

9992 ■ Society for Clinical and Medical Hair Removal
2424 American Ln.
Madison, WI 53704-3102
Ph:(608)443-2470
Fax:(608)443-2474
Co. E-mail: homeoffice@scmhr.org
URL: http://www.scmhr.org
Contact: Nedra D. Lockhart, Pres.

Description: Professional society of electrologists (persons engaged in the removal of superfluous hair by galvanic blend or short wave methods for cosmetic and medical purposes). Conducts continuing education and leadership development seminars. **Publications:** *SCME Directory of Membership* (annual).

DIRECTORIES OF EDUCATIONAL PROGRAMS

9993 ■ *Directory of Private Accredited Career Schools and Colleges of Technology*
Pub: Accrediting Commission of Career Schools and Colleges of Technology
Contact: Michale S. McComis, Exec. Dir.

Released: On web page. **Price:** Free. **Description:** Covers 3900 accredited post-secondary programs that provide training programs in business, trade, and technical fields, including various small business endeavors. Entries offer school name, address, phone, description of courses, job placement assistance, and requirements for admission. Arrangement is alphabetical.

REFERENCE WORKS

9994 ■ "Every Little Bit Helps" in *Black Enterprise* (Vol. 38, November 2007, No. 4, pp. 102)
Pub: Earl G. Graves Publishing Co. Inc.
Ed: Tennille M. Robinson. **Description:** After a career in the cosmetics industry, Tricialee Riley is marketing and advertising her new venture, the Polish Bar, a salon offering manicures, pedicures, makeup application, and waxing.

9995 ■ "Secret Ingredient" in *Entrepreneur* (Vol. 35, November 2007, No. 11, pp. 172)
Pub: Entrepreneur Media Inc.

Ed: Sara Wilson. **Description:** Ojon Corporation in Burlington, Ontario, Canada has developed a natural hair- and skin-care line from ojon oil. The oil, which has very good restorative effects on hair, is extracted from nuts found in ojon trees in the rainforests of Honduras. Details on how Ojon Corporation started and its growing venture in the market are outlined.

FRANCHISES AND BUSINESS OPPORTUNITIES

9996 ■ Women's Health Boutique
Women's Health Boutique Franchise System, Inc.
12715 Telge Rd.
Cypress, TX 77429
Free: 888-708-9982
Fax:(281)256-4100
Co. E-mail: w-h-bsales@w-h-b.com
URL: http://www.w-h-b.com

No. of Franchise Units: 13. **Founded:** 1991. **Franchised:** 1994. **Description:** Products and services related to pre and postnatal care, post-mastectomy, compression therapy, hair loss, incontinence, and skin care. **Equity Capital Needed:** $49,000 minimum start-up cash. **Financial Assistance:** Yes. **Training:** Yes.

ASSOCIATIONS AND OTHER ORGANIZATIONS

9997 ■ Allied Beauty Association
145 Traders Blvd. E, Units 26 and 27
Mississauga, ON, Canada L4Z 3L3
Ph:(905)568-0158
Free: 800-268-6644
Fax:(905)568-1581
Co. E-mail: abashows@abacanada.com
URL: http://www.abacanada.com
Contact: Marc E. Speir, Exec. Dir.
Description: Individuals and corporations engaged in the beauty industries. Promotes growth and development of members' businesses. Represents members' interests, conducts public relations campaigns and serves as a clearinghouse on the Canadian beauty industries. **Publications:** *Riben Nehrah Quarterly* (quarterly).

9998 ■ American Association of Cosmetology Schools
9927 E Bell Rd., Ste. 110
Scottsdale, AZ 85260
Ph:(480)281-0431
Free: 800-831-1086
Fax:(480)905-0993
Co. E-mail: jim@beautyschools.org
URL: http://www.beautyschools.org
Contact: Jim Cox, Exec. Dir.
Description: Owners and teachers in cosmetology schools. **Publications:** *CEA Update* (quarterly); *Salon City Star*; *Skin Inc.* .

9999 ■ American Health and Beauty Aids Institute
PO Box 19510
Chicago, IL 60619-0510
Ph:(708)633-6328
Fax:(708)633-6329
Co. E-mail: ahbai1@sbcglobal.net
URL: http://www.ahbai.org
Contact: Clyde Hammond, Chm.
Description: Minority-owned companies engaged in manufacturing and marketing health and beauty aids for the black consumer. Represents the interests of members and the industry before local, state, and federal governmental agencies. Assists with business development and economic progress within the minority community by providing informational and educational resources. Maintains speakers' bureau. Conducts annual Proud Lady Beauty Show. .

10000 ■ Intercoiffure America
1303 Campbell Rd.
Houston, TX 77055
Ph:(713)984-8800
Free: 800-442-3007
Fax:(713)935-4409
Co. E-mail: maryanne@visiblechanges.com
URL: http://www.intercoiffure.us
Contact: Lois Christie, Pres.
Description: Owners of beauty salons in the United States and Canada who meet the ethical standards set down by Intercoiffure. Seeks to make the women of America the best in hair fashion. .

10001 ■ National Accrediting Commission of Cosmetology Arts and Sciences
4401 Ford Ave., Ste. 1300
Alexandria, VA 22302
Ph:(703)600-7600
Fax:(703)379-2200
Co. E-mail: amirando@naccas.org
URL: http://www.naccas.org
Contact: Tony Mirando MS, Exec. Dir.
Description: Accrediting body for schools of cosmetology; presently there are 1030 accredited schools. Objectives are to: raise standards of cosmetology schools throughout the country; encourage use of modern educational methods and techniques; stimulate self-improvement by the schools. Sponsors standards and professional team training workshops. **Publications:** *Directory of Accredited Cosmetology Schools* (annual); *NACCAS Review* (3/year).

10002 ■ National Association of Barber Boards of America
2703 Pine St.
Arkadelphia, AR 71923
Ph:(501)682-2806
Fax:(501)682-5073
Co. E-mail: nabba@att.net
URL: http://www.nationalbarberboards.com
Contact: Charles Kirkpatrick, Exec. Dir.
Description: Represents state boards of barber examiners. Promotes the exchange of information among state barber boards and state agencies that examine, license, and regulate the barber industry. Improves standards and procedures for examining barbers and regulates the barber industry. Furthers continuing education and development of curricula for educating barbers. Devises procedures for ensuring that consumers are informed and protected. Maintains library. .

10003 ■ National Beauty Culturists' League
25 Logan Cir. NW
Washington, DC 20005-3725
Ph:(202)332-2695
Fax:(202)332-0940
Co. E-mail: nbcl@bellsouth.net
URL: http://www.nbcl.org
Contact: Dr. Katie B. Catalon, Pres.
Description: Beauticians, cosmetologists, and beauty products manufacturers. Encourages standardized, scientific, and approved methods of hair, scalp, and skin treatments. Offers scholarships and plans to establish a research center. Sponsors: National Institute of Cosmetology, a training course in operating and designing and business techniques. Maintains hall of fame; conducts research program. .

10004 ■ National - Interstate Council of State Boards of Cosmetology
7622 Briarwood Cir.
Little Rock, AR 72205
Ph:(501)227-8262
Fax:(501)227-8212
Co. E-mail: dnorton@nictesting.org
URL: http://www.nictesting.org
Contact: Kay Kendrick, Pres.
Description: Persons commissioned by 50 state governments as administrators of cosmetology laws and examiners of applicants for licenses to practice cosmetology. .

10005 ■ Professional Beauty Association | National Cosmetology Association
15825 N 71st St., Ste. 100
Scottsdale, AZ 85254
Ph:(480)281-0424
Free: 800-468-2274
Fax:(480)905-0708
Co. E-mail: info@probeauty.org
URL: http://www.probeauty.org
Contact: Max Wexler, Exec. Dir.
Description: Manufacturers and manufacturers' representatives of beauty and barber products, cosmetics, equipment, and supplies used in or resold by beauty salons or barbershops. Promotes the beauty industry; works to ensure product safety; disseminates information. Holds educational seminars; organizes charity events. **Publications:** *PBA Progress* (3/year).

DIRECTORIES OF EDUCATIONAL PROGRAMS

10006 ■ *Directory of Private Accredited Career Schools and Colleges of Technology*
Pub: Accrediting Commission of Career Schools and Colleges of Technology
Contact: Michale S. McComis, Exec. Dir.
Released: On web page. **Price:** Free. **Description:** Covers 3900 accredited post-secondary programs that provide training programs in business, trade, and technical fields, including various small business endeavors. Entries offer school name, address, phone, description of courses, job placement assistance, and requirements for admission. Arrangement is alphabetical.

REFERENCE WORKS

10007 ■ "Because He Is Still Growing: Horst Rechelbacher: Intelligent Nutrients Minneapolis" in *Inc.* (Volume 32, December 2010, No. 10)
Pub: Inc. Magazine
Ed: Mike Hoffman. **Description:** Horst Rechelbacher, founder of hair care company Aveda, and after selling Aveda to Estee Lauder, he is expanding into a nutraceuticals company offering hair care products that are organically grown.

10008 ■ *Doing Business with Beauty: Black Women, Hair Salons, and the Racial Enclave Economy*
Pub: Rowman and Littlefield Publishers, Inc.
Ed: Adia Harvey Wingfield. **Released:** June 28, 2008. **Price:** $19.95. **Description:** Factors that draw black women into the hair industry are examined. Interviews with hair salon owners explore aspects of owning a salon, owner-employee relationships, and the black female owner's struggle for autonomy and success in entrepreneurship.

10009 ■ *Enterprising Women in Urban Zimbabwe: Gender, Microbusiness, and Globalization*
Pub: Indiana University Press
Ed: Mary Johnson Osirim. **Released:** April 1, 2009. **Price:** $39.95. **Description:** An investigation into the business and personal experiences of women entrepreneurs in the microenterprise sector in Zimbabwe. Many of these women work as market traders, crocheters, seamstresses, and hairdressers.

10010 ■ "Secret Ingredient" in *Entrepreneur* (Vol. 35, November 2007, No. 11, pp. 172)
Pub: Entrepreneur Media Inc.
Ed: Sara Wilson. **Description:** Ojon Corporation in Burlington, Ontario, Canada has developed a natural hair- and skin-care line from ojon oil. The oil, which has very good restorative effects on hair, is extracted from nuts found in ojon trees in the rainforests of Honduras. Details on how Ojon Corporation started and its growing venture in the market are outlined.

10011 ■ "Verizon Small Business Awards Give Companies a Technology Edge" in *Hispanic Business* (July-August 2009, pp. 32)
Pub: Hispanic Business
Ed: Patricia Marroquin. **Description:** Verizon Wireless awards grants to twenty-four companies in California. The winning businesses ranged from barbershop to coffee shop, tattoo parlor to florist.

10012 ■ "V's Barbershop Opening in Bakerview Square in May" in *Bellingham Business Journal* (Vol. March 2010, pp. 2)
Pub: Sound Publishing Inc.
Description: Upscale barbershop franchise catering to men, V's Barbershop, will open a new location in Bakerview Square (its first in Washington) in 2010. The new location will include six chairs and will appear like an old-time barbershop with a contemporary flavor featuring real barber chairs, flat-screen TVs, and hot lather shaves using a straight-edge razor.

10013 ■ "What Moms Want" in *Marketing to Women* (Vol. 21, February 2008, No. 2, pp. 6)
Pub: EPM Communications, Inc.
Description: According to a survey conducted by Eureka's Spa, moms would rather have an experience gift than flowers or chocolate. The top five dream gifts include a spa day, a weekend getaway, maid service, a bathroom makeover or a getaway weekend with girlfriends.

STATISTICAL SOURCES

10014 ■ *RMA Annual Statement Studies*
Pub: Robert Morris Associates (RMA)
Released: Annual. **Price:** $175.00 2006-07 edition, $105.00. **Description:** Contains composite balance sheets and income statements for more than 360 industries, including the accounting, auditing, and bookkeeping industries. Also contains five years of comparative historical data for discerning trends. Includes 16 commonly used ratios, computed for most of the size groupings for nearly every industry.

TRADE PERIODICALS

10015 ■ *The Beauty Industry Report*
Pub: The Beauty Industry Report
Contact: Mike Nave, Editor & Publisher
E-mail: mikenave@aol.com
Released: Monthly. **Price:** $96, individuals. **Description:** Dedicated to the professional beauty salon and store industry. Recurring features include columns titled Guest Column.

10016 ■ *Haircut and Style*
Pub: Harris Publications Inc.
Released: Quarterly. **Price:** $3 single issue. **Description:** Fashion magazine featuring hair and make-up tips and trends.

10017 ■ *Modern Salon*
Pub: Vance Publishing Corp.
Contact: Michele Musgrove, Assoc. Publisher
E-mail: mmusgrove@vancepublishing.com
Released: Monthly. **Price:** $28; $37 Canada and Mexico; $98 other countries airmail; $44 other countries; $40 two years; $57 Canada two years;

$73 two years foreign; $50 3 years; $73 Canada 3 years; $98 two years foreign. **Description:** Magazine focusing on hairstyling salons for men and women.

10018 ■ *Salon Today Magazine*
Pub: Vance Publishing Corp.
Contact: Stacey Soble, Editor-in-Chief
E-mail: ssoble@vancepublishing.com
Released: Monthly. **Price:** $42; $75 two years; $98 3 years; $60 other countries; $111 other countries TYR; $100 other countries 3 years. **Description:** Management guide for beauty salon owners and managers.

10019 ■ *State of the Art*
Pub: State Service Systems Inc.
Contact: Erin Jacobs, Mktg. Coord.
Released: Monthly. **Description:** Magazine for the professional beauty industry.

VIDEOCASSETTES/ AUDIOCASSETTES

10020 ■ *Haircutting Basics*
Instructional Video
2219 C St.
Lincoln, NE 68502
Ph:(402)475-6570
Free: 800-228-0164
Fax:(402)475-6500
Co. E-mail: feedback@insvideo.com
URL: http://www.insvideo.com
Price: $29.95. **Description:** Teaches haircutting basics, including how to cut an outline, a one-level bob, a bi-leveled with bobbed back, long-layered, and a wedge. Available only in the U.S. **Availability:** VHS.

10021 ■ *Haircutting with Clippers—Basic Techniques*
Instructional Video
2219 C St.
Lincoln, NE 68502
Ph:(402)475-6570
Free: 800-228-0164
Fax:(402)475-6500
Co. E-mail: feedback@insvideo.com
URL: http://www.insvideo.com
Price: $24.95. **Description:** Teaches basic haircutting techniques using clippers, including the clipper over skin, fingers, and comb techniques, how to trim and shape beards, mustaches, and sideburns, how to taper men's hair, cutting the design line, cutting layers, the bob haircut, and the modern flattop. Available only in the U.S. **Availability:** VHS.

10022 ■ *My First Haircut*
Tapeworm Video Distributors
25876 The Old Road 141
Stevenson Ranch, CA 91381
Ph:(661)257-4904
Fax:(661)257-4820
Co. E-mail: sales@tapeworm.com
URL: http://www.tapeworm.com
Released: 1996. **Price:** $9.95. **Description:** Video footage of children getting their haircut helps prepare toddlers for their first haircut. **Availability:** VHS.

TRADE SHOWS AND CONVENTIONS

10023 ■ Beauty Fair
The Finnish Fair Corp.
Messuaukio 1
PO Box 21
FIN-00521 Helsinki, Finland
Ph:358 9 15091
Fax:358 9 1509218
Co. E-mail: info@finnexpo.fi
Released: Annual. **Audience:** General public. **Principal Exhibits:** Beauty and fashion, cosmetics and services; hair products and services; clothing, showes, bags, accessories, jewelry, education, and publications.

10024 ■ National Beauty Show - HAIRWORLD
National Cosmetology Association
401 N Michigan Ave., 22nd Floor
Chicago, IL 60611-4255
Ph:(312)527-6765
Free: 800-527-1683
Fax:(312)464-6118
Co. E-mail: nca1@ncacares.org
URL: http://www.behindthechairexchange.com/nca
Released: Annual. **Audience:** Salon owners and cosmetologists. **Principal Exhibits:** Hair products, cosmetics, and jewelry.

FRANCHISES AND BUSINESS OPPORTUNITIES

10025 ■ Cartoon Cuts
5501 NW 21st Ave., Ste. 410
Ft. Lauderdale, FL 33309
Ph:(954)653-CUTS
Free: 800-701-CUTS
Fax:(954)653-9074
No. of Company-Owned Units: 19. **Founded:** 1991. **Franchised:** 2001. **Description:** Hair salons for children. **Equity Capital Needed:** $97,000-$216,000. **Franchise Fee:** $25,000. **Financial Assistance:** Yes. **Training:** Yes.

10026 ■ Chatters Salon
274-28042 Hwy. 11
Red Deer County, AB, Canada T4S 2L4
Ph:(403)342-5055
Free: 888-944-5055
Fax:(403)347-7759
Co. E-mail: franchise@chatters.ca
URL: http://www.chatters.ca
No. of Franchise Units: 90. **No. of Company-Owned Units:** 8. **Founded:** 1988. **Franchised:** 1991. **Description:** Hair salon and beauty supply full salon services with extensive retail component. **Equity Capital Needed:** $400,000$700,000. **Franchise Fee:** $40,000.

10027 ■ City Looks
6465 Millcreek Dr., Ste. 210
Mississauga, ON, Canada L5N 5R6
Ph:(905)363-4105
Free: 800-363-4105
Fax:(952)995-3403
Co. E-mail: franchiseleads@regiscorp.com
URL: http://www.regisfranchise.com
No. of Franchise Units: 18. **No. of Company-Owned Units:** 2. **Description:** City Looks caters to women looking for an exceptional hair care experience. Located primarily in shopping malls and strip centers. City Looks is backed by the strength and support of Regis Corporation. **Equity Capital Needed:** $150,000 liquid assets; $400,000 net worth. **Franchise Fee:** $22,500 1st salon, each additional $12,500. **Training:** Provides training and ongoing support.

10028 ■ Cookie Cutters Haircuts for Kids
CC Franchising
212 W 10th St., Ste. F-185
Indianapolis, IN 46202
Ph:(317)334-1680
Fax:888-430-6378
No. of Franchise Units: 40. **Founded:** 1993. **Franchised:** 1995. **Description:** Children's interactive hair care. **Equity Capital Needed:** $200,000 net worth. **Franchise Fee:** $25,000. **Financial Assistance:** No. **Training:** Yes.

10029 ■ Cost Cutters Family Hair Care
The Barbers, A Div. of Regis Corp.
7201 Metro Blvd.
Minneapolis, MN 55439
Free: 888-888-7008
Fax:(952)947-7900
Co. E-mail: franchiseleads@regiscorp.com
URL: http://www.costcutters.com
No. of Franchise Units: 447. **No. of Company-Owned Units:** 364. **Founded:** 1963. **Franchised:** 1982. **Description:** A value priced, full-service salon concept that provides low-cost, no-frills hair services for the family. The franchisor created Cost Cutters to

meet the demand for providing the public with quality hair services and products at a moderate price. **Equity Capital Needed:** $300,000 net worth; $100,000 liquid. **Franchise Fee:** $22,500 1st, $12,500 additional. **Financial Assistance:** Equipment leasing program, and financing programs available through third party vendor. **Managerial Assistance:** 1 week managerial and technical training. Consultation available on set fee structure, and business management assistance available. **Training:** 1 week onsite training with ongoing support.

10030 ■ Fantastic Sams

50 Dunham Rd.
Beverly, MA 01915
Ph:(978)232-5600
Fax:888-315-4437

No. of Franchise Units: 1,216. **Founded:** 1974. **Franchised:** 1976. **Description:** Full service family hair salons. **Equity Capital Needed:** $115,000-$228,600. **Franchise Fee:** $30,000. **Financial Assistance:** No. **Training:** Yes.

10031 ■ First Choice Haircutters

Regis Corp.
6465 Millcreek Dr., Ste. 210
Mississauga, ON, Canada L5N 5R6
Free: 800-617-3961
Fax:(905)567-7000
Co. E-mail: franchiseleads@regiscorp.com
URL: http://www.firstchoice.com

No. of Franchise Units: 189. **No. of Company-Owned Units:** 260. **Founded:** 1980. **Franchised:** 1982. **Description:** Value-priced family hair care centers. High-volume, low-cost, a la carte hair care for men, women and children. **Equity Capital Needed:** $300,000 net worth; $100,000 liquid. **Franchise Fee:** $22,500/1st, $12,500 each additional. **Financial Assistance:** Yes. **Training:** Provides 1 week managerial and technical training, 1 week onsite training with support in all areas including real estate, grand opening, staffing, marketing and ongoing support.

10032 ■ Great Clips, Inc.

Great Clips, Inc.
7700 France Ave. 425
Minneapolis, MN 55435
Free: 800-947-1143
Fax:(952)844-3443
Co. E-mail: franchise@greatclips.com
URL: http://www.greatclips.com

No. of Franchise Units: 2,650. **Founded:** 1982. **Franchised:** 1983. **Description:** High-volume, quality hair salons that specialize in cuts and perms for the entire family. Unique and attractive decor and quality advertising. Emphasis on strong, hands-on support to franchisees. Definite opportunity for growth in a fast-growing industry. directors. **Equity Capital Needed:** $300,000 net worth; $50,000 liquid. **Franchise Fee:** $25,000. **Financial Assistance:** Third party lenders available upon request. **Training:** Training begins with New Franchisee Orientation & Training. This 5 day session covers all aspects of the Great Clips operating systems. All style and employee training is provided through our field staff and our area training centers.

10033 ■ Lemon Tree Family Hair Salon

Joan M. Cable's La Femmina Beauty Salons, Inc.
6800 Jericho Turnpike, Ste. 326
Syosset, NY 11753
Ph:(516)393-5860
Free: 800-345-9156
Fax:(516)393-5862
Co. E-mail: lemontree@lemontree.com
URL: http://www.lemontree.com

No. of Franchise Units: 61. **Founded:** 1976. **Franchised:** 1976. **Description:** Offers franchises for unisex hair care services. **Equity Capital Needed:** $62,000-$110,500. **Franchise Fee:** $20,000. **Financial Assistance:** One half of equipment cost and one half of franchise fee. **Training:** Includes 1 week of training at corporate headquarters and a company representative spends 1 week at salon grand opening.

10034 ■ Magicuts

6465 Millcreek Dr., Ste. 210
Mississauga, ON, Canada
Ph:(905)363-4105
Free: 888-888-7778
Fax:(952)995-3403
Co. E-mail: franchiseleads@regiscorp.com
URL: http://www.regisfranchise.com

No. of Franchise Units: 84. **No. of Company-Owned Units:** 131. **Founded:** 1981. **Franchised:** 1982. **Description:** Full service hair salons with professional services and products at affordable prices. **Equity Capital Needed:** $100,000 liquid assets; $300,000 net worth. **Franchise Fee:** $22,500 first salon; $12,500 each additional. **Training:** Full training and support.

10035 ■ Pro-Cuts

Regis Corp.
7201 Metro Blvd.
Minneapolis, MN 55439
Ph:(952)947-7394
Free: 888-888-7008
Fax:(952)947-7900

No. of Franchise Units: 165. **Founded:** 1982. **Franchised:** 1984. **Description:** Family hair care centers, providing quality haircuts for a low price. Also carrying a line of private-label, high-quality, hair care products exclusive to Pro-Cuts. **Equity Capital Needed:** $300,000 net worth; $100,000 liquid assets. **Franchise Fee:** $22,500. **Financial Assistance:** Third party financing available. **Managerial Assistance:** Assistance with staffing, and marketing. **Training:** Provides 1 week managerial and technical training, 1 week onsite, support in real estate, grand opening and ongoing support.

10036 ■ Regal Nails, Salon Spa

5150 Florida Blvd.
Baton Rouge, LA 70806
Free: 888-414-6245
Fax:800-422-4608
Co. E-mail: book@regalnails.com
URL: http://www.regalnails.com
Founded: 2006. **Description:** Nail salon.

10037 ■ Roosters Men's Grooming Centers

Roosters MGC Intl., LLC
5523 East Nine Mile Rd.
Warren, MI 48091
Ph:(763)201-1470
Free: (866)642-2625
Fax:(586)619-2167
Co. E-mail: joe@roostermgc.com
URL: http://www.roostersmgc.com

No. of Franchise Units: 50. **No. of Company-Owned Units:** 1. **Founded:** 1999. **Franchised:** 2002. **Description:** Men beauty salons supply cosmetic products and specialist in tanning. **Equity Capital Needed:** $100,000-$250,000. **Franchise Fee:** $35,000-$73,000. **Financial Assistance:** No. **Training:** Yes.

10038 ■ Snip N' Clip Haircut Shops

11427 Strang Line Rd.
Lenexa, KS 66215
Ph:(913)345-0077
Free: 800-622-6804
Fax:(913)345-1554
Co. E-mail: info@snipnclip.net
URL: http://www.snipnclip.com

No. of Franchise Units: 23. **No. of Company-Owned Units:** 40. **Founded:** 1976. **Franchised:** 1986. **Description:** Family hair salons. **Equity Capital Needed:** $75,100-$88,950, includes of $15,000 franchise fee & turn-key package. **Franchise Fee:** $15,000. **Training:** Onsite training.

10039 ■ Sport Clips

Sport Clips, Inc.
PMB 266
PO Box 3000
Georgetown, TX 78627-3000
Ph:(512)869-1201
Free: 800-872-4247

Fax:(512)868-4699
Co. E-mail: Sara.Clements@sportsclips.com
URL: http://www.sportclips.com

No. of Franchise Units: 750. **No. of Company-Owned Units:** 19. **Founded:** 1993. **Franchised:** 1995. **Description:** Men's hair care centers with sports theme. **Equity Capital Needed:** $100,000. **Franchise Fee:** $25,000-$49,500. **Financial Assistance:** No. **Training:** Initial and ongoing technical and management training by Sport Clips area Coaches.

10040 ■ Supercuts

Regis Corp.
6465 Millcreek Dr. Ste. 210
Mississauga, ON, Canada L5N 5R6
Ph:(905)363-4105
Free: 888-888-7778
Fax:(952)995-3403
Co. E-mail: franchiseleads@regiscorp.com
URL: http://www.regisfranchise.com

No. of Franchise Units: 15. **No. of Company-Owned Units:** 37. **Founded:** 1975. **Franchised:** 1978. **Description:** The franchise offers affordable hair care. **Equity Capital Needed:** $100,000 liquid assets; $300,000 net worth. **Franchise Fee:** $22,500 first salon; $12,500 each additional. **Training:** Initial and ongoing support.

10041 ■ Trade Secrets

Trade Secrets / Glamour Secrets
101 Jevlan Dr.
Woodbridge, ON, Canada L4L 8C2
Ph:(905)264-2799
Free: 888-264-7444
Fax:(905)264-2779
Co. E-mail: franchising@tradesecrets.ca
URL: http://www.tradesecrets.com

No. of Franchise Units: 44. **No. of Company-Owned Units:** 21. **Founded:** 1989. **Franchised:** 1990. **Description:** Trade Secrets provides full service salon and branded products for sale. **Equity Capital Needed:** $80,000 minimum. **Franchise Fee:** $25,000. **Financial Assistance:** Complete turn-key operation and financing available. **Training:** Offers 3 weeks training.

10042 ■ Treehouse Cuts Salon

8800 Kelly Dr.
Yorktown, IN 47396-0231
Free: 888-928-TREE
Fax:(219)271-9646

No. of Franchise Units: 7. **No. of Company-Owned Units:** 6. **Founded:** 1996. **Franchised:** 1999. **Description:** Family haircare salon. **Equity Capital Needed:** $75,000-$220,000. **Franchise Fee:** $22,500. **Financial Assistance:** No. **Training:** Yes.

10043 ■ The Yellow Balloon

12448 Ventura Blvd.
Studio City, CA 91604
Ph:(818)760-7141
URL: http://www.theyellowballoon.com

Founded: 1983. **Franchised:** 2000. **Description:** Hair salons for children. **Equity Capital Needed:** $55,000-$103,500. **Franchise Fee:** $25,000. **Royalty Fee:** 4%. **Financial Assistance:** No. **Training:** Provides 7 days at corporate headquarters. s.

COMPUTER SYSTEMS/ SOFTWARE

10044 ■ Hairshaping

Phillip-Roy Inc.
13064 Indian Rocks Rd.
Largo, FL 33774
Ph:(727)593-2700
Free: 800-255-9085
Fax:(727)595-2685
Co. E-mail: info@philliproy.com
URL: http://www.philliproy.com

Price: $145.00. **Description:** Available for PC computers.

10045 ■ Salon 2.0 - Salon and Spa Managment Software
E-Z Way Salon Software
1386 Newton Ave., SW
Atlanta, GA 30316
Ph:(404)835-7157
Free: 800-927-0260
Co. E-mail: info@grantparksoftware.com
URL: http://www.grantparksoftware.com
Price: $199. **Description:** Software program designed for small salons. Contains all the features of E-Z Way Salon Software (Basic). Advanced functions include an accounting module and a payroll system; an appointment book for viewing and printing appointments; sales history analysis; product recommendations; and referral tracking.

LIBRARIES

10046 ■ Aesthetics International Association Library
310 E. Interstate 30, Ste. B107
Garland, TX 75043
Ph:(469)429-9300
Free: 877-968-7539
Fax:(469)429-9301
URL: http://www.aestheticsassociation.com
Contact: Melissa Lawrence
Scope: Skin care, makeup, body therapy, spa treatments, permanent cosmetics, paramedical cosmetics. **Services:** Library not open to the public. **Holdings:** 250 volumes; 50 audio/visual programs.

10047 ■ Clairol Research Library
1 Blachley Rd.
Stamford, CT 06922
Ph:(203)357-5001
Free: 800-252-4765
Fax:(203)969-2577
URL: http://www.clairol.com
Contact: Linda Massoni, Libn.

Scope: Chemistry and technology of cosmetics, hair dyes and dyeing, personal care. **Services:** Library open to the public with restrictions. **Holdings:** 10,000 books; 6000 bound periodical volumes; 30 titles on microfilm. **Subscriptions:** 350 journals and other serials.

ASSOCIATIONS AND OTHER ORGANIZATIONS

10048 ■ American Association of Handwriting Analysts
4143 Lorna Ct. SE
Lacey, WA 98503
Ph:(360)455-4551
Free: 800-826-7774
Co. E-mail: aahatreasjane@aol.com
URL: http://aahahandwriting.com
Contact: Jane O'Brien, Treas.
Description: Persons who have completed recognized courses in handwriting analysis, passed examinations by a committee of the Association, and displayed proficiency in the science of analyzing character from handwriting are certified members; individuals who have passed an exam on the guiding principles of graphology are associate members. Those who are interested in graphology are affiliate members. Serves as a forum for the exchange of information on graphology and research in the field. Promotes professionalism in the "science of analyzing character through examination of all forms of writing." Seeks public recognition of handwriting analysis as an important aid in the solution of problems involving personality and identification of signatures or writing. Promotes research in handwriting analysis. .

10049 ■ American Handwriting Analysis Foundation
PO Box 460385
Escondido, CA 92046-0385
Ph:(760)489-0692
Free: 800-826-7774
Co. E-mail: ahafpresident@gmail.com
URL: http://www.ahafhandwriting.org
Contact: Debra Peddy CG, Pres.
Description: Individuals interested in handwriting analysis. Seeks to advance graphology (the art and science of determining qualities of the personality from the script) as a helping profession; provide certification program for members; establish a code of ethics; foster research in handwriting analysis and cooperation among all handwriting analysts and handwriting societies. Maintains research and educational programs. Maintains speakers' bureau. Disseminates resource information. **Publications:** *AHAF Journal* (bimonthly); *Guide to Self-Published Papers, 1978-1988* (annual); *International Bibliography of Graphological Journal Articles, 1968-1988*; *Manual for Graphological Researchers*; *Recommended Reading Dossier*; *Standard Terms for Handwriting Analysts: English Terms, Document Examination Terms, Health Terms, International Terms*; *Write Learning* .

10050 ■ Association of Forensic Document Examiners
5432 E Karen Dr.
Scottsdale, AZ 85254-8205
Co. E-mail: journal.jfde@gmail.com
URL: http://www.afde.org
Contact: Emily J. Will, Pres.
Description: Represents forensic document examiners and students of document examination. Sponsors

annual continuing education conferences and offers a certification program. **Publications:** *Journal of Forensic Document Examination* (annual).

10051 ■ International Graphoanalysis Society
842 5th Ave.
New Kensington, PA 15068
Ph:(724)472-9701
Fax:(509)271-1149
Co. E-mail: greg@igas.com
URL: http://www.igas.com
Contact: Greg Greco, Pres.
Description: Represents handwriting analysts and identification experts. Maintains hall of fame and speakers' bureau. Compiles statistics; conducts research programs, specialized education, and placement service. .

10052 ■ National Society for Graphology
250 W 57th St., Ste. 1228A
New York, NY 10107-1221
Ph:(212)265-1148
Co. E-mail: irenicnyc@aol.com
URL: http://www.handwriting.org/nsg/nsgmain.html
Contact: Janice Klein
Description: Professionally certified graphologists and individuals interested in Gestalt graphology. (Graphology is the study of handwriting for purposes of character analysis.) Promotes the study of graphology. Encourages individuals to train in graphology and seek professional status within the organization. .

TRADE PERIODICALS

10053 ■ *Journal of Graphoanalysis*
Pub: International Graphoanalysis Society
Description: Magazine on handwriting analysis.

VIDEOCASSETTES/ AUDIOCASSETTES

10054 ■ *Handwriting Analysis Course*
Cambridge Educational
c/o Films Media Group
132 West 31st Street, 17th Floor
Ste. 124
New York, NY 10001
Free: 800-257-5126
Fax:(609)671-0266
Co. E-mail: custserve@films.com
URL: http://www.cambridgeol.com
Released: 1990. **Price:** $350.00. **Description:** Two untitled tapes present detailed instruction on the techniques of analyzing handwriting. Includes two text books. **Availability:** VHS.

CONSULTANTS

10055 ■ All Handwriting Services L.L.C.
PO Box 204
Bountiful, UT 84011
Ph:(801)915-7715

Fax:(801)294-3201
Co. E-mail: allhandwriting@hotmail.com
URL: http://allhandwritingservicesllc.com
Contact: Linda Cropp, President
E-mail: allhandwriting@hotmail.com
Scope: Offers questioned document examination, letters of opinion, testimony, forgery detection, anonymous letters, psychological profiles, jury selection, behavior profiling for personnel selection and promotions, vocation selection, business compatibility reports, and litigation support. Qualified for district and federal courts. Industries served include legal, law enforcement, retail, manufacturing, business, and personnel departments. **Seminars:** Basics of Handwriting Analysis; Know Yourself and Others Through Handwriting Analysis; The Troubled Teen; Introduction to Handwriting Analysis; Pre-employment Screening and Handwriting Analysis; How to Hire a Document Examiner: Credentials, Expertise, Certifications, Fees; When to Hire document Examiner; Detect Violence in the Workplace Through Handwriting Analysis; The Dishonest/Abusive Personality.

COMPUTER SYSTEMS/ SOFTWARE

10056 ■ Handwriting Analyst
Riverside Publishing Company
3800 Golf Rd., Ste. 100
Rolling Meadows, IL 60008
Ph:(630)467-7000
Free: 800-323-9540
Fax:(630)467-7192
URL: http://www.riverpub.com
Price: $79.95, plus shipping. **Description:** Available for Apple Macintosh, Apple II, and IBM computers. System analyzes handwriting to describe personalities.

LIBRARIES

10057 ■ American Association of Handwriting Analysts Library
4143 Lorna Ct., SE
Lacey, WI 98503
Co. E-mail: aahatreasjane@aol.com
URL: http://wwww.aahahandwriting.com
Contact: Ernestine Wisnewski, Lib.Hd.
Scope: Handwriting analysis. **Services:** Library not open to the public. **Holdings:** 860 volumes.

10058 ■ Handwriting Analysis Research Library
PO Box 104
Greenfield, MA 01342-0104
Ph:(413)774-4667
URL: http://handwritinganalysisresearchlibrary.org
Contact: Joanne Garland
Scope: Graphology, handwriting, analysis, penmanship, questioned documents. **Services:** Interlibrary loan; copying; Library open to the public for reference use only. **Holdings:** 174 bound periodical

volumes; 791 research reports; 68,471 manuscripts, clippings, photocopies; 901 translated items; 4891

abstracts; archival records of 17 defunct handwriting analysis organizations (closed reserve); 126 reports;

377 manuscripts; 14 archives; 41 notebooks; 3 CD-ROMs. **Subscriptions:** 16 journals and other serials.

ASSOCIATIONS AND OTHER ORGANIZATIONS

10059 ■ American Hardware Manufacturers Association
801 N Plaza Dr.
Schaumburg, IL 60173
Ph:(847)605-1025
Fax:(847)605-1030
Co. E-mail: info@ahma.org
URL: http://www.ahma.org
Contact: Timothy S. Farrell, Pres./CEO
Description: Represents the hardware, home improvement, lawn and garden, paint and decorating, and related industries. **Publications:** *AHMA Eagle* (bimonthly); *AHMA Employee Relations Report* (monthly); *AHMA Issue Briefing* (monthly); *AHMA Washington Report* (monthly); *The Hard Fax International* (biweekly);Membership Directory (annual).

10060 ■ Builders Hardware Manufacturers Association
355 Lexington Ave., 15th Fl.
New York, NY 10017
Ph:(212)297-2122
Fax:(212)370-9047
Co. E-mail: bhma@kellencompany.com
URL: http://www.buildershardware.com
Contact: Don Baker, Pres.
Description: Manufacturers of builders' hardware, both contract and stock. Provides statistical services; maintains standardization program; sponsors certification programs for locks, latches, door closers and cabinet hardware. Maintains 12 product sections. .

10061 ■ Canadian Institute of Plumbing and Heating–L'Institut Canadien de Plomberie et de Chauffage
295 The West Mall, Ste. 330
Toronto, ON, Canada M9C 4Z4
Ph:(416)695-0447
Free: 800-639-2474
Fax:(416)695-0450
Co. E-mail: info@ciph.com
URL: http://www.ciph.com
Contact: Ralph Suppa BA, Sec.
Description: Manufacturers, distributors and wholesalers of plumbing and heating equipment and supplies. Promotes advancement of members' businesses; seeks to improve plumbing and heating practice and technology. Serves as a clearinghouse on the plumbing and heating industries; represents members' interests before government agencies; assists in the formation of industry standards; encourages increased use of hydronic heating systems. Sponsors educational and training programs for members; compiles industry statistics. **Publications:** *Pipeline* (quarterly).

10062 ■ Lumber and Building Materials Association of Ontario
5155 Spectrum Way, Unit 27
Mississauga, ON, Canada L4W 5A1
Ph:(905)625-1084
Free: 888-365-2626

Fax:(905)625-3006
Co. E-mail: dwcampbell@lbmao.on.ca
URL: http://www.lbmao.on.ca
Contact: David W. Campbell, Pres.
Description: Retailers of building supplies. Seeks to advance the lumber and building supplies industries. Facilitates communication and cooperation among members; represents members' interests before labor and industrial organizations, government agencies, and the public. **Publications:** *Directory of Ontario Lumber and Building Materials, Hardware and Home Improvement Retailers* (annual); *Reporter* (bimonthly).

10063 ■ National Lumber and Building Material Dealers Association
2025 M St. NW, Ste. 800
Washington, DC 20036-3309
Ph:(202)367-1169
Free: 800-634-8645
Fax:(202)367-2169
Co. E-mail: info@dealer.org
URL: http://www.dealer.org
Contact: Michael O'Brien CAE, Pres./CEO
Description: Represents more than 8,000 lumber and building material companies with over 400,000 employees, 20 state and regional associations and the industry's leading manufacturers and service providers. **Publications:** *Cost of Doing Business* (annual); *Forklift and You*; *NLBMDA Advocate* (monthly); *Nuts & Bolts*; *ProSales* (monthly); *Risk Management Best Practices*; *Your National Perspective* (quarterly).

10064 ■ North American Retail Hardware Association
6325 Digital Way, No. 300
Indianapolis, IN 46278-1787
Ph:(317)290-0338
Free: 800-772-4424
Fax:(317)328-4354
Co. E-mail: pfbowman@nrha.org
URL: http://www.nrha.org
Contact: Patty Bowman
Description: Represents independent family-owned hardware/home improvement retailers. Sponsors correspondence courses in hardware and building materials retailing; conducts annual cost-of-doing-business study. **Publications:** *Do-It-Yourself Retailing* (monthly).

REFERENCE WORKS

10065 ■ "Code Name: Investors: Go From Golden Idea to Agent of Invention" in *Black Enterprise* (Vol. 41, November 2010, No. 4, pp. 78)
Pub: Earl G. Graves Publishing Co. Inc.
Ed: Renita Burns. **Description:** Profile of Andre Woolery, inventor of a magnetic wristband that holds small nails, screws, drill bits, and small tools, allowing handymen to keep essential tools at hand while working.

10066 ■ *Directory of Home Center Operators & Hardware Chains*
Pub: Chain Store Guide
Released: Annual, Latest edition 2010. **Price:** $395, individuals Directory; $445, individuals online lite; $1,075, individuals online pro. **Covers:** 4,500 U.S. and Canadian companies which operate home centers, home center warehouses, lumber and building material outlets, specialty paint and home decorating stores, and kitchen and bath centers. Concentrates on companies with a minimum annual sales of one million dollars. **Entries Include:** Company name, address, phone, fax, 6,500 personnel e-mail address, web site, Internet order processing indicator, listing type, product lines, total sales, sales percentage per customer type, total selling square footage, total stores, units by type of store operated, units made by trade name, trading areas, projected openings and remodeling, distribution center locations, buying and/or marketing group name and location, number of nurseries operated, average number of check-outs, year founded, public company indicator, parent and subsidiary company information, division and branch office locations, key personnel, and number of locations by city. **Arrangement:** Geographical. **Indexes:** Product line, alphabetical, exclusions, state.

10067 ■ "Doing Good: Cause and Effect" in *Entrepreneur* (Vol. 36, February 2008, No. 2, pp. 23)
Pub: Entrepreneur Media Inc.
Description: Lisa Knoppe established Art for a Cause LLC that employs people with mental and physical disabilities. The company makes hand-painted tools and furniture to be sold at gift retailers and hardware stores.

10068 ■ "The Final Piece; Lowe's to Fill Last Big Parcel Near Great Lakes Crossing" in *Crain's Detroit Business* (March 10, 2008)
Pub: Crain Communications, Inc.
Ed: Daniel Duggan. **Description:** Silverman Development Co. is developing a Lowe's home-improvement store on the last major retail parcel near the intersection of I-75 and Joslyn Road, an area which was once desolate but is now home to several restaurants and other retail facilities.

10069 ■ "High Hopes: Ralph Mitchell's Picks Have Growth Potential" in *Black Enterprise* (Vol. 37, February 2007, No. 7, pp. 42)
Pub: Earl G. Graves Publishing Co. Inc.
Ed: Carolyn M. Brown. **Description:** Ralph Mitchell, president and senior financial advisor of Braintree-Carthage Financial Group, offers three recommendations: Toll Brothers, Home Depot, and Lowe's.

10070 ■ "Home Improvement Marketers Target Women With New Products, New Campaigns and Plenty of Pink" in *Marketing to Women* (March 2008)
Pub: EPM Communications, Inc.
Description: From creating tools that fit a woman's ergonomics to designs that fit a woman's fashion sense, home improvement is finding new ways in which to market to women.

10071 ■ "The Main Event" in *Canadian Business* **(Vol. 80, November 19, 2007, No. 23, pp. 28)**
Pub: Rogers Media

Ed: Zena Olijnyk. **Description:** U.S.-based Lowe's Companies, Inc. will be opening three stores in Canada in December 2007 and another three in 2008. The housing market crisis in the U.S. is the reason behind the home improvement store's Canadian expansion. The impacts of the expansion on Canadian home care stores and on the market competition are evaluated.

10072 ■ "Milwaukee Rolls Out Major Line Expansion" in *Contractor* **(Vol. 56, July 2009, No. 7, pp. 3)**
Pub: Penton Media, Inc.

Ed: Robert P. Mader. **Description:** Milwaukee Electric Tool Corp. introduced a new line of products that include corded tools and cordless tools, measurement instruments, and tool accessories. The products include four new Deep Cut Band Saws and the M12 Cordless 3/8-inch Impact Wrench.

10073 ■ "Most Popular Tools? The Survey Says" in *Contractor* **(Vol. 57, February 2010, No. 2, pp. 1)**
Pub: Penton Media, Inc.

Ed: Robert P. Mader. **Description:** According to a survey of individuals in the field, mechanical contractors are purchasing more of their tools at home centers and they are also increasingly working in the service, repair, and retrofit markets. The survey also found that the reciprocating saw is the most used corded power tool. Additional purchasing habits of mechanical contractors are listed.

10074 ■ "Profit Strong Rona to Maintain Acquisition Strategy" in *Globe & Mail* **(February 22, 2007, pp. B14)**
Pub: CTVglobemedia Publishing Inc.

Description: Canada-based Rona Inc., home improvement retailer that reported record annual profit in 2006, will continue its strategy of acquisitions. The company has reported profits of $190.6 million in 2006.

10075 ■ "Retail Briefs - Dollar Store Opens in Long Leaf Mall" in *Star-News* **(November 5, 2010)**
Pub: Star-News Media

Ed: Judy Royal. **Description:** Dollar Delight$ opened a new shop in Long Leaf Mall in Wilmington, North Carolina. The store will carry gift bags, balloons, party supplies, greeting cards, school supplies, health and beauty products, hardware, baby items, toys, Christmas goods, crafts, housewares and jewelry in its inventory.

STATISTICAL SOURCES

10076 ■ *The Home Improvement Market*
Pub: MarketResearch.com

Released: 1999. **Price:** $2750.00. **Description:** This study analyzes the growing market for do-it-yourself (DIY) home improvement in the United States.

10077 ■ *RMA Annual Statement Studies*
Pub: Robert Morris Associates (RMA)

Released: Annual. **Price:** $175.00 2006-07 edition, $105.00. **Description:** Contains composite balance sheets and income statements for more than 360 industries, including the accounting, auditing, and bookkeeping industries. Also contains five years of comparative historical data for discerning trends. Includes 16 commonly used ratios, computed for most of the size groupings for nearly every industry.

10078 ■ *Standard & Poor's Industry Surveys*
Pub: Standard & Poor's Corp.

Released: Annual. **Price:** $3633.00. **Description:** Two-volume book that examines the prospects for specific industries, including trucking. Also provides analyses of trends and problems, statistical tables and charts, and comparative company analyses.

TRADE PERIODICALS

10079 ■ *Building Products Digest*
Pub: Cutler Publishing Inc.
Contact: Alan Oakes, Publisher
E-mail: ajoakes@aol.com

Released: Monthly. **Price:** $24; $39 two years. **Description:** Magazine covering lumber yards, home centers, retailers, and wholesalers.

10080 ■ *Hardware Merchandising*
Pub: Rogers Media Publishing
Contact: David Chestnut, Publisher
E-mail: david.chestnut@rci.rogers.com

Ed: Frank Condron, Editor, frank.condron@rci.rogers.com. **Released:** Monthly. **Price:** $99 Canada 2 years; plus applicable taxes; $60 Canada plus applicable taxes; $85 U.S. **Description:** Trade magazine on hardware industry.

10081 ■ *Home Channel News*
Pub: Lebhar-Friedman, Inc.
Contact: Jeff Arlen, Publisher
E-mail: jarlen@homechannelnews.com

Released: 16/yr. **Price:** $189. **Description:** Business tabloid serving home center/building material retailers.

10082 ■ *Home Improvement Retailing*
Pub: Powershift Communications Inc.

Released: Bimonthly. **Price:** $76; $110 Canada plus applicable taxes. **Description:** Trade magazine for the home improvement retail and wholesale market.

10083 ■ *Southwestern Retailer*
Pub: Western Retail Implement and Hardware Association

Released: Monthly. **Description:** Farm implements and hardware magazine.

TRADE SHOWS AND CONVENTIONS

10084 ■ Ace Hardware Fall Convention and Exhibit
Ace Hardware Corp.
2200 Kensington Ct.
Oak Brook, IL 60523-2100
Ph:(630)990-6600
Fax:(708)990-0278
Co. E-mail: jlapi@acehardware.com
URL: http://www.acehardware.com

Released: Annual. **Audience:** Ace Hardware dealers. **Principal Exhibits:** Hardware-related products. **Dates and Locations:** 2011 Oct 15-17, Denver, CO.

10085 ■ Door and Hardware Institute Annual Convention and Exposition
Door and Hardware Institute
14150 Newbrook Dr., Ste. 200
Chantilly, VA 20151-2223
Ph:(703)222-2010
Fax:(703)222-2410
URL: http://www.dhi.org

Released: Annual. **Audience:** Industry distributors, sales representatives, and manufacturers; engineers; and facility administrators. **Principal Exhibits:** Doors, hardware, and speciality building products.

10086 ■ H2X Canada Hardware & Home Improvement Expo & Conference
Messe Frankfurt Inc. (Atlanta, Georgia)
1600 Parkwood Cir., Ste. 515
Atlanta, GA 30339
Ph:(770)984-8016
Fax:(770)984-8023
Co. E-mail: info@usa.messefrankfurt.com
URL: http://www.usa.messefrankfurt.com

Released: Annual. **Audience:** Volume buyers, including retailers and manufacturers' representatives. **Principal Exhibits:** Hardware, housewares, giftware, paint, wallcovering, and products for leisure living, and home improvement.

10087 ■ Northwestern Building Products Expo
Northwestern Lumber Association
1405 Lilac Dr. N, Ste. 130
Minneapolis, MN 55422
Ph:(763)544-6822
Free: 800-331-0193
Fax:(763)595-4060
Co. E-mail: nlassn@nlassn.org
URL: http://www.nlassn.org

Released: Annual. **Audience:** Retail lumber and building material dealers. **Principal Exhibits:** Any product or service that is ultimately sold or used by retail lumber and building material dealers.

10088 ■ Wisconsin Manufacturing & Technology Show
Expo Productions Inc.
510 Hartbrook Dr.
Hartland, WI 53029
Ph:(262)367-5500
Free: 800-367-5520
Fax:(262)367-9956
Co. E-mail: expo@execpc.com
URL: http://www.expoproductionsinc.com

Released: Biennial. **Audience:** Purchasing agents, presidents and CEOs of companies, and plant engineers. **Principal Exhibits:** Metal working machinery and related manufacturing equipment, supplies, and services machine tools. **Dates and Locations:** 2011 Oct 04-06, West Allis, WI.

FRANCHISES AND BUSINESS OPPORTUNITIES

10089 ■ Atlantic Mower Parts
Atlantic Mower Part Supplies Inc.
13421 SW 14 Pl.
Ft. Lauderdale, FL 33325
Ph:(954)474-4942
Fax:(954)475-0414

No. of Franchise Units: 12. **No. of Company-Owned Units:** 1. **Founded:** 1978. **Franchised:** 1988. **Description:** Hardware Stores. **Equity Capital Needed:** $45,000. **Franchise Fee:** $15,900. **Financial Assistance:** No. **Training:** Yes.

10090 ■ Matco Tools
Danaher Corp.
4403 Allen Rd.
Stow, OH 44224
Ph:(330)929-4949
Free: 800-368-6651
Fax:(330)926-5325
Co. E-mail: matcofh@franchisehub.com
URL: http://www.matcotools.com

No. of Franchise Units: 1,384. **No. of Company-Owned Units:** 6. **Founded:** 1979. **Franchised:** 1993. **Description:** Matco Tools is a provider of precision mechanics hand tools, service equipment, and diagnostic computers that are distributed through franchised mobile tool distributors. From well-stocked Matco Tools trucks, Matco Distributors provide weekly service to customers at their place of employment. **Equity Capital Needed:** $82,376-$191,819 total investment. **Franchise Fee:** None. **Financial Assistance:** Financing is available through Matco for qualified candidates. Matco can finance up to $63,000 of the total investment required. **Training:** All new Matco Distributors are required to attend and successfully complete the Matco Tools New Distributor Training Program. This training is presented in a 6 day classroom training in Stow, OH, and a 3 week on truck training with a designated trainer.

10091 ■ Snap-on Tools Co.
Snap-on Inc.
Franchise Recruiting
2801 80th St.
Kenosha, WI 53141-1410
Free: 877-4SN-APON
URL: http://www.snapon.com

No. of Franchise Units: 4,595. **No. of Company-Owned Units:** 85. **Founded:** 1920. **Franchised:** 1991. **Description:** Develops, produces & markets professional equipment & tools. **Equity Capital Needed:** Low cost start-up programs. **Franchise Fee:**

$5,000. **Financial Assistance:** A variety of financing options are available through Snap-on Credit LLC, an affiliate of Snap-on, or through other third-party resources. **Training:** Provides extensive classroom and field training in such areas as business management, product knowledge, sales, record keeping, and product merchandising. In addition to supplying a custom Windows-Based Dealer Software Package,

each dealer is assigned to a field manager who acts as both coach and business consultant.

10092 ■ Woodcraft Franchise, LLC
SBR, Inc.
1177 Rosemar Rd.
P.O. Box 245
Parkersburg, WV 26105
Ph:(304)422-5412

Fax:(304)485-1939
Co. E-mail: woodcraftfranchise@woodcraft.com
URL: http://www.woodcraft.com
No. of Franchise Units: 88. **No. of Company-Owned Units:** 4. **Founded:** 1928. **Franchised:** 1997. **Description:** Specialty retail store. **Equity Capital Needed:** $150,000 liquid capital; $503,300-$650,300 total investment. **Franchise Fee:** $50,000. **Financial Assistance:** No. **Training:** Yes.

REFERENCE WORKS

10093 ■ *Hat Life Directory*
Pub: Mint Publishing
Released: Annual, Latest edition 2010. **Price:** $84, individuals directory: U.S. orders only; $94, individuals directory: includes international delivery. **Covers:** About 1,000 hat manufacturers, wholesalers, renovators, and importers of men's headwear, plus trade suppliers listed (SIC 2253, 2352, 5036); includes about 120 Canadian manufacturers. **Entries Include:** Company name, address, phone, fax, trade and brand names. **Arrangement:** Classified by product.

VIDEOCASSETTES/ AUDIOCASSETTES

10094 ■ *Accessory Allure*
Cambridge Educational
c/o Films Media Group
132 West 31st Street, 17th Floor
Ste. 124
New York, NY 10001
Free: 800-257-5126
Fax:(609)671-0266
Co. E-mail: custserve@films.com
URL: http://www.cambridgeol.com
Released: 1987. **Price:** $29.95. **Description:** This video shows viewers how to make the most of their wardrobe by using scarves, earrings, hats, and other accessories. **Availability:** VHS.

CONSULTANTS

10095 ■ **Contex Analytical Inc.**
2032 Lurting Ave.
Bronx, NY 10461

Ph:(718)829-0080
Fax:(718)829-0080
Co. E-mail: teachtex@earthlink.net
Contact: Robert J. Beaulieu, President
E-mail: teachtex@earthlink.net
Scope: Provides professional consulting services to the apparel textile trades. These services include: textile and sewn products design engineering, textile and sewn products defect analysis, market research, and expert witness. Industries served: textile, apparel and other sewn products manufacturers; retail stores, government agencies, law firms, and insurance.

LIBRARIES

10096 ■ **Fashion Institute of Design & Merchandising–Cyril Magnin Resource and Research Center**
55 Stockton St., 5th Fl.
San Francisco, CA 94108-5829
Ph:(415)675-5200, x3361
Free: 800-422-3436
Fax:(415)296-7299
URL: http://fidm.edu
Contact: Jim Glenny, Lib.Dir.
Scope: Fashion design and merchandising, interior design, apparel manufacturing, advertising, merchandising, marketing. **Services:** Center not open to the public. **Holdings:** 4000 books; 800 AV programs; 1000 newspaper clipping files; 4000 videos, DVDs, and slides. **Subscriptions:** 200 journals and other serials.

10097 ■ **Fashion Institute of Design & Merchandising–Orange County Library**
17590 Gillette Ave.
Irvine, CA 92614-5610

Ph:(949)851-6200
Fax:(949)851-6808
Co. E-mail: rmarkman@fidm.com
URL: http://www.fidm.com
Contact: Rebecca Markman, Campus Libn.
Scope: Apparel manufacturing management, cosmetics and fragrance merchandising, fashion design, interior design, merchandise marketing, textile design, visual presentation and space design. **Services:** Library open to the public by appointment. **Holdings:** 3000 books; 130 bound periodical volumes; 40 pamphlet headings; 475 videotapes; 135 slide sets; 300 retail catalogs; 100 Annual reports; 50 CD-ROMs. **Subscriptions:** 80 journals and other serials; 8 newspapers.

10098 ■ **Fashion Institute of Technology–Gladys Marcus Library**
7th Ave. at 27th St.
E-Bldg. E502
New York, NY 10001-5992
Ph:(212)217-4340
Fax:(212)217-4371
Co. E-mail: greta_earnest@fitnyc.edu
URL: http://fitnyc.edu/library
Contact: Prof. N.J. Wolfe, Lib.Dir.
Scope: Costume, fashion, interior design, management engineering technology, fashion buying and merchandising, textiles, toy design, packaging design, advertising. **Services:** Interlibrary loan; copying; Library open to the public for reference use only by appointment. **Holdings:** 130,260 books; 113,265 nonprint units; 20,637 bound periodical volumes; 125,000 fashion slides; 4712 reels of microfilm; 438 CD-ROM serials and digital monographs. **Subscriptions:** 4000 journals and other serials.

ASSOCIATIONS AND OTHER ORGANIZATIONS

10099 ■ Council on Safe Transportation of Hazardous Articles
7803 Hill House Ct.
Fairfax Station, VA 22039-2043
Ph:(703)451-4031
Fax:(703)451-4207
Co. E-mail: mail@costha.com
URL: http://www.costha.com
Contact: Robert Heinrich, Pres.
Description: Participates in international harmonization efforts. Promotes regulatory compliance and safety in the hazardous materials transportation industry. Promotes the growth and development of its members as Hazardous Materials Professionals. **Publications:** *COSTHA Quarterly* (quarterly).

10100 ■ Dangerous Goods Advisory Council
1100 H St. NW, Ste. 740
Washington, DC 20005-5484
Ph:(202)289-4550
Fax:(202)289-4074
Co. E-mail: info@dgac.org
URL: http://www.dgac.org
Contact: Mr. Mike Morrissette, Pres.
Description: Represents shippers, carriers, and container manufacturers of hazardous materials, substances, and wastes, shipper and carrier associations. Works to promote safe transportation of these materials; provides assistance in answering regulatory questions, guidance to appropriate governmental resources, and advice in establishing corporate compliance and safety programs. Conducts seminars on domestic and international hazardous materials packaging and transporting; sponsors educational programs. Provides training courses. .

10101 ■ Environmental Industry Associations
4301 Connecticut Ave. NW, Ste. 300
Washington, DC 20008-2304
Ph:(202)244-4700
Free: 800-424-2869
Fax:(202)966-4824
Co. E-mail: membership@envasns.org
URL: http://www.environmentalisteveryday.org
Contact: Bruce Parker, Pres./CEO
Description: Compiles statistics; conducts research and educational programs. **Publications:** *Waste Industry News* (monthly).

10102 ■ National Solid Wastes Management Association
4301 Connecticut Ave. NW, Ste. 300
Washington, DC 20008-2304
Ph:(202)244-4700
Free: 800-424-2869
Fax:(202)966-4824
Co. E-mail: bparker@nswma.org
URL: http://www.nswma.org
Contact: Bruce J. Parker, Pres./CEO
Description: Commercial firms that collect and dispose solid wastes. Acts as a forum for the discussion of specific aspects of hazardous waste transport.

Promotes professionalism in the industry to minimize the risks to public health and safety. Aids in the development of industry laws and regulations. Fosters public understanding of waste transport and disposal through educational programs. Urges members to: comply with federal liability insurance requirements; employ drivers who have completed a comprehensive training program and obtained their Department of Transportation commercial vehicle operator's license and medical evaluation certificate; set limits on drivers' hours of service; and maintain transport vehicles in accordance with federal motor carrier safety regulations. **Publications:** *Legal Bulletin* (quarterly); *Manual of Recommended Safety Practices*; *Waste Industry News* (quarterly).

DIRECTORIES OF EDUCATIONAL PROGRAMS

10103 ■ Habitats and Ecosystems
Pub: ABC-CLIO
Contact: Mark Crawford, Author
Released: Published December 1999. **Price:** $75, individuals print; $51.95, individuals. **Covers:** A listing of more than 1,400 of the most hazardous pollution sites since 1980. **Entries Include:** Location. **Arrangement:** Geographical by state.

REFERENCE WORKS

10104 ■ Hazardous Waste Consultant—Directory of Commercial Hazardous Waste Management Facilities Issue
Pub: Elsevier Science
Released: Semiannual. **Publication Includes:** List of 170 licensed commercial facilities that treat and/or dispose of hazardous waste in North America. **Entries Include:** Facility name, address, phone, contact name, type of waste handled, methods of on-site treatment and/or disposal, Environmental Protection Agency permit status and identification number, restrictions, description of other services. **Arrangement:** Geographical. **Indexes:** Organization name.

10105 ■ "Uranium Energy Corp Provides an Update on Its Goliad Operations" in *Canadian Corporate News* (May 16, 2007)
Pub: Comtex News Network Inc.
Description: Complaints against Uranium Energy Corp. and its Goliad Project in South Texas have been dismissed. The Railroad Commission of Texas (RRC), the regulatory authority which oversees mineral exploration in Texas, concluded that Uranium Energy Corp.'s drilling activities on the Goliad Project have not contaminated certain water wells or the related aquifer.

10106 ■ WASTEC Product and Service Directory
Pub: Waste Equipment Technology Association
Released: Annual. **Covers:** About 250 member consultants, manufacturers, and distributors of waste handling, collection, and processing equipment;

coverage includes Canada. **Entries Include:** Company name, address, phone, e-mail, URL, products, contact name. **Arrangement:** Alphabetical, product category. **Indexes:** Product.

STATISTICAL SOURCES

10107 ■ Market for Medical Waste Management
Pub: Theta Corp. Reports
Released: 1995. **Price:** $1625.00. **Description:** examines the handling of medical waste, and provides a comprehensive analysis of 5 market segments: disposable products, hazardous waste, infectious waste, pathological waste, and sharps.

TRADE PERIODICALS

10108 ■ Chemical Week Price Report
Pub: Chemical Week Associates
Ed: David Hunter, Editor. **Released:** Weekly. **Price:** $675, U.S.; $750, elsewhere. **Description:** Covers weekly market trends concerning chemicals, and reports on price developments.

10109 ■ Environmental Engineering Science
Pub: Mary Ann Liebert Incorporated Publishers
Ed: Julia Stegemann, Editor, j.stegemann@ucl.ac.uk. **Released:** 12/yr. **Price:** $908 print and online; $1,367 other countries print and online; $700 online only; $2,074 institutions print and online; $2,275 institutions, other countries print and online; $1,592 institutions print only; $1,957 institutions, other countries print only; $1,462 institutions online only. **Description:** Journal on environmental and industrial waste technology.

10110 ■ Waste Age
Pub: Primedia Business
Contact: Jay Schlosser, National Sales
E-mail: jay.schlosser@penton.com
Ed: Stephen Ursery, Editor, steve.ursery@penton.com. **Released:** Monthly. **Description:** Waste removal and disposal magazine.

VIDEOCASSETTES/ AUDIOCASSETTES

10111 ■ AIDS/Hepatitis B: Handling and Processing Infectious Waste
American Society for Training and Development (ASTD)
1640 King St.
Box 1443
Alexandria, VA 22313-2043
Ph:(703)683-8100
Free: 800-628-2783
Fax:(703)683-8103
URL: http://www.astd.org
Released: 1989. **Price:** $250.00. **Description:** An overview for professional and environmental health workers on the proper disposal methods for infectious waste materials. **Availability:** VHS; 3/4U.

10112 ■ *The Global Dumping Ground: International Traffic in Hazardous Waste*
The Video Project
PO Box 411376
San Francisco, CA 94141-1376
Free: 800-4-PLANET
Fax:888-562-9012
Co. E-mail: support@videoproject.com
URL: http://www.videoproject.com
Released: 1990. **Price:** $99.95. **Description:** PBS Frontline report examines of the problem of exporting hazardous waste to countries with less-stringent regulations on disposal. **Availability:** VHS; 3/4U; Special order formats.

10113 ■ *Handling Hazardous Waste*
Learning Communications LLC
5520 Trabuco Rd.
Irvine, CA 92620
Free: 800-622-3610
Fax:(949)727-4323
Co. E-mail: sales@learncom.com
URL: http://www.learncomhr.com
Released: 1991. **Price:** $175.00. **Description:** A seven-module program designed to train workers how to deal effectively with hazardous waste. **Availability:** VHS; 3/4U.

10114 ■ *Hazard Management Safety Series*
Gulf Publishing Co.
PO Box 2608
Houston, TX 77252
Ph:(713)529-4301
Free: 800-231-6275
Fax:(713)520-4433
Co. E-mail: customerservices@gulfpub.com
URL: http://www.gulfpub.com
Released: 1991. **Price:** $375.00. **Description:** A four-tape series covering the safe management of hazardous materials, sites, and procedures. A workbook is included. **Availability:** VHS; 3/4U.

10115 ■ *Hazardous Waste*
Emergency Film Group
Detrick Lawrence Corp.
PO Box 1928
Edgartown, MA 02539
Ph:(508)627-8844
Free: 800-842-0999
Fax:(508)627-8863
Co. E-mail: info@efilmgroup.com
URL: http://www.efilmgroup.com
Released: 1989. **Price:** $330.00. **Description:** Find out the proper way to deal with hazardous waste. **Availability:** VHS; 3/4U.

10116 ■ *The New Superfund—What It Is, How It Does—A Series*
National Audiovisual Center
5301 Shawnee Rd.
Alexandria, VA 22312
Ph:(703)605-6000
Free: 800-553-6847
Fax:(703)321-8547
Co. E-mail: customerservice@ntis.gov
URL: http://www.ntis.gov/products/nac.aspx
Released: 1987. **Price:** $585.00. **Description:** The Environmental Protection Agency's new cleanup process is profiled in extensive detail. **Availability:** VHS; 3/4U.

TRADE SHOWS AND CONVENTIONS

10117 ■ Expo Yate Mundial - Mexico Boat Show
E.J. Krause & Associates, Inc.
6550 Rock Spring Dr., Ste. 500
Bethesda, MD 20817
Ph:(301)493-5500
Fax:(301)493-5705
Co. E-mail: ejkinfo@ejkrause.com
URL: http://www.ejkrause.com
Released: Annual. **Audience:** Public. **Principal Exhibits:** Powerboats, sailboats, sports and fishing equipment, marinas and resorts, financial and insurance, clothing, jewelry and lifestyle.

CONSULTANTS

10118 ■ American Waste Processing Ltd.
2100 W Madison St.
PO Box 306
Maywood, IL 60153-1744
Ph:(708)681-3999
Free: 800-841-6900
Fax:(708)681-5583
Co. E-mail: american@american-waste.com
Contact: William J. Vajdik, President
E-mail: american@american-waste.com
Scope: Consultants in hazardous waste management, treatment and disposal. Particular expertise in environmental audits, plant closures, treatment of waste on and off site, waste disposal, transportation, remedial action, complete clean up services and underground tank removal to include cleaning, excavating and disposal.

10119 ■ Analytical Consulting Services
2278 Woodsfield Ln. NE
Marietta, GA 30062
Ph:(770)565-0078
Fax:(770)565-0078
Co. E-mail: rbelote@analytical-consultants.com
URL: http://www.analytical-consultants.com
Contact: Richard H. Belote, Owner
E-mail: rbelote@analytical-consultants.com
Scope: Provides training and consulting services in accident or incident investigations, root cause analysis of complex problems, system safety, team membership and leadership, risk analysis, structured problem solving, nuclear safety assessment, and management oversight and risk tree analysis. Industries served: industries that deal with highly hazardous chemicals, substances or have substantial risk to their employees; emphasis on nuclear, petrochemical, government (OSHA), and military (ship and aircraft maintenance and overhaul). **Seminars:** Accident Investigation Workshop; Root Cause Analysis; Team Effectiveness Training; Process Safety Management; Occupational Accident Investigations; Incident/Accident Investigations (Nuclear industry); Root Cause Analysis of Operating Events (Nuclear industry); Report Writing and Oral Briefings; Advanced Techniques Upgrade for Basic Level Graduates; Process Safety Management Overview; OSHA 102 - Basic Accident Investigation (link to OSHA); OSHA 202 - Advanced Accident Investigation (link to OSHA); OSHA 141Legal Aspects of Inspection (link to OSHA); Occupational Accident Investigations; Occurrence Reporting (Department of Energy and Contractors).

10120 ■ Baxter & Woodman Inc.
8840 W 192nd St.
Mokena, IL 60448
Ph:(815)459-1260
Fax:(815)455-0450
Co. E-mail: info@baxterwoodman.com
URL: http://www.baxterwoodman.com
Contact: William B. Sprague Jr., Vice President
Scope: Provides municipalities, sanitary districts, and counties in Illinois and Wisconsin consulting engineering services specializing in water and wastewater treatment, wells, water mains, sanitary and storm sewers, flood control, roads, intersections, downtown transportation, UST remediation, GIS, SCADA systems, and general municipal engineering.

10121 ■ CH2M Hill Companies Ltd.
9191 S Jamaica St.
Englewood, CO 80112-5946
Ph:(720)286-2000
Free: 888-242-6445
Fax:(720)286-9250
Co. E-mail: feedback@ch2m.com
URL: http://www.ch2m.com
Contact: John Madia, Chief Human Resources Officer
E-mail: robert.card@atsch2m.com
Scope: International consulting firm of engineers, planners, economists and scientists in many technical fields. Services include general civil engineering; structural engineering; municipal and industrial waste water, solid waste and water resources management; construction management; toxic and hazardous

waste management; irrigation; transportation; and environmental studies. Serves private industries as well as government agencies. **Seminars:** Intranet Services.

10122 ■ Cosar Inc.
2231 Devine St.
PO Box 50334
Columbia, SC 29205
Ph:(803)771-9911
Fax:(803)256-8746
Contact: Carl O. Schulz, Principle
Scope: Services provided are: toxicology study protocol design or review, design of a toxicology testing strategy, placing of toxicology studies, monitoring of toxicology studies, data audits, data interpretation, and risk assessment. Also assists with expert testimony and litigation support, and literature searches and critical reviews. Offers GLP compliance assistance; hazardous waste site assessment; and petition, application, or registration support. Industries served: oil and chemical companies, medical device manufacturers, hazardous waste owners and operators, and engineering firms. **Seminars:** Toxicological Issues in the Development of an Occupational Health Standard for Formaldehyde; Reporting the Results of a Risk Assessment; What You Should Know About Performing a Risk Assessment.

10123 ■ Dangerous Goods Council Inc.
1040 Detwiler Dr.
PO Box 7325
York, PA 17404
Ph:(717)848-8840
Fax:(717)848-8841
Co. E-mail: hazmat@hazshipper.com
URL: http://www.hazshipper.com
Contact: Daine Wrobleski, Vice President
Scope: Offers a wide range of hazardous materials transportation regulatory compliance training programs. Provides awareness training, initial and recurrent training, and safety training. Materials used include: CFR 49, iCAO/IATA, HM 181, and emergency response guidebook. Firm gives seminars and in-house consultation. Training is accomplished through lecture, work projects, question-and-answer sessions and testing. These courses are designed to meet the training requirements of United States Department of Transportation Docket HM 126F. Also provides safety audits that comply with all OSHA, Dot, and FAA regulations. Industries served: manufacturing, industrial, and transportation. **Publications:** "PHMSA-02-11989 (HM-224C) and PHMSA-04-19886 (HM-224E): Hazardous Materials; Transportation of Lithium Batteries," 2008; "Hazardous Materials Regulations: Transportation of Compressed Oxygen, Other Oxidizing Gases and Chemical Oxygen Generators on Aircraft; correction," 2007; "Hazardous Materials: Security Requirements for Offerors and Transporters of Hazardous Materials," 2003. **Seminars:** Initial and recurrent training for dangerous goods; Awareness/familiarization training for dangerous goods; Safety training for dangerous goods, Hazmat Training. **Special Services:** Haz-Shipper^R.

10124 ■ Environmental Response Inc.
2131 Murfreesboro Pke., Ste. 209
Nashville, TN 37217
Ph:(615)399-1300
Fax:(615)822-8238
Contact: R. Terry McDaniel, President
Scope: Involved in hazardous waste management, specifically OSHA and E.P.A., and chemical and biological safety. Serves private industries as well as government agencies. **Seminars:** Training programs - Hazwoper, Sara-Sub-Title 3, Right-to-Know, and Site Specific.

10125 ■ Global Secure Training
10485 Theodore Green Blvd.
White Plains, MD 20695
Ph:(301)932-0994
Free: 800-258-7501
Fax:(301)934-9584
Co. E-mail: traininginfo@globalsecurecorp.com
Contact: Charles A. Hasper, CFO
E-mail: lmead@globalsecurecorp.com
Scope: Consultants in hazardous waste management. Specialists in the development of site specific, employee hazardous waste training to most major

industries dealing with hazardous waste, specifically the automobile and transportation industries. Industries served: Auto, manufacturing, and government agencies.

10126 ■ Kimmel & Associates
25 Page Ave.
Asheville, NC 28801
Ph:(828)251-9900
Fax:(828)251-9955
Co. E-mail: kimmel@kimmel.com
URL: http://www.kimmel.com
Contact: Paul Samuels, Vice President
E-mail: psamuels@atskimmel.com
Scope: Offers executive search and personnel consulting, management practices consultation, and merger and acquisition consultation. Industries served: general contracting, construction engineering, specialty contracting, environmental engineering firms, waste management, recycling, remedial or hazardous waste contractors, engineering consulting firms, and government agencies. **Publications:** "GRAY POWER can give you an EDGE," ENR magazine; "A Guide to Hiring Forwarder Talent," CNS Focus Magazine, 2004.

10127 ■ Michael Senew & Associates
6320 Capital Blvd., Ste. 116
Raleigh, NC 27616
Ph:(919)872-6601
Fax:(919)872-6626
Co. E-mail: msenew@martiniprint.com
URL: http://martiniprint.com
Contact: Michael Senew, President
E-mail: msenew@aol.com
Scope: A registered professional engineer and consultant specializing in manpower development and training. Publishes environmental, health safety, quality assurance, and human resource training materials as well as other short-run publications. On a consultant basis, will assist in the development of instructional programs and will provide complete editing, writing, graphic and printing support. Industries served: Environmental, safety, hazardous materials, educational, trainers and curriculum developers, and government agencies worldwide. **Publications:** "OSHA Regulations"; "Basic Industrial Processes"; "Hazard Communications"; "Worker Right-to-Know"; "DOT Regulations"; "EPA Regulations"; "Incident Management"; "Recovery Incineration and Disposal". **Seminars:** Brown fields awareness worker and implementation strategies; Environmental training, and safety training.

10128 ■ MVTL Laboratories Inc.
1126 N Front St.
New Ulm, MN 56073
Ph:(507)354-8517
Free: 800-782-3557
Fax:(507)359-2890
Co. E-mail: crc@mtvl.com
URL: http://www.mvtl.com
Contact: Jerry Balbach, President
E-mail: jbalbach@atsmvtl.com
Scope: Environmental consultants offering analytical consulting and field services in the following areas: air, water and wastewater, ground water, solid and hazardous waste, industrial hygiene and transportation and disposal of hazardous waste. **Publications:** "What You Need to Know About Salmonella," 2007; "The What, Where, Why of Nataymcin," Apr, 2007; "Why Gluten Testing is needed," Apr, 2007; "Sulfates in Your Well," 2007; "What Is Your Well Water Telling You".

10129 ■ OMI Government Relations Inc.
980 9th St., Ste. 430
Sacramento, CA 95814-2724
Ph:(916)447-4113
Fax:(916)444-7835
Co. E-mail: burnsdc@aol.com
Contact: Eric R. Carleson, Principle
E-mail: burnsdc@aol.com
Scope: Offers governmental affairs consulting services to trade and professional associations and corporations. Also offers general consulting services to nonprofit corporations. Industries served: radioactive waste disposal, toxic waste management, timber,

consumer information and credit reporting, construction, electronics, multi housing, laundry, manufacturing, retailing, pharmaceuticals, and government agencies.

10130 ■ Smyth Fivenson Co.
8513 Irvington Ave.
Irvine, CA 92604
Ph:(301)493-6600
Fax:(301)530-7557
URL: http://www.smythfivenson.com
Contact: Tom Somers, Principal
E-mail: tsomers@smythfivenson.com
Scope: A Human Resources consulting firm providing services to two business areas, both nationally. First, provides temporary human resource professionals to all industries. Second, Smyth Fivenson Co. performs recruiting and placement services for the environmental industry.

LIBRARIES

10131 ■ Air & Waste Management Association Collection
1 Gateway Ctr., 3rd Fl.
420 Ft. Duquesne Blvd.
Pittsburgh, PA 15222-1435
Ph:(412)232-3444
Free: 800-270-3444
Fax:(412)232-3450
Co. E-mail: info@awma.org
URL: http://www.awma.org
Contact: Andy Knopes, Pub.Dir.
Scope: Air pollution, hazardous waste management. **Services:** Copying; Library open to members of the association and students. **Holdings:** 200 books. **Subscriptions:** 1 journal.

10132 ■ Brown & Caldwell Library
201 N. Civic Dr.
Walnut Creek, CA 94596
Free: 800-727-2224
Fax:(925)937-9026
Co. E-mail: info@brwncald.com
URL: http://www.brownandcaldwell.com
Scope: Environmental engineering, water and wastewater treatment, civil engineering. **Services:** Library open to the public by appointment. **Holdings:** 4000 books; 100 bound periodical volumes; 8000 reports; 400 microfiche; 400 reels of microfilm; 700 vendor catalogs. **Subscriptions:** 100 journals and other serials.

10133 ■ Brown University–Center for Environmental Studies
135 Angell St.
Box 1943
Providence, RI 02912
Ph:(401)863-3449
Fax:(401)863-3503
Co. E-mail: patti_caton@brown.edu
URL: http://envstudies.brown.edu
Contact: Patricia-Ann Caton, Adm.Mgr.
Scope: Environmental issues. **Services:** Library open to the public for reference use only. **Holdings:** 500 books; 200 reports. **Subscriptions:** 7 journals and other serials.

10134 ■ California Department of Conservation–Division of Recycling–Resource Center (801 K)
801 K St.
MS-18-58
Sacramento, CA 95814-3530
Ph:(916)323-3836
Free: 800-REC-YCLE
Fax:(916)327-2144
Co. E-mail: doriis@calrecycle.ca.gov
URL: http://www.consrv.ca.gov
Contact: Patti Holmes, Lib.Coord.
Scope: Recycling, waste reduction, resource conservation. **Services:** Library open to the public with restrictions. **Holdings:** 300 books; 400 reports; 277 videocassettes. **Subscriptions:** 93 journals and other serials.

10135 ■ Center for Health, Environment and Justice Library
PO Box 6806
Falls Church, VA 22040-6806
Ph:(703)237-2249
Co. E-mail: chej@chej.org
URL: http://www.chej.org
Contact: Lois Marie Gibbs, Exec.Dir.
Scope: Waste management technology, health effects from exposure to toxic chemicals and hazardous wastes, environmental concerns. **Services:** Library open to the public by appointment. **Holdings:** 3500 volumes. **Subscriptions:** 850 journals and other serials.

10136 ■ CH2M Hill, Inc. Technical Library
3011 SW Williston Rd.
PO Box 147009
Gainesville, FL 32614-7009
Ph:(352)335-7991
Fax:(352)335-2959
Co. E-mail: mccourtney@ch2m.com
URL: http://www.ch2m.com/corporate/default_north_america.asp
Contact: Mary Courtney, Sr.Rec.Mgt.Spec.
Scope: Water supply, wastewater treatment and disposal, domestic and industrial waste treatment, solid and hazardous wastes disposal, environmental sciences, construction management, transportation. **Services:** Center not open to the public. **Holdings:** 6500 books; 243 bound periodical volumes; 3000 engineering reports; 2800 specifications; 500 reels of microfilm; 5500 microfiche; AV equipment; maps. **Subscriptions:** 150 journals and other serials.

10137 ■ Environmental Hazards Management Institute Library
10 Newmarket Rd.
Durham, NH 03821
Ph:(603)868-1496
Free: 800-558-EHMI
Fax:(603)868-1547
Co. E-mail: info@ehmi.org
URL: http://www.ehmi.org
Contact: Sue Brassett
Scope: Environmental health and safety, toxicology, mold prevention, public health and the environment, waste minimization, disaster prevention and homeland security, education. **Services:** Library open to the public. **Holdings:** 3000 books; 2000 bound periodical volumes; 300 reports; 60 manuscripts.

10138 ■ Illinois Sustainable Technology Center
1 Hazelwood Dr.
Champaign, IL 61820
Ph:(217)333-8957
Fax:(217)333-8944
Co. E-mail: library@istc.illinois.edu
URL: http://www.istc.illinois.edu
Contact: Laura L. Barnes, Libn.
Scope: Pollution prevention, hazardous waste, industrial process engineering, industrial audits, analytical chemistry, waste reduction, household hazardous waste, energy efficiency, renewable energy, alternative fuels, biodiesel. **Services:** Interlibrary loan; Library open to the public for reference use only. **Holdings:** 8000 books; 75 videotapes. **Subscriptions:** 250 journals and other serials; 1 newspaper.

10139 ■ Long Island Lighting Company Resource Center
131 Hoffman Ln.
Central Islip, NY 11722
Ph:(516)436-4003
Fax:(516)436-4036
Contact: Carolyn Jaskot, Curric.Rsrc.Spec.
Scope: Energy, electricity, public utilities, business management. **Services:** Library not open to the public. **Holdings:** 1570 books; 100 periodical titles; videocassettes; audiocassettes. **Subscriptions:** 30 journals and other serials; 2 newspapers.

10140 ■ Metcalf & Eddy, Inc.–Harry L. Kinsel Library
701 Edgewater Dr.
Wakefield, MA 01880-5371
Ph:(781)246-5200
Fax:(781)245-6293
Co. E-mail: richard_mansfield@metcalfeddy.com
URL: http://www.aecom.com
Contact: Richard Mansfield, Libn.
Scope: Environment, hazardous waste, drinking water, wastewater/sewage, civil engineering. **Services:** Interlibrary loan; Library open to the public by appointment. **Holdings:** 6000 books; 658 bound periodical volumes. **Subscriptions:** 234 journals and other serials; 3 newspapers.

10141 ■ Pennsylvania Environmental Council Library
1315 Walnut St., Ste. 532
Philadelphia, PA 19107
Ph:(215)545-4570
Fax:(215)545-4594
URL: http://www.pecpa.org
Contact: Don Welsh, Pres./CEO
Scope: Solid waste and energy issues, water issues, air pollution, transportation, growth management, land use, industrial sites reuse, mediation, population. **Services:** Copying; faxing; Library open to the public by appointment. **Holdings:** 400 books; 100 reports; 40 videotapes; 10 slide shows. **Subscriptions:** 200 journals and other serials.

10142 ■ Solid Waste Information Clearinghouse Library
1100 Wayne Ave., Ste. 700
PO Box 7219
Silver Spring, MD 20910
Ph:(301)585-2898
Free: 800-467-9262 (G0-SWANA)
Fax:(301)585-0297
Co. E-mail: info@swana.org
URL: http://www.swana.org
Contact: John Skinner, Exec.Dir./CEO
Scope: Municipal solid waste management - collection, disposal, planning; source reduction; transfer; recycling landfills - operations, gas; resource recovery. **Services:** Copying; Library open to the public by appointment. **Holdings:** 7500 documents; 50 newsletters. **Subscriptions:** 35 journals and other serials.

10143 ■ U.S. Environmental Protection Agency Headquarters Library
1200 Pennsylvania Ave., NW
Rm. 3340
Mailcode 3404T
Washington, DC 20460-0001
Ph:(202)566-0556
Fax:(202)566-0574
Co. E-mail: hqchemlibraries@epa.gov
URL: http://www.epa.gov/libraries/hqrepository.html
Scope: Water - pollution, quality, supply; air pollution; noise abatement; radiation; hazardous wastes; solid waste management; resource recovery; pesticides; chemistry and toxicology; social, economic, legislative, legal, administrative, and management aspects of environmental policy. **Services:** Interlibrary loan; SDI; Library open to the public with restrictions. **Holdings:** 16,000 books; 7000 hardcopy documents and technical reports; 400,000 documents and reports from the EPA and its predecessor agencies on microfiche; newspapers, abstracts and indexes, periodicals on microfilm. **Subscriptions:** 20 journals and other serials.

RESEARCH CENTERS

10144 ■ Environmental Hazards Management Institute
10 Newmarket Rd.
Durham, NH 03824
Ph:(603)868-1496

Free: 800—558-3464
Fax:(603)868-1547
Co. E-mail: aborner@ehmi.org
URL: http://www.ehmi.org
Contact: Alan John Borner, CEO
E-mail: aborner@ehmi.org
Scope: Natural and man-made disasters, global pandemic influenza preparedness or risk avoidance and societal continuity. **Services:** Compost Education Wheel; Household Hazardous Waste Wheel; Kidswheel, on hazardous household products; Water Sense Wheel, interactive tools that educate workers, community leaders, and homeowners. **Publications:** EHMI.University Blogs (daily). **Educational Activities:** Educational bookcovers; Mold Wheel; Seminars, training. **Awards:** EHMI Awards for Leadership.

10145 ■ The Nature Conservancy–Ohio Chapter
6375 Riverside Dr., Ste. 100
Dublin, OH 43017
Ph:(614)717-2770
Free: 877—TNC-OHIO
Fax:(614)717-2777
Co. E-mail: ohio@tnc.org
URL: http://www.nature.org/ourinitiatives/regions/
northamerica/unitedstates/ohio
Contact: Josh Knights, Exec.Dir.
E-mail: ohio@tnc.org
Scope: Owns and manages 35 preserves throughout Ohio to protect habitat; preserves serve as living laboratories to apply conservation science and methods. Current projects include Southern Appalachian forests (edge of Appalachia Preserve System); Ohio River Watershed/Drainage basin (Darby Creek Watershed); Lake Erie Watershed/Drainage basin (Grand River Watershed, Oak Openings Region, Akron Kames). Also studies invasive species and compatible agriculture. **Services:** Research use of preserves. **Publications:** Nature Conservancy Magazine (quarterly); Ohio Chapter Newsletter (semiannually). **Educational Activities:** Field trips and special events (monthly), throughout the state; Prescribed burn and land management training (occasionally).

10146 ■ University of Alabama–Environmental Institute
103 Bevill Research Bldg.
PO Box 870205
Tuscaloosa, AL 35487-0205
Ph:(205)348-1677
Co. E-mail: rpitt@eng.ua.edu
URL: http://ei.ua.edu
Contact: Prof. Robert Pitt PhD, Dir.
E-mail: rpitt@eng.ua.edu
Scope: Global change, focusing on the effects of elevated carbon dioxide levels on natural and managed ecosystems, quantifying the manifestation of these effects on a regional scale, and identifying and providing the information needed for evaluating the biological and ecological consequences of these effects on natural and human systems. **Services:** environmental science information; Information Resource Service, for government agencies and legislative committees; Waste reduction and pollution prevention technical support, to Alabama businesses and industry. **Publications:** NIGEC-Southeast Regional Center Annual Report (annually). **Educational Activities:** Seminars and conferences, to promote dialogue and information exchange on waste management and global environmental change issues; Symposium, on Global Climate Change Research.

10147 ■ University of Florida–Hinkley Center for Solid and Hazardous Waste Management
4635 NW 53rd Ave., Ste. 205
Gainesville, FL 32653
Ph:(352)392-6264

Fax:(352)846-0183
Co. E-mail: jschert@ufl.edu
URL: http://www.hinkleycenter.com
Contact: John D. Schert, Dir.
E-mail: jschert@ufl.edu
Scope: Construction and demolition debris, hazardous waste management, medical waste management, pollution prevention, socioeconomic issues, special wastes, waste reduction. **Services:** Information dissemination, publications listing. **Publications:** Annual Research Booklet; Newsletter (quarterly). **Educational Activities:** Exhibits at workshops and conferences; Research symposium (annually); Seminars.

10148 ■ University of Iowa–Center for Health Effects of Environmental Contamination
100 Oakdale Campus, Rm. N202 OH
Iowa City, IA 52242-5000
Ph:(319)335-4550
Fax:(319)335-4077
Co. E-mail: gene-parkin@uiowa.edu
URL: http://www.cheec.uiowa.edu
Contact: Gene Parkin PhD, Dir.
E-mail: gene-parkin@uiowa.edu
Scope: Fate and transport of toxic substances in the environment, radon and indoor air contaminants, nonpoint source chemical contamination of water supplies, and epidemiologic studies that relate the occurrence of diseases to contaminant exposure. **Services:** Develops and maintains environmental databases, that can be accessed by state agencies; Engineering, health, and laboratory consultations; Health assessments, at hazardous waste disposal sites; Responds to public inquiries, regarding health effects of exposure to environmental contaminants. **Publications:** Annual Report; Newsletter; Technical Report. **Educational Activities:** Educational seminars and conferences, on the causes and prevention of environmentally-induced disease.

10149 ■ University of Northern Iowa–Iowa Waste Reduction Center
BCS Bldg., Ste. 113
Cedar Falls, IA 50614-0185
Ph:(319)273-8905
Free: 800—422-3109
Fax:(319)273-6582
Co. E-mail: john.konefes@uni.edu
URL: http://www.iwrc.org
Contact: John Konefes, Dir.
E-mail: john.konefes@uni.edu
Scope: Environmentally safe ways to reduce and manage waste from small business, including hazardous waste, air emissions, used oil, air-conditioning and coolant waste, wastewater, and solid waste. **Services:** Consulting for the Iowa Automobile Dealers Service and painting technicians; Maintains mobile exhibits that travel to small companies and rural areas. **Publications:** The Closed Loop (quarterly); Point Source Newsletter. **Educational Activities:** Air permitting workshops and proper spray application technique training; Workshops in hazardous waste, laboratory and photoprocessing waste management, and solid waste management.

10150 ■ Western Region Hazardous Substance Research Center
204 Apperson Hall
Oregon State University
Corvallis, OR 97331-2302
Ph:(541)737-2751
Fax:(541)737-3099
Co. E-mail: lewis.semprini@oregonstate.edu
URL: http://wrhsrc.oregonstate.edu
Contact: Dr. Lewis Semprini, Dir.
E-mail: lewis.semprini@oregonstate.edu
Scope: Movement, fate, and effects of volatile organic compounds in soils and groundwater. Develops advanced physical, chemical, and biological processes for the removal of hazardous chemicals. **Services:** On-line searchable publications database; Technical assistance, regarding brownfields; Technical outreach services, for communities. **Publications:** Annual report; Journal articles.

START-UP INFORMATION

10151 ■ **"Organic Chain Scouting Tri-State Sites, Including Kenwood" in** *Business Courier* **(Vol. 27, December 3, 2010, No. 31, pp. 1)**
Pub: Business Courier
Ed: Tom Demeropolis. **Description:** Asheville, North Carolina-based Earth Fare has been planning to add a total of six stores in 2011, including the potential opening of more than one store in the Greater Cincinnati area market. Earth Fare has not named specific locations but Kenwood area was reportedly being considered for its first location. Insights on growing trends toward health food stores are also given.

10152 ■ **"Vitamins to Spice Up Food" in** *Philadelphia Business Journal* **(Vol. 28, October 2, 2009, No. 33, pp. 1)**
Pub: American City Business Journals
Ed: John George. **Description:** VitaminSpice, a startup company established by Ed Bukstel, makes a line of spice and vitamin blends that come in seasoning form. The form of the blends could facilitate easier ingestion of vitamins into people's diets. A reverse merger that will allow a publicly-traded company status for VitaminSpice will be accomplished by early October 2009.

ASSOCIATIONS AND OTHER ORGANIZATIONS

10153 ■ **Canadian Health Food Association–Association Canadienne des Aliements de Sante**
235 Yorkland Blvd., Ste. 302
Toronto, ON, Canada M2J 4Y8
Ph:(416)497-6939
Free: 800-661-4510
Fax:(416)497-3214
Co. E-mail: info@chfa.ca
URL: http://www.chfa.ca
Contact: Penelope Marrett, Pres./CEO
Description: Represents producers and distributors of health foods. Seeks to advance the health food industries. Facilitates communication and cooperation among members; represents the commercial and regulatory interests of the health food industries; sponsors educational and promotional programs. **Publications:** *The Natural Voice* (5/year).

10154 ■ **Health Information Resource Center**
1850 W Winchester Rd., Ste. 213
Libertyville, IL 60048
Ph:(847)816-8660
Free: 800-828-8225
Fax:(847)816-8662
Co. E-mail: info@fitnessday.com
URL: http://www.healthawards.com
Contact: Patricia Henze, Exec. Dir.
Description: Clearinghouse for consumer health information. Provides information and referral services to many organizations that use or produce consumer health information materials. Conducts

market research. **Publications:** *Consumer Health Information Online* (annual); *Consumer Health Information: The Professional Guide to the Nations' Best Consumer Health Information Programs and Materials* (annual); *Health and Medical Media '99* (annual); *The Health Events Calendar* (annual).

10155 ■ **National Association for the Specialty Food Trade**
136 Madison Ave., 12th Fl.
New York, NY 10016
Ph:(212)482-6440
Free: 800-627-3869
Fax:(212)482-6459
Co. E-mail: info@nasft.org
URL: http://www.specialtyfood.com
Contact: Ann Daw, Pres.
Description: Represents manufacturers, distributors, processors, importers, retailers, and brokers of specialty and gourmet foods. **Publications:** *Specialty Food Magazine* (10/year).

10156 ■ **Natural Products Association**
1773 T St. NW
Washington, DC 20009
Ph:(202)223-0101
Free: 800-966-6632
Fax:(202)223-0250
Co. E-mail: natural@npainfo.org
URL: http://www.npainfo.org
Contact: Ms. Sandra Jackson, Communications Mgr.
Description: Represents retailers, wholesalers, brokers, distributors and manufacturers of natural, nutritional, dietetic foods, supplements, services and natural body and home care products. .

REFERENCE WORKS

10157 ■ **"Bagging Profits; High-End Grocers Expand Despite Stale Economy" in** *Crain's Detroit Business* **(Vol. 24, March 24, 2008, No. 12, pp. 1)**
Pub: Crain Communications, Inc.
Ed: Nancy Kaffer. **Description:** Discusses the expansion plans of several high-end grocery stores in the Detroit area and the reasons why, despite the poor economy, these gourmet grocers are doing well. Statistical data included.

10158 ■ **"Ben & Jerry's Changing Some 'All Natural' Labels" in** *Ice Cream Reporter* **(Vol. 23, October 20, 2010, No. 11, pp. 1)**
Pub: Ice Cream Reporter
Description: Following criticism from the Center for Science in the Public Interest, Ben & Jerry's will omit the term 'All Natural' from its labeling, however the firm reports it will continue to use the most natural ingredients they can find for its products.

10159 ■ **"Beverage Brand Vies To Be the Latest Purple Prince" in** *Brandweek* **(Vol. 49, April 21, 2008, No. 16, pp. 20)**
Pub: VNU Business Media, Inc.
Ed: Becky Ebenkamp. **Description:** Profile on the new beverage product Purple and its founder, Ted Farnsworth; Purple is a drink that blends seven

antioxidant-rich juices to create what Mr. Farnsworth calls a "Cascade Effect" that boosts antioxidants' effectiveness. Mr. Farnsworth is marketing the brand's Oxygen Radical Absorbance Capability (ORAC) which is a value of 7,600 compared with orange juice's 1,200.

10160 ■ **"Canine Cuisine: Tips for a Healthful Diet" in** *Seattle Times* **(September 13, 2008, pp. D9)**
Pub: Associated Press
Description: The American Kennel Club recommends feeding dogs food with balanced essential nutrients, including proteins, carbohydrates, fats, vitamins, minerals, and water; types of food, feeding practices and what not to feed a dog is discussed.

10161 ■ **"Careers in Organic Food Preparation" in** *Occupational Outlook Quarterly* **(Vol. 54, Fall 2010, No. 3, pp. 3)**
Pub: U.S. Bureau of Labor Statistics
Ed: Adam Bibler. **Description:** Organic methods of food production, including methods that combine science with traditional farming practices, are outlined. Facts regarding careers in organic food preparation are presented.

10162 ■ **"Drink Up" in** *Black Enterprise* **(Vol. 38, March 2008, No. 8, pp. 50)**
Pub: Earl G. Graves Publishing Co. Inc.
Ed: Tennille H. Robinson. **Description:** Advice is given to an individual seeking to start a natural juice small business, along with information for finding a bottling company.

10163 ■ **"Earth Angels" in** *Playthings* **(Vol. 106, September 1, 2008, No. 8, pp. 10)**
Pub: Reed Business Information
Ed: Karyn M. Peterson. **Description:** ImagiPlay toy company has partnered with Whole Foods Market to distribute the company's wooden playthings across the country. The company's Earth-friendly business model is outlined.

10164 ■ **"Effort Is Growing to Offer Healthier Choices in Vending Machines" in** *Philadelphia Inquirer* **(July 29, 2011)**
Pub: Philadelphia Media Network Inc.
Ed: Don Sapatkin. **Description:** Since Boston's mayor announced a ban on the sale of all sugar sweetened beverages on city properties, it seems more cities, states, hospitals, businesses, and even park systems are following suit. Thus, vending machines are beginning to offer healthier snacks and drinks to consumers.

10165 ■ **"Essentially Organic Vending Takes Healthy Snacks to Ohio High School" in** *Entertainment Close-Up* **(September 13, 2011)**
Pub: Close-Up Media
Description: Essentially Organic Vending is offering students a healthy alternative for their snacking. The vending machines will be stocked with nutritious energy options.

10166 ■ "Hain Celestial Acquires Greek Gods Yogurt" in *Ice Cream Reporter* (Vol. 23, July 20, 2010, No. 8, pp. 1)
Pub: Ice Cream Reporter
Description: Hain Celestial Group acquired The Greek Gods LLC. Hain Celestial is a natural and organic products company and Greek Gods makes all natural, Greek-style yogurt and ice cream.

10167 ■ "Half Empty or Half Full" in *Crain's Chicago Business* (Vol. 31, March 24, 2008, No. 12, pp. 4)
Pub: Crain Communications, Inc.
Ed: Meghan Streit. **Description:** Lifeway Foods Inc., the health food company which manufactures a yogurt-like drink called kefir, is being negatively affected by the soaring price of milk; however, the fact that probiotics are picking up in the market may mean that Lifeway stands a good chance of bouncing back and the company's lower share price could be an opportunity for long-term investors who have a tolerance for risk.

10168 ■ "Healthy Fast Food Acquires Rights to U-Swirl Yogurt" in *Ice Cream Reporter* (Vol. 21, October 20, 2008, No. 11, pp. 5)
Pub: Ice Cream Reporter
Description: Healthy Fast Food Inc. will acquire worldwide rights to U-Swirl Frozen Yogurt; the firm will use the new acquisition to create a yogurt superstore in a cafe setting concept for its operations.

10169 ■ "High Growth Reported for the Natural Supermarket Pet Department Close-Up" in *Canadian Corporate News* (October 20, 2008)
Pub: Comtex News Network Inc.
Description: Leading natural supermarket chains have been outperforming mainstream grocers by carrying natural and organic pet products. Statistical data included.

10170 ■ "His Way" in *Inc.* (February 2008, pp. 90-97)
Pub: Gruner & Jahr USA Publishing
Ed: Stephanie Clifford. **Description:** Profile of Chris Reed, founder of a natural soda company, who undertook an initial public offering (IPO). Reed discusses the challenges he faced mediating with the Securities Exchange Commission regarding his firm's IPO.

10171 ■ "In the Raw: Karyn Calabrese Brings Healthy Dining to a New Sophisticated Level" in *Black Enterprise* (Vol. 41, September 2010)
Pub: Earl G. Graves Publishing Co. Inc.
Ed: Sonia Alleyne. **Description:** Profile of Karyn Calabrese whose businesses are based in Chicago, Illinois. Calabrese has launched a complete line of products (vitamins and beauty items), services (spa, chiropractic, and acupuncture treatments), and restaurants to bring health dining and lifestyles to a better level.

10172 ■ "Loseley Dairy Ice Cream" in *Ice Cream Reporter* (Vol. 23, November 20, 2010, No. 12, pp. 8)
Pub: Ice Cream Reporter
Description: Neil Burchell has been named managing director of Loseley Dairy Ice Cream, one of the UK's largest independent producers. Burchell, with over 30 years experience in the food industry, was recently managing director of Rachel's, the leading organic dairy foods company in the UK, where he is credited with driving a sixfold increase in sales.

10173 ■ "Medicine Men" in *Canadian Business* (Vol. 80, February 12, 2007, No. 4, pp. 19)
Pub: Rogers Media
Ed: Joe Castaldo. **Description:** The effort of HPI Health Products' owners Dong Pedersen and Kent Pedersen to popularize their pain reliever product 'Lakota' is discussed.

10174 ■ "Moms Give More Thought to Nutrition" in *Marketing to Women* (Vol. 21, February 2008, No. 2, pp. 8)
Pub: EPM Communications, Inc.
Description: Moms are thinking more about nutritional issues than they did in the past and spending more time reading labels in the grocery store. 74 percent of moms consider the nutritional content of foods purchased for their children more now than they did two years ago.

10175 ■ "Need Fiber in Your Diet? Pour Some Milk" in *Globe & Mail* (April 10, 2007, pp. B7)
Pub: CTVglobemedia Publishing Inc.
Ed: William Illsey Atkinson. **Description:** The growing market and demand for functional foods and neutraceuticals in Canada is discussed. The research being conducted by University of Manitoba's Richardson Centre for Functional Foods and Nutraceuticals to explore new health compounds in food is highlighted.

10176 ■ "Net Profits: Get a Social Life" in *Entrepreneur* (Vol. 35, October 2007, No. 10, pp. 140)
Pub: Entrepreneur Media Inc.
Ed: Amanda C. Kooser. **Description:** Social networking sites such as Facebook and MySpace have millions of users, a sign that social networking is a growing industry. One way to enter this industry is target marketing, like Med3Q, a site for health-conscious individuals had done. How Med3q is earning through online advertising and sponsors is explained.

10177 ■ "New Recipes Added to IAMS Naturals Pet Food Line" in *MMR* (Vol. 28, August 1, 2011, No. 11, pp. 17)
Pub: Racher Press Inc.
Description: Procter & Gamble Company's IAMS brand has created a new pet food line called IAMS Naturals for pet owners wishing to feed their pets natural, wholesome food. IAMS Sensitive Naturals has ocean fish and its first ingredient for dogs with sensitivities. IAMS Simple & Natural features chicken with no fillers.

10178 ■ "New Zealand Natural Ice Cream is Opening a Second U.S. Scoop Shop" in *Ice Cream Reporter* (Vol. 21, October 20, 2008, No. 11, pp. 7)
Pub: Ice Cream Reporter
Description: New Zealand Natural Ice Cream is opening a second store in California. The company is a market leader in New Zealand and has gained distribution through 300 outlets in California.

10179 ■ "A Nice Consistency" in *Inc.* (Vol. 31, January-February 2009, No. 1, pp. 94)
Pub: Mansueto Ventures LLC
Ed: Jason Del Rey. **Description:** PJ Madison spent almost a quarter of its revenue promoting its latest product, organic ice cream. The Texas-based firm saw sales increase dramatically.

10180 ■ "Organic Dairy Farmers Wanted" in *Canadian Business* (Vol. 80, April 23, 2007, No. 9, pp. 11)
Pub: Rogers Media
Ed: Wendy Glauser. **Description:** The growth of the Harmony Organic due to demand for organic dairy products is presented.

10181 ■ "Organic Dog Treats" in *Veterinary Economics* (Vol. 49, November 2008, No. 11, pp. 52)
Pub: Advanstar Communications Inc.
Description: Wet Noses all-natural dog treats come in six flavors: dogranola, pumpkin, sweet potato curry, apples and carrots, cheddar, and peanut butter and molasses. The treats are made without animal by-products, added chemicals, preservatives, corn, soy or wheat.

10182 ■ "Perry's Goes Organic" in *Ice Cream Reporter* (Vol. 22, December 20, 2008, No. 1, pp. 1)
Pub: Ice Cream Reporter
Description: Family-owned Perry's Ice Cream is starting a new line of organic ice cream in both vanilla and chocolate flavors. All Perry's products are made with milk and cream from local dairy farmers.

10183 ■ "R&R Launches Upscale Spoony's and Low Fat Dragon's Den" in *Ice Cream Reporter* (Vol. 23, August 20, 2010, No. 9, pp. 3)
Pub: Ice Cream Reporter
Description: European ice cream manufacturer R&R has acquired French ice cream maker Rolland and will position itself as an upscale challenger to brands like Ben & Jerry's.

10184 ■ "A Recipe for Change" in *Canadian Business* (Vol. 80, October 22, 2007, No. 21, pp. 25)
Pub: Rogers Media
Ed: Erin Pooley. **Description:** Market conditions have changed and customers around the world are demanding low-fat alternatives. Labor costs have risen and so did the price of foodstuffs. The impacts of this on fast food restaurants as well as the measures they have taken to cope with the new demands are discussed.

10185 ■ "Red Mango Set to Grow in Florida" in *Ice Cream Reporter* (Vol. 23, September 20, 2010, No. 10, pp. 2)
Pub: Ice Cream Reporter
Description: Red Mango will add 12 new locations throughout Florida. The stores offer healthy, nutritious frozen yogurt, smoothies and parfaits.

10186 ■ "Secaucus-Based Freshpet is Barking Up the Right Tree" in *Record* (September 8, 2011)
Pub: North Jersey Media Group
Ed: Rebecca Olles. **Description:** Freshpet produces a variety of nutritious, refrigerated pet foods and treats for cats and dogs. The firm introduced five new recipes and treats to its grain-free line called Vital line. The Vital line mimics the ancestral diets of dogs and cats.

10187 ■ "Sodexo Updates Healthy Vending Program" in *Entertainment Close-Up* (September 25, 2011)
Pub: Close-Up Media
Description: Sodexo launched its Your Health Your Way On-the-Go program for its vending machines across the nation.

10188 ■ "A Switch in the Kitchen" in *Barron's* (Vol. 88, March 24, 2008, No. 12, pp. 17)
Pub: Dow Jones & Company, Inc.
Description: Men are doing more kitchen duties, with 18 percent of meals at home being made by men in 2007 compared to 11 percent four years previously. Young wives, however, choose to forgo work and stay at home.

10189 ■ "Tapping the 'Well' in Wellness" in *Pet Product News* (Vol. 64, November 2010, No. 11, pp. 1)
Pub: BowTie Inc.
Ed: Wendy-Bedwell Wilson. **Description:** Healthy food and treats are among the leading wellness products being sought by customers from specialty retailers to keep their pets healthy. With this demand for pet wellness products, retailers suggest making sure that staff know key ingredients to emphasize to customers. Other insights into this trend and ways to engage customers are discussed.

10190 ■ "Waste Not" in *Entrepreneur* (Vol. 36, April 2008, No. 4, pp. 21)
Pub: Entrepreneur Media, Inc.
Ed: JJ Ramberg. **Description:** RecycleBank is a company that provides homes with carts in which recyclables are thrown. An identification chip measures the amount of recyclables and converts them into points, which can be redeemed in stores, such as Starbucks and Whole Foods. RecycleBank earns revenue from cities that save landfill waste spending with the use of the program.

10191 ■ "Yogun Fruz Adds First Location in Southern New York State" in *Ice Cream Reporter* (Vol. 23, September 20, 2010, No. 10, pp. 2)
Pub: Ice Cream Reporter
Description: Yogen Fruz signed a master franchise agreement to expand into the southern counties of

New York State. The firm offers a healthy and beneficial option to fast food and typical dessert choices.

STATISTICAL SOURCES

10192 ■ *The Organic Food and Beverage Market*
Pub: Rector Press, Ltd.
Contact: Lewis Sckolnick, Pres
Released: 2009. **Price:** Contact Rector Press.

10193 ■ *Outlook For The Health and Natural Food Market*
Pub: Business Trend Analysts, Inc.
Released: 2005-2006. **Price:** $3795.00. **Description:** Covers the U.S. market for health and natural foods. Offers historical, current, and projected sales data; consumer demographics; strategies for advertising and promotion; product mix; distribution methods and patterns; and profiles of large industry competitors.

10194 ■ *RMA Annual Statement Studies*
Pub: Robert Morris Associates (RMA)
Released: Annual. **Price:** $175.00 2006-07 edition, $105.00. **Description:** Contains composite balance sheets and income statements for more than 360 industries, including the accounting, auditing, and bookkeeping industries. Also contains five years of comparative historical data for discerning trends. Includes 16 commonly used ratios, computed for most of the size groupings for nearly every industry.

TRADE PERIODICALS

10195 ■ *Natural Foods Merchandiser*
Pub: New Hope Natural Media
Contact: Pamela Bond, Managing Editor
E-mail: pamela.bond@penton.com
Ed: Anna Soref, Editor, anna.soref@penton.com. **Released:** Monthly. **Description:** Natural foods industry trade magazine.

10196 ■ *No Salt Week-The Newsletter*
Pub: Prosperity & Profits Unlimited, Distribution Services
Contact: A. Doyle
Ed: A. Doyle, Editor. **Released:** Annual. **Price:** $2, U.S.; $3, Canada; $4, elsewhere. **Description:** Presents possibilities for herb and spice blends that contain no added salt. Also contains ideas for cooking and much more.

10197 ■ *Nutrition Action Healthletter*
Pub: Center for Science in the Public Interest
Ed: Stephen Schmidt, Editor. **Released:** 10/year. **Description:** Covers food and nutrition, the food industry, and relevant government regulations and legislation. Focuses on the connections among diet, lifestyle, and disease. Includes nutritional comparisons of food products, reader questions and answers, and health-promoting recipies.

10198 ■ *The Tan Sheet*
Pub: F-D-C Reports Inc.
Contact: Ramsey Baghdadi, Managing Editor
Ed: Christopher Walker, Editor. **Released:** Weekly, 50/year. **Price:** $2,020, U.S. print and web. **Description:** Provides "in-depth coverage of nonprescription pharmaceuticals and dietary supplement/nutritionals." Topics include congressional hearings and legislation, business and marketing news, FDA recalls and seizures, regular listing of product trademarks, and activities of FTC, CPSC, and FDA.

10199 ■ *Whole Foods*
Pub: WFC Inc.
Contact: Kaylynn Chiarello-Ebner, Ed./Assoc. Publisher
E-mail: kaylynnebner@wfcinc.com
Released: Monthly, 2 in May. **Price:** $70; $80 two years in U.S.; $80 Canada and Mexico; $195 other countries. **Description:** Natural product retailer magazine.

FRANCHISES AND BUSINESS OPPORTUNITIES

10200 ■ Berrybrook Farm Franchising Inc.
1257 East Blvd.
Charlotte, NC 28203
Ph:(704)334-6528
Fax:(704)334-2299
No. of Franchise Units: 1. **Founded:** 1972. **Franchised:** 2005. **Description:** Natural foods, supplements, health and beauty aids and juice bar deli. **Equity Capital Needed:** $95,000-$175,000. **Franchise Fee:** $25,000. **Royalty Fee:** 5%. **Financial Assistance:** No. **Training:** Provides 16 days at headquarters, 14 days onsite with ongoing support.

10201 ■ Booster Juice
8915-51 Ave., Ste. 205
Edmonton, AB, Canada T6E 5J3
Ph:(780)440-6770
Fax:(416)621-2880
Co. E-mail: franchise@boosterjuice.com
URL: http://www.boosterjuice.com
No. of Franchise Units: 260. **No. of Company-Owned Units:** 2. **Founded:** 1999. **Franchised:** 1999. **Description:** Serves fresh juice and sells a health food concept. **Equity Capital Needed:** $237,000-$265,000 turn-key, $85,000-&95,000 start-up capital required. **Franchise Fee:** $20,000. **Training:** Training includes 2 weeks at head office and ongoing support.

10202 ■ Sangster's Health Centres
2218 Hanselman Ave.
Saskatoon, SK, Canada S7L 6A4
Ph:(306)653-4481
Fax:(306)653-4688
No. of Franchise Units: 36. **No. of Company-Owned Units:** 5. **Founded:** 1971. **Franchised:** 1978. **Description:** Retail sale of vitamins, herbs, natural cosmetics, natural foods, body building and supplies, specializing in their own name-brand products and also national company brands. **Equity Capital Needed:** $30,000 minimum. **Franchise Fee:** $25,000. **Financial Assistance:** No. **Training:** Yes.

10203 ■ Smoothie King Franchises, Inc.
121 Park Pl.
Covington, LA 70433
Ph:(985)635-6973
Fax:(985)635-6987
No. of Franchise Units: 560. **No. of Company-Owned Units:** 1. **Founded:** 1973. **Franchised:** 1989. **Description:** Smoothie King centers offer guests the industry's first, original nutritional fruit and function based fresh-blended smoothies. Each "Lifestyle Center" also offers healthy retail product solutions, including sports beverages, energy bars, healthy snacks, vitamin supplements, herbs, minerals and other sports nutrition products. **Equity Capital Needed:** $50,000-$60,000. **Franchise Fee:** $25,000. **Financial Assistance:** Third party financing available. **Training:** Provides 1 day pre-opening (orientation), 14 days management training at Corporate store, 8 days store opening (14 days before open & 4 days after opening) onsite. Assistance in real estate, design and construction.

10204 ■ Uncle Louie G, Inc.
101M Ellis Rd.
Staten Island, NY 10307
Ph:(718)966-3763
Fax:(718)966-3764
No. of Company-Owned Units: 51. **Founded:** 1998. **Franchised:** 1999. **Description:** Handmade in state of the art factory. **Equity Capital Needed:** $30,000-$75,000 costs to open. **Franchise Fee:** $7,500. **Financial Assistance:** Yes. **Training:** Yes.

COMPUTERIZED DATABASES

10205 ■ *Consumer Buying Power*
The Nielsen Co.
770 Broadway
New York, NY 10003-9595
URL: http://www.claritas.com/sitereports/default.jsp
Description: Contains current-year estimates and 5-year projections of total household expenditures for more than 350 product categories, including goods and services, and 73 summary categories. Provides estimated potential consumer expenditures by store types for 41 retail store types, such as eating places; furniture; grocery; shoes; and sporting goods; as well as a breakdown of average household expenditures, such as apparel; education; electronic devices; food at home; furniture; major appliances; medical expenses; and personal care. Also includes average household expenditures for 53 Yellow Page headings. **Availability:** Online: The Nielsen Co. **Type:** Statistical.

LIBRARIES

10206 ■ American Dietetic Association–Knowledge Center
120 S. Riverside Plaza, Ste. 20000
Chicago, IL 60606-6995
Ph:(312)877-1600, x4864
Free: 800-877-1600
Co. E-mail: knowledge@eatright.org
URL: http://www.eatright.org/
Contact: Margaret Williams, Info.Spec./Libn.
Scope: Nutrition, dietetics, food service. **Services:** Interlibrary loan; copying; Library open to the public by appointment. **Holdings:** 3000 books. **Subscriptions:** 60 journals and other serials; 4 newspapers.

10207 ■ Geisinger Medical Center–Community Health Library
100 N. Academy Ave.
Danville, PA 17822-4401
Ph:(570)271-5638
Fax:(570)271-5635
Co. E-mail: chrl@geisinger.edu
URL: http://www.geisinger.edu
Contact: Patricia A Ulmer, Commun.Hea.Libn.
Scope: General medicine, nutrition, alternative and complementary medicine, pediatrics, cancer, AIDS. **Services:** Interlibrary loan. **Holdings:** 860 books; 200 audio/visual materials. **Subscriptions:** 14 journals and other serials.

10208 ■ Lemmen-Holton Cancer Pavilion Library
135 Michigan NE
330 Barclay Ave., NE
Grand Rapids, MI 49503
Ph:(616)391-1655
Fax:(616)391-3527
Co. E-mail: diane.hummel@spectrum-health.org
URL: http://www.spectrum-health.org/
Contact: Diane Hummel, Lib.Mgr.
Scope: Cancer. **Services:** Library open to the public. **Holdings:** Pamphlets.

10209 ■ New York Public Library–Mid-Manhattan Library–General Reference and Advisory Services/Health Information Center (455 5)
455 5th Ave. at 40th St.
New York, NY 10016
Ph:(212)340-0863
URL: http://www.nypl.org/branch/central/mml
Contact: Wol Sue Lee, Dept.Hd.
Scope: Consumer, health medicine, nursing, allied health. **Services:** Copying; Library open to the public. **Holdings:** 22,000 books and videocassettes; 4 VF of pamphlets. **Subscriptions:** 278 journals and other serials.

10210 ■ Price-Pottenger Nutrition Foundation Library
7890 Broadway
Lemon Grove, CA 91945
Ph:(619)462-7600
Free: 800-366-3748
Fax:(619)433-3136
Co. E-mail: info@ppnf.org
URL: http://www.ppnf.org/catalog/ppnf/ReferenceLibrary.htm
Contact: Joan Grinzi, Exec.Dir.
Scope: Nutrition, preventative medicine, health, natural farming and gardening, pesticides, fluoride, mercury, dental health, natural farming and gardening, natural pet care, traditional/historic diets, primitive diets, holistic medicine. **Services:** Copying; Library open to members only for reference use.

Holdings: 10,000 volumes; 18,000 film positives; 6000 glass lantern slides; scientific reprints; video and audio tapes; reports; archives. **Subscriptions:** Journals and other serials.

10211 ■ U.S.D.A.–National Agricultural Library–Food and Nutrition Information Center (10301)
10301 Baltimore Ave., Rm. 105
Beltsville, MD 20705-2351

Ph:(301)504-5414
Fax:(301)504-6409
URL: http://fnic.nal.usda.gov
Contact: Dennis Smith, Info.Ctr.Coord.
Scope: Human nutrition education, nutrition resources for USDA food and nutrition programs. **Services:** Interlibrary loan; Center open to the public with restricted lending. **Holdings:** 50,000 books; VF drawers. **Subscriptions:** 200 journals and other serials.

10212 ■ Voice for Animals, Inc. Library
PO Box 120095
San Antonio, TX 78212
Ph:(210)737-3138
Co. E-mail: voice@voiceforanimals.org
URL: http://www.voiceforanimals.org/

Scope: Animal rights; vegetarianism. **Services:** Library not open to the public. **Holdings:** 200 books; newsletters; videocassettes.

START-UP INFORMATION

10213 ■ **"Ahead of the Pack"** in *Small Business Opportunities* **(Fall 2010)**
Pub: Harris Publications Inc.
Description: Profile of an organic fast-food business that is carving out a niche that is gaining favor. Elevation Burger is a unique concept offering healthier burgers in sustainable buildings.

10214 ■ **"Organic Chain Scouting Tri-State Sites, Including Kenwood"** in *Business Courier* **(Vol. 27, December 3, 2010, No. 31, pp. 1)**
Pub: Business Courier
Ed: Tom Demeropolis. **Description:** Asheville, North Carolina-based Earth Fare has been planning to add a total of six stores in 2011, including the potential opening of more than one store in the Greater Cincinnati area market. Earth Fare has not named specific locations but Kenwood area was reportedly being considered for its first location. Insights on growing trends toward health food stores are also given.

10215 ■ **"Vitamins to Spice Up Food"** in *Philadelphia Business Journal* **(Vol. 28, October 2, 2009, No. 33, pp. 1)**
Pub: American City Business Journals
Ed: John George. **Description:** VitaminSpice, a startup company established by Ed Bukstel, makes a line of spice and vitamin blends that come in seasoning form. The form of the blends could facilitate easier ingestion of vitamins into people's diets. A reverse merger that will allow a publicly-traded company status for VitaminSpice will be accomplished by early October 2009.

ASSOCIATIONS AND OTHER ORGANIZATIONS

10216 ■ **Canadian Health Food Association–Association Canadienne des Aliements de Sante**
235 Yorkland Blvd., Ste. 302
Toronto, ON, Canada M2J 4Y8
Ph:(416)497-6939
Free: 800-661-4510
Fax:(416)497-3214
Co. E-mail: info@chfa.ca
URL: http://www.chfa.ca
Contact: Penelope Marrett, Pres./CEO
Description: Represents producers and distributors of health foods. Seeks to advance the health food industries. Facilitates communication and cooperation among members; represents the commercial and regulatory interests of the health food industries; sponsors educational and promotional programs. **Publications:** *The Natural Voice* (5/year).

10217 ■ **Canadian Restaurant and Foodservices Association–Association Canadienne des Restaurateurs et des Services Alimentaires**
316 Bloor St. W
Toronto, ON, Canada M5S 1W5
Ph:(416)923-8416

Free: 800-387-5649
Fax:(416)923-1450
Co. E-mail: info@crfa.ca
URL: http://www.crfa.ca
Contact: Garth Whyte, Pres./CEO
Description: Restaurant and food service corporations, hotels, caterers, and food service suppliers and educators. Seeks to create a favorable business environment for members. Represents members' interests before government; conducts trade research. Makes available group buying programs and other services to members; owns and operates three industry trade shows. **Publications:** *Canadian Foodservice Industry Operations Report* (biennial); *Foodservice Facts* (annual); *Legislation Guide* (quarterly).

10218 ■ **National Restaurant Association**
1200 17th St. NW
Washington, DC 20036
Ph:(202)331-5900
Free: 800-424-5156
Fax:(202)331-2429
URL: http://www.restaurant.org
Contact: Sally Smith, Chair
Description: Represents restaurants, cafeterias, clubs, contract foodservice management, drive-ins, caterers, institutional food services and other members of the foodservice industry; also represents establishments belonging to non-affiliated state and local restaurant associations in governmental affairs. Supports foodservice education and research in several educational institutions. Is affiliated with the Educational Foundation of the National Restaurant Association to provide training and education for operators, food and equipment manufacturers, distributors and educators. Has 300,000 member locations. **Publications:** *National Restaurant Association—Washington Report* (semimonthly).

REFERENCE WORKS

10219 ■ **"Beverage Brand Vies To Be the Latest Purple Prince"** in *Brandweek* **(Vol. 49, April 21, 2008, No. 16, pp. 20)**
Pub: VNU Business Media, Inc.
Ed: Becky Ebenkamp. **Description:** Profile on the new beverage product Purple and its founder, Ted Farnsworth; Purple is a drink that blends seven antioxidant-rich juices to create what Mr. Farnsworth calls a "Cascade Effect" that boosts antioxidants' effectiveness. Mr. Farnsworth is marketing the brand's Oxygen Radical Absorbance Capability (ORAC) which is a value of 7,600 compared with orange juice's 1,200.

10220 ■ **"Careers in Organic Food Preparation"** in *Occupational Outlook Quarterly* **(Vol. 54, Fall 2010, No. 3, pp. 3)**
Pub: U.S. Bureau of Labor Statistics
Ed: Adam Bibler. **Description:** Organic methods of food production, including methods that combine science with traditional farming practices, are outlined. Facts regarding careers in organic food preparation are presented.

10221 ■ **Directory of High Volume Independent Restaurants**
Pub: Chain Store Guide
Released: Annual, Latest edition 2010. **Price:** $1,375, individuals online pro plus; $1,075, individuals online pro; $445, individuals online lite. **Covers:** Approximately 4,400 independently owned restaurants with annual sales of at least $1 million. **Entries Include:** Company name, address, phone and fax numbers, e-mail and web addresses; total annual sales; average check amount; type of food service; menu type; alcohol types served; catering services indicator; food wholesaler name and location; year founded; key personnel with titles. **Arrangement:** Geographical. **Indexes:** Alphabetical, exclusions.

10222 ■ **"Drink Up"** in *Black Enterprise* **(Vol. 38, March 2008, No. 8, pp. 50)**
Pub: Earl G. Graves Publishing Co. Inc.
Ed: Tennille H. Robinson. **Description:** Advice is given to an individual seeking to start a natural juice small business, along with information for finding a bottling company.

10223 ■ **"Effort Is Growing to Offer Healthier Choices in Vending Machines"** in *Philadelphia Inquirer* **(July 29, 2011)**
Pub: Philadelphia Media Network Inc.
Ed: Don Sapatkin. **Description:** Since Boston's mayor announced a ban on the sale of all sugar sweetened beverages on city properties, it seems more cities, states, hospitals, businesses, and even park systems are following suit. Thus, vending machines are beginning to offer healthier snacks and drinks to consumers.

10224 ■ **"Essentially Organic Vending Takes Healthy Snacks to Ohio High School"** in *Entertainment Close-Up* **(September 13, 2011)**
Pub: Close-Up Media
Description: Essentially Organic Vending is offering students a healthy alternative for their snacking. The vending machines will be stocked with nutritious energy options.

10225 ■ **"Hain Celestial Acquires Greek Gods Yogurt"** in *Ice Cream Reporter* **(Vol. 23, July 20, 2010, No. 8, pp. 1)**
Pub: Ice Cream Reporter
Description: Hain Celestial Group acquired The Greek Gods LLC. Hain Celestial is a natural and organic products company and Greek Gods makes all natural, Greek-style yogurt and ice cream.

10226 ■ **"Healthy Fast Food Acquires Rights to U-Swirl Yogurt"** in *Ice Cream Reporter* **(Vol. 21, October 20, 2008, No. 11, pp. 5)**
Pub: Ice Cream Reporter
Description: Healthy Fast Food Inc. will acquire worldwide rights to U-Swirl Frozen Yogurt; the firm will use the new acquisition to create a yogurt superstore in a cafe setting concept for its operations.

10227 ■ **"In the Raw: Karyn Calabrese Brings Healthy Dining to a New Sophisticated Level"** in *Black Enterprise* **(Vol. 41, September 2010)**
Pub: Earl G. Graves Publishing Co. Inc.
Ed: Sonia Alleyne. **Description:** Profile of Karyn Calabrese whose businesses are based in Chicago, Il-

linois. Calabrese has launched a complete line of products (vitamins and beauty items), services (spa, chiropractic, and acupuncture treatments), and restaurants to bring health dining and lifestyles to a better level.

10228 ■ "New Zealand Natural Ice Cream is Opening a Second U.S. Scoop Shop" in *Ice Cream Reporter* **(Vol. 21, October 20, 2008, No. 11, pp. 7)**

Pub: Ice Cream Reporter

Description: New Zealand Natural Ice Cream is opening a second store in California. The company is a market leader in New Zealand and has gained distribution through 300 outlets in California.

10229 ■ "Organic Dairy Farmers Wanted" in *Canadian Business* **(Vol. 80, April 23, 2007, No. 9, pp. 11)**

Pub: Rogers Media

Ed: Wendy Glauser. **Description:** The growth of the Harmony Organic due to demand for organic dairy products is presented.

10230 ■ "R&R Launches Upscale Spoony's and Low Fat Dragon's Den" in *Ice Cream Reporter* **(Vol. 23, August 20, 2010, No. 9, pp. 3)**

Pub: Ice Cream Reporter

Description: European ice cream manufacturer R&R has acquired French ice cream maker Rolland and will position itself as an upscale challenger to brands like Ben & Jerry's.

10231 ■ "A Recipe for Change" in *Canadian Business* **(Vol. 80, October 22, 2007, No. 21, pp. 25)**

Pub: Rogers Media

Ed: Erin Pooley. **Description:** Market conditions have changed and customers around the world are demanding low-fat alternatives. Labor costs have risen and so did the price of foodstuffs. The impacts of this on fast food restaurants as well as the measures they have taken to cope with the new demands are discussed.

10232 ■ "Red Mango Set to Grow in Florida" in *Ice Cream Reporter* **(Vol. 23, September 20, 2010, No. 10, pp. 2)**

Pub: Ice Cream Reporter

Description: Red Mango will add 12 new locations throughout Florida. The stores offer healthy, nutritious frozen yogurt, smoothies and parfaits.

10233 ■ "Sodexo Updates Healthy Vending Program" in *Entertainment Close-Up* **(September 25, 2011)**

Pub: Close-Up Media

Description: Sodexo launched its Your Health Your Way On-the-Go program for its vending machines across the nation.

10234 ■ "Turmoil Means Changes For Retailers" in *The Business Journal-Serving Metropolitan Kansas City* **(Vol. 27, October 10, 2008, No. 4)**

Pub: American City Business Journals, Inc.

Ed: Suzanna Stagemeyer. **Description:** Impacts of the financial crisis on Kansas Metropolitan Area retailers are varied. Rob Dalzell, for instance, found it difficult to secure a loan for his new self-serve yogurt store Yummo. The trends in retailing in the area are examined further as well as ways in which local businesses are changing in an attempt to stay solvent during the economic downturn.

10235 ■ "Yogun Fruz Adds First Location in Southern New York State" in *Ice Cream Reporter* **(Vol. 23, September 20, 2010, No. 10, pp. 2)**

Pub: Ice Cream Reporter

Description: Yogen Fruz signed a master franchise agreement to expand into the southern counties of New York State. The firm offers a healthy and beneficial option to fast food and typical dessert choices.

TRADE PERIODICALS

10236 ■ *Chef*
Pub: Talcott Communication Corp.
Released: 11/yr. **Price:** $32; $47 two years; $64 3 years; $43 Canada; $96 other countries. **Description:** Food information for chefs.

10237 ■ *ConcepTrac*
Pub: Technomic Information Services
Ed: Eric Giandelone, Editor, egiandelone@technomic.com. **Released:** Monthly. **Price:** $395, individuals. **Description:** Provides news on chain restaurant development. Includes information on decor, atmosphere, service styles, cooking preparation methods, and unit economics.

10238 ■ *Cooking for Profit*
Pub: CP Publishing, Inc.
Released: Monthly. **Price:** $30; $55 two years; $52 Canada; $98 Canada 2 years; $85 other countries; $160 other countries 2 years. **Description:** Food service trade publication for owners/operators of food service businesses. Profiles successful operations, offers management tips, recipes with photos and step-by-step instructions, new and improved uses and maintenance of gas equipment.

10239 ■ *Foodservice and Hospitality Magazine*
Pub: Kostuch Publications Ltd.
Contact: Mitch Kostuch, Pres. and Gp. Publisher
E-mail: mkostuch@foodservice.ca
Released: Monthly. **Price:** $55 Canada; $80 U.S.; $100 other countries. **Description:** Magazine for restaurant and hotel operators.

10240 ■ *Le Chef du Service Alimentaire*
Pub: Le Chef D.S.A. Inc.
Contact: Johanne Talbot
E-mail: jtalbot@magazinelechef.com
Released: Bimonthly. **Price:** $44.95; $74.95 two years; $87.95 3 years. **Description:** Magazine serving the foodservice and restaurant industries in Quebec.

10241 ■ *Midwest Food Network*
Pub: Pinnacle Publishing Group
Contact: Anthony Fulton, Production
E-mail: afulton@midwestfoodservicenews.com
Released: Bimonthly. **Price:** $24 Free to qualified subscribers; $24 others. **Description:** Food service trade magazine featuring new products and suppliers and other industry news including food news, restaurant association updates, news of chefs, restaurant concepts, earnings, and openings and closings.

10242 ■ *No Salt Week-The Newsletter*
Pub: Prosperity & Profits Unlimited, Distribution Services
Contact: A. Doyle
Ed: A. Doyle, Editor. **Released:** Annual. **Price:** $2, U.S.; $3, Canada; $4, elsewhere. **Description:** Presents possibilities for herb and spice blends that contain no added salt. Also contains ideas for cooking and much more.

10243 ■ *Restaurant Business*
Pub: VNU Business Publications
Contact: Scott Allmendinger, Gp. Publisher
E-mail: sallmendinger@idealmediallc.com
Released: Monthly. **Price:** $119; $212 Canada; $468 other countries rest of the world. **Description:** Trade magazine for restaurants and commercial food service.

10244 ■ *Restaurant Hospitality*
Pub: Penton Media Inc.
Contact: Michael Sanson, Editor-in-Chief
E-mail: msanson@penton.com
Released: Monthly. **Description:** Dedicated to the success of full service restaurants and edited for chefs and other commercial foodservice professionals. Includes new food and equipment products and trends, menu and recipe ideas, industry news, new technology, food safety, emerging new concepts, consumer attitudes and trends, labor and training, and profiles of successful operations.

10245 ■ *Sunbelt Foodservice*
Pub: Shelby Publishing Company Inc.
Contact: Stormie Ellwanger, Director
E-mail: stormie@shelbypublishing.com
Released: Monthly. **Price:** $36; $60 two years. **Description:** Trade newspaper (tabloid) covering the food industry geared toward restaurant operators.

10246 ■ *Vegetarian Journal*
Pub: The Vegetarian Resource Group
Ed: Charles Stahler, Editor. **Released:** Quarterly. **Price:** $20, members; $32, Canada and Mexico; $42, elsewhere. **Description:** Focuses on the ethical and nutritional aspects of vegetarianism, as well as health, ecology, animal rights, and world hunger. Recurring features include product reviews, recipes, a calendar of events, and reviews of scientific and informational articles.

10247 ■ *Vegetarian Journal's Foodservice Update*
Pub: The Vegetarian Resource Group
Ed: Nancy Berkoff, R.D., Editor. **Released:** Quarterly. **Price:** $20, U.S. **Description:** Provides information about serving vegetarian meals in institutions. Includes advice and recipes.

VIDEOCASSETTES/ AUDIOCASSETTES

10248 ■ *Healthy Habits Video Series*
Cambridge Educational
c/o Films Media Group
132 West 31st Street, 17th Floor
Ste. 124
New York, NY 10001
Free: 800-257-5126
Fax:(609)671-0266
Co. E-mail: custserve@films.com
URL: http://www.cambridgeol.com
Price: $139.95. **Description:** Five-part series offering educational information and health tips on the importance of proper nutrition. Discusses such topics as cooking, cholesterol, good and bad foods, vitamins, and food allergies. **Availability:** VHS.

TRADE SHOWS AND CONVENTIONS

10249 ■ ApEx
Canadian Restaurant and Food Services Association
316 Bloor St. W.
Toronto, ON, Canada M5S 1W5
Ph:(416)923-8416
Free: 800-387-5649
Fax:(416)923-1450
Co. E-mail: info@crfa.ca
URL: http://www.crfa.ca
Audience: Trade. **Principal Exhibits:** Products and services for the restaurant and hospitality industry, as well as institutions, convenience stores, delis and bakeries. **Dates and Locations:** 2011 Apr 03-04, Moncton, NB.

10250 ■ International Restaurant & Foodservice Show of New York
Reed Exhibitions North American Headquarters
383 Main Ave.
Norwalk, CT 06851
Ph:(203)840-4800
Fax:(203)840-5805
Co. E-mail: export@reedexpo.com
URL: http://www.reedexpo.com
Released: Annual. **Principal Exhibits:** Equipment, supplies, and services for the food products, foodservice, restaurant, and institutional food service industries.

10251 ■ Michigan Restaurant Show
Michigan Restaurant Association
225 W. Washtenaw St.
Lansing, MI 48933
Ph:(517)482-5244
Free: 800-968-9668

Fax:(517)482-7663
URL: http://www.michiganrestaurant.org
Released: Annual. **Principal Exhibits:** Equipment, supplies, and services for the food service industry.

10252 ■ Natural Products Expo East
New Hope Natural Media
1401 Pearl St.
Boulder, CO 80302-5346
Ph:(303)939-8440
Fax:(303)998-9020
Co. E-mail: info@newhope.com
URL: http://www.newhope.com
Released: Annual. **Audience:** Retailers, wholesalers, distributors, and brokers from the natural products industry. **Principal Exhibits:** Natural, organic and environmentally sound products, including: alternative health care, vegetarian and allergy-free personal care recycled/recyclable products, biodegradable products, and organic meats. **Dates and Locations:** 2011 Sep 21-24, Baltimore, MD.

10253 ■ West Ex: The Rocky Mountain Regional Hospitality Exposition
Colorado Restaurant Association
430 E. 7th Ave.
Denver, CO 80203
Ph:(303)830-2972
Free: 800-522-2972
Fax:(303)830-2973
Co. E-mail: info@coloradorestaurant.com
URL: http://www.coloradorestaurant.com
Released: Annual. **Audience:** Food service and restaurant industry personnel. **Principal Exhibits:** Food service and lodging products, equipment, and services.

10254 ■ Western Food Service & Hospitality Expo Los Angeles
California Restaurant Association
1011 10th St.
Sacramento, CA 95814
Ph:(916)447-5793
Free: 800-765-4842
Fax:(916)447-6182
URL: http://www.calrest.org
Audience: Food service hospitality and lodging industry professionals. **Principal Exhibits:** Food, equipment, supplies, and services for food service and lodging industries. **Dates and Locations:** 2011 Aug 28-30, San Diego, CA.

CONSULTANTS

10255 ■ Birchfield Jacobs Foodsystems Inc.
519 N Charles St., Ste. 350A
Baltimore, MD 21201-5022
Ph:(410)528-8700
Fax:(410)528-6060
URL: http://www.birchfieldjacobs.com
Contact: Robert Jacobs, Principle
E-mail: rjacobs@atsbirchfieldjacobs.com
Scope: Food facilities design consultants for colleges; universities; schools; healthcare facilities; government; military; correctional; country clubs and restaurants. Services include facilities design; feasibility studies; operations analysis and master planning.

10256 ■ GEC Consultants Inc.
4604 Birchwood Ave.
Skokie, IL 60076-3835
Ph:(847)674-6310
Fax:(847)674-3946
Co. E-mail: experts@gecconsultants.com
URL: http://www.gecconsultants.com
Contact: Lloyd M. Gordon, CEO
E-mail: legal@gecconsultants.com
Scope: Consulting in all areas of bar and restaurant operations. Restaurant manager development appraises existing locations or sites. Studies the feasibility of projects. Develop new concepts. Assist in expanding, existing food operations, marketing, expert witness (legal) for hospitality/restaurant industry. **Publications:** "How You Can Fight Back to Minimize This Recession!"; "New Thoughts On Leases"; "The Use of Job Analysis to Actually Reduce

Payroll Costs"; "Do You Need a Feasibility Study?"; "Combat Negative Hospitality"; "How To Run A Successful Night club"; "Are Capitalists In Your Cabinet?"; "Marketing For The 21st Century"; "Profitability In The Banquet Industry"; "Starting a Restaurant, Bar or Catering Business"; "How To Find And Retain Suitable Employees"; "26 Things To Do To Plan A Restaurant"; "Wall Fabric or Paint: Decor Magic It's Your Call"; "The Art of Cafe Ambiance"; "Why You Need A Consultant". **Seminars:** How to increase restaurant profit, Member MSPC Speakers Bureau; Raising Capital for New Development and Expansion.

10257 ■ L G Anthony Associates
40 Wellington Blvd.
Reading, PA 19610
Ph:(610)670-0477
Contact: Louis G. Anthony, Owner
Scope: Provides food service facility planning, layout and design, including equipment selection and specification. Also offers management systems and operations analysis, such as the development of operating policies and procedures. Firm can design menu planning and recipe development, food selection and specification, work simplification, service, and quality control around current concepts in the field. Industries served: hospital, nursing home, restaurant, group homes; commercial and institutional food service industries. **Seminars:** Food Service Sanitation; Menu Planning; Work Simplification; Quality Control in Food Service.

10258 ■ Linda Lipsky Restaurant Consultants Inc.
216 Foxcroft Rd.
PO Box 489
Broomall, PA 19008
Ph:(610)325-3663
Free: 877-425-3663
Fax:(610)325-3329
Co. E-mail: lipsky@restaurantconsult.com
URL: http://www.restaurantconsult.com
Contact: Linda J. Lipsky, President
E-mail: lipsky@restaurantconsult.com
Scope: Helps food and beverage operations achieve their highest level of profits, product consistency and service quality. Concentrates on implementing cost cutting measures, developing training programs for both front and heart of the house employees, engineering menus, performing Spotter's reports and creating organizational manuals and procedures for restaurant, bar, hotel, banquet facility, country clubs, or caterer. Key areas of specialization include on site operations evaluations to identify in effective cost controls, flaws in the organizational structure and inadequacies of management systems, policies and procedures; profit enhancement as a result of implementing cost-cutting measures in all prime cost areas; server training, sales incentive training, and management training and evaluation programs; recipe documentation, cost analysis, menu pricing and menu copy writing; competitive market surveys and market positioning analysis, and bridge management. **Seminars:** Designing Menus for Maximum Sales and Profits; How to Maximize Your Check Average; Going Beyond Your Customer's Expectations; Seeing Your Restaurant Through a Customer's Eyes; Making the Best First and Last Impression; Basic Training in Kitchen Management Techniques; Basic Training in Bar Management Techniques; Make Every Labor Dollar Count; Back to Basics/More Than Shift Management; Conducting Your Own In-House Inspection; Basics of Sanitation Training for Kitchen Employees; Basics of Sanitation Training for Dining Room Employees.

FRANCHISES AND BUSINESS OPPORTUNITIES

10259 ■ Evos
609 S Howard Ave.
Tampa, FL 33606
Ph:(813)258-0005
Free: 877-888-3867

Fax:(727)391-2435
No. of Franchise Units: 5. **No. of Company-Owned Units:** 3. **Founded:** 1999. **Franchised:** 2006. **Description:** Healthy fast food. **Equity Capital Needed:** $350,000-$440,000. **Franchise Fee:** $35,000. **Royalty Fee:** 5.5%. **Financial Assistance:** Limited third party financing available. **Training:** Provides 4-6 weeks training at headquarters and ongoing support.

10260 ■ Ho-Lee-Chow
GCF Food Services Inc.
5415 Dundas St. W, Ste. 110
Toronto, ON, Canada M9B 1B5
Ph:(416)778-8028
Fax:(416)778-6818
Co. E-mail: holeechow@holeechow.com
URL: http://www.holeechow.com
No. of Franchise Units: 18. **No. of Company-Owned Units:** 3. **Founded:** 1989. **Franchised:** 1989. **Description:** Quick-food service industry catering fresh, attractive, delicious and healthful, low in additives and free of MSG, Chinese food with a quality product and impeccable standards of preparation and delivery. **Equity Capital Needed:** $175,000. **Franchise Fee:** Included in turn-key package. **Training:** Offers 4-6 weeks and ongoing support provided.

10261 ■ Indigos Fruit Smoothies
Indigos Franchising, Inc.
21551 Arbor Way
Boca Raton, FL 33433
Ph:(407)383-3872
No. of Franchise Units: 9. **Founded:** 2004. **Franchised:** 2004. **Description:** Retail smoothie/juice bar & healthy restaurant. **Equity Capital Needed:** $89,800-$272,000. **Franchise Fee:** $25,000. **Royalty Fee:** 6&. **Financial Assistance:** Limited third party financing available. **Training:** Includes 6 days training at headquarters, 7 days at franchisee's location and ongoing support.

10262 ■ Pockets Restaurant
1001 Green Bay Rd., Ste. 237
Winnetka, IL 60093
Ph:(847)242-0738
Fax:(847)242-0739
No. of Franchise Units: 2. **No. of Company-Owned Units:** 10. **Founded:** 1989. **Franchised:** 2007. **Description:** Fast food; healthy choices. **Equity Capital Needed:** $150,000 in liquid assets; $300,000 net worth. **Franchise Fee:** $25,000-$30,000. **Financial Assistance:** No. **Training:** Yes.

10263 ■ Subway
Franchise Sales Dept.
325 Bic Dr.
Milford, CT 06460
Ph:(203)877-4281
Free: 800-888-4848
Fax:(203)783-7325
Co. E-mail: franchise@subway.com
URL: http://www.subway.com
No. of Franchise Units: 33,000. **No. of Company-Owned Units:** 1. **Founded:** 1974. **Franchised:** 1974. **Description:** Submarine sandwich category with fresh, great tasting, made-for-you sandwiches and salads, many of which have 6 grams of fat or less. Offering a healthful alternative to fatty fast food has made Subway a popular destination for health-conscious consumers. **Equity Capital Needed:** $114,800-$258,300 total investment. **Franchise Fee:** $15,000. **Financial Assistance:** Third party financing, and equipment leasing is available for qualified franchisees. **Training:** Provides training and assistance to franchisees in all areas of business operation.

10264 ■ Vitality Juice, Java & Smoothie Bar
790 Florida St., Ste. 1
Mandeville, LA 70448
Ph:(985)674-6898
Fax:(985)674-4464
No. of Franchise Units: 4. **No. of Company-Owned Units:** 2. **Founded:** 2004. **Franchised:** 2005. **Description:** Smoothies, juices, coffee and vitamins.

Equity Capital Needed: $128,000-$393,500. **Franchise Fee:** $15,000-$35,000. **Royalty Fee:** 5%. **Financial Assistance:** Third party financing available. **Training:** Offers 2 weeks training at headquarters, 1 week onsite and ongoing as needed at any location.

COMPUTERIZED DATABASES

10265 ■ *Food Code - Recommendations of the United States Public Health Service Food and Drug Administration*
U.S. Department of Health and Human Services
10903 New Hampshire Ave.
Silver Spring, MD 20993-0002
Free: 888-INFO-FDA
URL: http://www.fda.gov
Description: Contains information on progress made in monitoring and preventing food borne diseases, including requirements for safeguarding public health. Provides clarification of the food code based on advances in science and reflective of new technologies. Corresponds in part to the printed version *Food Code*, but the electronic version includes 2 additional manuals. **Availability:** Online: U.S. Department of Health and Human Services; CD-ROM: U.S. Department of Commerce; Diskette: U.S. Department of Commerce. **Type:** Full text.

LIBRARIES

10266 ■ American Dietetic Association–Knowledge Center
120 S. Riverside Plaza, Ste. 20000
Chicago, IL 60606-6995
Ph:(312)877-1600, x4864
Free: 800-877-1600
Co. E-mail: knowledge@eatright.org
URL: http://www.eatright.org/
Contact: Margaret Williams, Info.Spec./Libn.
Scope: Nutrition, dietetics, food service. **Services:** Interlibrary loan; copying; Library open to the public by appointment. **Holdings:** 3000 books. **Subscriptions:** 60 journals and other serials; 4 newspapers.

10267 ■ California Culinary Academy Library
625 Polk St.
San Francisco, CA 94102
Ph:800-229-2433
Free: 888-897-3222
Co. E-mail: bgk@baychef.com
URL: http://www.baychef.com
Contact: Beth Klein, Dean, Lib.Svcs.
Scope: Culinary arts, nutrition, restaurant and hospitality industry. **Services:** Library open to the public by special appointment only. **Holdings:** 3500 books. **Subscriptions:** 90 journals and other serials.

10268 ■ City College of San Francisco Culinary Arts and Hospitality Studies Department–Alice Statler Library
50 Phelan Ave.
Statler Wing, Rm. 10
San Francisco, CA 94112
Ph:(415)239-3460
Fax:(415)239-3026
Co. E-mail: aniosi@ccsf.edu
URL: http://www.ccsf.edu/library/alice/statler.html
Contact: Andrea Niosi, Libn.
Scope: Public hospitality industries - hotels, motels, restaurants, catering services, cookery and nutrition; tourism; beverages. **Services:** Copying; Library open to the public for reference use only. **Holdings:** 10,000 books; 3500 pamphlets; 900 menus; videotapes; archives. **Subscriptions:** 80 journals and other serials.

10269 ■ Geisinger Medical Center–Community Health Library
100 N. Academy Ave.
Danville, PA 17822-4401
Ph:(570)271-5638
Fax:(570)271-5635
Co. E-mail: chrl@geisinger.edu
URL: http://www.geisinger.edu
Contact: Patricia A Ulmer, Commun.Hea.Libn.
Scope: General medicine, nutrition, alternative and complementary medicine, pediatrics, cancer, AIDS. **Services:** Interlibrary loan. **Holdings:** 860 books;

200 audio/visual materials. **Subscriptions:** 14 journals and other serials.

10270 ■ Lemmen-Holton Cancer Pavilion Library
135 Michigan NE
330 Barclay Ave., NE
Grand Rapids, MI 49503
Ph:(616)391-1655
Fax:(616)391-3527
Co. E-mail: diane.hummel@spectrum-health.org
URL: http://www.spectrum-health.org/
Contact: Diane Hummel, Lib.Mgr.
Scope: Cancer. **Services:** Library open to the public. **Holdings:** Pamphlets.

10271 ■ New York Public Library–Mid-Manhattan Library–General Reference and Advisory Services/Health Information Center (455 5)
455 5th Ave. at 40th St.
New York, NY 10016
Ph:(212)340-0863
URL: http://www.nypl.org/branch/central/mml
Contact: Wol Sue Lee, Dept.Hd.
Scope: Consumer, health medicine, nursing, allied health. **Services:** Copying; Library open to the public. **Holdings:** 22,000 books and videocassettes; 4 VF of pamphlets. **Subscriptions:** 278 journals and other serials.

10272 ■ Voice for Animals, Inc. Library
PO Box 120095
San Antonio, TX 78212
Ph:(210)737-3138
Co. E-mail: voice@voiceforanimals.org
URL: http://www.voiceforanimals.org/
Scope: Animal rights; vegetarianism. **Services:** Library not open to the public. **Holdings:** 200 books; newsletters; videocassettes.

ASSOCIATIONS AND OTHER ORGANIZATIONS

10273 ■ Academy of Doctors of Audiology
3493 Lansdowne Dr., Ste. 2
Lexington, KY 40517-1147
Free: (866)493-5544
Fax:(859)977-7441
Co. E-mail: info@audiologist.org
URL: http://www.audiologist.org
Contact: Bruce Vircks AuD, Pres.
Description: Individuals with graduate degrees in audiology who dispense hearing aids as part of a rehabilitative practice. Fosters and supports professional dispensing of hearing aids by qualified audiologists; encourages audiology training programs to include pertinent aspects of hearing aid dispensing in their curriculums; conducts seminars on the business aspects of the hearing aid industry. .

10274 ■ American Auditory Society
19 Mantua Rd.
Mount Royal, NJ 08061
Ph:(856)423-3118
Free: 800-638-6423
Fax:(856)423-3420
Co. E-mail: aas@talley.com
URL: http://www.amauditorysoc.org
Contact: Timothy D. Trine PhD, Pres.
Description: Audiologists, otolaryngologists, scientists, hearing aid industry professionals, and educators of hearing impaired people; individuals involved in industries serving hearing impaired people, including the amplification systems industry. Works to increase knowledge and understanding of: the ear, hearing, and balance; disorders of the ear, hearing, and balance; prevention of these disorders; habilitation and rehabilitation of individuals with hearing and balance dysfunction. **Publications:** *The Bulletin of the American Auditory Society* (3/year); *Ear and Hearing* (bimonthly); *Peer Reviewed Clinical Research Publication* .

10275 ■ HEAR Center
301 E Del Mar Blvd.
Pasadena, CA 91101
Ph:(626)796-2016
Fax:(626)796-2320
Co. E-mail: info@hearcenter.org
URL: http://www.hearcenter.org
Contact: Ellen Simon, Exec. Dir.
Description: Auditory and verbal program designed to help hearing-impaired children, infants, and adults lead normal and productive lives. Seeks to develop auditory techniques to aid people who have communication problems due to deafness; primary objectives include early identification of hearing loss in infants and children and early amplification. Operates a program involving: binaural hearing aids where appropriate; continuous exposure to sound; development of auditory perception; wide-range amplification; environmental stimulation. Provides services in: diagnosis and audiological evaluation; hearing aid evaluation and trial use; development of listening skills and articulation; speech therapy; hearing aid

dispensing; parent counseling. **Publications:** *Effectiveness of Early Detection and Auditory Stimulation on the Speech and Language of Hearing Impaired Children*; *Hear: A Four Letter Word*; *HEAR Center Proceedings* (periodic); *The Listener* (quarterly).

10276 ■ Hearing Industries Association
1444 I St. NW, Ste. 700
Washington, DC 20005
Ph:(202)449-1090
Fax:(202)216-9646
Co. E-mail: mspangler@bostrom.com
URL: http://www.hearing.org
Contact: Carole M. Rogin, Exec. Dir.
Description: Companies engaged in the manufacture and/or sale of electronic hearing aids, their component parts, and related products and services on a national basis. Cooperates in and contributes toward efforts to promote the number of hearing aid users; collects trade statistics; conducts market research activities, investigations, and studies in connection with hearing and hearing aids. .

10277 ■ International Hearing Society
16880 Middlebelt Rd., Ste. 4
Livonia, MI 48154-3374
Ph:(734)522-7200
Co. E-mail: kmennillo@ihsinfo.org
URL: http://ihsinfo.org
Contact: Kathleen Mennillo MBA, Exec. Dir.
Description: Hearing aid specialists who test hearing for the selection, adaptation, fitting, adjusting, servicing, and sale of hearing aids. Members counsel the hearing impaired and instruct them in care and use of hearing aids. Activities include: administration of a qualification program for screening persons designated as Hearing Instrument Specialists; administration of a consumer information program; publication of information and research concerning hearing health care; establishment of standards of education, equipment, and techniques in the fitting of hearing aids; cooperation with other professional organizations engaged in hearing health care; cooperation and consultation with government officials and agencies in the development of policies and legislation. Accredits seminars and workshops for the education of hearing aid specialists. Maintains the International Institute for Hearing Instruments Studies as the educational arm of the society. **Publications:** *The Hearing Professional* (quarterly).

REFERENCE WORKS

10278 ■ *Academy of Doctors of Audiology—Membership Directory*
Pub: Academy of Doctors of Audiology
Released: Annual. **Covers:** Nearly 250 member audiologists. **Entries Include:** Name, address, phone.

10279 ■ *Hearing Journal—Hearing Health Industry World Directory Issue*
Pub: Lippincott Williams & Wilkins
Contact: Christy Gonzales
Released: Annual, latest edition 2005, Published with December issue of HJ. **Price:** $124, individuals in

U.S.; $151, institutions in U.S.; $232, individuals international. **Covers:** Manufacturers and suppliers of hearing aids, earmolds, audiometers, testing equipment, calibrators, and accessory items; hearing aid repair laboratories; services; related publishers, trade associations, organizations; international coverage. **Entries Include:** Company name, address, phone, names and titles of executives, whether manufacturer or distributor, trade and brand names, list of products or services provided. **Arrangement:** Alphabetical. **Indexes:** Product (Trade name).

10280 ■ *International Hearing Society—Directory of Members*
Pub: International Hearing Society
Contact: Susan Stewart, Production Mgr.
Released: Annual, spring. **Price:** Free. **Covers:** 5,400 hearing instrument specialists and board certificants. **Entries Include:** Individual name, address, phone. **Arrangement:** Geographical, alphabetical.

TRADE PERIODICALS

10281 ■ *The Hearing Professional*
Pub: International Hearing Society
Contact: James Ogurek, President
Released: Bimonthly. **Price:** $35 U.S.; $45 elsewhere. **Description:** Magazine publishing technical articles and product announcements on hearing aids and hearing.

10282 ■ *The League Letter*
Pub: Center for Hearing and Communication
Price: Included in membership. **Description:** Reports on news and events of the The League for the Hard of Hearing. Recurring features include a calendar of events. Remarks: TTY available at (917)305-7999.

10283 ■ *Volta Voices*
Pub: Alexander Graham Bell Association for the Deaf and Hard of Hearing
Released: Bimonthly. **Price:** $7.50 single issue. **Description:** Magazine providing news and feature articles of interest to the deaf and hearing impaired-child, parent, adult and professional.

VIDEOCASSETTES/ AUDIOCASSETTES

10284 ■ *Extra Sense-Assistive Listening Devices for the Hearing Impaired*
House Ear Institute
2100 W. 3rd St.
Los Angeles, CA 90057
Ph:(213)483-4431
Free: 800-388-8612
Fax:(213)483-8789
Co. E-mail: info@hei.org
URL: http://www.hei.org
Released: 1985. **Price:** $30.00. **Description:** Nanette Fabray demonstrates "listening devices" which are used to help people with hearing impairments. **Availability:** VHS; 3/4U.

10285 ■ *Hearing Aids in Children and Adults*
House Ear Institute
2100 W. 3rd St.
Los Angeles, CA 90057
Ph:(213)483-4431
Free: 800-388-8612
Fax:(213)483-8789
Co. E-mail: info@hei.org
URL: http://www.hei.org
Released: 1985. **Price:** $30.00. **Description:** An explanation of how hearing aids work and what type is best for each kind of patient. **Availability:** VHS; 3/4U.

FRANCHISES AND BUSINESS OPPORTUNITIES

10286 ■ Miracle Ear
Amplifon
5000 Cheshire Lane N
Plymouth, MN 55446
Free: 800-234-7714
Fax:(763)268-4253
Co. E-mail: cejohns@miracle-ear.com
URL: http://www.miracle-ear.com
No. of Franchise Units: 916. **No. of Company-Owned Units:** 187. **Founded:** 1948. **Franchised:** 1983. **Description:** Manufacturer and retail sales of hearing aids. **Equity Capital Needed:** $112,500-$570,000; minimum $25,000 cash. **Franchise Fee:** $30,000. **Financial Assistance:** No. **Training:** Yes.

COMPUTERIZED DATABASES

10287 ■ *Health Devices Alerts*
ECRI Institute
5200 Butler Pike
Plymouth Meeting, PA 19462-1298
Ph:(610)825-6000
Fax:(610)834-1275
Co. E-mail: info@ecri.org
URL: http://www.ecri.org
Description: Contains information on more than 700,000 reported medical device problems, hazards, recalls, technology assessments, evaluations, and updates. Includes citations with abstracts, to English-language medical, legal, and technical literature, Action Items (AI) that ECRI has investigated, Problem Reporting Program (PRP) records from the U.S. Food and Drug Administration (FDA) voluntary reporting program, and Medical Device Reporting (MDR) records from the FDA's mandatory reporting system. Covers problems with diagnostic and therapeutic medical equipment, including radiological equipment, hospital furniture, implanted devices and related accessories, disposable medical products, and clinical laboratory reagents. Corresponds to *Health Devices Alerts*. Is indexed with ECRI's Universal Medical Device Nomenclature System (UMDNS). **Availability:** Online: ProQuest LLC, ECRI Institute, DIMDI, the German Institute of Medical Documentation and Information. **Type:** Bibliographic; Full text.

10288 ■ *Health Devices International Sourcebase*
ECRI Institute
5200 Butler Pike
Plymouth Meeting, PA 19462-1298
Ph:(610)825-6000
Fax:(610)834-1275
Co. E-mail: info@ecri.org
URL: http://www.ecri.org
Description: Provides information on more than 15,000 manufacturers and distributors of more than 66,000 new medical devices and equipment. Also includes service companies that buy, sell, and repair used equipment. Provides product name, code, and typical price range for diagnostic and therapeutic medical devices and materials, clinical laboratory equipment and reagents, systems and instruments for testing clinical equipment, and hospital furniture. Product records also contain references, if available, to brand-name evaluations or product specifications in other ECRI publications. Manufacturer information includes organization name and type, contact information, product names and codes, trade names,

number of employees and total sales, and names of executive officers. Service records contain organization name, contact information, service category (e. g., clinical laboratory, nuclear medicine), type of service offered (e.g., sales, parts, repairs), locations served, and names of service management personnel. Corresponds to the *Health Devices Sourcebook*. **Availability:** Online: ProQuest LLC, DIMDI, the German Institute of Medical Documentation and Information, ECRI Institute. **Type:** Directory.

LIBRARIES

10289 ■ Atlanta-Fulton Public Library System–Learning and Career Center
One Margaret Mitchell Sq., 4th Fl.
Atlanta, GA 30303
Ph:(404)730-1700
Fax:(404)730-1990
Co. E-mail: librarycomments@fultoncountyga.gov
URL: http://www.afpls.org
Contact: Daniel Asomah, Mgr., Lrng. and Career Ctr.
Scope: Literacy program, visually impaired assistance, hearing impaired assistance, test preparation materials. **Services:** Interlibrary loan; copying; free Wi-Fi; Library open to the public. **Subscriptions:** 10 journals and other serials.

10290 ■ Berks Deaf & Hard of Hearing Services Library
2045 Centre Ave.
Reading, PA 19605
Ph:(610)685-4520
Fax:(610)685-4526
Co. E-mail: lfisher@bdhhs.org
URL: http://www.bdhhs.org
Contact: Lori Fisher, Client Cons.
Scope: Deafness and hard of hearing. **Services:** Center open to the public. **Holdings:** 480 books; videotapes; patents; archives. **Subscriptions:** 4 journals and other serials; 2 newspapers.

10291 ■ Central Institute for the Deaf–Speech, Hearing and Education Library
4560 Clayton Ave.
St. Louis, MO 63110
Ph:(314)977-0268
Fax:(314)977-0030
Co. E-mail: sarlic@wusm.wustl.edu
URL: http://pacs.wustl.edu/pacs/pacsweb.nsf/CI-D?Open
Contact: Cathy Sarli, Libn./Cur.
Scope: Audiology, early childhood education, behavioral sciences, speech pathology, physiology, otolaryngology, education of the deaf, noise control, electro-acoustics, digital instrumentation, aural rehabilitation, neurophysiology. **Services:** Copying; Library open to the public for reference use only. **Holdings:** 5000 books; 1195 bound periodical volumes; 150 dissertations; 30 videotapes. **Subscriptions:** 70 journals and other serials.

10292 ■ New York Public Library–Mid-Manhattan Library–Accessibility Services (455 5)
455 5th Ave. at 40th St., 2nd Fl.
New York, NY 10016
Ph:(212)340-0863
URL: http://www.nypl.org/locations/mid-manhattan-library
Contact: Theresa Myrhol, Chf.Libn.
Scope: The disabled - vision impaired, hearing impaired, learning and mobility impaired. **Services:** Special equipment, including Kurzweil Personal Reader, available for use by appointment; TTY on circulation; Library open to the public. **Holdings:** 300 books; 7 VF drawers of pamphlets material concerning the disabled; zoom text (XTRA 7.0). **Subscriptions:** 20 journals and other serials.

10293 ■ Oregon Health Sciences University–Oregon Hearing Research Center
3181 SW Sam Jackson Park Rd.
Portland, OR 97239-3098
Ph:(503)494-8032

Fax:(503)494-5656
Co. E-mail: ohrc@ohsu.edu
URL: http://www.ohsu.edu/ohrc
Contact: Rachel Dresbeck, PhD, Dir.
Scope: Auditory science, hearing, tinnitus. **Services:** Library open to members of Academic community only. **Holdings:** 200 books; 500 bound periodical volumes. **Subscriptions:** 10 journals and other serials.

RESEARCH CENTERS

10294 ■ House Ear Institute
2100 W 3rd St.
Los Angeles, CA 90057
Ph:(213)483-4431
Free: 800—388-8612
Fax:(213)483-8789
Co. E-mail: info@hei.org
URL: http://www.hei.org
Contact: James D. Boswell, CEO
E-mail: info@hei.org
Scope: Cause, treatment, and prevention of hearing and balance disorders, including investigations on cochlear implants and auditory prostheses, electrophysiology, electron microscopy, anatomy, cellular and molecular biology, and psychoacoustics. **Services:** Safety Patrol, Bridging the Gap, Family Camp; Workshops for the Hearing Impaired; Young Adult Work Program. **Publications:** House Calls Magazine; Progress report. **Educational Activities:** Conference of Auditory Prostheses; Hearst Laboratory Internships for undergraduates; IHCON International Hearing Aid Research Conference; International Skullbase Congress; Meniere's Conference; Rupley Fellowships for graduate students; Seminars on Primary Care in Otology; Skullbase surgical dissection courses; Temporal Bone Surgical Dissection Courses (monthly).

10295 ■ Houston Ear Research Foundation
7737 Southwest Fwy., Ste. 630
Houston, TX 77074
Ph:(713)771-9966
Free: 800—843-0807
Fax:(713)771-0546
Co. E-mail: jgilden@houstoncochlear.org
URL: http://houstoncochlear.org/
Contact: Jan Gilden, Exec.Dir.
E-mail: jgilden@houstoncochlear.org
Scope: Provides candidacy testing to determine if adults and children are cochlear implant candidates; provides initial hook up and follow up reprogramming and testing for cochlear implant recipients; provides aural rehabilitation therapy for cochlear implant recipients. **Publications:** Newsletter (annually). **Educational Activities:** Aural rehabilitation therapy for adult and children cochlear implant recipients; Cochlear implant candidacy testing, provide all testing and counseling to determine if adult/child is cochlear implant candidates; Initial stimulation/reprogramming/follow-up testing/troubleshooting of cochlear implant, provide all initial hook up, follow-up reprogramming and testing with cochlear implant.

10296 ■ University of Michigan–Kresge Hearing Research Institute
Medical Science II, Rm. 4605
1150 W Medical Center Dr.
Ann Arbor, MI 48109-5616
Ph:(734)764-8110
Fax:(734)764-0014
Co. E-mail: schacht@umich.edu
URL: http://www.khri.med.umich.edu
Contact: Prof. Jochen Schacht PhD, Dir.
E-mail: schacht@umich.edu
Scope: Auditory physiology and pathology, including studies on the reception, coding and processing of complex speech signals by the auditory system, transduction processes of the inner ear, cochlear blood flow and inner ear metabolism, development of cochlear prostheses and appropriate speech processor schemes, immune mediated hearing loss, the effects of age and environmental stress factors on hearing, biochemistry and motility of hair cells, afferent and efferent transmitters of the inner ear, psychophysics of hearing in normal individuals, immunology and immune systems related to squamous cell carcinoma, mechanisms of sound, localization,

molecular biology and genetics of the inner ear, and human genetics (linkage studies). **Educational Activities:** Seminars (weekly).

10297 ■ University of Michigan–Kresge Hearing Research Institute–Auditory Anatomy Laboratory
1150 W Medical Center Dr.
Ann Arbor, MI 48109-5616
Ph:(734)763-0060
Fax:(734)764-0014
Co. E-mail: shuler@umich.edu
URL: http://www2.khri.med.umich.edu/research/ altschuler_lab
Contact: Prof. Richard A. Altschuler PhD, Dir.
E-mail: shuler@umich.edu
Scope: Molecular interventions to reduce acquired deafness, such as those resulting from noise or ototoxic drugs; central auditory pathways, neurotransmitters, receptors and channels in normal hearing function and how they change as a consequence of deafness and interventions to restore hearing; survival or restoration of auditory nerves following deafness; the risks of new otologic treatments and

devices, including cochlear and central nervous system prostheses. **Educational Activities:** Demonstrations and visitor participation programs.

10298 ■ University of Oklahoma–Keys Speech and Hearing Center
1200 N Stonewall
PO Box 26901
Oklahoma City, OK 73117
Ph:(405)271-4214
Fax:(405)271-3360
Co. E-mail: stephen-painton@ouhsc.edu
URL: http://www.ah.ouhsc.edu
Contact: Stephen Painton PhD
E-mail: stephen-painton@ouhsc.edu
Scope: Loudness and acoustic reflex, temporal integration and acoustic reflex, critical bands measured with pulsation pattern psychophysical technique, sensory scaling, absolute thresholds for frequency modulated signals, bone conduction vibrator calibration, bone conduction speech audiometry, intelligibility of distorted speech, electrocochleography, brain stem auditory-evoked responses, acoustic correlates of abnormal vocal quality, aerodynamics of

voice production, phonemic and morphologic studies of language of the communicatively impaired, assessment of receptive and expressive language abilities, and studies in childhood language disorders in children with attention deficit disorders.

10299 ■ University of Tulsa–Mary K. Chapman Center for Communicative Disorders
800 Tucker Dr.
Tulsa, OK 74104
Ph:(918)631-2504
Fax:(918)631-3668
Co. E-mail: paula_cadogan@utulsa.edu
URL: http://www.cas.utulsa.edu/commdis/
Contact: Paula Cadogan EdD, Ch.
E-mail: paula_cadogan@utulsa.edu

Scope: Communication disorders, including laryngectomy and speech, and language and hearing problems. Also conducts aid tests. **Services:** Speech, language, and clinical hearing assessments. **Educational Activities:** Graduate training; Route 66 Annual Conference, on communication disorders.

ASSOCIATIONS AND OTHER ORGANIZATIONS

10300 ■ **American Herb Association**
PO Box 1673
Nevada City, CA 95959
Ph:(530)265-9552
URL: http://www.ahaherb.com
Contact: Kathi Keville, Dir./Ed.
Description: Enthusiasts and specialists of medicinal herbs and herbal products. Seeks to increase knowledge and provide up-to-date scientific and experiential information on herbs. Offers a network to exchange data and resources among members nationwide. Maintains herb garden. **Publications:** *Directory of Mail-Order Medicinal Herb Products* .

10301 ■ **American Herbal Products Association**
8630 Fenton St., Ste. 918
Silver Spring, MD 20910-5606
Ph:(301)588-1171
Fax:(301)588-1174
Co. E-mail: ahpa@ahpa.org
URL: http://www.ahpa.org
Contact: Michael McGuffin, Pres.
Description: Represents growers, brokers, manufacturers, distributors, retailers, importers and related consultants of herbal products such as bulk ingredients, teas, dietary supplements, and body care products. Seeks to effectively deal with common interests and industry-related problems by acquiring, affecting and disseminating business and regulatory information. Represents industry to legislators, regulating agencies and media. Conducts trade promotion and research activities; compiles statistics. Publishes resource documents and provides educational programs. Maintains New Dietary Ingredient Database, based on FDA dockets, other databases under development. **Publications:** *Botanical Safety Handbook*; *Herbs of Commerce*; *St. John's Wart, Ephedra, Echinacea or Saw Palmetto* .

10302 ■ **Herb Growing and Marketing Network**
PO Box 245
Silver Spring, PA 17575-0245
Ph:(717)393-3295
Fax:(717)393-9261
Co. E-mail: herbworld@aol.com
URL: http://www.herbworld.com
Contact: Maureen Rogers, Dir.
Description: Herb retailers, wholesalers, and growers; manufacturers of related products; serious hobbyists. Provides information on all segments of the herb industry with an emphasis on marketing and locating wholesale sources. **Publications:** *The Herbal Green Pages* (annual); *Proceedings from 5th Annual Conference*; *Proceedings from 1st Annual Conference*; *Proceedings from 4th Annual Conference*; *Proceedings from 2nd Annual Conference*; *Proceedings from 3rd Annual Conference*; *Starting an Herb Business* .

10303 ■ **Herb Research Foundation**
5589 Arapahoe Ave., Ste. 205
Boulder, CO 80303
Ph:(303)449-2265
Fax:(303)449-7849
Co. E-mail: info@herbs.org
URL: http://www.herbs.org
Contact: Robert S. McCaleb, Pres./Founder
Description: Professionals in the health food industry, plant research scientists, herbal medicine practitioners and their patients, pharmacologists, herbal manufacturers and trade organizations, ethnobotanists, and interested consumers; scientists and students in the fields of pharmacognosy, botany, ethnobotany, and medicine. Encourages and supports research on the chemistry, pharmacology, and use of herbal folk medicines, teas, and other botanical products; provides a forum for discussion and cooperation among herbalists, physicians, health food advocates, and scientists. Works to form a liaison between the U.S. herbal movement and the worldwide scientific community. Disseminates research information on botanicals and serves as a source of information for the public and press on medicinal plants. Provides botanical literature research service. **Publications:** *Herbal Research News* (quarterly); *HerbalGram* (quarterly); *Herbs Companion* (bimonthly).

10304 ■ **Herb Society of America**
9019 Kirtland Chardon Rd.
Kirtland, OH 44094
Ph:(440)256-0514
Fax:(440)256-0541
Co. E-mail: herbs@herbsociety.org
URL: http://www.herbsociety.org
Contact: Ms. Katrinka Morgan, Exec. Dir.
Description: Represents scientists, educators, and others interested in botanical and horticultural research on herbs and the culinary, economic, decorative, fragrant, and historic use of herbs. Maintains herb gardens in arboreta and other public sites. Establishes and maintains gardens for the blind. Planned and funded the National Herb Garden, which was donated to the National Arboretum in Washington, DC. Promotes the knowledge, use and delight of herbs through educational programs, research, and sharing the experience of its members with the community. **Publications:** *The Beginners Herb Garden* (semiannual); *The Herb Society of America New Encyclopedia of Herbs and Their Uses*; *The Herb Society of America Newsletter* (quarterly); *The Herbarist* (annual).

10305 ■ **International Herb Association**
PO Box 5667
Jacksonville, FL 32247-5667
Ph:(904)614-7745
URL: http://www.iherb.org
Contact: Nancy Momsen, Pres.
Description: Herb professionals. Works to unite members for growth through promotion and education. Offers help with business concerns such as the packaging and labeling of herbal products, budgets and projections, computerized business problem solv-ing, and retail display and design. Maintains speakers' bureau. **Publications:** *IHA Membership Directory* (annual); *IHA Newsletter* (quarterly).

REFERENCE WORKS

10306 ■ **"Because He Is Still Growing: Horst Rechelbacher: Intelligent Nutrients Minneapolis" in** *Inc.* **(Volume 32, December 2010, No. 10)**
Pub: Inc. Magazine
Ed: Mike Hoffman. **Description:** Horst Rechelbacher, founder of hair care company Aveda, and after selling Aveda to Estee Lauder, he is expanding into a nutraceuticals company offering hair care products that are organically grown.

10307 ■ *Herb Society of America—Membership Directory and By-laws*
Pub: Herb Society of America Inc.
Contact: Katrinka Morgan, Exec. Dir.
E-mail: director@herbsociety.org
Released: Biennial, odd years. **Covers:** 3,000 scientists, educators, and others interested in botanical and horticultural research on herbs and the culinary, economic, decorative, fragrant, and historic use of herbs. **Entries Include:** Name, address, unit or region. **Arrangement:** By unit or region.

10308 ■ *Herbal Green Pages*
Pub: The Herb Growing & Marketing Network
Ed: Maureen Rogers, Editor. **Released:** Annual, August. **Covers:** Over 6,000 companies and individuals involved in herb growing, marketing, and related areas. **Entries Include:** Name, address, phone, contact, products or services, nature of business (wholesale, retail, etc.), catalog availability. **Arrangement:** Alphabetical. **Indexes:** Product, service, contact person, geographical.

TRADE PERIODICALS

10309 ■ *Kitchen Gardener*
Pub: Taunton Press Inc.
Released: Bimonthly. **Price:** $4.95 back issue; $3.50 shipping and handling. **Description:** Gardening magazine for people who take pleasure and pride in their gardens and the food they prepare from them. Contains how-to information on growing, cooking, and preserving vegetables, herbs, and fruits.

10310 ■ *No Salt Week-The Newsletter*
Pub: Prosperity & Profits Unlimited, Distribution Services
Contact: A. Doyle
Ed: A. Doyle, Editor. **Released:** Annual. **Price:** $2, U.S.; $3, Canada; $4, elsewhere. **Description:** Presents possibilities for herb and spice blends that contain no added salt. Also contains ideas for cooking and much more.

VIDEOCASSETTES/ AUDIOCASSETTES

10311 ■ *Herbs*
Emergency Training
PO Box 13896
Emory University
Dobbs University Center - 5th Floor
Fairlawn, OH 44334

Ph:(404)727-3853
Fax:(404)727-5667
Released: 1987. **Price:** $19.95. **Description:** The history, uses, and methods of growing herbs are given. **Availability:** VHS.

LIBRARIES

10312 ■ Abbey of Regina Laudis, Order of St. Benedict–Our Lady of the Rock Monastery–Priory Library (PO Box)
PO Box 425
Shaw Island, WA 98286
Ph:(360)468-2321
Co. E-mail: mhildegard@rockisland.com
URL: http://www.ourladyoftherock.com
Contact: Mother Therese Critchley, Pres.
Scope: Scripture, theology, patristics, musicology, ecclesiastical history, art, Japanese history and literature, oriental studies. **Services:** Library not open to the public. **Holdings:** 4000 books. **Subscriptions:** 12 journals and other serials.

10313 ■ American Herb Association Library
PO Box 1673
Nevada City, CA 95959-1673
Ph:(530)265-9552
URL: http://www.ahaherb.com
Contact: Kathi Keville, Dir./Ed.
Scope: Herbs, herbal products, antique herbs, flora. **Services:** Library not open to the public. **Holdings:** 1000 volumes. **Subscriptions:** 60 journals and other serials.

10314 ■ Carnegie-Mellon University–Hunt Institute for Botanical Documentation Library
5000 Forbes Ave.
Pittsburgh, PA 15213-3890
Ph:(412)268-7301
Fax:(412)268-5677
Co. E-mail: dwbrown@andrew.cmu.edu
URL: http://huntbot.andrew.cmu.edu
Contact: Charlotte A. Tancin, Libn.
Scope: Botanical history; plant taxonomy, including 15th- to 17th-century herbals; extensive collection of 18th- and 19th-century color plate works, floras, monographic works, and other works on natural history, plant exploration and introduction. **Services:** Interlibrary loan (limited); copying; Library open to the public for reference use only. **Holdings:** 29,000 books; 25,000 portraits; 30,000 watercolors, drawings and prints; 2000 autograph letters and manuscripts. **Subscriptions:** 275 journals and other serials.

10315 ■ Cleveland Botanical Garden–Eleanor Squire Library
11030 East Blvd.
Cleveland, OH 44106
Ph:(216)707-2812
Fax:(216)721-2056
Co. E-mail: info@cbgarden.org
URL: http://www.cbgarden.org/Learn/Library.html
Contact: Gary Esmonde, Libn.
Scope: Gardening, horticulture, landscape architecture, herbs, flower arranging, botany. **Services:** Library open to the public with paid admission (members may borrow); rare books open to the public by appointment for review, research, and study. **Holdings:** 17,000 books; seed and nursery catalogs; slides; botanical prints; 1000 rare books. **Subscriptions:** 50 journals and other serials.

10316 ■ Dittrick Medical History Center
Allen Memorial Medical Library
11000 Euclid Ave.
Cleveland, OH 44106-1714
Ph:(216)368-3643
Fax:(216)368-0165
Co. E-mail: laura.travis@case.edu
URL: http://www.cwru.edu/artsci/dittrick/site2
Contact: James M. Edmonson, Chf.Cur.
Scope: History of medicine. **Services:** Copying; photographic services; Library open to the public. **Holdings:** 35,000 books; 75,000 artifacts, Archives, and Image collections.

10317 ■ Florida State University Special Collections
Robert Manning Strozier Library
116 Honors Way
Tallahassee, FL 32306-2047
Ph:(850)644-3271
Fax:(850)644-1221
Co. E-mail: spc@reserves.lib.fsu.edu
URL: http://www.fsu.edu/lAtspeccoll/
Contact: Lucia Patrick, Hd., Spec.Coll.
Scope: Florida, Florida State University, early Americana, Confederate imprints, book arts, herbals, poetry, Napoleon, North Florida/South Georgia area business. **Services:** Collections open to the public.

10318 ■ Horticultural Society of New York Library
148 W. 37th St., 13th Fl.
New York, NY 10018-6976
Ph:(212)757-0915, x102
Fax:(212)246-1207
Co. E-mail: kpowis@hsny.org
URL: http://www.hsny.org
Contact: Katherine Powis, Libn.
Scope: Gardening; garden design and garden history; horticulture; landscape design; botanical illustration; flower arrangement. **Services:** Library open to the public for reference use only. **Holdings:** 6000 books; 3500 bound periodical volumes; 75 lin.ft. of institutional archives. **Subscriptions:** 120 journals and other serials.

10319 ■ Idaho State University–Idaho Museum of Natural History–Stirton-Kelson Library (Bldg.)
Bldg. 12, Rm. 205C
921 S. 8th Ave.
ISU Mail Stop 8096
Pocatello, ID 83209-0001
Ph:(208)282-2603
Fax:(208)282-5893
Co. E-mail: lohserne@isu.edu
URL: http://imnh.isu.edu/Collections/Library.htm
Contact: Dr. Skip Lohse, Acting Dir.
Scope: Paleontology, anthropology, biology, geology, herpetology, botany, natural history. **Services:** Interlibrary loan; Library open to University community and museum researchers. **Holdings:** 900 books; 2150 bound periodical volumes; 24,000 reprints; 1500 journals/government documents.

10320 ■ Kingwood Center Library
900 Park Ave., W.
Mansfield, OH 44906
Ph:(419)522-0211, x-108
Co. E-mail: cgleaves@kingwoodcenter.org
URL: http://www.kingwoodcenter.org/education_library.html
Contact: William W. Collins, Hd. Gardener
Scope: Horticulture, natural history. **Services:** Interlibrary loan; copying; Library open to the public. **Holdings:** 8500 books; 500 bound periodical volumes; 12 VF drawers of pamphlets, pictures, clippings; 600 current seed and nursery catalogs. **Subscriptions:** 100 journals and other serials.

10321 ■ Miami University–Walter Havighurst Special Collections Library
321 King Library
Oxford, OH 45056
Ph:(513)529-3324
Fax:(513)529-1719
Co. E-mail: stuckejh@muohio.edu
URL: http://www.lib.muohio.edu
Contact: Janet H. Stuckey, Spec.Coll.Libn.
Scope: Early children's literature books, book arts, James T. Farrel, Percy MacKaye, George Orwell, William Dean Howells, William H. McGuffey, William Faulkner, Rodolfo Usigli, Hamlin Garland. **Services:** Library open to the public for reference use only with identification. **Holdings:** 65,000 books; 2330 bound periodical volumes; literary annuals and gift books. **Subscriptions:** 13 journals and other serials.

10322 ■ New York Public Library–The Research Libraries - Humanities and Social Sciences Library–Arents Tobacco Collection (5th A)
5th Ave. & 42nd St., Rm. 328
New York, NY 10018-2788
Ph:(212)642-0110
Fax:(212)302-4815
Co. E-mail: arnref@nypl.org
URL: http://legacy.www.nypl.org/research/chss/spe/rbk/arents/tobacco.html
Contact: Sarah Augusta Dickson, Libn.
Scope: Tobacco, herbals, history, medicine, law, manufacture, marketing; smoking and health. **Services:** Open to qualified researchers by card of admission secured in Special Collections Office. **Holdings:** 13,000 books and manuscripts; 150,000 cards and pieces of ephemera. **Subscriptions:** 10 journals and other serials.

10323 ■ Pennsylvania Horticultural Society–McLean Library
100 N. 20th St., 5th Fl.
Philadelphia, PA 19103-1455
Ph:(215)988-8800
Fax:(215)988-8810
Co. E-mail: wiredgardener@pennhort.org
URL: http://www.pennsylvaniahorticulturalsociety.org
Contact: Janet Evans, Lib.Mgr.
Scope: Ornamental horticulture, botany, landscape design, garden history. **Services:** Interlibrary loan; photocopying; Garden Q&A (telephone plant information service); Library open to the public for reference use only (borrowing privileges for members and PHS staff). **Holdings:** 16,500 books; 4000 bound periodical volumes; 1000 slides; 250 videotapes on gardening. **Subscriptions:** 100 journals and other serials.

RESEARCH CENTERS

10324 ■ Alberta Agriculture and Rural Development–Crop Diversification Centre South
301 Horticultural Station Rd. E
Brooks, AB, Canada T1R 1E6
Ph:(403)362-1350
Fax:(403)362-1306
Co. E-mail: shelley.barkley@gov.ab.ca
URL: http://www1.agric.gov.ab.ca/$department/deptdocs.nsf/all/opp4386
Contact: Shelley Barkley
E-mail: shelley.barkley@gov.ab.ca
Scope: Greenhouse crop production, protection and utilization. Field research programs include potato crops emphasizing evaluation of new cultivars, development of production and management techniques suited to a short growing season. Research programs into special crops investigates dry beans and other pulse crops and corn emphasizing cultivar development and development of production and management techniques. The Centre is also home to soil and water management, plant pathology, weed control, entomology and food processing research programs. **Services:** Extension for agricultural industries. **Publications:** Annual report; Fruit Facts; Greenhouse Coverings; Program Trial Reports. **Educational Activities:** Field day and guided and self-guided tours (annually), in August; Grower meetings and seminars.

10325 ■ Herb Research Foundation
5589 Arapahoe Ave., Ste. 205
Boulder, CO 80303
Ph:(303)449-2265
Fax:(303)449-7849
Co. E-mail: info@herbs.org
URL: http://www.herbs.org
Contact: Robert S. McCaleb, Pres.
E-mail: info@herbs.org
Scope: Pharmacognosy, ethnobotany, and toxicology of medicinal plants. **Services:** Research services. **Publications:** Herb Research News (quarterly); HerbalGram; Herbs for Health; Information Services Catalog; Reports. **Educational Activities:** Literature research on many aspects of herb use (periodically); Technical information, on medicinal plants and professional literature searching and review.

10326 ■ Rodale Institute
611 Siegfriedale Rd.
Kutztown, PA 19530-9320
Ph:(610)683-1400
Fax:(610)683-8548
Co. E-mail: info@rodaleinst.org

URL: http://www.rodaleinstitute.org
Contact: Maria Rodale, Co-Chm.
E-mail: info@rodaleinst.org
Scope: Organic gardening and farming systems. Specific areas of interest include vegetables, apples, composting, cover crops, soil fertility and soil health, regenerative agriculture, legume screening, inter-

seeding, overseeding, weed control, nitrogen cycling, tillage systems, and perennial grains. **Publications:** Brochures; Fact sheets; Pamphlets; Technical Reports. **Educational Activities:** Field Days, open to farmers, researchers, and students; Internship program; Workshops. **Awards:** Paid Internships (annually).

ASSOCIATIONS AND OTHER ORGANIZATIONS

10327 ■ Cookware Manufacturers Association
PO Box 531335
Birmingham, AL 35253-1335
Ph:(205)592-0389
Fax:(205)599-5598
Co. E-mail: hrushing@usit.net
URL: http://www.cookware.org
Contact: Hugh J. Rushing, Exec. VP
Description: Represents manufacturers of cooking utensils and cooking accessories. Compiles statistics.

10328 ■ Fashion Group International
8 W 40th St., 7th Fl.
New York, NY 10018
Ph:(212)302-5511
Fax:(212)302-5533
Co. E-mail: cheryl@fgi.org
URL: http://www.fgi.org
Contact: Cheryl Ingersoll, Regional Dir.
Description: Fashion, apparel, accessories, beauty and home industries. Works to advance professionalism in fashion and its related lifestyle industries with a particular emphasis on the role and development of women. Provides a public forum for examination of important contemporary issues in fashion and the business of fashion. Works to present timely information regarding national and global trends and to attain greater recognition of women's achievements in business and to promote career opportunities in fashion.

10329 ■ Home Fashion Products Association
355 Lexington Ave., Ste. 1500
New York, NY 10017-6603
Ph:(212)297-2122
Fax:(212)370-9047
Co. E-mail: contactus@hfpaonline.org
URL: http://www.homefashionproducts.com
Contact: Katie Goshgarian, Exec. Dir.
Description: Manufacturers of curtains, draperies, bedding, rugs and related products. Sponsors annual scholarship for students attending accredited schools in home textiles. .

10330 ■ International Housewares Association
6400 Shafer Ct., Ste. 650
Rosemont, IL 60018
Ph:(847)292-4200
Fax:(847)292-4211
Co. E-mail: pbrandl@housewares.org
URL: http://www.housewares.org
Contact: Philip J. Brandl, Pres.
Description: Manufacturers and distributors of housewares and small appliances. Conducts annual market research survey of the housewares industry. Manages the international housewares show. **Publications:** *BusinessWatch* (monthly); *Housewares Mar-*ketWatch (quarterly); *IHA Reports* (bimonthly); *January Exhibitors Directory* (annual); *NHMA Reports Newsletter* (bimonthly).

REFERENCE WORKS

10331 ■ *American Edged Products Manufacturers Association—Annual Membership Directory*
Pub: American Edged Products Manufacturers Association
Contact: David W. Barrack, Exec. Dir.
E-mail: info@aepma.org
Released: Annual, September. **Price:** Free. **Covers:** Approximately 35 member manufacturers and suppliers of knives, scissors, and edged hand tools. **Entries Include:** Company name, address, phone, names and titles of key personnel, number of employees, products provided, year founded. **Arrangement:** Alphabetical. **Indexes:** Company name and personnel listing.

10332 ■ "Bedding a Leader in Kohl's Q1 Gains" in *Home Textiles Today* (Vol. 31, May 24, 2011, No. 13, pp. 1)
Pub: Reed Business Information
Description: Kohl's credited home furnishings, particularly bedding, as the leading source of its first-quarter sales and profit gains in 2011. Statistical data included.

10333 ■ "Bon-Ton Halves Q1 Losses, Show Operating Profit" in *Home Textiles Today* (Vol. 31, May 24, 2011, No. 13, pp. 7)
Pub: Reed Business Information
Ed: James Mammarella. **Description:** Bon-Ton Stores reported progress in its multi-year push to profitability, with soft home sales leading the way. Statistical data included.

10334 ■ "CGG Home Fashions to Show Hand-Loomed Textiles" in *Home Textiles Today* (Vol. 31, May 24, 2011, No. 13, pp. 4)
Pub: Reed Business Information
Description: CGG Home Fashions introduced textiles made from natural fibers and vegetable dyes for upscale industry use at the HD Expo in Las Vegas, Nevada.

10335 ■ "Colores Origenes: Martha Kruse" in *Advertising Age* (Vol. 77, November 13, 2006, No. 46, pp. S12)
Pub: Crain Communications, Inc.
Ed: Laurel Wentz. **Description:** Home Depot has created a range of Latin paint colors called Colores Origenes; the new line was originally intended to launch only at locations with heavily Hispanic patrons but the company decided to make the line available at all of their stores.

10336 ■ "A Counter Offer" in *Inc.* (February 2008, pp.)
Pub: Gruner & Jahr USA Publishing
Ed: Elaine Appleton Grant. **Description:** Online retailer offering a line of kitchen and home products has upgraded its Website in order to make the busi-ness more attractive to possible buyers of the company. The firm is asking $9.9 million and reported gross revenue of $12.7 in 2007. The owner suggests that a buyer add product lines geared towards more rooms of the home than currently offer on the retail site.

10337 ■ "Doing Good: Cause and Effect" in *Entrepreneur* (Vol. 36, February 2008, No. 2, pp. 23)
Pub: Entrepreneur Media Inc.
Description: Lisa Knoppe established Art for a Cause LLC that employs people with mental and physical disabilities. The company makes hand-painted tools and furniture to be sold at gift retailers and hardware stores.

10338 ■ "Dreamy Fortune: Pillow Biz Dreams of Sales Reaching $10 Million a Year" in *Small Business Opportunities* (Spring 2008)
Pub: Harris Publications Inc.
Ed: Stan Roberts. **Description:** Profile of Michale Lezberg, owner of a pillow factory. Lezberg shares insight into building his firm to a multi-million dollar a year business.

10339 ■ "Entrepreneur Says Spirituality Has Been a Key to Her Success" in *Business First Columbus* (Vol. 25, October 17, 2008, No. 8, pp. 1)
Pub: American City Business Journals
Ed: Scott Rawdon. **Description:** Profile of Carolyn Williams Francis, CEO of Williams Interior Designs Inc. She outlines her mantra for success in her furniture design business, but emphasizes that faith has taken her business to greater heights.

10340 ■ "Furniture Chain Moving to Harford" in *Baltimore Business Journal* (Vol. 27, January 22, 2010, No. 38, pp. 1)
Pub: American City Business Journals
Ed: David J. Sernovitz. **Description:** Manchester, Connecticut-based Bob's Discount Furniture signed a lease for 672,000 square feet of space in Harford County, Maryland. The site will become the discount furniture retailer's distribution center in mid-Atlantic US. As many as 200 jobs could be generated when the center opens.

10341 ■ "Home Helps Push Macy's to First-Quarter Profit" in *Home Textiles Today* (Vol. 31, May 24, 2011, No. 13, pp. 2)
Pub: Reed Business Information
Description: Macy's Inc. reported home goods as one of the three strong performing categories for first quarter 2011. Home goods sales, both big and small ticket items, have improved significantly for the retailer.

10342 ■ "Home Shows Signs of Life at Target" in *Home Textiles Today* (Vol. 31, May 24, 2011, No. 13, pp. 1)
Pub: Reed Business Information
Description: Retailer, Target, is experience a boost in sales for apparel and products for the home.

10343 ■ "Home Sits Out Q1 Surge at JCP" in *Home Textiles Today* **(Vol. 31, May 24, 2011, No. 13, pp. 1)**
Pub: Reed Business Information
Ed: James Mammarella. **Description:** JCPenney chairman and CEO, Mike Ullman, reported sales gains for first quarter 2011 in all products except home goods.

10344 ■ "Home Source Debuts Diesel Home Collection" in *Home Textiles Today* **(Vol. 31, May 24, 2011, No. 13, pp. 1)**
Pub: Reed Business Information
Ed: Carole Sloan. **Description:** Home Source is highlighting the debut collection of bed and bath products made by Diesel. These items interpret the jeans culture into home furnishings.

10345 ■ "Just Add Water and Lily Pads" in *Crain's Chicago Business* **(Vol. 31, April 28, 2008, No. 17, pp. 50)**
Pub: Crain Communications, Inc.
Ed: Phuong Ly. **Description:** Aquascape Inc., a major manufacturer of pond-building supplies, is using the recent drought in the South which hurt its business significantly to create a new product: an upscale, decorative version of the rain barrel which will collect rainwater to circulate through a pond or a fountain.

10346 ■ *LDB Interior Textiles Annual Buyers' Guide*
Pub: E.W. Williams Publications Co.
Contact: Philippa Hochschild, Publisher
Released: Annual, Latest edition 2010. **Covers:** Over 3,000 manufacturers, importers, and suppliers of home fashions products and services, decorative fabric converters, and alternative window coverings; fabricators; manufacturer's representatives; and others allied to the home fashions trade. **Entries Include:** For manufacturers, importers, converters, fabricators, and suppliers—Company name, address, phone, fax, contact, product line. For manufacturer's representatives—Name, address, phone, contact, lines carried. For others—Name, address, phone, fax. **Arrangement:** Classified by product/service. **Indexes:** Product.

10347 ■ "Liora Manne to Debut Fabric Line" in *Home Textiles Today* **(Vol. 31, May 24, 2011, No. 13, pp. 4)**
Pub: Reed Business Information
Description: Textile and product designer Liora Manne will debut her new decorative fabric collection at the Showtime in High Point, North Carolina in June 2011. More than 22 fabric patterns and solid colors using Manne's patented Lamontage textile design process will be featured and can be used for indoor/outdoor decorative fabrics, furniture, decorative pillows, upholstery and more.

10348 ■ *Martha, Inc.*
Pub: John Wiley and Sons, Inc.
Ed: Christopher Byron. **Released:** 2002. **Price:** $28.00. **Description:** Profile of Martha Stewart's rise from working class to a billionaire businesswoman is presented. The book covers Stewart's power struggles and personal conflicts as well as her triumphs.

10349 ■ "New Kittinger Showroom Twice the Size of the Last One" in *Business First Buffalo* **(December 7, 2007, pp. 4)**
Pub: American City Business Journals, Inc.
Ed: Tracey Drury. **Description:** Kittinger Furniture Company, an upscale furniture maker, has opened a 6,000 square foot retail outlet at the Transit Road, New York. The company's moved to attract suburban and affluent customers for its high-end furniture products.

10350 ■ "New Year's Resolutions: How Three Companies Came Up With Their 2008 Growth Strategies" in *Inc.* **(January 2008, pp. 47-49)**
Pub: Gruner & Jahr USA Publishing
Ed: Martha C. White. **Description:** Three companies share 2008 growth strategies; companies include a candle company, a voice mail and text messaging marketer, and hotel supplier of soap and shampoo.

10351 ■ "P/Kaufmann Sells Bennettsville" in *Home Textiles Today* **(Vol. 31, May 24, 2011, No. 13, pp. 6)**
Pub: Reed Business Information
Description: Decorative Screen Printers purchased the printing and finishing facility of P/Kaufmann in Bennettsville, South Carolina. However, the firm will continue its focus on its core business, a vat printing facility for home furnishings fabrics.

10352 ■ *The Pampered Chef*
Pub: Doubleday Broadway Publishing Group
Ed: Doris Christopher. **Description:** The Pampered Chef has been selling high quality kitchen tools through in-home cooking demonstration for twenty-five years. CEO and founder explains how she turned her one woman company into a a business with sales approaching $1 billion. Christopher shares her story by providing the foundation, strategies for entrepreneurs, setting priorities, knowing when to expand and when to slow growth, and dealing with adversity.

10353 ■ "Peking Launches Trina Turk Bedding Collection" in *Home Textiles Today* **(Vol. 31, May 24, 2011, No. 13, pp. 4)**
Pub: Reed Business Information
Description: Peking Handicraft is launching designer Trina Turk's bedding collection of four beds that reflect her approach to contemporary fabric design using color and prints with strong graphic effects.

10354 ■ "Procter Gambles on Wallpaper; Putting Paint On a Roll" in *Advertising Age* **(Vol. 77, September 18, 2006, No. 38, pp. 4)**
Pub: Crain Communications, Inc.
Ed: Jack Neff. **Description:** Procter & Gamble Co. has launched a new line of textured paints that are already applied to a wallpaper-like roll that can be hung without paste or wallpaper tools.

10355 ■ "Ross Stores Reports Spectacular First Quarter" in *Home Textiles Today* **(Vol. 31, May 24, 2011, No. 13, pp. 2)**
Pub: Reed Business Information
Ed: James Mammarella. **Description:** Retailer Ross Stores reported strong sales and profit gains for first quarter 2011, with their home department helping to lead the way.

10356 ■ "Sales at Furniture Showrooms Sink" in *Puget Sound Business Journal* **(Vol. 29, October 10, 2008, No. 25, pp. 1)**
Pub: American City Business Journals
Ed: Greg Lamm. **Description:** Furniture showrooms are seeing a drop in sales due to the bad economy. Buyer demand has also fallen because of the slumping real estate market.

10357 ■ "Shaw Joins Green Institute Launch" in *Home Textiles Today* **(Vol. 31, May 24, 2011, No. 13, pp. 4)**
Pub: Reed Business Information
Description: Shaw Industries Group joined the Green Products Innovation Institute, the first nonprofit institute of its kind in America. The institute promotes the concepts of reverse engineering, elimination of waste, safe chemistries, and closed loop technical nutrients.

10358 ■ "Sheets Makers Optimistic Amid Price, Delivery Issues" in *Home Textiles Today* **(Vol. 31, May 24, 2011, No. 13, pp. 8)**
Pub: Reed Business Information
Ed: Jill Rowen. **Description:** Retail sales of sheets and pillowcases dropped 4.7 percent in volume in 2009. Retailers pulled back inventory significantly in 2010. Statistical data included.

10359 ■ "Sunbrella Engages Consumers Via Social Media" in *Home Textiles Today* **(Vol. 31, May 24, 2011, No. 13, pp. 4)**
Pub: Reed Business Information
Description: Performance fabric brand Sunbrella is marketing to social media, such as Facebook and Twitter, in order to boost consumer interest and retailer support.

10360 ■ "Williams-Sonoma Beats Expectations in Q1" in *Home Textiles Today* **(Vol. 31, May 24, 2011, No. 13, pp. 2)**
Pub: Reed Business Information
Description: Both retail nameplates, Williams-Sonoma and Pottery Barn reported gains in 2011's first quarter, accredited to the way shoppers responded to new opening price point programs for several of its brands.

SOURCES OF SUPPLY

10361 ■ *Casual Living—Casual Outdoor Furniture and Accessory Directory Issue*
Pub: Reed Business Information
Contact: Cinde W. Ingram, Editor-in-Chief
E-mail: cwingram@reedbusiness.com
Released: Annual, Latest edition 2008. **Price:** $22.99, individuals; $55.99, Canada; $55.99, other countries; $138.99, individuals air delivery. **Publication Includes:** List of manufacturers, manufacturers' representatives, and suppliers of outdoor furniture, wicker and rattan furniture, and backyard accessories, such as barbecue grills, picnic accessories, outdoor lighting, cushions and pads, patio umbrellas, vinyl refinishing and maintenance products. **Entries Include:** Name of firm, address, phone, products. **Arrangement:** Alphabetical. **Indexes:** Organization name.

10362 ■ *Dallas Market Center—Permanent Directory*
Pub: Dallas Market Center Co.
Released: Semiannual, January and June. **Covers:** Representatives of manufacturers, importers, and wholesale distributors of residential and contract furniture, home furnishings, floor coverings, gifts and decorative accessories, jewelry, lamps, and lighting products. **Entries Include:** Firm name, mart address, phone. **Arrangement:** Classified by product/service. **Indexes:** Company name, product/service.

10363 ■ *Gifts & Tablewares—Directory Issue*
Pub: Business Information Group
Released: Annual, Latest edition 2010. **Price:** $46.95, individuals; $52.95, individuals; $57.95, other countries. **Publication Includes:** List of approximately 1,000 manufacturers and suppliers of gift, home decor, stationery, and tableware items in Canada. **Entries Include:** Company name, address, phone, fax, name, address, and phone of branches and showrooms; description of products and services; email and web sites. **Arrangement:** Alphabetical. **Indexes:** Product, brand name.

10364 ■ *Merchandise Mart Buyers Guide*
Pub: Hoyt Publishing
Contact: Kelly Harrison
Ed: Jennifer Woolford, Editor. **Released:** Semiannual, June and December. **Price:** $5. **Covers:** About 3,000 representatives of manufacturers, importers, and wholesale distributors of residential and contract furniture, home furnishings, floor coverings, gifts and accessories, lamps and lighting products, domestics, and small appliances. **Entries Include:** Firm name, mart address; alphabetical listings include phone. **Arrangement:** Alphabetical by company.

STATISTICAL SOURCES

10365 ■ *Tabletop Market*
Pub: Rector Press, Ltd.
Contact: Lewis Skolnick, Pres
Released: 2009. **Price:** Contact Rector Press. **Description:** Profiles the tabletop market, covering dinnerware, glassware, and flatware. Includes projections to the year 2000. Provides information on pricing, factors affecting demand, design trends, foreign trade, and distribution channels. Also contains profiles of leading marketers.

10366 ■ *The U.S. Tabletop Market*
Pub: MarketResearch.com
Released: 2000. **Price:** $1375.00. **Description:** This report explores the question of whether the situation may be changing as tabletop marketers embrace the trend toward more casual living. The report estimates industry sales over the last five years and gives

projections through 2004 based on close consideration of all relevant data and trends. growth with projections to 1996, the bridal market, market breakouts, leading marketers, consumer advertising and promotion, advertising expenditures and positioning, distribution, retail, pricing, and purchasing habits and attitudes. Also contains tables, charts, and examples of trade and consumer advertising.

TRADE PERIODICALS

10367 ■ *Casual Living*
Pub: Reed Business Information
Contact: Cinde W. Ingram, Editor-in-Chief
E-mail: cingram@casualliving.com
Released: Monthly. **Price:** $20; $4 single issue. **Description:** Trade magazine for the casual furnishings industry.

10368 ■ *The duPont Registry*
Pub: duPont Publishing Inc.
Released: Monthly. **Price:** $15.95; $25.95 Canada; $45.95 other countries. **Description:** Magazine featuring worldwide luxury homes for sale.

10369 ■ *Gifts & Decorative Accessories*
Pub: Sandow Media Corp.
Contact: Caroline Kennedy, Editor-in-Chief
E-mail: ckennedy@giftsanddec
Released: Monthly. **Price:** $36; $39 Canada; $135 other countries. **Description:** International magazine for retailers of gifts, greeting cards, decorative accessories, and stationery-related merchandise.

10370 ■ *Gifts & Tablewares*
Pub: Business Information Group
Contact: Brenda Bishop, Publisher
E-mail: bbishop@gifts-and-tableware.com
Released: 7/yr. **Price:** $43.95 Canada plus taxes; $49.95 in U.S.; $54.95 other countries. **Description:** Magazine featuring gifts, tableware, social stationery, housewares, and home accessories.

10371 ■ *Home Improvement Retailing*
Pub: Powershift Communications Inc.
Released: Bimonthly. **Price:** $76; $110 Canada plus applicable taxes. **Description:** Trade magazine for the home improvement retail and wholesale market.

10372 ■ *LDB Interior Textiles*
Pub: E.W. Williams Publications Co.
Contact: Wanda Jankowski, Editor-in-Chief
E-mail: wandaldb@ewwpi.com
Released: Monthly. **Price:** $72; $125 Canada; $150 elsewhere airmail; $100 two years; $7 single issue; $12 single issue, Canada; $18 single issue elsewhere. **Description:** Magazine for buyers of home fashions, including bed, bath and table linens, hard and soft window treatments, home fragrances, decorative pillows and home accessories, accent rugs, and decorative fabrics.

VIDEOCASSETTES/ AUDIOCASSETTES

10373 ■ *Home Decorating Combo*
Nancy's Notions Ltd.
333 Beichl Ave.
P.O. Box 683
Beaver Dam, WI 53916-0683
Ph:(920)887-7321
Free: 800-725-0361
Fax:800-255-8119
Co. E-mail: customerservice@nancysnotions.com
URL: http://www.nancysnotions.com
Released: 1987. **Description:** This video contains two programs on fabric-based home decoration: "Window Treatments" and "Instant Decorating." **Availability:** VHS.

10374 ■ *Home Improvement: Decorating*
S.I. Video Sales Group
PO Box 63745
Philadelphia, PA 19147

Ph:(267)519-2222
Co. E-mail: stann@sivideo.com
URL: http://www.sivideo.com
Price: $12.95. **Description:** Discusses basic decorating and design concepts to consider in making your house feel like a home. Also explains how to make the right choice in carpets for each room. **Availability:** VHS.

10375 ■ *Home Improvement: Interior Projects*
S.I. Video Sales Group
PO Box 63745
Philadelphia, PA 19147
Ph:(267)519-2222
Co. E-mail: stann@sivideo.com
URL: http://www.sivideo.com
Price: $12.95. **Description:** Learn how to install wall shelving and kitchen counter tops, repair holes and cracks in walls and ceilings, remove wallpaper, and more. **Availability:** VHS.

10376 ■ *Home Improvement Videos*
Do It Yourself, Inc./D.I.Y. Video Corp.
171 Grassy Knoll Way
Blowing Rock, NC 28605
Ph:(828)295-4610
Fax:(828)295-6901
Co. E-mail: roskind@boone.net
Released: 1986. **Price:** $19.95. **Description:** This is a series of in-depth home improvement instructions. Videos are available individually and a booklet comes with each one. **Availability:** VHS.

TRADE SHOWS AND CONVENTIONS

10377 ■ Accent on Design - A Division of the New York International Gift Fair
George Little Management, LLC (New York, New York)
1133 Westchester Ave., Ste. N136
White Plains, NY 10606
Ph:(914)421-3200
Free: 800-272-SHOW
Co. E-mail: cathy_steel@glmshows.com
URL: http://www.glmshows.com
Released: Annual. **Audience:** Buyers from specialty, department, and jewelry stores and; gift shops; interior designers; home products importers and distributors; mail order catalogs. **Principal Exhibits:** General giftware, tabletop and housewares, decorative and personal accessories, museum gifts, ethnic, traditional, country and contemporary design products, juvenile products, floral products and pet products.

10378 ■ Accent on Design - A Division of the San Francisco International Gift Fair
George Little Management, LLC (New York, New York)
1133 Westchester Ave., Ste. N136
White Plains, NY 10606
Ph:(914)421-3200
Free: 800-272-SHOW
Co. E-mail: cathy_steel@glmshows.com
URL: http://www.glmshows.com
Released: Semiannual. **Audience:** Specialty, department, stationery, jewelry, and juvenile stores, gift and gourmet shops, interior designers, importers/distributors of home products, museums. **Principal Exhibits:** Decorative accessories, lighting and home furnishings, housewares, stationery, tabletop, gourmet and general gift merchandise.

10379 ■ Charlotte Gift and Jewelry Show
Charlotte Gift and Jewelry Show
3710 Latrobe Dr., Ste. 110
Charlotte, NC 28211
Ph:(704)365-4150
Fax:(704)365-4154
Co. E-mail: michael@charlottegiftshow.com
URL: http://www.charlottegiftshow.com
Released: Quarterly. **Audience:** Trade buyers. **Principal Exhibits:** Gifts, housewares, jewelry, crafts, silk plants and flowers, tabletop, glassware, collectibles, accessories, home decorating accessories, basketry, and other related products.

10380 ■ H2X Canada Hardware & Home Improvement Expo & Conference
Messe Frankfurt Inc. (Atlanta, Georgia)
1600 Parkwood Cir., Ste. 515
Atlanta, GA 30339
Ph:(770)984-8016
Fax:(770)984-8023
Co. E-mail: info@usa.messefrankfurt.com
URL: http://www.usa.messefrankfurt.com
Released: Annual. **Audience:** Volume buyers, including retailers and manufacturers' representatives. **Principal Exhibits:** Hardware, housewares, giftware, paint, wallcovering, and products for leisure living, and home improvement.

10381 ■ International Bedding Exposition
International Sleep Products Association
501 Wythe St.
Alexandria, VA 22314-1917
Ph:(703)683-8371
Fax:(703)683-4503
Co. E-mail: ispa@sleepproducts.org
URL: http://www.sleepproducts.org
Released: Biennial. **Audience:** Bedding manufacturers, suppliers, and trade professionals. **Principal Exhibits:** Manufacturing supplies related to mattresses, including machinery, textiles foam, inner springs, fiber, hard goods, and soft goods.

10382 ■ International Fancy Food and Confection Show/Winter
National Association for the Specialty Food Trade, Inc.
120 Wall St., 27th Fl.
New York, NY 10005
Ph:(212)482-6440
Fax:(212)482-6459
URL: http://www.fancyfoodshows.com
Released: Annual. **Audience:** Retailers, brokers, importers, buyers, chefs, caterers and related personnel. **Principal Exhibits:** Pates, cheeses, specialty meats and seafood, condiments, sauces, mustards, vinegars, chocolates, fine candies, biscuits, cookies, cakes, jams, jellies, preserves, coffees, teas, fruits, nuts, special beverages, beer, wine, ice creams, desserts, and cooking accessories.

10383 ■ Supermarket Promotion Show
Association of Retail Marketing Services
10 Drs. James Parker Blvd., Ste. 103
Red Bank, NJ 07701-1500
Ph:(732)842-5070
Fax:(732)219-1938
Co. E-mail: info@goarms.com
URL: http://www.goarms.com
Released: Annual. **Audience:** Buyers of retail, consumer incentives. **Principal Exhibits:** Dinnerware, glassware, housewares, books, videos, games, sweepstakes, dolls, and plush toys suppliers.

CONSULTANTS

10384 ■ KV Marketing Inc.
12 Huntsville Rd.
Katonah, NY 10536-2002
Ph:(914)232-7566
Fax:(914)232-7848
Co. E-mail: pci19@optonline.net
URL: http://www.p-c-i.org
Contact: Meri Pollak, Mgr
E-mail: pci19@optonline.net
Scope: Provides international marketing expertise including market research and analysis, new product development, marketing plans, and general management assistance to both nonprofits and the commercial sectors.

FRANCHISES AND BUSINESS OPPORTUNITIES

10385 ■ Miracle Method Bath And Kitchen Restoration
5020 Mark Dabling Blvd.
Colorado Springs, CO 80918
Free: 800-444-8827

Fax:(719)594-9282
Co. E-mail: sales@miraclemethod.com
URL: http://www.miraclemethod.com
No. of Franchise Units: 125. **Founded:** 1977. **Franchised:** 1979. **Description:** Bath and kitchen refinishing business. **Equity Capital Needed:** $85,000-$123,000. **Franchise Fee:** $35,000. **Financial Assistance:** Financing of 50 percent of initial franchise fee subject to credit approval. **Training:** Includes 10 days training.

10386 ■ The Panhandler
Liv Canada Gift Group Inc.
294 Walker Dr., Unit 2
Brampton, ON, Canada L6T 4Z2
Ph:(905)790-9023
Free: (866)463-4124

Fax:(905)790-7059
Co. E-mail: franchises@franchisebancorp.com
URL: http://www.livcan.com
No. of Franchise Units: 25. **Founded:** 1970. **Franchised:** 1970. **Description:** Boutiques specializing in gift, home decor, and kitchen items. **Equity Capital Needed:** $140,000-$180,000. **Franchise Fee:** $25,000. **Financial Assistance:** No. **Training:** Yes.
s.

10387 ■ Pot Pourri Accent
216 Migneron
St. Laurent, QC, Canada H4T 1Y7
Ph:(514)341-4000
Fax:(514)341-4241
Co. E-mail: info@potpourri.ca
URL: http://www.potpourri.ca
No. of Franchise Units: 30. **No. of Company-Owned Units:** 4. **Founded:** 1990. **Franchised:**

1990. **Description:** The franchise specializes in retailing of kitchen items and decorations. **Equity Capital Needed:** $50,000-$100,000. **Franchise Fee:** $20,000-$30,000. **Training:** Yes.

10388 ■ Rafters Home Store
Franchise Bancorp Inc.
294 Walker Dr., Unit 2
Brampton, ON, Canada L6T 4Z2
Ph:(905)790-9023
Free: (866)463-4124
Fax:(905)790-7059
Co. E-mail: franchises@franchisebancorp.com
URL: http://www.livcan.com
No. of Franchise Units: 6. **Founded:** 1975. **Franchised:** 1975. **Description:** The franchise offers house ware and kitchen items. **Equity Capital Needed:** $200,000-$350,000. **Franchise Fee:** $25,000. **Training:** Yes.

ASSOCIATIONS AND OTHER ORGANIZATIONS

10389 ■ American Home Furnishings Alliance
317 W High Ave., 10th Fl.
High Point, NC 27260
Ph:(336)884-5000
Fax:(336)884-5303
Co. E-mail: acounts@ahfa.us
URL: http://www.ahfa.us
Contact: Andy Counts, CEO
Description: Furniture manufacturers seeking to provide a unified voice for the furniture industry and to aid in the development of industry personnel. Provides: market research data; industrial relations services; costs and operating statistics; transportation information; general management and information services. Compiles statistics; develops quarterly Econometric Forecast. **Publications:** *Furniture Executive* (monthly); *Human Resources Close-Up* (monthly); *Suppliers on Demand*;Membership Directory (annual).

10390 ■ Fashion Group International
8 W 40th St., 7th Fl.
New York, NY 10018
Ph:(212)302-5511
Fax:(212)302-5533
Co. E-mail: cheryl@fgi.org
URL: http://www.fgi.org
Contact: Cheryl Ingersoll, Regional Dir.
Description: Fashion, apparel, accessories, beauty and home industries. Works to advance professionalism in fashion and its related lifestyle industries with a particular emphasis on the role and development of women. Provides a public forum for examination of important contemporary issues in fashion and the business of fashion. Works to present timely information regarding national and global trends and to attain greater recognition of women's achievements in business and to promote career opportunities in fashion.

10391 ■ High Point Market Authority
164 S Main St., Ste. 700
High Point, NC 27260
Ph:(336)869-1000
Free: 800-874-6492
Co. E-mail: bcasey@highpointmarket.org
URL: http://www.highpointmarket.org
Contact: Kevin O'Connor, Pres.
Description: Furniture manufacturers and exhibition buildings working to create a cooperative business environment. .

10392 ■ Home Furnishings Independents Association
PO Box 420807
Dallas, TX 75342
Ph:(214)741-7632
Free: 800-942-4663

Fax:(214)742-9103
Co. E-mail: info@hfia.com
URL: http://www.hfia.com
Contact: Mary Frye, Pres.
Description: Retailers and suppliers of home furnishings organized to protect and advance industry and member interests and increase profitability. Conducts educational seminars; makes discount bank card and group health and life insurance programs available to members. .

10393 ■ International Furniture Rental Association
5229 College Hill Rd.
Woodstock, VT 05091
Co. E-mail: info@ifra.org
URL: http://www.ifra.org
Description: Companies whose major business is the leasing and rental of home furnishings and accessories; suppliers of products and services to these companies are associate members. Dedicated in upholding ethical standards of the furniture rental industry and providing quality products and service. Conducts industry exposition and statistical surveys. Promotes industry through nationwide consumer education program. Works to safeguard against adverse legislation and regulation. **Publications:** *Furniture Rental Association of America—Newsletter* (bimonthly).

10394 ■ International Furniture Transportation and Logistics Council
282 N Ridge Rd.
Brooklyn, MI 49230
Ph:(517)467-9355
Co. E-mail: russ111@comcast.net
URL: http://www.iftlc.org
Contact: Russ Matthews
Description: Represents and promotes furniture transportation logistics professionals. .

10395 ■ International Home Furnishings Representatives Association
PO Box 670
High Point, NC 27261
Ph:(336)889-3920
Fax:(336)802-1959
Co. E-mail: info@ihfra.org
URL: http://www.IHFRA.org
Contact: Kathy Parks, Exec. Dir.
Description: Local affiliated organizations of approximately 2,000 home furnishings representatives. Provides services to affiliates and individual members, including information exchange, listing manufacturers seeking representatives in all territories and representatives seeking manufacturers' lines in specific territories. Conducts certified home furnishings educational program. .

10396 ■ Kitchen Cabinet Manufacturers Association
1899 Preston White Dr.
Reston, VA 20191-5435
Ph:(703)264-1690

Fax:(703)620-6530
Co. E-mail: info@kcma.org
URL: http://www.kcma.org
Contact: C. Richard Titus, Exec. VP
Description: Serves as a national trade association representing cabinet and countertop manufacturers and suppliers to the industry. Promotes the cabinet manufacturing industry, develops standards for the industry, administers a testing and certification program, conducts education programs and meetings, provides management information and industry data, and engages in activities on behalf of members on legislative and regulatory issues. **Publications:** *Cabinet News* (bimonthly); *Directory of Certified Cabinet Manufacturers* (annual).

10397 ■ National Home Furnishings Association
3910 Tinsley Dr., Ste. 101
High Point, NC 27265-3610
Ph:(336)886-6100
Free: 800-888-9590
Fax:(336)801-6102
Co. E-mail: info@nhfa.org
URL: http://www.nhfa.org
Contact: Steve DeHaan, Exec. VP
Description: Provides business services to help retailers of home furnishings grow their businesses. Provides educational programs for retail sales managers and trainers, for middle management, for owners and executives, and for family businesses. **Publications:** *Home Furnishings Retailer* (8/year).

10398 ■ National Kitchen and Bath Association
687 Willow Grove St.
Hackettstown, NJ 07840
Ph:(908)852-0033
Free: 800-843-6522
Fax:(908)852-1695
Co. E-mail: feedback@nkba.org
URL: http://www.nkba.org
Contact: Bill Darcy, Exec. VP
Description: Manufacturers and firms engaged in retail kitchen sales; manufacturers' representatives and wholesale distributors; utilities, publications and other firms supplying products or services to the kitchen and bathroom industry. Protects and promotes the interest and welfare of members by fostering a better business climate in the industry. Awards titles of Certified Kitchen Designer and Certified Bathroom Designer to individuals with proven knowledge, ability and experience in the design, planning, and installation supervision of residential kitchens. Conducts kitchen and bathroom training schools throughout the country. Sponsors business management and consumer awareness programs. Maintains speakers' bureau and Hall of Fame. .

10399 ■ Summer and Casual Furniture Manufacturers Association
317 W High Ave.
High Point, NC 27260
Ph:(336)884-5000

Fax:(336)884-5303
Co. E-mail: jlogan@ahfa.us
URL: http://www.ahfa.us/divisions/scfma.asp
Contact: Joseph P. Logan, Exec. Dir.
Description: A division of American Home Furnishings Alliance. Manufacturers of household summer and casual furniture. Compiles trade statistics; provides legislative, technical, management, and marketing services. Conducts technical and marketing research. .

10400 ■ Upholstered Furniture Action Council

Box 2436
High Point, NC 27261
Ph:(336)885-5065
Fax:(336)885-5072
Co. E-mail: info@ufac.org
URL: http://www.ufac.org
Description: Conducts research and disseminates information regarding the development and adoption of voluntary guidelines for production of more cigarette-resistant upholstered furniture; educates the public in the safe use of smoking materials. Maintains speakers' bureau; compiles statistics. **Publications:** *UFAC: Action Guide* (annual).

REFERENCE WORKS

10401 ■ "Bedding a Leader in Kohl's Q1 Gains" in *Home Textiles Today* (Vol. 31, May 24, 2011, No. 13, pp. 1)

Pub: Reed Business Information
Description: Kohl's credited home furnishings, particularly bedding, as the leading source of its first-quarter sales and profit gains in 2011. Statistical data included.

10402 ■ "Bon-Ton Halves Q1 Losses, Show Operating Profit" in *Home Textiles Today* (Vol. 31, May 24, 2011, No. 13, pp. 7)

Pub: Reed Business Information
Ed: James Mammarella. **Description:** Bon-Ton Stores reported progress in its multi-year push to profitability, with soft home sales leading the way. Statistical data included.

10403 ■ "CGG Home Fashions to Show Hand-Loomed Textiles" in *Home Textiles Today* (Vol. 31, May 24, 2011, No. 13, pp. 4)

Pub: Reed Business Information
Description: CGG Home Fashions introduced textiles made from natural fibers and vegetable dyes for upscale industry use at the HD Expo in Las Vegas, Nevada.

10404 ■ "Colores Origenes: Martha Kruse" in *Advertising Age* (Vol. 77, November 13, 2006, No. 46, pp. S12)

Pub: Crain Communications, Inc.
Ed: Laurel Wentz. **Description:** Home Depot has created a range of Latin paint colors called Colores Origenes; the new line was originally intended to launch only at locations with heavily Hispanic patrons but the company decided to make the line available at all of their stores.

10405 ■ "A Counter Offer" in *Inc.* (February 2008, pp.)

Pub: Gruner & Jahr USA Publishing
Ed: Elaine Appleton Grant. **Description:** Online retailer offering a line of kitchen and home products has upgraded its Website in order to make the business more attractive to possible buyers of the company. The firm is asking $9.9 million and reported gross revenue of $12.7 in 2007. The owner suggests that a buyer add product lines geared towards more rooms of the home than currently offer on the retail site.

10406 ■ *Directory of Home Furnishings Retailers*

Pub: Chain Store Guide
Released: Annual, Published March, 2007. **Price:** $275, individuals online lite; $875, individuals online pro; $1,175, individuals online pro plus. **Covers:** 2,900 U.S. and Canadian companies operating 8,300 executives and buyers. Also covers 1,000 wholesale companies. **Entries Include:** Company name; physi-

cal address; mailing address; main phone number; main fax number; 1,430 executive e-mail and web addresses; total sales; industry sales; Internet order processing; Internet sales percentage; total units; units by trade name; total selling square footage; average number of checkouts; projected openings and remodeling; product lines; furniture styles; furniture price lines; trading areas; distribution center locations; services provided; products rented; private label credit card indicator; gallery names; primary wholesaler's name and location; parent company name and location; public company indicator; year founded; subsidiaries names and location; divisional office locations; key personnel with titles; store locations with addresses and manager's names. Wholesale listings also include import and export indicators. **Arrangement:** Geographical. **Indexes:** Alphabetical, product line, specialty, exclusions.

10407 ■ "Doing Good: Cause and Effect" in *Entrepreneur* (Vol. 36, February 2008, No. 2, pp. 23)

Pub: Entrepreneur Media Inc.
Description: Lisa Knoppe established Art for a Cause LLC that employs people with mental and physical disabilities. The company makes hand-painted tools and furniture to be sold at gift retailers and hardware stores.

10408 ■ "Dreamy Fortune: Pillow Biz Dreams of Sales Reaching $10 Million a Year" in *Small Business Opportunities* (Spring 2008)

Pub: Harris Publications Inc.
Ed: Stan Roberts. **Description:** Profile of Michale Lezberg, owner of a pillow factory. Lezberg shares insight into building his firm to a multi-million dollar a year business.

10409 ■ "Entrepreneur Says Spirituality Has Been a Key to Her Success" in *Business First Columbus* (Vol. 25, October 17, 2008, No. 8, pp. 1)

Pub: American City Business Journals
Ed: Scott Rawdon. **Description:** Profile of Carolyn Williams Francis, CEO of Williams Interior Designs Inc. She outlines her mantra for success in her furniture design business, but emphasizes that faith has taken her business to greater heights.

10410 ■ "Forget Your Pants, Calvin Klein Wants Into Your Bedroom" in *Globe & Mail* (March 31, 2007, pp. B4)

Pub: CTVglobemedia Publishing Inc.
Ed: Barrie McKenna. **Description:** The plans of Phillips-Van Heusen Corp. to open more Calvin Klein stores for selling the new ranges of clothing, personal care products, luggage and mattresses are discussed.

10411 ■ "Furniture Chain Moving to Harford" in *Baltimore Business Journal* (Vol. 27, January 22, 2010, No. 38, pp. 1)

Pub: American City Business Journals
Ed: David J. Sernovitz. **Description:** Manchester, Connecticut-based Bob's Discount Furniture signed a lease for 672,000 square feet of space in Harford County, Maryland. The site will become the discount furniture retailer's distribution center in mid-Atlantic US. As many as 200 jobs could be generated when the center opens.

10412 ■ "The Furniture Company Wanted to Sell Him Its Buildings-And Close Down. Should He Buy the Company, Too?" in *Inc.* (November 2007)

Pub: Gruner & Jahr USA Publishing
Ed: Alex Salkever. **Description:** Rick Detkowski, real estate investor, discusses his decision to purchase the furniture company housed in the buildings he was interested in buying. The property would have cost him between $500,000 to $1 million, he was able to purchase the property and business with its entire inventory of furniture, vehicles, and machinery for $1.8 million.

10413 ■ "Furniture Making May Come Back—Literally" in *Business North Carolina* (Vol. 28, March 2008, No. 3, pp. 32)

Pub: Business North Carolina
Description: Due to the weak U.S. dollar and the fact that lumber processors never left the country,

foreign furniture manufacturers are becoming interested in moving manufacturing plants to the U.S.

10414 ■ *Gift, Housewares & Home Textiles Buyers*

Pub: Briefings Media Group
Contact: Alan M. Douglas, President
E-mail: chart@douglaspublications.com
Released: Annual, latest edition 2011-2012. **Price:** $329, individuals directory price; $659, individuals directory/CD combo. **Covers:** 12,700 buyers in the gift, housewares, and textiles industry throughout the United States, Puerto Rico, the Virgin Islands, and Canada. **Entries Include:** Company name, address, phone, fax; e-mail; URL; names and titles of key personnel; financial data; branch/subsidiary names and addresses; products and/or services provided; price points; sales volume; type of stores; number of stores; divisions of parent companies; corporate buying offices. **Arrangement:** Geographical. **Indexes:** Store name, new listings, mail order, online retailer.

10415 ■ "Home Helps Push Macy's to First-Quarter Profit" in *Home Textiles Today* (Vol. 31, May 24, 2011, No. 13, pp. 2)

Pub: Reed Business Information
Description: Macy's Inc. reported home goods as one of the three strong performing categories for first quarter 2011. Home goods sales, both big and small ticket items, have improved significantly for the retailer.

10416 ■ "Home Shows Signs of Life at Target" in *Home Textiles Today* (Vol. 31, May 24, 2011, No. 13, pp. 1)

Pub: Reed Business Information
Description: Retailer, Target, is experience a boost in sales for apparel and products for the home.

10417 ■ "Home Sits Out Q1 Surge at JCP" in *Home Textiles Today* (Vol. 31, May 24, 2011, No. 13, pp. 1)

Pub: Reed Business Information
Ed: James Mammarella. **Description:** JCPenney chairman and CEO, Mike Ullman, reported sales gains for first quarter 2011 in all products except home goods.

10418 ■ "Home Source Debuts Diesel Home Collection" in *Home Textiles Today* (Vol. 31, May 24, 2011, No. 13, pp. 1)

Pub: Reed Business Information
Ed: Carole Sloan. **Description:** Home Source is highlighting the debut collection of bed and bath products made by Diesel. These items interpret the jeans culture into home furnishings.

10419 ■ "Liora Manne to Debut Fabric Line" in *Home Textiles Today* (Vol. 31, May 24, 2011, No. 13, pp. 4)

Pub: Reed Business Information
Description: Textile and product designer Liora Manne will debut her new decorative fabric collection at the Showtime in High Point, North Carolina in June 2011. More than 22 fabric patterns and solid colors using Manne's patented Lamontage textile design process will be featured and can be used for indoor/outdoor decorative fabrics, furniture, decorative pillows, upholstery and more.

10420 ■ *Market Resource Guide*

Pub: International Home Furnishings Center
Contact: Tom Loney, Vice President
Released: Semiannual, Latest edition 2011. **Price:** $25, individuals market resource guide & add $40 for shipments. **Publication Includes:** List of 80,000 manufacturers and distributors in the furniture industry who exhibit at the International Home Furnishings Market. **Entries Include:** Company name, address, phone; showroom name and location, president, vice president, dir. of marketing. **Arrangement:** Alphabetical.

10421 ■ "Martha Stewart Launches Macys Line" in *Marketing to Women* (Vol. 21, March 2008, No. 3, pp. 5)

Pub: EPM Communications, Inc.
Description: Martha Stewart launches an exclusive line of home decor called Wedgwood as part of her relationship with Macy's stores.

10422 ■ **"New Kittinger Showroom Twice the Size of the Last One"** in *Business First Buffalo* (December 7, 2007, pp. 4)

Pub: American City Business Journals, Inc.

Ed: Tracey Drury. **Description:** Kittinger Furniture Company, an upscale furniture maker, has opened a 6,000 square foot retail outlet at the Transit Road, New York. The company's moved to attract suburban and affluent customers for its high-end furniture products.

10423 ■ **"P/Kaufmann Sells Bennettsville"** in *Home Textiles Today* (Vol. 31, May 24, 2011, No. 13, pp. 6)

Pub: Reed Business Information

Description: Decorative Screen Printers purchased the printing and finishing facility of P/Kaufmann in Bennettsville, South Carolina. However, the firm will continue its focus on its core business, a vat printing facility for home furnishings fabrics.

10424 ■ **"Peking Launches Trina Turk Bedding Collection"** in *Home Textiles Today* (Vol. 31, May 24, 2011, No. 13, pp. 4)

Pub: Reed Business Information

Description: Peking Handicraft is launching designer Trina Turk's bedding collection of four beds that reflect her approach to contemporary fabric design using color and prints with strong graphic effects.

10425 ■ **"Procter Gambles on Wallpaper; Putting Paint On a Roll"** in *Advertising Age* (Vol. 77, September 18, 2006, No. 38, pp. 4)

Pub: Crain Communications, Inc.

Ed: Jack Neff. **Description:** Procter & Gamble Co. has launched a new line of textured paints that are already applied to a wallpaper-like roll that can be hung without paste or wallpaper tools.

10426 ■ **"Ross Stores Reports Spectacular First Quarter"** in *Home Textiles Today* (Vol. 31, May 24, 2011, No. 13, pp. 2)

Pub: Reed Business Information

Ed: James Mammarella. **Description:** Retailer Ross Stores reported strong sales and profit gains for first quarter 2011, with their home department helping to lead the way.

10427 ■ **"Sales at Furniture Showrooms Sink"** in *Puget Sound Business Journal* (Vol. 29, October 10, 2008, No. 25, pp. 1)

Pub: American City Business Journals

Ed: Greg Lamm. **Description:** Furniture showrooms are seeing a drop in sales due to the bad economy. Buyer demand has also fallen because of the slumping real estate market.

10428 ■ **"Shaw Joins Green Institute Launch"** in *Home Textiles Today* (Vol. 31, May 24, 2011, No. 13, pp. 4)

Pub: Reed Business Information

Description: Shaw Industries Group joined the Green Products Innovation Institute, the first nonprofit institute of its kind in America. The institute promotes the concepts of reverse engineering, elimination of waste, safe chemistries, and closed loop technical nutrients.

10429 ■ **"Sheets Makers Optimistic Amid Price, Delivery Issues"** in *Home Textiles Today* (Vol. 31, May 24, 2011, No. 13, pp. 8)

Pub: Reed Business Information

Ed: Jill Rowen. **Description:** Retail sales of sheets and pillowcases dropped 4.7 percent in volume in 2009. Retailers pulled back inventory significantly in 2010. Statistical data included.

10430 ■ **"Sunbrella Engages Consumers Via Social Media"** in *Home Textiles Today* (Vol. 31, May 24, 2011, No. 13, pp. 4)

Pub: Reed Business Information

Description: Performance fabric brand Sunbrella is marketing to social media, such as Facebook and Twitter, in order to boost consumer interest and retailer support.

10431 ■ **"Too Good to be Threw: The Complete Operations Manual for Resale and Consignment Shops"**

Pub: Katydid Press

Price: $69.95. **Description:** Revised edition covers all the information needfed to start and run a buy-outright or consignment shop, covering anything from clothing to furniture resale.

10432 ■ **"Williams-Sonoma Beats Expectations in Q1"** in *Home Textiles Today* (Vol. 31, May 24, 2011, No. 13, pp. 2)

Pub: Reed Business Information

Description: Both retail nameplates, Williams-Sonoma and Pottery Barn reported gains in 2011's first quarter, accredited to the way shoppers responded to new opening price point programs for several of its brands.

10433 ■ **"Women Take Care of a Home's Inside, Men Work on the Outside"** in *Marketing to Women* (Vol. 23, November 2010, No. 11, pp. 2)

Pub: EPM Communications, Inc.

Description: Women spend more time doing housework, caring for children, and talking on the telephone; while men's time is spent working, participating in sports, watching TV, and lawn maintenance.

STATISTICAL SOURCES

10434 ■ **RMA Annual Statement Studies**

Pub: Robert Morris Associates (RMA)

Released: Annual. **Price:** $175.00 2006-07 edition, $105.00. **Description:** Contains composite balance sheets and income statements for more than 360 industries, including the accounting, auditing, and bookkeeping industries. Also contains five years of comparative historical data for discerning trends. Includes 16 commonly used ratios, computed for most of the size groupings for nearly every industry.

10435 ■ **Standard & Poor's Industry Surveys**

Pub: Standard & Poor's Corp.

Released: Annual. **Price:** $3633.00. **Description:** Two-volume book that examines the prospects for specific industries, including trucking. Also provides analyses of trends and problems, statistical tables and charts, and comparative company analyses.

TRADE PERIODICALS

10436 ■ **Casual Living**

Pub: Reed Business Information

Contact: Cinde W. Ingram, Editor-in-Chief

E-mail: cingram@casualliving.com

Released: Monthly. **Price:** $20; $4 single issue. **Description:** Trade magazine for the casual furnishings industry.

10437 ■ **The duPont Registry**

Pub: duPont Publishing Inc.

Released: Monthly. **Price:** $15.95; $25.95 Canada; $45.95 other countries. **Description:** Magazine featuring worldwide luxury homes for sale.

10438 ■ **The Furniture Executive**

Pub: American Furniture Manufacturers Association

Ed: Pat Bowling, Editor, pbowling@afma4u.org. **Released:** Monthly. **Price:** Included in membership. **Description:** Reports on the activities of the American Furniture Manufacturers Association and on issues impacting the industry.

10439 ■ **Furniture Today**

Pub: Reed Business Information

Contact: Ray Allegrezza, Editor-in-Chief

E-mail: rallegrezza@reedbusiness.com

Released: 50/yr. **Price:** $127.48 U.S. and Canada; $244.49 other countries. **Description:** Furniture retailing and manufacturing magazine (tabloid).

10440 ■ **Furniture Transporter**

Pub: Bohman Industrial Traffic Consultants Inc.

Ed: Ray Bohman, Jr., Editor. **Released:** Monthly. **Description:** Reports important news and developments in shipping, packaging, and transporting that affect the furniture and allied products industries.

10441 ■ **Furniture World Magazine**

Pub: Towse Publishing Co.

Released: Semiannual. **Price:** $19; $29 Canada; $89 other countries; $39 three years. **Description:** Trade magazine covering marketing, finance, retail operations, and sales training for furniture retailers.

10442 ■ **Home Furnishings Retailer**

Pub: Home Furnishings Retailer

Ed: Mary Wynn Ryan, Editor. **Released:** 11/yr. **Price:** Free to qualified subscribers; $60; $80 Canada; $120 other countries. **Description:** Home Furnishings Retail Trade Journal.

10443 ■ **Home Improvement Retailing**

Pub: Powershift Communications Inc.

Released: Bimonthly. **Price:** $76; $110 Canada plus applicable taxes. **Description:** Trade magazine for the home improvement retail and wholesale market.

10444 ■ **Laminating Design and Technology**

Pub: Cygnus Business Media

Ed: Tim Fixmer, Editor. **Released:** Bimonthly. **Price:** $48; $68; $99 Canada and Mexico; $99 other countries. **Description:** Trade magazine covering decorative surface fashion and functionality.

TRADE SHOWS AND CONVENTIONS

10445 ■ **Fort Lauderdale Furniture and Accessory Market**

Karel Exposition Management Co.

3590 Mystic Pointe Dr.

Aventura, FL 33180

Ph:(305)792-9990

Fax:(305)792-9898

Co. E-mail: info@kemexpo.com

URL: http://www.kemexpo.com

Released: Annual. **Audience:** Furniture trade. **Principal Exhibits:** Furniture.

10446 ■ **Fort Lauderdale Home Design & Remodeling Show**

Home Show Management

1450 Madruga Ave., Ste. 301

Coral Gables, FL 33146

Ph:(305)667-9299

Free: 800-353-EXPO

Fax:(305)667-3266

Co. E-mail: info@homeshows.net

URL: http://www.homeshows.net

Released: Annual. **Audience:** Designers, decorators, builders, developers, contractors, and consumers. **Principal Exhibits:** Architecture, interior design, furnishings, home improvement, and remodeling equipment, supplies, and services. **Dates and Locations:** 2011 Jun 27-30, Broward County, FL.

10447 ■ **International Contemporary Furniture Fair**

George Little Management, LLC (New York, New York)

1133 Westchester Ave., Ste. N136

White Plains, NY 10606

Ph:(914)421-3200

Free: 800-272-SHOW

Co. E-mail: cathy_steel@glmshows.com

URL: http://www.glmshows.com

Released: Annual. **Audience:** Retailers, architects, interior designers, and manufacturers. **Principal Exhibits:** Contemporary furniture, lighting, wall coverings, floor coverings, textiles, and decorative accessories for the residential, home office, and contract markets. **Dates and Locations:** 2011 May 14-17, New York, NY.

10448 ■ **The Miami Home Design & Remodeling Show**

Home Show Management

1450 Madruga Ave., Ste. 301

Coral Gables, FL 33146

Ph:(305)667-9299

Free: 800-353-EXPO

Fax:(305)667-3266
Co. E-mail: info@homeshows.net
URL: http://www.homeshows.net
Released: Annual. **Audience:** Designers, decorators, builders, developers, contractors, and consumers. **Principal Exhibits:** Architecture, interior design, furnishings, home improvements, and remodeling equipment, supplies, and services. **Dates and Locations:** 2011 Sep 02-06, Miami Beach, FL.

10449 ■ Toronto International Home Furnishings Market
Quebec Furniture Manufacturers Association, Inc.
1111 St.-Urbain, Ste. 101
Montreal, QC, Canada H2Z 1Y6
Ph:(514)866-3631
Free: 800-361-6681
Fax:(514)871-9900
Co. E-mail: info@qfma.com
URL: http://www.qfma.com
Released: Annual. **Audience:** Trade only; retailers, designers, architects, and decorators. **Principal Exhibits:** Furniture, lamps, and accessories.

CONSULTANTS

10450 ■ KV Marketing Inc.
12 Huntsville Rd.
Katonah, NY 10536-2002
Ph:(914)232-7566
Fax:(914)232-7848
Co. E-mail: pci19@optonline.net
URL: http://www.p-c-i.org
Contact: Meri Pollak, Mgr
E-mail: pci19@optonline.net
Scope: Provides international marketing expertise including market research and analysis, new product development, marketing plans, and general management assistance to both nonprofits and the commercial sectors.

10451 ■ Riedel Marketing Group
5327 E Pinchot Ave.
Phoenix, AZ 85018-2963
Ph:(602)840-4948

Fax:(602)840-4928
Co. E-mail: ajr@4rmg.com
URL: http://www.4rmg.com
Contact: A. J. Riedel, Senior Partner
E-mail: ajr@4rmg.com
Scope: The house wares and food service industry strategic marketing planning experts. Help manufacturers of house wares and food products solve marketing problems and identify and exploit marketing opportunities. Provides a full-range of strategic marketing planning services including development of marketing strategy, development of fact-based sales presentations, category management, definition of market opportunities and new product development exclusively to the house wares and food service industries. **Publications:** "Your Key Consumer: Her Take on the International Home & Housewares Show," Mar, 2008; "What's Hot, What's Not: The Consumer Speaks," Mar, 2006; "HIPsters SPEAK: What We Love to Buy and Why," Apr, 2005; "Influentials: Who They Are and Why You Should Care," Jun, 2004; "The Seven Secrets to Selling More Housewares," Jan, 2003. **Seminars:** Consumers Speak: What We Love to Buy and Why, What Do Those Consumers Think; The Seven Secrets to Selling More House wares. **Special Services:** Home Trend Influentials Panel.

FRANCHISES AND BUSINESS OPPORTUNITIES

10452 ■ Bath Fitter
Bath Fitter Franchising, Inc.
27 Berard Dr., Ste. 2701
South Burlington, VT 05403
Ph:(450)472-0027
Free: 877-422-2322
Fax:(450)472-9490
URL: http://www.bathfitter.com
No. of Franchise Units: 97. **No. of Company-Owned Units:** 20. **No. of Operating Units:** 149. **Founded:** 1984. **Franchised:** 1992. **Description:** Sales and installation of custom-molded acrylic bathtub liners, made-to-measure acrylic bath walls, shower bases, shower walls and related accessories.

Equity Capital Needed: $190,000-$270,000. **Franchise Fee:** $40,000. **Financial Assistance:** No. **Training:** Provides 3 weeks at headquarters and 2 weeks at franchisees location with ongoing support.

10453 ■ Children's Lighthouse Franchise Co.
101 S Jennings
Fort Worth, TX 76104
Ph:(817)247-0886
Free: 888-338-4466
Fax:(817)887-5772
No. of Franchise Units: 30. **No. of Company-Owned Units:** 8. **Founded:** 1997. **Franchised:** 1999. **Description:** Childcare franchise. **Equity Capital Needed:** $150,000 minimum liquid assets; $500,000 net worth. **Franchise Fee:** $50,000. **Financial Assistance:** No. **Training:** Yes. s.

10454 ■ More Space Place
More Space Place, Inc.
5040 140th Ave. N
Clearwater, FL 33760
Free: 888-731-3051
Fax:(727)524-6382
No. of Franchise Units: 42. **No. of Company-Owned Units:** 5. **Founded:** 1985. **Franchised:** 1993. **Description:** Storage units and furniture designed to provide maximum space utilization. **Equity Capital Needed:** $40,000-$65,000 cash, $133,000-$203,000 total investment. **Franchise Fee:** $22,000-$29,500. **Financial Assistance:** Third party financing available. **Training:** Yes.

10455 ■ Verlo Mattress Factory Stores
VyMaC Corporation Co.
201 N Main St., Ste. 5
Fort Atkinson, WI 53538
Ph:(920)568-3100
Free: 800-229-8957
Fax:(920)568-3140
No. of Franchise Units: 61. **Founded:** 1958. **Franchised:** 1980. **Description:** Factory direct mattress manufacturer. **Equity Capital Needed:** $325,000 net worth; minimum $75,000 liquid. **Franchise Fee:** $50,000. **Financial Assistance:** Yes. **Training:** Yes. es.

START-UP INFORMATION

10456 ■ "Caring Concern" in *Small Business Opportunities* **(September 2010)**
Pub: Harris Publications Inc.
Description: Profile of Joshua Hoffman, founder and CEO of HomeWell Senior Care, Inc., provider of non-medical live-in and hourly personal care, companion-ship and homemaker services for seniors so they can remain in their own homes.

10457 ■ "Home: Where the Money Is!" in *Small Business Opportunities* **(May 2008)**
Pub: Harris Publications Inc.
Description: Profile of ComForcare, a franchise company that serves the senior population in America; a franchise can be started with one owner and add and build a team as it grows.

10458 ■ "This Biz Is Booming" in *Small Business Opportunities* **(Winter 2010)**
Pub: Harris Publications Inc.
Description: Non-medical home care is a $52 billion industry. Advice to start a non-medical home care business is provided, focusing on franchise FirstLight HomeCare, but showing that independent home care agencies are also successful.

ASSOCIATIONS AND OTHER ORGANIZATIONS

10459 ■ American Association for Homecare
2011 Crystal Dr., Ste. 725
Arlington, VA 22202
Ph:(703)836-6263
Fax:(703)836-6730
Co. E-mail: info@aahomecare.org
URL: http://www.aahomecare.org
Contact: Mr. Tyler Wilson, Pres./CEO
Description: Represents all elements of home care; dedicated to advancing value and practice of quality healthcare services at home. **Publications:** *AAHomecare Update* (weekly); *HME Answer Book* (quarterly).

10460 ■ American Hospital Association
155 N Wacker Dr.
Chicago, IL 60606
Ph:(312)422-3000
Fax:(312)422-4796
Co. E-mail: rich@aha.org
URL: http://www.aha.org
Contact: Richard Umbdenstock PhD, Pres./CEO
Description: Represents health care provider organizations. Seeks to advance the health of individuals and communities. Leads, represents, and serves health care provider organizations that are account-able to the community and committed to health improvement. **Publications:** *AHA News Now* (daily); *Guide to the Health Care Field* (annual); *Hospital Statistics* (annual); *Hospitals and Health Networks* (monthly).

10461 ■ Canadian Association of Nurses in Oncology–Association canadienne des infirmieres en oncologie
375 W 5th Ave., Ste. 201
Vancouver, BC, Canada V5Y 1J6
Ph:(604)874-4322
Fax:(604)874-4378
Co. E-mail: cano@malachite-mgmt.com
URL: http://www.cano-acio.ca
Contact: Jennifer Wiernikowski RN, Pres.
Description: Registered nurses in independent practice. Promotes improved public access to health care; seeks to increase the role of nurses in the delivery of health care services. Develops business and practice guidelines for members. Provides support and assistance to members; conducts educational programs to raise public awareness of nursing and other health care services; sponsors business and continuing professional development courses for members. Conducts lobbying activities; undertakes research projects; compiles statistics. **Publications:** *Canadian Oncology Nursing Journal* .

10462 ■ Canadian Home Care Association–Association Canadienne de Soins et Services a Domicile
10 Kingsbridge Garden Cir., Ste. 704
Mississauga, ON, Canada L5R 3K6
Ph:(905)361-2294
Fax:(905)361-3274
Co. E-mail: chca@cdnhomecare.ca
URL: http://www.cdnhomecare.ca
Contact: Donna Dill, Pres.
Description: Providers of home health care services. Promotes excellence in the practice of home care. Represents members' interests before medical organizations, government agencies, and the public. Conducts continuing professional development courses for home care personnel. Sponsors promotional programs. **Publications:** *Cnez Nous, At Home* (quarterly).

10463 ■ Canadian Nurses Foundation–Fondation des Infirmieres et Infirmiers du Canada
50 Driveway
Ottawa, ON, Canada K2P 1E2
Ph:(613)237-2133
Free: 800-361-8404
Fax:(613)237-3520
Co. E-mail: info@cnf-fiic.ca
URL: http://www.cnf-fiic.ca
Contact: Helene Sabourin, Exec. Dir.
Description: Promotes health and patient care in Canada. Fosters excellence in nursing through nursing research grants, scholarships, and specialty certification. **Publications:** *Foundation Focus* (semi-annual).

10464 ■ Canadian Society of Gastroenterology Nurses and Associates–Societe Canadienne des Infirmieres et Infirmiers en Gastroenterologie et Travailleurs Associes
No. 224 - 1540 Cornwall Rd.
Oakville, ON, Canada L6J 7W5
Ph:(905)829-8794
Free: (866)544-8794
Fax:(905)829-0242
Co. E-mail: palma@cag-acg.org
URL: http://www.csgna.com
Contact: Cindy James, Treas.
Description: Gastroenterology nurses, medical technicians, and sales representatives of medical equipment and pharmaceutical manufacturers. Promotes excellence in the teaching and practice of gastroenterological nursing. Facilitates communication among members; produces patient education materials. Conducts continuing professional education programs; maintains speakers' bureau.

10465 ■ National Association for Home Care and Hospice
228 7th St. SE
Washington, DC 20003
Ph:(202)547-7424
Fax:(202)547-3540
Co. E-mail: exec@nahc.org
URL: http://www.nahc.org
Contact: Andrea Devoti, Chair
Description: Represents providers of home health care, hospice, and homemaker-home health aide services; interested individuals and organizations. Develops and promotes high standards of patient care in home care services. Seeks to affect legislative and regulatory processes concerning home care services; gathers and disseminates home care industry data; develops public relations strategies; works to increase political visibility of home care services. Provides legal and accounting consulting services; conducts market research and compiles statistics. Sponsors educational programs for organizations and individuals concerned with home care services. **Publications:** *Caring* (monthly); *Hospice Forum* (biweekly); *NAHC Report* (weekly); *National Home Care and Hospice Directory* (annual).

10466 ■ National Health Council
1730 M St. NW, Ste. 500
Washington, DC 20036
Ph:(202)785-3910
Fax:(202)785-5923
Co. E-mail: info@nhcouncil.org
URL: http://www.nationalhealthcouncil.org
Contact: Myrl Weinberg, Pres.
Description: National association of voluntary and professional societies in the health field; national organizations and business groups with strong health interests. Seeks to improve the health of patients, particularly those with chronic diseases, through conferences, publications, policy briefings and special projects. Distributes printed material on health careers and related subjects. Promotes standardization of financial reporting for voluntary health groups. **Publications:** *Council Currents* (bimonthly); *Directory of Health Groups in Washington*; *Guide to America's Voluntary Health Agencies*; *Standards of Accounting and Reporting for Voluntary Health and Welfare Organizations*; *300 Ways to Put Your Talent to Work in the Health Field* .

10467 ■ National League for Nursing
61 Broadway, 33rd Fl.
New York, NY 10006
Ph:(212)363-5555
Free: 800-669-1656
Fax:(212)812-0391
Co. E-mail: generalinfo@nln.org
URL: http://www.nln.org
Contact: Judith A. Halstead PhD, Pres.-Elect
Description: Champions the pursuit of quality nursing education. A professional association of nursing faculty, education agencies, health care agencies, allied/public agencies, and public members whose mission is to advance quality nursing education that prepares the nursing workforce to meet the needs of diverse populations in an ever-changing health care environment. Serves as the primary source of information about every type of nursing education program, from the LVN and LPN to the EdD and PhD. There are 20 affiliated constituent leagues that provide a local forum for members. The National League for Nursing Accrediting Commission is an independent corporate affiliate of the NLN, responsible for providing accreditation services to all levels of nursing education. **Publications:** *Nursing Data Review* (annual); *Nursing Education Perspectives* (bimonthly); *Professional Development Bulletin* (biweekly); *State Approved Schools of Nursing - RN* (annual); *Undergraduate & Graduate Nursing Programs, 2nd Ed.* .

REFERENCE WORKS

10468 ■ "Advancing the Ball" in *Inside Healthcare* (Vol. 6, December 2010, No. 7, pp. 31)
Pub: RedCoat Publishing Inc.
Ed: Michelle McNickle. **Description:** Profile of Medicalodges an elder-care specialty company that provides both patient care and technology development. President and CEO of the firm believes that hiring good employees is key to growth for any small business.

10469 ■ "Breaking the Mold" in *Entrepreneur* (Vol. 37, September 2009, No. 9, pp. 87)
Pub: Entrepreneur Media, Inc.
Ed: Tracy Stapp. **Description:** Profiles of top franchise businesses in the United States are presented. Hey Buddy! Pet Supply Vending Co. offers pet supply vending machines. Home Health Mates, on the other hand, provides professional medical care at home.

10470 ■ *Case Management Resource Guide*
Pub: Access Intelligence L.L.C.
Released: Annual, latest edition 2005-2006. **Price:** $60, individuals for additional copy, per volume. **Entries Include:** Facility name, address, phone names and titles of key personnel; number of employees, geographical area served, type of service or programs provided branch office or parent organization name and phone, and credentials. **Database Covers:** In four regional volumes, lists 110,000 health care facilities and support services, including homecare, rehabilitation, psychiatric, and addiction treatment program; hospices, adult day care, and burn and cancer centers. **Arrangement:** Classified by service provided and location. **Indexes:** Company name, advertiser.

10471 ■ "Chemed's Vitas Aims to Acquire" in *Business Courier* (Vol. 27, July 9, 2010, No. 10, pp. 1)
Pub: Business Courier
Ed: James Ritchie. **Description:** Chemed Corporation's Vitas Healthcare Corporation is looking for smaller nonprofit hospices as it looks to become more streamlined in a tougher reimbursement environment. CFO David Williams syas they want to acquire these hospices as fast as they can integrate them.

10472 ■ "Connecting the Dots Between Wellness and Elder Care" in *Benefits and Compensation Digest* (Vol. 47, August 2010, No. 8, pp. 18)
Pub: International Foundation of Employee Benefit Plans
Ed: Sandra Timmermann. **Description:** Employees caring for aged and infirm parents deal with time and financial issues and other stresses. The connection between health status of caregivers and employers' health care costs could be aided by linking programs and benefits with wellness and caregiving.

10473 ■ "Elder Care Costs Surge" in *National Underwriter Life & Health* (Vol. 114, November 8, 2020, No. 21, pp. 25)
Pub: Summit Business Media
Ed: Trevor Thomas. **Description:** Nursing home and assisted living rates rose from 2009 to 2010, according to MetLife Mature Market Institute. Statistical data included.

10474 ■ "Elder Care, Rx Drugs Reforms Top Zoeller's Agenda" in *Times* (December 21, 2010)
Pub: The Times
Ed: Sarah Tompkins. **Description:** Indiana Attorney General Greg Zoeller is hoping to develop a program in the state that will help regulate care for the elderly; freeze medical licenses for doctors involved in criminal investigations; address illegal drug use; and to establish a program to help individuals dispose of old prescription medications easily at pharmacies.

10475 ■ "Elder-Care Seminar to Teach Ways to Avoid Falls" in *Virginian-Pilot* (November 25, 2010)
Pub: Virginian-Pilot
Ed: Amy Jeter. **Description:** ResCare HomeCare, a home health services firm, offers free seminars on helping to make residences safer for seniors prone to falling.

10476 ■ "EVMS Gets Grant to Train Providers for Elder Care" in *Virginian-Pilot* (October 29, 2010)
Pub: Virginian-Pilot
Ed: Elizabeth Simpson. **Description:** Eastern Virginia Medical School received a federal grant to train health providers in elder care. Details of the program are provided.

10477 ■ "Face Issues if Elder Care, Unemployment Collide" in *Atlanta Journal-Constitution* (December 26, 2010, pp. G1)
Pub: Atlanta Journal-Constitution
Ed: Amy Lindgren. **Description:** More issues arise during holiday for families with older members requiring care, including the issue of employment for those doing the caregiving.

10478 ■ "GeckoSystems Reduces Sensor Fusion Costs Due to Elder Care Robot Trials" in *Internet Wire* (December 14, 2010)
Pub: Comtex
Description: GeckoSystems International Corporation has been able to reduce the cost of its sensor fusion system while maintaining reliability and performance. The firm's ongoing first in-home elder care robot trials have sparked interest regarding its business model, technologies available for licensing, and joint domestic and international ventures.

10479 ■ *Healthcare Standards Directory*
Pub: ECRI Institute
Released: Annual, Latest edition 2009. **Price:** $650, individuals plus shipping and handling charges. **Covers:** Over 40,000 standards, guidelines, laws, and regulations from over 1,200 organizations. **Entries Include:** In 'Organizations and Their Standards' section—Organization name, address, phone, standards or guidelines, year of issue, price, catalog number, author, bibliographic information. **Indexes:** Keyword.

10480 ■ *Medical and Health Information Directory*
Pub: Gale
Released: Annual, Latest edition April 2011. **Price:** $1190, individuals set; $501, individuals per volume. **Covers:** In volume 1, more than 33,000 medical and health oriented associations, organizations, institutions, and government agencies, including health maintenance organizations (HMOs), preferred provider organizations (PPOs), insurance companies, pharmaceutical companies, research centers, and medical and allied health schools. In Volume 2, over 20,000 medical book publishers; medical periodicals, directories, audiovisual producers and services, medi-

cal libraries and information centers, electronic resources, and health-related internet search engines. In Volume 3, more than 40,500 clinics, treatment centers, care programs, and counseling/diagnostic services for 34 subject areas. **Entries Include:** Institution, service, or firm name, address, phone, fax, email and URL; many include names of key personnel and, when pertinent, descriptive annotation. Volume 3 was formerly listed separately as Health Services Directory. **Arrangement:** Classified by organization activity, service, etc. **Indexes:** Each volume has a complete alphabetical name and keyword index.

10481 ■ "New Elder Care Center to Focus on Residents with Failing Memories" in *Tulsa World* (November 30, 2010)
Pub: World Publishing
Ed: Robert Evatt. **Description:** People with Alzheimer's disease and other mental disorders require specialized care. Constant Care Management Company runs 'memory care' centers designed for the elderly with such conditions.

10482 ■ "Q&A With Devin Ringling: Franchise's Services Go Beyond Elder Care" in *Gazette* (October 2, 2010)
Pub: The Gazette
Ed: Bill Radford. **Description:** Profile of franchise, Interim HealthCare, in Colorado Springs, Colorado; the company offers home care services that include wound care and specialized feedings to shopping and light housekeeping. It also runs a medical staffing company that provides nurses, therapists and other health care workers to hospitals, prisons, schools and other facilities.

10483 ■ "Taking the Right Road" in *Entrepreneur* (Vol. 37, October 2009, No. 10, pp. 104)
Pub: Entrepreneur Media, Inc.
Ed: Jason Daley. **Description:** Joe Grubb's franchise of BrightStar Healthcare, a home health care provider, in Knoxville, Tennessee has grown into a $1 million business. Grubb, a former sales agent, experienced slow growth for his franchise and had to deal with cash flow issues during its first few months.

10484 ■ "VPA to Pay $9.5 Million to Settle Whistle-Blower Lawsuits" in *Crain's Detroit Business* (Vol. 26, January 11, 2010, No. 2, pp. 13)
Pub: Crain Communications, Inc.
Ed: Jay Greene. **Description:** According to Terrence Berg, first assistant with the U.S. Attorney's Office in Detroit, Voluntary Physicians Association, a local home health care company, has agreed to pay $9.5 million to settle four whistle-blower lawsuits; the agreement settles allegations that VPA submitted claims to TriCare, the Michigan Medicaid program and Medicare for unnecessary home visits, tests and procedures.

STATISTICAL SOURCES

10485 ■ *RMA Annual Statement Studies*
Pub: Robert Morris Associates (RMA)
Released: Annual. **Price:** $175.00 2006-07 edition, $105.00. **Description:** Contains composite balance sheets and income statements for more than 360 industries, including the accounting, auditing, and bookkeeping industries. Also contains five years of comparative historical data for discerning trends. Includes 16 commonly used ratios, computed for most of the size groupings for nearly every industry.

TRADE PERIODICALS

10486 ■ *Abbeyfield Houses Society of Canada Newsletter*
Pub: Abbeyfield Houses Society of Canada
Ed: Robert McMullan, Editor. **Released:** Quarterly. **Description:** Reports on news of Abbeyfield Houses Society of Canada, a provider of care and companionship for the elderly. Also features articles related to

aging, housing, and lifestyle in Canada and internationally. Recurring features include letters to the editor, and columns titled News of Local Societies and Bits 'n Bites.

10487 ■ *Adult Day Services Letter*
Pub: Health Resources Publishing
Contact: Beth-Ann Kerber, Managing Editor
Released: Monthly. **Price:** $97, individuals. **Description:** Provides crucial management information and serves as a link between adult day programs across the country.

10488 ■ *American Hospital Association—Ambulatory Outreach*
Pub: American Hospital Association
Ed: Glen Brown, Editor, gbrownl@aha.org. **Released:** Quarterly. **Price:** $85, members; $99, nonmembers. **Description:** Analyzes the factors influencing market supply, demand, and competition. Recurring features include statistics, details on the latest accreditation standards, reviews of current literature, education and technical assistance updates, news of research, and resources.

10489 ■ *Care Management Journals*
Pub: Springer Publishing Co.
Contact: Carol D. Austin, Editorial Advisory Board
Ed: F. Russell Kellogg, MD, Editor. **Released:** Quarterly. **Price:** $105 print only; $158 print & online; $95 online only; $265 institutions print only; $255 institutions online only; $383 institutions print & online. **Description:** Journal presenting research, analysis of current issues, and reports on programs in case management and current programs and policies in the long term home health care field.

10490 ■ *Caring*
Pub: National Association for Home Care
Contact: Hubert H. Humphrey, Vice President
Released: Monthly. **Description:** Journal concerning home care.

10491 ■ *Caring People*
Pub: National Association for Home Care
Contact: Val Halamandaris, Ed. and Publisher
Released: Monthly. **Description:** Magazine spotlighting individuals who care and service others.

10492 ■ *Home Health Care Management and Practice*
Pub: Sage Publications Inc.
Released: Bimonthly. **Price:** $499 institutions print & e-access; $549 institutions current volume print & all online content; $449 institutions e-access; $499 institutions all online content; $449 institutions content through 1998; $489 institutions print only; $160 print only; $90 institutions single print; $35 single print. **Description:** Journal covering issues and practical concerns in home health care.

10493 ■ *Home Health Care Services Quarterly*
Pub: Routledge Journals
Contact: William T. Wake MD, Editorial Board
Ed: Maria Aranda, PhD, Editor. **Released:** Quarterly. **Price:** $118 online; $124 print & online. **Description:** Professional journal.

10494 ■ *Home Health Line*
Pub: United Communications Group
Contact: Jason Huffman, Publisher
E-mail: jhuffman@decisionhealth.com
Released: Weekly, 48/yr. **Price:** $497. **Description:** Reports on Medicare, Medicaid, and other federal and managed care coverage and payment for home health care, including home health agencies, hospice care, home medical equipment, home infusion therapy, and the home care industry as a business.

10495 ■ *Home Healthcare Nurse*
Pub: Lippincott Williams & Wilkins
Contact: Carolyn J. Humphrey, Ed. Emeritus
Ed: Tina M. Marrelli, Editor, news@marelli.com. **Released:** 10/yr. **Price:** $59.91; $202.95 institutions; $148 other countries; $252.95 institutions, other countries; $39.99 in-training. **Description:** Magazine for the practicing professional nurse working in the home health, community health, and public health areas.

10496 ■ *Homecare Administrative HORIZONS*
Pub: Beacon Health Corp.
Contact: Diane J. Omdahl RN, MS, Editor-in-Chief
Released: Monthly. **Price:** $347, individuals. **Description:** Provides homecare agency management information on all kinds of business and personnel topics. Incorporates comprehensive how-to information, current regulatory requirements, and documentation strategies. Runs a series of articles, including how to move into managed care, how to manage and measure outcomes, how to survive scrutiny by medicare's fraud squad, strengthening agency/physician relationships, and personnel issues. Recurring features include columns titled Peaks & Valleys, Fine-tuning the Fundamentals, Clearing the Fog, and Higher Ground.

10497 ■ *Homecare DIRECTION*
Pub: Beacon Health Corp.
Contact: Diane J. Omdahl RN, MS, Editor-in-Chief
Released: Monthly. **Price:** $337. **Description:** Delivers timely regulatory information with how-to elements to apply to everyday care delivery. Equips agency patient care personnel with knowledge they need to deliver quality care and comply with medicare certification and reimbursement requirements. Offers valuable tips on interpreting medicare rules to justify care; how to create policies that reduce survey surprises, and documentation tips and examples. Recurring features include columns titled Documenting with Impact, Survey Sense, Looking for Direction, and From the Lamp Room.

10498 ■ *HomeCare Magazine*
Pub: Penton Media
Contact: Gregg Herring, Publisher
E-mail: greg.herring@penton.com
Released: Monthly. **Price:** $135 Canada; $150 two years Canada; $250 other countries; $250 two years and other countries. **Description:** Magazine serving home medical equipment suppliers, including independent and chain centers specializing in home care, pharmacies or chain drug stores with home care products, and joint-ventured hospital home health care businesses. Contains industry news and new product launches and marketing strategies.

10499 ■ *Hospital Home Health*
Pub: American Health Consultants Inc.
Contact: Lee Reinauer, Assoc. Managing Ed.
E-mail: lee.reinauer@ahepub.com
Released: Monthly. **Price:** $499, individuals $349/year, U.S.; $399 elsewhere. **Description:** Provides clinical, legal, and management information pertinent to hospital-based home health agencies. Also monitors government regulation and profiles successful or unique programs.

10500 ■ *Modern Healthcare*
Pub: Crain Communications Inc.
Contact: Paul Barr, News Ed.
E-mail: pbarr@crain.com
Ed: David Burda, Editor, dburda@crain.com. **Released:** Weekly. **Price:** $159; $249 Canada; $213 other countries. **Description:** Weekly business news magazine for healthcare management.

10501 ■ *NAHC Report*
Pub: National Association for Home Care & Hospice
Released: Weekly. **Price:** $325. **Description:** Reports on legislative, regulatory, judicial affairs, and research developments in the home care industry.

VIDEOCASSETTES/ AUDIOCASSETTES

10502 ■ *The Business of Caring*
Victoria International Corp.
1 Harts Cove, PO Box 14
New Castle, NH 03854
Ph:(603)436-1067
Fax:(603)433-4204
URL: http://www.victoriainternationalcorp.com
Released: 1987. **Description:** A series of programs for nursing professionals about patient care, consideration and relation to the family. Each program has nine episodes. **Availability:** VHS; 3/4U.

10503 ■ *Home Health Nursing: Nursing Diagnosis in the Home Health Setting*
AJN Video Library/Lippincott Williams & Wilkins
American Journal of Nursing
345 Hudson St., 16th Fl.
New York, NY 10014
Ph:(212)886-1200
Free: 800-256-4045
Fax:(212)886-1276
Co. E-mail: info@nursingcenter.com
URL: http://www.nursingcenter.com
Price: $195.00. **Description:** Features actual home health nurse visiting a patient to provide an overview of the entire nursing process, including information on patient assessment, patient history, goal setting, physical assessment, teaching the caregiver, and environmental assessment. Also furnishes a look at nursing diagnoses, including alteration in comfort, knowledge deficit and self-care deficit. **Availability:** VHS.

10504 ■ *Home Visits: The Nursing Bag*
AJN Video Library/Lippincott Williams & Wilkins
American Journal of Nursing
345 Hudson St., 16th Fl.
New York, NY 10014
Ph:(212)886-1200
Free: 800-256-4045
Fax:(212)886-1276
Co. E-mail: info@nursingcenter.com
URL: http://www.nursingcenter.com
Price: $195.00. **Description:** Provides instructional material for nursing students and home health providers on proper use of the nursing bag, including information on safety precautions, universal precautions when dealing with blood and body fluids, and supplies and equipment commonly found in the nursing bag. Also contains general guidelines for the care of the nursing bag, protection against loss or theft, and the history of the bag. **Availability:** VHS.

10505 ■ *Lazaris: Forgiving Yourself*
Tapeworm Video Distributors
25876 The Old Road 141
Stevenson Ranch, CA 91381
Ph:(661)257-4904
Fax:(661)257-4820
Co. E-mail: sales@tapeworm.com
URL: http://www.tapeworm.com
Released: 1985. **Price:** $29.95. **Description:** Insights of Lazaris, a non-physical entity that channels his message of love and fulfillment through Jach Pursel. **Availability:** VHS.

TRADE SHOWS AND CONVENTIONS

10506 ■ NAHC's Annual Meeting and Home Care and Hospice Expo
National Association for Home Care
228 7th St. SE
Washington, DC 20003
Ph:(202)547-7424
Fax:(202)547-3540
URL: http://www.nahc.org
Released: Annual. **Audience:** Home health professionals, hospital administrators, healthcare suppliers, consultants, and certified public accountants. **Principal Exhibits:** General home health products, emergency response systems, computers, uniforms, publications, surgical and medical supplies, pharmaceuticals, durable and home medical equipment. **Dates and Locations:** 2011 Mar 27-30, Washington, DC.

CONSULTANTS

10507 ■ Carol K. Revilock
1004 Tuxedo Ave.
Parma, OH 44134-1726
Ph:(216)749-2293
Contact: Duane M. Revilock, Principle
Scope: Offers health care consulting services, specializes in the following areas: home health care, geriatrics, non-profit organizations and staff development.

10508 ■ Family Home Care Inc.
10 W Sq., Lake Rd., Ste. 219
Bloomfield Hills, MI 48302
Ph:(248)338-1016
Fax:(248)338-1016
Contact: Marilyn LeVasseur, Principle
E-mail: marlevbri@aol.com
Scope: Provides seminars, programs or individual consultation for home healthcare, either Medicare or Medicaid, private pay or other insurances. The emphasis ranges from agency startup and encompasses any area of the home care agency, which includes financial, management, nursing, marketing, and public relations. Serves government agencies also.

10509 ■ Linda Berkowitz
1938 Soule Rd.
Clearwater, FL 33759
Ph:(727)726-7442
Fax:(727)785-7656
Co. E-mail: magicrb1216@yahoo.com
E-mail: magicrb1216@yahoo.com
Scope: Consultant in health care and employee and systems management.

10510 ■ R.D. Network Inc.
PO Box 375
Lafayette Hill, PA 19444
Ph:(215)482-4461
Free: 877-482-4991
Fax:(215)836-0378
Co. E-mail: info@rdnetwork.com
URL: http://www.rdnetwork.com
Contact: Melissa Altman, Principle
E-mail: info@rdnetwork.com
Scope: Dietitians, diet technicians, and certified dietary managers available nationwide and worldwide through an international registry for consulting positions to wellness and employee education programs, drug or alcohol rehabilitation, hospital, LTC, nutrition and labeling communications, nutrition consultation, weight control classes, healthcare staff supplementation, media and program development, and all nutrition and food-related needs. Expert witness and speakers bureau also available. Industries served: healthcare, food industry, food service, restaurateurs, supermarkets, pharmaceutical companies, home health agencies, insurance companies, HMOs, and government agencies. **Seminars:** Healthy Dining Etiquette for Executives and Sales Staff Diet and Wellness; Cardiovascular Nutrition; Starting a Nutrition Consulting Practice; AIDS and Diet Therapy; Nutrition Care for Your Parents in Their Elder Years; Increase Your Energy-Increase Your Sales.

10511 ■ United American Healthcare Corp.
303 E Wacker Dr., Ste. 1200
Chicago, IL 60601
Ph:(313)393-0200
Fax:(313)393-7944
Co. E-mail: sharris@uahc.com
URL: http://www.uahc.com
Contact: Emmett Moten,, Secretary
E-mail: sharris@uahc.com
Scope: Provides services to the health care industry, including information systems, claims processing, and strategic planning.

FRANCHISES AND BUSINESS OPPORTUNITIES

10512 ■ Accessible Home Health Care
210 N University Dr., Ste. 806
Coral Springs, FL 33071
Ph:(954)341-5600
Fax:(954)757-3009
No. of Franchise Units: 99. **No. of Company-Owned Units:** 1. **Founded:** 2001. **Franchised:** 2006. **Description:** Home health-care services. **Equity Capital Needed:** $55,000-$95,000. **Franchise Fee:** $39,500. **Royalty Fee:** 5%. **Financial Assistance:** Limited in-house financing available. **Training:** Provides 1 week training at headquarters, 2 days at franchisee's location and ongoing support.

10513 ■ AtWork HelpingHands Services
3215 John Sevier Hwy.
Knoxville, TN 37920
Free: 800-383-0804
Fax:(865)573-1171
No. of Franchise Units: 4. **Founded:** 1990. **Franchised:** 2003. **Description:** Non-medical in-home services & senior care. **Equity Capital Needed:** $70,000-$115,500. **Franchise Fee:** $21,000. **Royalty Fee:** 3-5%. **Financial Assistance:** No. **Training:** Offers 5+ days training at headquarters, 2-5 days at franchisee's location and ongoing support.

10514 ■ A Better Solution, Inc.
PO Box 653
Venice, FL 34284
Ph:(941)416-2540
Free: (866)480-9393
Co. E-mail: absivenice@earthlink.net
URL: http://www.abettersolutionusa.com
No. of Franchise Units: 3. **Founded:** 1998. **Franchised:** 2003. **Description:** A non-medical solution for our everyday needs. You will offer a staff of caring, experienced, dependable caregivers able to assist clients of all ages with non-medical needs. homemaking, companionship, transportation, meal planning, etc. **Equity Capital Needed:** $35,000-$65,000. **Franchise Fee:** $19,700. **Financial Assistance:** No. **Training:** 2 week training and on the job, in your live office location. Your comprehensive FL training class covers marketing and sales, recruitment, operations, scheduling, payroll, and client relations. Full ongoing support includes phone, onsite visits and website support.

10515 ■ BrightStar Healthcare
1790 Nations Dr., Ste. 103
Gurnee, IL 60031
Ph:877-689-6898
No. of Franchise Units: 243. **No. of Company-Owned Units:** 1. **Founded:** 2002. **Franchised:** 2005. **Description:** Medical/non-medical home care & medical staffing. **Equity Capital Needed:** $95,067-$162,158. **Franchise Fee:** $47,500. **Royalty Fee:** 5-7%. **Financial Assistance:** Yes. **Training:** Provides 10 days at headquarters, 10 days onsite with ongoing support.

10516 ■ Comfort Keepers
245 Fairview Mall Dr., Ste. 505
Toronto, ON, Canada M2J 4T1
Ph:(416)663-2930
Free: (866)363-0072
Fax:(416)498-7155
Co. E-mail: pdrutz@comfortkeepers.ca
URL: http://www.comfortkeepers.ca
No. of Franchise Units: 45. **No. of Company-Owned Units:** 1. **Founded:** 1998. **Franchised:** 1999. **Description:** Provides non-medical in-home care for the elderly and others who need assistance with daily living activities. Comfort Keepers believes and practices the philosophy of "Thinking Outside The Box". Our marketing and advertising methods are extremely proprietary and unlike anything else on the market. We have become one of the fastest growing new franchises in North America, as recognized by INC., Successful Franchises, Entrepreneur, Fortune, HGTV, and over 100 major newspapers. This is a business of caring - you can find businesses that are personally rewarding and you can find businesses that are financially rewarding, but it is not every day you can be in a business that can be both! **Equity Capital Needed:** $88,000-110,000. **Franchise Fee:** $39,500. **Training:** Yes.

10517 ■ GEM Health Care Services
383 Parkdale Ave., Ste. 304
Ottowa, ON, Canada K1Y 4R4
Ph:(613)761-7474
Free: 877-761-4361
Fax:(613)761-7738
Co. E-mail: carl.maynard@gemhealthcare.com
URL: http://www.gemhealthcare.com
No. of Company-Owned Units: 1. **Founded:** 1994. **Franchised:** 2006. **Description:** Health care agency. **Equity Capital Needed:** $97,500-$137,000. **Franchise Fee:** $37,500. **Training:** Provides 3 weeks training.

10518 ■ Home Care Assistance
HCAFranchise Corp.
148 Hawthorne Ave.
Palo Alto, CA 94301
Ph:(702)204-1436
Free: 800-536-2973
Fax:(650)462-6907
Co. E-mail: jj@homecareassistance.com
URL: http://www.hcafranchise.com
No. of Franchise Units: 42. **No. of Company-Owned Units:** 4. **Founded:** 2002. **Franchised:** 2004. **Description:** Home Care Assistance offers 'Assisted Living at Home' to seniors. We focus on 24/7 live-in service and offer exclusive 'We Will Be There' guarantee. Business model makes use of strong consumer advertising. Looking for franchisees with good business background. Serious business people wanting substantial business opportunity. **Equity Capital Needed:** $75,000-$150,000. **Franchise Fee:** $24,950. **Financial Assistance:** No. **Training:** 1 week at national training headquarters, and ongoing by phone and email.

10519 ■ Home Helpers
10700 Montgomery Rd., Ste. 300
Cincinnati, OH 45242
Free: (866)708-8921
Fax:(513)563-2691
Co. E-mail: inquiry@homehelpers.cc
URL: http://www.homehelpers.cc
No. of Franchise Units: 658. **Founded:** 1997. **Franchised:** 1997. **Description:** Non-medical, in-home companion care for the elderly, new mothers, and those recuperating from illness. **Equity Capital Needed:** $47,200-$86,400 total investment. **Franchise Fee:** $36,900. **Financial Assistance:** Financing available. **Training:** 5 Extensive raining includes operations, payroll, recruitment, accounting, scheduling and client relations. Teaches the industry's most advanced marketing program that includes print, TV, radio, media and referral programs.

10520 ■ Nurse Next Door Senior Care Services
5511 West Blvd., Ste. 320
Vancouver, BC, Canada V3M 3W6
Free: 877-330-1819
Fax:(604)228-4359
Co. E-mail: spahal@nursenextdoor.ca
URL: http://www.nursenextdoor.c0m
No. of Franchise Units: 47. **No. of Company-Owned Units:** 1. **Founded:** 2001. **Franchised:** 2007. **Description:** Home health care for seniors. **Equity Capital Needed:** $114,000-$138,000. **Franchise Fee:** $40,000. **Training:** 1 week training and ongoing support.

10521 ■ Retire-At-Home Services
1704 Carling Ave., Ste. 100
Ottawa, ON, Canada K2A 1C7
Free: 877-444-9001
Fax:877-444-9002
Co. E-mail: franchiseinfo@retireathome.com
URL: http://www.retireathome.com
No. of Franchise Units: 22. **No. of Company-Owned Units:** 1. **Founded:** 1994. **Franchised:** 2007. **Description:** In home healthcare for seniors. **Equity Capital Needed:** $59,500-$69,500. **Franchise Fee:** $35,000. **Training:** Provides 7 days training.

10522 ■ Right at Home
Right At Home, Inc.
6464 Center St., Ste. 150
Omaha, NE 68106
Ph:(402)697-7537
Fax:(402)697-0289
Co. E-mail: info@rightathome.org
URL: http://www.rightathome.net
No. of Franchise Units: 224. **Founded:** 1995. **Franchised:** 2000. **Description:** In home, senior care and supplemental staffing for the healthcare industry. **Equity Capital Needed:** $100,000-$200,000 net worth. **Franchise Fee:** $41,500. **Financial Assistance:** No. **Training:** A comprehensive program of pre-training, 2 week initial training program, and follow up onsite training visit. Full on-going support includes telephone, onsite visits and web site support.

10523 ■ Stay At Home
The Arden Group
9821 Cogdill Rd., Ste. 1
Knoxville, TN 37932
Ph:(865)692-1101
Free: 877-261-0793
Co. E-mail: info@StayHomeWeb.com
URL: http://www.StayHomeWeb.com
No. of Franchise Units: 10. **Description:** With over two decades of experience in non-medical in-home care, our founders led the way in establishing the industry, launching & successfully operating several home healthcare companies. The key to our success lies in genuine compassion for patients & commitment to uncompromising dependability, both for patients & franchise owners. Our training programs ensure owners are well prepared to capitalize on one of the country's fastest growing demographics. **Equity Capital Needed:** $49,900-$69,900. **Franchise Fee:** $35,900. **Financial Assistance:** No. **Training:** Our Quick Start, Immersion & Continuing Education programs are quick, easy & through. Each of our key business processessales, advertising, patient care, staffing, payroll, etc. is clearly documented using our easy to follow Stay At Home Process Maps.

10524 ■ Synergy Homecare
Synergy Homecare Franchising, LLC
1757 E Baseline Rd., Bldg. 6, Ste. 124
Gilbert, AZ 85234
Ph:(480)659-7771
Fax:(480)659-7713
Co. E-mail: info@synergyhealthcare.com
URL: http://www.synergyhealthcare.com
No. of Franchise Units: 80. **Founded:** 2000. **Franchised:** 2005. **Description:** Non-medical homecare services. **Equity Capital Needed:** $49,240-$99,540. **Franchise Fee:** $35,000. **Financial Assistance:** No. **Training:** Offers 1 week comprehensive training includes industry basics, business operations, office and employee management, client services, sales & marketing and profitability.

10525 ■ Tender Loving Care
Staff Builders, Inc.
PO Box 90002
Baton Rouge, LA 70879
Ph:(516)327-3361
Free: 800-444-4633
Fax:(516)358-3678
No. of Franchise Units: 248. **No. of Company-Owned Units:** 32. **Founded:** 1961. **Franchised:** 1987. **Description:** Home health care. **Equity Capital Needed:** $125,000-$135,000, includes franchise and working capital. **Franchise Fee:** $$29,500. **Financial Assistance:** Yes. **Training:** Yes.

10526 ■ Touching Hearts At Home
Touching Hearts, Inc.
2314 University Ave. W, Ste. 14
St. Paul, MN 55114
Ph:(651)236-8447
Free: 877-870-8750
Fax:(651)452-7829
Co. E-mail: contact@touchinghearts.com
URL: http://www.touchinghearts.com
No. of Franchise Units: 27. **No. of Company-Owned Units:** 1. **Founded:** 1998. **Franchised:** 2007. **Description:** Help seniors and people with disabilities remain independent by providing non-medical in-home care. Each franchise offers companionship, light housekeeping, laundry, meal preparation, transportation, and much more through a staff of dependable kind caregivers. **Equity Capital Needed:** Initial start-up $41,950-$60,000+. **Franchise Fee:** $29,500. **Financial Assistance:** No. **Training:** Comprehensive 5 day training gives you the knowledge, skills and tools required to run a successful

franchise. Outstanding ongoing support is provided through toll free number assistance, email, internal website discussion forum, HQ support staff, and regional and national seminars.

10527 ■ Visiting Angels
Living Assistance Services, Inc.
28 W Eagle Rd., Ste. 201
Havertown, PA 19083
Ph:(610)924-9663
Free: 800-365-4189
Fax:(610)924-9690
No. of Franchise Units: 409. **Founded:** 1992. **Franchised:** 1998. **Description:** Non-medical senior homecare. **Equity Capital Needed:** $55,285-$87,035. **Franchise Fee:** $28,950-$46,950. **Royalty Fee:** 3.5-2%. **Financial Assistance:** No. **Training:** Yes.

10528 ■ We Care Health Services Inc.
151 Bloor St. W, Ste. 602
Toronto, ON, Canada M5S 1S4
Ph:(416)922-7601
Free: 800-316-2212
Fax:(416)922-6280
Co. E-mail: larry_smith@wecare.ca
URL: http://www.wecare.ca
No. of Franchise Units: 20. **No. of Company-Owned Units:** 28. **Founded:** 1984. **Description:** Offers homecare services. **Equity Capital Needed:** $125,000-$150,000 investment required; $75,000-$90,000 start-up capital required. **Franchise Fee:** $40,000. **Training:** Offers 2 weeks training.

COMPUTERIZED DATABASES

10529 ■ *Health and Medical Care Archive*
University of Michigan
330 Packard St.
PO Box 1248
Ann Arbor, MI 48106-1248
Ph:(734)647-5000
Fax:(734)647-8200
Co. E-mail: netmail@icpsr.umich.edu
URL: http://www.icpsr.umich.edu
Description: Contains the archive of the Robert Wood Johnson Foundation. Features data on health care provided by researchers from universities, public and private agencies, with the aid of the Foundation grants. Included are evaluations of innovative health care delivery programs, investigations of access to and financing of medical care, surveys of health care professionals, and substance abuse surveys. **Availability:** Online: University of Michigan; CD-ROM: University of Michigan. **Type:** Full text.

10530 ■ *Home Healthcare Agency & Chains Directory*
F1RSTMARK Inc.
25 Vintinner Rd.
PO Box 1270
Campton, NH 03223
Ph:(603)726-4800
Free: 800-729-2600
Fax:(603)726-4840
Co. E-mail: leads@firstmark.com
URL: http://www.firstmark.com
Description: Contains listings for more than 8100 home healthcare agencies that provide service to people who have been discharged from hospitals and/or are otherwise in need of medical services at home, including elderly and chronically ill patients. Includes name, address, phone number, key contact name, type of ownership, staffing data and types of services provided. **Availability:** CD-ROM: F1RSTMARK Inc. **Type:** Directory.

10531 ■ *KINETIDEX System*
Thomson Reuters
6200 S Syracuse Way, Ste. 300
Greenwood Village, CO 80111-4740
Ph:(303)486-6444
Free: 800-525-9083
Fax:(303)486-6460
Co. E-mail: mdx.info@thomson.com
URL: http://www.micromedex.com
Description: Contains information on therapeutic drugs and drug dosages. For each drug, provides such information as recommended therapeutic levels, physical IV incompatibilities, clinically significant drug interactions, adverse effects, and guidelines for clinical monitoring. Designed for use by clinicians, enables the user to establish an optimal drug therapy regimen for any patient at any point in time based on age, various disease and physiologic states, multiple drug therapy, social habits, and drug absorption. Software facilitates calculation of drug dose, interval, peak, trough, and other critical pharmacokinetic parameters. Features tables for drug use in patients with renal dysfunction or liver disease as well as the ability to maintain a database of patient records for use in subsequent drug monitoring and drug utilization review. **Availability:** Online: Thomson Reuters; CD-ROM: Thomson Reuters. **Type:** Full text; Numeric.

LIBRARIES

10532 ■ Boone Hospital Center Medical Library
1600 E. Broadway
Columbia, MO 65201
Ph:(573)815-3504
Fax:(573)815-2629
URL: http://www.boone.org
Contact: J. Feintuch, Med.Libn.
Scope: Medicine, nursing. **Services:** Interlibrary loan; copying; document delivery; Library not open to the public. **Holdings:** 2500 books. **Subscriptions:** 225 journals and other serials.

10533 ■ El Camino Hospital–Health Library and Resource Center
Main Bldg., 1st Fl.
2500 Grant Rd.
Mountain View, CA 94040
Ph:(650)940-7210
Fax:(650)940-7174
Co. E-mail: healthlib@elcaminohospital.org
URL: http://www.elcaminohospital.org/Patient_Services/Health_Library
Contact: Jack Black, Sr.Libn.
Scope: Medicine, nursing, healthcare administration, caregiving, elder care. **Services:** Interlibrary loan; copying; Library open to the public. **Holdings:** 5500 books and videotapes. **Subscriptions:** 150 journals and other serials; 3 newspapers.

10534 ■ Virginia Commonwealth University–Virginia Center on Aging–Information Resources Center (730 E)
730 E. Broad St.
Theatre Row Building
Richmond, VA 23219
Ph:(804)828-1525
Fax:(804)828-7905
Co. E-mail: eansello@vcu.edu
URL: http://www.vcu.edu/vcoa
Contact: Dr. Edward F. Ansello, Dir.
Scope: Gerontology, mental health, sociology and the politics of aging, geriatrics, family relationships, long-term care, lifelong learning. **Services:** Library open to the public with restrictions. Audiovisual materials available to Virginia residents only. **Holdings:** 1500 books; 4 archives; 120 AV items. **Subscriptions:** 6 journals and other serials.

START-UP INFORMATION

10535 ■ *Starting and Running Your Own Horse Business*
Pub: Storey Publishing, LLC
Ed: Mary Ashby McDonald. **Released:** November 1, 2009. **Price:** $19.95. **Description:** Insight into starting and running a successful equestrian business is given. The book covers safety, tips for operating a riding school or horse camp, strategies for launching a carriage business, along with tax and insurance advice.

ASSOCIATIONS AND OTHER ORGANIZATIONS

10536 ■ American Driving Society
PO Box 278
Cross Plains, WI 53528
Ph:(608)237-7382
Fax:(608)237-6468
Co. E-mail: info@americandrivingsociety.org
URL: http://www.americandrivingsociety.org
Contact: John Freiburger, Pres.

Description: Persons interested in the sport of driving horses and carriages. Promotes horse and pony driving both competitively and for pleasure; creates and maintains public interest in driving events; organizes or facilitates the organization of driving events; establishes a list of qualified judges. Sponsors educational programs, judge's clinics, and a junior judging program; recognizes driving competitions. Maintains speakers' bureau. .

10537 ■ American Horse Council
1616 H St. NW, 7th Fl.
Washington, DC 20006
Ph:(202)296-4031
Fax:(202)296-1970
Co. E-mail: ahc@horsecouncil.org
URL: http://www.horsecouncil.org
Contact: James J. Hickey Jr., Pres.

Description: Equine breed registries, horse-related organizations, and commercial businesses; individuals with commercial interest in the equine industry; those who have a recreational and pleasure interest in the horse industry. Represents the horse industry before congress and federal agencies. Promotes equitable taxation and legislation; maintains liaison with government agencies and advises members of current national developments affecting the equine industry. Provides advisory, consulting, and referral services; offers tax and information service. Sponsors public affairs program on the contributions of the horse industry to the American economy and quality of life. Compiles statistics. .

10538 ■ American Horse Publications
49 Spinnaker Cir.
South Daytona, FL 32119
Ph:(386)760-7743

Fax:(386)760-7728
Co. E-mail: ahorsepubs@aol.com
URL: http://www.americanhorsepubs.org
Contact: Sandy Kucharski, Pres.

Description: Members are horse-oriented publications, professionals and businesses. Aims to improve the horse publication field and network within the equine publishing industry. .

10539 ■ American Youth Horse Council
577 N Boyero Ave.
Pueblo West, CO 81007
Ph:(719)594-9778
Free: 800-TRY-AYHC
Fax:(775)256-0382
Co. E-mail: info@ayhc.com
URL: http://www.ayhc.com
Contact: Jill Montgomery, Exec. Dir.

Description: Works as the umbrella organization providing resources and leadership to the youth horse industry. Promotes the youth horse industry and responsible equine management practices. Provides a forum for information exchange within the horse industry. Conducts educational forums for youth leaders. Establishes youth conference guidelines. **Publications:** *Horse Industry Handbook: A Guide to Equine Care and Management*; *Safety Manual*; *Youth Leaders Manual* .

10540 ■ Canadian Long Distance Riding Association
48 Long Stan Rd.
Whitchurch-Stouffville, ON, Canada L4A 1P5
Ph:(905)640-7915
Co. E-mail: secretary@caldra.net
URL: http://www.caldra.net
Contact: Kelli Hayhurst, Pres.

Description: Long distance horseback riding enthusiasts. Promotes increased participation in long distance horseback riding and other equestrian events. Serves as a clearinghouse on long distance horseback riding; sponsors educational and recreational programs.

10541 ■ Canadian Therapeutic Riding Association–Association Canadienne d'Equitation Therapeutique
5420 Hwy. 6 N, Ste. 11, R.R. No. 5
Guelph, ON, Canada N1H 6J2
Ph:(519)767-0700
Fax:(519)767-0435
Co. E-mail: ctra@golden.net
URL: http://www.cantra.ca
Contact: Lisa Burd

Description: Therapists with an interest in the use of equestrian activities to promote health and fitness. Seeks to advance the practice of therapeutic riding; promotes ongoing professional development of members. Serves as a clearinghouse on therapeutic horseback riding; sponsors research and educational programs.

10542 ■ CHA - Certified Horsemanship Association
4037 Iron Works Pkwy., Ste. 180
Lexington, KY 40511
Ph:(859)259-3399
Free: 800-399-0138
Fax:(859)255-0726
Co. E-mail: office@cha-ahse.org
URL: http://www.cha-ahse.org
Contact: Mr. Christy Landwehr, CEO

Description: Certifies riding instructors and trail guides, accredits equine facilities, maintains an active database of instructors and stables for the general public on the website. **Publications:** *CHA Composite Horsemanship Manual*; *Ready to Ride?*; *Riding Instructors Manual*; *Standards for Group Riding Programs* .

10543 ■ Equine Canada–Canada Hippique
2685, Queensview Dr., Ste. 100
Ottawa, ON, Canada K2B 8K2
Ph:(613)248-3433
Free: (866)282-8395
Fax:(613)248-3484
Co. E-mail: inquires@equinecanada.ca
URL: http://www.equinecanada.ca
Contact: Mike Gallagher, Pres.

Description: Participants in equestrian events; admirers of horses. Promotes increased interest and participation in equestrian sports. Sponsors competitions; compiles statistics.

10544 ■ Gladstone Equestrian Association
PO Box 469
Gladstone, NJ 07934
Ph:(908)453-3332
Fax:(908)453-3332
Co. E-mail: gladstoneeq@gladstonedriving.org
URL: http://www.gladstonedriving.org

Description: Individuals with an interest in carriage driving and other equestrian events and activities. Seeks to increase interest and participation in carriage driving and related sports. Sponsors competitions. .

10545 ■ Horsemanship Safety Association
5304 Reeve Rd.
Mazomanie, WI 53560
Ph:(608)767-2593
Fax:(608)767-2590
Co. E-mail: hoofbeat@midplains.net
URL: http://www.horsesafety.net
Contact: Ted Marthe

Description: Schools of horsemanship; equine programs at colleges and technical schools; riding instructors and students; medical personnel. To educate equestrians and instructors in safe horsemanship practices. Trains instructors in leadership techniques; conducts group and private lessons for children and adults; sponsors seminars and speaking engagements by certified clinicians. Conducts riding instructor clinics for adults. Certifies instructors at 4 levels: assistant riding instructor, horsemanship safety instructor, associate instructor, and clinic instructor. Certified instructors must renew certification every 3 years. Provides on-site consultation. Offers Expert Witness service. Compiles statistics; maintains speakers' bureau and placement service. Operates job placement services. **Publications:** *Equestrian Lifeguard's Manual*; *Horse Science Manual*; *HSA News* (quarterly).

10546 ■ InterCollegiate Horse Show Association
8125 Verbeck Dr.
Manlius, NY 13104
Co. E-mail: glihsa@aol.com
URL: http://www.ihsainc.com
Contact: George Lukemire, VP
Description: Colleges and universities; individuals. Promotes the education of students in horsemanship and sportsmanship. Provides a basis of competition for intercollegiate riders from beginning through advanced levels. Sponsors clinics, seminars, and other horse-oriented activities. **Publications:** *Regional Directory* (annual).

10547 ■ International Gay Rodeo Association
PO Box 460504
Aurora, CO 80046-0504
Co. E-mail: admin.assistant@igra.com
URL: http://www.igra.com
Contact: Tommy Channel, Admin. Asst.
Description: Gay rodeo associations in the United States and Canada. Promotes public interest in rodeo events and seeks to increase participation in rodeo by gay people. Facilitates communication and cooperation among members; sponsors competitions. **Publications:** *Safety Video*; *2005 Rodeo Resource Guidebook* .

10548 ■ International Jumper Futurity
PO Box 1445
Georgetown, KY 40324
Ph:(502)535-6787
Fax:(502)535-4412
Co. E-mail: yjcoffice@youngjumpers.com
URL: http://www.youngjumpers.com
Description: Owners, breeders, and trainers of sport horses. Promotes interest and participation in show jumping and other equestrian events; seeks to improve sport horse bloodlines. Serves as a clearinghouse on North American sport horses; recognizes outstanding equestrian riders, trainers, and breeders.

10549 ■ National Association of Competitive Mounted Orienteering
4309 Laura St. NW
Comstock Park, MI 49321
Ph:(616)784-1645
Co. E-mail: alisonannebennett@gmail.com
URL: http://www.nacmo.org
Contact: Alison Bennett, Pres.
Description: Horse enthusiasts with a special interest in wilderness-type riding. Promotes horseback riding and fellowship among members. Fosters regulation of the sport through a uniform rules system. Offers competitive and noncompetitive mounted orienteering activities. (Mounted orienteering combines horseback riding with map reading and direction-finding.) Provides assistance to members wishing to manage a ride, and informs members of ride dates and locations. Responds to discrepancies and complaints reported by members. Emphasizes competition through orientation skills as opposed to the speed of individual horses. Conducts charitable program. Compiles statistics. **Publications:** *Meadow Muffin Reports* (5/year); *NACMO How to Ride the Sport* .

10550 ■ North American Horsemen's Association
PO Box 223
Paynesville, MN 56362
Ph:(320)243-7250
Free: 800-328-8894
Fax:(320)243-7224
Co. E-mail: ark@lakedalelink.net
URL: http://www.arkagency-naha.com
Contact: Linda L. Liestman, Pres.
Description: Represents individual horse owners and clubs. Promotes interests of members. Encourages equine safety. Maintains a reference library of books, periodicals, and clippings on equine law and

safety in business issues. Gathers statistics, conducts research, maintains hall of fame, and provides educational programs. **Publications:** *Risk Reduction Program Catalog* (semiannual); *Yearbook of News* (annual).

10551 ■ United Professional Horsemen's Association
4059 Iron Works Pkwy., Ste. 2
Lexington, KY 40511
Ph:(859)231-5070
Fax:(859)255-2774
Co. E-mail: uphakgr@aol.com
URL: http://www.uphaonline.com
Contact: Bret Day, Pres.
Description: Professional horse trainers involved in the show horse industry; horse owners and breeders. Seeks to educate the public about show horses and improve the industry. Sponsors classics for Three- and Four-Year Olds. Maintains hall of fame. .

10552 ■ United States Dressage Federation
4051 Iron Works Pkwy.
Lexington, KY 40511
Ph:(859)971-2277
Fax:(859)971-7722
Co. E-mail: president@usdf.org
URL: http://www.usdf.org
Contact: George W. Williams, Pres.
Description: Members of local dressage organizations and other interested individuals. Promotes and encourages a high standard of accomplishment in dressage throughout the U.S., primarily through educational programs, and to improve understanding of dressage through educational clinics, forums, and seminars. (In dressage, a horse is trained to execute intricate and highly refined steps and maneuvers. Ideally, the signals from rider to horse are not visible to the spectator.) Certifies dressage instructors. **Publications:** *USDF Connection* (monthly); *USDF Directory* (annual).

10553 ■ United States Equestrian Federation
4047 Iron Works Pkwy.
Lexington, KY 40511-8483
Ph:(859)258-2472
Fax:(859)231-6662
Co. E-mail: lrawls@usef.org
URL: http://www.usef.org
Contact: Mr. David O'Connor, Pres.
Description: Individuals and horse shows. Promotes interest in equestrian sports; establishes and enforces rules governing equestrian competitions; maintains records and sanctions dates for competitions. Administers drugs and medication testing program and research. Provides general and specific assistance on equestrian sports in the U.S. as well as referrals. Conducts educational programs for licensed officials throughout the year. Licenses judges and stewards. National Federation of Equestrian Sports for the U.S. National Governing Body for Equestrian Sports (USOC). **Publications:** *Rule Book* (biennial).

10554 ■ United States Eventing Association
525 Old Waterford Rd. NW
Leesburg, VA 20176
Ph:(703)779-0440
Fax:(703)779-0550
Co. E-mail: info@useventing.com
URL: http://www.useventing.com
Contact: Jo Whitehouse, CEO
Description: Horsemen and others supporting the objectives of the USCTA. Formulates, distributes, and explains standards, rules, and regulations for the proper conduct of combined training instruction and equestrian combined training competitions. (A combined training competition is composed of two or all three of the following equestrian activities: dressage, cross-country, and show jumping; when all three activities are included the competition is called a horse trial or event.) Sponsors clinics. Assists to provide training opportunities for potential Olympic games competitors. Approves competitions; compiles records and statistics. **Publications:** *Rules for Combined Training* (biennial); *USCTA News* (bimonthly); *USCTA Omnibus* (quarterly).

10555 ■ United States Pony Clubs
4041 Iron Works Pkwy.
Lexington, KY 40511-8483
Ph:(859)254-7669
Fax:(859)233-4652
Co. E-mail: ceo@ponyclub.org
URL: http://www.ponyclub.org
Contact: Kevin Price, Exec. Dir./CEO
Description: Provides education in riding, mounted sports, horse management, and the care of horses and ponies. Grants certificates of proficiency. Promotes responsibility, moral judgment, leadership, and self-confidence in youth. Sponsors local, regional, and national competitions. Cooperates with the British Horse Society - Pony Club. Offers educational programs. Maintains 20 committees. **Publications:** *Pony Club News* (quarterly); *USPC Handbook and Rules for Eventing Competition* .

DIRECTORIES OF EDUCATIONAL PROGRAMS

10556 ■ *Directory of Private Accredited Career Schools and Colleges of Technology*
Pub: Accrediting Commission of Career Schools and Colleges of Technology
Contact: Michale S. McComis, Exec. Dir.
Released: On web page. **Price:** Free. **Description:** Covers 3900 accredited post-secondary programs that provide training programs in business, trade, and technical fields, including various small business endeavors. Entries offer school name, address, phone, description of courses, job placement assistance, and requirements for admission. Arrangement is alphabetical.

REFERENCE WORKS

10557 ■ *ARICP Directory of Certified Riding Instructors*
Pub: American Riding Instructors Association
Released: Quarterly. **Covers:** Horseback riding instructors who have passed written, practical and oral examinations to earn ARICP certification. **Arrangement:** Geographical.

10558 ■ "Can Turfway Park Stay in the Race?" in *Business Courier* (Vol. 26, January 8, 2010, No. 38, pp. 1)
Pub: American City Business Journals, Inc.
Ed: Jon Newberry. **Description:** Legalization of slot machine gambling in Kentucky could affect raceway Turfway Park and the state's thoroughbred industry. Thousands of farms and jobs in the industry could be lost if slot machine gambling is approved.

10559 ■ *Horse Industry Directory*
Pub: American Horse Council
Contact: James J. Hickey Jr., President
Released: Annual, Latest edition 2011. **Price:** $25, individuals; Free. **Covers:** Organizations concerned with all aspects of the horse industry, including breed registries, racing and showing organizations, transportation and sales companies, and rodeo/trail organizations and equine publications. **Entries Include:** Organization name, address, phone, names and titles of key personnel, e-mail & Internet addresses. **Arrangement:** Classified by service. **Indexes:** Organization name.

10560 ■ "Northwest Washington Fair Building Larger Horse Arena" in *Bellingham Business Journal* (Vol. March 2010, pp. 6)
Pub: Sound Publishing Inc.
Description: Northwest Washington Fair is building a new equestrian arena that will provide larger show space for the horse community. The existing arena will function as a warm-up arena when hosting large shows.

10561 ■ "Turfway Slowing its Gait" in *Business Courier* (Vol. 26, November 6, 2009, No. 28, pp. 1)
Pub: American City Business Journals, Inc.
Ed: Jon Newberry. **Description:** Kentucky's Turfway Park will be decreasing its weekly race schedule from five days to three days in the first two months of 2010,

and to four days in March 2010. The decision to make reductions in the schedule is attributed to the relocation of thoroughbred racing to states that allow casino gambling. As a result, Turfway Park's resources and purse money would be focused on less days.

TRADE PERIODICALS

10562 ■ Saddle & Bridle Magazine
Pub: Saddle & Bridle Inc.
Contact: Mary G. Bernhardt, Managing Editor
Ed: Jeffrey Thompson, Editor. **Released:** Monthly.
Price: $79; $119 two years; $179 three years; $79 other countries. **Description:** Publication for owners, trainers, breeders, and horse show managers of English show horses.

VIDEOCASSETTES/ AUDIOCASSETTES

10563 ■ Horsemanship, Vol. 1-3
ESPN Home Video
ESPN Plz., 935 Middle St.
Bristol, CT 06010
Ph:(860)766-2000
Fax:(860)585-2213
URL: http://www.espn.go.com
Released: 1995. **Price:** $29.95. **Description:** A fundamental training program for the novice viewer in horse riding and racing techniques, as well as care and grooming. Three volumes. **Availability:** VHS.

LIBRARIES

10564 ■ American Mustang and Burro Association Library
PO Box 608
Greenwood, DE 19950
Co. E-mail: in2horses4@yahoo.com
URL: http://www.ambainc.net
Contact: George W. Berrier, Jr., CEO
Scope: Wild horses and burros - history, care, general information, fiction. **Services:** Copying; Library open to the public. **Holdings:** Books; newspaper and magazine article files; artwork; sculpture.

10565 ■ American Saddlebred Museum Library
4083 Iron Works Pkwy.
Lexington, KY 40511
Ph:(859)259-2746, x-312
Fax:(859)255-4909
Co. E-mail: museum@asbmuseum.org
URL: http://www.americansaddlebredmuseum.org
Contact: Kim Skipton, Libn./Cur.
Scope: Saddlebred history, Saddlebred bloodlines, training, riding, driving, art. **Services:** Library not open to the public (museum members only). **Holdings:** 2400 volumes. **Subscriptions:** 4 journals and other serials.

10566 ■ American Suffolk Horse Association ASHA Library
4240 Goehring Rd.
Ledbetter, TX 78946-5004
Ph:(979)249-5795
Co. E-mail: suffolks@cvtx.com
URL: http://www.suffolkpunch.com
Contact: Mary Margaret M. Read, Sec.-Treas.
Scope: Suffolk horses. **Holdings:** 30 books.

10567 ■ Arabian Horse Owners Foundation–W.R. Brown Memorial Library
4101 N. Bear Canyon Rd.
Tucson, AZ 85749
Ph:(520)760-0682
Free: 800-892-0682
Co. E-mail: info@ahof.org
URL: http://www.arabianhorseowners.org/
Contact: Howard F. Shenk, Exec.Dir.
Scope: Arabian horses - history, breeding, use; horses in general - use, care, training, literature, history. **Services:** Copying; Library open to the public

by appointment. **Holdings:** 1200 books; 20 bound periodical volumes; films; photographs; Arabian show and sale programs. **Subscriptions:** 5 journals and other serials.

10568 ■ Arabian Horse Trust Library
12000 Zuni St.
Westminster, CO 80234
Ph:(303)450-4710
Fax:(303)450-4707
Contact: Linda Gruver
Scope: Arabian horses - breeding, history, bloodlines; horsemanship. **Services:** Copying; video viewing room; Library open to the public. **Holdings:** 1500 books; 160 bound periodical volumes; 18,000 horse photographs. **Subscriptions:** 43 journals and other serials.

10569 ■ Bay Meadows Racetrack–William P. Kyne Memorial Thoroughbred Racing Library
PO Box 5050
San Mateo, CA 94402
Ph:(650)574-7223
Co. E-mail: webmaster@baymeadows.com
URL: http://www.baymeadows.com/index.php
Contact: Rusty Mathieson, Asst.Libn.
Scope: Thoroughbred horses - racing, breeding, training, diseases, history; personalities in racing. **Services:** Copying; Library open to the public for reference use only. **Holdings:** 1681 books; 157 bound periodical volumes; photographs; national and international racing programs.

10570 ■ Bloodstock Research Information Services, Inc. Library
801 Corporate Dr., 3rd Fl.
PO Box 4097
Lexington, KY 40544-4097
Ph:(859)223-4444
Free: 800-354-9206
Fax:(859)223-7024
Co. E-mail: brisinfo@brisnet.com
URL: http://www.brisnet.com
Contact: Becky Seabrook
Scope: Thoroughbred horses, horse breeding, horse racing, horse and farm management. **Services:** Library not open to the public. **Holdings:** 1000 bound volumes. **Subscriptions:** 20 journals and other serials.

10571 ■ California State Polytechnic University–W.K. Kellogg Arabian Horse Library
3801 W. Temple Ave.
Bldg. 35, Rm. 207
Pomona, CA 91768-4080
Ph:(909)869-3081
Co. E-mail: mjpaul@csupomona.edu
URL: http://www.csupomona.edu/lAtwkkahl
Contact: Melissa J. Paul, Cur.
Scope: Arabian horses - history, breeding, use, pedigrees, literature. **Services:** Library open to the public for reference use only. **Holdings:** 9500 books; 760 bound periodical volumes; 5 VF drawers of club newsletters; 2 VF drawers of farm brochures; 124 videotapes; photographs; show programs; auction catalogs; films; negatives; manuscripts; prints; paintings; bronzes. **Subscriptions:** 50 journals and other serials.

10572 ■ Camelot Therapeutic Horsemanship–Camelot Library
23623 N. Scottsdale Rd., Ste. D3
PMB 259
Scottsdale, AZ 85255-3471
Ph:(480)515-1542
Fax:(480)515-1542
Co. E-mail: info@camelot-th.org
URL: http://www.camelot-th.org
Scope: Equines, therapeutic horsemanship, domestic animals, therapeutic use of animals, nature, chivalry, King Arthur. **Services:** Interlibrary loan; copying; Library open to the public by appointment. **Holdings:** 300 books.

10573 ■ Harness Racing Museum & Hall of Fame–Peter D. Haughton Memorial Library
240 Main St.
Goshen, NY 10924
Ph:(845)294-6330
Fax:(845)294-3463
Co. E-mail: director@harnessmuseum.com
URL: http://harnessmuseum.com
Contact: Gail Cunard, Dir.
Scope: History of Standardbred horses, history of harness racing, training horses, horses in literature, veterinary medicine. **Services:** Library open to members. **Holdings:** 8061 archival items; 389 books; 1165 bound periodical volumes; 4706 unbound periodicals, pamphlets, and other materials; 2431 videos; 5305 photographs; 1006 programs, newspapers, and other print and manuscript materials. **Subscriptions:** 10 journals and other serials; 5 newspapers.

10574 ■ Keeneland Association Library
Keeneland Race Course
4201 Versailles Rd.
Box 1690
Lexington, KY 40588-1690
Ph:(859)254-3412
Free: 800-456-3412
Fax:(859)255-2484
Co. E-mail: library@keeneland.com
URL: http://www.keeneland.com/visit/Lists/Copy/ research.aspx
Contact: Cathy C. Schenck, Libn.
Scope: Thoroughbred horse racing and breeding, horse sports. **Services:** Library open to the public for reference use only on limited schedule. **Holdings:** 10,000 books; 1000 bound periodical volumes; 1500 videocassettes; 225,000 photo negatives; 3000 files containing newspaper clippings; pamphlet file. **Subscriptions:** 35 journals and other serials.

10575 ■ Palomino Horse Breeders of America Library
15253 E. Skelly Dr.
Tulsa, OK 74116-2620
Ph:(918)438-1234
Fax:(918)438-1232
Co. E-mail: yellahrses@palominohba.com
URL: http://www.palominohba.com/
Contact: Beth Merley, Off.Mgr.
Scope: Horses and equine-related activities, the Palomino horse. **Services:** Library not open to the public.

10576 ■ University of Kentucky–Gluck Equine Research Center I John A. Morris Memorial Library
Gluck Equine Research Center, 2nd Fl.
1400 Nicholasville Rd.
Lexington, KY 40546-0099
Ph:(859)257-4757 x81147
Fax:(859)257-8542
Co. E-mail: ghale@email.uky.edu
URL: http://www.ca.uky.edu/gluck/ServLibrary.asp
Contact: Gracie Hale, Libn.
Scope: Equine veterinary medicine, horses and horse care. **Services:** Document delivery; SDI; Library open to the public for reference use only. **Holdings:** 300 books; 250 bound periodical volumes; 25 videotapes. **Subscriptions:** 20 journals and other serials.

10577 ■ University of Minnesota, Crookston Library
160 Kiehle Bldg.
2900 University Ave.
Crookston, MN 56716-5000
Ph:(218)281-8399
Fax:(218)281-8080
Co. E-mail: willi099@umn.edu
URL: http://www1.crk.umn.edu/library
Contact: Owen E. Williams, Dir. of Lib.Svcs.
Scope: Agriculture, horsemanship, business, foods, hospitality, hotel management. **Services:** Interlibrary loan; copying; wireless Internet; scanning; document delivery. **Holdings:** 32,265 books; 135 periodicals on microfilm; 1900 AV programs. **Subscriptions:** 766 journals and other serials; 55 newspapers.

RESEARCH CENTERS

10578 ■ Grayson-Jockey Club Research Foundation
821 Corporate Dr.
Lexington, KY 40503
Ph:(859)224-2850
Fax:(859)224-2853
Co. E-mail: ebowen@jockeyclub.com
URL: http://www.grayson-jockeyclub.org/
Contact: Edward L. Bowen, Pres.
E-mail: ebowen@jockeyclub.com
Scope: Horses, equine medical research, and horse health and care.

10579 ■ Michigan State University–Michigan State University Horse Teaching and Research Center
1290 Anthony
East Lansing, MI 48824
Ph:(517)355-8391
Co. E-mail: shelle@msu.edu
URL: http://www.msuarabians.com
Contact: Prof. John Shelle, Coord.
E-mail: shelle@msu.edu
Scope: Equine exercise physiology, nutrition, and management.

10580 ■ University of California, Davis–Center for Equine Health
School of Veterinary Medicine
1 Shields Ave.
Davis, CA 95616-8589
Ph:(530)752-6433
Fax:(530)752-9379
Co. E-mail: glferraro@ucdavis.edu
URL: http://www.vetmed.ucdavis.edu/ceh/default.cfm
Contact: Dr. Gregory L. Ferraro, Dir.
E-mail: glferraro@ucdavis.edu
Scope: Basic and clinical studies related to health and behavioral problems in horses. The Center's programs cover many areas of infectious and noninfectious disease research, including reproduction, genetics, musculoskeletal system, performance, medical and surgical diseases, respiratory conditions, nutrition, parasitology, and immunology. **Publications:** The Horse Report (quarterly); Research Review (annually); Specialty Publication (annually). **Educational Activities:** Seminars, tours.

10581 ■ University of Florida–Horse Research Center
2655 NW 100th St.
Ocala, FL 34475
Ph:(352)622-7084
Co. E-mail: esc@ifas.ufl.edu
URL: http://www.animal.ufl.edu/extension/equine/esc.shtml
Contact: Chris Cooper, Coord. of Res.Prog./Farm Mgr.
E-mail: esc@ifas.ufl.edu
Scope: Equine nutrition and reproductive physiology, including basic and applied studies on problems related to horse breeding and production, disease and parasite control, forage utilization, feeding systems, and breeding management. **Educational Activities:** FFA, 4-H, generation connection and other mentoring organizations (annually), events include land judging competitions and tours.

10582 ■ University of Kentucky–Horse Research Farm
900 W.P. Garrigus Bldg.
Department of Animal & Food Sciences
Lexington, KY 40546-0215
Ph:(859)257-2686
Fax:(859)257-2538
Co. E-mail: rharmon@uky.edu
URL: http://www.uky.edu/Ag/AnimalSciences/equine/horsefarm.html
Contact: Robert J. Harmon PhD, Ch.
E-mail: rharmon@uky.edu
Scope: Horse nutrition, growth, and exercise physiology.

START-UP INFORMATION

10583 ■ "Do Your Homework" in *Black Enterprise* **(Vol. 38, November 2007, No. 4, pp. 114)**
Pub: Earl G. Graves Publishing Co. Inc.
Ed: Tennille M. Robinson. **Description:** Preschool teacher seeks advice for starting a hotel resort and day spa.

ASSOCIATIONS AND OTHER ORGANIZATIONS

10584 ■ American Hotel and Lodging Association
1201 New York Ave. NW, No. 600
Washington, DC 20005-3931
Ph:(202)289-3100
Fax:(202)289-3199
Co. E-mail: informationcenter@ahla.com
URL: http://www.ahla.com
Contact: Joseph A. David, Pres./CEO
Description: Represents state lodging associations throughout the United States with some 13,000 property members worldwide, representing more than 1.7 million guest rooms. Provides its members with assistance in operations, education and communications and lobbies on Capitol Hill to provide a business climate in which the industry can continue to prosper. Individual state associations provide representation at the state level and offer many additional cost-saving benefits. **Publications:** *AH&LA Register* (10/year); *Lodging News* (biweekly).

10585 ■ American Hotel and Lodging Educational Foundation
1201 New York Ave. NW, No. 600
Washington, DC 20005-3931
Ph:(202)289-3100
Fax:(202)289-3199
Co. E-mail: cboatman@ahlef.org
URL: http://www.ahlef.org
Contact: Christa Boatman, Mgr. of Foundation Programs
Description: Provides financial support that enhances the stability, prosperity, and growth of the lodging industry through educational and research programs. **Publications:** *Lodging* (monthly).

10586 ■ Asian American Hotel Owners Association
7000 Peachtree Dunwoody Rd. NE, Bldg. 7
Atlanta, GA 30328
Ph:(404)816-5759
Free: 888-692-2462
Fax:(404)816-6260
Co. E-mail: info@aahoa.com
URL: http://www.aahoa.com
Contact: Fred Schwartz, Pres.
Description: Serves as advocacy, educational, and professional development group for Asian-American hotel owners. .

10587 ■ Canadian Resort Development Association
147 Liberty St.
Toronto, ON, Canada M6K 3G3
Ph:(416)960-4930
Free: 800-646-9205
Fax:(416)533-0591
Co. E-mail: crda@rogers.com
URL: http://www.crda.com
Contact: Ross Perlmutter, Exec. Dir.
Description: Owners and operators of resorts. Promotes Canada as a vacation destination; seeks to improve the quality of accommodation and service at Canadian resorts. Interacts with provincial and federal governments regarding legislation affecting the resort industries; facilitates exchange of information among members; represents members' interests; conducts research and educational programs. **Publications:** *Consumers' Guide to Timesharing and Resort Report* (semiannual); *Resort Report* (semiannual).

10588 ■ CDS International
440 Park Ave. S
New York, NY 10016
Ph:(212)497-3500
Fax:(212)497-3535
Co. E-mail: info@cdsintl.org
URL: http://www.cdsintl.org
Contact: Karl Geercken, Chm.
Description: Committed to the advancement of international career training opportunities customized to provide individuals with in-depth practical knowledge of other nations' business practices, cultures, and political traditions. Helps strengthen global cooperation and understanding amongst individuals, businesses, organizations and communities. Annually serves approximately 1,700 individuals from the United States, Germany, Japan, and almost 60 other nations around the globe in a wide variety of internship, fact-finding, and work-study programs. Provides opportunities for individuals to enhance their professional abilities cross-culturally in order to obtain and maintain the skills necessary for successful careers in global economy. Promotes international exchange to help strengthen cooperation between different cultures and nations. .

10589 ■ Green Hotels Association
PO Box 420212
Houston, TX 77242-0212
Ph:(713)789-8889
Fax:(713)789-9786
Co. E-mail: green@greenhotels.com
URL: http://greenhotels.com
Contact: Patricia Griffin, Pres./Founder
Description: Hotels, motels, inns, bed and breakfasts, and all other lodging establishments with an interest in protecting the environment. Encourages, promotes and supports ecological consciousness in the hospitality industry. **Publications:** *Greening Newsletter* (bimonthly); *Membership Conservation Guidelines and Ideas* (quadrennial).

10590 ■ Hospitality Financial and Technology Professionals
11709 Boulder Ln., Ste. 110
Austin, TX 78726
Ph:(512)249-5333
Free: 800-646-4387
Fax:(512)249-1533
Co. E-mail: membership@hftp.org
URL: http://www.hftp.org
Contact: Thomas G. Smith CHAE, Pres.
Description: Accountants, financial officers and MIS managers in 50 countries working in hotels, resorts, casinos, restaurants, and clubs. Develops uniform system of accounts. Conducts education, training, and certification programs; offers placement service; maintains hall of fame. **Publications:** *The Bottomline* (bimonthly).

10591 ■ Hospitality Sales and Marketing Association International
1760 Old Meadow Rd., Ste. 500
McLean, VA 22102
Ph:(703)506-3280
Fax:(703)506-3266
Co. E-mail: info@hsmai.org
URL: http://www.hsmai.org
Contact: Robert A. Gilbert CHME, Pres./CEO
Description: Represents professional society of individuals engaged in sales and marketing in hospitality, travel and tourism. Provides and manages educational programs, recognition programs, research, marketplace events, and publications for the members and the industry. Conducts major events, meetings, trade shows, and a series of strategy conferences. **Publications:** *HSMAI Marketing Review* (quarterly); *HSMAI Update* (bimonthly);Reports (periodic).

10592 ■ Hotel Brokers International
1420 NW Vivion Rd., Ste. 111
Kansas City, MO 64118
Ph:(816)505-4315
Fax:(816)505-4319
Co. E-mail: info@hbihotels.com
URL: http://www.hbihotels.com
Contact: Joseph R. McCann, Pres.
Description: Real estate brokers specializing in sales of and investments in hotel and motel properties. Members cooperate in the interchange of listings and data by computer, so the buying public will have information concerning all hotels available through the members of the association. Maintains speakers' bureau. **Publications:** *TransActions Recap* (annual).

10593 ■ Hotel Electronic Distribution Network Association
750 National Press Bldg.
529 14th St. NW
Washington, DC 20045
Ph:(202)204-8400

Fax:(703)223-9741
Co. E-mail: info@hedna.org
URL: http://www.hedna.org
Contact: Reed Hitchcock, Exec. Dir.
Description: Hotel distribution industry. Strives to increase hotel industry revenues and profitability from electronic distribution channels such as the Internet. .

10594 ■ IAHI, the Owners' Association
3 Ravinia Dr., Ste. 100
Atlanta, GA 30346
Ph:(770)604-5555
Free: 877-500-4244
Fax:(770)604-5684
URL: http://www.iahi.org
Contact: Eva Ferguson, Pres.
Description: Holiday Inn hotel owners and franchisees. Serves as liaison among members through owner committees. Sponsors programs in government relations and financial review; reviews corporate programs. Operates employment resume service. .

10595 ■ International Council on Hotel, Restaurant, and Institutional Education
2810 N Parham Rd., Ste. 230
Richmond, VA 23294
Ph:(804)346-4800
Fax:(804)346-5009
Co. E-mail: kmccarty@chrie.org
URL: http://www.chrie.org
Contact: Kathy McCarty, CEO
Description: Schools and colleges offering specialized education and training in hospitals, recreation, tourism and hotel, restaurant, and institutional administration; individuals, executives, and students. Provides networking opportunities and professional development. **Publications:** *Guide to Hospitality Education* (semiannual); *Hosteur Magazine* (biennial); *The Journal of Hospitality and Tourism Education* (quarterly); *The Journal of Hospitality and Tourism Research* (3/year); *Membership Directory and Research Guide* (annual).

10596 ■ Resort Hotel Association
2100 E Cary St., Ste. 3
Richmond, VA 23223
Ph:(804)525-2020
Fax:(804)525-2021
Co. E-mail: info@rhainsure.com
URL: http://www.resorthotelinsurance.com
Contact: Brooks W. Chase, Pres./CEO
Description: Represents resort and hotel owners. Develops and administers products and services customized for the hospitality industry. Offers both liability and property insurance programs. .

10597 ■ Unite Here
275 7th Ave.
New York, NY 10001-6708
Ph:(212)265-7000
Co. E-mail: ccarrera@unitehere.org
URL: http://www.unitehere.org
Contact: John W. Wilhelm, Pres.
Description: AFL-CIO. Helps improve working conditions, wages, and benefits across the U.S. and Canada. Organizes the unorganized in the industry. Works with employers to resolve issues in the workplace and in the relevant industry. **Publications:** *Catering Industry Employee* (monthly).

DIRECTORIES OF EDUCATIONAL PROGRAMS

10598 ■ *Directory of Private Accredited Career Schools and Colleges of Technology*
Pub: Accrediting Commission of Career Schools and Colleges of Technology
Contact: Michale S. McComis, Exec. Dir.
Released: On web page. **Price:** Free. **Description:** Covers 3900 accredited post-secondary programs that provide training programs in business, trade, and technical fields, including various small business endeavors. Entries offer school name, address, phone, description of courses, job placement assistance, and requirements for admission. Arrangement is alphabetical.

REFERENCE WORKS

10599 ■ "$50 Million Project for West Chester" in *Business Courier* (Vol. 24, December 14, 2008, No. 35, pp. 1)
Pub: American City Business Journals, Inc.
Ed: Laura Baverman. **Description:** Commercial developer Scott Street Partners is planning to invest $50 million for the development of a site south of the Streets of West Chester retail center. The 31-acre project will generate 1,200 jobs, and will bring in offices, restaurants and a hotel. The development plans and the features of the site are discussed as well.

10600 ■ "$100 Million Complex To Be Built...On a Bridge" in *Business Courier* (Vol. 27, November 12, 2010, No. 28, pp. 1)
Pub: Business Courier
Ed: Lucy May. **Description:** A development firm closed a deal with the Newport Southbank Bridge Company for a $100M entertainment complex that will be built on tope of the Purple People Bridge. The proposed project will cover 150,000 square feet with attractions such as restaurants, a boutique hotel, and pubs.

10601 ■ "2010 Book of Lists" in *Austin Business JournalInc.* (Vol. 29, December 25, 2009, No. 42, pp. 1)
Pub: American City Business Journals
Description: Rankings of companies and organizations within the business services, finance, healthcare, hospitality and travel, insurance, marketing and media, professional services, real estate, education and technology industries in Austin, Texas are presented. Rankings are based on sales, business size, and other statistics.

10602 ■ "2010 Book of Lists" in *Business Courier* (Vol. 26, December 26, 2009, No. 36, pp. 1)
Pub: American City Business Journals, Inc.
Description: Rankings of companies and organizations within the business services, education, finance, health care, hospitality and tourism, real estate, and technology industries in the Cincinnati, Ohio-Northern Kentucky area are presented. Rankings are based on sales, business size, or other statistics.

10603 ■ "2010 Book of Lists" in *Tampa Bay Business Journal* (Vol. 30, December 22, 2009, No. 53, pp. 1)
Pub: American City Business Journals
Description: Rankings of companies and organizations within the human resources, banking and finance, business services, healthcare, real estate, technology, hospitality and travel, and education industries in the Greater Tampa Bay area are presented. Rankings are based on sales, business size, and more.

10604 ■ "Atlific Adds Management of 4 Hotels to Its Portfolio in Fort McMurray" in *Canadian Corporate News* (May 16, 2007)
Pub: Comtex News Network Inc.
Description: Atlific Hotels & Resorts took over management for Merit Inn & Suites, The Merit Hotel, The Nomad Hotel and The Nomad Suites in Fort Mc-Murray. The company feels that they will be able to increase the hotels' abilities to promote their services through their vast network of sales personnel and marketing and e-commerce team.

10605 ■ "Benchmark Makes Granduca Entrance" in *Houston Business Journal* (Vol. 40, January 8, 2010, No. 35, pp. 2)
Pub: American City Business Journals
Ed: Jennifer Dawson. **Description:** Houston, Texas-based Interfin Company, owner of the Hotel Granduca, has tapped the services of Benchmark Hospitality International to manage the property. The hiring of Benchmark is part of Interfin's efforts to develop Granduca hotels in other markets. Statistical data included.

10606 ■ "Big Spenders" in *Hawaii Business* (Vol. 53, November 2007, No. 5, pp. 28)
Pub: Hawaii Business Publishing
Ed: Cathy S. Cruz-George. **Description:** Blackstone Group announced its acquisition of Hilton Hotels

Corp. valued at $26 billion in July 2007, one of the largest buyouts in the history of hotels. Blackstone now becomes the second most powerful landowners in Hawaii.

10607 ■ "Book of Lists 2010" in *Philadelphia Business Journal* (Vol. 28, December 25, 2009, No. 45, pp. 1)
Pub: American City Business Journals
Description: Rankings of companies and organizations within the banking, biotechnology, economic development, healthcare, hospitality, law and accounting, marketing and media, real estate, and technology industries in the Philadelphia, Pennsylvania area are presented. Rankings are based on sales, business size, and more.

10608 ■ "Building Targeted for Marriott in Violation" in *Business Journal-Milwaukee* (Vol. 28, December 24, 2010, No. 12, pp. A1)
Pub: Milwaukee Business Journal
Ed: Sean Ryan. **Description:** Milwaukee, Wisconsin's Department of Neighborhood Services has ordered structural improvements and safeguards for the Pioneer Building after three violations from structural failures were found. Pioneer was among the five buildings wanted by Jackson Street Management LLC to demolish for the new Marriott Hotel.

10609 ■ "Business Start-Up a Learning Experience for Young Bellingham Entrepreneur" in *Bellingham Herald* (July 18, 2010)
Pub: Bellingham Herald
Ed: Dave Gallagher. **Description:** Profile of 21-year-old entrepreneur, Chase Larabee, who developed an online program that helps airport fixed-based operators handle refueling, hotel and transportation reservations and other requests from private airplane pilots.

10610 ■ *Buying and Running a Guesthouse or Small Hotel*
Pub: Hot To Books Ltd.
Ed: Dan Marshall. **Released:** December 2007. **Price:** $30.00. **Description:** Teaches how to build and enjoy a lifestyle while running a guesthouse or small hotel.

10611 ■ "City Eyeing Tax Breaks for Arena" in *Boston Business Journal* (Vol. 29, June 3, 2011, No. 4, pp. 1)
Pub: American City Business Journals Inc.
Ed: Daniel J. Sernovitz. **Description:** Baltimore City is opting to give millions of dollars in tax breaks and construction loans to a group of private investors led by William Hackerman who is proposing to build a new arena and hotel at the Baltimore Convention Center. The project will cost $500 million with the state putting up another $400 million for the center's expansion.

10612 ■ "City Hopes Casino Will Be $333M Jackpot" in *Business First Buffalo* (October 5, 2007, pp. 1)
Pub: American City Business Journals, Inc.
Ed: James Fink. **Description:** Construction of the $333 million Seneca Buffalo Creek Casino, which includes a hotel, spa and restaurants, is schedule to begin in October 2007. The 5,000 square-foot casino is expected to generate revenue and provide 1,000 jobs for the City of Buffalo, New York.

10613 ■ "City Wooing Red Roof Inn for Return of Corporate HQ" in *Business First-Columbus* (October 19, 2007, pp. A1)
Pub: American City Business Journals, Inc.
Ed: **Description:** Department of Development of Columbus, Ohio offered Red Roof Inns Inc. a four-year, 40 percent jobs growth initiative to entice the company to move its corporate headquarters into the city from Dallas, Texas. The Watermark Island office building off Dublin Road and Grandview Avenue will be the headquarters of the company if it accepts the offer.

10614 ■ "City's Hilton Hotel Still Losing Money" in *Baltimore Business Journal* (Vol. 28, October 15, 2010, No. 23, pp. 1)
Pub: Baltimore Business Journal
Ed: Danile J. Sernovitz. **Description:** Baltimore, Maryland-owned Hilton Baltimore Convention Center Hotel has been expected by Baltimore Hotel Corpora-

tion to wrap up 2010 with a $9.8 million deficit after completing its first year in operation in the red. The forecast would mark the controversial project's third-straight year of losses.

10615 ■ "Click Here to Book" in *Caterer & Hotelkeeper* **(October 28, 2011, No. 288)**
Pub: Reed Reference Publishing
Ed: Ross Bentley. **Description:** Customers expectations are determined by the quality of a Website when booking hotel rooms.

10616 ■ "Clock Ticks On Columbia Sussex Debt" in *Business Courier* **(Vol. 27, July 30, 2010, No. 13, pp. 1)**
Pub: Business Courier
Ed: Dan Monk. **Description:** Cincinnati, Ohio-based Columbia Sussex Corporation has made plans to restructure a $1 billion loan bundle that was scheduled to mature in October 2010. The privately held hotel has strived in a weak hotel market to keep pace with its $3 billion debt load.

10617 ■ "Commercial Builders Take It on the Chin" in *Crain's Chicago Business* **(Vol. 31, April 28, 2008, No. 17, pp. 16)**
Pub: Crain Communications, Inc.
Ed: Alby Gallun. **Description:** Although the health care development sector has seen growth, the rest of Chicago's local commercial building industry has seen steep declines in the first quarter of this year. According to McGraw-Hill Construction, Chicago-area non-residential construction starts totaled $731 million in the quarter, a 60 percent drop from the year-earlier period. Volume in the retail, office and hotel markets fell by nearly 70 percent.

10618 ■ "Corporex Checks Into Hotel Niche" in *Business Courier* **(Vol. 24, October 12, 2008, No. 26, pp. 1)**
Pub: American City Business Journals, Inc.
Ed: Laura Baverman. **Description:** Corporex Companies Inc. is investing $900 million on select-service hotels ranging from $12 million to $20 million each, with eight hotels under construction and nine sites under contract.

10619 ■ "Corus Eases Off Ailing Condo Market; Office Developers Get Majority of 1Q Loans" in *Crain's Chicago Business* **(April 28, 2008)**
Pub: Crain Communications, Inc.
Ed: H. Lee Murphy. **Description:** Corus Bankshares Inc., a specialist in lending for the condominium high-rise construction market, is diversifying its portfolio by making loans to office developers and expects to be investing in hotels through the rest of the year. Corus' $7.57 billion loan portfolio is also discussed in detail as well as the company's earnings and share price. Statistical data included.

10620 ■ *Council on Hotel, Restaurant and Institutional Education—Member Directory and Resource Guide*
Pub: International Council on Hotel, Restaurant & Institutional Education
Contact: Kathy McCarthy, CEO
E-mail: kmccarty@chrie.org
Released: Biennial, March of even years. **Covers:** Over 2,000 educational programs and institutions in the hotel, restaurant, and tourism industries. **Entries Include:** Name, address, phone, fax. **Arrangement:** Alphabetical. **Indexes:** Geographical, membership category.

10621 ■ "A Crystal Ball" in *Business Journal Portland* **(Vol. 27, December 31, 2010, No. 44, pp. 1)**
Pub: Portland Business Journal
Ed: Wendy Culverwell. **Description:** McMenamins Pubs and Breweries has resumed construction of its Crystal Hotel project. The company has been working to convert a former bath house into a 51-room hotel. The hotel is expected to open in 2011.

10622 ■ "Deals Still Get Done at Drake's Coq d'Or" in *Crain's Chicago Business* **(Vol. 31, November 17, 2008, No. 46, pp. 35)**
Pub: Crain Communications, Inc.
Ed: Shia Kapos. **Description:** Chicago's infamous Coq d'Or, a restaurant and lounge located at the Drake Hotel, is still a favorite establishment for noted

executives but the eatery is now trying to cater to younger professionals through marketing and offering new beverages that appeal to that demographic. Many find it the perfect environment in which to close deals, relax or network.

10623 ■ "The Debt Mountain in Mid-Collapse" in *Canadian Business* **(Vol. 83, October 12, 2010, No. 17, pp. 28)**
Pub: Rogers Media Ltd.
Ed: Michael McCullough. **Description:** A growing real estate market has made Intrawest ULC's Whistler-Blackcomb resort a model for a booming industry for years. However, resorts are now required to manage themselves better because of the recession. Some mountains are also trimming the cost of labor and cutting peripheral services.

10624 ■ "DePaul To Train Hotel Leaders" in *Chicago Tribune* **(September 22, 2008)**
Pub: McClatchy-Tribune Information Services
Ed: Kathy Bergen. **Description:** With help from a $7.5 million grant from the Conrad N. Hilton Foundation, DePaul University will dramatically expand its role as a training ground for the tourism-industry with the opening of a School of Hospitality.

10625 ■ "Developers Await Hotel" in *The Business Journal-Portland* **(Vol. 25, July 11, 2008, No. 18, pp. 1)**
Pub: American City Business Journals, Inc.
Ed: Wendy Culverwell. **Description:** Developers are eager to start the construction of a new hotel at the Oregon Convention Center in Portland, Oregon as hey say that the project will help boost the convention center neighborhood. The project, called The Westin Portland at the Convention Center, is partly handled by Ashforth Pacific Inc.

10626 ■ "Discover the Wedding Location of Your Dreams" in *Benzinga.com* **(December 24, 2011)**
Pub: Benzinga.com
Ed: Benzinga Staff. **Description:** Ritz Carlton Hotel Company helps couples choose from their 70 wedding locations worldwide with wedding advisors to assist in planning.

10627 ■ "Doubletree Finds a Niche for Giving Back" in *Hotel and Motel Management* **(Vol. 225, July 2010, No. 8, pp. 6)**
Pub: Questex Media Group Inc.
Ed: Paul J. Heney. **Description:** Profile of Doubletree Hotel's community outreach programs that help employee volunteers work to educate children and the public about issues important to the environment.

10628 ■ "Embassy Suites Signs On: Dulski Building Developer Lands Anchor Tenant" in *Business First Buffalo* **(October 26, 2007, pp. 1)**
Pub: American City Business Journals, Inc.
Ed: James Fink. **Description:** Embassy Suites will open a 150-room hotel at the former Dulski Federal Office Building in Buffalo, New York. Bringing in Embassy Suite to the building is hoped to increase the interest of tenants at the building which is being renovated by Uniland Development Company and Acquest Development Company.

10629 ■ *Exceptional Service, Exceptional Profit: The Secrets of Building a Five-Star Customer Service Organization*
Pub: AMACOM
Ed: Leonard Inghilleri, Micah Solomon. **Released:** April 1, 2010. **Price:** $21.95. **Description:** Team of insiders share exclusive knowledge of the loyalty-building techniques pioneered by the world's most successful service leaders, including brick-and-mortar stars such as The Ritz-Carlton and Lexus and online success stories such as Netflix and CD Baby.

10630 ■ "F1 Makes Room(s) for Aspiring Entrepreneur" in *Austin Business Journal* **(Vol. 31, July 1, 2011, No. 17, pp. 1)**
Pub: American City Business Journals Inc.
Ed: Vicky Garza. **Description:** Formula One fan and graphic designer Danielle Crespo cashes in on the June 17, 2012 racing event in Austin, Texas via host-

ing a Website that allows users to book hotel rooms. She invested less than $100 and long hours on this enterprise which now has 74,000-plus visitors.

10631 ■ "Finding Room for Financing" in *The Business Journal-Serving Metropolitan Kansas City* **(Vol. 26, August 1, 2008, No. 47, pp. 1)**
Pub: American City Business Journals, Inc.
Ed: Rob Roberts. **Description:** Kansas City officials are expecting to receive financing recommendations for a new 1,000-room convention headquarters hotel. The $300-million project could be financed either through private ownership with public subsidies, or through public ownership with tax-exempt bond financing. Other views and information on the project and its expected economic impact, are presented.

10632 ■ "Founding Family Acquires Airport Marriott" in *Crain's Cleveland Business* **(Vol. 28, November 5, 2007, No. 44, pp. 3)**
Pub: Crain Communications, Inc.
Ed: Stan Bullard. **Description:** Big River Real Estate LLC, part of the Marriott family's investment fund, is the new owner of the Cleveland Airport Marriott; renovations estimated at about $11 million will ensure that the hotel meets Marriott's standards.

10633 ■ "A Gambling Man: Career Transitions that Put a Vegas Hotshot on Top" in *Black Enterprise* **(Vol. 37, October 2006, No. 3, pp. 89)**
Pub: Earl G. Graves Publishing Co. Inc.
Ed: Laura Egodigwe. **Description:** Interview with Lorenzo Creighton, president and chief operating officer of MGM Mirage's New York-New York Hotel and Casino. Creighton talks about his history and the challenges he faced since he didn't come from the casino industry.

10634 ■ "Grand Bohemian Hotel in Orlando, Fla. Takes Lead in Wedding Planning" in *Benzinga.com* **(August 4, 2011)**
Pub: Benzinga.com
Ed: Benzinga Staff. **Description:** MAD-Marketing launched a newly-designed Website for the Grand Bohemian Hotel in Orlando, Florida. The site features the hotel's wedding vanity site to help target prospective couples planning their weddings.

10635 ■ *Heads in Beds*
Pub: Prentice Hall PTR
Ed: Ivo Raza. **Released:** May 28, 2004. **Description:** Advice is given to help build brands, generate sales and grow profits through marketing for any hospitality or tourism business.

10636 ■ "Here's the Deal" in *Crain's Cleveland Business* **(Vol. 30, June 15, 2009, No. 23, pp. 14)**
Pub: Crain Communications, Inc.
Description: Incentives being offered by hotels, restaurants, golf courses and major chains in order to promote bookings for meetings or conferences in the Cleveland area are listed.

10637 ■ "Higher Thread Count for Metropole" in *Business Courier* **(Vol. 26, September 25, 2009, No. 22, pp. 1)**
Pub: American City Business Journals, Inc.
Ed: Lisa Biank Fasig, Lucy May. **Description:** Cincinnati Center City Development Corporation is under contract to buy the 225-unit apartment building called Metropole Apartments and 21c Museum Hotel is the lead candidate for the space. Advocates of some residents of the low-income rental complex complain that this move could leave them homeless.

10638 ■ "Host Your Dream Wedding at the Minneapolis Marriott Southwest" in *Benzinga.com* **(June 6, 2011)**
Pub: Benzinga.com
Ed: Benzinga Staff. **Description:** Minneapolis Marriott Southwest is helping engaged couples plan their wedding destination at their property. Details of wedding reception options are outlined.

10639 ■ "Hotel Confidential" in *Canadian Business* **(Vol. 80, Winter 2007, No. 24, pp. 91)**
Pub: Rogers Media
Ed: Erik Heinrich. **Description:** Celebrities such as Jason Priestley, Clint Eastwood, and Francis Ford Coppola have made investment in the hospitality industry. Investing in the hospitality industry has proved to be an excellent long-term investment and the venture also has a vanity aspect to it.

10640 ■ "Hotel Tax Eyed For Waukesha" in *The Business Journal-Milwaukee* **(Vol. 25, August 29, 2008, No. 49, pp. A1)**
Pub: American City Business Journals, Inc.
Ed: Rich Kirchen. **Description:** Midwest Airlines Center chairman Frank Gimbel wants Waukesha County to help in the funding of the $200-million expansion of the convention center through a hotel room tax. The Waukesha hotel industry is expected to oppose the new room tax. Other views and information on the planned new room tax in Waukesha are presented.

10641 ■ *Hotel & Travel Index*
Pub: Northstar Travel Media L.L.C.
Released: Quarterly, late February, May, August, November. **Price:** Free. **Covers:** over 110,000 hotels, resorts, inns, and guest houses, worldwide; hotel representatives and reservations services. **Entries Include:** All entries show company name, address, phone; hotel listings show rates, manager's name, hotel representative, telex, toll-free number, fax, automated CRT access codes, travel agency commission, and corporate rate. **Arrangement:** Geographical, alphabetical.

10642 ■ "Hotel Woes Reflect Area Struggle" in *Business Journal Serving Greater Tampa Bay* **(Vol. 30, December 3, 2010, No. 50, pp. 1)**
Pub: Tampa Bay Business Journal
Ed: Mark Holan. **Description:** Quality Inn and Suites in East Tampa, Florida has struggled against the sluggish economy but remained open to guests despite facing a foreclosure. The hotel project is the center of East Tampa's redevelopment plans and public officials defend the $650,000 investment in public amenities near the building.

10643 ■ "Hotels Get a Fill-Up" in *Crain's Detroit Business* **(Vol. 25, June 1, 2009, No. 22, pp. 1)**
Pub: Crain Communications Inc. - Detroit
Ed: Daniel Duggan. **Description:** Hot Rod Power Tour will have a $1 million economic impact on the area when it arrives in June 2009; the tour will bring 3,500 out-of-state custom vehicles to the event, whose owners will be needing hotel rooms.

10644 ■ "Hotels' Healthy Finish in '07" in *Crain's Chicago Business* **(Vol. 31, March 24, 2008, No. 12, pp. 16)**
Pub: Crain Communications, Inc.
Ed: Alby Gallun. **Description:** Chicago's hotel market saw mostly rising occupancies and room rates in the fourth quarter of 2007, reflecting continued strong demand from leisure and business travelers; however, due to the current state of the economy hoteliers face an increasingly uncertain outlook.

10645 ■ "Hotels Seeking Room Downtown" in *Crain's New York Business* **(Vol. 24, January 14, 2008, No. 2, pp. 32)**
Pub: Crain Communications, Inc.
Ed: Laura Koss-Feder. **Description:** In a rush to expand capacity in New York City, particularly lower Manhattan, the hotel industry plans to more than double the existing rooms in the area.

10646 ■ "How He Thinks" in *Canadian Business* **(Vol. 80, Winter 2007, No. 24, pp. 78)**
Pub: Rogers Media
Ed: Roger Martin. **Description:** Isadore Sharp sought to combine the best of the small hotel with the best of the large hotel so that he could provide his guests with the sense of intimacy and personalized service while also bringing a wide array of amenities.

Sharp decreed that there would be no customer service department at his hotel but every member of the staff are in charge of customer service.

10647 ■ *How to Open a Financially Successful Bed & Breakfast or Small Hotel*
Pub: Atlantic Publishing Company
Ed: Lora Arduser; Douglas R. Brow. **Released:** May 1, 2004. **Price:** $39.95. **Description:** Handbook with CD ROM demonstrates ways to set up, operate and manage a financially successful bed-and-breakfast or small hotel.

10648 ■ *How to Open and Operate a Bed & Breakfast, 8th Edition*
Pub: Globe Pequot Press
Ed: Jan Stankus. **Released:** January 1, 2007 (paperback). **Price:** $18.95 (paperback). **Description:** Handbook outlines how to set up and run a bed and breakfast, whether using a spare room of a home or a small inn.

10649 ■ *How to Start and Operate Your Own Bed-and-Breakfast: Down-To-Earth Advice from an Award-Winning B&B Owner*
Pub: Owl Books
Ed: Martha W. Murphy. **Released:** May 15, 1994. **Price:** $18.00. **Description:** Bed and breakfast owner shares tip for running a successful business.

10650 ■ "The Idea That Saved My Company" in *Inc.* **(October 2007, pp. 42)**
Pub: Gruner & Jahr USA Publishing
Description: Profile of Chip Conley, founder of seventeen boutique hotels in the San Francisco, California Bay Area. Conley learned to overcome depression and regain his entrepreneurial inspiration, which in turn saved his company. Abraham Maslow, author of "Toward of Psychology of Being" promoted Conley to write his own book, "Peak: How Great Companies Get Their Mojo From Maslow".

10651 ■ "Increased Competition Prompts Detroit Hotels to Make Upgrades" in *Crain's Detroit Business* **(Vol. 24, March 31, 2008, No. 13, pp. 1)**
Pub: Crain Communications, Inc.
Ed: Daniel Duggan. **Description:** Five Detroit hotels have recently undergone upgrades or are preparing for major construction projects due to a more competitive hospitality market in the city.

10652 ■ "Inland Snaps Up Rival REITs" in *Crain's Chicago Business* **(Vol. 31, November 17, 2008, No. 46, pp. 3)**
Pub: Crain Communications, Inc.
Ed: Alby Gallun. **Description:** Discusses Inland American Real Estate Trust Inc., a real estate investment trust that is napping up depressed shares of publicly traded competitors, a possible first step toward taking over these companies; however, with hotel and retail properties accounting for approximately 70 percent of its portfolio, the company could soon face its own difficulties.

10653 ■ "Inn at Saratoga Owners Buy Caribbean Hotel" in *Business Review, Albany New York* **(Vol. 34, November 2, 2007, No. 31, pp. 3)**
Pub: American City Business Journals, Inc.
Ed: Robin K. Cooper. **Description:** Bob Israel, owner of the Inn at Saratoga in Saratoga Springs, New York, made a $3 million to $4 million acquisition of the 22-room Mafolie Hotel and Restaurant in the Island of St. Thomas in the Caribbean. This is Israel's first real estate venture out of Saratoga Springs.

10654 ■ *INNside Scoop: Everything You Ever Wanted to Know About Bed & Breakfast Inns*
Pub: The B&B and Country Inn Marketplace
Ed: Maxine Pinson. **Released:** December 2002. **Description:** Guide for running a successful bread and breakfast inn.

10655 ■ "Kent Officials Seek Further KSU, City Unity" in *Crain's Cleveland Business* **(Vol. 28, December 3, 2007, No. 48, pp. 3)**
Pub: Crain Communications, Inc.
Ed: Jay Miller. **Description:** Kent State University and Portage County are searching for a developer who will use a three-acre parcel to bring new life to

the city's sagging downtown and create an area that will better link the town and the Kent State campus. The project will include a hotel and conference center as well as retail and restaurant space.

10656 ■ "The Lap of Eco-Luxury" in *Entrepreneur* **(Vol. 37, August 2009, No. 8, pp. 38)**
Pub: Entrepreneur Media, Inc.
Ed: Dina Mishev. **Description:** Founder Rob DesLauriers of the Terra Resort Group says that the natural world has taken very good care of him and that he wants to do his part to take care of it. The mattresses that their hotel uses are made from recycled steel springs and their TVs are Energy Star-approved. Their linens are made from organically grown cottons and their walls use by-products from coal burning.

10657 ■ "Laterooms and Octopus Travel Top Greenlight's Integrated Search Report for the Hotel Sector" in *Internet Wire* **(October 23, 2009)**
Pub: Comtex News Network, Inc.
Description: According to a research report conducted by Greenlight, the UK's leading independent Internet search marketing agency, the most visible hotel websites in natural search during June 2009 are premierinn.com, booking.com and laterooms.com; OctopusTravel.com generated the greatest share of the paid search section with 21 percent visibility. The report is focused on the hotel sector and covers the second quarter of 2009. Statistical data included.

10658 ■ "Latest Falls, Ontario Hotel Will Be 25-Story Westin" in *Business First Buffalo* **(October 19, 2007, pp. 1)**
Pub: American City Business Journals, Inc.
Ed: James Fink. **Description:** Niagara Falls, Ontario-based Canadian Niagara Hotels has announced the construction of a Westin Hotel on Robinson Street that is 25-stories high and has 518 suites starting in 2008. The scope of the $120 million construction project is expected to be completed in 2010.

10659 ■ "Leave It Behind; Novel Packing Strategy" in *Crain's Chicago Business* **(Vol. 31, April 21, 2008, No. 16, pp. 32)**
Pub: Crain Communications, Inc.
Ed: Sarah A. Klein. **Description:** Patrick Brady who investigates possible violations of the Foreign Corrupt Practices Act has a novel approach when traveling to frequent destinations which allows him to travel with only a carry-on piece of luggage: he leaves suits at dry cleaners in the places he visits most often and since he mainly stays at the same hotels, he also leaves sets of workout clothes and running shoes with hotel staff.

10660 ■ "Legacy Hotels Looks for a Buyer" in *Globe & Mail* **(March 2, 2007, pp. B3)**
Pub: CTVglobemedia Publishing Inc.
Ed: Elizabeth Church. **Description:** Legacy Hotels Real Estate Investment Trust, which has a portfolio of 25 properties, plans to sell its businesses. The shares of the real estate investment trust climbed $13.21, as the sales news was delivered.

10661 ■ "Like a Business Militia" in *Crain's Detroit Business* **(Vol. 25,**
Pub: Crain Communications Inc. - Detroit
Ed: Daniel Duggan. **Description:** Hotel executives are forming hotel committees and associations in Southeastern Michigan in the hopes of drawing more visitors to the region. Meetings are encouraging the use of promoting specific regions in ways that will secure multi-hotel events.

10662 ■ "Local Hotels Brace for Downturn" in *Crain's Chicago Business* **(Vol. 31, March 31, 2008, No. 13, pp. 3)**
Pub: Crain Communications, Inc.
Ed: Bob Tita. **Description:** Chicago hotels are seeing a noticeable drop in business-related guests so far this year due to a slumping national economy, tighter corporate expense budgets and higher airfares.

10663 ■ *Lodging Magazine—American Hotel and Motel Association Buyers Guide*
Pub: American Hotel & Lodging Association
Contact: Lawrence Wilhelm, Publisher
Ed: Philip Hayward, Editor. **Released:** Monthly, September. **Publication Includes:** List of about 4,000 suppliers to the hotel industry. **Entries Include:** Company name, address, phone, name of principal executive, list of products or services. **Arrangement:** Classified by product or service. **Indexes:** Alphabetical listing, categorical listings.

10664 ■ "Loop Hotel Plan Locks Up Funding" in *Crain's Chicago Business* (Vol. 31, March 24, 2008, No. 12, pp. 2)
Pub: Crain Communications, Inc.
Ed: Eddie Baeb. **Description:** Signaling further expansion in the downtown hotel market, the secured $395 million in financing will fund a 610-room luxury hotel operated by J.W. Marriott, a more upscale brand in the Marriott line.

10665 ■ "Luxe Hotels on a Budget" in *Inc.* (Volume 32, December 2010, No. 10, pp. 60)
Pub: Inc. Magazine
Ed: Adam Baer. **Description:** Off & Away Website allows users to vie for discounted hotel rooms at more than 100 luxury properties. To compete, uses buy $1 bids and each time an individual bids the price of the room goes up by 10 cents.

10666 ■ "Marriott Checks Out Hotel Prospect" in *The Business Journal-Serving Metropolitan Kansas City* (Vol. 27, November 14, 2008, No. 10)
Pub: American City Business Journals, Inc.
Description: Marriott International Inc. is planning to operate a hotel in Kansas City, Missouri and may take over the Kansas City Marriot Downtown although other hotel operators are interested in bidding on the project.

10667 ■ "Memphis Marriott Downtown Offers Wedding Reception Discounts to Soon-To-Be Newlyweds" in *Benzinga.com* (June 23, 2011)
Pub: Benzinga.com
Ed: Benzinga Staff. **Description:** Memphis Marriott Downtown in Memphis, Tennessee is offering wedding reception discounts to couples planning their weddings.

10668 ■ "More Details Emerge on Maersk Plan" in *Charlotte Business Journal* (Vol. 25, August 13, 2010, No. 21, pp. 1)
Pub: Charlotte Business Journal
Ed: Will Boye. **Description:** Children Klen Properties has announced the details of its redevelopment plan for a property in Charlotte, North Carolina. The plan includes office and retail space and residential units. The construction of a hotel has also been proposed.

10669 ■ "New Year's Resolutions: How Three Companies Came Up With Their 2008 Growth Strategies" in *Inc.* (January 2008, pp. 47-49)
Pub: Gruner & Jahr USA Publishing
Ed: Martha C. White. **Description:** Three companies share 2008 growth strategies; companies include a candle company, a voice mail and text messaging marketer, and hotel supplier of soap and shampoo.

10670 ■ "No Rooms for the Inn In This High-Rise" in *Chicago Tribune* (October 4, 2008)
Pub: McClatchy-Tribune Information Services
Ed: Ameet Sachdev; Jim Kirk. **Description:** Construction has stalled for several hotel expansion projects due to the economy which has caused a decline in occupancy and little growth in average daily room rates in downtown Chicago because consumers and businesses are becoming more cautious in the amount of money they spend on travel.

10671 ■ "Not Enough Room" in *Austin Business JournalInc.* (Vol. 29, November 13, 2009, No. 36, pp. A1)
Pub: American City Business Journals
Ed: Jacob Dirr. **Description:** Hotel and convention business in downtown Austin, Texas lost nearly $5.3 million when Dell Inc. relocated its annual convention

to Las Vegas. However, lack of capital caused the postponement of various hotel projects which need to be finished in order to attract well-attended conventions. Makeover projects on Austin's Waller Creek and Sixth Street are discussed.

10672 ■ "O'Loughlin Cuts $6 Million for Chesterfield Doubletree" in *Saint Louis Business Journal* (Vol. 32, September 2, 2011, No. 1, pp. 1)
Pub: Saint Louis Business Journal
Ed: Angela Mueller. **Description:** Lodging Hospitality Management (LHM) acquired the Doubletree Hotel and Conference Center in Chesterfield, Missouri and added it as the 18th hotel in its portfolio. LHM chairman and CEO Bob O'Loughlin plans to invest nearly $15 million in the hotel, including $9 for renovation.

10673 ■ "On the Green: Sheila Johnson Adds $35 Million Golf Resort To Her Expanding Portfolio" in *Black Enterprise* (January 2008)
Pub: Earl G. Graves Publishing Co. Inc.
Ed: Donna M. Owens. **Description:** Profile of Sheila Johnson, CEO of Salamander Hospitality LLC, made history when she purchased the Innisbrook Resort and Golf Club, making her the first African American woman to own this type of property. The resort includes four championship golf courses, six swimming pools, four restaurants, eleven tennis courts, three conference halls, and a nature preserve.

10674 ■ "Out With the Old? City Officials Investigating Options for New Hopkins Hotel" in *Crain's Cleveland Business* (October 22, 2007)
Pub: Crain Communications, Inc.
Ed: Jay Miller. **Description:** Cleveland officials have begun talks that could lead to a new hotel which would replace the aging, nine-story Sheraton Cleveland Hopkins Hotel at Cleveland Hopkins International Airport.

10675 ■ "Plan Your Next Event at Newport News Marriott at City Center" in *Benzinga.com* (July 29, 2011)
Pub: Benzinga.com
Ed: Benzinga Staff. **Description:** Newport News Marriott at City Center is promoting itself as the premier venue for business meetings, conventions and weddings.

10676 ■ "Plan Your Wedding with Cleveland Airport Marriott's Certified Event Planners" in *Benzinga.com* (February 2, 2011)
Pub: Benzinga.com
Ed: Benzinga Staff. **Description:** Cleveland's Airport Marriott makes wedding planning easy with its venue spaces and a full team of wedding planners.

10677 ■ "Plans for $160M Condo Resort in Wisconsin Dells Moves Forward" in *Commercial Property News* (March 18, 2008)
Pub: Nielsen Company
Description: Plans for the Grand Cambrian Resort in the Wisconsin Dells is discussed. The luxury condominium resort will include condos, townhomes, and condo-hotel style residences, two water parts, meeting space and indoor entertainment space, as well as a spa, four restaurants and retail offerings.

10678 ■ "Portland's Hilton For Sale" in *Business Journal Portland* (Vol. 27, October 22, 2010, No. 34, pp. 1)
Pub: Portland Business Journal
Ed: Wendy Culverwell. **Description:** Hilton Portland & Executive Tower, Portland's biggest hotel, is being sold by Cornerstone Real Estate Advisers LLC. Cornerstone hopes to close the deal for the 782-room complex by the end of 2010. Cornerstone contracted Jones Lang LaSalle to manage the sale, but terms to the deal are not available.

10679 ■ "Pre-Certified LEED Hotel Prototype Reduces Energy Use, Conserves Water" in *Contractor* (Vol. 57, January 2010, No. 1, pp. 3)
Pub: Penton Media, Inc.
Ed: Candace Roulo. **Description:** Marriott International Inc.'s LEED pre-certified prototype hotel will reduce a hotel's energy and water consumption by

25 percent and save owners approximately $100,000. Their Courtyard Settler's Ridge in Pittsburgh will be the first hotel built based on the prototype.

10680 ■ "'Pre-Sale' for Planned Could Mich Tower" in *Crain's Chicago Business* (Vol. 31, March 24, 2008, No. 12, pp. 14)
Pub: Crain Communications, Inc.
Ed: Eddie Baeb. **Description:** Condominium developer William Warman is planning to build a mixed-use tower at 300 North Michigan Avenue which would include a hotel, retail space, apartments and a parking garage. Mr. Warman is looking for investors to buy part or all of the space in order to make it easier to land financing.

10681 ■ "Prominent Hispanic Businessman Signs with Choice Hotels" in *Hispanic Business* (March 2008, pp. 36)
Pub: Hispanic Business
Ed: Melinda Burns. **Description:** Profile of John C. Lopez, who has signed an agreement with Choice Hotels International to build five new Cambria Suites in the U.S.; cost of the project will total $14 million.

10682 ■ "Prominent Hispanic Businessman Signs With Choice Hotels" in *Hispanic Business* (Vol. 30, March 2008, No. 3, pp. 36)
Pub: Hispanic Business
Ed: Melinda Burns. **Description:** Chairman of the board of Lopez Food Inc., John C. Lopez signs the agreement with Choice Hotels International to build five new Cambria suites in the USA. This is his first hotel venture and also the first Hispanic franchisee to enter into business with Choice Hotels.

10683 ■ "Real Opportunities: Don't Let Mortgage Mayhem Steer You Away From Sound Investments" in *Black Enterprise* (December 2007)
Pub: Earl G. Graves Publishing Co. Inc.
Ed: James A. Anderson. **Description:** Real estate investment trusts (REITs) that operate office buildings, industrial parks, shopping malls, hotels, hospitals, or other commercial properties may be a sound investment, despite the mortgage crisis facing the U.S. financial sector.

10684 ■ *Resort and Commercial Recreation—Membership Directory*
Pub: Resort and Commercial Recreation Association
Contact: Lisa Linden, Pres. Elect
E-mail: lisa.linden@rcra.org
Released: Annual, April. **Covers:** Approximately 600 professionals, educators, and students in the field of commercial recreation and leisure services. **Entries Include:** personal name, address, phone, corporate or university affiliation, and title, e-mail. **Arrangement:** Geographical.

10685 ■ "Restoring Grandeur" in *Business Courier* (Vol. 26, December 4, 2009, No. 32, pp. 1)
Pub: American City Business Journals, Inc.
Ed: Dan Monk. **Description:** Eagle Realty Group intends to spend more than $10 to restore the historic 12-story Phelps apartment building in Lytle Park in Cincinnati. Its president, Mario San Marco, expressed the need to invest in the building in order to maintain operations. The building could be restored into a hotel catering to executives and consultants.

10686 ■ "Revelations Derek Johnstone, Head Chef, Greywalls Hotel and Chez Roux" in *Caterer & Hotelkeeper* (October 28, 2011, No. 288)
Pub: Reed Reference Publishing
Description: Profile of Derek Johnstone, head chef at Greywalls Hotel and Chez Roux and his love for catering.

10687 ■ "Rise in Occupancy Rate Fuels Area Hotel Building Boom" in *Crain's Detroit Business* (Vol. 24, March 10, 2008, No. 10, pp. 14)
Pub: Crain Communications, Inc.
Ed: Jonathan Eppley. **Description:** Due to a rise in the region's yearly occupancy rate, a number of new hotel construction and renovation projects are slated for the Detroit area.

10688 ■ "Ritz Kapalua Sells 93 Suites for $176M to Fund Renovation" in *Commercial Property News* **(March 17, 2008)**
Pub: Nielsen Company

Description: Ritz-Carlton, Kapalua in Lahaina, Hawaii sold ninety-three of its units in order to fund renovations of 463 rooms and suites along with construction of a new spa and fitness center, new and expanded restaurants and pools and an environmental education center for children.

10689 ■ "Sales Gave W&S Record '07" in *Business Courier* **(Vol. 24, March 14, 2008, No. 49, pp. 1)**
Pub: American City Business Journals, Inc.

Ed: Jon Newberry. **Description:** Western & Southern Financial Group was able to achieve a record $365 million in net income thanks in large part to the double-digit increases in profits by its W&S Agency Group field offices and non-insurance businesses. The sale of their Integrated Investment Services Subsidiary and shares in several Marriot hotels also added to the record profit.

10690 ■ "Silverdome Bidders Bring New Proposals" in *Crain's Detroit Business* **(Vol. 24, March 17, 2008, No. 11, pp. 23)**
Pub: Crain Communications, Inc.

Ed: Daniel Duggan. **Description:** Discusses the seven plans which have been proposed as part of the third round of bidding for the Pontiac Silverdome; proposals range from Global Baseball Inc., a baseball league that would pit a team from every country against one another, to an Indian casino, a musical "hall of fame", a convention center, a horse track, a hotel and an indoor water park.

10691 ■ *So, You Want to Be an Innkeeper*
Pub: Chronicle Books LLC

Ed: JoAnn M. Bell; Susan Brown, Mary Davies; Pat Hardy. **Released:** March 2004. **Description:** Provides information for aspiring innkeepers, includes information on cottages, luxury properties, and spa services.

10692 ■ "Son of Sandman: Can Tom Gaglardi Really Outdo His Old Man?" in *Canadian Business* **(Vol. 80, Winter 2007, No. 24, pp. 106)**
Pub: Rogers Media

Ed: Calvin Leung. **Description:** Bob Gagliardi of Northland Properties started to learn about his family's business by working at a construction site at one of the high-rise buildings in downtown Vancouver. Gagliardi wants to expand their Moxie's restaurant chain and increase the market share of their Sandman hotel by 2018.

10693 ■ *Start and Run a Profitable Bed and Breakfast*
Pub: Self-Counsel Press Inc.

Ed: Monica Taylor, Richard Taylor. **Released:** October 1999. **Description:** Information for starting and running a successful bed and breakfast is presented.

10694 ■ "Survey Says Commercial Real Estate Headed for Turbulence" in *Commercial Property News* **(March 17, 2008)**
Pub: Nielsen Company

Description: Commercial real estate sector is declining due to the sluggish U.S. economy. According to a recent survey, national office, retail and hospitality markets are also on the decline.

10695 ■ "Tom Gaglardi" in *Canadian Business* **(Vol. 82, April 27, 2009, No. 7, pp. 56)**
Pub: Rogers Media

Ed: Calvin Leung. **Description:** Northland Properties Corporation president Tom Gaglardi believes that their business model of keeping much of operations in-house allows the firm to crate assets at a lesser price while commanding higher margins than their competitors. He believes that it is an ideal time to invest in the hospitality industry because of opportunities to purchase properties at low prices.

10696 ■ "Tourism Bureau Seeks Hotel Tax Hike" in *Baltimore Business Journal* **(Vol. 27, December 18, 2009, No. 32, pp. 1)**
Pub: American City Business Journals

Ed: Rachel Bernstein. **Description:** Baltimore, Maryland's tourism agency, Visit Baltimore, has proposed a new hotel tax that could produce $2 million annually for its marketing budget, fund improvements to the city's 30-year-old convention center and help it compete for World Cup soccer games. Baltimore hotel leaders discuss the new tax.

10697 ■ "Tourism Push Rising in Fall" in *Philadelphia Business Journal* **(Vol. 30, August 26, 2011, No. 28, pp. 1)**
Pub: American City Business Journals Inc.

Ed: Peter Van Allen. **Description:** Philadelphia is offering events for tourists this fall despite massive cuts for tourism promotion. Governor Tim Corbet slashed $5.5 million in funding for the state's tourism-promotion agencies which received $32 million in 2009. The agencies were forced to cooperate and fend for themselves using the hotel taxes that sustain them.

10698 ■ "Travel Tears" in *Crain's Chicago Business* **(Vol. 31, November 17, 2008, No. 46, pp. 3)**
Pub: Crain Communications, Inc.

Ed: Bob Tita. **Description:** Hotels, restaurants and conventions are seeing a decline in profits due to corporate travel cutbacks and the sagging economy. City and state revenues derived from taxes on tourism-related industries are also suffering.

10699 ■ "Unfilled Hotels Go All Out for Business Meetings" in *Crain's Detroit Business* **(Vol. 25, June 8, 2009, No. 23, pp. 9)**
Pub: Crain Communications Inc. - Detroit

Ed: Daniel Duggan. **Description:** Hotels in Michigan are offering discounts to companies holding business meetings at their properties. Details of competition and plans are included.

10700 ■ "'Unknown' Muted Grand Prix Impact" in *Boston Business Journal* **(Vol. 29, September 9, 2011, No. 18, pp. 3)**
Pub: American City Business Journals Inc.

Ed: Alexander Jackson. **Description:** Baltimore Grand Prix caught restaurateurs, hoteliers and street vendors in Baltimore, Maryland unprepared for the thousands of race fans who attended the inaugural event over Labor Day weekend. The race popularity is relatively unknown to them and some felt they were not able to make as much money as they had hoped.

10701 ■ *Upstart Guide to Owning and Managing a Bed and Breakfast*
Pub: Kaplan Publishing

Ed: Lisa Angowski Rogak. **Released:** November 1, 1994. **Description:** Guide for running a profitable bed and breakfast.

10702 ■ "Vegas in the D; Local Architects Collaborate On MGM Grand" in *Crain's Detroit Business* **(Vol. 23, October 1, 2007, No. 40, pp. 1)**
Pub: Crain Communications Inc. - Detroit

Ed: Daniel Duggan. **Description:** Local Detroit architects, Smith Group and Hamilton Anderson Associates are among the contractors vying for subcontracted architecture, construction and consulting contracts for the new MGM Grand Detroit casino and hotel.

10703 ■ "Vernon Revamp" in *Business Courier* **(Vol. 26, October 9, 2009, No. 24, pp. 1)**
Pub: American City Business Journals, Inc.

Ed: Dan Monk. **Description:** Al Neyer Inc. will redevelop the Vernon Manor Hotel as an office building for the Cincinnati Children's Hospital Medical Center. The project will cost $35 million and would generate a new investment vehicle for black investors who plan to raise $2.7 million in private offerings to claim majority ownership of the property after its renovations.

10704 ■ "Wal-Mart Doesn't Sell Council" in *The Business Journal-Serving Metropolitan Kansas City* **(Vol. 26, July 4, 2008, No. 43, pp. 1)**
Pub: American City Business Journals, Inc.

Ed: Steve Vockrodt. **Description:** Wal-Mart Stores Inc. announced that it will move the location of its annual convention from Kansas City, Missouri to Orlando, Florida. The change of venue came after Rick Hughes, Kansas City Convention and Visitors Association president rejected Wal-Mart's proposal to subsidize a new hotel in the downtown area that is needed for the event.

STATISTICAL SOURCES

10705 ■ *RMA Annual Statement Studies*
Pub: Robert Morris Associates (RMA)

Released: Annual. **Price:** $175.00 2006-07 edition, $105.00. **Description:** Contains composite balance sheets and income statements for more than 360 industries, including the accounting, auditing, and bookkeeping industries. Also contains five years of comparative historical data for discerning trends. Includes 16 commonly used ratios, computed for most of the size groupings for nearly every industry.

10706 ■ *Standard & Poor's Industry Surveys*
Pub: Standard & Poor's Corp.

Released: Annual. **Price:** $3633.00. **Description:** Two-volume book that examines the prospects for specific industries, including trucking. Also provides analyses of trends and problems, statistical tables and charts, and comparative company analyses.

TRADE PERIODICALS

10707 ■ *Cornell Hoospitality Quarterly*
Pub: Cornell University School of Hotel Administration

Ed: J. Bruce Tracey, Editor. **Released:** Quarterly. **Price:** $296 institutions combined print and electronic access; $290 institutions print only; $95 print & online; $31 single issue. **Description:** Magazine of applied research and ideas for hotel and restaurant managers.

10708 ■ *FIU Hospitality Review*
Pub: Florida International University
Contact: Joseph West, Publisher

Ed: Nestor Portocarrero, Editor. **Released:** Biennial. **Price:** $40; $60 libraries; $80 elsewhere. **Description:** Trade journal covering hospitality management.

10709 ■ *Hospitality Design*
Pub: Nielsen Business Media
Contact: Tara Mastrelli, Managing Editor
E-mail: tmastrelli@hdmag.com

Released: 10/yr. **Price:** $79; $94 Canada; $139 other countries by airmail. **Description:** Magazine covering design of restaurants, hotels, facilities, clubs, cruise ships, etc.

10710 ■ *Hospitality Law*
Pub: LRP Publications
Contact: David Light

Released: Monthly. **Price:** $217 plus $22 s/h. **Description:** Discusses legal issues pertaining to the hospitality industry, using actual cases as illustration. Offers articles on liability, contract law, tax codes, and legal trends relevant to the lodging industry. Recurring features include interviews, book reviews, notices of publications available, and columns titled Trends and Observations, Test Your Knowledge, Security, Legal Briefs, Legal Basics, and Employee Management.

10711 ■ *Hotel Business*
Pub: ICD Publications
Contact: Bruce Serlen, Exec. Ed.

Ed: Dennis Nessler, Editor, dennisn@hotelbusiness. com. **Released:** Biweekly. **Price:** $260 domestic; $315 Canada and Mexico; $695 other countries; $395 digital. **Description:** Trade magazine covering the hotel industry.

10712 ■ Hotel & Motel Management
Pub: Questex Media Group
Released: 21/yr. **Price:** $58.85; $81.40 Canada and Mexico; $143 other countries; $75 additional airmail shipping; Free to qualified subscribers. **Description:** Magazine (tabloid) covering the global lodging industry.

10713 ■ Hotelier
Pub: Kostuch Publications Ltd.
Contact: Rosanna Caira, Editor & Publisher
E-mail: rcaira@foodservice.ca
Released: 8/yr. **Price:** $25 Canada; $30 U.S.; $40 other countries. **Description:** Trade journal covering Canada's hotel industry.

10714 ■ HOTELS
Pub: Marketing & Technology Group
Released: Monthly. **Description:** Magazine covering management and operations as well as foodservice and design in the hospitality industry.

10715 ■ Journal of Hospitality Marketing & Management
Pub: Routledge Journals
Contact: Bonnie J. Knutson PhD, Editorial Board
Released: 8/yr. **Price:** $809 institutions print & online; $728 institutions online; $165 online. **Description:** Academic and industry journal dealing with marketing issues in the hospitality and leisure industries.

10716 ■ Lodging Magazine
Pub: American Hotel & Lodging Association
Contact: Edward J. McNeill Jr., Publisher
Released: Monthly. **Description:** Magazine directed to the management staff of hotels and motels.

10717 ■ Los Cabos Magazine
Pub: Promociones Tyson S.A. de C.V.
Contact: Joseph A. Tyson, Publisher
E-mail: tyson@loscabosguide.com
Released: Quarterly. **Price:** $21.95. **Description:** Magazine covering hotel, resort, restaurant and shopping information on the Mexican resort area of Los Cabos.

10718 ■ Newsline
Pub: Ontario Accommodation Association
Ed: Bruce M. Gravel, Editor. **Released:** Quarterly. **Price:** Included in membership. **Description:** Provides news of Association activities, government lobbying and regulatory changes.

VIDEOCASSETTES/ AUDIOCASSETTES

10719 ■ Inside Business Today
GPN Educational Media
1550 Executive Drive
Elgin, IL 60123
Ph:(402)472-2007
Free: 800-228-4630
Fax:800-306-2330
Co. E-mail: askgpn@smarterville.com
URL: http://www.shopgpn.com
Released: 1989. **Description:** Leaders in business and industry tell their success stories in this extensive series. **Availability:** VHS; 3/4U.

TRADE SHOWS AND CONVENTIONS

10720 ■ Annual Hotel, Motel, and Restaurant Supply Show of the Southeast
Leisure Time Unlimited, Inc.
708 Main St.
PO Box 332
Myrtle Beach, SC 29577
Ph:(843)448-9483
Free: 800-261-5591

Fax:(843)626-1513
Co. E-mail: dickensshow@sc.rr.com
Released: Annual. **Audience:** Hospitality industry, managers, and buyers. **Principal Exhibits:** Carpeting, furniture, coffee makers, produce companies, wine and beer and food companies, and services to motels, hotels, and restaurants.

10721 ■ ApEx
Canadian Restaurant and Food Services Association
316 Bloor St. W.
Toronto, ON, Canada M5S 1W5
Ph:(416)923-8416
Free: 800-387-5649
Fax:(416)923-1450
Co. E-mail: info@crfa.ca
URL: http://www.crfa.ca
Audience: Trade. **Principal Exhibits:** Products and services for the restaurant and hospitality industry, as well as institutions, convenience stores, delis and bakeries. **Dates and Locations:** 2011 Apr 03-04, Moncton, NB.

10722 ■ Arkansas Hospitality Association Convention & Exhibition
Arkansas Hospitality Association
603 S. Pulaski, PO Box 3866
Little Rock, AR 72203-3866
Ph:(501)376-2323
Fax:(501)376-6517
Co. E-mail: aha@arhospitality.org
URL: http://www.arhospitality.org
Released: Semiannual. **Audience:** Restaurant owners, motel and hotel owners and operators, and resort and recreational attraction trade professionals. **Principal Exhibits:** Food products, furniture, fixtures for hotels and restaurants, and telephones.

10723 ■ CENTREX Hotel & Restaurant Tradeshow
Manitoba Hotel Association
1505-155 Carlton St.
Winnipeg, MB, Canada R3C 3H8
Ph:(204)942-0671
Free: 888-859-9976
Fax:(204)942-6719
Co. E-mail: info@manitobahotelAssociation.ca
URL: http://www.manitobahotelAssociation.ca
Released: Annual. **Audience:** Representatives from hotels, restaurants, motels, bars, cabarets. **Principal Exhibits:** Hotel and restaurant food equipment, supplies, and services. **Dates and Locations:** 2011 Mar 20-21, Winnipeg, MB.

10724 ■ Florida International Restaurant & Hotel Expo
Florida International Medical Expo Inc.
3348 17th St.
Sarasota, FL 34235
Ph:(941)366-2554
Fax:(941)366-9861
Co. E-mail: info@fimeshow.com
URL: http://www.fimeshow.com
Released: Annual. **Audience:** Restaurant managers and owner/operators; hotel and motel managers and food service managers; and related food service professionals. **Principal Exhibits:** Restaurant, hotel, motel, leisure, hospitality, and bakery industries equipment, supplies, and services, including foods and beverages, furniture, paper goods and disposables, chemicals, computers, amenities, advertising, and trade publications.

10725 ■ HSMAI - Affordable Meetings West
George Little Management, LLC (New York, New York)
1133 Westchester Ave., Ste. N136
White Plains, NY 10606
Ph:(914)421-3200
Free: 800-272-SHOW
Co. E-mail: cathy_steel@glmshows.com
URL: http://www.glmshows.com
Released: Annual. **Audience:** Trade professionals. **Principal Exhibits:** Equipment, supplies, and services for the hospitality and marketing industry. **Dates and Locations:** 2011 Jun 15-16, Long Beach, CA.

10726 ■ IH/M & RS - International Hotel/Motel & Restaurant Show
George Little Management, LLC (New York, New York)
1133 Westchester Ave., Ste. N136
White Plains, NY 10606
Ph:(914)421-3200
Free: 800-272-SHOW
Co. E-mail: cathy_steel@glmshows.com
URL: http://www.glmshows.com
Released: Annual. **Audience:** Representatives from mass feeding, lodging, and healthcare industries. **Principal Exhibits:** Products and services for lodging and food serving properties, including: technology, uniforms, linens and bedding, tabletop accessories, guest amenities and services, food and beverages, cleaning maintenance, food service equipment and supplies, franchising information, finance and management furnishings and fixtures, fitness equipment, and leisure and entertainment services. **Dates and Locations:** 2011 Dec 12-15, New York, NY.

10727 ■ National Restaurant Association Restaurant and Hotel-Motel Show
National Restaurant Association Convention Office
1200 17th St., NW
Washington, DC 20036
Ph:(202)331-5900
Free: 800-424-5156
Fax:(202)331-2429
URL: http://www.restaurant.org
Released: Annual. **Audience:** Restaurant operators and owners, hotel and motel managers, food service managers, purchasing agents, and related food service professionals. **Principal Exhibits:** Food service equipment, supplies, and services and food and beverage products for the hospitality industry. Includes international cuisine pavilion. **Dates and Locations:** 2011 May 21-24, Chicago, IL.

10728 ■ Ocean City Hotel, Motel, and Restaurant Association Spring Trade Exposition
Ocean City Hotel, Motel, and Restaurant Association
4001 Philadelphia Ave.
PO Box 340
Ocean City, MD 21843-0340
Ph:(410)289-6733
Free: 800-OCO-CEAN
Fax:(410)289-5645
Co. E-mail: inquire@ocvisitor.com
URL: http://www.ocvisitor.com
Released: Annual. **Audience:** Trade and buyers. **Principal Exhibits:** Food products, restaurant equipment, bedding, laundry supplies, televisions (commercial), media, and any trade related items. **Dates and Locations:** 2011 Mar 06-07.

10729 ■ West Ex: The Rocky Mountain Regional Hospitality Exposition
Colorado Restaurant Association
430 E. 7th Ave.
Denver, CO 80203
Ph:(303)830-2972
Free: 800-522-2972
Fax:(303)830-2973
Co. E-mail: info@coloradorestaurant.com
URL: http://www.coloradorestaurant.com
Released: Annual. **Audience:** Food service and restaurant industry personnel. **Principal Exhibits:** Food service and lodging products, equipment, and services.

CONSULTANTS

10730 ■ Certified Housekeeping Consultants
115-01 Lefferts Blvd.
Jamaica, NY 11420-2488
Ph:(718)848-0200
Fax:(718)848-0203
Co. E-mail: finehousekeeping@att.net
URL: http://www.finehotelhousekeeping.com
Contact: Alfred Fine MHS, President
Scope: Housekeeping consulting services specializing in housekeeping operations, planning cost reduction, training linen inventory laundry, employee scheduling and budgeting. Serves the hotel, motel, and assisted living industries.

10731 ■ Cini-Little International Inc.
20251 Century Blvd., Ste. 375
Germantown, MD 20874-1114
Ph:(301)528-9700
Fax:(301)528-9711
Co. E-mail: info@cinilittle.com
URL: http://www.cinilittle.com
Contact: William V. Eaton, Principle
E-mail: weaton@atscinilittle.com
Scope: Offers a full range of independent management and design consulting services in all aspects of food service to industries such as hospitality, business, and health care. Services include feasibility studies and or operations analyses, food service programs and concepts, operational training programs and manuals, food service contractor selection, contract documents, review of contractor submittal and site inspections. Offers consulting in materials management, materials handling, vertical horizontal transport elevator escalator moving sidewalks to all segments of the construction, hospitality, health-care and related industries.

10732 ■ Clevenger Associates
11803 101st Avenue Ct. E, Ste. 203
Puyallup, WA 98373-3473
Ph:(253)841-7811
Fax:(253)841-7435
Co. E-mail: info@clevengerassoc.com
URL: http://www.clevengerassoc.com
Contact: Trine Loepfe, Mgr
E-mail: info@atsclevengerassoc.com
Scope: Offers food service and laundry/valet design and consulting. Will design new and remodeled space; specify equipment, and follow-up to ensure quality and likeness to specifications. Industries served: hotels, restaurants, clubhouses, health care, educational, institutional corrections, convention centers, business and industry.

10733 ■ Health Fitness Dynamics Inc.
1305 NE 23rd Ave., Ste. 2
Pompano Beach, FL 33062
Ph:(954)942-0049
Fax:(954)941-0854
Co. E-mail: hfd@hfdspa.com
URL: http://www.hfdspa.com
Contact: Patricia A. Monteson, Principle
E-mail: pattymonteson@atshfdspa.com
Scope: Firm offers spa consulting services in the following areas: program development, facility planning, feasibility and market studies, staffing requirements, product and equipment selection, coordinating of support departments, systems of operation, personnel, and on-going management. Industries served: hospitality, hotels and resorts, and health spas. **Publications:** "Spa News & Views: If The Spa Will Not Help Sell Rooms, Do Not Add A Spa," Spa Management, Mar, 2006; "Thinking of Jumping on the Spa Bandwagon Look Before You Leap"; "Spa Savvy-Best Practices for Hiring, Training & Retaining Your Staff". **Seminars:** Management Workshop; Managing a Revenue Generating Spa within a Resort; The Health Spa - Another Marketable and Complementary Dimension of a Resort; Planning and Managing a Health Spa in a Resort.

10734 ■ Hostline
School of Hotel Administration Library
Cornell University
G80 Statler Hall
Ithaca, NY 14853-6902
Ph:(607)254-4503
Fax:(607)255-0021
Co. E-mail: hostline@cornell.edu
URL: http://www.nestlelib.cornell.edu/hostline
Contact: Mihoko Hosoi, Mgr
E-mail: hostline@cornell.edu
Scope: Provides reference service for the hospitality industry in the following areas hotel management, franchising and management contracts, tourism and travel, food and beverage management, hospitality marketing and branding, real estate, technology updates, hospitality law, architecture and interior design, hospitality financial structures, cookery/food science/sanitation, hotel and restaurant accounting, human resource management and company background. Provides information on particular issues,

trends, and theories specific facts in statistics; references for quick updates and background review and referrals to other information sources. Access to the Hospitality Database, which indexes more than 80hospitality journals and newsletters; the Hotel School Library's collection of 26, 000 volumes and 1000 periodicals and newsletters; the Cornell University Library's holdings of seven million books and serial volumes and seven million microforms; multiple databases designed for the hospitality and general business and industry and academic experts. Expertise in gathering key information, providing published information, bibliographic citations and photocopied documents suited to the requested research topic.

10735 ■ Isaksen Foodservice Consultants Inc.
11228 Georgia Ave.
Silver Spring, MD 20902-2712
Ph:(301)933-2100
Fax:(301)933-2101
Co. E-mail: isaksen@erols.com
Contact: Rosemarie Kellinger, Vice President
Scope: Consultants to architects, developers, and owners regarding layout and design of food service equipment for health care, elder care, country clubs, bakeries, hotels, hospitals, restaurants, nursing homes, schools, prisons and other institutions, as well as government agencies. Also space planning, lighting and acoustic design, laundry layout and design and food service area construction and installation supervision services. **Publications:** "Contemporary Long Term Care," Oct, 1997; "Pantries Take on Non-Institutional Look"; "Hospitality Profiles," Nov, 1994; "Interview: Ron Isak sen of Isak sen Food services Strategies"; "Food service Equipment and Supplies Specialist," Sep, 1991; "Winning Kitchens Show Their Metal"; "Food service Equipment and Supplies Specialist," Jun, 1991; "Isak sen, Others Devote Time to Charity," Restaurants and Institutions, Feb, 1991; "Nothing Fishy About Proper Seafood Refrigeration," Food service Equipment and Supplies Specialist, Oct, 1990; "Seven Great Kitchen Design Ideas". **Seminars:** Recipe for Success: New Concepts in Nutrition for the Aging; Integration of Food Delivery Systems with Decentralized Cluster Concepts.

10736 ■ Nisonger Associates Inc.
202 Elm St.
Milford, OH 45150-1185
Ph:(513)248-1441
Fax:(513)248-1445
Co. E-mail: info@nisongerassoc.com
URL: http://www.nisongerassoc.com
Contact: Harry T. Nisonger, President
E-mail: nisongerai@aol.com
Scope: Food service consultants offering management and design services to the food service, lodging, health care, and leisure time industries, as well as to schools, private clubs and other institutions, and government agencies. Not only will the firm evaluate and prescribe, but it will take the project through the implementation process. Services include financial planning, menu development, facilities design, operations assessment, programming, systems studies, corporate valuations, contract and lease negotiations, consumer surveys, market and feasibility studies, prototype planning, and expert witness services. Construction division formed to provide clients with design or build services for fast track projects with cost efficiencies.

10737 ■ Protection Management Associates Inc.
8632 E Sells Dr., Ste. 302
Scottsdale, AZ 85251-2927
Ph:(480)949-5637
Fax:(602)994-0493
Contact: Loren E. Newland, President
Scope: Provides litigation support and expert witness services to corporations and facilities, designed to limit claims of negligence with respect to security adequacy. Performs security management assessments and audits designed to evaluate effectiveness of security design and administration. Industries served: hotels, hospitals, apartment houses, nursing homes, casinos and resorts, and government agen-

cies. **Publications:** "Hotel Protection Management: the Inn keepers Guide to Guest Protection and Reasonable Care".

10738 ■ Tarbutton Associates Inc.
1072 Laskin Rd.
Virginia Beach, VA 23451-6364
Ph:(757)422-2020
Fax:(757)422-2020
Co. E-mail: ltarbutton@aol.com
Contact: Dr. Kenton L. Tarbutton, President
E-mail: ltarbutton@aol.com
Scope: A consulting firm specializing in franchise consulting worldwide for expert witness court and legislative testimony as well as the sale or acquisition of franchising parent companies. **Publications:** "Franchising: The How-To Book," Prentice-Hall Inc. **Seminars:** 21st Century Management Techniques; Developing Your Business for Franchising; Developing People into Producers; The Franchising Possibilities.

FRANCHISES AND BUSINESS OPPORTUNITIES

10739 ■ Aloha Hotels and Resorts
PO Box 3347
Princeville, HI 96722
Ph:(808)826-6244
URL: http://franchisedirectory.ca
Description: Provides independent Inn, Hotel and Resort owners with the ability to obtain new sources of revenue. Membership in the Aloha Hotels and Resort chain brings a wide variety of benefits to the property owner. Aloha Hotel and Resort president has over 25 years of enhancing financial performance for 3 major hotel and resort chains. **Equity Capital Needed:** $1,000-$200,000 total investment; $1,000-$200,000 required cash liquidity. **Training:** Provides training an support programs. There is one assigned management team member to your property that is available to answer any questions and take you through the steps to become an Aloha Hotel and Resort member. There are many training and support areas that are included in your membership.

10740 ■ Baymont Inn & Suites
Baymont Franchise Systems
22 Sylvan Way
Parsippany, NJ 07054
Free: 800-758-8999
Fax:(973)753-8724
No. of Franchise Units: 254. **Founded:** 1974. **Franchised:** 1987. **Description:** Hotel chain. **Equity Capital Needed:** $195,870-$5,488,521 total investment. **Franchise Fee:** $26,000-$27,000. **Royalty Fee:** 5%. **Financial Assistance:** Limited third party and in-house financing available. **Training:** Provides 5 days at headquarters, 2 days at franchisee's location with ongoing support.

10741 ■ Choice Hotels Canada Inc.
5090 Explorer Dr., 5th Fl.
Mississauga, ON, Canada L4W 4T9
Ph:(905)602-2222
URL: http://www.franchisedirectory.ca
Description: Hotel chain in which applicants must have their own hotel asset or be prepared to buy or build. Choice provides marketing, reservation, sales and purchasing support. **Equity Capital Needed:** $2,000,000-$10,000,000 total investment; $1,000,000-$5,000,000 required cash liquidity. **Training:** Provides sales, marketing and operational training on an ongoing basis, both regionally and on a property-specific basis.

10742 ■ Choice Hotels International
10750 Columbia Pike
Silver Spring, MD 20901
Free: 800-547-0007
No. of Franchise Units: 6,077. **No. of Company-Owned Units:** 3. **Founded:** 1939. **Franchised:** 1972. **Description:** Hotel/motel franchise. Economy to mid-price to up-scale. **Equity Capital Needed:** $1,271,699-$14,641,600. **Franchise Fee:** $10,000-

$60,000. **Royalty Fee:** Varies. **Financial Assistance:** No. **Training:** Provides 1 week at headquarters and ongoing regional training.

10743 ■ Country Inns & Suites by Carlson
PO Box 59159
Minneapolis, MN 55459-8205
Ph:(763)212-2525
Free: 800-336-3301
No. of Franchise Units: 448. **No. of Company-Owned Units:** 9. **Founded:** 1987. **Franchised:** 1987. **Description:** Mid-priced lodging. **Equity Capital Needed:** $4,206,100-$6,542,300. **Franchise Fee:** $45,000. **Royalty Fee:** 4.5%. **Financial Assistance:** No. **Training:** Yes.

10744 ■ Days Inn Worldwide, Inc.
Wyndham Hotel Group
22 Sylvan Way
Parsippany, NJ 07054
Free: 888-222-7484
No. of Franchise Units: 1,662. **Founded:** 1970. **Franchised:** 1972. **Description:** Days Inn Worldwide is the licensor of Days Inn guest lodging facilities. **Equity Capital Needed:** Varies depending on project. **Franchise Fee:** $35,000/minimum, $350/room. **Financial Assistance:** No. **Training:** Yes.

10745 ■ Howard Johnson
Wyndham Hotel Group
22 Sylvan Way
Parsippany, NJ 07054
Free: 888-222-7484
No. of Franchise Units: 500+. **Founded:** 1954. **Franchised:** 1954. **Description:** Licensor of Howard Johnson guest lodging facilities. **Equity Capital Needed:** Varies depending upon project. **Franchise Fee:** $10,000 minimum; $100/room. **Financial Assistance:** Yes. **Training:** Yes.

10746 ■ Howard Johnson Canada Franchise Systems Limited
2904 South Sheridan Way, Ste. 101
Oakville, ON, Canada L6J 7L7
Ph:(905)829-4002
Free: 800-249-4656
Fax:(905)829-4716
Co. E-mail: glen.blake@fullhousefranchisesystems.ca
URL: http://www.howardjohnson.ca
No. of Franchise Units: 67. **Founded:** 1972. **Franchised:** 1991. **Description:** Master franchisor in Canada for Howard Johnson Plaza Hotels, Hotels, Inns and Express Inns. Howard Johnson is recognized as the leading mid-market brand for leisure and business travel. Services include advertising/ marketing, asset management services, franchise services and support, Preferred Alliance Group purchasing services, operations consulting and support, and quality assurance, training. **Equity Capital Needed:** $350,000. **Franchise Fee:** $35,000 or $350,000/room. **Training:** Yes.

10747 ■ Knights Inn
Wyndham Hotel Group
22 Sylvan Way
Parsippany, NJ 07054
Free: 888-222-7484
No. of Franchise Units: 229. **Founded:** 1972. **Franchised:** 1972. **Description:** Budget lodging. **Franchise Fee:** $15,000 or $150/room. **Financial Assistance:** Yes. **Training:** Yes.

10748 ■ Knights Inn Canada Franchise Systems Limited
2904 South Sheridan Way, Ste 101
Oakville, ON, Canada L6J 7L7
Ph:(905)829-4002
Free: 800-248-4656
Fax:(905)829-4716
Co. E-mail: glen.blake@fhfsl.ca
URL: http://www.knightsinn.ca
No. of Franchise Units: 20. **Founded:** 1999. **Franchised:** 2000. **Description:** Budget lodging brand appealing to value conscious frequent business and leisure/family travel. **Equity Capital Needed:** $250,000. **Franchise Fee:** $5,000. **Managerial Assistance:** Services include advertising/marketing, asset management services, and franchise services and support. **Training:** Provides training and ongoing support.

10749 ■ La Quinta Canada Inc.
Franchise Div.
135 Queens Plate Dr., Ste. 410
TOR, ON, Canada M9W 6V1
Free: 800-248-4656
URL: http://www.franchisedirectory.ca
Description: La Quinta brand is a high quality mid-priced, limited service product which appeals to both the business and leisure traveler and is franchised under two tiers: La Quinta Inn- A mid market, limited service property with the business and leisure traveler in mind - comfortable guest rooms with coffee maker, dataport phones, meeting facilities, swimming pool, complimentary continental breakfast. La Quinta Inn & Suites- All the benefits of a La Quinta Inn plus - two room suites with microwave, refrigerator, extra dataports, fitness center, guest laundry and more. La Quinta properties are multi level configurations with a minimum of 100 to 150 units per location. **Equity Capital Needed:** $750,000-$1,500,000 total investment; $500,000 required cash liquidity. **Franchise Fee:** $500,000. **Training:** Services include Marketing/ Advertising services, operational and revenue management support, asset management services, franchise services and support, AFM Preferred Alliance purchasing services, operations consulting and support, quality assurance, and training.

10750 ■ Mainstay Suites
Choice Hotels International
10750 Columbia Pike
Silver Spring, MD 20901
Free: 800-547-0007
Fax:(301)592-6205
No. of Franchise Units: 40. **No. of Company-Owned Units:** 3. **Founded:** 1996. **Franchised:** 1996. **Description:** Mid-priced extended-stay hotel. **Equity Capital Needed:** $300/room; $30,000 minimum. **Franchise Fee:** 4.5%GRR. **Financial Assistance:** Yes. **Training:** Yes.

10751 ■ Microtel Inn & Suites
Wyndham Hotel Group
22 Sylvan Way
Parsippany, NJ 07054
Free: 888-222-7484
No. of Franchise Units: 220. **Founded:** 1987. **Franchised:** 1987. **Description:** Budget sector hotel chain. **Equity Capital Needed:** $250,000-$600,000. **Franchise Fee:** $35,000. **Financial Assistance:** Yes. **Training:** Yes.

10752 ■ Motel 6
IBL, LTD
4001 International Pky.
Carrollton, TX 75007
Ph:(972)360-2547
Free: 888-842-2942
Fax:(972)360-5567
No. of Franchise Units: 406. **No. of Company-Owned Units:** 605. **Founded:** 1962. **Franchised:** 1996. **Description:** Budget lodging. **Equity Capital Needed:** $2,426,699-$3,177,399. **Franchise Fee:** $25,000. **Royalty Fee:** 4%. **Financial Assistance:** Yes. **Training:** Offers 1 week at headquarters and training available at franchisees location, annual convention with ongoing support.

10753 ■ Motel6Canada
77 Bloor St., Ste. 77
Toronto, ON, Canada M5S 1M2
Ph:(416)966-8387
Fax:(416)923-3654
Co. E-mail: motel6@realstarhospitality.ca
URL: http://www.motel6.com
No. of Franchise Units: 14. **No. of Company-Owned Units:** 1. **Founded:** 2003. **Franchised:** 2003. **Description:** Establishing franchised and corporate properties in all major cities across the country in the econompriced segment of the market. Providing franchisees with extensive and dedicated franchise services, national sales & marketing, training and purchasing power. **Franchise Fee:** $40,000. **Training:** Assistance with opening and ongoing support.

10754 ■ Ramada Worldwide
Wyndham Hotel Group
22 Sylvan Way
Parsippany, NJ 07054
Free: 888-222-7484
Fax:(993)496-5351
No. of Franchise Units: 965. **Founded:** 1954. **Franchised:** 1954. **Description:** Ramada Franchise Systems is licensor of Ramada guest lodging facilities. **Equity Capital Needed:** Varies depending on project. **Franchise Fee:** $35,000; $350/room. **Financial Assistance:** No. **Training:** Yes.

10755 ■ Realstar Hospitality
77 Bloor St. W, Ste. 2000
Toronto, ON, Canada M5S 1M2
Ph:(416)966-8387
Fax:(416)923-5424
Co. E-mail: Irwin.prince@realstarhospitality.ca
URL: http://www.realstargroup.com
Description: The master franchisor for Days Inn, Motel 6, Studio 6 and Novotel in Canada. Establishing franchised and corporate hotels across the country in the limited and full service sectors. Providing franchisees with extensive and dedicated franchise services, national sales & marketing, training and purchasing power.

10756 ■ Red Roof Inn
Accor North America
4001 International Pky.
Carrolton, TX 75007
Ph:(972)360-2547
Free: 888-842-2942
Fax:(972)360-5567
No. of Franchise Units: 95. **No. of Company-Owned Units:** 240. **Founded:** 1972. **Franchised:** 1996. **Description:** Economy lodging. **Equity Capital Needed:** $100,000-$500,000; $3,500,000 total investment. **Franchise Fee:** $30,000. **Financial Assistance:** No. **Training:** Yes.

10757 ■ The Residence Inn by Marriott
The Plamondon Cos.
321 Ballenger Ctr. Dr., Ste. 201
Fredrick, MD 21703
Ph:(301)380-5237
No. of Franchise Units: 106. **No. of Company-Owned Units:** 60. **Founded:** 1976. **Description:** Extended-stay hotels. **Equity Capital Needed:** $5,000,000, not including land. **Franchise Fee:** $400 per suite. **Financial Assistance:** No. **Training:** Yes.

10758 ■ Rodeway Inn
Choice Hotels Intl.
10750 Columbia Pike
Silver Spring, MD 20901
Free: 800-547-0007
Fax:(301)592-6205
Co. E-mail: franchise_sales@choicehotels.com
No. of Franchise Units: 146. **Founded:** 1964. **Franchised:** 1964. **Description:** Hotels. **Equity Capital Needed:** $125/room; $10,000 minimum. **Franchise Fee:** 3.5%GRR. **Royalty Fee:** $31 per room/month. **Financial Assistance:** Yes. **Training:** Yes.

10759 ■ Scottish Inns, Red Carpet Inns, Master Hosts Inns
Hospitality International, Inc.
1726 Montreal Cir.
Tucker, GA 30084
Ph:(770)270-1180
Free: 800-247-4677
Fax:800-813-6322
No. of Franchise Units: 259. **Founded:** 1982. **Franchised:** 1982. **Description:** Budget motels. Limited amenity lodging. **Equity Capital Needed:** Varies. **Franchise Fee:** $5,000-$12,500. **Financial Assistance:** No. **Training:** Yes.

10760 ■ Sleep Inn
Choice Hotels International
10750 Columbia Pike
Silver Spring, MD 20901
Free: 800-547-0007
Fax:(301)592-6205
Co. E-mail: franchise_info@choicehotels.com
No. of Franchise Units: 307. **Founded:** 1988. **Franchised:** 1988. **Description:** Motel with state-of-the-art guestrooms. **Equity Capital Needed:** $300/room; $40,000 minimum. **Franchise Fee:** 4.5%GRR. **Financial Assistance:** Third party assistance. **Training:** Yes.

10761 ■ Studio 6
Accor North America
4001 International Pky.
Carrollton, TX 75007
Ph:(972)360-2547
Free: 888-842-2942
Fax:(972)360-5567
No. of Franchise Units: 7. **No. of Company-Owned Units:** 34. **Founded:** 1998. **Franchised:** 1999. **Description:** Provider of lodging services. **Equity Capital Needed:** $100,000-$500,000; $3,500,000 total investment. **Franchise Fee:** $25,000. **Financial Assistance:** No. **Training:** Training and support provided.

10762 ■ Studio6Canada
77 Bloor St., W, Ste. 2000
Toronto, ON, Canada M5S 1M2
Ph:(416)966-8387
Fax:(416)923-5424
Co. E-mail: Studio6@realstarhospitality.com
URL: http://www.staystudio6.com
No. of Company-Owned Units: 1. **Founded:** 2003. **Franchised:** 2003. **Description:** Economy extended stay lodging and short term housing sector. Provides franchisees with extensive and dedicated franchise services, national sales & marketing, and purchasing power. **Franchise Fee:** $40,000. **Training:** Provides training, assistance with opening and ongoing support.

10763 ■ Super 8 Motels, Inc.
Wyndham Hotel Group
22 Sylvan Way
Parsippany, NJ 07054
Free: 888-222-7484
Fax:(973)753-8724
No. of Franchise Units: 1,980. **Founded:** 1974. **Franchised:** 1976. **Description:** Economy motels. **Equity Capital Needed:** Varies depending on project. **Franchise Fee:** $20,000+. **Financial Assistance:** Third party and in-house assistance available. **Training:** Offers 5 days at headquarters, 2 days at franchisees location, regional workshops, and customized property training 1-3 days.

10764 ■ Travelodge Hotels
Cendant Corp.
22 Sylvan Way
Parsippany, NJ 07054
Ph:888-223-4675
Free: 800-758-8999
Fax:(973)753-8724
No. of Franchise Units: 342. **Founded:** 1939. **Franchised:** 1966. **Description:** Hotels and motels. **Equity Capital Needed:** $189,849-$6,374,140. **Franchise Fee:** $36,000. **Royalty Fee:** 4.5%. **Financial Assistance:** Limited in-house and third party financing available. **Training:** Available at headquarters for 5 days, 2 days at franchisees location, regional workshops and customized property training 1-3 days.

10765 ■ Value Place
Value Place Franchise Services LLC
8621 E 21st St. N, Ste. 250
Wichita, KS 67206
Ph:(316)630-5505
Fax:(316)631-1333
No. of Franchise Units: 175. **No. of Company-Owned Units:** 43. **Founded:** 2003. **Franchised:** 2004. **Description:** Hotels/motels franchisor. **Equity Capital Needed:** $500,000 liquid; $1,000,000 or greater net worth. **Franchise Fee:** $49,600. **Financial Assistance:** No. **Training:** Yes.

10766 ■ Yogi Bear's Jellystone Park Camp-Resorts
Leisure Systems, Inc.
50 W TechneCenter Dr., Ste. G
Milford, OH 45150
Ph:(513)831-2100
Free: 800-626-3720
Fax:(513)576-8670
URL: http://www.jellystonefranchise.com
No. of Franchise Units: 71. **Founded:** 1969. **Franchised:** 1970. **Description:** Leisure Systems, Inc. holds an exclusive license to franchise Yogi Bear's Jellystone Park Camp/Resorts in the US and Canada. Presently, there are 70 units in the U.S. and 3 in Canada. **Equity Capital Needed:** $25,000+. **Franchise Fee:** $20,000. **Financial Assistance:** Yes. **Training:** Franchisees are required to attend a 5 day training program held at the home office in Cincinnati, OH. Additional onsite training is also conducted for a period of 2-3 days.

COMPUTER SYSTEMS/ SOFTWARE

10767 ■ Resort Data Processing
Resort Data Processing
PO Box 1170
Vail, CO 81658
Ph:(970)845-1140
Fax:(970)845-0150
Co. E-mail: info@resortdata.com
URL: http://www.resortdata.com
Price: Contact Resort Data for pricing. **Description:** Available for IBM computers and compatibles. System designed for hotels with less than 74 rooms. Options include a package with full accounts payable, general ledger, and financial reporting.

LIBRARIES

10768 ■ American Hotel & Lodging Association Information Center
1201 New York Ave. N.W., Ste. 600
Houston, TX 77204-3028
Ph:(202)289-3100
Free: 888-743-2515
Fax:(202)289-3199
Co. E-mail: informationcenter@ahla.com
URL: http://www.ahla.com
Contact: Lydia Westbrook, Res.Dir.
Scope: Hotels and restaurants; travel and tourism. **Services:** Library open to the public with restrictions by appointment only. **Holdings:** 2500 volumes; microfilms; archives. **Subscriptions:** 100 journals and other serials.

10769 ■ California Culinary Academy Library
625 Polk St.
San Francisco, CA 94102
Ph:800-229-2433
Free: 888-897-3222
Co. E-mail: bgk@baychef.com
URL: http://www.baychef.com
Contact: Beth Klein, Dean, Lib.Svcs.
Scope: Culinary arts, nutrition, restaurant and hospitality industry. **Services:** Library open to the public by special appointment only. **Holdings:** 3500 books. **Subscriptions:** 90 journals and other serials.

10770 ■ City College of San Francisco Culinary Arts and Hospitality Studies Department–Alice Statler Library
50 Phelan Ave.
Statler Wing, Rm. 10
San Francisco, CA 94112
Ph:(415)239-3460
Fax:(415)239-3026
Co. E-mail: aniosi@ccsf.edu
URL: http://www.ccsf.edu/library/alice/statler.html
Contact: Andrea Niosi, Libn.
Scope: Public hospitality industries - hotels, motels, restaurants, catering services, cookery and nutrition; tourism; beverages. **Services:** Copying; Library open

to the public for reference use only. **Holdings:** 10,000 books; 3500 pamphlets; 900 menus; videotapes; archives. **Subscriptions:** 80 journals and other serials.

10771 ■ Colorado Mountain College–Alpine Campus Library
1330 Bob Adams Dr.
Steamboat Springs, CO 80477
Ph:(970)870-4445
Free: 800-621-8559
Co. E-mail: dwillis@coloradomtn.edu
URL: http://www.coloradomtn.edu/current_students/library/about/alpine/
Contact: David Willis, Lib.Dir.
Scope: Small business, hotel and restaurant management, health and fitness, U.S. history and literature, American music, skiing. **Services:** Interlibrary loan; Library open to the public. **Holdings:** 30,000 books; 580 CDs; maps; state documents; CD-ROMs. **Subscriptions:** 225 journals and other serials; 15 newspapers.

10772 ■ Cornell University–The Nestle Library
G80 Statler Hall
School of Hotel Administration
Ithaca, NY 14853-6901
Ph:(607)255-3673
Fax:(607)255-0021
Co. E-mail: hotelref@cornell.edu
URL: http://www.hotelschool.cornell.edu/research/library
Contact: Donald Schnedeker, Dir.
Scope: Hotel, motel, and restaurant management, administration, accounting, quantity cookery, food facilities engineering, sanitation, advertising, sales promotion, public relations, marketing, hospitality law, franchising, real estate, tourist industry, resort development. **Services:** Interlibrary loan; Library open to the public by appointment on a fee basis. **Holdings:** 37,000 volumes; 17,000 microforms; 500 computer files; 1000 reels of microfilm; 16,500 microfiche; 1500 videos. **Subscriptions:** 500 serials; 12 newspapers.

10773 ■ Hospitality Sales and Marketing Association International–Research Library
1760 Old Meadow Rd., Ste. 500
McLean, VA 22102
Ph:(703)506-3280
Fax:(703)506-3266
Co. E-mail: bgilbert@hsmai.org
URL: http://www.hsmai.org
Contact: Robert A. Gilbert, Pres./CEO
Scope: Hotels, hospitality, travel and tourism, promotion, merchandising, public relations, marketing, direct mail, publicity, advertising, sales education, revenue management, internet marketing, distribution and channel management, travel and tourism. **Services:** Library open to members by appointment. **Holdings:** 200 volumes. **Subscriptions:** 22 journals and other serials.

10774 ■ Johnson & Wales University–Harborside Culinary Library
321 Harborside Blvd.
Providence, RI 02905
Ph:(401)598-1282
Fax:(401)598-1834
Co. E-mail: barbara.janson@jwu.edu
URL: http://www.jwu.edu
Contact: Barbara Janson, Hd.Libn.
Scope: Cookbooks, food service, menu planning, nutrition, professional management, catering and banquets, household manuals, canning, preserving and freezing, hotel and motel management. **Services:** Copying; Library open to the public. **Holdings:** 10,000 books; 700 menus. **Subscriptions:** 100 journals and other serials.

10775 ■ Johnson and Wales University Charleston Campus–Barry L. Gleim Library
701 E. Bay St.
Charleston, SC 29403
Ph:(843)727-3045

Fax:(843)727-3078
Co. E-mail: Joanne.Letendre@jwu.edu
Contact: Joanne N. Letendre
Scope: Culinary arts, food service, hospitality management, travel and tourism. **Services:** Library open to the public with restrictions. **Holdings:** 10,681 books; 1230 videos; 6 CD-ROMs. **Subscriptions:** 174 journals and other serials; 5 newspapers.

10776 ■ Oregon Lodging Association–Materials Library
8600 SW Salish Ln., Ste. 3
Wilsonville, OR 97070-9675
Ph:(503)783-2797
Fax:(503)783-2798
Co. E-mail: info@oregonlodging.com
URL: http://www.oregonlodging.com
Contact: Jeff Hampton, Pres./CEO
Scope: Hospitality. **Services:** Library open to lodging members. **Holdings:** 57 books; 86 videocassettes. **Subscriptions:** 1 journal.

10777 ■ Paul Smith's College of Arts and Sciences–Joan Weill Adirondack Library
Rte. 86 and 30
PO Box 265
Paul Smiths, NY 12970-0265
Ph:(518)327-6227
Free: 800-421-2605
Fax:(518)327-6016
Co. E-mail: nsurprenant@paulsmiths.edu
URL: http://www.paulsmiths.edu/library
Contact: Neil Surprenant, Dir., Lib.Svcs.
Scope: Hotel and restaurant management, chef training, culinary arts, forestry, urban tree management, environmental science, forest recreation, surveying, ecotourism, natural resources management, fisheries management, business management. **Services:** Interlibrary loan; copying; Library open to the public with restrictions. **Holdings:** 54,000 books; pamphlets. **Subscriptions:** 504 journals and other serials; 7 newspapers.

10778 ■ PKF Consulting Library
50 California St., 19th Fl.
San Francisco, CA 94111

Ph:(415)788-3102
Fax:(415)433-7844
Co. E-mail: thomas.callahan@pkfc.com
URL: http://www.pkfc.com/
Contact: Thomas E. Callahan
Scope: Hotel operations, travel, tourism. **Services:** Library not open to the public. **Subscriptions:** 15 journals and other serials; 4 newspapers.

10779 ■ South College Library
3904 Lonas Dr.
Knoxville, TN 37909
Ph:(865)251-1800
Co. E-mail: mmchugh@southcollegetn.edu
URL: http://www.southcollegetn.edu/library/
Contact: Mel McHugh, Hd.Libn.
Scope: Business, physical therapy, occupational therapy, administration, medical administration, legal administration, small business, secretarial science, paralegal, hotel and restaurant management. **Services:** Interlibrary loan; copying; SDI. **Holdings:** 6700 books; 10 VF drawers; 214 volumes on microfilm; 1 cabinet of microfiche. **Subscriptions:** 106 journals and other serials.

Ice Cream/Frozen Yogurt Shop

START-UP INFORMATION

10780 ■ **"Lee's Launches With Focus on Liqueur-based Ice Creams" in** *Ice Cream Reporter* **(Vol. 23, August 20, 2010, No. 9, pp. 6)**
Pub: Ice Cream Reporter
Description: Lee's Cream Liqueur Ice Cream Parlors launched their grand opening in Old Town Scottsdale in July, featuring premium liqueurs to create adult-only ice creams that can be served on their own or blended into exotic drinks.

10781 ■ **"Young Entrepreneur's Business Plan? An Ice Cream Boat? Really Floats: Maine at Work" in** *Portland Press Herald* **(August 9, 2010)**
Pub: Portland Press Herald
Ed: Ray Routhier. **Description:** Profile of Jake Viola, founder of and ice cream boat located near Portland, Maine. Viola is a sophomore at Yale University and sells ice cream from his pontoon boat on Little Sebago lake.

ASSOCIATIONS AND OTHER ORGANIZATIONS

10782 ■ **Allied Purchasing Company**
PO Box 1249
Mason City, IA 50402
Free: 800-247-5956
Fax:800-635-3775
Co. E-mail: brian@alliedpurchasing.com
URL: http://www.alliedpurchasing.com
Contact: Brian Janssen, Pres./CFO
Description: Represents dairies, ice cream plants and soft drink bottlers. Collaborates to obtain group purchasing rates on equipment, ingredients, services, and supplies. .

10783 ■ **Dairy Management, Inc.**
10255 W Higgins Rd., Ste. 900
Rosemont, IL 60018-5616
Ph:(847)627-3252
Free: 800-853-2479
Fax:(847)803-2077
Co. E-mail: marykateg@rosedmi.com
URL: http://www.dairyinfo.com
Contact: Joe Bavido
Description: Operates under the auspices of the United Dairy Industry Association. Milk producers, milk dealers, and manufacturers of butter, cheese, ice cream, dairy equipment, and supplies. Conducts programs of nutrition research and nutrition education in the use of milk and its products. **Publications:** *Dairy Council Digest* (bimonthly).

10784 ■ **Food Processing Suppliers Association**
1451 Dolley Madison Blvd., Ste. 101
McLean, VA 22101-3847
Ph:(703)761-2600

Fax:(703)761-4334
Co. E-mail: info@fpsa.org
URL: http://www.fpsa.org
Contact: David Seckman, Pres./CEO
Description: Manufacturers and distributors of dairy and food processing and packaging equipment, machinery, ingredients, and supplies. Provides marketing and technical services to member firms. Compiles market statistics. **Publications:** *IAFIS—Directory of Membership Products and Services* (biennial); *IAFIS—Reporter* (monthly).

10785 ■ **National Ice Cream Retailers Association**
1028 W Devon Ave.
Elk Grove Village, IL 60007
Ph:(847)301-7500
Free: (866)303-6960
Fax:(847)301-8402
Co. E-mail: info@nicyra.org
URL: http://www.nicra.org
Contact: Lynda Utterback, Exec. Dir.
Description: Represents frozen dessert retailers that operate ice cream and frozen yogurt dipping stores or parlors. Provides free and frank exchange of information among members so that all may improve their operations, increase profits and prosper. **Publications:** *NICRA Bulletin* (monthly); *NICRA Yearbook* (annual).

REFERENCE WORKS

10786 ■ **"7-Eleven Considers Private Label Ice Cream" in** *Ice Cream Reporter* **(Vol. 22, December 20, 2008, No. 1, pp. 1)**
Pub: Ice Cream Reporter
Description: 7-Eleven is considering the introduction of a private label of snack foods, including ice cream desserts.

10787 ■ **"Allied Brands Loses Baskin-Robbins Franchise Down Under" in** *Ice Cream Reporter* **(Vol. 23, November 20, 2010, No. 12, pp. 2)**
Pub: Ice Cream Reporter
Description: Dunkin Brands, worldwide franchisor of Baskin-Robbins, terminated the master franchise agreement for Australia held by the food marketer Allied Brands Services.

10788 ■ **"Also Active in the Fight Against Cancer is Dreyer's Grand Ice Cream" in** *Ice Cream Reporter* **(Vol. 23, October 20, 2010, No. 11, pp. 8)**
Pub: Ice Cream Reporter
Description: Dreyer's Grand Ice Cream partnered with Experience Project's BroadCause.com to raise awareness around pediatric cancer research.

10789 ■ **"B. Jannetta" in** *Ice Cream Reporter* **(Vol. 21, August 20, 2008, No. 9, pp. 8)**
Pub: Ice Cream Reporter
Description: B. Jannetta ice cream parlor, run by Owen and Nicola Hazel, is celebrating its 100th Anniversary. The ice cream parlor is believed to be the

oldest business still operating in its original shop in Saint Andrews. Owen and Nicola are the fourth generation to run the shop since Hazel's grandfather founded the business in 1908.

10790 ■ **"Baskin-Robbins Expanding in China and U.S." in** *Ice Cream Reporter* **(Vol. 21, August 20, 2008, No. 9, pp. 1)**
Pub: Ice Cream Reporter
Description: Baskin-Robbins will open its first store in Shanghai, China along with plans for 100 more shops in that country. They will also be expanding their market in the Dallas/Fort Worth, Texas area as well as Greater Cincinnati/Northern Kentucky regions.

10791 ■ **"Baskin-Robbins Expanding to South Texas" in** *Ice Cream Reporter* **(Vol. 23, July 20, 2010, No. 8, pp. 4)**
Pub: Ice Cream Reporter
Description: Baskin-Robbins will develop six new shops in south Texas after signing agreements with two franchisees.

10792 ■ **"Baskin-Robbins" in** *Ice Cream Reporter* **(Vol. 23, September 20, 2010, No. 10, pp. 6)**
Pub: Ice Cream Reporter
Description: Baskin-Robbins will feature an old favorite called Quarterback Crunch as its September Flavor of the Month. The item was created in 1978 and features vanilla ice cream with chocolate covered rice crunchies and a carmel ribbon.

10793 ■ **"Baskin-Robbins: New in U.S., Old in Japan" in** *Ice Cream Reporter* **(Vol. 23, August 20, 2010, No. 9, pp. 2)**
Pub: Ice Cream Reporter
Description: Baskin-Robbins is celebrating its first franchise in Japan.

10794 ■ **"Baskin-Robbins Reopens in New Orleans" in** *Ice Cream Reporter* **(Vol. 23, September 20, 2010, No. 10, pp. 3)**
Pub: Ice Cream Reporter
Description: Baskin-Robbins will open its first shop in New Orleans, Louisiana after Hurricane Katrina in 2005. The shop stands in the exact location of a Baskin-Robbins shop destroyed by Katrina.

10795 ■ **"Baskin-Robbins Tests New Upscale Concept" in** *Ice Cream Reporter* **(Vol. 21, September 20, 2008, No. 10, pp. 1)**
Pub: Ice Cream Reporter
Description: Baskin-Robbins is opening its new upscale store, Cafe 31 in an effort to invigorate its brand. The shop will serve fondues, cakes and other treats prepared by an in-store chef.

10796 ■ **"Ben & Jerry" in** *Ice Cream Reporter* **(Vol. 21, August 20, 2008, No. 9, pp. 7)**
Pub: Ice Cream Reporter
Description: Ben & Jerry's created a limited-batch ice cream to honor singer Elton John when he performed in Vermont. The treat was called "Goodbye Yellow Brick Road" and featured chocolate ice cream, peanut butter cookie dough, butter brickle, and white chocolate chunks.

Small Business Sourcebook • 29th Edition 705

10797 ■ "Ben & Jerry's Changing Some 'All Natural' Labels" in *Ice Cream Reporter* **(Vol. 23, October 20, 2010, No. 11, pp. 1)**
Pub: Ice Cream Reporter

Description: Following criticism from the Center for Science in the Public Interest, Ben & Jerry's will omit the term 'All Natural' from its labeling, however the firm reports it will continue to use the most natural ingredients they can find for its products.

10798 ■ "Ben & Jerry's Introduces 'Green' Freezer" in *Ice Cream Reporter* **(Vol. 21, October 20, 2008, No. 11, pp. 1)**
Pub: Ice Cream Reporter

Description: Ben & Jerry's describes its latest concept as a cleaner, greener freezer. The hydrocarbon-based freezer provides great environmental benefits by minimizing the freezer's impact on global warming.

10799 ■ "Blue Bell Breaks Ground in South Carolina" in *Ice Cream Reporter* **(Vol. 23, August 20, 2010, No. 9, pp. 3)**
Pub: Ice Cream Reporter

Description: Texas-based Blue Bell Creameries will open a new 2,000 square foot transfer facility in North Charleston, South Carolina. The facility will expand Blue Bell's distribution efforts in the state.

10800 ■ "Blue Bell Touts Non-Shrinkage" in *Ice Cream Reporter* **(Vol. 21, July 20, 2008, No. 8, pp. 1)**
Pub: Ice Cream Reporter

Description: Blue Bell Ice Cream is promoting its decision to keep their ice cream products in a full half-gallon container rather than downsizing the package. Thirty-second television ads contrast the move by other ice cream makers to offer less for the same money.

10801 ■ "Boston Globe" in *Ice Cream Reporter* **(Vol. 21, August 20, 2008, No. 9, pp. 7)**
Pub: Ice Cream Reporter

Description: Boston City Council approved an ordinance that will limit when ice cream vendors can announce their presence with music over loud speakers. The rules are simple: when the wheels stop moving, the jingles stop playing.

10802 ■ "Carvel" in *Ice Cream Reporter* **(Vol. 23, September 20, 2010, No. 10, pp. 7)**
Pub: Ice Cream Reporter

Description: Pamela Carvel, niece of Carvel founding soft serve has been barred from bringing any more lawsuits against her uncle's estate.

10803 ■ "Carvel Offers Franchisee Discount" in *Ice Cream Reporter* **(Vol. 21, August 20, 2008, No. 9, pp. 2)**
Pub: Ice Cream Reporter

Description: Carvel Ice Cream is offering new franchise opportunities in Florida, New Jersey, and New York. The company will offer incentive for new franchise owners.

10804 ■ "Cold Stone Creamery" in *Ice Cream Reporter* **(Vol. 22, January 20, 2009, No. 2, pp. 8)**
Pub: Ice Cream Reporter

Description: Franchise News reports that Cold Stone Creamery is looking for master franchisees to support its expansion into the North German market. The report notes that following its successful launch in Denmark, the firm is also preparing for expansion into France.

10805 ■ "Cold Stone Creamery Offers New Eight-Layer Ice Cream Cakes" in *Ice Cream Reporter* **(Vol. 23, October 20, 2010, No. 11, pp. 2)**
Pub: Ice Cream Reporter

Description: Cold Stone Creamery is introducing a new line of eight-layer ice cream cakes, which are crafted with three layers of ice cream, three layers of cake and two mid-layers of mix-ins and finished with frosting and a creative design.

10806 ■ "Cold Stone in Licensing Agreement with Turin Chocolates" in *Ice Cream Reporter* **(Vol. 22, December 20, 2008, No. 1, pp. 2)**
Pub: Ice Cream Reporter

Description: Cold Stone Creamery and Turin Chocolatier are teaming up to offer a new line of chocolate truffles under the Cold Stone label. The treats will feature four the most popular Cold Stone flavors: Coffee Lovers Only, Chocolate Devotion, Our Strawberry Blonde, and Peanut Butter Cup Perfection.

10807 ■ "CoolBrands" in *Canadian Business* **(Vol. 83, September 14, 2010, No. 15, pp. 25)**
Pub: Rogers Media Ltd.

Ed: Joe Castaldo. **Description:** CoolBrands International Inc.'s merger with Swisher International Inc., a US hygiene products and services company, has formally erased the last traces of the former ice cream company. CoolBrands began as a frozen yogurt stand in 1986 and flourished across the world. How the string of acquisitions and poor corporate governance led to its demise are cited.

10808 ■ "Dairy Queen Aims to Blitz Blizzberry" in *Ice Cream Reporter* **(Vol. 23, August 20, 2010, No. 9, pp. 1)**
Pub: Ice Cream Reporter

Description: International Diary Queens has filed a lawsuit to stop Yogubliz Inc. from using Blizzberry and Blizz Frozen Yogurt as the name of its shops because the name is so close to Dairy Queen's Blizzard frozen dessert.

10809 ■ "Dairy Queen Ends Effort Against Yogubliz" in *Ice Cream Reporter* **(Vol. 23, November 20, 2010, No. 12, pp. 1)**
Pub: Ice Cream Reporter

Description: Dairy Queen has stopped demands that Yogubliz Inc. change its Blizzberry and Blizz Frozen Yogurt shops because they sound too much like Dairy Queen's Blizzard frozen dessert treat. Dairy Queen feared consumers would confuse the two brands.

10810 ■ "Dean Foods" in *Ice Cream Reporter* **(Vol. 23, November 20, 2010, No. 12, pp. 8)**
Pub: Ice Cream Reporter

Description: The impact of higher commodity prices can be seen in the recent news from Dean Foods, the largest U.S. dairy company, which reported that rising butterfat and other dairy commodity costs have led to lower-than-expected quarterly profits after it cut prices to compete with private-label brands.

10811 ■ "Denali Asks Consumers to Name Next Moose Tracks Flavor" in *Ice Cream Reporter* **(Vol. 23, August 20, 2010, No. 9, pp. 4)**
Pub: Ice Cream Reporter

Description: Denali Flavors based in Michigan is inviting consumer to name its newest Moose Tracks version of ice cream flavors.

10812 ■ "Department of Agriculture" in *Ice Cream Reporter* **(Vol. 23, November 20, 2010, No. 12, pp. 8)**
Pub: Ice Cream Reporter

Description: Department of Agriculture notes that food price inflation for 2010 will be at its lowest since 1992.

10813 ■ "Dreyer's Grand Ice Cream" in *Ice Cream Reporter* **(Vol. 23, September 20, 2010, No. 10, pp. 8)**
Pub: Ice Cream Reporter

Description: Dreyer's Grand Ice Cream will add one hundred new manufacturing jobs at its plant in Laurel, Maryland and another 65 new hires before the end of 2010 and another 35 in 2011.

10814 ■ "Emack & Bolio" in *Ice Cream Reporter* **(Vol. 23, October 20, 2010, No. 11, pp. 8)**
Pub: Ice Cream Reporter

Description: Emack & Bolio's is engaging in scent marketing using various odors to help boost sales by attracting consumers with scents appropriate to their products.

10815 ■ "Fieldbrook Foods Acquired By Private Equity Firm" in *Ice Cream Reporter* **(Vol. 23, October 20, 2010, No. 11, pp. 1)**
Pub: Ice Cream Reporter

Description: Fieldbrook Foods Corporation, manufacturer of frozen novelty and ice cream products was acquired by Chicago-based private equity firm Arbor Investments. Arbor partnered with Herman 'Bing' Graffunder, a long-term dairy industry partner, in its acquisition of Fieldbrook.

10816 ■ "First Airport Location for Paciugo Gelato" in *Ice Cream Reporter* **(Vol. 23, October 20, 2010, No. 11, pp. 2)**
Pub: Ice Cream Reporter

Description: Paciugo Gelato and Caffee has partnered with airport concessions developer Airmail to open a shop in the Cleveland Hopkins International Airport. The firm will create a wide variety of choices for travelers.

10817 ■ "Fraser and Neave Acquires King's Creameries" in *Ice Cream Reporter* **(Vol. 23, November 20, 2010, No. 12, pp. 1)**
Pub: Ice Cream Reporter

Description: Fraser and Neave Ltd., a Singapore-based consumer products marketer, has entered a conditional agreement to acquire all outstanding shares of King's Creameries, the leading manufacturer and distributor of frozen desserts.

10818 ■ "Friendly Ice Cream Corporation" in *Ice Cream Reporter* **(Vol. 23, August 20, 2010, No. 9, pp. 8)**
Pub: Ice Cream Reporter

Description: Friendly Ice Cream Corporation appointed Andrea M. McKenna as vice president of marketing and chief marketing officer.

10819 ■ "Friendly" in *Ice Cream Reporter* **(Vol. 21, August 20, 2008, No. 9, pp. 8)**
Pub: Ice Cream Reporter

Description: Advertising Age presented Friendly's with the award, "Ad of the Day" for its television commercial depicting a Norman Rockwell-esque family transported to a psychedelic wonderland.

10820 ■ "Frozen Dessert Year in Review..." in *Ice Cream Reporter* **(Vol. 22, January 20, 2009, No. 2, pp. 1)**
Pub: Ice Cream Reporter

Description: Falling economy caused the closing of several ice cream plants across the U.S. in 2008. Top stories of interest to the industry are presented.

10821 ■ "Frozen Yogurt Market Heats Up Again" in *Houston Business Journal* **(Vol. 40, November 27, 2009, No. 29, pp. 1)**
Pub: American City Business Journals

Ed: Allison Wollam. **Description:** Frozen yogurt stores are being reestablished or expanding in new sites throughout Houston, Texas due to presumed oversupply of ice cream stores in the market. Among these stores are Berripop, BlueBerryHill, Fruituzy, and Tasti D-Lite. Suggestions for these stores to focus on frozen yogurts in order to distinguish them from stores offering other products such as specialty drink items and sandwiches are outlined.

10822 ■ "Gifford's Tops in Chocolate" in *Ice Cream Reporter* **(Vol. 21, August 20, 2008, No. 9, pp. 3)**
Pub: Ice Cream Reporter

Description: Gifford's Ice Cream was presented with two major awards at the World Dairy Expo: "World's Best Chocolate Ice Cream" and "Worlds Best Vanilla Ice Cream". Entries are judged on flavor, body and texture, color and appearance, melting quality, and quality assurance.

10823 ■ "Gillette Creamery" in *Ice Cream Reporter* **(Vol. 23, September 20, 2010, No. 10, pp. 8)**
Pub: Ice Cream Reporter

Description: Gillette family of Gillette Creamery in Ellenville have been Entrepreneurs of the Year in Ulster County, New York. Gillette is the largest supplier of ice cream products in Eastern New York.

10824 ■ "Golden Spoon Accelerates Expansion Here and Abroad" in *Ice Cream Reporter* **(Vol. 22, December 20, 2008, No. 1, pp. 2)**
Pub: Ice Cream Reporter
Description: Golden Spoon frozen yogurt franchise chain is developing 35 more locations in the Phoenix, Arizona area along with plans to open a store in Japan.

10825 ■ "Haagen-Dazs Recruits Shop Owners through Facebook" in *Ice Cream Reporter* **(Vol. 23, November 20, 2010, No. 12, pp. 1)**
Pub: Ice Cream Reporter
Description: Haagen-Dazs Shoppe Company is using Facebook, the leading social media, to recruit new franchises.

10826 ■ "Hain Celestial Acquires Greek Gods Yogurt" in *Ice Cream Reporter* **(Vol. 23, July 20, 2010, No. 8, pp. 1)**
Pub: Ice Cream Reporter
Description: Hain Celestial Group acquired The Greek Gods LLC. Hain Celestial is a natural and organic products company and Greek Gods makes all natural, Greek-style yogurt and ice cream.

10827 ■ "The Harris Teeter Grocery Chain Has Started a New Ice Cream Club for Shoppers" in *Ice Cream Reporter* **(Vol. 21, July 20, 2008)**
Pub: Ice Cream Reporter
Description: Store loyalty cards are being issued to Harris Teeter customers to purchase any variety of Ben & Jerry's, Haagen-Dazs, Dove, Starbucks, Ciao Bella, Clemmy's, Purely Decadent, So Delicious, Harris Teeter Naturals, HT Traders, Hunter Farms or Denali Ice Cream. One point is earned for every dollar spent, 30 total points earns a $5 electronic coupon towards the next purchase.

10828 ■ "Healthy Fast Food Acquires Rights to U-Swirl Yogurt" in *Ice Cream Reporter* **(Vol. 21, October 20, 2008, No. 11, pp. 5)**
Pub: Ice Cream Reporter
Description: Healthy Fast Food Inc. will acquire worldwide rights to U-Swirl Frozen Yogurt; the firm will use the new acquisition to create a yogurt superstore in a cafe setting concept for its operations.

10829 ■ "Herrell's Launches New Corporate Identity at Fancy Food Show" in *Ice Cream Reporter* **(Vol. 23, July 20, 2010, No. 8, pp. 3)**
Pub: Ice Cream Reporter
Description: Herrell's ice cream introduced a new corporate branding at the Summer 2010 Fancy Food Show last summer. Slightly Mad Communications advertising agency developed the new brand to reflect the era of the early 1970s.

10830 ■ "In Addition, Pinkberry Reports It Is Opening a New Shop in Sunnyvale, CA" in *Ice Cream Reporter* **(Vol. 23, October 20, 2010)**
Pub: Ice Cream Reporter
Description: Pinkberry opened a new shop in Sunnyvale, California, its fourth opening in the South Bay and its 101st location worldwide.

10831 ■ "International Dairy Queen" in *Ice Cream Reporter* **(Vol. 23, October 20, 2010, No. 11, pp. 7)**
Pub: Ice Cream Reporter
Description: International Dairy Queen will open more than 100 new outlets in China in 2011, adding to the current level of more than 300 outlets in that country.

10832 ■ "Kosher Ice Cream Features Traditional Jewish Ingredients" in *Ice Cream Reporter* **(Vol. 23, August 20, 2010, No. 9, pp. 5)**
Pub: Ice Cream Reporter
Description: Chozen Ice Cream is offering traditional Jewish dessert and snack foods using tradition Jewish ingredients to name items: regelach, coconut-almond macaroon, and chocolate matzo.

10833 ■ "Looking To Hire Young? Be Careful" in *Boston Business Journal* **(Vol. 30, November 19, 2010, No. 43, pp. 1)**
Pub: Boston Business Journal
Ed: Lisa van der Pool. **Description:** The Massachusetts Commission Against Discrimination (MCAD) has been using undercover job applicants to expose discrimination. Cabot's Ice Cream and Restaurant has been accused of denying older workers equal employment opportunities. MCAD has discovered unfair hiring practices such as hiring high school and college students.

10834 ■ "Loseley Dairy Ice Cream" in *Ice Cream Reporter* **(Vol. 23, November 20, 2010, No. 12, pp. 8)**
Pub: Ice Cream Reporter
Description: Neil Burchell has been named managing director of Loseley Dairy Ice Cream, one of the UK's largest independent producers. Burchell, with over 30 years experience in the food industry, was recently managing director of Rachel's, the leading organic dairy foods company in the UK, where he is credited with driving a sixfold increase in sales.

10835 ■ "MaggieMoo's Ice Cream and Treatery" in *Ice Cream Reporter* **(Vol. 23, September 20, 2010, No. 10, pp. 7)**
Pub: Ice Cream Reporter
Description: MaggieMoo's Ice Cream and Treatery has launched a new Website where visitors can learn about the brands newest ice cream innovations.

10836 ■ "Marble Slab Creamery" in *Ice Cream Reporter* **(Vol. 23, November 20, 2010, No. 12, pp. 7)**
Pub: Ice Cream Reporter
Description: Marble Slab Creamery is promoting its company by offering a New Year's Eve Sweepstakes.

10837 ■ "Menchie's Tops Restaurant Business' Future 50 List" in *Ice Cream Reporter* **(Vol. 23, August 20, 2010, No. 9, pp. 4)**
Pub: Ice Cream Reporter
Description: Menchie's, frozen yogurt shop, announced it placed first in the Restaurant Business Magazine's Future 50, ranking the franchise the fastest-growing in the food industry.

10838 ■ "Mini Melts" in *Ice Cream Reporter* **(Vol. 23, August 20, 2010, No. 9, pp. 8)**
Pub: Ice Cream Reporter
Description: Mini Melts appointed David S. Tade to position of director of sales USA in order to cultivate existing distributors and add new partners to its distribution network.

10839 ■ "Mini Melts Offers 'Win an Ice Cream Business' Contest" in *Ice Cream Reporter* **(Vol. 23, October 20, 2010, No. 11, pp. 3)**
Pub: Ice Cream Reporter
Description: Mini Melts USA launched a promotional program offering contestants the opportunity to win a Mini Melts ice cream business. The business is not a franchise and there are not royalty fees.

10840 ■ "MooBella Adds Two Airports" in *Ice Cream Reporter* **(Vol. 23, November 20, 2010, No. 12, pp. 5)**
Pub: Ice Cream Reporter
Description: MooBella Inc. has placed MooBella Ice Creamery machines in New England's Logan International Airport in Boston and in New Hampshire's Manchester-Boston Regional Airport.

10841 ■ "New CEO For Friendly's" in *Ice Cream Reporter* **(Vol. 23, September 20, 2010, No. 10, pp. 1)**
Pub: Ice Cream Reporter
Description: Friendly Ice Cream Corporation named Harsha V. Agadi as new chief executive officer. Agadi has 24 years experience in food service, most recently serving as CEO of Church's Chicken.

10842 ■ "New Zealand Natural Co-Branding with Mrs. Fields" in *Ice Cream Reporter* **(Vol. 23, November 20, 2010, No. 12, pp. 2)**
Pub: Ice Cream Reporter
Description: Mrs. Fields has partnered with a New Zealand firm to co-brand ice cream and cookies in Australian markets.

10843 ■ "New Zealand Natural Ice Cream is Opening a Second U.S. Scoop Shop" in *Ice Cream Reporter* **(Vol. 21, October 20, 2008, No. 11, pp. 7)**
Pub: Ice Cream Reporter
Description: New Zealand Natural Ice Cream is opening a second store in California. The company is a market leader in New Zealand and has gained distribution through 300 outlets in California.

10844 ■ "NexCen Brands Sells Chains and Will Liquidate" in *Ice Cream Reporter* **(Vol. 23, August 20, 2010, No. 9, pp. 1)**
Pub: Ice Cream Reporter
Description: NexCen Brands is closing the sale of its franchise businesses, which include the frozen dessert chains MaggieMoo's and Marbel Slab Creamery, to Global Franchise Group.

10845 ■ "A Nice Consistency" in *Inc.* **(Vol. 31, January-February 2009, No. 1, pp. 94)**
Pub: Mansueto Ventures LLC
Ed: Jason Del Rey. **Description:** PJ Madison spent almost a quarter of its revenue promoting its latest product, organic ice cream. The Texas-based firm saw sales increase dramatically.

10846 ■ "Oberweis Tests Home Ice Cream Delivery" in *Ice Cream Reporter* **(Vol. 21, November 20, 2008, No. 12, pp. 1)**
Pub: Ice Cream Reporter
Description: Oberwies Dairy launched its Treat Delivery Program in the Saint Louis area. The program allows customers to order milkshakes, ice cream cones, sundaes and scoops of ice cream and they are delivered to their home or office. Oberweis is a fourth generation family run business.

10847 ■ "Other First Place Winners From the Expo" in *Ice Cream Reporter* **(Vol. 23, September 20, 2010, No. 10, pp. 8)**
Pub: Ice Cream Reporter
Description: Sassy Cow Creamery, Columbus, Wisconsin; Stewarts, Saratoga Springs, New York; Purity Dairies, Nashville, Tennessee; Kemps, Cedarburg, Wisconsin, and Kelly Country Creamery also won first place awards for various categories at the 2010 World Dairy Expo.

10848 ■ "Penny Chapman" in *Canadian Business* **(Vol. 79, July 17, 2006, No. 14-15, pp. 75)**
Pub: Rogers Media
Ed: Erin Pooley. **Description:** Interview with Penny Chapman, president of Chapman's Ice Cream, who speaks about her journey from rags to riches.

10849 ■ "Perry's Goes Organic" in *Ice Cream Reporter* **(Vol. 22, December 20, 2008, No. 1, pp. 1)**
Pub: Ice Cream Reporter
Description: Family-owned Perry's Ice Cream is starting a new line of organic ice cream in both vanilla and chocolate flavors. All Perry's products are made with milk and cream from local dairy farmers.

10850 ■ "Pierre's Ice Cream" in *Ice Cream Reporter* **(Vol. 23, October 20, 2010, No. 11, pp. 8)**
Pub: Ice Cream Reporter
Description: Pierre's Ice Cream has started work on its new $8 million manufacturing facility in Cleveland, Ohio.

10851 ■ "Pinkberry" in *Ice Cream Reporter* **(Vol. 23, October 20, 2010, No. 11, pp. 6)**
Pub: Ice Cream Reporter
Description: Pinkberry introduced its new Fresh Fruit Bowl, a made-to-order dessert with fresh cut fruit and topped with signature P:inkberry Swirly Whip whipped cream.

10852 ■ "Private Label Manufacturers Association" in *Ice Cream Reporter* **(Vol. 23, July 20, 2010, No. 8, pp. 7)**
Pub: Ice Cream Reporter
Description: Branded frozen dessert manufacturers sold more frozen desserts in terms of sales volume and revenue and market share in 2009. Statistical details included.

10853 ■ "R&R Ice Cream" in *Ice Cream Reporter* **(Vol. 23, November 20, 2010, No. 12, pp. 8)**
Pub: Ice Cream Reporter
Description: R&R Ice Cream, the United Kingdom's largest ice cream manufacturer, has completed a private offering of senior secured notes that has raised 298 million (pounds sterling) to fund expansion and acquisitions.

10854 ■ "R&R Launches Upscale Spoony's and Low Fat Dragon's Den" in *Ice Cream Reporter* **(Vol. 23, August 20, 2010, No. 9, pp. 3)**
Pub: Ice Cream Reporter
Description: European ice cream manufacturer R&R has acquired French ice cream maker Rolland and will position itself as an upscale challenger to brands like Ben & Jerry's.

10855 ■ "Red Mango Set to Grow in Florida" in *Ice Cream Reporter* **(Vol. 23, September 20, 2010, No. 10, pp. 2)**
Pub: Ice Cream Reporter
Description: Red Mango will add 12 new locations throughout Florida. The stores offer healthy, nutritious frozen yogurt, smoothies and parfaits.

10856 ■ "Safeway" in *Ice Cream Reporter* **(Vol. 23, September 20, 2010, No. 10, pp. 8)**
Pub: Ice Cream Reporter
Description: Safeway supermarkets have upsized their private label ice cream to a full half gallon, thus reversing the trend where most brands were shrinking their containers.

10857 ■ "SBA Lauds Anchorage DQ Franchise" in *Alaska Business Monthly* **(Vol. 27, October 2011, No. 10, pp. 9)**
Pub: Alaska Business Publishing Company
Ed: Nancy Pounds. **Description:** US Small Business Administration (SBA) honored Greg Todd, operator of four DQ Grill and Chill eateries in Anchorage, Alaska. The firm has created 100 jobs since receiving SBA assistance.

10858 ■ "Silver Springs Creamery Opens Retail" in *Bellingham Business Journal* **(Vol. March 2010, pp. 3)**
Pub: Sound Publishing Inc.
Description: Eric Sundstrom, owner of Silver Springs Creamery, announced the opening of its on-site retail store that will sell the farm's goat and cow cheese, yogurt, ice cream and flesh milk.

10859 ■ "Styles" in *Ice Cream Reporter* **(Vol. 21, July 20, 2008, No. 8, pp. 6)**
Pub: Ice Cream Reporter
Description: British ice cream maker Styles is using sheep's milk in its new frozen dessert, Slim Ewe Iced Dessert. The products has all the natural taste, texture and health advantages of sheep's milk with less than 2.5 grams of fat and under 75 calories per serving.

10860 ■ "Target Gets Exclusive with Ben & Jerry's" in *Ice Cream Reporter* **(Vol. 23, July 20, 2010, No. 8, pp. 1)**
Pub: Ice Cream Reporter
Description: Target Corporation will launch two new Ben & Jerry's ice cream flavors at its retail stores in 49 states. The new ice cream flavors will be available in mini cups and pints and are called Berry Voluntary and Brownie Chew Gooder.

10861 ■ "Tastee-Freez Celebrates 60th Anniversary" in *Ice Cream Reporter* **(Vol. 23, July 20, 2010, No. 8, pp. 2)**
Pub: Ice Cream Reporter
Description: Tastee-Freez founders, Leo Moranz (inventor) and Harry Axene, an inventor partnered to market the soft-serve pump and freezer for serving frozen treats back in 1950.

10862 ■ "Tasti D-Lite Has Franchise Agreement for Australia" in *Ice Cream Reporter* **(Vol. 23, November 20, 2010, No. 12, pp. 3)**
Pub: Ice Cream Reporter
Description: Tasti D-Lite signed an international master franchise agreement with Friezer Australia

Pty. Ltd. and will open 30 units throughout Australia over the next five years.

10863 ■ "Thai Ice Cream Cremo Expanding to Middle East" in *Ice Cream Reporter* **(Vol. 23, September 20, 2010, No. 10, pp. 3)**
Pub: Ice Cream Reporter
Description: Thai-based frozen dessert manufacturer Chomthana, maker of Cremo brand ice cream, is expanding into the Middle East.

10864 ■ "To Help Maintain an Adequate Blood Supply During the Summer Months" in *Ice Cream Reporter* **(Vol. 21, August 20, 2008, No. 9, pp. 8)**
Pub: Ice Cream Reporter
Description: Friendly's and the American Red Cross have partnered to offer blood donors a coupon for one free carton of Friendly's ice cream in order to maintain an adequate supply during summer months.

10865 ■ "Tofutti Brands" in *Ice Cream Reporter* **(Vol. 23, September 20, 2010, No. 10, pp. 6)**
Pub: Ice Cream Reporter
Description: Tofutti Brands announced net sales at $4.5 million for second quarter 2010.

10866 ■ "U-Swirl Added to SBA's Franchise Registry" in *Ice Cream Reporter* **(Vol. 23, September 20, 2010, No. 10, pp. 1)**
Pub: Ice Cream Reporter
Description: Healthy Fast Food Inc., parent to the U-SWIRL Frozen Yogurt cafe chain announced that the U.S. Small Business Administration listed U-SWIRL Frozen Yogurt on its official franchise registry. This move will allow U-SWIRL the benefits of a streamlined review process for SBA financing.

10867 ■ "U-Swirl To Open in Salt Lake City Metro Market" in *Ice Cream Reporter* **(Vol. 23, November 20, 2010, No. 12, pp. 4)**
Pub: Ice Cream Reporter
Description: Healthy Fast Food Inc., parent company to U-SWIRL International Inc., the owner and franchisor of U-SWIRL Frozen Yogurt cafes signed a franchising area development agreement for the Salt Lake City metropolitan area with Regents Management and will open 5 cafes over a five year period.

10868 ■ "Unilever Acquiring Danish Operations of Diplom-Is Ice Cream" in *Ice Cream Reporter* **(Vol. 23, August 20, 2010, No. 9, pp. 1)**
Pub: Ice Cream Reporter
Description: Unilever will acquire Danish operations of the ice cream company Diplom-Is from Norwegian dairy group Tine.

10869 ■ "Unilever Acquiring EVGA's Ice Cream Brands in Greece" in *Ice Cream Reporter* **(Vol. 23, October 20, 2010, No. 11, pp. 1)**
Pub: Ice Cream Reporter
Description: Unilever will acquire the ice cream brands and distribution network of the Greek frozen dessert manufacturer EVGA.

10870 ■ "Unilever to Sustainably Source All Paper and Board Packaging" in *Ice Cream Reporter* **(Vol. 23, July 20, 2010, No. 8, pp. 1)**
Pub: Ice Cream Reporter
Description: Unilever, a leader in the frozen dessert market, has developed a new sustainable paper and board packaging sourcing policy that will reduce environmental impact by working with suppliers to source 75 percent of paper and board packaging from sustainably managed forests or from recycled material. Unilever is parent company to Breyers, Haagen-Dazs, Klondike, Popsicle and other ice cream brands.

10871 ■ "Velvet Ice Cream" in *Ice Cream Reporter* **(Vol. 23, November 20, 2010, No. 12, pp. 7)**
Pub: Ice Cream Reporter
Description: Velvet Ice Cream will open its Ye Olde Mill for private corporate parties around the holidays. Their facility can accommodate groups ranging from 30 to 125 individuals. The historic site houses the company headquarters, an ice cream museum, and a restaurant.

10872 ■ "Wells' Is Title Sponsor for Volleyball Championship" in *Ice Cream Reporter* **(Vol. 22, August 20, 2008, No. 9, pp. 4)**
Pub: Ice Cream Reporter
Description: Wells' Dairy was chosen to sponsor the 29th Annual National Association of Intercollegiate Athletics (NAIA) Volleyball National Championship to be held in Sioux City, Iowa. Blue Bunny will sponsor the 2008 NAIA Women's Volleyball National Championship, also a Wells' brand.

10873 ■ "YoCream" in *Ice Cream Reporter* **(Vol. 23, September 20, 2010, No. 10, pp. 6)**
Pub: Ice Cream Reporter
Description: YoCream reported a sales increase for third quarter 2010 at 15.6 percent and net income increasing 25 percent to $2,141,000 for that quarter.

10874 ■ "Yogun Fruz Adds First Location in Southern New York State" in *Ice Cream Reporter* **(Vol. 23, September 20, 2010, No. 10, pp. 2)**
Pub: Ice Cream Reporter
Description: Yogen Fruz signed a master franchise agreement to expand into the southern counties of New York State. The firm offers a healthy and beneficial option to fast food and typical dessert choices.

10875 ■ "Yogurtini" in *Ice Cream Reporter* **(Vol. 23, September 20, 2010, No. 10, pp. 7)**
Pub: Ice Cream Reporter
Description: Self-serve frozen yogurt chain, Yogurtini has opened its second store in Kansas City, Missouri.

TRADE PERIODICALS

10876 ■ *IDDBA Legis-Letter*
Pub: International Dairy-Deli-Bakery Association
Contact: Roberta Rush
Ed: Carol L. Christison, Editor, cchristison@iddba.org. **Price:** Included in membership. **Description:** Reports on legislative activity concerning the supermarket dairy-deli-bakery industry.

10877 ■ *The National Dipper*
Pub: The National Dipper
Price: Free to qualified subscribers. **Description:** Magazine catering to ice cream retail stores.

10878 ■ *WrapUp*
Pub: International Dairy-Deli-Bakery Association
Ed: Carol L Christison, Editor, cchristison@iddba.org. **Released:** Quarterly. **Price:** Included in membership. **Description:** Reports on news, activities, and topics of interest to the Association.

VIDEOCASSETTES/ AUDIOCASSETTES

10879 ■ *Ice Cream and Economics: Ben and Jerry's Homemade*
Ambrose Video Publishing, Inc.
145 W. 45th St., Ste. 1115
New York, NY 10036
Ph:(212)768-7373
Free: 800-526-4663
Fax:(212)768-9282
Co. E-mail: customerservice@ambrosevideo.com
URL: http://www.ambrosevideo.com
Released: 1989. **Price:** $69.95. **Description:** The story of the two men who started the successful ice cream company, Ben and Jerry's. **Availability:** VHS.

FRANCHISES AND BUSINESS OPPORTUNITIES

10880 ■ Abbott's Frozen Custard
4791 Lake Ave.
Rochester, NY 14612
Ph:(585)865-7400

Fax:(585)865-6034

No. of Franchise Units: 20. **No. of Company-Owned Units:** 5. **Founded:** 1902. **Franchised:** 1977. **Description:** Frozen custard. **Equity Capital Needed:** $120,000-$126,800. **Franchise Fee:** $19,000. **Royalty Fee:** $2.20/gallon. **Financial Assistance:** No. **Training:** Offers 1 week at headquarters and 1 week onsite with ongoing support.

10881 ■ All American Ice Cream & Frozen Yogurt Shops

The All American Specialty Restaurants, Inc.
1201 SW 12th Ave., Ste. 415
Portland, OR 97205
Ph:(503)224-6199
Free: 800-311-3930
Fax:(503)224-5042

No. of Franchise Units: 29. **Founded:** 1986. **Franchised:** 1987. **Description:** Retail shop selling frozen yogurt and ice cream. Majority of shops are in enclosed shopping centers. Upscale design. **Equity Capital Needed:** $35,000-$50,000. **Franchise Fee:** $6,000-$25,000. **Financial Assistance:** Yes. **Training:** Yes.

10882 ■ Andrew Smash

Smash International, Inc.
PO Box 12233
Eugene, OR 97440
Ph:(541)465-9088
Fax:(541)465-9088

No. of Company-Owned Units: 1. **Founded:** 1995. **Franchised:** 1998. **Description:** Meatless burger and smoothie restaurant. **Equity Capital Needed:** $100,000-$175,000. **Franchise Fee:** $10,000-$20,000. **Financial Assistance:** No. **Training:** Yes.

10883 ■ Angels Ice Cream and Hot Dog Franchise

Angels Franchising, Inc.
37252 Hwy. 26
Seaside, OR 97138
Ph:(503)717-9560
Fax:(503)717-9558

No. of Franchise Units: 40. **Founded:** 1999. **Franchised:** 2003. **Description:** Ice cream and hot dog restaurant. **Equity Capital Needed:** $50,000. **Franchise Fee:** $14,900-$19,900. **Financial Assistance:** Yes. **Training:** Yes.

10884 ■ Applegate Inc.

616 Grove St.
Upper Montclair, NJ 07043
Ph:(973)744-7000
Fax:(973)744-0334

No. of Franchise Units: 7. **No. of Company-Owned Units:** 1. **Founded:** 1848. **Franchised:** 2002. **Description:** Ice cream. **Equity Capital Needed:** $137,700-$322,000. **Franchise Fee:** $25,000. **Royalty Fee:** 5%. **Financial Assistance:** Third party financing available. **Training:** Offers 2 weeks training at headquarters, 1 week onsite and ongoing support.

10885 ■ Bahama Buck's Original Shaved Ice Co.

Bahama Buck's Franchise Corp.
5123 69th St.
Lubbock, TX 79424
Ph:(806)771-2189
Fax:(806)771-2190

No. of Franchise Units: 21. **No. of Company-Owned Units:** 3. **Founded:** 1989. **Franchised:** 1993. **Description:** Bahama Buck's serves gourmet shaved ice in over 70 different flavors and combinations. They also serve serve fresh-squeezed lemonades, limeades and many $155,000. **Equity Capital Needed:** $163,422-$463,884. **Franchise Fee:** $29,500. **Royalty Fee:** 6%. **Financial Assistance:** Third party financing available. **Training:** Provides 5 days training at headquarters and 5 days onsite.

10886 ■ Baskin-Robbins Ice Cream

Baskin-Robbins USA, Co.
130 Royall St.
Canton, MA 02021
Free: 800-777-9983

Fax:(781)737-4000

No. of Franchise Units: 3,456. **No. of Company-Owned Units:** 4. **Founded:** 1945. **Description:** Operates retail specialty ice cream and yogurt stores. **Equity Capital Needed:** $600,000 liquid assets; $1,200,000 net worth. **Franchise Fee:** $30,000. **Financial Assistance:** Yes. **Training:** Yes.

10887 ■ Ben and Jerry's

Ben and Jerry's Homemade, Inc.
30 Community Dr.
S Burlington, VT 05403
Ph:(802)846-1500
Fax:(802)846-1538

No. of Franchise Units: 302. **No. of Company-Owned Units:** 5. **Founded:** 1978. **Franchised:** 1981. **Description:** Franchised ice cream parlors. **Equity Capital Needed:** $175,250-$451,250. **Franchise Fee:** $37,000. **Royalty Fee:** 3%. **Financial Assistance:** Third party financing available. **Training:** Training includes 11 days at headquarters and 3-5 days onsite.

10888 ■ Blue Sky Creamery, Inc.

1323 XB Pl.
Ames, IA 50014
Ph:(515)268-4336
Free: 877-NIT-RO4U
Fax:(253)295-2755
Co. E-mail: info@blueskycreamery.net
URL: http://www.blueskycreamery.net

No. of Franchise Units: 4. **No. of Company-Owned Units:** 2. **Founded:** 2005. **Franchised:** 2005. **Description:** Franchisees use our patented Nitro Freeze technology to manufacture premium brand ice cream products. Franchisees operating Factory Stores manufacture and distribute our products within the exclusive territory to grocery stores, convenience stores, third party distributors, and to other franchisees operating Blue Sky Creamery Ice Cream Cafes. **Equity Capital Needed:** $35,000-$95,000 liquid; $300,000 minimum net worth. **Franchise Fee:** $25,000-$35,000. **Financial Assistance:** No. **Training:** Training program covering unit operations, accounting, food safety, manufacturing, marketing and advertising at headquarters with additional onsite, start-up and ongoing support.

10889 ■ Breeze Freeze

13340 Merriman Rd.
Livonia, MI 48150
Free: (866)472-6482
Fax:(734)414-6537

No. of Franchise Units: 31. **No. of Company-Owned Units:** 303. **Founded:** 2001. **Franchised:** 2004. **Description:** Frozen fruit drinks. **Equity Capital Needed:** $9,200-$94,300, express/kiosk option available. **Franchise Fee:** $5,000/$40,000. **Royalty Fee:** None. **Financial Assistance:** Limited third party financing assistance. **Training:** Offers 1-3 days at headquarters, 1-2 days at franchisees location with ongoing support.

10890 ■ Bruster's Real Ice Cream

730 Mulberry St.
Bridgewater, PA 15009
Ph:(724)774-4250
Fax:(724)774-0666

No. of Franchise Units: 227. **No. of Company-Owned Units:** 4. **Founded:** 1989. **Franchised:** 1993. **Description:** "Homemade" ice cream and yogurt shop. **Equity Capital Needed:** $100,000 minimum liquidity. **Franchise Fee:** $32,000. **Financial Assistance:** No. **Training:** Yes.

10891 ■ Carvel Ice Cream

Focus Brands, Inc.
200 Glenridge Point Pky., Ste. 200
Atlanta, GA 30342
Ph:(404)255-3250
Fax:(404)255-4978
URL: http://www.carvel.com

No. of Franchise Units: 449. **Founded:** 1934. **Franchised:** 1947. **Description:** Custom ice cream desserts and novelties. **Equity Capital Needed:** $100,000 liquid cash; $300,000 net worth. **Franchise Fee:** $30,000. **Financial Assistance:** Does not provide financing, but you will have access to the Carvel Development Network, which includes lend-

ers. **Training:** 2 week ice cream training school; access to the Carvel Development Network (real estate brokers, architects, lenders, contractors, etc.); Design & construction support & assistance; Grand opening support and toll-free hotline available.

10892 ■ Chocolate Chocolate Chocolate Co.

Abeis Chocolates Inc.
112 N Kirkwood Rd.
St. Louis, MO 63122
Ph:(314)832-2639

No. of Franchise Units: 11. **Founded:** 1981. **Franchised:** 2003. **Description:** Fine chocolates made fresh daily. **Equity Capital Needed:** $185,000. **Franchise Fee:** $20,000. **Financial Assistance:** No. **Training:** Yes.

10893 ■ Cold Stone Creamery

9311 E Via De Ventura
Scottsdale, AZ 85258
Ph:(480)362-4800
Fax:(480)362-4792
Co. E-mail: franchise@coldstonecreamery.com
URL: http://www.coldstonecreamery.com

No. of Franchise Units: 2,200. **No. of Company-Owned Units:** 22. **Founded:** 1988. **Franchised:** 1995. **Description:** Ice cream and desserts. **Equity Capital Needed:** $294,150-$438,850. **Franchise Fee:** $42,000. **Financial Assistance:** No. **Training:** 10 day training program at headquarters; ongoing support.

10894 ■ Culvers Frozen Custard

Culver Franchising System, Inc.
1240 Water St.
Prairie du Sac, WI 53578
Ph:(608)644-2130
Fax:(608)644-2626

No. of Franchise Units: 430. **No. of Company-Owned Units:** 9. **Founded:** 1984. **Franchised:** 1990. **Description:** Frozen custard and butter burgers. **Equity Capital Needed:** $350,000-$600,000. **Franchise Fee:** $55,000. **Financial Assistance:** No. **Training:** Yes.

10895 ■ Dairy Queen Canada Inc.

5045 S Service Rd., No. 3000
Box 430
Burlington, ON, Canada L7R 3Y3
Ph:(905)639-1492
Fax:(905)681-3623
Co. E-mail: tammie.verna@idq.com
URL: http://www.dairyqueen.com

No. of Franchise Units: 588. **Founded:** 1940. **Description:** Dairy Queen is on the move with a new look, a new menu, and a new attitude. We are a Berkshire Hathaway Company with more than 60 years of franchising. We offer a full line of hamburgers, sandwiches, and of course the traditional soft serve treats. **Equity Capital Needed:** $300,000+. **Franchise Fee:** $30,000-$45,000. **Training:** Yes.

10896 ■ Dippin' Dots Franchising Inc.

1640 McCracken Blvd., Ste. 100
Paducah, KY 42001
Ph:(270)575-6990
Fax:(270)575-6997
URL: http://www.dippindots.com

No. of Franchise Units: 486. **No. of Company-Owned Units:** 1. **Founded:** 1988. **Franchised:** 2000. **Description:** The franchise is a homemade ice cream shop including specialist ice cream, frozen yogurt and ices. **Equity Capital Needed:** $80,400-$235,300. **Franchise Fee:** $12,500. **Royalty Fee:** 4%. **Financial Assistance:** No. **Training:** Provides 3 days of training at corporate headquarters and 2 days onsite.

10897 ■ FreshBerry Natural Frozen Yogurt

8801 S Yale, Ste. 400
Tulsa, OK 74137
Ph:(918)488-9727
Fax:(918)497-1916

No. of Franchise Units: 16. **Founded:** 2007. **Franchised:** 2007. **Description:** Natural frozen yogurt, smoothies, and yogurt popsicles. **Equity Capital Needed:** $165,750-$386,200. **Franchise Fee:** $25,000. **Royalty Fee:** 6%. **Financial Assistance:** Limited third party financing available.

10898 ■ Fuzziwig's Candy Factory

Fuzziwig's Candy Factory Inc.
656 Main Ave.
Durango, CO 81301
Ph:(970)247-2770
Free: 877-247-2770
Fax:(970)247-2735
Co. E-mail: info@fuzziwigscandyfactory.com
URL: http://www.fuzziwigscandyfactory.com

No. of Franchise Units: 54. **No. of Company-Owned Units:** 12. **Founded:** 1995. **Franchised:** 2002. **Description:** Offers franchise in ice cream, candy and related business. **Equity Capital Needed:** Start-up cash $50,000-$75,000; Total investment $150,300-$284,250. **Franchise Fee:** $30,000. **Financial Assistance:** No financing provided, however franchisor does assist with business preparation and guidance through securing financing. **Training:** Training provided at one of three locations, choose the one nearest to you. Training covers: merchandising, marketing, customer service, inventory and cost control, record keeping, pre-opening training, ongoing support, regional and national meetings, web site support with current trends in the business.

10899 ■ Gelato Amare/ Jazzy Juices

11504 Hyde Pl.
Raleigh, NC 27614
Ph:(919)847-4435

No. of Franchise Units: 2. **Founded:** 1983. **Franchised:** 1986. **Description:** Serves Italian-style super-premium, low-fat, low-calorie ice cream made right in the store, with several flavors. Lactose-free. Also features all-natural, sugar-free frozen yogurt, espresso, cappuccino, cookies, light soups, salads and sandwiches. **Equity Capital Needed:** $75,000-$250,000. **Franchise Fee:** $18,900. **Financial Assistance:** No. **Training:** Yes.

10900 ■ Haagen-Dazs Shops

The Haagen-Dazs Shoppe Co, Inc.
500 S Washington Ave., Ste. 2040
Minneapolis, MN 55415
Ph:(612)337-3314
Free: 800-793-6872
Fax:(612)337-3301
Co. E-mail: development@haagendazsshoppecompany.com
URL: http://www.haagen-dazs.com

No. of Franchise Units: 252. **Founded:** 1961. **Franchised:** 1977. **Description:** Retail super-premium ice cream shops. **Equity Capital Needed:** $80,000 liquid; $200,000 net worth. **Franchise Fee:** $30,000. **Financial Assistance:** No. **Training:** 2 weeks of comprehensive training in operations, management and customer service at corporate training facility.

10901 ■ Happy and Healthy Products, Inc.

1600 S Dixie Hwy., Ste. 200
Boca Raton, FL 33432
Ph:(561)367-0739
Free: 800-764-6114
Fax:(561)368-5267

No. of Franchise Units: 56. **Founded:** 1991. **Franchised:** 1993. **Description:** 100%natural frozen fruit bars. **Equity Capital Needed:** $35,000-$85,000. **Franchise Fee:** $23,000. **Financial Assistance:** No. **Training:** Yes.

10902 ■ Hogi Yogi

Hogi Yogi Franchise Corp.
375 W 200 S, Ste. 300
Salt Lake City, UT 84101
Ph:(801)222-9004

No. of Franchise Units: 82. **No. of Company-Owned Units:** 4. **Founded:** 1989. **Franchised:** 1992. **Description:** Sandwiches, frozen yogurt, and fruit smoothies. **Equity Capital Needed:** Approximately $150,000. **Franchise Fee:** $15,000. **Financial Assistance:** No. **Training:** Yes. .

10903 ■ Juice Heaven

Juice Heaven Franchise Corp.
17834 Burbank Blvd., Ste. 229
Encino, CA 91316
Ph:(818)668-8488

Fax:(818)668-8489

No. of Franchise Units: 2. **Founded:** 1999. **Franchised:** 2002. **Description:** Franchise of beverages and fruit juice businesses. **Equity Capital Needed:** $88,500-$187,500. **Franchise Fee:** $20,000. **Financial Assistance:** No. **Training:** Yes.

10904 ■ Juice It Up! Franchise Corp.

17915 Sky Park Cir., Ste. J
Irvine, CA 92614
Ph:(949)475-0146
Free: 888-70J-UICE
Fax:(949)475-0137
Co. E-mail: lidiad@juiceitup.com
URL: http://www.juiceitup.com

No. of Franchise Units: 90. **No. of Company-Owned Units:** 5. **Founded:** 1995. **Franchised:** 1999. **Description:** The franchise offers ice cream, yogurt, smoothies, candy and beverages services. **Equity Capital Needed:** Net worth of $250,000 with $50,000 liquid. **Franchise Fee:** $20,000. **Financial Assistance:** Refer to lending sources. **Training:** Provides extensive training.

10905 ■ Juiceblendz International

2893 Executive Dr., Ste. 202
Weston, FL 33331
Free: (866)525-3639

No. of Franchise Units: 5. **No. of Company-Owned Units:** 1. **Founded:** 2005. **Franchised:** 1005. **Description:** Juice. **Equity Capital Needed:** $125,000 liquid; $350,000 net worth. **Franchise Fee:** $50,000. **Financial Assistance:** No. **Training:** Yes.

10906 ■ Kohr Bros. Frozen Custard & Smoothie Station

Kohr Bros. Franchise Systems, Inc.
2151 Richmond Rd., Ste. 200
Charlottesville, VA 22911
Ph:(434)975-1500
Fax:(434)975-1505
Co. E-mail: dennispoletti@kohrbros.com
URL: http://www.kohrbros.com

No. of Franchise Units: 37. **No. of Company-Owned Units:** 11. **Founded:** 1919. **Franchised:** 1994. **Description:** Frozen custard and related products. **Equity Capital Needed:** $250,000 liquid, $500,000 net worth, multiple units only. **Franchise Fee:** $27,500. **Financial Assistance:** No. **Training:** Yes.

10907 ■ La Paletera Franchise Systems, Inc.

3000 Weslayan Dr., Ste. 120
Houston, TX 77027
Ph:(713)622-9500
Fax:(713)621-8200

No. of Franchise Units: 30. **No. of Company-Owned Units:** 1. **Founded:** 1997. **Franchised:** 2003. **Description:** La Paletera is a food centre, which provides ice cream, yogurt, smoothies, fruit bars, candy and beverages. **Equity Capital Needed:** $45,000-$60,000. **Franchise Fee:** $28,000. **Financial Assistance:** Yes. **Training:** Yes.

10908 ■ La Paloma Gelateria & Cafe

1357 St. Clair Ave. W
Toronto, ON, Canada M6E 1C5
Ph:(416)656-2340
Fax:(416)656-8602
Co. E-mail: info@lapaloma.ca
URL: http://www.lapaloma.ca

No. of Franchise Units: 2. **No. of Company-Owned Units:** 2. **Founded:** 1967. **Franchised:** 2004. **Description:** Established in 1967, La Paloma is the most authentic Italian dessert experience. Over 40 years developing countless proprietary recipes, La Paloma is now franchising. "The ART of Italian Artisan Ice Cream". Our turnkey "Gelato Cafe" concept features over 40 flavours in-store to offer a taste of Italy that is unequalled. **Equity Capital Needed:** $250,000-$550,000 **Franchise Fee:** $25,000. **Training:** 2 weeks pre-opening at corporate head office.

10909 ■ MaggieMoo's Ice Cream & Treatery

Global Franchise Group
1346 Oakbrook Dr., Ste. 170
Norcross, GA 30093
Ph:(770)514-4500
Free: 800-524-6444

Fax:(770)514-4903
Co. E-mail: info@maggiemoos.com
URL: http://www.maggiemoos.com

No. of Franchise Units: 144. **Founded:** 1989. **Franchised:** 1997. **Description:** Unique & exciting retail shop, featuring homemade, super-premium ice cream, non-fat ice cream, sorbet, smoothies, custom-made cakes, homemade fudge, plus a line of specialty merchandise. We make our ice cream fresh in the store & serve it in fresh-baked waffle cones. Featuring over 40 mix-ins and folded in on a frozen granite slab to create 1,000s of great combos. Association with a marketable spokes character MAGGIEMOO-in a fun, contemporary store design. **Equity Capital Needed:** $250,000 net worth; $85,000 liquid. **Franchise Fee:** $25,000 first store. **Financial Assistance:** No. **Training:** Franchisees receive site selection assistance and, once site is ready, receive an extensive 11 day training program in a company owned store, followed by onsite assistance during the opening of their unit. Ongoing field support provided continuously throughout.

10910 ■ Marble Slab Creamery

Marble Slab Creamery, Inc.
1346 Oakbrook Dr., Ste. 170
Norcross, GA 30093
Ph:(770)514-4500
Free: 800-524-6444
Fax:(770)514-4903
Co. E-mail: chris@marbleslab.com
URL: http://www.marbleslab.com

No. of Franchise Units: 360. **Founded:** 1983. **Franchised:** 1984. **Description:** Marble Slab Creamery is a unique concept where ice cream is actually made fresh daily at each store. Customers can create their own ice cream fantasies by combining any flavor of superpremium ice cream with 'mixins' such as fresh fruit, candy, cookies or nuts. The ice cream & mixins are then folded together on a frozen marble slab & served on a freshly baked waffle cone. Other products include non-fat yogurt, ice cream pies/cakes, specialty coffees & bakery items. **Equity Capital Needed:** $250,000 net worth, $85,000 liquid. **Franchise Fee:** $25,000. **Financial Assistance:** No. **Managerial Assistance:** Maintains an ongoing business relationship with its franchisees, with assistance available in all phases of store operations. A complete operations manual is provided to all franchisees. Company field personnel visit stores on a regular basis to insure consistency of operations. **Training:** Marble Slab Creamery offers assistance in site selection, lease negotiation, architectural layout and construction supervision. There is a required 10 day training program in Houston, Texas, store opening assistance, continued field supervision, and advertising/public relations assistance.

10911 ■ Maui Wowi Hawaiian Coffees & Smoothies

Maui Wowi Franchising, Inc.
5445 DTC Pky., Ste. 1050
Greenwood Village, CO 80111
Ph:(303)781-7800
Free: 888-862-8555
Fax:(303)781-2438

No. of Franchise Units: 550. **Founded:** 1982. **Franchised:** 1997. **Description:** Hawaiian coffee & smoothie franchise. **Equity Capital Needed:** $150,000 net worth; $70,000 needed. **Franchise Fee:** $36,500 std/$59,500 empire. **Financial Assistance:** Yes. **Training:** Yes.

10912 ■ Mini Melts

www.minimelts.com
245 Asylum St.
Norwich, CT 06360
Ph:(860)889-7300
Fax:(860)887-1033
URL: http://H

No. of Franchise Units: 2,000+. **Founded:** 1996. **Franchised:** 1997. **Description:** Mini Melts ice cream product. **Equity Capital Needed:** $25,000-$1,000,000. **Franchise Fee:** $12,500-$200,000. **Financial Assistance:** No. **Training:** Yes.

10913 ■ Mister Softee, Inc.

Mr. Softee Inc.
901 E Clements Bridge Rd.
Runnemede, NJ 08078
Ph:(856)939-4103
Fax:(856)939-0490
URL: http://www.mistersoftee.com

No. of Franchise Units: 600. **Founded:** 1956. **Franchised:** 1958. **Description:** Retails soft ice cream from vehicles. **Equity Capital Needed:** Minimum $35,000 cash. **Franchise Fee:** $5,000. **Financial Assistance:** Yes. **Training:** Yes.

10914 ■ Paciugo Gelato

Paciugo Franchising, LP
1215 Viceroy Dr.
Dallas, TX 75247
Ph:(214)654-9501
Fax:(214)654-9509

No. of Franchise Units: 43. **No. of Company-Owned Units:** 1. **Founded:** 2000. **Franchised:** 2004. **Description:** Italian gelato. **Equity Capital Needed:** $192,500-$462,000. **Franchise Fee:** $30,000. **Financial Assistance:** No. **Training:** Yes.

10915 ■ Planet Smoothie

Petrus Brands
1425 Ellsworth Industrial Blvd. NW, Ste. 38
Atlanta, GA 30318
Ph:(404)856-4320
Fax:(404)856-4334

No. of Franchise Units: 124. **No. of Company-Owned Units:** 1. **Founded:** 1995. **Franchised:** 1995. **Description:** Smoothie franchise with nutritional products. **Equity Capital Needed:** $250,000 net worth; $80,000 liquid. **Franchise Fee:** $25,000. **Financial Assistance:** Relationships with multiple financial institutions with experience assisting franchisees. **Training:** Raving Brands University classroom and onsite training provided. From register to food preparation, from hiring staff to accounting procedures, you'll improve your management skills, setup your back office and develop an airtight sales and marketing plan.

10916 ■ Rita's Italian Ice

Rita's Water Ice Franchise Co., LLC
1210 Northbrook Dr., Ste. 310
Trevose, PA 19053
Ph:(215)876-9300
Free: 800-677-7482
Fax:(866)499-0974

No. of Franchise Units: 560. **No. of Company-Owned Units:** 1. **Founded:** 1984. **Franchised:** 1989. **Description:** Italian ice, custard, and gelatin. **Equity Capital Needed:** $100,000 liquid; $300,000 net worth. **Franchise Fee:** $35,000. **Financial Assistance:** Yes. **Training:** Training is divided into two phases, with 6 days at a corporate training center and 2 days at the franchisee's location for the grand opening. Training covers production, quality control, advertising concepts and strategies and general business practices.

10917 ■ Shake's Frozen Custard

PO Box 8700
Fayetteville, AR 72703
Ph:(479)587-9115
Free: (866)742-5648
Fax:(479)587-0780
Co. E-mail: info@shakesfrozencustard.com
URL: http://www.shakesfrozencustard.com

No. of Franchise Units: 44. **No. of Company-Owned Units:** 3. **Founded:** 1991. **Franchised:** 1998. **Description:** Frozen custard. **Equity Capital Needed:** $100,000 liquid; $500,000 net worth. **Franchise Fee:** $30,000. **Financial Assistance:** No. **Training:** 2 weeks at headquarters, 1 week at franchisees location and ongoing support.

10918 ■ Smoothie King Franchises, Inc.

121 Park Pl.
Covington, LA 70433
Ph:(985)635-6973
Fax:(985)635-6987

No. of Franchise Units: 560. **No. of Company-Owned Units:** 1. **Founded:** 1973. **Franchised:** 1989. **Description:** Smoothie King centers offer guests the industry's first, original nutritional fruit and function based fresh-blended smoothies. Each "Lifestyle Center" also offers healthy retail product solutions, including sports beverages, energy bars, healthy snacks, vitamin supplements, herbs, minerals and other sports nutrition products. **Equity Capital Needed:** $50,000-$60,000. **Franchise Fee:** $25,000. **Financial Assistance:** Third party financing available. **Training:** Provides 1 day pre-opening (orientation), 14 days management training at Corporate store, 8 days store opening (14 days before open & 4 days after opening) onsite. Assistance in real estate, design and construction.

10919 ■ Son's

319 W State St.
Quarryville, PA 17566
Ph:(717)786-5665
Fax:(717)786-5645

No. of Franchise Units: 2. **No. of Company-Owned Units:** 1. **Founded:** 2003. **Franchised:** 2004. **Description:** Gourmet Italian ice, ice cream, and sandwiches. **Equity Capital Needed:** $200,000-$350,000. **Franchise Fee:** $35,000. **Financial Assistance:** No. **Training:** Yes.

10920 ■ Surf City Squeeze

Kahala Corp.
9311 E Via De Ventura
Scottsdale, AZ 85258
Ph:(480)362-4800
Free: 800-438-2590

No. of Franchise Units: 137. **No. of Company-Owned Units:** 3. **Founded:** 1988. **Franchised:** 1994. **Description:** The franchise caters ice cream, yogurt, smoothies, candy and beverages. **Equity Capital Needed:** $82,700-$383,300. **Franchise Fee:** $30,000. **Royalty Fee:** 6%. **Financial Assistance:** Limited third party financing available. **Training:** Provides 1 week training at headquarters, 2 weeks at franchisee's location, and ongoing support.

10921 ■ TCBY

Mrs. Fields Famous Brands
1141 W 2400 S
Salt Lake City, UT 84119
Ph:(801)736-5600
Free: (866)643-9491
Fax:(801)736-1654
URL: http://www.tcby.com

No. of Franchise Units: 500. **No. of Company-Owned Units:** 2. **Founded:** 1981. **Franchised:** 1982. **Description:** yogurt treats. **Equity Capital Needed:** $191,300-$356,600 estimated initial investment. **Franchise Fee:** $25,000. **Financial Assistance:** No. **Training:** Yes.

10922 ■ Tropical Smoothie Cafe

Tropical Smoothie Franchise Development Corp.
12598 US Hwy. 98 W, Ste. 200
Destin, FL 32550
Free: 888-292-2522
Fax:(850)269-9845
Co. E-mail: scole@tropicalsmoothie.com
URL: http://www.tropicalsmoothie.com

No. of Franchise Units: 285. **No. of Company-Owned Units:** 1. **Founded:** 1997. **Franchised:** 1997. **Description:** Offers nutritional smoothies. **Equity Capital Needed:** $285,000-$385,000. **Franchise Fee:** $25,000. **Financial Assistance:** No. **Training:** Comprehensive training on operations, marketing & management of your business.

10923 ■ Wienerschnitzel/Tastee-Freez

Galardi Group, Inc.
7700 Irvine Center Dr., Ste. 550
Irvine, CA 92618
Ph:(949)892-2619
Free: 800-764-9353
Fax:(949)892-2615
Co. E-mail: KPeters@GalardiGroup.com
URL: http://www.tastee-freez.com

No. of Franchise Units: 370. **Founded:** 1950. **Franchised:** 1950. **Description:** Fast food, including soft-serve ice cream and desserts. Plans available for free-standing building/food court/seasonal stores considered. **Equity Capital Needed:** $150,000-$250,000 liquid; $1,200,000 total investment. **Franchise Fee:** $32,000. **Royalty Fee:** 4%. **Financial Assistance:** Yes. **Managerial Assistance:** Provides ongoing field support, marketing support, product development, area meetings, equipment advisor and store lay-out assistance. **Training:** Consists of 2 weeks at the corporate office - total operation and business training given.

10924 ■ Yogen Fruz

210 Shields Ct.
Markham, ON, Canada L3R 8V2
Ph:(905)479-8762
Fax:(905)479-5235

No. of Franchise Units: 61. **No. of Company-Owned Units:** 3. **Founded:** 1986. **Franchised:** 1987. **Description:** Frozen yogurt and frozen dairy-related treats. **Equity Capital Needed:** $135,679-$472,179. **Franchise Fee:** $25,000. **Royalty Fee:** 6%. **Financial Assistance:** Limited third party financing available. **Training:** Offers 1 week at headquarters and 1 week onsite.

ASSOCIATIONS AND OTHER ORGANIZATIONS

10925 ■ Association of Image Consultants International
100 E Grand Ave., Ste. 330
Des Moines, IA 50309
Ph:(515)282-5500
Fax:(515)243-2049
Co. E-mail: info@aici.org
URL: http://www.aici.org
Contact: Kimberly Law, Pres.
Description: Personal color, style, wardrobe, and image planning consultants. Promotes quality service for clients; aids in establishing working relations between retail stores and consultants; assists community colleges in offering accredited image consulting programs; maintains standards of professionalism for members in the image consulting industry. Provides continuing education and training; maintains speakers' bureau. .

REFERENCE WORKS

10926 ■ "1914 Proved to Be Key Year for Chevy" in *Automotive News* **(Vol. 86, October 31, 2011, No. 6488, pp. S18)**
Pub: Crain Communications Inc.
Ed: Jamie Lareau. **Description:** Chevy Bow Tie emblem was born in 1914, creating the brand's image that has carried through to current days.

10927 ■ "Another California Firm On Way" in *Austin Business Journal* **(Vol. 31, May 6, 2011, No. 9, pp. 1)**
Pub: American City Business Journals Inc.
Ed: Christopher Calnan. **Description:** Main Street Hub Inc. is planning to build a facility in Austin, Texas. The company helps businesses manage their online reputations. Main Street has selected Aquila Commercial LLC as its real estate broker.

10928 ■ *Birthing the Elephant: The Woman's Go-for-It! Guide to Overcoming the Big Challenges of Launching a Business*
Pub: Ten Speed Press
Ed: Karin Abarbanel; Bruce Freeman. **Released:** March 2008. **Price:** $15.95. **Description:** Advice for women entrepreneurs is given. The book explores the emotional challenges faced by women starting businesses, along with advice for reshaping image. This handbook helps women survive and succeed in business.

10929 ■ "Brand Imaging" in *Small Business Opportunities* **(November 2010)**
Pub: Harris Publications Inc.
Ed: Karen Harnesk. **Description:** Design and branding pro shares strategies and tips to help guide any small business' image development.

10930 ■ "The Buck Stops Here" in *Canadian Business* **(Vol. 81, November 10, 2008, No. 19, pp. 25)**
Pub: Rogers Media Ltd.
Ed: Sarka Halas. **Description:** Reputation strategist Leslie Gaines-Ross says that minimizing the damage

followed by the identification of what went wrong are the first steps that companies need to take when trying to salvage their reputation. Gaines-Ross states that it is up to the CEO to ensure the company's speedy recovery and they need to be at the forefront of the process.

10931 ■ "Deskside Story: As the Latest Buzzword Suggests, PR Firms Are Happy To Drop By" in *Inc.* **(December 2007, pp. 70, 73)**
Pub: Gruner & Jahr USA Publishing
Ed: Nitasha Tiku. **Description:** Setting up a meeting between a company's CEO and a journalist is known as deskside and is becoming popular again whereby a publicist offers clients deskside visits, briefings and alerts to help promote public relations for a company.

10932 ■ "Empowered" in *Harvard Business Review* **(Vol. 88, July-August 2010, No. 7-8, pp. 94)**
Pub: Harvard Business School Publishing
Ed: Josh Bernoff, Ted Schadler. **Description:** HERO concept (highly empowered and resourceful operative) which builds a connection between employees, managers, and IT is outlined. The resultant additional experience and knowledge gained by employees improves customer relationship management.

10933 ■ "Hopkins' Security, Reputation Face Challenges in Wake of Slaying" in *Baltimore Business Journal* **(Vol. 28, August 6, 2010, No. 13)**
Pub: Baltimore Business Journal
Ed: Gary Haber. **Description:** The slaying of Johns Hopkins University researcher Stephen Pitcairn has not tarnished the reputation of the elite school in Baltimore, Maryland among students. Maintaining Hopkins' reputation is important since it is Baltimore's largest employer with nearly 32,000 workers. Insights on the impact of the slaying among the Hopkins' community are also given.

10934 ■ *If You Have to Cry, Go Outside: And Other Things Your Mother Never Told You*
Pub: HarperOne
Ed: Kelly Cutrone. **Released:** February 2, 2010. **Price:** $22.99. **Description:** Women's mentor advices on how to make it in one of the most competitive industries in the world, fashion. She has kicked people out of fashion shows, forced some of reality television's shiny start to fire their friends, and built her own company which is one of the most powerful public relations firms in the fashion business.

10935 ■ "Increasing Building Work at Ryan Cos." in *Crain's Chicago Business* **(Vol. 34, May 23, 2011, No. 21, pp. 6)**
Pub: Crain Communications Inc.
Ed: Eddie Baeb. **Description:** Profile of Tim Hennelly, who is working to make Ryan Company known as a pure builder rather than a developer-builder.

10936 ■ "It's Time to Take Full Responsibility" in *Harvard Business Review* **(Vol. 88, October 2010, No. 10, pp. 42)**
Pub: Harvard Business School Publishing
Ed: Rosabeth Moss Kanter. **Description:** A case for corporate responsibility is cited, focusing on long-term impact and the effects of public accountability.

10937 ■ "Let Your Stuff Tell a Story: How to Edit Your Accessories to Showcase Your Personality" in *Charlotte Observer* **(February 8, 2007)**
Pub: Knight-Ridder/Tribune Business News
Ed: Nancy Brachey. **Description:** Tips to accessorize any home or office are presented; eliminating clutter is stressed.

10938 ■ *Media, Organizations and Identity*
Pub: Palgrave Macmillan
Ed: Lilie Chouliaraki, Mette Morsing. **Released:** January 19, 2010. **Price:** $90.00. **Description:** The mass media, press and television are a essential in the formation of corporate identity and the promotion of business image and reputation. This book offers a new perspective into the interrelationships between media and organizations over three dimensions: media as business, media in business and business in the media.

10939 ■ "Optima Public Relations Gains Partners" in *Alaska Business Monthly* **(Vol. 27, October 2011, No. 10, pp. 10)**
Pub: Alaska Business Publishing Company
Ed: Nancy Pounds. **Description:** OPrima Public Relations has partnered with Gogerty Marriott of Seattle and Seattle Design Group.

10940 ■ "Reputation Warfare" in *Harvard Business Review* **(Vol. 88, December 2010, No. 12, pp. 70)**
Pub: Harvard Business School Publishing
Ed: Leslie Gaines-Ross. **Description:** Steps are presented for addressing attacks on corporate public image. These include responding promptly, avoiding disproportionate displays of force, empowering employees to present the firm's position, and stockpiling credentials to bolster credence.

10941 ■ *Sarbanes-Oxley for Dummies, 2nd Ed.*
Pub: John Wiley and Sons, Inc.
Ed: Jill Gilbert Welytok. **Released:** February 2008. **Price:** $21.99. **Description:** Provides the latest Sarbanes-Oxley (SOX) legislation with procedures to safely and effectively reduce compliance costs. Topics include way to: establish SOX standards for IT professionals, minimize compliances costs for every aspect of a business, survive a Section 404 audit, avoid litigation under SOX, anticipate future rules and trends, create a post-SOX paper trail, increase a company's standing and reputation, work with SOX in a small business, meet new SOX standards, build a board that can't be bought, and to comply with all SOX management mandates.

10942 ■ "Timberland's CEO On Standing Up to 65,000 Angry Activists" in *Harvard Business Review* **(Vol. 88, September 2010, No. 9, pp. 39)**
Pub: Harvard Business School Publishing
Ed: Jeff Swartz. **Description:** Timberland Company avoided a potential boycott by taking a two-way approach. It addressed a supplier issue that posed a

threat to the environment, and launched an email campaign to keep Greenpeace activists informed of the development of a new supplier agreement.

10943 ■ "To Be Seen Is to Be Successful" in
Pet Product News **(Vol. 64, December 2010, No. 12, pp. 12)**
Pub: BowTie Inc.

Ed: David Arvin. **Description:** Guidelines on how pet business retailers can boost customer visibility are described considering that complacency could hamper retailers' efforts to effectively market their businesses. To enhance customer base and stand out from competing businesses, being different, strategic, creative, and differentiated is emphasized.

10944 ■ "Toss the Gum Before You Speak" in *Agency Sales Magazine* **(Vol. 39, July 2009, No. 7, pp. 34)**
Pub: MANA

Ed: Stephen D. Boyd. **Description:** When preparing to present to a prospective principal, a salesperson should anticipate the speaking situation and find out in advance the program events that occur around their speech. They should also practice their material in front of a friend or colleague.

10945 ■ "Vanity Plates" in *Canadian Business* **(Vol. 82, April 27, 2009, No. 7, pp. 26)**
Pub: Rogers Media

Ed: Andy Holloway. **Description:** Politicians in the U.S. called for the review of firms that availed of the bailout money but are under deals for naming rights of sports stadiums. Angus Reid's Corporate Reputation and Sponsorship Index found for example, that there is little correlation between sponsoring arenas on having a better brand image. It is suggested that firms who enter these deals build closer to people's homes.

10946 ■ "Voice: Rebuilding Trust" in *Business Strategy Review* **(Vol. 21, Summer 2010, No. 2, pp. 79)**
Pub: Wiley-Blackwell

Ed: David De Cremer. **Description:** The financial world's attempts to rebuild trust are charted. Three steps to jump-start that process are outlined.

10947 ■ "'We Had to Won the Mistakes'" in *Harvard Business Review* **(Vol. 88, July-August 2010, No. 7-8, pp. 108)**
Pub: Harvard Business School Publishing

Ed: Adi Ignatius. **Description:** Interview with Howard Schultz, CEO of Starbucks, covers topics that include investment in retraining, the impact of competition,

premium quality, authenticity, customer services, strategy development, work-and-life issues, and international presence.

10948 ■ *When the Headline Is You: An Insider's Guide to Handling the Media*
Pub: Jossey-Bass

Ed: Jeff Ansell, Jeff Lesson. **Price:** $29.95. **Description:** How-to guide for executives and other professionals whose high-visibility requires frequent interviews with the media. Tested techniques, tools, and insights for how to respond to all types of media in tough situation are provided. The books also reveals the lessons learned and the pitfalls to avoid by referencing actual news stores from around the world and provides exercises for readers who wish to sharpen their media-handling skills.

VIDEOCASSETTES/ AUDIOCASSETTES

10949 ■ *Building a Profitable Consulting Practice Series*
Instructional Video
2219 C St.
Lincoln, NE 68502
Ph:(402)475-6570
Free: 800-228-0164
Fax:(402)475-6500
Co. E-mail: feedback@insvideo.com
URL: http://www.insvideo.com

Description: Two-part business educational series by Howard Shenson offers tips on how to build a profitable consulting practice. Covers consulting opportunities, market strategies, proposal writing, contracting strategies, fee setting, disclosure, and collection techniques. **Availability:** VHS.

10950 ■ *The Professional Image*
Thomson South-Western
5191 Natorp Blvd.
Mason, OH 45040
Ph:(513)229-1020
Free: 800-543-0487

Released: 1985. **Description:** An instructional program for the business-person in how to choose the right sartorial look for success in the jobplace. **Availability:** VHS; 3/4U; Q.

CONSULTANTS

10951 ■ Bixler Consulting Group
200 Galleria Pky., Ste. 1425
Atlanta, GA 30339
Ph:(770)953-1653

Fax:(770)953-4560
Co. E-mail: info@bixlerconsulting.com
URL: http://www.bixlerconsulting.com
Contact: Tracy Penticuff, Vice President
E-mail: tpenticuff@atsbixlerconsulting.com
Scope: Offers executive coaching, leadership workshops, career transitioning programs to enable individuals and organizations to excel in a highly competitive, transforming marketplace. Target audience: mid-level to senior level leaders. Serves private industries as well as government agencies. **Publications:** "Professional Presence"; "Take Action!"; "The Professional Image"; "5 Steps to Professional Presence". **Special Services:** 360-Degree Feedback Report.

10952 ■ Lisa Cunningham & Associates
905 W End Ave., Ste. 64
New York, NY 10025-3530
Ph:(212)662-7783
Free: 800-662-7784
Fax:(212)662-7782
Contact: Lisa A. Cunningham, President
Scope: Image consulting firm providing unique in-depth professional image management solutions for corporations, retail businesses, and individuals. **Seminars:** Color Facts for Business Men and Women; Principles of Business Clothing Selection; Basic Grooming (for Hospitality Industries); Proper Fit and Business Do's and Dont's; Building Business Wardrobes; Business Casual Dress; Customer Service; Nonverbal Communications. Executive coachings: Offer high-level executives intensive coachings in one-on-one settings on Facial/Body Language; Vocal Intonation; Communications Styles; and Appearance, Grooming, and Wardrobe.

10953 ■ The Rothschild Image
13900 Tahiti Way, Ste. 308
Marina del Rey, CA 90292
Ph:(310)574-6018
Co. E-mail: info@rothschildimage.com
URL: http://www.rothschildimage.com
Contact: Ashley Rothschild, CEO
E-mail: ashley@rothschildimage.com
Scope: Image consultant offering advice through group exercises, lectures, wardrobe, and hair and makeup makeovers on how to discover the key components of a winning image. Specializes in designing the images of power brokers, politicians, and entrepreneurs, as well as clients at the start of their careers. **Publications:** "Is There an O'Neal Family Curse? - ABC News," Feb, 2007; "Can an Image Consultant Help You Dress for Success? - Wall Street Journal," Feb, 2006; "Reality Check - Paris Hilton & Amber Moore," Jan, 2004; "Britney's Mystery Man - Britney Spears," Dec, 2003; "People who need to redo their image," Jun, 2003; "Reshaping an Image," Jun, 2003; "Dress to Impress the World International Business Fashion," Apr, 2003. **Seminars:** S.T. A.R.POWER: A Professional Image Consultant Training Program.

START-UP INFORMATION

10954 ■ "Savvy Solutions" in *Black Enterprise* (Vol. 41, September 2010, No. 2, pp. 46)
Pub: Earl G. Graves Publishing Co. Inc.
Ed: Tennille M. Robinson. **Description:** Insight is given to help start an import and export business.

ASSOCIATIONS AND OTHER ORGANIZATIONS

10955 ■ **American Association of Exporters and Importers**
1050 17th St. NW, Ste. 810
Washington, DC 20036
Ph:(202)857-8009
Fax:(202)857-7843
Co. E-mail: hq@aaei.org
URL: http://www.aaei.org
Contact: Marianne Rowden, Pres./CEO
Description: Exporters and importers of goods, products, and raw materials; wholesalers and retailers; customs brokers and forwarders; banks; insurance underwriters; steamship companies; customs attorneys and others engaged directly or indirectly in dealing with exports and imports. Seeks fair and equitable conditions for world trade. Anticipates problems of interpretation of laws and regulations affecting members' businesses; gathers and disseminates data on world trade; supports and creates legislation promoting balanced international trade; works for fair administration of policy. Maintains liaison with government committees, agencies, and other trade policy groups. Testifies for exporters and importers before government and other official bodies. Studies problems concerning export and import; offers advice and support to members facing problems in their businesses; conducts forums and workshops on timely topics and developments; holds exporting and importing seminars. Operates extensive library of research information and government data, and records legal precedents. **Publications:** *International Trade Alert* (weekly).

10956 ■ **Council for International Tax Education**
PO Box 1012
White Plains, NY 10602
Ph:(914)328-5656
Free: 800-207-4432
Fax:(914)328-5757
Co. E-mail: info@citeusa.org
URL: http://www.citeusa.org
Contact: Diane Pastore, Exec. Dir.
Description: Corporations, professional firms, and individual tax advisors. Works to maximize members' understanding of U.S. tax incentives and other offshore benefits available to exporters. Conducts educational programs for companies that generate tax incentives for the export of U.S. goods. Holds seminars on international tax, export and cross-border lease finance, and incentives offered companies that set up manufacturing or operating sites abroad. .

10957 ■ **Foreign Credit Insurance Association**
125 Park Ave., 14th Fl.
New York, NY 10017
Ph:(212)885-1500
Fax:(212)885-1535
Co. E-mail: service@fcia.com
URL: http://www.fcia.com
Description: Represents marine, property, and casualty insurance companies. Insures companies against the risks of nonpayment by buyers for commercial and/or political reasons. Facilitates the financing of term credit sales, thus providing companies with support to meet competitive terms of payment offered by others. .

10958 ■ **Joint Industry Group**
111 Rockville Pike, Ste. 410
Rockville, MD 20850
Ph:(202)466-5490
Fax:(202)559-0131
Co. E-mail: jig@moinc.com
URL: http://www.jig.org
Contact: Megan Giblin, Chair
Description: Trade associations and business and professional firms engaged in international trade. Seeks to influence administration of customs and related trade laws to facilitate trade and encourage compliance. .

10959 ■ **National Association of Export Companies**
PO Box 3949
Grand Central Station
New York, NY 10163
Free: 877-291-4901
Fax:(646)349-9628
Co. E-mail: director@nexco.org
URL: http://www.nexco.org
Contact: Barney Lehrer, Pres.
Description: Established independent international trade firms, bilateral chambers of commerce, banks, law firms, accounting firms, trade associations, insurance companies, and product/service providers; export trading companies; export management companies. Promotes expansion of U.S. trade. Promotes the participation of members in international trade. Conducts educational programs. .

10960 ■ **National Foreign Trade Council**
1625 K St. NW, Ste. 200
Washington, DC 20006
Ph:(202)887-0278
Fax:(202)452-8160
Co. E-mail: nftcinformation@nftc.org
URL: http://www.nftc.org
Contact: William A. Reinsch, Pres.
Description: Manufacturers, exporters, importers, foreign investors, banks, transportation lines, and insurance, communication, law, accounting, service, and publishing firms. Works to promote and protect American foreign trade and investment. Areas of concern include the removal of arbitrary barriers to expansion of international trade and investment; a greater awareness by the government that this expansion is essential to the economic growth of the U.S.; the formation of a cohesive, consistent international economic policy. .

10961 ■ **Small Business Exporters Association of the United States**
1156 15th St. NW, Ste. 1100
Washington, DC 20005
Ph:(202)659-9320
Free: 800-345-6728
Fax:(202)872-8543
Co. E-mail: info@sbea.org
URL: http://www.sbea.org
Contact: James Morrison, Pres.
Description: Exporters with fewer than 500 employees, banks, insurance underwriters, carriers, custom brokers, trade associations, trade clubs, researchers, students, and individuals employed by federal or state agencies. Promotes interests of small and mid-size export companies. Informs public and governmental agencies of small business concerns and issues. Disseminates information to members on legislation that influences small export companies. Offers information on marketplace opportunities. Conducts educational and research programs. Operates extensive, interactive website. .

10962 ■ **U.S.-China Business Council**
1818 N St. NW, Ste. 200
Washington, DC 20036-2470
Ph:(202)429-0340
Fax:(202)775-2476
Co. E-mail: info@uschina.org
URL: http://www.uschina.org
Contact: Mr. John Frisbie, Pres.
Description: Represents American companies trading with and investing in the People's Republic of China (PRC). Established to facilitate the development of U.S.-China business relations. Provides representation, practical assistance, and up-to-date information to members. Provides business advisory services and sponsors briefings on China trade and investment subjects for member firms. Maintains offices in Washington, DC, in Beijing, and Shanghai. **Publications:** *China Business Review* (bimonthly); *China Market Intelligence* (weekly).

10963 ■ **United States Council for International Business**
1212 Avenue of the Americas
New York, NY 10036
Ph:(212)354-4480
Fax:(212)575-0327
Co. E-mail: membership@uscib.org
URL: http://www.uscib.org
Contact: Mr. Peter M. Robinson, Pres./CEO
Description: Serves as the U.S. National Committee of the International Chamber of Commerce. Enables multinational enterprises to operate effectively by representing their interests to intergovernmental and governmental bodies and by keeping enterprises advised of international developments having a major

impact on their operations. Serves as: U.S. representative to the International Organization of Employers; national affiliate to the U.S.A. Business and Industry Advisory Committee to the BIAC. Operates ATA Carnet export service, which enables goods to be shipped overseas duty-free for demonstration and exhibition. Sponsors seminars and luncheon briefings. **Publications:** *United States Council Foundation: Occasional Paper* .

10964 ■ **World Trade Centers Association**
420 Lexington Ave., Ste. 518
New York, NY 10170
Ph:(212)432-2626
Free: 800-937-8886
Fax:(212)488-0064
Co. E-mail: wtca@wtca.org
URL: http://www.wtcaonline.com
Contact: Ghazi Abu Nahl, Chm.

Description: Regular members are organizations involved in the development or operation of a World Trade Center (WTC). Affiliate members are Chambers of Commerce, clubs, exhibit facilities or other international trade related organizations. Encourages expansion of world trade and international business relationships. **Publications:** *WTCA News* (monthly); *WTCA Services Directory* (annual).

EDUCATIONAL PROGRAMS

10965 ■ **Import/Export Procedures and Documentation**
Seminar Information Service, Inc.
20 Executive Park, Ste. 120
Irvine, CA 92614
Ph:(949)261-9104
Free: 877-SEM-INFO
Fax:(949)261-1963
Co. E-mail: info@seminarinformation.com
URL: http://www.seminarinformation.com

Price: $2,095.00. **Description:** Obtain the skills necessary to deal with banks, freight forwarders, customs brokers, and foreign customers, as well as how to mark merchandise, use forms, licenses, and insurance documents for profitable and error-free passage. **Locations:** Chicago, IL; and San Francisco, CA.

DIRECTORIES OF EDUCATIONAL PROGRAMS

10966 ■ *AAPEX Export Interest Directory*
Pub: Motor & Equipment Manufacturers Association
Contact: Jeremy Denton, Exec. Dir.
E-mail: jdenton@mema.org

Released: Latest edition 2008. **Price:** Free. **Description:** Lists U.S. companies that are interested in overseas markets, and exhibited at AAPEX 2008.

10967 ■ *Directory of Private Accredited Career Schools and Colleges of Technology*
Pub: Accrediting Commission of Career Schools and Colleges of Technology
Contact: Michale S. McComis, Exec. Dir.

Released: On web page. **Price:** Free. **Description:** Covers 3900 accredited post-secondary programs that provide training programs in business, trade, and technical fields, including various small business endeavors. Entries offer school name, address, phone, description of courses, job placement assistance, and requirements for admission. Arrangement is alphabetical.

10968 ■ *International Directory of Importers—Food and Beverage*
Pub: International Directory of Importers

Released: Annual, latest edition 2009. **Price:** $320, individuals print; $320, individuals CD-ROM; $370, individuals print and CD-ROM. **Covers:** 7,200 major food and beverage importers around the world. **Entries Include:** Company name, address, phone, fax, email addresses when available, importing manager, year established.

10969 ■ *International Directory of Importers - Sporting Goods and Toys*
Pub: International Directory of Importers

Released: Annual, latest edition 2009. **Price:** $295, individuals print; $295, individuals CD-ROM; $345, individuals print and CD-ROM. **Covers:** 5,000 worldwide manufacturers, and importers trading sporting goods, toys, and commodities. **Entries Include:** Company name, address, phone, fax, email addresses when available, importing manager, year established. **Arrangement:** Alphabetical. **Indexes:** Alphabetical By country/company and by commodity.

REFERENCE WORKS

10970 ■ "Abroad, Not Overboard" in *Entrepreneur* (Vol. 36, April 2008, No. 4, pp. 68)
Pub: Entrepreneur Media, Inc.

Ed: Crystal Detamore-Rodman. **Description:** Export-Import Bank is an agency created by the U.S. government to help exporters get credit insurance and capital loans by providing them with loan guarantees. The bank, being criticized as supporting more the bigger exporters, has allotted to smaller businesses a bigger portion of the annual credit being approved.

10971 ■ "Advances in Pump Technology - Part Two" in *Contractor* (Vol. 57, February 2010, No. 2, pp. 22)
Pub: Penton Media, Inc.

Ed: Mark Eatherton. **Description:** Chinese and Japanese companies have come up with refrigerant based heat pump products that are air based which will significantly lower the installed cost of heat pump based systems. Some of these newer models have variable speed, soft start compressors and have the ability to perform high-efficiency heat pump operation on a modulating basis.

10972 ■ "Africa Rising" in *Harvard Business Review* (Vol. 86, September 2008, No. 9, pp. 36)
Pub: Harvard Business School Press

Ed: John T. Landry. **Description:** Review of the book entitled, "Africa Rising: How 900 Million African Consumers Offer More Than You Think" provides advice for marketing to those on the African continent.

10973 ■ "Ag Officials Employ Preventive Pest Control" in *Yakima Herald-Republic* (June 24, 2011)
Pub: Yakima Herald-Republic

Ed: Ross Courtney. **Description:** Washington State Department of Agriculture is placing vineyard traps for the European grapevine moth, an invasive species whose larvae eat grape buds and fruit clusters, thus exposing the vines to diseases that could destroy them.

10974 ■ "Airing It Out" in *The Business Journal-Serving Greater Tampa Bay* (Vol. 28, July 11, 2008, No. 29, pp. 1)
Pub: American City Business Journals, Inc.

Ed: Jane Meinhardt. **Description:** Flanders Corp. is planning to expand its business in Europe and Southeast Asia. The St. Petersburg, Florida-based company has about 2,800 employees and manufactures air filtration products for industrial and residential applications.

10975 ■ "All About The Benjamins" in *Canadian Business* (Vol. 81, September 29, 2008, No. 16, pp. 92)
Pub: Rogers Media Ltd.

Ed: David Baines. **Description:** Discusses real estate developer Royal Indian Raj International Corp., a company that planned to build a $3 billion "smart city" near the Bangalore airport; to this day nothing has ever been built. The company was incorporated in 1999 by Manoj C. Benjamin one investor, Bill Zack, has been sued by the developer for libel due to his website that calls the company a scam. Benjamin has had a previous case of fraud issued against him as well as a string of liabilities and lawsuits.

10976 ■ "All For One, None for All?" in *Canadian Business* (Vol. 83, October 12, 2010, No. 17, pp. 60)
Pub: Rogers Media Ltd.

Ed: Michael McCullogh. **Description:** The effect of the growth of Canada's overseas provincial trade offices on Canadian trade is discussed. Economic development commissions in the country have devised a single 'Consider Canada' campaign to pitch foreign investors. It is hoped that large cities will gain from banding together rather than competing against one another.

10977 ■ "Ampm Focus Has BP Working Overtime; New Convenience-Store Brand Comes to Chicago" in *Crain's Chicago Business* (April 28, 2008)
Pub: Crain Communications, Inc.

Ed: John T. Slania. **Description:** Britian's oil giant BP PLC is opening its ampm convenience stores in the Chicago market and has already begun converting most of its 78 Chicago-area gas stations to ampms. The company has also started to franchise the stores to independent operators. BP is promoting the brand with both traditional and unconventional marketing techniques such s real or simulated 3D snacks embedded in bus shelter ads and an in-store Guitar Hero contest featuring finalists from a recent contest at the House of Blues.

10978 ■ "An Amazing Race" in *Canadian Business* (Vol. 81, March 3, 2008, No. 3, pp. 25)
Pub: Rogers Media

Ed: Rachel Pulfer. **Description:** U.S. presidential candidates Barack Obama and Hilary Clinton lead the Democratic Part primaries while John McCain is a frontrunner at the Republican Party. These leading candidates have different plans for the U.S. economy which will affect Canada's own economy particularly concerning trade policies. The presidential candidates' proposals and the impacts of U.S. economic downturn on Canada are examined.

10979 ■ "And The Winner Is..." in *Canadian Business* (Vol. 81, March 3, 2008, No. 3, pp. 21)
Pub: Rogers Media

Ed: Joe Castaldo. **Description:** Thirty out of 141 Canadian chief executive officers think that Hilary Clinton would be best for U.S.-Canada relations if elected as U.S. president. Findings also revealed that 60 respondents believe that presidential candidate John McCain would be best on handling issues of international military-security. Views on the candidates' performance and their ability to deal with the declining U.S. economy as well as international trade issues are also given.

10980 ■ "Arizona Firms In Chicago Go For Gold With '08 Games" in *The Business Journal - Serving Phoenix and the Valley of the Sun* (Vol. 28, August 8, 2008, No. 49, pp. 1)
Pub: American City Business Journals, Inc.

Ed: Patrick O'Grady. **Description:** More than 20 U.S. athletes will wear Arizona-based eSoles LLC's custom-made insoles to increase their performance at the 2008 Beijing Olympics making eSoles one of the beneficiaries of the commercialization of the games. Translation software maker Auralog Inc saw a 60 percent jump in sales from its Mandarin Chinese language applications.

10981 ■ "A Baby Step to the South" in *Canadian Business* (Vol. 81, July 22, 2008, No. 12-13, pp. 21)
Pub: Rogers Media Ltd.

Ed: Jane Bao. **Description:** Canada's free trade agreement (FTA) with Colombia is seen as Canada's re-engagement with Latin America. Some politicians believe that the FTA is more of a political agreement than a trade agreement with Colombia. Key information on Canada's trade agreements, as well as trade with Colombia and Latin American countries, is presented.

10982 ■ Bad Samaritans: The Myth of Free Trade and the Secret History of Capitalism
Pub: Bloomsbury USA
Ed: Ha-Joon Chang. **Released:** 2009. **Price:** $26.95. **Description:** Economist challenges open-market proponents and believes that free trade would do more harm than good.

10983 ■ "The Believer" in Inc. (December 2007, pp. 130-138)
Pub: Gruner & Jahr USA Publishing
Ed: Leigh Buchanan. **Description:** Profile of Selena Cuffe, wine importer and socially conscious woman entrepreneur, who is focusing her talents on helping South Africa get wine products to America.

10984 ■ Benchmarking the Canadian Business Presence in East Asia
Pub: University of Toronto Press Inc.
Ed: A.E. Safarian; Wendy Dobson. **Released:** October 27, 1995. **Price:** $19.00. **Description:** Covers Canadian trade with East Asian economies.

10985 ■ "Betting On Volatile Materials" in Barron's (Vol. 88, July 14, 2008, No. 28, pp. M11)
Pub: Dow Jones & Co., Inc.
Ed: John Marshall. **Description:** Economic slowdowns in the U.S., Europe and China could cause sharp short-term declines in the materials sector. The S&P Materials sector is vulnerable to shifts in the flow of funds. Statistical data included.

10986 ■ "Beware this Chinese Export" in Barron's (Vol. 90, August 30, 2010, No. 35, pp. 21)
Pub: Barron's Editorial & Corporate Headquarters
Ed: Bill Alpert, Leslie P. Norton. **Description:** A look at 158 China reverse-merger stocks in the U.S. reveal that the median underperformed the index of U.S. listed Chinese companies by 75 percent in their first three years. These reverse merger stocks also lagged the Russell 2000 index of small cap stocks by 66 percent.

10987 ■ "Bottler Will Regain Its Pop" in Barron's (Vol. 88, March 17, 2008, No. 11, pp. 56)
Pub: Dow Jones & Company, Inc.
Ed: Alexander Eule. **Description:** Discusses he 30 percent drop in the share price of PepsiAmericas Inc. from their 2007 high which presents an opportunity to buy into the company's dependable U.S. market and fast growing Eastern European business. The bottler's Eastern European operating profits in 2007 grew to $101 million from $21 million in 2006.

10988 ■ "Bottom-Fishing and Speed-Dating in India" in Barron's (Vol. 88, March 24, 2008, No. 12, pp. M12)
Pub: Dow Jones & Company, Inc.
Ed: Elliot Wilson. **Description:** Indian stocks have fallen hard in 2008, with Mumbai's Sensex 30 down 30 percent from its January 2008 peak of 21,000 to 14,995 in March. The India Private Equity Fair 2008 attracted 140 of the world's largest private equity firms and about 24 of India's fastest-growing corporations. Statistical data included.

10989 ■ "Bountiful Barrels: Where to Find $140 Trillion" in Barron's (Vol. 88, July 14, 2008, No. 28, pp. 40)
Pub: Dow Jones & Co., Inc.
Ed: Andrew Bary. **Description:** Surge in oil prices has caused a large transfer of wealth to oil-producing countries thereby reshaping the global economy. Oil reserves of oil exporting countries are now valued at $140 trillion. Economist Stephen Jen believes that this wealth will be transformed into paper assets as these countries invest in global stocks and bonds.

10990 ■ "Brazil's New King of Food" in Barron's (Vol. 89, July 13, 2009, No. 28, pp. 28)
Pub: Dow Jones & Co., Inc.
Ed: Kenneth Rapoza. **Description:** Perdigao and Sadia's merger has resulted in the creation of Brasil Foods and the shares of Brasil Foods provides a play

on both Brazil's newly energized consumer economy and its role as a major commodities exporter. Brasil Foods shares could climb as much as 36 percent.

10991 ■ "Brewing a Love-Haiti Relationship" in The Business Journal - Serving Phoenix and the Valley of the Sun (Vol. 28, July 4, 2008, No. 44)
Pub: American City Business Journals, Inc.
Ed: Yvonne Zusel. **Description:** Jean and Alicia Marseille have ventured into a coffee distribution company called Ka Bel LLC which markets Marabou brand of coffee imported from Haiti. Part of the proceeds of the business is donated to entrepreneurs from Jean's country, Haiti. Details of the Marseille's startup business and personal mission to help are discussed.

10992 ■ "Brewing National Success" in Hawaii Business (Vol. 53, November 2007, No. 5, pp. 46)
Pub: Hawaii Business Publishing
Ed: Alex Salkever. **Description:** Kona Brewing Co. (KBC) is already selling its brews in four cities in Florida and 17 other states and Japan as well. KBC is currently forming a deal with Red Hook to produce Longboard Lager and other KBC brews at Red Hooks' brewery in New Hampshire. KBC's chief executive officer Mattson Davis shares KBC's practices for success.

10993 ■ Building Wealth in China: 36 True Stories of Chinese Millionaires and How They Made Their Fortunes
Pub: Crown Business Books
Ed: Ling, Zhu. **Released:** April 27, 2010. **Price:** $15.00. **Description:** Thirty-six of China's most successful and innovative entrepreneurs discuss valuable lessons for growing a business in China.

10994 ■ "Calendar" in Crain's Detroit Business (Vol. 26, January 18, 2010, No. 3, pp. 16)
Pub: Crain Communications, Inc.
Description: Listing of events includes seminars sponsored by the Detroit Economic Club as well as conferences dealing with globalization and marketing.

10995 ■ "Cambodia Calls" in Barron's (Vol. 89, July 27, 2009, No. 30, pp. M7)
Pub: Dow Jones & Co., Inc.
Ed: Leslie P. Norton. **Description:** Interest in frontier markets could jump if enthusiasm about growth in the developed world gathers steam. Cambodia is the latest market to get attention where a handful of investors are trying to set up funds. One investor believes that Cambodia is back open for business but others are still cautious about investing in the country.

10996 ■ "Can a Brazilian SUV Take On the Jeep Wrangler?" in Business Week (September 22, 2008, No. 4100, pp. 50)
Pub: McGraw-Hill Companies, Inc.
Ed: Helen Walters. **Description:** Profile of the Brazilian company TAC as well as the flourishing Brazilian car market; TAC has launched a new urban vehicle, the Stark, which has won prizes for innovation; the company uses local technology and manufacturing expertise.

10997 ■ Canada Business and Investment Opportunities Yearbook
Pub: USA International Business Publications
Released: March 20, 2009. **Price:** $149.95. **Description:** Yearbook contains basic information on export-import, investment and business opportunities in Canada.

10998 ■ Canada Investment and Business Guide
Pub: USA International Business Publications
Released: March 20, 2009. **Price:** $149.95. **Description:** Guide for conducting investment, export-import activity in Canada; includes strategic and business information, contacts regulations and more.

10999 ■ "Canada, Not China, Is Partner In Our Economic Prosperity" in Crain's Chicago Business (Vol. 31, April 14, 2008, No. 15, pp. 14)
Pub: Crain Communications, Inc.
Ed: Paul O'Connor. **Description:** In 2005 more than $500 billion in two-way trade crossed the friendly border between the Great Lakes states and Canadian provinces and for decades Canada is every Great Lakes State's number one and growing export market.

11000 ■ "CBC Chief: Future is Now" in Business Courier (Vol. 27, August 13, 2010, No. 15, pp. 1)
Pub: Business Courier
Ed: Lucy May. **Description:** Tom Williams, chairman of the Cincinnati Business Committee (CBC), maintains that politicians and business leaders must cooperate to ensure the competitiveness of the city for the 21st Century. Under Williams' leadership, the CBC has put emphasis on initiatives related to government efficiency, economic development, and public education. Williams' views on a proposed inland port are given.

11001 ■ "Cemex Paves a Global Road to Solid Growth" in Barron's (Vol. 88, March 10, 2008, No. 10, pp. 24)
Pub: Dow Jones & Company, Inc.
Ed: Sandra Ward. **Description:** Shares of Cemex are expected to perform well with the company's expected strong performance despite fears of a US recession. The company has a diverse geographical reach and benefits from a strong worldwide demand for cement.

11002 ■ "Cents and Sensibility" in Playthings (Vol. 107, January 1, 2009, No. 1, pp. 19)
Pub: Reed Business Information
Ed: Pamela Brill. **Description:** Recent concerns over safety, phthalate and lead paint and other toxic materials, as well as consumers going green, are issues discussed by toy manufacturers. Doll manufacturers also face increase labor and material costs and are working to design dolls that girls will love.

11003 ■ "Champion Enterprises Buys UK Company" in Crain's Detroit Business (Vol. 24, March 17, 2008, No. 11, pp. 4)
Pub: Crain Communications, Inc.
Ed: Daniel Duggan. **Description:** With the acquisition of ModularUK Building Systems Ltd., a steel-frame modular manufacturer, Champion Enterprises has continued its expansion outside the United States.

11004 ■ "Charlotte Pipe Launches Satirical Campaign" in Contractor (Vol. 57, January 2010, No. 1, pp. 6)
Pub: Penton Media, Inc.
Description: Charlotte Pipe and Foundry Co. launched an advertising campaign that uses social media and humor to make a point about how it can be nearly impossible to determine if imported cast iron pipes and fittings meet the same quality standards as what is made in the U.S. The campaign features 'pipe whisperers' and also spoofs pipe sniffing dogs.

11005 ■ "China Trade Deficit Costs California Jobs" in Sacramento Business Journal (Vol. 25, August 8, 2008, No. 23, pp. 1)
Pub: American City Business Journals, Inc.
Ed: Melanie Turner. **Description:** California topped the ranking of states with job losses because of the rising trade deficit with China, losing 325,800 jobs between 2001-2007. The U.S. has lost 2.3 million workers within the period. Other views and information on the job loses because of the trade deficit with China, are presented.

11006 ■ "China Vs. the World: Whose Technology Is It?" in Harvard Business Review (Vol. 88, December 2010, No. 12, pp. 94)
Pub: Harvard Business School Publishing
Ed: Thomas M Hout, Pankaj Ghemawat. **Description:** Examination of the regulation the Chinese government is implementing that require foreign

corporations wishing to do business in the country to give up their new technologies. These regulations avoid World Trade Organization technology transfer provisions and complicate the convergence of socialism and capitalism.

11007 ■ **"Chinese Fund Loans $33.5 Million to Prestolite"** in *Crain's Detroit Business* **(Vol. 26, January 18, 2010, No. 3, pp. 1)**
Pub: Crain Communications, Inc.
Ed: Ryan Beene. **Description:** Prestolite Electric Inc., a distributor of alternators and starter motors for commercial and heavy-duty vehicles, looked to China for fresh capital in order to fund new product launches.

11008 ■ **"City Slickers"** in *Canadian Business* **(Vol. 81, March 31, 2008, No. 5, pp. 36)**
Pub: Rogers Media
Ed: Joe Castaldo. **Description:** Richard Florida believes that the creative class drives the economy and the prosperity of countries depends on attracting and retaining these people. Florida has brought attention to developing livable and economically vibrant cities thanks in part to his promotional skills. However, he has also drawn critics who see his data on his theories as flimsy and inadequate.

11009 ■ **"Closed Minds and Open Skies"** in *Barron's* **(Vol. 88, March 10, 2008, No. 10, pp. 50)**
Pub: Dow Jones & Company, Inc.
Ed: Thomas Donlan. **Description:** American politicians have closed minds when it comes to fair trade. The American government must not interfere with the country's manufacturing industries or worry about outsourcing defense contracts to European aerospace company Airbus.

11010 ■ **"Coming: Cheaper Oil and a Stronger Buck"** in *Barron's* **(Vol. 88, March 24, 2008, No. 12, pp. 53)**
Pub: Dow Jones & Company, Inc.
Ed: Lawrence C. Strauss. **Description:** Carl C. Weinberg, the chief economist of High Frequency Economics, forecasts that Chinese economic growth will slow down and that oil prices will drop to $80 a barrel in 2008. He also believes that the US dollar will start rising the moment the Federal Reserve stops cutting interest rates.

11011 ■ **"Compelling Opportunities"** in *Barron's* **(Vol. 88, March 10, 2008, No. 10, pp. 39)**
Pub: Dow Jones & Company, Inc.
Ed: Neil A. Martin. **Description:** Michael L. Reynal, portfolio manager of Principal International Emerging Markets Fund, is bullish on the growth prospects of stocks in emerging markets. He is investing big on energy, steel, and transportation companies.

11012 ■ **"Coping With a Shrinking Planet"** in *Agency Sales Magazine* **(Vol. 39, December 2009, No. 11, pp. 46)**
Pub: MANA
Ed: Mark Young. **Description:** China and India are forcing big changes in the world and are posing a huge threat to U.S. manufacturers and their sales representatives. Reps may want to consider expanding into these territories. Helping sell American products out of the country presents an opportunity for economic expansion.

11013 ■ **"Cost Remains Top Factor In Considering Green Technology"** in *Canadian Sailings* **(June 30, 2008)**
Pub: Commonwealth Business Media
Ed: Julie Gedeon. **Description:** Improving its environmental performance remains a priority in the shipping industry; however, testing new technologies can prove difficult due to the harsh conditions that ships endure as well as installation which usually requires a dry dock.

11014 ■ **"CPR-CN Deal to Ease Vancouver Logjam"** in *Globe & Mail* **(January 27, 2006, pp. B4)**
Pub: CTVglobemedia Publishing Inc.
Ed: Brent Jang. **Description:** In a bid to lessen West coast port grid lock Canadian Pacific Railway Ltd and Canadian National Railway Co. has agreed to share tracks in the Vancouver region. This will allow the trains to operate more efficiently from the Vancouver Port.

11015 ■ **Currency Internationalization: Global Experiences and Implications for the Renminbi**
Pub: Palgrave Macmillan
Ed: Wensheng Peng, Chang Shu. **Released:** January 5, 2010. **Price:** $100.00. **Description:** A collection of academic studies relating to the potential internationalization of China's remninbi. It also discusses the increasing use of China's remninbi currency in international trade and finance.

11016 ■ **D & B Principal International Businesses**
Pub: Dun & Bradstreet Corp.
Contact: Danielle Woods
E-mail: woodsd@dnb.com.au
Released: Annual. **Price:** $595 commercial & library price. **Covers:** approximately 55,000 leading businesses in all lines, outside of the U.S., in 143 countries. **Entries Include:** Company name, address, phone, fax, D&B number, telex, up to six Standard Industrial Classification (SIC) code, line of business, sales volume (in U.S. currency), number of employees, parent company and location, executive name and title, year established, and import/export designation. **Arrangement:** Geographical. **Indexes:** Geographical, cross-referenced alphabetical, industry classification.

11017 ■ **"Dollar Doldrums; How American Companies are Beating the Currency Crunch"** in *Inc.* **(March 2008, pp. 45-46)**
Pub: Gruner & Jahr USA Publishing
Ed: Sarah Goldstein. **Description:** Despite the low American dollar, some exporters are seeing a growth in their businesses, while other have had to relocate operations and switch to U.S. supplier. Four business owners tell how they are dealing with the current economic conditions.

11018 ■ **"Don't Try This Offshore"** in *Harvard Business Review* **(Vol. 86, September 2008, No. 9, pp. 39)**
Pub: Harvard Business School Press
Ed: Description: Fictitious outsourcing scenario is presented, with contributors offering advice. The suggestions address the ease or complexity of offshoring business creativity, along with challenges and benefits.

11019 ■ **"Down the Tracks, a Whistle Is a Blowin'"** in *Barron's* **(Vol. 89, July 27, 2009, No. 30, pp. 36)**
Pub: Dow Jones & Co., Inc.
Ed: Jim McTague. **Description:** Higher numbers of freight-rail carloads are a sign that the economy is improving and it is no stretch to imagine that this is aided by the American Recovery and Reinvestment Act. It is also predicted that 2009 municipal bond issuance will be above $373 billion with at least $55 billion of it made up of Buy America Bonds that are subsidized by the federal government.

11020 ■ **"Dragon, but..."** in *Canadian Business* **(Vol. 81, December 8, 2008, No. 21, pp. 45)**
Pub: Rogers Media Ltd.
Ed: Matthew McLearn. **Description:** The greatest challenge in smooth trade relations between China and Canada is believed to be lukewarm relations with China over human rights issues. Australia on the other hand, has attracted huge Chinese outward direct investments because of strong trade relations.

11021 ■ **"Dreaming in Macau"** in *Canadian Business* **(Vol. 81, December 8, 2008, No. 21, pp. 65)**
Pub: Rogers Media Ltd.
Ed: Joe Chidley. **Description:** Key information, as well as views on the economic aspects of Macau are presented. Macau was once monopolized by Stanley Ho's Sociedad de Turismo e Diversoes de Macau, but the government transformed the area into a leisure-and-entertainment spot. Details about Cirque de Soleil are also presented.

11022 ■ **"EBay Finally Gaining Traction in China"** in *San Jose Mercury News* **(October 26, 2011)**
Pub: San Jose Mercury News
Ed: John Boudreau. **Description:** eBay has developed a new strategy in China that allows exporters of every type of merchandise to sell directly to eBays 97 million overseas users.

11023 ■ **Effect of the Overvalued Dollar on Small Exporters: Congressional Hearing**
Pub: DIANE Publishing Company
Ed: Donald Manzullo. **Released:** September 2002. **Price:** $30.00. **Description:** Congressional hearing: Witnesses: Dr. Lawrence Chimerine, Economist; Tony Raimondo, President and CEO, Behlen Manufacturing Company; Robert J. Weskamp, President, Wes-Tech, Inc.; Wayne Dollar, President, Georgia Farm Bureau; and Vargese George, President and CEO, Westex International, Inc. Appendix includes correspondence sent to committee on the overvalued dollar.

11024 ■ **"European Stocks on Deck"** in *Barron's* **(Vol. 89, July 27, 2009, No. 30, pp. M7)**
Pub: Dow Jones & Co., Inc.
Ed: Vito J. Racanelli. **Description:** European stocks are cheap and these trade at a discount to U.S. equities rarely seen in the past 40 years. This represents an opportunity for Americans and trends show that Europe's stocks outperform when there is a discrepancy between the price to earnings ratio in European stocks versus U.S. stocks and when sentiment on European equities are downbeat.

11025 ■ **"Europe's Meltdown"** in *Canadian Business* **(Vol. 83, June 15, 2010, No. 10, pp. 76)**
Pub: Rogers Media Ltd.
Ed: Bryan Borzykowski. **Description:** As European countries such as Greece, Spain, and Portugal struggle with debt problems, it is worth noting that its equities trade at a 30 percent discount to the U.S. and that a 10 percent drop in the Euro translates to a 10 percent rise in profitability for exporters. Investors may also want to focus on business-to-business operations rather than consumer-focused ones.

11026 ■ **"Event Stresses Cross-Border Cooperation"** in *Crain's Detroit Business* **(Vol. 24, March 31, 2008, No. 13, pp. 5)**
Pub: Crain Communications, Inc.
Ed: Chad Halcom. **Description:** According to John Austin, a senior fellow of The Brookings Institution, open immigration policies, better transportation and trade across the border and a cleanup of the Great Lakes will bring economic resurgence to Midwestern states and Canadian provinces with manufacturing economies.

11027 ■ **"Export Initiative Launched"** in *Philadelphia Business Journal* **(Vol. 28, December 11, 2009, No. 43, pp. 1)**
Pub: American City Business Journals
Ed: Athena D. Merritt. **Description:** The first initiative that came out of the partnership between the Export-Import Bank of the US, the city of Philadelphia, and the World Trade Center of Greater Philadelphia is presented. A series of export finance workshops have featured Ex-Im Bank resources that can provide Philadelphia businesses with working capital, insurance protection and buyer financing.

11028 ■ **"Export Opportunity"** in *Business Journal-Portland* **(Vol. 24, October 12, 2007, No. 33, pp. 1)**
Pub: American City Business Journals, Inc.
Ed: Matthew Kish. **Description:** U.S. dollar is weak, hitting an all-time low against the Euro, while the Canadian dollar is also performing well it hit parity for the first time after more than thirty years. The weak U.S. dollar is making companies that sell overseas benefit as it makes their goods cheaper to buy.

11029 ■ *Export Sales and Marketing Manual*
Pub: Export Institute
Contact: John R. Jagoe, Author
E-mail: jrj@exportinstitute.com
Released: Annual, Latest edition 24th; 2011. **Price:** $295, individuals print or CD; $395, other countries print & CD. **Publication Includes:** List of approximately 4,000 international trade contacts, including World Trade Centers, U.S. Department of Commerce Trade Specialists and Country Desk Officers, State International Trade offices, small business development centers, U.S. Customs services, U.S. Port Authorities, U.S. embassies, foreign trade associations in the U.S., and chambers of commerce in foreign countries, and foreign embassies and chambers of commerce in the U.S. **Entries Include:** Name, address, phone, fax, name and title of contact, geographical area served, products covered, description of services, and 1,200 internet addresses of export-related sites. Principal content of publication is a step-by-step program showing U.S. companies and entrepreneurs how to begin exporting or increase their existing overseas sales. **Arrangement:** Classified by product/service and export marketing functions. **Indexes:** General, international trade or export/import. Worksheets, graphs, flow charts, pricing and budgeting formats, international price quotations, export contracts, international shipping documents, samples of international correspondence, glossaries, index and illustrations.

11030 ■ *Exporters' Encyclopedia*
Pub: Dun & Bradstreet Corp.
Released: Annual, August; biweekly updates. **Publication Includes:** List of United States and foreign government agencies, international trade associations, and firms specializing in international business and trade research; covers about 220 countries. **Entries Include:** Country profile, communications, key contacts, trade regulations, documentation, marketing data, transportation, business travel. Principal content of publication is analysis of 220 export markets. **Arrangement:** Geographical.

11031 ■ "Fair Play? China Cheats, Carney Talks and Rankin Walks; Here's the Latest" in *Canadian Business* (Vol. 81, March 17, 2008, No. 4)
Pub: Rogers Media
Description: Discusses the World Trade Organization which says that China is breaking trade rules by taxing imports of auto parts at the same rate as foreign-made finished cars. Mark Carney first speech as the governor of the Bank of Canada made economists suspect a rate cut on overnight loans. Andre Rankin was ordered by the Ontario Securities Commission to pay $250,000 in investigation costs.

11032 ■ "Fed May Ban Amphibian Trade" in *Pet Product News* (Vol. 64, November 2010, No. 11, pp. 13)
Pub: BowTie Inc.
Description: U.S. Fish and Wildlife Service is seeking public input on a petition submitted by the conservation activist group Defenders of Wildlife. The petition involves possible classification of chytrid fungus-infected amphibians and amphibian eggs as 'injurious wildlife' under the Lacey Act. Interstate trading or importation of injurious wildlife into the U.S. is not allowed.

11033 ■ "Fight Against Fake" in *The Business Journal-Portland* (Vol. 25, July 18, 2008, No. 19, pp. 1)
Pub: American City Business Journals, Inc.
Ed: Erik Siemers. **Description:** Companies, such as Columbia Sportswear Co. and Nike Inc., are fighting the counterfeiting of their sportswear and footwear products through the legal process of coordinating with law enforcement agencies to raid factories. Most of the counterfeiting factories are in China and India. Other details on the issue are discussed.

11034 ■ "Finding A Higher Gear" in *Harvard Business Review* (Vol. 86, July-August 2008, No. 8, pp. 68)
Pub: Harvard Business School Press
Ed: Thomas A. Stewart; Anand P. Raman. **Description:** Anand G. Mahindra, the chief executive officer of Mahindra and Mahindra Ltd., discusses how his company fosters innovation, drawn from customer centricity, and how this will grow the company beyond India's domestic market.

11035 ■ "Fries With That?" in *Canadian Business* (Vol. 81, September 29, 2008, No. 16, pp. 33)
Pub: Rogers Media Ltd.
Ed: Calvin Leung. **Description:** Profile of Toronto-based New York Fries, which has four stores in South Korea, is planning to expand further as well as into Hong Kong and Macau; the company also has a licensee in the United Arab Emirates whom is also planning to expand.

11036 ■ *Fugitive Denim: A Moving Story of People and Pants in the Borderless World of Global Trade*
Pub: W.W. Norton & Company
Ed: Rachel Snyder. **Released:** April 2009. **Price:** $16.95. **Description:** In-depth study of the global production and processes of how jeans are designed, sewn, and transported as well as how the cotton for denim is grown, regulated, purchased and processed.

11037 ■ "Getting Rid of Global Glitches: Choosing Software For Trade Compliance" in *Black Enterprise* (Vol. 41, September 2010, No. 2, pp. 48)
Pub: Earl G. Graves Publishing Co. Inc.
Ed: Marcia Wade Talbert. **Description:** Compliance software for trading with foreign companies must be compatible with the U.S. Census Bureau's Automated Export System (www.aesdirect.gov). It has to be current with regulatory requirements for any country in the world. Whether owners handle their own compliance or hire a logistics company, they need to be familiar with this software in order to access reports and improve transparency and efficiency of theft supply chain.

11038 ■ "Global Market Could Be Silver Lining" in *Hispanic Business* (January-February 2008, pp. 14, 16, 18)
Pub: Hispanic Business
Description: Economic slowdown in the U.S. is expected to continue through 2008. However, the export sector should hold steady during the same period.

11039 ■ "Going the Distance" in *Hispanic Business* (July-August 2007, pp. 38-40, 42-43)
Pub: Hispanic Business
Ed: Keith Rosenblum. **Description:** Top Hispanic export companies are discussed; charts with exporters by sector as well as a complete listing that includes company name, CEO, number of employees, revenue information, export sales, growth, products and services and destinations are included.

11040 ■ "The Great Cleanup" in *Canadian Business* (Vol. 81, April 14, 2008, No. 6, pp. 50)
Pub: Rogers Media
Ed: Graham Silnicki. **Description:** China's rectification program includes the licensing of 100 percent of food producers and monitoring of 100 percent of raw materials for exports between August and December, 2007. There is a lot of money to be made for those who are willing to help China win its quality battle. PharmEng International Inc. is one of the companies that helps Chinese companies meet international quality standards.

11041 ■ "Grin and Bear It" in *Canadian Business* (Vol. 81, March 3, 2008, No. 3, pp. 53)
Pub: Rogers Media
Ed: Jeff Sanford. **Description:** Discusses the United States economic downturn, caused by the credit market crisis, which is expected to affect the Canadian economy, as Canada depend on the U.S. for 80 percent of its exports. Economist David Rosenberg thinks that in 2008, housing prices will decline by 15 percent and gross domestic product growth will slow to 0.8 percent. Other forecasts for Canadian economy are given.

11042 ■ "Headwinds From the New Sod Slow Aer Lingus" in *Barron's* (Vol. 88, March 10, 2008, No. 10, pp. M6)
Pub: Dow Jones & Company, Inc.
Ed: Sean Walters; Arindam Nag. **Description:** Aer Lingus faces a drop in its share prices with a falling US market, higher jet fuel prices, and lower long-haul passenger load factors. British media companies Johnston Press and Yell Group are suffering from weaker ad revenue and heavier debt payments due to the credit crunch.

11043 ■ "Hot For All The Wrong Reasons" in *Canadian Business* (Vol. 81, March 31, 2008, No. 5, pp. 19)
Pub: Rogers Media
Ed: Andrea Jezovit. **Description:** Soaring platinum prices are due to South Africa's platinum mining industry's safety issues and power supply disruptions that exacerbate the metal's supply problems. South Africa supplies 80 percent of the world's platinum. South Africa's power utility has said that it cannot guarantee the industry's power needs until 2013.

11044 ■ "How Bad Is It?" in *Hawaii Business* (Vol. 54, July 2008, No. 1, pp. 35)
Pub: Hawaii Business Publishing
Ed: Jolyn Okimoto Rosa. **Description:** Donald G. Horner, chief executive officer of First Hawaiian Bank, says that the current Hawaiian economic situation is a cyclical slowdown. Maurice Kaya, an energy consultant, says the slowdown is due to overdependence on imported fuels. Other local leaders, such as Constance H. Lau, also discuss their view on the current economic situation in Hawaii.

11045 ■ "How Exports Could Save America" in *Barron's* (Vol. 89, July 20, 2009, No. 29, pp. 15)
Pub: Dow Jones & Co., Inc.
Ed: Jonathan R. Laing. **Description:** Increase in US exports should help drive up the nation's economic growth, according to Wells Capital Management strategist Jim Paulsen. He believes US gross domestic product could grow by 3-3.5 percent annually starting in 2010 due to a more favorable trade balance.

11046 ■ "How High Can Soybeans Fly?" in *Barron's* (Vol. 88, March 10, 2008, No. 10, pp. M14)
Pub: Dow Jones & Company, Inc.
Ed: Kenneth Rapoza. **Description:** Prices of soybeans have risen to $14.0875 a bushel, up 8.3 percent for the week. Increased demand, such as in China and in other developing economies, and the investment-driven commodities boom are boosting prices.

11047 ■ "How to Secure U.S. Jobs" in *Gallup Management Journal* (October 27, 2011)
Pub: Gallup
Ed: Jim Clifton. **Description:** If America doubled its number of engaged customers globally, it could triple exports, which would create more good jobs and put the US economy back on track.

11048 ■ "How Two Flourishing Exporters Did It" in *Hispanic Business* (Vol. 30, July-August 2008, No. 7-8, pp. 46)
Pub: Hispanic Business, Inc.
Ed: Richard Kaplan. **Description:** Vigorous growth in export revenues posted by two Hispanic-owned export companies Compasa LLC and Ametza LLC is discussed; both firms have benefited from their closer locations to major Mexican markets, superior quality of their products, market knowledge and the relationships of trust developed with key business partners.

11049 ■ "Ill Winds; Cuba's Economy" in *The Economist* (Vol. 390, January 3, 2009, No. 8612, pp. 20)
Pub: The Economist Newspaper Inc.
Description: Cuba's long-term economic prospects remain poor with the economy forecasted to grow only 4.3 percent for the year, about half of the original forecast, due in part to Hurricane Gustav which caused $10 billion in damage and disrupted the food-supply network and devastated farms across the region; President Raul Castro made raising agricul-

tural production a national priority and the rise in global commodity prices hit the country hard. The only bright spot has been the rise in tourism which is up 9.3 percent over 2007.

11050 ■ **"Immigration Issues Frustrate Owners From Overseas" in** *The Business Journal-Serving Greater Tampa Bay* **(Vol. 28, August 15, 2008)**

Pub: American City Business Journals, Inc.

Ed: Margie Manning. **Description:** Investors who availed the E-2 visa program believe that the tightened restrictions on the visa program has trapped them in the United States. The E-2 investor visa program was designed to attract investors into the U.S., but restrictions were tightened after the September 11, 2001 attacks. Other views and information on E-2 and its impact on investors are presented.

11051 ■ *Import/Export for Dummies*

Pub: John Wiley and Sons, Inc.

Ed: John J. Capela. **Released:** June 2008. **Price:** $19.99. **Description:** Provides entrepreneurs and small- to medium-size businesses with information required to start exporting products globally and importing goods to the U.S. Topics covered include the ins and outs of developing or expanding operations to gain market share, with details on the top ten countries in which America trades, from Canada to Germany to China.

11052 ■ *Importers Manual USA*

Pub: World Trade Press

Contact: Edward Hinkelman, Author

Released: Biennial, latest edition 4, 2003. **Price:** $145, individuals Hardcover; $108.75, individuals Sale Price. **Publication Includes:** Lists of trade fairs, embassies, chambers of commerce, banks, and other sources of information on various aspects of international trade. **Entries Include:** Source name, address, phone, telex, description. Principal content of publication is information on importing to the U.S., including coverage of U.S. Customs, banking, laws, shipping, and insurance. **Indexes:** Product/service, geographical, source name.

11053 ■ **"Importers Share Safety Liability" in** *Feedstuffs* **(Vol. 80, January 21, 2008, No. 3, pp. 19)**

Pub: Miller Publishing Company, Inc.

Description: Pet food and toys containing lead paint are among products from China being recalled due to safety concerns. American Society for Quality's list of measures that outsourcing companies can take to help ensure safer products being imported to the U.S.

11054 ■ **"In China, Railways to Riches" in** *Barron's* **(Vol. 88, July 7, 2008, No. 27, pp. M9)**

Pub: Dow Jones & Co., Inc.

Ed: Assif Shameen. **Description:** Shares of Chinese railway companies look to benefit from multimillion-dollar investments aimed at upgrading the Chinese railway network. Investment in the sector is expected to reach $210 billion for the 2006-2010 period.

11055 ■ **"In India, A Gold-Price Threat?" in** *Barron's* **(Vol. 88, June 30, 2008, No. 26, pp. M12)**

Pub: Dow Jones & Co., Inc.

Ed: Melanie Burton. **Description:** Gold purchases in India are falling as record prices take its toll on demand. Gold imports to India fell by 52 percent in May 2008 from the previous year and local prices are higher by one-third from the previous year to 12,540 rupees for 10 grams.

11056 ■ **"Is the Sun Setting on Oil Sector's Heydey?" in** *Globe & Mail* **(January 25, 2007, pp. B3)**

Pub: CTVglobemedia Publishing Inc.

Ed: Shawn McCarthy. **Description:** The effects of fuel efficiency management policies of the United States on Canadian petroleum industry are discussed. Canada is the largest exporter of crude oil to America after the Middle East.

11057 ■ **"Is 'Tsunami' of Freight in our Future?" in** *Business Courier* **(Vol. 26, November 27, 2009, No. 31, pp. 1)**

Pub: American City Business Journals, Inc.

Ed: Dan Monk. **Description:** Freight companies are planning for cargo-container shipping facilities on the riverfront of Cincinnati in light of the completion of the $5 billion Panama Canal expansion in 2015. The city's capability to utilize the growth in freight has been under investigation by authorities.

11058 ■ **"It's Time To Swim" in** *Canadian Business* **(Vol. 81, March 3, 2008, No. 3, pp. 37)**

Pub: Rogers Media

Ed: Megan Harman. **Description:** Canadian manufacturers should consider Asian markets such as India and the United Arab Emirates as the U.S. economic downturn continues. Canada's shortage in skilled labor is also expected to negatively affect manufacturing industries. Ontario's plans to assist manufacturers are also presented.

11059 ■ **"Jobs, Export Surge Confirm Recovery" in** *Globe & Mail* **(March 10, 2007, pp. B5)**

Pub: CTVglobemedia Publishing Inc.

Ed: Heather Scoffield. **Description:** The increase in the number of jobs and exports that is forecast to reverse the slowdown in the Canadian economy is discussed.

11060 ■ **"Keeping Railcars 'Busy At All Times' At TTX" in** *Crain's Chicago Business* **(Vol. 31, April 28, 2008, No. 17, pp. 6)**

Pub: Crain Communications, Inc.

Ed: Bob Tita. **Description:** Profile of the president of Chicago railcar pool operator TTX Co. and his business plan for the company which includes improving fleet management and car purchasing through better use of data on railroad demand.

11061 ■ *Leonard's Guide—International Air Cargo Directory*

Pub: G.R. Leonard & Co.

Released: Latest edition 2011-2012. **Price:** $175, individuals print. **Covers:** Companies providing air cargo service from North America to international and domestic destinations.

11062 ■ **"Lightening the Load" in** *Crain's Cleveland Business* **(Vol. 28, October 8, 2007, No. 40, pp. 3)**

Pub: Crain Communications, Inc.

Ed: Jay Miller. **Description:** Companies reliant on barge deliveries are running well below capacity due to both the building up of silt at the bottom of the Cuyahoga River as well as the lower water levels which are causing a number of problems for the barges and big boats that deliver goods to the region.

11063 ■ **"Li'l Guy Rolls Up Into Bigger Company" in** *The Business Journal-Serving Metropolitan Kansas City* **(Vol. 26, September 12, 2008)**

Pub: American City Business Journals, Inc.

Ed: Suzanna Stagemeyer. **Description:** Li'l Guy Foods, a Mexican food company in Kansas City, Missouri, has merged with Tortilla King Inc. Li'l Guy's revenue in 2007 was $3.3 million, while a newspaper report said that Tortilla King's revenue in 2001 was $7.5 million. Growth opportunities for the combined companies and Li'l Guy's testing of the Wichita market are discussed.

11064 ■ **"Madeleine Paquin" in** *Canadian Business* **(Vol. 81, March 3, 2008, No. 3, pp. 92)**

Pub: Rogers Media

Ed: Regan Ray. **Description:** Madeleine Paquin, chief executive officer and president of Logistec Corp., talks about how she balanced her career and her life as a mother to two girls. Paquin thinks that working mothers need to focus on some things instead of trying to do everything. Her career in the marine cargo handling industry is also discussed.

11065 ■ **"Making Factory Tours Count" in** *Playthings* **(Vol. 107, January 1, 2009, No. 1, pp. 14)**

Pub: Reed Business Information

Ed: Malcolm Denniss. **Description:** The importance of touring an overseas toy supplier's manufacturing facility is stressed. Strategies for general factory visits are outlined in order to determine safety-related quality assurance issues in production.

11066 ■ *Managing Economies, Trade and International Business*

Pub: Palgrave Macmillan

Ed: Aidan O'Connor. **Released:** January 19, 2010. **Price:** $90.00. **Description:** An in-depth look at the areas that affect and influence international business, exploring specific issues businesses face in terms of economic development, trade law, and international marketing and management.

11067 ■ **"Marine Act Amendments Gain Parliamentary Approval" in** *Canadian Sailings* **(July 7, 2008)**

Pub: Commonwealth Business Media

Ed: Alex Binkley. **Description:** Changes to the Canada Marine Act provides better borrowing deals as well as an ability to tap into federal infrastructure funding for environmental protection measures, security improvements and other site enhancements.

11068 ■ **"Market Watch" in** *Barron's* **(Vol. 88, March 24, 2008, No. 12, pp. M18)**

Pub: Dow Jones & Company, Inc.

Ed: Ashraf Laidi; Marc Pado; David Kotok. **Description:** Latest measures implemented by the Federal Reserve to address the credit crisis did not benefit the US dollar, with the Japanese yen and the euro recouping earlier losses against the dollar. Goldman Sachs reported earnings of $3.23 per share, claiming a stronger liquidity position. The US markets bottomed early on 22 January 2007, according to evidence.

11069 ■ **"Melamine Analytical Methods Released" in** *Feedstuffs* **(Vol. 80, October 6, 2008, No. 41, pp. 2)**

Pub: Miller Publishing Company

Description: Romer Labs has released new validations for its AgraQuant Melamine enzyme-linked immunosorbent assay. The test kit screens for melamine in feed and diary products, including pet foods, milk and milk powder. Melamine by itself is nontoxic in low doses, but when combined with cyanuric acid it can cause fatal kidney stones. The Chinese dairy industry is in the midst of a huge melamine crisis; melamine-contaminated dairy and food products from China have been found in more than 20 countries.

11070 ■ **"Miami's 'Big Wheels' Keep Latin America Rolling" in** *Hispanic Business* **(July-August 2007, pp. 46-47)**

Pub: Hispanic Business

Ed: Frank Nelson. **Description:** Four top Hispanic owned exporters of tires are discussed. All four companies are based in Miami, Florida.

11071 ■ **"Minimizing Import Risks" in** *Canadian Sailings* **(July 7, 2008)**

Pub: Commonwealth Business Media

Ed: Jack Kohane. **Description:** New food and product safety laws may be enacted by Canada's Parliament; importers, retailers and manufacturers could face huge fines if the new laws are passed.

11072 ■ **"Mission to China" in** *Canadian Business* **(Vol. 81, December 8, 2008, No. 21, pp. 28)**

Pub: Rogers Media Ltd.

Ed: Andrew Wahl. **Description:** Canada China Business Council and the Council of the Federation visited China for a three-city trade mission. The trade mission aims to re-establish the strong relationship between China and Canada.

11073 ■ **"Montreal Port Head Lands CP Ships Deal" in** *Globe & Mail* **(January 5, 2006, pp. B4)**

Pub: CTVglobemedia Publishing Inc.

Description: The opinions of president Dominic Taddeo, on the positive impact of TUI AG's acquisition of CP Ships Ltd. on operations at Port of Montreal, are presented.

11074 ■ **"The Mood of a Nation"** in *Canadian Business* (Vol. 81, April 14, 2008, No. 6, pp. 56)
Pub: Rogers Media
Ed: Joe Castaldo. **Description:** Independent Fish Harvesters Inc. processes more kilograms a year and has had to hire more workers but its managers worry about how a slowdown in the U.S. economy will affect his business. A planned shopping complex in Mirabel Quebec, the manufacturing industry in Kitchener, Ontario, and a cattle farming business in Sarnia, Ontario are discussed to provide a snapshot of the challenges that business in Canada are facing as recession looms.

11075 ■ **"More Pain"** in *Canadian Business* (Vol. 81, December 24, 2007, No. 1, pp. 12)
Pub: Rogers Media
Ed: Lauren McKeon. **Description:** Manufacturing sector in Canada is sinking with a forecast by as much as 23 percent for 2008, which can be offset as manufacturers say they plan to increase productivity by 25 percent. Details on the sector's competitiveness, workforce, importing of machinery from the U.S. and financial needs for research and development are examined.

11076 ■ **"Mover and Sheika"** in *Conde Nast Portfolio* (Vol. 2, June 2008, No. 6, pp. 104)
Pub: Conde Nast Publications, Inc.
Ed: John Arlidge. **Description:** Profile of Princess Sheika Lubna who is the first female foreign trade minister in the Middle East, the United Arab Emirates biggest business envoy, paving the way for billions in new investment, and also a manufacturer of her own perfume line.

11077 ■ **"No Shortage of Challenges for Cross-Border Trade"** in *Canadian Sailings* (June 30, 2008)
Pub: Commonwealth Business Media
Ed: Kathlyn Horibe. **Description:** Pros and cons of the North American Free Trade Agreement are examined. The agreement between the U.S. and Canada concerning trade was an essential step toward securing economic growth for Canadian citizens. Two-way trade between the counties has tripled since the agreement and accounts for 7.1 million American and 3 million Canadian jobs.

11078 ■ *Official Export Guide*
Pub: UBM Global Trade
Contact: Alan Glass, Chm./Pres./CEO
Released: Annual, January; inter-edition supplements. **Price:** $449.50 sale price; $899 regular price. **Covers:** Customs officials, port authorities, embassies and consulates, chambers of commerce, foreign trade zones, and other organizations and agencies involved in international trade; prospective foreign buyers; related trade services. **Entries Include:** Generally, organization or company name, address, phone, phone, telex, fax, names and titles of key personnel. **Arrangement:** Geographical, then classified by service.

11079 ■ **"On the Itinerary: Your Future"** in *Entrepreneur* (Vol. 37, October 2009, No. 10, pp. 92)
Pub: Entrepreneur Media, Inc.
Ed: Joel Holland. **Description:** Josh Hackler's Spanish Vines imports and distributes wines from Spain while using Spanish culture to help market the wines. The business was hatched after Hackler signed up for a study-abroad program in Spain.

11080 ■ **"Online Fortunes"** in *Small Business Opportunities* (Fall 2008)
Pub: Entrepreneur Media Inc.
Description: Fifty hot, e-commerce enterprises for the aspiring entrepreneur to consider are featured; virtual assistants, marketing services, party planning, travel services, researching, web design and development, importing as well as creating an online store are among the businesses featured.

11081 ■ **"OPEC Exposed"** in *Hawaii Business* (Vol. 54, September 2008, No. 3, pp. 2)
Pub: Hawaii Business Publishing
Ed: Serena Lim. **Description:** Organization of the Petroleum Exporting Countries (OPEC) has said that their effort in developing an alternative energy source

has driven prices up. The biofuel sector is criticizing the statement, saying that a research study found that biofuels push petroleum prices down by 15 percent. Details on the effect of rising petroleum prices are discussed.

11082 ■ **"Open Skies: Opportunity, Challenge for Airlines"** in *Crain's Chicago Business* (April 21, 2008)
Pub: Crain Communications, Inc.
Ed: Paul Merrion. **Description:** Discusses the new aviation agreement between Europe and the United States known as Open Skies; the pact creates opportunities for U.S. carriers to fly to new destinations in Europe from more U.S. cities; it also allows carriers to fly between European cities, something they have not been able to do until now.

11083 ■ **"Parent Firm's Global Reach, Stricter Air Quality Rules Have Stock Smiling"** in *Crain's Cleveland Business* (October 15, 2007)
Pub: Crain Communications, Inc.
Ed: David Bennett. **Description:** Since Stock Equipment Co., a firm that makes industrial pollution control equipment, was acquired by Schenck Process Group, a diversified global manufacturer based in Germany, the company's orders from abroad have been on the rise. The purchase has opened the doors to regions such as Eastern and Central Europe, Latin America and Australia.

11084 ■ **"Paying for the Recession: Rebalancing Economic Growth"** in *Montana Business Quarterly* (Vol. 49, Spring 2011, No. 1, pp. 2)
Pub: Bureau of Business & Economic Research
Ed: Patrick M. Barkey. **Description:** Four key issues required to address in order to rebalance economic growth in America are examined. They include: savings rates, global trade imbalances, government budgets and most importantly, housing price correction.

11085 ■ **"Port Metro Vancouver Unveiled"** in *Canadian Sailings* (July 7, 2008)
Pub: Commonwealth Business Media
Description: Vancouver Fraser Port Authority is marketing the port as Port Metro Vancouver; Along with the new name the port has announced additional strategies for continued growth and launched a new logo.

11086 ■ **"Procter & Gamble Boosts Bet on Exclusive Brands"** in *Business Courier* (Vol. 27, July 9, 2010, No. 10, pp. 1)
Pub: Business Courier
Ed: Jon Newberry. **Description:** Procter & Gamble is creating more special versions of its brands such as Pringles and Pampers exclusively for retail partners such as Tesco in the U.K. The greater push towards this direction is seen as a way to regain market share.

11087 ■ **"Pulque with Flavor"** in *Canadian Business* (Vol. , pp.)
Pub: Rogers Media Ltd.
Ed: Augusta Dwyer. **Description:** Mexico-based Pulque Poliqhui, which has exported 20,000 bottles of Pulque into Canada in March 2008, plans to distribute in Ontario and Quebec. Pulque Poliqhui is introducing Cool Passion, a fruit-flavored version of pulque in Canada.

11088 ■ **"Q&A Interview With Perrin Beatty"** in *Canadian Business* (Vol. 80, October 8, 2007, No. 20, pp. 13)
Pub: Rogers Media
Description: Perrin Beatty, president and chief executive officer of the Canadian Chamber of Commerce, talks about his move from the Canadian Manufacturers and Exporters to his current organization. He also discusses the state of Canada's economy, as well as the need for leadership.

11089 ■ **"Recalls Cause Consumers to Put More Stock in Online Reviews"** in *Crain's Cleveland Business* (Vol. 28, November 12, 2007, No. 45)
Pub: Crain Communications, Inc.
Ed: Jack Neff. **Description:** Due to the string of product recalls over the last year, consumers are

looking at online product reviews to help them make purchasing decisions which could reshape marketing for a wide range of products.

11090 ■ **"Religious Revival"** in *Canadian Business* (Vol. 81, December 8, 2008, No. 21, pp. 57)
Pub: Rogers Media Ltd.
Ed: Paul Webster. **Description:** Canada-based lawyer Cyndee Todgham Cherniak believes that Canadians wishing to do business in China should have professional competence, as well as cultural and spiritual sensitivity. Chinese government officials also acknowledge the role of religion in China's economy.

11091 ■ **"Reportlinker Adds Report: Social Networks: Five Consumer Trends for 2009"** in *Wireless News* (October 23, 2009)
Pub: Close-Up Media
Description: "Social Networks: Five Consumer Trends for 2009," a new market research report by Reportlinker.com found that in the countries of Italy and Spain lag behind their European neighbors in Internet development. Since large numbers of consumers in these two countries remain offline, only a minimal portion of total advertising spending goes into Internet marketing, and those advertising campaigns are directed at the relatively young, affluent users. Statistical data included.

11092 ■ **"Reps Continue to Move to International Trade"** in *Agency Sales Magazine* (Vol. 39, September-October 2009, No. 9, pp. 24)
Pub: MANA
Ed: Jack Foster. **Description:** Sales representatives should get involved and look into international trade if they want to be successful in the future. The weak U.S. dollar, labor costs, and the low cost of transportation are factors that drive the trend towards international trade.

11093 ■ **"Research and Markets Adds Report: Asian - Internet Market"** in *Health and Beauty Close-Up* (January 19, 2010)
Pub: Close-Up Media
Description: Overview of Research and Markets new report regarding Internet marketing and e-commerce in the Asian region; statistical data included.

11094 ■ **"Riding the Export Wave: How To Find a Good Distributor Overseas"** in *Inc.* (January 2008, pp. 49)
Pub: Gruner & Jahr USA Publishing
Ed: Sarah Goldstein. **Description:** Small companies should contact the U.S. embassy in foreign companies in order to connect with the U.S. Commercial Service's Gold Key program that is designed to work with small and midsize exporters.

11095 ■ **"Rising in the East; Research and Development"** in *The Economist* (Vol. 390, January 3, 2009, No. 8612, pp. 47)
Pub: The Economist Newspaper Inc.
Description: Impressive growth of the technological research and development in Asian countries is discussed. Statistical data included.

11096 ■ **"Rough Trade"** in *Canadian Business* (Vol. 79, September 11, 2006, No. 18, pp. 31)
Pub: Rogers Media
Ed: Christina Campbell. **Description:** The divergence between trade policy agreements entered into by Chile and the Canadian government are highlighted. Canada-Chile Free Trade Agreement and the myth around the big benefits to be reaped by bilateral trade policy agreements are discussed.

11097 ■ **"Russian Renaissance"** in *Chicago Tribune* (September 22, 2008)
Pub: McClatchy-Tribune Information Services
Ed: Alex Rodriguez. **Description:** Winemakers from Russia are returning to the craft and quality of winemaking now that they are free from Soviet restraints.

11098 ■ **"Saudi Overtures"** in *The Business Journal-Portland* (Vol. 25, August 15, 2008, No. 23, pp. 1)

Pub: American City Business Journals, Inc.

Ed: Aliza Earnshaw. **Description:** Saudi Arabia's huge revenue from oil is creating opportunities for Oregon companies as the country develops new cities, industrial zones, and tourism centers. Oregon exported only $46.8 million worth of goods to Saudi Arabia in 2007 but the kingdom is interested in green building materials and methods, renewable energy and water quality control, and nanotechnology all of which Oregon has expertise in.

11099 ■ **"Sedo Keeps Trucking in Good Times and Bad"** in *Crain's Chicago Business* (Vol. 31, April 28, 2008, No. 17, pp. 35)

Pub: Crain Communications, Inc.

Ed: Samantha Stainburn. **Description:** Discusses Seko Worldwide Inc., an Itasca-based freight forwarder, and its complicated road to growth and expansion on a global scale.

11100 ■ **"Shaky on Free Trade"** in *Canadian Business* (Vol. 81, December 24, 2007, No. 1, pp. 29)

Pub: Rogers Media

Ed: Rachel Pulfer. **Description:** Rhetoric at the U.S. presidential elections seems to be pointing toward a weaker free trade consensus, with Democratic candidates being against the renewal of free trade deals, while Republican candidates seem to be for free trade.

11101 ■ **"Shopped Out; Retailing Gloom"** in *The Economist* (Vol. 390, January 3, 2009, No. 8612, pp. 26)

Pub: The Economist Newspaper Inc.

Description: Economic volatility in the retail sector is having an impact on a number of countries around the globe. Europe is experiencing hard economic times as well and unless businesses have a strong business plan banks feel unable to lend the money necessary to tide the retailers over. The falling pound has increased the cost of imported goods and small to midsize retail chains may not be able to weather such an unforgiving economic climate.

11102 ■ **"Sign of Progress"** in *Playthings* (Vol. 106, October 1, 2008, No. 9, pp. 4)

Pub: Reed Business Information

Ed: Cliff Annicelli. **Description:** The ramifications of the toy recalls in 2007 are discussed. Mandates for lead-free toys and other safety issues are having an impact on the American toy industry.

11103 ■ **"Slimmed-Down Supplier TI Automotive Relaunches"** in *Crain's Detroit Business* (Vol. 26, January 11, 2010, No. 2, pp. 14)

Pub: Crain Communications, Inc.

Ed: Robert Sherefkin. **Description:** TI Automotive Ltd., one of the world's largest suppliers of fuel storage and delivery systems, has reorganized the company by splitting it into five global divisions and is relaunching its brand which is now more focused on new technology.

11104 ■ **"Some Relief Possible Following Painful Week"** in *Barron's* (Vol. 88, July 14, 2008, No. 28, pp. M3)

Pub: Dow Jones & Co., Inc.

Ed: Kopin Tan. **Description:** Dow Chemical is offering a 74 percent premium to acquire Rohm & Haas' coatings and electronics materials operations. Frontline amassed a 5.6 percent stake in rival Overseas Shipholding Group and a merger between the two would create a giant global fleet with pricing power. Highlights of the U.S. stock market during the week that ended in July 11, 2008 are discussed. Statistical data included.

11105 ■ *A Splendid Exchange: How Trade Shaped the World*

Pub: Atlantic Monthly Press

Ed: William J. Bernstein. **Released:** 2009. **Price:** $30.00. **Description:** Chronicle of how commerce defined cultures and shaped history.

11106 ■ **"The Superpower Dilemma"** in *Canadian Business* (Vol. 83, August 17, 2010, No. 13-14, pp. 42)

Pub: Rogers Media Ltd.

Description: Canada has been an energy superpower partly because it controls the energy source and the production means, particularly of fossil fuels. However, Canada's status as superpower could diminish if it replaces petroleum exports with renewable technology for using sources of energy available globally.

11107 ■ **"Supply Chain Visibility A Two-Way Street"** in *Canadian Sailings* (July 7, 2008)

Pub: Commonwealth Business Media

Ed: Jack Kohane. **Description:** Canada is experiencing unprecedented market pressures due to globalization. Competition from foreign countries, demand for better and faster service from customers and shorter innovation cycles are some of the problems the country is facing regarding trade and the importing and exporting industry.

11108 ■ **"Tales of the City"** in *Canadian Business* (Vol. 81, December 8, 2008, No. 21, pp. 37)

Pub: Rogers Media Ltd.

Ed: Joe Chidley. **Description:** Key information on doing business in Hong Kong are shared by an entrepreneur, a consultant, an exporter, and a financier who were from Canada. Hong Kong hosts about 3,900 regional headquarters or offices of international companies.

11109 ■ **"The Three Amigos"** in *Canadian Business* (Vol. 81, March 17, 2008, No. 4, pp. 19)

Pub: Rogers Media

Ed: Rachel Pulfer. **Description:** Mexican president Felipe Calderon said that Mexico exported 30 percent more to Europe and 25 percent more to other countries in Latin America in 2006 in light of the downturn in the U.S. economy. Calderon made this announcement in a speech at Harvard University while protestors marched outside protesting against NAFTA.

11110 ■ **"Tied to Home: Female Owned Businesses Export Less, And It's Not Just Because They're Smaller"** in *Canadian Business* (April 14, 2008)

Pub: Rogers Media

Ed: Lauren McKeon. **Description:** Only 12 percent of small and midsized enterprises that are run by women export their products and services. Government agencies can be more proactive in promoting the benefits of exporting by including women in case studies and recruiting women as mentors. Exporting provides great growth potential especially for the service sector where women have an advantage.

11111 ■ **"Timken's Bearings Rolling in China, India"** in *Crain's Cleveland Business* (Vol. 28, October 29, 2007, No. 43, pp. 14)

Pub: Crain Communications, Inc.

Ed: David Bennett. **Description:** Canton-based Timken Co., a manufacturer of bearings and specialty metals, is seeing growing demand for its line of tapered roller bearings, which allow rail users to carry heavy car loads. The company is finding significant growth in China and India due to their rapidly growing rail markets.

11112 ■ **"To Keep Freight Rolling, Springfield Must Grease the Hub"** in *Crain's Chicago Business* (Vol. 31, April 21, 2008, No. 16, pp. 22)

Pub: Crain Communications, Inc.

Ed: Paul O'Connor. **Description:** Discusses the importance of upgrading Chicago's continental-hub freight rail system which is integral to moving international products as well as domestic ones. Global tonnage is expected to double by 2020 and unless more money is designated to upgrade the infrastructure the local and national economy will suffer.

11113 ■ **"Too Much Precaution About Biotech Corn"** in *Barron's* (Vol. 88, March 17, 2008, No. 11, pp. 54)

Pub: Dow Jones & Company, Inc.

Ed: Mark I. Schwartz. **Description:** In the U.S., 90 percent of cultivated soybeans are biotech varietals as well as 60 percent of the corn. Farmers have significantly reduced their reliance on pesticides in the growing of biotech corn. Biotech cotton cultivation has brought hundreds of millions of dollars in net financial gains to farmers. The European Union has precluded the cultivation or sale of biotech crops within its border.

11114 ■ **"Top 50 Exporters"** in *Hispanic Business* (Vol. 30, July-August 2008, No. 7-8, pp. 42)

Pub: Hispanic Business, Inc.

Ed: Hildy Medina. **Description:** Increases in exports revenues reported by food exporters and green companies in a time of economic slowdown in the U.S are described. Food exporters have benefited from the growth of high-volume grocery stores in underdeveloped countries and the German governments' promotion of solar energy has benefited the U.S. solar heating equipment and solar panel manufactures.

11115 ■ **"Top Private Companies"** in *Baltimore Business Journal* (Vol. 28, August 27, 2010, No. 16, pp. 1)

Pub: Baltimore Business Journal

Ed: Gary Haber. **Description:** The combined revenue of the 100 largest private firms in Maryland's Baltimore region dropped from about $22.7 billion in 2008 to $21 billion in 2009, an annual decrease of more than 7 percent. To survive the recession's impact, these firms resorted to strategies such as government contracting and overseas expansion. How these strategies affected the revenue of some firms is described.

11116 ■ *Trade with Italy*

Pub: Italy-America Chamber of Commerce Inc.

Contact: Franco De Angelis, Exec. Ed.

Released: Biennial, Latest edition 2009. **Price:** $150. **Covers:** more than 6,600 importers and exporters to and from the United States. **Entries Include:** Company name, address, phone, fax, name and title of contact, products or services; importer listings show brand names and firms represented; listings for U.S. companies in Italy show address and name of Italian representative. **Arrangement:** Classified by activity. **Indexes:** Commodity, brand name, exporter name.

11117 ■ **"Trade Winds"** in *Canadian Sailings* (June 30, 2008)

Pub: Commonwealth Business Media

Ed: Peter Malkovsky. **Description:** Trade between Canada and the United States is discussed as well as legislation concerning foreign trade and the future of this trade relationship.

11118 ■ **"Transborder Short-Sea Shipping: Hurdles Remain"** in *Canadian Sailings* (June 30, 2008)

Pub: Commonwealth Business Media

Ed: Kathlyn Horibe. **Description:** Legislation that would exempt non-bulk commercial cargo by water in the Great Lakes region from U.S. taxation is discussed.

11119 ■ **"The Transparent Supply Chain"** in *Harvard Business Review* (Vol. 88, October 2010, No. 10, pp. 76)

Pub: Harvard Business School Publishing

Ed: Steve New. **Description:** Examination of the use of new technologies to create a transparent supply chain, such as next-generation 2D bar codes in clothing labels that can provide data on a garment's provenance.

11120 ■ **"Tweaking On-Board Activities, Equipment Saves Fuel, Reduces CO_2"** in *Canadian Sailings* (June 30, 2008)

Pub: Commonwealth Business Media

Description: Optimizing ship activities and equipment uses less fuel and therefore reduces greenhouse gas emissions. Ways in which companies are implementing research and development techniques in order to monitor ship performance and analyze data in an attempt to become more efficient are examined.

11121 ■ "Uncle Volodya's Flagging Christmas Spirit; Russia" in *The Economist* (Vol. 390, January 3, 2009, No. 8612, pp. 22)
Pub: The Economist Newspaper Inc.
Description: Overview of Russia's struggling economy as well as unpopular government decisions such as raising import duties on used foreign vehicles so as to protect Russian carmakers.

11122 ■ *Understanding Exporting in the Small and Micro Enterprise*
Pub: Nova Science Publishers, Inc.
Ed: Densil A. Williams. **Released:** April 1, 2009. **Price:** $79.00. **Description:** An examination into the reasons why some small and micro locally-owned businesses choose to sell a portion of their goods abroad while others facing similar market conditions remain focused on the domestic market.

11123 ■ "U.S. Targets China's Exported Paper" in *Globe & Mail* (March 31, 2007, pp. B5)
Pub: CTVglobemedia Publishing Inc.
Ed: Barrie McKenna. **Description:** The prospects of the rise in duties on goods imported into the United States, due to the levy of duties on imports of Chinese paper, are discussed.

11124 ■ "Up On The Farm" in *Canadian Business* (Vol. 81, March 31, 2008, No. 5, pp. 23)
Pub: Rogers Media
Ed: John Gray. **Description:** Agricultural products have outperformed both energy and metal and even the prospect of a global economic slowdown does not seem to hinder its prospects. The Organization for Economic Cooperation and Development sees prices above historic equilibrium levels during the next ten years given that fuel and fertilizers remain high and greater demand from India and China remain steady

11125 ■ "Venture Gap" in *Canadian Business* (Vol. 81, March 17, 2008, No. 4, pp. 82)
Pub: Rogers Media
Ed: Joe Castaldo. **Description:** Money raised by Canadian venture capitalist firms has been declining since 2001. A strong venture capital market is important if Canada is to build innovative companies. Fixing Canada's tax policy on foreign investments is a start in reviving the industry.

11126 ■ "Wake-Up Call" in *Canadian Business* (Vol. 80, October 8, 2007, No. 20, pp. 58)
Pub: Rogers Media
Ed: Andrea Mandel-Campbell. **Description:** The need for Canadian companies to develop global marketing strategies is discussed. Thomas Caldwell, chairman of Caldwell Securities, believes the country's average performance in global markets should be a cause for alarm. The factors affecting the country's current economic state is also presented.

11127 ■ "We May Finally Find the Silver Lining" in *Crain's Detroit Business* (Vol. 24, April 7, 2008, No. 14, pp. 8)
Pub: Crain Communications, Inc.
Ed: Description: Discusses a possible economic turnaround for Michigan which could be brought forth with such things as the new film initiative incentives which may make filming in the state more appealing than filming in Canada due to the weakened state of the dollar and more exportation from Michigan companies.

11128 ■ "Wegmans Uses Database for Recall" in *Supermarket News* (Vol. 56, September 22, 2008, No. 38)
Pub: Penton Business Media, Inc.
Ed: Carol Angrisani. **Description:** Wegmans used data obtained through its loyalty card that, in turn, sent automated telephone calls to every customer who had purchased tainted pet food when Mars Petcare recalled dog food products.

11129 ■ *What Has EX-IM Bank Done for Small Business Lately?: Congressional Hearing*
Pub: DIANE Publishing Company
Ed: Donald A. Manzullo. **Description:** Covers Congressional hearing: Witnesses: Philip Merrill, President and CEO, Export Import Bank of the U.S.; Victoria Hadfield, President, Semiconductor Equipment and Materials International (SEMI), North America; and Michael Vaden, President and CEO, Rutland Plastic Technologies, Inc. Attachments: April 1, 2005, letter to Chairman Philip Merrill from Semiconductor Manufacturing International Corporation (SMIC); Attachment A - Chronology of SMIC Transaction; Attachment B-Appendices; Appendix A: March 21, 2005, letter from EX-IM Chairman Philip Merrill to Congressman Donald A. Manzullo from the State of Illinois; and Appendix B: Congressional letter written on SMIC and equipment suppliers behest. Includes charts and tables.

11130 ■ "What'll You Have Tonight?" in *Barron's* (Vol. 88, July 4, 2008, No. 28, pp. 22)
Pub: Dow Jones & Co., Inc.
Ed: Neil A. Martin. **Description:** Shares of Diageo could rise by 30 percent a year from June 2008 after it slipped due to U.S. sales worries. The company also benefits from the trend toward more premium alcoholic beverage brands worldwide especially in emerging markets.

11131 ■ "Who Produces for Whom in the World Economy?" in *Canadian Journal of Economics* (Vol. 44, November 2011, No. 4, pp. 1403)
Pub: Blackwell Publishers Ltd.
Ed: Guillaume Daudin, Christine Rifflart, Danielle Schweisguth. **Description:** For two decades, the share of trade in inputs, also called vertical trade, has been dramatically increasing. In reallocating trade flows to their original input-producing industries and countries, the article suggests a new measure of international trade: 'value-added trade' and makes it possible to answer the question, 'who produces for whom?'

11132 ■ "Why Change?" in *Canadian Business* (Vol. 80, October 8, 2007, No. 20, pp. 9)
Pub: Rogers Media
Ed: Joe Chidley. **Description:** The need for economic change in Canada is discussed. Despite the country's economic growth and low unemployment rate, economic reform is needed in order to maximize its economic potential in the future. Other reasons for the need to further develop its economy, such as the rise of manufacturing and service industries in Asia and the emergence of regional trade pacts in South America are also tackled.

11133 ■ "Why You Aren't Buying Venezuelan Chocolate. " in *Harvard Business Review* (Vol. 88, December 2010, No. 12, pp. 25)
Pub: Harvard Business School Publishing
Ed: Rohit Deshpande. **Description:** The concept of provenance paradox is defined as the preconceived notions consumers have about the country of origin of a given product, which can pose significant difficulties for emerging markets. Five strategies are presented for combating this problem, including building on historic events that have informed cultural perspectives.

11134 ■ "Winning Gold" in *The Business Journal-Milwaukee* (Vol. 25, August 8, 2008, No. 46, pp. A1)
Pub: American City Business Journals, Inc.
Ed: Rich Rovito. **Description:** Johnson Controls Inc. of Milwaukee, Wisconsin is taking part in the 2008 Beijing Olympics with the installation of its sustainable control equipment and technology that monitor over 58,000 points in 18 Olympic venues. Details of Johnson Controls' green products and sustainable operations in China are discussed.

11135 ■ "With Whom Do You Trade? Defensive Innovation and the Skill-Bias" in *Canadian Journal of Electronics* (Vol. 43, November 2010)
Pub: Journal of the Canadian Economics Association
Ed: Pushan Dutt, Daniel Traca. **Description:** Examination into whether increased trade with ineffective

protection of intellectual property has contributed to the skill-deepening of the 1980s. An index of effective protection of intellectual property at the country level, combining data on protection of patents and rule of law are presented. An industry-specific version of this index is given using as weights each country's trade share in the total trade of the industry. A decline is seen in this trade-weighted index, owing to a rise in trade with countries with low effective protection of intellectual property, which explains 29 percent of the rise within-industry skill-intensity.

11136 ■ *Your Guide to Canadian Export Financing: Successful Techniques for Financing Your Exports from Canada*
Pub: Productive Publications
Ed: Iain Williamson. **Released:** December 31, 2000. **Description:** Canadian export financing is covered.

TRADE PERIODICALS

11137 ■ *Bacard's Global Investor*
Pub: Ferney Scribes Inc.
Ed: Andre Bacard, Editor. **Released:** Monthly. **Price:** $129, U.S.. **Description:** Provides monthly updates of select no-load global and international funds, model portfolios, foreign market graphs, monthly analysis and current recommendations. Recurring features include news of research and a column titled Mutual Fund in the Spotlight.

11138 ■ *CUBANEWS*
Pub: Target Research
Contact: Larry Luxner
Ed: Larry Luxner, Editor. **Released:** Monthly. **Price:** $429, individuals; $199 academic institutions. **Description:** Covers business and economic issues involving Cuba, including an economic overview, monthly developments, and industrial analysis.

11139 ■ *Export Finance Letter Quarterly–Export Finance Guide News*
Pub: Richard Barovick
Contact: Richard Barovick, Editor & Publisher
E-mail: editor@exportsourcebook.com
Released: Quarterly. **Price:** $156, individuals. **Description:** Provides news and information on exporting.

11140 ■ *The Export Practitioner*
Pub: Gilston-Kalin Communications, LLC
Contact: Terry Gilston
Ed: Sam Gilston, Editor. **Released:** Monthly. **Price:** $499.00, individuals 499/year; $998.00, two years for print edition. **Description:** Focuses on regulatory policy and legal trends regarding export of products and services. Covers planning strategies for marketability.

11141 ■ *ImportCar*
Pub: Babcox
Contact: Valli Pantuso, Advertising Svcs.
E-mail: vpantuso@babcox.com
Released: Monthly. **Description:** Magazine focusing on import specialist repair shops that derive more than 50% of revenue from servicing import nameplates.

11142 ■ *International Trade Reporter*
Pub: Bureau of National Affairs Inc.
Contact: Linda G. Botsford, Managing Editor
Released: Weekly. **Price:** $1,159. **Description:** Covers current international trade policies of the U.S. and of major U.S. trading partners. Topics include bilateral negotiations, customs, export/import policy, foreign investment, standards, taxation, and other related issues. Recurring features include a calendar of events, reports of meetings, and notices of publications available.

11143 ■ *Ottawa Letter*
Pub: CCH Canadian Ltd.
Contact: Anna Wong
E-mail: awong@cch.ca
Released: Biweekly. **Price:** $920. **Description:** Reports on current events and topics of Canada, such as free trade, human rights, employment, and defense. Also provides statistics, lending, and foreign exchange rates.

COMPUTERIZED DATABASES

11144 ■ *International Trade Reporter*
The Bureau of National Affairs Inc.
1801 S Bell St.
Arlington, VA 22202
Free: 800-372-1033
Co. E-mail: customercare@bna.com
URL: http://www.bna.com
Description: Contains current information on developments in international trade and actions of U.S. courts and federal agencies related to imports and exports. Covers import competition and restrictions, export financing, trade agreements and negotiations, and foreign investment in the United States. Provides current information on the World Trade Organization, APEC, the European Union, and NAFTA. Covers such topics as export incentives, import relief, agricultural trade, financing, trade in services, taxation, balance of trade, foreign investments and more. **Availability:** Online: Thomson Reuters, The Bureau of National Affairs Inc. **Type:** Full text.

11145 ■ *U.S. Exports of Merchandise*
U.S. Census Bureau
4600 Silver Hill Rd.
Washington, DC 20233
Ph:(301)763-4636
Free: 800-923-8282
Co. E-mail: comments@census.gov
URL: http://www.census.gov/foreign-trade
Description: Contains monthly data for U.S. exports by International Harmonized System Commodity Classification codes (HS-Based Schedule B). Covers quantity, value, and shipping weight by country of destination, U.S. customs district of exportation, and transportation method. Includes totals for each commodity, country of destination, and exportation district. **Availability:** CD-ROM: U.S. Census Bureau. **Type:** Statistical.

LIBRARIES

11146 ■ The Economist Intelligence Unit Information Center
111 W. 57th St.
New York, NY 10019
Ph:(212)554-0600
Fax:(212)586-1181
Co. E-mail: newyork@eiu.com
URL: http://www.eiu.com
Contact: Beth Kilmer
Scope: Foreign investment, International trade, economics, finance, forecasting, critical issues monitoring. **Services:** Interlibrary loan; copying. **Holdings:** Economist Intelligence Unit publications (complete set); corporate directories; databases for the United Nations, the World Bank, and major regional economic organizations. **Subscriptions:** 7 newspapers.

11147 ■ Export-Import Bank of the United States Library
811 Vermont Ave., NW
Washington, DC 20571
Ph:(202)565-3946
Free: 800-565-3946
Fax:(202)565-3931
Co. E-mail: research@exim.gov
URL: http://www.exim.gov/about/links.cfm
Contact: Eugene Ferguson, Libn.
Scope: Export finance, world economics, U.S. and foreign business, trade statistics, International banking, insurance, law, country risk. **Services:** Interlibrary loan; SDI; daily news briefing; weekly and monthly subject briefings; Library open to the public for reference use only with prior appointment. **Holdings:** 15,000 books and pamphlets; 20,000 documents; 300 lin.ft. of archives. **Subscriptions:** 250 journals and other serials; 10 newspapers.

11148 ■ U.S. International Trade Commission–National Library of International Trade
500 E St., SW
USITC Bldg., 3rd Fl.
Washington, DC 20436
Ph:(202)205-2630
URL: http://www.usitc.gov/press_room/usitc_services.htm
Scope: U.S. trade policy, International trade, foreign trade statistics, tariffs. **Services:** Interlibrary loan except for legislative histories and archival copies of ITC publications; copying; Library open to the public. **Holdings:** 100,000 volumes. **Subscriptions:** 2500 journals and other serials.

RESEARCH CENTERS

11149 ■ The Heritage Foundation–Asian Studies Center
214 Massachusetts Ave. NE
Washington, DC 20002-4999
Ph:(202)546-4400
Fax:(202)546-8328
Co. E-mail: info@heritage.org
URL: http://www.heritage.org/about/departments/asianstudies.cfm
Contact: Walter Lohman, Dir.
E-mail: info@heritage.org
Scope: International trade and economics, U.S.-Asian relations, U.S. and Western security interests in Asia and the Pacific, U.S. policy towards China and Korea, U.S. interests in the Philippines, U.S. policy regarding the Association of Southeast Asian Nations, and the future of the U.S.-Japan relationship. **Services:** Expert testimony, before Congress and party platform committees. **Publications:** Asian Studies Center Backgrounders; Executive Memoranda Series; U.S. and Asia Statistical Handbook. **Educational Activities:** Heritage Lectures and seminars; Public diplomacy engagements, in the United States and throughout Asia.

ASSOCIATIONS AND OTHER ORGANIZATIONS

11150 ■ National Business Incubation Association
20 E Circle Dr., No. 37198
Athens, OH 45701-3571
Ph:(740)593-4331
Fax:(740)593-1996
Co. E-mail: info@nbia.org
URL: http://www.nbia.org
Contact: Mr. David Monkman, Pres./CEO

Description: Incubator developers and managers; corporate joint venture partners, venture capital investors; economic development professionals. (Incubators are business assistance programs providing business consulting services and financing assistance to start-up and fledgling companies.) Helps newly formed businesses to succeed. Educates businesses and investors on incubator benefits; offers specialized training in incubator formation and management. Conducts research and referral services; compiles statistics; maintains speakers' bureau; publishes information relevant to business incubation and growing companies. **Publications:** *NBIA Insights* (monthly); *NBIA Memberabilia* (bi-weekly); *NBIA Review* (bimonthly).

REFERENCE WORKS

11151 ■ "Funding Drought Stalls Biotech Incubators" in *Saint Louis Business Journal* (Vol. 31, July 29, 2011, No. 49, pp. 1)
Pub: Saint Louis Business Journal
Ed: Angela Mueller. **Description:** Economic slow-down took its toll on cash-strapped startups that fill incubators such as the Bio-Research and Development Growth (BRDG) Park in Creve Coeur, Missouri and the Center for Emerging Technologies in Midtown St. Louis. BRDG put a hold on construction of of its two buildings.

11152 ■ "Start-Up Pointers" in *Inside Business* (Vol. 13, September-October 2011, No. 5, pp. Y3)
Pub: Great Lakes Publishing Company
Description: Four tips to help entrepreneurs with startup firms are provided by Youngstown Business Incubator.

TRADE PERIODICALS

11153 ■ *Entrepreneur Magazine*
Pub: Entrepreneur Media Inc.
Contact: Rieva Lesonsky, Editorial Dir.
Released: Monthly. **Price:** $11.97. **Description:** Magazine covering small business management and operation.

11154 ■ *Entrepreneurship Theory and Practice*
Pub: Baylor University
Released: Bimonthly. **Price:** $511 institutions Americas, print & online; $394 institutions UK, print & online; $772 institutions, other countries print & online; $500 institutions Europe print & online; $129 Americas, print & online; $122 other countries UK, print & online; $122 Europe (non-euro zone) print & online; $182 Europe (non-euro zone) print & online; $465 institutions Americas, online only. **Description:** Journal of the United States Association for Small Business and Entrepreneurship.

11155 ■ *Minority Business Entrepreneur*
Pub: Minority Business Entrepreneur
Contact: Ginger Conrad, Publisher
E-mail: gconrad@mbemag.com
Released: Bimonthly. **Price:** $18; $30 two years. **Description:** Business magazine for ethnic minority and women business owners.

11156 ■ *Small Business Opportunities*
Pub: Harris Publications Inc.
Contact: Melissa Zinker
E-mail: melissa@harris-pub.com
Ed: Susan Rakowski, Editor, sr@harris-pub.com. **Released:** Bimonthly, (plus 4 special editions). **Price:** $14.97 U.S. and Canada; $29.94 other countries. **Description:** How-to magazine for small business owners.

ASSOCIATIONS AND OTHER ORGANIZATIONS

11157 ■ American Library Association
50 E Huron St.
Chicago, IL 60611
Ph:(312)944-6780
Free: 800-545-2433
Fax:(312)440-9374
Co. E-mail: ala@ala.org
URL: http://www.ala.org
Contact: Mr. Keith Michael Fiels, Exec. Dir.

Description: Librarians, libraries, trustees, friends of libraries, and others interested in the responsibilities of libraries in the educational, social, and cultural needs of society. Promotes and improves library service and librarianship. Establishes standards of service, support, education, and welfare for libraries and library personnel; promotes the adoption of such standards in libraries of all kinds; safeguards the professional status of librarians; encourages the recruiting of competent personnel for professional careers in librarianship; promotes popular understanding and public acceptance of the value of library service and librarianship. Works in liaison with federal agencies to initiate the enactment and administration of legislation that will extend library services. Offers placement services. **Publications:** *American Libraries* (bimonthly); *Booklist* (biweekly).

11158 ■ American Society for Information Science and Technology
1320 Fenwick Ln., Ste. 510
Silver Spring, MD 20910
Ph:(301)495-0900
Fax:(301)495-0810
Co. E-mail: asis@asis.org
URL: http://www.asis.org
Contact: Richard B. Hill, Exec. Dir.

Description: Information specialists, scientists, librarians, administrators, social scientists, and others interested in the use, organization, storage, retrieval, evaluation, and dissemination of recorded specialized information. Seeks to improve the information transfer process through research, development, application, and education. Provides a forum for the discussion, publication, and critical analysis of work dealing with the theory, practice, research, and development of elements involved in communication of information. Members are engaged in a variety of activities and specialties including classification and coding systems, automatic and associative indexing, machine translation of languages, special librarianship and library systems analysis, and copyright issues. Sponsors National Auxiliary Publications Service, which provides reproduction services and a central depository for all types of information. Maintains placement service. Sponsors numerous special interest groups. Conducts continuing education programs and professional development workshops. **Publications:** *Handbook and Directory* (annual); *Journal of the American Society for Information Science and Technology* (monthly).

11159 ■ ARMA International - Canadian Region
PO Box 6000
Fredericton, NB, Canada E3B 5H1
Ph:(506)453-5618
Co. E-mail: bernita.cogswell@gnb.ca
URL: http://www.arma.org
Contact: Bernita Cogswell, Region Mgr.

Description: Information management professionals. Promotes professional advancement of members and seeks to insure adherence to high standards of ethics and practice within the field of information management. Represents members' interests, conducts continuing professional development programs and serves as a clearinghouse on information management.

11160 ■ Canadian Association for Information Science–L'Association Canadienne des Sciences de l'Information
University of Western Ontario
Faculty of Information & Media Studies
45 Willcocks St., No. 335
Toronto, ON, Canada M5S 1C7
Ph:(416)978-4664
Co. E-mail: nadia.caidi@utoronto.ca
URL: http://www.cais-acsi.ca
Contact: Nadia Caidi, Pres.

Description: Institutions and individuals interested in the various aspects of information science, including information production, storage, and dissemination. Serves as a forum for dialogue and exchange of ideas concerned with the theory and practice of all factors involved in the communication of information. **Publications:** *Canadian Journal of Information and Library Science* (quarterly).

11161 ■ Information Technology Association of Canada–Association Canadienne de la Technologie de l'Information
5090 Explorer Dr., Ste. 801
Mississauga, ON, Canada L4W 4T9
Ph:(905)602-8345
Fax:(905)602-8346
Co. E-mail: kgupta@itac.ca
URL: http://www.itac.ca
Contact: Karna Gupta, CEO/Pres.

Description: Corporations producing information technologies and related components. Promotes growth and development in the domestic information technology industry. Represents members' interests; conducts research; maintains advocacy programs. Operates hall of fame; compiles statistics.

11162 ■ National Federation of Abstracting and Information Services
1518 Walnut St., Ste. 1004
Philadelphia, PA 19102-3403
Ph:(215)893-1561
Fax:(215)893-1564
Co. E-mail: blawlor@nfais.org
URL: http://www.nfais.org
Contact: Bonnie Lawlor, Exec. Dir.

Description: Represents major abstracting and indexing service organizations, online vendors, CD-ROM vendors, and related organizations. Aims to improve the extent and quality of the documentation and use of the world's literature through research programs, publications, and seminars. Works to develop communications, cooperation, and coordination among all segments of the information processing and dissemination community, including primary publishers, libraries, commercial and industrial abstracting and indexing services, data analysis centers, information dissemination centers, and people teaching or undertaking research in the abstracting and indexing field. Serves as a communication forum for its members through meetings, workshops, committee activities, and formal publications. Provides programs that are designed to: facilitate communication among members; conduct research projects useful to the abstracting and indexing community; provide educational programs for the information-science community; act as a collective voice for member services. Compiles statistics. **Publications:** *Guide to Database Distribution*; *NFAIS Newsletter* (bimonthly).

11163 ■ Special Libraries Association
331 S Patrick St.
Alexandria, VA 22314-3501
Ph:(703)647-4900
Fax:(703)647-4901
Co. E-mail: janice@sla.org
URL: http://www.sla.org
Contact: Janice R. Lachance, CEO

Description: International association of information professionals who work in specialized information environments such as business, research, government, universities, newspapers, museums, and institutions. Seeks to advance the leadership role of information professionals through learning, networking and advocacy. Offers consulting services to organizations that wish to establish or expand a library or information services. Conducts strategic learning and development courses, public relations, and government relations programs. Provides employment services. Operates knowledge exchange on topics pertaining to the development and management of special libraries. **Publications:** *Information Outlook* (8/year); *SLA Connections* (monthly).

REFERENCE WORKS

11164 ■ *Conquering Information Chaos in the Growing Business: IBM Solutions for Managing Information in an On Demand World*
Pub: Maximum Press

Ed: Jim Hoskins. **Released:** April 2005. **Price:** $29.95. **Description:** Information management is critical to any business.

11165 ■ *Contingency Planning and Disaster Recovery: A Small Business Guide*
Pub: John Wiley & Sons, Incorporated

Ed: Donna R. Childs, Stefan Dietrich. **Released:** October 2002. **Description:** Four keys issues to help a business plan for disasters include: preparation, response, recovery, and sample IT solutions in order to secure property and confidential data files and covers the six types of disasters: human errors, equipment failures, third-party failures, environmental hazards, fires and other structural catastrophes, and terrorism and sabotage.

11166 ■ Directory of Libraries in Canada–Repertoire des bibliotheques canadiennes
Pub: Grey House Publishing Canada Inc.
Released: Annual, Latest edition 2011. **Price:** $275, individuals Hardcover. **Covers:** Over 6,700 libraries, library associations, library schools and technician programs, archives, periodicals, provincial library agencies, government libraries, regional systems, and library services suppliers (wholesalers, binders, subscription agencies, etc.) in Canada. **Entries Include:** Library or firm name, address, phone, fax, TDD, e-mail; names and titles of key personnel and contact, description of collection, services offered to the public; budget range; computers and automated systems in use; publications and url addresses. **Arrangement:** Library schools are geographical; other lists are alphabetical. **Indexes:** Geographical, subject, personal name.

11167 ■ International Literary Market Place
Pub: Information Today Inc.
Contact: Thomas H. Hogan, Publisher/Pres.
Released: Annual, Latest edition 2012. **Price:** $289, individuals softbound; $260.10, individuals first time standing order. **Covers:** Over 10,500 publishers in over 180 countries outside the United States and Canada, and about 1,499 trade and professional organizations related to publishing abroad; includes major printers, binders, typesetters, book manufacturers, book dealers, libraries, literary agencies, translators, book clubs, reference books and journals, periodicals, prizes, and international reference section. **Entries Include:** For publishers—Name, address, phone, fax, telex, names and titles of key personnel, branches, type of publications, subjects, ISBN prefix. Listings for others include similar information but less detail. **Arrangement:** Classified by business activities, then geographical. **Indexes:** Company name, subject, type of publication.

TRADE PERIODICALS

11168 ■ The DATA BASE for Advances in Information Systems
Pub: Association for Computing Machinery
Contact: Dr. Dorothy Liedner, Co-Ed.
E-mail: d.leidner@tcu.edu
Released: Quarterly. **Price:** $20, Included in membership; $14, students; $38, nonmembers. **Description:** Presents articles on practical research relating to business uses of information systems.

11169 ■ Data Base Alert
Pub: PBI Media L.L.C.
Ed: Judy Duke, Editor. **Released:** Monthly. **Description:** Provides updates on publicly available online services. Contains a listing of distributors of new or revised data bases with data bases listed alphabetically under the appropriate distributor along with information about pricing, updates, and number of records. Remarks: Newsletter is part of DataBase Directory Service, which includes an annual directory and supplement.

11170 ■ Dat@Line
Pub: Dun & Bradstreet
Ed: Jean Fitzgerald, Editor, fitzjean@mail.dnb.com. **Released:** 4/year. **Price:** Free. **Description:** Informs online users of database contents and applications. Also provides general information on Dun & Bradstreet. Recurring features include new product announcements, a calendar of training sessions and trade shows, and a page highlighting unique online database applications at a particular company or organization. Also includes columns titled Q&A Corner and Tips and Techniques.

11171 ■ FEDLINK Technical Notes
Pub: Federal Library and Information Network
Contact: Susan M. Tarr, Exec. Dir.
Released: Monthly. **Price:** Included in membership. **Description:** Carries technical information about the Federal Library and Information Center Committee

and its network component FEDLINK, its programs and services, and items of interest to those in library science and information fields.

11172 ■ The Information Advisor
Pub: Find/SVP
Ed: Robert I. Berkman, Editor, rberkman@javanet.com. **Released:** Monthly, plus Quarterly Knowledge Management Supplement. **Price:** $165, U.S.; $175, Canada and foreign. **Description:** Supplies business data users information on comparing and evaluating competing information sources. Provides comparison charts, reviews, advice on data reliability, and quality for both online and print business information produced in the U.S., Europe, Asia, and Latin America.

11173 ■ Information Management
Pub: Idea Group Publishing
Ed: Mehdi Khosrowpour, D.B.A., Editor. **Released:** Semiannual, 2/year. **Price:** $40, U.S.; $60, individuals only in USA; $46, Canada. **Description:** Follows trends and issues in the field of information technology and information resources technology. Strives to "enhance the overall knowledge and understanding of effective information resources management in the 1990s and beyond." Recurring features include interviews, news of research, a calendar of events, book reviews, news of product releases, and columns titled Technology Talk, An Information Management Tool, and End User Attitudes.

11174 ■ Information Standards Quarterly
Pub: National Information Standards Organization
Contact: Patricia R. Harris
Released: Quarterly. **Price:** $130, U.S.; $165, elsewhere. **Description:** NISO's newsletter, *Information Standards Quarterly* (ISQ), features timely standards-related news, information about implementation of standards, and updates on standards-in-development. The January issue features an annual "State of the Standards" which reports on the status of each standard in NISO's program.

11175 ■ Information Today
Pub: Information Today Inc.
Contact: Michael V. Zarrello, Advertising Dir
E-mail: mzarrello@infotoday.com
Released: 11/yr. **Price:** $84.95; $112 Canada and Mexico; $160 two years; $122 outside North America. **Description:** User and producer magazine (tabloid) covering electronic and optical information services.

11176 ■ Journal of the American Society for Information Science and Technology
Pub: John Wiley & Sons Inc.
Contact: Blaise Cronin, Editor-in-Chief
E-mail: bcronin@indiana.edu
Released: Monthly. **Price:** $2,331 institutions print only; $2,471 institutions, Canada print only; $2,590 institutions, other countries print only. **Description:** International journal serves as a forum for discussion and experimentation concerning the theory and practice of communicating information. Covers computer technology, operations research, librarianship, communications, management, information storage and retrieval, reprography, and systems design. Also includes *Perspectives*, a journal within a journal, containing collections of papers analyzing a single topic.

11177 ■ LIMS/Letter
Pub: LIMS/Letter
Ed: Helen Gillespie, Editor. **Released:** Quarterly. **Price:** $139, U.S.; $144, Canada and Mexico; $159, elsewhere; $399, institutions. **Description:** Provides information for Laboratory Information Management Systems (LIMS) professionals. Recurring features include interviews, case studies, invited articles, trends, and a calendar of events.

11178 ■ Ottawa Letter
Pub: CCH Canadian Ltd.
Contact: Anna Wong
E-mail: awong@cch.ca
Released: Biweekly. **Price:** $920. **Description:** Reports on current events and topics of Canada, such as free trade, human rights, employment, and defense. Also provides statistics, lending, and foreign exchange rates.

11179 ■ Third Indicator
Pub: Bibliographical Center for Research, Rocky Mountain Region Inc.
Ed: Cheryl Burkert, Editor, cburkert@bcr.org. **Released:** Bimonthly. **Price:** $30, individuals Free to BCR/OCLC libraries; $30/year to others; $6, single issue. **Description:** Provides articles and information concerning the Online Computer Library Center (OCLC) and library automation.

TRADE SHOWS AND CONVENTIONS

11180 ■ Special Libraries Association Information Revolution
Special Libraries Association
331 South Patrick St.
Alexandria, VA 22314-3501
Ph:(703)647-4900
Fax:(703)647-4901
Co. E-mail: sla@sla.org
URL: http://www.sla.org
Released: Annual. **Audience:** Information managers and librarians. **Principal Exhibits:** Library equipment, supplies, and services, including computers and software, Database information.

CONSULTANTS

11181 ■ A. Davis Grant & Co.
295 Pierson Ave.
Edison, NJ 08837-3118
Ph:(732)463-1414
Fax:(732)494-3626
Co. E-mail: info@adg.net
URL: http://www.adg.net
Contact: Allan D. Grossman, Senior Partner
E-mail: allan@adg.net
Scope: Executive search firm dealing exclusively in the field of information systems and technology.

COMPUTERIZED DATABASES

11182 ■ DIALOG Bluesheets
ProQuest LLC
2250 Perimeter Park Dr., Ste. 300
Morrisville, NC 27560
Ph:(919)804-6400
Free: 800-334-2564
Fax:(919)804-6410
Co. E-mail: contact@dialog.com
URL: http://www.dialog.com
Description: Contains descriptions and guidelines for searching all databases that are currently accessories online through DIALOG. Corresponds to DIALOG's printed Bluesheets, excluding sample records. For each database, provides database name and subject, file label, file description, identifiers, sources, print counterparts, dates covered (on DIALOG), file size, update frequency, database content, document types indexed, geographic coverage of source data, special features, DIALINDEX acronyms, producer name, address, telephone number, DIALMAIL electronic mail address, geographic restrictions, disclaimer, basic index field names and search codes, display codes, search suffix, name of field, indexing, notes, limited fields, sortable fields, MAP fields, bluesheet status, date of printed bluesheet, and online bluesheet status. Includes sources of data and the origin of the information contained in the databases. Additional features include type of records contained in the database; availability of CD-ROM, Alerts, Classroom Instruction Protection, document delivery through a specific supplier, and annual accession number ranges, if applicable. Includes up-to-date rate information. **Availability:** Online: ProQuest LLC, ProQuest LLC; CD-ROM: ProQuest LLC. **Type:** Directory; Numeric.

11183 ■ Information Today
Information Today Inc.
143 Old Marlton Pke.
Medford, NJ 08055
Ph:(609)654-6266
Free: 800-300-9868

Fax:(609)654-4309
Co. E-mail: custserv@infotoday.com
URL: http://www.infotoday.com
Description: Contains the complete text of *Information Today*, a monthly newspaper covering developments in the electronic information industry. Covers online databases and services, optical disk products and technologies, telecommunications systems, and computer equipment for information storage and retrieval. Includes business news, analyses of industry trends, and a calendar of conferences and events. **Availability:** Online: Information Today Inc. **Type:** Full text.

11184 ■ *InformationWeek*
United Business Media Ltd.
600 Community Dr.
Manhasset, NY 11030
Ph:(516)562-5000
Fax:(516)562-7830
Co. E-mail: inquiries@ubm-us.com
URL: http://www.ubmtechnology.com
Description: Contains the complete text of *InformationWeek*, a weekly newspaper covering companies, individuals, products, and events in the computer and communications industries. **Availability:** Online: United Business Media Ltd., LexisNexis Group. **Type:** Full text.

11185 ■ *Library Literature & Information Science Full Text*
EBSCO Publishing
10 Estes St.
Ipswich, MA 01938
Ph:(978)356-6500
Free: 800-653-2726
Fax:(978)356-6565
Co. E-mail: information@ebscohost.com
URL: http://www.ebscohost.com/wilson
Description: Contains more than 240,000 citations and indexing to more than 400 English and foreign language periodicals and journals, monographs, conference proceedings, pamphlets, and library school theses, as well as full text of articles from January 1994. Includes reviews of books, periodicals, and audiovisual materials in the library and information science area. Features periodical indexing from 1984. Provides hotlinks to websites featured in the articles. **Availability:** Online: EBSCO Publishing, Wolters Kluwer Health, Wolters Kluwer Health. **Type:** Bibliographic; Full text.

LIBRARIES

11186 ■ CD Research, Ltd.–Library Services
8 Dexter Saunders Rd.
North Scituate, RI 02857
Ph:(401)273-4070
Contact: Derryl R. Johnson, Info. Broker
Scope: Library and information services. **Services:** SDI; Library not open to the public. **Holdings:** 5000 volumes.

11187 ■ Decision Information Services, Ltd. Library
2130 Hanover St.
Palo Alto, CA 94306
Ph:(650)856-3666
Fax:(415)494-3737
Contact: Ulla Mick, Pres.
Scope: Management of information work; information needs and behaviors; information technology; microcomputers; participatory planning; policy studies. **Holdings:** 500 books; 5000 papers and reports. **Subscriptions:** 200 journals and other serials.

11188 ■ Grosvenor Barber and Associates Library
724 Miller Ave.
Great Falls, VA 22066
Ph:(703)759-6587
Fax:(703)759-9233
Co. E-mail: 71460.1506@compuserve.com
Contact: Grosvenor Barber, Pres.
Scope: Business, technology, information sources, health data. **Services:** Library not open to the public. **Holdings:** 600 bound volumes. **Subscriptions:** 20 journals and other serials.

11189 ■ Seek Information Service Library
2318 Bancroft Ave., Ste. B
Los Angeles, CA 90039
Ph:(323)660-0091
Free: 800-722-SEEK
Fax:(323)660-0678
Co. E-mail: seek@seekinfo.com
URL: http://www.seekinfo.com
Scope: Information retrieval. **Services:** Copying; SDI; Library not open to the public. **Holdings:** Figures not available.

11190 ■ UMI InfoStore
789 E. Eisenhower Pkwy.
PO Box 1346
Ann Arbor, MI 48106-1346
Ph:(734)761-4700

Free: 800-521-0600
Co. E-mail: info@proquest.com
URL: http://il.proquest.com/en-US/products/brands
Contact: Elyse Eisner, Prod.Mgr.
Scope: Information services, document retrieval, translation. **Services:** Library not open to the public. **Holdings:** Figures not available. **Subscriptions:** 15,000 journals and other serials.

11191 ■ University of California, Los Angeles–Department of Education & Information Studies–Multimedia & Information Technology Lab (102A)
102A GSE & IS Bldg.
Mailbox 951520
Los Angeles, CA 90095-1520
Ph:(310)206-9263
Fax:(310)206-4460
Co. E-mail: kbotello@ucla.edu
URL: http://is.gseis.ucla.edu/resources/MIT_lab/lab/
Contact: Keri Botello, Dir.
Scope: Librarianship, information access, information Organization, information science, information retrieval systems, informatics, online searching, bibliography, history of printing, archives, preservation. **Services:** Library open to the public for reference use only. **Holdings:** 4000 books; 400 bound periodical volumes; 100 reports. **Subscriptions:** 55 journals and other serials.

RESEARCH CENTERS

11192 ■ Stanford University–Center for Information Technology
Computer Science Department
Stanford, CA 94305
Ph:(650)723-0934
Fax:(650)725-7411
Co. E-mail: genesereth@stanford.edu
URL: http://logic.stanford.edu/cit/cit.html
Contact: Michael R. Genesereth
E-mail: genesereth@stanford.edu
Scope: Multimedia technology, integration technology, information capture, and human-computer interaction, focusing on the development of advanced information technology, including computer technology appropriate to the encoding, storage, communication, manipulation, and use of information in digital form.

ASSOCIATIONS AND OTHER ORGANIZATIONS

11193 ■ EIFS Industry Members Association
513 W Broad St., Ste. 210
Falls Church, VA 22046-3257
Free: 800-294-3462
Fax:(703)538-1736
Co. E-mail: eifsinfo@eima.com
URL: http://www.eima.com
Contact: David A. Johnston, Exec. Dir.
Description: Represents the exterior insulation and finish systems industry. Aims to improve the exterior insulation industry and to widen the use of its products through collective action. Conducts educational and research programs. .

11194 ■ Insulation Contractors Association of America
1321 Duke St., Ste. 303
Alexandria, VA 22314
Ph:(703)739-0356
Fax:(703)739-0412
Co. E-mail: icaa@insulate.org
URL: http://www.insulate.org
Description: Residential and commercial insulation contractors; manufacturing and supplier associates. Seeks to develop industry standards; promotes energy conservation in old and new buildings through proper specifications and applications of insulation; represents interests of the industry at all government levels; promotes exchange of information among insulation contractors. Sponsors seminars, field surveys, and research. **Publications:** *Insulation Contractors Association of America—Bulletin* (periodic); *Insulation Contractors Report* (bimonthly); *Insulation Industry Buyer's Guide* (annual).

11195 ■ National Insulation Association
12100 Sunset Hills Rd., Ste. 330
Reston, VA 20190
Ph:(703)464-6422
Fax:(703)464-5896
Co. E-mail: mjones@insulation.org
URL: http://www.insulation.org
Contact: Michele M. Jones, Exec. VP/CEO
Description: Insulation contractors, distributors, and manufacturers. **Publications:** *Insulation Outlook* (monthly); *National Industries and Commercial Standards Manual*; *NIA News* (monthly); *Safety Handbook* .

11196 ■ North American Insulation Manufacturers Association
44 Canal Center Plz., Ste. 310
Alexandria, VA 22314
Ph:(703)684-0084
Fax:(703)684-0427
URL: http://www.naima.org
Contact: Mike Lawrence, Chm.
Description: Manufacturers of fiberglass, rock wool, and slag wool insulation products. Promotes energy efficiency and environmental preservation through the use of fiberglass, rock wool, and slag wool insulation products. Encourages safe production and use of insulation materials. .

REFERENCE WORKS

11197 ■ *National Insulation Association—Membership Directory and Resource Guide*
Pub: National Insulation Association
Contact: Michele M. Jones, President
Released: Annual, fall. **Covers:** About 600 member manufacturers, distributors, and contractors involved in the commercial and industrial insulation and asbestos abatement industries. **Entries Include:** Company name, address, phone, names and titles of key personnel, subsidiary and branch names and locations, products and services. **Arrangement:** Alphabetical by company, classified by, product/service. **Indexes:** Product/service, subject, geographical.

TRADE PERIODICALS

11198 ■ *Roofing Contractor*
Pub: BNP Media
Contact: Jill Bloom, Gp. Publisher
E-mail: blooj@bnpmedia.com
Released: Monthly. **Price:** $25 Free to qualified subscribers; $5; $5 single issue. **Description:** Trade magazine on roofing and insulation.

START-UP INFORMATION

11199 ■ "Docs Prop Up Health Insurer" in
***Business First-Columbus* (December 14, 2007, pp. A1)**
Pub: American City Business Journals, Inc.
Ed: Carrie Ghose. **Description:** Doctors and executives supporting Physicians Assurance Corporation, a startup health insurer in Central Ohio, were required to raise $2.5 million before they could apply for a license from the state Department of Insurance. The company, which hopes to acquire its license by January 2007, will focus on doctor's offices and businesses with two to ninety-nine employees.

11200 ■ "Startup Makes Attempt to 'Reform' Health Insurance" in *Austin Business JournalInc.* (Vol. 29, January 15, 2010, No. 45, pp. 1)
Pub: American City Business Journals
Ed: Sandra Zaragoza. **Description:** Health insurance provider ETMG LLC of Austin, Texas plans to act as a managing general agent and a third-party administrator that can facilitate customized plans for small businesses and sole proprietors. According to CEO Mark Adams, profitability is expected for ETMG, which have also clinched $1.5 million worth of investments. Entities that have agreed to do business with ETMG are presented.

ASSOCIATIONS AND OTHER ORGANIZATIONS

11201 ■ American Association of Insurance Management Consultants
Texas Insurance Consulting
8980 Lakes at 610 Dr., Ste. 100
Houston, TX 77054
Ph:(713)664-6424
Co. E-mail: thomas.braniff@aaimco.com
URL: http://www.aaimco.com
Contact: Mr. Thomas M. Braniff, Pres.
Description: Consists of individuals who devote a substantial portion of their services to insurance consulting, risk management activities, legal representation relating to insurance issues; as well as education and professional development training, employment consulting, and other technical and management advice to the insurance industry. Advises and assists the insurance industry and seeks to achieve professional recognition for insurance management consultants. Mediates the exchange of ideas; sets standards of service and performance; maintains a code of ethics; offers a referral service and a series of educational conferences and seminars. Operates speakers' bureau; offers placement services; compiles statistics. .

11202 ■ American Association of Insurance Services
1745 S Naperville Rd.
Wheaton, IL 60189-8132
Ph:(630)681-8347
Free: 800-564-AAIS

Fax:(630)681-8356
Co. E-mail: info@aaisonline.com
URL: http://www.aaisonline.com
Contact: Mr. Paul Baiocchi, Pres./CEO
Description: Property and casualty insurance companies; mutual, stock, and reciprocal companies. Develops loss costs, rules, forms, and statistical services for property and casualty insurance. Licensed in all states, the District of Columbia, and the Commonwealth of Puerto Rico. .

11203 ■ American Association of Managing General Agents
150 S Warner Rd., Ste. 156
King of Prussia, PA 19406
Ph:(610)225-1999
Fax:(610)225-1996
Co. E-mail: bernie@aamga.org
URL: http://www.aamga.org
Contact: Bernd G. Heinze Esq., Exec. Dir.
Description: Managing general agents of insurance companies. Conducts specialized education programs; compiles statistics. **Publications:** *Communique* (quarterly).

11204 ■ American Council of Life Insurers
101 Constitution Ave. NW, Ste. 700
Washington, DC 20001-2133
Ph:(202)624-2000
Free: 877-674-4659
Co. E-mail: webadmin@acli.com
URL: http://www.acli.com
Contact: Frank A. Keating, Pres./CEO
Description: Represents the interests of legal reserve life insurance companies in legislative, regulatory and judicial matters at the federal, state and municipal levels of government and at the NAIC. Member companies hold majority of the life insurance in force in the United States. **Publications:** *Investment Bulletins* (quarterly); *Life Insurance Fact Book* (annual).

11205 ■ American Institute for CPCU
720 Providence Rd., Ste. 100
Malvern, PA 19355-3433
Free: 800-644-2101
Fax:(610)640-9576
Co. E-mail: customerservice@cpcuiia.org
URL: http://www.aicpcu.org
Contact: Peter L. Miller MBA, Pres./CEO
Purpose: Determines qualifications for professional certification of insurance personnel; conducts examinations and awards designation of Chartered Property Casualty Underwriter (CPCU). **Publications:** *CPCU/IIA Catalogue* (annual); *Malvern Examiner* (annual).

11206 ■ American Insurance Association
2101 L St. NW, Ste. 400
Washington, DC 20037
Ph:(202)828-7100
Fax:(202)293-1219
Co. E-mail: info@aiadc.org
URL: http://www.aiadc.org/aiapub
Contact: Leigh Ann Pusey, Pres./CEO
Description: Represents companies providing property and casualty insurance and suretyship. Monitors and reports on economic, political, and

social trends; serves as a clearinghouse for ideas, advice, and technical information. Represents members' interests before state and federal legislative and regulatory bodies; coordinates members' litigation. **Publications:** *Automobile Insurance Laws*; *Claims Administration Digest*; *Guide to Campaign Laws*; *State Rating Guide*; *Summary of States Regulations and Laws Affecting General Contractors*; *Termination and Renewal of Property/Casualty Insurance Policies* .

11207 ■ American Risk and Insurance Association
716 Providence Rd.
Malvern, PA 19355-3402
Ph:(610)640-1997
Fax:(610)725-1007
Co. E-mail: aria@theinstitutes.org
URL: http://www.aria.org
Contact: Mr. Anthony Biacchi, Exec. Dir.
Description: Comprises of academics, individual insurance industry representatives, students, and retirees. Works to emphasize research relevant to the operational concerns and functions of insurance professionals. **Publications:** *Journal of Risk and Insurance* (quarterly); *Risk Management and Insurance Review* (semiannual).

11208 ■ Canadian Association of Mutual Insurance Companies–Association Canadienne des Compagnies d'Assurance Mutuelles
311 Ave. McArthur, Ste. 205
Ottawa, ON, Canada K1L 6P1
Ph:(613)789-6851
Fax:(613)789-7665
Co. E-mail: nlafreniere@camic.ca
URL: http://www.camic.ca
Contact: Normand Lafreniere, Pres.
Description: Mutual insurance companies. Seeks to advance the insurance industry. Facilitates communication and cooperation among members; represents members' commercial interests before government agencies and the public.

11209 ■ Canadian Board of Marine Underwriters
2233 Argentia Rd., Ste. 100
Mississauga, ON, Canada L5N 2X7
Ph:(905)826-4768
Fax:(905)826-4873
Co. E-mail: cbmu@cbmu.com
URL: http://www.cbmu.com/HOME/default.asp
Contact: Claudio Verconich, Pres.
Description: Marine underwriters. Promotes professional development of members; seeks to advance the practice of marine insurance underwriting. Serves as a forum for the exchange of information among members; conducts continuing professional education courses. **Publications:** *The Log* (biennial).

11210 ■ Canadian Independent Adjusters' Association–Association Canadienne Des Experts Independants
Centennial Ctre.
5401 Eglinton Ave. W, Ste. 100
Etobicoke, ON, Canada M9C 5K6

Ph:(416)621-6222
Free: 877-255-5589
Fax:(416)621-7776
Co. E-mail: info@ciaa-adjusters.ca
URL: http://www.ciaa-adjusters.ca
Contact: Patricia M. Battle, Exec. Dir.
Description: Independent insurance adjusters. Represents the collective interests of independent adjusters to government, industry and the public on a provincial, regional and national level. Promotes continuing professional development of members; encourages adherence to high standards of ethics and practice in the industry. Conducts educational programs. **Publications:** *Canadian Independent Adjuster* (bimonthly); *Canadian Independent Adjusters' Claims Manual* (annual).

11211 ■ Canadian Life and Health Insurance Association–Association Canadienne des Compagnies d'Assurances de Personnes
1 Queen St. E, Ste. 1700
Toronto, ON, Canada M5C 2X9
Ph:(416)777-2221
Free: 800-268-8099
Fax:(416)777-1895
URL: http://www.clhia.ca
Contact: George Mohacsi, Chm.
Description: Life and health insurance companies. Seeks to advance the insurance industry; promotes adherence to high standards of ethics and practice among members. Serves as a forum for the exchange of information among members; represents the collective interests of the life and health insurance industries. **Publications:** *Policyholder Tax Manual* .

11212 ■ Conference of Consulting Actuaries
3880 Salem Lake Dr., Ste. H
Long Grove, IL 60047-5292
Ph:(847)719-6500
Fax:(847)719-6506
Co. E-mail: conference@ccactuaries.org
URL: http://www.ccactuaries.org
Contact: Adam J. Reese, Pres.
Description: Full-time consulting actuaries or governmental actuaries. Develops and maintains structure and programs to reinforce, enhance, or add to members' knowledge and skills; this includes continuing education, through diverse delivery methods, for all practice areas and for consulting and business skills. **Publications:** *The Proceedings* (annual).

11213 ■ Consumer Credit Industry Association
6300 Powers Ferry Rd., Ste. 600-286
Atlanta, GA 30339
Ph:(312)939-2242
Co. E-mail: sbrandt@cciaonline.com
URL: http://www.cciaonline.com
Contact: Stephanie Brandt, Dir.
Description: Insurance companies underwriting consumer credit insurance in areas of life insurance, accident and health insurance, and property insurance. **Publications:** *Consumer Credit Insurance Association—Annual Meeting Proceedings* (annual); *Consumer Credit Insurance Association—Digest Bulletin* (periodic); *Consumer Credit Insurance Association—Information Bulletin* (periodic); *Consumer Credit Insurance Association—Legislative Bulletin* (periodic).

11214 ■ Council of Insurance Agents and Brokers
701 Pennsylvania Ave. NW, Ste. 750
Washington, DC 20004-2608
Ph:(202)783-4400
Fax:(202)783-4410
Co. E-mail: ciab@ciab.com
URL: http://www.ciab.com
Contact: H. Wade Reece, Dir.
Description: Represents the interests of the leading commercial property and casualty insurance agencies and brokerage firms in the U.S. and around the world. **Publications:** *For Your Benefit* (monthly); *Leader's Edge* (bimonthly).

11215 ■ CPCU Society
720 Providence Rd.
Malvern, PA 19355-3402
Ph:(610)251-2727
Free: 800-932-2728

Fax:(610)251-2780
Co. E-mail: membercenter@cpcusociety.org
URL: http://www.cpcusociety.org
Contact: James R. Marks, CEO
Description: Serves as a professional society of individuals who have passed national examinations of the American Institute for Chartered Property Casualty Underwriters, have 3 years of work experience, have agreed to be bound by a code of ethics, and have been awarded CPCU designation. Promotes education, research, social responsibility, and professionalism in the field. Holds seminars, symposia, and workshops. **Publications:** *CPCU News* (5/year); *CPCU Yearbook* (annual).

11216 ■ GAMA International
2901 Telestar Ct., Ste. 140
Falls Church, VA 22042-1205
Free: 800-345-2687
Fax:(703)770-8182
Co. E-mail: gamamail@gamaweb.com
URL: http://www.gamaweb.com
Contact: Kenneth G. Gallacher, Pres.-Elect
Description: Provides world-class education and training resources for individuals, companies and organizations involved with the recruitment and development of field managers, representatives and staff in the life insurance and financial services industry; advocates of the value-added role of field management and representatives in the ethical distribution of life insurance and financial products and services industry. **Publications:** *GAMA International Journal* (bimonthly).

11217 ■ Independent Financial Brokers of Canada–Courtiers Indenpendants en Securite Financiere
306-30 Eglinton Ave. W
Mississauga, ON, Canada L5R 3E7
Ph:(905)279-2727
Free: 888-654-3333
Fax:(905)276-7295
URL: http://www.ifbc.ca
Contact: John Dargie, Chm./Pres.
Description: Represents members' interests. Conducts educational programs. **Publications:** *The Independent* (quarterly).

11218 ■ Independent Insurance Agents and Brokers of America
127 S Peyton St.
Alexandria, VA 22314
Free: 800-221-7917
Fax:(703)683-7556
Co. E-mail: info@iiaba.org
URL: http://www.iiaba.net
Contact: Beth Montgomery, VP
Description: Sales agencies handling property, fire, casualty, and surety insurance. Organizes technical and sales courses for new and established agents. Sponsors Independent Insurance Agent Junior Classic Golf Tournament. **Publications:** *Independent Agent* (monthly); *Insurance News and Views* (weekly).

11219 ■ Insurance Brokers Association of Canada–Association des courtiers d'assurances du Canada
18 King St. E, Ste. 1210
Toronto, ON, Canada M5C 1C4
Ph:(416)367-1831
Fax:(416)367-3687
Co. E-mail: ibac@ibac.ca
URL: http://www.ibac.ca
Contact: Dan Danyluk, CEO
Description: Insurance brokers. Promotes advancement of the insurance brokerage industry. Represents members' interests. Conducts educational and training programs for members' staff.

11220 ■ Insurance Bureau of Canada–Bureau D'Assurance du Canada
PO Box 121
Toronto, ON, Canada M5G 2C8
Ph:(416)362-2031
Free: 800-387-2880

Fax:(416)644-4961
Co. E-mail: memberservices@ibc.ca
URL: http://www.ibc.ca
Contact: Don Forgeron, Pres./CEO
Description: Trade association of the private property and casualty insurance industry. Works with members to improve communication with the public, government, news media, and other industry associations. Identifies and monitors legal and policy issues affecting the industry; conducts public opinion research; campaigns on a range of issues in order to reduce losses and increase public understanding of P&C insurance; promotes safety on the road, at work and at home. Gathers statistical data on insurance loss experience. **Publications:** *Between the Lines; Comment* (periodic); *Facts of the General Insurance Industry of Canada* (periodic); *Perspective: Financial Affairs, Regulatory Affairs* (quarterly).

11221 ■ Insurance Consumer Affairs Exchange
PO Box 746
Lake Zurich, IL 60047
Ph:(847)991-8454
Co. E-mail: nbrebner@icae.com
URL: http://icae.com
Contact: Nancy Brebner, Exec. Dir.
Description: Voluntary, professional group of consumer affairs specialists from insurance companies, insurance regulators, and consumer information centers. Provides opportunities to exchange ideas for improving communication between insurers, consumers, and regulators. **Publications:** *Catalyst* (semiannual); *Resource Manual* .

11222 ■ Insurance Information Institute
110 William St.
New York, NY 10038
Ph:(212)346-5500
Co. E-mail: members@iii.org
URL: http://www.iii.org
Contact: Dr. Robert P. Hartwig CPCU, Pres.
Description: Property and casualty insurance companies. Provides information and educational services to mass media, educational institutions, trade associations, businesses, government agencies, and the public. **Publications:** *I.I.I. Insurance Daily*; *Insurance Handbook for Reporters* .

11223 ■ Insurance Institute of America
720 Providence Rd., Ste. 100
Malvern, PA 19355-3433
Free: 800-644-2101
Fax:(610)640-9576
Co. E-mail: customerservice@theinstitutes.org
URL: http://www.aicpcu.org
Description: Sponsors educational programs for property and liability insurance personnel. Conducts exams and awards certificates and diplomas. **Publications:** *Succeed* (annual).

11224 ■ Insurance Marketing and Communications Association
4916 Point Fosdick Dr. NW, No. 180
Gig Harbor, WA 98335
Ph:(206)219-9811
Fax:(866)210-2481
Co. E-mail: info@imcanet.com
URL: http://www.imcanet.com
Contact: September J. Seibert, Exec. Dir.
Description: Advertising, marketing, public relations, and sales promotion executives of property and casualty insurance companies. Provides members with a forum for enhancing their knowledge of marketing and communications techniques and strategies, so that they can attain the highest standards of professional excellence in serving the information needs of their policyholders, employees, producers and the general public. **Publications:** *UPDATE* (quarterly).

11225 ■ National Association of Health Underwriters
2000 N 14th St., Ste. 450
Arlington, VA 22201
Ph:(703)276-0220

Fax:(703)841-7797
Co. E-mail: info@nahu.org
URL: http://www.nahu.org
Contact: Janet Trautwein, Exec. VP/CEO
Description: Insurance agents and brokers engaged in the promotion, sale, and administration of disability income and health insurance. Sponsors advanced health insurance underwriting and research seminars. Testifies before federal and state committees on pending health insurance legislation. Sponsors Leading Producers Roundtable Awards for leading salesmen. Maintains a speakers' bureau and a political action committee. **Publications:** *Health Insurance Underwriter* (monthly).

11226 ▪ National Association of Insurance and Financial Advisors
2901 Telestar Ct.
Falls Church, VA 22042-1205
Ph:(703)770-8100
Free: 877-866-2432
Co. E-mail: membersupport@naifa.org
URL: http://www.naifa.org
Contact: Susan B. Waters EDM, CEO
Description: Federation of states and local associations representing 75,000 financial planners, life insurance agents, general agents, and managers; associate members are independent insurance agents, general managers of life companies and other life and health insurance professionals. Supports and maintains the highest principles and standards of life and health insurance. Promotes high ethical standards. Informs the public, render community service, and promotes public goodwill. Sponsors public service programs. Offers educational programs. .

11227 ▪ National Association of Insurance Women International
9343 E 95th Ct. S
Tulsa, OK 74133
Ph:(918)294-3700
Free: 800-766-6249
Fax:(918)294-3711
Co. E-mail: joinnaiw@naiw.org
URL: http://www.naiw.org
Contact: Linda Wilson, Pres.
Description: Insurance industry professionals. Promotes continuing education and networking for the professional advancement of its members. Offers education programs, meetings, services, and leadership opportunities. Provides a forum to learn about other disciplines in the insurance industry. **Publications:** *Today's Insurance Professionals* (quarterly).

11228 ▪ National Association of Professional Insurance Agents
400 N Washington St.
Alexandria, VA 22314
Ph:(703)836-9340
Fax:(703)836-1279
Co. E-mail: web@pianet.org
URL: http://www.pianet.com
Contact: Leonard Brevik, Exec. VP
Description: Represents independent agents in all 50 states, Puerto Rico and the District of Columbia. Represents members' interests in government and industry; provides educational programs; compiles statistics; conducts research programs; develops products/services unique to independent agencies; provides information and networking opportunities. **Publications:** *Consumer Brochures for Your Clients*; *PIA Connection* (monthly).

11229 ▪ Physician Insurers Association of America
2275 Research Blvd., Ste. 250
Rockville, MD 20850
Ph:(301)947-9000
Fax:(301)947-9090
Co. E-mail: batchinson@piaa.us
URL: http://www.piaa.us
Contact: Brian Atchinson, Pres./CEO
Description: Physician liability insurance companies, including domestic physician and dental liability insurers, international affiliates, and reinsurers. Seeks to further the best interests of member companies in areas related to physician liability insurance. Focuses

on the availability and affordability of professional liability insurance and the effective delivery of quality healthcare. Conducts research and educational programs; monitors and advocates for legislation. **Publications:** *The Physician Insurer* (quarterly); *PIAA Membership Directory* (annual); *Research Notes* (quarterly).

11230 ▪ Property Casualty Insurers Association of America
2600 S River Rd.
Des Plaines, IL 60018-3286
Ph:(847)297-7800
Fax:(847)297-5064
Co. E-mail: jeffrey.brewer@pciaa.net
URL: http://www.pciaa.net
Contact: David A. Sampson, Pres.
Description: Independent property and casualty insurance companies. Provides advocacy and technical information. Maintains 32 committees, including political action. Conducts educational programs; compiles statistics. **Publications:** *Individual State Profile* (annual); *Legislative Reporter* (biweekly); *State Insurance Department Directory* (annual).

11231 ▪ Risk and Insurance Management Society
1065 Ave. of the Americas, 13th Fl.
New York, NY 10018
Ph:(212)286-9292
Co. E-mail: membership@rims.org
URL: http://www.rims.org
Contact: Scott Clark, Pres./Dir.
Description: Business association serving corporate risk and insurance managers. Dedicated to advancing the practice of risk management, a discipline that protects physical, financial, and human resources. **Publications:** *Annual Risk Management Buyers Guide* (annual); *Compensation and Benefits Survey*; *RIMSCANADA* (quarterly); *RIMSCOPE* (monthly); *Risk Management* (monthly).

11232 ▪ Society of Financial Service Professionals
19 Campus Blvd., Ste. 100
Newtown Square, PA 19073-3239
Ph:(610)526-2500
Free: 800-392-6900
Fax:(610)527-1499
Co. E-mail: info@financialpro.org
URL: http://www.financialpro.org
Contact: James J. Tyrpak, Chm.
Description: Represents the interests of financial advisers. Fosters the development of professional responsibility. Assists clients to achieve personal and business-related financial goals. Offers educational programs, online professional resources and networking opportunities. **Publications:** *Journal of Financial Service Professionals* (bimonthly).

11233 ▪ Society of Insurance Financial Management
PO Box 9001
Mount Vernon, NY 10552
Ph:(914)966-3180
Fax:(914)966-3264
Co. E-mail: sifm@cinn.com
URL: http://www.sifm.org
Contact: Edward J. Majkowski, Pres.
Description: Insurance company officers and employees in financial management departments. .

REFERENCE WORKS

11234 ▪ "2010 Book of Lists" in *Austin Business JournalInc.* (Vol. 29, December 25, 2009, No. 42, pp. 1)
Pub: American City Business Journals
Description: Rankings of companies and organizations within the business services, finance, healthcare, hospitality and travel, insurance, marketing and media, professional services, real estate, education and technology industries in Austin, Texas are presented. Rankings are based on sales, business size, and other statistics.

11235 ▪ "Abroad, Not Overboard" in *Entrepreneur* (Vol. 36, April 2008, No. 4, pp. 68)
Pub: Entrepreneur Media, Inc.
Ed: Crystal Detamore-Rodman. **Description:** Export-Import Bank is an agency created by the U.S. government to help exporters get credit insurance and capital loans by providing them with loan guarantees. The bank, being criticized as supporting more the bigger exporters, has allotted to smaller businesses a bigger portion of the annual credit being approved.

11236 ▪ "All-Star Advice 2010" in *Black Enterprise* (Vol. 41, October 2010, No. 3, pp. 97)
Pub: Earl G. Graves Publishing Co. Inc.
Ed: Renita Burns, Sheiresa Ngo, Marcia Wade Talbert. **Description:** Financial experts share tips on real estate, investing, taxes, insurance and debt management.

11237 ▪ "The Annual Entitlement Lecture: Trustees of Medicare and Social Security Issue Another Dismal Report" in *Barron's* (March 31, 2008)
Pub: Dow Jones & Company, Inc.
Ed: Thomas G. Donlan. **Description:** Expenditures on Medicare hospital insurance and the revenues available to pay for it have led to a gap of capital valued at $38.6 trillion. Slashing the benefits or raising taxes will not solve the gap which exists unless the government saves the money and invests it in private markets.

11238 ▪ "Anthem Leading the Way in Social Tech Revolution" in *Inside Business* (Vol. 13, September-October 2011, No. 5, pp. 1B3)
Pub: Great Lakes Publishing Company
Ed: Ryan Clark. **Description:** Anthem Blue Cross and Blue Shield is leading the way in social technology. The firm's social media initiatives to promote itself are outlined.

11239 ▪ "An Apple a Day" in *Entrepreneur* (Vol. 36, February 2008, No. 2, pp. 19)
Pub: Entrepreneur Media Inc.
Ed: Mark Henricks. **Description:** Businesses are handling rising health coverage costs by providing employees with wellness programs, which include smoking-cessation programs, consumer-directed plans for savings on premiums, and limited medical care plans. Details on the growing trend regarding employee health coverage are discussed.

11240 ▪ "Are Prepaid Legal Services Worthwhile?" in *Contractor* (Vol. 56, December 2009, No. 12, pp. 31)
Pub: Penton Media, Inc.
Ed: Susan Linden McGreevy. **Description:** Companies' provision of legal insurance as an employee benefit in the United States is discussed. Stoppage of premium payment halts employee coverage. It also does not cover all kinds of personal issues.

11241 ▪ "Are You Overinsured? Some Policies May Not Offer Much Additional Benefit" in *Black Enterprise* (Vol. 38, March 2008, No. 8, pp. 126)
Pub: Earl G. Graves Publishing Co. Inc.
Ed: Tamara E. Holmes. **Description:** Travel insurance, identity-theft insurance, specific disease or health condition insurance policies are described. Advice is given to help determine if you are over-insured.

11242 ▪ "Baldwin Connelly Partnership Splits" in *Business Journal Serving Greater Tampa Bay* (Vol. 30, November 19, 2010, No. 48, pp. 1)
Pub: Tampa Bay Business Journal
Ed: Alexis Muellner. **Description:** The fast-growing insurance brokerage Baldwin Connelly is now breaking up after five years. Two different entrepreneurial visions have developed within the organization and founders Lowry Baldwin and John Connell will not take separate tracks. Staffing levels in the firm are expected to remain the same.

11243 ■ "Bank Forces Brooke Founder To Sell His Holdings" in *The Business Journal-Serving Metropolitan Kansas City* (October 10, 2008)
Pub: American City Business Journals, Inc.
Ed: James Dornbrook. Description: Robert Orr who is the founder of Brooke Corp., a franchise of insurance agencies, says that he was forced to sell virtually all of his stocks in the company by creditors. First United Bank held the founder's stock as collateral for two loans worth $5 million and $7.9 million, which were declared in default in September 2008. Details of the selling of the company's stocks are provided.

11244 ■ "Bankruptcy Claims Brooke, Gives Franchisees Hope" in *The Business Journal-Serving Metropolitan Kansas City* (October 31, 2008)
Pub: American City Business Journals, Inc.
Ed: James Dornbrook; Steve Vockrodt. Description: Insurer Brooke Corp. was required to file for Chapter 11 bankruptcy for a deal to sell all of its assets to businessmen Terry Nelson and Lysle Davidson. The new Brooke plans to share contingency fees with franchisees. The impacts of the bankruptcy case on Brooke franchisees are discussed.

11245 ■ *Best's Key Rating Guide*
Pub: A.M. Best Co.
Released: Annual, Latest edition 2010. Price: $180, individuals regular service; shipping/handling (16.95); $800, individuals full service; online; $900, individuals full service; print/online. Covers: Financial and operating characteristics on over 3,400 major property/casualty insurance companies, over 1,650 major life and health insurance companies. Entries include: Company name, city, state, phone, officers' names and titles, date founded, principal lines of business, capitalization, states in which licensed, Best's ratings for previous five years, other key financial ratios and tests. Arrangement: Alphabetical.

11246 ■ "Bills Raise Blues Debate; An Unfair Edge or Level Playing Field?" in *Crain's Detroit Business* (Vol. 24, January 21, 2008, No. 3)
Pub: Crain Communications Inc. - Detroit
Ed: Sherri Begin. Description: Changes in Michigan state law would change the way health insurance can be sold to individuals. Michigan Blue Cross Blue Shield is working to keep its tax-exempt status while staying competitive against for-profit insurers and nonprofit HMOs.

11247 ■ "Blue Cross Confronts Baby Blues" in *Marketing to Women* (Vol. 21, March 2008, No. 3, pp. 3)
Pub: EPM Communications, Inc.
Description: Blue Cross of California has launched a Maternity Depression Program aimed at educating mothers suffering from postpartum depression.

11248 ■ "Blue Cross to Put Kiosk in Mall" in *News & Observer* (November 9, 2010)
Pub: News & Observer
Ed: Alan M. Wolf. Description: Blue Cross and Blue Shield of North Carolina has placed a kiosk in Durham's Streets of Southpoint in order to market its health insurance.

11249 ■ "Brooke Agents Claim Mistreatment" in *The Business Journal-Serving Metropolitan Kansas City* (Vol. 27, October 24, 2008, No. 7, pp. 1)
Pub: American City Business Journals, Inc.
Ed: James Dornbrook. Description: Franchisees of Brooke Corp., an insurance franchise, face uncertainty as their bills remain unpaid and banks threaten to destroy their credit. The company bundled and sold franchisee loans to different banks, but the credit crunch left the company with massive debts and legal disputes.

11250 ■ *Business Insurance—Agent/Broker Profiles Issue*
Pub: Business Insurance
Contact: Paul D. Winston, Editorial Dir.
E-mail: pwinston@businessinsurance.com
Released: Annual, Latest edition 2008. Publication Includes: List of top 10 insurance agents/brokers worldwide specializing in commercial insurance. En-

tries Include: Firm name, address, phone, fax, branch office locations, year established, names of subsidiaries, gross revenues, premium volume, number of employees, principal officers, percent of revenue generated by commercial retail brokerage, acquisitions. Arrangement: Alphabetical by company. Indexes: Geographical.

11251 ■ "Businesses Balk at 1099 Provision in Health Reform Law" in *Baltimore Business Journal* (Vol. 28, August 13, 2010, No. 14, pp. 1)
Pub: Baltimore Business Journal
Ed: Scott Dance. Description: Small business advocates and accountants have criticized the Internal Revenue Service Form 1099 provision in the health care reform law as not worth the cost of time and money. Critics believe the policy would create a deluge of the documents that is too much for the companies or the IRS to handle. Details of the provision are also discussed.

11252 ■ "Businesses Keep a Watchful Eye on Worker's Comp" in *The Business Journal-Serving Greater Tampa Bay* (September 5, 2008)
Pub: American City Business Journals, Inc.
Ed: Jane Meinhardt. Description: Pending a ruling from the Florida Supreme Court that could uphold the 2003 changes on workers' compensation law, the outcome would include restrictions on claimant attorneys' fees and allow the competitive workers' compensation insurance rates to remain low. However, insurance rates are expected to go up if the court overturns the changes.

11253 ■ "Cerner Works the Business Circuit" in *Business Journal-Serving Metropolitan Kansas City* (Vol. 26, October 5, 2007, No. 4, pp. 1)
Pub: American City Business Journals, Inc.
Ed: Rob Roberts. Description: Cerner Corporation is embracing the coming of the electronic medical record exchange by creating a regional health information organization (RHIO) called the CareEntrust. The RHIO convinced health insurers to share claims data with patients and clinicians. At the Center Health Conference, held October 7 to 10, Cerner will demonstrate the software it developed for CareEntrust to the 40,000 healthcare and information technology professionals.

11254 ■ "Changes Sought to Health Law" in *Baltimore Business Journal* (Vol. 28, July 30, 2010, No. 12, pp. 1)
Pub: Baltimore Business Journal
Ed: Kent Hoover. Description: Business groups that opposed health care reform are working to undo parts of the new laws even before they go into effect. Business groups are gaining support for one legislative fix, which is repealing the law's provision that requires all businesses to file 1099 forms with the IRS any time they pay more than $600 a year to another business.

11255 ■ "CNinsure Offers Safety in Numbers" in *Barron's* (Vol. 90, September 13, 2010, No. 37, pp. 29)
Pub: Barron's Editorial & Corporate Headquarters
Ed: Teresa Rivas. Description: China's insurance holding company CNinsure has a long growth future due to the nascent insurance market in the country. It has also been diversifying its offerings and it has a broad network in the nation. The shares of the company are trading cheaply at nearly 14 times its 2011 earnings, and is considered a good point for investors.

11256 ■ "Connecting the Dots Between Wellness and Elder Care" in *Benefits and Compensation Digest* (Vol. 47, August 2010, No. 8, pp. 18)
Pub: International Foundation of Employee Benefit Plans
Ed: Sandra Timmermann. Description: Employees caring for aged and infirm parents deal with time and financial issues and other stresses. The connection

between health status of caregivers and employers' health care costs could be aided by linking programs and benefits with wellness and caregiving.

11257 ■ "Consulting Firm Goes Shopping" in *Crain's Chicago Business* (Vol. 31, April 28, 2008, No. 17, pp. 45)
Pub: Crain Communications, Inc.
Ed: Phuong Ly. Description: Clark & Wamberg LLC was created last year after the merger of Clark Inc. to a Dutch insurance conglomerate. Clark Inc. was a life insurance and benefits consultancy which had been on a downslide, returning just 5.6 percent a year to shareholders. In contrast Clark & Wamberg posted first-year revenue of $106.8 million, fueled by business from its executive compensation and health care clients.

11258 ■ "Continuously Monitoring Workers' Comp Can Limit Costs" in *Crain's Cleveland Business* (Vol. 28, October 8, 2007, No. 40, pp. 21)
Pub: Crain Communications, Inc.
Ed: Michael Lagnoni. Description: When operating without a plan for managing its workers' compensation program, a company risks losing money. For most companies workers' compensation insurance premiums are often reduced to an annual budget entry but employers who are actively involved in the management of their programs are more likely to experience reductions in premiums and limit indirect costs associated with claims.

11259 ■ "Controversial Bill Could Raise Rates for Homeowners" in *Orlando Business Journal* (Vol. 26, January 22, 2010, No. 34, pp. 1)
Pub: American City Business Journals
Ed: Oscar Pedro Musibay; Christopher Boyd. Description: Florida Senate Bill 876 and its companion House Bill 447 are pushing for the deregulation of rates in the state's home insurance market. The bill is being opposed by consumer advocates as it could mean higher rates for homeowner insurance policies.

11260 ■ "Cost of Md. Health Plan Not Known" in *Baltimore Business Journal* (Vol. 28, September 3, 2010, No. 17, pp. 1)
Pub: Baltimore Business Journal
Ed: Emily Mullin. Description: United States health reform is seen to result in increased health insurance prices in Maryland. However, health care reform advocates claim a new marketplace and increased competition will help keep costs down.

11261 ■ "Courting Canadian Customers Confounds Car Dealers" in *Business First Buffalo* (November 9, 2007, pp. 1)
Pub: American City Business Journals, Inc.
Ed: James Fink. Description: Strength of the Canadian dollar has led to an influx of potential customers for the Western New York automobile industry, but franchising restrictions and licensing as well as insurance issues have limited the potential of having larger sales figures. Border and trade issues that affect the car industry in WNY are also discussed.

11262 ■ "CreFirst To Reward Doctors for Reducing Costs, Improving Care" in *Baltimore Business Journal* (Vol. 28, June 4, 2010, No. 4, pp. 1)
Pub: Baltimore Business Journal
Ed: Scott Graham. Description: CareFirst Blue Cross Blue Shield plans to introduce a program that dangles big financial rewards to physicians who change the way they deliver primary care by improving the health of their sickest patients while reducing costs. The company will soon begin recruiting primary care physicians in Maryland, Washington DC, and Northern Virginia.

11263 ■ "Crop Insurance Harvest Prices in 2011" in *Farm Industry News* (November 9, 2011)
Pub: Penton Business Media Inc.
Ed: Gary Schnitkey. Description: Risk Management Agency (RMA) reported harvest prices for corn and soybean grown in the Midwest with corn at $6.32 per

bushel, 31 cents higher than the project $6.01; soybeans were at $12.14 per bushel, down $1.35 from the projected price of $13.49.

11264 ■ "Cutting Health Care Costs: the 3-Legged Stool" in HR Specialist (Vol. 8, September 2010, No. 9, pp. 1)
Pub: Capitol Information Group Inc.
Description: Employer spending on health insurance benefits to employees is investigated.

11265 ■ "Diana Bonta: Keeping People Healthy and Thriving" in Hispanic Business (Vol. 30, April 2008, No. 4, pp. 30)
Pub: Hispanic Business
Ed: Leanndra Martinez. **Description:** Diana Bonta serves as vice president of public affairs for Kaiser Permanente and is a strong advocate for health reform and improving access to health care. In order to better serve the underinsured and uninsured, she directs Kaiser's Community Benefit division that devoted $369 million last year to this cause.

11266 ■ Dictionary of Real Estate Terms
Pub: Barron's Educational Series, Incorporated
Ed: Jack P. Friedman, Jack C. Harris, J. Bruce Lindeman. **Released:** October 2008. **Price:** $13.99. **Description:** More than 2,500 real estate terms relating to mortgages and financing, brokerage law, architecture, rentals and leases, property insurance, and more.

11267 ■ "Discovery Communications" in Workforce Management (Vol. 88, December 14, 2009, No. 13, pp. 17)
Pub: Crain Communications, Inc.
Ed: Jeremy Smerd. **Description:** Discovery Communications provides its employees a wealth of free health services via a comprehensive work-site medical clinic that is available to its employees and their dependents. Overview of the company's innovative approach to healthcare is presented.

11268 ■ "Doctors Eye Rating Plan With Caution" in The Business Journal-Portland (Vol. 25, July 4, 2008, No. 17, pp. 1)
Pub: American City Business Journals, Inc.
Ed: Robin J. Moody. **Description:** Doctors in Portland, Oregon are wary of a new Providence Health Plan system that rates their performance on patients with certain medical conditions. The system is expected to discourage wasteful procedures, thereby, saving employers' money. Other mechanics of the rating system are also discussed.

11269 ■ "Doctors, Health Insurers Squabble Over Who Sends Patients the Bill" in Baltimore Business Journal (Vol. 27, February 6, 2010)
Pub: American City Business Journals
Ed: Scott Graham. **Description:** Issue of allowing patients to send reimbursement checks to physicians who are not part of their health insurer's provider network is being debated in Maryland. Details on the proposed Maryland bill and the arguments presented by doctors and insurers are outlined.

11270 ■ "Doctor's Orders" in Canadian Business (Vol. 79, November 20, 2006, No. 23, pp. 73)
Pub: Rogers Media
Ed: Jeff Sanford. **Description:** George Cohon, the founder of McDonald's in Canada and Russia, speaks about the Canadian market and the experience of starting McDonald's in Canada.

11271 ■ "Doctors Warn of Problems" in Austin Business JournalInc. (Vol. 29, December 4, 2009, No. 39, pp. 1)
Pub: American City Business Journals
Ed: Sandra Zaragoza. **Description:** Texas physicians have voiced their concern regarding the potential cuts in Medicare reimbursement rates due to the 21 percent cut imposed by Centers for Medicare and Medicaid at the start of 2010. Experts believe the large cuts would result in the closure of some physician practices. Details of the Texas Medical Association's stand on the health reform bill are examined.

11272 ■ "Doing Without" in Baltimore Business Journal (Vol. 28, June 11, 2010, No. 5, pp. 1)
Pub: Baltimore Business Journal
Ed: Scott Graham. **Description:** Maryland Health Care Commission report figures have shown only 47,661 small businesses provided some level of health coverage to 381,517 employees in 2009. These numbers are down from 51,283 employers who offered benefits to 407,983 employees in 2008 to highlight a disturbing trend in Maryland's small-group insurance market. Reasons for the drop are discussed.

11273 ■ "E-Medical Records Save Money, Time in Ann Arbor" in Crain's Detroit Business (Vol. 24, January 21, 2008, No. 3, pp. 6)
Pub: Crain Communications Inc. - Detroit
Ed: Jay Greene. **Description:** Ann Arbor Area Health Information Exchange is improving patient outcomes by sharing clinical and administrative data in electronic medical record systems.

11274 ■ "Elder Care Costs Surge" in National Underwriter Life & Health (Vol. 114, November 8, 2020, No. 21, pp. 25)
Pub: Summit Business Media
Ed: Trevor Thomas. **Description:** Nursing home and assisted living rates rose from 2009 to 2010, according to MetLife Mature Market Institute. Statistical data included.

11275 ■ "Employer Jobless Tax Could Rise" in Sacramento Business Journal (Vol. 28, May 27, 2011, No. 13, pp. 1)
Pub: Sacramento Business Journal
Ed: Kathy Robertson. **Description:** The government of California is facing an estimated $16 billion deficit in its unemployment insurance fund. Unemployment insurance spending has exceeded employer contributions to the fund. Statistics on unemployment insurance is included.

11276 ■ "Employers Tied in Knots" in Sacramento Business Journal (Vol. 25, August 15, 2008, No. 24, pp. 1)
Pub: American City Business Journals, Inc.
Ed: Kathy Robertson. **Description:** Conflicting laws on same sex marriage have been posing problems for companies, and insurers in California. The court ruling that allowed gay marriages has created differences between state and federal laws. Federal laws on same-sex spouse taxation are also seen to complicate the issue.

11277 ■ "Employers Waking Up to Effects of Workers' Sleep Problems" in Crain's Cleveland Business (Vol. 28, December 3, 2007, No. 48, pp. 18)
Pub: Crain Communications, Inc.
Ed: Jennifer Keirn. **Description:** Employers are beginning to realize that poor sleep quality can impact their bottom lines with higher health care costs and more lost-time accidents. The National Institutes of Health estimates that sleep deprivation, sleep disorders and excessive daytime sleepiness add about $15 billion to our national health care bill and cost employers $50 billion in lost productivity.

11278 ■ "Experts Take the Temp of Obama Plan" in The Business Journal-Serving Metropolitan Kansas City (Vol. 27, November 14, 2008, No. 10)
Pub: American City Business Journals, Inc.
Ed: Rob Roberts. **Description:** Kansas City, Missouri-based employee benefits experts say president-elect Barack Obama's health care reform plan is on track. Insurance for children and capitalization for health information technology are seen as priority areas. The plan is aimed at reducing the number of uninsured people in the United States.

11279 ■ "Export Initiative Launched" in Philadelphia Business Journal (Vol. 28, December 11, 2009, No. 43, pp. 1)
Pub: American City Business Journals
Ed: Athena D. Merritt. **Description:** The first initiative that came out of the partnership between the Export-Import Bank of the US, the city of Philadelphia, and

the World Trade Center of Greater Philadelphia is presented. A series of export finance workshops have featured Ex-Im Bank resources that can provide Philadelphia businesses with working capital, insurance protection and buyer financing.

11280 ■ "Firms Sue Doracon to Recoup More Than $1M in Unpaid Bills" in Baltimore Business Journal (Vol. 28, July 9, 2010, No. 9, pp. 1)
Pub: Baltimore Business Journal
Ed: Scott Dance. **Description:** Concrete supplier Paul J. Rach Inc., Selective Insurance Company, and equipment leasing firm Colonial Pacific Leasing Corporation intend to sue Baltimore, Maryland-based Doracon Contracting Inc. for $1 million in unpaid bills. Doracon owed Colonial Pacific $794,000 and the equipment is still in Doracon's possession. Selective Insurance and Paul J. Rach respectively seek $132,000 and $88,000.

11281 ■ "For All It's Worth" in Entrepreneur (Vol. 36, April 2008, No. 4, pp. 46)
Pub: Entrepreneur Media, Inc.
Ed: Farnoosh Torabi. **Description:** Discusses the federal estate tax system requires that 45 percent of the money beyond $2 million be given to the government. Ways on how to minimize the effects of estate tax on assets include: creating bypass trusts for married couples; setting up an irrevocable life insurance trust to avoid taxation of estate for insurance benefactors; and having annual gift tax exclusion.

11282 ■ "Generational Savvy" in Hawaii Business (Vol. 54, August 2008, No. 2, pp. 135)
Pub: Hawaii Business Publishing
Ed: Jolyn Okimoto Rosa. **Description:** Lawrence Takeo Kagawa founded Security Insurance Agency, later renamed Occidental Underwriters of Hawaii Ltd., in 1933 to provide insurance to Asian-Americans in Hawaii at lower premiums. Details on the company's history, growth investment products and Transamerica Life products and 75 years of family-run business are discussed.

11283 ■ Green Your Small Business: Profitable Ways to Become an Ecopreneur
Pub: McGraw-Hill
Ed: Scott Cooney. **Released:** November 7, 2008. **Price:** $19.95 paperback. **Description:** Advice and guidance is given to help any entrepreneur start, build or grow a green business, focusing on green business basics, market research and financing, as well as handling legal and insurance issues.

11284 ■ "Greenberg Sues U.S. Over AIG Rescue" in Wall Street Journal Eastern Edition (November 22 , 2011, pp. C3)
Pub: Dow Jones & Company Inc.
Ed: Liam Pleven, Serena Ng. **Description:** Former Chief Executive Officer of American International Group Inc., Maurice R. 'Hank' Greenberg, has filed a lawsuit against the United States and the Federal Reserve Bank of New York on behalf of shareholders and his company, Starr International Company Inc., claiming that the government was wrong in taking control of the insurance giant and used it to move tens of millions of dollars to the trading partners of AIG.

11285 ■ "Harleysville Eyes Growth After Nationwide Deal" in Philadelphia Business Journal (Vol. 30, October 7, 2011, No. 34, pp. 1)
Pub: American City Business Journals Inc.
Ed: Jeff Blumenthal. **Description:** Harleysville Group announced growth plans after the company was sold to Columbus, Ohio-based Nationwide Mutual Insurance Company for about $1.63 billion. Nationwide gained an independent agency platform in 32 states with the Harleysville deal.

11286 ■ "Health Alliance Could Sell Group" in Business Courier (Vol. 27, June 18, 2010, No. 7, pp. 1)
Pub: Business Courier
Ed: James Ritchie. **Description:** Health Alliance could sell the 31-doctor Greater Cincinnati Associated Physicians Group. The group has seen several

members withdraw ever since the group filed a complaint asking to be released from services to Health Alliance.

11287 ■ "Health Care Braces for Federal Cuts" in *Boston Business Journal* **(Vol. 29, August 19, 2011, No. 15, pp. 1)**
Pub: American City Business Journals Inc.

Ed: Scott Dance. **Description:** The healthcare industry in Baltimore is expecting negative effects from the federal debt ceiling on Medicare and Medicaid spending. Medicare funds are expected to be slashed and could impact hospitals and doctors.

11288 ■ "Health Care of the Future" in *Business Journal Serving Greater Tampa Bay* **(Vol. 30, November 19, 2010, No. 48, pp. 1)**
Pub: Tampa Bay Business Journal

Ed: Margie Manning. **Description:** Information about accountable care organizations (ACO), which are integrated care systems with doctors and hospitals working closely together to handle patient care, is provided. The Patient Protection and Affordable Care Act paved the way for ACOs as Medicare demonstration projects.

11289 ■ "Health Centers Plan Expansion" in *Crain's Detroit Business* **(Vol. 25, June 15, 2009, No. 24, pp. 3)**
Pub: Crain Communications Inc. - Detroit

Ed: Jay Greene. **Description:** Detroit has five federally qualified health centers that plan to receive over $3 million in federal stimulus money that will be used to expand projects that will care for uninsured patients.

11290 ■ "Health Insurance Dilemmas" in *Hispanic Business* **(January-February 2008, pp. 58)**
Pub: Hispanic Business

Ed: Anna Davison. **Description:** Small business owners discussed the challenges they face providing health insurance to employees.

11291 ■ "Health IT Regulations Generate Static Among Providers" in *Philadelphia Business Journal* **(Vol. 28, January 29, 2010, No. 50, pp. 1)**
Pub: American City Business Journals

Ed: John George. **Description:** US Centers for Medicaid and Medicare Services and the Office of the National Coordinator for Health Information Technology have proposed rules regarding the meaningful use of electronic health records. The rules must be complied with by hospitals and physicians to qualify for federal stimulus funds.

11292 ■ "Health Reform Could Expand HSA-Based Plans" in *Workforce Management* **(Vol. 88, December 14, 2009, No. 13, pp. 6)**
Pub: Crain Communications, Inc.

Ed: Jeremy Smerd. **Description:** HSA-qualified plans are the cheapest insurance plans on the market as they have a higher deductible but cost less upfront. If health care reform passes, HSA-qualified plans should benefit greatly.

11293 ■ "Health Reform How-To" in *Business Courier* **(Vol. 26, December 11, 2009, No. 33, pp. 1)**
Pub: American City Business Journals, Inc.

Ed: James Ritchie. **Description:** Greater Cincinnati health care leaders shared views about the health care reform bill. Respondents included the Cincinnati Visiting Nurse's Wallen Falberg, healthcare consultant Hirsch Cohen, Greater Cincinnati Health Council's Coleen O'Toole, Employer Health Care Alliance's Sharron DiMario, Legal Aid Society of Greater Cincinnati's Col Owens, Christ Hospital's Susan Croushore, and Humana of Ohio's Tim Cappel.

11294 ■ "Healthcare: How To Get a Better Deal" in *Inc.* **(November 2007, pp. 34)**
Pub: Gruner & Jahr USA Publishing

Ed: Sarah Goldstein. **Description:** Things to consider when choosing an insurance carrier for your employees are explored.

11295 ■ "Here's How Buffett Spent 2007" in *Barron's* **(Vol. 88, March 10, 2008, No. 10, pp. 48)**
Pub: Dow Jones & Company, Inc.

Ed: Andrew Bary. **Description:** Earnings of Berkshire Hathaway may decline in 2008 due to a tighter insurance market, but its portfolio is expected to continue growing. Warren Buffett purchased $19.1 billion worth of stocks in 2007.

11296 ■ "Home Sweet Home" in *Canadian Business* **(Vol. 79, October 9, 2006, No. 20, pp. 22)**
Pub: Rogers Media

Ed: Peter Shawn Taylor. **Description:** Changes being made in the management of mortgage insurance business in Canada are critically analyzed.

11297 ■ "Hospital Fighting for Its Life; Board of St. Anthony Scrambles to Stem Losses" in *Crain's Chicago Business* **(April 28, 2008)**
Pub: Crain Communications, Inc.

Ed: Mike Colias. **Description:** Chicago's Catholic health chain was looking to sell the money-losing hospital St. Anthony Hospital on the West Side but with the financial picture improving and no merger offers in the works the investment bank hired to shop the hospital is hoping to operate the 111-year-old facility as an independent entity. St. Anthony serves as a "safety net" for the region since an increasing number of its patients are uninsured or on public aid, which pays far less than commercial insurers.

11298 ■ "Hospitals See Major Shift To Outpatient Care" in *The Business Journal-Milwaukee* **(Vol. 25, September 12, 2008, No. 51, pp. A1)**
Pub: American City Business Journals, Inc.

Ed: Corrinne Hess. **Description:** Statistics show that the revenue of Wisconsin hospitals from outpatient medical care is about to surpass revenue from hospital patients who stay overnight. This revenue increase is attributed to new technology and less-invasive surgery. Trends show that the shift toward outpatient care actually started in the late 1980s and early 1990s.

11299 ■ "How to Maximize Your Investment Income" in *Contractor* **(Vol. 56, December 2009, No. 12, pp. 33)**
Pub: Penton Media, Inc.

Ed: Irv Blackman. **Description:** Private placement life insurance (PPLI) can minimize taxes and protect assets. PPLI is a form of variable universal insurance that is offered privately. Risk of insurance company illiquidity is avoided as investments are placed in separate accounts.

11300 ■ *How to Start a Home-Based Senior Care Business: Check-in-Care, Transportation Services, Shopping and Cooking*
Pub: The Globe Pequot Press

Ed: James L. Ferry. **Released:** January 1, 2010. **Price:** $18.95. **Description:** Information is provided to start a home-based senior care business.

11301 ■ "How a Unique Culture Proposition Became a USP" in *Business Strategy Review* **(Vol. 21, Spring 2010, No. 1, pp. 52)**
Pub: Wiley-Blackwell

Ed: Adam Kingl. **Description:** How can you transform the way you do things into a compelling sales proposition? Zurich Insurance has created a Unique Culture Proposition which may be its Unique Selling Point.

11302 ■ "Humana: Take Pay Cut or Get Out" in *Business Courier* **(Vol. 24, February 1, 2008, No. 43, pp. 1)**
Pub: American City Business Journals, Inc.

Ed: James Ritchie. **Description:** Insurer Humana Inc. is removing some surgery centers from its network for refusing to welcome the new payment system. Evendale Surgery Center and the Surgery Center of Cincinnati will be removed from the network because they resist the newly imposed lower rates. Speculations over Humana's decision are discussed.

11303 ■ "IBC Reverses Member Slide" in *Philadelphia Business Journal* **(Vol. 30, September 23, 2011, No. 32, pp. 1)**
Pub: American City Business Journals Inc.

Ed: John George. **Description:** Health insurer Independence Blue Cross (IBC) added more than 40,000 members across all product lines since the start of 2011. It has 2.2 million members in Pennsylvania's Philadelphia region and 3.1 million members across the U.S. Services and other growth-related plans of IBC are covered.

11304 ■ "Impressive Numbers: Companies Experience Substantial Increases in Dollars, Employment" in *Hispanic Business* **(July-August 2007)**
Pub: Hispanic Business

Ed: Derek Reveron. **Description:** Profiles of five fastest growing Hispanic companies reporting increases in revenue and employment include Brightstar, distributor of wireless products; Greenway Ford Inc., a car dealership; Fred Loya Insurance, auto insurance carrier; and Group O, packaging company; and Diverse Staffing, Inc., an employment and staffing firm.

11305 ■ "Injured Workers Caught in the Middle" in *Sacramento Business Journal* **(Vol. 28, June 10, 2011, No. 15, pp. 1)**
Pub: Sacramento Business Journal

Ed: Kelly Johnson. **Description:** A bill that would extend the cap on disability payments to nearly five years is in the works, but employers and insurance companies fear it would increase their costs. Proponents of the bill say, however, that it would correct unfairness suffered by the employees. Features of the bill are discussed as well as its effects on both parties and the State of California.

11306 ■ "Insurance Firm Consolidates Offices; Integro Finds the Right Price Downtown" in *Crain's New York Business* **(January 14, 2008)**
Pub: Crain Communications, Inc.

Description: Integro insurance brokers is relocating its headquarters to 1 State Street Plaza, where it will consolidate its operations in March. The firm feels that the upscale design will provide an appropriate setting for entertaining clients and an engaging work environment for employees.

11307 ■ "Insurance: Marathon Effort" in *Canadian Business* **(Vol. 80, January 29, 2007, No. 3, pp. 11)**
Pub: Rogers Media

Ed: Jeff Sanford. **Description:** The efforts of the insurance firm ING Canada Inc. to manage its relations with its customers are described. The enhancement of the insurance services provided by the company is discussed.

11308 ■ "An Insurance Roll-Up In Danger of Unraveling" in *Barron's* **(Vol. 88, March 17, 2008, No. 11, pp. 51)**
Pub: Dow Jones & Company, Inc.

Ed: Bill Alpert. **Description:** Shares of National Financial Partners have fallen below their initial offering price as sputtering sales and management turnover leave many investors wondering. One of the company's star brokers is being sued for their "life settlement" contracts while another broker is being pursued by the IRS for unpaid taxes.

11309 ■ "Insuraprise Growing Fast" in *Austin Business Journal* **(Vol. 31, April 22, 2011, No. 7, pp. 1)**
Pub: American City Business Journals Inc.

Ed: Sandra Zaragoza. **Description:** Austin, Texas-based Insuraprise Inc. is finalizing the purchase of a 24,000-square-foot office at 12116 Jekel Circle. The firm, with 23 salespeople and sales that are growing nearly 300 percent over the past 18 months, will now have room to grow. Insuraprise plans to hire 35 new salespersons for its call center.

11310 ■ "Insurer Buys Foundation's Uptown HQ" in *Charlotte Business Journal* **(Vol. 25, December 17, 2010, No. 39, pp. 1)**
Pub: Charlotte Business Journal

Ed: Will Boye. **Description:** Charlotte, North Carolina-based Synergy Coverage Solutions has purchased the three-story building owned by Foundations For the Carolinas for slightly more than $3 million. Synergy plans to relocate its operation in the uptown building by August 2011.

11311 ■ "Insurers No Longer Paying Premium for Advertising" in *Brandweek* **(Vol. 49, April 21, 2008, No. 16, pp. SR3)**
Pub: VNU Business Media, Inc.

Ed: Eric Newman. **Description:** Insurance companies are cutting their advertising budgets after years of accelerated double-digit growth in spending due to the economic downturn, five years of record-breaking ad spend and a need to cut expenditures as claims costs rise and a competitive market keeps premiums in place. Statistical data included.

11312 ■ "Insurers Warn Brokers" in *Sacramento Business Journal* **(Vol. 25, August 22, 2008, No. 25, pp. 1)**
Pub: American City Business Journals, Inc.

Ed: Kathy Robertson. **Description:** Sacramento, California-based health plans have warned insurance brokers not to combine two different kinds of insurance products or they will be stricken from the sales network. The health plans also asked employers to promise not to combine plans with self-insurance. Such schemes are seen to destroy lower-premium health products.

11313 ■ "Internet Marketing 2.0: Closing the Online Chat Gap" in *Agent's Sales Journal* **(November 2009, pp. 14)**
Pub: Summit Business Media

Ed: Jeff Denenholz. **Description:** Advice regarding the implementation of an Internet marketing strategy for insurance agencies includes how and why to incorporate a chat feature in which a sales agent can communicate in real-time with potential or existing customers. It is important to understand if appropriate response mechanisms are in place to convert leads into actual sales.

11314 ■ "Is Hawaii Ready for Universal Health Care?" in *Hawaii Business* **(Vol. 53, February 2008, No. 8, pp. 26)**
Pub: Hawaii Business Publishing

Description: Representative Lyn Finnegan does not believe that a universal health is good for Hawaii as health insurance for everyone will be difficult to achieve. Representative John M. Mizuno says that House Bill 1008 introduced in the state was a landmark for Hawaii as it will provide the people with health care insurance. Other details about their opinion on the topic are presented.

11315 ■ "Is There a Doctor In the House?" in *Black Enterprise* **(Vol. 41, December 2010, No. 5, pp. 42)**
Pub: Earl G. Graves Publishing Co. Inc.

Ed: Renita Burns. **Description:** Health insurance premiums have increased between 15 percent and 20 percent for small business owners, making it one of the most expensive costs. Ways to evaluate a health plan's costs and effectiveness are examined.

11316 ■ "The Keeper of Records" in *Black Enterprise* **(Vol. 41, December 2010, No. 5, pp. 54)**
Pub: Earl G. Graves Publishing Co. Inc.

Ed: Denise Campbell. **Description:** Medical billing and coding, submission of claims to health insurance companies and Medicare or Medicaid for payment is one of the fastest growing disciplines in healthcare.

11317 ■ *King of Capital*
Pub: John Wiley and Sons, Inc.

Ed: Amey Stone; Mike Brewster. **Released:** 2004. **Price:** $16.95. **Description:** Biography of Sandy Weill describes how he became a billionaire business giant by creating successful companies from smaller, sometimes failing firms; creating successful new products where none previously existed; and making deals no one thought possible. He is also responsible for changing the landscape of the banking industry and insurance business when he created Citigroup in 1998, the world's largest financial services firm.

11318 ■ "Labor Pains" in *Canadian Business* **(Vol. 79, August 14, 2006, No. 16-17, pp. 80)**
Pub: Rogers Media

Description: Canada's employment insurance is analyzed in view of the growing shortage of labor.

11319 ■ "Law Allows Captive Insurance Companies to Form in State" in *Crain's Detroit Business* **(Vol. 24, March 31, 2008, No. 13, pp. 29)**
Pub: Crain Communications, Inc.

Description: Discusses new legislation allowing the formation of captive insurance companies in the state of Michigan; these companies are subsidiaries of non-insurers that are formed primarily to insure some or all of the risks of its parent company.

11320 ■ "Leave Policies: How to Avoid Leave-Related Lawsuits" in *Employee Benefit News* **(Vol. 25, December 1, 2011, No. 15, pp. 12)**
Pub: SourceMedia Inc.

Ed: John F. Galvin. **Description:** Tips for employers when adding disability and maternity leave benefits to workers are outlined, with focus on ways to avoid leave-related lawsuits.

11321 ■ "Lifetime Planning with a Twist" in *Contractor* **(Vol. 56, July 2009, No. 7, pp. 40)**
Pub: Penton Media, Inc.

Ed: Irv Blackman. **Description:** Private Placement Life Insurance lets wealthy investors make their investment gains tax-free and can be set up so investors can make tax-free loans from the policy. This can be used on a younger member of the family as a wealth-building strategy if the investor is uninsurable.

11322 ■ "Local Hospitals Wage Wars on 'Bounce-Backs'" in *Business Courier* **(Vol. 27, July 30, 2010, No. 13, pp. 1)**
Pub: Business Courier

Ed: James Ritchie. **Description:** Health care organizations in Greater Cincinnati area have tried a number of care and follow up programs, primarily focused on congestive heart failure to prevent readmissions to hospitals. Hospital administrators have made the averting of bounce-backs a priority due to new federal government plans on reimbursement.

11323 ■ "Luster Lost" in *Saint Louis Business Journal* **(Vol. 32, September 16, 2011, No. 3, pp. 1)**
Pub: Saint Louis Business Journal

Ed: E.B. Solomont. **Description:** Express Cripts shares have plunged 22.71 percent since late July amid regulatory concerns, as the luster of the second-largest deal announced for 2011 wore off. Express Scripts has become the largest pharmacy benefit manager in the country after the $29 billion deal to take rival Medco Health Solutions.

11324 ■ *Managing Health Benefits in Small and Mid-Sized Organizations*
Pub: Amacom

Ed: Patricia Halo. **Released:** July 1999. **Description:** Comprehensive guide for developing health care plans for companies employing between 50 and 5,000 employees in order to provide employees with better health care at lower prices.

11325 ■ "Markel American Insurance Company Announces Wedding and Special Event Insurance for Consumers" in *Benzinga.com* **(February 16, 2011)**
Pub: Benzinga.com

Ed: Benzinga Staff. **Description:** Markel American Insurance Company, headquartered in Waukesha, Wisconsin has launched its new special event insurance and wedding insurance to protect both liabilities and cancellations associated with these events.

11326 ■ "Maryland Hospitals Cope with Rare Drop in Patient Admissions" in *Boston Business Journal* **(Vol. 29, September 23, 2011, No. 20, pp. 1)**
Pub: American City Business Journals Inc.

Ed: Scott Dance. **Description:** Admissions to Maryland hospitals have dropped to less than 700,000 in fiscal year 2010 and initial figures for fiscal 2011 show in-patient admissions are now nearing 660,000. The decline can be partly attributed to new ways health insurers are paying hospitals for care and to the financial reward hospitals get for cutting back on admissions.

11327 ■ "The Massachusetts Mess: Good Health Care Is Expensive" in *Barron's* **(Vol. 89, July 27, 2009, No. 30, pp. 39)**
Pub: Dow Jones & Co., Inc.

Ed: Thomas G. Donlan. **Description:** Massachusetts' mandatory health insurance has produced the highest rate of insurance coverage among the states but the state is now unable to afford its dream of universal coverage just three years after they enacted it. This supposed model for federal health-care reform is turning out to be a joke.

11328 ■ "Meadowbrook CEO Sees 20 Percent Growth With New Acquisition" in *Crain's Detroit Business* **(Vol. 24, March 10, 2008, No. 10, pp. 4)**
Pub: Crain Communications, Inc.

Ed: Jay Greene. **Description:** Discusses the major turnaround of Meadowbrook Insurance Group after Robert Cubbin became CEO and implemented a new business strategy.

11329 ■ "Meadowbrook To Acquire ProCentury in $272.6 Million Deal" in *Crain's Detroit Business* **(Vol. 24, February 25, 2008, No. 8, pp. 4)**
Pub: Crain Communications Inc. - Detroit

Description: Meadowbrook Insurance Group, based in Southfield, Michigan reports its proposed acquisition of ProCentury Corporation based in Columbus, Ohio. Meadowbrook provides risk-management to agencies, professional and trade associations and small-to-midsize businesses.

11330 ■ "Medicaid Insurers See Growth in Small Business Market" in *Boston Business Journal* **(Vol. 31, July 15, 2011, No. 25, pp. 1)**
Pub: Boston Business Journal

Ed: Julie M. Donnelly. **Description:** BMC HealthNet Plan announced plans to launch small business products to serve small businesses that are priced out of rising premium rates at large Massachusetts insurers. BMC joined competitors CeltiCare Health Plan and Neighborhood Health Plan in augmenting its core business.

11331 ■ "Medicare Plans Step Up Battle for Subscribers" in *Sacramento Business Journal* **(Vol. 28, October 21, 2011, No. 34, pp. 1)**
Pub: Sacramento Business Journal

Ed: Kathy Robertson. **Description:** California's market for health plans have become increasingly competitive as more than 313,000 seniors try to figure out the best plans to meet their needs for 2012. Health plans are rated on Medicare materials to help consumers distinguish among the Medicare health maintenance organizations (HMOs).

11332 ■ "The Moody Blues" in *Entrepreneur* **(Vol. 36, April 2008, No. 4, pp. 87)**
Pub: Entrepreneur Media, Inc.

Ed: Mark Henricks. **Description:** Depression among employees can affect their productivity and cost the company. Businesses with a workforce that is likely to have depression should inform their employees about the health benefits covered by insurance. Other details on how to address depression concerns among employees are discussed.

11333 ■ "More Businesses Will Shift Health Costs to Workers" in *Business Review, Albany New York* **(Vol. 34, November 16, 2007, No. 33, pp. 1)**
Pub: American City Business Journals, Inc.

Ed: Barbara Pinckney. **Description:** Survey conducted by consulting firm Benetech Inc. showed that sixty percent of employers are planning to increase payroll deductions to pay for health insurance premiums. More than ninety percent of the employers prefer HMO plans, followed by Preferred Provider Organizations. Other details of the survey are discussed.

11334 ■ "More Small Businesses Willing to Fund Employees' Benefits" in *Baltimore Business Journal* **(Vol. 28, June 18, 2010, No. 6, pp. 1)**
Pub: Baltimore Business Journal
Ed: Scott Graham. **Description:** An increasing number of small businesses in Maryland are tapping into potentially cheaper self-funded health plans instead of providing fully insured benefits to employees through traditional health plans. Self-funded health plans charge employers for health care up to a specified level. Economic implications of self-funded plans to small businesses are discussed.

11335 ■ "Most States Have High-Risk Health Insurance Pools" in *Crain's Detroit Business* **(Vol. 24, March 24, 2008, No. 12, pp. 31)**
Pub: Crain Communications, Inc.
Ed: Jay Greene. **Description:** High-risk health insurance pools, designed to cover individuals with medical conditions that essentially make them otherwise uninsurable, are being debated by the Senate Health Policy Committee; the pool concept is supported by Blue Cross Blue Shield of Michigan and contested by a number of consumer groups and competing health insurers.

11336 ■ "Nationwide Bank Ready for December Conversion" in *Business First-Columbus* **(October 12, 2007, pp. A1)**
Pub: American City Business Journals, Inc.
Ed: Adrian Burns. **Description:** Nationwide Bank will increase marketing to its customers, including the 45,000 that came from the acquisition of Nationwide Federal Credit Union in December 2006. Upgrading its online banking system and Website will bring the company and its services closer to clients. The influence of the insurance industry on the bank's marketing strategy is also examined.

11337 ■ "New Database Brings Doctors Out of the Dark" in *Business Courier* **(Vol. 26, October 23, 2009, No. 26, pp. 1)**
Pub: American City Business Journals, Inc.
Ed: James Ritchie. **Description:** A database created by managed care consulting firm Praesentia allows doctors in Cincinnati to compare average reimbursements from health insurance companies to doctors in different areas. Specialist doctors in the city are paid an average of $172.25 for every office consultation.

11338 ■ "New Health Law, Lack of Docs Collide on Cape Cod" in *Boston Business Journal* **(Vol. 27, October 12, 2007, No. 37, pp. 1)**
Pub: American City Business Journals Inc.
Ed: Mark Hollmer. **Description:** There is a shortage of primary care providers at Outer Cape Health Services in Massachusetts, with the isolation of the area and as physicians look for higher paying careers in specialty positions. The Commonwealth Health Insurance Connector Authority is pushing for a new health insurance law and is working with Cape Cod Chamber of Commerce to conduct outreach programs.

11339 ■ "North American Pet Health Insurance Market Poised for Growth" in *Pet Product News* **(Vol. 64, December 2010, No. 12, pp. 4)**
Pub: BowTie Inc.
Ed: David Lummis. **Description:** The pet health insurance market is expected to further grow after posting about $350 million in sales in 2009, a gain of more than $40 million. Pet insurance firms have offered strategies such as product humanization in response to this growth forecast. Meanwhile, pet insurance shoppers have been provided more by insurance firms with wider choices.

11340 ■ "Norvax University Health Insurance Sales Training and Online Marketing Conference" in *Internet Wire* **(January 27, 2010)**
Pub: Comtex News Network, Inc.
Description: Overview of the Norvax University Marketing and Sales Success Conference Tour which includes insurance sales training seminars, proven and innovative online marketing techniques and a host of additional information and networking opportunities.

11341 ■ "Now the Real Work Begins" in *Baltimore Business Journal* **(Vol. 28, October 15, 2010, No. 23, pp. 1)**
Pub: Baltimore Business Journal
Ed: Emily Mullin. **Description:** The Henry J. Kaiser Family Foundation's survey shows nearly 53 percent of Americans remain confused about health care reform and it was up to the states to educate the people. However, Maryland is still trying to figure out how to conduct the campaign without guidance or funding from the Federal government.

11342 ■ "Open Enrollment: Staying Healthy During Enrollment Season" in *Employee Benefit News* **(Vol. 25, November 1, 2011, No. 14, pp. 41)**
Pub: SourceMedia Inc.
Ed: Shana Sweeney. **Description:** Tips for staying healthy during your benefit open enrollment period are outlined.

11343 ■ "Passing It On: Using Life Insurance as an Estate Planning Tool" in *Inc.* **(October 2007, pp. 47-49)**
Pub: Gruner & Jahr USA Publishing
Ed: Elaine Appleton Grant. **Description:** Permanent life insurance policies can be used to cover estate taxes for heirs inheriting large estates, while allowing them time to sell any small business. Six tips are included to assist in choosing the right policy.

11344 ■ "Patients to Elect to Cut Care" in *The Business Journal-Serving Metropolitan Kansas City* **(Vol. 27, November 21, 2008, No. 11, pp. 1)**
Pub: American City Business Journals, Inc.
Ed: Rob Roberts. **Description:** Patients in Kansas City, Missouri are cutting down on health care services due to the economic crisis. A decline in diagnostic procedures has been observed at Northland Cardiology. Elective reconstructive procedures have also been reduced by 25 percent. Additional information and statistics regarding the healthcare sector is included.

11345 ■ "Patricia Hemingway Hall; President, Chief Operating Officer, Health Care Service Corp." in *Crain's Chicago Business* **(May 5, 2008)**
Pub: Crain Communications, Inc.
Ed: Mike Colias. **Description:** Profile of Patricia Hemingway Hall who is the president and chief operating officer of Health Care Service Corp., a new strategy launched by Blue Cross & Blue Shield of Illinois; the new endeavor will emphasize wellness rather than just treatment across its four health plans.

11346 ■ "PCH Gets Trauma Center Status" in *The Business Journal - Serving Phoenix and the Valley of the Sun* **(Vol. 28, July 11, 2008, No. 45)**
Pub: American City Business Journals, Inc.
Ed: Angela Gonzales. **Description:** Phoenix Children's Hospital has been allowed by the Arizona Department of Health Services to launch the state's first trauma center for children. The trauma center is expected to cost the hospital $7 million a year.

11347 ■ "The People Puzzle; Re-Training America's Workers" in *The Economist* **(Vol. 390, January 3, 2009, No. 8612, pp. 32)**
Pub: The Economist Newspaper Inc.
Description: With thousands of workers losing their jobs, America is now facing the task of getting them back to work. With an overall unemployment rate of 6.7 percent, the federal government has three main ways for leading workers back to employment: training them for new jobs, providing unemployment insurance in order to replace lost wages during the period of job-hunting; and matching employers who desire a skill with workers who have that skill. Specialized staffing agencies provide employers and potential employees with the help necessary to find a job in some of the more niche markets.

11348 ■ "Planning a Wedding Fit for a Royal? Read This First, Urge Legal and General" in *Benzinga.com* **(April 21, 2011)**
Pub: Benzinga.com
Ed: Benzinga Staff. **Description:** When planning a wedding, the author suggests checking life insurance to be sure you are covered for any situations that may arise.

11349 ■ "Prescription for Health: Choosing the Best Healthcare Plan" in *Black Enterprise* **(Vol. 38, July 2008, No. 12, pp. 48)**
Pub: Earl G. Graves Publishing Co. Inc.
Ed: Tamara E. Holmes. **Description:** According to a survey of small-business owners conducted by Sure-Payroll Inc., 20 percent of respondents have had a prospective employee refuse a job offer because healthcare benefits did not come with it. Cost is not the only reason many small-business owners do not offer these benefits. Guidelines to help take some of the confusion out of the guesswork that comes with trying to find the proper fit concerning healthcare benefits are outlined.

11350 ■ "The Price of Citizenship" in *Canadian Business* **(Vol. 79, August 14, 2006, No. 16-17, pp. 13)**
Pub: Rogers Media
Ed: Jack Mintz. **Description:** Safety and insurance benefits provided by the Canadian government to Canadian passport holders returning from Lebanon, is discussed.

11351 ■ "Public Health Care Funding and the Montana Economy" in *Montana Business Quarterly* **(Vol. 49, Spring 2011, No. 1, pp. 23)**
Pub: Bureau of Business & Economic Research
Ed: Gregg Davis. **Description:** Montana has more baby boomers and veterans per capita than any other state in the nation. The role of public health in the state is a crucial part of the state's economy.

11352 ■ "Recovery on Tap for 2010?" in *Orlando Business Journal* **(Vol. 26, January 1, 2010, No. 31, pp. 1)**
Pub: American City Business Journals
Ed: Melanie Stawicki Azam, Richard Bilbao, Christopher Boyd, Anjali Fluker. **Description:** Economic forecasts for Central Florida's leading business sectors in 2010 are presented. These sectors include housing, film and TV, sports business, law, restaurants, aviation, tourism and hospitality, banking and finance, commercial real estate, retail, health care, insurance, higher education, and manufacturing. According to some local executives, Central Florida's economy will slowly recover in 2010.

11353 ■ "Rich or Poor, Hospitals Must Work Together" in *Crain's Chicago Business* **(Vol. 31, April 28, 2008, No. 17, pp. 22)**
Pub: Crain Communications, Inc.
Description: Chicago=area safety-net hospitals that serve the poor, uninsured and underinsured are struggling to stay open while wealthier areas compete to build advanced facilities for the expensive surgical procedures their privately insured patients can afford. If these safety-net hospitals close, their patients, many of them in ambulances, will show up at the remaining hospitals resulting in a strain that will test the ability of hospitals across the region to care for all of their patients. Hospitals need to address the threats to the local health care system before it slips into crisis since the current every-hospital-for-itself approach that pays off big for some will eventually will make losers of everyone.

11354 ■ "RPA Preps for Building Radiant Conference, Show" in *Contractor* **(Vol. 57, January 2010, No. 1, pp. 5)**
Pub: Penton Media, Inc.
Description: Radiant Panel Association is accepting registrations for its Building Radiant 2010 Conference and Trade Show. The conference will discuss radiant heating as well as insurance and other legal matters for mechanical contractors.

11355 ■ "A Safety Net in Need of Repair" in *The Economist* **(Vol. 390, January 3, 2009, No. 8612, pp. 33)**
Pub: The Economist Newspaper Inc.
Description: America's unemployment-insurance scheme is outdated and skimpy compared to other industrialized countries despite the fact that Americans tend to work harder at returning to the job market; the benefits are lower and available for a smaller amount of time and less unemployed workers are even able to collect these benefits. Statistical data included.

11356 ■ **"Sluggish Market Gives Hospitals the Financial Chills" in** *The Business Journal-Serving Greater Tampa Bay* **(Vol. 28, August 1, 2008)**

Pub: American City Business Journals, Inc.

Ed: Margie Manning. **Description:** Operating margins for hospitals in the Tampa Bay, Florida area have been reduced from 2 percent in 2006 to 0.8 percent in 2007 due to a weaker US economy. Total margins, on the other hand, rose from 2.9 percent to 3.3 percent in the same period.

11357 ■ **"Small Biz Owners Are Tapping Into Health Savings Plans" in** *Small Business Opportunities* **(Fall 2007)**

Pub: Harris Publications Inc.

Ed: Michael L. Corne. **Description:** Health savings accounts were developed by Golden Rule, a United Healthcare company. Today, more than 40 percent of the company's customers are covered by health savings account plans.

11358 ■ *Small Business Access and Alternatives to Health Care: Congressional Hearing*

Pub: DIANE Publishing Company

Ed: Donald A. Manzullo. **Released:** July 2006. **Price:** $35.00. **Description:** Congressional hearings regarding the health care crisis facing America's small businesses is discussed.

11359 ■ **"Small Businesses Changing Their Health Plan Preferences" in** *Boston Business Journal* **(Vol. 29, June 24, 2011, No. 7, pp. 1)**

Pub: American City Business Journals Inc.

Ed: Scott Dance. **Description:** Small businesses in Maryland are shifting from traditional health plans to the consumer-oriented health savings accounts or HSAs. Health insurance industry experts say the change is indicative of the insurance buyers' desire to be more thrifty and discerning in their health care purchases.

11360 ■ **"Small, But Mighty" in** *Employee Benefit News* **(Vol. 25, November 1, 2011, No. 14, pp. 32)**

Pub: SourceMedia Inc.

Ed: Andrea Davis. **Description:** Three consulting firms are facing the challenge of helping clients understand the new health care reform in a tight economy.

11361 ■ **"The Smell of Fear: Is a Bottom Near?" in** *Barron's* **(Vol. 88, March 17, 2008, No. 11, pp. M3)**

Pub: Dow Jones & Company, Inc.

Ed: Kopin Tan. **Description:** Liquidity problems at Bear Stearns frightened investors in markets around the world due to the fear of the prospects of a big bank's failure. Shares of health maintenance organizations got battered led by WellPoint, and Humana but longer-term investors who could weather short-term volatility may find value here. The value of J. Crew shares is also discussed.

11362 ■ *Starting and Running Your Own Horse Business*

Pub: Storey Publishing, LLC

Ed: Mary Ashby McDonald. **Released:** November 1, 2009. **Price:** $19.95. **Description:** Insight into starting and running a successful equestrian business is given. The book covers safety, tips for operating a riding school or horse camp, strategies for launching a carriage business, along with tax and insurance advice.

11363 ■ **"Steeling for Battle" in** *Crain's Chicago Business* **(Vol. 31, April 21, 2008, No. 16, pp. 3)**

Pub: Crain Communications, Inc.

Ed: Bob Tita. **Description:** Discusses contract negotiations between the United Steelworkers union and ArcelorMittal USA Inc., the nation's largest steelmaker, and U.S. Steel Corp., the third-largest; the union sees these negotiations as the best chance in two decades to regain lost ground but industry experts predict the companies will try to reduce

benefits, demand a separate, lower wage scale for new hires and look for relief from the rising costs for retirees' health insurance coverage.

11364 ■ **"Struggling States Slashing Health Care For Poor" in** *Chicago Tribune* **(January 15, 2009)**

Pub: McClatchy-Tribune Information Services

Ed: Noam N. Levey. **Description:** Health officials warn that even the huge federal rescue plan may not be enough to restore health services being eliminated due to the economic crisis.

11365 ■ **"Survivorship Policies: Planning a Policy for Two" in** *Employee Benefit News* **(Vol. 25, November 1, 2011, No. 14, pp. 20)**

Pub: SourceMedia Inc.

Ed: Marli D. Riggs. **Description:** Survivorship insurance is becoming an added benefit high net worth individuals and executives should consider when evaluating life insurance policies.

11366 ■ **"Sutter, CHW Reject Blue Cross Deal" in** *Sacramento Business Journal* **(Vol. 25, August 15, 2008, No. 24, pp. 1)**

Pub: American City Business Journals, Inc.

Ed: Kathy Robertson. **Description:** California-based Sutter Health and Catholic Healthcare West have rejected the $11.8 million class action settlement in connection with contract rescissions between California hospitals and Anthem Blue Cross. Blue Cross can halt the settlement if not enough hospitals accept it. The deal covers all hospitals that owe money due to rescinded Blue Cross coverage.

11367 ■ **"Symbility Solutions Joins Motion Computing Partner Program" in** *Canadian Corporate News* **(May 14, 2007)**

Pub: Comtex News Network Inc.

Description: Symbility Solutions Inc., a wholly owned subsidiary of Automated Benefits Corp., announced an agreement with Alliance Partner of Motion Computing, a leader in wireless communications and mobile computing, in which both companies will invest in a sales and marketing strategy that focuses specifically on the insurance market.

11368 ■ **"Taking Full Advantage: What You Need To Know During Open-Enrollment Season" in** *Black Enterprise* **(Vol. 38, November 2007, No. 4)**

Pub: Earl G. Graves Publishing Co. Inc.

Ed: Donald Jay Korn. **Description:** Employees can change or enroll in new insurance benefits during the fall season. It is important to assess each plan offered and to determine your deductible. Statistical data included.

11369 ■ **"Tenacious Trailblazer" in** *Hispanic Business* **(Vol. 30, April 2008, No. 4, pp. 26)**

Pub: Hispanic Business

Ed: Melinda Burns. **Description:** Dr. Sandra Hernandez has been named as Hispanic Business Woman of the Year for her pioneering work in health care reform. Dr. Hernandez is the first Hispanic and the first woman to serve as public health director for the city and county of San Francisco.

11370 ■ **"Thousands Balk at Health Law Sign-Up Mandate" in** *Boston Business Journal* **(Vol. 27, November 9, 2007, No. 41, pp. 1)**

Pub: American City Business Journals Inc.

Ed: Mark Hollmer. **Description:** About 100,000 Massachusetts residents have not signed up for insurance plans created as part of the state's health care reform law. Insurers have underestimated the number of new customers signing up for insurance and come close to risking penalties if they do not get insurance by the end of 2007. The Commonwealth Health Insurance Connector Authority's deadline to buy insurance before penalties kick in is November 15, 2007.

11371 ■ **"Top 50 In Total Revenue" in** *Canadian Business* **(Vol. 81, Summer 2008, No. 9, pp. 119)**

Pub: Rogers Media Ltd.

Description: Table showing the top 50 Canadian companies in terms of total revenue is presented. Manulife Financial Corp. topped the list with revenue

of 34.5 billion. The financial services firm is the 6th largest provider of life insurance in the world and the second largest in North America.

11372 ■ **"United Insurance To Grow St. Pete's Corporate Base" in** *The Business Journal-Serving Greater Tampa Bay* **(August 29, 2008)**

Pub: American City Business Journals, Inc.

Ed: Margie Manning. **Description:** United Insurance Holdings LC is on its way to becoming a public company by agreeing in a reverse merger with FMG Acquisition Corp. The $104.3 million agreement will provide the company's St. Petersburg operations the opportunity to grow. The other impacts of the proposed reverse merger are examined.

11373 ■ **"UnitedHealthcare Resists Prognosis" in** *The Business Journal-Serving Metropolitan Kansas City* **(Vol. 26, August 29, 2008, No. 51)**

Pub: American City Business Journals, Inc.

Ed: Rob Roberts. **Description:** Saint Luke's Hospital Systems terminated UnitedHealthcare from its insurance provider network on July 25, 2008. Negotiators with both parties have stopped speaking, and employees under UnitedHealthcare plans will have to pay higher bills unless Saint Luke's reconsiders its decision. The parties' previous negotiations are discussed.

11374 ■ **"VPA to Pay $9.5 Million to Settle Whistle-Blower Lawsuits" in** *Crain's Detroit Business* **(Vol. 26, January 11, 2010, No. 2, pp. 13)**

Pub: Crain Communications, Inc.

Ed: Jay Greene. **Description:** According to Terrence Berg, first assistant with the U.S. Attorney's Office in Detroit, Voluntary Physicians Association, a local home health care company, has agreed to pay $9.5 million to settle four whistle-blower lawsuits; the agreement settles allegations that VPA submitted claims to TriCare, the Michigan Medicaid program and Medicare for unnecessary home visits, tests and procedures.

11375 ■ **"W&S to Trim Rich Retirement Plan" in** *Business Courier* **(Vol. 27, October 15, 2010, No. 24, pp. 1)**

Pub: Business Courier

Ed: Dan Monk. **Description:** Insurance firm Western & Southern Financial Group announced that it will reduce the pension benefits of its 4,000 associates by more than 30 percent starting January 1, 2011. The move is expected to reduce annual retirement payments by several thousand dollars per associate. Western is a Fortune 500 company and has $34 billion in total assets.

11376 ■ **"We Have a Budget, Too" in** *Entrepreneur* **(Vol. 37, October 2009, No. 10, pp. 89)**

Pub: Entrepreneur Media, Inc.

Ed: Craig Matsuda. **Description:** One human resources executive at a financial services company claims that health care issues are as costly and irritating for companies as they are for the employees. Health care vendors and insurers try as much as possible to maximize profits, while companies exert much effort to maximize benefits for their workers.

11377 ■ **"Week on the Web" in** *Crain's Detroit Business* **(Vol. 25, June 22, 2009, No. 25, pp. 19)**

Pub: Crain Communications Inc. - Detroit

Description: Blue Cross Blue Shield of Michigan, in a class-action lawsuit, will pay about 100 families whose children were either denied coverage for autism treatment or paid for treatment out of pocket. The settlement is worth about $ million.

11378 ■ **"What Choice Did I Have?" in** *Entrepreneur* **(Vol. 37, October 2009, No. 10, pp. 88)**

Pub: Entrepreneur Media, Inc.

Ed: Craig Matsuda. **Description:** Profile of a worker at a financial services company who acquired first hand knowledge concerning the relationship between health insurance costs and coverage. The worker's son got severely ill, forcing the worker to spend above what is covered by health insurance.

11379 ■ "Work At It!" in *Hawaii Business* (Vol. 53, October 2007, No. 4, pp. 44)

Pub: Hawaii Business Publishing

Ed: Cathy S. Cruz-George. Description: Employers in Hawaii are mitigating the effects of rising health-care costs by giving their employees health insurance and offering wellness programs. Employer-based health insurance has increases by 87 percent in the United States over the 2000-2006 period. Wellness programs that address different aspects of employees' health, such as food consumption, drug compliance and smoking habits, are discussed.

11380 ■ "The Worst-Run Industry in Canada: Health Care" in *Canadian Business* (Vol. 83, October 12, 2010, No. 17, pp. 39)

Pub: Rogers Media Ltd.

Ed: Rachel Mendleson. Description: Most Canadians believe that the problem of the country's health care system is rooted in insufficient funding, demographic overload, or corporate profiteering. However, health economists and policy analysts think the real issues is mismanagement, as the pervasive inefficiency is affecting the system's structure.

11381 ■ "Year-End Tax Tips" in *Hawaii Business* (Vol. 53, December 2007, No. 6, pp. 136)

Pub: Hawaii Business Publishing

Ed: Kathleen Bryan. Description: Tax planning tips for the end of 2007, in relation to the tax breaks that are scheduled to expire, are presented. Among the tax breaks that will be expiring at the 2007 year-end are sales tax deduction in the state and local level, premiums on mortgage insurance, and deduction on tuition. The impacts of these changes are discussed.

11382 ■ "Young Adults Choose to go Without Health Insurance" in *Business Review, Albany New York* (Vol. 34, November 30, 2007, No. 35, pp. 1)

Pub: American City Business Journals, Inc.

Ed: Barbara Pinckney. Description: U.S. Census Bureau revealed that in 2006, 19 million people between the ages of 18 and 34 were without health insurance, or 40 percent of the uninsured individuals in the country. College graduation usually means the end of health coverage, since most fresh graduates opt to not get any health insurance plan. Solutions to this growing issue are also addressed.

STATISTICAL SOURCES

11383 ■ *RMA Annual Statement Studies*

Pub: Robert Morris Associates (RMA)

Released: Annual. Price: $175.00 2006-07 edition, $105.00. Description: Contains composite balance sheets and income statements for more than 360 industries, including the accounting, auditing, and bookkeeping industries. Also contains five years of comparative historical data for discerning trends. Includes 16 commonly used ratios, computed for most of the size groupings for nearly every industry.

11384 ■ *Standard & Poor's Industry Surveys*

Pub: Standard & Poor's Corp.

Released: Annual. Price: $3633.00. Description: Two-volume book that examines the prospects for specific industries, including trucking. Also provides analyses of trends and problems, statistical tables and charts, and comparative company analyses.

TRADE PERIODICALS

11385 ■ *AAIS Viewpoint*

Pub: American Association of Insurance Services (AAIS)

Contact: Joseph S. Harrington

E-mail: joeh@aaisonline.com

Released: Quarterly, 4/Year (Mid-Feb., May, Aug., and Nov.). Price: Included in membership. Description: Contains news of current insurance issues, AAIS activities, insurance legislation, and other subjects of interest.

11386 ■ *Barger & Wolen Newsletter*

Pub: Barger & Wolen

Contact: Larry Golub, Managing Editor

Released: Quarterly. Price: Free. Description: Discusses current events in the legal field relating to insurance. Carries decision briefs.

11387 ■ *Best's Review*

Pub: A.M. Best Company, Inc.

Contact: Dennis Gorski, Managing Editor

Ed: Lynna Goch, Editor. Released: Monthly. Price: $50. Description: Magazine covering issues and trends for the management personnel of life/health insurers, the agents, and brokers who market their products.

11388 ■ *BestWeek Life/Health Edition*

Pub: A.M. Best Co.

Ed: Brendan Noonan, Editor. Released: Weekly. Description: Contains annotated news articles and staff-written perspectives on current events in the life/health insurance industry. Reports on legislative developments, new products, and corporate changes. Recurring features include news of industry meetings and comparative operating results.

11389 ■ *BestWeek Property/Casualty Editions*

Pub: A.M. Best Co.

Ed: Brendan Noonan, Editor. Released: Weekly. Description: Contains articles and staff-written perspectives on current events in the property/casualty and life/health insurance industries, statistical studies and special reports by A.M Best financial analysts. Reports on legislative developments, industry meetings, new products, and corporate changes. Recurring features include comparative operating results and news of industry regulation.

11390 ■ *Business Insurance*

Pub: Crain Communications Inc.

Contact: Paul D. Winston, Assoc. Publisher/Editorial Dir.

Ed: Regis J. Coccia, Editor. Released: Weekly. Price: $125; $219 two years; $69 digital; $130 Canada and Mexico; $234 Canada and Mexico 2 years. Description: International newsweekly reporting on corporate risk and employee benefit management news.

11391 ■ *Healthcare Corporate Finance News*

Pub: Irving Levin Associates Inc.

Contact: Stephen M. Monroe, Managing Editor

Ed: Gretchen S. Swanson, Editor. Released: Monthly. Price: $495. Description: Reports on the growth strategies of managed care providers, hospitals, drug companies, medical device manufacturers, and other healthcare organizations. Also reports on the latest deals in the healthcare sector, and how healthcare companies are doing on Wall Street.

11392 ■ *Insurance Daily*

Pub: SNL Financial L.C.

Contact: Reid Nagle, Publisher

Ed: Will Retzer, Editor. Released: Daily. Description: Provides information on the insurance industry. Features news releases, filings, and news on top-performing stocks, insider trades, ownership filings, and legislative issues.

11393 ■ *Insurance Forum*

Pub: Insurance Forum Inc.

Contact: Ann I. Belth, Business Mgr

Ed: Joseph M. Belth, Editor. Released: Monthly. Price: $90 plus 6%sales tax. Description: Provides analyses and information on the insurance business.

11394 ■ *Insurance Industry Litigation Reporter*

Pub: Thomson West

Ed: Jason Schossler, Editor. Released: Monthly. Price: $2683.56, individuals. Description: "Follows insurance disputes involving triggers of coverage, occurrence, exclusions, foreseeability, duty to defend, bad faith allegations and emerging judicial theories of recovery such as risk contribution, emotional distress and enhanced risk of future injury." Reprints complete texts of key decisions and pleadings.

11395 ■ *Insurance Institute of Southern Alberta Newsletter*

Pub: Insurance Institute of Southern Alberta

Ed: Released: 5/year. Price: Included in membership. Description: Covers insurance education.

11396 ■ *The Insurance Journal of the West*

Pub: Wells Publishing Inc.

Contact: Dena Kaplan, Assoc. Publisher, Advertising

E-mail: dkaplan@insurancejournal.com

Released: Semimonthly. Price: $195; $295 other countries; $295 two years; $495 other countries 2 years. Description: Trade journal covering insurance.

11397 ■ *The Insurance M&A Newsletter*

Pub: SNL Financial L.C.

Ed: John Racine, Editor. Released: Biweekly. Price: $998, individuals. Description: Features articles and financial information on insurance mergers and acquisitions activity. Covers insurance companies, insurance brokers and agencies, managed care companies, and hospital administrators.

11398 ■ *Insurance Weekly*

Pub: SNL Financial L.C.

Contact: Pat LaBua

Ed: Mike Deane, Editor. Released: Weekly. Description: Summarizes events, market activity, and regulatory filings affecting insurance companies and insurance brokers.

11399 ■ *The John Liner Letter*

Pub: Standard Publishing Corp.

Contact: John C. Cross

Ed: Robert Montgomery, Editor. Released: Monthly. Price: $262, U.S.; $340.60, elsewhere. Description: Provides risk management and technical insurance advice for business firms, such as broadening coverage, cutting costs, and anticipating special insurance problems.

11400 ■ *Journal of Financial Service Professionals*

Pub: Society of Financial Service Professionals

Contact: John T. Adney, Assoc. Ed.

Ed: Kenn Beam Tacchino, Editor. Released: Bi-monthly. Price: $20 single issue; $90; $115 institutions; $45 members. Description: Magazine focusing on life and health insurance and financial services.

11401 ■ *Journal of Insurance Regulation*

Pub: National Association of Insurance Commissioners

Ed: Lars Powell, Editor, jireditor@ualr.edu. Released: Quarterly. Price: $70; $85 other countries. Description: Forum for research and public policy analysis of topics dealing with the control of insurance companies/markets by regulatory bodies.

11402 ■ *Personal Perspective*

Pub: Insurance Marketing and Management Services

Contact: George Nordhaus, Publisher

Ed: Pamela Grieman, Editor. Released: 4/year. Description: Provides a resource for insurance agents to explain homeowners, auto, personal property, health, and life coverages and related issues to clients. Recurring features include news of research and a column titled Short Shots.

11403 ■ *Reinsurance News*

Pub: Society of Actuaries

Contact: Joe Adduci

E-mail: jadduci@soa.org

Ed: Bernard Goebel, Editor, goebelb@towers.com. Released: 3-4/year. Price: Included in membership; $25, nonmembers U.S. Description: Encourages the professional development of Society members in the field of reinsurance. Recurring features include letters to the editor, news of research, news of educational opportunities, and a calendar of events.

11404 ■ *The Risk Report*

Pub: International Risk Management Institute Inc.

Contact: Jack P. Gibson, President

Released: Monthly. Price: $199, individuals. Description: Deals with risk management and commercial insurance. Monitors trends in loss exposures, insurance pricing, and coverage. Suggests techniques for reducing insurance costs, and provides detailed policy analyses.

11405 ■ *Small Talk*
Pub: Society of Actuaries
Contact: Terry M. Long FSA, Chairperson
E-mail: tlong@lewisellis.com
Ed: James R. Thompson, FSA, Editor, jimthompson@ameritech.net. **Released:** 2-3/year. **Price:** Included in membership; $10, nonmembers U.S. **Description:** The purpose of the Smaller Insurance Company newsletter shall be to encourage and facilitate the professional development of its members through activities such as meetings, seminars, and the generation and dissemination of literature pertaining to the unique problems that face actuaries employed by smaller life insurance companies. The Section focuses on methods, techniques and solutions that do not require the more extensive actuarial resources available to large companies, and provides a forum where professionals working in a smaller company environment can discuss their special concerns. The Section newsletter is small talk.

11406 ■ *Society of Financial Service Professionals—Society Page*
Pub: Society of Financial Service Professionals
Ed: Maryanne Mennite, Editor. **Released:** Quarterly. **Price:** Included in membership. **Description:** Reports Society and member news, notices of the Society's upcoming conferences and seminars, and continuing education information.

11407 ■ *Today's Insurance Professionals*
Pub: National Association of Insurance Women (International)
Contact: Melissa Cobbs, Dir. of Communications/Ed.
E-mail: editor@naiw.org
Released: Quarterly. **Price:** $15; $5 single issue. **Description:** Magazine on insurance and professional development topics for men and women in the risk and insurance field.

VIDEOCASSETTES/ AUDIOCASSETTES

11408 ■ *Business Insurance: A Sales Skills Introduction*
Custom Communications
1661 Greenview Dr. SW
Rochester, MN 55902-4215
Ph:(507)288-5522
Free: 800-274-8258
Fax:(507)287-0757
Co. E-mail: info@custom-alarm.com
URL: http://www.custom-alarm.com
Description: Designed to develop the vital sales skills an agent needs to make a smooth transition into the lucrative area of business insurance. **Availability:** VHS; 3/4U.

11409 ■ *Going Bare: Crisis in Insurance*
New Jersey Network
25 S. Stockton St.
P.O. Box 777
Trenton, NJ 08625-0777
Ph:(609)777-5000
Free: 800-792-8645
Fax:(973)643-4004
Co. E-mail: njnvideo@njn.org
URL: http://www.njn.net
Released: 1988. **Description:** Examines the history of the insurance industry, price wars between insurance companies, and small businesses who are without liability insurance because of extremely high premiums. **Availability:** VHS; 3/4U.

11410 ■ *Telephone Techniques: A Complete Program for the Insurance Professional*
Custom Communications
1661 Greenview Dr. SW
Rochester, MN 55902-4215
Ph:(507)288-5522
Free: 800-274-8258

Fax:(507)287-0757
Co. E-mail: info@custom-alarm.com
URL: http://www.custom-alarm.com
Description: This program is designed to help insurance agents improve their telephone selling techniques. **Availability:** VHS; 3/4U.

TRADE SHOWS AND CONVENTIONS

11411 ■ Annual NAIW Convention - National Association of Insurance Women International
National Association of Insurance Women International
9343 E. 95th Ct. S.
Tulsa, OK 74133
Ph:(918)294-3700
Free: 800-766-6249
Fax:(918)743-1968
Co. E-mail: joinnaiw@naiw.org
URL: http://www.naiw.org
Released: Annual. **Principal Exhibits:** Equipment, supplies, and services for insurance industry professionals. **Dates and Locations:** 2011 Jun 05-08, Flamingo, NV.

11412 ■ CPCU Conferment Ceremony
American Institute for CPCU
720 Providence Rd.
PO Box 3016
Malvern, PA 19355-0716
Ph:(610)644-2100
Free: 800-644-2101
Fax:(610)640-9576
Co. E-mail: cserv@cpcuiia.org
URL: http://www.aicpcu.org
Released: Annual. **Principal Exhibits:** Exhibits for insurance personnel and Chartered Property Casualty Underwriters (CPCUs).

CONSULTANTS

11413 ■ Analytical Engineering Services Corp.
3102 Drogue Ct.
Annapolis, MD 21403
Ph:(410)268-7133
Fax:(410)268-9581
Co. E-mail: acipriani@fticonsulting.com
Contact: A. Cipriani, President
E-mail: acipriani@fticonsulting.com
Scope: Offers engineering accident analysis with expertise in vehicle accident reconstruction for autos, trucks, bus, pedestrian, bicycles, motorcycles, etc.; fire origin and cause for vehicular, residential, commercial, boiler or furnace related fires; and product liability for guarding, failure analysis, warnings and labels, etc. Industries served: insurance and legal. **Seminars:** Vehicle Accident Reconstruction, Principles, Case Studies.

11414 ■ Financial Computer Support Inc.
16 Commerce Dr.
Oakland, MD 21550-3940
Ph:(301)334-1800
Free: 877-432-2267
Fax:(301)334-1896
Co. E-mail: fcsitechsupport@morningstar.com
Contact: David Huxford, Principal
Scope: Independent user group which provides computer and administrative support for financial planners, money managers, and insurance agents. Serves finance and insurance industries. **Publications:** "Check Out Carmen Petote," Jul, 2006; "Control the Information Flow with Rep Level Access," Feb, 2005.

11415 ■ Forensic Accident Investigations Inc.
6971 N Federal Hwy., Ste. 405
Boca Palm Professional Plz.
Boca Raton, FL 33487
Ph:(561)703-3881

Fax:(561)995-7168
Co. E-mail: rmcelroy@forensicaccident.com
URL: http://www.forensicaccident.com
Contact: Robert C. McElroy, President
E-mail: rmcelroy@forensicaccident.com
Scope: Accident reconstruction/investigation, product failure and liability analysis, industrial standard and safety research, regulatory compliance, design/maintenance defects, mechanical inspections, preservation of evidence pertaining to collisions/insurance fraud, documentation/determinations regarding occupant restraint function/usage, mechanical systems failure/evaluation. Biomechanical analysis and research, perception/reaction and time-distance analysis, human factors, crash worthiness evaluations, 2-D and 3-D computer simulation and/or animation. **Seminars:** Bicycle Pedestrian Collision Investigation, North Florida, Jan, 2005; Safety Wins Defensive Driving Training, Homestead, Nov, 2004; Human Factors in Traffic Crash Reconstruction, North Florida, Nov, 2004; Collision Reconstruction Technology and Application, Burlington, Aug, 2003; Intelligent Vehicle Initiative, On board Safety Technology Workshop, Washington, Aug, 2003; Contemporary Accident Reconstruction; Accident Reconstruction; Accident Investigation, Reconstruction, Interpretation and the Law; Commercial Vehicle Collision Investigation; Accident Reconstruction and Event Data Recorders; EDR User Perspectives on Parameters and Data Accessibility: Independent Investigator Consultant Accident Reconstruction; Retread Procedures for Commercial Tires; EDR Transportation Event Data Recorders. **Special Services:** PC-Crash and PC-Rect Simulation; AI Tools: SLAM, Linear Momentum, Equations; SAE Databases: MOVE, Stapp, Accident Reconstruction; CAD:Designer, AutoSketch; Page-Maker, MGI VideoWave. NHTSA Database Research, Autotrack Database Research; VDO Accident Data Recorder; North American Crash Analysis Center.

11416 ■ Limra International Inc.
300 Day Hill Rd.
Windsor, CT 06095-1783
Ph:(860)688-3358
Free: 800-235-4672
Fax:(860)298-9555
Co. E-mail: hdrescher@limra.com
URL: http://www.limra.com
Contact: Gary Aluise, Senior VP
E-mail: galuise@atslimra.com
Scope: A research and management consulting organization specializing in insurance marketing. Company research services apply scientific techniques to the areas of performance appraisal, manpower utilization, employee and consumer opinion sampling, and market analysis. Management consultation services include strategic planning, field cost controls and a computer modeling service. Also offers financial services consulting including defining distribution strategy, developing a distribution channel, organizational development and operations consulting. **Publications:** "28 Ways to Improve Your Sales Performance"; "Advanced Selection Interview Guide"; "LIMRA's Market Facts"; "Looking Ahead"; "Cross Selling". **Seminars:** Compensation and Motivation Plans that Deliver Results, Bangkok, Aug, 2009; Sales Compensation Seminar, Simsbury, May, 2009; Growth by Design; Strategic Marketing Review. **Special Services:** Career Profile™.

11417 ■ National Insurance Professionals Corp.
1040 NE Hostmark St., Ste. 200
Poulsbo, WA 98370-7454
Ph:(360)697-3611
Free: 800-275-6472
Fax:(360)697-3688
Co. E-mail: kathy_schufreider@rpsvcs.com
URL: http://www.nipc.com
Contact: Jamie Augustine, Mgr
E-mail: jamie_augustine@atsrpsins.com
Scope: Program administrators for alternative specialty markets. Includes social service agencies and bicycle tour operators. Provides retail and wholesale insurance brokers access to specialty insurance carriers.

11418 ■ R.D. Network Inc.
PO Box 375
Lafayette Hill, PA 19444
Ph:(215)482-4461
Free: 877-482-4991
Fax:(215)836-0378
Co. E-mail: info@rdnetwork.com
URL: http://www.rdnetwork.com
Contact: Melissa Altman, Principle
E-mail: info@rdnetwork.com
Scope: Dietitians, diet technicians, and certified dietary managers available nationwide and worldwide through an international registry for consulting positions to wellness and employee education programs, drug or alcohol rehabilitation, hospital, LTC, nutrition and labeling communications, nutrition consultation, weight control classes, healthcare staff supplementation, media and program development, and all nutrition and food-related needs. Expert witness and speakers bureau also available. Industries served: healthcare, food industry, food service, restaurateurs, supermarkets, pharmaceutical companies, home health agencies, insurance companies, HMOs, and government agencies. **Seminars:** Healthy Dining Etiquette for Executives and Sales Staff Diet and Wellness; Cardiovascular Nutrition; Starting a Nutrition Consulting Practice; AIDS and Diet Therapy; Nutrition Care for Your Parents in Their Elder Years; Increase Your Energy-Increase Your Sales.

11419 ■ Strack Vaughan L.L.C.
4833 Rugby Ave., Ste. 201
Bethesda, MD 20814-3035
Ph:(301)654-7778
Fax:(301)951-0063
Contact: Janice Hartmann, Partner
Scope: Business and financial planning consultants providing services in mergers and acquisitions, strategic planning, and tax planning. Serves insurance agencies and the graphic arts industry.

FRANCHISES AND BUSINESS OPPORTUNITIES

11420 ■ Paul Davis Systems Canada, Ltd.
38 Crockford Blvd.
Scarborough, ON, Canada M1R 3C2
Ph:(416)299-8890
Free: 800-661-5975
Fax:(416)299-8510
Co. E-mail: steve@pds.ca
URL: http://www.pds.ca
No. of Franchise Units: 58. **Founded:** 1985. **Franchised:** 1986. **Description:** Insurance claims and qualified restoration contractor across Canada and the U.S. **Equity Capital Needed:** $100,000. **Franchise Fee:** $25,000-$45,000. **Training:** Offers 3 weeks training.

COMPUTERIZED DATABASES

11421 ■ Best's Statement File - Property/Casualty - United States
A.M. Best Company Inc.
Ambest Rd.
Oldwick, NJ 08858
Ph:(908)439-2200
Free: 800-424-2378
Fax:(908)439-3296
Co. E-mail: customer_service@ambest.com
URL: http://www.ambest.com
Description: Contains 11 years of annual and six years of quarterly statutory filing data on some 4100 U.S. property and casualty insurance companies. For each company, provides complete information from the NAIC annual statement, including assets, liability and surplus, expenses, premiums written by line, exhibit of life insurance, stock and bond summary, and quality and maturity of bonds. Includes *Best's Review, BestWeek,* and *BestAlert Service.* Also includes a one-year subscription to *Best's Review* magazine. **Availability:** CD-ROM: A.M. Best Company Inc. **Type:** Numeric; Directory.

11422 ■ National Underwriter Life & Health
Summit Business Media
5081 Olympic Blvd.
Erlanger, KY 41018
Ph:(859)692-2100
Free: 800-543-0874
Fax:(859)692-2000
URL: http://www.summitbusinessmedia.com
Description: Provides information pertinent to the life and health insurance industry, including current events coverage, trade association meetings, new product introductions, technology updates, and coverage of state, federal, and legislative affairs. Searchable by date, author, keywords, and headlines. Corresponds to the print journal of the same name. **Availability:** Online: LexisNexis Group, Dow Jones & Company Inc., Summit Business Media. **Type:** Full text.

11423 ■ National Underwriter Property & Casualty
Summit Business Media
5081 Olympic Blvd.
Erlanger, KY 41018
Ph:(859)692-2100
Free: 800-543-0874
Fax:(859)692-2000
URL: http://www.summitbusinessmedia.com
Description: Provides information pertinent to the property and casualty insurance industry, including current events coverage, trade association meetings, new product introductions, technology updates, and in-depth coverage of state, federal and legislative affaires pertaining to the insurance industry. Coverage also includes risk management, employee benefits, stocks and marketing, and industry trends. Corresponds to the print journal of the same name. **Availability:** Online: LexisNexis Group, Dow Jones & Company Inc., Summit Business Media. **Type:** Full text.

11424 ■ Sage Property & Casualty
Vertafore Inc.
11831 N Creek Pky. N
Bothell, WA 98011
Free: 800-444-4813
Fax:(425)402-9569
Co. E-mail: information@vertafore.com
URL: http://www.vertafore.com
Description: Contains information for insurance agents, including information on property, casualty, benefits and human relations. Also includes commercial lines coverage analysis, industry profiles, coverage recommendations, markets, coverage checklists and risk surveys, customer service brochure templates, form letters and proposal templates. Also includes GL and WC classification tables with SIC and NAICS cross-references. **Availability:** Online: Vertafore Inc. **Type:** Full text.

COMPUTER SYSTEMS/SOFTWARE

11425 ■ Agency Accounting
Insurance Technology Consultants
681 S Parker St., Ste. 260
Orange, CA 92868
Ph:(714)836-0671
Fax:(714)836-0737
URL: http://www.itc-systems.com
Price: $20,000 Windows based licensing fee and maintenance and $600 per month. **Description:** Available for Windows 95, 98 NT and MICRO-based operating systems. System provides general agents with accounting and policy maintenance capabilities.

11426 ■ Agency Information Management System
Insurance Rating Systems, Inc.
433 Kitty Hawk, Ste. 211
PO Box 2576
Universal City, TX 78148
Ph:800-456-7595
Free: 800-876-1466
Fax:(210)658-2220
URL: http://www.irsaims.com
Price: Description: Windows 95/98 based agency management system. Combining the standard navigational tools and conventions of the windows operating system with an SQL data base, MARS offers complete customer and financial management yet is simple to use.

LIBRARIES

11427 ■ American Institute for Chartered Property Casualty Underwriters–Insurance Institute of America | Nancy W. Spellman Memorial Library
720 Providence Rd.
Malvern, PA 19355-0725
Ph:(610)644-2101
Fax:(610)640-9576
Co. E-mail: irc@cpcuiia.org
URL: http://www.aicpcu.org/
Contact: Adam Carmichael, Dir.
Scope: Insurance, risk management, economics, management, accounting, continuing education. **Services:** Copying; Library open to the public. **Holdings:** 9500 books. **Subscriptions:** 150 journals and other serials.

11428 ■ American Insurance Association Law Library
2101 L St. NW, Ste. 400
Washington, DC 20037
Ph:(202)828-7100
Fax:(202)293-1219
Co. E-mail: info@aiadc.org
URL: http://www.aiadc.org
Contact: Allen K. Haddox, Libn.
Scope: Property and casualty insurance, law, healthcare policy. **Services:** Library open to the public by appointment. **Holdings:** 30,000 volumes; 215 VF drawers; reports; archives; proceedings. **Subscriptions:** 130 journals and other serials; 11 newspapers.

11429 ■ Buset & Partners Library
1121 Barton St.
Thunder Bay, ON, Canada P7B 5N3
Ph:(807)623-2500
Free: (866)532-8738
Fax:(807)622-7808
Co. E-mail: cenns@buset-partners.com
URL: http://www.buset-partners.com
Contact: Carolyn Enns, Libn.
Scope: Law - real estate, labor, corporate, commercial, family, personal injury, insurance; civil litigation, wills and estates, employment, municipal, environmental. **Services:** Library not open to the public. **Holdings:** 2100 books; 3 bound periodical volumes. **Subscriptions:** 7 journals and other serials; 3 newspapers.

11430 ■ Colonial Life & Accident Insurance Company–Archives and Library
1200 Colonial Life Blvd.
PO Box 1365
Columbia, SC 29202
Ph:(803)798-7000
Free: 800-325-4368
Fax:800-880-9325
URL: http://www.coloniallife.com/
Scope: Insurance - life, health; employee benefits. **Holdings:** Figures not available.

11431 ■ Erie Insurance Group Corporate Library
100 Erie Insurance Pl.
Erie, PA 16530
Ph:(814)451-5000
Fax:(814)451-5060
URL: http://www.erieinsurance.com/
Contact: Judith A. Knapp, Supv.
Scope: Insurance; management; law. **Services:** Interlibrary loan; copying; SDI; Library open to the public by appointment. **Holdings:** 1200 books; 1000 archival materials. **Subscriptions:** 150 journals and other serials; 10 newspapers.

11432 ■ Golden Rule Insurance Co. Library
7440 Woodland Dr.
Indianapolis, IN 46278-1719
Ph:(317)715-7111
URL: http://www.goldenrule.com
Contact: Ellen Laden, Dir., PR
Scope: Insurance. **Services:** Library not open to the public. **Holdings:** 400 books; 500 reports; archives; videos. **Subscriptions:** 50 journals and other serials; 7 newspapers.

11433 ■ Hartford Conservatory–Carolyn B. Taylor Library
834 Asylum Ave.
Hartford, CT 06105
Ph:(860)246-2588
Fax:(860)249-6330
Co. E-mail: mhuntington@hartfordconservatory.org
URL: http://www.hartfordconservatory.org
Contact: Marilynn Huntington
Scope: Music (classical and jazz), dance, theater. **Services:** Interlibrary loan; Library open to the public for reference use only. **Holdings:** 1600 books and bound periodical volumes; 5114 music scores; 400 pieces of sheet music; 4800 sound recordings; 130 compact discs. **Subscriptions:** 10 journals and other serials.

11434 ■ Insurance Information Institute Library
110 William St.
New York, NY 10038
Ph:(212)346-5500
URL: http://www.iii.org
Contact: Madine Singer, Libn.
Scope: Property and casualty insurance and allied subjects. **Services:** Library open to the public by appointment only. **Holdings:** 2000 books. **Subscriptions:** 75 journals and other serials.

11435 ■ Insurance Institute of Ontario Library
18 King St. E., 16th Fl.
Toronto, ON, Canada M5C 1C4
Ph:(416)362-8586
Fax:(416)362-8081
Co. E-mail: gtamail@insuranceinstitute.ca
URL: http://cip.iic-iac.org/About/Ontario.asp
Contact: Livia Tersigni, Mgr.
Scope: Property and casualty insurance. **Services:** Library open to members. **Holdings:** 250 books; 12 serials; 6 other cataloged items. **Subscriptions:** 29 journals and other serials.

11436 ■ LeBoeuf, Lamb, Greene & MacRae Law Library
1 Riverfront Plaza
Newark, NJ 07102-5490
Ph:(973)643-8000
Fax:(973)643-6111
Co. E-mail: spierson@llgm.com
URL: http://www.llgm.com/Home.aspx
Contact: Stephanie Fox Pierson, Leg.Info.Rsrcs.Mgr.
Scope: Law - insurance, public utilities, corporate. **Services:** Library not open to the public. **Holdings:** 3000 books. **Subscriptions:** 20 journals and other serials; 8 newspapers.

11437 ■ LIMRA International–InfoCenter
300 Day Hill Rd.
Windsor, CT 06095
Ph:(860)688-3358
Free: 800-235-4672
Fax:(860)298-9555
URL: http://www.limra.com
Contact: James Kerley, Pres.
Scope: Life insurance, financial services, industrial psychology, statistical methods. **Services:** Interlibrary loan; Library open to members and to others upon application. **Holdings:** 6000 books; 150 VF drawers of clippings, pamphlets, documents. **Subscriptions:** 300 journals and other serials.

11438 ■ Manulife Financial–Canadian Division Law Library
500 King St., N.
Waterloo, ON, Canada N2J 4C6
Ph:(519)747-7000

Fax:(519)747-6325
Co. E-mail: tina_pedersen@manulife.com
Contact: Tina Pedersen, Leg.Info.Spec.
Scope: Canadian insurance law. **Services:** Library not open to the public. **Holdings:** 800 books; 1000 bound periodical volumes; 10 reports; CD-ROMs. **Subscriptions:** 70 journals and other serials.

11439 ■ McKenna Long & Aldridge LLP Law Library
1900 K St. NW, Lower Level
Washington, DC 20006-1108
Ph:(202)496-7752
Fax:(202)496-7756
Co. E-mail: kmartin@mckennalong.com
URL: http://www.mckennalong.com
Contact: Kate Martin, Dir. of Lib.Svcs.
Scope: Law - government contracts, environmental, litigation, food and drug, International, health care, labor, insurance, energy. **Services:** Interlibrary loan; Library not open to the public. **Holdings:** 15,000 books; 5000 bound periodical volumes. **Subscriptions:** 400 journals and other serials.

11440 ■ Metropolitan Life Insurance Company–Corporate Information Center & Library
200 Park Ave.
New York, NY 10166
Ph:(212)922-9100
Fax:(212)922-9195
URL: http://www.metlife.com/
Scope: Insurance, management. **Services:** Interlibrary loan; archives open to researchers by appointment. **Holdings:** 65,000 volumes. **Subscriptions:** 47 journals and other serials; 3 newspapers.

11441 ■ National Association of Insurance Commissioners–NAIC Support and Services Office–Research Library (2301)
2301 McGee, Ste. 800
Kansas City, MO 64108-2662
Ph:(816)842-3600
Fax:(816)783-8269
Co. E-mail: reslib@naic.org
URL: http://www.naic.org
Contact: Sandra Hollis, Res.Lib.Svcs.Mgr.
Scope: Insurance - regulation, law, business. **Services:** Library not open to the public. **Holdings:** 13,000 volumes; reports; microfiche and microfilm. **Subscriptions:** 160 journals and other serials.

11442 ■ Parker, Smith & Feek, Inc. Library
2233 112th Ave., NE
Bellevue, WA 98004
Ph:(425)709-3600
Free: 800-457-0220
Fax:(425)709-7460
URL: http://www.psfinc.com
Contact: Sherri Monteith, Info.Spec.
Scope: Insurance. **Services:** Library open to clients. **Holdings:** 100 books; 400 reports. **Subscriptions:** 125 journals and other serials; 7 newspapers.

11443 ■ Property Casualty Insurers Association of America Library
2600 S. River Rd.
Des Plaines, IL 60118-3286
Ph:(847)297-7800
Fax:(847)297-5064
URL: http://www.pciaa.net/web/sitehome.nsf/main
Contact: Holly Grossman
Scope: Insurance, law. **Services:** Interlibrary loan. **Holdings:** 4000 books. **Subscriptions:** 250 journals and other serials; 6 newspapers.

11444 ■ Protape, Inc. Library
1540 Broadway
New York, NY 10036
Contact: Richard Sobelsohn
Scope: Accounting, law, real estate, English, math, insurance, travel, taxation, stock broker, medical billing, claims adjusting, private investigation, paralegal. **Services:** Library not open to the public. **Holdings:** 25,000 books; 250 bound periodical volumes. **Subscriptions:** 65 journals and other serials; 20 newspapers.

11445 ■ Ropers Majeski Kohn & Bentley Library
1001 Marshall St., Ste. 300
Redwood City, CA 94063
Ph:(650)364-8200
Fax:(650)780-1701
Co. E-mail: ccallahan@rmkb.com
URL: http://www.rmkb.com
Contact: Carmen Callahan, Off.Mgr.
Scope: Law - California, federal, insurance; civil litigation; legal reference. **Services:** Library not open to the public. **Holdings:** 4000 books; 400 bound periodical volumes; 175 reports; 1000 archival items; CD-ROMs. **Subscriptions:** 9 journals and other serials; 5 newspapers.

11446 ■ Society of Insurance Research Library
631 Eastpointe Dr.
Shelbyville, IN 46176
Ph:(317)398-3684
Fax:(317)642-0535
Co. E-mail: sir.mail@comcast.net
URL: http://www.sirnet.org
Contact: Ed Budd, Exec.Dir.
Scope: Insurance research. **Services:** Library open to the public. **Holdings:** 12 bound periodical volumes.

11447 ■ Swidler Berlin Shereff Friedman, LLP Library
3000 K St., NW, Ste. 300
Washington, DC 20007
Ph:(202)424-7500
Fax:(202)424-7645
Co. E-mail: lspeer@swidlaw.com
URL: http://www.bingham.com/bingham/default.asp
Contact: Laura Speer, Dir., Lib.Svcs.
Scope: Law - communications, insurance, energy, bankruptcy, the environment, government affairs, antitrust, litigation, corporate, intellectual property. **Services:** Library not open to the public. **Holdings:** 1800 volumes.

11448 ■ XL Global Services Corporate Library
70 Seaview Ave.
Stamford, CT 06902-6036
Ph:(203)964-5216
Fax:(203)964-0763
Co. E-mail: diane.fischer@xlgroup.com
Contact: Diane Fischer, Info.Rsrcs.Mgr.
Scope: Reinsurance, insurance. **Services:** Interlibrary loan; Library not open to the public. **Holdings:** 200 books. **Subscriptions:** 200 journals and other serials; 3 newspapers.

RESEARCH CENTERS

11449 ■ Insurance Research Council
718 Providence Rd.
Malvern, PA 19355
Ph:(610)644-2212
Fax:(610)640-5388
Co. E-mail: corum@cpcuiia.org
URL: http://www.ircweb.org
Contact: David Corum, VP
E-mail: corum@cpcuiia.org
Scope: Property-casualty insurance and public policy issues, including studies of insurance fraud, auto insurance reform, catastrophic automobile injuries, compensation for auto injuries, catastrophic losses and damage mitigation, fire following earthquakes, attorney involvement in insurance claims, drinking and driving, and the performance of the auto accident compensation system. Performs research through surveys, computer modeling, and claims data analysis. **Publications:** Auto Injury Study (5/year); Public Attitude Monitor (annually).

11450 ■ Society of Insurance Research
631 Eastpointe Dr.
Shelbyville, IN 46176
Ph:(317)398-3684
Co. E-mail: sir.mail@comcast.net
URL: http://www.sirnet.org
Contact: Ed Budd, Exec.Dir.
E-mail: sir.mail@comcast.net
Scope: Stimulates insurance research through the interchange of ideas on research methodology. **Pub**

lications: S.I.R. News. **Educational Activities:** Conference (annually); Workshops (annually).

11451 ■ University of Georgia–Center for Insurance Education and Research
206 Brooks Hall
Terry College of Business
Athens, GA 30602-6255
Ph:(706)542-4290

Fax:(706)542-4295
Co. E-mail: rhoyt@terry.uga.edu
URL: http://www.terry.uga.edu/insurance
Contact: Dr. Robert E. Hoyt, Dir.
E-mail: rhoyt@terry.uga.edu

Scope: Insurance industry. **Educational Activities:** Insurance Managers Seminar (annually). **Awards:** Research grants (periodically).

START-UP INFORMATION

11452 ■ "Five Low-Cost Home Based Startups" in *Women Entrepreneur* **(December 16, 2008)**
Pub: Entrepreneur Media Inc.
Ed: Lesley Spencer Pyle. **Description:** During tough economic times, small businesses have an advantage over large companies because they can adjust to economic conditions more easily and without having to go through corporate red tape that can slow the implementation process. A budding entrepreneur may find success by taking inventory of his or her skills, experience, expertise and passions and utilizing those qualities to start a business. Five low-cost home-based startups are profiled. These include starting an online store, a virtual assistant service, web designer, sales representative and a home staging counselor.

11453 ■ *How to Open and Operate a Financially Successful Redesign, Redecorating, and Home Staging Business: With Companion CD-ROM*
Pub: Atlantic Publishing Group, Inc.
Ed: Mary Larsen; Teri B. Clark. **Released:** January 2008. **Price:** $39.95 paperback. **Description:** Questions are asked to help individuals determine if they should launch their own redesign or real estate staging firm.

11454 ■ *How to Start a Home-Based Interior Design Business*
Pub: Globe Pequot Press
Ed: Nita Phillips. **Released:** January 2006.

11455 ■ *Interior Design Business*
Pub: Globe Pequot Press
Ed: Suzanne DeWalt; Nita B. Phillips. **Released:** January 2006. **Price:** $18.95. **Description:** Tips for starting and running a home-based interior design business are given.

11456 ■ "No Place Like Home" in *Small Business Opportunities* **(Winter 2010)**
Pub: Harris Publications Inc.
Ed: Description: Five reasons to start a home-staging business in any economy are listed. Home staging is listed as the top emerging career on Website, Careerbuilder.com.

ASSOCIATIONS AND OTHER ORGANIZATIONS

11457 ■ American Floorcovering Alliance
210 W Cuyler St.
Dalton, GA 30720
Ph:(706)278-4101
Free: 800-288-4101
Fax:(706)278-5323
Co. E-mail: afa@americanfloor.org
URL: http://www.americanfloor.org
Contact: Wanda J. Ellis, Exec. Dir.
Description: Floorcovering manufacturers and companies providing services or supplies to the floor covering industry. Promotes the floor covering industry. Provides insurance programs for members. **Publications:** *Floor Covering Weekly* (weekly); *Floor Focus* (monthly); *Floor Tek Source Guide* (biennial); *Industry Profile* (quarterly).

11458 ■ Association of University Interior Designers
Ohio State University
Office of Student Life
Facility Management and Logistics
Columbus, OH 43210
URL: http://www.auid.org
Contact: Julie Lenczycki, Pres.
Description: In-house interior designers associated with universities. Serves as an educational forum to share ideas and concerns of interior design relating to universities and colleges. .

11459 ■ Council for Interior Design Accreditation
206 Grandville Ave., Ste. 350
Grand Rapids, MI 49503
Ph:(616)458-0400
Fax:(616)458-0460
Co. E-mail: info@accredit-id.org
URL: http://www.accredit-id.org
Contact: Holly Mattson, Exec. Dir.
Description: Formed by Interior Design Educators Council and American Society of Interior Designers. Administers voluntary plan for the special accreditation of interior design education programs offered at institutions of higher learning throughout the U.S. and its possessions and Canada; emphasizes the use of accreditation procedures to assure that the purposes and accomplishments of programs of interior design education meet the needs of society, students, and the interior design profession; recognized by the Council for Higher Education Accreditation as a national accrediting agency for programs in interior design in schools throughout the country. .

11460 ■ Home Fashion Products Association
355 Lexington Ave., Ste. 1500
New York, NY 10017-6603
Ph:(212)297-2122
Fax:(212)370-9047
Co. E-mail: contactus@hfpaonline.org
URL: http://www.homefashionproducts.com
Contact: Katie Goshgarian, Exec. Dir.
Description: Manufacturers of curtains, draperies, bedding, rugs and related products. Sponsors annual scholarship for students attending accredited schools in home textiles. .

11461 ■ Interior Design Society
164 S Main St., Fl. 8
High Point, NC 27260
Ph:(336)884-4437
Free: 888-884-4469
Fax:(336)885-3291
Co. E-mail: info@interiordesignsociety.org
URL: http://www.interiordesignsociety.org
Contact: Pamela G. White, CEO
Description: Represents independent designers and decorators, retail designers and sales people, design-oriented firms, and manufacturers. Grants accreditation and recognition to qualified residential interior designers and retail home furnishing stores. Conducts educational seminars in design, sales training, and marketing. Offers products and publications for designers and a correspondence course for home furnishing sales people. **Publications:** *Design for Success* (monthly); *Portfolio* (quarterly); *Residential Interior Design Books and Designer Tools* .

11462 ■ International Association of Lighting Designers
Merchandise Mart, Ste. 9-104
Chicago, IL 60654
Ph:(312)527-3677
Fax:(312)527-3680
Co. E-mail: iald@iald.org
URL: http://www.iald.org
Contact: Marsha L. Turner CAE, Exec. VP
Description: Represents professionals, educators, students, and others working in the field of lighting design worldwide. Promotes the benefits of quality lighting design and emphasizes the potential impact of lighting on architectural design and environmental quality. Furthers professional standards of lighting designers and seeks to increase their function in the interior design industry. Sponsors national awards program, summer intern program for qualified college students interested in lighting design as a profession, and career development lectures and seminars. **Publications:** *e-Reflections* (monthly); *International Association of Lighting Designers—Membership Directory* (annual); *Why Hire an IALD Lighting Designer?* .

11463 ■ International Furnishings and Design Association
150 S Warner Rd., Ste. 156
King of Prussia, PA 19406
Ph:(610)535-6422
Fax:(610)535-6423
Co. E-mail: info@ifda.com
URL: http://www.ifda.com
Contact: Janet Stevenson, Pres.
Description: Represents individuals engaged in design, production, distribution, education, promotion and editorial phases of the interior furnishings industry and related fields. Founded IFDA Educational Foundation in 1968. Conducts charitable programs; maintains speakers' bureau. **Publications:** *IFDA Network* (quarterly).

11464 ■ International Interior Design Association
222 Merchandise Mart, Ste. 567
Chicago, IL 60654
Ph:(312)467-1950
Free: 888-799-4432
Fax:(312)467-0779
Co. E-mail: iidahq@iida.org
URL: http://www.iida.org
Contact: Peter Conant, Pres.-Elect
Description: Represents professional interior designers, including designers of commercial, healthcare, hospitality, government, retail, residential facilities; educators; researchers; representatives of allied manufacturing sources. Conducts research, student

programs and continuing education programs for members. Has developed a code of ethics for the professional design membership. **Publications:** *GRAction* .

11465 ■ National Council for Interior Design Qualification

1602 L St. NW, Ste. 200
Washington, DC 20036-2581
Ph:(202)721-0220
Fax:(202)721-0221
Co. E-mail: inquiries@ncidq.org
URL: http://www.ncidq.org
Contact: Jeffrey F. Kenney, Exec. Dir.

Description: Independent organization of state and provincial regulatory bodies. Provides the public with the means to identify those interior designers who have demonstrated the minimum level of competence needed to practice in this profession. Provides a professional examination in interior design. Endeavors to maintain the most advanced examining procedures, and to update continually the examination to reflect expanding professional knowledge and design development techniques to protect the health, safety and welfare of the public. Seeks acceptance of the NCIDQ examination as a universal standard by which to measure the competency of interior designers practicing as professionals. **Publications:** *Continuing Education; The Mark of a Professional; QLetter* (semiannual).

11466 ■ National Kitchen and Bath Association

687 Willow Grove St.
Hackettstown, NJ 07840
Ph:(908)852-0033
Free: 800-843-6522
Fax:(908)852-1695
Co. E-mail: feedback@nkba.org
URL: http://www.nkba.org
Contact: Bill Darcy, Exec. VP

Description: Manufacturers and firms engaged in retail kitchen sales; manufacturers' representatives and wholesale distributors; utilities, publications and other firms supplying products or services to the kitchen and bathroom industry. Protects and promotes the interest and welfare of members by fostering a better business climate in the industry. Awards titles of Certified Kitchen Designer and Certified Bathroom Designer to individuals with proven knowledge, ability and experience in the design, planning, and installation supervision of residential kitchens. Conducts kitchen and bathroom training schools throughout the country. Sponsors business management and consumer awareness programs. Maintains speakers' bureau and Hall of Fame. .

11467 ■ Organization of Black Designers

300 M St. SW, Ste. N110
Washington, DC 20024
Ph:(202)659-3918
Co. E-mail: info@obd.org
URL: http://www.core77.com/OBD/welcome.html
Contact: David H. Rice, Founder/Chm.

Description: African American designers holding college degrees who are practicing graphic advertising, industrial, fashion, textile, and interior design. Provides forum for discussion and educational programs, business, career and economic development. Sponsors competitions and speakers' bureau. **Publications:** *DesigNation* (biennial); *OBData* .

11468 ■ Paint and Decorating Retailers Association

1401 Triad Center Dr.
St. Peters, MO 63376-7353
Ph:(636)326-2636
Co. E-mail: info@pdra.org
URL: http://www.pdra.org
Contact: Jeff Baggaley, Pres.

Description: Serves as a trade association of locally-owned paint and decorating stores in the U.S., Canada and around the world. Offers professional advice, personal service and quality products for every paint, wall covering, window treatment and floor covering project. **Publications:** *Decorating Registry* (annual); *Gold Book* (annual); *Paint and Decorating Retailer* (monthly).

11469 ■ Painting and Decorating Contractors of America

1801 Park 270 Dr., Ste. 220
St. Louis, MO 63146
Ph:(314)514-7322
Free: 800-332-PDCA
Fax:(314)514-9417
Co. E-mail: rgreene@pdca.org
URL: http://www.pdca.org
Contact: Richard Greene, CEO

Description: Painting and wall covering contractors. Operates educational and charitable programs. Compiles statistics. **Publications:** *Hazardous Waste Handbook; Painting and Wallcovering Contractor* (bimonthly); *PDCA Directory* (annual).

11470 ■ Window Covering Manufacturers Association

355 Lexington Ave., 15th Fl.
New York, NY 10017
Ph:(212)297-2122
URL: http://www.wcmanet.org

Description: Represents corporations engaged in the manufacture or assembly of Venetian blinds, vertical blinds, pleated shades, or their components. Promotes the use, utility, image, and attractiveness of the products and services offered by the window covering industry. .

DIRECTORIES OF EDUCATIONAL PROGRAMS

11471 ■ *Directory of Private Accredited Career Schools and Colleges of Technology*

Pub: Accrediting Commission of Career Schools and Colleges of Technology

Contact: Michale S. McComis, Exec. Dir.

Released: On web page. **Price:** Free. **Description:** Covers 3900 accredited post-secondary programs that provide training programs in business, trade, and technical fields, including various small business endeavors. Entries offer school name, address, phone, description of courses, job placement assistance, and requirements for admission. Arrangement is alphabetical.

REFERENCE WORKS

11472 ■ "Colores Origenes: Martha Kruse" in *Advertising Age* (Vol. 77, November 13, 2006, No. 46, pp. S12)

Pub: Crain Communications, Inc.

Ed: Laurel Wentz. **Description:** Home Depot has created a range of Latin paint colors called Colores Origenes; the new line was originally intended to launch only at locations with heavily Hispanic patrons but the company decided to make the line available at all of their stores.

11473 ■ "Entrepreneur Says Spirituality Has Been a Key to Her Success" in *Business First Columbus* (Vol. 25, October 17, 2008, No. 8, pp. 1)

Pub: American City Business Journals

Ed: Scott Rawdon. **Description:** Profile of Carolyn Williams Francis, CEO of Williams Interior Designs Inc. She outlines her mantra for success in her furniture design business, but emphasizes that faith has taken her business to greater heights.

11474 ■ "First the Merger: Then, The Culture Clash. How To Fix the Little Things That Can Tear a Company Apart" in *Inc.* (January 2008)

Pub: Gruner & Jahr USA Publishing

Ed: Elaine Appleton Grant. **Description:** Ways three CEOs handled the culture classes that followed after company mergers; companies profiled include Fuel Outdoor, an outdoor advertising company; Nelson, an interior design and architecture firm; and Beber Silverstein, an ad agency.

11475 ■ *Floor Covering Weekly—Annual Product Source Guide*

Pub: FCW

Contact: Santiago Montero, Editor & Publisher

E-mail: smontero@hearst.com

Released: Annual, Latest edition 2011. **Price:** $66, Canada; $61, individuals; $101, two years; $184, out of country. **Publication Includes:** Lists of manufac-

turers and importers of carpet, rugs, carpet cushion, fiber, resilient wood, and ceramic floor coverings; separate listing of distributors by state, retail groups and associations. **Entries Include:** For manufacturers—Company name, address, phone, regional sales offices, names and titles of key personnel, local distributors, products. For distributors—Company name, address, phone, manufacturers represented. **Arrangement:** Alphabetical. **Indexes:** Geographical by distributor.

11476 ■ *Home Staging for Dummies*

Pub: John Wiley and Sons, Inc.

Ed: Christine Rae; Janice Saunders Maresh. **Released:** May 2008. **Price:** $19.99. **Description:** Guide shows how to make improvements room by room in order to generate a higher profit on home sales. The book offers tips to clear clutter and show the home's best features, inspire curb appeal, and how to depersonalize and neutralize every room.

11477 ■ "How to Declutter Your Life Closet Cleanup: Putting a Lid on Clutter" in *Atlanta Journal-Constitution* (May 1, 2011)

Pub: Atlanta Journal-Constitution

Ed: Felicia Feaster. **Description:** The annual Closets and Home Organization Convention and Expo spotlights new products and services designed to help people get organized at home or the workplace. The organization sector is holding steady despite the recession and is expected to expand into garage organization.

11478 ■ "Inside the Googleplex" in *Canadian Business* (Vol. 79, November 6, 2006, No. 22, pp. 59)

Pub: Rogers Media

Ed: Christina Campbell. **Description:** The views of Clive Wilkinson, a designer, on relationship between interior design and employee's productivity are presented.

11479 ■ "Intel Joins Movement to Turn Cube Farms Into Wide-Open Spaces" in *Sacramento Business Journal* (Vol. 28, May 27, 2011, No. 13, pp. 1)

Pub: Sacramento Business Journal

Ed: Melanie Turner. **Description:** Intel Corporation has remodeled its facility in Folsom, California. The renovation has required some workers to give up their cubicles. Comments from executives are included.

11480 ■ *Interior Design—Buyers Guide Issue*

Pub: Cahners Publishing Co.

Contact: Carol Cisco, Sales Mgr.

E-mail: ccisco@reedbusiness.com

Released: published 15 times a year. **Price:** $64.95, individuals 12 issues, annual rate for subscribers; $87, individuals 12 issues, annual rate for subscribers; $87, individuals Other country. **Publication Includes:** Lists of 4,000 manufacturers and suppliers of furniture, furnishings, and services to contract and residential designers; trade buildings and marts; trade associations; carpet guide. **Entries Include:** Company name, address, phone, fax. **Arrangement:** Alphabetical. **Indexes:** Keyword, product, geographical. Calendar of industry events; reference book index.

11481 ■ "Let Your Stuff Tell a Story: How to Edit Your Accessories to Showcase Your Personality" in *Charlotte Observer* (February 8, 2007)

Pub: Knight-Ridder/Tribune Business News

Ed: Nancy Brachey. **Description:** Tips to accessorize any home or office are presented; eliminating clutter is stressed.

11482 ■ "Make a Resolution: ADA Training" in *HRMagazine* (Vol. 54, January 2009, No. 1, pp. 81)

Pub: Society for Human Resource Management

Ed: Victoria Zellers. **Description:** Americans with Disabilities Act (ADA) Amendments Act took effect January 1, 2009. The ADA Amendments Act means that more applicants and employees are eligible for reasonable accommodations and that employers need to develop a new ADA compliance strategy.

11483 ■ **"Monday Organizer: Clean and De-Clutter in 15 Minutes" in** *Tulsa World* **(June 13, 2011)**
Pub: McClatchy Company

Ed: Kim Brown. **Description:** New weekly series highlights practical tips and helpful ideas to simply life by taking 15 minutes to de-clutter your home or office. Paper clutter can be eliminated in 15 minutes by gathering up newspapers and magazines to recycle; sort mail as soon as you receive it and throw away any junk mail at that time. If watching TV, use commercial time to accomplish small tasks.

11484 ■ *Peggy's Corner: The Art of Staging*
Pub: Eaton-Moghannam Publishing

Ed: Peggy Selinger-Eaton; Gayla Moghannam. **Released:** June 2005. **Description:** Techniques to enhance the value of any home are given. Seven principles of staging a home for sale include making a great first impression, maximizing space and eliminating clutter, using lighting for open spacious feeling, de-emphasize flaws, make the home appealing to buyers with varied tastes, creating warmth, and modernizing the home.

11485 ■ **"Procter Gambles on Wallpaper; Putting Paint On a Roll" in** *Advertising Age* **(Vol. 77, September 18, 2006, No. 38, pp. 4)**
Pub: Crain Communications, Inc.

Ed: Jack Neff. **Description:** Procter & Gamble Co. has launched a new line of textured paints that are already applied to a wallpaper-like roll that can be hung without paste or wallpaper tools.

11486 ■ **"Staging a Martini-and-GQ Lifestyle; Faux Possessions Play to Buyer's Aspirations" in** *Crain's Chicago Business* **(April 21, 2008)**
Pub: Crain Communications, Inc.

Ed: Kevin Davis. **Description:** Due to the competition of the slumping housing market, home stagers are becoming more prominent and are using creative ways to make an impression beyond de-cluttering, painting and cleaning by using accents such as casually placed magazines, candles and table settings.

SOURCES OF SUPPLY

11487 ■ *Interior Design Sourcebook*
Pub: Omnigraphics Inc.

Ed: Susan A. Lewis, Editor. **Released:** Irregular. **Price:** $22.50, individuals. **Covers:** 15 chapters covers all interior design resources for academics and professionals, including, competitions and scholarships, magazines and publishers, trade associations, governmental agencies and research centers, conferences, design theory, programming and planning, furniture, finishes and textiles, building and interior systems, project types, visual communication methods, and business and professional practice. **Entries Include:** Publication name, topic, address, phone number. **Arrangement:** Subject. **Indexes:** Name, organization, subject.

TRADE PERIODICALS

11488 ■ *Architectural Digest*
Pub: Conde Nast Publications Inc.

Contact: Guilio Capua, VP & Publisher

Released: Monthly. **Price:** $24; $36 two years; $59.95 Canada; $67.95 other countries surface mail. **Description:** Magazine on interior design, art, and antiques.

11489 ■ *ARIDO*
Pub: Association of Registered Interior Designers of Ontario

Ed: Lori Theoret, Editor, ltheoret@arido.on.ca. **Released:** 6/yr. **Price:** Included in membership. **Description:** Covers issues affecting the interior design profession. Contains information on association news as well as design resources. Recurring features include letters to the editor, research news, a calendar of events, technical and business articles, and columns titled Viewpoint and Announcements. Available via fax only.

11490 ■ *Award Magazine*
Pub: Canada Wide Magazines & Communications Ltd.

Contact: Anne Rose, Exec. Ed.

E-mail: arose@canadawide.com

Ed: Kim Mah, Editor, kmah@canadawide.com. **Released:** Bimonthly. **Price:** $22.34 plus HST. **Description:** Trade magazine for architects, developers, interior designers, and related professionals.

11491 ■ *CAUS News*
Pub: Color Association of the United States (CAUS)

Ed: Released: Bimonthly. **Price:** Included in membership. **Description:** Explores aspects of color design, discussing applications to a wide variety of fields, including fashion, textiles, interior decorating, environmental construction, marketing, and advertising. Contains news of research, book reviews, and editorials. Recurring features include letters to the editor, news of members, and a calendar of events.

11492 ■ *Chicago Home and Garden*
Pub: Chicago Home & Garden

Ed: Jan Parr, Editor, jparr@chicagomag.com. **Released:** Quarterly. **Price:** $9.95; $25; $35 other countries. **Description:** Magazine covering home and garden style in the Chicago, IL, area.

11493 ■ *Contract*
Pub: VNU eMedia Inc.

Released: Monthly. **Description:** Magazine serving the commercial and institutional interior design and furnishings field.

11494 ■ *Country Home*
Pub: Meredith Corp.

Released: Monthly, 10/yr. **Price:** $4.95 newsstand; $21.97 two years. **Description:** Magazine furnishing information on American interior design, architecture, antiques and collectibles, gardening, art, and culinary endeavor.

11495 ■ *Country Sampler*
Pub: Country Sampler Group

Contact: Elizabeth Preston, Assoc. Ed.

Ed: Donna Marcel, Editor. **Released:** Bimonthly. **Price:** $19.96 U.S.; $29.96 Canada; $49.96 other countries. **Description:** Country arts, crafts, interior design, and lifestyle magazine.

11496 ■ *Hospitality Design*
Pub: Nielsen Business Media

Contact: Tara Mastrelli, Managing Editor

E-mail: tmastrelli@hdmag.com

Released: 10/yr. **Price:** $79; $94 Canada; $139 other countries by airmail. **Description:** Magazine covering design of restaurants, hotels, facilities, clubs, cruise ships, etc.

11497 ■ *House Beautiful*
Pub: Hearst Magazines

Contact: Stephen Drucker, Editor-in-Chief

Price: $10; $15 two years. **Description:** Magazine focusing on architecture, building, interior decorating, gardening, and landscaping.

11498 ■ *Interior Design*
Pub: Reed Business Information

Contact: Helene Oberman, Managing Editor

E-mail: hoberman@interiordesign.net

Released: 15/yr. **Price:** $59.95; $87 Canada; $187 other countries. **Description:** Interior designing and furnishings magazine.

11499 ■ *LDB Interior Textiles*
Pub: E.W. Williams Publications Co.

Contact: Wanda Jankowski, Editor-in-Chief

E-mail: wandaldb@ewwpi.com

Released: Monthly. **Price:** $72; $125 Canada; $150 elsewhere airmail; $100 two years; $7 single issue; $12 single issue, Canada; $18 single issue elsewhere. **Description:** Magazine for buyers of home fashions, including bed, bath and table linens, hard and soft window treatments, home fragrances, decorative pillows and home accessories, accent rugs, and decorative fabrics.

11500 ■ *Metropolitan Home*
Pub: Hachette Filipacchi Media U.S. Inc.

Contact: Deborah Burns, VP/Publisher

Released: 10/yr. **Price:** $16 two years; $10; $22 Canada; $29 other countries. **Description:** Magazine on home interior design and decorating.

11501 ■ *Old-House Interiors*
Pub: Gloucester Publishers

Contact: Bill O'Donnell, Publisher

E-mail: bodonnell@oldhouseinteriors.com

Released: Bimonthly. **Price:** $24; $32 Canada; $38 other countries; $42 two years; $58 Canada 2 years; $70 other countries 2 years. **Description:** Consumer magazine covering interior design for period homes.

VIDEOCASSETTES/ AUDIOCASSETTES

11502 ■ *The Art of Interior Decorating*
Cambridge Educational
c/o Films Media Group
132 West 31st Street, 17th Floor
Ste. 124
New York, NY 10001
Free: 800-257-5126
Fax:(609)671-0266
Co. E-mail: custserve@films.com
URL: http://www.cambridgeol.com

Released: 1988. **Price:** $49.95. **Description:** Learn professional techniques for decorating a room or a whole house. Discusses colors, style, furniture, and accessories. A workbook is included. **Availability:** VHS.

11503 ■ *Feng Shui Today*
Tapeworm Video Distributors
25876 The Old Road 141
Stevenson Ranch, CA 91381
Ph:(661)257-4904
Fax:(661)257-4820
Co. E-mail: sales@tapeworm.com
URL: http://www.tapeworm.com

Price: $19.95. **Description:** Interior designer Jami Lin presents Feng Shui an interior decorating style with spirit. **Availability:** VHS.

TRADE SHOWS AND CONVENTIONS

11504 ■ **Accent on Design - A Division of the New York International Gift Fair**
George Little Management, LLC (New York, New York)
1133 Westchester Ave., Ste. N136
White Plains, NY 10606
Ph:(914)421-3200
Free: 800-272-SHOW
Co. E-mail: cathy_steel@glmshows.com
URL: http://www.glmshows.com

Released: Annual. **Audience:** Buyers from specialty, department, and jewelry stores and; gift shops; interior designers; home products importers and distributors; mail order catalogs. **Principal Exhibits:** General giftware, tabletop and housewares, decorative and personal accessories, museum gifts, ethnic, traditional, country and contemporary design products, juvenile products, floral products and pet products.

11505 ■ **Accent on Design - A Division of the San Francisco International Gift Fair**
George Little Management, LLC (New York, New York)
1133 Westchester Ave., Ste. N136
White Plains, NY 10606
Ph:(914)421-3200
Free: 800-272-SHOW
Co. E-mail: cathy_steel@glmshows.com
URL: http://www.glmshows.com

Released: Semiannual. **Audience:** Specialty, department, stationery, jewelry, and juvenile stores, gift and gourmet shops, interior designers, importers/distributors of home products, museums. **Principal Exhibits:**

Decorative accessories, lighting and home furnishings, housewares, stationery, tabletop, gourmet and general gift merchandise.

11506 ■ Chicago Design Show

Merchandise Mart Properties Inc.
222 Merchandise Mart, Ste. 470
Chicago, IL 60654
Free: 800-677-6278
URL: http://www.merchandisemart.com
Released: Annual. **Audience:** Interior design trade professionals and consumers. **Principal Exhibits:** Contemporary design in furniture, fashion, food.

11507 ■ Fort Lauderdale Home Design & Remodeling Show

Home Show Management
1450 Madruga Ave., Ste. 301
Coral Gables, FL 33146
Ph:(305)667-9299
Free: 800-353-EXPO
Fax:(305)667-3266
Co. E-mail: info@homeshows.net
URL: http://www.homeshows.net
Released: Annual. **Audience:** Designers, decorators, builders, developers, contractors, and consumers. **Principal Exhibits:** Architecture, interior design, furnishings, home improvement, and remodeling equipment, supplies, and services. **Dates and Locations:** 2011 Jun 27-30, Broward County, FL.

11508 ■ The Miami Home Design & Remodeling Show

Home Show Management
1450 Madruga Ave., Ste. 301
Coral Gables, FL 33146
Ph:(305)667-9299
Free: 800-353-EXPO
Fax:(305)667-3266
Co. E-mail: info@homeshows.net
URL: http://www.homeshows.net
Released: Annual. **Audience:** Designers, decorators, builders, developers, contractors, and consumers. **Principal Exhibits:** Architecture, interior design, furnishings, home improvements, and remodeling equipment, supplies, and services. **Dates and Locations:** 2011 Sep 02-06, Miami Beach, FL.

CONSULTANTS

11509 ■ A.P. Designs

33 Merrall Dr., Ste. 1
Lawrence, NY 11559
Ph:(516)239-2931
Fax:(516)239-2932
Contact: Ann Pollack, President
Scope: Provides interior design business services. Industries served: All industries and individuals requiring interior design services.

11510 ■ Chambers Ltd.

1800 Washington Blvd., Ste. 111
Baltimore, MD 21230
Ph:(410)727-4535
Fax:(410)727-6982
Co. E-mail: rsnellinger@chambersusa.com
URL: http://www.chambersusa.com
Contact: Robert Doyle, Vice President
E-mail: rdoyle@atschambersusa.com
Scope: Performs architecture, interior design, planning and consulting work for the club, residential, commercial, banking, industrial, hotel, health care, restaurant, governmental and educational communities.

11511 ■ Ogden Roemer Wilkerson Architecture

2950 E Barnett Rd.
Medford, OR 97504
Ph:(541)779-5237
Fax:(541)772-8472
Co. E-mail: office@orwarch.com
URL: http://www.orwarchitecture.com
Contact: Warren Barnhart, Mgr
E-mail: ken@atsorwarch.com
Scope: Consultants active in architecture interior design, planning, as well as city, urban and site and master planning. Specific expertise in schools, hospitals, assisted living facilities and historic building evaluation.

FRANCHISES AND BUSINESS OPPORTUNITIES

11512 ■ Deck the Walls

Franchise Concepts, Inc.
101 S Hanley Rd., No. 1280
St. Louis, MO 63105
Free: 800-543-3325
Co. E-mail: franinfo@FCIbiz.com
URL: http://www.deckthewalls.com
No. of Franchise Units: 19. **Founded:** 1979. **Franchised:** 1981. **Description:** Art and custom framing retail stores located in regional malls. **Equity Capital Needed:** $112,535-$178,108 total investment. **Franchise Fee:** $30,000. **Royalty Fee:** 6%. **Financial Assistance:** Third party financing available. **Managerial Assistance:** Conventions, workshops, private trade shows, newsletters & national credit card program. **Training:** Classroom and in-store training prepare franchisees for all aspects of business, including custom framing. Support includes: site, lease, construction aid; national buying power; vendor network and national marketing.

11513 ■ Decor & You, Inc.

900 Main St. S, Bldg. 2
Southbury, CT 06488
Ph:(203)264-3500
Free: 800-477-3326
Fax:(203)264-5095
Co. E-mail: info@decorandyou.com
URL: http://www.decorandyou.com
No. of Franchise Units: 160. **Founded:** 1994. **Franchised:** 1998. **Description:** State of the art computerized sampling and personalized services from professionally trained interior decorators. **Equity Capital Needed:** $56,000-$79,000 Decor Designers; $207,000-$225,000 Regional Dev.; $185,000-$200,000 Terr. Dir. **Franchise Fee:** $25,000/$150,000/$85,000. **Financial Assistance:** No. **Managerial Assistance:** Franchisees are provided with a Regional director to support them through the developmental stages of their growing businesses and provide coaching and problem-solving assistance while tracking and nurturing the success of each franchise. **Training:** 4 phase training program for all franchisees. All aspects of the decorating business are covered, including color and design, trends, product knowledge, client development, follow-up skills, advertising and virtual decorating through computer graphics.

COMPUTER SYSTEMS/ SOFTWARE

11514 ■ Design Your Own Home

MCS Investments, Inc.
PO Box 23333
Eugene, OR 97402
Ph:(541)431-0592
Free: 800-451-4871
Fax:(541)431-0592
Co. E-mail: sales@theliquidateher.com
URL: http://www.theliquidateher.com
Price: Description: Offers several design programs, including Architecture, Interiors, Landscape, and Libraries. Provides methods for determining structural details and drawing floor plans.

11515 ■ Microspot Interiors

Microspot Interiors Pro
418 S Military Tr.
Deerfield Beach, FL 33441
Ph:(561)395-9996
Free: 800-622-7568
Fax:(561)395-9941
Co. E-mail: sales@microspot.com
URL: http://www.macroenter.com
Price: $229.00. **Description:** Available for Apple Macintosh and Macintosh Plus computers. System provides an interior design program. Formerly Microspot Interiors.

LIBRARIES

11516 ■ American Intercontinental University Library

12655 W. Jefferson Blvd.
Los Angeles, CA 90066
Ph:(310)302-2111
Co. E-mail: nkleban@la.aiuniv.edu
URL: http://la.aiuniv.edu/about_aiu/library.aspx
Contact: Eric Zakem, Libn.
Scope: Fashion, busines, commercial art, costume history, interior design, information technology, criminal justice, media production. **Services:** Copying; Library not open to the public. **Holdings:** 25,000 books; 225 bound periodical volumes; 25,000 microfiche; fashion clipping file. **Subscriptions:** 200 journals and other serials; 15 newspapers.

11517 ■ City College of City University of New York–Art Visual Resources Library

Compton-Goethals, Rm. 245A
160 Convent Ave.
New York, NY 10031
Ph:(212)650-7175
Fax:(212)650-7604
Co. E-mail: artimage@ccny.cuny.edu
URL: http://www1.ccny.cuny.edu/library/art_resources/index.cfm
Contact: Ching-Jung Chen, Cur.
Scope: Art, architecture, design. **Services:** Library not open to the public. **Holdings:** 100,000 slides.

11518 ■ Conde Nast Publications Library and Information Services

4 Times Sq., 17th Fl.
New York, NY 10036
Ph:(212)286-2860
URL: http://www.condenastdigital.com
Contact: Sarah Chubb, Pres.
Scope: Fashion, houses, gardens, home furnishings, interior design, health, personalities, photographs. **Holdings:** 7000 volumes. **Subscriptions:** 200 journals and other serials; 4 newspapers.

11519 ■ Craigdarroch Castle

1050 Joan Crescent
Victoria, BC, Canada V8S 3L5
Ph:(250)592-5323
Fax:(250)592-1099
Co. E-mail: info@thecastle.ca
URL: http://www.thecastle.ca
Contact: Bruce Davies, Cur.
Scope: Nineteenth Century European and North American domestic material. **Services:** Library open by appointment to serious researchers only. **Holdings:** Photographs; documents; memorabilia; electronic records; graphic materials; microforms; moving images; sound recordings; textual records.

11520 ■ CUH2A, Inc. Library

211 Carnegie Ctr.
Princeton, NJ 08540-6298
Ph:(609)452-1212
Fax:(609)419-8137
Co. E-mail: smoss@cuh2a.com
URL: http://www.cuh2a.com
Contact: Susan Moss, Mgr., Info.Rsrcs.Libn
Scope: Architecture, engineering, graphic arts, interior design. **Services:** Interlibrary loan; copying; SDI; Library open to the public for reference use only. **Holdings:** 2500 books. **Subscriptions:** 124 journals and other serials; 2 newspapers.

11521 ■ Fashion Institute of Technology–Gladys Marcus Library

7th Ave. at 27th St.
E-Bldg. E502
New York, NY 10001-5992
Ph:(212)217-4340
Fax:(212)217-4371
Co. E-mail: greta_earnest@fitnyc.edu
URL: http://fitnyc.edu/library
Contact: Prof. N.J. Wolfe, Lib.Dir.
Scope: Costume, fashion, interior design, management engineering technology, fashion buying and merchandising, textiles, toy design, packaging design, advertising. **Services:** Interlibrary loan; copying; Library open to the public for reference use only

by appointment. **Holdings:** 130,260 books; 113,265 nonprint units; 20,637 bound periodical volumes; 125,000 fashion slides; 4712 reels of microfilm; 438 CD-ROM serials and digital monographs. **Subscriptions:** 4000 journals and other serials.

11522 ■ Furniture Library Association Library
1009 N. Main St.
High Point, NC 27262
Ph:(336)883-4011
Fax:(336)883-6579
Co. E-mail: info@furniturelibrary.com
URL: http://www.furniturelibrary.com
Contact: Carl Vuncannon, Cur.
Scope: Early architecture; design - interior, furniture, fabric; furniture styles, 1600 to present. **Services:** Photographing; Library open to the public. **Holdings:** 7000 books; bound periodical volumes, including over 100 years of furniture catalogs; Furniture World; trade journals. **Subscriptions:** 10 journals and other serials.

11523 ■ Harrington College of Design–Design Library
200 W. Madison St., 2nd Fl.
Chicago, IL 60606-3433
Ph:(312)939-4975
Free: (866)590-4423
Co. E-mail: elaine@interiordesign.edu
URL: http://www.interiordesign.edu
Contact: Elaine Lowenthal, Lib.Dir.
Scope: Architecture, design, building materials, furniture, decorative arts, modern design. **Services:** Interlibrary loan; copying; Library open to the public by appointment for reference use only with referral from another Library. **Holdings:** 22,000 books; 900 bound periodical volumes; 23,000 slides; 450 videotapes; 35,000 digital images. **Subscriptions:** 125 journals and other serials.

11524 ■ Hillwood Museum & Gardens–Art Research Library
4155 Linnean Ave., NW
Washington, DC 20008
Ph:(202)243-3953
Fax:(202)966-7846
Co. E-mail: plynagh@hillwoodmuseum.org
URL: http://www.hillwoodmuseum.org/resources/library.html
Contact: Pat Lynagh, Asst.Libn.
Scope: Art - decorative, French, Russian; Russian imperial history; interior design. **Services:** Copying; Library open to the public by appointment. **Holdings:** 30,000 volumes; 16,000 auction catalogs; pamphlets. **Subscriptions:** 30 journals and other serials.

11525 ■ Illinois Institute of Art/ Schaumburg–Learning Resource Center
1000 N. Plaza Dr., Ste. 100
Schaumburg, IL 60173-4913
Ph:(847)619-3450
Free: 800-314-3450
URL: http://www.artinstitutes.edu/schaumburg/
Scope: Graphic design, interior design, applied art and design, furniture history. **Services:** Interlibrary loan. **Holdings:** Books; slides; periodicals; videotapes; DVDs; CD-ROMs. **Subscriptions:** 175 journals and other serials.

11526 ■ Leo A. Daly Company Library
1357 Kapiolani Blvd., Ste. 1230
Honolulu, HI 96814-4537
Ph:(808)521-8889
Fax:(808)521-3757
Co. E-mail: info@leoadaly.com
URL: http://www.leoadaly.com
Contact: Donna L. Ching, Dir. of Bus.Dev.
Scope: Structural engineering, precast and prestressed concrete, architecture, planning, interior design. **Services:** Library not open to the public; reference services for librarians and qualified researchers. **Holdings:** 2500 books; 33 bound periodical volumes; 46 VF drawers of clippings, archives, photographs, manufacturers' literature; slides; maps. **Subscriptions:** 75 journals and other serials; 6 newspapers.

11527 ■ University of Nevada, Las Vegas–Architecture Studies Library
Box 454049
4505 Maryland Pkwy.
Las Vegas, NV 89154-4049
Ph:(702)895-1959
Fax:(702)895-1975
Co. E-mail: jeanne.brown@unlv.edu
URL: http://www.library.unlv.edu/arch/index.html
Contact: Jeanne M. Brown, Hd., Arch.Stud.
Scope: Architecture - history, design, theory, and criticism; landscape architecture; interior design; construction; urban planning. **Services:** Interlibrary loan; copying; Library open to the public. **Holdings:** 25,000 volumes; 600 videos/DVDs; archives; microfiche and microfilm. **Subscriptions:** 150 journals and other serials.

11528 ■ Watkins College of Art, Design, & Film Library
2298 Rosa L. Parks Blvd.
Nashville, TN 37228
Ph:(615)277-7427
Fax:(615)383-4849
Co. E-mail: library@watkins.edu
URL: http://www.watkins.edu/library
Contact: Lisa Williams, Libn.
Scope: Film, fine arts, interior design, graphic design, photography. **Services:** Library open to the public for reference use only. **Holdings:** 11,600 books; 1200 videotapes and films. **Subscriptions:** 50 journals and other serials; 11 newspapers.

11529 ■ Woodbury University Library
7500 Glenoaks Blvd.
Burbank, CA 91504-1052
Ph:(818)252-5201
Fax:(818)767-4534
Co. E-mail: jennifer.rosenfeld@woodbury.edu
URL: http://library.woodbury.edu
Contact: Nedra Peterson, Dir.
Scope: Business and management, International business, art, architecture, interior design, fashion marketing and design, psychology, animation. **Services:** Interlibrary loan; copying; Library open to the public for reference use only. **Holdings:** 65,000 books; 3070 bound periodical volumes; 17,401 slides; 2000 DVD/VHS. **Subscriptions:** 300 journals and other serials; 5 newspapers.

START-UP INFORMATION

11530 ■ *101 Internet Businesses You Can Start from Home: How to Choose and Build Your Own Successful E-Business*
Pub: Maximum Press
Ed: Susan Sweeney. **Released:** June 2006. **Price:** $29.95. **Description:** Guide for starting and growing an Internet business; information for developing a business plan, risk levels, and promotional techniques are included.

11531 ■ *How to Start an Internet Sales Business*
Pub: Lulu.com
Ed: Dan Davis. **Released:** August 2005. **Price:** $19.95. **Description:** Small business guide for launching an Internet sales company. Topics include business structure, licenses, and taxes.

11532 ■ *"Online Fortunes" in Small Business Opportunities* (Fall 2008)
Pub: Entrepreneur Media Inc.
Description: Fifty hot, e-commerce enterprises for the aspiring entrepreneur to consider are featured; virtual assistants, marketing services, party planning, travel services, researching, web design and development, importing as well as creating an online store are among the businesses featured.

11533 ■ *Start Your Own Net Services Business*
Pub: Entrepreneur Press
Released: February 1, 2009. **Price:** $17.95. **Description:** Web design, search engine marketing, new-media online, and blogging, are currently the four most popular web services available. This book provides information to start a net service business.

11534 ■ *Starting an Ebay Business for Canadians for Dummies*
Pub: John Wiley & Sons, Incorporated
Ed: Marsha Collier; Bill Summers. **Released:** February 2007. **Price:** $35.99. **Description:** Tips for turning a hobby into a successful online eBay company.

11535 ■ *Starting a Yahoo! Business for Dummies*
Pub: John Wiley & Sons, Incorporated
Ed: Rob Snell. **Released:** June 2006. **Price:** $24.99. **Description:** Rob Snell offers advice for turning online browsers into buyers, increase online traffic, and build an online store from scratch.

11536 ■ *Starting a Yahoo! Business For Dummies*
Pub: John Wiley & Sons, Incorporated
Ed: Rob Snell. **Released:** May 27, 2006. **Price:** $24.99. **Description:** Advice helps turn Web browsers into buyers, boost online traffic, and information to launch a profitable online business.

11537 ■ *"Startup Aims to Cut Out Coupon Clipping" in The Business Journal-Serving Metropolitan Kansas City* (Vol. 26, August 15, 2008, No. 49)
Pub: American City Business Journals, Inc.
Ed: Suzanna Stagemeyer. **Description:** TDP Inc., who started operations 18 months ago, aims to transform stale coupon promotions using technology by digitizing the entire coupon process. The process is expected to enable consumers to hunt coupons online where they will be automatically linked to loyalty cards. Other views and information on TDP and its services are presented.

ASSOCIATIONS AND OTHER ORGANIZATIONS

11538 ■ **Internet Society**
1775 Wiehle Ave., Ste. 201
Reston, VA 20190-5158
Ph:(703)439-2120
Fax:(703)326-9881
Co. E-mail: isoc@isoc.org
URL: http://www.isoc.org
Contact: Lynn St. Amour, Pres.
Description: Technologists, developers, educators, researchers, government representatives, and business people. Seeks to ensure global cooperation and coordination for the Internet and related internetworking technologies and applications. Supports the development and dissemination of standards for the Internet. Promotes the growth of Internet architecture and Internet-related education and research. Encourages assistance to technologically developing countries in implementing local Internet infrastructures. **Publications:** *ISOC Forum* (monthly); *ISP Column* .

11539 ■ **World Organization of Webmasters**
PO Box 1743
Folsom, CA 95630
Ph:(916)989-2933
Fax:(916)987-3022
Co. E-mail: info@joinwow.org
URL: http://webprofessionals.org
Contact: Bill Cullifer, Exec. Dir.
Description: Individuals who create, manage, market, or maintain websites. Seeks to advance the profession of website creation and management; promotes the online industries. Represents members' interests; facilitates communication and cooperation among members. .

DIRECTORIES OF EDUCATIONAL PROGRAMS

11540 ■ *Internet Industry Almanac*
Pub: Computer Industry Almanac Inc.
Contact: Dr. Egil Juliussen PhD, Author
Price: $50, individuals paperback; $60, individuals hardcover. **Publication Includes:** Lists of Internet companies; Internet publications; Internet research and testing companies; Internet conferences; Internet people; Internet resource directory; Internet publishers; Internet associations and organizations; and Internet conference companies. Principal content of publication is information about the Internet industry, including a definition of the Internet, employment data, Internet humor, salary information, Internet market forecasts, and technology forecasts. **Arrangement:** By industry.

REFERENCE WORKS

11541 ■ *10 Steps to Successful Social Networking for Business*
Pub: American Society for Training and Development
Ed: Darin Hartley. **Released:** July 1, 2010. **Price:** $19.95. **Description:** Designed for today's fast-paced, need-it-yesterday business environment and for the thousands of workers who find themselves faced with new assignments, responsibilities, and requirements and too little time to learn what they must know.

11542 ■ *"The 40-Year-Old Intern" in Entrepreneur* (Vol. 37, October 2009, No. 10, pp. 90)
Pub: Entrepreneur Media, Inc.
Ed: Kristin Ladd. **Description:** Brian Kurth's VocationVacation is an internship program aimed at helping people experience their dream job. The website, launched in January 2004, matches people with businesses that allow them to experience their fantasy jobs.

11543 ■ *"529.com Wins Outstanding Achievement in Web Development" in Investment Weekly* (November 14, 2009, pp. 152)
Pub: Investment Weekly News
Description: Web Marketing Association's 2009 WebAward for Financial Services Standard of Excellence and Investment Standard of Excellence was won by 529.com, the website from Upromise Investments, Inc., the leading administrator of 529 college savings plans.

11544 ■ *"Aiming at a Moving Web Target" in Entrepreneur* (Vol. 37, August 2009, No. 8, pp. 30)
Pub: Entrepreneur Media, Inc.
Ed: Dan O'Shea. **Description:** Rapidly increasing numbers of businesspeople are web surfing on mobile phones. To make a website that is accessible to people on the move, the main page should be light on images and graphics and the most important information should be put near the top. A more intensive route is to create a separate mobile-specific website.

11545 ■ *"Airlines Mount PR Push to Win Public Support Against Big Oil" in Advertising Age* (Vol. 79, July 14, 2008, No. 7, pp. 1)
Pub: Crain Communications, Inc.
Ed: Michael Bush. **Description:** Top airline executives from competing companies have banded together in a public relations plan in which they are sending e-mails to their frequent fliers asking for aid in lobbying legislators to put a restriction on oil speculation.

11546 ■ *"All About The Benjamins" in Canadian Business* (Vol. 81, September 29, 2008, No. 16, pp. 92)
Pub: Rogers Media Ltd.
Ed: David Baines. **Description:** Discusses real estate developer Royal Indian Raj International Corp., a company that planned to build a $3 billion "smart

city" near the Bangalore airport; to this day nothing has ever been built. The company was incorporated in 1999 by Manoj C. Benjamin one investor, Bill Zack, has been sued by the developer for libel due to his website that calls the company a scam. Benjamin has had a previous case of fraud issued against him as well as a string of liabilities and lawsuits.

11547 ■ "All Those Applications, and Phone Users Just Want to Talk" in *Advertising Age* **(Vol. 79, August 11, 2008, No. 31, pp. 18)**
Pub: Crain Communications, Inc.
Ed: Mike Vorhaus. **Description:** Although consumers are slowly coming to text messaging and other data applications, a majority of those Americans surveyed stated that they simply want to use their cell phones to talk and do not care about other activities. Statistical data included.

11548 ■ "Analyzing the Analytics" in *Entrepreneur* **(Vol. 37, October 2009, No. 10, pp. 42)**
Pub: Entrepreneur Media, Inc.
Ed: Mikal E. Belicove. **Description:** Startups can maximize Web analytics by using them to monitor traffic sources and identify obstacles to converting them into targeted behaviors . Startups should set trackable Web site goals and continuously track traffic and conversion rates.

11549 ■ "Anything Could Happen" in *Inc.* **(March 2008, pp. 116-123)**
Pub: Gruner & Jahr USA Publishing
Ed: Max Chafkin. **Description:** Profile of Evan Williams, founder of Blogger and Twitter, a new type of technology idea; Williams answers ten questions and share insight into growing both of his companies.

11550 ■ "Apparel Apparatchic at Kmart" in *Barron's* **(Vol. 88, March 17, 2008, No. 11, pp. 16)**
Pub: Dow Jones & Company, Inc.
Description: Kmart began a nationwide search for women to represent the company in a national advertising campaign. Contestants need to upload their photos to Kmart's website and winners will be chosen by a panel of celebrity judges. The contest aims to reverse preconceived negative notions about the store's quality and service.

11551 ■ "Apps For Anybody With an Idea" in *Advertising Age* **(Vol. 79, October 20, 2008, No. 39, pp. 29)**
Pub: Crain Communications, Inc.
Ed: Beth Snyder Bulik. **Description:** Apple's new online App Store is open to anyone with an idea and the ability to write code and many of these developers are not only finding a sense of community through this venue but are also making money since the sales are split with Apple, 30/70 in the developer's favor.

11552 ■ "Are Offline Pushes Important to E-Commerce?" in *DM News* **(Vol. 31, September 14, 2009, No. 23, pp. 10)**
Pub: Haymarket Media, Inc.
Description: With the importance of Internet marketing and the popularity of ecommerce increasing experts debate the relevance of more traditional channels of advertising.

11553 ■ "Attention, Please" in *Entrepreneur* **(Vol. 36, April 2008, No. 4, pp. 52)**
Pub: Entrepreneur Media, Inc.
Ed: Andrea Cooper. **Description:** Gurbaksh Chahal created his own company ClickAgents at the age of 16, and sold it two years later for $40 million to ValueClick. He then founded BlueLithium, an online advertising network on behavioral targeting, which Yahoo! Inc. bought in 2007 for $300 million. Chahal, now 25, talks about his next plans and describes how BlueLithium caught Yahoo's attention.

11554 ■ "Attorney Internet Marketing Services Launched by SEO Advantage at SEOLegal.com" in *Internet Wire* **(October 5, 2009)**
Pub: Comtex News Network, Inc.
Description: SEO Advantage, an Internet marketing and website designer firm, has extended its services to the legal industry.

11555 ■ "Attract More Online Customers: Make Your Website Work Harder for You" in *Black Enterprise* **(Vol. 37, November 2006, No. 4, pp. 66)**
Pub: Earl G. Graves Publishing Co. Inc.
Ed: Description: Having an impressive presence on the Internet has become crucial. Detailed advice on making your website serve your business in the best way possible is included.

11556 ■ "Auto Show Taps Moms" in *Marketing to Women* **(Vol. 21, April 2008, No. 4, pp. 3)**
Pub: EPM Communications, Inc.
Description: Teamed with Mother Proof, an online site which features automotive content aimed at moms, the Chicago Auto Show will present a full day of programming with the emphasis on mom.

11557 ■ "avVaa World Health Care Products Rolls Out Internet Marketing Program" in *Health and Beauty Close-Up* **(September 18, 2009)**
Pub: Close-Up Media
Description: avVaa World Health Care Products, Inc., a biotechnology company, manufacturer and distributor of nationally branded therapeutic, natural health care and skin products, has signed an agreement with Online Performance Marketing to launch of an Internet marketing campaign in order to broaden its presence online. The impact of advertising on the Internet to generate an increase in sales is explored.

11558 ■ "The Bankrate Double Pay" in *Barron's* **(Vol. 88, March 24, 2008, No. 12, pp. 27)**
Pub: Dow Jones & Company, Inc.
Ed: Neil A. Martin. **Description:** Shares of Bankrate may rise as much as 25 percent from their level of $45.08 a share due to a strong cash flow and balance sheet. The company's Internet business remains strong despite weakness in the online advertising industry and is a potential takeover target.

11559 ■ "Banks Fall Short in Online Services for Savvy Traders" in *Barron's* **(Vol. 88, March 17, 2008, No. 11, pp. 35)**
Pub: Dow Jones & Company, Inc.
Ed: Theresa W. Carey. **Description:** Banc of America Investment Services, WellsTrade, and ShareBuilder are at the bottom of the list of online brokerages because they offer less trading technologies and product range. Financial shoppers miss out on a lot of customized tools and analytics when using these services.

11560 ■ "BayTSP, NTT Data Corp. Enter Into Reseller Pact to Market Online IP Monitoring" in *Professional Services Close-Up* **(Sept. 11, 2009)**
Pub: Close-Up Media
Description: Due to incredible interest from distributors and content owners across Asia, NTT Data Corp. will resell BayTSP's online intellectual property monitoring, enforcement, business intelligence and monetization services in Japan.

11561 ■ "Be Wary of Legal Advice on Internet, Lawyers Warn" in *Crain's Detroit Business* **(Vol. 24, September 22, 2008, No. 38, pp. 16)**
Pub: Crain Communications, Inc.
Ed: Harriet Tramer. **Description:** While some lawyers feel that the proliferation of legal information on the Internet can point people in the right direction, others maintain that it simply results in giving false hope, may bring about confusion or worse yet, it sometimes makes their jobs even harder.

11562 ■ "Being all a-Twitter" in *Canadian Business* **(Vol. 81, December 8, 2008, No. 21, pp. 22)**
Pub: Rogers Media Ltd.
Ed: Andrew Wahl. **Description:** Marketing experts suggest that advertising strategies have to change along with new online social media. Companies are advised to find ways to incorporate social software because workers and customers are expected to continue its use.

11563 ■ "Blacks Go Broadband: High Speed Internet Adoption Grows Among African Americans" in *Black Enterprise* **(Vol. 38, February 2008)**
Pub: Earl G. Graves Publishing Co. Inc.
Ed: Cliff Hocker. **Description:** Number of black households using broadband Internet services tripled since 2005 according to a survey conducted by Pew Internet and American Life Project.

11564 ■ "Blockbuster Launches Internet Movie Downloads to Compete Against Netflix, Others" in *Chicago Tribune* **(December 3, 2008)**
Pub: McClatchy-Tribune Information Services
Ed: Eric Benderoff. **Description:** Blockbuster Inc., the DVD rental giant, has launched a new service that delivers movies to their customer's homes via the Internet in an attempt to compete against Netflix and other competitors.

11565 ■ "Blog Buzz Heralds Arrival of IPhone 2.0" in *Advertising Age* **(Vol. 79, June 9, 2008, No. 40, pp. 8)**
Pub: Crain Communications, Inc.
Ed: Abbey Klaasen. **Description:** Predictions concerning the next version of the iPhone include a global-positioning-system technology as well as a configuration to run on a faster, 3G network.

11566 ■ "Boom has Tech Grads Mulling Their Options" in *Globe & Mail* **(March 14, 2006, pp. B1)**
Pub: CTVglobemedia Publishing Inc.
Ed: Grant Robertson. **Description:** Internet giant Google Inc. has stepped up its efforts to hire the talented people, in Canada, at Waterloo University in southern Ontario, to expand its operations. The details of the job market and increasing salaries are analyzed.

11567 ■ "Borders Previews New Web Site" in *Crain's Detroit Business* **(Vol. 23, October 8, 2007, No. 41, pp. 4)**
Pub: Crain Communications Inc. - Detroit
Ed: Sheena Harrison. **Description:** Borders Group Inc. previewed its new Website that allows customers to buy items that include the Magic Shelf, a virtual bookcase that displays available recommended books, movies and music.

11568 ■ "Bottoms Up!" in *Entrepreneur* **(Vol. 36, April 2008, No. 4, pp. 128)**
Pub: Entrepreneur Media, Inc.
Ed: Amanda C. Kooser. **Description:** Jill Bernheimer launched her online alcohol business Domaine547 in 2007, and encountered challenges as legal issues over the licensing and launching of the business took about seven months to finish. Domain547 features blog and forum areas. Marketing strategy that connects to the social community is one of the ways to reach out to customers.

11569 ■ "Branding Your Way" in *Canadian Business* **(Vol. 80, February 12, 2007, No. 4, pp. 31)**
Pub: Rogers Media
Ed: Erin Pooley. **Description:** The trend in involving consumers in brand marketing by seeking their views through contests or inviting them to produce and submit commercials through Internet is discussed.

11570 ■ "Break Up the Gang?" in *Canadian Business* **(Vol. 81, November 10, 2008, No. 19, pp. 24)**
Pub: Rogers Media Ltd.
Ed: Andrew Wahl. **Description:** Nortel Networks Corporation announced they will their Metro Ethernet Network division, suggesting desperation on the part of the company. Some analysts suggest the division is promising, if still unprofitable.

11571 ■ "Brite-Strike Tactical Launches New Internet Marketing Initiatives" in *Internet Wire* **(September 15, 2009)**
Pub: Comtex News Network, Inc.
Description: Brite-Strike Tactical Illumination Products, Inc. has enlisted the expertise of Internet marketing guru Thomas J. McCarthy to help revamp the company's Internet campaign. An outline of the Internet marketing strategy is provided.

11572 ■ "Broadband Reaches Access Limits in Europe" in *Information Today* **(Vol. 26, February 2009, No. 2, pp. 22)**
Pub: Information Today, Inc.

Ed: Jim Ashling. **Description:** Eurostat (the Statistical Office of the European communities) reports results from is survey regarding Internet use by businesses throughout its 27-member states. Iceland, Finland and the Netherlands provide the most access at broadband speeds, followed by Belgium, Spain and France.

11573 ■ "BusinessOnLine Launches a New Web-Based Search Engine Optimization Tool" in *Internet Wire* **(October 19, 2009)**
Pub: Comtex News Network, Inc.

Description: First Link Checker, a complimentary new search engine optimization tool that helps site owners optimize their on-page links by understanding which of those links are actually being counted in Google's relevancy algorithm, was developed by BusinessOnLine, a rapidly growing Internet marketing agency. This tool will make it easy for the average web master to ensure that their internal link structure is optimized.

11574 ■ "Campaigner Survey: 46 Percent of Small Businesses Use Email Marketing" in *Wireless News* **(November 21, 2009)**
Pub: Close-Up Media

Description: Almost half (46 percent) of small businesses surveyed by Campaigner's 2009 State of Small Business Online Marketing, say that they rely on email marketing to help them find new customers, keep existing ones and grow their businesses. The survey also found that 36 percent of small businesses plan to begin using email marketing over the next year. The trend to utilize Internet marketing tools is allowing small businesses to grow faster and generate higher revenues than those that are not using these mediums.

11575 ■ "Canadians Keep Memories in 'Inboxes' Instead of Shoe Boxes; MSN Canada" in *Canadian Corporate News* **(May 14, 2007)**
Pub: Comtex News Network Inc.

Description: According to an MSN Canada online poll, 76 percent of Canadians are creating 'virtual shoeboxes' with their email inboxes and archiving important messages, photos, and documents.

11576 ■ "CarTango Lauches Site for Women" in *Marketing to Women* **(Vol. 21, April 2008, No. 4, pp. 5)**
Pub: EPM Communications, Inc.

Description: CarTango.com is an Internet site that seeks to overcome what women say are dismissive or pushy salespeople by allowing the shoppers the chance to decide what they want before inviting dealers to compete for their business.

11577 ■ "Cell Phone the Ticket on American Airlines" in *Chicago Tribune* **(November 14, 2008)**
Pub: McClatchy-Tribune Information Services

Ed: Julie Johnsson. **Description:** American Airlines is testing a new mobile boarding pass at O'Hare International Airport. Travelers on American can board flights and get through security checkpoints by flashing a bar code on their phones. Passengers must have an Internet-enabled mobile device and an active e-mail address in order to utilize this service.

11578 ■ "Charlotte Pipe Launches Satirical Campaign" in *Contractor* **(Vol. 57, January 2010, No. 1, pp. 6)**
Pub: Penton Media, Inc.

Description: Charlotte Pipe and Foundry Co. launched an advertising campaign that uses social media and humor to make a point about how it can be nearly impossible to determine if imported cast iron pipes and fittings meet the same quality standards as what is made in the U.S. The campaign features 'pipe whisperers' and also spoofs pipe sniffing dogs.

11579 ■ "Chris Curtis Preaches the Gospel of Internet Success" in *Black Enterprise* **(Vol. 38, March 2008, No. 8, pp. 56)**
Pub: Earl G. Graves Publishing Co. Inc.

Ed: Anthony Calypso. **Description:** Profile of the Web Business Ownership Series, a collection of 20 free seminars that help small businesses learn about the Web development process.

11580 ■ *Cisco Network Design Solutions for Small-Medium Businesses*
Pub: Cisco Press

Ed: Peter Rybaczyk. **Released:** August 2004. **Price:** $55.00. **Description:** Solutions for computer networking professionals using computer networks within a small to medium-sized business. Topics cover not only core networking issues and solutions, but security, IP telephony, unified communications, customer relations management, wireless LANs, and more.

11581 ■ "A Class Act" in *Hawaii Business* **(Vol. 53, March 2008, No. 9, pp. 25)**
Pub: Hawaii Business Publishing

Ed: Cathy S. Cruz-George. **Description:** UBoost is a startup company that offers online content for the educational magazine 'Weekly Reader'. The website features quizzes and allows users to accumulate points and redeem rewards afterward. Other details about the company are discussed.

11582 ■ "ClickFuel Launches New Products to Help Small and Mid-Sized Businesses Bolster Their Brand Online" in *Internet Wire* **(Dec. 3, 2009)**
Pub: Comtex News Network, Inc.

Description: Boostability, a provider of Enterprise Search Engine Optimization (SEO) software technology, has partnered with ClickFuel, a firm that designs, tracks and manages Internet marketing campaigns in order to leverage Boostability's technology in order to deliver comprehensive SEO solutions to small and mid-size businesses; three new products will also become available for these business clients to help them manage all facets of their online presence.

11583 ■ "ClickFuel Unveils Internet Marketing Tools for Small Businesses" in *Internet Wire* **(October 19, 2009)**
Pub: Comtex News Network, Inc.

Description: ClickFuel, a firm that manages, designs and tracks marketing campaigns has unveiled a full software suite of affordable services and technology solutions designed to empower small business owners and help them promote and grow their businesses through targeted Internet marketing campaigns.

11584 ■ *Clicking Through: A Survival Guide for Bringing Your Company Online*
Pub: Bloomberg Press

Ed: Jonathan I. Ezor. **Released:** October 1999. **Description:** Summary of legal compliance issues faced by small companies doing business on the Internet, including copyright and patent laws.

11585 ■ "CN to Webcast 2007 Analyst Meeting in Toronto May 23-24" in *Canadian Corporate News* **(May 16, 2007)**
Pub: Comtex News Network Inc.

Description: Canadian National Railway Company (CN) broadcast its analyst meeting in Toronto with a webcast which focused on CN's opportunities, strategies, and financial outlook through the year 2010.

11586 ■ "Comcast Launches New Home Security Service, Developed in Portland" in *The Oregonian* **(June 7, 2011)**
Pub: McClatchy-Tribune Regional News

Ed: Mike Rogoway. **Description:** Comcast introduced its new high-end home security system that provides 24-hour monitoring and control of homes and utilities, along with Web and mobile access.

11587 ■ *The Complete Guide to Google Adwords: Secrets, Techniques, and Strategies You Can Learn to Make Millions*
Pub: Atlantic Publishing Company

Released: December 1, 2010. **Price:** $24.95. **Description:** Google AdWords, when it launched in 2002 signaled a fundamental shift in what the Inter-

net was for so many individuals and companies. Learning and understanding how Google AdWords operates and how it can be optimized for maximum exposure, boosting click through rates, conversions, placement, and selection of the right keywords, can be the key to a successful online business.

11588 ■ "Connections: United We Gab" in *Entrepreneur* **(Vol. 35, October 2007, No. 10, pp. 60)**
Pub: Entrepreneur Media Inc.

Ed: Mike Hogan. **Description:** T-Mobile and AT&T introduced dual-mode service to consumers, helping them to switch between cellular and Wi-Fi networks easily. These services, such as Hotspot@Home, reduces the cost of long distance calls by routing them over the Internet with the use of WiFi. Benefits of dual mode service, such as lower hardware price and better call coverage are given.

11589 ■ "Contec Innovations Inc.: MovieSet.com First to Mobilize Content Using BUZmob" in *Canadian Corporate News* **(May 16, 2007)**
Pub: Comtex News Network Inc.

Description: Contec Innovations Inc., a provider of mobile infrastructure software, announced that MovieSet.com is the first Internet portal to mobilize their content using BUZmob, the company's new mobile publishing service that allows content publishers to enable mobile access to their feed-based content on any mobile device or network in real-time.

11590 ■ "Conversations with Customers" in *Business Journal Serving Greater Tampa Bay* **(Vol. 31, December 31, 2010, No. 1, pp. 1)**
Pub: Tampa Bay Business Journal

Description: Tampa Bay, Florida-based businesses have been using social media to interact with customers. Forty percent of businesses have been found to have at least one social media platform to reach customers and prospects.

11591 ■ "Coping with the Web" in *Agency Sales Magazine* **(Vol. 39, December 2009, No. 11, pp. 52)**
Pub: MANA

Ed: Karen Saunders. **Description:** When branding your company on the Internet, strategy should first be discussed with the website designer and the target and niche audience should also be defined. Describing "what" and "how" the product or service is offering is also important. In addition, perception, the logo, and the tag line are some elements that are needed to create a brand.

11592 ■ "Cox Opens Norfolk Mall Kiosk; Wireless Service Not Ready" in *Virginian-Pilot* **(September 20, 2010)**
Pub: Virginian-Pilot

Ed: Carolyn Shapiro. **Description:** Cox Communications opened a kiosk at MacArthur Center that will sell wireless telephone devices and plans.

11593 ■ "Cross Atlantic Commodities Launches National Internet Marketing Programs" in *Manufacturing Close-Up* **(September 8, 2009)**
Pub: Close-Up Media

Description: Profile of the Internet campaign recently launched by Cross Atlantic Commodities, Inc., a manufacturer of specialty beauty and health products.

11594 ■ *Crossing the Chasm: Marketing and Selling Disruptive Products to Mainstream Customers*
Pub: HarperInformation

Ed: Geoffrey A. Moore. **Released:** September 2002. **Price:** $17.95. **Description:** A guide for marketing in high-technology industries, focusing on the Internet.

11595 ■ "Cyber Thanksgiving Online Shopping a Growing Tradition" in *Marketing Weekly News* **(December 12, 2009, pp. 137)**
Pub: Investment Weekly News

Description: According to e-commerce analysts, Thanksgiving day is becoming increasingly important to retailers in terms of online sales. Internet marketers are realizing that consumers are already searching for Black Friday sales and if they find deals on the products they are looking for, they are highly likely to make their purchase on Thanksgiving day instead of waiting.

11596 ■ "Datran Media Executives to Lead Industry Debates Across Q1 Conferences" in *Internet Wire* **(January 22, 2010)**
Pub: Comtex News Network, Inc.
Description: Datran Media, an industry-leading digital marketing technology company, will be sending members of its management team to several conferences in the early part of the first quarter of 2010; discussions will include Internet marketing innovations, e-commerce and media distribution.

11597 ■ *Design and Launch Your eCommerce Business in a Week*
Pub: Entrepreneur Press
Ed: Jason R. Rich. **Released:** July 2008. **Price:** $17.95. **Description:** Guide to help anyone start an online business in one week; included tips for Website design.

11598 ■ *Design and Launch Your Online Boutique in a Week*
Pub: Entrepreneur Press
Ed: Melissa Campanelli. **Released:** June 2008. **Price:** $17.95. **Description:** Guide to start an online boutique includes information on business planning, Website design and funding.

11599 ■ "Designing Events Updates Online Suite" in *Wireless News* **(October 25, 2009)**
Pub: Close-Up Media
Description: Designing Events, an outsourcing and consulting firm for conferences and meetings, announced the release of an update to its Designing Events Online suite of web-based management and marketing tools; features include enhanced versions of online registration and collaboration, content management, session development, social media and conference websites.

11600 ■ *Designing Websites for Every Audience*
Pub: F & W Publications, Incorporated
Ed: Ilise Benun. **Released:** January 2003. **Description:** Twenty-five case studies targeting six difference audiences are used to help a business design, or make over, a Website.

11601 ■ *Digital Divide: Civic Engagement, Information Poverty, and the Internet Worldwide*
Pub: Cambridge University Press
Ed: Pippa Norris. **Released:** January 22, 2010. **Price:** $28.99. **Description:** The expansive growth of the Internet is intensifying existing inequalities between the information rich and poor. The book examines the evidence for access and use of the Internet in 179 countries and discusses the global divide that is evident between industrialized and developing societies.

11602 ■ "Diving Into Internet Marketing" in *American Agent and Broker* **(Vol. 81, December 2009, No. 12, pp. 24)**
Pub: Summit Business Media
Ed: Steve Anderson. **Description:** Internet marketing is becoming an essential tool for most businesses; advice is provided regarding the social networking opportunities available for marketing one's product or service on the Internet.

11603 ■ "Do-It-Yourself Portfolio Management" in *Barron's* **(Vol. 89, July 13, 2009, No. 28, pp. 25)**
Pub: Dow Jones & Co., Inc.
Ed: Mike Hogan. **Description:** Services of several portfolio management web sites are presented. These web sites include MarketRiders E.Adviser, TD Ameritrade and E*Trade.

11604 ■ "Don't' Hate the Cable Guy" in *Saint Louis Business Journal* **(Vol. 31, August 5, 2011, No. 50, pp. 1)**
Pub: Saint Louis Business Journal
Ed: Angela Mueller. **Description:** Charter Communications named John Birrer as senior vice president of customer experience. The company experienced problems with its customer services.

11605 ■ *Double or Nothing: How Two Friends Risked It All to Buy One of Las Vegas' Legendary Casinos*
Pub: HarperBusiness
Ed: Tom Breitling, with Cal Fussman. **Released:** March 2008. **Price:** $24.95. **Description:** Founders of a successful Internet travel agency share their experience from startup to selling the company.

11606 ■ "Drive Traffic To Your Blog" in *Women Entrepreneur* **(January 13, 2009)**
Pub: Entrepreneur Media Inc.
Ed: Lesley Spencer Pyle. **Description:** Internet social networking has become a vital component to marketing one's business. Tips are provided on how to establish a blog that will attract attention to one's business and keep one's customers coming back for more.

11607 ■ "The Easy Route" in *Entrepreneur* **(Vol. 36, April 2008, No. 4, pp. 60)**
Pub: Entrepreneur Media, Inc.
Ed: Amanda C. Kooser. **Description:** Buyer's guide of wireless office routers is presented. All products included in the list use the latest draft-n technology. Price and availability of the products are provided.

11608 ■ *EBay Income: How ANYONE of Any Age, Location, and/or Background Can Build a Highly Profitable Online Business with eBay (Revised 2nd Edition)*
Pub: Atlantic Publishing Company
Released: December 1, 2010. **Price:** $24.95. **Description:** A complete overview of eBay is given and guides any small company through the entire process of creating the auction and auction strategies, photography, writing copy, text and formatting, multiple sales, programming tricks, PayPal, accounting, creating marketing, merchandising, managing email lists, advertising plans, taxes and sales tax, best time to list items and for how long, sniping programs, international customers, opening a storefront, electronic commerce, buy-it now pricing, keywords, Google marketing and eBay secrets.

11609 ■ *Electronic Commerce*
Pub: Course Technology
Ed: Gary Schneider, Bryant Chrzan, Charles McCormick. **Released:** May 1, 2010. **Price:** $117.95. **Description:** E-commerce can open the door to more opportunities than ever before for small business. Packed with real-world examples and cases, the book delivers comprehensive coverage of emerging online technologies and trends and their influence on the electronic marketplace. It details how the landscape of online commerce is evolving, reflecting changes in the economy and how business and society are responding to those changes. Balancing technological issues with the strategic business aspects of successful e-commerce, the new edition includes expanded coverage of international issues, social networking, mobile commerce, Web 2.0 technologies, and updates on spam, phishing, and identity theft.

11610 ■ *Electronic Commerce: Technical, Business, and Legal Issues*
Pub: Prentice Hall PTR
Ed: Oktay Dogramaci; Aryya Gangopadhyay; Yelena Yesha; Nabil R. Adam. **Released:** August 1998. **Description:** Provides insight into the goals of using the Internet to grow a business in the areas of networking and telecommunication, security, and storage and retrieval; business areas such as marketing, procurement and purchasing, billing and payment, and supply chain management; and legal aspects such as privacy, intellectual property, taxation, contractual and legal settlements.

11611 ■ *Emerging Business Online: Global Markets and the Power of B2B Internet Marketing*
Pub: FT Press
Ed: Lara Fawzy, Lucas Dworksi. **Released:** October 1, 2010. **Price:** $49.99. **Description:** An introduction into ebocube (emerging business online), a comprehensive proven business model for Internet B2B marketing in emerging markets.

11612 ■ "Empowered" in *Harvard Business Review* **(Vol. 88, July-August 2010, No. 7-8, pp. 94)**
Pub: Harvard Business School Publishing
Ed: Josh Bernoff, Ted Schadler. **Description:** HERO concept (highly empowered and resourceful operative) which builds a connection between employees, managers, and IT is outlined. The resultant additional experience and knowledge gained by employees improves customer relationship management.

11613 ■ "Endeca Gears Up for Likely IPO Bid" in *Boston Business Journal* **(Vol. 31, July 1, 2011, No. 23, pp. 1)**
Pub: Boston Business Journal
Ed: Kyle Alspach. **Description:** Endeca Inc. is readying itself for its plans to register as a public company. The search engine technology leader is enjoying continued growth with revenue up by 30 percent in 2010 while its expansion trend makes it an unlikely candidate for an acquisition.

11614 ■ "Entrepreneur Column" in *Entrepreneur* **(September 24, 2009)**
Pub: Entrepreneur Media, Inc.
Ed: Allen Moon. **Description:** In an attempt to compete with Google, Microsoft and Yahoo have entered a partnership to merge their search services; advice on the best ways to get noticed on this new search engine entitled Bing, is provided.

11615 ■ *The Facebook Effect: The Inside Story of the Company That Is Connecting the World*
Pub: Simon & Shuster
Ed: David Kirkpatrick. **Released:** June 8, 2010. **Price:** $26.00. **Description:** There's never been a Website like Facebook: more than 350 million people have accounts, and if the growth rate continues, by 2013 every Internet user worldwide will have his or her own page. No one's had more access to the inner workings of the phenomenon than Kirkpatrick, a senior tech writer at Fortune magazine. Written with the full cooperation of founder Mark Zuckerberg, the book follows the company from its genesis in a Harvard dorm room through its successes over Friendster and MySpace, the expansion of the user base, and Zuckerberg's refusal to sell.

11616 ■ "Fast Fact: Women's Online Habits" in *Marketing to Women* **(Vol. 22, July 2009, No. 7, pp. 1)**
Pub: EPM Communications, Inc.
Description: Lists the Internet habits of women. Statistical data included.

11617 ■ "Fast Revival Unlikely For Indian 'Net Stocks" in *Barron's* **(Vol. 88, July 7, 2008, No. 27, pp. 12)**
Pub: Dow Jones & Co., Inc.
Ed: Leslie P. Norton. **Description:** Shares of Indian Internet companies Rediff.com and Sify are not likely to stage a rebound due to weak financial results. Rediff.com shares have declined 39.2 percent in 2008, while Sify shares are down 35.8 percent.

11618 ■ "Financo Panel Lauds Product, Online Marketing" in *Home Textiles Today* **(Vol. 31, January 25, 2010, No. 3, pp. 1)**
Pub: Reed Business Information, Inc.
Ed: James Mammarella. **Description:** Overview of the Financo Annual Merchandising Industry Chief Executives Event during which there was much discussion on the merits of e-commerce, online marketing as well as the traditional methods of brand recognition and retailing.

11619 ■ "Fitter from Twitter" in *Boston Business Journal* **(Vol. 30, December 17, 2010, No. 47, pp. 1)**
Pub: Boston Business Journal
Ed: Lisa van der Pool. **Description:** Small businesses are increasing their use of the Twitter microblogging platform to attract and retain customers. Lisa Johnson, who owns Modern Pilates studios, managed to raise awareness of her personal brand nationally through the social media platform.

11620 ■ "Five Low-Cost Home Based Startups" in *Women Entrepreneur* (December 16, 2008)
Pub: Entrepreneur Media Inc.
Ed: Lesley Spencer Pyle. **Description:** During tough economic times, small businesses have an advantage over large companies because they can adjust to economic conditions more easily and without having to go through corporate red tape that can slow the implementation process. A budding entrepreneur may find success by taking inventory of his or her skills, experience, expertise and passions and utilizing those qualities to start a business. Five low-cost home-based startups are profiled. These include starting an online store, a virtual assistant service, web designer, sales representative and a home staging counselor.

11621 ■ "Fly Phishing" in *Canadian Business* (Vol. 80, October 22, 2007, No. 21, pp. 42)
Pub: Rogers Media
Ed: Andy Holloway. **Description:** Symantec Corporation's report shows consumers and companies have effectively installed network defenses that prevent unwanted access. Phishing packages are readily available and are widely used. Other details of the Internet Security Threat Report are presented.

11622 ■ "The Folly of Google's Latest Gambit" in *Barron's* (Vol. 89, July 13, 2009, No. 28, pp. 23)
Pub: Dow Jones & Co., Inc.
Ed: Eric J. Savitz. **Description:** Google will enter the operating systems business with the introduction of the Google Chrome OS but its success is dubious because the project is still a year or so away while Microsoft will release an updated version of Windows by then; another problem is that Google already has another OS called Android which will overlap with the Chrome OS's market.

11623 ■ "For MySpace, A Redesign to Entice Generation Y" in *The New York Times* (October 27, 2010, pp. B3)
Pub: The New York Times Company
Ed: Miguel Helft. **Description:** MySpace is redesigning its Website in order to attract individuals from the Generation Y group.

11624 ■ "ForeSee Finds Satisfaction On Web Sites, Bottom Line" in *Crain's Detroit Business* (Vol. 24, February 25, 2008, No. 8, pp. 3)
Pub: Crain Communications Inc. - Detroit
Ed: Tom Henderson. **Description:** Ann Arbor-based ForeSee Results Inc. evaluates user satisfaction on Web sites. The company expects to see an increase of 40 percent in revenue for 2008 with plans to expand to London, Germany, Italy and France by the end of 2009.

11625 ■ "Forsys Metals Corporation Goes "Live" With Q4's On-Demand Disclosure Management Software" in *Canadian Corporate News* (May 16, 2007)
Pub: Comtex News Network Inc.
Description: Forsys Metals Corp. selected Q4 Web Systems to automate its corporate website disclosure with Q4's software platform which also automates and simplifies many of the administrative tasks that Forsys was doing manually, allowing them to focus their internal resources on the business.

11626 ■ "The Fort" in *Hawaii Business* (Vol. 53, November 2007, No. 5, pp. 19)
Pub: Hawaii Business Publishing
Ed: Jason Ubay. **Description:** DRFortress' flagship data center The Fort located at Honolulu's Airport Industrial Park provides companies a place to store their servers in an ultra-secure environment. Anything stored in here that requires power has a back up and in case of an outage generators can supply power up to 80 hrs. The Fort caters to major carriers and Internet service providers.

11627 ■ "Fresh Direct's Crisis" in *Crain's New York Business* (Vol. 24, January 14, 2008, No. 2, pp. 3)
Pub: Crain Communications, Inc.
Ed: Lisa Fickenscher. **Description:** Freshdirect, an Internet grocery delivery service, finds itself under siege from federal immigration authorities, customers

and labor organizations due to its employment practice of hiring illegals. At stake is the grocer's reputation as well as its ambitious growth plans, including an initial public offering of its stock.

11628 ■ "The Frugal Billionaire" in *Canadian Business* (Vol. 79, Winter 2006, No. 24, pp. 63)
Pub: Rogers Media
Ed: Joe Castaldo. **Description:** The achievements of David Cheriton are described, along with his investments in various firms, including Google Inc.

11629 ■ "Funbrain Launches Preschool Content" in *Marketing to Women* (Vol. 21, March 2008, No. 3, pp. 3)
Pub: EPM Communications, Inc.
Description: Funbrain.com launches The Moms and Kids Playground, a section of the website devoted to activities and games for moms and kids aged 2 to 6; content aims at building early computer skills and to teach basic concepts such as counting and colors.

11630 ■ "Generation Y Chooses the Mobile Web" in *PR Newswire* (November 24, 2010)
Pub: PR Newswire Association LLC
Description: Generation Y individuals between the ages of 18 - 27 use their mobile phones to browse the Internet more often than a desktop or laptop computer, according to a survey conducted by Opera, a Web browser company.

11631 ■ "Get Online or Be Left Behind" in *Women In Business* (Vol. 61, August-September 2009, No. 4, pp. 33)
Pub: American Business Women's Association
Ed: Diane Stafford. **Description:** Technology's significance for the connectivity purposes among business people is discussed. Details on the use of wireless tools and online social media to boost technology IQ are presented.

11632 ■ "Get Them Talking" in *Entrepreneur* (Vol. 36, February 2008, No. 2, pp. 50)
Pub: Entrepreneur Media Inc.
Ed: Heather Clancy. **Description:** Yelp.com is an Internet search site that presents businesses across the U.S., sorted according to the number of customer reviews they have received. One to five stars are used by the reviewers, or yelpers, to rate businesses. Details on how the International Orange day spa benefited from Yelp are discussed.

11633 ■ "Giants Now Admit They Roam Planet Earth; Time To Buy?" in *Barron's* (Vol. 88, March 31, 2008, No. 13, pp. 39)
Pub: Dow Jones & Company, Inc.
Ed: Eric J. Savitz. **Description:** Oracle's third-quarter results showed that top-line growth fell short of expectations but the company is expected to fare better than most applications companies in the downturn. Google had a flat growth in the number of people who click their online ads. The time for investors in the tech sector with a long-term horizon has arrived.

11634 ■ "Go Beyond Local Search With Hyper-Local" in *Women Entrepreneur* (October 30, 2008)
Pub: Entrepreneur Media Inc.
Ed: Lena West. **Description:** According to Forrester Research, as much as $500 billion in local spending in 2007 was influenced by the Internet and industry analysts report that consumers spend approximately 80 percent of their income within 50 miles of their home. Discussion of ways in which to capitalize on the hyper-local trend that is being driven by greater Internet connectivity and use of the web to find information is provided.

11635 ■ "Google Edges into Wireless E-Mail" in *Globe & Mail* (February 19, 2007, pp. B5)
Pub: CTVglobemedia Publishing Inc.
Ed: Simon Avery. **Description:** Google Inc. has introduced a free mobile e-mail service in Canada. The mobile users can read, send, and search messages using the new software.

11636 ■ "Google, MySpace Deal Hits Snag" in *Globe & Mail* (February 7, 2007, pp. B11)
Pub: CTVglobemedia Publishing Inc.
Ed: Julia Angwin; Kevin J. Delaney. **Description:** MySpace's intention to partner with eBay which is delaying the finalization of its $900 million online advertising deal signed with Google Inc. is discussed.

11637 ■ "Google Places a Call to Bargain Hunters" in *Advertising Age* (Vol. 79, September 29, 2008, No. 36, pp. 13)
Pub: Crain Communications, Inc.
Ed: Abbey Klaassen. **Description:** Google highlighted application developers who have created tools for its Android mobile phone in the device's unveiling; applications such as ShopSavvy and CompareEverywhere help shoppers to find bargains by allowing them to compare prices in their local areas and across the web.

11638 ■ *The Google Story: Inside the Hottest Business, Media, and Technology Success of Our Time*
Pub: Random Housing Publishing Group
Ed: David A. Vise; Mark Malseed. **Price:** $26.00.

11639 ■ "Google's Next Stop: Below 350?" in *Barron's* (Vol. 88, March 10, 2008, No. 10, pp. 17)
Pub: Dow Jones & Company, Inc.
Ed: Jacqueline Doherty. **Description:** Share prices of Google Inc. are expected to drop from their level of $433 each to below $350 per share. The company is expected to miss its earnings forecast for the first quarter of 2008, and its continued aggressive spending on non-core areas will eventually bring down earnings.

11640 ■ "Googly Eyed" in *Entrepreneur* (Vol. 36, February 2008, No. 2, pp. 48)
Pub: Entrepreneur Media Inc.
Ed: Mike Hogan. **Description:** Linux has developed desktops that boot into the Google toolbar and applications. These desktops include: Zonbu, Everex gPCTC2502, and Asus Eee PC 4G mini laptop. Details on the applications of these desktops are discussed.

11641 ■ "Graceful Landing" in *Entrepreneur* (Vol. 37, November 2009, No. 11, pp. 59)
Pub: Entrepreneur Media, Inc.
Ed: Mikal E. Belicove. **Description:** Successful marketers regularly use Website landing pages to capture qualified leads and make sales. It is believed that an effective landing page devoted to a single product or service offering can significantly boost leads and conversion rates. Organizations can create a top-notch landing page by anticipating customer expectations and focusing on a clear call to action.

11642 ■ *Groundswell: Winning in a World Transformed by Social Technologies*
Pub: Harvard Business School Press
Ed: Charlene Li; Josh Bernoff. **Released:** April 21, 2008. **Price:** $29.95. **Description:** Individuals are using online social technologies such as blogs, social networking sites, YouTube, and podcasts to discuss products and companies, write their own news, and find their own deals. When consumers you've never met are rating your company's products in public forums with which you have no experience or influence, your company is vulnerable. This book teaches the tools and data necessary to turn this treat into an opportunity.

11643 ■ *Grown Up Digital: How the Net Generation Is Changing Your World*
Pub: The McGraw-Hill Companies
Ed: Don Tapscott. **Released:** 2009. **Price:** $27.95. **Description:** As baby boomers retire, business needs to understand what makes the Internet work for business.

11644 ■ "Growth of Free Dailies Dropping" in *Globe & Mail* (March 24, 2007, pp. B7)
Pub: CTVglobemedia Publishing Inc.
Ed: Grant Robertson. **Description:** The decrease in the readership of free newspapers in Canada, in view of growing preference for online news, is discussed.

11645 ■ "A Hacker in India Hijacked His Website Design and Was Making Good Money Selling It" in *Inc.* (December 2007, pp. 77-78, 80)
Pub: Gruner & Jahr USA Publishing
Ed: Darren Dahl. **Description:** John Anton, owner of an online custom T-shirt business and how a company in India was selling software Website templates identical to his firm's Website.

11646 ■ "Happy Blogging" in *Black Enterprise* (Vol. 38, January 2008, No. 6, pp. 47)
Pub: Earl G. Graves Publishing Co. Inc.
Ed: Sonya A. Donaldson. **Description:** Individual seeks advice for setting up a Website and starting a blog; Squarespace and Weebly both offer Web design.

11647 ■ "Harlequin Leads the Way" in *Marketing to Women* (Vol. 22, July 2009, No. 7, pp. 1)
Pub: EPM Communications, Inc.
Description: Although the publishing industry has been slow to embrace new media options, the Internet is now a primary source for reaching women readers. Harlequin has been eager to court their female consumers over the Internet and often uses women bloggers in their campaigns strategies.

11648 ■ "Harley-Davidson Moves to Unconventional Marketing Plan" in *Business Journal-Milwaukee* (Vol. 28, November 26, 2010, No. 8, pp. A1)
Pub: Milwaukee Business Journal
Ed: Rich Rovito. **Description:** Harley Davidson Inc. hired Boulder, Colorado-based Victors & Spoils, an agency that specializes in crowdsourcing, to implement a new creative marketing model. Under the plan, Harley Davidson will draw on the ideas of its brand enthusiasts to help guide the brand's marketing direction.

11649 ■ "Harnessing the Wisdom of Crowds" in *Entrepreneur* (Vol. 37, September 2009, No. 9, pp. 74)
Pub: Entrepreneur Media, Inc.
Ed: Mark Henricks. **Description:** Online customer service business Get Satisfaction has registered growth. The business enables customers to search for answers to common product questions. Customers use the service to post questions, complaints, and even product ideas.

11650 ■ "Has Microsoft Found a Way to Get at Yahoo?" in *Advertising Age* (Vol. 79, July 7, 2008, No. 26, pp. 4)
Pub: Crain Communications, Inc.
Ed: Abbey Klaassen. **Description:** Microsoft's attempt to acquire Yahoo's search business is discussed as is Yahoo's plans for the future at a time when the company's shares have fallen dangerously low.

11651 ■ "Help for Job Seekers" in *Crain's Detroit Business* (Vol. 26, January 18, 2010, No. 3, pp. 14)
Pub: Crain Communications, Inc.
Description: CareerWorks is aimed at helping those who are in career transition or are looking for new jobs; this weekly collection of news, advertising and information includes weekly stories, events and the highlighting of a person who has successfully made the transition from one profession to another. On the Website, readers are welcome to post an anonymous resume in order to attract employers.

11652 ■ "A Home's Identity in Black and White" in *Crain's Chicago Business* (Vol. 31, April 21, 2008, No. 16, pp. 35)
Pub: Crain Communications, Inc.
Ed: Lisa Bertagnoli. **Description:** Real estate agents are finding that showing customers a written floor plan is a trend that is growing since many buyers feel that Online virtual tours distort a room. Although floor plans cost up to $500 to have drawn up, they clearly show potential buyers the exact dimensions of rooms and how they connect.

11653 ■ "Hoover's Mobile, MobileSP Now Available" in *Information Today* (Vol. 26, February 2009, No. 2, pp. 29)
Pub: Information Today, Inc.
Description: Hoover's Inc. introduced its Hoover's Mobile for iPhone, BlackBerry and Windows Mobile smartphones along with Hoover's MobileSP for BlackBerry and Windows Mobile. Both products allow users to access customer, prospect, and partner information; analyze competitors; prepare for meetings; and find new opportunities. In addition, MobileSP adds one-click calling to executives, GPS-enabled location searches, advanced search and list building, and a custom call queue and a 'save to contacts' capabilities.

11654 ■ "How to Boost Your Super Bowl ROI" in *Advertising Age* (Vol. 80, December 7, 2009, No. 41, pp. 3)
Pub: Crain's Communications
Ed: Abbey Klaassen. **Description:** Internet marketing is essential, even for the corporations that can afford to spend $3 million on a 30-second Super Bowl spot; last year, Super Bowl advertising reached an online viewership of 99.5 million while 98.7 million people watched the game on television validating the idea that public relations must go farther than a mere television ad campaign. Social media provides businesses with a longer shelf life for their ad campaigns. Advice is also given regarding ways in which to strategize a smart and well-thought plan for utilizing the online marketing options currently available.

11655 ■ *How to Get Rich on the Internet*
Pub: Morgan James Publishing, LLC
Ed: Ted Ciuba. **Released:** August 2004. **Price:** $19.95. **Description:** Interviews with successful Internet entrepreneurs provide insight into marketing products and services online using minimal investment. The importance of a sound marketing ad campaign using the Internet is discussed; maintaining a database and Website will automatically carry out business transactions daily. Suggestions for various types of businesses to run online are given.

11656 ■ *How to Make Money with Social Media: Using New and Emerging Media to Grow Your Business*
Pub: FT Press
Ed: Jamie Turner, Reshma Shah. **Released:** October 1, 2010. **Price:** $24.99. **Description:** Marketers, executives, entrepreneurs are shown more effective ways to utilize Internet social media to make money. This guide brings together both practical strategies and proven execution techniques for driving maximum value from social media marketing.

11657 ■ "How to Make Your Website Really Sell" in *Entrepreneur* (Vol. 37, September 2009, No. 9, pp. 79)
Pub: Entrepreneur Media, Inc.
Ed: David Port. **Description:** Advice on how to succeed in Internet marketing is presented. Offering visitors purchase incentives on the home page is encouraged. Delivery of customized landing pages and content is also recommended.

11658 ■ "How Marketers Can Tap the Web" in *Sales and Marketing Management* (November 12, 2009)
Pub: Nielsen Business Media, Inc.
Description: Internet marketing strategies require careful planning and tools in order to track success. Businesses are utilizing this trend to attract new clients as well as keep customers they already have satisfied. Advice on website development and design is provided.

11659 ■ "How Not to Build a Website" in *Women Entrepreneur* (December 24, 2008)
Pub: Entrepreneur Media Inc.
Ed: Erica Ruback; Joanie Reisen. **Description:** Tips for producing a unique and functional Website are given as well as a number of lessons a pair of entrepreneurs learned while trying to launch their networking website, MomSpace.com.

11660 ■ *How to Open and Operate a Financially Successful Bookstore on Amazon and Other Web Sites: With Companion CD-ROM*
Pub: Atlantic Publishing Company
Released: December 1, 2010. **Price:** $39.95. **Description:** This book was written for every used book aficionado and bookstore owner who currently wants to take advantage of the massive collection of online resources available to start and run your own online bookstore business.

11661 ■ "How to Ramp Up Marketing in a Downturn" in *Entrepreneur* (Vol. 37, July 2009, No. 7, pp. 55)
Pub: Entrepreneur Media, Inc.
Ed: Jeff Wuorio. **Description:** How businesses can save money while boosting their marketing efforts during a down economy is discussed. Using price-driven marketing, online social networks, and cause-driven marketing are among the suggested ways companies can attract more customers. Guarantees and warrantees, as well as contests, can also be used as marketing tools.

11662 ■ *How to Use the Internet to Advertise, Promote, and Market Your Business or Web Site: With Little or No Money*
Pub: Atlantic Publishing Company
Released: December 1, 2010. **Price:** $24.95. **Description:** Information is given to help build, promote, and make money from your Website or brick and mortar store using the Internet, with minimal costs.

11663 ■ "Hunter and the Hunted" in *Canadian Business* (Vol. 81, Summer 2008, No. 9, pp. 12)
Pub: Rogers Media Ltd.
Ed: Thomas Watson. **Description:** Brian Hunter, a partner in oil and gas engineering firm Montane Resources, invested his life savings in Vancouver-based Canacord Capital Corp. Details of the asset-backed commercial paper fiasco and Hunter's use of Facebook to encourage other investors to participate in his claim against the mortgage company are presented.

11664 ■ "iControl Networks Powers Comcast's XFINITY (Reg) Home Security Service" in *Benzinga.com* (June 9, 2011)
Pub: Benzinga.com
Ed: Benzinga Staff. **Description:** Comcast's XFINITY Home Security Service is powered by iControl Networks' OpenHome (TM) software platform. The service provides intrusion and fire protection along with interactive features such as home monitoring, home management, and energy management services with Web and mobile access.

11665 ■ *I'm on LinkedIn - Now What? (Second Edition): A Guide to Getting the Most Out of LinkedIn*
Pub: Happy About
Ed: Diane Danielson. **Released:** January 7, 2009. **Price:** $19.95. **Description:** Designed to help get the most out of LinkedIn, the popular business networking site and follows the first edition and includes the latest and great approaches using LinkedIn. With over 32 million members there is a lot of potential to find and develop relationships to help in your business and personal life, but many professionals find themselves wondering what to do once they sign up. This book explains the different benefits of the system and recommends best practices (including LinkedIn Groups) so that you get the most out of LinkedIn.

11666 ■ "Image Conscious" in *Canadian Business* (Vol. 81, March 17, 2008, No. 4, pp. 36)
Pub: Rogers Media
Ed: Andrew Wahl. **Description:** Idee Inc. is testing an Internet search engine for images that does not rely on tags but compares its visual data to a database of other images. The company was founded and managed by Leila Boujnane as an off-shoot of their risk-management software firm. Their software has already been used by image companies to track copyrighted images and to find images within their own archives.

11667 ■ **"Impressive Numbers: Companies Experience Substantial Increases in Dollars, Employment" in** *Hispanic Business* **(July-August 2007)**
Pub: Hispanic Business
Ed: Derek Reveron. **Description:** Profiles of five fastest growing Hispanic companies reporting increases in revenue and employment include Brightstar, distributor of wireless products; Greenway Ford Inc., a car dealership; Fred Loya Insurance, auto insurance carrier; and Group O, packaging company; and Diverse Staffing, Inc., an employment and staffing firm.

11668 ■ **"In Print and Online" in** *Marketing to Women* **(Vol. 22, August 2009, No. 8, pp. 3)**
Pub: EPM Communications, Inc.
Description: Seventeen magazine is unifying its print and Online editions with complementary content, a strategy that seems to be working as every aspect of Seventeen drives the reader to another component.

11669 ■ *Information Technology for the Small Business: How to Make IT Work For Your Company*
Pub: TAB Computer Systems, Incorporated
Ed: T.J. Benoit. **Released:** June 2006. **Price:** $17.95. **Description:** Basics of information technology to help small companies maximize benefits are covered. Topics include pitfalls to avoid, email and Internet use, data backup, recovery and overall IT organization.

11670 ■ **"Ingrian and Channel Management International Sign Distribution Agreement" in** *Canadian Corporate News* **(May 16, 2007)**
Pub: Comtex News Network Inc.
Description: Channel Management International (CMI), a Canadian channel management and distribution company, and Ingrian Networks, Inc., the leading provider of data privacy solutions, announced a Canadian distribution agreement to resell Ingrian encryption solutions to the Canadian market.

11671 ■ **"Inside Intel's Effectiveness System for Web Marketing" in** *Advertising Age* **(Vol. 81, January 25, 2010, No. 4, pp. 4)**
Pub: Crain's Communications
Ed: Beth Snyder Bulik. **Description:** Overview of Intel's internally developed program called Value Point System in which the company is using in order to evaluate and measure online marketing effectiveness.

11672 ■ **"Inside an Online Bazaar" in** *Entrepreneur* **(Vol. 37, September 2009, No. 9, pp. 38)**
Pub: Entrepreneur Media, Inc.
Ed: Kara Ohngren. **Description:** Etsy.com is a website that provides a marketplace for handmade products. The site has attracted more than 250,000 sellers since its launch in 2005. Site features and services are also supplied.

11673 ■ **"Internet Marketing 2.0: Closing the Online Chat Gap" in** *Agent's Sales Journal* **(November 2009, pp. 14)**
Pub: Summit Business Media
Ed: Jeff Denenholz. **Description:** Advice regarding the implementation of an Internet marketing strategy for insurance agencies includes how and why to incorporate a chat feature in which a sales agent can communicate in real-time with potential or existing customers. It is important to understand if appropriate response mechanisms are in place to convert leads into actual sales.

11674 ■ **"Internet Marketing Agency .Com Marketing Wins National Awards for Web Design and SEO" in** *Marketing Weekly News* **(Jan. 2, 2010)**
Pub: Investment Weekly News
Description: Internet marketing agency .Com Marketing has won two bronze awards for its exceptional quality web services; the company is a full-service interactive marketing and advertising agency that specializes in a variety of online services including web design, social media marketing and press releases.

11675 ■ **"Internet Marketing and Social Media Knowledge Vital for SMBs" in** *Internet Wire* **(November 24, 2009)**
Pub: Comtex News Network, Inc.
Description: Small and medium-size businesses must learn to market themselves over the Internet in order to succeed and grow in today's marketplace. Web Marketing Today offers the largest source of the most important information concerning doing business on the Internet including e-commerce, email marketing and social networking opportunities.

11676 ■ **"Internet and Mobile Media" in** *MarketingMagazine* **(Vol. 115, September 27, 2010, No. 13, pp. 60)**
Pub: Rogers Publishing Ltd.
Description: Market data covering the Internet and mobile media in Canada is given.

11677 ■ **"Into the Groove: Fine-Tune Your Biz By Getting Into the Good Habit Groove" in** *Small Business Opportunities* **(Spring 2008)**
Pub: Harris Publications Inc.
Description: Profile of Ty Freyvogel and his consulting firm Freyvogel Communications. Freyvogel serves the telecommunications need of Fortune 500 and mid-sized businesses.

11678 ■ **"Into the Light: Making Our Way Through the Economic Tunnel" in** *Agency Sales Magazine* **(Vol. 39, August 2009, No. 8, pp. 26)**
Pub: MANA
Ed: Michael Dotson. **Description:** Ways in which to avoid business stagnation brought about by the economic downturn, is presented. Being different, being a puzzle solver, and knowing the competition are among the things marketing personnel should do in order to wade through the economic downturn. Marketing via direct mail and the Internet also recommended.

11679 ■ **"Intrepid Souls: Meet a Few Who've Made the Big Leap" in** *Crain's Chicago Business* **(Vol. 31, November 10, 2008, No. 45, pp. 26)**
Pub: Crain Communications, Inc.
Ed: Meredith Landry. **Description:** Advice is given from entrepreneurs who have launched businesses in the last year despite the economic crisis. Among the types of businesses featured are a cooking school, a child day-care center, a children's clothing store and an Internet-based company.

11680 ■ **"Israeli Spam Law May Have Global Impact" in** *Information Today* **(Vol. 26, February 2009, No. 2, pp. 28)**
Pub: Information Today, Inc.
Ed: David Mirchin. **Description:** Israels new law, called Amendment 40 of the Communications Law, will regulate commercial solicitations including those sent without permission via email, fax, automatic phone dialing systems, or short messaging technologies.

11681 ■ **"It Was a Very Good Year...To Be Ted Rogers" in** *Canadian Business* **(Vol. 80, Winter 2007, No. 24, pp. 121)**
Pub: Rogers Media
Ed: Andrew Wahl. **Description:** Ted Rogers had a banner year in 2007 as Rogers Communications Inc. (RCI) took in huge profits from its phone and wireless business and his personal wealth grew sixty-seven percent to $7.6 billion. Rogers has record of betting on technologies that get the best returns relative to the investment in the marketplace such as its use of the GSM network and its cable hybrid fiber coaxial network.

11682 ■ **"It's a New Game: Killerspin Pushes Table Tennis to Extreme Heights" in** *Black Enterprise* **(Vol. 37, October 2006, No. 3, pp. 73)**
Pub: Earl G. Graves Publishing Co. Inc.
Ed: Bridget McCrea. **Description:** Profile of Robert Blackwell and his company Killerspin L.L.C., which is popularizing the sport of table tennis. Killerspin has

hit $1 million in revenues due to product sales primarily generated through the company's website, magazines, DVDs, and event ticket sales.

11683 ■ **"It's Not About the G1; Google Just Wants You to Use the Mobile Web" in** *Advertising Age* **(Vol. 79, September 29, 2008, No. 36, pp. 32)**
Pub: Crain Communications, Inc.
Ed: Abbey Klaassen. **Description:** Google's Android is the first serious competitor to Apple's iPhone; the company says that its goal is to simplify the mobile market and get wireless subscribers to use the mobile Internet and purchase smartphones.

11684 ■ **"Jay Berkowitz to Present Making Social Media Money Seminar at Affiliate Summit West" in** *Entertainment Close-Up* **(January 15, 2010)**
Pub: Close-Up Media
Description: Highlights of Jay Berkowitz's conference, "Making Social Media Make Money" include ways in which to develop Internet marketing strategies that will maximize Website traffic and convert that traffic to sales.

11685 ■ **"Johnny Royal of Luthier Society Unveils Archimedes 1.0 Trailer" in** *Internet Wire* **(October 22, 2009)**
Pub: Comtex News Network, Inc.
Description: Luthier Society, a social media and viral branding agency, has released the first viral video for the company's ROI weighted-value software platform named Archimedes 1.0; users of the software will be able to determine the depth of their outreach efforts, saturation rate, value of their Internet presence and the geo-spatial location of their audience; this will give a true, monetized value for ROI (Return on Investment) in social media marketing.

11686 ■ **"Johnson Publishing Expands: Moving Into Television and Internet To Extend Brand" in** *Black Enterprise* **(October 2007)**
Pub: Earl G. Graves Publishing Co. Inc.
Ed: Tamara E. Holmes. **Description:** Johnson Publishing Company has followed the lives of black families in both Ebony and Jet magazines. The media firm has expanded its coverage by developing entertainment content for television, the Internet and other digital arenas.

11687 ■ **"Johnson's Taps Online Animation" in** *Marketing to Women* **(Vol. 21, April 2008, No. 4, pp. 3)**
Pub: EPM Communications, Inc.
Description: Johnson's has launched a new integrated campaign for its baby lotion in an effort to appeal to the growing number of moms online.

11688 ■ **"JumpTV to Hold Conference Call to Discuss Q1 Results and Annual General Meeting" in** *Canadian Corporate News* **(May 16, 2007)**
Pub: Comtex News Network Inc.
Description: Profile of JumpTv, the world's leading broadcaster of ethnic television over the Internet, and the results of a conference that discussed their first quarter 2007 financial report as well as the company's business goals. Statistical data included.

11689 ■ **"Kawasaki's New Top Gun" in** *Brandweek* **(Vol. 49, April 21, 2008, No. 16, pp. 18)**
Pub: VNU Business Media, Inc.
Description: Discusses Kawasaki's marketing plan which included designing an online brochure in which visitors could create a video by building their own test track on a grid and then selecting visual special effects and musical overlay. This engaging and innovative marketing technique generated more than 166,000 unique users within the first three months of being launched.

11690 ■ **"Keeping Up With the Joneses: Outfitting Your Company With Up-To-Date Technology is Vital" in** *Black Enterprise* **(November 2007)**
Pub: Earl G. Graves Publishing Co. Inc.
Ed: Sonya A. Donaldson. **Description:** Small businesses, whether home-based or not, need to keep up with new technological developments including hardware, software, and the Internet.

11691 ■ "Kid-Friendly Business Sources" in *Black Enterprise* (Vol. 37, January 2007, No. 6, pp. 40)
Pub: Earl G. Graves Publishing Co. Inc.
Ed: Carolyn M. Brown. **Description:** Financial or business camps are a great way to encourage a child who interested in starting his or her own business. A number of these camps are available each year including Kidpreneurs Conference and Bull and Bear Investment Camp. Other resources are available online. Resources included.

11692 ■ "Kids, Computers and the Social Networking Evolution" in *Canadian Business* (Vol. 81, October 27, 2008, No. 18, pp. 93)
Pub: Rogers Media Ltd.
Ed: Penny Milton. **Description:** Social networking was found to help educate students in countries like the U.S., Canada and Mexico. Schools that embrace social networking teach students how to use computers safely and responsibility in order to counter threats to children on the Internet.

11693 ■ "Kuno Creative to Present B2B Social Media Campaign Webinar" in *Entertainment Close-Up* (August 25, 2011)
Pub: Close-Up Media
Description: Kuno Creative, an inbound marketing agency, will host Three Steps of a Successful B2B Social Media Campaign. The firm is a provider of Website development, branding, marketing strategy, public relations, Internet marketing, and inbound marketing.

11694 ■ "Last Founder Standing" in *Conde Nast Portfolio* (Vol. 2, June 2008, No. 6, pp. 124)
Pub: Conde Nast Publications, Inc.
Ed: Kevin Maney. **Description:** Interview with Amazon CEO Jeff Bezos in which he discusses the economy, the company's new distribution center and the hiring of employees for it, e-books, and the overall vision for the future of the firm.

11695 ■ "Laterooms and Octopus Travel Top Greenlight's Integrated Search Report for the Hotel Sector" in *Internet Wire* (October 23, 2009)
Pub: Comtex News Network, Inc.
Description: According to a research report conducted by Greenlight, the UK's leading independent Internet search marketing agency, the most visible hotel websites in natural search during June 2009 are premierinn.com, booking.com and laterooms.com; OctopusTravel.com generated the greatest share of the paid search section with 21 percent visibility. The report is focused on the hotel sector and covers the second quarter of 2009. Statistical data included.

11696 ■ "Lavante, Inc. Joins Intersynthesis, Holistic Internet Marketing Company" in *Internet Wire* (November 5, 2009)
Pub: Comtex News Network, Inc.
Description: Lavante, Inc., the leading provider of on-demand vendor information and profit recovery audit solutions for Fortune 1000 companies has chosen Intersynthesis, a new holistic Internet marketing firm, as a provider of pay for performance services. Lavante believes that Intersynthesis' expertise and knowledge combined with their ability to develop integrated strategies, will help them fuel more growth.

11697 ■ "Leading Ohio Internet Marketing Firm Announces Growth in September" in *Marketing Weekly News* (September 26, 2009, pp. 24)
Pub: Investment Weekly News
Description: Despite a poor economy, Webbed Marketing, a leading social media marketing and search engine optimization firm in the Midwest, has added five additional professionals to its fast-growing team. The company continues to win new business, provide more services and hire talented employees.

11698 ■ "Legal Aid: Sample Legal Documents can Lower Your Attorney Fees" in *Black Enterprise* (Vol. 37, October 2006, No. 3, pp. 210)
Pub: Earl G. Graves Publishing Co. Inc.
Ed: Tamara E. Holmes. **Description:** FreeLegalForms.net provides thousands of free legal forms.

These forms are not a substitute for consultation with an attorney but the sample documents can help save you time and money.

11699 ■ "Legislating the Cloud" in *Information Today* (Vol. 28, October 2011, No. 9, pp. 1)
Pub: Information Today, Inc.
Description: Internet and telecommunications industry leaders are asking for legislation to address the emerging market in cloud computing. Existing communications laws do not adequately govern the modern Internet.

11700 ■ "Let the Online Games Begin" in *Canadian Business* (Vol. 80, January 29, 2007, No. 3, pp. 23)
Pub: Rogers Media
Ed: Andy Holloway. **Description:** The trends pertaining to the promotion of the products and services of different Canadian companies on the internet are discussed.

11701 ■ "Make It Easy" in *Entrepreneur* (Vol. 36, May 2008, No. 5, pp. 49)
Pub: Entrepreneur Media, Inc.
Ed: Mike Hogan. **Description:** Zoho has a Planner that keep contacts, notes and reminders and a DB & Reports feature for reports, data analysis and pricing comparisons. WebEx WebOffice Workgroup supports document management and templates for contacts lists, time sheets and sales tracking. Other online data manages are presented.

11702 ■ "Making It Click" in *Barron's* (Vol. 88, March 17, 2008, No. 11, pp. 31)
Pub: Dow Jones & Company, Inc.
Ed: Theresa W. Carey. **Description:** Listing of 23 online brokers that are evaluated based on their trade experience, usability, range of offerings, research amenities, customer service and access, and costs. TradeStation Securities takes the top spot followed by thinkorswim by just a fraction.

11703 ■ "Managing the Facebookers; Business" in *The Economist* (Vol. 390, January 3, 2009, No. 8612, pp. 10)
Pub: Economist Newspaper Ltd.
Description: According to a report from PricewaterhouseCoopers, a business consultancy, workers from Generation Y, also known as the Net Generation, are more difficult to recruit and integrate into companies that practice traditional business acumen. 61 percent of chief executive managers say that they have trouble with younger employees who tend to be more narcissistic and more interested in personal fulfillment with a need for frequent feedback and an overprecise set of objectives on the path to promotion which can be hard for managers who are used to a different relationship with their subordinates. Older bosses should prepare to make some concessions to their younger talent since some of the issues that make them happy include cheaper online ways to communicate and additional coaching, both of which are good for business.

11704 ■ "Mapping the Social Internet" in *Harvard Business Review* (Vol. 88, July-August 2010, No. 7-8, pp. 32)
Pub: Harvard Business School Publishing
Description: Chart compares and contrasts online social networks in selected countries.

11705 ■ "Marketing Management Analytics Announces MMA Digital" in *Internet Wire* (January 26, 2010)
Pub: Comtex News Network, Inc.
Description: Innovator and pioneer in marketing effectiveness, Marketing Management Analytics, is offering a new service called MMA Digital; using this service companies will be able to more accurately measure the effects of digital media alongside other marketing tools in order to better understand and leverage the drivers of online marketing success.

11706 ■ "A Matter of Online Trust" in *Entrepreneur* (Vol. 37, August 2009, No. 8, pp. 35)
Pub: Entrepreneur Media, Inc.
Ed: Mikal E. Belicove. **Description:** Startup websites should make their potential customers feel confident to do business with them. To build customer's trust,

the website should have an attractive and professional design, clear and simple navigation, error-free copy, and physical address, telephone number, and e-mail address.

11707 ■ "McD's Warms Up For Olympics Performance" in *Advertising Age* (Vol. 79, July 7, 2008, No. 26, pp. 8)
Pub: Crain Communications, Inc.
Ed: Description: Overview of McDonald's marketing plans for the company's sponsorship of the Olympics which includes a website, an alternate-reality game, names featured on U.S. athletes and on-the-ground activities.

11708 ■ "Microsoft's Big Gamble" in *Canadian Business* (Vol. 81, March 3, 2008, No. 3, pp. 13)
Pub: Rogers Media
Ed: Andrew Wahl. **Description:** Microsoft Corp. is taking a big risk in buying Yahoo, as it is expected to pay more than $31 a share to finalize the acquisition. The deal would be seven and a half times bigger than any other that Microsoft has entered before, an execution of such deal is also anticipated to become a challenge for Microsoft. Recommendations on how Microsoft should handle the integration of the two businesses are given.

11709 ■ "Milk Producers Target Moms" in *Marketing to Women* (Vol. 21, January 2008, No. 1, pp. 3)
Pub: EPM Communications, Inc.
Description: In an attempt to encourage moms to serve milk with meals, the American Dairy Association partners with the New York State Dietetic Association to promote milk via a new logo, website and contest.

11710 ■ *Million Dollar Website: Simple Steps to Help You Compete with the Big Boys-Even on a Small Business Budget*
Pub: Prentice Hall Press
Ed: Lori Culwell. **Released:** May 9, 2010. **Price:** $19.95. **Description:** Resource for any small business owner wishing to build a successful Website in order to compete with big box stores.

11711 ■ "Mobile: Juanes Fans Sing for Sprint" in *Advertising Age* (Vol. 79, November 3, 2008, No. 41, pp. 22)
Pub: Crain Communications, Inc.
Ed: Laurel Wentz. **Description:** Marketers are appealing to the Hispanic market since they are more prone to use their cell phones to respond to contests, download videos, ringtones, or other data activity. Sprint recently sponsored a contest inviting people to sing like Colombian megastar Juanes; the participants filmed and sent their videos using their cell phones rather than laptops or camcorders illustrating the Hispanic overindex on mobile-phone technology. The contest generated hundreds of thousands of dollars in additional fee revenue, as monthly downloads increased 63 percent.

11712 ■ "Mobility: So Happy Together" in *Entrepreneur* (Vol. 35, October 2007, No. 10, pp. 64)
Pub: Entrepreneur Media Inc.
Ed: Heather Clancy. **Description:** Joshua Burnett, CEO and founder of 9ci, uses index cards to keep track of what he needs to do despite the fact that he has a notebook computer, cell phone and PDA. Kim Hahn, a media entrepreneur, prefers jotting her ideas down in a spiral notebook, has a team that would organize her records for her, and a personal assistant that would keep track of changes to her schedule. Reasons why these entrepreneurs use old-fashioned methods along with new technology are given.

11713 ■ "Moosylvania Releases Latest XL Marketing Trends Report" in *Wireless News* (October 6, 2009)
Pub: Close-Up Media
Description: Moosylvania, a digital promotion and branding agency that also has an on-site research facility, has released its 2nd XL Marketing Trends Report which focuses on digital video; the study defines the top digital video trends marketers must

focus on now and well into the future and notes that in 2010, Mobile Web Devices, such as smart phones will outnumber computers in this country. Statistical data included.

11714 ■ "More Leading Retailers Using Omniture Conversion Solutions to Boost Sales and Ecommerce Performance" in *Internet Wire* **(Sept. 22,2009)**
Pub: Comtex News Network, Inc.
Description: Many retailers are utilizing Omniture conversion solutions to improve the performance of their ecommerce businesses; recent enhancements to Omniture Merchandising and Omniture Recommendations help clients drive increased conversion to their Internet ventures.

11715 ■ "Most Viewed Stories, Videos on farmindustrynews.com in 2010" in *Farm Industry News* **(January 4, 2011)**
Pub: Penton Business Media Inc.
Description: The top ten most popularly viewed stories and videos presented on farmindustrynews.com Website are listed.

11716 ■ "Moving Pitchers" in *Entrepreneur* **(Vol. 37, December 2009, No. 12, pp. 46)**
Pub: Entrepreneur Media, Inc.
Ed: Gwen Moran. **Description:** Online videos have become accessible for business development and marketing due to the decline in production costs and the growth in viewership. Research company comScore reveals that 153 million Internet users in the U.S. watched an online video in August 2009. The benefits of using online videos to further market one's company are explained.

11717 ■ "Navigate to Better Direct Response Messaging Through Search Marketing" in *DM News* **(Vol. 32, January 18, 2010, No. 2, pp. 26)**
Pub: Haymarket Media, Inc.
Ed: Mark Simon. **Description:** Important lessons to apply when utilizing Internet marketing schemes include telling your customers you have what they want to buy, provide them with discounts or ways to save additional money and drive them to a customized destination like an Online store.

11718 ■ "The Neighborhood Watch" in *Hawaii Business* **(Vol. 53, March 2008, No. 9, pp. 36)**
Pub: Hawaii Business Publishing
Ed: David K. Choo. **Description:** OahuRe.com offers information on Hawaii real estate market, with spreadsheets and comparative market analysis page, which shows properties that are active, sold, or in escrow. Other details about OahuRe.com are discussed. A list of other top real estate websites in Hawaii and in the U.S. in general is provided.

11719 ■ "Net Connections" in *Black Enterprise* **(Vol. 38, July 2008, No. 12, pp. 28)**
Pub: Earl G. Graves Publishing Co. Inc.
Ed: Anthony S. Calypso. **Description:** Marketers are making strategic partnerships with online social networks in an attempt to gain further market reach. The value of these networks appears to be on the rise forcing media companies to recalculate their strategies for delivering products to customers.

11720 ■ "Netflix Gets No Respect" in *Barron's* **(Vol. 89, July 27, 2009, No. 30, pp. 26)**
Pub: Dow Jones & Co., Inc.
Ed: Tiernan Ray. **Description:** Netflix met expectations when they announced their second quarter sales but their shares still fell by almost 10 percent. Analysts say their entry into the "streaming video" business is a mixed bag since customers are increasingly buying the cheaper monthly plan and this is dragging the economics of the business.

11721 ■ "A Network of One: Local Writer Adds Web Interviews to Creative Output" in *La Crosse Tribune* **(September 14, 2009)**
Pub: La Crosse Tribune
Ed: Geri Parlin. **Description:** Profile of Andrew Revels, a freelance and aspiring writer, who has created a website in order to help gain attention for his

own writing as well as for other local artists, musicians and comedians. His latest endeavor includes interviewing local talent and broadcasting the interviews on his site each week.

11722 ■ "Networking Web Sites: a Two-Edged Sword" in *Contractor* **(Vol. 56, October 2009, No. 10, pp. 52)**
Pub: Penton Media, Inc.
Ed: H. Kent Craig. **Description:** People need to be careful about the information that they share on social networking Web sites. They should realize that future bosses, coworkers, and those that might want to hire them might read those information. Posting on these sites can cost career opportunities and respect.

11723 ■ "The New Guard" in *Entrepreneur* **(Vol. 36, February 2008, No. 2, pp. 46)**
Pub: Entrepreneur Media Inc.
Ed: Amanda C. Kooser. **Description:** A natural language search engine is being developed by Powerset for better online searching. Zannel Inc. offers Instant Media Messaging platform, which allows for social networking using phones. Ning is an online platform that allows users to customize and control their social networks.

11724 ■ "New IPhone Also Brings New Way of Mobile Marketing" in *Advertising Age* **(Vol. 79, June 16, 2008, No. 24, pp. 23)**
Pub: Crain Communications, Inc.
Ed: Abbey Klaasen. **Description:** Currently there are two kinds of applications for the iPhone and other mobile devices: native applications that allow for richer experiences and take advantage of features that are built into a phone and web applications, those that allow access to the web through specific platforms. Marketers are interested in creating useful experiences for customers and opening up the platforms which will allow them to do this.

11725 ■ "New Recession-Proof Internet Marketing Package Allows Businesses to Ramp Up Web Traffic and Profits" in *PR Newswire* **(Jan. 25, 2010)**
Pub: PR Newswire Association, LLC
Description: Profile of Reel Web Design, a leading marketing firm in New York City that caters to small to medium sized businesses with smaller budgets that need substantial return on investment; Reel Web Design offers video production and submission, web design and maintenance and press release writing among additional services.

11726 ■ "New Sony HD Ads Tout Digital" in *Brandweek* **(Vol. 49, April 21, 2008, No. 16, pp. 5)**
Pub: VNU Business Media, Inc.
Description: Looking to promote Sony Electronics' digital imaging products, the company has launched another campaign effort known as HDNA, a play on the words high-definition and DNA; originally Sony focused the HDNA campaign on their televisions, the new ads will include still and video cameras as well and marketing efforts will consist of advertising in print, Online, television spots and publicity at various venues across the country.

11727 ■ "New TurnHere Survey Reveals Online Video Trends" in *Internet Wire* **(October 22, 2009)**
Pub: Comtex News Network, Inc.
Description: TurnHere, Inc., the leading online video marketing services company, released the findings of its recent survey regarding current and future trends in online video among marketing agencies and brand recognition; the report found that online video has and will continue to play a prominent role in the realm of marketing edging out both search and email marketing campaigns. Additional highlights and statistical data included.

11728 ■ "A New Way to Tell When to Fold" in *Barron's* **(Vol. 88, July 7, 2008, No. 27, pp. 27)**
Pub: Dow Jones & Co., Inc.
Ed: Theresa W. Carey. **Description:** Overview of the Online trading company SmartStops, a firm that aims to tell investors when to sell the shares of a particular company. The company's Web site categorizes

stocks as moving up, down, or sideways, and calculates exit points for individual stocks based on an overall market trend.

11729 ■ "New Ways to Catch a Thief" in *Barron's* **(Vol. 88, March 10, 2008, No. 10, pp. 37)**
Pub: Dow Jones & Company, Inc.
Ed: Theresa W. Carey. **Description:** Online brokerage firms employ different methods to protect the accounts of their customers from theft. These methods include secure Internet connections, momentary passwords, and proprietary algorithms.

11730 ■ "Nine Sectors to Watch: Telecom" in *Canadian Business* **(Vol. 81, December 24, 2007, No. 1, pp. 44)**
Pub: Rogers Media
Ed: Andrew Wahl. **Description:** Forecasts on the Canadian telecommunications industry for 2008 are presented. Details on consumer spending growth, the popularity of broadband, and activities in the wireless sector are also discussed.

11731 ■ "Nobody Knows What To Do" in *Barron's* **(Vol. 88, March 17, 2008, No. 11, pp. 40)**
Pub: Dow Jones & Company, Inc.
Ed: Mark Veverka. **Description:** Attendees of the South by Southwest Interactive conference failed to get an insight on how to make money on the Web from former Walt Disney CEO Michael Eisner when Eisner said there's no proven business model for financing projects. Eisner said he finances his projects with the help of his connections to get product-placement deals.

11732 ■ "Norvax University Health Insurance Sales Training and Online Marketing Conference" in *Internet Wire* **(January 27, 2010)**
Pub: Comtex News Network, Inc.
Description: Overview of the Norvax University Marketing and Sales Success Conference Tour which includes insurance sales training seminars, proven and innovative online marketing techniques and a host of additional information and networking opportunities.

11733 ■ "Note to Marketers: A Viral Video Has a Life of Its Own" in *Advertising Age* **(Vol. 80, October 5, 2009, No. 33, pp. 29)**
Pub: Crain's Communications
Ed: Ken Wheaton. **Description:** Internet marketers do not decide whether or not an online video goes viral. It is the audience that decides what online videos to spread and such fare is usually passed around due to its content being downright witty or creative or so laughably bad that the audience wants to share it.

11734 ■ "Nothing Plus Nothing" in *Entrepreneur* **(Vol. 37, October 2009, No. 10, pp. 25)**
Pub: Entrepreneur Media, Inc.
Ed: Joe Robinson. **Description:** Jason Fried and David Heinemeier Hansson of Web application firm 37signals believe that free Web services will never become profitable in the long term. They believe that Web service providers should charge a fair price on such services.

11735 ■ "Nowspeed and OneSource to Conduct Webinar" in *Internet Wire* **(December 14, 2009)**
Pub: Comtex News Network, Inc.
Description: OneSource, a leading provider of global business information, and Nowspeed, an Internet marketing agency, will conduct a webinar titled "How to Develop Social Media Content That Gets Results" in order to provide marketers insight into how to develop and optimize effective social media content to get consumer results that translate into purchases and lead generation.

11736 ■ "Nowspeed's David Reske to Speak at SolidWorks World 2010 in Anaheim" in *Internet Wire* **(January 7, 2010)**
Pub: Comtex News Network, Inc.
Description: David Reske, managing director at Nowspeed, an Internet marketing agency based in the Boston area, will be presenting at SolidWorks

World 2010; the convention's presentation will focus on proven methodologies, practical tips and real-world case studies in order to help attendees leverage the powerful Internet marketing innovations that are proving effective for businesses.

11737 ■ "Obama Plan May Boost Maryland Cyber Security" in *Boston Business Journal* **(Vol. 29, May 20, 2011, No. 2, pp. 1)**
Pub: American City Business Journals Inc.
Ed: Scott Dance. **Description:** May 12, 2011 outline of the cyber security policies of President Obama may improve the cyber security industry in Maryland as the state is home to large defense and intelligence activities. Details of the proposed policies are discusses as well as their advantages to companies that deal in developing cyber security plans for other companies.

11738 ■ "Office Retooled" in *Canadian Business* **(Vol. 80, March 26, 2007, No. 7, pp. 67)**
Pub: Rogers Media
Ed: Andrew Wahl. **Description:** The merits and demerits of using new Google Apps Premier Edition are presented.

11739 ■ "Oh, Behave!" in *Entrepreneur* **(Vol. 36, April 2008, No. 4, pp. 87)**
Pub: Entrepreneur Media, Inc.
Ed: Gwen Moran. **Description:** Online social networks can pose awkward situations for users. These include instances such as getting a link request from someone you do not know, having a contact post embarrassing information on your site, and a contact asking you to be refer him to one of your business contacts. Tips on how to deal with these situations are discussed.

11740 ■ "Omniture's Next Version of SearchCenter Delivers Landing Page Optimization" in *Internet Wire* **(September 24, 2009)**
Pub: Comtex News Network, Inc.
Description: Omniture, Inc., a leading provider of online business optimization software, has announced a new release of Omniture SearchCenter; this latest version will allow search engine marketers to test landing pages across campaigns and ad groups.

11741 ■ "On Target" in *Canadian Business* **(Vol. 81, July 22, 2008, No. 12-13, pp. 45)**
Pub: Rogers Media Ltd.
Ed: Calvin Leung. **Description:** Companies such as LavalifePRIME, a dating website devoted to singles 45 and older, discuss the value of marketing and services aimed at Canada's older consumers. One-third of Canada's 33 million people are 50-plus, controlling 77 percent of the countries wealth.

11742 ■ "Online Marketing and Promotion of Canadian Films via Social Media Tools" in *CNW Group* **(January 27, 2010)**
Pub: Comtex News Network, Inc.
Description: Telefilm Canada announced the launch of a pilot initiative aimed at encouraging the integration of online marketing and the use of social media tools into means of distribution ahead of a films' theatrical release. During this pilot phase Web-Cine 360 will target French-language feature films.

11743 ■ "Online Postings Really Influence Older Women" in *Marketing to Women* **(Vol. 22, July 2009, No. 7, pp. 8)**
Pub: EPM Communications, Inc.
Description: Women over the age of 55 are more likely to be swayed to purchase a product by referrals from others, including Online postings by strangers. Another key influence is associated with the brand's ability to address their lifestyle needs.

11744 ■ "Online Self-Publishing Services" in *Black Enterprise* **(Vol. 37, November 2006, No. 4, pp. 90)**
Pub: Earl G. Graves Publishing Co. Inc.
Description: Profiles of five online self-publishing services.

11745 ■ "Orbitz Adds Parent Panel" in *Marketing to Women* **(Vol. 21, March 2008, No. 3, pp. 5)**
Pub: EPM Communications, Inc.
Description: Orbitz introduces the Orbitz Parent Panel in an attempt to better connect with traveling families.

11746 ■ "Ordering Pizza Hut From Your Facebook Page?" in *Advertising Age* **(Vol. 79, November 10, 2008, No. 42, pp. 50)**
Pub: Crain Communications, Inc.
Ed: Emily Bryson York. **Description:** Fast-food chains are experimenting with delivery/takeout services via social networks such as Facebook and iPhone applications. This also allows the chains to build valuable databases of their customers.

11747 ■ "Our Gadget of the Week" in *Barron's* **(Vol. 88, March 24, 2008, No. 12, pp. 47)**
Pub: Dow Jones & Company, Inc.
Ed: Tiernan Ray. **Description:** Review of the $299 Apple Time Capsule, which is a 500-megabyte hard disk drive and a Wi-Fi router, rolled into one device. The device allows users to create backup files without the need for sophisticated file management software.

11748 ■ "Our Gadget of the Week: Mostly, I Liked It" in *Barron's* **(Vol. 88, July 14, 2008, No. 28, pp. 31)**
Pub: Dow Jones & Co., Inc.
Ed: Jay Palmer. **Description:** Review of the Apple iPhone 3G, which costs $199, has better audio and is slightly thicker than its predecessor; using the 3G wireless connection makes going online faster but drains the battery faster too.

11749 ■ "Our World with Black Enterprise" in *Black Enterprise* **(Vol. 37, February 2007, No. 7, pp. 145)**
Pub: Earl G. Graves Publishing Co. Inc.
Description: Our World with Black Enterprise is a television broadcast that features roundtable discussions and interviews with important African American figures.

11750 ■ *Overcoming Barriers to Entrepreneurship in the United States*
Pub: Lexington Books
Ed: Diana Furchtgott-Roth. **Released:** March 28, 2008. **Price:** $24.95. **Description:** Real and perceived barriers to the founding and running of small businesses in America are discussed. Each chapter outlines how policy and economic environments can hinder business owners and offers tips to overcome these obstacles. Starting with venture capital access in Silicon Valley during the Internet bubble, the book goes on to question the link between personal wealth and entrepreneurship, examines how federal tax rates affect small business creation and destruction, explains the low rate of self-employment among Mexican immigrants, and suggests ways pension coverage can be increased in small businesses.

11751 ■ "Pagetender LLC Releases Website Design Package for HubSpot Users" in *Internet Wire* **(September 30, 2009)**
Pub: Comtex News Network, Inc.
Description: Profile of Pagetender LLC, a Certified HubSpot partner, who announced a Website Design Package marketed specifically for HubSpot Owner and Marketer users. This packaged was developed for small to medium sized businesses that want a website designed or their current site redesigned on HubSpot's Content Management System. Companies that would like a more robust site have the option of adding Flash development, ecommerce and photo galleries.

11752 ■ "Partnering for Success" in *Art Business News* **(Vol. 36, October 2009, No. 10, pp. 4)**
Pub: Summit Business Media
Ed: Jennifer Dulin Wiley. **Description:** In such a volatile economy many savvy artists and gallery owners are turning to out-of-the-box partnerships for continued success; these partnerships are also

pervading the Internet, especially with such social media networks as Facebook and Twitter where artists and businesses can develop a loyal following.

11753 ■ "Paterson Plots Comeback With Internet IPO" in *Globe & Mail* **(February 20, 2006, pp. B1)**
Pub: CTVglobemedia Publishing Inc.
Ed: Grant Robertson. **Description:** The initial public offering plans of chief executive officer Scott Paterson of JumpTV.com are presented.

11754 ■ "People; E-Commerce, Online Games, Mobile Apps" in *Advertising Age* **(Vol. 80, October 19, 2009, No. 35, pp. 14)**
Pub: Crain's Communications
Ed: Nat Ives. **Description:** Profile of People Magazine and the ways in which the publisher is moving its magazine forward by exploring new concepts in a time of declining newsstand sales and advertising pages; among the strategies are e-commerce such as the brand People Style Watch in which consumers are able highlight clothing and jewelry and then connect to retailers' sites and a channel on Taxi TV, the network of video-touch screens in New Your City taxis.

11755 ■ "People; E-Commerce, Online Games, Mobile Apps: This Isn't Your Mom's People" in *Advertising Age* **(Vol. 80, October 19, 2009, No. 35)**
Pub: Crain's Communications
Ed: Nat Ives. **Description:** Profile of People Magazine and the ways in which the publisher is moving its magazine forward by exploring new concepts in a time of declining newsstand sales and advertising pages; among the strategies are e-commerce such as the brand People Style Watch in which consumers are able highlight clothing and jewelry and then connect to retailers' sites and a channel on Taxi TV, the network of video-touch screens in New Your City taxis.

11756 ■ "Pet-Food Crisis a Boon to Organic Players" in *Advertising Age* **(Vol. 78, April 9, 2007, No. 15, pp. 3)**
Pub: Crain Communications, Inc.
Ed: Jack Neff. **Description:** In the wake of the pet-food recall crisis, the natural-and-organic segment of the market is gaining recognition and sales; one such manufacturer, Blue Buffalo, has not only seen huge sale increases but also has witnessed a 50-60 percent increase in traffic to the brand's website which has led to the decision to move up the timetable for the brand's first national ad campaign.

11757 ■ "Philanthropy Good For Business" in *Crain's Detroit Business* **(Vol. 24, February 18, 2008, No. 7, pp. 14)**
Pub: Crain Communications Inc. - Detroit
Ed: Sheena Harrison. **Description:** Profile of Burce McCully, founder of Dynamic Edge Inc., and his views on philanthropy as a key to any small company's success. The Ann Arbor, Michigan information technology firm has volunteered and raised funds for many causes since 1999 when the company was founded.

11758 ■ *Planet Google: One Company's Audacious Plan to Organize Everything We Know*
Pub: Free Press
Ed: Randall Stross. **Released:** 2009. **Price:** $26.00. **Description:** The book examines Google, the leader in Internet search engines.

11759 ■ "Planning Your Next Move in Ad Land" in *Advertising Age* **(Vol. 81, January 4, 2009, No. 1, pp. 1)**
Pub: Crain's Communications
Description: Overview of the challenges that ad agencies face today and will face in the years to come; highlights include problems occurring in various industries, Internet marketing innovations and the social media landscape.

11760 ■ "PMA Launches Online Education Program" in *Contractor* **(Vol. 56, October 2009, No. 10, pp. 8)**
Pub: Penton Media, Inc.
Description: Plumbing & Mechanical Association of Georgia launched an online program that covers technical and business management that will help

contractors run their businesses. Future courses will include math for plumbers, graywater systems, and recession-proofing your business.

11761 ■ "PopCap Games Achieves Significant Increase in Return on Ad Spend With Omniture SearchCenter" in *Internet Wire* (September 15, 2009)
Pub: Comtex News Network, Inc.
Description: PopCap Games, a leading computer games provider, is using Omniture SearchCenter together with Omniture SiteCatalyst to increase revenue from its search engine marketing campaign. Omniture, Inc. is a leading provider of Internet business optimization software.

11762 ■ "Pro Teams Shift Ad Budgets; Naming Rights Deals Near $1 Billion" in *Brandweek* (Vol. 49, April 21, 2008, No. 16, pp. 18)
Pub: VNU Business Media, Inc.
Ed: Barry Janoff. **Description:** More and more professional sports marketers are spending less of their advertising budgets on traditional media outlets such as television, print and radio; the growing trend in sports marketing is in utilizing new media venues such as the Internet in which innovative means are used to encourage interaction with fans.

11763 ■ "Promote Your Business Through New Media" in *Business Week* (November 5, 2009)
Pub: McGraw-Hill Companies
Ed: Karen E. Klein. **Description:** Traditional public relations strategies are becoming more and more outdated due to the rapid shift in Internet marketing opportunities. Ideas for marketing your company online are presented.

11764 ■ "Punta Gorda Interested in Wi-Fi Internet" in *Charlotte Observer* (February 1, 2007)
Pub: Knight-Ridder/Tribune Business News
Ed: Steve Reilly. **Description:** Punta Gorda officials are developing plans to provide free wireless Internet services to businesses and residents.

11765 ■ "Q&A Patrick Pichette" in *Canadian Business* (Vol. 81, October 13, 2008, No. 17, pp. 6)
Pub: Rogers Media Ltd.
Ed: Andrew Wahl. **Description:** Patrick Pichette finds challenge in taking over the finances of an Internet company that has a market cap of about $140 billion. He feels, however, that serving as Google's chief financial officer is nothing compared to running Bell Canada Enterprises (BCE). Pichette's other views on Google and BCE are presented.

11766 ■ "Quantivo Empowers Online Media Companies to Immediately Expand Audiences and Grow Online Profits" in *Internet Wire* (Nov. 18, 2009)
Pub: Comtex News Network, Inc.
Description: Quantivo, the leader in on-demand Behavioral Analytics, has launched a new solution that includes 22 of the most critical Internet audience behavior insights as out-of-the-box reports; Internet marketers need to understand their audience, what they want and how often to offer it to them in order to gain successful branding and campaigns online.

11767 ■ "The Question: Who Do You Think Is the Most Genuine?" in *Advertising Age* (Vol. 79, July 7, 2008, No. 26, pp. 4)
Pub: Crain Communications, Inc.
Ed: Ken Wheaton. **Description:** According to a survey conducted by Harris Interactive Reputation Quotient, Johnson & Johnson was deemed the most genuine brand. Google came in second followed by UPS.

11768 ■ "Quickoffice's MobileFiles Pro App Enables Excel Editing On-the-Go" in *Information Today* (Vol. 26, February 2009, No. 2, pp. 31)
Pub: Information Today, Inc.
Description: Quickoffice Inc. introduced MobileFiles Pro, which features editable Microsoft Office functionality for the iPone and iPod touch. The application al-

lows users to edit and save Microsoft Excel files in .xls format, transfer files to and from PC and Mac desktops via Wi-Fi, and access and synchronize with Apple MobileMe accounts.

11769 ■ "Recalls Cause Consumers to Put More Stock in Online Reviews" in *Crain's Cleveland Business* (Vol. 28, November 12, 2007, No. 45)
Pub: Crain Communications, Inc.
Ed: Jack Neff. **Description:** Due to the string of product recalls over the last year, consumers are looking at online product reviews to help them make purchasing decisions which could reshape marketing for a wide range of products.

11770 ■ "Reply! Grows at Unprecedented Rate, Rips Beta Off Its Marketplace" in *Marketing Weekly News* (September 19, 2009, pp. 149)
Pub: Investment Weekly News
Description: Profile of Reply.com, a leader in locally-targeted Internet marketing, announced significant growth in terms of revenue, enhanced features and services and new categories since launching its beta Reply! Marketplace platform. Even in the face of an economic downturn, the company has posted over 50 percent revenue growth in the Real Estate and Automotive categories.

11771 ■ "Reportlinker Adds Report: Social Networks: Five Consumer Trends for 2009" in *Wireless News* (October 23, 2009)
Pub: Close-Up Media
Description: "Social Networks: Five Consumer Trends for 2009," a new market research report by Reportlinker.com found that in the countries of Italy and Spain lag behind their European neighbors in Internet development. Since large numbers of consumers in these two countries remain offline, only a minimal portion of total advertising spending goes into Internet marketing, and those advertising campaigns are directed at the relatively young, affluent users. Statistical data included.

11772 ■ "Reportlinker.com Adds Report: GeoWeb and Local Internet Markets: 2008 Edition" in *Entertainment Close-Up* (September 11, 2009)
Pub: Close-Up Media
Description: Reportlinker.com is adding a new market research report that is available in its catalogue: GeoWeb and Local Internet Markets - 2008 Edition; highlights include the outlook for consumer mapping services and an examination of monetizing services and an analysis the development outlook for geospacial Internet market, also referred to as the Geoweb.

11773 ■ "Research and Markets Adds Report: Asian - Internet Market" in *Health and Beauty Close-Up* (January 19, 2010)
Pub: Close-Up Media
Description: Overview of Research and Markets new report regarding Internet marketing and e-commerce in the Asian region; statistical data included.

11774 ■ "Research and Markets Adds Report: Cyprus: Convergence, Broadband and Internet Market" in *Wireless News* (September 4, 2009)
Pub: Close-Up Media
Description: Overview of a new report by Research and Markets entitled, "Cyprus Convergence, Broadband and Internet Market - Overview, Statistics and Forecasts." Highlights include information regarding broadband accounts which now account for the majority of household Internet connections.

11775 ■ "Research and Markets Adds Report: Ghana: Convergence, Broadband and Internet Market" in *Wireless News* (September 4, 2009)
Pub: Close-Up Media
Description: Overview of a new report by Research and Markets entitled, "Ghana Convergence, Broadband and Internet Market - Overview, Statistics and Forecasts." Ghana was among the first countries in Africa connected to the Internet and to introduce

ADSL broadband services; however, only 30 of the 140 licensed ISP's are operational making the sector highly competitive.

11776 ■ "Research and Markets Adds Report: The U.S. Mobile Web Market" in *Entertainment Close-Up* (December 10, 2009)
Pub: Close-Up Media
Description: Highlights of the new Research and Markets report "The U.S. Mobile Web Market: Taking Advantage of the iPhone Phenomenon" include: mobile Internet marketing strategies; the growth of mobile web usage; the growth of revenue in the mobile web market; and a look at Internet business communications, social media and networking.

11777 ■ "Research and Markets Adds Report: USA - Internet Market - Analysis, Statistics and Forecasts" in *Wireless News* (January 15, 2010)
Pub: Close-Up Media
Description: According to Research and Markets new report concerning the United State's Internet market, e-commerce and Online advertising are expected to recover strongly in 2010.

11778 ■ "Research Reports: How Analysts Size Up Companies" in *Barron's* (Vol. 88, March 17, 2008, No. 11, pp. M13)
Pub: Dow Jones & Company, Inc.
Ed: Anita Peltonen. **Description:** Shares of Applied Industrial Technologies are ranked Market Perform while the shares of Google get a buy rating. Salix Pharmaceuticals gets a Sell/Above-Average risk rating. The shares of Dune Energy, Franklin Resources, Internet Brands, Piper Jaffray, and Texas Instruments are also rated.

11779 ■ "Resource Line" in *Black Enterprise* (Vol. 37, January 2007, No. 6, pp. 6)
Pub: Earl G. Graves Publishing Co. Inc.
Description: Interactive Media Editor, Philana Patterson, writes a column for blackenterprise.com that offers advice and provides resources for entrepreneurs, corporate executives, business owners, and budding investors.

11780 ■ "The Right Time for REITs" in *Barron's* (Vol. 88, July 14, 2008, No. 28, pp. 32)
Pub: Dow Jones & Co., Inc.
Ed: Mike Hogan. **Description:** Discusses the downturn in U.S. real estate investment trusts so these are worth considering for investment. Several Websites that are useful for learning about real estate investment trusts for investment purposes are presented.

11781 ■ "Ring Ka-Ching" in *Canadian Business* (Vol. 79, November 6, 2006, No. 22, pp. 106)
Pub: Rogers Media
Description: A brief profile of Jajah including its web activated telephone services is presented.

11782 ■ "Rise Interactive, Internet Marketing Agency, Now Offers Custom Google Analytics Installation" in *Internet Wire* (September 29, 2009)
Pub: Comtex News Network, Inc.
Description: In order to optimize a client's return of investment, Rise Interactive, a full-service Internet marketing agency, now offers custom Google Analytics installation to its customers; the installation process includes identifying an Internet marketing campaign's unique key performance indicators, translating them to actions one will perform on a website and configuring the analytical tool to ensure the customized advertising campaign goals are set and properly tracked.

11783 ■ "Rise Interactive, Internet Marketing Agency, Now Offers Social Media Training and Advisory Services" in *Internet Wire* (Nov. 4, 2009)
Pub: Comtex News Network, Inc.
Description: Profile of Rise Interactive, a full-service Internet marketing agency which has recently added social media to its list of offerings; the agency touts that its newest service gives their clients the power to

have ongoing communication with current and potential customers on the sites they are most actively visiting.

11784 ■ **"Ritchie Bros. Breaks Record for Internet Sales at Fort Worth Site During Multi-Million Dollar Unreserved Auction" in** *Canadian Corporate News*

Pub: Comtex News Network Inc.

Description: Ritchie Bros. Auctioneers, the world's largest auctioneer of trucks and industrial equipment, conducted a large unreserved auction at its permanent auction facility in Fort Worth, Texas, in which the company broke the record for Internet sales with bidders using the company's online bidding service, rbauctionBid-Live. Internet bidders purchased more than 440 lots in the auction.

11785 ■ **"ROIonline Announces Streaming Video Products" in** *Marketing Weekly News* **(December 5, 2009, pp. 155)**

Pub: Investment Weekly News

Description: ROIonline LLC, an Internet marketing firm serving business-to-business and the industrial marketplace, has added streaming video options to the Internet solutions it offers its clients; due to the huge increase of broadband connections, videos are now commonplace on the Internet and can often convey a company's message in a must more efficient, concise and effective way that will engage a website's visitor thus delivering a high return on a company's investment.

11786 ■ **"The Rypple Effect; Performance Management" in** *The Economist* **(Vol. 390, January 3, 2009, No. 8612, pp. 48)**

Pub: The Economist Newspaper Inc.

Description: New companies such as Rypple, a new, web-based service, claim that they can satisfy the Net Generation's need for frequent assessments while easing the burden this creates for management.

11787 ■ **"Save the Date" in** *Mergers & Acquisitions: The Dealmaker's Journal* **(March 1, 2008)**

Pub: SourceMedia, Inc.

Description: Listing of conferences and forums that deal with business and investing, particularly with mergers and acquisitions. Includes dates, locations and Internet addresses.

11788 ■ ***The Savvy Gal's Guide to Online Networking (Or What Would Jane Austen Do?)***

Pub: Booklocker.com Inc.

Ed: Diane K. Daneilson, Lindsey Pollak. **Released:** August 10, 2007. **Price:** $14.95. **Description:** It is a truth universally acknowledged that a woman in search of a fabulous career must be in want of networking opportunities. Or so Jane Austen would say if she were writing, or more likely, blogging today. So begins the must-read guide to networking in the 21st Century. Authors and networking experts share the nuts, bolts and savvy secrets that businesswomen need in order to use technology to build professional relationships.

11789 ■ **"Say Goodbye to Voicemail" in** *Agency Sales Magazine* **(Vol. 39, November 2009, No. 10, pp. 3)**

Pub: MANA

Description: Salespeople should think twice before leaving a voicemail. The emerging modern etiquette is to send a text message or to e-mail the customer or client. Communication suggestions for both salespeople and their principals are presented.

11790 ■ **"Scitable Puts Nature Education on the Map" in** *Information Today* **(Vol. 26, February 2009, No. 2, pp. 29)**

Pub: Information Today, Inc.

Description: Nature Education, a division of the Nature Publishing Group, released its first product, Scitable, a free online resource for undergraduate biology students and educators. The service includes over 180 overviews of key genetics concepts as well as social networking features, including groups and

functionality, that lets students work with classmates and others. Teachers can use the service to set up public or private groups for students.

11791 ■ **"Search and Discover New Opportunities" in** *DM News* **(Vol. 31, December 14, 2009, No. 29, pp. 13)**

Pub: Haymarket Media, Inc.

Ed: Chantal Tode. **Description:** Although other digital strategies are gaining traction in Internet marketing, search marketing continues to dominate this advertising forum. Companies like American Greetings, which markets e-card brands online, are utilizing social networking sites and affiliates to generate a higher demand for their products.

11792 ■ ***The Search: How Google and Its Rival Rewrote the Rules of Business and Transformed Our Culture***

Pub: Penguin Group Incorporated

Ed: John Battelle. **Released:** October 3, 2006. **Price:** $14.95. **Description:** Provides a history of Internet search technology.

11793 ■ ***The SEO Manifesto: A Practical and Ethical Guide to Internet Marketing and Search Engine Optimization***

Pub: Cape Project Management Inc.

Ed: Dan Tousignant, Pamela Gobiel. **Released:** December 5, 2011. **Price:** $14.99. **Description:** Comprehensive guide for each phase of launching an online business; chapters include checklists, process descriptions, and examples.

11794 ■ **"Shaw, Telus Take Up Battle Positions" in** *Globe & Mail* **(January 1, 2006, pp. B1)**

Pub: CTVglobemedia Publishing Inc.

Ed: Catherine McKLean. **Description:** The competition between Shaw Communications Inc. and Telus Corp. over voice over Internet protocol offer for customers is presented.

11795 ■ **"Sherwin-Williams Workers Forgo Travel for Virtual Trade Show" in** *Crain's Cleveland Business* **(Vol. 28, October 15, 2007, No. 41)**

Pub: Crain Communications, Inc.

Ed: John Booth. **Description:** Overview of Cyber-Coating 2007, a cutting-edge virtual three-dimensional trade show that exhibitors such as Sherwin-Williams Co.'s Chemical Coatings Division will take part in by chatting verbally or via text messages in order to exchange information and listen to pitches just like they would on an actual trade show floor.

11796 ■ **"Shipping 2.0" in** *Entrepreneur* **(Vol. 36, April 2008, No. 4, pp. 54)**

Pub: Entrepreneur Media, Inc.

Ed: Heather Clancy. **Description:** Doggypads.com contacted with Web 2.0 service provider Shipwire to handle its warehouse concerns. The service works by paying a rent to Shipwire and they will store the client's items. The client's customers can continue to order from the client's website and Shipwire will take care of delivery. Doggypads was able to save up on costs by using Shipwire.

11797 ■ **"Shoestring-Budget Marketing" in** *Women Entrepreneur* **(January 5, 2009)**

Pub: Entrepreneur Media Inc.

Ed: Maria Falconer. **Description:** Pay-per-click search engine advertising is the traditional type of e-marketing that may not only be too expensive for certain kinds of businesses but also may not attract the quality customer base a business looking to grow needs to find. Social networking websites have become a mandatory marketing tool for business owners who want to see growth in their sales; tips are provided for utilizing these networking websites in order to gain more visibility on the Internet which can, in turn, lead to the more sales.

11798 ■ **"Show and Tell" in** *Entrepreneur* **(Vol. 36, May 2008, No. 5, pp. 54)**

Pub: Entrepreneur Media, Inc.

Ed: Heather Clancy. **Description:** FreshStart Telephone uses recorded video testimonials of customers, by using Pure Digital Flip Video that downloads

content directly to the computer, and uploads it in the company's website to promote their wireless phone service.

11799 ■ **"Silverpop Recognized for Email Marketing Innovations by Econsultancy" in** *Marketing Weekly News* **(January 23, 2010, pp. 124)**

Pub: Investment Weekly News

Description: Econsultancy, a respected source of insight and advice on digital marketing and e-commerce, recognized Silverpop, the world's only provider of both marketing automation solutions and email marketing specifically tailored to the unique needs of B2C and B2B marketers at Econsultancy's 2009 Innovation Awards.

11800 ■ ***SMEs and New Technologies: Learning E-Business and Development***

Pub: Palgrave Macmillan

Ed: Banji Oyelaran-Oyeyinka; Kaushalesh Lal. **Released:** October 2006. **Price:** $85.00. **Description:** Adoption and learning of new information technologies in developing nations is covered. New technologies are opening opportunities for small companies in these countries.

11801 ■ **"Social Media: Communicate the Important Stuff" in** *Agency Sales Magazine* **(Vol. 39, November 2009, No. 10, pp. 52)**

Pub: MANA

Ed: Jack Foster. **Description:** Social media such as Twitter or Facebook allows businesses to communicate with their customers over great distances but this technology can take away from the personal touch. For those that want to implement these tools in their marketing plans, they should first find out which social media networks their target audience use and give their customers reasons to become fans.

11802 ■ **"Social Media, E-Mail Remain Challenging for Employees" in** *Workforce Management* **(Vol. 88, December 14, 2009, No. 13, pp. 4)**

Pub: Crain Communications, Inc.

Ed: Ed Frauenheim. **Description:** Examining the impact of Internet social networking and the workplace; due to the power of these new technologies, it is important that companies begin to set clear policies regarding Internet use and employee privacy.

11803 ■ **"Social Networkers for Hire" in** *Black Enterprise* **(Vol. 40, December 2009, No. 5, pp. 56)**

Pub: Earl G. Graves Publishing Co., Inc.

Ed: Brittany Hutson. **Description:** Companies are utilizing social networking sites in order to market their brand and personally connect with consumers and are increasingly looking to social media specialists to help with this task. Aliya S. King is one such web strategist, working for ICED Media by managing their Twitter, Facebook, YouTube and Flickr accounts for one of their publicly traded restaurant clients.

11804 ■ **"Social Networking Site for Moms" in** *Marketing to Women* **(Vol. 21, March 2008, No. 3, pp. 3)**

Pub: EPM Communications, Inc.

Description: The Cradle is a social networking site devoted to pregnancy and new parenthood.

11805 ■ **"The Solution" in** *Entrepreneur* **(Vol. 37, October 2009, No. 10, pp. 71)**

Pub: Entrepreneur Media, Inc.

Ed: Jennifer Wang. **Description:** Ford's 2010 Transit Connect is a compact commercial van developed specifically for small business owners. The compact van offers an integrated in-dash computer system providing a cellular broadband connection.

11806 ■ **"A Sports Extravaganza - To Go" in** *Canadian Business* **(Vol. 79, June 19, 2006, No. 13, pp. 21)**

Pub: Rogers Media

Ed: Andy Holloway. **Description:** Television broadcasting industry in Canada utilizing advanced technologies like mobile television and internet protocol television in broadcasting major sports events. Large number of new technologies are being invented to support increasing demand.

11807 ■ "State Efforts to Boost Contract Efficiency Hurt Smaller Firms" in *Boston Business Journal* **(Vol. 27, November 9, 2007, No. 41, pp. 1)**

Pub: American City Business Journals Inc.

Ed: Lisa van der Pool. **Description:** Massachusetts Operational Services Division, which provides state-wide telecommunications and data infrastructure contracts, announced that it is cutting the list of companies on the new contract from twelve to six. The cost-cutting efforts began in 2005, after a review by an independent consultant advised the state to adopt strategies that would save millions of dollars.

11808 ■ "Sticking to Stories; Havey Ovshinksy Changes Method, Keeps the Mission" in *Crain's Detroit Business* **(Vol. 24, March 31, 2008)**

Pub: Crain Communications, Inc.

Ed: Daniel Duggan. **Description:** Profile of Harvey Ovshinsky, an award-winning documentary filmmaker who has reinvented his work with corporations who want to market themselves with the transition to digital media. His company, HKO Media, takes Ovshinsky's art of storytelling and enhances it through multimedia operations on the Internet through a joint venture with a man he once mentored, Bob Kernen.

11809 ■ "Stimulating Fare at the SBA" in *Barron's* **(Vol. 89, July 20, 2009, No. 29, pp. 12)**

Pub: Dow Jones & Co., Inc.

Ed: Jim McTague. **Description:** Internet access at the Small Business Administration slowed down on 7 July 2009, apparently caused by employees streaming videos of the Michael Jackson tribute. The agency claims that the event did not disrupt its operations.

11810 ■ "Stretch Your Advertising Dollars" in *Women Entrepreneur* **(January 27, 2009)**

Pub: Entrepreneur Media Inc.

Ed: Rosalind Resnick. **Description:** During such poor economic times, most businesses are having to cut their advertising budgets; tips for targeting your advertising dollars toward the customer base most likely to buy your product are given.

11811 ■ "Study: New Moms Build A Lot of Brand Buzz" in *Brandweek* **(Vol. 49, April 21, 2008, No. 16, pp. 7)**

Pub: VNU Business Media, Inc.

Description: According to a new survey which sampled 1,721 pregnant women and new moms, this demographic is having 109 word-of-mouth conversations per week concerning products, services and brands. Two-thirds of these conversations directly involve brand recommendations. The Internet is driving these word-of-mouth, or W-O-M, conversations among this segment, beating out magazines, television and other forms of media.

11812 ■ "Success Products" in *Black Enterprise* **(Vol. 37, February 2007, No. 7, pp. 135)**

Pub: Earl G. Graves Publishing Co. Inc.

Ed: Tanisha A. Sykes. **Description:** Using innovative resources that are already at your fingertips instead of trying to reach out to companies first is a great way to discover whether you have a viable idea or product. Be motivated to start an e-newsletter letting people know about your products and attend conferences like The Motivation Show, the world's largest exhibition of motivational products and services related to performance in business.

11813 ■ *Success Secrets of Social Media Marketing Superstars*

Pub: Entrepreneur Press

Ed: Mitch Meyerson. **Released:** June 1, 2010. **Price:** $21.95. **Description:** Provides access to the playbooks of social media marketers who reveal their most valuable strategies and tactics for standing out in the new online media environment.

11814 ■ "Tale of the Tape: IPhone Vs. G1" in *Advertising Age* **(Vol. 79, October 27, 2008, No. 40, pp. 6)**

Pub: Crain Communications, Inc.

Ed: Rita Chang. **Description:** T-Mobile's G1 has been positioned as the first serious competitor to Apple's iPhone. G1 is the first mobile phone to run on the Google-backed, open-source platform Android.

11815 ■ "A Taxing Proposition" in *Black Enterprise* **(Vol. 37, January 2007, No. 6, pp. 6)**

Pub: Earl G. Graves Publishing Co. Inc.

Description: Learn how to avoid tax problems on Black Enterprise's website, blackenterprise.com.

11816 ■ "Tee Off Online" in *Black Enterprise* **(Vol. 37, January 2007, No. 6, pp. 52)**

Pub: Earl G. Graves Publishing Co. Inc.

Ed: James C. Johnson. **Description:** The E-Com Resource Center is one of many resources that are available for those interested in starting an e-commerce business. One of the first steps is to create a business plan, of which there are free samples available at BPlans.com.

11817 ■ "Texas Fold 'Em" in *Canadian Business* **(Vol. 79, October 9, 2006, No. 20, pp. 44)**

Pub: Rogers Media

Ed: John Gray. **Description:** New policies of the United States law makers for the online casino industries that could force many of them out of business are discussed.

11818 ■ "Things Really Clicking for Macy's Online" in *Business Courier* **(Vol. 24, November 30, 2008, No. 33, pp. 1)**

Pub: American City Business Journals, Inc.

Ed: Lisa Biank Fasig. **Description:** Retailer Macy's online division Macys.com are projecting sales at $1billion in 2007, compared to $620 million in 2006. Macy's new online features and products and the growth of online retail sector are also discussed.

11819 ■ "Thomas Industrial Network Unveils Custom SPEC" in *Entertainment Close-Up* **(March 3, 2011)**

Pub: Close-Up Media

Description: Thomas Industrial Network assists custom manufacturers and industrial service providers a complete online program called Custom SPEC which includes Website development and Internet exposure.

11820 ■ "Tim Armstrong" in *Canadian Business* **(Vol. 81, July 21, 2008, No. 11, pp. 10)**

Pub: Rogers Media Ltd.

Ed: Calvin Leung. **Description:** Interview with Tim Armstrong who is the president of advertising and commerce department of Google Inc. for North America; the information technology company executive talked about the emerging trends and changes to YouTube made by the company since its acquisition in 2006.

11821 ■ "Time for a Little Pruning" in *Barron's* **(Vol. 89, July 6, 2009, No. 27, pp. 13)**

Pub: Dow Jones & Co., Inc.

Ed: Dimitra DeFotis. **Description:** Investors are advised to avoid the shares of Whole Foods, American Tower, T. Rowe Price, Iron Mountain, Intuitive Surgical, Salesforce.com, and Juniper Networks due to their high price to earnings ratios. The shares of Amazon.com, Broadcom, and Expeditors International of Washington remain attractive to investors despite their high price to earnings ratios due to their strong growth.

11822 ■ "To Blog, Or Not To Blog" in *Canadian Business* **(Vol. 80, December 25, 2006, No. 1, pp. 15)**

Pub: Rogers Media

Ed: Andy Holloway. **Description:** The growing use of weblogs for internet marketing by business enterprises is discussed.

11823 ■ "The Top Mistakes of Social Media Marketing" in *Agency Sales Magazine* **(Vol. 39, November 2009, No. 9, pp. 42)**

Pub: MANA

Ed: Pam Lontos; Maurice Ramirez. **Description:** One common mistake in social media marketing is having more than one image on the Internet because this ruins a business' credibility. Marketers need to put out messages that are useful to their readers and to keep messages consistent.

11824 ■ "Traits that Makes Blogs Attractive to Book Publishers" in *Marketing to Women* **(Vol. 22, July 2009, No. 7, pp. 1)**

Pub: EPM Communications, Inc.

Description: Book publishers are finding a beneficial relationship between themselves and women bloggers on the Internet. A high visitor count, frequent updates and active readership are criteria for identifying the blogs with the most clout and therefore providing the greatest benefit to publishers.

11825 ■ "Transform Your Life" in *Black Enterprise* **(Vol. 37, January 2007, No. 6, pp. 14)**

Pub: Earl G. Graves Publishing Co. Inc.

Description: Through the magazine, television and radio programs, events, and the website, the various platforms of Black Enterprise will provide the tools necessary to achieve success in business ventures, career aspirations, and personal goals.

11826 ■ *Twitterville: How Businesses Can Thrive in the New Global Neighborhoods*

Pub: Portfolio Hardcover

Ed: Shel Israel. **Price:** $23.95. **Description:** Twitter is the most rapidly adopted communication tool in history, going from zero to ten million users in just over two years. On Twitter, word can spread faster than wildfire. Companies no longer have the option of ignoring the conversation. Unlike other hot social media spaces, Twitterville is dominated by professionals, not students. And despite its size, it still feels like a small town. Twitter allows people to interact much the way they do face-to-face, honestly and authentically.

11827 ■ "Two Field Service Management Solutions" in *Contractor* **(Vol. 56, November 2009, No. 11, pp. 37)**

Pub: Penton Media, Inc.

Ed: William Feldman; Patti Feldman. **Description:** Bella Solutions Field Service Software v. 4.2 is a web based solution for HVAC service contractors that enables scheduling of emergency, one-time, multi-visit or periodically recurring jobs with drag and drop appointments. VaZing is another web based solution that costs $99 per month for contractors. It can handle line-item discounting and invoices aside from scheduling.

11828 ■ "Unlimited Priorities Strengthens Executive Team" in *Entertainment Close-Up* **(November 1, 2011)**

Pub: Close-Up Media

Description: Founder and president of Unlimited Priorities Corporation, Iris L. Hanney, added two executive level professionals to her team. The new employees will help increase the firm's capabilities in social media and information technology.

11829 ■ "Up To Code? Website Eases Compliance Burden for Entrepreneurs" in *Black Enterprise* **(Vol. 38, March 2008, No. 8, pp. 48)**

Pub: Earl G. Graves Publishing Co. Inc.

Ed: Robin White-Goode. **Description:** Business.gov is a presidential E-government project created to help small businesses easily find, understand, and comply with laws and regulations pertaining to a particular industry.

11830 ■ "Use Social Media to Enhance Brand, Business" in *Contractor* **(Vol. 56, December 2009, No. 12, pp. 14)**

Pub: Penton Media, Inc.

Ed: Elton Rivas. **Description:** Advice on how plumbing contractors should use online social networks to increase sales is presented including such issues as clearly defining goals and target audience. An additional advantage to this medium is that advertisements can easily be shared with other users.

11831 ■ "Utah Technology Council: Social Media Is Here to Stay; Embrace It" in *Wireless News* **(December 14, 2009)**
Pub: Close-Up Media
Description: Social media outlets such as Facebook and Twitter are blurring the lines between advertising, public relations, branding and marketing; businesses must stop thinking in terms of traditional marketing versus Internet marketing if they want to succeed in today's marketing climate.

11832 ■ "Verizon's Big Gamble Comes Down to the Wire" in *Globe & Mail* **(February 3, 2007, pp. B1)**
Pub: CTVglobemedia Publishing Inc.
Ed: Catherine McLean. **Description:** The launch of a new broadband service by Verizon Communications Inc. based on fibre optic cable technology is discussed. The company has spent $23 billion for introducing the new service.

11833 ■ "A View to a Killer Business Model" in *Black Enterprise* **(Vol. 40, December 2009, No. 5, pp. 50)**
Pub: Earl G. Graves Publishing Co., Inc.
Ed: Sonya A. Donaldson. **Description:** Profile of Gen2Media Corp., a production, technology and Internet marketing firm based in Florida with offices in New York; Gen2Media is utilizing the advances in technology to now include video in its online marketing offerings.

11834 ■ "The Virtual Office" in *Canadian Business* **(Vol. 80, April 9, 2007, No. 8, pp. 64)**
Pub: Rogers Media
Ed: Andrew Wahl. **Description:** The business operation of Eloqua which runs all its IT systems using its own online software is discussed.

11835 ■ "Virtus.com Wins 'Best of Industry' WebAward for Excellence in Financial Services" in *Investment Weekly News* **(October 24, 2009)**
Pub: Investment Weekly News
Description: Web Marketing Association honored Virtus.com, the Website of Virtus Investment Partners, Inc., for Outstanding Achievement in Web Development and Acsys Interactive was awarded the Financial Services Standard of Excellence Award for developing the site. The site was part of a rebranding effort and is a one-stop portal for both financial advisors and their investors.

11836 ■ "Vistaprint Survey Indicates that Online Marketing Taking Hold Among Small Businesses" in *Internet Wire* **(December 10, 2009)**
Pub: Comtex News Network, Inc.
Description: According to a comprehensive survey from Vistaprint N.V., small businesses are very likely to increase their use of Internet marketing strategies such as paid and organic search, email marketing, social media networking and custom websites over the next year. Trends continue to show that more small businesses are indeed adapting to the changing marketplace and are more willing to diversify their marketing strategies than ever before.

11837 ■ "Vonage V-Phone: Use Your Laptop to Make Calls Via the Internet" in *Black Enterprise* **(Vol. 37, January 2007, No. 6, pp. 52)**
Pub: Earl G. Graves Publishing Co. Inc.
Ed: James C. Johnson. **Description:** Overview of the Vonage V-Phone, which is small flash drive device that lets you make phone calls through a high-speed Internet connection and plugs into any computer's USB port. Business travels may find this product to be a wonderful solution as it includes 250MB of memory and can store files, digital photos, MP3s, and more.

11838 ■ "Web-Based Marketing Excites, Challenges Small Business Use" in *Colorado Springs Business Journal* **(January 20, 2010)**
Pub: Dolan Media Co.
Ed: Becky Hurley. **Description:** Business-to-business and consumer-direct firms alike are using the fast-

changing Web technologies to increase sales, leads and track consumer behavior but once a company commits to an Online marketing plan, experts believe, they must be prepared to consistently tweak and overhaul content and distribution vehicles in order to keep up.

11839 ■ "Web-Based Solutions Streamline Operations" in *Contractor* **(Vol. 56, December 2009, No. 12, pp. 28)**
Pub: Penton Media, Inc.
Ed: William Feldman; Patti Feldman. **Description:** Sage Project Lifecycle Management is a Web-based service platform for plumbing and HVAC contractors. It enables effective workflow and document management. Projectmates, on the other hand, is a Web-based enterprise-wide solution for managing both commercial plumbing and HVAC projects.

11840 ■ "Web Biz Brulant Surfing for Acquisition Candidates" in *Crain's Cleveland Business* **(Vol. 28, December 3, 2007, No. 48, pp. 6)**
Pub: Crain Communications, Inc.
Ed: Chuck Soder. **Description:** Brulant Inc., a provider of web development and marketing services, is looking to acquire other companies after growing for five years straight. The company is one of the largest technology firms in Northeast Ohio.

11841 ■ "The Web Gets Real" in *Canadian Business* **(Vol. 79, July 17, 2006, No. 14-15, pp. 19)**
Pub: Rogers Media
Ed: Andrew Wahl. **Description:** Ron Lake's efforts of bringing the virtual and physical worlds more closely together by using Geographic Markup Language (GML) are presented.

11842 ■ "Web Sight: Do You See What I See?" in *Entrepreneur* **(Vol. 35, October 2007, No. 10, pp. 58)**
Pub: Entrepreneur Media Inc.
Ed: Heather Clancy. **Description:** Owners of Trunkt, a boutique in New York that showcases independent designs, have created a new style of Website called Trunkt.org. The Website allows buyers to select the products they want to see and designers can choose anytime which of their items will be displayed on the site. An explanation of the strategy that helped bring Trunkt closer to its clients is presented.

11843 ■ "Web Site Focuses on Helping People Find Jobs, Internships with Area Businesses" in *Crain's Detroit Business* **(Vol. 26, Jan. 4, 2010)**
Pub: Crain Communications, Inc.
Ed: Dustin Walsh. **Description:** DetroitIntern.com, LLC is helping metro Detroit college students and young professionals find career-advancing internships or jobs with local businesses.

11844 ■ "Web Traffic Numbers Facing Scrutiny" in *Boston Business Journal* **(Vol. 27, November 2, 2007, No. 40, pp. 1)**
Pub: American City Business Journals Inc.
Ed: Jesse Noyes. **Description:** Interactive Advertising Bureau (IAB) held a summit meeting with major industry players in an effort to create more transparent standards for measuring Internet traffic. The terms at issue were registered users, unique visitors, time spent and retention.

11845 ■ "Webadvertising" in *MarketingMagazine* **(Vol. 115, September 27, 2010, No. 13, pp. 70)**
Pub: Rogers Publishing Ltd.
Description: Website advertising in Canada is examined.

11846 ■ "Website Backup Made Simple" in *Inc.* **(Vol. 33, September 2011, No. 7, pp. 52)**
Pub: Inc. Magazine
Ed: John Brandon. **Description:** Tools to back up content on a Website are profiled. Vaultpress works only with sites that run on the WordPress publishing platform and CodeGuard works with a variety of publishing platforms and hosting services.

11847 ■ "Website Triples Traffic in Three Weeks Using Press Releases" in *PR Newswire* **(January 5, 2010)**
Pub: PR Newswire Association, LLC
Description: Irbtrax, an Internet marketing firm, concluded a comprehensive study revealing that online press release submission services offer measurable Website traffic-building results.

11848 ■ "Website for Women 50+ Launches" in *Marketing to Women* **(Vol. 21, April 2008, No. 4, pp. 5)**
Pub: EPM Communications, Inc.
Description: Vibrantnation.com is an online community targeting women over age 50; members can share recommendations on a variety of topics such as vacation spots, retailers and financial issues.

11849 ■ "Wendy Turner; Vice-President and General Manager, Vocalo.org" in *Crain's Chicago Business* **(Vol. 31, May 5, 2008, No. 18, pp. 22)**
Pub: Crain Communications, Inc.
Ed: Kevin McKeough. **Description:** Profile of Wendy Turner who is a leader at Vocalo, a combination of talk radio and Web site, where listeners can set up profile pages similar to those on Facebook.

11850 ■ "What You Look Like Online" in *Black Enterprise* **(Vol. 37, January 2007, No. 6, pp. 56)**
Pub: Earl G. Graves Publishing Co. Inc.
Ed: Marcia A. Reed-Woodard. **Description:** Of 100 executive recruiters 77 percent stated that they use search engines to check the backgrounds of potential job candidates, according to a survey conducted by ExecuNet. Of those surveyed 35 percent stated that they eliminate potential candidates based on information they find online so it is important to create a positive Web presence which highlights professional image qualities.

11851 ■ "What's In Your Toolbox" in *Women In Business* **(Vol. 61, August-September 2009, No. 4, pp. 7)**
Pub: American Business Women's Association
Ed: Mimi Kopulos. **Description:** Business owners are increasingly turning to using social networking websites, such as Facebook, LinkedIn and Twitter, to promote their companies. The number of adult social media users has increased from 8 percent in 2005 to 35 percent in 2009.

11852 ■ "Why-Max?" in *Canadian Business* **(Vol. 81, July 22, 2008, No. 12-13, pp. 19)**
Pub: Rogers Media Ltd.
Ed: Andrew Wahl. **Description:** Nascent technology known as LTE (Long Term Evolution) is expected to challenge Intel's WiMax wireless technology as the wireless broadband standard. LTE , which is believed to be at least two years behind WiMax in development, is likely to be supported by wireless and mobile-phone carriers. Views and information on WiMax and LTE are presented.

11853 ■ "Why Some Get Shaften By Google Pricing" in *Advertising Age* **(Vol. 79, July 14, 2008, No. 7, pp. 3)**
Pub: Crain Communications, Inc.
Ed: Abbey Klaassen. **Description:** Google's search advertising is discussed as well as the company's pricing structure for these ads.

11854 ■ "Why Women Blog and What They Read" in *Marketing to Women* **(Vol. 22, July 2009, No. 7, pp. 8)**
Pub: EPM Communications, Inc.
Description: Listing of topics that are visited the most by female Internet users. Statistical data included.

11855 ■ "Wi-Fi Finds Its Way Despite Nixed Plan for Free System" in *Crain's Cleveland Business* **(Vol. 28, November 12, 2007, No. 45, pp. 3)**
Pub: Crain Communications, Inc.
Ed: Jay Miller. **Description:** Discusses the issues facing Cleveland and Northeast Ohio concerning their proposal to offer citizens wireless Internet services for free or a small fee.

11856 ■ **"Wi-Fi On Steroids: Will WiMAX Provide the Juice For Souped-Up Connections?" in** *Black Enterprise* **(November 2007)**
Pub: Earl G. Graves Publishing Co. Inc.
Ed: Fiona Haley. **Description:** WiMAX, Worldwide Interoperability for Microwave Access in the U.S. WiMax is technology that moves data and connects faster and at greater distances than before.

11857 ■ *Wikinomics: How Mass Collaboration Changes Everything*
Pub: Penguin Group Incorporated
Ed: Don Tapscott; Anthony D. Williams. **Released:** April 2008. **Price:** $27.95. **Description:** Research and information about the every changing world of the Internet is provided to help small businesses.

11858 ■ **"Will the Force Be With Salesforce?" in** *Barron's* **(Vol. 88, March 24, 2008, No. 12, pp. 20)**
Pub: Dow Jones & Company, Inc.
Ed: Mark Veverka. **Description:** Shares of Salesforce.com are likely to drop from the $44.83-a-share level in the face of a deteriorating economy and financial sector and thus lower demand for business software. The company is unlikely to deliver on its ambitious earnings forecasts for 2008 especially with strengthening competition from Oracle.

11859 ■ *Winner Take All: How Competitiveness Shapes the Fate of Nations*
Pub: Basic Books
Ed: Richard J. Elkus Jr. **Released:** 2009. **Price:** $27.00. **Description:** American government and misguided business practices has allowed the U.S. to fall behind other countries in various market sectors such as cameras and televisions, as well as information technologies. It will take a national strategy for America to regain its lead in crucial industries.

11860 ■ **"Wireless: Full Service" in** *Entrepreneur* **(Vol. 35, October 2007, No. 10, pp. 60)**
Pub: Entrepreneur Media Inc.
Ed: Amanda C. Kooser. **Description:** Palm Foleo, the $599 smart phone enables users to access and compose email, browse the Internet, view documents and play Powerpoint files. It weighs 2.5 pounds and has a 10-inch screen. Other features, such as built-in WiFi are described.

11861 ■ **"Wireless Provider's Star Grows $283 Million Brighter" in** *Hispanic Business* **(July-August 2007, pp. 60)**
Pub: Hispanic Business
Description: Profile of Brightstar Corporation, the world's largest wireless phone distribution and supply chain reported record growth in 2007.

11862 ■ **"Women Clicking to Earn Virtual Dollars" in** *Sales and Marketing Management* **(November 11, 2009)**
Pub: Nielsen Business Media, Inc.
Ed: Stacy Straczynski. **Description:** According to a new report from Internet marketing firm Q Interactive, women are increasingly playing social media games where they are able to click on an ad or sign up for a promotion to earn virtual currency. Research is showing that this kind of marketing may be a potent tool, especially for e-commerce and online stores.

11863 ■ **"Words at Work" in** *Information Today* **(Vol. 26, February 2009, No. 2, pp. 25)**
Pub: Information Today, Inc.
Description: Current new buzzwords include the following: digital amnesia, or overload by availability, speed and volume of digital information; maternal profiling, a form a discrimination against women; recipe malpractice, a reminder that just because you can turn on a stove it doesn't make you a chef; ringxiety, the act when everyone reaches for their cell phone when one rings; verbing, the practice of turning good nouns into verbs.

11864 ■ **"WordStream Announces a Pair of Firsts for SEO and PPC Keyword Research Tools" in** *Internet Wire* **(November 10, 2009)**
Pub: Comtex News Network, Inc.
Description: WordSteam, Inc., a provider of pay-per-click (PPC) and search engine optimization (SEO) solutions for continuously expanding and optimizing search marketing efforts has released two new features in their flagship Keyword Management solution; these tools will allow marketers to analyze data from paid search, organic search and estimated totals from keyword suggestion tools side-by-side.

11865 ■ **"Work Smarter" in** *Entrepreneur* **(Vol. 36, April 2008, No. 4, pp. 70)**
Pub: Entrepreneur Media, Inc.
Ed: Amanda C. Kooser. **Description:** Online applications that address a business' particular needs are presented. These web applications offer email services, collaboration services of sharing and editing documents and presentations, and tie-ups with online social networking sites. Details on various web applications are provided.

11866 ■ **"Xtium Has Its Head in the Clouds" in** *Philadelphia Business Journal* **(Vol. 30, September 23, 2011, No. 32, pp. 1)**
Pub: American City Business Journals Inc.
Ed: Peter Key. **Description:** Philadelphia-based cloud computing firm Xtium LLC received an $11.5 million first-round investment from Boston-Massachusetts-based OpenView Venture Partners. Catering to midsize businesses and unit of bigger firms, Xtium offers disaster-recovery, hosting, and managed-information-technology-infrastructure services.

11867 ■ **"The Yahoo Family Tree" in** *Conde Nast Portfolio* **(Vol. 2, June 2008, No. 6, pp. 34)**
Pub: Conde Nast Publications, Inc.
Ed: Blaise Zerega. **Description:** Yahoo, founded in 1994 by Stanford students Jerry Yang and David Filo, is still an Internet powerhouse. The company's history is also outlined as well as the reasons in which Microsoft desperately wants to acquire the firm.

11868 ■ **"Yahoo! - Microsoft Pact: Alive Again?" in** *Barron's* **(Vol. 89, July 27, 2009, No. 30, pp. 8)**
Pub: Dow Jones & Co., Inc.
Ed: Mark Veverka. **Description:** Yahoo! reported higher than expected earnings in the second quarter of 2009 under CEO Carol Bartz who has yet to articulate her long-term vision and strategy for turning around the company. The media reported that Yahoo! and Microsoft are discussing an advertising-search partnership which should benefit both companies.

11869 ■ **"You Are What They Click" in** *Entrepreneur* **(Vol. 37, July 2009, No. 7, pp. 43)**
Pub: Entrepreneur Media, Inc.
Ed: Mikal Belicove. **Description:** Hiring the right website design firm is the first stage in building an online business, and this involves various factors such as price, technical expertise, and talent. Writing a request for proposal (RFP) detailing the website's details, which include purpose, budget and audience, is the first step the process. Other tips in finding the right web designer are given.

11870 ■ **"Your Annual Business Tune-Up" in** *Business Week* **(December 28, 2006)**
Pub: McGraw-Hill Companies
Ed: Karen E. Klein. **Description:** Interview with entrepreneurial expert, Ty Freyvogel, founder of EntrpreneursLab.com. Freyvogel gives tips on how a thorough review of existing systems, vendors, customers, and employees could help keep an entrepreneur's business not only safe but highly successful in the upcoming year.

11871 ■ **"Zen and the Art of Twitter Maintenance" in** *Agency Sales Magazine* **(Vol. 39, September-October 2009, No. 9, pp. 48)**
Pub: MANA
Ed: Terry Brock. **Description:** Online social networks such as Twitter, LinkedIn, and Facebook should be used to stay in touch with business relationships, especially customers. There should be a focus on making customers happy and building the bottomline when using these tools.

11872 ■ **"Zeon Solutions Teams with Endeca for SaaS Version of Endeca InFront" in** *Entertainment Close-Up* **(October 25, 2011)**
Pub: Close-Up Media
Description: Zeon Solutions, an enterprise e-commerce and Website development firm announced a special licensing partnership with Endecca Technologies. Endeca is an information management software company that provides small and mid-size retailers with high-performance Customer Experience Management technology.

TRADE PERIODICALS

11873 ■ *Association for Computing Machinery*
Pub: Special Interest Group on Data Communication
Ed: Martha Steenstrup, Editor. **Released:** Quarterly. **Price:** $50. **Description:** Serves as a forum for computing professionals in the data communications field. Focuses on network architecture, including the Internet, network protocols, and distributed systems.

11874 ■ *Data Base Alert*
Pub: PBI Media L.L.C.
Ed: Judy Duke, Editor. **Released:** Monthly. **Description:** Provides updates on publicly available online services. Contains a listing of distributors of new or revised data bases with data bases listed alphabetically under the appropriate distributor along with information about pricing, updates, and number of records. **Remarks:** Newsletter is part of DataBase Directory Service, which includes an annual directory and supplement.

11875 ■ *Information Today*
Pub: Information Today Inc.
Contact: Michael V. Zarrello, Advertising Dir
E-mail: mzarrello@infotoday.com
Released: 11/yr. **Price:** $84.95; $112 Canada and Mexico; $160 two years; $122 outside North America. **Description:** User and producer magazine (tabloid) covering electronic and optical information services.

11876 ■ *Internet Marketing Report*
Pub: Progressive Business Publications
Ed: Alan Field, Editor. **Released:** Semimonthly. **Price:** $299, individuals. **Description:** Communicates the latest news and trends in website marketing. g.

11877 ■ *Internet Telephone–Green Data Centers*
Pub: Information Gatekeepers Inc.
Ed: Tony Carmona, Editor. **Released:** Monthly. **Price:** $695, U.S. and Canada; $745, elsewhere. **Description:** Provides marketing and technology information on new developments in the internet telephone industry on a worldwide basis.

11878 ■ *ISP Business–IPTB*
Pub: Information Gatekeepers Inc.
Ed: Rebecca Jackson, Editor. **Released:** Monthly. **Price:** $695, U.S. and Canada; $745, elsewhere. **Description:** Covers news of the business aspects of Internet service providers worldwide. Includes information on finances, marketing, mergers and acquisitions, joint ventures, technologies, customer billing and service, new products, and international developments.

11879 ■ *Larry Chase's Web Digest for Marketers (WDFM)*
Pub: Chase Online Marketing Strategies,Inc
Contact: Larry Chase, Exec. Editor
E-mail: larry@wdfm.com
Ed: Mary Gillen, Editor. **Released:** Weekly. **Price:** Free. **Description:** Delivers 15 short reviews of business-related websites every issue. **Remarks:** America Online, Inc.

11880 ■ *Medicine on the Net*
Pub: COR Healthcare Resources
Contact: Joyce Flory
Ed: Bridget Meaney, Editor. **Released:** Monthly. **Price:** $147, U.S. and Canada; $159, elsewhere. **Description:** Spotlights developing issues in the use of the Internet by medical professionals. Recurring features include letters to the editor, interviews, news of research, and book reviews.

11881 ■ *Online*
Pub: Online, A Division of Information Today Inc.
Ed: Marydee Ojala, Editor, marydee@infotoday.com.
Released: Bimonthly. **Price:** $129.50; $243 two years; $145 Canada and Mexico; $172 other countries. **Description:** Professional magazine covering online and CD-ROM databases with practical how-to articles covering the entire online industry.

11882 ■ *Worldgram Newsletter*
Pub: Worldprofit Inc.
Ed: Dr. Jeffrey Lant, Editor, drjlant@worldprofit.com.
Released: Bimonthly. **Price:** Free. **Description:** Internet newsletter with a marketing focus for businesses. Also offers tips on how to profit from the World Wide Web.

VIDEOCASSETTES/ AUDIOCASSETTES

11883 ■ *Computer Communication Networks*
Stoney-Wolf Productions, Inc.
130 West Columbia Ct.
PO Box 460
Chaska, MN 55318
Ph:(952)556-0075
Free: 800-237-7583
Fax:(952)361-4217
Co. E-mail: stoneywolf@montana.com
URL: http://www.stoneywolf.com
Price: $75.00. **Description:** Outlines principles involving computer communications networks. Also discusses basic computer terms and illustrates the layouts for some of the more popular communications cable networks in use. Includes training test with answer key. **Availability:** VHS; 3/4U.

11884 ■ *Internet Gateway Environments and Technology*
University of Arizona
University Teaching Center
1600 E. 1st St.
PO Box 210102
Tucson, AZ 85721-0129
Ph:(520)621-7788
Fax:(520)626-7314
URL: http://www.utc.arizona.edu
Released: 1989. **Price:** $280.00. **Description:** The design and implementation of internet gateways are demonstrated. **Availability:** VHS; EJ; 3/4U.

CONSULTANTS

11885 ■ Construction Computing Solutions Inc.
40 Orchard Ct.
Brick, NJ 08724-4396
Ph:(732)899-4319
Fax:(732)899-1921
Co. E-mail: constructioncomputing@comcast.net
URL: http://www.ccspcs.com
Contact: Gerry Bierbrauer, President
E-mail: gerryb@ccswebservices.com
Scope: Links home and small business customers, contractors and engineers with their PC system's hardware and software to achieve the maximum productivity that the hardware and software allow. Offers individual and network PC consulting services for home users, small (0-10 user) to medium (10-50 user) businesses, and construction and engineering companies in the tri-state area in the following general areas: Evaluation of computer needs, hardware, software and training, sales and installation of hardware and software as needed, sales, set up and training on construction specific software, training for and/or administration of software and network functions, internet sales, set up, access, email, and web pages.

11886 ■ Law Offices of Robert J. Keller, P.C.
Farragut Sta.
PO Box 33428, Farragut Sta.
Washington, DC 20033-3428
Ph:(202)223-2100

Fax:(202)223-2121
Co. E-mail: rjk@telcomlaw.com
URL: http://www.telcomlaw.com
Contact: Robert J. Keller, CEO
E-mail: rjk@telcomlaw.com
Scope: Specializes in telecommunications law, policy, and regulation, with particular emphasis on wireless telecommunications, new and emerging technologies, transactions involving FCC-regulated entities and licensees, and the special legal and regulatory issues relating to toll free telephone numbers. Experience in representing clients before the Federal Communications Commission, federal courts, and state and federal regulatory agencies.

FRANCHISES AND BUSINESS OPPORTUNITIES

11887 ■ Auction it Today Inc.
5424 E Grand River Ave., Ste. 101
Howell, MI 48843
Ph:(810)225-0555
Free: (866)216-3666
Fax:(810)225-8231
Co. E-mail: franchise@auction-itTODAY.com
URL: http://www.auction-itToday.com
No. of Franchise Units: 105. **No. of Company-Owned Units:** 1. **Founded:** 2004. **Franchised:** 2005. **Description:** Takes the hassles out of selling on eBay. Handle the entire eBay selling process for individuals, businesses, charities, estates etc. Sell everything from small antiques and collectibles to heavy equipment and real estate. **Equity Capital Needed:** $19,000-$105,000. **Franchise Fee:** $14,000-$22,000. **Royalty Fee:** Varies. **Financial Assistance:** Secured financing for entire package, which is available to qualified individuals. Offers financing up to 80% of the total package. **Training:** Provides training, marketing, merchandising, and sales program with hands on experience in one of our stores, with ongoing phone and email support.

11888 ■ Instantfx Web Services
Expetec Corp.
12 2nd Ave., SW
Aberdeen, SD 57401
Free: 888-297-2292
Fax:(605)225-5176
No. of Franchise Units: 70. **Founded:** 1992. **Franchised:** 2004. **Description:** Web design and hosting services. **Equity Capital Needed:** $13,300-$16,200, total investment. **Franchise Fee:** $12,500. **Financial Assistance:** No. **Training:** Yes.

11889 ■ Pak Mail
7173 S Havan St., Ste. 600
Centennial, CO 80112
Free: 800-833-2821
Fax:800-336-7363
Co. E-mail: sales@pakmail.org
URL: http://www.pakmail.com
No. of Franchise Units: 500. **Founded:** 1983. **Franchised:** 1984. **Description:** One-stop shop offers the customer a convenient location to send packages, make copies, send or receive a fax or rent a private mailbox. **Equity Capital Needed:** $130,000-$164,300. **Franchise Fee:** $29,950. **Financial Assistance:** Third party finance packages. **Managerial Assistance:** Offers assistance with site selection, lease negotiation, build-out & merchandising, operations processes, & marketing programs and ongoing networking. **Training:** Provides training, education & ongoing support to build your business.

11890 ■ The Utility Company Ltd.
One Hines Rd., Ste. 101
Kanata, ON, Canada K2K 3C7
Ph:(613)591-9800
Fax:(613)591-3966
Co. E-mail: abradley@theutilitycompany.com
URL: http://www.theutilitycompany.com
No. of Franchise Units: 57. **No. of Company-Owned Units:** 1. **Founded:** 2006. **Franchised:** 2006. **Description:** Supplier of information technology delivered as a utility service to small and medium businesses, providing the required hardware, software and service for a monthly fee per user. Our Connected Office service suite empowers people to

operate, communicate and manage their business more effectively. **Equity Capital Needed:** $45,119-$70,357. **Franchise Fee:** $39,000. **Royalty Fee:** 7%. **Training:** Yes.

11891 ■ WSI Internet
1660 Tech Ave., Unit 2
Mississauga, ON, Canada L4W 5S9
Ph:(905)678-7588
Free: 888-678-7588
Fax:(905)678-7242
Co. E-mail: wsileads@wsiworld.com
URL: http://www.wsicorporate.com
No. of Franchise Units: 83. **Founded:** 1995. **Franchised:** 1996. **Description:** Provides full service internet solutions. Helps operate internet consultancy franchise. **Equity Capital Needed:** $49,700. **Franchise Fee:** $49,700. **Financial Assistance:** No. **Training:** Yes.

LIBRARIES

11892 ■ Gartner IRC
56 Top Gallant Rd.
Stamford, CT 06904
Ph:(203)964-0096
URL: http://www.gartner.com
Scope: Information technology, computers, system design, telecommunications. **Services:** SDI; Center not open to the public (client research only). **Holdings:** 3000 items. **Subscriptions:** 1200 journals and other serials.

11893 ■ International Data Corp.–IDC Library
2131 Landings Dr.
Mountain View, CA 94043
Ph:(650)962-6481
Fax:(650)691-0531
Co. E-mail: slake@idc.com
URL: http://www.idc.com
Contact: Sara Lake, Mgr.Lib.Svcs.
Scope: Information technology. **Services:** Center not open to the public. **Holdings:** 350 books; 250 subject files. **Subscriptions:** 70 journals and other serials.

11894 ■ LexisNexis Technical Library
9595 Springboro Pike
Miamisburg, OH 45342
Ph:(937)865-6800
Fax:(937)865-1655
Co. E-mail: technical.library@lexisnexis.com
Contact: Patricia J. Carter, Mgr.
Scope: Online industry. **Services:** Interlibrary loan; Library not open to the public. **Holdings:** 6000 volumes. **Subscriptions:** 100 journals and other serials; 2 newspapers.

11895 ■ Queens Borough Public Library–Information Services Division
89-11 Merrick Blvd.
Jamaica, NY 11432
Ph:(718)990-0778
Fax:(718)658-8342
Co. E-mail: thomas.w.galante@queenslibrary.org
URL: http://www.queenslibrary.org
Contact: Thomas W. Galante, CEO/Lib.Dir.
Scope: General. **Services:** Interlibrary loan; copying; email reference; faxing to New York State residents; Library open to the public. **Holdings:** 1000 volumes; partial depository for federal government documents; state and city documents.

11896 ■ University of Michigan–Information and Library Studies Library
Hatcher Graduate Library, Rm. 209
Ann Arbor, MI 48109-1205
Ph:(734)764-3166
Co. E-mail: cerebus@umich.edu
URL: http://www.lib.umich.edu
Contact: Donna Hayward, Assoc.Libn.
Scope: Library science, history of libraries, history of publishing, history of bookselling, history of the book, bibliography, children's literature, online information services, information technology, storage and retrieval, micrographics, human computer interaction, archives and records management, information policy, information economics. **Services:** Interlibrary

loan; Library open to the public. **Holdings:** 63,259 books; 701 dissertations; 453 reels of microfilm; 7020 sheets of microfiche; 20 AV programs; 22 CD-ROMs; 30,000 monographs; 400 serials; 300 periodicals. **Subscriptions:** 589 journals and other serials.

RESEARCH CENTERS

11897 ■ Bibliographical Center for Research–Rocky Mountain Region
14394 E Evans Ave.
Aurora, CO 80014-1478
Ph:(303)751-6277
Free: 800—397-1552
Fax:(303)751-9787
Co. E-mail: bbailey@bcr.org
URL: http://www.bcr.org

Contact: Brenda Bailey-Hainer, Pres./CEO
E-mail: bbailey@bcr.org
Scope: Development of improved library techniques and improved means of document delivery, information retrieval systems, Internet technology, and use of microcomputers and Internet technology in libraries. Center is the hub of a regional network that links libraries to automated literature databases and major computerized bibliographic cooperatives. **Publications:** Action for Libraries Newsletter (monthly); Annual Report; Third Indicator Technical Newsletter (monthly). **Educational Activities:** Information retrieval training sessions and information technology workshops.

11898 ■ Pennsylvania State University at Harrisburg–Pennsylvania State Data Center
777 W Harrisburg Pike
Middletown, PA 17057-4898

Ph:(717)948-6336
Fax:(717)948-6754
Co. E-mail: pasdc@psu.edu
URL: http://pasdc.hbg.psu.edu
Contact: Sue Copella, Dir.
E-mail: pasdc@psu.edu
Scope: Data collection and analysis, including a decennial and economic census, population estimates and projections, migration flows, commutation patterns, housing school district data, geographic information systems, on-line systems, economic impacts of smoking, county to county migration flows, AIDS studies, and health insurance. **Services:** Demographic and socioeconomic data, via telephone requests. **Publications:** County Data Books; Estimates (annually); State Abstract. **Educational Activities:** Conference (annually); PASDC User Conference; Regional workshops, on census basics, CD-ROMS, on-line systems, and GIS.

ASSOCIATIONS AND OTHER ORGANIZATIONS

11899 ■ Canadian Securities Institute–Institut Canadien des Valeurs Mobilieres
200 Wellington St. W, 15th Fl.
Toronto, ON, Canada M5V 3C7
Ph:(416)364-9130
Free: (866)866-2601
Fax:(416)359-0486
Co. E-mail: customer_support@csi.ca
URL: http://www.csi.ca
Contact: Roberta Wilton, Pres./CEO
Description: Stock exchanges, brokers, and other investment professionals. Promotes increased public understanding of securities investment. Serves as a network linking members; sponsors educational programs.

11900 ■ Canadian ShareOwners Association
4 King St. W, Ste. 806
Toronto, ON, Canada M5H 1B6
Ph:(416)595-9600
Free: 800-268-6881
Fax:(416)595-0400
Co. E-mail: customercare@shareowner.com
URL: http://www.shareowner.com/index.html
Contact: John T. Bart, Founder/Pres.
Description: Investors in securities. Promotes successful investment by independent investors. Conducts educational programs; sponsors research. **Publications:** *Share Owner* (bimonthly).

11901 ■ CFA Institute
560 Ray C. Hunt Dr.
Charlottesville, VA 22903-2981
Ph:(434)951-5499
Free: 800-247-8132
Fax:(434)951-5262
Co. E-mail: info@cfainstitute.org
URL: http://www.cfainstitute.org
Contact: John D. Rogers CFA, Pres./CEO

Description: Security and financial analyst association whose members are practicing investment analysts. Includes private, voluntary self-regulation program in which members are enrolled. Internationally renowned for its rigorous Chartered Financial Analyst curriculum and examination program, which has more than 86,000 candidates from 143 countries enrolled for exams. In addition, it is internationally recognized for its investment performance standards, which investment firms use to document and report investment results, as well as for its Code of Ethics and Standards of Professional Conduct. **Publications:** *AIMR Exchange* (bimonthly); *AIMR Membership Directory* (annual); *Financial Analysts Journal* (bimonthly).

11902 ■ Investment Adviser Association
1050 17th St. NW, Ste. 725
Washington, DC 20036-5514
Ph:(202)293-4222

Fax:(202)293-4223
Co. E-mail: info@investmentadviser.org
URL: http://www.investmentadviser.org
Contact: Mr. David G. Tittsworth, Exec. Dir./VP
Description: Federally registered investment adviser firms. Represents the interests of the investment management profession before legislative and regulatory bodies. .

11903 ■ Investment Management Consultants Association
5619 DTC Pkwy., Ste. 500
Greenwood Village, CO 80111
Ph:(303)770-3377
Fax:(303)770-1812
Co. E-mail: imca@imca.org
URL: http://www.imca.org
Contact: Sean Walters CAE, Exec. Dir./CEO
Description: Consultants, money managers, and others in the investment management consultant business. Seeks to increase public awareness of investment management consultants, provide educational programs to members, and encourage high business standards. Operates consulting industry certification program. Maintains a legislative network with state and federal legislative information affecting the industry. **Publications:** *Essentials of Investment Consulting*; *Ethical Considerations for Consultants*; *The Facts About Investing*; *IMCA Practice Management Standards*; *IMCA Reporting Standards* (semiannual); *The Journal of Investment Consulting* (semiannual); *The Monitor* (bimonthly); *Wealth Management Course* .

11904 ■ National Investment Company Service Association
8400 Westpark Dr., 2nd Fl.
McLean, VA 22102
Ph:(508)485-1500
Fax:(508)485-1560
Co. E-mail: info@nicsa.org
URL: http://www.nicsa.org
Contact: Theresa Hamacher CFA, Pres.
Description: Mutual fund investment managers, distributors, custodians, transfer agents, accounting and legal firms, broker/dealers, and general providers of services and products to the mutual fund industry. Seeks to address future service needs and trends by providing a forum on operational and technological developments. **Publications:** *NICSA News* (quarterly);Membership Directory (annual).

11905 ■ National Investor Relations Institute
8020 Towers Crescent Dr., Ste. 250
Vienna, VA 22182
Ph:(703)506-3570
Fax:(703)506-3571
Co. E-mail: info@niri.org
URL: http://www.niri.org
Contact: Jeffrey D. Morgan, Pres./CEO
Description: Executives engaged in investor relations. Identifies the role of the investor relations practitioner; protects a free and open market with equity and access to investors of all kinds; improves communication between corporate management and shareholders, present and future. Holds professional

development seminars and conducts research programs. Maintains placement service and speakers' bureau; compiles statistics. **Publications:** *Investor Relations Weekly* (weekly); *IR Update* (monthly); *Roster* (annual); *Standards of Practice for Investor Relations* (periodic).

11906 ■ National Society of Compliance Professionals
22 Kent Rd.
Cornwall Bridge, CT 06754
Ph:(860)672-0843
Fax:(860)672-3005
Co. E-mail: info@nscp.org
URL: http://www.nscp.org
Contact: Joan Hinchman, Exec. Dir.
Description: Professionals in brokerage houses, investment advisers, accounting and law firms, and banks, who are responsible for compliance with government and other regulations. Provides access to accounting and legal expertise. Provides a forum for exchange between members. Monitors new state and federal laws and regulations. Offers interpretive and practical assistance in compliance matters. Conducts educational programs. **Publications:** *NSCP Currents* (bimonthly); *NSCP Hotline Memo* (monthly).

11907 ■ New York Society of Security Analysts
1540 Broadway, Ste. 1010
New York, NY 10036-2714
Ph:(212)541-4530
Fax:(212)541-4677
Co. E-mail: webaccess@nyssa.org
URL: http://www.nyssa.org
Contact: Amy Geffen PhD, Pres./CEO
Description: Security analysts and portfolio managers employed primarily in New York by brokerage houses, banks, insurance companies, mutual funds and other financial institutions. Conducts educational forums on topics relating to the securities markets. Maintains placement service. **Publications:** *Corporate Governance Handbook*; *NYSSA News* (monthly).

11908 ■ North American Securities Administrators Association
750 1st St. NE, Ste. 1140
Washington, DC 20002-8034
Ph:(202)737-0900
Fax:(202)783-3571
Co. E-mail: ri@nasaa.org
URL: http://www.nasaa.org
Contact: Russ Iuculano, Exec. Dir.
Description: Represents the interests of the state, provincial and territorial securities administrators in the U.S., Canada, Mexico and Puerto Rico. Provides support to its members in government relations and with federal regulators, industry SROs and other groups. .

11909 ■ Securities Industry and Financial Markets Association
120 Broadway, 35th Fl.
New York, NY 10271-0080
Ph:(212)313-1200

Fax:(212)313-1301
Co. E-mail: inquiry@sifma.org
URL: http://www.sifma.org
Contact: T. Timothy Ryan Jr., Pres./CEO

Description: Represents more than 650 member firms of all sizes, in all financial markets in the U.S. and around the world. Enhances the public's trust and confidence in the markets, delivering an efficient, enhanced member network of access and forward-looking services, as well as premiere educational resources for the professionals in the industry and the investors whom they serve. Maintains offices in New York City and Washington, DC. **Publications:** *Securities Industry Association—Directory and Guide* (annual); *Securities Industry Association—Foreign Activity Report* (quarterly); *Securities Industry Association—Yearbook*; *Securities Industry Trends* (quarterly).

11910 ■ Security Traders Association

80 Broad St., 5th Fl.
New York, NY 10004
Ph:(203)202-7680
Fax:(203)202-7681
Co. E-mail: sta@securitytraders.org
URL: http://securitytraders.info
Contact: Jim Toes, Pres./CEO

Description: Brokers and dealers handling listed and OTC securities, stocks and bonds, and all securities. Conducts educational programs. Promotes the interests of members throughout the global financial markets. Provides representation of these interests in the legislative, regulatory and technological processes. Fosters goodwill and high standards of integrity in accord with the association's founding principle. .

11911 ■ Stable Value Investment Association

1025 Connecticut Ave. NW, Ste. 1000
Washington, DC 20036
Ph:(202)580-7620
Fax:(202)580-7621
Co. E-mail: info@stablevalue.org
URL: http://stablevalue.org
Contact: Marc Magnoli, Chm.

Description: Pension plan sponsors, investment managers, banks, life insurance companies and consultants. Promotes retirement savings and educates individuals on the role that stable value funds can play in achieving a financially secure retirement. .

REFERENCE WORKS

11912 ■ "3Par: Storing Up Value" in *Barron's* (Vol. 90, August 30, 2010, No. 35, pp. 30)

Pub: Barron's Editorial & Corporate Headquarters

Ed: Mark Veverka. **Description:** Dell and Hewlett Packard are both bidding for data storage company 3Par. The acquisition would help Dell and Hewlett Packard provide customers with a one-stop shop as customers move to a private cloud in the Internet.

11913 ■ "13D Filings" in *Barron's* (Vol. 88, March 10, 2008, No. 10, pp. M11)

Pub: Dow Jones & Company, Inc.

Description: Barington Capital and Clinton Group sent a letter to Dillard's demanding a list of the company's stockholders. Elliott Associates announced that it is prepared to take over Packeteer for $5.50 a share. Strongbow capital suggested a change in leadership in Duckwall-ALCO Stores.

11914 ■ "13D Filings: Investors Report to the SEC" in *Barron's* (Vol. 88, March 31, 2008, No. 13, pp. M10)

Pub: Dow Jones & Company, Inc.

Description: Obrem Capital Management wants Micrel to rescind Micrel's shareholder-rights plan and to boost its board to six members from five. Patricia L. Childress plans to nominate herself to the board of Sierra Bancorp, and Luther King Capital Management may consider a competing acquisition proposal for Industrial Distribution Group.

11915 ■ "A 16-Year Housing Slump? It Could Happen" in *Barron's* (Vol. 88, March 17, 2008, No. 11, pp. 27)

Pub: Dow Jones & Company, Inc.

Ed: Gene Epstein. **Description:** Housing remains a good protection against inflation but over very long periods. Inflation-adjusted stock prices did even better but have greater volatility. Commodities, on the other hand, underperformed both housing and stocks as inflation hedges. House prices tend to rise faster than the consumer price index is because land is inherently limited.

11916 ■ "$50 Million Project for West Chester" in *Business Courier* (Vol. 24, December 14, 2008, No. 35, pp. 1)

Pub: American City Business Journals, Inc.

Ed: Laura Baverman. **Description:** Commercial developer Scott Street Partners is planning to invest $50 million for the development of a site south of the Streets of West Chester retail center. The 31-acre project will generate 1,200 jobs, and will bring in offices, restaurants and a hotel. The development plans and the features of the site are discussed as well.

11917 ■ "75 Most Powerful Blacks on Wall Street" in *Black Enterprise* (Vol. 37, October 2006, No. 3, pp. 136)

Pub: Earl G. Graves Publishing Co. Inc.

Ed: Carolyn M. Brown. **Description:** Profiles of seventy-five African American top executives. The listing is a compilation of the brightest and best venture capitalists, asset managers, CEOs, traders, and investment bankers.

11918 ■ "The 100 Most Bullish Stocks" in *Canadian Business* (Vol. 81, Summer 2008, No. 9, pp. 81)

Pub: Rogers Media Ltd.

Ed: Megan Harman; Lauren McKeon. **Description:** 100 of the most bullish stocks are taken from the list of the 500 best-performing stocks. The idea is to narrow the list help investors in their investment decisions since it is difficult to choose from a large list. Analysts rate the companies with 5 being the most bullish and 1 the least. Other details of the roster are presented.

11919 ■ "401(k) Keys to Stable Value" in *Barron's* (Vol. 88, March 10, 2008, No. 10, pp. 40)

Pub: Dow Jones & Company, Inc.

Ed: Tom Sullivan. **Description:** Stable-value funds offer investors stability in a period of volatility in financial markets, attracting $888 million in funds. The Securities and Exchange Commission approved the launch of actively managed exchange-traded funds.

11920 ■ "529.com Wins Outstanding Achievement in Web Development" in *Investment Weekly* (November 14, 2009, pp. 152)

Pub: Investment Weekly News

Description: Web Marketing Association's 2009 WebAward for Financial Services Standard of Excellence and Investment Standard of Excellence was won by 529.com, the website from Upromise Investments, Inc., the leading administrator of 529 college savings plans.

11921 ■ "2008: Year of the Rat Race" in *Mergers & Acquisitions: The Dealmaker's Journal* (March 1, 2008)

Pub: SourceMedia, Inc.

Ed: Danelle Fugazy. **Description:** Although China still presents opportunities to Western investors, many are discovering that much more research needs to be done concerning doing business in that country before investing there becomes truly mainstream. According to one source, there are at least 300,000 small state-owned enterprises in China and millions of middle-market privately owned companies; the Chinese stock market can only handle about 50 to 70 IPOs a year and lists about 1,500 companies at a time.

11922 ■ "2010 Book of Lists" in *Austin Business JournalInc.* (Vol. 29, December 25, 2009, No. 42, pp. 1)

Pub: American City Business Journals

Description: Rankings of companies and organizations within the business services, finance, healthcare, hospitality and travel, insurance, marketing and media, professional services, real estate, education and technology industries in Austin, Texas are presented. Rankings are based on sales, business size, and other statistics.

11923 ■ "2010 Book of Lists" in *Business Courier* (Vol. 26, December 26, 2009, No. 36, pp. 1)

Pub: American City Business Journals, Inc.

Description: Rankings of companies and organizations within the business services, education, finance, health care, hospitality and tourism, real estate, and technology industries in the Cincinnati, Ohio-Northern Kentucky area are presented. Rankings are based on sales, business size, or other statistics.

11924 ■ "2010 Book of Lists" in *Tampa Bay Business Journal* (Vol. 30, December 22, 2009, No. 53, pp. 1)

Pub: American City Business Journals

Description: Rankings of companies and organizations within the human resources, banking and finance, business services, healthcare, real estate, technology, hospitality and travel, and education industries in the Greater Tampa Bay area are presented. Rankings are based on sales, business size, and more.

11925 ■ "A Conversation With; Ron Gatner, Jones Lang LaSalle" in *Crain's Detroit Business* (Vol. 24, October 6, 2008, No. 40, pp. 9)

Pub: Crain Communications, Inc.

Description: Interview with Ron Gatner who is a corporate real estate adviser with the real estate company Jones Lang LaSalle as well as the company's executive vice president and part of the tenant advisory team; Gatner speaks about the impact that the Wall Street crisis is having on the commercial real estate market in Detroit.

11926 ■ "A Good Step, But There's a Long Way to Go" in *Business Week* (September 22, 2008, No. 4100, pp. 10)

Pub: McGraw-Hill Companies, Inc.

Ed: James C. Cooper. **Description:** Despite the historic action by the U.S. government to nationalize the mortgage giants Freddie Mac and Fannie Mae, rising unemployment rates may prove to be an even bigger roadblock to bringing back the economy from its downward spiral. The takeover is meant to restore confidence in the credit markets and help with the mortgage crisis but the rising rate in unemployment may make many households unable to take advantage of any benefits which arise from the bailout. Statistical data included.

11927 ■ "ABM Janitorial Services Receives Service Excellence Award from Jones Lang LaSalle" in *Investment Weekly News* (July 16, 2011, pp. 75)

Pub: News RX

Description: ABM Janitorial Services was awarded the 2010 Jones Lang LaSalle Distinction award in the category of Service Excellence. LaSalle is a leading financial and professional services firm that specializes in real estate services and investment management. The program recognizes supplier partners who play a vital role in LaSalle's aim to provide the highest quality of services, value and innovation to clients.

11928 ■ "ACE Agrees to Pay Out $266 Million to Investors" in *Globe & Mail* (February 17, 2006, pp. B1)

Pub: CTVglobemedia Publishing Inc.

Ed: Brent Jang. **Description:** Canada-based commercial aviation firm ACE Aviation Holdings has agreed to pay 266 million dollars to its investors after filing a bankruptcy one year ago. Complete details of this pay off are discussed.

11929 ■ "ACE Back in Unfriendly Skies" in *Globe & Mail* **(February 14, 2006, pp. B17)**
Pub: CTVglobemedia Publishing Inc.
Ed: Brent Jang. **Description:** ACE Aviation Holdings Inc. reported $258 million profit for 2005. The opinions of analysts on the share price of the company for 2006 are presented.

11930 ■ "Achieve Tampa Bay Thrown a Lifeline in Proposed Merger" in *Tampa Bay Business Journal* **(Vol. 30, January 22, 2010, No. 5, pp. 1)**
Pub: American City Business Journals
Ed: Margie Manning. **Description:** Mental Health Care Inc. proposed a merger with Achieve Tampa Bay Inc. The former proposes to administer the latter's operations and take over its assets while paying its debts.

11931 ■ "AdvacePierre Heats Up" in *Business Courier* **(Vol. 27, October 29, 2010, No. 26, pp. 1)**
Pub: Business Courier
Ed: John Newberry. **Description:** Bill Toler, chief executive officer of AdvancePierre Foods, is aiming for more growth and more jobs. The company was formed after the merger of Pierre Foods with two Oklahoma-based food processing companies. Toler wants to expand production and is set to start adding employees in the next 6-12 months.

11932 ■ "Advertising May Take a Big Hit in Southwest/AirTran Merger" in *Baltimore Business Journal* **(Vol. 28, October 1, 2010, No. 21, pp. 1)**
Pub: Baltimore Business Journal
Ed: Gary Haber. **Description:** Advertising on television stations and the publishing industry in Baltimore could drop as a result of the merger between rival discount airlines Southwest Airlines and AirTran Airways. Southwest is among the top advertisers in the U.S., spending $126 million in 2009. No local jobs are expected to be affected because neither airline uses a local advertising firm.

11933 ■ "After Price Cuts, Competition GPS Makers Lose Direction" in *Brandweek* **(Vol. 49, April 21, 2008, No. 16, pp. 16)**
Pub: VNU Business Media, Inc.
Ed: Steve Miller. **Description:** Garmin and TomTom, two of the leaders in portable navigation devices, have seen lowering revenues due to dramatic price cuts and unexpected competition from the broadening availability of personal navigation on mobile phones. TomTom has trimmed its sales outlook for its first quarter while Garmin's stock dropped 40 percent since February.

11934 ■ "Ag Firms Harvest Revenue Growth" in *The Business Journal-Serving Metropolitan Kansas City* **(Vol. 26, July 18, 2008, No. 45, pp. 1)**
Pub: American City Business Journals, Inc.
Ed: Steve Vockrodt. **Description:** Five of the biggest agricultural companies in the Kansas City area, except one, reported multibillion-dollar revenue increases in 2007. The companies, which include Lansing Trade Group, posted a combined $9.5 billion revenue growth. The factors that affected the revenue increase in the area's agricultural companies, such as prices and high demand, are also examined.

11935 ■ "Aggenix Completes Merger with German Giant" in *Houston Business Journal* **(Vol. 40, December 25, 2009, No. 33, pp. 2)**
Pub: American City Business Journals
Ed: Mary Ann Azevedo. **Description:** Agennix Inc. has completed its transformation into a German company after Germany-based GPC Biotech merged into the former publicly traded Agennix AG. One quarter of Agennix's 60 employees will remain in Houston. Details on Agennix's drug trials are examined.

11936 ■ "AIC To Buy $350M of Real Estate" in *Austin Business JournalInc.* **(Vol. 28, November 14, 2008, No. 35, pp. 1)**
Pub: American City Business Journals
Ed: Kate Harrington. **Description:** Austin-based AIC Ventures LP is planning to buy $350 million worth of commercial real estate. The company's move will double its acquisitions. It is also planning to acquire 30 assets for its eight fun in 2009 from middle-market companies.

11937 ■ "AIG Fixed; Is Michigan Next?" in *Crain's Detroit Business* **(Vol. 24, September 22, 2008, No. 38, pp. 1)**
Pub: Crain Communications, Inc.
Ed: Jay Greene. **Description:** Michigan's economic future is examined as is the mortgage buyout plan and American International Group Inc.'s takeover by the U.S. government.

11938 ■ "Air Canada Boss Gains $3.5 Million in Options" in *Globe & Mail* **(January 19, 2007, pp. B5)**
Pub: CTVglobemedia Publishing Inc.
Ed: Brent Jang. **Description:** Air Canada chairman Robert Milton's sale of 200,000 shares in stock options is discussed.

11939 ■ "Alberta's Runaway Train" in *Canadian Business* **(Vol. 80, December 25, 2006, No. 1, pp. 17)**
Pub: Rogers Media
Ed: Andrew Nikiforuk. **Description:** The high revenue brought about by the growth in the number of oil sand plants in Canada and the simultaneous burden on infrastructure and housing is discussed.

11940 ■ "Algoma Resolves Hedge Fund Fight" in *Globe & Mail* **(March 8, 2006, pp. B1)**
Pub: CTVglobemedia Publishing Inc.
Ed: Greg Keenan. **Description:** Algoma Steel Inc. has ended a dispute with Paulson and Co., a New York hedge fund, by offering to pay $200 million special dividend, appointing new directors, and continue to go for a sale.

11941 ■ "Algoma Shares Soar on Growing Sale Rumors" in *Globe & Mail* **(February 13, 2007, pp. B1)**
Pub: CTVglobemedia Publishing Inc.
Ed: Andrew Willis; Greg Keenan. **Description:** The stock prices of Algoma Steel Inc. have touched record high of $40 on the Toronto Stock Exchange. The growing rumors about the possible takeover bid is the major reason for the stock price growth.

11942 ■ "All About The Benjamins" in *Canadian Business* **(Vol. 81, September 29, 2008, No. 16, pp. 92)**
Pub: Rogers Media Ltd.
Ed: David Baines. **Description:** Discusses real estate developer Royal Indian Raj International Corp., a company that planned to build a $3 billion "smart city" near the Bangalore airport; to this day nothing has ever been built. The company was incorporated in 1999 by Manoj C. Benjamin one investor, Bill Zack, has been sued by the developer for libel due to his website that calls the company a scam. Benjamin has had a previous case of fraud issued against him as well as a string of liabilities and lawsuits.

11943 ■ "All Eyes On Iris" in *Canadian Business* **(Vol. 81, July 22, 2008, No. 12-13, pp. 20)**
Pub: Rogers Media Ltd.
Ed: Jack Mintz. **Description:** Provincial governments in Canada are believed to be awaiting Alberta Finance Minister Iris Evans' financial and investment policies as well as Evans' development of a new saving strategy. Alberta is the only Canadian province that is in position to invest in sovereign wealth funds after it eliminated its debt in 2005.

11944 ■ *All the Money in the World: How the Forbes 400 Make - and Spend - Their Fortunes*
Pub: AMACOM
Ed: Peter W. Bernstein; Annalyn Swan. **Released:** September 2007. **Description:** A fascinating and historical breakdown of the 400 richest Americans according to Forbes magazine. The book examines how the list's members actually make and spend their money. Illustrating the text with charts and informational sidebars, readers are given the opportunity to look at both production and consumption and insights in social and historical context.

11945 ■ "All Revved Up" in *Barron's* **(Vol. 90, September 13, 2010, No. 37, pp. 18)**
Pub: Barron's Editorial & Corporate Headquarters
Ed: Christopher C. Williams. **Description:** Shares of Advance Auto Parts has returned 55 percent in a span of three years and the stock could still reach the mid-60s by 2011 from its price of 46.07 in the second week of September 2010. The shares are trading at just 13 times the 2011 earnings.

11946 ■ "All-Star Advice 2010" in *Black Enterprise* **(Vol. 41, October 2010, No. 3, pp. 97)**
Pub: Earl G. Graves Publishing Co. Inc.
Ed: Renita Burns, Sheiresa Ngo, Marcia Wade Talbert. **Description:** Financial experts share tips on real estate, investing, taxes, insurance and debt management.

11947 ■ "Alto Ventures Retains Investor Relations Professional" in *Canadian Corporate News* **(May 16, 2007)**
Pub: Comtex News Network Inc.
Description: Alto Ventures Ltd., a gold exploration and development company with a portfolio of eleven properties in the Canadian Shield, announced that it has engaged the consulting services of Mark Prosser in order to focus on increasing investor awareness and exposure to the investment community through the dissemination of corporate information to a network of North American and European institutions, retail brokerage firms, and private investors.

11948 ■ "Amit Wadhwaney" in *Canadian Business* **(Vol. 80, March 12, 2007, No. 6, pp. 22)**
Pub: Rogers Media
Ed: Rachel Pulfer. **Description:** Manager of Third Avenue International Value Fund, Amit Wadhwaney, shares his views on buying Canadian agricultural and forestry stocks.

11949 ■ "Analysts: More Mergers for the Region's Hospitals" in *Boston Business Journal* **(Vol. 30, October 15, 2010, No. 36, pp. 1)**
Pub: Boston Business Journal
Ed: Julie M. Donnelly. **Description:** A number of hospitals in Boston, Massachusetts are engaging in mergers and acquisitions. Caritas Christi Health Care is set to be purchased by Cerberus Capital Management. The U.S. healthcare reform law is seen to drive the development.

11950 ■ "Analysts Not Fazed By Constellation's Halt to New Nuclear Plants" in *Baltimore Business Journal* **(Vol. 28, October 22, 2010, No. 24)**
Pub: Baltimore Business Journal
Ed: Scott Dance. **Description:** Wall Street analysts believe that Constellation Energy Group Inc.'s decision to pull out of the nuclear construction business would not change their outlook on the company. New nuclear power had been one of Constellation's long-term goals, but the company pulled the plug on the project. It is believed that most investors were not expecting any payoff from the venture.

11951 ■ "And In This Briefcase" in *Mergers & Acquisitions: The Dealmaker's Journal* **(March 1, 2008)**
Pub: SourceMedia, Inc.
Description: ACG San Diego decided to address the impact the changes in the economy will have on potential private equity transactions as well as what criteria private equity firms are looking for when assessing a company. At the opening of the chapter's 2008 breakfast meeting, real-world case studies were utilized with the audiences' participation in order to assess pre-deal risk scenarios.

11952 ■ "The Annual Entitlement Lecture: Trustees of Medicare and Social Security Issue Another Dismal Report" in *Barron's* **(March 31, 2008)**
Pub: Dow Jones & Company, Inc.
Ed: Thomas G. Donlan. **Description:** Expenditures on Medicare hospital insurance and the revenues available to pay for it have led to a gap of capital

valued at $38.6 trillion. Slashing the benefits or raising taxes will not solve the gap which exists unless the government saves the money and invests it in private markets.

11953 ■ "Another Man's Pain" in *Canadian Business* **(Vol. 80, October 22, 2007, No. 21, pp. 33)**
Pub: Rogers Media
Ed: Andy Holloway. **Description:** U.S. financial collapse can have a positive impact on Canadian investors. Graphs on the total number of home foreclosures in the U.S. from January to August 2007, as well as foreclosure market by type, are presented.

11954 ■ "Apartment Market Down, Not Out" in *Crain's Detroit Business* **(Vol. 24, October 6, 2008, No. 40, pp. 9)**
Pub: Crain Communications, Inc.
Ed: Daniel Duggan. **Description:** Detroit's apartment market is considered to have some of the strongest fundamentals of any apartment market in the country with relatively low vacancy rates and a relatively low supply of new units compared with demand. Investors continue to show interest in the buildings but the national lending market is making it difficult to invest in the city.

11955 ■ "Apartment Tower in River North Fetches More Than $90 Million" in *Crain's Chicago Business* **(Vol. 34, October 24, 2011, No. 42, pp. 17)**
Pub: Crain Communications Inc.
Ed: Alby Gallun. **Description:** Apartment tower in River North was sold for over $90 million to a Texas pension fund adviser. Details are included.

11956 ■ *Are the Rich Necessary? Great Economic Arguments and How They Reflect Our Personal Values*
Pub: Axios Press
Ed: Hunter Lewis. **Released:** 2007. **Price:** $20.00. **Description:** Investment advisor argues whether today's economic system promotes greed. Each chapter of the book poses a question and then he answers.

11957 ■ "Are We There Yet?" in *Business Courier* **(Vol. 24, April 4, 2008, No. 52, pp. 1)**
Pub: American City Business Journals, Inc.
Ed: Lucy May; Dan Monk. **Description:** Groundbreaking for The Banks project happened in April 2, 2008, however, the future of the development remains uncertain due to some unresolved issues such as financing. Developers Harold A. Dawson Co. and Carter still have to pass final financing documents to Hamilton County and Cincinnati. The issue of financial commitment for the central riverfront project is examined.

11958 ■ "Are You Ready for Dow 20,000?" in *Barron's* **(Vol. 88, March 24, 2008, No. 12, pp. 26)**
Pub: Dow Jones & Company, Inc.
Ed: Jonathan R. Laing. **Description:** Stock strategist James Finucane forecasts that the Dow Jones Industrial Average will rise from its 12,361 level to as high as 20,000 from 2008 to 2009. He believes that stock liquidation and a buildup of cash provide the perfect conditions for a huge rally.

11959 ■ "Are You Ready To Do It Yourself? Discipline and Self-Study Can Help You Profit From Online Trading" in *Black Enterprise* **(Feb. 2008)**
Pub: Earl G. Graves Publishing Co. Inc.
Ed: Steve Garmhausen. **Description:** Steps to help individuals invest in stocks online is given by an expert broker. Discount brokerage houses can save money for online investors.

11960 ■ "As Capital Gains Tax Hike Looms, Merger Activity Percolates" in *Baltimore Business Journal* **(Vol. 28, August 27, 2010, No. 16, pp. 1)**
Pub: Baltimore Business Journal
Ed: Scott Dance. **Description:** Concerns for higher capital gains taxes in 2011 have been provoking buyers and sellers to engage in mergers and acquisi-

tions activity, which is expected to gain momentum before the end of 2010. Companies that had saved cash during the recession have been taking advantage of the buyer's market. Other trends in local and national mergers and acquisitions activity are presented.

11961 ■ "Asia Breathes a Sigh of Relief" in *Business Week* **(September 22, 2008, No. 4100, pp. 32)**
Pub: McGraw-Hill Companies, Inc.
Ed: Bruce Einhorn; Theo Francis; Chi-Chu Tschang; Moon Ihlwan; Hiroko Tashiro. **Description:** Foreign bankers, such as those in Asia, that had been investing heavily in the United States began to worry as the housing crisis deepened and the impact on Freddie Mac and Fannie Mae became increasingly clear. Due to the government bailout, however, central banks will most likely continue to buy American debt.

11962 ■ "'The Asian Decade'" in *Hawaii Business* **(Vol. 53, January 2008, No. 7, pp. 19)**
Pub: Hawaii Business Publishing
Ed: Cathy S. Cruz-George. **Description:** Chaney Brooks, a Hawaiian real estate company, has affiliated with commercial real estate network NAI Global. The NAI partnership will improve Hawaii's international business, particularly its Asian investments. Hawaii's diverse workforce is evaluated, with regards to being an asset for international businesses.

11963 ■ *Association for Investment Management & Research—Membership Directory*
Pub: CFA Institute
Contact: John D. Rogers, CEO & Pres.
Released: Annual, January. **Price:** $150 per year. **Covers:** 38,000 security and financial analysts who are practicing investment analysis. **Entries Include:** Name, firm affiliation and address, phone, fax, e-mail. **Arrangement:** Alphabetical.

11964 ■ "ATS Secures Investment From Goldman Sachs" in *The Business Journal - Serving Phoenix and the Valley of the Sun* **(Vol. 29, September 26, 2008, No. 4, pp. 1)**
Pub: American City Business Journals, Inc.
Ed: Patrick O'Grady. **Description:** Goldman Sachs made an investment to American Traffic Solutions Inc. (ATS) which will allow it to gain two seats on the board of the red-light and speed cameras maker. The investment will help ATS maintain its rapid growth which is at 83 percent over the past 18 months leading up to September 2008.

11965 ■ "Attorney Guides Biotech Company in $6 Million Initial Public Offering" in *Miami Daily Business Review* **(March 26, 2008)**
Pub: ALM Media Inc.
Description: In order to raise capital to engage in a full-scale trial of MyoCell to receive clinical approval, Bioheart Inc., launched an initial public offering. Bioheart researches and develops cell therapies to treat heart damage.

11966 ■ "Au Revoir Or Goodbye?" in *Barron's* **(Vol. 88, July 14, 2008, No. 28, pp. 5)**
Pub: Dow Jones & Co., Inc.
Ed: Alan Abelson. **Description:** Former Senator Phil Gramm's opinion that the U.S. is a "nation of whiners" as they moan about recession is another example of the disconnection between Washington and Wall Street on one hand and the real world on the other. It would be a catastrophe for most of the world if Fannie Mae and Freddie Mac were to go under and take their trillions of mortgage debt with them.

11967 ■ "Auction-Rate Cash Frees Up" in *The Business Journal-Portland* **(Vol. 25, August 15, 2008, No. 23, pp. 1)**
Pub: American City Business Journals, Inc.
Ed: Aliza Earnshaw. **Description:** FEI Co. and RadiSys Corp. have received notices that UBS AG will buy back the auction-rate securities that were sold to them in around two years from 2008. FEI had $110.1 million invested in auction-rate securities while RadiSys holds $62.8 million of these securities.

11968 ■ "Austin Ventures: Is It a VC Firm?" in *Austin Business Journal* **(Vol. 31, June 17, 2011, No. 15, pp. 1)**
Pub: American City Business Journals Inc.
Ed: Christopher Calnan. **Description:** Investment firm Austin Ventures could lose its classification as a venture capital firm under a new definition of venture capital by the Securities and Exchange Commission. The reclassification could result in additional expenses for Austin Ventures, which has two-thirds of its investments in growth equity transactions.

11969 ■ "Auto Supplier Stock Battered In Wake Of Wall Street Woes" in *Crain's Detroit Business* **(Vol. 24, September 29, 2008, No. 39, pp. 4)**
Pub: Crain Communications, Inc.
Ed: Ryan Beene. **Description:** Due to the volatility of the stock market and public perception of the $700 billion banking bailout, auto suppliers are now facing a dramatic drop in their shares. Statistical data included.

11970 ■ "Awaiting a Call from Deutsche Telekom" in *Barron's* **(Vol. 90, September 6, 2010, No. 36, pp. M5)**
Pub: Barron's Editorial & Corporate Headquarters
Ed: Vito J. Racanelli. **Description:** Deutsche Telekom's (DT) T-Mobile USA Unit has settled in the number four position in the market and the parent company will need to decide if it will hold onto the company in the next 12-18 months from September 2010. T-Mobile's rivals will make critical improvements during this time and DT has the option to upgrade T-Mobile at the cost of improvements to its other units.

11971 ■ "BABs in Bond Land" in *Barron's* **(Vol. 89, July 6, 2009, No. 27, pp. 14)**
Pub: Dow Jones & Co., Inc.
Ed: Jim McTague. **Description:** American Recovery and Reinvestment Act has created taxable Build America Bonds (BAB) to finance new construction projects. The issuance of the two varieties of taxable BABs is expected to benefit the municipal bond market.

11972 ■ "Back in the Race" in *Barron's* **(Vol. 88, March 17, 2008, No. 11, pp. 43)**
Pub: Dow Jones & Company, Inc.
Ed: Leslie P. Norton. **Description:** Katherine Schapiro was able to get Sentinel International Equity's Morningstar classification to blended fund from a value fund rating after joining Sentinel from her former jobs at Strong Overseas Fund. Schapiro aims to benefit from the global rebalancing as the U.S.'s share of the world economy shrinks.

11973 ■ "Back Talk with Chris Gardner" in *Black Enterprise* **(Vol. 37, January 2007, No. 6, pp. 112)**
Pub: Earl G. Graves Publishing Co. Inc.
Ed: Kenneth Meeks. **Description:** Profile of with Chris Gardner and his Chicago company, Gardner Rich L.L.C., a multimillion-dollar investment firm. During an interview, Gardner discusses his rise from homelessness. His story became a book, The Pursuit of Happyness and was recently released as a film starring Will Smith.

11974 ■ "Back on Track-Or Off the Rails?" in *Business Week* **(September 22, 2008, No. 4100, pp. 22)**
Pub: McGraw-Hill Companies, Inc.
Ed: Peter Coy; Tara Kalwarski. **Description:** Discusses the possible scenarios the American economy may undergo due to the takeover of Fannie Mae and Freddie Mac. Statistical data included.

11975 ■ "Bad-Loan Bug Bites Mid-Tier Banks; More Pain, Tighter Lending Standards Ahead, CEOs Say" in *Crain's Chicago Business* **(May 5, 2008)**
Pub: Crain Communications, Inc.
Ed: Steve Daniels. **Description:** Mid-sized commercial banks form the bedrock of Chicago's financial-services industry and they are now feeling the results of the credit crisis that has engulfed the nation's largest banks and brokerages. Commercial

borrowers are seeing tighter terms on loans and higher interest rates while bank investors are unable to forecast lenders' earnings performance from quarter to quarter. Statistical data included.

11976 ■ **"Bad Loans Start Piling Up"** in *Crain's New York Business* **(Vol. 24, January 7, 2008, No. 1, pp. 2)**
Pub: Crain Communications, Inc.
Ed: Tom Fredrickson. **Description:** Problems in the subprime mortgage industry have extended to other lending activities as evidenced by bank charge-offs on bad commercial and industrial loans which have more than doubled in the third quarter.

11977 ■ **Bad Money**
Pub: Viking Press/Penguin Group
Ed: Kevin Phillips. **Released:** April 15, 2008. **Description:** How the financial sector has hijacked the American economy, aided by Washington's ruinous faith in the efficiency of markets.

11978 ■ **"Bad Paper"** in *Canadian Business* **(Vol. 80, November 19, 2007, No. 23, pp. 34)**
Pub: Rogers Media
Ed: Al Rosen. **Description:** The Canadian government froze the market for non-bank asset-backed commercial paper (ABCP) August 2007, which means holders will be unable to withdraw investments. The crisis and value of ABCP are discussed.

11979 ■ **"Bailout Forgets the 'Little Guys'"** in *The Business Journal-Milwaukee* **(Vol. 25, September 26, 2008, No. 53, pp. A1)**
Pub: American City Business Journals, Inc.
Ed: Rich Kirchen. **Description:** Community Bankers of Wisconsin and the Wisconsin Bankers Association are urging members to approach congressional representatives and remind them to include local banks in building the $700 billion bailout plan. WBA president and CEO Kurt Bauer thinks that it is only fair to include smaller institutions in the bailout. The initial bailout plan and its benefit for the smaller banks are examined.

11980 ■ **"Bailout May Force Cutbacks, Job Losses"** in *The Business Journal - Serving Phoenix and the Valley of the Sun* **(Vol. 29, September 26, 2008, No. 4, pp. 1)**
Pub: American City Business Journals, Inc.
Ed: Mike Sunnucks. **Description:** Economists say the proposed $700 billion bank bailout could affect Arizona businesses as banks could be forced to reduce the amount and number of loans it has thereby forcing businesses to shrink capital expenditures and then jobs. However, the plan could also stimulate the economy by taking bad loans off banks balance sheets according to another economist.

11981 ■ **"Baking Up Bigger Lance"** in *Charlotte Business Journal* **(Vol. 25, December 3, 2010, No. 37, pp. 1)**
Pub: Charlotte Business Journal
Ed: Ken Elkins. **Description:** Events that led to the merger between Charlotte, North Carolina-based snack food manufacturer Lance Inc. and Pennsylvania-based pretzel maker Snyder's of Hanover Inc. are discussed. The merger is expected to help Lance in posting a 70 percent increase in revenue, which reached $900 million in 2009. How the merger would affect Snyder's of Hanover is also described.

11982 ■ **"Bank Bullish on Austin"** in *Austin Business JournalInc.* **(Vol. 29, November 13, 2009, No. 36, pp. A1)**
Pub: American City Business Journals
Ed: Kate Harrington. **Description:** American Bank's presence in Austin, Texas has been boosted by new management and a new 20,000 square foot building. This community bank intends to focus on building relationship with commercial banking customers. American Bank also plans to extend investment banking, treasury management, and commercial lending services.

11983 ■ **"Bank Forces Brooke Founder To Sell His Holdings"** in *The Business Journal-Serving Metropolitan Kansas City* **(October 10, 2008)**
Pub: American City Business Journals, Inc.
Ed: James Dornbrook. **Description:** Robert Orr who is the founder of Brooke Corp., a franchise of insur-

ance agencies, says that he was forced to sell virtually all of his stocks in the company by creditors. First United Bank held the founder's stock as collateral for two loans worth $5 million and $7.9 million, which were declared in default in September 2008. Details of the selling of the company's stocks are provided.

11984 ■ **"Bank Sticks to Rate Rise Script but 'Modest' is the Salient Word"** in *Globe & Mail* **(January 25, 2006, pp. B5)**
Pub: CTVglobemedia Publishing Inc.
Ed: Heather Scoffield. **Description:** The reasons behind the decision of Bank of Canada to increase interest rate, which is posted at 3.5 percent, are presented.

11985 ■ **"Banking Bailout: Boost or Bust?"** in *Crain's Detroit Business* **(Vol. 24, September 29, 2008, No. 39, pp. 1)**
Pub: Crain Communications, Inc.
Ed: Amy Lane. **Description:** Economic insiders discuss the banking bailout and how it might impact the state of Michigan.

11986 ■ **"A Banking Play Without Banking Plagues"** in *Barron's* **(Vol. 88, March 31, 2008, No. 13, pp. 26)**
Pub: Dow Jones & Company, Inc.
Ed: Jack Willoughby. **Description:** Fiserv's shares have been dragged down by about 20 percent which presents an appealing entry point since the shares could rise by 30 percent or more by 2009. The company enables banks to post and open new checks and keeps track of loans which are not discretionary processes of banks.

11987 ■ **"The Bankrate Double Pay"** in *Barron's* **(Vol. 88, March 24, 2008, No. 12, pp. 27)**
Pub: Dow Jones & Company, Inc.
Ed: Neil A. Martin. **Description:** Shares of Bankrate may rise as much as 25 percent from their level of $45.08 a share due to a strong cash flow and balance sheet. The company's Internet business remains strong despite weakness in the online advertising industry and is a potential takeover target.

11988 ■ **"Bankruptcies Shoot Up 68 Percent"** in *Sacramento Business Journal* **(Vol. 25, July 18, 2008, No. 20, pp. 1)**
Pub: American City Business Journals, Inc.
Ed: Kathy Robertson. **Description:** Personal bankruptcy in the Sacramento area rose by 68 percent for the first half of 2008 while business bankruptcies rose by 50 percent for the same period. The numbers of consumer bankruptcy reflects the effect of high debt, rising mortgage costs, and declining home values on U.S. households.

11989 ■ **"Bankruptcy Blowback"** in *Business Week* **(September 22, 2008, No. 4100, pp. 36)**
Pub: McGraw-Hill Companies, Inc.
Ed: Jessica Silver-Greenberg. **Description:** Changes to bankruptcy laws which were enacted in 2005 after banks and other financial institutions lobbied hard for them are now suffering the consequences of the laws which force more troubled borrowers to let their homes go into foreclosure; lenders suffer financially every time they have to take on a foreclosure and the laws in which they lobbied so hard to see enacted are now becoming a problem for these lending institutions. Details of the changes in the laws are outlined as are the affects on the consumer, the economy and the lenders.

11990 ■ **"Banks Fall Short in Online Services for Savvy Traders"** in *Barron's* **(Vol. 88, March 17, 2008, No. 11, pp. 35)**
Pub: Dow Jones & Company, Inc.
Ed: Theresa W. Carey. **Description:** Banc of America Investment Services, WellsTrade, and ShareBuilder are at the bottom of the list of online brokerages because they offer less trading technologies and product range. Financial shoppers miss out on a lot of customized tools and analytics when using these services.

11991 ■ **"Banks Fret About Gist Of Bailout"** in *The Business Journal-Serving Metropolitan Kansas City* **(Vol. 27, September 26, 2008, No. 2)**
Pub: American City Business Journals, Inc.
Ed: James Dornbrook. **Description:** Banks from the Kansas City area hope that the proposed $700 billion bailout will not send the wrong message. UMB Financial Corp. chairman says that he hopes that the bailout would benefit companies that were more risk restrained and punish those that took outsized risk. Other bank executives' perceptions on the planned bailout are given.

11992 ■ **"Banks Seeing Demand for Home Equity Loans Slowing"** in *Crain's Cleveland Business* **(Vol. 28, December 3, 2007, No. 48, pp. 1)**
Pub: Crain Communications, Inc.
Ed: Shawn A. Turner. **Description:** Discusses the reasons for the decline in demand for home equity loans and lines of credit. Statistical data included.

11993 ■ **"Barbarians Set Bar Low With Lowly Canadian Telco"** in *Globe & Mail* **(March 31, 2007, pp. B1)**
Pub: CTVglobemedia Publishing Inc.
Ed: Derek DeCloet. **Description:** The efforts of the private equity fund Kohlberg, Kravis, Roberts and Co. to acquire the Canadian telecommunications firm BCE are described.

11994 ■ **"Bargain Hunting In Vietnam"** in *Barron's* **(Vol. 88, July 14, 2008, No. 28, pp. M6)**
Pub: Dow Jones & Co., Inc.
Ed: Elliot Wilson. **Description:** Vietnam's economy grew by just 6.5 percent for the first half of 2008 and its balance of payments ballooned to $14.4 billion. The falling stock prices in the country is a boon for bargain hunters and investing in the numerous domestic funds is one way of investing in the country. Some shares that investors are taking an interest in are also discussed.

11995 ■ **"Barron's Lipper Fund Listings"** in *Barron's* **(Vol. 89, July 13, 2009, No. 28, pp. 19)**
Pub: Dow Jones & Co., Inc.
Description: Statistical tables are presented which show the assets and return of mutual funds up to a ten year period. The listing covers funds with at least $200 million in assets.

11996 ■ **"BASF Launches $4.9 Billion Bid for Rival Engelhard"** in *Globe & Mail* **(January 4, 2006, pp. B7)**
Pub: CTVglobemedia Publishing Inc.
Ed: Mike Esterl; Steve Levine. **Description:** The plans of BASF AG, to acquire Engelhard Corp. for $4.9 billion, are presented.

11997 ■ **"Battered U.S. Auto Makers in Grip of Deeper Sales Slump"** in *Globe & Mail* **(April 4, 2007, pp. B1)**
Pub: CTVglobemedia Publishing Inc.
Ed: Greg Keenan. **Description:** The fall in Canadian sales and market share of Ford Motor Co., General Motors Corp. and Chrysler Group is discussed.

11998 ■ **"Battle of the Titans"** in *Canadian Business* **(Vol. 81, March 17, 2008, No. 4, pp. 15)**
Pub: Rogers Media
Ed: Rachel Pulfer. **Description:** Regulatory authorities in Canada gave Thomson Corp and Reuters Group PLC the permission to go ahead with their merger. The merged companies could eclipse Bloomberg LP's market share of 33 percent. Authorities also required Thomson and Reuters to sell some of their databases to competitors.

11999 ■ **"BCE's Aliant Trust Spinoff Valued at About $8.5 Billion"** in *Globe & Mail* **(March 8, 2006, pp. B1)**
Pub: CTVglobemedia Publishing Inc.
Ed: Catherine McLean. **Description:** The details pertaining to the spinoff of Aliant Inc.'s landline business into an income trust by BCE Inc. are presented. The trust is valued at $8.5 billion.

12000 ■ "BDC Launches New Online Business Advice Centre" in *Internet Wire* **(July 13, 2010)**
Pub: Comtex
Description: The Business Development Bank of Canada (BDC) offers entrepreneurs the chance to use their new online BDC Advice Centre in order to seek advice regarding the challenges of entrepreneurship. Free online business tools and information to help both startups and established firms are also provided.

12001 ■ "The Bear Arrives - With Bargain Hunters" in *Barron's* **(Vol. 88, July 7, 2008, No. 27, pp. M3)**
Pub: Dow Jones & Co., Inc.
Ed: Kopin Tan. **Description:** US stock markets have dropped 20 percent below their highs, entering the bear market at the end of June 2008. It was also the worst performance of the stock markets during June. Wine maker Constellation Brands, however, reported a 50 percent rise in net income for the first quarter of 2008.

12002 ■ "Bear Market Tough On Investors" in *The Business Journal-Milwaukee* **(Vol. 25, July 4, 2008, No. 41, pp. A1)**
Pub: American City Business Journals, Inc.
Ed: Rich Kirchen. **Description:** Public companies and their investors in the Milwaukee area suffered as the bear market took hold of the Wisconsin stock market. There were 18 stocks out of the 36 publicly traded stocks that have fallen into the bear market, meaning a 20 percent decline from the market peak in the fall of 2007. The impacts of the bear market on investors are evaluated.

12003 ■ "The Bear's Back" in *Barron's* **(Vol. 88, July 7, 2008, No. 27, pp. 17)**
Pub: Dow Jones & Co., Inc.
Ed: Randall W. Forsyth; Vito Racanelli. **Description:** US stock markets have formally entered the bear market after the Dow Jones Industrial Average dropped 20 percent from its high as of June 2008. Investors remain uncertain as to how long the bear market will persist, especially with the US economy on the edge of recession.

12004 ■ "The Beauty of Banking's Big Ugly" in *Barron's* **(Vol. 89, July 27, 2009, No. 30, pp. 31)**
Pub: Dow Jones & Co., Inc.
Ed: Andrew Bary. **Description:** Appeal of the shares of Citigroup comes from its sharp discount to its tangible book value and the company's positive attributes include a strong capital position, high loan-loss reserves, and their appealing global-consumer. The shares have the potential to generate nice profits and decent stock gains as the economy turns.

12005 ■ "Beer Stocks Rally on Anheuser, InBev Report" in *Globe & Mail* **(February 16, 2007, pp. B3)**
Pub: CTVglobemedia Publishing Inc.
Ed: Keith McArthur. **Description:** The stock prices of beer manufacturing industries have increased considerably after impressive profit reports from Anheuser Busch Cos Inc. and InBev SA. Complete analysis in this context is presented.

12006 ■ "Behind the Numbers: When It Comes to Earnings, Look for Quality, Not Just Quantity" in *Black Enterprise* **(July 2008, pp. 35)**
Pub: Earl G. Graves Publishing Co. Inc.
Ed: Chris Keenan. **Description:** It is important for investors to examine the quality of a company's earnings rather than fixate on the quantity of those earnings. Advice is given regarding issues investors can look at when trying to determine the potential growth of a firm.

12007 ■ "Being Big By Design" in *Canadian Business* **(Vol. 82, April 27, 2009, No. 7, pp. 39)**
Pub: Rogers Media
Ed: Andrew Wahl. **Description:** Gennum expects that its planned acquisition of Tundra Semiconductor will expand its market presence and leverage its

research and development better than working alone. The proposed friendly acquisition could challenge Zarlink Semiconductor as the largest Canadian semiconductor firm in terms of revenue. The merger could expand Gennum's addressable market to about $2 billion.

12008 ■ "Beltway Monitor" in *Mergers & Acquisitions: The Dealmaker's Journal* **(March 1, 2008)**
Pub: SourceMedia, Inc.
Description: Discusses in detail The Foreign Investment and National Security Act of 2007 which was put into legislation due to the initially approved acquisition of certain U.S. ports by Dubai Ports World which set off a firestorm of controversy.

12009 ■ "Bertha's Birth Stirs Juice" in *Barron's* **(Vol. 88, July 14, 2008, No. 28, pp. M11)**
Pub: Dow Jones & Co., Inc.
Ed: Tom Sellen. **Description:** Price of frozen concentrated orange juice, which has risen to four-month highs of $1.3620 in July 2008 is due, in part, to the hurricane season that has come earlier than normal in the far eastern Atlantic thereby possibly harming the 2008-2009 Florida orange crop. Future tropical-storm development will affect the prices of this commodity.

12010 ■ "Best Cash Flow Generators" in *Canadian Business* **(Vol. 82, Summer 2009, No. 8, pp. 40)**
Pub: Rogers Media
Ed: Calvin Leung. **Description:** Agrium Inc. and FirstService Corporation are in the list of firms that are found to have the potential to be the best cash flow generators in Canada. The list also includes WestJet Airlines Ltd., which accounts for 385 flights each day. More than 80 percent of analysts rate the airline stocks a Buy.

12011 ■ "Best Defensive Stocks" in *Canadian Business* **(Vol. 81, Summer 2008, No. 9, pp. 67)**
Pub: Rogers Media Ltd.
Ed: Calvin Leung. **Description:** Stocks of the companies presented have market capitalization of greater than $1 billion and dividend gains of at least 2 percent. A table showing the average one-year total return of the stocks is provided.

12012 ■ "The Best Five-Month Run Since 1938" in *Barron's* **(Vol. 89, August 3, 2009, No. 31, pp. M3)**
Pub: Dow Jones & Co., Inc.
Ed: Kopin Tan. **Description:** US stock markets ended July 2009 registering the highest five-month rise since 1938. The shares of Cablevision could rise as the company simplifies its structure and spins off its Madison Square Garden unit. The shares of Potash Corp. could fall as the company faces lower earnings due to falling potash purchases.

12013 ■ "Best Growth Stocks" in *Canadian Business* **(Vol. 82, Summer 2009, No. 8, pp. 28)**
Pub: Rogers Media
Ed: Calvin Leung. **Description:** Canadian stocks that are considered as the best growth stocks, and whose price-earnings ratio is less than their earnings growth rate, are suggested. Suggestions include pharmaceutical firm Paladin Labs, which was found to have 13 consecutive years of revenue growth. Paladin Labs acquires or licenses niche drugs and markets them in Canada.

12014 ■ "Best Income Trust" in *Canadian Business* **(Vol. 81, Summer 2008, No. 9, pp. 69)**
Pub: Rogers Media Ltd.
Ed: Calvin Leung. **Description:** Table showing five-year annualized growth rate and one-year stock performance of real estate investment trusts firms in Canada is presented. Calgary-based Boardwalk REIT is projected to grow the fastest among North American REITs over the next two years. Other details on the stock performance analysis are presented.

12015 ■ "Best Income Trusts" in *Canadian Business* **(Vol. 82, Summer 2009, No. 8, pp. 36)**
Pub: Rogers Media
Ed: Calvin Leung. **Description:** Boardwalk REIT and Can. Apartment Properties REIT are among the income trusts in Canada that are found to have the potential as a good investment. Suggested income trusts also include the Yellow Pages Income Fund, which recently reported a 19.4 percent yield. The income trusts however, are expected to be affected by the Conservatives' tax that will take effect in 2011.

12016 ■ "Best Managed Companies (Canada)" in *Canadian Business* **(Vol. 82, Summer 2009, No. 8, pp. 38)**
Pub: Rogers Media
Ed: Calvin Leung. **Description:** Agrium Inc. and Barrick Gold Corporation are among those that are found to be the best managed companies in Canada. Best managed companies also include software firm Open Text Corporation, which has grown annual sales by 75 percent and annual profits by 160 percent since 1995. Open Text markets software that allow firms to manage word-based data, and has 46,000 customers in 114 countries.

12017 ■ "Best Managed Companies" in *Canadian Business* **(Vol. 81, Summer 2008, No. 9, pp. 71)**
Pub: Rogers Media Ltd.
Ed: Calvin Leung. **Description:** Table showing the five-year annualized growth rate and one-year stock performance of companies that have grown their cash flow per share at an annualized rate of 15 percent or more over the past five years. Analysts project that the cash flow trend will continue. Other details of the stock performance index are presented.

12018 ■ "Best Turnaround Stocks" in *Canadian Business* **(Vol. 81, Summer 2008, No. 9, pp. 65)**
Pub: Rogers Media Ltd.
Ed: Calvin Leung. **Description:** Share prices of Sierra Wireless Inc. and EXFO Electro Optical Engineering Inc. have fallen over the past year but have good chance at a rebound considering that the companies have free cash flow and no long-term debt. One-year stock performance analysis of the two companies is presented.

12019 ■ "Best Value Stocks" in *Canadian Business* **(Vol. 82, Summer 2009, No. 8, pp. 30)**
Pub: Rogers Media
Ed: Calvin Leung. **Description:** Canadian companies that are believed to have the best value stocks are suggested. Suggestions include publishing firm Glacier Media, which has reported a four-fold growth in sales in the last three years. While publishers like Glacier Media face challenges such as declining circulation, the firm's industry diversification is expected to help it weather the economic downturn.

12020 ■ "Bet on China" in *Canadian Business* **(Vol. 80, November 5, 2007, No. 22, pp. 30)**
Pub: Rogers Media
Ed: Thomas Watson. **Description:** Former U.S. Federal Reserve Board head, Alan Greenspan, warns that contraction will happen in the Chinese market. However, the economic success of China does not seem to be at the point of ending, as the country remains the largest market for mobile telecommunications. Forecasts for Chinese trading and investments are provided.

12021 ■ "Bet on the Subcontinent" in *Canadian Business* **(Vol. 81, April 14, 2008, No. 6, pp. 27)**
Pub: Rogers Media
Ed: Calvin Leung. **Description:** Morgan Stanley Capital International India Index is down 28 percent for the first half of 2008 but this index rebounded 6 percent in 2002 then skyrocketed 65 percent in 2003. The economic reforms in the 1990's have created a growing middle class and households that can afford

discretionary items will grow from eight million to 94 million by 2025. India's equity market could outperform developed markets if its economy grows at its current rate.

12022 ■ "Betting Big, Winning Big" in *Barron's* **(Vol. 88, March 17, 2008, No. 11, pp. 49)**
Pub: Dow Jones & Company, Inc.

Ed: Lawrence C. Strauss. **Description:** Bruce Berkowitz explains that the reason that his portfolio is concentrated is because getting more positions makes the portfolio more average compared to putting the money into your 10th or 20th-best idea. Berkowitz' picks include Berkshire Hathaway, WellCare Health Plus, Sears Holdings, and Mohawk Industries.

12023 ■ "Betting on a Happy Ending" in *Barron's* **(Vol. 88, July 7, 2008, No. 27, pp. 14)**
Pub: Dow Jones & Co., Inc.

Ed: Dimitra DeFotis. **Description:** Shares of Time Warner, priced at $14.69 each, appear under-priced as financial analysts discount the value of the company. The company should be worth more than $20 a share as the company is spinning off Time Warner Cable.

12024 ■ "Betting On Volatile Materials" in *Barron's* **(Vol. 88, July 14, 2008, No. 28, pp. M11)**
Pub: Dow Jones & Co., Inc.

Ed: John Marshall. **Description:** Economic slowdowns in the U.S., Europe and China could cause sharp short-term declines in the materials sector. The S&P Materials sector is vulnerable to shifts in the flow of funds. Statistical data included.

12025 ■ "Beware this Chinese Export" in *Barron's* **(Vol. 90, August 30, 2010, No. 35, pp. 21)**
Pub: Barron's Editorial & Corporate Headquarters

Ed: Bill Alpert, Leslie P. Norton. **Description:** A look at 158 China reverse-merger stocks in the U.S. reveal that the median underperformed the index of U.S. listed Chinese companies by 75 percent in their first three years. These reverse merger stocks also lagged the Russell 2000 index of small cap stocks by 66 percent.

12026 ■ "Beware the Ides of March" in *Canadian Business* **(Vol. 81, April 14, 2008, No. 6, pp. 13)**
Pub: Rogers Media

Ed: Jeff Sanford. **Description:** Financial troubles of Bear Stearns in March, 2008 was part of the credit crunch that started in the summer of 2007 in the U.S. when subprime mortgages that were written for people who could barely afford the payments started defaulting. The bankruptcy protection given to 20 asset backed commercial paper trusts is being fought by the investors in these securities who could stand to lose 40 percent of their money under the agreement.

12027 ■ "Beware of Rotting Money" in *Barron's* **(Vol. 89, July 13, 2009, No. 28, pp. 31)**
Pub: Dow Jones & Co., Inc.

Ed: Thomas G. Donlan. **Description:** Inflation can take hold of a country and do it great harm; it is caused by people, most particularly central bankers in charge of the world's reserve currency. Arrogant economists pushed the belief that the government can engineer the economy and it is argued that there is trouble ahead when the government tries to control the economy.

12028 ■ "Beyond Microsoft and Yahoo!: Some M&A Prospects" in *Barron's* **(Vol. 88, March 17, 2008, No. 11, pp. 39)**
Pub: Dow Jones & Company, Inc.

Ed: Eric J. Savitz. **Description:** Weak quarterly earnings report for Yahoo! could pressure the company's board to cut a deal with Microsoft. Electronic Arts is expected to win its hostile $26-a-share bid for Take-Two Interactive Software. Potential targets and buyers for mergers and acquisitions are mentioned.

12029 ■ "The Big 50" in *Canadian Business* **(Vol. 81, Summer 2008, No. 9, pp. 125)**
Pub: Rogers Media Ltd.

Description: Large publicly held corporations are ranked based on market capitalization and stock performance. Potash Corp. of Saskatchewan topped the roster with 169.3 percent of return and even surpassing its 2007 result of 107 percent. A table showing the 2008 rankings of the companies is presented.

12030 ■ "Big Gains Brewing at Anheuser-Busch InBev" in *Barron's* **(Vol. 90, August 30, 2010, No. 35, pp. 34)**
Pub: Barron's Editorial & Corporate Headquarters

Ed: Christopher C. Williams. **Description:** Anheuser-Busch InBev is realizing cost synergies and it posted better than expected returns two years after the merger that formed the company. One analyst believes its American depositary receipt could be worth as much as 72 in a year.

12031 ■ "Big Losses Mount for Hospitals" in *Baltimore Business Journal* **(Vol. 27, October 23, 2009, No. 24, pp. 1)**
Pub: American City Business Journals

Ed: Scott Graham. **Description:** Reported losses by nine of the 22 hospitals in the Greater Baltimore area during fiscal 2009 have proven that the health care industry is not immune to the recession. The rising costs of doing business and losses in the stock market have strongly affected the financial status of hospitals.

12032 ■ *The Big Rich: The Rise and Fall of the Greatest Texas Oil Fortunes*
Pub: Penguin Group USA Inc.

Ed: Bryan Burrough. **Released:** 2009. **Price:** $29.95. **Description:** The story of the great 20th Century oilmen offers lessons on the value of confidence, grit and guile.

12033 ■ "Big Sell-Off At Sunwest" in *The Business Journal-Portland* **(Vol. 25, July 25, 2008, No. 20, pp. 1)**
Pub: American City Business Journals, Inc.

Ed: Robin J. Moody. **Description:** Oregon's largest operator of assisted living facilities Sunwest Management Inc. is expected to sell 132 of its properties. The planned sale, which is believed to be worth more than $1 billion, will help Sunwest pay creditors and investors. Other views and information on the planned sale, as well as on Sunwest's services which include adult day care, are presented.

12034 ■ "Big Trouble at Sony Ericsson" in *Barron's* **(Vol. 88, March 24, 2008, No. 12, pp. M9)**
Pub: Dow Jones & Company, Inc.

Ed: Angelo Franchini. **Description:** Sony Ericsson is facing trouble as it warned that its sales and net income before taxes will fall by nearly half for the first quarter of 2008. The joint venture of Sony and Ericsson has a global mobile phone market share of nine percent as of 2007, fourth largest in the world.

12035 ■ "Biotechs Are Using Back Door to Go Public" in *Boston Business Journal* **(Vol. 31, May 27, 2011, No. 18, pp. 1)**
Pub: Boston Business Journal

Ed: Julie M. Donnelly. **Description:** Members of Massachusetts' biotechnology sector have been engaging in reverse mergers as an alternative to initial public offerings. Reverse mergers provide access to institutional investors and hedge funds.

12036 ■ "Biovail Hits SAC With $4.6 Billion Suit" in *Globe & Mail* **(February 23, 2006, pp. B1)**
Pub: CTVglobemedia Publishing Inc.

Ed: Shawn McCarthy. **Description:** The details of Biovail Corp.'s securities fraud case against SAC Management LLC are presented.

12037 ■ "Black Diamond Holdings Corp. Receives SEC Approval" in *Canadian Corporate News* **(May 16, 2007)**
Pub: Comtex News Network Inc.

Description: Black Diamond Holdings, Corp., a British Columbia domiciled company and its two wholly owned subsidiaries are engaged in the bottling,

importation, distribution, marketing, and brand creation of premium spirits and wines to worldwide consumers, announced that it has completed the SEC review process and has applied to list for trading in the United States on the OTC.BB.

12038 ■ "Blackstone Set to Sell Stake" in *Globe & Mail* **(March 17, 2007, pp. B6)**
Pub: CTVglobemedia Publishing Inc.

Ed: Tennille Tracy. **Description:** The plan of Blackstone Group to sell 10 percent of its stake to raise $4 billion and its proposal to go for initial public offering is discussed.

12039 ■ "Blackstone's Outlook Still Tough" in *Barron's* **(Vol. 88, March 17, 2008, No. 11, pp. 19)**
Pub: Dow Jones & Company, Inc.

Ed: Andrew Bary. **Description:** Earnings for the Blackstone Group may not recover soon since the company's specialty in big leveraged buyouts is floundering and may not recover until 2009. The company earns lucrative incentive fees on its funds but those fees went negative in the fourth quarter of 2007 and there could be more fee reversals in the future.

12040 ■ "A Bleak Earnings View" in *Barron's* **(Vol. 88, March 10, 2008, No. 10, pp. 15)**
Pub: Dow Jones & Company, Inc.

Description: Analysts expect consumer discretionary profits in the S&P 500 to drop 8.4 percent in the first quarter of 2008. A less confident consumer is expected to pull profits down, putting forecasts of earnings growth in the S&P 500 at risk. Statistical data included.

12041 ■ "Bloody Monday for Bear?" in *Barron's* **(Vol. 88, March 17, 2008, No. 11, pp. M14)**
Pub: Dow Jones & Company, Inc.

Ed: Steven M. Sears. **Description:** Shares of Bear Stearns could slip further at the start of the trading week unless the company is bought out or bolstered by some other development over the weekend. Prices of the company's shares in the options market suggests about a 30 percent chance that the stock falls below $20 before March expirations expire.

12042 ■ "Blue-Collar Broker" in *Boston Business Journal* **(Vol. 31, July 15, 2011, No. 25, pp. 1)**
Pub: Boston Business Journal

Ed: Tim McLaughlin. **Description:** Richard F. Connolly Jr. was ranked 91st in Barron's latest annual ranking of top financial advisers and his team at Morgan Stanley Smith Barney oversee an estimated $3.7 billion in assets. However, anyone who knew him knows that he's just a blue-collar broker from Woburn who loves golf.

12043 ■ "BMW Makes Bet on Carbon Maker" in *Wall Street Journal Eastern Edition* **(November 19 , 2011, pp. B3)**
Pub: Dow Jones & Company Inc.

Ed: Christoph Rauwald. **Description:** Eight months ago, Volkswagen AG acquired a 10 percent holding in carbon-fiber maker SGL Carbon SE. Its rival BMW AG is catching up by acquiring 15.2 percent stake in SGL as it seeks alliances like the rest of the industry in order to share industrial costs of new product development.

12044 ■ "BMW Revs Up for a Rebound" in *Barron's* **(Vol. 89, July 13, 2009, No. 28, pp. M7)**
Pub: Dow Jones & Co., Inc.

Ed: Jonathan Buck. **Description:** Investors may like BMW's stocks because the company has maintained its balance sheet strength and has an impressive production line of new models that should boost sales in the next few years. The company's sales are also gaining traction, although their vehicle delivery was down 1.7 percent year on year on June 2009, this was still the best monthly sales figure for 2009.

12045 ■ "Boar Market: Penny-Wise Consumers Favoring Pork" in *Crain's Chicago Business* **(Vol. 31, April 14, 2008, No. 15, pp. 4)**
Pub: Crain Communications, Inc.

Ed: Bruce Blythe. **Description:** Interview with Alan Cole who is the president of Cedar Hill Associates

Inc. and who discusses ways in which his company is taking advantage of the record highs of oil and natural gas as well as his overall outlook on the market.

12046 ■ "Board This Powertrain" in *Barron's* **(Vol. 89, July 27, 2009, No. 30, pp. 30)**
Pub: Dow Jones & Co., Inc.

Ed: Naureen S. Malik. Description: Siemens' American Depositary Receipts have risen 60 percent from their March 2009 low and they should continue heading higher. The company has solid earnings and revenue growth since they lead in growing markets such as alternative energy and health-care infrastructure. Their shares also look cheap at 1.9 times book value.

12047 ■ "Boeing Earns Its Wings With Strong Quarter" in *Crain's Chicago Business* **(Vol. 31, April 28, 2008, No. 17, pp. 4)**
Pub: Crain Communications, Inc.

Ed: Daniel Rome Levine. Description: Interview with Michael A. Crowe, the senior managing director at Mesirow Financial Investment Management, who discusses highlights from the earnings season so far, his outlook for the economy and the stock market as well as what his company is purchasing. Mr. Crowe also recommends shares of five companies.

12048 ■ "BofA May Part With U.S. Trust" in *Boston Business Journal* **(Vol. 31, May 20, 2011, No. 17, pp. 1)**
Pub: Boston Business Journal

Ed: Tim McLaughlin. Description: Bank of America Corporation is willing to sell its U.S. Trust private banking division to improve its capital ratio. The unit remains to be the corporation's core asset and posted $696 million revenue in the first quarter 2010 in contract with Merrill Lynch Global Wealth Management's $3.5 billion. Analysts say that U.S. Trust would fetch more than $3 billion.

12049 ■ "BofA Will Reach the Top with Countrywide Deal" in *Business North Carolina* **(Vol. 28, March 2008, No. 3, pp. 36)**
Pub: Business North Carolina

Description: Bank of America, headquartered in Charlotte, North Carolina, will add Countrywide to its let of credits. Countrywide is the largest U.S. mortgage lender. Statistical data included.

12050 ■ *Bonds - the Other Market*
Pub: AuthorHouse

Ed: George L. Fulton. Released: March 16, 2005. Price: $15.50. Description: Professional bond broker provides fundamental information to help investors choose the bond market an alternative to the stock market. The book describes the various types of bonds available, including treasury bonds, issued by the U.S. Government; municipal bonds, issued by a municipal authority of a local or state government; and corporate bonds, issued by corporations. Risk vs. reward in bond investing is also covered.

12051 ■ "Bonds v. Stocks: Who's Right About Recession?" in *Barron's* **(Vol. 90, August 23, 2010, No. 34, pp. M3)**
Pub: Barron's Editorial & Corporate Headquarters

Ed: Kopin Tan. Description: The future of treasury securities and stocks should the U.S. enter or avoid a recession are discussed. The back to school business climate and BHP Billiton's bid for Potash Corporation of Saskatchewan are also discussed.

12052 ■ "Book of Lists 2010" in *Philadelphia Business Journal* **(Vol. 28, December 25, 2009, No. 45, pp. 1)**
Pub: American City Business Journals

Description: Rankings of companies and organizations within the banking, biotechnology, economic development, healthcare, hospitality, law and accounting, marketing and media, real estate, and technology industries in the Philadelphia, Pennsylvania area are presented. Rankings are based on sales, business size, and more.

12053 ■ "The Book On Indigo" in *Canadian Business* **(Vol. 81, July 22, 2008, No. 12-13, pp. 29)**
Pub: Rogers Media Ltd.

Ed: Thomas Watson. Description: Indigo Books & Music Inc. reported record sales of $922 million resulting in a record net profit of $52.8 million for the 2008 fiscal year ended March 29, 2008. Earnings per share were $2.13, greater than Standard & Poor's expected $1.70 per share. Additional information concerning Indigo Books is presented.

12054 ■ "Boring Bonds Gain Pizzazz as Investors Flock to Debt Issues" in *Baltimore Business Journal* **(Vol. 28, June 11, 2010, No. 5, pp. 1)**
Pub: Baltimore Business Journal

Ed: Gary Haber. Description: Companies and nonprofit organizations have increased the pace of bond offerings in order to take advantage of the bonds' appeal among willing investors. Companies mostly issued corporate bonds to replace existing debt at lower interest rates and save them money from interest payments.

12055 ■ "Boston Hedge Fund Pours Money Into Real Estate Projects" in *Charlotte Business Journal* **(Vol. 25, December 3, 2010, No. 37, pp. 1)**
Pub: Charlotte Business Journal

Ed: Will Boye. Description: Boston-based hedge fund Baupost Group has been financing real estate project in Charlotte, North Carolina including more than 80 acres just north of uptown. Aside from purchasing the $23.8 million note for the Rosewood Condominiums from Regions Financial Corporation, the Baupost Group is also negotiating with Regions to buy the $93.9 million debt of the EipCentre real estate project.

12056 ■ "Bottler Will Regain Its Pop" in *Barron's* **(Vol. 88, March 17, 2008, No. 11, pp. 56)**
Pub: Dow Jones & Company, Inc.

Ed: Alexander Eule. Description: Discusses he 30 percent drop in the share price of PepsiAmericas Inc. from their 2007 high which presents an opportunity to buy into the company's dependable U.S. market and fast growing Eastern European business. The bottler's Eastern European operating profits in 2007 grew to $101 million from $21 million in 2006.

12057 ■ "Bottom-Fishing and Speed-Dating in India" in *Barron's* **(Vol. 88, March 24, 2008, No. 12, pp. M12)**
Pub: Dow Jones & Company, Inc.

Ed: Elliot Wilson. Description: Indian stocks have fallen hard in 2008, with Mumbai's Sensex 30 down 30 percent from its January 2008 peak of 21,000 to 14,995 in March. The India Private Equity Fair 2008 attracted 140 of the world's largest private equity firms and about 24 of India's fastest-growing corporations. Statistical data included.

12058 ■ "Bountiful Barrels: Where to Find $140 Trillion" in *Barron's* **(Vol. 88, July 14, 2008, No. 28, pp. 40)**
Pub: Dow Jones & Co., Inc.

Ed: Andrew Bary. Description: Surge in oil prices has caused a large transfer of wealth to oil-producing countries thereby reshaping the global economy. Oil reserves of oil exporting countries are now valued at $140 trillion. Economist Stephen Jen believes that this wealth will be transformed into paper assets as these countries invest in global stocks and bonds.

12059 ■ "Bracing for a Bear of a Week" in *Barron's* **(Vol. 88, March 17, 2008, No. 11, pp. 24)**
Pub: Dow Jones & Company, Inc.

Ed: Jacqueline Doherty. Description: JPMorgan Chase and the Federal Reserve Bank of New York's opening of a line of credit to Bear Stearns cut the stock price of Bear Stearns by 47 percent to 30 followed by speculation of an imminent sale. JP Morgan may be the only potential buyer for the firm and some investors say Bears could be sold at $20 to $30. Bears prime assets include its enormous asset base worth $395 billion.

12060 ■ "Brazil's New King of Food" in *Barron's* **(Vol. 89, July 13, 2009, No. 28, pp. 28)**
Pub: Dow Jones & Co., Inc.

Ed: Kenneth Rapoza. Description: Perdigao and Sadia's merger has resulted in the creation of Brasil Foods and the shares of Brasil Foods provides a play on both Brazil's newly energized consumer economy and its role as a major commodities exporter. Brasil Foods shares could climb as much as 36 percent.

12061 ■ "Brief: US-Business/eBay Earnings Rise 31 Per Cent" in *Denver Post* **(July 21, 2011)**
Pub: Denver Post

Ed: Andy Goldberg. Description: eBay's strong performance in second quarter 2011 is being attributed to Paypal online payments division. eBay's online auction sites reported gross merchandise volume up 34 percent. Statistical data included.

12062 ■ "Briefly" in *Crain's Detroit Business* **(Vol. 25, June 15, 2009, No. 24, pp. 18)**
Pub: Crain Communications Inc. - Detroit

Ed: Tom Henderson, Jay Greene. Description: Details of the merger between PI= anning Alternatives Ltd. and Oakland Wealth Management are highlighted. The two investment advisory firms will have a combined staff of 12 and will maintain two offices.

12063 ■ "Bristol-Myers Close to Settling Lawsuit" in *Globe & Mail* **(January 23, 2006, pp. B6)**
Pub: CTVglobemedia Publishing Inc.

Ed: Barbara Martinez. Description: The details of shareholder case against Bristol-Myers Squibb Co. are presented. The dispute is over the company's claim on the efficiency of Vanlev drug.

12064 ■ "Brooke Agents Claim Mistreatment" in *The Business Journal-Serving Metropolitan Kansas City* **(Vol. 27, October 24, 2008, No. 7, pp. 1)**
Pub: American City Business Journals, Inc.

Ed: James Dornbrook. Description: Franchisees of Brooke Corp., an insurance franchise, face uncertainty as their bills remain unpaid and banks threaten to destroy their credit. The company bundled and sold franchisee loans to different banks, but the credit crunch left the company with massive debts and legal disputes.

12065 ■ "Builders, Unions Aim to Cut Costs; Pushing Changes to Regain Share of Residential Market; Seek Council's Help" in *Crain's New York Business*
Pub: Crain Communications, Inc.

Ed: Erik Engquist. Description: Union contractors and workers are worried about a decline in their market share for housing so they intend to ask the City Council to impose new safety and benefit standards on all contractors to avoid being undercut by nonunion competitors.

12066 ■ "Building Confidence" in *Black Enterprise* **(Vol. 38, January 2008, No. 6, pp. 50)**
Pub: Earl G. Graves Publishing Co. Inc.

Ed: Marcia A. Reed-Woodard. Description: Patriot Management in Chicago offers courses at its Investment Management Training Academy for the institutional asset management and investment sector. Classes are designed to help build investor confidence amid the scandals that hit the financial, investment and asset management industry.

12067 ■ "Building Portfolios for a World of 2.5 Percent Gains" in *Barron's* **(Vol. 88, July 7, 2008, No. 27, pp. L9)**
Pub: Dow Jones & Co., Inc.

Ed: Karen Hube. Description: Interview with Harold Evenski whom is a financial planner running a fee-only planning practice; he continues to caution investors against pursuing short-term gains and focusing on long-term trends. He advises investors against investing in commodity and real estate stocks and is concerned about the possible effects of high inflation.

12068 ■ "Burned Investors Fire Back" in *Canadian Business* **(Vol. 80, April 23, 2007, No. 9, pp. 12)**

Pub: Rogers Media

Ed: Geoff Kirbyson; Dan Lett. **Description:** The details of the oppression remedy suit filed by investors on Maple Leaf Distillers Inc. and Protos International are presented.

12069 ■ "Business Still Expected To Take Hit In 2008" in *Business Journal-Serving Phoenix and the Valley of the Sun* **(December 28, 2007)**

Pub: American City Business Journals, Inc.

Ed: Chris Casacchia. **Description:** Community banks are expected to suffer through 2008 due to the subprime mortgage and credit crisis. Meanwhile, the asset devaluation of big banks and global investment companies are higher than that of smaller banks. Third and fourth quarter losses of banks, including Bear Sterns, are discussed.

12070 ■ "Business Through Hollywood's Lens" in *Harvard Business Review* **(Vol. 88, October 2010, No. 10, pp. 146)**

Pub: Harvard Business School Publishing

Ed: Batia Wiesnefeld, Gino Cattani. **Description:** The authors contend that businesses are likely to be portrayed as villains in movies because corruption has higher entertainment draw. However, movies also depict popular opinion, which encourages businesses to be accountable and to help build communities.

12071 ■ "C.A. Bancorp Inc. (TSX:BKP) Announces First Quarter 2007 Financial Results" in *Canadian Corporate News* **(May 16, 2007)**

Pub: Comtex News Network Inc.

Ed: Description: Financial report for the first quarter of 2007 for C.A. Bancorp Inc., a publicly traded Canadian merchant bank and asset manager providing investors access to a range of private equity and alternative asset class investment opportunities. Statistical data and highlights included.

12072 ■ "Calming Customers" in *The Business Journal-Portland* **(Vol. 25, August 29, 2008, No. 25, pp. 1)**

Pub: American City Business Journals, Inc.

Ed: Kirsten Grind; Rob Smith. **Description:** Credit unions and banks in the Portland area are reaching out to clients in an effort to reassure them on the security of their money and the firms' financial stability. Roy Whitehead of Washington Federal Savings, for instance, wrote 41,000 customers of the bank to reassure them. The strategies of different banks and credit unions to answer their client's worries are discussed

12073 ■ "Cambodia Calls" in *Barron's* **(Vol. 89, July 27, 2009, No. 30, pp. M7)**

Pub: Dow Jones & Co., Inc.

Ed: Leslie P. Norton. **Description:** Interest in frontier markets could jump if enthusiasm about growth in the developed world gathers steam. Cambodia is the latest market to get attention where a handful of investors are trying to set up funds. One investor believes that Cambodia is back open for business but others are still cautious about investing in the country.

12074 ■ *Canada Business and Investment Opportunities Yearbook*

Pub: USA International Business Publications

Released: March 20, 2009. **Price:** $149.95. **Description:** Yearbook contains basic information on export-import, investment and business opportunities in Canada.

12075 ■ *Canada Investment and Business Guide*

Pub: USA International Business Publications

Released: March 20, 2009. **Price:** $149.95. **Description:** Guide for conducting investment, export-import activity in Canada; includes strategic and business information, contacts regulations and more.

12076 ■ "Canadian Banks Too Timid in China, Beijing Tells Flaherty" in *Globe & Mail* **(January 22, 2007, pp. B1)**

Pub: CTVglobemedia Publishing Inc.

Ed: Steven Chase. **Description:** The article discusses Canadian banks' investments on China according to the views of federal Finance Minister Jim Flaherty.

12077 ■ *Canadian Multinationals and International Finance*

Pub: International Specialized Book Services, Inc.

Ed: Greg Marchildon. **Released:** October 1, 1992. **Price:** $190.00. **Description:** Seven stories that explore the role of Canadian multinational enterprise in world finance, trade and direct investment.

12078 ■ "Canadian Satellite Investors Scoop Up Stratos" in *Globe & Mail* **(March 20, 2007, pp. B4)**

Pub: CTVglobemedia Publishing Inc.

Ed: Simon Avery. **Description:** The proposed acquisition of Stratos Global Corp. by CIP Canada Investment Inc. for $229 million is discussed.

12079 ■ "The Canadians Are Coming!" in *Canadian Business* **(Vol. 80, October 22, 2007, No. 21, pp. 15)**

Pub: Rogers Media

Ed: Rachel Pulfer. **Description:** Toronto-Dominion Bank declared its acquisition of the New Jersey-based Commerce Bancorp for C$8.5 billion. Royal Bank of Canada has scooped up Trinidad-based Financial Group for C$2.2 billion. Details of the foreign acquisitions, as well as the impact of high Canadian dollars on the mergers are discussed.

12080 ■ "Candidates Won't Bash Fed; Rate Cuts Bash Savers" in *Barron's* **(Vol. 88, March 24, 2008, No. 12, pp. 31)**

Pub: Dow Jones & Company, Inc.

Ed: Jim McTague. **Description:** Candidates in the 2008 US presidential election, like the current administration, do not and will not bash the Federal Reserve. The Federal Reserve's aggressive interest rate cuts hurt the incomes of people depending on their savings accounts.

12081 ■ "Capital Position" in *Business Journal-Milwaukee* **(Vol. 28, December 24, 2010, No. 12, pp. A1)**

Pub: Milwaukee Business Journal

Ed: Rich Kirchen. **Description:** Canada-based BMO Financial Group has purchased Marshall and Isley Corporation (M and I), which dominated lending among Wisconsin businesses for decades. The sale of M and I will enable other banks to recruit M and I's customers but BMO Financial remains a stronger competitor since it possesses a more potent capital position.

12082 ■ "Capturing Generation Y: Ready, Set, Transform" in *Credit Union Times* **(Vol. 21, July 14, 2010, No. 27, pp. 20)**

Pub: Summit Business Media

Ed: Senthil Kumar. **Description:** The financial services sector recognizes that Generation Y will have a definite impact on the way business is conducted in the future. The mindset of Generation Y is social and companies need to use networking tools such as Facebook in order to reach this demographic.

12083 ■ "The Case of the Deflated IPO" in *Boston Business Journal* **(Vol. 29, June 24, 2011, No. 7, pp. 1)**

Pub: American City Business Journals Inc.

Ed: Scott Dance. **Description:** IPO market is on the rebound from the recession but for some companies in Maryland, the time is not yet ripe to go public. One of the companies that chooses to wait for better timing is SafeNet Inc. and it is eyeing some possible acquisitions while doing so.

12084 ■ "Cash Flow Myths" in *Canadian Business* **(Vol. 80, March 12, 2007, No. 6, pp. 25)**

Pub: Rogers Media

Ed: Al Rosen. **Description:** Expert advice to Canadian investors about understanding the cash flow statements of companies before investing money is presented.

12085 ■ "Catch the Wind to Hold Investor Update Conference Call on October 18, 2011" in *CNW Group* **(October 4, 2011)**

Pub: CNW Group

Description: Catch the Wind Ltd., providers of laser-based wind sensor products and technology, held a conference call for analysts and institutional investors. The high-growth technology firm is headquartered in Manassas, Virginia.

12086 ■ "Cemex Paves a Global Road to Solid Growth" in *Barron's* **(Vol. 88, March 10, 2008, No. 10, pp. 24)**

Pub: Dow Jones & Company, Inc.

Ed: Sandra Ward. **Description:** Shares of Cemex are expected to perform well with the company's expected strong performance despite fears of a US recession. The company has a diverse geographical reach and benefits from a strong worldwide demand for cement.

12087 ■ "Centrue Sets Down New Roots in St. Louis; Bank Looks to Expand in Exurbs of Chicago" in *Crain's Chicago Business* **(May 5, 2008)**

Pub: Crain Communications, Inc.

Ed: H. Lee Murphy. **Description:** Centrue Financial Corp. has moved its headquarters from Ottawa to suburban St. Louis in search of higher-growth markets. The banks acquisitions and expansion plans are also discussed.

12088 ■ "CEO Pay: The Details" in *Crain's Detroit Business* **(Vol. 25, June 22, 2009, No. 25, pp.)**

Pub: Crain Communications Inc. - Detroit

Description: Total compensation packages for CEOs at area companies our outlined. These packages include salary, bonuses, stock awards, and options.

12089 ■ "CEOs Gone Wild" in *Canadian Business* **(Vol. 79, August 14, 2006, No. 16-17, pp. 15)**

Pub: Rogers Media

Ed: Thomas Watson. **Description:** Stock investment decisions of chief executive officers of metal companies in Canada, are discussed.

12090 ■ "Certified Financial Planner Board of Standards Reacts to Jobs Program" in *Professional Services Close-Up* **(September 14, 2011)**

Pub: Close-Up Media Inc.

Description: Certified Financial Planner Board of Standards Consumer Advocate, Eleanor Blayney, believe that people should be looking inward at their own ability to change their employment future. She shares tips for the job market to help out.

12091 ■ "CGB Purchases Illinois Grain-Fertilizer Firm" in *Farm Industry News* **(December 2, 2011)**

Pub: Penton Business Media Inc.

Description: CGB Enterprises Inc. bought Twomey Company's grain and fertilizer assets. The purchase includes eight locations and a barge loading terminal near Gladstone, Illinois and storage capacity of 51 million bushels and 18,000 tons of liquid fertilizer.

12092 ■ *Chain of Blame: How Wall Street Caused the Mortgage and Credit Crisis*

Pub: John Wiley & Sons, Inc.

Ed: Paul Muolo, Mathew Padilla. **Released:** 2009. **Price:** $27.95. **Description:** The book describes how risky loans given irresponsibly put big investment banks at the center of the subprime crisis.

12093 ■ "Challenges Await Quad in Going Public" in *Milwaukee Business Journal* **(Vol. 27, January 29, 2010, No. 18, pp. A1)**

Pub: American City Business Journals

Ed: Rich Rovito. **Description:** Sussex, Wisconsin-based Quad/Graphics Inc.'s impending acquisition of rival Canadian World Color Press Inc. will transform it into a publicly held entity for the first time. Quad has operated as a private company for nearly 40 years and will need to adjust to changes, such as the way management shares information with Quad/Graphics' employees. Details of the merger are included.

12094 ■ **"Change of Plans"** in *Entrepreneur* (Vol. 35, November 2007, No. 11, pp. 74)
Pub: Entrepreneur Media Inc.
Ed: C.J. Prince. **Description:** Companies should provide 401K plans that meet employee needs and demographics, with new technology allowing providers to lower their own costs. Details on finding a plans that appeal to employees are examined.

12095 ■ *The Changing Geography of Banking and Finance*
Pub: Springer Publishing Company
Ed: Pietro Alessandrini, Michele Fratianni, Alberto Zazzaro. **Released:** May 1, 2009. **Price:** $139.00. **Description:** The two contrasting trends that have emerged from the integration and consolidation processes of the banking industry in both Europe and the United States in the 1990s is examined.

12096 ■ **"Chemed's Vitas Aims to Acquire"** in *Business Courier* (Vol. 27, July 9, 2010, No. 10, pp. 1)
Pub: Business Courier
Ed: James Ritchie. **Description:** Chemed Corporation's Vitas Healthcare Corporation is looking for smaller nonprofit hospices as it looks to become more streamlined in a tougher reimbursement environment. CFO David Williams syas they want to acquire these hospices as fast as they can integrate them.

12097 ■ **"Chuck's Big Chance"** in *Barron's* (Vol. 89, July 13, 2009, No. 28, pp. L3)
Pub: Dow Jones & Co., Inc.
Ed: Leslie P. Norton. **Description:** Charles Schwab is cutting prices and rolling out new products to lure customers and the company is well positioned to benefit from Wall Street's misery. Their shares are trading at just 17 times earnings, which should be at least at a multiple of 20.

12098 ■ **"CIBC Spends $1.1 Billion on Caribbean Expansion"** in *Globe & Mail* (March 14, 2006, pp. B1)
Pub: CTVglobemedia Publishing Inc.
Ed: Sinclair Stewart. **Description:** Canadian Imperial Bank of Commerce (CIBC), the fifth-largest bank of Canada, is planning to spend $1.1billion to buy major share of Barbados-based First Caribbean International Bank. The details of the acquisition plan are presented.

12099 ■ **"Citadel Hires Three Lehman Execs"** in *Chicago Tribune* (October 2, 2008)
Pub: McClatchy-Tribune Information Services
Ed: James P. Miller. **Description:** Citadel Investment Group LLC, Chicago hedge-fund operator, has hired three former senior executives of bankrupt investment banker Lehman Brothers Holding Inc. Citadel believes that the company's hiring spree will help them to further expand the firm's capabilities in the global fixed income business.

12100 ■ **"Citi Ruling Could Chill SEC, Street Legal Pacts"** in *Wall Street Journal Eastern Edition* (November 29, 2011, pp. C1)
Pub: Dow Jones & Company Inc.
Ed: Jean Eaglesham, Chad Bray. **Description:** A $285 million settlement was reached between the Securities and Exchange Commission and Citigroup Inc. over allegations the bank misled investors over a mortgage-bond deal. Now, Judge Jed S. Rakoff has ruled against the settlement, a decision that will affect the future of such attempts to prosecute Wall Street fraud. Rakoff said that the settlement was "neither fair, nor reasonable, nor adequate, nor in the public interest."

12101 ■ **"Citigroup Moves to Buy Japan's Nikko"** in *Globe & Mail* (March 7, 2007, pp. B12)
Pub: CTVglobemedia Publishing Inc.
Ed: Jonathan Soble; Dan Wilchins. **Description:** Citigroup Inc. offered $10.8 billion to acquire troubled Nikko Cordial Corp., Japan's largest securities firm.

12102 ■ **"Clash of the Titans"** in *Canadian Business* (Vol. 80, March 12, 2007, No. 6, pp. 27)
Pub: Rogers Media
Ed: Andrew Wahl. **Description:** The frequent allegations of Google Inc. and Microsoft Corp. against each other over copyright and other legal issues, with a view to taking away other's market share, is discussed.

12103 ■ **"A Click In the Right Direction: Website Teaches Youth Financial Literacy"** in *Black Enterprise* (Vol. 38, December 2007, No. 5)
Pub: Earl G. Graves Publishing Co. Inc.
Ed: Nicole Norfleet. **Description:** Profile of Donald Lee Robinson who launched SkillsThatClick, a Website that teaches young individuals ages 12 to 15 about money management. Robinson shares how he used his Navy career as a model for designing the site.

12104 ■ **"Climbing the Wall of Worry, Two Steps at a Time"** in *Barron's* (Vol. 89, July 13, 2009, No. 28, pp. L16)
Pub: Dow Jones & Co., Inc.
Ed: Brian Blackstone. **Description:** Statistical table that shows the performance of different mutual funds for the second quarter of 2009 is presented. The data shows that on average, the 8,272 diversified equity funds gained 17 percent for this quarter.

12105 ■ **"Cloudy Future for VMware?"** in *Barron's* (Vol. 90, September 13, 2010, No. 37, pp. 21)
Pub: Barron's Editorial & Corporate Headquarters
Ed: Jonathan R. Laing. **Description:** VMWare dominated the virtualization market for years, but it may be ending as it faces more competition from rivals that offer cloud computing services. The company's stocks are also expensive and are vulnerable to the smallest mishap.

12106 ■ **"CMO Nicholson Exits Pepsi as Share Declines"** in *Advertising Age* (Vol. 79, July 7, 2008, No. 26, pp. 4)
Pub: Crain Communications, Inc.
Ed: Natalie Zmuda. **Description:** Cie Nicholson, the chief marketing officer at Pepsi-Cola UK, is leaving the company at a time when its market share is down; the brand, which was known for its dynamic marketing, has diverted much of its attention from its core brands and shifted attention to the ailing Gatorade brand as well as Sobe Life Water and Amp.

12107 ■ **"CN 'Extremely Optimistic' After Record Profit"** in *Globe & Mail* (January 24, 2007, pp. B3)
Pub: CTVglobemedia Publishing Inc.
Ed: Brent Jang. **Description:** The increase in Canadian National Railway Co.'s profits to $2.1 billion despite a harsh winter is discussed.

12108 ■ **"CN to Webcast 2007 Analyst Meeting in Toronto May 23-24"** in *Canadian Corporate News* (May 16, 2007)
Pub: Comtex News Network Inc.
Description: Canadian National Railway Company (CN) broadcast its analyst meeting in Toronto with a webcast which focused on CN's opportunities, strategies, and financial outlook through the year 2010.

12109 ■ **"CNinsure Offers Safety in Numbers"** in *Barron's* (Vol. 90, September 13, 2010, No. 37, pp. 29)
Pub: Barron's Editorial & Corporate Headquarters
Ed: Teresa Rivas. **Description:** China's insurance holding company CNinsure has a long growth future due to the nascent insurance market in the country. It has also been diversifying its offerings and it has a broad network in the nation. The shares of the company are trading cheaply at nearly 14 times its 2011 earnings, and is considered a good point for investors.

12110 ■ **"Coca-Cola Looks Ready to Pause"** in *Barron's* (Vol. 88, March 10, 2008, No. 10, pp. 18)
Pub: Dow Jones & Company, Inc.
Ed: Michael Santoli. **Description:** Shares of Coca-Cola are expected to turn sideways or experience a slight drop from $59.50 each to the mid-50 level. The company has seen its shares jump 40 percent since 2006, when it was in a series of measures to improve profitability.

12111 ■ **"Cogeco Profit Jumps 47 Percent in First Quarter"** in *Globe & Mail* (January 13, 2006, pp. B3)
Pub: CTVglobemedia Publishing Inc.
Ed: Catherine McLean. **Description:** The reasons behind 47 percent increase in first quarter 2006 profits for Cogeco Inc. are presented.

12112 ■ **"Coherent Laying Off 144 As It Prepares To Shut Auburn Plant"** in *Sacramento Business Journal* (Vol. 25, August 1, 2008, No. 22, pp. 1)
Pub: American City Business Journals, Inc.
Ed: Melanie Turner. **Description:** Sacramento, California-based Coherent Inc. is planning to lay off 144 workers at its Auburn facility. Coherent has been cutting payroll and its real estate holdings. Statistics on the company's earnings are also provided.

12113 ■ *A Colossal Failure of Common Sense: The Inside Story of the Collapse of Lehman Brothers*
Pub: Crown Business
Ed: Lawrence G. McDonald, Patrick Robinson. **Released:** 2009. **Price:** $27.00. **Description:** Former employee of Lehman Brothers details the failure of leadership that led to the demise of the company.

12114 ■ **"Columbia's JPB Raising $175M to Acquire Companies, Real Estate"** in *Boston Business Journal* (Vol. 29, May 27, 2011, No. 3, pp. 1)
Pub: American City Business Journals Inc.
Ed: Gary Haber. **Description:** JPB Enterprises is preparing to raise $175 million in its goal of acquiring companies and real estate that are major names in America. The $75 million will be raised for a buyout fund that will target wide range of industries while the $100 million will be used for land investment projects in the Florida Panhandle. Baltimore firms are expected to benefit from this deal.

12115 ■ **"Coming: Cheaper Oil and a Stronger Buck"** in *Barron's* (Vol. 88, March 24, 2008, No. 12, pp. 53)
Pub: Dow Jones & Company, Inc.
Ed: Lawrence C. Strauss. **Description:** Carl C. Weinberg, the chief economist of High Frequency Economics, forecasts that Chinese economic growth will slow down and that oil prices will drop to $80 a barrel in 2008. He also believes that the US dollar will start rising the moment the Federal Reserve stops cutting interest rates.

12116 ■ **"Coming Soon: Bailouts of Fannie and Freddie"** in *Barron's* (Vol. 88, July 14, 2008, No. 28, pp. 14)
Pub: Dow Jones & Co., Inc.
Ed: Jonathan R. Laing. **Description:** Assurances from the government that Fannie Mae and Freddie Mac are adequately capitalized and able to carry on their duties as guarantors or owners of over $5 trillion of U.S. home mortgages are designed to keep both entities afloat until they attempt to raise $10 billion in new equity. The government would assume any losses in a bailout and owners of the banks' papers would profit as yields drop.

12117 ■ **"Commodities: Who's Behind the Boom?"** in *Barron's* (Vol. 88, March 31, 2008, No. 13, pp. 3)
Pub: Dow Jones & Company, Inc.
Ed: Gene Epstein. **Description:** Proliferation of mutual funds and exchange traded funds tied to commodities indexes has helped speculative buying reach unusual levels. Index funds are estimated to account for 40 percent of all bullish bets on commodities. Commodities could drop by 30 percent as speculators retreat. Statistical data included.

12118 ■ **"Commodity Speculation: Over the Top?"** in *Barron's* (Vol. 89, July 13, 2009, No. 28, pp. 22)
Pub: Dow Jones & Co., Inc.
Ed: Gene Epstein. **Description:** Commodity Futures Trading Commission is planning to impose position limits on speculators of oil and other commodities as energy costs rebound from their lows. These regulations make much sense and these position limits

would greatly diminish the cash commitment of the commodity index traders if these were imposed on speculators and swaps dealers properly.

12119 ■ "Compelling Opportunities" in *Barron's* **(Vol. 88, March 10, 2008, No. 10, pp. 39)**
Pub: Dow Jones & Company, Inc.
Ed: Neil A. Martin. **Description:** Michael L. Reynal, portfolio manager of Principal International Emerging Markets Fund, is bullish on the growth prospects of stocks in emerging markets. He is investing big on energy, steel, and transportation companies.

12120 ■ "Competition At Last?" in *Canadian Business* **(Vol. 81, July 22, 2008, No. 12-13, pp. 7)**
Pub: Rogers Media Ltd.
Description: Competition Policy Review Panel's 'Compete to Win' report revealed that Canada is being 'hollowed-out' by foreign acquisitions. The panel investigated competition and foreign investment policies in Canada. Key information on the report, as well as views on the Investment Canada Act and the Competition Act, is presented.

12121 ■ "Competition To Provide Liquidity on the New York Stock Exchange" in *Business Horizons* **(November-December 2007, pp. 513)**
Pub: Elsevier Technology Publications
Ed: Robert Battalio, Robert Jennings. **Description:** Provision of liquidity at the New York Stock Exchange is studied. On-floor traders enjoy some advantages in providing liquidity compared to off-floor traders. The NYSE is justified in implementing measures designed to level the playing field between on- and off-floor traders.

12122 ■ "Competitors Line Up to Save Failing Banks" in *The Business Journal - Serving Phoenix and the Valley of the Sun* **(Vol. 28, July 25, 2008, No. 47, pp. 1)**
Pub: American City Business Journals, Inc.
Ed: Chris Casacchia. **Description:** Financial institutions in Arizona are positioning themselves as possible buyers in the event of failure of one of their competitors. These banks have already approached the Federal Deposit Insurance Corp. about their ability to take over their more troubled competitors.

12123 ■ "Comtech's Winning Streak" in *Crain's New York Business* **(Vol. 24, January 7, 2008, No. 1, pp. 3)**
Pub: Crain Communications, Inc.
Description: Comtech Telecommunications Corp., a designer and manufacturer of equipment that helps military track troops and vehicles on the field, has been one of the stock market's biggest winners over the past decade. Statistical data included.

12124 ■ "Connect the Thoughts" in *Canadian Business* **(Vol. 81, October 27, 2008, No. 18, pp. 8)**
Pub: Rogers Media Ltd.
Ed: Jeff Sanford. **Description:** Thomas Homer-Dixon believes the financial crisis that hit Wall Street is a systemic crisis and may result in the reconfiguration of financial markets in ways that people may never understand. He also thinks the U.S. may borrow against its assets, making it a weaker nation.

12125 ■ "Conquering Your Fear of Fees" in *Entrepreneur* **(Vol. 37, October 2009, No. 10, pp. 86)**
Pub: Entrepreneur Media, Inc.
Ed: Rosalind Resnick. **Description:** Entrepreneurs should study money management charges carefully before investing. They should understand how different forms of investments work and how much money managers and mutual funds charge for their services.

12126 ■ "Consumers Finding It Harder to Get and Keep Credit" in *Chicago Tribune* **(January 10, 2009)**
Pub: McClatchy-Tribune Information Services
Ed: Susan Chandler. **Description:** Five tips to maintain a good credit rating in these economic times are outlined and discussed.

12127 ■ "Conversation Starters for the Holiday" in *Barron's* **(Vol. 89, July 6, 2009, No. 27, pp. 7)**
Pub: Dow Jones & Co., Inc.
Ed: Michael Santoli. **Description:** Investors are concerned that the US will experience high inflation due to low interest rates and improved money supply. US consumer spending has increased to 70 percent of gross domestic product, brought by health-care spending increases, while savings rates have risen to 6.9 percent.

12128 ■ "A Conversation With Money Manager William Vellon" in *Crain's Chicago Business* **(Vol. 31, November 17, 2008, No. 46, pp. 4)**
Pub: Crain Communications, Inc.
Ed: Mike Colias. **Description:** Interview with William Vellon, the executive vice-president of Kingsbury Capital Investment Advisors; Vellon discusses ways in which the government can help the financial sector, his client base and bargains that investors should consider.

12129 ■ "Cool on Chicago Office Properties" in *Crain's Chicago Business* **(Vol. 31, March 31, 2008, No. 13, pp. 16)**
Pub: Crain Communications, Inc.
Ed: Eddie Baeb. **Description:** Investors predict values on Chicago office buildings to drop 1.3 percent over the next year.

12130 ■ "CoolBrands" in *Canadian Business* **(Vol. 83, September 14, 2010, No. 15, pp. 25)**
Pub: Rogers Media Ltd.
Ed: Joe Castaldo. **Description:** CoolBrands International Inc.'s merger with Swisher International Inc., a US hygiene products and services company, has formally erased the last traces of the former ice cream company. CoolBrands began as a frozen yogurt stand in 1986 and flourished across the world. How the string of acquisitions and poor corporate governance led to its demise are cited.

12131 ■ "Copper Giant to Spin Off Silver Assets" in *Globe & Mail* **(February 27, 2006, pp. B1)**
Pub: CTVglobemedia Publishing Inc.
Ed: Sinclair Stewart; Andrew Willis. **Description:** The reasons behind the sale of silver mining assets by Codelco are presented.

12132 ■ "Copper, Zinc Prices Hammered" in *Globe & Mail* **(February 3, 2007, pp. B7)**
Pub: CTVglobemedia Publishing Inc.
Ed: John Partridge. **Description:** The decline in the global prices of copper and zinc metals in January 2007 is discussed. Copper prices fell by 12 percent while zinc prices dropped by 6.3 percent.

12133 ■ "Copy Karachi?" in *Barron's* **(Vol. 88, June 30, 2008, No. 26, pp. 5)**
Pub: Dow Jones & Co., Inc.
Ed: Randall W. Forsyth. **Description:** Karachi bourse had a historic 8.6 percent one-day gain because the bourse banned short-selling for a month and announced a 30 billion rupee fund to stabilize the market. The shares of General Motors are trading within the same values that it had in 1974. The reasons for this decline are discussed.

12134 ■ "Copycat" in *Canadian Business* **(Vol. 79, October 23, 2006, No. 21, pp. 53)**
Pub: Rogers Media
Ed: Andrew Wahl. **Description:** The conversion of BCE Inc. into an income trust for tax advantages, soon after the transition of its business rival Telus Corp. into an income trust, is discussed.

12135 ■ "Corn May Get Shucked By Soy" in *Barron's* **(Vol. 88, March 31, 2008, No. 13, pp. M12)**
Pub: Dow Jones & Company, Inc.
Ed: Angie Pointer. **Description:** Acreage allotted to soybeans could jump by 12 percent from 2007's 63.6 million as the price for soybeans reaches record highs. Corn acreage could drop by 6.7 percent as other crops expand and higher fertilizer prices shift farmers away from corn.

12136 ■ "Corporate Elite Show Resilience" in *The Business Journal-Serving Greater Tampa Bay* **(Vol. 28, August 1, 2008, No. 32, pp. 1)**
Pub: American City Business Journals, Inc.
Ed: Margie Manning; Alexis Muellner. **Description:** Stocks of the largest public companies in Tampa Bay, Florida, outperformed the S&P 500 index by 28 percent in the first half of 2008. The escalation is attributed to the growth orientation of the companies in the area and the lack of exposure to the real estate and financial services sectors.

12137 ■ "Corporex Checks Into Hotel Niche" in *Business Courier* **(Vol. 24, October 12, 2008, No. 26, pp. 1)**
Pub: American City Business Journals, Inc.
Ed: Laura Baverman. **Description:** Corporex Companies Inc. is investing $900 million on select-service hotels ranging from $12 million to $20 million each, with eight hotels under construction and nine sites under contract.

12138 ■ "Corus Eases Off Ailing Condo Market; Office Developers Get Majority of 1Q Loans" in *Crain's Chicago Business* **(April 28, 2008)**
Pub: Crain Communications, Inc.
Ed: H. Lee Murphy. **Description:** Corus Bankshares Inc., a specialist in lending for the condominium high-rise construction market, is diversifying its portfolio by making loans to office developers and expects to be investing in hotels through the rest of the year. Corus' $7.57 billion loan portfolio is also discussed in detail as well as the company's earnings and share price. Statistical data included.

12139 ■ "Cost Cuts Lead Dealers to Record Profits" in *Globe & Mail* **(March 24, 2006, pp. B3)**
Pub: CTVglobemedia Publishing Inc.
Ed: Omar El Akkad. **Description:** The reasons behind posting of $4.3 billion profit by Canadian securities sector, for 2005, are presented.

12140 ■ "Countdown" in *Canadian Business* **(Vol. 81, March 3, 2008, No. 3, pp. 27)**
Pub: Rogers Media
Ed: Al Rosen. **Description:** According to a recent poll only 42 percent of portfolio managers in Canada are aware that the country is planning to adopt the International Financial Reporting Standards beginning 2011. The shift to the new standards will have significant impacts on investment values and will be the biggest revolution in Canadian financial reporting. The effects of the transition on portfolio managers and investors are analyzed.

12141 ■ "CPI, Coal Lead Local Stock Decline" in *Saint Louis Business Journal* **(Vol. 32, October 14, 2011, No. 7, pp. 1)**
Pub: Saint Louis Business Journal
Ed: Greg Edwards. **Description:** Coal companies and CPI Corporation were among those whose stocks have declined in St. Louis, Missouri. The stocks of local firms have plunged by 28 percent during the first nine months of 2011.

12142 ■ "CPI Corporation Acquires Assets of Bella Pictures" in *Benzinga.com* **(January 28, 2011)**
Pub: Benzinga.com
Ed: Benzinga Staff. **Description:** CPI Corporation acquired assets of Bella Pictures Inc., a leading provider of branded wedding photography services. Details of the acquisition are explained.

12143 ■ "Crain's Picks Top '08 Stocks" in *Crain's New York Business* **(Vol. 24, January 7, 2008, No. 1, pp. 3)**
Pub: Crain Communications, Inc.
Ed: Aaron Elstein. **Description:** Listing of five stocks that Crain's believes can deliver solid gains for shareholders.

12144 ■ *Crash Proof 2.0: How to Profit From the Economic Collapse*
Pub: John Wiley & Sons, Inc.
Ed: Peter D. Schiff. **Released:** September 22, 2009. **Price:** $27.95. **Description:** Factors that will affect financial stability in the coming years are explained. A three step plan to battle the current economic downturn is also included.

12145 ■ *Creating Capitalism Joint-Stock Enterprise in British Politics and Culture, 1800-1870*

Pub: Royal Historical Society

Ed: James Taylor. **Released:** October 2006. **Price:** $80.00. **Description:** The growth of joint-stock business in Victorian Britain is discussed, particularly the resistance to it.

12146 ■ **"The Credit Crisis Continues"** in *Barron's* (Vol. 88, March 10, 2008, No. 10, pp. M12)

Pub: Dow Jones & Company, Inc.

Ed: Randall W. Forsyth. **Description:** Short-term Treasury yields dropped to new cyclical lows in early March 2008, with the yield for the two-year Treasury note falling to 1.532 percent. Spreads of the mortgage-backed securities of Fannie Mae and Freddie Mac rose on suspicion of collapses in financing.

12147 ■ **"Credit Crisis Puts Market in Unprecedented Territory"** in *Crain's New York Business* (Vol. 24, January 7, 2008, No. 1, pp. 14)

Pub: Crain Communications, Inc.

Ed: Aaron Elstein. **Description:** Banks are being forced to take enormous losses due to investors who are refusing to buy anything linked to subprime mortgages and associated securities.

12148 ■ **"Credit-Market Crisis Batters Origen Financial's Bottom Line"** in *Crain's Detroit Business* (Vol. 24, March 31, 2008, No. 13, pp. 4)

Pub: Crain Communications, Inc.

Ed: Description: Overview of the effect the credit-market crisis has had on Origen Financial Inc., a company that underwrites and services loans for manufactured housing. CEO Ronald Klein didn't think Origen would be affected by the collapse due to its sound operations but the company's share price dropped considerably causing its auditors to warn that the company's existence could be in jeopardy.

12149 ■ **"Credit Unions Cast Wary Eye at Paulson Plan, But Not Panicking Yet"** in *The Business Review Albany* (Vol. 35, April 11, 2008, No. 1)

Pub: The Business Review

Ed: Barbara Pinckney. **Description:** Credit unions are suspicious of US Treasury Secretary Henry Paulson's plan to establish a single federally insured depository institution charter for all institutions covered by federal deposit insurance. The charter would replace national banks, federal savings associations, and federal credit union charters.

12150 ■ **"Crime and Punishment"** in *Canadian Business* (Vol. 81, December 24, 2007, No. 1, pp. 21)

Pub: Rogers Media

Ed: Joe Castaldo. **Description:** Cmpass Inc.'s survey of 137 Canadian chief executive officers showed that they want tougher imposition of sentences on white-collar criminals, as they believe that the weak enforcement of securities laws gives an impression that Canada is a country where it is easy to get away with fraud.

12151 ■ *Currency Internationalization: Global Experiences and Implications for the Renminbi*

Pub: Palgrave Macmillan

Ed: Wensheng Peng, Chang Shu. **Released:** January 5, 2010. **Price:** $100.00. **Description:** A collection of academic studies relating to the potential internationalization of China's remninbi. It also discusses the increasing use of China's remninbi currency in international trade and finance.

12152 ■ **"Customers Turned Off? Not at Best Buy"** in *Barron's* (Vol. 88, March 24, 2008, No. 12, pp. 29)

Pub: Dow Jones & Company, Inc.

Ed: Sandra Ward. **Description:** Shares of Best Buy, trading at $42.41 each, are expected to rise to an average of $52 a share due to the company's solid fundamentals. The company's shares have fallen 20

percent from their 52-week high and are attractive given the company's bright prospects in the video game sector and high-definition video.

12153 ■ **"CVRD Inco Strike Shuts Sudbury Mines"** in *Globe & Mail* (April 2, 2007, pp. B1)

Pub: CTVglobemedia Publishing Inc.

Ed: Andy Hoffman. **Description:** The closure of nickel mining operations at the Sudbury mines due to the strike by employees of CVRD Inco Ltd. is described. The prospects of a rise in the prices of nickel are discussed, besides the production of metals in Canada.

12154 ■ **"Cyclicals, Your Day Is Coming"** in *Barron's* (Vol. 89, July 27, 2009, No. 30, pp. 24)

Pub: Dow Jones & Co., Inc.

Ed: Dimitra DeFotis. **Description:** Cyclical stocks are likely to be big winners when the economy improves and 13 stocks that have improving earnings, decent balance sheets, and dividends are presented. These candidates include U.S. Steel, Alcoa, Allegheny Tech, Dow Chemical, and Nucor.

12155 ■ **"Danaher to Acquire Tectronix"** in *Canadian Electronics* (Vol. 22, November-December 2007, No. 7, pp. 1)

Pub: CLB Media Inc.

Description: Leading supplier of measurement, test and monitoring equipment Tektronix will be acquired by Danaher Corporation for $2.8 billion. Tektronix products are expected to complement Danaher's test equipment sector. The impacts of the deal on Tektronix shareholders and Danaher's operations are discussed.

12156 ■ **"Dancing With Giants: Acquisition and Survival of the Family Firm"** in *Family Business Review* (Vol. 19, December 2006, No. 4, pp. 289)

Pub: Family Firm Institute Inc.

Ed: Adam Steen, Lawrence S. Welch. **Description:** Responses of family firms to mergers and acquisitions are analyzed taking the example of the takeover of an Australian wine producer and family firm.

12157 ■ **"Darkness Falling..."** in *Barron's* (Vol. 89, July 20, 2009, No. 29, pp. 13)

Pub: Dow Jones & Co., Inc.

Description: Newsletter writer Arch Crawford believes that market indicators signal a possible downturn in US stock markets. High risk areas also include China and Japan .

12158 ■ **"Data Dispel Some Notions About Value of Stock Buybacks"** in *Crain's Cleveland Business* (Vol. 28, November 19, 2007, No. 46, pp. 9)

Pub: Crain Communications, Inc.

Ed: Megan Johnston. **Description:** According to new research on buybacks and their benefits, companies engaged in stock buybacks frequently do not enjoy a nice boost in their share prices despite the conventional wisdom that states that investors like stock buybacks.

12159 ■ *Data Driven Investing: Professional Edition*

Pub: Data Driven Publishing, LLC

Ed: Mitchell R. Hardy; Bill Matson. **Released:** 2004. **Description:** Investment concepts and trading techniques are explored in a simple and practical way. The book covers the unreliability of financial markets due to malpractices, appalling analysis, insider training and more. Information is based on data and common sense and easy to use for beginner as well as professional.

12160 ■ **"Dating Games"** in *Canadian Business* (Vol. 79, September 25, 2006, No. 19, pp. 23)

Pub: Rogers Media

Ed: John Gray. **Description:** Increasing stock option scandals in Canada and American companies is discussed.

12161 ■ **"David Azrieli"** in *Canadian Business* (Vol. 82, April 27, 2009, No. 7, pp. 54)

Pub: Rogers Media

Ed: Alex Mlynek. **Description:** David Azrieli wants to take advantage of opportunities, revealing that he has increased his portfolio nearly every recession. Azrieli has recently purchased properties of General Electric near the Toronto airport for about $100 million. He believes the economy will rebound in the second half of 2009.

12162 ■ **"A Day Late and a Dollar Short"** in *Indoor Comfort Marketing* (Vol. 70, March 2011, No. 3, pp. 30)

Pub: Industry Publications Inc.

Ed: Philip J. Baratz. **Description:** A discussion involving futures options and fuel oil prices is presented.

12163 ■ **"Deal Braces Cramer for Growth Run"** in *The Business Journal-Serving Metropolitan Kansas City* (Vol. 26, July 4, 2008, No. 43, pp. 1)

Pub: American City Business Journals, Inc.

Ed: James Dornbook. **Description:** Gardner, Kansas-based Cramer Products Inc. bought 100 percent of the stocks of Louisville, Kentucky-based Active Ankle Inc. from 26 private investors increasing its revenue by 20 percent. The latter is the second largest vendor of Cramer. Other details of the merger are presented.

12164 ■ **"Deal or No Deal?"** in *Canadian Business* (Vol. 80, January 15, 2007, No. 2, pp. 38)

Pub: Rogers Media

Ed: Andrew Wahl; Zena Olijnkyk; Jeff Sanford; Erin Pooley. **Description:** The trends in the stock prices of companies like Loblaw Companies Ltd., Domtar Inc. and Biovail Corp., from January 2006 to January 2007, are analyzed.

12165 ■ **"The Deal - Rhymes With Steal - Of A Lifetime"** in *Barron's* (Vol. 88, March 24, 2008, No. 12, pp. 24)

Pub: Dow Jones & Company, Inc.

Ed: Andrew Bary. **Description:** JPMorgan Chase's impending acquisition of Bear Stearns for $2.50 a share is a huge steal for the former. JPMorgan is set to acquire a company with a potential annual earnings of $1 billion while the Federal Reserve funds Bear's illiquid assets by providing $30 billion in non-recourse loans.

12166 ■ **"Dean Foods"** in *Ice Cream Reporter* (Vol. 23, November 20, 2010, No. 12, pp. 8)

Pub: Ice Cream Reporter

Description: The impact of higher commodity prices can be seen in the recent news from Dean Foods, the largest U.S. dairy company, which reported that rising butterfat and other dairy commodity costs have led to lower-than-expected quarterly profits after it cut prices to compete with private-label brands.

12167 ■ **"Death Spiral"** in *Business Journal Serving Greater Tampa Bay* (Vol. 30, October 29, 2010, No. 45, pp. 1)

Pub: Tampa Bay Business Journal

Ed: Margie Manning. **Description:** Bay Cities Bank has started working on the loan portfolio of its acquisition, Progress Bank of Florida. Regulators closed Progress Bank in October 2010 after capital collapsed due to charge-offs and increases in the provision for future loan losses.

12168 ■ **"Debutante NYSE Soars 20 Percent"** in *Globe & Mail* (March 9, 2006, pp. B1)

Pub: CTVglobemedia Publishing Inc.

Ed: John Partridge. **Description:** The debutant share trading of NYSE Group Inc. is discussed. The prices rose by 20 percent before closing.

12169 ■ **"Decision CEO Cool to Acquisitions"** in *Globe & Mail* (April 19, 2007, pp. B6)

Pub: CTVglobemedia Publishing Inc.

Ed: Andy Hoffman. **Description:** The increase in the shares of Denison Mines Corp. due to hike in Uranium prices is discussed.

12170 ■ "Decline in Assets Is Costly for Advisers" in *The Business Journal-Serving Metropolitan Kansas City* (Vol. 27, October 24, 2008)
Pub: American City Business Journals, Inc.
Ed: James Dornbrook. **Description:** Financial advisers in the Kansas City, Missouri area are forced to cut costs as their assets have decreased sharply due to the huge drop in stock prices. American Century Investments was forced to diversify into foreign assets and cut 90 jobs as its assets dropped to $84 billion. Diversification has softened the impact of the steep decline in stock prices for Waddell & Reed Financial Inc.

12171 ■ *A Demon of Our Own Design: Markets, Hedge Funds, and the Perils of Financial Innovation*
Pub: John Wiley and Sons, Inc.
Ed: Richard Bookstaber. **Released:** December 2008. **Price:** $16.95 paperback. **Description:** Longtime hedge-fund manager offers his take on a market and investment system that he believes is needlessly complex owing to investment banks, hedge funds, innovation, regulation, and safeguards and further compounded by investor and market instabilities. These complexities could create a large-scale disaster.

12172 ■ "Detecting Crookery" in *Canadian Business* (Vol. 80, February 12, 2007, No. 4, pp. 23)
Pub: Rogers Media
Ed: Al Rosen. **Description:** Expert advice to Canadian investors on proper financial reporting is presented and ways to protect their investments are discussed.

12173 ■ "Deutsche Bank Joins the Club" in *Barron's* (Vol. 88, March 31, 2008, No. 13, pp. M6)
Pub: Dow Jones & Company, Inc.
Ed: Arindam Nag. **Description:** Deutsche Bank's tangible leverage has worsened sharply in the past year from 2.1 percent to 2.3 percent during 2002-2006 to only 1.6 percent. The bank has also been accumulating a lot of illiquid assets and its Level-3 assets are three times its tangible equity.

12174 ■ *The Dhandho Investor: The Low Risk Value Method to High Returns*
Pub: John Wiley and Sons Inc.
Ed: Mohnish Pabrai. **Released:** April 2007. **Price:** $27.95. **Description:** Value investing is described using the Dhandho capital allocation framework for successfully investing in the stock market.

12175 ■ "Diana Sands; Vice-President of Investor Relations, Boeing Co." in *Crain's Chicago Business* (Vol. 31, May 5, 2008, No. 18, pp. 32)
Pub: Crain Communications, Inc.
Ed: John Rosenthal. **Description:** Profile of Diana Sands who is the vice-president of investor relations at Boeing Co. which entails explaining the company's performance to securities analysts and institutional investors.

12176 ■ "Diary of a Short-Seller" in *Conde Nast Portfolio* (Vol. 2, June 2008, No. 6, pp. 44)
Pub: Conde Nast Publications, Inc.
Ed: Jesse Eisinger. **Description:** Profile of David Einhorn who is a fund manager that spoke out against finance company Allied Capital whose stock fell nearly 20 percent the day after Einhorn's critique; Einhorn subsequently had to contend with attacks against his credibility as well as investigations by the S.E.C.; Einhorn's experience illuminates our current economic crisis.

12177 ■ "Diaz Announces Financial and Operating Results for the First Three Months of 2007" in *Canadian Corporate News* (May 16, 2007)
Pub: Comtex News Network Inc.
Description: Diaz Resources Ltd., an oil and gas exploration and production company, announced its financial results during the first quarter of 2007 which

were hampered by lower gas prices and declining production volumes but anticipates the financial results should steadily improve in the second quarter of 2007.

12178 ■ "Dick Haskayne" in *Canadian Business* (Vol. 81, March 31, 2008, No. 5, pp. 72)
Pub: Rogers Media
Ed: Andy Holloway. **Description:** Dick Haskayne says that he learned a lot about business from his dad who ran a butcher shop where they had to make a decision on buying cattle and getting credit. Haskayne says that family, friends, finances, career, health, and infrastructure are benchmarks that have to be balanced.

12179 ■ *Dictionary of Finance, Investment and Banking*
Pub: Palgrave Macmillan
Ed: Erik Banks. **Released:** 2010. **Price:** $42.95. **Description:** Comprehensive dictionary covering terms used in finance, investment and banking sectors.

12180 ■ "A Different Kind of Waiting List" in *Canadian Business* (Vol. 80, April 9, 2007, No. 8, pp. 17)
Pub: Rogers Media
Ed: Erin Pooley. **Description:** The adverse impact on drug companies' profitability due to regulatory delays in approving drugs is discussed.

12181 ■ "Different This Time?" in *Canadian Business* (Vol. 81, April 14, 2008, No. 6, pp. 38)
Pub: Rogers Media
Ed: Matthew McClearn. **Description:** Irving Fisher believed that the low interest rates of the 1920's spurred investors to borrow and use the money to speculate with the proceeds thereby increasing the debt to unmanageable levels prior to the stock market crash in Oct. 29, 1929. The U.S. economic conditions in 1929 and U.S. economic conditions in 2008 are discussed.

12182 ■ "Digging Deep for Gold" in *Barron's* (Vol. 88, March 24, 2008, No. 12, pp. 49)
Pub: Dow Jones & Company, Inc.
Ed: Suzanne McGee. **Description:** David Iben, manager of the Nuveen Tradewinds Value Opportunities Fund, looks for value in companies and industries where the consensus of analysts is negative. He started investing in gold stocks well before gold prices started to rise.

12183 ■ *The Directory of Venture Capital and Private Equity Firms: 2009*
Pub: Grey House Publishing
Ed: Laura Mars-Proietti. **Released:** April 1, 2009. **Price:** $450.00. **Description:** Updated and expanded edition that includes new entries offering access to more than 3,500 domestic and international venture capital and private equity firms; detailed contact information and extensive data on investments and funds is included.

12184 ■ "Disappearing Act" in *Globe & Mail* (April 21, 2007, pp. B1)
Pub: CTVglobemedia Publishing Inc.
Ed: David Parkinson. **Description:** The effects of the buyout of BCE Inc. on the trends of stock prices at the Toronto Stock Exchange are described.

12185 ■ "Discount Beers Take Fizz Out Of Molson" in *Globe & Mail* (February 10, 2006, pp. B3)
Pub: CTVglobemedia Publishing Inc.
Ed: Omar El Akkad. **Description:** The reasons behind the decline in profits by 60 percent for Molson Coors Brewing Co., during fourth quarter 2005, are presented.

12186 ■ "Diversity Stock Indexes" in *Hispanic Business* (September 2007, pp. 28)
Pub: Hispanic Business
Description: Presentation of the Hispanic Business Stock Index shows the current value of fifteen Hispanic companies through August 2007.

12187 ■ "DiversityStockIndexes" in *Hispanic Business* (October 2007, pp. 68)
Pub: Hispanic Business
Description: Two proprietary stock indexes of interest to Hispanic businesses are presented.

12188 ■ "Dividing to Conquer" in *Barron's* (Vol. 88, March 31, 2008, No. 13, pp. 22)
Pub: Dow Jones & Company, Inc.
Ed: Andrew Bary. **Description:** Altria's spin off of Philip Morris International could unlock substantial value for both domestic and international cigarette concerns. The strong brands and ample payouts from both companies will most likely impress investors.

12189 ■ "Do-It-Yourself Portfolio Management" in *Barron's* (Vol. 89, July 13, 2009, No. 28, pp. 25)
Pub: Dow Jones & Co., Inc.
Ed: Mike Hogan. **Description:** Services of several portfolio management web sites are presented. These web sites include MarketRiders E.Adviser, TD Ameritrade and E*Trade.

12190 ■ "Do the Math" in *Canadian Business* (Vol. 79, October 9, 2006, No. 20, pp. 17)
Pub: Rogers Media
Ed: Al Rosen. **Description:** Faulty practices followed by regulators in Canadian stock market are discussed. The need for authorities to protect investors against these frauds are emphasized.

12191 ■ "Doctor's Orders" in *Canadian Business* (Vol. 79, November 20, 2006, No. 23, pp. 73)
Pub: Rogers Media
Ed: Jeff Sanford. **Description:** George Cohon, the founder of McDonald's in Canada and Russia, speaks about the Canadian market and the experience of starting McDonald's in Canada.

12192 ■ "DoEs and DonEts" in *Canadian Business* (Vol. 79, July 17, 2006, No. 14-15, pp. 29)
Pub: Rogers Media
Ed: Andy Holloway; Erin Pooley; Thomas Watson. **Description:** Strategic tips for planning systematic investments, in order to make life more enjoyable after retirement, are elucidated.

12193 ■ "Dofasco Quarterly Profit Plunges on Lower Steel Prices, Rising Costs" in *Globe & Mail* (February 4, 2006, pp. B3)
Pub: CTVglobemedia Publishing Inc.
Ed: Shirley Won. **Description:** Dofasco Inc. posted 71% decline in profits for fourth quarter 2005. The revenue drop is attributed to fall in steel prices.

12194 ■ "Dofasco Warms to New Thyssen Bid" in *Globe & Mail* (January 4, 2006, pp. B1)
Pub: CTVglobemedia Publishing Inc.
Ed: Greg Keenan. **Description:** The details on ThyssenKrupp AG's bid for Dofasco Inc., at $63 a share, are presented.

12195 ■ "The Dogs of TSX" in *Canadian Business* (Vol. 81, Summer 2008, No. 9, pp. 77)
Pub: Rogers Media Ltd.
Ed: Calvin Leung. **Description:** Table showing the one-year stock performance of the ten highest dividend-yielding stocks on the S&P/TSX 60 Composite Index is presented. This technique is similar to the 'Dogs of the Dow' approach. The idea in this investment strategy is to buy equal amounts of stocks from these companies and selling them a year later, and then repeat the process.

12196 ■ "The Dominance of Doubt" in *Barron's* (Vol. 89, July 13, 2009, No. 28, pp. M3)
Pub: Dow Jones & Co., Inc.
Ed: Description: Five straight down days leading up to July 10, 2009 in the U.S. stock market reminds one strategist of 1982 when there was a feeling that things could never be the same again. One analyst is

bullish on the stocks of Apple Inc. and sees the stocks rising to at least 180 in 12 months. The prospects of the shares of GM and Ford are also discussed.

12197 ■ "Don't Bet Against The House" in Barron's (Vol. 88, July 14, 2008, No. 28, pp. 20)

Pub: Dow Jones & Co., Inc.

Ed: Sandra Ward. **Description:** Shares of Nasdaq OMX have lost more than 50 percent of their value from November 2007 to July 2008 but the value of these shares could climb 50 percent on the strength of world security exchanges. Only 15 percent of the company's revenues come from the U.S. and the shares are trading at 12.5 times the amount expected for 2008.

12198 ■ "Don't Count Your Millions Yet" in Business Courier (Vol. 24, January 11, 2008, No. 40, pp. 1)

Pub: American City Business Journals, Inc.

Ed: Steve Watkins. **Description:** Merger and acquisition deals have been difficult to complete since 2007 largely due to a weaker economy and the credit crunch. Buyers have become more cautious because of the state of the economy and capital has become tougher to obtain because of the credit market crisis. The trends in mergers and acquisitions are analyzed further.

12199 ■ "Don't Expect Quick Fix" in The Business Journal-Serving Metropolitan Kansas City (Vol. 27, October 3, 2008, No. 3, pp. 1)

Pub: American City Business Journals, Inc.

Ed: James Dornbrook. **Description:** United States governmental entities cannot provide a quick fix solution to the current financial crisis. The economy requires a systemic change in the way people think about credit. The financial services industry should also focus on core lending principles.

12200 ■ "Don't Get Lulled by the Calm" in Barron's (Vol. 89, July 27, 2009, No. 30, pp. M13)

Pub: Dow Jones & Co., Inc.

Ed: Steven M. Sears. **Description:** Options traders expect volatility to return in the fall of 2009 and to bring correlation with it. September and October are typically the most volatile months and the trick is to survive earnings season.

12201 ■ "Don't' Hang Up On FairPoint" in Barron's (Vol. 88, July 7, 2008, No. 27, pp. M5)

Pub: Dow Jones & Co., Inc.

Ed: Fleming Meeks. **Description:** Shares of FairPoint Communications, priced at $6.63 each, are undervalued and should be worth over $12 each. The company increased its size by more than five times by acquiring Verizon's local telephone operations in Vermont, New Hampshire, and Maine, but must switch customers in those areas into their system by the end of September 2007.

12202 ■ "Dow Jones Gives Apple-Loving Sales Professionals a Boost" in Information Today (Vol. 26, February 2009, No. 2, pp. 30)

Pub: Information Today, Inc.

Description: Dow Jones Sales Triggers for iPhone and iPod program helps sales professionals stay current to prospects and customers in their fields by providing real-time news on business changes, including management moves, mergers, and new investments. The application presents events that trigger best opportunities and allows users to look up companies and executives to retrieve information.

12203 ■ "Downtown Bank Got High Marks for Irwin Purchase, Is Looking For More" in Business Courier (Vol. 27, September 3, 2010, No. 18, pp. 1)

Pub: Business Courier

Ed: Steve Watkins. **Description:** First Financial Bancorp is looking to acquire more troubled banks following its purchase of Irwin Union Bank. The bank has reported a $383 million bargain purchase gain during the third quarter of 2009.

12204 ■ "Downtown Retail Site Sold to ATCO" in Austin Business JournalInc. (Vol. 29, November 20, 2009, No. 37, pp. 1)

Pub: American City Business Journals

Ed: Kate Harrington. **Description:** New York-based real estate company ATCO Advisory Services purchased a 13,700 square foot retail space in Austin, Texas from 360 Condominiums. The selection of the retail space, named the Shops at 360 has been attributed to the local tenant mix and its location in downtown Austin. Meanwhile, ATCO may continue investing in the area in the near future.

12205 ■ "Drilling Deep and Flying High" in Barron's (Vol. 88, June 30, 2008, No. 26, pp. 34)

Pub: Dow Jones & Co., Inc.

Ed: Kenneth Rapoza. **Description:** Shares of Petrobras could rise another 25 percent if the three deepwater wells that the company has found proves as lucrative as some expect. Petrobras will become an oil giant if the reserves are proven.

12206 ■ "Drug-Maker Plans IPO" in Business Courier (Vol. 24, November 23, 2008, No. 32, pp. 1)

Pub: American City Business Journals, Inc.

Ed: James Ritchie; Steve Watkins. **Description:** Xanodyne Pharmaceuticals Inc. filed plans with the Securities and Exchange Commission on November 9, 2007 for an initial public offering. The company, with annual sales of $75 million, had lost $222 million since it was founded in 2001.

12207 ■ "Drug, Seed Firms Offer Antidote For Inflation" in Crain's Chicago Business (Vol. 31, April 21, 2008, No. 16, pp. 4)

Pub: Crain Communications, Inc.

Ed: Daniel Rome Levine. **Description:** Interview with Jerrold Senser, the CEO of Institutional Capital LLC in Chicago, in which he discusses the ways that the company is adjusting to the economic slowdown and rising inflation, his favorite firms for investment and his prediction of an economic turnaround; he also recommends five companies he feels are worth investing in.

12208 ■ "Drug Trial Halt at YM Sets Stage for Selloff" in Globe & Mail (January 31, 2007, pp. B3)

Pub: CTVglobemedia Publishing Inc.

Ed: Leonard Zehr. **Description:** The decision of YM Biosciences Inc. to stop its trial of cancer drug tesmilifene and stocks following government concern over the safety of the drug is discussed.

12209 ■ "Dueling Visions" in Barron's (Vol. 89, July 27, 2009, No. 30, pp. 13)

Pub: Dow Jones & Co., Inc.

Ed: Michael Santoli. **Description:** Goldman Sachs' market strategists believe the stock market has entered a "sustained-rally" mode while Morgan Stanley's strategist believes this is a "rally to sell into". What is not known in the stock market is how much of a "V"-shaped recovery in earning the market rebound has already priced in.

12210 ■ "Dynamic Duo" in Barron's (Vol. 88, March 10, 2008, No. 10, pp. 45)

Pub: Dow Jones & Company, Inc.

Ed: Shirley A. Lazo. **Description:** General Dynamics, the world's sixth-largest military contractor, raised its dividend payout by 20.7 percent from 29 cents to 35 cents a share. Steel Dynamics, producer of structural steel and steel bar products, declared a 2-for-1 stock split and raised its quarterly dividend by 33 percent to a split-adjusted 10 cents a share.

12211 ■ "easyhome Ltd. Discovers Employee Fraud at an Easyfinancial Kiosk Company" in Internet Wire (October 14, 2010)

Pub: Comtex

Description: Canada's leading merchandise leasing company and provider of financial services, easyhome Ltd., reported employee fraud totaling $3.4 million that was perpetrated against the firm's easyfinancial services business.

12212 ■ "eBay Business Looking Up" in Zacks (July 26, 2011)

Pub: Comtex News Network Inc.

Ed: Sejuti Banerjea. **Description:** eBay reported solid revenue growth for 2011 second quarter, keeping in line with the Zacks Consensus Estimate, and third quarter earnings are expected to be higher. eBay's new strategy is to direct traffic to bigger sellers with improved customer service, making this good for eBay businesses.

12213 ■ "eBay Inc. Completes Acquisition of Zong" in Benzinga.com (October 29, 2011)

Pub: Benzinga.com

Ed: Benzinga Staff. **Description:** eBay Inc. acquired Zong, a provider of payments through mobile carrier billing. Terms of the agreement are outlined.

12214 ■ "Economic Distance and the Survival of Foreign Direct Investments" in Academy of Management Journal (Vol. 50, No. 5, October 2007)

Pub: Academy of Management

Ed: Eric W.K. Tsang, Paul S.L. Yip. **Description:** Study was undertaken to assess the relationship between economic disparities of various countries and foreign direct investments, focusing on Singapore. Results revealed that economic distance has a definite impact on foreign direct investment hazard rates.

12215 ■ "Economic Prognosis" in Barron's (Vol. 89, July 13, 2009, No. 28, pp. 11)

Pub: Dow Jones & Co., Inc.

Ed: Karen Hube. **Description:** Loomis Sayles Bond Fund manager Dan Fuss believes that the economy is bottoming and that recovery will be long and drawn out. Fuss guesses that the next peak in 10-year Treasury yields will be about 6.25%in around 4 and a half or five years ahead of 2009.

12216 ■ "An Educated Play on China" in Barron's (Vol. 88, June 30, 2008, No. 26, pp. M6)

Pub: Dow Jones & Co., Inc.

Ed: Mohammed Hadi. **Description:** New Oriental Education & Technology Group sells English-language courses to an increasingly competitive Chinese workforce that values education. The shares in this company have been weighed down by worries on the impact of the Beijing Olympics on enrollment and the Sichuan earthquake. These shares could be a great way to get exposure to the long-term growth in China.

12217 ■ "Effect of Oil Prices on the Economy" in Canadian Business (Vol. 81, September 15, 2008, No. 14-15, pp. 5)

Pub: Rogers Media Ltd.

Ed: Joe Chidley. **Description:** Rise of oil prices above $100 in February 2008 and $140 in July signals the birth of a "new economy" according to commentators; this shift is causing uneasiness from oil industry professionals who are unsure of how this trend could be sustained. Oil dropped below $120 in August, which could slow down global economic growth followed by oil demand, then oil prices.

12218 ■ "Egg Fight: The Yolk's on the Short" in Barron's (Vol. 88, July 7, 2008, No. 27, pp. 20)

Pub: Dow Jones & Co., Inc.

Ed: Christopher C. Williams. **Description:** Shares of Cal-Maine Foods, the largest egg producer and distributor in the US, are due for a huge rise because of the increase in egg prices. Short sellers, however, continue betting that the stock, priced at $31.84 each, will eventually go down.

12219 ■ "The Emerging Capital Market for Nonprofits" in Harvard Business Review (Vol. 88, October 2010, No. 10, pp. 110)

Pub: Harvard Business School Publishing

Ed: Robert S. Kaplan, Allen S. Grossman. **Description:** Demonstration of how nonprofits can use intermediaries to grow their organizational structures, giving them improved scale and impact is offered.

Some intermediaries play a mutual-fund role and conduct due diligence, while others act as venture capital funds and implement strategy.

12220 ■ "The Emperor Strikes Back" in
Canadian Business **(Vol. 80, March 26, 2007, No. 7, pp. 48)**
Pub: Rogers Media
Ed: Rachel Pulfer. **Description:** The financial performance of Fairfax Financial Holdings Ltd. in 2006 is presented. The efforts of chief executive Prem Watsa to lead the company towards growth track are also presented.

12221 ■ "Empire of the Sun" in *Canadian Business* **(Vol. 82, April 27, 2009, No. 7, pp. 42)**
Pub: Rogers Media
Ed: Jeff Sanford. **Description:** Suncor Energy Inc. and Petro-Canada announced on March 23, 2009 plans for a merger. The $19 billion merger will result in Suncor keeping their brand name and 60 percent of the company while Pe= tro-Canada will hold 40 percent. The new Suncor now has 7.5 billion barrels of proved and probable reserves of oil and could account for as much as 25 percent of North American production by 2025.

12222 ■ "EnCana Axes Spending on Gas Wells" in *Globe & Mail* **(February 16, 2006, pp. B1)**
Pub: CTVglobemedia Publishing Inc.
Ed: Dave Ebner. **Description:** The reasons behind EnCana Corp.'s cost spending measures by $300 million on natural gas wells are presented. The company projects 2 percent cut in gas and oil sales for 2006.

12223 ■ "End of the Beginning" in *Canadian Business* **(Vol. 81, November 10, 2008, No. 19, pp. 17)**
Pub: Rogers Media Ltd.
Ed: David Wolf. **Description:** The freeze in the money markets and historic decline in equity markets around the world finally forced governments into aggressive coordinated action. The asset price inflation brought on by cheap credit will now work in reverse and the tightening of credit will be difficult economically. Canada is exposed to the fallout everywhere, given that the U.S, the U.K. and Japan buy 30 percent of Canada's output.

12224 ■ "End of an Era" in *Barron's* **(Vol. 88, July 7, 2008, No. 27, pp. 3)**
Pub: Dow Jones & Co., Inc.
Ed: Alan Abelson. **Description:** June 2008 was a very bad month for US stocks, with investors losing as much as 41.9 percent in the first half of 2008 signaling an end to the financial environment that prevailed around the world since the 1980's. The US job market lost 62,000 jobs in June 2008.

12225 ■ "Endeca Gears Up for Likely IPO Bid" in *Boston Business Journal* **(Vol. 31, July 1, 2011, No. 23, pp. 1)**
Pub: Boston Business Journal
Ed: Kyle Alspach. **Description:** Endeca Inc. is readying itself for its plans to register as a public company. The search engine technology leader is enjoying continued growth with revenue up by 30 percent in 2010 while its expansion trend makes it an unlikely candidate for an acquisition.

12226 ■ "Energy Firms Face Stricter Definitions" in *Globe & Mail* **(March 26, 2007, pp. B3)**
Pub: CTVglobemedia Publishing Inc.
Ed: David Ebner. **Description:** The Alberta Securities Commission has imposed strict securities regulations on oil and gas industries. Energy industries will have to submit revenue details to stake holders.

12227 ■ "Energy, MLPs: Pipeline to Profits" in *Barron's* **(Vol. 89, July 27, 2009, No. 30, pp. 9)**
Pub: Dow Jones & Co., Inc.
Ed: Dimitra DeFotis. **Description:** Energy master limited partnership stocks are range-bound in the next few months from July 2009 but there are there

are some opportunities that remain. These include Energy Transfer Equity, Enterprise GP holdings, NuStar GP Holdings, and Plains All American Pipeline.

12228 ■ "Energy Slide Slows Fourth Quarter Profits" in *Globe & Mail* **(April 13, 2007, pp. B9)**
Pub: CTVglobemedia Publishing Inc.
Ed: Angela Barnes. **Description:** The decrease in the fourth quarter profits of several companies across various industries in Canada, including mining and manufacturing, due to global decrease in oil prices, is discussed.

12229 ■ "Engine of Growth: U.S. Industry Funk hasn't Hurt Cummins or Its Investors" in *Barron's* **(Vol. 88, July 14, 2008, No. 28, pp. 43)**
Pub: Dow Jones & Co., Inc.
Ed: Shirley A. Lazo. **Description:** Engine maker Cummins increased its quarterly common dividend by 40 percent to 17.5 cents per share from 12.5 cents. CVS Caremark's dividend saw a hike of 18.4 percent from 9.5 cents to 11.25 cents per share while its competitor Walgreen is continuing its 75th straight year of dividend distribution and its 33rd straight year of dividend hikes.

12230 ■ *Entrepreneurial Small Business*
Pub: McGraw-Hill
Ed: Jerry Katz; Richard P. Green. **Released:** January 4, 2008. **Price:** $139.43. **Description:** Students are provided a vision of small business in today's marketplace. The book focuses on the distinctive nature of starting and running small companies, including personal independence with financial security, rather than market dominance with wealth.

12231 ■ "An Equity Fund of Their Own" in *Entrepreneur* **(Vol. 35, October 2007, No. 10, pp. 68)**
Pub: Entrepreneur Media Inc.
Ed: Lee Gimpel. **Description:** About 100 new private equity funds have formed since 2002, proof that private equity investing is becoming popular among companies. There is also an increase in competition to close deals owing to the large number of investors that companies can choose; advantages of smaller funds over the larger one is explained.

12232 ■ "Essential Releases Record First Quarter Results" in *Canadian Corporate News* **(May 14, 2007)**
Pub: Comtex News Network Inc.
Description: The first quarter of 2007 saw record financial performance despite numerous challenges for Essential Energy Services Trust. Statistical data included.

12233 ■ "ETF Score Card" in *Barron's* **(Vol. 89, July 13, 2009, No. 28, pp. 51)**
Pub: Dow Jones & Co., Inc.
Description: Statistical table is presented which shows the net assets of various exchange-traded funds is presented. The table also shows the total return of these funds up to a three-year time period.

12234 ■ "European Stocks on Deck" in *Barron's* **(Vol. 89, July 27, 2009, No. 30, pp. M7)**
Pub: Dow Jones & Co., Inc.
Ed: Vito J. Racanelli. **Description:** European stocks are cheap and these trade at a discount to U.S. equities rarely seen in the past 40 years. This represents an opportunity for Americans and trends show that Europe's stocks outperform when there is a discrepancy between the price to earnings ratio in European stocks versus U.S. stocks and when sentiment on European equities are downbeat.

12235 ■ "Europe's Meltdown" in *Canadian Business* **(Vol. 83, June 15, 2010, No. 10, pp. 76)**
Pub: Rogers Media Ltd.
Ed: Bryan Borzykowski. **Description:** As European countries such as Greece, Spain, and Portugal struggle with debt problems, it is worth noting that its equities trade at a 30 percent discount to the U.S. and that a 10 percent drop in the Euro translates to a

10 percent rise in profitability for exporters. Investors may also want to focus on business-to-business operations rather than consumer-focused ones.

12236 ■ "Even Gold Gets Tarnished When Everyone Wants Cash" in *Globe & Mail* **(February 28, 2007, pp. B1)**
Pub: CTVglobemedia Publishing Inc.
Ed: John Partridge. **Description:** The impact of fall in Chinese equities on the United States stock market and metal prices, including gold, is discussed.

12237 ■ "Everyone Out of the Pool" in *Barron's* **(Vol. 89, July 20, 2009, No. 29, pp. 18)**
Pub: Dow Jones & Co., Inc.
Ed: Sandra Ward. **Description:** Shares of Pool Corp. could drop as continued weakness in the housing market weakens the market for swimming pool equipment. The company's shares are trading at $18.29, about 20 times projected 2009 earnings of $0.91 a share.

12238 ■ "The Evolution of Corporate Social Responsibility" in *Business Horizons* **(November-December 2007, pp. 449)**
Pub: Elsevier Technology Publications
Ed: Philip L. Cochran. **Description:** Corporate social responsibility is now perceived as vital in enhancing the profitability of businesses while improving their reputation. It has changed business practices such as philanthropy, investment, and entrepreneurship.

12239 ■ "Expect a Rally as Waders Dive In" in *Barron's* **(Vol. 89, July 20, 2009, No. 29, pp. 11)**
Pub: Dow Jones & Co., Inc.
Ed: Vito J. Racanelli. **Description:** US stock markets may experience a rally in the autumn of 2009 as skeptical investors start to return to the market. The Standard & Poor's Index may jump to the 1025-1050 point levels during this rally.

12240 ■ "Experts: Market Shaky But Resilient" in *The Business Journal-Serving Metropolitan Kansas City* **(Vol. 27, September 19, 2008, No. 1)**
Pub: American City Business Journals, Inc.
Ed: Steve Vockrodt. **Description:** Investment advisers believe that the local investors in Kansas City who have a long-term approach towards their portfolios may come out even or even experience gains despite the Wall Street financial crisis. The impacts of the crisis are expected to take time to reach the area of Kansas City. The potential impacts of the Wall Street meltdown are examined further.

12241 ■ *Facing Financial Dysfunction*
Pub: Infinity Publishing
Ed: Bert Whitehead. **Released:** April 2004. **Description:** Handbook to help individuals manage their finances, investments, taxes and retirement.

12242 ■ "Fairfax Announces Acquisition of William Ashley" in *Benzinga.com* **(August 16, 2011)**
Pub: Benzinga.com
Ed: Benzinga Staff. **Description:** Fairfax Financial Holdings Limited acquired the family-owned William Ashley China company, leader within the dinnerware and wedding registry industries and was the first company in North America to introduce a computerized wedding registry system.

12243 ■ "Falling Local Executive Pay Could Suggest a Trend" in *Tampa Bay Business Journal* **(Vol. 30, January 15, 2010, No. 4, pp. 1)**
Pub: American City Business Journals
Ed: Margie Manning. **Description:** Tampa Bay, Florida-based Raymond James Financial Inc. and MarineMax Inc.'s proxy statements have shown the decreasing compensation of the companies' highest paid executives. The falling trend in executive compensation was a result of intensified shareholder scrutiny and the economy.

12244 ■ "Falling Markets' Nastiest Habits" in *Barron's* **(Vol. 88, July 7, 2008, No. 27, pp. 7)**
Pub: Dow Jones & Co., Inc.
Ed: Michael Santoli. **Description:** US market conditions reflect a bear market, with the S&P 500 index falling 20 percent below its recent high as of June 2008. The bear market is expected to persist in the immediate future, although bear market rallies are likely to occur.

12245 ■ "Falling Share Prices Will Convince Big Oil Producers to Pay Up to Drill" in *Globe & Mail* **(April 21, 2007, pp. B1)**
Pub: CTVglobemedia Publishing Inc.
Ed: Boyd Erman. **Description:** The effect of the increase in operational costs and the decline in share prices, on the exploration of petroleum deposits in Canada, is described.

12246 ■ *A Family Matter: A Guide to Operating Your Personal Estate*
Pub: Brown Books Publishing Group
Ed: William A. Verkest. **Released:** May 2003. **Price:** $22.95 **Description:** Guidebook to financial management of personal assets is presented. Important documents must be maintained in a safe, secure place for family members or attorneys to access when necessary. The author suggests that a personal diary be kept with important information regarding records of investment accounts and financial summaries for every year in order to calculate taxes and manage financial matters more efficiently.

12247 ■ "Family Matters: Founding Family Firms and Corporate Political Activity" in *Business and Society* **(December 2007, pp. 395-428)**
Pub: Sage Publications USA
Ed: Michael Hadani. **Description:** The impact of publicly traded family founding firms and their inclination for corporate political activity is examined. Publicly traded family founding firms are more predisposed to engage in corporate political activity when the founder is in an executive position. Details of these findings are reported.

12248 ■ "Fannie and Freddie: How They'll Change" in *Business Week* **(September 22, 2008, No. 4100, pp. 30)**
Pub: McGraw-Hill Companies, Inc.
Ed: Jane Sasseen. **Description:** Three possible outcomes of the fate of struggling mortgage giants Freddie Mac and Fannie Mae after the government bailout are outlined.

12249 ■ "Fast Revival Unlikely For Indian 'Net Stocks" in *Barron's* **(Vol. 88, July 7, 2008, No. 27, pp. 12)**
Pub: Dow Jones & Co., Inc.
Ed: Leslie P. Norton. **Description:** Shares of Indian Internet companies Rediff.com and Sify are not likely to stage a rebound due to weak financial results. Rediff.com shares have declined 39.2 percent in 2008, while Sify shares are down 35.8 percent.

12250 ■ "February Hot for Mutual Fund Sales" in *Globe & Mail* **(March 3, 2006, pp. B10)**
Pub: CTVglobemedia Publishing Inc.
Ed: Keith Damsell. **Description:** The details on Canadian mutual fund sector, which posted $4.7 billion for February 2005, are presented.

12251 ■ "The Fed Still Has Ammunition" in *Barron's* **(Vol. 90, August 30, 2010, No. 35, pp. M9)**
Pub: Barron's Editorial & Corporate Headquarters
Ed: Randall W. Forsyth. **Description:** Federal Reserve chairman Ben Bernanke said the agency still has tools to combat deflation and a second downturn but these strategies are not needed at this time. The prospects of the Federal Open Market Committee's purchasing of treasuries are also discussed.

12252 ■ "Fed Tackles Bear of a Crisis" in *Barron's* **(Vol. 88, March 17, 2008, No. 11, pp. M10)**
Pub: Dow Jones & Company, Inc.
Ed: Randall W. Forsyth. **Description:** Emergency funding package for Bear Stearns from the Federal Reserve Bank of New York through JPMorgan Chase

is one of the steps taken by the central bank shore up bank liquidity. Prior to the emergency funding, the central bank announced the Term Securities Lending Facility to allow dealers to borrow easily saleable Treasuries in exchange for less-liquid issues.

12253 ■ "Federal Bailout, Three Years Later" in *Business Owner* **(Vol. 35, September-October 2011, No. 5, pp. 6)**
Pub: DL Perkins Company
Description: State of the economy and small business sector three years after the government stimulus and bailout programs were instituted.

12254 ■ "Fees Come Down; Markets Come Down More" in *Barron's* **(Vol. 89, July 13, 2009, No. 28, pp. L8)**
Pub: Dow Jones & Co., Inc.
Ed: J.R. Brandstrader. **Description:** Investors spent less on mutual fund fees in 2009 than they did in the last 25 years. These fees include administration, accounting, and legal expense. Despite the popularity of money market funds which has contributed to this decline, the short-term yields of these funds fell in the last year.

12255 ■ "Fertilizer for Growth" in *Canadian Business* **(Vol. 83, September 14, 2010, No. 15, pp. 76)**
Pub: Rogers Media Ltd.
Ed: Bryan Borzykowski. **Description:** Australian-based BHP Billiton launches a C$38.5 billion hostile takeover bid for Saskatchewan-based Potash Corporation and some investors immediately bought Potash stock at C$130. However, Potash has resisted BHP's offer and announced a plan to try to stop the deal.

12256 ■ "A Few Points of Contention" in *Barron's* **(Vol. 88, July 14, 2008, No. 28, pp. 3)**
Pub: Dow Jones & Co., Inc.
Ed: Michael Santoli. **Description:** Headline inflation tends to revert to the lower core inflation, which excludes food and energy in its calculation over long periods. Prominent private equity figures believe that regulators should allow more than the de facto 10 percent to 25 percent limit of commercial banks to hasten the refunding of the financial sector.

12257 ■ "Fieldbrook Foods Acquired By Private Equity Firm" in *Ice Cream Reporter* **(Vol. 23, October 20, 2010, No. 11, pp. 1)**
Pub: Ice Cream Reporter
Description: Fieldbrook Foods Corporation, manufacturer of frozen novelty and ice cream products was acquired by Chicago-based private equity firm Arbor Investments. Arbor partnered with Herman 'Bing' Graffunder, a long-term dairy industry partner, in its acquisition of Fieldbrook.

12258 ■ "Fifth Third CEO Kabat: A World of Difference" in *Business Courier* **(Vol. 26, January 1, 2010, No. 37, pp. 1)**
Pub: American City Business Journals, Inc.
Ed: Steve Watkins. **Description:** CEO Kevin Kabat of Cincinnati-based Fifth Third Bancorp believes that the bank's assets of $111 billion and stock value of more than $10 indicate the recovery from the low stock prices posted in February 2009. He attributes the recovery from the federal government's stress test finding in May 2009 that Fifth Third needs to generate $1.1 billion.

12259 ■ "Fifth Third Spinoff" in *Business Courier* **(Vol. 27, July 16, 2010, No. 11, pp. 1)**
Pub: Business Courier
Ed: Dan Monk, Steve Watkins. **Description:** Electronic-funds transfer company Fifth Third Solutions (FTPS), a spinoff of Fifth Third Bancorp, is seeking as much as 200,000 square feet of new office space in Ohio. The bank's sale of 51 percent ownership stake to Boston-based Advent International Corporation has paved the way for the growth of FTPS. How real estate brokers' plans have responded to FTPS' growth mode is discussed.

12260 ■ "The Final Say" in *Hispanic Business* **(Vol. 30, March 2008, No. 3, pp. 52)**
Pub: Hispanic Business
Ed: Hildy Medina. **Description:** Vice-Chairwoman of the pensions and investments committee and Illinois State Senator Iris Martinez is the first Hispanic

woman to be elected Senator and is advocating for pension funds to include Hispanic money managers and minority- and female-owned businesses in the investment plans.

12261 ■ "Finalist: BlackEagle Partners L.L.C." in *Crain's Detroit Business* **(Vol. 24, March 24, 2008, No. 12, pp. 12)**
Pub: Crain Communications, Inc.
Ed: Brent Snavely. **Description:** Overview of private-equity firm, BlackEagle Partners L.L.C., an upstart that acquired Rockford Products Corp. in order to improve the performance of the company who does business with several major tier-one automotive suppliers; Rockford manufactures highly engineered chassis and suspension components for automakers and the automotive aftermarket.

12262 ■ "Finally, Justice" in *Canadian Business* **(Vol. 82, April 27, 2009, No. 7, pp. 12)**
Pub: Rogers Media
Ed: John Gray. **Description:** Former investment adviser Alex Winch feels that he was vindicated with the Canadian Court's ruling that Livent Inc. founders Garth Drabinsky and Myron Gottlieb were guilty of fraud. Drabinsky filed a libel case on Winch over Winch's letter that complained over Livent's accounting procedures. Winch also criticized the inconsistent accounting during Drabinsky's term as chief executive of another firm.

12263 ■ "The Finance Function In A Global Corporation" in *Harvard Business Review* **(Vol. 86, July-August 2008, No. 8, pp. 108)**
Pub: Harvard Business School Press
Ed: Mihir A. Desai. **Description:** Designing and implementing a successful finance function in a global setting is discussed. Additional topics include the internal capital market, managing risk and budgeting capital internationally.

12264 ■ "Financial Education: Boomer's Spending Hurts Retirement" in *Employee Benefit News* **(Vol. 25, November 1, 2011, No. 14, pp. 18)**
Pub: SourceMedia Inc.
Ed: Ann Marsh. **Description:** Financial planners and employers need to educate clients and employees about retirement planning. Boomers are spending money that should be saved for their retirement.

12265 ■ *Financing Growth: Strategies, Capital Structure, and M and A Transactions*
Pub: John Wiley & Sons, Inc.
Ed: Kenneth H. Marks, Larry E. Robbins, Gonzalo Fernandez, John P. Funkhouser, D.L. Williams. **Released:** September 1, 2009. **Price:** $95.00. **Description:** Guide for emerging growth and middle market companies includes information to help understand and apply the basics of corporate finance using empirical data and actual company cases to illustrate capital structures and financing approaches.

12266 ■ *Financing Your Small Business*
Pub: Barron's Educational Series, Incorporated
Ed: Robert Walter. **Released:** December 2003. **Description:** Tips for raising venture capital, dealing with bank officials, and initiating public offerings of stock shares for small business.

12267 ■ "Finding Good Bets Down on the Farm" in *Crain's Chicago Business* **(Vol. 31, March 24, 2008, No. 12, pp. 4)**
Pub: Crain Communications, Inc.
Ed: Daniel Rome Levine. **Description:** Interview with money manager Jeff James, the portfolio manager for Driehaus Capital Management LLC, who discusses the Federal Reserve and recommends several companies in which to make investments.

12268 ■ "Finding the Voice of the Marketplace" in *Mergers & Acquisitions: The Dealmaker's Journal* **(March 1, 2008)**
Pub: SourceMedia, Inc.
Description: Companies oftentimes are unable to achieve their strategic goals through acquisition due, in part, to not understanding the target's market and its position in the marketplace.

12269 ■ **"Finger-Pointing Time" in** *Barron's* **(Vol. 88, March 10, 2008, No. 10, pp. 9)**
Pub: Dow Jones & Company, Inc.
Ed: Michael Santoli. **Description:** Discusses who is to blame for the financial crisis brought about by the credit crunch in the United States; the country's financial markets will eventually digest this crisis but will bottom out first before the situation improves.

12270 ■ **"First Financial Aiming for Banking Big Leagues" in** *Business Courier* **(Vol. 26, December 4, 2009, No. 32, pp. 1)**
Pub: American City Business Journals, Inc.
Ed: Steve Watkins. **Description:** First Financial Bancorp could dominate the community banking market of Greater Cincinnati after buying failed banks with the supervision of the FDIC. Details of the transactions are presented.

12271 ■ **"First the Merger: Then, The Culture Clash. How To Fix the Little Things That Can Tear a Company Apart" in** *Inc.* **(January 2008)**
Pub: Gruner & Jahr USA Publishing
Ed: Elaine Appleton Grant. **Description:** Ways three CEOs handled the culture classes that followed after company mergers; companies profiled include Fuel Outdoor, an outdoor advertising company; Nelson, an interior design and architecture firm; and Beber Silverstein, an ad agency.

12272 ■ **"First U.S. :M-Press Tiger with Inline Screen Printing" in** *American Printer* **(Vol. 128, June 1, 2011, No. 6)**
Pub: Penton Media Inc.
Description: Graphic Tech located in California bought :M-Press Tiger, the first in North America with an inline screen printing unit.

12273 ■ **"FIS-Metavante Deal Paying Off for Many" in** *Business Journal-Milwaukee* **(Vol. 28, December 17, 2010, No. 11, pp. A1)**
Pub: Milwaukee Business Journal
Ed: Rich Kirchen. **Description:** Jacksonville, Florida-based Fidelity National Information Services Inc., also known as FIS, has remained committed to Milwaukee, Wisconsin more than a year after purchasing Metavante Technologies Inc. FIS has transferred several operations into Metropolitan Milwaukee and has continued its contribution to charitable organizations in the area.

12274 ■ *The Flaw of Averages: Why We Underestimate Risk in the Face of Uncertainty*
Pub: John Wiley & Sons, Inc.
Ed: Sam L. Savage. **Released:** June 3, 2009. **Price:** $22.95. **Description:** Personal and business plans are based on uncertainties on a daily basis. The common avoidable mistake individuals make in assessing risk in the face of uncertainty is defined. The explains why plans based on average assumptions are wrong, on average, in areas as diverse as finance, healthcare, accounting, the war on terror, and climate change.

12275 ■ **"A Flawed Yardstick for Banks" in** *Barron's* **(Vol. 88, July 14, 2008, No. 28, pp. M6)**
Pub: Dow Jones & Co., Inc.
Ed: Arindam Nag. **Description:** Return on equity is no longer the best measure for investors to judge banks by in a post-subprime-crises world. Investors should consider the proportion of a bank's total assets that are considered risky and look out for any write-downs of goodwill when judging a bank's financial health.

12276 ■ **"Florida's Housing Gloom May Add To Woes of National City" in** *Crain's Cleveland Business* **(Vol. 28, October 29, 2007, No. 43, pp. 1)**
Pub: Crain Communications, Inc.
Ed: Shawn A. Turner. **Description:** Already suffering by bad loans in the troubled mortgage market, National City Corp. is attempting to diversify its geographic presence beyond the slow-growth industrial Midwest by acquiring two Florida firms. Analysts worry that the acquisitions may end up making National City vulnerable to a takeover if the housing slump continues and credit quality becomes more of an issue for the bank.

12277 ■ **"Flying High?" in** *Canadian Business* **(Vol. 80, April 9, 2007, No. 8, pp. 42)**
Pub: Rogers Media
Ed: Thomas Watson. **Description:** The increase in Bombardier Inc.'s income by 30 percent to $112 million and increase in its share prices are discussed. The caution of analysts about its accounting methods that may adversely hit the company in future, too is discussed.

12278 ■ *Fooling Some of the People All of the Time*
Pub: John Wiley & Sons, Inc.
Ed: David Einhorn. **Released:** March 10, 2010. **Price:** $29.95. **Description:** A chronicle of the ongoing saga between author, David Einhorn's hedge fund, Greenlight Capital, and Allied Capital, a leader in the private finance industry.

12279 ■ *Fool's Gold: How the Bold Dream of a Small Tribe at J.P. Morgan Was Corrupted by Wall Street Greed*
Pub: Free Press
Ed: Gillian Tett. **Released:** 2009. **Price:** $26.00. **Description:** An explanation of how swaps and CDOs, which were invented by J.P. Morgan, ended up creating more risk not controlling it.

12280 ■ **"For Baxter, A Lingering PR Problem; Ongoing Focus On Heparin Deaths Ups Heat On CEO" in** *Crain's Chicago Business* **(April 21, 2008)**
Pub: Crain Communications, Inc.
Ed: Mike Colias. **Description:** Baxter International Inc.'s recall of the blood-thinning medication heparin has exposed the company to costly litigation and put the perils of overseas drug manufacturing in the spotlight. Wall Street investors predict that an indefinite halt in production of the drug should not hurt the company's bottom line since heparin represents a tiny sliver of the business. Since Baxter began recalling the drug in January its shares have continued to outpace most other medical stocks.

12281 ■ **"For Buffet Fans, the Price Is Right" in** *Barron's* **(Vol. 89, July 13, 2009, No. 28, pp. 17)**
Pub: Dow Jones & Co., Inc.
Ed: Andrew Bary. **Description:** Shares of Warren Buffett's Berkshire Hathaway have fallen to $85,000 and these are cheap since they are trading at just 1.2 times estimated book value and are well below its peak of $149,000. One fan of the stock expects it to top $110,000 in the next year from June 2009.

12282 ■ **"For Gilead, Growth Beyond AIDS" in** *Barron's* **(Vol. 88, June 30, 2008, No. 26, pp. 18)**
Pub: Dow Jones & Co., Inc.
Ed: Jay Palmer. **Description:** First-quarter 2008 revenue for Gilead Sciences grew by 22 percent and an earnings gain of 19 percent thanks to their HIV-treatment drugs that comprised over two-thirds of the company's sales in 2007. An analyst has a 12-month target from June, 2008 of 65 per share. The factors behind the company's prospects are also discussed.

12283 ■ **"For Kenwood, Cavalry Could Be Close" in** *Business Courier* **(Vol. 26, October 2, 2009, No. 23, pp. 1)**
Pub: American City Business Journals, Inc.
Ed: Dan Monk. **Description:** New York-based Black-Rock Inc. is believed to be participating in the settlement liens at Kenwood Towne Place, a mixed-use development site in Cincinnati, Ohio. BlackRock may play a key role as an advisor or investor representative to an unnamed investors.

12284 ■ **"For Sale: Old Florida Panache" in** *The Business Journal-Serving Greater Tampa Bay* **(Vol. 28, July 4, 2008, No. 28, pp. 1)**
Pub: American City Business Journals, Inc.
Ed: Jane Meinhardt. **Description:** Linger Lodge, owned by real estate investor and developer Martin Kaplan and Senator Michael Bennett, is now on the market for a sealed bid process facilitated by Levin & Associates. The business partners bought the riverfront property for about $3 million in 2005. Other details on the sale of the property are presented.

12285 ■ **"Ford Canada's Edsel of a Year: Revenue Plummets 24 Percent in '05" in** *Globe & Mail* **(February 2, 2006, pp. B1)**
Pub: CTVglobemedia Publishing Inc.
Ed: Greg Keenan. **Description:** Ford Motor Company of Canada Ltd. posted 24% decline in revenues for 2005. The drop in earnings is attributed to plant shutdown in Oaksville, Canada.

12286 ■ **"Foreign (In)Direct Investment and Corporate Taxation" in** *Canadian Journal of Economics* **(Vol. 44, November 2011, No. 4, pp. 1497)**
Pub: Blackwell Publishers Ltd.
Ed: Georg Wamser. **Description:** Foreign investments of multinational firms are often complex in that they involve conduit entities. In particular, a multinational can pursue either a direct or an indirect investment strategy, where the latter involves an intermediate corporate entity and is associated with enhanced opportunities for international tax planning. As a consequence, in the case of indirect investments, the role of corporate taxation in destination countries may change. An investigation into the effects of corporate taxation on foreign investment decisions of German multinationals, taking explicitly into account that firms choose in a first stage the investment regime, (direct vs. indirect) is provided.

12287 ■ **"Former Mayor Driving $500 Million Real Estate Equity Fund" in** *The Business Journal - Serving Phoenix and the Valley of the Sun* **(Vol. 28, August 15, 2008, No. 50, pp. 1)**
Pub: American City Business Journals, Inc.
Ed: Jan Buchholz. **Description:** Paul John, the former mayor of Phoenix, is establishing a $500 million real estate asset management fund. The fund is dubbed Southwest Next Capital Management and has attracted three local partners, namely Joseph Meyer, Jay Michalowski, and James Mullany, who all have background in finance and construction.

12288 ■ **"The Four Cheapest Plays in Emerging Markets" in** *Barron's* **(Vol. 89, July 27, 2009, No. 30, pp. 34)**
Pub: Dow Jones & Co., Inc.
Ed: Lawrence C. Strauss. **Description:** Portfolio manager Arjun Divecha of the GMO Emerging Markets III Fund says that the main thing in investing in emerging markets is getting the country right since getting it wrong makes it harder to add value. Divecha says that the four countries that they are positive on are Turkey, Russia, South Korea, and Thailand.

12289 ■ **"Franchising Lures Boomers" in** *Business Journal-Portland* **(Vol. 24, November 9, 2007, No. 36, pp. 1)**
Pub: American City Business Journals, Inc.
Ed: Wendy Culverwell. **Description:** Popularity of franchising has increased, and investors belonging to the baby boom generation contribute largely to this growth. The number of aging baby boomers is also increasing, particularly in Oregon, which means further growth of franchises can be expected. Reasons why franchising is a good investment for aging baby boomers are given.

12290 ■ **"Francois Joly" in** *Canadian Business* **(Vol. 79, September 11, 2006, No. 18, pp. 146)**
Pub: Rogers Media
Ed: Andy Holloway. **Description:** President and chief operating officer of Desjardins Financial Security, Francois Joly speaks about his interests and emphasizes the need to be passionate about work.

12291 ■ **"Fraser and Neave Acquires King's Creameries" in** *Ice Cream Reporter* **(Vol. 23, November 20, 2010, No. 12, pp. 1)**
Pub: Ice Cream Reporter
Description: Fraser and Neave Ltd., a Singapore-based consumer products marketer, has entered a conditional agreement to acquire all outstanding shares of King's Creameries, the leading manufacturer and distributor of frozen desserts.

12292 ■ "Fraud Alleged at Norshield; Investors Out $215 Million" in *Globe & Mail* (March 8, 2007, pp. B1)
Pub: CTVglobemedia Publishing Inc.

Ed: Paul Waldie. **Description:** The investigation of the diversion of $215 million in investors' money by the management of Norshield Asset Management (Canada) Ltd. is described.

12293 ■ "Freak Weather Dampens Intrawest Forecast" in *Globe & Mail* (February 8, 2006, pp. B3)
Pub: CTVglobemedia Publishing Inc.

Ed: Peter Kennedy. **Description:** Intrawest Corp. dropped its earnings forecast by 7 percent. The impact of weather on earnings is discussed.

12294 ■ "Friends With Money" in *Canadian Business* (Vol. 81, Summer 2008, No. 9, pp. 22)
Pub: Rogers Media Ltd.

Description: Two of the most well connected managers in Canadian capital markets Rob Farquharson and Brian Gibson will launch Panoply Capital Asset Management in June. The investment management company aims to raise a billion dollars from institutions and high-net worth individuals.

12295 ■ "From Buyout to Busted" in *Business Week* (September 22, 2008, No. 4100, pp. 18)
Pub: McGraw-Hill Companies, Inc.

Ed: Emily Thornton; Deborah Stead. **Description:** Bankruptcy filings by private equity-backed companies are at a record high with 134 American firms taken private (or invested in) by buyout firms that have filed for protection this year under Chapter 11; this is 91 percent higher when the previous year, which had set a record when 70 of such companies filed for protection under Chapter 11.

12296 ■ "From Fastenal, a Boost" in *Barron's* (Vol. 89, July 20, 2009, No. 29, pp. M13)
Pub: Dow Jones & Co., Inc.

Ed: Shirley A. Lazo. **Description:** Fastenal increased its semi-annual common payout from $0.35 to $0.37 a share. Core Laboratories declared a special dividend of $0.75 a share along with its quarterly payout of $0.10. Ryder System and Landstar System raised their payouts to $0.23 and $0.045 a share respectively.

12297 ■ "The Frugal Billionaire" in *Canadian Business* (Vol. 79, Winter 2006, No. 24, pp. 63)
Pub: Rogers Media

Ed: Joe Castaldo. **Description:** The achievements of David Cheriton are described, along with his investments in various firms, including Google Inc.

12298 ■ "Full-Court Press for Apple" in *Barron's* (Vol. 88, March 24, 2008, No. 12, pp. 47)
Pub: Dow Jones & Company, Inc.

Ed: Mark Veverka. **Description:** Apple Inc. is facing more intellectual property lawsuits in 2008, with 30 patent lawsuits filed compared to 15 in 2007 and nine in 2006. The lawsuits, which involve products such as the iPod and the iPhone, present some concern for Apple's shareholders.

12299 ■ "Funds "Friend" Facebook" in *Barron's* (Vol. 89, July 27, 2009, No. 30, pp. 30)
Pub: Dow Jones & Co., Inc.

Ed: Leslie P. Norton. **Description:** Mutual-fund companies are the latest entrants to the "social media" space and several companies have already set up Facebook and Twitter pages. The use of this technology pose special challenges for compliance and regulators especially since the Financial Industry Regulatory Authority reminds companies that advertising, sales and literature are governed by regulations.

12300 ■ "The Future of Private Equity" in *Canadian Business* (Vol. 80, March 26, 2007, No. 7, pp. 19)
Pub: Rogers Media

Ed: Jack Mintz. **Description:** The impact growing Canadian economy and competition in global business on the performance of private equity funds is analyzed.

12301 ■ "Future's Brighter for Financial Stocks" in *Barron's* (Vol. 89, July 20, 2009, No. 29, pp. 14)
Pub: Dow Jones & Co., Inc.

Ed: Jacqueline Doherty. **Description:** Shares of US financial companies are projected to rise as their earnings start to normalize. Earnings of these companies have been hurt by credit losses but have been bolstered by one-time gains.

12302 ■ "Futures Shock for the CME" in *Crain's Chicago Business* (Vol. 31, November 10, 2008, No. 45, pp. 8)
Pub: Crain Communications, Inc.

Ed: Ann Saphir. **Description:** Chicago-based CME Group Inc., the largest futures exchange operator in the U.S., is facing a potentially radically altered regulatory landscape as Congress weighs sweeping reform of financial oversight. The possible merger of the CFTC and the Securities and Exchange Commission are among CME's concerns. Other details of possible regulatory measures are provided.

12303 ■ "Futures of the Street" in *Barron's* (Vol. 88, June 30, 2008, No. 26, pp. 27)
Pub: Dow Jones & Co., Inc.

Ed: Michael Santoli. **Description:** Prospects of the securities industry in terms of jobs and profit sources are discussed. Suggestions on what the industry needs with regards to its use of capital are also discussed.

12304 ■ "Gas Glut Pummels Prices" in *Barron's* (Vol. 89, July 27, 2009, No. 30, pp. M8)
Pub: Dow Jones & Co., Inc.

Ed: Christine Buurma. **Description:** Natural gas-futures prices have fallen 73 percent and the glut of output from onshore gas fields and the weak demand signals that a rebound is not near. An analyst expects U.S. production to show increasingly steep declines but the oversupply situation is not good for prices.

12305 ■ "Gateway Delays Start" in *The Business Journal-Serving Metropolitan Kansas City* (Vol. 27, October 31, 2008, No. 8, pp. 1)
Pub: American City Business Journals, Inc.

Ed: Rob Roberts. **Description:** Economic problems caused, in part, by the Wall Street crisis has resulted in the setback of a proposed mixed-use redevelopment project, The Gateway. The $307 million project, which includes the Kansas Aquarium, will be delayed due to financing problems. Details of the project are given.

12306 ■ "GE Looking to Extend Hot Streak" in *Business Courier* (Vol. 24, January 25, 2008, No. 42, pp. 1)
Pub: American City Business Journals, Inc.

Ed: John Newberry. **Description:** GE Aviation has enjoyed strong revenues and sales due to increase aircraft engine orders. It has an engine backlog order of $19 million as of the end of 2007. Data on the aviation company's revenues, operating profit and total engine orders for the year 2004 to 2007 are presented.

12307 ■ "GeckoSystems Reduces Sensor Fusion Costs Due to Elder Care Robot Trials" in *Internet Wire* (December 14, 2010)
Pub: Comtex

Description: GeckoSystems International Corporation has been able to reduce the cost of its sensor fusion system while maintaining reliability and performance. The firm's ongoing first in-home elder care robot trials have sparked interest regarding its business model, technologies available for licensing, and joint domestic and international ventures.

12308 ■ "General Motors Can't Kick Incentives-But They Work" in *Advertising Age* (Vol. 79, July 7, 2008, No. 26, pp. 3)
Pub: Crain Communications, Inc.

Ed: Jean Halliday. **Description:** General Motors Corp. was able to maintain their market share just as Toyota Motor Corp. was beginning to pass the manufacturer; GM lured in customers with a sales incentive that they heavily advertised and subsequently helped build demand; investors, however, were not impressed and GM shares were hammered to their lowest point in 50 years after analysts speculated the company might go bankrupt.

12309 ■ "Generation Y - An Opportunity for a Fresh Financial Start" in (September 11, 2010, pp. 241)
Pub: VerticalNews

Description: Eleanor Blayney, the consumer advocate for the Certified Financial Planner Board of Standards, offers a financial strategy for Generation Y individuals starting their financial planning. The first segment of the non-profit's Lifelong Financial Strategies initiative is called 'Starting Out', and focuses on ways Generation Y people can avoid pitfalls of earlier generations by making smart financial decisions.

12310 ■ "Genzyme: Underrated Oversold" in *Barron's* (Vol. 88, March 24, 2008, No. 12, pp. 58)
Pub: Dow Jones & Company, Inc.

Ed: Johanna Bennett. **Description:** Shares of bio-technology company Genzyme appear oversold and underrated at their $71.86 level. The company's finances are on a solid foundation, with revenues over $3.8 billion in 2007 and forecasts of $4.5-4.7 billion in revenue for 2008.

12311 ■ "Get It While Its Hot" in *Canadian Business* (Vol. 80, January 15, 2007, No. 2, pp. 49)
Pub: Rogers Media

Ed: John Gray. **Description:** The rise in the demand for processed uranium and increase in the number of investors interested to invest in metal industries is discussed.

12312 ■ "Get Off The Rollercoaster" in *Michigan Vue* (Vol. 13, July-August 2008, No. 4, pp. 19)
Pub: Entrepreneur Media Inc.

Ed: Donald N. Hobley Jr. **Description:** Benefits of creating and implementing a solid financial plan during these rocky economic times are examined. Things to keep in mind before meeting with a financial planner include risk assessment, investment goals, the length of time required to meet those goals and the amount of money one has available to invest.

12313 ■ "Getting In on the Ground Floor" in *Barron's* (Vol. 89, July 27, 2009, No. 30, pp. 32)
Pub: Dow Jones & Co., Inc.

Ed: Jacqueline Doherty. **Description:** Shares of Ava-lonBay Communities have fallen 61 percent in the past two and a half years to July 2009 but at $56, the stock is trading near the asset value. The shares could rise as the economy improves and if the recovery takes longer, investors will be rewarded with a yield of 3.5 percent.

12314 ■ "Getting More Out of Retirement" in *Agency Sales Magazine* (Vol. 39, November 2009, No. 10, pp. 48)
Pub: MANA

Ed: Joshua D. Mosshart. **Description:** Overview of the Tax Increase Prevention and Reconciliation Act, which lets employees convert to a Roth IRA in 2010. The benefits of conversion depend on age and wealth and it is best to consult a tax advisor to determine the best strategy for retirement planners.

12315 ■ "Giant Garages Could Rise Up Downtown" in *Business Courier* (Vol. 27, October 22, 2010, No. 25, pp. 1)
Pub: Business Courier

Ed: Dan Monk. **Description:** More than 2,500 new parking spaces could rise up to the eastern edge of downtown Cincinnati, Ohio as public and private investors collect resources for new garage projects. These projects are expected to accommodate almost 1,500 monthly parkers who will lose access at Broadway Commons due to the construction of Harrah's casino.

12316 ■ "Giants Now Admit They Roam Planet Earth; Time To Buy?" in *Barron's* **(Vol. 88, March 31, 2008, No. 13, pp. 39)**
Pub: Dow Jones & Company, Inc.
Ed: Eric J. Savitz. **Description:** Oracle's third-quarter results showed that top-line growth fell short of expectations but the company is expected to fare better than most applications companies in the downturn. Google had a flat growth in the number of people who click their online ads. The time for investors in the tech sector with a long-term horizon has arrived.

12317 ■ "Give Me Liberty With DirecTV" in *Barron's* **(Vol. 89, July 13, 2009, No. 28, pp. M5)**
Pub: Dow Jones & Co., Inc.
Ed: Fleming Meeks. **Description:** Shares of Liberty Entertainment look cheap at $25.14 and the same goes for DirecTV at $23.19. A merger between the two companies was announced and the deal will likely close by September 2009. Barclays Capital has a target of $30 for Liberty Media and $32 for DirecTV.

12318 ■ "Global Good Time" in *Canadian Business* **(Vol. 80, January 15, 2007, No. 2, pp. 53)**
Pub: Rogers Media
Ed: Thomas Watson. **Description:** Speculations on the stock prices of global emerging markets for 2007 are presented.

12319 ■ "Global Steel Makers Circle Stelco" in *Globe & Mail* **(April 19, 2007, pp. B3)**
Pub: CTVglobemedia Publishing Inc.
Ed: Greg Keenan. **Description:** The details of the take over bids offered to Stelco Inc. are presented. Due to these bids the shares of Stelco Inc rose up to 70 percent.

12320 ■ "Gold Handshake" in *Canadian Business* **(Vol. 79, September 11, 2006, No. 18, pp. 25)**
Pub: Rogers Media
Ed: John Gray. **Description:** Goldcorp Inc.'s company's planned takeover of Glamis Gold Ltd. is discussed. Implications of the merger on its investors are presented.

12321 ■ "Gold Still Has That Glitter" in *Barron's* **(Vol. 89, July 20, 2009, No. 29, pp. M8)**
Pub: Dow Jones & Co., Inc.
Ed: Allen Sykora. **Description:** Gold prices appear to be ready for an increase starting in the fall of 2009 due to an increase in demand. The price of the August 2009 gold contract fell to as low as $904.08 an ounce before recovering to $937.50.

12322 ■ "A Golden Retirement?" in *Canadian Business* **(Vol. 81, December 8, 2008, No. 21, pp. 7)**
Pub: Rogers Media Ltd.
Ed: Paul Webster. **Description:** Canada Pension Plan Investment Board (CPPIB) is believed to have suffered heavy losses in global stock markets. CPPIB has moved aggressively into stock markets after independent managers started handling the funds in 2000.

12323 ■ "Goldeye Completes Private Placement" in *Canadian Corporate News* **(May 16, 2007)**
Pub: Comtex News Network Inc.
Description: Goldeye, a Canadian mineral exploration company acquiring, exploring, and advancing properties in Chile and Canada, announced that it has completed a partially brokered private placement for gross proceeds of $1,232,660 which will be used to finance exploration on Goldeye's mineral properties in Chile and for administrative expenses, and working capital.

12324 ■ "A Good Book Is Worth a Thousand Blogs" in *Barron's* **(Vol. 88, July 14, 2008, No. 28, pp. 42)**
Pub: Dow Jones & Co., Inc.
Ed: Gene Epstein. **Description:** Nine summer book suggestions on economics are presented. The list includes 'The Revolution' by Ron Paul, 'The Forgotten Man' by Amity Shales, 'The Commitments of Traders Bible' by Stephen Briese, and 'Economic Facts and Fallacies' by Thomas Sowell.

12325 ■ "Good Going, Partners: Energy-Asset Firms Do Their Parents Proud" in *Barron's* **(Vol. 89, July 27, 2009, No. 30, pp. M8)**
Pub: Dow Jones & Co., Inc.
Ed: Shirley A. Lazo. **Description:** Four master limited partnerships boosted their dividends. Sunoco Logistics raised theirs by 11.2 percent, El Paso Pipeline by 12 percent, Holly Energy upped their dividends by a penny, and Western Gas hiked their dividend to 31 cents per unit.

12326 ■ "A Good Sign for Commercial Real Estate" in *Austin Business JournalInc.* **(Vol. 29, December 18, 2009, No. 41, pp. 1)**
Pub: American City Business Journals
Ed: Kate Harrington. **Description:** Factors that could contribute to the reemergence of the commercial mortgage-backed securities market in Texas are discussed. These securities can potentially boost the commercial real estate market statewide as well as nationwide. Commercial mortgage-backed securities origination in 2009 is worth less that $1 billion, compared with $238 billion in 2008.

12327 ■ "Good Things Happen When We Buy Local" in *Crain's Detroit Business* **(Vol. 24, October 6, 2008, No. 40, pp. 7)**
Pub: Crain Communications, Inc.
Description: Michigan is facing incredibly difficult economic times. One way in which each one of us can help the state and the businesses located here is by purchasing our goods and services from local vendors. The state Agriculture Department projected that if Michigan households earmarked $10 per week in their grocery purchases to made-in-Michigan products, this would generate $30 million a week in economic impact.

12328 ■ "Goodwill Haunts Local Companies; Bad Buyouts During Boom Times Producing Big Writedowns" in *Crain's Chicago Business* **(Apr. 28, 2008)**
Pub: Crain Communications, Inc.
Ed: Ann Saphir. **Description:** Many companies are having to face the reality that they overpaid for acquisitions made in better economic times; investors often dismiss such one-time charges as mere accounting adjustments but writeoffs related to past acquisitions can signal future problems because they mean the expected profits that justified the purchase have not materialized. Writeoffs are particularly worrisome for firms with a lot of debt and whose banks require them to have enough assets to back up their borrowings.

12329 ■ "Google's Next Stop: Below 350?" in *Barron's* **(Vol. 88, March 10, 2008, No. 10, pp. 17)**
Pub: Dow Jones & Company, Inc.
Ed: Jacqueline Doherty. **Description:** Share prices of Google Inc. are expected to drop from their level of $433 each to below $350 per share. The company is expected to miss its earnings forecast for the first quarter of 2008, and its continued aggressive spending on non-core areas will eventually bring down earnings.

12330 ■ "Government Intervention" in *Canadian Business* **(Vol. 79, November 6, 2006, No. 22, pp. 116)**
Pub: Rogers Media
Description: The effects of income trust tax on economic conditions and investment of Canada are presented.

12331 ■ "Graduates to the TSX in 2008" in *Canadian Business* **(Vol. 81, Summer 2008, No. 9, pp. 79)**
Pub: Rogers Media Ltd.
Ed: Calvin Leung. **Description:** Table showing the market capitalization and stock performance of the companies that jumped to the TSX Venture Exchange is presented. The 17 companies that made the leap to the list will have an easier time raising capital, although leeway must be made in investing since they are still new businesses.

12332 ■ "The Great Deleveraging" in *Canadian Business* **(Vol. 81, October 13, 2008, No. 17, pp. 45)**
Pub: Rogers Media Ltd.
Ed: Jeff Sanford. **Description:** 'Hell Week' of financial crisis on Wall Street is believed to have started with the downgrade of AIG Inc.'s credit rating. AIG is a major player in the credit derivatives market, and its bankruptcy would have affected firms on Wall Street.

12333 ■ "The Great Fall" in *Barron's* **(Vol. 88, March 10, 2008, No. 10, pp. 5)**
Pub: Dow Jones & Company, Inc.
Ed: Alan Abelson. **Description:** Discusses the US economy is considered to be in a recession, with the effects of the credit crisis expected to intensify as a result. Inflation is estimated at 4.3 percent in January 2008, while 63,000 jobs were lost in February 2008.

12334 ■ "The Great Moderation" in *Canadian Business* **(Vol. 80, February 12, 2007, No. 4, pp. 25)**
Pub: Rogers Media
Ed: David Wolf. **Description:** Caution over the changes to stock inventory levels and their adverse impact on the Canadian economy is discussed.

12335 ■ "Great Stocks Cheap" in *Canadian Business* **(Vol. 80, January 15, 2007, No. 2, pp. 31)**
Pub: Rogers Media
Ed: Calvin Leung. **Description:** The stock performance of top 10 international companies like Furgo, Moody's Investor Service, Adidas Group and Nestle is analyzed.

12336 ■ "Green Assets Powering Boralex Shares" in *Globe & Mail* **(March 30, 2007, pp. B10)**
Pub: CTVglobemedia Publishing Inc.
Ed: Richard Blackwell. **Description:** The impact of econ-friendly power plant portfolio on the stock performance of Kingsey Falls-based Boralex Inc. is analyzed.

12337 ■ "The Green Trap" in *Canadian Business* **(Vol. 80, April 9, 2007, No. 8, pp. 19)**
Pub: Rogers Media
Ed: Al Rosen. **Description:** Expert advice to companies on investing in environmental-friendly measures is presented.

12338 ■ "Greenberg Sues U.S. Over AIG Rescue" in *Wall Street Journal Eastern Edition* **(November 22 , 2011, pp. C3)**
Pub: Dow Jones & Company Inc.
Ed: Liam Pleven, Serena Ng. **Description:** Former Chief Executive Officer of American International Group Inc., Maurice R. 'Hank' Greenberg, has filed a lawsuit against the United States and the Federal Reserve Bank of New York on behalf of shareholders and his company, Starr International Company Inc., claiming that the government was wrong in taking control of the insurance giant and used it to move tens of millions of dollars to the trading partners of AIG.

12339 ■ "Greener Pastures" in *Canadian Business* **(Vol. 80, February 12, 2007, No. 4, pp. 69)**
Pub: Rogers Media
Ed: Thomas Watson. **Description:** The effort of venture capitalists, including chief executive officer of Fun Technologies Lorne Abony, in successful running of several ventures in diverse fields is discussed.

12340 ■ "A Greenish Light for Financial-Sector Funds" in *Barron's* **(Vol. 88, March 24, 2008, No. 12, pp. 52)**
Pub: Dow Jones & Company, Inc.

Ed: Tom Sullivan. **Description:** Financial sector funds have lost value in 2008 through 17 March, and investors are advised to reduce investments in the financial sector. Exchange-traded funds present a good way to own financial stocks.

12341 ■ "Greg Stringham" in *Canadian Business* **(Vol. 81, March 3, 2008, No. 3, pp. 8)**
Pub: Rogers Media

Ed: Michelle Magnan. **Description:** Canadian Association of Petroleum Producers' Greg Stringham thinks that the new royalty plan will result in companies pulling out their investments for Alberta's conventional oil and gas sector. Stringham adds that Alberta is losing its competitive advantage and companies must study their cost profiles to retrieve that advantage. The effects of the royalty system on Alberta's economy are examined further.

12342 ■ "A Gripping Read: Bargains & Noble" in *Barron's* **(Vol. 88, March 17, 2008, No. 11, pp. 20)**
Pub: Dow Jones & Company, Inc.

Ed: Jonathan R. Laing. **Description:** Barnes & Noble's earnings forecast for the fiscal year ending in January, 2008 to be $1.70 to $1.90 per share which is way lower than the $2.12 analyst consensus. The company also said that sales at stores one-year old or older dropped 0.5 percent in the fourth quarter. However, the shares are now cheap at 4.9 times enterprise value with some analysts putting a price target of 41 per share.

12343 ■ "Grote Company Puts Final Wrap on Sandwich-Making Line" in *Business First-Columbus* **(October 26, 2007, pp. A1)**
Pub: American City Business Journals, Inc.

Ed: Dan Eaton. **Description:** Grote Company acquired Oxfordshire, England-based Advanced Food Technology Ltd., giving the Ohio-based food cutting equipment company a manufacturing base in Europe. This is the company's second deal in four months. Details on Grote Company's plan to tap into the prepared fresh sandwich market are discussed.

12344 ■ *Grow Your Money: 101 Easy Tips to Plan, Save and Invest*
Pub: HarperBusiness

Ed: Jonathan D. Pond. **Released:** December 2007. **Price:** $26.95. **Description:** In what should be required reading for anyone entering the work world, the author offers helpful investment and financial definitions, debt-management strategies, retirement and home ownerships considerations and more.

12345 ■ "Growing Subscriber Base Fuels Roger's Rosy Outlook for 2007" in *Globe & Mail* **(February 16, 2007, pp. B3)**
Pub: CTVglobemedia Publishing Inc.

Ed: Catherine McLean. **Description:** Canada-based Rogers Communications Inc. has projected increased profits for the 2007 fiscal year. The company has increased its market share by 14 percent with fourth quarter revenues of $176 million.

12346 ■ "Growth Back on CIBC's Agenda" in *Globe & Mail* **(March 3, 2006, pp. B1)**
Pub: CTVglobemedia Publishing Inc.

Ed: Sinclair Stewart. **Description:** The details on business growth of Canadian Imperial Bank of Commerce, which posted $547 million profit for first quarter 2006, are presented.

12347 ■ "Hain Celestial Acquires Greek Gods Yogurt" in *Ice Cream Reporter* **(Vol. 23, July 20, 2010, No. 8, pp. 1)**
Pub: Ice Cream Reporter

Description: Hain Celestial Group acquired The Greek Gods LLC. Hain Celestial is a natural and organic products company and Greek Gods makes all natural, Greek-style yogurt and ice cream.

12348 ■ "Half Empty or Half Full" in *Crain's Chicago Business* **(Vol. 31, March 24, 2008, No. 12, pp. 4)**
Pub: Crain Communications, Inc.

Ed: Meghan Streit. **Description:** Lifeway Foods Inc., the health food company which manufactures a yogurt-like drink called kefir, is being negatively affected by the soaring price of milk; however, the fact that probiotics are picking up in the market may mean that Lifeway stands a good chance of bouncing back and the company's lower share price could be an opportunity for long-term investors who have a tolerance for risk.

12349 ■ "Handleman Liquidation Leaves Questions For Shareholders" in *Crain's Detroit Business* **(Vol. 24, October 6, 2008, No. 40, pp. 4)**
Pub: Crain Communications, Inc.

Ed: Nancy Kaffer. **Description:** Discusses Handleman Co., a Troy-based music distribution company, and their plan of liquidation and dissolution as well as how shareholders will be affected by the company's plan. Handleman filed its plan to liquidate and dissolve assets with the Securities and Exchange Commission in mid-August, following several quarters of dismal earnings.

12350 ■ "Hank and Ben: Hedgies' BFFs" in *Barron's* **(Vol. 88, March 31, 2008, No. 13, pp. 50)**
Pub: Dow Jones & Company, Inc.

Ed: Tom Sullivan. **Description:** David Ballin of Alternative Investment Solutions says that everything in the financial markets is tainted and beaten-up which presents an extraordinary opportunity for hedge funds as long as they back up their decisions with sharp and intensive research. He adds that money managers should short suspect stocks and go long on undeservedly battered stocks in the same sector.

12351 ■ "Hank Paulson On the Housing Bailout and What's Ahead" in *Business Week* **(September 22, 2008, No. 4100, pp. 19)**
Pub: McGraw-Hill Companies, Inc.

Ed: Maria Bartiromo. **Description:** Interview with Treasury Secretary Henry Paulson in which he discusses the bailout of Fannie Mae and Freddie Mac as well as the potential impact on the American economy and foreign interests and investments in the country. Paulson has faith that the government's actions will help to stabilize the housing market.

12352 ■ "Happy New Year, Celestica?" in *Canadian Business* **(Vol. 80, January 15, 2007, No. 2, pp. 25)**
Pub: Rogers Media

Ed: Andrew Wahl. **Description:** Speculations on the performance of the electronics manufacturing company Celestica Inc. in 2007, which has been labelled as a 'sick' company in recent times, are presented.

12353 ■ "A Harbinger?" in *The Business Journal-Milwaukee* **(Vol. 25, August 29, 2008, No. 49, pp. A1)**
Pub: American City Business Journals, Inc.

Ed: Rich Kirchen. **Description:** Stock prices of Marshall & Ilsley Corp. (M&I) and MGIC Investment Corp. are expected to rebound after insiders were reported to have bought stocks of the companies. M&I director David Lubar bought $4.3 million, while MGIC CEO and chairman Curt Culver bought 20,000 stocks of MGIC. Other views and information on the insiders' purchase of stocks are presented.

12354 ■ "Harleysville Eyes Growth After Nationwide Deal" in *Philadelphia Business Journal* **(Vol. 30, October 7, 2011, No. 34, pp. 1)**
Pub: American City Business Journals Inc.

Ed: Jeff Blumenthal. **Description:** Harleysville Group announced growth plans after the company was sold to Columbus, Ohio-based Nationwide Mutual Insurance Company for about $1.63 billion. Nationwide gained an independent agency platform in 32 states with the Harleysville deal.

12355 ■ "Hartco Income Fund Announces the Completion of the CompuSmart Strategic Review" in *Canadian Corporate News* **(May 14, 2007)**
Pub: Comtex News Network Inc.

Description: Hartco Income Fund announced that it has completed the process of exploring strategic options for CompuSmart and found that it should implement a plan to sell select stores and assets while consolidating remaining CompuSmart locations over the next sixty days.

12356 ■ "Has Microsoft Found a Way to Get at Yahoo?" in *Advertising Age* **(Vol. 79, July 7, 2008, No. 26, pp. 4)**
Pub: Crain Communications, Inc.

Ed: Abbey Klaassen. **Description:** Microsoft's attempt to acquire Yahoo's search business is discussed as is Yahoo's plans for the future at a time when the company's shares have fallen dangerously low.

12357 ■ "Hastily Enacted Regulation Will Not Cure Economic Crisis" in *Crain's Chicago Business* **(Vol. 31, May 5, 2008, No. 18, pp. 18)**
Pub: Crain Communications, Inc.

Ed: Stephen P. D'Arcy. **Description:** Policymakers are looking for ways to respond to what is possibly the greatest financial crisis of a generation due to the collapse of the housing market, the credit crisis and the volatility of Wall Street.

12358 ■ "Have High-Tech Tax Credits Helped or Hurt Hawaii?" in *Hawaii Business* **(Vol. 53, December 2007, No. 6, pp. 28)**
Pub: Hawaii Business Publishing

Description: Presents the opinons of Channel Capital LLC's Walter R. Roth and Hawaii Venture Capital Association's Bill Spencer concerning the impacts of tax credits. Roth thinks that Act 221 appeals to investors who can earn despite business failure while Spencer thinks that the legislation promotes investments in innovative technology firms. The need to support tax credits is also discussed.

12359 ■ "Have I Got a Deal For You" in *Canadian Business* **(Vol. 83, October 12, 2010, No. 17, pp. 65)**
Pub: Rogers Media Ltd.

Ed: Bryan Borzykowski. **Description:** U.S. automobile market currently has more than three players, providing investors with a number of investment options. The sector is still mired in uncertainty, but people believe that these companies can only grow from this point forward. However, investors should use due diligence before jumping into the market.

12360 ■ "Hawaii's Identity Crisis" in *Hawaii Business* **(Vol. 53, November 2007, No. 5, pp. 10)**
Pub: Hawaii Business Publishing

Ed: Kelli Abe Trifonovitch. **Description:** Some Hawaiians have shown that the Superferry controversy makes it seem to the rest of the world as if they do not know what they are doing, and intensifies several issues regarding the stability of investing in Hawaii. With or without the Superferry, there is still no evidence that investors are afraid to put their money in Hawaii.

12361 ■ "Hawaii's Top Twenty Financial Advisors" in *Hawaii Business* **(Vol. 53, February 2008, No. 8, pp. 32)**
Pub: Hawaii Business Publishing

Description: Listing of Hawaii's top 20 financial advisors is presented. Details on the methodology used to create the rankings are discussed.

12362 ■ "HB Diversity Stock Index" in *Hispanic Business* **(March 2008, pp. 10)**
Pub: Hispanic Business

Ed: **Description:** Presentation of the Hispanic Business Diversity Stock Index as of February 1, 2008, which includes 54 publicly traded companies. Statistical data included.

12363 ■ **"HBDiversity Stock Index" in** *Hispanic Business* (July-August 2007, pp. 58)
Pub: Hispanic Business
Description: Listing of 43 Hispanic companies, their stock symbol, value and change over a six month period, January 3, 2007 through July 6, 2007.

12364 ■ **"HBDiversityStockIndex" in** *Hispanic Business* (January-February 2008, pp. 10)
Pub: Hispanic Business
Description: Presentation of the Hispanic Business Diversity Stock Index for 2007, which includes 54 publicly traded companies.

12365 ■ **"Headwinds From the New Sod Slow Aer Lingus" in** *Barron's* (Vol. 88, March 10, 2008, No. 10, pp. M6)
Pub: Dow Jones & Company, Inc.
Ed: Sean Walters; Arindam Nag. **Description:** Aer Lingus faces a drop in its share prices with a falling US market, higher jet fuel prices, and lower long-haul passenger load factors. British media companies Johnston Press and Yell Group are suffering from weaker ad revenue and heavier debt payments due to the credit crunch.

12366 ■ **"Health Care Leads Sectors Attracting Capital" in** *Hispanic Business* (Vol. 30, March 2008, No. 3, pp. 14)
Pub: Hispanic Business
Ed: Scott Williams. **Description:** Discusses the capital gains of Hispanic-owned companies and other Hispanic leaders in the investment and retail fields in the year 2007. Sectors like health care, media, food and technology saw a healthy flow of capital due to successful mergers, acquisitions and increased private equity investments.

12367 ■ **"HealthTronics Eager to Buy" in** *Austin Business JournalInc.* (Vol. 28, September 12, 2008, No. 26, pp. 1)
Pub: American City Business Journals
Ed: Laura Hipp. **Description:** HealthTronics Inc., an Austin, Texas urology equipment company has repeated its offer to buy Endocare Inc., an Irvine, California tumor technology firm for $26.9 million. The proposal has been revised to allow Endocare shareholders to choose between HealthTronics cash or shares. Endocare has not commented on the offer.

12368 ■ **"Heart Test No Boom for BG Medical" in** *Boston Business Journal* (Vol. 31, June 17, 2011, No. 21, pp. 1)
Pub: Boston Business Journal
Ed: Julie M. Donnelly. **Description:** The Galectin-3 test failed to boost stock prices of its manufacturer, BG Medicine, which has fallen to $6.06/share. The company hopes that its revenue will be boosted by widespread adoption of an automated and faster version of the test, which diagnoses for heart failure.

12369 ■ **"The Heat Is On" in** *Crain's Chicago Business* (Vol. 31, April 28, 2008, No. 17, pp. 4)
Pub: Crain Communications, Inc.
Ed: Steve Daniels. **Description:** Discusses Nicor Inc., a natural-gas utility serving 2 million customers in Chicago's suburbs, and its potential acquirers; shares of the company have dropped 17 percent this year making Nicor the second-worst among 31 utilities in an index tracked by Standrd & Poor's. Statistical data included.

12370 ■ **"Heat's On, but Glacier Not Retreating" in** *Globe & Mail* (January 26, 2006, pp. B3)
Pub: CTVglobemedia Publishing Inc.
Ed: Grant Robertson. **Description:** The details on Glacier Ventures International Corp., which acquired Hollinger International Inc.'s assets, are presented.

12371 ■ **"Hedge-Fund Titan Cohen Plans Bid for Dodgers" in** *Wall Street Journal Eastern Edition* (November 25 , 2011, pp. C3)
Pub: Dow Jones & Company Inc.
Ed: Matthew Futterman, Gregory Zuckerman. **Description:** Steven A. Cohen, the founder and head of hedge-fund SAC Capital Advisors LLC is looking to make an offer at the bankruptcy auction for the financially-troubled Los Angeles Dodgers baseball team.

12372 ■ **"Hello, 9000! The Dow's Run Is Far From Over" in** *Barron's* (Vol. 89, July 27, 2009, No. 30, pp. 20)
Pub: Dow Jones & Co., Inc.
Ed: Andrew Bary. **Description:** Another 10 percent gain is possible for the rest of 2009 as the Dow Jones Industrial Average moved above 9000 level for the week ending July 24, 2009. Blue chip stocks could do well in the next 10 years.

12373 ■ **"Here are the Stocks of the Decade" in** *Business Courier* (Vol. 26, December 18, 2009, No. 34, pp. 1)
Pub: American City Business Journals, Inc.
Ed: Steve Watkins. **Description:** Listing of companies with stocks that made big gains since December 1999 to November 30, 2009 is presented.

12374 ■ **"Here's How Buffett Spent 2007" in** *Barron's* (Vol. 88, March 10, 2008, No. 10, pp. 48)
Pub: Dow Jones & Company, Inc.
Ed: Andrew Bary. **Description:** Earnings of Berkshire Hathaway may decline in 2008 due to a tighter insurance market, but its portfolio is expected to continue growing. Warren Buffett purchased $19.1 billion worth of stocks in 2007.

12375 ■ **"The Hidden Tax" in** *Canadian Business* (Vol. 81, April 14, 2008, No. 6, pp. 28)
Pub: Rogers Media
Ed: Al Rosen. **Description:** Accounting fraud could take out a sizable sum from one's retirement fund when computed over a long period of time. The much bigger tax on savings is the collective impact of the smaller losses that do not attract the attention they deserve. Ensuring that investors are not unnecessarily taxed 2 percent of their total investments every year outweighs the benefit of a 2 percent reduction in personal tax rates.

12376 ■ **"H.I.G. Capital Announces Acquisition of Next Generation Vending" in** *Benzinga.com* (October 29, 2011)
Pub: Benzinga.com
Ed: Benzinga Staff. **Description:** H.I.G. Capital LLC, a leader in global private investments, acquired Next Generation Vending and Food Service Inc.. Next Generation is a provider of vending services for corporate and institutional clients in Northeastern United States.

12377 ■ **"High Hopes: Ralph Mitchell's Picks Have Growth Potential" in** *Black Enterprise* (Vol. 37, February 2007, No. 7, pp. 42)
Pub: Earl G. Graves Publishing Co. Inc.
Ed: Carolyn M. Brown. **Description:** Ralph Mitchell, president and senior financial advisor of Braintree-Carthage Financial Group, offers three recommendations: Toll Brothers, Home Depot, and Lowe's.

12378 ■ **"High Marks: Parker Hannifin's Stock Lauded by Wall Street Journal" in** *Crain's Cleveland Business* (Vol. 28, November 5, 2007, No. 44)
Pub: Crain Communications, Inc.
Description: According to The Wall Street Journal, Parker Hannifin Corp., a manufacturer of motion and control equipment, is one of eight stocks that are attractively priced and continuously showing growth.

12379 ■ **"High-Yield Turns Into Road Kill" in** *Barron's* (Vol. 88, July 7, 2008, No. 27, pp. M7)
Pub: Dow Jones & Co., Inc.
Ed: Emily Barrett. **Description:** High-yield bonds have returned to the brink of collapse after profits have recovered from the shock brought about by the collapse of Bear Stearns. The high-yield bond market could decline again due to weakness in the automotive sector, particularly in Ford and General Motors.

12380 ■ **"Higher Freight Rates Keep CPR Rolling in Profit" in** *Globe & Mail* (February 1, 2006, pp. B3)
Pub: CTVglobemedia Publishing Inc.
Ed: Brent Jang. **Description:** Canadian Pacific Railway Ltd. posted $135.4 million in revenues for fourth quarter 2005. The company's earnings projections for 2006 and workforce reduction plans are presented.

12381 ■ **"The Hired Guns" in** *Business Courier* (Vol. 26, November 13, 2009, No. 29, pp. 1)
Pub: American City Business Journals, Inc.
Ed: Lisa Biank Fasig. **Description:** YourForce has nearly 6,000 retired scientists and researchers who work together in helping Procter & Gamble (P&G) and other companies in addressing various project needs. Operating as an online innovation community, YourEncore is a result of P&G's Connect + Develop program.

12382 ■ **"His Way" in** *Inc.* (February 2008, pp. 90-97)
Pub: Gruner & Jahr USA Publishing
Ed: Stephanie Clifford. **Description:** Profile of Chris Reed, founder of a natural soda company, who undertook an initial public offering (IPO). Reed discusses the challenges he faced mediating with the Securities Exchange Commission regarding his firm's IPO.

12383 ■ **"Hispantelligence Report" in** *Hispanic Business* (March 2008, pp. 8)
Pub: Hispanic Business
Description: Listing of the Hispanic Business Stock Index covering Hispanic owned businesses; stock symbol, previous 30-day, year-to-date and one year performance is presented.

12384 ■ **"A History of Neglect" in** *Canadian Business* (Vol. 79, September 11, 2006, No. 18, pp. 21)
Pub: Rogers Media
Ed: Al Rosen. **Description:** Faulty practices being followed by auditors and regulators of Canada are discussed. The need for appropriate steps to protect investors against these frauds are emphasized.

12385 ■ **"Hit the Books" in** *Black Enterprise* (Vol. 38, July 2008, No. 12, pp. 42)
Pub: Earl G. Graves Publishing Co. Inc.
Ed: Mellody Hobson. **Description:** Four books that deal with investing are discussed as is the idea that reading even 15 minutes a day from one of these books will give you tools that far exceed what you can learn from magazines and the business section of your daily newspaper.

12386 ■ **"Hits and Misses" in** *Canadian Business* (Vol. 80, December 25, 2006, No. 1, pp. 69)
Pub: Rogers Media
Ed: Calvin Leung. **Description:** The performance of stocks of several Canadian companies is discussed.

12387 ■ **"Hitting Bottom?" in** *Barron's* (Vol. 88, March 24, 2008, No. 12, pp. 21)
Pub: Dow Jones & Company, Inc.
Ed: Jacqueline Doherty. **Description:** Brokerage houses and banks may stabilize in 2008 as a result of regulatory responses brought about by the near-collapse of Bear Stearns. Some of their shares may rise by as much as 20 percent from 2008 to 2009.

12388 ■ **"Hold the IPhone" in** *Canadian Business* (Vol. 80, January 15, 2007, No. 2, pp. 22)
Pub: Rogers Media
Ed: Andrew Wahl. **Description:** The rise in the price of shares of Apple Inc. after the introduction of its new product, the iPhone, is discussed.

12389 ■ **"Hold Your Nose, Say 'Da'" in** *Canadian Business* (Vol. 79, September 11, 2006, No. 18, pp. 151)
Pub: Rogers Media
Ed: Thomas Watson. **Description:** The changing business environment and investment opportunities in Russia despite its instable democracy are discussed. Russia's potential and its ability to attract productive investment are presented.

12390 ■ **"Hollinger Shares Plummet on Reports" in** *Globe & Mail* (March 10, 2007, pp. B5)
Pub: CTVglobemedia Publishing Inc.
Ed: Richard Blackwell. **Description:** The fall in the share prices of Hollinger Inc. to 49 percent soon after the company filed its annual statements is discussed.

12391 ■ "A Home of Her Own" in *Hawaii Business* **(Vol. 53, October 2007, No. 4, pp. 51)**

Pub: Hawaii Business Publishing

Ed: Maria Torres-Kitamura. **Description:** It was observed that the number of single women in Hawaii purchasing their own home has increased, as that in the whole United States where the percentage has increased from 14 percent in 1995 to 22 percent in 2006. However, First Hawaiian Bank's Wendy Lum thinks that the trend will not continue in Hawaii due to lending restrictions. The factors that women consider in buying a home of their own are presented.

12392 ■ "Home Sweet Home?" in *Canadian Business* **(Vol. 79, September 11, 2006, No. 18, pp. 17)**

Pub: Rogers Media

Ed: David Wolf. **Description:** Fading attractiveness of the Canadian stock market for its domestic investors is discussed. Changing investor's trends toward cross-border investments are presented.

12393 ■ "Homebuilders Continue to be Our Nemesis" in *Contractor* **(Vol. 56, July 2009, No. 7, pp. 50)**

Pub: Penton Media, Inc.

Ed: Bob Mader. **Description:** Homebuilders rank high on the greed scale along with Wall Street brokers. There is this one instance when a builder gave copies of another contractor's quotes that have just been blackened out and another instance when one builder let other bidders visit a site while the current mechanical contractor is working.

12394 ■ "Honesty Doesn't Pay" in *Canadian Business* **(Vol. 79, Winter 2006, No. 24, pp. 28)**

Pub: Rogers Media

Ed: Al Rosen. **Description:** The effects of the outlook of financial analysts and investment bankers, on their career prospects, are described.

12395 ■ "Hong Kong's Boom in IPO" in *Barron's* **(Vol. 89, July 13, 2009, No. 28, pp. M7)**

Pub: Dow Jones & Co., Inc.

Ed: Nick Lord. **Description:** Hong Kong's IPO (initial public offering) market is booming with 13 Chinese IPOs already on the market for the year as July 2009. One of them is Bawang International which raised $214 million after generating $9 billion in order which makes it 42 times oversubscribed.

12396 ■ "Hospital Revenue Healthier in 2009" in *Orlando Business Journal* **(Vol. 26, February 5, 2010, No. 36, pp. 1)**

Pub: American City Business Journals

Ed: Melanie Stawicki Azam. **Description:** Orlando Health, Health Central and Adventist Health System are Florida-based hospital systems that generated the most profits in 2009. Orlando Health had the highest profit in 2009 at $73.3 million, contrary to about $31 million in losses in 2008. The increased profits are attributed to stock market recovery, cost-cutting initiatives, and rising patient volumes.

12397 ■ "Hot For All The Wrong Reasons" in *Canadian Business* **(Vol. 81, March 31, 2008, No. 5, pp. 19)**

Pub: Rogers Media

Ed: Andrea Jezovit. **Description:** Soaring platinum prices are due to South Africa's platinum mining industry's safety issues and power supply disruptions that exacerbate the metal's supply problems. South Africa supplies 80 percent of the world's platinum. South Africa's power utility has said that it cannot guarantee the industry's power needs until 2013.

12398 ■ "Hotel Confidential" in *Canadian Business* **(Vol. 80, Winter 2007, No. 24, pp. 91)**

Pub: Rogers Media

Ed: Erik Heinrich. **Description:** Celebrities such as Jason Priestley, Clint Eastwood, and Francis Ford Coppola have made investment in the hospitality industry. Investing in the hospitality industry has proved to be an excellent long-term investment and the venture also has a vanity aspect to it.

12399 ■ *House of Cards*

Pub: Doubleday, a Division of Random House

Ed: William D. Cohan. **Released:** March 10, 2009. **Price:** $27.95. **Description:** The fall of Bear Stearns and the beginning of the Wall Street Collapse.

12400 ■ *House of Cards: A Tale of Hubris and Wretched Excess on Wall Street*

Pub: Anchor Press

Ed: William D. Cohan. **Released:** February 9, 2010. **Price:** $16.95. **Description:** A historical account of the events leading up to the Bear Stearns implosion.

12401 ■ "How to Avoid the Three Big Mistakes" in *Barron's* **(Vol. 88, March 10, 2008, No. 10, pp. 30)**

Pub: Dow Jones & Company, Inc.

Ed: Karen Hube. **Description:** Investors, particularly those having retirement investments, are advised to diversify their investments, refrain from market timing, and minimize payments to maximize investment gains. An investor committing these mistakes could lose as much as $375,000 dollars over ten years.

12402 ■ "How to Beat the Pros" in *Canadian Business* **(Vol. 81, Summer 2008, No. 9, pp. 59)**

Pub: Rogers Media Ltd.

Ed: Calvin Leung. **Description:** Table showing the results of the Investor 500 beat the S&P/TSX composite index is presented. The average total return, best performing stocks and total return of the 2007 stock screen are provided.

12403 ■ *How Come That Idiot's Rich and I'm Not?*

Pub: Crown Publishing/Random House

Ed: Robert Shemin. **Released:** April 2009. **Price:** $13.95. **Description:** The book shows the average person not only how to get rich, but to create, connect and contribute greatly.

12404 ■ "How CoolBrand's Thrills Turned to Chills" in *Globe & Mail* **(January 25, 2007, pp. B1)**

Pub: CTVglobemedia Publishing Inc.

Ed: Keith McArthur. **Description:** The key reasons behind the sudden share price fall of ice cream giant CoolBrands International Inc. are discussed.

12405 ■ "How to Deal" in *Canadian Business* **(Vol. 81, November 10, 2008, No. 19, pp. 36)**

Pub: Rogers Media Ltd.

Ed: Calvin Leung. **Description:** The Great Depression, Japan's Lost Decade, and the Swedish Banking Crisis is compared to the 2008 financial crisis in the U.S. The chances for recession in the U.S. are discussed along with investment strategies to survive.

12406 ■ "How Foreigners Could Disrupt U.S. Markets" in *Barron's* **(Vol. 90, September 13, 2010, No. 37, pp. 30)**

Pub: Barron's Editorial & Corporate Headquarters

Ed: Jim McTague. **Description:** An informal meeting by the House Homeland Security Panel concluded that U.S. stock exchanges and related trading routes can be the subject of attacks from rogue overseas traders. A drop in funding for the U.S. Department of Defense is discussed.

12407 ■ "How High Can Soybeans Fly?" in *Barron's* **(Vol. 88, March 10, 2008, No. 10, pp. M14)**

Pub: Dow Jones & Company, Inc.

Ed: Kenneth Rapoza. **Description:** Prices of soybeans have risen to $14.0875 a bushel, up 8.3 percent for the week. Increased demand, such as in China and in other developing economies, and the investment-driven commodities boom are boosting prices.

12408 ■ "How Interest Rate Changes Affect You" in *Agency Sales Magazine* **(Vol. 39, September-October 2009, No. 9, pp. 50)**

Pub: MANA

Ed: Lee Eisinberg. **Description:** Falling interest rates make the prices of previously issued bonds rise and new issues are offered at lower rates. For stock investors, rising interest rates can have a positive or negative effect. Terminologies related to investing are explained.

12409 ■ "How Investors React When Women Join Boards" in *Harvard Business Review* **(Vol. 88, July-August 2010, No. 7-8, pp. 24)**

Pub: Harvard Business School Publishing

Ed: Andrew O'Connell. **Description:** Research reveals a cognitive bias in blockholders regarding the presence of women on boards of directors despite evidence showing that diversity improves results.

12410 ■ *How to Make Money in Stocks: A Winning System in Good Times and Bad*

Pub: The McGraw-Hill Companies

Ed: William J. O'Neil. **Released:** June 12. 2009. **Price:** $16.95. **Description:** The bestselling guide to buying stocks, from the founder of Investor's Business Daily. The technique is based on a study of the greatest stock market winners dating back to 1953 and includes a seven-step process for minimizing risk, maximizing return, and finding stocks that are ready to perform.

12411 ■ "How to Maximize Your Investment Income" in *Contractor* **(Vol. 56, December 2009, No. 12, pp. 33)**

Pub: Penton Media, Inc.

Ed: Irv Blackman. **Description:** Private placement life insurance (PPLI) can minimize taxes and protect assets. PPLI is a form of variable universal insurance that is offered privately. Risk of insurance company illiquidity is avoided as investments are placed in separate accounts.

12412 ■ "How Not to Raise Bank Capital" in *Barron's* **(Vol. 88, June 30, 2008, No. 26, pp. M6)**

Pub: Dow Jones & Co., Inc.

Ed: Sean Walters. **Description:** French bank Natixis wants to raise 1 billion euros from cash provided by their two major owners. Natixis will reimburse Banque Populaire and Caisses d'Epargne with hybrid securities so this move will not benefit Natixis' core Tier 1 ratio. This has also given the impression that the company is afraid of a full rights issue which could shake investors' faith in the bank.

12413 ■ "How Our Picks Beat The Bear" in *Barron's* **(Vol. 88, July 14, 2008, No. 28, pp. 18)**

Pub: Dow Jones & Co., Inc.

Ed: Andrew Bary. **Description:** Performance of the stocks that Barron's covered in the first half of 2008 is discussed; some of the worst picks and most rewarding pans have been in the financial sector while the best plays were in the energy, materials, and the transportation sectors.

12414 ■ "How to Play the Tech Mergers" in *Barron's* **(Vol. 90, August 30, 2010, No. 35, pp. 18)**

Pub: Barron's Editorial & Corporate Headquarters

Ed: Tiernan Ray. **Description:** The intense bidding by Hewlett-Packard and Dell for 3Par was foreseen in a previous Barron's cover story and 3Par's stock has nearly tripled since reported. Other possible acquisition targets in the tech industry include Brocade Communication Systems, NetApp, Xyratex, and Isilon Systems.

12415 ■ *How to Protect and Manage Your 401K: Shield, Save, and Grow Your Money, Guard Against Corporate Corruption, Do What It Takes to Protect Your Future*

Pub: Career Press, Incorporated

Ed: Elizabeth Opalka. **Released:** May 2003. **Description:** Ways to protect and manage 401(K) investments.

12416 ■ "How Sweet It Will Be" in *Barron's* **(Vol. 89, July 13, 2009, No. 28, pp. M13)**

Pub: Dow Jones & Co., Inc.

Ed: Debbie Carlson. **Description:** Raw sugar experienced a rally in the first half of 2009 and the long term outlook for sugar prices is still good. However, there is a likely near-term correction due to the onset of Brazilian harvest that could be 20.7 percent higher for 2009 as compared to the previous year and October contracts could fall to 15.61 cents per pound.

12417 ■ "HSBC Canada Posts 8.8 Percent Profit Gain in 2006" in Globe & Mail (February 20, 2007, pp. B14)
Pub: CTVglobemedia Publishing Inc.
Ed: Andrew Willis. Description: HSBC Bank Canada reported profits of $497 million in 2006. The financial results of the company for 2006 are presented.

12418 ■ "The Human Element" in Canadian Business (Vol. 80, April 23, 2007, No. 9, pp. 78)
Pub: Rogers Media
Ed: Jeff Sanford. Description: The effects of human resource programs on stocks and investor relations are presented.

12419 ■ "Huntington's Future At a Crossroads" in Crain's Cleveland Business (Vol. 30, June 22, 2009, No. 24, pp. 1)
Pub: Crain Communications, Inc.
Ed: Arielle Kass. Description: Despite Huntington Bancshares plans to expand in the Cleveland, Ohio area, experts wonder if the bank will be able to take advantage of the area's growth in the long run. Statistical data included.

12420 ■ "Ian Gordon" in Canadian Business (Vol. 81, Summer 2008, No. 9, pp. 10)
Pub: Rogers Media Ltd.
Ed: Matthew McClearn. Description: Bolder Investment Partners' Ian Gordon discussed the economic theory promulgated by Russian economist Nikolai Kondratieff. The cycle begins with a rising economy then followed by deflationary depression. Details of his views on the Kondratieff cycle and its application to the current economy are presented.

12421 ■ "Identity Crisis: The Battle For Your Data" in Canadian Business (Vol. 81, March 17, 2008, No. 4, pp. 12)
Pub: Rogers Media
Description: Nigel Brown explains that businesses must protect their data through encryption and tightening up access to data. Brown also points out that banks and merchants bear most of the costs for identity fraud and leaves individuals with a lot of pain and heartache in clearing their name.

12422 ■ "If You Go Into the Market Today..." in Canadian Business (Vol. 82, Summer 2009, No. 8, pp. 18)
Pub: Rogers Media
Ed: Jeff Sanford. Description: Opinions of experts and personalities who are known to have bear attitudes towards the economy were presented in the event 'A Night with the Bears' in Toronto in April 2009. Known bears that served as resource persons in the event were Nouriel Roubini, Eric Sprott, Ian Gordon, and Meredith Whitney. The bears were observed to have differences regarding consumer debt.

12423 ■ "An Ill Wind: Icelandic Bank Failures Chill Atlantic Canada" in Canadian Business (Vol. 81, November 10, 2008, No. 19, pp. 10)
Pub: Rogers Media Ltd.
Ed: Charles Mandel. Description: Bank failures in Iceland have put a stop to flights ferrying Icelanders to Newfoundland to purchase Christmas gifts, thereby threatening Newfoundland's tourism industry. The credit of Newfoundland's fisheries is also being squeezed since most of Atlantic Canadian seafood processors hold lines of credit from Icelandic banks.

12424 ■ "Ill Winds; Cuba's Economy" in The Economist (Vol. 390, January 3, 2009, No. 8612, pp. 20)
Pub: The Economist Newspaper Inc.
Description: Cuba's long-term economic prospects remain poor with the economy forecasted to grow only 4.3 percent for the year, about half of the original forecast, due in part to Hurricane Gustav which caused $10 billion in damage and disrupted the food-supply network and devastated farms across the region; President Raul Castro made raising agricultural production a national priority and the rise in global commodity prices hit the country hard. The only bright spot has been the rise in tourism which is up 9.3 percent over 2007.

12425 ■ "Immigrants Trapped in Forex Mess" in Boston Business Journal (Vol. 27, October 5, 2007, No. 36, pp. 1)
Pub: American City Business Journals Inc.
Ed: Jackie Noblett. Description: U. S. Commodity Futures Trading Commission and Swiss Federal Banking Commission are jointly working on the case of Tradex Swiss AG. Investors have filed lawsuits to recover their money. Details of the illegal operation of the Forex company are discussed.

12426 ■ "Immigration Issues Frustrate Owners From Overseas" in The Business Journal-Serving Greater Tampa Bay (Vol. 28, August 15, 2008)
Pub: American City Business Journals, Inc.
Ed: Margie Manning. Description: Investors who availed the E-2 visa program believe that the tightened restrictions on the visa program has trapped them in the United States. The E-2 investor visa program was designed to attract investors into the U.S., but restrictions were tightened after the September 11, 2001 attacks. Other views and information on E-2 and its impact on investors are presented.

12427 ■ "The Impact of Acquisitions On the Productivity of Inventors at Semiconductor Firms" in Academy of Management Journal (October 2007)
Pub: Academy of Management
Ed: Rahul Kapoor, Kwanghui Lim. Description: Study examined the relation between knowledge-based and incentive-based outlook in explaining the impact of acquisitions on the productivity of inventors at acquired semiconductor firms. Results showed a definite relation between the two perspectives.

12428 ■ "The Impact of Brand Quality on Shareholder Wealth" in Journal of Marketing (Vol. 75, September 2011, No. 5, pp. 88)
Pub: American Marketing Association
Ed: Sundar G. Bharardwaj, Kapil R. Tuli, Andre Bonfrer. Description: The effects of brand quality on idiosyncratic risk, systematic risk, and stock returns are investigated. Findings reveal that unexpected changes in brand quality negatively associated with idiosyncratic risk changes and positively related to stock returns. However, unexpected changes in brand quality will reduce shareholder wealth due to positive relationship with changes n systematic risk.

12429 ■ "Imports Frothing Up Beer Market" in Globe & Mail (February 16, 2006, pp. B4)
Pub: CTVglobemedia Publishing Inc.
Ed: Andy Hoffman. Description: The reasons behind the rise in market share of beer imports, in Canada, are presented.

12430 ■ "In the Bag?" in Canadian Business (Vol. 81, March 3, 2008, No. 3, pp. 57)
Pub: Rogers Media
Ed: Calvin Leung. Description: American stocks are beginning to appear cheap amidst the threat of a worldwide economic slowdown, United States economic crisis and declining stock portfolios. Investors looking for bargain stocks should study the shares of Apple and Oshkosh Corp. Evaluation of other cheap-looking stocks such as the shares of Coach and 3M is also given.

12431 ■ "In China, Railways to Riches" in Barron's (Vol. 88, July 7, 2008, No. 27, pp. M9)
Pub: Dow Jones & Co., Inc.
Ed: Assif Shameen. Description: Shares of Chinese railway companies look to benefit from multimillion-dollar investments aimed at upgrading the Chinese railway network. Investment in the sector is expected to reach $210 billion for the 2006-2010 period.

12432 ■ "In India, A Gold-Price Threat?" in Barron's (Vol. 88, June 30, 2008, No. 26, pp. M12)
Pub: Dow Jones & Co., Inc.
Ed: Melanie Burton. Description: Gold purchases in India are falling as record prices take its toll on demand. Gold imports to India fell by 52 percent in

May 2008 from the previous year and local prices are higher by one-third from the previous year to 12,540 rupees for 10 grams.

12433 ■ "In Praise of How Not to Invest" in Barron's (Vol. 89, July 13, 2009, No. 28, pp. 11)
Pub: Dow Jones & Co., Inc.
Ed: Vito J. Racanelli. Description: One research study found that the shares of companies that have growing market shares and expanding asset bases underperform. This is contrary to the widely held premise that stock prices for these companies rise. It is argued that this result is caused by these companies' tendency to sacrifice profitability to grab market share and this is reflected in their stock prices.

12434 ■ "In the Public Eye" in Entrepreneur (Vol. 35, November 2007, No. 11, pp. 75)
Pub: Entrepreneur Media Inc.
Ed: David Worrell. Description: The market for initial public offerings (IPOs) was booming in 2007 and strong fundamentals for companies that would like to go public are needed. The basics that companies should review before planning an IPO are outlined.

12435 ■ "In Sickness and In Wealth Management" in Hispanic Business (Vol. 30, March 2008, No. 3, pp. 28)
Pub: Hispanic Business
Ed: Rick Munarriz. Description: Discusses the investment and wealth management firms owned and operated by Hispanics. There are only a handful of these firms owned by Hispanics, as most of them prefer capital preservation by investing in hard assets like cash and real estate than in capital appreciation.

12436 ■ "In Sickness and in Wealth Management" in Hispanic Business (March 2008, pp. 28, 30)
Pub: Hispanic Business
Ed: Rick Munarriz. Description: Financial advice is offered by experts, Myrna Rivera and Samuel Ramirez Jr., with an overview of Hispanic-owned investment firms.

12437 ■ "In Surging Oil Industry, Good Fortune Comes In Stages" in Barron's (Vol. 88, July 7, 2008, No. 27, pp. 12)
Pub: Dow Jones & Co., Inc.
Ed: Sandra Ward. Description: Shares of US land oil and gas driller Helmerich and Payne, priced at $69 each, are estimated to be at peak levels. The shares are trading at 17 times 2008 earnings and could be in for some profit taking.

12438 ■ "In the Wake of Pet-Food Crisis, Iams Sales Plummet Nearly 17 Percent" in Advertising Age (Vol. 78, May 14, 2007, No. 18, pp. 3)
Pub: Crain Communications, Inc.
Ed: Jack Neff. Description: Although the massive U.S. pet-food recall impacted more than 100 brands, Procter & Gamble Co.'s Iams lost more sales and market share than any other industry player. According to Information Resources Inc. data, the brand's sales dropped 16.5 percent in the eight-week period ended April 22. Many analysts feel that the company could have handled the crisis in a better manner.

12439 ■ "In With the Good" in Canadian Business (Vol. 80, November 5, 2007, No. 22, pp. 22)
Pub: Rogers Media
Ed: Jack Mintz. Description: Restriction on foreign direct investment in Canada is unlikely to materialize despite Minister of Industry Jim Prentice's opinion that new rules be set in Ottawa regarding foreign state-owned businesses. Reasons why governments would not unreasonably regulate foreign investments are investigated.

12440 ■ "Inflation Woes: Secure Your Portfolio Against Rising Prices" in Black Enterprise (Vol. 37, January 2007, No. 6, pp. 40)
Pub: Earl G. Graves Publishing Co. Inc.
Ed: Donald Jay Korn. Description: Inflation has a huge impact on investing and it is important to take the steady increase on cost into account when looking at your financial goals and investing in your future. Statistical data included.

12441 ■ **"Inland Snaps Up Rival REITs"** in *Crain's Chicago Business* (Vol. 31, November 17, 2008, No. 46, pp. 3)
Pub: Crain Communications, Inc.
Ed: Alby Gallun. **Description:** Discusses Inland American Real Estate Trust Inc., a real estate investment trust that is napping up depressed shares of publicly traded competitors, a possible first step toward taking over these companies; however, with hotel and retail properties accounting for approximately 70 percent of its portfolio, the company could soon face its own difficulties.

12442 ■ **"Inmet Selling Nunavut Mining Properties"** in *Globe & Mail* (February 15, 2006, pp. B6)
Pub: CTVglobemedia Publishing Inc.
Ed: Allan Robinson. **Description:** The details on Wolfden Resources Inc.'s acquisition of mining assets of Inmet Mining Corp. are presented.

12443 ■ **"Insider"** in *Canadian Business* (Vol. 81, March 3, 2008, No. 3, pp. 96)
Pub: Rogers Media
Description: History of gold usage and gold trading is presented in a timeline. Gold was a symbol of power and wealth in 2500 B.C., and in 1500 B.C., it became the first currency to be recognized internationally. Other remarkable events in the gold industry and laws that covered gold are discussed.

12444 ■ **"An Insurance Roll-Up In Danger of Unraveling"** in *Barron's* (Vol. 88, March 17, 2008, No. 11, pp. 51)
Pub: Dow Jones & Company, Inc.
Ed: Bill Alpert. **Description:** Shares of National Financial Partners have fallen below their initial offering price as sputtering sales and management turnover leave many investors wondering. One of the company's star brokers is being sued for their "life settlement" contracts while another broker is being pursued by the IRS for unpaid taxes.

12445 ■ **"Intangible Assets"** in *Canadian Business* (Vol. 79, July 17, 2006, No. 14-15, pp. 17)
Pub: Rogers Media
Ed: Al Rosen. **Description:** Need for investors to check the actual worth of a company and not to get carried away by the inflated claims made by the company is emphasized.

12446 ■ **"International ETFs: Your Passport to the World"** in *Barron's* (Vol. 89, July 13, 2009, No. 28, pp. L10)
Pub: Dow Jones & Co., Inc.
Ed: John Hintze. **Description:** International exchange traded funds give investors more choices in terms of investment plays and there are 174 U.S. ETF listings worth $141 billion as of July 2009. Suggestions on how to invest in these funds based on one's conviction on how the global economy will unfold are presented.

12447 ■ **"International Nickel Ventures Corporation Reports Results for the First Quarter 2007"** in *Canadian Corporate News* (May 16, 2007)
Pub: Comtex News Network Inc.
Description: Profile of International Nickel Ventures Corporation (INV) including its financial report for the first quarter of fiscal 2007, its partnership and possible acquisition of Teck Cominco Limited, and its plans for the future. Statistical data included.

12448 ■ *The Internationalization of Asset Ownership in Europe*
Pub: Cambridge University Press
Ed: Harry Huizinga, Lars Jonung. **Released:** November 2005. **Price:** $112.00. **Description:** Ten financial experts provide analysis of the growth and the implications of foreign ownership in Europe's financial markets.

12449 ■ **"Investment Bank Predicts Shakeup in Farm Equipment Industry"** in *Farm Industry News* (November 16, 2011)
Pub: Penton Business Media Inc.
Ed: Jodie Wehrspann. **Description:** Farming can expect to see more mergers and acquisitions in the agricultural equipment industry, as it appears to be in the early stages of growth over the next few years.

12450 ■ *Investment Counsel Association of America—Directory of Member Firms*
Pub: Investment Adviser Association
Contact: David G. Tittsworth, Exec. Dir.
E-mail: david.tittsworth@investmentadviser.org
Released: Annual. **Price:** Free. **Covers:** over 300 member investment counseling firms. **Entries Include:** Name and address of firm; contact, number of clients, assets under management, staff, type of account, minimum account and fee.

12451 ■ **"Investment Firms Unite: Coalition Fights New Tax Law"** in *Black Enterprise* (Vol. 38, December 2007, No. 5, pp. 52)
Pub: Earl G. Graves Publishing Co. Inc.
Ed: Joyce Jones. **Description:** Minorities working in private equity, real estate and investment management firms have united to form the Access to Capital Coalition to oppose legislation that they feel would adversely affect their ability to attract investments and executives. Details of the group are included.

12452 ■ **"Investment Manager Disciplined"** in *Sacramento Business Journal* (Vol. 25, July 4, 2008, No. 18, pp. 1)
Pub: American City Business Journals, Inc.
Ed: Mark Anderson. **Description:** Community Capital Management's David A. Zwick is permanently barred by the Securities and Exchange Commission (SEC) from associating with any broker or dealer, after investigations revealed that he took part in paying kickbacks to a bond trader. Other views and information on Community Capital, and on the SEC investigation on Zwick, are presented.

12453 ■ **"Investors Finding Bay Area Deals"** in *Tampa Bay Business Journal* (Vol. 29, November 6, 2009, No. 46, pp. 1)
Pub: American City Business Journals
Ed: Margie Manning. **Description:** Private equity investors have found dozens of privately held companies in Tampa Bay area in Florida in which to invest $84 million fresh equity. Revenue generation, growth, solid management teams are some of the factors found by the investors on these companies which span a range of sizes and industries.

12454 ■ **"An Investor's Guide to This Year's Inc. 500"** in *Inc.* (October 2007, pp. 34)
Pub: Gruner & Jahr USA Publishing
Description: Three investment firms specializing in growth companies provide insight into today's market.

12455 ■ **"Investors Lost Patience A Long Time Ago"** in *Globe & Mail* (January 21, 2006, pp. B5)
Pub: CTVglobemedia Publishing Inc.
Ed: Konrad Yakabuski. **Description:** The financial impasse at Quebecor World Inc., under chief executive officer Pierre Karl Peladeau, is discussed.

12456 ■ **"Investors Shrug Off the Turmoil"** in *Globe & Mail* (March 1, 2007, pp. B1)
Pub: CTVglobemedia Publishing Inc.
Ed: Geoffrey York. **Description:** The decision of Chinese investors to continue to buy stocks despite the decade's biggest market crash is discussed. The rise in the stock price indexes of China is described.

12457 ■ **"Investors Sue Jackson Properties for Fraud, Breach of Contract"** in *The Business Journal - Serving Phoenix and the Valley of the Sun* (Vol. 28, July 18, 2008, No. 46, pp. 1)
Pub: American City Business Journals, Inc.
Ed: Jan Buchholz. **Description:** Investors sued Jackson Properties EVB Inc. and Jackson Properties EVB LLC for fraud and breach of contract over a botched housing development deal. The investors also filed a complaint before the Arizona Corporation Commission. The investors stand to lose $8 million from the halted development deal.

12458 ■ **"Is this a Buying Opportunity?"** in *Canadian Business* (Vol. 82, April 27, 2009, No. 7, pp. 46)
Pub: Rogers Media
Ed: Andy Holloway. **Description:** Home prices in Canada are down by as much as 14.2 percent in 2009 compared to prices in 2008, making homes

more affordable now. Some housing experts believe that homes are still good investments as prices of rent and properties always recover. Meanwhile, a survey found that Canadians under 35 plan to buy a home within two years.

12459 ■ **"Is the VIX in Denial?"** in *Barron's* (Vol. 88, July 7, 2008, No. 27, pp. M12)
Pub: Dow Jones & Co., Inc.
Ed: Lawrence McMillan. **Description:** Volatility Index (VIX) of the Chicago Board Options Exchange did not rise significantly despite the drop in the US stock markets, rising to near 25. This market decline, however, will eventually result in investor panic and the rise of the VIX.

12460 ■ **"It Could Be Worse"** in *Barron's* (Vol. 89, July 27, 2009, No. 30, pp. 5)
Pub: Dow Jones & Co., Inc.
Ed: Alan Abelson. **Description:** Media sources are being fooled by corporate America who is peddling an economic recovery rather than reality as shown by the report of a rise in existing home sales which boosted the stock market even if it was a seasonal phenomenon. The phrase "things could be worse" sums up the reigning investment philosophy in the U.S. and this has been stirring up the market.

12461 ■ **"It Takes More Than One"** in *Black Enterprise* (Vol. 38, July 2008, No. 12, pp. 38)
Pub: Earl G. Graves Publishing Co. Inc.
Ed: James A. Anderson. **Description:** Interview with Eric Small, the CEO of SBK-Brooks Investment Corp., whom discusses the importance of versatility when trying to find the best investment choices; the primary factors investors should be mindful of; his current stock picks; and recommendations for investing in an uncertain and volatile market.

12462 ■ **"Itochu Joins KKR in Samson Buyout"** in *Wall Street Journal Eastern Edition* (November 25 , 2011, pp. B7)
Pub: Dow Jones & Company Inc.
Description: Samson Investment Company is the target of a $7.2 billion leveraged buyout by a consortium led by US investment firm Kohlberg Kravis Roberts & Company and Tokyo-based Itochu Corporation, part of the consortium is coming in on the deal for a 25 percent holding, for which it will pay $1.04 billion.

12463 ■ **"It's Good to be Goldman"** in *Barron's* (Vol. 89, July 20, 2009, No. 29, pp. 5)
Pub: Dow Jones & Co., Inc.
Ed: Randall W. Forsyth. **Description:** Profits of Goldman Sachs rose to $3.44 billion in the second quarter of 2009, aided by federal financial stimulus programs. CIT Group is facing bankruptcy and may need up to $6 billion to survive. The federal economic stimulus programs are benefiting Wall Street more than the US economy itself.

12464 ■ **"It's Time to Wise Up: Income Trusts"** in *Canadian Business* (Vol. 79, November 6, 2006, No. 22, pp. 24)
Pub: Rogers Media
Ed: Mark Rosen. **Description:** The effects bogus financial reporting of income trusts on investors are analyzed.

12465 ■ **"Ivernia Mine Closing Could Boost Lead"** in *Globe & Mail* (April 4, 2007, pp. B5)
Pub: CTVglobemedia Publishing Inc.
Ed: Andy Hoffman. **Description:** The closing of Ivernia Inc.'s mine in view of government investigation into alleged lead contamination at the port of Esperance is discussed. The likely increase in the price of lead is also discussed.

12466 ■ **"Jamieson Eyes $175 Million Trust IPO"** in *Globe & Mail* (March 7, 2006, pp. B1)
Pub: CTVglobemedia Publishing Inc.
Ed: Sinclair Stewart; Leonard Zehr. **Description:** The reasons behind $175 million initial public offering plans of Jamieson Laboratories Ltd. are presented.

12467 ■ **"Jean Coutu Resuscitates Bottom Line"** in *Globe & Mail* (January 11, 2006, pp. B5)
Pub: CTVglobemedia Publishing Inc.
Ed: Bertrand Marotte. **Description:** The details on Jean Coutu Group (PJC) Inc., which posted $30.8 million profits for second quarter 2005, are presented.

12468 ■ **"Jet Sales Put Bombardier Back in Black"** in *Globe & Mail* **(March 30, 2006, pp. B1)**

Pub: CTVglobemedia Publishing Inc.

Ed: Bertrand Morotte. **Description:** The details on Bombardier Inc., which posted 20 percent rise in shares following $86 million profit for fourth quarter 2005, are presented.

12469 ■ **"Judge Gives RIM One Last Chance"** in *Globe & Mail* **(February 25, 2006, pp. B5)**

Pub: CTVglobemedia Publishing Inc.

Ed: Barrie McKenna; Paul Waldie. **Description:** United States District Court Judge James Spencer offers more time for Research In Motion Ltd. (RIM) to settle the patent infringement dispute with NTP Inc. RIM's shares increase by 6.2 percent following the decision.

12470 ■ **"The Judgment Deficit"** in *Harvard Business Review* **(Vol. 88, September 2010, No. 9, pp. 44)**

Pub: Harvard Business School Publishing

Ed: Amar Bhide. **Description:** The importance of individual, decentralized initiative and judgment in the capitalist system is outlined. While financial models have their use, they cannot always account appropriately for the inherent uncertainty in economic decision making.

12471 ■ **"Juiced on Energy"** in *Barron's* **(Vol. 88, July 14, 2008, No. 28, pp. 33)**

Pub: Dow Jones & Co., Inc.

Ed: Leslie P. Norton. **Description:** Brad Evans and his team at Heartland Value Plus were able to outperform their peers by significantly under-committing to financials and overexposing themselves with energy stocks. Brad Evans believes that there is a lot of value left in energy stocks such as natural gas.

12472 ■ **"Julie Holzrichter; Managing Director of Operations, CME Group Inc."** in *Crain's Chicago Business* **(Vol. 31, May 5, 2008, No. 18)**

Pub: Crain Communications, Inc.

Ed: Ann Saphir. **Description:** Profile of Julie Holzrichter who works as the managing director of operations for CME Group Inc. and is known as a decisive leader able to intercept and solve problems.

12473 ■ **"Just Hang Up"** in *Barron's* **(Vol. 88, March 10, 2008, No. 10, pp. 45)**

Pub: Dow Jones & Company, Inc.

Ed: Tiernan Ray. **Description:** Sprint's shares are expected to continue falling while the company attempts to attract subscribers by cutting prices, cutting earnings in the process. The company faces tougher competition from better-financed AT&T and Verizon Communications.

12474 ■ **"KC Presents Healthy Market for Medical REIT"** in *Business Journal-Serving Metropolitan Kansas City* **(Vol. 26, November 30, 2007)**

Pub: American City Business Journals, Inc.

Ed: Rob Roberts. **Description:** Medical Properties Trust, the only real estate investment trust that specializes in buying hospitals, is planning to invest in Kansas City due to its fast growing hospital market. The company owns 29 properties nationwide and is still planning to increase its portfolio.

12475 ■ **"Keeping the Faith in Fuel-Tech"** in *Barron's* **(Vol. 88, March 24, 2008, No. 12, pp. 20)**

Pub: Dow Jones & Company, Inc.

Ed: Christopher C. Williams. **Description:** Shares of air pollution control company Fuel-Tech remain on track to reach $40 each from their $19 level due to a continued influx of contracts. The stock has suffered from lower-than-expected quarterly earnings and tougher competition but stand to benefit from increased orders.

12476 ■ **"Kid Rock"** in *Canadian Business* **(Vol. 81, Summer 2008, No. 9, pp. 54)**

Pub: Rogers Media Ltd.

Ed: John Gray. **Description:** Damien Reynolds is the founder, chairman and chief executive officer of Vancouver-based Longview Capital Partners. The investment bank, founded in 2005, is one of the fastest-growing companies in British Columbia. The recent economic downturn has battered the stocks of the company and its portfolio of junior miners.

12477 ■ *King of Capital*

Pub: John Wiley and Sons, Inc.

Ed: Amey Stone; Mike Brewster. **Released:** 2004. **Price:** $16.95. **Description:** Biography of Sandy Weill describes how he became a billionaire business giant by creating successful companies from smaller, sometimes failing firms; creating successful new products where none previously existed; and making deals no one thought possible. He is also responsible for changing the landscape of the banking industry and insurance business when he created Citigroup in 1998, the world's largest financial services firm.

12478 ■ **"The King of Kincardine"** in *Canadian Business* **(Vol. 79, October 9, 2006, No. 20, pp. 101)**

Pub: Rogers Media

Ed: Paul Webster. **Description:** Motives of Duncan Hawthorne, president and chief executive officer of Bruce Power Ltd., behind investing in nuclear power plant in Ontario, Canada through private financing are discussed.

12479 ■ **"Land on Boardwalk"** in *Canadian Business* **(Vol. 82, April 27, 2009, No. 7, pp. 19)**

Pub: Rogers Media

Ed: Calvin Leung. **Description:** Boardwalk REIT remains as one of the most attractive real estate investment trusts in Canada, with 73 percent of analysts rating the firm a Buy. Analyst Neil Downey believes that good management, as well as a good business model, makes Boardwalk a good investment. Downey is concerned however, that a worsening of Alberta's economy could significantly impact Boardwalk.

12480 ■ **"The Last Ingredient?"** in *Canadian Business* **(Vol. 81, October 13, 2008, No. 17, pp. 88)**

Pub: Rogers Media Ltd.

Ed: Rachel Pulfer. **Description:** Views and information on Cookie Jar Group's plan to acquire rights for Strawberry Shortcake and the Care Bears are discussed. The move would make Cookie Jar a major player in the global children's entertainment market. Cookie Jar chief executive, Michael Hirsh is believed to be securing funds for the planned $195 million acquisition.

12481 ■ **"The Latin Beat Goes On"** in *Barron's* **(Vol. 88, July 7, 2008, No. 27, pp. L5)**

Pub: Dow Jones & Co., Inc.

Ed: Tom Sullivan. **Description:** Latin American stocks have outperformed other regional markets due to rising commodities prices and favorable economic climate. Countries such as Brazil, Mexico, Chile, and Peru provide investment opportunities, while Argentina and Venezuela are tougher places to invest.

12482 ■ **"Laugh or Cry?"** in *Barron's* **(Vol. 88, March 24, 2008, No. 12, pp. 7)**

Pub: Dow Jones & Company, Inc.

Ed: Alan Abelson. **Description:** Discusses the American economy which is just starting to feel the effect of the credit and housing crises. JPMorgan Chase purchased Bear Stearns for $2 a share, much lower than its share price of $60, while quasi-government entities Fannie Mae and Freddie Mac are starting to run into trouble.

12483 ■ **"Leaders and Lagards"** in *Barron's* **(Vol. 89, July 13, 2009, No. 28, pp. 14)**

Pub: Dow Jones & Co., Inc.

Ed: J.R. Brandstrader. **Description:** Statistical table that shows the returns of different mutual funds in different categories that include U.S. stock funds, sector funds, world equity funds, and mixed equity funds is presented. The data presented is for the second quarter of 2009.

12484 ■ **"Leaders Weigh In On Fannie Mae, Freddie Mac Failure, Fed Bailout"** in *The Business Journal - Serving Phoenix and the Valley of the Sun* **(Vol. 28, September 12, 2008, No. 53, pp. 1)**

Pub: American City Business Journals, Inc.

Ed: Chris Casacchia; Mike Sunnucks; Jan Buchholz. **Description:** Fannie Mae and Freddie Mac's federal takeover was a move to help stabilize the financial market and it helped bring down interest rates in the past week. Local executives from Arizona's Phoenix area share their thoughts on the immediate effect of the takeover and its upside and downside.

12485 ■ **"Lean on Me"** in *Entrepreneur* **(Vol. 36, February 2008, No. 2, pp. 40)**

Pub: Entrepreneur Media Inc.

Ed: Farnoosh Torabi. **Description:** Investing in tax liens is booming with the growth in the number of homeowners missing property tax payments. Details on how to bid for and when to redeem tax liens are outlined.

12486 ■ **"Leasing Midway; Look for Higher Parking Fees, More Retail Under Private Airport Operator"** in *Crain's Chicago Business* **(May 5, 2008)**

Pub: Crain Communications, Inc.

Ed: Paul Merrion. **Description:** According to experts, bids for the first privatization of a major U.S. airport could run as high as $3.5 billion. Information-gathering and negotiations will soon get under way with some or all of the six major international investor groups that recently expressed interest in running Midway.

12487 ■ **"Legg's Compensation Committee Chair Defends CEO Fetting's Pay"** in *Boston Business Journal* **(Vol. 29, July 22, 2011, No. 11, pp. 1)**

Pub: American City Business Journals Inc.

Ed: Gary Haber. **Description:** Legg Mason Inc. CEO Mark R. Fetting has been awarded $5.9 million pay package and he expects to receive questions regarding it in the coming shareholders meeting. However, Baltimore, Maryland-based RKTL Associates chairman emeritus Harold R. Adams believes Fetting has done a tremendous job in bringing Legg's through a tough market.

12488 ■ **"Lehman's Hail Mary Pass"** in *Business Week* **(September 22, 2008, No. 4100, pp. 28)**

Pub: McGraw-Hill Companies, Inc.

Ed: Matthew Goldstein; David Henry; Ben Levison. **Description:** Overview of Lehman Brothers' CEO Richard Fuld's plan to keep the firm afloat and end the stock's plunge downward; Fuld's strategy calls for selling off a piece of the firm's investment management business.

12489 ■ **"Lenders Capitalize on a Thinning Bulge Bracket"** in *Mergers & Acquisitions: The Dealmaker's Journal* **(March 1, 2008)**

Pub: SourceMedia, Inc.

Description: Regardless of what the economic markets look like, private equity firms will continue to invest capital and mid-market finance firms are becoming very attractive acquisition opportunities since not as much capital is needed to buy them.

12490 ■ **"Lenders"** in *The Business Journal - Serving Phoenix and the Valley of the Sun* **(Vol. 28, July 25, 2008, No. 47, pp. 1)**

Pub: American City Business Journals, Inc.

Ed: Jan Buchholz. **Description:** Private equity lender Investor Mortgage Holdings Inc. has continued growing despite the crisis surrounding the real estate and financial industries and has accumulated a $700 million loan portfolio. Private lending has become increasingly important in financing real estate deals as commercial credit has dried up.

12491 ■ **"Lending Idea Gets Mixed Review"** in *Tampa Bay Business Journal* **(Vol. 29, October 30, 2009, No. 45, pp. 1)**

Pub: American City Business Journals

Ed: Kent Hoover, Margie Manning. **Description:** Tampa Bay area, Florida's community banks have expressed disapproval to the proposal of President Obama to increase lending to small business, wherein the government will provide cheap capital through US Treasury Troubled Asset Relief Program (TARP). The banks were hesitant on the plan because of the strings attached to TARP.

12492 ■ "Less Malaise in Malaysia" in *Barron's* **(Vol. 88, March 17, 2008, No. 11, pp. M12)**
Pub: Dow Jones & Company, Inc.
Ed: Assif Shameen. Description: Shares of Malaysia's Bursa have been in freefall while the Malaysia government prolongs its pitch to sell a 10 percent stake of the exchange to NYSE Euronext. Asian bourses had produced very good returns for five years and charge some of the highest fees for exchanges. A key growth driver for Asian bourses could be the derivatives markets and exchange-traded funds.

12493 ■ "Let Us Count the Ways" in *Barron's* **(Vol. 88, July 7, 2008, No. 27, pp. M10)**
Pub: Dow Jones & Co., Inc.
Ed: Bennet Sedacca. Description: Investors are advised to remain cautious after the drop in stock prices in June 2008. The stock markets remain in the downtrend after reaching a peak in October 2007 and are on the verge of a collapse.

12494 ■ *Let's Buy a Company: How to Accelerate Growth Through Acquisitions*
Pub: Career Press, Incorporated
Ed: H. Lee Rust. Released: January 2006. Price: $18.99 (US), $25.95 (Canadian). Description: Advice for negotiating terms and pricing as well as other aspects of mergers and acquisitions in small companies.

12495 ■ "Lifebank Grants Stock Options" in *Canadian Corporate News* **(May 16, 2007)**
Pub: Comtex News Network Inc.
Description: Lifebank, a biomedical service company that provides processing cryogenic storage of umbilical cord blood stem cells, announced that, under its stock option plan, it has granted incentive stock options to directors, officers, and consultants of the company.

12496 ■ "A Lifetime of Making Deals" in *Crain's Detroit Business* **(Vol. 24, March 24, 2008, No. 12, pp. 11)**
Pub: Crain Communications, Inc.
Ed: Tom Henderson. Description: Profile of Walter "Bud" Aspatore who received Crain's Lifetime Achievement Award for mergers and acquisitions; Aspatore is chairman and co-founder of Amherst Partners L.L.C., an investment banking firm that does evaluations and financings, specializes in turnarounds and advises private and public companies on mergers and acquisitions.

12497 ■ "Lifetime Planning with a Twist" in *Contractor* **(Vol. 56, July 2009, No. 7, pp. 40)**
Pub: Penton Media, Inc.
Ed: Irv Blackman. Description: Private Placement Life Insurance lets wealthy investors make their investment gains tax-free and can be set up so investors can make tax-free loans from the policy. This can be used on a younger member of the family as a wealth-building strategy if the investor is uninsurable.

12498 ■ "A Limited Sphere of Influence" in *Mergers & Acquisitions: The Dealmaker's Journal* **(March 1, 2008)**
Pub: SourceMedia, Inc.
Ed: Ken MacFadyen. Description: Changes to the interest rate has had little impact on the mergers and acquisitions market since the federal funds rate does not link directly to the liquidity available to the M&A market; lenders are looking at cash flows and are likely to remain cautious due to other factors impacting the market.

12499 ■ "Listen to Bond Market on Tembec" in *Globe & Mail* **(January 25, 2006, pp. B1)**
Pub: CTVglobemedia Publishing Inc.
Ed: Derek DeCloet. Description: The feasibility of Tembec Inc.'s restructuring efforts is discussed.

12500 ■ "Listen Up: There's a Revolution in the Cubicle" in *Barron's* **(Vol. 89, July 27, 2009, No. 30, pp. 18)**
Pub: Dow Jones & Co., Inc.
Ed: Jay Palmer. Description: Plantronics will be among the first beneficiaries when the unified communications revolution arrives in the office. Plantron-

ics' shares could rise to around 30 in 2009 from the 20s as of July 2009. Unified communications could create a huge new multimillion-dollar market for Plantronics.

12501 ■ "The Little Biotech that Could" in *Barron's* **(Vol. 89, July 27, 2009, No. 30, pp. 19)**
Pub: Dow Jones & Co., Inc.
Ed: Christopher C. Williams. Description: OSI Pharmaceuticals' shares is a compelling investment bet among small biotech firms due to its Tarceva anticancer drug which has a 23 percent market share as well as their strong balance sheet. OSI is planning to expand the use of Tarceva which could re-ignite sales and one analyst expects the shares to trade in the 40s one year from July 2009.

12502 ■ "A Load of Bull?" in *Canadian Business* **(Vol. 82, Summer 2009, No. 8, pp. 12)**
Pub: Rogers Media
Ed: Joe Castaldo. Description: Some experts and analysts believe that the improvement of some economic indicators in Canada suggest an economic recovery. A survey of Russell Investment in March 2009 found that 60 percent of investment managers are bullish on Canadian stocks. Some experts like Mike Zyblock, however, remain cautious on the economy.

12503 ■ "Loblaw Posts 40 Percent Profit Drop as it Scrambles to Lower Costs" in *Globe & Mail* **(February 9, 2006, pp. B1)**
Pub: CTVglobemedia Publishing Inc.
Ed: Marina Strauss. Description: The reasons behind 40 percent decline in profits for Lobalaw Companies Ltd., for fourth quarter 2005, are presented.

12504 ■ "A Local Affair: Decisions for Tops Again Being Made at Amherst HQ" in *Business First Buffalo* **(December 7, 2007, pp. 3)**
Pub: American City Business Journals, Inc.
Ed: James Fink. Description: Tops Market LLC merged with Morgan Stanley Private Equity and names its new CEO, Frank Curci. The company headquarters moved to its new location in Amherst, New York.

12505 ■ "Local Firms Will Feel Impact Of Wall St. Woes" in *The Business Journal-Milwaukee* **(Vol. 25, September 19, 2008, No. 52, pp. A1)**
Pub: American City Business Journals, Inc.
Ed: Rich Kirchen. Description: Wall Street's crisis is expected to affect businesses in Wisconsin, in terms of decreased demand for services and products and increased financing costs. Businesses in Milwaukee area may face higher interest rates and tougher loan standards. The potential impacts of the Wall Street crisis on local businesses are examined further.

12506 ■ "Local TV Hits Media Radar Screen" in *Business Courier* **(Vol. 27, July 2, 2010, No. 9, pp. 1)**
Pub: Business Courier
Ed: Dan Monk. Description: Fort Wright, Kentucky-based broadcasting company Local TV LLC has acquired 18 television stations since its founding in 2007, potentially boosting its chances of becoming a media empire. In the last twelve months that ended in March 2010, Local TV LLC has posted total revenues of $415 million. How Local TV LLC has entered into cost-sharing deals with other stations is also discussed.

12507 ■ "Locally Based Stocks Escape Worst of Market's Turmoil" in *Crain's Detroit Business* **(Vol. 24, September 22, 2008, No. 38, pp. 4)**
Pub: Crain Communications, Inc.
Ed: Daniel Duggan. Description: Locally-based companies did not take as big a hit as might be expected with the shock to the financial markets last week; this is due mainly to the fact that the region does not have heavy exposure to energy or capital markets.

12508 ■ "Long - And Leery" in *Barron's* **(Vol. 88, March 31, 2008, No. 13, pp. 47)**
Pub: Dow Jones & Company, Inc.
Ed: Jack Willoughby. Description: Tom Claugus' Bay Resource Partners hedge fund has returned 20 percent annually since it started in 1993. Claugus says that he is as aggressively long as he has ever been despite the dangers of the U.S. market. Claugus' stock picks include Canadian Natural Resources, NII Holdings, and Discover Financial.

12509 ■ "A Look Ahead Into 2007" in *Canadian Business* **(Vol. 80, December 25, 2006, No. 1, pp. 40)**
Pub: Rogers Media
Description: The 2007 forecasts for various industrial sectors like telecom, information technology, manufacturing, retail, financial and energy among others is discussed.

12510 ■ "Looking For Financing?" in *Hispanic Business* **(Vol. 30, July-August 2008, No. 7-8, pp. 16)**
Pub: Hispanic Business, Inc.
Ed: Frank Nelson. Description: Investment firms want to know about businesses that need funding for either expansion or acquisition; companies fitting this profile are interviewed and their perceptions are discussed. Investment firms need businesses to be realistic in their expectations and business plans which show spending of funds and expected benefits, long term goals, track record and strong management teams.

12511 ■ "Looking For Good Buys" in *Black Enterprise* **(Vol. 38, November 2007, No. 4, pp. 39)**
Pub: Earl G. Graves Publishing Co. Inc.
Ed: Steve Garmhausen. Description: Lower interest rates mean consumers generally have more money to spend, which could spur economic growth in the retail sector of the U.S.

12512 ■ "Loonie Tunes: When Will the Dollar Rise Again?" in *Canadian Business* **(Vol. 81, November 10, 2008, No. 19, pp. 62)**
Pub: Rogers Media Ltd.
Ed: Joe Castaldo. Description: The Canadian dollar has weakened against the U.S. Dollar as the U.S. financial crisis rocked global markets. A currency strategist says that the strength of the U.S. dollar is not based on people's optimism on the U.S. economy but on a structural demand where U.S. non-financial corporations have been repatriating greenbacks from foreign subsidiaries.

12513 ■ "Lotus Starts Slowly, Dodges Subprime Woes" in *Crain's Detroit Business* **(Vol. 24, April 14, 2008, No. 15, pp. 3)**
Pub: Crain Communications, Inc.
Ed: Tom Henderson. Description: Discusses Lotus Bancorp Inc. and their business plan, which although is not right on target due to the subprime mortgage meltdown, is in a much better position than its competitors due to the quality of their loans.

12514 ■ "Lower Prices No Shoo-In as Telcos Near Deregulation" in *Globe & Mail* **(March 28, 2007, pp. B1)**
Pub: CTVglobemedia Publishing Inc.
Ed: Catherine McLean. Description: The fall in market share and low quality of service among other issues that may disallow telecommunication industries in Canada from setting their phone rates is discussed.

12515 ■ "Loyalty Pays" in *Entrepreneur* **(Vol. 36, February 2008, No. 2, pp. 63)**
Pub: Entrepreneur Media Inc.
Ed: David Worrell. Description: Michael Vadini, chief executive officer of Titan Technology Partners looks after his stockholders and investors by making sure that they are protected from risk. Having been affected by the downturn in the technology industry between 2001 and 2004, Vadini granted his investors a liquidity preference. Details regarding his actions to retain investor loyalty are discussed.

12516 ■ "Lundin Deal Leaves Nickel Market Thin" in *Globe & Mail* **(April 5, 2007, pp. B4)**
Pub: CTVglobemedia Publishing Inc.
Ed: Andy Hoffman. **Description:** The likely acquisition of Rio Narcea Gold Mines Ltd. by Lundin Mining Corp. and the decreasing number of nickel mining companies on the list of Toronto Stock Exchange are discussed.

12517 ■ "Luster Lost" in *Saint Louis Business Journal* **(Vol. 32, September 16, 2011, No. 3, pp. 1)**
Pub: Saint Louis Business Journal
Ed: E.B. Solomont. **Description:** Express Cripts shares have plunged 22.71 percent since late July amid regulatory concerns, as the luster of the second-largest deal announced for 2011 wore off. Express Scripts has become the largest pharmacy benefit manager in the country after the $29 billion deal to take rival Medco Health Solutions.

12518 ■ "Lux Coffees, Breads Push Chains to React" in *Advertising Age* **(Vol. 77, June 26, 2006, No. 26, pp. S14)**
Pub: Crain Communications, Inc.
Ed: Kate MacArthur. **Description:** Fast-food giants such as McDonald's, Burger King, Dunkin' Donuts and Subway have adjusted their menus in order to become more competitive with gourmet coffee shops and bakeries like Panera Bread and Starbucks which have taken a large share in the market. Statistical data included.

12519 ■ "Magna Banks on Big Cash Hoard" in *Globe & Mail* **(March 1, 2006, pp. B3)**
Pub: CTVglobemedia Publishing Inc.
Ed: Greg Keenan. **Description:** The details on Magna International Inc., which posted decline in profits at $639 million for 2005, are presented.

12520 ■ "Magna Shares Sink on Tepid Outlook" in *Globe & Mail* **(January 13, 2006, pp. B1)**
Pub: CTVglobemedia Publishing Inc.
Ed: Greg Keenan. **Description:** The impact of Magna International Inc.'s sales projection for 2006, on its shares, is discussed.

12521 ■ "Making It Click" in *Barron's* **(Vol. 88, March 17, 2008, No. 11, pp. 31)**
Pub: Dow Jones & Company, Inc.
Ed: Theresa W. Carey. **Description:** Listing of 23 online brokers that are evaluated based on their trade experience, usability, range of offerings, research amenities, customer service and access, and costs. TradeStation Securities takes the top spot followed by thinkorswim by just a fraction.

12522 ■ "M&I Execs May Get Golden Parachutes" in *Business Journal-Milwaukee* **(Vol. 28, December 31, 2010, No. 14, pp. A3)**
Pub: Milwaukee Business Journal
Ed: Rich Kirchen. **Description:** Marshall and Isley Corporation's top executives have a chance to receive golden-parachute payments it its buyer, BMO Financial Group, repays the Troubled Asset Relief Program (TARP) loan on behalf of the company. One TARP rule prevents golden-parachute payments to them and the next five most highly paid employees of TARP recipients.

12523 ■ "M&T On the March?" in *Baltimore Business Journal* **(Vol. 28, November 12, 2010, No. 27, pp. 1)**
Pub: Baltimore Business Journal
Ed: Gary Haber. **Description:** Information on the growth of M&T Bank, as well as its expansion plans are presented. M&T recently acquired Wilmington Trust and took over $500 million in deposits from the failed K Bank. Analysts believe that M&T would continue its expansion through Washington DC and Richmond, Virginia, especially after a bank executive acknowledged that the markets in those areas are attractive.

12524 ■ "Many Roads Lead to Value" in *Barron's* **(Vol. 88, March 10, 2008, No. 10, pp. 46)**
Pub: Dow Jones & Company, Inc.
Ed: Lawrence C. Strauss. **Description:** David J. Williams, lead manager of Excelsior Value & Restructuring Fund, invests in struggling companies and those

companies whose turnarounds show promise. Morgan Stanley, Lehman Brothers, and Petroleo Brasileiro are some of the companies he holds shares in, while he has unloaded shares of Citigroup, Freddie Mac, and Sallie Mae.

12525 ■ "Market Recoups Its Losses - And Its Optimism" in *Barron's* **(Vol. 89, July 20, 2009, No. 29, pp. M3)**
Pub: Dow Jones & Co., Inc.
Ed: Kopin Tan. **Description:** US stock markets gained heavily in the third week of July 2009, rising by about 7 percent during the week. The shares of human resource management companies could be overpriced as they are trading at very high price-earnings multiples. Baxter International faces a class-action suit due to its alleged conspiracy with CSL to fix blood-plasma product prices.

12526 ■ "Market Volatility and Your Retirement" in *Agency Sales Magazine* **(Vol. 39, August 2009, No. 8, pp. 48)**
Pub: MANA
Ed: Joshua D. Mosshart. **Description:** Strategies for retirees in managing investments amid market volatility are presented. Retirees should keep their withdrawal assumptions conservative, maintain sensible asset allocation, review and rebalance their portfolio and allow a financial professional to guide them. Insights on market volatility are also given.

12527 ■ "Market Watch: A Sampling of Advisory Opinion" in *Barron's* **(Vol. 88, March 17, 2008, No. 11, pp. M10)**
Pub: Dow Jones & Company, Inc.
Ed: Paul Schatz; William Gibson; Michael Darda. **Description:** S&P 500 bank stocks were down 46 percent from their 2007 peak while the peak to through fall in 1989-1990 was just over 50 percent. This suggests that the bottom on the bank stocks could be near. The Federal Reserve Board announced they will lend up to $200 billion to primary lenders in exchange other securities.

12528 ■ "Market Watch" in *Barron's* **(Vol. 88, March 24, 2008, No. 12, pp. M18)**
Pub: Dow Jones & Company, Inc.
Ed: Ashraf Laidi; Marc Pado; David Kotok. **Description:** Latest measures implemented by the Federal Reserve to address the credit crisis did not benefit the US dollar, with the Japanese yen and the euro recouping earlier losses against the dollar. Goldman Sachs reported earnings of $3.23 per share, claiming a stronger liquidity position. The US markets bottomed early on 22 January 2007, according to evidence.

12529 ■ "Markets Defy the Doomsayers" in *Barron's* **(Vol. 88, March 24, 2008, No. 12, pp. M5)**
Pub: Dow Jones & Company, Inc.
Ed: Leslie P. Norton. **Description:** US stock markets registered strong gains, with the Dow Jones Industrial Average rising 3.43 percent on the week to close at 12,361.32, in a rally that may be seen as short-covering. Shares of Hansen Natural are poised for further drops with a slowdown in the energy drink market.

12530 ■ "Markets in Disarray...Fundamentals Still Strong?" in *Hispanic Business* **(October 2007, pp. 14, 16, 18)**
Pub: Hispanic Business
Ed: Dr. Juan B. Solana. **Description:** Quarterly economic forecast is presented, covering credit, interest rates, home prices, stock market, and what lies ahead.

12531 ■ "The Market's (Very) Tender Spring Shoots" in *Barron's* **(Vol. 88, March 31, 2008, No. 13, pp. M3)**
Pub: Dow Jones & Company, Inc.
Ed: Kopin Tan. **Description:** Expansion in price-earnings multiples and a lower credit-default risk index has encouraged fans of the spring-awakening theory. Shares of industrial truckers have gone up 32 percent in 2008 and some shares are pushing five-year highs brought on by higher efficiency and earnings from more load carried. The prospects of the shares of Foot Locker are also discussed.

12532 ■ *The Match King: Ivar Kreuger, the Financial Genius Behind a Century of Wall Street Scandals*
Pub: Basic Books
Ed: Frank Portnoy. **Released:** 2009. **Price:** $26.95. **Description:** Ivar Kreuger, the so-called Match King, used a pyramid scheme to become the financier to European leaders.

12533 ■ "Meadowbrook CEO Sees 20 Percent Growth With New Acquisition" in *Crain's Detroit Business* **(Vol. 24, March 10, 2008, No. 10, pp. 4)**
Pub: Crain Communications, Inc.
Ed: Jay Greene. **Description:** Discusses the major turnaround of Meadowbrook Insurance Group after Robert Cubbin became CEO and implemented a new business strategy.

12534 ■ "Meadowbrook To Acquire ProCentury in $272.6 Million Deal" in *Crain's Detroit Business* **(Vol. 24, February 25, 2008, No. 8, pp. 4)**
Pub: Crain Communications Inc. - Detroit
Description: Meadowbrook Insurance Group, based in Southfield, Michigan reports its proposed acquisition of ProCentury Corporation based in Columbus, Ohio. Meadowbrook provides risk-management to agencies, professional and trade associations and small-to-midsize businesses.

12535 ■ "Media Industry Collection Agency Completes Acquisition" in *Collections & Credit Risk* **(Vol. 15, December 1, 2010, No. 11, pp. 22)**
Pub: SourceMedia Inc.
Description: Media Receivable Management Inc. (MRM) will take over the collection operations at Borden, Jones & Mitchell, in Miami, Florida. MRM clients are basically magazine and electronic media publishers.

12536 ■ "The Medium 150" in *Canadian Business* **(Vol. 81, Summer 2008, No. 9, pp. 129)**
Pub: Rogers Media Ltd.
Description: Medium-sized companies are ranked based on market capitalization and stock performance. Timminico Ltd. topped the roster with 1,294.2 percent returns, while Petrominerales Ltd. ranked second with 325.4 percent. A table showing the 2008 rankings of the companies is presented.

12537 ■ *Medium Sized Firms and Economics Growth*
Pub: Nova Science Publishers, Incorporated
Ed: Janez Prasniker. **Released:** April 2005. **Price:** $130.00. **Description:** Medium sized companies should have a more definitive presence in modern microeconomic theory, the theory of entrepreneurship, and the theory of financial markets.

12538 ■ "Meet the Gatekeepers" in *Crain's Chicago Business* **(Vol. 30, February 2007, No. 6, pp. 40)**
Pub: Crain Communications, Inc.
Ed: Kate Ryan. **Description:** Recruiters at big investment banking firms agree that the way to get your foot in the door requires common sense issues such as not answering your phone in the middle of an interview, proofreading your cover letter, and research. Interviews with three top executives give more insight and advice.

12539 ■ "Merger Brings New Force to Hispanic Marketing Industry" in *Hispanic Business* **(July-August 2007, pp. 60)**
Pub: Hispanic Business
Description: Merger between Latin Force LLC, a marketing strategy firm and Geoscape International Inc., a consumer intelligence and data analytics company is discussed.

12540 ■ *Mergers and Acquisitions from A to Z*
Pub: Amacom
Ed: Andrew J. Sherman, Milledge A. Hart. **Released:** January 2006. **Price:** $35.00. **Description:** Guide for the entire process of mergers and acquisitions, including taxes, accounting, laws, and projected financial gain.

12541 ■ "Mettle Detector" in *Canadian Business* **(Vol. 79, July 17, 2006, No. 14-15, pp. 63)**
Pub: Rogers Media
Ed: Calvin Leung. **Description:** The difficulties faced in completing the Certified Financial Analyst course, and the rewards one can expect after its completion, are discussed.

12542 ■ "MF Global Moved Clients' Funds to BNY Mellon" in *Wall Street Journal Eastern Edition* **(November 19 , 2011, pp. B2)**
Pub: Dow Jones & Company Inc.
Ed: Aaron Lucchetti. **Description:** Since the collapse of securities brokerage MF Global Holdings Ltd., one question has remained: where did the hundreds of millions of dollars in customers' accounts go? It has been revealed that MF Global moved those millions from its own brokerage unit to Bank of New York Mellon Corporation in August of this year, just two months before filing for bankruptcy protection.

12543 ■ "MFS Survey: Generation X/Y Perplexed and Conservative about Future Investing" in *Wireless News* **(November 16, 2010)**
Pub: Close-Up Media Inc.
Description: Generation X and Y tend to have a conservative approach to investing according to a survey conducted by MFS Investment Management. Statistical data included.

12544 ■ "Micro-Cap Companies" in *Canadian Business* **(Vol. 81, Summer 2008, No. 9, pp. 157)**
Pub: Rogers Media Ltd.
Description: Micro-cap companies have lower than $221 million in terms of market capitalization. Burnaby, British Columbia-based Fancamp Exploration Ltd. topped the roster with 1,116.7 percent in return. A table showing the 2008 rankings of the companies is presented.

12545 ■ "Microsoft Goes Macrosoft" in *Barron's* **(Vol. 89, July 27, 2009, No. 30, pp. 25)**
Pub: Dow Jones & Co., Inc.
Ed: Mark Veverka. **Description:** Microsoft reported a weak quarter on the heels of a tech rally which suggests the economy has not turned around. Marc Andreesen describes his new venture-capital fund as focused on 'classic tech' and that historical reference places him in the annals of the last millennium.

12546 ■ "Microsoft's Big Gamble" in *Canadian Business* **(Vol. 81, March 3, 2008, No. 3, pp. 13)**
Pub: Rogers Media
Ed: Andrew Wahl. **Description:** Microsoft Corp. is taking a big risk in buying Yahoo, as it is expected to pay more than $31 a share to finalize the acquisition. The deal would be seven and a half times bigger than any other that Microsoft has entered before, an execution of such deal is also anticipated to become a challenge for Microsoft. Recommendations on how Microsoft should handle the integration of the two businesses are given.

12547 ■ "Millions Needed To Finish First Place" in *The Business Journal-Milwaukee* **(Vol. 25, August 15, 2008, No. 47, pp. A1)**
Pub: American City Business Journals, Inc.
Ed: Rich Kirchen. **Description:** First Place on the River condominium project in Milwaukee, Wisconsin, needs $18.2 million before it can be completed. A total of $6.8 million have already been spent since the project went into receivership on 31 January 2008.

12548 ■ "Mine Woes Could Rouse Zinc" in *Barron's* **(Vol. 88, July 7, 2008, No. 27, pp. M12)**
Pub: Dow Jones & Co., Inc.
Ed: Andrea Hotter. **Description:** Prices of zinc could increase due to supply problems in producing countries such as Australia and China. London Metal Exchange prices for the metal have dropped about 36 percent in 2008.

12549 ■ "Mining Executive Telfer Pocketed Millions" in *Globe & Mail* **(April 5, 2007, pp. B4)**
Pub: CTVglobemedia Publishing Inc.
Ed: Andy Hoffman. **Description:** The issue of huge compensation for former executive of both Goldcorp Inc. and UrAsia Energy Ltd., Ian Telfer, for his efficient management of stock options is discussed.

12550 ■ "Mining Goldman for Insight" in *Barron's* **(Vol. 89, July 20, 2009, No. 29, pp. M8)**
Pub: Dow Jones & Co., Inc.
Ed: Steven M. Sears. **Description:** Methods of investing in options for companies with earnings estimates from Goldman Sachs are discussed. These methods take advantage of increased volatility generated by earnings revisions.

12551 ■ "Minor-League Baseball's Sliders Plan Stock Offering" in *Crain's Detroit Business* **(Vol. 25, June 15, 2009, No. 24, pp. 3)**
Pub: Crain Communications Inc. - Detroit
Ed: Bill Shea. **Description:** New minor-league baseball team is raising funds to build a new stadium in Waterford Township, Michigan because banks are unwilling to provide loans for the project. Owners of the Midwest Sliders in Ypsilanti, Michigan are waiting for the federal Securities and Exchange Commission to approve a Regulation A public offering.

12552 ■ "Misguided" in *Canadian Business* **(Vol. 81, July 22, 2008, No. 12-13, pp. 30)**
Pub: Rogers Media Ltd.
Ed: Al Rosen. **Description:** Canada's securities regulations are discussed; differing views on using principles-based and rules-based securities regulations are also presented.

12553 ■ "Misplaced Trust" in *Canadian Business* **(Vol. 79, October 23, 2006, No. 21, pp. 65)**
Pub: Rogers Media
Ed: John Gray. **Description:** The reasons for the drop in the share prices of the income trusts of Retrocom Investment Management Inc. are analyzed.

12554 ■ "Missing MF Global Funds Could Top $1.2 Billion" in *Wall Street Journal Eastern Edition* **(November 22 , 2011, pp. A1)**
Pub: Dow Jones & Company Inc.
Ed: Aaron Lucchetti, Dan Strumpf. **Description:** As the investigation into the collapse of securities brokerage MF Global Holdings Ltd. continues, the question of what happened to customers' funds has to be answered. Now, it is believed that the actual amount of missing funds is much more than the $600 million originally thought, and could be well over $1.2 billion.

12555 ■ "A Mixed-Bag Quarter" in *Barron's* **(Vol. 88, July 7, 2008, No. 27, pp. 19)**
Pub: Dow Jones & Co., Inc.
Ed: Shirley A. Lazo. **Description:** Seven component companies of the Dow Jones Industrial Average increased their dividend payouts in the second quarter of 2008 despite the weak performance of the index. Five companies in the Dow Jones Transportation index and three in the Dow Jones Utilities also increased their dividends.

12556 ■ "Modern-Day Midas Hasn't Lost Touch" in *Globe & Mail* **(January 19, 2006, pp. B4)**
Pub: CTVglobemedia Publishing Inc.
Ed: Shirley Won. **Description:** The investment plans of chief executive officer Rob McEwen of U.S. Gold Corp. are presented.

12557 ■ "Molson Coors Ends Ill-Fated Foray Into Brazil" in *Globe & Mail* **(January 17, 2006, pp. B1)**
Pub: CTVglobemedia Publishing Inc.
Ed: Andy Hoffman. **Description:** The details of loss incurred by Molson Coors Brewing Co., from the sale of Cervejarias Kaiser SA to Fomento Economico Mexicano S.A. de C.V., are presented.

12558 ■ "Molycorp Funds Wind Energy Technology Company" in *Manufacturing Close-Up* **(September 19, 2011)**
Pub: Close-Up Media
Description: Molycorp Inc., producer of rare earth oxides (REO) and a REO producer outside of China, announced it will invest in Boulder Wind Power, which has designed a rare earth magnet powered wind turbine generator. This new generator can produce electricity as low as $0.04 per Kilowatt Hour. Boulder Wind Power's patented wind turbine technology allows for use of rare earth permanent magnets that do not require dysprosium, which is relatively scarce.

12559 ■ "Moms Mull Money" in *Marketing to Women* **(Vol. 21, February 2008, No. 2, pp. 6)**
Pub: EPM Communications, Inc.
Description: According to a survey by Countrywide Bank, women, especially mothers, are more concerned about their financial fitness than men.

12560 ■ "Money Man" in *Canadian Business* **(Vol. 80, January 15, 2007, No. 2, pp. 67)**
Pub: Rogers Media
Ed: Jeff Sanford. **Description:** A profile of Donald A. Guloien, chief investment officer of Manulife Financial and chief executive officer of Global Investment Management, is presented.

12561 ■ "Monsanto Acquires Targeted-Pest Control Technology Start-Up; Terms Not Disclosed" in *Benzinga.com* **(, 2011)**
Pub: Benzinga.com
Ed: Benzinga Staff. **Description:** Monsanto Company acquired Beelogics, a firm that researches and develops biological tools that control pests and diseases. Research includes a product that will help protect bee health.

12562 ■ "Montreal Exchange Buoyed by U.S. Takeover Moves" in *Globe & Mail* **(March 16, 2007, pp. B1)**
Pub: CTVglobemedia Publishing Inc.
Ed: Sinclair Stewart. **Description:** The rise in the share prices of Montreal Exchange due to the derivatives exchange's bid to acquire the Chicago Board of Trade is discussed. The trends pertaining to the consolidation of global stock markets are described.

12563 ■ "Moody and Paranoid" in *Barron's* **(Vol. 88, March 10, 2008, No. 10, pp. M14)**
Pub: Dow Jones & Company, Inc.
Ed: Steven M. Sears. **Description:** Discusses the options market which remains liquid but is cautious of possible failures, especially for financial companies. Investors are in absolute fear when trading with options involving the financial sector.

12564 ■ "More Gains in the Pipeline" in *Barron's* **(Vol. 89, August 3, 2009, No. 31, pp. M5)**
Pub: Dow Jones & Co., Inc.
Ed: Fleming Meeks. **Description:** Shares of El Paso Corp. could recover as the company concludes a deal with a private-equity group to fund pipeline construction. The company's shares are trading at $10.06 and could move up to $12 as bad news has already been priced into the stock.

12565 ■ "More Jobs Moving Out of City" in *Business Courier* **(Vol. 24, March 14, 2008, No. 49, pp. 1)**
Pub: American City Business Journals, Inc.
Ed: Steve Watkins; Laura Baverman. **Description:** UBS Financial Services Inc. is moving Gradison to Kenwood Town Place in Sycamore Township a year after UBS acquired Gradison. The township does not have a tax on earnings so the move will save Gradison's employees the 2.1 percent Cincinnati tax.

12566 ■ "More Questions Face Huntington" in *Business First-Columbus* **(December 7, 2007, pp. A3)**
Pub: American City Business Journals, Inc.
Ed: Adrian Burns. **Description:** Marty Adams' abrupt resignation has lead to speculation that he was dismissed by the bank in relation to the unexpected run-in with the subprime mortgage fiasco. Analysis

predict Columbus-based Huntington Bancshares Inc. might be targeted for acquisition. Details on the company's revenues and shares of stock prices are presented.

12567 ■ "Mortgage Mess Continues To Trigger Bids To Ease Crisis" in *Business First-Columbus* **(December 14, 2007, pp. A1)**
Pub: American City Business Journals, Inc.
Ed: Adrian Burns. **Description:** Measures to prevent foreclosures in Ohio are presented. On December 6, 2007, the Bush Administration started a national incentive that will establish a streamlined process for modifying loans. Some have questioned the proposal, since it is expected the plan will only help about 90,000 of the 1.8 million borrowers. According to Ohio Treasurer, Richard Cordray, one of the state's objectives is to calm the markets on Wall Street.

12568 ■ "Mortgage Mess: How To Determine Your Exposure To the Subprime Crisis" in *Black Enterprise* **(Vol. 38, November 2007, No. 4, pp. 46)**
Pub: Earl G. Graves Publishing Co. Inc.
Ed: Ilana Polyak. **Description:** Stocks and mutual funds have experienced declines because of the subprime crisis. Morningstar's Website can help investors research firms in which they have invested; if a fund is named high yield or high income or in the financial services sector, investments will have greater exposure to the mess.

12569 ■ "Mortgage Securities Drop Hits Home" in *The Business Journal-Serving Metropolitan Kansas City* **(Vol. 27, October 17, 2008, No. 5)**
Pub: American City Business Journals, Inc.
Ed: Rob Roberts. **Description:** Sale of commercial mortgage-backed securities (CMBS) in Kansas City, Missouri have declined. The area may avoid layoffs if the United States government succeeds in stabilizing the economy. Major CMBS players in the area include Midland Loan Services Inc. and KeyBank Real Estate Capital.

12570 ■ "A Motorola Spinoff Is No Panacea" in *Barron's* **(Vol. 88, March 31, 2008, No. 13, pp. 19)**
Pub: Dow Jones & Company, Inc.
Ed: Mark Veverka. **Description:** Motorola's plan to try and spinoff their handset division is bereft of details as to how or specifically when in 2009 the spinoff would occur. There's no reason to buy the shares since there's a lot of execution risk to the plan. Motorola needs to hire a proven cellphone executive and develop a compelling new cellphone platform.

12571 ■ "Move Marks KKR's Latest Push into Retail" in *Globe & Mail* **(March 13, 2007, pp. B17)**
Pub: CTVglobemedia Publishing Inc.
Ed: Heather Burke. **Description:** Investment giant Kohlberg Kravis Roberts and Co. has finalized a deal to acquire retail store chain Dollar General Corp. for an estimated 6.9 billion dollars. The company will be entering lucrative retail market by this acquisition.

12572 ■ "Mover and Sheika" in *Conde Nast Portfolio* **(Vol. 2, June 2008, No. 6, pp. 104)**
Pub: Conde Nast Publications, Inc.
Ed: John Arlidge. **Description:** Profile of Princess Sheika Lubna who is the first female foreign trade minister in the Middle East, the United Arab Emirates biggest business envoy, paving the way for billions in new investment, and also a manufacturer of her own perfume line.

12573 ■ "'Mr. CEO, Please Do Elaborate On Your Firm's Metrics'" in *Business Courier* **(Vol. 24, February 29, 2008, No. 47, pp. 1)**
Pub: American City Business Journals, Inc.
Ed: Jon Newberry. **Description:** Discusses a rogue caller who goes by the name of Joe Herrick, Steven Nissan and Joe Harris has joined in over a dozen conference calls, asking chief executive officers on their plans and commenting on the companies' opera-

tions. The mystery caller attempts to pass himself off as a financial analyst. Transcripts of some conference calls, in which the rogue caller is involved, are provided.

12574 ■ "Mr. Deeds" in *Canadian Business* **(Vol. 81, March 31, 2008, No. 5, pp. 24)**
Pub: Rogers Media
Ed: Thomas Watson. **Description:** Ron Sandler has the right experience to save Northern Rock PLC get through its liquidity problems. Sandler is known for saving Lloyd's of London in the mid-90's and he is not afraid to make enemies. Ron Sandler's assignment to help Northern Rock comes at a time when the health of the U.K. housing is not great.

12575 ■ "MTI Faces Touch Choices" in *The Business Review Albany* **(Vol. 35, April 4, 2008, No. 53, pp. 1)**
Pub: The Business Review
Ed: Richard A. D'Errico. **Description:** Mechanical Technology Inc.'s auditor, PricewaterhouseCoopers LLP is concerned about the company's limited current cash and its $105 million accumulated deficit. MTI has already sold 1.45 million of its PlugPower Inc. shares, but still considers to sell more of the Plug stock. The problems at MTI and the difficult decisions it has to face to solve them are examined.

12576 ■ "Muddy Portfolio Raises a Question: Just What Is National City Worth?" in *Crain's Detroit Business* **(Vol. 24, April 7, 2008, No. 14)**
Pub: Crain Communications, Inc.
Ed: Jay Miller. **Description:** National City Bank is looking at strategies to help it deal with its credit and loan problems which are reflected in its falling stock price. One possible solution is a merger with another bank, however most national banks are facing their own home-loan portfolio issues and may be unable to tackle another company's unresolved problems. Statistical data included.

12577 ■ "The Murky Tale of a Failed Fund" in *Globe & Mail* **(January 3, 2006, pp. B1)**
Pub: CTVglobemedia Publishing Inc.
Ed: Bertrand Marotte. **Description:** The opinions of chief executive officer John Xanthoudakis of Norshield Financial Group, on controversy surrounding the company's handling of investors' money, are presented.

12578 ■ "Mutual Fund Sales of $23.4 Billion Best Since 2001" in *Globe & Mail* **(January 5, 2006, pp. B3)**
Pub: CTVglobemedia Publishing Inc.
Ed: Omar El Akkad. **Description:** The details on $23.4 billion net sales of mutual fund sector, in Canada, are presented.

12579 ■ "Myths of Deleveraging" in *Barron's* **(Vol. 90, August 23, 2010, No. 34, pp. M14)**
Pub: Barron's Editorial & Corporate Headquarters
Ed: Gene Epstein. **Description:** The opposite is true against reports about deleveraging or the decrease in credit since inflation-adjusted-investment factories and equipment rose 7.8 percent in the first quarter of 2010. On consumer deleveraging, sales of homes through credit is weak but there is a trend towards more realistic homeownership and consumer spending on durable goods rose 8.8 percent.

12580 ■ "Naked Investing" in *Canadian Business* **(Vol. 80, January 15, 2007, No. 2, pp. 27)**
Pub: Rogers Media
Ed: Al Rosen. **Description:** The need for Canadian investors to learn important facts about income trusts before investing in them is discussed.

12581 ■ "Nancy Hughes Anthony" in *Canadian Business* **(Vol. 81, October 13, 2008, No. 17, pp. 104)**
Pub: Rogers Media Ltd.
Ed: Andy Holloway. **Description:** Profile of Nancy Hughes Anthony, who believes her experience operating large enterprises as a public servant helped her earn positions that ultimately brought her to her current position as chief executive and president of

the Canadian Bankers Association. She also thinks there should be more public-private sector coordination within industries.

12582 ■ "Nanoready?" in *Entrepreneur* **(Vol. 36, May 2008, No. 5, pp. 20)**
Pub: Entrepreneur Media, Inc.
Ed: Andrea Cooper. **Description:** Experts predict that the medicine and energy sectors are among those that will see nanotechnology innovations in the coming years, and that nanotechnology will produce significant commercial value in new products. Some entrepreneurs are investing in nanotech and are partnering with universities. Details on nanotech funding concerns are discussed.

12583 ■ "Nautilus Fights For Its Life" in *Business Journal-Portland* **(Vol. 24, November 23, 2007, No. 38, pp. 1)**
Pub: American City Business Journals, Inc.
Ed: Matthew Kish. **Description:** Shareholders meeting will determine whether four members at Nautilus Inc. will be ousted and control given to New York firm Sherborne Investors LP. The decision on December 18, 2007 is crucial since the investor's record is varied. For some it has significantly increased shares, while others have ended in near-bankruptcy stages.

12584 ■ "Need Grub? Start Texting at Kroger" in *Business Courier* **(Vol. 24, December 21, 2008, No. 36, pp. 1)**
Pub: American City Business Journals, Inc.
Ed: Laura Baverman. **Description:** Discusses the University of Cincinnati which is teaming up to release a technology platform called Macopay that would link a cell phone to a bank account and allow a person to make payments at participating retailers by sending a text message. Details with regard to the new service and its growth potential are discussed.

12585 ■ "Needed: A Strategy; Banking In China" in *The Economist* **(Vol. 390, January 3, 2009, No. 8612, pp. 54)**
Pub: The Economist Newspaper Inc.
Description: International banks are competing for a role in China but are finding obstacles in their paths such as a reduction in the credit their operations may receive from Chinese banks and the role they can play in the public capital markets which remain limited.

12586 ■ *Nelson Information's Directory of Investment Research*
Pub: Nelson Information
Released: Annual, December. **Price:** $750, individuals print. **Covers:** Over 7,000 firms; 14,000 public companies; and 9,000 analysts. **Entries Include:** Name, address, phone, fax, names and titles of key personnel, five-year operating summary, description of business.

12587 ■ *Nerds on Wall Street: Math, Machines and Wired Markets*
Pub: John Wiley & Sons, Inc.
Ed: David J. Leinweber. **Released:** May 27, 2009. **Price:** $39.95. **Description:** The history of technology and how it will transform investing and trading on Wall Street is outlined.

12588 ■ "Nestle Acquires Waggin' Train Dog Treat Company" in *Pet Product News* **(Vol. 64, November 2010, No. 11, pp. 7)**
Pub: BowTie Inc.
Description: Vevey, Switzerland-based Nestle has acquired South Carolina-based dog treat firm Waggin' Train LLC from private equity firm VMG Partners in September 2010. Waggin' Train LLC, which will be operated as a wholly owned subsidiary, is expected to fill a gap in Nestle's dog treat product portfolio.

12589 ■ "Netflix Gets No Respect" in *Barron's* **(Vol. 89, July 27, 2009, No. 30, pp. 26)**
Pub: Dow Jones & Co., Inc.
Ed: Tiernan Ray. **Description:** Netflix met expectations when they announced their second quarter sales but their shares still fell by almost 10 percent. Analysts say their entry into the "streaming video"

business is a mixed bag since customers are increasingly buying the cheaper monthly plan and this is dragging the economics of the business.

12590 ■ "The New Arsenal of Risk Management" in *Harvard Business Review* **(Vol. 86, September 2008, No. 9, pp. 92)**
Pub: Harvard Business School Press

Ed: Kevin Bueler; Andrew Freeman; Ron Hulme. **Description:** Goldman Sachs Group Inc. is used to illustrate methods for successful risk management. The investment bank's business principles, partnerships, and oversight practices are discussed.

12591 ■ "New Century's Fall Has a New Culprit" in *Barron's* **(Vol. 88, March 31, 2008, No. 13, pp. 20)**
Pub: Dow Jones & Company, Inc.

Ed: Jonathan R. Laing. **Description:** Court examiner Michael Missal reports that New Century Financial's auditor contributed to New Century's demise by its negligence in permitting improper and imprudent practices related to New Century's accounting processes. New Century's bankruptcy filing is considered the start of the subprime-mortgage crisis.

12592 ■ "New Drug Could Revitalize Amgen" in *Barron's* **(Vol. 88, July 7, 2008, No. 27, pp. 23)**
Pub: Dow Jones & Co., Inc.

Ed: Johanna Bennett. **Description:** Shares of the biotechnology company Amgen could receive a boost from the release of the anti-osteoporosis drug denosumab. The shares, priced at $48.84 each, are trading at 11 times expected earnings for 2008 and could also be boosted by cost cutting measures.

12593 ■ "A New Kid on the Block" in *Barron's* **(Vol. 88, March 17, 2008, No. 11, pp. 58)**
Pub: Dow Jones & Company, Inc.

Ed: Thomas G. Donlan. **Description:** Discusses the Federal Reserve which has offered to lend $100 billion in cash to banks and $200 billion in Treasuries to Wall Street investment banks that have problems with liquidity. The reluctance of the banks to lend money to meet a margin call on securities that could still depreciate is the reason why the agency is going into the direct loan business.

12594 ■ "New Law Lets Shareholders Play Hardball With Firms" in *Globe & Mail* **(January 2, 2006, pp. B1)**
Pub: CTVglobemedia Publishing Inc.

Ed: Janet McFarland. **Description:** Business lawyer Wes Voorheis discusses about the launching of Bill 198 by plaintiffs' lawyers on behalf of ordinary retail investors.

12595 ■ "New Money" in *Entrepreneur* **(Vol. 36, February 2008, No. 2, pp. 62)**
Pub: Entrepreneur Media Inc.

Ed: C.J. Prince. **Description:** Tips on how to handle business finance, with regard to the tightened credit standards imposed by leading institutions, are provided. These include: selling receivables, margining blue chips, and selling purchase orders.

12596 ■ "The New Nimble" in *Barron's* **(Vol. 90, August 30, 2010, No. 35, pp. S12)**
Pub: Barron's Editorial & Corporate Headquarters

Ed: Suzanne McGee. **Description:** Financial advisors are making investments based on short-lived market trends due to the uncertainty in the long-term market. This strategy can be demanding and advisors should only try it if they are confident about their skill in spotting short-term trends.

12597 ■ "The New Risk Tolerance" in *Entrepreneur* **(Vol. 37, September 2009, No. 9, pp. 66)**
Pub: Entrepreneur Media, Inc.

Ed: Rosalind Resnick. **Description:** Offers advice on where to invest personal money in the United States. One could lose money from investing in gold and treasuries. High-quality corporate bonds and Treasury Inflation-Protected Securities are seen as ideal investments.

12598 ■ "New Thinking for a New Financial Order" in *Harvard Business Review* **(Vol. 86, September 2008, No. 9, pp. 26)**
Pub: Harvard Business School Press

Ed: Diana Farell. **Description:** Factors driving the current global economy are analyzed with a focus on the influence of new public and private sectors and the impact of unregulated markets.

12599 ■ "A New Way to Tell When to Fold" in *Barron's* **(Vol. 88, July 7, 2008, No. 27, pp. 27)**
Pub: Dow Jones & Co., Inc.

Ed: Theresa W. Carey. **Description:** Overview of the Online trading company SmartStops, a firm that aims to tell investors when to sell the shares of a particular company. The company's Web site categorizes stocks as moving up, down, or sideways, and calculates exit points for individual stocks based on an overall market trend.

12600 ■ "New Ways to Catch a Thief" in *Barron's* **(Vol. 88, March 10, 2008, No. 10, pp. 37)**
Pub: Dow Jones & Company, Inc.

Ed: Theresa W. Carey. **Description:** Online brokerage firms employ different methods to protect the accounts of their customers from theft. These methods include secure Internet connections, momentary passwords, and proprietary algorithms.

12601 ■ "The Next Government Bailout?" in *Barron's* **(Vol. 88, March 10, 2008, No. 10, pp. 21)**
Pub: Dow Jones & Company, Inc.

Ed: Jonathan Laing. **Description:** Fannie Mae may need a government bailout as it faces huge hits brought about by the effects of the housing crisis. The shares of the government-sponsored enterprise have dropped 65 percent since the housing crisis began.

12602 ■ "Nightmare on Wall Street" in *Canadian Business* **(Vol. 80, November 19, 2007, No. 23, pp. 33)**
Pub: Rogers Media

Ed: Thomas Watson. **Description:** Merrill Lynch Stanley O'Neal resigned after the company experienced a $2.2 billion loss in third quarter 2007. Citigroup's Charles Prince will also be leaving due to the crisis involving subprime mortgages and collaterized debt obligations. Forecasts for the stock market are supplied.

12603 ■ "Nine Sectors to Watch: Energy" in *Canadian Business* **(Vol. 81, December 24, 2007, No. 1, pp. 54)**
Pub: Rogers Media

Ed: Jeff Sanford. **Description:** One of the concerns in the petroleum industry is the fear of decline in production in many oilfields, as analysts predict the world will be pumping 17 percent less by 2025. Details on the continuing rise in demand and increase in prices are discussed.

12604 ■ "Nine Sectors to Watch: Gold" in *Canadian Business* **(Vol. 81, December 24, 2007, No. 1, pp. 53)**
Pub: Rogers Media

Ed: John Gray. **Description:** Turmoil in the financial markets, triggered by the meltdown in subprime mortgages, has pushed the price of gold to more than $840 an ounce in November 2007. Details on investor interest in gold and prediction on price trends in trade are discussed.

12605 ■ "No Surprises" in *Canadian Business* **(Vol. 79, September 25, 2006, No. 19, pp. 49)**
Pub: Rogers Media

Ed: Jeff Sanford. **Description:** The increasing income trust sector in Canada is discussed.

12606 ■ "Nonprofit NAIC Acquires Software Developer as For-Profit Arm" in *Crain's Detroit Business* **(Vol. 25, June 22, 2009, No. 25, pp. 10)**
Pub: Crain Communications Inc. - Detroit

Ed: Sherri Begin Welch. **Description:** Details of National Association of Investors Corporation's acquisition of a Massachusetts investment software developer in order to offer more products to investment clubs and individual investors nationwide.

12607 ■ "Nortel Outlook Shows Recovery Won't Come Quickly" in *Globe & Mail* **(March 20, 2007, pp. B4)**
Pub: CTVglobemedia Publishing Inc.

Ed: Catherine McLean. **Description:** The forecast about the unlikely recovery of Nortel Networks Corp. from decrease in its share prices is discussed.

12608 ■ "Nortel Plays Big to Settle Lawsuits" in *Globe & Mail* **(February 9, 2006, pp. B1)**
Pub: CTVglobemedia Publishing Inc.

Ed: Catherine McLean. **Description:** The details on Nortel Networks Corp.'s settlement of cases with shareholders are presented.

12609 ■ "Northern Overexposure" in *Canadian Business* **(Vol. 79, August 14, 2006, No. 16-17, pp. 36)**
Pub: Rogers Media

Description: Fall in revenue from foreign film productions in Canada due to its overexposure, and incentives offered by other nations to foreign film productions, are discussed.

12610 ■ "Not In My Backyard" in *Entrepreneur* **(Vol. 36, May 2008, No. 5, pp. 42)**
Pub: Entrepreneur Media, Inc.

Ed: Farnoosh Torabi. **Description:** More investors are turning to overseas real estate investments as the U.S. market sees a slowdown. Analysts say that risk-averse investors opt for funds with record of strong returns and U.S. real estate investment trusts that partner with foreign businesses for transparency purposes. Other details about foreign real estate investments are discussed.

12611 ■ "A Novel Fix for the Credit Mess" in *Barron's* **(Vol. 88, March 31, 2008, No. 13, pp. 10)**
Pub: Dow Jones & Company, Inc.

Ed: Michael Santoli. **Description:** Due to the common bank-leverage factor of 10, the $250 billion of lost bank capital would have supported $2.5 trillion in lending capacity. Jeffrey Lewis suggests onerous regulations on bank-holding companies that own 10 to 25 percent, as they are partly to blame. Statistical data included.

12612 ■ "Now in Play, Score Keeps Head Up and Stick on Ice" in *Globe & Mail* **(January 20, 2007, pp. B5)**
Pub: CTVglobemedia Publishing Inc.

Ed: Grant Robertson. **Description:** The hike in the shares of Score Media Inc. due to its new services is presented.

12613 ■ "Now That's Rich" in *Canadian Business* **(Vol. 80, February 12, 2007, No. 4, pp. 92)**
Pub: Rogers Media

Ed: Thomas Watson. **Description:** The effort of chief executive officer of Stelco Inc. Rodney Mott in resolving the issue of financial loss of the company by taking up backdating options for share price is discussed.

12614 ■ "Now You See It..." in *Canadian Business* **(Vol. 81, November 10, 2008, No. 19, pp. 20)**
Pub: Rogers Media Ltd.

Ed: Sharda Prashad. **Description:** Total return swaps were offered by Deutsche Bank AG and UBS AG to foreign investors for them to avoid paying taxes on the proceeds of their shares of Fording Canadian Coal Trust when Teck Cominco offered to buy the company. This means that the Canadian government is losing tax revenue from foreigners and it is argued that a simpler tax system would avoid this practice.

12615 ■ "NStar Feels the Heat" in *Cape Cod Times* **(September 30, 2011)**
Pub: Cape Cod Media Group

Ed: Patrick Cassidy. **Description:** Massachusetts energy officials wish to delay a merger between NStar and Northeast Utilities until it is clear how the partnership would meet the state's green energy goals. Governor Deval Patrick supports the proposed Nantucket Sound wind farm.

12616 ■ **"Nuclear Plans May Stall on Uranium Shortage"** in *Globe & Mail* (March 22, 2007, pp. B4)
Pub: CTVglobemedia Publishing Inc.
Ed: Shawn McCarthy. **Description:** The poor investments in uranium production and enrichment despite growing demand for it for nuclear energy is discussed.

12617 ■ **"Number of Mechanic's Liens Triple Since 2005"** in *The Business Journal - Serving Phoenix and the Valley of the Sun* (Vol. 28, August 22, 2008, No. 51, pp. 1)
Pub: American City Business Journals, Inc.
Ed: Jan Buchholtz. **Description:** Experts are blaming the mortgage and banking industries for the tripling of mechanic's liens that were filed in Arizona from 2005 through August 6, 2008. The rise in mechanic's liens is believed to indicate stress in the real estate community. Other views and information on the rise of mechanic's liens filed in Arizona are presented.

12618 ■ **"The Numbers Speak For Themselves"** in *Barron's* (Vol. 88, July 14, 2008, No. 28, pp. 16)
Pub: Dow Jones & Co., Inc.
Ed: Bill Alpert. **Description:** Discusses quant fund managers versus traditional long-short equity funds after quants outperformed traditional funds in the year 2000. Causes for the underperformance are outlined and statistical data is included.

12619 ■ **"Nvidia Shares Clobbered After Gloomy Warning"** in *Barron's* (Vol. 88, July 7, 2008, No. 27, pp. 25)
Pub: Dow Jones & Co., Inc.
Ed: Eric J. Savitz. **Description:** Shares of graphics chip manufacturer Nvidia suffered a 30 percent drop in its share price after the company warned that revenue and gross margin forecasts for the quarter ending July 27, 2008 will be below expectations. Stan Glasgow, chief operating officer of Sony Electronics, believes the US economic slowdown will not affect demand for the company's products. Statistical data included.

12620 ■ **"Nvidia's Picture Brighter Than Stock Price Indicates"** in *Barron's* (Vol. 88, March 24, 2008, No. 12, pp. 46)
Pub: Dow Jones & Company, Inc.
Ed: Eric J. Savitz. **Description:** Shares of graphics chip maker Nvidia, priced at $18.52 each, do not indicate the company's strong position in the graphics chip market. The company's shares have dropped due to fears of slower demand for PCs, but the company is not as exposed to broader economic forces.

12621 ■ **"N.Y. Investors Reject AnorMed Board Proposal"** in *Globe & Mail* (February 21, 2006, pp. B11)
Pub: CTVglobemedia Publishing Inc.
Ed: Leonard Zehr. **Description:** The reasons behind the denial of investors over the restructuring plans of AnorMed are presented.

12622 ■ **"Nymex Dissidents Rattle Sabers"** in *Crain's Chicago Business* (Vol. 31, April 21, 2008, No. 16, pp. 2)
Pub: Crain Communications, Inc.
Ed: Ann Saphir. **Description:** Two groups of New York Mercantile Exchange members say they have more than enough votes to stop CME Group Inc.'s $10 billion deal to acquire the oil and metals exchange and they are threatening a proxy fight if the Chicago exchange doesn't raise its offer.

12623 ■ **"OccuLogix Shares Plummet 65 Percent"** in *Globe & Mail* (February 4, 2006, pp. B5)
Pub: CTVglobemedia Publishing Inc.
Ed: Leonard Zehr. **Description:** The shares of OccuLogix drop by 65%in Canada. The decline in share price is attributed to failure of blood filtering system.

12624 ■ **"October 2009: Recovery Plods Along"** in *Hispanic Business* (October 2009, pp. 10-11)
Pub: Hispanic Business
Ed: Dr. Juan Solana. **Description:** Economist reports on a possible economic recovery which will not be allowed to rely on a strong domestic demand in order

to sustain it. Consumers, looking to counterbalance years of leverage financing based on unrealistic, ever-increasing home and portfolio valuations, are saving rather than spending money.

12625 ■ **"Off the RIM"** in *Canadian Business* (Vol. 80, January 15, 2007, No. 2, pp. 7)
Pub: Rogers Media
Ed: John Gray. **Description:** The reasons for the rise and fall in stock prices of the software company, Research In Motion Ltd., from September 2006 to January 2007, are analyzed.

12626 ■ **"Office Market May Turn Down"** in *Crain's New York Business* (Vol. 24, January 14, 2008, No. 2, pp. 26)
Pub: Crain Communications, Inc.
Description: Although still dominated by Wall Street, the downturn in the economy is raising fears that the continuing fallout from the subprime mortgage crisis could result in layoffs that will derail the office market.

12627 ■ **"Oil Patch Expects Richer Shell Offer"** in *Globe & Mail* (January 3, 2006, pp. B1)
Pub: CTVglobemedia Publishing Inc.
Ed: Andrew Willis; Patrick Brethour. **Description:** The concerns investors over the feasibility of Royal Dutch Shell PLC's acquisition of Shell Canada Ltd., for $7.6 billion, are presented. Shell Canada Ltd. reports rise in shares by ten percent.

12628 ■ **"Oil Picks and Pans"** in *Canadian Business* (Vol. 79, August 14, 2006, No. 16-17, pp. 67)
Pub: Rogers Media
Ed: Graham Scott. **Description:** A survey on investments in Canadian energy companies and the inflation caused by oil price hike, are discussed.

12629 ■ **"The Oilman"** in *Canadian Business* (Vol. 79, Winter 2006, No. 24, pp. 64)
Pub: Rogers Media
Ed: Michelle Magnan. **Description:** The achievements of David Werklund, the chairman of the CCS Income Trust, are described.

12630 ■ **"Oil's Going Down, Down, Down"** in *Canadian Business* (Vol. 79, October 9, 2006, No. 20, pp. 148)
Pub: Rogers Media
Ed: Ian McGugan. **Description:** Strategies for investors to benefit from the fall in global crude oil prices are discussed.

12631 ■ **"Ok, So Now What?"** in *Canadian Business* (Vol. 79, November 6, 2006, No. 22, pp. 113)
Pub: Rogers Media
Ed: Calvin Leung. **Description:** Details of healthy income-generating corporations, such as Cedar Fair L.P., are presented.

12632 ■ **"The Old Railway is on a Roll"** in *Globe & Mail* (January 26, 2006, pp. B1)
Pub: CTVglobemedia Publishing Inc.
Description: The reasons behind 5 percent rise in shares for Canadian National Railway Co. are presented.

12633 ■ **"Olympus is Urged to Revise Board"** in *Wall Street Journal Eastern Edition* (November 28, 2011, pp. B3)
Pub: Dow Jones & Company Inc.
Ed: Phred Dvorak. **Description:** Koji Miyata, once a director on the board of troubled Japanese photographic equipment company, is urging the company to reorganize its board, saying the present group should resign their board seats but keep their management positions. The company has come under scrutiny for its accounting practices and costly acquisitions.

12634 ■ **"On tap: More Could Get MEGA Credits; Need to Look Outside State May Be Cut"** in *Crain's Detroit Business* (April 7, 2008)
Pub: Crain Communications, Inc.
Ed: Amy Lane. **Description:** In order to qualify for Michigan Economic Growth Authority tax credits Michigan businesses may no longer have to shop

outside the state due to a new bill which has already passed the state Senate and will move on to the House; the bill, along with further changes to the MEGA program, is designed to provide incentives for investments that would add relevance and make Michigan more competitive.

12635 ■ **"On the Trail of the Bear"** in *Canadian Business* (Vol. 81, March 17, 2008, No. 4, pp. 28)
Pub: Rogers Media
Ed: Thomas Watson. **Description:** Discusses the conservative rule of thumb which is to invest in equity markets when a five to ten percent market rally is sustained for more than a few months. Bear markets on the S&P 500 bear markets in the 20th century only lasts over a year based on average. It is also good to remember that bear markets are followed by bulls that exceed the previous market highs.

12636 ■ **"One-Time Area Trust Executive Finds Trouble in N.H."** in *The Business Journal-Serving Metropolitan Kansas City* (September 12, 2008)
Pub: American City Business Journals, Inc.
Ed: Steve Vockrodt. **Description:** About 200 investors, some from Missouri's Kansas City area, claim that they had conducted business with Noble Trust Co.. The trust company was placed under New Hampshire Banking Department's conservatorship after $15 million was discovered to be missing from its account. It is alleged that the money was lost in a Colorado Ponzi scheme.

12637 ■ **"Online Forex Broker Tadawul FX Intros Arabic Website"** in *Entertainment Close-Up* (June 23, 2011)
Pub: Close-Up Media
Description: Online forex broker, Tadawul FX, launched its Arabic language Website, noting that the Middle East is a key market for the investment firm.

12638 ■ **"Open the Telecom Market"** in *Canadian Business* (Vol. 80, April 23, 2007, No. 9, pp. 80)
Pub: Rogers Media
Description: The effects of federal telecommunication law on foreign investments in telecommunication industry are presented.

12639 ■ **"Operation Fusion"** in *Black Enterprise* (Vol. 38, November 2007, No. 4, pp. 30)
Pub: Earl G. Graves Publishing Co. Inc.
Ed: Tara C. Walker. **Description:** Entrepreneur Albert H. Frazier tells how he combined three separate acquisitions in order to create Goods Movement Inc.:-W&H Systems Inc., a systems integrator and material handler supplier and North American Conveyor Inc. which fabricates and installs conveyor and sort equipment systems for the U.S. Postal Service and Total Transportation Services, a third-party logistics provider.

12640 ■ **"Opportunity Now Lies at Short End of the Market"** in *Barron's* (Vol. 88, June 30, 2008, No. 26, pp. M9)
Pub: Dow Jones & Co., Inc.
Ed: Michael S. Derby. **Description:** Renewed credit concerns and the lesser chance of a Federal Reserve interest rate hike boosted the bond market. Some portfolio managers are more bullish on short-dated securities as they expect the market to adjust to a more appropriate outlook.

12641 ■ **"An Opportunity for Patience"** in *Barron's* (Vol. 88, June 30, 2008, No. 26, pp. M5)
Pub: Dow Jones & Co., Inc.
Ed: Fleming Meeks. **Description:** Shares of Louisiana-Pacific are near their 52-week low at $8.95 per share making them look like a better buy than

they were at $11.51 in May, 2008. The company is a to player in a cyclical business and its balance sheet is sound compared to its peers with net debt at just $84 million or 20 percent of total capital.

12642 ■ "Optimize.ca Supplies Free Online Financial Advice" in *Entertainment Close-Up* **(October 9, 2010)**
Pub: Close-Up Media Inc.
Description: Optimize.ca provides free online financial advice, focusing on instant savings for their mutual funds and other banking products while improving rates of return and overall financial health.

12643 ■ "Oracle: No Profit of Doom" in *Barron's* **(Vol. 88, March 31, 2008, No. 13, pp. 40)**
Pub: Dow Jones & Company, Inc.
Ed: Mark Veverka. **Description:** Oracle's revenues grew by 21 percent but fell short of expectation and their profits came in at the low-end of expectations. The company's shares dropped 8 percent but investors are advised to pay more attention to the company's earnings expansion rather than revenue growth in a slow economy. Nokia's Rick Simonson points out that their markets in Asia and particularly India is growing so they are not as affected by the U.S. economic conditions.

12644 ■ "The Oracle's Endgame; Wrigley Investment Isn't What Many Call a Classic Buffett Play" in *Crain's Chicago Business* **(May 5, 2008)**
Pub: Crain Communications, Inc.
Ed: Ann Saphir. **Description:** Discusses Warren Buffett's deal with Mars Inc. to buy Wm. Wrigley Jr. Co., a move which would make Mr. Buffett a minority shareholder in a privately held company, a departure from his typical investment strategy. Mr. Buffett's Berkshire Hathaway Inc. agreed to provide $4.4 billion to help finance the $23 billion deal to pay another $2.1 billion for an equity stake in the company once it became a subsidiary of Mars.

12645 ■ "OSC Eyes New Tack on Litigation" in *Globe & Mail* **(April 9, 2007, pp. B1)**
Pub: CTVglobemedia Publishing Inc.
Ed: Janet McFarland. **Description:** The efforts of the Ontario Securities Commission to set up a tribunal for the investigation and control of securities fraud are described. The rate of the conviction of corporate officials in cases heard by the courts is discussed.

12646 ■ "Ottawa Attacks!" in *Canadian Business* **(Vol. 79, November 6, 2006, No. 22, pp. 21)**
Pub: Rogers Media
Ed: Jeff Sanford. **Description:** The effects of new tax policy developed by Jim Flaherty, Finance Minister of Canada, on income trusts are presented.

12647 ■ "Our Rich Past: a Guide to Some of Canada's Historic Fortunes" in *Canadian Business* **(Vol. 80, Winter 2007, No. 24, pp. 131)**
Pub: Rogers Media
Ed: Graham F. Scott. **Description:** Donald Alexander Smith rose through the ranks at Hudson's Bay Company to become the company's principal shareholder. John Wilson McConnell started his career at the Standard Chemical Company but later shifted to selling stocks and receiving equity stocks in return for his endorsement. Bud McDougald is well known for his deal making skills before he died in 1978.

12648 ■ "Out of Fashion" in *Barron's* **(Vol. 88, March 17, 2008, No. 11, pp. 48)**
Pub: Dow Jones & Company, Inc.
Ed: Robin Goldwyn Blumenthal. **Description:** Shares of Perry Ellis International and G-III Apparel Group have taken some beating in the market despite good growth earnings prospects. Perry Ellis sees earnings growth of 8 to 11 percent for fiscal 2009, while G-III Apparel expects earnings growth of 25 percent.

12649 ■ "Over A Barrel" in *Canadian Business* **(Vol. 81, July 21, 2008, No. 11, pp. 13)**
Pub: Rogers Media Ltd.
Ed: Thomas Watson. **Description:** Analysts predict that the skyrocketing price of fuel will cause a crackdown in the market as purported in the peak oil

theory. It is forecasted that the price of oil will reach $200 per barrel. Details of the effect of the increasing oil prices on the market are presented.

12650 ■ "Over a Barrel" in *Canadian Business* **(Vol. 80, February 12, 2007, No. 4, pp. 52)**
Pub: Rogers Media
Ed: Andrew Nikoforuk. **Description:** The potential of tar sands of Alberta in becoming the largest source of oil in the world and huge investments of Canadian companies to mine for the oil there are discussed.

12651 ■ "Owner of IT Firm MK2 Tying Future to Software" in *Crain's Cleveland Business* **(Vol. 30, June 15, 2009, No. 23, pp. 3)**
Pub: Crain Communications, Inc.
Ed: Chuck Soder. **Description:** Donald Kasper, owner of MK2 Technologies LLC of Cleveland, Ohio discusses his recent acquisition of a portion of ProSource Solution. The move will help expand the two companies' custom software development plans.

12652 ■ "Packaging Firm Wraps Up Remake; Overseas Plants Help Firm Fatten Margins" in *Crain's New York Business* **(January 7, 2008)**
Pub: Crain Communications, Inc.
Description: Sealed Air Corp., a packaging manufacturer, has seen its share price fall nearly 20 percent over the past two years, making it one of the worst performers in the packaging sector.

12653 ■ "Pain Ahead as Profit Pressure Increases" in *Crain's Chicago Business* **(Vol. 31, May 5, 2008, No. 18, pp. 4)**
Pub: Crain Communications, Inc.
Ed: Daniel Rome Levine. **Description:** Interview with David Klaskin, the chairman and chief investment officer at Oak Ridge Investments LLC, who discusses the outlook for the economy and corporate earnings, particularly in the housing and auto industries, the impact of economic stimulus checks, the weakness of the dollar and recommendations of stocks that individual investors may find helpful.

12654 ■ "P&G's Iams Finds Itself in a Pet-Food Dogfight" in *Advertising Age* **(Vol. 78, March 5, 2007, No. 10, pp. 6)**
Pub: Crain Communications, Inc.
Ed: Jack Neff. **Description:** Proctor & Gamble Co.'s Iams has been slow to embrace the trend toward foods for pets that appear fit for human consumption. Competitors such as Nestle Purina have made big gains with its colorful premium Beneful brand and dry nuggets that look like chunks of vegetables and meat. Statistical data included.

12655 ■ *Panic! The Story of Modern Financial Insanity*
Pub: W.W. Norton & Company
Ed: Michael Lewis. **Released:** 2009. **Price:** $27.95. **Description:** Two decades of stock market crashes are outlined.

12656 ■ *Paper Fortunes: Modern Wall Street: Where It's Been and Where It's Going*
Pub: St. Martin's Press LLC
Ed: Roy C. Smith. **Released:** 2010. **Price:** $35.00. **Description:** Comprehensive history of Wall Street and lessons learned with insight into ways Wall Street will reinvent itself in this new economy.

12657 ■ *Partnership: Small Business Start-Up Kit*
Pub: Nova Publishing Company
Ed: Daniel Sitarz. **Released:** November 2005. **Price:** $29.95. **Description:** Guidebook detailing partnership law by state covering the formation and use of partnerships as a business form. Information on filing requirements, property laws, legal liability, standards, and the new Revised Uniform Partnership Act is covered.

12658 ■ *The Partnership: The Making of Goldman Sachs*
Pub: Penguin Group USA Inc.
Ed: Charles D. Ellis. **Released:** 2009. **Price:** $37.95. **Description:** The history of Goldman Sachs is presented, along with a chronicle of Wall Street.

12659 ■ "Patchy Oil Profits" in *Canadian Business* **(Vol. 80, February 12, 2007, No. 4, pp. 89)**
Pub: Rogers Media
Ed: Michelle Magnan. **Description:** The fall in fourth-quarter earnings of several oil and gas companies in Canada, in view of rise in their expenditure, is discussed.

12660 ■ "Paterson Plots Comeback With Internet IPO" in *Globe & Mail* **(February 20, 2006, pp. B1)**
Pub: CTVglobemedia Publishing Inc.
Ed: Grant Robertson. **Description:** The initial public offering plans of chief executive officer Scott Paterson of JumpTV.com are presented.

12661 ■ "Patience May Pay Off" in *Barron's* **(Vol. 89, July 13, 2009, No. 28, pp. 30)**
Pub: Dow Jones & Co., Inc.
Ed: Johanna Bennett. **Description:** New CEO Craig Herkert can turn around Supervalu and their shares could double to $30 in three years from June 2009 according to one investment officer. Herkert knows how to run a lean and tight operation since he has worked for Albertsons and Wal-Mart in the past.

12662 ■ "PC Connection Acquires Cloud Software Provider" in *New Hampshire Business Review* **(Vol. 33, March 25, 2011, No. 6, pp. 8)**
Pub: Business Publications Inc.
Description: Merrimack-based PC Connection Inc. acquired ValCom Technology, a provider of cloud-based IT service management software. Details of the deal are included.

12663 ■ "Peak Performer" in *Canadian Business* **(Vol. 81, October 13, 2008, No. 17, pp. 30)**
Pub: Rogers Media Ltd.
Ed: Andrea Jezovit. **Description:** Jerry Del Missier's promotion as president of Barclays Capital (BarCap) has made him the likely successor to BarCap chief executive Bob Diamond. Diamond believes the technology Jerry Del Missier built on BarCap is producing record performance for the company. Public opinion on Jerry Del Missier, as well as his views, is discussed.

12664 ■ "Penny Chief Shops For Shares" in *Barron's* **(Vol. 88, July 7, 2008, No. 27, pp. 29)**
Pub: Dow Jones & Co., Inc.
Ed: Teresa Rivas. **Description:** Myron Ullman III, chairman and chief executive officer of J.C. Penney, purchased $1 million worth of shares of the company. He now owns 393,140 shares of the company and an additional 1,282 on his 401(k) plan.

12665 ■ "A Perfect Predator: Brookfield Asset Management Isn't Brash" in *Canadian Business* **(Vol. 83, July 20, 2010, No. 11-12, pp. 50)**
Pub: Rogers Media Ltd.
Ed: Joanna Pachner. **Description:** Brookfield Asset Management CEO Bruce Flatt manages $108 billion worth of real estate and the company has become one of the world's biggest prime real estate owners since he became leader. Flatt says their goal is to earn a 12-15 percent compound annual return per share and that they would shrink in size if it meant reaching that goal.

12666 ■ "The Perks of Going Public" in *Austin Business Journal* **(Vol. 31, July 15, 2011, No. 19, pp. A17)**
Pub: American City Business Journals Inc.
Ed: Christopher Calnan. **Description:** HomeAway Inc. launched a $216 million initial public offering. Austin Ventures has generated more than $32 million from the IPO.

12667 ■ "Pet Food Insider Sold Shares Before Recall" in *Globe & Mail* **(April 10, 2007, pp. B1)**
Pub: CTVglobemedia Publishing Inc.
Ed: Keith McArthur. **Description:** The issue related the selling of share units by Mark Weins, chief financial officer of pet food firm Menu Foods Income Fund, just before the recall of contaminated pet food is discussed.

12668 ■ **"Peter Bynoe Trades Up"** in *Black Enterprise* (Vol. 38, July 2008, No. 12, pp. 30)
Pub: Earl G. Graves Publishing Co. Inc.
Ed: Alexis McCombs. **Description:** Chicago-based Loop Capital Markets L.L.C. has named Peter Bynoe managing director of corporate finance. Bynoe was previously a senior partner at the law firm DLA Piper U.S. L.L.P., where he worked on stadium deals.

12669 ■ **"PetSmart: A Barking Buy"** in *Barron's* (Vol. 89, July 6, 2009, No. 27, pp. 15)
Pub: Dow Jones & Co., Inc.
Ed: Jay Palmer. **Description:** Shares of PetSmart could climb from $21.70 to about $28 due to the company's improving profits, cash flow, and product portfolio. The company's shares are trading at 14 times projected 2010 earnings of $1.64 a share.

12670 ■ **"Phillips Edison Launches $1.8B Retail REIT"** in *Business Courier* (Vol. 27, October 15, 2010, No. 24, pp. 1)
Pub: Business Courier
Ed: Dan Monk. **Description:** Retail center operator Phillips Edison & Company is organizing a real estate investment trust (REIT) to raise $1.8 billion to finance the planned purchase of 150 grocery-centered shopping centers around the U.S. The offering would be Phillips largest. Phillips Edison employesss 174 workers and operates 250 shopping centers nationwide.

12671 ■ **"Phoenix Company Realizing Dream of Global Growth"** in *The Business Journal - Serving Phoenix and the Valley of the Sun* (Vol. 28, July 18, 2008, No. 46, pp. 1)
Pub: American City Business Journals, Inc.
Ed: Chris Casacchia. **Description:** Phoenix, Arizona-based lubricant maker DreamBrands Inc. is realizing global growth. The company, which has been generating interest from institutional investors, is seeking a second round of funding. Details of the company's products and marketing plans are also discussed.

12672 ■ **"Picking a 529 College Savings Plan"** in *Black Enterprise* (Vol. 37, February 2007, No. 7, pp. 46)
Pub: Earl G. Graves Publishing Co. Inc.
Ed: Carolyn M. Brown. **Description:** Advice is given to help choose the right college savings plan.

12673 ■ **"Place Restrictions on Your Stock Shares"** in *Business Owner* (Vol. 35, July-August 2011, No. 4, pp. 14)
Pub: DL Perkins Company
Description: It is critical for any small business owner to be certain that the buyer or recipient of any part of the company represents that the stock is being acquired or given for investment purposes only.

12674 ■ **"A Place in the Sun"** in *Canadian Business* (Vol. 81, July 22, 2008, No. 12-13, pp. 56)
Pub: Rogers Media Ltd.
Description: Experts believe that it is the best time for Canadians to own a retirement home in the U.S., where real estate prices are up to 50 percent below their peak. Other views concerning the economic conditions occurring in the United States, as well as on the implications for Canadians planning to invest in the country are presented.

12675 ■ **"Planning Ahead: Steven Taylor Mulls a Second Career After Retirement"** in *Black Enterprise* (Vol. 37, November 2006, No. 4, pp. 82)
Pub: Earl G. Graves Publishing Co. Inc.
Ed: Sheryl Nance Nash. **Description:** Many workers are unprepared for retirement. Profile of Steven Taylor, a soon to retire dietary correctional officer who looked to Walt Clark, president of Clark Capital Financial in Maryland, to assess his retirement goals. Detailed advice and statistical data included.

12676 ■ **"Playing Citigroup's Woes"** in *Barron's* (Vol. 88, March 31, 2008, No. 13, pp. M7)
Pub: Dow Jones & Company, Inc.
Ed: Steven M. Sears. **Description:** Citigroup's first-quarter earnings estimate was slashed to a $1.15-per-share-loss from 28 cents. A strategist recom-

mends buying the company's shares at Sept. 20, 2008 put and selling a Sept. 17.50 put with a maximum profit of $166 if the shares is at or below $17.50 at expiration.

12677 ■ **"Playing Defense"** in *Crain's Chicago Business* (Vol. 31, November 10, 2008, No. 45, pp. 4)
Pub: Crain Communications, Inc.
Ed: Monee Fields-White. **Description:** Chicago's money managers are increasingly investing in local companies such as Caterpillar Inc., a maker of construction and mining equipment, Kraft Foods Inc. and Baxter International Inc., a manufacturer of medical products, in an attempt to bolster their portfolios. These companies have a history of surviving tough economic times.

12678 ■ **"PNC Begins Search for New Local HQ"** in *Baltimore Business Journal* (Vol. 28, June 4, 2010, No. 4, pp. 1)
Pub: Baltimore Business Journal
Ed: Daniel J. Sernovitz. **Description:** PNC Financial Services Group Inc. is searching for a new headquarters building in Greater Baltimore, Maryland. The company is seeking about 150,000 square feet for its regional operations. However, PNC could also end up moving out of Baltimore for space in the surrounding suburbs.

12679 ■ **"Point, Click, Buy"** in *Barron's* (Vol. 90, September 6, 2010, No. 36, pp. 11)
Pub: Barron's Editorial & Corporate Headquarters
Ed: Vito J. Racanelli. **Description:** Non-travel online retail sales from January to July 2010 increased nine percent which indicates that online shopping for the coming holidays will be good. Online sales are outpacing traditional shopping, but pricing is still critical.

12680 ■ **"Polite Conversation"** in *Mergers & Acquisitions: The Dealmaker's Journal* (March 1, 2008)
Pub: SourceMedia, Inc.
Description: In January, industry leaders and dealmakers met at Davos to discuss topics ranging from the possibility of a recession to what lies ahead in the deal market.

12681 ■ **"Portfolio: Written in the Polls"** in *Entrepreneur* (Vol. 35, October 2007, No. 10, pp. 74)
Pub: Entrepreneur Media Inc.
Ed: Scott Bernard Nelson. **Description:** Ibbotsen Associates looked at trends in the U.S. presidential elections to see if the election has something to do with stock market behavior. It was found that election years beat non-election years in the stock market by nearly three percentage points each year. Details of the presidential elections' impact on the stock market are given.

12682 ■ **"Powder River Reports First Quarter Revenues Over 5 Million"** in *Canadian Corporate News* (May 16, 2007)
Pub: Comtex News Network Inc.
Description: Financial report for Powder River Basin Gas Corp., a revenue generating producer, marketer, and acquirer of crude oil and natural gas properties. Statistical data included.

12683 ■ **"The Power of Alumni Networks"** in *Harvard Business Review* (Vol. 88, October 2010, No. 10, pp. 34)
Pub: Harvard Business School Publishing
Ed: Lauren H. Cohen, Christopher J. Malloy. **Description:** Research indicates that members of alumni associations tend to invest in similar ways; implications for the mutual funds sector are discussed.

12684 ■ **"Power In the Boardroom"** in *Black Enterprise* (Vol. 38, February 2008, No. 7, pp. 112)
Pub: Earl G. Graves Publishing Co. Inc.
Ed: Derek T. Dingle. **Description:** Comprehensive list of Black corporate directors for 250 of the largest companies in the U.S.; these leaders play a critical role in business development.

12685 ■ **"The Power of Innovation"** in *Canadian Business* (Vol. 81, March 17, 2008, No. 4, pp. 57)
Pub: Rogers Media
Ed: Andrew Wahl. **Description:** Canada ranks badly in terms innovation yardsticks that directly translate to economic growth such as business R&D as a percentage of GDP and R&D per capita. Canada's reliance on natural resources does not provide incentives to innovate unlike smaller countries with little natural resources. Canada could spur innovation through regulations that encourage industrial research.

12686 ■ **"Power Partnerships"** in *Business Courier* (Vol. 27, October 22, 2010, No. 25, pp. 1)
Pub: Business Courier
Ed: Lucy May. **Description:** The $400 million Harrah's casino and the $47 million redevelopment and expansion of Washington Park are project aimed at boosting the economy in downtown Cincinnati, Ohio. These projects will be done in cooperation with the National Association for the Advancement of Colored People. Insights into the role of minority-owned businesses in regional economic development are explored.

12687 ■ *PPC's Guide to Choosing Retirement Plans for Small Businesses*
Pub: Practitioners Publishing Company
Released: June 2004. **Price:** $119.00. **Description:** Guide to evaluate and select retirement plans for small business.

12688 ■ **"Pre-Deal Trades More Common in Canada, Study Finds"** in *Globe & Mail* (March 23, 2007, pp. B5)
Pub: CTVglobemedia Publishing Inc.
Ed: John Kipphoff; Joe Schneider. **Description:** The results of the study conducted by Measuredmarkets Inc. to examine the impact of merger activity on insider trading of the companies are presented.

12689 ■ **"A Precious Resource: Investing In the Fate of Fresh Water"** in *Black Enterprise* (Vol. 38, February 2008, No. 7, pp. 44)
Pub: Earl G. Graves Publishing Co. Inc.
Ed: Charles Keenan. **Description:** Despite rising oil prices, water may become the most precious commodity in years to come because the world's supply of drinkable water is dwindling.

12690 ■ *Principles of Private Firm Valuation*
Pub: John Wiley & Sons, Incorporated
Ed: Stanley J. Feldman. **Released:** April 2005. **Price:** $85.00. **Description:** Tools and techniques to correctly perform private firm valuation, including value and how to measure it, valuing control, determining the size of the marketability discount, creating transparency and the implications for value, the value of tax pass-through entities versus a C corporation, etc.

12691 ■ **"Private Equity Firm Links First Arizona Deal"** in *Business Journal-Serving Phoenix and the Valley of the Sun* (November 2, 2007)
Pub: American City Business Journals, Inc.
Ed: Chris Cassacchia. **Description:** Pacific Investment Partners and Your Source Financial launched a $10 million fund and signed their first deal. The two companies acquires a minority stake in Dreambrands Inc. for $3 million. Dreambrands is using the capital to market its personal lubricant product Carrageenana.

12692 ■ **"Private Equity Firms Focus on Failing Banks"** in *Baltimore Business Journal* (Vol. 28, July 16, 2010, No. 10, pp. 1)
Pub: Baltimore Business Journal
Ed: Gary Haber. **Description:** Four deals in which assets of failed banks were acquired by private equity firms have been approved by the Federal Deposit Insurance Corporation in the past couple of years. Bay Bank FSK, for example, purchased Bay National Bank's assets in July 2010. Forecasts on more private equity acquisitions in the community banking industry are given.

12693 ■ **"Private Equity Firms Shopping Valley For Deals"** in *The Business Journal - Serving Phoenix and the Valley of the Sun* (Vol. 29, September 19, 2008, No. 3, pp. 1)
Pub: American City Business Journals, Inc.
Ed: Mike Sunnucks. Description: Private equity firms from California, Boston, New York, and overseas are expected to invest in growth-oriented real estate markets that include Phoenix. Real estate experts revealed that privately held investment and acquisition firms are looking to invest in real estate markets hit by the housing crisis. Views and information on private equity firms' real estate investments are presented.

12694 ■ **"Private Pitfalls"** in *Canadian Business* (Vol. 80, October 22, 2007, No. 21, pp. 34)
Pub: Rogers Media
Ed: Al Rosen. Description: Guidelines on how minority shareholders can avoid drawbacks at the time of purchase, during ownership, and when selling shares are discussed; contractual protection, sales taxation and share price are also presented. Investment in a private company entails knowing the party you are buying share from.

12695 ■ **"Private TV Industry's Profit Climbs Four Percent"** in *Globe & Mail* (March 29, 2006, pp. B6)
Pub: CTVglobemedia Publishing Inc.
Ed: Simon Tuck. Description: The private television industry in Canada is experiencing 4 percent increase in its profits, i.e. $242.2 millions. The revenues of CTV contributed more to this increase in profits.

12696 ■ **"Profico Takes Itself Off the Market"** in *Globe & Mail* (March 14, 2006, pp. B1)
Pub: CTVglobemedia Publishing Inc.
Ed: Deborah Yedlin; Dave Ebner. Description: Profico Energy Management Ltd., Canada's largest junior energy explorer, has backed off its potential acquisition plans. The decreased prices of the natural gas are the main reasons that caused Profico to back off from the acquisition plan.

12697 ■ **"Profit Predictions Look Too Plump"** in *Barron's* (Vol. 88, March 31, 2008, No. 13, pp. 37)
Pub: Dow Jones & Company, Inc.
Ed: Johanna Bennett. Description: Full-year forecast points to a 14 percent gain for 2008 but the second-half profit increases would have to grow at a fast rate and peak at 61 percent in the fourth quarter to achieve this. Trends in the U.S. economic conditions are also discussed.

12698 ■ **"Proof That Good Entrepreneurs Can Make Bad Investors"** in *Inc.* (October 2007, pp. 77-78)
Pub: Gruner & Jahr USA Publishing
Ed: Norm Brodsky. Description: Information for small business owners is offered to help decide which investments are right for them.

12699 ■ **"A Property Rights Analysis of Newly Private Firms"** in *Business Ethics Quarterly* (Vol. 21, July 2011, No. 3, pp. 445)
Pub: Society for Business Ethics
Ed: Marguerite Schneider, Alix Valenti. Description: A key factor in the decision to convert a publicly owned company to private status is the expectation that value will be create, providing the firm with rent. These rents have implications regarding the property rights of the firm's capital-contributing constituencies. The article identifies and analyzes the types of rent associated with the newly private firm. Compared to public firms, going private allows owners the potential to partition part of the residual risk to bond holders and employees, rendering them to be co-residual risk bearers with owners.

12700 ■ **"PRWT Service Acquires Pharmaceutical Plant: Firm Wins Multimillion-Dollar Contract with Merck"** in *Black Enterprise* (March 2008)
Pub: Earl G. Graves Publishing Co. Inc.
Ed: Tamara E. Holmes. Description: PRWT Services Inc. expanded through its acquisition of a chemical manufacturing plant in New Jersey. The Whitehouse

Station, part of Merck & Co. Inc. produces active pharmaceutical ingredients for antibiotics, making PRWT the first minority-owned company in the U.S. to manufacture active pharmaceutical ingredients.

12701 ■ **"Public Opinion"** in *Entrepreneur* (Vol. 36, April 2008, No. 4, pp. 28)
Pub: Entrepreneur Media, Inc.
Ed: Aliza Sherman. Description: According to a 2007 report from Group and Organization Management, women in top positions can lead publicly traded companies to stock price and earnings growth. Some women business owners say that going public has provided them with the capital to grow. Details on the potential of women-managed publicly traded companies are discussed.

12702 ■ **"Pulte May Be Bouncing Back From Stock-Price Doldrums"** in *Crain's Detroit Business* (Vol. 23, October 8, 2007, No. 41, pp. 4)
Pub: Crain Communications Inc. - Detroit
Ed: Daniel Duggan. Description: Pulte Homes saw a jump in its stocks due to Citigroup's analysts rating Pulte and other builders higher due to strong balance sheets.

12703 ■ *The Pursuit of Happyness*
Pub: HarperCollins Publishers Inc.
Ed: Chris Gardner. Released: May 2006. Price: $25.95. Description: Rags-to-riches saga of a homeless father who raised and cared for his son on the streets of San Francisco and worked to become a powerful leader on Wall Street.

12704 ■ **"Put It on MasterCard"** in *Barron's* (Vol. 89, July 27, 2009, No. 30, pp. 16)
Pub: Dow Jones & Co., Inc.
Ed: Bill Alpert. Description: Shares of MasterCard trade at a discount at just 15 times its anticipated earnings and some believe that these shares may be a better play in an economic recovery. The prospects of these shares are compared with those of Visa.

12705 ■ **"Putting SogoTrade Through Its Paces"** in *Barron's* (Vol. 89, July 27, 2009, No. 30, pp. 27)
Pub: Dow Jones & Co., Inc.
Ed: Theresa W. Carey. Description: SogoTrade options platform streams options quotes in real time and lets users place a trade in several ways. The site also features notable security tactics and is a reasonable choice for bargain-seekers. OptionsXpress' Xtend platform lets users place trades and get real time quotes.

12706 ■ **"Putting the World at Your Fingertips"** in *Barron's* (Vol. 88, July 7, 2008, No. 27, pp. L13)
Pub: Dow Jones & Co., Inc.
Ed: Neil A. Martin. Description: Currency-traded exchange funds allow investors to diversify their assets and take advantage of investment opportunities such as speculation and hedging. Investors can use these funds to build positions in favor of or against the US dollar.

12707 ■ **"Q&A: David Labistour"** in *Canadian Business* (Vol. 81, March 17, 2008, No. 4, pp. 10)
Pub: Rogers Media
Ed: Lauren McKeon. Description: David Labistour says that the difference between being a co-op retailer and a corporate-owned retailer in the case of Mountain Equipment Co-op (MEC) is that the company is owned by their customers and not by shareholders. Labistour also says that MEC works with their factories to ensure that these maintain ethical standards in the manufacturing process.

12708 ■ **"Qualcomm Could Win Big as the IPhone 3G Calls"** in *Barron's* (Vol. 88, July 4, 2008, No. 28, pp. 30)
Pub: Dow Jones & Co., Inc.
Ed: Eric J. Savitz. Description: Apple iPhone 3G's introduction could widen the smartphone market thereby benefiting handset chipmaker Qualcomm in the process. Qualcomm Senior V.P., Bill Davidson

sees huge potential for his company's future beyond phones with their Snapdragon processor. The prospects of Sun Microsystems' shares are also discussed.

12709 ■ **"Quality at Bargain Prices"** in *Black Enterprise* (Vol. 41, December 2010, No. 5, pp. 30)
Pub: Earl G. Graves Publishing Co. Inc.
Ed: James A. Anderson. Description: Monica L. Walker, CEO of Holland Capital Management, suggests investors to watch prevailing trends in the financial market and to focus on using bottom-up analysis to identify companies meeting their investment criteria.

12710 ■ *The Quants*
Pub: Crown Business Books
Ed: Scott Patterson. Released: January 25, 2011. Price: $16.00. Description: The story of four rich and powerful men, along with Jim Simons, the founder of the most successful hedge fund in history and how they felt and what they thought in the days and weeks during the crash of Wall Street.

12711 ■ **"Quarreling Parties Keep Schenectady Redevelopment Plan In Limbo"** in *The Business Review Albany* (Vol. 35, April 4, 2008, No. 53)
Pub: The Business Review
Ed: Michael DeMasi. Description: First National Bank of Scotia chairman Louis H. Buhrmaster opposes the Erie Boulevard design project. as it could negatively affect access to the bank. Buhrmaster, aslo a vice president for Schenectady Industrial Corp, prohibits environmental assessment at the former American Locomotive property. The issues affecting the progress of the planned redevelopment at Schenectady are analyzed

12712 ■ **"Quebecor World Cuts Dividend"** in *Globe & Mail* (January 20, 2006, pp. B1)
Pub: CTVglobemedia Publishing Inc.
Description: The reasons behind the decrease in dividend by Quebecor World Inc., and its impact on investors, are discussed.

12713 ■ **"A Questionable Chemical Romance"** in *Barron's* (Vol. 88, July 14, 2008, No. 28, pp. 28)
Pub: Dow Jones & Co., Inc.
Ed: Andrew Bary. Description: Dow Chemical paid $78-a-share for the surprise takeover of Rohm & Haas. The acquisition is reducing Dow Chemical's financial flexibility at a time when chemical companies are being affected by high costs and a weak U.S. economy.

12714 ■ **"Quick Earnings Revival Unlikely"** in *Barron's* (Vol. 88, June 30, 2008, No. 26, pp. 31)
Pub: Dow Jones & Co., Inc.
Ed: Johanna Bennett. Description: Analysts are pushing back their prediction of a U.S. economy turnaround to 2009. A recession in the first half of 2008 may not have happened but unemployment is rising and house prices continue to fall.

12715 ■ *Raising Capital*
Pub: Greenwood Publishing Group, Inc.
Ed: David Nour. Released: March 1, 2009. Price: $39.95. Description: An overview to help entrepreneurs find capital for starting and maintaining a small business is presented. The author shows how to develop long-term relationships with financial partners and ways to attract financing to fund the startup and growth phases of any business. Entrepreneurs tell how they raised money from friends, family, angel investors, banks and venture capitalists and private equity firms.

12716 ■ **"Raising Money: the Bond that Lasts"** in *Entrepreneur* (Vol. 35, October 2007, No. 10, pp. 73)
Pub: Entrepreneur Media Inc.
Ed: Crystal Detamore-Rodman. Description: Tax-exempt bonds can be the solution to long-term financing needs of entrepreneurs. However, high initial costs may discourage some entrepreneurs to apply

for these bonds, with transactions usually costing $3 mor more. How tax-exempt bonds work, and how rules vary with different states are discussed.

12717 ■ "Ralcorp Investigated for Rejecting ConAgra Bid" in *Saint Louis Business Journal* **(Vol. 32, September 16, 2011, No. 3, pp. 1)**
Pub: Saint Louis Business Journal
Ed: Evan Binns. **Description:** New York-based Levi & Korsinsky started investigating Ralcorp Holidngs Inc. after it rejected ConAgra Foods Inc.'s third and latest takeover bid of $5.17 billion. The investigation would determine whether Ralcorp's directors had acted on behalf of shareholders' best interest.

12718 ■ "R&R Ice Cream" in *Ice Cream Reporter* **(Vol. 23, November 20, 2010, No. 12, pp. 8)**
Pub: Ice Cream Reporter
Description: R&R Ice Cream, the United Kingdom's largest ice cream manufacturer, has completed a private offering of senior secured notes that has raised 298 million (pounds sterling) to fund expansion and acquisitions.

12719 ■ "R&R Launches Upscale Spoony's and Low Fat Dragon's Den" in *Ice Cream Reporter* **(Vol. 23, August 20, 2010, No. 9, pp. 3)**
Pub: Ice Cream Reporter
Description: European ice cream manufacturer R&R has acquired French ice cream maker Rolland and will position itself as an upscale challenger to brands like Ben & Jerry's.

12720 ■ "Raptor Opens Consultancy" in *Austin Business Journal* **(Vol. 31, July 8, 2011, No. 18, pp. 1)**
Pub: American City Business Journals Inc.
Ed: Christopher Calnan. **Description:** Boston hedge fund operator Raptor Group launched Raptor Accelerator, a consulting business providing sales and advisory services to early-stage companies in Central Texas. Aside from getting involved with the startups in which the Raptor Group invests, Raptor Accelerator will target firms operating in the sports, media, entertainment, and content technology sectors.

12721 ■ "Ratio-Cination" in *Canadian Business* **(Vol. 79, October 23, 2006, No. 21, pp. 164)**
Pub: Rogers Media
Ed: Ian McGugan. **Description:** Tips for investors, on how to make market observations before selecting companies for purchasing stocks, are presented.

12722 ■ "The RBC Dynasty Continues" in *Globe & Mail* **(January 30, 2006, pp. B1)**
Pub: CTVglobemedia Publishing Inc.
Ed: Gordon Pitts. **Description:** The details on business growth of Royal Bank of Canada, under chief executive officer Gordon Nixon, are presented.

12723 ■ "RBC's Hot Foreign Operations Contribute to Record Profit" in *Globe & Mail* **(March 3, 2007, pp. B3)**
Pub: CTVglobemedia Publishing Inc.
Ed: Andrew Willis. **Description:** Royal Bank of Canada posted 27.6 percent growth in the final quarter of 2006. The bank posted $1.49 billion in profits.

12724 ■ "Ready for the Back Burner" in *Barron's* **(Vol. 88, March 17, 2008, No. 11, pp. 47)**
Pub: Dow Jones & Company, Inc.
Ed: Vito J. Racanelli. **Description:** McDonald's has promised to return $15 billion to $17 billion to shareholders in 2007-2009 but headwinds are rising for the company. December, 2007 same-store sales were flat and the company's traffic growth in the U.S. is slowing. Its shares are likely to trade in tandem with the market until recession fears recede.

12725 ■ "Ready for a Rally?" in *The Economist* **(Vol. 390, January 3, 2009, No. 8612, pp. 54)**
Pub: The Economist Newspaper Inc.
Description: Analysts predict that the recession could end by 2010. The current economic crisis is presented in detail.

12726 ■ "Real Estate's New Reality" in *Entrepreneur* **(Vol. 37, July 2009, No. 7, pp. 32)**
Pub: Entrepreneur Media, Inc.
Ed: Rosalind Resnick. **Description:** Investing in real estate is still an advisable move, as long as investors are prepared to hold on to the property and there is a rent roll to provide a decent return on investment. Among the key considerations when investing in real estate is the property's expenses and cash flow. Other suggestions for future real estate investors are given.

12727 ■ "Real Opportunities: Don't Let Mortgage Mayhem Steer You Away From Sound Investments" in *Black Enterprise* **(December 2007)**
Pub: Earl G. Graves Publishing Co. Inc.
Ed: James A. Anderson. **Description:** Real estate investment trusts (REITs) that operate office buildings, industrial parks, shopping malls, hotels, hospitals, or other commercial properties may be a sound investment, despite the mortgage crisis facing the U.S. financial sector.

12728 ■ "Recent Deals Signal an M&A Resurgence" in *Austin Business JournalInc.* **(Vol. 29, January 22, 2010, No. 46, pp. 1)**
Pub: American City Business Journals
Ed: Jacob Dirr. **Description:** The acquisition of at least six Austin, Texas technology companies reflects the growing acquisition activity in the US. Corporations have bought 86 companies and spent $7.3 billion during the fourth quarter of 2009. Insights into the impact of the acquisition activity to Austin's entrepreneurial energy are also given.

12729 ■ "Recession Fears Power Gold" in *Barron's* **(Vol. 88, March 17, 2008, No. 11, pp. M14)**
Pub: Dow Jones & Company, Inc.
Ed: Melanie Burton. **Description:** Gold prices have been more attractive as the U.S. dollar weakens and the Dow Jones Industrial Average has slipped almost 10 percent in 2008. The rate cuts from the Federal Reserve Board has also spurred inflation fears adding upward pressure to the price of the metal.

12730 ■ "Recession Management" in *Canadian Business* **(Vol. 81, March 3, 2008, No. 3, pp. 62)**
Pub: Rogers Media
Ed: Joe Castaldo. **Description:** Some companies such as Capital One Financial Corp. are managing their finances as if a recession has already taken place to prepare themselves for the looming economic downturn. Intel Corp., meanwhile shows how increasing its investments during a recession could be advantageous. Tips on how companies can survive a recession are provided.

12731 ■ "Recovery on Tap for 2010?" in *Orlando Business Journal* **(Vol. 26, January 1, 2010, No. 31, pp. 1)**
Pub: American City Business Journals
Ed: Melanie Stawicki Azam, Richard Bilbao, Christopher Boyd, Anjali Fluker. **Description:** Economic forecasts for Central Florida's leading business sectors in 2010 are presented. These sectors include housing, film and TV, sports business, law, restaurants, aviation, tourism and hospitality, banking and finance, commercial real estate, retail, health care, insurance, higher education, and manufacturing. According to some local executives, Central Florida's economy will slowly recover in 2010.

12732 ■ "Red October" in *Canadian Business* **(Vol. 81, December 8, 2008, No. 21, pp. 61)**
Pub: Rogers Media Ltd.
Ed: Mitch Moxley. **Description:** Analysts predict that Chinese stock market traders practice prudence amidst the challenging financial conditions in stock markets. The Chinese stock markets imploded in the last 12 months, losing two-thirds of its value.

12733 ■ "Reduce the Risk of Failed Financial Judgments" in *Harvard Business Review* **(Vol. 86, July-August 2008, No. 8, pp. 24)**
Pub: Harvard Business School Press
Ed: Robert G. Eccles; Edward J. Fiedl. **Description:** Utilization of business consultants, evaluators, ap-

praisers, and actuaries to decrease financial management risks is discussed.

12734 ■ "Regarding Warren" in *Canadian Business* **(Vol. 80, November 5, 2007, No. 22, pp. 29)**
Pub: Rogers Media
Ed: Jeff Sanford. **Description:** Berkshire Hathaway's Warren Buffet believes that investing in energy shares is profitable, however, he warns investors about volatility in prices. Buffet, the second richest man in the world, forecasts that the value of the Canadian dollar will continue to rise. Buffet's investments are also discussed.

12735 ■ "Regent's Signal, Once Powerful, Fading From Local Scene" in *Business Courier* **(Vol. 27, June 4, 2010, No. 5, pp. 1)**
Pub: Business Courier
Ed: Dan Monk. **Description:** Los Angeles, California-based Oaktree Capital Management bought former Regent Communications Inc. from Chapter 11 bankruptcy and transformed it into Townsquare Media Inc., a privately held firm. Regent's corporate presence has faded fast in Cincinnati, Ohio as its operations wind down. Insights on Regent's failed business model are also given.

12736 ■ "REIT's Decry Foreign Limits on Investment" in *Globe & Mail* **(March 29, 2007, pp. B4)**
Pub: CTVglobemedia Publishing Inc.
Ed: Elizabeth Church. **Description:** The planned legislation by Canadian government for regulation foreign investments by real estate investment trusts is discussed.

12737 ■ "Reports of Banks' Revival were Greatly Exaggerated" in *Barron's* **(Vol. 88, July 7, 2008, No. 27, pp. L14)**
Pub: Dow Jones & Co., Inc.
Ed: Jack Willoughby. **Description:** Performance of mutual funds improved for the second quarter of 2008 compared to the previous quarter, registering an average gain of 0.13 percent; funds focusing on natural resources rose the highest, their value rising by an average of 24.50 percent.

12738 ■ "A Research Firm With More Than One Foe" in *Globe & Mail* **(February 24, 2006, pp. B1)**
Pub: CTVglobemedia Publishing Inc.
Ed: Shawn McCarthy. **Description:** The details of Biovail Corp.'s securities fraud case against Gradient Analytics Inc. are presented.

12739 ■ "Research Reports" in *Barron's* **(Vol. 89, July 20, 2009, No. 29, pp. M12)**
Pub: Dow Jones & Co., Inc.
Description: Shares of Bank of the Ozarks, Broadpoint Gleacher Securities Group, Halozyme Therapeutics, and Take Two Interactive are rated as Buy. The shares of Fluor and PetMed Express are rated as Outperform, while those of Humana and Janus Capital Group are rated as Hold and Underweight respectively.

12740 ■ "Research Reports: How Analysts Size Up Companies" in *Barron's* **(Vol. 88, March 17, 2008, No. 11, pp. M13)**
Pub: Dow Jones & Company, Inc.
Ed: Anita Peltonen. **Description:** Shares of Applied Industrial Technologies are ranked Market Perform while the shares of Google get a buy rating. Salix Pharmaceuticals gets a Sell/Above-Average risk rating. The shares of Dune Energy, Franklin Resources, Internet Brands, Piper Jaffray, and Texas Instruments are also rated.

12741 ■ "Retail Woes: The Shoe Doesn't Fit for Gerald Loftin's Stock Picks" in *Black Enterprise* **(Vol. 38, July 2008, No. 12, pp. 40)**
Pub: Earl G. Graves Publishing Co. Inc.
Ed: Steve Garmhausen. **Description:** Each of the three stocks that Gerald Loftin picked in May 2007 have lost money; DSW, the designer shoe retailer, fell by 63.7 percent; paint and coatings retailer Sherwin-Williams Co. fell by 7.2 percent; and Verizon Communications Inc. fell by 1.4 percent. Statistical data included.

12742 ■ *Retire Dollar Smart*
Pub: Trafford Publishing
Ed: Jim Miller. **Released:** July 2006. **Price:** $25.99. **Description:** The difference between savings and investments and their importance is examined, along with four rules for converting good investments into even greater ones. Contingency plans for healthcare costs as well as ways to manage taxes on investments are discussed. Five methods to control the costs of investing and saving include the use of smart strategies; getting independent, accurate, complete information; investing passively; asking for a discount; and taking off your blinders. Ten steps for designing a foolproof retirement investment portfolio are also provided.

12743 ■ "Return to Wealth; Bank Strategy" in *The Economist* (Vol. 390, January 3, 2009, No. 8612, pp. 56)
Pub: The Economist Newspaper Inc.
Description: UBS' strategy to survive these trying economic times is presented. Statistical data included. UBS has a stronger balance-sheet than most of its investment-banking peers and has reduced its portfolio.

12744 ■ *Rich Dad, Poor Dad*
Pub: Warner Books Inc.
Ed: Robert Kiyosaki with Sharon Lechter. **Price:** $16.95. **Description:** What the wealthy teach their children about money that others do not.

12745 ■ *Rich Dad, Poor Dad: What the Rich Teach Their Kids About Money-That the Poor and Middle Class Do Not!*
Pub: Time Warner Paperbacks
Ed: Robert T. Kiyosaki; Sharon L. Lechter. **Released:** December 5, 2002. **Price:** $16.95. **Description:** Personal finance expert shares his economic perspective through exposure to a pair of disparate influences: his own highly education but fiscally unstable father and the multimillionaire eighth-grade dropout father of his closest friend.

12746 ■ *Rich Dad's Increase Your Financial IQ: Get Smarter with Your Money*
Pub: Business Plus
Ed: Robert T. Kiyosaki. **Released:** $16.99. **Price:** March 26, 2008. **Description:** Author describes his five key principles of financial knowledge to help readers build wealth.

12747 ■ "The Right Time for REITs" in *Barron's* (Vol. 88, July 14, 2008, No. 28, pp. 32)
Pub: Dow Jones & Co., Inc.
Ed: Mike Hogan. **Description:** Discusses the downturn in U.S. real estate investment trusts so these are worth considering for investment. Several Websites that are useful for learning about real estate investment trusts for investment purposes are presented.

12748 ■ "RIM's Options Story Under Fire" in *Globe & Mail* (March 16, 2007, pp. B1)
Pub: CTVglobemedia Publishing Inc.
Ed: Janet McFarland. **Description:** The investigation of the backdating of options by Research In Motion Ltd. is discussed. The analysis of the backdating of company's options issues by Professor Erik Lie from the University of Iowa is presented.

12749 ■ "Risk Management Starts at the Top" in *Business Strategy Review* (Vol. 21, Spring 2010, No. 1, pp. 18)
Pub: Wiley-Blackwell
Ed: Paul Strebel, Hongze Lu. **Description:** Authors question why, at the end of 2008, Citigroup, Merrill Lynch and UBS had well over $40 billion in sub-prime write-downs and credit losses, while some of their competitors were much less exposed. Their research into the situation revealed correlations of great import to today's firms.

12750 ■ "Rob McEwen" in *Canadian Business* (Vol. 80, Winter 2007, No. 24, pp. 138)
Pub: Rogers Media
Ed: John Gray. **Description:** Rob McEwen's interest in gold started with his father who was in the investment industry and was always talking about the value

of gold. McEwen believes that there is a lot of room to innovate in mining and that Canada should be a leader in this field.

12751 ■ "Rock Festival: High Spirited Conventioneers Celebrate Their Good Fortune" in *Canadian Business* (Vol. 81, March 31, 2008, No. 5)
Pub: Rogers Media
Ed: Jeff Sanford. **Description:** Soaring prices of commodities in the mining industry have been very good for the attendees of the 76th annual conference of the Prospectors & Developers Association of Canada. A speaker at the conference expects commodity prices to come off a bit but not fall dramatically as it did in the 1980's.

12752 ■ "Rogue's Gallery" in *Canadian Business* (Vol. 81, November 10, 2008, No. 19, pp. 44)
Pub: Rogers Media Ltd.
Ed: Rachel Pulfer. **Description:** Laissez-faire capitalism or poor oversight of Fannie Mae and Freddie Mac are causes for the financial crisis in the U.S., depending or Democrat or Republican viewpoint. Events leading up to the 2008 financial crisis are covered.

12753 ■ "Roundtable - The Auto Sector Shifts Gears" in *Mergers & Acquisitions: The Dealmaker's Journal* (March 1, 2008)
Pub: SourceMedia, Inc.
Description: Industry professionals discuss the current state of the automotive sector as well as what they predict for the future of the industry; also provides information for investors about opportunities in the sector.

12754 ■ "RS Information Systems Signs Buyout Deal" in *Black Enterprise* (February 2008)
Pub: Earl G. Graves Publishing Co. Inc.
Ed: Alan Hughes. **Description:** Details of the RS Information Systems buyout by Wyle, a privately held provider of high-tech aerospace engineering, testing, and research services.

12755 ■ "Ryder's Shock Absorbers Are In Place" in *Barron's* (Vol. 88, March 24, 2008, No. 12, pp. 19)
Pub: Dow Jones & Company, Inc.
Ed: Christopher C. Williams. **Description:** Shares of Ryder System Inc. are expected to continue rising on the back of rising earnings, forecast at $5.20 a share for 2009. The shares of the truck freight company hit a 52-week high of $62.27 each and may reach $70 a share.

12756 ■ "SABMiller Deal Hit by Tax Ruling" in *Wall Street Journal Eastern Edition* (November 21 , 2011, pp. B9)
Pub: Dow Jones & Company Inc.
Ed: David Fickling, Simon Zekaria. **Description:** SABMiller PLC, the giant brewer in the United Kingdom, is acquiring Australian beer icon Foster's Group Ltd. for US$9.9 billion, but will have to come up with another A$582 million following a tax ruling by the Australian Taxation Office in order that shareholders of Foster's don't lose.

12757 ■ *Safety Net*
Pub: Crown Business Books
Ed: James Glassman. **Released:** February 22, 2011. **Price:** $23.00. **Description:** Ways to build a financial investment strategy that protects you, while ensuring growth in a strong financial future are presented.

12758 ■ "St. Elizabeth Fights for Share at St. Lukes" in *Business Courier* (Vol. 27, November 12, 2010, No. 28, pp. 1)
Pub: Business Courier
Ed: James Ritchie. **Description:** Key information on how St. Elizabeth Healthcare helps partner St. Luke's Hospitals increase market share in the healthcare industry are presented. Some of St. Luke's hospitals, such as the St. Elizabeth Fort Thomas in Kentucky, are struggling with low occupancy rates, prompting St. Elizabeth to invest about $24 million to help St. Luke's increase its market share.

12759 ■ "Sales Gave W&S Record '07" in *Business Courier* (Vol. 24, March 14, 2008, No. 49, pp. 1)
Pub: American City Business Journals, Inc.
Ed: Jon Newberry. **Description:** Western & Southern Financial Group was able to achieve a record $365 million in net income thanks in large part to the double-digit increases in profits by its W&S Agency Group field offices and non-insurance businesses. The sale of their Integrated Investment Services Subsidiary and shares in several Marriot hotels also added to the record profit.

12760 ■ "Sales of Pension Income Targeted by Senator" in *Wall Street Journal Eastern Edition* (November 21 , 2011, pp. C7)
Pub: Dow Jones & Company Inc.
Ed: Leslie Scism. **Description:** Senator Tom Harkin is concerned about a widening business in which retirees and veterans sell pension income to investors in the secondary market. The business provides major profits for middlemen. Harkin wants those who are considering such a sale to have adequate information provided and knowledge in order to avoid unscrupulous dealings.

12761 ■ "Samll Fortunes" in *Business Courier* (Vol. 27, July 23, 2010, No. 12, pp. 1)
Pub: Business Courier
Ed: Steve Watkins. **Description:** Small banks in Cincinnati, Ohio have been faring well despite the economic crisis, a survey has revealed. Sixty percent of local small banks have capital levels above 15.8 percent median. But regulators are seen to close more banks in 2010 than since the financial crises began.

12762 ■ "Satellite Down, Stock Up: Raytheon Is On Target With Ten Percent Dividend Increase" in *Barron's* (Vol. 88, March 31, 2008, No. 13)
Pub: Dow Jones & Company, Inc.
Ed: Shirley A. Lazo. **Description:** Raytheon hiked their quarterly dividend to 28 cents per share from 25.5 cents. Aircastle slashed their quarterly common dividend by 64 percent for them to retain additional capital that can be used to increase their liquidity position.

12763 ■ "Save the Date" in *Mergers & Acquisitions: The Dealmaker's Journal* (March 1, 2008)
Pub: SourceMedia, Inc.
Description: Listing of conferences and forums that deal with business and investing, particularly with mergers and acquisitions. Includes dates, locations and Internet addresses.

12764 ■ "A Say on Pay" in *Canadian Business* (Vol. 82, April 27, 2009, No. 7, pp. 14)
Pub: Rogers Media
Ed: Joe Castaldo. **Description:** A COMPAS Inc. survey of 134 Canadian chief executive officers found that 44 percent agree that CEO compensation should be subject to a non-binding vote. The respondents were also divided on whether to allow shareholders to exercise retroactive clawbacks on executive compensation if firm performance turns out to be worse than projected.

12765 ■ *Schaum's Outline Financial Management, Third Edition*
Pub: McGraw-Hill
Ed: Jae K. Shim; Joel G. Siegel. **Released:** May 2007. **Price:** $22.95 (CND). **Description:** Rules and regulations governing corporate finance, including the Sarbanes-Oxley Act are discussed.

12766 ■ "Schwab: Lower Returns Ahead" in *Barron's* (Vol. 89, July 13, 2009, No. 28, pp. L4)
Pub: Dow Jones & Co., Inc.
Ed: Leslie P. Norton. **Description:** Charles Schwab says that 8 percent to 10 percent equity-market returns are not realistic these days and that 4 percent to 5 percent are more realistic in the next four to five years from 2009. Schwab expects inflation to be close to 10 percent per annum in a couple of years.

12767 ■ "Score One for 'Barron's'" in *Barron's* (Vol. 89, July 13, 2009, No. 28, pp. 14)

Pub: Dow Jones & Co., Inc.

Ed: Andrew Bary. **Description:** 57 companies that were bullishly covered on 'Barron's' for the first half of 2009 were up an average of 20.4 percent compared to the 10.2 percent gain in the relevant market indexes. The bearish stock picks by 'Barron's' were down 3.4 percent compared to a 6.4 percent for the benchmarks.

12768 ■ "Scotiabank Targets More Baby Boomers" in *Globe & Mail* (March 4, 2006, pp. B5)

Pub: CTVglobemedia Publishing Inc.

Ed: Elizabeth Church. **Description:** Bank of Nova Scotia posted $844 million profit for first quarter 2006. The plans of the bank to achieve baby boomer client base are presented.

12769 ■ "Scottsdale Bank Plans 4Q Opening" in *The Business Journal - Serving Phoenix and the Valley of the Sun* (Vol. 28, August 15, 2008, No. 50)

Pub: American City Business Journals, Inc.

Ed: Chris Casacchia. **Description:** Arizona's Department of Financial Institutions has approved Scottsdale Business Bank, a community bank which plans to open in the fourth quarter of 2008. The bank, which is to be located near McCormick Ranch in Scottsdale, Arizona, will cater to small business owners in the professional sector, such as accountants and doctors.

12770 ■ "Screening for the Best Stock Screens" in *Barron's* (Vol. 90, September 13, 2010, No. 37, pp. 36)

Pub: Barron's Editorial & Corporate Headquarters

Ed: Mike Hogan. **Description:** Pros and cons of the new and revised stock screening tools from Zack, Finviz.com, and GuruFocus are discussed. FinVix.com is more capable for screening through stocks and the service is free.

12771 ■ "Sears' Lampert Solid in Game of Valuation Chicken" in *Globe & Mail* (February 25, 2006, pp. B2)

Pub: CTVglobemedia Publishing Inc.

Ed: Eric Reguly. **Description:** The feasibility of share value of Sears Canada Inc., following Sears Holdings Corp.'s acquisition, is discussed.

12772 ■ "SEC Doesn't Buy Biovail's Claims" in *Barron's* (Vol. 88, March 31, 2008, No. 13, pp. 20)

Pub: Dow Jones & Company, Inc.

Ed: Bill Alpert. **Description:** Overstatement of earnings and chronic fraudulent conduct has led the SEC to file a stock fraud suit against Biovail, Eugene Melnyk and three others present or former employees of Biovail. Melnyk had the firm file suit in 2006 that blames short-sellers and stock researchers for the company's drop in share price.

12773 ■ "SEC Report On Rating Agencies Falls Short" in *Barron's* (Vol. 88, July 14, 2008, No. 28, pp. 35)

Pub: Dow Jones & Co., Inc.

Ed: Jack Willoughby. **Description:** The Securities and Exchange Commissions report on credit-rating firms should have drawn attention to the slipshod practices in the offerings of collateralized debt obligations. The report fell short of prescribing correctives for the flawed system of these agencies' relationship with their clients.

12774 ■ *The Secret of Exiting Your Business Under Your Terms!*

Pub: Outskirts Press, Incorporated

Ed: Gene H. Irwin. **Released:** August 2005. **Price:** $29.95. **Description:** Topics include how to sell a business for the highest value, tax laws governing the sale of a business, finding the right buyer, mergers and acquisitions, negotiating the sale, and using a limited auction to increase future value of a business.

12775 ■ "A Security Risk?" in *Canadian Business* (Vol. 80, October 22, 2007, No. 21, pp. 36)

Pub: Rogers Media

Ed: Joe Castaldo. **Description:** Garda World Security Corporation declared a C$1.5 million loss in the second quarter of 2007. The company's securities have been falling since June and hit a 52-week low of $15.90 in September. Details of the physical and cash-handling firm's strategy to integrate its acquisitions are discussed.

12776 ■ "Selling Michigan; R&D Pushed as Reason For Chinese To Locate In State" in *Crain's Detroit Business* (Vol. 24, January 14, 2008)

Pub: Crain Communications Inc. - Detroit

Ed: Marti Benedetti. **Description:** Southeast Michigan Economic Development organizations are working to develop relationships with Chinese manufacturers so they will locate their automotive research and development operations in the state.

12777 ■ "Selling Pressures Rise in China" in *Barron's* (Vol. 88, March 10, 2008, No. 10, pp. M9)

Pub: Dow Jones & Company, Inc.

Ed: Mohammed Hadi. **Description:** There are about 1.6 trillion yuan worth of shares up for sale in Chinese stock markets in 2008, adding to the selling pressures in these markets. The Chinese government has imposed restrictions to prevent a rapid rise in selling stocks.

12778 ■ "Sense of Discovery" in *Business Journal Portland* (Vol. 27, November 19, 2010, No. 38, pp. 1)

Pub: Portland Business Journal

Ed: Erik Siemers. **Description:** Tigard, Oregon-based Exterro Inc. CEO Bobby Balachandran announced plans to go public without the help of an institutional investor. Balachandran believes Exterro could grow to a $100 million legal compliance software company in the span of three years. Insights on Exterro's growth as market leader in the $1 billion legal governance software market are also given.

12779 ■ "Sentiment Split on Financials" in *Barron's* (Vol. 88, March 24, 2008, No. 12, pp. M14)

Pub: Dow Jones & Company, Inc.

Ed: Steven M. Sears. **Description:** Experts in the financial sector are split as to whether or not the worst of the financial crisis brought on by the credit crunch is over. Some options traders are trading on are defensive puts, expecting the worst, while investors buying calls are considered as bullish.

12780 ■ "Serious Signal Flashing?" in *Barron's* (Vol. 88, July 7, 2008, No. 27, pp. 11)

Pub: Dow Jones & Co., Inc.

Description: Discusses the Hindenburg Omen, named after the airship disaster of May 1937, which is considered a predictor of market crashes and has appeared twice in June 2008. There is a 25 percent probability that the US stock market will suffer a crash in the July-October 2008 period.

12781 ■ "Seven Ways to Fail Big" in *Harvard Business Review* (Vol. 86, September 2008, No. 9, pp. 82)

Pub: Harvard Business School Press

Ed: Paul B. Carroll; Chunka Mui. **Description:** Seven factors involved in business failures are identified, and ways to avoid them are described. These factors include flawed financial engineering, hurrying into consolidation, and investing in technology that is not a good fit.

12782 ■ "A Shallow Pool" in *Canadian Business* (Vol. 81, Summer 2008, No. 9, pp. 44)

Pub: Rogers Media Ltd.

Ed: Joe Castaldo. **Description:** Bank of Canada projected in its 'Monetary Policy Report' a growth rate of 1.4 percent in 2008 and does not expect the economy to fully recover until mid-2010. The Cana-

dian stock market has been recovering although slowly with just a 1.6 percent gain by April 30. Other details on the Canadian equity market are presented.

12783 ■ "Shanghai Butterfly" in *Canadian Business* (Vol. 80, March 12, 2007, No. 6, pp. 69)

Pub: Rogers Media

Ed: Thomas Watson. **Description:** The volatile nature of Shanghai stock markets and its impact on investors and the economy is discussed.

12784 ■ "Shipwreck Floats Nickel's Boat" in *Globe & Mail* (January 24, 2007, pp. B1)

Pub: CTVglobemedia Publishing Inc.

Ed: John Partridge. **Description:** The rise in the price of nickel to $38,300 a tonne following a shipwreck in which 1,000 tonnes of the metal was lost is discussed.

12785 ■ "Shopped Out; Retailing Gloom" in *The Economist* (Vol. 390, January 3, 2009, No. 8612, pp. 26)

Pub: The Economist Newspaper Inc.

Description: Economic volatility in the retail sector is having an impact on a number of countries around the globe. Europe is experiencing hard economic times as well and unless businesses have a strong business plan banks feel unable to lend the money necessary to tide the retailers over. The falling pound has increased the cost of imported goods and small to midsize retail chains may not be able to weather such an unforgiving economic climate.

12786 ■ "Shoppes of Kenwood Files Chap. 11" in *Business Courier* (Vol. 26, December 18, 2009, No. 34, pp. 1)

Pub: American City Business Journals, Inc.

Ed: Jon Newberry. **Description:** Shoppes of Kenwood filed for Chapter 11 reorganization in US Bankruptcy Court just as the property was scheduled to be offered at a sheriff's auction. Details of the filing are included.

12787 ■ "Shorts Story" in *Barron's* (Vol. 89, July 6, 2009, No. 27, pp. 16)

Pub: Dow Jones & Co., Inc.

Ed: Gene Epstein. **Description:** Shares of Compass Minerals, J2 Global Communications, K12, Middleby, and Pactiv should be shorted by investors. These companies suffer from weaknesses in their business models, making them vulnerable to a share price decline.

12788 ■ "Should the Fed Regulate Wall Street?" in *Barron's* (Vol. 88, March 24, 2008, No. 12, pp. M15)

Pub: Dow Jones & Company, Inc.

Ed: Randall W. Forsyth. **Description:** Greater regulation of the financial sector by the Federal Reserve is essential for it to survive the crisis it is experiencing. The resulting regulation could be in complete contrast with the deregulation the sector previously experienced.

12789 ■ "Should I or Shouldn't I?" in *Indoor Comfort Marketing* (Vol. 70, February 2011, No. 2, pp. 30)

Pub: Industry Publications Inc.

Ed: Philip J. Baratz. **Description:** Investment tips are shared for investing in futures options.

12790 ■ "Silver Standard Reports First Quarter 2007 Results" in *Canadian Corporate News* (May 14, 2007)

Pub: Comtex News Network Inc.

Description: Silver Standard Resources Inc. reports a first quarter loss of $1.6 million compared with the first quarter of 2006 in which the loss was $1.1 million. Statistical data included.

12791 ■ "A Simple Old Reg that Needs Dusting Off" in *Barron's* (Vol. 88, June 30, 2008, No. 26, pp. 35)

Pub: Dow Jones & Co., Inc.

Ed: Gene Epstein. **Description:** Senator Joe Lieberman has a point when he accused speculators of inflating the prices of food and fuel futures but introducing legislation to address speculation has an alternative. The senator's committee should instead demand that the Commodity Futures Trading Commission enforce position limits on the maximum number of contracts in a given market per speculative entity.

12792 ■ "Six Great Stock Funds for the Long Haul" in *Barron's* **(Vol. 89, July 13, 2009, No. 28, pp. L5)**
Pub: Dow Jones & Co., Inc.
Ed: Lawrence C. Strauss; Tom Sullivan. **Description:** Six mutual funds that have solid long-term performance, transparency, savvy stock picking, and discipline are presented. The managers of these funds are also evaluated. These funds include the T. Rowe Price Emerging Market Stock Fund, Fairholme, and Dodge & Cox Stock.

12793 ■ "Six Things You Can Do To Ride Out A Turbulent Market" in *Hispanic Business* **(Vol. 30, March 2008, No. 3, pp. 20)**
Pub: Hispanic Business
Ed: Hildy Medina; Michael Bowker. **Description:** Top financial experts' views on managing investment portfolios during turbulent periods in the stock market are reported. Experts prefer investing in health care, short term investments, international bonds and preferred stocks or just maintain cash until such times as the market settles.

12794 ■ "Six Things You Can Do To Ride Out a Turbulent Market" in *Hispanic Business* **(March 2008, pp. 20-21)**
Pub: Hispanic Business
Ed: Hildy Medina, Michael Bowker. **Description:** Experts in the financial industry suggest shifting portfolios; investing in cash; thinking long-term for market investments; investing in foreign bonds, covered calls and preferred stocks; and to rebalance a portfolio in order to survive the downturn in the stock market.

12795 ■ "Skinner's No Drive-Thru CEO" in *Crain's Chicago Business* **(Vol. 31, April 28, 2008, No. 17, pp. 1)**
Pub: Crain Communications, Inc.
Ed: David Sterrett. **Description:** Profile of James Skinner who was named CEO for McDonald's Corp. in November 2004 and has proved to be a successful leader despite the number of investors who doubted him when he came to the position. Mr. Skinner has overseen three years of unprecedented sales growth and launched the biggest menu expansion in 30 years.

12796 ■ "Skype Ltd. Acquired GroupMe" in *Information Today* **(Vol. 28, October 2011, No. 9, pp. 12)**
Pub: Information Today, Inc.
Description: Skype Ltd. acquired GroupMe, a group messaging company that allows users to form impromptu groups where they can text message, share data, and make conference calls for free and is supported on Android, iPhone, BlackBerry, and Windows phones.

12797 ■ "The Skype's the Limit" in *Canadian Business* **(Vol. 80, February 12, 2007, No. 4, pp. 70)**
Pub: Rogers Media
Ed: Gerry Blackwell. **Description:** The increase in the market share of Skype Technologies S.A.'s Internet phone service to 171 million users is discussed.

12798 ■ "Sleeman Cuts Again as Cheap Suds Bite" in *Globe & Mail* **(March 3, 2006, pp. B3)**
Pub: CTVglobemedia Publishing Inc.
Ed: Andy Hoffman. **Description:** The details on 5 percent employee reduction at Sleeman Breweries Ltd., which posted 86 percent decline in profits for fourth quarter 2005, are presented.

12799 ■ "A Slice of Danish; Fixing Finance" in *The Economist* **(Vol. 390, January 3, 2009, No. 8612, pp. 55)**
Pub: The Economist Newspaper Inc.
Description: Denmark's mortgage-holders and the county's lending system is presented.

12800 ■ "Slow but Steady into the Future" in *Barron's* **(Vol. 88, July 7, 2008, No. 27, pp. M)**
Pub: Dow Jones & Co., Inc.
Ed: Mark Veverka. **Description:** Investors are advised to maintain their watch on the shares of business software company NetSuite. The company's chief executive officer, Zach Nelson, claims that the company has a 10-year lead on its competitors with the development of software-as-a service.

12801 ■ "The Small 300" in *Canadian Business* **(Vol. 81, Summer 2008, No. 9, pp. 137)**
Pub: Rogers Media Ltd.
Description: Small cap-companies are ranked based on market capitalization and stock performance. Calgary-based Grande Cache Coal Corp. topped the roster with 1,000 percent of return resulting from strong sales. A table showing the 2008 rankings of the companies is presented.

12802 ■ "Small is Bountiful for Intuit" in *Barron's* **(Vol. 90, September 13, 2010, No. 37, pp. 22)**
Pub: Barron's Editorial & Corporate Headquarters
Ed: Mark Veverka. **Description:** Finance software maker Intuit wants to tap the underserved small business market. One analyst sees Intuit's shares rising 25 percent to 55 percent in the next 12 months from September 2010.

12803 ■ "Small Firms Punch Ticket for Growth" in *Houston Business Journal* **(Vol. 40, January 29, 2010, No. 38, pp. 1)**
Pub: American City Business Journals
Ed: Allison Wollam. **Description:** Independent ticket agencies anticipate growth as American and Canadian authorities approved a merger between Ticketmaster and concert promoter Live Nation. Expansion of service offerings and acquisition of venues have also been done by independent ticket agencies in light of the merger. Details of the merger are included.

12804 ■ "Smart Investor's Shopping List: Coke, Walgreen, Drill Bits; A Conversation with Money Manager Paula Dorion-Gray" in *Crain's Chicago Business*
Pub: Crain Communications, Inc.
Ed: Bruce Blythe. **Description:** Interview with Paula Dorion-Gray, president of Dorion-Gray Retirement Planning Inc., discusses the state of the investing environment, favored industries, industries to avoid, and her approach towards investing.

12805 ■ "Smart Medicine" in *Canadian Business* **(Vol. 80, February 26, 2007, No. 5, pp. 73)**
Pub: Rogers Media
Ed: Zena Olijnyk. **Description:** The stock price stability and future earnings prospects of Canadian biotechnology firm YM Biosciences are analyzed.

12806 ■ "The Smell of Fear: Is a Bottom Near?" in *Barron's* **(Vol. 88, March 17, 2008, No. 11, pp. M3)**
Pub: Dow Jones & Company, Inc.
Ed: Kopin Tan. **Description:** Liquidity problems at Bear Stearns frightened investors in markets around the world due to the fear of the prospects of a big bank's failure. Shares of health maintenance organizations got battered led by WellPoint, and Humana but longer-term investors who could weather short-term volatility may find value here. The value of J. Crew shares is also discussed.

12807 ■ *The Snowball: Warren Buffett and the Business of Life*
Pub: Bantam Books
Ed: Alice Schroeder. **Released:** 2009. **Price:** $35.00.
Description: The first authorized biography of Warren Buffett provides deep and timely insight into the psyche of the billionaire investor.

12808 ■ "A Socko Payout Menu: Rural Phone Carrier Plots to Supercharge Its Shares" in *Barron's* **(Vol. 88, June 30, 2008, No. 26, pp. M5)**
Pub: Dow Jones & Co., Inc.
Ed: Shirley A. Lazo. **Description:** CenturyTel boosted its quarterly common payout to 70 cents from 6.75 cents per share die to its strong cash flows and solid

balance sheet. Eastman Kodak's plan for a buyback will be partially funded by its $581 million tax refund. CME Group will buyback stocks through 2009 worth $1.1 billion.

12809 ■ "Software's Last Hurrah" in *Canadian Business* **(Vol. 81, December 24, 2007, No. 1, pp. 27)**
Pub: Rogers Media
Ed: Andrew Wahl. **Description:** Canada's software industry could be facing a challenge with IBM's acquisition of Cognos, which was the country's last major independent business intelligence company and was IBM's largest acquisition ever. Next in line to Cognos in terms of prominence is Open Text Corporation, which could also be a possible candidate for acquisition, as analysts predict.

12810 ■ "Solace for the Freshly Flaherty'd" in *Canadian Business* **(Vol. 79, November 6, 2006, No. 22, pp. 114)**
Pub: Rogers Media
Ed: Ian McGugan. **Description:** Tips to manage investments with relation to cash distribution tax on income trusts are presented.

12811 ■ "Somanetics to Buy Back Up to $15 Million of Common Shares" in *Crain's Detroit Business* **(Vol. 24, April 7, 2008, No. 14, pp. 4)**
Pub: Crain Communications, Inc.
Ed: Tom Henderson. **Description:** Somanetics Corp., a company that manufactures and markets noninvasive devices for monitoring blood oxygen levels in the brain and elsewhere in the body during surgery, plans to buy back up to $15 million worth of its common shares. Statistical data included on the company's current and past earnings and stock prices as well as its plans to increase revenue.

12812 ■ "Some Big Biotechs Buying Own Stock" in *Boston Business Journal* **(Vol. 30, November 5, 2010, No. 41, pp. 1)**
Pub: Boston Business Journal
Ed: Julie M. Donnelly. **Description:** Biotechnology companies such as Biogen Idec and Genzyme Corporation are conducting stock buybacks as they look to invest their cash holdings. Other analysts see the buybacks as reluctance in committing to longer-term investments.

12813 ■ "Some Relief Possible Following Painful Week" in *Barron's* **(Vol. 88, July 14, 2008, No. 28, pp. M3)**
Pub: Dow Jones & Co., Inc.
Ed: Kopin Tan. **Description:** Dow Chemical is offering a 74 percent premium to acquire Rohm & Haas' coatings and electronics materials operations. Frontline amassed a 5.6 percent stake in rival Overseas Shipholding Group and a merger between the two would create a giant global fleet with pricing power. Highlights of the U.S. stock market during the week that ended in July 11, 2008 are discussed. Statistical data included.

12814 ■ "Something to Like" in *Canadian Business* **(Vol. 81, April 14, 2008, No. 6, pp. 22)**
Pub: Rogers Media
Ed: Jack Mintz. **Description:** Jim Flaherty's policy on tax-free savings account (TFSA) will allow Canadians to accumulate wealth at a much faster rate and these accounts could be especially good for people who are subject to high effective taxes on savings. Investors should put their money into a Registered Retirement Savings Plan (RRSP) when it comes to risky investments but the TFSA is better than an RRSP if investors expect very high taxes on withdrawals from their RRSP.

12815 ■ "S.O.S. Sorting Out Subprime" in *Black Enterprise* **(Vol. 38, November 2007, No. 4, pp. 76)**
Pub: Earl G. Graves Publishing Co. Inc.
Ed: Trevor Delaney. **Description:** Subprime distress in the housing market is discussed and the impact it has put on investors.

12816 ■ **"The Spark's Back in Sanyo"** in *Barron's* **(Vol. 88, March 31, 2008, No. 13, pp. M9)**
Pub: Dow Jones & Company, Inc.
Ed: Jay Alabaster. **Description:** Things are looking up for Sanyo Electric after its string of calamities that range from major losses brought on by earthquake damage to its semiconductor operations and its near collapse and bailout. The company looks poised for a rebound as they are on track for their first net profit since 2003 and could beat its earnings forecast for 2008.

12817 ■ **"Spectre of Iran War Spooks Oil Markets"** in *Globe & Mail* **(March 28, 2007, pp. B1)**
Pub: CTVglobemedia Publishing Inc.
Ed: Shawn McCarthy. **Description:** The increase in the price of crude oil by $5 a barrel to reach $68 in the United States following speculation over war against Iran, is discussed.

12818 ■ **"Spotlight on Pensions"** in *Business Horizons* **(Vol. 51, March-April 2008, No. 2, pp. 105)**
Pub: Elsevier Advanced Technology Publications
Ed: Laureen A. Maines. **Description:** Perceptions of pension burden and risk among financial statement users is likely to increase with changes in pension accounting. These perceptions might affect decisions on pension commitments and investments.

12819 ■ **"Spread Your Wings"** in *Canadian Business* **(Vol. 81, March 17, 2008, No. 4, pp. 31)**
Pub: Rogers Media
Ed: Megan Harman. **Description:** Financing from angel investors is one avenue that should be explored by startups. Angel investors are typically affluent individuals who invest their own money. Angel investors usually want at least 10 times their initial investment within eight years but they benefit the businesses through their help in decision-making and the industry expertise they provide.

12820 ■ **"Sprint Tries to Wring Out Positives"** in *The Business Journal-Serving Metropolitan Kansas City* **(Vol. 26, August 8, 2008, No. 48)**
Pub: American City Business Journals, Inc.
Ed: Suzanna Stagemeyer. **Description:** Sprint Nextel Corp. reported that 901,000 subscribers left the company in the quarter ending June 30, 2008; fewer than the nearly 1.1 million it lost in the previous quarter. Customer turnover also dropped to just less than 2 percent, compared to 2.45 percent in the first quarter of 2008.

12821 ■ **"Stand-Up Guy"** in *Barron's* **(Vol. 88, July 7, 2008, No. 27, pp. L11)**
Pub: Dow Jones & Co., Inc.
Ed: Suzanne McGee. **Description:** James O'Shaughnessy, a mutual fund manager with O'Shaughnessy Asset Management, is bullish on both financial and energy stocks. He was formerly involved with Bear Stearns until he left the firm in March 2008.

12822 ■ **"State of Play"** in *Canadian Business* **(Vol. 79, June 19, 2006, No. 13, pp. 25)**
Pub: Rogers Media
Ed: Andrew Wahl; Zena Olijnyk; Jeff Sanford. **Description:** Top 100 information technology companies in Canada are ranked by their market capitalization as of June 1. The statistics that show the revenues of these companies are also presented.

12823 ■ **"State Shock Prices Take Large Tumble"** in *The Business Journal-Milwaukee* **(Vol. 25, September 12, 2008, No. 51, pp. A1)**
Pub: American City Business Journals, Inc.
Ed: Rich Rovito. **Description:** Weak economic times have caused the stocks of most publicly traded companies in Wisconsin to dip in 2008. Companies that appeared on the worst performing stocks list also experienced drops in share price to as much as 70 percent. Information about the companies that experienced increases in stock prices is also presented. Statistical data included.

12824 ■ **"Stay Calm, Bernanke Urges Markets"** in *Globe & Mail* **(March 1, 2007, pp. B1)**
Pub: CTVglobemedia Publishing Inc.
Ed: Brian McKenna. **Description:** The views of Ben Bernanke, the chief of the United States Federal Reserve Board, on the future trends of the United States' economy are presented. The effect of the global stock market trends on the American stock markets is discussed.

12825 ■ **"Stelco Investors Told Their Stock Now Worthless"** in *Globe & Mail* **(January 23, 2006, pp. B4)**
Pub: CTVglobemedia Publishing Inc.
Ed: Greg Keenan. **Description:** The reasons behind Ontario Superior Court's approval of Stelco Inc.'s restructuring proposal are presented.

12826 ■ **"The Stem Cell Revolution"** in *Canadian Business* **(Vol. 79, November 20, 2006, No. 23, pp. 31)**
Pub: Rogers Media
Ed: Erin Pooley. **Description:** The commercial prospects and the future of stem cell therapeutics are presented. The use of stem cell therapy to heal the chronic conditions of patients is also discussed.

12827 ■ **"STMicroelectronics"** in *Canadian Electronics* **(Vol. 23, February 2008, No. 1, pp. 1)**
Pub: CLB Media Inc.
Description: STMicroelectronics, a semiconductor maker, revealed that it plans to acquire Genesis Microchip Inc. Genesis develops image and video processing systems. It was reported that the acquisition has been approved by Genesis' Board of Directors. It is expected that Genesis will enhance STMicroelectronics' technological capabilities.

12828 ■ **"Stock Analysts' Pans"** in *Canadian Business* **(Vol. 81, Summer 2008, No. 9, pp. 75)**
Pub: Rogers Media Ltd.
Ed: Calvin Leung. **Description:** Table showing the one-year stock performance of companies that are least loved by analysts and are rated either to be a Hold or Sell. These companies should not be included in the investment portfolio, at least in the short term.

12829 ■ **"Stock Car Racing"** in *Canadian Business* **(Vol. 81, September 15, 2008, No. 14-15, pp. 29)**
Pub: Rogers Media Ltd.
Ed: Thomas Watson. **Description:** Some analysts predict a Chapter 11-style tune-up making GM and Ford a speculative turnaround stock. However, the price of oil could make or break the shares of the Big Three U.S. automobile manufacturers and if oil goes up too high then a speculative stock to watch is an electric car company called Zenn Motor Co.

12830 ■ **"Stock Delisting Could Hamper First Mariner"** in *Boston Business Journal* **(Vol. 29, July 29, 2011, No. 12, pp. 1)**
Pub: American City Business Journals Inc.
Ed: Gary Haber. **Description:** Possible delisting of First Mariner Bancorp from the Nasdaq stock exchange could adversely impact the bank's ability to attract institutional investors. Some institutions limit their investments to companies trading on the Nasdaq.

12831 ■ **"Stockgroup Completes US $4.5 Million Financing"** in *Canadian Corporate News* **(May 16, 2007)**
Pub: Comtex News Network Inc.
Description: Stockgroup, a financial media company focused on collaborative technologies and user-generated content, will use the proceeds of the private placement for acquisitions and general working capital.

12832 ■ **"Street Beaters: How the Top Stock Earners on Our List Pulled It Off"** in *Canadian Business* **(Vol. 80, Winter 2007, No. 24, pp. 135)**
Pub: Rogers Media
Ed: Jeff Sanford. **Description:** Shares of Research in Motion Ltd. jumped 163 percent in 2007 after setting their patent dispute. ShawCor Ltd.'s stocks rose 99.6 percent while Onex Corporation's shares reached a high of $41.25 in 2007 from its $25 average in 2006.

12833 ■ *Street Fighters: The Last 72 Hours of Bears Stearns, the Toughest Firm on Wall Street*
Pub: Portfolio
Ed: Kate Kelly. **Released:** 2009. **Price:** $25.95. **Description:** An account of the investment bank, Bears Stearns fight for survival is documented.

12834 ■ **"Stressed Out: 7 Banks Rated 'At Riks'"** in *Saint Louis Business Journal* **(Vol. 32, September 16, 2011, No. 3, pp. 1)**
Pub: Saint Louis Business Journal
Ed: Greg Edwards. **Description:** St. Louis, Missouri has seven banks that are well above the 100 percent level that is considered 'at risk' based on a risk measurement called the Texas ratio. The banks are the Sun Security bank, 1st Advantage Bank, Superior Bank, Truman Bank, Reliance Bank, St. Louis Bank and Meramec Valley Bank.

12835 ■ **"Stretch Your Last Dollar Or Invest It?"** in *Business Owner* **(Vol. 35, November-December 2011, No. 6, pp. 4)**
Pub: DL Perkins Company
Description: Should small business owners cut expenses or invest in a downturned economy? Difficult times can be an opportunity to build a business brad.

12836 ■ **"Struggling Community Banks Find Little Help In Wall Street Bailout"** in *Crain's Detroit Business* **(Vol. 24, September 29, 2008)**
Pub: Crain Communications, Inc.
Ed: Tom Henderson. **Description:** Both public and private Michigan bands have been hit hard by poorly performing loan portfolios and although their problems were not caused by high-risk securities but by a longtime statewide recession and a housing slump, these community banks have little hope of seeing any of the bailout money that has been allotted for the larger institutions.

12837 ■ **"Stymiest's RBC Compensation Triggers Shareholder Outrage"** in *Gl obe & Mail* **(January 28, 2006, pp. B3)**
Pub: CTVglobemedia Publishing Inc.
Ed: Sinclair Stewart. **Description:** The concerns of shareholders over the issue of Royal Bank of Canada's $6.6 million pay package for chief executive officer Barbara Stymiest, in 2004, are presented.

12838 ■ **"Subprime Hits Huntington"** in *Business First-Columbus* **(November 23, 2007, pp. A1)**
Pub: American City Business Journals, Inc.
Ed: Adrian Burns. **Description:** Huntington Bancshares Inc. picked up a $1.5 billion exposure to the country's subprime mortgage mess. It caused the bank to set aside $450 million to cover increases in loan losses. When Huntington acquired Sky Financial, it absorbed a 17-year relationship Sky had with Franklin Credit Corporation, which is a subprime lender and servicer.

12839 ■ *The Subprime Solution: How Today's Global Financial Crisis Happened, and What to Do About It*
Pub: Princeton University Press
Ed: Robert J. Shiller. **Released:** 2009. **Price:** $16.95. **Description:** Yale economist discusses the worldwide financial crisis and offers plans to reform the system.

12840 ■ **"Sudbury Waits With Future Up in the Air"** in *Globe & Mail* **(February 22, 2006, pp. B1)**
Pub: CTVglobemedia Publishing Inc.
Ed: Wendy Stueck. **Description:** The takeover of Falconbridge Ltd., by Inco Ltd Sudbury, is in the process with uncertainty. The transaction has been a long overdue.

12841 ■ "Suiting Up; Yes, You're Smart, But Can You Look the Part" in *Crain's Chicago Business* **(Vol. 30, February 2007, No. 6, pp. 39)**
Pub: Crain Communications, Inc.
Ed: Kate Ryan. Description: For investment bankers, fashion is a must. Advice for men and women included.

12842 ■ "The Suits Look Better Than the Shares" in *Barron's* **(Vol. 88, March 31, 2008, No. 13, pp. 25)**
Pub: Dow Jones & Company, Inc.
Ed: Bill Alpert. Description: Jos. A. Bank's inventory has increased sharply raising questions about the company's growth prospects. The company's shares have already dropped significantly from 46 to 23 and could still continue its slide. The company is also battling a class action suit where plaintiffs allege that the Bank inventories were bloated.

12843 ■ "Sullivan Led Bucyrus through Unforgettable Year" in *Business Journal-Milwaukee* **(Vol. 28, December 17, 2010, No. 11, pp. A1)**
Pub: Milwaukee Business Journal
Ed: Rich Rovito. Description: Bucyrus International's president and CEO, Tim Sullivan, was chosen as Milwaukee, Wisconsin's Executive of the Year for 2010. Sullivan led Bucyrus through a year of dramatic change which started with the acquisition of the mining business of Terex Corporation and culminating with a deal to sell Caterpillar Inc.

12844 ■ "Summit, Lions Gate are in Talks to Merge Studios" in *Wall Street Journal Eastern Edition* **(November 29, 2011, pp. B2)**
Pub: Dow Jones & Company Inc.
Ed: Erica Orden, Michelle Kung. Description: Movie studio Summit Entertainment LLC is in talks with television producer Lions Gate Entertainment Corporation about a possible merger. Previous talks have taken place, but no deal was ever reached. Such a deal would create a large, independent studio able to compete in the market with the big Hollywood giants.

12845 ■ "Sun Capital Partners Affiliate Acquires Timothy's Coffees" in *Miami Daily Business Review* **(March 26, 2008)**
Pub: ALM Media Inc.
Description: An affiliate of Sun Capital Partners acquired Timothy's Coffees of the World. Timothy's operates and franchises 166 stores offering coffees, muffins, and Michel's Baguette products.

12846 ■ "Surprise Package" in *Business Courier* **(Vol. 27, June 25, 2010, No. 8, pp. 1)**
Pub: Business Courier
Ed: Dan Monk, Jon Newberry, Steve Watkins. Description: More than 60 percent of the chief executive officers (CEOs) in Greater Cincinnati's 35 public companies took a salary cut in 2009, but stock grants resulted in large paper gains for the CEOs. The salary cuts show efforts of boards of directors to observe austerity. Statistics on increased values of stock awards for CEOs, median pay for CEOs, and median shareholder return are also presented.

12847 ■ "A Survival Guide for Crazy Times" in *Canadian Business* **(Vol. 81, March 3, 2008, No. 3, pp. 61)**
Pub: Rogers Media
Ed: David Wolf. Description: Investors should ensure that their portfolios are positioned defensively more than the average as the U.S. and Canadian markets face turbulent times. They should not assume that U.S. residential property is a good place to invest only because prices have dropped and the Canadian dollar is showing strength. Other tips that investors can use during unstable periods are supplied.

12848 ■ "Surviving the Storm" in *Canadian Business* **(Vol. 81, July 22, 2008, No. 12-13, pp. 50)**
Pub: Rogers Media Ltd.
Ed: Jeff Sanford. Description: Investment adviser Harry Dent and finance professor Paul Marsh discuss their views and forecasts on the United States'

economic condition. Dent believes advisors should concentrate on wealth preservation rather than on returns. Other views regarding U.S. economic conditions are also presented.

12849 ■ "Sweet Harmony" in *Canadian Business* **(Vol. 82, April 27, 2009, No. 7, pp. 6)**
Pub: Rogers Media
Description: Canada will harmonize its 5 percent federal goods and services tax wit the 8 percent provincial sales tax effective July 1, 2010. Meanwhile, provinces like Ontario and Quebec have switched the sales taxes that are charged in new investments into a value-added tax. The conversion has led to an 11 percent increase in investments in Quebec and the three other provinces that made the conversion.

12850 ■ "Sweet Spot" in *Canadian Business* **(Vol. 79, November 20, 2006, No. 23, pp. 25)**
Pub: Rogers Media
Ed: John Gray. Description: The plans of Kinross Gold Corp., to acquire the stake of Bema Gold Corp., are discussed. Under the terms of the deal Kinross is offering Bema stockholders 0.441 of a Kinross share for each of Bema shares.

12851 ■ "A Swifter, Better Marketplace" in *Barron's* **(Vol. 89, July 13, 2009, No. 28, pp. M13)**
Pub: Dow Jones & Co., Inc.
Ed: Eric W. Noll. Description: Listed-derivatives market is moving towards greater trading through computerized systems with an emphasis on speed and innovation. The market for listed options is also being changed by new techniques from other markets such as algorithmic trading, dark pools, and new-order priority systems.

12852 ■ "Swinging For the Fences" in *Academy of Management Journal* **(October 2007, pp. 1055)**
Pub: Academy of Management
Ed: William Gerard Sanders, Donald C. Hambrick. Description: Study examines managerial risk-taking vis-a-vis stock options of the company; results reveal that stock options instigate CEOs to take unwise risks that could bring huge losses to the company.

12853 ■ "Sykes Group Targets GunnAllen" in *The Business Journal-Serving Greater Tampa Bay* **(Vol. 28, September 5, 2008, No. 37, pp. 1)**
Pub: American City Business Journals, Inc.
Ed: Margie Manning. Description: GAH Holdings LLC. a newly formed investment company by John H. Sykes of Sykes Enterprises Inc., will add capital to Tampa Bay Area investment banking firm GunnAllen Holdings Inc. The capital infusion is to aid GunnAllen Holdings in expanding and diversifying as GAH becomes its largest shareholder.

12854 ■ "Sykes Shift from GunnAllen to New Venture" in *Tampa Bay Business Journal* **(Vol. 30, December 18, 2009, No. 52, pp. 1)**
Pub: American City Business Journals
Ed: Margie Manning. Description: Tampa, Florida's entrepreneur John H. Sykes acquired Pointe Capital Inc., a GunnAllen Holdings Inc. subsidiary, through his JHS Capital Holdings Inc. and changed the name to JHS Capital Advisors Inc. Sykes will become president and CEO of JHS Capital Advisors and will relocate its corporate headquarters to Tampa, Florida.

12855 ■ "Take a Flyer on Choice" in *Canadian Business* **(Vol. 79, October 23, 2006, No. 21, pp. 163)**
Pub: Rogers Media
Description: The variations in the stock market prices of companies like Nike Inc. and Black & Decker Corp. from October 2005-06 are discussed.

12856 ■ "Take It to the Bank" in *Barron's* **(Vol. 89, July 13, 2009, No. 28, pp. 20)**
Pub: Dow Jones & Co., Inc.
Ed: Jim McTague. Description: Banks are one of the safest place to put one's principal due to the temporary increase in the Federal Deposit Insurance Corp.'s insurance of bank accounts up to $250,000 and also because of the Cdars (Certificates of

Deposit Registry Service) program which spreads the deposit to several banks thereby making the account covered as if the money was deposited at multiple banks.

12857 ■ "Take the Wheel: the Pension Protection Act Doesn't Mean You Can Sit Back and Relax" in *Black Enterprise* **(October 2007)**
Pub: Earl G. Graves Publishing Co. Inc.
Ed: Mellody Hobson. Description: Pension Protection Act provides multiple benefits and tax advantages for retirement, however the investment options and contribution rates are very conservative.

12858 ■ "Takeover Frenzy Stokes Steel Stocks" in *Globe & Mail* **(February 7, 2006, pp. B1)**
Pub: CTVglobemedia Publishing Inc.
Description: The impact of merger speculations, on shares of steel companies such as Ipsco Inc., is discussed.

12859 ■ "Taking Collections" in *Investment Dealers' Digest* **(Vol. 75, October 9, 2009, No. 38, pp. 19)**
Pub: SourceMedia, Inc.
Ed: Aleksandrs Rozens. Description: Although the nation's debt-collection industry has grown with increased reliance by consumers on credit, valuations of these firms have lessened due to the economy which has hurt some of the success of these firms in obtaining the debt back from consumers who are experiencing trying economic times.

12860 ■ "Taking the Over-the-Counter Route to US" in *Barron's* **(Vol. 88, July 7, 2008, No. 27, pp. 24)**
Pub: Dow Jones & Co., Inc.
Ed: Eric Uhlfelder. Description: Many multinational companies have left the New York Stock Exchange and allowed their shares to trade over-the-counter. The companies have taken advantage of a 2007 SEC rule allowing publicly listed foreign companies to change trading venues if less than 5 percent of global trading volume in the past 12 months occurred in the US.

12861 ■ "Taking a Pounding; Recession Fears Weigh Down Steakhouse Operator Morton's" in *Crain's Chicago Business* **(March 31, 2008)**
Pub: Crain Communications, Inc.
Ed: Monee Fields-White. Description: Morton's Restaurant Group Inc. has seen a 50 percent drop in shares in the past six months due to the economy and cutbacks in corporate expense accounts; business customers provide the restaurant about 80 percent of its revenue.

12862 ■ "Tanganyika Announces First Quarter 2007 Results" in *Canadian Corporate News* **(May 14, 2007)**
Pub: Comtex News Network Inc.
Description: Tanganyika Oil Company Ltd., announced the interim operating and financial results for the first quarter ending March 31, 2007. Statistical data included.

12863 ■ "Tao of Downfall" in *International Journal of Entrepreneurship and Small Business* **(Vol. 11, August 31, 2010, No. 2, pp. 121)**
Pub: Publishers Communication Group
Ed: Wenxian Zhang, Ilan Alon. Description: Through historical reviews and case studies, this research seeks to understand why some initially successful entrepreneurs failed in the economic boom of past decades. Among various factors contributing to their downfall are a unique political and business environment, fragile financial systems, traditional cultural influences and personal characteristics.

12864 ■ "Tax Credit Crunch" in *Miami Daily Business Review* **(March 26, 2008)**
Pub: ALM Media Inc.
Ed: Paula Iuspa-Abbott. Description: Uncertainty is growing over the future of the low-income housing project in South Florida and the tax credit program that helps fuel the projects.

12865 ■ **"The Tech 100" in** *Canadian Business* **(Vol. 81, July 21, 2008, No. 11, pp. 48)**
Pub: Rogers Media Ltd.
Ed: Calvin Leung. **Description:** Absolute Software Corp. Day4 Energy Inc., Sandvine Corp., Norsat International Inc. and Call Genie Inc. are the five technology firms included in the annual ranking of top companies in Canada by market capitalization. The services and the one-year total return potential of the companies are presented.

12866 ■ **"Tech Godfather Steve Walker Winding Down Howard Venture Fund" in** *Baltimore Business Journal* **(Vol. 27, December 11, 2009, No. 31)**
Pub: American City Business Journals
Ed: Scott Dance. **Description:** Steve Walker, president of venture capital fund firm Walker Ventures, will be closing the Howard County, Maryland-based firm as the economic situation is finding it difficult to recover investor's money. According to Walker, the economy also constrained investors from financing venture funds. Despite the closure, Walker will continue his work in the local angel investing community.

12867 ■ **"Tech Investing: March's Long Road" in** *Canadian Business* **(Vol. 80, January 29, 2007, No. 3, pp. 67)**
Pub: Rogers Media
Ed: Calvin Leung. **Description:** The efforts of March Networks, a manufacturer of digital surveillance equipment, from the decline in the price of its shares at the beginning of the year 2007 are described.

12868 ■ **"Tech's Payout Problem" in** *Barron's* **(Vol. 90, September 13, 2010, No. 37, pp. 19)**
Pub: Barron's Editorial & Corporate Headquarters
Ed: Andrew Bary. **Description:** Big tech companies have the potential to be good dividend payers, but instead just hoard their cash for acquisitions and share buybacks. If these companies offered more dividends, they could boost their shares and attract more income-oriented investors.

12869 ■ **"Tektronix Buys Arbor Networks for Security Business" in** *eWeek* **(August 9, 2010)**
Pub: Ziff Davis Enterprise
Description: Tektronix Communications, provider of communications test and network intelligence solutions will acquire Arbor Networks. The deal will help Tektronix build a brand in security. Details of the transaction are included.

12870 ■ **"TerraVest Income Fund Releases 2007 First Quarter Financial Results" in** *Canadian Corporate News* **(May 14, 2007)**
Pub: Comtex News Network Inc.
Description: Overview of TerraVest Income Fund's financial results for the quarter ended March 31, 2007 in which the net earnings increased 36.7 percent to $3.7 million from the 2006 first quarter. Statistical data included.

12871 ■ **"That's About It for Quantitative Easing" in** *Barron's* **(Vol. 89, July 20, 2009, No. 29, pp. M11)**
Pub: Dow Jones & Co., Inc.
Ed: Brian Blackstone. **Description:** US Federal Reserve appears to have decided to halt quantitative easing, causing bond prices to drop and yields to rise. The yield for the 1-year Treasury bond rose more than 0.3 percentage point to about 3.65 percent.

12872 ■ **"The End of the Line for Line Extensions?" in** *Advertising Age* **(Vol. 79, July 7, 2008, No. 26, pp. 3)**
Pub: Crain Communications, Inc.
Ed: Description: After years of double-digit growth, some of the most heavily extended personal-care products have slowed substantially or even declined in the U.S. Unilever's Dove and P&G's Pantene and Olay are two such brands that have been affected. Statistical data included.

12873 ■ **"The File On...Skoda Minotti" in** *Crain's Cleveland Business* **(Vol. 28, October 8, 2007, No. 40, pp. 26)**
Pub: Crain Communications, Inc.
Ed: Kimberly Bonvissuto. **Description:** Overview of Skoda Minotti, the accounting and financial services firm located in Mayfield Village; the company has 140 employees and an expanded slate of services.

12874 ■ **"The REIT Stuff" in** *Canadian Business* **(Vol. 80, March 26, 2007, No. 7, pp. 72)**
Pub: Rogers Media
Description: The stock performance of various real estate investment trusts in Canada is analyzed.

12875 ■ **"Theme Park Sale has Vendor Upside" in** *Tampa Bay Business Journal* **(Vol. 29, October 23, 2009, No. 44, pp. 1)**
Pub: American City Business Journals
Ed: Margie Manning. **Description:** Private equity firm The Blackstone Group has concluded its $2.7 billion purchase of Busch Entertainment Corporation. Aside from enhanced business opportunities in Florida's Tampa Bay area, new attractions might be built in the Busch Gardens and Adventure Island properties that will be acquired by Blackstone. Blackstone's other plans are also discussed.

12876 ■ **"There's More Upside in Germany" in** *Barron's* **(Vol. 90, September 6, 2010, No. 36, pp. M7)**
Pub: Barron's Editorial & Corporate Headquarters
Ed: Jonathan Buck. **Description:** Germany's stocks have gone up since the beginning of 2010, and investors can still benefit. These stocks will benefit from Germany's stellar economic performance and the relative weakness of the Euro. The prospects of the shares of Daimler and Hochtief are discussed.

12877 ■ **"TheStree.com: Study Abroad" in** *Entrepreneur* **(Vol. 35, October 2007, No. 10, pp. 44)**
Pub: Entrepreneur Media Inc.
Ed: Farnoosh Torabi. **Description:** Businessmen who wish to pursue foreign investments should study the country in which they will operate. Some investors do their research by completely exposing themselves to their prospective country, while others prefer studying the market home-based. Details of how investors pick their country and the different ways of investing in foreign land are presented.

12878 ■ **"They Have Issues: New Black-Owned Investment Bank Nets $90 Million In Managed Issues" in** *Black Enterprise* **(Vol. 38, March 2008)**
Pub: Earl G. Graves Publishing Co. Inc.
Ed: Marcia A. Wade. **Description:** Castle Oak Securities LP has co-managed multiple deals for more than 35 blue-chip clients. Their first deal earned $300 million for General Electric Capital Corporation and Castle Oak has since co-managed nine more deals with GE Capital, seven for Citigroup, six for American Express, and three for Goldman Sachs.

12879 ■ **"They're Hopping Mad" in** *Canadian Business* **(Vol. 80, October 22, 2007, No. 21, pp. 20)**
Pub: Rogers Media
Description: Alberta Review Panel is calling for a 20 percent increase in oil and gas development taxes. SABMiller and Molson Coors Brewing Company combined its U.S. and Puerto Rican operations, though the deal is still subject to regulatory approvals. Montreal Exchange Inc. filed for approval of the trade of Montreal Climate Exchange futures contracts.

12880 ■ **"They've Fallen, But They Can Get Up" in** *Barron's* **(Vol. 88, March 10, 2008, No. 10, pp. 43)**
Pub: Dow Jones & Company, Inc.
Ed: Kopin Tan. **Description:** Shares of senior housing companies present buying opportunities to investors because of their low prices. Companies such as Brookdale Senior Living are not as dependent on housing prices but have suffered declines in share prices.

12881 ■ **"Things Will Improve, or Not: a Chartered Financial Analyst Explains It All" in** *Canadian Business* **(Vol. 81, November 10, 2008)**
Pub: Rogers Media Ltd.
Description: Myles Zyblock expects the global economic slowdown to deepen over the next six to nine months. Zyblock addressed the Toronto CFA Society at their annual dinner in October 2008. He stressed a tight correlation between the credit ratio and asset prices and predicts the S&P 500 to be up by 11 percent by October 2009.

12882 ■ *This Is Not Your Parents' Retirement: A Revolutionary Guide for a Revolutionary Generation*
Pub: Entrepreneur Press
Ed: Patrick P. Astre. **Released:** July 2005. **Price:** $19.95 (US), $26.95 (Canadian). **Description:** Mutual funds, stocks, bonds, insurance products, and tax strategies for retirement planning.

12883 ■ **"Time to Change Direction" in** *Canadian Business* **(Vol. 79, October 23, 2006, No. 21, pp. 21)**
Pub: Rogers Media
Ed: Jack Mintz. **Description:** The decision of BCE Inc. to get converted into an income trust is discussed. The economic factors responsible for the conversion of firms to income trusts are analyzed.

12884 ■ **"Time to Engage Europe" in** *Canadian Business* **(Vol. 79, June 19, 2006, No. 13, pp. 19)**
Pub: Rogers Media
Ed: Jack Mintz. **Description:** European and Canadian governments improved their trade and investment relations with the March 18, 2004 frame work to develop a Trade and Investment Enhancement Agreement. Still there is lot of opportunities to solve tax and trade issues.

12885 ■ **"Time to Leave the Party?" in** *Barron's* **(Vol. 88, March 24, 2008, No. 12, pp. M16)**
Pub: Dow Jones & Company, Inc.
Ed: Andrea Hotter. **Description:** Prices of commodities such as gold, copper, crude oil, sugar, cocoa, and wheat have fallen from their all-time highs set in the middle of March 2008. Analysts, however, caution that this decline in prices may be temporary, and that a banking crisis may trigger new price rises in commodities.

12886 ■ **"Time for a Little Pruning" in** *Barron's* **(Vol. 89, July 6, 2009, No. 27, pp. 13)**
Pub: Dow Jones & Co., Inc.
Ed: Dimitra DeFotis. **Description:** Investors are advised to avoid the shares of Whole Foods, American Tower, T. Rowe Price, Iron Mountain, Intuitive Surgical, Salesforce.com, and Juniper Networks due to their high price to earnings ratios. The shares of Amazon.com, Broadcom, and Expeditors International of Washington remain attractive to investors despite their high price to earnings ratios due to their strong growth.

12887 ■ **"A Timely Boon for Small Investors" in** *Barron's* **(Vol. 88, March 24, 2008, No. 12, pp. 48)**
Pub: Dow Jones & Company, Inc.
Ed: Theresa W. Carey. **Description:** Nasdaq Data Store's new program called Market Replay allows investors to accurately track stock price movements. The replay can be as long as a day of market time and allows investors to determine whether they executed stock trades at the best possible price.

12888 ■ **"Tiptoeing Beyond Treasuries" in** *Barron's* **(Vol. 88, March 31, 2008, No. 13, pp. M6)**
Pub: Dow Jones & Company, Inc.
Ed: Michael S. Derby. **Description:** Risk-free assets like treasuries are still a good place for cash even if market conditions have calmed down and Treasury yields are low. Investors looking for yield and safety might want to consider Treasury inflation-indexed securities that are attractive given new inflation pressures.

12889 ■ **"To Give and Receive: How to Pass On 401k Assets and Manage an Inheritance"** in *Black Enterprise* (Vol. 38, October 2007, No. 3)
Pub: Earl G. Graves Publishing Co. Inc.
Ed: Steven Garmhausen. **Description:** Without proper planning, heirs could pay large tax bills to the government unless assets are managed properly. A common error is to avoid updating account records to reflect the names of designated beneficiaries.

12890 ■ **"To Sell or Not To Sell"** in *Inc.* (December 2007, pp. 80)
Pub: Gruner & Jahr USA Publishing
Ed: Patrick J. Sauer. **Description:** Owner of a private equity discusses the challenges he faces when deciding to sell his family's business.

12891 ■ **"To Thine Own Self"** in *Entrepreneur* (Vol. 35, November 2007, No. 11, pp. 50)
Pub: Entrepreneur Media Inc.
Ed: Torabi Farnoosh. **Description:** Self-directed individual retirement account (IRA) provides more investment options as payoff from this can be higher than an average mutual fund. Details on how to manage self-directed IRAs are discussed.

12892 ■ **"Tofutti Brands"** in *Ice Cream Reporter* (Vol. 23, September 20, 2010, No. 10, pp. 6)
Pub: Ice Cream Reporter
Description: Tofutti Brands announced net sales at $4.5 million for second quarter 2010.

12893 ■ **"A Tonic for Irrationality"** in *Barron's* (Vol. 89, July 13, 2009, No. 28, pp. 12)
Pub: Dow Jones & Co., Inc.
Description: Financial-personality assessment being introduced by Barclays Wealth, measures six personality aspects related to financial behavior through a profile that measures such traits including risk tolerance, composure and perceived financial expertise. The profile helps the company create a portfolio that are structured to meet their client's personality needs.

12894 ■ **"Too Much Precaution About Biotech Corn"** in *Barron's* (Vol. 88, March 17, 2008, No. 11, pp. 54)
Pub: Dow Jones & Company, Inc.
Ed: Mark I. Schwartz. **Description:** In the U.S., 90 percent of cultivated soybeans are biotech varietals as well as 60 percent of the corn. Farmers have significantly reduced their reliance on pesticides in the growing of biotech corn. Biotech cotton cultivation has brought hundreds of millions of dollars in net financial gains to farmers. The European Union has precluded the cultivation or sale of biotech crops within its border.

12895 ■ **"Too Much too Soon"** in *Barron's* (Vol. 89, July 27, 2009, No. 30, pp. 33)
Pub: Dow Jones & Co., Inc.
Ed: Leslie P. Norton. **Description:** Shares of hhgregg have risen 85 percent in the year leading up to July 2009 and analysts believe the stock could hit 25. However, their 113 outlets are concentrated in states where unemployment is above 10 percent and expanding into areas already overstored. Competition is also rife and credit availability is still tight.

12896 ■ **"Tool-o-Rama"** in *Barron's* (Vol. 90, September 6, 2010, No. 36)
Pub: Barron's Editorial & Corporate Headquarters
Description: New trading tool features from several online brokers are discussed. The new features from Fidelity, ChoiceTrade, JunoTrade and TradeKing are examined. Investors can now screen exchanged traded funds in the same way as stocks with Fidelity, while ChoiceTrade can run in any browser without the need to install additional plug-ins.

12897 ■ **"Top 10 Retirement Mistakes and How to Avoid Them"** in *Canadian Business* (Vol. 83, July 20, 2010, No. 11-12, pp. 39)
Pub: Rogers Media Ltd.
Ed: Jacqueline Nelson, Angelina Chapin. **Description:** Some of the top retirement mistakes is relying on selling one's house to find a retirement. Other mistakes are paying too much for investments and

planning to work in retirement since no one can be sure that they will be healthy enough to accomplish this. Suggestions to avoid these pitfalls are discussed.

12898 ■ **"Top 50 By 1-Year Return"** in *Canadian Business* (Vol. 81, Summer 2008, No. 9, pp. 121)
Pub: Rogers Media Ltd.
Description: Table showing the top 50 Canadian companies ranked in terms of one-year return is presented. Toronto, Canada-based Timminco Ltd. topped the roster with a 1,294.2 percent in one-year return. However, the share prices of the company were affected by the recent controversy in its silicon purification process.

12899 ■ **"Top 50 By 5-Year Return"** in *Canadian Business* (Vol. 81, Summer 2008, No. 9, pp. 123)
Pub: Rogers Media Ltd.
Description: Table showing the rankings of the top 50 Canadian companies in terms of five-year return is presented. Silver Wheaton Corp. topped the roster with a 178.5 percent in five-year return. The company's share prices have skyrocketed despite increasing silver prices.

12900 ■ **"Top 50 in the Capital Market"** in *Canadian Business* (Vol. 81, Summer 2008, No. 9, pp. 117)
Pub: Rogers Media Ltd.
Description: Research in Motion Ltd. topped the list of companies in Canada in terms of market capitalization. The company's share prices surge to 119.8 percent in the year ended April 4. A table showing the top 50 Canadian companies in terms of market capitalization is presented.

12901 ■ **"Top 50 In Profits"** in *Canadian Business* (Vol. 81, Summer 2008, No. 9, pp. 116)
Pub: Rogers Media Ltd.
Description: Royal Bank of Canada topped the Investor 500 by profits list despite the slower economic growth in Canada and the U.S. The bank was in the runner-up position in the 2007. RBC's growth strategy is through hefty acquisitions in the U.S.A. A table ranking the top 50 companies in Canada in terms of profits is presented.

12902 ■ **"Top 50 In Total Revenue"** in *Canadian Business* (Vol. 81, Summer 2008, No. 9, pp. 119)
Pub: Rogers Media Ltd.
Description: Table showing the top 50 Canadian companies in terms of total revenue is presented. Manulife Financial Corp. topped the list with revenue of 34.5 billion. The financial services firm is the 6th largest provider of life insurance in the world and the second largest in North America.

12903 ■ **"Top Law Firms Join Forces"** in *Business Journal Portland* (Vol. 27, December 3, 2010, No. 40, pp. 1)
Pub: Portland Business Journal
Ed: Andy Giegerich. **Description:** Law Firms Powell PC and Roberts Kaplan LLP will forge a collaboration, whereby 17 Roberts Kaplan attorneys will join the Portland, Oregon-based office of Lane Powell. The partnership is expected to strengthen the law firms' grip on Portland's banking clients.

12904 ■ **"A Torch in the Darkness"** in *Canadian Business* (Vol. 83, August 17, 2010, No. 13-14, pp. 66)
Pub: Rogers Media Ltd.
Ed: Joe Castaldo. **Description:** Research In Motion (RIM) unveiled the BlackBerry Touch, featuring a touch screen as well as a physical keyboard, in an attempt to repel competitors and expand share in the consumer smart phone market. RIM shares have fallen 43 percent from its peak in 2009.

12905 ■ **"Tory or Liberal, Blue or Red, the Impact of the Election is All in Your Head"** in *Globe & Mail* (January 14, 2006, pp. B19)
Pub: CTVglobemedia Publishing Inc.
Ed: Derek DeCloet. **Description:** The effect of the outcome of 2006 Canadian federal elections on stock markets is discussed.

12906 ■ **"Toy Story"** in *Forbes* (Vol. 180, October 15, 2007, No. 8, pp. 102)
Pub: Forbes Inc.
Description: Three voluntary recalls of Chinese-made toys were announced by American toymakers, sending Mattel stocks plummeting.

12907 ■ **"Toyota Marks Record Profit Sales"** in *Globe & Mail* (February 7, 2007, pp. B10)
Pub: CTVglobemedia Publishing Inc.
Ed: Martin Fackler. **Description:** The record quarterly sales and earnings reported by Japanese automaker Toyota Motor Corp. are discussed. The company sold 2.16 million vehicles during the quarter while registering 426.8 billion yen in profits.

12908 ■ **"The Trader's Edge"** in *Barron's* (Vol. 88, March 31, 2008, No. 13, pp. 56)
Pub: Dow Jones & Company, Inc.
Ed: Dan McGuire. **Description:** There is a $3,000 a year annual limit to deducting investor's losses and normal investment expenses are purportedly deductible as miscellaneous expenses on Schedule A only to the extent that they exceed two percent of adjusted gross income. Professional gamblers who can use Schedule C are unable deduct a net gaming loss against income from any other sources.

12909 ■ **"Trading Down at the Supermarket"** in *Barron's* (Vol. 88, July 14, 2008, No. 28, pp. 36)
Pub: Dow Jones & Co., Inc.
Ed: Alexander Eule. **Description:** Shares of Ralcorp Holdings are cheap at around $49.95 after slipping 20 percent prior to their acquisition of Post cereals from Kraft. Some analysts believe its shares could climb over 60 percent to $80 as value-seeking consumers buy more private label products.

12910 ■ **"Transcontinental to Exchange Assets with Quad/Graphics"** in *American Printer* (Vol. 128, August 1, 2011, No. 8)
Pub: Penton Media Inc.
Description: Transcontinental Inc. and Quad/Graphics Inc. entered into an agreement where Transcontinental will indirectly acquire all shares of Quad Graphics Canada Inc.

12911 ■ **"Treasuries Buffeted by Stocks"** in *Barron's* (Vol. 89, July 27, 2009, No. 30, pp. M9)
Pub: Dow Jones & Co., Inc.
Ed: Randall W. Forsyth. **Description:** Warren Buffett favors equities over long-term government bonds or stocks even with the Dow index at an eight-month high. The 10-year Treasury was up two basis points to 3.67 percent as of July 24, 2009. Corporate bond issuance hit a record $1.79 trillion for the first half of 2009.

12912 ■ **"Treasuries Rally Despite Huge Supply"** in *Barron's* (Vol. 89, July 13, 2009, No. 28, pp. M10)
Pub: Dow Jones & Co., Inc.
Ed: Randall W. Forsyth. **Description:** Prices of U.S. Treasuries were sent higher and their yields lower despite four auctions of coupon securities because of the strong appetite for government securities around the world. The reopening of the 10-year note in the week ending July 10, 2009 drew the strongest bidding since 1995.

12913 ■ **"A Trend Is His Friend"** in *Barron's* (Vol. 89, July 27, 2009, No. 30, pp. 28)
Pub: Dow Jones & Co., Inc.
Ed: Eric Uhlfelder. **Description:** Global Diversified Program fund under Quality Capital Management is managed through a trading system called the Advanced Resource Allocator which rebalances short-term tactical moves to gather quick profits. CEO Aref Karim's allocations are based on risk and he says their sentiments toward the market conditions are agnostic.

12914 ■ **"The Trials of Brian Hunter"** in *Canadian Business* (Vol. 81, March 3, 2008, No. 3, pp. 64)
Pub: Rogers Media
Ed: Thomas Watson. **Description:** Brian Hunter was a considered a brilliant trader in Wall Street before he was blamed for the fall of the Amaranth hedge fund.

Some people blame Hunter for placing bets based on unpredictable weather when he was a trader for Amaranth Advisors LLC. The accusation against Hunter that he conspired to manipulate natural gas prices is also discussed.

12915 ■ *The Trillion Dollar Meltdown: Easy Money, High Rollers, and the Great Credit Crash*
Pub: Public Affairs

Ed: Charles R. Morris. **Released:** 2009. **Price:** $22.95. **Description:** Former banker believes that Wall Street and the financial community have too much power in America. He estimates that writedowns and defaults of residential mortgages, commercial mortgages, junk bonds, leveraged loans, credit cards, and complex securitized bonds could reach $1 trillion.

12916 ■ **"Trilogy Metals Inc.: Private Placement" in *Canadian Corporate News* (May 16, 2007)**
Pub: Comtex News Network Inc.

Description: Trilogy Metals Inc. announces a private placement of 10,000,000 units at $0.08 per unit in an effort to raise total gross proceeds of $800,000 which will be allocated to working capital, new acquisitions, and to service existing debt.

12917 ■ **"Trust Buyouts Not My Fault, Flaherty Says" in *Globe & Mail* (April 3, 2007, pp. B1)**
Pub: CTVglobemedia Publishing Inc.

Ed: Tara Perkins; Doug Saunders; Steven Chase. **Description:** The causes of the acquisition of Canadian firms by foreign investors are discussed by the Canadian Finance Minister Jim Flaherty.

12918 ■ **"Trust Distrust" in *Canadian Business* (Vol. 79, July 17, 2006, No. 14-15, pp. 61)**
Pub: Rogers Media

Ed: John Gray. **Description:** The need to frame better trust deeds in order to protect the investor's money as well as their returns is examined.

12919 ■ **"TUSK Announces 2007 First Quarter Results" in *Canadian Corporate News* (May 14, 2007)**
Pub: Comtex News Network Inc.

Description: TUSK Energy Corp. announced its financial and operating results for the first quarter ending March 31, 2007.

12920 ■ **"TV Revenue Slide Hits CanWest Profit" in *Globe & Mail* (January 13, 2006, pp. B3)**
Pub: CTVglobemedia Publishing Inc.

Ed: Grant Robertson. **Description:** CanWest Global Communications Corp. posted drop in profits by 14 percent for first quarter 2006. The downward trend in profits is attributed to low television revenues.

12921 ■ **"UBS Buys Out Canadian Partner" in *Globe & Mail* (January 20, 2006, pp. B1)**
Pub: CTVglobemedia Publishing Inc.

Ed: Andrew Willis. **Description:** The details on UBS AG's acquisition of UBS Securities Canada Inc. are presented.

12922 ■ *Ultimate Startup Directory: Expert Advice and 1,500 Great Startup Ideas*
Pub: Entrepreneur Press

Ed: James Stephenson. **Released:** February 2007. **Price:** $30.95 (CND). **Description:** Startup opportunities in over 30 industries are given, along with information on investment, earning potential, skills, legal requirements and more.

12923 ■ **"Understanding the Economy: People Worry That a Recession Is Coming" in *Inc.* (December 2007, pp. 103-104)**
Pub: Gruner & Jahr USA Publishing

Ed: Joseph H. Ellis. **Description:** It is suggested that by the time a recession arrives, the worst economic damage has already occurred.

12924 ■ **"Understanding the Fed" in *Black Enterprise* (Vol. 38, December 2007, No. 5, pp. 66)**
Pub: Earl G. Graves Publishing Co. Inc.

Ed: Steve Garmhausen. **Description:** The Federal Reserve System along with twelve regional banks regulates the value of money through the law of supply and demand. The Feds increase or decrease the supply of dollars in circulation which makes them cheap or expensive.

12925 ■ **"An Unfair Knock on Nokia" in *Barron's* (Vol. 88, March 10, 2008, No. 10, pp. 36)**
Pub: Dow Jones & Company, Inc.

Ed: Mark Veverka. **Description:** Discusses the decision by the brokerage house Exane to recommend a Sell on Nokia shares, presumably due to higher inventories, which is unfounded. The news that the company's inventories are rising is not an indicator of falling demand for its products. The company is also benefiting from solid management and rising market share.

12926 ■ **"Unify Corp. Back in the Black, Poised to Grow" in *Sacramento Business Journal* (Vol. 25, August 29, 2008, No. 26, pp. 1)**
Pub: American City Business Journals, Inc.

Ed: Melanie Turner. **Description:** It was reported that Unify Corp. returned to profitability in the fiscal year ended April 30, 2008 with a net income of $1.6 million, under the guidance of Todd Wille. Wille, who took over as the company's chief executive officer in October 2000, was named as Turnaround CEO of the Year in June 2008 for his efforts.

12927 ■ **"Unilever Acquiring Danish Operations of Diplom-Is Ice Cream" in *Ice Cream Reporter* (Vol. 23, August 20, 2010, No. 9, pp. 1)**
Pub: Ice Cream Reporter

Description: Unilever will acquire Danish operations of the ice cream company Diplom-Is from Norwegian dairy group Tine.

12928 ■ **"Unilever Acquiring EVGA's Ice Cream Brands in Greece" in *Ice Cream Reporter* (Vol. 23, October 20, 2010, No. 11, pp. 1)**
Pub: Ice Cream Reporter

Description: Unilever will acquire the ice cream brands and distribution network of the Greek frozen dessert manufacturer EVGA.

12929 ■ **"U.S. Economy's Underlying Strengths Limit Recession Threat" in *Hispanic Business* (Vol. 30, April 2008, No. 4, pp. 14)**
Pub: Hispanic Business

Ed: Dr. Juan B. Solana. **Description:** Large and small businesses as well as consumers and policy-makers are attempting to identify the areas of risk and loss created by the economic crisis; analysts are now estimating that U.S. mortgage losses could reach the $380 to $400 billion mark. Also discusses the falling of wages and the rising of unemployment. Statistical data included.

12930 ■ **"Universal Energy Group Releases March 31, 2007 Financial Statements" in *Canadian Corporate News* (May 14, 2007)**
Pub: Comtex News Network Inc.

Description: Universal Energy Group Ltd., a company that sells electricity and natural gas to small to mid-size commercial and small industrial customers as well as residential customers, announced the release of its March 31, 2007 financial statements. Management's analysis and discussion of the company's financial condition and results of operations are listed. Statistical data included.

12931 ■ **"Unpleasant Surprise" in *Barron's* (Vol. 88, March 24, 2008, No. 12, pp. 60)**
Pub: Dow Jones & Company, Inc.

Ed: Shirley A. Lazo. **Description:** Discusses the $175 million that footwear company Genesco received in a settlement with Finish Line and UBS is

considered as a stock distribution and is taxable as dividend income. Railroad company CSX raised its quarterly common payout from 15 cents to 18 cents.

12932 ■ **"The Upside of Fear and Loathing" in *Barron's* (Vol. 88, March 24, 2008, No. 12, pp. 11)**
Pub: Dow Jones & Company, Inc.

Ed: Michael Santoli. **Description:** Fear and risk aversion prevalent among investors may actually serve to cushion the decline and spark a rally in US stock prices. Surveys of investors indicate rising levels of anxiety and bearishness, indicating a possible positive turnaround.

12933 ■ **"US Airways Stock Up 5 Percent on Day Merger Try Ends" in *Charlotte Observer* (February 1, 2007)**
Pub: Knight-Ridder/Tribune Business News

Ed: Steve Harrison. **Description:** US Airways stock rose 5 percent on the day Doug Parker, CEO, cancelled his offer to purchase Delta Air Lines.

12934 ■ **"USAmeriBank Deals for Growth" in *The Business Journal-Serving Greater Tampa Bay* (Vol. 28, September 26, 2008, No. 40, pp. 1)**
Pub: American City Business Journals, Inc.

Ed: Margie Manning. **Description:** It is believed that the pending $14.9 million purchase of Liberty Bank by USAmeriBank could be at the forefront of a trend. Executives of both companies expect the deal to close by the end of 2008. USAmeriBank will have $430 million in assets and five offices in Pinellas, Florida once the deal is completed.

12935 ■ *Using Other People's Money To Get Rich: Secrets, Techniques, and Strategies Investors Use Every Day Using OPM*
Pub: Atlantic Publishing Company

Ed: Eric J. Leech. **Released:** December 2009. **Price:** $24.95 paperback. **Description:** Discussion showing individuals how to invest using other people's money.

12936 ■ **"Valener Announces that Gaz Metro has Achieved a Key Step in Acquiring CVPS" in *CNW Group* (September 30, 2011)**
Pub: CNW Group

Description: Valener Inc., which owns about 29 percent of Gaz Metro Ltd. Partnership, announced that Gaz Metro welcomes the sale of Central Vermont Public Service Corporation (CVPS). Valener owns an indirect interest of 24.5 percent in the wind power projects jointly developed by Beaupre Eole General Partnership and Boralex Inc. on private lands in Quebec. Details of the deal are included.

12937 ■ **"Valenti: Roots of Financial Crisis Go Back to 1998" in *Crain's Detroit Business* (Vol. 24, October 6, 2008, No. 40, pp. 25)**
Pub: Crain Communications, Inc.

Ed: Tom Henderson; Nathan Skid. **Description:** Interview with Sam Valenti III who is the chairman and CEO of Valenti Capital L.L.C., a wealth-management firm; Valenti discusses in detail the history that led up to the current economic crisis as well as his prediction for the future of the country.

12938 ■ **"V&J Scores Partnership with Shaq" in *Business Journal-Milwaukee* (Vol. 25, October 12, 2007, No. 2, pp. A1)**
Pub: American City Business Journals, Inc.

Ed: Rich Kirchen. **Description:** O'Neal Franchise Group has agreed to a partnership with V&J Foods of Milwaukee to handle Auntie Anne's shops in New York, South Africa, Michigan, and the Caribbean. V&J O'Neal Enterprises will open six Auntie Anne's soft pretzel shops in Detroit towards the end of 2007. Planned international ventures of the partnership are presented.

12939 ■ **"Venture Gap" in *Canadian Business* (Vol. 81, March 17, 2008, No. 4, pp. 82)**
Pub: Rogers Media

Ed: Joe Castaldo. **Description:** Money raised by Canadian venture capitalist firms has been declining since 2001. A strong venture capital market is important if Canada is to build innovative companies. Fixing Canada's tax policy on foreign investments is a start in reviving the industry.

12940 ■ **"Virtus.com Wins 'Best of Industry' WebAward for Excellence in Financial Services" in** *Investment Weekly News* **(October 24, 2009)**
Pub: Investment Weekly News
Description: Web Marketing Association honored Virtus.com, the Website of Virtus Investment Partners, Inc., for Outstanding Achievement in Web Development and Acsys Interactive was awarded the Financial Services Standard of Excellence Award for developing the site. The site was part of a rebranding effort and is a one-stop portal for both financial advisors and their investors.

12941 ■ **"Vista-Based NCV Bought by Canteen Vending" in** *North County Times* **(October 18, 2011)**
Ed: Pat Maio. **Description:** Details of North Carolina-based Canteen Vending Services' acquisition of NCV Refreshment Services, are given.

12942 ■ **"Vital Signs: The Big Picture" in** *Canadian Business* **(Vol. 81, Summer 2008, No. 9, pp. 153)**
Pub: Rogers Media Ltd.
Description: Results of the Investor 500 showing percentage of companies with positive returns, most actively traded companies over the past six months and market capitalization by industry are presented. Stock performance and revenues of publicly held corporations in Canada are also provided.

12943 ■ **"Vitamins to Spice Up Food" in** *Philadelphia Business Journal* **(Vol. 28, October 2, 2009, No. 33, pp. 1)**
Pub: American City Business Journals
Ed: John George. **Description:** VitaminSpice, a start-up company established by Ed Bukstel, makes a line of spice and vitamin blends that come in seasoning form. The form of the blends could facilitate easier ingestion of vitamins into people's diets. A reverse merger that will allow a publicly-traded company status for VitaminSpice will be accomplished by early October 2009.

12944 ■ **"Vive La Resistance: Competing Logics and the Consolidation of U.S. Community Banking" in** *Academy of Management Journal* **(August 2007)**
Pub: Academy of Management
Ed: Christopher Marquis, Michael Lounsbury. **Description:** Ways in which competing logics facilitate resistance to institutional change is presented, highlighting on banking professionals' resistance to large, national banks acquisitions of smaller, local banks.

12945 ■ **"Voice: Rebuilding Trust" in** *Business Strategy Review* **(Vol. 21, Summer 2010, No. 2, pp. 79)**
Pub: Wiley-Blackwell
Ed: David De Cremer. **Description:** The financial world's attempts to rebuild trust are charted. Three steps to jump-start that process are outlined.

12946 ■ **"Wachovia Gears Up for Major Arizona Expansion" in** *Business Journal-Serving Phoenix and the Valley of the Sun* **(Vol. 5, Oct. 5, 2007)**
Pub: American City Business Journals, Inc.
Ed: Chris Casacchia. **Description:** Wachovia, America's fourth-largest bank is finalizing a deal to build its Arizona headquarters in downtown Phoenix. The bank plans to add an additional 100 employees by June 2008 and double its financial network to 30 offices in four years. Wachovia will also convert fifteen World Savings Bank branches it acquired in 2006 through Golden West Financial Corporation.

12947 ■ **"Wait for the Call" in** *Canadian Business* **(Vol. 80, April 9, 2007, No. 8, pp. 74)**
Pub: Rogers Media
Ed: Andrew Wahl. **Description:** The effort of chief executive of BCE Inc. Michael Sabia to deal with rumors about the company's private equity deal with Kohlberg Kravis Roberts & Co. is discussed.

12948 ■ **"Wait a Minute!" in** *Entrepreneur* **(Vol. 37, September 2009, No. 9, pp. 76)**
Pub: Entrepreneur Media, Inc.
Ed: Jennifer Wang. **Description:** Advice on how entrepreneurs in the United States should secure funding in view of the economic crisis is presented. Enough interest should be stimulated so as to secure a follow-up meeting. Investors should be asked questions that would encourage them to tell stories related to the downturn.

12949 ■ **"Walk This Way" in** *Barron's* **(Vol. 90, August 23, 2010, No. 34, pp. 13)**
Pub: Barron's Editorial & Corporate Headquarters
Ed: Christopher C. Williams. **Description:** Crocs and Skechers are selling very popular shoes and sales show no signs of winding down. The shares of both companies are attractively prices.

12950 ■ **"Wall Street Is No Friend to Radical Innovation" in** *Harvard Business Review* **(Vol. 88, July-August 2010, No. 7-8, pp. 28)**
Pub: Harvard Business School Publishing
Ed: Julia Kirby. **Description:** Research indicates that investors are skittish about backing a business that proposes significant changes to its product or service status quo.

12951 ■ **"W&S to Trim Rich Retirement Plan" in** *Business Courier* **(Vol. 27, October 15, 2010, No. 24, pp. 1)**
Pub: Business Courier
Ed: Dan Monk. **Description:** Insurance firm Western & Southern Financial Group announced that it will reduce the pension benefits of its 4,000 associates by more than 30 percent starting January 1, 2011. The move is expected to reduce annual retirement payments by several thousand dollars per associate. Western is a Fortune 500 company and has $34 billion in total assets.

12952 ■ **"Want People to Save? Force Them" in** *Harvard Business Review* **(Vol. 88, September 2010, No. 9, pp. 36)**
Pub: Harvard Business School Publishing
Ed: Dan Ariely. **Description:** Contrasts in U.S. attitudes towards savings and government regulation with those of Chile, where all employees are required to save 11 percent of their salary in a retirement account, are highlighted.

12953 ■ **"Want Some of This?" in** *Canadian Business* **(Vol. 80, April 9, 2007, No. 8, pp. 71)**
Pub: Rogers Media
Ed: Jeff Sanford. **Description:** The economic impact of growing private equity in Canada is discussed.

12954 ■ **"Water Works Spinoff Could Make Big Splash" in** *Business Courier* **(Vol. 24, October 19, 2008, No. 27, pp. 1)**
Pub: American City Business Journals, Inc.
Ed: Dan Monk. **Description:** Cincinnati, Ohio city manager Milton Dohoney proposed to spin off the city-owned Greater Cincinnati Water Works into a regionally focused water district that could allow the city to receive millions of dollars in annual dividends. A feasibility study is to be conducted by a team of outside consultants and city staffers and is expected to be finished by summer of 2008.

12955 ■ **"The Way to the Market's Heart?" in** *Canadian Business* **(Vol. 80, March 26, 2007, No. 7, pp. 74)**
Pub: Rogers Media
Ed: Erin Pooley. **Description:** The financial and stock performance of Canadian biotechnology companies Medicure Inc. and Angiotech Pharmaceuticals Inc. are analyzed.

12956 ■ **"The Wealth Portfolio" in** *Canadian Business* **(Vol. 79, Winter 2006, No. 24, pp. 146)**
Pub: Rogers Media
Ed: Jeff Sanford. **Description:** The trends pertaining to the pricing of shares of public enterprises, at the Montreal stock exchange, are described.

12957 ■ **"A Week of the Worst Kind of Selling" in** *Barron's* **(Vol. 88, June 30, 2008, No. 26, pp. M3)**
Pub: Dow Jones & Co., Inc.
Ed: Kopin Tan. **Description:** In the week that ended in June 27, 2008 the selloff in the U.S. stock market was brought on by mounting bank losses and the spread of economic slowdown on top of high oil prices. The 31 percent decrease in the share price of Ingersoll-Rand since October 2007 may have factored in most of its risks. The company has completed its acquisition of Trane to morph into a refrigeration-equipment company.

12958 ■ *A Weekend with Warren Buffett: And Other Shareholder Meeting Adventures*
Pub: Basic Books/Perseus Books Group
Ed: Randy Cepuch. **Released:** February 23, 2007.
Price: $23.95. **Description:** Financial writer and personal investor relates his experiences attending various shareholder meetings, reviewing each meeting and grading its educational value. The book is essential for those hoping to learn more about the way companies invest and do business.

12959 ■ **"Welcome to the Neighborhood" in** *Hawaii Business* **(Vol. 53, October 2007, No. 4, pp. 48)**
Pub: Hawaii Business Publishing
Ed: Jolyn Okimoto Rosa. **Description:** Finance Factors is planning to build branches in Manoa, and Liliha, as part of its strategy to position itself in high-yield areas. The company chose Manoa and Liliha due to thee sites' rich deposits. Its strategy with regards to the branches' location and to the building design is discussed.

12960 ■ **"Wells Fargo Will Soon Lead Local Banks in Deposits" in** *Austin Business JournalInc.* **(Vol. 28, December 5, 2008, No. 38, pp. A1)**
Pub: American City Business Journals
Ed: Christopher Calnan. **Description:** Acquisition of Wachovia Corporation by Wells Fargo and Company will leave the latter as the top bank for deposits in Austin, Texas. The merged bank will have deposits of more than $ billion, more than the $3.9 billion deposits Bank of America maintains in the area.

12961 ■ **"Welsh Meat Sales on the Rise" in** *Farmer's Weekly* **(March 28, 2008, No. 320)**
Pub: Reed Business Information
Description: Due, in part, to marketing efforts, retail sales of Welsh lamb and beef rose significantly in the first two months of 2008.

12962 ■ **"Wenzel Downhole Tools Ltd. Announces First Quarter Results for 2007" in** *Canadian Corporate News* **(May 14, 2007)**
Pub: Comtex News Network Inc.
Description: Wenzel Downhole Tools Ltd., a manufacturer, renter, and seller of drilling tools used in gas and oil exploration, announced its financial results for the first quarter ended March 31, 2007 which includes achieved revenues of $14.5 million. Statistical data included.

12963 ■ **"Weyerhaeuser's REIT Decision Shouldn't Scare Investors Away" in** *Barron's* **(Vol. 88, June 30, 2008, No. 26, pp. 18)**
Pub: Dow Jones & Co., Inc.
Ed: Christopher Williams. **Description:** Weyerhaeuser Co.'s management said that a conversion to a real estate investment trust was not likely in 2009 since the move is not tax-efficient as of the moment and would overload its non-timber assets with debt. The company's shares have fallen by 19.5 percent. However, the company remains an asset-rich outfit and its activist shareholder is pushing for change.

12964 ■ **"What Enforcement?" in** *Canadian Business* **(Vol. 81, December 24, 2007, No. 1, pp. 26)**
Pub: Rogers Media
Ed: Al Rosen. **Description:** Securities enforcement in Canada needs to be improved in order to tackle white collar crimes that influence investors' opinion of the country. There have been high-profile cases where investigations have not been initiated. Details

on the responsibilities of the securities commissions and the need for enforcement mandate in a separate agency are discussed.

12965 ■ **"What Ever Happened to TGIF?"** in *Barron's* (Vol. 88, March 10, 2008, No. 10, pp. M3)
Pub: Dow Jones & Company, Inc.
Ed: Kopin Tan. **Description:** US stock markets fell in early March 2008 to their lowest level in 18 months, venturing close to entering a bear market phase. The S&P 500 has dropped an average of 0.78 percent on Fridays for 2008.

12966 ■ **"What Has Sergey Wrought?"** in *Barron's* (Vol. 89, July 13, 2009, No. 28, pp. 8)
Pub: Dow Jones & Co., Inc.
Ed: Alan Abelson. **Description:** Sergey Aleynikov is a computer expert that once worked for Goldman Sachs but he was arrested after he left the company and charged with theft for bringing with him the code for the company's proprietary software for high-frequency trading. The stock market has been down for four straight weeks as of July 13, 2009 which reflects the reality of how the economy is still struggling.

12967 ■ **"What Recovery?"** in *Canadian Business* (Vol. 82, April 27, 2009, No. 7, pp. 18)
Pub: Rogers Media
Ed: Rachel Pulfer. **Description:** U.S. markets have rallied on the end of March 2009 but experts and analysts believe that it could be short-lived. Market rallies were found to be common during recessions and are not indicative of economic recovery. Meanwhile, it is believed that employment will be a key factor that will determine the U.S. economic recovery.

12968 ■ **"What'll You Have Tonight?"** in *Barron's* (Vol. 88, July 4, 2008, No. 28, pp. 22)
Pub: Dow Jones & Co., Inc.
Ed: Neil A. Martin. **Description:** Shares of Diageo could rise by 30 percent a year from June 2008 after it slipped due to U.S. sales worries. The company also benefits from the trend toward more premium alcoholic beverage brands worldwide especially in emerging markets.

12969 ■ **"What's In a Name?"** in *Barron's* (Vol. 88, March 17, 2008, No. 11, pp. 7)
Pub: Dow Jones & Company, Inc.
Ed: Alan Abelson. **Description:** Eliot Spitzer's resignation incidentally caused the stock market to go up by 400 points. The Federal Reserve Board's new Term Securities Lending Facility provides liquidity to the big lenders by funneling $200 billion in the form of 28-day loans of Treasuries. The analysis of Paul Brodsky and Lee Quaintance of QB Partners on the demand for commodities is also discussed.

12970 ■ **"What's More Important: Stag or Inflation?"** in *Barron's* (Vol. 88, July 14, 2008, No. 28, pp. M8)
Pub: Dow Jones & Co., Inc.
Ed: Randall W. Forsyth. **Description:** Economists are divided on which part of stagflation, an economic situation in which inflation and economic stagnation occur simultaneously and remain unchecked for a period of time, is more important. Some economists say that the Federal government is focusing on controlling inflation while others see the central bank as extending its liquidity facilities to the financial sector.

12971 ■ **"When to Roll Over"** in *Black Enterprise* (Vol. 37, November 2006, No. 4, pp. 50)
Pub: Earl G. Graves Publishing Co. Inc.
Ed: Carolyn M. Brown. **Description:** Being proactive and rolling over your funds if you own stock of your former employee will give you more control over your money, especially if the company merges or is sold.

12972 ■ **"Where Are the Vultures?"** in *Mergers & Acquisitions: The Dealmaker's Journal* (March 1, 2008)
Pub: SourceMedia, Inc.
Ed: Ken MacFadyen. **Description:** Although the real estate market is distressed, not many acquisitions

are being made by distress private equity investors; this is due, in part, to the difficulty in assessing real estate industry firms since it is a sector which is so localized.

12973 ■ **"Where the Money Is"** in *Conde Nast Portfolio* (Vol. 2, June 2008, No. 6, pp. 113)
Pub: Conde Nast Publications, Inc.
Description: Revenue generated from treatments for common brain disorders that are currently on the market are listed.

12974 ■ **"Where Next?"** in *Business Strategy Review* (Vol. 21, Summer 2010, No. 2, pp. 20)
Pub: Blackwell Publishers Ltd.
Description: The emergence of large, vibrant and seemingly unstoppable new markets has been the good news story for the past decade. Brazil, Russia, India and China (BRIC) are among those emerging into the economic light. Amid the turbulence and rapid growth, new and various markets will continue to emerge. For investors and business leaders, the critical question is simple: where next?

12975 ■ **"Where Oil-Rich Nations Are Placing Their Bets"** in *Harvard Business Review* (Vol. 86, September 2008, No. 9, pp. 119)
Pub: Harvard Business School Press
Ed: Rawi Abdelal; Ayesha Khan; Tarun Khanna. **Description:** Investment strategies of the Gulf Cooperation Council nations are examined in addition to how these have impacted the global economy and capitalism.

12976 ■ **"Where to Stash Your Cash"** in *Barron's* (Vol. 88, March 17, 2008, No. 11, pp. 41)
Pub: Dow Jones & Company, Inc.
Ed: Mike Hogan. **Description:** Investors are putting their money in money-market mutual funds seeking fractionally better yields and a safe haven from the uncertainties that was brought about by subprime lending. These funds, however, are hovering near 3.20 percent which is less than the 4 percent inflation rate.

12977 ■ **"Where To Look for Income"** in *Women In Business* (Vol. 63, Summer 2011, No. 2, pp. 50)
Pub: American Business Women's Association
Ed: William J. Lynott. **Description:** Advice on ways to invest in the US market are presented, with information on Certificates of Deposit and Money Markets included.

12978 ■ **"Whiplashed? That's a Bullish Sign"** in *Barron's* (Vol. 88, March 31, 2008, No. 13, pp. 34)
Pub: Dow Jones & Company, Inc.
Ed: Richard W. Arms. **Description:** Huge volatility often occurs just ahead of a substantial rally, according to an analysis of the volatility in the Dow Jones Index since 2000. The Average Percentage Change based on a 10-day moving average of volatility is a way to measure the level of fear in the market and reveals when buying or selling have been overdone.

12979 ■ **"Whistling Past the Graveyard?"** in *Barron's* (Vol. 88, March 17, 2008, No. 11, pp. 15)
Pub: Dow Jones & Company, Inc.
Ed: Michael Santoli. **Description:** Discusses the Federal Reserve's move to provide $200 billion to the system which can be seen as an effort to avoid the liquidity problems that Bear Stearns suffered. The Federal Reserve's move seems to frighten investors rather than reassure them.

12980 ■ **"Who Gets the Last Laugh?"** in *Barron's* (Vol. 88, March 31, 2008, No. 13, pp. 17)
Pub: Dow Jones & Company, Inc.
Ed: Leslie P. Norton. **Description:** Nord/LB will take a charge of 82.5 million euros to cover potential losses apparently related to Vatas' refusal to take the shares of Remote MDx Inc. after buying the shares. Remote MDx's main product is an ankle bracelet to monitor criminals; the firm has lost over half of its market cap due to the Nord/LB troubles and questions about its revenues.

12981 ■ **"Why Intel Should Dump Its Flash-Memory Business"** in *Barron's* (Vol. 88, March 10, 2008, No. 10, pp. 35)
Pub: Dow Jones & Company, Inc.
Ed: Eric J. Savitz. **Description:** Intel Corp. must sell its NAND flash-memory business as soon as it possibly can to the highest bidder to focus on its PC processor business and take advantage of other business opportunities. Apple should consider a buyback of 10 percent of the company's shares to lift its stock.

12982 ■ **"Why It Pays to be in the Boardroom"** in *Globe & Mail* (January 16, 2006, pp. B1)
Pub: CTVglobemedia Publishing Inc.
Ed: Janet McFarland. **Description:** The reasons behind higher stock compensation for board directors, in Canada, are presented. The survey is conducted by Patrick O'Callaghan & Associates and Korn/Ferry International.

12983 ■ **"Why the Rally Should Keep Rolling...for Now"** in *Barron's* (Vol. 89, July 27, 2009, No. 30, pp. M3)
Pub: Dow Jones & Co., Inc.
Ed: Kopin Tan. **Description:** Stocks rallied for the second straight week as of July 24, 2009 and more companies reported better than expected earnings but the caveat is that companies are beating estimates chiefly by slashing expenses and firing workers. The regulatory risks faced by CME Group and the IntercontinentalExchange are discussed as well as the shares of KKR Private Equity Investors LP.

12984 ■ **"Why the Rout in Financials Isn't Over"** in *Barron's* (Vol. 88, June 30, 2008, No. 26, pp. 23)
Pub: Dow Jones & Co., Inc.
Ed: Robin Goldwyn Blumenthal. **Description:** Top market technician Louise Yamada warns that the retreat in the shares of financial services is not yet over based on her analysis of stock charts. Yamada's analysis of the charts of Citigroup, Fifth Third Bancorp and Merrill Lynch are discussed together with the graphs for these shares. Statistical data included.

12985 ■ **"Why WestJet's Culture Guru Chooses to Fly Under the Radar"** in *Globe & Mail* (January 22, 2007, pp. B1)
Pub: CTVglobemedia Publishing Inc.
Ed: Brent Jang. **Description:** The views of co-founder Donald Bell of WestJet Airlines Ltd. on company's shares and services are presented.

12986 ■ **"Wielding a Big Ax"** in *Barron's* (Vol. 89, July 13, 2009, No. 28, pp. 26)
Pub: Dow Jones & Co., Inc.
Ed: Shirley A. Lazo. **Description:** Weyerhaeuser cut their quarterly common payout by 80 percent from 25 cents to a nickel a share which they said will help them preserve their long-term value and improve their performance. Paccar also cut their quarterly dividend by half to nine cents a share. Walgreen however, boosted their quarterly dividend by 22.2 percent to 13.75 cents a share.

12987 ■ **"The Wild West"** in *Canadian Business* (Vol. 80, January 15, 2007, No. 2, pp. 57)
Pub: Rogers Media
Ed: David Baines. **Description:** The impact of the introduction of regulations by the British Columbia Securities Commission on trading of securities by investors is discussed.

12988 ■ **"Will the Force Be With Salesforce?"** in *Barron's* (Vol. 88, March 24, 2008, No. 12, pp. 20)
Pub: Dow Jones & Company, Inc.
Ed: Mark Veverka. **Description:** Shares of Salesforce.com are likely to drop from the $44.83-a-share level in the face of a deteriorating economy and financial sector and thus lower demand for business software. The company is unlikely to deliver on its ambitious earnings forecasts for 2008 especially with strengthening competition from Oracle.

12989 ■ **"Wind Point Partners Closes Southfield HQ" in** *Crain's Detroit Business* **(Vol. 26, January 18, 2010, No. 3, pp. 18)**
Pub: Crain Communications, Inc.
Ed: Tom Henderson. **Description:** Wind Point Partners, a private-equity firm that expanded its headquarters to Southfield in 1997, has closed down its Michigan operations opting to move its headquarters back to Illinois.

12990 ■ *Wine Investment for Portfolio Diversification: How Investing in Wine Can Yield Greater Returns than Stocks and Bonds*
Pub: Wine Appreciation Guild, Ltd.
Ed: Mahesh Kumar. **Released:** October 2005. **Price:** $45.00. **Description:** Analysis of the performance of investments in fine wines, particularly Bordeaux, is presented. History verifies that wine has traditionally been a sound investment offering a higher expected return over the market relative to its overall contribution of risk. Wine can be used as an effective means of diversifying one's portfolio.

12991 ■ **"With the Indian Market, You Take the Good With the Bad" in** *Globe & Mail* **(March 23, 2007, pp. B11)**
Pub: CTVglobemedia Publishing Inc.
Ed: David Parkinson. **Description:** The performance of Bombay Stock Exchange in the month of February 2007 is analyzed. The impact of growing economy on the stock market performance is also analyzed.

12992 ■ **"With Mine Approval, Crystallex's Value as Target Seen on Rise" in** *Globe & Mail* **(March 28, 2006, pp. B3)**
Pub: CTVglobemedia Publishing Inc.
Ed: Wendy Stueck. **Description:** Crystallex International Corp. obtains Venezuelan Ministry of Basic Industry and Mining's authorization on Las Cristinas mining project. The impact of the approval, which posted rise in shares by 21 percent for the company, is discussed.

12993 ■ **"Wobbling Economy" in** *The Business Journal-Serving Metropolitan Kansas City* **(Vol. 27, September 26, 2008, No. 2, pp. 1)**
Pub: American City Business Journals, Inc.
Ed: Rob Roberts. **Description:** Real estate developers in Kansas City Metropolitan Area are worried of the possible impacts of the crisis at Wall Street. They expect tightening of the credit market, which will result in difficulty of financing their projects. The potential effects of the Wall Street crisis are examined further.

12994 ■ **"Woes Portend Consumer Shift" in** *The Business Journal-Serving Metropolitan Kansas City* **(Vol. 27, September 26, 2008, No. 2, pp. 1)**
Pub: American City Business Journals, Inc.
Ed: Suzanna Stagemeyer. **Description:** Black Bamboo owner Tim Butt believes that prolonged tightening of the credit market will result in consumer spending becoming more cash-driven that credit card driven. The financial crisis has already constricted spending among consumers. Forecasts for the US economy are provided.

12995 ■ *The Working Man and Woman's Guide to Becoming a Millionaire*
Pub: Prentiss Publishing
Ed: Al Herron. **Released:** November 2006. **Description:** President and CEO of a Century 21 office in Dallas, Texas shares insight into financial security and commitment to community.

12996 ■ **"A World of Opportunity: Foreign Markets Offer Diversity to Keen Investors" in** *Canadian Business* **(Vol. 81, Summer 2008, No. 9)**
Pub: Rogers Media Ltd.
Ed: Andrew Wahl. **Description:** International Monetary Fund projected in its 'World Economy Outlook' that there is a 25 percent chance that a global recession will occur in 2008 and 2009. Global growth rate is forecasted at 3.7 percent in 2008. Inflation in Asia emerging markets and forecasts on stock price indexes are presented.

12997 ■ **"World's Best CEOs" in** *Barron's* **(Vol. 88, March 24, 2008, No. 12, pp. 33)**
Pub: Dow Jones & Company, Inc.
Ed: Andrew Bary. **Description:** Listing of the 30 best chief executive officers worldwide which was compiled through interviews with investors and analysts, analysis of financial and stock market performance, and leadership and industry stature.

12998 ■ **"The Worst Lies Ahead for Wall Street; More Losses Certain" in** *Crain's New York Business* **(Vol. 24, January 21, 2008, No. 3, pp. 1)**
Pub: Crain Communications, Inc.
Ed: Aaron Elstein. **Description:** Due to the weakening economy, many financial institutions will face further massive losses forcing them to borrow more at higher interest rates and dragging down their earnings for years to come. The effects on commercial real estate and credit card loans are also discussed as well as the trend to investing in Asia and the Middle East.

12999 ■ **"Xstrata's Takeover Bid Comes Up Short in Shareholder's Eyes" in** *Globe & Mail* **(March 27, 2007, pp. B16)**
Pub: CTVglobemedia Publishing Inc.
Ed: Andy Hoffman. **Description:** The share holders of LionOre Mining International have expressed dissatisfaction over $4.6 billion take over by Xstrata PLC. Share holders are demanding more prices for share value.

13000 ■ **"Yahoo! - Microsoft Pact: Alive Again?" in** *Barron's* **(Vol. 89, July 27, 2009, No. 30, pp. 8)**
Pub: Dow Jones & Co., Inc.
Ed: Mark Veverka. **Description:** Yahoo! reported higher than expected earnings in the second quarter of 2009 under CEO Carol Bartz who has yet to articulate her long-term vision and strategy for turning around the company. The media reported that Yahoo! and Microsoft are discussing an advertising-search partnership which should benefit both companies.

13001 ■ **"YoCream" in** *Ice Cream Reporter* **(Vol. 23, September 20, 2010, No. 10, pp. 6)**
Pub: Ice Cream Reporter
Description: YoCream reported a sales increase for third quarter 2010 at 15.6 percent and net income increasing 25 percent to $2,141,000 for that quarter.

13002 ■ **"You Won't Go Broke Filling Up On These Stocks" in** *Barron's* **(Vol. 88, July 14, 2008, No. 28, pp. 38)**
Pub: Dow Jones & Co., Inc.
Ed: Assif Shameen. **Description:** Due to high economic growth, pro-business policies and a consumption boom, the Middle East is a good place to look for equities. The best ways in which to gain exposure to this market include investing in the real estate industry and telecommunications markets as well as large banks that serve corporations and consumers.

13003 ■ *Young Bucks: How to Raise a Future Millionaire*
Pub: Thomas Nelson Inc.
Ed: Troy Dunn. **Released:** November 2007. **Price:** $17.99. **Description:** Advice is given to parents to teach their children how to save money, invest wisely and even start their own business.

13004 ■ **"Young People Speak Out On Credit Union Board Involvement" in** *Credit Union Times* **(Vol. 21, July 14, 2010, No. 27, pp. 20)**
Pub: Summit Business Media
Ed: Myriam Di Giovanni. **Description:** Results of a Credit Union Times survey of Generation Y individuals about serving on Credit Union boards across the country are examined.

13005 ■ **"Your 2010 Windfall" in** *Small Business Opportunities* **(July 2010)**
Pub: Harris Publications Inc.
Description: Make this a year of fiscal health and wealth. A survey says most will strive to save this year.

13006 ■ **"Your Exposure to Bear Stearns" in** *Barron's* **(Vol. 88, March 17, 2008, No. 11, pp. 45)**
Pub: Dow Jones & Company, Inc.
Ed: Tom Sullivan; Jack Willoughby. **Description:** Bear Stearns makes up 5.5 percent of Pioneer Independence's portfolio, 1.4 percent of Vanguard Windsor II's portfolio, 1.2 percent of Legg Mason Value Trust, about 1 percent of Van Kampen Equity & Income, and 0.79 percent of Putnam Fund for Growth & Income. Ginnie Mae securities are now trading at 1.78 percentage points over treasuries due to the mortgage crises.

13007 ■ **"Your Startup may be Worth Less than You Think" in** *Entrepreneur* **(Vol. 37, October 2009, No. 10, pp. 96)**
Pub: Entrepreneur Media, Inc.
Ed: Asheesh Advani. **Description:** Valuations of startups at the idea stage are dropping due to the effects of the recession. This drop is due to the decreasing availability of investment capital, the reduction in portfolio values of investors, and the increase in early stage startups.

13008 ■ **"Zell Takes a Gamble on Tribune" in** *Globe & Mail* **(April 3, 2007, pp. B1)**
Pub: CTVglobemedia Publishing Inc.
Ed: Sinclair Stewart. **Description:** The purchase of the majority share in Tribune Co. by Samuel Zell is described. Samuel Zell's plans to keep the company's assets intact are discussed.

13009 ■ **"Zucker Closes Deal on HBC With Sweeter Takeover Offer" in** *Globe & Mail* **(January 27, 2006, pp. B1)**
Pub: CTVglobemedia Publishing Inc.
Ed: Marina Strauss; Sinclair Stewart; Jacquie McNish. **Description:** Jerry Zucker, vice-president of InterTech Group Inc., has finalized a deal to buy retail store Hudson Bay Co, for 1.1 billion dollars. The shares will be purchased at a rate of 15.25 dollars per share in an all cash transaction. Complete details of the buyout are discussed.

13010 ■ **"Zucker's HBC Shakeup Imminent" in** *Globe & Mail* **(February 20, 2006, pp. B3)**
Pub: CTVglobemedia Publishing Inc.
Ed: Marina Strauss. **Description:** The plans of investor Jerry Zucker to revamp Hudson's Bay Co., upon its acquisition, are presented.

TRADE PERIODICALS

13011 ■ *Bacard's Global Investor*
Pub: Ferney Scribes Inc.
Ed: Andre Bacard, Editor. **Released:** Monthly. **Price:** $129, U.S.. **Description:** Provides monthly updates of select no-load global and international funds, model portfolios, foreign market graphs, monthly analysis and current recommendations. Recurring features include news of research and a column titled Mutual Fund in the Spotlight.

13012 ■ *Banking & Financial Services Policy Report*
Pub: Aspen Publishers
Contact: Shulte Roth
Released: 12/yr. **Price:** $689 with free standard shipping on U.S prepaid orders. **Description:** Journal covering topics related to the converging banking and financial services industries.

13013 ■ *Barron's*
Pub: Dow Jones & Company Inc.
Contact: Edwin A. Finn Jr., Ed., Pres.
Released: Weekly (Mon.). **Price:** $149 print & online; $99 print only; $79 online only. **Description:** Business and finance magazine.

13014 ■ *Bernie Shaeffer's Option Advisor*
Pub: Schaeffer's Investment Research Inc.
Contact: Bernie Schaeffer, Sr. Ed.
E-mail: bschaeffer@sir-inc.com
Released: Monthly, 12/year. **Price:** $149, U.S. $149/year, U.S.; $225, Canada; $225, Canada. **Description:** Makes both aggressive and conservative recommendations on listed stock options for the individual investor. Reports on news pertinent to the

options market including new options listings, and suggested brokerage firms. **Remarks:** Subscription includes a telephone hotline service and approximately six special bulletins per year.

13015 ■ Bert Dohmen's Wellington Letter
Pub: Dohmen Capital Research Institute
Ed: Bert Dohmen-Ramirez, Editor. **Released:** Monthly. **Price:** $350, U.S.; $385, elsewhere. **Description:** Provides a comprehensive monthly analysis of the major U.S. and world investments.

13016 ■ The Bowser Directory of Small Stocks
Pub: R. Max Bowser
Ed: Cindy Bowser, Editor. **Released:** Monthly. **Price:** $89, U.S. and Canada; $138, elsewhere. **Description:** Provides extensive information on stocks valued at $3/share or less.

13017 ■ Chartcraft Weekly Service
Pub: Chartcraft Inc.
Contact: John Grey
Ed: Michael Burke, Editor. **Released:** Weekly. **Price:** $256. **Description:** Offers recommendations to investors in New York and American Stock Exchange securities, including buy and sell signals and relative strength. Discusses industry groups and option indexes. Lists more than 1,400 stocks and includes point and figure of each stock covered.

13018 ■ The COINfidential Report
Pub: Bale Publications
Ed: Don Bale, Jr., Editor. **Released:** Bimonthly, except July and August. **Price:** $19.95, individuals; $99 lifetime subscription. **Description:** Features coin, stock and bullion market forecasts and analyses, plus inside information and best coin and stock bets. Recurring features include interviews, book reviews, and notices of publications available.

13019 ■ Consensus, National Futures & Financial Weekly
Pub: Consensus Inc.
Contact: Sharon Buchko
Ed: Robert E. Salva, Editor, rsalva@aol.com. **Released:** Weekly. **Price:** $365, U.S.; $395, Canada; $595, elsewhere; $295 online. **Description:** Presents market letters, special reports, and buy/sell advice from over 100 sources. Covers all stock and financial markets, metals, agricultural markets, livestock, grains, and oilseeds. Recurring features include graphic CONSENSUS Index of Bullish Market Opinion, CONSENSUS review of major indexes, Commitments of Traders reports, Futures Market Trading Facts, and a calendar of events.

13020 ■ Conversion Watch
Pub: SNL Financial L.C.
Contact: John Racine
Ed: **Released:** Irregular. **Price:** $1200, per year. **Description:** Informs readers by fax whenever new activity is announced. Provides all relevant data on conversion related filings and important conversion dates. Recurring features include news of research and a calendar of events.

13021 ■ Fitch Insights
Pub: Fitch IPCA Inc.
Contact: Stephen W. Joynt, Pres./CEO
Released: Monthly. **Description:** Provides ratings actions, comments, criteria, and surveillance via fax. Includes explanations of ratings decisions as well as Fitch's views on market actions and events.

13022 ■ Ford Investment Management Report
Pub: Ford Investor Services Inc.
Ed: David C. Morse, Editor. **Released:** Monthly. **Price:** $288. **Description:** Summarizes financial and market data for 2,680 common stocks in the Ford Data Base to provide investment managers with information for selection. Includes news of research, investment reviews, and special study reports covering research projects.

13023 ■ FXC Newsletter
Pub: FXC Investors Corp.
Ed: Francis Curzio, Editor. **Released:** Semimonthly. **Price:** $119 one year, online; $129 one year, print; $210 two years, online; $230 two years, print. **De-**

scription: Reports on the securities of companies that have the potential for extreme capital appreciation. Offers news of research for investors with risk capital, conservative and speculative investment recommendations, and performance reports.

13024 ■ Global Investment Magazine
Pub: Investment Media Inc.
Released: Biweekly. **Price:** $995; $1,075 other countries. **Description:** Professional journal for the securities and investment industry.

13025 ■ The Grandich Letter
Pub: Grandich Publications
Ed: Peter Grandich, Editor, peter@grandich.com. **Released:** Bimonthly. **Price:** $99. **Description:** Covers markets in banking and finance, commodities, bonds, currencies, energy, estate planning, business, futures, economics, metals, insurance, medical research, new issues, oil, gas, mining, options, penny stocks, precious metals, real estate, securities, taxes and tax shelters, technology, and treasury bills.

13026 ■ Hulbert Financial Digest
Pub: Hulbert Financial Digest
Contact: John Kimble, Chief Analyst
Ed: Mark Hulbert, Editor. **Released:** Monthly. **Price:** $135 $59/intro year; $37.50/five month trial; $59 introductory price. **Description:** Provides performance ratings on more than 400 portfolios recommended by more than 145 financial newsletters, calculated on the basis of model portfolios constructed according to each newsletter's advice. Includes a timing scoreboard, analysis of newsletter performance, list of mutual funds most frequently recommended for sale or purchase, a stock market sentiment index, and a question and answer section.

13027 ■ Investor, U.S.A.
Pub: Seahorse Financial Advisers Inc.
Ed: Edvard Jorgensen, Editor, edvard@seahorseadvisers.com. **Released:** Monthly. **Description:** Discusses investment from a global perspective. Recurring features include portfolio updates and columns titled Market Performances, Timing Indicators, and Investment Strategy.

13028 ■ Investors Intelligence
Pub: Chartcraft Inc.
Ed: Michael Burke, Editor. **Released:** Biweekly. **Price:** $184. **Description:** Serves as a comprehensive and authoritative Stock Market Advisory Service dedicated to bringing the investor facts, original projections, and a cross section of the recommendations of other leading Services.

13029 ■ John Bollinger's Capital Growth Letter
Pub: Bollinger Capital Management Inc.
Ed: John Bollinger, Editor. **Released:** Monthly. **Price:** $300 $225/year; $300, two years. **Description:** Provides investors with specific investment advice on stocks, bonds, precious metals, oil, and the dollar. Contains in-depth analysis, charts, and forecasts, with investment recommendations based on a technically driven Asset Allocation model developed by John Bollinger.

13030 ■ The Journal of Investing
Pub: Aspen Publishers Inc.
Contact: Brian Bruce, Editor-in-Chief
Released: Quarterly. **Price:** $756 institutions; $1,285 institutions 2 years. **Description:** Trade journal covering investing.

13031 ■ The Konlin Letter
Pub: Kon-Lin Research & Analysis Corp.
Ed: Konrad Kuhn, Editor. **Released:** Monthly. **Price:** $95, individuals $95/year. **Description:** Provides investment advice on stocks under $10, especially Emerging Growth and Special Situations stock poised for Explosive Price Appreciation Potential. Makes specific buy and sell recommendations and monitors a broad range of technical indicators for the best possible market timing advice.

13032 ■ The Lancz Letter
Pub: Alan B. Lancz & Associates Inc.
Contact: Alan Lancz
Ed: Alan B. Lancz, Editor. **Released:** 15-17/year. **Price:** $250, U.S.; $275, Canada E-mail; $300, elsewhere domestic prices by e-mail; $450, else-

where two year. domestic prices by e-mail. **Description:** Gives current advice on stocks, bonds, precious metals, currencies and other related investment vehicles. Analyzes interest rate and general investment trends and suggests investments for both aggressive and conservative investors. Recurring features include portfolio performance statistics and columns titled Investor's Corner and New Recommendations. **Remarks:** Subscription includes occasional special issues.

13033 ■ Louis Navellier's Emerging Growth
Pub: Navellier-MPT Review Inc.
Contact: Martha Seitchek
Ed: Louis G. Navellier, Editor. **Released:** Monthly. **Price:** $995 $995/year; $1795, two years online. **Description:** Provides extensive quantitative analysis on nearly 400 stocks and the market environment. Offers 15 model portfolios.

13034 ■ Lovejoy's MarketBrief Hotline
Pub: Lovejoy Corp.
Ed: David Luciano, Editor. **Released:** Monthly. **Price:** $195. **Description:** Gives fundamental, technical, and psychological investment analysis of stocks, mutual funds, and industries transformed into ratings (Buy, Sell & Hold). Provides timing strategy for stock, bond, and gold markets. Recurring features include letters to the editor. **Remarks:** Available through email.

13035 ■ MMA Cycles Report
Pub: Merriman Market Analyst
Ed: Raymond A. Merriman, Editor. **Released:** 17/year. **Price:** $249, U.S.; $249, other countries plus 10%for postal delivery. **Description:** Presents summaries and strategies on the stock market, precious metals, T-bonds, currencies, and grains.

13036 ■ Money Fund Report
Pub: iMoneyNet Inc.
Contact: Peter Crane, Managing Editor
E-mail: pcrane@imoneynet.com
Ed: Connie Bugbee, Editor, cbugbee@imoneynet.com. **Released:** Weekly. **Price:** $2,695, individuals. **Description:** Publishes weekly data on more than 1,600 taxable and tax-free money market mutual funds. Provides summary of money fund activity, including average 7-day, 30-day, 7-day compound yields, assets, and average maturities. Includes 13-week trend analysis, industry commentary, and fund profiles.

13037 ■ The Moneychanger
Pub: Little Mountain Corp.
Contact: Franklin Sanders, Editor
Ed: Franklin Sanders, Editor. **Released:** Monthly. **Price:** $95, individuals. **Description:** Makes investment recommendations congruent with the editors' attempts to help Christians prosper with their principles intact in an age of monetary and moral chaos. Focuses on the gold and silver markets. Recurring features include interviews and columns titled Current Market Projections and Unforgettable (quotes and commentary).

13038 ■ The MoneyLetter
Pub: MPL Communications Inc.
Released: Semimonthly. **Description:** Designed to offer financial planning advice and investment and tax-planning strategies to a broad range of investors. Recommends specific stocks, bonds, mutual funds, and occasional esoteric investments. Provides specific columns aimed at particular types of investors: conservative, growth-oriented, "value" investors, and the smaller investor. Also offers items on tax-saving strategies, portfolio management, real estate investment, and stock market trends. Recurring features include letters to the editor and updates on previous recommendations. **Remarks:** Toll-free telephone number in the U.S. is 800-222-4863.

13039 ■ NYSE Weekly Stock Buys
Pub: Elton Stephens Investments
Ed: Elton Stephens, Editor. **Released:** Weekly. **Description:** Identifies stocks with increases in dividends, earnings, and price appreciation.

13040 ■ The Option Strategist
Pub: McMillan Analysis Corp.
Contact: Lawrence G. McMillan
Ed: Lawrence G. McMillan, Editor. **Released:** 24/ year. **Price:** $295, individuals $250/year. **Description:** Discusses options on stocks, indices, and futures. Includes investment recommendations and educational articles.

13041 ■ The Review of Securities & Commodities Regulation
Pub: Standard & Poor's
Ed: Michael O. Finkelstein, Editor, mofinkelstein@ hotmail.com. **Released:** Semimonthly. **Price:** $1,197. **Description:** Professional magazine covering current laws and regulations affecting the securities and futures industry.

13042 ■ Sadoff Investment Management
Pub: Bryan Sadoff
Contact: John Kenney
Ed: Ronald Sadoff, Editor. **Released:** 12/year. **Description:** Provides stock and bond market summaries and trends, advice on when and how to invest for optimum growth and minimal risk. Interprets losses or gains in the stock market as resulting from the changes in four environments: monetary, psychological, technical, and the economic/business cycle. Recurring features include a model portfolio.

13043 ■ The Secured Lender
Pub: Commercial Finance Association
Contact: Michele Ocejo, Exec. Ed.
E-mail: mocejo@cfa.com
Released: Bimonthly. **Price:** $32 members domestic; $60 nonmembers domestic; $38 members international; $65 nonmembers international. **Description:** Trade magazine for the asset-based financial services industry.

13044 ■ SNL Financial Services Daily
Pub: SNL Financial L.C.
Contact: John W. Milligan, Editor-in-Chief
E-mail: jmilligan@snl.com
Ed: Released: Daily. **Description:** Summarizes by email or fax daily news headlines on finance companies, mortgage banks, investment advisors, and brokers/dealers, plus dividend and earnings announcements, stock highlights and index values, registration statements, and ownership filings.

13045 ■ Special Investment Situations
Pub: George W. Southerland
Ed: George W. Southerland, Editor. **Released:** Monthly. **Description:** Provides stock market investment recommendations. Focuses on companies that offer the prospect of a substantial capital gain in a relatively short time with comparatively small risk. Includes a description of the company, pertinent financial data, and factors influencing the recommendation. Also updates previous recommendations.

13046 ■ Standard & Poor's The Outlook
Pub: Standard & Poor's
Ed: Released: 48/year. **Description:** Supplies investment advice, recommending specific stocks and reviewing past recommendations and carries company profiles. Recurring features include columns titled In the Limelight, 5-Star Stock of the Month, Stocks for Total Return, and Statistical Highlights.

13047 ■ Stock Market Focus
Pub: Ned Davis Research Inc.
Ed: Tim Hayes, Editor, tim@ndr.com. **Released:** Semimonthly. **Description:** Advises on timing model readings and offers strategy for market timing. Covers technical analysis of the stock market and monetary conditions. Includes charts.

13048 ■ Timer Digest
Pub: James H. Schmidt
Ed: James H. Schmidt, Editor. **Released:** 18/year. **Price:** $175, individuals; $175, individuals Internet only; $225, individuals Internet & print. **Description:** Compiles and ranks the performance of intermediate and long-term stock market, gold, and bond timing signals by monitoring advisory services. Includes articles on mutual fund switch programs, fidelity sector funds, Dow Jones Industrials, and profiles of investment advisors of 80 services. Remarks: Sub-

scription includes a telephone hotline service. It monitors over 100 of the nations leading market timing models, ranking the top stock, bond, and gold timers according to the performance of their recommendations over the previous 52

13049 ■ Vickers Weekly Insider Report
Pub: Vickers Stock Research Corp.
Contact: Debbie Plonski
Ed: Richard Cuneo, Editor, rcuneo@argusmail.com. **Released:** Weekly. **Price:** $176, individuals. **Description:** Reports on stock insider transactions and maintains portfolios based on insider buy signals-96 up 68%.

13050 ■ The Wall Street Digest
Pub: Donald H. Rowe
Contact: Donald H. Rowe, Editor & Publisher
Released: Monthly. **Price:** $99, individuals $150/ year; $175, two years. **Description:** Covers major investment areas, including stocks and bonds; foreign currencies; gold, silver, and other precious metals; real estate; tax shelters; and estate planning. Recurring features include a digest of the month's best investment and financial seminars, newsletter reviews, and statistics.

13051 ■ Washington Weekly
Pub: Securities Industry and Financial Markets Association
Ed: Peter Roberson, Editor, proberson@bondmarkets.com. **Released:** Weekly, during Congressional sessions. **Price:** Included in membership. **Description:** Provides information on legislative activity relating to the municipal, corporate, and government securities and asset-backed securities markets. Analyzes taxes, budget, and banking issues.

13052 ■ Whisper on Wall Street
Pub: George Brooks
Ed: George Brooks, Editor. **Released:** 5-8/year. **Description:** Covers investments on all exchanges as well as emerging companies, promising speculations, and special situations.

13053 ■ The Yamamoto Forecast
Pub: The Yamamoto Forecast
Ed: Irwin T. Yamamoto, Editor. **Released:** Monthly. **Description:** Analyzes and reports on undervalued stocks, selling at bargain prices and ready to emerge, market timing and economy.

VIDEOCASSETTES/ AUDIOCASSETTES

13054 ■ Ask for the Order. . .and Get It!
Dartnell Corp.
2222 Sedwick Drive, Ste. 101
Durham, NC 27713
Free: 800-233-8720
Fax: 800-508-2592
Co. E-mail: customerservice@dartnellcorp.com
URL: http://www.dartnellcorp.com
Released: 1972. **Description:** Hammers home a key principle of salesmanship—to get an order you must ask for it; from the "Tough-Minded Salesmanship" series. **Availability:** VHS; 3/4U; Special order formats.

13055 ■ Bonds: Types, Terminology & Principles
Instructional Video
2219 C St.
Lincoln, NE 68502
Ph:(402)475-6570
Free: 800-228-0164
Fax:(402)475-6500
Co. E-mail: feedback@insvideo.com
URL: http://www.insvideo.com
Price: $29.95. **Description:** Provides information on bonds, including the different types available, terminology, basic market principles, and how to be a knowledgeable creditor. **Availability:** VHS.

13056 ■ The Cold Call
Video Arts, Inc.
c/o Aim Learning Group
8238-40 Lehigh
Morton Grove, IL 60053-2615

Free: 877-444-2230
Fax:(416)252-2155
Co. E-mail: service@aimlearninggroup.com
URL: http://www.aimlearninggroup.com
Released: 1976. **Price:** $695.00. **Description:** This program demonstrates the specific skills and disciplines of telephone selling, and the dangers of ignoring them. **Availability:** VHS; 8mm; 3/4U; Special order formats.

13057 ■ Commodities: The Professional Trader
American Media, Inc.
4621 121st St.
Urbandale, IA 50323-2311
Ph:(515)224-0919
Free: 888-776-8268
Fax:(515)327-2555
Co. E-mail: custsvc@ammedia.com
URL: http://www.ammedia.com
Released: 1982. **Description:** This series offers traders a strategy for success that is based on a consensus of advice from winning speculators. **Availability:** VHS; 3/4U.

13058 ■ The Competitive Edge
Film Library/National Safety Council California Chapter
4553 Glencoe Ave., Ste. 150
Marina Del Rey, CA 90292
Ph:(310)827-9781
Free: 800-421-9585
Fax:(310)827-9861
Co. E-mail: California@nsc.org
URL: http://www.nsc.org/nsc_near_you/FindYourLocalChapter/Pages/California.aspx
Released: 1989. **Description:** This program emphasizes finding out your customer's most immediate concern, and selling to that concern. **Availability:** VHS; 3/4U.

13059 ■ Financial Business Services
Morris Video
12881 Knott St.
Garden Grove, CA 92841
Ph:(310)533-4800
Fax:(310)320-3171
Released: 1983. **Price:** $24.95. **Description:** Money management careers are explored, including investment counselors, securities brokers, trust officers and mortgage underwriters. **Availability:** VHS.

13060 ■ A Happy Beginning
Resources for Education & Management, Inc.
1804 Montreal Ct., Ste. A
Tucker, GA 30084
Released: 1971. **Description:** An examination of closing the sale, asking for the order, and answering the customer's objections. How to become a confident sale closer. **Availability:** VHS; 3/4U.

13061 ■ How to Close the Sale
Dartnell Corp.
2222 Sedwick Drive, Ste. 101
Durham, NC 27713
Free: 800-233-8720
Fax: 800-508-2592
Co. E-mail: customerservice@dartnellcorp.com
URL: http://www.dartnellcorp.com
Released: 1981. **Description:** This program shows salespeople how to ask for the order, and how to get it. **Availability:** VHS; 3/4U; Special order formats.

13062 ■ How to Take the Butt Out of a Sales Rebuttal
Dartnell Corp.
2222 Sedwick Drive, Ste. 101
Durham, NC 27713
Free: 800-233-8720

Fax:800-508-2592
Co. E-mail: customerservice@dartnellcorp.com
URL: http://www.dartnellcorp.com
Released: 1967. **Description:** A look at how to cope with the difficult problem of rebutting a customer's objection-without being objectionable. **Availability:** VHS; 3/4U; Special order formats.

13063 ■ *Investing for Women by Women*
Tapeworm Video Distributors
25876 The Old Road 141
Stevenson Ranch, CA 91381
Ph:(661)257-4904
Fax:(661)257-4820
Co. E-mail: sales@tapeworm.com
URL: http://www.tapeworm.com
Released: 1996. **Price:** $34.95. **Description:** Discusses stock market investing and retirement planning options for women. **Availability:** VHS.

13064 ■ *Joy of Stocks: The Forbes Guide to the Stock Market*
MGM Home Entertainment
2500 Broadway
Santa Monica, CA 90404-6061
Ph:(310)449-3000
Fax:(310)449-3100
URL: http://www.mgmhomevideo.com
Released: 1983. **Description:** This introductory video to the stock market is divided into ten instructional segments. **Availability:** VHS.

13065 ■ *Knowing the Prospect*
Resources for Education & Management, Inc.
1804 Montreal Ct., Ste. A
Tucker, GA 30084
Released: 1971. **Description:** Shows the relationship of product or service benefits to the sales prospect's personal goals, and illustrates the value of knowing a prospect's needs. Ignores the fast-talking sales pitch. **Availability:** VHS; 3/4U.

13066 ■ *Louis Rukeyser's Wall Street Investment Seminar*
PBS Home Video
Catalog Fulfillment Center
PO Box 751089
Charlotte, NC 28275-1089
Ph:800-531-4727
Free: 800-645-4PBS
Co. E-mail: info@pbs.org
URL: http://www.pbs.org
Released: 1986. **Description:** This seminar on value investment, market strategy, and mutual fund investing features the latest moneymaking ideas for individual investors. Also included are presentations by 12 of the nation's leading stock market professionals. **Availability:** VHS; 3/4U.

13067 ■ *Making It Live*
Resources for Education & Management, Inc.
1804 Montreal Ct., Ste. A
Tucker, GA 30084
Released: 1971. **Description:** This tape demonstrates a key to sales success-knowing your product or service and telling your story with enthusiasm and conviction. **Availability:** VHS; 3/4U.

13068 ■ *The Making of a Salesman*
Exec-U-Service Associates
4326 US Highway 1
Princeton, NJ 08540
Released: 1984. **Description:** Provides basic material to enhance a sales training program. All programs are available individually. **Availability:** VHS; 3/4U; Special order formats.

13069 ■ *More Awkward Customers*
Video Arts, Inc.
c/o Aim Learning Group
8238-40 Lehigh
Morton Grove, IL 60053-2615
Free: 877-444-2230

Fax:(416)252-2155
Co. E-mail: service@aimlearninggroup.com
URL: http://www.aimlearninggroup.com
Released: 1973. **Description:** This program shows the importance of knowing your stock and services so that you can deal professionally with awkward customers. **Availability:** 3/4U.

13070 ■ *Mutual Funds, Options, Commodities, & Collectibles*
Instructional Video
2219 C St.
Lincoln, NE 68502
Ph:(402)475-6570
Free: 800-228-0164
Fax:(402)475-6500
Co. E-mail: feedback@insvideo.com
URL: http://www.insvideo.com
Price: $24.95. **Description:** Seminar-style program features six experts as they discuss what every investor needs to know about mutual funds, options, and commodities. **Availability:** VHS.

13071 ■ *Nightly Business Report: How Wall Street Works—The NBR Guide to Investing in the Financial Markets*
PBS Home Video
Catalog Fulfillment Center
PO Box 751089
Charlotte, NC 28275-1089
Ph:800-531-4727
Free: 800-645-4PBS
Co. E-mail: info@pbs.org
URL: http://www.pbs.org
Released: 1990. **Price:** $19.95. **Description:** A thorough, basic look at the workings and terminology of the stock market. Includes much background information on getting started in the investment world. **Availability:** VHS; 3/4U.

13072 ■ *Overcoming Objections*
Film Library/National Safety Council California Chapter
4553 Glencoe Ave., Ste. 150
Marina Del Rey, CA 90292
Ph:(310)827-9781
Free: 800-421-9585
Fax:(310)827-9861
Co. E-mail: California@nsc.org
URL: http://www.nsc.org/nsc_near_you/FindYourLocalChapter/Pages/California.aspx
Released: 198?. **Description:** This film emphasizes the importance of understanding the customer's point of view. **Availability:** VHS; 3/4U.

13073 ■ *The Perfect Sale*
Skillsoft
107 Northeastern Blvd.
Nashua, NH 03062
Free: 877-545-5763
Co. E-mail: info@netg.com
URL: http://www.skillsoft.com/
Released: 1984. **Description:** This program emphasizes the art of selling from approach to close. **Availability:** VHS; 3/4U.

13074 ■ *Prescription for Complaints*
Video Arts, Inc.
c/o Aim Learning Group
8238-40 Lehigh
Morton Grove, IL 60053-2615
Free: 877-444-2230
Fax:(416)252-2155
Co. E-mail: service@aimlearninggroup.com
URL: http://www.aimlearninggroup.com
Released: 1975. **Price:** $695.00. **Description:** This program shows a six-step, objective method for dealing with customer complaints. **Availability:** VHS; 8mm; 3/4U; Special order formats.

13075 ■ *Presenting the Story*
Resources for Education & Management, Inc.
1804 Montreal Ct., Ste. A
Tucker, GA 30084
Released: 1971. **Description:** How a salesman can best communicate benefits to a customer. Emphasis is on preparation of the story and practice. **Availability:** VHS; 3/4U.

13076 ■ *Self-Motivation in Selling*
Learning Communications LLC
5520 Trabuco Rd.
Irvine, CA 92620
Free: 800-622-3610
Fax:(949)727-4323
Co. E-mail: sales@learncom.com
URL: http://www.learncomhr.com
Released: 1979. **Description:** A look at how to avoid sales slumps and maintain peak performances. Four untitled programs cover frustrations and turndowns, seeking feedback, how to keep personal problems from affecting performance, and how sales managers can keep their people motivated. **Availability:** VHS; 3/4U.

13077 ■ *So You Want to Be a Success at Selling?*
Video Arts, Inc.
c/o Aim Learning Group
8238-40 Lehigh
Morton Grove, IL 60053-2615
Free: 877-444-2230
Fax:(416)252-2155
Co. E-mail: service@aimlearninggroup.com
URL: http://www.aimlearninggroup.com
Released: 1982. **Price:** $790.00. **Description:** Four videos that describe the fundamental skills of selling, from the initial research to the close. Part 1 focuses on the preparation, including client research and product knowledge. Part 2 looks at the skills and techniques of sales presentation. Part 3 shows how to deal with problem clients. Part 4 demonstrates the tactics for successfully closing a sale. Also available as a complete seminar kit. **Availability:** VHS; 8mm; 3/4U; Special order formats.

13078 ■ *The Stock Market*
Silver Mine Video Inc.
31316 Via Colinas, Ste. 104
Westlake Village, CA 91362-3905
Ph:(818)707-0300
URL: http://www.quicksilverrecords.zoomshare.com
Released: 1984. **Price:** $29.95. **Description:** An introduction to the world of investments, featuring a history of the stock market, and defining commonly used financial terms. **Availability:** VHS.

13079 ■ *Wall Street Week: An Investment Primer*
PBS Home Video
Catalog Fulfillment Center
PO Box 751089
Charlotte, NC 28275-1089
Ph:800-531-4727
Free: 800-645-4PBS
Co. E-mail: info@pbs.org
URL: http://www.pbs.org
Released: 1987. **Description:** A two-part investment introduction from the popular financial TV program with Louis Rukeyser, dealing with stocks, bonds, futures, commodities, options and more. **Availability:** VHS; 3/4U.

13080 ■ *When You're Turned Down—Turn On!*
Dartnell Corp.
2222 Sedwick Drive, Ste. 101
Durham, NC 27713
Free: 800-233-8720
Fax:800-508-2592
Co. E-mail: customerservice@dartnellcorp.com
URL: http://www.dartnellcorp.com
Released: 1977. **Description:** Examines the question: When is a turndown a true rejection and when is it just a disguised objection?; from the "Tough—Minded Salesmanship" series. **Availability:** VHS; 3/4U; Special order formats.

13081 ■ *Your Money Series*
Cambridge Educational
c/o Films Media Group
132 West 31st Street, 17th Floor
Ste. 124
New York, NY 10001
Free: 800-257-5126

Fax:(609)671-0266
Co. E-mail: custserve@films.com
URL: http://www.cambridgeol.com
Released: 1987. **Price:** $99.80. **Description:** Roma Sim, a board member of the National Association of Securities School, shows people how they can make their money grow. **Availability:** VHS.

TRADE SHOWS AND CONVENTIONS

13082 ■ The Bond Market Association - Fixed Income Summit Expo on E-Commerce & Technology
Flagg Management, Inc.
353 Lexington Ave.
New York, NY 10016
Ph:(212)286-0333
Fax:(212)286-0086
Co. E-mail: flaggmgmt@msn.com
URL: http://www.flaggmgmt.com
Released: Annual. **Audience:** Bond Market Association members, government bond officers, fixed income brokers and dealers. **Principal Exhibits:** Online services, Internet systems, fixed-income trading and executions systems, real-time systems, Internet and other new products and solutions; online trading and execution systems; bond market services; online research and global markets information.

13083 ■ Futures and Options Expo
Futures Industry Association
2001 Pennsylvania Ave. NW, Ste. 600
Washington, DC 20006
Ph:(202)466-5460
Fax:(202)296-3184
Co. E-mail: msaunders@futuresindustry.org
URL: http://www.futuresindustry.org
Released: Annual. **Audience:** Futures commission merchants, futures exchanges, clearing houses, brokers, commodity trading advisors, banks, and money managers. **Principal Exhibits:** Equipment, supplies, and services for the futures, options and derivatives industries.

CONSULTANTS

13084 ■ Bedford Associates Inc.
211 Greenwood Ave., Ste. 2-2
PO Box 221
Bethel, CT 06801
Ph:(203)846-0230
Fax:(203)846-1487
Co. E-mail: nick.kroot@bedford.com
URL: http://www.bedford.com
Contact: Stacy Luce, Mgr
E-mail: jose.badia@atsbedford.com
Scope: Offers expertise in the areas of computer information systems design and management. Services include airline systems consulting; transaction processing facility (TPF) and airline control system (ALCS) services; system development and maintenance; step by step (SST) and C-view sales, support and maintenance; supplemental staffing (either on site or remotely); web development services.

13085 ■ De Bellas & Co.
2700 Post Oak Blvd., Ste. 1400
Houston, TX 77056
Ph:(949)859-3332
Fax:(949)859-9333
Co. E-mail: info@debellas.com
URL: http://www.debellas.com
Contact: Royal J. Brown, Vice President
E-mail: rbrown@debellas.com
Scope: Provides merger, acquisition and financial advisory services to staffing and information technology services businesses and professional employer service organizations. **Publications:** "Tools to Take Advantage of the Current IT Staffing M and A Market," 2005; "Healthcare Staffing: Buy, Sell or Build," 2005.

13086 ■ DST International
27 Melcher St., 1st Fl.
Boston, MA 02210-1516
Ph:(617)482-8800
Fax:(617)482-8878
Co. E-mail: boston@dstintl.com
URL: http://www.dstinternational.com
Contact: Robert Evans, Principle
E-mail: rhonda.lepsch@atsdstintl.com
Scope: Firm specializing in asset management systems and work management systems. Asset management systems designed to satisfy the solution requirements needed by fund managers, dealers, settlement staff, custodians and record keepers operating as international asset managers, from front office simulation, opinion management and modeling functions, through data management, dealing and settlement to custody and corporate actions.

13087 ■ Financial Computer Support Inc.
16 Commerce Dr.
Oakland, MD 21550-3940
Ph:(301)334-1800
Free: 877-432-2267
Fax:(301)334-1896
Co. E-mail: fcsitechsupport@morningstar.com
Contact: David Huxford, Principal
Scope: Independent user group which provides computer and administrative support for financial planners, money managers, and insurance agents. Serves finance and insurance industries. **Publications:** "Check Out Carmen Petote," Jul, 2006; "Control the Information Flow with Rep Level Access," Feb, 2005.

13088 ■ Integrated Business Information Systems Ltd.
22 Colonial Pl.
New Haven, CT 06515
Ph:(203)397-1523
Fax:(203)397-1523
Contact: Dr. Michael L. Schneider, Principle
E-mail: mischni@idt.net
Scope: Provides financial and marketing software applications, design and development for PC LAN, Wang VS and IBM AS or 400 computers. Offers sales and support for several software products from other vendors, including Tele-magic, Real world, Lotus Notes and Power Builder. Industries served: Finance, marketing, investment, airlines, insurance and reinsurance worldwide. **Publications:** "Future Scope".

13089 ■ International Institute of Trading Mastery Inc.
102-A Commonwealth Ct.
Cary, NC 27511
Ph:(919)466-0043
Free: 800-385-4486
Fax:(919)466-0408
Co. E-mail: info@iitm.com
URL: http://www.iitm.com
Contact: Van K. Tharp, President
E-mail: mel@iitm.com
Scope: Teaches individual investors and traders the mental skills to become more successful. Trains traders to overcome fears and perform more consistently. Provides private counseling to CTAs, traders, brokers and floor traders worldwide. **Publications:** "New Series Research on New Ways to Manage Your Portfolio," Jun, 2010; "Gold Trend The Pause That Refreshes," Jun, 2010; "At the Half-way Mark: A Project Marathon Update," Jun, 2010; "Traders and Mistakes Part 3 Rule Based Discretionary Traders," Jun, 2010; "What Can You Do When the Markets Go Wild," May, 2010; "While Everyone Was Nervous, One Great Trader Took 100R from the Market Last Week," May, 2010; "Risk Calculation or Profit Factor," Apr, 2010; "Insidious Stress," Mar, 2010; "Should I Change My Figures For My Specific Market," Mar, 2010; "Volatility Highs and Lows," Jan, 2010; "Cause and Effect: Thinking Differently for Traders," Jan, 2010; "The Peak Performance Course for Investors and Traders"; "Trade Your Way to Financial Freedom"; "Financial Freedom Through Electronic Day Trading"; "Safe Strategies for Financial Freedom"; "Another Structural Change in the Market". **Seminars:** Peak Performance 101 Trading Course, Embassy Suites, Apr, 2007; Blue print for Trading Success, Embassy Suites, Apr, 2007; Highly Effective ETF and Mutual Fund Techniques, Crab tree Marriott, Mar, 2007; Professional E-Mini Futures Tactics, Crab tree Marriott, Mar, 2007; How To Design A Winning Trading System That Fits You; Infinite Wealth Workshop; Simulate Your Trading System and Position Sizing, Stock Market, Options, Electronic Day Trading; How to Develop a Winning Trading System That Fits You.

13090 ■ The Investor Intelligence Group
96 10th St.
Garden City, NY 11530
Ph:(516)248-1871
Fax:(516)248-6642
Co. E-mail: john_rhein3@yahoo.com
Contact: John Rhein, Owner
Scope: Provides expertise in investor relations, publishing, venture capital and lecturer.

13091 ■ Kauffman & Drebing Registered Investment Advisors
230 S Broad St., Ste. 5
Philadelphia, PA 19102
Ph:(215)546-8016
Contact: Neil B. Kauffman, President
Scope: Offers objective personal financial planning. Also conducts seminars on personal financial planning and provides investment management consulting for institutions.

13092 ■ Paul J. Litteau Consulting Services
516 S Kennicott Ave.
Arlington Heights, IL 60005
Ph:(847)255-4275
Fax:(847)255-1334
Contact: Paul J. Litteau, Owner
Scope: Securities consultancy whose clients include domestic and foreign governmental bodies, securities broker-dealers and related financial services organizations. Specializes in the areas of registration, administration, operations, regulatory reporting, training, and regulatory compliance. Also serves attorneys and other parties, including government agencies in securities-related litigation and arbitration particularly in regard to liability and damages in the U.S.

13093 ■ Scan Management Inc.
320 Spangler School Rd.
PO Box 4835
Gettysburg, PA 17325-8639
Ph:(717)359-7473
Fax:(717)359-7082
Co. E-mail: scanmngt@supernet.com
Contact: Budd Hallberg, President
E-mail: scanmngt@supernet.com
Scope: Consultants to the futures and securities industry. Provides services to institutions and corporations involved in using the futures market as a risk management tool. Conduct compliance audits - hedging and reporting audits and due diligence audits on use of derivative products. Clients include professional, corporate and institutional organizations in both the public and private sector, as well as government agencies. Also provides expert witness testimony.

13094 ■ SS & C Technologies
33 W Monroe, Ste. 420
Chicago, IL 60603-2401
Ph:(312)443-7501
Free: 800-234-0556
Fax:(312)443-7509
Co. E-mail: solution@sscinc.com
URL: http://www.ssctech.com
Contact: Stephen V. R. Whitman, Senior VP
E-mail: swhitman@atssscinc.com
Scope: Software development, consulting service, and turnkey systems provides servicing the investment/private wealth management, the financial/accounting services, and other markets requiring technical systems integration solutions. **Special Services:** Sun Solaris/MS NT Server Platforms. Software partners with Lotus Notes; Microsoft; Sybase; Ardent (Universe); and others.

13095 ■ Towneley Capital Management Inc.
23197 La Cadena Dr., Ste. 103
Laguna Hills, CA 92653-1484
Ph:(949)837-3580
Free: 800-545-4442

Fax:(949)837-3604
Co. E-mail: gretchen@towneley.com
URL: http://www.towneley.com
Contact: Wesley G. McCain, Chairman of the Board
E-mail: marnie@atstowneley.com
Scope: Offers investment counseling and mutual fund management services. Industries served: All. **Publications:** "Stock Market Extremes and Portfolio Performance".

13096 ■ VRTRADER.com
PO Box 1451
Sedona, AZ 86339
Ph:(928)282-1275
Fax:(480)607-5243
Co. E-mail: mark.vrtrader@gmail.com
URL: http://www.vrtrader.com
Contact: Mark Leibovit, Principle
E-mail: mark@vrsurvey.com
Scope: Offers individual stock selection and overall market timing services. Offers stock pick telephone hotline service and online e-mail service.

FRANCHISES AND BUSINESS OPPORTUNITIES

13097 ■ High Touch - High Tech
PO Box 8495
Asheville, NC 28814
Free: 800-444-4968
No. of Franchise Units: 144. **No. of Company-Owned Units:** 25. **Founded:** 1990. **Franchised:** 1993. **Description:** Mobile hands-on science experiments for children. **Equity Capital Needed:** $42,375-$46,100. **Franchise Fee:** $35,000. **Royalty Fee:** 7%. **Financial Assistance:** Assistance with franchise fee. **Training:** Provides 5 day training at regional programming office.

COMPUTERIZED DATABASES

13098 ■ ABA Banking Journal
Simmons-Boardman Publishing Corp.
345 Hudson St., 12th Fl.
New York, NY 10014
Ph:(212)620-7200
Free: 800-895-4389
URL: http://www.simmonsboardman.com
Description: Contains the complete text of *ABA Banking Journal*, a magazine on commercial bank operation and management. Covers employee relations, recruiting, and training; installment, mortgage, commercial, and industrial lending; correspondent, foreign, and retail banking; deposit gathering; bank cards; asset and liability management; data processing and telecommunications; security; government relations; and legal and regulatory developments. Also provides a calendar of ABA-sponsored courses, seminars, and workshops. **Availability:** Online: LexisNexis Group, Intuit Inc., Simmons-Boardman Publishing Corp. **Type:** Full text.

13099 ■ American Banker Financial Publications
SourceMedia Inc.
1 State St. Plz., 27th Fl.
New York, NY 10004
Ph:(212)803-8200
Free: 800-221-1809
Fax:(212)843-9600
Co. E-mail: custserv@AmericanBanker.com
URL: http://www.americanbanker.com
Description: Provides full text of the daily financial services newspaper and other financial newsletters which follow trends, developments, and news in banking and related financial areas. Includes topics such as capital markets, bank regulation, insurance letters, and public finance letters. **Availability:** Online: ProQuest LLC. **Type:** Full text.

13100 ■ Banking Information Source
ProQuest LLC
789 E Eisenhower Pky.
PO Box 1346
Ann Arbor, MI 48106-1346
Ph:(734)761-4700
Free: 800-521-0600

Fax:(734)761-6450
Co. E-mail: info@proquest.com
URL: http://www.proquest.com
Description: Contains more than 575,000 citations with abstracts, and full text articles, to articles and other published materials dealing with the management and marketing of financial services by banks, credit unions, insurance companies, investment and real estate firms, thrift institutions, and government agencies. Covers advertising, pricing, sales, marketing, pricing, personnel development and compensation, facilities planning, and product innovations. Pulled from more than 500 industry sources, including journals, newspapers, newsletters, reports, Bank Marketing Association's Golden Coin Awards competition entries, Stonier Theses, and School of Bank Marketing papers. Citations also provided for banking-related articles from *American Banker*, *The Wall Street Journal*, and *The New York Times*. **Availability:** Online: ProQuest LLC, ProQuest LLC, LexisNexis Group, ProQuest LLC. **Type:** Bibliographic; Full text.

13101 ■ Barron's Online
Dow Jones & Company Inc.
1 World Financial Ctr.
200 Liberty St.
New York, NY 10281
Ph:(212)416-2000
Fax:(212)416-4348
Co. E-mail: info@dowjones.com
URL: http://www.dowjones.com
Description: Provides the complete text of *Barron's*, providing articles and reports covering worldwide financial markets. Includes market data, news and market commentary, interviews, statistics, tools and resources (including specific analysis of online investing). Available as a stand-alone subscription product. **Availability:** Online: Dow Jones & Company Inc. **Type:** Full text; Numeric; Statistical.

13102 ■ Best's Statement File - Property/Casualty - United States
A.M. Best Company Inc.
Ambest Rd.
Oldwick, NJ 08858
Ph:(908)439-2200
Free: 800-424-2378
Fax:(908)439-3296
Co. E-mail: customer_service@ambest.com
URL: http://www.ambest.com
Description: Contains 11 years of annual and six years of quarterly statutory filing data on some 4100 U.S. property and casualty insurance companies. For each company, provides complete information from the NAIC annual statement, including assets, liability and surplus, expenses, premiums written by line, exhibit of life insurance, stock and bond summary, and quality and maturity of bonds. Includes *Best's Review*, *BestWeek*, and *BestAlert Service*. Also includes a one-year subscription to *Best's Review* magazine. **Availability:** CD-ROM: A.M. Best Company Inc. **Type:** Numeric; Directory.

13103 ■ BlockDATA
Thomson Reuters
3 Times Sq.
New York, NY 10036
Ph:(646)223-4000
Co. E-mail: salesinquires@thomsonreuters.com
URL: http://thomsonreuters.com/products_services/financial
Description: Provides information on the 400 most active listed, over-the-counter (OTC), and foreign securities traded on the AutEx Trading Information System (described in a separate entry). Includes industry profiles and trends as well as three months of trades data for comparative analysis. **Availability:** Online: Thomson Reuters, Thomson Reuters. **Type:** Full text; Numeric.

13104 ■ The Bond Buyer Online
Investcorp International Inc.
1 State St. Plaza, 27th Fl.
New York, NY 10004
Ph:(212)803-8200

Free: 800-221-1809
Co. E-mail: custserv@sourcemedia.com
URL: http://www.sourcemedia.com
Description: Contains more than 259,000 articles reporting news and information on the fixed-income securities market. Provides information on municipal bond issues available for negotiated and competitive bidding in each state, including name of borrowing entity, purpose of issue, issue and maturity dates, amount, interest cost to borrower, and underwriter. Also covers bond sales by state, results of bond elections, proposed bond issues, federal laws and regulations affecting the taxable and tax-exempt bond markets and U.S. Treasury bonds and securities, as well as news and commentary on events, economic trends, and government policies affecting the municipal bond market. Corresponds to *The Bond Buyer*. NOTE: On DIALOG, includes the complete text of *MUNIWEEK*, from 1986 to date. **Availability:** Online: Investcorp International Inc., ProQuest LLC, ProQuest LLC, ProQuest LLC. **Type:** Directory; Full text.

13105 ■ BondWatch
Thomson Reuters
3 Times Sq.
New York, NY 10036
Ph:(646)223-4000
Co. E-mail: salesinquires@thomsonreuters.com
URL: http://thomsonreuters.com/products_services/financial
Description: Contains real-time data as well as graphs and analyses of prices and yields for U.S. government bonds, bills, and notes. Includes MOR 2600 hedge fund managers; more than 14,000 managers of fixed income assets with 41,000 contacts; more than 7900 North American mutual funds, variable annuities, and pension funds with fixed income holdings representing over $1.9 trillion; and more than 13,200 non-U.S. mutual funds and pension funds with fixed income holdings representing over $617 billion. **Availability:** Online: Thomson Reuters. **Type:** Numeric; Full text.

13106 ■ Business Wire
Berkshire Hathaway Inc.
44 Montgomery St., 39th Fl.
San Francisco, CA 94104
Ph:(415)986-4422
Free: 800-227-0845
Fax:(415)788-5335
Co. E-mail: SF_sales_group@bizwire.com
URL: http://www.businesswire.com
Description: Contains more than 1.4 million records that make up the complete text of press releases from public and private companies and other organizations, such as hospitals and universities. Covers new products, stock offerings, mergers, legal actions, financial information, personnel changes, and company announcements of general interest. Includes headline recaps hourly plus recaps of high tech headlines in some systems. Records include company name, headline, publication date, ticker symbol, byline; dateline, time, word count (usually less than 500), and text, including contact information. Covers industries such as banking, computers, telecommunications, entertainment, aviation, biotechnology, and mining; general news and features; some international events; and sports. **Availability:** Online: Thomson Reuters, Mzinga Inc., ProQuest LLC, Dow Jones & Company Inc., LexisNexis Group, Bloomberg LP. **Type:** Full text.

13107 ■ CANNEX
CANNEX Financial Exchanges Ltd.
1200 Bay St., Ste. 1001
Toronto, ON, Canada M5R 2A5
Ph:(416)926-0882
Free: 800-387-1269
Fax:(416)926-0706
Co. E-mail: cannex@cannex.com
URL: http://www.cannex.com
Description: Contains current interest and product information for Term Deposits/GICs (Certificates of Deposit), mortgages, RRSPs (IRAs), annuities, RRIFs (similar to annuities), and savings and checking account products offered by banks, trust companies, savings and loans, and life insurance companies

in Australia, New Zealand, the U.S. and Canada. **Availability:** Online: CANNEX Financial Exchanges Ltd. **Type:** Numeric.

13108 ■ *Capital Stock*

Haver Analytics
60 E 42nd St.
New York, NY 10165
Ph:(212)986-9300
Fax:(212)986-5857
Co. E-mail: data@haver.com
URL: http://www.haver.com

Description: Contains more than 2000 annual time series covering all of the information contained in *Fixed Reproducible Tangible Wealth in the United States* by The Bureau of Economic Analysis. Detailed estimates by industry and by type of equipment or structure. **Availability:** Online: Haver Analytics. **Type:** Time series.

13109 ■ *CNQ Market Data Feed*

TMX Group Inc.
Exchange Tower, 3rd Fl.
130 King St. W
Toronto, ON, Canada M5X 1J2
Ph:(416)947-4670
Free: 888-873-8392
Fax:(416)947-4662
Co. E-mail: info@tsx.com
URL: http://www.tmx.com

Description: Provides each trade and bid/ask quote for all stocks, options, and futures listed on the Toronto Stock Exchange, Montreal Exchange, Vancouver Stock Exchange, and Alberta Stock Exchange. **Availability:** Online: TMX Group Inc. **Type:** Numeric.

13110 ■ *Dial-Data*

Track Data Corp.
95 Rockwell Pl.
Brooklyn, NY 11217
Ph:(718)522-7373
Free: 800-367-5968
Co. E-mail: info@trackdata.com
URL: http://www.trackdata.com

Description: A database system that contains current and historical data on securities, options, and commodities. Comprises the following three files. Securities—contains data from 1970 to date on more than 12,000 stocks, warrants, rights, bonds, and government issues. Includes both fundamental (e.g., earnings, shares outstanding) and technical data for all issues from the New York Stock Exchange (NYSE), American Stock Exchange (AMEX), NASDAQ Over-The-Counter market, International Stock Exchange (London), Montreal Exchange, Toronto Exchange, and government issues. Data items available include daily price and volume for NYSE and AMEX bonds; daily bid, ask, and yield for government issues; coupon and maturity data for both; and open, high, low, close, and volume interest data for all exchanges. Splits and dividends are reported on the evening of the day they occur. Options—contains data on all options listed on NYSE; Chicago Board Options Exchange (CBOE); AMEX; Philadelphia Exchange; and Pacific Stock Exchange (PSE). Daily price, volume, high, low, open, and close interest data as well as fundamental and technical data are available on all underlying securities from 1973 to date. Commodities—contains daily price, volume, high, low, open, and close interest data by contract on all commodities from the following exchanges: CBOE; Chicago Board of Trade (CBOT); Chicago Mercantile Exchange (CME); Commodity Exchange, Inc.; International Monetary Exchange; Kansas City Board of Trade; Mid America Exchange; Minneapolis Grain Exchange; New York Coffee, Sugar, and Cocoa Exchange; New York Cotton Exchange; New York Futures Exchange; New York Mercantile Exchange; and Winnipeg Grain Exchange. Covers commodities from 1963 to date, with selected cash series data from 1959 to date. Also includes 200 indexes and statistics on the daily or weekly performance of the securities market. Primary sources include NYSE, Dow Jones, Standard & Poor's, Value Line, and daily market summaries compiled from MERLIN data. Indexes and statistics date from 1972, with some data from 1970. **Availability:** Online: Track Data Corp. **Type:** Numeric.

13111 ■ *Dialog Finance and Banking Newsletters*

ProQuest LLC
2250 Perimeter Park Dr., Ste. 300
Morrisville, NC 27560
Ph:(919)804-6400
Free: 800-334-2564
Fax:(919)804-6410
Co. E-mail: contact@dialog.com
URL: http://www.dialog.com

Description: Provides access to more than 30 newsletters and journals published by publishers in the financial services industry. Covers more than 151,000 records. Includes publications from Euromoney Publications, Securities Data Publishing, Investment Dealers Digest, and Phillips Business Information. Includes such publications as: *Asset-Backed Securities Week. Bank Automation News. Bank Investment Marketing. Bank Loan Report. Central European Finance. Credit Risk Management Report. Employee Benefit News. Euromoney. Financial Planning. Financial Services Report. Investment Management Weekly. Mergers & Acquisitions Journal. On Wall Street. Mutual Fund Market News. Private Equity Week. Retail Delivery Systems News. Variable Annuity Market News. Venture Capital Journal.* **Availability:** Online: ProQuest LLC. **Type:** Full text.

13112 ■ *Dividend Record*

Standard & Poor's
55 Water St.
New York, NY 10041
Ph:(212)438-2000
Free: 800-523-4534
Fax:(212)438-7375
Co. E-mail: questions@standardandpoors.com
URL: http://www.standardandpoors.com

Description: Contains dividend disbursement data for more than 22,000 equity securities listed on the New York Stock Exchange (NYSE) and American Stock Exchange (AMEX), the NASDAQ market and the Toronto and Montreal stock exchanges. Also contains data on American Depository Receipts, mutual funds, closed-end investment companies, limited partnerships, and real-estate investment trusts. Comprised of and stock and cash dividend announcements, including initial dividends, dividends resumed, increase or decrease in dividends, omitted or suspended dividends, and additional, extra, special, or optional dividends. Also includes announcements of stock splits, stock redemptions, tender offers, rights offerings, spin-offs, stock exchange rulings, and due bill information. Provides, for each dividend, its declaration date, ex-dividend date, stock-of-record date, and payment date, as well as the amount of the dividend. Sources include the stock exchanges, National Association of Securities Dealers (NASD), and company information. Corresponds to Standard & Poor's printed *Dividend Record* services. **Availability:** Online: Standard & Poor's. **Type:** Numeric.

13113 ■ *EDR Sanborn Maps*

Environmental Data Resources Inc.
440 Wheelers Farms Rd.
Milford, CT 06461
Ph:(203)783-0300
Free: 800-352-0050
Fax:(203)231-6802
Co. E-mail: jhan@edrnet.com
URL: http://www.edrnet.com

Description: Contains more than 1.2 million Sanborn fire insurance maps covering the history of some 12,000 cities and towns in the United States from 1866 to the present. Enables users to search by latitude and longitude. **Availability:** Online: Environmental Data Resources Inc. **Type:** Image.

13114 ■ *EIU ViewsWire*

The Economist Group
26 Red Lion Sq.
London WC1R 4HQ, United Kingdom
Ph:44 20 7576 8181

Fax:44 20 7576 8476
Co. E-mail: london@eiu.com
URL: http://www.eiu.com

Description: Provides up to 150 articles daily covering practical business intelligence, including key events, market issues, impending crises, and the business and regulatory environment in emerging and International markets. Covers information from more than 195 countries. Includes: Briefings: critical political, economic, and business changes around the world organized by the topics of company, economy, finance, politics, regulations, and industry. Forecasts: Country updates-continuously updated overviews of GDP, inflation, demand, investment, fiscal policy, interest rates, currency, external accounts, and the political scene in more than 190 countries. Consensus forecasts-monthly currency, interest rate, and equity market short-term outlooks provided by multinational companies and investment banks. Country risk summary-political and credit risk ratings and analysis for 100 countries. Five-year forecasts—quarterly growth, inflation, and trade indicators for 60 countries. Forecast summaries—quarterly key economic indicators and business watchlist. Background: facts and figures on current conditions in more than 190 countries. Key economic indicators—quarterly statistics on growth, trade, reserves, and currencies. Basic data and country fact sheet-population data, per capita GDP, political structure, taxes, foreign trade and policy issues. Trade, tax and forex regulations-Connecticut updated full regulatory profiles on 60 countries. **Availability:** Online: The Economist Group, Thomson Reuters, Financial Times Ltd., LexisNexis Group. **Type:** Full text; Numeric.

13115 ■ *Extel Financial Cards from Primark*

Thomson Reuters
3 Times Sq.
New York, NY 10036
Ph:(646)223-4000
Co. E-mail: salesinquires@thomsonreuters.com
URL: http://thomsonreuters.com/products_services/
 financial

Description: Contains descriptive and financial information on quoted, major unquoted and other large companies worldwide. Subjects include board of directors; company name and contact information; company organization; consolidated balance sheet; director's reports; principal activities; registrar, bankers, and auditors; share capital details; and SIC codes and descriptions. Also provides 30 key financial data elements, including pre-tax profit, premium income, turnover, dividend information, share capital, capital employed, assets, market capitalization and borrowing. Enables user to search by country, company name and in both local and U.S. currencies. **Availability:** Online: ProQuest LLC. **Type:** Directory; Full text; Numeric.

13116 ■ *Ford Equity Research Databases*

Ford Equity Research Inc.
11722 Sorrento Valley Rd., Ste. I
San Diego, CA 92121
Ph:(858)755-1327
Free: 800-842-0207
Fax:(858)455-6316
Co. E-mail: info@fordequity.com
URL: http://www.fordequity.com

Description: Contains more than 200 financial data items for each of 4000 leading common stocks. Primary data include company name, CUSIP number, ticker symbol, quality rating, growth persistence rating, 12-month earnings per share, normal earnings per share, dividend rate, projected earnings growth rate, standard deviation of annual earnings, book value, debt/equity ratio, end-of-month share price, previous month share price, shares outstanding, percent of shares held by institutions, beta, quarterly earnings series for the past 4 quarters, an estimate for the coming quarter, an industry classification, and company annual revenues. Derived data include the past month price gain, market capitalization, total assets, cash flow per share, price/earnings ratio, current/normal earnings ratio, dividend payout ratio, dividend yield, total return, price/book value ratio, preferred equity, return on equity, plowback on equity, and the results of intrinsic value and earnings trend analysis performed by Ford. Includes the U.S. Daily Current Database, U.S. Historical Database, International Database, and International Historical Database. **Availability:** Online: Thomson Reuters; Diskette: Ford Equity Research Inc;Magnetic Tape: Ford Equity Research Inc. **Type:** Numeric.

13117 ■ *IGM CorporateWatch*
informa global markets
Graybar Bldg., Ste. 615
420 Lexington Ave.
New York, NY 10170
Ph:(212)509-5802
Fax:(212)949-4189
Co. E-mail: sales@informagm.com
URL: http://www.informagm.com/gml
Description: Contains news and analyses of developments in the US new issue market, Eurobonds, and private placements. Provides information from the United States, Europe, and the Asia-Pacific region. Covers corporate securities, equities, emerging markets, and international debt. Provides commentary and analysis, summary tables of recent deals, reporting of market developments and deal launches, bond and loan news, bond and credit news, and more. **Availability:** Online: Thomson Reuters, informa global markets. **Type:** Full text; Numeric.

13118 ■ *MarketScope*
Standard & Poor's
55 Water St.
New York, NY 10041
Ph:(212)438-2000
Free: 800-523-4534
Fax:(212)438-7375
Co. E-mail: questions@standardandpoors.com
URL: http://www.standardandpoors.com
Description: A financial information service that contains descriptive and financial data on more than 9500 companies, reports and analysis of the stock and bond markets, and financial investment news. Comprised of the following 2 section: Reference Section—contains descriptive information for each company, including background information, commentaries on future prospects, earnings and dividend projections (for 1100 major companies), and sales and earnings data by lines of business. Also contains current and historical statistical data (updated daily), including price range, price/earnings ratio, earnings per share, dividends, yield, and book value. Corporate and market developments are incorporated throughout the day. Also provides Stock Appreciation Ranking System (STARS), using 1 to 5 stars to rank the investment status of approximately 1100 stocks. Action Section—includes commentaries on current market activity (updated 7 times a day); economic analysis and projections, including EconomyWatch and MoneyWatch, by Standard & Poor's chief economist; analyses of developments that influence a company or industry group (updated continuously, throughout the day); MarketMovers, identification of active and volatile stock issues and rationale for their movements (updated continuously, throughout the day); interest rates for Federal funds, Treasury Bills, Treasury Notes, Treasury Bonds, and broker loan rates (updated at least 5 times a day); technical indicators; and high-yielding investment-grade municipal bonds. Data updated daily include stock allocation model, takeover candidates, and dollar, treasury, and international commentaries (provided by MMS International); a calendar of expected initial public stock offerings, indicating lead underwriter, business description, number of shares in offering, and expected price; performance data on new stocks for a 3-month period following initial public offering, including gain or loss percentage, recent bid, initial offering price, date of public offering, and stock symbol; an economic calendar, with forecasts of selected indicators; changes in key economic indicators, including comments by Standard & Poor's chief economist on key economic events and their impact; recommendations on specific stocks to buy for achieving 4 investment goals: long-term growth, emerging growth, income/total return, and speculative/cyclical; a master list of recommended stocks; *Fair Value*, Standard & Poor's proprietary quantitative stock valuation system; and Platinum Portfolio, which combines top rated stocks from *Fair Value* and STARS. **Availability:** Online: Dow Jones & Company

Inc., Track Data Corp., TD AMERITRADE Holding Corp., Bloomberg LP, Thomson Reuters, Standard & Poor's. **Type:** Numeric; Full text.

13119 ■ *Mergers Unleashed*
Investcorp International Inc.
1 State St. Plaza, 27th Fl.
New York, NY 10004
Ph:(212)803-8200
Free: 800-221-1809
Co. E-mail: custserv@sourcemedia.com
URL: http://www.sourcemedia.com
Description: Contains the complete text of *Mergers & Acquisitions Report* and *Mergers & Acquisitions Journal*. Covers pending and ongoing deals as well as insights into industry trends, strategies, and the firms and individuals involved. **Availability:** Online: LexisNexis Group, Investcorp International Inc. **Type:** Full text.

13120 ■ *Municipal Futures Data-Line*
Thomson Reuters
22 Thomson Pl.
Boston, MA 02210
Ph:(617)856-2900
Free: 800-367-8215
Fax:(617)856-5610
Co. E-mail: clientservice@tm3.com
URL: http://www.tm3.com
Description: Contains charts, graphs, and commentary on the municipal and Treasury cash and derivative markets. Provides data to analyze hedge and arbitrage strategies and municipal futures contract options. Includes a bond buyer index estimate, valuation of the municipal futures contract, and technical indicators. **Availability:** Online: Thomson Reuters. **Type:** Full text; Numeric.

13121 ■ *Municipal Market Data-Line*
Thomson Reuters
22 Thomson Pl.
Boston, MA 02210
Ph:(617)856-2900
Free: 800-367-8215
Fax:(617)856-5610
Co. E-mail: clientservice@tm3.com
URL: http://www.tm3.com
Description: Contains charts, graphs, and commentary on the municipal and Treasury markets. Provides analyses of municipal values, yields, and supply. Includes a daily municipal market index, daily commentary, technical indicators, and details of new issues. **Availability:** Online: Thomson Reuters. **Type:** Full text; Numeric.

13122 ■ *Mutual Fund Activity*
Haver Analytics
60 E 42nd St.
New York, NY 10165
Ph:(212)986-9300
Fax:(212)986-5857
Co. E-mail: data@haver.com
URL: http://www.haver.com
Description: Contains monthly and weekly data from the Investment Company Institute publication *Trends in Mutual Fund Activity*. Covers assets, sales, liquidity, redemptions, and cash flows. Contains 250 monthly series classified by 18 investment objectives. Data on money markets are also available including taxable and tax-exempt funds. **Availability:** Online: Haver Analytics. **Type:** Time series.

13123 ■ *opTrack Service*
Track Data Corp.
95 Rockwell Pl.
Brooklyn, NY 11217
Ph:(718)522-7373
Free: 800-367-5968
Co. E-mail: info@trackdata.com
URL: http://www.trackdata.com
Description: Provides real-time strategies and analyses for index and equity options as well as daily, weekly, and monthly graphs of the underlying securities price movement. Includes a directory of ticker symbols for the 6000 securities covered. **Availability:** Online: Track Data Corp. **Type:** Full text.

13124 ■ *Pink Sheets*
OTC Markets Group Inc.
304 Hudson St., 2nd Fl.
New York, NY 10013
Ph:(212)896-4400
Fax:(212)868-3848
Co. E-mail: info@otcmarkets.com
URL: http://www.otcmarkets.com
Description: Contains information on current prices of NASDAZ and non-NASDAZ over-the-counter securities. Covers new and updated issues of more than 15,000 U.S. and foreign companies. Provides listings for NYSE and AMEX securities for off the board trading. Includes a list of market makers for these issues. **Availability:** Online: Solera Holdings Inc., Bloomberg LP, OTC Markets Group Inc. **Type:** Full text; Numeric.

13125 ■ *Quarterly Financial Report*
Haver Analytics
60 E 42nd St.
New York, NY 10165
Ph:(212)986-9300
Fax:(212)986-5857
Co. E-mail: data@haver.com
URL: http://www.haver.com
Description: Contains statistics on the financial position of U.S. corporations aggregated by Industry from the *Quarterly Financial Report* and financial ratios for Manufacturing corporations. Includes quarterly data of income statements and balance sheet items for all Manufacturing, large mining, and trade corporations. Covers 8700 surveyed corporations, classified by Industry and asset size. **Availability:** Online: Haver Analytics. **Type:** Time series.

13126 ■ *Securities Law Daily*
The Bureau of National Affairs Inc.
1801 S Bell St.
Arlington, VA 22202
Free: 800-372-1033
Co. E-mail: customercare@bna.com
URL: http://www.bna.com
Description: Contains reports the latest developments in securities and futures law. Covers state and federal legislative, regulatory, and judicial actions affecting securities, commodities, and corporate activities. Includes coverage of U.S. Congress, state and federal courts, the Commodities Futures Trading Commission, and the Securities and Exchange Commission (SEC). Addresses such topics as insider trading, mutual funds, SEC regulation, investment advisors, global markets, and more. **Availability:** Online: Thomson Reuters, The Bureau of National Affairs Inc. **Type:** Full text.

13127 ■ *Securities Regulation & Law Report*
The Bureau of National Affairs Inc.
1801 S Bell St.
Arlington, VA 22202
Free: 800-372-1033
Co. E-mail: customercare@bna.com
URL: http://www.bna.com
Description: Contains the complete text of *Securities Regulation & Law Report*, covering federal and state regulations and laws on securities and futures trading and accounting. Includes corporate governance and attorney responsibility, enforcement activities, commodity futures regulation, and accounting standards and practices. Provides information on the most recent court cases, legal precedents, administrative opinions, and legislative and regulatory proposals and actions. Provides authoritative information on preparing, reviewing, and auditing financial statements filed with the SEC. Sources include Securities and Exchange Commission, Commodities Futures Trading Commission, industry, courts, and Congress. **Availability:** Online: Thomson Reuters, LexisNexis Group, The Bureau of National Affairs Inc. **Type:** Full text.

13128 ■ *SNL Financial Banks & Thrifts Module*
SNL Financial LC
One SNL Plaza
PO Box 2124
Charlottesville, VA 22902
Ph:(434)977-1600

Fax:(434)977-4466
Co. E-mail: support@snl.com
URL: http://www.snl.com

Description: Provides Information on more than 120,000 branches of banks and thrifts. Includes major exchange, OTC and pinksheet traded commercial banks and thrifts; GAAP balance sheet; detailed asset quality, loan and deposit composition, capital adequacy, and banking-specific performance and profitability ratios; mutual-to-stock thrift conversion data; historical financial data from the FDIC (Call Report), OTS (TFR), Federal Reserve (Y-9) and credit union regulatory agency filings; financial soundness ratings and regulatory enforcement actions; CRA ratings; Links to Uniform Bank Performance Reports (UBPR); and banking transactions. **Availability:** Online: SNL Financial LC. **Type:** Full text; Directory; Numeric; Statistical.

13129 ■ SNL Financial North American Real Estate Module
SNL Financial LC
One SNL Plaza
PO Box 2124
Charlottesville, VA 22902
Ph:(434)977-1600
Fax:(434)977-4466
Co. E-mail: support@snl.com
URL: http://www.snl.com

Description: Provides information on more than 40,000 publicly traded and private REITs (Real Estate Investment Trusts) and selected REOCs (Real Estate Operating Companies) in North America. Includes GAAP balance sheet, income statement, cash flow statement and debt composition; key financial ratios; NAV, NAV per share and price/NAV ratios; analyst consensus estimates for EPS, FFO, and AFFO. Includes property name, location and ownership percentage, size of property and demographic information. Offers Information on capital issues giving detailed description for each company's individual capital issues including preferred operating partnership units. Includes access to searchable database of SEC documents. **Availability:** Online: SNL Financial LC. **Type:** Directory; Numeric; Statistical.

13130 ■ Trendvest Ratings
Trendvest Management Inc.
923 First Colonial Rd., No. 1805
Virginia Beach, VA 23454
Ph:(757)412-4301
Fax:(757)412-4302
Co. E-mail: editor@trendvest.com
URL: http://www.trendvest.com

Description: Contains investment ratings for common stocks and aggregate indicators for the stock, bond, and gold markets. For each stock or market, provides a single numeric rating (e.g., 234 or -28) based on such factors as market values and market price momentum. High positive ratings indicate opportunities for buying; low negative ratings, for selling. Database service enables the user to download up to 50 data items for some 6000 common stocks for analysis and portfolio management. **Availability:** Online: Trendvest Management Inc. **Type:** Full text; Numeric.

13131 ■ U.S. Weekly Statistics
Haver Analytics
60 E 42nd St.
New York, NY 10165
Ph:(212)986-9300
Fax:(212)986-5857
Co. E-mail: data@haver.com
URL: http://www.haver.com

Description: Contains weekly financial and economic series aggregated from DAILY plus aggregate reserves, official reserve assets, bank assets and liabilities, commercial paper outstanding, money supply, bank credit, unemployment claims, car and truck production by firm, and production of raw steel, coal, and lumber. Also includes complete commitment of traders' data from the Commodity Futures Trading Commission. **Availability:** Online: Haver Analytics. **Type:** Statistical; Numeric.

13132 ■ Value Line DataFile
Value Line Inc.
220 E 42nd St., 6th Fl.
New York, NY 10017
Ph:(212)907-1500
Free: 800-531-1425
Fax:(212)907-1992
Co. E-mail: vlcr@valueline.com
URL: http://www.valueline.com

Description: Provides annual and quarterly financial histories and projections in the U.S., Canada, Europe, and Asia. Includes more than 80 industry composites. Includes stock market information and other financial business data. Covers more than 7500 securities listed on the major North American stock exchanges, NASDAQ, and OTC markets. The following time series are available: annual data since 1955; quarterly data from 1963 to date; full 10-Q data from 1985. Also features a composite of financial data for industrial companies. Information is obtained from company quarterly and annual financial statements. Also available as Datafile II, for Microsoft Access and Borland Paradox formats, offering a more limited data set. **Availability:** Online: Thomson Reuters, FactSet Research Systems Inc., Citigroup Inc., GIT Satellite LLC. **Type:** Time series; Numeric.

13133 ■ Value Line Electronic Convertibles
Value Line Inc.
220 E 42nd St., 6th Fl.
New York, NY 10017
Ph:(212)907-1500
Free: 800-531-1425
Fax:(212)907-1992
Co. E-mail: vlcr@valueline.com
URL: http://www.valueline.com

Description: Contains evaluation data for approximately 600 convertible securities. Includes price, yield, premium, issue size, liquidity, and maturity. Enables the user to perform calculations to evaluate the effects of changes in prices, common dividends, quality ratings, and interest rates. **Availability:** Online: Value Line Inc. **Type:** Numeric.

13134 ■ Value Line Estimates and Projections File
Value Line Inc.
220 E 42nd St., 6th Fl.
New York, NY 10017
Ph:(212)907-1500
Free: 800-531-1425
Fax:(212)907-1992
Co. E-mail: vlcr@valueline.com
URL: http://www.valueline.com

Description: Contains projected performance ratings and estimates of earnings-per-share, dividends-per-share, sales/revenue ratios, and 3-to-5 year growth in dividends per share for the 1700 common stocks that appear in the Value Line Investment Survey. Includes analysis of more than 70 variables, including investment measures (e.g., timeliness, safety, financial strength), price performance indicators (e.g., beta, stability, growth), estimates of price growth persistence and earnings predictability, quarterly estimates of sales and earnings-per-share, and projected growth rates and annual estimates. **Availability:** Online: Thomson Reuters, FactSet Research Systems Inc., GIT Satellite LLC. **Type:** Numeric.

LIBRARIES

13135 ■ Alberta Securities Commission Library
300-5th Ave. SW, 4th Fl.
Calgary, AB, Canada T2P 3C4
Ph:(403)297-6454
Free: 877-355-0585
Fax:(403)297-6156
Co. E-mail: inquiries@asc.ca
URL: http://www.albertasecurities.com
Contact: Yanming Fei, Libn.

Scope: Securities legislation, corporate law. **Services:** Library not open to the public. **Holdings:** Figures not available.

13136 ■ Ballard Spahr LLP Library
601 13th St. NW, Ste. 1000, S.
Washington, DC 20005
Ph:(202)661-2200
Fax:(202)661-2299
Co. E-mail: proctor@ballardspahr.com
URL: http://www.ballardspahr.com/
Contact: David J. Proctor, Dir. of Lib./Res.

Scope: Law; public utilities, taxation; municipal bonds; real estate. **Services:** Interlibrary loan; Library not open to the public. **Holdings:** 5000 volumes.

13137 ■ BMO Nesbitt Burns Library
1 First Canadian Place, 3rd Fl.
PO Box 150
Toronto, ON, Canada M5X 1H3
Ph:(416)359-4587
Fax:(416)359-5394
Co. E-mail: library@bmonb.com
Contact: Dani Breen, Mgr.

Scope: Investment. **Services:** Library not open to the public. **Holdings:** 200 books; 1000 reports; 32 online databases. **Subscriptions:** 200 journals and other serials, 6 newspapers.

13138 ■ CMA Ontario–Member Services Centre
70 University Ave., Ste. 101
Toronto, ON, Canada M5J 2M4
Ph:(416)204-3142
Fax:(416)977-1365
Co. E-mail: msc@cma-ontario.org
Contact: Patricia Black, Mgr., Member Svcs.Ctr.

Scope: Accounting, management, finance, strategy, taxation, investments. **Services:** Copying; SDI; Library not open to the public. **Holdings:** 2069 books; 267 videocassettes; 184 audiocassettes; 6 videodiscs. **Subscriptions:** 53 journals and other serials; 2 newspapers.

13139 ■ Compass Lexecon Library
332 S. Michigan Ave., Ste. 1300
Chicago, IL 60604
Ph:(312)322-0845
Fax:(312)322-0881
Co. E-mail: cgriffin@lexecon.com
Contact: Christine Griffin, Rec./Off.Svcs.Mgr.

Scope: Economics, securities, finance, government, business, reference. **Services:** Library not open to the public. **Subscriptions:** 54 journals and other serials; 5 newspapers.

13140 ■ Dechert LLP Library
1775 I St., NW
Washington, DC 20006-2401
Ph:(202)261-7909
Fax:(202)261-3333
Co. E-mail: david.lang@dechert.com
Contact: David W. Lang, Libn.

Scope: Law - antitrust, investment and securities, litigation. **Services:** Interlibrary loan; Library not open to the public. **Holdings:** 6000 volumes. **Subscriptions:** 50 journals and other serials; 6 newspapers.

13141 ■ Dresdner RCM Global Investors–Research Library
4 Embarcadero Center, Ste. 2900
San Francisco, CA 94111
Ph:(415)954-5338
Fax:(415)364-2325
Contact: Biff Moshe

Scope: Investment. **Services:** Interlibrary loan; Library not open to the public. **Holdings:** 230 books. **Subscriptions:** 400 journals and other serials; 10 newspapers.

13142 ■ Fenwick & West LLP Law Library
Silicon Valley Center
801 California St.
Mountain View, CA 94041-2008
Ph:(650)988-8500

Fax:(650)938-5200
Co. E-mail: library@fenwick.com
URL: http://www.fenwick.com
Contact: Sharon McNally Lahey, Lib.Mgr.
Scope: Securities, corporate, employment, International taxation, intellectual property. **Services:** Interlibrary loan; copying; Library not open to the public. **Holdings:** 10,000 books. **Subscriptions:** 350 journals and other serials; 8 newspapers.

13143 ■ Fidelity Management & Research Company–Fixed Income Research Center
82 Devonshire St., I39A
Boston, MA 02109
Ph:(603)791-7750
Fax:(617)476-9818
Contact: Susan L. Johnson, Dir.
Scope: Investments and securities, economics and business conditions. **Services:** Center not open to the public.

13144 ■ Fulbright & Jaworski L.L.P. Library
801 Pennsylvania Ave., NW
Washington, DC 20004-2604
Ph:(202)662-4601
Fax:(202)662-4643
Co. E-mail: jweiss@fulbright.com
URL: http://www.fulbright.com
Contact: Judith M. Weiss, Libn.
Scope: Law - antitrust, bankruptcy, criminal, investment and securities, labor, patents. **Services:** Interlibrary loan; Library not open to the public. **Holdings:** 23,000 volumes; microforms; CD-ROMs. **Subscriptions:** 1200 journals and other serials.

13145 ■ General Electric Company–G.E. Asset Management Information Center
3003 Summer St.
Stamford, CT 06904
Ph:(203)326-2404
Fax:(203)326-4026
Co. E-mail: mildred.lorenti@corporate.ge.com
Contact: Mildred Lorenti
Scope: Business, investment, finance. **Services:** Center not open to the public. **Holdings:** 1300 books. **Subscriptions:** 150 journals and other serials; 10 newspapers.

13146 ■ Gibson, Dunn & Crutcher Law Library
200 Park Ave.
New York, NY 10166-0193
Ph:(212)351-4005
Fax:(212)351-6262
Co. E-mail: sraber@gibsondunn.com
Contact: Steven Raber, Know. & Info. NY Mgr.
Scope: Securities, corporate, litigation. **Services:** Interlibrary loan; copying; Library not open to the public. **Subscriptions:** 250 journals and other serials; 20 newspapers.

13147 ■ Huddleston, Bolen LLP Law Library
611 3rd Ave.
PO Box 2185
Huntington, WV 25701
Ph:(304)529-6181
Fax:(304)522-4312
Co. E-mail: laldridge@huddlestonbolen.com
URL: http://www.huddlestonbolen.com/
Contact: Lauren Aldridge, Law Libn.
Scope: Taxation/estate, corporate/securities/banking, federal litigation, labor. **Services:** Library not open to the public. **Holdings:** 35,000 books.

13148 ■ Investment Company Institute Library
1401 H St. NW
Washington, DC 20005
Ph:(202)326-5800
Co. E-mail: ianthe.zabel@ici.org
URL: http://www.ici.org
Contact: John V. Murphy, Chm.
Scope: Mutual funds; state, federal and International mutual fund regulations; mutual fund legislation; mutual fund research; "back office" operations; marketing. **Services:** Library not open to the public. **Holdings:** 500 books; 400 government documents; 150 other cataloged items; ICI historical data and publications. **Subscriptions:** 225 journals and other serials; 10 newspapers.

13149 ■ Ontario Teachers' Pension Plan Board–Knowledge Centre
5650 Yonge St., Ste. 800
North York, ON, Canada M2M 4H5
Ph:(416)730-3770
Fax:(416)730-3773
Co. E-mail: inquiry@otpp.com
URL: http://www.otpp.com/wps/wcm/connect/otpp_en/home
Contact: Laurie Alberico, Mgr.
Scope: Pension management, investment, economics, finance. **Services:** Library not open to the public. **Holdings:** 900 books. **Subscriptions:** 30 journals and other serials.

13150 ■ Power Budd LLP Law Library
First Canadian Place, Ste. 7210
Toronto, ON, Canada M5X 1C7
Ph:(416)642-8580
Fax:(416)640-2777
Co. E-mail: lrhodes@powerbudd.com
Contact: Lesley Rhodes, Libn.
Scope: Energy, environmental and corporate law. **Services:** Library not open to the public. **Holdings:** Figures not available.

13151 ■ Sanford C. Bernstein & Company Information Resources
1345 Ave. of the Americas
New York, NY 10105
Ph:(212)486-5800
Fax:(212)969-2293
URL: http://www.alliancebernstein.com
Contact: Jill Kerr, Mgr., Info.Rsrcs.
Scope: Investments - finance and corporation. **Services:** Interlibrary loan; Library open to SLA members only. **Holdings:** Business directories, research materials, and newspapers. **Subscriptions:** 10 journals and other serials; 3 newspapers.

13152 ■ Scudder, Stevens & Clark Library
2 International Pl., Fl. 12
Boston, MA 02110-4103
Ph:(617)295-2282
Fax:(617)443-7063
Scope: Investments. **Services:** Interlibrary loan; Library not open to the public. **Holdings:** 1750 volumes; 135 drawers of 10K reports, clippings, and pamphlets; microfilm. **Subscriptions:** 200 journals and other serials.

13153 ■ Stearns Weaver Miller Weissler Alhadeff & Sitterson Library
150 W. Flagler St., Ste. 2200
Miami, FL 33130
Ph:(305)789-3251
Fax:(305)789-3395
Co. E-mail: jkorman@stearnsweaver.com
URL: http://www.stearnsweaver.com
Contact: Jeanne S. Korman, Dir. of Lib.Svcs.
Scope: Law - Florida, securities, banking, labor and immigration, corporate, litigation, land use, municipal law. **Services:** Interlibrary loan; copying; Library not open to the public. **Holdings:** 20,000 books. **Subscriptions:** 200 journals and other serials; 10 newspapers.

RESEARCH CENTERS

13154 ■ New York University–Glucksman Institute
Stern School of Business
44 W 4th St.
New York, NY 10012
Ph:(212)998-0700
Fax:(212)995-4220
Co. E-mail: wsilber@stern.nyu.edu
URL: http://w4.stern.nyu.edu/glucksman
Contact: Prof. William L. Silber, Dir.
E-mail: wsilber@stern.nyu.edu
Scope: Equities, bonds, futures, options, and other financial instruments and the markets in which they are traded. Research topics include implied volatility in options, bank fee structures, and changing character of stock prices.

ASSOCIATIONS AND OTHER ORGANIZATIONS

13155 ■ Accredited Gemologists Association
3315 Juanita St.
San Diego, CA 92105
Ph:(619)501-5444
Co. E-mail: 5444@accreditedgemologists.org
URL: http://accreditedgemologists.org
Contact: Donna Hawrelko FGA, Pres.
Description: Gemologists. Promotes the advancement of the science of gemology. Conducts research and educational programs. **Publications:** *Certified Gemological Lab Directory* (annual).

13156 ■ American Gem Trade Association
3030 LBJ Fwy., Ste. 840
Dallas, TX 75234
Ph:(214)742-4367
Free: 800-972-1162
Fax:(214)742-7334
Co. E-mail: info@agta.org
URL: http://www.agta.org
Contact: Douglas K. Hucker, CEO
Description: Represents suppliers of natural colored gemstones; retail jewelers and jewelry manufacturers. Promotes natural colored gemstones; encourages high ethical standards among members and within the industry. Seeks to establish closer communication within the industry; works to protect consumers from fraud and to create a greater awareness of natural colored gemstones. Conducts seminars; maintains speakers' bureau. **Publications:** *AGTA Newsletter* (quarterly); *AGTA Source Directory* (biennial).

13157 ■ American Hatpin Society
2505 Indian Creek Rd.
Diamond Bar, CA 91765-3307
Co. E-mail: info@americanhatpinsociety.com
URL: http://www.americanhatpinsociety.com
Contact: Jodi Lenocker, Pres.
Description: Collectors of hatpins. Promotes collection, preservation, and restoration of hatpins and related fashion accessories. Serves as a clearinghouse on hatpins and their history; facilitates exchange of information among members; conducts educational programs. .

13158 ■ Canadian Gemmological Association
55 Queen St. E, No. 1301
Toronto, ON, Canada M5C 1R6
Ph:(647)466-2436
Fax:(416)366-6519
Co. E-mail: info@canadiangemmological.com
URL: http://www.canadiangemmological.com
Contact: Duncan Parker BA, Pres.
Description: Jewelers and gemmologists. Promotes excellence in the practice of gemmology. Conducts continuing professional development programs for members; sponsors educational courses; sets and maintains standards of practice and competence for gemmologists. **Publications:** *Be a Professional Gemmologist*; *Canadian Gemmologist* (quarterly); *Canadian Professional Gemmology Course* .

13159 ■ Canadian Institute of Gemmology
PO Box 57010
Vancouver, BC, Canada V5K 5G6
Ph:(604)530-8569
Free: 800-924-2211
Co. E-mail: info@cigem.ca
URL: http://www.cigem.ca
Contact: J. Wolf Kuehn MA
Description: Gemmologists and others with an interest in gemmology and gemmology training. Conducts educational programs in gem appreciation, gemology, gem identification, diamond grading and jewelry history and design; gathers and disseminates information to trade bodies and the public. **Publications:** *Gemmology Canada* (quarterly).

13160 ■ Canadian Jewellers Association
27 Queen St. E, Ste. 600
Toronto, ON, Canada M5C 2M6
Ph:(416)368-7616
Free: 800-580-0942
Fax:(416)368-1986
Co. E-mail: cja@canadianjewellers.com
URL: http://www.canadianjewellers.com
Contact: J. David Ritter, Pres./CEO
Description: National trade association for the jewelry industry in Canada, with both retail and supply members. Offers educational courses, information on Kimberley Process, Canadian Diamond Code of Conduct and source for Canadian diamond suppliers. **Publications:** *At a Glance* .

13161 ■ Diamond Council of America
3212 W End Ave., Ste. 202
Nashville, TN 37203
Ph:(615)385-5301
Free: 877-283-5669
Fax:(615)385-4955
URL: http://www.diamondcouncil.org
Contact: Terry Chandler, Pres./CEO
Description: Retail jewelry firms and suppliers of gemstones. Firms operating approximately 4900 retail jewelry stores; associated manufacturers and importers. Offers courses in "gemology" and "diamontology" to employees of member firms; bestows titles of Certified Diamontologist and Guild Gemologist upon those completing courses and examinations. Supplies members with advertising and educational materials, sales tools, displays, ad copy, radio and television scripts, and merchandise plans. **Publications:** *Diamond Council of America—Directory* (annual).

13162 ■ Indian Diamond and Colorstone Association
56 W 45th St., Ste. 705
New York, NY 10036
Ph:(212)921-4488
Fax:(212)768-7935
Co. E-mail: idcany@gmail.com
URL: http://www.idcany.org
Contact: Sushil Goyal, Pres.
Description: Diamond and colorstone dealers of Indian descent and others who work with diamonds and gemstones from India. Promotes the growth and awareness of the Indian gem industry in the U.S.

Publications: *IDCA By-Laws Directory* (annual); *IDCA Pocket Directory* (periodic);Membership Directory (annual).

13163 ■ Jewelers of America
52 Vanderbilt Ave., 19th Fl.
New York, NY 10017-3827
Ph:(646)658-0246
Free: 800-223-0673
Fax:(646)658-0256
Co. E-mail: info@jewelers.org
URL: http://www.jewelers.org
Contact: Matthew A. Runci, Pres./CEO
Description: Retailers of jewelry, watches, silver, and allied merchandise. Conducts surveys and compiles statistics. Conducts educational programs. Provides information to consumers. .

13164 ■ Jewelers' Security Alliance
6 E 45th St.
New York, NY 10017
Free: 800-537-0067
Fax:(212)808-9168
Co. E-mail: jsa2@jewelerssecurity.org
URL: http://www.jewelerssecurity.org
Contact: John J. Kennedy, Pres.
Description: Advocates for crime prevention in the jewelry industry. Provides crime information and assistance to the jewelry industry and law enforcement. **Publications:** *Annual Report on Crime Against the Jewelry Industry in U.S.* (annual); *JSA Manual of Jewelry Security* (biennial); *JSA Newsletter* (quarterly);Bulletins (periodic).

13165 ■ Jewelers Vigilance Committee
25 W 45th St., Ste. 1406
New York, NY 10036
Ph:(212)997-2002
Fax:(212)997-9148
Co. E-mail: clg@jvclegal.org
URL: http://www.jvclegal.org
Contact: Cecilia L. Gardner Esq., Pres./CEO/Gen. Counsel
Description: Represents manufacturers, importers, wholesalers, and retailers. Combats deceptive trade practices and misleading advertising. Aims to develop and maintain high trade standards. Provides advice on markings and assists in prosecution of violations of marking, advertising, and related jewelry industry laws. **Publications:** *Manufacturers' Legal Handbook*

13166 ■ Jewellers Vigilance Canada
27 Queen St. E, Ste. 600
Toronto, ON, Canada M5C 2M6
Ph:(416)368-4840
Free: 800-636-9536
Fax:(416)368-5552
Co. E-mail: info@jewellersvigilance.ca
URL: http://www.jewellersvigilance.ca
Contact: Phyllis Richard, Exec. Dir.
Description: Strives to promote ethical practices within the jewelry industry. Offers educational programs and handles complaints from consumers. **Publications:** *Action Update* (quarterly).

13167 ■ Jewelry Information Center
52 Vanderbilt Ave., 19th Fl.
New York, NY 10017
Ph:(646)658-0246
Free: 800-223-0673
Fax:(646)658-0256
Co. E-mail: info@jic.org
URL: http://www.jic.org
Contact: David Bouffard, Chm.
Description: Represents retailers, wholesalers, and manufacturers of fine jewelry products. Conducts industry-wide promotional and educational programs; sponsors marketing seminars and consumer-oriented programs on radio, television, and print media. **Publications:** *LINK* (3/year).

13168 ■ Manufacturing Jewelers and Suppliers of America
57 John L. Dietsch Sq.
Attleboro Falls, MA 02763
Ph:(401)274-3840
Free: 800-444-6572
Fax:(401)274-0265
Co. E-mail: info@mjsa.org
URL: http://www.mjsa.org
Contact: David W. Cochran, Pres./CEO
Description: Represents American manufacturers and suppliers within the jewelry industry. Seeks to foster long-term stability and prosperity of the jewelry industry. Provides leadership in government affairs and industry education. **Publications:** *Buyers Guide* (biennial); *MJSA Journal* (monthly).

13169 ■ National Association of Jewelry Appraisers
PO Box 18
Rego Park, NY 11374-0018
Ph:(718)896-1536
Fax:(718)997-9057
Co. E-mail: office@najaappraisers.com
URL: http://www.najaappraisers.com
Contact: Ms. Gail Brett Levine GG, Exec. Dir.
Description: Gem and jewelry appraisers, jewelers, importers, brokers, manufacturers, gemological students, and others professionally interested in jewelry appraisal. Seeks to recognize and make available to the public the services of highly qualified, experienced, independent, and reliable jewelry appraisers. Conducts seminars on jewelry appraisal techniques, methods, and pricing for members and the public. Supports legislation to establish minimum standards of competency and licensing of jewelry appraisers; maintains code of professional ethics. Operates appraiser referral program; sponsors ongoing public relations campaign. Offers equipment discounts, new appraisal forms, travel discounts, insurance, and professional aids for members only. Compiles statistics. **Publications:** *National Association of Jewelry Appraisers—Membership Directory* (annual).

13170 ■ Women's Jewelry Association
52 Vanderbilt Ave., 19th Fl.
New York, NY 10017-3827
Ph:(212)687-2722
Fax:(646)355-0219
Co. E-mail: info@womensjewelry.org
URL: http://wjamarion.memberlodge.com
Contact: Kendra Bridel Weinman, Pres.
Description: Represents those involved in jewelry design, manufacture, retail, and advertising. Aims to: enhance the status of women in the jewelry industry; make known the contribution of women to the industry; provide a network for women involved with fine jewelry. Maintains hall of fame. **Publications:** *Jewelry Association Newsletter* (semiannual).

DIRECTORIES OF EDUCATIONAL PROGRAMS

13171 ■ *Directory of Private Accredited Career Schools and Colleges of Technology*
Pub: Accrediting Commission of Career Schools and Colleges of Technology
Contact: Michale S. McComis, Exec. Dir.
Released: On web page. **Price:** Free. **Description:** Covers 3900 accredited post-secondary programs that provide training programs in business, trade, and technical fields, including various small business endeavors. Entries offer school name, address, phone, description of courses, job placement assistance, and requirements for admission. Arrangement is alphabetical.

REFERENCE WORKS

13172 ■ "Former Apprentice Candidate Launches Jewelry Line" in *Black Enterprise* (Vol. 37, October 2006, No. 3, pp. 36)
Pub: Earl G. Graves Publishing Co. Inc.
Ed: Philana Patterson. **Description:** Star of the second season of NBC's The Apprentice, Stacie J, has launched a line of jewelry and accessories which will be sold at Claire's stores nationwide.

13173 ■ *Gems & Jewelry Appraising: Techniques of Professional Practice*
Pub: GemStone Press
Ed: Anna M. Miller; Gail Brett Levine. **Released:** August 28, 2008. **Price:** $39.99 paperback. **Description:** Comprehensive book for practicing appraisers, would-be appraisers; provides extension information about the profession.

13174 ■ "Gold Still Has That Glitter" in *Barron's* (Vol. 89, July 20, 2009, No. 29, pp. M8)
Pub: Dow Jones & Co., Inc.
Ed: Allen Sykora. **Description:** Gold prices appear to be ready for an increase starting in the fall of 2009 due to an increase in demand. The price of the August 2009 gold contract fell to as low as $904.08 an ounce before recovering to $937.50.

13175 ■ "High-End Jeweler Loses Street Sparkle" in *Houston Business Journal* (Vol. 40, November 27, 2009, No. 29, pp. 1)
Pub: American City Business Journals
Ed: Allison Wollam. **Description:** High-end jeweler Bailey Banks & Biddle's 7,000 square foot prototype store in Houston, Texas' CityCentre will be ceasing operations despite its parent company's filing for Chapter 11 protection from creditors. According to the bankruptcy filing, parent company Finlay Enterprises Inc. of New York intends to auction off its business and assets. Finlay has 67 Bailey Banks locations throughout the US.

13176 ■ *Lapidary Journal—Annual Buyers' Directory Issue*
Pub: Lapidary Journal
Contact: Donna Kraidman
E-mail: donna.kraidman@primedia.com
Ed: Merle White, Editor. **Released:** Annual, latest edition 2011. **Price:** $29.95, individuals. **Publication Includes:** List of 4,000 suppliers and retailers of gem-cutting and jewelry making and mineral collecting equipment, beads, fossils, minerals, and gems; gem and mineral clubs, bead societies, museums, schools, and shops. **Entries Include:** Company or organization name, address, phone. **Arrangement:** Classified by product and service. **Indexes:** Product/service, geographical, alphabetical by dealers.

13177 ■ "Midas Touch" in *Entrepreneur* (Vol. 36, April 2008, No. 4, pp. 160)
Pub: Entrepreneur Media, Inc.
Ed: Sara Wilson. **Description:** Lana Fertelmeister is a model-turned-jewelry designer. Her company, Lana Jewelry, designs fine jewelry for women. Her jewelry line is available in more than 100 stores worldwide and has been worn by celebrities like Cameron Diaz and Sandra Bullock.

13178 ■ "Modern Bride Unveiled Exclusively at JCPenney" in *Benzinga.com* (February 3, 2011)
Pub: Benzinga.com
Ed: Benzinga Staff. **Description:** JCPenney created its new Modern Bride concept in its bridal find jewelry departments. The new shopping experience is a collaboration between the retailer and Conde Nast catering to the bridal customer.

13179 ■ "Retail Briefs - Dollar Store Opens in Long Leaf Mall" in *Star-News* (November 5, 2010)
Pub: Star-News Media
Ed: Judy Royal. **Description:** Dollar Delight$ opened a new shop in Long Leaf Mall in Wilmington, North Carolina. The store will carry gift bags, balloons, party supplies, greeting cards, school supplies, health and beauty products, hardware, baby items, toys, Christmas goods, crafts, housewares and jewelry in its inventory.

13180 ■ "Shop Around" in *Houston Chronicle* (December 7, 2010, pp. 3)
Pub: Houston Chronicle
Ed: Tara Dooley. **Description:** Profile of Diana Candida and Maria Martinez who partnered to open Beatniks, a shop carrying vintage clothing, art from various artists, dance shoes, and jewelry.

13181 ■ "The Silvery Moon Moves to Larger Space" in *Bellingham Business Journal* (Vol. March 2010, pp. 5)
Pub: Sound Publishing Inc.
Description: Jewelry store, the Silvery Moon, moved to a larger location in order to expand its business. The new location was chosen because it offers the firm more visibility. The store offers find silver and gold pieces and specializes in Pacific Northwest native jewelry.

13182 ■ "Sylvie Collection Offers a Feminine Perspective and Voice in Male Dominated Bridal Industry" in *Benzinga.com* (October 29, 2011)
Pub: Benzinga.com
Ed: Benzinga Staff. **Description:** Bridal jewelry designer Sylvie Levine has created over 1,000 customizable styles of engagement rings and wedding bands and is reaching out to prospective new brides through a new Website, interactive social media campaign and monthly trunk show appearances.

13183 ■ "Women Prioritize Luxury Spending" in *Marketing to Women* (Vol. 22, July 2009, No. 7, pp. 8)
Pub: EPM Communications, Inc.
Description: In 2008, women spent 7 percent less on luxury items than in the previous year, according to Unity Marketing. Some luxury items, such as facial care products, are faring better than others. Statistical data included.

SOURCES OF SUPPLY

13184 ■ *Colored Stone—Tucson Show Guide Issue*
Pub: Lapidary Journal
Released: Annual, January; Latest edition 2009. **Covers:** Approximately 2,000 companies that exhibit at the Tucson Gem Shows, selling minerals, fossils, gems, jewelry, beads, and jewelry making supplies. **Entries Include:** Company name, address, phone; location of booth at show; geographical area served; product/service provided. **Arrangement:** Alphabetical. **Indexes:** Product/service, name, geographic.

STATISTICAL SOURCES

13185 ■ *The Precious and Fashion Jewelry Market*
Pub: Business Trend Analysts, Inc.
Released: 2003. **Price:** $1695.00. **Description:** Statistical report and analysis of the *Trends* jewelry industry, including past, present, and projected sales figures. Report also discusses key issues of interest to the industry, such as import penetration and export markets, consumer demographics and buying habits, strategies and ideas for advertising and promotions, distribution and supply, and the economics of the industry. Provides company profiles of industry leaders.

13186 ■ *RMA Annual Statement Studies*
Pub: Robert Morris Associates (RMA)
Released: Annual. **Price:** $175.00 2006-07 edition, $105.00. **Description:** Contains composite balance sheets and income statements for more than 360

industries, including the accounting, auditing, and bookkeeping industries. Also contains five years of comparative historical data for discerning trends. Includes 16 commonly used ratios, computed for most of the size groupings for nearly every industry.

TRADE PERIODICALS

13187 ■ *The Diamond Registry Bulletin*
Pub: Joseph Schlussel
Ed: Joseph Schlussel, Editor. **Released:** Monthly. **Description:** Supplies current data on the present and future outlook of the diamond market. Provides information concerning trends in jewelry and investment companies and actual wholesale prices by size, quality, and shape for certified and commercial diamonds. Recurring features include reviews of fashion trends, diamond sales boosters, quotes, and anecdotes.

13188 ■ *The Jewelry Appraiser*
Pub: National Association of Jewelry Appraisers Inc.
Ed: Gail Breit Leving, Editor. **Released:** Quarterly. **Price:** Included in membership. **Description:** Provides information on jewelry and gem appraising. Carries items on current appraisal practices and standards, and a wholesale price guide titled the Price Reporter. Recurring features include editorials, news of research, letters to the editor, news of new products, news of members, book reviews, a calendar of events, and columns titled News and Views, Industry News, and Association News.

13189 ■ *MJSA Benchmark*
Pub: Manufacturing Jewelers & Suppliers of America
Contact: Rich Youmans, Publisher
Ed: Tina Wojtkielo, Editor. **Released:** Monthly. **Price:** Included in membership. **Description:** Informs members of association news, as well as jewelry manufacturing industry events and issues.

13190 ■ *National Jeweler*
Pub: Nielsen Business Media
Contact: Teresa Novellino, Exec. Ed.
E-mail: tnovellino@nationaljeweler.com
Released: Semimonthly. **Price:** $10 single issue cover; $89 U.S.; $104 Canada; $330 other countries airmail only. **Description:** Jewelry industry magazine.

13191 ■ *Watch & Jewelry Review*
Pub: Golden Bell Press
Released: 10/yr. **Price:** $19.50; $35 two years; $60 other countries; $115 two years other countries. **Description:** Magazine on watches and clocks.

TRADE SHOWS AND CONVENTIONS

13192 ■ Beijing International Jewellery Fair
Neway International Trade Fairs Ltd.
9/F, Fortis Tower
77 Gloucester Rd.
Wan Chai, People's Republic of China
Ph:852 2561 5566
Fax:852 2811 9156
Co. E-mail: info@newayfairs.com
URL: http://www.newayfairs.com
Principal Exhibits: Jewellery, gemstones, jewellry materials, and manufacturing.

13193 ■ International Jewelry Fair/General Merchandise Show - Fall
Helen Brett Enterprises, Inc.
5111 Academy Dr.
Lisle, IL 60532-2171
Ph:(630)241-9865
Free: 800-541-8171
Fax:(630)241-9870
URL: http://www.gift2jewelry.com
Released: Semiannual. **Audience:** Wholesale buyers. **Principal Exhibits:** Jewelry and related items. **Dates and Locations:** 2011 May 21-24, New Orleans, LA.

13194 ■ Jewelers International Showcase
Jewelers International Showcase, Inc.
6421 Congress Ave., Ste. 105
Boca Raton, FL 33487
Ph:(561)998-0209
URL: http://www.jisshow.com
Released: 3/year. **Audience:** Professional jewelers, manufacturers, wholesale importers, and buyers from retail jewelry stores primarily from Florida, Latin America and Caribbean countries. **Principal Exhibits:** Fine jewelry, fashion jewelry, and related products and services to jewelry trade members.

13195 ■ Memphis Gift and Jewelry Show Fall
Helen Brett Enterprises, Inc.
5111 Academy Dr.
Lisle, IL 60532-2171
Ph:(630)241-9865
Free: 800-541-8171
Fax:(630)241-9870
URL: http://www.gift2jewelry.com
Released: Semiannual. **Audience:** Wholesale buyers. **Principal Exhibits:** Giftware and jewelry, apparel, home decor, novelties, silk flowers, fine/costume jewelry and accessories. **Dates and Locations:** 2011 Aug 27-29, Memphis, TN.

13196 ■ Mid-South Jewelry & Accessories Fair Spring
Helen Brett Enterprises, Inc.
5111 Academy Dr.
Lisle, IL 60532-2171
Ph:(630)241-9865
Free: 800-541-8171
Fax:(630)241-9870
URL: http://www.gift2jewelry.com
Released: Semiannual. **Audience:** Wholesale buyers. **Principal Exhibits:** Fine/costume jewelry, apparel, leathers, silks, beaded items, home decor, novelties. **Dates and Locations:** 2011 Apr 09-11, Memphis, TN.

13197 ■ New Orleans Gift and Jewelry Show Spring
Helen Brett Enterprises, Inc.
5111 Academy Dr.
Lisle, IL 60532-2171
Ph:(630)241-9865
Free: 800-541-8171
Fax:(630)241-9870
URL: http://www.gift2jewelry.com
Released: Semiannual. **Audience:** Wholesale buyers. **Principal Exhibits:** Giftware and jewelry, apparel, home decor, rugs, silk plants, fine jewelry, costume jewelry, loose gemstones.

13198 ■ Shanghai International Jewellery Fair
Neway International Trade Fairs Ltd.
9/F, Fortis Tower
77 Gloucester Rd.
Wan Chai, People's Republic of China
Ph:852 2561 5566
Fax:852 2811 9156
Co. E-mail: info@newayfairs.com
URL: http://www.newayfairs.com
Principal Exhibits: Jewellery, gemstones, jewellery materials and production.

FRANCHISES AND BUSINESS OPPORTUNITIES

13199 ■ Fast-Fix Jewelry and Watch Repairs
1300 NW 17th Ave., Ste. 170
Delray Beach, FL 33445
Ph:(561)330-6060
Free: 800-359-0407
Fax:(561)330-6062
Co. E-mail: franchise@fastfix.com
URL: http://www.fastfix.com
No. of Franchise Units: 2. **Founded:** 1984. **Franchised:** 1987. **Description:** Jewelry and watch repairs. **Equity Capital Needed:** $188,000-380,000. **Franchise Fee:** $40,000. **Training:** Provides 10 days initial training and 5 days onsite.

13200 ■ Hannoush Jewelers
Hannoush Franchise Corp.
134 Capital Dr.
West Springfield, MA 01089
Ph:(413)846-4640
Fax:(413)788-7588
No. of Franchise Units: 20. **No. of Company-Owned Units:** 52. **Founded:** 1980. **Franchised:** 1995. **Description:** Fine jewelry sales. **Equity Capital Needed:** $291,000-$717,000. **Franchise Fee:** $20,000. **Royalty Fee:** 4%. **Financial Assistance:** No. **Training:** Offers 2 weeks at headquarters, 3 months at franchisees location as needed with ongoing support.

LIBRARIES

13201 ■ Gemological Institute of America–Richard T. Liddicoat Gemological Library and Information Center
The Robert Mouawad Campus
5345 Armada Dr.
Carlsbad, CA 92008
Ph:(760)603-4046
Free: 800-421-7250, x-4046
Fax:(760)603-4256
Co. E-mail: library@gia.edu
URL: http://www.gia.edu
Contact: Dona Mary Dirlam, Dir.
Scope: Gemology, mineralogy, geology in relation to gem deposits, mining of gem deposits, jewelry history, jewelry manufacturing, lapidary (the art of cutting gems). **Services:** Library open to the public with restrictions. **Holdings:** 38,000 volumes; 92,500 digital assets; 1200 videos/DVDs. **Subscriptions:** 250 periodicals.

ASSOCIATIONS AND OTHER ORGANIZATIONS

13202 ■ Center on Education and Training for Employment
Ohio State University
1900 Kenny Rd.
Columbus, OH 43210-1016
Ph:(614)292-6991
Free: 800-848-4815
Fax:(614)292-1260
Co. E-mail: kelsey.28@osu.edu
URL: http://www.cete.org
Contact: Robert Mahlman, Dir.
Description: Aims to increase the ability of diverse agencies, institutions, and organizations to solve educational problems relating to individual career planning, preparation, and progression. Conducts occupational analyses and staff training programs. Evaluates programs and agencies and provides technical assistance. Researches identified problems or needs. Develops databases, information systems, and occupational curricula. **Publications:** *Cente-Gram* (quarterly).

13203 ■ National Training and Simulation Association
2111 Wilson Blvd., Ste. 400
Arlington, VA 22201-3061
Ph:(703)247-9471
Fax:(703)243-1659
Co. E-mail: prowe@ndia.org
URL: http://www.trainingsystems.org
Contact: Patrick Rowe, Dir. of Membership Services
Description: Represents the business interests of manufacturers of simulation systems, computer-based training systems, and training support systems; providers of contract training and other related training support services. Promotes the growth, development, and application of military training systems, products, and services. Seeks to contribute to the operational readiness and combat effectiveness of the armed forces of the U.S. and its allies; assist in fulfilling the training requirements of related federal agencies; enhance public education and training; increase understanding and appreciation of training systems technologies and services. Fosters communication between government and industry regarding requirements and procurement issues and policies; promotes responsibility and integrity among members. Compiles statistics; conducts research and educational programs. **Publications:** *NTSA Training Industry News* (bimonthly); *NTSA Training 2012* (biennial); *NTSA Yearbook* (annual).

REFERENCE WORKS

13204 ■ *Career Information Center*
Pub: Macmillan Reference USA
Released: Biennial, Latest edition 9th; December 2006. **Price:** $494, individuals. **Description:** Organized into 13 occupational clusters (comprising 13 volumes and an index volume). Each volume includes a section listing accredited occupational educational

and vocational institutions. A second section lists more than 700 occupational profiles and over 3,000 organizations with jobs in the field of work with which the volume is concerned. **Entries Include:** For institutions—Name, address, programs and degrees offered. For organizations—Name, address. **Arrangement:** By Career Area/Industry. **Indexes:** Each volume contains a general index, and a master index to the entire series appears in a 13th volume.

13205 ■ "Home Grown" in *Hawaii Business* (Vol. 53, November 2007, No. 5, pp. 51)
Pub: Hawaii Business Publishing
Ed: Jolyn Okimoto Rosa. **Description:** Discusses a program that focuses on Native Hawaiian entrepreneurs and offers business training at the Kapiolani Community College; upon completion of the program, participants may apply for a loan provided by the Office of Hawaiian Affairs (OHA) to help them start their business. OHA plans to present the restructured loan program in November 2007, with aims of shortening the loan process.

13206 ■ "Mitch D'Olier" in *Hawaii Business* (Vol. 53, November 2007, No. 5, pp. 27)
Pub: Hawaii Business Publishing
Ed: Cathy S. Cruz-George. **Description:** Mitch D'Olier chief executive officer of Kaneohe Ranch/ Harold K.L. Castle Foundation thinks that achievement gaps are a nationwide problem and that the Knowledge is Power Program is one of the programs that focuses on achievement gaps in some communities across the US. He also provides his insights on education in Hawaii and the current shortage of teachers.

13207 ■ "Up Against the Ropes: A Professional Coach May Help" in *Black Enterprise* (Vol. 37, December 2006, No. 5, pp. 72)
Pub: Earl G. Graves Publishing Co. Inc.
Ed: Description: Executive coaching is now a $1 billion industry. The coaching process itself and traits to look for in a coach are discussed.

SOURCES OF SUPPLY

13208 ■ *Tech Directions—Annual Buyers' Guide*
Pub: Prakken Publications Inc.
Contact: Tonya L. White, Advertising Sales Rep.
E-mail: tonya@techdirections.com
Released: Annual, April. **Publication Includes:** Directory of manufacturers and suppliers of equipment and materials to industrial and vocational/technical schools, community colleges, and universities. **Entries Include:** Company name, address, phone, fax, logo, e-mail, web address, product descriptions. **Arrangement:** Classified by subject. **Indexes:** Company name.

TRADE PERIODICALS

13209 ■ *FERA—Focus*
Pub: FERA Inc.
Ed: John A. Seeley, Editor. **Released:** 3/year. **Price:** Free. **Description:** Discusses consulting work and

research on evaluation of corporate training, human resource development programs, community-based social services, and educational programs.

13210 ■ *TD Magazine*
Pub: American Society for Training & Development
Contact: Juana Llorens, Managing Editor
E-mail: jllorens@astd.org
Released: Monthly. **Price:** $89 members; $150 nonmembers outside US; $300 institutions. **Description:** Magazine on training and development.

13211 ■ *Training Media Review*
Pub: TMR Publications
Contact: William C. Ellet, Editor & Publisher
E-mail: wellet@tmreview.com
Released: Bimonthly. **Price:** $229 print and online; $189 online only; $25 trial subscription. **Description:** Provides information for business trainers. Recurring features include software, video, Internet, and book reviews. Remarks: Also available online with searchable database of all reviews.

RESEARCH CENTERS

13212 ■ Academy for Educational Development–National Institute for Work and Learning
1825 Connecticut Ave. NW
Washington, DC 20009
Ph:(202)464-3798
Fax:(202)884-8422
Co. E-mail: icharner@aed.org
URL: http://www.niwl.org
Contact: Ivan Charner, VP/Dir.
E-mail: icharner@aed.org
Scope: Collaborative efforts among employers, educators, unions, service organizations, and government to resolve work and learning problems. Projects focus on youth development, work life transitions, and productive aging; critical skills, including youth transition from school to work; employment in the fast food industry, community service award programs for youth; access and barriers to adult education and training; computers in the workplace and impact of new technologies on women; analysis of education and training needs of workingwomen; employment-based tuition assistance; relationship between unemployment insurance and retraining; older workers and the labor movement; education planning and career development; and the role of postsecondary education in a changing economy. **Publications:** Policy papers; Reports. **Educational Activities:** Career Passport Program, to assist young people in resume preparation; Forums; Governmental Process Seminars (10/year); Training workshops and consultations, for businesses and community-based operations; Training, for adults to provide education information and advice to other adults.

13213 ■ Brandeis University–Center for Youth and Communities
Heller Bldg., 3rd Fl., MS 035
415 South St.
Waltham, MA 02454

Ph:(781)736-4835
Free: 800—343-4705
Fax:(781)736-3729
Co. E-mail: curnan@brandeis.edu
URL: http://cyc.brandeis.edu
Contact: Prof. Susan P. Curnan, Dir.
E-mail: curnan@brandeis.edu

Scope: Youth development policy and programs, including education, workforce, family and community connections, management and leadership in nonprofit organizations. **Publications:** Anthology; CYD Journal (occasionally); Reports. **Educational Activities:** Practitioner training (annually), on project-based learning, case management, evaluation, nonprofit management; Program Management and Evaluation; Research and consultation, for multiple clients - continuous.

13214 ■ Florida State University–Center for Human Resource Management
821 Academic Way
Department of Management
College of Business
PO Box 3061110
Tallahassee, FL 32306-1110
Ph:(850)644-7848
Fax:(850)644-7843
Co. E-mail: pperrewe@cob.fsu.edu
URL: http://www.cob.fsu.edu/man/hrcenter
Contact: Dr. Pamela Perrewe, Dir.
E-mail: pperrewe@cob.fsu.edu

Scope: Human resource policies, including training, compensation, staffing, personnel behavior, and benefits. **Services:** Contract research; Technical assistance, to small and medium-sized businesses; Training assistance. **Educational Activities:** Conference (semiannually), on special personnel topics; Workshops, for personnel professionals to earn accreditation in their fields.

13215 ■ Human Resources Research Organization
66 Canal Center Plz., Ste. 700
Alexandria, VA 22314-1591
Ph:(703)549-3611
Fax:(703)549-9025
Co. E-mail: webmaster@humrro.orgg
URL: http://www.humrro.org
Contact: William J. Strickland PhD, Pres./CEO
E-mail: webmaster@humrro.orgg

Scope: Training, training device requirements, instructional technology, recruitment and workforce analysis, personnel selection and classification, ability testing, simulation and modeling, system and job analysis, cognitive task analysis, performance appraisal, assessment centers, and program evaluation.

REFERENCE WORKS

13216 ■ **"Annapolis Seeks City Market Vendors"** in *Boston Business Journal* (Vol. 29, June 10, 2011, No. 5, pp. 3)
Pub: American City Business Journals Inc.
Ed: Daniel J. Sernovitz. **Description:** The city of Annapolis, Maryland is planning to revive the historical landmark Market House and it is now accepting bids from vendors until June 10, 2011. The city hopes to reopen the facility by July 2011 for a six-month period after which it will undergo renovations.

13217 ■ **"At Wine Kiosk, Show ID, Face Camera, Swipe Card and Blow"** in *Pittsburgh Post-Gazette* (November 28, 2010)
Pub: Pittsburgh-Post Gazette
Ed: Dennis B. Roddy. **Description:** New technology installed on wine kiosks enables sellers to abide by the law. This technology tests blood alcohol levels and warns people if they have recently used a mouthwash before testing.

13218 ■ **"Blue Cross to Put Kiosk in Mall"** in *News & Observer* (November 9, 2010)
Pub: News & Observer
Ed: Alan M. Wolf. **Description:** Blue Cross and Blue Shield of North Carolina has placed a kiosk in Durham's Streets of Southpoint in order to market its health insurance.

13219 ■ **"Border Boletin: UA to Take Lie-Detector Kiosk to Poland"** in *Arizona Daily Star* (September 14, 2010)
Pub: Arizona Daily Star
Ed: Brady McCombs. **Description:** University of Arizona's National Center for Border Security and Immigration Research will send a team to Warsaw, Poland to show border guards from 27 European Union countries the center's Avatar Kiosk. The Avatar technology is designed for use at border ports and airports to assist Customs officers detect individuals who are lying.

13220 ■ **"Boston Globe"** in *Ice Cream Reporter* (Vol. 21, August 20, 2008, No. 9, pp. 7)
Pub: Ice Cream Reporter
Description: Boston City Council approved an ordinance that will limit when ice cream vendors can announce their presence with music over loud speakers. The rules are simple: when the wheels stop moving, the jingles stop playing.

13221 ■ **"Cox Opens Norfolk Mall Kiosk; Wireless Service Not Ready"** in *Virginian-Pilot* (September 20, 2010)
Pub: Virginian-Pilot
Ed: Carolyn Shapiro. **Description:** Cox Communications opened a kiosk at MacArthur Center that will sell wireless telephone devices and plans.

13222 ■ **"Eagle's Wine Kiosk Is Area's 1st"** in *Pittsburgh Post-Gazette* (October 28, 2010)
Pub: Pittsburgh-Post Gazette
Ed: Bob Batz Jr. **Description:** Giant Eagle Market District store at Settlers Ridge opened the first self-

serve wine kiosk in Western Pennsylvania. The kiosk will have a built-in breathalyzer panel to ensure safety.

13223 ■ **"easyhome Ltd. Discovers Employee Fraud at an Easyfinancial Kiosk Company"** in *Internet Wire* (October 14, 2010)
Pub: Comtex
Description: Canada's leading merchandise leasing company and provider of financial services, easyhome Ltd., reported employee fraud totaling $3.4 million that was perpetrated against the firm's easyfinancial services business.

13224 ■ **"Fire Destroys Veterans' Kiosk"** in *Houston Chronicle* (November 24, 2010, pp. 14)
Pub: Houston Chronicle
Description: A leaking propane heater is believed to have started a fire that destroyed a kiosk near the Vietnam Veterans Memorial in Washington DC. The kiosk, manned by volunteers from the Rolling Thunder veterans group, provide education to the public about those individuals still missing from the Vietnam War.

13225 ■ **"Floral-Design Kiosk Business in Colorado Springs Blossoming"** in *Colorado Springs Business Journal* (September 24, 2010)
Pub: Dolan Media Newswires
Ed: Monica Mendoza. **Description:** Profile of Shellie Greto and her mother Jackie Martin who started a wholesale flower business in their garage. The do-it-yourself floral arrangement firm started a kiosk business in supermarkets called Complete Design.

13226 ■ **"Generous Donations Fund Repairs for Benton Trail Kiosk"** in *Morning Sentinel* (December 22, 2010)
Pub: Morning Sentinel
Ed: Scott Monroe. **Description:** The new kiosk at the entrance to a trail off Benton Avenue was paid for through donations and community contributions after the original was destroyed by vandals. The new kiosk's material was donated by the Huhtamaki manufacturing firm.

13227 ■ **"IF Challenges Atlanta's Vending Monopoly"** in *Benzinga.com* (July 28, 2011)
Pub: Benzinga.com
Ed: Benzinga Staff. **Description:** A lawsuit was filed by The Institute for Justice to challenge Atlanta's unconstitutional vending monopoly on behalf of two Atlanta street vendors.

13228 ■ **"iMozi Integrates Esprida LiveControl for Advanced DVD Kiosk Hardware"** in *Wireless News* (December 20, 2010)
Pub: Close-Up Media Inc.
Description: Provider of self-service entertainment technology, iMozi Canada has partnered with Esprida to make its automated DVD Kiosk solutions Esprida-enabled. Esprida develops remote device management solutions and will offer enhanced capabilities and to improve customer experience for users.

13229 ■ **"Kiosk Outfit ecoATM Now Recycling Video Games"** in *San Diego Union-Tribune* (October 7, 2010)
Pub: San Diego Union-Tribune
Ed: Mike Freeman. **Description:** ecoATM makes automated kiosks to buy back cell phones will now include video games as part of their recycling business.

13230 ■ **"LCB Puts a Cork in Kiosk Wine Sales"** in *Times Leader* (December 22, 2010)
Pub: Wilkes-Barre Publishing Company
Ed: Andrew M. Seder. **Description:** The Pennsylvania Liquor Control Board closed down thirty Pronto Wine Kiosks located in supermarkets throughout the state. The Board cited mechanical and technological issues such as products not dispensing.

13231 ■ **"LCB Turning Off Wine Vending Machines"** in *Pittsburgh Post-Gazette* (September 20, 2011)
Pub: PG Publishing Company
Ed: Tracie Mauriello. **Description:** Grocery store shoppers will no longer be able to purchase a bottle of wine from wine kiosks in Pennsylvania.

13232 ■ **"Pet Kiosk Offers Search Options"** in *Times-News* (October 14, 2010)
Pub: Times-News Publishing Company
Ed: Roselee Papandrea. **Description:** Chameleon Pet Kiosk located at the Spay and Neuter Clinic of Alamance County in Burlington, North Carolina allows users to see and read about animals available for adoption at the center.

13233 ■ **"Public Media Works to Launch DVD Kiosk Operations in Toronto, Canada"** in *Internet Wire* (November 15, 2010)
Pub: Comtex
Description: Public Media Works Inc. along with its EntertainmentXpress Inc., have partnered with Spot Venture Distribution Inc. and Signifi Solutions Inc., both headquartered in Toronto, Canada, to manage and expand the Spot DVD movie and game kiosk business in greater Toronto and other Canadian locations.

13234 ■ **"Titan to Become New York's Largest Provider of Phone Kiosk Advertising"** in *Marketing Weekly News* (September 11, 2010, pp. 150)
Pub: VerticalNews
Description: Titan will acquire from Verizon 1,900 payphones at 1,300 phone kiosk locations in New York City, New York. This transaction will triple the firm's inventory of New York Phone Kiosk media to over 5,000 advertising faces. Details are included.

13235 ■ **"'Unknown' Muted Grand Prix Impact"** in *Boston Business Journal* (Vol. 29, September 9, 2011, No. 18, pp. 3)
Pub: American City Business Journals Inc.
Ed: Alexander Jackson. **Description:** Baltimore Grand Prix caught restaurateurs, hoteliers and street vendors in Baltimore, Maryland unprepared for the thousands of race fans who attended the inaugural

event over Labor Day weekend. The race popularity is relatively unknown to them and some felt they were not able to make as much money as they had hoped.

13236 ■ "Ventura Police Install Electronic Kiosk to Access Services" in *Ventura County Star* (October 28, 2010)

Pub: Ventura County Star

Description: Ventura Police Department installed a kiosk in the front lobby of its building in order to provide services to the public. The kiosk allows access to the Department's Website; to retrieve a collision report, file an abandoned vehicle report, receive a permit for an oversized vehicle, or filing a citizen's complaint; information can be obtained about alarms, programs and permits; users can pay a parking ticket and review calls for services on an interactive map.

13237 ■ "A Wireless Makes 8 Store-In-Store Kiosk Acquisitions" in *Wireless News* (October 16, 2010)

Pub: Close-Up Media Inc.

Description: A Wireless, a retailer for Verizon Wireless has acquired eight of Verizon's retail kiosks that are positioned in home appliance and electronics stores.

FRANCHISES AND BUSINESS OPPORTUNITIES

13238 ■ Breeze Freeze

13340 Merriman Rd.
Livonia, MI 48150
Free: (866)472-6482
Fax:(734)414-6537

No. of Franchise Units: 31. **No. of Company-Owned Units:** 303. **Founded:** 2001. **Franchised:** 2004. **Description:** Frozen fruit drinks. **Equity Capital Needed:** $9,200-$94,300, express/kiosk option available. **Franchise Fee:** $5,000/$40,000. **Royalty Fee:** None. **Financial Assistance:** Limited third party financing assistance. **Training:** Offers 1-3 days at headquarters, 1-2 days at franchisees location with ongoing support.

13239 ■ California Quivers

5284 Eastgate Mall
San Diego, CA 92121
Ph:(858)558-1300
Fax:(858)558-1200

No. of Franchise Units: 3. **No. of Company-Owned Units:** 10. **Founded:** 1997. **Franchised:** 2004. **Description:** Carts serving fruit ices, hot dogs and coffee. **Equity Capital Needed:** $45,000-$149,300. **Franchise Fee:** $22,500. **Royalty Fee:** 6%. **Financial Assistance:** No. **Training:** Offers training 1 week at headquarters and ongoing support.

13240 ■ Cena

12501 N Hwy. 395, Ste. 3
Spokane, WA 99218
Ph:(509)448-1725

Free: 888-667-2362
Fax:(509)448-9380

No. of Franchise Units: 10. **No. of Company-Owned Units:** 1. **Founded:** 2004. **Franchised:** 2005. **Description:** Meal preparation/assembly center and wine shop. **Equity Capital Needed:** $148,400-$205,500; express/kiosk option available. **Franchise Fee:** $30,000. **Royalty Fee:** 5%. **Financial Assistance:** No. **Training:** Provides 4 days training at headquarters, 3 days onsite and ongoing support.

13241 ■ Frankitude

21 NW Miami Ct.
Miami, FL 33128
Ph:(305)371-9875
Free: 877-275-8778

No. of Franchise Units: 1. **No. of Company-Owned Units:** 1. **Founded:** 2006. **Franchised:** 2006. **Description:** Hot dogs, salads, panini, and wraps. **Equity Capital Needed:** $170,200-$325,000 (Express/kiosk option available). **Franchise Fee:** $25,000. **Royalty Fee:** 6%. **Financial Assistance:** No. **Training:** Offers 2+ weeks training at headquarters, 1+ weeks onsite and ongoing support.

13242 ■ Indigos Fruit Smoothies

Indigos Franchising, Inc.
21551 Arbor Way
Boca Raton, FL 33433
Ph:(407)383-3872

No. of Franchise Units: 9. **Founded:** 2004. **Franchised:** 2004. **Description:** Retail smoothie/juice bar & healthy restaurant. **Equity Capital Needed:** $89,800-$272,000. **Franchise Fee:** $25,000. **Royalty Fee:** 6&. **Financial Assistance:** Limited third party financing available. **Training:** Includes 6 days training at headquarters, 7 days at franchisee's location and ongoing support.

13243 ■ Motion Golf LLC

55 Lane Rd.
Fairfield, NJ 07004
Free: (866)-585-6033

No. of Company-Owned Units: 3. **Founded:** 2006. **Franchised:** 2007. **Description:** Golf swing analysis, instruction, and club fitting. **Equity Capital Needed:** $250,000 (Express/kiosk option available). **Franchise Fee:** $79,500. **Royalty Fee:** 6%. **Financial Assistance:** Limited third party financing available. **Training:** 1 week at franchisee's location.

13244 ■ Mr. Payroll Check Cashing

Cash America Intl.
1600 W 7th St.
Fort Worth, TX 76102
Free: 800-322-3250
Fax:(817)570-1738
URL: http://www.cashamerica.com

No. of Franchise Units: 113. **No. of Company-Owned Units:** 6. **Founded:** 1988. **Franchised:** 1990. **Description:** Operates as a financial services

kiosk inside a busy retail business, such as a grocery and convenience stores. Our pre-fabricated 48 square foot kiosk is space efficient and helps retailers increase sales from check cashing customers. Franchisees may be owners of such retail businesses or can operate as subtenants. Services include check cashing, money orders, wire transfers, bill payments, pre-paid phones and ancillary services. **Equity Capital Needed:** $75,300-$326,500. **Franchise Fee:** $10,000. **Royalty Fee:** 10%+. **Financial Assistance:** Third party financing available. **Training:** Offers 4 days at headquarters, 1-2 days at franchisees location with ongoing support.

13245 ■ Mr. Pickle's Sandwich Shop

670 Auburn-Folsom Rd., Ste. 106-571
Auburn, CA 95603
Ph:(916)746-7727
Fax:(916)746-7787

No. of Franchise Units: 24. **Founded:** 1996. **Franchised:** 2006. **Description:** Sandwiches, soups, and salads. **Equity Capital Needed:** $249,000 (Express/kiosk option available). **Franchise Fee:** $25,000. **Royalty Fee:** None. **Financial Assistance:** No. **Training:** 2 weeks training included at franchisee's location and ongoing support.

13246 ■ Printwell Management Inc.

1200 St. Laurent Blvd.
Ottawa, ON, Canada K1K 3B8
Ph:(613)744-2001
Free: (866)9PR-INT9
Fax:(613)744-6555
Co. E-mail: info@printwell.ca
URL: http://www.printwell.ca

No. of Franchise Units: 15. **No. of Company-Owned Units:** 1. **Founded:** 2002. **Franchised:** 2005. **Description:** A unique shopping mall-based business offering onsite inkjet cartridge refills, as well as the sale of a variety of inkjet and laser toner cartridges. Printwell has award-winning designed kiosks and offers turnkey operations, as well as an extensive franchisee training program. We can save our customers money and yet maintain a quality product, with an extremely high profit level. We are a popular destination for the printing needs of local businesses and mall customers **Equity Capital Needed:** $110,000-$180,000. **Franchise Fee:** $25,000. **Training:** Provides 3 weeks training.

13247 ■ Smash Hit Subs

Orion Food Systems
2930 W Maple
Sioux Falls, SD 57101
Ph:(605)336-6961
Free: 800-648-6227
Fax:(605)336-0141

No. of Franchise Units: 1,300. **No. of Company-Owned Units:** 12. **Founded:** 1984. **Franchised:** 1986. **Description:** Sub sandwiches. **Equity Capital Needed:** $25,000. **Franchise Fee:** $4,950. **Financial Assistance:** Yes. **Training:** Yes.

ASSOCIATIONS AND OTHER ORGANIZATIONS

13248 ■ American Nursery and Landscape Association
1200 G St., NW
Ste. 800
Washington, DC 20005
Ph:(202)789-2900
Fax:(202)789-1893
Co. E-mail: cbeirne@anla.org
URL: http://www.anla.org
Contact: Robert J. Dolibois CAE, Exec. VP
Description: Vertical organization of wholesale growers; landscape firms; garden centers; mail order nurseries; suppliers. Promotes the industry and its products. Offers management and consulting services and public relations programs. Provides government representation and bank card plan for members. Maintains hall of fame. .

13249 ■ American Seed Trade Association
1701 Duke St., Ste. 675
Alexandria, VA 22314
Ph:(703)837-8140
Fax:(703)837-9365
Co. E-mail: info@amseed.org
URL: http://www.amseed.com
Contact: Kelly Keithly, Chm.
Description: Breeders, growers, assemblers, conditioners, wholesalers, and retailers of grain, grass, vegetable, flower, and other seed for planting purposes. **Publications:** *Corn and Sorghum Proceedings* (annual); *Soybean Seed Proceedings* (annual).

13250 ■ Association of Professional Landscape Designers
4305 N Sixth St., Ste. A
Harrisburg, PA 17110
Ph:(717)238-9780
Fax:(717)238-9985
Co. E-mail: admin@apld.org
URL: http://www.apld.org
Contact: Patricia St. John, Pres.
Description: Landscape design professionals, students; and interested others. Works to improve status and establish professional credentials for landscape designers. International and regional continuing education opportunities. Offers certification programs. .

13251 ■ Independent Turf and Ornamental Distributors Association
174 Crestview Dr.
Bellefonte, PA 16823-8516
Ph:(717)243-7677
Free: 877-326-5995
Fax:(814)335-2452
Co. E-mail: info@itoda.org
URL: http://www.itoda.org
Contact: Patricia E. Heuser, Exec. Dir.
Description: Wholesale suppliers of lawn and turf chemicals, fertilizers, and equipment. Represents members' interests. Conducts educational programs. Provides consulting services. Maintains speakers' bureau; compiles statistics. .

13252 ■ New York State Turf and Landscape Association
1 Prospect Ave.
White Plains, NY 10607
Ph:(914)993-9455
Fax:(914)993-9051
Co. E-mail: nystla@aol.com
URL: http://www.nystla.com
Contact: Joseph Tinelli, Pres.
Description: Landscaping and grounds keeping professionals. Promotes the landscaping industry. **Publications:** *Installation*; *Irrigation*; *Mantenimiento* (monthly).

13253 ■ North American Flowerbulb Wholesalers Association
2424 Hwy. 72/221 E
Greenwood, SC 29649
Ph:(864)229-1618
Fax:(864)229-5719
Co. E-mail: nafwa1@aol.com
URL: http://www.nafwa.com
Contact: Jack C. De Vroomen, Sec.-Treas.
Description: Wholesalers and dealers of flower bulbs and related floricultural commodities. .

REFERENCE WORKS

13254 ■ "All the Trimmings" in *Green Industry Pro* (Vol. 23, March 2011, No. 3, pp. 29)
Pub: Cygnus Business Media
Ed: Gregg Wartgow. **Description:** When choosing lawn mowing equipment, it is advised to purchase commercial-grade 21-inch walk mowers rather than less expensive consumer-grade mowers. John Deere is reentering the commercial 21-inch walk behind mower market after a five-year hiatus.

13255 ■ "Best Turnaround Stocks" in *Canadian Business* (Vol. 82, Summer 2009, No. 8, pp. 32)
Pub: Rogers Media
Ed: Calvin Leung. **Description:** Canadian companies that are believed to have the potential for the best turnaround stocks are presented. Suggested stocks include those of Migao Corporation, which is rated by most research firms as a Buy. Migao produces potash-based fertilizers for the Chinese market.

13256 ■ "Hey, You Can't Do That" in *Green Industry Pro* (Vol. 23, September 2011)
Pub: Cygnus Business Media
Ed: Rod Dickens. **Description:** Manufacturers of landscape equipment are making better use of energy resources, such as the use of fuel-injection systems instead of carburetors, lightweight materials, better lubricants, advanced battery technology, and innovative engine designs.

13257 ■ "Precision Crop Control with Valley Irrigation/CropMetrics Partnership" in *Farm Industry News* (January 6, 2011)
Pub: Penton Business Media Inc.
Description: Irrigation systems have become a precision farming tool since partnering with agronomic software systems to apply products across the field by prescription. Valley Irrigation and CropMetrics have partnered in order to variably control water, fertilizer and other crop management products through a center pivot irrigation system.

TRADE PERIODICALS

13258 ■ *Landscape Trades*
Pub: Landscape Ontario Horticultural Trades Association
Contact: Lee Ann Knudsen, Publisher
E-mail: lak@landscapeontario.com
Released: 9/yr (not published Feb., Aug., and Dec.).
Price: $43.58; $78.74 two years; $110.24 3 years.
Description: Landscape/nursery magazine.

13259 ■ *Pacific Coast Nurseryman and Garden Supply Dealer*
Pub: Cox Publishing Company Inc.
Contact: Kathleen Pyle, Managing Editor
Released: Monthly. **Price:** $30; $50 two years; $45 Canada; $45 other countries surface mail. **Description:** Business management magazine for professionals in the environmental horticulture industry.

FRANCHISES AND BUSINESS OPPORTUNITIES

13260 ■ Nite Time Decor Inc.
The Decor Group
PO Box 5183
Lubbock, TX 79408-5183
Free: (866)321-4077
Fax:(806)722-9627
No. of Franchise Units: 37. **Founded:** 1986. **Franchised:** 1999. **Description:** Landscape lighting products and services. **Equity Capital Needed:** $37,500-$74,350. **Franchise Fee:** $16,900. **Royalty Fee:** 5%. **Financial Assistance:** Assistance with franchise fee. **Training:** Includes 4 days training at headquarters and ongoing support.

13261 ■ Outdoor Lighting Perspectives Franchise, Inc.
2924 Emerywood Parkway, Ste. 101
Richmond, VA 23294
Ph:(704)841-2666
Free: 800-722-4668
Fax:(704)341-8182
Co. E-mail: tiffany@outdoorlights.com
URL: http://www.olpfranchise.com
No. of Franchise Units: 70. **No. of Company-Owned Units:** 1. **Founded:** 1995. **Franchised:** 1998. **Description:** Design and installation of landscape lighting. **Equity Capital Needed:** $69,000-$102,000. **Franchise Fee:** $49,000. **Financial Assistance:** No. **Managerial Assistance:** Access to corporate personnel at all times. **Training:** 5 days of training at corporate location and 3 days within ninety days of start-up in that city. Product & technical training at manufacturing plant shortly after start-up.

START-UP INFORMATION

13262 ■ *How to Open and Operate a Financially Successful Landscaping, Nursery or Lawn Service Business: With Companion CD-ROM*
Pub: Atlantic Publishing Company
Ed: Lynn Wasnak. **Released:** June 1, 2009. **Price:** $39.95. **Description:** Guide provides understanding of the basic concepts of starting and running a service business, focusing on the operation of a small nursery, landscaping, or lawn service or combining the three operations. It also offers tips for running the business from the home.

13263 ■ *How to Start a Home-Based Landscaping Business*
Pub: Globe Pequot Press
Ed: Owen E. Dell. **Released:** December 2005. **Price:** $18.95. **Description:** Guide to starting and running a home-based landscaping business.

13264 ■ *How to Start and Run a Home-Based Landscaping Business*
Pub: Globe Pequot Press
Ed: Owen E. Dell. **Released:** December 2005. **Price:** $18.95. **Description:** Guide to starting and running a successful home-based landscaping business, including tips for marketing on the Internet.

13265 ■ *"Some Good Earners: Preparing Prison Inmates to Start Businesses Upon Their Release" in Inc. (Vol. 31, January-February 2009, No. 1)*
Pub: Mansueto Ventures LLC
Ed: Mike Hoffman. **Description:** Prison Entrepreneurship Program (PEP) is a nonprofit organization that works with the Texas Department of Criminal Justice to teach entrepreneurship to prison inmates. Profiled is Hans Becker, owner of Armadillo Tree and Shrub in Dallas; Becker studied the PEP program while serving five years in prison and started his successful company when released.

13266 ■ *Start Your Own Lawn Care Business: Your Step-by-Step Guide to Success*
Pub: Entrepreneur Press
Ed: Eileen Figure Sandlin. **Released:** March 2007. **Price:** $17.95. **Description:** Steps for starting and running a lawn care service.

13267 ■ *Start Your Own Lawn Care or Landscaping Business*
Pub: Entrepreneur Press
Ed: Eileen Figure Sandlin. **Released:** May 2007. **Price:** $19.95 (CND). **Description:** Advice for starting a lawn care and landscaping business is given.

ASSOCIATIONS AND OTHER ORGANIZATIONS

13268 ■ **American Society of Consulting Arborists**
9707 Key W Ave., Ste. 100
Rockville, MD 20850
Ph:(301)947-0483
Fax:(301)990-9771
Co. E-mail: asca@mgmtsol.com
URL: http://www.asca-consultants.org
Contact: Alan Jones, Pres.
Description: Arboriculture professionals who possess extensive technical knowledge and experience including skills in the areas of written and oral communications, consulting ethics, expert witness activities, and practice management. Allows members to provide independent diagnoses, opinions, appraisal of value, and condition evaluation on trees for clients in the legal, insurance, and development communities as well as the general public. .

13269 ■ **American Society of Landscape Architects**
636 Eye St. NW
Washington, DC 20001-3736
Ph:(202)898-2444
Free: 888-999-ASLA
Fax:(202)898-1185
Co. E-mail: nsomerville@asla.org
URL: http://www.asla.org
Contact: Nancy C. Somerville, Exec. VP/CEO
Description: Professional society of landscape architects. Promotes the advancement of education and skill in the art of landscape architecture as an instrument in service to the public welfare. Seeks to strengthen existing and proposed university programs in landscape architecture. Offers counsel to new and emerging programs; encourages state registration of landscape architects. Sponsors annual educational exhibit. Offers placement service; conducts specialized education and research. **Publications:** *ASLA Members Handbook* (monthly); *Landscape Architecture Magazine* (monthly); *Landscape Architecture News Digest - LAND Online* (biweekly).

13270 ■ **Association of Professional Landscape Designers**
4305 N Sixth St., Ste. A
Harrisburg, PA 17110
Ph:(717)238-9780
Fax:(717)238-9985
Co. E-mail: admin@apld.org
URL: http://www.apld.org
Contact: Patricia St. John, Pres.
Description: Landscape design professionals, students; and interested others. Works to improve status and establish professional credentials for landscape designers. International and regional continuing education opportunities. Offers certification programs. .

13271 ■ **Canadian Nursery Landscape Association–Association Candienne des Pepinieristes et des Paysagistes**
RR No. 4, Sta. Main
7856 5th Line S
Milton, ON, Canada L9T 2X8
Ph:(905)875-1399
Free: 888-446-3499
Fax:(905)875-1840
Co. E-mail: info@canadanursery.com
URL: http://www.canadanursery.com
Contact: Victor Santacruz CAE, Exec. Dir.
Description: Growers, retail garden centers, lawn care and gardening services, sod growers, landscape, construction, and maintenance contractors, and other horticultural industries. Promotes expansion of the nursery and related industries. Devises standards and develops and administers tests to ensure competence in nursery production, garden supply retailing, landscape contracting, and construction and maintenance. Makes available support and services to members including discount insurance policies and merchant credit cards, educational programs, and representation before government agencies. Sponsors research; compiles statistics. **Publications:** *CNLA Newsbrief* (bimonthly); Directory (annual).

13272 ■ **Canadian Society of Landscape Architects–L'Association des architects paysagistes du Canada**
PO Box 13594
Ottawa, ON, Canada K2K 1X6
Free: (866)781-9799
Fax:(866)871-1419
Co. E-mail: info@csla.ca
URL: http://www.csla.ca
Contact: Elizabeth A. Sharpe, Interim Exec. Dir.
Description: National association of landscape architects. Represents and promotes members' interests at national and international levels; develops and supports national activities and programs implemented by members. Maintains accreditation program; makes available professional liability insurance program. **Publications:** *Landscapes/Paysages* . **Telecommunication Services:** electronic mail, paulette@csla.ca.

13273 ■ **Independent Turf and Ornamental Distributors Association**
174 Crestview Dr.
Bellefonte, PA 16823-8516
Ph:(717)243-7677
Free: 877-326-5995
Fax:(814)335-2452
Co. E-mail: info@itoda.org
URL: http://www.itoda.org
Contact: Patricia E. Heuser, Exec. Dir.
Description: Wholesale suppliers of lawn and turf chemicals, fertilizers, and equipment. Represents members' interests. Conducts educational programs. Provides consulting services. Maintains speakers' bureau; compiles statistics. .

13274 ■ **International Society of Arboriculture**
PO Box 3129
Champaign, IL 61826-3129
Ph:(217)355-9411
Free: 888-472-8733
Fax:(217)355-9516
Co. E-mail: isa@isa-arbor.com
URL: http://www.isa-arbor.com
Contact: Jim Skiera, Exec. Dir.
Description: Individuals engaged in commercial, municipal, and utility arboriculture; city, state, and national government employees; municipal and com-

mercial arborists; others interested in shade tree welfare. Disseminates information on the care and preservation of shade and ornamental trees. Supports research projects at educational institutions. **Publications:** *Arborist News* (bimonthly); *Diseases of Trees and Shrubs* .

13275 ■ Landscape Architecture Foundation
818 18th St. NW, Ste. 810
Washington, DC 20006
Ph:(202)331-7070
Fax:(202)331-7079
Co. E-mail: rfigura@lafoundation.org
URL: http://www.lafoundation.org
Contact: Barbara Deutsch, Exec. Dir.

Description: Serves as an education and research vehicle for the landscape architecture profession in the U.S. Combines the capabilities of landscape architects, interests of environmentalists, and needs of agencies and resource foundations. Provides for the preparation and dissemination of educational and scientific information through publications, exhibits, lectures, and seminars. Solicits and expends gifts, legacies, and grants. Established an endowment fund for professorships at colleges and universities. Sponsors California Landscape Architectural Student Scholarship Fund. Conducts a study of the profession to establish goals in terms of education, research needs, practice, and formulation of public policy. **Publications:** *American Landscape Report* (quarterly).

13276 ■ New York State Turf and Landscape Association
1 Prospect Ave.
White Plains, NY 10607
Ph:(914)993-9455
Fax:(914)993-9051
Co. E-mail: nystla@aol.com
URL: http://www.nystla.com
Contact: Joseph Tinelli, Pres.

Description: Landscaping and grounds keeping professionals. Promotes the landscaping industry. **Publications:** *Installation*; *Irrigation*; *Mantenimiento* (monthly).

13277 ■ North American Flowerbulb Wholesalers Association
2424 Hwy. 72/221 E
Greenwood, SC 29649
Ph:(864)229-1618
Fax:(864)229-5719
Co. E-mail: nafwa1@aol.com
URL: http://www.nafwa.com
Contact: Jack C. De Vroomen, Sec.-Treas.

Description: Wholesalers and dealers of flower bulbs and related floricultural commodities. .

13278 ■ Outdoor Power Equipment Institute
341 S Patrick St.
Alexandria, VA 22314
Ph:(703)549-7600
Fax:(703)549-7604
Co. E-mail: kreamy@opei.org
URL: http://www.opei.org
Contact: Bill Harley, Pres./CEO

Description: Manufacturers of lawn mowers, garden tractors, snow throwers, utility vehicles, chainsaws, motor tillers, shredder/grinders, edger/trimmers, leaf vacuums, log splitters, stump cutters, chippers and sprayers, and major components. Compiles statistics and forecasting information; sponsors industry trade shows; produces comprehensive consumer education materials on safety and other industry issues; hosts' annual member meeting; represents members' interests on important legislative and regulatory issues. **Publications:** *Export-Import Report* (quarterly); *SmartBrief* (weekly); *Traffic Report* (monthly);Membership Directory (annual).

13279 ■ Professional Landcare Network
950 Herndon Pkwy., Ste. 450
Herndon, VA 20170
Ph:(703)736-9666
Free: 800-395-2522
Fax:(703)736-9668
Co. E-mail: info@landcarenetwork.org
URL: http://www.landcarenetwork.org
Contact: Gerald J. Grossi, Pres.

Description: Landscape contractors. Works to represent, lead and unify the interior and exterior landscape industry by working together on a national basis; addressing environmental and legislative issues; and creating increased opportunities in business. Provides forum to encourage members' profitability, personal growth and professional advancement. **Publications:** *Landscape Contractor News* (monthly).

13280 ■ Turf and Ornamental Communicators Association
PO Box 156
New Prague, MN 56071
Ph:(952)758-6340
Fax:(952)758-5813
Co. E-mail: toca@gardnerandgardnercommunications.com
URL: http://www.toca.org
Contact: Den Gardner, Exec. Dir.

Description: Editors, writers, photographers, public relations and advertising practitioners involved in green industry communications (turf and ornamental). Promotes communications excellence within trade and consumer media. Maintains speakers' bureau. .

REFERENCE WORKS

13281 ■ "Accelerator Welcomes First Hispanic Firms" in Business Courier (Vol. 27, August 13, 2010, No. 15, pp. 1)
Pub: Business Courier

Ed: Lucy May. **Description:** The Minority Business Accelerator (MBA) initiative of the Cincinnati USA Regional Chamber in Ohio has included Hispanic-owned firms Best Upon Request and Vivian Llambi and Associates Inc. to its portfolio. Vivian Llambi and Associates is a design, landscape architecture and civil engineering specialist. Prior to these firms' membership, MBA was limited to black-owned companies.

13282 ■ "Active Sales" in Green Industry Pro (Vol. 23, September 2011)
Pub: Cygnus Business Media

Ed: Gregg Wartgow. **Description:** Craig den Hartog, owner of Emerald Magic Lawn Care located in Holtsville, New York, describes the various marketing tactics he has developed to increase sales in the current economic environment. Statistical data included.

13283 ■ "All the Trimmings" in Green Industry Pro (Vol. 23, March 2011, No. 3, pp. 29)
Pub: Cygnus Business Media

Ed: Gregg Wartgow. **Description:** When choosing lawn mowing equipment, it is advised to purchase commercial-grade 21-inch walk mowers rather than less expensive consumer-grade mowers. John Deere is reentering the commercial 21-inch walk behind mower market after a five-year hiatus.

13284 ■ American Society of Consulting Arborists—Membership Directory
Pub: American Society of Consulting Arborists
Contact: Beth W. Palys, Exec. Dir.
E-mail: bpalys@mgmtsol.com

Released: Annual, March. **Price:** Free. **Covers:** About 400 persons specializing in the growth and care of urban shade and ornamental trees; includes expert witnesses and monetary appraisals. **Entries Include:** Name, address, phone, fax. **Arrangement:** Geographical. **Indexes:** Alphabetical.

13285 ■ "Be Innovative In Other Ways" in Green Industry Pro (Vol. 23, March 2011, No. 3, pp. 4)
Pub: Cygnus Business Media

Ed: Rod Dickens. **Description:** Emphasis is put on the importance of putting the customer first in order to successfully market any product or service. Six marketing ideas are presented to promote a landscaping business.

13286 ■ "Customer Retention is Proportionate to Employee Retention" in Green Industry Pro (Vol. 23, September 2011)
Pub: Cygnus Business Media

Description: Presented in a question-answer format, information is provided to help retain customers as well as keeping workers happy.

13287 ■ "Customized Before Custom Was Cool" in Green Industry Pro (July 2011)
Pub: Cygnus Business Media

Ed: Gregg Wartgow. **Description:** Profile of Turf Care Enterprises and owner Kevin Vogeler, who discusses his desire to use more natural programs using little or no chemicals in 1986. At that time, that sector represented 20 percent of his business, today it shares 80 percent.

13288 ■ "Deep in the Heart of Drought" in Green Industry Pro (Vol. 23, October 2011)
Pub: Cygnus Business Media

Ed: Gregg Wartgow. **Description:** Challenges faced by landscape contractors during the recent drought in Texas are explored. Despite these challenges, opportunity for contractors providing irrigation services has risen.

13289 ■ "Dozens 'Come Alive' in Downtown Chicago" in Green Industry Pro (July 2011)
Pub: Cygnus Business Media

Ed: Gregg Wartgow. **Description:** Highlights from the Come Alive Outside training event held in Chicago, Illinois July 14-15, 2011 are shared. Nearly 80 people representing 38 landscape companies attended the event that helps contractors review their services and find ways to sell them in new and various ways.

13290 ■ "Finding a Way to Continue Growing" in Green Industry Pro (Vol. 23, March 2011, No. 3, pp. 31)
Pub: Cygnus Business Media

Description: Profile of Brett Lemcke, VP of R.M. Landscape located in Rochester, New York. Lemcke tells how his Landscape Industry Certified credentials helped him to grow his business and beat out his competition.

13291 ■ "Five Distinct Divisions, One Collective Focus" in Green Industry Pro (Vol. 23, October 2011)
Pub: Cygnus Business Media

Ed: Gregg Wartgow. **Description:** Profile of ACLS Inc., an amalgamation of All Commercial Landscape Service (commercial maintenance), All Custom Landscape Service (design/build), Fresno Tree Service, Certified Water Consulting (irrigation), and Tractor Service (disking and flailing services on everything from one-acre lots to hundreds of acres of open land). The firm discusses its rebranding effort in order to increase sales.

13292 ■ "Forward Motion" in Green Industry Pro (July 2011)
Pub: Cygnus Business Media

Ed: Gregg Wartgow. **Description:** Several landscape contractors have joined this publication's Working Smarter Training Challenge over the last year. This process is helping them develop ways to improve work processes, boost morale, drive out waste, reduce costs, improve customer service, and be more competitive.

13293 ■ "Gain the 'Come Alive Outside' Selling Edge" in Green Industry Pro (July 2011)
Pub: Cygnus Business Media

Ed: Jim Paluch. **Description:** Marketing the 'Come Alive Outside' slogan can help landscapers to increase their market share by identifying and applying these elements to each customer as well as their workers.

13294 ■ "The Green Industry Jobs Gap" in Green Industry Pro (Vol. 23, October 2011)
Pub: Cygnus Business Media

Ed: Gregg Wartgow. **Description:** According to the U.S. Bureau of Labor Statistics, the landscaping industry employs over 829,000 workers. According to another private study, the industry would employ more if they were able to find more people interested in performing the required work.

13295 ■ "Hey, You Can't Do That" in *Green Industry Pro* (Vol. 23, September 2011)
Pub: Cygnus Business Media

Ed: Rod Dickens. Description: Manufacturers of landscape equipment are making better use of energy resources, such as the use of fuel-injection systems instead of carburetors, lightweight materials, better lubricants, advanced battery technology, and innovative engine designs.

13296 ■ "How to Dominate in Residential Maintenance" in *Green Industry Pro* (Vol. 23, October 2011)
Pub: Cygnus Business Media

Ed: Gregg Wartgow. Description: Lawn care services were ranked among the most expendable consumer expenditures, according to the National Retail Federation data accumulated in early 2011. This makes it critical for any landscape firm to target sales efforts toward higher-income households and higher-value homes.

13297 ■ "How To Turn Your Efforts Into Results" in *Green Industry Pro* (Vol. 23, September 2011)
Pub: Cygnus Business Media

Ed: Bob Coulter. Description: Working Smarter Training Challenge teaches that leaders are able to carry out solutions directly into their organization, develop skills and drive business results in key areas by creating a culture of energized workers who are able to take ownership of their performance as well as the performance of the company as a whole.

13298 ■ "Labor of Love" in *Green Industry Pro* (Vol. 23, March 2011, No. 3, pp. 14)
Pub: Cygnus Business Media

Ed: Gregg Wartgow. Description: Profile of CLS Landscape Management in Chino, California and its owner who started the company when he was 21 years old. Kevin Davis built his landscape firm into a $20 million a year business without using any dedicated salesperson.

13299 ■ "The Price of Profitability" in *Green Industry Pro* (Vol. 23, March 2011, No. 3, pp. 18)
Pub: Cygnus Business Media

Ed: Tony Bass. Description: Profit Builder Process is used to help landscaping companies be more competitive. Landscape contractors report pricing among their largest challenges and although the economy is improving, homeowners are paying closer attention to quality and service.

13300 ■ "Rediscovering the Land of Opportunity" in *Green Industry Pro* (July 2011)
Pub: Cygnus Business Media

Ed: Gregg Wartgow. Description: Landscape contractors need to discover new strategies that will generate leads and convert those leads into sales.

13301 ■ "Take Control of Your Company's Finances" in *Green Industry Pro* (Vol. 23, March 2011, No. 3, pp. 24)
Pub: Cygnus Business Media

Ed: Gregg Wartgow. Description: Understanding that when certain leading indicators that affect the outcome of certain lagging indicators are aligned, companies will be able to take control of their firm's finances. Ways to improve the processes that drive financial performance for landscape firms are outlined.

13302 ■ "Take This Job and Love It" in *Green Industry Pro* (Vol. 23, October 2011)
Pub: Cygnus Business Media

Ed: Gregg Wartgow. Description: Details of the lawsuit filed by the Professional Landcare Network (PLANET) against the U.S. Department of Labor are explained. Challenges faced by landscape firms because of employment costs are outlined. Statistical data included.

13303 ■ "Time to Fight Back" in *Green Industry Pro* (Vol. 23, March 2011, No. 3, pp. 8)
Pub: Cygnus Business Media

Ed: Rod Dickens. Description: Lawn care operators in the United States must learn from Canada that a shift to socialism will impact their industry in a negative way. Government regulation over the application of control products regarding environmental health in Canada has been a death sentence for small lawn care businesses.

13304 ■ "Urban Tree Service" in *New Hampshire Business Review* (Vol. 33, March 25, 2011, No. 6, pp. 35)
Pub: Business Publications Inc.

Description: Urban Tree Service received the Professional Communications Award from the Tree Care Industry Association for excellence in marketing and communications.

13305 ■ "Way More Than Mowing" in *Green Industry Pro* (Vol. 23, September 2011)
Pub: Cygnus Business Media

Ed: Rod Dickens. Description: Shipp Shape Lawn Services located in Sylvester, Georgia now offers aeration, fertilizing and weed control, mulching, yard renovation, flowerbed maintenance, landscaping, as well as irrigation repairs and installation in order to diversify the business and stay competitive.

STATISTICAL SOURCES

13306 ■ *RMA Annual Statement Studies*
Pub: Robert Morris Associates (RMA)

Released: Annual. Price: $175.00 2006-07 edition, $105.00. Description: Contains composite balance sheets and income statements for more than 360 industries, including the accounting, auditing, and bookkeeping industries. Also contains five years of comparative historical data for discerning trends. Includes 16 commonly used ratios, computed for most of the size groupings for nearly every industry.

TRADE PERIODICALS

13307 ■ *Arboriculture Consultant*
Pub: American Society of Consulting Arborists
Contact: Beth W. Palys, Exec. Dir.
Released: Quarterly. Description: Contains information on trees.

13308 ■ *California Garden*
Pub: San Diego Floral Association
Released: Bimonthly. Description: Magazine on floriculture and horticulture.

13309 ■ *Country Home*
Pub: Meredith Corp.
Released: Monthly, 10/yr. Price: $4.95 newstand; $21.97 two years. Description: Magazine furnishing information on American interior design, architecture, antiques and collectibles, gardening, art, and culinary endeavor.

13310 ■ *Fairchild Tropical Garden Views*
Pub: Fairchild Tropical Botanic Garden
Ed: Susan Knorr, Editor, sknorr@excel.net. Released: Quarterly. Price: Included in membership. Description: Provides information on tropical gardening. Includes news on botanical garden and horticulture, list of classes, and a calendar of events.

13311 ■ *Fuchsia Flash*
Pub: Northwest Fuchsia Society
Ed: Ken Gronert, Editor, editor@nwfuchsia.com. Released: Monthly. Price: $12; $16, out of country. Description: Provides information for individuals who cultivate fuchsia flowers worldwide.

13312 ■ *Garden Design*
Pub: Bonnier Corp.
Contact: Bill Marken, Editor-in-Chief
Ed: Sarah Kinbar, Editor. Released: 8/yr. Price: $11.97 7 issues; $19.97 Canada 7 issues; $32.97 other countries 7 issues. Description: Magazine on garden design, featuring individual gardens, design trend stories, design history, profiles, horticulture coverage, and book reviews.

13313 ■ *Horticulture*
Pub: FW Media Inc.
Contact: Patty Craft, Publisher & Editorial Dir.
Released: 8/yr. Price: $19.95; $39.95 Canada; $39.95 other countries. Description: Magazine for the amateur gardener.

13314 ■ *LAND*
Pub: American Society of Landscape Architects
Ed: Susan Hines, Editor, shines@asla.org. Released: Biweekly, 26 issues/year. Price: Included in membership. Description: Carries news and monitors developments in landscape architecture, environmental design, and related fields. Focuses on public policy, education, and other areas affecting landscape architecture.

13315 ■ *Landscape Architect and Specifier News*
Pub: Landscape Communications Inc.
Contact: Stephen Kelly, Sen. Ed.
E-mail: skelly@landscapeonline.com
Released: Monthly. Description: Trade magazine covering landscape architecture and planning for professionals.

13316 ■ *Landscape Architecture*
Pub: American Society of Landscape Architects
Contact: Lisa Schultz, Assoc. Ed.
E-mail: lschultz@asla.org
Ed: Bradford McKee, Editor, bmckee@asla.org. Released: Monthly. Price: $59 nonmembers; $99 nonmembers international; $75 institutions library; $125 institutions library, international; $50 students; $70 students, other countries. Description: Professional magazine covering land planning and design.

13317 ■ *The Landscape Contractor*
Pub: Illinois Landscape Contractor Association
Contact: Rick Reuland, Publisher
Released: Monthly. Price: $75; $150 out of state. Description: Magazine for the landscape trade.

13318 ■ *Landscape Journal*
Pub: University of Wisconsin Press
Contact: Arnold Alanen, Consulting Ed.
Ed: Lance Neckar, Editor. Released: 2/yr. Price: $225 institutions and libraries; print & online; $198 institutions and libraries; online; $72 print & online; $65 online only. Description: Scholarly journal covering research, investigation, and technical information on landscape architecture.

13319 ■ *Landscape Management*
Pub: Questex Media Group
Contact: Ron Hall, Editor-in-Chief
E-mail: rhall@questex.com
Released: 12/yr. Price: $46 domestic; $69 Canada and Mexico; $89 other countries. Description: Magazine for professionals in landscape, grounds management and lawn care, construction, and maintenance.

13320 ■ *Landscape Trades*
Pub: Landscape Ontario Horticultural Trades Association
Contact: Lee Ann Knudsen, Publisher
E-mail: lak@landscapeontario.com
Released: 9/yr (not published Feb., Aug., and Dec.). Price: $43.58; $78.74 two years; $110.24 3 years. Description: Landscape/nursery magazine.

13321 ■ *Lawn & Landscape Magazine*
Pub: G.I.E. Media, MC
Contact: Kevin Gilbride, Publisher
E-mail: kgilbride@gie.net
Ed: Chuck Bowen, Editor, cbowen@gie.net. Released: Monthly. Price: $15 U.S., Canada, and Mexico; $35; $100 other countries South America/Europe. Description: Business management magazine for lawn and landscape contracting professionals.

13322 ■ *Pro*
Pub: Cygnus Business Media
Contact: Rick A. Monogue, Publisher
E-mail: rick.monogue@cygnuspub.com
Released: 9/yr. Description: Magazine for landscape service firms.

13323 ■ *Tree City USA Bulletin*
Pub: National Arbor Day Foundation
Contact: John E. Rosenow, Publisher
Ed: James R. Fazio, Editor. **Released:** Bimonthly.
Price: $3, single issue; $15 membership subscription. **Description:** Provides tree planting and care instructions and information.

13324 ■ *Virginia Native Plant Society Bulletin*
Pub: Virginia Native Plant Society
Ed: Nancy Sorrells, Editor, lotswife@adelphia.net.
Released: 5/year. **Price:** $30, Included in membership. **Description:** Examines the native plants of Virginia and their habitats and provides information on botany.

VIDEOCASSETTES/ AUDIOCASSETTES

13325 ■ *Garden Pond Basics*
Karol Media
Hanover Industrial Estates
375 Stewart Rd.
PO Box 7600
Wilkes Barre, PA 18773-7600
Ph:(570)822-8899
Free: 800-526-4773
Co. E-mail: sales@karolmedia.com
URL: http://www.karolmedia.com
Released: 1997. **Price:** $14.95. **Description:** Provides instruction on care and maintenance of garden ponds. **Availability:** VHS.

13326 ■ *Groundskeeping Series*
AMS Distributors, Inc.
PO Box 658
Lady Lake, FL 32158
Free: 800-424-3464
Fax:(352)750-5635
Co. E-mail: orders@vpats.com
URL: http://www.vpats.com
Released: 1986. **Description:** A series of instruction on the art of industrial groundskeeping. **Availability:** VHS; 3/4U.

13327 ■ *Landscape Equipment Safety for the 90s*
American Nurseryman Publishing Co.
Book Dept.
223 W. Jackson Blvd., Ste. 500
Chicago, IL 60606
Ph:(312)427-7339
Free: 800-422-7147
Fax:(312)427-7346
Co. E-mail: books@amerinursery.com
URL: http://www.amerinursery.com
Released: 1991. **Price:** $64.99. **Description:** Series of programs updating OSHA information and federal regulations for landscape equipment use. **Availability:** VHS.

13328 ■ *Landscape Tools: Use and Safety*
American Nurseryman Publishing Co.
Book Dept.
223 W. Jackson Blvd., Ste. 500
Chicago, IL 60606
Ph:(312)427-7339
Free: 800-422-7147
Fax:(312)427-7346
Co. E-mail: books@amerinursery.com
URL: http://www.amerinursery.com
Released: 1989. **Price:** $94.99. **Description:** Demonstrates the proper use of 12 landscape tools, emphasizing safety rules. **Availability:** VHS.

13329 ■ *Lawns*
Emergency Training
PO Box 13896
Emory University
Dobbs University Center - 5th Floor
Fairlawn, OH 44334
Ph:(404)727-3853
Fax:(404)727-5667
Released: 1987. **Price:** $19.95. **Description:** A total guide to lawn care, from seeding to watering and everything in between. **Availability:** VHS.

13330 ■ *Master Gardener Series*
RMI Media
1365 N. Winchester St.
Olathe, KS 66061-5880
Ph:(913)768-1696
Free: 800-745-5480
Fax:800-755-6910
Co. E-mail: actmedia@act.org
URL: http://www.actmedia.com
Released: 1987. **Description:** Provides information on gardening and landscaping. **Availability:** VHS; 3/4U.

TRADE SHOWS AND CONVENTIONS

13331 ■ **American Society of Landscape Architects Annual Meeting and Expo**
American Society of Landscape Architects
636 Eye St. NW
Washington, DC 20001-3736
Ph:(202)898-2444
Free: 800-999-2752
Fax:(202)898-1185
Co. E-mail: info@asla.org
URL: http://www.asla.org
Released: Annual. **Audience:** Landscape architects and trade professionals. **Principal Exhibits:** Irrigation supplies, outdoor lighting, park and playground equipment, paving and ground cover, street and park furniture, landscape maintenance equipment, computer hardware and software, architectural finishing materials, construction materials, historic preservation services, surveying and mapping equipment, and related equipment, supplies, and services. **Dates and Locations:** 2011 Oct 30 - Nov 02, San Diego, CA; 2012 Sep 28 - Oct 01, Phoenix, AZ.

13332 ■ **International Conference on Oral and Maxillofacial Surgery**
Kenes International
Rue de Chantepoulet 1-3
PO Box 1726
CH-1211 Geneva, Switzerland
Ph:41 22 9080488
Fax:41 22 9069140
Co. E-mail: kenesinternational@kenes.com
URL: http://www.kenes.com
Released: Biennial. **Audience:** Medical professionals. **Principal Exhibits:** Oral and maxillofacial surgery, including diseases, injuries, and defects.

13333 ■ **International Society of Arboriculture Annual Conference and Industrial Trade Show**
International Society of Arboriculture
PO Box 3129
Champaign, IL 61826
Ph:(217)355-9411
Fax:(217)355-9516
Co. E-mail: isa@isa-arbor.com
URL: http://www.isa-arbor.com
Released: Annual. **Audience:** Arborists. **Principal Exhibits:** Chippers, bucket trucks, chain saws, hand tools, computer software and hardware, consulting services, and tree and lawn care products.

CONSULTANTS

13334 ■ **Boone's Landscaping Nursery Corp.**
736 Grathwol Dr.
Wilmington, NC 28405-1241
Ph:(281)684-7037
Co. E-mail: boone@booneslandscaping.com
URL: http://www.booneslandscaping.com
Contact: Kay C. Boone, Vice President
Scope: Offers landscaping consultation with particular expertise in land scaping design. Additional expertise available in nursery design, development, and maintenance, water gardening and aquatic plants, and bonsai gardens. Licensed landscape contractor.

13335 ■ **Erin Services Inc.**
111 Travelers Way
PO Box 1048
Saint Simons Island, GA 31522-5632
Ph:(912)638-9916
Free: 800-862-5361
Fax:(912)638-5701
Co. E-mail: dennisd@ns.technonet.com
Contact: Dennis J. Donnelly III, President
E-mail: dennis179@yahoo.com
Scope: Offers assistance in technical proposal production, marketing, and research. Industries served: Food service, janitorial, landscaping, hospitality and lodging, parks, and recreational.

13336 ■ **Forman & Biller Tree Expert Co.**
856 N Harrison St.
Arlington, VA 22205
Ph:(703)522-3141
Contact: James E. Biller, Owner
Scope: Consulting arbores providing tree care for residential and commercial properties.

13337 ■ **Jobs In Horticulture Inc.**
57 Rosedown Blvd.
PO Box 521731
Debary, FL 32713-4115
Ph:(386)753-0996
Free: 800-428-2474
Fax:(386)753-0997
Co. E-mail: info@hortjobs.com
URL: http://www.hortjobs.com
Contact: Joan Ferrell, Principal
E-mail: joan@hortjobs.com
Scope: Career consulting and career services with emphasis on horticulture.

13338 ■ **Richard L. Baldwin, Horticultural Consultant**
215 Virginia Dr.
Ventura, CA 93003
Ph:(805)643-8406
Scope: Provides diagnosis of plant disorders and management, construction and maintenance recommendations for horticulture, including playing fields. Also offers arboriculture consultation, including hazardous conditions, evaluation of loss, and related landscape research. Services include consultation on production of ornamental plants, including turf grass and management of landscape plants. **Seminars:** Pruning Fruit Trees; Propagation of Fruit Trees; Diagnosing Plant Disorders; Pest Control on Ornamental Plants; Turf grass Fertilization.

13339 ■ **Western Arborists Inc.**
502 W Rte. 66, Ste. 20
Glendora, CA 91740-4370
Ph:(626)963-1171
Fax:(626)963-8243
Contact: James W. Walker, President
E-mail: sharon.juliussen@verizon.net
Scope: Offers consulting on tree disease and insect problems. Also provides appraisal services covering damage or value of trees lost.

FRANCHISES AND BUSINESS OPPORTUNITIES

13340 ■ **Birthflowers.com, Inc.**
161 Swint Ave.
Milledgeville, GA 31061
Ph:(478)452-0008
No. of Franchise Units: 1. **No. of Company-Owned Units:** 1. **Founded:** 1995. **Franchised:** 2005. **Description:** Landscaping and design. **Equity Capital Needed:** $4,000. **Franchise Fee:** $7,000. **Financial Assistance:** Yes. **Training:** Yes.

13341 ■ **Clintar Groundskeeping Services**
Truserve Groundcare Inc.
70 Esna Park Dr., Unit 1
Markham, ON, Canada L3R 1E3
Ph:(905)943-9530
Free: 800-361-3542

Fax:(905)943-9529
Co. E-mail: info@clintar.com
URL: http://www.clintar.com
No. of Franchise Units: 21. **Founded:** 1973. **Franchised:** 1984. **Description:** Grounds keeping services including landscape maintenance, snow and ice control, power sweeping, light construction, tree care and irrigation maintenance. **Equity Capital Needed:** $100,000-$125,000; $50,000-$60,000 cash. **Franchise Fee:** $40,000. **Financial Assistance:** No. **Training:** Yes.

13342 ■ The Gardener
300 John St., Unit 329
Thornhill, ON, Canada L3T 5W4
Ph:(905)889-1532
Free: 800-970-6947
Fax:(905)889-3265
Co. E-mail: info@the-gardener.com
URL: http://www.thegardener.ca
No. of Franchise Units: 32. **Founded:** 1994. **Franchised:** 1994. **Description:** The company franchises residential landscape maintenance and snow removal services. **Equity Capital Needed:** $50,000. **Franchise Fee:** $25,000. **Financial Assistance:** Yes. **Training:** Comprehensive and ongoing support.

13343 ■ IntelliTurf
PO Box 8685
Atlanta, GA 31106
Free: 800-429-2971
Fax:(859)201-1164
Co. E-mail: franchise@intelliturf.com
URL: http://www.IntelliTurf.com
No. of Company-Owned Units: 1. **Founded:** 1997. **Franchised: Description:** Design & installation of custom, synthetic golf surfaces that look, play & feel like natural grass. The applications include, swimming pools, outdoor courts, croquet fields, soccer fields, and indoor putting surfaces. **Equity Capital Needed:** $60,000. **Franchise Fee:** $32,000. **Financial Assistance:** No. **Training:** Offers initial training at corporate headquarters in Atlanta and at franchisee's location.

13344 ■ Nite Time Decor Inc.
The Decor Group
PO Box 5183
Lubbock, TX 79408-5183
Free: (866)321-4077
Fax:(806)722-9627
No. of Franchise Units: 37. **Founded:** 1986. **Franchised:** 1999. **Description:** Landscape lighting products and services. **Equity Capital Needed:** $37,500-$74,350. **Franchise Fee:** $16,900. **Royalty Fee:** 5%. **Financial Assistance:** Assistance with franchise fee. **Training:** Includes 4 days training at headquarters and ongoing support.

13345 ■ Professional Polish, Inc
Professional Polish, Inc.
5450 E Loop 820 S
Ft. Worth, TX 76119
Ph:(817)572-7353
Free: 800-5610-6193
Fax:(817)561-6193
No. of Franchise Units: 28. **No. of Company-Owned Units:** 1. **Founded:** 1981. **Franchised:** 1986. **Description:** Janitorial, lawn, landscape and light building maintenance service at the local level. **Equity Capital Needed:** $10,000$150,000. **Franchise Fee:** $4,500-$50,000. **Financial Assistance:** Yes. **Training:** Yes.

13346 ■ Sunshine Grounds Care
22 Coles Cres
Orangeville, ON, Canada L9W 2Z2
Ph:(647)338-9435
Free: 800-361-5296
Fax:800-909-9515
Co. E-mail: info@sunshinebrands.ca
URL: http://www.sunshinegroundscare.com
No. of Franchise Units: 17. **No. of Company-Owned Units:** 1. **Founded:** 1987. **Franchised:** 2004. **Description:** Commercial and residential property maintenance and landscape design and construction. **Equity Capital Needed:** $76,000-$96,000. **Franchise Fee:** $19,000. **Training:** Provides 1 week initial training and ongoing.

13347 ■ Tuff Turf Inc.
6822 W Grovers Ave.
Glendale, AZ 85308
Ph:(602)290-0499
Free: (866)431-2468
Fax:(602)548-5567
No. of Franchise Units: 6. **Founded:** 1998. **Franchised:** 2002. **Description:** Selling and installing synthetic turf. **Equity Capital Needed:** $35,900-$65,100. **Franchise Fee:** $19,500. **Financial Assistance:** Yes. **Training:** Yes.

COMPUTER SYSTEMS/ SOFTWARE

13348 ■ Advance Grower Solutions–Nursery/ Greenhouse Accounting Software
Doane Agricultural Services Co.
4900 SW Griffith Dr., Ste. 248
Beaverton, OR 97005
Ph:(503)646-5581
Free: 800-367-7082
Fax:(503)646-0622
URL: http://www.advgrower.com/
Price: Prices vary depending on modules needed. **Description:** Available for IBM computers and compatibles. System provides accounting and report capabilities for nursery and landscaping businesses.

LIBRARIES

13349 ■ American Horticultural Society Library
7931 E. Boulevard Dr.
Alexandria, VA 22308
Ph:(703)768-5700
Free: 800-777-7931
Fax:(703)768-8700
Co. E-mail: tunderwood@ahs.org
URL: http://www.ahs.org/
Contact: Tom Underwood, Exec.Off.
Scope: Horticulture. **Services:** Library open to the public by appointment. **Holdings:** 5000 books.

13350 ■ American Society of Landscape Architects–Professional Practice Library
636 Eye St., NW
Washington, DC 20001-3736
Ph:(202)216-2354
Fax:(202)898-1185
Co. E-mail: mkoenig@asla.org
URL: http://www.asla.org/LibraryAndResearchServices.aspx
Contact: Marlene Koenig, Libn.
Scope: Landscape architecture, landscape design, sustainable design, urban planning and development, land use and design, land planning, the environment, gardens, historic preservation. **Services:** Interlibrary loan; Library open to the public by appointment. **Holdings:** 2000 books; 1000 non-book items. **Subscriptions:** 130 journals and other serials.

13351 ■ The Arboretum at Flagstaff–Transition Zone Horticultural Institute Library
4001 S. Woody Mountain Rd.
Flagstaff, AZ 86001-8775
Ph:(928)774-1442
Fax:(928)774-1441
Co. E-mail: steve.yoder@nau.edu
URL: http://www.thearb.org
Contact: Steve Yoder, Exec.Dir.
Scope: Horticulture, forestry, botany, ecology, Colorado Plateau, environmental education, nonprofit management. **Services:** Library open to arboretum members and researchers by appointment for reference use only. **Holdings:** 3000 books, 3000 images. **Subscriptions:** 5 journals and other serials.

13352 ■ Birmingham Botanical Gardens Library
2612 Lane Park Rd.
Birmingham, AL 35223
Ph:(205)414-3920

Fax:(205)414-3922
Co. E-mail: hopel@bham.lib.al.us
URL: http://www.bbgardens.org/library.php
Contact: Hope Long, Lib.Dir.
Scope: Horticulture, botany, floriculture, gardens and gardening, landscaping, flower arranging and children's books, organic gardening, insects, animals, nature crafts. **Services:** Copying; printing (black and white, color); faxing; Library open to the public. **Holdings:** 7000 circulating books; 870 reference books; 450 children's books; 100 CD-ROMs; DVDs. **Subscriptions:** 60 journals and other serials.

13353 ■ Carol R. Johnson & Associates, Inc. Library
115 Broad St.
Boston, MA 02110-3032
Ph:(617)896-2500
Fax:(617)896-2340
Co. E-mail: info@crja.com
URL: http://www.crja.com
Contact: Jane Lewis, Libn.
Scope: Landscape architecture, horticulture, parks and recreation, design. **Services:** Copying; Library open to the public by appointment. **Holdings:** 2000 books; technical data; product literature; reports. **Subscriptions:** 170 journals and other serials.

13354 ■ Chicago Park District–Garfield Park Conservatory
300 N. Central Park Ave.
Chicago, IL 60624-1945
Ph:(312)746-5100
Fax:(773)638-1777
URL: http://www.garfield-conservatory.org/
Contact: Mary Eysenbach, Dir.
Scope: Horticulture. **Services:** Library not open to the public. **Holdings:** 600 books. **Subscriptions:** 2 journals and other serials.

13355 ■ Cleveland Botanical Garden–Eleanor Squire Library
11030 East Blvd.
Cleveland, OH 44106
Ph:(216)707-2812
Fax:(216)721-2056
Co. E-mail: info@cbgarden.org
URL: http://www.cbgarden.org/Learn/Library.html
Contact: Gary Esmonde, Libn.
Scope: Gardening, horticulture, landscape architecture, herbs, flower arranging, botany. **Services:** Library open to the public with paid admission (members may borrow); rare books open to the public by appointment for review, research, and study. **Holdings:** 17,000 books; seed and nursery catalogs; slides; botanical prints; 1000 rare books. **Subscriptions:** 50 journals and other serials.

13356 ■ Georgia State Botanical Garden of Georgia Library
Callaway Bldg.
University of Georgia
2450 S. Milledge Ave.
Athens, GA 30605
Ph:(706)542-1244
Fax:(706)542-3091
Co. E-mail: garden@uga.edu
URL: http://www.uga.edu/botgarden/faccallaway.html
Contact: Karen Kulp, Libn.
Scope: Plants, gardening, horticulture, botany, conservation, ethnobotany, landscape design, floral crafts. **Services:** Library open to the public for reference use only. **Holdings:** 2000 books; 85 videotapes; CD-ROMs; archives; manuscripts. **Subscriptions:** 14 journals and other serials.

13357 ■ Horticultural Society of New York Library
148 W. 37th St., 13th Fl.
New York, NY 10018-6976
Ph:(212)757-0915, x102

Fax:(212)246-1207
Co. E-mail: kpowis@hsny.org
URL: http://www.hsny.org
Contact: Katherine Powis, Libn.
Scope: Gardening; garden design and garden history; horticulture; landscape design; botanical illustration; flower arrangement. **Services:** Library open to the public for reference use only. **Holdings:** 6000 books; 3500 bound periodical volumes; 75 lin.ft. of institutional archives. **Subscriptions:** 120 journals and other serials.

13358 ■ Morton Arboretum–Sterling Morton Library
4100 Illinois Rte. 53
Lisle, IL 60532-1293
Ph:(630)968-0074
Fax:(630)719-7950
Co. E-mail: library@mortonarb.org
URL: http://www.mortonarb.org/sterling-morton-library.html
Contact: Michael Stieber, Lib.Adm.
Scope: Botany, horticulture, dendrology, botanical art and illustration, arboriculture, landscape architecture, natural history, ecology and the environment. **Services:** Interlibrary loan; copying; SDI; Library open to the public. **Holdings:** 28,000 volumes; 1000 nursery and seed catalogs. **Subscriptions:** 800 journals and other serials.

13359 ■ Ontario Association of Landscape Architects Library
3rd Church St., Ste. 4017
Toronto, ON, Canada M5E 1M2
Ph:(416)231-4181
Fax:(416)231-2679
Co. E-mail: info@oala.ca
URL: http://www.oala.ca
Contact: Ronda Kellington, Adm.
Scope: Landscape architecture. **Services:** Library open to OALA members and interns only. **Holdings:** 250 books; 50 serials; 100 reports; archives; videos and audio tapes. **Subscriptions:** 12 journals and other serials.

13360 ■ U.S. National Arboretum Library
3501 New York Ave., NE
Washington, DC 20002-1958
Ph:(202)245-2726
Fax:(202)245-4575
Co. E-mail: everlyr@ars.usda.gov
URL: http://www.usna.usda.gov/
Contact: Robin Everly, Lib.
Scope: Botany, taxonomy, floristics, horticulture, gardening, plant genetics and breeding. **Services:** Interlibrary loan (through National Agricultural Library only); Library open to the public by appointment for onsite research only. **Holdings:** 10,000 books; 500 periodical titles. **Subscriptions:** 165 journals and other serials.

13361 ■ U.S. National Park Service–Blue Ridge Parkway–Archives (199 H)
199 Hemphill Knob Rd.
Asheville, NC 28803-8686
Ph:(828)271-4779

Fax:(828)271-4313
Co. E-mail: jackie_holt@nps.gov
URL: http://www.nps.gov/blri
Contact: Jackie Holt, Cur.
Scope: Blue Ridge Parkway - history, development, design, construction, landscape, resource management. **Services:** Archives open to researchers by appointment only. **Holdings:** 350,000 archives.

13362 ■ University of Alberta–Devonian Botanic Garden Library
Edmonton, AB, Canada T6G 2E1
Ph:(770)987-3054, x2240
Fax:(780)987-4141
Co. E-mail: rbelland@ualberta.ca
URL: http://www.devonian.ualberta.ca
Contact: Rene Belland, Cur.
Scope: Horticulture, botany, gardening, landscape design, natural history, plant diversity, conservation. **Services:** Library open to the public with restrictions. **Holdings:** 1000 books; reports; manuscripts; archives. **Subscriptions:** 6 journals and other serials.

13363 ■ University of Nevada, Las Vegas–Architecture Studies Library
Box 454049
4505 Maryland Pkwy.
Las Vegas, NV 89154-4049
Ph:(702)895-1959
Fax:(702)895-1975
Co. E-mail: jeanne.brown@unlv.edu
URL: http://www.library.unlv.edu/arch/index.html
Contact: Jeanne M. Brown, Hd., Arch.Stud.
Scope: Architecture - history, design, theory, and criticism; landscape architecture; interior design; construction; urban planning. **Services:** Interlibrary loan; copying; scanners; Library open to the public. **Holdings:** 25,000 volumes; 600 videos/DVDs; archives; microfiche and microfilm. **Subscriptions:** 150 journals and other serials.

RESEARCH CENTERS

13364 ■ Landscape Architecture Foundation
818 18th St. NW, Ste. 810
Washington, DC 20006
Ph:(202)331-7070
Fax:(202)331-7079
Co. E-mail: bdeutsch@lafoundation.org
URL: http://www.lafoundation.org
Contact: Barbara Deutsch, Exec.Dir.
E-mail: bdeutsch@lafoundation.org
Scope: Landscape planning, land use planning and design, environmental planning, landscape change, landscape intervention, place-based land use planning, public participation processes. **Publications:** American Landscape Report (quarterly); Land & Community Design Case Study Series (quarterly). **Educational Activities:** Conferences; Seminars, workshops.

13365 ■ The Nature Conservancy in Maine
14 Maine St., Ste. 401
Brunswick, ME 04011
Ph:(207)729-5181

Fax:(207)729-4118
Co. E-mail: naturemaine@tnc.org
URL: http://www.nature.org/ourinitiatives/regions/northamerica/unitedstates/maine
Contact: Mike Tetreault, Exec.Dir.
E-mail: naturemaine@tnc.org
Scope: Impact of threats on natural communities with intention of abating threats and adapting to climate changes; identifies rare plants and animals and the lands where they live; works with private and public landowners who voluntarily protect terrestrial, freshwater and marine resources; acquires conservation easements or management agreements which protect habitats, and purchases lands; manages and conserves privately-owned nature preserves; applies market-based solutions and encourages collaborative problem-solving.

13366 ■ University of Guelph–Arboretum
Guelph, ON, Canada N1G 2W1
Ph:(519)824-4120
Fax:(519)763-9598
Co. E-mail: awatson@uoguelph.ca
URL: http://www.uoguelph.ca/arboretum
Contact: Prof. Alan P. Watson, Dir.
E-mail: awatson@uoguelph.ca
Scope: Botany, fine arts, horticulture, landscape architecture, nature interpretation, ecology, and zoology. **Services:** Annual one day plant sale; Nature Interpretation Programs. **Publications:** The Green Web; A Life Zone Approach to School Yard Naturalization; Ontario Tree Atlas; Seasonal Program. **Educational Activities:** Horticultural and zoological adult programs; Special events and conservation-related symposia.

13367 ■ University of Pennsylvania–Morris Arboretum
100 E Northwestern Ave.
Philadelphia, PA 19118
Ph:(215)247-5777
Fax:(215)248-4439
Co. E-mail: info@morrisarboretum.org
URL: http://www.business-services.upenn.edu/arboretum
Contact: Paul W. Meyer, Dir.
E-mail: info@morrisarboretum.org
Scope: Taxonomy, pests and diseases of woody plants, history of landscape architecture, and flora of Pennsylvania, including exploration and introduction of plants from Asia, integrated pest management for ornamental plants, field studies of rare and endangered species. **Services:** Plant clinic. **Publications:** Annual report; Morris Arboretum Newsletter (quarterly). **Educational Activities:** Adult Education Courses, in horticulture and botany and opportunities for graduate research in taxonomy, phytopathology, and landscape architecture on a 166-acre tract with a living collection of 13,000 plants representing 2,500 taxa; Community Service Program; Development Courses, for arborists; Internships; Teacher Training, for Philadelphia and suburban teachers; Workshops and Symposia.

Lawn Maintenance Service

START-UP INFORMATION

13368 ▪ *How to Open and Operate a Financially Successful Landscaping, Nursery or Lawn Service Business: With Companion CD-ROM*
Pub: Atlantic Publishing Company
Ed: Lynn Wasnak. **Released:** June 1, 2009. **Price:** $39.95. **Description:** Guide provides understanding of the basic concepts of starting and running a service business, focusing on the operation of a small nursery, landscaping, or lawn service or combining the three operations. It also offers tips for running the business from the home.

13369 ▪ *Start Your Own Lawn Care or Landscaping Business*
Pub: Entrepreneur Press
Ed: Eileen Figure Sandlin. **Released:** May 2007. **Price:** $19.95 (CND). **Description:** Advice for starting a lawn care and landscaping business is given.

ASSOCIATIONS AND OTHER ORGANIZATIONS

13370 ▪ **Outdoor Power Equipment Institute**
341 S Patrick St.
Alexandria, VA 22314
Ph:(703)549-7600
Fax:(703)549-7604
Co. E-mail: kreamy@opei.org
URL: http://www.opei.org
Contact: Bill Harley, Pres./CEO
Description: Manufacturers of lawn mowers, garden tractors, snow throwers, utility vehicles, chainsaws, motor tillers, shredder/grinders, edger/trimmers, leaf vacuums, log splitters, stump cutters, chippers and sprayers, and major components. Compiles statistics and forecasting information; sponsors industry trade shows; produces comprehensive consumer education materials on safety and other industry issues; hosts' annual member meeting; represents members' interests on important legislative and regulatory issues. **Publications:** *Export-Import Report* (quarterly); *SmartBrief* (weekly); *Traffic Report* (monthly);Membership Directory (annual).

REFERENCE WORKS

13371 ▪ **"Active Sales"** in *Green Industry Pro* (Vol. 23, September 2011)
Pub: Cygnus Business Media
Ed: Gregg Wartgow. **Description:** Craig den Hartog, owner of Emerald Magic Lawn Care located in Holtsville, New York, describes the various marketing tactics he has developed to increase sales in the current economic environment. Statistical data included.

13372 ▪ **"All the Trimmings"** in *Green Industry Pro* (Vol. 23, March 2011, No. 3, pp. 29)
Pub: Cygnus Business Media
Ed: Gregg Wartgow. **Description:** When choosing lawn mowing equipment, it is advised to purchase commercial-grade 21-inch walk mowers rather than less expensive consumer-grade mowers. John Deere is reentering the commercial 21-inch walk behind mower market after a five-year hiatus.

13373 ▪ **"Be Innovative In Other Ways"** in *Green Industry Pro* (Vol. 23, March 2011, No. 3, pp. 4)
Pub: Cygnus Business Media
Ed: Rod Dickens. **Description:** Emphasis is put on the importance of putting the customer first in order to successfully market any product or service. Six marketing ideas are presented to promote a landscaping business.

13374 ▪ **"Customer Retention is Proportionate to Employee Retention"** in *Green Industry Pro* (Vol. 23, September 2011)
Pub: Cygnus Business Media
Description: Presented in a question-answer format, information is provided to help retain customers as well as keeping workers happy.

13375 ▪ **"Customized Before Custom Was Cool"** in *Green Industry Pro* (July 2011)
Pub: Cygnus Business Media
Ed: Gregg Wartgow. **Description:** Profile of Turf Care Enterprises and owner Kevin Vogeler, who discusses his desire to use more natural programs using little or no chemicals in 1986. At that time, that sector represented 20 percent of his business, today it shares 80 percent.

13376 ▪ **"Deep in the Heart of Drought"** in *Green Industry Pro* (Vol. 23, October 2011)
Pub: Cygnus Business Media
Ed: Gregg Wartgow. **Description:** Challenges faced by landscape contractors during the recent drought in Texas are explored. Despite these challenges, opportunity for contractors providing irrigation services has risen.

13377 ▪ **"Dozens 'Come Alive' in Downtown Chicago"** in *Green Industry Pro* (July 2011)
Pub: Cygnus Business Media
Ed: Gregg Wartgow. **Description:** Highlights from the Come Alive Outside training event held in Chicago, Illinois July 14-15, 2011 are shared. Nearly 80 people representing 38 landscape companies attended the event that helps contractors review their services and find ways to sell them in new and various ways.

13378 ▪ **"Finding a Way to Continue Growing"** in *Green Industry Pro* (Vol. 23, March 2011, No. 3, pp. 31)
Pub: Cygnus Business Media
Description: Profile of Brett Lemcke, VP of R.M. Landscape located in Rochester, New York. Lemcke tells how his Landscape Industry Certified credentials helped him to grow his business and beat out his competition.

13379 ▪ **"Five Distinct Divisions, One Collective Focus"** in *Green Industry Pro* (Vol. 23, October 2011)
Pub: Cygnus Business Media
Ed: Gregg Wartgow. **Description:** Profile of ACLS Inc., an amalgamation of All Commercial Landscape Service (commercial maintenance), All Custom Landscape Service (design/build), Fresno Tree Service, Certified Water Consulting (irrigation), and Tractor Service (disking and flailing services on everything from one-acre lots to hundreds of acres of open land). The firm discusses its rebranding effort in order to increase sales.

13380 ▪ **"Forward Motion"** in *Green Industry Pro* (July 2011)
Pub: Cygnus Business Media
Ed: Gregg Wartgow. **Description:** Several landscape contractors have joined this publication's Working Smarter Training Challenge over the last year. This process is helping them develop ways to improve work processes, boost morale, drive out waste, reduce costs, improve customer service, and be more competitive.

13381 ▪ **"Gain the 'Come Alive Outside' Selling Edge"** in *Green Industry Pro* (July 2011)
Pub: Cygnus Business Media
Ed: Jim Paluch. **Description:** Marketing the 'Come Alive Outside' slogan can help landscapers to increase their market share by identifying and applying these elements to each customer as well as their workers.

13382 ▪ **"The Green Industry Jobs Gap"** in *Green Industry Pro* (Vol. 23, October 2011)
Pub: Cygnus Business Media
Ed: Gregg Wartgow. **Description:** According to the U.S. Bureau of Labor Statistics, the landscaping industry employs over 829,000 workers. According to another private study, the industry would employ more if they were able to find more people interested in performing the required work.

13383 ▪ **"Hey, You Can't Do That"** in *Green Industry Pro* (Vol. 23, September 2011)
Pub: Cygnus Business Media
Ed: Rod Dickens. **Description:** Manufacturers of landscape equipment are making better use of energy resources, such as the use of fuel-injection systems instead of carburetors, lightweight materials, better lubricants, advanced battery technology, and innovative engine designs.

13384 ▪ **"How to Dominate in Residential Maintenance"** in *Green Industry Pro* (Vol. 23, October 2011)
Pub: Cygnus Business Media
Ed: Gregg Wartgow. **Description:** Lawn care services were ranked among the most expendable consumer expenditures, according to the National Retail Federation data accumulated in early 2011. This makes it critical for any landscape firm to target sales efforts toward higher-income households and higher-value homes.

13385 ▪ **"How To Turn Your Efforts Into Results"** in *Green Industry Pro* (Vol. 23, September 2011)
Pub: Cygnus Business Media
Ed: Bob Coulter. **Description:** Working Smarter Training Challenge teaches that leaders are able to carry out solutions directly into their organization,

develop skills and drive business results in key areas by creating a culture of energized workers who are able to take ownership of their performance as well as the performance of the company as a whole.

13386 ■ "Labor of Love" in *Green Industry Pro* **(Vol. 23, March 2011, No. 3, pp. 14)**
Pub: Cygnus Business Media
Ed: Gregg Wartgow. **Description:** Profile of CLS Landscape Management in Chino, California and its owner who started the company when he was 21 years old. Kevin Davis built his landscape firm into a $20 million a year business without using any dedicated salesperson.

13387 ■ "The Price of Profitability" in *Green Industry Pro* **(Vol. 23, March 2011, No. 3, pp. 18)**
Pub: Cygnus Business Media
Ed: Tony Bass. **Description:** Profit Builder Process is used to help landscaping companies be more competitive. Landscape contractors report pricing among their largest challenges and although the economy is improving, homeowners are paying closer attention to quality and service.

13388 ■ "Rediscovering the Land of Opportunity" in *Green Industry Pro* **(July 2011)**
Pub: Cygnus Business Media
Ed: Gregg Wartgow. **Description:** Landscape contractors need to discover new strategies that will generate leads and convert those leads into sales.

13389 ■ "Take Control of Your Company's Finances" in *Green Industry Pro* **(Vol. 23, March 2011, No. 3, pp. 24)**
Pub: Cygnus Business Media
Ed: Gregg Wartgow. **Description:** Understanding that when certain leading indicators that affect the outcome of certain lagging indicators are aligned, companies will be able to take control of their firm's finances. Ways to improve the processes that drive financial performance for landscape firms are outlined.

13390 ■ "Take This Job and Love It" in *Green Industry Pro* **(Vol. 23, October 2011)**
Pub: Cygnus Business Media
Ed: Gregg Wartgow. **Description:** Details of the lawsuit filed by the Professional Landcare Network (PLANET) against the U.S. Department of Labor are explained. Challenges faced by landscape firms because of employment costs are outlined. Statistical data included.

13391 ■ "Time to Fight Back" in *Green Industry Pro* **(Vol. 23, March 2011, No. 3, pp. 8)**
Pub: Cygnus Business Media
Ed: Rod Dickens. **Description:** Lawn care operators in the United States must learn from Canada that a shift to socialism will impact their industry in a negative way. Government regulation over the application of control products regarding environmental health in Canada has been a death sentence for small lawn care businesses.

13392 ■ "Way More Than Mowing" in *Green Industry Pro* **(Vol. 23, September 2011)**
Pub: Cygnus Business Media
Ed: Rod Dickens. **Description:** Shipp Shape Lawn Services located in Sylvester, Georgia now offers aeration, fertilizing and weed control, mulching, yard renovation, flowerbed maintenance, landscaping, as well as irrigation repairs and installation in order to diversify the business and stay competitive.

SOURCES OF SUPPLY

13393 ■ *Yard & Garden*
Pub: Cygnus Business Media
Contact: Rick A. Monogue, Publisher
E-mail: rick.monogue@cygnuspub.com
Ed: Robert Warde, Editor, robert.warde@cygnuspub.com. **Released:** Irregular, Latest edition October 2010. **Publication Includes:** Lists of about 33,000 dealers, retailers, and distributors of lawn and garden power equipment. **Entries Include:** Product name,

description and photograph, name and address of distributor or manufacturer. **Arrangement:** Classified by type of product.

TRADE PERIODICALS

13394 ■ *The Avant Gardener*
Pub: Horticultural Data Processors
Ed: Thomas Powell, Editor. **Released:** Monthly. **Price:** $24 year. **Description:** Contains information on such subjects as indoor and outdoor plants, edible plants, new products, methods of cultivation, breeding and growing techniques, pest control, fertilizers, and landscaping. Recurring features include several special issues per year on specific topics.

13395 ■ *Landscape Management*
Pub: Questex Media Group
Contact: Ron Hall, Editor-in-Chief
E-mail: rhall@questex.com
Released: 12/yr. **Price:** $46 domestic; $69 Canada and Mexico; $89 other countries. **Description:** Magazine for professionals in landscape, grounds management and lawn care, construction, and maintenance.

13396 ■ *Lawn & Landscape Magazine*
Pub: G.I.E. Media, MC
Contact: Kevin Gilbride, Publisher
E-mail: kgilbride@gie.net
Ed: Chuck Bowen, Editor, cbowen@gie.net. **Released:** Monthly. **Price:** $15 U.S., Canada, and Mexico; $35; $100 other countries South America/Europe. **Description:** Business management magazine for lawn and landscape contracting professionals.

13397 ■ *Pro*
Pub: Cygnus Business Media
Contact: Rick A. Monogue, Publisher
E-mail: rick.monogue@cygnuspub.com
Released: 9/yr. **Description:** Magazine for landscape service firms.

VIDEOCASSETTES/ AUDIOCASSETTES

13398 ■ *The Home Gardener*
RMI Media
1365 N. Winchester St.
Olathe, KS 66061-5880
Ph:(913)768-1696
Free: 800-745-5480
Fax:800-755-6910
Co. E-mail: actmedia@act.org
URL: http://www.actmedia.com
Released: 1987. **Description:** A series that provides basic instruction in ornamental horticulture. **Availability:** VHS; 3/4U.

13399 ■ *The Home Gardener, Revised Edition*
Coast Telecourses
11460 Warner Ave.
Fountain Valley, CA 92708-2597
Ph:(714)241-6109
Free: 800-547-4748
Fax:(714)241-6286
Co. E-mail: coastlearning@coastline.edu
URL: http://www.coastlearning.org
Released: 1976. **Description:** A series about the fundamentals of indoor and outdoor gardening, planting for patios and balconies, gardening in containers, and simple landscaping. **Availability:** VHS; 3/4U; Q.

13400 ■ *Landscape Equipment Safety for the 90s*
American Nurseryman Publishing Co.
Book Dept.
223 W. Jackson Blvd., Ste. 500
Chicago, IL 60606
Ph:(312)427-7339
Free: 800-422-7147

Fax:(312)427-7346
Co. E-mail: books@amerinursery.com
URL: http://www.amerinursery.com
Released: 1991. **Price:** $64.99. **Description:** Series of programs updating OSHA information and federal regulations for landscape equipment use. **Availability:** VHS.

13401 ■ *Landscape Tools: Use and Safety*
American Nurseryman Publishing Co.
Book Dept.
223 W. Jackson Blvd., Ste. 500
Chicago, IL 60606
Ph:(312)427-7339
Free: 800-422-7147
Fax:(312)427-7346
Co. E-mail: books@amerinursery.com
URL: http://www.amerinursery.com
Released: 1989. **Price:** $94.99. **Description:** Demonstrates the proper use of 12 landscape tools, emphasizing safety rules. **Availability:** VHS.

13402 ■ *Landscaping & Ground Covers*
Cambridge Educational
c/o Films Media Group
132 West 31st Street, 17th Floor
Ste. 124
New York, NY 10001
Free: 800-257-5126
Fax:(609)671-0266
Co. E-mail: custserve@films.com
URL: http://www.cambridgeol.com
Released: 1987. **Description:** A instructional series about caring for lawns and landscaping cover. **Availability:** VHS.

13403 ■ *Lawn Care for the North American Gardener*
Film Ideas, Inc.
308 N. Wolf Rd.
Wheeling, IL 60090
Ph:(874)419-0255
Free: 800-475-3456
Fax:(874)419-8933
Co. E-mail: info@filmideas.com
URL: http://www.filmideas.com
Released: 1992. **Price:** $89.00. **Description:** Provides simple prescriptions that will help make your lawn green and healthy. **Availability:** VHS.

13404 ■ *Lawn and Garden*
RMI Media
1365 N. Winchester St.
Olathe, KS 66061-5880
Ph:(913)768-1696
Free: 800-745-5480
Fax:800-755-6910
Co. E-mail: actmedia@act.org
URL: http://www.actmedia.com
Released: 1987. **Description:** This instructional series takes the viewer from basic to advanced gardening. **Availability:** VHS; 3/4U.

13405 ■ *Lawns*
Emergency Training
PO Box 13896
Emory University
Dobbs University Center - 5th Floor
Fairlawn, OH 44334
Ph:(404)727-3853
Fax:(404)727-5667
Released: 1987. **Price:** $19.95. **Description:** A total guide to lawn care, from seeding to watering and everything in between. **Availability:** VHS.

13406 ■ *Lawns: Planting and Maintenance*
RMI Media
1365 N. Winchester St.
Olathe, KS 66061-5880
Ph:(913)768-1696
Free: 800-745-5480
Fax:800-755-6910
Co. E-mail: actmedia@act.org
URL: http://www.actmedia.com
Released: 1980. **Description:** The topics of this program on how to seed a lawn and then how to maintain it include: liming and moss control, raking, thatching, mowing and trimming. **Availability:** VHS; 3/4U; Special order formats.

TRADE SHOWS AND CONVENTIONS

13407 ■ Builders St. Charles Home Show
Home Builders Association of Greater St. Louis
10104 Old Olive St. Rd.
St. Louis, MO 63141
Ph:(314)994-7700
Fax:(314)432-7185
URL: http://www.stlhba.com
Released: Annual. **Audience:** General public and construction industry. **Principal Exhibits:** Home remodeling equipment and supplies, lawn and garden equipment, swimming pools, home furnishings, model homes and kitchen and bath. **Dates and Locations:** 2011 Apr 08-10, St. Charles, MO.

13408 ■ Green Industry and Equipment Expo
PLANET, The Professional Landcare Network
950 Herndon Parkway, Ste. 450
Herndon, VA 20170
Ph:(703)736-9666
Free: 800-395-2522
Fax:(703)736-9668
Co. E-mail: info@gieonline.com
URL: http://www.landcarenetwork.org
Released: Annual. **Audience:** Lawn care professionals, landscape contractors, grounds managers. **Principal Exhibits:** Lawn care equipment, supplies, and services, including fertilizers, weed control materials, insurance information, and power equipment. **Dates and Locations:** 2011 Oct 27-29.

CONSULTANTS

13409 ■ All Seasons Tree Service Inc.
998 New Loudon Rd.
PO Box 303
Latham, NY 12110
Ph:(518)783-7363
Fax:(518)783-8937
Co. E-mail: info@allseasonstree.com
URL: http://www.allseasonstree.com
Contact: Richard C. Johnson, President
E-mail: treeguy333@aol.com
Scope: Offers counsel on the development of tree care and lawn care programs for maintenance as well as on damage appraisals for trees and shrubs. **Seminars:** All Seasons Lawn Care Program; All Seasons Organic Lawn Care Program.

13410 ■ The Caretakers Inc.
5657 W Maple Rd.
West Bloomfield, MI 48322
Ph:(248)626-3300
Contact: Thomas Mann, President
Scope: Landscape maintenance consulting services to establish level and quality of exterior grounds maintenance for commercial, industrial, condominium and town home clients. Includes screening of prospective qualified contractors to perform various grounds maintenance services including, but not restricted to the following: lawn mowing, tree and shrub, fertilization, weed control, pruning and snow removal and control. Also assists with selection of both equipment and personnel. Industries served: Commercial and industrial, property owners, developers of high grade corporate headquarters, multitenant and single tenant commercial and industrial properties and business parks as well as government agencies. **Seminars:** Selection of the Right Landscape Management Contractor.

13411 ■ Dinsmore Tree & Landscape Service
113 Stoneyside Ln.
Saint Louis, MO 63132-4123
Ph:(314)991-0796
Contact: Lewis E. Dinsmore, Owner
Scope: Offers outdoor environmental consulting including plant maintenance programs, landscaping and pre-construction planning where trees involved, plant appraisal and evaluation for insurance, tax and legal implications.

13412 ■ Forest City Tree Protection Company Inc.
1884 S Green Rd.
South Euclid, OH 44121-4246
Ph:(216)381-1700
Free: 800-332-8733
Fax:(216)381-1894
Co. E-mail: forestcitytree@hotmail.com
URL: http://www.forestcitytree.com
Contact: Thomas Mugridge, Gen Mgr
E-mail: lauren@lanphearsupply.com
Scope: Provides complete tree care/arboricultural services to home owners and commercial establishments. Work includes: Diagnosis, appraisals, planting recommendations, small and large tree planting, insect and disease management, fertilizing, pruning, removals, cabling and bracing. Serves private industries as well as government agencies. **Seminars:** Evaluating Trees and Damage to Trees, 1987; Tree Fertilization, 1987; Knots, Ropes and Rigging, 1987; Tree Appraisal, 1985; Trees, People and the Law, 1985. **Special Services:** Lanphear Supply[R].

13413 ■ Forman & Biller Tree Expert Co.
856 N Harrison St.
Arlington, VA 22205
Ph:(703)522-3141
Contact: James E. Biller, Owner
Scope: Consulting arbores providing tree care for residential and commercial properties.

13414 ■ Fred J. Robinson & Associates Inc.
7680 Eillie Pl.
Mentor, OH 44060-7154
Ph:(440)255-4471
Fax:(440)255-4822
Co. E-mail: fjrtree@lightstream.net
Contact: Fred J. Robinson, Owner
E-mail: fjrtree@lightstream.net
Scope: Provides information concerning trees: health, appraised value, pest management and both care and preservation. Consults with architects, landscape architects, attorneys, insurance adjusters, government agencies and engineers in addition to tree owners.

13415 ■ North Haven Gardens Inc.
7700 Northaven Rd.
Dallas, TX 75230
Ph:(214)363-5316
Fax:(214)360-1555
Co. E-mail: plantquestion@nhg.com
URL: http://www.nhg.com
Contact: Muriel Pinkus, Secretary
E-mail: lpinkus@atsnhg.com
Scope: Landscape architects offering the following services: Exterior landscape maintenance; interior scape and maintenance; design consultation; budgeting, cost estimates and scheduling; master plans; construction drawings, documents and specifications; bid packages; contract administration; garden decorations. Serves both public and private sectors. **Seminars:** Gardening 101, Jan, 2008.

13416 ■ Plantscape Inc.
3101 Liberty Ave.
Pittsburgh, PA 15201-1415
Ph:(412)281-6352
Free: 800-303-1380
Fax:(412)281-4775
Co. E-mail: info@plantscape.com
URL: http://www.plantscape.com
Contact: Cindy Urbach, Vice President
E-mail: thorowitz@atsplantscape.com
Scope: Firm provides a full range of interior and exterior landscape services to the Pittsburgh business commercial market.

13417 ■ Richard L. Baldwin, Horticultural Consultant
215 Virginia Dr.
Ventura, CA 93003
Ph:(805)643-8406
Scope: Provides diagnosis of plant disorders and management, construction and maintenance recommendations for horticulture, including playing fields. Also offers arboriculture consultation, including hazardous conditions, evaluation of loss, and related landscape research. Services include consultation on production of ornamental plants, including turf grass and management of landscape plants. **Seminars:** Pruning Fruit Trees; Propagation of Fruit Trees; Diagnosing Plant Disorders; Pest Control on Ornamental Plants; Turf grass Fertilization.

13418 ■ TruGreen LandCare
951 N Ridge Ave.
Lombard, IL 60148
Ph:(630)629-9660
Free: 877-526-3227
URL: http://www.trugreenlandcare.com
Contact: Thomas C. Graham, CEO
Scope: Landscape management company providing full service grounds care programs. Also provides consulting services to clients, landscape architects, building and property managers, and developers on contract and specification development, as well as design related consultation regarding long range cost impacts of various landscape design features. Also consulting on water management programs. Industries served building property and facilities management.

13419 ■ Western Arborists Inc.
502 W Rte. 66, Ste. 20
Glendora, CA 91740-4370
Ph:(626)963-1171
Fax:(626)963-8243
Contact: James W. Walker, President
E-mail: sharon.juliussen@verizon.net
Scope: Offers consulting on tree disease and insect problems. Also provides appraisal services covering damage or value of trees lost.

13420 ■ W.S. Moore Consulting
1206 Brighton Ave.
PO Box 9527
Berkeley, CA 94709
Ph:(510)524-1163
Free: 800-359-3435
Fax:(510)524-8085
Co. E-mail: mooreconsult@earthlink.net
URL: http://www.moorenewhomeowners.com
Contact: Dr. Wayne S. Moore, President
Scope: Active in the marketing of horticulture and gardening-related products, including pest-control products.

FRANCHISES AND BUSINESS OPPORTUNITIES

13421 ■ Clean Cut Lawn and Garden Services
24701–108th Ave.
Maple Ridge, BC, Canada V2W 1G7
Ph:(604)467-9273
Free: (866)974-7277
Fax:(604)466-2892
Co. E-mail: kelly@cleancutcanada.com
URL: http://www.cleancutcanada.com
No. of Company-Owned Units: 1. **Founded:** 2006. **Franchised:** 2006. **Description:** Lawn and garden service. **Equity Capital Needed:** $38,500. **Franchise Fee:** $10,000. **Royalty Fee:** 5%. **Financial Assistance:** Government guaranteed financing available-OAC. **Training:** Provides 5 days hands on training and ongoing support.

13422 ■ Clintar Groundskeeping Services
Truserve Groundcare Inc.
70 Esna Park Dr., Unit 1
Markham, ON, Canada L3R 1E3
Ph:(905)943-9530
Free: 800-361-3542
Fax:(905)943-9529
Co. E-mail: info@clintar.com
URL: http://www.clintar.com
No. of Franchise Units: 21. **Founded:** 1973. **Franchised:** 1984. **Description:** Grounds keeping services including landscape maintenance, snow and ice control, power sweeping, light construction, tree care and irrigation maintenance. **Equity Capital Needed:** $100,000-$125,000; $50,000-$60,000 cash. **Franchise Fee:** $40,000. **Financial Assistance:** No. **Training:** Yes.

13423 ■ Environmental Factor Inc.

85 Chambers Dr., Unit 8
Ajax, ON, Canada L1Z 1E2
Ph:(905)686-9909
Fax:(905)686-0357
URL: http://www.environmentalfactor.com
No. of Franchise Units: 7. **No. of Company-Owned Units:** 1. **Founded:** 1991. **Franchised:** 2001. **Description:** Non-chemical lawn care company **Equity Capital Needed:** $30,000-$40,000. **Franchise Fee:** $20,000. **Training:** Initial and ongoing one on one training. g.

13424 ■ Jim's Mowing Canada Inc.

1515 Pemberton Ave., Ste. 105
North Vancouver, BC, Canada V7P 2S3
Ph:(604)990-0714
Fax:(604)990-0724
Co. E-mail: info@jimsmowing.ca
URL: http://www.jimsmowing.ca
No. of Franchise Units: 2,460. **Founded:** 1989. **Description:** Lawn and garden franchise. **Equity Capital Needed:** $35,000. **Franchise Fee:** $490.00/month. **Training:** Ongoing support provided.

13425 ■ Lawn Doctor, Inc.

142 State Rte. 34
Holmdel, NJ 07733
Free: (866)529-6362
Fax:(732)946-0002
Co. E-mail: franchiseinformation@lawndoctor.com
URL: http://www.lawndoctor.com
No. of Franchise Units: 460. **Founded:** 1967. **Franchised:** 1967. **Description:** Automated lawn-care service, all-natural and regular fertilizer. **Equity Capital Needed:** $65,000-$80,000 initial investment; $27,000-$40,000 liquid capital required. **Franchise Fee:** $25,000. **Royalty Fee:** 10%. **Financial Assistance:** Yes. **Managerial Assistance:** Ongoing operations support, seminars and group meetings. Two-year new dealer support assistance. **Training:** Field and classroom intensive training program.

13426 ■ Naturalawn of America

1 E Church St.
Frederick, MD 21701
Ph:(301)694-5440
Free: 800-989-5444
Fax:(301)846-0320
No. of Franchise Units: 61. **No. of Company-Owned Units:** 5. **Founded:** 1986. **Franchised:** 1989. **Description:** Franchises organic-based lawn care services. **Equity Capital Needed:** Ability to secure a credit line of $150,000 and have a minimum net worth of $250,000. **Franchise Fee:** $29,500. **Financial Assistance:** Yes. **Training:** No.

13427 ■ NiteLites Outdoor Lighting Franchise

NiteLites Franchise Systems, Inc.
6107 Market Ave.
Franklin, OH 45005
Ph:(513)425-5510
Free: (866)648-3548
Fax:(513)433-0242
No. of Franchise Units: 33. **No. of Company-Owned Units:** 6. **Founded:** 1988. **Franchised:** 2004. **Description:** Outdoor/landscape lighting professionals. **Equity Capital Needed:** $75,000; minimum net worth of $300,000. **Franchise Fee:** $84,000$165,000. **Financial Assistance:** No. **Training:** Yes.

13428 ■ Nutri-Lawn

2077 Dundas St. E.
Mississauga, ON, Canada L4X 1M2
Ph:(416)620-7100
Free: 800-396-6096
URL: http://www.franchisedirectory.ca
No. of Franchise Units: 2. **No. of Company-Owned Units:** 1. **Description:** Ecology friendly lawn care. **Equity Capital Needed:** $120,000-$130,000 total investment. **Franchise Fee:** $40,000. **Training:** Provides 1 week initial training, onsite for 1 week and ongoing support.

13429 ■ Scotts Lawn Service

E.G. Systems, Inc.
14111 Scottslawn Rd.
Marysville, OH 43041
Free: 800-264-8973
Fax:(937)644-7422
No. of Franchise Units: 85. **No. of Company-Owned Units:** 86. **Founded:** 1984. **Franchised:** 1985. **Description:** Residential and commercial lawn care. **Equity Capital Needed:** $84,400-$299,500. **Franchise Fee:** to $25,000-$105,000. **Royalty Fee:** 6-10%. **Financial Assistance:** Limited in-house financing available. **Training:** Offers 1 week at headquarters, 1 week at franchisees location, annual business/operations training with ongoing training as needed.

13430 ■ Spectrum Home Services

SHS Franchising
9690 S 300 W, Ste 320 G-H
Sandy, UT 84070
Ph:(801)957-5671
Free: 800-496-5993
Fax:(801)957-5291
Co. E-mail: spectrumhomeserv@qwest.net
URL: http://www.spectrumhomeservice.com
No. of Franchise Units: 35. **Founded:** 2000. **Franchised:** 2004. **Description:** Full service senior care. Multiple profit centers such as homemaking, personal care, maintenance, yard care and relocation services increase your bottom line. **Equity Capital Needed:** $66,380-$104,433. **Franchise Fee:** $36,000. **Financial Assistance:** Third party financing available. **Training:** Includes 1 week training at headquarters and 1 week at franchisee's location with ongoing support.

13431 ■ Spring-Green Lawn Care Corp.

11909 Spaulding School Dr.
Plainfield, IL 60544
Free: 800-777-8608
Fax:(815)436-9056
Co. E-mail: nancysg@ix.netcom.com
URL: http://www.spring-green.com
No. of Franchise Units: 126. **No. of Company-Owned Units:** 5. **Founded:** 1977. **Franchised:** 1977. **Description:** National network of lawn and tree care businesses. **Equity Capital Needed:** $60,000 or $125,000. **Franchise Fee:** $30,000-$40,000 or $60,000-$80,000. **Financial Assistance:** Lease options on equipment and computer packages. **Training:** Initial training at headquarters covering areas of marketing, operations and computer system Besides, on-going training is offered through field visits, regional meetings, professional development programs, intranet, website, telephone and newsletters.

13432 ■ Turf Logic Inc.

92 Caplan Ave., Ste. 241
Barrie, ON, Canada L4N 0Z7
Ph:(705)812-1363
Free: (866)239-4056
Fax:(705)733-0090
Co. E-mail: franchisesales@turflogic.ca
URL: http://www.turflogic.ca
No. of Franchise Units: 8. **Founded:** 2004. **Franchised:** 2005. **Description:** An opportunity to get involved in pesticide-free lawn care, the fastest growing sector of the green trades industry. With several years of professional turf experience, Turf Logic provides you with proven programs, exclusive products and high-tech equipment in a protected territory. **Equity Capital Needed:** $50,000. **Franchise Fee:** $25,000. **Training:** Provides 2 weeks training.

13433 ■ Weed Man - USA

Turf Holdings, Inc.
1255 Terwillegar Ave., Ste. 6
Oshawa, ON, Canada L1J 7A4
Ph:(905)579-4000
Free: 888-321-9333
Fax:(905)579-5772
URL: http://www.weed-man.com
No. of Franchise Units: 366. **Founded:** 1970. **Franchised:** 1976. **Description:** Residential lawn care services. **Equity Capital Needed:** $65,980-$82,940. **Franchise Fee:** $20,000-$34,000. **Financial Assistance:** No. **Training:** Yes.

RESEARCH CENTERS

13434 ■ Kansas State University–John C. Pair Horticultural Center

1901 E 95th St. S
Haysville, KS 67060-8351
Ph:(316)788-0492
Fax:(316)788-3844
Co. E-mail: jgriffin@oznet.ksu.edu
URL: http://www.oznet.ksu.edu/rc_hefw
Contact: Dr. Jason J. Griffin, Dir.
E-mail: jgriffin@oznet.ksu.edu
Scope: Ornamental trees and shrubs, vegetable crops, and turfgrass. **Publications:** Newsletter (semiannually). **Educational Activities:** Group tours (periodically); Open House (annually); Ornamental Field Day; Vegetable Twilight Tour.

13435 ■ North Carolina Department of Agriculture and Consumer Services–Sandhills Research Station

2148 Windblow Rd.
Jackson Springs, NC 27281-9124
Ph:(910)974-4673
Fax:(910)974-4462
Co. E-mail: sandhills.resst@ncagr.gov
URL: http://www.ncagr.gov/Research/srs.htm
Contact: Jeff Chandler, Res.Oper.Mgr.
E-mail: sandhills.resst@ncagr.gov
Scope: Peaches, nectarines, plums, blueberries, peanuts, peppers, soybeans, brambles, strawberries, and turf, including ground covers, soil fertility, plant breeding, and weed, insect, disease, and nematode control. **Educational Activities:** Turfgrass Field Day (biennially), to promote turfgrass management; Small Fruits Field Day (biennially), focuses on research related to strawberries, brambles and blueberries; Peach Field Day.

13436 ■ University of Arizona–Karsten Turfgrass Research Facility

2101 E Roger Rd.
Tucson, AZ 85719
Ph:(520)318-7142
Fax:(520)621-7186
Co. E-mail: dkopec@cals.arizona.edu
URL: http://turf.arizona.edu/karsten.htm
Contact: Dr. David M. Kopec
E-mail: dkopec@cals.arizona.edu
Scope: Turfgrass management focusing on water conservation and irrigation management, wastewater research, nitrogen fate, turfgrass development and evaluation, and herbicide efficacy. **Services:** Troubleshooting and consulting. **Publications:** Annual Turfgrass and Ornamentals Research Summary. **Educational Activities:** Conferences, trade shows, seminars, workshops, and educational programs; Turfgrass field day.

13437 ■ University of Guelph–Guelph Turfgrass Institute

328 Victoria Rd. S
RR No. 2
Guelph, ON, Canada N1H 6H8
Ph:(519)767-5009
Fax:(519)766-1704
Co. E-mail: info@guelphturfgrass.ca
URL: http://www.guelphturfgrass.ca
Contact: Prof. Rob Witherspoon, Dir.
E-mail: info@guelphturfgrass.ca
Scope: Turfgrass production and management, including soil science, growth regulation, toxicology, environmental research, disease etiology and management, insect control, weed control, and turfgrass physiology, seed production, and nutrition. **Services:** Consulting, through the Institute and through Ontario Ministry of Agriculture and Food. **Publications:** Annual Research Report; GTI advisor (biweekly). **Educational Activities:** GTI Research Field Day (biennially), in August; Independent study correspondence courses; short courses, workshops and seminars; Ontario Turfgrass Symposium (annually), in February; Turf Managers Course (annually), in February.

ASSOCIATIONS AND OTHER ORGANIZATIONS

13438 ■ National Limousine Association
49 S Maple Ave.
Marlton, NJ 08053
Ph:(856)596-3344
Free: 800-652-7007
Fax:(856)596-2145
Co. E-mail: patricia.nelson@limo.org
URL: http://www.limo.org
Contact: Ms. Patricia A. Nelson, Exec. Dir.
Description: Limousine owners and operators; limousine manufacturers and suppliers to the industry. Seeks to: promote and advance industry professionalism and the common interests of members; increase use of chauffeured transportation in both business and public sectors. Monitors legislation and organizes lobbying activities. Sponsors seminars on safety/regulatory issues and management techniques. **Publications:** Membership Directory (periodic).

REFERENCE WORKS

13439 ■ "21st Century Filling Station" in *Austin Business JournalInc.* **(Vol. 29, December 11, 2009, No. 40, pp. 1)**
Pub: American City Business Journals
Ed: Jacob Dirr. **Description:** Clean Energy Fuels Corporation announced plans for the construction of a $1 million, 17,000 square foot compressed natural gas fueling station at or near the Austin-Bergstrom International Airport (ABIA). Clean Energy Fuels hopes to encourage cab and shuttle companies in the ABIA to switch from gasoline to natural gas.

13440 ■ "Business Start-Up a Learning Experience for Young Bellingham Entrepreneur" in *Bellingham Herald* **(July 18, 2010)**
Pub: Bellingham Herald
Ed: Dave Gallagher. **Description:** Profile of 21-year-old entrepreneur, Chase Larabee, who developed an online program that helps airport fixed-based operators handle refueling, hotel and transportation reservations and other requests from private airplane pilots.

13441 ■ "Capital Metro May Soon Seek Contractor to Replace Star Tran" in *Austin Business Journal* **(Vol. 31, June 10, 2011, No. 14, pp. 1)**
Pub: American City Business Journals Inc.
Ed: Vicky Garza. **Description:** Capital Metropolitan Transportation Authority may be forced to contract out its bus services provided by StarTran Inc. as early as September 2012 following legislation approved by the Texas legislature. The bill originates in a report by the Sunset Advisory Commission. Details are included.

13442 ■ "Funkhouser Wants Region to Get On Board Light Rail" in *Business Journal-Serving Metropolitan Kansas City* **(November 30, 2007)**
Pub: American City Business Journals, Inc.
Ed: Suzanna Stagemeyer. **Description:** Mark Funhouser, Mayor of Kansas City, is planning to construct a regional multimodal public transit system. A previous light rail plan was rescinded due to logistical, financial and legal problems. Details of the light transit plans are discussed.

13443 ■ How to Start a Home-Based Senior Care Business: Check-in-Care, Transportation Services, Shopping and Cooking
Pub: The Globe Pequot Press
Ed: James L. Ferry. **Released:** January 1, 2010. **Price:** $18.95. **Description:** Information is provided to start a home-based senior care business.

13444 ■ "MV Transportation Winds $133M Contract" in *Black Enterprise* **(Vol. 38, November 2007, No. 4, pp. 30)**
Pub: Earl G. Graves Publishing Co. Inc.
Ed: Marcia A. Wade. **Description:** MV Transportation won a $133 million contract to operate 139 fixed-route buses in the San Gabriel and Pomona valley areas of California.

13445 ■ "Professional Help: Cross That Off Your To-Do List" in *Inc.* **(November 2007, pp. 89-90, 92)**
Pub: Gruner & Jahr USA Publishing
Ed: Alison Stein Wellner. **Description:** Small business owners are finding that it pays to hire someone to takeover the personal tasks of daily living, including hiring a personal assistant, chauffeur, chef, stylist, pet caregiver, or concierge service.

13446 ■ "Taxis Are Set to Go Hybrid" in *Philadelphia Business Journal* **(Vol. 30, September 16, 2011, No. 31, pp. 1)**
Pub: American City Business Journals Inc.
Ed: Natalie Kostelni. **Description:** Taxis are going hybrid in several major states such as New York, California and Maryland where it is mandated, but it is yet to happen in Philadelphia, Pennsylvania with the exception of one taxi company. Freedom Taxi is awaiting Philadelphia Parking Authority's sign off.

STATISTICAL SOURCES

13447 ■ RMA Annual Statement Studies
Pub: Robert Morris Associates (RMA)
Released: Annual. **Price:** $175.00 2006-07 edition, $105.00. **Description:** Contains composite balance sheets and income statements for more than 360 industries, including the accounting, auditing, and bookkeeping industries. Also contains five years of comparative historical data for discerning trends. Includes 16 commonly used ratios, computed for most of the size groupings for nearly every industry.

TRADE PERIODICALS

13448 ■ In the Driver's Seat
Pub: Ontario Safety League
Ed: Terry Thompson, Editor. **Released:** Monthly. **Price:** Included in membership. **Description:** Commercial driver safety newsletter.

13449 ■ LCT
Pub: Bobit Business Media
Contact: Heidi Dimaya, Production Mgr
E-mail: heidi@lctmag.com
Ed: Martin Romjue, Editor, martin@lctmag.com. **Released:** Monthly. **Price:** $24. **Description:** Magazine for the limousine service industry. 1 Magazine for the limousine service industry.

LIBRARIES

13450 ■ Alabama Department of Transportation–Research & Development Bureau–Research Library (1409)
1409 Coliseum Blvd.
Montgomery, AL 36110
Ph:(334)206-2210
Fax:(334)264-2042
Co. E-mail: harrisi@dot.state.al.us
URL: http://www.dot.state.al.us/docs
Contact: Jeffrey W. Brown, Res. & Dev.Engr.
Scope: Transportation. **Services:** Interlibrary loan; Library not open to the public. **Holdings:** 1000 books; 5000 reports. **Subscriptions:** 8 journals and other serials.

13451 ■ California State Department of Motor Vehicles–Licensing Operations Division - Research and Development Branch–Traffic Safety Research Library (2415)
2415 1st Ave., MS F-126
Sacramento, CA 95818
Ph:(916)657-3079
Fax:(916)657-8589
Co. E-mail: dluong@dvm.ca.gov
Contact: Douglas Luong, Staff Svcs.Anl.
Scope: Automobile transportation. **Services:** Copying; Library not open to the public. **Holdings:** 500 books; 10,000 bound periodical volumes; reports; manuscripts. **Subscriptions:** 20 journals and other serials.

13452 ■ Connecticut Department of Transportation–ConnDOT Library and Information Center
2800 Berlin Tpke.
Newington, CT 06111-4116
Ph:(860)594-3035
Fax:(860)594-3039
Co. E-mail: betty.ambler@po.state.ct.us
URL: http://www.ct.gov/dot/site/default.asp
Contact: Betty Ambler, Libn.
Scope: Transportation. **Services:** Interlibrary loan; copying; Library open to the public by appointment. **Holdings:** 10,000 books; 10,000 reports.

13453 ■ Kansas Department of Transportation Library
700 S.W. Harrison St.
Eisenhower State Office Bldg., 4th Fl., W.
Topeka, KS 66603-3745
Ph:(785)291-3854
Fax:(785)291-3717
Co. E-mail: library@ksdot.org
Contact: Marie Manthe, Libn.
Scope: Transportation. **Services:** Interlibrary loan; Library open to the public. **Holdings:** 3000 books; 20,000 reports; 175 CD-ROMs; 100 videos **Subscriptions:** 100 journals and other serials.

13454 ■ Kentucky Transportation Center Library
University of Kentucky
176 Raymond Bldg.
Lexington, KY 40506-0281
Ph:(859)257-2155
Free: 800-432-0719
Fax:(859)257-1815
Co. E-mail: lwhayne@engr.uky.edu
URL: http://www.kyt2.com/
Contact: Laura Whayne, Libn.
Scope: Transportation. **Services:** Interlibrary loan; copying; Library open to the public. **Holdings:** 6000 books; 9000 reports; 800 videotapes. **Subscriptions:** 300 journals and other serials.

13455 ■ Missouri Highway and Transportation Department–Division of Materials Library
PO Box 270
Jefferson City, MO 65102-0270
Ph:(573)751-6735
Fax:(573)526-5636
Co. E-mail: michael.meyerhoff@mail.modot.state.mo.us
URL: http://www.modot.org/
Contact: Mona Scott
Scope: Transportation. **Services:** Library not open to the public. **Holdings:** Figures not available.

13456 ■ Montana Department of Transportation Library
2701 Prospect Ave.
PO Box 201001
Helena, MT 59620-1001
Ph:(406)444-6338
Fax:(406)444-7204
Co. E-mail: ssillick@mt.gov
URL: http://www.mdt.mt.gov/research/unique/services.shtml
Contact: Susan Sillick
Scope: Transportation. **Services:** Interlibrary loan; copying. **Holdings:** 10,000 items; reports; CD-ROMs; video. **Subscriptions:** 10 journals and other serials.

13457 ■ New Jersey Department of Transportation–Research Library
1035 Parkway Ave.
PO Box 600
Trenton, NJ 08625-0600
Ph:(609)530-5289
Fax:(609)530-2052
Co. E-mail: library@dot.state.nj.us
URL: http://www.state.nj.us/transportation/refdata/library/
Contact: Carol Paszamant, Libn.
Scope: Transportation. **Services:** Interlibrary loan; Library open to the public by appointment. **Holdings:** 300 books; 11,000 reports. **Subscriptions:** 50 journals and other serials.

13458 ■ North Carolina Department of Transportation–Research and Development Library
PO Box 25201
Raleigh, NC 27611
Ph:(919)715-2463
Fax:(919)715-0137
Co. E-mail: rhhall@dot.state.nc.us
URL: http://www.ncdot.org/
Contact: Bob Hall
Scope: Transportation. **Services:** Interlibrary loan; copying; Library open to the public for reference use

only. **Holdings:** 11,209 books; 20,021 reports; 132 videos. **Subscriptions:** 57 journals and other serials.

13459 ■ North Dakota Department of Transportation–Materials and Research Division Library
300 Airport Rd.
Bismarck, ND 58504-6005
Ph:(701)328-6901
Fax:(701)328-0310
Co. E-mail: gweisger@nd.gov
Contact: Gerri Weisgerber, Adm. Staff Off.
Scope: Transportation. **Services:** Library not open to the public. **Holdings:** 6600 reports. **Subscriptions:** 5 journals and other serials.

13460 ■ South Carolina Department of Transportation Library
955 Park St., Rm. 110
Columbia, SC 29202
Ph:(803)737-9897
Fax:(803)737-0824
Co. E-mail: adcockda@dot.state.sc.us
URL: http://www.dot.state.sc.us
Contact: Ann Adcock, Mgr.
Scope: Transportation, engineering, mass transit. **Services:** Interlibrary loan; transportation related research; Library open to the public. **Holdings:** 5500 books; 90 bound periodical volumes; 1900 reports; 250 videos. **Subscriptions:** 41 journals and other serials; 10 newspapers.

13461 ■ Vermont Agency of Transportation–Policy and Planning Division Library
133 State St.
Montpelier, VT 05633
Ph:(802)828-2544
Fax:(802)828-3983
Contact: Sandy Aja
Scope: Transportation. **Holdings:** Figures not available.

ASSOCIATIONS AND OTHER ORGANIZATIONS

13462 ■ American Apparel and Footwear Association
1601 N Kent St., Ste. 1200
Arlington, VA 22209
Ph:(703)797-9037
Free: 800-520-2262
Fax:(703)522-6741
Co. E-mail: pcarty@apparelandfootwear.org
URL: http://www.apparelandfootwear.org
Contact: Kevin M. Burke, Pres./CEO
Description: Manufacturers of infants', children's, boys', girls', juniors', men's, and women's wearing apparel; associate members are suppliers of fabrics, equipment, accessories, and services to the apparel industry. Operates the Apparel Foundation; offers placement service through newsletter. Compiles statistics. **Publications:** *AAFA Directory of Members and Associate Members* (annual); *Technical Advisory Committee Bulletin* (periodic).

13463 ■ The Hosiery Association
7421 Carmel Executive Park, Ste. 200
Charlotte, NC 28226
Ph:(704)365-0913
Fax:(704)362-2056
Co. E-mail: thainfo@hosieryassociation.com
URL: http://www.hosieryassociation.com
Contact: Sally Kay, Pres.
Description: Hosiery manufacturers and suppliers. Develops standards for hosiery measurement. Sponsors annual "Celebrate Hosiery" to educate consumers on hosiery varieties. Conducts field visitations for assistance in technical areas. Compiles statistics; conducts research programs. Operates Group Purchasing Program. **Publications:** *Hosiery News* (monthly); *Industry Directory of Manufacturers, Marketers, Distributors, Suppliers* (periodic); *THA Directory of Hosiery Manufacturers and Mill Suppliers* (periodic); *THA Directory of Hosiery Mill Suppliers* (periodic).

13464 ■ Intimate Apparel Square Club
326 Field Rd.
Clinton Corners, NY 12514

Ph:(845)758-5752
Fax:(845)758-2546
Co. E-mail: amasry@yahoo.com
URL: http://thehugaward.org
Contact: Adam Masry, Sec.
Description: Members of the women's and children's intimate apparel industry. Works with other charity groups in the greater New York City area. Strives to "help those who cannot help themselves". Provides support to needy medical school students and makes contributions to children's organizations and rehabilitation clinics, primarily Rusk Institute. .

REFERENCE WORKS

13465 ■ "The Bottom Line" in *Retail Merchandiser* (Vol. 51, July-August 2011, No. 4, pp. 60)
Pub: Phoenix Media Corporation
Description: Hanky Panky believes that comfort and style don't have to be mutually exclusive when designing their line of intimate apparel for women. The lingerie retailer was launched in 1977.

13466 ■ "Pink Label: Victoria's Sales Secret" in *Advertising Age* (Vol. 79, July 7, 2008, No. 26, pp. 4)
Pub: Crain Communications, Inc.
Ed: Natalie Zmuda. **Description:** Victoria Secret's Pink label accounted for roughly 17 percent of the retailer's total sales last year. The company is launching a Collegiate Collection which will be promoted by a campus tour program.

SOURCES OF SUPPLY

13467 ■ *Canadian Apparel Directory*
Pub: Canadian Apparel Federation
Contact: Bob Kirke, Exec. Dir.
E-mail: bkirke@apparel.ca
Released: Biennial, May/June. **Price:** $132, members; $350, nonmembers. **Publication Includes:** Lists of Canadian industry suppliers, and manufacturers of apparel. **Entries Include:** Company name, address, phone, fax, names and titles of key personnel, name and title of contact, product/service, description

of company business activities. **Arrangement:** Alphabetical. **Indexes:** Trade name, product/service, geographical.

TRADE SHOWS AND CONVENTIONS

13468 ■ Denver Apparel and Accessory Market
Denver Merchandise Mart
451 E. 58th Ave., Ste. 4270
Denver, CO 80216-8470
Ph:(303)292-6278
Free: 800-289-6278
Fax:(303)297-8473
Co. E-mail: info@denvermart.com
URL: http://www.denvermart.com
Released: 5/yr. **Audience:** Retailers of women's, children's, and men's apparel and accessories. **Principal Exhibits:** Women's, men's, and children's apparel and accessories. **Dates and Locations:** 2011 Aug 26-29, Denver, CO.

13469 ■ Florida Fashion Focus Show
Southern Apparel Exhibitors, Inc.
1856 Sheridan St.
Evanston, IL 60201
Ph:(847)475-1856
Free: 888-249-1377
Co. E-mail: info@saemiami.com.
URL: http://www.saemiami.com
Released: 5/yr. **Audience:** Trade buyers. **Principal Exhibits:** Ladies ready-to-wear clothing; handbags, jewelry, and accessories. Order-writing for future delivery.

13470 ■ Women's and Children's Apparel and Accessories Mart
Dallas Market Center Co.
Attn: SG Marketing Mgr.
2100 Stemmons Fwy.
Dallas, TX 75207
Ph:(214)655-6100
Free: 800-325-6587
Fax:(214)655-6238
Co. E-mail: info@dmcmail.com
Audience: Apparel and accessories and home furnishings retailers. **Principal Exhibits:** Regional Merchandising Mart servicing department and specialty store buyers nationwide.

ASSOCIATIONS AND OTHER ORGANIZATIONS

13471 ■ American Beverage Licensees
5101 River Rd., Ste. 108
Bethesda, MD 20816-1560
Ph:(301)656-1494
Free: 800-656-3241
Fax:(301)656-7539
Co. E-mail: info@ablusa.org
URL: http://www.ablusa.org
Contact: John Bodnovich, Exec. Dir.

Description: Federation of associations of alcohol beverage retailers. .

13472 ■ National Association of Beverage Importers
National Press Bldg.
529 14th St. NW, Ste. 1183
Washington, DC 20045
Ph:(202)393-6224
Fax:(202)393-6594
Co. E-mail: beverageimportersinfo@nabi-inc.org
URL: http://www.nabi-inc.org
Contact: William T. Earle, Pres.

Description: Represents importers of alcoholic beverages. Compiles and reports statistics from Bureau of Census and Internal Revenue sources. **Publications:** *Statistics and Member Letter* (periodic).

13473 ■ National Beer Wholesalers Association
1101 King St., Ste. 600
Alexandria, VA 22314-2944
Ph:(703)683-4300
Free: 800-300-6417
Fax:(703)683-8965
Co. E-mail: info@nbwa.org
URL: http://www.nbwa.org
Contact: Craig A. Purser CAE, Pres.

Description: Independent wholesalers of malt beverages and affiliates of the malt beverage industry. Conducts specialized education programs. **Publications:** *NBWA Beer Perspectives* (biweekly).

13474 ■ Wine and Spirits Wholesalers of America
805 15th St. NW, Ste. 430
Washington, DC 20005
Ph:(202)371-9792
Fax:(202)789-2405
Co. E-mail: membership@wswa.org
URL: http://www.wswa.org
Contact: Craig Wolf, Pres./CEO

Description: Represents wholesale distributors of domestic and imported wine and distilled spirits. **Publications:** *Upfront* (monthly); *WSWA Member Roster and Industry Directory* (annual).

REFERENCE WORKS

13475 ■ "Beer Stocks Rally on Anheuser, InBev Report" in *Globe & Mail* (February 16, 2007, pp. B3)
Pub: CTVglobemedia Publishing Inc.
Ed: Keith McArthur. **Description:** The stock prices of beer manufacturing industries have increased considerably after impressive profit reports from Anheuser Busch Cos Inc. and InBev SA. Complete analysis in this context is presented.

13476 ■ *Beverage Industry—Annual Manual Issue*
Pub: BNP Media
Released: Annual, Latest edition 2010. **Publication Includes:** List of over 1,700 companies supplying equipment and materials to the soft drink, beer, wine, bottled water, and juice industries; industry associations; bottling and supply franchise companies; beer importers distributors; manufacturers' representatives; soft drink distributors. **Entries Include:** For suppliers—Company name, address, phone, code to indicate products. For associations—Name, address, phone, name of president; some association listings also include meeting date and location and names of other executives. For franchise companies—Name, address, phone, names and titles of executives, number of plants, number of franchised plants, products, foreign involvement. For beer importers and distributors—Name, address, phone, names and titles of key executives, brands handled. For manufacturers' representatives—Name, address, phone, names of contacts, market areas, products represented. **Arrangement:** State associations and supplier associations are geographical; other listings are alphabetical. **Indexes:** Trade name, product/service.

13477 ■ *Beverage Marketing Directory*
Pub: Beverage Marketing Corp.
Contact: Brian Sudano, Mng. Dir.
Released: Annual, Latest edition 33rd; 2011. **Price:** $1,435, individuals softcover or in PDF format; $5,495, individuals database on CD-ROM; $5,495, Canada database on CD-ROM. **Covers:** Over 25,500 beer wholesalers, wine and spirits wholesalers, soft drink bottlers and franchisors, breweries, wineries, distilleries, alcoholic beverage importers, bottled water companies; and trade associations, government agencies, micro breweries, juice, coffee, tea, milk companies, and others concerned with the beverage and bottling industries; coverage includes Canada. **Entries Include:** Beverage and bottling company listings contain company name, address, phone, names of key executives, number of employees, brand names, and other information, including number of franchisees, number of delivery trucks, sales volume. Suppliers and related companies and organizations listings include similar but less detailed information. **Arrangement:** Geographical. **Indexes:** Personnel, supplier's product, company name.

13478 ■ "Black Diamond Holdings Corp. Receives SEC Approval" in *Canadian Corporate News* (May 16, 2007)
Pub: Comtex News Network Inc.
Description: Black Diamond Holdings, Corp., a British Columbia domiciled company and its two wholly owned subsidiaries are engaged in the bottling, importation, distribution, marketing, and brand creation of premium spirits and wines to worldwide consumers, announced that it has completed the SEC review process and has applied to list for trading in the United States on the OTC.BB.

13479 ■ "Booze Makers Battle Over Turkey Day" in *Advertising Age* (Vol. 78, October 29, 2007, No. 43, pp. 4)
Pub: Crain Communications, Inc.
Ed: Jeremy Mullman. **Description:** Beer and wine marketers are jockeying for position in regards to the Thanksgiving holiday.

13480 ■ "Bottoms Up!" in *Entrepreneur* (Vol. 36, April 2008, No. 4, pp. 128)
Pub: Entrepreneur Media, Inc.
Ed: Amanda C. Kooser. **Description:** Jill Bernheimer launched her online alcohol business Domaine547 in 2007, and encountered challenges as legal issues over the licensing and launching of the business took about seven months to finish. Domain547 features blog and forum areas. Marketing strategy that connects to the social community is one of the ways to reach out to customers.

13481 ■ "Cheap Thrills: Where to Look When You're Craving a Low-Price Wine" in *Chicago Tribune* (January 12, 2009)
Pub: McClatchy-Tribune Information Services
Ed: Bill Daley. **Description:** Wines priced $15 and above are being hit the hardest by the economic downturn while cheaper wines, specifically those priced between $3 and $6, are seeing a growth in sales.

13482 ■ "Day-Care Center Owner to Argue Against Liquor Store Opening Nearby" in *Chicago Tribune* (March 13, 2008)
Pub: McClatchy-Tribune Information Services
Ed: Matthew Walberg. **Description:** NDLC's owner feels that Greenwood Liquors should not be granted its liquor license due to the claim that the NDLC is not only a day-care center but also a school that employs state-certified teachers.

13483 ■ "Discount Beers Take Fizz Out Of Molson" in *Globe & Mail* (February 10, 2006, pp. B3)
Pub: CTVglobemedia Publishing Inc.
Ed: Omar El Akkad. **Description:** The reasons behind the decline in profits by 60 percent for Molson Coors Brewing Co., during fourth quarter 2005, are presented.

13484 ■ "Executive Decision: Damn the Profit Margins, Sleeman Declares War on Buck-a-Beer Foes" in *Globe & Mail* (January 28, 2006, pp. B3)
Pub: CTVglobemedia Publishing Inc.
Ed: Andy Hoffman. **Description:** The cost savings plans of chief executive officer John Sleeman of Sleeman Breweries Ltd. are presented.

13485 ■ **"First Venture Reports Proprietary Yeasts Further Reduce Ethyl Carbamate in Sake"** in *Canadian Corporate News* (May 16, 2007)
Pub: Comtex News Network Inc.
Description: First Ventures Technologies Corp., a biotechnology company that develops and commercializes advanced yeast products, confirmed that two of their proprietary yeasts used in the making of sake have yielded reductions in ethyl carbamate compared to previous sake brewing trials.

13486 ■ **"Grape Expectations"** in *Canadian Business* (Vol. 80, March 12, 2007, No. 6, pp. 55)
Pub: Rogers Media
Ed: Andrea Jezvovit. **Description:** The emergence of Nova Scotia as one of the leading wine-making places in Canada, in view of its favorable climate for growing grapes, is discussed.

13487 ■ **"Hike in Md.'s Alcohol Tax May Be Hard For Lawmakers to Swallow"** in *Baltimore Business Journal* (Vol. 28, November 19, 2010, No. 28)
Pub: Baltimore Business Journal
Ed: Emily Mullin. **Description:** Maryland's General Assembly has been reluctant to support a dime-per-drink increase in alcohol tax that was drafted in the 2009 bill if the tax revenue goes into a separate fund. The alcohol tax increase is considered unnecessary by some lawmakers and business leaders due to impending federal spending boosts.

13488 ■ **"Homes, Not Bars, Stay Well Tended"** in *Advertising Age* (Vol. 79, January 28, 2008, No. 4, pp. 8)
Pub: Crain Communications, Inc.
Ed: Jeremy Mullman. **Description:** Due to the downturn in the economy, consumers are drinking less at bars and restaurants; however, according to the Distilled Spirits Council of the United States, they are still purchasing expensive liquor to keep in their homes.

13489 ■ **"Imports Frothing Up Beer Market"** in *Globe & Mail* (February 16, 2006, pp. B4)
Pub: CTVglobemedia Publishing Inc.
Ed: Andy Hoffman. **Description:** The reasons behind the rise in market share of beer imports, in Canada, are presented.

13490 ■ **"Labatt to Swallow Lakeport"** in *Globe & Mail* (February 2, 2007, pp. B1)
Pub: CTVglobemedia Publishing Inc.
Ed: Keith McArthur. **Description:** The decision of Labatt Brewing Company Ltd. to acquire Lakeport Brewing Income Fund for $201.4 million is discussed.

13491 ■ **"Lawyers Cash In On Alcohol"** in *Business Journal Portland* (Vol. 27, November 19, 2010, No. 38, pp. 1)
Pub: Portland Business Journal
Ed: Andy Giegerich. **Description:** Oregon-based law firms have continued to corner big business on the state's growing alcohol industry as demand for their services increased. Lawyers, who represent wine, beer and liquor distillery interests, have seen their workload increased by 20 to 30 percent in 2009.

13492 ■ **"Leinie's Charts National Craft Beer Rollout"** in *The Business Journal-Milwaukee* (Vol. 25, August 29, 2008, No. 49, pp. A1)
Pub: American City Business Journals, Inc.
Ed: Rich Rovito. **Description:** Jacob Leinenkugel Brewing Co. is expected to complete the national rollout of its craft beer brands, while the launch of a new beer is prepared for this fall. The rollout is will likely benefit MillerCoors LLC, and will leave Alaska as the only state without Leinenkugel beer. Other views and information on Leinenkugel's national rollout are presented.

13493 ■ **"Liquor Stores Sips on Growth Cocktail"** in *Globe & Mail* (February 6, 2006, pp. B5)
Pub: CTVglobemedia Publishing Inc.
Ed: Omar El Akkad. **Description:** The business growth plans of Liquor Stores Income Fund are presented.

13494 ■ **"Little Cheer in Holiday Forecast for Champagne"** in *Advertising Age* (Vol. 88, November 17, 2008, No. 43, pp. 6)
Pub: Crain Communications, Inc.
Ed: Jeremy Mullman. **Description:** Due to a weak economy that has forced consumers to trade down from the most expensive alcoholic beverages as well as a weak U.S. dollar that has driven already lofty Champagne prices higher, makers of the French sparkling wine are anticipating a brutally slow holiday season.

13495 ■ **"MillerCoors Needs the Quickie Mart"** in *Crain's Chicago Business* (Vol. 32, November 16, 2009, No. 46, pp. 2)
Pub: Crain Communications, Inc.
Ed: David Sterrett. **Description:** Power Marts convenience store owner Sam Odeh says that Chicago-based MillerCoors LLC has done a poor job at promoting its brand, keeping its signs up to date and stocking the shelves at his stores. He complains that the company's service has been awful and the marketing pathetic. Convenience stores accounted for more than $14 billion in beer sales in the past year.

13496 ■ **"Moet, Rivals Pour More Ad Bucks Into Bubbly"** in *Advertising Age* (Vol. 88, September 3, 2007, No. 35, pp. 4)
Pub: Crain Communications, Inc.
Ed: Jeremy Mullman. **Description:** In an attempt to revive sluggish sales, champagne companies are raising their advertising budgets, transforming themselves from light-spending seasonal players to year-round heavyweights in the advertising world.

13497 ■ **"On the Itinerary: Your Future"** in *Entrepreneur* (Vol. 37, October 2009, No. 10, pp. 92)
Pub: Entrepreneur Media, Inc.
Ed: Joel Holland. **Description:** Josh Hackler's Spanish Vines imports and distributes wines from Spain while using Spanish culture to help market the wines. The business was hatched after Hackler signed up for a study-abroad program in Spain.

13498 ■ **"The Price Is Right: What You Can Learn From the Wine Industry"** in *Advertising Age* (Vol. 88, February 11, 2008, No. 6, pp. 14)
Pub: Crain Communications, Inc.
Ed: Lenore Skenazy. **Description:** In California a wine study was conducted in which participants' brains were hooked up to an MRI so researchers could watch what was happening in both the taste centers as well as the pleasure centers; the participants were given three different wines but were told that the samples were from a variety of wines that differed radically in price; surprisingly, the differences did not affect the taste centers of the brain, however, when the participants were told that a sample was more expensive, the pleasure centers were greatly affected.

13499 ■ **"Sobering Consequences"** in *The Business Journal-Milwaukee* (Vol. 25, July 11, 2008, No. 42, pp. A1)
Pub: American City Business Journals, Inc.
Ed: Rich Rovito. **Description:** Milwaukee Mayor Tom Barrett and Wisconsin Governor Jim Doyle met with MillerCoors management in an effort to convince the company to locate its corporate headquarters in the city. The company is expected to announce its decision by mid-July 2008. It was revealed that the decision-making process is focusing on determining an optimal location for the headquarters.

13500 ■ **"A Very Good Year for Beer"** in *Entrepreneur* (Vol. 37, October 2009, No. 10, pp. 18)
Pub: Entrepreneur Media, Inc.
Ed: Jennie Dorris. **Description:** Americans are shifting to craft beers, as shown by the almost 6 percent rise in craft beer sales in 2008. Mass-market domestic brand sales grew 0.6 percent while imported beer sales declined by 3.4 percent.

13501 ■ **"What'll You Have Tonight?"** in *Barron's* (Vol. 88, July 4, 2008, No. 28, pp. 22)
Pub: Dow Jones & Co., Inc.
Ed: Neil A. Martin. **Description:** Shares of Diageo could rise by 30 percent a year from June 2008 after it slipped due to U.S. sales worries. The company

also benefits from the trend toward more premium alcoholic beverage brands worldwide especially in emerging markets.

13502 ■ **"Wirtz Partners With California Liquor Wholesaler To Expand Reach"** in *Chicago Tribune* (December 17, 2008)
Pub: McClatchy-Tribune Information Services
Ed: Mike Hughlett. **Description:** Young's Market Co. and Wirtz Beverage Group have tentatively agreed to a joint venture that will give both companies a larger reach in the wine and liquor distribution business.

SOURCES OF SUPPLY

13503 ■ *Beverage World—Buyers Guide Issue*
Pub: Beverage World
Contact: Jeff Cioletti, Editor-in-Chief
E-mail: jcioletti@beverageworld.com
Released: Annual, Latest edition June 2008. **Publication Includes:** List of suppliers to the beverage industry. **Entries Include:** Company name, address. **Arrangement:** Classified by product.

STATISTICAL SOURCES

13504 ■ *RMA Annual Statement Studies*
Pub: Robert Morris Associates (RMA)
Released: Annual. **Price:** $175.00 2006-07 edition, $105.00. **Description:** Contains composite balance sheets and income statements for more than 360 industries, including the accounting, auditing, and bookkeeping industries. Also contains five years of comparative historical data for discerning trends. Includes 16 commonly used ratios, computed for most of the size groupings for nearly every industry.

13505 ■ *The U.S. Liquor Market*
Pub: Business Trend Analysts, Inc.
Released: 2004-2005. **Price:** $1695.00. **Description:** Tracks the size and growth of the U.S. liquor market, covering all types of white and dark distilled spirits, cordials, liqueurs, cognac, brandy, and more.

TRADE PERIODICALS

13506 ■ *Beverage Dynamics*
Pub: Beverage Information Group
Contact: Richard Brandes, Editor-in-Chief
E-mail: rbrandes@m2media360.com
Released: Bimonthly. **Price:** $20 print version; $50 Canada and Mexico print version; $130 print version; $30 print & digital version; $60 Canada and Mexico print & digital version; $140 other countries print & digital version. **Description:** Trade magazine on beverage and food retail business.

13507 ■ *Beverage World*
Pub: Beverage World
Contact: Andrew Kaplan, Managing Editor
Released: Monthly. **Price:** $99. **Description:** Trade magazine for corporate, marketing, distribution, production, and purchasing top and middle management in the multi-product beverage industry.

13508 ■ *Modern Brewery Age*
Pub: Business Journals Inc.
Contact: Mac R. Brighton, Chm., COO
E-mail: macb@busjour.com
Released: Bimonthly. **Price:** $125. **Description:** Magazine for the wholesale and brewing industry.

FRANCHISES AND BUSINESS OPPORTUNITIES

13509 ■ **Bevinco**
505 Consumers Rd., Ste. 510
Toronto, ON, Canada M2J 4V8
Ph:(416)490-6266
Free: 888-238-4626
Fax:(416)490-6899
Co. E-mail: info@bevinco.com

URL: http://www.bevinco.com
No. of Franchise Units: 250. **No. of Company-Owned Units:** 1. **Founded:** 1987. **Franchised:** 1991. **Description:** Liquor inventory control system for bars, restaurants, hotels, clubs, etc. **Equity Capital Needed:** $40,000. **Franchise Fee:** $40,000. **Financial Assistance:** Up to $10,000 for qualified candidates. **Training:** 7 days corporate training in Toronto, 5-10 days regional training with state master franchise.

LIBRARIES

13510 ■ Distilled Spirits Council of the U.S. Library
1250 Eye St. NW, Ste. 400
Washington, DC 20005
Ph:(202)628-3544
Fax:(202)682-8888
URL: http://www.discus.org/

Scope: Distilled spirits industry, prohibition, temperance movement, alcoholism, liquor laws, alcohol and health/safety issues, moderate drinking, drinking customs. **Services:** Interlibrary loan; copying; Library open to researchers with prior approval. **Holdings:** 3500 volumes; 72 VF drawers of information on subjects and organizations. **Subscriptions:** 225 journals and other serials.

ASSOCIATIONS AND OTHER ORGANIZATIONS

13511 ■ Association of Authors' Representatives
676A 9th Ave., Ste. 312
New York, NY 10036
Ph:(212)840-5777
Co. E-mail: administrator@aaronline.org
URL: http://www.aaronline.org
Contact: Jody Klein, Admin. Sec.
Description: Literary and dramatic agents who market books, plays, and other literary and dramatic material. .

13512 ■ Association of Talent Agents
9255 Sunset Blvd., Ste. 930
Los Angeles, CA 90069
Ph:(310)274-0628
Fax:(310)274-5063
Co. E-mail: shellie@agentassociation.com
URL: http://www.agentassociation.com
Contact: Sandy Bresler, Pres.
Description: Talent agencies that have clients in the Screen Actors Guild, American Federation of Television and Radio Artists, Directors Guild of America, Writers Guild of America, East, and Writers Guild of America, West. Negotiates terms of franchise agreements with these guilds and maintains liaison with their representatives. Assists members with contract problems, interpretations, rulings, residual matters, and arbitrations. Employs legal counsel to prepare opinions upon request and to file briefs in arbitrations and labor commission hearings. Maintains liaison with labor commission representatives in San Francisco and Los Angeles, CA, and intervenes on behalf of individual members having special problems. Conducts seminars and symposia. **Publications:** *Employment Law* .

REFERENCE WORKS

13513 ■ *International Literary Market Place*
Pub: Information Today Inc.
Contact: Thomas H. Hogan, Publisher/Pres.
Released: Annual, Latest edition 2012. **Price:** $289, individuals softbound; $260.10, individuals first time standing order. **Covers:** Over 10,500 publishers in over 180 countries outside the United States and Canada, and about 1,499 trade and professional organizations related to publishing abroad; includes major printers, binders, typesetters, book manufacturers, book dealers, libraries, literary agencies, translators, book clubs, reference books and journals, periodicals, prizes, and international reference section. **Entries Include:** For publishers—Name, address, phone, fax, telex, names and titles of key personnel, branches, type of publications, subjects, ISBN prefix. Listings for others include similar information but less detail. **Arrangement:** Classified by business activities, then geographical. **Indexes:** Company name, subject, type of publication.

TRADE PERIODICALS

13514 ■ *Fiction Writer's Guideline*
Pub: Fiction Writer's Connection
Contact: Blythe Camenson, Editor & Dir.
E-mail: bcamenson@aol.com
Released: Enewsletter. **Price: Description:** Offers practical advice and support on writing and getting published. Recurring features include interviews, book reviews, and Advice From agents and editors and Writing Tips.

13515 ■ *Publishers Weekly*
Pub: Publishers Weekly
Contact: Sonia Jaffe Robbins, Managing Editor
Released: Weekly. **Price:** $249.99; $299.99 Canada; $399.99 other countries air delivery. **Description:** Magazine for publishers.

13516 ■ *Writer's Digest*
Pub: FW Media Inc.
Contact: Nancy Miller, Advertising Sales Rep.
E-mail: nancymiller@fwmedia.com
Released: 8/yr. **Price:** $19.96; $29.96 Canada including GST/HST; $29.96 other countries surface delivery. **Description:** Professional magazine for writers.

ASSOCIATIONS AND OTHER ORGANIZATIONS

13517 ■ Associated Locksmiths of America
3500 Easy St.
Dallas, TX 75247
Ph:(214)819-9733
Free: 800-532-2562
Fax:(214)819-9736
URL: http://www.aloa.org
Contact: Hans Mejlshede CML, Pres.
Description: Retail locksmiths; associate members are manufacturers and distributors of locks, keys, safes, and burglar alarms. Aims to educate and provide current information to individuals in the physical security industry. Maintains information and referral services for members; offers insurance and bonding programs. Holds annual five-day technical training classes and 3-day technical exhibit. Maintains museum. **Publications:** *Keynotes* (monthly).

13518 ■ Lock Museum of America
230 Main St., Rte. 6
PO Box 104
Terryville, CT 06786-0104
Ph:(860)589-6359
Fax:(860)589-6359
Co. E-mail: thomasnsc@aol.com
URL: http://www.lockmuseum.com
Contact: Thomas F. Hennessy Jr., Pres./Asst. Curator
Description: Locksmiths, lock collectors, lock and key manufacturers, and builders. Seeks to preserve and exhibit the colonial American craft of lock, key, and security device making. Maintains hall of fame and museum. **Publications:** *Newsletter and Historical Research Series* (quarterly).

13519 ■ Security Hardware Distributors Association
105 Eastern Ave., Ste. 104
Annapolis, MD 21403
Ph:(410)940-6346
Fax:(410)263-1659
Co. E-mail: info@shda.org
URL: http://associationdatabase.com/aws/SHDA/pt/
sp/Home_Page
Contact: Steve Dyson, Pres.
Description: Wholesalers of locksmith supplies; associate members are manufacturers of locks and locksmith supplies. **Publications:** *SHDA Unlocked* (monthly).

DIRECTORIES OF EDUCATIONAL PROGRAMS

13520 ■ *Directory of Private Accredited Career Schools and Colleges of Technology*
Pub: Accrediting Commission of Career Schools and Colleges of Technology
Contact: Michale S. McComis, Exec. Dir.
Released: On web page. **Price:** Free. **Description:** Covers 3900 accredited post-secondary programs

that provide training programs in business, trade, and technical fields, including various small business endeavors. Entries offer school name, address, phone, description of courses, job placement assistance, and requirements for admission. Arrangement is alphabetical.

REFERENCE WORKS

13521 ■ "Eve in the Sky: A Look at Security Tech from All Angles" in *Bellingtham Business Journal* (October 2008, pp. 23)
Pub: Sun News Inc.
Ed: Lance Henderson. **Description:** High tech solutions to security issues in any company are not the only things to be considered; a low-tech evaluation of a building and its security fixtures, such as door knobs, locks, doors and windows as well as lighting are important aspects to security any office.

13522 ■ "SECO Manufacturing" in *Point of Beginning* (Vol. , 2008, No. , pp.)
Pub: BNP Media
Description: Seco Manufacturing's 3015-Series lock features an all-metal tilting holder with an improved brass front locking lever for improved security for any building.

13523 ■ "Vandal-Resistant Mortise Locks" in *Building Design and Construction* (Vol. 49, September 1, 2008, No. 12, pp. 78)
Pub: Reed Business Information
Description: Stanley Security Solutions offers mortise locks with a vandal-resistant feature that includes a clutch mechanism designed to break away when excessive force is applied either by kicking or standing on the lever. Once the mortise lock breaks away it can be easily reset to its original position without sustaining damage.

TRADE PERIODICALS

13524 ■ *American Lock Collectors Association Newsletter*
Pub: American Lock Collectors Association
Ed: Robert Dix, Editor, dixlock@aol.com. **Released:** Bimonthly. **Price:** $18, U.S.; $22, Canada; $30, elsewhere. **Description:** Provides information on the collecting, history, buying, selling, and trading of antique and unusual locks, keys, handcuffs, and locking devices. Carries announcements and reports of collector shows.

13525 ■ *Keynotes*
Pub: Associated Locksmiths of America
Contact: Jennifer Brown, Advertising Mgr
Released: Monthly. **Description:** Trade magazine for locksmiths and other security specialists.

13526 ■ *National Locksmith*
Pub: National Publishing Company Inc.
Contact: Jeffery Adair, Sales & Mktg. Dir.
Ed: Greg Mango, Editor. **Released:** 13/yr. **Description:** Magazine focusing on physical security and locksmithing.

TRADE SHOWS AND CONVENTIONS

13527 ■ ALOA Security Expo
Associated Locksmiths of America Inc.
3500 Easy St.
Dallas, TX 75247
Ph:(214)819-9733
Free: 800-532-2562
Fax:(214)827-1810
Co. E-mail: media@aloa.org
URL: http://www.aloa.org
Audience: Retailers, wholesalers and manufacturers of physical security products. **Principal Exhibits:** Physical security products, including: locks, safes, door hardware, alarms and related products and services.

FRANCHISES AND BUSINESS OPPORTUNITIES

13528 ■ Pop-A-Lock
SystemForward America, Inc.
1018 Harding St., Ste. 101
Lafayette, LA 70503
Ph:(337)233-6211
Co. E-mail: michaelkleimeyer@systemforward.com
URL: http://www.popalock.com
No. of Franchise Units: 220. **Founded:** 1991. **Franchised:** 1994. **Description:** Mobile locksmith/car unlocking service. There is no build-out required with quick to market/revenue generation. Your employees provide our mobile tech services to commercial & residential customers, and national accounts. **Equity Capital Needed:** $50,000 and up, based on territory population. **Franchise Fee:** $29,000. **Financial Assistance:** Third party, SBA National Franchise Registry. **Training:** Offers new franchisee business training, employee advanced technical training including state-of-the-art dispatch service. Provides ongoing technical updates, public relations and marketing, business analysis, and National Accounts Support-mentor program.

LIBRARIES

13529 ■ Lock Museum of America Inc. Library
PO Box 104
230 Main St., Rte. 6
Terryville, CT 06786-0104
Ph:(860)589-6359
Fax:(860)589-6359
Co. E-mail: thomasnsc@aol.com
URL: http://www.lockmuseum.com/
Contact: Thomas F. Hennessy, Cur.
Scope: Locks, keys, ornate hardware. **Services:** Copying; Library open to the public. **Holdings:** 1000 books; 500 bound periodical volumes; 1200 patents; patent indexes, 1790-1977.

ASSOCIATIONS AND OTHER ORGANIZATIONS

13530 ■ Leather Apparel Association
4705 Center Blvd., Ste. 806
Long Island City, NY 11109
Ph:(718)606-0767
Fax:(718)606-6345
Co. E-mail: info@leatherassociation.com
URL: http://www.leatherapparelassociation.com
Contact: Richard Harrow, Exec. Dir.
Description: Manufacturers, retailers, tanners, cleaners, and other individuals involved in the leather garment industry. Seeks to increase the sales of leather clothing through public relations, consumer education, and business support services. Marketing programs focus on fashion videos, media tours, press kits, brochures, hangtags, manufacturing and cleaning guidelines, and market research. Conducts seminars. .

13531 ■ Leather Industries of America
3050 K St. NW, Ste. 400
Washington, DC 20007
Ph:(202)342-8497
Fax:(202)342-8583
Co. E-mail: info@leatherusa.com
URL: http://www.leatherusa.com
Description: Represents the interests of the American tanner and leather suppliers. Provides environmental, technical, education, statistical and marketing services. **Publications:** *Dictionary of Leather Terminology* (periodic); *Leather Facts*; *Leather Industries of America's Member Directory and Buyer's Guide* (annual); *Technical Bulletin* (periodic); *U.S. Leather Industries Statistics* (annual).

13532 ■ National Luggage Dealers Association
1817 Elmdale Ave.
Glenview, IL 60026
Ph:(847)998-6869
Fax:(847)998-6884
Co. E-mail: inquiry@nlda.com
URL: http://www.nlda.com
Description: Represents retailers of luggage, leather goods, gifts, and handbags. Buying group producing promotional materials. **Publications:** *Christmas Catalog* (annual);Membership Directory (annual).

REFERENCE WORKS

13533 ■ Leather Manufacturer Directory
Pub: Shoe Trades Publishing Co.
Released: Annual, Latest edition 2008. **Price:** $61, individuals. **Covers:** Tanneries, leather finishers, and hide processors and their suppliers in the United States and Canada. **Entries Include:** Company name, address, phone, names of executives, list of products or services and over 300 companies classified by their goods and services. **Arrangement:** Tanners and hide processors are geographical; suppliers are classified by product. **Indexes:** Tanners, classifications, hide processors.

13534 ■ "Packing Chic" in Black Enterprise (Vol. 38, February 2008, No. 7, pp. 154)
Pub: Earl G. Graves Publishing Co. Inc.
Ed: Sonai Alleyne. **Description:** Profile of Angela Theodora's leather overnight bags that offer a variety of smart compartments for the business traveler.

STATISTICAL SOURCES

13535 ■ RMA Annual Statement Studies
Pub: Robert Morris Associates (RMA)
Released: Annual. **Price:** $175.00 2006-07 edition, $105.00. **Description:** Contains composite balance sheets and income statements for more than 360 industries, including the accounting, auditing, and bookkeeping industries. Also contains five years of comparative historical data for discerning trends. Includes 16 commonly used ratios, computed for most of the size groupings for nearly every industry.

TRADE PERIODICALS

13536 ■ Travel Goods Showcase
Pub: Travel Goods Association
Contact: Michele Marini Pittinger, President
Released: Periodic, 5/yr. **Description:** Magazine featuring domestic luggage, leather goods, and handbags.

TRADE SHOWS AND CONVENTIONS

13537 ■ Canadian Luggage, Leathergoods, Handbags and Accessories Show
Pro-Sho Inc.
15 Lesmill Rd. Unit 7
East Toronto, ON, Canada M3B 2T3
Ph:(416)229-2060
Free: 800-896-7469
Fax:(416)223-2826
Co. E-mail: prosho@meteorshows.com
URL: http://www.llhashows.com
Released: Annual. **Audience:** Luggage, leather goods, and handbag retailers. **Principal Exhibits:** Luggage, leather goods, handbags, and travel accessories. **Dates and Locations:** 2011 Apr 10-12, Toronto, ON.

FRANCHISES AND BUSINESS OPPORTUNITIES

13538 ■ Leather Medic
5565 Lee St., Ste. 1
Lehigh Acres, FL 33971
Free: 888-561-0423
Fax:(239)561-5715
Co. E-mail: klife@leathermedic.com
URL: http://www.leathermedic.com
No. of Franchise Units: 35. **No. of Company-Owned Units:** 1. **Founded:** 1988. **Description:** Repairing and refinishing leather furniture. **Equity Capital Needed:** $47,500. **Franchise Fee:** $47,500. **Financial Assistance:** In-house financing available. **Training:** Offers 2 weeks of one-on-one training.

ASSOCIATIONS AND OTHER ORGANIZATIONS

13539 ■ American Lumber Standard Committee
PO Box 210
Germantown, MD 20875-0210
Ph:(301)972-1700
Fax:(301)540-8004
Co. E-mail: alsc@alsc.org
URL: http://www.alsc.org
Contact: T.D. Searles, Pres.

Description: Members appointed by the Department of Commerce to represent producers, consumers, and specifiers of softwood lumber. Establishes and maintains standards for size, grade, and other matters; elects an independent board of review to approve softwood lumber grading rules and accredit agencies that audit treating plants and accredit agencies that audit pallet, box and crate manufacturers for international trade. .

13540 ■ American Walnut Manufacturers Association
1007 N 725 W
West Lafayette, IN 47906-9431
Co. E-mail: jackson@purdue.edu
URL: http://www.walnutassociation.org
Contact: Liz Jackson, Exec. Dir.

Description: Manufacturers of hardwood veneer and lumber, especially American black walnut. Seeks to improve the sale of products made from hardwoods through advertising, promotion, sales education and product improvement; also promotes good forest management. .

13541 ■ APA: The Engineered Wood Association
7011 S 19th St.
Tacoma, WA 98466
Ph:(253)565-6600
Fax:(253)565-7265
Co. E-mail: marilyn.lemoine@apawood.org
URL: http://www.apawood.org
Contact: Dennis Hardman, Pres.

Description: Manufacturers of structural panel products, oriented strand board and composites. Conducts trade promotion through advertising, publicity, merchandising, and field promotion. Maintains quality supervision in accordance with U.S. product standards, APA performance standards, and APA trademarking. Conducts research to improve products, applications, and manufacturing techniques. Sponsors Engineered Wood Research Foundation; compiles statistics. **Publications:** *Engineered Wood Journal*; *Management Report* (monthly).

13542 ■ Hardwood Manufacturers Association
665 Rodi Rd., Ste. 305
Pittsburgh, PA 15235
Ph:(412)244-0440

Fax:(412)244-9090
Co. E-mail: ljovanovich@hardwood.org
URL: http://www.hmamembers.org
Contact: Linda Jovanovich

Description: Represents manufacturers of hardwood lumber and hardwood products. Conducts national consumer promotion program. **Publications:** *HMA Link* (monthly).

13543 ■ Hardwood Plywood and Veneer Association
1825 Michael Faraday Dr.
Reston, VA 20190
Ph:(703)435-2900
Fax:(703)435-2537
Co. E-mail: hpva@hpva.org
URL: http://www.hpva.org
Contact: Mr. Kip Howlett, Pres.

Description: Manufacturers and finishers of hardwood plywood; manufacturers and sales agents of veneer; suppliers of glue, machinery, and other products related to the industry; stocking distributors. Conducts laboratory testing of plywood, adhesives, finishes, flamespread, formaldehyde emissions, structural, and smoke density. Performs glue bond, flamespread, formaldehyde emissions, and structural listing services. Provides public relations, advertising, marketing, and technical services to members. Represents the industry in legislative matters and keeps members informed on tariff and trade actions. **Publications:** *Hardwood Plywood*; *Hardwood Plywood and Veneer News* (monthly); *Where to Buy Hardwood Plywood, Veneer, and Engineered Hardwood Flooring Membership Directory* (annual).

13544 ■ International Wood Products Association
4214 King St.
Alexandria, VA 22302
Ph:(703)820-6696
Fax:(703)820-8550
Co. E-mail: info@iwpawood.org
URL: http://www.iwpawood.org
Contact: Brent J. McClendon CAE, Exec. VP

Description: Importers, processors, manufacturers, and distributors of imported wood products; steamship companies; customs brokers; etc. Membership figure represents participants from 30 countries. Promotes acceptance and use of imported wood products; develops product standards; compiles statistics; supports good forestry management. **Publications:** *Imported Wood: The Guide to Applications, Sources and Trends* (annual).

13545 ■ National Hardwood Lumber Association
PO Box 34518
Memphis, TN 38184-0518
Ph:(901)377-1818
Free: 800-933-0318
Fax:(901)399-7581
Co. E-mail: membership@nhla.com
URL: http://www.nhla.com
Contact: Mark Barford, Exec. Dir.

Description: United States, Canadian and International hardwood lumber and veneer manufacturers, distributors and consumers. Inspects hardwood

lumber. Maintains inspection training school. Conducts management and marketing seminars for the hardwood industry. Promotes research in hardwood timber management and utilization. Promotes public awareness of the industry. **Publications:** *Hardwood Matters* (monthly).

13546 ■ National Lumber and Building Material Dealers Association
2025 M St. NW, Ste. 800
Washington, DC 20036-3309
Ph:(202)367-1169
Free: 800-634-8645
Fax:(202)367-2169
Co. E-mail: info@dealer.org
URL: http://www.dealer.org
Contact: Michael O'Brien CAE, Pres./CEO

Description: Represents more than 8,000 lumber and building material companies with over 400,000 employees, 20 state and regional associations and the industry's leading manufacturers and service providers. **Publications:** *Cost of Doing Business* (annual); *Forklift and You*; *NLBMDA Advocate* (monthly); *Nuts & Bolts*; *ProSales* (monthly); *Risk Management Best Practices*; *Your National Perspective* (quarterly).

13547 ■ North American Wholesale Lumber Association
3601 Algonquin Rd., Ste. 400
Rolling Meadows, IL 60008
Ph:(847)870-7470
Free: 800-527-8258
Fax:(847)870-0201
Co. E-mail: info@nawla.org
URL: http://www.lumber.org
Contact: Gary Vitale, Pres.

Description: Wholesale distributors of lumber, wood products, and complementary products. Aids members with procedure for settling trade disputes. Provides weeklong course for wholesale lumber traders. Compiles statistics. Provides networking opportunities at regional, and annual meetings, trade show, and NAWLA Traders Market. **Publications:** *North American Wholesale Lumber Association— Membership Bulletin* (monthly).

13548 ■ Northeastern Lumber Manufacturers Association
PO Box 87A
Cumberland, ME 04021
Ph:(207)829-6901
Fax:(207)829-4293
Co. E-mail: info@nelma.org
URL: http://www.nelma.org
Contact: Jeff Easterling, Pres.

Description: Manufacturers of hardwood and softwood lumber and timber products in the New England states, New York, and Pennsylvania. Promotes the interests of the northeastern lumber manufacturing industry. Encourages uniformity, efficiency, and economy in the manufacture, gradation, distribution, and use of lumber and timber products. Encourages the use of lumber and timber products and the conservation and renewal of forest resources by improved forest utilization and practices. Conducts economic research on forest and other industry problems, and technical and other investigations of the properties and uses of wood. Collects and disseminates statistics and other economic information. Presents the views of the industry to other organizations, the government, and the public. Sponsors annual two-week training school for softwood lumber graders. **Publications:** *Dimensional Lumber; Eastern White Pine; Northeastern Lumber Manufacturers Association—Buyer's Guide and Membership Directory* (annual); *Standard Grading Rules for Northeastern Lumber* .

13549 ■ Northwestern Lumber Association
5905 Golden Valley Rd., No. 110
Minneapolis, MN 55422
Ph:(763)544-6822
Free: 888-544-6822
Fax:(763)595-4060
Co. E-mail: psiewert@nlassn.org
URL: http://www.nlassn.org
Contact: Paula Siewert, Pres.
Description: Building materials dealers in Iowa, Minnesota, North Dakota, South Dakota and Wisconsin; associate members are distributors, manufacturers, and allied industries. **Publications:** *Building Products Connection* (bimonthly); *Dealer Reference Manual and Buyers' Guide* (annual); *Northwestern Scene* (monthly).

13550 ■ Southeastern Lumber Manufacturers Association
200 Greencastle Rd.
Tyrone, GA 30290
Ph:(770)631-6701
Fax:(770)631-6720
Co. E-mail: wendy@slma.org
URL: http://www.slma.org
Contact: Debbie Burns, Pres.
Description: Independent southeastern lumber manufacturers. Represents and coordinates efforts of membership to alleviate local, regional, and national problems that affect independent southeastern lumber manufacturing industry. Conducts marketing and promotional activities. .

13551 ■ Western Building Material Association
PO Box 1699
Olympia, WA 98507
Ph:(360)943-3054
Fax:(360)943-1219
Co. E-mail: casey@wbma.org
URL: http://www.wbma.org
Contact: Casey Voorhees, Exec. Dir.
Description: Retail lumber and building material dealers in states of Alaska, Hawaii, Idaho, Montana, Oregon, and Washington. Seeks to further and protect the interests of retail lumber dealers. Services include: classes, workshops, and seminars; group insurance and pension; printing of business forms; government and legislative action; information clearinghouse; training courses for personnel. Maintains a learning resource center. Conducts educational programs. **Publications:** *Western Building Material Association—Management Guide* (monthly); *Western Building Material Association—Newsletter* (monthly); *Western News* (monthly).

13552 ■ Western Red Cedar Lumber Association
1501-700 W Pender St.
Pender Pl. 1, Business Bldg.
Vancouver, BC, Canada V6C 1G8
Ph:(604)684-0266
Free: (866)778-9096
Fax:(604)687-4930
Co. E-mail: wrcla@wrcla.org
URL: http://www.wrcla.org
Description: Represents producers of Western Red Cedar lumber products. Aims to help consumers understand cedar's long-term benefits and special features. Provides information on how to use cedar properly. **Publications:** *Where to Buy Western Red Cedar* (annual).

13553 ■ Western Wood Products Association
522 SW 5th Ave., Ste. 500
Portland, OR 97204-2122
Ph:(503)224-3930

Fax:(503)224-3934
Co. E-mail: info@wwpa.org
URL: http://www2.wwpa.org
Contact: Kevin Binam, Pres./CEO
Description: Represents lumber manufacturers in 12 Western states and Alaska. Delivers lumber grade inspection and quality control, technical support, product/market support and statistical services to Western sawmills. .

REFERENCE WORKS

13554 ■ "Bad News for Canada: U.S. New-Home Starts Sink" in *Globe & Mail* (February 17, 2007, pp. B7)
Pub: CTVglobemedia Publishing Inc.
Ed: Tavia Grant. **Description:** The new-home construction in the United States dropped by 14.3 percent in January 2007. The sinking construction activity shows significant impact on the Canadian factories and lumber companies.

13555 ■ "Blueprint for Profit: Family-Run Lumberyard Sets Sites On Sales of $100 Million a Year" in *Small Business Opportunities* (Jan. 2008)
Pub: Harris Publications Inc.
Ed: Stan Roberts. **Description:** Profile of family-run lumberyard whose owner shares insight into the challenges of competing with big box operations like Home Depot and Lowe's.

13556 ■ *Directory of Home Center Operators & Hardware Chains*
Pub: Chain Store Guide
Released: Annual, Latest edition 2010. **Price:** $395, individuals Directory; $445, individuals online lite; $1,075, individuals online pro. **Covers:** 4,500 U.S. and Canadian companies which operate home centers, home center warehouses, lumber and building material outlets, specialty paint and home decorating stores, and kitchen and bath centers. Concentrates on companies with a minimum annual sales of one million dollars. **Entries Include:** Company name, address, phone, fax, 6,500 personnel e-mail address, web site, Internet order processing indicator, listing type, product lines, total sales, sales percentage per customer type, total selling square footage, total stores, units by type of store operated, units made by trade name, trading areas, projected openings and remodeling, distribution center locations, buying and/or marketing group name and location, number of nurseries operated, average number of check-outs, year founded, public company indicator, parent and subsidiary company information, division and branch office locations, key personnel, and number of locations by city. **Arrangement:** Geographical. **Indexes:** Product line, alphabetical, exclusions, state.

13557 ■ "Furniture Making May Come Back—Literally" in *Business North Carolina* (Vol. 28, March 2008, No. 3, pp. 32)
Pub: Business North Carolina
Description: Due to the weak U.S. dollar and the fact that lumber processors never left the country, foreign furniture manufacturers are becoming interested in moving manufacturing plants to the U.S.

13558 ■ "Goldbelt Inc.: Targeting Shareholder Development" in *Alaska Business Monthly* (Vol. 27, October 2011, No. 10, pp. 108)
Pub: Alaska Business Publishing Company
Ed: Tracy Kalytiak. **Description:** Profile of Goldbelt Inc., the company that has changed its original focus of timber to real estate to tourism and then to government contracting opportunities.

13559 ■ *International Wood Products Association—Directory*
Pub: International Wood Products Association
Contact: Brent J. McClendon CAE, Exec. VP
Released: Annual, summer. **Covers:** Includes 220 U.S. importers, overseas suppliers, and service providers to the imported wood products industry. **Entries Include:** Company name, address, phone,

names of executives, list of products or services, fax, e-mail addresses, URL. **Arrangement:** Classified by type of membership.

13560 ■ "Lumber Rebounds" in *Business Journal Portland* (Vol. 26, December 11, 2009, No. 40, pp. 1)
Pub: American City Business Journals Inc.
Ed: Erik Siemers. **Description:** Oregon's lumber industry could be boosted as wood consumption across the country is expected to increase by 11 percent or 34.5 billion board feet in 2010.

13561 ■ "The Main Event" in *Canadian Business* (Vol. 80, November 19, 2007, No. 23, pp. 28)
Pub: Rogers Media
Ed: Zena Olijnyk. **Description:** U.S.-based Lowe's Companies, Inc. will be opening three stores in Canada in December 2007 and another three in 2008. The housing market crisis in the U.S. is the reason behind the home improvement store's Canadian expansion. The impacts of the expansion on Canadian home care stores and on the market competition are evaluated.

13562 ■ *Merchant Magazine—Buyers Guide*
Pub: Cutler Publishing Inc.
Contact: Alan Oakes, Publisher
E-mail: ajoakes@aol.com
Released: Monthly. **Price:** $3, U.S. per issue; $18, U.S. per year. **Publication Includes:** List of over 400 suppliers of lumber and home improvement goods in 13 western states. **Entries Include:** Company name and phone. **Arrangement:** Geographical.

13563 ■ *Mid-America Lumbermens Association—Buyer's Guide and Dealer Directory*
Pub: Mid-America Lumbermens Association
Released: Annual, Latest edition 2011. **Price:** $150, nonmembers plus shipping; Free; $30, members additional copies. **Covers:** Lumber and building material suppliers nationwide and retail lumber dealers in Arkansas, Kansas, Missouri, Nebraska, Oklahoma; retail associations, national building industry associations, and line yards. **Entries Include:** For dealers—Company name, address, phone, names of contacts. For suppliers—Company name, address, phone, fax, toll free number, email, URL, representative's names. **Arrangement:** Alphabetical for suppliers; geographical for dealers. **Indexes:** Product, brand name, supplier, retail dealer.

13564 ■ "Montana's Manufacturing Industry" in *Montana Business Quarterly* (Vol. 49, Spring 2011, No. 1, pp. 29)
Pub: Bureau of Business & Economic Research
Ed: Todd A. Morgan, Charles E. Keegan III, Colin B. Sorenson. **Description:** Manufacturing remains a vital part of Montana's economy despite the recession and decline in the production of wood products. Statistical data included.

13565 ■ *National Hardwood Lumber Association—Members*
Pub: National Hardwood Lumber Association
Contact: Mark Barford, Exec. Dir.
Released: Annual, January. **Covers:** 2,000 United States, Canadian, and foreign hardwood lumber manufacturers, distributors, and consumers. **Entries Include:** Company, address, headquarters location if a plant or branch office. **Arrangement:** Separate geographical sections for active, associate, and sustaining members.

13566 ■ *North American Building Material Distribution Association—Membership Directory*
Pub: North American Building Material Distribution Association
Released: Annual. **Covers:** About 200 wholesale distributors of building products who are members, and 150 manufacturers in that field who are associate members and over 800 of their locations. **Entries Include:** Company name, address, phone, fax, name of principal executive, products offered. **Arrangement:** Geographical. **Indexes:** Alphabetical.

13567 ■ *Panel World—Directory and Buyers' Guide Issue*
Pub: Hatton-Brown Publishers Inc.
Contact: Rhonda Thomas
E-mail: rhonda@hattonbrown.com
Released: Annual, Latest edition January 2011. **Covers:** List of manufacturers and suppliers of machinery, equipment, and supplies, including veneers and panels, to the woodworking industry; trade associations. **Entries Include:** For companies—Name, address, phone, fax, e-mail, website address. For associations—Name, address, phone, fax, e-mail, website, annual meeting dates, key contacts. **Arrangement:** Separate geographical sections for machinery manufacturers and veneer/panel manufacturers. **Indexes:** Product, machine manufacturers.

13568 ■ "Pulp Friction: Spin Off Mills to Boost Wood Products" in *Globe & Mail* (February 18, 2006, pp. B3)
Pub: CTVglobemedia Publishing Inc.
Ed: Peter Kennedy. **Description:** The reasons behind the decision of chief executive officer Jim Shepherd of Canfor Corp. to sell pulp mills are presented.

13569 ■ *Where to Buy Hardwood Plywood, Veneer, and Engineered Hardwood Flooring Buyers' Guide*
Pub: Hardwood Plywood & Veneer Association
Released: Annual, Latest edition 2011. **Price:** Free. **Covers:** About 196 member manufacturers of veneer and hardwood plywood, prefinishers and their suppliers. Also includes wholesale stocking distributors. **Entries Include:** Company name, address, phone, name and title of sales contact, list of products and services. **Arrangement:** Classified by type of manufacturer or member.

STATISTICAL SOURCES

13570 ■ *RMA Annual Statement Studies*
Pub: Robert Morris Associates (RMA)
Released: Annual. **Price:** $175.00 2006-07 edition, $105.00. **Description:** Contains composite balance sheets and income statements for more than 360 industries, including the accounting, auditing, and bookkeeping industries. Also contains five years of comparative historical data for discerning trends. Includes 16 commonly used ratios, computed for most of the size groupings for nearly every industry.

13571 ■ *Standard & Poor's Industry Surveys*
Pub: Standard & Poor's Corp.
Released: Annual. **Price:** $3633.00. **Description:** Two-volume book that examines the prospects for specific industries, including trucking. Also provides analyses of trends and problems, statistical tables and charts, and comparative company analyses.

TRADE PERIODICALS

13572 ■ *APA—The Engineered Wood Association—Management Journal*
Pub: APA—The Engineered Wood Association
Contact: Maria Johnsen
Ed: Jack Merry, Editor, jack.merry@apawood.org.
Released: Semiannual. **Description:** Provides news influencing the use or acceptance of structural panels. Covers subjects including economic outlook, promotional programs and other activities of the Association, and legislative developments.

13573 ■ *Ask NELMA Newsletter*
Pub: Northeastern Lumber Manufacturers Association
Contact: D. Reynolds
Ed: Donna J. Reynolds, Editor. **Released:** Monthly. **Description:** Discusses the growth, harvesting, production, and marketing of Northeastern lumber. Includes news of federal and state activities and of business of the Association.

13574 ■ *Building Products Digest*
Pub: Cutler Publishing Inc.
Contact: Alan Oakes, Publisher
E-mail: ajoakes@aol.com
Released: Monthly. **Price:** $24; $39 two years. **Description:** Magazine covering lumber yards, home centers, retailers, and wholesalers.

13575 ■ *The Lumber Co-Operator*
Pub: Northeastern Retail Lumber Association
Contact: Jeff Sacks
E-mail: jsacks@nrla.org
Released: Bimonthly. **Price:** $40; $50 Canada; $35 nonmembers groups of five or more. **Description:** Trade publication serving the building material industry in the Northeast and Canada.

13576 ■ *The Merchant Magazine*
Pub: Cutler Publishing Inc.
Contact: Chuck Casey, Advertising Mgr
E-mail: ccasey@building-products.com
Released: Monthly. **Price:** $22; $36 two years. **Description:** Lumber and building materials magazine for the retailer and wholesaler of lumber & building materials.

13577 ■ *Northwestern Scene*
Pub: Northwestern Lumber Association
Contact: Melanie Hultman
Ed: Gary L. Smith, Editor. **Released:** Monthly. **Price:** Included in membership. **Description:** Concentrates on providing retail lumber dealers in Iowa, Minnesota, North Dakota, and South Dakota with information and news relating to the lumber industry. Also contains information of interest to distributors, manufacturers, and allied industries. Recurring features include news of members, news of research, reports of industry developments and trends, and notices of Association activities and events.

13578 ■ *Panel World*
Pub: Hatton-Brown Publishers Inc.
Contact: Jennifer McCary, Sen. Assoc. Ed.
E-mail: jmccary@hattonbrowwn.com
Ed: Rich Donnell, Editor, rich@hattonbrown.com. **Released:** Bimonthly. **Price:** $50; $60 Canada; $24.95 full online; $9.95 limited online; $95 other countries. **Description:** Business magazine serving the worldwide veneer, plywood, and panel board industry.

13579 ■ *Random Lengths Weekly Report*
Pub: Random Lengths Publications Inc.
Ed: Burrle Elmore, Editor. **Released:** Weekly. **Price:** $345, U.S.; $357, Canada by mail; $289. **Description:** Covers the North American softwood markets, including lumber, plywood, oriented strand board, and related products. Includes price guides. Recurring features include a calendar of events and notices of publications available.

TRADE SHOWS AND CONVENTIONS

13580 ■ Lumbermen's Association of Texas Convention
Lumbermen's Association of Texas
816 Congress Ave., Ste. 1250
Austin, TX 78701
Ph:(512)472-1194
Free: 800-749-5862
Fax:(512)472-7378
Co. E-mail: latadmin@lat.org
URL: http://www.lat.org
Released: Annual. **Audience:** Retail lumber and building material dealers. **Principal Exhibits:** Lumber, building materials, hardware, and related products. **Dates and Locations:** 2011 Apr 07-09, Fort Worth, TX.

13581 ■ Mississippi Lumber Manufacturers Association Convention and Trade Show
Mississippi Lumber Manufacturers Association
PO Box 5241
Jackson, MS 39296-5241
Ph:(601)982-1731
Fax:(601)982-5263
Co. E-mail: sylvianapper@bellsouth.net
URL: http://www.mslumbermfg.org
Released: Annual. **Audience:** Mill members, lumber and mill producers, business related firms, wholesalers and producers in other states. **Principal Exhibits:** Lumber manufacturing equipment, supplies, and services.

13582 ■ Northwestern Building Products Expo
Northwestern Lumber Association
1405 Lilac Dr. N, Ste. 130
Minneapolis, MN 55422
Ph:(763)544-6822
Free: 800-331-0193
Fax:(763)595-4060
Co. E-mail: nlassn@nlassn.org
URL: http://www.nlassn.org
Released: Annual. **Audience:** Retail lumber and building material dealers. **Principal Exhibits:** Any product or service that is ultimately sold or used by retail lumber and building material dealers.

CONSULTANTS

13583 ■ Lee Resources International Inc.
104 Maxwell Ave., Ste. 349
PO Box 942
Greenwood, SC 29648-0942
Ph:(864)229-0600
Free: 800-277-7888
Fax:877-230-6329
Co. E-mail: info@leeresources.com
URL: http://www.leeresources.com
Contact: Andy Johnston, Principle
E-mail: andy@atsleeresources.com
Scope: Consulting service assists clients in the lumber and building supply industry to improve organizational productivity. Specializes in site selection; site planning; facility design and specification; equipment requirements and procurement; personnel needs and job descriptions; inventory assortment; Proforma P and L budgets; initial capitalization requirements. **Publications:** "The Artichoke Factor"; "Customer Care"; "The Impact Selling System"; "Time Out"; "You Can Sell More Professionally"; "You Can Build a Better You"; "You Can Prospect More Creatively"; "You Can Manage and Motivate"; "The Secrets of Power Negotiating"; "Take Charge of Your Life"; "Swim with the Sharks Without Being Eaten Alive"; "The Psychology of Winning"; "The Psychology of Selling"; "The Management Advantage"; "The 7 Habits of Highly Effective People"; "Even Further Up the Organization"; "Defrosting Telephone Cold Calls"; "Guide to Everyday Negotiating". **Seminars:** Developing Your Sales Process; I Dare You; Relationship Selling; Time Management; Customer Service; Protecting Your Margins; Business Development.

LIBRARIES

13584 ■ National Hardwood Lumber Association Library
Box 34518
6830 Raleigh-LaGrange Rd.
Memphis, TN 38184-0518
Ph:(901)377-1818
Free: 800-933-0318
Fax:(901)399-7581
Co. E-mail: m.barford@nhla.com
URL: http://www.nhla.com
Contact: Mark Barford, Exec.Dir.
Scope: Hardwood lumber; grading rules. **Services:** Copying; Library open to members of NHLA. **Holdings:** 2500 volumes.

13585 ■ Society of Wood Science and Technology
PO Box 6155
Monona, WI 53716-6155
Ph:(608)577-1342
Fax:(608)467-8979
Co. E-mail: vicki@swst.org
URL: http://www.swst.org
Contact: Vicki Herian, Exec.Dir.
Scope: Wood and fiber science. **Services:** Library open to the public. **Holdings:** 30 periodicals. **Subscriptions:** 880 journals and other serials.

13586 ■ Texas Forest Service–Texas Forest Products Laboratory Library
Box 310
Lufkin, TX 75902

Ph:(936)639-8180
URL: http://texasforestservice.tamu.edu
Contact: Susan Shockley, Staff Asst.
Scope: Wood science, forest products technology and utilization. **Services:** Copying; Library open to the public for reference use only.

13587 ■ U.S.D.A. Forest Service–Forest Products Laboratory Library
One Gifford Pinchot Dr.
Madison, WI 53726-2398
Ph:(608)231-9313
Fax:(608)231-9311
Co. E-mail: pdl_fpl_library@fs.fed.us
URL: http://www.fpl.fs.fed.us/products/library/index. php
Contact: Julie Blankenburg, Supv.Libn.
Scope: Forest products utilization, energy from wood, paper and pulp, wood engineering, wood processing and protection, timber, wood products economics. **Services:** Interlibrary loan; copying (limited); Library open to the public. **Holdings:** 56,300 books and bound periodical volumes; 30,300 technical reports; 20,000 bulletins, reports, reprints; 6200 patents; 5900 microforms. **Subscriptions:** 340 journals.

13588 ■ Weyerhaueser Company–Archives
NP-190
PO Box 9777
Federal Way, WA 98063-9777

Ph:(253)924-5051
Fax:(253)924-7863
Co. E-mail: megan.moholt@weyerhaeuser.com
URL: http://www.weyerheauser.com
Contact: Megan Moholt, Archv.

Scope: Weyerhaeuser Company, forest products, logging, lumber manufacturing, pulp/paperboard, Pacific Northwest. **Services:** Archives open to the public on a limited basis with restrictions. **Holdings:** 3000 cubic feet and 128 lin.ft. of archival material including correspondence and office files, 1900-2008, ledgers, journals, Annual and financial reports, biographical files, speeches of company executives and personnel, company publications, minute books of the company, photographs of company facilities and operations, photographs of logging in the Northwest, films, oral history interviews, artifacts and memorabilia, maps, archives. **Subscriptions:** n/a

RESEARCH CENTERS

13589 ■ Hardwood Plywood and Veneer Association
1825 Michael Faraday Dr.
Reston, VA 20190-5304
Ph:(703)435-2900

Fax:(703)435-2537
Co. E-mail: khowlett@hpva.org
URL: http://www.hpva.org/home
Contact: Kip Howlett, Pres.
E-mail: khowlett@hpva.org

Scope: Manufacture and structure of hardwood plywood, veneer, glue bond, flamespread, finishes, and adhesives. Reviews federal and military specifications and foreign standards affecting hardwood plywood and laminated hardwood flooring. Provides in-plant inspection and verification. Testing facilities and services include fire and smoke tests, racking strength test, large-scale structural test, formaldehyde emission testing, moisture content tests, linear variation tests, specific gravity tests on plywood, veneer, or lumber, non-volatile solids tests, ash determination on flours, viscosity determinations on liquids, and finish tests. **Services:** Planting of hardwood trees. **Publications:** Hardwood Plywood & E-News (semimonthly); HPMA Testing and Inspection and Listed Products Manual (annually); Where to Buy Hardwood Plywood and Veneer Directory (annually). **Educational Activities:** Semiannual conventions; Workshops.

ASSOCIATIONS AND OTHER ORGANIZATIONS

13590 ■ Aluminum Extruders Council
1000 N Rand Rd., Ste. 214
Wauconda, IL 60084
Ph:(847)526-2010
Fax:(847)526-3993
Co. E-mail: mail@aec.org
URL: http://www.aec.org
Contact: Rand A. Baldwin CAE, Pres.
Description: Manufacturers of extruded aluminum shapes and their suppliers. Compiles statistics; provides technical assistance and develops markets. Conducts workshops for management, sales, and plant personnel. **Publications:** *Aluminum Extrusion*; *Buyer's Guide*; *Executive Report* (bimonthly); *Publications Catalog* .

13591 ■ American Machine Tool Distributors' Association
7361 Calhoun Pl., Ste. 320
Rockville, MD 20855
Ph:(301)738-1200
Fax:(301)738-9499
Co. E-mail: info@amtda.org
URL: http://www.amtda.org
Contact: Peter A. Borden, Pres.
Description: Distributors and builders of manufacturing technology. Offers technical training, sales training and management. Compiles statistics. **Publications:** *Tool Talk* (10/year); *US Machine Tool Consumption Report* (monthly).

13592 ■ Canadian Foundry Association–Association des Fonderies Canadiennes
1 Nicholas St., Ste. 1500
Ottawa, ON, Canada K1N 7B7
Ph:(613)789-4894
Fax:(613)789-5957
Co. E-mail: judy@foundryassociation.ca
URL: http://www.foundryassociation.ca
Contact: David Seyler, Pres.
Description: Foundries. Seeks to advance the metals and forging industries. Serves as a forum for the exchange of information among members; represents members' interests before labor and industrial organizations, government agencies, and the public.

13593 ■ Canadian Welding Bureau–Le Bureau Canadien de Soudage
8260 Parkhill Dr.
Milton, ON, Canada L9T 5V7
Free: 800-844-6790
Fax:(905)542-1318
Co. E-mail: info@cwbgroup.org
URL: http://eng.cwbgroup.org
Contact: Doug Luciani, Pres./CEO
Description: Participants include welding organizations, consumable manufacturers, welding inspectors, welders and welding educators and trainers. Seeks to ensure maintenance of high standards of practice and compliance to accepted workmanship standards in the welding profession. Provides welding certification for fabricating and manufacturing companies and manufacturers of steel building systems, welding inspection companies and metal products inspectors, and welding consumables. Conducts ISO 9000, 14000 quality training and education. Holds examinations. (Quasar Division) Provides training and education study material and software. Conducts education and training of welding personnel (Learning Centre). **Publications:** *CWB NET* (periodic).

13594 ■ Fabricators and Manufacturers Association International
833 Featherstone Rd.
Rockford, IL 61107-6301
Ph:(815)399-8775
Free: 888-394-4362
Co. E-mail: info@fmanet.org
URL: http://www.fmanet.org
Contact: Gerald Shankel, Pres./CEO
Description: People involved in the metal forming and fabricating industry. Disseminates technological information on the fabrication of sheet, coil, tube, pipe, plate, and structural metal shapes. Conducts continuing education conferences. Maintains technical information center. **Publications:** *The Fabricator: Journal of Metal Forming and Fabricating Technology* (monthly); *Member Connections* (bimonthly); *Practical Welding Today* (bimonthly); *Stamping Journal* (monthly).

13595 ■ Precision Metalforming Association
6363 Oak Tree Blvd.
Independence, OH 44131-2556
Ph:(216)901-8800
Fax:(216)901-9190
Co. E-mail: dsansone@pma.org
URL: http://www.metalform.com
Contact: David Sansone, Exec. Dir.
Description: Represents the metalforming industry of North America; the industry that creates precision metal products using stamping, fabricating and other value-added processes. Its member companies include metal stampers, fabricators, spinners, slide formers and roll formers, as well as suppliers of equipment, materials and services to the industry. Members are located in 30 countries, with the majority found in North America; in 41 states of the United States as well as Canada and Mexico. Conducts technical and educational programs, compiles statistics, offers training systems, and provides legislative and regulatory assistance to members. **Publications:** *MetalForming* (monthly); *PMA Update* .

13596 ■ Society of Manufacturing Engineers
One SME Dr.
Dearborn, MI 48121
Ph:(313)425-3000
Free: 800-733-4763
Fax:(313)425-3400
Co. E-mail: service@sme.org
URL: http://www.sme.org
Contact: Mark C. Tomlinson, Exec. Dir./Gen. Mgr.
Description: Professional society of manufacturing engineers, practitioners and management executives concerned with manufacturing technologies for improved productivity. Seeks to advance the science of manufacturing through the continuing education of manufacturing engineers, practitioners and management. Conducts expositions, international seminars and clinics. **Publications:** *Composites in Manufacturing* (quarterly); *Electronics Manufacturing: SME's Quarterly on Electronics Manufacturing Technology* (quarterly); *Finishing Line: AFP/SME's Quarterly on Finishing and Coatings Technology* (quarterly); *Journal of Manufacturing Systems* (quarterly); *Manufacturing Engineering* (monthly); *SME News* (bimonthly); *Vision: SME's Quarterly on Vision Technology* (quarterly).

13597 ■ Specialty Tools and Fasteners Distributors Association
PO Box 44
Elm Grove, WI 53122
Ph:(262)784-4774
Free: 800-352-2981
Fax:(262)784-5059
Co. E-mail: info@stafda.org
URL: http://www.stafda.org
Contact: Georgia H. Foley, Exec. Dir.
Description: Distributors and suppliers of power tools, power-actuated tools, anchors, fastening systems, diamond drilling, and related construction equipment. Encourages legal, ethical, and friendly business relations within the industry. Collects and disseminates information pertinent to the industry; develops more effective, economical, and profitable distribution. **Publications:** *Trade News* (monthly);*Membership Directory* (annual).

13598 ■ Tooling, Manufacturing and Technologies Association
PO Box 2204
Farmington Hills, MI 48333-2204
Ph:(248)488-0300
Free: 800-969-9682
Fax:(248)488-0500
Co. E-mail: rob@thetmta.com
URL: http://www.thetmta.com
Contact: Robert J. Dumont, Pres./CEO
Description: Manufacturers of dies, jigs, fixtures, molds, gages, tools, special machinery, and related products; suppliers of die tryout, machining, and experimental and designing service. **Publications:** *TMTA Talk* (monthly).

13599 ■ United States Cutting Tool Institute
1300 Sumner Ave.
Cleveland, OH 44115-2851
Ph:(216)241-7333
Fax:(216)241-0105
Co. E-mail: uscti@uscti.com
URL: http://www.uscti.com
Contact: Steve Morency, Pres.
Description: Manufacturers of rotary metal cutting tools. Objectives are to: promote the manufacture and sale of rotary metal cutting tools in the U.S. and in foreign markets; promote the standardization of sizes, dimensions, and tolerances in cooperation with the American National Standards Institute, American Society of Mechanical Engineers , and other engineering organizations; increase the use of metal cut-

ting tools and allied products. **Publications:** *Drilled Holes for Tapping*; *Standards and Dimensions for Ground Thread Taps*;Membership Directory (periodic).

DIRECTORIES OF EDUCATIONAL PROGRAMS

13600 ■ *Directory of Private Accredited Career Schools and Colleges of Technology*
Pub: Accrediting Commission of Career Schools and Colleges of Technology
Contact: Michale S. McComis, Exec. Dir.
Released: On web page. **Price:** Free. **Description:** Covers 3900 accredited post-secondary programs that provide training programs in business, trade, and technical fields, including various small business endeavors. Entries offer school name, address, phone, description of courses, job placement assistance, and requirements for admission. Arrangement is alphabetical.

REFERENCE WORKS

13601 ■ *AMT—Member Product Directory*
Pub: Association For Manufacturing Technology AMT
Contact: Douglas K. Woods, President
E-mail: dwoods@amtonline.org
Released: Annual, winter. **Covers:** Machine tools and related products built by members of the Association for Manufacturing Technology. **Entries Include:** Company name, address, phone, telex, fax, e-mail, website, and product specifications. **Arrangement:** Product type; company name. **Indexes:** Product type (in English, French, Spanish, German, Japanese, Italian, Portuguese, Chinese).

13602 ■ **"The Consequences of Tardiness"** in *Modern Machine Shop* (Vol. 84, August 2011, No. 3, pp. 34)
Pub: Gardner Publications
Ed: Wayne S. Chaneski. **Description:** Five point addressing motivating factors behind employees who are tardy and those who choose to be on time in the workplace are shared.

13603 ■ **"Customer Service Center Will Rise in Indian Land"** in *Charlotte Observer* (February 4, 2007)
Pub: Knight-Ridder/Tribune Business News
Ed: Taylor Bright. **Description:** Kennametal is building a new customer service center in Lancaster County, North Carolina. Kennametal makes metal tools and parts, specializing in metals highly resistant to heat.

13604 ■ *Cutting Tool Engineering—Superabrasives Directory Issue*
Pub: CTE Publications Inc.
Ed: Don Nelson, Editor, dnelson@jwr.com. **Released:** Annual, November. **Covers:** Nearly 400 manufacturers and distributors of industrial diamond and superabrasive products and related equipment. **Entries Include:** Company name, address, phone, key personnel. **Arrangement:** Alphabetical. **Indexes:** Product.

13605 ■ *Dun and Bradstreet's Industrial Guide*
Pub: Dun & Bradstreet Corp.

13606 ■ **"Engineering Services Supplier Launches 'Robotic Renaissance'"** in *Modern Machine Shop* (Vol. 84, September 2011, No. 4, pp. 46)
Pub: Gardner Publications
Description: Profile of Applied Manufacturing Technologies (AMT) new hiring initiative that supports continuing growth in the robotics industry. AMT is located in Orion, Michigan and supplies factory automation design, engineering and process consulting services.

13607 ■ **"Evaluate Your Process and Do It Better"** in *Modern Machine Shop* (Vol. 84, October 2011, No. 5, pp. 34)
Pub: Gardner Publications
Ed: Wayne S. Chaneski. **Description:** In order to be more competitive, many machine shops owners are

continually looking at their processes and procedures in order to be more competitive.

13608 ■ **"Getting the Word Out"** in *Modern Machine Shop* (Vol. 84, September 2011, No. 4, pp. 16)
Pub: Gardner Publications
Ed: Derek Korn. **Description:** Many times machine shops create devices to streamline their own machining processes and find these devices can be used by other shops, thus developing a marketable product. Tips for this process are outlined.

13609 ■ **"Insert Grade Coating Improves Tool Live"** in *Modern Machine Shop* (Vol. 84, October 2011, No. 5, pp. 124)
Pub: Gardner Publications
Ed: Emily K. Tudor. **Description:** Profile of Sumitomo Electric Carbide's AC420K insert that is a CVD-coated carbide grade that features layers of TiCN and Al.sub.2 O.sub.3 for wear, chipping and heat resistance.

13610 ■ **"Lincoln Electric Installs Large Wind Tower"** in *Modern Machine Shop* (Vol. 84, October 2011, No. 5, pp. 42)
Pub: Gardner Publications
Description: Lincoln Electric, a welding product manufacturer, constructed a 443-foot-tall wind tower at its plant in Euclid, Ohio. The tower is expected to generate as much as 10 percent of the facility's energy and save as much as $500,000 annually in energy costs.

13611 ■ *Machine Tool Reference Guide*
Pub: Machinery Dealers National Association
Released: Every five years. **Price:** $19.95, individuals; $29.95, nonmembers. **Covers:** Nearly 1,000 metalworking machine tool manufacturers; international coverage. **Entries Include:** Company name, address, phone, fax, product/service provided. **Arrangement:** Alphabetical. **Indexes:** Company name, type of equipment.

13612 ■ **"A Model Machine for Titanium"** in *Modern Machine Shop* (Vol. 84, October 2011, No. 5, pp. 84)
Pub: Gardner Publications
Ed: Peter Zelinski. **Description:** Researchers have developed a machine tool that controls vibration in order to mill titanium more productively. In-depth information on the machine tool as well as understanding the processes involved in milling titanium is covered.

13613 ■ **"Pedal to the Medal"** in *Small Business Opportunities* (Summer 2010)
Pub: Harris Publications Inc.
Ed: Chuck Green. **Description:** Profile of Darlene Miller who became and partner and eventually took over Permac Industries, a firm that specializes in precision machine products.

13614 ■ **"Sandvik Expands Energy-Saving Program"** in *Modern Machine Shop* (Vol. 84, September 2011, No. 4, pp. 48)
Pub: Gardner Publications
Description: Sandvik Coromant, based in Fair Lawn, New Jersey, expanded its Sustainable Manufacturing Program that originally was developed to help Japanese-based firms reduce electricity consumption by 15 percent after the recent earthquake that cause loss of electrical power. The program now provides energy reduction through the Sandvick cutting tool technology, application techniques and productivity increases.

13615 ■ **"Tempering Urgency Within Your Shop"** in *Modern Machine Shop* (Vol. 84, October 2011, No. 5, pp. 16)
Pub: Gardner Publications
Ed: Derek Korn. **Description:** Because machine shops operate under an environment of urgency, patience can commingle with the pressure to produce products efficiently and timely.

13616 ■ **"To Be or Not To Be an S Corporation"** in *Modern Machine Shop* (Vol. 84, September 2011, No. 4, pp. 38)
Pub: Gardner Publications
Ed: Irving L. Blackman. **Description:** The definitions of both C corporations and S corporations are defined to help any machine shop discover which best suits the owner's business plan.

13617 ■ *Used Machinery Buyer's Guide*
Pub: Machinery Dealers National Association
Released: Annual, Latest edition 2011. **Price:** Free. **Covers:** 450 member dealers in used capital equipment. **Entries Include:** Company name, address, phone, names of executives, telex number, telefax. **Arrangement:** Geographical, Alphabetical, specialty. **Indexes:** Company name, types of equipment.

13618 ■ **"A Virtual Jog Mode for CAM"** in *Modern Machine Shop* (Vol. 84, November 2011, No. 6, pp. 22)
Pub: Gardner Publications
Ed: Edwin Gasparraj. **Description:** In many cases, CAM programming required a specific, user-defined path. Siemens PLMs Generic Motion Controller is an alternative that defines the tool path within CAM. The program is a virtual 'teach' mode that enables the user to capture cutter locations by jogging machines axes within CAM.

13619 ■ **"What Do Your ISO Procedures Say?"** in *Modern Machine Shop* (Vol. 84, September 2011, No. 4, pp. 34)
Pub: Gardner Publications
Ed: Wayne S. Chaneski. **Description:** ISO 9000 certification can be time-consuming and costly, but it is a necessary step in developing a quality management system that meets both current and potential customer needs.

13620 ■ **"What Is In Your Company Library?"** in *Modern Machine Shop* (Vol. 84, October 2011, No. 5, pp. 60)
Pub: Gardner Publications
Ed: Mike Lynch. **Description:** A good company library in any machine shop can help keep employees productive. Safety as well as information are critical to complete any task in a shop.

13621 ■ **"What Makes for an Effective, Production-Oriented VMC?"** in *Modern Machine Shop* (Vol. 84, November 2011, No. 6, pp. 24)
Pub: Gardner Publications
Ed: Derek Korn. **Description:** When a machine shop's existing VMC only offers a modest spindle performance and slow, non-cutting functions, the latest VMC technology for high-volume production that minimizes cycle times and maximizes competitiveness could be helpful. Makino's new Production Standard (PS) series of VMCs provides not only a number of standard features to shrink cycle times, but also design elements that can effectively support a shops production elements are defined.

SOURCES OF SUPPLY

13622 ■ *Aluminum Extrusion Press Directory*
Pub: The Aluminum Association Inc.
Released: Irregular. **Price:** $70, members; $135, nonmembers. **Covers:** Locations of 496 aluminum presses at 217 plants in 148 US companies; details on extruders, locations, press sizes, anodizing, painting and billet casting facilities. **Entries Include:** Names of extruders and plant addresses.

13623 ■ *Utillaje*
Pub: Utillaje Inc.
Released: Monthly. **Covers:** Over 10,000 listings of manufacturing and industrial equipment listed by over 300 sellers throughout North, Central, and South America. Equipment includes new, used, and rebuilt machinery, chemical/food, as well as electrical equipment. **Entries Include:** Company name, location, phone number, fax number, description of services and products provided. **Arrangement:** Classified by product. **Indexes:** Name, geographical.

STATISTICAL SOURCES

13624 ■ *RMA Annual Statement Studies*
Pub: Robert Morris Associates (RMA)
Released: Annual. **Price:** $175.00 2006-07 edition, $105.00. **Description:** Contains composite balance sheets and income statements for more than 360 industries, including the accounting, auditing, and bookkeeping industries. Also contains five years of comparative historical data for discerning trends. Includes 16 commonly used ratios, computed for most of the size groupings for nearly every industry.

TRADE PERIODICALS

13625 ■ *American Machinist*
Pub: Penton Media Inc.
Released: Monthly. **Price:** $90 Canada; $153 Canada 2 years; $112.50 other countries; $175.50 other countries 2 years. **Description:** Magazine serving the metalworking marketplace, consisting of plants in industries primarily engaged in manufacturing durable goods and other metal products.

13626 ■ *American Tool, Die & Stamping News*
Pub: Eagle Publications Inc.
Released: Bimonthly. **Price:** $60 other countries; $110 other countries two years. **Description:** Magazine focusing on tool, die, stamping, moldmaking and EDMing.

13627 ■ *Die Casting Engineer*
Pub: North American Die Casting Association
Contact: Melisa Twarog, Advertising & Promotions managing editorager
Released: 6/yr. **Price:** $60 U.S., Canada, and Mexico; $120 U.S., Canada, and Mexico two years; $270 other countries two years; $135 other countries. **Description:** Trade magazine serving the die casting industry.

13628 ■ *The Fabricator*
Pub: The Croydon Group Ltd.
Contact: Eric Lundin, Sen. Ed.
E-mail: ericl@thefabricator.com
Released: Monthly. **Price:** Free to qualified subscribers. **Description:** Trade journal covering the metalforming and fabricating industry.

13629 ■ *Machining Science & Technology*
Pub: Taylor & Francis Group Journals
Contact: Said Jahanmir, Exec. Ed.
E-mail: sjahanmir@nist.gov
Released: 4/yr. **Price:** $242 print only; $836 institutions online only; $880 institutions print & online; $700 institutions print & online; $664 institutions online only; $194 print only. **Description:** Trade Journal publishing scientific and technical papers related to machining and machining processes on all materials.

13630 ■ *Metalforming*
Pub: Precision Metalforming Association
Contact: Andy Flando, Publisher
E-mail: aflando@pma.org
Ed: Brad Kuvin, Editor, bkuvin@pma.org. **Released:** Monthly. **Price:** $40 North America; $225 other countries; Free to qualified subscribers. **Description:** Serving those who add value to sheetmetal.

13631 ■ *Modern Casting Magazine*
Pub: American Foundry Society
Contact: Alfred Spada, Editor-in-Chief
E-mail: aspada@afsinc.org
Released: Monthly. **Price:** $40; $5 single issue; $50; $75 by mail. **Description:** Magazine on metal casting plants and pattern shops.

13632 ■ *Practical Welding Today*
Pub: The Croydon Group Ltd.
Released: Bimonthly. **Price:** Free to qualified subscribers. **Description:** Trade magazine covering instructional and educational information on welding.

13633 ■ *Production Technology News*
Pub: Advantage Business Media
Contact: Tom Lynch, Gp. Publisher
E-mail: tom.lynch@advantagemedia.com
Released: Monthly, 9/yr. **Price:** $64 Free to qualified subscribers; $109 U.S.; $109 Canada; $10 Mexico; $10 single issue. **Description:** Trade publication reporting on product innovations in manufacturing and production. Features news on products, tools, equipment, manufacturing software, CAD/CAM, controls and their application in the process of metal cutting, metal forming and fabrication, tooling, welding, materials and coatings, grinding and finishing, robotics and quality control.

13634 ■ *Tooling & Production*
Pub: Nelson Publishing Inc.
Released: Monthly. **Description:** Magazine concerning metalworking.

TRADE SHOWS AND CONVENTIONS

13635 ■ METALFORM Mexico
Precision Metalforming Association
6363 Oak Tree Blvd.
Independence, OH 44131-2500
Ph:(216)901-8800
Fax:(216)901-9190
Co. E-mail: pma@pma.org
URL: http://www.metalforming.com
Released: Annual. **Audience:** Metal stampers, and spinnings and fabricated parts industry. **Principal Exhibits:** Presses and stamping equipment, tooling and fabricating machines, management aids, and related materials.

CONSULTANTS

13636 ■ Machine Tool Sales Co.
2694 Dorchester Rd.
PO Box 71
Birmingham, MI 48009
Ph:(248)614-0063
Fax:(248)822-4175
Co. E-mail: tom@tshipley.cnchost.com
URL: http://www.tshipley.cnchost.com
Contact: Thomas E. Shipley, President
E-mail: tom@tshipley.cnchost.com
Scope: Offers complete marketing service for metal working, computer, and machine automation fields. **Seminars:** Precision Grinding Seminar; Radio for Industrial Advertising - What It Needs to Do; What's Wrong With Metalworking Marketing?.

LIBRARIES

13637 ■ Erico Inc.–Information Resources Center
34600 Solon Rd.
Solon, OH 44139
Ph:(440)248-0100
Fax:(440)248-0723
URL: http://www.erico.com/library.asp
Scope: Engineering, science and technology, materials, metals, research and development, sales, marketing, personnel. **Services:** Interlibrary loan; copying; Center open to the public with restrictions. **Holdings:** 6000 books; 2000 patents; 500 manuscripts; standards; specifications. **Subscriptions:** 100 journals and other serials; 5 newspapers.

RESEARCH CENTERS

13638 ■ Lehigh University–Institute for Metal Forming
Materials Science & Engineering Department
5 E Packer Ave.
Bethlehem, PA 18015-1657
Ph:(610)758-4252
Fax:(610)758-4244
Co. E-mail: wzm2@lehigh.edu
URL: http://www.lehigh.edu/IAtinimf
Contact: Prof. Wojciech Z. Misiolek, Dir.
E-mail: wzm2@lehigh.edu
Scope: Metal forming processes, including basic and applied studies on inclusion and void behavior during deformation, deep drawing analysis, flow and fracture of composite materials, forming of composites, including superconducting wire limit analysis of axisymmetric plastic forming processes, forging and extrusion of powder metal preforms, and modeling of friction behavior. Provides advance instruction in principles of metal forming, research training for graduate students, and assistance to industry in solutions of forming problems. **Publications:** Reports.

START-UP INFORMATION

13639 ■ *55 Surefire Food-Related Businesses: You Can Start for Under $5000*
Pub: Entrepreneur Press
Ed: Cheryl Kimball. **Released:** March 1, 2009. **Price:** $17.95. **Description:** Advice is given to start 55 various food-related companies and goes beyond restaurant or catering services. Home-based, retail and mail order ventures are covered, as well as food safety and standards.

13640 ■ *An Eye for Winners*
Pub: DIANE Publishing Co.
Ed: Lillian Vernon. **Released:** 1999. **Price:** $23.00.

13641 ■ *How to Start a Home-Based Mail Order Business*
Pub: Globe Pequot Press
Ed: Georganne Fiumara. **Released:** January 2005. **Price:** $17.95. **Description:** Step-by-step guide for starting and growing a home-based mail order business. Information about equipment, pricing, online marketing, are included along with worksheets and checklists for planning.

ASSOCIATIONS AND OTHER ORGANIZATIONS

13642 ■ Catalog and Multichannel Marketing Council
1120 Ave. of the Americas
New York, NY 10036-6700
Ph:(212)768-7277
Fax:(212)302-6714
Co. E-mail: customerservice@the-dma.org
URL: http://www.the-dma.org
Contact: G. Steven Dapper, Chm.
Description: Catalog houses, catalog printers, and list brokers; members of Direct Marketing Association. Aims to keep members abreast of legislative and legal matters concerning the industry, exchange up-to-date ideas on graphics, production, and lists and share the benefits of consumer-oriented publicity projects about catalogs in newspapers and magazines. Provides representation in Congress on legislative and postal matters. Conducts workshops. **Publications:** *Current and Crossroads* (monthly); *DMA Insider* (quarterly).

13643 ■ Direct Marketing Association
1120 Ave. of the Americas
New York, NY 10036-6700
Ph:(212)768-7277
Fax:(212)302-6714
Co. E-mail: presiden@the-dma.org
URL: http://www.the-dma.org
Contact: Lawrence M. Kimmel Jr., Pres./CEO
Description: Manufacturers, wholesalers, public utilities, retailers, mail order firms, publishers, schools, clubs, insurance companies, financial organizations, business equipment manufacturers, paper and envelope manufacturers, list brokers, compilers, managers, owners, computer service bureaus, advertising agencies, letter shops, research organizations, printers, lithographers, creators and producers of direct mail and direct response advertising. Studies consumer and business attitudes toward direct mail and related direct marketing statistics. Offers Mail Preference Service for consumers who wish to receive less mail advertising, Mail Order Action Line to help resolve difficulties with mail order purchases and Telephone Preference Service for people who wish to receive fewer telephone sales calls. Maintains hall of fame; offers placement service; compiles statistics. Sponsors several three-day Basic Direct Marketing Institutes, Advanced Direct Marketing Institutes and special interest seminars and workshops. Maintains Government Affairs office in Washington, DC. Operates Direct Marketing Educational Foundation. **Publications:** *The DMA Insider* (quarterly); *Politically Direct* (quarterly).

REFERENCE WORKS

13644 ■ *Direct Marketing List Source*
Pub: SRDS
Contact: Debbie Dunkleberger, Director
E-mail: ddunk@srds.com
Released: Annual. **Price:** $750 annual unlimited single-user. **Covers:** Over 38,000 mailing lists composed of business persons and firms, general consumers, and rural and farm consumers, plus cooperative mailings, card decks, and package insert programs. Includes separate sections for new listings, mailing list brokers, compilers, managers; and suppliers of products and services to the direct mail industry (e.g., lettershops, etc.); and an international counterpart to all of the above. **Entries Include:** For mailing lists—Title of list; name, address, phone of owner, manager, or broker, and name of contact; description of list, and its arrangement, maintenance, quantity, etc.; specific identification of source of list; addressing selections, method of delivery, schedules; mailing services offered; restrictions on use of list; price. For brokers and compilers—Firm name, address, phone, names of principal personnel, types of lists handled, fees and deposit mailing services offered, association memberships. **Arrangement:** Lists arranged by market classification (safety, literature and book buyers, etc.), by list name within classifications; managers, compilers, and brokers are alphabetical; suppliers classified by service. **Indexes:** Subject/market classification, list title/list owner.

13645 ■ *The Directory of Mail Order Catalogs*
Pub: Grey House Publishing
Contact: Leslie MacKenzie, Publisher
Released: Annual, Latest edition 2011. **Price:** $395, individuals; $250, libraries. **Covers:** Over 13,000 mail order firms and the catalogs they offer. **Entries Include:** Company, address and phone for catalog orders, fax, description of merchandise offered; names of buyers, company president, marketing and production manager; size of catalog, price and frequency of catalog, availability of mailing list, number of employees, sales volume. **Arrangement:** Type of catalog or merchandise offered. **Indexes:** Company name, product, online.

13646 ■ *Mail Order in the Internet Age*
Pub: Morgan James Publishing, LLC
Ed: Ted Ciuba. **Released:** May 2004. **Price:** $19.95. **Description:** Direct response market, or mail order, for marketing and selling a product or service is discussed, with emphasis on how direct marketing compares favorably to other methods in terms of speed, ease, profitability, and affordability. Advice is given for writing ads; seminars to attend; and newsletters, mailing lists and magazines in which to subscribe.

13647 ■ **"Netflix vs. Blockbuster" in** *Inc.* **(October 2007, pp. 32)**
Pub: Gruner & Jahr USA Publishing
Description: Nexflix, the mail-order DVD rental service, is losing market share to Blockbuster, even after matching prices to that of its competitors. Entrepreneurs are asked how they would run Netflix to gain back market share.

13648 ■ **"Up, Up and Away" in** *Small Business Opportunities* **(November 2007)**
Pub: Harris Publications Inc.
Ed: Stan Roberts. **Description:** Profile of Miniature Aircraft USA, a mail order business providing kits to build flying machines priced from $500 to $2,500.

STATISTICAL SOURCES

13649 ■ *Mail Service Pharmacy Market*
Pub: MarketResearch.com
Released: 1999. **Price:** $3250.00 (Online). **Description:**

13650 ■ *RMA Annual Statement Studies*
Pub: Robert Morris Associates (RMA)
Released: Annual. **Price:** $175.00 2006-07 edition, $105.00. **Description:** Contains composite balance sheets and income statements for more than 360 industries, including the accounting, auditing, and bookkeeping industries. Also contains five years of comparative historical data for discerning trends. Includes 16 commonly used ratios, computed for most of the size groupings for nearly every industry.

13651 ■ *Standard & Poor's Industry Surveys*
Pub: Standard & Poor's Corp.
Released: Annual. **Price:** $3633.00. **Description:** Two-volume book that examines the prospects for specific industries, including trucking. Also provides analyses of trends and problems, statistical tables and charts, and comparative company analyses.

TRADE PERIODICALS

13652 ■ *Business Mailers Review*
Pub: Sedgwick Publishing
Ed: Kate Phelan Muth, Editor, muth@erols.com. **Released:** Biweekly, 25/year. **Price:** $377, U.S. and Canada year; $392, elsewhere year. **Description:** Concerned with the monitoring of the U.S. Postal Service, private carriers, and suppliers. Offers volume mailers, traffic managers, parcel shippers, and operators of letter-shops news of current developments in

the field of business mailings. Reports on new technologies and products, rate changes, metering alternatives, and relevant legislative activity. Recurring features include interviews and news of research.

13653 ■ *Direct Marketing Magazine*
Pub: Hoke Communications Inc.
Released: Monthly. **Price:** $60; $6 single issue. **Description:** Direct response advertising magazine.

13654 ■ *DM News*
Pub: DM News
Contact: Rose Gordon, Sen. Ed.
E-mail: rose.gordon@dmnews.com
Released: Weekly. **Price:** $148; $198 Canada; $228 other countries; $265 two years; $355 Canada 2 years; $395 other countries 2 years. **Description:** Tabloid newspaper for publishers, fund raisers, financial marketers, catalogers, package goods advertisers and their agencies, and other marketers who use direct mail, mail order advertising, catalogs, or other direct response media to sell their products or services.

TRADE SHOWS AND CONVENTIONS

13655 ■ Direct Marketing Association Annual Conference & Exhibition
Direct Marketing Association
1120 Ave. of the Americas
New York, NY 10036-6700
Ph:(212)768-7277
Free: 800-255-0006
Fax:(212)302-6714
Co. E-mail: customerservice@the-dma.org
URL: http://www.the-dma.org
Released: Annual. **Audience:** Trade professionals. **Principal Exhibits:** Printers, list brokers, envelope manufacturers, telephone marketing companies, computers and other equipment, supplies, and services for direct marketing. **Dates and Locations:** 2011 Oct 01-06, Boston, MA.

CONSULTANTS

13656 ■ Jeffrey Lant Associates Inc.
50 Follen St., Ste. 507
PO Box 38
Cambridge, MA 02138
Ph:(617)547-6372
Fax:(617)547-0061
Co. E-mail: drjlant@worldprofit.com
URL: http://www.jeffreylant.com
Contact: Sandy Hunter, Director of Information Technology
E-mail: sandi@atsworldprofit.com
Scope: Firm sets up businesses online, design websites and assists with marketing. **Publications:** "E-mail El Dorado," JLA Publications, 1998; "Web Wealth: How to Turn the World Wide Web Into a Cash Hose for Your Business. Whatever You're Selling," 1997; "Multi-Level Money," JLA Publications, 1994; "No More Cold Calls," JLA Publications, 1997; "Cash Copy"; "How to make at least $100000 a year"; "E-Money". **Seminars:** Business and personal development, including Establishing and Operating Your Successful Consulting Business; Successfully Promoting Your Small Business and Professional Practice; Succeeding in Your Mail Order Business; Successfully Raising Money for Your Nonprofit Organization from Foundations, Corporations and Individuals; Money Making Marketing: Finding the People Who Need What You're Selling and Making Sure They Buy It; Getting Corporations, Foundations, and Individuals to Give You the Money Your Nonprofit Organization Needs.

13657 ■ Leon Gelfond & Associates
17266 Boca Club Blvd., Apt. 1606
Boca Raton, FL 33487-1279
Ph:(561)995-0865
Contact: Renee M. Gelfond, Principle
Scope: Consultants offering services in mail order, fulfillment, data processing, shipping and warehousing, printing, and book packaging. Primarily serving the publishing industry. Also has the capabilities and facilities for providing clients with a complete mail order package, from the creation to the printing and mailing of the promotion. Serves government also.

LIBRARIES

13658 ■ Direct Marketing Association Library & Resource Center
1120 Ave. of the Americas
New York, NY 10036-6700
Ph:(212)768-7277
Fax:(212)302-6714
Co. E-mail: lrc@the-dma.org
URL: http://www.the-dma.org
Contact: Terri Bartlett
Scope: Direct response advertising and marketing, including media applications (direct mail, catalog, telemarketing, print, interactive media, television), markets (business-to-business, consumer) and management basics. **Services:** Center open to non-members on a fee basis. **Holdings:** 1500 bound portfolios of direct marketing ECHO Awards campaigns. **Subscriptions:** 50 journals, magazines, and newsletters.

START-UP INFORMATION

13659 ■ *How to Start a Home-Based Consulting Business: Define Your Specialty Build a Client Base Make Yourself Indispensable*
Pub: The Globe Pequot Press

Ed: Bert Holtje. **Released:** January 10, 2010. **Price:** $18.95. **Description:** Everything needed for starting and running a successful consulting business from home.

13660 ■ *Starting and Running a Coaching Business*
Pub: How To Books

Ed: Aryanne Oade. **Released:** August 9, 2010. **Price:** $26.00. **Description:** Guide for the comprehensive, practical and personalized process of starting and running a coaching business is presented.

ASSOCIATIONS AND OTHER ORGANIZATIONS

13661 ■ **American Management Association**
1601 Broadway
New York, NY 10019-7420
Ph:(212)586-8100
Free: 877-566-9441
Fax:(212)903-8168
Co. E-mail: customerservice@amanet.org
URL: http://www.amanet.org
Contact: Edward T. Reilly, Pres./CEO

Purpose: Maintains a publishing program providing tools individuals use to extend learning beyond the classroom in a process of life-long professional growth and development through education. **Publications:** *Management Review* (monthly); *The Take-Charge Assistant* (monthly).

13662 ■ **Association of Management Consulting Firms**
370 Lexington Ave., Ste. 2209
New York, NY 10017
Ph:(212)262-3055
Fax:(212)262-3054
Co. E-mail: info@amcf.org
URL: http://www.amcf.org/amcf
Contact: John Furth, Pres./CEO

Description: Trade association for consulting organizations that provide a broad range of managerial services to commercial, industrial, governmental, and other organizations and individuals. Seeks to unite management-consulting firms in order to develop and improve professional standards and practice in the field. Offers information and referral services on management consultants; administers public relations program. Conducts research. Monitors regulatory environment. **Publications:** *15th Annual Operating Ratios for Management Consulting Firms: A Resource for Benchmarking* (annual).

13663 ■ **International Association for Time Use Research**
University of Oxford
Dept. of Sociology
Manor Road Bldg.
Oxford OX1 3UQ, United Kingdom
Co. E-mail: kimberly.fisher@sociology.ox.ac.uk
URL: http://iatur.timeuse.org
Contact: Prof. Michael Bittman, Pres.

Description: The International Association for Time Use Research (IATUR) facilitates exchange of ideas, methodology, and data collection techniques among researchers and compilers of official statistics on the patterns of daily activities and changes in people's behaviours over time. **Publications:** *Electronic International Journal for Time Use Research* (annual); *Fifteenth Reunion of the International Association for Time Use Research Amsterdam* (periodic); *Time Use Methodology: Towards Consensus* .

13664 ■ **Professional and Technical Consultants Association**
PO Box 2261
Santa Clara, CA 95055
Ph:(408)971-5902
Free: 800-74-PATCA
Fax:(866)746-1053
Co. E-mail: info@patca.org
URL: http://www.patca.org
Contact: Jerry W. Rice, Pres.

Description: Represents Independent consultants active in the support of business, industry, and government. Serves as a referral service to aid independent consultants in marketing their services as well as to assist those seeking their services. **Publications:** *PATCA Directory of Consultants* (annual); *PATCA Survey of Rates and Business Practices* (biennial).

13665 ■ **Turnaround Management Association**
150 S Wacker Dr., Ste. 900
Chicago, IL 60606
Ph:(312)578-6900
Fax:(312)578-8336
Co. E-mail: info@turnaround.org
URL: http://www.turnaround.org
Contact: Linda Delgadillo CAE, Exec. Dir.

Description: Practitioners (interim managers, consultants, corporate managers and professional advisors), academics, students, attorneys and judges, commercial lenders and legislative personnel. Promotes the image and credibility of the turnaround profession; fosters professional development and networking opportunities for turnaround executives; serves as a clearinghouse of information and research pertinent to the profession. Conducts networking forums; offers educational and credentialing programs. **Publications:** *Professional Fees in Bankruptcy Handbook* .

REFERENCE WORKS

13666 ■ **"Auxis Introduces Services for Government Contracting" in** *Entertainment Close-Up* **(December 22, 2010)**
Pub: Close-Up Media

Description: Profile of Auxis Inc., a management consulting and outsourcing company has launched a new service for companies involved in or bidding for government contracts. Details of the program are provided.

13667 ■ **"Benchmark Makes Granduca Entrance" in** *Houston Business Journal* **(Vol. 40, January 8, 2010, No. 35, pp. 2)**
Pub: American City Business Journals

Ed: Jennifer Dawson. **Description:** Houston, Texas-based Interfin Company, owner of the Hotel Granduca, has tapped the services of Benchmark Hospitality International to manage the property. The hiring of Benchmark is part of Interfin's efforts to develop Granduca hotels in other markets. Statistical data included.

13668 ■ **Consultants and Consulting Organizations Directory**
Pub: Gale

Released: Annual, New edition expected 37th; February, 2012. **Price:** $1,392, individuals. **Covers:** Over 26,000 firms, individuals, and organizations active in consulting. **Entries Include:** Individual or organization name, address, phone, fax, e-mail, URL, specialties, founding date, branch offices, names and titles of key personnel, number of employees, financial data, publications, seminars and workshops. **Arrangement:** By broad subject categories. **Indexes:** Subject, geographical, organization name.

13669 ■ *D & B Consultants Directory*
Pub: Dun & Bradstreet Corp.
Contact: Sara Mathew, Chm./CEO

Released: Annual, Latest edition September, 2008. **Covers:** Top 30,000 U.S. consulting firms in more than 200 areas of specialization. **Entries Include:** Firm name, address, phone, sales, number of employees, year established, description of service, other locations, names and titles of key personnel, reference to parent company, D&B DUNS number, trade name, consulting activity, owned companies clientele, territory served, number of accounts, stock exchange symbol and indicator for publicly owned companies. **Arrangement:** Complete consultants profiles appear in the consultants alphabetical section. Companies are cross-referenced geographically and by activity. **Indexes:** All companies with a primary or secondary Standard Industrial Classification (SIC) code of 8748 "Business Consulting Services," as well as those companies whose type of business description includes the word "consult." All companies must have a phone number and be either a headquarters or single location.

13670 ■ *Franchise: Freedom or Fantasy*
Pub: iUniverse

Ed: Mitchell York. **Released:** June 22, 2009. **Price:** $13.95. **Description:** Successful franchisee and professional certified coach guides individuals through the many steps involved in deciding whether or not to buy a franchise and how to do it correctly.

13671 ■ **"Leadership: The Couch in the Corner Office: Surveying the Landscape of the CEO Psyche" in** *Inc.* **(January 2008, pp. 33-34)**
Pub: Gruner & Jahr USA Publishing

Description: Profile of Leslie G. Mayer, founder of the Leadership Group, a firm that provides assistance to CEOs of firms by offering a deep understanding of the relationships, insecurities, and blind spots that can weaken strong leadership.

13672 ■ Leading at a Higher Level
Pub: FT Press
Ed: Ken Blanchard. **Released:** November 2006. **Price:** $26.99. **Description:** Tips, advice and techniques from a management consultant to help entrepreneurs create a vision for their company; includes information on manager-employee relationships.

13673 ■ The Management Myth: Why the "Experts" Keep Getting It Wrong
Pub: W.W. Norton & Company
Ed: Matthew Stewart. **Released:** August 10, 2009. **Price:** $27.95. **Description:** An insider's perspective on the management consulting industry, which reveals the high fees and incompetent consultants.

13674 ■ The Mirror Test: How to Breathe New Life Into Your Business
Pub: Grand Central Publishing
Ed: Jeffrey W. Hayzlett. **Released:** May 10, 2010. **Price:** $24.99. **Description:** Consultant and author, Jeffrey Hayzlett, explains why a business is not doing well and asks the questions that most business managers are afraid to ask.

13675 ■ Professional and Technical Consultants Association—Directory of Consultants
Pub: Professional and Technical Consultants Association
Contact: Martin A. Van Derpool, Chm. of Directory
E-mail: martin@martinconsult.com
Released: Annual, January; Latest edition 2009-2010. **Covers:** More than 350 consultants involved in computer technology, management, marketing, manufacturing, engineering, etc. **Entries Include:** Individual or firm name, address, phone, specialties, degrees held. **Arrangement:** Alphabetical. **Indexes:** Specialty, geographical.

13676 ■ The Sticking Point Solution: 9 Ways to Move Your Business from Stagnation to Stunning Growth in Tough Economic Times
Pub: Vanguard Press
Ed: Jay Abraham. **Released:** May 10, 2010. **Price:** $25.95. **Description:** Renowned business consultant, Jay Abraham, reveals the nine ways even successful businesses get stuck, hit plateaus, and fail to achieve their dreams and he explains how to get unstuck and create exponential growth.

STATISTICAL SOURCES

13677 ■ RMA Annual Statement Studies
Pub: Robert Morris Associates (RMA)
Released: Annual. **Price:** $175.00 2006-07 edition, $105.00. **Description:** Contains composite balance sheets and income statements for more than 360 industries, including the accounting, auditing, and bookkeeping industries. Also contains five years of comparative historical data for discerning trends. Includes 16 commonly used ratios, computed for most of the size groupings for nearly every industry.

TRADE PERIODICALS

13678 ■ Consultants News
Pub: Kennedy Information
Contact: Wayne Cooper, CEO
E-mail: editor@kennedyinfo.com
Released: Monthly. **Price:** $349, U.S. and Canada; $399, elsewhere. **Description:** The authoritative voice of the consulting industry, covering news, analysis, practice advice, proprietary data and opinion.

13679 ■ Innovative Leader
Pub: Winston J. Brill & Associates
Contact: Winston J. Brill
E-mail: wbrill@winstonbrill.com
Released: Monthly. **Price:** Free. **Description:** Serves as a resource for managers on creativity and productivity.

13680 ■ The Journal for Quality and Participation
Pub: American Society for Quality
Released: 4/yr. **Price:** $49 members domestic, individuals; $78 members international, individuals; $71 members includes GST individual, Canada; $83 nonmembers domestic, individuals; $93 nonmembers international, individuals; $93 nonmembers Canadian, includes GST individual. **Description:** Journal covering total quality management and employee involvement processes.

13681 ■ Make It A Winning Life
Pub: Wolf Rinke Associates,Inc.
Ed: Wolf J. Rinke, Ph.D., Editor, wolfrinke@aol.com. **Released:** Bimonthly. **Price:** Free. **Description:** Features ideas and strategies to help individuals succeed faster and improve the quality of their life. Remarks: America Online, Inc.

13682 ■ Management Report for Nonunion Organizations
Pub: John Wiley and Sons Inc.
Ed: Sarah Magee, Editor. **Released:** Monthly. **Price:** $995, U.S.; $995, Canada and Mexico; $1067, elsewhere. **Description:** Features news on current activities; employers' responses; NLRB rulings; court cases; pending legislation; government policies; and advice and opinions from Alfred T. DeMaria, "one of the country's foremost labor lawyers" representing management. Includes information on preventive tactics on how to handle human resources and labor issues without risking unionization, a campaign workshop on what the laws and regulations mean in terms of day-to-day management, white-collar organizing, and questions and answers on common problems.

13683 ■ Productivity Software
Pub: Worldwide Videotex
Released: Monthly. **Price:** $150. **Description:** Provides information on computer software.

VIDEOCASSETTES/ AUDIOCASSETTES

13684 ■ Building a Profitable Consulting Practice Series
Instructional Video
2219 C St.
Lincoln, NE 68502
Ph:(402)475-6570
Free: 800-228-0164
Fax:(402)475-6500
Co. E-mail: feedback@insvideo.com
URL: http://www.insvideo.com
Description: Two-part business educational series by Howard Shenson offers tips on how to build a profitable consulting practice. Covers consulting opportunities, market strategies, proposal writing, contracting strategies, fee setting, disclosure, and collection techniques. **Availability:** VHS.

13685 ■ Creativity in Management
Video Arts, Inc.
c/o Aim Learning Group
8238-40 Lehigh
Morton Grove, IL 60053-2615
Free: 877-444-2230
Fax:(416)252-2155
Co. E-mail: service@aimlearninggroup.com
URL: http://www.aimlearninggroup.com
Price: $149.00. **Description:** John Cleese presents the five steps for building an effective and creative work team. **Availability:** VHS.

13686 ■ The 21st Century Manger
Karol Media
Hanover Industrial Estates
375 Stewart Rd.
PO Box 7600
Wilkes Barre, PA 18773-7600
Ph:(570)822-8899

Free: 800-526-4773
Co. E-mail: sales@karolmedia.com
URL: http://www.karolmedia.com
Released: 1997. **Price:** $69.95. **Description:** Four-volume series discusses the new era of management. **Availability:** VHS.

CONSULTANTS

13687 ■ Advanced Benefits & Human Resources
9350-F Snowden River Pky., Ste. 222
Columbia, MD 21045
Ph:(410)290-9037
Fax:(410)740-2568
Co. E-mail: hrb@abhr.com
Contact: Linda Polacek, President
Scope: Provides human resource consulting to high technology businesses. Offers services in the areas of human resources, benefits, and training. Creates, maintains, or updates current human resource functions.

13688 ■ Advent Management International Ltd.
411 Old Baltimore Pke.
Chadds Ford, PA 19317-9444
Ph:(610)506-6311
Free: 800-726-7985
Fax:(413)618-5273
Co. E-mail: johnr@getresults.com
URL: http://www.getresults.com
Contact: John J. Reddish, President
E-mail: johnr@getresults.com
Scope: Works with leaders and members of their teams who want to become their personal best to master growth, manage change and facilitate succession. Services include: strategic, succession, operational and marketing planning; process improvement and project management, standards certification preparation, merchant banking; executive search, and management development. Primary industries served: manufacturing, professional services, IT, industrial distribution and B2B e-commerce. **Publications:** "Boomer Succession: A Philosophy For Letting Go"; "Strategic Fees: Planning & Pricing Your Future"; "Succession and Peace of Mind"; "Who Comes Next: Succession Issues For Business Owners"; "Finding Pockets: Buying A Business"; "Valuing The Closely Held Company: Which Way Is Best"; "How to Buy a Business"; "The Business Leader: Responsibilities"; "Responsibilities of Owners In A Smaller Business"; "Valuing The Closely Held Company: Which Way Is Best"; "The Seven Signs of Business Trouble: And What They Mean"; "How To Avoid Cash Flow Problems"; "Bankruptcies And Turnarounds". **Seminars:** How To Get More From Any Workshop.

13689 ■ Advisory Management Services Inc.
9600 E 129th St., Ste. B
Kansas City, MO 64149-1025
Ph:(816)765-9611
Fax:(816)765-7447
Co. E-mail: amsi1@mindspring.com
Contact: Hal Wood, President
Scope: A management consulting and training firm specializing in employee relations, management and staff training, organizational development, strategic planning, and continuous quality improvement.

13690 ■ The Alliance Management Group Inc.
38 Old Chester Rd., Ste. 300
Gladstone, NJ 07934
Ph:(908)234-2344
Fax:(908)234-0638
Co. E-mail: kathy@strategicalliance.com
URL: http://www.strategicalliance.com
Contact: Dan G. Watson, Senior Partner
E-mail: gene@atsstrategicalliance.com
Scope: The firm enables leading companies to maximize the value of their strategic alliances, mergers and acquisitions. Offers services in partner evaluation process, a planning and negotiating program, mergers and acquisition integration, management issues, the turnaround or termination of poorly performing alliances, and a competitive strategic analysis program. **Publications:** "Effective Practices For Sourcing Innovation," Jan-Feb, 2009; "Intellectual

Property Issues in Collaborative Research Agreements," Nov-Dec, 2008; "Building University Relationships in China," Sep-Oct, 2008; "Reinventing Corporate Growth: Implementing the Transformational Growth Model"; "The Strongest Link"; "Allocating Patent Rights in Collaborative Research Agreements"; "Protecting Know-how and Trade Secrets in Collaborative Research Agreements," Aug, 2006; "Sourcing External Technology for Innovation," Jun, 2006. **Special Services:** "Want, Find, Get, Manage" Model[R]; "Want, Find, Get, Manage" Framework[R]; WFGM Framework[R]; The Alliance Implementation Program[R]; WFGM Paradigm[R]; WFGM Model[R]; "Want, Find, Get, Manage" Paradigm[R], Transformational Growth[R]; T-growth[R].

13691 ■ Alliance Management International Ltd.
PO Box 470691
Cleveland, OH 44147-0691
Ph:(440)838-1922
Fax:(440)740-1434
Co. E-mail: bob@bgruss.com
Contact: Ken Gruss, Mgr
E-mail: bgruss@cox.net
Scope: A consulting company that helps to form national and international strategic alliances. Handles alliances between companies forming joint ventures. Staff specialized in small company-large company alliance, alliance assessment and analysis, and alliance strategic planning. **Seminars:** Joint Business Planning; Developing a Shared Vision; Current and New/Prospective Partner Assessment; Customer Service; Sales Training; Leader and Management Skills.

13692 ■ Anderson/Roethle Inc.
700 N Water St., Ste. 1100
Milwaukee, WI 53202-4221
Ph:(414)276-0070
Fax:(414)276-4364
Co. E-mail: info@anderson-roethle.com
URL: http://www.anderson-roethle.com
Contact: James H. Hunter, Managering Director
E-mail: jimh@atsanderson-roethle.com
Scope: Provides merger, acquisition and divestiture advisory services. Offers strategic planning, valuations and specialized M and A advisory services.

13693 ■ Apex Innovations Inc.
700 W 47th St., Ste. 300
PO Box 15208
Kansas City, MO 64112-1805
Ph:(913)254-0250
Fax:(913)254-0320
Co. E-mail: sales@apex-innovations.com
URL: http://www.apex-innovations.com
Contact: Connie Fox, Dir of Human Resources
Scope: A firm of business operations and technology professionals providing solutions nationwide for business needs. Provides a bridge between operations and technology for clients in manufacturing, insurance, banking and government. Offers services in business planning, assessment, education, business performance improvement, change management and the planning, and implementation management of solutions. **Special Services:** i-INFO.EPR[TM]; i-INFO. WORKS[TM]; i-INFO Classes[TM].

13694 ■ Arnold S. Goldin & Associates Inc.
5030 Champion Blvd., Ste. G-6231
Boca Raton, FL 33496
Ph:(561)994-5810
Fax:(561)994-5860
Co. E-mail: arnold@goldin.com
URL: http://www.goldin.com
Contact: Arnold S. Goldin, Principle
E-mail: arnold@goldin.com
Scope: An accounting and management consulting firm. Serves clients worldwide. Provides management services. Handles monthly write-ups and tax returns.

13695 ■ Associated Enterprises Ltd.
183 Pauls Ln.
Bailey, CO 80421-1122
Ph:(303)988-6695

Fax:(303)838-0658
Co. E-mail: ael@aelgroup.biz
Contact: Lawrence J. Rouse, President
E-mail: ael@aelgroup.biz
Scope: General management consulting in all disciplines plus specialty in franchise and franchisee development programs. Additional specialties include economic research, analysis, and forecasting, financial management, business planning, and financing packaging, involving equity, debt, SBA 7A loans, 501 or 504 program development, and federal, state, and local program packages. Also experienced with litigation support, marketing, and audiovisual services. Serves private industries as well as government agencies.

13696 ■ Associated Management Services Inc.
8701 Georgia Ave., Ste. 705
Silver Spring, MD 20910-3713
Ph:(301)588-9694
Fax:(301)588-2113
Co. E-mail: info@amsihq.com
URL: http://www.amsihq.com
Contact: Kelly Kim, Treasurer
E-mail: samuelklatt@atsaol.com
Scope: Small business management firm offers consultation in the following areas: accounting, auditing, bookkeeping services, business advisory services and tax preparation for individuals, government agencies, and businesses and computer training and software applications.

13697 ■ Association of Home-Based Women Entrepreneurs
PO Box 31561
Saint Louis, MO 63131-1561
Ph:(314)805-9519
Fax:(314)909-8179
Co. E-mail: aschaefer@advbizsol.com
URL: http://www.hbwe.org
Contact: Sue Lunnemann, Treasurer
E-mail: sue@atssl-solutions.biz
Scope: Organization dedicated to women working from home-based offices. Focuses on the needs and interests of women doing their own business. It also focuses on business-related programs and issues, networking, leads and mentoring for professional growth in a dynamic and friendly atmosphere. **Publications:** "Taking Your Business International"; "Dressing For Success"; "Web 2.0 The Future of the Internet"; "Assertiveness Skills for Women in Business". **Seminars:** Making Connections, Jul, 2008; One Inch Wide, One Mile Deep, Jun, 2008; Accelerating Your Business, May, 2008; Change is Good, Apr, 2008; Pyro Marketing, Jan, 2007; Twenty Five Key Steps To Maintaining A Successful Home-Based Business, Nov, 2006.

13698 ■ Aurora Management Partners Inc.
4485 Tench Rd., Ste. 340
Suwanee, GA 30024
Ph:(770)904-5209
Co. E-mail: rturcotte@auroramp.com
URL: http://www.auroramp.com
Contact: William A. Barbee, Director
E-mail: abarbee@atsauroramp.com
Scope: Firm specializes in turnaround management and reorganization consulting. Firm develop strategic initiatives, organize and analyze solutions, deal with creditor issues, review organizational structure and develop time frames for decision making. Turnaround services offered include Recovery plans and their implementation, Viability analysis, Crisis management, Financial restructuring, Corporate and organizational restructuring, Facilities rationalization, Liquidation management, Loan workout, Litigation support and Expert testimony, Contract renegotiation, Sourcing loan refinancing and Sourcing equity investment. **Publications:** "TMA Turnaround of the Year Award, Small Company, Honorable Mention," Nov, 2005; "Back From The Brink - Bland Farms," Progressive Farmer, Oct, 2004; "New Breed of Turnaround Managers," Catalyst Magazine, Aug, 2004; "Key Performance Drivers - Bland Farms," The Produce News, Apr, 2004; "Corporate Governance: Averting Crisis's Before They Happen," ABJ journal, Feb, 2004.

13699 ■ Automated Accounting
23325 Gerbera St.
Moreno Valley, CA 92553
Ph:(951)653-5053
Co. E-mail: autoacc@earthlink.net
Contact: Gary Capolino, Owner
Scope: A business management consulting firm that caters to small businesses. Offers software installation services, tax preparation services and business plan advisory services. **Publications:** "Inflated Real Estate Prices. . .How Did This Happen," Moreno Valley Magazine, Aug, 2005.

13700 ■ Bahr International Inc.
PO Box 795
Gainesville, TX 76241
Ph:(940)665-2344
Fax:(940)665-2359
Co. E-mail: info@bahrintl.com
URL: http://www.bahrintl.com
Contact: C. Charles Bahr III, Chairman of the Board
Scope: Offers consulting in general management, corporate polices and culture, and strategic and long-range planning. Provides management audits and reports and profit improvement programs. High level strategic marketing, advertising strategy/tactics, turnaround consulting and management.

13701 ■ Beacon Management Group Inc.
1000 W McNab Rd., Ste. 150
Pompano Beach, FL 33069-4719
Ph:(954)782-1119
Free: 800-771-8721
Fax:(954)969-2566
Co. E-mail: md@beaconmgmt.com
URL: http://www.beaconmgmt.com
Contact: Chris Roy, Treasurer
E-mail: md@beaconmgmt.com
Scope: Specializes in change management, organized workplaces, multicultural negotiations and dispute resolutions and internet based decision making.

13702 ■ Benchmark Consulting Group Inc.
283 Franklin St., Ste. 400
PO Box 126
Boston, MA 02110-3100
Ph:(617)482-7661
Fax:(617)423-2158
Co. E-mail: werobb35@aol.com
Contact: Walter E. Robb III, President
E-mail: werobb35@aol.com
Scope: Provides financial and management services to companies. Helps companies grow through debt, equity sourcing and restructuring, business valuation, acquisition and divestiture, computer information systems and improved operation profitability.

13703 ■ BioSciCon Inc.
14905 Forest Landing Cir.
Rockville, MD 20850-3924
Ph:(301)610-9130
Fax:(301)610-7662
Co. E-mail: info@bioscicon.com
URL: http://www.bioscicon.com
Contact: Olivera Markovic, Director
E-mail: info@bioscicon.com
Scope: Sponsoring development of the technology of the Pap test accuracy via introduction of a new bio-marker that enhances visibility of abnormal cells on Pap smears or mono-layers of cervical cells obtained in solution. Conducts clinical trials for assessment of the test efficacy and safety, manufactures research tools for conduct of trials, and markets IP to license manufacturing, marketing, sales and distribution rights of the new technology line of products. **Publications:** "Cervical Acid Phosphates: A Biomarker of Cervical Dysplasia and Potential Surrogate Endpoint for Colposcopy," 2004; "Enhancing Pap test with a new biological marker of cervical dysplasia," 2004; "A cytoplasmic biomarker for liquid-based Pap," The FACEB Journal Experimental Biology, 2004; "Pap test and new biomarker-based technology for enhancing visibility of abnormal cells," 2004. **Special Services:** MarkPap[R]; PreservCyt[R].

13704 ■ Blankinship & Associates Inc.
322 C St.
Davis, CA 95616-7617
Ph:(530)757-0941
Fax:(530)757-0940
Co. E-mail: blankinship@envtox.com
URL: http://www.h2osci.com
Contact: Michael Blankinship, Principal
E-mail: mike@atsenvtox.com
Scope: Specializes in assisting water resource and conveyance, golf and production, protection and enhancement of natural resources. **Publications:** "Air Blast Sprayer Calibration and Chlorpyrifos Irrigation Study," Oct, 2007; "How Green is your golf course," Prosper Magazine, 2007. **Seminars:** CDFG Wildlands IPM Seminar, Oct, 2009.

13705 ■ BPT Consulting Associates Ltd.
12 Parmenter Rd., Ste. B-6
Londonderry, NH 03053
Ph:(603)437-8484
Free: 888-278-0030
Fax:(603)434-5388
Co. E-mail: bptcons@tiac.net
Contact: John Kuczynski, President
E-mail: bptcons@tiac.net
Scope: Provides management consulting expertise and resources to cross-industry clients with services for: Business Management consulting, People/Human Resources Transition and Training programs, and a full cadre of multi-disciplined Technology Computer experts. Virtual consultants with expertise in e-commerce, supply chain management, organizational development, and business application development consulting.

13706 ■ Bran Management Services Inc.
2106 High Ridge Rd.
Louisville, KY 40207-1128
Ph:(502)896-1632
Contact: Robert C. Braverman, CEO
Scope: Offers management consulting services to companies in manufacturing, distribution and services to help them cope with growth and change. Helps small businesses create and identify product strategies. Services include developing international business opportunities; turnaround management; sales and marketing development; business planning; acquisitions and mergers.

13707 ■ Business Improvement Architects
33 Riderwood Dr.
Toronto, ON, Canada M2L 2X4
Ph:(416)444-8225
Free: (866)346-3242
Fax:(416)444-6743
Co. E-mail: info@bia.ca
URL: http://www.bia.ca
Contact: Susan Lee, Principle
E-mail: slee@atsbia.ca
Scope: Provides the following services: strategic planning, leadership development, innovation and project and quality management. Specialize in strategic planning, change management, leadership assessment, and development of skills. **Publications:** "Avoiding Pit falls to Innovation"; "Create a New Dimension of Performance with Innovation"; "The Power of Appreciation in Leadership"; "Why It Makes Sense To Have a Strategic Enterprise Office"; "Burning Rubber at the Start of Your Project"; "Accounting for Quality"; "How Pareto Charts Can Help You Improve the Quality of Business Processes"; "Managing Resistance to Change". **Seminars:** The Innovation Process. . .From Vision to Reality, San Diego, Oct, 2007; Critical Thinking, Kuala Lump or, Sep, 2007; Critical Thinking, Brunei, Sep, 2007; Delivering Project Assurance, Auckland, Jun, 2007; From Crisis to Control: A New Era in Strategic Project Management, Prague, May, 2007; What Project Leaders Need to Know to Help Them Sleep Better At Night, London, May, 2007; Innovation Process. . .From Vision To Reality, Orlando, Apr, 2007. **Special Services:** Project Planning Tool™.

13708 ■ ByrneMRG
22 Isle of Pines Dr.
Hilton Head Island, SC 29928
Ph:(215)630-7411

Free: 888-816-8080
Co. E-mail: info@byrnemrg.com
URL: http://www.byrnemrg.com
Contact: Patrick J. Boyle, CEO
E-mail: pjboyle@byrnemrg.com
Scope: Firm specializes in management consulting, including department management, equipment evaluation and selection, project management, research and development planning; and database design and management. **Publications:** "Implementing Solutions to Everyday Issues".

13709 ■ C. Clint Bolte & Associates
809 Philadelphia Ave.
Chambersburg, PA 17201-1268
Ph:(717)263-5768
Fax:(717)263-8954
Co. E-mail: clint@clintbolte.com
URL: http://www.clintbolte.com
Contact: C. Clint Bolte, Principle
E-mail: cbolte3@comcast.net
Scope: Provides management consulting services to firms involved with the printing industry. Services include outsourcing studies, graphics supply chain management studies, company and equipment valuations, plant layout services, litigation support, fulfillment warehouse consulting and product development services. **Publications:** "UV Cost Savings Environmental Advantage"; "Possible Quebecor World Fall Out"; "80-20 Rule for Managing"; "Options Available in Starting Up a Mailing Operation"; "High Volume Print Buyers at Print 2009"; "Diversifying With Mailing & Fulfillment Services"; "New Business Model Needed for Magazine News stand Distribution"; "Purchasing Incentives Can Be Costly.."; "In-Plant New Product Opportunity for 2009: Tran promo Printing"; "Possible Quebecor World Fall Out"; "Offshore Print Evolution"; "Benefits of Third Party Lease Review"; "Unique Information Fulfillment Opportunities for In-Plant Printers"; "Tough Competition Forces New Strategic Realities for In-Plants"; "Direct Mail Industry Group Files Interpretive Ruling Requests with the Ssta"; "Interesting Opportunities Amid the Gray Clouds of 2007 Postal Rate Increases"; "Time to Break Through the Glass Ceiling," the Seybold Report, May, 2006; "Challenges and Opportunities Presented By Postal Rate Increases," the Seybold Report, May, 2006; "Packaging Roll Sheeting Comes of Age," the Seybold Report, May, 2006; "Diversifying with Mailing and Fulfillment Services," the Seybold Report, Jan, 2006. **Seminars:** How to compete with the majors.

13710 ■ Carelli & Associates
17 Reid Pl.
Delmar, NY 12054
Ph:(518)439-0233
Fax:(518)439-3006
Co. E-mail: anneobriencarelli@yahoo.com
URL: http://www.carelli.com
Contact: Dr. Anne Obrien Carelli, Owner
E-mail: anneobriencarelli@yahoo.com
Scope: Provides writing and editing services to industry and businesses, health care and educational institutions, and government agencies. Also provides program management in creating and disseminating publications and in implementing related training. Assists organizations in designing and implementing team-based management. Offers supervisory skills training and problem-solving work sessions for managers. Individual Consultation are provided for managers, CEOs, potential supervisors including 360 degree assessments. **Publications:** "The Truth About Supervision: Coaching, Teamwork, Interviewing, Appraisals, 360 degree Assessments, and Recognition". **Seminars:** Supervisory Skills Training Series; Problem-Solving Work Sessions for Managers; Effective Leadership.

13711 ■ The Center for Organizational Excellence Inc.
15204 Omega Dr., Ste. 300
Rockville, MD 20850
Ph:(301)948-1922
Free: 877-674-3923
Fax:(301)948-2158
Co. E-mail: results@center4oe.com
URL: http://www.center4oe.com
Contact: Kirstin Austin, Mgr
E-mail: kaustin@atscenter4oe.com
Scope: An organizational effectiveness consulting firm specializing in helping organizations achieve

results through people, process, and performance. Service areas include organizational performance systems, leadership systems, customer systems, and learning systems.

13712 ■ Center for Personal Empowerment
102 N Main St., Ste. 1
Columbia, IL 62236-1702
Ph:(618)281-3565
Free: 888-657-1530
Fax:(618)476-7083
Co. E-mail: personalempowerment@wholenet.net
Contact: Cherri Hendrix, Vice President
Scope: Private consultations and trainings to educate on how to determine which emotions, events, beliefs from the past prevent you from achieving success. Methods used include time line therapy, news linguistic programming and hypnosis. Behavior modification through NLP trainings. **Seminars:** NLP Practitioner Training; Hypnosis Certification Training; Lifemap Seminars.

13713 ■ Century Business Services Inc.
6050 Oak Tree Blvd. S, Ste. 500
Cleveland, OH 44131-6951
Ph:(216)525-1947
Fax:(216)447-9007
Co. E-mail: info@cbiz.com
URL: http://www.cbiz.com
Contact: Steven L. Gerard, CEO
E-mail: gdufour@cbiz.com
Scope: A business consulting and tax services firm providing financial, consulting, tax and business services through seven groups: Financial management, tax advisory, construction and real estate, health-care, litigation support, capital resource and CEO outsource. **Publications:** "FAS 154: Changes in the Way We Report Changes," 2006; "Equity-Based Compensation: How Much Does it Really Cost Your Business," 2006; "Preventing Fraud - Tips for Nonprofit Organizations"; "Today's Workforce and Nonprofit Organizations: Meeting a Critical Need"; "IRS Highlights Top Seven Form 990 Errors". **Seminars:** Health Care - What the Future Holds; Consumer Driven Health Plans; Executive Plans; Health Savings Accounts; Healthy Wealthy and Wise; Legislative Update; Medicare Part D; Retirement Plans.

13714 ■ CFO Service
112 Chester Ave.
Saint Louis, MO 63122
Ph:(314)757-2940
Contact: John D. Skae, President
E-mail: jds217@aol.com
Scope: A group of professional executives that provide upper management services to companies that cannot support a full time COO or CFO. Provides clients in the areas of business planning, company policies, contract negotiations, safety policies, product and service pricing, loans management, taxes, cost analysis, loss control and budgeting.

13715 ■ Chamberlain & Cansler Inc.
2251 Perimeter Park Dr.
Atlanta, GA 30341
Ph:(770)457-5699
Contact: Charles L. Cansler, Owner
Scope: Firm specializes in strategic planning; profit enhancement; small business management; interim management; crisis management; turnarounds.

13716 ■ Chartered Management Co.
125 S Wacker Dr.
Chicago, IL 60606
Ph:(312)214-2575
Contact: William B. Avellone, President
Scope: Operations improvement consultants. Specializes in strategic planning; feasibility studies; management audits and reports; profit enhancement; start-up businesses; mergers and acquisitions; joint ventures; divestitures; interim management; crisis management; turnarounds; business process re-engineering; venture capital; and due diligence.

13717 ■ Claremont Consulting Group
4525 Castle Ln.
La Canada, CA 91011-1436
Ph:(818)249-0584

Fax:(818)249-5811
Contact: Donald S. Remer, Partner
E-mail: amruskin@compuserve.com
Scope: Consulting, coaching, training, and litigation support in project management, engineering management, system engineering and cost estimating. **Publications:** "What Every Engineer Should Know About Project Management"; "100%product-oriented work breakdown structures and their importance to system engineering". **Seminars:** Project Management, System Engineering and Cost Estimating.

13718 ■ Colmen Menard Company Inc.
The Woods, 994 Old Eagle School Rd., Ste. 1000
Wayne, PA 19087
Ph:(484)367-0300
Fax:(484)367-0305
Co. E-mail: cmci@colmenmenard.com
URL: http://www.colmenmenard.com
Contact: David W. Menard, Managing Director
E-mail: dmenard@atscolmenmenard.com
Scope: Merger and acquisition corporate finance and business advisory services for public and private companies located in North America. **Publications:** "Success in Selling a Troubled Company," Nov, 2002; "Savvy Dealmakers," May, 2001; "Truisms," M&A Today, Nov, 2000.

13719 ■ Consulting & Conciliation Service
2830 I St., Ste. 301
Sacramento, CA 95816
Ph:(916)396-0480
Free: 888-898-9780
Fax:(916)441-2828
Co. E-mail: service@azurewings.net
Contact: Jane A. McCluskey, Principle
E-mail: service@azurewings.net
Scope: Offers consulting and conciliation services. Provides pre-mediation counseling, training and research on preparing for a peaceful society, mediation and facilitation, and preparation for shifts in structure, policy and personnel. Offers sliding scale business rates and free individual consultation. **Publications:** "Native America and Tracking Shifts in US Policy"; "Biogenesis: A Discussion of Basic Social Needs and the Significance of Hope". **Seminars:** Positive Approaches to Violence Prevention: Peace building in Schools and Communities.

13720 ■ The Consulting Exchange
1770 Mass Ave., Ste. 288
PO Box 391050
Cambridge, MA 02140
Ph:(617)576-2100
Free: 800-824-4828
Co. E-mail: gday@consultingexchange.com
URL: http://www.cx.com
Contact: Geoffrey Day, President
E-mail: gday@consultingexchange.com
Scope: A consultant referral service for management and technical consultants. Serves a local, regional and international client base. **Publications:** "Looking for a Consultant? Success Points for Finding the Right One," Boston Business Journal, Jun, 2001; "Getting Full Value From Consulting is in Your Hands," Mass High Tech, May, 1998; "Developing Knowledge-Based Client Relationships, The Future of Professional Services"; "The Consultant's Legal Guide"; "The Business of Consulting: The Basics and Beyond".

13721 ■ The Corlund Group L.L.C.
101 Federal St., Ste. 310
Boston, MA 02110
Ph:(617)423-9364
Fax:(617)423-9371
Co. E-mail: info@corlundgroup.com
URL: http://www.corlundgroup.com
Contact: Deborah J. Cornwall, Managing Director
E-mail: dcornwall@atscorlundgroup.com
Scope: Boutique firm offering services in the areas of leadership, governance, and change with a particular focus on CEO and senior executive succession planning, including assessment, development, and orchestrating succession processes with management and Boards of Directors. Also Board governance effectiveness. **Publications:** "Are You Rolling the Dice on CEO Succession?" Center for Healthcare Governance, 2006; "Leadership Due

Diligence: The Neglected Governance Frontier," Directorship, Sep, 2001; "Leadership Due Diligence: Managing the Risks," The Corporate Board, Aug, 2001; "Succession: The need for detailed insight," Directors and Boards, 2001; "CEO Succession: Who's Doing Due Diligence?," 2001.

13722 ■ Corporate Consulting Inc.
3333 Belcaro Dr.
Denver, CO 80209-4912
Ph:(303)698-9292
Fax:(303)698-9292
Co. E-mail: corpcons@compuserve.com
Contact: Devereux C. Josephs, President
E-mail: corpcons@compuserve.com
Scope: Specializes in feasibility studies, organizational development, small business management, mergers and acquisitions, joint ventures, divestitures, interim management, crisis management, turnarounds, financing, appraisals valuations and due diligence studies.

13723 ■ COTC Technologies Inc.
172 E Industrial Blvd.
PO Box 7615
Pueblo, CO 81007-4406
Ph:(719)547-0938
Free: 888-547-0938
Fax:(719)547-1105
Contact: Karen Renz, CFO
E-mail: karen@atscotc-consulting.com
Scope: Provides software consulting services to organizations that require assistance with their HP3000 computer system. Provides systems analysis, programming, operations support, and system management. Also provides PC software and hardware support and consulting. Additionally provides various training for the HP3000 computer system. Industries served: healthcare, aerospace procurement, aerospace proposal activities, and HP3000 computer systems.

13724 ■ Crystal Clear Communications Inc.
1633 W Winslow Dr., Ste. 210
Mequon, WI 53092
Ph:(262)240-0072
Fax:(262)240-0073
Co. E-mail: contact@crystalclear1.com
URL: http://www.crystalclear1.com
Contact: Chez Fogel, Principle
E-mail: chfogel@atscrystalclear.com
Scope: Specialize in helping executives identify impediments to success, and then develop strategies to surmount them. Serves to identify core problems, suggest appropriate business changes, work with the organization to support these changes, and help executives articulate the behavior that will uphold these changes. Specializes in strategic planning; organizational development; small business management; executive coaching. **Publications:** "Weakest Link"; "Aware Leadership"; "Integrity"; "When Your Plate is Full"; "Problem Solving"; "Strategic Thinking".

13725 ■ David G. Schantz
29 Wood Run Cir.
Rochester, NY 14612-2271
Ph:(716)723-0760
Fax:(716)723-8724
Co. E-mail: daveschantz@yahoo.com
URL: http://www.daveschantz.freeservers.com
E-mail: daveschantz@yahoo.com
Scope: Provides industrial engineering services for photofinishing labs, including amateur-wholesale, professional, commercial, school, and package.

13726 ■ Development Resource Consultants
PO Box 118
Rancho Cucamonga, CA 91729
Ph:(909)902-7655
Fax:(909)476-6942
Co. E-mail: drc@gotodrc.com
URL: http://www.gotodrc.com
Contact: Jerry R. Frey, Partner
E-mail: jfrey@atsgotodrc.com
Scope: Specializes in office re-organization, employee training in office organization, communication skills, sales training and career counseling. **Publications:** "Institute of Management Consultants Southern California Chapter," Jan, 2006.

13727 ■ Donna Cornell Enterprises Inc.
68 N Plank Rd., Ste. 204
Newburgh, NY 12550-2122
Ph:(845)565-0088
Free: 888-769-3792
Fax:(845)565-0084
Co. E-mail: rc@cornellcareercenter.com
Contact: Donna Cornell, President
E-mail: rc@cornellcareercenter.com
Scope: Offers services in career consultant, professional search, job placement and national professional search. **Publications:** "The Power of the Woman Within"; "Juggling it All!"; "Journey: A Woman's Guide to Success"; "Shatter the Traditions".

13728 ■ DRI Consulting
2 Otter Ln.
North Oaks, MN 55127-6436
Ph:(651)415-1400
Free: (866)276-4600
Fax:(651)415-9968
Co. E-mail: dric@dric.com
URL: http://www.dric.com
Contact: Dr. Heather Mortensen, Principle
E-mail: heathermortensen@atsdric.com
Scope: Licensed psychologists providing organization and management consulting. Developing leaders, managers and individuals through coaching, business strategy, career development, crisis management, policy consultation and technology optimization.

13729 ■ Dropkin & Co.
390 George St.
New Brunswick, NJ 08901
Ph:(732)828-3211
Fax:(732)828-4118
Co. E-mail: murray@dropkin.com
URL: http://www.dropkin.com
Contact: Mel Nusbaum, Principle
E-mail: mel@atsdropkin.com
Scope: Firm specializes in feasibility studies; business management; business process re-engineering; and team building, health care and housing. **Publications:** "Bookkeeping for Nonprofits," Jossey Bass, 2005; "Guide to Audits of Nonprofit Organizations," PPC; "The Nonprofit Report," Warren, Gorham & Lamont; "The Budget Building Book for Nonprofits," Jossey-Bass; "The Cash Flow Management Book for Nonprofits," Jossey-Bass.

13730 ■ Dubuc Lucke & Company Inc.
120 W 5th St.
Cincinnati, OH 45202-2713
Ph:(513)579-8330
Fax:(513)241-6669
Contact: Kenneth E. Dubuc, President
Scope: Provides consulting services in the areas of profit enhancement; small business management; mergers and acquisitions; joint ventures; divestitures; interim management; crisis management; turnarounds; appraisals; valuations; due diligence; and international trade.

13731 ■ The DuMond Group
5282 Princeton Ave.
Westminster, CA 92683-2753
Ph:(714)373-0610
Contact: David L. Dumond, Principle
Scope: Human resources and executive search consulting firm that specializes in organizational development; small business management; employee surveys and communication; performance appraisals; and team building.

13732 ■ Dunelm International
437 Colebrook Ln.
Bryn Mawr, PA 19010-3216
Ph:(610)989-0144
Fax:(610)964-9524
Co. E-mail: jecdunelm@worldnet.att.net
Contact: John E. Crowther, President
E-mail: jecdunelm@dunelm.org.uk
Scope: Firm specializes in feasibility studies; start-up businesses; interim management; crisis management; turnarounds; business process re-engineering; sales forecasting; supply chain solution and project management.

13733 ■ Everett & Co.

3126 S Franklin St.
Englewood, CO 80113
Ph:(303)761-7999
Fax:(303)781-8296
Contact: Wayne Everett, Principle
Scope: Provides strategic real estate solutions and project management.

13734 ■ Family Business Institute Inc.

904 Steffi Ct.
Lawrenceville, GA 30044-6933
Ph:(770)952-4085
Fax:(770)432-6660
Co. E-mail: asktheexpert@family-business-experts.
 com
URL: http://www.family-business-experts.com
Contact: Wayne Rivers, President
E-mail: don@family-business-experts.com
Scope: Assists families in business to achieve personal, family, and organizational goals by meeting challenges that are unique to family-owned businesses. Provides coordinated and integrated assessments and solutions for family issues and needs; for company finance and for human resource and operational requirements. **Publications:** "Professional Intervention in the Family Owned Business"; "Building Consensus in a Family Business"; "Professionalizing Family Business Management"; "Recognizing generations - know them by their weekends"; "Succession planning tactics"; "Succession Planning Obstacles in Family Business"; "Succession: three ways to ease the transition"; "Pruning the family business tree"; "Responsibility diffusion - the most critical impediment to successfully growing any kind of business"; "Breaking Up is Hard to Do: Divorce in the Family Business".

13735 ■ FCP Consulting

500 Sutter St., Ste. 507
San Francisco, CA 94102-1114
Ph:(415)956-5558
Fax:(415)956-5722
Contact: Cox Ferrall, President
Scope: Management consulting in Business-To-Business sales.

13736 ■ First Strike Management Consulting Inc.

401 Loblolly Ave.
PO Box 1188
Little River, SC 29566-1188
Ph:(843)385-6338
Fax:(843)390-1004
Co. E-mail: fsmc.hq@fsmc.com
URL: http://www.fsmc.com
Contact: J.D. Lewis, President
E-mail: jd.lewis@fsmc.com
Scope: Offers proposal management and program management services. Specializes in enterprise systems, management systems, and staff augmentation. Serves the following industries: Nuclear/Fossil Power, Petro-Chemical, Aerospace and Defense, Telecommunications, Engineering and Construction, Information Technology, Golf Course Construction/Management, Utility Engineering/Construction, Civil Works, and Housing Development. **Publications:** "Project Management for Executives"; "Project Risk Management"; "Project Communications Management"; "Winning Proposals, Four Computer Based Training (CBT) courses"; "Principles of Program Management". **Seminars:** Preparing Winning Proposals in Response to Government RFPs.

13737 ■ Freese & Associates Inc.

PO Box 814
Chagrin Falls, OH 44022-0814
Ph:(440)564-9183
Fax:(440)564-7339
Co. E-mail: tfreese@freeseinc.com
URL: http://www.freeseinc.com
Contact: James H. Muir, Principle
E-mail: tfreese@freeseinc.com
Scope: A management consulting firm offering advice in all forms of business logistics. Consulting services are in the areas of strategic planning; network analysis, site selection, facility layout and design, outsourcing, warehousing, transportation and customer service. Typical projects include 3PL marketing surveys; third party outsourcing selection; operational audits; competitive analysis; inventory management; due diligence; and implementation project management. **Publications:** "Building Relationships is Key to Motivation," Distribution Center Management, Apr, 2006; "Getting Maximum Results from Performance Reviews," WERC Sheet, Oct, 2003; "SCM: Making the Vision a Reality," Supply Chain Management Review, Oct, 2003; "Contents Under Pressure," DC Velocity, Aug, 2003; "When Considering Outsourcing, It's Really a Financial Decision," Inventory Management Report, Mar, 2003. **Seminars:** WERC/CAWS Warehousing in China Conference, Sep, 2008; CSCMP Annual Conference, Denver, Oct, 2008; Keys to Retaining and Motivating Your Associates, Dallas, Mar, 2006; The Value and Challenges of Supply Chain Management, Dubai, Feb, 2006; Best Practices in Logistics in China, Jun, 2005; Keys to Motivating Associates, Dallas, May, 2005; The Goal and the Way of International Cooperation in Logistics, Jenobuk, Apr, 2005.

13738 ■ Global Business Consultants

200 Lake Hills Rd.
PO Box 776
Pinehurst, NC 28374-0776
Ph:(910)295-5991
Fax:(910)295-5991
Co. E-mail: gbc@pinehurst.net
Contact: Gerd Hofielen, Partner
E-mail: mcoin@atsyourculturecoach.com
Scope: Firm specializes in human resources management; project management; software development; and international trade. Offers litigation support. **Publications:** "Culture to Culture: Mission Trip Do's and Don'ts," Jul, 2005; "Rules of the Game: Global Business Protocol". **Seminars:** Cross-Cultural Training.

13739 ■ Global Technology Transfer L.L.C.

1500 Dixie Hwy.
Park Hills, KY 41011-2819
Ph:(859)431-1262
Fax:(859)431-5148
Co. E-mail: arzembrodt@worldnet.att.net
Contact: Michelle Hartley, CFO
Scope: Firm specializes in product development; quality assurance; new product development; and total quality management focusing on household chemical specialties, especially air fresheners. Utilizes latest technology from global resources. Specializes in enhancement products for home and automobile.

13740 ■ Great Lakes Consulting Group Inc.

54722 Little Flower Trl.
Mishawaka, IN 46545
Ph:(574)287-4500
Fax:(574)233-2688
Contact: James E. Schrager, President
Scope: Provides consulting services in the areas of strategic planning; feasibility studies; start-up businesses; small business management; mergers and acquisitions; joint ventures; divestitures; interim management; crisis management; turnarounds; business process re-engineering; venture capital; and international trade.

13741 ■ Great Western Association Management Inc.

7995 E Prentice Ave., Ste. 100
Greenwood Village, CO 80111
Ph:(303)770-2220
Fax:(303)770-1614
Co. E-mail: info83@gwami.com
URL: http://www.gwami.com
Contact: Sheryl Pitts, Principle
E-mail: kwojdyla@atsgwami.com
Scope: Provides clients with products and services to effectively manage existing and startup, for- and not-for-profit organizations. Clients select from a menu of services including association development and public relations, conferences and seminars, financial management, membership communications, and governance. Expertise also includes association strategic planning, compliance, lobbying, meeting planning, fundraising, marketing and communications. Serves national, regional and state organizations. **Seminars:** Site selection; Creative program development; Contract negotiations; On-site conference management; Trade show management; Travel and logistics.

13742 ■ The Greystone Group Inc.

440 N Wells, Ste. 570
Chicago, IL 60610
Ph:(616)451-8880
Fax:(616)451-9180
Co. E-mail: consult@greystonegp.com
E-mail: consult@greystonegp.com
Scope: Firm specializes in strategic planning and communications; organizational development; start-up businesses; business management; mergers and acquisitions; joint ventures; divestitures; business process re-engineering.

13743 ■ Grimmick Consulting Services

455 Donner Way
San Ramon, CA 94582
Ph:(925)735-1036
Fax:(925)735-1100
Co. E-mail: hank@grimmickconsulting.com
URL: http://www.grimmickconsulting.com
Contact: Henry Grimmick, President
E-mail: hank@grimmickconsulting.com
Scope: Provides consulting services in the areas of strategic planning; organizational assessment; organizational development; leadership and management development Baldridge criteria, process improvement and balanced scorecards and team dynamics.

13744 ■ Harvey A. Meier Co.

410 W Nevada St., Billings Ranch, Ste. 245
Ashland, OR 97520-1043
Ph:(509)458-3210
Fax:(541)488-7905
Co. E-mail: harvey@harveymeier.com
URL: http://www.harveymeier.com
Contact: Harvey A. Meier, President
E-mail: harvey@harveymeier.com
Scope: Firm provides service to chief executive officers and board of directors. Specializes in interim management, strategic planning, financial planning and organization governance. **Publications:** "The D'Artagnan Way".

13745 ■ Hewitt Development Enterprises

18 Lindley Ave.
North Kingstown, RI 02852
Ph:(305)372-0941
Free: 800-631-3098
Fax:(305)372-0941
Co. E-mail: info@hewittdevelopment.com
URL: http://www.hewittdevelopment.com
Contact: Robert G. Hewitt, Principal
E-mail: bob@hewittdevelopment.com
Scope: Specializes in strategic planning; profit enhancement; start-up businesses; interim management; crisis management; turnarounds; production planning; just-in-time inventory management; and project management. Serves senior management (CEOs, CFOs, division presidents, etc.) and acquirers of distressed businesses.

13746 ■ Hickey & Hill Inc.

1009 Oak Hill Rd., Ste. 201
Lafayette, CA 94549-3812
Ph:(925)906-5331
Contact: Edwin L. Hill, CEO
Scope: Firm provides management consulting services to companies in financial distress. Expertise area: Corporate restructuring and turnaround.

13747 ■ hightechbiz.com

4209 Santa Monica Blvd., Ste. 201
PO Box 189
Los Angeles, CA 90029-3027
Ph:(323)913-3355
Free: 877-648-4753
Fax:(323)913-3355
Contact: Jack Potter, Principal
Scope: A full service marketing agency specializing in integrated marketing solutions. Services include: marketing surveys; positioning surveys; strategic and tactical plans; implementation plans; management consulting; product brochures; product catalogs;

product packaging; product data sheets; direct mail programs; media research; competitive research; complete creative; production and film; media placement; corporate identity; in-house creative; public relations.

13748 ■ Holt Capital
1916 Pike Pl., Ste. 12-344
Seattle, WA 98101
Ph:(206)484-0403
Fax:(206)789-8034
Co. E-mail: info@holtcapital.com
URL: http://www.holtcapital.com
Contact: David Brazeau, Principle
E-mail: mjholt@holtcapital.com
Scope: Registered investment advisory firm. Services include: Debt planning, private equity, mergers, divestitures and acquisitions, transaction support services. Connects companies with capital. **Publications:** "Early Sales Key to Early-Stage Funding"; "Financial Transactions: Who Should Be At Your Table"; "Get the Deal Done: The Four Keys to Successful Mergers and Acquisitions"; "Is Your First Paragraph a Turn-off"; "Bubble Rubble: Bridging the Price Gap for an Early-Stage Business"; "Are You Ready For The new Economy"; "Could I Get Money or Jail Time With That The Sarbanes-Oxley Act Of 2002 gives early-stage companies More Risks". **Seminars:** Attracting Private Investors; Five Proven Ways to Finance Your Company; How to Get VC Financing; Venture Packaging; How to Finance Company Expansion.

13749 ■ Human Resource Specialties Inc.
3 Monroe Pky., Ste. 900
PO Box 1733
Lake Oswego, OR 97035
Ph:(503)697-3329
Free: 800-354-3512
Fax:(503)636-1594
Co. E-mail: info@hrspecialties.com
URL: http://www.hrspecialties.com
Contact: Elaine W. Ankersen, Mgr
E-mail: elainea@atshrspecialties.com
Scope: Provides human resources assistance to organizations. Offers preparation of affirmative action plans, support documents, and adverse impact studies of personnel activities. Also offers customized consultations in small business services, diversity and discrimination, and investigations, complaints and grievances. Provides investigations, including allegations of unfair treatment, equal employment opportunity (EEO) and racial or sexual harassment. Offers customized web-based training (webinars) on a variety of HR, EEO and AAP-related topics.

13750 ■ I.H.R. Solutions
3333 E Bayaud Ave., Ste. 219
Denver, CO 80209
Ph:(303)588-4243
Fax:(303)978-0473
Co. E-mail: dhollands@ihrsolutions.com
Contact: Deborah Hollands, President
E-mail: dhollands@ihrsolutions.com
Scope: Provides joint-venture and start-up human resource consulting services as well as advice on organization development for international human capital. Industries served: high-tech and telecommunications.

13751 ■ IMC Consulting & Training
901 McHenry Ave., Ste. A
Modesto, CA 95350
Ph:(209)572-2271
Fax:(209)572-2862
Co. E-mail: info@imc-1.net
URL: http://www.imc-1.net
Contact: Ed Stout, Principle
E-mail: michael@imc-1.net
Scope: Firm helps businesses and professionals identify, develop and market their selling proposition to increase profits. Services include B-to-B surveys, direct marketing, media relations, planning and strategy, sales management, training and leadership coaching. **Publications:** "Consultant Earns Advanced Certificate," Hccsc Business Review, Dec, 2004; "Adapting to Change - the New Competitive Advantage," Business Journal, Jul, 2004; "Loyalty Marketing Can Divide New Business," Jun, 2004; "Eleven

Major Marketing Mistakes," Jul, 2003; "Planning to Win or Racing to Fail," Jun, 2003. **Seminars:** Negotiating High Profit Sales; How to Write Winning Proposals, Modesto Chamber of Commerce, Oct, 2007; Winning the 2nd Half: A 6-month Plan to Score New Customers and Profits.

13752 ■ The Institute for Management Excellence
PO Box 5459
Lacey, WA 98509-5459
Ph:(360)412-0404
Co. E-mail: pwoc@itstime.com
URL: http://www.itstime.com
Contact: Michael Anthony, Director
E-mail: btaylor@itstime.com
Scope: Management consulting and training focuses on improving productivity, using practices and creative techniques. Practices based on the company's theme: It's time for new ways of doing business. Industries served: public sector, law enforcement, finance or banking, non profit, computers or high technology, education, human resources, utilities. **Publications:** "Income Without a Job," 2008; "The Other Side of Midnight, 2000: An Executive Guide to the Year 2000 Problem"; "Concordance to the Michael Teachings"; "Handbook of Small Business Advertising"; "The Personality Game"; "How to Market Yourself for Success". **Seminars:** The Personality Game; Power Path Seminars; Productivity Plus; Sexual Harassment and Discrimination Prevention; Worker's Comp Cost Reduction; Americans with Disabilities Act; In Search of Identify: Clarifying Corporate Culture.

13753 ■ Interminds & Federer Resources Inc.
106 E 6th St., Ste. 310
Austin, TX 78701-3659
Ph:(512)476-8800
Fax:(512)476-8811
URL: http://www.interminds.com
Contact: Salvador Apud, Partner
E-mail: sapud@atsintegra100.com
Scope: Firm specializes in feasibility studies; startup businesses; small business management; mergers and acquisitions; joint ventures; divestitures; interim management; crisis management; turnarounds; production planning; team building; appraisals and valuations.

13754 ■ Interpersonal Coaching & Consulting
1516 W Lake St., Ste. 2000S
Minneapolis, MN 55408
Ph:(612)381-2494
Fax:(612)381-2494
Co. E-mail: mail@interpersonal-coaching.com
URL: http://www.interpersonal-coaching.com
Contact: Mary Belfry, Partner
E-mail: mail@interpersonal-coaching.com
Scope: Provides coaching and consulting to businesses and organizations. Assesses the interpersonal workplace through interviews, assessment instruments and individual group settings. Experienced as a therapist for over a decade. **Seminars:** Sexual harassment and discrimination issues.

13755 ■ Joel Greenstein & Associates
6212 Nethercombe Ct.
McLean, VA 22101
Ph:(703)893-1888
Co. E-mail: jgreenstein@contractmasters.com
Contact: Joel Greenstein, Principle
E-mail: jgreenstein@contractmasters.com
Scope: Provides services to minority and women-owned businesses and government agencies. Specializes in interpreting federal, agency-specific acquisition regulations and contract terms and conditions. Offers assistance with preparing technical, cost proposals and sealed bids.

13756 ■ Johnston Co.
1646 Massachusetts Ave., Ste. 22
Lexington, MA 02420
Ph:(781)862-7595

Fax:(781)862-9066
Co. E-mail: info@johnstoncompany.com
URL: http://www.johnstoncompany.com
Contact: Terry Sugrue, Mgr
E-mail: tzsugrue@atshotmail.com
Scope: Firm specializes in management audits and reports; start-up businesses; small business management; mergers and acquisitions; joint ventures; divestitures; interim management; crisis management; turnarounds; cost controls; financing; venture capital; controller services; financial management, strategic and advisory services. **Publications:** "Why are board meetings such a waste of time," Boston Business Journal, Apr, 2004.

13757 ■ Keiei Senryaku Corp.
19191 S Vermont Ave., Ste. 530
Torrance, CA 90502-1049
Ph:(310)366-3331
Free: 800-951-8780
Fax:(310)366-3330
Co. E-mail: takenakaes@earthlink.net
Contact: Kurt Miyamoto, President
Scope: Offers consulting services in the areas of strategic planning; feasibility studies; profit enhancement; organizational development; start-up businesses; mergers and acquisitions; joint ventures; divestitures; executive searches; sales management; and competitive analysis.

13758 ■ Koch Group Inc.
240 E Lake St., Ste. 300
Addison, IL 60101-2874
Ph:(630)941-1100
Free: 800-470-7845
Fax:(630)941-3865
Co. E-mail: info@kochgroup.com
URL: http://www.kochgroup.com
Contact: Charissa Pachucki, Treasurer
E-mail: rgg@atskochgroup.com
Scope: Provides industrial marketing consulting services to small to mid-sized manufacturers. Primary assistance includes industrial market research and analysis, identification of potential markets, strategic planning and plan implementation, market planning, sales analysis, competitor analysis. Specializes in assisting manufacturers identify, recruit, and manage agents and reps and developing website for business promotion. **Seminars:** Niche Marketing; Regional Industrial Association Recruiting; Strategic Marketing for Manufacturers; Strategic Marketing; How To Identify, Screen, Interview and Select High Quality Agents; Basics of Industrial Market Research; Elements of Industrial Marketing; Trade Adjustment Assistance For Firms; Developing New Business; Selecting An Industrial Web Site Developer; Strategic Selling; Pick Your Customer; Strategic and Tactical Marketing.

13759 ■ Kostka & Company Inc.
9 Wild Rose Ct.
Cromwell, CT 06416
Ph:(860)257-1045
Co. E-mail: mail@mmgnet.com
URL: http://www.mmgnet.com
Contact: Tom Steiner, Managing Partner
E-mail: peterpk@gmail.com
Scope: Areas of expertise: management consulting, global technology sourcing, complex project management, SKU management and new product introduction, application development, medical point-of-sale, multi-touch user interface, made-to-order management systems and Smartphone ERP connectivity. Clients include global fortune 500 companies as well as small and medium-sized businesses and startups.

13760 ■ Kroll Zolfo Cooper L.L.C.
777 S Figueroa St., 24th Fl.
Los Angeles, CA 90017
Ph:(212)561-4000
Fax:(212)948-4226
Co. E-mail: mwyse@krollzolfocooper.com
URL: http://www.krollzolfocooper.com
Contact: Stephen F. Cooper, Principal
E-mail: scooper@kroll.com
Scope: Firm provides accounting consulting services to businesses. Specializes in restructuring and turnaround consulting; interim and crisis management; performance improvement; creditor advisory; cross-border restructuring and corporate finance.

13761 ■ Lupfer & Associates
92 Glen St.
Natick, MA 01760-5646
Ph:(508)655-3950
Fax:(508)655-7826
Co. E-mail: donlupfer@aol.com
Contact: Donald Lupfer, President
E-mail: don.lupfer@lupferassociates.com
Scope: Assists off shore hi-tech companies in entering United States markets and specializes in channel development for all sorts of products. Perform MARCOM support for hi-tech United States clients. **Publications:** "What's Next For Distribution-Feast or Famine"; "The Changing Global Marketplace"; "Making Global Distribution Work". **Seminars:** How to do Business in the United States.

13762 ■ Management Resource Partners
181 2nd Ave., Ste. 542
San Mateo, CA 94401
Ph:(650)401-5850
Fax:(650)401-5850
Contact: John C. Roberts, Principle
Scope: Firm specializes in strategic planning; small business management; mergers and acquisitions; joint ventures; divestitures; interim management; crisis management; turn around; venture capital; appraisals and valuations.

13763 ■ Management Strategies
1000 S Old Woodward, Ste. 105
Birmingham, MI 48009
Ph:(248)258-2756
Fax:(248)258-3407
Co. E-mail: bob@hois.com
Contact: Robert E. Hoisington, President
E-mail: bob@hois.com
Scope: Firm specializes in strategic planning; feasibility studies; profit enhancement; organizational studies; start up businesses; turnarounds; business process re engineering; industrial engineering; marketing; ecommerce.

13764 ■ Marketing Leverage Inc.
2022 Laurel Oak
Palm City, FL 34990
Free: 800-633-1422
Fax:(772)659-8664
Co. E-mail: lkelly@marketingleverage.com
URL: http://www.marketingleverage.com
Contact: Genina Gravlin, Principle
E-mail: davery@atsmarketingleverage.com
Scope: Consulting and research firm focusing on the targeting, retention and satisfaction of customers. Consulting is offered for due diligence; marketing and customer retention strategy; program design and implementation. Research services offered help clients determine service improvements that increase customer loyalty; boosting sales through better understanding buyer motivations; increasing the odds of product acceptance through new product concept testing; and improving the effectiveness of advertising, collateral, publications through audience evaluation. Clients include top financial services, insurance, health care, technology and management services organizations. **Publications:** "Creating Strategic Leverage"; "Exploring Corporate Strategy"; "Competitive Advantage"; "Breakpoint and Beyond "; "Competitive Strategy ". **Seminars:** Best Practices in Brainstorming; Getting Results in the Real World; Finding the Leverage in Your Customer Strategy; The Role of Communications in Building Customer Loyalty; Building a Customer Centered Relationship and Making it Pay. **Special Services:** The Marketing Leverage Win/Loss Tracking System™.

13765 ■ May Toy Lukens
3226 NE 26th Ct.
Renton, WA 98056
Ph:(425)891-3226
Contact: May T. Lukens, Principle
Scope: Provides training to teach people to think of ways to improve their operations continuously by changing the way they think. Industries served: All, particularly financial. Operational analysis and training. **Seminars:** Seminars and workshops in maximizing resource utilization and staff potential.

13766 ■ McCreight & Company Inc.
36 Grove St., Ste. 4
New Canaan, CT 06840-5329
Ph:(203)801-5000
Fax:(866)646-8339
Co. E-mail: roc@implementstrategy.com
URL: http://www.implementstrategy.com
Contact: Laraine Mehr-Turlis, CFO
E-mail: jas@atsimplementstrategy.com
Scope: The firm assist the global clients with strategy implementation involving large scale change, including mergers, divestitures, alliances, and new business launches. Along with the alliance partners, focus on issues that energize or constrain strategic change including: plans and goals; transition design; management competence; organization structure, effectiveness, and staffing; roles and responsibilities; management processes; information management and technology; and change management effectiveness. **Publications:** "The Board's Role in Strengthening M&A Success," Boardroom Briefing, 2008; "Creating the Future," Ask Magazine, 2007; "Strategy Implementation Insights," Mccreight and Company Inc., Oct, 2007; "Sustaining Growth," Deloitte and Ct Technology Council, Jul, 2006; "A Four Phase Approach to Succession Planning," Southern Connecticut Newspapers Inc., 2005; E perspective; Board Effectiveness Insights; and Information Technology Insights. **Seminars:** Successful Mergers and Acquisitions - An Implementation Guide; Global 100One-Face-to-the-Customer; Implementation of Strategic Change.

13767 ■ McDonald Consulting Group Inc.
1900 W Park Dr., Ste. 280
Westborough, MA 01581
Ph:(952)841-6357
Fax:(507)664-9389
Co. E-mail: rmcdonald@mcdonaldconsultinggroup.com
URL: http://www.mcdonaldconsultinggroup.com
Contact: Ron A. McDonald, President
E-mail: rmcdonald@mcdonaldconsultinggroup.com
Scope: A management consulting firm specializing in assisting insurance companies improve operations. Provides services in the areas of strategic planning; profit enhancement; organizational development; interim management; crisis management; turnarounds; business process re-engineering; benefits and compensation planning and total quality management. **Publications:** "Improving Customer Focus through Organizational Structure," AASCIF News; "Changing Strategies in Hard Markets," The National Underwriter; "Moving Beyond Management 101: Postgraduate Time Management for Executives," The National Underwriter; "A New Attitude: 3 Clients Improved Results Through Our Fundamental Change Process," Bests Review; "How to Organize Your Company Around Your Customers," Bests Review. **Seminars:** How to establish "expense allowable"; How to design an incentive compensation plan around a units core success measures.

13768 ■ McShane Group Inc.
2345 York Rd., Ste. 102
Timonium, MD 21093
Ph:(410)560-0077
Fax:(410)560-2718
Co. E-mail: tmcshane@mcshanegroup.com
URL: http://www.mcshanegroup.com
Contact: Richard D. Montgomery, Principle
E-mail: rdm@atsmcshanegroup.com
Scope: Turnaround consulting and crisis management firm. Specializes in due diligence services, interim management, strategic business realignments, business sale and asset depositions and debt restructuring. Industries served: technology, financial, retail, distribution, medical, educational, manufacturing, contracting, environmental and health care.

13769 ■ Medical Imaging Consultants Inc.
1037 US Highway 46, Ste. G-2
Clifton, NJ 07013-2445
Ph:(973)574-8000
Free: 800-589-5685
Fax:(973)574-8001
Co. E-mail: info@micinfo.com
URL: http://www.micinfo.com
Contact: Dr. Philip A. Femano, President
E-mail: phil@micinfo.com
Scope: Provides professional support services for radiology management and comprehensive continuing education programs for radiologic technologists. Management services include resource-critical database logistics; customer registration in educational programs; educational program development and Category A accreditation; national agency notification (e.g., ASRT, SNM-TS) of CE credits earned; meeting planning; manpower assessment; market research; expert witness; think-tank probes and executive summaries of industry issues. **Seminars:** Sectional Anatomy and Imaging Strategies; CT Cross-Trainer; CT Registry Review Program; MR Cross Trainer; MRI Registry Review Program; Digital Mammography Essentials for Technologists; Radiology Trends for Technologists.

13770 ■ Medical Outcomes Management Inc.
132 Central St., Ste. 215
Foxborough, MA 02035-2422
Ph:(508)543-0050
Fax:(508)543-1919
Co. E-mail: info@mom-inc.com
Contact: Vinit P. Nair, Mgr
E-mail: vinit@atsmom-inc.com
Scope: Management and technology consulting firm providing a specially focused group of services such as disease management programs and pharmacoeconomic studies. Services include clinical and educational projects, medical writing and editing, marketing and sales projects, disease registries, educational seminars, strategic planning projects, managed care organizations; and pharmaceutical and biotechnology companies. **Publications:** "Treatment of acute exacerbation's of chronic bronchitis in patients with chronic obstructive pulmonary disease: A retrospective cohort analysis logarithmically extended release vs. Azithromycin," 2003; "A retrospective analysis of cyclooxygenase-II inhibitor response patterns," 2002; "DUE criteria for use of regional urokinase infusion for deep vein thrombosis,"2002; "The formulary management system and decision-making process at Horizon Blue Cross Blue Shield of New Jersey," Pharmaco therapy, 2001. **Seminars:** Economic Modeling as a Disease Management Tool, Academy of Managed Care Pharmacy, Apr, 2005; Integrating Disease State Management and Economics, Academy of Managed Care Pharmacy, Oct, 2004; Clinical and economic outcomes in the treatment of peripheral occlusive diseases, Mar, 2003.

13771 ■ Mefford, Knutson & Associates Inc.
6437 Lyndale Ave. S, Ste. 103
Richfield, MN 55423-1465
Ph:(612)869-8011
Free: 800-831-0228
Fax:(612)869-8004
Co. E-mail: info@mkaonline.net
URL: http://www.mkaonline.net
Contact: Jennifer Thompson, Director
E-mail: jthompson@atsmkaonline.com
Scope: A consulting and licensed business brokerage firm specializing in start-up businesses; strategic planning; mergers and acquisitions; joint ventures; divestitures; business process re-engineering; personnel policies and procedures; market research; new product development and cost controls.

13772 ■ Midwest Computer Group L.L.C.
6060 Franks Rd.
House Springs, MO 63051-1101
Ph:(636)677-0287
Fax:(636)677-0287
Co. E-mail: sales@mcgcomputer.com
URL: http://www.mcgcomputer.com
Contact: Jeffrey A. Sanford, Mgr
E-mail: jeffrey@atsmcgcomputer.com
Scope: Firm specializes in helping businesses create accounting, marketing and business information systems; software development; and database design and management.

13773 ■ Miller, Hellwig Associates

150 W End Ave.
New York, NY 10023-5713
Ph:(212)799-0471
Fax:(212)877-0186
Co. E-mail: millerhelwig@earthlink.net
Contact: Ernest C. Miller, President
Scope: Consulting services in the areas of start-up businesses; small business management; employee surveys and communication; performance appraisals; executive searches; team building; personnel policies and procedures; market research. Also involved in improving cross-cultural and multi-cultural relationships, particularly with Japanese clients. **Seminars:** Objectives and standards/recruiting for boards of directors.

13774 ■ Navarro, Kim & Associates

529 N Charles St., Ste. 202
Baltimore, MD 21201
Ph:(410)837-6317
Fax:(410)837-6294
Co. E-mail: bnavarro@sprynet.com
Contact: Beltran Navarro, Director
E-mail: bnavarro@sprynet.com
Scope: Specializes in bridging the gap between firms and non-traditional ethnic communities, especially in community development and institutional building.

13775 ■ New Commons

545 Pawtucket Ave., Studio 106A
PO Box 116
Pawtucket, RI 02860
Ph:(401)351-7110
Fax:(401)351-7158
Co. E-mail: info@newcommons.com
URL: http://www.newcommons.com
Contact: Robert Leaver, Principal
E-mail: rleaver@atsnewcommons.com
Scope: Builder of agile human networks to champion innovation and mobilize change; to pursue business opportunities; to custom design agile organizations and communities, to foster civic engagement. Clients include organizations on-profits, corporations, government agencies, educational institutions; networks-Trade/professional groups, IT services collaborations, service-sharing collectives; and communities- municipalities, states and statewide agencies, regional collaborations. **Publications:** "Plexus Imperative," Sep, 2005; "Creating 21st Century Capable Innovation Systems," Aug, 2004; "Call to Action: Building Providences Creative and Innovative Economy"; "Getting Results from Meetings"; "The Entrepreneur as Artist," Commonwealth Publications; "Leader and Agent of Change," Commonwealth Publications; "Achieving our Providence: Lessons of City-Building," Commonwealth Publications. **Seminars:** Introduction to Social Computing (Web 2.0), Jan, 2009; Every Company Counts, Jun, 2009; Facilitating for Results; Story-Making and Story-Telling.

13776 ■ Nightingale Associates

7445 Setting Sun Way
Columbia, MD 21046-1261
Ph:(410)381-4280
Fax:(410)381-4280
Co. E-mail: fredericknightingale@nightingaleassociates.net
URL: http://www.nightingaleassociates.net
Contact: Frederick C. Nightingale, Managing Director
E-mail: fredericknightingale@nightingaleassociates.net
Scope: Management training and consulting firm offering the following skills: productivity and accomplishment; leadership skills for the experienced manager; management skills for the new manager; leadership and teambuilding; supervisory development; creative problem solving; real strategic planning; providing superior customer service; international purchasing and supply chain management; negotiation skills development and fundamentals of purchasing. **Seminars:** Productivity and Accomplishment Management Skills for the New Manager; Leadership and Team building; Advanced Management; Business Process Re engineering; Strategic Thinking; Creative Problem Solving; Customer Service; International Purchasing and Materials Management; Fundamentals of Purchasing; Negotiation Skills Development; Providing superior customer service; Leadership skills for the experienced manager.

13777 ■ Organization Counselors Inc.

44 W Broadway, Ste. 1102
PO Box 987
Salt Lake City, UT 84101
Ph:(801)363-2900
Fax:(801)363-0861
Co. E-mail: jpanos@xmission.com
Contact: John E. Panos, President
E-mail: jpanos@xmission.com
Scope: Organizational development; employee surveys and communication; outplacement; team building; total quality management and continuous improvement. **Seminars:** Correcting Performance Problems; Total Quality Management; Employee Selection; Performance Management.

13778 ■ P2C2 Group Inc.

4101 Denfeld Ave.
Kensington, MD 20895-1514
Ph:(301)942-7985
Fax:(301)942-7986
Co. E-mail: info@p2c2group.com
URL: http://www.p2c2group.com
Contact: Jim Kendrick, President
E-mail: kendrick@p2c2group.com
Scope: Works with clients on the business side of federal program and project management. Services include program/project planning and optimization; acquisition strategy and work statements; IT Capital Planning and Investment Control (CPIC); business cases - new, revisions, critiques; budget analysis - cost benefits- alternatives; CPIC, SELC, and security documentation; research, metrics, analysis, and case studies. Consulting support helping to: Define or redefine programs; strengthen portfolio management; identify alternatives for lean budgets; improve capital planning and investment; develop better plans and documentation, and evaluate performance of existing program investments. **Publications:** "OMB 300s Go Online," Federal Sector Report, Mar, 2007; "Using Risk-Adjusted Costs for Projects," Federal Sector Report, Feb, 2007; "Make Better Decisions Using Case Studies," Federal Sector Report, Jan, 2007; "PMO Performance Measurement & Metrics"; "Executive Sponsors for Projects"; "ABCs of the Presidential Transition"; "Financial Systems and Enterprise Portfolio Management"; "The Future of CPIC"; "Critical Factors for Program and Project Success"; "Using Risk-Adjusted Costs for Projects"; "Tactics for a Successful Year of CPIC"; "Operational Analysis Reviews"; "Successful IT Strategic Planning"; "Information Technology Investment Management". **Seminars:** How to Hire a Management Consultant and Get the Results You Expect.

13779 ■ Papa and Associates Inc.

200 Consumers Rd., Ste. 305
Toronto, ON, Canada M2J 4R4
Ph:(416)512-7272
Fax:(416)512-2016
Co. E-mail: ppapa@papa-associates.com
URL: http://www.papa-associates.com
Contact: Roxanne Wilson, Mgr
E-mail: ppapa@atspapa-associates.com
Scope: Firm provides broad based management consulting services in the areas of quality assurance, environmental, health and safety and integrated management systems.

13780 ■ Parker Consultants Inc.

230 Mason St.
Greenwich, CT 06830-6633
Ph:(203)869-9400
Contact: William P. Hartl, Chairman of the Board
Scope: Firm specializes in strategic planning; organizational development; small business management; performance appraisals; executive searches; team building; and customer service audits.

13781 ■ Partners for Market Leadership Inc.

400 Galleria Pky., Ste. 1500
Atlanta, GA 30339
Ph:(770)850-1409
Free: 800-984-1110
Co. E-mail: dcarpenter@market-leadership.com
URL: http://www.market-leadership.com
Contact: Nancy Surdyka, Mgr
E-mail: nsurdyka@atsmarket-leadership.com
Scope: Boutique consulting firm focused on assisting clients to develop sustainable market leadership in geographic, practice area and/or industry markets. Provides consulting on market leadership, revenue enhancement, strategic development and change facilitation. Additional services are offered to legal, accounting, valuation and financial firms.

13782 ■ Performance Consulting Associates Inc.

3700 Crestwood Pky., Ste. 100
Duluth, GA 30096
Ph:(770)717-2737
Fax:(770)717-7014
Co. E-mail: info@pcaconsulting.com
URL: http://www.pcaconsulting.com
Contact: Robert Wilson, Mgr
E-mail: wilson@atspcaconsulting.com
Scope: Maintenance consulting and engineering firm specializing in production planning, project management, team building, and re-engineering maintenance. **Publications:** "Does Planning Pay," Plant Services, Nov, 2000; "Asset Reliability Coordinator," Maintenance Technology, Oct, 2000; "Know What it is You Have to Maintain," Maintenance Technology; May, 2000; "Does Maintenance Planning Pay," Maintenance Technology, Nov, 2000.; "What is Asset Management?"; "Implementing Best Business Practices".

13783 ■ Performance Consulting Group Inc.

8031 SW 35th Terr.
Miami, FL 33155-3443
Ph:(305)264-5577
Fax:(305)264-9079
Contact: Patrick J. O'Brien, President
Scope: Firm provides consulting services in the areas of strategic planning; profit enhancement; product development; and production planning.

13784 ■ R.E. Moulton Inc.

50 Doaks Ln.
Marblehead, MA 01945
Ph:(781)631-1325
Fax:(781)631-2165
Co. E-mail: mike_lee@remoultoninc.com
URL: http://www.oneamerica.com/wps/wcm/connect/REMoulton
Contact: Reynolds E. Moulton Jr., Chairman of the Board
E-mail: dick@atsremoultoninc.com
Scope: Offers underwriting services, marketing solutions, claims administration and adjudication; policy and commission administration; and risk management solutions to clients. Supplementary service s include risk management and employee assistance. Clients include individuals, business men, employers and finance professionals.

13785 ■ Richard J. Jones Consulting Services

9195 White Oak Ln.
Westerville, OH 43082-9679
Ph:(614)895-7101
Co. E-mail: rjjcs@aol.com
Contact: Richard J. Jones, Owner
Scope: Small manufacturing management consulting firm specializing in development, organization and management from start-up through production of goods and services.

13786 ■ Rose & Crangle Ltd.

117 N 4th St.
PO Box 285
Lincoln, KS 67455
Ph:(785)524-5050
Fax:(785)524-3130
Co. E-mail: rcltd@nckcn.com
URL: http://www.roseandcrangle.com
Contact: Jeanne Crangle, Principle
E-mail: rcltd@nckcn.com
Scope: Firm provides evaluation, planning and policy analyzes for universities, associations, foundations, governmental agencies and private companies

engaged in scientific, technological or educational activities. Special expertise in the development of new institutions. Special skills in providing planning and related group facilitation workshops. **Publications:** "Preface to Bulgarian Integration Into Europe and NATO: Issues of Science Policy And research Evaluation Practice," Ios Press, 2006; "Allocating Limited National Resources for Fundamental Research," 2005.

13787 ■ Rothschild Strategies Unlimited L.L.C.

19 Thistle Rd.
PO Box 7568
Norwalk, CT 06851-1909
Ph:(203)846-6898
Fax:(203)847-1426
Co. E-mail: bill@strategyleader.com
URL: http://www.strategyleader.com
Contact: William Rothchild, CEO
E-mail: billrothschild@atsoptonline.net
Scope: Consults with senior management and business level strategy teams to develop overall strategic direction, set priorities and creates sustainable competitive advantages and differentiators. Enables organizations to enhance their own strategic thinking and leadership skills so that they can continue to develop and implement profitable growth strategies. **Publications:** "Putting It All Together-a guide to strategic thinking"; "Competitive Advantage"; "Ristaker, Caretaker, Surgeon & Undertaker four faces of strategic leadership"; "The Secret to GE's Success"; "Having the Right Strategic Leader and Team". **Seminars:** Who is going the WRONG way?; Learning from your Successes and Failures. **Special Services:** StrategyLeader[R].

13788 ■ Schneider Consulting Group Inc.

50 S Steele St., Ste. 390
Denver, CO 80209
Ph:(303)320-4413
Fax:(303)320-5795
Contact: Kim Schneider Malek, Vice President
E-mail: kim@atsscgfambus.com
Scope: Assists family-owned and privately-held business transition to the next generation and/or to a more professionally managed company, turn around consulting for small and medium size companies.

13789 ■ Scott Ashby Teleselling Inc.

1102 Ben Franklin Dr., Ste. 309
Sarasota, FL 34236
Ph:(941)388-4283
Fax:(941)388-5240
Co. E-mail: rscottashby@netscape.net
URL: http://www.scottashbyteleselling.com
Contact: R. Scott Ashby, Owner
E-mail: rscottashby@netscape.net
Scope: Provides consulting services and customized training programs that emphasize consultative telephone selling techniques. **Publications:** "How Will the Internet Affect Teleselling Programs?"; "When is Telemarketing Really Not Telemarketing?"; "The Future of Account Management Telesales". **Seminars:** Start-Up Educational, Planning and Strategy Development; Existing Program Audit, Evaluation, State-of-the-Art Best Practices Comparison, Tracking and Measurement Review, Systems and Procedures Analysis, and Optional Selling Skills; Develop New or Revised Consultative Telephone Selling; Helping Clients Build Relationship and Grow Their Business by Phone.

13790 ■ Sklar and Associates Inc.

242 Laurel Bay Dr.
Murrells Inlet, SC 29576
Ph:(202)257-5061
Fax:(843)651-3090
Co. E-mail: sklarincdc@aol.com
URL: http://www.sklarinc.com
Contact: Tim Sklar, President
Scope: Provides consulting services for business acquisitions, business development and project finance. Provides audit oversight services to listed corporations on Sarbanes-Oxley compliance. Services include: Due diligence analyses and corporate governance. Industries served: transportation sectors, energy sector and commercial real estate

industries. **Seminars:** Financial Analysis in MBA; Emerging Company Finance; Due Diligence in Business Acquisition; Business Valuation.

13791 ■ Straightline Services Inc.

11 Centre St., Ste. 10
Salem, CT 06420-3845
Ph:(860)889-7929
Fax:(860)885-1894
Co. E-mail: straitln@aol.com
Contact: Wayne J. S. France CPCM, President
Scope: Design and implementation of organizational infrastructure, business plans and troubleshooting. Emphasizes on operations with a central and field or satellite offices. Industries served: Construction, resorts, Indian tribes, academies, small-medium sized business, mostly privately held.

13792 ■ Strategic MindShare Consulting

1401 Brickell Ave., Ste. 640
Miami, FL 33131
Ph:(305)377-2220
Fax:(305)377-2280
Co. E-mail: dee@strategicmindshare.com
URL: http://www.strategicmindshare.com
Contact: Cynthia R. Cohen, President
E-mail: cohen@strategicmindshare.com
Scope: Firm specializes in strategic planning; feasibility studies; profit enhancement; organizational development; start-up businesses; mergers and acquisitions; joint ventures; divestitures; interim management; crisis management; turnarounds; new product development and competitive analysis. **Publications:** "Top Ten CEO Burning Issues for 2005"; "Top Ten Consumer Behavioral Trends for 2005"; "The Influence Factors"; "New Profit Opportunities for Retailers and Consumer Product Companies".

13793 ■ TC International Marketing Inc.

11 Iliffe House, Iliffe Ave.
Leicester LE2 5LS, United Kingdom
Ph:(845)258-7482
Fax:(845)986-2130
Co. E-mail: tcintl@warwick.net
Contact: Graeme Wright, Partner
Scope: Business expansion consulting including feasibility studies, mergers and acquisitions, divestment, market research and strategizing.

13794 ■ Trendzitions Inc.

25691 Atlantic Ocean Dr., Ste. B13
Lake Forest, CA 92630-8842
Ph:(949)727-9100
Free: 800-266-2767
Fax:(949)727-3444
Co. E-mail: ctooker@trendzitions.com
URL: http://www.trendzitions.com
Contact: Christian Tooker, President
E-mail: ctooker@atstrendzitions.com
Scope: Provides services in the areas of communications consulting, project management, construction management, and furniture procurement. Offers information on spatial uses, building codes, ADA compliance and city ordinances. Also offers budget projections.

13795 ■ Turnaround Inc.

3415 A St. NW
Gig Harbor, WA 98335
Ph:(253)857-6730
Fax:(253)857-6344
Co. E-mail: info@turnround-inc.com
URL: http://www.turnaround-inc.com
Contact: Miles Stover, President
E-mail: mstover@turnaround-inc.com
Scope: Firm provides interim executive management assistance and management advisory to small, medium and family-owned businesses that are not meeting their goals. Services include acting as an interim executive or on-site manager. Extensive practices in arena of bankruptcy management. **Publications:** "How to Identify Problem and Promising Management"; "How to Tell if Your Company is a Bankruptcy Candidate"; "Signs that Your Company is in Trouble"; "The Turnaround Specialist: How to File a Petition Under 11 USC 11". **Seminars:** Competitive Intelligence Gathering.

13796 ■ ValueNomics Value Specialists

50 W San Fernando St., Ste. 600
San Jose, CA 95113
Ph:(408)200-6400
Fax:(408)200-6401
Co. E-mail: info@amllp.com
Contact: Jeff A. Stegner, Partner
Scope: Consulting is offered in the areas of financial management, process re-engineering, growth business services; governance, risk/compliance, SOX readiness and compliance, SAS 70, enterprise risk management, system security, operational and internal audit; business advisory services; valuation services; CORE assessment; contract assurance; transaction advisory services, IT solutions and litigation support services. **Publications:** "Dueling Appraisers: How Differences in Input and Assumptions May Control the Value," Apr, 2005; "The Business of Business Valuation and the CPA as an expert witness"; "The Business of Business Valuation," McGraw-Hill Professional Publishers Inc.

13797 ■ Via Nova Consulting

1228 Winburn Dr.
Atlanta, GA 30344
Ph:(404)761-7484
Fax:(404)762-7123
Scope: Consulting services in the areas of strategic planning; privatization; executive searches; market research; customer service audits; new product development; competitive intelligence; and Total Quality Management (TQM).

13798 ■ Vision Management

149 Meadows Rd.
Lafayette, NJ 07848-3120
Ph:(973)702-1116
Fax:(973)702-8311
Contact: Norman L. Naidish, President
Scope: Firm specializes in profit enhancement; strategic planning; business process reengineering; industrial engineering; facilities planning; team building; inventory management; and total quality management (TQM). **Publications:** "To increase profits, improve quality," Manufacturing Engineering, May, 2000.

13799 ■ Walker & Associates

255 N Madison Ave.
PO Box 701
Pasadena, CA 91102
Ph:(626)396-9593
Fax:(626)396-9222
Co. E-mail: info@waa.bz
URL: http://www.waa.bz
Contact: Rodney D. Walker, Principal
E-mail: rodney@waa.bz
Scope: A management consulting firm with services that include fund development, grant writing, executive coaching, board development, diversity training, organizational assessment, organizational development, strategic planning, marketing and public relations, nonprofit start-up assistance, and workshops and training. **Publications:** "Program Evaluation"; "Grant Writing"; "Financial Management"; "Risk Management"; "Strategic Planning"; "Capacity Building". **Seminars:** Strategic Planning That Makes Sense; Fundraising Essentials; Best Practices for Executive Directors; Effective Program Evaluation That Makes Sense; Marketing Your Nonprofit; How Nonprofits Can Thrive In Turbulent Times.

13800 ■ Weich & Bilotti Inc.

600 Worcester Rd., 4th Fl.
Framingham, MA 01702
Ph:(508)663-1600
Fax:(508)663-1682
Co. E-mail: info@weich-bilotti.com
URL: http://www.weich-bilotti.com
Contact: Mervyn D. Weich, President
E-mail: mweich@weich-bilotti.com
Scope: Specializes in business plans, venture capital, computer information systems, turnaround/interim management, retail consulting, start-up process, college recruiting and IS and IT personnel.

13801 ■ Wheeler and Young Inc.
33 Peter St.
Markham, ON, Canada L3P 2A5
Ph:(905)471-5709
Fax:(905)471-9989
Co. E-mail: wheeler@ericwheeler.ca
URL: http://www.ericwheeler.ca
Contact: Eric S. Wheeler, Managing Partner
E-mail: ewheeler@yorku.ca
Scope: Provides consulting services to high-tech companies on the implementation of software development processes; quality management systems (including ISO 9000 compliance) and business management systems. Offers business management and knowledge-management services to organizations. Industries served: Knowledge-based industries, including software and hardware development, medical and legal professionals, information service providers.

13802 ■ William E. Kuhn & Associates
234 Cook St.
Denver, CO 80206-5305
Ph:(303)322-8233
Fax:(303)331-9032
Co. E-mail: billkuhn1@cs.com
Contact: William E. Kuhn, Owner
E-mail: billkuhn1@cs.com
Scope: Firm specializes in strategic planning; profit enhancement; small business management; mergers and acquisitions; joint ventures; divestitures; human resources management; performance appraisals; team building; sales management; appraisals and valuations. **Publications:** "Creating a High-Performance Dealership," Office SOLUTIONS & Office DEALER, Jul-Aug, 2006.

13803 ■ Zogby International
150 SE 2nd Ave., Ste. 600
Miami, FL 33131
Ph:(315)624-0200
Free: 877-462-7655
Fax:(315)624-0210
Co. E-mail: marketing@zogby.com
URL: http://www.zogby.com
Contact: Stephanie Vogel, COO
Scope: Specializes in providing market research and analysis services. **Publications:** "Just who are you calling anyway"; "All of this leads to a very basic question". **Seminars:** The Research Authority, Oct, 2006; Christian Science Monitor Break fast, Oct, 2006.

FRANCHISES AND BUSINESS OPPORTUNITIES

13804 ■ Belron Canada Inc.
8288 Boul, PIE-IX
Montreal, QC, Canada H1Z 3T6
Ph:(514)593-3824
Fax:(514)593-6404
Co. E-mail: palessi@belroncanada.com
URL: http://www.belroncanada.com
No. of Franchise Units: 204. **No. of Company-Owned Units:** 190. **Founded:** 1965. **Franchised:** 1982. **Description:** Provides services and solutions for auto glass repair and replacement. Operates under four retail banners - Apple Auto Glass, Speedy Glass, Lebeau Vitres d'autos, DURO vitres d'autos - and conducts its wholesale activities under the Vanfax and Technicentre Plus trade names. It also offers claims management services. **Equity Capital Needed:** $40,000-$90,000. **Franchise Fee:** $10,000.

13805 ■ Clean First Time, Inc.
8810 Commodity Cir., Ste. 7
Orlando, FL 32819
Free: (866)390-2532
Fax:(407)352-1443
No. of Franchise Units: 15. **No. of Company-Owned Units:** 1. **Founded:** 2003. **Franchised:** 2004. **Description:** New home construction cleaning. **Equity Capital Needed:** $12,000-$150,000. **Franchise Fee:** $12,000-$150,000. **Royalty Fee:** 7%. **Financial Assistance:** Limited in-house financing

available. **Training:** Includes 3-5 days training at headquarters, 3-5 days at franchisee's location and ongoing support.

13806 ■ Cleaning Consultant Services Inc.
PO Box 1273
Seattle, WA 98111
Ph:(206)682-9748
No. of Franchise Units: 2. **No. of Company-Owned Units:** 3. **Founded:** 1976. **Franchised:** 1978. **Description:** Support services to those who own, manage and/or supervise cleaning operations. **Equity Capital Needed:** $7,500. **Franchise Fee:** $2,500. **Managerial Assistance:** Manuals and onsite visits provided. **Training:** 2-3 days at out training site in Seattle, WA.

13807 ■ Manufacturing Management Associates
700 Commerce Dr., Ste. 500
Oak Brook, IL 60523
Ph:(630)575-8700
No. of Franchise Units: 8. **No. of Company-Owned Units:** 1. **Founded:** 1982. **Franchised:** 1993. **Description:** Has built its reputation providing small to mid-sized manufacturing and distribution companies with the technical and advisory services they need to achieve their individual business goals. Areas of expertise include manufacturing systems and network technology, process flow (JIT), quality (TQC), cost management, human resource change management, ISO 9000 certification preparation and work cell design/factory layout. days of training in Chicago, IL. Will also assist the franchisee in sales and marketing efforts to promote the success of the franchise. Other notable benefits include potential client leads, alliances with industry experts, project management methodologies, proprietary computer software systems, reference proposals and R & D. **Equity Capital Needed:** $14,900-$49,450. **Franchise Fee:** $10,000. **Financial Assistance:** No. **Training:** An intensive 8 day seminar in Chicago, IL, where the franchisee will be exposed to a working office and receive extensive training in the policies of running a successful franchise. The franchisee will receive a thorough explanation of proven methodologies, as well as training in proprietary software and business systems.

13808 ■ Sandler Training
Sandler Systems, Inc.
300 Red Brook Blvd., Ste. 400
Owings Mills, MD 21117
Ph:(410)559-2005
Free: 800-669-3537
Fax:(410)753-8270
Co. E-mail: Etaylor@sandler.com
URL: http://www.sandler.com
No. of Franchise Units: 235. **Founded:** 1969. **Franchised:** 1983. **Description:** No. 1 Rated Management Training Franchise by Entrepreneur Magazine 2001. The franchise offered consists of the right to operate a Sandler Sales Institute business devoted to a distinctive style of training persons in the fields of sales and sales management, management consulting, human relations, leadership development, and methods of teaching such subjects through ongoing training, seminars and workshops. **Equity Capital Needed:** $82,150-$98,750. **Franchise Fee:** $68,000. FAS No. **Training:** Toll-free hotline for training support, frequent initial training schools, quarterly training conferences, training and operating manuals, newsletter, promotional materials, lead generation, leader's guides.

13809 ■ Turbo Leadership Systems Ltd.
36280 NE Wilsonville Rd.
Newberg, OR 97132
Ph:(503)625-1867
Fax:(503)625-2699
No. of Company-Owned Units: 1. **Founded:** 1985. **Franchised:** 1995. **Description:** Management training and team building training. **Equity Capital Needed:** $49,000. **Franchise Fee:** $39,000. **Financial Assistance:** No. **Training:** Yes.

COMPUTERIZED DATABASES

13810 ■ *Business & Management Practices*
Cengage Learning Inc.
27500 Drake Rd.
Farmington Hills, MI 48331-3535

Ph:(248)699-4253
Free: 800-877-4253
Fax:(248)699-8069
Co. E-mail: galeord@gale.com
URL: http://gale.cengage.com
Description: Provides access to more than 831,000 records from more than 1200 management sources, and selected records from more than 300 Business and Industry sources. Includes information on how companies and managers make decisions, implement new technology, plan for the future, and expand. Includes definitions of key terms in business methodology and management issues. Contains book reviews, how-to articles, interviews, speeches, and surveys. Includes case studies, practical applications and guidelines. Defines more than 400 searchable management concept terms. Indexes include company and industry names, product codes and names and geographic codes. Available as part of the RDS Business Suite. **Availability:** Online: Cengage Learning Inc., Alacra Inc., LexisNexis Group, Nerac Inc., Thomson Reuters, Wolters Kluwer Health, ProQuest LLC, GENIOS - German Business Information/Deutsche Wirtschaftsdatenbank GmbH. **Type:** Full text; Bibliographic.

LIBRARIES

13811 ■ American Society for Training and Development ASTD Information Center
1640 King St.
PO Box 1443
Alexandria, VA 22313-2043
Ph:(703)683-8100
Free: 800-628-2783
Fax:(703)683-1523
Co. E-mail: customercare@astd.org
URL: http://www.astd.org
Contact: Greg Bindner, Mgr.
Scope: Human resource development - general, management, training, career development, Organization development, consulting skills. **Services:** Library open to national members of the Society. **Holdings:** 3000 bound volumes. **Subscriptions:** 60 journals and other serials.

13812 ■ CMA Ontario–Member Services Centre
70 University Ave., Ste. 101
Toronto, ON, Canada M5J 2M4
Ph:(416)204-3142
Fax:(416)977-1365
Co. E-mail: msc@cma-ontario.org
Contact: Patricia Black, Mgr., Member Svcs.Ctr.
Scope: Accounting, management, finance, strategy, taxation, investments. **Services:** Copying; SDI; Library not open to the public. **Holdings:** 2069 books; 267 videocassettes; 184 audiocassettes; 6 videodiscs. **Subscriptions:** 53 journals and other serials; 2 newspapers.

13813 ■ Hanley-Wood, LLC Library
426 S. Westgate St.
Addison, IL 60101-4546
Ph:(630)543-0870
Fax:(630)543-3112
URL: http://www.hanleywood.com
Contact: Kimberly Last, Libn.
Scope: Concrete, cement, masonry, construction, home building. **Services:** Interlibrary loan; copying. **Holdings:** 3000 books; 120 bound periodical volumes. **Subscriptions:** 100 journals and other serials.

13814 ■ Management Consultants International, Inc. Library
3904 Creekside Pl.
Burnaby, BC, Canada V5G 4P9
Ph:(604)434-7184
Scope: Management of videotex, electronic international banking, telecommunications, electronic publishing, point-of-sale systems, broadcasting. **Holdings:** 200 bound volumes. **Subscriptions:** 25 journals and other serials.

**13815 ■ Right Management
Consultants–Corporate Research Center**
1818 Market St., 33rd Fl.
Philadelphia, PA 19103
Ph:(215)988-1588
Free: 800-237-4448
Co. E-mail: contactus@right.com
URL: http://www.right.com
Scope: Career management, executives, change
management, human resource issues. **Services:**
Interlibrary loan; Center not open to the public. **Holdings:** 700 books. **Subscriptions:** 70 journals and
other serials; 4 newspapers.

**13816 ■ Strategic Account Management
Association–Resource Search Library**
33 N. LaSalle St., Ste. 3700
Chicago, IL 60602

Ph:(312)251-3131
Fax:(312)251-3132
URL: http://www.strategicaccounts.org/search/re-
  sourcesearch.asp
Contact: Elisabeth Cornell, Dir. of Educ. and Rsrcs.
Scope: National and global account management
programs, account managers, strategic account
management, strategic partnering and alliances,
cross-functional teams, channel conflict, supply chain
management, internal selling, customer viewpoint,
value-added selling, account planning, account
segmentation, compensation. **Services:** Library not
open to the public (numerous sample documents
available to non-members, and most can be purchased). **Holdings:** 1500 documents, periodicals,
audiocassettes, case studies, white papers, research
studies, books, reports, archives, PDFs, and presentation materials. **Subscriptions:** 1 journal; 3 newsletters.

**13817 ■ University of Kentucky–Business &
Economics Information Center**
B&E Info. Ctr., Rm. 116
335-BA Gatton College of Business & Economics
Lexington, KY 40506-0034
Ph:(859)257-5868
Fax:(859)323-9496
Co. E-mail: mrazeeq@pop.uk.edu
URL: http://www.uky.edu//Provost/academicpro-
  grams.html
Contact: Michael A. Razeeq, Bus.Ref.Libn.

Scope: Business, economics, business management, marketing, finance, accounting. **Services:**
Library open to the public for reference use only.

ASSOCIATIONS AND OTHER ORGANIZATIONS

13818 ■ Manufacturers' Agents for the Foodservice Industry
1199 Euclid Ave.
Atlanta, GA 30307
Ph:(404)214-9474
Fax:(404)522-0132
Co. E-mail: info@mafsi.org
URL: http://www.mafsi.org
Contact: Alison Cody, Exec. Dir.

Description: Independent manufacturers' representative firms selling equipment, furnishings, and supplies to dealers and users. Sponsors annual mini manufacturer sales meetings. Conducts specialized education programs. **Publications:** *Outfront* (quarterly); *Principles of Decision*;Membership Directory (annual).

13819 ■ Manufacturers' Agents National Association
16 A Journey, Ste. 200
Aliso Viejo, CA 92656-3317
Ph:(949)859-4040
Free: 877-626-2776
Fax:(949)855-2973
Co. E-mail: mana@manaonline.org
URL: http://www.manaonline.org
Contact: Charles Cohon, Pres./CEO

Description: Manufacturers' agents in all fields representing two or more manufacturers on a commission basis; associate members are manufacturers and others interested in improving the agent-principal relationship. Maintains code of ethics and rules of business and professional conduct; issues model standard form of agreement. **Publications:** *MANA Matters* (monthly); *Manufacturers' Agents National Association—Special Report* (periodic).

13820 ■ Manufacturers Representatives of America
1111 Jupiter Rd., Ste. 204D
Plano, TX 75074
Ph:(972)422-0428
Fax:(972)422-7351
Co. E-mail: assnhqtrs@aol.com
URL: http://www.mra-reps.com
Contact: Eric Rud, Pres.

Description: Independent manufacturers' representatives handling paper and plastic disposable products and sanitary supplies. Aims to improve agent sales skills, market coverage and customer service and to establish more effective agent/principal communications. .

13821 ■ Manufacturers Representatives Educational Research Foundation
8329 Cole St.
Arvada, CO 80005
Ph:(303)463-1801

Fax:(303)379-6024
Co. E-mail: certify@mrerf.org
URL: http://www.mrerf.org
Contact: Ms. Susannah E. Hart, Exec. Dir.

Description: Sponsored by 35 national and state associations of manufacturers' representatives, distributors and manufacturers. Promotes the profession of outsourced field sales through academic research and publication; disseminates research findings on the role of manufacturers' representatives to academic institutions; provides a forum for the exchange of information. Operates professional certification program for agency owners and sales people. Also provides educational programs for manufacturers who outsource field sales. **Publications:** *New Directions in Inside Sales*; *Synergistic Selling for the 21st Century* (periodic).

13822 ■ NAGMR
16A Journey, Ste. 200
Aliso Viejo, CA 92656
Ph:(949)859-4040
Fax:(949)855-2973
Co. E-mail: lball@manaonline.org
URL: http://www.nagmr.com
Contact: Jim Lewis, Membership Committee

Description: Consumer products brokers specializing in selling drug, health, beauty aids, and nonfood products to food chains and the same products and grocery items to the nonfood market. .

DIRECTORIES OF EDUCATIONAL PROGRAMS

13823 ■ New England Manufacturers Directory
Pub: Harris InfoSource
Contact: Linda Vermillion, Sr. Product Mgr., Headquarters
E-mail: lindav@harrisinfo.com

Released: Annual, March; Latest edition 2009. **Covers:** Over 30,600 manufacturers. **Entries Include:** Names and titles of key personnel, company name and address, annual sales, date of establishment, employment size, import/export involvement, sic, plant size, headquarters, phone, fax, and toll-free number. **Arrangement:** Alphabetical, geographical, SIC code, product.

13824 ■ Scott's Directories
Pub: Scott's Directories

Ed: Barbara Peard, Editor. **Released:** Annual, February; latest edition 2007 edition. **Price:** $899, individuals CD; pinpointer; $1,799, individuals CD; profiler; $3,499, individuals CD; prospector; $849, individuals online; pinpointer. **Covers:** 58,000 manufacturers throughout Canada. **Entries Include:** Company name, address, phone, fax, telex, names and titles of key personnel, number of employees, parent or subsidiary companies, North American Standard Industrial (NAICS) code, product, export interest, and year established.

REFERENCE WORKS

13825 ■ Manufacturers' Agents National Association—Directory of Manufacturers' Sales Agencies
Pub: Manufacturers' Agents National Association
Contact: Bryan Shirley, Pres./CEO
E-mail: bryan@manaonline.org

Ed: Helen Degli-Angeli, Editor, helen@manaonline. org. **Released:** Online Directory. **Covers:** 4,000 independent agents and firms representing manufacturers and other businesses in specified territories on a commission basis, including consultants and associate member firms interested in the manufacturer/ agency method of marketing. **Entries Include:** For manufacturers—Company name, address, phone, fax, E-mail, URL, name of contact, product. For agencies—Agency name, address, phone, fax, E-mail, URL, name of contact, warehouse facilities, territory covered, number of field sales representatives, branch office location, year established, date of joining association. **Arrangement:** Separate alphabetical sections for manufacturers and agencies. **Indexes:** Geographic, target industries.

TRADE PERIODICALS

13826 ■ Agency Sales Magazine
Pub: Manufacturers' Agents National Association

Ed: Jack Foster, Editor, jfoster@manaonline.org. **Released:** Monthly. **Price:** $79; $89 Canada; $102 other countries. **Description:** Magazine for manufacturers' agents and manufacturers. Includes tax developments and tips, management aids for manufacturers and agents, legal bulletins, trend-identifying market data, classified ads.

13827 ■ The Representative
Pub: NAGMR Consumer Products Sales Agencies
Contact: Jack M. Springer

Released: Quarterly. **Price:** Included in membership. **Description:** Contains Association, industry, and tax information for consumer product brokers who specialize in selling drug, health, and non-food products and beauty aids to food and drug chains and mass merchandisers. Recurring features include news of members, a calendar of events.

13828 ■ UAMR Confidential Bulletin
Pub: United Association of Manufacturers' Representatives (UAMR)

Ed: Karen Mazzola, Editor. **Released:** Monthly. **Price:** Included in membership. **Description:** Covers product lines offered for representation in all fields. Provides details of the company and product, type of accounts to be serviced, and the areas open for representation. Subscription includes bulletin of lines for representatives, articles on rep business, and trade show listings.

TRADE SHOWS AND CONVENTIONS

13829 ■ National Association of General Merchandise Representatives Annual Convention
National Association of General Merchandise Representatives NAGMR
c/o MANA
One Spectrum Pointe, Ste. 150
Lake Forest, CA 92630
Ph:(636)527-7115

Fax:(636)527-2116
Co. E-mail: rotto@nationalsalessolutions.com
URL: http://www.nagmr.org
Released: Annual. **Audience:** Sales representatives and trade professionals. **Principal Exhibits:** Health and beauty aids that are sold in drug stores.

RESEARCH CENTERS

13830 ■ Manufacturers Representatives Educational Research Foundation
8329 Cole St.
Arvada, CO 80005
Ph:(303)463-1801

Fax:(303)379-6024
Co. E-mail: susannah@mrerf.org
URL: http://www.mrerf.org
Contact: Susannah E. Hart, Exec.Dir.
E-mail: susannah@mrerf.org
Scope: Role and profession of outsourced sales. **Educational Activities:** Executive Education and Certification (annually), certified professional manufacturers' representative program held each year, involves 3 annual sessions followed by an exam process; Professional Sales Certification (bimonthly), certified sales professional designation earned by attending professional selling seminar and taking written and verbal exam.

ASSOCIATIONS AND OTHER ORGANIZATIONS

13831 ■ American Boat Builders and Repairers Association
50 Water St.
Warren, RI 02885
Ph:(401)247-0318
Fax:(401)247-0074
Co. E-mail: mamaral@abbra.org
URL: http://www.abbra.org
Contact: Doug Domenie, Pres.
Description: Boat yards, marinas, and sailmakers. Seeks to: develop and encourage high standards of service and conduct within the industry; foster and promote the common business and professional interests of members; provide a forum for the discussion of problems and the exchange of experiences and ideas. **Publications:** *Boatyard and Marinas Operators Manual; Capstan* (monthly); *Environmental Briefing; Gel Coat Blister Repair* .

13832 ■ American Boat and Yacht Council
613 3rd St., Ste. 10
Annapolis, MD 21403
Ph:(410)990-4460
Fax:(410)990-4466
URL: http://www.abycinc.org
Contact: Mr. Skip Burdon, Pres./CEO
Description: Consists of boatbuilders, boat owners, boat yards, dealerships, educational institutions, equipment and accessory manufacturers, government agencies, insurance companies, law firms, marinas, marine retailers, service technicians, surveyors and trade associations. Develops the consensus-based safety standards for the design, construction, equipage, maintenance and repair of small craft and their systems through 18 project technical committees. **Publications:** *American Boat and Yacht Council—News* (quarterly); *Rules and Regulations for Recreational Boats* (periodic); *Standards and Technical Information Reports for Small Craft* (annual); *USCG Compliance Guidelines* (periodic).

13833 ■ Association of Marina Industries
50 Water St.
Warren, RI 02885
Free: (866)367-6622
Fax:(401)247-0074
Co. E-mail: malves@marinaassociation.org
URL: http://www.marinaassociation.org
Contact: Jim Frye, Pres./Chm.
Description: Marinas and other boat storage facilities. Promotes growth and professional development among members and their employees. Gathers and disseminates business and technical information of interest to members. Conducts continuing professional education courses for marina personnel in areas including management, facilities maintenance and environmental protection. **Publications:** *Dock Lines* (biweekly); *Practices and Products for Clean Marinas* .

13834 ■ Boat Owners Association of the United States
880 S Pickett St.
Alexandria, VA 22304
Ph:(703)823-9550
Free: 800-395-2628
Fax:(703)461-2847
Co. E-mail: mail@boatus.com
URL: http://www.boatus.com
Contact: Richard Schwartz, Chm./Founder
Description: Represents owners or prospective owners of recreational boats. Independent, consumer service organization offering representation, benefits, and programs for boat owners. Services include: legislative and regulatory representation on issues affecting boaters' interests; marine insurance; magazines; trailering club; marina discounts; long-term boat financing; boating regulations and forms service; charter and group travel services; sale and chartering exchange; marine surveyor and admiralty lawyer reference service; assistance with individual boating problems and towing reimbursement; association flag. Maintains Consumer Protection Bureau, which utilizes comprehensive consumer experience files to pursue individual complaints. **Publications:** *BOAT U.S. Magazine* (bimonthly); *Boat U.S. Trailering Magazine* (bimonthly); *Equipment Catalog* (annual); *Seaworthy* (quarterly).

13835 ■ Inland Seas Education Association
100 Dame St.
Suttons Bay, MI 49682
Ph:(231)271-3077
Fax:(231)271-3088
Co. E-mail: isea@schoolship.org
URL: http://www.greatlakeseducation.org
Contact: Jay Zelenock, Pres.
Description: Individuals concerned with the stewardship of the Great Lakes. Develops leadership, understanding, and commitment needed for long-term stewardship of the Great Lakes. Provides shipboard educational programs where people of all ages can gain first-hand training and experience in the Great Lakes ecosystem. Offers aquatic science, environmental awareness, and sail training classes. **Publications:** *Schoolship Log* (quarterly).

13836 ■ International Shipmasters Association
514 Jaycox Rd.
Avon Lake, OH 44012-2219
Ph:(440)933-4376
Co. E-mail: grskuggen@oh.rr.com
URL: http://www.shipmaster.org
Contact: George R. Skuggen, Grand Lodge Sec.
Description: Represents licensed marine officers operating on the Great Lakes. Promotes legislation to increase greater safety, health, and welfare of Great Lakes transportation and navigation. .

13837 ■ Marine Retailers Association of America
PO Box 725
Boca Grande, FL 33921
Ph:(941)964-2534

Fax:(941)531-6777
Co. E-mail: mraa@mraa.com
URL: http://www.mraa.com
Contact: Phil Keeter, Pres.
Description: Marine retail dealers, marine manufacturers and accessory distributors, and marine services. Disseminates information and promotes activities and programs for the betterment of recreational boating. Co-sponsors dealer management seminars to improve professional management skills. Maintains speakers' bureau; compiles statistics. **Publications:** *Bearings* (monthly).

13838 ■ National Marine Bankers Association
231 S LaSalle St., Ste. 2050
Chicago, IL 60604
Ph:(312)946-6260
Co. E-mail: bmcardle@nmma.org
URL: http://www.marinebankers.org
Contact: Bernice McArdle, Mgr.
Description: Banks, savings institutions, and financial service firms that extend credit to consumers, retailers, and manufacturers of recreational boating equipment. Provides a forum in which lenders can exchange information on developing recreational boating loan programs. Promotes the extension of credit to recreational boating manufacturers, retailers, and consumers. Educates financial institutions on correct methods of underwriting and securing consumer loans and wholesale financing through Marine Lender Workshops. Compiles national statistics on marine financing. **Publications:** *Business of Pleasure Boats* (quarterly); *Lender's Boating Handbook; Summary of Annual Marine Lending Survey* (annual).

13839 ■ National Marine Distributors Association
37 Pratt St.
Essex, CT 06426
Ph:(860)767-7898
Fax:(860)767-7932
Co. E-mail: executivedirector@nmdaonline.com
URL: http://www.nmdaonline.com
Contact: Nancy Cueroni, Exec. Dir.
Description: Wholesale distributors of marine accessories and hardware to the Pleasure Boating Industry. .

13840 ■ National Marine Electronics Association
7 Riggs Ave.
Severna Park, MD 21146
Ph:(410)975-9425
Free: 800-808-6632
Fax:(410)975-9450
Co. E-mail: info@nmea.org
URL: http://www.nmea.org
Contact: David J. Hayden, Pres./Exec. Dir.
Description: Manufacturers, retail service dealers, distributors, educational institutions, and organizations associated with sales and service of marine electronics. Promotes the education and advancement of the marine electronics industry and the market which it serves. .

13841 ■ National Marine Manufacturers Association
231 S LaSalle, Ste. 2050
Chicago, IL 60604
Ph:(312)946-6200
Co. E-mail: webmaster@nmma.org
URL: http://www.nmma.org
Description: Members of Association of Marine Engine Manufacturers, National Association of Boat Manufacturers, and National Association of Marine Products and Services; manufacturers of pleasure boats, marine engines, outboard motors, and boating products. Compiles statistics and provides specialized training for designers of yachts. Sponsors consumer boat shows. .

13842 ■ Northwest Marine Trade Association
1900 N Northlake Way, No. 233
Seattle, WA 98103-9087
Ph:(206)634-0911
Fax:(206)632-0078
Co. E-mail: info@nmta.net
URL: http://www.nmta.net
Contact: George Harris, Pres.
Description: Sole proprietorships, firms, partnerships, or corporations engaged in the sales, service, distribution, and construction of boats, engines, and accessories; allied businesses. Seeks to further the interests of members; to promote public interest in boating; to cooperate with similar organizations; to develop local and state legislation beneficial to the industry and the boating public. Produces and sponsors boat shows; serves as legislative consultant and watchdog for the industry; conducts seminars and management and sales workshops; maintains advertising and public relations programs for the industry; commissions special studies and reports; conducts social activities. **Publications:** *Northwest Marine Trade Association—Membership Directory* (annual); *Water Life* (monthly).

13843 ■ Personal Watercraft Industry Association
444 N Capitol St., Ste. 645
Washington, DC 20001
Ph:(202)737-9768
Fax:(202)628-4716
Co. E-mail: info@pwia.org
URL: http://www.pwia.org
Contact: Dave Dickerson, Exec. Dir.
Description: Represents the four U.S. personal watercraft manufacturers. Works to ensure that personal watercraft (PWC) and personal watercraft users are treated fairly when local, state, and federal government officials consider boating regulations; supports and actively advocates for reasonable regulations, strong enforcement of boating and navigation laws, and mandatory boating safety education for all PWC operators. **Publications:** *An Environmental Guide for Personal Watercraft Operators*; *Riding Rules for Personal Watercraft* .

DIRECTORIES OF EDUCATIONAL PROGRAMS

13844 ■ *Directory of Private Accredited Career Schools and Colleges of Technology*
Pub: Accrediting Commission of Career Schools and Colleges of Technology
Contact: Michale S. McComis, Exec. Dir.
Released: On web page. **Price:** Free. **Description:** Covers 3900 accredited post-secondary programs that provide training programs in business, trade, and technical fields, including various small business endeavors. Entries offer school name, address, phone, description of courses, job placement assistance, and requirements for admission. Arrangement is alphabetical.

REFERENCE WORKS

13845 ■ *American Boat and Yacht Council—Membership List*
Pub: American Boat & Yacht Council Inc.
Contact: Skip Burdon, President
Price: Free. **Covers:** Over 4,000 marine engineers, marine underwriters, naval architects, marine surveyors, manufacturers and designers of small boats and

related equipment, attorneys, boat owners, and Coast Guard, Navy, and state government personnel. **Entries Include:** Name, address, phone, fax, email. **Arrangement:** Alphabetical.

13846 ■ "Bellingham Boatbuilder Norstar Yachts Maintains Family Tradition" in *Bellingham Business Journal* (Vol. February 2010, pp. 12)
Pub: Sound Publishing Inc.
Ed: Isaac Bonnell. **Description:** Profile of Norstar Yachts and brothers Gary and Steve Nordtvedt who started the company in 1994. The company recently moved its operations to a 12,000 square foot space in the Fairhaven Marine Industrial Park.

13847 ■ "Boat Sales Sputter as Cash-Strapped Buyers Drift Away" in *Puget Sound Business Journal* (Vol. 29, August 15, 2008, No. 17, pp. 1)
Pub: American City Business Journals
Ed: Greg Lamm. **Description:** Boat sales in Washington fell by 44 percent in the second quarter of 2008. The decline is attributed to the soft economy, which has given customers second thoughts on purchasing recreational water vehicles.

13848 ■ *BUC Used Boat Price Guide*
Pub: BUC International Corp.
Released: Semiannual, Latest edition 97th, 2008. **Price:** $95, individuals volume 1; $85, individuals volume 2; $69, individuals volume 3; $215, individuals three volume set. **Covers:** Current market price for about 3,500 manufacturers of outboard, inboard, outdrives, sailboats, houseboats, and custom boats as well as approximately 20 manufacturers of boat trailers. In three volumes—Volume 1 covers 1994-2003; volume 2 covers 1982-1993; volume 3 covers 1905-1981. **Entries Include:** Listings for manufacturers still in business include company name, city and state, and Coast Guard identification code; defunct manufacturer listings show city in which last operated. All listings show boat and engine manufacturer's complete specifications. **Arrangement:** Alphabetical by manufacturer name. **Indexes:** Company, trade name.

13849 ■ "Half a World Away" in *Tampa Bay Business Journal* (Vol. 30, December 4, 2009, No. 50, pp. 1)
Pub: American City Business Journals
Ed: Jane Meinhardt. **Description:** Enterprise Florida has offered four trade grants for Florida's marine industry businesses to give them a chance to tap into the Middle East market at the Dubai International Boat Show on March 9 to 13, 2010. The grants pay for 50 percent of the exhibition costs for the qualifying business.

13850 ■ *Marine Products Directory*
Pub: Underwriters Laboratories Inc.
Contact: Susan Druktenis, Asst. Mgr.
Released: Annual, Latest edition 2010. **Price:** $40, individuals. **Covers:** Companies that have qualified to use the UL listing mark or classification marking on or in connection with products which have been found to be in compliance with UL's requirements. Coverage includes foreign companies which manufacture for distribution in the United States. **Entries Include:** Company name, city, zip code, UL file number, and type of product. **Arrangement:** Classified by type of product. There is a separate section listing a limited number of trade names or trademarks authorized to use UL certification without mention of company name. **Indexes:** Company name.

13851 ■ *National Marine Representatives Association—Directory*
Pub: National Marine Representatives Association
Contact: Chris Kelly, President
Released: Annual, January. **Price:** members; $10 Addl. Copy; $20 Hard Copy. **Covers:** Approximately 400 independent representatives selling pleasure craft and other small boats, motors, and marine accessories. **Entries Include:** Name, address, phone, fax, e-mail, manufacturers represented, territories covered, customer classifications. **Arrangement:** Alphabetical. **Indexes:** Geographical.

13852 ■ *Pacific Boating Almanac*
Pub: Prostar Publications Inc.
Ed: Peter L. Griffes, Editor. **Released:** Annual, Latest edition 2006. **Price:** $26.95, individuals. **Covers:** Over 3,000 marine facilities serving recreational boating in California, Oregon, Washington, British Columbia, Alaska, and Mexico's Baja area. **Entries Include:** Name of facility, address, phone, name of owner, list of services. **Arrangement:** Geographical in four volumes: Volume 1, Pacific Northwest; volume 2, Pacific Northwest and Alaska; volume 3, Northern California the Delta; volume 4, Southern California and Baja.

13853 ■ *Portbook*
Pub: Portbook Publications Inc.
Contact: Sandra Squire, Publisher
Released: Annual, March. **Price:** $4, individuals mail copies; Free. **Covers:** Marinas, yacht clubs, boatyards, dealers, marine supply stores, repair facilities, other services for yachtsmen; also includes provisioning information, restaurants, marine and medical emergency numbers; editions available for Annapolis, Maryland; and for Newport and Narragansett Bay, Rhode Island. **Entries Include:** Company name, address, phone, products or services; keyed to map of area. **Arrangement:** Alphabetical. **Indexes:** Product/service.

13854 ■ *Quimby's Cruising Guide*
Pub: Waterways Journal Inc.
Contact: Nelson Spencer, Publisher
E-mail: hnspencer@waterwaysjournal.net
Released: Annual, latest edition 2009. **Price:** $39, individuals plus S&H. **Covers:** Fuel stations and other harbor services for over 650 pleasure boat marinas, harbors, and clubs on the Mississippi, Monongahela, Allegheny, Ohio, Illinois, Tennessee, Cumberland, Arkansas, St. Croix, Kentucky, Muskingum, Missouri, Alabama, Black Warrior, GIWW East, Kanawha, and Apalachicola-Chattahoochee-Flint Rivers, and the Tennessee/Tombigbee Waterway, GIWW West. **Entries Include:** For facilities—Store, company, or facility name, location, phone, product or service provided. For harbors—Name, owner name, address, phone, depth, description. **Arrangement:** By river name, then by river mile. **Indexes:** City name.

13855 ■ *World Maritime Directory*
Pub: Maritime Activity Reports Inc.
Released: Annual. **Price:** $149 plus s/h. **Publication Includes:** List of several hundred manufacturers and suppliers of products used in the design, construction, and repair of commercial and naval vessels; international coverage. **Entries Include:** Company name, address, phone, fax, e-mail, URL, and products provided.

STATISTICAL SOURCES

13856 ■ *RMA Annual Statement Studies*
Pub: Robert Morris Associates (RMA)
Released: Annual. **Price:** $175.00 2006-07 edition, $105.00. **Description:** Contains composite balance sheets and income statements for more than 360 industries, including the accounting, auditing, and bookkeeping industries. Also contains five years of comparative historical data for discerning trends. Includes 16 commonly used ratios, computed for most of the size groupings for nearly every industry.

13857 ■ *The U.S. Market for Pleasure Boats*
Pub: Business Trend Analysts, Inc.
Released: 2003. **Price:** $1695.00. **Description:** This in-depth investigation of the pleasure boat industry tracks current and projected sales (to 2011) of cabin cruisers, houseboats, sailboats, runabouts, center consoles, pontoon boats, canoes, rowboats, and other pleasure craft.

TRADE PERIODICALS

13858 ■ *Boating Magazine*
Pub: Hachette Filipacchi Media U.S. Inc.
Released: Monthly. **Price:** $22 two years print; $14 print; $24 other countries; $32 other countries 2 years. **Description:** Magazine reporting on boat tests, new gear, electronics, and sport fishing for pleasure power boaters.

13859 ■ *The duPont Registry*
Pub: duPont Publishing Inc.
Released: Bimonthly. **Price:** $29.95; $49.95 Canada; $89.95 other countries. **Description:** Magazine featuring worldwide luxury sail and sport boats for sale.

13860 ■ *Inter/Port*
Pub: National Marine Manufacturers Association
Contact: Daniel T. Green
Ed: Dan Green, Editor, dgreen@nmma.org. **Released:** Monthly. **Description:** Provides information on boating legislation, market research, marine engineering, and other subjects of significance to pleasure-boating equipment manufacturers. Recurring features include financial news of industry firms, items on personnel.

13861 ■ *Power and Motoryacht*
Pub: Primedia
Contact: Capt. Richard Thiel, Editor-in-Chief
E-mail: richard.thiel@powerandmotoryacht.com
Released: Monthly. **Price:** $11.97; $19.97 two years; $23.97 Canada; $43.97 Canada two years; $35.97 other countries; $67.97 two years and other countries. **Description:** Magazine for owners of large power-boats.

13862 ■ *Powerboat Magazine*
Pub: Powerboat Magazine
Released: Monthly, Nov./Dec. combined issue. **Price:** $19.97 6 issues; $34.97 12 issues; $25.97 Canada 6 issues; $46.97 Canada; $31.97 other countries 6 issues; $58.97 other countries. **Description:** Magazine reporting news and trends in performance boating. Includes test reports on boats; technical reports on marine products, hull construction, and safety equipment; and water skiing and boat racing news.

13863 ■ *Sailing World*
Pub: Miller Sports Group L.L.C.
Contact: Sally Helme, Publisher
E-mail: sally.helme@bonniercorp.com
Ed: John Burnham, Editor. **Released:** 9/yr. **Price:** $14.97; $23.97 Canada; $36.97 other countries. **Description:** Magazine on performance sailing.

13864 ■ *Soundings*
Pub: Dominion Enterprises
Ed: William Sisson, Editor. **Released:** Monthly. **Price:** $24.97; $46.97 Canada; $66.97 other countries; $39.97 two years; $83.97 Canada 2 years; $123.97 other countries 2 years. **Description:** News magazine for recreational boaters.

13865 ■ *Soundings Trade Only*
Pub: Soundings Publications L.L.C.
Contact: Melanie Winters, Staff Writer
E-mail: m.winters@tradeonlytoday.com
Ed: Tom Hubbard, Editor, t.hubbard@tradeonlytoday.com. **Released:** Monthly. **Price:** Free to qualified subscribers; $9.95 print and digital; $41.95; $73.95 two years. **Description:** Trade magazine for the recreational boating industry.

13866 ■ *WoodenBoat*
Pub: WoodenBoat Publications Inc.
Contact: Carl Cramer, Publisher
E-mail: carl@woodenboat.com
Ed: Matthew Murphy, Editor, matt@woodenboat.com. **Released:** Bimonthly. **Price:** $32; $59 two years; $85 three years; $37 Canada; $64 Canada two years; $45 other countries. **Description:** Magazine covering the design, building, care, preservation, and use of wooden boats, including commercial and pleasure, old and new, sail and power.

13867 ■ *Yachting*
Pub: Time4 Media Inc.
Contact: Gary De Sanctis, Publisher
Released: 7/yr. **Price:** $16; $26 Canada; $46 other countries. **Description:** Yachting magazine for affluent, experienced sail and power yachtsmen.

VIDEOCASSETTES/ AUDIOCASSETTES

13868 ■ *Navigating with Marine Electronics: A Guide to DC*
Bennett Marine Video
2321 Abbot Kinney Blvd., Top Fl.
Venice, CA 90291
Ph:(310)827-8064
Free: 800-733-8862
Fax:(310)827-8074
Co. E-mail: questions@bennettmarine.com
URL: http://www.bennettmarine.com
Released: 1986. **Description:** A comprehensive review of new and traditional electronic items available to boaters, including battery chargers, converters, VHF ship-to-shore radios, radio direction finders, radar, sonar, autopilots, navigation computers, radar detectors and more. **Availability:** VHS.

13869 ■ *Teaching Kids How to Sail*
Victory Multimedia
222 N. Sepulveda Blvd., Ste. 1306
El Segundo, CA 90245
Ph:(310)416-9140
Fax:(310)416-9839
Co. E-mail: RFVictory@juno.com
Price: $19.95. **Description:** Presents the basics of seamanship, docking, tacking, jibbing, and man overboard rescue. **Availability:** VHS.

TRADE SHOWS AND CONVENTIONS

13870 ■ **Annual Spring New Products Show**
Pacific Expositions
1600 Kapiolani Blvd. 1660
Honolulu, HI 96814-3801
Ph:(808)945-3594
Fax:(808)946-6399
Co. E-mail: info@prohawaii.com
URL: http://www.hawaiibid.com
Released: Annual. **Audience:** Trade professionals, buyers, and general public. **Principal Exhibits:** Boats; sport and leisure vehicles; new products and services.

13871 ■ **Atlanta Boat Show**
National Marine Manufacturers Association (Miami Chapter)
9050 Pines Blvd., No. 305
Pembroke Pines, FL 33024
Ph:(954)441-3220
Fax:(954)430-4171
Released: Annual. **Audience:** General public. **Principal Exhibits:** Powerboats, sailboats, fishing boats, water ski boats, pontoon boats, houseboats, personal watercraft, inflatable and more. Exhibits also include marine accessories, services and a showcase on outdoor travel section featuring lodges, marinas and boating resorts.

13872 ■ **Cincinnati Travel, Sports, and Boat Show**
Hart Productions, Inc.
2234 Bauer Rd., Ste. B
Batavia, OH 45103
Ph:(513)797-7900
Free: 877-704-8190
Fax:(513)797-1013
URL: http://www.hartproductions.com
Released: Annual. **Audience:** General public. **Principal Exhibits:** Showcasing a world of travel and recreation featuring vacation travel exhibits, boats, sporting goods, fishing and hunting equipment and seminars. **Dates and Locations:** 2011 Jan 14-23, Cincinnati, OH.

13873 ■ **Detroit Boat Show**
Michigan Boating Industries Association
32398 5 Mile Rd.
Livonia, MI 48154-6109
Ph:(734)261-0123
Free: 800-932-2628
Fax:(734)261-0880
Co. E-mail: boatmichigan@mbia.org
URL: http://www.mbia.org
Released: Annual. **Audience:** Trade professionals and general public. **Principal Exhibits:** Boats, fishing equipment, boat-related accessories, charter rentals, nautical attire, trailer and outboard motors, and personal watercraft.

13874 ■ **Eastern Sports & Outdoor Show**
Reed Exhibitions North American Headquarters
383 Main Ave.
Norwalk, CT 06851
Ph:(203)840-4800
Fax:(203)840-5805
Co. E-mail: export@reedexpo.com
URL: http://www.reedexpo.com
Released: Annual. **Audience:** General public. **Principal Exhibits:** Recreational vehicles, boats, hunting and fishing equipment, clothing, and related outdoor products, resorts, SUVs, retailers and manufacturers, motorcycles, ATVs, travel and tourism.

13875 ■ **Fort Lauderdale International Boat Show**
Yachting Promotions, Inc.
1115 NE, 9th Ave.
Fort Lauderdale, FL 33304
Ph:(954)764-7642
Free: 800-940-7642
Fax:(954)462-4140
Co. E-mail: info@showmanagement.com
URL: http://www.showmanagement.com
Released: Annual. **Audience:** Trade professionals and general public. **Principal Exhibits:** Boats and marine equipment, supplies, and services. **Dates and Locations:** 2011 Oct 27-31, Fort Lauderdale, FL.

13876 ■ **Fort Wayne Sports, Vacation, and Boat Show**
Trio Enterprises, Inc.
3624 Maxim Dr.
Fort Wayne, IN 46815
Ph:(219)483-2638
Free: 800-446-2638
Fax:(219)484-0876
Released: Annual. **Audience:** General public. **Principal Exhibits:** Recreational vehicles, boats, and travel and vacation information.

13877 ■ **Kansas Sports, Boat, & Travel Show**
Industrial Expositions, Inc.
1675 Larimer St., No.700
PO Box 480084
Denver, CO 80248-0084
Ph:(303)892-6800
Free: 800-457-2434
Fax:(303)892-6322
Co. E-mail: info@iei-expos.com
URL: http://www.iei-expos.com/
Released: Annual. **Audience:** General public. **Principal Exhibits:** Recreational vehicles, boats, sports equipment, and travel destination information; fishing and hunting equipment, supplies, and services.

13878 ■ **Miami International Boat Show and Strictly Sail**
National Marine Manufacturers Association (Miami Chapter)
9050 Pines Blvd., No. 305
Pembroke Pines, FL 33024
Ph:(954)441-3220
Fax:(954)430-4171
Released: Annual. **Audience:** Marine manufacturers, distributors, and dealers; and general public. **Principal Exhibits:** Boats (power and sail), engines and accessories, fishing and water sport accessories.

13879 ■ **Portland Boat Show**
O'Loughlin Trade Shows (Portland, Oregon)
PO Box 80750
Portland, OR 97280
Ph:(503)246-8291
Free: 800-343-6973
Fax:(503)246-1066
URL: http://www.oloughlintradeshows.com
Released: Annual. **Audience:** General public. **Principal Exhibits:** Boats and motors, water sporting goods, clothing, and marine accessories.

13880 ■ **Seattle International Boat Show**
Northwest Marine Trade Association
1900 N Northlake Way, Ste. 233
Seattle, WA 98103-9087
Ph:(206)634-0911

Fax:(206)632-0078
Co. E-mail: info@nmta.net
URL: http://www.nmta.net
Released: Annual. **Audience:** General public. **Principal Exhibits:** Power boats, sail boats, marine accessories, and related exhibits.

13881 ■ Tacoma Dome Boat Show
O'Loughlin Trade Shows (Tacoma, Washington)
PO Box 110849
Tacoma, WA 98411-0849
Ph:(253)756-2121
Fax:(253)756-6898
URL: http://www.otsusa.com
Released: Annual. **Audience:** General public. **Principal Exhibits:** Boats and motors, marine electronics, and accessories. **Dates and Locations:** 2011 Mar 17-20, Tacoma, WA.

13882 ■ Yacht and Brokerage Show
Yachting Promotions, Inc.
1115 NE, 9th Ave.
Fort Lauderdale, FL 33304
Ph:(954)764-7642
Free: 800-940-7642
Fax:(954)462-4140
Co. E-mail: info@showmanagement.com
URL: http://www.showmanagement.com
Released: Annual. **Audience:** Trade and general public. **Principal Exhibits:** Yachts and the industry's leading yacht brokerage firms. **Dates and Locations:** 2011 Feb 17-21, Miami, FL.

CONSULTANTS

13883 ■ Halcrow HPA
22 Cortlandt St. 31st Fl.
New York, NY 10007
Ph:(212)608-3990
Fax:(212)566-5059
Co. E-mail: pking@halcrow.com
URL: http://www.han-padron.com
Contact: Russell MacDonald, Director
E-mail: pierre.desautels@atshalcrowyolles.com
Scope: A full service engineering firm specializing in projects in the marine environment. Offers a unique range of services that include such specialties as underwater inspection and maritime security.

13884 ■ J-U-B Engineers Inc.
250 S Beechwood Ave., Ste. 201
Boise, ID 83709-0944
Ph:(208)376-7330
Free: 888-582-2647
Fax:(208)323-9336
Co. E-mail: info@jub.com
URL: http://www.jub.com
Contact: Brian Deeter, Mgr
E-mail: brd@atsjub.com
Scope: Offers consulting engineering services in the following areas civil, structural and sanitary engineering airports, bridges, buildings, land developments, drainage, highways, irrigation, fishery facilities, marine facilities, sewerage facilities including master planning, modeling, collection system design, treatment plant planning and design, storm drainage, structures, sub divisions, water treatment supply, storm and distribution; boundary and topographic surveying by GPS methods and planning subdivisions, housing, commercial, industrial, city. Serves private clients, industries, public utilities and governmental agencies including, but not limited to municipalities, counties, state, federal, road districts, water and sewer districts. **Publications:** "Idaho Engineering Firm of the Year," McGraw-Hill Companies, 2005.

LIBRARIES

13885 ■ Alaska Marine Safety Education Association Library
2924 Halibut Point Rd.
Sitka, AK 99835
Ph:(907)747-3287

Fax:(907)747-3259
Co. E-mail: amsea@amsea.org
URL: http://www.amsea.org
Contact: Deborah Roesch, Off.Mgr.
Scope: Marine - survival, casualty news, safety studies, casualties, safety curriculum; land survival. **Services:** Copying; Library open to the public. **Holdings:** 200 books; 200 reports; 50 videos. **Subscriptions:** 10 journals and other serials.

13886 ■ Antique Boat Museum, Inc.–Lou Smith Library and Marion Clayton Link Archives
750 Mary St.
Clayton, NY 13624
Ph:(315)686-4104, x-225
Fax:(315)686-2775
Co. E-mail: dmiller@abm.org
URL: http://www.abm.org/collections.asp
Contact: Dan Miller, Cur.
Scope: Freshwater nautical history, St. Lawrence River and Seaway history, boat building and restoration. **Services:** Copying; Library open to the public with restrictions on a limited schedule (appointment suggested; research for non-members is $20 per hour). **Holdings:** 1500 books; 2500 periodicals (1900 to present); 4000 photographs; 100 charts and maps; 20 oral history tapes; 12 VF drawers of boat plans, parts and equipment information, engine manuals, and boat manufacturers catalogs; 7 VF drawers of clippings; historic postcard files. **Subscriptions:** 25 journals and other serials; 17 newsletters.

13887 ■ Canadian Coast Guard Library
Canada Bldg.
344 Slater St., Ste. 737
Ottawa, ON, Canada K1A 0N7
Ph:(613)998-1801
Fax:(613)993-8659
Contact: Ginette Dion, Sr.Info.Off.
Scope: Marine; marine engineering; naval architecture; ships; CCGS Data Books; ship specifications - construction; instrument manuals; ships - tests, trials. **Services:** Interlibrary loan; copying. **Holdings:** Technical reports; manuals; technical drawings; photographs; documents.

13888 ■ Chesapeake Bay Maritime Museum–Howard I. Chapelle Memorial Library
PO Box 636
St. Michaels, MD 21663
Ph:(410)745-2916
Fax:(410)745-6088
Co. E-mail: plesher@cbmm.org
URL: http://www.cbmm.org
Contact: Pete Lesher, Chf.Cur.
Scope: Chesapeake Bay history and marine life; boat construction, maintenance, handling; waterfowl; voyages and travel; naval and sailing craft history; ship models; steamboat history; Maryland history; Virginia history. **Services:** Library open to the public with restrictions. **Holdings:** 9800 volumes; 150 lin.ft. of archives; 200 taped oral histories. **Subscriptions:** 18 journals and other serials.

13889 ■ Deer Isle-Stonington Historical Society Library
416 Sunset Rd.
Deer Isle, ME 04627-0652
Ph:(207)367-8978
Co. E-mail: judyhill@acadia.net
Contact: Becke Thompson, Pres.
Scope: Marine vessels, steamboats and yachts, early children's books and school books. **Services:** Library open to the public. **Holdings:** 200 books; early scrapbooks; file of clippings on local subjects; diaries; photographs; archives; microfilm.

13890 ■ The Library at the Mariners' Museum
100 Museum Dr.
Newport News, VA 23606-3759
Ph:(757)591-7782

Fax:(757)591-7310
Co. E-mail: library@marinersmuseum.org
URL: http://www.marinersmuseum.org/library
Contact: Susan Berg, Dir.
Scope: Shipping, shipbuilding, navigation, merchant marine, navies, exploration and travel, whaling, yachting, maritime history. **Services:** Copying; Library open to the public. **Holdings:** 78,000 volumes; 10,000 bound periodical volumes; 600,000 photographs; 500 logbooks and journals; 60 microfilm; 5000 charts and maps; 700 newspaper clippings and journals; 1 million manuscripts; ships' papers; 10,000 plans and drawings; tapes; atlases; 1500 magazines, journals and newsletters. **Subscriptions:** 250 journals and other serials.

13891 ■ Maine Maritime Academy–Nutting Memorial Library
Box C-1
Pleasant St.
Castine, ME 04420-1001
Ph:(207)326-2263
Fax:(207)326-2261
Co. E-mail: bhall@mma.edu
URL: http://sisportal.mma.edu/default.aspx
Contact: Brent Hall, Lib.Dir.
Scope: Marine engineering, marine transportation, nautical science, maritime management, International business and logistics, engineering technology, power engineering, yacht operations, boat yard management, ocean studies, oceanography. **Services:** Interlibrary loan; copying; Library open to the public. **Holdings:** 68,213 books; 5616 maps and charts; 109,610 government documents. **Subscriptions:** 470 journals and newspapers.

13892 ■ Marine Museum at Fall River, Inc. Library
70 Water St.
Fall River, MA 02721
Ph:(508)674-3533
Fax:(508)674-3534
Co. E-mail: staff@marineuseum.org
URL: http://www.marinemuseum.org
Contact: Dr. Edwin L. Dunbaugh, Libn./Hist.
Scope: History of steam power-driven watercraft. **Services:** Library not open to the public. **Holdings:** 2000 books; 125 bound periodical volumes; 5000 photographic plates; 1000 glass slides. **Subscriptions:** 3 journals and other serials.

13893 ■ Mystic Seaport Museum, Inc.–G.W. Blunt White Library
95 Greenmanville Ave.
Mystic, CT 06355
Ph:(860)572-5367
Co. E-mail: collections@mysticseaport.org
URL: http://library.mysticseaport.org
Contact: Paul J. O'Pecko, Lib.Dir.
Scope: American maritime history, shipbuilding, vessel registration, yachting, naval architecture, fisheries. **Services:** Interlibrary loan; Library open to the public for research and reference use only. **Holdings:** 70,000 books; 5000 bound periodical volumes; 1200 logbooks; 2000 reels of microfilm; 9000 charts and maps; 100,000 ship plans. **Subscriptions:** 392 journals and other serials.

13894 ■ Robert Weinstein Maritime Historical Collection
1851 Stearns Dr.
Los Angeles, CA 90035-4629
Ph:(213)936-0558
Fax:(213)936-1661
Contact: Robert Weinstein, Owner
Scope: Sailing ships of all countries and trades. **Services:** Library not open to the public. **Holdings:** 250,000 original and copy photographs, glass negatives, clippings, post cards.

ASSOCIATIONS AND OTHER ORGANIZATIONS

13895 ■ American Marketing Association
311 S Wacker Dr., Ste. 5800
Chicago, IL 60606
Ph:(312)542-9000
Free: 800-262-1150
Fax:(312)542-9001
Co. E-mail: info@ama.org
URL: http://www.marketingpower.com
Contact: George Day, Chm.

Description: Serves as a professional society of marketing and market research executives, sales and promotion managers, advertising specialists, academics, and others interested in marketing. Fosters research; sponsors seminars, conferences, and student marketing clubs; provides educational placement service and doctoral consortium. **Publications:** *American Marketing Association—Proceedings* (annual); *Journal of Marketing* (bimonthly); *Journal of Marketing Research* (bimonthly); *Journal of Public Policy and Marketing* (semiannual); *Marketing Academics at AMA* (bimonthly); *Marketing Health Service* (quarterly); *Marketing Matters* (biweekly); *Marketing Research* (quarterly).

13896 ■ Marketing Research Association
110 National Dr., 2nd Fl.
Glastonbury, CT 06033-1212
Ph:(860)682-1000
Fax:(860)682-1050
Co. E-mail: email@mra-net.org
URL: http://www.mra-net.org
Contact: Elisa Galloway, Pres.

Description: Companies and individuals involved in any area of opinion and marketing research, such as data collection, research, or as an end-user. **Publications:** *Blue Books Research Service Directory* (annual); *Recruiting and Facility Management Qualitative Handbook* .

LEGISLATIVE ASSISTANCE

13897 ■ Office of the Governor–Economic Development and Tourism Division–Economic Information Clearinghouse (PO Bo)
PO Box 12428
PO Box 12728
Austin, TX 78711
Ph:(512)463-2000
Free: 800-888-0511
Fax:(512)463-1849
URL: http://www.governor.state.tx.us/

Description: Program attempts to ensure that each state agency awards 10 percent of all purchases of articles, supplies, commodities, materials, or services to small businesses.

DIRECTORIES OF EDUCATIONAL PROGRAMS

13898 ■ Quirk's Marketing Research Review Data Processing and Statistical Analysis Directory Issue
Pub: Quirk Enterprises Inc.

Ed: Joe Rydhom, Editor, joe@quirks.com. **Released:** Annual, March. **Publication Includes:** List of companies that provides data processing and statistical analysis services for the marketing research industry. **Entries Include:** Company name, address, phone, description of product. **Arrangement:** Alphabetic.

13899 ■ Quirk's Marketing Research Review—Directory of Customer Satisfaction Research Providers Issue
Pub: Quirk Enterprises Inc.

Ed: Joe Rydhom, Editor, joe@quirks.com. **Released:** Annual, October. **Publication Includes:** List of companies that offer customer satisfaction research services for the marketing research industry. **Entries Include:** Company name, address, phone, description of service.

REFERENCE WORKS

13900 ■ "The AHA Moment" in *Hispanic Business* (December 2010)
Pub: Hispanic Business

Ed: Rebecca Vallaneda. **Description:** An interview with Gisela Girard on how competitive market conditions push buttons. Girard stepped down from her 18-month position as chairwoman the Association of Hispanic Advertising Agencies. She has more than 20 years of experience in advertising and research marketing.

13901 ■ "Bar Hopping: Your Numbers At a Glance" in *Inc.* (January 2008, pp. 44-45)
Pub: Gruner & Jahr USA Publishing

Ed: Michael Fitzgerald. **Description:** Software that helps any company analyze data include Crystal Xcelsius, a program that takes data from Excel documents and turns them into animated gauges, charts and graphs; CashView, a Web-based application that tracks receivables and payables; iDashboards, a Web-based programs that produces animated gauges, maps, pie charts and graphs; Corda Human Capital Management, that transforms stats like head count, productivity, and attrition into graphs and dials; NetSuite, a Web-based application that tracks key indicators; and Cognos Now, that gauges, dials, and graphs data.

13902 ■ "Because Kids Need To Be Heard: Tina Wells: Buzz Marketing Group: Voorhees, New Jersey" in *Inc.* (Volume 32, December 2010)
Pub: Inc. Magazine

Ed: Tamara Schweitzer. **Description:** Profile of Tina Wells, founder and CEO of Buzz Marketing Group, who writes a tween book series called Mackenzie Blue to reach young girls.

13903 ■ Bradford's International Directory of Marketing Research Agencies
Pub: Business Research Services Inc.

Released: Biennial, Latest edition 30th. **Price:** $95, individuals in-print; $95, individuals CD-ROM; $125, individuals in print and CD-ROM. **Covers:** Over 2,300 marketing research agencies worldwide. Includes domestic and international demographic data and professional association contacts. **Entries Include:** Company name, address, phone, name and title of contact, date founded, number of employees, description of products or services, e-mail, URL. **Arrangement:** Geographical. **Indexes:** Alphabetical by company.

13904 ■ Business Marketing Association—Membership & Resource Directory
Pub: Business Marketing Association

Contact: Rick Kean

Released: Annual, January. **Covers:** Over 4,500 member business communications professionals in fields of advertising, marketing communications, and marketing; their service and supply companies are listed in the "Marketing Resources" section. **Entries Include:** For individuals—Name, title, company with which affiliated, address, phone. For companies—Name, address, phone, contact, description of products or services. **Arrangement:** Individuals are alphabetical within chapter; companies are classified by product or service. **Indexes:** Alpha, company, chapter.

13905 ■ "Decoding Demand Opportunities" in *Business Strategy Review* (Vol. 21, Spring 2010, No. 1, pp. 64)
Pub: Wiley-Blackwell

Ed: Erich Joachimsthaler, Markus Pfeiffer. **Description:** Classic marketing techniques, such as the use of focus groups or ethnographies, miss the enormous opportunities that can be leveraged once companies commit to understanding consumers in the context of life experiences.

13906 ■ "Funny Business" in *Canadian Business* (Vol. 82, April 27, 2009, No. 7, pp. 27)
Pub: Rogers Media

Ed: Rachel Pulfer. **Description:** Companies are advised to use humor in marketing to drive more revenue. IBM Canada, for example, commissioned Second City Communications for a marketing campaign that involved humor. While IBM Canada declined to give sales or traffic figures, firm executives rank the marketing campaign as an overall success.

13907 ■ "Harley-Davidson Moves to Unconventional Marketing Plan" in *Business Journal-Milwaukee* (Vol. 28, November 26, 2010, No. 8, pp. A1)
Pub: Milwaukee Business Journal

Ed: Rich Rovito. **Description:** Harley Davidson Inc. hired Boulder, Colorado-based Victors & Spoils, an agency that specializes in crowdsourcing, to implement a new creative marketing model. Under the plan, Harley Davidson will draw on the ideas of its brand enthusiasts to help guide the brand's marketing direction.

13908 ■ "I Hear You're Interested In a..." in *Inc.* **(January 2008, pp. 40-43)**
Pub: Gruner & Jahr USA Publishing
Ed: Leah Hoffmann. **Description:** Four tips to help any small business generate sales leads online are examined.

13909 ■ "Ideas at Work: Sparkling Innovation" in *Business Strategy Review* **(Vol. 21, Summer 2010, No. 2, pp. 07)**
Pub: Wiley-Blackwell
Ed: Julian Birkinshaw, Peter Robbins. **Description:** GlaxoSmithKline faced a situation common to large global organizations: how to allocate marketing resources to smaller, regional brands. The company's approach to worldwide marketing that led to the development of a unique and productive network is outlined.

13910 ■ *Integration Marketing: How Small Businesses Become Big Businesses and Big Businesses Become Empires*
Pub: John Wiley & Sons, Inc.
Ed: Mark Joyner. **Released:** May 1, 2009. **Price:** $22.95. **Description:** Leading Internet marketing expert offers a marketing methodology to grow any business.

13911 ■ *Marketing for Dummies*
Pub: John Wiley & Sons Inc.
Ed: Alexander Hiam, Editor. **Released:** latest edition 3rd; Published October, 2009. **Price:** $21.99, individuals paperback. **Publication Includes:** Marketing web sites, marketing consultants, trade associations, market researchers, and other experts. **Entries Include:** Individual or company name, address, phone number, web site address (where applicable). Principal content of publication is articles on marketing strategies.

13912 ■ *Marketing for Entrepreneurs*
Pub: FT Press
Ed: Jurgen Wolff. **Released:** December 9, 2010. **Price:** $24.99. **Description:** This text identifies marketing as the entire process of researching, creating, distributing and selling a product or service. It isn't about theory and metrics, rather it is a practical guide that starts with the basics of all marketing aspects.

13913 ■ *The Markets Directory*
Pub: The Markets Directory
Contact: James Roxton, Publisher
E-mail: jim.roxton@marketsdirectory.com
Released: Annual. **Entries Include:** Company name, address, phone, fax, contact name, line of business, facilities. **Database Covers:** Over 7,000 service organizations implementing marketing research projects for marketing professionals in the U.S. and around the world.

13914 ■ "Mars Advertising's Orbit Grows as Other Ad Segments Fall" in *Crain's Detroit Business* **(Vol. 25, June 1, 2009, No. 22, pp. 10)**
Pub: Crain Communications Inc. - Detroit
Ed: Bill Shea. **Description:** An electrical fire burned at Mars Advertising's headquarters in Southfield, Michigan. The company talks about its plans for regrouping and rebuilding. The family firm specializes in in-store marketing that targets consumers already in the buying mode.

13915 ■ "Miller's Crossroad" in *Canadian Business* **(Vol. 83, September 14, 2010, No. 15, pp. 58)**
Pub: Rogers Media Ltd.
Ed: Joe Castaldo. **Description:** Future Electronics founder and billionaire Robert Miller shares the secret of Future's unique operating model, which is based on inventory and market research. Miller attributes much of the company's success to its privately held status that enables quick movement against competitors.

13916 ■ "Network Marketing Strategies for Marketing Professionals" in *Black Enterprise* **(Vol. 38, October 2007, No. 3, pp. 70)**
Pub: Earl G. Graves Publishing Co. Inc.
Description: Network marketing programs are redefining the sales business and leveraging opportunities in the ever-expanding global, highly networked, and ultra-specialized marketplace.

13917 ■ *Qualitative Research Consultants Association—Membership Directory*
Pub: Qualitative Research Consultants Association
Contact: Ricardo Lopez
Released: Annual, Spring. **Covers:** About 600 qualitative market and social researchers and consultants. **Entries Include:** Company name, address, phone, name of contact, specialties, areas. **Arrangement:** Alphabetical. **Indexes:** Geographical.

13918 ■ *Research Alert*
Pub: EPM Communications Inc.
Contact: Ira Mayer, Pres.
Released: Annual, latest edition 2005. **Price:** $389, individuals. **Publication Includes:** Companies and abstracts of marketing studies that analyze trends, consumer buying habits, lifestyles, and prospective markets. **Entries Include:** Company name, address, phone, name and title of contact, products or services, summary of key findings. Principal content is a collection of consumer marketing studies. **Arrangement:** Classified by subject.

13919 ■ "Research and Markets Adds Report: Vending Machines" in *Travel and Leisure Close-Up* **(October 20, 2011)**
Pub: Close-Up Media
Description: Research and Markets has added "Vending Machines – Global Strategic Business Report" to its lineup. The report analyzes globally installed vending machines in US million dollars by the following product types: Beverage, Food, Cigarette, and Other Products (includes personal and health care products, contraceptives, books, magazines).

13920 ■ *Researching Company Financial Information*
Pub: MarketResearch.com
Released: Edition V. **Price:** $59, individuals. **Description:** Helps readers learn how to research and understand financial data from companies, as well as compile in-depth financial data on competitors in order to get a better picture of the competition. **Publication Includes:** A directory of corporate financial info sources.

13921 ■ "Ric Elis/Dan Feldstein" in *Charlotte Business Journal* **(Vol. 25, December 31, 2010, No. 41, pp. 6)**
Pub: Charlotte Business Journal
Ed: Ken Elkins. **Description:** Charlotte, North Carolina-based Internet marketing firm Red Ventures has grown significantly. General Atlantic has purchased stakes in Red Ventures.

13922 ■ "The Rise of Pompei" in *Retail Merchandiser* **(Vol. 51, September-October 2011, No. 5, pp. 13)**
Pub: Phoenix Media Corporation
Description: Soho creative consulting group follows its C3 philosophy to create an invigorated brand experience that transforms customers from consumers to empowered buyers. Pompei AD is a leading creative consultancy that specializes in design and branding for retail, museum, hospitality, and other sectors.

13923 ■ "Security Alert: Data Server" in *Entrepreneur* **(Vol. 36, February 2008, No. 2, pp. 28)**
Pub: Entrepreneur Media Inc.
Ed: Amanda C. Kooser. **Description:** Michael Kogon is the founder of Definition 6, a technology consulting and interactive marking firm. He believes in the philosophy that the best way to keep sensitive data safe is not to store it. Details on the security policies of his firm are discussed.

13924 ■ "Sophistication in Research in Marketing" in *Journal of Marketing* **(Vol. 75, July 2011, No. 4, pp. 155)**
Pub: American Marketing Association
Ed: Donald R. Lehmann, Leigh McAlister, Richard Staelin. **Description:** A look at the current imbalance in the research in marketing is presented. The level of analytical rigor has risen in articles published in marketing academic journals but other desirable characteristics, such as communicability, relevance, and simplicity have been downplayed.

13925 ■ "Strength In Numbers" in *Black Enterprise* **(Vol. 38, January 2008, No. 6, pp. 53)**
Pub: Earl G. Graves Publishing Co. Inc.
Description: According to recent studies geared to advertisers, African Americans represent a demographic that drives style and consumer trends. The African American buying power is expected to increase to $1.1 trillion by 2011. Beyond Demographics helps clients identify ways to value and measure investments within the black community.

13926 ■ *The Unofficial Guide to Starting a Small Business*
Pub: John Wiley & Sons, Incorporated
Ed: Marcia Layton Turner. **Released:** October 2004. **Price:** $16.99. **Description:** Information and tools for starting a small business, covering the start-up process, from market research, to business plans, to marketing programs.

13927 ■ "Why You Need a New-Media 'Ringmaster'" in *Harvard Business Review* **(Vol. 88, December 2010, No. 12, pp. 78)**
Pub: Harvard Business School Publishing
Ed: Patrick Spenner. **Description:** The concept of ringmaster is applied to brand marketing. This concept includes integrative thinking, lean collaboration skills, and high-speed decision cycles.

13928 ■ "Your Turn in the Spotlight" in *Inc.* **(Volume 32, December 2010, No. 10, pp. 57)**
Pub: Inc. Magazine
Ed: John Brandon. **Description:** Examples of three video blogs created by entrepreneurs to promote their businesses and products are used to show successful strategies. Wine Library TV promotes a family's wine business; SHAMA.TV offers marketing tips and company news; and Will It Blend? promotes sales of a household blender.

TRADE PERIODICALS

13929 ■ *ADM Flash*
Pub: Association of Directory Marketing
Ed: Nancy Augustine, Editor, naugustine@admworks. org. **Released:** 10/year. **Price:** Free. **Description:** Features information about marketing directories.

13930 ■ *Alert!*
Pub: Marketing Research Association
Contact: Betsy Peterson
Ed: Paul Melillo, Editor, paul.melillo@mra-net.org. **Released:** Monthly. **Price:** Included in membership. **Description:** Provides information about marketing industry events, trends in marketing research, management techniques, association events, and legislative activities affecting the marketing industry. Recurring features include news of research, a calendar of events, reports of meetings, news of educational opportunities, job listings, notices of publications available, business opportunities, and facilities for sale.

13931 ■ *The Gauge*
Pub: Delahaye Medialink
Contact: Katharine Delahaye Paine, Publisher
E-mail: kpaine@delahaye.com
Ed: William Teunis Paarlberg, Editor, wpaarlberg@ aol.com. **Released:** Bimonthly. **Price:** $75. **Description:** Provides information on and evaluates marketing communications activities of companies. Recurring features include interviews, news of research, and a calendar of events.

13932 ■ *Internet Marketing Report*
Pub: Progressive Business Publications
Ed: Alan Field, Editor. **Released:** Semimonthly.
Price: $299, individuals. **Description:** Communicates the latest news and trends in website marketing. g.

13933 ■ *Journal of Marketing Research*
Pub: American Marketing Association
Ed: Tulin Erdem, Editor, terdem@stern.nyu.edu. **Released:** Bimonthly. **Price:** $85 additional 7%GST pay for Canadian residents; $125 institutions additional 7%GST pay for Canadian residents; $115 other countries; $160 institutions, other countries. **Description:** Peer-reviewed journal concentrates on marketing research.

13934 ■ *Larry Chase's Web Digest for Marketers (WDFM)*
Pub: Chase Online Marketing Strategies,Inc
Contact: Larry Chase, Exec. Editor
E-mail: larry@wdfm.com
Ed: Mary Gillen, Editor. **Released:** Weekly. **Price:** Free. **Description:** Delivers 15 short reviews of business-related websites every issue. **Remarks:** America Online, Inc.

13935 ■ *Marketing Magazine*
Pub: Rogers Media Publishing
Contact: Lucy Collin, Publisher
E-mail: lucy.collin@marketingmag.rogers.com
Released: 41/yr. **Price:** $95 Canada; $55 students. **Description:** Weekly newsmagazine for consumer and business marketers and their suppliers, including ad agencies, the media, and auxiliary companies from graphics to event marketing.

13936 ■ *Marketing Management*
Pub: American Marketing Association
Contact: Sally Schmitz, Production Mgr
E-mail: sschmitz@ama.org
Ed: Gordon Wyner, Editor, gwyner@comcast.net. **Released:** Bimonthly. **Price:** $90 taxes extra for Canadian residents; $120 institutions taxes extra for Canadian residents; $120 other countries; $165 institutions. **Description:** Publication focusing on strategic marketing.

13937 ■ *Marketing News*
Pub: American Marketing Association
Contact: Sally Schmitz, Production Mgr
E-mail: sschmitz@ama.org
Released: 16/yr. **Price:** $35 members; $100 nonmembers; $130 institutions libraries and corporations; $3 single issue individuals; $5 single issue institutions; $140 institutions, other countries extra for air delivery. **Description:** Business magazine focusing on current marketing trends.

13938 ■ *Marketing Research*
Pub: American Marketing Association
Contact: Sally Schmitz, Production Mgr
E-mail: sschmitz@ama.org
Ed: Chuck Chakrapani, Editor, chakrapani@research.ryerson.ca. **Released:** Quarterly. **Price:** $85 additional 7%GST pay for Canadian residents; $125 institutions additional 7%GST pay for Canadian residents; $115 other countries; $160 institutions, other countries. **Description:** For the professional whose primary interest is in marketing research.

13939 ■ *Research Alert*
Pub: EPM Communications Inc.
Contact: Ira Mayer, President/Publisher
Ed: Barbara Perrin, Editor, bperrin@epmcom.com. **Released:** 24/year. **Price:** $389, individuals $369/year, U.S. and Canada; $429 elsewhere. **Description:** Summarizes the most current consumer marketing research reports. Includes complete contact, methodology, and price information.

13940 ■ *SRIC-BI News*
Pub: Business Intelligence Program
Ed: Judith Clay Lhamon, Editor. **Released:** Monthly. **Description:** Reports research being performed in technical, market, and management areas. Analyzes early signs of potential social, political, economic, and technological change, and, relating these developments to one another, suggests possible implications for BIP's clients.

13941 ■ *Survey Research*
Pub: Survey Research Laboratory
Contact: Diane O'Rourke, Managing Editor
E-mail: dianeo@srl.uic.edu
Ed: Lisa Kelly-Wilson, Editor, lisakw@srl.uic.edu. **Released:** 3/year. **Price:** $15, individuals; $60 organizations; $600 patrons (up to 60 copies of each issue). **Description:** Contains descriptions of current survey research projects by academic and not-for-profit survey research organizations; news from survey research centers; descriptions of recent methodological publications on survey Current Research, Personnel Notes, and New Methodological Publications.

13942 ■ *The Top 100 List*
Pub: Luce Press Clippings
Ed: Richard Weiner, Editor. **Description:** Presents marketing information and demographics from newspapers, magazines, and other media on U.S. cities.

VIDEOCASSETTES/ AUDIOCASSETTES

13943 ■ *Marketing Research*
GPN Educational Media
1550 Executive Drive
Elgin, IL 60123
Ph:(402)472-2007
Free: 800-228-4630
Fax:800-306-2330
Co. E-mail: askgpn@smarterville.com
URL: http://www.shopgpn.com
Released: 1988. **Price:** $69.95. **Description:** Looks at the format, systematic approach and the informal, casual methods of marketing research, and how companies make their marketing decisions. **Availability:** VHS.

CONSULTANTS

13944 ■ Adam Market Research Inc.
2246 University Square Mall, Ste. C
Tampa, FL 33612
Ph:(813)875-4005
Fax:(813)875-4055
Co. E-mail: adam.market.research@worldnet.att.net
Contact: Mark R. Segal, President
Scope: Offers a variety of market research interviewing services.

13945 ■ American Cut Crystal Corp.
1150 Broadway
Hewlett, NY 11557
Ph:(516)569-1300
Fax:(516)569-5656
Contact: Marvin Wolf, President
Scope: Provides a wide range of marketing research services, both to consumer and business-to-business, as well as to government agencies. Specialties include new product development, market studies, psychologically probing qualitative research and trend spotting.

13946 ■ Bowman R&C Projects
8613 W Richardson Rd.
Pasco, WA 99301-1611
Ph:(509)544-9520
Fax:(509)544-9514
Contact: Carol H. Bowman, President
Scope: Active in the design and analysis of primary marketing research. Industries served: Catalog, retail, direct marketing, and service-oriented businesses.

13947 ■ Brink & Associates Inc.
2325 N Glebe Rd.
Arlington, VA 22207
Ph:(703)312-5244
Fax:(703)312-5246
Co. E-mail: info@brinkassociates.net
URL: http://www.brinkassociates.net
Contact: Melinda Williams, Mgr
Scope: A full-service healthcare consulting company. Provides services in clinical operations, research, hospital administration, marketing, and communications.

13948 ■ Brown Koff & Fried Inc.
111 Madison Ave.
New York, NY 10016-7416
Ph:(212)779-4600
Fax:(212)779-2714
Contact: Michael Brown, President
Scope: Marketing research firm offering a wide range of services, many of them customized to suit the needs of each specific client.

13949 ■ The Browning Group
1300 Clay St., Ste. 600
Oakland, CA 94612
Ph:(510)635-3878
Fax:(510)464-8001
Co. E-mail: partners@browninggroup.com
URL: http://www.browninggroup.com
Contact: Paul Cohune, Managing Director
E-mail: pcohune@atsbrowninggroup.com
Scope: Offers marketing research, strategic planning, and program implementation services for travel, hospitality, specialty retail, restaurant and food service, real estate, office products, and health services. **Seminars:** 21st Century Maxims; Meeting The Business Challenges of the 21st Century, 2006; Vision Marketing Workshop for marketing staff, management and senior management of client organizations; Getting to Real.

13950 ■ The Chatham Group Inc.
47 George Ryder Rd.
PO Box 780
Chatham, MA 02633
Ph:(508)945-2675
Fax:(508)945-4888
Co. E-mail: info@chathamgroup.com
URL: http://www.chathamgroup.com
Contact: Frederick T. Miller, President
E-mail: miller@atschathamgroup.com
Scope: Management consulting firm specializing in the areas of strategy, competitive positioning, governance, and organizational effectiveness. The philosophy of CGI is based on three tenets: information driven strategy, multi-discipline teams to assure requisite expertise, and state of the art applications of knowledge and technology. Principal industries served: advertising and public relations, arts, cultural education, health, minority entrepreneurs, philanthropy, professional firms, service, social service, and government agencies. **Seminars:** Board development, planning, and management.

13951 ■ Construction Resources Inc.
120 Spring Water Rd.
Poland, ME 04274
Ph:(207)998-2747
Fax:(207)998-5733
Co. E-mail: tommuller@fairpoint.net
Contact: Thomas A. Muller, President
E-mail: tom.muller@maineairparks.com
Scope: Provides services to existing and startup businesses in the areas of market research, leads and analysis; introduces new products and product lines to the market; writes business plans; refers clients to financing sources and negotiates loans.

13952 ■ Consumer Research Corp.
445 Butler Sq.
Minneapolis, MN 55403
Ph:(612)332-8741
Fax:(612)332-8617
Co. E-mail: crc@conresco.com
URL: http://www.conresco.com
Contact: David L. Frey, President
E-mail: dfrey@conresco.com
Scope: Offers comprehensive market research and planning for every phase of marketing, including strategic planning, consumer and marketing research, acquisition analysis, trade research, opinion polls,

retail site location, communications research and focus groups. Serves private industries as well as government agencies.

13953 ■ The Coxe Group Inc.
Securities Bldg., 1904 3rd Ave., Ste. 229
Seattle, WA 98101-1194
Ph:(206)467-4040
Fax:(206)467-4038
Co. E-mail: info@coxegroup.com
URL: http://www.coxegroup.com
Contact: Thomas Kvan, Principle
E-mail: ssilverman@atscoxegroup.com
Scope: Offers counsel in organization management, marketing planning, market research, financial management, ownership transition, and mergers/acquisitions. Exclusively serves the design community, i.e. architects, engineers, planners, etc. worldwide. **Publications:** "Being a Real Architect Means Being a Conscientious Practitioner, Spring," 2008; "Those Without Courage Step Aside, Summer," 2008; "So You're Starting a Practice," 2007; "Practice Made Simple," 2006; "Observations From Prague," 2005; "Tips for Anticipating and Strategizing for the Next Ten Years," 2005; "Cultural Understanding the First Step to Successful Offshoring Strategy," 2005; "Sell, Acquire, Merge: Another Perspective," 2005; "Architects Advised to Get Smart About Design Competitions," 2004; "Architect's Essentials of Ownership Transition," John Wiley And Qmp; Sons Inc, 2002; "Architect's Essentials of Starting a Design Firm," John Wiley and Sons Inc, 2002; "So You're Starting a Practice". **Seminars:** Marketing Coordinators Clinic; Leadership Development Programs; Clinic for Marketing Professionals; Advanced Marketing Workshop; Effective Negotiations; Marketing Workshop; Project Management Workshop; Project Process Workshop; Selling Skills Clinic.

13954 ■ Creative Research International Inc.
4950 Yonge St., Ste. 1002
North York, ON, Canada M2N 6K1
Ph:(416)250-8500
Fax:(416)250-8515
Co. E-mail: info@crii.com
Contact: Robert J. Stewart, Vice President
E-mail: bob@atscrii.com
Scope: Custom research firm specializing in design, implementation, analysis and reporting of all types of public opinion, marketing and advertising research. Multi-disciplinary professional staff to handle government, commercial assignments, large or small studies, marketing models, and group interviews. Conducts syndicated studies on social values.

13955 ■ Customer Perspectives
213 W River Rd.
Hooksett, NH 03106-2628
Ph:(603)647-1300
Free: 800-277-4677
Fax:(603)647-0900
Co. E-mail: info@customerperspectives.com
URL: http://www.customerperspectives.com
Contact: Laura Sevigny, Operations Mgr
Scope: A market research consultancy specializing in mystery shopping. **Special Services:** Customer Perspectives™.

13956 ■ The Fairfield Factor Inc.
30 Main St., Ste. 407
Danbury, CT 06810-3040
Ph:(203)798-8850
Fax:(203)798-8779
Co. E-mail: mail@fairfieldfactor.com
URL: http://www.fairfieldfactor.com
Contact: Tanner Louis, Mgr
E-mail: artk@fairfieldfactor.com
Scope: Marketing consulting and research firm that offers business-to-business communications for high technology and industrial markets; copy writing that naturally communicates the value and benefits of the latest advances in product design, materials, assembly and electronic components, information technologies, manufacturing equipment and systems, packaging and allied support services across a broad spectrum of applications; knowledgeable and experienced in all high-tech sectors: medical device and other precision-sensitive industries are a particular focus; concept development and proposal writing for

new business initiatives; market research; competitive intelligence; marketing and sales presentations; news releases and public relations with targeted distribution to all industry-relevant print and electronic media; development and promotion strategies and services for high technology trade show organizers and publishers.

13957 ■ Goldhaber Research Associates L.L.C.
1525 Amherst Manor Dr., Ste. 907
Williamsville, NY 14221
Ph:(716)689-3311
Fax:(716)689-3342
Co. E-mail: employment@goldhaber.com
URL: http://www.goldhaber.com
Contact: Paul Leiner, Principle
E-mail: paul@atsgoldhaber.com
Scope: Full service market research company that specializes in custom-designed market studies, public opinion research and communication research. Industries served: Business, finance, real estate development, politics entertainment arts and the legal profession. **Publications:** "Organizational Communication". **Seminars:** Design and Development of a Product Warning System.

13958 ■ Ilium Associates Inc.
600 108th Ave. NE, Ste. 660
Bellevue, WA 98004-5110
Ph:(425)646-6525
Free: 800-874-6525
Fax:(425)646-6522
Co. E-mail: ilium@ilium.com
URL: http://www.ilium.com
E-mail: ilium@ilium.com
Scope: Marketing consultants active in market research and analysis, marketing planning, product and packaging design and graphics, as well as architectural design, graphics, signage, electronics. Industries served: transportation, real estate development, architecture, manufacturing, software publishing and government agencies worldwide.

13959 ■ Industrial Technology Consultants
PO Box 100589
Denver, CO 80250-0589
Ph:(303)422-3431
Fax:(303)997-8977
Co. E-mail: drlynn@iindustrialtechnologyconsultants. net
URL: http://www.industrialtechnologyconsultants.net
Contact: Nan R. Schouweiler, CEO
E-mail: nanno@atsindustrialtechnologyconsultants. net
Scope: Designs; develops and utilizes specific research models which identify multi-million dollar opportunities. Models are provided for: Mergers and Acquisitions; Research and Development of New Technologies and Products; Competitor Evaluations; Market Assessments; Sales and Forecast Models and Distribution Channel Strategies. **Seminars:** Proprietary Marketing Intelligence Research Gathering Techniques; How to Insulate Your Organization Against Competitive Data Gathering; Industrial Expionage Techniques and Strategies; New Business Development; Competitive Marketing Intelligence; Customer Strategic Intelligence Research.

13960 ■ Irwin Broh & Associates Inc.
1011 E Touhy Ave., Ste. 450
Des Plaines, IL 60018
Ph:(847)297-7515
Fax:(847)297-7847
Co. E-mail: info@irwinbroh.com
URL: http://www.irwinbroh.com
Contact: Ron Malek, Principle
E-mail: tjackowiak@atsirwinbroh.com
Scope: Offers research services in market strategy, acquisition, market and customer analysis, new products, customer satisfaction, advertising, and market segmentation studies. Provides both custom and syndicated research. Industries served: sporting goods, recreation, marine, outdoor power equipment, publishing hardware, industrial products, and government in the United States.

13961 ■ Ken Berwitz Marketing Research
9 S Main St.
PO Box 464
Marlboro, NJ 07746-1539
Ph:(732)780-5657
Fax:(732)780-5657
Co. E-mail: kbmr@optonline.net
Contact: Ken Berwitz, President
Scope: Conducts market research specializing in focus group research. Work involves both qualitative and quantitative methods. Industries served: manufacturers, communications, insurance, and advertising. **Publications:** "The Hopelessly Partisan Guide to American Politics: An Irreverent Look at the Private Lives of Republicans and Democrats," Select Books, Sep, 2006; "Ken Berwitz marketing research Guide".

13962 ■ Harold L. Kestenbaum P.C.
1425 Rexcorp Plz., E Twr., 15th Fl.
Uniondale, NY 11556
Ph:(516)745-0099
Fax:(516)745-0293
Co. E-mail: hkestenbaum@farrellfritz.com
URL: http://www.franchiseatty.com
Contact: Harold L. Kestenbaum, Principal
E-mail: hkesten@worldnet.att.net
Scope: Provides consulting services for startup and existing franchisors. Services include feasibility studies, determination of franchise format, business plan development, capital resources, manual preparation and legal services. Practices franchise law and provides marketing services as well. Serves all industries. **Publications:** "Four tips to starting a successful franchise".

13963 ■ Kidfacts Research
3331 W Big Beaver Rd.
Troy, MI 48084
Ph:(248)816-6772
Fax:(248)816-6778
Co. E-mail: kidfacts@kidfacts.com
Contact: Dana Blackwell, Principle
Scope: Market research firm specializes in qualitative research with children, teens and parents. Expertise in toys and games, food and beverages, clothing, computer software, electronic interactive media, television, entertainment and advertising research. Services include research, analysis and report presentation.

13964 ■ Lynn Greenberg Associates
36 Country Ridge Rd.
Scarsdale, NY 10583
Ph:(914)478-1296
Fax:(914)472-4051
Co. E-mail: lgaresearch@cs.com
URL: http://www.lynngreenberg.com
Contact: Lynn P. Greenberg, President
Scope: Marketing research firm offering strategic planning services and research involving both qualitative and quantitative methods. Experienced with focus groups, interviewing, new product development and marketing, packaging, and advertising. The children's market is a specialty. **Seminars:** The Art of the Immediate Debrief; What you Don't Learn in Moderating School; Report Writing Alternatives; Sharing Secrets of Success; Taking your Business to the Next Level; The New Normal Consumer: Understanding the Consumer in Uncertain Times.

13965 ■ Maritz Inc.
1375 N Hwy. Dr.
PO Box 26102
Fenton, MO 63099
Ph:(636)827-4000
Free: 877-462-7489
Fax:(636)827-3312
Co. E-mail: info@maritz.com
URL: http://www.maritz.com
Contact: Liz Bachmann, Principle
E-mail: liz.bachmann@atsmaritz.com
Scope: Offers sales and marketing services including employee recognition programs, incentive travel programs, learning programs, loyalty marketing, marketing research, meetings and events organization, sales incentives and sponsorship marketing. Industries served: consumer, industrial, medical and

healthcare. **Seminars:** Creating a Successful Health and Productivity Strategy, Mar, 2009; Coaching Your Sales Team to Higher Levels of Performance, Nov, 2005.

13966 ■ Mark Clements Research Inc.
25 Barker St., Ste. 309
Mount Kisco, NY 10549
Ph:(212)221-2470
Fax:(212)221-7628
Co. E-mail: information@markclementsresearch.com
URL: http://www.markclementsresearch.com
Contact: Martin J. Feldman, VP of Sales
E-mail: mjfharvey@aol.com
Scope: Marketing research consultants active in marketing management, sales and product research for magazines, manufacturers, media ad agencies and associations. Studies individually designed, quantitative or qualitative, to answer clients needs and problems.

13967 ■ Mayeri Research Inc.
134 West 92nd St.
New York, NY 10025
Ph:(707)944-8585
Free: 888-282-0155
Fax:(707)581-1721
Co. E-mail: inetpoll@internetpoll.com
URL: http://www.internetpoll.com
Contact: Harriet Mayeri, Principal
E-mail: ray@atsmayeriresearch.com
Scope: Specializes in the design, execution and analysis of research us in gone-on-one computer-conducted interviewing and online interviewing via the internet and e-mail. **Special Services:** Internet Poll™; The Internet Poll™; EmailPoll™; The Email Poll™.

13968 ■ Musicals Tonight Inc.
455 Vallejo St.
San Francisco, CA 94133
Ph:(212)362-5620
Co. E-mail: contactus@musicalstonight.org
URL: http://www.musicalstonight.org
Contact: Melvin Miller, President
Scope: A not-for-profit theatre company involved in theatrical productions for the revival of neglected musicals in a manner affordable to most audience members.

13969 ■ Opinion Research of California
917 Pine Ave.
Long Beach, CA 90813-4325
Ph:(562)432-0474
Fax:(562)432-6911
Contact: Donald L. McGrew, President
Scope: Marketing research consultants offering survey research and statistical testing.

13970 ■ Paul A. Warner Associates Inc.
5600 Roswell Rd., Ste. 300 N
Atlanta, GA 30342
Ph:(404)239-0101
Fax:(404)237-1235
Co. E-mail: john@pwarner.com
URL: http://www.pwarner.com
Contact: Paul A. Warner, President
E-mail: paul@atspwarner.com
Scope: Marketing research and marketing consulting in African-American and urban culture markets. **Special Services:** Qualitative Research; Quantitative Research.

13971 ■ The Performance Group Inc.
233 Main St.
PO Box 828
Mount Vernon, IN 47620-1839
Ph:(812)838-9814
Fax:(812)838-8076
Co. E-mail: wb@pgiresearch.com
Contact: Walter E. Babcock Jr., President
E-mail: wb@pgiresearch.com
Scope: Marketing research firm.

13972 ■ Psychological Insights Inc.
2000 N Ocean Blvd., Ste. 102
Boca Raton, FL 33431-7818
Ph:(561)750-1123
Fax:(561)750-1102
Contact: Renee H. Frengut, President
Scope: Offers advertising, media, new product, and market research services aimed at a mature market.

13973 ■ Research USA Inc.
180 N Wacker Dr., Ste. 202
Chicago, IL 60606
Ph:(847)762-7850
Free: 800-863-4800
Fax:(312)658-0085
Co. E-mail: info@researchusainc.com
URL: http://www.researchusainc.com
Contact: Lawrence Tootikian, CEO
E-mail: cj@atsresearchusainc.com
Scope: Provides marketing research expertise to publications, associations, and businesses in the entire World.

13974 ■ The Spectrem Group Inc.
641 W Lake St., Ste. 402
Chicago, IL 60661
Ph:(312)382-8284
Fax:(312)382-8283
Co. E-mail: info@spectrem.com
URL: http://www.spectrem.com
Contact: Tom Wynn, Managering Director
E-mail: twynn@atsspectrem.com
Scope: Provides strategic consulting and market research services to financial services clients sewing the affluent and retirement markets. **Publications:** "Affluent Market Insights," 2009; "Ultra Rich Invest Far More Aggressively Than Other Wealthy Individuals," Nov, 2007.

13975 ■ Sumerford System Seven L.L.C.
333 Singing Quail Trl.
Haslet, TX 76052
Ph:(817)439-0928
Co. E-mail: w2@sumerford7.com
URL: http://www.sumerford7.com
Contact: Kenneth Scott Sumerford, President
Scope: Offers marketing services especially marketing databases, market research and direct marketing and information systems for small companies. Provides off-the-shelf marketing software and develops custom software applications. Provides services in Web site creation, web page enhancement, web page design and content, e commerce, and database programming. Industries served: manufacturing, sales and marketing organizations, real estate agents, office managers, and small business owners. **Publications:** "One True Friend," 2007. **Special Services:** Sumerford Marketing Database 1™; Sumerford Real Estate1™.

13976 ■ Technology Management Associates Inc.
1699 Wall St., Ste. 515
Mount Prospect, IL 60056
Ph:(312)984-5050
Fax:(312)984-5057
Co. E-mail: jogucwa@techmanage.com
URL: http://www.techmanage.com
Contact: Joanne F. Gucwa, President
E-mail: jogucwa@techmanage.com
Scope: Offers research and development strategic planning, high-technology business analysis, industrial marketing, sales strategy, environmental expertise, and general management consulting. Assists organizations in reaching their business goals more efficiently and more profitably. Serves entrepreneurs, governments, associations, and international management clients worldwide. **Publications:** "Three Indisputable Truths About Business Intelligence and The Internet"; "Beyond Customer Satisfaction"; "Keys to Creating Successful New Products"; "Increased Profitability By Building Customer Loyalty"; "Global-scale partnering and business alliances"; "10 Keys to Collecting Information"; "The Thinking Manager's Toolbox: Effective Processes for Problem Solving and Decision Making"; "My Say"; "Successful Project Management"; "Thinking Through the Privatization Option"; "Your Marketing Mindset"; "Intellectual Capital: The New Wealth of Organizations"; "Lean and Meaningful"; "Nuts!: Southwest Airlines' Crazy Recipe for Business and Personal Success"; "If Aristotle Ran General Motors: The New Soul of Business"; "Real Time: Preparing for the Age of the Never

Satisfied Customer"; "Webonomics: Nine Essential Principles for Growing your Business on the World Wide Web"; "Asia Rising"; "Customer Centered Growth: Five Proven Strategies for Building Competitive Advantage"; "Cybercorp: The New Business Revolution"; "Net Gain: Expanding Markets Through Virtual Communities"; "Strategic Cost Management"; "Three Indisputable Truths About Business Intelligence and the Internet"; "Leveraging Technology To Build Customer Loyalty"; "Practical and Effective Customer Satisfaction Studies".

13977 ■ Vertex Consultants Inc.
111 Queen St. E, Ste. 501
Toronto, ON, Canada M5C 1S2
Ph:(416)968-9397
Fax:(416)920-6975
Co. E-mail: mnesbitt@vertexconsultants.com
URL: http://www.vertexconsultants.com
Contact: Lynn Gadue, Accounting Manager
E-mail: lynn.gadue@atsvertexconsulting.com
Scope: A management consultancy whose practice focus is on the intersection between strategy and implementation. Committed to helping clients identify and implement profitable change. Core services include: Assisting insetting and evolving effective strategy; assisting in the implementation of strategy throughout the organization; and research.

13978 ■ Young & Associates Inc.
121 E Main St.
PO Box 711
Kent, OH 44240
Ph:(330)678-0524
Free: 800-525-9775
Fax:(330)678-6219
Co. E-mail: online@younginc.com
URL: http://www.younginc.com
Contact: Stephen Clinton, Vice President
E-mail: sclinton@younginc.com
Scope: Provides a variety of management consulting, outsourcing, educational, and research services, including strategic planning, risk management, capital planning, mergers and acquisitions, internal audit, branching and expansion, loan review, information technology, marketing, market research, human resources planning and management, site/location feasibility studies, development of business plans, and organizational analysis and development and regulatory compliance. Specialists in small and mid-size companies. Industries served: financial institutions, manufacturers (business-to-business and consumer), banking, healthcare (hospitals and practitioners), retailers, and services. **Publications:** "An Avalanche of New Compliance Regulations," Oct, 2009; "Fair Lending Risk Assessment," May, 2009. **Special Services:** The Compliance Monitoring System™; Compliance Monitoring Update Service™; The Compliance Review Program™; Compliance Review Program Update Service™.

FRANCHISES AND BUSINESS OPPORTUNITIES

13979 ■ Fransurvey.com
Franchise Research Institute
PO Box 6385
Lincoln, NE 68506-0385
Free: 800-410-5205
Fax:(402)477-3898
Description: Complete market research services.

LIBRARIES

13980 ■ Advertising Research Foundation Information Center
432 Park Ave., S.
New York, NY 10016
Ph:(212)751-5656
Fax:(212)319-5265
Co. E-mail: mihui@thearf.org
URL: http://www.thearf.org
Contact: Mi hui Pak
Scope: Market research, advertising, research methods, media research. **Services:** Library open to members. **Holdings:** 3000 volumes; 2000 vertical files of clippings, reports, surveys. **Subscriptions:** 110 journals and other serials.

13981 ■ BayerDiag, a Bayer Company Library
63 North St.
Medfield, MA 02052
Ph:(508)359-3538
Fax:(508)359-3442
Co. E-mail: kathleen.mccabe.b@bayer.com
URL: http://www.bayerdiag.com/
Contact: Kathleen E. McCabe, Mgr. of Info.Ctrs.
Scope: Clinical medicine, market research, engineering, biotechnology, business. **Services:** Center not open to the public. **Holdings:** 3000 books; 3500 periodical volumes; 28,000 patents; 850 research reports. **Subscriptions:** 425 journals and other serials.

13982 ■ Business Trend Analysts Library
2171 Jericho Tpke., Ste. 200
Commack, NY 11725
Ph:(631)462-5454
Free: 800-866-4648
Fax:(631)462-1842
Co. E-mail: sales@bta-ler.com
URL: http://www.businesstrendanalysts.com
Contact: J. Marquardt, Libn.
Scope: Marketing, business, economics. **Services:** Library not open to the public. **Holdings:** 200 reports. **Subscriptions:** 400 journals and other serials; 8 newspapers.

13983 ■ Clapp and Mayne Library
8401 Colesville Rd., Ste. 425
Silver Spring, MD 20910-3363
Ph:(301)495-9572
URL: http://www.nbr-bd.org/nbrweb/Support/supportPage1.htm
Scope: Marketing research, economics. **Services:** Library open to the public with restrictions. **Holdings:** 4000 books; 1000 reports. **Subscriptions:** 10 journals and other serials.

13984 ■ Elrick and Lavidge Library
3 Westbrook Corporate Center, Ste. 600
Westchester, IL 60154
Ph:(708)449-5300
Fax:(708)449-4498
Contact: Theresa Litoborski, Libn.
Scope: Market research, marketing, consumer behavior, business and management, industry, statistics. **Services:** Interlibrary loan; Library not open to the public. **Holdings:** 300 books; 7 VF drawers of pamphlets; 2 drawers of maps; 100 directories; 283 telephone directories; census publications. **Subscriptions:** 50 journals and other serials.

13985 ■ Frankel & Company Information Center
111 E. Wacker Dr.
Chicago, IL 60601
Ph:(312)552-5197
Fax:(312)552-5424
Co. E-mail: Karen_trimberger@frankel.com
Contact: Karen Trimberger
Scope: Marketing, sales promotion. **Services:** Interlibrary loan; center open to the public by appointment. **Holdings:** 20 books. **Subscriptions:** 100 journals and other serials; 5 newspapers.

13986 ■ General Mills Business Information Center
PO Box 1113
Minneapolis, MN 55440-1113
Ph:(763)764-7747
Fax:(763)764-4742
Co. E-mail: pat.ewald@genmills.com
Contact: Pat Ewald, Mgr.
Scope: Business, marketing, food industry. **Services:** Center not open to the public. **Holdings:** 800 books; 22,000 internal marketing research reports, electronic, hardcopy and microfiche. **Subscriptions:** 180 journals and other serials; 5 newspapers.

13987 ■ IIMI Information Center
4205 K St.
Philadelphia, PA 19124
Ph:(215)537-1790
Contact: Albert C. Vara
Scope: Marketing; food research; job location; population studies; multicultural sources; area studies; African-American, Asian-American, and Hispanic writers; company personnel information. **Services:** Library not open to the public. **Holdings:** 2700 books; 95 bound periodical volumes; 1990 reports; manuscripts; 16 VF drawers of documents and reports; 2000 microfiche. **Subscriptions:** 54 journals and other serials; 6 newspapers.

13988 ■ Marketemps–Marketing Intelligence Center
3435 Ocean Park Blvd., Ste. 112
Santa Monica, CA 90405
Ph:(310)471-5590
Fax:(310)471-0932
Contact: Clifford S. Lightfoot, Prin.
Scope: Marketing intelligence, new product development, growth industries, market trends, technology assessment, technology transfer, commercialization, trade shows. **Services:** Provides marketing outsourcing services and executive recruiting; center open to the public on fee basis. **Holdings:** 500 books; 200 reports and presentations, start-up businesses. **Subscriptions:** 40 journals and other serials; 5 newspapers.

13989 ■ MORPACE International Library
31700 Middlebelt Rd., Ste. 200
Farmington Hills, MI 48334-2373
Ph:(248)737-5300
Fax:(248)737-5326
Co. E-mail: information@morpace.com
URL: http://www.morpace.com/
Contact: Patricia Watkins, Mgr. of Info.Rsrcs.
Scope: Market, automotive, and consumer research. **Services:** Library not open to the public. **Holdings:** 4000 proprietary reports and surveys. **Subscriptions:** 125 journals and other serials; 7 newspapers.

13990 ■ Ricerca Biosciences–Information Services
7528 Auburn Rd.
PO Box 1000
Concord, OH 44077-1000
Ph:(440)357-3300
Free: 888-742-3722
Fax:(440)763-4797
Co. E-mail: info@ricerca.com
URL: http://www.ricerca.com
Contact: R. Ian Lennox, Chm./CEO
Scope: Pharmaceuticals, chemistry, agriculture, business, biotechnology, engineering, management, marketing research, finance. **Services:** Library not open to the public. **Holdings:** 2000 books; 2500 bound periodical volumes; 3000 reels of microfilm. **Subscriptions:** 50 journals and other serials.

13991 ■ Silver Burdett & Ginn–Editorial Library
299 Jefferson Rd.
Parsippany, NJ 07054
Ph:(973)739-8000
Fax:(973)898-0114
Scope: General education, publishing, market research. **Services:** Library not open to the public. **Holdings:** 10,000 books. **Subscriptions:** 150 journals and other serials.

13992 ■ The Vineyard–Real Estate, Shopping Center & Urban Development Information Center
100 W. Shaw Ave.
Fresno, CA 93704
Ph:(209)222-0182
Contact: Richard Erganian, Info.Dir.
Scope: Real estate, shopping centers, urban and regional planning, architecture, mortgage financing, market research, landscaping. **Services:** Library open to real estate developers. **Holdings:** 3000 books; 500 bound periodical volumes; 2000 other cataloged items; 30 real estate transcripts; 50 shopping center development transcripts; 20 appraisal tapes and cassettes; 25 income property reports and transcripts; 150 video cassettes. **Subscriptions:** 25 journals and other serials; 5 newspapers.

Martial Arts Studio

ASSOCIATIONS AND OTHER ORGANIZATIONS

13993 ■ American Amateur Karate Federation
445 S Figueroa St., Ste. 2600
Los Angeles, CA 90071
Free: 888-939-8882
Fax:888-939-8555
Co. E-mail: office@aakf.org
URL: http://www.aakf.org
Contact: Mr. Robert Graves
Description: Represents karate clubs and schools representing over 20000 individuals. Serves as a national governing body for karate. Seeks to improve the physical and mental health of the public through the practice of karate; promotes public understanding of karate. Establishes competition standards such as rules, judging, and athlete qualifications. Sets ranking standards in accordance with international standards. Sanctions and conducts national competitions including the All America Karate Championship; recognizes karate practitioners. Plans and executes karate development programs. Sponsors U.S. team development camp, national summer training course, U.S. regional instructor program, championship ranking and judging programs, and examiner qualification program. **Publications:** *Ranking and Examination Guide* (periodic); *Times Newsletter* (monthly).

13994 ■ American Kenpo Karate International
PO Box 768
Evanston, WY 82931
Ph:(307)789-4124
Co. E-mail: akki@allwest.net
URL: http://www.akki.com
Contact: Mr. Paul Mills, Pres./Founder
Description: Seeks to preserve, honor, and elevate the strength of Kenpo Karate. Sponsors competitions. Maintains educational, charitable, and research programs, children's services, and a speakers' bureau. *1st Level Club Manual; 1st Level Knife Manual; Kenpo Karate-Works; Professional Business Guide* .

13995 ■ Canadian Kendo Federation–Federation Canadienne de Kendo
8013 Hunter St.
Burnaby, BC, Canada V5A 2B8
Ph:(604)420-0438
Fax:(604)420-1971
Co. E-mail: hokusa@kendo-canada.com
URL: http://kendo-canada.com
Contact: Hiro Okusa, Pres.
Description: Kendo enthusiasts. Promotes increased interest and participation in Kendo, a Japanese form of swordsmanship. Facilitates creation of Kendo clubs; conducts educational programs; sponsors competitions. **Publications:** *Kendo Referee Handbook* .

13996 ■ International Traditional Karate Federation
1930 Wilshire Blvd., Ste. 503
Los Angeles, CA 90057-3603
Ph:(213)483-8262

Fax:(213)483-4060
Co. E-mail: office@itkf.org
URL: http://www.itkf.org
Description: Represents national karate federations. Provides international rules, regulations, and competition standards for traditional karate; sanctions international competitions and seminars. **Publications:** *Official Circular* (biweekly).

13997 ■ Tomiki Aikido of the Americas
5752 S Kingston Way
Englewood, CO 80111
Ph:(303)740-7424
Co. E-mail: nettles@tomiki.org
URL: http://www.tomiki.org
Contact: Seiji Tanaka, Chm./Dir.
Description: Fosters international amateur sports competition. Seeks to introduce and promote the Japanese martial art Aikido by organizing training camps, exhibitions, and tournaments around the world. Promotes international and intercultural exchange, education, and understanding. **Publications:** *The Aikido Times* (quarterly).

13998 ■ United States Judo Association
PO Box 1880
Tarpon Springs, FL 34688-1880
Free: 877-411-3409
Fax:888-276-3432
Co. E-mail: membership@usja-judo.org
URL: http://www.usja-judo.org
Contact: Gary S. Goltz, Pres.
Description: Amateur judo athletes and coaches. Promotes the recreational and physical benefits of judo; advocates practice of the sport to develop sportsmanship, good citizenship, and mental well-being. Encourages public interest and participation in Judo. Seeks the advancement of amateur judo competition in the U.S. and worldwide. Maintains National Judo Hall of Fame. Sanctions local, state, and regional tournaments. Offers training and certification program for coaches and referees. **Publications:** *American Judo Magazine* (quarterly).

13999 ■ U.S. Taekwondo Union
1 Olympic Plz.
Colorado Springs, CO 80909
Ph:(719)866-4632
Fax:(719)866-4642
Co. E-mail: david.askinas@usa-taekwondo.us
URL: http://www.usa-taekwondo.us
Contact: David Askinas, CEO
Description: A member of the United States Olympic Committee and the national governing body for the sport of Taekwondo. Amateur Taekwondo athletes and instructors. Promotes Taekwondo programs in the U.S. and represents the U.S. in the Olympics and World Championships and other international competitions under sanction of the World Taekwondo Federation. Offers referee and coaching certification programs; conducts seminars. Sponsors competitions; selects national Olympic Taekwondo teams. **Publications:** *U.S. Referee Seminar; U.S. Taekwondo Journal* (annual); *USTU Club Newsletter* (bimonthly).

14000 ■ U.S.A. Karate Federation
1550 Ritchie Rd.
Stow, OH 44224
Co. E-mail: usakarate@usakarate.us
URL: http://www.usakarate.org
Contact: Patrick M. Hickey, Pres.
Description: Individuals, corporations, sports organizations, and karate clubs. Serves as a national federation for karate in the U.S. Seeks to promote karate as a sport and to advance karate performance and instruction; certifies karate instructors. Organizes competitions, selects U.S. a national karate team. Conducts classes for karate students and masters. Conducts research; compiles statistics; maintains hall of fame and speakers' bureau. .

14001 ■ World Martial Arts Association
Redeemer St. John's Church
939 - 83rd St.
Brooklyn, NY 11228
Ph:(718)833-9039
URL: http://www.wmaa.com
Contact: Michael T. Dealy
Description: Persons interested in the martial arts. Purpose is to teach, promote, and grade the technical aspects of martial arts such as judo, karate, tae kwon do, kung fu, jujitsu, and aikido. .

14002 ■ Zen-do Kai Martial Arts
PO Box 186
Johnstown, NY 12095
Ph:(518)762-1589
Fax:(518)762-1589
Co. E-mail: director@zdkusa.com
URL: http://www.zdkusa.com
Contact: Michael J. Campos, Dir.
Description: Martial art clubs. Teaches Shotokan, Shokukai, Uechi-Ryu, Pentjak-Silat, and Tae Kwon Do styles of karate. Sponsors tournaments and anti-rape and police training seminars. Conducts demonstrations of the martial arts. Organizes martial arts sports production. Conducts instructor training programs. Provides guest instructors and seminars; maintains hall of fame and speakers' bureau; sponsors competitions. Offers children's services and charitable program. **Publications:** *The Warrior* (quarterly).

TRADE PERIODICALS

14003 ■ *Black Belt Magazine*
Pub: Ohara
Ed: Jim Coleman, Editor. **Released:** Monthly. **Price:** $24; $45 two years; $36 Canada; $69 Canada two years; $48 other countries; $93 other countries two years. **Description:** Self-defense magazine featuring various martial arts, including how-to's, historical and current events in the martial arts. Audience ranges from pre-teens to 50's.

14004 ■ *T'ai Chi*
Pub: Wayfarer Publications
Contact: Marvin Smalheiser, Editor & Publisher
Released: Bimonthly. **Price:** $20; $5.99 single issue U.S.; $6.25 single issue international; $30 other

countries; $30 two years; $50 other countries two years. **Description:** A magazine for practitioners of T'ai Chi and related martial arts, health and fitness disciplines.

14005 ■ *The Warrior*
Pub: Zen-Do Kai Martial Arts Association

Ed: Michael J. Campos, Editor. **Released:** Quarterly. **Description:** Reports on activities of the Association and its member clubs, Karate philosophy, and other material of interest to members. Recurring features include tournament news and announcements of special events.

14006 ■ *The World of ASP*
Pub: American Self-Protection Association (ASP)

Ed: Nellie Baltazzi, Editor, ebaltazzi@aol.com. **Released:** Quarterly. **Price:** Included in membership. **Description:** Encourages the development of self-defense and physical fitness programs in YMCAs (Young Men's Christian Associations) and schools across the U.S. Highlights research conducted in the field of combative arts. Recurring features include notices of publications available, news of members, and announcements of upcoming radio, television, and group presentations.

VIDEOCASSETTES/ AUDIOCASSETTES

14007 ■ *Daito-Ryu Revelations*
Keen Media
857 Pulpit Rock Circle N.
Colorado Springs, CO 80918
Ph:(719)593-2155
Free: 800-363-5336
Fax:(719)593-2888
Co. E-mail: jim@keenmedia.com
URL: http://www.keenmedia.com

Released: 1995. **Price:** $99. **Description:** Two-part set features advanced martial arts instruction from master Seigo Okamoto. **Availability:** VHS.

14008 ■ *Daito-Ryu Secrets*
Keen Media
857 Pulpit Rock Circle N.
Colorado Springs, CO 80918
Ph:(719)593-2155
Free: 800-363-5336

Fax:(719)593-2888
Co. E-mail: jim@keenmedia.com
URL: http://www.keenmedia.com
Released: 1995. **Price:** $99. **Description:** Two-part set features martial arts instruction from master Seigo Okamoto. **Availability:** VHS.

14009 ■ *Guide to Karate-Do*
ESPN Home Video
ESPN Plz., 935 Middle St.
Bristol, CT 06010
Ph:(860)766-2000
Fax:(860)585-2213
URL: http://www.espn.go.com
Price: $19.95. **Description:** James Coffman, 7th degree black belt champion, teaches the discipline of Okinawan Shorin-Ryu karate. **Availability:** VHS.

14010 ■ *Tao of Karate*
Videomaker
PO Box 4591
Chico, CA 95927
Ph:(530)891-8410
Free: 800-284-3226
Fax:(530)891-8443
Co. E-mail: customerservice@videomaker.com
URL: http://www.videomaker.com
Price: $9.99. **Description:** Provides an introductory lesson in karate. **Availability:** VHS.

Masonry, Stonework, and Plastering Contractors

ASSOCIATIONS AND OTHER ORGANIZATIONS

14011 ■ American Society of Civil Engineers
1801 Alexander Bell Dr.
Reston, VA 20191-4400
Ph:(703)295-6300
Free: 800-548-2723
Fax:(703)295-6333
Co. E-mail: pnatale@asce.org
URL: http://www.asce.org
Contact: Patrick J. Natale, Exec. Dir.
Description: Enhances the welfare of humanity by advancing the science and profession of engineering. Offers continuing education courses and technical specialty conferences. Develops technical codes and standards. Works closely with Congress, the White House and federal agencies to build sound national policy on engineering issues. Supports research of new civil engineering technology and material. Informs the public about various engineering-related topics. **Publications:** *ASCE Publications Information* (bimonthly); *Civil Engineering* (monthly); *Emerging Technology* (bimonthly); *Manuals and Reports on Engineering Practice* (periodic); *Worldwide Projects* (quarterly).

14012 ■ Association of the Wall and Ceiling Industries International
513 W Broad St., Ste. 210
Falls Church, VA 22046
Ph:(703)538-1600
Fax:(703)534-8307
Co. E-mail: info@awci.org
URL: http://www.awci.org
Contact: Brent Allen, Pres.
Description: Acoustical tile, drywall, demountable partitions, lathing and plastering, fireproofing, light-gauge steel framing, stucco and exterior insulation finish systems contractors, suppliers and manufacturers. **Publications:** *Construction Dimensions Magazine* (monthly); *Information Resources* .

14013 ■ Brick Industry Association
1850 Centennial Park Dr., Ste. 301
Reston, VA 20191
Ph:(703)620-0010
Fax:(703)620-3928
Co. E-mail: brickinfo@bia.org
URL: http://www.gobrick.com
Contact: J. Gregg Borchelt, Pres./CEO
Description: Manufacturers and distributors of clay brick. Promotes clay brick with the goal of increasing its market share. **Publications:** *Annual Sales and Marketing Report* (annual); *BIA News* (monthly); *Brick in Architecture* (quarterly); *Directory of Manufacturers* (annual).

14014 ■ Building Stone Institute
PO Box 419
5 Riverside Dr., Bldg. 2
Chestertown, NY 12817
Ph:(518)803-4336
Free: (866)786-6313

Fax:(518)803-6313
Co. E-mail: jane@buildingstoneinstitute.org
URL: http://www.buildingstoneinstitute.org
Contact: Jane Bennett, Exec. VP
Description: Represents natural stone quarriers, fabricators, installers, dealers, importers, expo and restorers. Serves as a clearinghouse of information for architects, contractors, and masons. Promotes the use of natural stone. **Publications:** *Building Stone Magazine* (quarterly); *Stone Information Manual*; *Who's Who in the Stone Business* (annual)-;Newsletter (monthly).

14015 ■ Ceilings and Interior Systems Construction Association
405 Illinois Ave., Unit 2B
St. Charles, IL 60174
Ph:(630)584-1919
Fax:(866)560-8537
Co. E-mail: cisca@cisca.org
URL: http://www.cisca.org
Contact: Bill Shannon, Pres.
Description: International trade association for the advancement of the interior commercial construction industry. Provides quality education, resources and a forum for communication among its members. **Publications:** *Ceiling Systems* .

14016 ■ Indiana Limestone Institute of America
400 Stone City Bank Bldg.
Bedford, IN 47421
Ph:(812)275-4426
Fax:(812)279-8682
Co. E-mail: todd@iliai.com
URL: http://www.iliai.com
Contact: Todd Schnatzmeyer, Exec. Dir.
Description: Conducts promotional and technical services for the Indiana limestone industry; sponsors research; establishes standards; offers technical service in product use to architects, builders and owners. Maintains speakers' bureau; conducts specialized education. .

14017 ■ International Institute for Lath and Plaster
PO Box 1663
Lafayette, CA 94549
Ph:(925)283-5160
Fax:(925)283-5161
Co. E-mail: frank@lpinst.org
URL: http://www.iilp.org
Contact: Frank E. Nunes, Sec.
Description: Industry-wide federation of lathing and plastering contractors, labor organizations, and manufacturers of lathing and plastering supplies. Promotes use of lath and plaster. .

14018 ■ International Masonry Institute
The James Brice House
42 East St.
Annapolis, MD 21401
Ph:(410)280-1305
Free: 800-803-0295

Fax:(301)261-2855
Co. E-mail: masonryquestions@imiweb.org
URL: http://www.imiweb.org
Contact: Joan Baggett Calambokidis, Pres.
Description: Joint labor/management trust fund of the International Union of Bricklayers and Allied Craftworkers and union masonry contractors. Aims for the advancement of quality masonry construction through national and regional training, promotion, advertising and labor management relations programs in the U.S. and Canada. Provides support and materials for local/regional masonry promotion groups in the U.S. and Canada, and cooperates with national groups and organizations promoting the industry. Sponsors craft training and research programs. Offers educational programs. Maintains museum. **Publications:** *IMI Today* (bimonthly).

14019 ■ Mason Contractors Association of America
1481 Merchant Dr.
Algonquin, IL 60102
Ph:(224)678-9709
Free: 800-536-2225
Fax:(224)678-9714
URL: http://www.masoncontractors.org
Contact: Jeff Buczkiewicz, Exec. Dir.
Description: Masonry construction firms. Conducts specialized education and research programs. Compiles statistics. .

14020 ■ The Masonry Society
3970 Broadway, Ste. 201-D
Boulder, CO 80304-1135
Ph:(303)939-9700
Fax:(303)541-9215
Co. E-mail: info@masonrysociety.org
URL: http://www.masonrysociety.org
Contact: Mr. Phillip J. Samblanet, Exec. Dir.
Description: Represents individuals interested in the art and science of masonry. Serves as professional, technical, and educational association dedicated to the advancement and knowledge of masonry. Gathers and disseminates technical information. **Publications:** *The Masonry Society Journal*; *2011 MSJC - Masonry Building Code Requirements and Specifications for Masonry Construction* (triennial).

14021 ■ National Concrete Masonry Association
13750 Sunrise Valley Dr.
Herndon, VA 20171-4662
Ph:(703)713-1900
Fax:(703)713-1910
Co. E-mail: rthomas@ncma.org
URL: http://www.ncma.org
Contact: Robert D. Thomas, Pres.
Description: Manufacturers of concrete masonry units (concrete blocks), segmental retaining wall units and paving block; associate members are machinery, cement and aggregate manufacturers. Conducts testing and research on masonry units and masonry assemblies. Compiles statistics. **Publications:** *CM News* (monthly).

14022 ■ Precast/Prestressed Concrete Institute
200 W Adams St., No. 2100
Chicago, IL 60606
Ph:(312)786-0300
Fax:(312)621-1114
Co. E-mail: info@pci.org
URL: http://www.pci.org
Contact: James G. Toscas, Pres.
Description: Manufacturers, suppliers, educators, engineers, technicians and others interested in the design and construction of prestressed concrete. Compiles statistics. Maintains 17 committees, including marketing, technical and research committees. **Publications:** *Journal of the Precast/Prestressed Concrete Institute* (bimonthly).

14023 ■ Tile Council of North America
100 Clemson Research Blvd.
Anderson, SC 29625
Ph:(864)646-8453
Fax:(864)646-2821
Co. E-mail: info@tileusa.com
URL: http://www.tileusa.com
Contact: Kathy Snipes
Description: Manufacturers of domestic ceramic tile for floors, walls, and related products. Promotes increase in the marketability of ceramic tile. Conducts testing program on tile and tile installation materials. Supervises international licensing program with 16 licensees. Compiles statistics. **Publications:** *Directory of Manufacturers of Ceramic Tile and Related Products* (annual); *Handbook for Ceramic Tile Installation* (annual); *TileFlash* (monthly).

DIRECTORIES OF EDUCATIONAL PROGRAMS

14024 ■ *Directory of Private Accredited Career Schools and Colleges of Technology*
Pub: Accrediting Commission of Career Schools and Colleges of Technology
Contact: Michale S. McComis, Exec. Dir.
Released: On web page. **Price:** Free. **Description:** Covers 3900 accredited post-secondary programs that provide training programs in business, trade, and technical fields, including various small business endeavors. Entries offer school name, address, phone, description of courses, job placement assistance, and requirements for admission. Arrangement is alphabetical.

REFERENCE WORKS

14025 ■ *Association of the Wall and Ceiling Industries International—Buyer's Guide*
Pub: Association of the Wall and Ceiling Industries International
Contact: Brenton C. Stone, Assoc. Publisher
Ed: Laura M. Porinchak, Editor. **Released:** Annual, August. **Price:** $10, members; $20, nonmembers. **Covers:** Manufacturers and suppliers of products and equipment used in the wall and ceiling, asbestos removal, and related industries; relevant trade associations and publishers allied with the industry; coverage includes Canada. **Entries Include:** Name, address, phone; description of product or service. **Arrangement:** Alphabetical. **Indexes:** Product.

14026 ■ *Brick Industry Association—Membership Directory*
Pub: Brick Industry Association
Released: Annual. **Covers:** Brick distributors, brick manufacturers, and related service providers throughout the U.S. and Canada. **Entries Include:** Company name, address, phone, name of principal executives, list of products or services. **Arrangement:** Alphabetical by personnel.

14027 ■ "Firms Sue Doracon to Recoup More Than $1M in Unpaid Bills" in *Baltimore Business Journal* (Vol. 28, July 9, 2010, No. 9, pp. 1)
Pub: Baltimore Business Journal
Ed: Scott Dance. **Description:** Concrete supplier Paul J. Rach Inc., Selective Insurance Company, and equipment leasing firm Colonial Pacific Leasing

Corporation intend to sue Baltimore, Maryland-based Doracon Contracting Inc. for $1 million in unpaid bills. Doracon owed Colonial Pacific $794,000 and the equipment is still in Doracon's possession. Selective Insurance and Paul J. Rach respectively seek $132,000 and $88,000.

14028 ■ "Housing Slide Picks Up Speed" in *Crain's Chicago Business* (Vol. 31, April 21, 2008, No. 16, pp. 2)
Pub: Crain Communications, Inc.
Ed: Eddie Baeb. **Description:** According to Tracy Cross & Associates Inc., a real estate consultancy, sales of new homes in the Chicago area dropped 61 percent from the year-earlier period which is more bad news for homebuilders, contractors and real estate agents who are eager for an indication that market conditions are improving.

STATISTICAL SOURCES

14029 ■ *RMA Annual Statement Studies*
Pub: Robert Morris Associates (RMA)
Released: Annual. **Price:** $175.00 2006-07 edition, $105.00. **Description:** Contains composite balance sheets and income statements for more than 360 industries, including the accounting, auditing, and bookkeeping industries. Also contains five years of comparative historical data for discerning trends. Includes 16 commonly used ratios, computed for most of the size groupings for nearly every industry.

TRADE PERIODICALS

14030 ■ *CM News*
Pub: National Concrete Masonry Association
Contact: Ms. Randi Hertzberg, Adv.Mgr.
E-mail: hertzberg@worldnet.att.net
Ed: Heidi Lorence, Editor, hlorence@ncma.org. **Released:** Monthly. **Price:** Free. **Description:** Focuses on the manufacturing and marketing of concrete masonry products and the managment of production plants. Covers legislative and regulatory developments, production and marketing developments, and new products and services of interest to the industry. Also reports the news and activities of the Association. Recurring features include news of research, news of members, and a calendar of events.

14031 ■ *Stone Magazine*
Pub: Tile and Stone Inc.
Contact: Dave Anderson, Publisher/CEO
Ed: Eemrson Schwartkopf, Editor. **Released:** Monthly. **Description:** International trade publication covering the natural stone industry (marble, granite and other dimensional stone).

14032 ■ *TMS Journal*
Pub: The Masonry Society
Ed: John Chrysler, Editor. **Released:** Annual. **Price:** $55, individuals; $60, out of area. **Description:** Presents news of the activities of this Society, devoted to the use of masonry. Contains information on codes and standards, testing, research and development, education and training, inspection, quality control, construction, and public relations.

14033 ■ *Walls & Ceilings*
Pub: BNP Media
Released: Monthly. **Description:** Trade magazine for contractors, suppliers, and distributors of drywall, plaster, stucco, EIFS, acoustics, metal framing, and ceilings.

VIDEOCASSETTES/ AUDIOCASSETTES

14034 ■ *Basic Masonry*
Bergwall Productions, Inc.
1 DIckinson Drive, Brandywine BUilding 5, Ste. 105
PO Box 1481
Chadds Ford, PA 19317
Ph:(610)361-0334
Free: 800-934-8696

Fax:(610)361-0092
URL: http://www.bergwall.com
Released: 1987. **Price:** $359.00. **Description:** The basics of masonry construction are demonstrated. Also available on a single tape at the same cost. **Availability:** VHS.

14035 ■ *Masonry Block Explained*
Bergwall Productions, Inc.
1 DIckinson Drive, Brandywine BUilding 5, Ste. 105
PO Box 1481
Chadds Ford, PA 19317
Ph:(610)361-0334
Free: 800-934-8696
Fax:(610)361-0092
URL: http://www.bergwall.com
Released: 1989. **Price:** $1289.00. **Description:** The function, use, and composition of masonry is examined. Also available on a single tape at the same cost. **Availability:** VHS.

TRADE SHOWS AND CONVENTIONS

14036 ■ Construction Directions
Association of the Wall and Ceiling Industries International
513 W. Broad St., Ste. 210
Falls Church, VA 22046
Ph:(703)538-1600
Fax:(703)534-8307
Co. E-mail: info@awci.org
URL: http://www.awci.org
Released: Annual. **Audience:** Contractors, architects, distributors, and suppliers in the wall and ceiling industries. **Principal Exhibits:** Construction equipment, materials, and tools.

14037 ■ MCAA's Masonry Showcase & MCAA Annual Convention
Mason Contractors Association of America
33 S. Roselle Rd., Ste. 101
Schaumburg, IL 60193
Ph:(847)301-0001
Free: 800-536-2225
Fax:(847)301-1110
Co. E-mail: info@masoncontractors.com
URL: http://www.masoncontractors.org
Released: Annual. **Audience:** Mason contractors and related industry officials. **Principal Exhibits:** Masonry equipment, supplies, and services.

14038 ■ World of Concrete
Hanley-Wood Exhibitions
8600 Freeport Parkway
Irving, TX 75063
Ph:(972)536-6300
Free: 800-869-8522
Fax:(972)536-6301
URL: http://www.hanley-wood.com
Released: Annual. **Audience:** Concrete contractors, developers, architects, engineers, distributors, dealers, and precast, and ready-mix producers. **Principal Exhibits:** Equipment and services for the construction industry.

FRANCHISES AND BUSINESS OPPORTUNITIES

14039 ■ A-1 Concrete Leveling Inc.
388 S Main St., Ste. 402
Akron, OH 44311
Free: 888-675-3835
Fax:(330)253-1261
No. of Franchise Units: 47. **Founded:** 1992. **Franchised:** 1993. **Description:** Concrete leveling service. **Equity Capital Needed:** $115,500-$145,900 total investment. **Franchise Fee:** $85,000. **Royalty Fee:** 6%. **Financial Assistance:** Limited third-party financing available. **Training:** Provides 1 week at headquarters, 2 weeks of onsite and ongoing support including newsletter, meetings toll-free phone line, Internet, security/safety procedures, and field operations/evaluations.

14040 ■ Case Handyman & Remodeling Services LLC
Case Design/Remodeling Inc.
North Plz., Ste. 40
4701 Sangamore Rd.
Bethesda, MD 20816
Ph:(301)229-4600
Free: 800-426-9434
Fax:(301)229-2089
Co. E-mail: info@casehandyman.com
URL: http://www.casehandyman.com
No. of Franchise Units: 45. **No. of Company-Owned Units:** 5. **Founded:** 1992. **Franchised:** 1997. **Description:** Handyman services. **Equity Capital Needed:** $105,000-$150,000. **Franchise Fee:** $25,000. **Royalty Fee:** 4-6%. **Financial Assistance:** No. **Training:** Includes 3 weeks training at headquarters, 2 days at franchisee's location and ongoing support.

14041 ■ Concrete Raising of America
2855 South 166th St.
New Berlin, WI 53151
Ph:(262)827-5000
Free: 800-270-0011
Fax:(262)827-5005
No. of Franchise Units: 18. **No. of Company-Owned Units:** 3. **Founded:** 1947. **Franchised:** 1995. **Description:** Concrete raising, stabilizing and repair. **Equity Capital Needed:** $75,000 liquid preferred, most purchase equipment via lease-to-own programs. **Franchise Fee:** Up to $25,000. **Financial Assistance:** Yes. **Training:** Yes.

14042 ■ Precision Concrete Cutting
Datigen.com, Inc.
3191 N Canyon Rd.
Provo, UT 84604
Ph:(801)830-4060
Free: 800-833-7770
No. of Franchise Units: 29. **No. of Company-Owned Units:** 6. **Founded:** 1992. **Franchised:** 2002. **Description:** Trip hazard removal of sidewalks. **Equity Capital Needed:** Minimum cash investment of $140,000-$164,500. **Franchise Fee:** $65,000. **Royalty Fee:** 8%. **Financial Assistance:** Third party financing available. **Training:** Offers 1 week at headquarters and 1 week at franchisee' location with ongoing support.

14043 ■ Systems Paving Franchising Inc.
System's Paving, Inc.
1600 Dove St., Ste. 250
Newport Beach, CA 92660
Ph:(949)263-8300
Fax:(949)263-0452
No. of Franchise Units: 6. **No. of Company-Owned Units:** 9. **Founded:** 1992. **Franchised:** 2001. **Description:** Offers services like marketing, sales, and installation of paving stones. **Equity Capital Needed:**

$39,950-$120,800. **Franchise Fee:** $14,800-$17,800. **Royalty Fee:** 6%. **Financial Assistance:** No. **Training:** Offers 10-12 days at headquarters, 10 days at franchisees location, and ongoing for new employees.

LIBRARIES

14044 ■ Brick Industry Association Library
1850 Centennial Park Dr., Ste. 301
Reston, VA 20191
Ph:(703)620-0010
Fax:(703)620-3928
Co. E-mail: brickinfo@bia.org
URL: http://www.gobrick.com
Scope: Engineering and research pertinent to masonry construction. **Services:** Library open to the public with approval from Engineering Department. **Holdings:** 2500 volumes. **Subscriptions:** 10 journals and other serials.

14045 ■ Foundation of the Wall & Ceiling Industry–John H. Hampshire Memorial Library
513 W Broad St., Ste. 210
Falls Church, VA 22046
Ph:(703)538-1600
Fax:(703)534-8307
Co. E-mail: smith@awci.org
URL: http://www.awci.org/thefoundation.shtml
Contact: Don Smith, Dir., Tech.Svcs.
Scope: Construction - specifications and standards, management, and law; asbestos removal; fire standards; insulation. **Services:** Copying; Library open to the public. **Holdings:** 10,000 volumes; 3000 books; 500 unbound reports; manufacturers' catalogs. **Subscriptions:** 100 journals and other serials.

14046 ■ Hanley-Wood, LLC Library
426 S. Westgate St.
Addison, IL 60101-4546
Ph:(630)543-0870
Fax:(630)543-3112
URL: http://www.hanleywood.com
Contact: Kimberly Last, Libn.
Scope: Concrete, cement, masonry, construction, home building. **Services:** Interlibrary loan; copying. **Holdings:** 3000 books; 120 bound periodical volumes. **Subscriptions:** 100 journals and other serials.

14047 ■ LaFarge Canada Inc. Technical Library
6150 Royalmount Ave.
Montreal, QC, Canada H4P 2R3
Ph:(514)738-1202
Fax:(514)738-1124
Co. E-mail: library@accent.net
URL: http://www.lafargenorthamerica.com/wps/portal/
Contact: Irene M. Paulmier, Hd.Libn.
Scope: Cement; concrete; engineering; physical sciences. **Services:** Library not open to the public. **Holdings:** Figures not available.

14048 ■ National Concrete Masonry Association Library
13750 Sunrise Valley Dr.
Herndon, VA 20171-4662
Ph:(703)713-1900
Fax:(703)713-1910
Co. E-mail: jthompson@ncma.org
URL: http://www.ncma.org
Contact: Jason Thompson, Dir. of Engr.
Scope: Concrete masonry and related topics. **Services:** Library not open to the public. **Holdings:** 1000 volumes; 10,000 journal articles. **Subscriptions:** 40 journals and other serials; 10 newspapers.

RESEARCH CENTERS

14049 ■ National Concrete Masonry Association–Research and Development Laboratory
13750 Sunrise Valley Dr.
Herndon, VA 20171-4662
Ph:(703)713-1900
Fax:(703)713-1910
Co. E-mail: rthomas@ncma.org
URL: http://www.ncma.org/lab/Pages/default.aspx
Contact: Robert D. Thomas, Pres.
E-mail: rthomas@ncma.org
Scope: Construction materials, energy, construction methods, and manufacturing methods. **Services:** Consulting services for developmental research of new products for concrete masonry industry. **Publications:** C/M News (monthly); Engineering Bulletins (bimonthly).

14050 ■ University of Manitoba–W.R. McQuade Laboratory
Ag & Civil Engineering Bldg.
A250-96 Dafoe Rd.
Winnipeg, MB, Canada R3T 2N2
Ph:(204)474-8506
Fax:(204)474-7519
Co. E-mail: muftia@cc.umanitoba.ca
URL: http://www.isiscanada.com
Contact: Dr. Aftab Mufti, Pres.
E-mail: muftia@cc.umanitoba.ca
Scope: Large scale static and dynamic testing of steel, concrete, masonry, timber and fiber reinforced polymer (FRP) structures and components; structural health monitoring of infrastructure; civionics testing; fiber optic sensors; field testing of structures. Projects include testing of full scale steel free bridge decks; glass fiber reinforced polymer (GFRP) utility poles and towers; FRP strengthened timber beams in controlled environmental conditions; and durability of concrete subject to chemical attack. **Publications:** Design manuals; Innovator Newsletter (biennially). **Educational Activities:** Conference (annually); Workshops, seminars.

START-UP INFORMATION

14051 ■ *Becoming a Personal Trainer for Dummies*
Pub: John Wiley & Sons, Incorporated
Ed: Melyssa Michael, Linda Formichelli. **Released:** October 2004. **Price:** $19.99 (US), $25.99 (Canadian). **Description:** Legal and tax issues involved in starting and running a personal trainer firm. The book offers suggestions for incorporating massage and nutritional services.

ASSOCIATIONS AND OTHER ORGANIZATIONS

14052 ■ American Massage Therapy Association
500 Davis St., Ste. 900
Evanston, IL 60201-4695
Ph:(847)864-0123
Free: 877-905-0577
Fax:(847)864-5196
Co. E-mail: info@amtamassage.org
URL: http://www.amtamassage.org
Contact: Shelly Johnson, Exec. Dir.
Description: Massage therapists and massage schools. Promotes standards for the profession, has a Code of Ethics, and supports chapter efforts for state regulation of massage. Sponsors National Massage Therapy Awareness Week to promote public education on the benefits of massage; offers educational literature. Supports research on the efficacy of massage. Offers free Find A Message Therapists National locator service to help consumers and healthcare professionals find qualified, professional massage therapists. **Publications:** *AMTA's Find a Massage Therapist/Experience the Benefits of Massage*; *Massage Therapy*; *Massage Therapy Journal* (quarterly); *Sports Massage*; *Stress* .

14053 ■ American Organization for Bodywork Therapies of Asia
1010 Haddonfield-Berlin Rd., Ste. 408
Voorhees, NJ 08043-3514
Ph:(856)782-1616
Fax:(856)782-1653
Co. E-mail: office@aobta.org
URL: http://www.aobta.org
Contact: Wayne Mylin, Pres.
Description: Professional Asian Bodywork Therapy (ABT) practitioners, teachers, schools and programs; interested individuals. (Asian bodywork therapy is a form of therapeutic bodywork which utilizes theories and techniques directly and derived from ancient and traditional Chinese medicine, as well as evolving forms which stem from that 'root'. ABT focuses on balancing the Qi flow in the body, utilizing many techniques.) Identifies qualified practitioners; serves as a legal entity representing members when dealing with the government, especially in terms of establishing professional status. Sets educational standards for all styles of Asian bodywork including acupres-

sure, Tuina, Amma, Chi Nei Tsang, Nuad bo Rarn, and Shiatsu, among others. Sponsors speakers' bureau; conducts educational programs. .

14054 ■ American Society of Hand Therapists
15000 Commerce Pkwy., Ste. C
Mount Laurel, NJ 08054
Ph:(856)380-6856
Fax:(856)439-0525
Co. E-mail: asht@asht.org
URL: http://www.asht.org
Contact: Jerry Coverdale OTR, Pres.
Description: Registered and licensed occupational and physical therapists specializing in hand therapy and committed to excellence and professionalism in hand rehabilitation. Works to promote research, publish information, improve treatment techniques, and standardize hand evaluation and care. Fosters education and communication between therapists in the U.S. and abroad. Compiles statistics; conducts research and education programs and continuing education seminars. **Publications:** *Journal of Hand Therapy* (quarterly).

14055 ■ Associated Bodywork and Massage Professionals
25188 Genesee Trail Rd., Ste. 200
Golden, CO 80401
Ph:(303)674-8478
Free: 800-458-2267
Fax:800-667-8260
Co. E-mail: expectmore@abmp.com
URL: http://www.abmp.com
Description: Professional massage therapists and bodyworkers, sports massage therapists, skin care professionals, reflexologists, energy practitioners, etc.; massage therapy schools; affiliated organizations. Promotes massage and bodywork. Seeks to improve the image of massage therapy and bodywork, and to educate the public about its benefits. Fosters greater credibility and cooperation with the medical profession. Encourages ethical practices, high standards of professional conduct, and continuing education. Provides members with low-cost liability insurance coverage and product discounts. **Publications:** *ABMP Massage Marketplace* (annual); *ABMP Successful Business Handbook*; *ABMP Touch Resource Guide*; *Body Sense* (biennial); *Different Strokes* (bimonthly); *Massage and Bodywork* (bimonthly); *The Massage Educator* (quarterly); *Skin Deep* (bimonthly).

14056 ■ International Association of Infant Massage
PO Box 6370
Ventura, CA 93006
Ph:(805)644-8524
Free: 800-248-5432
Fax:(805)830-1729
Co. E-mail: iaim4us@aol.com
URL: http://www.iaim.ws
Contact: Andrea M. Kelly, CEO for Marketing/Communications
Description: Parents, caregivers. Works to promote nurturing touch, positive interactive contact, and com-

munication through massage. Trains and certifies individuals to teach parents and caregivers to massage their babies. .

14057 ■ National Association of Nurse Massage Therapists
PO Box 232
West Milton, OH 45383
Ph:(937)698-4128
Free: 800-262-4017
Fax:(937)698-6153
Co. E-mail: info@nanmt.org
URL: http://www.nanmt.org
Contact: Deborah Shields, Pres.
Description: Nurses and other healthcare professionals who practice massage therapy. Promotes the integration of massage and other therapeutic forms of body work into existing healthcare practice. Promotes Nurse Massage Therapists as specialists within the nursing profession. Establishes standards of professional practice and criteria for national certification of Nurse Massage Therapists. Educates the medical community and the general public about bodywork therapies. Monitors legislation. **Publications:** *NANMT News* (quarterly).

REFERENCE WORKS

14058 ■ "Do Your Homework" in *Black Enterprise* (Vol. 38, November 2007, No. 4, pp. 114)
Pub: Earl G. Graves Publishing Co. Inc.
Ed: Tennille M. Robinson. **Description:** Preschool teacher seeks advice for starting a hotel resort and day spa.

14059 ■ "How I Did It: Jack Ma" in *Inc.* (January 2008, pp. 94-102)
Pub: Gruner & Jahr USA Publishing
Ed: Rebecca Fannin. **Description:** Profile of Jack Ma, who started as a guide and interpreter for Western tourists in Hangzhou. Ma used the Internet to build Alibaba.com, China's largest business-to-business site and one of the hottest IPOs in years.

14060 ■ "Want a Facial With That Steak?" in *Charlotte Observer* (February 5, 2007)
Pub: Knight-Ridder/Tribune Business News
Ed: Jen Aronoff. **Description:** Profile of Burke Myotherapy Massage & Spa and Schell's Bistro. Lynn Shell moved her massage therapy business into a 106-year old home that had been used as a restaurant. She opened her own eatery on the first floor and offers massage therapy upstairs.

SOURCES OF SUPPLY

14061 ■ *Massage*
Pub: Enterprise Publishing
Contact: Martin Ashley, Author
Released: Triennial, Latest edition 5th Edition. **Price:** $25.95, individuals. **Publication Includes:** Approximately 1,000 organizations involved in the massage industry, including schools, associations, massage equipment suppliers, bodywork organizations,

and massage marketing companies in the United States. **Entries Include:** For schools—Name, address, phone, hours of training required, number of in-class hours required, cost, financial aid availability, subjects covered, unique aspects of school or curriculum. For others—Name, address, phone, description of products/services offered. Principal content of publication is information on becoming a successful massage therapist. **Arrangement:** Schools are geographical by state, then alphabetical. Others are classified by line of business, then alphabetical. **Indexes:** Alphabetical list of schools.

TRADE PERIODICALS

14062 ■ *Journal of Spiritual Bodywork*
Pub: Spiritual Massage Healing Ministry
Contact: Mary L. Brewster
E-mail: maryella1@earthlink.net
Released: Quarterly. **Description:** Trade magazine covering massage and spirituality.

VIDEOCASSETTES/ AUDIOCASSETTES

14063 ■ *Acupressure Massage (Shiatsu)*
Aspen Publishers
7201 McKinney Circ.
Frederick, MD 21704
Ph:(301)698-7100
Free: 800-234-1660
Fax:800-901-9075
URL: http://www.aspenpublishers.com
Released: 1980. **Description:** Shiatsu, a Japanese healing and rejuvenating massage, is demonstrated and explained. **Availability:** VHS; 3/4U.

14064 ■ *Advanced Shiatsu Massage*
Artistic Video
c/o Long Island School of Tai-Chi-Chuan
87 Tyler Ave.
Sound Beach, NY 11789-2639
Ph:(631)744-5999
Free: 888-982-4244
Fax:(631)744-5993
Co. E-mail: service@movementsofmagic.com
URL: http://www.movementsofmagic.com
Released: 1991. **Price:** $39.95. **Description:** Understand the techniques of fine Oriental massage after viewing this video. **Availability:** VHS.

14065 ■ *Back Shiatsu for Lovers*
Acupressure Institute
1533 Shattuck Ave.
Berkeley, CA 94709
Ph:(510)845-1059
Free: 800-442-2232
Fax:(510)845-1496
Co. E-mail: info@acupressureinstitute.com
URL: http://www.acupressureinstitute.com
Price: $29.95. **Description:** Presents how to eroticize your partner with a full-body back massage. **Availability:** VHS.

14066 ■ *Complete Body Massage*
Aspen Publishers
7201 McKinney Circ.
Frederick, MD 21704
Ph:(301)698-7100
Free: 800-234-1660
Fax:800-901-9075
URL: http://www.aspenpublishers.com
Released: 1980. **Description:** A complete massage based on traditional Swedish techniques is explained and demonstrated in detail. **Availability:** VHS; 3/4U.

14067 ■ *Healthy Massage Series*
ESPN Home Video
ESPN Plz., 935 Middle St.
Bristol, CT 06010
Ph:(860)766-2000
Fax:(860)585-2213
URL: http://www.espn.go.com
Released: 1989. **Price:** $19.95. **Description:** Three easy-to-follow educational tapes teach proper technique in both Swedish and Oriental (Accupressure) method. Part 1 covers the scalp, face, neck and chest; Part 2 covers the back; Part 3 covers the legs and feet. **Availability:** VHS.

14068 ■ *Holistic Massage—The Caring Touch*
American Educational Products, LLC
401 Hickory St.
PO Box 2121
Fort Collins, CO 80522
Ph:(970)484-7445
Free: 800-289-9299
Fax:(970)484-1198
Co. E-mail: custserv@amep.com
URL: http://www.amep.com
Released: 1981. **Description:** Instructor Rachel Harris, PhD., teaches how to give and receive a nude massage. **Availability:** VHS.

14069 ■ *Massage for Health*
Video Collectibles
PO Box 385
Lewiston, NY 14092-0385
Free: 800-268-3891
Fax:800-269-8877
Co. E-mail: info@collectablesdirect.com
URL: http://www.collectablesdirect.com
Released: 1988. **Price:** $24.95. **Description:** A step-by-step guide to Western style/Swedish massage techniques for the entire body. Fifty effective stroke techniques are demonstrated, as well as simple methods of self-massage and stress relaxation. Includes a massage handbook and bottle of professional massage oil. In HiFi Stereo. **Availability:** VHS; 8mm.

14070 ■ *Relaxing Touch: A Guide to the Healing Art of Massage Therapy*
ESPN Home Video
ESPN Plz., 935 Middle St.
Bristol, CT 06010
Ph:(860)766-2000
Fax:(860)585-2213
URL: http://www.espn.go.com
Released: 1988. **Price:** $29.95. **Description:** A method of full body massage is demonstrated for the amateur. Viewers learn stress-relieving techniques for consenting adults. **Availability:** VHS.

14071 ■ *Shiatsu Massage*
Artistic Video
c/o Long Island School of Tai-Chi-Chuan
87 Tyler Ave.
Sound Beach, NY 11789-2639
Ph:(631)744-5999
Free: 888-982-4244
Fax:(631)744-5993
Co. E-mail: service@movementsofmagic.com
URL: http://www.movementsofmagic.com
Released: 1987. **Price:** $39.95. **Description:** A complete demonstration of a full body massage is given. **Availability:** VHS.

14072 ■ *Therapeutic Massage for Sports and Fitness*
Cambridge Educational
c/o Films Media Group
132 West 31st Street, 17th Floor
Ste. 124
New York, NY 10001
Free: 800-257-5126
Fax:(609)671-0266
Co. E-mail: custserve@films.com
URL: http://www.cambridgeol.com
Price: $39.95. **Description:** Comprehensive, step-by-step instruction in all phases of deep-muscle massage. **Availability:** VHS.

14073 ■ *Touch for Health*
Chinese for Affirmative Action
The Kuo Bldg.
17 Walter U. Lum Pl.
San Francisco, CA 94108
Ph:(415)274-6750
Fax:(415)397-8770
Co. E-mail: info@caasf.org
URL: http://www.caasf.org
Released: 197?. **Price:** $39.95. **Description:** The system of muscle testing and acupressure massage is demonstrated by Doctor of Chiropractic Medicine, John Thie. **Availability:** VHS; 3/4U.

FRANCHISES AND BUSINESS OPPORTUNITIES

14074 ■ Elements Therapeutic Massage
Elements Therapeutic Massage Inc.
9092 S Ridgeline Blvd., Ste. A
Highlands Ranch, CO 80129
Ph:(303)663-0880
Free: 877-663-0880
Fax:(303)663-1617
No. of Franchise Units: 113. **Founded:** 2000. **Franchised:** 2006. **Description:** Professional, affordable, therapeutic massage. **Equity Capital Needed:** $70,000 cash; $140,387-$336,187. **Franchise Fee:** $34,000. **Financial Assistance:** Yes. **Training:** Yes.

14075 ■ Hand and Stone Massage and Facial Spa
1830 Hooper Ave.
Toms River, NJ 08753
Ph:(732)255-9300
Fax:(732)255-9205
No. of Company-Owned Units: 47. **Founded:** 2004. **Franchised:** 2006. **Description:** Massage therapy spas. **Equity Capital Needed:** $304,802-$402,522. **Franchise Fee:** $39,000. **Royalty Fee:** 5%. **Financial Assistance:** Limited third party financing available. **Training:** Offers 3 weeks at headquarters, 1 week onsite with ongoing support.

14076 ■ Massage Envy
14350 N 87th St., Ste. 200
Scottsdale, AZ 85260
Ph:(480)366-4100
No. of Franchise Units: 693. **Founded:** 2001. **Franchised:** 2003. **Description:** Therapeutic massage services. **Equity Capital Needed:** $343,025-$567,985. **Franchise Fee:** $45,000. **Royalty Fee:** 5%. **Financial Assistance:** Limited third party financing available. **Training:** Offers 5 days at headquarters, 5 days onsite and ongoing training and support as requested.

ASSOCIATIONS AND OTHER ORGANIZATIONS

14077 ■ ADR Institute of Canada
234 Eglinton Ave. E, Ste. 405
Toronto, ON, Canada M4P 1K5
Ph:(416)487-4733
Free: 877-475-4353
Fax:(416)487-4429
Co. E-mail: admin@adrcanada.ca
URL: http://www.adrcanada.ca
Contact: Mary Anne Harnick, Exec. Dir.
Description: Professionals providing arbitration and mediation services. Promotes the professional advancement of members; seeks to raise awareness of arbitration and services. Makes available arbitration and mediation rules and services to parties wishing to resolve disputes; works with regional affiliate institutes to set standards. Offers educational programs.

14078 ■ American Arbitration Association
1633 Broadway, 10th Fl.
New York, NY 10019
Ph:(212)716-5800
Free: 800-778-7879
Fax:(212)716-5905
Co. E-mail: websitemail@adr.org
URL: http://www.adr.org
Contact: William K. Slate II, Pres./CEO
Description: Works to achieve the resolution of disputes through the use of mediation, arbitration, democratic elections, and other voluntary methods. Provides administrative services for arbitrating, mediating, or negotiating disputes and impartial administration of elections. Maintains National Roster of Arbitrators and Mediators for referrals to parties involved in disputes. Conducts skill-building sessions to promote a more complete understanding of conflict resolution processes. **Publications:** *Dispute Resolution Journal* (quarterly);Newsletter (monthly).

14079 ■ Association for Conflict Resolution
12100 Sunset Hills Rd., Ste. 130
Reston, VA 20190
Ph:(703)234-4141
Fax:(703)435-4390
Co. E-mail: membership@acrnet.org
URL: http://www.acrnet.org
Contact: Lou Gieszl, Pres.
Description: Professional organization dedicated in enhancing the practice and public understanding of conflict resolution. **Publications:** *ACResolution* (quarterly).

14080 ■ Center for Dispute Settlement
1666 Connecticut Ave. NW
Washington, DC 20009-1039
Ph:(202)265-9572
Fax:(202)332-3951
Co. E-mail: administrator@cdsusa.org
URL: http://www.cdsusa.org
Contact: Linda R. Singer, Founder/Pres.
Description: Seeks to design, implement, and evaluate programs that apply mediation and other dispute resolution techniques to government, interpersonal, community, business, and institutional problems. Manages complaint center and operates service for the mediation of disputes. Offers consulting and training services. .

14081 ■ Grace Contrino Abrams Peace Education Foundation
1900 Biscayne Blvd.
Miami, FL 33132
Ph:(305)576-5075
Free: 800-749-8838
Fax:(305)576-3106
Co. E-mail: lloyd@peace-ed.org
URL: http://www.peace-ed.org
Contact: Lloyd Van Bylevett, Pres.
Description: Teachers, counselors, and school administrators; clergy and laypersons; interested others. Works to educate students, parents, and teachers on creative and nonviolent methods of resolving conflict. Develops and disseminates grade-specific curricula on nonviolent conflict resolution and mediation for preschool through high school students. Maintains the Training Institute for Conflict Resolution, Mediation, and Peacemaking. Conducts workshops and seminars; maintains speakers' bureau. Sponsors contests. **Publications:** *Prepared for Action: Responding Effectively to Crisis in Your School* .

14082 ■ Institute for Mediation and Conflict Resolution
384 E 149th St., Ste. 330
Bronx, NY 10455
Ph:(718)585-1190
Co. E-mail: trich@imcr.org
URL: http://www.imcr.org
Contact: Titus Rich Jr., Dir. of Mediation
Description: Agency, supported by foundation grants and contracts, to which community disputants can turn for assistance in resolving differences on a voluntary basis. Seeks to: mediate community conflicts; train people in mediation techniques and conflict resolution skills; design dispute settlement systems. Facilitates discussion on current trends in dispute resolution. **Publications:** *F.Y.I.* (quarterly).

14083 ■ International Ombudsman Institute–Institut International de l'Ombusdman
PO Box 20
1015 Vienna, Austria
Ph:43 1 5129388
Fax:43 1 5129388
Co. E-mail: loi@volksanw.qv.at
URL: http://www.law.ualberta.ca/centres/ioi
Contact: Mrs. Diane Callan, Admin.
Description: Ombudsman offices, complaint handling organizations, institutions, libraries, and individuals in 74 countries. Promotes concept of ombudsmanship and supports research and educational efforts in the field. Disseminates information about ombudsmanship; participates in seminars concerning the ombudsman concept.

14084 ■ National Academy of Arbitrators
1 N Main St., Ste. 412
Cortland, NY 13045
Ph:(607)756-8363
Fax:888-317-1729
Co. E-mail: naa@naarb.org
URL: http://www.naarb.org
Contact: Roberta Golick, Pres.
Description: Labor-management arbitrators. Works to improve general understanding of the nature and use of arbitration as a means of settling labor disputes. Conducts research and educational programs. .

DIRECTORIES OF EDUCATIONAL PROGRAMS

14085 ■ *Martindale-Hubbell International Dispute Resolution Directory*
Pub: Martindale-Hubbell Inc.
Contact: Claire Trigger
E-mail: claire.trigger@martindale.com
Released: Annual. **Price:** $250, individuals. **Covers:** Service providers in over 90 countries of international arbitration and dispute resolution at both international levels and within the individual's national jurisdiction; Professionals and their credentials. **Entries Include:** Contact information. **Arrangement:** In three main sections.

TRADE PERIODICALS

14086 ■ *Conflict Resolution & Mediation*
Pub: Jossey-Bass Publishers
Ed: Jon Jenkins, Editor. **Released:** Quarterly. **Price:** $40 U.S. **Description:** Publication offering information on applications, techniques, and concerns in the family mediation field.

14087 ■ *Dispute Resolution Journal*
Pub: American Arbitration Association
Ed: Susan Zuckerman, Editor, zuckermans@adr.org. **Released:** Quarterly. **Price:** $150; $164 Canada; $183 other countries. **Description:** Professional journal.

14088 ■ *Labor Arbitration in Government*
Pub: American Arbitration Association
Released: Monthly. **Price:** $142. **Description:** Periodical covering arbitrator awards, statutes and collective bargaining, absenteeism, grievances, drug and alcohol abuse, and layoffs. Contains arbitrator and subject indexes.

14089 ■ *Ohio State Journal on Dispute Resolution*
Pub: Ohio State University
Contact: Nancy Hardin Rogers, Board of Advisor
Released: Quarterly. **Price:** $50; $60 other countries. **Description:** Professional legal journal covering alternative dispute resolution.

CONSULTANTS

14090 ■ Consulting & Conciliation Service
2830 I St., Ste. 301
Sacramento, CA 95816
Ph:(916)396-0480
Free: 888-898-9780
Fax:(916)441-2828
Co. E-mail: service@azurewings.net
Contact: Jane A. McCluskey, Principle
E-mail: service@azurewings.net
Scope: Offers consulting and conciliation services. Provides pre-mediation counseling, training and research on preparing for a peaceful society, mediation and facilitation, and preparation for shifts in structure, policy and personnel. Offers sliding scale business rates and free individual consultation. **Publications:** "Native America and Tracking Shifts in US Policy"; "Biogenesis: A Discussion of Basic Social Needs and the Significance of Hope". **Seminars:** Positive Approaches to Violence Prevention: Peace building in Schools and Communities.

COMPUTERIZED DATABASES

14091 ■ Daily Labor Report
The Bureau of National Affairs Inc.
1801 S Bell St.
Arlington, VA 22202
Free: 800-372-1033
Co. E-mail: customercare@bna.com
URL: http://www.bna.com
Description: Contains the complete text of Daily Labor Report, covering legislative, regulatory, and judicial activities related to labor relations and employment practices. Covers fair employment practices, immigration, pension benefits, collective bargaining, arbitration, Social Security reform, occupational safety, and job training. Includes actions relating to the Occupational Safety and Health Act, National Labor Relations Board decisions, and other labor-related federal agency directives. **Availability:** Online: Thomson Reuters, The Bureau of National Affairs Inc. **Type:** Full text.

14092 ■ Government Employee Relations Report
The Bureau of National Affairs Inc.
1801 S Bell St.
Arlington, VA 22202
Free: 800-372-1033
Co. E-mail: customercare@bna.com
URL: http://www.bna.com
Description: Contains detailed reporting and coverage of federal, state, and local issues and developments in public-sector employment. Covers subjects of interest to government employees, such as collective bargaining, merit pay and salaries, union organizing, work and family issues and more. Provides information on new legislative, regulatory, and legal developments affecting government workers. Also includes economic statistics (e.g., consumer price index, earnings, hours of work). **Availability:** Online: Thomson Reuters, The Bureau of National Affairs Inc. **Type:** Full text.

LIBRARIES

14093 ■ American Arbitration Association–Library and Information Center on the Resolution of Disputes
1633 Broadway
New York, NY 10019-6708
Ph:(212)716-5800
Fax:(212)716-5905
Co. E-mail: referencedesk@adr.org
URL: http://www.adr.org
Contact: Laura Ferris Brown, Dir., Lib.Svcs.
Scope: Arbitration, mediation, and other forms of alternative dispute resolution - general, commercial, International, labor, environmental, maritime, insurance, medical and health, employment, mandatory arbitration. **Services:** Interlibrary loan (to LLAGNY members); copying; Library open to the public on a fee basis (free to AAA ADR Information Package

subscribers and AAA Library Services Subscribers). **Holdings:** 24,000 titles; arbitration awards. **Subscriptions:** 240 journals and other serials.

14094 ■ The Peace Center Library
102 W. Maple Ave.
Langhorne, PA 19047-2820
Ph:(215)750-7220
Fax:(215)750-9237
Co. E-mail: info@thepeacecenter.org
URL: http://www.thepeacecenter.org
Scope: Conflict resolution, violence prevention, peacemaking, multiculturalism, mediation, parenting. **Services:** Library open by appointment. **Holdings:** 200 books; curricula; videos; articles relating to violence prevention, conflict resolution, mediation, parenting, cooperative games, and peace issues.

14095 ■ York University–Centre for Research in Work and Society
276 York Lanes
4700 Keele St.
Toronto, ON, Canada M3J 1P3
Ph:(416)736-2100 x70494
Co. E-mail: paszter@yorku.ca
URL: http://www.yorku.ca/crws
Contact: Dr. Norene Pupo, Dir.
Scope: Work and society, unions, arbitration. **Services:** Library open to students, faculty and staff; open by appointment only from May to August. **Holdings:** 500 books; journals; primary and secondary documents and sources.

RESEARCH CENTERS

14096 ■ Center for Dispute Settlement
1666 Connecticut Ave. NW
Washington, DC 20009-1039
Ph:(202)265-9572
Fax:(202)332-3951
Co. E-mail: administrator@cdsusa.org
URL: http://www.cdsusa.org
Contact: Linda R. Singer, Pres.
E-mail: administrator@cdsusa.org
Scope: Designs, implements, and evaluates alternative methods of dispute resolution, including studies, mediation, and training in dispute resolution in public and private organizations and businesses. **Services:** Dispute Resolution Center; Mediation, Facilitation. **Publications:** Reports. **Educational Activities:** Training programs in mediation and negotiation.

14097 ■ Center for Policy Research
1570 Emerson St.
Denver, CO 80218
Ph:(303)837-1555
Fax:(303)837-1557
Co. E-mail: jspearson@centerforpolicyresearch.org
URL: http://www.centerforpolicyresearch.org
Contact: Dr. Jessica Pearson, Dir.
E-mail: jspearson@centerforpolicyresearch.org
Scope: Problems in legal, social, and human services, including studies on mediation, alternatives to litigation, child abuse, legal needs of the poor, child support, welfare, and education reform. **Publications:** Reports, papers, articles.

14098 ■ Harvard University–Harvard Negotiation Project
513 Pound Hall
Harvard Law School
1563 Massachusetts Ave.
Cambridge, MA 02138
Ph:(617)495-1684
Fax:(617)495-7818
Co. E-mail: jsebenius@hbs.edu
URL: http://www.pon.harvard.edu/research_projects/harvard-negotiation-project/hnp
Contact: Prof. James K. Sebenius, Dir.
E-mail: jsebenius@hbs.edu
Scope: Seeks to improve the theory and practice of negotiation, mediation, and conflict resolution in the contexts of business, labor disputes, and international conflicts. **Educational Activities:** Negotiation Workshop (semiannually), one-week intensive course on negotiation offered each June and November.

14099 ■ Northwestern University–Dispute Resolution Research Center
Jacobs Ctr. 371
J.L. Kellogg School of Management
2001 Sheridan Rd.
Evanston, IL 60208-2001
Ph:(847)491-8068
Fax:(847)467-5700
Co. E-mail: jmbrett@kellogg.northwestern.edu
URL: http://www.kellogg.northwestern.edu/research/drrc
Contact: Prof. Jeanne M. Brett PhD, Dir.
E-mail: jmbrett@kellogg.northwestern.edu
Scope: Dispute resolution, including the causes of disputes, negotiation processes, fair settlements, and the role of third parties. Conducts interdisciplinary studies in game theory, procedural justice, behavioral decision theory, and dispute systems design. Projects focus on judgment, group negotiation, tactics in negotiation, alternative dispute resolution, environmental dispute resolution, ethics, and cross-cultural negotiations. **Publications:** Teaching Materials; Working Paper Series. **Educational Activities:** Negotiation teaching workshops; Negotiation Teaching Certificate Program; Practitioner workshops; Problem solving workshops; Research seminar series; Seminars, for managers and lawyers.

14100 ■ Pennsylvania State University–Center for Research in Conflict and Negotiation
475 Business Bldg.
Smeal College of Business
University Park, PA 16802
Ph:(814)865-3822
Fax:(814)865-0123
Co. E-mail: b9g@psu.edu
URL: http://www.smeal.psu.edu/crcn
Contact: Dr. Barbara Gray, Dir.
E-mail: b9g@psu.edu
Scope: Conflict and dispute resolution, emphasizing international joint venture negotiations; multi-party disputes; game theoretic models of negotiating; bargaining experiments, arbitration, and mediation; organizational conflicts and teambuilding; environmental conflict; the effect of individual cognitions, emotions, and language patterns on negotiations; cross-cultural negotiations; and management of diversity. **Services:** Consulting; Mediation programs. **Publications:** CRCN Newsletter; Working Paper Series. **Educational Activities:** Practitioners' Conferences; Seminar series; Negotiations training for organizations (periodically), provides team building workshops and negotiations training and training on collaborative problem solving, and collaborative leadership for public, private and NGO organizations.

14101 ■ Syracuse University–Program on the Analysis and Resolution of Conflicts
400 Eggers Hall
Maxwell School of Citizenship & Public Affairs
Syracuse, NY 13244-1020
Ph:(315)443-2367
Fax:(315)443-3818
Co. E-mail: roleary@maxwell.syr.edu
URL: http://www.maxwell.syr.edu/parc
Contact: Rosemary O'Leary PhD, Co-Dir.
E-mail: roleary@maxwell.syr.edu
Scope: Conflict and conflict resolution, including peacekeeping, negotiation, mediation, studies on family violence, alternative dispute resolution methods, computational modeling, mediation training programs, community organizing efforts, prevention of disputes through increased public participation in environmental issues, nonviolent means of protest, geopolitical ideologies, foreign policy decision making during crises, de-escalation achievements in U.S.-Soviet and Arab-Israeli relations, cognitive mapping for international negotiations, ethnic and culture conflicts, and gender problems, including the empowerment of women using dispute resolution services. **Services:** Outreach programs; Training and consulting services. **Publications:** Articles; Newsletter; Occasional papers; Reprint series; Working Paper Series. **Educational Activities:** Conferences; Public forums, workshops; Summer Institute on Creative Conflict Resolution.

ASSOCIATIONS AND OTHER ORGANIZATIONS

14102 ■ Advanced Medical Technology Association
701 Pennsylvania Ave. NW, Ste. 800
Washington, DC 20004-2654
Ph:(202)783-8700
Fax:(202)783-8750
Co. E-mail: info@advamed.org
URL: http://www.advamed.org
Contact: Stephen J. Ubl, Pres./CEO
Description: Represents domestic (including U.S. territories and possessions) manufacturers of medical devices, diagnostic products, and healthcare information systems. Develops programs and activities on economic, technical, medical, and scientific matters affecting the industry. Gathers and disseminates information concerning the United States and international developments in legislative, regulatory, scientific or standards-making areas. Conducts scientific and educational seminars and programs. **Publications:** *Health Industry Manufacturers Association—Directory* (annual); *In Brief* (monthly).

14103 ■ Association for the Advancement of Medical Instrumentation
4301 N Fairfax Dr., Ste. 301
Arlington, VA 22203-1633
Ph:(703)525-4890
Free: 800-332-2264
Fax:(703)276-0793
Co. E-mail: mlogan@aami.org
URL: http://www.aami.org
Contact: Mary Logan JD, Pres./CEO
Description: Clinical engineers, biomedical equipment technicians, physicians, hospital administrators, consultants, engineers, manufacturers of medical devices, nurses, researchers and others interested in medical instrumentation. Works to improve the quality of medical care through the application, development, and management of technology. Maintains placement service. Offers certification programs for biomedical equipment technicians and clinical engineers. Produces numerous standards and recommended practices on medical devices and procedures. Offers educational programs. **Publications:** *Biomedical Instrumentation and Technology* (bimonthly);Catalog (annual).

14104 ■ Dental Trade Alliance
2300 Clarendon Blvd., Ste. 1003
Arlington, VA 22201
Ph:(703)379-7755
Fax:(703)931-9429
Co. E-mail: info@dentaltradealliance.org
URL: http://www.dentaltradealliance.org
Contact: Bret Wise, Chm.
Description: Represents dental manufacturers, dental dealers, dental laboratories, dental market service providers and dental publications. **Publications:** *Dental Trade Newsletter* (bimonthly).

14105 ■ Health Industry Distributors Association
310 Montgomery St.
Alexandria, VA 22314-1516
Ph:(703)549-4432
Free: 800-549-4432
Fax:(703)549-6495
Co. E-mail: rowan@hida.org
URL: http://www.hida.org
Contact: Matthew J. Rowan, Pres./CEO
Description: Represents distributors of medical, laboratory, surgical, and other health care equipment and supplies to hospitals, physicians, nursing homes, and industrial medical departments. Conducts sales training, management seminars, and research through the HIDA Educational Foundation. **Publications:** Membership Directory (annual).

14106 ■ Hearing Industries Association
1444 I St. NW, Ste. 700
Washington, DC 20005
Ph:(202)449-1090
Fax:(202)216-9646
Co. E-mail: mspangler@bostrom.com
URL: http://www.hearing.org
Contact: Carole M. Rogin, Exec. Dir.
Description: Companies engaged in the manufacture and/or sale of electronic hearing aids, their component parts, and related products and services on a national basis. Cooperates in and contributes toward efforts to promote the number of hearing aid users; collects trade statistics; conducts market research activities, investigations, and studies in connection with hearing and hearing aids. .

14107 ■ Independent Medical Distributors Association
5204 Fairmount Ave.
Downers Grove, IL 60515
Ph:(630)655-9280
Free: (866)463-2937
Fax:(630)493-0798
Co. E-mail: imda@imda.org
URL: http://www.imda.org
Contact: Katie Swartz, Exec. Dir.
Description: Represents sales, marketing and distribution organizations focused on bringing innovative medical technologies to market. Employs salespeople who are technically sophisticated, and who enjoy long-standing relationships with clinicians in their territories. **Publications:** *IMDA—Update* (monthly).

DIRECTORIES OF EDUCATIONAL PROGRAMS

14108 ■ *Hospital Telephone Directory*
Pub: UNICOL Inc.
Released: Annual, Latest edition 2011. **Price:** $119, individuals. **Covers:** Almost 7,000 hospitals and medical centers in the U.S. **Entries Include:** name, address and telephone number. **Arrangement:** Geographical. **Indexes:** Alphabetical.

REFERENCE WORKS

14109 ■ *Advanced Medical Technology Association—Directory*
Pub: Advanced Medical Technology Association
Released: Monthly. **Covers:** About 1,100 member manufacturers of medical devices, diagnostic products, and health information systems and products. **Entries Include:** For public site—Company name plus hyperlinks to company websites. For private member site—Company name, address, phone, name of official representative or correspondent; product or service provided, plus hyperlinks to company websites. **Arrangement:** Alphabetical.

14110 ■ *Association for the Advancement of Medical Instrumentation—Membership Directory*
Pub: Association for the Advancement of Medical Instrumentation
Covers: 6,500 physicians, clinical engineers, biomedical engineers and technicians, nurses, researchers, and medical equipment manufacturers. **Entries Include:** Name, title, affiliation, office address, phone, code for occupational specialization. **Arrangement:** Alphabetical. **Indexes:** Specialty, geographical, job function.

14111 ■ "Bovie Medical Makes Electrosurgical Strike" in *The Business Journal-Serving Greater Tampa Bay* (Vol. 28, August 22, 2008, No. 35)
Pub: American City Business Journals, Inc.
Ed: Margie Manning. **Description:** Bovie Medical Group, which manufactures electrosurgical products, is planning to sell its manufacturing plant in the Tyrone Industrial Park and to purchase the former Harland Clarke facility. The moves are expected to boost the efficiency and the development of new products. Other information on Bovie Medical Group is presented.

14112 ■ "Ending the Ebola Death Sentence" in *Canadian Business* (Vol. 83, August 17, 2010, No. 13-14, pp. 22)
Pub: Rogers Media Ltd.
Ed: Michael McCullough. **Description:** US Army Medical Research Institute of Infectious Diseases made a $140 million agreement with Tekmira Pharmaceuticals Corporation to develop both a drug delivery system and delivery technology for curing the Ebola virus. Tekmira's delivery technology, which has been shown to halt Ebola in laboratory animals, might be the key to finding a cure.

14113 ■ "Ethics and the End of Life" in *Crain's Chicago Business* (Vol. 34, October 24, 2011, No. 42, pp. 31)
Pub: Crain Communications Inc.
Ed: Lisa Bertagnoli. **Description:** Technology has enabled doctors to provide more and better methods for helping patients, however end of life issues faced by medical ethicists are discussed.

14114 ■ "Finalist: Private Company, Less Than $100M" in Crain's Detroit Business (Vol. 25, June 22, 2009, No. 25)
Pub: Crain Communications Inc. - Detroit
Ed: Sherri Begin Welch. **Description:** Profile of family-owned Guardian Alarm Company is presented. The firm has expanded to include medical monitoring and video equipment of doors and windows.

14115 ■ "Former Synthes Officers Receive Prison Sentences" in Wall Street Journal Eastern Edition (November 22 , 2011, pp. B4)
Pub: Dow Jones & Company Inc.
Ed: Peter Loftus. **Description:** Michael D. Huggins, formerly chief operating officer of medical-device maker Synthes Ltd., and Thomas B. Higgins, formerly the president of Synthes spine unit, were given prison sentences of nine months while a third executive, John J. Walsh, formerly director of regulatory and clinical affairs in the spine division, was given a five-month sentence for their involvement in the promotion of the unauthorized use of a bone cement produced by the company.

14116 ■ "The Game of Operation" in Crain's Chicago Business (Vol. 31, April 28, 2008, No. 17, pp. 26)
Pub: Crain Communications, Inc.
Ed: Samantha Stainburn. **Description:** Revenue at Medline Industries Inc., a manufacturer of medical products, has risen 12 percent a year since 1976, reaching $2.81 billion last year. Growth at the company is due to new and increasingly sophisticated operations by surgeons which brings about the need for more specialized tools.

14117 ■ "GeckoSystems Reduces Sensor Fusion Costs Due to Elder Care Robot Trials" in Internet Wire (December 14, 2010)
Pub: Comtex
Description: GeckoSystems International Corporation has been able to reduce the cost of its sensor fusion system while maintaining reliability and performance. The firm's ongoing first in-home elder care robot trials have sparked interest regarding its business model, technologies available for licensing, and joint domestic and international ventures.

14118 ■ "Growing at the Margins" in Business Journal Serving Greater Tampa Bay (Vol. 30, November 5, 2010, No. 46, pp. 1)
Pub: Tampa Bay Business Journal
Ed: Margie Manning. **Description:** Jabil Circuit Inc. has reported an increase in revenues from its smart phones and medical devices. The company has been focusing on its core services such as making smart phone parts and medical devices.

14119 ■ Health Devices Sourcebook
Pub: ECRI Institute
Released: Annual, Latest edition 2011. **Price:** $475, individuals. **Covers:** Over 6,800 suppliers of patient care equipment, medical and surgical instruments, implants, clinical laboratory equipment and supplies, medical and hospital disposable supplies, and testing instruments; also lists companies that service, recondition, lease, or buy and sell used equipment; coverage includes U.S. and Canada. **Entries Include:** Company name, address, phone, toll-free phone, fax, toll-free fax, URL, e-mail, total sales, names of key executives and contacts, product categories handled, trade names, methods of distribution, typical pricing, annual volume. Price of directory includes custom updates upon request. **Arrangement:** Alphabetical. **Indexes:** Product listings, manufacturers' product lines, service company profiles, product categories (by number), product categories (alphabetic), product categories (by specialty), manufacturers addresses (geographic), trade names, equipment services, numerical listings, executive contacts, bioterrorism and emergency preparedness.

14120 ■ "Heart Hospitals Analyzed" in Philadelphia Business Journal (Vol. 30, September 2, 2011, No. 29, pp. 1)
Pub: American City Business Journals Inc.
Ed: John George. **Description:** Centers for Medicare and Medicaid Services (CMS) released updated data on mortality rates for heart attack patients as hospitals

in Pennsylvania. Doylestown Hospital posted the lowest mortality rates with 10.9 percent, tying the fourth best in the entire nation. Other details on the CMS data are presented.

14121 ■ "Heart Test No Boom for BG Medical" in Boston Business Journal (Vol. 31, June 17, 2011, No. 21, pp. 1)
Pub: Boston Business Journal
Ed: Julie M. Donnelly. **Description:** The Galectin-3 test failed to boost stock prices of its manufacturer, BG Medicine, which has fallen to $6.06/share. The company hopes that its revenue will be boosted by widespread adoption of an automated and faster version of the test, which diagnoses for heart failure.

14122 ■ "Hospitals Try to Buy Smarter" in Crain's Detroit Business (Vol. 25, June 1, 2009, No. 22, pp. M025)
Pub: Crain Communications Inc. - Detroit
Ed: Jay Greene. **Description:** Hospitals in southeast Michigan are using bulk discount purchasing of medical and non-medical supplies through group purchasing organizations in order to cut costs.

14123 ■ "Inventive Doctor New Venture Partner" in Houston Business Journal (Vol. 40, January 29, 2010, No. 38, pp. A2)
Pub: American City Business Journals
Ed: Ford Gunter. **Description:** Dr. Billy Cohn, a surgeon from Houston, Texas has been named as venture partner for venture firm Sante Ventures LLC of Austin, Texas. Cohn will be responsible for seeing marketable developing technologies in the medical industry. The motivation for Cohn's naming as venture partner is his development of a minimally invasive therapy for end-stage renal disease.

14124 ■ "Medical Connectors: Meeting the Demands of Reliability, Portability, Size and Cost" in Canadian Electronics (February 2008)
Pub: CLB Media Inc.
Ed: Murtaza Fidaali, Ted Worroll. **Description:** Component manufacturers who serve the medical industry need to ensure component reliability in order to maintain patient safety. Because of this, connectors in medical equipment are becoming more versatile. It is concluded that these manufacturers are facing challenges meeting the medical industry standards or reliability, miniaturization, portability, and cost.

14125 ■ "Medical Market a Healthy Alternative" in Crain's Cleveland Business (Vol. 30, June 1, 2009, No. 21, pp. 3)
Pub: Crain Communications, Inc.
Ed: Dan Shingler. **Description:** Manufacturing for the Medical Market: Requirements for Supply Chain Entry, was an event held in Northeast Ohio. Representatives from various health systems addressed 250 area manufacturers about their future medical supply needs.

14126 ■ "Mentor Medical Device Maker's Partnerships Open New Opportunities" in Crain's Cleveland Business (Vol. 30, June 22, 2009, No. 24)
Pub: Crain Communications, Inc.
Ed: Chuck Soder. **Description:** Frantz Medical Development Ltd. develops medical devices based on ideas from outside inventors. The company wants to manufacture the innovations at its Mentor campus.

14127 ■ "Oakland County Hopes Auto Suppliers Can Drive Medical Industry Growth" in Crain's Detroit Business (March 10, 2008)
Pub: Crain Communications, Inc.
Ed: Chad Halcom. **Description:** Oakland County officials are hoping to create further economic development for the region by pairing health care companies and medical device makers with automotive suppliers in an attempt to discover additional crossover technology.

14128 ■ "Playing Defense" in Crain's Chicago Business (Vol. 31, November 10, 2008, No. 45, pp. 4)
Pub: Crain Communications, Inc.
Ed: Monee Fields-White. **Description:** Chicago's money managers are increasingly investing in local

companies such as Caterpillar Inc., a maker of construction and mining equipment, Kraft Foods Inc. and Baxter International Inc., a manufacturer of medical products, in an attempt to bolster their portfolios. These companies have a history of surviving tough economic times.

14129 ■ "SAGE Publications Announced a Partnership with Which Medical Device" in Information Today (Vol. 28, November 2011, No. 10, pp. 15)
Pub: Information Today, Inc.
Description: SAGE Publications has partnered with Which Medical Device to offer insights, tutorials, and reviews of medical devices.

14130 ■ Scott's Canadian Dental Directory
Pub: Business Information Group
Released: Biennial, Latest edition 2010. **Price:** $239, individuals Plus Applicable Taxes + S/H; $289, individuals CD-pinpointer; $599, individuals CD-profiler; $3,999, individuals CD-prospector. **Covers:** Approximately 18,000 dentists, dental suppliers, and dental laboratories and associations in Canada. **Entries Include:** Name, address, phone, names and titles of key personnel, biographical data (for dentists), geographical area served. **Arrangement:** For dentists—Same information available in geographical and alphabetical sections. For others—Classified by line of business, then alphabetical.

14131 ■ "Somanetics to Buy Back Up to $15 Million of Common Shares" in Crain's Detroit Business (Vol. 24, April 7, 2008, No. 14, pp. 4)
Pub: Crain Communications, Inc.
Ed: Tom Henderson. **Description:** Somanetics Corp., a company that manufactures and markets noninvasive devices for monitoring blood oxygen levels in the brain and elsewhere in the body during surgery, plans to buy back up to $15 million worth of its common shares. Statistical data included on the company's current and past earnings and stock prices as well as its plans to increase revenue.

14132 ■ "Sterotaxis Needs $10 Million in 60 Days" in Saint Louis Business Journal (Vol. 32, October 7, 2011, No. 6, pp. 1)
Pub: Saint Louis Business Journal
Ed: E.B. Solomont. **Description:** Medical device firm Stereotaxis signed a loan modification deal with Silicon Valley Bank. The company suffered massive losses during second quarter 2011. Under the deal, the company waived the minimum tangible net work covenant of the original loan in exchange for reduction in its credit line.

14133 ■ "Survey: Most Approve of Donating Used Pacemakers to Medically Underserved" in Crain's Detroit Business (Vol. 25, June 1, 2009)
Pub: Crain Communications Inc. - Detroit
Description: According to a survey conducted by University of Michigan Cardiovascular Center, 87 percent of those with pacemakers and 71 percent of the general population would donate the device to patients in underserved nations.

14134 ■ "UMKC, Hospital Drill Down on Deal" in The Business Journal-Serving Metropolitan Kansas City (Vol. 26, July 18, 2008, No. 45, pp. 1)
Pub: American City Business Journals, Inc.
Ed: Rob Roberts. **Description:** University of Missouri Kansas City and Children's Mercy Hospital are negotiating the hospital's potential acquisition of the university's School of Dentistry building. The deal would transfer the 240,000-square foot dental school building to Children's Mercy. Plans for a new dental school building for the UMKC are also presented.

14135 ■ "Zit Zapper Lands New Funding" in Houston Business Journal (Vol. 40, November 27, 2009, No. 29, pp. 1)
Pub: American City Business Journals
Ed: Mary Ann Azevedo. **Description:** Tyrell Inc. of Houston, Texas generated $20 million in funds for making a cheaper version of its acne-removing Zeno device. The upcoming product, Zeno Mini, will be targeted to a mass market with a price tag of about

$89. In 2005, the original Zeno acne treatment device could only be bought through medical offices and spas at about $225.

STATISTICAL SOURCES

14136 ■ *The Market for Dental Equipment and Supplies*
Pub: MarketResearch.com
Released: 2007. **Price:** $2495.00. **Description:** This report quantifies market trends through 2009 for all types of dental equipment for professional use. A special section of the report examines relevant trends in the two major end-use markets for professional dental products-dental offices and dental laboratories.

14137 ■ *RMA Annual Statement Studies*
Pub: Robert Morris Associates (RMA)
Released: Annual. **Price:** $175.00 2006-07 edition, $105.00. **Description:** Contains composite balance sheets and income statements for more than 360 industries, including the accounting, auditing, and bookkeeping industries. Also contains five years of comparative historical data for discerning trends. Includes 16 commonly used ratios, computed for most of the size groupings for nearly every industry.

14138 ■ *Standard & Poor's Industry Surveys*
Pub: Standard & Poor's Corp.
Released: Annual. **Price:** $3633.00. **Description:** Two-volume book that examines the prospects for specific industries, including trucking. Also provides analyses of trends and problems, statistical tables and charts, and comparative company analyses.

14139 ■ *Trends in Noninvasive and Minimally Invasive Medical Device Market*
Pub: MarketResearch.com
Released: 2006. **Price:** $4850.00. **Description:**

TRADE PERIODICALS

14140 ■ *24x7*
Pub: Ascend Media
Contact: Stephen Noonoo, Assoc. Ed.
E-mail: snoonoo@ascendmedia.com
Released: Monthly. **Price:** Free to qualified subscribers. **Description:** Trade magazine covering maintenance and repair of medical, computer and telecommunications technology within healthcare enterprises.

14141 ■ *AAMI News*
Pub: Association for the Advancement of Medical Instrumentation
Ed: Steve Campbell, Editor, scampbell@aami.org. **Released:** Monthly. **Price:** Included in membership; $160, nonmembers; $195, other countries. **Description:** Covers Association programs, policies, and meetings. Reports on AAMI standards program and publications in the Standards Monitor section as well as regulatory and legislative proposals or actions. Recurring features include news of educational opportunities and a calendar of events.

14142 ■ *Biomedical Instrumentation & Technology*
Pub: Elsevier
Contact: Vicki Cummins, Advertising Mgr
E-mail: vcummins@aami.org
Released: Bimonthly. **Price:** $182; $211 out of country; $219 institutions; $252 out of country. **Description:** Peer-reviewed journal for clinical engineers, biomedical equipment technicians, and other medical technology professionals.

14143 ■ *Biomedical Safety & Standards*
Pub: Lippincott Williams & Wilkins
Ed: Timothy Baker, Editor. **Released:** Semimonthly, 22/year. **Price:** $349.98, individuals in USA; $699.98, institutions in USA; $548.96, individuals other countries; $949.96, institutions in other countries. **Description:** Reports on biomedical safety and standards. Provides information on safety hazards, product recalls, product and facilities standards, legal actions, legislation and regulations, hospital safety, and biomedical equipment technician activities. Recurring features include news of research, book reviews, and a calendar of events.

14144 ■ *Bioscience Technology*
Pub: Advantage Business Media
Released: Monthly. **Description:** Journal covering life science research and biotechnology products.

14145 ■ *Dental Economics*
Pub: PennWell Corp.
Released: Monthly. **Price:** $132; $179 Canada and Mexico; $248 other countries; $211 two years; $312 Canada and Mexico; $428 other countries two years. **Description:** Magazine featuring business-related articles for dentists.

14146 ■ *Dentaletter*
Pub: MPL Communications Inc.
Contact: John Hobez, Managing Editor
Ed: Dr. Brian Waters, Editor. **Released:** 11/year. **Price:** $119. **Description:** Publishes news of dental research. Also covers related web sites.

14147 ■ *Devices & Diagnostics Letter*
Pub: FDA News
Ed: Nick Wakeman, Editor. **Released:** Weekly. **Price:** $1,047, U.S., Canada, and Mexico; $1,087, elsewhere. **Description:** Seeks to provide executives in the industry with information on regulatory developments regarding medical devices and in vitro diagnostic products. Reports on the Food and Drug Administration (FDA), the Health Care Financing Administration, and Congress. Discusses a variety of issues, including manufacturing practices, compliance and inspection programs, defect reporting, labeling and testing rules, and performance standards. Recurring features include news of research and reports of meetings.

14148 ■ *Healthcare Corporate Finance News*
Pub: Irving Levin Associates Inc.
Contact: Stephen M. Monroe, Managing Editor
Ed: Gretchen S. Swanson, Editor. **Released:** Monthly. **Price:** $495. **Description:** Reports on the growth strategies of managed care providers, hospitals, drug companies, medical device manufacturers, and other healthcare organizations. Also reports on the latest deals in the healthcare sector, and how healthcare companies are doing on Wall Street.

14149 ■ *In Brief. . .*
Pub: Advanced Medical Technology Association
Contact: John Arnold
Ed: John Arnold, Editor, jarnold@aduamed.org. **Released:** Semimonthly. **Description:** Covers regulatory, legislative, and standards activities related to the medical device, health care information systems, and the diagnostic products industries. Remarks: Also available via e-mail.

14150 ■ *Journal of Nuclear Cardiology*
Pub: Springer-Verlag New York Inc.
Released: Bimonthly. **Price:** $369 institutions print online; $442.80 institutions print enhanced access. **Description:** Official journal of the American Society of Nuclear Cardiology (ASNC). Covers all aspects of nuclear cardiology including interpretation, diagnosis, radiopharmaceuticals, and imaging equipment.

14151 ■ *Medical Devices, Diagnostics & Instrumentation Reports - The Gray Sheet*
Pub: F-D-C Reports Inc.
Contact: Jaimie Kelley, Managing Editor
Ed: Mary Houghton, Editor. **Released:** Weekly. **Price:** $1,860. **Description:** Covers the medical device and diagnostics field, including FDA regulations; policies and congressional reform initiatives concerning premarket approvals and 501(k) exemptions; new products; business start-ups and financial deals; international developments; and technology reimbursement. Recurring features include columns titled In Brief, Financings In Brief, Device Approvals, Recalls & FDA Seizures, and MDDI Stock Index.

14152 ■ *Medical Imaging*
Pub: Ascend Media
Contact: Debra Britton, Art Dir.
E-mail: dbritton@ascendmedia.com
Released: Monthly. **Description:** Trade magazine covering medical imaging technology for healthcare professionals.

14153 ■ *MEEN Imaging Technology News*
Pub: Reilly Communications Group
Contact: Dave Fornell, Assoc. Ed.
E-mail: dfornell@sgcmail.com
Released: 9/yr. **Description:** Trade magazine (tabloid) serving users and buyers of medical imaging technologies and services.

14154 ■ *Proofs*
Pub: PennWell Corp.
Contact: Mark Hartley, Group Editorial Dir.
E-mail: markh@pennwell.com
Released: 5/yr. **Price:** $17; $55 Canada and Mexico; $164 other countries air-mailed out of country. **Description:** Magazine for the executive, marketing, sales, and service personnel of dental distributor and dental manufacturer organizations.

14155 ■ *Warning Letter Bulletin*
Pub: Washington Information Source
Contact: Kenneth Reid, Editor & Publisher
Released: Biweekly. **Price:** $799. **Description:** Digests warnings issued by the U.S. Food and Drug Administration (FDA) to companies that are allegedly violating the law. Recurring features include news of research, calendar of events, reports of meetings, and book reviews.

14156 ■ *Wednesday in Washington*
Pub: American Association for Homecare
Ed: Released: Weekly, via fax, email or mail. **Price:** Included in membership. **Description:** Informs members of developments in government agencies, state legislatures, and on Capitol Hill, as well as any other pertinent information that affects the home medical equipment services and homecare industries. Remarks: Available in print, e-mail, or fax format.

TRADE SHOWS AND CONVENTIONS

14157 ■ American Academy of Implant Dentistry Annual Meeting
American Academy of Implant Dentistry
211 E. Chicago Ave., Ste. 750
Chicago, IL 60611
Ph:(312)335-1550
Fax:(312)335-9090
Co. E-mail: info@aaid-implant.org
URL: http://www.aaid-implant.org
Released: Annual. **Audience:** Dentists. **Principal Exhibits:** Dental equipment, supplies, and services. **Dates and Locations:** 2011 Oct 19-22, Las Vegas, NV; 2012 Oct 03-06, Washington, DC.

14158 ■ Association for the Advancement of Medical Instrumentation Annual Conference and Expo
Association for the Advancement of Medical Instrumentation AAMI
4301 N. Fairfax Dr., Ste. 301
Arlington, VA 22203
Ph:(703)525-4890
Free: 800-332-2264
Fax:(703)276-0793
Co. E-mail: customerservice@aami.org
URL: http://www.aami.org
Released: Annual. **Audience:** Biomedical equipment technicians, clinical engineers, hospital administrators, manufacturers, students, government personnel, nurses, equipment engineers. **Principal Exhibits:** Over 66 product categories of medical device technologies, products and services.

14159 ■ Chicagoland
Advanstar Communications
641 Lexington Ave., 8th Fl.
New York, NY 10022
Ph:(212)951-6600
Fax:(212)951-6793
Co. E-mail: info@advantstar.com
URL: http://www.advantstar.com
Audience: Disabled consumers, seniors, rehab and healthcare professionals, hospital personnel, special educators, dealers and representatives. **Principal Exhibits:** Wheelchairs, assistive technology, personal care products, support organizations, and daily living aids.

CONSULTANTS

14160 ■ Colucci, Blendow & Johnson
643 Main St., Ste. 7
PO Box 10
Half Moon Bay, CA 94019-1988
Ph:(650)712-0103
Fax:(650)712-0105
Co. E-mail: exsearch@ix.netcom.com
Contact: Bart A. Colucci, President
Scope: Executive search consultants in the medical technology area that includes pharmaceuticals, medical equipment and device manufacturers, biotechnology, therapeutic supplies, diagnostic laboratory equipment and supplies, diagnostic imaging equipment and supplies, medical services, chemicals, cosmetic and toiletries, dental, veterinarian, and agricultural genetics companies.

14161 ■ John C. Palmer Associates Inc.
54 W Shore Dr.
Pennington, NJ 08534-2121
Ph:(609)737-3213
Fax:(609)737-2797
Contact: John C. Palmer, President
Scope: Provides management consulting specializing in executive selection. Particular expertise in search assignments in the biomedical, pharmaceutical, medical device and instrumentation segments of the health care industry. Offers services in locating, selecting and evaluating candidates for middle and upper management line and staff positions.

FRANCHISES AND BUSINESS OPPORTUNITIES

14162 ■ BioPed Footcare Centres
2150 Winston Park Dr. Ste. 21
Oakville, ON, Canada L6H 5V1
Ph:(905)829-0505
Free: (866)424-6733
Fax:(905)829-5199
Co. E-mail: nekets@bioped.com
URL: http://www.bioped.com
No. of Franchise Units: 49. **Founded:** 1980. **Franchised:** 1985. **Description:** Provides aid to people of all ages requiring comfort or relief from lower limb disorders through the design and manufacture of high quality, biomechanical designed, foot support systems and footwear. **Equity Capital Needed:** $162,000-$225,000. **Franchise Fee:** $29,700.

14163 ■ MEDIchair Ltd.
500-1121 Centre St NW
Calgary, AB, Canada T2E 7K6
Ph:(403)204-1419
Free: 800-667-0087
Fax:(403)204-1409
Co. E-mail: development@medichair.com
URL: http://www.medichair.com
No. of Franchise Units: 67. **No. of Company-Owned Units:** 3. **Founded:** 1985. **Description:** MEDIchair Franchise offer sales, rentals and services of Home Medical Equipments. **Equity Capital Needed:** $400,000. **Franchise Fee:** $50,000. **Training:** Initial and ongoing support provided.

COMPUTERIZED DATABASES

14164 ■ *Health Devices International Sourcebase*
ECRI Institute
5200 Butler Pike
Plymouth Meeting, PA 19462-1298
Ph:(610)825-6000
Fax:(610)834-1275
Co. E-mail: info@ecri.org
URL: http://www.ecri.org
Description: Provides information on more than 15,000 manufacturers and distributors of more than 66,000 new medical devices and equipment. Also includes service companies that buy, sell, and repair used equipment. Provides product name, code, and typical price range for diagnostic and therapeutic medical devices and materials, clinical laboratory equipment and reagents, systems and instruments for testing clinical equipment, and hospital furniture. Product records also contain references, if available, to brand-name evaluations or product specifications in other ECRI publications. Manufacturer information includes organization name and type, contact information, product names and codes, trade names, number of employees and total sales, and names of executive officers. Service records contain organization name, contact information, service category (e. g., clinical laboratory, nuclear medicine), type of service offered (e.g., sales, parts, repairs), locations served, and names of service management personnel. Corresponds to the *Health Devices Sourcebook*. **Availability:** Online: ProQuest LLC, DIMDI, the German Institute of Medical Documentation and Information, ECRI Institute. **Type:** Directory.

14165 ■ *WinMDR—Medical Device Register on Disk*
Canon Communications L.L.C.
11444 W Olympic Blvd., Ste. 900
Los Angeles, CA 90064
Ph:(310)445-4200
Fax:(310)445-4299
Co. E-mail: info@cancom.com
URL: http://www.ubmcanon.com
Contact: Thanh Nguyen, Tech. Admin.
E-mail: than.nguyen@cancom.com
Released: Published 2006. **Entries Include:** Name, address, phone, fax, e-mail and Web site addresses for manufacturers and companies; current executives; company background; FDA codes and descriptions of products. **Database Covers:** The entire 2-volume print edition of the MDR on CDROM; More than 17,600 companies and 82,000 products searchable by supplier, product category, location, keyword, or trade name.

LIBRARIES

14166 ■ Sentron Medical Inc.–Senmed Medical Ventures Library
4445 Lake Forest Dr., No. 600
Cincinnati, OH 45242-3798
Ph:(513)563-3240
Fax:(513)563-3261
URL: http://www.senmed.com/organization.htm
Contact: Rosanne Wohlwender
Scope: Biotechnology, medical devices and diagnostics, technology transfer, pharmaceuticals, venture capital, licensing. **Services:** Library not open to the public. **Holdings:** 800 books; 50 reports. **Subscriptions:** 100 journals and other serials; 2 newspapers.

RESEARCH CENTERS

14167 ■ ECRI Institute
5200 Butler Pike
Plymouth Meeting, PA 19462-1298
Ph:(610)825-6000
Fax:(610)834-1275
Co. E-mail: info@ecri.org
URL: http://www.ecri.org
Contact: Jeffrey C. Lerner PhD, Pres./CEO
E-mail: info@ecri.org
Scope: Improvement of safety, performance, reliability, and cost effectiveness of health care technology; quality of health care; health care environmental management; and risk management. **Services:** Litigation support and expert witness services; Technical assistance in accident investigation and clinical engineering; Technical assistance to health care facilities in planning, specification, evaluation, procurement and management of medical equipment. **Publications:** Clinical Laboratory Product Comparison System (monthly); Health Devices (monthly); Health Technology Trends (monthly); Risk Management Reporter (monthly). **Educational Activities:** Annual conference, seminars, distance learning, audio and web conferences.

14168 ■ University of Wisconsin—Madison–Medical Instrumentation Laboratory
1550 Engineering Dr.
Madison, WI 53706
Ph:(608)263-1574
Fax:(608)265-9239
Co. E-mail: webster@engr.wisc.edu
Contact: Prof. John G. Webster PhD
E-mail: webster@engr.wisc.edu
Scope: Medical electrodes, medical amplifiers, radio frequency microwave, and cryohepatic ablation, electromuscular incapacitating device safety, objective measurement of hot flashes.

ASSOCIATIONS AND OTHER ORGANIZATIONS

14169 ■ American Health Information Management Association
233 N Michigan Ave., 21st Fl.
Chicago, IL 60601
Ph:(312)233-1100
Free: 800-335-5535
Fax:(312)233-1090
Co. E-mail: info@ahima.org
URL: http://www.ahima.org
Contact: Bonnie S. Cassidy MPA, Pres.
Description: Registered record administrators; accredited record technicians with expertise in health information management, biostatistics, classification systems, and systems analysis. Sponsors Independent Study Programs in Medical Record Technology and coding. Conducts annual qualification examinations to credential medical record personnel as Registered Record Administrators (RRA), Accredited Record Technicians (ART) and Certified Coding Specialists (CCS). Maintains Foundation of Research and Education Library, Scholarships and loans. **Publications:** *From the Couch: Official Newsletter of the Mental Health Record Section of the American Medical Record Association* (quarterly); *Journal of AHIMA* (10/year); *Leader: AHIMA Volunteer* (quarterly); *QA Section Connection* (bimonthly); *Spectrum* (quarterly).

14170 ■ International Claim Association
1155 15th St. NW, Ste. 500
Washington, DC 20005
Ph:(202)452-0143
Fax:(202)530-0659
Co. E-mail: cmurphy@claim.org
URL: http://www.claim.org
Contact: Christopher Murphy, Exec. Dir.
Description: Claim executives and administrators representing companies writing life, health, or accident insurance. Promotes efficiency, effectiveness and high standards of performance in claim administration by member companies. Provides a forum for research, education and the exchange of ideas relating to various aspects of claim administration. **Publications:** *ICA News* (quarterly); *International Claim Association—Annual Report* (annual).

REFERENCE WORKS

14171 ■ "New York Collection Agency's Bribery Case Resolved" in *Collections & Credit Risk* (Vol. 15, August 1, 2010, No. 7, pp. 19)
Pub: SourceMedia Inc.
Description: Criminal conviction and civil settlement in a bribery case and Medicaid scam involving H.I.S. Holdings Inc. and owner Deborah Kantor is examined.

TRADE PERIODICALS

14172 ■ *Materials Management in Health Care*
Pub: Health Forum L.L.C.
Contact: Mary Grayson, Editorial Dir.
E-mail: mgrayson@healthforum.com
Released: Monthly. **Description:** Trade magazine for purchasers, managers, and manufacturers of health care equipment and supplies.

14173 ■ *Reimbursement Advisor*
Pub: Aspen Publishers Inc.
Ed: Dennis Barry, Esq., Editor. **Released:** Monthly. **Price:** $485, individuals. **Description:** Provides information on health care spending and Medicare reimbursement. Deals with universal health insurance, physician payments, preventative services, and the industry's regulations.

COMPUTERIZED DATABASES

14174 ■ *HMO and Chains Directory*
F1RSTMARK Inc.
25 Vintinner Rd.
PO Box 1270
Campton, NH 03223
Ph:(603)726-4800
Free: 800-729-2600
Fax:(603)726-4840
Co. E-mail: leads@firstmark.com
URL: http://www.firstmark.com
Description: Contains information on more than 64 Health Maintenance Organization chains, which provide prepaid, comprehensive health coverage for hospital and physician services. Includes more than 4600 executives and other decision makers. **Availability:** CD-ROM: F1RSTMARK Inc. **Type:** Directory.

14175 ■ *State Health Care Regulatory Developments*
The Bureau of National Affairs Inc.
1801 S Bell St.
Arlington, VA 22202
Free: 800-372-1033
Co. E-mail: customercare@bna.com
URL: http://www.bna.com
Description: Contains information on health care regulatory news and developments in the United States. Subjects include community-based care, home care, emergency care, infectious diseases, managed care, insurance, laboratories, Medicaid, mental health, medical waste, nursing homes, pharmaceuticals, physician services, professional licensing, provider relationships, worker protection and compensation. Entries are organized by state, topic, and register citation. **Availability:** Online: The Bureau of National Affairs Inc., Thomson Reuters. **Type:** Full text.

RESEARCH CENTERS

14176 ■ American University–National Center for Health Fitness
Nebraska Hall, Lower Level
4400 Massachusetts Ave. NW
Washington, DC 20016-8037
Ph:(202)885-6275
Fax:(202)885-6288
Co. E-mail: nchfaa@american.edu
URL: http://www.american.edu/academic.depts/cas/health/nchf/index.html
Contact: Dr. Robert C. Karch, Exec.Dir.
E-mail: nchfaa@american.edu
Scope: Worksite health promotion programs, focusing on costs, benefits, and cost-effectiveness, and including international health promotion and special populations. **Services:** Consulting. **Educational Activities:** Health/fitness specialist training; International Institute for Health Promotion Conference (annually). **Awards:** Dean Meyerson Award, for Leadership in Health Promotion.

ASSOCIATIONS AND OTHER ORGANIZATIONS

14177 ■ American Association of Bioanalysts
906 Olive St., Ste. 1200
St. Louis, MO 63101-1448
Ph:(314)241-1445
Fax:(314)241-1449
URL: http://www.aab.org
Contact: Mark S. Birenbaum PhD, Admin.
Description: Professional organization of directors, owners, managers, supervisors, technologists and technicians of bioanalytical clinical laboratories devoting their efforts to clinical laboratory procedure and testing. Sponsors Proficiency Testing Service open to individuals engaged in the clinical laboratory field. Provides specialized education and representation before federal and state legislatures and regulatory agencies. **Publications:** *AAB Bulletin* (quarterly); *AAB Update* (periodic); *Andrology and Embryology Review Course Manual; General Knowledge for the Clinical Lab Director; QA Manual for POLs and Industries and Hospital Labs* .

14178 ■ American Association for Laboratory Accreditation
5301 Buckeystown Pike, Ste. 350
Frederick, MD 21704
Ph:(301)644-3248
Fax:(301)662-2974
Co. E-mail: punger@a2la.org
URL: http://www.a2la.org
Contact: Peter Unger, Pres./CEO
Description: Represents individuals, associations, corporations, universities, laboratories, research institutes and government agencies interested in improving the quality of laboratories. Accredits testing laboratories, certifies laboratory reference materials and registers quality systems. **Publications:** *A2LA News* (quarterly).

14179 ■ American Board of Bioanalysis
906 Olive St., Ste. 1200
St. Louis, MO 63101-1448
Ph:(314)241-1445
Fax:(314)241-1449
Co. E-mail: abb@abbcert.org
URL: http://www.aab.org/aab/American_Board_of_
   Bioanalysis.asp
Description: Certifying agency consisting of scientists, educators, and recognized authorities in the clinical laboratory field. Certifies clinical laboratory directors at two levels depending on qualifications, including High Complexity or Moderate Complexity Clinical Laboratory Director. Also certifies Technical Consultants, two levels of supervisor (Technical and General), and Bioanalyst Laboratory Manager (BLM).

14180 ■ American Clinical Laboratory Association
1100 New York Ave. NW, Ste. 725 W
Washington, DC 20005
Ph:(202)637-9466

Fax:(202)637-2050
Co. E-mail: info@clinical-labs.org
URL: http://www.acla.com
Contact: Alan Mertz, Pres.
Description: Corporations, partnerships, or individuals owning or controlling one or more independent clinical laboratory facilities operating for a profit and licensed under the Clinical Laboratories Improvement Act of 1967 or the Clinical Laboratories Improvement Amendment of 1988, or accredited by the Medicare program. Promotes the development of uniformly high quality laboratory testing; eliminates the present inequalities in the standards applied to different segments of the clinical laboratory market; discourages the enactment of restrictive legislative or regulatory policies that may impede the free flow of commerce or operate to the detriment of the public. Examines federal and state health care and laboratory regulatory and legislative proposals and submits comments and opinions to the appropriate agencies or legislative bodies. **Publications:** *Results* (monthly).

14181 ■ American Medical Technologists
10700 W Higgins Rd., Ste. 150
Rosemont, IL 60018
Ph:(847)823-5169
Free: 800-275-1268
Fax:(847)823-0458
Co. E-mail: membership@amt1.com
URL: http://www.amt1.com
Contact: Christopher A. Damon JD, Exec. Dir.
Description: Represents medical technologists, medical laboratory technicians, medical assistants, medical administrative specialists, dental assistants, office laboratory technicians, phlebotomy technicians, laboratory consultants, and allied health instructors. Provides allied health professionals with professional certification services and membership programs to enhance their professional and personal growth. Aims to issue certification credentials to medical and dental assistants, clinical laboratory personnel, laboratory consultants, and allied health instructors. **Publications:** *AMT Events and Continuing Education Supplement* (quarterly); *Continuing Education Topics & Issues* (3/year).

14182 ■ American Society for Clinical Laboratory Science
2025 M St. NW, Ste. 800
Washington, DC 20036
Ph:(202)367-1174
Fax:(301)657-2909
Co. E-mail: ascls@ascls.org
URL: http://www.ascls.org
Contact: Linda Smith, Pres.-Elect
Description: Primarily clinical laboratory personnel who have an associate or baccalaureate degree and clinical training and specialists who hold at least a master's degree in one of the major fields of clinical laboratory science such as bacteriology, mycology, or biochemistry; also includes technicians, specialists, and educators with limited certificates and students enrolled in approved programs of clinical laboratory studies and military medical technology schools. Promotes and maintains high standards in clinical laboratory methods and research and advances

standards of education and training of personnel. Conducts educational program of seminars and workshops. Approves programs of continuing education and maintains records on participation in continuing education programs for members. **Publications:** *Clinical Laboratory Science* (quarterly).

14183 ■ American Society for Clinical Pathology
33 W Monroe, Ste. 1600
Chicago, IL 60603
Ph:(312)541-4999
Free: 800-267-2727
Fax:(312)541-4998
Co. E-mail: info@ascp.org
URL: http://www.ascp.org
Contact: John E. Tomaszewski MD, Pres.
Description: Works to promote public health and safety by the appropriate application of pathology and laboratory medicine. Provides educational programs for pathologists and laboratory professionals throughout the year, certification for laboratory professionals, and publishes scientific journals and reference textbooks. **Publications:** *ASCP Member News* (monthly); *Laboratory Medicine* (monthly); *Pathology Patterns* (semiannual); *Pathology Today* (bimonthly).

14184 ■ Canadian Society for Medical Laboratory Science–Societe Canadienne de Science de Laboratoire Medical
PO Box 2830
LCD 1
Hamilton, ON, Canada L8N 3N8
Ph:(905)528-8642
Free: 800-263-8277
Fax:(905)528-4968
Co. E-mail: alison@csmls.org
URL: http://www.csmls.org
Contact: Goldie Fagan, Pres.
Description: Laboratory technologists in 20 countries. Seeks to maintain high standards of medical laboratory technology to insure effective and economical laboratory services. Promotes the interests of medical laboratory technologists. Emphasizes the importance of continuing education; sponsors courses. Communicates with government authorities concerning issues affecting members. Offers insurance program to members. Organizes national medical laboratory week annually. **Publications:** *Annual Roster* (annual); *Canadian Journal of Medical Laboratory Science* (bimonthly); *Catalogs of Continuing Education; Guidelines for Laboratory Safety* .

14185 ■ Clinical Laboratory Management Association
401 N Michigan Ave., Ste. 2200
Chicago, IL 60611
Ph:(312)321-5111
Fax:(312)673-6927
Co. E-mail: info@clma.org
URL: http://www.clma.org
Contact: C. Anne Pontius, Pres.
Description: Individuals holding managerial or supervisory positions with clinical laboratories; persons engaged in education of such individuals;

manufacturers or distributors of equipment or services to clinical laboratories. Objectives are: to enhance management skills and promote more efficient and productive department operations; to further exchange of professional knowledge, new technology, and colleague experience; to encourage cooperation among those engaged in management or supervisory functions. Activities include: workshops, seminars, and expositions; dissemination of information about legislation and other topics. **Publications:** *Clinical Leadership Management Review* (bimonthly).

14186 ■ Clinical and Laboratory Standards Institute
940 W Valley Rd., Ste. 1400
Wayne, PA 19087-1898
Ph:(610)688-0100
Free: 877-447-1888
Fax:(610)688-0700
Co. E-mail: customerservice@clsi.org
URL: http://www.clsi.org
Contact: Glen Fine MS, Exec. VP
Description: Government agencies, professional societies, clinical laboratories, and industrial firms with interests in medical testing. Purposes are to promote the development of national and international standards for medical testing and to provide a consensus mechanism for defining and resolving problems that influence the quality and cost of health-care work performed. .

14187 ■ National Accrediting Agency for Clinical Laboratory Sciences
5600 N River Rd., Ste. 720
Rosemont, IL 60018-5119
Ph:(773)714-8880
Fax:(773)714-8886
Co. E-mail: info@naacls.org
URL: http://www.naacls.org
Contact: Peggy Simpson MS, Pres.
Description: Independently accredits academic programs in hospitals, colleges, and universities for the following health professional classifications: Clinical Laboratory Scientist/Medical Technologist, Clinical Laboratory Technician/Medical laboratory Technician, Cytogenetic Technologist, Histologic Technician, Histotechnologist, Pathologists' Assistant. Independently approves academic programs in hospitals and colleges for the following: Phlebotomist, Clinical Assistant. Establishes standards for quality educational programs; determines if hospitals and colleges are maintaining standards through self-study and on-site visits. Provides workshops for program officials on self-study and accreditation. **Publications:** *NAACLS News* (quarterly); *NAACLS Program Approval Guide*; *National Accrediting Agency for Clinical Laboratory Sciences—Annual Report* (annual); *National Accrediting Agency for Clinical Laboratory Sciences—Standards* .

DIRECTORIES OF EDUCATIONAL PROGRAMS

14188 ■ *Directory of Private Accredited Career Schools and Colleges of Technology*
Pub: Accrediting Commission of Career Schools and Colleges of Technology
Contact: Michale S. McComis, Exec. Dir.
Released: On web page. **Price:** Free. **Description:** Covers 3900 accredited post-secondary programs that provide training programs in business, trade, and technical fields, including various small business endeavors. Entries offer school name, address, phone, description of courses, job placement assistance, and requirements for admission. Arrangement is alphabetical.

REFERENCE WORKS

14189 ■ *Directory of International and Regional Organizations Conducting Standards-Related Activities*
Pub: National Technical Information Service
Ed: Breitenberg Maureen, Editor. **Covers:** 338 international and regional organizations which conduct standardization, certification, laboratory accreditation, and other standards-related activities.

Entries Include: Description, scope of each organization, national affiliations of members, U.S. Participants, restrictions on membership, availability of any standards in English.

14190 ■ "Ending the Ebola Death Sentence" in *Canadian Business* (Vol. 83, August 17, 2010, No. 13-14, pp. 22)
Pub: Rogers Media Ltd.
Ed: Michael McCullough. **Description:** US Army Medical Research Institute of Infectious Diseases made a $140 million agreement with Tekmira Pharmaceuticals Corporation to develop both a drug delivery system and delivery technology for curing the Ebola virus. Tekmira's delivery technology, which has been shown to halt Ebola in laboratory animals, might be the key to finding a cure.

14191 ■ "HER's: the Future is Free" in *Benzinga.com* (October 29, 2011)
Pub: Benzinga.com
Ed: Benzinga Staff. **Description:** In order to create and maintain electronic health records that connects every physician and hospital it is essential to create a reliable, easy-to-use, certified Web-based ambulatory ERH using an ad-supported model. eBay seems to be the company showing the most potential for improving services to physicians and consumers, but requires sellers to pay fees based upon sales price.

14192 ■ "mChip: Claros Diagnostics" in *Inc.* (Vol. 33, November 2011, No. 9, pp. 42)
Pub: Inc. Magazine
Ed: Christine Lagorio. **Description:** Harvard University researchers have developed a device called the mChip that produces accurate blood tests in about 10 minutes. Plans to apply for FDA approval for the mChip in the US should happen in 2012.

14193 ■ *Medical and Health Information Directory*
Pub: Gale
Released: Annual, Latest edition April 2011. **Price:** $1190, individuals set; $501, individuals per volume. **Covers:** In volume 1, more than 33,000 medical and health oriented associations, organizations, institutions, and government agencies, including health maintenance organizations (HMOs), preferred provider organizations (PPOs), insurance companies, pharmaceutical companies, research centers, and medical and allied health schools. In Volume 2, over 20,000 medical book publishers; medical periodicals, directories, audiovisual producers and services, medical libraries and information centers, electronic resources, and health-related internet search engines. In Volume 3, more than 40,500 clinics, treatment centers, care programs, and counseling/diagnostic services for 34 subject areas. **Entries Include:** Institution, service, or firm name, address, phone, fax, email and URL; many include names of key personnel and, when pertinent, descriptive annotation. Volume 3 was formerly listed separately as Health Services Directory. **Arrangement:** Classified by organization activity, service, etc. **Indexes:** Each volume has a complete alphabetical name and keyword index.

STATISTICAL SOURCES

14194 ■ *RMA Annual Statement Studies*
Pub: Robert Morris Associates (RMA)
Released: Annual. **Price:** $175.00 2006-07 edition, $105.00. **Description:** Contains composite balance sheets and income statements for more than 360 industries, including the accounting, auditing, and bookkeeping industries. Also contains five years of comparative historical data for discerning trends. Includes 16 commonly used ratios, computed for most of the size groupings for nearly every industry.

TRADE PERIODICALS

14195 ■ *A2LA Today*
Pub: American Association for Laboratory Accreditation
Ed: Teresa Barnett, Editor. **Released:** 4/year. **Price:** Free. **Description:** Updates the latest accreditation actions. Provides information on improving the quality of test data.

14196 ■ *AAB Bulletin*
Pub: American Association of Bioanalysts (AAB)
Contact: LeAnn Hampton
Ed: Mark S. Birenbaum, Ph.D., Editor. **Released:** Quarterly. **Price:** Included in membership. **Description:** Addresses legislative and regulatory issues and scientific developments. Contains commentary, news from other laboratory professionals, regional activities, and continuing education programs. Recurring features include interviews, news of research, a calendar of events, reports of meetings, news of educational opportunities, and job listings.

14197 ■ *AIDS Policy and Law*
Pub: LRP Publications
Ed: Frank Baran, Editor. **Released:** Biweekly, 22/year. **Price:** $497, U.S. plus $39.50 s/h. **Description:** Reports on federal, state, and local news pertaining to the Acquired Immune Deficiency Syndrome (AIDS) virus. Discusses fair employment practices, litigation, legislation, regulation, policy guidelines, case studies, and interviews. Recurring features include news of research and summaries of state and federal legislation.

14198 ■ *AIDS Research and Human Retroviruses*
Pub: Mary Ann Liebert Incorporated Publishers
Contact: Thomas Hope PhD, Editor-in-Chief
Released: Monthly. **Price:** $676 print and online; $795 other countries print and online; $622 online only; $4,080 institutions print and online; $4,572 institutions, other countries print and online; $3,246 institutions print only; $3,399 institutions, other countries print only; $3,892 institutions online only. **Description:** Peer-reviewed journal on the multidisciplinary study of retrovirus associated diseases with emphasis on AIDS.

14199 ■ *Bulletin of Experimental Treatments for AIDS BETA*
Pub: San Francisco AIDS Foundation
Contact: Liz Highleyman, Copy Ed.
Ed: Reilly O'Neal, Editor. **Released:** Biennial. **Description:** Magazine reporting medical information about treatment for HIV infection.

14200 ■ *Laboratory Compliance Insider*
Pub: Brownstone Publishers Inc.
Contact: John M. Striker, Publisher
Ed: Kevin Lamberson, Editor. **Released:** Monthly. **Price:** $357, individuals print; $385, individuals electronic; $437, individuals electronic and print combination. **Description:** Features information for laboratory managers on compliance with regulatory requirements set by the federal Health Care Financing Administration (HFCA). Recurring features include ready-to-use compliance plan language, billing and coding guidelines, and model forms.

14201 ■ *Laboratory Medicine*
Pub: American Society for Clinical Pathology
Contact: Frank H. Wians PhD, Editor-in-Chief
Released: Monthly. **Price:** $115 print and online; $115 other countries print and online; $190 other countries print and online, expedited; $20 other countries single copies; $15 single issue; $140 institutions print and online; $140 institutions, other countries print and online; $190 institutions, other countries print and online, expedited. **Description:** Professional journal covering medical technology and pathology.

14202 ■ *Laboratory Product News*
Pub: Business Information Group
Contact: Anita Havas-Stainton, Assoc. Publisher
E-mail: ahavas-stainton@labcanada.com
Released: 7/yr. **Price:** $66 in U.S.; $36 Canada applicable taxes; $105 other countries. **Description:** Magazine (tabloid) featuring laboratory equipment, instruments, and materials.

14203 ■ *Medical Laboratory Observer MLO*
Pub: Nelson Publishing Inc.
Contact: Vern Nelson, Group Publisher
E-mail: vnelson@nelsonpub.com
Ed: Carren Bersch, Editor, cbersch@nelsonpub.com. **Released:** Monthly. **Description:** Magazine for clinical laboratory professionals.

14204 ■ *NAACLS News*
Pub: National Accrediting Agency for Clinical Laboratory Sciences
Ed: Megan Hennessy Eggert, Editor, mheggert@juno.com. **Released:** 3/year. **Price:** Included in membership; $25, nonmembers. **Description:** Provides news of the activities of the Agency as well as issues related to laboratory scientists.

14205 ■ *Translational Research*
Pub: Mosby Inc.
Contact: Jeffrey Laurence MD, Editor-in-Chief
Released: Monthly. **Price:** $252; $121 students; $333 other countries; $171 students, other countries; $633 institutions; $731 institutions, other countries. **Description:** Journal providing information to physicians, academic clinical scientists, and laboratory consultants with an interest in clinical investigation and research.

VIDEOCASSETTES/ AUDIOCASSETTES

14206 ■ *AIDS/Hepatitis B: Handling and Processing Infectious Waste*
American Society for Training and Development (ASTD)
1640 King St.
Box 1443
Alexandria, VA 22313-2043
Ph:(703)683-8100
Free: 800-628-2783
Fax:(703)683-8103
URL: http://www.astd.org
Released: 1989. **Price:** $250.00. **Description:** An overview for professional and environmental health workers on the proper disposal methods for infectious waste materials. **Availability:** VHS; 3/4U.

14207 ■ *AIDS: The Workplace and the Law*
Phoenix Learning Group
2349 Chaffee Dr.
St. Louis, MO 63146-3306
Ph:(314)569-0211
Free: 800-221-1274
Fax:(314)569-2834
URL: http://www.phoenixlearninggroup.com
Released: 1988. **Price:** $600.00. **Description:** Dionne Warwick, in her official capacity as U.S. Ambassador of Health, hosts this look at the deadly disease and what ordinary people can do to stop its destructive spread. **Availability:** VHS; 8mm; 3/4U.

14208 ■ *Laboratory Technician Training*
Williams Learning Network
15400 Calhoun Dr.
Rockville, MD 20855-2762
Fax:(301)315-6880
Co. E-mail: mait@willearn.com
URL: http://www.willearn.com
Description: Twenty-six part laboratory technician training program that offers instruction in all areas of chemical training that provides a solid understanding of chemical fundamentals as well as of laboratory equipment and procedures. Each section comes with 10 textbooks and an instructor guide. **Availability:** VHS.

TRADE SHOWS AND CONVENTIONS

14209 ■ American Association for Laboratory Animal Science Conference & Exhibits
American Association for Laboratory Animal Science
9190 Crestwyn Hills Dr.
Memphis, TN 38125-8538
Ph:(901)754-8620
Fax:(901)753-0046
Co. E-mail: info@aalas.org
URL: http://www.aalas.org/
Released: Annual. **Audience:** Research veterinarians, medical doctors, PhDs, laboratory animal technicians, and commercial animal breeders. **Principal Exhibits:** Pharmaceuticals and laboratory animal facility equipment and supplies. **Dates and Locations:** 2011 Oct 02-06, San Diego, CA.

14210 ■ American Medical Technologists Convention
American Medical Technologists
10700 W. Higgins, Ste. 150
Rosemont, IL 60018
Ph:(847)823-5169
Free: 800-275-1268
Fax:(847)823-0458
Co. E-mail: mail@amt1.com
URL: http://www.amt1.com
Released: Annual. **Audience:** Clinical laboratory technologists and directors and medical assistants. **Principal Exhibits:** Clinical laboratory books, equipment, supplies, and services.

14211 ■ CLMA/ASCP Annual Conference and Exhibition ThinkLab
Clinical Laboratory Management Association
401 N. Michigan Ave., Ste. 2200
Chicago, IL 60611
Ph:(312)321-5111
Fax:(312)673-6927
Co. E-mail: info@clma.org
URL: http://www.clma.org
Released: Annual. **Audience:** Directors, managers, supervisors, healthcare executives and educators responsible for laboratories and clinical systems mgmt in hospitals health systems, group. **Principal Exhibits:** Laboratory devices manufacturers, laboratory information systems, coagulation homeostasis, publishers, autoimmune disease testing, bacteriology, allergy testing, chemistry systems.

14212 ■ United States and Canadian Academy of Pathology Convention & Exhibits
United States and Canadian Academy of Pathology
3643 Walton Way Extension
Augusta, GA 30909
Ph:(706)733-7550
Fax:(706)733-8033
Co. E-mail: iap@uscap.org
URL: http://www.uscap.org
Released: Annual. **Audience:** General pathologists, veterinary pathologists, toxicologists, pediatric pathologists, osteopathic pathologists, oncologists, and immunologists. **Principal Exhibits:** Medical equipment, laboratory supplies, and medical books. **Dates and Locations:** 2011 Feb 28 - Mar 02, San Antonio, TX.

CONSULTANTS

14213 ■ Barry Page Consulting
1304 Buckingham Rd.
Garner, NC 27529-4706
Ph:(919)779-3037
Fax:(919)779-9682
Co. E-mail: bioservice@compuserve.com
Contact: Barry F. Page, Owner
E-mail: bfjpage@aol.com
Scope: Provides consulting for laboratory operations, product and process troubleshooting, technical file preparation, and product submissions. Expert knowledge of domestic and international standards and requirements for risk assessment, material characterization, biological evaluation, product sterilization, sterilization residuals, and the changing regulatory requirements for medical devices. On site supervision and training for laboratory operations.

FRANCHISES AND BUSINESS OPPORTUNITIES

14214 ■ DNA Services of America
130 Fifth Ave., 10th Fl.
New York, NY 10011-4399
Ph:(212)242-4399
Description: Own a high-demand, innovative business that serves the growing needs of Americans by offering members of your community peace of mind through evidence provided by DNA identification test results for paternity, family relationship establishment, infidelity testing and forensic DNA. **Equity Capital Needed:** $49,175-$97,100 total investment. **Training:** Offers a complete, proven business system, ongoing support, and thorough training.

COMPUTERIZED DATABASES

14215 ■ *The American Hospital Directory*
American Hospital Directory
4350 Brownsboro Rd., Ste. 110
Louisville, KY 40207
Fax:(502)899-7738
Co. E-mail: inbox@ahd.com
URL: http://www.ahd.com
Price: Free. **Entries Include:** Hospital name, address, phone, fax, characteristics, financial statistics, services, accreditation status, utilization statistics, hospital web page. **Database Covers:** Comparative data on hospitals in the U.S.

14216 ■ *Diagnostic Imaging Centers and Chains Directory*
F1RSTMARK Inc.
25 Vintinner Rd.
PO Box 1270
Campton, NH 03223
Ph:(603)726-4800
Free: 800-729-2600
Fax:(603)726-4840
Co. E-mail: leads@firstmark.com
URL: http://www.firstmark.com
Description: Provides listings of more than 6100 diagnostic imaging centers and 900 chains throughout the United States, which includes the name of executive director and/or medical director. Covers centers performing MRI, CT scan, mammography, ultrasound, vascular, nuclear medicine, and X-ray imaging procedures. Facilities may be freestanding or may be in clinics or large medical groups. **Availability:** CD-ROM: F1RSTMARK Inc. **Type:** Directory.

14217 ■ *Health Devices International Sourcebase*
ECRI Institute
5200 Butler Pike
Plymouth Meeting, PA 19462-1298
Ph:(610)825-6000
Fax:(610)834-1275
Co. E-mail: info@ecri.org
URL: http://www.ecri.org
Description: Provides information on more than 15,000 manufacturers and distributors of more than 66,000 new medical devices and equipment. Also includes service companies that buy, sell, and repair used equipment. Provides product name, code, and typical price range for diagnostic and therapeutic medical devices and materials, clinical laboratory equipment and reagents, systems and instruments for testing clinical equipment, and hospital furniture. Product records also contain references, if available, to brand-name evaluations or product specifications in other ECRI publications. Manufacturer information includes organization name and type, contact information, product names and codes, trade names, number of employees and total sales, and names of executive officers. Service records contain organization name, contact information, service category (e. g., clinical laboratory, nuclear medicine), type of service offered (e.g., sales, parts, repairs), locations served, and names of service management personnel. Corresponds to the *Health Devices Sourcebook*. **Availability:** Online: ProQuest LLC, DIMDI, the German Institute of Medical Documentation and Information, ECRI Institute. **Type:** Directory.

14218 ■ *KINETIDEX System*
Thomson Reuters
6200 S Syracuse Way, Ste. 300
Greenwood Village, CO 80111-4740
Ph:(303)486-6444
Free: 800-525-9083
Fax:(303)486-6460
Co. E-mail: mdx.info@thomson.com
URL: http://www.micromedex.com
Description: Contains information on therapeutic drugs and drug dosages. For each drug, provides such information as recommended therapeutic levels, physical IV incompatibilities, clinically significant drug interactions, adverse effects, and guidelines for clinical monitoring. Designed for use by clinicians, enables the user to establish an optimal drug therapy regimen for any patient at any point in time based on age, various disease and physiologic states, multiple

drug therapy, social habits, and drug absorption. Software facilitates calculation of drug dose, interval, peak, trough, and other critical pharmacokinetic parameters. Features tables for drug use in patients with renal dysfunction or liver disease as well as the ability to maintain a database of patient records for use in subsequent drug monitoring and drug utilization review. **Availability:** Online: Thomson Reuters; CD-ROM: Thomson Reuters. **Type:** Full text; Numeric.

14219 ■ *Smoking and Health Resource Library*
U.S. Centers for Disease Control and Prevention
4770 Buford Hwy.
MS K-50
Atlanta, GA 30341
Ph:(404)639-3311
Free: 800-331-3435
Fax:(404)232-3299
Co. E-mail: tobaccoinfo@cdc.gov
URL: http://www.cdc.gov/tobacco
Description: Contains more than 57,000 citations, with some abstracts, to worldwide scientific and technical literature on tobacco, tobacco use, and smoking. Sources include scientific and translated journals, technical reports, bibliographies, books and book chapters, conference proceedings, government documents, policy and legal documents, editorials, letters and patents. Also available as part of the Chronic Disease Prevention (CDP) File CD-ROM (described in a separate entry). **Availability:** Online: U.S. National Library of Medicine, U.S. Centers for Disease Control and Prevention. **Type:** Bibliographic.

14220 ■ *State Health Care Regulatory Developments*
The Bureau of National Affairs Inc.
1801 S Bell St.
Arlington, VA 22202
Free: 800-372-1033
Co. E-mail: customercare@bna.com
URL: http://www.bna.com
Description: Contains information on health care regulatory news and developments in the United States. Subjects include community-based care, home care, emergency care, infectious diseases, managed care, insurance, laboratories, Medicaid, mental health, medical waste, nursing homes, pharmaceuticals, physician services, professional licensing, provider relationships, worker protection and compensation. Entries are organized by state, topic, and register citation. **Availability:** Online: The Bureau of National Affairs Inc., Thomson Reuters. **Type:** Full text.

LIBRARIES

14221 ■ BloodCenter of Wisconsin–Benz Oil Library
PO Box 2178
Milwaukee, WI 53201-2178
Ph:(414)937-6112
Fax:(414)937-6332
Co. E-mail: marylou.rice@bcw.edu
URL: http://www.bcw.edu
Contact: Mary L. Rice, Libn.
Scope: Hematology, immunology, cell biology, clinical medicine. **Services:** Interlibrary loan; copying; Library not open to the public. **Holdings:** 925 books; 3400 bound periodical volumes. **Subscriptions:** 100 journals and other serials; 1 newspaper.

14222 ■ Canadian Society for Medical Laboratory Science Library
PO Box 2830, LCD1
Hamilton, ON, Canada L8N 3N8
Ph:(905)528-8642, x8698
Free: 800-263-8277
Fax:(905)528-4968
URL: http://www.csmls.org
Contact: Lucy Agro, Coord., CE
Scope: Laboratory technology, laboratory standards. **Services:** Library not open to the public. **Holdings:** 291 standards; 125 modules.

RESEARCH CENTERS

14223 ■ American Federation for Medical Research
900 Cummings Ctr., Ste. 221-U
Beverly, MA 01915
Ph:(978)927-8330
Fax:(978)524-8890
Co. E-mail: afmr@prri.com
URL: http://www.afmr.org
Contact: Sharma S. Prabhakar, Pres.
E-mail: afmr@prri.com
Scope: Cardiovascular medicine, dermatology, endocrinology, gastroenterology, genetics, hematology, immunology, connective tissue disease, infectious disease, metabolism, neoplastic disease, patient care, pulmonary medicine. **Services:** Information assistance, on membership status, files, and national abstracting processing. **Publications:** Journal of Investigative Medicine (bimonthly). **Educational Activities:** Scientific programs (annually); Specialized education programs. **Awards:** AFMR Foundation Awards.

14224 ■ Indiana University-Purdue University at Indianapolis–Center for Alzheimer's Disease and Related Disorders
550 N University Blvd., Ste. 1710
Indianapolis, IN 46202
Ph:(317)944-4000
Free: 888—944-3627
Fax:(317)274-5873
Co. E-mail: mfarlow@iupui.edu
URL: http://www.research.iu.edu/centers/cadrnd.html
Contact: Martin R. Farlow MD, Dir.
E-mail: mfarlow@iupui.edu
Scope: Alzheimer's Disease and related neuropsychiatric disorders characterized by memory loss and mood disorders in the older adult.

14225 ■ Public Health Institute
555 12th St., 10th Fl.
Oakland, CA 94607
Ph:(510)285-5500
Fax:(510)285-5501
Co. E-mail: mpittman@phi.org
URL: http://www.phi.org
Contact: Mary A. Pittman, Pres./CEO
E-mail: mpittman@phi.org
Scope: Public health issues, including drug and alcohol problems, occupational and environmental health, nutrition and physical activity, population issues, maternal and child health, violence prevention, reproductive health, leadership development, and public health policy development. **Educational Activities:** Annual California Cancer Registries Conference (annually).

14226 ■ University of California, San Francisco–Center for AIDS Prevention Studies
50 Beale St., Ste. 1300
San Francisco, CA 94105
Ph:(415)597-9100
Fax:(415)597-9213
Co. E-mail: steve.morin@ucsf.edu
URL: http://www.caps.ucsf.edu
Contact: Steve Morin PhD, Dir.
E-mail: steve.morin@ucsf.edu
Scope: Methods to change AIDS high risk behavior. Activities include developing and testing AIDS prevention strategies for at-risk populations, promoting multidisciplinary research on the prevention of HIV disease, funding pilot studies on minority issues in AIDS, and operating the CAPS International Visiting Scholars Program, which brings scholars from Africa, Asia, Eastern Europe, and Latin America to work with CAPS scientists in developing AIDS prevention research protocols. **Publications:** Prevention Fact Sheets. **Educational Activities:** CAPS conference (annually).

Medical Supplies Store

START-UP INFORMATION

14227 ■ "Hot Market Opportunity" in *Small Business Opportunities* (January 2011)
Pub: Harris Publications Inc.
Ed: Description: Mobility products for seniors give this small business a $3 million lift. Profile of 101 Mobility, the nation's first full-service sales, service and installation provider of mobility and accessibility products and equipment including stair lifts, auto lifts, ramps, porch lifts, power wheelchairs and scooters as well as other medical equipment such as walkers, hospital beds and more.

ASSOCIATIONS AND OTHER ORGANIZATIONS

14228 ■ Advanced Medical Technology Association
701 Pennsylvania Ave. NW, Ste. 800
Washington, DC 20004-2654
Ph:(202)783-8700
Fax:(202)783-8750
Co. E-mail: info@advamed.org
URL: http://www.advamed.org
Contact: Stephen J. Ubl, Pres./CEO
Description: Represents domestic (including U.S. territories and possessions) manufacturers of medical devices, diagnostic products, and healthcare information systems. Develops programs and activities on economic, technical, medical, and scientific matters affecting the industry. Gathers and disseminates information concerning the United States and international developments in legislative, regulatory, scientific or standards-making areas. Conducts scientific and educational seminars and programs. **Publications:** *Health Industry Manufacturers Association—Directory* (annual); *In Brief* (monthly).

14229 ■ American Association for Homecare
2011 Crystal Dr., Ste. 725
Arlington, VA 22202
Ph:(703)836-6263
Fax:(703)836-6730
Co. E-mail: info@aahomecare.org
URL: http://www.aahomecare.org
Contact: Mr. Tyler Wilson, Pres./CEO
Description: Represents all elements of home care; dedicated to advancing value and practice of quality healthcare services at home. **Publications:** *AAHomecare Update* (weekly); *HME Answer Book* (quarterly).

REFERENCE WORKS

14230 ■ "Beaumont Outsources Purchasing as Route to Supply Cost Savings" in *Crain's Detroit Business* (Vol. 25, June 1, 2009, No. 22)
Pub: Crain Communications Inc. - Detroit
Ed: Jay Greene. **Description:** William Beaumont Hospitals in Royal Oak have begun outsourcing the purchasing of supplies in order to cut costs. So far,
Beaumont is the only hospital in southeast Michigan to outsource its purchasing department. Other hospitals employ their own purchasing supply workers.

14231 ■ Emergency Medical Services Magazine—Buyers Guide Issue
Pub: Cygnus Business Media
Released: Annual, September; Latest edition 2011. **Publication Includes:** Lists of about 1,000 manufacturers, suppliers, and distributors of equipment and other products used in emergency medical services; coverage includes Canada. Also covers 50 emergency medical service associations, state agencies, and meetings, workshops, and other conferences of interest. **Entries Include:** For companies—Company name, address, phone, fax, toll-free, E-mail address, name of principal executive, product/service. For associations—Name, address, phone, name of director, number of members, description of membership, publications, meeting time. **Arrangement:** Alphabetical. **Indexes:** Product/service.

14232 ■ "GeckoSystems Reduces Sensor Fusion Costs Due to Elder Care Robot Trials" in *Internet Wire* (December 14, 2010)
Pub: Comtex
Description: GeckoSystems International Corporation has been able to reduce the cost of its sensor fusion system while maintaining reliability and performance. The firm's ongoing first in-home elder care robot trials have sparked interest regarding its business model, technologies available for licensing, and joint domestic and international ventures.

14233 ■ Health Devices Sourcebook
Pub: ECRI Institute
Released: Annual, Latest edition 2011. **Price:** $475, individuals. **Covers:** Over 6,800 suppliers of patient care equipment, medical and surgical instruments, implants, clinical laboratory equipment and supplies, medical and hospital disposable supplies, and testing instruments; also lists companies that service, recondition, lease, or buy and sell used equipment; coverage includes U.S. and Canada. **Entries Include:** Company name, address, phone, toll-free phone, fax, toll-free fax, URL, e-mail, total sales, names of key executives and contacts, product categories handled, trade names, methods of distribution, typical pricing, annual volume. Price of directory includes custom updates upon request. **Arrangement:** Alphabetical. **Indexes:** Product listings, manufacturers' product lines, service company profiles, product categories (by number), product categories (alphabetic), product categories (by specialty), manufacturers addresses (geographic), trade names, equipment services, numerical listings, executive contacts, bioterrorism and emergency preparedness.

14234 ■ "HER's: the Future is Free" in *Benzinga.com* (October 29, 2011)
Pub: Benzinga.com
Ed: Benzinga Staff. **Description:** In order to create and maintain electronic health records that connects every physician and hospital it is essential to create a
reliable, easy-to-use, certified Web-based ambulatory ERH using an ad-supported model. eBay seems to be the company showing the most potential for improving services to physicians and consumers, but requires sellers to pay fees based upon sales price.

14235 ■ "Hospitals Try to Buy Smarter" in *Crain's Detroit Business* (Vol. 25, June 1, 2009, No. 22, pp. M025)
Pub: Crain Communications Inc. - Detroit
Ed: Jay Greene. **Description:** Hospitals in southeast Michigan are using bulk discount purchasing of medical and non-medical supplies through group purchasing organizations in order to cut costs.

14236 ■ Medical Device Register
Pub: Canon Communications L.L.C.
Contact: Jessica Moody
E-mail: jmoody@greyhouse.com
Released: Annual, Latest edition 2007. **Price:** $325, individuals; $499, individuals online. **Covers:** More than 65,000 U.S. Manufacturers of medical devices and clinical laboratory products; includes OEM manufacturers. **Entries Include:** For manufacturers—Company name, address, phone, fax, telex, names and titles of key personnel, ownership, medical product sales volume, number of employees, method of distribution, medical product subsidiaries; public company listings include annual revenues and net income. **Arrangement:** Alphabetical. **Indexes:** Product (includes suppliers names, addresses, phone numbers, prices, trade names, product specifications, and advertising), manufacturer, keyword, trade name, OEM manufacturer profile.

14237 ■ "Mentor Medical Device Maker's Partnerships Open New Opportunities" in *Crain's Cleveland Business* (Vol. 30, June 22, 2009, No. 24)
Pub: Crain Communications, Inc.
Ed: Chuck Soder. **Description:** Frantz Medical Development Ltd. develops medical devices based on ideas from outside inventors. The company wants to manufacture the innovations at its Mentor campus.

14238 ■ "Survey: Most Approve of Donating Used Pacemakers to Medically Underserved" in *Crain's Detroit Business* (Vol. 25, June 1, 2009)
Pub: Crain Communications Inc. - Detroit
Description: According to a survey conducted by University of Michigan Cardiovascular Center, 87 percent of those with pacemakers and 71 percent of the general population would donate the device to patients in underserved nations.

TRADE PERIODICALS

14239 ■ Homecare DIRECTION
Pub: Beacon Health Corp.
Contact: Diane J. Omdahl RN, MS, Editor-in-Chief
Released: Monthly. **Price:** $337. **Description:** Delivers timely regulatory information with how-to elements to apply to everyday care delivery. Equips agency patient care personnel with knowledge they need to deliver quality care and comply with medicare

certification and reimbursement requirements. Offers valuable tips on interpreting medicare rules to justify care; how to create policies that reduce survey surprises, and documentation tips and examples. Recurring features include columns titled Documenting with Impact, Survey Sense, Looking for Direction, and From the Lamp Room.

14240 ■ *The League Letter*
Pub: Center for Hearing and Communication
Price: Included in membership. **Description:** Reports on news and events of the The League for the Hard of Hearing. Recurring features include a calendar of events. Remarks: TTY available at (917)305-7999.

14241 ■ *OrthoKinetic Review*
Pub: Novicom Inc.
Released: Bimonthly. **Description:** Magazine featuring new products and services available in the podiatric field.

14242 ■ *Physical Therapy Products*
Pub: Novicom Inc.
Contact: Jody Rich, Gp. Publisher
E-mail: jrich@allied360.com
Ed: Stephen Noonoo, Editor, snoonoo@allied360. com. **Released:** Monthly. **Price:** Free to qualified subscribers. **Description:** Magazine featuring new products and services available in the physical therapy field.

14243 ■ *Surgical Products*
Pub: Advantage Business Media
Contact: Noreen Costelloe, Publisher
E-mail: noreen.costelloe@advantgemedia.com
Ed: Amanda McGowan, Editor, amanda.mcgowan@ advantagemedia.com. **Released:** Bimonthly. **Description:** Magazine on products, technology, equipment, and supplies for operating rooms, intensive care/coronary care units, central supply (in hospitals), and surgicenters.

TRADE SHOWS AND CONVENTIONS

14244 ■ American Academy of Implant Dentistry Annual Meeting
American Academy of Implant Dentistry
211 E. Chicago Ave., Ste. 750
Chicago, IL 60611
Ph:(312)335-1550
Fax:(312)335-9090
Co. E-mail: info@aaid-implant.org
URL: http://www.aaid-implant.org
Released: Annual. **Audience:** Dentists. **Principal Exhibits:** Dental equipment, supplies, and services. **Dates and Locations:** 2011 Oct 19-22, Las Vegas, NV; 2012 Oct 03-06, Washington, DC.

14245 ■ Chicagoland
Advanstar Communications
641 Lexington Ave., 8th Fl.
New York, NY 10022
Ph:(212)951-6600
Fax:(212)951-6793
Co. E-mail: info@advantstar.com
URL: http://www.advanstar.com
Audience: Disabled consumers, seniors, rehab and healthcare professionals, hospital personnel, special educators, dealers and representatives. **Principal Exhibits:** Wheelchairs, assistive technology, personal care products, support organizations, and daily living aids.

14246 ■ North Carolina Medical Society Annual Meeting
North Carolina Medical Society
PO Box 27167
Raleigh, NC 27611
Ph:(919)833-3836
Fax:(919)833-2023
URL: http://www.ncmedsoc.org
Released: Annual. **Audience:** Physicians. **Principal Exhibits:** Medical equipment, supplies, and services.

14247 ■ Southern Medical Association Annual Scientific Assembly
Southern Medical Association
35 Lakeshore Dr.
Birmingham, AL 35209
Ph:(205)945-1840
Free: 800-423-4992
Fax:(205)945-1830
URL: http://www.sma.org
Released: Annual. **Audience:** Doctors, students, residents, and related professionals. **Principal Exhibits:** Medical equipment and pharmaceutical products.

CONSULTANTS

14248 ■ Colucci, Blendow & Johnson
643 Main St., Ste. 7
PO Box 10
Half Moon Bay, CA 94019-1988
Ph:(650)712-0103
Fax:(650)712-0105
Co. E-mail: exsearch@ix.netcom.com
Contact: Bart A. Colucci, President
Scope: Executive search consultants in the medical technology area that includes pharmaceuticals, medical equipment and device manufacturers, biotechnology, therapeutic supplies, diagnostic laboratory equipment and supplies, diagnostic imaging equipment and supplies, medical services, chemicals, cosmetic and toiletries, dental, veterinarian, and agricultural genetics companies.

14249 ■ Harry Schwartz & Associates
100 E Hartsdale Ave.
PO Box 1169
Hartsdale, NY 10530
Ph:(914)725-1642
Fax:(914)725-1134
Contact: Harry Schwartz, President
Scope: Provides public relations and marketing assistance to many entities in the healthcare field, including physician groups, hospitals, manufacturers and sellers of pharmaceuticals and hospital supplies. **Publications:** "Scrip Pharmaceutical Executive"; "Physician's Management".

FRANCHISES AND BUSINESS OPPORTUNITIES

14250 ■ Relax the Back Corp.
6 Centerpoint Dr., Ste. 350
La Palma, CA 90638
Ph:(714)523-2870
Free: 800-290-2225
Fax:(714)523-2980
No. of Franchise Units: 101. **Founded:** 1984. **Franchised:** 1989. **Description:** Ergonomic and back care retailers. **Equity Capital Needed:** $500,000 net worth; $100,000 liquid. **Franchise Fee:** $49,500. **Royalty Fee:** 5%. **Financial Assistance:** Third party financing available. **Training:** Provides 14 days training at headquarters, 4 days at franchisee's location, 2 days of regional training and ongoing support.

14251 ■ Sona MedSpa
Sona MedSpa Intl., Inc.
10710 Sikes Pl., Ste. 120
Charlotte, NC 28277
Ph:(615)591-5040
Fax:(615)591-5041
Co. E-mail: info@sonamedspa.com
URL: http://www.sonamedspa.com
No. of Franchise Units: 40. **No. of Company-Owned Units:** 5. **Founded:** 1997. **Franchised:** 2002. **Description:** Sona offers FDA approved laser hair removal & skin rejuvenation treatments performed by trained, certified medical personnel. We provide safe, effective treatments using the most advanced technology equipment & technologies. **Equity Capital Needed:** $409,200-$824,900. **Franchise Fee:** $59,500. **Royalty Fee:** 7.5%. **Financial Assistance:** Third party financing available. **Training:** Provides 14 days training at headquarters, 6 days at franchisee's location, regional training, web-based training, monthly webcasts and ongoing support.

COMPUTERIZED DATABASES

14252 ■ *The American Hospital Directory*
American Hospital Directory
4350 Brownsboro Rd., Ste. 110
Louisville, KY 40207
Fax:(502)899-7738
Co. E-mail: inbox@ahd.com
URL: http://www.ahd.com
Price: Free. **Entries Include:** Hospital name, address, phone, fax, characteristics, financial statistics, services, accreditation status, utilization statistics, hospital web page. **Database Covers:** Comparative data on hospitals in the U.S.

14253 ■ *Health Devices Alerts*
ECRI Institute
5200 Butler Pike
Plymouth Meeting, PA 19462-1298
Ph:(610)825-6000
Fax:(610)834-1275
Co. E-mail: info@ecri.org
URL: http://www.ecri.org
Description: Contains information on more than 700,000 reported medical device problems, hazards, recalls, technology assessments, evaluations, and updates. Includes citations with abstracts, to English-language medical, legal, and technical literature, Action Items (AI) that ECRI has investigated, Problem Reporting Program (PRP) records from the U.S. Food and Drug Administration (FDA) voluntary reporting program, and Medical Device Reporting (MDR) records from the FDA's mandatory reporting system. Covers problems with diagnostic and therapeutic medical equipment, including radiological equipment, hospital furniture, implanted devices and related accessories, disposable medical products, and clinical laboratory reagents. Corresponds to *Health Devices Alerts*. Is indexed with ECRI's Universal Medical Device Nomenclature System (UMDNS). **Availability:** Online: ProQuest LLC, ECRI Institute, DIMDI, the German Institute of Medical Documentation and Information. **Type:** Bibliographic; Full text.

14254 ■ *Health Devices International Sourcebase*
ECRI Institute
5200 Butler Pike
Plymouth Meeting, PA 19462-1298
Ph:(610)825-6000
Fax:(610)834-1275
Co. E-mail: info@ecri.org
URL: http://www.ecri.org
Description: Provides information on more than 15,000 manufacturers and distributors of more than 66,000 new medical devices and equipment. Also includes service companies that buy, sell, and repair used equipment. Provides product name, code, and typical price range for diagnostic and therapeutic medical devices and materials, clinical laboratory equipment and reagents, systems and instruments for testing clinical equipment, and hospital furniture. Product records also contain references, if available, to brand-name evaluations or product specifications in other ECRI publications. Manufacturer information includes organization name and type, contact information, product names and codes, trade names, number of employees and total sales, and names of executive officers. Service records contain organization name, contact information, service category (e. g., clinical laboratory, nuclear medicine), type of service offered (e.g., sales, parts, repairs), locations served, and names of service management personnel. Corresponds to the *Health Devices Sourcebook*. **Availability:** Online: ProQuest LLC, DIMDI, the German Institute of Medical Documentation and Information, ECRI Institute. **Type:** Directory.

14255 ■ *Medical Device Register*
UBM plc
11444 W Olympic Blvd.
Los Angeles, CA 90064
Ph:(310)445-4200
Fax:(310)445-4299
Co. E-mail: info@ubm.com
URL: http://www.ubmcanon.com
Description: Contains information on more than 82,000 medical devices produced by 13,600 U.S. based Companies and 4000 European Companies.

Provides profiles identifying whether the Manufacturers are the original equipment Manufacturers, distributors, or end Product Manufacturers. Includes information on new product and product recall alerts, customized mailing lists and event alerts and postings. **Availability:** Online: UBM plc; CD-ROM: UBM plc. **Type:** Directory.

LIBRARIES

14256 ■ Association of Tongue Depressors Library
c/o Matthew Schorr
100 E. Maple St.
Teaneck, NJ 07666
Ph:(201)387-6969
Fax:(201)387-6969
Contact: Matthew Schorr, Sec.
Scope: Health care, medical products, marketing. **Holdings:** 280 volumes.

14257 ■ BayerDiag, a Bayer Company Library
63 North St.
Medfield, MA 02052
Ph:(508)359-3538
Fax:(508)359-3442
Co. E-mail: kathleen.mccabe.b@bayer.com
URL: http://www.bayerdiag.com/
Contact: Kathleen E. McCabe, Mgr. of Info.Ctrs.
Scope: Clinical medicine, market research, engineering, biotechnology, business. **Services:** Center not

open to the public. **Holdings:** 3000 books; 3500 periodical volumes; 28,000 patents; 850 research reports. **Subscriptions:** 425 journals and other serials.

14258 ■ ECRI Institute Library
5200 Butler Pike
Plymouth Meeting, PA 19462
Ph:(610)825-6000
Fax:(610)834-1275
Co. E-mail: info@ecri.org
URL: http://www.ecri.org
Contact: Evelyn Kuserk, Lib.Supv.
Scope: Medical devices, biomedical engineering, hospital safety, health services research, health technology assessment. **Services:** Interlibrary loan; Library not open to the public. **Holdings:** 11,000 books; 470 VF drawers of technical reports and evaluation data. **Subscriptions:** 2000 journals and other serials.

14259 ■ Harvard University–School of Medicine–The Libraries of the Massachusetts Eye and Ear Infirmary (243 C)
243 Charles St.
Boston, MA 02114
Ph:(617)573-3196
Fax:(617)573-3370
Co. E-mail: judith_nims@meei.harvard.edu
URL: http://www.masseyeandear.org/about-us/library-resources/
Contact: Judith Nims, Lib.Dir.
Scope: Ophthalmology, otolaryngology. **Services:** Interlibrary loan; copying; Library blog; Library open

to the public for reference use only. **Holdings:** 7000 volumes; 11,000 bound periodical volumes; 300 stereophotographs of diseases of the eye; 130 cubic feet of archival materials; 40 cubic feet of manuscripts; 2000 rare books. **Subscriptions:** 130 journals and other serials.

14260 ■ U.S. Food & Drug Administration–Center for Devices & Radiological Health–Library HFZ-46 (9200)
9200 Corporate Blvd.
Rockville, MD 20850
Ph:(301)827-6901
Fax:(301)594-2352
Co. E-mail: hba@cdrh.fda.gov
URL: http://www.fda.gov/cdrh
Contact: Harriet Albersheim, Chf.Libn.
Scope: Medical devices, artificial organs, biomedical engineering, biomaterials, radiology, radiobiology, radiation, nuclear medicine, radiological health, radiation protection, radiation hazards, emission, microwaves, ultrasonics, lasers. **Services:** Interlibrary loan; Library open to the public for reference use only. **Holdings:** 7000 books; periodical titles (bound and microfilm). **Subscriptions:** 700 journals and other serials.

ASSOCIATIONS AND OTHER ORGANIZATIONS

14261 ■ Association for Healthcare Documentation Integrity
4230 Kiernan Ave., Ste. 130
Modesto, CA 95356
Ph:(209)527-9620
Free: 800-982-2182
Fax:(209)527-9633
Co. E-mail: ahdi@ahdionline.org
URL: http://www.ahdionline.org
Contact: Wendy Carriegan, Dir. of Admin.
Description: Medical transcriptionists, their supervisors, teachers and students of medical transcription, owners and managers of medical transcription services, and other interested health personnel. Provides information about the profession of medical transcription and gives continuing education for medical transcriptionists. Advocates professional recognition of medical transcriptionists in county, state, and national medical societies and in health care facilities nationwide. Sponsors voluntary certification/ credentialing program. Offers updates on developments in medicine and curricula, and on new transcription methods and equipment; sponsors and encourages research in the field. Establishes guidelines for education of medical transcriptionists. **Publications:** *Health Data Matrix* (bimonthly); *Vitals* (weekly).

REFERENCE WORKS

14262 ■ "Help Wanted: 100 Hospitals IT Workers" in *Business Courier* **(Vol. 27, October 8, 2010, No. 23, pp. 1)**
Pub: Business Courier
Ed: James Ritchie. **Description:** Hospitals in the Greater Cincinnati area are expected to hire more than 100 information technology (IT) workers to help digitize medical records. Financial incentives from the health care reform bill encouraged investments in electronic medical record systems, increasing the demand for IT workers that would help make information exchange across the healthcare system easier.

14263 ■ "Providers Ride First Wave of eHealth Dollars" in *Boston Business Journal* **(Vol. 31, June 10, 2011, No. 20, pp. 1)**
Pub: Boston Business Journal
Ed: Julie M. Donnelly. **Description:** Health care providers in Massachusetts implementing electronic medical records technology started receiving federal stimulus funds. Beth Israel Deaconess Medical Center was the first hospital to qualify for the funds.

LIBRARIES

14264 ■ American Health Information Management Association–FORE Library
233 N. Michigan Ave., 21st Fl.
Chicago, IL 60601
Ph:(312)233-1803
Fax:(312)253-7060
Co. E-mail: library.services@ahima.org
URL: http://www.ahimafoundation.org/PolicyResearch/LibraryServices.aspx
Contact: Nadine Caputo, MS, Dir. of R&D
Scope: Medical records; codes and coding - classification of disease. **Services:** Document delivery; Library not open to the public. **Holdings:** 1100 books. **Subscriptions:** 130 journals and other serials.

14265 ■ Davenport University–Thomas F. Reed, Jr. Memorial Library
4123 W. Main St.
Kalamazoo, MI 49006
Ph:(616)382-2835
Free: 800-632-8928
Fax:(269)382-2657
Co. E-mail: kz_linc@davenport.edu
URL: http://www.davenport.edu/
Contact: Judith J. Bosshart, Dir.
Scope: Business, data processing, administrative services, accounting, humanities, paralegal, medical records, healthcare administration, computer and information processing. **Services:** Interlibrary loan; copying; faxing; Library open to the public for reference use only. **Holdings:** 14,200 books; 995 videotapes. **Subscriptions:** 12,000 journals and other serials; 6 newspapers.

14266 ■ Florida A&M University–Frederick S. Humphries Science Research Center Library
401-501 Science Research Center
309 Pershing St.
Tallahassee, FL 32307
Ph:(850)599-3393
Fax:(850)599-3422
Co. E-mail: william.nichols@famu.edu
URL: http://www.famu.edu/index.
cfma=library&p=ScienceResearch
Contact: William Nichols, Assoc.Univ.Libn.
Scope: Pharmacy, allied health, physics, computer science, environmental science, respiratory therapy, physical therapy, healthcare management, medical records administration, occupational therapy. **Services:** Interlibrary loan; copying; SDI; Library open to the public. **Holdings:** 5989 bound periodical volumes; 915 print and online journals; 791 microcards; 24,102 monographs. **Subscriptions:** 697 journals and other serials; 5 newspapers.

START-UP INFORMATION

14267 ■ **"Courier Service Delivers Big Profits and Top-Notch Customer Service" in** *Small Business Opportunities* **(November 2007)**
Pub: Harris Publications Inc.
Description: Profile of Relay Express, a courier franchising business started by three friends in 1986. The company focuses on customer service and calls them every 19 minutes to report on progress of a parcel until it is delivered.

ASSOCIATIONS AND OTHER ORGANIZATIONS

14268 ■ **Canadian Courier and Logistics Association–Association Canadienne des Enterprises de Messagerie**
660 Eglinton Ave. E, Unit 119, Box 333
Toronto, ON, Canada M4G 3K2
Ph:(416)696-9995
Free: 877-766-6604
Fax:(416)696-9993
Co. E-mail: dturnbull@canadiancourier.org
URL: http://www.canadiancourier.org
Contact: David Turnbull, Pres./CEO
Description: Courier services and shipping and delivery companies. Promotes growth and development of the shipping and delivery industries. Facilitates communication and cooperation among members; represents members' interests before trade and labor organizations, government agencies, and the public. **Publications:** *E-News* (bimonthly).

14269 ■ **Messenger Courier Association of America**
750 National Press Bldg.
529 14th St. NW
Washington, DC 20045
Ph:(202)785-3298
Fax:(202)223-9741
Co. E-mail: bdecaprio@mcaa.com
URL: http://www.mcaa.com
Contact: Bob DeCaprio, Exec. Dir.
Description: Trade organization of local and international messenger courier companies. Addresses issues facing the industry, including municipal traffic ordinances that impede industry operations. Works to establish driver pools and to develop centralized core computer service bureaus for smaller courier companies. Provides training, discount purchasing programs, and legislative and regulatory issue monitoring. Conducts educational and research programs; compiles statistics. **Publications:** *Who's Who in the Messenger Courier Industry* (annual).

14270 ■ **National Association of Professional Process Servers**
PO Box 4547
Portland, OR 97208-4547
Ph:(503)222-4180
Free: 800-477-8211
Fax:(503)222-3950
Co. E-mail: administrator@napps.org
URL: http://www.napps.org
Contact: Gary A. Crowe, Admin.
Description: Individuals and companies who serve summonses, complaints, subpoenas, and other legal documents. Goals are to: promote and upgrade the process-serving industry; establish high moral and ethical standards for the industry; monitor legislation at the state and federal level; assist in the formation and continuation of state associations representing the industry. Seeks to improve relations between process servers and members of the legal community such as attorneys, judges, clerks, and court officers. Assists with service of process in foreign countries through the Hague Service Convention; makes discount insurance programs available to members. **Publications:** *Annual Seminar Conferences*; *The Docket Sheet* (bimonthly); *Membership Directory and Civil Rules Guide* (semiannual).

REFERENCE WORKS

14271 ■ *The Concierge Manual: A Step-by-Step Guide to Starting Your Own Concierge Service or Lifestyle Management Company*
Pub: New Road Publishing
Ed: Katharine C. Giovanni. **Released:** September 9, 2010. **Price:** $23.00. **Description:** Answering some of the biggest questions about the logistics of running a concierge business, this guide provides all the tools necessary to create a successful concierge, lifestyle management, errand service, or personal assistant company.

14272 ■ **"Pocket Change?" in** *Inc.* **(Vol. 30, December 2008, No. 12, pp. 28)**
Pub: Mansueto Ventures LLC
Ed: Ryan McCarthy. **Description:** Owner of a chain of nine retail billiard showrooms grew his business by starting to deliver pool tables for Sears. The company, consisting of seven retail locations and two warehouses, is now for sale. Details are included.

FRANCHISES AND BUSINESS OPPORTUNITIES

14273 ■ **AIM Mail Centers**
Amailcenter Franchise Corp.
15550-D Rockfield Blvd.
Irvine, CA 92618
Ph:(949)837-4145
Free: 800-669-4246
Fax:(949)837-4537
No. of Franchise Units: 66. **Founded:** 1985. **Franchised:** 1989. **Description:** Business service center. **Equity Capital Needed:** $132,100-$211,400, including working capital. **Franchise Fee:** $26,900. **Royalty Fee:** 5%. **Financial Assistance:** Yes. **Training:** Yes.

14274 ■ **Fastway Couriers (Canada)**
300-1687 West Broadway
Vancouver, BC, Canada V6J 1X2
Ph:(604)739-2520
Free: 877-739-2520
Fax:(604)739-2560
Co. E-mail: info@fastway.ca
URL: http://www.fastway.ca
Founded: 1983. **Franchised:** 1984. **Description:** Sole Regional Franchise rights for each city are awarded to only one entrepreneur who enters the business of franchising, not package distribution. Cities are then divided into territories which are awarded to Courier Franchisees who conduct the actual distribution of packages. **Equity Capital Needed:** Regional $200,000-$700,000; Courier $8,000+ van. **Training:**

14275 ■ **Parcel Plus**
International Center For Entrepreneurial Development
12715 Telge Rd.
Cypress, TX 77429
Free: 888-280-2053
Fax:(281)256-4178
Co. E-mail: ppsales@iced.net
URL: http://www.parcelplus.com
No. of Franchise Units: 67. **Founded:** 1986. **Franchised:** 1988. **Description:** Offer packaging, freight, cargo, crating and international shipping in a retail setting. **Equity Capital Needed:** $152,200-$198,400. **Franchise Fee:** $35,000. **Royalty Fee:** 6%. **Financial Assistance:** No. **Training:** Owners attend 4 days classroom training and visit existing locations.

ASSOCIATIONS AND OTHER ORGANIZATIONS

14276 ■ National Golf Foundation
1150 S U.S. Hwy. 1, Ste. 401
Jupiter, FL 33477
Ph:(561)744-6006
Free: 888-275-4643
Fax:(561)744-6107
Co. E-mail: general@ngf.org
URL: http://www.ngf.org
Contact: Dr. Joseph F. Beditz, Pres./CEO
Description: Golf-oriented businesses including: equipment and apparel companies; golf facilities; golf publications; golf course architects, developers and builders; companies offering specialized services to the golf industry; golf associations; teachers, coaches and instructors and other interested individuals. Serves as a market research and strategic planning organization for the golf industry and promotes public golf course development in the U.S. Provides information and consulting services for golf course planning, construction, and operation. Conducts golf course development and operations seminars including the National Institute of Golf Management. **Publications:** *Golf Facilities in the U.S.* (annual); *Golf Industry Report* (bimonthly).

14277 ■ Professional Putters Association
28 Sioux Trail
Ransom Canyon, TX 79366
Ph:(434)237-7888
Co. E-mail: joe@proputters.com
URL: http://www.proputters.com
Contact: Joe Aboid, Commissioner
Description: Persons over age 18 who compete in national putting tournaments sanctioned by the Association; "Putt Putt" golf course franchise owners, managers, and suppliers. Seeks to recognize, develop, and reward the skills and abilities of America's putters. Sponsors competitions; compiles statistics; presents awards national, regional and local titles and cash prizes. Produces Putt-Putt Golf Courses Championship currently airing on ESPN Series, a television sports show of three half-hour segments. **Publications:** *Putt Putt World* (biennial).

14278 ■ United States Golf Association
PO Box 708
Far Hills, NJ 07931
Ph:(908)234-2300
Free: 800-223-0041
Fax:(908)234-9687
Co. E-mail: membership@usga.org
URL: http://www.usga.org
Contact: James B. Hyler Jr., Pres.
Description: Regularly organized golf clubs and golf courses. Serves as governing body for golf in the United States. Turfgrass Visiting Service promotes scientific work in turf management. Provides data on rules, handicapping, amateur status, tournament procedure, turf maintenance, and golf balls and implements. Administers Golf House Museum, a collection of memorabilia including clubs of champions, the Moon Club, and paintings, insignia, and portraits of USGA champions. Sponsors USGA Research and Educational Fund. Conducts 13 annual national championships and research programs; sponsors teams for international competitions. **Publications:** *Golf Journal* (9/year).

TRADE SHOWS AND CONVENTIONS

14279 ■ FUN Expo
Reed Exhibitions North American Headquarters
383 Main Ave.
Norwalk, CT 06851
Ph:(203)840-4800
Fax:(203)840-5805
Co. E-mail: export@reedexpo.com
URL: http://www.reedexpo.com
Released: Annual. **Principal Exhibits:** Amusement and recreation products for family and location based entertainment centers, small amusement parks and family oriented businesses such as bowling centers, skating rinks, sports parks, miniature golf courses, golf driving ranges, family restaurants, resorts and other entertainment/recreation businesses. **Dates and Locations:** 2011 Mar 01-03, Las Vegas, NV.

FRANCHISES AND BUSINESS OPPORTUNITIES

14280 ■ Monster Mini Golf
400 Harris St.
Providence, RI 02909
Ph:(401)454-8100
No. of Franchise Units: 27. **Founded:** 2004. **Franchised:** 2005. **Description:** Family entertainment center featuring glow-in-the-dark mini golf. **Equity Capital Needed:** $390,000-$471,000. **Franchise Fee:** $30,000. **Royalty Fee:** 7%. **Financial Assistance:** Limited third party financing available. **Training:** Offers 2-4 weeks at headquarters, 2 weeks onsite with ongoing support.

DIRECTORIES OF EDUCATIONAL PROGRAMS

14281 ■ *Directory of Private Accredited Career Schools and Colleges of Technology*
Pub: Accrediting Commission of Career Schools and Colleges of Technology
Contact: Michale S. McComis, Exec. Dir.
Released: On web page. **Price:** Free. **Description:** Covers 3900 accredited post-secondary programs that provide training programs in business, trade, and technical fields, including various small business endeavors. Entries offer school name, address, phone, description of courses, job placement assistance, and requirements for admission. Arrangement is alphabetical.

REFERENCE WORKS

14282 ■ **"A Digital Makeover for the Modeling Business" in** *Inc.* **(February 2008, pp. 82-86, 88-89)**
Pub: Gruner & Jahr USA Publishing
Ed: David H. Freedman. **Description:** Ways the Ford Modeling Agency is using the online You Tube to realign its business are presented. Products to help a firm grow its presence on the Internet are included.

14283 ■ **"Fashionistas Weigh in on the Super-Thin" in** *Charlotte Observer* **(February 7, 2007)**
Pub: Knight-Ridder/Tribune Business News
Ed: Crystal Dempsey. **Description:** Council of Fashion Designers of America held a panel discussion regarding the weight and ages of models used to highlight clothing.

VIDEOCASSETTES/ AUDIOCASSETTES

14284 ■ *Modeling, Commercials, & Acting*
Educational Video Network
1401 19th St.
Huntsville, TX 77340
Ph:(936)295-5767
Free: 800-762-0060
Fax:(936)294-0233
URL: http://www.evndirect.com
Price: $49.95. **Description:** Features interviews from TV stars, models, and Hollywood agents who offer advice on how to get started in acting and modeling, including tips on photo preparation, resume writing, and agents. **Availability:** VHS.

14285 ■ *Modeling Made Easy*
Videoactive Co.
2522 Hyperion Ave.
Los Angeles, CA 90027-3317
Ph:(323)669-8544
Free: 800-927-2949
Co. E-mail: bill@videoactive.com
URL: http://www.videoactive.com
Description: In-depth instructional video on modeling techniques, including runway techniques for both men and women, breaking into modeling, the different types of modeling, and tips on the fashion show. Features Jill Donnellan, model, actress, and former Miss Bermuda. **Availability:** VHS.

START-UP INFORMATION

14286 ■ *Foreclosure Cleanout Business: High Profits – Low Start Up Cost*
Pub: James R. Tolliver
Ed: James Tolliver. **Released:** October 11, 2011. **Price:** $17.99. **Description:** Foreclosure cleanout business is booming. This manual teaches how to start a foreclosure firm, who to contact, what to charge, services provided and more.

ASSOCIATIONS AND OTHER ORGANIZATIONS

14287 ■ **Council of Real Estate Brokerage Managers**
430 N Michigan Ave.
Chicago, IL 60611-4011
Ph:(312)321-4414
Free: 800-621-8738
Fax:(312)329-8882
Co. E-mail: info@crb.com
URL: http://www.crb.com
Contact: Matthew Ferrara, CEO
Description: Represents managers, brokers and owners, serving nearly 7,000 members through superior educational programming, products and publications. Exemplifies professional achievement and recognition in real estate brokerage management. Bestows CRB (Certified Real Estate Brokerage Manager) designation on members who have completed courses conducted by REBMC. **Publications:** *e-Connections Newsletter* (monthly); *Real Estate Business Magazine* (bimonthly).

14288 ■ **Mortgage Bankers Association**
1717 Rhode Island Ave. NW, Ste. 400
Washington, DC 20036
Ph:(202)557-2700
Free: 800-793-6222
Co. E-mail: membership@mortgagebankers.org
URL: http://www.mortgagebankers.org
Contact: Michael D. Berman CMB, Chm.
Description: Principal lending and investor interests in the mortgage finance field, including mortgage banking firms, commercial banks, life insurance companies, title companies, and savings and loan associations. Seeks to improve methods of originating, servicing, and marketing loans of residential and income-producing properties through industry education and cooperation with federal agencies and the Congress. Holds clinics on all aspects of the mortgage finance business. Sponsors School of Mortgage Banking, and correspondence courses and web-based training on mortgage subjects for member personnel. Collects statistics and conducts research on the industry. **Publications:** *Mortgage Bankers Performance Study* (quarterly); *Mortgage Banking: The Magazine of Real Estate Finance* (monthly); *National Delinquency Survey* (quarterly).

14289 ■ **Mortgage Insurance Companies of America**
1425 K St. NW, Ste. 210
Washington, DC 20005

Ph:(202)682-2683
Fax:(202)842-9252
Co. E-mail: info@privatemi.com
URL: http://www.privatemi.com
Contact: Jeff Lubar, Dir. of Communications
Description: U.S. and Australian mortgage insurance companies united to provide a forum for discussion of industrywide standards, and for representation before Congress and federal and state regulatory agencies that reviews housing-related legislation. Compiles statistics. **Publications:** *PrivateMI Perspective* (quarterly).

14290 ■ **National Association of Mortgage Brokers**
7900 Westpark Dr., Ste. T309
McLean, VA 22102
Ph:(703)342-5900
Fax:(703)342-5905
Co. E-mail: rdeloach@namb.org
URL: http://www.namb.org
Contact: Michael J. D'Alonzo CMC, Pres.
Description: Mortgage brokers seeking to increase professionalism and to foster business relationships among members. Offers three levels of professional certification. Focuses on education and government affairs. .

14291 ■ **National Association of Professional Mortgage Women**
PO Box 451718
Garland, TX 75045
Free: 800-827-3034
Co. E-mail: napmw1@aol.com
URL: http://www.napmw.org
Contact: Gary Tumbiolo, Pres.
Description: Supports professional and personal development for individuals in the mortgage lending industry. Aims to maintain high standards of professional conduct and to encourage the educational advancement of women in the industry. Believes in equal recognition and professional opportunities for women. Offers professional designations through the Institute of Mortgage Lending. .

14292 ■ **National Association of Real Estate Brokers**
5504 Brentwood Stair Rd.
Fort Worth, TX 76112
Ph:(817)446-7715
Fax:(817)446-7744
Co. E-mail: wvincent.wimbish@nareb.com
URL: http://www.nareb.com
Contact: Vincent Wimbish, Pres.
Description: Members of the real estate industry. Research, educational and certification programs include: Real Estate Management Brokers Institute; National Society of Real Estate Appraisers; Real Estate Brokerage Institute; United Developers Council. Encourages unity among those who are engaged in real estate. Promotes and maintains high standards of conduct. Protects the public against unethical, improper, or fraudulent practices connected with the real estate business. Conducts research; compiles statistics on productivity, marketing and development. Gives members license to use "Realtist" symbol.

Sponsors educational seminars. Maintains Willis E. Carson Library. **Publications:** *Realtist Membership Directory* (annual).

14293 ■ **National Association of Review Appraisers and Mortgage Underwriters**
810 N Farrell Dr.
Palm Springs, CA 92262
Ph:(760)327-5284
Fax:(760)327-5631
Co. E-mail: support@assoc-hdqts.org
URL: http://www.naramu.org
Contact: Dr. Bill Merrell, Advisory Council
Description: Real estate professionals and mortgage underwriters who aid in determining value of property. Acts as umbrella group for real estate appraisers. Conducts educational seminars; maintains speakers' bureau; operates placement service. **Publications:** Membership Directory (annual).

REFERENCE WORKS

14294 ■ "The 35 Year Mortgage-Built to Last Time" in *Globe & Mail* (March 17, 2006, pp. B1)
Pub: CTVglobemedia Publishing Inc.
Ed: Patrick Brethour. **Description:** The 35-year mortgage has arrived in Canada. The plan will give an opportunity to the first-time buyers into the real estate market. Details of the new mortgage are analyzed.

14295 ■ "A Good Step, But There's a Long Way to Go" in *Business Week* (September 22, 2008, No. 4100, pp. 10)
Pub: McGraw-Hill Companies, Inc.
Ed: James C. Cooper. **Description:** Despite the historic action by the U.S. government to nationalize the mortgage giants Freddie Mac and Fannie Mae, rising unemployment rates may prove to be an even bigger roadblock to bringing back the economy from its downward spiral. The takeover is meant to restore confidence in the credit markets and help with the mortgage crisis but the rising rate in unemployment may make many households unable to take advantage of any benefits which arise from the bailout. Statistical data included.

14296 ■ "AIG Fixed; Is Michigan Next?" in *Crain's Detroit Business* (Vol. 24, September 22, 2008, No. 38, pp. 1)
Pub: Crain Communications, Inc.
Ed: Jay Greene. **Description:** Michigan's economic future is examined as is the mortgage buyout plan and American International Group Inc.'s takeover by the U.S. government.

14297 ■ "All Bubbles Must Burst" in *Canadian Business* (Vol. 83, August 17, 2010, No. 13-14, pp. 12)
Pub: Rogers Media Ltd.
Ed: Matthew McClearn. **Description:** Canada's housing markets is showing signs of cooling down as home and condo sales both fell for the first time in 16 years. The Canadian government has fueled the

market over an extended period through Canada Mortgage and Housing Corporation's role in insuring mortgage lenders against risk of defaults.

14298 ■ "Antwerpen Takes on Chrysler Financial Over Foreclosure Sales" in *Baltimore Business Journal* **(Vol. 28, July 30, 2010, No. 12, pp. 1)**
Pub: Baltimore Business Journal
Ed: Gary Haber. **Description:** Antwerpen Motorcars Ltd. aims to fight the scheduled foreclosure sale of real estate it leases in Baltimore County, including the showroom for its Hyundai dealership on Baltimore National Pike in Catonsville, Maryland. The company is planning to file papers in court to stop the scheduled August 11, 2010 auction sought by Chrysler Financial Services Americas LLC.

14299 ■ "Apartment Market Down, Not Out" in *Crain's Detroit Business* **(Vol. 24, October 6, 2008, No. 40, pp. 9)**
Pub: Crain Communications, Inc.
Ed: Daniel Duggan. **Description:** Detroit's apartment market is considered to have some of the strongest fundamentals of any apartment market in the country with relatively low vacancy rates and a relatively low supply of new units compared with demand. Investors continue to show interest in the buildings but the national lending market is making it difficult to invest in the city.

14300 ■ "Asia Breathes a Sigh of Relief" in *Business Week* **(September 22, 2008, No. 4100, pp. 32)**
Pub: McGraw-Hill Companies, Inc.
Ed: Bruce Einhorn; Theo Francis; Chi-Chu Tschang; Moon Ihlwan; Hiroko Tashiro. **Description:** Foreign bankers, such as those in Asia, that had been investing heavily in the United States began to worry as the housing crisis deepened and the impact on Freddie Mac and Fannie Mae became increasingly clear. Due to the government bailout, however, central banks will most likely continue to buy American debt.

14301 ■ "Au Revoir Or Goodbye?" in *Barron's* **(Vol. 88, July 14, 2008, No. 28, pp. 5)**
Pub: Dow Jones & Co., Inc.
Ed: Alan Abelson. **Description:** Former Senator Phil Gramm's opinion that the U.S. is a "nation of whiners" as they moan about recession is another example of the disconnection between Washington and Wall Street on one hand and the real world on the other. It would be a catastrophe for most of the world if Fannie Mae and Freddie Mac were to go under and take their trillions of mortgage debt with them.

14302 ■ "Back on Track-Or Off the Rails?" in *Business Week* **(September 22, 2008, No. 4100, pp. 22)**
Pub: McGraw-Hill Companies, Inc.
Ed: Peter Coy; Tara Kalwarski. **Description:** Discusses the possible scenarios the American economy may undergo due to the takeover of Fannie Mae and Freddie Mac. Statistical data included.

14303 ■ "Bad-Loan Bug Bites Mid-Tier Banks; More Pain, Tighter Lending Standards Ahead, CEOs Say" in *Crain's Chicago Business* **(May 5, 2008)**
Pub: Crain Communications, Inc.
Ed: Steve Daniels. **Description:** Mid-sized commercial banks form the bedrock of Chicago's financial-services industry and they are now feeling the results of the credit crisis that has engulfed the nation's largest banks and brokerages. Commercial borrowers are seeing tighter terms on loans and higher interest rates while bank investors are unable to forecast lenders' earnings performance from quarter to quarter. Statistical data included.

14304 ■ "Bad Loans Start Piling Up" in *Crain's New York Business* **(Vol. 24, January 7, 2008, No. 1, pp. 2)**
Pub: Crain Communications, Inc.
Ed: Tom Fredrickson. **Description:** Problems in the subprime mortgage industry have extended to other lending activities as evidenced by bank charge-offs on bad commercial and industrial loans which have more than doubled in the third quarter.

14305 ■ "Bailout May Force Cutbacks, Job Losses" in *The Business Journal - Serving Phoenix and the Valley of the Sun* **(Vol. 29, September 26, 2008, No. 4, pp. 1)**
Pub: American City Business Journals, Inc.
Ed: Mike Sunnucks. **Description:** Economists say the proposed $700 billion bank bailout could affect Arizona businesses as banks could be forced to reduce the amount and number of loans it has thereby forcing businesses to shrink capital expenditures and then jobs. However, the plan could also stimulate the economy by taking bad loans off banks balance sheets according to another economist.

14306 ■ "Bankruptcies Swell" in *The Business Journal-Portland* **(Vol. 25, July 4, 2008, No. 17, pp. 1)**
Pub: American City Business Journals, Inc.
Ed: Andy Giegerich. **Description:** Individual and business bankruptcy filings in Portland, Oregon had increased. The rising gas and food prices, mortgage crisis and tightening lending standards are seen as causes of bankruptcies. Statistics on bankruptcy filings are also provided.

14307 ■ "Bankruptcy Blowback" in *Business Week* **(September 22, 2008, No. 4100, pp. 36)**
Pub: McGraw-Hill Companies, Inc.
Ed: Jessica Silver-Greenberg. **Description:** Changes to bankruptcy laws which were enacted in 2005 after banks and other financial institutions lobbied hard for them are now suffering the consequences of the laws which force more troubled borrowers to let their homes go into foreclosure; lenders suffer financially every time they have to take on a foreclosure and the laws in which they lobbied so hard to see enacted are now becoming a problem for these lending institutions. Details of the changes in the laws are outlined as are the affects on the consumer, the economy and the lenders.

14308 ■ "Banks Seeing Demand for Home Equity Loans Slowing" in *Crain's Cleveland Business* **(Vol. 28, December 3, 2007, No. 48, pp. 1)**
Pub: Crain Communications, Inc.
Ed: Shawn A. Turner. **Description:** Discusses the reasons for the decline in demand for home equity loans and lines of credit. Statistical data included.

14309 ■ "Best Income Trust" in *Canadian Business* **(Vol. 81, Summer 2008, No. 9, pp. 69)**
Pub: Rogers Media Ltd.
Ed: Calvin Leung. **Description:** Table showing five-year annualized growth rate and one-year stock performance of real estate investment trusts firms in Canada is presented. Calgary-based Boardwalk REIT is projected to grow the fastest among North American REITs over the next two years. Other details on the stock performance analysis are presented.

14310 ■ "Beware the Ides of March" in *Canadian Business* **(Vol. 81, April 14, 2008, No. 6, pp. 13)**
Pub: Rogers Media
Ed: Jeff Sanford. **Description:** Financial troubles of Bear Stearns in March, 2008 was part of the credit crunch that started in the summer of 2007 in the U.S. when subprime mortgages that were written for people who could barely afford the payments started defaulting. The bankruptcy protection given to 20 asset backed commercial paper trusts is being fought by the investors in these securities who could stand to lose 40 percent of their money under the agreement.

14311 ■ "Bills Would Regulate Mortgage Loan Officers" in *Crain's Detroit Business* **(Vol. 24, February 25, 2008, No. 8, pp. 9)**
Pub: Crain Communications Inc. - Detroit
Ed: Amy Lane. **Description:** New legislation in Michigan, if passed, would create a registration process for mortgage loan officers in the state in order to address the mortgage loan crisis.

14312 ■ "BofA Will Reach the Top with Countrywide Deal" in *Business North Carolina* **(Vol. 28, March 2008, No. 3, pp. 36)**
Pub: Business North Carolina
Description: Bank of America, headquartered in Charlotte, North Carolina, will add Countrywide to its

let of credits. Countrywide is the largest U.S. mortgage lender. Statistical data included.

14313 ■ "Bottom's Up" in *Barron's* **(Vol. 88, July 14, 2008, No. 28, pp. 25)**
Pub: Dow Jones & Co., Inc.
Ed: Jonathan R. Laing. **Description:** Economist Chip Case believes that home prices are nearing a bottom based on his analysis of the history of the housing market; surprisingly, in the past the housing market has rebounded after a quarter from a massive housing start drop. The drop in early stage delinquencies is another sign of the housing market's recovery.

14314 ■ "Business Still Expected to Take Hit in 2008" in *Business Journal-Serving Phoenix and the Valley of the Sun* **(December 28, 2007)**
Pub: American City Business Journals, Inc.
Ed: Chris Casacchia. **Description:** Community banks in 2008 are still projected to suffer from the repercussions of the subprime mortgage and credit crises. Meanwhile, the asset devaluation of big banks and global investment companies are higher than that of smaller banks. The third quarter and fourth quarter losses of banks such as Bear Stearns are discussed as well.

14315 ■ "Business Still Expected To Take Hit In 2008" in *Business Journal-Serving Phoenix and the Valley of the Sun* **(December 28, 2007)**
Pub: American City Business Journals, Inc.
Ed: Chris Casacchia. **Description:** Community banks are expected to suffer through 2008 due to the subprime mortgage and credit crisis. Meanwhile, the asset devaluation of big banks and global investment companies are higher than that of smaller banks. Third and fourth quarter losses of banks, including Bear Sterns, are discussed.

14316 ■ *Chain of Blame: How Wall Street Caused the Mortgage and Credit Crisis*
Pub: John Wiley & Sons, Inc.
Ed: Paul Muolo, Mathew Padilla. **Released:** 2009. **Price:** $27.95. **Description:** The book describes how risky loans given irresponsibly put big investment banks at the center of the subprime crisis.

14317 ■ "Citi Ruling Could Chill SEC, Street Legal Pacts" in *Wall Street Journal Eastern Edition* **(November 29, 2011, pp. C1)**
Pub: Dow Jones & Company Inc.
Ed: Jean Eaglesham, Chad Bray. **Description:** A $285 million settlement was reached between the Securities and Exchange Commission and Citigroup Inc. over allegations the bank misled investors over a mortgage-bond deal. Now, Judge Jed S. Rakoff has ruled against the settlement, a decision that will affect the future of such attempts to prosecute Wall Street fraud. Rakoff said that the settlement was "neither fair, nor reasonable, nor adequate, nor in the public interest."

14318 ■ "Coming Soon: Bailouts of Fannie and Freddie" in *Barron's* **(Vol. 88, July 14, 2008, No. 28, pp. 14)**
Pub: Dow Jones & Co., Inc.
Ed: Jonathan R. Laing. **Description:** Assurances from the government that Fannie Mae and Freddie Mac are adequately capitalized and able to carry on their duties as guarantors or owners of over $5 trillion of U.S. home mortgages are designed to keep both entities afloat until they attempt to raise $10 billion in new equity. The government would assume any losses in a bailout and owners of the banks' papers would profit as yields drop.

14319 ■ "Condominium Sales Fall to a Seven-Year Low" in *Crain's Chicago Business* **(Vol. 31, November 10, 2008, No. 45, pp. 2)**
Pub: Crain Communications, Inc.
Ed: Alby Gallun. **Description:** Downtown Chicago condominium market is experiencing the lowest number of sales in years due to the tightening of the mortgage lending market, the Wall Street crisis and the downturn in the economy. The supply of new condos is soaring, the result of the building boom of

2005 and 2006; many developers are finding it difficult to pay off construction loans and fear foreclosure on their properties. Additional information and statistical data related to the downtown condominium market is provided.

14320 ■ "Contingent Offers: Weighing the Risk" in *Crain's Chicago Business* **(Vol. 31, April 21, 2008, No. 16, pp. 48)**
Pub: Crain Communications, Inc.
Ed: Darci Smith. **Description:** Interview with Greer Haseman, the broker-owner of Town Square Associates, who discusses contingent offers in a challenging housing market.

14321 ■ "Cornered by Credit; As $1 Billion in Loans Come Due, Will Landlords Find Funds?" in *Crain's Detroit Business* **(October 6, 2008)**
Pub: Crain Communications, Inc.
Ed: Daniel Duggan. **Description:** Conduit loans are used by many real estate investors and are normally issued in 7- to 10-year terms with balloon payments due at the end, requiring the full balance to be paid upon maturity. Many building owners may find their properties going into foreclosure as these loans mature next year since these loans cannot be extended like typical loans and the credit crisis along with falling property values is making it more difficult to secure new sources of funding. Possible solutions to this problem are also explored.

14322 ■ "Corporate Elite Show Resilience" in *The Business Journal-Serving Greater Tampa Bay* **(Vol. 28, August 1, 2008, No. 32, pp. 1)**
Pub: American City Business Journals, Inc.
Ed: Margie Manning; Alexis Muellner. **Description:** Stocks of the largest public companies in Tampa Bay, Florida, outperformed the S&P 500 index by 28 percent in the first half of 2008. The escalation is attributed to the growth orientation of the companies in the area and the lack of exposure to the real estate and financial services sectors.

14323 ■ "Cost of Home Purchase Loans are Higher for Hispanics" in *Hispanic Business* **(October 2007, pp. 88)**
Pub: Hispanic Business
Description: Home loans for Hispanics generally are offered at a higher interest rate. Statistical data included.

14324 ■ "Crash Pads" in *Business Courier* **(Vol. 24, November 2, 2008, No. 29, pp. 1)**
Pub: American City Business Journals, Inc.
Ed: Jon Newberry. **Description:** Francisca Webster accumulated $4 million in mortgage debt in about 2 months. She filed a lawsuit against her tax preparer and her mortgage broker contending that the defendants had breached their fiduciary duties to her and made fraudulent misrepresentations to her. The other details of the case are supplied.

14325 ■ "The Credit Crisis Continues" in *Barron's* **(Vol. 88, March 10, 2008, No. 10, pp. M12)**
Pub: Dow Jones & Company, Inc.
Ed: Randall W. Forsyth. **Description:** Short-term Treasury yields dropped to new cyclical lows in early March 2008, with the yield for the two-year Treasury note falling to 1.532 percent. Spreads of the mortgage-backed securities of Fannie Mae and Freddie Mac rose on suspicion of collapses in financing.

14326 ■ "Critics: Efforts to Fix Loans Won't Stop Foreclosure Wave" in *Business First Columbus* **(Vol. 25, November 14, 2008, No. 12, pp. A1)**
Pub: American City Business Journals
Ed: Adrian Burns. **Description:** Efforts by U.S. banks to help homeowners pay mortgages are seen to have little if any impact on foreclosures. Banks have announced plans to identify and aid troubled borrowers. Statistical data included.

14327 ■ "Delinquent Properties on the Rise" in *Business Courier* **(Vol. 27, June 11, 2010, No. 6, pp. 1)**
Pub: Business Courier
Ed: Dan Monk. **Description:** Reports show that Cincinnati now ranks in the U.S. Top 20 for its delinquency rate on securitized commercial real

estate loans. In December 2009, the region ranked 28th out of 50 cities studied by Trepp LLC. As of May 30, 2010, more than $378 million in commercial mortgage-backed security loans were more than 60 days past due.

14328 ■ "Detroit Residential Market Slows; Bright Spots Emerge" in *Crain's Detroit Business* **(Vol. 24, October 6, 2008, No. 40, pp. 11)**
Pub: Crain Communications, Inc.
Ed: Daniel Duggan. **Description:** Discusses the state of the residential real estate market in Detroit; although condominium projects receive the most attention, deals for single-family homes are taking place in greater numbers due to financing issues. Buyers can purchase a single family home with a 3.5 percent down payment compared to 20 percent for some condo deals because of the number of first-time homebuyer programs under the Federal Housing Administration.

14329 ■ "Developer Wins Bout with Bank in Roundabout Way" in *Tampa Bay Business Journal* **(Vol. 30, January 29, 2010, No. 6, pp. 1)**
Pub: American City Business Journals
Ed: Janet Leiser. **Description:** Developer Donald E. Phillips of Phillips Development and Realty LLC won against the foreclosure filed by First Horizon National Corporation, which is demanding the company to fully pay its $2.9 million loan. Phillips requested that his company pay monthly mortgage and extend the loan's maturity date.

14330 ■ *Dictionary of Real Estate Terms*
Pub: Barron's Educational Series, Incorporated
Ed: Jack P. Friedman, Jack C. Harris, J. Bruce Lindeman. **Released:** October 2008. **Price:** $13.99. **Description:** More than 2,500 real estate terms relating to mortgages and financing, brokerage law, architecture, rentals and leases, property insurance, and more.

14331 ■ "Docs Might Hold Cure for Real Estate, Banks" in *Baltimore Business Journal* **(Vol. 28, November 5, 2010, No. 26, pp. 1)**
Pub: Baltimore Business Journal
Ed: Gary Haber. **Description:** Health care providers, including physicians are purchasing their office space instead of renting it as banks lower interest rates to 6 percent on mortgages for medical offices. The rise in demand offers relief to the commercial real estate market. It has also resulted in a boom in building new medical offices.

14332 ■ "Downtown Evens Tenant Ledger" in *The Business Journal-Serving Metropolitan Kansas City* **(Vol. 26, July 11, 2008, No. 44, pp. 1)**
Pub: American City Business Journals, Inc.
Ed: Rob Roberts. **Description:** Financial services company PricewaterhouseCoopers will relocate its office from the Broadway building, but it will not leave downtown as it signs a long-term lease for a 27,000 square feet of space in Town Pavilion. Town Pavilion is the biggest multitenant office building in downtown. Downtown's market competitiveness is also examined.

14333 ■ "East-Side Real Estate Forum Detours To Grand Rapids" in *Crain's Detroit Business* **(Vol. 24, October 6, 2008, No. 40, pp. 17)**
Pub: Crain Communications, Inc.
Ed: Daniel Duggan. **Description:** Tom Wackerman was elected chairman of the University of Michigan-Urban Land Institute Real Estate Forum and proposed that the annual conference be held in Grand Rapids due to the brisk economic activity he was finding there; although the idea was initially met with resistance, the plan to introduce East-siders to the West side began receiving more enthusiasm due to the revitalization of the area, which was once considered to have a bleak outlook. Many are hoping to learn the lessons of those who were able to change a negative economic climate into a positive one in which the cooperation of private business and government can work together to accomplish goals.

14334 ■ "Easy to be Queasy" in *Canadian Business* **(Vol. 81, December 24, 2007, No. 1, pp. 25)**
Pub: Rogers Media
Ed: Jack Mintz. **Description:** Canada could be facing a slowdown in economic growth for 2008 as the country's economy depends on the U.S. economy, which is still facing recession in the subprime market. Details on Canada's economic growth, the impact of the weak U.S. dollar, increase in the unemployment rate, and decline in tax revenue are explored.

14335 ■ "Economy Peddles Rent In This Cycle" in *The Business Journal-Serving Metropolitan Kansas City* **(Vol. 26, August 8, 2008, No. 48)**
Pub: American City Business Journals, Inc.
Ed: Ashlee Kieler. **Description:** Rental demand for apartment units in downtown Kansas City, Missouri, is increasing due to the housing crisis, lack of real estate development, and increasing popularity of the downtown area. The downtown area has 7,378 multifamily units as of June 2008, of which 4,114 are rentals.

14336 ■ "Exposed?" in *Mergers & Acquisitions: The Dealmaker's Journal* **(March 1, 2008)**
Pub: SourceMedia, Inc.
Ed: Jerry Abejo. **Description:** State-run pension plans' contributions are declining due to a loss of tax revenue from plummeting home values.

14337 ■ "Fannie and Freddie: How They'll Change" in *Business Week* **(September 22, 2008, No. 4100, pp. 30)**
Pub: McGraw-Hill Companies, Inc.
Ed: Jane Sasseen. **Description:** Three possible outcomes of the fate of struggling mortgage giants Freddie Mac and Fannie Mae after the government bailout are outlined.

14338 ■ "FBI Initiates Fraud Inquiry Into Mortgage Lenders" in *Miami Daily Business Review* **(March 26, 2008)**
Pub: ALM Media Inc.
Description: FBI has launched investigations into Countrywide Financial, the nation's largest mortgage lender, along with sixteen other firms, tied to the subprime mortgage crisis.

14339 ■ "Fifth Third Grapples With Account Snafu" in *Business Courier* **(Vol. 24, December 7, 2008, No. 34, pp. 1)**
Pub: American City Business Journals, Inc.
Ed: Jon Newberry. **Description:** Fifth Third Bank's vendor committed an error which led to a badly damaged credit score for Brett and Karen Reloka. The couple reported the incident to the bank and are still waiting for action to be taken. A major outourced services vendor caused paid-off mortgages to be reported delinquent.

14340 ■ "Final Player In Big Mortgage Fraud Operation Gets Jail Time" in *Boston Business Journal* **(Vol. 31, May 27, 2011, No. 18, pp. 3)**
Pub: Boston Business Journal
Ed: Galen Moore. **Description:** Real estate broker Ralp Appolon has been sentenced to 70 months in prison for wire fraud. Appolon was part of a group that falsified information about property purchase prices. A total of ten mortgage lenders have become victims of the group.

14341 ■ "Finger-Pointing Time" in *Barron's* **(Vol. 88, March 10, 2008, No. 10, pp. 9)**
Pub: Dow Jones & Company, Inc.
Ed: Michael Santoli. **Description:** Discusses who is to blame for the financial crisis brought about by the credit crunch in the United States; the country's financial markets will eventually digest this crisis but will bottom out first before the situation improves.

14342 ■ "First-Time Homebuyer Credit May Add Some Momentum to Market" in *Crain's Cleveland Business* **(Vol. 30, May 18, 2009, No. 20)**
Pub: Crain Communications, Inc.
Ed: Stan Bullard. **Description:** Federal tax credits for first-time homebuyers have increased the number of homes being sold. Details of the tax credit are defined.

14343 ■ **"A Flawed Yardstick for Banks"** in *Barron's* (Vol. 88, July 14, 2008, No. 28, pp. M6)
Pub: Dow Jones & Co., Inc.
Ed: Arindam Nag. **Description:** Return on equity is no longer the best measure for investors to judge banks by in a post-subprime-crises world. Investors should consider the proportion of a bank's total assets that are considered risky and look out for any write-downs of goodwill when judging a bank's financial health.

14344 ■ *The Foreclosure of America: Life Inside Countrywide Home Loans and the Selling of the American Dream*
Pub: Berkley Trade/Penguin Group (USA) Inc.
Ed: Adam Michaelson. **Released:** April 6, 2010. **Price:** $16.00. **Description:** An inside look at Countrywide Home Loans and the mortgage crisis.

14345 ■ **"Foreclosures Crisis Expected to Significantly Drain Wealth"** in *Black Enterprise* (Vol. 41, September 2010, No. 2, pp. 24)
Pub: Earl G. Graves Publishing Co. Inc.
Description: African American communities will lose billions in wealth because of the current foreclosure crisis. Statistical data included.

14346 ■ **"FTC Takes Aim At Foreclosure 'Rescue' Firm"** in *The Business Journal-Serving Greater Tampa Bay* (Vol. 28, September 19, 2008, No. 39)
Pub: American City Business Journals, Inc.
Ed: Michael Hinman. **Description:** United Home Savers LLP has been ordered to halt its mortgage foreclosure rescue services after the Federal Trade Commission accused it of deceptive advertising. The company is alleged to have charged customers $1,200 in exchange for unfulfilled promises to keep them in their homes.

14347 ■ **"GM's Mortgage Unit Deal Brings in $9 Billion"** in *Globe & Mail* (March 24, 2006, pp. B3)
Pub: CTVglobemedia Publishing Inc.
Ed: Shawn McCarthy. **Description:** General Motors Corp. sells General Motors Acceptance Corp.'s commercial real estate division to Kohlberg Kravis Roberts & Co. Five Mile Capital Partners LLC and Goldman Sachs Capital Partners. The reasons behind the deal are presented.

14348 ■ **"A Good Sign for Commercial Real Estate"** in *Austin Business JournalInc.* (Vol. 29, December 18, 2009, No. 41, pp. 1)
Pub: American City Business Journals
Ed: Kate Harrington. **Description:** Factors that could contribute to the reemergence of the commercial mortgage-backed securities market in Texas are discussed. These securities can potentially boost the commercial real estate market statewide as well as nationwide. Commercial mortgage-backed securities origination in 2009 is worth less that $1 billion, compared with $238 billion in 2008.

14349 ■ *Grow Your Money: 101 Easy Tips to Plan, Save and Invest*
Pub: HarperBusiness
Ed: Jonathan D. Pond. **Released:** December 2007. **Price:** $26.95. **Description:** In what should be required reading for anyone entering the work world, the author offers helpful investment and financial definitions, debt-management strategies, retirement and home ownerships considerations and more.

14350 ■ **"Hank Paulson On the Housing Bailout and What's Ahead"** in *Business Week* (September 22, 2008, No. 4100, pp. 19)
Pub: McGraw-Hill Companies, Inc.
Ed: Maria Bartiromo. **Description:** Interview with Treasury Secretary Henry Paulson in which he discusses the bailout of Fannie Mae and Freddie Mac as well as the potential impact on the American economy and foreign interests and investments in the country. Paulson has faith that the government's actions will help to stabilize the housing market.

14351 ■ **"Hastily Enacted Regulation Will Not Cure Economic Crisis"** in *Crain's Chicago Business* (Vol. 31, May 5, 2008, No. 18, pp. 18)
Pub: Crain Communications, Inc.
Ed: Stephen P. D'Arcy. **Description:** Policymakers are looking for ways to respond to what is possibly the greatest financial crisis of a generation due to the collapse of the housing market, the credit crisis and the volatility of Wall Street.

14352 ■ **"Hollander 95 Project Getting Bigger"** in *Boston Business Journal* (Vol. 29, September 23, 2011, No. 20, pp. 1)
Pub: American City Business Journals Inc.
Ed: Gary Haber. **Description:** Hollander 95 Business Park is in for a huge change as its new owners plan a $50 million expansion which calls for building as many as eight more buildings or a total of more than 500,000 square feed. FRP Development bought the site for $4.35 million at a foreclosure sale in July 2010 and is now seeking city approval for an Industrial Planned Unit Development designation.

14353 ■ **"Home Builder, Four Others, Face Sentencing"** in *Business Courier* (Vol. 27, November 26, 2010, No. 30, pp. 1)
Pub: Business Courier
Ed: Jon Newberry. **Description:** Home builder Bernie Kurlemann was convicted on November 10, 2010 on six felony counts and faces up to 65 years in prison due to his part in a 2006 Warren County mortgage fraud scheme. Four other business people have pleaded guilty to related charges, and all are awaiting sentencing in early 2011.

14354 ■ **"Home Prices Sag"** in *Crain's Chicago Business* (Vol. 31, April 28, 2008, No. 17, pp. 3)
Pub: Crain Communications, Inc.
Ed: Alby Gallun. **Description:** Since the slump in the housing market is continuing with no sign of recovery, Chicago-area home prices are poised for an even steeper drop this year. In 2007, the region's home prices fell nearly 5 percent and according to a forecast by Fiserv Inc., they will decline 8.1 percent this year and another 2.2 percent in 2009. Statistical data included.

14355 ■ **"Home Sweet Home"** in *Canadian Business* (Vol. 79, October 9, 2006, No. 20, pp. 22)
Pub: Rogers Media
Ed: Peter Shawn Taylor. **Description:** Changes being made in the management of mortgage insurance business in Canada are critically analyzed.

14356 ■ **"Homeownership: Still the American Dream?"** in *Gallup Management Journal* (May 5, 2011)
Pub: Gallup
Description: The mortgage finance system is broken. Housing prices continue to fall. Foreclosures are expected to increase in the coming months. However, Gallup's chief economist does not believe this is the end of the American dream of owning one's own home.

14357 ■ **"Hotel Woes Reflect Area Struggle"** in *Business Journal Serving Greater Tampa Bay* (Vol. 30, December 3, 2010, No. 50, pp. 1)
Pub: Tampa Bay Business Journal
Ed: Mark Holan. **Description:** Quality Inn and Suites in East Tampa, Florida has struggled against the sluggish economy but remained open to guests despite facing a foreclosure. The hotel project is the center of East Tampa's redevelopment plans and public officials defend the $650,000 investment in public amenities near the building.

14358 ■ **"Housing Hedge"** in *Canadian Business* (Vol. 79, July 17, 2006, No. 14-15, pp. 66)
Pub: Rogers Media
Ed: Jeff Sanford. **Description:** The idea of starting a hedge scheme for housing is presented using the advent of pension schemes as an example to follow.

14359 ■ **"Housing Slide Picks Up Speed"** in *Crain's Chicago Business* (Vol. 31, April 21, 2008, No. 16, pp. 2)
Pub: Crain Communications, Inc.
Ed: Eddie Baeb. **Description:** According to Tracy Cross & Associates Inc., a real estate consultancy, sales of new homes in the Chicago area dropped 61 percent from the year-earlier period which is more bad news for homebuilders, contractors and real estate agents who are eager for an indication that market conditions are improving.

14360 ■ **"How About Trying a Foreclosure Tax?"** in *Crain's Detroit Business* (Vol. 24, January 28, 2008, No. 4, pp. 9)
Pub: Crain Communications Inc. - Detroit
Ed: Mark Goodell. **Description:** According to a recent study, local communities could see a $100 million decrease in property tax revenues, and the state could lose as much as $12 million in lower sales tax proceeds. Experts discuss options for Michigan's government to institute a foreclosure tax.

14361 ■ *How to Start, Operate and Market a Freelance Notary Signing Agent Business*
Pub: Gom Publishing, LLC
Ed: Victoria Ring. **Released:** September 2004. **Price:** $8.18. **Description:** Due to the changes in the 2001 Uniform Commercial Code allowing notary public agents to serve as a witness to mortgage loan closings (eliminating the 2-witness requirement under the old code), notaries are working directly for mortgage, title and signing companies as mobile notaries.

14362 ■ **"Hunter and the Hunted"** in *Canadian Business* (Vol. 81, Summer 2008, No. 9, pp. 12)
Pub: Rogers Media Ltd.
Ed: Thomas Watson. **Description:** Brian Hunter, a partner in oil and gas engineering firm Montane Resources, invested his life savings in Vancouver-based Canacord Capital Corp. Details of the asset-backed commercial paper fiasco and Hunter's use of Facebook to encourage other investors to participate in his claim against the mortgage company are presented.

14363 ■ **"In Control: Tips For Navigating a Buyer's Market"** in *Black Enterprise* (Vol. 38, December 2007, No. 5, pp. 64)
Pub: Earl G. Graves Publishing Co. Inc.
Ed: Erinn R. Johnson. **Description:** Tips are given to help would-be home buyers. The importance of finding a good real estate agent is stressed.

14364 ■ **"Independence's Day Keeps on Getting Brighter"** in *Business Courier* (Vol. 27, June 11, 2010, No. 6, pp. 1)
Pub: Business Courier
Ed: Lucy May. **Description:** Reports show that residential and commercial development continues in Independence, Kentucky despite the recession, with a 144-unit apartment complex under construction. The city recorded 152 new-home closings in 2009, or 25 percent of all new homes closed in Boone, Campbell, and Kenton counties.

14365 ■ **"The Influencers"** in *Entrepreneur* (Vol. 36, March 2008, No. 3, pp. 66)
Pub: Entrepreneur Media Inc.
Ed: Andrea Cooper. **Description:** Among the 25 people, events, and trends that will influence business in 2008 are: the 2008 U.S. presidential elections, climate change, China, weakening U.S. dollar, mortgage crisis, generational shift, Bill Drayton, and Bill Gates. Other 2008 influencers are presented.

14366 ■ **"It Could Be Worse"** in *Barron's* (Vol. 89, July 27, 2009, No. 30, pp. 5)
Pub: Dow Jones & Co., Inc.
Ed: Alan Abelson. **Description:** Media sources are being fooled by corporate America who is peddling an economic recovery rather than reality as shown by the report of a rise in existing home sales which boosted the stock market even if it was a seasonal phenomenon. The phrase "things could be worse" sums up the reigning investment philosophy in the U.S. and this has been stirring up the market.

14367 ■ "Latest Volley Tries to Press Port Group" in *Business Courier* (Vol. 26, November 20, 2009, No. 30, pp. 1)
Pub: American City Business Journals, Inc.
Ed: Dan Monk. **Description:** Subcontractors filed a new legal argument to force the Port of Greater Cincinnati Development Authority to pursue default claim against Bank of America. The bank issued letters of credit to guarantee bond payments in addition to holding the mortgage of the Kenwood Towne Place. Details of the claim are discussed.

14368 ■ "Laugh or Cry?" in *Barron's* (Vol. 88, March 24, 2008, No. 12, pp. 7)
Pub: Dow Jones & Company, Inc.
Ed: Alan Abelson. **Description:** Discusses the American economy which is just starting to feel the effect of the credit and housing crises. JPMorgan Chase purchased Bear Stearns for $2 a share, much lower than its share price of $60, while quasi-government entities Fannie Mae and Freddie Mac are starting to run into trouble.

14369 ■ "Law Firms See Improvement in Financing Climate" in *Sacramento Business Journal* (Vol. 28, October 14, 2011, No. 33, pp. 1)
Pub: Sacramento Business Journal
Ed: Kathy Robertson. **Description:** Sacramento, California-based Weintraub Genshlea Chediak Law Corporation has helped close 26 financing deals worth more than $1.6 billion in 2010, providing indication of improvement in Sacramento's economy. Lawyers have taken advantage of low interest rates to make refinancing agreements and help clients get new funds.

14370 ■ "Lean on Me" in *Entrepreneur* (Vol. 36, February 2008, No. 2, pp. 40)
Pub: Entrepreneur Media Inc.
Ed: Farnoosh Torabi. **Description:** Investing in tax liens is booming with the growth in the number of homeowners missing property tax payments. Details on how to bid for and when to redeem tax liens are outlined.

14371 ■ "Leaning Tower" in *Business Courier* (Vol. 27, June 4, 2010, No. 5, pp. 1)
Pub: Business Courier
Ed: Jon Newberry. **Description:** New York-based developer Armand Lasky, owner of Tower Place Mall in downtown Cincinnati, Ohio has sued Birmingham, Alabama-based Regions Bank to prevent the bank's foreclosure on the property. Regions Bank claims Lasky was in default on an $18 million loan agreement. Details on the mall's leasing plan is also discussed.

14372 ■ "Lehman's Hail Mary Pass" in *Business Week* (September 22, 2008, No. 4100, pp. 28)
Pub: McGraw-Hill Companies, Inc.
Ed: Matthew Goldstein; David Henry; Ben Levison. **Description:** Overview of Lehman Brothers' CEO Richard Fuld's plan to keep the firm afloat and end the stock's plunge downward; Fuld's strategy calls for selling off a piece of the firm's investment management business.

14373 ■ "Lenders Get Boost from Low Rates" in *Saint Louis Business Journal* (Vol. 32, September 9, 2011, No. 2, pp. 1)
Pub: Saint Louis Business Journal
Ed: Greg Edwards. **Description:** St. Louis, Missouri-based lenders have benefitted from record low mortgage interest rates. Housing loan applications have increased in view of the development.

14374 ■ "Local Commercial Real Estate Foreclosures Continue to Rise" in *Baltimore Business Journal* (Vol. 28, October 1, 2010, No. 21, pp. 1)
Pub: Baltimore Business Journal
Ed: Daniel J. Sernovitz. **Description:** Foreclosures of commercial real estate across the Greater Baltimore area have continued to rise. The region is now host to about $2 billion worth of commercial properties that carry a maturing debt or have been fore-

closed. Commercial real estate owners are unable to finance their debts because banks have become stricter in passing out loans.

14375 ■ "Lotus Starts Slowly, Dodges Subprime Woes" in *Crain's Detroit Business* (Vol. 24, April 14, 2008, No. 15, pp. 3)
Pub: Crain Communications, Inc.
Ed: Tom Henderson. **Description:** Discusses Lotus Bancorp Inc. and their business plan, which although is not right on target due to the subprime mortgage meltdown, is in a much better position than its competitors due to the quality of their loans.

14376 ■ "A Matter of Perspective" in *Business Journal-Portland* (Vol. 24, November 2, 2007, No. 35, pp. 1)
Pub: American City Business Journals, Inc.
Ed: Andy Giegerich. **Description:** Oregon Governor Ted Kulongoski assembled the Mortgage Lending Work Group, made up of members of the mortgage industry and consumer groups, to recommend possible bills for the Oregon Senate and House to consider. How its members try to balance philosophical differences in mortgage lending rules is discussed.

14377 ■ "Mequon Plan On Tracks, Bucks Housing Trend" in *The Business Journal-Milwaukee* (Vol. 25, September 26, 2008, No. 53, pp. A1)
Pub: American City Business Journals, Inc.
Ed: Pete Millard. **Description:** Insight Development Group plans to build condominium units and single-family homes despite the residential market downturn. The Orchard Glen project, a planned development in Mequon, is a $22 million project which will include 38 condos and 12 single-family homes. Details of the project are provided.

14378 ■ "More Questions Face Huntington" in *Business First-Columbus* (December 7, 2007, pp. A3)
Pub: American City Business Journals, Inc.
Ed: Adrian Burns. **Description:** Marty Adams' abrupt resignation has lead to speculation that he was dismissed by the bank in relation to the unexpected run-in with the subprime mortgage fiasco. Analysis predict Columbus-based Huntington Bancshares Inc. might be targeted for acquisition. Details on the company's revenues and shares of stock prices are presented.

14379 ■ *Mortgage Industry Directory*
Pub: Thomson Financial
Ed: Paul Muolo, Editor, paul.muolo@thomsonmedia.com. **Released:** Annual, latest edition 14th, 2008. **Price:** $529, individuals. **Covers:** Approximately 700 mortgage industry leaders, profiles, and 700 top bank, S&L and credit union mortgage holders, including industry rankings. **Entries Include:** Organization name, address, phone plus complete data on all aspects of the mortgage industry.

14380 ■ "Mortgage Mess Continues To Trigger Bids To Ease Crisis" in *Business First-Columbus* (December 14, 2007, pp. A1)
Pub: American City Business Journals, Inc.
Ed: Adrian Burns. **Description:** Measures to prevent foreclosures in Ohio are presented. On December 6, 2007, the Bush Administration started a national incentive that will establish a streamlined process for modifying loans. Some have questioned the proposal, since it is expected the plan will only help about 90,000 of the 1.8 million borrowers. According to Ohio Treasurer, Richard Cordray, one of the state's objectives is to calm the markets on Wall Street.

14381 ■ "Mortgage Mess: How To Determine Your Exposure To the Subprime Crisis" in *Black Enterprise* (Vol. 38, November 2007, No. 4, pp. 46)
Pub: Earl G. Graves Publishing Co. Inc.
Ed: Ilana Polyak. **Description:** Stocks and mutual funds have experienced declines because of the subprime crisis. Morningstar's Website can help investors research firms in which they have invested; if a fund is named high yield or high income or in the financial services sector, investments will have greater exposure to the mess.

14382 ■ "Mortgage Securities Drop Hits Home" in *The Business Journal-Serving Metropolitan Kansas City* (Vol. 27, October 17, 2008, No. 5)
Pub: American City Business Journals, Inc.
Ed: Rob Roberts. **Description:** Sale of commercial mortgage-backed securities (CMBS) in Kansas City, Missouri have declined. The area may avoid layoffs if the United States government succeeds in stabilizing the economy. Major CMBS players in the area include Midland Loan Services Inc. and KeyBank Real Estate Capital.

14383 ■ "Mortgages Going Under" in *Black Enterprise* (Vol. 41, December 2010, No. 5, pp. 20)
Pub: Earl G. Graves Publishing Co. Inc.
Description: Nearly one-fifth of the country's homeowners are underwater in their mortgages, which means they owe more on their home than the home's worth. Statistical data included.

14384 ■ "Myths of Deleveraging" in *Barron's* (Vol. 90, August 23, 2010, No. 34, pp. M14)
Pub: Barron's Editorial & Corporate Headquarters
Ed: Gene Epstein. **Description:** The opposite is true against reports about deleveraging or the decrease in credit since inflation-adjusted-investment factories and equipment rose 7.8 percent in the first quarter of 2010. On consumer deleveraging, sales of homes through credit is weak but there is a trend towards more realistic homeownership and consumer spending on durable goods rose 8.8 percent.

14385 ■ "Neighborhood Watch" in *Baltimore Business Journal* (Vol. 28, July 23, 2010, No. 11, pp. 1)
Pub: Baltimore Business Journal
Ed: Daniel J. Sernovitz. **Description:** Maryland government and housing leaders are set to spend $100 million in federal funding to stem the increase in foreclosures in the area. The federal funding is seen as inadequate to resolve the problem of foreclosures.

14386 ■ "New Century's Fall Has a New Culprit" in *Barron's* (Vol. 88, March 31, 2008, No. 13, pp. 20)
Pub: Dow Jones & Company, Inc.
Ed: Jonathan R. Laing. **Description:** Court examiner Michael Missal reports that New Century Financial's auditor contributed to New Century's demise by its negligence in permitting improper and imprudent practices related to New Century's accounting processes. New Century's bankruptcy filing is considered the start of the subprime-mortgage crisis.

14387 ■ "New Rule Rankles In Jersey" in *Philadelphia Business Journal* (Vol. 30, September 16, 2011, No. 31, pp. 1)
Pub: American City Business Journals, Inc.
Ed: Jeff Blumenthal. **Description:** A new rule in New Jersey which taxes out-of-state companies that conduct business in the state earned the ire of several banks, mortgage lenders and credit card companies and prompted opponents to threaten to file lawsuits. The new rule is an amendment to New Jersey Division of Taxation's corporate business tax regulation and is retroactive to 2002. Details are given.

14388 ■ "The Next Government Bailout?" in *Barron's* (Vol. 88, March 10, 2008, No. 10, pp. 21)
Pub: Dow Jones & Company, Inc.
Ed: Jonathan Laing. **Description:** Fannie Mae may need a government bailout as it faces huge hits brought about by the effects of the housing crisis. The shares of the government-sponsored enterprise have dropped 65 percent since the housing crisis began.

14389 ■ "Nightmare on Wall Street" in *Canadian Business* (Vol. 80, November 19, 2007, No. 23, pp. 33)
Pub: Rogers Media
Ed: Thomas Watson. **Description:** Merrill Lynch Stanley O'Neal resigned after the company experienced a $2.2 billion loss in third quarter 2007. Citi-

group's Charles Prince will also be leaving due to the crisis involving subprime mortgages and collaterized debt obligations. Forecasts for the stock market are supplied.

14390 ■ "Nine Sectors to Watch: Gold" in *Canadian Business* **(Vol. 81, December 24, 2007, No. 1, pp. 53)**
Pub: Rogers Media
Ed: John Gray. **Description:** Turmoil in the financial markets, triggered by the meltdown in subprime mortgages, has pushed the price of gold to more than $840 an ounce in November 2007. Details on investor interest in gold and prediction on price trends in trade are discussed.

14391 ■ "Number of Mechanic's Liens Triple Since 2005" in *The Business Journal - Serving Phoenix and the Valley of the Sun* **(Vol. 28, August 22, 2008, No. 51, pp. 1)**
Pub: American City Business Journals, Inc.
Ed: Jan Buchholtz. **Description:** Experts are blaming the mortgage and banking industries for the tripling of mechanic's liens that were filed in Arizona from 2005 through August 6, 2008. The rise in mechanic's liens is believed to indicate stress in the real estate community. Other views and information on the rise of mechanic's liens filed in Arizona are presented.

14392 ■ "October 2009: Recovery Plods Along" in *Hispanic Business* **(October 2009, pp. 10-11)**
Pub: Hispanic Business
Ed: Dr. Juan Solana. **Description:** Economist reports on a possible economic recovery which will not be allowed to rely on a strong domestic demand in order to sustain it. Consumers, looking to counterbalance years of leverage financing based on unrealistic, ever-increasing home and portfolio valuations, are saving rather than spending money.

14393 ■ "Office Market May Turn Down" in *Crain's New York Business* **(Vol. 24, January 14, 2008, No. 2, pp. 26)**
Pub: Crain Communications, Inc.
Description: Although still dominated by Wall Street, the downturn in the economy is raising fears that the continuing fallout from the subprime mortgage crisis could result in layoffs that will derail the office market.

14394 ■ "OK, Bring in the Lawyers" in *Crain's Chicago Business* **(Vol. 31, November 17, 2008, No. 46, pp. 26)**
Pub: Crain Communications, Inc.
Ed: Daniel Rome Levine. **Description:** Bankruptcy attorneys are finding the economic and credit crisis a benefit for their businesses due to the high number of business owners and mortgage holders that are need of their services. One Chicago firm is handling ten times the number of cases they did the previous year and of that about 80 percent of their new clients are related to the real estate sector.

14395 ■ "Optimism Index" in *Black Enterprise* **(Vol. 41, September 2010, No. 2, pp. 24)**
Pub: Earl G. Graves Publishing Co. Inc.
Description: According to a Pew Research Center report, 81 percent of African Americans expect to improve their finances in 2011. Blacks have carried a disproportionate share of job losses and housing foreclosures in the recession that began in 2007.

14396 ■ "Past Due: $289 Million in Loans" in *Saint Louis Business Journal* **(Vol. 32, September 23, 2011, No. 4, pp. 1)**
Pub: Saint Louis Business Journal
Ed: Evans Binns. **Description:** New York-based Trepp LLC research found about $289 million in local commercial mortgage-backed securities loans on 20 properties delinquent in payments by 30 days or more as of August 31, 2011. The report also placed the delinquency rate for St. Louis at that time at 9.64 percent.

14397 ■ "Paying for the Recession: Rebalancing Economic Growth" in *Montana Business Quarterly* **(Vol. 49, Spring 2011, No. 1, pp. 2)**
Pub: Bureau of Business & Economic Research
Ed: Patrick M. Barkey. **Description:** Four key issues required to address in order to rebalance economic

growth in America are examined. They include: savings rates, global trade imbalances, government budgets and most importantly, housing price correction.

14398 ■ "A Place in the Sun" in *Canadian Business* **(Vol. 81, July 22, 2008, No. 12-13, pp. 56)**
Pub: Rogers Media Ltd.
Description: Experts believe that it is the best time for Canadians to own a retirement home in the U.S., where real estate prices are up to 50 percent below their peak. Other views concerning the economic conditions occurring in the United States, as well as on the implications for Canadians planning to invest in the country are presented.

14399 ■ "Private Equity Firms Shopping Valley For Deals" in *The Business Journal - Serving Phoenix and the Valley of the Sun* **(Vol. 29, September 19, 2008, No. 3, pp. 1)**
Pub: American City Business Journals, Inc.
Ed: Mike Sunnucks. **Description:** Private equity firms from California, Boston, New York, and overseas are expected to invest in growth-oriented real estate markets that include Phoenix. Real estate experts revealed that privately held investment and acquisition firms are looking to invest in real estate markets hit by the housing crisis. Views and information on private equity firms' real estate investments are presented.

14400 ■ "Race, Not Income, Played Role in Subprime Loans" in *Black Enterprise* **(Vol. 40, July 2010, No. 12, pp. 26)**
Pub: Earl G. Graves Publishing Co. Inc.
Ed: Deborah Creighton Skinner. **Description:** African Americans were 80 percent more likely than whites to receive a subprime loan and were almost 20 percent more likely to go into foreclosure, according to a study done by the National Community Reinvestment Coalition. Statistical data included.

14401 ■ "Ready for a Rally?" in *The Economist* **(Vol. 390, January 3, 2009, No. 8612, pp. 54)**
Pub: The Economist Newspaper Inc.
Description: Analysts predict that the recession could end by 2010. The current economic crisis is presented in detail.

14402 ■ "Real Estate Defaults Top $300M" in *Business Courier* **(Vol. 26, January 15, 2010, No. 39, pp. 1)**
Pub: American City Business Journals, Inc.
Ed: Dan Monk. **Description:** Cincinnati commercial real estate owners defaulting in securitized loans reached $306 million at the end of 2009. The trend has lifted the region's default rate to nearly 9 percent. National average for commercial real estate default is examined.

14403 ■ "Real Estate Vets Take Times In Stride" in *The Business Journal-Serving Metropolitan Kansas City* **(Vol. 26, July 25, 2008, No. 46)**
Pub: American City Business Journals, Inc.
Ed: Rob Roberts. **Description:** Kansas City, Missouri's real estate industry veterans like Allen Block believe that the challenges faced by the industry in the 1980s, when the Federal Reserve Board controlled the money supply to slow down inflation, were worse than the challenges faced today. Other views, trends and information on the real estate industry of the city, are presented.

14404 ■ "Real Estate Woes Mount for State's Smaller Banks" in *Boston Business Journal* **(Vol. 27, November 30, 2007, No. 44, pp. 1)**
Pub: American City Business Journals Inc.
Ed: Craig M. Douglas. **Description:** Massachusetts banking industry is facing a steep increase on loan defaults such as in home mortgages and condominium projects, contrary to public belief that the local industry is safe from the real estate meltdown. The dollar value of local banks' nonperforming loans doubled in 2007, and is rising statewide. Other banking issues in the state are discussed.

14405 ■ "Red Tape Ties Detroit Housing Rehab Plan" in *Crain's Detroit Business* **(Vol. 24, September 22, 2008, No. 38, pp. 1)**
Pub: Crain Communications, Inc.
Ed: Ryan Beene. **Description:** Venture-capital firm Wilherst Oxford LLC is a Florida-based company that has purchased 300 inner-city homes which were in foreclosure in Detroit. Wilherst Oxford is asking the city to forgive the existing tax and utility liens so the firm can utilize the money for home improvements. The city, however, is reluctant but has stated that they are willing to negotiate.

14406 ■ "Regulation Papered Over" in *Charlotte Business Journal* **(Vol. 25, November 5, 2010, No. 33, pp.)**
Pub: Charlotte Business Journal
Ed: Adam O'Daniel. **Description:** County courts in North Carolina are having challenges coping with its oversight and regulation duties as it becomes too busy with foreclosure cases. Clerks in some county courts have presided over foreclosure hearings because of the flooding of foreclosure cases.

14407 ■ "Revitalizing Real Estate: Couple Sails Through Sea of Housing Woes" in *Black Enterprise* **(Vol. 38, February 2008, No. 7, pp. 50)**
Pub: Earl G. Graves Publishing Co. Inc.
Ed: Ayana Dixon. **Description:** Owner, Christopher Gablin and Regina Mincey-Garlin offer a broad range of real estate-related services to clients in order to not only survive, but thrive in today's market.

14408 ■ "Rogue's Gallery" in *Canadian Business* **(Vol. 81, November 10, 2008, No. 19, pp. 44)**
Pub: Rogers Media Ltd.
Ed: Rachel Pulfer. **Description:** Laissez-faire capitalism or poor oversight of Fannie Mae and Freddie Mac are causes for the financial crisis in the U.S., depending or Democrat or Republican viewpoint. Events leading up to the 2008 financial crisis are covered.

14409 ■ "Rules Will Tighten, Bankers are Told: House Panel Chairman Expects More Regulation" in *Charlotte Observer* **(February 6, 2007)**
Pub: Knight-Ridder/Tribune Business News
Ed: Binyamin Appelbaum. **Description:** House Financial Services Committee will impose more federal regulation on banks offering mortgages.

14410 ■ "Servicers Back National Effort" in *Business First-Columbus* **(October 19, 2007, pp. A1)**
Pub: American City Business Journals, Inc.
Ed: Adrian Burns. **Description:** Ohio is having difficulty convincing mortgage companies to sign a compact containing guidelines when working with troubled borrowers. Many of Ohio's mortgage companies are supporting a national initiative to respond to the mortgage crisis instead.

14411 ■ "A Shallow Pool" in *Canadian Business* **(Vol. 81, Summer 2008, No. 9, pp. 44)**
Pub: Rogers Media Ltd.
Ed: Joe Castaldo. **Description:** Bank of Canada projected in its 'Monetary Policy Report' a growth rate of 1.4 percent in 2008 and does not expect the economy to fully recover until mid-2010. The Canadian stock market has been recovering although slowly with just a 1.6 percent gain by April 30. Other details on the Canadian equity market are presented.

14412 ■ "'Short Sales,' A Sign of Housing Troubles, Start Popping Up" in *The Business Review Albany* **(Vol. 35, April 11, 2008, No. 1, pp. 1)**
Pub: The Business Review
Ed: Michael DeMasi. **Description:** Discusses the number of short sales, where homeowners ask banks to forgive part of their mortgages to sell the properties, which is starting to increase in the Albany, New York area. Real estate agents in the area are taking up crash courses in short selling.

14413 ■ "Six Leading Economists on What to Expect in the Year Ahead: Derek Holt; Housing" in *Canadian Business* (December 24, 2007)

Pub: Rogers Media

Ed: Derek Holt. **Description:** The Canadian subprime mortgage market could take a different turn from that of the U.S. as laws governing Canada's mortgage market indirectly limit the probability of a slowdown. Details on how Canada avoided the slowdown in the housing market and forecasts of new homes for 2008 are discussed.

14414 ■ "A Slice of Danish; Fixing Finance" in *The Economist* (Vol. 390, January 3, 2009, No. 8612, pp. 55)

Pub: The Economist Newspaper Inc.

Description: Denmark's mortgage-holders and the county's lending system is presented.

14415 ■ "S.O.S. Sorting Out Subprime" in *Black Enterprise* (Vol. 38, November 2007, No. 4, pp. 76)

Pub: Earl G. Graves Publishing Co. Inc.

Ed: Trevor Delaney. **Description:** Subprime distress in the housing market is discussed and the impact it has put on investors.

14416 ■ "State Barks At Servicers Over Reluctance To Back Compact" in *Business First-Columbus* (2007, pp.)

Pub: American City Business Journals, Inc.

Ed: Adrian Burns. **Description:** State of Ohio asked members of the mortgage industry to back a compact as a way to prevent foreclosures. Mortgage services denied the state's request. Other measures to help borrowers avoid foreclosure are investigated.

14417 ■ "State Targets Credit Fixers" in *Business Journal-Portland* (Vol. 24, October 12, 2007, No. 33, pp. 1)

Pub: American City Business Journals, Inc.

Ed: Andy Giegerich, Justin Matlick. **Description:** Number of companies that offer quick fix to consumers is growing; the State of Oregon is considering rules to target them. A group working on a study in the state's mortgage lending regulations could craft bills to be examined for legislative session in February 2008.

14418 ■ "Struggling Community Banks Find Little Help In Wall Street Bailout" in *Crain's Detroit Business* (Vol. 24, September 29, 2008)

Pub: Crain Communications, Inc.

Ed: Tom Henderson. **Description:** Both public and private Michigan bands have been hit hard by poorly performing loan portfolios and although their problems were not caused by high-risk securities but by a longtime statewide recession and a housing slump, these community banks have little hope of seeing any of the bailout money that has been allotted for the larger institutions.

14419 ■ "Stuck With Two Mortgages; The Nightmare When Buyers Upgrade" in *Crain's Chicago Business* (Vol. 31, April 21, 2008, No. 16)

Pub: Crain Communications, Inc.

Ed: Darci Smith. **Description:** Discusses the problem a number of people are facing due to the slump in the housing market: being stuck with two mortgages when they move because their former homes have not sold. Many thought they could afford to move to a larger home, anticipating significant equity appreciation that did not occur; now they are left with lowering their price and competing with the host of new developments.

14420 ■ "Subprime Hits Huntington" in *Business First-Columbus* (November 23, 2007, pp. A1)

Pub: American City Business Journals, Inc.

Ed: Adrian Burns. **Description:** Huntington Bancshares Inc. picked up a $1.5 billion exposure to the country's subprime mortgage mess. It caused the bank to set aside $450 million to cover increases in loan losses. When Huntington acquired Sky Financial, it absorbed a 17-year relationship Sky had with Franklin Credit Corporation, which is a subprime lender and servicer.

14421 ■ "Subprime Lenders Under Fire: Does the NAACP Have a Viable Case?" in *Black Enterprise* (Vol. 38, October 2007, No. 3, pp. 31)

Pub: Earl G. Graves Publishing Co. Inc.

Ed: Trevor Delaney. **Description:** NAACP filed a lawsuit charging a number of mortgage lenders with 'institutionalized systematic racism'. Lenders named in the suit include Accredited Home Lenders, Ameriquest Mortgage Company, BNC Mortgage, Citigroup, Encore Credit, First Franklin Financial Corporation, Fremont Investment and Loan, HSBC Finance Corporation, Long Beach Mortgage Company, Option One Mortgage Corporation, Washington Mutual Inc., and WMC Mortgage Corporation. Details of the lawsuit are included.

14422 ■ "Subprime Problems Loom" in *The Business Journal-Portland* (Vol. 25, August 29, 2008, No. 25, pp. 1)

Pub: American City Business Journals, Inc.

Ed: Wendy Culverwell. **Description:** Over half of subprime mortgages in Portland are resetting by the end of 2008, which will cause more problems to the local real estate market. The inventory of unsold homes has also been increasing for over a year. Forecasts for the Portland housing market in relation to mortgage resets are supplied.

14423 ■ "Sunwest Vies To Stave Off Bankruptcy" in *The Business Journal-Portland* (Vol. 25, August 15, 2008, No. 23, pp. 1)

Pub: American City Business Journals, Inc.

Ed: Robin J. Moody. **Description:** Sunwest Management Inc. is teetering on the edge of bankruptcy as creditors start foreclosure on nine of their properties. This could potentially displace residents of the assisted living operator. Sunwest is trying to sell smaller packages of properties to get a $100 million bridge loan to maintain operations.

14424 ■ "Survival Guide: There Can Be an Upside to Managing a Downturn" in *Canadian Business* (Vol. 81, November 10, 2008, No. 19, pp. 54)

Pub: Rogers Media Ltd.

Ed: Sharda Prashad. **Description:** Canada-based Foxy is already limiting its exposure to retailers who could be a credit problem in case of recession. Retirement Life Communities is entering into fixed-rate and fixed-term loans for them to have sufficient financing to grow. Business owners need to realize that customers want more for less.

14425 ■ "Tampa Bay's CMBS Exposure Looms Large" in *Tampa Bay Business Journal* (Vol. 30, December 4, 2009, No. 50, pp. 1)

Pub: American City Business Journals

Ed: Margie Manning. **Description:** Tampa, Florida's metropolitan statistical area have listed 50 to 601 commercial mortgage-backed securities loans as delinquent with a total delinquent loan balance of $439 million. The total was 9.7 percent of the $4.5 billion loans outstanding and was higher than the delinquency rate in New York and Los Angeles.

14426 ■ *The Trillion Dollar Meltdown: Easy Money, High Rollers, and the Great Credit Crash*

Pub: Public Affairs

Ed: Charles R. Morris. **Released:** 2009. **Price:** $22.95. **Description:** Former banker believes that Wall Street and the financial community have too much power in America. He estimates that writedowns and defaults of residential mortgages, commercial mortgages, junk bonds, leveraged loans, credit cards, and complex securitized bonds could reach $1 trillion.

14427 ■ "Try, Try Again" in *Baltimore Business Journal* (Vol. 28, August 20, 2010, No. 15, pp. 1)

Pub: Baltimore Business Journal

Ed: Gary Haber. **Description:** Customers' refinancing of mortgages has boosted Baltimore, Maryland mortgage banking business. The housing decline has resulted in a decrease in the number of people looking for new mortgages.

14428 ■ "Unions Pony Up $1 Million for McBride Stimulus" in *Saint Louis Business Journal* (Vol. 31, July 29, 2011, No. 49, pp. 1)

Pub: Saint Louis Business Journal

Ed: Evan Binns. **Description:** Carpenters District Council of Greater St. Louis and International Brotherhood of Electrical Workers Local 1 were among the nine unions that agreed to split the cost of nearly $1 million in incentives for homebuyers who purchase homes in McBride communities. McBride & Son has spent over $100,000 to promote the incentive program.

14429 ■ "U.S. Economy's Underlying Strengths Limit Recession Threat" in *Hispanic Business* (Vol. 30, April 2008, No. 4, pp. 14)

Pub: Hispanic Business

Ed: Dr. Juan B. Solana. **Description:** Large and small businesses as well as consumers and policymakers are attempting to identify the areas of risk and loss created by the economic crisis; analysts are now estimating that U.S. mortgage losses could reach the $380 to $400 billion mark. Also discusses the falling of wages and the rising of unemployment. Statistical data included.

14430 ■ "Valenti: Roots of Financial Crisis Go Back to 1998" in *Crain's Detroit Business* (Vol. 24, October 6, 2008, No. 40, pp. 25)

Pub: Crain Communications, Inc.

Ed: Tom Henderson; Nathan Skid. **Description:** Interview with Sam Valenti III who is the chairman and CEO of Valenti Capital L.L.C., a wealth-management firm; Valenti discusses in detail the history that led up to the current economic crisis as well as his prediction for the future of the country.

14431 ■ "What's Ahead for Fannie and Fred?" in *Barron's* (Vol. 90, August 30, 2010, No. 35, pp. 26)

Pub: Barron's Editorial & Corporate Headquarters

Ed: Jonathan R. Laing. **Description:** A meeting presided by Treasury Secretary Timothy Geithner discussed the future of Fannie Mae and Freddie Mac. The two government sponsored enterprises were mismanaged and reforming these two agencies is critical.

14432 ■ "Where Are the Vultures?" in *Mergers & Acquisitions: The Dealmaker's Journal* (March 1, 2008)

Pub: SourceMedia, Inc.

Ed: Ken MacFadyen. **Description:** Although the real estate market is distressed, not many acquisitions are being made by distress private equity investors; this is due, in part, to the difficulty in assessing real estate industry firms since it is a sector which is so localized.

14433 ■ "Where to Stash Your Cash" in *Barron's* (Vol. 88, March 17, 2008, No. 11, pp. 41)

Pub: Dow Jones & Company, Inc.

Ed: Mike Hogan. **Description:** Investors are putting their money in money-market mutual funds seeking fractionally better yields and a safe haven from the uncertainties that was brought about by subprime lending. These funds, however, are hovering near 3.20 percent which is less than the 4 percent inflation rate.

14434 ■ "The Worst Lies Ahead for Wall Street; More Losses Certain" in *Crain's New York Business* (Vol. 24, January 21, 2008, No. 3, pp. 1)

Pub: Crain Communications, Inc.

Ed: Aaron Elstein. **Description:** Due to the weakening economy, many financial institutions will face further massive losses forcing them to borrow more at higher interest rates and dragging down their earnings for years to come. The effects on commercial real estate and credit card loans are also discussed as well as the trend to investing in Asia and the Middle East.

14435 ■ **"You Better Shop Around: Four Steps to Getting the Best Deal On a Home Loan" in** *Black Enterprise* **(Vol. 40, July 2010, No. 12, pp. 78)**
Pub: Earl G. Graves Publishing Co. Inc.
Ed: Tara-Nicholle Nelson. **Description:** Four steps to help anyone seeking a mortgage for a home purchase are listed.

14436 ■ **"Your Exposure to Bear Stearns" in** *Barron's* **(Vol. 88, March 17, 2008, No. 11, pp. 45)**
Pub: Dow Jones & Company, Inc.
Ed: Tom Sullivan; Jack Willoughby. **Description:** Bear Stearns makes up 5.5 percent of Pioneer Independence's portfolio, 1.4 percent of Vanguard Windsor II's portfolio, 1.2 percent of Legg Mason Value Trust, about 1 percent of Van Kampen Equity & Income, and 0.79 percent of Putnam Fund for Growth & Income. Ginnie Mae securities are now trading at 1.78 percentage points over treasuries due to the mortgage crises.

TRADE PERIODICALS

14437 ■ *Commercial Mortgage Alert*
Pub: Harrison Scott Publications Inc.
Contact: Andrew Albert, Publisher
E-mail: tferris@hspnews.com
Ed: Thomas J. Ferris, Editor. **Released:** 48/year. **Price:** $2,797, U.S., Canada and elsewhere. **Description:** Covers the commercial mortgage market. Recurring features include a calendar of events and a column titled The Grapevine. Remarks: Available via email in PDF format. Sold with the CMBS Database.

14438 ■ *Inside MBS & ABS*
Pub: Inside Mortgage Finance Publications Inc.
Contact: John Bancroft, Managing Editor
E-mail: jbancroft@imfpubs.com
Released: Weekly, 48 times/year. **Price:** $1,997, individuals. **Description:** Covers the mortgage-related securities market and secondary mortgage market, including regulatory and market developments. Also covers ABS and CMBS markets. Recurring features include interviews, news of research, and exclusive market statistics.

14439 ■ *Inside Mortgage Finance*
Pub: Inside Mortgage Finance Publications Inc.
Contact: John Bancroft, Managing Editor
E-mail: jbancroft@imfpubs.com
Released: Weekly, 48 times/year. **Price:** $1,097, individuals. **Description:** Contains coverage and analysis of market trends and developments affecting the residential (primary) mortgage market. Includes extensive data on mortgage originations and servicing as well as secondary market activity.

14440 ■ *Mortgage Banking Magazine*
Pub: Mortgage Bankers Association of America
Contact: Janet Hewitt, Editor-in-Chief
E-mail: jhewitt@mortgagebankers.org
Released: Monthly. **Price:** $65 members; $75 non-members; $90 other countries. **Description:** Magazine of the real estate finance industry.

14441 ■ *Mortgage Technology*
Pub: SourceMedia Inc.
Contact: Timothy Murphy, Gp. Publisher
E-mail: tim.murphy@thomsonmedia.com
Ed: Anthony Garritano, Editor. **Released:** Monthly. **Price:** $88 U.S.; $108 Canada; $108 other countries. **Description:** Magazine covering technological trends and developments within the mortgage industry.

14442 ■ *National Mortgage News*
Pub: SourceMedia Inc.
Contact: Brian Collins, Bureau Ch.
Released: Weekly. **Description:** Newspaper for mortgage lenders and investment bankers.

VIDEOCASSETTES/ AUDIOCASSETTES

14443 ■ *Financial Business Services*
Morris Video
12881 Knott St.
Garden Grove, CA 92841

Ph:(310)533-4800
Fax:(310)320-3171
Released: 1983. **Price:** $24.95. **Description:** Money management careers are explored, including investment counselors, securities brokers, trust officers and mortgage underwriters. **Availability:** VHS.

TRADE SHOWS AND CONVENTIONS

14444 ■ **The Bond Market Association - Fixed Income Summit Expo on E-Commerce & Technology**
Flagg Management, Inc.
353 Lexington Ave.
New York, NY 10016
Ph:(212)286-0333
Fax:(212)286-0086
Co. E-mail: flaggmgmt@msn.com
URL: http://www.flaggmgmt.com
Released: Annual. **Audience:** Bond Market Association members, government bond officers, fixed income brokers and dealers. **Principal Exhibits:** Online services, Internet systems, fixed-income trading and executions systems, real-time systems, Internet and other new products and solutions; online trading and execution systems; bond market services; online research and global markets information.

14445 ■ **National Association of Review Appraisers and Mortgage Underwriters Convention - National Conference & Expo**
National Association of Review Appraisers and Mortgage Underwriters
1224 N Nokomis NE
Alexandria, MN 56308-5072
Ph:(320)763-6870
Fax:(320)763-9290
URL: http://iami.org/nara
Released: Annual. **Audience:** Appraisers, mortgage loan officers, review appraisers, and other trade professionals. **Principal Exhibits:** Real estate-related information and services.

CONSULTANTS

14446 ■ **Hilbren Consulting Services Inc.**
287 Valencia Dr.
Monroe Township, NJ 08831
Ph:(732)545-7913
Fax:(732)220-8188
Co. E-mail: info@hilbren.com
URL: http://www.hilbren.com
Contact: Gary L. Tinkel, President
E-mail: gtinkel@hilbren.com
Scope: Provides the commercial banking and brokerage industries with expertise in designing and implementing financial systems. Backgrounds include foreign exchange, funds transfer, offshore loans, money markets and Euro dollar systems working with both front and back office operations. Also provide a full range of professional services including project management, feasibility studies, systems analysis, programming and support.

14447 ■ **ICDI Inc.**
250 N Wymore Rd.
Winter Park, FL 32789-3455
Ph:(407)622-2532
Fax:(407)290-2532
Contact: Cindy Bishop, Mgr
Scope: Conducts land title searches, judgment, tax lien or unadjusted contractual changes searches and asset searches. Specializes in title insurance needs. Serves counties in central Florida. Works with mortgage lenders, real estate sales, owners, potential buyers, and any other company or individual needing land title work.

14448 ■ **James Quinn Agency Inc.**
513 W Park Ave., RR 1
PO Box 420
Greenwood, MS 38930-2945
Ph:(662)453-9269

Fax:(662)453-3269
Co. E-mail: amadeus8@bellsouth.net
Contact: Edwina Quinn, Secretary
E-mail: jlquinn@atsnicrosted.com
Scope: Offers a wide range of real estate appraisal and brokerage services involving residential, commercial, industrial and agricultural properties. Also provides investment analysis and feasibility studies. Serves attorneys, accountants, banks, mortgage lenders, trustees for estates and individual investors on land development, financing and valuation matters. Available for expert witness testimony.

14449 ■ **M. S. Franks & Company Inc.**
11 La Cuesta Rd.
Orinda, CA 94563-2303
Ph:(925)254-1469
Fax:(925)254-7783
Co. E-mail: msf@msfranksco.com
URL: http://www.msfranksco.com
Contact: Michael Franks, Owner
E-mail: msf@msfranksco.com
Scope: Offers services in cash management, check processing, general ledger, financial reporting, loan processing, international, branch operations and merger integrations. Specializes in operations design to financial service companies with a focus on impact analysis, user requirements, work flow analysis and design, project communications, development of training programs and material, project management. **Seminars:** Facilitating Great Meetings; Creating Great Project Documentation; Producing Great Meeting Notes.

FRANCHISES AND BUSINESS OPPORTUNITIES

14450 ■ **Centum Financial Group Inc.**
700-1199 West Pender St.
Vancouver, BC, Canada V6E 2R1
Ph:(604)606-2133
Free: 888-257-3940
Fax:(604)257-3949
Co. E-mail: paul_therien@centum.ca
URL: http://www.centum.ca
No. of Franchise Units: 260. **No. of Company-Owned Units:** 1. **Founded:** 2002. **Franchised:** 2002. **Description:** Mortgage broker firms. **Equity Capital Needed:** Minimal to $10,000. **Franchise Fee:** Contact for more information. **Training:** Yes.

14451 ■ **Realty Direct**
Realty Direct Franchise Corp.
44075 Pipeline Plz., Ste. 320
Ashburn, VA 20147
Ph:(703)327-2428
Free: 800-359-5220
Fax:(703)852-3508
Co. E-mail: franchise@realtydirect.com
URL: http://www.realtydirect.com
No. of Franchise Units: 10. **Founded:** 2001. **Franchised:** 2004. **Description:** Full service discount residential brokerage company. Our model provides for a quick start-up in a local market. Our quality program and streamlined operations provide our franchisees with the tools they need to provide residential brokerage services to their clients. Our discount service approach, full-service quality, and our technology focus set us apart from other discount brokerages. **Equity Capital Needed:** $39,600-$67,700. **Franchise Fee:** $19,900. **Financial Assistance:** No. **Training:** 1 week of intense detailed training, 1 day of onsite training and ongoing support via Area Representatives.

COMPUTERIZED DATABASES

14452 ■ *ABA Banking Journal*
Simmons-Boardman Publishing Corp.
345 Hudson St., 12th Fl.
New York, NY 10014
Ph:(212)620-7200
Free: 800-895-4389
URL: http://www.simmonsboardman.com
Description: Contains the complete text of *ABA Banking Journal*, a magazine on commercial bank operation and management. Covers employee rela-

tions, recruiting, and training; installment, mortgage, commercial, and industrial lending; correspondent, foreign, and retail banking; deposit gathering; bank cards; asset and liability management; data processing and telecommunications; security; government relations; and legal and regulatory developments. Also provides a calendar of ABA-sponsored courses, seminars, and workshops. **Availability:** Online: LexisNexis Group, Intuit Inc., Simmons-Boardman Publishing Corp. **Type:** Full text.

14453 ■ American Banker Financial Publications
SourceMedia Inc.
1 State St. Plz., 27th Fl.
New York, NY 10004
Ph:(212)803-8200
Free: 800-221-1809
Fax:(212)843-9600
Co. E-mail: custserv@AmericanBanker.com
URL: http://www.americanbanker.com
Description: Provides full text of the daily financial services newspaper and other financial newsletters which follow trends, developments, and news in banking and related financial areas. Includes topics such as capital markets, bank regulation, insurance letters, and public finance letters. **Availability:** Online: ProQuest LLC. **Type:** Full text.

14454 ■ Barron's Online
Dow Jones & Company Inc.
1 World Financial Ctr.
200 Liberty St.
New York, NY 10281
Ph:(212)416-2000
Fax:(212)416-4348
Co. E-mail: info@dowjones.com
URL: http://www.dowjones.com
Description: Provides the complete text of *Barron's*, providing articles and reports covering worldwide financial markets. Includes market data, news and market commentary, interviews, statistics, tools and resources (including specific analysis of online investing). Available as a stand-alone subscription product. **Availability:** Online: Dow Jones & Company Inc. **Type:** Full text; Numeric; Statistical.

14455 ■ BlockDATA
Thomson Reuters
3 Times Sq.
New York, NY 10036
Ph:(646)223-4000
Co. E-mail: salesinquires@thomsonreuters.com
URL: http://thomsonreuters.com/products_services/financial
Description: Provides information on the 400 most active listed, over-the-counter (OTC), and foreign securities traded on the AutEx Trading Information System (described in a separate entry). Includes industry profiles and trends as well as three months

of trades data for comparative analysis. **Availability:** Online: Thomson Reuters, Thomson Reuters. **Type:** Full text; Numeric.

14456 ■ Business Wire
Berkshire Hathaway Inc.
44 Montgomery St., 39th Fl.
San Francisco, CA 94104
Ph:(415)986-4422
Free: 800-227-0845
Fax:(415)788-5335
Co. E-mail: SF_sales_group@bizwire.com
URL: http://www.businesswire.com
Description: Contains more than 1.4 million records that make up the complete text of press releases from public and private companies and other organizations, such as hospitals and universities. Covers new products, stock offerings, mergers, legal actions, financial information, personnel changes, and company announcements of general interest. Includes headline recaps hourly plus recaps of high tech headlines in some systems. Records include company name, headline, publication date, ticker symbol, byline; dateline, time, word count (usually less than 500), and text, including contact information. Covers industries such as banking, computers, telecommunications, entertainment, aviation, biotechnology, and mining; general news and features; some international events; and sports. **Availability:** Online: Thomson Reuters, Mzinga Inc., ProQuest LLC, Dow Jones & Company Inc., LexisNexis Group, Bloomberg LP. **Type:** Full text.

14457 ■ CANNEX
CANNEX Financial Exchanges Ltd.
1200 Bay St., Ste. 1001
Toronto, ON, Canada M5R 2A5
Ph:(416)926-0882
Free: 800-387-1269
Fax:(416)926-0706
Co. E-mail: cannex@cannex.com
URL: http://www.cannex.com
Description: Contains current interest and product information for Term Deposits/GICs (Certificates of Deposit), mortgages, RRSPs (IRAs), annuities, RRIFs (similar to annuities), and savings and checking account products offered by banks, trust companies, savings and loans, and life insurance companies in Australia, New Zealand, the U.S. and Canada. **Availability:** Online: CANNEX Financial Exchanges Ltd. **Type:** Numeric.

14458 ■ Mortgage Delinquency Rates
Haver Analytics
60 E 42nd St.
New York, NY 10165
Ph:(212)986-9300
Fax:(212)986-5857
Co. E-mail: data@haver.com
URL: http://www.haver.com
Description: Provides information on quarterly delinquency rates of one- to four-unit residential

mortgage loans reported by the Mortgage Brokers Association. Data for the total United States and Census regions begin in 1972. Data for states and Census divisions begin in 1979. **Availability:** Online: Haver Analytics. **Type:** Numeric.

14459 ■ Securities Law Daily
The Bureau of National Affairs Inc.
1801 S Bell St.
Arlington, VA 22202
Free: 800-372-1033
Co. E-mail: customercare@bna.com
URL: http://www.bna.com
Description: Contains reports the latest developments in securities and futures law. Covers state and federal legislative, regulatory, and judicial actions affecting securities, commodities, and corporate activities. Includes coverage of U.S. Congress, state and federal courts, the Commodities Futures Trading Commission, and the Securities and Exchange Commission (SEC). Addresses such topics as insider trading, mutual funds, SEC regulation, investment advisors, global markets, and more. **Availability:** Online: Thomson Reuters, The Bureau of National Affairs Inc. **Type:** Full text.

14460 ■ U.S. Banker Online
Investcorp International Inc.
1 State St. Plaza, 27th Fl.
New York, NY 10004
Ph:(212)803-8200
Free: 800-221-1809
Co. E-mail: custserv@sourcemedia.com
URL: http://www.sourcemedia.com
Description: Contains the complete text of *United States Banker*, a magazine covering competitive, regulatory, and technological developments in banking investment products, asset/liability management, fair lending, home banking, consolidation, branch automation, and bank management issues. **Availability:** Online: ProQuest LLC, Investcorp International Inc. **Type:** Full text.

14461 ■ U.S. Weekly Statistics
Haver Analytics
60 E 42nd St.
New York, NY 10165
Ph:(212)986-9300
Fax:(212)986-5857
Co. E-mail: data@haver.com
URL: http://www.haver.com
Description: Contains weekly financial and economic series aggregated from DAILY plus aggregate reserves, official reserve assets, bank assets and liabilities, commercial paper outstanding, money supply, bank credit, unemployment claims, car and truck production by firm, and production of raw steel, coal, and lumber. Also includes complete commitment of traders' data from the Commodity Futures Trading Commission. **Availability:** Online: Haver Analytics. **Type:** Statistical; Numeric.

ASSOCIATIONS AND OTHER ORGANIZATIONS

14462 ■ American Motorcyclist Association
13515 Yarmouth Dr.
Pickerington, OH 43147-8214
Ph:(614)856-1900
Free: 800-262-5646
Fax:(614)856-1920
Co. E-mail: ama@ama-cycle.org
URL: http://www.ama-cycle.org
Contact: Stan Simpson, Chm.
Description: Represents motorcycle enthusiasts. Acts as a rulemaking body for motorcycle competition. Promotes highway safety. Maintains museum and hall of fame. **Publications:** *American Motorcycle Association—Action* (bimonthly).

14463 ■ Motorcycle Industry Council
2 Jenner St., Ste. 150
Irvine, CA 92618-3806
Ph:(949)727-4211
Fax:(949)727-3313
Co. E-mail: ciannello@mic.org
URL: http://www.mic.org
Contact: Carole Iannello
Description: Manufacturers and distributors of motorcycles and allied industries. Maintains liaison with state and federal governments. Operates collection of research documents, federal and state government documents, and trade publications. Compiles statistics. .

REFERENCE WORKS

14464 ■ *Achieving Planned Innovation: A Proven System for Creating Successful New Products and Services*
Pub: Simon and Schuster
Ed: Frank R. Bacon. **Released:** August 2007. **Price:** $16.95. **Description:** Planned innovation is a disciplined and practical step-by-step sequence of procedures for reaching the intended destination point: successful products. This easy-to-read book explains the system along with an action-oriented program for continuous success in new-product innovations. Five steps outlined include: a disciplined reasoning process; lasting market orientation; proper selection criteria that reflect both strategic and tactical business objectives and goals along with dynamic matching of resources to present and future opportunities, and positive and negative requirements before making major expenditures; and proper organizational staffing. The author explains what to do and evaluating the potential of any new product or service, ranging from ventures in retail distribution to the manufacture of goods as diverse as bicycles, motorcycles, aerospace communication and navigation equipment, small business computers, food packaging, and medical products.

14465 ■ "Harley-Davidson Moves to Unconventional Marketing Plan" in *Business Journal-Milwaukee* (Vol. 28, November 26, 2010, No. 8, pp. A1)
Pub: Milwaukee Business Journal
Ed: Rich Rovito. **Description:** Harley Davidson Inc. hired Boulder, Colorado-based Victors & Spoils, an agency that specializes in crowdsourcing, to implement a new creative marketing model. Under the plan, Harley Davidson will draw on the ideas of its brand enthusiasts to help guide the brand's marketing direction.

14466 ■ "Local Shops' Wares Sound Good To Boomers Needing Some Fun" in *Crain's Cleveland Business* (Vol. 30, May 18, 2009, No. 20, pp. 5)
Pub: Crain Communications, Inc.
Ed: Dan Shingler. **Description:** Dr. Z Amplification, who makes amplifiers for guitars and SuperTrapp Performance Exhausts, producer of tunable exhausts for motorcycles, are seeing increased sales as baby boomers look to add enjoyment to their lives.

14467 ■ "MANAfest Provides Reps with Tools for the Future" in *Agency Sales Magazine* (Vol. 39, September-October 2009, No. 9, pp. 36)
Pub: MANA
Ed: Jack Foster. **Description:** Former Harley Davidson director of communications Ken Schmidt was the keynote speaker at the MANAfest conference; he discussed how the company delivered itself from bankruptcy. Selling Power magazine publisher Gerhard Gschwandtner also made a presentation; he believes that there will be opportunities for sales people involved in relationship selling.

14468 ■ "A New Way to Arrive in Style" in *Inc.* (Vol. 33, September 2011, No. 7, pp. 54)
Pub: Inc. Magazine
Ed: Matthew Rist. **Description:** EagleRider is a franchise offering various two-wheeled rentals, including BMWs and Harley-Davidsons at more than 100 locations worldwide.

14469 ■ "Wowing Her Customers" in *Women In Business* (Vol. 61, August-September 2009, No. 4, pp. 34)
Pub: American Business Women's Association
Ed: Kathleen Leighton. **Description:** Gail Worth, together with her brother, bought her parents' Harley-Davidson motorcycle dealership in Grandview, Missouri. She eventually had the dealership to herself when her brother broke out of the partnership. Gail says she is comfortable in a man's world kind of business and has expanded the business with a 10-acre site.

STATISTICAL SOURCES

14470 ■ *RMA Annual Statement Studies*
Pub: Robert Morris Associates (RMA)
Released: Annual. **Price:** $175.00 2006-07 edition, $105.00. **Description:** Contains composite balance sheets and income statements for more than 360 industries, including the accounting, auditing, and bookkeeping industries. Also contains five years of comparative historical data for discerning trends. Includes 16 commonly used ratios, computed for most of the size groupings for nearly every industry.

TRADE PERIODICALS

14471 ■ *American Motorcyclist*
Pub: American Motorcyclist Association
Contact: Grant Parsons, Managing Editor
E-mail: gparsons@ama-cycle.org
Released: Monthly. **Price:** $15 nonmembers. **Description:** Magazine covering motorcycling in America. Publication of the American Motorcyclist Association.

14472 ■ *Cycle News*
Pub: CN Publishing
Contact: Henny Ray Abrams, Contributing Ed.
Released: Weekly. **Price:** $45 include online; $150 other countries include online; $80 two years include online; $29.95 online edition only. **Description:** Newspaper (tabloid) for motorcycle enthusiasts.

14473 ■ *Cycle World*
Pub: Hachette Filipacchi Media U.S. Inc.
Contact: Larry Little, Sen. VP/Publisher
Released: Monthly. **Price:** $12; $35 other countries. **Description:** Magazine on street, dirt, dual-purpose, and all-terrain motorcylces. Covering tests, aftermarket products, parts and accessories, competition, personalities, travel, and nostalgia.

14474 ■ *Dealernews*
Pub: Advanstar Communications
Contact: Mary Slepicka, Assoc. Publisher/Editorial Dir.
E-mail: mslepicka@dealernews.com
Released: Monthly. **Description:** Magazine covering dealers of motorcycles, ATV/off-road vehicles, watercraft, other powersport vehicles, and related aftermarket and apparel products.

14475 ■ *Motorcycle Industry Magazine*
Pub: Industry Shopper Publishing Inc.
Contact: Rick Campbell, Editor & Publisher
E-mail: rick@atv-industry.com
Released: Monthly. **Price:** $180 other countries. **Description:** Trade magazine covering the motorcycle industry.

14476 ■ *The Motorcyclist's Post*
Pub: The Motorcyclist's Post
Ed: Leo Castell, Editor, lcastell@snet.net. **Released:** Monthly. **Price:** $25; $45 two years. **Description:** Tabloid newspaper covering motorcycle activities and legislation.

TRADE SHOWS AND CONVENTIONS

14477 ■ Minneapolis International Motorcycle Show
Advanstar Communications
641 Lexington Ave., 8th Fl.
New York, NY 10022
Ph:(212)951-6600

Fax:(212)951-6793
Co. E-mail: info@advantstar.com
URL: http://www.advanstar.com
Audience: Public: Motorcycle, watercraft and ATV enthusiasts. **Principal Exhibits:** A marketplace where manufacturers can display and sell their products such as motorcycles, all-terrain vehicles (ATV), scooters, watercraft, apparel, parts and accessories.

14478 ■ Seattle International Motorcycle Show
Advanstar Communications
641 Lexington Ave., 8th Fl.
New York, NY 10022
Ph:(212)951-6600
Fax:(212)951-6793
Co. E-mail: info@advantstar.com
URL: http://www.advanstar.com
Audience: Motorcycle, watercraft and ATV enthusiasts. **Principal Exhibits:** A marketplace where manufacturers and retailers can display and sell their products such as motorcycles, all-terrain vehicles (ATV), scooters, watercraft, apparel, parts and accessories. **Dates and Locations:** 2011 Dec 10-12, Seattle, WA.

14479 ■ Southern California International Motorcycle Show
Advanstar Communications
641 Lexington Ave., 8th Fl.
New York, NY 10022
Ph:(212)951-6600
Fax:(212)951-6793
Co. E-mail: info@advantstar.com
URL: http://www.advanstar.com
Audience: Public: Motorcycle, watercraft, and ATV enthusiasts. **Principal Exhibits:** A marketplace where manufacturers and retailers can display and sell their products such as motorcycles, all-terrain vehicles (ATV), scooters watercraft, apparel, parts and accessories.

14480 ■ TUP 2011
Romexpo S.A.
65-67 Marasti Blvd.
PO Box 32-3
R-011465 Bucharest, Romania
Ph:40 21 2025700
Fax:40 21 2077070
Co. E-mail: romexpo@romexpo.org
URL: http://www.romexpo.org
Audience: Utilities professionals, general public.
Principal Exhibits: Services and public utilities.

LIBRARIES

14481 ■ Antique Automobile Club of America–AACA Library & Research Center, Inc.
501 W. Governor Rd.
PO Box 417
Hershey, PA 17033
Ph:(717)534-2082
Fax:(717)534-9101
Co. E-mail: critter@aacalibrary.org
URL: http://www.aacalibrary.org
Contact: Christopher Ritter, Hd.Libn.

Scope: Automobiles, automotive history, automobile restoration, commercial vehicles, trucks, motorcycles. **Services:** Copying; Library open to the public. **Holdings:** 6000 books; 300 bound periodical volumes; 400,000 pieces of sales literature, owners and shop manuals; 70 reels of microfilm; 3000 microfiche; 15 drawers of blueprints; paint chips; photographs; sheet music; memorabilia; maps; postcards. **Subscriptions:** 220 journals and other serials.

Movie Theatre Operation

ASSOCIATIONS AND OTHER ORGANIZATIONS

14482 ■ Independent Film and Television Alliance
10850 Wilshire Blvd., 9th Fl.
Los Angeles, CA 90024-4321
Ph:(310)446-1000
Fax:(310)446-1600
Co. E-mail: rburt@ifta-online.org
URL: http://www.ifta-online.org
Contact: Lloyd Kaufman, Chm.
Description: Trade association for the worldwide independent film and television industry. Contributes to negotiations with foreign producer associations; develops standardized theatrical, TV and video contracts for international distribution. Established and maintains the IFTA International Arbitration Tribunal, a system through which prominent entertainment attorneys throughout the world assist members and consenting clients in reaching equitable and binding agreements. Facilitates the formulation of policies, standardized private practices and language contracts and the exchange of information and experience among members. Produces the American Film Market (AFM), the largest international motion picture trade event in the world. .

14483 ■ Motion Picture Association of America
15301 Ventura Blvd., Bldg. E
Sherman Oaks, CA 91403-5585
Ph:(818)995-6600
Fax:(818)285-4403
URL: http://www.mpaa.org
Contact: Robert Pisano, Pres./Interim CEO
Description: Represents principal producers and distributors of motion pictures in the U.S. Serves as an advocate of the American motion picture, home video, and television industries; activities also include preserving and protecting the rights of copyright owners; fighting censorship and restrictive attacks on First Amendment rights of motion picture, television, and home video producers; and directing anti-piracy programs to protect U.S. films, television programming, and home video throughout the U.S. .

14484 ■ Motion Picture Theatre Associations of Canada–Federation des Associations de proprietaires de cinemas du Canada
1235 Bay St., Ste. 400
Toronto, ON, Canada M5R 3K4
Ph:(416)969-7057
Fax:(416)969-8916
Co. E-mail: mptac.ca@ca.inter.net
URL: http://www.mptac.ca
Contact: Adina Lebo, Exec. Dir.
Description: Cinema associations. Promotes a business climate beneficial to members. Functions as a trade association for exhibitors in the motion picture industry. Conducts research; sponsors competitions; compiles industry statistics. **Publications:** *Cinescope* (monthly).

14485 ■ National Association of Theatre Owners
750 1st St. NE, Ste. 1130
Washington, DC 20002
Ph:(202)962-0054
Fax:(202)962-0370
Co. E-mail: nato@natodc.com
URL: http://www.natoonline.org
Contact: Tony Kerasotes, Chm.
Description: Owners, operators and executives of motion picture theaters. Provides services to assist theater owners in successfully operating their theaters including monitoring legislative and technological advancements; compiles statistics. **Publications:** *Encyclopedia of Exhibition* (annual).

REFERENCE WORKS

14486 ■ "AMC Scouts Downtown for New HQ" in *Business Journal-Serving Metropolitan Kansas City* (Vol. 26, October 19, 2007, No. 6, pp. 1)
Pub: American City Business Journals, Inc.
Ed: Jim Davis. **Description:** AMC Entertainment Inc. is seeking a new 100,000 square foot office in downtown Kansas City. The new headquarters is expected to bring additional employment and revenue to the city. AMC's stay on Main Street since 2002 is discussed.

14487 ■ "Are Movie Theaters Doomed?" in *Business Horizons* (November-December 2007, pp. 491)
Pub: Elsevier Technology Publications
Ed: Jon Silver, John McDonnell. **Description:** Theater operators must embrace new technologies and more diverse target markets if they are to stem the decline in theatergoers. Movie theaters remain highly vulnerable to trends in the home entertainment industry.

14488 ■ "Calling An Audible" in *The Business Journal-Milwaukee* (Vol. 25, August 1, 2008, No. 45, pp. A1)
Pub: American City Business Journals, Inc.
Ed: David Dedge. **Description:** Tough economic conditions are forcing entertainment businesses in Milwaukee, Wisconsin, to try new business strategies to keep attracting customers. These strategies include keeping prices steady despite increasing costs and new sales promotions.

14489 ■ "Deltona to Get First Movie Theater, Shopping Center" in *Orlando Business Journal* (Vol. 26, December 4, 2009, No. 26, pp. 1)
Pub: American City Business Journals
Ed: Anjali Fluker. **Description:** Epic Theaters Inc. revealed plans to build a new 900,000 square foot retail center anchored by a 12-screen movie theater in the city of Deltona in Volusia County, Florida by 2010. The project, dubbed Deltona Village, would provide the city with its first movie theater and shopping center.

14490 ■ "EX3D to Launch In-Theater Vending Machines for Stylish RealD 3D Glasses" in *Entertainment Close-Up* (August 16, 2011)
Pub: Close-Up Media
Description: Marchon3d has partnered with Cinemark and UltraStar Cinemas to install vending machines selling Marchon3D's line of patented, curved RealD 3D compatible eyeglasses.

14491 ■ "Feldman Pushing Past 'Pain' of Cost Overruns, Delays at Colonie Center" in *Business Review, Albany New York* (November 9, 2007)
Pub: American City Business Journals, Inc.
Ed: Michael DeMasi. **Description:** Details of major improvements at Colonie Center are presented. The total cost for these projects increased by $15 million, and the construction of the nearly ten-story theater in the mall is experiencing delays. According to Larry Feldman, chairman of Feldman Mall Properties, which owns a minority stake in the mall, the cost overruns have pushed the company's renovation costs to around $85 million.

14492 ■ *Film Journal International—Equipment, Concessions & Services Guide*
Pub: Sunshine Group Worldwide Ltd.
Contact: Kevin Lally, Exec. Ed.
E-mail: kevin.lally@nielsen.com
Released: Annual, Latest edition 2008. **Publication Includes:** Lists of about 300 manufacturers and suppliers of equipment, products, and services for the theatrical motion picture and concession industries; more than 20 film processors, and over 200 dealers and distributors of equipment and supplies. **Entries Include:** Company name, address, phone, names and titles of key personnel, products or services. **Arrangement:** Separate alphabetical sections for manufacturers and processors; dealers are geographical. **Indexes:** Product/service.

14493 ■ "Ghouls, Goblins, and Harry Potter: Cashing In On Halloween" in *Inc.* (Vol. 33, October 2011, No. 8, pp. 24)
Pub: Inc. Magazine
Ed: Darren Dahl. **Description:** Costume Craze, an online costume retailer reports $13.2 million in sales last year. Originally the family business started out as a software company called StaticAdvantage, but switched gears.

14494 ■ *Motion Picture TV and Theatre Directory*
Pub: Motion Picture Enterprises Publications Inc.
Contact: Neal R. Pilzer, Publisher
Released: Semiannual, spring and fall. **Price:** $22.53, individuals each, within New York; $20.79, individuals each, outside New York. **Covers:** Companies providing products and services to the motion picture and television industries. All listings are paid. **Entries Include:** Company name, address, phone. **Arrangement:** Classified by product or service. **Indexes:** Alphabetical.

14495 ■ *The Pixar Touch: The Making of a Company*
Pub: Pantheon Books
Ed: David A. Price. **Released:** 2009. **Price:** $27.95.
Description: Profile of how Pixar's founders turned their computer-animated films into a successful movie studio.

14496 ■ **"Sneak Preview: Alamo Revamp" in** *Austin Business Journal Inc.* **(Vol. 28, December 12, 2008, No. 39, pp. 1)**
Pub: American City Business Journals
Ed: Sandra Zaragoza. **Description:** Austin, Texas-based Alamo Drafthouse Cinemas is planning to build a new Circle C Ranch. The new theater will showcase digital projectors and the latest sound systems to show 3-D movies. The company is in lease negotiations with developer Stratus Properties Inc.

14497 ■ **"Stars Shine Downtown" in** *The Business Journal-Serving Metropolitan Kansas City* **(Vol. 26, August 29, 2008, No. 51, pp. 1)**
Pub: American City Business Journals, Inc.
Ed: Rob Roberts. **Description:** Movie chain AMC Entertainment Inc. renews its lease for 97,000 square feet of space at Ten Main Center. HNTB Federal Services Corp., meanwhile, is to take up 42,000 square feet at an office building located at 120 W. 12th St. The leases' impacts on downtown office market are examined.

14498 ■ *Theatre Directory*
Pub: Theatre Communications Group
Released: Annual, Latest edition 2007-2008. **Price:** $14.95, individuals each. **Covers:** Approximately 450 not-for-profit profession theatres, and over 100 arts resource organizations. **Entries Include:** For theatres—company name, address, business and box office phone and fax numbers, name and title of 3 primary staff members, e-mail and web addresses, season, union contracts and special interests. For resource organizations—company name, address, business phone and fax numbers, name and title of contact, e-mail and web addresses, and a brief description of the organization. **Arrangement:** Classified by activity or service. **Indexes:** Special interest, personnel, theatre by state.

STATISTICAL SOURCES

14499 ■ *RMA Annual Statement Studies*
Pub: Robert Morris Associates (RMA)
Released: Annual. **Price:** $175.00 2006-07 edition, $105.00. **Description:** Contains composite balance sheets and income statements for more than 360 industries, including the accounting, auditing, and bookkeeping industries. Also contains five years of comparative historical data for discerning trends. Includes 16 commonly used ratios, computed for most of the size groupings for nearly every industry.

TRADE PERIODICALS

14500 ■ *Boxoffice Magazine*
Pub: Media Enterprises L.P.
Contact: Lyle Homes, Editor-in-Chief
Released: Monthly. **Price:** $59.95; $64.95 Canada; $125 other countries. **Description:** Trade magazine for the motion picture exhibition industry; including news of film distribution and exhibition, film reviews, and technical articles.

14501 ■ *Film Comment*
Pub: Film Society of Lincoln Center
Contact: Laura Kern, Managing Editor
E-mail: lkern@filmlinc.com
Ed: Gavin Smith, Editor, editor@filmlinc.com. **Released:** Bimonthly. **Price:** $29.95; $35.95 institutions and libraries; $40 Canada and Mexico; $45 institutions, Canada and Mexico libraries; $60 other countries; $70 institutions, other countries libraries. **Description:** Motion picture magazine.

14502 ■ *Film Journal International*
Pub: Sunshine Group Worldwide Ltd.
Contact: Kevin Lally, Exec. Ed.
E-mail: kevin.lally@nielsen.com
Released: Monthly. **Price:** $65; $100 two years. **Description:** Magazine addressing interests of the motion picture industry.

VIDEOCASSETTES/AUDIOCASSETTES

14503 ■ *Inside Business Today*
GPN Educational Media
1550 Executive Drive
Elgin, IL 60123
Ph:(402)472-2007
Free: 800-228-4630
Fax:800-306-2330
Co. E-mail: askgpn@smarterville.com
URL: http://www.shopgpn.com
Released: 1989. **Description:** Leaders in business and industry tell their success stories in this extensive series. **Availability:** VHS; 3/4U.

CONSULTANTS

14504 ■ **Stage Equipment & Lighting Inc.**
9207 Palm River Rd., Ste. 108
Tampa, FL 33610
Ph:(305)891-2010
Free: 800-597-2010
Fax:(305)893-2828
Co. E-mail: info@seal-fla.com
URL: http://www.seal-fla.com
Contact: Vivian Gill, President
Scope: Offers creative services for presentations, staging, and lighting, including systems designs, installation supervision, seminars for personnel, theatrical equipment maintenance and lighting for all forms of presentations and presentation facilities, theaters, television, film, audiovisuals, meetings, and product presentations.

FRANCHISES AND BUSINESS OPPORTUNITIES

14505 ■ **Actor's Garage**
152 Ryder Rd.
Manhasset, NY 11030
Ph:(516)627-7211
Fax:(516)627-7230
No. of Franchise Units: 3. **No. of Company-Owned Units:** 13. **Founded:** 2004. **Franchised:** 2006. **Description:** Children's acting schools. **Equity Capital Needed:** $30,600-$31,700. **Franchise Fee:** $24,000. **Royalty Fee:** 9%. **Financial Assistance:** Limited third party financing available. **Training:** Provides 5 days at headquarters with ongoing support.

14506 ■ **Kidstage**
PO Box 1072
Appleton, WI 54912
Ph:(920)915-0044
Free: 877-415-5115
Fax:(920)735-6572
No. of Franchise Units: 14. **No. of Company-Owned Units:** 3. **Founded:** 1996. **Franchised:** 2003. **Description:** Drama classes and performance opportunities. **Equity Capital Needed:** $14,000. **Franchise Fee:** $12,500. **Financial Assistance:** Yes. **Training:** Yes.

LIBRARIES

14507 ■ **Academy of Motion Picture Arts and Sciences—Margaret Herrick Library**
Fairbanks Center for Motion Picture Studies
333 S. La Cienega Blvd.
Beverly Hills, CA 90211
Ph:(310)247-3020
Fax:(310)859-9619
Co. E-mail: lmehr@oscars.org
URL: http://www.oscars.org/library/index.html
Contact: Linda Harris Mehr, Dir.
Scope: Motion picture history, biography, and production. **Services:** Copying; photographic reproduction; Library open to the public for reference use only; special collections open to the public by appointment. **Holdings:** 32,000 books; 2400 periodical titles; 1875 VF drawers of clippings on film productions, individuals, general subject, festivals, awards, Academy his-

tory; 70,000 scripts; 10 million photographs; 35,000 posters. **Subscriptions:** 200 journals and other serials; 3 newspapers.

14508 ■ **American Film Institute—Louis B. Mayer Library**
2021 N. Western Ave.
Box 27999
Los Angeles, CA 90027-1657
Ph:(323)856-7654
Fax:(323)467-4578
URL: http://www.afi.com/about/library.aspx
Contact: Caroline Sisneros, Libn.
Scope: Moving pictures, television, video, cable, satellite. **Services:** Copying; Library open to the public. Indexing Service (microfiche); Film Production Index, 1930-1969 (card). **Holdings:** 14,000 books; 900 bound periodical volumes; 6000 motion picture and television scripts; 44 oral history transcripts; 535 seminar transcripts; 600 seminar audiotapes; 75 reels of microfilm. **Subscriptions:** 100 journals and other serials (approximately); 5 newspapers.

14509 ■ **Hollywood Film Archive Library**
8391 Beverly Blvd. PMB 321
Hollywood, CA 90048
Ph:(323)655-4968
Co. E-mail: cabaret66@aol.com
Contact: D. Richard Baer, Dir.
Scope: Motion pictures, television, video. **Services:** Library open to the public by appointment only. **Holdings:** 2400 volumes; 6000 motion picture stills; Monthly Film Bulletin, 1934 to present; Motion Picture Exhibitor, 1931-1972; Motion Picture Herald, 1944-1960; Boxoffice, 1960 to present.

14510 ■ **John E. Allen Motion Picture Archives**
PO Box 452
Newfoundland, PA 18445
Ph:(570)676-4152
Fax:(570)676-9194
Co. E-mail: jeainc@gmail.com
URL: http://www.allenarchive.com/wordpress/
Contact: Beverley Allen, Archv.
Scope: Motion pictures, 1896-1980s; general coverage with wide subject base, actuality and dramatic. **Services:** Copying; archives open to the public by appointment on fee basis. **Holdings:** 25 million feet of 35mm and 16mm film.

14511 ■ **Motion Picture Association of America Library**
15301 Ventura Blvd., Bldg. E
Sherman Oaks, CA 91403
Ph:(818)995-6600
Fax:(818)285-4403
URL: http://www.mpaa.org
Scope: Theatrical motion pictures - history, finance, censorship, content. **Services:** Library available to qualified persons for consultation by mail or telephone. **Holdings:** 3000 volumes. **Subscriptions:** 20 journals and other serials.

14512 ■ **University of Southern California Library—Cinematic Arts Library**
Doheny Memorial Library, Ground Fl.
3550 Trousdale Pkwy.
Los Angeles, CA 90089-0185
Ph:(213)740-3994
Co. E-mail: shanson@usc.edu
URL: http://www.usc.edu/isd/libraries/locations/cinema_tv/
Contact: Stephen Hanson, Dir.
Scope: Motion pictures, television, radio. **Services:** Interlibrary loan (limited); copying; Library open to the public for reference use only. **Holdings:** 22,000 volumes; 250 reels of microfilm; 427 cartridges of videotape of David Wolper productions, 1962-1972; teleplay collection; screenplay collection; 1700 reels and cartridges of audiotape; 1200 soundtracks and original cast recordings. **Subscriptions:** 220 journals and other serials.

RESEARCH CENTERS

14513 ■ Theatre Historical Society of America
York Theatre Bldg., 2nd Fl.
152 N York St.
Elmhurst, IL 60126-2806

Ph:(630)782-1800
Fax:(630)782-1802
Co. E-mail: thrhistsoc@aol.com
URL: http://www.historictheatres.org
Contact: Richard J. Sklenar, Exec.Dir.
E-mail: thrhistsoc@aol.com
Scope: American theater, including all buildings designed or regularly used for exhibition of stage or motion picture presentations and theater equipment and personnel. Acts as a clearinghouse for theater research. **Services:** Research assistance to both members and nonmembers. **Publications:** Marquee (quarterly). **Educational Activities:** Annual convention and theater tour. **Awards:** Jeffery Weiss Memorial Writing Competition.

ASSOCIATIONS AND OTHER ORGANIZATIONS

14514 ■ American Moving and Storage Association
1611 Duke St.
Alexandria, VA 22314-3406
Ph:(703)683-7410
Free: 888-849-AMSA
Fax:(703)683-7527
Co. E-mail: info@moving.org
URL: http://www.moving.org
Contact: Jaime Barnhart, Dir. of Conferences
Description: Local, intrastate, interstate, and international movers who transport household goods, office and institutional equipment, and high-value products. Sponsors Household Goods Dispute Settlement Program which handles consumer complaints between consumers and interstate moving companies. **Publications:** *AMSA Membership Directory* (annual); *Direction* (monthly); *Government Traffic News* (monthly); *The Moving World* (biweekly); *Transportation Fact Book* (annual).

REFERENCE WORKS

14515 ■ "For His Bigness of Heart: Larry O'Toole: Gentle Giant Moving, Somerville, Massachusetts" in *Inc.* (Volume 32, December 2010)
Pub: Inc. Magazine
Description: Profile of Larry O'Toole, owners of Gentle Giant Moving Company, where his company charges more, but in return consumers receive a higher quality service.

14516 ■ "KXAN Seeks Larger Studio, Office Space" in *Austin Business Journal* (Vol. 31, May 27, 2011, No. 12, pp. A1)
Pub: American City Business Journals Inc.
Ed: Cody Lyon. **Description:** Austin NBC affiliate KXAN Television is opting to sell its property north of downtown and relocate to another site. The station is now inspecting possible sites to house its broadcasting facility and employees totaling as many as 200 people. Estimated cost of the construction of the studios and offices is $13 million plus another million in moving the equipment.

STATISTICAL SOURCES

14517 ■ *RMA Annual Statement Studies*
Pub: Robert Morris Associates (RMA)
Released: Annual. **Price:** $175.00 2006-07 edition, $105.00. **Description:** Contains composite balance sheets and income statements for more than 360 industries, including the accounting, auditing, and bookkeeping industries. Also contains five years of comparative historical data for discerning trends. Includes 16 commonly used ratios, computed for most of the size groupings for nearly every industry.

FRANCHISES AND BUSINESS OPPORTUNITIES

14518 ■ Craters & Freighters
Craters & Freighters Franchise Co.
331 Corporate Cir., No. J
Golden, CO 80401
Free: 800-949-9931
Fax:(303)399-8190
Co. E-mail: franchise@CratersAndFreighters.com
URL: http://www.CratersAndFreighters.com
No. of Franchise Units: 66. **Founded:** 1990. **Franchised:** 1991. **Description:** As "speciality freight handlers," the Company serves an up-scale market on art galleries, museums, estate liquidators, interior decorators and a host of other clients to fulfill their specialized needs in moving a multitude of large, delicate and valuable freight shipments. **Equity Capital Needed:** $137,200-$204,500. **Franchise Fee:** $31,500. **Royalty Fee:** 5%. **Financial Assistance:** Third party financing assistance available. **Training:** Offers training at headquarters 10 days, 2-3 days at franchisees location, 2 days annual convention with ongoing support.

14519 ■ Mobile Attic Franchising Company
Mobile Attic, Inc.
246 Larkin Rd.
Elba, AL 36323
Ph:(334)897-1346
Free: (866)874-8474
Fax:(334)897-1349
No. of Franchise Units: 40. **No. of Company-Owned Units:** 4. **Founded:** 2000. **Franchised:** 2004. **Description:** Portable self-storage. **Equity Capital Needed:** $250,000+. **Financial Assistance:** Yes. **Training:** Yes.

14520 ■ Moving Solutions Franchise LLC
115 W Eagle Rd.
Havertown, PA 19083
Ph:(610)853-2600
Fax:(610)853-2600
No. of Franchise Units: 6. **No. of Company-Owned Units:** 1. **Founded:** 1996. **Franchised:** 2005. **Description:** Move management and relocation services. **Equity Capital Needed:** $29,300-$40,700. **Franchise Fee:** $9,000-$29,000. **Financial Assistance:** No. **Training:** Yes.

14521 ■ Two Men and a Truck
Two Men and a Truck Intl., Inc.
3400 Belle Chase Way
Lansing, MI 48911
Ph:(517)394-7210
Free: 800-345-1070
Co. E-mail: shirleyk@twomenandatruck.com
URL: http://www.twomenandatruck.com
No. of Franchise Units: 221. **Founded:** 1985. **Franchised:** 1989. **Description:** One of the largest local-moving franchises in the U.S. High-growth unique profitable market niche. No experience necessary. Strong and steady year-round market, regardless of economy. Nationally recognized name and logo. Industry-wide leadership position with a proven operating system of success. Award winning advertising and marketing support. Franchisee Advisory Council - TEAM, rated in Entrepreneur Magazine top 500. Excellent opportunity for women and men. **Equity Capital Needed:** $158,000-$430,910. **Franchise Fee:** $45,000. **Financial Assistance:** No. **Training:** Training at Stick Men University: marketing, moving logistics, employee issues, computerized franchise management system "Movers Who Care" and more. Ongoing support: unlimited consulting, onsite visits, monthly training, advanced training, custom ads, annual convention and much more.

14522 ■ Two Men and a Truck Canada
245 Yorkland Blvd., Ste. 100
Toronto, ON, Canada M2J 4W9
Ph:(416)646-0486
Fax:(416)490-1456
Co. E-mail: franchise@twomenandatruck.ca
URL: http://www.twomenandatruck.ca
No. of Franchise Units: 15. **No. of Company-Owned Units:** 2. **Founded:** 2005. **Franchised:** 2005. **Description:** Moving service. **Equity Capital Needed:** $177,500$406,000. **Franchise Fee:** $35,000. **Training:** Provides 3 weeks training.

ASSOCIATIONS AND OTHER ORGANIZATIONS

14523 ■ American String Teachers Association
4155 Chain Bridge Rd.
Fairfax, VA 22030
Ph:(703)279-2113
Fax:(703)279-2114
Co. E-mail: asta@astaweb.com
URL: http://www.astaweb.com
Contact: Donna Sizemore Hale, Exec. Dir.
Description: Promotes excellence in string and orchestra teaching and playing, together with the National School Orchestra Association. Pursues its mission through: an open sharing of ideas; benefits, services, and activities responsive to the needs of all members; development of strong state leadership and chapters; enhancing the image and visibility of string teaching and study; advocacy for string education; and an inclusive community of string teachers and players. **Publications:** *ASTA eNews* (monthly).

14524 ■ Association for Technology in Music Instruction
312 E Pine St.
Missoula, MT 59802
Co. E-mail: jimf@soundtree.com
URL: http://www.atmionline.org
Contact: James Frankel, Pres.
Description: University professors, public school teachers, music industry professionals, and research laboratory personnel. Seeks to increase public awareness of computer-based music systems. Provides a forum for publishing research; facilitates the exchange of information among users of computers in music instruction; aids music teachers in implementing computer-based systems in music education. Serves as a research clearinghouse in the field. **Publications:** *ATMI Music Technology Directory* (annual); *Technology Directory* (annual).

14525 ■ Canadian Federation of Music Teachers' Associations–Federation Canadienne des Professeurs de Musique
302-550 Berkshire Dr.
London, ON, Canada N6J 3S2
Ph:(519)471-6051
Fax:(519)471-9126
Co. E-mail: bernadette_bullock@rogers.com
URL: http://www.cfmta.org
Contact: Bernadette Bullock, Sec.-Treas.
Description: Private music teachers. Promotes music education in Canada. Organizes performances and competitions. Sponsors Canada Music Week and Young Artists' series. **Publications:** *The Canadian Music Teacher* (3/year); *The Canadian Music Teacher: Canada Music Week Edition* (annual).

14526 ■ Canadian University Music Society–Societe de Musique des Universites Canadiennes
10 Morrow Ave., Ste. 202
Toronto, ON, Canada M6R 2J1
Ph:(416)538-1650

Fax:(416)489-1713
Co. E-mail: membership@cums-smuc.ca
URL: http://www.cums-smuc.ca
Contact: Lynn Cavanagh, Pres.
Description: Represents university music schools and professors, graduate students, and independent scholars. **Publications:** *Intersections* (semiannual).

14527 ■ International Association for Jazz Education
PO Box 70213
San Diego, CA 92167-1213
Ph:(619)223-2069
Co. E-mail: lessons@apassion4jazz.net
URL: http://www.apassion4jazz.net/iaje.html
Contact: DC DowDell
Description: Music teachers from grade school through college, professional musicians, and others; students from junior high through college; libraries; individuals from the music industry. Fosters and promotes understanding, appreciation, and artistic performance of jazz music; disseminates educational and professional news. Encourages the adoption of curricula that will explore contemporary composition, arrangement, and improvisation; cooperation with all organizations dedicated to the development of musical culture in America. Maintains hall of fame. .

14528 ■ International Computer Music Association
1819 Polk St., Ste. 330
San Francisco, CA 94109
Fax:(734)878-3031
Co. E-mail: icma@umich.edu
URL: http://www.computermusic.org
Contact: Tae Hong Park, Pres.
Description: Composers, computer software and hardware developers, researchers and musicians. Works to advance individuals and institutions involved in the technical, creative and performance aspects of computer music. Provides networking opportunities; sponsors research and projects; holds competitions. .

14529 ■ MENC: The National Association for Music Education
1806 Robert Fulton Dr.
Reston, VA 20191
Ph:(703)860-4000
Free: 800-336-3768
Fax:(703)860-1531
Co. E-mail: mbrserv@menc2.org
URL: http://www.menc.org
Contact: Michael A. Butera, Exec. Dir.
Description: Comprised of music educators, administrators, supervisors, consultants, and music education majors in colleges. Publishes materials for music educators, presents conferences, compiles statistics. **Publications:** *Journal of Music Teacher Education* (semiannual); *Journal of Research in Music Education* (quarterly); *Music Educators Journal* (bimonthly); *Teaching Music* (bimonthly).

14530 ■ Music Publishers' Association of the United States
243 5th Ave., Ste. 236
New York, NY 10016

Ph:(212)327-4044
Co. E-mail: admin@mpa.org
URL: http://www.mpa.org
Contact: Lauren Keiser, Pres.
Description: Publishers of music intended for educational and concert purposes. Promotes trade and commerce; encourages understanding of and compliance with copyright laws to protect musical works against piracy and infringement. .

14531 ■ Music Teachers National Association
441 Vine St., Ste. 3100
Cincinnati, OH 45202-3004
Ph:(513)421-1420
Free: 888-512-5278
Fax:(513)421-2503
Co. E-mail: mtnanet@mtna.org
URL: http://www.mtna.org
Contact: Dr. Gary L. Ingle, Exec. Dir./CEO
Description: Professional society of independent and collegiate music teachers committed to furthering the art of music through programs that encourage and support teaching, performance, composition, and scholarly research. .

14532 ■ NAMM - The International Music Products Association
5790 Armada Dr.
Carlsbad, CA 92008
Ph:(760)438-8001
Free: 800-767-6266
Fax:(760)438-7327
Co. E-mail: info@namm.org
URL: http://www.namm.org
Contact: Tom Schmitt, Chm./CEO
Description: Retailers of musical instruments and allied products, manufacturers, distributors, jobbers, wholesalers and publishers of print music. Holds several professional development seminars in various locations around the country and 2 major trade shows. **Publications:** *Cost of Doing Business Survey* (annual); *Music USA* (annual); *Playback* (bimonthly).

14533 ■ National Association of School Music Dealers
14070 Proton Rd., Ste. 100
Dallas, TX 75244-3601
Ph:(972)233-9107
Fax:(972)490-4219
Co. E-mail: office@nasmd.com
URL: http://www.nasmd.com
Contact: Joel Menchey, Pres.
Description: Retail music stores and companies engaged in sales, service and repair of band and orchestra instruments to elementary and secondary schools and colleges. **Publications:** *NASMD Newsletter* (quarterly).

14534 ■ National Association of Schools of Music
11250 Roger Bacon Dr., Ste. 21
Reston, VA 20190-5248
Ph:(703)437-0700

Fax:(703)437-6312
Co. E-mail: info@arts-accredit.org
URL: http://nasm.arts-accredit.org
Contact: Don Gibson, Pres.
Description: Serves as an accrediting agency for music educational programs. Compiles statistics. .

14535 ■ National Association for the Study and Performance of African-American Music
809 E Gladwick St.
Carson, CA 90746
Co. E-mail: webmaster@naspaam.org
URL: http://www.naspaam.org
Contact: Ina Allen, Pres.
Description: Fosters the creation, study, and promotion of black-derived music in education. Seeks to heighten public awareness of the problems faced by black music educators and students and to increase public understanding of those problems. Provides a forum for the discussion of concerns. Coordinates and disseminates materials concerning black-derived music in order to assist music teachers in teaching black music and students. Encourages blacks to aspire to leadership positions and to demand inclusion in the development and presentation of Music Educators National Conference activities, including participation in MENC's regional conferences. Sponsors collegiate and high school gospel choir competitions. Compiles list of music, books, and related music materials by blacks. **Publications:** *Con Brio* (quarterly).

14536 ■ National Association of Teachers of Singing
9957 Moorings Dr., Ste. 401
Jacksonville, FL 32257
Ph:(904)992-9101
Fax:(904)262-2587
Co. E-mail: info@nats.org
URL: http://www.nats.org
Contact: Vernon Yenne, Pres.
Description: Serves as a professional society of teachers of singing. Encourages the highest standards of the vocal art and of ethical principles in the teaching of singing. Promotes vocal education and research at all levels, both for the enrichment of the general public and for the professional advancement of the talented. **Publications:** *Journal of Singing* (5/year);Membership Directory (biennial).

14537 ■ Organization of American Kodaly Educators
1612 29th Ave. S
Moorhead, MN 56560
Ph:(218)227-6253
Fax:(218)277-6254
Co. E-mail: oakeoffice@oake.org
URL: http://www.oake.org
Contact: Joy Nelson, Pres.
Description: Represents music educators, students, organizations, schools, and libraries interested in the Kodaly concept of music education. Zoltan Kodaly (1882-1967), Hungarian composer and educator, originated a concept of music education that seeks to develop the sensibilities, intellectual facilities, and skills of children, with the intention of creating a musically educated public. Objectives are: to encourage communication and cooperation among Kodaly educators; to encourage musical and human growth; to provide a forum for comment on the impact of the Kodaly concept; to recognize, identify, and convey the multicultural musical heritage of American society; to contribute to and encourage the aesthetic education of the child. Conducts clinics and other small unit activities. **Publications:** *Kodaly Concept of Music Education; Kodaly Envoy* (quarterly); *OAKE Research Collection Vol. 1; The Owl Sings; Sourwood Mountain; Who Was Kodaly: OAKE Monograph No. 1* .

REFERENCE WORKS

14538 ■ American Musicological Society—Directory
Pub: American Musicological Society Inc.
Contact: Robert Judd, Exec. Dir.
Released: Annual, February. **Covers:** About 5,000 members and subscribers to the society's Journal. **Entries Include:** Name, address, phone, fax, and e-

mail. **Arrangement:** Members are alphabetical; subscribers are geographical.

14539 ■ Directory of Festivals, Schools and Workshops
Pub: Chamber Music America
Ed: Leonard Levine, Editor. **Released:** Annual, Latest edition 2011. **Covers:** over 150 chamber music workshops and schools for students, young professionals, and adult amateurs; international listings. **Entries Include:** Name, location or address, description of program and participants sought, procedure for auditions, type of accommodations and recreational facilities, dates, age requirements, and fees as of spring 2000. **Arrangement:** Geographical. **Indexes:** Alphabetical by state, alphabetical by program.

14540 ■ Directory of Nationally Certified Teachers
Pub: Music Teachers National Association
Contact: Marcie Lindsey, Director
E-mail: amt@mtna.org
Released: Annual, April. **Covers:** 4,300 nationally certified music teachers, searchable by instrument or type of education. **Entries Include:** Teacher name, address, phone, specialty. **Arrangement:** Geographical.

14541 ■ Instrumentalist—Buyer's Guide Issue
Pub: Instrumentalist Co.
Released: Annual, July. **Publication Includes:** List of about 460 companies associated with the music business. **Entries Include:** Name and address. Paid listings include additional data. **Arrangement:** Classified by product or service. **Indexes:** Product/service.

14542 ■ Instrumentalist—Directory of Summer Music Camps, Clinics, and Workshops Issue
Pub: Instrumentalist Co.
Released: Annual, Latest edition 2009. **Price:** $2.50. **Publication Includes:** List of nearly 250 summer music camps, clinics, and workshops in the United States; limited Canadian and foreign coverage. **Entries Include:** Camp name, location, name of director, opening and closing dates, tuition fees, courses offered. **Arrangement:** Geographical.

14543 ■ National Association of Schools of Music—Directory
Pub: National Association of Schools of Music
Released: Annual. **Price:** $20, individuals. **Covers:** Approximately 630 college and university departments of music and music conservatories accredited by the association. **Entries Include:** School name, address, type of membership, description of music program, name of chief administrator, phone, degree or other study programs offered in music. **Arrangement:** Alphabetical.

14544 ■ National Opera Association—Membership Directory
Pub: National Opera Association
Contact: Dr. Robert Hansen, Exec. Dir.
Released: Semiannual. **Covers:** About 675 music and singing teachers, singers, directors, and about 300 schools, colleges, and organizations interested in opera; international coverage. **Entries Include:** Name, address, phone, activity or occupation. **Arrangement:** Alphabetical within membership divisions. **Indexes:** Geographical.

14545 ■ "Sound Fundamentals" in *Hispanic Business* (September 2007, pp. 12, 14, 16)
Pub: Hispanic Business
Ed: Michael T. Mena. **Description:** Profile of Ozomatli, a Los Angeles-based multicultural, multi-ethnic musical group that has topped Billboard's Latin Pop chart without relying on record sales. Members explain how they run the group like a small business.

SOURCES OF SUPPLY

14546 ■ Music Trades—Purchaser's Guide to the Music Industry Issue
Pub: Music Trades Corp.
Ed: Brian T. Majeski, Editor, brian@musictrades.com. **Released:** Annual, Latest edition 2010; New edition expected 2012. **Price:** $16, individuals per year. **Pub-**

lication Includes: List of 3,000 musical instrument manufacturers and wholesalers, publishers of sheet music, and manufacturers of musical accessories; international coverage. **Entries Include:** Company name, address, phone, names of executives, trade and brand names, products or services. **Arrangement:** Alphabetical.

TRADE PERIODICALS

14547 ■ Accordionists and Teachers Guild—Bulletin
Pub: Accordionists and Teachers Guild, International
Contact: Joan Sommers, President
Ed: Julia Cortinas, Editor, jcortina@uiuc.edu. **Released:** 4/year. **Price:** Included in membership. **Description:** Focuses on accordion teaching and performing. Carries items on concerts, recitals, new music, conventions, and the activities of the Guild and its members.

14548 ■ Acoustic Guitar Magazine
Pub: Acoustic Guitar
Contact: David A. Lusterman, Publisher
Released: 8/yr. **Price:** $29.95. **Description:** Magazine for professional and amateur acoustic guitar enthusiasts offering advice on choosing, maintaining, and playing acoustic guitar.

14549 ■ American Music Teacher
Pub: Music Teachers National Association
Contact: Marcie Gerrietts Lindsey, Dir. of Publishing
E-mail: mlindsey@mtna.org
Released: Bimonthly. **Price:** $6 single issue domestic; $30 nonmembers; $40 other countries; $24 libraries; $7 single issue international. **Description:** Magazine.

14550 ■ American Suzuki Journal
Pub: Suzuki Association of Americas
Ed: Robert F. Bennett, Editor, editor@suzukiassociation.org. **Released:** Quarterly. **Price:** $56 members and Canada; $39 U.S. and Canada associate. **Description:** Music education journal.

14551 ■ AMS Newsletter
Pub: American Musicological Society Inc.
Ed: Kristen Lavoie, Editor. **Released:** Semiannual, in February and August. **Price:** Included in membership. **Description:** Serves members of this Association, which is a constituent member of the American Council of Learned Societies. Reports on committee and chapter activities and on items of general interest to musicologists. Recurring features include news of research, fellowships, grants, awards, and significant musical publications.

14552 ■ ATMI International Newsletter
Pub: Association for Technology in Music Instruction (ATMI)
Ed: **Released:** Quarterly. **Price:** Included in membership. **Description:** Discusses computer-based education in music, music synthesis, and music instruction and music classroom management using computers. Reports calls for information and new products of interest to members. Recurring features include book reviews, news of research, and a calendar of events.

14553 ■ British Journal of Music Education
Pub: Cambridge University Press
Contact: Dr. Stephanie Pitts, Book Review Ed.
E-mail: s.e.pitts@sheffield.ac.uk
Ed: Dr. Pamela Burnard, Editor. **Released:** 3/yr. **Price:** $128 institutions online & print; $116 institutions online; $220 institutions online & print; $198 institutions online. **Description:** Peer-reviewed journal focusing on current issues in music education.

14554 ■ Clavier
Pub: Instrumentalist Co.
Contact: James T. Rohner, Publisher
Released: Monthly, 10/yr except June and August. **Price:** $17; $25 two years; $9 students; $32 3 years. **Description:** Trade magazine for keyboard performers, teachers, and students.

14555 ■ Contemporary A Cappella News
Pub: Contemporary A Cappella Society of America
Ed: Amy Malkoff, Editor. **Price:** Free. **Description:**
Internet newsletter addressing various types and
styles of a cappella music worldwide. Recurring
features include interviews, a calendar of events, job
listings, recording and concert reviews, and notices
of publications available.

14556 ■ Down Beat
Pub: Maher Publications Inc.
Contact: Kevin Maher, Publisher
Released: Monthly. **Price:** $48.99 two years; $26.99;
$48.99 other countries; $92.99 other countries two
years; $37.99 Canada; $70.99 Canada two years.
Description: Magazine edited for the learning musi-
cian.

14557 ■ Journal of Music Teacher Education
Pub: MENC: The National Association for Music
   Education
Contact: Linda Brown
E-mail: lindab@menc.org
Ed: Janice Killian, Editor. **Released:** Semiannual.
Price: $34 institutions e-access. **Description:**
Journal for music educators.

**14558 ■ Journal of Research in Music
Education**
Pub: MENC: The National Association for Music
   Education
Contact: Ella Wilcox
E-mail: ellaw@menc.org
Ed: Wendy L. Sims, Editor, simsw@missouri.edu.
Released: Quarterly. **Description:** Scholarly publica-
tion.

14559 ■ Kodaly Envoy
Pub: Organization of American Kodaly Educators
Contact: Tom Michalek, Advertising Editor
E-mail: t-michalek@cox.net
Ed: Kim Vitray, Editor, kvitray@sbcglobal.net. **Released:** Quarterly. **Price:** Included in membership.
Description: Promotes the use of Kodaly music
education, a teaching approach founded by Hungarian composer, teacher, and ethnomusicologist, Zoltan
Kodaly (1882-1967). The Kodaly approach is for
general and choral music education. Recurring
features include book reviews, news of members, a
calendar of events, news of research, and feature
articles.

**14560 ■ Kodaly Society of Canada, Alla
Breve**
Pub: Kodaly Society of Canada
Contact: Maureen MacDougall, Advertising Ed.
E-mail: macdoume@staff.ednet.ns.ca
Ed: Moira Szabo, Editor, mszabo@uvic.ca. **Re-
leased:** Semiannual. **Description:** Trade journal
covering music education.

14561 ■ MASTA notes
Pub: American String Teachers Association with
   National School Orchestra Association—Michigan
   Chapter (MASTA w/NSOA)
Ed: Molly Rebeck, Editor, momokay@home.com. **Re-
leased:** Quarterly. **Price:** Included in membership.
Description: Reports on news, events, programs,
and workshops for members of the Michigan chapter
of the American String Teachers Association. Recur-
ring features include a calendar of events.

14562 ■ Music Educators Journal
Pub: MENC: The National Association for Music
   Education
Contact: Patrick Freer, Ch./Academic Ed.
E-mail: pfreer@gsu.edu
Released: 4/yr. **Description:** Journal covering all
levels of music education. Published on alternate
months with Teaching Music.

14563 ■ Music Trades
Pub: Music Trades Corp.
Contact: Paul A. Majeski, Publisher
E-mail: paul@musictrades.com
Ed: Brian T. Majeski, Editor, brian@musictrades.com.
Released: Monthly. **Price:** $45 foreign; $23 two years
domestic; $16 domestic. **Description:** Music trade
magazine.

14564 ■ Percussion News
Pub: Percussive Arts Society
Contact: Hillary Henry, Managing Editor
E-mail: teresa@pas.org
Ed: Rick Mattingly, Editor, rick@pas.org. **Released:**
6/year. **Price:** Included in membership. **Description:**
Provides membership activity news and includes
classified advertisements and industry news.

14565 ■ Tri-M News
Pub: Tri-M Music Honor Society
Contact: John Mahlmann, Exec. Dir.
Released: Semiannual. **Price:** Included in membership. **Description:** Publishes news of chapter events
and projects and scholarship information. Announces
individual awards as well as chapter activities, new
and reactivated chapters, and member achievements.

VIDEOCASSETTES/ AUDIOCASSETTES

14566 ■ Cello for Beginners
Calprod Pro Film/Video Production, Inc.
730 S. Central Ave., Ste. 209
Glendale, CA 91204
Ph:(818)548-8822
Fax:(818)548-4499
Co. E-mail: info@profilmvideo.com
URL: http://www.profilmvideo.com
Description: Introductory lessons cover posture,
notes, hand positions, reading music, breathing, play-
ing the instrument, and more. **Availability:** VHS.

14567 ■ Clarinet for Beginners
Calprod Pro Film/Video Production, Inc.
730 S. Central Ave., Ste. 209
Glendale, CA 91204
Ph:(818)548-8822
Fax:(818)548-4499
Co. E-mail: info@profilmvideo.com
URL: http://www.profilmvideo.com
Description: Introductory lessons cover posture,
notes, hand positions, reading music, breathing, play-
ing the instrument, and more. **Availability:** VHS.

14568 ■ Flute for Beginners
Calprod Pro Film/Video Production, Inc.
730 S. Central Ave., Ste. 209
Glendale, CA 91204
Ph:(818)548-8822
Fax:(818)548-4499
Co. E-mail: info@profilmvideo.com
URL: http://www.profilmvideo.com
Price: $19.95. **Description:** Introductory lessons
cover posture, notes, hand positions, reading music,
breathing, playing the instrument, and more. **Avail-
ability:** VHS.

14569 ■ Kids Play Harmonica Overnight
Cambridge Educational
c/o Films Media Group
132 West 31st Street, 17th Floor
Ste. 124
New York, NY 10001
Free: 800-257-5126
Fax:(609)671-0266
Co. E-mail: custserve@films.com
URL: http://www.cambridgeol.com
Description: Introductory lessons include an il-
lustrated booklet and a Hohner Harmonica. **Avail-
ability:** VHS.

14570 ■ Piano for Quitters
Leslie T. McClure
PO Box 1223
Pebble Beach, CA 93953
Ph:(831)656-0553
Fax:(831)656-0555
Co. E-mail: leslie@411videoinfo.com
URL: http://www.411videoinfo.com
Released: 1998. **Price:** $29.95. **Description:** Mark
Almond provides instruction for those who have previ-
ously tried to learn piano-playing. **Availability:** VHS.

14571 ■ Play Blues Piano Overnight
Calprod Pro Film/Video Production, Inc.
730 S. Central Ave., Ste. 209
Glendale, CA 91204

Ph:(818)548-8822
Fax:(818)548-4499
Co. E-mail: info@profilmvideo.com
URL: http://www.profilmvideo.com
Description: Presents seven lessons that include
simple to use practice card and practice audio tape.
Availability: VHS.

14572 ■ Play Guitar Overnight—Rock
Cambridge Educational
c/o Films Media Group
132 West 31st Street, 17th Floor
Ste. 124
New York, NY 10001
Free: 800-257-5126
Fax:(609)671-0266
Co. E-mail: custserve@films.com
URL: http://www.cambridgeol.com
Description: Introductory lessons focus on style and
soloing techniques. Also includes simple to use song-
book and practice audio tape. **Availability:** VHS.

14573 ■ Play Harmonica Overnight
Cambridge Educational
c/o Films Media Group
132 West 31st Street, 17th Floor
Ste. 124
New York, NY 10001
Free: 800-257-5126
Fax:(609)671-0266
Co. E-mail: custserve@films.com
URL: http://www.cambridgeol.com
Description: Introductory lessons include illustrated
booklet and a Hohner Harmonica. **Availability:** VHS.

14574 ■ Play Piano Overnight
Calprod Pro Film/Video Production, Inc.
730 S. Central Ave., Ste. 209
Glendale, CA 91204
Ph:(818)548-8822
Fax:(818)548-4499
Co. E-mail: info@profilmvideo.com
URL: http://www.profilmvideo.com
Description: Introductory lessons include simple to
use practice card and practice audio tape. **Avail-
ability:** VHS.

14575 ■ Saxophone for Beginners
Calprod Pro Film/Video Production, Inc.
730 S. Central Ave., Ste. 209
Glendale, CA 91204
Ph:(818)548-8822
Fax:(818)548-4499
Co. E-mail: info@profilmvideo.com
URL: http://www.profilmvideo.com
Description: Introductory lessons cover posture,
notes, hand positions, reading music, breathing, play-
ing the instrument, and more. **Availability:** VHS.

14576 ■ Snare Drum for Beginners
Calprod Pro Film/Video Production, Inc.
730 S. Central Ave., Ste. 209
Glendale, CA 91204
Ph:(818)548-8822
Fax:(818)548-4499
Co. E-mail: info@profilmvideo.com
URL: http://www.profilmvideo.com
Description: Introductory lessons cover posture,
notes, hand positions, reading music, breathing, play-
ing the instrument, and more. **Availability:** VHS.

14577 ■ Trombone for Beginners
Calprod Pro Film/Video Production, Inc.
730 S. Central Ave., Ste. 209
Glendale, CA 91204
Ph:(818)548-8822
Fax:(818)548-4499
Co. E-mail: info@profilmvideo.com
URL: http://www.profilmvideo.com
Price: $19.95. **Description:** Introductory lessons
cover posture, notes, hand positions, reading music,
breathing, playing the instrument, and more. **Avail-
ability:** VHS.

14578 ■ Trumpet for Beginners
Calprod Pro Film/Video Production, Inc.
730 S. Central Ave., Ste. 209
Glendale, CA 91204
Ph:(818)548-8822

Fax:(818)548-4499
Co. E-mail: info@profilmvideo.com
URL: http://www.profilmvideo.com
Price: $19.95. **Description:** Introductory lessons cover posture, notes, hand positions, reading music, breathing, playing the instrument, and more. **Availability:** VHS.

14579 ■ Tuba for Beginners
Calprod Pro Film/Video Production, Inc.
730 S. Central Ave., Ste. 209
Glendale, CA 91204
Ph:(818)548-8822
Fax:(818)548-4499
Co. E-mail: info@profilmvideo.com
URL: http://www.profilmvideo.com
Price: $19.95. **Description:** Introductory lessons cover posture, notes, hand positions, reading music, breathing, playing the instrument, and more. **Availability:** VHS.

14580 ■ Viola for Beginners
Calprod Pro Film/Video Production, Inc.
730 S. Central Ave., Ste. 209
Glendale, CA 91204
Ph:(818)548-8822
Fax:(818)548-4499
Co. E-mail: info@profilmvideo.com
URL: http://www.profilmvideo.com
Price: $19.95. **Description:** Introductory lessons cover posture, notes, hand positions, reading music, breathing, playing the instrument, and more. **Availability:** VHS.

14581 ■ Violin for Beginners
Calprod Pro Film/Video Production, Inc.
730 S. Central Ave., Ste. 209
Glendale, CA 91204
Ph:(818)548-8822
Fax:(818)548-4499
Co. E-mail: info@profilmvideo.com
URL: http://www.profilmvideo.com
Price: $19.95. **Description:** Introductory lessons cover posture, notes, hand positions, reading music, breathing, playing the instrument, and more. **Availability:** VHS.

14582 ■ Vladimir Ashkenazy
Tapeworm Video Distributors
25876 The Old Road 141
Stevenson Ranch, CA 91381
Ph:(661)257-4904
Fax:(661)257-4820
Co. E-mail: sales@tapeworm.com
URL: http://www.tapeworm.com
Released: 1996. **Price:** $19.95. **Description:** Documents the life and career of the pianist and conductor. Also provides excerpts of his tour in Russia, Switzerland, Sweden, and Germany. **Availability:** VHS.

TRADE SHOWS AND CONVENTIONS

14583 ■ American Choral Directors Association National Conference
American Choral Directors Association
545 Couch Dr.
PO Box 2720
Oklahoma City, OK 73102-2207
Ph:(405)232-8161
Fax:(405)232-8162
Co. E-mail: acda@acdaonline.org
URL: http://www.acdaonline.org
Released: Biennial. **Audience:** Choral directors.
Principal Exhibits: Choral music and supplies.

14584 ■ American Harp Society National Conference
American Harp Society
PO Box 38334
Los Angeles, CA 90038-0334
Ph:(323)469-3050

Fax:(323)469-3050
Co. E-mail: execsecretary@harpsociety.org
URL: http://www.harpsociety.org
Released: Annual. **Audience:** Professional and amateur harpists and students. **Principal Exhibits:** Harps and related materials. **Dates and Locations:** 2012 Jun 30 - Jul 03, New York, NY.

14585 ■ College Music Society National Conference
The College Music Society
312 E. Pine St.
Missoula, MT 59802
Ph:(406)721-9616
Free: 800-729-0235
Fax:(406)721-9419
Co. E-mail: cms@music.org
URL: http://www.music.org
Released: Annual. **Audience:** Publishers, record companies, related trade professionals, college and university music faculty. **Principal Exhibits:** Music publishers, instrument manufacturers, music retailers, non-profit associations, music hardware and software manufacturers. **Dates and Locations:** 2011 Oct 20-23, Richmond, VA; 2012 Nov 15-18, San Diego, CA.

14586 ■ European Congress on Psychiatry
Kenes International
Rue de Chantepoulet 1-3
PO Box 1726
CH-1211 Geneva, Switzerland
Ph:41 22 9080488
Fax:41 22 9069140
Co. E-mail: kenesinternational@kenes.com
URL: http://www.kenes.com
Released: Annual. **Audience:** Medical professionals.
Principal Exhibits: Psychiatry and neuropsychiatry.

14587 ■ MENC National In-Service Conference
MENC National Association for Music Education
1806 Robert Fulton Dr.
Reston, VA 20191
Ph:(703)860-4000
Free: 800-336-3768
Fax:(703)860-1531
URL: http://www.menc.org
Released: Biennial. **Audience:** Music educators teaching in public and private schools and colleges.
Principal Exhibits: Music education equipment, supplies, and services.

14588 ■ The Midwest Clinic An International Band and Orchestra Conference
The Midwest Clinic
828 Davis St., Ste. 100
Evanston, IL 60201
Ph:(847)424-4163
Fax:(847)424-5185
Co. E-mail: info@midwestclinic.org
URL: http://www.midwestclinic.org
Released: Annual. **Audience:** Trade professionals.
Principal Exhibits: Music instruments and publications, supplies, and services, universities, military organizations, fund raisers, music publishers. **Dates and Locations:** 2011 Dec 14-17, Chicago, IL.

14589 ■ New York State School Music Association Winter Conference
New York State School Music Association
718 Plain Rd.
Westbury, NY 11590-5931
Free: 888-NYS-SMA1
Fax:(516)997-1700
Co. E-mail: executive@nyssma.org
URL: http://www.nyssma.org
Released: Annual. **Audience:** Music teachers and general public. **Principal Exhibits:** Music publishers, musical instruments, fund-raising materials, and educational materials.

14590 ■ Texas Music Educators Association Clinic/Convention
Texas Music Educators Association
PO Box 140465
Austin, TX 78714-0465
Ph:(512)452-0710
Free: 888-318-TMEA

Fax:(512)451-9213
URL: http://www.tmea.org
Released: Annual. **Audience:** Music teachers. **Principal Exhibits:** Music publishers, uniform/gowns, recruitment, photographers, software.

FRANCHISES AND BUSINESS OPPORTUNITIES

14591 ■ Arcadia Academy of Music
661 Chrislea Rd., Unit 7
Woodbridge, ON, Canada L4L 8A3
Ph:(905)850-3701
Fax:(905)850-8489
Co. E-mail: maurizio@arcadiamusicacademy.com
URL: http://www.arcadiamusicacademy.com
No. of Franchise Units: 9. **No. of Company-Owned Units:** 1. **Founded:** 1984. **Franchised:** 1998. **Description:** Music school. **Equity Capital Needed:** $60,000 and up leasehold/equipment. **Franchise Fee:** $20,000. **Training:** Yes.

COMPUTERIZED DATABASES

14592 ■ Jazz Greats from Louis Armstrong to Duke Ellington
Technology Dynamics Corp.
1601 N Sepulveda Blvd., Ste. 374
PO Box 219
Manhattan Beach, CA 90267
Ph:(310)406-1803
Fax:(310)406-0833
Co. E-mail: contact@tdcinteractive.com
URL: http://www.tdcinteractive.net
Description: Contains information on the important pioneers of American jazz, including Jelly Roll Morton, Duke Ellington, Louis Armstrong, Coleman Hawkins, Billie Holiday, Count Basie, Benny Goodman, and Art Tatum. Covers the history, development, and influences of jazz music. Includes recordings, text, and video discussions. **Availability:** CD-ROM: Technology Dynamics Corp. **Type:** Full text.

LIBRARIES

14593 ■ American Conservatory of Music–Robert R. McCormick Memorial Library
252 Wildwood Rd.
Hammond, IN 46324
Ph:(219)931-6000
Co. E-mail: registrar@americanconservatory.edu
URL: http://www.americanconservatory.edu/library.html
Contact: Mary Ellen Newson, Reg.
Scope: Music - piano, organ, strings, woodwinds, percussion, brass, opera, lieder, classical guitar, jazz.
Services: Copying; Library not open to the public.
Holdings: 15,628 books and music scores; 563 bound periodical volumes; 276 dissertations; 2784 discs; 584 audio and video tapes.

14594 ■ American Music Center Collection at the New York Public Library for the Performing Arts
Dorothy and Lewis B. Cullman Center
40 Lincoln Center Plaza
New York, NY 10023-7498
Ph:(212)870-1630
Fax:(212)366-5265
Co. E-mail: performingarts@nypl.org
URL: http://www.amc.net
Contact: Jacqueline Z. Davis, Exec.Dir.
Scope: Works of contemporary American composers. **Services:** Interlibrary loan; Library open to the public on a limited schedule (call for appointment).
Holdings: 55,000 published and unpublished scores; 15,000 recordings; 8000 tapes; 7000 files of composers' biographies; 4000 CDs.

14595 ■ Andy Warhol Museum–Archives Study Center
117 Sandusky St.
Pittsburgh, PA 15212-5890
Ph:(412)237-8300

Fax:(412)237-8340
Co. E-mail: wrbicanm@warhol.org
URL: http://www.warhol.org/collections/archives.html
Contact: Matt Wrbican, Archv.

Scope: Andy Warhol, pop art movement, journalism, rock music, celebrity culture, fashion. **Services:** Archives is open to researchers by appointment. **Holdings:** Business records; scrapbooks; photographs; audiocassettes; videotapes; published materials; books; art work; clothing; posters; correspondence; personal objects; 4000 audio tapes.

14596 ■ Bagaduce Music Lending Library
PO Box 829, 5 Music Library Ln.
Blue Hill, ME 04614
Ph:(207)374-5454
Fax:(207)374-2733
Co. E-mail: library@bagaducemusic.org
URL: http://www.bagaducemusic.org/
Contact: Sean Schmeits, Exec.Dir.

Scope: Printed music - choral, keyboard, instrumental, popular and classical vocals. **Services:** Library open to the public. **Holdings:** 200,000 pieces of sheet music, scores, collections, and anthologies. **Subscriptions:** 2 journals and other serials.

14597 ■ Baylor University–Crouch Fine Arts Library
1 Bear Pl., No. 97148
Waco, TX 76798
Ph:(254)710-2164
Fax:(254)710-3116
Co. E-mail: sha_towers@baylor.edu
URL: http://www.baylor.edu/lib/FineArts
Contact: Sha Towers, Mus. and Fine Arts Libn.

Scope: Musicology, music theory, church music, instrumental and orchestral music, historical sets (collected), music education, vocal music, monuments of music, visual arts architecture. **Services:** Library open to the public. **Holdings:** 50,000 books; 4300 bound periodical volumes; 650 microforms; 75,000 musical items; 23,000 phonograph records; 17,000 compact disc recordings; 5000 videocassettes, 500 DVDs, and 200 laser discs; 6300 audiocassettes. **Subscriptions:** 200 journals and other serials.

14598 ■ Berklee College of Music–Stan Getz Library
1140 Boylston St.
Boston, MA 02115
Ph:(617)747-2258
Free: 800-237-5533
Fax:(617)747-2047
Co. E-mail: pengle@berklee.edu
URL: http://library.berklee.edu
Contact: Paul Engle, Dir. of Lib.Svcs.

Scope: Core music, jazz, core humanities, commercial music. **Services:** Library open to the public with restrictions. **Holdings:** 24,837 books; 19,573 scores; 27,500 sound recordings; 3315 videos. **Subscriptions:** 215 journals and other serials.

14599 ■ Brown University–Orwig Music Library
Box A
One Young Orchard Ave.
Providence, RI 02912
Ph:(401)863-3759
Co. E-mail: orwig@brown.edu
URL: http://dl.lib.brown.edu/libweb/about/orwig/
Contact: Ned Quist, Hd.Mus.Libn.

Scope: Music. **Services:** Interlibrary loan; Library open to persons affiliated with Brown University. **Holdings:** 30,000 volumes; 25,000 scores; 43,000 sound recordings; 1100 videos. **Subscriptions:** 225 journals and other serials.

14600 ■ California University of Pennsylvania–Louis L. Manderino Library | Special Collections
250 University Ave., Rm. 435
California, PA 15419
Ph:(724)938-5926

Fax:(724)938-5901
Co. E-mail: nolf@cup.edu
URL: http://www.library.calu.edu
Contact: Alber Pokol, Libn.

Scope: Rare books, art, music. **Services:** Library open to the public by appointment.

14601 ■ Cambridge Public Library–Audio-Visual Department
449 Broadway
Cambridge, MA 02138
Ph:(617)349-4040
URL: http://www.cambridgema.gov/cpl/Services/Collections/AudioVisual.aspx
Contact: Susan Flannery, Dir.

Scope: Music - piano, jazz. **Services:** Interlibrary loan; Library open to the public. **Holdings:** 7000 books, bound periodicals, music scores; 75 full orchestral scores; 15,724 sound recordings; 500 videocassettes; 8000 music CDs; 12,000 DVDs.

14602 ■ Catholic University of America Music Library
101 Ward Hall
620 Michigan Ave., NE
Washington, DC 20064
Ph:(202)319-5424
Fax:(202)319-4735
Co. E-mail: saylor@cua.edu
URL: http://libraries.cua.edu/music
Contact: Maurice Saylor, Libn.

Scope: Musicology, music education, performance. **Services:** Interlibrary loan; copying; Library open to the public with restrictions. **Holdings:** 25,000 books and score; 4605 bound periodical volumes; 12,917 pieces of music; 16,256 sound recordings; 5000 CDs; 309 LDs; 15,000 long-playing records; 200 DVDs; 300 laser discs. **Subscriptions:** 150 journals.

14603 ■ Chapman University–Albert Schweitzer Institute Library
1 University Dr.
Orange, CA 92866
Ph:(714)997-6636
Fax:(714)532-6078
Co. E-mail: meyer@chapman.edu
URL: http://www.chapman.edu/SchweitzerInstitute/
Contact: Marvin Meyer, Libn.

Scope: Albert Schweitzer's life and works. **Services:** Interlibrary loan. **Holdings:** Books.

14604 ■ Chicago Public Library–Visual & Performing Arts Division–Music Information Center (Harol)
Harold Washington Library Center
400 S. State St., 8th Fl.
Chicago, IL 60605
Ph:(312)747-4850
URL: http://www.chipublib.org/branch/details/library/harold-washington/p/Vpa
Contact: Richard Schwegel

Scope: History and theory of music, biographies of musicians and composers, music education, opera, musical comedy, sacred music, popular music, discography, music business, musical instruments, vocal and instrumental pedagogy, music therapy, folk music, composition and orchestration, arranging. **Services:** Interlibrary loan; copying; listening/viewing Center; practice rooms; music chamber; Center open to the public. **Holdings:** 49,800 books; 8025 bound periodical volumes; 67,000 bound volumes of music; 30,000 pieces of music; 15 VF drawers of pamphlets and clippings; 6102 microfiche of music; 2220 reels of microfilm of periodicals; 169,000 phonograph records, compact discs, audiocassettes; 3900 music videos; 334 laserdiscs; 4250 photographs; 51,957 uncatalogued scores. **Subscriptions:** 561 journals and other serials.

14605 ■ Cleveland Institute of Music–Robinson Music Library
11021 East Blvd.
Cleveland, OH 44106
Ph:(216)795-3114

Fax:(216)791-3063
Co. E-mail: jean.toombs@case.edu
URL: http://www.cim.edu/
Contact: Jean S. Toombs, Dir.

Scope: Music - performance materials, scores, analytical works, bibliographies, biographies. **Services:** Interlibrary loan; Library open to staff and students only. **Holdings:** 52,000 books and scores; 27,000 audio/visual materials. **Subscriptions:** 110 journals and other serials; 2 newspapers.

14606 ■ Concord Free Public Library–Music Collection
129 Main St.
Concord, MA 01742
Ph:(978)318-3377
Fax:(978)318-3344
URL: http://www.concordlibrary.org/
Contact: Barbara Powell, Lib.Dir.

Scope: Music. **Services:** Interlibrary loan; Library open to the public for reference use only. **Holdings:** 1500 books and bound periodical volumes; 375 music scores; 4450 sound recordings.

14607 ■ Conservatoire de Musique de Quebec–Bibliotheque
270 rue St. Amable
Quebec, QC, Canada G1R 5G1
Ph:(418)643-2190
Fax:(418)644-9658
Co. E-mail: cmq_bib@conservatoire.gouv.qc.ca
URL: http://www.conservatoire.gouv.qc.ca/quebec/index.asp
Contact: Pierre Plante, Hd. Music Libn.

Scope: Classical music, orchestral music. **Services:** Library open to the public for reference use only. **Holdings:** 65,000 books. **Subscriptions:** 33 journals and other serials; 1 newspaper.

14608 ■ Curtis Institute of Music–Milton L. Rock Resource Center
1726 Locust St.
Philadelphia, PA 19103
Ph:(215)893-5265
Fax:(215)717-3170
Co. E-mail: elizabeth.walker@curtis.edu
URL: http://www.curtis.edu/html/10000.shtml
Contact: Elizabeth Walker, Dir. of Lib.Info.Rsrcs.

Scope: Music orchestral, chamber, solo instrumental, vocal. **Services:** Interlibrary loan; Library open to the public by appointment only. **Holdings:** 9797 books; 55,255 scores; 858 LPs; 2996 audio tapes; 682 videotapes; 486 videodiscs; 1231 DVDs; 17,617 compact discs; 5368 microfiche; 72 reels of microfilm. **Subscriptions:** 70 journals and other serials.

14609 ■ Edinboro University–Baron-Forness Library | Special Collections
200 Tartan Rd., 7th Fl.
Edinboro, PA 16444
Ph:(814)732-2415
Fax:(814)732-2883
Co. E-mail: obringer@edinboro.edu
URL: http://www.edinboro.edu/departments/library
Contact: Prof. David Obringer, Archv. & Ref.Libn.

Scope: Music, art, education, Pennsylvania history, Civil War regimental history, rare books. **Services:** Interlibrary loan; tutoring; Library open to the public with restrictions. **Holdings:** 3000 volumes; prints.

14610 ■ Grinnell College–Burling Library–Listening Room (1111)
1111 Sixth Ave.
Grinnell, IA 50112-1690
Ph:(641)269-3365
Fax:(641)269-4283
Co. E-mail: jonesran@grinnell.edu
URL: http://www.lib.grinnell.edu/collections/ListeningRoom.html
Contact: Randye Jones, Listening Rm.Supv.

Scope: Music. **Services:** Library open to the public with restrictions (public may use items in-house, unless space is needed by students or faculty). **Holdings:** 25,000 cataloged titles in compact disc, LP record, cassette tape, and videocassettes formats; 6000 cataloged titles in DVD and VHS formats.

14611 ■ Hardin-Simmons University–Smith Music Library
Caldwell Hall
2200 Hickory
Box 16195
Abilene, TX 79689
Ph:(915)670-1565
Co. E-mail: sickbert@hstux.edu
URL: http://rupert.alc.org/library
Contact: Murl Sickbert, Mus.Libn.
Scope: Music. **Services:** Interlibrary loan. **Holdings:** Scores; collected works of various composers; recordings; basic music books; listening equipment.

14612 ■ Hartford Conservatory–Carolyn B. Taylor Library
834 Asylum Ave.
Hartford, CT 06105
Ph:(860)246-2588
Fax:(860)249-6330
Co. E-mail: mhuntington@hartfordconservatory.org
URL: http://www.hartfordconservatory.org
Contact: Marilynn Huntington
Scope: Music (classical and jazz), dance, theater. **Services:** Interlibrary loan; Library open to the public for reference use only. **Holdings:** 1600 books and bound periodical volumes; 5114 music scores; 400 pieces of sheet music; 4800 sound recordings; 130 compact discs. **Subscriptions:** 10 journals and other serials.

14613 ■ Interlochen Center for the Arts–Frederick and Elizabeth Ludwig Fennell Music Library
4000 S. M-137 Hwy.
PO Box 199
Interlochen, MI 49643
Ph:(231)276-7230
Co. E-mail: admission@interlochen.org
URL: http://www.interlochen.org
Contact: Laurie Lake, Dir., Mus.Lib.
Scope: Music. **Services:** Copying; Library open to the public for reference use only. **Holdings:** 8175 orchestra titles; 6525 band titles; 4675 choir titles; 985 jazz band titles; 37,725 solo and small ensemble titles; 10,275 recordings; 6565 study score titles.

14614 ■ John Brown University Music Library
2000 W. University St.
Siloam Springs, AR 72761
Ph:(479)524-7266
Co. E-mail: twubbena@jbu.edu
URL: http://www.jbu.edu/academics/cfa/music/facilities/cathedral.asp
Contact: Mrs. Terri R. Wubbena, Mus.Ch.
Scope: Music. **Services:** Library open to the public. **Holdings:** 1000 music scores; 2400 music sound recordings on LPs and CDs.

14615 ■ Kenyon College–Olin Library–Visual Image Collection (Kenyo)
Kenyon College
103 College Dr.
Gambier, OH 43022-9623
Ph:(740)427-5193
Co. E-mail: zhouy@kenyon.edu
URL: http://lbis.kenyon.edu
Contact: Yan Zhou, Vis.Rsrcs.Cur.
Scope: Painting, sculpture, architecture, furniture, theater, history, music, religion, psychology, historical biography, sociology. **Services:** Collection not open to the public. **Holdings:** Slides. **Subscriptions:** 2 journals and other serials.

14616 ■ Knox College–Center for the Fine Arts Music Library
Ford Center for the Fine Arts, Rm. 226
Galesburg, IL 61401
Ph:(309)341-7249
Co. E-mail: jdouglas@knox.edu
URL: http://www.knox.edu/Library/Inside-the-Library.html
Contact: Jeff Douglas, Lib.Dir.
Scope: Classical music, jazz, world music. **Services:** Library open to the public. **Holdings:** CD-ROMs; vinyl record albums; printed music scores; reference works.

14617 ■ Lawrence University–Seeley G. Mudd Library–Music Collections (711 E)
711 E. Boldt Way
Appleton, WI 54911
Ph:(920)832-6995
Co. E-mail: antoinette.powell@lawrence.edu
URL: http://www.lawrence.edu/library/music/collection.shtml
Contact: Antoinette Powell, Mus.Libn.
Scope: Music - instrumental solo, chamber works, orchestral, piano, vocal, classical, jazz, Western art, world music, musical theater, opera. **Services:** Interlibrary loan. **Holdings:** 12,000 scores; 10,000 LPs; 4500 compact discs; 8000 books on music; 400 music videotapes. **Subscriptions:** 80 journals and other serials.

14618 ■ Lenox Library Association–Music Department
18 Main St.
Lenox, MA 01240
Ph:(413)637-0197
Fax:(413)637-2115
Co. E-mail: alafave@lenoxlib.org
URL: http://lenoxlib.org
Contact: Amy Lafave, Mus. and Ref.Libn.
Scope: Music. **Services:** Interlibrary loan; Library open to the public. **Holdings:** 1300 books and bound periodical volumes; 850 music scores; 950 music parts; 60 librettos; 5700 sound recordings; 4000 CD-ROM; 1800 musical scores; 400 LPs; 300 audiocassettes; 250 videocassettes. **Subscriptions:** 5 journals and other serials.

14619 ■ Library of Congress–Music Division
101 Independence Ave., SE
James Madison Memorial Bldg., Rm. LM 113
Washington, DC 20540-4710
Ph:(202)707-5507
Fax:(202)707-0621
URL: http://www.loc.gov/rr/perform
Contact: Jon Newsom, Chf.
Scope: Music and music literature, dance, and theater of the world, emphasizing Western civilization, American music, opera and librettos, and chamber music; music organizations; literature about music in various languages (excepting Hebraic and Asiatic). **Services:** Interlibrary loan (limited); listening facilities in the Performing Arts Reading Room. **Holdings:** 20.5 million items; manuscripts, scores, correspondence, and personal papers of musicians; printed books and music; microforms. **Subscriptions:** 1000 journals.

14620 ■ Longy School of Music–Bakalar Music Library
1 Follen St.
Cambridge, MA 02138
Ph:(617)876-0956, x1540
Co. E-mail: roy.rudolph@longy.edu
URL: http://www.longy.edu/library_bakalar/library_home.htm
Contact: Roy Rudolph, Lib.Dir.
Scope: Music - piano, string chamber, general. **Services:** Interlibrary loan; copying; Library open to the public for reference use only with letter from a music librarian. **Holdings:** 4300 books; 11,000 music scores; 9000 sound recordings; 150 videos and DVDs. **Subscriptions:** 30 journals and other serials.

14621 ■ Manhattan School of Music–Peter Jay Sharp Library
120 Claremont Ave.
New York, NY 10027
Ph:(212)749-2802
Co. E-mail: library@msmnyc.edu
URL: http://www.msmnyc.edu/libraries/
Contact: Peter Caleb, Dir. of Lib.Svcs.
Scope: Music. **Services:** Interlibrary loan; copying; Library open to the public by appointment or via METRO card. **Holdings:** 18,000 books; 20,000 CDs; 9000 LPs; 2500 DVDs; 50,000 music scores. **Subscriptions:** 107 paper journals.

14622 ■ Mannes College of Music–Harry Scherman Music Library
150 W. 85th St.
New York, NY 10024
Ph:(212)580-0210, x4803
Co. E-mail: scarcele@newschool.edu
URL: http://library.newschool.edu/scherman
Contact: Ed Scarcelle, Dir.
Scope: Music. **Services:** Interlibrary loan; copying; Library open to the public for reference use only upon application for specific materials. **Holdings:** 8529 books; 31,298 scores; 9000 phonograph records; 2000 compact discs; 152 videocassettes; 300 video recordings. **Subscriptions:** 74 journals and other serials.

14623 ■ Mount Holyoke College Library–Music and Dance Library
50 College St.
South Hadley, MA 01075-6404
Ph:(413)538-6261
Co. E-mail: kmehl@mtholyoke.edu
URL: http://www.mtholyoke.edu
Contact: Karen Mehl, Circ.Mgr.
Scope: Music, dance. **Services:** Interlibrary loan; copying; Library open to the public for reference use only. **Holdings:** 4600 books and bound periodical volumes; 6948 music scores.

14624 ■ New England Conservatory of Music–Harriet M. Spaulding Library
33 Gainsborough St.
Boston, MA 02115
Ph:(617)585-1250
Fax:(617)585-1245
Co. E-mail: jean.morrow@necmusic.edu
URL: http://necmusic.edu/study-nec/libraries/spaulding-library
Contact: Jean A. Morrow, Dir. of Libs.
Scope: Music and music literature. **Services:** Interlibrary loan; copying; Library open to the public for reference use only. **Holdings:** 85,000 books and scores; 55,000 sound recordings; 1000 video recordings; 250 theses; 500 reels of microfilm; publications and documents on Boston musical life and history of the conservatory. **Subscriptions:** 300 journals and other serials.

14625 ■ Nipawin School Division–Education Resource Centre
Box 2044
Nipawin, SK, Canada S0E 1E0
Ph:(306)862-4616
Fax:(306)862-9733
Co. E-mail: verda.hoppe-nsd@saskschools.ca
Scope: Music, special education. **Services:** Interlibrary loan. **Holdings:** 10,000 books; 1500 videotapes; 1000 recordings. **Subscriptions:** 10 journals and other serials.

14626 ■ Ohio Wesleyan University–Kinnison Music Library
Sanborn Hall, Rm. 303
Delaware, OH 43105
Ph:(740)368-3715
Co. E-mail: paszabo@owu.edu
URL: http://go.owu.edu/lAtlibrweb/libmusic.htm
Contact: Peter Szabo, Mus.Libn.
Scope: Music. **Services:** Interlibrary loan; copying; Library open to the public. **Holdings:** 15,000 items - 6000 books; 1184 bound periodical volumes; 1500 CD-ROMs; 4500 LPs. **Subscriptions:** 34 journals and other serials.

14627 ■ Orchestras Canada Resource Centre
460 College St.
Toronto, ON, Canada M6G 1A1
Ph:(416)366-8834
Fax:(416)366-1780
Co. E-mail: info@oc.ca
URL: http://orchestrascanada.org/resources/
Contact: Katherine Carleton, Exec.Dir.
Scope: Music, arts education, orchestral training. **Services:** Library not open to the public. **Holdings:** Books; reports. **Subscriptions:** Available to members only.

14628 ■ Percussive Arts Society Library
110 W. Washington St., Ste. A
Indianapolis, IN 46204
Ph:(317)974-4488
Fax:(317)974-4499
Co. E-mail: percarts@pas.org
URL: http://www.pas.org
Contact: Otice Sircy, Cur./Libn.
Scope: Percussion instruments and music reference. **Services:** Library open to the public for reference use only. **Holdings:** 5000 archival materials; manuscripts. **Subscriptions:** 50 journals and other serials.

**14629 ■ Portland Public Library–Art/
Audiovisual Department**
5 Monument Sq.
Portland, ME 04101
Ph:(207)871-1725
Fax:(207)871-1703
Co. E-mail: audiovisual@portland.lib.me.us
URL: http://www.portlandlibrary.com
Contact: Stephen J. Podgajny, Exec.Dir.
Scope: Music. **Services:** Interlibrary loan; copying; Library open to the public. **Holdings:** 2500 books and bound periodical volumes; 7 file drawers of sheet music; 9500 sound recordings; 3600 videocassettes. **Subscriptions:** 16 journals and other serials.

14630 ■ St. Norbert Arts Centre Archives
PO Box 175
Winnipeg, MB, Canada R3V 1L6
Ph:(204)269-0564
Fax:(204)261-1927
Co. E-mail: snac@snac.mb.ca
URL: http://www.snac.mb.ca
Contact: Gerry Atwell, Dir.
Scope: Art - visual art, music, theater, and dance. **Services:** Archives open to the public. **Holdings:** Graphic materials; textual records.

14631 ■ San Francisco Conservatory of Music Library
50 Oak St.
San Francisco, CA 94102
Ph:(415)503-6253
Fax:(415)503-6299
Co. E-mail: library@sfcm.edu
URL: http://www.sfcm.edu/departments/library.aspx
Contact: Kevin McLaughlin, Hd.Libn.
Scope: Music. **Services:** Interlibrary loan; Library open to the public by appointment for reference use only. **Holdings:** 16,500 books; 50,000 musical scores; 75 bound periodical volumes; 2250 tapes; 16,500 phonograph records and CDs. **Subscriptions:** 77 journals and other serials.

**14632 ■ San Francisco Public
Library–Bernard Osher Foundation–Art,
Music & Recreation Center (100 L)**
100 Larkin St.
San Francisco, CA 94102
Ph:(415)557-4525
Fax:(415)557-4524
Co. E-mail: info@sfpl.org
URL: http://www.sfpl.org/librarylocations/main/art/art.htm
Contact: Mark Hall, Fl.Mgr.
Scope: Arts - visual, graphic; sports and recreation; photography; architecture; arts and crafts; performing arts; music - orchestral, chamber, opera, popular, folk, jazz. **Services:** Center open to the public. **Holdings:** Books; serials; scores.

14633 ■ Settlement Music School–Blanche Wolf Kohn Library
416 Queen St.
PO Box 63966
Philadelphia, PA 19147
Ph:(215)320-2600
Fax:(215)551-0483
Contact: Jean Peoples
Scope: Music. **Services:** Library open to students, faculty, staff, alumni, and noted musicians. **Holdings:** 10,000 record albums; books; 10,000 scores; 100,000 pieces of classical sheet music.

14634 ■ State University of New York at Buffalo Music Library
112 Baird Hall
Buffalo, NY 14260-4750
Ph:(716)645-2923
Fax:(716)645-3906
Co. E-mail: musique@buffalo.edu
URL: http://library.buffalo.edu/music/
Contact: Nancy Nuzzo, Dir.
Scope: Music - history, theory, performance; jazz history; new music; computer composition. **Services:** Interlibrary loan; copying; Library open to the public. **Holdings:** 40,000 books; 23,000 bound periodical volumes; 89,000 scores and parts; 41,000 sound recordings; 8000 microforms; 2100 slides and photographs; 1000 videos. **Subscriptions:** 1400 journals and other serials.

14635 ■ Sweet Briar College–Junius P. Fishburn Music Library
134 Chapel Rd.
PO Box 1200
Sweet Briar, VA 24595
Ph:(434)381-6138
Fax:(434)381-6173
Co. E-mail: jgjaffe@sbc.edu
URL: http://www.cochran.sbc.edu
Contact: John Jaffe, Dir., Lib. & Integ.Lrng.Rsrcs.
Scope: Music. **Services:** Interlibrary loan; Library open to the public. **Holdings:** 12,000.

14636 ■ Temple University–Esther Boyer College of Music–New School Institute - Alice Tully Library (1715)
1715 N. Broad St., Rock Hall Rm. 102
Philadelphia, PA 19101
Ph:(215)204-6950
Fax:(215)204-5528
URL: http://www.library.temple.edu/about/libraries
Contact: Millie Bai, Supv.
Scope: Music, music literature. **Services:** Library not open to the public. **Holdings:** 400 books; 5000 scores; 200 recordings; archival materials of the Curtis String Quartet.

14637 ■ Tiger Hills Arts Association–Music Resource Library
PO Box 58
Holland, MB, Canada R0G 0X0
Ph:(204)526-2063
Fax:(204)526-2105
Co. E-mail: thaa@escape.ca
URL: http://www.tigerhillsarts.com/
Contact: Denise Walleyn, Exec.Dir.
Scope: Music - vocal, guitar, recorder; arts; music teaching. **Services:** Copying; Library open to the public. **Holdings:** Figures not available.

14638 ■ Toronto Reference Library–Performing Arts Centre
789 Yonge St., 5th Fl.
Toronto, ON, Canada M4W 2G8
Ph:(416)393-7131
Fax:(416)393-7147
Co. E-mail: mmilne@torontopubliclibrary.ca
URL: http://www.torontopubliclibrary.ca/books-video-music/specialized-collection s/
Contact: Mary Shantz, Mgr.
Scope: Music, dance, film, theatre. **Services:** Library open to the public. **Holdings:** 17,000 LPs; 12,000 CDs; 47,000 music scores; 11,000 photographs; 4000 original stage drawings; prints; engravings; Canadian theatre and concert programs; clippings; archival materials; Canadian sheet music; microfiche; microfilm. **Subscriptions:** 150 journals and other serials.

14639 ■ U.S. Armed Forces School of Music Reference Library
1420 Gator Blvd.
Norfolk, VA 23521-2617
Ph:(757)462-7511
Fax:(757)464-7294
Co. E-mail: gysgt-jon.fishman@cnet.navy.mil
Contact: Jon Fishman, Gy.Sgt.
Scope: Music - analysis, conducting, composition, counterpoint, harmony, theory, instruments; jazz; military music. **Services:** Library open to the public with restrictions. **Holdings:** 5200 books; 2600 scores;

7000 phonograph records; 765 compact discs; 110 song books; 1900 reel-to-reel tapes; 467 cassette tapes; 350 archives. **Subscriptions:** 30 journals and other serials.

14640 ■ University of California, Los Angeles Music Library
1102 Schoenberg Music Bldg.
Box 951490
Los Angeles, CA 90095-1490
Ph:(310)825-4882
Fax:(310)206-7322
Co. E-mail: music-ref@library.ucla.edu
URL: http://www2.library.ucla.edu/libraries/Music/index.cfm
Contact: Gordon Theil, Hd.
Scope: Music, musicology, ethnomusicology, music education. **Services:** Interlibrary loan; copying; Library open to the public. **Holdings:** 182,816 volumes (books & scores); 6476 reels of microfilm; 18,454 microfiche; 67,500 sound recordings (CD and LP); 950 video recordings (disc and cassette). **Subscriptions:** 1267 journals and other serials.

14641 ■ University of Cincinnati–College Conservatory of Music–Gorno Memorial Music Library (Carl)
Carl Blegen Library
PO Box 210152
Cincinnati, OH 45221-0152
Ph:(513)556-1970
Fax:(513)556-3777
Co. E-mail: mark.palkovic@uc.edu
URL: http://www.libraries.uc.edu/libraries/ccm/index.html
Contact: Mark Palkovic, Hd., CCM Lib.
Scope: Music performance, history, and theory; musicology; dance; theater arts; music education. **Services:** Interlibrary loan; copying; Library open to the public for reference use only. **Holdings:** 38,000 bound volumes; 72,000 scores; 55,000 sound recordings; 6000 microforms. **Subscriptions:** 550 journals and other serials.

14642 ■ University of Nevada, Las Vegas Music Library
Beam Music Center
4505 S. Maryland Pkwy.
Las Vegas, NV 89154
Ph:(702)895-2541
Co. E-mail: music.library@unlv.edu
URL: http://www.unlv.edu
Contact: Cheryl Taranto, Hd.Mus.Libn.
Scope: Music. **Services:** Interlibrary loan; copying; document delivery; Library open to the public. **Holdings:** 35,000 volumes; 11,000 recordings (compact discs, LPs, audiocassettes); 1200 videos; 9000 books. **Subscriptions:** 156 journals and other serials.

14643 ■ University of North Carolina at Greensboro–Special Collections & Rare Books, Jackson Library–Cello Music Collections (222B)
222B Jackson Library
PO Box 26170
Greensboro, NC 27402-6170
Ph:(336)334-5246
Fax:(336)334-5399
Co. E-mail: bill_finley@uncg.edu
URL: http://library.uncg.edu/info/depts/scua/collections/cello
Contact: William K. Finley, Hd.
Scope: Luigi Silva, Elizabeth Cowling, Rudolf Matz, Maurice Eisenberg, Janos Scholz; history and teaching of the cello. **Services:** Copying (limited); collection open to the public for research. **Holdings:** 300 books, including 20 bound periodical volumes and 80 bound volumes of chamber music; 240 boxes of manuscripts and printed scores, representing 4300 indexed items; 100 boxes of archival materials, including photographs, teaching notes, and correspondence.

14644 ■ University of North Carolina School of the Arts–Semans Library
UNC School of the Arts
1533 S. Main St.
Winston-Salem, NC 27127
Ph:(336)770-3270
Fax:(336)770-3271
Co. E-mail: rebeccab@uncsa.edu
URL: http://www.uncsa.edu/library
Contact: Rebecca Brown, Hd. of Access Svcs.
Scope: Music, art and design, theater, film, dance, humanities. **Services:** Interlibrary loan; Library open to the public. **Holdings:** 111,000 books; 9000 bound periodical volumes; 50,000 music scores; 45,000 sound recordings; 5200 DVDs and videos. **Subscriptions:** 470 journals and other serials; 25 newspapers.

14645 ■ University of Redlands–Armacost Library | Special Collections
1200 E. Colton Ave.
PO Box 3080
Redlands, CA 92373-0999
Ph:(909)748-8022
Fax:(909)335-5392
Co. E-mail: les_canterbury@redlands.edu
URL: http://www.redlands.edu/library.asp
Contact: Les Canterbury, Interim Lib.Dir.
Scope: Music, literature, religion, East Asia. **Services:** Interlibrary loan; copying; Library open to the public with restrictions. **Holdings:** 208,503 book; 314,219 microforms; 168,228 documents. **Subscriptions:** 18,953 journals and other serials.

14646 ■ Vandercook College of Music–Harry Ruppel Memorial Library
3140 S. Federal St.
Chicago, IL 60616-3731
Ph:(312)225-6288, x-301
Fax:(312)225-5211
Co. E-mail: rdeland@vandercook.edu
URL: http://www.vandercook.edu/library
Contact: Rob DeLand, Hd.Libn.
Scope: Music and music education, education. **Services:** Interlibrary loan; listening facilities; Library open to alumni and associates of Vandercook College and one neighboring institution (Illinois Institute of Technology identification necessary). **Holdings:** 14,653; volumes; 7166 books; 3461 sound recordings; 381 videotapes; 43 CD-ROMs; 2183 scores; 987 archives. **Subscriptions:** 84 journals and other serials.

14647 ■ Weill-Lenya Research Center
7 E. 20th St.
New York, NY 10003
Ph:(212)505-5240

Fax:(212)353-9663
Co. E-mail: wlrc@kwf.org
URL: http://www.kwf.org/kwf/foundation/weill-lenya-research-center
Contact: Dave Stein, Archv.
Scope: Life and work of composer Kurt Weill and Lotte Lenya, musicology, music theory, theater history, 20th-century culture, Weimar Republic culture, women's studies, Jewish studies, emigre studies. **Services:** Copying at staff discretion; lending photos for reprinting; Library open to the public by appointment. **Holdings:** Books; printed music; music manuscripts; scripts; correspondence; audio and video recordings; films; programs; photographs; posters; press clippings; business records; personal papers. **Subscriptions:** 1 journal.

14648 ■ Western Connecticut State University–Ruth A. Haas Library
Midtown Campus
181 White St.
Danbury, CT 06810
Ph:(203)837-9100
Fax:(203)837-9108
Co. E-mail: oharae@wcsu.edu
URL: http://library.wcsu.edu/web/about/units/haas/
Contact: Ed O'Hara, Dir.
Scope: Music. **Services:** Interlibrary loan; Library open to the public for reference use only. **Holdings:** 175,000 volumes; 359 bound periodical volumes; 4712 music scores; 3084 sound recordings; 8 reels of microfilm; 8700 media titles. **Subscriptions:** 23 journals and other serials.

14649 ■ Westminster Choir College–Rider University–Talbott Library (101 W)
101 Walnut Ln.
Princeton, NJ 08540
Ph:(609)921-7100
Fax:(609)497-0243
Co. E-mail: sszalewicz@rider.edu
URL: http://www.rider.edu/15478_5846.htm
Contact: Stan Szalewicz, Libn.
Scope: Music - choral, vocal, keyboard, sacred. **Services:** Interlibrary loan (fee); copying; Library open to the public with fee for circulation for area residents. **Holdings:** 67,000 books; 29,000 scores; 23,000 sound and video recordings; college archives; 5400 choral music titles; 80,000 choral music reference. **Subscriptions:** 170 journals and other serials.

RESEARCH CENTERS

14650 ■ American Institute of Musical Studies
28 E 69th St.
Kansas City, MO 64113

Ph:(816)268-3657
Co. E-mail: aimsgraz@gmail.com
URL: http://www.aimsgraz.com/
Contact: Thomas King, Dir.
E-mail: aimsgraz@gmail.com
Scope: Music and music studies, focusing on advancing young singers, pianists, and instrumentalists toward a professional career. **Educational Activities:** Hands-on training programs.

14651 ■ Council for Research in Music Education
School of Music
University of Illinois
1114 W Nevada St.
Urbana, IL 61801
Ph:(217)333-1027
Fax:(217)244-8136
Co. E-mail: crme@illinois.edu
URL: http://www.crme.illinois.edu
Contact: Tina Happ, Bus.Mgr.
E-mail: crme@illinois.edu
Scope: Music education. **Publications:** Bulletin of the Council for Research in Music Education (quarterly). **Awards:** Outstanding Dissertation Award (Music Education).

14652 ■ Florida State University–Center for Music Research
College of Music - KMU 218
Tallahassee, FL 32306-1180
Ph:(850)644-5787
Fax:(850)644-2033
Co. E-mail: jgeringer@fsu.edu
URL: http://www.music.fsu.edu/Music-Research-Centers/Center-for-Music-Research
Contact: Prof. John M. Geringer, Dir.
E-mail: jgeringer@fsu.edu
Scope: Music, music education, music therapy development through scholarly inquiry. Provides space and facilities to develop applications of research to music performance, teaching, therapy, and analysis. Develops new technology and applications in teaching and research. **Educational Activities:** Seminars; Workshops.

14653 ■ Rutgers University–Institute of Jazz Studies
John Cotton Dana Library
185 University Ave.
Newark, NJ 07102
Ph:(973)353-5595
Fax:(973)353-5944
Co. E-mail: dmorgens@andromeda.rutgers.edu
URL: http://newarkwww.rutgers.edu/IJS
Contact: Dan Morgenstern, Dir.
E-mail: dmorgens@andromeda.rutgers.edu
Scope: Jazz and related music, oral history, ethnomusicology, Afro-American history, and sound documentation. **Publications:** Annual Review of Jazz Studies (periodically); Studies in Jazz Monograph Series. **Educational Activities:** Conferences; Jazz from the Archives (weekly), weekly radio program on WBGO-FM Newark; Research Roundtable (monthly); Seminars (occasionally).

ASSOCIATIONS AND OTHER ORGANIZATIONS

14654 ■ American School Band Directors' Association
PO Box 696
Guttenberg, IA 52052
Ph:(563)252-2500
Co. E-mail: asbda@alpinecom.net
URL: http://www.asbda.com
Contact: Monte Dunnum, Natl. Pres.

Description: Persons actively engaged in teaching instrumental music at the elementary, junior high or senior high school level; affiliates are persons no longer engaged in active teaching; associates are commercial firms dealing in products used by members. Seeks to improve instruction of instrumental music in the schools, the equipment used in instrumental music, music materials and methods, audiovisual aids, and acoustics of musical instruments used in school instructional programs. **Publications:** *ASBDA Directory and Handbook* (annual).

14655 ■ Early Music America
2366 Eastlake Ave. E, No. 429
Seattle, WA 98102
Ph:(206)720-6270
Free: 888-722-5288
Fax:(206)720-6290
Co. E-mail: info@earlymusic.org
URL: http://www.earlymusic.org
Contact: Maria V. Coldwell, Exec. Dir.

Description: Serves and strengthens the early music community in North America. Compiles statistics. Conducts educational programs. **Publications:** *Early Music America* magazine (quarterly); *EMA Electronic Bulletin* (quarterly);Membership Directory (annual).

14656 ■ Music Industries Association of Canada–Association Canadiene Des Industries De La Musique
505 Consumers Rd., Ste. 807
Toronto, ON, Canada M2J 4V8
Ph:(416)490-1871
Free: 877-490-6422
Fax:(416)490-0369
Co. E-mail: barbara@miac.net
URL: http://www.miac.net
Contact: Barbara Cole, Exec. Dir.

Description: Manufacturers, distributors, and retailers of musical instruments, accessories, sound reinforcement products, and published music. Promotes and represents members' interests. **Publications:** *MIAC E-News* (monthly).

14657 ■ National Association of School Music Dealers
14070 Proton Rd., Ste. 100
Dallas, TX 75244-3601
Ph:(972)233-9107

Fax:(972)490-4219
Co. E-mail: office@nasmd.com
URL: http://www.nasmd.com
Contact: Joel Menchey, Pres.

Description: Retail music stores and companies engaged in sales, service and repair of band and orchestra instruments to elementary and secondary schools and colleges. **Publications:** *NASMD Newsletter* (quarterly).

REFERENCE WORKS

14658 ■ "AllHipHop.com's Founders Thought a Weeklong Event Would Raise the Company'" in *Inc.* (February 2008, pp. 48-51)
Pub: Gruner & Jahr USA Publishing

Ed: Kermit Pattison. **Description:** Co-founders Greg Watkins and Chuck Creekmur, planned a weeklong festival to promote their company, AllHipHop.com; the event nearly ruined the firm. The online firm provides news about hip hop artists and the industry and is updated daily.

14659 ■ The Big Payback: The History of the Business of Hip-Hop
Pub: New American Library/Penguin Group

Ed: Dan Charnas. **Price:** $24.95. **Description:** The complete history of hip-hop music is presented, by following the money and the relationship between artist and merchant. In its promise of economic security and creative control for black artist-entrepreneurs, it is the culmination of dreams of black nationalists and civil rights leaders.

14660 ■ "The Book On Indigo" in *Canadian Business* (Vol. 81, July 22, 2008, No. 12-13, pp. 29)
Pub: Rogers Media Ltd.

Ed: Thomas Watson. **Description:** Indigo Books & Music Inc. reported record sales of $922 million resulting in a record net profit of $52.8 million for the 2008 fiscal year ended March 29, 2008. Earnings per share were $2.13, greater than Standard & Poor's expected $1.70 per share. Additional information concerning Indigo Books is presented.

14661 ■ "Handleman Liquidation Leaves Questions For Shareholders" in *Crain's Detroit Business* (Vol. 24, October 6, 2008, No. 40, pp. 4)
Pub: Crain Communications, Inc.

Ed: Nancy Kaffer. **Description:** Discusses Handleman Co., a Troy-based music distribution company, and their plan of liquidation and dissolution as well as how shareholders will be affected by the company's plan. Handleman filed its plan to liquidate and dissolve assets with the Securities and Exchange Commission in mid-August, following several quarters of dismal earnings.

14662 ■ How to Market and Sell Your Art, Music, Photographs, and Handmade Crafts Online
Pub: Atlantic Publishing Group, Inc.

Ed: Lee Rowley. **Released:** May 2008. **Price:** $24.95. **Description:** The book provides all the basics for starting and running an online store selling arts,

crafts, photography or music. There are more than 300 Websites listed to help anyone market and promote their arts and/or crafts online.

14663 ■ Music Trades—Purchaser's Guide to the Music Industry Issue
Pub: Music Trades Corp.

Ed: Brian T. Majeski, Editor, brian@musictrades.com. **Released:** Annual, Latest edition 2010; New edition expected 2012. **Price:** $16, individuals per year. **Publication Includes:** List of 3,000 musical instrument manufacturers and wholesalers, publishers of sheet music, and manufacturers of musical accessories; international coverage. **Entries Include:** Company name, address, phone, names of executives, trade and brand names, products or services. **Arrangement:** Alphabetical.

14664 ■ "Sound Fundamentals" in *Hispanic Business* (September 2007, pp. 12, 14, 16)
Pub: Hispanic Business

Ed: Michael T. Mena. **Description:** Profile of Ozomatli, a Los Angeles-based multicultural, multi-ethnic musical group that has topped Billboard's Latin Pop chart without relying on record sales. Members explain how they run the group like a small business.

14665 ■ "Universal Music Sues Grooveshark's Parent" in *Wall Street Journal Eastern Edition* (November 22 , 2011, pp. B5)
Pub: Dow Jones & Company Inc.

Ed: Ethan Smith. **Description:** Escape Media Group Inc., the parent company of online-music service Grooveshark, and seven of its executives have been sued by Universal Music Group, which alleges patent infringement involving its sound recordings. The executives are alleged to have uploaded thousands of songs onto Grooveshark.

14666 ■ "Welcome to Babesland" in *Women In Business* (Vol. 62, June 2010, No. 2, pp. 33)
Pub: American Business Women's Association

Ed: Leigh Elmore. **Description:** Music group, Four Bitchin' Babes will be performing at the 2010 American Business Women's Association's National Women's Leadership Conference. The group has been in the industry for 20 years and has released nine albums. The Four Bitchin' Babes consist of Sally Fingerett, Nancy Moran, Deirdre Flint, and Debi Smith.

STATISTICAL SOURCES

14667 ■ The Market for Musical Instruments
Pub: Business Trend Analysts, Inc.

Released: 2002-2003. **Price:** $1695.00.

14668 ■ RMA Annual Statement Studies
Pub: Robert Morris Associates (RMA)

Released: Annual. **Price:** $175.00 2006-07 edition, $105.00. **Description:** Contains composite balance sheets and income statements for more than 360 industries, including the accounting, auditing, and bookkeeping industries. Also contains five years of comparative historical data for discerning trends. Includes 16 commonly used ratios, computed for most of the size groupings for nearly every industry.

14669 ■ *Standard & Poor's Industry Surveys*
Pub: Standard & Poor's Corp.
Released: Annual. **Price:** $3633.00. **Description:** Two-volume book that examines the prospects for specific industries, including trucking. Also provides analyses of trends and problems, statistical tables and charts, and comparative company analyses.

TRADE PERIODICALS

14670 ■ *Acoustic Guitar Magazine*
Pub: Acoustic Guitar
Contact: David A. Lusterman, Publisher
Released: 8/yr. **Price:** $29.95. **Description:** Magazine for professional and amateur acoustic guitar enthusiasts offering advice on choosing, maintaining, and playing acoustic guitar.

14671 ■ *American Music*
Pub: University of Illinois Press
Contact: Jennifer DeLapp Birkett, Multimedia Review Ed.
Ed: Michael Hicks, Editor, michael_hicks@byu.edu.
Released: Quarterly. **Price:** $47 print or online; $52 print online; $99 institutions print or online; $109 institutions print online; $25 students online. **Description:** Scholarly journal devoted to American music.

14672 ■ *Down Beat*
Pub: Maher Publications Inc.
Contact: Kevin Maher, Publisher
Released: Monthly. **Price:** $48.99 two years; $26.99; $48.99 other countries; $92.99 other countries two years; $37.99 Canada; $70.99 Canada two years. **Description:** Magazine edited for the learning musician.

14673 ■ *Drum Business*
Pub: Modern Drummer Publications Inc.
Contact: Kevin W. Kearns, Vice President
E-mail: kevk@moderndrummer.com
Released: Monthly. **Price:** $29.97 U.S. and Canada individual. **Description:** Magazine focusing on helping drum retailers with information on merchandising, management, product description and review, and sales technique.

14674 ■ *Harmonica Happenings*
Pub: Society for the Preservation and Advancement of the Harmonica Inc.
Contact: Doug Tate, President
E-mail: dougtate@istal.com
Ed: George Davis, Editor, gdavis9@ix.netcom.com.
Released: Quarterly. **Description:** Promotes appreciation for harmonica music. Contains material of interest to harmonica players, with profiles of and interviews with musicians, instructional material, and news notes. Recurring features include letters to the editor, editorials on professional harmonicists.

14675 ■ *ITG Journal*
Pub: International Trumpet Guild (ITG)
Contact: David C. Jones, ITG Treasurer
Released: 4/year. **Price:** Included in membership. **Description:** Carries news of interest to trumpet players, teachers, and students. Contains book reviews, record reviews, and listings of new publications and recordings, and occassionally includes sheet music and CD recordings. Also carries articles on trumpet pedagogy, players of note, musical analysis, and historical instruments.

14676 ■ *MASTA notes*
Pub: American String Teachers Association with National School Orchestra Association—Michigan Chapter (MASTA w/NSOA)
Ed: Molly Rebeck, Editor, momokay@home.com. **Released:** Quarterly. **Price:** Included in membership. **Description:** Reports on news, events, programs, and workshops for members of the Michigan chapter of the American String Teachers Association. Recurring features include a calendar of events.

14677 ■ *Music Inc.*
Pub: Maher Publications Inc.
Contact: Kevin Maher, Publisher
Released: 11/yr. **Price:** $17. **Description:** Magazine serving retailers of music and sound products.

14678 ■ *Music Trades*
Pub: Music Trades Corp.
Contact: Paul A. Majeski, Publisher
E-mail: paul@musictrades.com
Ed: Brian T. Majeski, Editor, brian@musictrades.com.
Released: Monthly. **Price:** $45 foreign; $23 two years domestic; $16 domestic. **Description:** Music trade magazine.

14679 ■ *NAMM PlayBack*
Pub: National Association of Music Merchants (NAMM)
Released: Bimonthly. **Price:** Included in membership. **Description:** Published to keep member retailers and manufacturers of musical instruments apprised of industry news and Association trade shows. Also publicizes the Association's educational services and membership benefits. Recurring features include a calendar of events, reports of meetings, and notices of publications available.

14680 ■ *Premiere Guitar*
Pub: Gearhead Communications, LLC
Contact: Adam Moore, Sen. Ed.
E-mail: adam@premierguitar.com
Released: Monthly. **Price:** $24.95 1 issue free; $39.95 two years 3 issues free. **Description:** Consumer magazine covering equipment, services, and supplies for professional, performing musicians.

14681 ■ *Sheet Music Magazine*
Pub: Piano Today
Released: Quarterly. **Price:** $47.44 two years; $24.97. **Description:** Magazine containing sheet music, musical "how to" articles, and information on new keyboard products.

VIDEOCASSETTES/AUDIOCASSETTES

14682 ■ *Vladimir Ashkenazy*
Tapeworm Video Distributors
25876 The Old Road 141
Stevenson Ranch, CA 91381
Ph:(661)257-4904
Fax:(661)257-4820
Co. E-mail: sales@tapeworm.com
URL: http://www.tapeworm.com
Released: 1996. **Price:** $19.95. **Description:** Documents the life and career of the pianist and conductor. Also provides excerpts of his tour in Russia, Switzerland, Sweden, and Germany. **Availability:** VHS.

TRADE SHOWS AND CONVENTIONS

14683 ■ **American Choral Directors Association National Conference**
American Choral Directors Association
545 Couch Dr.
PO Box 2720
Oklahoma City, OK 73102-2207
Ph:(405)232-8161
Fax:(405)232-8162
Co. E-mail: acda@acdaonline.org
URL: http://www.acdaonline.org
Released: Biennial. **Audience:** Choral directors. **Principal Exhibits:** Choral music and supplies.

14684 ■ **College Music Society National Conference**
The College Music Society
312 E. Pine St.
Missoula, MT 59802
Ph:(406)721-9616
Free: 800-729-0235
Fax:(406)721-9419
Co. E-mail: cms@music.org
URL: http://www.music.org
Released: Annual. **Audience:** Publishers, record companies, related trade professionals, college and university music faculty. **Principal Exhibits:** Music publishers, instrument manufacturers, music retail-

ers, non-profit associations, music hardware and software manufacturers. **Dates and Locations:** 2011 Oct 20-23, Richmond, VA; 2012 Nov 15-18, San Diego, CA.

14685 ■ **European Congress on Psychiatry**
Kenes International
Rue de Chantepoulet 1-3
PO Box 1726
CH-1211 Geneva, Switzerland
Ph:41 22 9080488
Fax:41 22 9069140
Co. E-mail: kenesinternational@kenes.com
URL: http://www.kenes.com
Released: Annual. **Audience:** Medical professionals. **Principal Exhibits:** Psychiatry and neuropsychiatry.

14686 ■ **MENC National In-Service Conference**
MENC National Association for Music Education
1806 Robert Fulton Dr.
Reston, VA 20191
Ph:(703)860-4000
Free: 800-336-3768
Fax:(703)860-1531
URL: http://www.menc.org
Released: Biennial. **Audience:** Music educators teaching in public and private schools and colleges. **Principal Exhibits:** Music education equipment, supplies, and services.

14687 ■ **The NAMM Show**
NAMM I International Music Products Association
5790 Armada Dr.
Carlsbad, CA 92008
Ph:(760)438-8001
Free: 800-767-6266
Fax:(760)438-7327
Co. E-mail: info@namm.com
URL: http://www.namm.com
Released: Annual. **Audience:** Retail music merchants; manufacturers of musical instruments and accessories; manufacturers of acoustical equipment; sheet music publishers. **Principal Exhibits:** Musical instruments and accessories, acoustical equipment, and sheet music publications. **Dates and Locations:** 2012 Jan 19-22, Nashville, TN; 2013 Jan 17-20, Nashville, TN.

14688 ■ **New York State School Music Association Winter Conference**
New York State School Music Association
718 Plain Rd.
Westbury, NY 11590-5931
Free: 888-NYS-SMA1
Fax:(516)997-1700
Co. E-mail: executive@nyssma.org
URL: http://www.nyssma.org
Released: Annual. **Audience:** Music teachers and general public. **Principal Exhibits:** Music publishers, musical instruments, fund-raising materials, and educational materials.

14689 ■ **Texas Music Educators Association Clinic/Convention**
Texas Music Educators Association
PO Box 140465
Austin, TX 78714-0465
Ph:(512)452-0710
Free: 888-318-TMEA
Fax:(512)451-9213
URL: http://www.tmea.org
Released: Annual. **Audience:** Music teachers. **Principal Exhibits:** Music publishers, uniform/gowns, recruitment, photographers, software.

CONSULTANTS

14690 ■ **Jess Barker, Document Research/Retrieval L.L.C.**
209A S Macoupin St.
Gillespie, IL 62033-1605
Ph:(217)839-3219
Free: 888-316-3773

Fax:877-522-7537
Co. E-mail: documentretrieval@frontiernet.net
URL: http://www.documentresearch.biz
Contact: James Barker, Principle

Scope: A full service title search company that provides Title Reports to investors who are interested in making offers on properties.

FRANCHISES AND BUSINESS OPPORTUNITIES

14691 ■ Music Go Round
Winmark Corp.
605 Highway 169 N., Ste. 400
Minneapolis, MN 55441
Free: 800-592-8049
URL: http://www.musicgoround.com

No. of Franchise Units: 33. **Founded:** 1986. **Franchised:** 1994. **Description:** Sales of new, used, and consignment musical instruments. **Equity Capital Needed:** $253,450-$325,100; approximately 30% cash requirement. **Franchise Fee:** $25,000. **Financial Assistance:** No in-house financing available; support provided in developing a three year business plan and cash flow analysis for use in securing financing. **Training:** Training program includes product acquisition, inventory management, retail store operations, employee management, and ongoing support.

LIBRARIES

14692 ■ Alberta Band Association–Music Lending Library
10612-124 St., Ste. 206
Edmonton, AB, Canada T5N 1S4
Ph:(780)488-2263
Free: 877-687-4239
Fax:(780)488-4132
URL: http://albertabandassociation.com/library.php
Contact: Neil Corlett, Mng.Dir.

Scope: Music. **Services:** Library not open to the public. **Holdings:** Concert band titles, scores, methods, and recordings.

14693 ■ Andy Warhol Museum–Archives Study Center
117 Sandusky St.
Pittsburgh, PA 15212-5890
Ph:(412)237-8300
Fax:(412)237-8340
Co. E-mail: wrbicanm@warhol.org
URL: http://www.warhol.org/collections/archives.html
Contact: Matt Wrbican, Archv.

Scope: Andy Warhol, pop art movement, journalism, rock music, celebrity culture, fashion. **Services:** Archives is open to researchers by appointment. **Holdings:** Business records; scrapbooks; photographs; audiocassettes; videotapes; published materials; books; art work; clothing; posters; correspondence; personal objects; 4000 audio tapes.

14694 ■ Bagaduce Music Lending Library
PO Box 829, 5 Music Library Ln.
Blue Hill, ME 04614
Ph:(207)374-5454
Fax:(207)374-2733
Co. E-mail: library@bagaducemusic.org
URL: http://www.bagaducemusic.org/
Contact: Sean Schmeits, Exec.Dir.

Scope: Printed music - choral, keyboard, instrumental, popular and classical vocals. **Services:** Library open to the public. **Holdings:** 200,000 pieces of sheet music, scores, collections, and anthologies. **Subscriptions:** 2 journals and other serials.

14695 ■ California University of Pennsylvania–Louis L. Manderino Library I Special Collections
250 University Ave., Rm. 435
California, PA 15419
Ph:(724)938-5926

Fax:(724)938-5901
Co. E-mail: nolf@cup.edu
URL: http://www.library.calu.edu
Contact: Alber Pokol, Libn.

Scope: Rare books, art, music. **Services:** Library open to the public by appointment.

14696 ■ Chicago Public Library–Visual & Performing Arts Division–Music Information Center (Harol)
Harold Washington Library Center
400 S. State St., 8th Fl.
Chicago, IL 60605
Ph:(312)747-4850
URL: http://www.chipublib.org/branch/details/library/
harold-washington/p/Vpa
Contact: Richard Schwegel

Scope: History and theory of music, biographies of musicians and composers, music education, opera, musical comedy, sacred music, popular music, discography, music business, musical instruments, vocal and instrumental pedagogy, music therapy, folk music, composition and orchestration, arranging. **Services:** Interlibrary loan; copying; listening/viewing Center; practice rooms; music chamber; Center open to the public. **Holdings:** 49,800 books; 8025 bound periodical volumes; 67,000 bound volumes of music; 30,000 pieces of music; 15 VF drawers of pamphlets and clippings; 6102 microfiche of music; 2220 reels of microfilm of periodicals; 169,000 phonograph records, compact discs, audiocassettes; 3900 music videos; 334 laserdiscs; 4250 photographs; 51,957 uncatalogued scores. **Subscriptions:** 561 journals and other serials.

14697 ■ Conservatoire de Musique de Quebec–Bibliotheque
270 rue St. Amable
Quebec, QC, Canada G1R 5G1
Ph:(418)643-2190
Fax:(418)644-9658
Co. E-mail: cmq_bib@conservatoire.gouv.qc.ca
URL: http://www.conservatoire.gouv.qc.ca/quebec/
index.asp
Contact: Pierre Plante, Hd. Music Libn.

Scope: Classical music, orchestral music. **Services:** Library open to the public for reference use only. **Holdings:** 65,000 books. **Subscriptions:** 33 journals and other serials; 1 newspaper.

14698 ■ Edinboro University–Baron-Forness Library I Special Collections
200 Tartan Rd., 7th Fl.
Edinboro, PA 16444
Ph:(814)732-2415
Fax:(814)732-2883
Co. E-mail: obringer@edinboro.edu
URL: http://www.edinboro.edu/departments/library
Contact: Prof. David Obringer, Archv. & Ref.Libn.

Scope: Music, art, education, Pennsylvania history, Civil War regimental history, rare books. **Services:** Interlibrary loan; tutoring; Library open to the public with restrictions. **Holdings:** 3000 volumes; prints.

14699 ■ Grinnell College–Burling Library–Listening Room (1111)
1111 Sixth Ave.
Grinnell, IA 50112-1690
Ph:(641)269-3365
Fax:(641)269-4283
Co. E-mail: jonesran@grinnell.edu
URL: http://www.lib.grinnell.edu/collections/Listenin-
gRoom.html
Contact: Randye Jones, Listening Rm.Supv.

Scope: Music. **Services:** Library open to the public with restrictions (public may use items in-house, unless space is needed by students or faculty). **Holdings:** 25,000 cataloged titles in compact disc, LP record, cassette tape, and videocassettes formats; 6000 cataloged titles in DVD and VHS formats.

14700 ■ Hardin-Simmons University–Smith Music Library
Caldwell Hall
2200 Hickory
Box 16195
Abilene, TX 79689

Ph:(915)670-1565
Co. E-mail: sickbert@hstux.edu
URL: http://rupert.alc.org/library
Contact: Murl Sickbert, Mus.Libn.

Scope: Music. **Services:** Interlibrary loan. **Holdings:** Scores; collected works of various composers; recordings; basic music books; listening equipment.

14701 ■ John Brown University Music Library
2000 W. University St.
Siloam Springs, AR 72761
Ph:(479)524-7266
Co. E-mail: twubbena@jbu.edu
URL: http://www.jbu.edu/academics/cfa/music/facili-
ties/cathedral.asp
Contact: Mrs. Terri R. Wubbena, Mus.Ch.

Scope: Music. **Services:** Library open to the public. **Holdings:** 1000 music scores; 2400 music sound recordings on LPs and CDs.

14702 ■ Kenyon College–Olin Library–Visual Image Collection (Kenyo)
Kenyon College
103 College Dr.
Gambier, OH 43022-9623
Ph:(740)427-5193
Co. E-mail: zhouy@kenyon.edu
URL: http://lbis.kenyon.edu
Contact: Yan Zhou, Vis.Rsrcs.Cur.

Scope: Painting, sculpture, architecture, furniture, theater, history, music, religion, psychology, historical biography, sociology. **Services:** Collection not open to the public. **Holdings:** Slides. **Subscriptions:** 2 journals and other serials.

14703 ■ Lawrence University–Seeley G. Mudd Library–Music Collections (711 E)
711 E. Boldt Way
Appleton, WI 54911
Ph:(920)832-6995
Co. E-mail: antoinette.powell@lawrence.edu
URL: http://www.lawrence.edu/library/music/collec-
tion.shtml
Contact: Antoinette Powell, Mus.Libn.

Scope: Music - instrumental solo, chamber works, orchestral, piano, vocal, classical, jazz, Western art, world music, musical theater, opera. **Services:** Interlibrary loan. **Holdings:** 12,000 scores; 10,000 LPs; 4500 compact discs; 8000 books on music; 400 music videotapes. **Subscriptions:** 80 journals and other serials.

14704 ■ Nipawin School Division–Education Resource Centre
Box 2044
Nipawin, SK, Canada S0E 1E0
Ph:(306)862-4616
Fax:(306)862-9733
Co. E-mail: verda.hoppe-nsd@saskschools.ca

Scope: Music, special education. **Services:** Interlibrary loan. **Holdings:** 10,000 books; 1500 videotapes; 1000 recordings. **Subscriptions:** 10 journals and other serials.

14705 ■ Ohio Wesleyan University–Kinnison Music Library
Sanborn Hall, Rm. 303
Delaware, OH 43105
Ph:(740)368-3715
Co. E-mail: paszabo@owu.edu
URL: http://go.owu.edu/lAtlibrweb/libmusic.htm
Contact: Peter Szabo, Mus.Libn.

Scope: Music. **Services:** Interlibrary loan; copying; Library open to the public. **Holdings:** 15,000 items - 6000 books; 1184 bound periodical volumes; 1500 CD-ROMs; 4500 LPs. **Subscriptions:** 34 journals and other serials.

14706 ■ St. Norbert Arts Centre Archives
PO Box 175
Winnipeg, MB, Canada R3V 1L6
Ph:(204)269-0564

Fax:(204)261-1927
Co. E-mail: snac@snac.mb.ca
URL: http://www.snac.mb.ca
Contact: Gerry Atwell, Dir.
Scope: Art - visual art, music, theater, and dance. **Services:** Archives open to the public. **Holdings:** Graphic materials; textual records.

14707 ■ San Francisco Public Library–Bernard Osher Foundation–Art, Music & Recreation Center (100 L)
100 Larkin St.
San Francisco, CA 94102
Ph:(415)557-4525
Fax:(415)557-4524
Co. E-mail: info@sfpl.org
URL: http://www.sfpl.org/librarylocations/main/art/art.htm
Contact: Mark Hall, Fl.Mgr.
Scope: Arts - visual, graphic; sports and recreation; photography; architecture; arts and crafts; performing arts; music - orchestral, chamber, opera, popular, folk, jazz. **Services:** Center open to the public. **Holdings:** Books; serials; scores.

14708 ■ Sweet Briar College–Junius P. Fishburn Music Library
134 Chapel Rd.
PO Box 1200
Sweet Briar, VA 24595

Ph:(434)381-6138
Fax:(434)381-6173
Co. E-mail: jgjaffe@sbc.edu
URL: http://www.cochran.sbc.edu
Contact: John Jaffe, Dir., Lib. & Integ.Lrng.Rsrcs.
Scope: Music. **Services:** Interlibrary loan; Library open to the public. **Holdings:** 12,000.

14709 ■ University of Nevada, Las Vegas Music Library
Beam Music Center
4505 S. Maryland Pkwy.
Las Vegas, NV 89154
Ph:(702)895-2541
Co. E-mail: music.library@unlv.edu
URL: http://www.unlv.edu
Contact: Cheryl Taranto, Hd.Mus.Libn.
Scope: Music. **Services:** Interlibrary loan; copying; document delivery; Library open to the public. **Holdings:** 35,000 volumes; 11,000 recordings (compact discs, LPs, audiocassettes); 1200 videos; 9000 books. **Subscriptions:** 156 journals and other serials.

14710 ■ University of North Carolina School of the Arts–Semans Library
UNC School of the Arts
1533 S. Main St.
Winston-Salem, NC 27127
Ph:(336)770-3270

Fax:(336)770-3271
Co. E-mail: rebeccab@uncsa.edu
URL: http://www.uncsa.edu/library
Contact: Rebecca Brown, Hd. of Access Svcs.
Scope: Music, art and design, theater, film, dance, humanities. **Services:** Interlibrary loan; Library open to the public. **Holdings:** 111,000 books; 9000 bound periodical volumes; 50,000 music scores; 45,000 sound recordings; 5200 DVDs and videos. **Subscriptions:** 470 journals and other serials; 25 newspapers.

14711 ■ Weill-Lenya Research Center
7 E. 20th St.
New York, NY 10003
Ph:(212)505-5240
Fax:(212)353-9663
Co. E-mail: wlrc@kwf.org
URL: http://www.kwf.org/kwf/foundation/weill-lenya-research-center
Contact: Dave Stein, Archv.
Scope: Life and work of composer Kurt Weill and Lotte Lenya, musicology, music theory, theater history, 20th-century culture, Weimar Republic culture, women's studies, Jewish studies, emigre studies. **Services:** Copying at staff discretion; lending photos for reprinting; Library open to the public by appointment. **Holdings:** Books; printed music; music manuscripts; scripts; correspondence; audio and video recordings; films; programs; photographs; posters; press clippings; business records; personal papers. **Subscriptions:** 1 journal.

ASSOCIATIONS AND OTHER ORGANIZATIONS

14712 ■ American Institute of Organbuilders
PO Box 35306
Canton, OH 44735
Ph:(330)806-9011
Co. E-mail: robert_sullivan@pipeorgan.org
URL: http://www.pipeorgan.org
Contact: Robert Sullivan, Exec. Sec.
Description: Professional builders and service technicians of pipe organs. Advances the art of pipe organ building by encouraging discussion, inquiry, and research; furthers knowledge regarding pipe organ building through lectures and the exchange of information. Conducts examinations and small-group training seminars. **Publications:** *AIO Service Manual*; *Apprenticeship and Training Policy Manual*; *Journal of American Organbuilding* (quarterly); *Membership List* (annual).

14713 ■ American Musical Instrument Society
1106 Garden St.
Hoboken, NJ 07030
Ph:(201)656-0107
Co. E-mail: j2kopp@aol.com
URL: http://www.amis.org
Contact: Stewart A. Carter, Pres.
Description: Individuals, museums, and other institutions interested in all aspects of musical instruments (both Western and non-Western) through demonstrations, papers, slides, and meetings. **Publications:** Newsletter (semiannual).

14714 ■ Associated Pipe Organ Builders of America
PO Box 155
Chicago Ridge, IL 60415
Ph:(660)747-3066
Free: 800-473-5270
URL: http://www.apoba.com
Description: Manufacturers of pipe organs and pipe organ parts. Aims to expand and perfect the art of pipe organ building in the U.S. Sponsors educational programs and speakers' bureau. Compiles marketing statistics. **Publications:** *Success Stories: Five Pipe Organ Projects Summarized* .

14715 ■ International Association of Piano Builders and Technicians
4444 Forest Ave.
Kansas City, KS 66106
Ph:(913)432-9975
Fax:(913)432-9986
Co. E-mail: iapbt@ptg.org
URL: http://www.ptg.org/iapbt
Contact: Kerry Cooper, Pres.
Description: Works as worldwide association of piano service organizations and individuals. Seeks to form and maintain a worldwide fellowship of piano technicians and rebuilders. Provides a means of exchange of technical information and related subjects and for cooperation in scientific research to improve the quality of pianos. Exchange of information is on a voluntary basis. .

14716 ■ National Association of Professional Band Instrument Repair Technicians
PO Box 51
Normal, IL 61761
Ph:(309)452-4257
Fax:(309)452-4825
Co. E-mail: napbirt@napbirt.org
URL: http://www.napbirt.org
Description: Aims to offer continuing education in the field of band instrument repair. Promotes technical integrity in the craft. Conducts self-evaluation programs, local parts and services exchange programs, and problem solution services. Surveys tools and procedures to improve work quality. Serves as liaison between manufacturers/suppliers and technicians by providing a technical audience for the introduction and evaluation of new products and policies. Has established a code of ethics. Provides placement service. Holds hands-on training sessions per year. .

14717 ■ Piano Manufacturers Association International
14070 Proton Rd., Ste. 100, LB9
Dallas, TX 75244
Ph:(972)233-9107
Fax:(972)490-4219
Co. E-mail: mad@madcrouch.com
URL: http://www.pianonet.com
Description: Manufacturers of pianos and parts suppliers. Compiles monthly unit shipment and dollar volume reports. Supports National Piano Foundation. .

14718 ■ Piano Technicians Guild
4444 Forest Ave.
Kansas City, KS 66106
Ph:(913)432-9975
Fax:(913)432-9986
Co. E-mail: ptg@ptg.org
URL: http://www.ptg.org
Contact: Ms. Barbara J. Cassaday, Exec. Dir.
Description: Piano tuners and technicians. Conducts technical institutes at conventions, seminars and local chapter meetings. Promotes public education in piano care; maintains liaison with piano manufacturers and teachers. Maintains hall of fame. **Publications:** *Piano Technicians Journal* (monthly).

DIRECTORIES OF EDUCATIONAL PROGRAMS

14719 ■ *Directory of Private Accredited Career Schools and Colleges of Technology*
Pub: Accrediting Commission of Career Schools and Colleges of Technology
Contact: Michale S. McComis, Exec. Dir.
Released: On web page. **Price:** Free. **Description:** Covers 3900 accredited post-secondary programs that provide training programs in business, trade, and technical fields, including various small business endeavors. Entries offer school name, address, phone, description of courses, job placement assistance, and requirements for admission. Arrangement is alphabetical.

TRADE PERIODICALS

14720 ■ *Acoustic Guitar Magazine*
Pub: Acoustic Guitar
Contact: David A. Lusterman, Publisher
Released: 8/yr. **Price:** $29.95. **Description:** Magazine for professional and amateur acoustic guitar enthusiasts offering advice on choosing, maintaining, and playing acoustic guitar.

14721 ■ *Premiere Guitar*
Pub: Gearhead Communications, LLC
Contact: Adam Moore, Sen. Ed.
E-mail: adam@premierguitar.com
Released: Monthly. **Price:** $24.95 1 issue free; $39.95 two years 3 issues free. **Description:** Consumer magazine covering equipment, services, and supplies for professional, performing musicians.

TRADE SHOWS AND CONVENTIONS

14722 ■ The Midwest Clinic An International Band and Orchestra Conference
The Midwest Clinic
828 Davis St., Ste. 100
Evanston, IL 60201
Ph:(847)424-4163
Fax:(847)424-5185
Co. E-mail: info@midwestclinic.org
URL: http://www.midwestclinic.org
Released: Annual. **Audience:** Trade professionals. **Principal Exhibits:** Music instruments and publications, supplies, and services, universities, military organizations, fund raisers, music publishers. **Dates and Locations:** 2011 Dec 14-17, Chicago, IL.

RESEARCH CENTERS

14723 ■ University of Hartford–Acoustics Laboratory
College of Engineering, Technology & Architecture
200 Bloomfield Ave.
West Hartford, CT 06117
Ph:(860)768-4792
Free: 800—766-4024
Co. E-mail: celmer@hartford.edu
URL: http://uhaweb.hartford.edu/celmer/lab.htm
Contact: Dr. Robert D. Celmer, Dir.
E-mail: celmer@hartford.edu
Scope: Noise and vibration control, machine diagnostics, musical instrument analysis, psychoacoustics, architectural acoustics, sound system design, optimization and materials testing, hearing loss, as well as sound quality design and optimization.

ASSOCIATIONS AND OTHER ORGANIZATIONS

14724 ■ Professional Beauty Association l Nail Manufacturers Council
15825 N 71st St., Ste. 100
Scottsdale, AZ 85254
Ph:(480)281-0424
Free: 800-468-2274
Fax:(480)905-0708
Co. E-mail: info@probeauty.org
URL: http://www.probeauty.org/about/committees/nmc
Contact: Bruce Selan, Chm.
Description: Division of American Beauty Association. Nail product manufacturers and marketers. Promotes unity within the nail product industry. Works to: elevate safety standards; maintain high ethical standards in advertising; increase public awareness of nail care. Lobbies the government concerning issues that affect the industry. Acts as a forum for the exchange of information. Maintains safety guidelines.

DIRECTORIES OF EDUCATIONAL PROGRAMS

14725 ■ *Directory of Private Accredited Career Schools and Colleges of Technology*
Pub: Accrediting Commission of Career Schools and Colleges of Technology
Contact: Michale S. McComis, Exec. Dir.
Released: On web page. **Price:** Free. **Description:** Covers 3900 accredited post-secondary programs that provide training programs in business, trade, and technical fields, including various small business endeavors. Entries offer school name, address, phone, description of courses, job placement assistance, and requirements for admission. Arrangement is alphabetical.

REFERENCE WORKS

14726 ■ "Every Little Bit Helps" in *Black Enterprise* (Vol. 38, November 2007, No. 4, pp. 102)
Pub: Earl G. Graves Publishing Co. Inc.
Ed: Tennille M. Robinson. **Description:** After a career in the cosmetics industry, Tricialee Riley is marketing and advertising her new venture, the Polish Bar, a salon offering manicures, pedicures, makeup application, and waxing.

TRADE SHOWS AND CONVENTIONS

14727 ■ Beauty Prague
Expona spol. s.r.o.
Masovicka 263/22
CZ-142 00 Praha, Czech Republic
Ph:42 271 961305
Fax:42 274 869807
Co. E-mail: expona@expona.cz
Audience: professionals mostly. **Principal Exhibits:** National Championships in make-up and nail-design.

CONSULTANTS

14728 ■ Contempo Nails
108 W Avenida Gaviota
San Clemente, CA 92672
Ph:(949)498-7060
Fax:(949)498-3962
Contact: Diane Day, President
Scope: Provides consulting on all aspects of sculptured acrylic nail application and care; use of acrylic nails and nail products to improve hand appearance, enhance self-image and self-confidence, prevent nail biting and other hand-related nervous disorders.

FRANCHISES AND BUSINESS OPPORTUNITIES

14729 ■ Atir Natural Nail Care Clinic
1301 Jamestown Rd., Ste. 101
Williamsburg, VA 23185
Ph:(757)258-0696
Fax:(757)258-8999
No. of Franchise Units: 6. **No. of Company-Owned Units:** 2. **Founded:** 2004. **Franchised:** 2004. **Description:** Natural manicures & pedicures. **Equity Capital Needed:** $200,000-$288,000. **Franchise Fee:** $34,000. **Royalty Fee:** 6%. **Financial Assistance:** No. **Managerial Assistance:** Offers 4 weeks manager training at training clinic **Training:** Offers 7 days at headquarters, 3 days at franchisees location with ongoing support.

ASSOCIATIONS AND OTHER ORGANIZATIONS

14730 ■ Au Pair in America
9 W Broad St., River Plz.
Stamford, CT 06902
Ph:(203)399-5000
Free: 800-928-7247
Fax:(203)399-5592
Co. E-mail: aupair.info@aifs.org
URL: http://www.aupairinamerica.com
Contact: Ruth Ferry, Sr. VP/Dir.

Description: A program of the American Institute for Foreign Study, Inc. International youth exchange program organized to promote cross-cultural understanding and cooperation between American families and Western European young adults by providing the opportunity for young people overseas to learn about American culture and family life while living in the U.S. Arranges for foreigners between the ages of 18 and 26 to reside in the U.S. for a year while caring for the children of a host family; participants serve as an "au pair," or equal person, in the host family's household. Has developed a reciprocal program which allows young Americans to travel to Europe. .

14731 ■ International Nanny Association
PO Box 1299
Hyannis, MA 02601
Ph:(713)526-2670
Free: 888-878-1477
Fax:(508)638-6462
Co. E-mail: info@nanny.org
URL: http://www.nanny.org
Contact: Wendy Sachs, Co-Pres.

Description: An educational association for nannies and those who educate, place, employ, and support professional in-home child care. Membership is open to those who are directly involved with the in-home child care profession, including nannies, nanny employers, nanny placement agency owners (and staff), nanny educators, and providers of special services related to the nanny profession. **Publications:** *A Nanny for Your Family*; *Beyond Peanut Butter and Jelly*; *Directory of Nanny Training Programs, Placement Agencies and Special Services* (annual); *INAVision* (quarterly); *Recommended Practices for Nannies*; *So You Want to Be a Nanny* .

DIRECTORIES OF EDUCATIONAL PROGRAMS

14732 ■ *Directory of Private Accredited Career Schools and Colleges of Technology*
Pub: Accrediting Commission of Career Schools and Colleges of Technology
Contact: Michale S. McComis, Exec. Dir.

Released: On web page. **Price:** Free. **Description:** Covers 3900 accredited post-secondary programs that provide training programs in business, trade, and technical fields, including various small business endeavors. Entries offer school name, address, phone, description of courses, job placement assistance, and requirements for admission. Arrangement is alphabetical.

REFERENCE WORKS

14733 ■ "Domestic Workers Organize!" in *WorkingUSA* (Vol. 11, December 2008, No. 4, pp. 413)
Pub: Blackwell Publishers Ltd.

Ed: Eileen Boris, Premilla Nadasen. **Description:** History of domestic workers in the U.S. is examined. The article challenges the long-standing assumption that these, primarily women of color cleaners, nannies, and elder care providers are unable to organize and assesses the possibilities and limitations of recent organizing efforts. The nature of the occupation, its location in the home, the isolated character of the work, informal arrangements with employers, and exclusions from labor law protection, has fostered community-based, social movement organizing to build coalitions, reform legislation and draw public attention to the plight of domestic workers.

VIDEOCASSETTES/ AUDIOCASSETTES

14734 ■ *Day Care Grows Up*
Films for the Humanities & Sciences
132 West 31st Street
New York, NY 10001
Ph:(609)671-1000
Free: 800-257-5126
Fax:(609)671-0266
Co. E-mail: custserv@films.com
URL: http://www.films.com

Released: 1991. **Price:** $159.00. **Description:** Discusses the new attitudes and measures being taken to increase the quality of childcare in the U.S. **Availability:** VHS.

FRANCHISES AND BUSINESS OPPORTUNITIES

14735 ■ A+ Nannies Inc.
6730 E McDowell Rd., Ste. 133
Scottsdale, AZ 85257
Ph:(480)690-7558
Fax:888-202-7738

No. of Franchise Units: 6. **No. of Company-Owned Units:** 4. **Founded:** 2001. **Franchised:** 2007. **Description:** Nanny referral service. **Equity Capital Needed:** $39,250-$53,000. **Franchise Fee:** $28,000. **Royalty Fee:** 6%. **Financial Assistance:** In-house assistance available. **Training:** Offers 4 days training at headquarters and ongoing support.

14736 ■ Absolute Best Care Nanny Agency
Absolute Best Care Franchising LLC
274 Madison Ave.
New York, NY 10016
Ph:(212)481-5705
Fax:(212)481-5706

No. of Franchise Units: 5. **No. of Company-Owned Units:** 2. **Founded:** 2002. **Franchised:** 2006. **Description:** Placement agency for nannies, baby nurses, housekeepers and sitters. **Equity Capital Needed:** $66,990-$74,240. **Franchise Fee:** $49,900. **Royalty Fee:** 8.5%. **Financial Assistance:** No. **Managerial Assistance:** Co-op advertising, ad slicks, and regional advertising. **Training:** Offers 1 week at headquarters and 1 week onsite with ongoing support.

14737 ■ Nanny Poppinz Corporate, Inc.
121 Delmar Ave.
Fort Myers Beach, FL 33931
Ph:(954)775-6017
Fax:(954)752-6708

No. of Franchise Units: 3. **No. of Company-Owned Units:** 2. **Founded:** 1999. **Franchised:** 2004. **Description:** Nanny agency franchise. **Equity Capital Needed:** $65,000-$107,000. **Franchise Fee:** $35,000. **Financial Assistance:** No. **Training:** Yes.

START-UP INFORMATION

14738 ■ "Best In Show" in *Pet Product News*
(Vol. 64, November 2010, No. 11, pp. 20)
Pub: BowTie Inc.

Ed: Lizett Bond. **Description:** Cherrybrook Premium Pet Supplies offers an expanded array of quality holistic products and is staffed by people who possess wide knowledge of these products. Aside from receiving the Outstanding Holistic Approach award, Cherrybrook has opened three stores in New Jersey. How a holistic approach to service kept customers coming back is discussed.

ASSOCIATIONS AND OTHER ORGANIZATIONS

14739 ■ Acupuncture Foundation of Canada Institute–Institute de la Fondation D'Acupuncture du Canada
2131 Lawrence Ave. E, Ste. 204
Scarborough, ON, Canada M1R 5G4
Ph:(416)752-3988
Fax:(416)752-4398
Co. E-mail: afciweb@afcinstitute.com
URL: http://www.afcinstitute.com
Contact: Cheryll A. Kwok, Exec. Dir.
Description: Promotes acupuncture's legitimate place in health care by initiating and supporting research in acupuncture.

14740 ■ Alexander Technique International
1692 Massachusetts Ave., 3rd Fl.
Cambridge, MA 02138
Ph:(617)497-5151
Free: 888-668-8996
Fax:(617)497-2615
Co. E-mail: alexandertechnique@verizon.net
URL: http://www.ati-net.com
Contact: Jen Fries, Admin. Asst.
Description: Worldwide organization of Alexander technique teachers, students and supporters of the technique, created to promote and advance the work discovered by F.M. Alexander. Alexander Technique can improve health by overcoming harmful habits that cause stress and pain which often restrict physical and mental capabilities. **Publications:** *E-Communique*; *The ExChange* .

14741 ■ American Reflexology Certification Board
PO Box 141553
Grand Rapids, MI 49514
Ph:(303)933-6921
Fax:(303)904-0460
Co. E-mail: info@arcb.net
URL: http://www.arcb.net
Contact: Michael Rainone, Pres.
Description: Works to protect the public; promotes advancement of field through recognition of competent reflexologists meeting national standards; provides National Board Certified Reflexologist certification. **Publications:** *Reflexology Today* (semiannual).

14742 ■ American Reiki Master Association
PO Box 130
Lake City, FL 32056-0130
Ph:(904)755-9638
Co. E-mail: american_reiki@yahoo.com
URL: http://members.atlantic.net/lAtarma
Contact: Cheri L. Robertson, Pres.
Description: Promotes the Reiki therapy technique as a method of natural healing; offers training and certification. .

14743 ■ International Chiropractic Pediatric Association
327 N Middletown Rd.
Media, PA 19063
Ph:(610)565-2360
Free: 800-670-KIDS
Fax:(610)565-3567
Co. E-mail: info@icpa4kids.com
URL: http://www.icpa4kids.com
Contact: Dr. Jeanne Ohm, Exec. Coor.
Description: Chiropractors and chiropractic students with an interest in family wellness care. Seeks to advance the study, teaching, and practice of family based chiropractic; promotes continuing professional development of members. Serves as a clearinghouse on family health; sponsors research and educational programs; formulates standards of study for the family practitioner. **Publications:** *Pathways to Family Wellness* (quarterly).

14744 ■ International Society for the Study of Ghosts and Apparitions
Penthouse N
29 Washington Sq. W
New York, NY 10011-9180
Co. E-mail: theghostpost@yahoo.com
URL: http://www.phantasm.mynetcologne.de/issga.
  html
Contact: Dr. Jeanne Keyes Youngson, Pres./Founder
Description: Professional ghost hunters; individuals interested in ghosts and apparitions. Provides information on ghosts, apparitions, and other phenomena. Sponsors private tours in Greenwich Village, NY, led by the president of the society. Compiles statistics; conducts research. .

14745 ■ Reflexology Association of America
PO Box 714
Chepachet, RI 02814
Ph:(980)234-0159
Fax:(401)568-6449
Co. E-mail: inforaa@reflexology-usa.org
URL: http://www.reflexology-usa.org
Contact: Ms. Alison Gingras, Pres.
Description: Promotes and supports reflexology ("the systematic, manual stimulation of the reflex maps located on the feet, hands and outer ears that resemble the shape of the human body"). **Publications:** *Guidelines to Setting up a Reflexology Association*; *How do Reflexologists Earn a Living?*; *Reflexology Across America* (quarterly); *State Leadership Training Manual*; *State Organizational Development Guidelines* .

14746 ■ Reiki Alliance
PO Box 451
Belchertown, MA 01007
Ph:(413)323-4381
Co. E-mail: info@reikialliance.com
URL: http://www.reikialliance.com
Contact: Gerri Jackson
Description: Teachers of Reiki, the Usui System of Reiki Healing. Supports teachers of the Usui System Of Reiki Healing in 40 countries. Promotes exchange among teachers and students; provides member referrals; supports workshops for additional teacher training. Sponsors annual Global Gathering. **Publications:** *Reiki Alliance Membership Newsletter* (3/year); *Student Book* .

REFERENCE WORKS

14747 ■ *The Secrets of Spiritual Marketing: A Complete Guide for Natural Therapists*
Pub: O Books
Ed: Lawrence Ellyard. **Released:** November 1, 2009. **Price:** $24.95. **Description:** Strategies for marketing and advertising a natural therapy business are examined.

STATISTICAL SOURCES

14748 ■ *The U.S. Market for Vitamin, Minerals, and Herbal Supplements*
Pub: Business Trend Analysts, Inc.
Released: 2002. **Price:** $2495.00. **Description:** Tracks historical, current, and projected sales trends (to 2006) for all types of nutritional supplements, on a product-by-product basis.

TRADE PERIODICALS

14749 ■ *Aquarian Alternatives*
Pub: Aquarian Research Foundation
Contact: Judy Rosenblum
Ed: Art Rosenblum, Editor, artr@juno.com. **Released:** Varies. **Description:** Concerned with alternative lifestyles, new-age and positive future information, and related subjects arising from "a concern for peace and love in the world." Recurring features include book reviews, a calendar of events, and news of research.

14750 ■ *Body Soul Magazine*
Pub: Martha Stewart Living Omnimedia
Contact: Katie Spear
Released: 8/yr. **Price:** $20. **Description:** New Age Journal reports on leading-edge ideas in the areas of health, natural living, self-improvement, psychology, publishing and music. It is written for readers who are not limited by conventional thinking and are seeking to improve their lives and society.

14751 ■ *Geocosmic Magazine*
Pub: National Council for Geocosmic Research Inc.
Contact: Arlene Nimark, Advertising Mgr
Ed: Leigh Westin, Editor. **Released:** Semiannual. **Price:** $10 depending on size. **Description:** Trade magazine on astrology and cosmology.

14752 ■ *Journal of Spiritual Bodywork*
Pub: Spiritual Massage Healing Ministry
Contact: Mary L. Brewster
E-mail: maryella1@earthlink.net
Released: Quarterly. **Description:** Trade magazine covering massage and spirituality.

14753 ■ *Light Lines*
Pub: L/L Research
Contact: Jim McCarty
Ed: Jim McCarty, Editor, jim@llresearch.org. **Released:** Quarterly, 4/year (spring, summer, winter, and fall). **Price:** Free. **Description:** Provides news of interest regarding metaphysical evolution.

14754 ■ *Revelations of Awareness*
Pub: Cosmic Awareness Communications
Ed: Avaton, Editor, avaton@aol.com. **Released:** Monthly. **Price:** Included in membership. **Description:** Consists of a series of questions submitted by readers which are answered through channelings from a force describing itself as Cosmic Awareness or 'Universal Mind'. Offers deeply spiritual, yet practical and current information that can be applied to the daily life of the reader on such topics as holistic health, philosophy, and unsolved mysteries. Recurring features include letters to the editor, news of research, book reviews, notices of publications available, reports of meetings, and a calendar of events. Exposes UFO and New World Order conspiracies.

14755 ■ *SCP Journal*
Pub: SCP Journal
Contact: Tal Brooke, Pres./Ed.
Released: Quarterly. **Price:** $25; $35 out of country. **Description:** Magazine covering spiritual phenomena and cultural trends such as near-death experiences, deep ecology, Gaia, witchcraft, and UFOs. Analyzes spiritual trends from a Christian perspective.

14756 ■ *Soaring Spirit*
Pub: Office for History of Science and Technology
Contact: Tara Sutphen
Ed: Dick Sutphen, Editor. **Released:** Biennial. **Description:** Magazine covering metaphysical New Age philosophy with complete catalog listing of Valley of the Sun products.

14757 ■ *Triangles*
Pub: Lucis Trust
Contact: Sarah McKechue
Released: Quarterly. **Price:** Free. **Description:** Contains articles regarding the Triangles Network of Light, a service activity for men and women of goodwill who believe in the power of thought. Concerned with the principles of brotherhood, the one humanity, and with the global community preparing for the New Age and the Reappearance of the Christ. Reports on organizations and movements of interest to Network members. Recurring features include editorials and news from Network units.

VIDEOCASSETTES/ AUDIOCASSETTES

14758 ■ *Caroline Myss' The Energetics of Healing*
PBS Home Video
Catalog Fulfillment Center
PO Box 751089
Charlotte, NC 28275-1089
Ph:800-531-4727
Free: 800-645-4PBS
Co. E-mail: info@pbs.org
URL: http://www.pbs.org
Released: 1998. **Price:** $49.95. **Description:** Dr. Caroline Myss takes you on a guided tour of your energy anatomy, a vast network that determines how your body functions and heals. Three hours on two videocassettes. **Availability:** VHS.

TRADE SHOWS AND CONVENTIONS

14759 ■ *ESP - Psychic Expo and Psychic, Mystics, and Seers Fair*
Impact Event Management
Newcastle upon Tyne
Box 65060
Toronto, ON, Canada M4K 3Z2
Ph:(416)461-5306
Fax:(416)461-8460
URL: http://www.impact-events.co.uk
Released: Semiannual, and mid-October. **Audience:** General public. **Principal Exhibits:** Psychr, tarot astrology readings and information, including occult books, computerized fortune telling, holistic health information and supplies, and mind awareness information.

14760 ■ *Great San Francisco Crystal Fair*
Pacific Crystal Guild
PO Box 1371
Sausalito, CA 94966-1371
Ph:(415)383-7837
Co. E-mail: sfxtl@earthlink.net
URL: http://www.crystalfair.com
Released: 3/yr. **Audience:** Mineralogists, geologists, collectors, new agers, and general public. **Principal Exhibits:** Gems, minerals, jewelry, and metaphysical healing tools.

LIBRARIES

14761 ■ *As-You-Like-It Library*
2200 NW Market St., L-05
Seattle, WA 98107

Ph:(206)329-1794
Co. E-mail: contact@seattlemetaphysicallibrary.org
URL: http://www.seattlemetaphysicallibrary.org
Contact: Margaret Bartley, Exec.Dir.
Scope: Alternative and complementary health, spirituality, metaphysics, astrology, psychology, alchemy, occult and secret societies, unidentified flying objects, consciousness expansion, world religions and lineage teachings, future science, ancient civilizations, parapsychology, unexplained phenomena, self-help, feminist, Goddess and gender studies, conspiratorial political history, cryptozoology, meditation, yoga, Hindu studies, Chinese philosophy, Ancient Near East, alternative science, magic, Manly P. Hall, spiritual communities (EST, Course in Miracles, Scientology, Divine Life, Rajneesh). **Services:** Library open to the public. **Holdings:** 13,000 books; 200 cassette tapes; 400 video tapes; DVDs.

14762 ■ *Astrological Research Library of Canada*
240 Crestwood Rd.
Thurnhill, ON, Canada L4J 1A9
Ph:(905)889-0793
Scope: Astrology, astronomy, metaphysical systems, divinatory sciences, myth and magic, healing, parapsychology. **Services:** Library open to the public by appointment. **Holdings:** 12,000 books; 5000 bound periodical volumes; 2000 slides and charts. **Subscriptions:** 12 journals and other serials.

14763 ■ *Bastyr University Library*
14500 Juanita Dr., NE
Kenmore, WA 98028
Ph:(425)602-3020
Fax:(425)602-3188
Co. E-mail: library@bastyr.edu
URL: http://www.bastyr.edu/library
Contact: Jane D. Saxton, MLIS, Dir. of Lib.Svcs.
Scope: Complementary and alternative medicine, acupuncture and traditional Chinese medicine, naturopathic medicine, nutrition, health psychology, exercise science, primary care medicine, homeopathy, midwifery, herbal science, botanical medicine. **Services:** Interlibrary loan; copying; Library open to the public for reference use only. **Holdings:** 21,000 books; 4000 CD/audiocassettes; 800 DVD/videocassettes; online databases. **Subscriptions:** 250 journals and other serials.

14764 ■ *Geisinger Medical Center–Community Health Library*
100 N. Academy Ave.
Danville, PA 17822-4401
Ph:(570)271-5638
Fax:(570)271-5635
Co. E-mail: chrl@geisinger.edu
URL: http://www.geisinger.edu
Contact: Patricia A Ulmer, Commun.Hea.Libn.
Scope: General medicine, nutrition, alternative and complementary medicine, pediatrics, cancer, AIDS. **Services:** Interlibrary loan. **Holdings:** 860 books; 200 audio/visual materials. **Subscriptions:** 14 journals and other serials.

START-UP INFORMATION

14765 ■ **"David Maus Debuting New Dealership"** in *Orlando Business Journal* (Vol. 26, February 5, 2010, No. 36, pp. 1)
Pub: American City Business Journals
Ed: Anjali Fluker. **Description:** Automotive dealers David Maus Automotive Group and Van Tuyl Automotive Investment Group will launch David Maus Chevrolet in Sanford, Florida in fall 2010. The 12-acre site of the Chevy dealership will be located adjacent to the David Maus Toyota dealership. The new store is expected to generate nearly 125 new jobs.

ASSOCIATIONS AND OTHER ORGANIZATIONS

14766 ■ **1953-54 Buick Skylark Club**
51 Statesville Quarry Rd.
Lafayette, NJ 07848
Ph:(973)383-6035
Fax:(973)383-6035
Co. E-mail: buick5354@aol.com
URL: http://www.skylarkclub.org
Contact: JoAnne DePeppo, Corresponding Sec.
Description: Owners and admirers of Buick Skylark automobiles built in 1953 and 1954. Promotes preservation and maintenance of classic Buicks. Serves as a clearinghouse on 1953 and 1954 Buick Skylarks; facilitates communication and good fellowship among members. .

14767 ■ **American Automotive Leasing Association**
675 N Washington St., Ste. 410
Alexandria, VA 22314
Ph:(703)548-0777
Fax:(703)548-1925
Co. E-mail: sederholm@aalafleet.com
URL: http://www.aalafleet.com
Contact: Pamela Sederholm, Exec. Dir.
Purpose: Represents the commercial automotive fleet leasing and management industry. .

14768 ■ **American International Automobile Dealers Association**
211 N Union St., Ste. 300
Alexandria, VA 22314
Ph:(703)519-7800
Free: 800-462-4232
Fax:(703)519-7810
Co. E-mail: membership@aiada.org
URL: http://www.aiada.org
Contact: Jim Smail, Chm.
Description: Trade association for America's international nameplate automobile dealerships and their employees who sell and service automobiles manufactured in the U.S. and abroad. Works to preserve a free market for international automobiles in the U.S. and is dedicated to increasing public awareness of the benefits the industry provides. **Publications:** *AIADA's Showroom* (9/year).

14769 ■ **Canadian Automobile Dealers Association–Corporation des associations de detaillants d'automobiles**
85 Renfrew Dr.
Markham, ON, Canada L3R 0N9
Ph:(905)940-4959
Free: 800-463-5289
Fax:(905)940-6870
Co. E-mail: mail@cada.ca
URL: http://www.cada.ca
Contact: Luc Duval, Chm.
Description: Automobile dealers. Seeks to advance the automotive and automotive services industries. Facilitates communication and cooperation among members; represents members' interests before industrial organizations and government agencies. **Publications:** *Newsline* (monthly).

14770 ■ **Ford Motor Minority Dealers Association**
16000 W 9 Mile Rd., Ste. 603
Southfield, MI 48075
Ph:(248)557-2500
Free: 800-247-0293
Fax:(248)557-2882
Co. E-mail: fmmdafacts@aol.com
URL: http://www.fmmda.org
Contact: Dr. A.V. Fleming, Exec. Dir./CEO
Description: Minority-owned car dealerships. Promotes professional standards of minority dealerships. Strives to increase the number of minority dealerships. .

14771 ■ **National Association of Fleet Resale Dealers**
2521 Brown Blvd.
Arlington, TX 76006
Ph:(817)649-5858
Fax:(817)649-5866
Co. E-mail: jd@niada.com
URL: http://www.nafrd.com
Contact: Mitch Pomerantz, Pres.
Description: Used car wholesalers dealing exclusively with large fleets. Encourages members to employ effective marketing methods and to conduct businesses soundly and ethically. Seeks a favorable public image of wholesale used cars and the used car industry. Serves as a forum for exchange of ideas and information; monitors legislation. **Publications:** *Inside Tracks* (quarterly); *NAFRD Resource Guide* (annual).

14772 ■ **National Association of Minority Automobile Dealers**
8201 Corporate Dr., Ste. 550
Lanham, MD 20785
Ph:(301)306-1614
Fax:(301)306-1493
Co. E-mail: damon.lester@namad.org
URL: http://www.namad.org
Contact: Damon Lester, Pres.
Description: Automobile dealers. Acts as liaison between membership, the federal government, the community, and industry representatives; seeks to better the business conditions of its members on an ongoing basis. Serves as a confidential spokesperson for dealers. Offers business analysis, financial counseling, and short- and long-term management planning. Conducts research programs; compiles statistics. .

14773 ■ **National Auto Auction Association**
5320 Spectrum Dr., Ste. D
Frederick, MD 21703
Ph:(301)696-0400
Fax:(301)631-1359
Co. E-mail: naaa@naaa.com
URL: http://www.naaa.com
Contact: Jay Cadigan, Pres.
Description: Owners/operators of wholesale automobile and truck auctions; associate members are car and truck manufacturers, insurers of checks and titles, car and truck rental companies, publishers of auto price guide books, and others connected with the industry. Maintains hall of fame. **Publications:** *National Auto Auction Association—Membership Directory* (annual); *On the Block* (quarterly).

14774 ■ **National Automobile Dealers Association**
8400 Westpark Dr.
McLean, VA 22102
Ph:(703)821-7000
Free: 800-252-6232
Fax:(703)821-7234
Co. E-mail: nadainfo@nada.org
URL: http://www.nada.org
Contact: Phillip D. Brady, Pres.
Description: Franchised new car and truck dealers. Provides representation for franchised new car and truck dealers in the areas of government, industry, and public affairs. Offers management services and retirement and insurance programs to member dealers. Maintains National Automobile Dealers Charitable Foundation. **Publications:** *AutoExec* (monthly); *DEAC Report* (quarterly); *NADA Headlines* (daily).

14775 ■ **National Independent Automobile Dealers Association**
2521 Brown Blvd.
Arlington, TX 76006
Ph:(817)640-3838
Free: 800-682-3837
Fax:(817)649-5866
Co. E-mail: mike@niada.com
URL: http://www.niada.com
Contact: Mr. Michael R. Linn, CEO
Description: Individuals, companies, or corporations licensed by their states as dealers to buy and sell used motor vehicles; associate members are businesses related to or associated with the buying or selling of motor vehicles. Gathers and disseminates information relative to the used car industry; represents used car dealers before regulatory and legislative bodies; provides educational and other programs to help used car dealers understand their responsibilities; works for the betterment of the automobile industry. Works closely with local and state independent automobile dealers' associations and others concerning dealers and the public. Maintains code of fair dealing for members. Conducts seminars, meet-

ings, and professional training programs. Maintains speakers' bureau; services for children, and charitable programs. Sponsors competitions; compiles statistics. **Publications:** *Dealer Connection* (quarterly); *Used Car Dealer* (monthly); *Used Car Industry Report* (annual).

14776 ■ Used Truck Association
325 Country Club Dr., Ste. A
Stockbridge, GA 30281
Free: 877-438-7882
Co. E-mail: contact@uta.org
URL: http://www.uta.org
Contact: Rick Clark, Pres.

Description: Truck dealerships with substantial used truck sales; truck manufacturers. Promotes professionalism among members; works to elevate the image of the used truck sales business. Monitors federal regulatory developments affecting used truck sales; conducts lobbying activities. .

REFERENCE WORKS

14777 ■ "$3 Million in Repairs Prep Cobo for Auto Show" in *Crain's Detroit Business* **(Vol. 26, January 4, 2010, No. 1, pp. 1)**
Pub: Crain Communications, Inc.

Ed: Nancy Kaffer. **Description:** Overview of the six projects priced roughly at $3 million which were needed in order to host the North American International Auto Show; show organizers stated that the work was absolutely necessary to keep the show in the city of Detroit.

14778 ■ "The 490 Made Chevy a Bargain Player" in *Automotive News* **(Vol. 86, October 31, 2011, No. 6488, pp. S22)**
Pub: Crain Communications Inc.

Ed: David Phillips. **Description:** The first Chevrolet with the 490 engine was sold in 1913, but it was too expensive for masses. In 1914 the carmaker launched a lower-priced H-series of cars competitively priced. Nameplates such as Corvette, Bel Air, Camaro and Silverado have defined Chevrolet through the years.

14779 ■ "1914 Proved to Be Key Year for Chevy" in *Automotive News* **(Vol. 86, October 31, 2011, No. 6488, pp. S18)**
Pub: Crain Communications Inc.

Ed: Jamie Lareau. **Description:** Chevy Bow Tie emblem was born in 1914, creating the brand's image that has carried through to current days.

14780 ■ "2011 FinOvation Awards" in *Farm Industry News* **(January 19, 2011)**
Pub: Penton Business Media Inc.

Ed: Jodie Wehrspann. **Description:** The 2011 FinOvation Award winners are announced, covering new products that growers need for corn and soybean crops. Winners range from small turbines and a fuel-efficient pickup to a Class 10 combine and drought-tolerant hybrids.

14781 ■ "A123-Fisker Deal May Mean 540 Jobs" in *Crain's Detroit Business* **(Vol. 26, January 18, 2010, No. 3, pp. 4)**
Pub: Crain Communications, Inc.

Ed: Dustin Walsh. **Description:** Manufacturing plants in Livonia and Romulous may be hiring up to 540 skilled workers due to a contract that was won by A123 Systems Inc. that will result in the company supplying lithium-ion batteries to Fisker Automotive Inc. to be used in their Karma plug-in hybrid electric vehicle.

14782 ■ "Ad Firms Stew Over Lost Car Biz; Diversifying Business Is Uphill Battle" in *Crain's Detroit Business* **(Vol. 23, July 30, 2007, No. 31)**
Pub: Crain Communications, Inc.

Ed: Jean Halliday. **Description:** Struggling Detroit automakers are breaking their tradition of loyalty and moving their advertising accounts to agencies in Los Angeles, San Francisco, and Boston; This has Detroit's advertising community very worried.

14783 ■ "Antwerpen Takes on Chrysler Financial Over Foreclosure Sales" in *Baltimore Business Journal* **(Vol. 28, July 30, 2010, No. 12, pp. 1)**
Pub: Baltimore Business Journal

Ed: Gary Haber. **Description:** Antwerpen Motorcars Ltd. aims to fight the scheduled foreclosure sale of real estate it leases in Baltimore County, including the showroom for its Hyundai dealership on Baltimore National Pike in Catonsville, Maryland. The company is planning to file papers in court to stop the scheduled August 11, 2010 auction sought by Chrysler Financial Services Americas LLC.

14784 ■ "Auction Company Grows with Much Smaller Sites" in *Automotive News* **(Vol. 86, October 31, 2011, No. 6488, pp. 23)**
Pub: Crain Communications Inc.

Ed: Arlena Sawyers. **Description:** Auction Broadcasting Company has launched auction sites and is expanding into new areas. The family-owned business will provide auctions half the size traditionally used. The firm reports that 40 percent of the General Motors factory-owned vehicles sold on consignment were purchased by online buyers, up 30 percent over 2010.

14785 ■ "Auto Bankruptcies Could Weaken Defense" in *Crain's Detroit Business* **(Vol. 25, June 8, 2009, No. 23, pp. 1)**
Pub: Crain Communications Inc. - Detroit

Ed: Chad Halcom. **Description:** Bankruptcy and supplier consolidation of General Motors Corporation and Chrysler LLC could interfere with the supply chains of some defense contractors, particularly makers of trucks and smaller vehicles.

14786 ■ "Auto Show Aims to Electrify" in *Crain's Detroit Business* **(Vol. 26, January 11, 2010, No. 2, pp. 1)**
Pub: Crain Communications, Inc.

Ed: Ryan Beene. **Description:** Overview of the North American International Auto show include sixteen production and concept vehicles including eight from the Detroit 3. High-tech battery suppliers as well as hybrid and electric vehicles will highlight the show.

14787 ■ "Auto Show Taps Moms" in *Marketing to Women* **(Vol. 21, April 2008, No. 4, pp. 3)**
Pub: EPM Communications, Inc.

Description: Teamed with Mother Proof, an online site which features automotive content aimed at moms, the Chicago Auto Show will present a full day of programming with the emphasis on mom.

14788 ■ "Autoline Goes West" in *Michigan Vue* **(Vol. 13, July-August 2008, No. 4, pp. 6)**
Pub: Entrepreneur Media Inc.

Ed: Dave Gibbons. **Description:** Profile of Blue Sky Productions, a Detroit-based production company that produces the nationally syndicated television series "Autoline", which traditionally probes inside the Detroit auto industry; the company recently decided to shoot in Southern California, an area that now has an immense auto industry but has been virtually ignored by the media. Blue Sky originally slated four shows but ended up producing eleven due to the immense amount of material they discovered concerning the state of California's auto market.

14789 ■ "Automotive Trouble" in *Canadian Business* **(Vol. 82, April 27, 2009, No. 7, pp. 11)**
Pub: Rogers Media

Ed: Thomas Watson. **Description:** The likely effects of a possible bailout of the U.S. automotive industry are examined. Some experts believe that a bailout will be good for the automotive industry and on the U.S. economy. Others argue however, that the nationalization may have a negative impact on the industry and on the economy.

14790 ■ "Bankruptcies" in *Crain's Detroit Business* **(Vol. 24, October 6, 2008, No. 40, pp. 26)**
Pub: Crain Communications, Inc.

Description: Current businesses that have filed for Chapter 7 or 11 protection in U.S. Bankruptcy Court include an auto dealership, a gun range and a grocery service.

14791 ■ "Battered U.S. Auto Makers in Grip of Deeper Sales Slump" in *Globe & Mail* **(April 4, 2007, pp. B1)**
Pub: CTVglobemedia Publishing Inc.

Ed: Greg Keenan. **Description:** The fall in Canadian sales and market share of Ford Motor Co., General Motors Corp. and Chrysler Group is discussed.

14792 ■ "Because He Is Always On the Accelerator: Jay Rogers: Local Motors, Chandler, Arizona" in *Inc.* **(Volume 32, December 2010, No. 10)**
Pub: Inc. Magazine

Description: Profile of Jay Rogers, founder of Local Motors, who manufactures cars, including the Phoenix Rally Fighter made from lightweight composites rather than steel.

14793 ■ "Black On Black Business: Moorehead Buys Hank Aaron's Toyota Dealership" in *Black Enterprise* **(Vol. 38, February 2008, No. 7, pp. 28)**
Pub: Earl G. Graves Publishing Co. Inc.

Ed: Brenda Porter. **Description:** In a move to expand his automotive business, Thomas A. Moorehead, CEO of BMW/MINI of Sterling, Georgia bought Hank Aaron's Toyota automobile dealership in McDonough, Georgia. Moorehead stated that he will call the new store Toyota of McDonough.

14794 ■ "BMW Makes Bet on Carbon Maker" in *Wall Street Journal Eastern Edition* **(November 19 , 2011, pp. B3)**
Pub: Dow Jones & Company Inc.

Ed: Christoph Rauwald. **Description:** Eight months ago, Volkswagen AG acquired a 10 percent holding in carbon-fiber maker SGL Carbon SE. Its rival BMW AG is catching up by acquiring 15.2 percent stake in SGL as it seeks alliances like the rest of the industry in order to share industrial costs of new product development.

14795 ■ "BMW Revs Up for a Rebound" in *Barron's* **(Vol. 89, July 13, 2009, No. 28, pp. M7)**
Pub: Dow Jones & Co., Inc.

Ed: Jonathan Buck. **Description:** Investors may like BMW's stocks because the company has maintained its balance sheet strength and has an impressive production line of new models that should boost sales in the next few years. The company's sales are also gaining traction, although their vehicle delivery was down 1.7 percent year on year on June 2009, this was still the best monthly sales figure for 2009.

14796 ■ "Bob Johnson Opens Car Dealership: Plans To Provide a Bridge To Create More Minority Owners" in *Black Enterprise* **(December 2007)**
Pub: Earl G. Graves Publishing Co. Inc.

Ed: Wendy Isom, Jeff Fortson. **Description:** Robert L. Johnson, founder of RLJ Companies and majority owner of RLJ-McLarty Automotive Landers Automotive Partnership which carries Chrysler, Dodge, Ford, Jeep, Scion, and Toyota vehicles has a plan to create opportunity for minority car dealers.

14797 ■ "Brand Police Keep the Lines Distinct at GM" in *Automotive News* **(Vol. 86, October 31, 2011, No. 6488, pp. 3)**
Pub: Crain Communications Inc.

Ed: Mike Colias. **Description:** Joel Ewanick, marketing chief at General Motors, is working to keep General Motor's four brands distinct within their brands.

14798 ■ "Buick Prices Verano Below Rival Luxury Compacts" in *Automotive News* **(Vol. 86, October 31, 2011, No. 6488, pp. 10)**
Pub: Crain Communications Inc.

Ed: Mike Colias. **Description:** General Motors's Verano will compete with other luxury compacts such as the Lexus IS 250 and the Acura TSX, but will be prices significantly lower coming in with a starting price of $23,470, about $6,000 to $10,000 less than those competitors.

14799 ■ "Burning Issues: Four of Today's Hottest Energy Topics" in *Canadian Business* (Vol. 83, August 17, 2010, No. 13-14, pp. 45)
Pub: Rogers Media Ltd.

Description: A look at four issues dominating Canada's energy industry is presented. These issues are lack of transmission capacity and difficulty in transferring power across provincial boundaries, the management of intermittency of renewable generation, techniques that would clean up the Alberta's oil sands, and the impending massive use of electric cars in North America.

14800 ■ *Buyology: Truth and Lies About Why We Buy*
Pub: Doubleday, a Division of Random House

Ed: Martin Lindstrom. **Released:** 2009. **Price:** $24.95. **Description:** Marketers study brain scans to determine how consumers rate Nokia, Coke, and Ford products.

14801 ■ "Can a Brazilian SUV Take On the Jeep Wrangler?" in *Business Week* (September 22, 2008, No. 4100, pp. 50)
Pub: McGraw-Hill Companies, Inc.

Ed: Helen Walters. **Description:** Profile of the Brazilian company TAC as well as the flourishing Brazilian car market; TAC has launched a new urban vehicle, the Stark, which has won prizes for innovation; the company uses local technology and manufacturing expertise.

14802 ■ "Canadian Vehicle Sales Accelerate in April, but U.S. Goes on Bumpy Ride" in *Globe & Mail* (May 2, 2007, pp. B7)
Pub: CTVglobemedia Publishing Inc.

Ed: Greg Keenan. **Description:** The increase in Canadian vehicle sales to 169,280 in April 2007, but decline in their sales in the United States due to slump in housing sector are discussed.

14803 ■ "Car Dealer Closings: Immoral, Slow-Death" in *Crain's Detroit Business* (Vol. 25, June 8, 2009, No. 23)
Pub: Crain Communications Inc. - Detroit

Ed: Daniel Duggan. **Description:** Colleen McDonald discusses the closing of her two Chrysler dealerships located in Taylor and Livonia, Michigan, along with her Farmington Hills store, Holiday Chevrolet.

14804 ■ "Car Dealers Shift Gears to Survive" in *Puget Sound Business Journal* (Vol. 29, November 14, 2008, No. 30, pp. 1)
Pub: American City Business Journals

Ed: Gregg Lamm. **Description:** Washington-based automobile dealers are offering incentives such as repairs, parts and used cars in order to supplement the decline in new car sales.

14805 ■ "Car Trouble" in *Canadian Business* (Vol. 80, October 22, 2007, No. 21, pp. 27)
Pub: Rogers Media

Ed: Thomas Watson. **Description:** Contract between General Motors Corporation and the United Auto Workers Union has created a competitive arm for the U.S. Big Three automakers. Data on the market and production data of car companies are presented.

14806 ■ "CarBiz Inc. Speaking At NABD" in *Canadian Corporate News* (May 14, 2007)
Pub: Comtex News Network Inc.

Description: CarBiz Inc., a leading provider of software, consulting, and training solutions to the United States' automotive industry, had two of its executive officers speak at the National Alliance of Buy Here - Pay Here Dealers (NABD), a conference that draws over 2,000 dealers, service providers, and experts from across the United States.

14807 ■ "CarTango Lauches Site for Women" in *Marketing to Women* (Vol. 21, April 2008, No. 4, pp. 5)
Pub: EPM Communications, Inc.

Description: CarTango.com is an Internet site that seeks to overcome what women say are dismissive or pushy salespeople by allowing the shoppers the chance to decide what they want before inviting dealers to compete for their business.

14808 ■ "CAW Hopes to Beat Xstrata Deadline" in *Globe & Mail* (January 30, 2007, pp. B3)
Pub: CTVglobemedia Publishing Inc.

Ed: Andy Hoffman. **Description:** The decision of Canadian Auto Workers to strike work at Xstrata PLC over wage increase is discussed.

14809 ■ "Charged Up for Sales" in *Charlotte Business Journal* (Vol. 25, October 15, 2010, No. 30, pp. 1)
Pub: Charlotte Business Journal

Ed: Susan Stabley. **Description:** Li-Ion Motors Corporation is set to expand its production lines of electric cars in Sacramento, California. The plan is seen to create up to 600 jobs. The company's total investment is seen to reach $500 million.

14810 ■ "Chinese Fund Loans $33.5 Million to Prestolite" in *Crain's Detroit Business* (Vol. 26, January 18, 2010, No. 3, pp. 1)
Pub: Crain Communications, Inc.

Ed: Ryan Beene. **Description:** Prestolite Electric Inc., a distributor of alternators and starter motors for commercial and heavy-duty vehicles, looked to China for fresh capital in order to fund new product launches.

14811 ■ "Combat Mission: Rebuffed, BAE Systems Fights Army Contract Decision" in *Business Courier* (Vol. 26, September 25, 2009)
Pub: American City Business Journals, Inc.

Ed: Jon Newberry. **Description:** BAE Systems filed a complaint with the US Government Accountability Office after the US Army issued an order to BAE's competitor for armoured trucks which is potentially worth over $3 billion. Hundreds of jobs in Butler County, Ohio hinge on the success of the contract protest.

14812 ■ "Consumers Like Green, But Not Mandates" in *Business Journal-Milwaukee* (Vol. 28, December 10, 2010, No. 10, pp. A1)
Pub: Milwaukee Business Journal

Ed: Sean Ryan. **Description:** Milwaukee, Wisconsin consumers are willing to spend more on green energy, a survey has revealed. Respondents also said they will pay more for efficient cars and appliances. Support for public incentives for homeowners and businesses that reduce energy use has also increased.

14813 ■ "Courting Canadian Customers Confounds Car Dealers" in *Business First Buffalo* (November 9, 2007, pp. 1)
Pub: American City Business Journals, Inc.

Ed: James Fink. **Description:** Strength of the Canadian dollar has led to an influx of potential customers for the Western New York automobile industry, but franchising restrictions and licensing as well as insurance issues have limited the potential of having larger sales figures. Border and trade issues that affect the car industry in WNY are also discussed.

14814 ■ "Dealer Gets a Lift with Acquisitions at Year's End" in *Crain's Detroit Business* (Vol. 26, January 11, 2010, No. 2, pp. 3)
Pub: Crain Communications, Inc.

Ed: Ryan Beene. **Description:** Alta Equipment Co., a forklift dealer, closed 2009 with a string of acquisitions expecting to double the firm's employee headcount and triple its annual revenue. Alta Lift Truck Services, Inc., as the company was known before the acquisitions, was founded in 1984 as Michigan's dealer for forklift manufacturer Yale Materials Handling Corp.

14815 ■ "Dealers Fight To Steer Course" in *The Business Journal-Serving Metropolitan Kansas City* (Vol. 27, November 7, 2008, No. 9, pp. 1)
Pub: American City Business Journals, Inc.

Ed: Steve Vockrodt. **Description:** One local automobile dealer says that their sales are down by 30 to 40 percent and that car financing is now in the low 60 percentile from 85 to 88 percent. The National Automobile Dealers Association says that 700 dealerships are likely to be lost for 2008.

14816 ■ "Dealers Trying Not to Fold" in *Business First Columbus* (Vol. 25, December 5, 2008, No. 15, pp. A1)
Pub: American City Business Journals

Ed: Dan Eaton. **Description:** Increase in the number of automobile dealer closures in Ohio is seen to impact the state's economy. The trend of consolidation is forecasted to adversely affect employment and sales. Statistical data included.

14817 ■ "Despite Gloom, Auto Sales Saw Gains in 2005" in *Globe & Mail* (January 5, 2006, pp. B1)
Pub: CTVglobemedia Publishing Inc.

Ed: Greg Keenan. **Description:** An overview of positve automotive sales in Canada, for 2005, is presented.

14818 ■ "Detroit 3's Fall Would Be a Big One in Ohio" in *Business First Columbus* (Vol. 25, November 28, 2008, No. 14, pp. A1)
Pub: American City Business Journals

Ed: Dan Eaton. **Description:** Ohio's economy will suffer huge negative effects in the event of a failure of one or more of the automotive companies, General Motors Corporation, Ford Motor Company, or Chrysler LLC. The state is home to 97,900 jobs in the automotive industry and is a vital link to the industry's supply network.

14819 ■ "The Doomsday Scenario" in *Conde Nast Portfolio* (Vol. 2, June 2008, No. 6, pp. 91)
Pub: Conde Nast Publications, Inc.

Ed: Jeffrey Rothfeder. **Description:** Detroit and the U.S. auto industry are discussed as well as the ramifications of the demise of this manufacturing base. Similarities and differences between the downfall of the U.S. steel business and the impact it had on Pittsburg, Pennsylvania is also discussed.

14820 ■ "Everyone Has a Story Inspired by Chevrolet" in *Automotive News* (Vol. 86, October 31, 2011, No. 6488, pp. S003)
Pub: Crain Communications Inc.

Ed: Keith E. Crain. **Description:** Besides being a great ad slogan, 'Baseball, Hot Dogs, Apple Pie and Chevrolet', the brand conjures up memories for most everyone in our society. Louis Chevrolet had a reputation as a race car driver and lent his name to the car that has endured for 100 years.

14821 ■ "Extra Rehab Time Boosts M-B's Off-Lease Profits" in *Automotive News* (Vol. 86, October 31, 2011, No. 6488, pp. 22)
Pub: Crain Communications Inc.

Ed: Arlena Sawyers. **Description:** Mercedes-Benz Financial Services USA is holding on to off-lease vehicles in order to recondition them and the move is boosting profits for the company.

14822 ■ "Fair Play? China Cheats, Carney Talks and Rankin Walks; Here's the Latest" in *Canadian Business* (Vol. 81, March 17, 2008, No. 4)
Pub: Rogers Media

Description: Discusses the World Trade Organization which says that China is breaking trade rules by taxing imports of auto parts at the same rate as foreign-made finished cars. Mark Carney first speech as the governor of the Bank of Canada made economists suspect a rate cut on overnight loans. Andre Rankin was ordered by the Ontario Securities Commission to pay $250,000 in investigation costs.

14823 ■ "Fighting Detroit" in *Baltimore Business Journal* (Vol. 27, January 22, 2010, No. 38, pp. 1)
Pub: American City Business Journals

Ed: Daniel J. Sernovitz. **Description:** Baltimore, Maryland-based car dealers could retrieve their franchises from car manufacturers, Chrysler LLC and General Motors Corporation, through a forced arbitration. A provision in a federal budget mandates the arbitration. The revoking of franchises has been attributed to the car manufacturers' filing of bankruptcy protection.

14824 ■ **"Finalist: Private Company, $100M-$1B"** in *Crain's Detroit Business* (Vol. 25, June 22, 2009, No. 25)
Pub: Crain Communications Inc. - Detroit
Ed: Chad Halcom. **Description:** Profile of U.S. Farathane Corporation, the Sterling Heights, Michigan-based automotive plastic components maker. The company's CFO discusses ways they are coping with the cutbacks at major automobile factories.

14825 ■ **"Florin Car Dealers Drive Plan"** in *Sacramento Business Journal* (Vol. 25, August 22, 2008, No. 25, pp. 1)
Pub: American City Business Journals, Inc.
Ed: Melanie Turner. **Description:** Automobile dealers in Sacramento, California are working with the city and the business district in planning for future redevelopment in Florin Road. The move stemmed from pressure from the Elk Grove Auto Mall, high fuel prices and the credit crunch. The area has suffered business closures recently.

14826 ■ **"Former Chrysler Dealers Build New Business Model"** in *Crain's Detroit Business* (Vol. 25, June 22, 2009, No. 25, pp. 3)
Pub: Crain Communications Inc. - Detroit
Ed: Daniel Duggan. **Description:** Joe Ricci is one of 14 Detroit area dealerships whose franchises have been terminated. Ricci and other Chrysler dealers in the area are starting new businesses or switching to new franchises.= Ricci's All American Buyer's Service will be located in Dearborn and will sell only used cars.

14827 ■ **"Former Football Pro Closes Doors of Car Dealership"** in *Black Enterprise* (Vol. 38, March 2008, No. 8, pp. 28)
Pub: Earl G. Graves Publishing Co. Inc.
Ed: Brenda Porter. **Description:** Aenease Williams automobile dealerships closed their doors in Louisiana due to low sales. Williams, a former NFL safety retired in 2005. According to an expert, the image of the Lincoln as a luxury brand has been diminished.

14828 ■ **"Former Schaefer and Strohminger Dealerships to Hit Auction Block"** in *Baltimore Business Journal* (Vol. 28, September 10, 2010)
Pub: Baltimore Business Journal
Ed: Gary Haber. **Description:** Maryland's real estate developers have a chance to vie for almost 11 acres of prime Baltimore County real estate that are on the auction block. The five properties were once home to Schaefer and Strohminger car dealerships and were located in the county's busiest areas. Other potential uses for the properties are also discussed.

14829 ■ **"From American Icon to Global Juggernaut"** in *Automotive News* (Vol. 86, October 31, 2011, No. 6488, pp. S003)
Pub: Crain Communications Inc.
Ed: Peter Brown. **Description:** Chevrolet celebrates its 100th Anniversary. The brand revolutionized its market with affordable cars that bring technology to the masses. Chevys have been sold in 140 countries and the company is responding to a broader market.

14830 ■ **"Fuel for Thought"** in *Canadian Business* (Vol. 81, April 14, 2008, No. 6, pp. 18)
Pub: Rogers Media
Ed: John Gray. **Description:** Discusses a web poll of 133 CEOs and other business leaders that shows that they predict oil prices to increase to US $113 per barrel over the 2008 to 2010 timeframe. Most of the respondents did not favor cutting gas taxes but this group wants the government to cut taxes on fuel-efficient vehicles and increase subsidies to local transit systems.

14831 ■ **"Full Speed Ahead: How to Get the Most Out of Your Company Vehicles"** in *Entrepreneur* (Vol. 37, October 2009, No. 10, pp. 78)
Pub: Entrepreneur Media, Inc.
Ed: Jill Amadio. **Description:** Methods of saving costs on purchasing and maintaining vehicles are described. Tips include shopping online, choosing hybrid vehicles, and choosing cars with incentives and lower insurance costs.

14832 ■ **"Future Autoworkers will Need Broader Skills"** in *Crain's Detroit Business* (Vol. 25, June 8, 2009, No. 23, pp. 13)
Pub: Crain Communications Inc. - Detroit
Ed: Ryan Beene. **Description:** Auto industry observers report that new workers in the industry will need advanced skills and educational backgrounds in engineering and technical fields because jobs in the factories will become more technology-based and multidisciplinary.

14833 ■ **"General Motors Can't Kick Incentives-But They Work"** in *Advertising Age* (Vol. 79, July 7, 2008, No. 26, pp. 3)
Pub: Crain Communications, Inc.
Ed: Jean Halliday. **Description:** General Motors Corp. was able to maintain their market share just as Toyota Motor Corp. was beginning to pass the manufacturer; GM lured in customers with a sales incentive that they heavily advertised and subsequently helped build demand; investors, however, were not impressed and GM shares were hammered to their lowest point in 50 years after analysts speculated the company might go bankrupt.

14834 ■ **"GM-Chrysler Merger Could Cull Dealerships From Coast to Coast"** in *Globe & Mail* (February 20, 2007, pp. B17)
Pub: CTVglobemedia Publishing Inc.
Ed: Greg Keenan. **Description:** General Motors Corp. is planning to acquire Chrysler Group. The challenges before the possible merger are presented.

14835 ■ **"GM-Chrysler Merger: Just a Bigger Mess?"** in *Globe & Mail* (February 17, 2007, pp. B3)
Pub: CTVglobemedia Publishing Inc.
Ed: Barrie McKenna; Greg Keenan. **Description:** The General Motors Corp. is negotiating talks to acquire DaimlerChrysler AG's Chrysler Group. The five reasons for the possible merger of the companies are presented.

14836 ■ **"GM Flexes Muscles With New Camaro Concept"** in *Globe & Mail* (January 10, 2006, pp. B15)
Pub: CTVglobemedia Publishing Inc.
Ed: Greg Keenan. **Description:** General Motors Corp., has displayed the new concept car Chevrolet Camaro, at the North American International Auto Show in Detroit. The features of this automobile manufactured at the company's assembly plant in Quebec are discussed.

14837 ■ **"GM Is On the Road Again"** in *Canadian Business* (Vol. 83, September 14, 2010, No. 15, pp. 14)
Pub: Rogers Media Ltd.
Ed: Thomas Watson. **Description:** Former General Motors CEO Rick Wagoner has been credited for single-handedly putting the automaker back on track before he was forced to resign and GM was restructured by the government. GM earned $2.19 billion the first half of 2010 after losing more than $80 billion in the three years leading up to its failure. GM's comeback is discussed.

14838 ■ **"GM Releases 2010 Product Guide, Ends Production of Medium-Duty Trucks"** in *Contractor* (Vol. 56, July 2009, No. 7, pp. 5)
Pub: Penton Media, Inc.
Ed: Candace Roulo. **Description:** General Motors will cease production of the Chevrolet Kodiak and GMC Topkick by July 31, 2009. Their 2010 Product Guide for the U.S. still has four remaining brands including the Buick, Cadillac, Chevrolet, and GMC.

14839 ■ **"GM's Decision to Boot Dealer Prompts Sale"** in *Baltimore Business Journal* (Vol. 27, November 6, 2009, No. 26, pp. 1)
Pub: American City Business Journals
Ed: Daniel J. Sernovitz. **Description:** General Motors Corporation's (GM) decision to strip Baltimore's Anderson Automotive Group Inc. of its GM franchise has prompted the owner, Bruce Mortimer, to close the automotive dealership and sell the land to a developer. The new project could make way for new homes, a shopping center and supermarket.

14840 ■ **"GM's Volt Woes Cast Shadow on E-Cars"** in *Wall Street Journal Eastern Edition* (November 28, 2011, pp. B1)
Pub: Dow Jones & Company Inc.
Ed: Sharon Terlep. **Description:** The future of electric cars is darkened with the government investigation by the National Highway Traffic Safety Administration into General Motor Company's Chevy Volt after two instances of the car's battery packs catching fire during crash tests conducted by the Agency.

14841 ■ **"Greening the Auto Industry"** in *Business Journal-Serving Phoenix & the Valley of the Sun* (Vol. 30, July 23, 2010, No. 46, pp. 1)
Pub: Phoenix Business Journal
Ed: Patrick O'Grady. **Description:** Thermo Fluids Inc. has been recycling used oil products since 1993 and could become Arizona's first home for oil filter recycling after retrofitting its Phoenix facility to include a compaction machine. The new service could help establish Thermo Fluids as a recycling hub for nearby states.

14842 ■ **"Have I Got a Deal For You"** in *Canadian Business* (Vol. 83, October 12, 2010, No. 17, pp. 65)
Pub: Rogers Media Ltd.
Ed: Bryan Borzykowski. **Description:** U.S. automobile market currently has more than three players, providing investors with a number of investment options. The sector is still mired in uncertainty, but people believe that these companies can only grow from this point forward. However, investors should use due diligence before jumping into the market.

14843 ■ **"High-Yield Turns Into Road Kill"** in *Barron's* (Vol. 88, July 7, 2008, No. 27, pp. M7)
Pub: Dow Jones & Co., Inc.
Ed: Emily Barrett. **Description:** High-yield bonds have returned to the brink of collapse after profits have recovered from the shock brought about by the collapse of Bear Stearns. The high-yield bond market could decline again due to weakness in the automotive sector, particularly in Ford and General Motors.

14844 ■ **"Hispantelligence Report"** in *Hispanic Business* (July-August 2007, pp. 18)
Pub: Hispanic Business
Description: Presentation of the Hispanic Business Stock Index shows the current value of fifteen Hispanic companies from January 3 through July 6, 2007. Results of a survey covering Hispanic household spending on new automobiles are also included. Statistical data included.

14845 ■ **"How Much Profit is Enough?"** in *Automotive News* (Vol. 86, October 31, 2011, No. 6488, pp. 12)
Pub: Crain Communications Inc.
Ed: Keith Crain. **Description:** Workers at the big three automobile companies are unhappy about the issues of class wealth, like the high compensations offered to CEOs.

14846 ■ **"Hyannis Mercedes Franchise Sold"** in *Cape Cod Times* (December 2, 2010)
Pub: Cape Cod Times
Ed: Sarah Shemkus. **Description:** Trans-Atlantic Motors franchise has been sold to Mercedes-Benz of Westwood.

14847 ■ **"Hyundai Enters Minivan Market"** in *Globe & Mail* (February 15, 2006, pp. B7)
Pub: CTVglobemedia Publishing Inc.
Ed: Greg Keenan. **Description:** The reasons behind the launch of minivan by Hyundai Auto Canada Inc. are presented.

14848 ■ **"Hyundai's Hitting Its Stride"** in *Barron's* (Vol. 89, July 20, 2009, No. 29, pp. M7)
Pub: Dow Jones & Co., Inc.
Ed: Assif Shameen. **Description:** Hyundai Motors has kept growing by producing better products, enabling it to increase its sales and market share

despite the weaker automotive market. The shares of Hyundai and Kia are poised to rise due to their improved finances.

14849 ■ **"Impressive Numbers: Companies Experience Substantial Increases in Dollars, Employment"** in *Hispanic Business* (July-August 2007)

Pub: Hispanic Business

Ed: Derek Reveron. Description: Profiles of five fastest growing Hispanic companies reporting increases in revenue and employment include Brightstar, distributor of wireless products; Greenway Ford Inc., a car dealership; Fred Loya Insurance, auto insurance carrier; and Group O, packaging company; and Diverse Staffing, Inc., an employment and staffing firm.

14850 ■ **"Japan-Brand Shortages Will Linger Into '12"** in *Automotive News* (Vol. 86, October 31, 2011, No. 6488, pp. 1)

Pub: Crain Communications Inc.

Ed: Amy Wilson, Mark Rechtin. Description: Floods in Thailand and the tsunami in Japan have caused shortages of Japanese-brand vehicle parts. These shortages are expected to linger into 2012.

14851 ■ **"J.C. Watts First Black John Deere Dealer"** in *Black Enterprise* (Vol. 37, November 2006, No. 4, pp. 36)

Pub: Earl G. Graves Publishing Co. Inc.

Ed: Kiara Ashanti. Description: Profile of former Congressman J.C. Watts Jr., a man who grew up in rural America and is the first African American to own a John Deere Dealership.

14852 ■ **"KC Plants Downshift"** in *The Business Journal-Serving Metropolitan Kansas City* (Vol. 27, November 7, 2008, No. 9, pp. 1)

Pub: American City Business Journals, Inc.

Ed: James Dornbrook. Description: Discusses Ford Motor Co. and General Motors' factories in the region; Ford Motor Co. removed the second shift on the F-150 line at the Kansas City Assembly Plant but added a shift to the production of the Ford Escape and Mercury Mariner in an attempt to avoid layoffs. One spokesman for General Motors, however, states that they cannot guarantee that they won't make any production cuts and layoffs in the future.

14853 ■ **"LatinWorks Cozies Up to Chevy in Detroit"** in *Austin Business Journal* (Vol. 31, August 12, 2011, No. 23, pp. A1)

Pub: American City Business Journals Inc.

Ed: Sandra Zaragoza. Description: Hispanic marketing agency LatinWorks opened an office in Detroit to better serve its client Chevrolet and to potentially secure more contracts from its parent company General Motors, whose offices are located nearby.

14854 ■ **"The Lithium Deficit"** in *Canadian Business* (Vol. 82, April 27, 2009, No. 7, pp. 17)

Pub: Rogers Media

Ed: Joe Castaldo. Description: Experts are concerned that there may not be enough lithium available to support the expected rise in demand for the natural resource. Lithium is used in lithium ion batteries, the standard power source for electric and hybrid vehicles. Experts believe that the demand for lithium can only be measured once the technology is out in the market.

14855 ■ **"Local Auto Suppliers Upbeat as Detroit 3's Prospects Trend Up"** in *Crain's Cleveland Business* (Vol. 30, June 8, 2009, No. 22, pp. 1)

Pub: Crain Communications, Inc.

Ed: Dan Shingler. Description: According to the Center for Automotive Research located in Ann Arbor, Michigan, if Detroit automakers can hold their market share, they will end up producing more vehicles as the market recovers.

14856 ■ **"Local Dealers Fear Shortages in Car Supply"** in *Boston Business Journal* (Vol. 29, May 13, 2011, No. 1, pp. 1)

Pub: American City Business Journals Inc.

Ed: Scott Dance. Description: The earthquake and tsunami in Japan are seen to impact the automobile dealers in Baltimore, Maryland. Automobile supply in

the area is seen to decrease dramatically during the summer sales season. Shortage of transmission parts and paint colors is also forecasted.

14857 ■ **"Local Green Technology on Display"** in *Crain's Detroit Business* (Vol. 26, January 18, 2010, No. 3, pp. 1)

Pub: Crain Communications, Inc.

Ed: Ryan Beene. Description: Detroit's 2010 North American International Auto Show put the newest, most innovative green technologies on display showing that the Southeast Michigan automobile industry is gaining traction with its burgeoning e-vehicle infrastructure. Think, a Norwegian electric city-car manufacturer is eyeing sites in Southeast Michigan in which to locate its corporate headquarters and technical center for its North American branch.

14858 ■ **"A Look At Three Gas-Less Cars"** in *Hispanic Business* (Vol. 30, September 2008, No. 9, pp. 90)

Pub: Hispanic Business, Inc.

Ed: Daniel Soussa. Description: Three major car manufacturers, Chevrolet, BMW, and Honda, are giving market leader Toyota competition for the next generation of eco-friendly car. The latest and most advanced of the gasoline-less cars designed by the three firms, namely, the Chevrolet Volt, BMW's Hydrogen 7, and the Honda FCX Clarity, are reviewed.

14859 ■ **"Luxe Men Are In Style"** in *Brandweek* (Vol. 49, April 21, 2008, No. 16, pp. 12)

Pub: VNU Business Media, Inc.

Description: According to a recent survey by Unity Marketing, among 1,300 luxury shoppers found that men spent an average of $2,401 on fashion items over a three-month period which is nearly $1,000 more than women. Men also spring for more luxury items such as vehicles and memberships to exclusive clubs.

14860 ■ **"McIntosh Family Sells Car Dealership"** in *Black Enterprise* (Vol. 38, December 2007, No. 5)

Pub: Earl G. Graves Publishing Co. Inc.

Ed: Brenda Porter. Description: Seattle's McIntosh family sold its Kirkland Chrysler Jeep dealership to private equity firm Cerberus Capital Management. Details of the deal are given.

14861 ■ **"Mercury (1939-2010)"** in *Canadian Business* (Vol. 83, June 15, 2010, No. 10, pp. 27)

Pub: Rogers Media Ltd.

Ed: Steve Maich. Description: Ford's Mercury brand of cars began in 1939 and it was designed by Ford to attract a wealthier clientele. Mercury was mentioned in a 1949 song by K.C. Douglas and was driven in the movie, "Rebel Without a Cause". However, the brand was too expensive for the mass market and not exclusive enough through the years, so Ford Motor Company decided to discontinue the brand in 2010.

14862 ■ **"The New Frontier"** in *Crain's Detroit Business* (Vol. 26, January 18, 2010, No. 3, pp. S025)

Pub: Crain Communications, Inc.

Ed: Richard Truett; Bradford Wernle. Description: Due to the changing consumer preference resulting from new fuel-efficiency standards, concern about climate change and higher gasoline prices, Detroit car designers are beginning to shift focus onto smaller vehicles.

14863 ■ **"New Life for Porsche's VW Dreams"** in *Barron's* (Vol. 89, July 6, 2009, No. 27, pp. 9)

Pub: Dow Jones & Co., Inc.

Ed: Vito J. Racanelli. Description: Porsche and Volkswagen moved closer to a merger after the Qatar Investment Authority offered to take a stake in Porsche. The QIA could take up to a 30 percent stake in Porsche and purchase all Volkswagen calls for up to $6 billion.

14864 ■ **"Next Generation Audi TT Hits Canadian Streets"** in *Canadian Corporate News* (May 16, 2007)

Pub: Comtex News Network Inc.

Description: Audi Canada prepares for the launch of the highly anticipated 2008 Audi TT, recipient of the 2007 World Car Design of the Year due to its contemporary look, powerful engine, and innovative technology, with a multiple touch-point marketing campaign.

14865 ■ **"Nine Sectors to Watch: Automotive"** in *Canadian Business* (Vol. 81, December 24, 2007, No. 1, pp. 47)

Pub: Rogers Media

Ed: Thomas Watson. Description: Forecasts on the Canadian automotive sector for 2008 are presented. Details on contract concessions made by American unions, the industry's Big Three (General Motors, Chrysler, and Ford) operations in Canada, and Canadian Auto Workers demand for higher wages are also discussed.

14866 ■ **"Nissan Unveils Family Concept Car"** in *Marketing to Women* (Vol. 21, February 2008, No. 2, pp. 3)

Pub: EPM Communications, Inc.

Description: Nissan displayed its latest design for the ultimate family vehicle at the 2008 North American International Auto Show in Detroit. The Nissan Forum targets families with older children.

14867 ■ **"No End to the Nightmare; America's Car Industry"** in *The Economist* (Vol. 390, January 3, 2009, No. 8612, pp. 46)

Pub: The Economist Newspaper Inc.

Description: Detroit's struggling auto industry and the government loan package is discussed as well as the United Auto Worker union, which is loathed by Senate Republicans.

14868 ■ **"No Frills - And No Dodge"** in *Crain's Detroit Business* (Vol. 24, September 22, 2008, No. 38, pp. 3)

Pub: Crain Communications, Inc.

Ed: Bradford Wernie. Description: Chrysler LLC is in the middle of a business plan known as Project Genesis, a five-year strategy in which the company will reduce the dealer count by combining its Jeep, Chrysler and Dodge brands under one rooftop wherever possible. Not every dealer will be able to arrange this deal because of the investment required to expand stores in which have low-overhead; many of these stores feel that low-overhead structures are more likely to survive difficult times than the larger stores in which the Genesis consolidation plan intends to implement.

14869 ■ **"O'Reilly Will Soup Up KC Warehouse"** in *The Business Journal-Serving Metropolitan Kansas City* (Vol. 26, August 15, 2008, No. 49)

Pub: American City Business Journals, Inc.

Ed: Rob Roberts. Description: O'Reilly Automotive Inc. plans to construct a 215,000-square foot warehouse in Kansas City. The move is expected to triple the size of the company's distribution center. Other views and information on the planned warehouse construction, are presented.

14870 ■ **"Pain Ahead as Profit Pressure Increases"** in *Crain's Chicago Business* (Vol. 31, May 5, 2008, No. 18, pp. 4)

Pub: Crain Communications, Inc.

Ed: Daniel Rome Levine. Description: Interview with David Klaskin, the chairman and chief investment officer at Oak Ridge Investments LLC, who discusses the outlook for the economy and corporate earnings, particularly in the housing and auto industries, the impact of economic stimulus checks, the weakness of the dollar and recommendations of stocks that individual investors may find helpful.

14871 ■ **"Penske Opens Its First Smart Car Dealership In Bloomfield Hills"** in *Crain's Detroit Business* (Vol. 24, January 21, 2008, No. 3)

Pub: Crain Communications Inc. - Detroit

Ed: Sheena Harrison. Description: Information about Penske Automotive Group's Smart Car addition to its dealership lineup. Smart Car pricing starts at $11,590, with more than 30,000 individuals reserving vehicles.

14872 ■ **"Porsche Raises VW Stake, Makes Bid for Firm"** in *Globe & Mail* **(March 26, 2007, pp. B5)**
Pub: CTVglobemedia Publishing Inc.
Ed: Chad Thomas. Jeremy Van Logan. **Description:** Automobile giant Porsche AG has increased its stake in Volkswagen AG to $54 billion recently. The company is planning a merger by claiming 30%stake under German law.

14873 ■ **"Providing Expertise Required to Develop Microsystems"** in *Canadian Electronics* **(Vol. 23, February 2008, No. 1, pp. 6)**
Pub: CLB Media Inc.
Ed: Ian McWalter. **Description:** CMC Microsystems, formerly Canadian Microelectronics Corporation, is focused on empowering microelectronics and Microsystems research in Canada. Microsystems offers the basis for innovations in the fields of science, environment, technology, automotives, energy, aerospace and communications technology. CMC's strategy in developing Microsystems in Canada is described.

14874 ■ **"Put It In Drive"** in *Entrepreneur* **(Vol. 36, April 2008, No. 4, pp. 31)**
Pub: Entrepreneur Media, Inc.
Ed: Jill Amadio. **Description:** Commercial vehicle models for 2008 are presented. These new models are more user- and environment-friendly. Features and prices of car models and tips to consider before purchasing are presented.

14875 ■ **"Realities May Blur Vision"** in *The Business Journal-Serving Metropolitan Kansas City* **(Vol. 27, September 19, 2008, No. 1, pp. 1)**
Pub: American City Business Journals, Inc.
Ed: Rob Roberts. **Description:** Vision Metcalf is a study by Kansas City that depicts how Metcalf Avenue could look like if redeveloped. Redevelopment plans for the Metcalf corridor include a 20-story mixed-use building on a vacant car dealership. The challenges that the redevelopment plans will face are also analyzed.

14876 ■ **"Reply! Grows at Unprecedented Rate, Rips Beta Off Its Marketplace"** in *Marketing Weekly News* **(September 19, 2009, pp. 149)**
Pub: Investment Weekly News
Description: Profile of Reply.com, a leader in locally-targeted Internet marketing, announced significant growth in terms of revenue, enhanced features and services and new categories since launching its beta Reply! Marketplace platform. Even in the face of an economic downturn, the company has posted over 50 percent revenue growth in the Real Estate and Automotive categories.

14877 ■ **"Ron Carpenter"** in *Crain's Cleveland Business* **(Vol. 30, June 29, 2009, No. 25, pp. 12)**
Pub: Crain Communications, Inc.
Ed: Dan Shingler. **Description:** Profile of Ron Carpenter, owner of Production Tool Company located in Twinsburg, Ohio. Carpenter was forced to lay off half of his staff of 14 workers after the auto business tanked. He believes it was the single most difficult decision he had to make as a manager.

14878 ■ **"Ross: There's Still Money In the Auto Industry"** in *Crain's Detroit Business* **(Vol. 24, January 28, 2008, No. 4, pp. 12)**
Pub: Crain Communications Inc. - Detroit
Ed: Brent Snavely. **Description:** Wilbur Ross, chairman and CEO of WL Ross and Company LLC, a private equity firm, predicts U.S. vehicle sales will fall by about 750,000 in 2008, but continues to look for supplier bargains.

14879 ■ **"Sellers Shift Gears"** in *Crain's Detroit Business* **(Vol. 25, June 22, 2009, No. 25, pp. 3)**
Pub: Crain Communications Inc. - Detroit
Description: Of the 14 new car Chrysler dealerships in the Detroit area who had franchises terminated, Joe Ricci of Dearborn will sell used cars at his new

business called All American Buyer's Service; Lochmoor Automotive Group in Detroit will focus on Mahindra & Mahindra trucks; Mt. Clemens Dodge, Clinton Township is also selling Mahindra & Mahindra trucks; and Monicatti Chrysler Jeep, Sterling Heights, will offer service along with selling used cars.

14880 ■ **"Selling Michigan; R&D Pushed as Reason For Chinese To Locate In State"** in *Crain's Detroit Business* **(Vol. 24, January 14, 2008)**
Pub: Crain Communications Inc. - Detroit
Ed: Marti Benedetti. **Description:** Southeast Michigan Economic Development organizations are working to develop relationships with Chinese manufacturers so they will locate their automotive research and development operations in the state.

14881 ■ **"Slimmer Interiros Make Small Cars Seem Big"** in *Automotive News* **(Vol. 86, October 31, 2011, No. 6488, pp. 16)**
Pub: Crain Communications Inc.
Ed: David Sedgwick. **Description:** Cost-conscious buyers want luxury car amenities in their smaller vehicles, so automakers are rethinking interiors. Style, efficiency and value could be the next trend in vehicles.

14882 ■ **"Small is the New Big in Autos"** in *Globe & Mail* **(February 16, 2006, pp. B3)**
Pub: CTVglobemedia Publishing Inc.
Ed: Greg Keenan. **Description:** The reasons behind the introduction of subcompact cars by companies such as Ford Motor Co. are presented. The automobiles were unveiled at Canadian International Auto Show in Toronto.

14883 ■ **"Smart Car Sales Take Big Hit in Recession"** in *Business Journal-Milwaukee* **(Vol. 28, December 10, 2010, No. 10, pp. A1)**
Pub: Milwaukee Business Journal
Ed: Stacey Vogel Davis. **Description:** Sales of smart cars in Milwaukee declined in 2010. Smart Center Milwaukee sold only 52 new cars through October 2010. Increased competition is seen as a reason for the decline in sales.

14884 ■ **"Solidarity UAW Forever"** in *Crain's Detroit Business* **(Vol. 25, June 1, 2009, No. 22, pp. M001)**
Pub: Crain Communications Inc. - Detroit
Ed: Ryan Beene. **Description:** United Auto Workers union has made it difficult for certain businesses to move to Michigan. Discussion is made about the issues involved and changes that need to be made in the way labor and management do business.

14885 ■ **"The Solution"** in *Entrepreneur* **(Vol. 37, October 2009, No. 10, pp. 71)**
Pub: Entrepreneur Media, Inc.
Ed: Jennifer Wang. **Description:** Ford's 2010 Transit Connect is a compact commercial van developed specifically for small business owners. The compact van offers an integrated in-dash computer system providing a cellular broadband connection.

14886 ■ **"Speed Reader"** in *Crain's Chicago Business* **(Vol. 30, February 2007, No. 6, pp. 58)**
Pub: Crain Communications, Inc.
Ed: Laura Bianchi. **Description:** Interview with Paul Tamraz, president and CEO of Motor Werkes, which carries luxury vehicle lines like BMW, Porsche, and Mercedes-Benz. Tamraz discusses the importance of keeping up to speed with not only U.S. business but what is happening around the world.

14887 ■ **"Steering Toward Profitability"** in *Black Enterprise* **(Vol. 41, December 2010, No. 5, pp. 72)**
Pub: Earl G. Graves Publishing Co. Inc.
Ed: Alan Hughes. **Description:** Systems Electro Coating LLC had to make quick adjustments when auto manufacturers were in a slump. The minority father-daughter team discuss their strategies during the auto industry collapse.

14888 ■ **"Stimulus 'Loser' Won't Build Plant in Mass."** in *Boston Business Journal* **(Vol. 30, November 5, 2010, No. 41, pp. 1)**
Pub: Boston Business Journal
Ed: Kyle Alspach. **Description:** Boston-Power Inc. no longer plans to build an electric vehicle battery plant in Massachusetts after it failed to obtain stimulus funds from the federal government. The company is instead looking to build a lithium-ion battery plant in China and possibly Europe.

14889 ■ **"Stock Car Racing"** in *Canadian Business* **(Vol. 81, September 15, 2008, No. 14-15, pp. 29)**
Pub: Rogers Media Ltd.
Ed: Thomas Watson. **Description:** Some analysts predict a Chapter 11-style tune-up making GM and Ford a speculative turnaround stock. However, the price of oil could make or break the shares of the Big Three U.S. automobile manufacturers and if oil goes up too high then a speculative stock to watch is an electric car company called Zenn Motor Co.

14890 ■ **"Suppliers May Follow Fiat"** in *Crain's Detroit Business* **(Vol. 25, June 15, 2009, No. 24, pp. 1)**
Pub: Crain Communications Inc. - Detroit
Ed: Ryan Beene. **Description:** Italian suppliers to Fiat SpA are looking toward Detroit after the formation of Chrysler Group LLC, the Chrysler-Fiat partnership created from Chrysler's bankruptcy. The Italian American Alliance for Business and Technology is aware of two Italy-based powertrain component suppliers that are considering a move to Detroit.

14891 ■ **"The 'Supply Side' of the Auto Industry"** in *Montly Labor Review* **(Vol. 133, September 2010, No. 9, pp. 72)**
Pub: Bureau of Labor Statistics
Description: Restructuring and geographic change in the automobile industry is discussed.

14892 ■ **"The Tata Way"** in *Business Strategy Review* **(Vol. 21, Summer 2010, No. 2, pp. 14)**
Pub: Wiley-Blackwell
Description: Tata Motors is one of the world's most talked-about companies. Its new ultra-low-cost Nano car is being heralded as the people's car. Vice chairman, Ravi Kant, talks about India and its emerging markets.

14893 ■ **"There's More Upside in Germany"** in *Barron's* **(Vol. 90, September 6, 2010, No. 36, pp. M7)**
Pub: Barron's Editorial & Corporate Headquarters
Ed: Jonathan Buck. **Description:** Germany's stocks have gone up since the beginning of 2010, and investors can still benefit. These stocks will benefit from Germany's stellar economic performance and the relative weakness of the Euro. The prospects of the shares of Daimler and Hochtief are discussed.

14894 ■ **"This Just In"** in *Crain's Detroit Business* **(Vol. 25, June 1, 2009, No. 22, pp. 1)**
Pub: Crain Communications Inc. - Detroit
Description: Three veterans of the auto industry have partnered to create, Revitalizing Michigan, a nonprofit dedicated to help manufacturers improve their processes. The firm is seeking federal, state and private grants to fund the mission.

14895 ■ **"Toyota Marks Record Profit Sales"** in *Globe & Mail* **(February 7, 2007, pp. B10)**
Pub: CTVglobemedia Publishing Inc.
Ed: Martin Fackler. **Description:** The record quarterly sales and earnings reported by Japanese automaker Toyota Motor Corp. are discussed. The company sold 2.16 million vehicles during the quarter while registering 426.8 billion yen in profits.

14896 ■ **"Trillium Turmoil"** in *Canadian Business* **(Vol. 81, December 8, 2008, No. 21, pp. 16)**
Pub: Rogers Media Ltd.
Ed: Jeff Sanford. **Description:** Ontario's manufacturing success in the past was believed to have been built by the 1965 Canada-U.S. automotive pact and

by advantages such as low-cost energy. The loss of these advantages along with the challenging economic times has hurt Ontario's manufacturing industry.

14897 ■ "Uncle Volodya's Flagging Christmas Spirit; Russia" in *The Economist* **(Vol. 390, January 3, 2009, No. 8612, pp. 22)**
Pub: The Economist Newspaper Inc.
Description: Overview of Russia's struggling economy as well as unpopular government decisions such as raising import duties on used foreign vehicles so as to protect Russian carmakers.

14898 ■ *Why GM Matters: Inside the Race to Transform an American Icon*
Pub: Walker & Company
Ed: William J. Holstein. **Released:** 2009. **Price:** $26.00. **Description:** A timely examination of General Motors Corporation and the problems it is facing.

14899 ■ "With Traffic Jam in Super Bowl, Can Any Auto Brand Really Win?" in *Advertising Age* **(Vol. 81, December 6, 2010, No. 43, pp. 1)**
Pub: Crain Communications, Inc.
Ed: Rupal Parekh, Brian Steinberg. **Description:** Car marketers are doubling down for Super Bowl XLV in Arlington, Texas and asking their ad agencies to craft commercials unique enough to break through the clutter and to capture viewers' attention.

14900 ■ "Worry No. 1 at Auto Show" in *Crain's Detroit Business* **(Vol. 24, January 21, 2008, No. 3, pp. 1)**
Pub: Crain Communications Inc. - Detroit
Ed: Brent Snavely. **Description:** Recession fears clouded activity at the 2008 Annual North American International Auto Show. Automakers are expecting to see a drop in sales due to slow holiday retail spending as well as fallout from the subprime lending crisis.

14901 ■ "Xstrata and CAW Get Tentative Deal" in *Globe & Mail* **(February 2, 2007, pp. B3)**
Pub: CTVglobemedia Publishing Inc.
Ed: Andy Hoffman. **Description:** The agreement between Xstrata PLC and Canadian Auto Workers union over wage hike is discussed.

14902 ■ "ZF Revving Up Jobs, Growth" in *Business Courier* **(Vol. 26, November 6, 2009, No. 28, pp. 1)**
Pub: American City Business Journals, Inc.
Ed: Jon Newberry. **Description:** Proposed $96 million expansion of German-owned automotive supplier ZF Steering systems LLC is anticipated to generate 299 jobs in Boone County, Kentucky. ZF might invest $90 million in equipment, while the rest will go to building and improvements.

STATISTICAL SOURCES

14903 ■ *RMA Annual Statement Studies*
Pub: Robert Morris Associates (RMA)
Released: Annual. **Price:** $175.00 2006-07 edition, $105.00. **Description:** Contains composite balance sheets and income statements for more than 360 industries, including the accounting, auditing, and bookkeeping industries. Also contains five years of comparative historical data for discerning trends. Includes 16 commonly used ratios, computed for most of the size groupings for nearly every industry.

14904 ■ *Standard & Poor's Industry Surveys*
Pub: Standard & Poor's Corp.
Released: Annual. **Price:** $3633.00. **Description:** Two-volume book that examines the prospects for specific industries, including trucking. Also provides analyses of trends and problems, statistical tables and charts, and comparative company analyses.

TRADE PERIODICALS

14905 ■ *AIADA News–Auto Dealer*
Pub: American International Automobile Dealers Association (AIADA)
Contact: Lori W. Barnes
Ed: Lori McMahon, Editor. **Released:** Monthly. **Description:** Offers international auto dealers current news on the issues impacting the business.

14906 ■ *Automotive Industries*
Pub: Reed Business Information (New York, New York)
Released: Monthly. **Price:** $88 in North America; $168 other countries airmail. **Description:** Magazine serving original equipment manufacturers in the automotive industry.

14907 ■ *Automotive News*
Pub: Crain Communications Inc. (Detroit, Michigan)
Contact: Keith E. Crain, Editor-in-Chief
E-mail: kcrain@crain.com
Released: Weekly. **Price:** $159 print and digital online; $99 digital/online; $199 data center only; $24.95 1 month, website access only; $14.95 1 week, website access only. **Description:** Tabloid reporting on all facets of the automotive and truck industry, as well as related businesses.

14908 ■ *AutoWeek*
Pub: Crain Communications Inc. (Detroit, Michigan)
Contact: KC Crain, VP/Gp. Publisher
E-mail: kccrain@crain.com
Released: Weekly. **Price:** $29.95 26 issues. **Description:** Magazine for car enthusiasts, includes news coverage and features on vehicles, personalities, and events. Provides coverage of Formula One, CART, NASCAR, and IMSA races.

14909 ■ *Car and Driver*
Pub: Hachette Filipacchi Media U.S. Inc.
Contact: Eddie Alterman, VP/Ed.-in-Ch.
Released: Monthly. **Price:** $10; $16 two years. **Description:** Magazine for automotive enthusiasts.

14910 ■ *FDA Newsletter*
Pub: Ford Dealers Alliance
Ed: **Released:** Bimonthly. **Price:** Included in membership. **Description:** Covers factory-dealer relations focusing on factory encroachment on dealer equity in their own franchise. Discusses fleet subsidies, sales agreements, terminations, add points, warranty administration, and product distribution. Examines individual dealer problems. Recurring features include letters to the editor, news of research, book reviews, reports of meetings, and interviews.

14911 ■ *Hemmings Motor News*
Pub: Hemmings Motor News
Released: Quarterly. **Price:** $56.14 Canada 4th class; $108.52 Canada 2 years, 4th class; $94.24 Canada priority mail; $184.71 Canada priority mail, 2 years; $31.95 4th class; $59.95 two years 4th class; $86.95 priority mail; $169.95 two years priority mail; $163.95 by mail Asia, Africa, Australia or New Zealand; $118.95 by mail Central America. **Description:** Trade magazine on the world's largest antique, classic, vintage, muscle, street rod, and special interest auto marketplace.

14912 ■ *Motor Trend*
Pub: PRIMEDIA Los Angeles
Released: Monthly. **Price:** $10; $18 two years; $22 Canada; $42 Canada 2 years; $34 other countries. **Description:** Consumer automotive publication.

14913 ■ *Road & Track*
Pub: Hachette Filipacchi Media U.S. Inc.
Released: Monthly. **Price:** $10; $16 two years; $48 other countries. **Description:** Automotive magazine.

14914 ■ *Used Car Dealer*
Pub: National Independent Automobile Dealers Association
Ed: Jena Barton, Editor, jena@niada.com. **Released:** Monthly. **Price:** $80 nonmembers. **Description:** Association magazine for dealers who buy and sell used cars.

14915 ■ *Vehicle Leasing Today*
Pub: National Vehicle Leasing Association
Ed: Chris Brown, Editor, chris.brown@bobit.com. **Released:** Quarterly, Winter, Spring, Summer and Fall. **Price:** $39 per year. **Description:** Trade magazine covering the consumer and commercial automobile leasing markets.

14916 ■ *Ward's Auto World*
Pub: Ward's Communications
Contact: Drew Winter, Sen. Ed.
E-mail: dwinter@wardsauto.com
Released: Monthly. **Price:** $69 U.S.A and Mexico; $85 Canada; $104 other countries. **Description:** Business magazine containing news and analysis for middle and upper management within all disciplines of the automotive OEM.

VIDEOCASSETTES/ AUDIOCASSETTES

14917 ■ *Auto Buyer Alert*
Tapeworm Video Distributors
25876 The Old Road 141
Stevenson Ranch, CA 91381
Ph:(661)257-4904
Fax:(661)257-4820
Co. E-mail: sales@tapeworm.com
URL: http://www.tapeworm.com
Released: 1996. **Price:** $14.95. **Description:** Presents car buying tips on when to buy, how to make trade-ins, financing, and more. **Availability:** VHS.

14918 ■ *Get the Upper Hand*
Tapeworm Video Distributors
25876 The Old Road 141
Stevenson Ranch, CA 91381
Ph:(661)257-4904
Fax:(661)257-4820
Co. E-mail: sales@tapeworm.com
URL: http://www.tapeworm.com
Price: $19.95. **Description:** Presents a guideline for buying and leasing a new or used vehicle. **Availability:** VHS.

14919 ■ *The Insider's Guide to Buying and Leasing Automobiles*
Tapeworm Video Distributors
25876 The Old Road 141
Stevenson Ranch, CA 91381
Ph:(661)257-4904
Fax:(661)257-4820
Co. E-mail: sales@tapeworm.com
URL: http://www.tapeworm.com
Released: 1997. **Price:** $19.95. **Description:** Discusses how to save on new car purchases, tricks of the trade, and lease language. **Availability:** VHS.

TRADE SHOWS AND CONVENTIONS

14920 ■ Great American Trucking Show
Sellers Expositions
222 Pearl St., Ste. 300
New Albany, IN 47150
Ph:(812)949-9200
Free: 800-558-8767
Fax:(812)949-9600
URL: http://www.sellersexpo.com
Audience: Truck owners and operators, exempt haulers, company drivers and truck drivers for hire, aftermarket parts purchasers, purchasing agents, mechanics, fleet owner. **Principal Exhibits:** Trucks and related equipment, supplies, and services.

14921 ■ New England International Auto Show
Paragon Group, Inc.
873 Worcester St.
Wellesley, MA 02482
Ph:(781)237-5533
Free: 800-258-8912
Fax:(781)237-0407
Co. E-mail: inquiry@paragonexpo.com
URL: http://www.paragonexpo.com
Released: Annual. **Audience:** General public. **Principal Exhibits:** New model domestic, import, and specialty cars and light trucks, and accessories.

14922 ■ North American International Auto Show
North American International Auto Show
1900 W. Big Beaver Rd., Ste. 100
Troy, MI 48084

Ph:(248)643-0250
Fax:(248)647-0784
Co. E-mail: naiasmail@dada.orr
URL: http://www.naias.com
Released: Annual. **Audience:** General public and trade; automotive analysts, executives, media. **Principal Exhibits:** New automobiles and trucks, concept cars, manufacturer-related displays.

14923 ■ San Diego International Auto Show
Liberty Productions
8170 Adams Drive
PO Box 4097
Hummelstown, PA 17036
Ph:(717)566-6100
Fax:(717)566-7868
URL: http://www.autoshowusa.com
Released: Annual. **Audience:** General public. **Principal Exhibits:** Equipment, supplies, and services.

14924 ■ Service Specialists Association Annual Convention
Service Specialists Association
4015 Marks Rd., Ste. 2B
Medina, OH 44256
Ph:(330)725-7160
Free: 800-763-5717
Fax:(330)722-5638
Co. E-mail: trucksvc@aol.com
URL: http://www.truckservice.org
Released: Annual. **Audience:** Trade-Heavy Duty Aftermarket. **Principal Exhibits:** Exhibits related to truck repair operations, rebuilding departments, individuals who have maintained shop equipment such as hydraulic press or heat treating furnace.

14925 ■ West Virginia International Auto Show
Liberty Productions
8170 Adams Drive
PO Box 4097
Hummelstown, PA 17036
Ph:(717)566-6100
Fax:(717)566-7868
URL: http://www.autoshowusa.com
Released: Annual. **Audience:** Car enthusiasts. **Principal Exhibits:** Hundreds of new model domestic and imported automobiles.

CONSULTANTS

14926 ■ ASC Retail Consulting
10 Iverness Center Pky., Ste. 320
Birmingham, AL 35242-4818
Ph:(205)995-5300
Free: 800-633-4767
Fax:(205)995-5360
Co. E-mail: martincic@hoffman.ds.adp.com
URL: http://www.ascconsulting.com
Contact: Sam Yelverton, Principle
E-mail: martincic@hoffman.ds.adp.com
Scope: Offers management consulting for auto dealers, distributors and manufacturers specializing in service, parts and body shop departments. Industries served: Automotive retail, wholesale and manufacturers. **Publications:** "Competitive and Profitable"; "Controlling Service Expense". **Special Services:** Applied Service Management™; Automated Service Pricing; Customized Solutions.

FRANCHISES AND BUSINESS OPPORTUNITIES

14927 ■ J.D. Byrider
J.D. Byrider Systems, Inc.
12802 Hamilton Crossing Blvd.
Carmel, IN 46032
Ph:(317)249-3000
Free: 800-947-4532
Fax:(317)249-3001
No. of Franchise Units: 123. **No. of Company-Owned Units:** 12. **Founded:** 1989. **Franchised:** 1989. **Description:** Used car sales and finance. **Equity Capital Needed:** $267,550-$1,933,000. **Franchise Fee:** $35,000-$50,000. **Financial Assistance:** Yes. **Training:** Yes.

14928 ■ Rent 'N Drive
Rent 'n Drive Franchising LLC
1440 Plumridge Rd.
Lincoln, NE 68527
Ph:(402)467-4994
Fax:(402)466-3819
No. of Franchise Units: 1. **No. of Company-Owned Units:** 1. **Founded:** 1990. **Franchised:** 1996. **Description:** Used car, van, and truck rentals. **Equity Capital Needed:** $83,000-$189,000, depending on fleet size. **Franchise Fee:** $7,500. **Financial Assistance:** No. **Training:** Yes. Yes.

14929 ■ Thrifty Car Sales Inc.
5310 E 31st St., CIMS 1130
Tulsa, OK 74135
Free: 877-289-2583
Fax:(918)669-2654
URL: http://www.thriftycarsales.com
No. of Franchise Units: 51. **Founded:** 1998. **Franchised:** 1998. **Description:** Deals with car sales. **Equity Capital Needed:** $765,000-$4,000,000. **Franchise Fee:** $35,000. **Royalty Fee:** $110+/vehicle. **Financial Assistance:** Yes. **Training:** Available at headquarters, with ongoing support.

COMPUTERIZED DATABASES

14930 ■ *Automotive News*
Crain Communications Inc.
1155 Gratiot Ave.
Detroit, MI 48207
Ph:(313)446-6000
Free: 800-678-2427
Fax:(313)446-1616
Co. E-mail: info@crain.com
URL: http://www.crain.com
Description: Contains the complete text of *Automotive News*, a weekly newspaper on the automotive industry. Covers news and analyses of production, dealers and dealerships, personnel, service management, law, sales, marketing, advertising, reviews of relevant books, and announcements and reviews of new models. Numeric data from this database is also available in Automotive News Time Series. **Availability:** Online: Crain Communications Inc., LexisNexis Group, ProQuest LLC. **Type:** Full text.

14931 ■ *AutoSite Pro*
Autobytel Inc.
18872 MacArthur Blvd.
Irvine, CA 92612
Ph:(949)225-4500
Fax:(949)757-8920
Co. E-mail: consumercare@autobytel.com
URL: http://www.autobytel.com
Description: Provides the data and reporting capabilities needed by auto professionals for complex vehicle option pricing analysis across all U.S. business people. Supports as a pricing reporting engine designed to increase productivity by retrieving and analyzing attribute information. **Availability:** Online: Autobytel Inc. **Type:** Full text; Numeric; Directory.

14932 ■ *Highway Vehicles Safety Database*
SAE International
400 Commonwealth Dr.
Warrendale, PA 15096-0001
Ph:(724)776-4841
Free: 877-606-7323
Fax:(724)776-0790
Co. E-mail: CustomerService@sae.org
URL: http://www.sae.org
Description: Contains more than 70,000 document summaries (detailed abstracts and bibliographies) of technical papers, journal articles, magazine articles, standards and specifications, Technology books, and research reports relating to highway vehicle safety. Covers topics related to passenger cars, vans, minivans, trucks, buses, and motorcycles, and such safety issues as crashworthiness, stability, vehicle control, human factors, safety equipment, crash impact, occupant protection, collision avoidance, restraint systems, human response, design, testing, modeling, reconstruction, and research. Includes extensive coverage of publications from the United States, Japan, Germany, Italy, the United Kingdom, France, Korea, Brazil, Canada, and other countries.

All information is translated from the original language into English. **Availability:** Online: SAE International; CD-ROM: SAE International. **Type:** Bibliographic.

14933 ■ *Tire Business*
Crain Communications Inc.
1155 Gratiot Ave.
Detroit, MI 48207
Ph:(313)446-6000
Free: 800-678-2427
Fax:(313)446-1616
Co. E-mail: info@crain.com
URL: http://www.crain.com
Description: Contains news, features, articles, and up-to-date industry information for dealers and businesses in the automotive tire industry. Includes daily news headlines, feature articles on automotive service and management issues, and industry brochures and company material. Includes detailed tire market information, including material on the largest marketing groups, retail chains, commercial dealerships, and more. Includes company market share information, customer loyalty details, tire production data, tire markets, and other market data. Includes classified advertisements, job postings, story archives, and more. **Availability:** Online: Crain Communications Inc. **Type:** Full text; Numeric.

COMPUTER SYSTEMS/ SOFTWARE

14934 ■ Black Book, Inc.
Black Book
PO Box 758
Gainesville, GA 30503
Ph:(770)532-4111
Free: 800-554-1026
Fax:800-357-3444
URL: http://www.blackbookusa.com
Description: Available for IBM computers and MS-DOS compatibles. System provides including cost and retail, options, and finance and lease payments. pricing information on cars and light trucks, including cost and retail, options, and finance and lease payments.

14935 ■ F & I Billing System
American Systems Corp.
1632 Denniston Ave.
Pittsburgh, PA 15217-1458
Ph:(412)421-4446
Fax:(412)421-4446
URL: http://americansystemscorp.com/
Price: Contact American Systems for pricing. **Description:** Available for all personal computers. Program for automobile dealers. Calculates monthly payments and prints retail delivery forms.

LIBRARIES

14936 ■ American Automobile Association Research Library
1000 AAA Dr.
Heathrow, FL 32746-5060
Ph:(407)444-7965
Fax:(407)444-7759
Co. E-mail: rinesta@aaasouth.com
URL: http://www.aaasouth.com
Contact: Renaldo Inesta, Div.Mgr.
Scope: Travel guide books; market studies; highway and traffic safety; driver education; automobiles - history, statistics, insurance. **Services:** Interlibrary loan; Library open to researchers with permission. **Holdings:** 10,000 books; 20 VF drawers of pamphlets; reports. **Subscriptions:** 100 journals and other serials.

14937 ■ Crain Communications Information Center
1155 Gratiot Ave.
Detroit, MI 48207
Ph:(313)446-0367
Fax:(313)259-3319
Co. E-mail: detinfo@crain.com
URL: http://www.crain.com
Contact: Corinne M. Young, Info.Ctr.Mgr.
Scope: Automotive; company information. **Services:** Copying; Library not open to the public. **Holdings:**

2000 books; 1000 bound periodical volumes; 300 reports; archival items; microfiche; microfilm. **Subscriptions:** 52 journals and other serials; 13 newspapers.

14938 ■ National Association of Fleet Administrators–Fleet Information Resources Center
125 Village Boulevard
Suite 200
Princeton, NJ 08540
Ph:(609)720-0882
Fax:(609)452-8004

Co. E-mail: firc@nafa.org
URL: http://www.nafa.org
Contact: Joseph Dunne, Dir., Educ.
Scope: Automotive fleet management, leasing, automotive safety programs, alternative fuels, fleet industry laws and regulations. **Services:** Interlibrary loan; copying; Library open to the public by appointment. **Holdings:** 7000 records, including books, manuals, reports, and videotapes. **Subscriptions:** 45 journals and other serials.

14939 ■ UAW-Daimler Chrysler–Technology Training Center–Resource Library (3675)
3675 E. Outer Dr.

Detroit, MI 48234
Ph:(313)369-6169
Fax:(313)369-6111
Co. E-mail: akoroscik@ucntc.org
Contact: Alexandra Koroscik

Scope: Automobile industry and skilled trades. **Services:** Interlibrary loan; copying; Library not open to the public. **Holdings:** 2000 books; reports; standards; manuals. **Subscriptions:** 80 journals and other serials; 7 newspapers.

ASSOCIATIONS AND OTHER ORGANIZATIONS

14940 ■ Specialized Information Publishers Association
8229 Boone Blvd., Ste. 260
Vienna, VA 22182
Ph:(703)992-9339
Free: 800-356-9302
Fax:(703)992-7512
URL: http://sipaonline.com
Contact: Guy D. Cecala, Pres.

Purpose: Aims to further the professional, economic, and organizational interest of members and their employees. Plans include: conducting research and preparing reports; representing members before federal agencies and monitoring legislation; holding seminars and workshops for members. **Publications:** *Directory of Members and Industry Suppliers*; *Hotline* (biweekly); *How To Launch A Newsletter*, *Newsletter Publishers' Guidebook*; *The Ultimate Guide to Newsletter Publishing* .

EDUCATIONAL PROGRAMS

14941 ■ Creating Successful Newsletters
EEI Communications
66 Canal Center Plz., Ste. 200
Alexandria, VA 22314
Ph:(703)683-7453
Free: 888-253-2762
Fax:(703)683-7310
Co. E-mail: train@eeicom.com
URL: http://www.eeicom.com/training

Price: $745.00. **Description:** Covers development of audience profile, understanding publishing goals, writing and editing skills, and publication design. **Locations:** Alexandria, VA.

14942 ■ Writing News
EEI Communications
66 Canal Center Plz., Ste. 200
Alexandria, VA 22314
Ph:(703)683-7453
Free: 888-253-2762
Fax:(703)683-7310
Co. E-mail: train@eeicom.com
URL: http://www.eeicom.com/training

Price: $745.00. **Description:** Covers current techniques for newsletter and news periodical writing, including using more compelling reporting techniques; avoiding common grammar and punctuation errors in condensed writing; formulating dynamic leads and conclusions; understanding and using tone to convey news appropriately; using spoken and printed quotations correctly; checking statistics and logical generalizations; and finding resources for research and story ideas. **Locations:** Silver Spring, MD; and Alexandria, VA.

DIRECTORIES OF EDUCATIONAL PROGRAMS

14943 ■ *Directory of Private Accredited Career Schools and Colleges of Technology*
Pub: Accrediting Commission of Career Schools and Colleges of Technology
Contact: Michale S. McComis, Exec. Dir.
Released: On web page. **Price:** Free. **Description:** Covers 3900 accredited post-secondary programs that provide training programs in business, trade, and technical fields, including various small business endeavors. Entries offer school name, address, phone, description of courses, job placement assistance, and requirements for admission. Arrangement is alphabetical.

REFERENCE WORKS

14944 ■ *Oxbridge Directory of Newsletters*
Pub: Oxbridge Communications Inc.
Released: Annual, Latest edition 2011. **Price:** $995, individuals print version; $1,195, individuals CD-ROM single user; $1,995, individuals print and CD-ROM. **Covers:** Approximately 15,000 newsletters in the U.S. and Canada. **Entries Include:** Publication name, publisher name, address, phone; names of editor and other key personnel; description of contents and types of material used, year founded, frequency, advertising and subscription rates, print method, page size, number of pages. **Arrangement:** Classified by subject. **Indexes:** Title, geographical, publisher.

14945 ■ *Standard Periodical Directory*
Pub: Oxbridge Communications Inc.
Ed: Deborah Striplin, Editor, dstriplin@oxbridge.com. **Released:** Annual, Latest edition January 2011. **Price:** $1,995, individuals print version; $1,995, single issue CD-ROM single user; $2,995, individuals print and CD-ROM. **Covers:** 63,000 magazines, journals, newsletters, directories, house organs, association publications, etc., in the United States and Canada. **Entries Include:** Publication current and former title; publisher name, address, phone; names and titles of key personnel; circulation and advertising rates; description of contents; ISSN, year founded, frequency; subscription rates, print method, page size, number of pages. **Arrangement:** Classified by subject. **Indexes:** Subject, title.

14946 ■ *Ulrich's Periodicals Directory*
Pub: R.R. Bowker L.L.C.
Released: Annual, Latest edition 2010. **Price:** $1,260, individuals Hardcover, 4 volumes. **Covers:** Nearly 200,000 current periodicals and newspapers published worldwide. **Entries Include:** In main list— Publication title; Dewey Decimal Classification number, Library of Congress Classification Number (where applicable), CODEN designation (for sci-tech serials), British Library Document Supply Centre shelfmark number, country code, ISSN; subtitle, language(s) of text, year first published, frequency, subscription prices, sponsoring organization, publishing company name, address, phone, fax, e-mail and website addresses, editor and publisher names; regular features (reviews, advertising, abstracts, bibliographies, trade literature, etc.), indexes, circulation, format, brief description of content; availability of microforms and reprints; whether refereed; CD-ROM availability with vendor name; online availability with service name; services that index or abstract the periodical, with years covered; advertising rates and contact; right and permissions contact name and phone; availability through document deliver **Arrangement:** Main listing is classified by subject; U.S. general daily and weekly newspapers are listed in a separate volume; lists of cessations, online services, and CD-ROM vendors are alphabetical. **Indexes:** Cessations, subjects, title (including variant, former, and ceased titles), ISSN, periodicals available on CD-ROM, online periodical title, refereed serial, and international organization publication title.

TRADE PERIODICALS

14947 ■ *How To Be Your Own Publisher Update*
Pub: Bibliotheca Press
Contact: A. Doyle
Ed: A. Doyle, Editor. **Released:** Annual. **Price:** $12.95, U.S.; $15.95, Canada; $19.95, other countries. **Description:** Acts as a reference for self publishers. Distributed by Prosperity & Profits Unlimited Distribution Services, PO Box 416, Denver, CO, 80201.

14948 ■ *Independent Publisher Online*
Pub: Jenkins Group Inc.
Contact: Jim Barnes, Managing Editor
E-mail: jimb@bookpublishing.com
Released: Monthly. **Description:** Online magazine containing book reviews and articles about independent publishing.

14949 ■ *Newsletter Communications*
Pub: The Newsletter Factory
Contact: Tondra Bowen, President
Ed: **Released:** Quarterly. **Price: Description:** Provides news and information to help professionals use newsletters for effective communications. Scope includes creating, enhancing, and/or improving newsletters of varying types, sizes, and purposes. Also spotlights design, editorial, and production topics.

14950 ■ *The Newsletter on Newsletters*
Pub: Newsletter on Newsletters
Contact: Marlene Jensen, Publisher
E-mail: jensen@newsletterbiz.com
Released: 22/year. **Price:** $275, U.S. and Canada; $295, elsewhere. **Description:** Informs readers about all aspects of the newsletter and specialized information industry. Profiles new newsletters and publishers, reports on mergers and acquisitions in the industry, offers advice on marketing, editing, design, management, and online publishing and marketing.

14951 ■ *Oregon Publisher*
Pub: Oregon Newspaper Publishers Association
Contact: LeRoy Yorgason, Publisher
E-mail: leroy@orenews.com
Ed: David Merrill, Editor, dmerrill@orenews.com. **Released:** Every other month. **Price:** Included in

membership. **Description:** Covers journalism and publishing topics.

14952 ■ *Publishing Executive*
Pub: North American Publishing Co.
Contact: Noelle Skodzinski, Editorial Dir.
E-mail: nskodzinski@napco.com

Released: 10/yr. **Description:** Trade magazine covering current trends in print production of magazines, catalogs, books, direct mail, corporate publishing, and advertising agencies.

VIDEOCASSETTES/ AUDIOCASSETTES

14953 ■ *Introduction to Desktop Publishing*
RMI Media
1365 N. Winchester St.
Olathe, KS 66061-5880
Ph:(913)768-1696
Free: 800-745-5480
Fax:800-755-6910
Co. E-mail: actmedia@act.org
URL: http://www.actmedia.com

Released: 1987. **Price:** $89.95. **Description:** Computer expert and consultant Julie Gomoll explains what desktop publishing is, how it can be used, and who should use it. **Availability:** VHS; 3/4U.

14954 ■ *Introduction to PageMaker*
RMI Media
1365 N. Winchester St.
Olathe, KS 66061-5880
Ph:(913)768-1696
Free: 800-745-5480
Fax:800-755-6910
Co. E-mail: actmedia@act.org
URL: http://www.actmedia.com

Released: 1987. **Price:** $89.95. **Description:** Introduces viewers to Aldus PageMaker 3.0 software capability and operation. Assuming no prior knowledge of publishing or printing, shows how to create a sample four-page newsletter. **Availability:** VHS; 3/4U.

CONSULTANTS

14955 ■ Editorial Code and Data Inc.
814 Wolverine Dr., Ste. 2
Walled Lake, MI 48390
Ph:(248)926-5187
Fax:(248)926-6047
Co. E-mail: monique@marketsize.com
URL: http://www.marketsize.com
Contact: Joyce P. Simkin, Mgr
E-mail: monique@marketsize.com

Scope: Provides data and computer services primarily to the publishing industry, with specialization in statistical data drawn from government sources. Services include data acquisition, analysis, formatting, and typesetting, archiving of computer data on CD-ROM, custom data display, search, and printing software, information brokering services, and related services such as design, writing, and data processing design. Industries served: publishing, in-house printing, non-profit organizations, government agencies, utilities, and manufacturing. **Publications:** "Market Share Reporter"; "Encyclopedia of Products & Industries"; "Economic Indicators Handbook"; "American Salaries and Wages Survey"; "Dun and Bradstreet & Gale: Industrial Handbook"; "Reference American Cost of Living Survey".

14956 ■ Heidelberg Graphics
2 Stansbury Ct.
Chico, CA 95928
Ph:(530)342-6582

Fax:(530)342-6582
Co. E-mail: service@heidelberggraphics.com
URL: http://www.heidelberggraphics.com
Contact: Larry S. Jackson, Owner

Scope: Offers services including scans, disc conversions, layouts, editing and printing for books, catalogs and magazines. Provides the codes on paper, disk, film, embedded in designs, or in variable labeling and personalized printing. Serves private industries as well as government agencies. **Publications:** "Chronicles of the Clandestine Knights: Hyacinth Blue," 2003; "A Book of Thoughts II," 2001; "Historic Shot Glasses: The pre-Prohibition," 1992; "After the War," 1981; "Phantasm," 1980.

14957 ■ The K.S. Giniger Company Inc.
1045 Park Ave.
New York, NY 10028
Ph:(212)369-6692
Fax:(212)269-6692
Co. E-mail: bernicecullinan@verizon.net
Contact: Kenneth Seeman Giniger, President

Scope: Consultants on book publishing to publishers of books, magazines and newsletters, direct sales organizations, government agencies, educational organizations, financial and investment institutions; public relations and advertising agencies. Clients in the United States, Canada, Mexico, England, Denmark, France, Spain, Switzerland, Germany, Israel, Singapore and Australia.

14958 ■ Moseley Associates Inc.
6 Bart Bull Rd.
Middletown, NY 10941
Ph:(212)988-2834
Fax:(212)717-2435
Co. E-mail: pwadams@consultmoseley.com
URL: http://www.consultmoseley.com
Contact: Cameron S. Moseley, Chairman of the Board
E-mail: pwadams@consultmoseley.com

Scope: Management consultants to the publishing industry-commercial and nonprofit-in the United States and international markets. Expertise in publishing areas: books, periodicals and non-print media. Consulting in all aspects of the publishing process: management studies, business planning, organization evaluation, research and development, financial analysis, editorial, marketing, market research, sales, production, warehousing and distribution, order fulfillment and related operations. Also has expertise with organization and operating technology for new publishing and information service enterprises, as well as acquisitions, divestitures, and mergers. Extensive experience in appraisals of books, magazines and learning materials; and of entire publishing firms. Has worked with government agencies. **Publications:** "Is This the End of Publishing? As We Know It," Jun, 2007; "US School Publishing," Apr, 2001; "A Century of Progress," Jun, 2006; "Technology in Publishing: A Century of Progress," Against the Grain, May, 2001; "Why I Don't Read Electronic Journals: An Iconoclast Speaks Out," Sep, 1997; "Post-Traumatic Shock Syndrome, Or, Surviving the Merger," Jun, 2009; "Familiar and Unfamiliar Quotations," Apr, 2009.

14959 ■ Stillman H. Publishers Inc.
21405 Woodchuck Ln.
Boca Raton, FL 33428
Ph:(561)482-6343
Contact: Herbert Stillman, President

Scope: Offers consulting services in the following areas: management, start ups, profit maximization, world wide negotiating, interim management, corporate debt resolution.

FRANCHISES AND BUSINESS OPPORTUNITIES

14960 ■ Coffee News
Coffee News USA, Inc.
120 Linden St.
Bangor, ME 04402-8444

Ph:(207)941-0860
Fax:(207)941-1050
Co. E-mail: bill@coffeenews.com
URL: http://www.coffeenewsusa.com

No. of Franchise Units: 802. **Founded:** 1988. **Franchised:** 1995. **Description:** Weekly publication for distribution in coffee shops and restaurants. **Equity Capital Needed:** $6,000 per franchise, plus a one-time training fee of $2,500 for first franchise. **Franchise Fee:** $8,500. **Financial Assistance:** Visa/MasterCard. **Managerial Assistance:** Newsletter published every two months and full line of products available for purchase. **Training:** Quarterly training sessions, open to all franchisees and personal mentor program.

14961 ■ Disciple's Directory, Inc.
PO Box 100
Wilmington, MA 01887
Free: 800-696-2344
Fax:(978)657-5411

No. of Franchise Units: 6. **No. of Company-Owned Units:** 2. **Founded:** 1984. **Franchised:** 1998. **Description:** Church telephone directories. **Equity Capital Needed:** $7,500. **Franchise Fee:** $7,500. **Financial Assistance:** Yes. **Training:** Yes.

14962 ■ My City Daily
9333 N Meridian St., Ste. 115
Indianapolis, IN 46260
Ph:(317)571-1525

No. of Franchise Units: 3. **No. of Company-Owned Units:** 1. **Founded:** 2006. **Franchised:** 2006. **Description:** Local daily newsletter. **Equity Capital Needed:** $74,200. **Franchise Fee:** $22,900. **Royalty Fee:** None. **Financial Assistance:** No. **Training:** Provides 4 days training at headquarters, 3 days at franchisee's location and ongoing support.

COMPUTERIZED DATABASES

14963 ■ *Daily Brief Services*
Oxford Analytica Ltd.
5 Alfred St.
Oxford OX1 4EH, United Kingdom
Ph:44 1865 261600
Fax:44 1865 242018
URL: http://www.oxan.com

Description: Contains Oxford Analytica's *Daily Brief* Database. Includes six regional daily briefs and two sectoral daily briefs, as well as the Daily Brief World Service. Provides analysis of key social, political, business, economic, and financial events in 140 countries worldwide. Provides interdisciplinary analyses that evaluate complex geopolitical, macroeconomic, and social developments within a coherent political/social/economic global framework. Lets users apply political and economic research to the assessment and management of risks and opportunities. Provides four to five articles assessing the implications of the most important National and International developments each week day with a six month information embargo. Provides four years of historical daily briefs for comparison and analysis of trends and events. Allows users to set up custom information profiles and receive e-mail alerts when relevant material appears. **Availability:** Online: Oxford Analytica Ltd. **Type:** Full text.

14964 ■ *Oxbridge Directory of Newsletters*
Oxbridge Communications Inc.
186 5th Ave.
New York, NY 10010
Ph:(212)741-0231
Free: 800-955-0231
Fax:(212)633-2938
Co. E-mail: info@oxbridge.com
URL: http://www.oxbridge.com

Description: Contains information on more than 15,000 newsletters in more than 250 categories that are published in the United States and Canada. For each newsletter, provides title, publisher, address, editorial description, advertising rates, contact name, circulation, and frequency. Includes coverage of looseleaf publications, bulletins, and fax letters. Corresponds to the print *Oxbridge Directory of Newsletters*. **Availability:** CD-ROM: Oxbridge Communications Inc. **Type:** Directory.

ASSOCIATIONS AND OTHER ORGANIZATIONS

14965 ■ Toy Industry Association
1115 Broadway, Ste. 400
New York, NY 10010
Ph:(212)675-1141
Co. E-mail: info@toyassociation.org
URL: http://www.toyassociation.org
Contact: Bryan Stockton, Chm.
Description: Provides business services to U.S. manufacturers and importers of toys. Manages American International Toy Fair; represents the industry before Federal, State and Local government on issues of importance; provides legal and legislative counsel; conducts educational programs; compiles industry statistics. **Publications:** *American International Toy Fair Official Directory* (annual); *Toy Challenges and Opportunities* (annual).

SOURCES OF SUPPLY

14966 ■ Souvenirs, Gifts & Novelties Magazine—Buyer's Guide Issue
Pub: Kane Communications Inc.
Contact: Scott C. Borowsky, Asst. Ed.
Released: 8/year. **Price:** $40, U.S. (one year); $50, individuals (one year), foreign and Canadian rate. **Publication Includes:** List of 1,000 manufacturers, wholesalers, and importers of souvenirs, gifts, apparel, toys, jewelry novelty, and candle items. **Entries Include:** Company name, address, phone, products, whether firm is manufacturer, wholesaler, or importer. **Arrangement:** Classified by product. **Indexes:** Alphabetical.

TRADE PERIODICALS

14967 ■ The Toy Book
Pub: Adventure Publishing Group Inc.
Contact: Jonathan Samet, Group Publisher
E-mail: jsamet@adventurepub.com
Released: Monthly. **Price:** $48; $200 other countries airmail only; $80 two years; $56 Canada and Mexico; $100 3 years. **Description:** Tabloid for buyers in the toy and hobby industries.

VIDEOCASSETTES/ AUDIOCASSETTES

14968 ■ Gift and Bazaar Projects, Part 2
RMI Media
1365 N. Winchester St.
Olathe, KS 66061-5880
Ph:(913)768-1696
Free: 800-745-5480

Fax:800-755-6910
Co. E-mail: actmedia@act.org
URL: http://www.actmedia.com
Released: 1981. **Description:** Lee Maher shows how to make fun items and novelties, including kitchen witches, woven fabric baskets, decorated kitchen brooms and other imaginative creations. **Availability:** VHS; 3/4U; Special order formats.

TRADE SHOWS AND CONVENTIONS

14969 ■ Boston Gift Show
Urban Expositions
1395 S. Marietta Pkwy., Bldg. 400, Ste. 210
Marietta, GA 30067
Ph:(678)285-3976
Free: 800-318-2238
Released: Annual. **Audience:** Specialty and department store retailers, importer/export firms, distributors, gift shops, mail-order/catalog, houses and boutique. **Principal Exhibits:** Stationery, gourmet products and foods, toys, general gifts, floral items, decorative and personal accessories, souvenirs, jewelry, traditional and contemporary crafts, and tabletop items. Features Handmade and Made in New England sections.

14970 ■ International Association of Fairs and Expositions Trade Show
International Association of Fairs and Expositions
3043 E. Cairo
Springfield, MO 65802
Ph:(417)862-5771
Free: 800-516-0313
Fax:(417)862-0156
Co. E-mail: iafe@fairsandexpos.com
URL: http://www.fairsandexpos.com
Released: Annual. **Audience:** Fair managers, staffs, and board members; carnival owners and staffs; concessionaires; talent and other agencies related to the fair industry. **Principal Exhibits:** Talent agencies, concessionaires, novelties, amusement devices, insurance, ribbons, plaques, attractions, and equipment. Products and services for the fair industry.

FRANCHISES AND BUSINESS OPPORTUNITIES

14971 ■ Precious Prints Baby Art, Inc.
20 Stonepath Cres.
Stittsville, ON, Canada K2S 1S4
Ph:(613)599-7999
Free: (866)907-7999
Co. E-mail: info@preciousprints.ca
URL: http://www.preciousprints.ca
No. of Franchise Units: 2. **No. of Company-Owned Units:** 1. **Founded:** 2004. **Franchised:** 2007. **Description:** Precious Prints Baby Art creates lasting

memories for new parents and grandparents in a unique and wonderful way. Precious Prints are three dimensional impressions of baby's and children's hands and feet in all their tiny perfection. We are offering turn-key franchises; perfect for a stay-at-home parent, or retired couple. **Equity Capital Needed:** $15,500. **Training:** 3 days mandatory training in Ottawa.

14972 ■ Watch It! Inc.
10544B-82 Ave.
Edmonton, AB, Canada T6E 2A4
Ph:(780)435-2824
Free: 877-404-2824
Fax:(780)434-5039
Co. E-mail: partner@watchit.ca
URL: http://www.watchit.ca
No. of Franchise Units: 17. **No. of Company-Owned Units:** 6. **Founded:** 1999. **Franchised:** 2004. **Description:** Watch It! Is a cool and funky retail boutique that offers a wide selection of premium brand name watches, sunglasses and accessories. With its trademarked names, a consistent look and feel across stores, low start-up costs and operating procedures that are polished and efficient, purchasing a Watch It franchise is a sensible investment. **Equity Capital Needed:** $200,000-$350,000. **Franchise Fee:** $33,000. **Training:** Yes.

LIBRARIES

14973 ■ Haystack Mountain School of Crafts Library
PO Box 518
Deer Isle, ME 04627-0518
Ph:(207)348-2306
Fax:(207)348-2307
Co. E-mail: haystack@haystack-mtn.org
URL: http://www.haystack-mtn.org/
Scope: Fine arts, ceramics, weaving, glassblowing, flat glass, jewelry, surface and textile design, wood, blacksmithing, printmaking, papermaking, weaving. **Services:** Library open to the public on a limited basis. **Holdings:** 1000 books. **Subscriptions:** 20 journals and other serials.

14974 ■ Museum of Contemporary Craft Library
724 NW Davis St.
Portland, OR 97209
Ph:(503)223-2654
Fax:(503)223-0190
Co. E-mail: info@museumofcontemporarycraft.org
URL: http://www.museumofcontemporarycraft.org/
Contact: Linda Brower, Treas.
Scope: Ceramics and pottery, weaving and textiles, Pacific Northwest craftsmen, contemporary designers, metalwork and jewelry, contemporary glass, sculpture, woodworking, architecture. **Services:** Library open during Museum hours. **Holdings:** 420 books; 74 bound and 125 unbound periodical volumes.

START-UP INFORMATION

14975 ■ "Bond Hill Cinema Site To See New Life" in *Business Courier* **(Vol. 27, October 29, 2010, No. 26, pp. 1)**
Pub: Business Courier
Ed: Dan Monk. **Description:** Avondale, Ohio's Corinthian Baptist Church will redevelop the 30-acre former Showcase Cinema property to a mixed-use site that could feature a college, senior home, and retail. Corinthian Baptist, which is one of the largest African-American churches in the region, is also planning to relocate the church.

14976 ■ *How to Start a Home-Based Senior Care Business: Develop a Winning Business Plan*
Pub: The Globe Pequot Press
Ed: James L. Ferry. **Released:** January 10, 2010. **Price:** $18.95. **Description:** Everything needed to know in order to start and run a profitable, ethical, and satisfying senior care business from your home. Information covers writing a good business plan, marketing services to families, creating a fee structure, and developing a network of trusted caregivers and service providers.

ASSOCIATIONS AND OTHER ORGANIZATIONS

14977 ■ American College of Health Care Administrators
1321 Duke St., Ste. 400
Alexandria, VA 22314
Ph:(202)536-5120
Fax:(866)874-1585
Co. E-mail: mgrachek@achca.org
URL: http://www.achca.org
Contact: Marianna Kern Grachek, Pres./CEO
Description: Persons actively engaged in the administration of long-term care facilities, such as nursing homes, retirement communities, assisted living facilities, and sub-acute care programs. Administers professional certification programs for assisted living, sub-acute and nursing home administrators. Works to elevate the standards in the field and to develop and promote a code of ethics and standards of education and training. Seeks to inform allied professions and the public that good administration of long-term care facilities calls for special formal academic training and experience. Encourages research in all aspects of geriatrics, the chronically ill, and administration. Maintains placement service. Holds special education programs; facilitates networking among administrators. **Publications:** *ACHCA E-News* (biweekly).

14978 ■ American Health Care Association
1201 L St. NW
Washington, DC 20005
Ph:(202)842-4444
Fax:(202)842-3860
Co. E-mail: hr@ahca.org
URL: http://www.ahcancal.org/Pages/Default.aspx
Contact: Mark Parkinson, Pres./CEO
Description: Federation of state associations of long-term health care facilities. Promotes standards for professionals in long-term health care delivery and quality care for patients and residents in a safe environment. Focuses on issues of availability, quality, affordability, and fair payment. Operates as liaison with governmental agencies, Congress, and professional associations. Compiles statistics. **Publications:** *AHCA Notes* (monthly); *Provider: For Long Term Care Professionals* (monthly).

14979 ■ American Hospital Association
155 N Wacker Dr.
Chicago, IL 60606
Ph:(312)422-3000
Fax:(312)422-4796
Co. E-mail: rich@aha.org
URL: http://www.aha.org
Contact: Richard Umbdenstock PhD, Pres./CEO
Description: Represents health care provider organizations. Seeks to advance the health of individuals and communities. Leads, represents, and serves health care provider organizations that are accountable to the community and committed to health improvement. **Publications:** *AHA News Now* (daily); *Guide to the Health Care Field* (annual); *Hospital Statistics* (annual); *Hospitals and Health Networks* (monthly).

14980 ■ American Medical Directors Association
11000 Broken Land Pkwy., Ste. 400
Columbia, MD 21044
Ph:(410)740-9743
Free: 800-876-2632
Fax:(410)740-4572
Co. E-mail: info@amda.com
URL: http://www.amda.com
Contact: Lorraine Tarnove, Exec. Dir.
Description: Physicians providing care in long-term facilities including nursing homes. Sponsors continuing medical education in geriatrics and medical administration. Promotes improved long-term care. **Publications:** *Caring for the Ages* (monthly); *JAMDA* (9/year); *State Network News* (quarterly).

14981 ■ American Seniors Housing Association
5225 Wisconsin Ave. NW, Ste. 502
Washington, DC 20015
Ph:(202)237-0900
Fax:(202)237-1616
Co. E-mail: dschless@seniorshousing.org
URL: http://www.seniorshousing.org
Contact: David S. Schless, Pres.
Description: Members are engaged in all aspects of the development and operation of housing for older adults, including construction, finance, and management of the housing. Represents the interests of firms participating in seniors housing and has played an integral role in seniors housing advocacy. Focuses on long-term care policy, state regulations, and other issues concerned with this topic. **Publications:** *The Seniors Housing Construction Trends Report*; *Seniors Housing Legal Notes*; *Seniors Housing Research Notes*; *Seniors Housing Statistical Handbook*; *Seniors Housing Update* .

14982 ■ Assisted Living Federation of America
1650 King St., Ste. 602
Alexandria, VA 22314-2747
Ph:(703)894-1805
Fax:(703)894-1831
Co. E-mail: rgrimes@alfa.org
URL: http://www.alfa.org
Contact: Richard Grimes MEd, Pres./CEO
Description: Providers of assisted living, state associations of providers, and others interested or involved in the industry. Promotes the interests of the assisted living industry and works to enhance the quality of life for the population it serves. Provides a forum for assisted living providers to unite, exchange information, and interact. Encourages the development of high standards for the industry. Promotes the concept of assisted living facilities with public and private agencies and other professionals. Works to educate providers and the public and increase national awareness of assisted living. Sponsors speakers' bureau, conferences, educational opportunities, trade show, research & training products. **Publications:** *ALFA Alert* (weekly); *ALFA Executive Portfolio: Inside the Minds of the Leaders in Assisted Living and Senior Housing*; *Assisted Living Executive* (9/year); *Guide to Choosing an Assisted Living Residence* .

14983 ■ Association of Jewish Aging Services
316 Pennsylvania Ave. SE, Ste. 402
Washington, DC 20003
Ph:(202)543-7500
Fax:(202)543-4090
Co. E-mail: info@ajas.org
URL: http://www.ajas.org
Contact: Martin Goetz MBA, Chm.
Description: Represents charitable Jewish homes and nursing homes; retirement and housing units; independent and assisted living, geriatric hospitals, and special facilities for Jewish aged and chronically ill. Conducts institutes and conferences; undertakes legislative activities; compiles statistics. Conducts studies and maintains demographic and other information on Jewish aging. Publishes journals and periodicals on aging. **Publications:** *Journal on Jewish Aging* (semiannual).

14984 ■ Beverly Foundation
1120 Pennsylvania St. NE
Albuquerque, NM 87110
Ph:(505)222-0620
Co. E-mail: info@beverlyfoundation.org
URL: http://www.beverlyfoundation.org
Contact: Don Pearson, Chm.
Description: Aims to enhance the quality of life and care until the last moment of life, thus bettering the well being of older adults, their caregivers, and their families. Engages in research, education and demonstration. Addresses special concerns through programs such as: mobility and transportation within the community; service delivery and care support within institutional and home settings; life enrichment of the body, mind, and spirit for those who live independently

and in institutions. Provides technical and informational assistance to professionals, caregivers, and families. Influences other organizations and groups through communication, collaboration, and limited financial support to program partners. Funds activities through efficient use of its own resources and the contributions of others. .

14985 ■ Center for the Study of Aging of Albany
706 Madison Ave.
Albany, NY 12208
Ph:(518)465-6927
Fax:(518)462-1339
Co. E-mail: iapaas@aol.com
URL: http://www.centerforthestudyofaging.org
Description: Participants include behavioral scientists, educators, gerontologists, physicians, and other health professionals. Promotes education, research, and training; provides leadership in the field of health and fitness for older people. Includes: programs for volunteers and professionals in aging, gerontology, geriatrics, wellness, physical fitness, and mental health; consultant services include adult day care, nutrition, physical and mental fitness, nursing home, housing, and retirement; speakers' bureau. Develops national and international conferences on health, fitness, and prevention. Provides expert assistance in research, institutional and community program development, planning, and organization; offers consultation addressing the development of library resource centers and collections of books on aging. Conducts seminars and offers information and referral services. .

14986 ■ Foundation Aiding the Elderly
PO Box 254849
Sacramento, CA 95865-4849
Ph:(916)481-8558
Free: 877-481-8558
Fax:(916)481-2239
Co. E-mail: caroleh@4fate.org
URL: http://www.4fate.org
Contact: Carole Herman, Pres./Chair
Description: Assists the public with relatives and friends in long-term care nursing homes. Provides awareness of the existence of, and potential for, abuse, neglect, and lack of dignity of the elderly in nursing homes. Initiates action to make improvements. Raises funds to bring about nursing home reform. Offers referrals for senior issues and advocates for legislation. .

14987 ■ Health Industry Distributors Association
310 Montgomery St.
Alexandria, VA 22314-1516
Ph:(703)549-4432
Free: 800-549-4432
Fax:(703)549-6495
Co. E-mail: rowan@hida.org
URL: http://www.hida.org
Contact: Matthew J. Rowan, Pres./CEO
Description: Represents distributors of medical, laboratory, surgical, and other health care equipment and supplies to hospitals, physicians, nursing homes, and industrial medical departments. Conducts sales training, management seminars, and research through the HIDA Educational Foundation. **Publications:** Membership Directory (annual).

14988 ■ LeadingAge
2519 Connecticut Ave. NW
Washington, DC 20008-1520
Ph:(202)783-2242
Fax:(202)783-2255
Co. E-mail: info@leadingage.org
URL: http://www.leadingage.org
Contact: William L. Minnix Jr., Pres./CEO
Description: Works to advance the vision of healthy, affordable and ethical aging services for America. Represents 5,600 mission-driven, not-for-profit nursing homes, continuing care retirement communities, assisted living and senior housing facilities, and community service organizations throughout the U.S. **Publications:** Aging Services: The Not-for-Profit Difference; FutureAge (bimonthly); HCBS Report (monthly); Savings and Solutions (bimonthly).

14989 ■ National Association of Boards of Examiners of Long Term Care Administrators
1444 I St. NW, No. 700
Washington, DC 20005-6542
Ph:(202)712-9040
Fax:(202)216-9646
Co. E-mail: nab@bostrom.com
URL: http://www.nabweb.org
Contact: Randy Lindner, Pres./CEO
Description: State boards responsible for licensing nursing homes administrators. Produces exam to test the competence of nursing home administrators; operates continuing education review service; disseminates information and educational materials on nursing home administration. **Publications:** NAB/AIT Preceptor's Domains of Practice Internship Manual; NAB Study Guide: How To Prepare For the Nursing Home Administrators Examination; RC/AL AIT Preceptor's Domains of Practice Internship Manual; RC/AL Study Guide: How to Prepare for the Residential Care/Assisted Living Administrators Examination .

14990 ■ National Association of Directors of Nursing Administration in Long Term Care
Reed Hartman Tower
11353 Reed Hartman Hwy., Ste. 210
Cincinnati, OH 45241
Ph:(513)791-3679
Free: 800-222-0539
Fax:(513)791-3699
Co. E-mail: bzynurse1@aol.com
URL: http://www.nadona.org
Contact: Sherrie Dornberger, Pres.
Description: Directors, assistant directors, and former directors of nursing in long term care. Aims are: to create and establish an acceptable ethical standard for practices in long term care nursing administration and to promote and encourage research in the profession; to develop and provide a consistent program of education and certification for the positions of director, associate director, and assistant director; to promote a positive image of the long-term health care industry. Encourages members to share concerns and experiences; sponsors research programs. Advocates legislation pertaining to the practice of professional nursing. Maintains speakers' bureau. .

14991 ■ National Association of Professional Geriatric Care Managers
3275 W Ina Rd., Ste. 130
Tucson, AZ 85741-2198
Ph:(520)881-8008
Fax:(520)325-7925
Co. E-mail: kboothroyd@napgcm.org
URL: http://www.caremanager.org
Contact: Kaaren Boothroyd, Exec. Dir.
Description: Promotes quality services and care for elderly citizens. Provides referral service and distributes information to individuals interested in geriatric care management. Maintains referral network. **Publications:** GCM Journal (quarterly); Inside GCM (quarterly);Membership Directory (annual).

14992 ■ National Association of State United for Aging and Disabilities
1201 15th St. NW, Ste. 350
Washington, DC 20005
Ph:(202)898-2578
Fax:(202)898-2583
Co. E-mail: info@nasuad.org
URL: http://www.nasuad.org
Contact: Irene Collins, Pres.
Description: Public interest organization that provides information, technical assistance, and professional development support to State Units on Aging. (A state unit is an agency of state government designated by the governor and state legislature to administer the Older Americans Act and to serve as a focal point for all matters relating to older people.) Serves as organized channel for officially designated state leadership in aging to exchange information and mutual experiences, and to join together for appropriate action on behalf of the elderly. Services include: information on federal policy and program developments in aging; training and technical as-

sistance on a wide range of program and management issues; liaison with organizations representing the public and private sectors. .

14993 ■ National Consumer Voice for Quality Long-Term Care
1001 Connecticut Ave. NW, Ste. 425
Washington, DC 20036
Ph:(202)332-2275
Fax:(202)332-2949
Co. E-mail: info@theconsumervoice.org
URL: http://www.theconsumervoice.org
Contact: Sarah F. Wells MA, Exec. Dir.
Description: National, state and local consumer/citizen groups and individuals seeking nursing home and board and care reform. Seeks to provide a consumer voice at the national, state, and local levels in the development and implementation of the long-term care system. Provides a platform through which groups can keep informed of current movements for change and can make their views known. Conducts seminars and training programs and utilizes a speakers' bureau consisting of advocates from around the country. Serves as a clearinghouse for information on nursing home and board care issues, and publishes consumer books and pamphlets. Maintains speakers' bureau; conducts research and advocacy programs. **Publications:** Avoiding Physical Restraint Use: New Standards in Care; Nursing Home Staffing: A Guide for Residents, Families, Friends, and Caregivers; Nursing Homes: Getting Good Care There (bimonthly); Piecing Together Quality Long-Term Care: A Consumer's Guide to Choices and Advocacy; Quality Care Advocate (quarterly); Where Do I Go From Here? A Guide for Nursing Home Residents, Families, and Friends a Consulting on Attorney .

14994 ■ National Institute on Community-Based Long-Term Care
National Council on Aging
1901 I St. NW, 4th Fl.
Washington, DC 20036
Ph:(202)479-1200
Fax:(202)479-0735
Co. E-mail: info@ncoa.org
URL: http://www.ncoa.org/strengthening-community-organizations
Description: Serves as a unit of the National Council on Aging. Seeks to promote a comprehensive long-term care system that will integrate home-and community-based services, enabling older adults to live in their own homes as long as it is medically, socially, and economically feasible. Serves as information clearinghouse for long-term care professionals. Advocates public policies that support home and community-based services. Maintains speakers' bureau; offers educational sessions; compiles statistics. **Publications:** Care Management Standards; NCOA Networks (bimonthly); Perspective on Aging (periodic).

14995 ■ New England Gerontological Association
1 Cutts Rd.
Durham, NH 03824-3102
Ph:(603)868-5757
Co. E-mail: info@negaonline.org
URL: http://www.negaonline.org
Contact: Dr. Eugene E. Tillock, Exec. Dir.
Description: Promotes the study of the aging process. Conducts educational programs in aging, health service administration and long-term care administration. Computer Assisted Home Study Programs for CEU credits are made available. .

REFERENCE WORKS

14996 ■ "$20M Aimed at Affordable Los Angeles Seniors Housing" in Commercial Property News (March 17, 2008)
Pub: Nielsen Company

Description: Grand Plaza Apartments in Los Angeles, California will be renovated in order to maintain housing for over 400 low-income seniors. Details of plans are included.

14997 ■ "Advancing the Ball" in *Inside Healthcare* **(Vol. 6, December 2010, No. 7, pp. 31)**
Pub: RedCoat Publishing Inc.
Ed: Michelle McNickle. **Description:** Profile of Medicalodges an elder-care specialty company that provides both patient care and technology development. President and CEO of the firm believes that hiring good employees is key to growth for any small business.

14998 ■ "Analysts Not Too Sad Over Gemunder" in *Business Courier* **(Vol. 27, August 6, 2010, No. 14, pp. 1)**
Pub: Business Courier
Ed: James Ritchie. **Description:** Analysts and investors do not understand why Omnicare chief executive officer (CEO) Joel Gemunder suddenly retired after nearly thirty years with the Covington, Kentucky company. They believe that new leadership might invigorate the firm, which provides pharmacy and related services to the long-term care industry.

14999 ■ "Chemed's Vitas Aims to Acquire" in *Business Courier* **(Vol. 27, July 9, 2010, No. 10, pp. 1)**
Pub: Business Courier
Ed: James Ritchie. **Description:** Chemed Corporation's Vitas Healthcare Corporation is looking for smaller nonprofit hospices as it looks to become more streamlined in a tougher reimbursement environment. CFO David Williams syas they want to acquire these hospices as fast as they can integrate them.

15000 ■ "Connecting the Dots Between Wellness and Elder Care" in *Benefits and Compensation Digest* **(Vol. 47, August 2010, No. 8, pp. 18)**
Pub: International Foundation of Employee Benefit Plans
Ed: Sandra Timmermann. **Description:** Employees caring for aged and infirm parents deal with time and financial issues and other stresses. The connection between health status of caregivers and employers' health care costs could be aided by linking programs and benefits with wellness and caregiving.

15001 ■ "Domestic Workers Organize!" in *WorkingUSA* **(Vol. 11, December 2008, No. 4, pp. 413)**
Pub: Blackwell Publishers Ltd.
Ed: Eileen Boris, Premilla Nadasen. **Description:** History of domestic workers in the U.S. is examined. The article challenges the long-standing assumption that these, primarily women of color cleaners, nannies, and elder care providers are unable to organize and assesses the possibilities and limitations of recent organizing efforts. The nature of the occupation, its location in the home, the isolated character of the work, informal arrangements with employers, and exclusions from labor law protection, has fostered community-based, social movement organizing to build coalitions, reform legislation and draw public attention to the plight of domestic workers.

15002 ■ "Elder Care Costs Surge" in *National Underwriter Life & Health* **(Vol. 114, November 8, 2020, No. 21, pp. 25)**
Pub: Summit Business Media
Ed: Trevor Thomas. **Description:** Nursing home and assisted living rates rose from 2009 to 2010, according to MetLife Mature Market Institute. Statistical data included.

15003 ■ "Elder Care, Rx Drugs Reforms Top Zoeller's Agenda" in *Times* **(December 21, 2010)**
Pub: The Times
Ed: Sarah Tompkins. **Description:** Indiana Attorney General Greg Zoeller is hoping to develop a program in the state that will help regulate care for the elderly; freeze medical licenses for doctors involved in criminal investigations; address illegal drug use; and to establish a program to help individuals dispose of old prescription medications easily at pharmacies.

15004 ■ "Elder-Care Seminar to Teach Ways to Avoid Falls" in *Virginian-Pilot* **(November 25, 2010)**
Pub: Virginian-Pilot
Ed: Amy Jeter. **Description:** ResCare HomeCare, a home health services firm, offers free seminars on helping to make residences safer for seniors prone to falling.

15005 ■ "EVMS Gets Grant to Train Providers for Elder Care" in *Virginian-Pilot* **(October 29, 2010)**
Pub: Virginian-Pilot
Ed: Elizabeth Simpson. **Description:** Eastern Virginia Medical School received a federal grant to train health providers in elder care. Details of the program are provided.

15006 ■ "Face Issues if Elder Care, Unemployment Collide" in *Atlanta Journal-Constitution* **(December 26, 2010, pp. G1)**
Pub: Atlanta Journal-Constitution
Ed: Amy Lindgren. **Description:** More issues arise during holiday for families with older members requiring care, including the issue of employment for those doing the caregiving.

15007 ■ "GeckoSystems Reduces Sensor Fusion Costs Due to Elder Care Robot Trials" in *Internet Wire* **(December 14, 2010)**
Pub: Comtex
Description: GeckoSystems International Corporation has been able to reduce the cost of its sensor fusion system while maintaining reliability and performance. The firm's ongoing first in-home elder care robot trials have sparked interest regarding its business model, technologies available for licensing, and joint domestic and international ventures.

15008 ■ *Health Care Careers Directory*
Pub: American Medical Association
Released: Annual, Latest edition 2010-2011. **Price:** $30, individuals Softbound. **Covers:** More than 8,600 health career educational programs in over 82 health occupations at 2,700 sponsoring institutions. **Entries Include:** Occupational descriptions, employment characteristics, and information on education programs, such as length, curriculum, and prerequisites. **Arrangement:** Classified by occupation, then geographical. **Indexes:** Institution name, program name.

15009 ■ "New Elder Care Center to Focus on Residents with Failing Memories" in *Tulsa World* **(November 30, 2010)**
Pub: World Publishing
Ed: Robert Evatt. **Description:** People with Alzheimer's disease and other mental disorders require specialized care. Constant Care Management Company runs 'memory care' centers designed for the elderly with such conditions.

15010 ■ "Novi Eyed for $11 Million, 100-Bed Medilodge" in *Crain's Detroit Business* **(Vol. 25, June 1, 2009, No. 22, pp. M032)**
Pub: Crain Communications Inc. - Detroit
Description: Novi, Michigan is one of the cities being considered for construction of a new 110-bed skilled nursing facility. Details of the project are included.

15011 ■ "Nursing Home Group Put on the Block" in *Globe & Mail* **(February 23, 2006, pp. B1)**
Pub: CTVglobemedia Publishing Inc.
Ed: Elizabeth Church. **Description:** The reasons behind the decision of Exetendicare Inc. to go for sale are presented.

15012 ■ "Priority: Business For Sale" in *Inc.* **(January 2008, pp. 28)**
Pub: Gruner & Jahr USA Publishing
Ed: Elaine Appleton Grant. **Description:** Profile of an employment agency providing registered nurses to hospitals and nursing homes. The company began as an temporary placement agency for IT professionals and is now for sale at the asking price of $4.2 million.

15013 ■ *Provider—LTC Buyers' Guide Issue*
Pub: American Health Care Association
Released: Annual, August; latest edition 2008. **Price:** $48, individuals; $61, Canada and Mexico; $85, other countries. **Publication Includes:** List of several hundred manufacturers and suppliers of products and services to the long-term care industry. **Entries Include:** Company name, address, phone, products or services. **Arrangement:** Classified by product or service. **Indexes:** Product/service.

15014 ■ "Renewed Vision" in *Hawaii Business* **(Vol. 54, August 2008, No. 2, pp. 49)**
Pub: Hawaii Business Publishing
Ed: Jason Ubay. **Description:** Saint Francis Healthcare System of Hawaii, ranked 81 in Hawaii's top 250 companies for 2008, has been rebranding to focus on senior community healthcare and sold some of its operations, which explains the decline in gross sales from $219.5M in 2006 to $122.7M in 2007. The system's senior services and home hospice service expansion are provided.

15015 ■ "Silver Dollars" in *Small Business Opportunities* **(September 2008)**
Pub: Entrepreneur Media Inc.
Description: Profile of Always Best Care Senior Services, a franchise created by Michael Newman, which offers non-medical In-Home Care, Personal Emergency Response Systems, and Assisted Living Placement Services to seniors; the company offers franchisees the opportunity to fill what is oftentimes a void for the seniors and their families in the community.

15016 ■ "Small Is Best, Says Housing Officials" in *Business First Buffalo* **(November 16, 2007, pp. 1)**
Pub: American City Business Journals, Inc.
Ed: Tracey Drury. **Description:** Nonprofit organizations in some parts of the U.S. are moving senior citizens from larger institutions into smaller housing. The benefits of smaller housing for the elderly are evaluated.

15017 ■ "They've Fallen, But They Can Get Up" in *Barron's* **(Vol. 88, March 10, 2008, No. 10, pp. 43)**
Pub: Dow Jones & Company, Inc.
Ed: Kopin Tan. **Description:** Shares of senior housing companies present buying opportunities to investors because of their low prices. Companies such as Brookdale Senior Living are not as dependent on housing prices but have suffered declines in share prices.

15018 ■ "Trisun Healthcare Eager to Add Centers" in *Austin Business JournalInc.* **(Vol. 28, August 22, 2008, No. 23, pp. 1)**
Pub: American City Business Journals
Ed: Kate Harrington. **Description:** Austin-based nursing and rehabilitation centers operator Trisun Healthcare plans to build more facilities as part of a growth strategy that can expand beyond Texas. Trisun has 16 facilities along the corridor from San Antonio to Temple, and projects to have three more in Texas in 2008.

15019 ■ "VA Seeking Bidders for Ft. Howard" in *Baltimore Business Journal* **(Vol. 28, June 25, 2010, No. 7, pp. 1)**
Pub: Baltimore Business Journal
Ed: Daniel J. Sernovitz. **Description:** The Veterans Affairs Maryland Health Care Systems has requested proposals from developers to build a retirement community at Fort Howard in Baltimore County. The historic site, which has about 36 mostly vacant buildings, could become the home to hundreds of war veterans. Details of the proposed development are discussed.

STATISTICAL SOURCES

15020 ■ *RMA Annual Statement Studies*
Pub: Robert Morris Associates (RMA)
Released: Annual. **Price:** $175.00 2006-07 edition, $105.00. **Description:** Contains composite balance sheets and income statements for more than 360 industries, including the accounting, auditing, and bookkeeping industries. Also contains five years of comparative historical data for discerning trends. Includes 16 commonly used ratios, computed for most of the size groupings for nearly every industry.

15021 ■ *Standard & Poor's Industry Surveys*
Pub: Standard & Poor's Corp.
Released: Annual. **Price:** $3633.00. **Description:** Two-volume book that examines the prospects for specific industries, including trucking. Also provides analyses of trends and problems, statistical tables and charts, and comparative company analyses.

TRADE PERIODICALS

15022 ■ Abbeyfield Houses Society of Canada Newsletter
Pub: Abbeyfield Houses Society of Canada

Ed: Robert McMullan, Editor. **Released:** Quarterly. **Description:** Reports on news of Abbeyfield Houses Society of Canada, a provider of care and companionship for the elderly. Also features articles related to aging, housing, and lifestyle in Canada and internationally. Recurring features include letters to the editor, and columns titled News of Local Societies and Bits 'n Bites.

15023 ■ Abstracts in Social Gerontology
Pub: EBSCO Publishing Inc.

Released: Quarterly. **Price:** $685 institutions print only; $179 print only; $189 institutions single print issue; $58 single print issue. **Description:** Annotated bibliography of books, journal articles, and documents relevant to social gerontology.

15024 ■ AHCA Notes
Pub: American Health Care Association

Ed: Nathan Childs, Editor, nchilds@ahca.org. **Released:** Monthly, 12/year. **Price:** Included in membership. **Description:** Presents information on nursing homes, assisted living, and residential care facilities. Covers legislation on prescription drug prices, nurse assistant training, certification enforcement, Medicare/Medicaid and long term care requirements, and legal activities.

15025 ■ The Capsule Newsletter
Pub: Children of Aging Parents
Contact: Lorraine Sailor

Ed: Lorraine Sailor, Editor. **Released:** Bimonthly. **Price:** Included in membership; Free; $100. **Description:** Contains articles and informational notices on the concerns and issues of elderly persons and those who care for them. Provides organizations, resources, and services to help caregivers of elderly.

15026 ■ Clinical Gerontologist
Pub: Routledge Journals
Contact: Daniel L. Segal PhD, Assoc. Ed.

Released: Quarterly. **Price:** $108 online; $113 print & online. **Description:** Contains practical information and research on assessment and intervention of mental health needs of aged patients.

15027 ■ Contemporary Long Term Care
Pub: Leisure Publications Inc.

Released: Monthly, 11/yr. **Price:** $80; $95 Canada and Mexico; $130 two years; $129 other countries. **Description:** Magazine covering the long term healthcare trade.

15028 ■ Elderly Health Services Letter
Pub: Health Resources Publishing
Contact: Beth-Ann Kerber, Managing Editor

Released: Monthly. **Price:** $147, individuals. **Description:** Predicts future trends in hospital based health care services for the elderly.

15029 ■ Housing for Seniors Report
Pub: CD Publications
Contact: Carol Solomon

Ed: Marcella Kogan, Editor. **Released:** Monthly. **Price:** $297/year. **Description:** Provides news and practical suggestions concerning the production, management, marketing and other business aspects of housing for the elderly. Coverage includes nursing homes, apartment projects, and retirement communities; also government-operated programs. Recurring features include news of research.

15030 ■ Long Term Care
Pub: Ontario Long Term Care Association
Contact: Michael Murton
E-mail: murton@murtonco.com

Released: Quarterly. **Price:** $15 Canada; $27 Canada two years; $21; $33 two years; $4.95 single issue. **Description:** Professional magazine for long term care owners, managers, and staff.

15031 ■ Physical Medicine and Rehabilitation Clinics of North America
Pub: Elsevier
Contact: Prof. George H. Kraft MD, Consulting Ed.
Released: Quarterly. **Price:** $540 institutions, other countries; $345 other countries; $175 students, other countries; $414 institutions; $122 students; $280 Canada; $230; $175 students, Canada; $540 institutions, Canada. **Description:** Journal for long-term care professionals.

15032 ■ Quality Care Advocate
Pub: The National Consumer Voice for Quality Long-Term Care
Released: Bimonthly. **Price:** Included in membership; $45, nonmembers. **Description:** Reports on current efforts at federal, state, and local levels to achieve better quality nursing homes and other long-term care facilities in the U.S. Discusses current legislation and regulations, summarizes current litigation proceedings and past court cases related to long term care, and evaluates the effectiveness of various direct advocacy campaigns. Recurring features include news of research and notices of publications available.

15033 ■ Topics in Geriatric Rehabilitation TGR
Pub: Lippincott Williams & Wilkins
Ed: Carole B. Lewis, PhD, Editor. **Released:** Quarterly. **Price:** $105.49; $395.49 institutions; $197.73 other countries; $536.73 institutions, other countries. **Description:** Journal presenting clinical, basic, and applied research, as well as theoretical information, for the health care professional practicing in the area of geriatric rehabilitation.

VIDEOCASSETTES/ AUDIOCASSETTES

15034 ■ Activities of Daily Living
AJN Video Library/Lippincott Williams & Wilkins
American Journal of Nursing
345 Hudson St., 16th Fl.
New York, NY 10014
Ph:(212)886-1200
Free: 800-256-4045
Fax:(212)886-1276
Co. E-mail: info@nursingcenter.com
URL: http://www.nursingcenter.com
Price: $285.00. **Description:** Part of the Functional Assessment of the Elderly nursing training series. Teaches methods on assessing an elderly client's functions as changed by age and pathophysiology and how to use assessment data to plan appropriate nursing interventions. Contains information on activities of daily life, including eating, ambulating, toileting, grooming, climbing stairs, shopping, keeping house, interacting with others, and traveling. Also discusses how the cardiovascular, respiratory, neuromuscular, gastrointestinal, and genitourinary systems affect daily functions. Includes study guide. Approved for CE credit. **Availability:** VHS.

15035 ■ Advance Directives and the Elderly: Making Decisions about Treatment Limitations
University of Maryland
Video Press
100 N. Greene St., Ste. 300
Baltimore, MD 21201-1082
Ph:(410)706-5497
Free: 800-328-7450
Fax:(410)706-8471
Co. E-mail: videopressmail@som.umaryland.edu
URL: http://www.videopress.org
Price: $150.00. **Description:** Discusses with three nursing home residents their wishes to limit treatment. Covers artificial feeding, CPR, and use of antibiotics. **Availability:** VHS.

15036 ■ Agitation, Aggression and Violence
University of Maryland
Video Press
100 N. Greene St., Ste. 300
Baltimore, MD 21201-1082
Ph:(410)706-5497
Free: 800-328-7450

Fax:(410)706-8471
Co. E-mail: videopressmail@som.umaryland.edu
URL: http://www.videopress.org
Price: $150.00. **Description:** Part of the Nursing Home Mental Health Series. Details verbal and physical aggression in the nursing home, outlining an approach that stresses proper assessment, early recognition, specific interventions, and avoidance of future episodes. **Availability:** VHS.

15037 ■ Alleviating Stress Associated with Nursing Home Admission
University of Maryland
Video Press
100 N. Greene St., Ste. 300
Baltimore, MD 21201-1082
Ph:(410)706-5497
Free: 800-328-7450
Fax:(410)706-8471
Co. E-mail: videopressmail@som.umaryland.edu
URL: http://www.videopress.org
Price: $300.00. **Description:** Examines the anxiety and stress patients and their families face when admission into a nursing home is necessary. Three residents discuss their fears and anxieties prior to being admitted into the nursing home and how they have adjusted their lives. Emphasis is placed on how staff can ease the transition. **Availability:** VHS.

15038 ■ Alzheimer's Disease: Effects on Communication
American Society for Training and Development (ASTD)
1640 King St.
Box 1443
Alexandria, VA 22313-2043
Ph:(703)683-8100
Free: 800-628-2783
Fax:(703)683-8103
URL: http://www.astd.org
Released: 1986. **Price:** $250.00. **Description:** A program for professionals about the signs and symptoms of Alzheimer's disease and how to determine the nature of communicative changes in patients. **Availability:** VHS; 3/4U.

15039 ■ The Business of Caring
Victoria International Corp.
1 Harts Cove, PO Box 14
New Castle, NH 03854
Ph:(603)436-1067
Fax:(603)433-4204
URL: http://www.victoriainternationalcorp.com
Released: 1987. **Description:** A series of programs for nursing professionals about patient care, consideration and relation to the family. Each program has nine episodes. **Availability:** VHS; 3/4U.

15040 ■ Comprehensive Care of Elderly
Lippincott Williams & Wilkins
Department of Audiovisual Media
530 Walnut St.
Philadelphia, PA 19106
Ph:(215)521-8300
Free: 800-638-3030
Fax:(215)521-8902
Co. E-mail: info@lww.com
URL: http://www.lww.com
Released: 1986. **Description:** A nurse-training series for the care of elderly patients. **Availability:** VHS; 3/4U.

15041 ■ Coping and Home Safety Tips for Caregivers of the Elderly
Jefferson Area Board for Aging
674 Hillsdale Dr., Ste. 9
Charlottesville, VA 22901
Ph:(434)817-5222
Fax:(434)817-5230
Co. E-mail: jabacares@gmail.com
URL: http://www.jabacares.org
Released: 1989. **Price:** $89.95. **Description:** Designed for family caregivers and home care workers, this videotape demonstrates ways in which to help older people with chronic physical and mental dysfunction in their daily activities. Includes a manual. **Availability:** VHS.

15042 ■ *Foundations in Long-Term Care*
University of Maryland
Video Press
100 N. Greene St., Ste. 300
Baltimore, MD 21201-1082
Ph:(410)706-5497
Free: 800-328-7450
Fax:(410)706-8471
Co. E-mail: videopressmail@som.umaryland.edu
URL: http://www.videopress.org
Price: $1000.00. **Description:** Module 1 of the Elder-Core Training Modules series. Contains four sessions: One East—Portrait of a Nursing Home; Understanding Your Elderly Patient; Caring for Disordered Behavior in the Nursing Home; and Working with Families in Long-Term Care. **Availability:** VHS.

15043 ■ *A Germs' Guide to Hitchhiking: Infection Control Rule of Thumb*
Moonbeam Publications, Inc.
PO Box 5150
Traverse City, MI 49696
Ph:(616)922-0533
Free: 800-445-2391
Fax:800-334-9789
Co. E-mail: custserv@moonbeampublications.com
URL: http://www.moonbeampublications.com
Released: 1987. **Price:** $250.00. **Description:** A program for hospital staff on controlling the spread of infection in a hospital. Discusses the six conditions necessary for infections to spread. **Availability:** VHS; 3/4U.

15044 ■ *The More We Get Together*
Filmakers Library, Inc.
124 E. 40th St.
New York, NY 10016
Ph:(212)808-4980
Free: 800-555-9815
Fax:(212)808-4983
URL: http://www.filmakers.com
Released: 1986. **Description:** Provides information on working with very old, disoriented, nursing home patients. **Availability:** VHS; 3/4U.

TRADE SHOWS AND CONVENTIONS

15045 ■ American Association of Homes and Services for the Aging Convention
American Association of Homes and Services for the Aging
2519 Connecticut Ave. NW
Washington, DC 20008
Ph:(202)783-2242
Fax:(202)783-2255
Co. E-mail: info@aahsa.org
Released: Annual. **Audience:** Professionals, administrators, and invited guests. **Principal Exhibits:** Equipment, supplies, and services for housing and long-term care facilities for the aged.

15046 ■ American Health Care Association Annual Convention and Exposition
American Health Care Association
1201 L St. NW
Washington, DC 20005
Ph:(202)842-4444
Fax:(202)842-3860
URL: http://www.ahca.org
Released: Annual. **Audience:** Long-term care and nursing home owners and administrators. **Principal Exhibits:** Supplies for the long-term healthcare industry. **Dates and Locations:** 2011 Sep 18-21, Las Vegas, NV; 2012 Oct 07-10, Tampa, FL; 2013 Oct 06-09, Phoenix, AZ.

15047 ■ Senior Housing South
Merchandise Mart Properties Inc.
222 Merchandise Mart, Ste. 470
Chicago, IL 60654
Free: 800-677-6278
URL: http://www.merchandisemart.com
Released: Annual. **Principal Exhibits:** Equipment, supplies, and services for the planning, building, design and management of long-term care facilities.

CONSULTANTS

15048 ■ Charlotte Eliopoulos Considine, PhD
11104 Glen Arm Rd.
Glen Arm, MD 21057
Ph:(410)668-7055
Free: 800-690-1150
Fax:(410)668-7718
Scope: Offers holistic-focused consultation and educational programs to long-term care facilities and geriatric care agencies. Services include workshop presentation, assistance in integrating alternative complementary therapies, and planning and development of new programs. Industries served: long-term care facilities, assisted living, and hospitals. **Publications:** "Gerontological Nursing, 5th edition," Lippincott, 2001; "Nursing Administration Manual for LTCF, 5th edition," Health Education Network, 2001; "Manual of Gerontologic Nursing," Mosby, 1995; "Integrating Alternative and Conventional Care: Holistic Care of Chronic Conditions," Mosby; "Relationship of Faith and Healing". **Seminars:** Alternative therapies in LTC, Holistic Chronic Care Nursing, Gerontological Nursing Update; LTC Clinical and Managerial Updates; Geriatric Care.

15049 ■ Diversified Health Resources Inc.
875 N Michigan Ave., Ste. 3250
Chicago, IL 60611-1901
Ph:(312)266-0466
Fax:(312)266-0715
Contact: Andrea R. Rozran, President
E-mail: yablon@ix.netcom.com
Scope: Offers health care consulting for hospitals, nursing homes including homes for the aged, and other health related facilities and companies. Specializes in planning and marketing. Also conducts executive searches for top level health care administrative positions. Serves private industries as well as government agencies. **Publications:** "City Finance".

15050 ■ Helen Tredway
1638 Rd. W
RR 1
Neosho Rapids, KS 66864-8700
Ph:(620)343-3637
Fax:(620)342-8175
Scope: Nursing consultant to nursing homes. Offers services in service education. **Seminars:** Meeting the Needs of the Nursing Home Nurse; Adult Day Care.

15051 ■ Nutrition Entrepreneurs
9212 Delphi Rd. SW
Olympia, WA 98512
Ph:(360)956-1367
Free: 800-861-9406
Fax:(360)956-1367
Co. E-mail: nedpg@aol.com
URL: http://www.nedpg.org
Contact: Vanessa Cavallaro, Director
Scope: Serves as the clearinghouse for nutrition entrepreneurs throughout the U.S. and Canada. Members provide consultation to a variety of clients which include consumers, medical clinics, physician's offices, outpatient departments of hospitals, restaurants, corporations, long-term care facilities, television, radio-television-print media, supermarkets, and food companies. In addition, many members produce and market nutrition related products. Industries served: Acute and long term health care settings, all forms of media, consumer and professional education, corporate wellness, entrepreneurial production and marketing of products for consumers and/or professionals. **Publications:** "Time is Money: Finding Balance in Your Life," 2007; "The Future is Now: Focusing Your Vision," 2007; "Financial Planning 101," 2006; "Marketing Your Private Practice for Dietitians"; "Drawing the Line on Calories, Carbs, and Fat"; "Is Your Personality Type Making You Fat?". **Seminars:** Public Policy Workshop, 2009; Thriving in a Virtual Business Landscape: FNCE 2007; NE Teleconferences 2007.

15052 ■ Professional Healthcare Associates Inc.
422 Morris Ave., Ste. 1
Long Branch, NJ 07740
Ph:(732)229-4545

Free: 800-634-2498
Fax:(732)229-9647
Co. E-mail: czagury@vistapubl.com
Contact: John J. Barney, Principle
E-mail: czagury@vistapubl.com
Scope: Offers health care consulting services in the areas of geriatric service development; grant funding research, development and application preparation; and system development and strategic planning for nursing. Additional work in education and training for health care professionals in management training, clinical areas, and writing skills. Other services include manuscript development, editing, publishing and marketing of books, journals and articles related to health care, human services and women's issues. Industries served: health care, long term care, human services, and municipal government agencies. **Publications:** "Nurse Entrepreneur Building the Bridge of Opportunity".

15053 ■ Protection Management Associates Inc.
8632 E Sells Dr., Ste. 302
Scottsdale, AZ 85251-2927
Ph:(480)949-5637
Fax:(602)994-0493
Contact: Loren E. Newland, President
Scope: Provides litigation support and expert witness services to corporations and facilities, designed to limit claims of negligence with respect to security adequacy. Performs security management assessments and audits designed to evaluate effectiveness of security design and administration. Industries served: hotels, hospitals, apartment houses, nursing homes, casinos and resorts, and government agencies. **Publications:** "Hotel Protection Management: the Inn keepers Guide to Guest Protection and Reasonable Care".

15054 ■ Sarah G. Burger
3403 Woodley Rd. NW
Washington, DC 20016-5030
Ph:(202)966-3025
Co. E-mail: sgburger@rcu.com
Contact: Sarah G. Burger, President
E-mail: sgburger@rcu.com
Scope: Nursing consultant in management and supervision of long-term patient care facilities. Works with individuals and families making decisions about the combination of services needed for long-term care in the community or in institutions. **Seminars:** Chemical and Physical Restraint Reduction; Working with the Minimum DataSet.

FRANCHISES AND BUSINESS OPPORTUNITIES

15055 ■ Age Advantage Home Care Franchising Inc.
9461 Grossmont Summit Dr., Ste. E
La Mesa, CA 91941
Ph:(619)660-8881
Free: 877-433-0141
Fax:(619)660-8882
No. of Franchise Units: 1. **No. of Company-Owned Units:** 1. **Founded:** 1998. **Franchised:** 2006. **Description:** In-home senior care. **Equity Capital Needed:** $36,500-$67,200. **Franchise Fee:** $24,900. **Royalty Fee:** 3%. **Financial Assistance:** Limited third party financing available.

15056 ■ Home Instead Senior Care
Home Instead, Inc.
13323 California St.
Omaha, NE 68154
Ph:(402)498-4466
Free: 888-484-5759
Fax:(402)498-5757
Co. E-mail: franinfo@homeinstead.com
URL: http://www.homeinstead.com
No. of Franchise Units: 587. **No. of Company-Owned Units:** 1. **Founded:** 1994. **Franchised:** 1995. **Description:** Non-medical companionship and homecare services for elderly people. **Equity Capital**

Needed: $55,000-$70,000. **Franchise Fee:** $39,000. **Financial Assistance:** No. **Training:** Pre-training program, 1 week initial training, and posttraining field visits.

COMPUTERIZED DATABASES

15057 ■ *Consumer InSite*
Thomson Reuters
610 Opperman Dr.
Eagen, MN 55122
Free: 800-477-4300
Co. E-mail: gale.contentlicensing@cengage.com
URL: http://www.insite2.gale.com
Description: Focuses on consumer behavior, political opinion, contemporary lifestyles, leisure activities, and trends in popular culture. Provides the full text and summaries from more than 350 widely read North American newsstand titles and specialty magazines; derived from Magazine Database. Contains approximately 600,000 articles, including entertainment reviews of books, films, video, theatre, concerts, musical recordings, hotels, and restaurants, consumer buyer's guides, columns, editorials, product evaluations, biographies, speeches, interviews, and obituaries. **Availability:** Online: Thomson Reuters. **Type:** Full text.

15058 ■ *Health & Wellness InSite*
Thomson Reuters
610 Opperman Dr.
Eagen, MN 55122
Free: 800-477-4300
Co. E-mail: gale.contentlicensing@cengage.com
URL: http://www.insite2.gale.com
Description: Contains complete information about health, medicine, fitness, and nutrition. Provides access to 170 of the world's leading professional and consumer health publications, including *The Lancet* and *Nutrition Today;* 550 health and medical pamphlets; 200,000 health-related articles from more than 3000 other publications; and 1800 overviews of different diseases and medical conditions published by Clinical Reference Systems, Ltd. Includes six medical reference books: *Columbia University College of Physicians & Surgeons Complete Home Medical Guide; Mosby's Medical, Nursing, and Allied Health Dictionary; Consumer Health Information Source Book; The People's Book of Medical Tests; USP DI-Vol. II Advice for the Patient; Drug Information in Lay Language;* and *The Complete Directory for People With Chronic Illness..* Allows searches by article title, article type, author, company name, person discussed in the article, publication name, publication date range, publication type, target audience, ticker symbol, words in the title, and words that appear anywhere in the article. **Availability:** Online: Thomson Reuters. **Type:** Full text.

15059 ■ *State Health Care Regulatory Developments*
The Bureau of National Affairs Inc.
1801 S Bell St.
Arlington, VA 22202
Free: 800-372-1033
Co. E-mail: customercare@bna.com
URL: http://www.bna.com
Description: Contains information on health care regulatory news and developments in the United States. Subjects include community-based care, home care, emergency care, infectious diseases, managed care, insurance, laboratories, Medicaid, mental health, medical waste, nursing homes, pharmaceuticals, physician services, professional licensing, provider relationships, worker protection and compensation. Entries are organized by state, topic, and register citation. **Availability:** Online: The Bureau of National Affairs Inc., Thomson Reuters. **Type:** Full text.

LIBRARIES

15060 ■ American College of Health Care Administrators–ACHCA Information Center
12100 Sunset Hills Rd., Ste. 130
Reston, VA 20190
Ph:(703)739-7900

Fax:(866)874-1585
Co. E-mail: info@achca.org
URL: http://www.achca.org
Contact: Anita Bell, Off.Coord.
Scope: Long-term care, gerontology. **Services:** Center open to ACHCA members only. **Holdings:** 100 books; governmental statistical reports. **Subscriptions:** 125 journals and other serials.

15061 ■ Anderson Area Medical Center Library
800 N. Fant St.
Anderson, SC 29621
Ph:(864)261-1253
Fax:(864)261-1552
Contact: Beth Addis
Scope: Medicine, nursing. **Services:** Interlibrary loan, literature searches. **Holdings:** 750 books. **Subscriptions:** 125 journals and other serials; 2 newspapers.

15062 ■ Arkansas Aging Foundation Information Center
706 S. Pulaski St.
Little Rock, AR 72201-3927
Ph:(501)376-6083
Contact: Ed Doman, Pres.
Scope: Health promotion; seniors - enhancing independent living, health issues, activities. **Services:** Copying. **Holdings:** Monthly newspaper. **Subscriptions:** 1 newspaper.

15063 ■ Clemson University–College of Health, Education & Human Development–Learning Resource Center (309 E)
309 Edwards Hall Clemson
Box 34074
Clemson, SC 29634
Ph:(864)656-5495
Fax:(864)656—168
Co. E-mail: marches@clemson.edu
URL: http://www.hehd.clemson.edu/
Contact: Dr. Michael J. Padilla, Dir.
Scope: Nursing, health. **Services:** Photocopying. **Holdings:** 250 books; 400 videotapes; 30 software.

15064 ■ Evangelical Lutheran Good Samaritan Society–Resource Library
PO Box 5038
Sioux Falls, SD 57117-5038
Ph:(605)362-3270
Co. E-mail: cnelson2@good-sam.com
URL: http://www.good-sam.com/
Contact: Crystal Gering Nelson, Rsrc.Lib.Coord.
Scope: Nursing home care. **Holdings:** 771 videos; 556 books; 48 cassettes; 193 DVDs; 6 CDs. **Subscriptions:** 25 journals and other serials.

15065 ■ Genesis Medical Center–Illini Campus–Perlmutter Library of the Health Sciences (855 I)
855 Illini Dr., Ste. 102
Silvis, IL 61282
Ph:(309)792-4360
Fax:(309)792-4362
Co. E-mail: tharpb@genesishealth.com
Contact: Barb Tharp, Libn.
Scope: Clinical medicine, healthcare management, nursing. **Services:** Interlibrary loan; literature searches; PUBMED training; Library open to the public. **Holdings:** 1600 books; 500 video recordings. **Subscriptions:** 225 journals and other serials.

15066 ■ Lexington Medical Center–LMC Health Library
2720 Sunset Blvd.
West Columbia, SC 29169
Ph:(803)791-2000
URL: http://www.lexmed.com/
Scope: Medicine, nursing, and allied health sciences. **Holdings:** Figures not available.

15067 ■ Mercy Medical Center Health Sciences Library
2700 Stewart Pkwy.
Roseburg, OR 97470
Ph:(541)677-2144

Fax:(541)677-4391
Co. E-mail: carolkibbey@chiwest.com
URL: http://www.mercyrose.org/index.html
Contact: Carol Kibbey, Med.Libn.
Scope: Medicine, nursing, patient education, allied health. **Services:** Interlibrary loan; copying; Library open to the public. **Holdings:** 250 books; 50 bound periodical volumes. **Subscriptions:** 25 journals and other serials.

15068 ■ Mid-Columbia Medical Center–Planetree Health Resource Center
200 E. 4th St.
The Dalles, OR 97058
Ph:(541)296-8444
Fax:(541)296-6054
Co. E-mail: micheles@mcmc.net
URL: http://www.mcmc.net/library
Contact: Michele Spatz, Dir.
Scope: Consumer health, medicine, cancer, complementary therapies, smoking cessation, violence prevention and conflict resolution. **Services:** Interlibrary loan; copying; Library open to the public. **Holdings:** 3600 books; 981 clipping files; 350 audio/visual items; teaching tools. **Subscriptions:** 53 journals and other serials; 2 newspapers.

15069 ■ Millcreek Community Hospital/ LECOM Medical Library
5515 Peach St.
Erie, PA 16509
Ph:(814)868-8118
Fax:(814)868-7708
Co. E-mail: rschnick@lecom.edu
URL: http://www.millcreekcommunityhospital.com
Contact: Robert Schnick, Dir., LECOM Hea.Sys.Libs.
Scope: Family practice, orthopedic surgery, internal medicine, osteopathic medicine, obstetrics, gynecology. **Services:** Interlibrary loan; photocopying; information consultation; Library not open to the public. **Holdings:** 550 books; 9000 periodical back issues. **Subscriptions:** 110 journals and other serials.

15070 ■ Princeton Community Hospital Library
122 12th St.
PO Box 1369
Princeton, WV 24740-1369
Ph:(304)487-7246
Fax:(304)487-2161
Co. E-mail: mperdue@pchonline.org
URL: http://www.pchonline.org
Contact: Melinda Perdue, Libn.
Scope: Medicine, nursing, and allied health sciences. **Services:** Library open to the public. **Holdings:** 400 books. **Subscriptions:** 12 journals and other serials.

15071 ■ Reedsburg Area Medical Center Medical Library
2000 N. Dewey Ave.
Reedsburg, WI 53959
Ph:(608)768-6275
Fax:(608)524-2104
URL: http://www.ramchealth.com
Contact: Win Byers, Chm.
Scope: Family practice, nursing, surgery. **Services:** Interlibrary loan; research; copying; Library open to the public for reference use only. **Holdings:** 120 books. **Subscriptions:** 20 journals and other serials.

15072 ■ Resource Centre for the Aging Family Library
1133 7th Ave. SW
Calgary, AB, Canada T2P 1B2
Ph:(403)705-3226
Fax:(403)264-7047
Co. E-mail: resource@kerbycentre.com
Contact: Judy Caban, Libn.
Scope: Seniors' health, caregiving (including the "sandwich generation"), elder abuse, terminal care, retirement. **Services:** Interlibrary loan; copying; SDI; Library open to the public. **Holdings:** 1850 volume; 150 videocassettes. **Subscriptions:** 50 journals and other serials; 3 newspapers.

15073 ■ Southwest Health Center Medical Library
1400 East Side Rd.
Platteville, WI 53818
Ph:(608)348-2331
Fax:(608)342-5011
Co. E-mail: library@southwesthealth.org
URL: http://www.southwesthealth.org/index.php
Scope: Medicine, nursing, and allied health sciences. **Services:** Interlibrary loan; copying; Library open to the public. **Holdings:** 500 books. **Subscriptions:** 80 journals and other serials.

15074 ■ Toronto Rehabilitation Institute Library
University Centre
550 University Ave.
Toronto, ON, Canada M5G 2A2
Ph:(416)597-3422, x3000
Fax:(416)591-6515
Co. E-mail: millman-wilson.doreen@torontorehab.on.ca
URL: http://www.torontorehab.on.ca
Contact: Doreen Millman-Wilson, Mgr.Lib.Svcs.
Scope: Gerontology, acquired brain injury, stroke rehabilitation, long term care, complex continuing care, spinal cord injury. **Services:** Interlibrary loan; copying; document delivery; Library open to the public for reference use only. **Holdings:** 4200 books; 1500 bound periodical volumes; 200 videotapes. **Subscriptions:** 120 journals and other serials.

15075 ■ United Way 2-1-1–Information & Referral Service
PO Box 7548
Madison, WI 53707-7548
Ph:(608)246-4350
Fax:(608)246-4349
Co. E-mail: sandye@uwdc.org
URL: http://www.unitedwaydanecounty.org
Contact: Sandy Erickson, Dir.
Scope: Geriatrics, medical care. **Services:** Community resource telephone line providing information and referral services for Dane County.

15076 ■ University of South Florida–College of Medicine–Suncoast Gerontology Center - The Eastern Star Library on Alzheimer's Disease (12901)
12901 Bruce B. Downs Blvd., MDC 50
Tampa, FL 33612-4799
Ph:(813)974-4355
Free: 800-633-4563
Fax:(813)974-4251
Co. E-mail: jardila@hsc.usf.edu
URL: http://hsc.usf.edu/suncoast/alzheimer/index.html
Contact: Jill Ardila, Clin.Res.Coord.
Scope: Alzheimer's disease, aging, caregiving, long-term care, mental health, dementia. **Services:** Interlibrary loan; copying; SDI; Library open to the public for reference use only. **Holdings:** 800 books; 450 reports; 50 archival materials; 25 videocassettes. **Subscriptions:** 6 journals and other serials.

15077 ■ UPMC Braddock Health Sciences Library
400 Holland Ave.
Braddock, PA 15104
Ph:(412)784-4238
Fax:(412)784-4989
Co. E-mail: haughaj@msx.upmc.edu
URL: http://braddock.upmc.com/
Contact: Amy Haugh, MLS, Dir.
Scope: Clinical medicine, clinical psychiatry, clinical nursing, clinical geriatrics. **Services:** Interlibrary loan; copying; SDI; Library open to the public with restrictions. **Holdings:** 500 books; 1000 bound periodical volumes; 34 microfiche titles. **Subscriptions:** 80 journals and other serials.

15078 ■ Virginia Commonwealth University–Virginia Center on Aging–Information Resources Center (730 E)
730 E. Broad St.
Theatre Row Building
Richmond, VA 23219
Ph:(804)828-1525

Fax:(804)828-7905
Co. E-mail: eansello@vcu.edu
URL: http://www.vcu.edu/vcoa
Contact: Dr. Edward F. Ansello, Dir.
Scope: Gerontology, mental health, sociology and the politics of aging, geriatrics, family relationships, long-term care, lifelong learning. **Services:** Library open to the public with restrictions. Audiovisual materials available to Virginia residents only. **Holdings:** 1500 books; 4 archives; 120 AV items. **Subscriptions:** 6 journals and other serials.

15079 ■ Western Illinois Area Agency on Aging–Greta J. Brook Elderly Living and Learning Facility
729 34th Ave.
Rock Island, IL 61201
Ph:(309)793-6800
Free: 800-322-1051
Fax:(309)793-6807
Co. E-mail: firststopforseniors@wiaaa.org
URL: http://www.wiaaa.org
Contact: Janice Stille, Exec.Dir.
Scope: Gerontology, Senior Housing, Family Caregiving, Medicare, Medicaid, Social Security, Retirement Planning, Intergenerational Programs, Program Development. **Services:** Interlibrary loan; Center open to the public (Senior Computer Center open to those fifty years of age or older; classes on Tuesdays 10am to noon or 1pm to 3pm). **Holdings:** 1108 books; 260 videotapes; 130 audio/visual materials; 35 DVDs and CDs. **Subscriptions:** 3 journals and other serials, 13 periodicals.

RESEARCH CENTERS

15080 ■ Center for Health Care Strategies
200 American Metro Blvd., Ste. 119
Hamilton, NJ 08619
Ph:(609)528-8400
Fax:(609)586-3679
Co. E-mail: ssomers@chcs.org
URL: http://www.chcs.org
Contact: Stephen A. Somers PhD, Pres./CEO
E-mail: ssomers@chcs.org
Scope: Development and implementation of effective health and social policy for all Americans. **Publications:** Case studies (monthly); Fact sheets (monthly); Policy and issue briefs (monthly); Reports (monthly); Resource papers (monthly); Technical assistance tools (monthly).

15081 ■ Center for the Study of Aging, Inc.
706 Madison Ave.
Albany, NY 12208-3604
Ph:(518)465-6927
Fax:(518)462-1339
Co. E-mail: csa@centerforthestudyofaging.org
URL: http://www.centerforthestudyofaging.org
Contact: Sara Harris, Exec.Dir.
E-mail: csa@centerforthestudyofaging.org
Scope: Social and medical research on aging, including physical activity and aging, housing for the elderly, geriatric cardiology, nutrition, mental health, oral history, public policy, caregiving, prevention, rural aging, and respite care for the frail elderly. **Services:** Consulting; Information and referral services, education and training, and fitness programming. **Publications:** Lifelong Health and Fitness Newsletter (quarterly). **Educational Activities:** International Conferences on Physical Activity, Aging, Sports, and Prevention of Illness and Maintenance of Well-being. **Awards:** Outstanding Leadership and Research in Physical Activity and Aging Award, presented at International Conference.

15082 ■ Research Institute on Aging
6105 Montrose Rd.
Rockville, MD 20852-4881
Ph:(301)770-8449
Fax:(301)770-8455
Co. E-mail: cohen-mansfield@hebrew-home.org
URL: http://www.researchinstituteonaging.org
Contact: Jiska Cohen-Mansfield, Dir.
E-mail: cohen-mansfield@hebrew-home.org
Scope: Gerontology, aging, and older adult, focusing on dementia care and prevention of decline in later years. Research topics in dementia care include pain

indicators in non-communicative elderly; non-drug individualized treatment of agitation for AD persons; self-identity in older persons suffering from dementia; agitated behaviors among the elderly; staff stress; back injuries among staff caretakers; the preferences of nursing home residents regarding life-sustaining treatments; standardized assessment of the physical and emotional states of nursing home residents; sleep patterns of nursing home residents; the use of physical restraints in the nursing home; the use of psychotropic medication in the nursing home; medical and nursing home resident decision making in end-of-life care. Research topics related to prevention of decline include loneliness in the older adult, exercise practice in community elderly, intergenerational programs, and the use of technology and the older adult. **Publications:** Monograph series; Papers in professional journals. **Educational Activities:** Hurwitz Lecture Series.

15083 ■ Sherbrooke University–Research Centre on Aging–Centre de Recherche sur le Vieillissement
1036, rue Belvedere Sud
Sherbrooke, QC, Canada J1H 4C4
Ph:(819)829-7131
Fax:(819)829-7141
Co. E-mail: communication@cdrv.ca
URL: http://www.csss-iugs.ca/cdrv/index.php?L=en
E-mail: communication@cdrv.ca
Scope: Biology of aging, oxidative stress, biosignalisation, rehabilitation, validation of measurement tools and methods, psychological distress, cognitive decline, family caregivers, quality of care, integrated services, Alzheimer's disease, diabetes, nutrition, epidemiology and prevention of functional decline, physical activity, gait and balance, psycho-sociology of aging, sleep disorders, medicine consumption, actualization of potential, psychological well-being, abuse and crime issues, road safety, consent, ethics, tissue regeneration, energy and lipid metabolism, telerehabilitation, emotion recognition, continuity of care, hobbies, social participation, memory, long-term consequences of cerebrovascular accident, professional practice in gerontology, etc. **Educational Activities:** Lunch time scientific conferences, every 2 weeks, Sept.-May; Research Day (annually). **Awards:** Grants.

15084 ■ University of Arizona–Arizona Center on Aging
1821 E Elm St.
Tucson, AZ 85719-4324
Ph:(520)626-5800
Fax:(520)626-5801
Co. E-mail: mfain@aging.arizona.edu
URL: http://aging.medicine.arizona.edu
Contact: Dr. Mindy Fain, Co-Dir.
E-mail: mfain@aging.arizona.edu
Scope: Long-term care, retirement communities, minority elderly, health and long-term care policy, and aging. Conducts applied research in service delivery system development and provides technical assistance and research dissemination. **Publications:** Monographs; Papers. **Educational Activities:** Caregiver and Alzheimer's training.

15085 ■ University of Massachusetts at Boston–Gerontology Institute
Wheatley Bldg., 3rd Fl., Rm. 124A
100 Morrissey Blvd.
Boston, MA 02125-3393
Ph:(617)287-7300
Fax:(617)287-7080
Co. E-mail: ellen.bruce@umb.edu
URL: http://www.geront.umb.edu
Contact: Ellen Bruce, Dir.
E-mail: ellen.bruce@umb.edu
Scope: Aging social policy, including health care, economics, security, long-term care, productive aging, systems delivery, older women's issues, pension assistance, retirement, older drivers, demographics and minority issues. **Publications:** Journal of Aging & Social Policy (quarterly). **Educational Activities:** Osher Life Long Learning Institute (daily), lifelong learning program for people aged 50 and over, which

offers non-credit courses, lectures, social events, and trips; Seminars, conferences, special events and forums, open to the public.

START-UP INFORMATION

15086 ■ *Becoming a Personal Trainer for Dummies*
Pub: John Wiley & Sons, Incorporated
Ed: Melyssa Michael, Linda Formichelli. **Released:** October 2004. **Price:** $19.99 (US), $25.99 (Canadian). **Description:** Legal and tax issues involved in starting and running a personal trainer firm. The book offers suggestions for incorporating massage and nutritional services.

ASSOCIATIONS AND OTHER ORGANIZATIONS

15087 ■ American Association of Nutritional Consultants
400 Oakhill Dr.
Winona Lake, IN 46590
Free: 888-828-2262
Fax:(574)268-2120
Co. E-mail: registrar@aanc.net
URL: http://www.aanc.net
Description: Professional nutritional consultants. Seeks to create a forum for exchange of nutritional information. Offers benefits such as car rental and laboratory discounts. .

15088 ■ American Dietetic Association
120 S Riverside Plz., Ste. 2000
Chicago, IL 60606-6995
Ph:(312)899-0040
Free: 800-877-1600
Fax:(312)899-4817
Co. E-mail: pbabjak@eatright.org
URL: http://www.eatright.org
Contact: Patricia M. Babjak, CEO
Description: Represents food and nutrition professionals. Promotes nutrition, health and well-being. **Publications:** *Dieting for Dummies, 2nd Edition*; *The Healthy Beef Cookbook*; *Journal of the American Dietetic Association* (monthly); *365 Days of Healthy Eating from the American Dietetic* .

15089 ■ American Nutrition Association
PO Box 262
Western Springs, IL 60558
Ph:(708)246-3663
Co. E-mail: contact@americannutritionassociation.org
URL: http://www.AmericanNutritionAssociation.org
Description: Aims to promote optimal health through nutrition and wellness education. Performs at the cutting edge of science-based nutrition, educating both laypeople and professionals about the health benefits of nutrition and wellness. Hosts hundreds of expert nutrition presentations in Chicago from such luminaries in the healthcare field as Nobel Laureate Linus Pauling. Engages in numerous other nutrition outreach programs, such as: over 30 years of quarterly Nutrition Digest Children's nutrition programs in local schools. **Publications:** *Nutrition Digest* .

15090 ■ Canadian Foundation for Dietetic Research–Fondation Canadienne de la Recherche en Dietetique
480 University Ave., Ste. 604
Toronto, ON, Canada M5G 1V2
Ph:(519)267-0755
Fax:(416)596-0603
Co. E-mail: cfdr@dietitians.ca
URL: http://cfdr.ca
Contact: Isla Horvath MA, Exec. Dir.
Description: Dietitians and other individuals with an interest in nutrition. Seeks to advance dietetic research. Provides support and assistance to nutrition research projects. Conducts educational programs. **Publications:** *Keeping In Touch* (3/year). **Telecommunication Services:** electronic mail, ihorvath_cfdr@dietitians.ca.

15091 ■ Canadian Health Food Association–Association Canadienne des Aliments de Sante
235 Yorkland Blvd., Ste. 302
Toronto, ON, Canada M2J 4Y8
Ph:(416)497-6939
Free: 800-661-4510
Fax:(416)497-3214
Co. E-mail: info@chfa.ca
URL: http://www.chfa.ca
Contact: Penelope Marrett, Pres./CEO
Description: Represents producers and distributors of health foods. Seeks to advance the health food industries. Facilitates communication and cooperation among members; represents the commercial and regulatory interests of the health food industries; sponsors educational and promotional programs. **Publications:** *The Natural Voice* (5/year).

15092 ■ Canadian Nutrition Society–Societe Canadienne de Nutrition
310-2175 Sheppard Ave., E
Toronto, ON, Canada M2J 1W8
Ph:(416)491-7188
Free: 888-414-7188
Fax:(416)491-1670
Co. E-mail: info@cns-scn.ca
URL: http://www.cns-scn.ca
Contact: Katherine Gray-Donald, Pres.-Elect
Description: Dieticians and other scientists and health care professionals with an interest in nutrition. Seeks to advance the study and practice of the nutritional sciences. Serves as a forum for the exchange of information among members; sponsors research and educational programs.

15093 ■ Dietary Managers Association
406 Surrey Woods Dr.
St. Charles, IL 60174
Ph:(630)587-6336
Free: 800-323-1908
Fax:(630)587-6308
Co. E-mail: info@dmaonline.org
URL: http://www.dmaonline.org
Contact: Ricky Clark CDM, Chm.
Description: Dietary managers united to maintain a high level of competency and quality in dietary departments through continuing education. Provides educational programs and placement service. **Publications:** *Accounting and Finance Fundamentals*; *Alzheimer's Disease*; *Diet Therapy for the Dietary Manager*, *Dietary Manager* (bimonthly); *DMA Master Track Human Resource*; *DMA Master Track Operations Management*; *Managing Foodservice Operations* .

15094 ■ Dietetics in Health Care Communities
2219 Cardinal Dr.
Waterloo, IA 50701
Ph:(319)235-0991
Fax:(319)235-7224
Co. E-mail: dhccdpg@mchsi.com
URL: http://www.dhccdpg.org
Contact: Cynthia Piland RD, Chair
Description: A special interest group of the American Dietetic Association. Dietitians employed in extended care facilities, nursing homes, homecare, and a variety of food service operations. Disseminates information; assists in solving their problems in the field. Conducts workshops; offers networking opportunities for professionals. **Publications:** *The Consultant Dietitian* (quarterly); *Inservice Manual* .

15095 ■ Dietitians of Canada–Les Dietetistes du Canada
480 University Ave., Ste. 604
Toronto, ON, Canada M5G 1V2
Ph:(416)596-0857
Fax:(416)596-0603
Co. E-mail: centralinfo@dietitians.ca
URL: http://www.dietitians.ca
Contact: Marsha Sharp, CEO
Description: Leads and supports members to promote health and well being through expertise in food and nutrition. **Publications:** *Canadian Journal of Dietetic Practice and Research* (quarterly).

15096 ■ International Union of Nutritional Sciences
University of Hawaii
Cancer Research Center of Hawaii
1236 Lauhala St., Ste. 407
Honolulu, HI 96813
Ph:(808)564-5861
Fax:(808)564-2982
Co. E-mail: suzanne@crch.hawaii.edu
URL: http://www.iuns.org
Contact: Prof. Rekia Belahsen, Sec. Gen.
Description: Promotes advancement in nutrition science, research and development through international cooperation at the global level. Encourages communication and collaboration among nutrition scientists as well as to disseminate information in nutritional sciences through modern communication technology. .

15097 ■ National Eating Disorder Information Centre
200 Elizabeth St., ES 7-421
Toronto, ON, Canada M5G 2C4
Ph:(416)340-4156
Free: (866)633-4220

Fax:(416)340-4736
Co. E-mail: nedic@uhn.on.ca
URL: http://www.nedic.ca
Contact: Merryl Bear MD, Dir.

Description: Provides information and resources on causes, symptoms of, and therapeutic and health care treatments for eating disorders and the preoccupation with food and weight. Aims to raise awareness on eating disorders through conducting lectures and workshops. **Publications:** Bulletin (5/year).

15098 ■ National Food Service Management Institute

University of Mississippi
6 Jeanette Philips Dr.
PO Drawer 188
University, MS 38677-0188
Ph:(662)915-7658
Free: 800-321-3054
Fax:800-321-3061
Co. E-mail: nfsmi@olemiss.edu
URL: http://www.nfsmi.org
Contact: Dr. Katie Wilson, Exec. Dir.

Description: Seeks to be the leader in providing education, research, and resources to promote excellence in child nutrition programs. Provides information, conducts applied research, and offers training and education opportunities using appropriate technology. **Publications:** *Insight* (quarterly); *Mealtime Memo for Child Care* (bimonthly); *Resource Guide*; *Update* (semiannual).

REFERENCE WORKS

15099 ■ *Everything is Possible: Life and Business Lessons from a Self-Made Billionaire and the Founder of Slim-Fast*

Pub: Newmarket Press

Ed: S. Daniel Abraham. **Released:** February 10, 2010. **Price:** $24.95. **Description:** A profile of the founder of Slim-Fast nutritional diet drink used to help people lose weight.

15100 ■ "Experts Strive to Educate on Proper Pet Diets" in *Pet Product News* (Vol. 64, November 2010, No. 11, pp. 40)

Pub: BowTie Inc.

Ed: John Hustace Walker. **Description:** Pet supply manufacturers have been bundling small mammal food and treats with educational sources to help retailers avoid customer misinformation. This action has been motivated by the customer's quest to seek proper nutritional advice for their small mammal pets.

15101 ■ "Food as Nature Intended" in *Pet Product News* (Vol. 64, November 2010, No. 11, pp. 30)

Pub: BowTie Inc.

Ed: Nikki Moustaki. **Description:** Dog owners have been extending their health-consciousness to their pets by seeking natural products that will address their pets' raw food diet. Retailers response to this trend are outlined.

15102 ■ "In the Raw: Karyn Calabrese Brings Healthy Dining to a New Sophisticated Level" in *Black Enterprise* (Vol. 41, September 2010)

Pub: Earl G. Graves Publishing Co. Inc.

Ed: Sonia Alleyne. **Description:** Profile of Karyn Calabrese whose businesses are based in Chicago, Illinois. Calabrese has launched a complete line of products (vitamins and beauty items), services (spa, chiropractic, and acupuncture treatments), and restaurants to bring health dining and lifestyles to a better level.

15103 ■ "Kubicki Juggles Lineup at Vianda" in *Business Courier* (Vol. 26, December 11, 2009, No. 33, pp. 1)

Pub: American City Business Journals, Inc.

Ed: Dan Monk. **Description:** Cincinnati real estate developer Chuck Kubicki replaced the management team of Vianda LLC and cancelled contracts with two vendors that caused a surge of customer complaints. Vianda is a direct-response marketing firm that sells and distributes dietary supplements for wellness and sexual performance.

15104 ■ "Making It Work" in *Pet Product News* (Vol. 64, December 2010, No. 12, pp. S8)

Pub: BowTie Inc.

Ed: Kerri Chladnicek. **Description:** How focusing on service and flexibility allowed New Jersey-based pet supply store B.C. Woof to achieve success is discussed. B.C. Woof began as a pet-sitting business which eventually concentrated on natural foods. Aside from conducting a do-it-yourself approach in food formulation for customers, B.C. Woof has also been guiding customers on nutrients they need for their pets.

15105 ■ "Must Work for Food" in *Pet Product News* (Vol. 64, November 2010, No. 11, pp. 24)

Pub: BowTie Inc.

Ed: Wendy Bedwell-Wilson. **Description:** Pet supply retailers can benefit from stocking foods and treats that address obesity, which according to the American Veterinary Medical Association, has become the most prevalent nutritional disorder in dogs. With the rise in dog obesity, products like work-for-their food toys have been sought by dog owners.

15106 ■ "No-Shed Dogs Lead the Way to Big Growth" in *Business Courier* (Vol. 26, January 8, 2010, No. 38, pp. 1)

Pub: American City Business Journals, Inc.

Ed: Lucy May. **Description:** Ed Lukacevic of Grant County, Kentucky is developing Dinovite, a dietary supplement that minimizes shedding and scratching in dogs. Statistical data included.

15107 ■ "Supplements Mix Nutrition With Convenience" in *Pet Product News* (Vol. 64, November 2010, No. 11, pp. 44)

Pub: BowTie Inc.

Ed: Karen Shugart. **Description:** Pet supply manufacturers have been making supplements and enhanced foods that improve mineral consumption, boost bone density, and sharpen appetite in herps. Customers seem to enjoy the convenience as particular herps demands are being addressed by these offerings. Features of other supplements and enhanced foods for herps are described.

15108 ■ "Sustaining Health" in *Pet Product News* (Vol. 64, November 2010, No. 11, pp. 28)

Pub: BowTie Inc.

Ed: Angela Pham. **Description:** How pet supply retailers have responded to dog owners' interest in health supplements and their ingredients is discussed. Dog owners are showing interest in the ingredients inside the supplements and are reading labels. Retailers must now prove the beneficial effects of these ingredients in order to make the sale.

TRADE PERIODICALS

15109 ■ *American Journal of Clinical Nutrition*

Pub: American Society for Nutrition

Contact: Darren T. Early, Managing Editor

Released: Monthly. **Price:** $510 institutions print and online U.S.; $490 institutions online U.S.; $205 print and online U.S.; $180 online U.S.; $60 students online U.S.; $535 institutions, Canada and Mexico print and online; $490 institutions, Canada and Mexico online only; $560 other countries print and online; $490 other countries online only. **Description:** Peer-reviewed journal publishing basic and clinical studies relevant to human nutrition.

15110 ■ *Better Nutrition Magazine*

Pub: Active Interest Media

Contact: Joanna Shirk, Publisher

E-mail: jshirk@aimmedia.com

Ed: Nicole Brechka, Editor, nbrechka@aimmedia.com. **Released:** Monthly. **Description:** Magazine focusing on 'all-natural dietary and lifestyle approaches to optimal nutrition and health.

15111 ■ *Eating Well Magazine*

Pub: Eating Well Inc.

Contact: Diane De Spirlet, Advertising Dir

E-mail: diane@eatingwell.com

Released: Bimonthly. **Price:** $14.97; $24.97 Canada; $34.97 other countries. **Description:** Food magazine with emphasis on delicious low-fat cooking and sensible nutrition.

15112 ■ *Journal of Culinary Science & Technology*

Pub: Taylor & Francis Group Ltd.

Contact: John M. Antun PhD, Co-Ed.

Released: Quarterly. **Price:** $78 online; $82 print & online. **Description:** The Journal of Culinary Science & Technology covers current developments in fine and applied culinary science research.

15113 ■ *Journal of Nutrition*

Pub: American Society for Nutrition

Released: Monthly. **Price:** $670 institutions online only; domestic & foreign; $710 institutions print online; $760 institutions, other countries print online; $200 print online; $255 other countries print online; $180 online only; domestic & foreign; $40 members print online; $80 members print online; and other countries. **Description:** Peer-reviewed journal covering on all aspects of experimental nutrition.

15114 ■ *No Salt Week-The Newsletter*

Pub: Prosperity & Profits Unlimited, Distribution Services

Contact: A. Doyle

Ed: A. Doyle, Editor. **Released:** Annual. **Price:** $2, U.S.; $3, Canada; $4, elsewhere. **Description:** Presents possibilities for herb and spice blends that contain no added salt. Also contains ideas for cooking and much more.

15115 ■ *Nutrition Reviews*

Pub: International Life Sciences Institute

Contact: Naomi Fukagawa MD, Editor-in-Chief

Released: Monthly. **Price:** $214 print online; $396 institutions print online; $360 institutions online; $208 European, print online; $262 institutions European, print online; $227 institutions European, online; $139 other countries print online; $514 institutions, other countries print online; $445 institutions, other countries online. **Description:** Journal providing information on developments in nutrition, dietetics, food science, and nutrition science policy.

15116 ■ *Nutrition Today*

Pub: Lippincott Williams & Wilkins

Contact: Kathleen M. Phelan, Publisher

E-mail: kathleen.phelan@wolterskluwer.com

Ed: Johanna Dwyer, Editor. **Released:** Bimonthly. **Price:** $87.99; $279 institutions; $49.98 in-training; $174 other countries; $396 institutions, other countries. **Description:** Health science journal.

15117 ■ *The Tan Sheet*

Pub: F-D-C Reports Inc.

Contact: Ramsey Baghdadi, Managing Editor

Ed: Christopher Walker, Editor. **Released:** Weekly, 50/year. **Price:** $2,020, U.S. print and web. **Description:** Provides "in-depth coverage of nonprescription pharmaceuticals and dietary supplement/nutritionals." Topics include congressional hearings and legislation, business and marketing news, FDA recalls and seizures, regular listing of product trademarks, and activities of FTC, CPSC, and FDA.

15118 ■ *Topics in Clinical Nutrition TICN*

Pub: Lippincott Williams & Wilkins

Ed: Judith A. Gilbride, PhD, Editor. **Released:** Quarterly. **Price:** $98.99; $354.49 institutions; $197.73 other countries; $453.73 institutions, other countries. **Description:** Peer-reviewed journal addressing the challenges and problems of dietitians and others involved in dietary care in a health care setting.

VIDEOCASSETTES/ AUDIOCASSETTES

15119 ■ *Chow! A Nutrition Curriculum*

Sunburst Technology
1550 Executive Dr.
Elgin, IL 60123
Free: 888-492-8817
Fax:888-800-3028
Co. E-mail: service@sunburst.com
URL: http://www.sunburst.com

Released: 1998. **Price:** $99.95. **Description:** Educates middle school viewers about the importance of a healthy diet. Includes teacher's guide. **Availability:** VHS.

15120 ■ *Diet and Cancer*
Discovery Education
One Discovery Pl.
Silver Spring, MD 20910
Ph:(847)328-6700
Free: 800-323-9084
Fax:(847)328-6706
URL: http://www.discoveryeducation.com
Released: 1988. **Price:** $295.00. **Description:** The latest research on the relationship between diet and cancer is reviewed and viewers are instructed on how they may change their eating habits to reduce the risk of cancer. **Availability:** VHS; 3/4U.

15121 ■ *The Diet Maze*
RMI Media
1365 N. Winchester St.
Olathe, KS 66061-5880
Ph:(913)768-1696
Free: 800-745-5480
Fax:800-755-6910
Co. E-mail: actmedia@act.org
URL: http://www.actmedia.com
Released: 1987. **Description:** Doctors and nutritionists rate various diets and discuss the role of family and overweight camps in helping dieters. **Availability:** VHS; 3/4U.

15122 ■ *8 Weeks to Optimum Health*
Tapeworm Video Distributors
25876 The Old Road 141
Stevenson Ranch, CA 91381
Ph:(661)257-4904
Fax:(661)257-4820
Co. E-mail: sales@tapeworm.com
URL: http://www.tapeworm.com
Released: 1996. **Price:** $19.95. **Description:** Dr. Andrew Weil discusses his easy to follow program of exercise, diet, vitamins and meditation drawn from medical techniques from around the world. **Availability:** VHS.

15123 ■ *Good Fat/Bad Fat: The No-Nonsense Cholesterol Guide*
CA Working Group/We Do the Work
1611 Telegraph Ave Suite 1550
Oakland, CA 94612
Ph:(510)268-9675
Fax:(510)268-3606
Co. E-mail: info@theworkinggroup.org
URL: http://www.pbs.org/livelyhood
Price: $24.95. **Description:** William Castelli, M.D., of the Framingham Heart Group discusses cholesterol and offers ways to dramatically lower your cholesterol level. He covers the causes, methods of detection, treatments, and tips on nutrition and fitness. **Availability:** VHS.

15124 ■ *Good Food for Good Health*
First Light Video Publishing
2321 Abbot Kinney Blvd., Top Fl.
Venice, CA 90291
Ph:(310)577-8581
Free: 800-262-8862
Fax:(310)574-0886
Co. E-mail: sales@firstlightvideo.com
URL: http://www.firstlightvideo.com
Price: $275.00. **Description:** Introductory program for children explains the basics of nutritional health and the principles of the new food pyramid. **Availability:** VHS; 3/4U.

15125 ■ *Nutrition for Better Health*
Encyclopedia Britannica
331 N. LaSalle St.
Chicago, IL 60654
Ph:(312)347-7159
Free: 800-323-1229
Fax:(312)294-2104
URL: http://www.britannica.com
Released: 1984. **Price:** $99.00. **Description:** Profiles good health through proper nutrition. Contains information on how overeating can hurt the body and how to avoid obesity, osteoporosis, hypertension, and heart disease. **Availability:** VHS; 3/4U; SVS.

15126 ■ *Nutrition: Eat and Be Healthy*
Milner-Fenwick, Inc.
119 Lakefront Dr.
Hunt Valley, MD 21030-2216
Free: 800-432-8433
Fax:(410)252-6316
Co. E-mail: patiented@milner-fenwick.com
URL: http://www.milner-fenwick.com
Released: 1994. **Price:** $250.00. **Description:** Introduces the USDA food-guide pyramid and provides suggestions for preparing meals that meet nutritional guidelines. **Availability:** VHS.

15127 ■ *Nutrition Facts: The New Food Label with Supermarket Savvy's Leni Reed*
Family Experiences Productions, Inc.
PO Box 5879
Austin, TX 78763-5879
Ph:(512)494-0338
Fax:(512)494-0340
Co. E-mail: todd@fepi.com
URL: http://www.fepi.com
Released: 1994. **Price:** $39.95. **Description:** Registered dietitian Leni Reed explains components of standardized food labels and their relationship to daily nutritional needs. **Availability:** VHS.

15128 ■ *Nutrition for Wellness*
AJN Video Library/Lippincott Williams & Wilkins
American Journal of Nursing
345 Hudson St., 16th Fl.
New York, NY 10014
Ph:(212)886-1200
Free: 800-256-4045
Fax:(212)886-1276
Co. E-mail: info@nursingcenter.com
URL: http://www.nursingcenter.com
Price: $250.00. **Description:** Part of the Lifestyles for Wellness Series. Features a clinical nutritionist who explains what a nutrient is, making it clear why good nutrition is so important to good health. She offers tips on how to choose the right and proper amounts of foods from the four food groups and also discusses food quality and developing new habits for wellness. **Availability:** VHS.

15129 ■ *Nutrition for You*
Educational Activities, Inc.
PO Box 87
Baldwin, NY 11510
Free: 800-797-3223
Fax:(516)623-9282
URL: http://www.edact.com
Price: $79.00. **Description:** Outlines the effects that nutrition has on the body, emphasizing the importance of good nutrition. Covers how proteins, carbohydrates, vitamins, minerals, and water affect the diet. Also contains information about anorexia and bulimia, nutritional importance of limiting fat, salt, and sugar intake, and adequate fiber intake. Includes teacher's guide, interactive video masters, and reproducible masters. **Availability:** VHS.

15130 ■ *Nutritional Aspects of the AIDS Patient*
American Society for Training and Development (ASTD)
1640 King St.
Box 1443
Alexandria, VA 22313-2043
Ph:(703)683-8100
Free: 800-628-2783
Fax:(703)683-8103
URL: http://www.astd.org
Released: 1989. **Price:** $250.00. **Description:** A program for professionals about the nutritional problems associated with care and support of HIV patients. **Availability:** VHS; 3/4U.

15131 ■ *Nutritional Assessment of the Elderly*
AJN Video Library/Lippincott Williams & Wilkins
American Journal of Nursing
345 Hudson St., 16th Fl.
New York, NY 10014
Ph:(212)886-1200
Free: 800-256-4045

Fax:(212)886-1276
Co. E-mail: info@nursingcenter.com
URL: http://www.nursingcenter.com
Price: $285.00. **Description:** Discusses the effects of human aging on nutritional assessment, enabling the health provider to identify the need for nutritional intervention much quicker. Provides information on the importance of a thorough history, normal physiological aging, socioeconomic status, acute and chronic illness, genetics, accessibility of care, climate, and individual nutritional habits. Demonstrates different measuring methods, including anthropometric, biochemical, hematologic, immune functions, oral, polypharmacy, psychosocial factors, and functional status. Includes study guide. **Availability:** VHS.

15132 ■ *Shopping for Health*
Family Experiences Productions, Inc.
PO Box 5879
Austin, TX 78763-5879
Ph:(512)494-0338
Fax:(512)494-0340
Co. E-mail: todd@fepi.com
URL: http://www.fepi.com
Released: 1997. **Description:** Four-volume series on women's nutrition and health issues. **Availability:** VHS.

TRADE SHOWS AND CONVENTIONS

15133 ■ California Dietetic Association Meeting
California Dietetic Association
7740 Manchester Ave., Ste. 102
Playa Del Rey, CA 90293-8499
Ph:(310)822-0177
Fax:(310)823-0264
Co. E-mail: bridget@dietitian.org
URL: http://www.dietitian.org
Released: Annual. **Audience:** Nutrition and dietetic professionals. **Principal Exhibits:** Food and nutrition services. **Dates and Locations:** 2011 Apr 28-30, Pasadena, CA.

15134 ■ Soho Expo
National Nutritional Foods Association, Southeast Region
5309 Lime St.
New Port Richey, FL 34652
Ph:(727)846-0320
Fax:(727)848-7654
Co. E-mail: senpa@southeastnpa.org
URL: http://www.nnfase.org
Released: Annual. **Audience:** Industry - owners/staff natural/health food stores. **Principal Exhibits:** Nutritional foods and related equipment, supplies, and services.

CONSULTANTS

15135 ■ Augusta Nutrition Consultants
4833 Mcgahee Rd.
PO Box 799
Evans, GA 30809-0799
Ph:(706)860-8935
Fax:(706)860-8932
Co. E-mail: reblack@mindspring.com
Contact: Rebecca F. Black, Principle
E-mail: reblack@mindspring.com
Scope: Provides nutrition consultation for individuals, groups, businesses, health departments, hospitals, private physicians, health maintenance organizations and prepaid group plans. **Publications:** "Lactation Specialist Self-Study Series," 1995.

15136 ■ Center for Lifestyle Enhancement - Columbia Medical Center of Plano
3901 W 15th St.
Plano, TX 75075
Ph:(972)596-6800

Fax:(972)519-1299
Co. E-mail: mcp.cle@hcahealthcare.com
URL: http://www.medicalcenterofplano.com
Contact: Doug Browning, Vice President
E-mail: boesdorfer@hcahealthcare.com

Scope: Provides professional health counseling in the areas of general nutrition for weight management, eating disorders, diabetic education, cholesterol reduction and adolescent weight management. Offers work site health promotion and preventive services. Also coordinates speaker's bureau, cooking classes and physician referrals. Industries served: education, insurance, healthcare, retail or wholesale, data processing and manufacturing throughout Texas. **Seminars:** Rx Diet and Exercise; Smoking Cessation; Stress Management; Health Fairs; Fitness Screenings; Body Composition; Nutrition Analysis; Exercise Classes; Prenatal Nutrition; SHAPEDOWN; Successfully Managing Diabetes; Gourmet Foods for Your Heart; The Aging Heart; Heart Smart Saturday featuring Day of Dance; Weight-Loss Management Seminars; The Right Stroke for Men; Peripheral Artery Disease Screening; Menstruation: The Cycle Begins; Boot Camp for New Dads; Grand parenting 101: Caring for Kids Today; Teddy Bear Camp; New Baby Day Camp; Safe Sitter Baby-Sitting Class.

15137 ■ Debra F. Latimer Nutrition and Diabetes Associates L.L.C.
11999 Katy Fwy., Ste. 150-H
Houston, TX 77062
Ph:(713)795-0876
Fax:(713)432-7989
Co. E-mail: dfl.nutrition@sbcglobal.net
URL: http://www.debraflatimer.com
Contact: Debra F. Latimer, Owner
E-mail: dfl.nutrition@sbcglobal.net

Scope: Provides medical nutrition therapy on individual and group bases. Plans and conducts corporate wellness programs. Consultant to service and food manufacturing industries, as well as government agencies. Specializes in diabetes and renal education and management, weight management and compulsive eating disorders. **Seminars:** Diabetes-Self Management and Training Program, Houston, Jul, 2007; Preventive and Treatment Plans for Cardiac Care; Pre and Post-natal Nutrition; Premenstrual Syndrome; Eating for the Health of It; Weight Management and Wellness Program; Supermarket Nutrition Tours; Diabetes education and training. The Diabetes-Self Management and Education Program.

15138 ■ Krumkill Stables
460 Krumkill Rd.
Albany, NY 12203
Ph:(518)482-8704
Fax:(518)482-7672
Co. E-mail: diet_farm@yahoo.com
URL: http://www.krumkillstables.com
Contact: Jean M. Bigaouette, Owner
E-mail: diet_farm@yahoo.com

Scope: Full service facility offering care for horses. Other services include taking riding lessons, organizing summer camps and offering trial rides.

15139 ■ Margaret L. Mikkola
5 Nashoba Rd.
PO Box 659
Acton, MA 01720
Ph:(978)264-9040
Fax:(978)264-9040
Co. E-mail: mmikkola@verizon.net
E-mail: mmikkola@verizon.net

Scope: Nutrition consultant provides expertise for individuals and groups regarding food/health related issues.

15140 ■ NRH Nutrition Consultants Inc.
334 Hollywood Ave.
PO Box 630169
Little Neck, NY 11363
Ph:(718)229-0606

Fax:(718)631-4336
Co. E-mail: foodscount@aol.com
URL: http://www.thenutritionexperts.com
Contact: Annette B. Natow, President
E-mail: jhjne@aol.com

Scope: Registered dietitians and nutritionists providing services as translators of nutrition concepts and information. Serves private industries as well as government agencies. **Publications:** "The Fat Counter"; "The Complete Food Counter"; "The Healthy Whole foods Counter"; "The Cholesterol Counter"; "The Calorie Counter"; "The Diabetes, Carbohydrate and Calorie Counter"; "The Most Complete Food Counter"; "The Complete Food Counter"; "The Fat Counter"; "The Ultimate Carbohydrate Counter "; "The Vitamin and Mineral Food Counter"; "The Protein Counter"; "The Healthy Heart Food Counter"; "The Eating Out Food Counter"; "The Fat Attack Plan"; "Get Skinny the Smart Way: Your Personalized Weight Attack Plan".

15141 ■ R.D. Network Inc.
PO Box 375
Lafayette Hill, PA 19444
Ph:(215)482-4461
Free: 877-482-4991
Fax:(215)836-0378
Co. E-mail: info@rdnetwork.com
URL: http://www.rdnetwork.com
Contact: Melissa Altman, Principle
E-mail: info@rdnetwork.com

Scope: Dietitians, diet technicians, and certified dietary managers available nationwide and worldwide through an international registry for consulting positions to wellness and employee education programs, drug or alcohol rehabilitation, hospital, LTC, nutrition and labeling communications, nutrition consultation, weight control classes, healthcare staff supplementation, media and program development, and all nutrition and food-related needs. Expert witness and speakers bureau also available. Industries served: healthcare, food industry, food service, restaurateurs, supermarkets, pharmaceutical companies, home health agencies, insurance companies, HMOs, and government agencies. **Seminars:** Healthy Dining Etiquette for Executives and Sales Staff Diet and Wellness; Cardiovascular Nutrition; Starting a Nutrition Consulting Practice; AIDS and Diet Therapy; Nutrition Care for Your Parents in Their Elder Years; Increase Your Energy-Increase Your Sales.

15142 ■ VitaFlo Consultant
7707 Paragon Rd., Ste. 105
Centerville, OH 45459-4041
Ph:(937)436-1985
Co. E-mail: monica.cengia@vitaflo.co.uk
Contact: Monica A. Cengia, President
E-mail: monica.cengia@vitaflo.co.uk

Scope: Registered dietitian offers nutritional assessments and consultations. Also provides individualized nutrition counseling, wellness programs, nutrition education programs, long-term health-care counseling, and media presentations. Industries served: long-term health-care, hospitals, universities, private businesses, health clubs/spas, physicians' offices, food industry, radio, television, and newspaper. **Seminars:** Fresh Start for Healthy Lifestyle Changes in 2007.

FRANCHISES AND BUSINESS OPPORTUNITIES

15143 ■ The Dentist Choice, Inc.
Choice Corporation, Inc.
33971 Selva Rd., Ste. 200
Dana Point, CA 92629
Free: 888-757-1333
Fax:(949)443-2074

No. of Franchise Units: 120. **No. of Company-Owned Units:** 1. **Founded:** 1994. **Franchised:** 1994. **Description:** Dental health services. **Equity Capital Needed:** $60,000. **Franchise Fee:** $45,000. **Financial Assistance:** Yes. **Training:** Provides 1 week at headquarters and ongoing support.

15144 ■ General Nutrition Centers
GNC Franchising, Inc.
300 Sixth Ave.
Pittsburgh, PA 15222

Ph:(412)3388-2503
Free: 800-766-7099
Fax:(412)402-7105
Co. E-mail: livewell@gncfranchising.com
URL: http://www.gncfranchising.com

No. of Franchise Units: 2,014. **No. of Company-Owned Units:** 3,799. **Founded:** 1935. **Franchised:** 1988. **Description:** Retailer of vitamins, minerals, herbs and sports nutrition supplements. GNC is the provider of products & information for personal health enhancement. **Equity Capital Needed:** $132,681-$182,031. **Franchise Fee:** $40,000. **Financial Assistance:** Offers direct company financing to qualified individuals. **Training:** 3 weeks training including 1 week intensive training class at corporate headquarters.

15145 ■ Griswold Special Care
Griswold Special Care, Inc.
717 Bethlehem Pike, Ste. 300
Erdenheim, PA 19073
Ph:(215)402-0200
Fax:(215)402-0202
URL: http://www.griswoldspecialcare.com

No. of Franchise Units: 137. **No. of Company-Owned Units:** 9. **Founded:** 1982. **Franchised:** 1984. **Description:** Non-medical homecare. **Equity Capital Needed:** $72,325-$95,300. **Franchise Fee:** $39,500. **Royalty Fee:** 3-4%. **Financial Assistance:** Third party financing available. **Training:** Provides 1 week at corporate headquarters, 2-4 days onsite with ongoing training in the field and free annual workshop series.

15146 ■ The Hungry Heart
Hungry Heart Franchise, LLC
28202 Cabot Rd., Ste. 300
Laguna Niguel, CA 92677
Free: 877-486-4797
Fax:(714)280-9755

No. of Franchise Units: 5. **No. of Company-Owned Units:** 1. **Founded:** 1996. **Franchised:** 2006. **Description:** A caring approach to out of control eating. **Equity Capital Needed:** $43,000-$57,000. **Franchise Fee:** $24,500. **Financial Assistance:** No. **Training:** Yes.

COMPUTERIZED DATABASES

15147 ■ Health & Wellness InSite
Thomson Reuters
610 Opperman Dr.
Eagen, MN 55122
Free: 800-477-4300
Co. E-mail: gale.contentlicensing@cengage.com
URL: http://www.insite2.gale.com

Description: Contains complete information about health, medicine, fitness, and nutrition. Provides access to 170 of the world's leading professional and consumer health publications, including *The Lancet* and *Nutrition Today*; 550 health and medical pamphlets; 200,000 health-related articles from more than 3000 other publications; and 1800 overviews of different diseases and medical conditions published by Clinical Reference Systems, Ltd. Includes six medical reference books: *Columbia University College of Physicians & Surgeons Complete Home Medical Guide*; *Mosby's Medical, Nursing, and Allied Health Dictionary*; *Consumer Health Information Source Book*; *The People's Book of Medical Tests*; *USP DI-Vol. II Advice for the Patient*; *Drug Information in Lay Language*; and *The Complete Directory for People With Chronic Illness.*. Allows searches by article title, article type, author, company name, person discussed in the article, publication name, publication date range, publication type, target audience, ticker symbol, words in the title, and words that appear anywhere in the article. **Availability:** Online: Thomson Reuters. **Type:** Full text.

LIBRARIES

15148 ■ American Dietetic Association–Knowledge Center
120 S. Riverside Plaza, Ste. 20000
Chicago, IL 60606-6995
Ph:(312)877-1600, x4864

Free: 800-877-1600
Co. E-mail: knowledge@eatright.org
URL: http://www.eatright.org/
Contact: Margaret Williams, Info.Spec./Libn.
Scope: Nutrition, dietetics, food service. **Services:** Interlibrary loan; copying; Library open to the public by appointment. **Holdings:** 3000 books. **Subscriptions:** 60 journals and other serials; 4 newspapers.

15149 ■ American Institute for Biosocial and Medical Research, Inc. Library
4117 S. Meridian
Puyallup, WA 98373
Ph:(253)286-2888
Fax:(253)286-2451
Co. E-mail: aibmrinfo@aibmr.com
URL: http://www.aibmr.com
Contact: Kathryn Millhorn, Dir., Lib.Svcs.
Scope: Behavioral science - eating disorders, abnormal behavior, learning disabilities, behavior disorders; mental illness; biochemistry; environmental health; nutrition; psychology; sociology; criminology; medicine; organic chemistry; botanical pharmacognosy; photobiology; neurology; toxicology. **Services:** Library not open to the public. **Holdings:** 10,330 books; 350 periodicals; 60,000 reference papers. **Subscriptions:** 303 journals and other serials; 3 newspapers.

15150 ■ Bastyr University Library
14500 Juanita Dr., NE
Kenmore, WA 98028
Ph:(425)602-3020
Fax:(425)602-3188
Co. E-mail: library@bastyr.edu
URL: http://www.bastyr.edu/library
Contact: Jane D. Saxton, MLIS, Dir. of Lib.Svcs.
Scope: Complementary and alternative medicine, acupuncture and traditional Chinese medicine, naturopathic medicine, nutrition, health psychology, exercise science, primary care medicine, homeopathy, midwifery, herbal science, botanical medicine. **Services:** Interlibrary loan; copying; Library open to the public for reference use only. **Holdings:** 21,000 books; 4000 CD/audiocassettes; 800 DVD/videocassettes; online databases. **Subscriptions:** 250 journals and other serials.

15151 ■ Beech-Nut Nutrition Corporation Library
102 Church St.
Canajoharie, NY 13317
Ph:(518)673-3251
Fax:(518)673-3259
URL: http://www.beechnut.com
Contact: Joan Caska, Libn.
Scope: Nutrition, pediatrics, food chemistry. **Services:** Library not open to the public. **Holdings:** 1000 books. **Subscriptions:** 31 journals and other serials.

15152 ■ California Culinary Academy Library
625 Polk St.
San Francisco, CA 94102
Ph:800-229-2433
Free: 888-897-3222
Co. E-mail: bgk@baychef.com
URL: http://www.baychef.com
Contact: Beth Klein, Dean, Lib.Svcs.
Scope: Culinary arts, nutrition, restaurant and hospitality industry. **Services:** Library open to the public by special appointment only. **Holdings:** 3500 books. **Subscriptions:** 90 journals and other serials.

15153 ■ Campbell Soup Company Research Information Center
1 Campbell Pl.
Camden, NJ 09103-1799
Ph:(856)342-4800
Fax:(856)342-3878
URL: http://www.campbellsoup.com
Scope: Food technology, biochemistry, microbiology, nutrition. **Services:** Interlibrary loan; Library not open to the public. **Holdings:** 5000 books; 2200 bound periodical volumes; 3500 patents. **Subscriptions:** 250 journals and other serials.

15154 ■ Cleveland Health Sciences Library
Sch. of Medicine, Robbins Bldg.
2109 Adelbert Rd.
Cleveland, OH 44106-4914
Ph:(216)368-4540
Co. E-mail: virginia.saha@case.edu
URL: http://www.case.edu/chsl/homepage.htm
Contact: Virginia G. Saha, Dir.
Scope: Medicine, dentistry, nursing, biology, nutrition. **Services:** Interlibrary loan; copying; SDI; scanning and digitization; Library open to the public for reference use only. **Holdings:** 425,000 books and journal volumes; 3752 microfiche; 1000 lin.ft. of archives; 500 CD-ROMs; 2634 audio/visual programs; 51,433 slides. **Subscriptions:** 14,642 journals and other serials (91 print, 14,551 electronic).

15155 ■ Dairy Management Inc.–Information Resources
10255 W. Higgins, Ste. 900
Rosemont, IL 60018-5616
Ph:(847)803-2000
Fax:(847)803-2077
Co. E-mail: ronalds@rosedmi.com
Contact: Ronald Stoner, Dir.
Scope: Dairy products, food, nutrition. **Services:** Interlibrary loan; technical background information; Library not open to the public. **Holdings:** 3000 books. **Subscriptions:** 300 journals and other serials.

15156 ■ Geisinger Medical Center–Community Health Library
100 N. Academy Ave.
Danville, PA 17822-4401
Ph:(570)271-5638
Fax:(570)271-5635
Co. E-mail: chrl@geisinger.edu
URL: http://www.geisinger.edu
Contact: Patricia A Ulmer, Commun.Hea.Libn.
Scope: General medicine, nutrition, alternative and complementary medicine, pediatrics, cancer, AIDS. **Services:** Interlibrary loan. **Holdings:** 860 books; 200 audio/visual materials. **Subscriptions:** 14 journals and other serials.

15157 ■ General Mills, Inc. Betty Crocker Kitchens Library
PO Box 9452
Minneapolis, MN 55440
Ph:(612)330-8877
Free: 800-446-1898
Fax:(763)764-8330
URL: http://www.bettycrocker.com
Scope: Cookery. **Services:** Center not open to the public. **Holdings:** 9000 books. **Subscriptions:** 81 journals and other serials.

15158 ■ The Gottesman Libraries at Teachers College
Columbia University
525 W. 120th St.
Box 69
New York, NY 10027
Ph:(212)678-3494
Fax:(212)678-3029
URL: http://library.tc.columbia.edu
Scope: Education, psychology, health sciences, nutrition, nursing, communications, computing, technology, speech and language pathology, audiology. **Services:** Interlibrary loan; consultations; eReserves; bibliographic instruction; course-specific instruction; Library open to the public with METRO cards. **Holdings:** 566,457 monograph and serial volumes; 224,227 microforms; 6679 nonprint materials; 3694 cubic feet of manuscript material; 93,639 photographs; 8361 titles in microform; 5251 computer files; sound recordings; 65 cartographic; 2345 graphic; 1488 audio; 2781 film and video. **Subscriptions:** 2104 journals and other serials.

15159 ■ Kellogg Company–Kellogg Information Center
2 Hamblin Ave., E.
Battle Creek, MI 49016-3423
Ph:(269)961-6917

Fax:(269)565-1227
Co. E-mail: liz.scalia@kellogg.com
URL: http://www.kelloggs.com
Contact: Liz Scalia
Scope: Food science and nutrition. **Services:** Document delivery (for Kellogg employees); Center not open to the public. **Holdings:** 3000 books. **Subscriptions:** 115 journals and other serials.

15160 ■ Kraft Foods, Inc.–Technical Information Center
801 Waukegan Rd.
Glenview, IL 60025
Ph:(847)646-3509
Fax:(847)646-5150
URL: http://www.kraft.com
Contact: David Jourdan
Scope: Food technology, dairy science, nutrition, microbiology, packaging. **Services:** Library not open to the public. **Holdings:** 8600 books; 800 bound periodical volumes; 8600 reels of microfilm; 42,000 research reports. **Subscriptions:** 325 journals and other serials.

15161 ■ Lemmen-Holton Cancer Pavilion Library
135 Michigan NE
330 Barclay Ave., NE
Grand Rapids, MI 49503
Ph:(616)391-1655
Fax:(616)391-3527
Co. E-mail: diane.hummel@spectrum-health.org
URL: http://www.spectrum-health.org/
Contact: Diane Hummel, Lib.Mgr.
Scope: Cancer. **Services:** Library open to the public. **Holdings:** Pamphlets.

15162 ■ National College of Natural Medicine Library
Academic Bldg. 1st Fl.
049 SW Porter St.
Portland, OR 97201
Ph:(503)552-1542
Fax:(503)219-9709
Co. E-mail: circulation@ncnm.edu
URL: http://www.ncnm.edu/library/
Contact: Rick Severson, Lib.Dir.
Scope: Naturopathy, homeopathy, nutrition, physiotherapy, botanical medicine, Chinese medicine, acupuncture, clinical and basic sciences. **Services:** Interlibrary loan; copying; Library open to the public with restrictions. **Holdings:** 14,000 books, videos, and audiotapes; 1000 bound periodical volumes. **Subscriptions:** 140 journals and other serials.

15163 ■ National Eating Disorder Information Centre
ES 7-421
200 Elizabeth St.
Toronto, ON, Canada M5G 2C4
Ph:(416)340-4156
Free: (866)633-4220
Fax:(416)340-4736
Co. E-mail: nedic@uhn.on.ca
URL: http://www.nedic.ca
Contact: Merryl Bear, Dir.
Scope: Eating disorders, food preoccupation, weight preoccupation, support groups. **Services:** Centre open to the public. **Holdings:** 50 books. **Subscriptions:** 250 journals and other serials.

15164 ■ New York Public Library–Mid-Manhattan Library–General Reference and Advisory Services/Health Information Center (455 5)
455 5th Ave. at 40th St.
New York, NY 10016
Ph:(212)340-0863
URL: http://www.nypl.org/branch/central/mml
Contact: Wol Sue Lee, Dept.Hd.
Scope: Consumer, health medicine, nursing, allied health. **Services:** Copying; Library open to the public. **Holdings:** 22,000 books and videocassettes; 4 VF of pamphlets. **Subscriptions:** 278 journals and other serials.

15165 ■ PepsiCo–The Information Center
617 W. Main St.
Barrington, IL 60010
Ph:(847)304-2064
Fax:(847)304-2062
Co. E-mail: sharon.lazzara@pepsico.com
Contact: Sharon Lazzara, Info.Anl.
Scope: Food, nutrition, exercise physiology, beverages. **Services:** Interlibrary loan; copying (limited). **Holdings:** 3000 books. **Subscriptions:** 200 journals and other serials.

15166 ■ Price-Pottenger Nutrition Foundation Library
7890 Broadway
Lemon Grove, CA 91945
Ph:(619)462-7600
Free: 800-366-3748
Fax:(619)433-3136
Co. E-mail: info@ppnf.org
URL: http://www.ppnf.org/catalog/ppnf/ReferenceLibrary.htm
Contact: Joan Grinzi, Exec.Dir.
Scope: Nutrition, preventative medicine, health, natural farming and gardening, pesticides, fluoride, mercury, dental health, natural farming and gardening, natural pet care, traditional/historic diets, primitive diets, holistic medicine. **Services:** Copying; Library open to members only for reference use. **Holdings:** 10,000 volumes; 18,000 film positives; 6000 glass lantern slides; scientific reprints; video and audio tapes; reports; archives. **Subscriptions:** Journals and other serials.

15167 ■ Ross Products Division–Abbott Laboratories–Resource Center (625 C)
625 Cleveland Ave.
Columbus, OH 43215
Ph:(614)624-3800
Fax:(614)727-3800
Co. E-mail: rosswebmaster@abbott.com
URL: http://abbottnutrition.com
Contact: Mary-Jeanne Metz, Mgr., Div.Info.Rsrcs.
Scope: Nutrition, food technology, business, analytical chemistry. **Services:** Current Awareness. **Holdings:** 3500 books; 6000 bound periodical volumes. **Subscriptions:** 350 journals and other serials.

15168 ■ Tufts University–Hirsh Health Sciences Library
145 Harrison Ave.
Boston, MA 02111
Ph:(617)636-6705
Fax:(617)636-4039
Co. E-mail: eric.albright@tufts.edu
URL: http://www.library.tufts.edu/hsl/index.html
Contact: Eric D. Albright, Dir.
Scope: Medicine, dentistry, veterinary medicine, nutrition. **Services:** Interlibrary loan; copying; online databases searching; SDI; Library open to the public by subscription. **Holdings:** 47,227 books; 160,127 bound periodical volumes; 581 audiotapes; 292 slide titles; reels of microfilm; microcards; 255 videotapes; phonograph records; video discs. **Subscriptions:** 921 journals and other serials; 19,000 electronic journals and other serials.

15169 ■ Unilever Foods R&D Information Center
800 Sylvan Ave.
Englewood Cliffs, NJ 07632-3201
Ph:(732)894-7569
Fax:(732)627-8506
Co. E-mail: john.troisi@unilever.com
Contact: Karla Cicciari, Info.Spec.
Scope: Nutrition, food technology, cookery, food microbiology, food analysis. **Services:** Interlibrary loan. **Holdings:** 10,000 books; company reports and patents on microfiche; archives; microfilm. **Subscriptions:** 300 journals and other serials.

15170 ■ U.S.D.A.–Agricultural Research Service–Western Regional Research Center Library (800 B)
800 Buchanan St.
Albany, CA 94710
Ph:(510)559-5603

Fax:(510)559-5766
Co. E-mail: howard.zhang@ars.usda.gov
URL: http://www.ars.usda.gov/AboutUs/AboutUs.htm?modecode=53-25-00-00
Contact: Howard Q. Zhang, Ctr.Dir.
Scope: Cereals, fruits and vegetables, field crops, food technology, chemistry, nutrition. **Services:** Interlibrary loan; copying; SDI; Library open to the public by appointment. **Holdings:** Figures not available.

15171 ■ U.S.D.A.–National Agricultural Library–Food and Nutrition Information Center (10301)
10301 Baltimore Ave., Rm. 105
Beltsville, MD 20705-2351
Ph:(301)504-5414
Fax:(301)504-6409
URL: http://fnic.nal.usda.gov
Contact: Dennis Smith, Info.Ctr.Coord.
Scope: Human nutrition education, nutrition resources for USDA food and nutrition programs. **Services:** Interlibrary loan; Center open to the public with restricted lending. **Holdings:** 50,000 books; VF drawers. **Subscriptions:** 200 journals and other serials.

15172 ■ U.S. Food & Drug Administration–Biosciences Library–CFSAN Branch Library (5100)
5100 Paint Branch Pkwy.
HFS-678
College Park, MD 20740
Ph:(301)436-2163
Fax:(301)436-2653
Co. E-mail: cfsanlib@fda.hhs.gov
Contact: Lee S. Bernstein, Br.Mgr.
Scope: Chemistry, analytical chemistry, toxicology, food technology, nutrition, medicine, biology, cosmetics. **Services:** Interlibrary loan; Library open to the public. **Holdings:** 1000 books; 500 reports, documents, pamphlets; 16,000 cartridges of microfilm. **Subscriptions:** 100 journals and other serials.

15173 ■ University of California, Berkeley–Marian Koshland Bioscience and Natural Resources Library
2101 Valley Life Sciences Bldg., No. 6500
Berkeley, CA 94720-6500
Ph:(510)642-2531
Fax:(510)642-8217
Co. E-mail: bweil@library.berkeley.edu
URL: http://www.lib.berkeley.edu/BIOS
Contact: Beth Weil, Hd.Libn.
Scope: Agriculture, anatomy, botany, cell biology, environmental sciences, molecular biology, biology, nutrition, pest management, physiology, forestry, entomology, paleontology. **Services:** Interlibrary loan (through General Library); copying; Library open to the public for reference use with restricted circulation; printing; scanning. **Holdings:** 542,000 volumes; 50,633 pamphlets and reprints; 1543 reels of microfilm; 24,005 microfiche. **Subscriptions:** 6500 journals and other serials; 10,000 e-journals.

15174 ■ University of Hawaii–John A. Burns School of Medicine–Health Sciences Library (651 I)
651 Ilalo St., MEB
Honolulu, HI 96813
Ph:(808)692-0810
Fax:(808)692-1244
Co. E-mail: hslinfo@hawaii.edu
URL: http://www.hawaii.edu/hslib
Contact: Virginia Tanji, Lib.Dir.
Scope: Public health, health services planning and administration, quantitative health sciences, health education, clinical medicine. **Services:** Interlibrary loan; copying; document delivery; Library open to the public. **Holdings:** 12,000 books; 1200 bound periodical volumes. **Subscriptions:** 70 journals and other serials.

15175 ■ University of Nebraska—Lincoln–C.Y. Thompson Library
38th and Holdrege Sts., East Campus
Lincoln, NE 68583-0717
Ph:(402)472-4401

Fax:(402)472-7005
Co. E-mail: cytmail@unlnotes.unl.edu
URL: http://libraries.unl.edu/cyt
Contact: Rebecca Bernthal, Liaison Libn.
Scope: Agriculture, natural resources, home economics, textiles, wildlife conservation, human development, family therapy, nutrition, food science, applied sciences, speech pathology, audiology, special education, dentistry, dental hygiene, oral surgery. **Services:** Interlibrary loan; copying; Library open to the public. **Holdings:** 187,399 books; 181,237 bound periodical volumes; 49,116 microforms. **Subscriptions:** 14,789 journals and other serials; 3 newspapers.

RESEARCH CENTERS

15176 ■ Center for Medical Consumers
239 Thompson St.
New York, NY 10012
Ph:(212)674-7105
Fax:(212)674-7100
Co. E-mail: centerformedicalconsumers@gmail.com
URL: http://medicalconsumers.org
Contact: Arthur Aaron Levin, Dir.
E-mail: centerformedicalconsumers@gmail.com
Scope: Mainstream and alternative medical treatments. **Publications:** HealthFacts (monthly).

15177 ■ Columbia University–Institute of Human Nutrition
College of Physicians & Surgeons, Ste. 1512
Presbyterian Hospital
630 W 168th St.
New York, NY 10032
Ph:(212)305-4808
Fax:(212)305-3079
Co. E-mail: nutrition@mail.cumc.columbia.edu
URL: http://www.cumc.columbia.edu
Contact: Richard J. Deckelbaum MD, Dir.
E-mail: nutrition@mail.cumc.columbia.edu
Scope: Atherosclerosis, lipoprotein-receptor-cell interaction; lipid emulsion metabolism; free fatty acids and cell lipid metabolism; basic retinoid and vitamin A physiology, biochemistry, and molecular biology; food and nutrition policy and law; intestinal ion transport mechanisms; enteric nervous system; human lipoprotein metabolism; lipolytic enzymes and endothelial cell biology; atherosclerosis; mineral metabolism and toxicology; carbohydrate and lipid metabolism, obesity, diabetes mellitus, food intake regulation; calcium metabolism; vascular cell biology; pathogenesis of thrombosis; regulation of intracellular cholesterol metabolism; endocytic pathways in macrophages; cholestryl ester transfer; protein structure/function and mutagenesis; regulation of gene expression; molecular nutrition; molecular mechanisms of carcinogenesis.

15178 ■ Ohio State University–Food Industries Center
Howlett Hall, Ste. 140
2001 Fyffe Rd.
Columbus, OH 43210-1007
Ph:(614)292-7004
Free: 800—752-2751
Fax:(614)688-5459
Co. E-mail: alvarez.23@osu.edu
URL: http://foodindustries.osu.edu
Contact: Dr. Valente B. Alvarez, Dir.
E-mail: alvarez.23@osu.edu
Scope: Food industries (plant and animal products), including technology, processing, engineering, marketing, food service, and food science and nutrition. Serves as the focal point of food activities on campus, including University-food industry cooperation, research coordination, and service programs. Maintains the Endowed Chair in Food Industries. **Publications:** Annual Reports; Bulletins; Newsletter Quarterly (quarterly). **Educational Activities:** Better Process Control School; Seminars.

15179 ■ University of Florida–Center for Nutritional Sciences
201 Food Science & Human Nutrition Bldg.
PO Box 110370
Gainesville, FL 32611
Ph:(352)392-2133

Fax:(352)392-1008
Co. E-mail: cousins@ufl.edu
URL: http://nutritionalsciences.centers.ufl.edu/default.
  aspx
Contact: Dr. Robert J. Cousins, Dir.
E-mail: cousins@ufl.edu
Scope: Nutritional sciences, including bioavailability of vitamins and minerals, bioinstrumentation in nutrition research, dietary regulation of gene expression, neonatal and developmental nutrition, trace elements and defense mechanisms, mechanisms of nutrient absorption, neuroendocrine control of food intake,

hormonal control of nutrient metabolism, metabolic studies with stable isotopes, animal models for total parenteral nutrition, nutritional status assessment in man and domestic animals, and nutritional anthropology. **Educational Activities:** Graduate Program; Graduate Research Assistantships; Seminars (periodically), on nutrition.

15180 ■ University of Texas Southwestern Medical Center at Dallas—Center for Human Nutrition
5323 Harry Hines Blvd.
Dallas, TX 75390-9052

Ph:(214)648-2890
Fax:(214)648-8955
Co. E-mail: nutrition@utsouthwestern.edu
URL: http://www.utsouthwestern.edu/utsw/cda/
  dept27712/files/40245.html
Contact: Prof. Scott M. Grundy PhD, Dir.
E-mail: nutrition@utsouthwestern.edu
Scope: Human nutrition. Investigates the preventive effects of vitamins C and E on atherosclerosis.

ASSOCIATIONS AND OTHER ORGANIZATIONS

15181 ■ Business and Institutional Furniture Manufacturer's Association
678 Front Ave. NW, Ste. 150
Grand Rapids, MI 49504-5368
Ph:(616)285-3963
Fax:(616)285-3765
Co. E-mail: email@bifma.org
URL: http://www.bifma.org
Contact: Thomas Reardon, Exec. Dir.
Description: Organized group of furniture manufacturers and suppliers addressing issues of common concern to the contract furnishings industry. Works to develop, expand, and promote work environments that enhance the productivity and comfort of customers. **Publications:** *The Download* (quarterly).

15182 ■ International Interior Design Association
222 Merchandise Mart, Ste. 567
Chicago, IL 60654
Ph:(312)467-1950
Free: 888-799-4432
Fax:(312)467-0779
Co. E-mail: iidahq@iida.org
URL: http://www.iida.org
Contact: Peter Conant, Pres.-Elect
Description: Represents professional interior designers, including designers of commercial, healthcare, hospitality, government, retail, residential facilities; educators; researchers; representatives of allied manufacturing sources. Conducts research, student programs and continuing education programs for members. Has developed a code of ethics for the professional design membership. **Publications:** *GRAction* .

15183 ■ MTM Association for Standards and Research
1111 E Touhy Ave.
Des Plaines, IL 60018
Ph:(847)299-1111
Fax:(847)299-3509
Co. E-mail: webmaster@mtm.org
URL: http://www.mtm.org
Description: Persons interested in the fields of industrial engineering, industrial psychology, and human engineering. Conducts research at accredited institutions on human motion (the physical movement of body and limb), with emphasis on examining: internal velocity, acceleration, tension, and control characteristics of a given motion under several conditions; external regularities of given groups of motion as they vary under several conditions of performance; the proper use of motion information in measuring, controlling, and improving manual activities. Also studies ergonomics and the effects of workplace environment on productivity. Provides information on fatigue, optimum methods of performance, the effect of practice on motion performance, and the use of motion information for determining allowances and predicting total performance time. Has developed computer programs for the application of Methods Time Measurement (MTM) and MTM-based work measurement systems. Conducts training courses and testing for certification of practitioners and instructors in all Association MTM Systems. Develops and makes available specialized productivity management services. .

REFERENCE WORKS

15184 ■ "Bridging the Ingenuity Gap" in *Canadian Business* (Vol. 79, November 6, 2006, No. 22, pp. 12)
Pub: Rogers Media
Ed: Rachel Pulfer. **Description:** The views of Patrick Whitney, director of Illinois Institute of Technology's Institute of design, on globalization and business design methods are presented.

15185 ■ "Colores Origenes: Martha Kruse" in *Advertising Age* (Vol. 77, November 13, 2006, No. 46, pp. S12)
Pub: Crain Communications, Inc.
Ed: Laurel Wentz. **Description:** Home Depot has created a range of Latin paint colors called Colores Origenes; the new line was originally intended to launch only at locations with heavily Hispanic patrons but the company decided to make the line available at all of their stores.

15186 ■ "Fabulous New Office Furniture: Ways to Revamp Your Workspace" in *Inc.* (Vol. 33, September 2011, No. 7, pp. 51)
Pub: Inc. Magazine
Ed: Nadine Heintz. **Description:** Various new looks to revamp any office space are highlighted including a table lamp by designer Peter Stathis for Joby.

15187 ■ "Inside the Googleplex" in *Canadian Business* (Vol. 79, November 6, 2006, No. 22, pp. 59)
Pub: Rogers Media
Ed: Christina Campbell. **Description:** The views of Clive Wilkinson, a designer, on relationship between interior design and employee's productivity are presented.

15188 ■ "Intel Joins Movement to Turn Cube Farms Into Wide-Open Spaces" in *Sacramento Business Journal* (Vol. 28, May 27, 2011, No. 13, pp. 1)
Pub: Sacramento Business Journal
Ed: Melanie Turner. **Description:** Intel Corporation has remodeled its facility in Folsom, California. The renovation has required some workers to give up their cubicles. Comments from executives are included.

15189 ■ "Let Your Stuff Tell a Story: How to Edit Your Accessories to Showcase Your Personality" in *Charlotte Observer* (February 8, 2007)
Pub: Knight-Ridder/Tribune Business News
Ed: Nancy Brachey. **Description:** Tips to accessorize any home or office are presented; eliminating clutter is stressed.

15190 ■ "Make a Resolution: ADA Training" in *HRMagazine* (Vol. 54, January 2009, No. 1, pp. 81)
Pub: Society for Human Resource Management
Ed: Victoria Zellers. **Description:** Americans with Disabilities Act (ADA) Amendments Act took effect January 1, 2009. The ADA Amendments Act means that more applicants and employees are eligible for reasonable accommodations and that employers need to develop a new ADA compliance strategy.

15191 ■ "Procter Gambles on Wallpaper; Putting Paint On a Roll" in *Advertising Age* (Vol. 77, September 18, 2006, No. 38, pp. 4)
Pub: Crain Communications, Inc.
Ed: Jack Neff. **Description:** Procter & Gamble Co. has launched a new line of textured paints that are already applied to a wallpaper-like roll that can be hung without paste or wallpaper tools.

15192 ■ "Shore Total Office Liquidates Massive Supply of Bank Furniture and Used Furniture" in *Internet Wire* (June 21, 2010)
Pub: Comtex
Description: Shore Total Office, located in San Diego, California, is liquidating quality bank furniture and used furniture to customers hoping to outfit their facilities with stylish new furnishings. Shore Total Office is a leading supplier of high quality office furniture and designs.

TRADE PERIODICALS

15193 ■ *Human Factors and Ergonomics Society Bulletin*
Pub: Human Factors and Ergonomics Society
Released: Monthly. **Description:** Recurring features include letters to the editor, news of research, a calendar of events, reports of meetings, news of educational opportunities, job listings, and notices of publications available.

15194 ■ *IE News: Ergonomics*
Pub: Institute of Industrial Engineers
Ed: Wendy Kavanagh, Editor. **Released:** Quarterly. **Price:** Included in membership. **Description:** Focuses on ergonomics (human factors) in the work place, the development of ergonomic standards, and case studies. Recurring features include a calendar of events, reports of meetings, and columns titled Message from the Director, Academic Roundup: Update, and Message from the Editor.

15195 ■ *Interior Design*
Pub: Reed Business Information
Contact: Helene Oberman, Managing Editor
E-mail: hoberman@interiordesign.net
Released: 15/yr. **Price:** $59.95; $87 Canada; $187 other countries. **Description:** Interior designing and furnishings magazine.

15196 ■ *Today's Facility Manager*
Pub: Group C Communications Inc.
Contact: Heidi Schwartz, Ed./Co-Publisher
E-mail: schwartz@groupc.com
Released: Monthly. **Description:** Tabloid for facility design and management.

CONSULTANTS

15197 ■ Alfred Swenson Pao-Chi Chang Architects

1104 S Wabash Ave., Ste. 601
Chicago, IL 60605
Ph:(312)431-1720
Fax:(312)431-1721
URL: http://www.swensonchangcasina.com
Contact: Alfred Swenson, Partner
E-mail: alfred_swenson@swensonchangcasina.com
Scope: Expertise and is internationally recognized in providing architectural theory and conceptual design for small, mid-rise, high-rise and ultra-tall buildings, offer traditional architectural services.

15198 ■ Building Design Service

350 Kresge Ln., Ste. B
Sparks, NV 89431-6435
Ph:(775)356-7870
Contact: Brian A. Beecher, President
Scope: Building design consultants with additional expertise in mine plant and facility design, structural and miscellaneous steel detailing and construction estimating.

15199 ■ Carmichael Associates

4255 Auburn St.
Wichita, KS 67220
Ph:(316)681-1535
Fax:(316)681-1548
Co. E-mail: joewmc@aol.com
Contact: Joe William Carmichael, President
E-mail: joewmc@aol.com
Scope: Architectural consultant active in legal assistance, library design, church design, health care projects, nursing homes, clinics, apartments, governmental buildings, renovations and remodeling work, residential and commercial, heavy truck maintenance and operations design, and small college buildings and planning.

15200 ■ Cassway/Albert Ltd.

1528 Walnut St., Ste. 1100
Philadelphia, PA 19102
Ph:(215)545-4900
Fax:(215)545-8222
Co. E-mail: cal@icdc.com
Contact: Elliot J. Rothschield, Principle
Scope: Consultants in architecture, landscape architecture, urban planning, interior design, and space planning.

15201 ■ Hewitt Architects

101 Stewart St., Ste. 200
Seattle, WA 98101-1048
Ph:(206)624-8154
Fax:(206)626-0541
Co. E-mail: information@hewittseattle.com
URL: http://www.hewittarchitects.com
Contact: Timothy L. Spelman, Principle
E-mail: spelman@atshewittarchitects.com
Scope: Multi-disciplinary firm with architecture, design and landscape architecture expertise specializing in new construction and renovation of administrative, waterfront, transportation facilities, urban residential and mixed-use complexes; master plan development for urban centers, village concepts, destination resorts, office parks/campuses, shopping facilities and transportation/multi-modal facilities.

15202 ■ The Hezner Corp.

678 Broadway St., Ste. 100
Libertyville, IL 60048-2324
Ph:(847)918-3800
Fax:(847)549-7633
Co. E-mail: info@hezner.com
URL: http://www.hezner.biz
Contact: Scott K. Hezner, Vice President
E-mail: kurth@atshezner.biz
Scope: Architectural design and internal layout design of financial institutions-banks, savings and loan associations, credit unions, and commercial facilities. Recommends practical procedures and practices, site plans and floor plans. Serves private industries as well as government, particularly the United States.

15203 ■ HLW International L.L.P.

115 Fifth Ave., 5th Fl.
New York, NY 10003-1004
Ph:(212)353-4600
Fax:(212)353-4666
Co. E-mail: jgering@hlw.com
URL: http://www.hlw.com
Contact: Ted Hammer, V Chm Bd
E-mail: thammer@atshlw.com
Scope: Provides a growing portfolio of comprehensive services for many diverse projects located throughout the United States and the world, including architecture, engineering, planning, interior design, and consulting. As part of its expanding practice, offers a series of next-generation services, which provide clients with expertise outside the realm of traditional disciplines: workplace management, strategic facilities planning and design/build. **Publications:** "Interior Design". **Seminars:** Rehabilitation of Office Facilities; R&D Facilities Costs and Cost Analysis; Renovation of R&D Buildings and Labs; Trends and New Developments for Medical Research Facilities; New Technologies for R&D Building Systems; New Labs for Pharmaceutical, Biotechnology, Medical Device and Personal Care Products. **Special Services:** Workplace ED/GE.

15204 ■ Marconi Designs

985 University Ave., Ste. 22
PO Box 320926
Los Gatos, CA 95032-0115
Ph:(408)807-8330
Fax:(408)841-7234
Co. E-mail: patricia@marconidesigns.com
URL: http://www.wahlichusa.com/design
Contact: Patricia A. Wahli, Owner
E-mail: patricia@marconidesigns.com
Scope: Provides interior design, space planning and facility design for commercial office buildings of any size. Renovation, remodel and reconfiguration of personnel workspaces and existing buildings the firms specialties. Tenant improvements for new and existing office space also handled. Industries served electronics, medical, banking industries and government agencies in California, statewide, with emphasis on San Francisco Bay Area.

15205 ■ Michaels Associates Design Consultants Inc.

14809 N 73rd St.
Scottsdale, AZ 85260-3113
Ph:(480)998-7476
Fax:(480)998-9390
Co. E-mail: info@madeline.com
URL: http://www.madcinc.com
Contact: David Leroy Michaels, Vice President
E-mail: david@atsmadcinc.com
Scope: Twenty year specialization in all areas of library (public, academic, corporate and national) programming and planning, including needs assessments and interior and graphic design. Michaels Associates expertise also includes ADA audits, furniture and product design for offices, lighting and graphic design. **Publications:** "Forum III: Physical Spaces for the E-ssential Library," 2003; "Library facility Planning"; "Library Administration & Management"; "Enhance Security With Effective Interior Planning and Design"; "Designing for Technology in Todays Libraries". **Seminars:** Library Environments: Changing to Fit New Technologies and Services, Dowling College, Long Island, NY, Nov, 2004; Reconfiguration Strategies Library Space for the E-Library, Information Futures Institute, San Francisco, CA, Sep, 2004; Creative Learning Seminars; Library Interior Planning & Design; Accessible, Healthy, Imaginative Spaces: Old & New; Fresh Looks for Library Interiors; The Future is Now: Library Planning &Design for the 21st Century; ADA Furnishings Response for Today's Libraries; Lighting & Libraries; Library Planning Based on New Functional Space Guidelines; Crime Prevention through Environmental Design.

15206 ■ Pinnix Design Inc.

2507 Goldcup Ln.
PO Box 8004
Reston, VA 20191-4219
Ph:(703)620-1167

Fax:(703)715-0811
Contact: Van L. Pinnix, President
E-mail: vlpinnix@sprynet.com
Scope: Architecture, bio-remediation, provides services in commercial interior design, space planning, architectural interior design, construction, specifications, procurement and installation management for commercial, institutional and industrial spaces. Serves private industries, particularly construction, as well as government agencies in the mid-Atlantic, northern and southeastern United States.

15207 ■ Site Design Group Ltd.

888 S Michigan Ave., Ste. 1000
Chicago, IL 60605
Ph:(312)427-7240
Fax:(312)427-7241
Co. E-mail: ecwong@site-design.com
URL: http://www.site-design.com
Contact: Juli Ordower, Mgr
E-mail: fksit@atssite-design.com
Scope: An architectural/engineering consulting firm with experience in food facilities design; interior design; landscape planning and plant/office layout and design. Serves a wide variety of industries and government agencies. **Publications:** "Wilderness Experiences inspire Urban design," Apr, 2004; "A Cultural Revolution: In Chicago's Chinatown, carving a public space out of an urban wasteland," Landscape Architecture, Jul, 2002; "Chinatown returns to center stage," Chicago Tribune, Jan, 2002; "An el of a tour," Chicago Magazine, Dec, 2000; "Chinatown cheers new park on river," Chicago Sun-Times, Sep, 1999; "Gateway to a greener China town," Chicago Sun-Times, Aug, 1998; "When does home remodeling become big rehab," News Chicago, Sep, 1987.

15208 ■ Vinod H. Dholakia-Architect P.C.

107-16 Jamaica Ave.
Richmond Hill, NY 11418-2239
Ph:(718)805-6790
Fax:(718)805-6790
Co. E-mail: vinodarchitect@msn.com
E-mail: vinodarchitect@msn.com
Scope: Architect and interior designer of residential, commercial stores, offices and restaurants and industrial buildings and spaces including zoning analysis and code compliance, space planning, lighting design, graphic design and furniture and furnishings selections. Active in new and renovation conversion projects. Industries served home owners, businesses, real estate investors and developers, retail corporations and government agencies.

15209 ■ Walsh Bishop Associates

900 N 3rd St.
Minneapolis, MN 55401
Ph:(612)338-8799
Free: 888-871-5615
Fax:(612)337-5785
Co. E-mail: info@walshbishop.com
URL: http://www.walshbishop.com
Contact: Keith O'Brien, Principle
E-mail: robert.walsh@atswalshbishop.com
Scope: Firm committed to providing customer solutions through architecture, interior design and facility management services. Those services include, master planning, landscape design, strategic facility planning, tenant services, programming, project management and food service design. Walsh Bishop is a 50-person firm located in downtown Minneapolis specializing in the areas of corporate, industrial, commercial, hospitality, entertainment, and housing projects locally and nationally.

FRANCHISES AND BUSINESS OPPORTUNITIES

15210 ■ California Closet Company

1000 4th St., Ste. 800
San Rafael, CA 94901
Ph:(415)256-8500
Free: 800-241-3222

Fax:(415)256-8501

No. of Franchise Units: 77. **Founded:** 1978. **Franchised:** 1982. **Description:** Custom closet design, manufacture, and installation. **Equity Capital Needed:** $127,500-$377,000 total investment. **Franchise Fee:** $40,000. **Royalty Fee:** 6%. **Financial Assistance:** No. **Training:** Includes training at headquarters, franchisees location, mentor training with ongoing support.

COMPUTERIZED DATABASES

15211 ■ *Art Index*
EBSCO Publishing
10 Estes St.
Ipswich, MA 01938
Ph:(978)356-6500
Free: 800-653-2726
Fax:(978)356-6565
Co. E-mail: information@ebscohost.com
URL: http://www.ebscohost.com/wilson

Description: Contains more than 870,000 citations to articles, reproductions, and book reviews in 400 periodicals, yearbooks, and museum bulletins published worldwide. Covers archaeology, architecture, art history, city planning, crafts, landscape architecture, film, fine arts, folk art, graphic arts, industrial design, interior design, and photography. Corresponds to *Art Index*. **Availability:** Online: EBSCO Publishing, Wolters Kluwer Health, Wolters Kluwer Health. **Type:** Bibliographic.

LIBRARIES

15212 ■ Tech-U-Fit Corporation Library
400 Madison St., No. 210
Alexandria, VA 22314
Ph:(703)549-0512
Fax:(703)548-0780
Contact: John Molino

Scope: Engineering, psychology, human factors engineering, ergonomics. **Holdings:** 200 volumes.

RESEARCH CENTERS

15213 ■ Western Michigan University–Human Performance Institute
Department of Industrial & Manufacturing Engineering
College of Engineering & Applied Sciences
4601 Campus Dr.
Kalamazoo, MI 49008-5336
Ph:(269)276-3360
Co. E-mail: tycho.fredericks@wmich.edu
URL: http://www.wmich.edu/ime/facilities/hpi.html
Contact: Dr. Tycho Fredericks, Dir.
E-mail: tycho.fredericks@wmich.edu
Scope: Ergonomics, work analysis and design, human capabilities in the workplace, job safety, and product design. Research focuses on analysis of job requirements such as strength, coordination, reaction time flexibility and dexterity, heart rate variations, oxygen use, and environmental factors. **Services:** In-house presentations and ergonomic audits. **Educational Activities:** Public workshops.

ASSOCIATIONS AND OTHER ORGANIZATIONS

15214 ■ Business Technology Association
12411 Wornall Rd., Ste. 200
Kansas City, MO 64145
Ph:(816)941-3100
Free: 800-505-2821
Fax:(816)941-4838
Co. E-mail: info@bta.org
URL: http://www.bta.org
Contact: Tom Ouellette, Pres.
Description: Dealers and resellers of office equipment and networking products and services. Offers 60 seminars on management, service, technology, and business systems. Conducts research, provides business-supporting services and benefits, including insurance, and legal counsel. **Publications:** *BTA Membership Directory* (annual); *Business Owner* (bimonthly); *Office Technology* (monthly).

15215 ■ Information Technology Industry Council
1101 K St. NW, Ste. 610
Washington, DC 20005
Ph:(202)737-8888
Fax:(202)638-4922
Co. E-mail: kkriner@itic.org
URL: http://www.itic.org
Contact: Dean Garfield, Pres./CEO
Description: Represents manufacturers of information technology products. Serves as secretariat and technology for ANSI-accredited standards committee x3 information technology group. Conducts public policy programs; compiles industry statistics. **Publications:** *Washington Letter* (biweekly).

15216 ■ ISDA - Association of Storage and Retrieval Professionals
750 Holiday Dr., Bldg. 9, Ste. 500
Pittsburgh, PA 15220
Free: 877-921-3501
Fax:(412)921-3525
Co. E-mail: elborne@isdanet.net
URL: http://www.isdanet.net
Description: Independent dealers of office filing systems and microfilm equipment. Aims to promote the development of the filing systems industry, and to maintain a high standard of ethics among members. Distributes information, encourages better business methods, and promotes the services of members to consumers. Sponsors dealer management and sales training programs. .

15217 ■ Print Services and Distribution Association
401 N Michigan Ave., Ste. 2200
Chicago, IL 60611
Free: 800-230-0175
Fax:(312)673-6880
Co. E-mail: psda@psda.org
URL: http://www.psda.org
Contact: Mr. Matt Sanderson, Exec. VP
Description: Independent distributors, manufacturers and suppliers to the forms, business printing and document management industries. Sponsors educa-

tional and channel marketing programs. Compiles statistics. **Publications:** *PERF Print Report* (quarterly); *Print Solutions Weekly* (weekly); *Who's Who in the Business Printing and Document Management Industry* (annual).

15218 ■ School and Office Products Network
3131 Elbee Rd.
Dayton, OH 45439
Ph:(937)610-3333
URL: http://www.schoolandofficenetwork.org
Contact: Dee Dee Hunt, Sec.
Description: Manufacturers, wholesaler and service merchandisers, importers, retailers, commercial/contract stationers, manufacturers' representatives, and associated individuals. Promotes the advancement of the school, office, and home office product industry through an annual trade show, research initiations and other benefits and services. .**Telecommunication Services:** electronic mail, stevej@shopa.org.

REFERENCE WORKS

15219 ■ "Bringing Charities More Bang for Their Buck" in *Crain's Chicago Business* (Vol. 34, May 23, 2011, No. 21, pp. 31)
Pub: Crain Communications Inc.
Ed: Lisa Bertagnoli. **Description:** Marcy-Newberry Association connects charities with manufacturers in order to use excess items such as clothing, janitorial and office supplies.

15220 ■ "Firm Stays In the 'Family'; After Owner's Death, Employees Buy Company" in *Crain's Detroit Business* (Vol. 24, January 28, 2008)
Pub: Crain Communications Inc. - Detroit
Ed: Chad Halcom. **Description:** Sterling Office Systems Inc., distributor of photocopiers and other office machines was purchased from the owner's family after his demise. The new owners would like to hit $1.75 million in sales their first year.

15221 ■ "A Labelmaker with Style" in *Inc.* (Vol. 33, October 2011, No. 8, pp. 48)
Pub: Inc. Magazine
Ed: John Brandon. **Description:** Epson's first labelmaker, the LabelWorks LW-400 offers many design options and has a full QWERTY keyboard that allows users to create and print labels in various sizes.

15222 ■ *Orion Blue Book—Copier*
Pub: Orion Research Corp.
Contact: Roger Rohrs, Publisher
Released: Annual, Latest edition 2007. **Price:** $130, individuals hardbound or CD. **Publication Includes:** List of manufacturers of copiers and other office equipment. **Entries Include:** Company name, address, phone. Principal content of publication is a listing of 3,091 office equipment products with the original retail value, value paid to customer on trade-in when in mint condition, and average value paid to customer on trade-in. **Arrangement:** Alphabetical.

15223 ■ "Staples Advantage Receives NJPA National Contract for Janitorial Supplies" in *Professional Services Close-Up* (April 22, 2011)
Pub: Close-Up Media
Description: Staples Advantage, the business-to-business division of Staples Inc. was awarded a contract for janitorial supplies to members of the National Joint Powers Alliance (NJPA). NJPA is a member-owned buying cooperative serving public and private schools, state and local governments, and nonprofit organizations.

STATISTICAL SOURCES

15224 ■ *The American Demand for Office Furniture and Anticipated Trends–Aktrin*
Pub: AKTRIN Furniture Research
Ed: Stephan Wille. **Released:** 2008. **Price:** $785.00 (paper).

15225 ■ *Office Furniture Market*
Pub: Business Trend Analysts
Released: 2008. **Price:** $3000.00. **Description:** Offers statistical analysis of the office furniture trade, including sales data and past performance, projections to the year 2000, labor trends in white-collar occupations, new product and design innovations, methods for distribution, construction and remodeling trends, pricing, industry economic structure, and strategies for advertising and promotions. Profiles of major companies in the industry are also included.

15226 ■ *RMA Annual Statement Studies*
Pub: Robert Morris Associates (RMA)
Released: Annual. **Price:** $175.00 2006-07 edition, $105.00. **Description:** Contains composite balance sheets and income statements for more than 360 industries, including the accounting, auditing, and bookkeeping industries. Also contains five years of comparative historical data for discerning trends. Includes 16 commonly used ratios, computed for most of the size groupings for nearly every industry.

FRANCHISES AND BUSINESS OPPORTUNITIES

15227 ■ California Closet Company
1000 4th St., Ste. 800
San Rafael, CA 94901
Ph:(415)256-8500
Free: 800-241-3222
Fax:(415)256-8501
No. of Franchise Units: 77. **Founded:** 1978. **Franchised:** 1982. **Description:** Custom closet design, manufacture, and installation. **Equity Capital Needed:** $127,500-$377,000 total investment. **Franchise Fee:** $40,000. **Royalty Fee:** 6%. **Financial Assistance:** No. **Training:** Includes training at headquarters, franchisees location, mentor training with ongoing support.

15228 ■ Island Ink-Jet Systems Inc.
244 4th St.
Courtney, BC, Canada V9N 1G6
Ph:(250)897-0067
Free: 877-446-5538
Fax:(250)897-1573
Co. E-mail: franchise@islandinkjet.com
URL: http://www.islandinkjet.com
No. of Franchise Units: 250. **Founded:** 1995. **Franchised:** 1977. **Description:** Inkjet refill mall location and area service centers. **Equity Capital Needed:** Minimum $50,000; total investment $100,000+. **Franchise Fee:** $29,000. **Financial Assistance:** No. **Training:** Yes.

15229 ■ PostNet Canada
1819 Wazee St.
Denver, CO 80202
Ph:(905)773-0504

Free: 800-841-7171
Fax:(303)771-7133
Co. E-mail: info@postnethq.ca
URL: http://www.postnet.ca/own
No. of Franchise Units: 25. **Founded:** 2004. **Franchised:** 2004. **Description:** Offers an array of high demand services and products, tailored to meet the needs of small business owners and today's busy consumer. We like to think of PostNet as an entrepreneur's store, helping the small office, home office and small business owners get what they need, when they need it. At the same time, PostNet caters to the general consumer, offering a host of products and services to help them complete their personal business needs quickly and efficiently. **Equity Capital Needed:** $175,000 investment required; $60,000 start-up capital required. **Franchise Fee:** $35,000. **Training:** Provides 8 days training and ongoing support.

15230 ■ Proforma
8800 E Pleasant Valley Rd.
Independence, OH 44131
Ph:(216)520-8400
Free: 800-825-1525
Fax:(216)520-8474
Co. E-mail: franchise@proforma.com
URL: http://www.connectwithperforma.com
No. of Franchise Units: 723. **Founded:** 1978. **Franchised:** 1986. **Description:** Franchises business service operations that handle business forms, commercial printing, computer supplies, office supplies, and computers. **Equity Capital Needed:** $19,500. **Franchise Fee:** $19,500. **Financial Assistance:** No. **Training:** 1 week franchise training at headquarters, local development agent support, ongoing classroom and regional training. Local and national campaigns. Regional meetings and annual national conventions.

START-UP INFORMATION

15231 ■ *Complete Idiot's Guide to Starting an Ebay Business*
Pub: Penguin Books (USA) Incorporated
Ed: Barbara Weltman, Malcolm Katt. **Released:** February 2008. **Price:** $19.95 (US), $29.00 (Canadian). **Description:** Guide for starting an eBay business includes information on products to sell, how to price merchandise, and details for working with services like PayPal, and how to organize fulfillment services.

15232 ■ *Design and Launch an Online Travel Business in a Week*
Pub: Entrepreneur Press
Ed: Charlene Davis. **Released:** May 1, 2009. **Price:** $17.95. **Description:** Guide providing techniques and professional advice for starting an online travel business. Tips are given to build a Website, find qualified providers and to set up a payment system.

15233 ■ *Design and Launch Your Online Boutique in a Week*
Pub: Entrepreneur Press
Ed: Melissa Campanelli. **Released:** June 26, 2008. **Price:** $17.95. **Description:** Tips for starting an online boutique in a short amount of time are given. The books shows how to build the online boutique with designer goods or your own product, ways to create eye-catching content, online tools to handle payments and accept orders, marketing and advertising techniques, and customer service.

15234 ■ *EBay Business Start-up Kit: 100s of Live Links to All the Information and Tools You Need*
Pub: NOLO
Ed: Richard Stim. **Released:** July 2008. **Price:** $24.99. **Description:** Interactive kit that connects user directly to EBay is presented.

15235 ■ *eBay Business the Smart Way*
Pub: AMACOM
Ed: Joseph T. Sinclair. **Released:** June 6, 2007. **Price:** $17.95. **Description:** eBay commands ninety percent of all online auction business. Computer and software expert and online entrepreneur shares information to help online sellers get started and move merchandise on eBay. Tips include the best ways to build credibility, find products to sell, manage inventory, create a storefront Website, and more.

15236 ■ *EBay Income: How ANYONE of Any Age, Location, and/or Background Can Build a Highly Profitable Online Business with eBay (Revised 2nd Edition)*
Pub: Atlantic Publishing Company
Released: December 1, 2010. **Price:** $24.95. **Description:** A complete overview of eBay is given and guides any small company through the entire process of creating the auction and auction strategies, photography, writing copy, text and formatting, multiple sales, programming tricks, PayPal, accounting, creating marketing, merchandising, managing email lists, advertising plans, taxes and sales tax,

best time to list items and for how long, sniping programs, international customers, opening a storefront, electronic commerce, buy-it now pricing, keywords, Google marketing and eBay secrets.

15237 ■ *How to Open and Operate a Financially Successful Bookstore on Amazon and Other Web Sites: With Companion CD-ROM*
Pub: Atlantic Publishing Company
Released: December 1, 2010. **Price:** $39.95. **Description:** This book was written for every used book aficionado and bookstore owner who currently wants to take advantage of the massive collection of online resources available to start and run your own online bookstore business.

15238 ■ *How to Use the Internet to Advertise, Promote, and Market Your Business or Web Site: With Little or No Money*
Pub: Atlantic Publishing Company
Released: December 1, 2010. **Price:** $24.95. **Description:** Information is given to help build, promote, and make money from your Website or brick and mortar store using the Internet, with minimal costs.

15239 ■ *"Online Fortunes" in* Small Business Opportunities *(Fall 2008)*
Pub: Entrepreneur Media Inc.
Description: Fifty hot, e-commerce enterprises for the aspiring entrepreneur to consider are featured; virtual assistants, marketing services, party planning, travel services, researching, web design and development, importing as well as creating an online store are among the businesses featured.

15240 ■ *"Power Up" in* Entrepreneur *(Vol. 35, November 2007, No. 11, pp. 140)*
Pub: Entrepreneur Media Inc.
Ed: Amanda C. Kooser. **Description:** PowerSeller is a status in the Internet company eBay, wherein sellers average at least $1,000 in sales per month for three consecutive months. There are five tiers in the PowerSeller status, which ranges from Bronze to Titanium. Launching startups at eBay can help entrepreneurs pick up a wide customer base, but getting and maintaining PowerSeller status is a challenge.

15241 ■ *Selling Online: Canada's Bestselling Guide to Becoming a Successful E-Commerce Merchant*
Pub: John Wiley and Sons Canada Ltd.
Ed: Jim Carroll; Rick Broadhead. **Released:** September 6, 2002. **Description:** Helps individuals build online retail enterprises; this updated version includes current tools, information and success strategies, how to launch an online storefront, security, marketing strategies, and mistakes to avoid.

15242 ■ *Start Your Own Business on eBay, 2nd Edition*
Pub: Entrepreneur Press
Ed: Jacquelyn Lynn. **Released:** May 2007. **Price:** $19.95. **Description:** Tips for starring a new online business on eBay are shared.

15243 ■ *Start Your Own Net Services Business*
Pub: Entrepreneur Press
Released: February 1, 2009. **Price:** $17.95. **Description:** Web design, search engine marketing, new-media online, and blogging, are currently the four most popular web services available. This book provides information to start a net service business.

15244 ■ *Starting an Ebay Business for Canadians for Dummies*
Pub: John Wiley & Sons, Incorporated
Ed: Marsha Collier; Bill Summers. **Released:** February 2007. **Price:** $35.99. **Description:** Tips for turning a hobby into a successful online eBay company.

15245 ■ *"Tee Off Online" in* Black Enterprise *(Vol. 37, January 2007, No. 6, pp. 52)*
Pub: Earl G. Graves Publishing Co. Inc.
Ed: James C. Johnson. **Description:** The E-Com Resource Center is one of many resources that are available for those interested in starting an e-commerce business. One of the first steps is to create a business plan, of which there are free samples available at BPlans.com.

15246 ■ *"Virtual Playground" in* Entrepreneur *(Vol. 36, March 2008, No. 3, pp. 112)*
Pub: Entrepreneur Media Inc.
Ed: Amanda C. Kooser. **Description:** The growing number of children visiting virtual worlds provides opportunity for entrepreneurs to start online businesses catering to this market. Entrepreneurs need to be aware of the Children's Online Privacy Protection Act with regard to collecting children's information. Details of other things to know about with reference to these businesses are examined.

ASSOCIATIONS AND OTHER ORGANIZATIONS

15247 ■ Internet Society
1775 Wiehle Ave., Ste. 201
Reston, VA 20190-5158
Ph:(703)439-2120
Fax:(703)326-9881
Co. E-mail: isoc@isoc.org
URL: http://www.isoc.org
Contact: Lynn St. Amour, Pres.
Description: Technologists, developers, educators, researchers, government representatives, and business people. Seeks to ensure global cooperation and coordination for the Internet and related internetworking technologies and applications. Supports the development and dissemination of standards for the Internet. Promotes the growth of Internet architecture and Internet-related education and research. Encourages assistance to technologically developing countries in implementing local Internet infrastructures. **Publications:** *ISOC Forum* (monthly); *ISP Column* .

REFERENCE WORKS

15248 ■ *"Analyzing the Analytics" in* Entrepreneur *(Vol. 37, October 2009, No. 10, pp. 42)*
Pub: Entrepreneur Media, Inc.
Ed: Mikal E. Belicove. **Description:** Startups can maximize Web analytics by using them to monitor

traffic sources and identify obstacles to converting them into targeted behaviors . Startups should set trackable Web site goals and continuously track traffic and conversion rates.

15249 ■ "Attract More Online Customers: Make Your Website Work Harder for You" in *Black Enterprise* **(Vol. 37, November 2006, No. 4, pp. 66)**
Pub: Earl G. Graves Publishing Co. Inc.
Ed: Description: Having an impressive presence on the Internet has become crucial. Detailed advice on making your website serve your business in the best way possible is included.

15250 ■ "Babynut.com to Shut Down" in *Bellingham Business Journal* **(Vol. February 2010, pp. 3)**
Pub: Sound Publishing Inc.
Description: Saralee Sky and Jerry Kilgore, owners of Babynut.com will close their online store. The site offered a free online and email newsletter to help mothers through pregnancy and the first three years of their child's life. Products being sold at clearance prices include organic and natural maternity and nursing clothing, baby and toddler clothes, books on pregnancy, and more.

15251 ■ "Best Buy's CEO On Learning to Love Social Media" in *Harvard Business Review* **(Vol. 88, December 2010, No. 12, pp. 43)**
Pub: Harvard Business School Publishing
Ed: Brian J. Dunn. **Description:** Effective utilization of online social networks to enhance brand identity, connect with consumers, and address bad publicity scenarios is examined.

15252 ■ "Boom and Bust in the Book Biz" in *Canadian Business* **(Vol. 83, August 17, 2010, No. 13-14, pp. 16)**
Pub: Rogers Media Ltd.
Ed: Jordan Timm. **Description:** Electronic book marketplace is booming with Amazon.com's e-book sales for the Kindle e-reader exceeding the hardcover sales. Kobo Inc. has registered early success with its Kobo e-reader and has partnered with Hong Kong telecom giant on an e-book store.

15253 ■ "Bottoms Up!" in *Entrepreneur* **(Vol. 36, April 2008, No. 4, pp. 128)**
Pub: Entrepreneur Media, Inc.
Ed: Amanda C. Kooser. **Description:** Jill Bernheimer launched her online alcohol business Domaine547 in 2007, and encountered challenges as legal issues over the licensing and launching of the business took about seven months to finish. Domain547 features blog and forum areas. Marketing strategy that connects to the social community is one of the ways to reach out to customers.

15254 ■ "Brite-Strike Tactical Launches New Internet Marketing Initiatives" in *Internet Wire* **(September 15, 2009)**
Pub: Comtex News Network, Inc.
Description: Brite-Strike Tactical Illumination Products, Inc. has enlisted the expertise of Internet marketing guru Thomas J. McCarthy to help revamp the company's Internet campaign. An outline of the Internet marketing strategy is provided.

15255 ■ *Building Buzz to Beat the Big Boys*
Pub: Greenwood Publishing Group, Inc.
Ed: Steve O'Leary; Kim Sheehan. **Released:** March 30, 2008. **Price:** $39.95. **Description:** Seventy to eighty percent of small retail stores fail within the first five years of opening due to competition from big-box retailers and online stores. Service providers and small retailers should capitalize on the fact that they are local and can connect on a personal level with customers in a way the big stores cannot. Word of mouth marketing methods are very critical to any small retail or service company. This book is designed to help any small business compete against large competitors.

15256 ■ "Business Forecast: Stormy and Successful" in *Women In Business* **(Vol. 62, June 2010, No. 2, pp. 12)**
Pub: American Business Women's Association
Ed: Kathleen Leighton. **Description:** Stormy Simon, vice president of customer service at Overstock.com

is a self-made career woman who started out as a temporary employee in the company in 2001. She was not able to attend college because she had two sons to care for after her divorce. Simon got involved in advertising and media buying and shares her love for business.

15257 ■ *The Complete Guide to Google Adwords: Secrets, Techniques, and Strategies You Can Learn to Make Millions*
Pub: Atlantic Publishing Company
Released: December 1, 2010. **Price:** $24.95. **Description:** Google AdWords, when it launched in 2002 signaled a fundamental shift in what the Internet was for so many individuals and companies. Learning and understanding how Google AdWords operates and how it can be optimized for maximum exposure, boosting click through rates, conversions, placement, and selection of the right keywords, can be the key to a successful online business.

15258 ■ "A Counter Offer" in *Inc.* **(February 2008, pp.)**
Pub: Gruner & Jahr USA Publishing
Ed: Elaine Appleton Grant. **Description:** Online retailer offering a line of kitchen and home products has upgraded its Website in order to make the business more attractive to possible buyers of the company. The firm is asking $9.9 million and reported gross revenue of $12.7 in 2007. The owner suggests that a buyer add product lines geared towards more rooms of the home than currently offer on the retail site.

15259 ■ "Cyber Thanksgiving Online Shopping a Growing Tradition" in *Marketing Weekly News* **(December 12, 2009, pp. 137)**
Pub: Investment Weekly News
Description: According to e-commerce analysts, Thanksgiving day is becoming increasingly important to retailers in terms of online sales. Internet marketers are realizing that consumers are already searching for Black Friday sales and if they find deals on the products they are looking for, they are highly likely to make their purchase on Thanksgiving day instead of waiting.

15260 ■ "Cyberwise" in *Black Enterprise* **(Vol. 41, September 2010, No. 2, pp. 49)**
Pub: Earl G. Graves Publishing Co. Inc.
Ed: Marcia Wade Talbert. **Description:** Advice is given to assist in selling an online store called theupscalegaragesale.com. A listing of business brokers specializing in the sale of Internet businesses is included.

15261 ■ "Dear Customer: Managing E-Mail Campaigns" in *Inc.* **(March 2008, pp. 58-59)**
Pub: Gruner & Jahr USA Publishing
Ed: Ryan Underwood. **Description:** Internet services that help firms manage their online business including email marketing, to manage subscriber lists, comply with spam regulations, monitor bouncebacks, and track potential customers are profiled. Constant Contact, MobileStorm Stun, Campaign Monitor, Pop Commerce, Emma, and StrongMail E-mail Server are among software and services highlighted.

15262 ■ "Dots Sings To New Tune With Its Radio Station" in *Crain's Cleveland Business* **(Vol. 30, June 15, 2009, No. 23, pp. 7)**
Pub: Crain Communications, Inc.
Description: Dots LLC, a women's clothing retailer, has launched an online radio station on its Website. The station plays the in-store music to customers while they are shopping online.

15263 ■ *The Ebay Seller's Tax and Legal Answer Book*
Pub: AMACOM
Ed: Cliff Ennico. **Released:** April 30, 2007. **Price:** $19.95. **Description:** Helps sellers using Ebay to file taxes properly, while saving money.

15264 ■ *Ebay the Smart Way: Selling, Burying, and Profiting on the Web's Number One Auction Site*
Pub: AMACOM
Ed: Joseph T. Sinclair. **Released:** May 2007. **Price:** $17.95. **Description:** Resource to help individuals sell, buy and profit using the Internet auction site Ebay.

15265 ■ *The Facebook Era: Tapping Online Social Networks to Build Better Products, Reach New Audiences, and Sell More Stuff*
Pub: Prentice Hall
Ed: Clara Shih. **Price:** $24.99. **Description:** The '90s were about the World Wide Web of information and the power of linking Web pages. Today it's about the World Wide Web of people and the power of the social graph. Online social networks are fundamentally changing the way we live, work, and interact. They offer businesses immense opportunities to transform customer relationships for profit: opportunities that touch virtually every business function, from sales and marketing to recruiting, collaboration to executive decision-making, product development to innovation.

15266 ■ "Full Speed Ahead: How to Get the Most Out of Your Company Vehicles" in *Entrepreneur* **(Vol. 37, October 2009, No. 10, pp. 78)**
Pub: Entrepreneur Media, Inc.
Ed: Jill Amadio. **Description:** Methods of saving costs on purchasing and maintaining vehicles are described. Tips include shopping online, choosing hybrid vehicles, and choosing cars with incentives and lower insurance costs.

15267 ■ "Get Sold On eBay" in *Entrepreneur* **(Vol. 36, March 2008, No. 3, pp. 94)**
Pub: Entrepreneur Media Inc.
Ed: Marcia Layton Turner. **Description:** Entrepreneurs are increasingly using eBay to sell products. Some tips to start selling products through eBay include: starting with used items, developing a niche to sell specific products, and researching product pricing. Other tips with regard to starting an eBay business are covered.

15268 ■ "Google Book Search Tosses Magazines Into the Mix" in *Information Today* **(Vol. 26, February 2009, No. 2, pp. 31)**
Pub: Information Today, Inc.
Description: Google Book Search expanded services to include magazines...

15269 ■ "The Greening of Lunch" in *Entrepreneur* **(Vol. 37, October 2009, No. 10, pp. 44)**
Pub: Entrepreneur Media, Inc.
Ed: Deborah Song. **Description:** Kids Konserve is a self-funded online business selling reusable and recycled lunch kits for kids. The company also aims to increase awareness about waste reduction.

15270 ■ *How to Market and Sell Your Art, Music, Photographs, and Handmade Crafts Online*
Pub: Atlantic Publishing Group, Inc.
Ed: Lee Rowley. **Released:** May 2008. **Price:** $24.95. **Description:** The book provides all the basics for starting and running an online store selling arts, crafts, photography or music. There are more than 300 Websites listed to help anyone market and promote their arts and/or crafts online.

15271 ■ "Inside an Online Bazaar" in *Entrepreneur* **(Vol. 37, September 2009, No. 9, pp. 38)**
Pub: Entrepreneur Media, Inc.
Ed: Kara Ohngren. **Description:** Etsy.com is a website that provides a marketplace for handmade products. The site has attracted more than 250,000 sellers since its launch in 2005. Site features and services are also supplied.

15272 ■ *Internet Industry Almanac*
Pub: Computer Industry Almanac Inc.
Contact: Dr. Egil Juliussen PhD, Author
Price: $50, individuals paperback; $60, individuals hardcover. **Publication Includes:** Lists of Internet companies; Internet publications; Internet research and testing companies; Internet conferences; Internet people; Internet resource directory; Internet publishers; Internet associations and organizations; and Internet conference companies. Principal content of publication is information about the Internet industry, including a definition of the Internet, employment

data, Internet humor, salary information, Internet market forecasts, and technology forecasts. **Arrangement:** By industry.

15273 ■ "It's a Hit" in *Entrepreneur* **(Vol. 36, March 2008, No. 3, pp. 110)**
Pub: Entrepreneur Media Inc.
Ed: John Jantsch. **Description:** Entrepreneurs use the Web to market business and keeping relevant content in the Website is important to address questions from customers. Other considerations in marketing businesses online include: interacting with site visitors, using Web applications for project collaboration and file storage, and encouraging customers to post reviews.

15274 ■ "It's a New Game: Killerspin Pushes Table Tennis to Extreme Heights" in *Black Enterprise* **(Vol. 37, October 2006, No. 3, pp. 73)**
Pub: Earl G. Graves Publishing Co. Inc.
Ed: Bridget McCrea. **Description:** Profile of Robert Blackwell and his company Killerspin L.L.C., which is popularizing the sport of table tennis. Killerspin has hit $1 million in revenues due to product sales primarily generated through the company's website, magazines, DVDs, and event ticket sales.

15275 ■ "Jo-Ann Fabric and Craft Stores Joins ArtFire.com to Offer Free Online Craft Marketplace" in *Internet Wire* **(January 26, 2010)**
Pub: Comtex News Network, Inc.
Description: Jo-Ann Fabric and Craft Stores has entered into a partnership with ArtFire.com which will provide sewers and crafters all the tools they need in order to make and sell their products from an online venue.

15276 ■ "Last Founder Standing" in *Conde Nast Portfolio* **(Vol. 2, June 2008, No. 6, pp. 124)**
Pub: Conde Nast Publications, Inc.
Ed: Kevin Maney. **Description:** Interview with Amazon CEO Jeff Bezos in which he discusses the economy, the company's new distribution center and the hiring of employees for it, e-books, and the overall vision for the future of the firm.

15277 ■ "A Life of Spice" in *Entrepreneur* **(Vol. 37, September 2009, No. 9, pp. 46)**
Pub: Entrepreneur Media, Inc.
Ed: Jason Daley. **Description:** Matt and Bryan Walls have successfully grown their Atlanta, Georgia-based Snorg Tees T-shirt company. The company has expanded its product offering and redesigned its Website to be more user-friendly. The company has registered between $5 and 10 million in 2008.

15278 ■ "Luxe Hotels on a Budget" in *Inc.* **(Volume 32, December 2010, No. 10, pp. 60)**
Pub: Inc. Magazine
Ed: Adam Baer. **Description:** Off & Away Website allows users to vie for discounted hotel rooms at more than 100 luxury properties. To compete, uses buy $1 bids and each time an individual bids the price of the room goes up by 10 cents.

15279 ■ "Navigate to Better Direct Response Messaging Through Search Marketing" in *DM News* **(Vol. 32, January 18, 2010, No. 2, pp. 26)**
Pub: Haymarket Media, Inc.
Ed: Mark Simon. **Description:** Important lessons to apply when utilizing Internet marketing schemes include telling your customers you have what they want to buy, provide them with discounts or ways to save additional money and drive them to a customized destination like an Online store.

15280 ■ "The Next Dimension" in *Entrepreneur* **(Vol. 35, November 2007, No. 11, pp. 62)**
Pub: Entrepreneur Media Inc.
Ed: Heather Clancy. **Description:** Entrepreneurs can make use of virtual worlds like Second Life to promote their products or services. Details and cautions on the use of virtual worlds are discussed.

15281 ■ "The One Thing You Must Get Right When Building a Brand" in *Harvard Business Review* **(Vol. 88, December 2010, No. 12, pp. 80)**
Pub: Harvard Business School Publishing
Ed: Patrick Barwise, Sean Meehan. **Description:** Four uses for new media include: communicating a clearly defined customer promise, creating trust via delivering on the promise, regularly improving on the promise, and innovating past what is familiar.

15282 ■ "Online Reverse Auctions: Common Myths Versus Evolving Reality" in *Business Horizons* **(September-October 2007, pp. 373)**
Pub: Elsevier Technology Publications
Ed: Tobias Schoenherr, Vincent A. Mabert. **Description:** Common misconceptions about online reverse auctions are examined based on the data obtained from 30 case study companies. Strategies for maintaining a good buyer-supplier relationship and implications for firms and supply managers are presented.

15283 ■ "Online Security Crackdown: Scanning Service Oversees Site Security at David's Bridal" in **(Vol. 84, July 2008, No. 7, pp. 46)**
Pub: Chain Store Age
Ed: Samantha Murphy. **Description:** Online retailers are beefing up security on their Websites. Cyber thieves use retail systems in order to gain entry to consumer data. David's Bridal operates over 275 bridal showrooms in the U.S. and has a one-stop wedding resource for new brides planning weddings.

15284 ■ "Optimize.ca Supplies Free Online Financial Advice" in *Entertainment Close-Up* **(October 9, 2010)**
Pub: Close-Up Media Inc.
Description: Optimize.ca provides free online financial advice, focusing on instant savings for their mutual funds and other banking products while improving rates of return and overall financial health.

15285 ■ *The Power of Social Networking: Using the Whuffie Factor to Build Your Business*
Pub: Crown Business Books
Ed: Tara Hunt. **Released:** May 4, 2010. **Price:** $15.00. **Description:** This book shows how any small business can harness its power by increasing whuffie, the store of social capital that is the currency of the digital world. Blogs and social networks such as Facebook and Twitter are used to help grow any small firm.

15286 ■ "Retail Franchises to Start Now" in *Entrepreneur* **(Vol. 37, August 2009, No. 8, pp. 88)**
Pub: Entrepreneur Media, Inc.
Ed: Tracy Stapp. **Description:** Listing of retail franchises is presented and is categorized based on their products sold. The total cost of the franchise and the website are also included as well as additional statistical data.

15287 ■ "Ric Elis/Dan Feldstein" in *Charlotte Business Journal* **(Vol. 25, December 31, 2010, No. 41, pp. 6)**
Pub: Charlotte Business Journal
Ed: Ken Elkins. **Description:** Charlotte, North Carolina-based Internet marketing firm Red Ventures has grown significantly. General Atlantic has purchased stakes in Red Ventures.

15288 ■ "Search and Discover New Opportunities" in *DM News* **(Vol. 31, December 14, 2009, No. 29, pp. 13)**
Pub: Haymarket Media, Inc.
Ed: Chantal Tode. **Description:** Although other digital strategies are gaining traction in Internet marketing, search marketing continues to dominate this advertising forum. Companies like American Greetings, which markets e-card brands online, are utilizing social networking sites and affiliates to generate a higher demand for their products.

15289 ■ "Shipping 2.0" in *Entrepreneur* **(Vol. 36, April 2008, No. 4, pp. 54)**
Pub: Entrepreneur Media, Inc.
Ed: Heather Clancy. **Description:** Doggypads.com contacted with Web 2.0 service provider Shipwire to handle its warehouse concerns. The service works by paying a rent to Shipwire and they will store the client's items. The client's customers can continue to order from the client's website and Shipwire will take care of delivery. Doggypads was able to save up on costs by using Shipwire.

15290 ■ "Tell Us What You Really Think Collecting Customer Feedback" in *Inc.* **(Vol. 30, December 2008, No. 12, pp. 52)**
Pub: Mansueto Ventures LLC
Ed: Ryan Underwood. **Description:** According to a recent survey, nearly 77 percent of online shoppers review consumer-generated reviews of products before making a purchase.

15291 ■ "Things Really Clicking for Macy's Online" in *Business Courier* **(Vol. 24, November 30, 2008, No. 33, pp. 1)**
Pub: American City Business Journals, Inc.
Ed: Lisa Biank Fasig. **Description:** Retailer Macy's online division Macys.com are projecting sales at $1billion in 2007, compared to $620 million in 2006. Macy's new online features and products and the growth of online retail sector are also discussed.

15292 ■ *Titanium EBay: A Tactical Guide to Becoming a Millionaire PowerSeller*
Pub: Penguin Group Incorporated
Ed: Skip McGrath. **Released:** June 2006. **Price:** $24.95. **Description:** Advice is given to help anyone selling items on eBay to become a Power Seller, an award presented based on monthly gross merchandise sales.

15293 ■ "Traffic's Up: Website's Down Preventing Costly Crashes" in *Inc.* **(March 2008, pp. 55-56)**
Pub: Gruner & Jahr USA Publishing
Ed: Darren Dahl. **Description:** Grid Web hosting protects a small company's Website when a sudden burst of Internet traffic hits enabling it to continue rather than be crippled. Options can vary in cost from $4 to $1,000 monthly and include using a shared server, grid server, virtual private server, or a dedicated server. The article explains each option.

15294 ■ "Understanding Persuasive Online Sales Messages from eBay Auctions" in *Business Communication Quarterly* **(December 2007, pp. 482)**
Pub: Sage Publications USA
Ed: Barbara Jo White, Daniel Clapper, Rita Noel, Jenny Fortier, Pierre Grabolosa. **Description:** eBay product listings were studied to determine the requirements of persuasive sales writing. Potential sellers should use the proper keywords and make an authentic description with authentic photographs of the item being auctioned.

15295 ■ "Uptick in Clicks: Nordstrom's Online Sales Surging" in *Puget Sound Business Journal* **(Vol. 29, August 22, 2008, No. 18, pp. 1)**
Pub: American City Business Journals
Ed: Gregg Lamm. **Description:** Nordstrom Inc.'s online division grew its sales by 15 percent in the second quarter of 2008, compared to 2007's 4.3 percent in overall decline. The company expects their online net sales to reach $700 million in 2008 capturing eight percent of overall sales.

15296 ■ "Web Sight: Do You See What I See?" in *Entrepreneur* **(Vol. 35, October 2007, No. 10, pp. 58)**
Pub: Entrepreneur Media Inc.
Ed: Heather Clancy. **Description:** Owners of Trunkt, a boutique in New York that showcases independent designs, have created a new style of Website called Trunkt.org. The Website allows buyers to select the products they want to see and designers can choose anytime which of their items will be displayed on the site. An explanation of the strategy that helped bring Trunkt closer to its clients is presented.

15297 ■ "White Cat Media Tells You Where to Get a Bargain. Now It's Shopping for $1.5 Million" in *Inc.* (March 2008, pp. 48)
Pub: Gruner & Jahr USA Publishing
Ed: Athena Schindelheim. **Description:** Profile of White Cat Media which runs two shopping Websites: SheFinds.com for fashion and beauty items, and MomFinds.com for mothers. The New York City firm reported revenues for 2007 at $400,000 and is looking for funding capital in the amount of $1.7 million.

15298 ■ "Women Clicking to Earn Virtual Dollars" in *Sales and Marketing Management* (November 11, 2009)
Pub: Nielsen Business Media, Inc.
Ed: Stacy Straczynski. **Description:** According to a new report from Internet marketing firm Q Interactive, women are increasingly playing social media games where they are able to click on an ad or sign up for a promotion to earn virtual currency. Research is showing that this kind of marketing may be a potent tool, especially for e-commerce and online stores.

15299 ■ "Women Workers Spend Lunchtime on Fridays Shopping Online" in *Marketing to Women* (Vol. 23, November 2010, No. 11, pp. 8)
Pub: EPM Communications, Inc.
Description: Forty percent of women shop online during work hours, particularly on Fridays. The largest number of women make these purchases during their lunch break. Demographics are included.

15300 ■ "You Are What They Click" in *Entrepreneur* (Vol. 37, July 2009, No. 7, pp. 43)
Pub: Entrepreneur Media, Inc.
Ed: Mikal Belicove. **Description:** Hiring the right website design firm is the first stage in building an online business, and this involves various factors such as price, technical expertise, and talent. Writing a request for proposal (RFP) detailing the website's details, which include purpose, budget and audience, is the first step the process. Other tips in finding the right web designer are given.

15301 ■ "Young Entrepreneur Gets Some Recognition and Some Help for College" in *Philadelphia Inquirer* (August 30, 2010)
Pub: Philadelphia Inquirer
Ed: Susan Snyder. **Description:** Profile of Zachary Gosling, age 18, who launched an online auction Website from his bedroom, using advertising and sponsorship funds rather than charging fees to users.

TRADE PERIODICALS

15302 ■ *Online*
Pub: Online, A Division of Information Today Inc.
Ed: Marydee Ojala, Editor, marydee@infotoday.com.
Released: Bimonthly. **Price:** $129.50; $243 two years; $145 Canada and Mexico; $172 other countries. **Description:** Professional magazine covering online and CD-ROM databases with practical how-to articles covering the entire online industry.

15303 ■ *Spotlights*
Pub: Internet/Media Strategies Inc.
Released: Weekly. **Description:** Analyzes business opportunities on the Internet and other technologies.

FRANCHISES AND BUSINESS OPPORTUNITIES

15304 ■ TheYardSale.com
10700 Montgomery Rd., Ste. 300
Cincinnati, OH 45242
Free: 800-291-0771
Fax:(513)563-2691
Franchised: 2005. **Description:** Selling items on Ebay for others. **Equity Capital Needed:** $10,000. **Franchise Fee:** $15,900 1st, $11,900 2nd. **Financial Assistance:** Yes. **Training:** Yes.

LIBRARIES

15305 ■ Alabama A & M University–J.F. Drake Memorial Learning Resources Center
4900 Meridian St.
Normal, AL 35762
Ph:(256)372-4747
Fax:(256)372-5764
URL: http://www.aamu.edu/library/
Contact: Veronica Acklin, Adm.Sec.

Scope: Education, business and economics, agriculture, the sciences, computer science, literature. **Services:** Interlibrary loan; copying; media services; Center open to the public (courtesy card must be purchased for check out of materials by persons not enrolled at the university or at one of the cooperating institutions). **Holdings:** 236,147 books; 25,517 bound periodical volumes; 5044 AV programs; 20,869 periodicals on microfilm; 1053 college catalogs; various telephone directories; 16,166 ERIC microfiche; 141,376 government documents; *Wall Street Journal* on microfiche (11,643). **Subscriptions:** 1657 journals and other serials; 93 newspapers; 359 microfilm subscriptions.

START-UP INFORMATION

15306 ■ **"Franchises with an Eye on Chicago" in** *Crain's Chicago Business* **(Vol. 34, March 14, 2011, No. 11, pp. 20)**
Pub: Crain Communications Inc.
Description: Profiles of franchise companies seeking franchisees for the Chicago area include: Extreme Pita, a sandwich shop; Hand and Stone, offering massage, facial and waxing services; Molly Maid, home-cleaning service; Primrose Schools, private accredited schools for children 6 months to 6 hears and after-school programs; Protect Painters, residential and light-commercial painting contractor; and Wingstop, a restaurant offering chicken wings in nine flavors, fries and side dishes.

15307 ■ *How to Start a Faux Painting or Mural Business, Second Edition*
Pub: Allworth Press
Ed: Rebecca Pittman. **Released:** October 1, 2010. **Price:** $24.95. **Description:** Updated and expanded to cover better ways to advertise, innovative supplies (such as Venetian plasters and stained cements), unique bidding and studio setups required for new plasters and varnishes.

ASSOCIATIONS AND OTHER ORGANIZATIONS

15308 ■ **American Coatings Association**
1500 Rhode Island Ave. NW
Washington, DC 20005
Ph:(202)462-6272
Fax:(202)462-8549
Co. E-mail: npca@paint.org
URL: http://www.paint.org
Contact: J. Andrew Doyle, Pres.
Description: Manufacturers of paints and chemical coatings; suppliers of raw materials and equipment. Conducts: statistical surveys; research, government, and public relations programs. Provides management information programs and management and technician development programs. Compiles statistics. **Publications:** *Insider News; Member Services Directory; Technical Bulletin; Trademark Directory* (periodic).

15309 ■ **Wallcoverings Association**
401 N Michigan Ave., Ste. 2200
Chicago, IL 60611
Ph:(312)321-5166
Fax:(312)673-6928
Co. E-mail: info@wallcoverings.org
URL: http://www.wallcoverings.org
Contact: Phil Tarullo, Pres.
Description: Manufacturers, converters, distributors and suppliers in the wallcoverings industry. .

DIRECTORIES OF EDUCATIONAL PROGRAMS

15310 ■ *Rauch Guide to the U.S. Paint Industry*
Pub: Grey House Publishing
Released: latest edition 6th; published August, 2010.
Price: $595, individuals softcover. **Covers:** Ap-

proximately 800 industry manufacturers with sales estimates, products, mergers and acquisitions, divestitures, and other information for the 400 largest companies. **Entries Include:** Company name, address, description of products and services, branch office and location, financial date, number of employees.

REFERENCE WORKS

15311 ■ **"Contractors Must be Lead Certified by April 2010" in** *Contractor* **(Vol. 57, February 2010, No. 2, pp. 3)**
Pub: Penton Media, Inc.
Description: Contractors should be trained and certified to comply with the U.S. Environmental Protection Agency's Lead Renovation, Repair, and Painting regulation if they work on housing built before 1978 by April 2010. Contractors with previous lead abatement training must be trained and certified under this new program.

15312 ■ *Decorating Registry*
Pub: Paint and Decorating Retailers Association
Contact: Michael Austin, Managing Editor
E-mail: mike@pdra.org
Released: Annual, July. **Publication Includes:** List of about 1,500 manufacturers, manufacturers' representatives, distributors, and suppliers of decorating merchandise; a comprehensive trademark and brand name directory; associations, societies, and trade shows related to the home decorating industry. **Entries Include:** For companies and manufacturer representatives—Firm name, address, phone, fax, name and title of contact, trademark, brand names. For associations—Name, address, phone, statement of purpose or description of service, key personnel, trade shows sponsored with dates and locations. Principal content of publication is decorative products (coatings, wallcoverings, window treatments, flooring, sundries). **Arrangement:** Alphabetical. **Indexes:** Brand and trade name.

15313 ■ *Directory of Home Center Operators & Hardware Chains*
Pub: Chain Store Guide
Released: Annual, Latest edition 2010. **Price:** $395, individuals Directory; $445, individuals online lite; $1,075, individuals online pro. **Covers:** 4,500 U.S. and Canadian companies which operate home centers, home center warehouses, lumber and building material outlets, specialty paint and home decorating stores, and kitchen and bath centers. Concentrates on companies with a minimum annual sales of one million dollars. **Entries Include:** Company name, address, phone, fax, 6,500 personnel e-mail address, web site, Internet order processing indicator, listing type, product lines, total sales, sales percentage per customer type, total selling square footage, total stores, units by type of store operated, units made by trade name, trading areas, projected openings and remodeling, distribution center locations, buying and/or marketing group name and location, number of nurseries operated, average number of check-outs, year founded, public company indica-

tor, parent and subsidiary company information, division and branch office locations, key personnel, and number of locations by city. **Arrangement:** Geographical. **Indexes:** Product line, alphabetical, exclusions, state.

15314 ■ **"Local Dealers Fear Shortages in Car Supply" in** *Boston Business Journal* **(Vol. 29, May 13, 2011, No. 1, pp. 1)**
Pub: American City Business Journals Inc.
Ed: Scott Dance. **Description:** The earthquake and tsunami in Japan are seen to impact the automobile dealers in Baltimore, Maryland. Automobile supply in the area is seen to decrease dramatically during the summer sales season. Shortage of transmission parts and paint colors is also forecasted.

15315 ■ **"Retail Woes: The Shoe Doesn't Fit for Gerald Loftin's Stock Picks" in** *Black Enterprise* **(Vol. 38, July 2008, No. 12, pp. 40)**
Pub: Earl G. Graves Publishing Co. Inc.
Ed: Steve Garmhausen. **Description:** Each of the three stocks that Gerald Loftin picked in May 2007 have lost money; DSW, the designer shoe retailer, fell by 63.7 percent; paint and coatings retailer Sherwin-Williams Co. fell by 7.2 percent; and Verizon Communications Inc. fell by 1.4 percent. Statistical data included.

15316 ■ **"Synthetic Drywall Rots Mechanical Parts" in** *Contractor* **(Vol. 56, December 2009, No. 12, pp. 50)**
Pub: Penton Media, Inc.
Ed: Bob Mader. **Description:** Chinese-made synthetic drywalls have been found to corrode mechanical and electrical products in homes. Drywalls always contain a certain amount of sulfur. The hydrogen sulfide gas component of synthetic drywalls causes copper and silver sulfide corrosion.

15317 ■ **"Why Women Blog and What They Read" in** *Marketing to Women* **(Vol. 22, July 2009, No. 7, pp. 8)**
Pub: EPM Communications, Inc.
Description: Listing of topics that are visited the most by female Internet users. Statistical data included.

SOURCES OF SUPPLY

15318 ■ *Gold Book*
Pub: Paint and Decorating Retailers Association
Contact: Michael Austin, Managing Editor
E-mail: mike@pdra.org
Released: Annual, Latest edition 2007. **Price:** $15, individuals per copy. **Covers:** Companies that manufacture/distribute wallcovering collections and related products. Ie. Window treatments, stencils. **Entries Include:** Name, address, phone, name and title of contact, subsidiary and branch names and locations, product/services provided, collection characteristics (vinyl, pre-pasted, strippable, scrubbable), expiration dates, distributor information for U.S., Canada, and Puerto Rico. **Arrangement:** Alphabetical. **Indexes:** Product/service.

STATISTICAL SOURCES

15319 ■ *Outlook for the Paints and Coatings Industry*
Pub: Business Trend Analysts, Inc.
Released: 2007-2008. **Price:** $2495.00. **Description:** This comprehensive report quantifies current and projected sales (through 2015) of architectural coatings, OEM product finishes, special-purpose coatings, and miscellaneous allied paint products.

15320 ■ *Paints and Coatings*
Pub: Business Trend Analysts, Inc.
Released: 1998. **Price:** $1495.00. **Description:** Profiles the paints and coatings market, covering interior and exterior trade paints, solvent and water-based paints, varnishes, stains, lacquers, OEM product finishes, powder coatings, and paint thinners and removers. Includes projections to the year 2001 on a product-by-product basis. Provides information on the paint retailing industry, distribution, pricing, and advertising. Also contains profiles of major manufacturers.

15321 ■ *RMA Annual Statement Studies*
Pub: Robert Morris Associates (RMA)
Released: Annual. **Price:** $175.00 2006-07 edition, $105.00. **Description:** Contains composite balance sheets and income statements for more than 360 industries, including the accounting, auditing, and bookkeeping industries. Also contains five years of comparative historical data for discerning trends. Includes 16 commonly used ratios, computed for most of the size groupings for nearly every industry.

TRADE PERIODICALS

15322 ■ *Paint & Decorating Retailer Magazine*
Pub: Paint and Decorating Retailers Association
Released: Monthly. **Price:** Free to qualified subscribers. **Description:** Magazine serving retailers of paint and decorating products.

LIBRARIES

15323 ■ Sherwin-Williams Automotive Finishes Corporation Library
4440 Warrensville Center Rd.
Warrensville Heights, OH 44128-2837
Free: 800-798-5872
URL: http://www.sherwin-automotive.com
Contact: Elizabeth Rinz, Mgr.

Scope: Paint, polymers, pigments, coatings. **Services:** Interlibrary loan.

START-UP INFORMATION

15324 ■ "Franchises with an Eye on Chicago" in *Crain's Chicago Business* (Vol. 34, March 14, 2011, No. 11, pp. 20)
Pub: Crain Communications Inc.
Description: Profiles of franchise companies seeking franchisees for the Chicago area include: Extreme Pita, a sandwich shop; Hand and Stone, offering massage, facial and waxing services; Molly Maid, home-cleaning service; Primrose Schools, private accredited schools for children 6 months to 6 hears and after-school programs; Protect Painters, residential and light-commercial painting contractor; and Wingstop, a restaurant offering chicken wings in nine flavors, fries and side dishes.

15325 ■ How to Start a Faux Painting or Mural Business, Second Edition
Pub: Allworth Press
Ed: Rebecca Pittman. **Released:** October 1, 2010. **Price:** $24.95. **Description:** Updated and expanded to cover better ways to advertise, innovative supplies (such as Venetian plasters and stained cements), unique bidding and studio setups required for new plasters and varnishes.

ASSOCIATIONS AND OTHER ORGANIZATIONS

15326 ■ American Coatings Association
1500 Rhode Island Ave. NW
Washington, DC 20005
Ph:(202)462-6272
Fax:(202)462-8549
Co. E-mail: npca@paint.org
URL: http://www.paint.org
Contact: J. Andrew Doyle, Pres.
Description: Manufacturers of paints and chemical coatings; suppliers of raw materials and equipment. Conducts: statistical surveys; research, government, and public relations programs. Provides management information programs and management and technician development programs. Compiles statistics. **Publications:** *Insider News*; *Member Services Directory*; *Technical Bulletin*; *Trademark Directory* (periodic).

15327 ■ American Subcontractors Association
1004 Duke St.
Alexandria, VA 22314-3588
Ph:(703)684-3450
Free: 888-374-3133
Fax:(703)836-3482
Co. E-mail: asaoffice@asa-hq.com
URL: http://www.asaonline.com
Contact: Timmy McLaughlin, Pres.
Description: Construction subcontractors of trades and specialties such as foundations, concrete, masonry, steel, mechanical, drywall, electrical, painting, plastering, roofing and acoustical. Formed to deal with issues common to subcontractors. Works with other segments of the construction industry in promoting ethical practices, beneficial legislation and education of construction subcontractors and suppliers. Manages the Foundation of the American Subcontractors Association (FASA). **Publications:** *Action ASA* (monthly); *The Contractor's Compass* (quarterly).

15328 ■ National Guild of Professional Paperhangers
136 S Keowee St.
Dayton, OH 45402
Ph:(937)222-6477
Free: 800-254-6477
Fax:(937)222-5794
Co. E-mail: ngpp@ngpp.org
URL: http://www.ngpp.org
Contact: Ms. Elsie Kapteina CP, Pres.
Description: Paperhangers united to promote use of wallcoverings; upgrade the skills of paperhangers and the quality of materials; foster unity among members; encourage good business practices and ethics in the industry. Conducts charitable programs. Sponsors educational programs. **Publications:** *American Painting Contractor*, *Jobsite*; *Paint Pro* .

15329 ■ Paint and Decorating Retailers Association
1401 Triad Center Dr.
St. Peters, MO 63376-7353
Ph:(636)326-2636
Co. E-mail: info@pdra.org
URL: http://www.pdra.org
Contact: Jeff Baggaley, Pres.
Description: Serves as a trade association of locally-owned paint and decorating stores in the U.S., Canada and around the world. Offers professional advice, personal service and quality products for every paint, wall covering, window treatment and floor covering project. **Publications:** *Decorating Registry* (annual); *Gold Book* (annual); *Paint and Decorating Retailer* (monthly).

15330 ■ Painting and Decorating Contractors of America
1801 Park 270 Dr., Ste. 220
St. Louis, MO 63146
Ph:(314)514-7322
Free: 800-332-PDCA
Fax:(314)514-9417
Co. E-mail: rgreene@pdca.org
URL: http://www.pdca.org
Contact: Richard Greene, CEO
Description: Painting and wall covering contractors. Operates educational and charitable programs. Compiles statistics. **Publications:** *Hazardous Waste Handbook*; *Painting and Wallcovering Contractor* (bimonthly); *PDCA Directory* (annual).

15331 ■ Wallcoverings Association
401 N Michigan Ave., Ste. 2200
Chicago, IL 60611
Ph:(312)321-5166
Fax:(312)673-6928
Co. E-mail: info@wallcoverings.org
URL: http://www.wallcoverings.org
Contact: Phil Tarullo, Pres.
Description: Manufacturers, converters, distributors and suppliers in the wallcoverings industry. .

DIRECTORIES OF EDUCATIONAL PROGRAMS

15332 ■ Directory of Private Accredited Career Schools and Colleges of Technology
Pub: Accrediting Commission of Career Schools and Colleges of Technology
Contact: Michale S. McComis, Exec. Dir.
Released: On web page. **Price:** Free. **Description:** Covers 3900 accredited post-secondary programs that provide training programs in business, trade, and technical fields, including various small business endeavors. Entries offer school name, address, phone, description of courses, job placement assistance, and requirements for admission. Arrangement is alphabetical.

REFERENCE WORKS

15333 ■ American Painting Contractor—Buyers' Guide
Pub: Briefings Media Group
Released: Annual, Latest edition 2011. **Publication Includes:** List of more than 600 manufacturers of products, tools, and equipment for the paint and wallcoverings application industry. **Entries Include:** Name, address, phone, fax, e-mail, URL, and contact name; some listings include logo and products. **Arrangement:** Alphabetical by product. **Indexes:** Product.

15334 ■ "Colores Origenes: Martha Kruse" in *Advertising Age* (Vol. 77, November 13, 2006, No. 46, pp. S12)
Pub: Crain Communications, Inc.
Ed: Laurel Wentz. **Description:** Home Depot has created a range of Latin paint colors called Colores Origenes; the new line was originally intended to launch only at locations with heavily Hispanic patrons but the company decided to make the line available at all of their stores.

15335 ■ "Contractors Must be Lead Certified by April 2010" in *Contractor* (Vol. 57, February 2010, No. 2, pp. 3)
Pub: Penton Media, Inc.
Description: Contractors should be trained and certified to comply with the U.S. Environmental Protection Agency's Lead Renovation, Repair, and Painting regulation if they work on housing built before 1978 by April 2010. Contractors with previous lead abatement training must be trained and certified under this new program.

15336 ■ "Local Dealers Fear Shortages in Car Supply" in *Boston Business Journal* (Vol. 29, May 13, 2011, No. 1, pp. 1)
Pub: American City Business Journals Inc.
Ed: Scott Dance. **Description:** The earthquake and tsunami in Japan are seen to impact the automobile

dealers in Baltimore, Maryland. Automobile supply in the area is seen to decrease dramatically during the summer sales season. Shortage of transmission parts and paint colors is also forecasted.

15337 ■ *Painting and Wallcovering Contractor—PDCA Roster*
Pub: Painting & Decorating Contractors of America
Released: Annual, August. **Publication Includes:** Roster of about 3,500 member contractors engaged in painting, decorating, drywall, wallcovering, and special coatings application. **Entries Include:** Company name, address, phone, fax, name of principal executive. **Arrangement:** By geographic council or chapter.

15338 ■ "Procter Gambles on Wallpaper; Putting Paint On a Roll" in *Advertising Age* (Vol. 77, September 18, 2006, No. 38, pp. 4)
Pub: Crain Communications, Inc.
Ed: Jack Neff. **Description:** Procter & Gamble Co. has launched a new line of textured paints that are already applied to a wallpaper-like roll that can be hung without paste or wallpaper tools.

15339 ■ "Software Solutions Increase Productivity" in *Contractor* (Vol. 57, February 2010, No. 2, pp. 26)
Pub: Penton Media, Inc.
Ed: William Feldman; Patti Feldman. **Description:** Singletouch is a real-time data capture solution for mechanical and other contractors that work in jobs that require materials and workload tracking. Contractors get information on extreme weather and sudden changes in the cost of materials. The OptimumHVAC optimization software by Optimum Energy is designed to optimize energy savings in commercial buildings.

15340 ■ "Synthetic Drywall Rots Mechanical Parts" in *Contractor* (Vol. 56, December 2009, No. 12, pp. 50)
Pub: Penton Media, Inc.
Ed: Bob Mader. **Description:** Chinese-made synthetic drywalls have been found to corrode mechanical and electrical products in homes. Drywalls always contain a certain amount of sulfur. The hydrogen sulfide gas component of synthetic drywalls causes copper and silver sulfide corrosion.

15341 ■ "Troubled Project In Court" in *The Business Journal-Portland* (Vol. 25, July 25, 2008, No. 20, pp. 1)
Pub: American City Business Journals, Inc.
Ed: Wendy Culverwell. **Description:** Views and information on Salpare Bay's Hayden Island project, as well as on financing problems and cases associated with the project, are presented. Construction of luxurious waterside condominiums stopped last fall, after the discovery of financing problems and subcontractors and other parties started filing claims and counterclaims.

SOURCES OF SUPPLY

15342 ■ *Decorating Registry*
Pub: Paint and Decorating Retailers Association
Contact: Michael Austin, Managing Editor
E-mail: mike@pdra.org
Released: Annual, July. **Publication Includes:** List of about 1,500 manufacturers, manufacturers' representatives, distributors, and suppliers of decorating merchandise; a comprehensive trademark and brand name directory; associations, societies, and trade shows related to the home decorating industry. **Entries Include:** For companies and manufacturer representatives—Firm name, address, phone, fax, name and title of contact, trademark, brand names. For associations—Name, address, phone, statement of purpose or description of service, key personnel, trade shows sponsored with dates and locations.

Principal content of publication is decorative products (coatings, wallcoverings, window treatments, flooring, sundries). **Arrangement:** Alphabetical. **Indexes:** Brand and trade name.

STATISTICAL SOURCES

15343 ■ *RMA Annual Statement Studies*
Pub: Robert Morris Associates (RMA)
Released: Annual. **Price:** $175.00 2006-07 edition, $105.00. **Description:** Contains composite balance sheets and income statements for more than 360 industries, including the accounting, auditing, and bookkeeping industries. Also contains five years of comparative historical data for discerning trends. Includes 16 commonly used ratios, computed for most of the size groupings for nearly every industry.

TRADE PERIODICALS

15344 ■ *Painting & Wallcovering Contractor*
Pub: Finan Publishing Company Inc.
Contact: Sharon Steele, Publisher
E-mail: ssteele@protectivecoatings.com
Ed: Mary Chollet-Lordan, Editor, pwc_editor@verizon.net. **Released:** Bimonthly. **Price:** $54.95 other countries; $104.90 two years. **Description:** Magazine covering painting and decorating industry-current research; new trends in techniques and products; and commercial, industrial, institutional, and residential application.

CONSULTANTS

15345 ■ Historic Exterior Paint Colors Consulting
3661 Waldenwood Dr.
Ann Arbor, MI 48105
Ph:(734)668-0298
Co. E-mail: robs@umich.edu
URL: http://www.historichousecolors.com
Contact: Robert Schweitzer, Owner
E-mail: robs@umich.edu
Scope: Provides exterior paint color consulting services. Provides services for historic, contemporary, new, commercial and residential services; museums. **Publications:** "Proof that Paint Color Lends Detail," Arts and Crafts Homes, 2006; "Bungalow Colors-Exteriors," Gibbs-Smith Publishers, 2002; "Color Scheming," Design NJ, 2002; "Colonial Revival Homes," Victorian Homes, Feb, 2003; "America's Favorite Homes"; "Color a New World," 60s Ranch Color Makeover, Romantic Homes, Aug, 2001; "How Shall I Paint my House," American Bungalow, 1999; "Color Concepts and Bungalow Basics," Cottages & Bungalows.

FRANCHISES AND BUSINESS OPPORTUNITIES

15346 ■ Certapro Painters
The Franchise Company
150 Green Tree Rd.
Oaks, PA 19456
Free: 800-689-7494
Fax:(610)650-9997
No. of Franchise Units: 325. **Founded:** 1992. **Franchised:** 1992. **Description:** Residential and commercial painting franchise. **Equity Capital Needed:** $129,000-$156,000. **Franchise Fee:** $50,000. **Financial Assistance:** No. **Training:** 2 weeks of training prior to start-up; quarterly training in field. Advance training is also provided.

15347 ■ Color World Housepainting Inc.
420 W Olentangy St., No. B
Powell, OH 43065
Ph:(614)581-1652
Free: 877-724-6877
Fax:(614)861-7751
No. of Franchise Units: 2. **No. of Company-Owned Units:** 6. **Founded:** 1997. **Franchised:** 2007. **Description:** Residential & commercial painting. **Equity Capital Needed:** $25,000-$110,000. **Franchise Fee:** $25,000. **Royalty Fee:** 5%. **Financial Assistance:** Limited inhouse financing available. **Training:** Includes 2 weeks training.

15348 ■ Hester Painting & Decorating
Hester Decorating
7340 N Monticello Ave.
Skokie, IL 60076
Free: 877-437-8371
Fax:(847)677-5139
Co. E-mail: info@hesterdecorating.com
URL: http://www.hesterfranchising.com
No. of Company-Owned Units: 2. **Founded:** 1968. **Franchised:** 2007. **Description:** Painting and faux finishing company. No painting experience is needed. Based on 39 years experience, the Hester Painting & Decorating franchise program provides training program, estimating software, professional marketing system, and exclusive faux finish showroom. **Franchise Fee:** $50,000. **Financial Assistance:** No. **Training:** Provides 9 days management training at headquarters covering award winning business systems along with over 3 weeks of hands on training for your staff at training facility and at your new showroom. You will learn approximately 30 faux and decorative finishing techniques.

15349 ■ The Painting Pros
1624-C Cross Beam Dr.
Charlotte, NC 28217
Ph:(704)424-5555
Fax:(704)424-1111
No. of Franchise Units: 7. **No. of Company-Owned Units:** 5. **Founded:** 2003. **Franchised:** 2006. **Description:** Residential and commercial painting contractor. **Franchise Fee:** $15,000-$50,000. **Financial Assistance:** Yes. **Training:** Yes.

15350 ■ Protect Painters
Protect Painters Development, LLC
3948 Ranchero Dr.
Ann Arbor, MI 48108
Free: 888-464-4242
Co. E-mail: franchiseinfo@protectpainters.com
URL: http://www.protectpainters.com
No. of Franchise Units: 32. **Founded:** 1995. **Franchised:** 1997. **Description:** Painting service. **Equity Capital Needed:** $73,050-$88,800. **Franchise Fee:** $14,900. **Financial Assistance:** Third party financing available. **Training:** 8-10 days hands-on training courses. Ongoing support includes marketing, sales, weekly analysis of marketing and production, weekly teleconferences, workshops, personal visits and regional meetings.

LIBRARIES

15351 ■ Sherwin-Williams Automotive Finishes Corporation Library
4440 Warrensville Center Rd.
Warrensville Heights, OH 44128-2837
Free: 800-798-5872
URL: http://www.sherwin-automotive.com
Contact: Elizabeth Rinz, Mgr.
Scope: Paint, polymers, pigments, coatings. **Services:** Interlibrary loan.

START-UP INFORMATION

15352 ■ "Fun And Easy Gold Mines" in *Small Business Opportunities* **(Fall 2008)**
Pub: Entrepreneur Media Inc.
Description: Twenty-five businesses that cater to the booming children's market are profiled; day care services, party planning, special events video-making, tutoring, personalized children's toys and products and other services geared toward the kids market are included.

ASSOCIATIONS AND OTHER ORGANIZATIONS

15353 ■ Clowns of America International
PO Box 1171
Englewood, FL 34295-1171
Ph:(941)474-4351
Free: 877-816-6941
URL: http://www.coai.org
Contact: Tom King, Pres.
Description: Professional and amateur clowns, magicians, puppeteers, jugglers, and others who present a humorous program for the circus, radio, television, stage, and screen; friends of clowns and persons interested in clowning as a profession or hobby. Includes activities such as: training sessions, and entertaining in parades and shows. Provides entertainment for charitable organizations and events. Promotes first week of August as National Clown Week. **Publications:** *The New Calliope* (bimonthly).

REFERENCE WORKS

15354 ■ "Green It Like You Mean It" in *Special Events Magazine* **(Vol. 28, February 1, 2009, No. 2)**
Pub: Special Events Magazine
Ed: Christine Landry. **Description:** Eco-friendly party planners offer advice for planning and hosting green parties or events. Tips include information for using recycled paper products, organic food and drinks. The Eco Nouveau Fashion Show held by Serene Star Productions reused old garments to create new fashions as well as art pieces from discarded doors and window frames for the show; eco-friendly treats and gift bags were highlighted at the event.

15355 ■ "Holiday Parties to Take a Hit in Hard Times" in *Philadelphia Business Journal* **(Vol. 28, November 6, 2009, No. 38, pp. 1)**
Pub: American City Business Journals
Ed: Peter van Allen. **Description:** Companies are cutting expenses in view of the economic downturn and are changing the way holiday parties will be held. Sixty-two percent of firms will still hold parties in 2009, but last minute decisions about reduced-cost parties are being made.

15356 ■ "How I Did It: Laurel Touby Mediabistro" in *Inc.* **(March 2008, pp. 124-126)**
Pub: Gruner & Jahr USA Publishing
Ed: Eric Schine. **Description:** Profile of Laurel Touby and her business plan; Touby started Mediabistro as

a series of parties that turned into an influential job listing and training Website for journalists. Last year she sold it for $23 million.

15357 ■ "Party Animals" in *Business Review, Albany New York* **(Vol. 34, November 16, 2007, No. 33, pp. 1)**
Pub: American City Business Journals, Inc.
Ed: Donna Abbott Viahos. **Description:** Total Events LLC, an event planning firm founded by Richard Carrier, generated sales from $13,000 to $1.5 million in eight years. Fine Affairs Inc. generates more than a million of revenues a year. Both companies provide party planning, organizing and decorating, wedding, galas, bar mitzvahs and other event planning.

TRADE PERIODICALS

15358 ■ *Balloons & Parties Magazine*
Pub: PartiLife Publications
Contact: Mark Zettler, Publisher
Released: Quarterly. **Price:** $16.95 two years; $9.95. **Description:** Magazine for balloon and party professionals and retailers of party goods.

15359 ■ *Linking Ring*
Pub: International Brotherhood of Magicians
Contact: B.J. Hickman, Advertising Mgr
Released: Monthly. **Price:** Free to qualified subscribers. **Description:** Membership journal for magicians.

15360 ■ *Magic*
Pub: Stagewrite Publishing Inc.
Contact: Stan Allen, Founding Ed.
Released: Monthly. **Price:** $54; $103 two years; $74 Canada; $82 Mexico; $143 two years for Canada; $159 two years for Mexico; $89 out of country airmail. **Description:** Trade journal for magicians and magic enthusiasts.

VIDEOCASSETTES/ AUDIOCASSETTES

15361 ■ *The Art of Magic*
PBS Home Video
Catalog Fulfillment Center
PO Box 751089
Charlotte, NC 28275-1089
Ph:800-531-4727
Free: 800-645-4PBS
Co. E-mail: info@pbs.org
URL: http://www.pbs.org
Released: 1998. **Price:** $29.98. **Description:** Documentary takes a look at the history and evolution of illusion and magic, from its beginning in ancient temples to the modern Las Vegas entertainment extravaganzas. Two hours and 30 minutes on two videocassettes. **Availability:** VHS.

15362 ■ *Magic: The Sleeveless Way*
Silver Mine Video Inc.
31316 Via Colinas, Ste. 104
Westlake Village, CA 91362-3905

Ph:(818)707-0300
URL: http://www.quicksilverrecords.zoomshare.com
Released: 1985. **Price:** $29.95. **Description:** A detailed demonstration of how to perform magic tricks with common household items. **Availability:** VHS.

FRANCHISES AND BUSINESS OPPORTUNITIES

15363 ■ Complete Music
7877 L St.
Omaha, NE 68154
Ph:(402)339-0001
Free: 800-843-3966
Fax:(402)898-1777
No. of Franchise Units: 170. **No. of Company-Owned Units:** 2. **Founded:** 1974. **Franchised:** 1981. **Description:** Mobile entertainment service. Entertainment for special events. Franchise owners hire and train a staff of DJ's to perform at these events. **Equity Capital Needed:** $15,000-$35,000. **Franchise Fee:** $18,000$35,500. **Financial Assistance:** Partial assistance available to qualified individuals. **Managerial Assistance:** Initial training, ongoing support. **Training:** 10 days at corporate office, covering day-to-day operations, including marketing, training of staff, hiring procedures, etc. Additional 4 day onsite provided.

15364 ■ Cool Daddy's
4188 Roswell Rd.
Atlanta, GA 30342
Ph:(404)352-9996
Fax:(404)352-9106
No. of Franchise Units: 1. **No. of Company-Owned Units:** 1. **Founded:** 2000. **Franchised:** 2005. **Description:** Frozen drink party rentals & entertainment. **Equity Capital Needed:** $105,000-$187,500. **Franchise Fee:** $25,000. **Royalty Fee:** 6%. **Financial Assistance:** Limited third party financing available. **Training:** Provides 2 weeks at headquarters. 1 week at franchisee's location, with ongoing support.

15365 ■ Grove Recreations, Inc.
1207 Hillside Dr. N
N Myrtle Beach, SC 29582
Ph:(843)249-2118
Fax:(849)249-2118
No. of Franchise Units: 37. **No. of Company-Owned Units:** 4. **Founded:** 1977. **Description:** Recreation and entertainment service. **Equity Capital Needed:** $200,000-$450,000. **Financial Assistance:** Yes. **Training:** Yes.

15366 ■ The Party Image
Pampered Girls, Inc.
2007 Oakview Dr.
Round Rock, TX 78681
Ph:(512)218-9390
Fax:(512)218-9970
No. of Company-Owned Units: 3. **Founded:** 2005. **Franchised:** 2006. **Description:** Spa atmosphere parties for young girls. **Equity Capital Needed:**

$46,000-$80,000. **Franchise Fee:** $20,000. **Financial Assistance:** Third party financing available. **Training:** Yes. Yes.

15367 ■ Party Land
5215 Militia Hill Rd.
Plymouth Meeting, PA 19462
Ph:(610)941-6200
Free: 800-778-9563
Fax:(610)941-6301
Co. E-mail: jbarry@partyland.com
URL: http://www.partyland.com

No. of Franchise Units: 43. **Founded:** 1986. **Franchised:** 1988. **Description:** Retail party supply stores. **Equity Capital Needed:** $280,000. **Franchise Fee:** $35,000. **Royalty Fee:** 5%. **Financial Assistance:** Third party financing available. **Training:** 1 week training.

RESEARCH CENTERS

15368 ■ International Clown Hall of Fame Museum and Research Center, Inc.
640 S 84th St., Ste. 526

West Allis, WI 53214
Ph:(414)290-0105
Fax:(414)290-0106
Co. E-mail: contact@theclownmuseum.org
URL: http://www.theclownmuseum.org
Contact: Terese M. Hall
E-mail: contact@theclownmuseum.org

Scope: Clowns and clowning. **Publications:** Newsletter (quarterly). **Educational Activities:** Workshops, seminars, special events, and live performances.

START-UP INFORMATION

15369 ■ **"Fun And Easy Gold Mines" in** *Small Business Opportunities* **(Fall 2008)**
Pub: Entrepreneur Media Inc.
Description: Twenty-five businesses that cater to the booming children's market are profiled; day care services, party planning, special events video-making, tutoring, personalized children's toys and products and other services geared toward the kids market are included.

ASSOCIATIONS AND OTHER ORGANIZATIONS

15370 ■ **National Association of Casino Party Operators**
PO Box 5626
South San Francisco, CA 94083
Free: 888-922-0777
Co. E-mail: info@casinoparties.com
URL: http://www.nactpo.com
Contact: Mike Miller, Dir.
Description: Casino party operators, party planners, party rental shop owners, theme party and special events operators, and others involved in casino party rental business. Strives to strengthen the casino and theme party industry and advance the industry into more geographical markets. Promotes members' interests. .

REFERENCE WORKS

15371 ■ **"2011 Summer Wedding and Party Tips and Must Have's" in** *Benzinga.com* **(June 17, 2011)**
Pub: Benzinga.com
Ed: Benzinga Staff. **Description:** Tips for hosting garden parties and get-togethers, but focusing on wedding receptions are provided.

15372 ■ **"Green It Like You Mean It" in** *Special Events Magazine* **(Vol. 28, February 1, 2009, No. 2)**
Pub: Special Events Magazine
Ed: Christine Landry. **Description:** Eco-friendly party planners offer advice for planning and hosting green parties or events. Tips include information for using recycled paper products, organic food and drinks. The Eco Nouveau Fashion Show held by Serene Star Productions reused old garments to create new fashions as well as art pieces from discarded doors and window frames for the show; eco-friendly treats and gift bags were highlighted at the event.

15373 ■ **"Holiday Bloom: Event Designer Collin Abraham Heightens Glamour With Florals" in** *Black Enterprise* **(Vol. 41, November 2010, No. 4)**
Pub: Earl G. Graves Publishing Co. Inc.
Ed: Sean Drakes. **Description:** Profile of Collin Abraham, who works out of his Harlem boutique to arrange unique floral pieces to complement the social gatherings and main events he plans for his clients.

15374 ■ **"Holiday Parties to Take a Hit in Hard Times" in** *Philadelphia Business Journal* **(Vol. 28, November 6, 2009, No. 38, pp. 1)**
Pub: American City Business Journals
Ed: Peter van Allen. **Description:** Companies are cutting expenses in view of the economic downturn and are changing the way holiday parties will be held. Sixty-two percent of firms will still hold parties in 2009, but last minute decisions about reduced-cost parties are being made.

15375 ■ **"Holy Wasabi! Sushi Not Just For Parents Anymore" in** *Chicago Tribune* **(March 13, 2008)**
Pub: McClatchy-Tribune Information Services
Ed: Christopher Borrelli. **Description:** Wicker Park cooking school, The Kid's Table, specializes in cooking classes for pre-teens; Elena Marre who owns the school was surprised when she was asked to plan a children's party in which she would teach a course in sushi making. More and more adolescents and small children are eating sushi.

15376 ■ **"How I Did It: Laurel Touby Mediabistro" in** *Inc.* **(March 2008, pp. 124-126)**
Pub: Gruner & Jahr USA Publishing
Ed: Eric Schine. **Description:** Profile of Laurel Touby and her business plan; Touby started Mediabistro as a series of parties that turned into an influential job listing and training Website for journalists. Last year she sold it for $23 million.

15377 ■ **"Interbrand's Creative Recruiting" in** *Business Courier* **(Vol. 27, November 12, 2010, No. 28, pp. 1)**
Pub: Business Courier
Ed: Dan Monk. **Description:** Global brand consulting firm Interbrand uses a creative recruitment agency to attract new employees into the company. Interbrand uses themed parties to attract prospective employees. The 'Alice In Wonderland' tea party for example, allowed the company to hire five new employees.

15378 ■ **"On Your Marks, American Airlines, Now Vote!" in** *Benzinga.com* **(, 2011)**
Pub: Benzinga.com
Ed: Benzinga Staff. **Description:** Wedding planner, Aviva Samuels, owner of Kiss the Planner boutique wedding and event planning agency in Florida, says that winning this contest would help her increase her knowledge base and provide in-depth, personal experience offering more destination wedding destinations.

15379 ■ **"Party Animals" in** *Business Review, Albany New York* **(Vol. 34, November 16, 2007, No. 33, pp. 1)**
Pub: American City Business Journals, Inc.
Ed: Donna Abbott Viahos. **Description:** Total Events LLC, an event planning firm founded by Richard Carrier, generated sales from $13,000 to $1.5 million in eight years. Fine Affairs Inc. generates more than a million of revenues a year. Both companies provide party planning, organizing and decorating, wedding, galas, bar mitzvahs and other event planning.

15380 ■ **"Plan Your Wedding with Cleveland Airport Marriott's Certified Event Planners" in** *Benzinga.com* **(February 2, 2011)**
Pub: Benzinga.com
Ed: Benzinga Staff. **Description:** Cleveland's Airport Marriott makes wedding planning easy with its venue spaces and a full team of wedding planners.

15381 ■ **Tent Rental Directory**
Pub: Industrial Fabrics Association International
Contact: Jan Schieffer, Managing Editor
Released: Annual, May. **Covers:** Over 200 manufacturing and rental firms of party, fair, and commercial tents; international coverage. **Entries Include:** Company name, address, phone, name of contact, product or service provided. **Arrangement:** Geographical.

15382 ■ **"Velvet Ice Cream" in** *Ice Cream Reporter* **(Vol. 23, November 20, 2010, No. 12, pp. 7)**
Pub: Ice Cream Reporter
Description: Velvet Ice Cream will open its Ye Olde Mill for private corporate parties around the holidays. Their facility can accommodate groups ranging from 30 to 125 individuals. The historic site houses the company headquarters, an ice cream museum, and a restaurant.

TRADE PERIODICALS

15383 ■ **The Polar Bear ROARS**
Pub: Polar Bear Alumni Association (PBAA)
Contact: Leeann Faust
Ed: Leeann Faust, Editor, lfaust@columbus.rr.com. **Released:** Quarterly. **Price:** Included in membership; $8 /year. **Description:** Provides news of current events regarding reunion information, memories of alumni, history of school and articles about alumni and faculty. Recurring features include reports of reunions.

15384 ■ **Singles in the Suburbs Newsletter**
Pub: Singles in the Suburbs Inc.
Contact: James Mackey, President
Ed: Sarah Regan, Editor. **Released:** Monthly. **Price:** $30, individuals. **Description:** Lists events that the club will be holding in the next calendar month. The events are planned to provide a low-pressure, casual way for singles to meet and socialize.

FRANCHISES AND BUSINESS OPPORTUNITIES

15385 ■ **Plan Ahead Events**
2121 Vista Pky.
West Palm Beach, FL 33411
Ph:(561)868-1368
Free: 877-866-1750
No. of Franchise Units: 64. **Founded:** 2007. **Franchised:** 2007. **Description:** Event planning. **Equity Capital Needed:** $36,255-$57,645. **Franchise Fee:** $29,900. **Royalty Fee:** $300/month. **Financial As-**

sistance: Third party financing available. **Training:** Provides 1 week at headquarters, 1 week at franchisee's location and ongoing support. .

ASSOCIATIONS AND OTHER ORGANIZATIONS

15386 ■ National Pawnbrokers Association
PO Box 508
Keller, TX 76244
Ph:(817)337-8830
Fax:(817)337-8875
Co. E-mail: info@nationalpawnbrokers.org
URL: http://www.nationalpawnbrokers.org
Contact: Dana Meinecke, Exec. Dir.
Description: Pawnbrokers and interested others. Seeks to educate and inform the public on the pawnbroking industry. Provides continuing education on technological changes. **Publications:** *Buyers Guide* (periodic); *National Pawnbroker* (quarterly); *Pawnbroker News* (periodic).

REFERENCE WORKS

15387 ■ "B-N Pawn Shop Auctions Off Jimmy Hoffa's Rifle" in *Pantagraph* (September 14, 2010)
Pub: The Pantagraph
Ed: Ryan Denham. **Description:** Midwest Exchange pawn shop located in IAA Drive in Bloomington, Illinois auctioned a rifle once belonging to Jimmy Hoffa.

15388 ■ "Boyd's Pawn Shop Looks More Like a Mini-Mall With Plenty For Sale" in *The Hawk Eye* (January 2, 2011)
Pub: McClatchy-Tribune Information Services
Ed: Rex L. Troute. **Description:** Profile of Brian Boyd, aka 'the king of pawn' and his shop located in West Burlington, Iowa. Boyd also operates a redemption center at the rear of his shop and collects nearly 42 million cans and bottles annually.

15389 ■ "BRIEF: Montana Street Pawn Shop Closing Doors" in *Montana Standard* (November 6, 2010)
Pub: Montana Standard
Ed: John Grant Emeigh. **Description:** First National Pawn located in Butte, Montana will close its doors after losing its lease. Co-owner Pat Evenson reported the lease situation coupled with the economy prompted the decision to close.

15390 ■ "Detroit Pawn Shop to be Reality TV Venue" in *UPI NewsTrack* (July 10, 2010)
Pub: United Press International-USA
Description: TruTV will present a new series called 'Hardcore Pawn' to compete with the History Channel's successful show 'Pawn Stars'. The show will feature American Jewelry and Loan in Detroit, Michigan and its owner Les Gold, who runs the store with his wife and children.

15391 ■ "Family Feud: Pawn Shop Empire Stalls with Transition to Second Generation" in *Billings Gazette* (December 19, 2010)
Pub: Billings Gazette
Ed: Jan Falstad. **Description:** Profile of Ben L. Brown Sr. and his pawn shop located in Billings, Montana is presented. Brown discusses his plan to transition his business to his children.

15392 ■ "Gold Still Has That Glitter" in *Barron's* (Vol. 89, July 20, 2009, No. 29, pp. M8)
Pub: Dow Jones & Co., Inc.
Ed: Allen Sykora. **Description:** Gold prices appear to be ready for an increase starting in the fall of 2009 due to an increase in demand. The price of the August 2009 gold contract fell to as low as $904.08 an ounce before recovering to $937.50.

15393 ■ "Pawn Shop Plan Snubbed by Citizen Group" in *North County Times* (October 14, 2010)
Pub: North County Times
Ed: Ray Huard. **Description:** A citizens advisory group is against the opening of an upscale pawn shop in downtown Oceanside, California. The group contends that a pawn shop does not fit the plans for revitalizing the area.

15394 ■ "Waco Pawn Shop Owners Say Reality Isn't Much Like 'Pawn Stars' TV Show" in *Waco Tribune-Herald* (August 15, 2010)
Pub: Waco Tribune-Herald
Ed: Mike Copeland. **Description:** Area pawn shop owners report that the television show on cable TV does not represent the true life operations of a pawn shop. The Las Vegas shop represented on TV boasts 30 employees and 21 on-call experts, which is not the case in reality.

Payroll Preparation Service

ASSOCIATIONS AND OTHER ORGANIZATIONS

15395 ■ American Payroll Association
660 N Main Ave., Ste. 100
San Antonio, TX 78205-1217
Ph:(210)226-4600
Free: 800-398-8681
Fax:(210)226-4027
Co. E-mail: apa@americanpayroll.org
URL: http://www.americanpayroll.org
Contact: Daniel J. Maddux, Exec. Dir.
Description: Payroll employees. Works to increase members' skills and professionalism through education and mutual support. Represents the interest of members before legislative bodies. Conducts training courses. Operates speakers' bureau; conducts educational programs. Administers the certified payroll professional program of recognition. **Publications:** *APA Basic Guide to Payroll* (annual); *APA Directory* (annual); *APA Guide to Payroll Practice and Management*; *Guide to Global Payroll Management*; *Payroll Currently* (biweekly); *The Payroll Source* (annual); *Your Paycheck Factbook* .

15396 ■ Canadian Payroll Association–Association canadienne de la paie
250 Bloor St. E, Ste. 1600
Toronto, ON, Canada M4W 1E6
Ph:(416)487-3380
Free: 800-387-4693
Fax:(416)487-3384
Co. E-mail: membership@payroll.ca
URL: http://www.payroll.ca
Contact: Patrick Culhane, Pres./CEO
Description: Represents the payroll community in Canada; offers education programs, advocacy efforts, products and services to help members enhance and adapt payroll operations, meet new legislative requirements, address changing workplace needs and take advantage of emerging technologies. **Publications:** *CPA E-Source* (bimonthly); *Dialogue Magazine* (bimonthly).

REFERENCE WORKS

15397 ■ "DHS Finalizes Rules Allowing Electronic I-9s" in *HR Specialist* (Vol. 8, September 2010, No. 9, pp. 5)
Pub: Capitol Information Group Inc.
Description: U.S. Department of Homeland Security issued regulations that give employers more flexibility to electronically sing and store I-9 employee verification forms.

15398 ■ *Employer Legal Forms Simplified*
Pub: Nova Publishing Company
Ed: Daniel Sitarz. **Released:** August 2007. **Price:** $24.95. **Description:** Business reference containing the following forms needed to handle employees in any small business environment: application, notice, confidentiality, absence, federal employer forms and notices, and many payroll forms. All forms are included on a CD that comes in both PDF and text formats. Adobe Acrobat Reader software is also included on the CD. The forms are valid in all fifty states and Washington, DC.

15399 ■ "May I Handle That For You?" in *Inc.* (March 2008, pp. 40, 42)
Pub: Gruner & Jahr USA Publishing
Ed: Taylor Mallory. **Description:** According to a recent survey, 53 percent of all companies outsource a portion of their human resources responsibilities. Ceridian, Administaff, Taleo, KnowledgeBank, and CheckPoint HR are among the companies profiled.

15400 ■ "More Businesses Will Shift Health Costs to Workers" in *Business Review, Albany New York* (Vol. 34, November 16, 2007, No. 33, pp. 1)
Pub: American City Business Journals, Inc.
Ed: Barbara Pinckney. **Description:** Survey conducted by consulting firm Benetech Inc. showed that sixty percent of employers are planning to increase payroll deductions to pay for health insurance premiums. More than ninety percent of the employers prefer HMO plans, followed by Preferred Provider Organizations. Other details of the survey are discussed.

15401 ■ "Privacy Concern: Are 'Group' Time Sheets Legal?" in *HR Specialist* (Vol. 8, September 2010, No. 9, pp. 4)
Pub: Capitol Information Group Inc.
Description: Under the Fair Labor Standards Act (FLSA) employers are required to maintain and preserve payroll or other records, including the number of hours worked, but it does not prescribe a particular order or form in which these records must be kept.

15402 ■ *QuickBooks X for Dummies*
Pub: John Wiley & Sons, Incorporated
Ed: Stephen L. Nelson. **Released:** November 2006. **Price:** $21.99. **Description:** Key features of QuickBooks software for small business are introduced. Invoicing and credit memos, recoding sales receipts, accounting, budgeting, taxes, payroll, financial reports, job estimating, billing, tracking, data backup, are among the features.

15403 ■ "What to Pay Your Top Team" in *Inc.* (March 2008, pp. 108-112, 114)
Pub: Gruner & Jahr USA Publishing
Ed: Jennifer Gill. **Description:** In-depth examination to help business owners decide if they paying their executives properly. A guide to executive salaries at private companies is presented. Statistical data included.

TRADE PERIODICALS

15404 ■ *Keep Up to Date on Payroll*
Pub: Progressive Business Publications
Contact: Ken Thorne
Ed: Ken Thorne, Editor, thorne@pbp.com. **Released:** Semimonthly. **Price:** $230, individuals. **Description:** Presents the latest on federal and state tax laws and unemployment insurance. Recurring features include interviews, a calendar of events, news of educational opportunities, and columns titled Law and Reg Update, Real Problems/Real Solutions, and Sharpen Your Judgment.

15405 ■ *Payroll Legal Alert*
Pub: Alexander Hamilton Institute Inc.
Contact: Alice Gilman
Ed: Alice Gilman, ESQ, Editor. **Released:** Monthly. **Price:** $99. **Description:** Covers aspects of payroll operations, including key tax and benefits laws, regulations, rulings, and cases. Includes new trends in tax law, ideas on benefits, wage and hour traps, and unemployment issues.

15406 ■ *Payroll Manager's Letter*
Pub: Aspen Publishers Inc.
Contact: Brendan Johnston
Released: Semimonthly. **Price:** $325, individuals. **Description:** Provides information payroll professionals require to comply with IRS, SSA, and other government regulations. Includes reports on court cases and their impact on payroll, relevant technology updates, and innovations in the payroll field. Recurring features include interviews and annual updates on Forms W-2 and W-4, tax rates, and per diems.

FRANCHISES AND BUSINESS OPPORTUNITIES

15407 ■ Universal Payroll Company
290 Main St., Ste. 300
Alpharetta, GA 30009
Ph:(770)778-6148
Free: (866)652-5500
Fax:(770)421-8171
Description: Full service payroll company.

COMPUTER SYSTEMS/ SOFTWARE

15408 ■ Aatrix Top Pay
Aatrix Software
2100 Library Cir.
Grand Forks, ND 58201
Ph:(701)746-6017
Free: 800-426-0854
Fax:(701)787-0594
URL: http://www.aatrix.com
Price: Contact Aatrix. **Description:** Handles payroll calculations and tax deductions for both salaried and hourly employees.

15409 ■ ABS Payroll System
American Business Systems, Inc.
315 Littleton Rd.
Chelmsford, MA 01824
Ph:(978)250-9600
Free: 800-356-4034

Fax:(978)250-8027
Co. E-mail: sales@abs-software.com
URL: http://www.abs-software.com
Description: Available for Windows XP, 2000, NT, ME, 98, or 95 platforms. Payroll and management system including an employee database driving payroll processing. System provides audit reports, and user-defined earnings and deduction categories.

15410 ■ ACCESS Payroll–Warren Computer Center
Software Design, Inc.
1945 Mitchell Ave.
Waterloo, IA 50702
Ph:(319)232-9504
Free: 800-553-0002
Fax:(319)232-8903
Co. E-mail: warren@warrencomputer.com
URL: http://www.warrencomputer.com
Contact: John Warren, Pres
Description: Available for IBM computers and MS-DOS compatibles. Payroll package featuring employee, company, and governmental reporting information and a master record for each employee.

15411 ■ Comprehensive Integrated Payroll System: CHIPS–Donald R. Frey and Company, Inc.
Donald R. Frey & Co., Inc.
40 N Grand Ave., Ste. 303
Ft. Thomas, KY 41075
Ph:(859)441-6566
Free: 800-659-3739
Fax:(859)441-7152
Co. E-mail: drfrey@drfrey.com
URL: http://www.drfrey.com
Description: CHIPS (CompreHensive Integrated Payroll System) is designed to provide the special functional and reporting capabilities required for fund based accounting operations.

15412 ■ CompuSystems, Inc.
1 Science Ct.
Columbia, SC 29203-9344
Ph:(803)735-7700
Free: 800-800-6472
Fax:800-800-8355
URL: http://www.misyshealth.com
Description: Available for MS-DOS compatibles. System maintaining employee records, and printing checks, check register, monthly reports, quarterly reports, annual reports, W-2 forms, and 1099 forms.

15413 ■ Custom Payroll
LPI Datasmith, Inc.
10020 Fontana
Overland Park, KS 66207
Ph:(913)381-9118
Fax:(913)381-9118
URL: http://www.datasmithpayroll.com
Contact: Dave Land
Price: Contact Datasmith product cost. **Description:** Contact Datasmith product cost

15414 ■ DacEasy Payroll–Sage Software SB, Inc.
DacEasy, Inc.
1505 Pavilion Place
Norcross, GA 30093
Ph:(770)724-4000
Free: 800-322-3279
Fax:(972)713-6331
Co. E-mail: dachelp@daceasy.com
URL: http://www.daceasy.com/
Price: Contact DacEasy for Pricing. **Description:**

15415 ■ Open Systems Payroll System
Open Systems Holdings Corp.
4301 Dean Lakes Blvd.
Shakopee, MN 55379
Ph:(952)403-5700
Free: 800-328-2276
Fax:(952)496-2495
Co. E-mail: info@osas.com
URL: http://www.osas.com
Description: Available for CP/M, MP/M environments. System designed for meeting government reporting requirements for hourly and salaried employees. Features check processing, withholding and department reporting, payroll processing, and labor expense distribution and reporting by department.

15416 ■ Ultimate Payroll
Aatrix Software
2100 Library Cir.
Grand Forks, ND 58201
Ph:(701)746-6017
Free: 800-426-0854
Fax:(701)746-4393
URL: http://www.aatrix.com
Contact: Steve Lunseth, Pres
Price: Contact Aatrix. **Description:** Available for Apple Macintosh computers. Features payroll functions as well as restaurant tips reporting, unlimited pay rates, piecework, and deductions. Also prints information on federal forms, and tracks check amounts, sick, vacation, and holiday pay.

LIBRARIES

15417 ■ Ernst & Young Center for Business Knowledge Libraries
1220 Skylight Office Twr.
1660 W. 2nd St.
Cleveland, OH 44113
Ph:(216)737-1355
Fax:(216)622-0199
Scope: Accounting, auditing, management, consulting. **Services:** Interlibrary loan; copying; Center not open to the public. **Holdings:** 1000 volumes. **Subscriptions:** 500 journals and other serials; 15 newspapers.

15418 ■ Ernst & Young Library
875 E. Wisconsin Ave.
Milwaukee, WI 53202
Ph:(414)273-5900
URL: http://www.ey.com
Contact: Julie Porter, Sr.Mgr.
Scope: Taxation, tax law, accounting, auditing. **Services:** Performs searches on fee basis for clients only. **Holdings:** 1200 books. **Subscriptions:** 35 journals and other serials.

15419 ■ International Public Management Association for Human Resources–HR Center
1617 Duke St.
Alexandria, VA 22314
Ph:(703)549-7100
Fax:(703)684-0948
Co. E-mail: nreichenberg@ipma-hr.org
URL: http://www.ipma-hr.org
Contact: Neil Reichenberg, Exec.Dir.
Scope: Public sector human resource management - classification, job analysis, policies and procedures, personnel, separation and retirement; wage and salary administration; employee relations; benefits; test development; total quality management. **Services:** Center not open to the public. **Holdings:** 500 volumes. **Subscriptions:** 12 newsletters.

15420 ■ Mercer–Information Research Centre
161 Bay St.
PO Box 501
Toronto, ON, Canada M5J 2S5
Ph:(416)868-2005
Fax:(416)868-7171
Co. E-mail: jo-anne.weiler@mercer.com
Contact: Jo-Anne Weiler, Mgr.
Scope: Employee benefits, pensions, human resources consulting, financial planning, strategic planning, salary administration, executive compensation, group insurance benefits. **Services:** Interlibrary loan. **Holdings:** 2500 books; 450 subject files; company financial reports. **Subscriptions:** 180 journals and other serials; 3 newspapers.

RESEARCH CENTERS

15421 ■ University of Waterloo–Centre for Accounting Research and Education
School of Accounting & Finance
200 University Ave. W
Waterloo, ON, Canada N2L 3G1
Ph:(519)888-4567
Fax:(519)888-7562
Co. E-mail: jbarnett@uwaterloo.ca
URL: http://accounting.uwaterloo.ca/research/care. html
Contact: James (Jim) Barnett, Dir.
E-mail: jbarnett@uwaterloo.ca
Scope: Assurance services, financial accounting, finance, management accounting and information systems, and taxation. Encourages interdisciplinary research at the University, including research in ethics. **Publications:** Working Papers (occasionally).

ASSOCIATIONS AND OTHER ORGANIZATIONS

15422 ■ Alliance of Area Business Publications
1970 E Grand Ave., Ste. 330
El Segundo, CA 90245
Ph:(310)364-0193
Fax:(310)364-0196
Co. E-mail: info@bizpubs.org
URL: http://www.bizpubs.org
Contact: C. James Dowden, Exec. Dir.

Description: Local area business publications. Encourages high journalistic standards among area business publications. Acts as a forum for the exchange of ideas and information, especially on common issues such as editorial excellence, postal regulations, government regulations, and advertising. Compiles statistics of business patterns in markets of members and engages in cooperative member market research. **Publications:** Newsletter (monthly).

15423 ■ American Business Media
675 3rd Ave., 7th Fl.
New York, NY 10017-5704
Ph:(212)661-6360
Fax:(212)370-0736
Co. E-mail: info@abmmail.com
URL: http://www.americanbusinessmedia.com
Contact: Clark Pettit, Pres./CEO

Description: Represents global business-to-business information providers. Members include producers of print and online magazines, newsletters and databases, as well as trade shows, conferences, seminars and other ancillary media. Exists to advance the common interests of business-to-business media organizations. Focuses on governmental affairs, promotion of the industry, best practices, and ethical standards. Its 200 plus member companies represent upwards of 1200 print publications, 1350 websites, and 850 trade shows, serving 181 industries and reaching 90 million readers. **Publications:** *Business Media Matters* (monthly); *E-News* (weekly).

15424 ■ American Court and Commercial Newspapers
PO Box 5337
Arlington, VA 22205
Ph:(703)237-9806
Fax:(703)237-9808
Co. E-mail: info@pnrc.net
URL: http://www.pnrc.net
Contact: Mark W.C. Stodder, Pres.

Description: Newspapers of general circulation devoted to lawyers and courts, financial and real estate professionals, contractors, and business interests. Functions as an advertising medium for business and legal vendors, marketers, advertising agencies, and related businesses. Operates speakers' bureau; conducts research reports. Compiles statistics. .

15425 ■ American Society of Magazine Editors
810 7th Ave., 24th Fl.
New York, NY 10019
Ph:(212)872-3700
Fax:(212)906-0128
Co. E-mail: asme@magazine.org
URL: http://www.magazine.org/asme
Contact: Nina Link, CEO/Pres.

Description: Represents magazine editors. Sponsors annual editorial internship program for college juniors and the National Magazine Awards. .

15426 ■ American Society of Media Photographers
150 N 2nd St.
Philadelphia, PA 19106
Ph:(215)451-2767
Fax:(215)451-0880
Co. E-mail: mopsik@asmp.org
URL: http://www.asmp.org
Contact: Eugene Mopsik, Exec. Dir.

Description: Professional society of freelance photographers. Works to evolve trade practices for photographers in communications fields. Provides business information to photographers and their potential clients; promotes ethics and rights of members. Holds educational programs and seminars. Compiles statistics. **Publications:** *ASMP Bulletin* (quarterly).

15427 ■ Association of Alternative Newsweeklies
1156 15th St. NW, Ste. 905
Washington, DC 20005
Ph:(202)289-8484
Fax:(202)289-2004
Co. E-mail: web@aan.org
URL: http://www.altweeklies.com
Contact: Mr. Mark Zusman, Pres.

Description: Members include Village Voice, L.A. Weekly, Chicago Reader and Washington City Paper. Provides members with information and communication relevant to the business of publishing an alternative newspaper. Holds annual convention. Compiles financial standards report, publishes monthly newsletter and administers annual editorial awards contest. .

15428 ■ Audit Bureau of Circulations
48 W Seegers Rd.
Arlington Heights, IL 60005-3913
Ph:(224)366-6939
Fax:(224)366-6949
Co. E-mail: service@accessabc.com
URL: http://www.accessabc.com
Contact: Michael J. Lavery, Pres./Managing Dir.

Description: Represents advertisers, advertising agencies, and publishers of daily and weekly newspapers, farm publications, consumer magazines, and business publications in the United States and Canada. Issues standardized statements on the circulation of publisher members; verifies the figures shown in these statements by auditors' examination of publishers' records; disseminates circulation data. Provides academic associate support; conducts

forums and seminars. **Publications:** *Audit Report and Publisher's Statements* (annual); *Canadian Circulation of U.S. Magazines* (annual); *County Penetration Reports* (semiannual); *FAS-FAX Reports* (semiannual); *Periodical Statement Library* (semiannual).

15429 ■ Book and Periodical Council
192 Spadina Ave., Ste. 107
Toronto, ON, Canada M5T 2C2
Ph:(416)975-9366
Fax:(416)975-1839
Co. E-mail: info@thebpc.ca
URL: http://www.bookandperiodicalcouncil.ca
Contact: Anne McClelland, Exec. Dir.

Description: Associations representing writers, editors, and publishers of books and periodicals and manufacturers, distributors, and sellers and lenders of printed materials. Promotes improved market conditions for Canadian publications and seeks to insure availability of a representative range of Canadian books and periodicals. Works to strengthen book and periodical distribution systems; supports development of new and existing Canadian-owned publishing companies; serves as a forum for discussion of industry issues.

15430 ■ Canadian Association of Journalists–L'Association Canadienne des Journalistes
Algonquin College
1106 Wellington St.
Ottawa, ON, Canada K1Y 4V3
Ph:(613)526-8061
Co. E-mail: canadianjour@magma.ca
URL: http://www.caj.ca
Contact: John Dickins, Exec. Dir.

Description: Professional organization representing the interests of journalists in Canada. Promotes high professional standards. Disseminates information. **Publications:** *Media* (3/year).

15431 ■ Canadian Business Press
2100 Banbury Crescent
Oakville, ON, Canada L6H 5P6
Ph:(905)844-6822
Co. E-mail: torrance@cbp.ca
URL: http://www.cbp.ca
Contact: Trish Torrance, Exec. Dir.

Description: Business publishers. Promotes the business press as a communications medium and source of information on Canadian business, industry, professions, and government. Works to improve standards among members; represents members' interests before government agencies; facilitates communication among members. Gathers and disseminates information; makes available technical assistance to members; serves as arbitrator in conflicts involving members. Sponsors competitions. **Publications:** *Baker's Journal*; *Canadian Contractor*; *Computing Canada* (biweekly); *Marketing* (weekly); *Wings* (semimonthly).

15432 ■ Canadian Circulation Management Association–Association Canadienne de Gerance de Tirage
298 Highfield St.
Moncton, NB, Canada E1C 5R6
Ph:(506)854-7091
Fax:(506)855-1334
Co. E-mail: dorman@nbnet.nb.ca
URL: http://www.ccmanet.ca
Contact: Dave Dorman, Sec.-Treas.

Description: Circulation managers employed by publishing companies. Promotes professional development of members; seeks to advance the publishing industry. Facilitates exchange of information among members; conducts educational programs.

15433 ■ Canadian Community Newspapers Association
890 Yonge St., Ste. 200
Toronto, ON, Canada M4W 3P4
Ph:(416)482-1090
Free: 877-305-2262
Fax:(416)482-1908
Co. E-mail: info@ccna.ca
URL: http://www.communitynews.ca
Contact: John Hinds, CEO

Description: Community newspapers. Promotes growth and development of small newspapers. Represents the interests of community newspapers before labor and industrial organizations, government agencies, and the public. Conducts educational and promotional activities. **Publications:** The Publisher (10/year).

15434 ■ Canadian Copyright Institute
192 Spadina Ave., Ste. 107
Toronto, ON, Canada M5T 2C2
Ph:(416)975-1756
Fax:(416)975-1839
Co. E-mail: info@thecci.ca
URL: http://www.canadiancopyrightinstitute.ca
Contact: Anne McClelland, Admin.

Description: Creators, producers, and distributors of copyrighted works. Encourages a more complete understanding of copyright laws among members and the public. Consults with government and judicial bodies regarding reform of copyright laws. Conducts and sponsors research on copyright laws worldwide. Works with organizations pursuing similar goals to improve copyright legislation and enforcement. **Publications:** Copyright Reform Legislation Reporting Service (periodic).

15435 ■ Canadian Newspaper Association–Association Canadienne des Journaux
890 Yonge St., Ste. 200
Toronto, ON, Canada M4W 3P4
Ph:(416)923-3567
Free: 877-305-2262
Fax:(416)923-7206
Co. E-mail: info@newspaperscanada.ca
URL: http://www.newspaperscanada.ca
Contact: John Hinds, Pres./CEO

Description: Daily newspapers. Promotes the growth and ongoing vitality of printed news media. Represents members' interests before government agencies, labor and industrial organizations, and the public. **Publications:** CNA Members' Bulletin (periodic).

15436 ■ Canadian University Press
920 Yonge St., Ste. 503
Toronto, ON, Canada M4W 3C7
Ph:(416)962-2287
Free: (866)250-5595
Fax:(416)966-3699
Co. E-mail: president@cup.ca
URL: http://www.cup.ca
Contact: James Michael McDonald, Pres.

Description: Student newspapers. Serves as a communication and support network for members; promotes exchange of news and features among members; seeks to develop journalistic skills among Canadian students; provides mechanism for sharing of national advertising by members. Encourages

cultural diversity in Canadian student media. Conducts political action caucuses. **Publications:** House Organ (monthly); This Week and More (weekly).

15437 ■ City and Regional Magazine Association
1970 E Grand Ave., Ste. 330
El Segundo, CA 90245
Ph:(310)364-0193
Fax:(310)364-0196
Co. E-mail: administrator@list.citymag.org
URL: http://www.citymag.org
Contact: C. James Dowden, Exec. Dir.

Description: City and regional consumer-oriented magazines; related businesses involved in printing, advertising, and circulation. Strives to gain presence in the marketplace and command an increased following among national advertisers. Serves as a channel of communication between city and regional consumer magazines and coordinates research projects. Distributes information; creates press materials. Compiles statistics. .

15438 ■ International Newsmedia Marketing Association
PO Box 740186
Dallas, TX 75374
Ph:(214)373-9111
Fax:(214)373-9112
Co. E-mail: megan.deleon@inma.org
URL: http://www.inma.org
Contact: Earl J. Wilkinson, Exec. Dir./CEO

Description: Represents individuals engaged in marketing, circulation, research, and public relations of newspapers. Conducts conferences; holds newspaper executives marketing and strategic planning seminars. .

15439 ■ Magazine Publishers of America
810 7th Ave., 24th Fl.
New York, NY 10019
Ph:(212)872-3700
Co. E-mail: mpa@magazine.org
URL: http://www.magazine.org
Contact: Nina Link, Pres./CEO

Description: Publishers of more than 1000 consumer and other magazines issued not less than four times a year. Activities include: Advertising Marketing Department to promote magazines as an advertising medium; Washington office to report on federal legislation and postal rates and regulations; Consumer Marketing Department to provide information services and assistance to members in all areas of circulation marketing. Conducts member surveys on magazine finance, paper usage, and compensation. Administers Publishers Information Bureau and Media Credit Association. **Publications:** Newsletter of International Publishing; Washington Newsletter .

15440 ■ Magazines Canada
425 Adelaide St. W, Ste. 700
Toronto, ON, Canada M5V 3C1
Ph:(416)504-0274
Fax:(416)504-0437
Co. E-mail: info@magazinescanada.ca
URL: http://www.magazinescanada.ca
Contact: Ms. Barbara Zatyko, Gen. Mgr./Publisher

Description: Magazine publishers. Promotes growth of magazine circulation and advancement of the publishing industries. Represents members' interests before government agencies and provides support and assistance to magazine publishers.

15441 ■ National Association of Hispanic Publications
529 14th St. NW, Ste. 1126
Washington, DC 20045
Ph:(202)662-7250
Fax:(202)662-7251
Co. E-mail: mgomez@nahp.org
URL: http://www.nahp.org
Contact: Mary Ann Gomez, Exec. Dir.

Description: Newspapers, magazines, and other periodicals published in Spanish (or bilingually in English and Spanish) in the United States. Promotes adherence to high standards of ethical and professional standards by members; advocates continuing professional development of Hispanic journalists and publishers. Provides technical assistance to members

in areas including writing and editing skills, circulation and distribution methods, attracting advertisers, obtaining financing, design and layout, and graphic arts. Conducts public service programs including voter registration drives. **Publications:** The Hispanic Press (quarterly).

15442 ■ North American Snowsports Journalists Association
460 Sarsons Rd.
Kelowna, BC, Canada V1W 1C2
Ph:(250)764-2143
Fax:(250)764-2145
Co. E-mail: nasja@shaw.ca
URL: http://www.nasja.org
Contact: Phil Johnson, Pres.

Description: Newspaper, magazine, book, television, radio writers and broadcasters, and photographers who report on skiing and other snow sports. Covers skiing and other snow sports. **Publications:** The Inside Edge (quinquennial); NASJA Directory (annual).

15443 ■ Periodical and Book Association of America
481 8th Ave., Ste. 526
New York, NY 10001
Ph:(212)563-6502
Fax:(212)563-4098
Co. E-mail: lscott@pbaa.net
URL: http://www.pbaa.net
Contact: Lisa W. Scott, Exec. Dir.

Description: Magazine and paperback publishers concerned with single copy or newsstand sales. Carries out concerted action in areas of publishing, production, and sales. .

15444 ■ Printing Industries of America
200 Deer Run Rd.
Sewickley, PA 15143
Ph:(412)741-6860
Free: 800-910-4283
Fax:(412)741-2311
Co. E-mail: printing@printing.org
URL: http://www.printing.org
Contact: Michael Makin, Pres./CEO

Description: Commercial printing firms (lithography, letterpress, gravure, platemakers, typographic houses); allied firms in the graphic arts. Provides extensive management services for member companies, including government relations, industry research and statistical information, technology information and assistance, and management education and publications. Compiles statistical and economic data, including annual ratio study that provides a benchmark for printers to compare profits as a basis for improving individual member company and industry profits. Provides reporting system on provisions, rates, and other matters relating to union contracts in effect throughout the industry. Sponsors annual Premier Print Awards Competition. .

15445 ■ Publishers Information Bureau
810 7th Ave., 24th Fl.
New York, NY 10019
Ph:(212)872-3700
Co. E-mail: pib@magazine.org
URL: http://www.magazine.org
Contact: Wayne Eadie, Pres.

Purpose: Measures the amount and type of advertising in magazines and reports this information monthly through printed and electronic formats; service prepared by TNSMI/Competitive Media Reporting (contracting agent). .

15446 ■ Society of Publication Designers
27 Union Sq. W, Ste. 207
New York, NY 10003
Ph:(212)223-3332
Fax:(212)223-5880
Co. E-mail: mail@spd.org
URL: http://www.spd.org
Contact: Nathalie Kirsheh, Pres.

Description: Represents art directors, designers, editors, photographers and illustrators with the responsibility of layout and design of consumer, business and professional publications and newspapers. Holds speakers' luncheons and auctions. **Publications:** GRIDS (quarterly); Solid Gold .

REFERENCE WORKS

15447 ■ "Advertising May Take a Big Hit in Southwest/AirTran Merger" in *Baltimore Business Journal* (Vol. 28, October 1, 2010, No. 21, pp. 1)
Pub: Baltimore Business Journal

Ed: Gary Haber. **Description:** Advertising on television stations and the publishing industry in Baltimore could drop as a result of the merger between rival discount airlines Southwest Airlines and AirTran Airways. Southwest is among the top advertisers in the U.S., spending $126 million in 2009. No local jobs are expected to be affected because neither airline uses a local advertising firm.

15448 ■ "Analyst Questions CanWest Papers' Viability" in *Globe & Mail* (January 14, 2006, pp. B3)
Pub: CTVglobemedia Publishing Inc.

Ed: Grant Robertson. **Description:** The opinions of analyst Tim Casey of BMO Nesbitt Burns Inc. over the prospects of two newspapers Dose and National Post of CanWest Global Communications Corp., which planned cost restructuring efforts, are presented.

15449 ■ "Best Value Stocks" in *Canadian Business* (Vol. 82, Summer 2009, No. 8, pp. 30)
Pub: Rogers Media

Ed: Calvin Leung. **Description:** Canadian companies that are believed to have the best value stocks are suggested. Suggestions include publishing firm Glacier Media, which has reported a four-fold growth in sales in the last three years. While publishers like Glacier Media face challenges such as declining circulation, the firm's industry diversification is expected to help it weather the economic downturn.

15450 ■ "Calista Sells Rural Newspapers" in *Alaska Business Monthly* (Vol. 27, October 2011, No. 10, pp. 8)
Pub: Alaska Business Publishing Company

Ed: Nancy Pounds. **Description:** Calista sold its six newspapers, a magazine, shoppers and its printing house. Details of the sales are given.

15451 ■ "Canadians Love Their Magazines" in *MarketingMagazine* (Vol. 115, September 27, 2010, No. 13, pp. 42)
Pub: Rogers Publishing Ltd.

Description: Market data covering magazine published or consumed in Canada is presented.

15452 ■ "A Class Act" in *Hawaii Business* (Vol. 53, March 2008, No. 9, pp. 25)
Pub: Hawaii Business Publishing

Ed: Cathy S. Cruz-George. **Description:** UBoost is a startup company that offers online content for the educational magazine 'Weekly Reader'. The website features quizzes and allows users to accumulate points and redeem rewards afterward. Other details about the company are discussed.

15453 ■ "Community Newspapers" in *MarketingMagazine* (Vol. 115, September 27, 2010, No. 13, pp. 38)
Pub: Rogers Publishing Ltd.

Description: Market data for the newspaper industry in Canada is presented.

15454 ■ "Copyright Clearance Center (CCC) Partnered with cSubs" in *Information Today* (Vol. 28, November 2011, No. 10, pp. 14)
Pub: Information Today, Inc.

Description: Copyright Clearance Center (CCC) partnered with cSubs to integrate CCC's point-of-content licensing solution RightsLink Basic directly into cSubs workflow. The partnership will allow cSubs' customers a user-friendly process for obtaining permissions. Csubs is a corporate subscription management service for books, newspapers, and econtent.

15455 ■ "Crain's Makes Ad Sales, Custom Marketing Appointments" in *Crain's Chicago Business* (Vol. 34, October 24, 2011, No. 42, pp. 13)
Pub: Crain Communications Inc.

Description: Crain's Chicago Business announced key appointments in its sales department: David Denor has been named first director of custom marketing services and Kate Van Etten will succeed Denor as advertising director.

15456 ■ "Crain's Nabs 15 Press Club Awards" in *Crain's Cleveland Business* (Vol. 30, June 29, 2009, No. 25, pp. 6)
Pub: Crain Communications, Inc.

Description: Crain's Cleveland Business was honored with 15 awards at the Ohio Excellence in Journalism competition conducted by the Press Club of Cleveland.

15457 ■ "Daily Newspapers" in *MarketingMagazine* (Vol. 115, September 27, 2010, No. 13, pp. 32)
Pub: Rogers Publishing Ltd.

Description: Market data covering the newspaper industry in Canada is examined.

15458 ■ *Directory of Small Press—Magazine Editors and Publishers*
Pub: Dustbooks

Ed: Len Fulton, Editor. **Released:** Annual, Latest edition 42nd; 2011-2012. **Price:** $49.95, individuals online; $21, individuals CD-ROM. **Covers:** About 7,500 publishers and editors. **Entries Include:** Individual name, title of press or magazine, address and phone number. **Arrangement:** Alphabetical.

15459 ■ "EBSCO Adds New Features to EBSCOhost Content Viewer" in *Information Today* (Vol. 26, February 2009, No. 2, pp. 31)
Pub: Information Today, Inc.

Description: EBSCOhost Content Viewer historical digital archive collection provides a visual overview of a displayed document, highlighting search keywords on the page as well as providing a document map that shows the number of times a given keyword is mentioned in a periodical, monograph, article, or other document. For periodical content, the viewer lets users browse multiple issues in a volume without leaving the interface; features include zoom and pan technology similar to online maps.

15460 ■ *The Facebook Effect: The Inside Story of the Company That Is Connecting the World*
Pub: Simon & Shuster

Ed: David Kirkpatrick. **Released:** June 8, 2010. **Price:** $26.00. **Description:** There's never been a Website like Facebook: more than 350 million people have accounts, and if the growth rate continues, by 2013 every Internet user worldwide will have his or her own page. No one's had more access to the inner workings of the phenomenon than Kirkpatrick, a senior tech writer at Fortune magazine. Written with the full cooperation of founder Mark Zuckerberg, the book follows the company from its genesis in a Harvard dorm room through its successes over Friendster and MySpace, the expansion of the user base, and Zuckerberg's refusal to sell.

15461 ■ "FCC Adopts New Media Ownership Rules" in *Black Enterprise* (Vol. 38, March 2008, No. 8, pp. 26)
Pub: Earl G. Graves Publishing Co. Inc.

Ed: Joyce Jones. **Description:** Federal Communications Commission approved a ruling that lifts a ban on newspaper and/or broadcast cross ownership. Because of declining sales in newspaper advertising and readership the ban will allow companies to share local news gathering costs across multiple media platforms.

15462 ■ *Freelancing for Journalists*
Pub: Routledge

Ed: Diana Harris. **Released:** January 1, 2010. **Price:** $110.00. **Description:** Comprehensive guide showing the specific skills required for those wishing to freelance in newspapers, magazines, radio, television, and as online journalists.

15463 ■ *Gale Directory of Publications and Broadcast Media*
Pub: Gale

Released: Annual, Latest edition April 2011. **Price:** $1,297, individuals. **Covers:** Approximately 57,000 publications and broadcasting stations, including newspapers, magazines, journals, radio stations, television stations, radio/television/cable networks, syndicates and cable systems in the U.S. and Canada. Newsletters and directories are excluded. **Entries Include:** For publications—Title, publishing and editorial addresses, phone, fax, description, names of editor, publisher, and advertising manager, base advertising rate, page specifications, subscription rate, circulation, frequency, ISSN, former names, additional contacts. For broadcast media—Call letters or cable system name, address, phone, fax, format, networks, owner, date founded, former call letters, operating hours, names and titles of key personnel, local programming, wattage, ad rates, additional contacts. **Arrangement:** Geographical. **Indexes:** Title; radio station format; publisher; geographic market; lists of agricultural, college, foreign language, Jewish, fraternal, black, women's, Hispanic, religious, general circulation, and trade and technical publications (by subject and/or geographical as needed); daily newspaper; daily periodical; free circulation newspaper; and shopping guides (each geographical); list of feature editors at daily newspapers with 50,000 or more circulation.

15464 ■ "Galvanizing the Scientific Community" in *Information Today* (Vol. 26, February 2009, No. 2, pp. 20)
Pub: Information Today, Inc.

Ed: Barbara Brynko. **Description:** Profile of John Haynes, newly appointed vice president of publishing for the American Institute of Physics; the Institute consists of ten organizations specializing in STM publishing as well as providing publishing services for over 170 science and engineering journals.

15465 ■ "Google Book Search Tosses Magazines Into the Mix" in *Information Today* (Vol. 26, February 2009, No. 2, pp. 31)
Pub: Information Today, Inc.

Description: Google Book Search expanded services to include magazines...

15466 ■ "Growth of Free Dailies Dropping" in *Globe & Mail* (March 24, 2007, pp. B7)
Pub: CTVglobemedia Publishing Inc.

Ed: Grant Robertson. **Description:** The decrease in the readership of free newspapers in Canada, in view of growing preference for online news, is discussed.

15467 ■ "Health Care Leads Sectors Attracting Capital" in *Hispanic Business* (March 2008, pp. 14-16, 18)
Pub: Hispanic Business

Ed: Scott Williams. **Description:** U. S. Hispanic healthcare, media, and food were the key industries in the U.S. gaining investors in 2007.

15468 ■ "Help for Job Seekers" in *Crain's Detroit Business* (Vol. 26, January 4, 2010, No. 1, pp. 14)
Pub: Crain Communications, Inc.

Description: CareerWorks is weekly paper targeting readers who are in a career transition or are looking for new employment.

15469 ■ *How to Get Rich*
Pub: Ebury Press

Ed: Felix Dennis. **Released:** 2008. **Price:** $25.95. **Description:** Publisher of Maxim, The Week, and Stuff magazines, discusses the mistakes he made running his companies. He didn't understand that people who buy computer gaming magazines wanted a free game with each copy, as one of his rivals was offering. And he laments not diversifying into television and exploiting the Internet.

15470 ■ "Ideas at Work: Total Communicator" in *Business Strategy Review* (Vol. 21, Autumn 2010, No. 3, pp. 10)
Pub: Blackwell Publishers Ltd.

Ed: Stuart Crainer. **Description:** Vittorio Colao has been chief executive of Vodafone Group for two years. He brings to the company special experience as CEO of RCS MediaGroup in Milan, which publishes newspapers, magazines and books in Italy, Spain and France. Prior to RCS, he held other positions within Vodaphone. Colao shares his views on business, the global economy and leading Vodafone.

15471 ■ "In Print and Online" in *Marketing to Women* **(Vol. 22, August 2009, No. 8, pp. 3)**
Pub: EPM Communications, Inc.
Description: Seventeen magazine is unifying its print and Online editions with complementary content, a strategy that seems to be working as every aspect of Seventeen drives the reader to another component.

15472 ■ "Integral USA Magazine Sponsors Eco-Fashion in the Park" in *Entertainment Close-Up* **(September 2, 2011)**
Pub: Close-Up Media
Description: Integral Magazine sponsored Eco-Fashion in the Park, a fashion show for the fashion conscious. Eleven independent designers will show their eco-friendly fashions at the event.

15473 ■ *International Directory of Little Magazines and Small Presses*
Pub: Dustbooks
Ed: Len Fulton, Editor. **Released:** Annual, Latest edition 47th; 2011-2012. **Price:** $65, individuals CD-ROM (3 directories); $49.95, individuals online; $30, individuals CD-ROM. **Covers:** Over 4,000 small, independent magazines, presses, and papers. **Entries Include:** Name, address, size, circulation, frequency, price, type of material used, number of issues or books published annually, and other pertinent data. **Arrangement:** Alphabetical. **Indexes:** Subject, regional.

15474 ■ "It's a New Game: Killerspin Pushes Table Tennis to Extreme Heights" in *Black Enterprise* **(Vol. 37, October 2006, No. 3, pp. 73)**
Pub: Earl G. Graves Publishing Co. Inc.
Ed: Bridget McCrea. **Description:** Profile of Robert Blackwell and his company Killerspin L.L.C., which is popularizing the sport of table tennis. Killerspin has hit $1 million in revenues due to product sales primarily generated through the company's website, magazines, DVDs, and event ticket sales.

15475 ■ "Joe Wikert, General Manager, O'Reilly Technology Exchange" in *Information Today* **(Vol. 26, February 2009, No. 2, pp. 21)**
Pub: Information Today, Inc.
Ed: Jamie Babbitt. **Description:** Joe Wikert, general manager of O'Reilly Technology Exchange discusses his plans to develop a free content model that will evolve with future needs. O'Reilly's major competitor is Google. Wikert plans to expand the firm's publishing program to include print, online, and in-person products and services.

15476 ■ "Johnson Publishing Expands: Moving Into Television and Internet To Extend Brand" in *Black Enterprise* **(October 2007)**
Pub: Earl G. Graves Publishing Co. Inc.
Ed: Tamara E. Holmes. **Description:** Johnson Publishing Company has followed the lives of black families in both Ebony and Jet magazines. The media firm has expanded its coverage by developing entertainment content for television, the Internet and other digital arenas.

15477 ■ "Knight Sold as Industry Struggles" in *Globe & Mail* **(March 14, 2006, pp. D1)**
Pub: CTVglobemedia Publishing Inc.
Ed: Christopher Rowland. **Description:** McClatchy Co. said that it would buy Knight Ridder Inc. for $4.5 billion, which is a newspaper giant in United States. The details of McClatchy acquisition plans for Knight Ridder news syndicate are analyzed.

15478 ■ "Lessons From My Father" in *Crain's Chicago Business* **(Vol. 31, November 10, 2008, No. 45, pp. 28)**
Pub: Crain Communications, Inc.
Ed: Rance Crain. **Description:** Rance Crain discusses his father, G.D. Crain Jr., who founded Crain Communications Inc. during the Great Depression. Advice is given for sustaining a business, even one that seems to be failing, during tough economic times.

15479 ■ *Library and Book Trade Almanac*
Pub: Information Today Inc.
Released: Annual, Latest edition 56th; June 2011. **Price:** $229, individuals hardbound; plus $17 shipping and handling charges; $206.10, individuals first time standing order. **Publication Includes:** Lists of accredited library schools; scholarships for education in library science; library organizations; library statistics; publishing and bookselling organizations. **Entries Include:** Directory listings give name of institution, address, phone, fax, name of officer or contact, publications; scholarship listings include requirements, value of grant, contact name. Principal content is articles and special reports on topics of interest to those in library/information science and publishers; international reports; annual reports from federal agencies and libraries and from national associations; information on legislation, funding, etc. **Arrangement:** Topical. **Indexes:** Organization; subject.

15480 ■ "Life's Work: Ben Bradlee" in *Harvard Business Review* **(Vol. 88, September 2010, No. 9, pp. 128)**
Pub: Harvard Business School Publishing
Ed: Alison Beard. **Description:** Newspaper publisher Ben Bradlee discusses factors that lead to success, including visible supervisors, enthusiasm, appropriate expansion, and the importance in truth in reporting.

15481 ■ "Media Giant Remakes Itself: Job Cuts Signal Journal Sentinel's Focus on New Products" in *Business Journal-Milwaukee* **(Oct. 12, 2007)**
Pub: American City Business Journals, Inc.
Ed: Rich Kirchen. **Description:** Milwaukee Journal Sentinel is reducing its workforce by offering separation pay, and is willing to consider layoffs if the separation program fails. The downsizing is a result of lowered revenue, which was caused by the decline in printed news demand and increase in online competition. Strategies that the Journal Sentinel are employing, such as developing new products, to increase revenue are presented.

15482 ■ "Media Industry Collection Agency Completes Acquisition" in *Collections & Credit Risk* **(Vol. 15, December 1, 2010, No. 11, pp. 22)**
Pub: SourceMedia Inc.
Description: Media Receivable Management Inc. (MRM) will take over the collection operations at Borden, Jones & Mitchell, in Miami, Florida. MRM clients are basically magazine and electronic media publishers.

15483 ■ *Media, Organizations and Identity*
Pub: Palgrave Macmillan
Ed: Lilie Chouliaraki, Mette Morsing. **Released:** January 19, 2010. **Price:** $90.00. **Description:** The mass media, press and television are a essential in the formation of corporate identity and the promotion of business image and reputation. This book offers a new perspective into the interrelationships between media and organizations over three dimensions: media as business, media in business and business in the media.

15484 ■ "Media Wars" in *Canadian Business* **(Vol. 83, August 17, 2010, No. 13-14, pp. 32)**
Pub: Rogers Media Ltd.
Ed: Thomas Watson. **Description:** Canada's newspaper industry has changed considerably with The Globe, under Philip Crawley, positioned as corporate Canada's newspaper of record. However, the National Post under Paul Godfrey is making a comeback by re-launching it as the flagship of a national chain of so-called digital first news organizations.

15485 ■ *Mississippi News Media Directory*
Pub: News Media Directories
Released: Annual, Latest edition 2010. **Price:** $45, individuals; $65, individuals CD; $85, individuals Combo-Directory and CD. **Covers:** Newspapers, periodicals, radio and television broadcasting stations, and press services operating in Mississippi. **Entries Include:** Publisher or company name, address, phone, names and titles of key personnel,

publication title, call letters, hours of operation, and frequency. **Arrangement:** Classified by type of media. **Indexes:** Title, call letters, county index.

15486 ■ "Moms Are Still Shopping" in *Marketing to Women* **(Vol. 21, February 2008, No. 2, pp. 1)**
Pub: EPM Communications, Inc.
Description: According to a monthly poll by Parenting Magazine, although the economic signs worsen many moms are still shopping. Statistical data included.

15487 ■ "Murdock Lifer Mans Main Street Journal" in *Advertising Age* **(Vol. 79, July 7, 2008, No. 26, pp. 1)**
Pub: Crain Communications, Inc.
Ed: Nat Ives. **Description:** Profile of Les Hinton, the U.K. executive who was chosen by Rupert Murdoch to run Dow Jones and The Wall Street Journal; Hinton discusses The Wall Street Journal's unique spot in American business which has helped it survive a dwindling newspaper industry.

15488 ■ "New Beginnings for VIBE" in *Black Enterprise* **(Vol. 37, November 2006, No. 4, pp. 34)**
Pub: Earl G. Graves Publishing Co. Inc.
Ed: Mashaun D. Simon. **Description:** Danyel Smith replaced Mimi Valdes as editor-in-chief of VIBE magazine after the Wicks Group, private equity firm focused on selected segments of the media, communications, and information industries, purchased the magazine.

15489 ■ "New Sony HD Ads Tout Digital" in *Brandweek* **(Vol. 49, April 21, 2008, No. 16, pp. 5)**
Pub: VNU Business Media, Inc.
Description: Looking to promote Sony Electronics' digital imaging products, the company has launched another campaign effort known as HDNA, a play on the words high-definition and DNA; originally Sony focused the HDNA campaign on their televisions, the new ads will include still and video cameras as well and marketing efforts will consist of advertising in print, Online, television spots and publicity at various venues across the country.

15490 ■ "Paper Tigers" in *Conde Nast Portfolio* **(Vol. 2, June 2008, No. 6, pp. 84)**
Pub: Conde Nast Publications, Inc.
Ed: Roger Lowenstein. **Description:** Newspapers are losing their advertisers and readers and circulation today is equal to that of 1950, a time when the U.S. population was half its present size.

15491 ■ "PD Targeting Audience Growth with Web Initiatives" in *Crain's Cleveland Business* **(Vol. 30, June 29, 2009, No. 25, pp. 1)**
Pub: Crain Communications, Inc.
Ed: Kathy Ames Carr. **Description:** Plain Dealer's publisher C.Z. Egger has his news organization focusing on online offerings in order to build circulation of its newspaper. The 167-year-old paper boasts 1,305,203 readers in print and online weekly.

15492 ■ "People; E-Commerce, Online Games, Mobile Apps" in *Advertising Age* **(Vol. 80, October 19, 2009, No. 35, pp. 14)**
Pub: Crain's Communications
Ed: Nat Ives. **Description:** Profile of People Magazine and the ways in which the publisher is moving its magazine forward by exploring new concepts in a time of declining newsstand sales and advertising pages; among the strategies are e-commerce such as the brand People Style Watch in which consumers are able highlight clothing and jewelry and then connect to retailers' sites and a channel on Taxi TV, the network of video-touch screens in New Your City taxis.

15493 ■ "People; E-Commerce, Online Games, Mobile Apps: This Isn't Your Mom's People" in *Advertising Age* **(Vol. 80, October 19, 2009, No. 35)**
Pub: Crain's Communications
Ed: Nat Ives. **Description:** Profile of People Magazine and the ways in which the publisher is moving its magazine forward by exploring new concepts in a

time of declining newsstand sales and advertising pages; among the strategies are e-commerce such as the brand People Style Watch in which consumers are able highlight clothing and jewelry and then connect to retailers' sites and a channel on Taxi TV, the network of video-touch screens in New Your City taxis.

15494 ■ **"Playboy to Target Lucrative India Market With No-Nudes Version" in** *Globe & Mail* **(January 2, 2006, pp. B2)**
Pub: CTVglobemedia Publishing Inc.

Ed: Anand Giridharadas. **Description:** The planning of Chicago based Playboy Enterprises Inc. to target lucrative India market with no nudes version, in order to increase its market shares is discussed.

15495 ■ **"Printing Company Edwards Brothers Grapples With a Shrinking Market" in** *Crain's Detroit Business* **(Vol. 26, Jan. 4, 2010)**
Pub: Crain Communications, Inc.

Ed: Bill Shea. **Description:** Overview of the publishing industry, which has seen a huge decline in revenue; Edwards Brothers, Inc., a family printing business that was founded 117 years ago is struggling due to a variety of factors, many of which are explored.

15496 ■ **"Pro Teams Shift Ad Budgets; Naming Rights Deals Near $1 Billion" in** *Brandweek* **(Vol. 49, April 21, 2008, No. 16, pp. 18)**
Pub: VNU Business Media, Inc.

Ed: Barry Janoff. **Description:** More and more professional sports marketers are spending less of their advertising budgets on media outlets such as television, print and radio; the growing trend in sports marketing is in utilizing new media venues such as the Internet in which innovative means are used to encourage interaction with fans.

15497 ■ **"Publishing Technology Introduces IngentaConnect Mobile" in** *Information Today* **(Vol. 26, February 2009, No. 2, pp. 33)**
Pub: Information Today, Inc.

Description: College undergraduates will find Publishing Technology's newest publisher product, IngentaConnect Mobile helpful. The product allows users to read articles and abstracts on mobile devices. According to a recent study, 73 percent of young adults with wireless hand-held devices use them to access non-voice data on any given day.

15498 ■ **"Reducing the Book's Carbon Footpring" in** *American Printer* **(Vol. 128, July 1, 2011, No. 7)**
Pub: Penton Media Inc.

Description: Green Press Initiative's Book Industry Environmental Council is working to achieve a 20 percent reduction in the book industry's carbon footprint by 2020. The Council is made up of publishers, printers, paper suppliers, and non-governmental organizations.

15499 ■ **"Renren Partners With Recruit to Launch Social Wedding Services" in** *Benzinga.com* **(June 7, 2011)**
Pub: Benzinga.com

Ed: Benzinga Staff. **Description:** Renren Inc. and Recruit Company Ltd. partnered to build a wedding social media catering to engaged couples and newlyweds in China. The platform will integrate online wedding related social content and offline media such as magazine and wedding exhibitions.

15500 ■ *Standard Periodical Directory*
Pub: Oxbridge Communications Inc.

Ed: Deborah Striplin, Editor, dstriplin@oxbridge.com. **Released:** Annual, Latest edition January 2011. **Price:** $1,995, individuals print version; $1,995, single issue CD-ROM single user; $2,995, individuals print and CD-ROM. **Covers:** 63,000 magazines, journals, newsletters, directories, house organs, association publications, etc. , in the United States and Canada. **Entries Include:** Publication current and former title; publisher name, address, phone; names and titles of key personnel; circulation and advertising rates; description of contents; ISSN, year founded, fre-

quency; subscription rates, print method, page size, number of pages. **Arrangement:** Classified by subject. **Indexes:** Subject, title.

15501 ■ **"Storytelling Star of Show for Scripps" in** *Business Courier* **(Vol. 26, November 13, 2009, No. 29, pp. 1)**
Pub: American City Business Journals, Inc.

Ed: Dan Monk. **Description:** Rich Boehne, CEO Of the EW Scripps Company in Cincinnati has authorized a new training program in storytelling for employees at Scripps' 10 television stations. He believes that the training will improve the quality of broadcasting content. His plans to improve quality of newspaper content are also discussed.

15502 ■ **"Study: New Moms Build A Lot of Brand Buzz" in** *Brandweek* **(Vol. 49, April 21, 2008, No. 16, pp. 7)**
Pub: VNU Business Media, Inc.

Description: According to a new survey which sampled 1,721 pregnant women and new moms, this demographic is having 109 word-of-mouth conversations per week concerning products, services and brands. Two-thirds of these conversations directly involve brand recommendations. The Internet is driving these word-of-mouth, or W-O-M, conversations among this segment, beating out magazines, television and other forms of media.

15503 ■ **"The Superfluous Position" in** *Entrepreneur* **(Vol. 37, July 2009, No. 7, pp. 62)**
Pub: Entrepreneur Media, Inc.

Description: Profile of an anonymous editor at a multimedia company that publishes tourism guides who shares his experiences in dealing with an officemate who was promoted as creative manager of content. Everyone was irritated by this person, who would constantly do something to justify his new title. The biggest problem was the fact that this person didn't have a clear job description.

15504 ■ **"Survey: More Buyers Expect to Spend Less in Most Media" in** *Advertising Age* **(Vol. 79, July 7, 2008, No. 26, pp. 3)**
Pub: Crain Communications, Inc.

Ed: Megan McIlroy. **Description:** Marketers are decreasing their budgets for advertising in television, radio, newspaper and outdoor due to the economic downturn. Statistical data concerning advertising agencies and marketers included.

15505 ■ **"Swedes Swoop In To Save Time4" in** *Advertising Age* **(Vol. 78, January 29, 2007, No. 5, pp. 4)**
Pub: Crain Communications, Inc.

Ed: Nat Ives. **Description:** Overview of Stockholm's Bonnier Group, a family-owned publisher that is looking to expand its U.S. presence; Bonnier recently acquired a number of Time Inc. magazines.

15506 ■ **"To JM On Its 75th Anniversary" in** *Journal of Marketing* **(Vol. 75, July 2011, No. 4, pp. 129)**
Pub: American Marketing Association

Ed: Ruth M. Bolton. **Description:** How the Journal of Marketing influenced the marketing science and practice is presented. The Marketing Science Institute's 50th anniversary coincides with the journal's 75th anniversary and both have collaborated to tackle important marketing issues identified in MSI's priorities. The mind-set of managers worldwide was also influenced by ideas in the journal's articles.

15507 ■ **"Transform Your Life" in** *Black Enterprise* **(Vol. 37, January 2007, No. 6, pp. 14)**
Pub: Earl G. Graves Publishing Co. Inc.

Description: Through the magazine, television and radio programs, events, and the website, the various platforms of Black Enterprise will provide the tools necessary to achieve success in business ventures, career aspirations, and personal goals.

15508 ■ **"A Turn in the South" in** *The Economist* **(Vol. 390, January 3, 2009, No. 8612, pp. 34)**
Pub: The Economist Newspaper Inc.

Description: Overview of Charleston, South Carolina, a region that lost its navy base in 1996, which had provided work for more than 22,000 people; the

city developed a plan called Noisette in order to redevelop the area and today the economy is healthier and more diversified than it was a decade ago. Charleston was described as among the best cities for doing business by Inc. Magazine and seems to be handling the downturn of the economy fairly well. Statistical data regarding growth, business and population is included.

15509 ■ *Ulrich's Periodicals Directory*
Pub: R.R. Bowker L.L.C.

Released: Annual, Latest edition 2010. **Price:** $1,260, individuals Hardcover, 4 volumes. **Covers:** Nearly 200,000 current periodicals and newspapers published worldwide. **Entries Include:** In main list—Publication title; Dewey Decimal Classification number, Library of Congress Classification Number (where applicable), CODEN designation (for sci-tech serials), British Library Document Supply Centre shelfmark number, country code, ISSN; subtitle, language(s) of text, year first published, frequency, subscription prices, sponsoring organization, publishing company name, address, phone, fax, e-mail and website addresses, editor and publisher names; regular features (reviews, advertising, abstracts, bibliographies, trade literature, etc.), indexes, circulation, format, brief description of content; availability of microforms and reprints; whether refereed; CD-ROM availability with vendor name; online availability with service name; services that index or abstract the periodical, with years covered; advertising rates and contact; right and permissions contact name and phone; availability through document deliver **Arrangement:** Main listing is classified by subject; U.S. general daily and weekly newspapers are listed in a separate volume; lists of cessations, online services, and CD-ROM vendors are alphabetical. **Indexes:** Cessations, subjects, title (including variant, former, and ceased titles), ISSN, periodicals available on CD-ROM, online periodical title, refereed serial, and international organization publication title.

15510 ■ *The Weather Channel*
Pub: Harvard Business School Press

Ed: Frank Batten with Jeffrey L. Cruikshank. **Released:** 2002. **Price:** $29.95. **Description:** Frank Batten illustrates the power of a resourceful growth strategy along with details the journey he successfully took his small, private newspaper into the cable industry.

15511 ■ **"Welch's Uses Taste Strips in Ads" in** *Marketing to Women* **(Vol. 21, April 2008, No. 4, pp. 3)**
Pub: EPM Communications, Inc.

Description: Welch's is positioning its 139-year-old brand in a new and inventive way with a new marketing campaign in which print ads will feature a tamper-evident flavor pouch that contains a dissolving taste strip flavored with Welch's grape juice.

STATISTICAL SOURCES

15512 ■ *RMA Annual Statement Studies*
Pub: Robert Morris Associates (RMA)

Released: Annual. **Price:** $175.00 2006-07 edition, $105.00. **Description:** Contains composite balance sheets and income statements for more than 360 industries, including the accounting, auditing, and bookkeeping industries. Also contains five years of comparative historical data for discerning trends. Includes 16 commonly used ratios, computed for most of the size groupings for nearly every industry.

TRADE PERIODICALS

15513 ■ *Canastota Bee-Journal*
Pub: Eagle Newspapers

Contact: David Tyler, Gen Mgr

E-mail: dtyler@cnylink.com

Released: Weekly (Wed.). **Price:** $28 in-state (NY); $45 two years in-state (NY); $60 3 years; in-state (NY); $33 out of state out-of-state; $60 out of state 2 years; out-of-state; $79 out of state 3 years; out-of-state; $28 out of country; $46 out of country 2 years;

$63 out of country; $23 senior rate in-county. **Description:** Community newspaper serving the Syracuse suburban towns of Lenox, Lincoln, and Canastota.

15514 ■ ENT
Pub: 1105 Media Inc.
Contact: Scott Bekker, Editor-in-Chief
E-mail: sbekker@entmag.com
Released: 18/yr. **Price:** $54.95 Canada and Mexico; $64.95 other countries. **Description:** Publication providing news and analysis for Windows NT enterprise users.

15515 ■ Granville Sentinel
Pub: Gannett Co.
Released: Weekly. **Description:** Community newspaper serving the Granville, OH, area.

15516 ■ Hamilton/Morrisville Tribune
Pub: Eagle Newspapers
Contact: Richard K. Keene, President
Released: Weekly (Wed.). **Price:** $25 in-state, one year; $30 out-of-state, one year; $28 in-state outside Ononandoga and Madison Counties; $23 senior in-county, one year; $19 college, one year; $99 outside the U.S., one year; $15 Syracuse parent, one year; $10 prime for senior citizens, one year. **Description:** Community newspaper serving the Syracuse suburban communities of Hamilton, Madison, Eaton, Lebanon, and Morrisville.

15517 ■ How To Be Your Own Publisher Update
Pub: Bibliotheca Press
Contact: A. Doyle
Ed: A. Doyle, Editor. **Released:** Annual. **Price:** $12.95, U.S.; $15.95, Canada; $19.95, other countries. **Description:** Acts as a reference for self publishers. Distributed by Prosperity & Profits Unlimited Distribution Services, PO Box 416, Denver, CO, 80201.

15518 ■ Independent Publisher Online
Pub: Jenkins Group Inc.
Contact: Jim Barnes, Managing Editor
E-mail: jimb@bookpublishing.com
Released: Monthly. **Description:** Online magazine containing book reviews and articles about independent publishing.

15519 ■ La Jolla Village News
Pub: San Diego Community Newspaper Group
Contact: Julie Mannis Hoisington, Publisher
E-mail: jmannis@sdnews.com
Ed: John Gregory, Editor, ljvn@sdnews.com. **Released:** Semiannual, weekly on web. **Description:** Community newspaper.

15520 ■ Publishing Executive
Pub: North American Publishing Co.
Contact: Noelle Skodzinski, Editorial Dir.
E-mail: nskodzinski@napco.com
Released: 10/yr. **Description:** Trade magazine covering current trends in print production of magazines, catalogs, books, direct mail, corporate publishing, and advertising agencies.

15521 ■ Redlands Daily Facts
Pub: Donrey Media Group
Contact: Christina Brock, Managing Editor
E-mail: christina.brock@inlandnewspapers.com
Released: Daily (eve.), Sunday (morn.). **Price:** $35 by mail. **Description:** General interest newspaper.

15522 ■ Wireless Week
Pub: Wireless Week
Contact: Holly Hoffer, Publisher
E-mail: holly.hoffer@advantagemedia.com
Released: Weekly. **Description:** Trade tabloid covering the wireless industry including cellular, paging, satellite, and microwave.

TRADE SHOWS AND CONVENTIONS

15523 ■ Folio Show
Cowles Event Management
11 River Bend Dr. South
PO Box 4232
Stamford, CT 06907
Ph:(203)358-3751
Released: 3/yr. **Audience:** Magazine and book publishing trades. **Principal Exhibits:** Publishing supplies, paper, printing equipment, color separators, fulfillment houses, lists, and related equipment, supplies, and services to the magazine and book publishing trades. **Dates and Locations:** 2011 Jun 07-09, New York, NY.

CONSULTANTS

15524 ■ B. Paolucci Inc.
39 Kane Ave.
Larchmont, NY 10538
Ph:(914)834-9594
Fax:(914)833-9106
Contact: Bert Paolucci, President
Scope: Offers publishing expertise such as working with magazine publishers and printers to get most efficient production and distribution at best price, soliciting printing bids, negotiating contracts, developing cost reduction programs, and economic analyses of new technologies. Serves the private sector as well as government agencies. **Seminars:** How to Solicit Printing Bids and Negotiate Printing Contracts.

15525 ■ Capell & Associates
601 Central Ave.
PO Box 742
Barnegat Light, NJ 08006
Ph:(202)572-8774
Fax:(609)494-7369
Co. E-mail: contact@capellandassociates.com
URL: http://www.capellandassociates.com
Contact: E. Daniel Capell, President
E-mail: dan_capell@att.net
Scope: Specialized consulting firm focused on direct marketing, magazine publishing and circulation. Consulting services include due diligence, circulation audits, benchmarking and list rental analysis. **Seminars:** Circulation for the Non-Circulator.

15526 ■ Heidelberg Graphics
2 Stansbury Ct.
Chico, CA 95928
Ph:(530)342-6582
Fax:(530)342-6582
Co. E-mail: service@heidelberggraphics.com
URL: http://www.heidelberggraphics.com
Contact: Larry S. Jackson, Owner
Scope: Offers services including scans, disc conversions, layouts, editing and printing for books, catalogs and magazines. Provides the codes on paper, disk, film, embedded in designs, or in variable labeling and personalized printing. Serves private industries as well as government agencies. **Publications:** "Chronicles of the Clandestine Knights: Hyacinth Blue," 2003; "A Book of Thoughts II," 2001; "Historic Shot Glasses: The pre-Prohibition," 1992; "After the War," 1981; "Phantasm," 1980.

15527 ■ J. S. Eliezer Associates Inc.
300 Atlantic St., 7th Fl.
Stamford, CT 06901-3513
Ph:(203)658-1300
Fax:(203)658-1301
Co. E-mail: dmckenna@jseliezer.com
URL: http://www.jseliezer.com
Contact: Mark J. Vallely, Principle
E-mail: jeliezer@atsjseliezer.com
Scope: Management and market research consultants offering design and implementation of manufacturing strategy, feasibility analysis and systems analysis, as well as management information systems and prepress systems; manufacturing proposals analysis, negotiations and contracts; paper purchasing strategy and contract negotiations; catalog distribution effectiveness analysis. Serves the publishing and catalog industries.

15528 ■ James Peter Associates Inc.
PO Box 772
Tenafly, NJ 07670
Ph:(201)568-0760
Fax:(201)568-2959
Co. E-mail: bertholtje@compuserve.com
Contact: Herbert F. Holtje, Principle
E-mail: bholtje@atsattmail.com
Scope: Consults with publishers and industry on such projects for total book production from conception through writing, design and illustration to camera-ready copy, video tapes and programmed instruction. Also works with businesses and non-profit organizations to develop books and periodical publications.

15529 ■ The K.S. Giniger Company Inc.
1045 Park Ave.
New York, NY 10028
Ph:(212)369-6692
Fax:(212)269-6692
Co. E-mail: bernicecullinan@verizon.net
Contact: Kenneth Seeman Giniger, President
Scope: Consultants on book publishing to publishers of books, magazines and newsletters, direct sales organizations, government agencies, educational organizations, financial and investment institutions; public relations and advertising agencies. Clients in the United States, Canada, Mexico, England, Denmark, France, Spain, Switzerland, Germany, Israel, Singapore and Australia.

15530 ■ Moseley Associates Inc.
6 Bart Bull Rd.
Middletown, NY 10941
Ph:(212)988-2834
Fax:(212)717-2435
Co. E-mail: pwadams@consultmoseley.com
URL: http://www.consultmoseley.com
Contact: Cameron S. Moseley, Chairman of the Board
E-mail: pwadams@consultmoseley.com
Scope: Management consultants to the publishing industry-commercial and nonprofit-in the United States and international markets. Expertise in publishing areas: books, periodicals and non-print media. Consulting in all aspects of the publishing process: management studies, business planning, organization evaluation, research and development, financial analysis, editorial, marketing, market research, sales, production, warehousing and distribution, order fulfillment and related operations. Also has expertise with organization and operating technology for new publishing and information service enterprises, as well as acquisitions, divestitures, and mergers. Extensive experience in appraisals of books, magazines and learning materials; and of entire publishing firms. Has worked with government agencies. **Publications:** "Is This the End of Publishing? As We Know It," Jun, 2007; "US School Publishing," Apr, 2001; "A Century of Progress," Jun, 2006; "Technology in Publishing: A Century of Progress," Against the Grain, May, 2001; "Why I Don't Read Electronic Journals: An Iconoclast Speaks Out," Sep, 1997; "Post-Traumatic Shock Syndrome, Or, Surviving the Merger," Jun, 2009; "Familiar and Unfamiliar Quotations," Apr, 2009.

FRANCHISES AND BUSINESS OPPORTUNITIES

15531 ■ AroundAbout Community Magazines Inc.
1025 Rose Creek Dr., Ste. 340
Woodstock, GA 30189
Ph:(770)516-7105
Fax:(770)516-4809
No. of Franchise Units: 6. **No. of Company-Owned Units:** 3. **Founded:** 1996. **Franchised:** 2003. **Description:** Direct-mail community magazine. **Equity Capital Needed:** $49,151-$69,797 total investment; $250,000 net worth, $100,000 cash liquidity. **Franchise Fee:** $37,500. **Royalty Fee:** 6%. **Financial Assistance:** No. **Training:** Provides 2 weeks at headquarters, 1 week onsite with ongoing support.

15532 ■ The Bingo Bugle Newspaper
Frontier Publications, Inc.
PO Box 527
Vashon, WA 98070
Ph:(206)463-5656

Fax:(206)463-5630

No. of Franchise Units: 47. **Founded:** 1980. **Franchised:** 1980. **Description:** Sell franchises for the Bingo Bugle Newspaper nationally. The Bingo Bugle is a monthly publication for bingo players. desktop publishing, typesetting and paste-up, bookkeeping and billing, distribution and multiple-edition advertising. **Equity Capital Needed:** $9,070-$15,020. **Franchise Fee:** $5,000. **Royalty Fee:** 8%. **Financial Assistance:** No. **Training:** Yes.

15533 ■ EasyChair Media LLC
800 Third St.
Windsor, CO 80550-5424
Free: 800-741-6308
Fax:800-438-2150

No. of Franchise Units: 1. **No. of Company-Owned Units:** 5. **Founded:** 2000. **Franchised:** 2002. **Description:** Regional & city publications. **Equity Capital Needed:** $32,700-$36,700. **Franchise Fee:** $10,000-$20,000. **Royalty Fee:** None. **Financial Assistance:** No. **Training:** Offers 2-3 days at headquarters, 2-3 weeks at franchisees location with ongoing support.

15534 ■ Homes & Land
Endurance Business Media
1830 E Park Ave.
Tallahassee, FL 32310
Free: 800-458-9250
Fax:(850)575-9567
Co. E-mail: franchise@homesandland.com
URL: http://www.homesandland.com

No. of Franchise Units: 260. **No. of Company-Owned Units:** 29. **Founded:** 1973. **Franchised:** 1984. **Description:** Network of more than 250 magazines, publishing approximately 60 million magazines covering thousands of communities across the U.S. and Canada. **Equity Capital Needed:** Minimum $50,000 liquid assets; $150,000 net worth. **Franchise Fee:** $27,000. **Financial Assistance:** No. **Training:** 1 week of classroom training at corporate office, and continued support with workshops, toll-free number, marketing materials and more.

15535 ■ TheHomeMag
1732 SE 47th Ter.
Cape Coral, FL 33904
Ph:(239)549-6960
Fax:(239)549-5462

No. of Franchise Units: 17. **No. of Company-Owned Units:** 5. **Founded:** 2002. **Franchised:** 2006. **Description:** Home improvement magazine. **Equity Capital Needed:** $108,575-$135,575. **Franchise Fee:** $19,000-$34,000. **Royalty Fee:** 5.5%.

Financial Assistance: No. **Training:** Offers 1 week training at headquarters and at franchisee's location upon request.

COMPUTERIZED DATABASES

15536 ■ *Daily Brief Services*
Oxford Analytica Ltd.
5 Alfred St.
Oxford OX1 4EH, United Kingdom
Ph:44 1865 261600
Fax:44 1865 242018
URL: http://www.oxan.com

Description: Contains Oxford Analytica's *Daily Brief* Database. Includes six regional daily briefs and two sectoral daily briefs, as well as the Daily Brief World Service. Provides analysis of key social, political, business, economic, and financial events in 140 countries worldwide. Provides interdisciplinary analyses that evaluate complex geopolitical, macroeconomic, and social developments within a coherent political/social/economic global framework. Lets users apply political and economic research to the assessment and management of risks and opportunities. Provides four to five articles assessing the implications of the most important National and International developments each week day with a six month information embargo. Provides four years of historical daily briefs for comparison and analysis of trends and events. Allows users to set up custom information profiles and receive e-mail alerts when relevant material appears. **Availability:** Online: Oxford Analytica Ltd. **Type:** Full text.

15537 ■ *Ethnic NewsWatch: A History*
ProQuest LLC
789 E Eisenhower Pky.
PO Box 1346
Ann Arbor, MI 48106-1346
Ph:(734)761-4700
Free: 800-521-0600
Fax:(734)761-6450
Co. E-mail: info@proquest.com
URL: http://www.proquest.com

Description: Contains more than 300,000 articles from newspapers, magazines and journals of the ethnic, minority and native press from 1959 to 1989. Covers various disciplines and subject areas, including the arts, media, popular culture, education, ethnic and cultural studies, history, journalism, political science, and social sciences. **Availability:** Online: ProQuest LLC. **Type:** Full text; Directory.

15538 ■ *NewsFile Collection*
NewsBank Inc.
4501 Tamiami Trail N, Ste. 316
Naples, FL 34103

Ph:(802)875-2910
Free: 800-762-8182
Fax:(802)875-2904
Co. E-mail: sales@newsbank.com
URL: http://www.newsbank.com

Description: Provides more than 70,000 news articles annually from more than 500 newspapers and other regional, national, and International news sources; including data from the defunct CD NewsBank database. Offers a total of more than 500,000 articles. Includes graphics, maps, illustrations, charts, and tables. **Availability:** Online: NewsBank Inc. **Type:** Full text.

LIBRARIES

15539 ■ Hanley-Wood, LLC Library
426 S. Westgate St.
Addison, IL 60101-4546
Ph:(630)543-0870
Fax:(630)543-3112
URL: http://www.hanleywood.com
Contact: Kimberly Last, Libn.

Scope: Concrete, cement, masonry, construction, home building. **Services:** Interlibrary loan; copying. **Holdings:** 3000 books; 120 bound periodical volumes. **Subscriptions:** 100 journals and other serials.

15540 ■ Magazine Publishers of America Information Center
810 Seventh Ave., 24th Fl.
New York, NY 10019
Ph:(212)872-3745
Co. E-mail: infocenter@magazine.org
URL: http://www.magazine.org
Contact: Deborah Martin, Dir. of Info.Svcs.

Scope: Magazine publishing and advertising. **Services:** Open only to MPA members, advertisers, and agencies by appointment. **Holdings:** Books; magazine publishers research reports; circulation reports; magazine advertising expenditures statistics; 400 vertical files of information on markets and media. **Subscriptions:** 150 journals and other serials.

15541 ■ Reader's Digest Association–Editorial Research Library
1 Reader Digest Rd.
Pleasantville, NY 10570
Ph:(914)244-5289
Fax:(914)238-0534
URL: http://www.rd.com
Contact: Ann DiCesare, Hd.Libn.

Scope: General reference, current news, Reader's Digest. **Services:** Interlibrary loan (limited); libraries not open to the public. **Holdings:** 10,000 books; archival materials. **Subscriptions:** 350 journals and other serials; 20 newspapers.

REFERENCE WORKS

15542 ■ *How to Start a Home-Based Senior Care Business: Check-in-Care, Transportation Services, Shopping and Cooking*
Pub: The Globe Pequot Press
Ed: James L. Ferry. **Released:** January 1, 2010. **Price:** $18.95. **Description:** Information is provided to start a home-based senior care business.

15543 ■ **"Professional Help: Cross That Off Your To-Do List" in** *Inc.* **(November 2007, pp. 89-90, 92)**
Pub: Gruner & Jahr USA Publishing
Ed: Alison Stein Wellner. **Description:** Small business owners are finding that it pays to hire someone to takeover the personal tasks of daily living, including hiring a personal assistant, chauffeur, chef, stylist, pet caregiver, or concierge service.

15544 ■ **"Q&A With Devin Ringling: Franchise's Services Go Beyond Elder Care" in** *Gazette* **(October 2, 2010)**
Pub: The Gazette
Ed: Bill Radford. **Description:** Profile of franchise, Interim HealthCare, in Colorado Springs, Colorado; the company offers home care services that include wound care and specialized feedings to shopping and light housekeeping. It also runs a medical staffing company that provides nurses, therapists and other health care workers to hospitals, prisons, schools and other facilities.

TRADE PERIODICALS

15545 ■ *Fulton Pennysaver*
Pub: Scotsman Community Publications
Released: Weekly (Mon.). **Description:** Shopper.

FRANCHISES AND BUSINESS OPPORTUNITIES

15546 ■ **Foot Solutions, Inc.**
Foot Solutions, Inc.
2359 Windy Hill Rd., Ste. 400
Marietta, GA 30067
Ph:(770)955-0099
Free: (866)338-2597
Fax:(770)953-6270
No. of Franchise Units: 229. **No. of Company-Owned Units:** 1. **Founded:** 2000. **Franchised:** 2000. **Description:** Personalized and custom designed products. **Equity Capital Needed:** $40,000 start-up retail store front, mobile unit $25,000. **Franchise Fee:** $32,500 retail/$28,500 mobile. **Financial Assistance:** No. **Training:** Yes.

15547 ■ **Instant Imprints**
Instant Imprints Franchising, Inc.
5897 Oberlin Dr., Ste. 200
San Diego, CA 92121
Ph:(858)642-4848
Free: 800-542-3437
Fax:(858)453-6513
No. of Franchise Units: 60. **No. of Company-Owned Units:** 1. **Founded:** 1992. **Franchised:** 2002. **Description:** Offers Personalized shopping services. **Equity Capital Needed:** $50,000-$60,000 liquid; $193,000 total cost. **Franchise Fee:** $29,500. **Financial Assistance:** No. **Training:** Yes.

START-UP INFORMATION

15548 ■ **"Monsanto Acquires Targeted-Pest Control Technology Start-Up; Terms Not Disclosed" in *Benzinga.com* (, 2011)**
Pub: Benzinga.com
Ed: Benzinga Staff. **Description:** Monsanto Company acquired Beelogics, a firm that researches and develops biological tools that control pests and diseases. Research includes a product that will help protect bee health.

15549 ■ **"New Businesses" in *Arkansas Business* (Vol. 28, June 27, 2011, No. 26, pp. 35)**
Pub: Arkansas Business Publishing Group
Ed: Nathan Vandiver. **Description:** Profile of United Pest Control the new business co-owned by Roddy McCaskill Jr., Graham Smith, Chuck Collins and Scott Hurley. The firm focuses on education and the use of nontoxic chemicals.

15550 ■ **"Termite Trouble" in *Arkansas Business* (Vol. 28, March 28, 2011, No. 13, pp. 5)**
Pub: Arkansas Business Publishing Group
Description: Thomas Pest Control of Little Rock, Arkansas has had liens placed against it by the Internal Revenue Service. The owner's daughter took over the business after her father passed away and is trying to rectify the situation.

ASSOCIATIONS AND OTHER ORGANIZATIONS

15551 ■ **Association of Applied IPM Ecologists**
PO Box 1119
Coarsegold, CA 93614
Ph:(559)761-1064
Co. E-mail: director@aaie.net
URL: http://www.aaie.net
Contact: Cliff Ohmart, Pres.
Description: Professional agricultural pest management consultants, entomologists, and field personnel. Promotes the implementation of integrated pest management in agricultural and urban environments. Provides a forum for the exchange of technical information on pest control. Offers placement service.

15552 ■ **National Pest Management Association International**
10460 N St.
Fairfax, VA 22030
Ph:(703)352-6762
Free: 800-678-6722
Fax:(703)352-3031
Co. E-mail: info@pestworld.org
URL: http://www.pestworld.org
Contact: Mr. Robert F. Lederer, Exec. VP
Description: Represents firms engaged in control of insects, rodents, birds, and other pests, in or around structures, through use of insecticides, rodenticides, miticides, fumigants, and non-chemical methods. Provides advisory services on control procedures, new products, and safety and business administration practices. Promotes June as National Pest Control Month. Sponsors research, periodic technical and management seminars. **Publications:** *National Pest Control Association—Technical Release* (monthly); *National Pest Management Association—Series of Management Reports* (periodic); *Pest Gazette* (quarterly).

15553 ■ **Responsible Industry for a Sound Environment**
1156 15th St. NW, Ste. 400
Washington, DC 20005
Ph:(202)872-3860
Fax:(202)355-1467
Co. E-mail: kreardon@pestfacts.org
URL: http://www.pestfacts.org
Contact: Angela B. Jamison, Pres.
Description: Manufacturers, formulators, distributors, and representatives of the specialty pesticides industry. Promotes the environmental, health, and safety benefits of the proper use of specialty pesticides. .

REFERENCE WORKS

15554 ■ **"Ag Officials Employ Preventive Pest Control" in *Yakima Herald-Republic* (June 24, 2011)**
Pub: Yakima Herald-Republic
Ed: Ross Courtney. **Description:** Washington State Department of Agriculture is placing vineyard traps for the European grapevine moth, an invasive species whose larvae eat grape buds and fruit clusters, thus exposing the vines to diseases that could destroy them.

15555 ■ **"Autumn Rat Control Essential for Poultry Units" in *Poultry World* (Vol. 165, September 2011, No. 9, pp. 32)**
Pub: Reed Business Information Inc.
Description: Dr. Alan Buckle discusses the use of rodenticides control, focusing on poultry units.

15556 ■ **"Bedbugs Are Here, But Help Is At Hand" in *Register-Guard* (June 26, 2011)**
Pub: The Register-Guard
Ed: Diane Dietz. **Description:** A survey conducted by the National Pest Control Association found that 95 percent of its 7,000 members have treated buildings for bed bugs. That number is up 25 percent from 2000.

15557 ■ **"Bountiful Exterminator Indicted for Unlawful Pesticide Use" in *Standard-Examiner* (February 3, 2011)**
Pub: Standard-Examiner
Ed: Bryon Saxton. **Description:** Bugman Pest and Lawn Inc. indicted Coleman Nocks and his business, Bugman Pest and Lawn Inc. for three counts of unlawful use of the pesticide Fumitoxin, resulting in the death of two little girls.

15558 ■ **_Crop Protection Handbook_**
Pub: Meister Media Worldwide
Contact: Gary T. Fitzgerald, Chm./CEO
Released: Annual, Latest edition 2011; New edition expected 2012. **Price:** $189, individuals print & CD; $89, individuals print/CD, discounted price. **Covers:** Manufacturers and suppliers of fertilizers, pesticides, and related equipment and services used in agribusiness. **Entries Include:** Company name, address, phone, fax numbers, e-mail address, trade and brand names, product information. **Arrangement:** Alphabetical.

15559 ■ **"Don't Let the Bed Bugs Bite" in *Yuma Sun* (April 22, 2011)**
Pub: The Yuma Sun
Ed: Mara Knaub. **Description:** Bug specialists note that bed bugs are returning. Exterminators say that eliminating these pests can be costly. Most bed bugs are picked up while traveling.

15560 ■ **"Faulkner Pest Service Has Been Providing Quality Pest Control Solutions for 23 Years" in *OfficialSpin* (September 30, 2011)**
Pub: SPIN
Description: Profile of Faulkner Pest Service, which has been providing pest control services in Amarillo for twenty-three years.

15561 ■ **"Hearing Damage Leads to Settlement" in *Register-Guard* (August 13, 2011)**
Pub: The Register-Guard
Ed: Karen McCowan. **Description:** Cynergy Pest Control lost a court battle when a rural Cottage Grove man was granted a $37,000 settlement after his hearing was damaged by the pest control companies method to eradicate gophers, using blasts in his neighbor's yard.

15562 ■ **"Suncoast Pest Control Introduces New Website" in *Entertainment Close-Up* (March 16, 2011)**
Pub: Close-Up Media
Description: Florida pest control company, Suncoast Pest Control, launched a new Website to better serve their customers. The new Website will allow users to reach local Florida pest control professionals 24 hours a day.

15563 ■ **"US Hygiene Adds Bed Bug Fix to Its Line of Highly Effective Cleaning and Pest Control Products" in *Benzinga.com* (October 29, 2011)**
Pub: Benzinga.com
Ed: Benzinga Staff. **Description:** US Hygiene LLC introduced its newest product called Bed Bug Fix, which is a naturally-derived, nontoxic insecticide that kills a multitude of bugs including bed bugs and dust mites. The product is safe to use around children, plants and pets.

STATISTICAL SOURCES

15564 ■ **_RMA Annual Statement Studies_**
Pub: Robert Morris Associates (RMA)
Released: Annual. **Price:** $175.00 2006-07 edition, $105.00. **Description:** Contains composite balance

sheets and income statements for more than 360 industries, including the accounting, auditing, and bookkeeping industries. Also contains five years of comparative historical data for discerning trends. Includes 16 commonly used ratios, computed for most of the size groupings for nearly every industry.

TRADE PERIODICALS

15565 ■ *Biological Control*
Pub: Academic Press
Ed: H.K. Kaya, Editor. **Released:** 9/yr. **Price:** $472 for European countries and Iran; $49,200 for Japan; $366 all countries except Europe, Japan, and Iran. **Description:** Journal containing information on the means of reducing or mitigating pets and pest effects through the use of natural enemies.

15566 ■ *Common Sense Pest Control Quarterly*
Pub: Bio-Integral Resource Center
Released: 4/year. **Price:** $30, individuals U.S. and Canada; $50, institutions U.S. and Canada; $40, individuals els ewhere; $60, institutions elsewhere. **Description:** Presents information regarding least-toxic pest management in layperson's terms. Evaluates alternative strategies for many pest problems still being treated exclusively with pesticides. Discusses such concerns as least-toxic management of pests on indoor plants, pests that damage paper, controlling fleas and ticks on pets, and garden pants, pests that damage paper, controlling fleas and ticks on pets, and garden pests. Recurring features include letters to the editor, interviews, news of research, book reviews, and notices of

15567 ■ *The IPM Practitioner*
Pub: Bio-Integral Resource Center
Released: 10/year. **Price:** Included in membership; $35, individuals; $60 business and institution; $60, two years. **Description:** Supports the Center in its efforts to publish information on all aspects of environmentally-sound pest control. Investigates the least-toxic methods of controlling pests in agriculture, urban landscapes and structures, greenhouse and general horticulture, forestry, medical/veterinary, range, and other settings. Recurring features include letters to the editor, interviews, news of research, reports of meetings, news of educational opportunities and job listings, notices and reviews of publications available, and a calendar of events. Contains yearly listings of products

15568 ■ *Pest Control Technology*
Pub: G.I.E. Media, MC
Contact: Dan Moreland, Publisher
E-mail: dmoreland@gie.net
Ed: Jodi Dorsch, Editor, jdorsch@gie.net. **Released:** Monthly. **Price:** $35 print and digital; $45 Canada and Mexico print and digital; $88 other countries print and digital. **Description:** Magazine for the pest control industry.

15569 ■ *Pest Management Professional*
Pub: Advanstar Communications, Inc.
Contact: George Casey, Publisher
E-mail: george.casey@questex.com
Released: Monthly. **Price:** $45 U.S.; $69 Canada and Mexico; $106 other countries. **Description:** Magazine serving pest control specialists.

15570 ■ *Pesticide Biochemistry and Physiology*
Pub: Elsevier Science B.V.
Ed: J.M. Clark, Editor. **Released:** 9/yr. **Price:** $206,000 institutions Japan; $1,975 institutions European countries and Iran; $1,498 institutions for all countries except Europe, Japan and Iran; $85,000 Japan; $816 European countries and Iran; $621 for all countries except Europe and Japan; $131 students European countries and Iran; $115 students for all countries except Europe, Japan and Iran; $13,600 students Japan. **Description:** Journal publishing scientific articles pertaining to the mode action of plant protection agents, such as insecticides, fungicides, herbicides, similar compounds including nonlethal pest control agents, biosynthesis of phermones, hormones, and plant resistance agents.

15571 ■ *Pesticide & Toxic Chemical News*
Pub: CRC Press L.L.C.
Ed: Jeffrey Winograd, Editor, jwinograd@crcpress.com. **Released:** Daily. **Price:** $887. **Description:** Provides news and analysis of chemical regulatory and legislative developments. Covers Environmental Protection Agency and other national and international organization activities and research.

15572 ■ *Tri-Ology*
Pub: Florida Department of Agriculture and Consumer Services
Contact: Dr. Greg Hodges, Bureau Ch.
E-mail: hodgesg@doacs.state.fl.us
Released: Monthly. **Description:** Government scientific publication covering plant pests and disease. Online only.

VIDEOCASSETTES/AUDIOCASSETTES

15573 ■ *Rat*
Vanguard International Cinema, Inc.
359 SOuth Hewitt St., Ste. 535
Los Angeles, CA 90013
Ph:(949)258-2000
Free: 800-218-7888
Fax:(213)599-7260
Co. E-mail: info@vanguardcinema.com
URL: http://www.vanguardcinema.com
Released: 1997. **Price:** $19.98. **Description:** Documentary uses humor and horror to reveal the struggle of man against rats in New York City. **Availability:** VHS.

TRADE SHOWS AND CONVENTIONS

15574 ■ Florida Pest Management Association Convention and Exposition
Florida Pest Management Association
6882 Edgewater Commerce Pkwy.
Orlando, FL 32810
Ph:(407)293-8627
Free: 800-426-4829
Fax:(407)292-0918
Co. E-mail: info@flpma.org
URL: http://www.flpma.org
Released: Annual. **Audience:** Pest control operators and companies. **Principal Exhibits:** Equipment, services, and supplies for the chemical industry.

CONSULTANTS

15575 ■ Pest Pros Inc.
10086 1st St.
PO Box 188
Plainfield, WI 54966-0188
Ph:(715)335-4046
Fax:(715)335-4746
Co. E-mail: pestpros@uniontel.net
URL: http://www.pestprosinc.com
Contact: Randy M. Van Haren, President
E-mail: pestpros@uniontel.net
Scope: Offers agricultural consulting involving fertility and pesticide recommendations, soil microbe assay and contract research.

FRANCHISES AND BUSINESS OPPORTUNITIES

15576 ■ Critter Control
Critter Franchise
9435 E Cherry Bend Rd.
Traverse City, MI 49684
Free: 800-Cri-tter
No. of Franchise Units: 105. **No. of Company-Owned Units:** 100. **Founded:** 1983. **Franchised:** 1987. **Description:** Animal & wildlife control services. **Equity Capital Needed:** $5,000. **Franchise Fee:** $18,000-$36,000. **Financial Assistance:** Yes. **Training:** Yes.

15577 ■ Mosquito Squad
2924 Emerywood Pkwy., Ste. 101
Richmond, VA 23294
Free: 800-722-4668
No. of Franchise Units: 27. **Description:** Pest control for residential and commercial. **Equity Capital Needed:** $32,000-$58,000. **Franchise Fee:** $17,500. **Financial Assistance:** No. **Training:** Yes.

15578 ■ MosquitoNix
12655 N Central Expy., Ste. 425
Dallas, TX 75243
Ph:(972)934-3131
Fax:(972)934-1055
No. of Franchise Units: 8. **No. of Company-Owned Units:** 2. **Founded:** 2003. **Franchised:** 2004. **Description:** Pest-control misting system. **Equity Capital Needed:** $130,000-$213,000. **Franchise Fee:** $25,000-$55,000. **Royalty Fee:** 5%. **Financial Assistance:** No. **Training:** Offers 5 days at headquarters and ongoing support.

15579 ■ Terminix Termite & Pest Control
3635 Knight Rd., Ste. 7
Memphis, TN 38118
Ph:(901)363-1132
Free: 800-441-5390
Fax:(901)363-8541
URL: http://www.terminix.com
No. of Franchise Units: 137. **No. of Company-Owned Units:** 329. **Founded:** 1927. **Franchised:** 1927. **Description:** Commercial, industrial and residential pest control and termite protection. **Equity Capital Needed:** $24,700-$85,300. **Franchise Fee:** $25,000-$50,000. **Royalty Fee:** 7-10%. **Financial Assistance:** No. **Training:** 1 week at headquarters, infield training and ongoing self-tutorial.

15580 ■ Truly Nolen
Truly Nolen of America, Inc.
3636 East Speedway
Tucson, AZ 85716
Ph:(520)322-4055
Free: 800-458-3664
Fax:(520)322-4010
Co. E-mail: truly@truly.com
URL: http://trullyfranchise.com
No. of Franchise Units: 13. **No. of Company-Owned Units:** 65. **Founded:** 1938. **Franchised:** 1996. **Description:** Environmentally friendly pest and insect control. **Equity Capital Needed:** varies. **Franchise Fee:** $10,000-$45,000. **Financial Assistance:** Yes. **Training:** Yes.

COMPUTERIZED DATABASES

15581 ■ *Integrated Pest Management Reviews*
Springer Science Business Media BV
Van Godewijckstraat 30
NL-3311 GX Dordrecht, Netherlands
Ph:31 78 657 6000
Fax:31 78 657 6555
URL: http://www.springer.com
Description: Contains reviews and papers on all aspects of pest management. Includes coverage of all ranges of pests, including insects, weeds, pathogens, mammals, birds, nematodes, and mollusks. Contains detailed information on chemical control, host resistance, biological control, socio-economic issues, implementation, and extension. Contains material on several systems, including forestry, agriculture, veterinary, medical, and domestic systems. Includes the most recent research findings, reviews of pest control chemicals, and more. Publication ceased in December 2002; an archive of back issues is available. **Availability:** Online: Springer Science Business Media BV. **Type:** Full text; Properties.

15582 ■ *National Pesticide Information Retrieval System*
Purdue University
1435 Win Hentschel Blvd., Ste. 207
West Lafayette, IN 47906
Ph:(765)494-6616

Fax:(765)494-9727
Co. E-mail: info@ceris.purdue.edu
URL: http://ceris.purdue.edu
Description: Contains five separate databases with detailed information on pesticides and pesticide-related chemicals. Provides three dictionaries with vocabularies relevant to pesticides and pesticide science. Includes the following databases: Federal and State Pesticide Product Information Provides federal pesticide product data such as federal brand names, EPA registration numbers, federal restricted use status, registration action dates, types of pests controlled by product, and more. Includes state information such as active ingredients per percentage, product formulations, use type classification, states registering, and product summary reports. Pesticide Document Management System (PDMS) - Contains information on pesticide research documents, with information such as research subjects, research laboratory codes and project numbers, research guidelines, study document types, accession numbers, and active ingredients. Includes PDMS summary reports containing lists and tables of submitters, pending registrations, chemicals, and guidelines. Data Submitter's List - Provides information such as first submitters names, chemicals, types of data, and more. Tolerance Index-Residue Tolerances Provides data on tolerances for pesticides and pest-controlling chemicals. Includes information such as commodities for which a tolerance or exemption exits, parts-per-million levels, petitions numbers, and federal register dates. Provides citations to the relevant sections of the U.S. Code of Federal Regulations. Federal Register Archive - Includes citations and full-text articles from the Federal Register on pesticide-related issues. **Availability:** Online: Purdue University, Wolters Kluwer Health; CD-ROM: Wolters Kluwer Health. **Type:** Full text; Numeric.

LIBRARIES

15583 ■ California Department of Pesticide Regulation Library
1001 I St.
PO Box 4015
Sacramento, CA 95812-4015
Ph:(916)324-3556
Fax:(916)324-1719
Co. E-mail: ckawamoto@cdpr.ca.gov
URL: http://www.cdpr.ca.gov/
Scope: Pesticides. **Services:** Library not open to the public. **Holdings:** 76,000 volumes. **Subscriptions:** 150 journals and other serials.

15584 ■ National Pest Management Association Library
10460 North St.
Fairfax, VA 22030
Ph:(703)352-6762
Fax:(703)352-3031
Co. E-mail: cmannes@pestworld.org
URL: http://www.pestworld.org
Contact: Greg Baumann, VP, Tech.Svcs.
Scope: Entomology, pest control. **Services:** Library not open to the public. **Holdings:** 2000 volumes. **Subscriptions:** 10 journals and other serials.

15585 ■ Rachel Carson Council Library
PO Box 10779
Silver Spring, MD 20914
Ph:(301)593-7507
Fax:(301)593-7508
Co. E-mail: rccouncil@aol.com
URL: http://www.rachelcarsoncouncil.org
Contact: Dr. Diana Post, Exec.Dir.
Scope: Pesticides, toxic substances, government regulation, pest management programs, alternatives to toxic chemical pesticides. **Services:** Copying (limited); Library open to the public by appointment. **Holdings:** 2000 books; 1500 documents and unbound reports; 50 drawers of specialized files; Environmental Protection Agency Pesticide Product Information and Registry of Toxic Effects of Chemical Substances materials on microfiche. **Subscriptions:** 85 journals and other serials.

15586 ■ U.S. Environmental Protection Agency–Andrew W. Breidenbach Environmental Research Center Library
26 W. Martin Luther King Dr.
Cincinnati, OH 45268
Ph:(513)569-7703
Fax:(513)569-7709
Co. E-mail: garza.david@epa.gov
URL: http://www.epa.gov/oarmcinc/library.htm
Contact: David Garza, Hd.Libn., ASRC Corp.
Scope: Water - pollution, quality, research; hazardous waste; chemistry; environmental studies; biotechnology. **Services:** Interlibrary loan; cataloging. **Holdings:** 20,000 books; 200,000 reports on microfiche; 6000 documents. **Subscriptions:** 700 journals and other serials.

15587 ■ U.S. Environmental Protection Agency–National Enforcement Investigations Center Environmental Forensics Library
Bldg. 25, E2, Denver Federal Ctr.
PO Box 25227
Denver, CO 80225-0227
Ph:(303)462-9352
Fax:(303)462-9354
Co. E-mail: neic-library@epamail.epa.gov
URL: http://www.epa.gov/libraries/neic.html
Contact: Jannie Morgan, Task Order Proj.Off.
Scope: Environmental law, water quality, industrial and agricultural pollution abatement practices, air and water pollution, hazardous wastes, chemistry. **Services:** Interlibrary loan (OCLC=EOB); Library open to the public by appointment. **Holdings:** 7300 volumes; 760,000 microforms; EPA technical reports; R&D reports; conference documents. **Subscriptions:** 100 journals and other serials.

RESEARCH CENTERS

15588 ■ Bio-Integral Resource Center
PO Box 7414
Berkeley, CA 94707
Ph:(510)524-2567
Fax:(510)524-1758
Co. E-mail: birc@igc.org
URL: http://www.birc.org
Contact: William Quarles PhD, Exec.Dir.
E-mail: birc@igc.org
Scope: Integrated pest management (IPM) and least-toxic methods of pest control. Components of IPM include: monitoring, determining injury levels, spot treatment, selecting least disruptive treatment for non-target organisms, and evaluating results. **Services:** Consulting service. **Publications:** Common Sense Pest Control Quarterly (quarterly); IPM Practitioner (10/year). **Educational Activities:** Training courses and lectures, on integrated pest management.

15589 ■ Cornell University–Cornell Cooperative Extension–New York State Integrated Pest Management Program
NYSAES
630 W North St.
Geneva, NY 14456
Ph:(315)787-2208
Fax:(315)787-2360
Co. E-mail: dar11@cornell.edu
URL: http://www.nysipm.cornell.edu
Contact: Prof. Donald A. Rutz, Dir.
E-mail: dar11@cornell.edu
Scope: Management alternatives for farmers; maintaining productivity and decreasing risks to the environment; computers and electronic weather equipment to assist with pest management decisions on potatoes, sweet corn, onions, tomatoes, apples, and grapes; pesticide reduction; and biological controls to combat pests; and management alternatives for schools, homes, parks and golf courses. **Publications:** Annual report; Articles; Brochures; Cornell Urban IPM News (quarterly); IPM Today (monthly); Manuals.

15590 ■ Kerr Center for Sustainable Agriculture, Inc.
PO Box 588
Poteau, OK 74953
Ph:(918)647-9123
Fax:(918)647-8712
Co. E-mail: mailbox@kerrcenter.com
URL: http://www.kerrcenter.com
Contact: James E. (Jim) Horne PhD, Pres./CEO
E-mail: mailbox@kerrcenter.com
Scope: Fertility management and soil health; water management; nutrient cycling and waste management; insect, disease, and predator management; weed management; biological diversity; plant and animal adaptation; energy use and conservation; effects of farm decisions on people; and economic and biological accounting. **Services:** Field days and ranch tours; Speakers. **Publications:** Kerr Center Newsletter. **Educational Activities:** Conferences; Workshops and seminars.

15591 ■ Ohio State University–Laboratory for Pest Control Application Technology
Ohio Agriculture Research & Development Center
1680 Madison Ave.
Wooster, OH 44691
Ph:(330)263-3931
Fax:(330)263-3686
Co. E-mail: downer.2@osu.edu
URL: http://www.oardc.ohio-state.edu/lpcat
Contact: Dr. Roger A. Downer, Hd.
E-mail: downer.2@osu.edu
Scope: Pest control agents, pest control application technology, and the basic processes and biological responses of the pesticide delivery system. Insecticides (conventional, biological, and hormonal), fungicides, plant growth regulators, nematicides, and herbicides are all studied in relation to various cropping systems used in growing corn, soybeans, fruit, vegetables, and turf. Research objectives are aimed at reducing involuntary pesticide exposure to humans, nontarget plants, or other organisms and developing improved procedures for pesticide application, formulation technology and pesticide waste management. Develops pesticide risk/benefit computer models to assist regulatory decision making. **Educational Activities:** Seminars and professional meetings.

15592 ■ Purdue University–Center for Urban and Industrial Pest Management
Department of Entomology
901 W State St.
West Lafayette, IN 47907
Ph:(765)494-4564
Fax:(765)494-0535
Co. E-mail: gbennett@purdue.edu
URL: http://extension.entm.purdue.edu/urban/home.html
Contact: Dr. Gary Bennett, Coord.
E-mail: gbennett@purdue.edu
Scope: Pest management, especially cockroach and termite control. **Educational Activities:** Conferences; workshops, seminars, and correspondence courses; Undergraduate and graduate degree programs in urban and industrial pest management in conjunction with the School of Agriculture at the Universe.

15593 ■ University of Florida–Institute of Food and Agricultural Sciences–Florida Medical Entomology Laboratory
200 9th St. SE
Vero Beach, FL 32962
Ph:(772)778-7200
Co. E-mail: wjt@ufl.edu
URL: http://fmel.ifas.ufl.edu
Contact: Walter J. Tabachnick PhD, Dir.
E-mail: wjt@ufl.edu
Scope: Biology and control of biting insects and other arthropods with emphasis on transmitters of disease and pest annoyances. Studies the entomological aspects of public health, veterinary science, sanitation, mosquito control, drainage and irrigation design, and wetlands management. **Services:** State Organizations and Districts Assistance. **Educational Activi-**

ties: International Symposium (biennially), on Host Regulated Developmental Mechanisms in vector Anthropods; Training, for students, in medical entomology.

START-UP INFORMATION

15594 ■ *101 Best Businesses for Pet Lovers*
Pub: Sourcebooks, Inc.
Ed: Nicholas Nigro. **Released:** September 2007.
Price: $18.95. **Description:** Advice for any individual wishing to start a business providing goods and services to pet lovers.

15595 ■ "Groomers Eye Profit Growth
Through Services" in *Pet Product News* (Vol. 64, December 2010, No. 12, pp. 26)
Pub: BowTie Inc.
Ed: Kathleen M. Mangan. **Description:** Pet groomers can successfully offer add-on services by taking into account insider customer knowledge, store image, and financial analysis in the decision-making process. Many pet groomers have decided to add services such as spa treatments and training due to a slump in the bathing and grooming business. How some pet groomers gained profitability through add-on services is explored.

15596 ■ "Keeping Customers Satisfied" in *Pet Product News* (Vol. 64, December 2010, No. 12, pp. 10)
Pub: BowTie Inc.
Ed: Devon McPhee. **Description:** Windsor, California-based Debbie's Pet Boutique, recipient of Pet Product News International's Outstanding Customer Service Award, has been dedicated to combining topnotch grooming services with a robust retail selection. These features might gain return customers for Debbie's Pet Boutique.

15597 ■ *Pet Care Business*
Pub: Globe Pequot Press
Ed: Kathy Salzberg. **Released:** March 2006. **Price:** $18.95. **Description:** Guide for starting and running a pet care business such as professional groomer, dog walker, pet sitter, or obedience training; issues regarding zoning, insurance, and health are discussed.

15598 ■ "Succeed With the Right
Equipment" in *Pet Product News* (Vol. 64, November 2010, No. 11, pp. 42)
Pub: BowTie Inc.
Ed: Sandi Cain. **Description:** Grooming shop owners have been focusing on obtaining ergonomic, durable, and efficient products such as restraints, tables, and tubs. These products enhance the way grooming tasks are conducted. Ways pet supply manufacturers have responded to this trend are examined.

ASSOCIATIONS AND OTHER ORGANIZATIONS

15599 ■ National Association of Professional Pet Sitters
15000 Commerce Pkwy., Ste. C
Mount Laurel, NJ 08054
Ph:(856)439-0324
Fax:(856)439-0525
Co. E-mail: napps@ahint.com
URL: http://www.petsitters.org
Contact: Felicia Lembesis, Exec. Dir.
Description: Owners or employees of pet-sitting services; professionals or businesses in related fields. Promotes professional and ethical standards in pet sitting and fosters cooperation among members of the pet-care industry. Serves as a network for the exchange of ideas and information on pet sitting and current industry practices. Disseminates information educating the pet-owning public on the advantages of leaving pets in a home environment and how to choose a reliable sitter. .

15600 ■ National Dog Groomers Association of America
PO Box 101
Clark, PA 16113-0101
Ph:(724)962-2711
Fax:(724)962-1919
Co. E-mail: ndga@nationaldoggroomers.com
URL: http://www.nationaldoggroomers.com
Contact: Jeffrey L. Reynolds, Exec. Dir.
Description: Dog groomers and supply distributors organized to upgrade the profession. Conducts state and local workshops; sponsors competitions and certification testing. Makes groomer referrals. .

15601 ■ Pet Care Services Association
2670 Academy Blvd.
Colorado Springs, CO 80917
Ph:(719)667-1600
Free: 877-570-7788
Fax:(719)667-0116
Co. E-mail: membership@petcareservices.org
URL: http://www.petcareservices.org
Contact: Joan Saunders, CEO
Description: Persons or firms that board pets; kennel suppliers; others interested in the facility boarding kennel industry. Seeks to upgrade the industry through accreditation educational programs, seminars and conventions. Provides insurance resources for members and supplies pet care information to the public. Promotes code of ethics and accreditation program for recognition and training of superior kennel operators. Compiles boarding facility statistics. **Publications:** *All About Dog Daycare*; *Pet Service Journal* (bimonthly).

15602 ■ Pet Industry Joint Advisory Council
1140 19th St. NW, Ste. 300
Washington, DC 20036
Ph:(202)452-1525
Free: 800-553-7387
Fax:(202)452-1516
Co. E-mail: info@pijac.org
URL: http://www.pijac.org
Contact: James P. Heim, Chm.
Description: Pet retailers, manufacturers and distributors; companion animal suppliers; pet industry trade associations. Works to monitor federal and state regulations and legislation affecting the industry.

Sponsors research projects and industry-related educational programs. **Publications:** *Our Pets, Our Health*; *PetLetter* (periodic); *Tips on Travel With Your Pets* .

DIRECTORIES OF EDUCATIONAL PROGRAMS

15603 ■ *Directory of Private Accredited Career Schools and Colleges of Technology*
Pub: Accrediting Commission of Career Schools and Colleges of Technology
Contact: Michale S. McComis, Exec. Dir.
Released: On web page. **Price:** Free. **Description:** Covers 3900 accredited post-secondary programs that provide training programs in business, trade, and technical fields, including various small business endeavors. Entries offer school name, address, phone, description of courses, job placement assistance, and requirements for admission. Arrangement is alphabetical.

REFERENCE WORKS

15604 ■ "Bark Up The Right Tree" in *Small Business Opportunities* (Winter 2009)
Pub: Entrepreneur Media Inc.
Description: Profile of Central Bark, a daycare company catering to pets that offers franchise opportunities and is expanding rapidly despite the economic downturn; the company's growth strategy is also discussed.

TRADE PERIODICALS

15605 ■ *Pet Services Journal*
Pub: The Pet Care Services Association
Contact: Angela Ashmore, Membership Coord.
Ed: Tracy Sellars, Editor, tracy@abka.com. **Released:** Bimonthly. **Price:** Included in membership. **Description:** Publishes articles related to the pet services industry and the Association. Contains information on animal health and kennel and grooming shop operation. Carries regional and national news on new products and programs, and kennel and shop profiles. Recurring features include editorials, news of research, letters to the editor, news of members, and columns titled From the Director's Desk, Message from the President.

VIDEOCASSETTES/ AUDIOCASSETTES

15606 ■ *Maintenance and Show Grooming*
Aspen Publishers
7201 McKinney Circ.
Frederick, MD 21704
Ph:(301)698-7100
Free: 800-234-1660
Fax:800-901-9075
URL: http://www.aspenpublishers.com
Released: 1990. **Description:** This tape features a complete visual text on the basics of daily show horse care. **Availability:** VHS.

15607 ■ *Maintenance and Show Grooming for Your Cat*

Bergwall Productions, Inc.
1 DIckinson Drive, Brandywine BUilding 5, Ste. 105
PO Box 1481
Chadds Ford, PA 19317
Ph:(610)361-0334
Free: 800-934-8696
Fax:(610)361-0092
URL: http://www.bergwall.com
Released: 1990. **Description:** Top cat expert Jim Costello gives a complete grooming program for long-haired cats, and pointers for cats with shorter hair. **Availability:** VHS.

TRADE SHOWS AND CONVENTIONS

15608 ■ Super Zoo

World Wide Pet Industry Association, Inc.
135 West Lemon Avenue
Monrovia, CA 91016
Ph:(626)447-2222
Free: 800-999-7295
Fax:(626)447-8350
Co. E-mail: info@wwpsa.com
URL: http://www.wwpsa.com
Released: Annual. **Audience:** Pet retailers, grooming shops, kennels, and veterinary clinic owners and other trade professionals. **Principal Exhibits:** Pet care foods, equipment, products and services. **Dates and Locations:** 2011 Sep 13-15, Las Vegas, NV.

FRANCHISES AND BUSINESS OPPORTUNITIES

15609 ■ Aussie Pet Mobile

85 Enterprise Dr., Ste. 400
Aliso Viejo, CA 92656
Ph:(949)234-0680
Fax:(949)234-0688
No. of Franchise Units: 335. **No. of Company-Owned Units:** 8. **Founded:** 1996. **Franchised:** 1996. **Description:** Pet grooming service in a specially-designed "Aussie Pet Mobile" trailer. **Equity Capital Needed:** $65,000-$140,000. **Franchise Fee:** $29,000 core territory, $20,000 additional territory. **Financial Assistance:** No. **Training:** Yes.

15610 ■ Camp Bow Wow

D.O.G. Development, LLC
1877 Broadway, Ste. 101
Boulder, CO 80302
Ph:(720)259-2250
Fax:(866)821-0412
Co. E-mail: CC@campbowwow.com
URL: http://www.campbowwow.tv
No. of Franchise Units: 200. **No. of Company-Owned Units:** 1. **Founded:** 2000. **Franchised:** 2002. **Description:** We provide doggy day camp, as well as overnight boarding for travelers. We utilize consistent start-up and operations systems that keep the franchise locations similar in look and customer experience. We oversee the growth of the company in a thoughtful, strategic manner that allows franchises to be successful in each location. **Equity Capital Needed:** Cash investment $80,000 liquid; $300,000-$600,000 total investment; minimum net

worth $100,000. **Franchise Fee:** $50,000. **Financial Assistance:** No. **Training:** 4 weeks of training and ongoing support.

15611 ■ Canine Campus

3116 Karen Pl.
Colorado Springs, CO 80907
Ph:(719)448-9600
Fax:(719)448-0496
No. of Company-Owned Units: 1. **Founded:** 1999. **Franchised:** 2004. **Description:** Day care, boarding, grooming & training services for dogs. **Equity Capital Needed:** $71,500-$182,300. **Franchise Fee:** $30,000. **Royalty Fee:** 4%. **Financial Assistance:** No. **Training:** Offers 7 days training at headquarters, 7 days at franchisee's location and ongoing support.

15612 ■ Dogtopia

4920 Wyaconda Rd.
North Bethesda, MD 20852
Free: 888-364-8674
Fax:(240)514-0214
No. of Franchise Units: 20. **No. of Company-Owned Units:** 3. **Founded:** 2001. **Franchised:** 2004. **Description:** Dog day care, boarding, and spa services. **Equity Capital Needed:** $243,1 00-$458,500. **Franchise Fee:** $40,000. **Royalty Fee:** 7%. **Financial Assistance:** Limited third party financing available.

15613 ■ Groomer On The Go

44 E Beaver Creek Rd., Unit 4
Richmond Hill, ON, Canada L4B 1G8
Ph:(905)707-7440
Free: 877-GRO-OM55
Fax:(905)889-1680
Co. E-mail: info@groomeronthego.com
URL: http://www.groomeronthego.com
No. of Franchise Units: 2. **Founded:** 2005. **Franchised:** 2005. **Description:** Groomer On The Go is a low cost with high profit potential mobile pet grooming franchise that taps into Canada's $3 billion booming pet industry. Delivering quality pet grooming with the ultimate in convenience for the owner and the one-on-one attention for the pet. No grooming experience required. **Equity Capital Needed:** $50,000. **Franchise Fee:** $24,995. **Training:** Provides 3 weeks comprehensive training.

15614 ■ Happy Tails Dog Spa

Happy to Be Here, Inc.
8528-F Tyco Rd.
Vienna, VA 22182
Ph:(703)821-1777
Fax:(703)821-1778
No. of Franchise Units: 6. **No. of Company-Owned Units:** 2. **Founded:** 2002. **Franchised:** 2005. **Description:** Luxury dog daycare and boarding services. **Equity Capital Needed:** $50,000 cash available; $120,000-$200,000 total investment. **Franchise Fee:** $35,000. **Financial Assistance:** No. **Training:** Yes.

15615 ■ Kennelwood Pet Resorts

1875 Lackland Hill Pky.
St. Louis, MO 63146
Free: 877-447-4173
Fax:(314)446-1001
Co. E-mail: franchise@kennelwood.com
URL: http://www.kennelwood.com
No. of Company-Owned Units: 6. **Founded:** 1974. **Franchised:** 2007. **Description:** Provides pets a safe & healthy vacation & lots of fun and attention. All resorts are full-service facilities offering a wide variety

of services, including all suite pet accommodations, grooming, personalized play time. **Equity Capital Needed:** $250,000. **Franchise Fee:** $55,000. **Financial Assistance:** Third party financial assistance available. **Training:** As part of our system, you will have the assistance & support of the entire franchisor organization, with access to our trained team, our established trademarks & operating systems, & full selection of tools & services designed to get you started & keep your business running efficiently.

15616 ■ Laund-UR-Mutt

Pet Pioneers, Inc.
12512-B W. Ken Caryl Ave.
Littleton, CO 80127
Ph:(303)470-1540
No. of Franchise Units: 3. **Founded:** 1992. **Franchised:** 1993. **Description:** Self-service dog grooming. **Equity Capital Needed:** $150,000. **Franchise Fee:** $25,000. **Royalty Fee:** 5%/month. **Financial Assistance:** No. **Training:** Offers 1 week at headquarters, 1 week at franchisee's location and ongoing support.

15617 ■ Pet Supplies 'Plus'

22670 Haggerty Rd.
Farmington Hills, MI 48335
Ph:(248)374-1900
Free: (866)477-7748
Fax:(248)374-7900
No. of Franchise Units: 239. **Founded:** 1988. **Franchised:** 1989. **Description:** Discount pet food and supplies. **Equity Capital Needed:** $500,000-$600,000. **Franchise Fee:** $25,000. **Royalty Fee:** $2,000 +/month. **Financial Assistance:** Third party financing available. **Training:** Provides 4 weeks training at headquarters.

15618 ■ Preppy Pet

Preppy Pet Franchises
57 West Michigan St.
Orlando, FL 32806
Ph:(407)420-1060
Free: 877-377-9738
Fax:(407)420-1068
No. of Franchise Units: 17. **No. of Company-Owned Units:** 1. **Founded:** 2003. **Franchised:** 2006. **Description:** Overnight dog boarding and day care. **Equity Capital Needed:** $127,750. **Franchise Fee:** $34,500. **Financial Assistance:** Yes. **Training:** Yes.

15619 ■ Ryan's Pet Food

Ryan's Pet Food, Inc.
70 Don Caster Rd.
Thornhille, ON, Canada L3T 1L3
Ph:(905)771-9227
Fax:(905)795-8903
No. of Franchise Units: 14. **No. of Company-Owned Units:** 24. **Founded:** 1979. **Franchised:** 1993. **Description:** Specialty pet foods and products. **Equity Capital Needed:** $95,000 inclusive; opening inventory, initial fee, leaseholds and working capital. **Franchise Fee:** $25,000. **Financial Assistance:** Yes. **Training:** Yes.

15620 ■ U-Wash Doggie

Total Pet Inc.
23013 Soledad Canyon Rd.
Santa Clarita, CA 91350
Ph:(818)846-9600
Fax:(661)297-2029
No. of Franchise Units: 1. **No. of Company-Owned Units:** 5. **Founded:** 1992. **Franchised:** 1997. **Description:** Self and full service pet grooming. **Equity Capital Needed:** $98,000. **Franchise Fee:** $15,000. **Financial Assistance:** No. **Training:** Yes.

START-UP INFORMATION

15621 ■ *101 Best Businesses for Pet Lovers*
Pub: Sourcebooks, Inc.
Ed: Nicholas Nigro. **Released:** September 2007.
Price: $18.95. **Description:** Advice for any individual wishing to start a business providing goods and services to pet lovers.

15622 ■ **"Biz Pays Tribute: Franchise Helps Owners Grieve and Honor Their Beloved Pets" in** *Small Business Opportunities* **(November 2007)**
Pub: Harris Publications Inc.
Description: Paws and Remember is a franchise company that provides pet cremation and memorial products while assisting veterinary clinics and other pet specialists to help clients when they lose a pet.

REFERENCE WORKS

15623 ■ *Minding Your Dog Business: A Practical Guide to Business Success for Dog Professionals*
Pub: Dogwise Publishing
Ed: Veronica Boutelle, Rikke Jorgensen. **Released:** June 1, 2010. **Price:** $19.95. **Description:** Setting up and running a successful dog-related business is an achievement in itself, but the real test is to build success and growth for the long haul.

ASSOCIATIONS AND OTHER ORGANIZATIONS

15624 ■ National Association of Dog Obedience Instructors
PO Box 1439
Socorro, NM 87801
Ph:(505)850-5957
URL: http://www.nadoi.org
Contact: Helen Cariotis, Pres.
Description: Dog obedience instructors who have met certain standards as established by the association. Promotes improved dog obedience instruction. Endorses instructors; serves as a network for communication among members. Maintains speakers' bureau. **Publications:** *FORWARD* (quarterly); *NADOI News* (bimonthly).

DIRECTORIES OF EDUCATIONAL PROGRAMS

15625 ■ Directory of Private Accredited Career Schools and Colleges of Technology
Pub: Accrediting Commission of Career Schools and Colleges of Technology
Contact: Michale S. McComis, Exec. Dir.
Released: On web page. **Price:** Free. **Description:** Covers 3900 accredited post-secondary programs that provide training programs in business, trade, and technical fields, including various small business endeavors. Entries offer school name, address, phone, description of courses, job placement assistance, and requirements for admission. Arrangement is alphabetical.

REFERENCE WORKS

15626 ■ Minding Your Dog Business: A Practical Guide to Business Success for Dog Professionals
Pub: Dogwise Publishing
Ed: Veronica Boutelle, Rikke Jorgensen. **Released:** June 1, 2010. **Price:** $19.95. **Description:** Setting up and running a successful dog-related business is an achievement in itself, but the real test is to build success and growth for the long haul.

TRADE PERIODICALS

15627 ■ Miniature Donkey Talk
Pub: Pheasant Meadow Farm
Ed: Bonnie Gross, Editor. **Released:** Bimonthly. **Price:** $32 by mail 1st class; $60 two years mailed 1st class; $35 Canada; $65 Canada 2 years; $55 other countries. **Description:** Trade magazine covering animal health care, management, and training.

15628 ■ Your Dog
Pub: Tufts University
Contact: Linda Ross D.V.M., Editor-in-Chief
Ed: Gloria Parkinson, Editor. **Released:** Monthly. **Price:** $20, individuals. **Description:** Publishes medi-

cal and behavioral advice and tips on dogs by veterinarians. Recurring features include columns titled My Dog and Chewing It Over.

VIDEOCASSETTES/ AUDIOCASSETTES

15629 ■ Advanced Training for Your Retriever
Stoney-Wolf Productions, Inc.
130 West Columbia Ct.
PO Box 460
Chaska, MN 55318
Ph:(952)556-0075
Free: 800-237-7583
Fax:(952)361-4217
Co. E-mail: stoneywolf@montana.com
URL: http://www.stoneywolf.com
Released: 1993. **Price:** $19.95. **Description:** Professional dog trainer and hunting guide Mike Mathiot provides continued training for retrievers. In this installment he covers steadying, decoys, blind retrieves, pattern work, cover, and distance. Contains actual hunting footage. **Availability:** VHS.

15630 ■ Ask Dr. Jim about Dogs
Tapeworm Video Distributors
25876 The Old Road 141
Stevenson Ranch, CA 91381
Ph:(661)257-4904
Fax:(661)257-4820
Co. E-mail: sales@tapeworm.com
URL: http://www.tapeworm.com
Released: 1994. **Price:** $19.95. **Description:** Veterinarian Jim Humphries discusses crate training puppies and adult dogs, spay and neutering, lyme disease, pet health insurance, overweight pets, and more. **Availability:** VHS.

15631 ■ Beginning Training for Your Retriever
Stoney-Wolf Productions, Inc.
130 West Columbia Ct.
PO Box 460
Chaska, MN 55318
Ph:(952)556-0075
Free: 800-237-7583
Fax:(952)361-4217
Co. E-mail: stoneywolf@montana.com
URL: http://www.stoneywolf.com
Released: 1993. **Price:** $19.95. **Description:** Mike Mathiot, professional dog trainer and hunting guide, illustrates techniques for training your hunting dog including obedience, voice and whistle commands, and water retrieving. **Availability:** VHS.

15632 ■ Caring for Your Dog
CinemaNow
4553 Glencoe Ave., Ste. 200
Marina Del Rey, CA 90292
Co. E-mail: sales@cinemanow.com
URL: http://www.cinemanow.com
Released: 1987. **Price:** $29.95. **Description:** Canine experts offer advice on dealing with dogs, from health care to achieving emotional stability. **Availability:** VHS.

15633 ■ Cats and Dogs
PBS Home Video
Catalog Fulfillment Center
PO Box 751089
Charlotte, NC 28275-1089
Ph:800-531-4727
Free: 800-645-4PBS
Co. E-mail: info@pbs.org
URL: http://www.pbs.org
Released: 1985. **Description:** This series explores all aspects of human-pet relationships, with tips on pet care, visits to feline and canine clinics, grooming, obedience and nutrition. **Availability:** VHS; 3/4U.

15634 ■ Dog Care
Karol Media
Hanover Industrial Estates
375 Stewart Rd.
PO Box 7600
Wilkes Barre, PA 18773-7600
Ph:(570)822-8899
Free: 800-526-4773
Co. E-mail: sales@karolmedia.com
URL: http://www.karolmedia.com
Released: 1987. **Price:** $9.95. **Description:** Pet authority Dr. Michael Fox offers this complete guide to dog care, from selecting and training a puppy to grooming and massaging a grown canine. **Availability:** VHS.

15635 ■ The Mentally Sound Dog
Tapeworm Video Distributors
25876 The Old Road 141
Stevenson Ranch, CA 91381
Ph:(661)257-4904
Fax:(661)257-4820
Co. E-mail: sales@tapeworm.com
URL: http://www.tapeworm.com
Description: Explains how to shape, train, and change canine behavior. **Availability:** VHS.

15636 ■ Raising Your Dog with the Monks of New Skete
PBS Home Video
Catalog Fulfillment Center
PO Box 751089
Charlotte, NC 28275-1089
Ph:800-531-4727
Free: 800-645-4PBS
Co. E-mail: info@pbs.org
URL: http://www.pbs.org
Released: 1998. **Price:** $64.95. **Description:** The Monks of New Skete present a unique view of the bond between dogs and humans and how this relationship can be used in the successful training of a puppy to bring out the best sides of both dog and human. Two hours and 53 minutes on three videocassettes. **Availability:** VHS.

15637 ■ Secret of Training Dogs
Video Collectibles
PO Box 385
Lewiston, NY 14092-0385
Free: 800-268-3891

Fax:800-269-8877
Co. E-mail: info@collectablesdirect.com
URL: http://www.collectablesdirect.com
Price: $24.95. **Description:** Video features the top ten fundamentals of dog training proven through solid research. **Availability:** VHS.

15638 ■ Training Dogs the Barbara Woodhouse Way
Video Collectibles
PO Box 385
Lewiston, NY 14092-0385
Free: 800-268-3891
Fax:800-269-8877
Co. E-mail: info@collectablesdirect.com
URL: http://www.collectablesdirect.com
Price: $39.95. **Description:** From the BBC series starring Barbara Woodhouse, practical, step-by-step training procedures for your dog (and you). **Availability:** VHS.

15639 ■ Training the Family Dog
CinemaNow
4553 Glencoe Ave., Ste. 200
Marina Del Rey, CA 90292
Co. E-mail: sales@cinemanow.com
URL: http://www.cinemanow.com
Released: 198?. **Price:** $19.99. **Description:** Keep that hound in check with this instructional video. **Availability:** VHS.

15640 ■ TTouch for Dogs and Puppies
Cambridge Educational
c/o Films Media Group
132 West 31st Street, 17th Floor
Ste. 124
New York, NY 10001
Free: 800-257-5126
Fax:(609)671-0266
Co. E-mail: custserve@films.com
URL: http://www.cambridgeol.com
Description: Presents a holistic approach to help solve behavioral problems and have a healthier, more obedient animal. **Availability:** VHS.

FRANCHISES AND BUSINESS OPPORTUNITIES

15641 ■ Bark Busters
PO Box 2558
Garibaldi Highlands, BC, Canada V0N 1T0

Ph:(604)815-0905
Free: (866)418-4584
Fax:(604)815-1808
Co. E-mail: franchise.inquiries@barkbusters.ca
URL: http://www.barkbusters.ca
No. of Franchise Units: 30. **Founded:** 1989. **Franchised:** 1994. **Description:** Dog training company. **Equity Capital Needed:** $55,000-$65,000. **Franchise Fee:** $33,000. **Training:** Provides 23 days training.

15642 ■ Bark Busters Home Dog Training
Dingo Inc.
250 W Lehow Ave., Ste. B
Englewood, CO 80110
Free: 877-300-2275
Fax:(720)283-2819
URL: http://www.barkbusters.com
No. of Franchise Units: 227. **No. of Operating Units:** 352. **Founded:** 1989. **Franchised:** 1994. **Description:** In-home dog training. **Equity Capital Needed:** $69,100-$97,100 total investment; $200,000 net worth, $12,500-$39,400 cash liquidity. **Franchise Fee:** $37,500. **Royalty Fee:** 8%. **Financial Assistance:** Third party financing available. **Training:** Offers 120 hours at headquarters with ongoing support.

15643 ■ Canine Dimensions
Davidson and Michaels LLC
PO Box 1192
Marlton, NJ 08053
Ph:(813)935-5087
Fax:(813)425-5799
No. of Franchise Units: 1. **No. of Company-Owned Units:** 1. **Founded:** 2007. **Franchised:** 2007. **Description:** Dog training. **Equity Capital Needed:** $44,050-$50,050. **Franchise Fee:** $22,500. **Financial Assistance:** No. **Training:** Yes.

15644 ■ Ryan's Pet Food
Ryan's Pet Food, Inc.
70 Don Caster Rd.
Thornhille, ON, Canada L3T 1L3
Ph:(905)771-9227
Fax:(905)795-8903
No. of Franchise Units: 14. **No. of Company-Owned Units:** 24. **Founded:** 1979. **Franchised:** 1993. **Description:** Specialty pet foods and products.

Equity Capital Needed: $95,000 inclusive; opening inventory, initial fee, leaseholds and working capital. **Franchise Fee:** $25,000. **Financial Assistance:** Yes. **Training:** Yes.

LIBRARIES

15645 ■ American Kennel Club Library
260 Madison Ave., 4th Fl.
New York, NY 10016
Ph:(212)696-8245
Fax:(212)696-8281
Co. E-mail: library@akc.org
URL: http://www.akc.org/about/library/index.cfm
Contact: Barbara Kolk, Libn.
Scope: Dogs - breeds, training, health, literature, art. **Services:** Copying; Library open to the public by appointment. **Holdings:** 18,000 volumes; VF drawers of clippings; videocassettes; fine art collection; 5 dissertations. **Subscriptions:** 300 journals and other serials.

15646 ■ National Animal Control Association–Research Library
PO Box 480851
Kansas City, MO 64148
Ph:(913)768-1319
Fax:(913)768-1378
Co. E-mail: naca@nacanet.org
URL: http://www.nacanet.org
Contact: John Mays, Exec.Dir.
Scope: Animal control, bites and attacks, rabies, euthanasia, humane education, officer training. **Services:** Copying; Library open to the public. **Holdings:** 85 books; 50 bound periodical volumes; 10,000 reports; videocassettes. **Subscriptions:** 15 journals and other serials; 1 newspaper.

15647 ■ U.S. Dept. of Defense–Central Repository for Military Working Dog Records–Archives (DOD D)
DOD Dog Center
Lackland AFB, TX 78236-5000
Ph:(512)671-3402
Scope: Military working dogs - training, working assignments, veterinary records.

START-UP INFORMATION

15648 ■ *101 Best Businesses for Pet Lovers*
Pub: Sourcebooks, Inc.

Ed: Nicholas Nigro. **Released:** September 2007.
Price: $18.95. **Description:** Advice for any individual wishing to start a business providing goods and services to pet lovers.

15649 ■ **"Big Bucks In Pet-ty Cash"** in *Small Business Opportunities* (Fall 2008)
Pub: Entrepreneur Media Inc.

Description: Twenty-five ways in which to start a business that caters to pets by either creating a product or a service that pet owners desire are profiled.

15650 ■ **"Birdcage Optimization"** in *Pet Product News* (Vol. 64, November 2010, No. 11, pp. 54)
Pub: BowTie Inc.

Description: Manufacturers have been emphasizing size, security, quality construction, stylish design, and quick cleaning when guiding consumers on making birdcage options. Selecting a birdcage is gaining importance considering that cage purchases have become the highest expense associated with owning a bird. Other avian habitat trends are also examined.

15651 ■ **"Capture New Markets"** in *Pet Product News* (Vol. 64, December 2010, No. 12, pp. 12)
Pub: BowTie Inc.

Ed: Ethan Mizer. **Description:** Flea and tick treatments are among the product categories that can be offered in order to clinch new markets. With the help of manufacturers, pet store retailers are encouraged to educate themselves about these products considering that capturing markets involves variations in customer perceptions. Retailers would then be deemed as resources and sources for these products.

15652 ■ **"Come Together"** in *Pet Product News* (Vol. 64, December 2010, No. 12, pp. 28)
Pub: BowTie Inc.

Ed: Lizett Bond. **Description:** Pet supply retailers have posted improved sales and improved customer service by bundling their offerings. Bundling pertains to grouping related items such as collars and leashes into a single unit for marketing purposes. Aside from providing convenience and enhanced product information to customers, bundling has facilitated more efficient purchases.

15653 ■ **"Experts Strive to Educate on Proper Pet Diets"** in *Pet Product News* (Vol. 64, November 2010, No. 11, pp. 40)
Pub: BowTie Inc.

Ed: John Hustace Walker. **Description:** Pet supply manufacturers have been bundling small mammal food and treats with educational sources to help retailers avoid customer misinformation. This action has been motivated by the customer's quest to seek proper nutritional advice for their small mammal pets.

15654 ■ **"Fed May Ban Amphibian Trade"** in *Pet Product News* (Vol. 64, November 2010, No. 11, pp. 13)
Pub: BowTie Inc.

Description: U.S. Fish and Wildlife Service is seeking public input on a petition submitted by the conservation activist group Defenders of Wildlife. The petition involves possible classification of chytrid fungus-infected amphibians and amphibian eggs as 'injurious wildlife' under the Lacey Act. Interstate trading or importation of injurious wildlife into the U.S. is not allowed.

15655 ■ **"Food as Nature Intended"** in *Pet Product News* (Vol. 64, November 2010, No. 11, pp. 30)
Pub: BowTie Inc.

Ed: Nikki Moustaki. **Description:** Dog owners have been extending their health-consciousness to their pets by seeking natural products that will address their pets' raw food diet. Retailers response to this trend are outlined.

15656 ■ **"Helping Customers Fight Pet Waste"** in *Pet Product News* (Vol. 64, November 2010, No. 11, pp. 52)
Pub: BowTie Inc.

Ed: Sandy Robins. **Description:** Pet cleaning products manufacturers have been enjoying high sales figures by paying attention to changing pet ownership trends and environmental awareness. Meanwhile, the inclusion of user-friendly features in these products has also been boosted by the social role of pets and the media attention to pet waste. How manufacturers have been responding to this demand is explored.

15657 ■ **"Making It Work"** in *Pet Product News* (Vol. 64, December 2010, No. 12, pp. S8)
Pub: BowTie Inc.

Ed: Kerri Chladnicek. **Description:** How focusing on service and flexibility allowed New Jersey-based pet supply store B.C. Woof to achieve success is discussed. B.C. Woof began as a pet-sitting business which eventually concentrated on natural foods. Aside from conducting a do-it-yourself approach in food formulation for customers, B.C. Woof has also been guiding customers on nutrients they need for their pets.

15658 ■ **"Must Work for Food"** in *Pet Product News* (Vol. 64, November 2010, No. 11, pp. 24)
Pub: BowTie Inc.

Ed: Wendy Bedwell-Wilson. **Description:** Pet supply retailers can benefit from stocking foods and treats that address obesity, which according to the American Veterinary Medical Association, has become the most prevalent nutritional disorder in dogs. With the rise in dog obesity, products like work-for-their food toys have been sought by dog owners.

15659 ■ **"Nestle Acquires Waggin' Train Dog Treat Company"** in *Pet Product News* (Vol. 64, November 2010, No. 11, pp. 7)
Pub: BowTie Inc.

Description: Vevey, Switzerland-based Nestle has acquired South Carolina-based dog treat firm Waggin' Train LLC from private equity firm VMG Partners

in September 2010. Waggin' Train LLC, which will be operated as a wholly owned subsidiary, is expected to fill a gap in Nestle's dog treat product portfolio.

15660 ■ **"North American Pet Health Insurance Market Poised for Growth"** in *Pet Product News* (Vol. 64, December 2010, No. 12, pp. 4)
Pub: BowTie Inc.

Ed: David Lummis. **Description:** The pet health insurance market is expected to further grow after posting about $350 million in sales in 2009, a gain of more than $40 million. Pet insurance firms have offered strategies such as product humanization in response to this growth forecast. Meanwhile, pet insurance shoppers have been provided more by insurance firms with wider choices.

15661 ■ **"Online Pet Medication Store Supports Free Vaccinations for Cats"** in *Internet Wire* (August 31, 2010)
Pub: Comtex

Description: Pethealth Inc., The Petango Store will help to support The Humane Society of Tampa Bay's efforts by offering free feline vaccinations for the cat's entire lifetime that is adopted between September 1, 2010 and February 28, 2010. The cat must be one year or older at time of adoption.

15662 ■ **"Perfecting Customer Services"** in *Pet Product News* (Vol. 64, November 2010, No. 11, pp. 18)
Pub: BowTie Inc.

Description: Pet supply retailers are encouraged to emphasize customer experience and sales representatives' knowledge of the store's product offerings to foster repeat business. Employee protocols could be implemented to improve customer interaction. Other guidelines on developing a pet supply retail environment that advances repeat business are presented.

15663 ■ **"Pet Food Bank 'Shares the Love'"** in *Pet Product News* (Vol. 64, December 2010, No. 12, pp. 6)
Pub: BowTie Inc.

Description: Winston-Salem, North Carolina-based nonprofit Share the Love Pet Food Bank has donated 60,000 pounds of pet food since its establishment in 2009. It has been linking pet food manufacturers and rescue groups to supply unsold pet food to needy animals. The nonprofit intends to reach out to more animal welfare groups by building more warehouses.

15664 ■ **"Promotions Create a Path to Better Profit"** in *Pet Product News* (Vol. 64, December 2010, No. 12, pp. 1)
Pub: BowTie Inc.

Ed: Joan Hustace Walker. **Description:** Pet store retailers can boost small mammal sales by launching creative marketing and promotions such as social networking and adoption days.

15665 ■ **"Rest Easy, Retailers"** in *Pet Product News* (Vol. 64, December 2010, No. 12, pp. S1)
Pub: BowTie Inc.

Ed: Wendy Bedwell-Wilson. **Description:** Pointers on how retailers can market all-natural beds and bedding products for pets are provided. The demand for these pet beds and bedding products has been increasing as customers become aware of the benefits of natural rest and relaxation products.

15666 ■ "Roundtable: Functional Foods and Treats" in Pet Product News (Vol. 64, December 2010, No. 12, pp. S1)
Pub: BowTie Inc.

Description: Executives and business owners from the pet supplies industries deliberate on the role of functional foods in the retail sector. Functional foods pertain to foods with specified health benefits. Insight into marketing functional foods and convincing pet owners to make the transition to these products is examined.

15667 ■ "Smarts Drive Sales" in Pet Product News (Vol. 64, December 2010, No. 12, pp. 1)
Pub: BowTie Inc.

Ed: Karen Shugart. Description: Retailers could make smart decisions by deciding how to best attract customers into their stores or resolving whether to nurture in-store or buy herps (reptiles) from suppliers. Paying attention to these smart decisions could help boost customer interest in herps and address customer demands.

15668 ■ "Solutions for the Frustrating Feline" in Pet Product News (Vol. 64, November 2010, No. 11, pp. 46)
Pub: BowTie Inc.

Ed: Lori Luechtefeld. Description: Products that can help customers deal with problematic cat behaviors, such as out-of-the-box urination and scratching are described. Information on such products including litter box deodorants and disposable scratchers is provided. Feline territorial behaviors can also be addressed by pheromone products that can calm hyperactive cats.

15669 ■ "Supplements Mix Nutrition With Convenience" in Pet Product News (Vol. 64, November 2010, No. 11, pp. 44)
Pub: BowTie Inc.

Ed: Karen Shugart. Description: Pet supply manufacturers have been making supplements and enhanced foods that improve mineral consumption, boost bone density, and sharpen appetite in herps. Customers seem to enjoy the convenience as particular herps demands are being addressed by these offerings. Features of other supplements and enhanced foods for herps are described.

15670 ■ "Sustaining Health" in Pet Product News (Vol. 64, November 2010, No. 11, pp. 28)
Pub: BowTie Inc.

Ed: Angela Pham. Description: How pet supply retailers have responded to dog owners' interest in health supplements and their ingredients is discussed. Dog owners are showing interest in the ingredients inside the supplements and are reading labels. Retailers must now prove the beneficial effects of these ingredients in order to make the sale.

15671 ■ "Tapping the 'Well' in Wellness" in Pet Product News (Vol. 64, November 2010, No. 11, pp. 1)
Pub: BowTie Inc.

Ed: Wendy-Bedwell Wilson. Description: Healthy food and treats are among the leading wellness products being sought by customers from specialty retailers to keep their pets healthy. With this demand for pet wellness products, retailers suggest making sure that staff know key ingredients to emphasize to customers. Other insights into this trend and ways to engage customers are discussed.

15672 ■ "Teachable Moments: Worth Every Penny" in Pet Product News (Vol. 64, December 2010, No. 12, pp. 34)
Pub: BowTie Inc.

Ed: Cheryl Reeves. Description: Pet bird retailers can attain both outreach to customers and enhanced profitability by staging educational events such as the annual Parrot Palooza event of Burlington, New Jersey-based Bird Paradise. Aside from attracting a global audience, Parrot Palooza features seminars, workshops, classes, and bird-related contests.

15673 ■ "To Be Seen Is to Be Successful" in Pet Product News (Vol. 64, December 2010, No. 12, pp. 12)
Pub: BowTie Inc.

Ed: David Arvin. Description: Guidelines on how pet business retailers can boost customer visibility are described considering that complacency could hamper retailers' efforts to effectively market their businesses. To enhance customer base and stand out from competing businesses, being different, strategic, creative, and differentiated is emphasized.

15674 ■ "Tradeshow Attendance Incentives Add Up" in Pet Product News (Vol. 64, December 2010, No. 12, pp. 14)
Pub: BowTie Inc.

Ed: Mark E. Battersby. Description: Pointers on how pet specialty retailers can claim business travel tax and income tax deductions for expenses paid or incurred in participation at tradeshows, conventions, and meetings are presented. Incentives in form of these deductions could allow pet specialty retailers to gain business benefits, aside from the education and enjoyment involved with the travel.

15675 ■ "Young Adult, Childless May Help Fuel Post-Recession Rebound" in Pet Product News (Vol. 64, November 2010, No. 11, pp. 4)
Pub: BowTie Inc.

Description: Pet industry retailers and marketers are encouraged to tap into the young adult and childless couple sectors to boost consumer traffic and sales to pre-recession levels. Among young adult owners, pet ownership increased from 40 percent in 2003 to 49 percent in 2009. Meanwhile, the childless couple sector represented 63 percent of all dog/cat owners in 2009.

ASSOCIATIONS AND OTHER ORGANIZATIONS

15676 ■ American Pet Products Association
255 Glenville Rd.
Greenwich, CT 06831
Ph:(203)532-0000
Free: 800-452-1225
Fax:(203)532-0551
Co. E-mail: bob@americanpetproducts.org
URL: http://www.appma.org
Contact: Robert L. Vetere, Pres.

Description: U.S. Manufacturers and importers of pet products. Provides public relations program to promote pet ownership and pet care. Sponsors the association's annual National Pet Products Trade Show; publishes the National Pet Owner's Survey, the association's research study in the pet industry. .

15677 ■ Pet Food Institute
2025 M St. NW, Ste. 800
Washington, DC 20036-2422
Ph:(202)367-1120
Fax:(202)367-2120
Co. E-mail: info@petfoodinstitute.org
URL: http://www.petfoodinstitute.org

Description: Represents the manufacturers of 97% of the commercial pet food produced in the United States. Serves as the voice of the industry before legislative and regulatory bodies at both the federal and state levels. .

15678 ■ Pet Industry Distributors Association
2105 Laurel Bush Rd., Ste. 200
Bel Air, MD 21015-5200
Ph:(443)640-1060
Fax:(443)640-1031
Co. E-mail: pida@ksgroup.org
URL: http://www.pida.org
Contact: Steven T. King, Pres.

Description: Strives to enhance the well-being of the pet product wholesaler-distributor. Promotes partnerships between suppliers and customers. Fosters the human-companion animal bond. Publications: PIDA Bulletin (bimonthly); Roster (annual).

15679 ■ Pet Industry Joint Advisory Council
1140 19th St. NW, Ste. 300
Washington, DC 20036
Ph:(202)452-1525
Free: 800-553-7387
Fax:(202)452-1516
Co. E-mail: info@pijac.org
URL: http://www.pijac.org
Contact: James P. Heim, Chm.

Description: Pet retailers, manufacturers and distributors; companion animal suppliers; pet industry trade associations. Works to monitor federal and state regulations and legislation affecting the industry. Sponsors research projects and industry-related educational programs. Publications: Our Pets, Our Health; PetLetter (periodic); Tips on Travel With Your Pets .

15680 ■ World Pet Association
135 W Lemon Ave.
Monrovia, CA 91016-2809
Ph:(626)447-2222
Free: 800-999-7295
Fax:(626)447-8350
Co. E-mail: info@wpamail.org
URL: http://www.wwpia.org
Contact: Doug Poindexter CAE, Pres.

Description: Manufacturers, retailers and distributors of pet food and services and of avian, aquarium and companion animal care products, equipment and services. Seeks to advance the economic interests of members; promotes responsible pet ownership. Conducts trade shows, certificate training courses and seminars for pet shop retailers, grooming establishments and veterinary clinics. .

REFERENCE WORKS

15681 ■ "AAAFCO Unveils Pet Food Resource" in Feedstuffs (Vol. 83, August 29, 2011, No. 35, pp. 15)
Pub: Miller Publishing Company

Description: The Association of American Feed Control Officials has launched a Website called The Business of Pet Food, which will address frequently asked questions about U.S. regulatory requirements for pet food. The site serves as an initial reference for anyone wishing to start a pet food business because it provides information and guidance.

15682 ■ "Add Aquatics to Boost Business" in Pet Product News (Vol. 64, December 2010, No. 12, pp. 20)
Pub: BowTie Inc.

Ed: David Lass. Description: Pet stores are encouraged to add aquatics departments to increase profitability through repeat sales. This goal can be realized by sourcing, displaying, and maintaining high quality live fish. Other tips regarding the challenges associated with setting up an aquatics department are presented.

15683 ■ "Aquatic Medications Engender Good Health" in Pet Product News (Vol. 64, November 2010, No. 11, pp. 47)
Pub: BowTie Inc.

Ed: Madelaine Heleine. Description: Pet supply manufacturers and retailers have been exerting consumer education and preparedness efforts to help aquarium hobbyists in tackling ornamental fish disease problems. Aquarium hobbyists have been also assisted in choosing products that facilitate aquarium maintenance before disease attacks their pet fish.

15684 ■ "Best In Show" in Pet Product News (Vol. 64, November 2010, No. 11, pp. 20)
Pub: BowTie Inc.

Ed: Lizett Bond. Description: Cherrybrook Premium Pet Supplies offers an expanded array of quality holistic products and is staffed by people who possess wide knowledge of these products. Aside from receiving the Outstanding Holistic Approach award, Cherrybrook has opened three stores in New Jersey. How a holistic approach to service kept customers coming back is discussed.

15685 ■ "Bits 'n' Pieces: Shelter Gives Out Pet Food to Keep Animals At Home" in *Columbian* (January 19, 2009)
Pub: The Columbian
Ed: Elisa Williams. **Description:** Lend a Paw program gives surplus food to pet owners in need; since August 2008 they distributed over 7,000 pounds of dry and wet food to shelters and pet owners.

15686 ■ "Breaking the Mold" in *Entrepreneur* (Vol. 37, September 2009, No. 9, pp. 87)
Pub: Entrepreneur Media, Inc.
Ed: Tracy Stapp. **Description:** Profiles of top franchise businesses in the United States are presented. Hey Buddy! Pet Supply Vending Co. offers pet supply vending machines. Home Health Mates, on the other hand, provides professional medical care at home.

15687 ■ "Canine Cuisine: Tips for a Healthful Diet" in *Seattle Times* (September 13, 2008, pp. D9)
Pub: Associated Press
Description: The American Kennel Club recommends feeding dogs food with balanced essential nutrients, including proteins, carbohydrates, fats, vitamins, minerals, and water; types of food, feeding practices and what not to feed a dog is discussed.

15688 ■ "Elanco Challenges Bayer's Advantage, K9 Advantix Ad Claims" in *Pet Product News* (Vol. 64, November 2010, No. 11, pp. 11)
Pub: BowTie Inc.
Description: Elanco Animal Health has disputed Bayer Animal Health's print and Web advertising claims involving its flea, tick, and mosquito control products Advantage and K9 Advantix. The National Advertising Division of the Council of Better Business Bureaus recommended the discontinuation of ads, while Bayer Animal Health reiterated its commitment to self-regulation.

15689 ■ "Foods for Thought" in *Pet Product News* (Vol. 64, December 2010, No. 12, pp. 16)
Pub: BowTie Inc.
Ed: Maddy Heleine. **Description:** Manufacturers have been focused at developing species-specific fish foods due to consumer tendency to assess the benefits of the food they feed their fish. As retailers stock species-specific fish foods, manufacturers have provided in-store items and strategies to assist in efficiently selling these food products. Trends in fish food packaging and ingredients are also discussed.

15690 ■ "Fromm Family Foods Converts Old Feed Mill Into Factory for Gourmet Pet Food" in *Wisconsin State Journal* (August 3, 2011)
Pub: Capital Newspapers
Ed: Barry Adams. **Description:** Fromm Family Foods, a gourmet cat and dog food company spent $10 million to convert an old feed mill into a pet food manufacturing facility. The owner forecasts doubling or tripling its production of 600 tons of feed per week in about five years.

15691 ■ "Give This Pooch a Home" in *Advertising Age* (Vol. 78, August 13, 2007, No. 32, pp. 4)
Pub: Crain Communications, Inc.
Ed: Kimberly D. Williams. **Description:** Overview of FlexPetz, a pet-sharing program that targets customers that live in metropolitan areas and travel frequently, who want to have a dog but cannot care for one on a full time basis.

15692 ■ "High Growth Reported for the Natural Supermarket Pet Department Close-Up" in *Canadian Corporate News* (October 20, 2008)
Pub: Comtex News Network Inc.
Description: Leading natural supermarket chains have been outperforming mainstream grocers by carrying natural and organic pet products. Statistical data included.

15693 ■ "Howl-o-ween" in *Decatur Daily* (October 25, 2011)
Pub: Decatur Daily
Ed: Catherine Godbey. **Description:** Animal Friends Humane Society provides free pet food and cat litter to Meals on Wheels clients.

15694 ■ "Importers Share Safety Liability" in *Feedstuffs* (Vol. 80, January 21, 2008, No. 3, pp. 19)
Pub: Miller Publishing Company, Inc.
Description: Pet food and toys containing lead paint are among products from China being recalled due to safety concerns. American Society for Quality's list of measures that outsourcing companies can take to help ensure safer products being imported to the U.S.

15695 ■ "In the Wake of Pet-Food Crisis, Iams Sales Plummet Nearly 17 Percent" in *Advertising Age* (Vol. 78, May 14, 2007, No. 18, pp. 3)
Pub: Crain Communications, Inc.
Ed: Jack Neff. **Description:** Although the massive U.S. pet-food recall impacted more than 100 brands, Procter & Gamble Co.'s Iams lost more sales and market share than any other industry player. According to Information Resources Inc. data, the brand's sales dropped 16.5 percent in the eight-week period ended April 22. Many analysts feel that the company could have handled the crisis in a better manner.

15696 ■ "Keeping Customers Satisfied" in *Pet Product News* (Vol. 64, December 2010, No. 12, pp. 10)
Pub: BowTie Inc.
Ed: Devon McPhee. **Description:** Windsor, California-based Debbie's Pet Boutique, recipient of Pet Product News International's Outstanding Customer Service Award, has been dedicated to combining topnotch grooming services with a robust retail selection. These features might gain return customers for Debbie's Pet Boutique.

15697 ■ "Marketer Bets Big on U.S.'s Growing Canine Obsession" in *Advertising Age* (Vol. 79, April 14, 2008, No. 15, pp. 14)
Pub: Crain Communications, Inc.
Ed: Emily Bryson York. **Description:** Overview of FreshPet, a New Jersey company that began marketing two brands of refrigerated dog food-Deli Fresh and FreshPet Select-which are made from fresh ingredients such as beef, rice and carrots. The company projects continued success due to the amount of money consumers spend on their pets as well as fears derived from the 2007 recalls that inspired consumers to look for smaller, independent manufacturers that are less likely to source ingredients from China.

15698 ■ "Melamine Analytical Methods Released" in *Feedstuffs* (Vol. 80, October 6, 2008, No. 41, pp. 2)
Pub: Miller Publishing Company
Description: Romer Labs has released new validations for its AgraQuant Melamine enzyme-linked immunosorbent assay. The test kit screens for melamine in feed and diary products, including pet foods, milk and milk powder. Melamine by itself is nontoxic in low doses, but when combined with cyanuric acid it can cause fatal kidney stones. The Chinese dairy industry is in the midst of a huge melamine crisis; melamine-contaminated dairy and food products from China have been found in more than 20 countries.

15699 ■ "Menu Foods Seeks Answers in Death of Ten Pets" in *Globe & Mail* (March 19, 2007, pp. B2)
Pub: CTVglobemedia Publishing Inc.
Ed: Thomas M. Burton. **Description:** The failure of Menu Foods Inc. to ascertain the cause of ten deaths of house pets, which were fed its food products, prompting the government to recall the products from the market, is discussed.

15700 ■ *Minding Your Dog Business: A Practical Guide to Business Success for Dog Professionals*
Pub: Dogwise Publishing
Ed: Veronica Boutelle, Rikke Jorgensen. **Released:** June 1, 2010. **Price:** $19.95. **Description:** Setting up and running a successful dog-related business is an achievement in itself, but the real test is to build success and growth for the long haul.

15701 ■ "New Recipes Added to IAMS Naturals Pet Food Line" in *MMR* (Vol. 28, August 1, 2011, No. 11, pp. 17)
Pub: Racher Press Inc.
Description: Procter & Gamble Company's IAMS brand has created a new pet food line called IAMS Naturals for pet owners wishing to feed their pets natural, wholesome food. IAMS Sensitive Naturals has ocean fish and its first ingredient for dogs with sensitivities. IAMS Simple & Natural features chicken with no fillers.

15702 ■ "Options Abound in Winter Wares" in *Pet Product News* (Vol. 64, November 2010, No. 11, pp. 1)
Pub: BowTie Inc.
Ed: Maggie M. Shein. **Description:** Pet supply manufacturers emphasize creating top-notch construction and functional design in creating winter clothing for pets. Meanwhile, retailers and pet owners seek human-inspired style, quality, and versatility for pets' winter clothing. How retailers generate successful sales of pets' winter clothing outside of traditional brand marketing is also examined.

15703 ■ "Organic Dog Treats" in *Veterinary Economics* (Vol. 49, November 2008, No. 11, pp. 52)
Pub: Advanstar Communications Inc.
Description: Wet Noses all-natural dog treats come in six flavors: dogranola, pumpkin, sweet potato curry, apples and carrots, cheddar, and peanut butter and molasses. The treats are made without animal by-products, added chemicals, preservatives, corn, soy or wheat.

15704 ■ "P&G's Iams Finds Itself in a Pet-Food Dogfight" in *Advertising Age* (Vol. 78, March 5, 2007, No. 10, pp. 6)
Pub: Crain Communications, Inc.
Ed: Jack Neff. **Description:** Proctor & Gamble Co.'s Iams has been slow to embrace the trend toward foods for pets that appear fit for human consumption. Competitors such as Nestle Purina have made big gains with its colorful premium Beneful brand and dry nuggets that look like chunks of vegetables and meat. Statistical data included.

15705 ■ "Paws That Refresh" in *Prepared Foods* (Vol. 177, August 2008, No. 8, pp. 35)
Pub: BNP Media
Description: Wellness Pet Food is offering enhanced dog foods to meet the dietary needs of both large and small dots.

15706 ■ *Pet Age—Sourcebook Issue*
Pub: H.H. Backer Associates Inc.
Contact: Karen Long MacLeod, Editor-in-Chief
E-mail: klmacleod@hhbacker.com
Released: Annual, December; latest edition 2007. **Publication Includes:** Lists of manufacturers and distributors of pet food, equipment, and accessories; companion animal suppliers, including livestock wholesalers and brokers; manufacturers' representatives; and trade associations. **Entries Include:** For manufacturers—Company name, address, phone, fax, e-mail, URL, name of principal executive, date established, brokers, and wholesalers—Company name, address, phone, fax, e-mail, URL, name of principal executive, date established, principal activity, products by type, modes of sale or distribution, size of sales staff, geographical area served. For associations—Organization name, address, phone, chief officers, purposes and activities, annual meeting date, dues, types of membership, number of members, publications. **Arrangement:** Distributors are geographical; others are alphabetical within separate sections. **Indexes:** Brand name, livestock, product.

15707 ■ "Pet-Food Crisis a Boon to Organic Players" in *Advertising Age* (Vol. 78, April 9, 2007, No. 15, pp. 3)
Pub: Crain Communications, Inc.
Ed: Jack Neff. **Description:** In the wake of the pet-food recall crisis, the natural-and-organic segment of the market is gaining recognition and sales; one such manufacturer, Blue Buffalo, has not only seen huge sale increases but also has witnessed a 50-60

percent increase in traffic to the brand's website which has led to the decision to move up the timetable for the brand's first national ad campaign.

15708 ■ "Pet-Food Industry Too Slow" in *Advertising Age* **(Vol. 78, March 26, 2007, No. 13, pp. 29)**

Pub: Crain Communications, Inc.

Ed: Description: Many crisis-communications experts believe that the pet-food industry mishandled the problem by waiting almost a month to recall the 60 million "wet-food" products after numerous consumer complaints. Experts site that the first 24 to 49 hours are the most important in dealing with a crisis of this nature.

15709 ■ "Pet Treats Recalled in Widening Salmonella Scare" in *Seattle Times* **(January 2009, pp. A2)**

Pub: Associated Press

Ed: Ricardo Alonso-Zaldivar. **Description:** PetSmart recalled seven varieties of its Grreat Choice dog biscuits due to contaminated dog biscuits. Dogs rarely get salmonella illness, but owners can pick up the bacteria when feeding pets.

15710 ■ "PetSmart: A Barking Buy" in *Barron's* **(Vol. 89, July 6, 2009, No. 27, pp. 15)**

Pub: Dow Jones & Co., Inc.

Ed: Jay Palmer. **Description:** Shares of PetSmart could climb from $21.70 to about $28 due to the company's improving profits, cash flow, and product portfolio. The company's shares are trading at 14 times projected 2010 earnings of $1.64 a share.

15711 ■ "The Progressive Pet Shop: Showcasing Strays" in *Animals' Agenda* **(March-April 1993, pp. 34)**

Pub: Animal Rights Network Inc.

Ed: Athena Rhiannon Schaffer. **Description:** Brothers Pets stopped selling cats and dogs in order to donate kennel space to the Aspen Hill, Maryland animal shelter. The events leading to this small business decision and its success are presented.

15712 ■ "Secaucus-Based Freshpet is Barking Up the Right Tree" in *Record* **(September 8, 2011)**

Pub: North Jersey Media Group

Ed: Rebecca Olles. **Description:** Freshpet produces a variety of nutritious, refrigerated pet foods and treats for cats and dogs. The firm introduced five new recipes and treats to its grain-free line called Vital line. The Vital line mimics the ancestral diets of dogs and cats.

15713 ■ "Shipping 2.0" in *Entrepreneur* **(Vol. 36, April 2008, No. 4, pp. 54)**

Pub: Entrepreneur Media, Inc.

Ed: Heather Clancy. **Description:** Doggypads.com contacted with Web 2.0 service provider Shipwire to handle its warehouse concerns. The service works by paying a rent to Shipwire and they will store the client's items. The client's customers can continue to order from the client's website and Shipwire will take care of delivery. Doggypads was able to save up on costs by using Shipwire.

15714 ■ "To Catch Up, Colgate May Ratchet Up Its Ad Spending" in *Advertising Age* **(Vol. 81, December 6, 2010, No. 43, pp. 1)**

Pub: Crain Communications, Inc.

Ed: Jack Neff. **Description:** Colgate-Palmolive Company has been losing market share in the categories of toothpaste, deodorant, body wash, dish soap and pet food.

15715 ■ "Want to Unleash the Next Best Seller? Think Like a Dog" in *Advertising Age* **(Vol. 79, March 10, 2008, No. 10, pp. 14)**

Pub: Crain Communications, Inc.

Ed: Lenore Skenazy. **Description:** Cott Corp. has launched a new product, fortified water for pets, in flavors ranging from peanut butter to parsley to spearmint.

15716 ■ "Wegmans Uses Database for Recall" in *Supermarket News* **(Vol. 56, September 22, 2008, No. 38)**

Pub: Penton Business Media, Inc.

Ed: Carol Angrisani. **Description:** Wegmans used data obtained through its loyalty card that, in turn, sent automated telephone calls to every customer who had purchased tainted pet food when Mars Petcare recalled dog food products.

15717 ■ "What's Next, Pup Tents in Bryant Park?" in *Advertising Age* **(Vol. 78, January 29, 2007, No. 5, pp. 4)**

Pub: Crain Communications, Inc.

Ed: Stephanie Thompson. **Description:** Designers such as Ralph Lauren, Juicy Couture, Burberry and Kiehl's have been expanding their businesses with new clothing lines for pets. Packaged Facts, a division of MarketResearch.com, predicts that pet expenditures will continue to grow in the years to come.

STATISTICAL SOURCES

15718 ■ *The Pet Food Market*

Pub: Rector Press, Ltd.

Contact: Lewis Sckolnick, Pres

Released: 2009. **Price:** Contact Rector Press.

15719 ■ *The U.S. Market for Pet Supplies and Pet Care Products, 5th Edition*

Pub: MarketResearch.com

Released: 2003. **Price:** $2250.00. **Description:** by Packaged Facts. Analyzes the dynamics of the pet supplies and accessories market. Covers a wide range of pets, but concentrates on dogs, cats, birds, and fish. Pinpoints the major factors impacting market growth. Includes sales projections to 1996; leading marketers; the competitive situation; new-product development; distribution channels, including distributors and rack jobbers; the retail level, including independent pet shops, supermarkets, drug chains, military exchanges, veterinarian offices, discount stores, and warehouse clubs; and consumer usage, including data on pet ownership.

TRADE PERIODICALS

15720 ■ *Dog World*

Pub: Bowtie, Inc.

Contact: Allan Reznik, Editor-in-Chief

Ed: Maureen Kochan, Editor. **Released:** Monthly. **Price:** $15; $27 other countries. **Description:** Magazine serving breeders, exhibitors, hobbyists and professionals in kennel operations, groomers, veterinarians, animal hospitals/clinics and pet suppliers.

15721 ■ *PIDA Bulletin*

Pub: Pet Industry Distributors Association (PIDA)

Contact: Maria Gurner

Ed: Mary Ann O'Brian, Editor. **Released:** Bimonthly. **Price:** Included in membership. **Description:** Deals with the pet industry, including companion animals, pet products manufacturers, assistance dogs, and animal welfare. Recurring features include news of research, a calendar of events, reports of meetings, news of educational opportunities, and notices of publications available.

15722 ■ *Reptiles*

Pub: Bowtie, Inc.

Ed: Russ Case, Editor. **Released:** Monthly. **Price:** $14.99 print; $26.99 other countries. **Description:** Consumer magazine covering reptile and amphibian care.

VIDEOCASSETTES/ AUDIOCASSETTES

15723 ■ *Ask Dr. Jim about Cats*

Tapeworm Video Distributors

25876 The Old Road 141

Stevenson Ranch, CA 91381

Ph:(661)257-4904

Fax:(661)257-4820

Co. E-mail: sales@tapeworm.com

URL: http://www.tapeworm.com

Released: 1994. **Price:** $19.95. **Description:** Veterinarian Jim Humphries discusses how to chose a cat, nutrition and obesity, vaccinations, behavior problems, human allergies, and more. **Availability:** VHS.

15724 ■ *Ask Dr. Jim about Dogs*

Tapeworm Video Distributors

25876 The Old Road 141

Stevenson Ranch, CA 91381

Ph:(661)257-4904

Fax:(661)257-4820

Co. E-mail: sales@tapeworm.com

URL: http://www.tapeworm.com

Released: 1994. **Price:** $19.95. **Description:** Veterinarian Jim Humphries discusses crate training puppies and adult dogs, spay and neutering, lyme disease, pet health insurance, overweight pets, and more. **Availability:** VHS.

15725 ■ *Escape*

Tapeworm Video Distributors

25876 The Old Road 141

Stevenson Ranch, CA 91381

Ph:(661)257-4904

Fax:(661)257-4820

Co. E-mail: sales@tapeworm.com

URL: http://www.tapeworm.com

Released: 1996. **Price:** $19.95. **Description:** Explains basic camping methods such as packing for the trip, finding the perfect campsite, building a fire, safeguarding food, and more. **Availability:** VHS.

15726 ■ *Freshwater Aquarium Basics*

Karol Media

Hanover Industrial Estates

375 Stewart Rd.

PO Box 7600

Wilkes Barre, PA 18773-7600

Ph:(570)822-8899

Free: 800-526-4773

Co. E-mail: sales@karolmedia.com

URL: http://www.karolmedia.com

Released: 1997. **Price:** $14.95. **Description:** Provides instruction on the care and maintenance of aquariums. **Availability:** VHS.

15727 ■ *Raising Your Dog with the Monks of New Skete*

PBS Home Video

Catalog Fulfillment Center

PO Box 751089

Charlotte, NC 28275-1089

Ph:800-531-4727

Free: 800-645-4PBS

Co. E-mail: info@pbs.org

URL: http://www.pbs.org

Released: 1998. **Price:** $64.95. **Description:** The Monks of New Skete present a unique view of the bond between dogs and humans and how this relationship can be used in the successful training of a puppy to bring out the best sides of both dog and human. Two hours and 53 minutes on three videocassettes. **Availability:** VHS.

15728 ■ *Show off Your Dog-Grooming Basics*

Tapeworm Video Distributors

25876 The Old Road 141

Stevenson Ranch, CA 91381

Ph:(661)257-4904

Fax:(661)257-4820

Co. E-mail: sales@tapeworm.com

URL: http://www.tapeworm.com

Released: 1997. **Price:** $19.95. **Description:** Breeder/exhibitor Ena Lane demonstrates grooming techniques such as proper brushing methods, bathing, blow drying, ironing, trimming, and the top knot. **Availability:** VHS.

15729 ■ *Understanding Cats*

PBS Home Video

Catalog Fulfillment Center

PO Box 751089

Charlotte, NC 28275-1089

Ph:800-531-4727

Free: 800-645-4PBS
Co. E-mail: info@pbs.org
URL: http://www.pbs.org
Released: 1998. **Price:** $19.98. **Description:** Cat expert Roger Tabor examines why cats behave the way they do. Covers both understanding and caring for cats. **Availability:** VHS.

TRADE SHOWS AND CONVENTIONS

15730 ■ Pet Industry Christmas Trade Show
H.H. Backer Associates Inc.
18 S. Michigan Ave., No. 1100
Chicago, IL 60603-3233
Ph:(312)578-1818
Fax:(312)578-1819
Co. E-mail: hhbacker@hhbacker.com
URL: http://www.hhbacker.com
Released: Annual. **Audience:** Pet store owners, managers, gift stores. **Principal Exhibits:** Pet supplies, gift products, lawn and garden products. **Dates and Locations:** 2011 Oct 14-16, Rosemont, IL.

15731 ■ Super Zoo
World Wide Pet Industry Association, Inc.
135 West Lemon Avenue
Monrovia, CA 91016
Ph:(626)447-2222
Free: 800-999-7295
Fax:(626)447-8350
Co. E-mail: info@wwpsa.com
URL: http://www.wwpsa.com
Released: Annual. **Audience:** Pet retailers, grooming shops, kennels, and veterinary clinic owners and other trade professionals. **Principal Exhibits:** Pet care foods, equipment, products and services. **Dates and Locations:** 2011 Sep 13-15, Las Vegas, NV.

FRANCHISES AND BUSINESS OPPORTUNITIES

15732 ■ Global Pet Foods
Franchise Bancorp, Inc.
294 Walker Dr., Ste. 2
Brampton, ON, Canada L6T 4Z2
Ph:(905)790-9023
Free: (866)463-4124
Fax:(905)790-7059
Co. E-mail: franchises@franchisebancorp.com
URL: http://www.globalpetfoods.com
No. of Franchise Units: 130. **No. of Company-Owned Units:** 3. **Founded:** 1976. **Franchised:** 1976. **Description:** Pet food store specializing in natural and wholesome pet foods with a full range of pet care accessories. We offer unprecedented support to all of our franchise owners while encouraging them to personalize their business for their market.

Equity Capital Needed: $160,000-$220,000. **Franchise Fee:** $30,000. **Training:** Training and support throughout franchise term.

15733 ■ Multi-Menu
1700 Boul. St-Elzear W, Ste. 105
Laval, QC, Canada H7L 3N2
Ph:(450)682-5056
Free: 877-462-0056
Fax:(450)682-5054
Co. E-mail: multimenu@multimenue.ca
URL: http://www.multimenu.ca
No. of Franchise Units: 170. **Founded:** 1996. **Description:** Pet food and accessories franchise and free home delivery of exclusive products. **Equity Capital Needed:** $12,000. **Franchise Fee:** $7,000. **Royalty Fee:** None. **Training:** Ongoing support and training.

15734 ■ Pet Supplies 'Plus'
22670 Haggerty Rd.
Farmington Hills, MI 48335
Ph:(248)374-1900
Free: (866)477-7748
Fax:(248)374-7900
No. of Franchise Units: 239. **Founded:** 1988. **Franchised:** 1989. **Description:** Discount pet food and supplies. **Equity Capital Needed:** $500,000-$600,000. **Franchise Fee:** $25,000. **Royalty Fee:** $2,000 +/month. **Financial Assistance:** Third party financing available. **Training:** Provides 4 weeks training at headquarters.

15735 ■ Petland
Petland, Inc.
250 Riverside St.
Chillicothe, OH 45601
Free: 800-221-5935
Fax:(740)775-2575
Co. E-mail: franchise@petland.com
URL: http://www.petland.com
No. of Franchise Units: 194. **No. of Company-Owned Units:** 5. **Founded:** 1967. **Franchised:** 1971. **Description:** Retailing of pets for hobbies and ownership. **Equity Capital Needed:** $95,000 liquid; $200,000 net worth. **Franchise Fee:** $30,000. **Financial Assistance:** Petland will assistant for financing including preparation of a comprehensive business plan/loan request package and introduce candidate to lenders. **Managerial Assistance:** Field representative visits to retail store. **Training:** 5 weeks of training, including 1 week of onsite training. Training comprised of classroom, hands-on in corporate training store, 1 week in new store prior to opening and 1 week of post-opening training. Video and audio training tapes and comprehensive operating manuals Bi-annual franchise meetings, monthly marketing guides.

15736 ■ Pets Are Inn
Pets Are Inn, Inc.
5100 Edina Industrial Blvd., Ste. 208
Minneapolis, MN 55439

Ph:(952)944-8298
Free: (866)343-0086
No. of Franchise Units: 19. **Founded:** 1982. **Franchised:** 1986. **Description:** Pet boarding service without kennels or cages. **Equity Capital Needed:** $49,950-$75,150. **Franchise Fee:** $35,000. **Royalty Fee:** 5-10%. **Financial Assistance:** In-house and third party limited financing available. **Training:** Provides 5 days at headquarters, 1 day at franchisee's location, weekly, monthly & quarterly "checkups" at owner's location.

15737 ■ Ruffin's Pet Centres Inc.
109 Industrial Ct.
Dunnville, ON, Canada N1A 2X5
Ph:(905)774-7079
Fax:(905)774-1096
Co. E-mail: franchise@ruffinspet.com
URL: http://www.ruffinspet.com
No. of Franchise Units: 11. **Founded:** 1981. **Franchised:** 1987. **Description:** Offers a combination of a traditional pet shop with the convenience of a pet food store. **Equity Capital Needed:** $85,000-$105,000. **Franchise Fee:** $20,000. **Training:** As required.

15738 ■ Ryan's Pet Food
Ryan's Pet Food, Inc.
70 Don Caster Rd.
Thornhill, ON, Canada L3T 1L3
Ph:(905)771-9227
Fax:(905)795-8903
No. of Franchise Units: 14. **No. of Company-Owned Units:** 24. **Founded:** 1979. **Franchised:** 1993. **Description:** Specialty pet foods and products. **Equity Capital Needed:** $95,000 inclusive; opening inventory, initial fee, leaseholds and working capital. **Franchise Fee:** $25,000. **Financial Assistance:** Yes. **Training:** Yes.

15739 ■ Wild Bird Center
Wild Bird Centers of America, Inc.
7370 MacArthur Blvd.
Glen Echo, MD 20812
Ph:(301)229-9585
Free: 800-WIL-BIRD
Fax:(301)320-6154
No. of Franchise Units: 95. **No. of Company-Owned Units:** 1. **Founded:** 1985. **Franchised:** 1990. **Description:** Franchises "one-stop" bird seed and supply stores. **Equity Capital Needed:** $94,900-$149,300. **Franchise Fee:** 3.5%-5.5% of gross sales. **Financial Assistance:** No. **Training:** Yes.

15740 ■ Wild Birds Unlimited, Inc.
11711 N College Ave., Ste. 146
Carmel, IN 46032
Free: 888-730-7108
Fax:(317)208-7110
No. of Franchise Units: 260. **Founded:** 1981. **Franchised:** 1983. **Description:** Retail outlets for birdseed, bird feeders and gift items. **Equity Capital Needed:** $93,121-$147,936. **Franchise Fee:** $18,000. **Royalty Fee:** 4%. **Financial Assistance:** Third party financing available. **Training:** Training available 6 days at headquarters, 2 days at franchisee's location, 5 days at annual meeting and ongoing support.

START-UP INFORMATION

15741 ■ *101 Best Businesses for Pet Lovers*
Pub: Sourcebooks, Inc.
Ed: Nicholas Nigro. **Released:** September 2007.
Price: $18.95. **Description:** Advice for any individual wishing to start a business providing goods and services to pet lovers.

15742 ■ *Pet Care Business*
Pub: Globe Pequot Press
Ed: Kathy Salzberg. **Released:** March 2006. **Price:** $18.95. **Description:** Guide for starting and running a pet care business such as professional groomer, dog walker, pet sitter, or obedience training; issues regarding zoning, insurance, and health are discussed.

15743 ■ "Pet Project Pays Off" in *Small Business Opportunities* (March 2011)
Pub: Harris Publications Inc.
Ed: Vicki Gerson. **Description:** Pet sitting goes big time, reporting $40 million annually for Camp Bow Wow. Pet-oriented businesses are recession-proof because of Americans love for pampering their canines.

ASSOCIATIONS AND OTHER ORGANIZATIONS

15744 ■ National Association of Professional Pet Sitters
15000 Commerce Pkwy., Ste. C
Mount Laurel, NJ 08054
Ph:(856)439-0324
Fax:(856)439-0525
Co. E-mail: napps@ahint.com
URL: http://www.petsitters.org
Contact: Felicia Lembesis, Exec. Dir.
Description: Owners or employees of pet-sitting services; professionals or businesses in related fields. Promotes professional and ethical standards in pet sitting and fosters cooperation among members of the pet-care industry. Serves as a network for the exchange of ideas and information on pet sitting and current industry practices. Disseminates information educating the pet-owning public on the advantages of leaving pets in a home environment and how to choose a reliable sitter. .

15745 ■ Pet Care Services Association
2670 Academy Blvd.
Colorado Springs, CO 80917
Ph:(719)667-1600
Free: 877-570-7788
Fax:(719)667-0116
Co. E-mail: membership@petcareservices.org
URL: http://www.petcareservices.org
Contact: Joan Saunders, CEO
Description: Persons or firms that board pets; kennel suppliers; others interested in the facility boarding kennel industry. Seeks to upgrade the industry through accreditation educational programs, seminars and conventions. Provides insurance resources for members and supplies pet care information to the public. Promotes code of ethics and accreditation program for recognition and training of superior kennel operators. Compiles boarding facility statistics. **Publications:** *All About Dog Daycare*; *Pet Service Journal* (bimonthly).

15746 ■ Pet Care Trust
2105 Laurel Bush Blvd., Ste. 200
Bel Air, MD 21015
Ph:(443)640-1060
Fax:(443)640-1031
Co. E-mail: marci@ksgroup.org
URL: http://www.petsintheclassroom.org
Contact: Mr. Steven T. King, Exec. Dir.
Purpose: Promotes public understanding regarding the value of and the right to enjoy companion animals; enhances society's knowledge about companion animals through research and education; promotes professionalism among members of the companion animal community. Compiles statistics. Provides animals in the classroom teacher education workshops. .

15747 ■ Pet Sitters International
201 E King St.
King, NC 27021
Ph:(336)983-9222
Fax:(336)983-5266
Co. E-mail: info@petsit.com
URL: http://www.petsit.com
Contact: Patti J. Moran, Pres.
Description: Represents professional pet sitters. Serves as an educational organization for professional pet sitters and advocates of at-home pet care. Promotes, recognizes and supports excellence in pet sitting. Provides a forum of communication for members who share a common vision of excellence in at-home pet care. **Publications:** *Pet Owner's World* (biennial); *The World of Professional Pet Sitting* (bimonthly).

REFERENCE WORKS

15748 ■ "Bark Up The Right Tree" in *Small Business Opportunities* (Winter 2009)
Pub: Entrepreneur Media Inc.
Description: Profile of Central Bark, a daycare company catering to pets that offers franchise opportunities and is expanding rapidly despite the economic downturn; the company's growth strategy is also discussed.

15749 ■ "Making It Work" in *Pet Product News* (Vol. 64, December 2010, No. 12, pp. S8)
Pub: BowTie Inc.
Ed: Kerri Chladnicek. **Description:** How focusing on service and flexibility allowed New Jersey-based pet supply store B.C. Woof to achieve success is discussed. B.C. Woof began as a pet-sitting business which eventually concentrated on natural foods. Aside from conducting a do-it-yourself approach in food formulation for customers, B.C. Woof has also been guiding customers on nutrients they need for their pets.

15750 ■ *Minding Your Dog Business: A Practical Guide to Business Success for Dog Professionals*
Pub: Dogwise Publishing
Ed: Veronica Boutelle, Rikke Jorgensen. **Released:** June 1, 2010. **Price:** $19.95. **Description:** Setting up and running a successful dog-related business is an achievement in itself, but the real test is to build success and growth for the long haul.

15751 ■ "Professional Help: Cross That Off Your To-Do List" in *Inc.* (November 2007, pp. 89-90, 92)
Pub: Gruner & Jahr USA Publishing
Ed: Alison Stein Wellner. **Description:** Small business owners are finding that it pays to hire someone to takeover the personal tasks of daily living, including hiring a personal assistant, chauffeur, chef, stylist, pet caregiver, or concierge service.

TRADE PERIODICALS

15752 ■ *The Voice*
Pub: The Voice of Florida
Ed: Ray Brasted, Editor. **Released:** Monthly. **Price:** $25. **Description:** Paper for persons with disabilities and referral resources.

FRANCHISES AND BUSINESS OPPORTUNITIES

15753 ■ Central Bark Doggy Day Care
BVI, Inc.
3699 N Dixie Hwy.
Oakland Park, FL 33334
Free: (866)799-2275
Fax:(954)568-3669
No. of Franchise Units: 29. **Founded:** 1997. **Franchised:** 2004. **Description:** Canine care facility. **Equity Capital Needed:** $60,000+ $150,000-$250,000 investment. **Franchise Fee:** $40,000. **Financial Assistance:** No. **Training:** Yes.

15754 ■ In Home Pet Services Inc.
88-25 247th St.
Bellerose, NY 11426
Ph:(718)347-7387
No. of Franchise Units: 5. **No. of Company-Owned Units:** 1. **Founded:** 2001. **Franchised:** 2005. **Description:** Pet sitting & dog walking services. **Equity Capital Needed:** $7,200-$31,100. **Franchise Fee:** $6,000. **Royalty Fee:** 5%. **Financial Assistance:** No. **Training:** Includes 1 week training at headquarters.

15755 ■ Pet-Tenders
Pet-Tenders International, Inc.
PO Box 23622
San Diego, CA 92193

Ph:(619)298-3033
No. of Franchise Units: 4. **No. of Company-Owned Units:** 1. **Founded:** 1983. **Franchised:** 1990. **Description:** In-home pet and house sitting service. **Equity Capital Needed:** $2,000-$5,400. **Franchise Fee:** $8,500. **Financial Assistance:** Yes. **Training:** Yes.

15756 ■ Preppy Pet
Preppy Pet Franchises
57 West Michigan St.
Orlando, FL 32806
Ph:(407)420-1060
Free: 877-377-9738

Fax:(407)420-1068
No. of Franchise Units: 17. **No. of Company-Owned Units:** 1. **Founded:** 2003. **Franchised:** 2006. **Description:** Overnight dog boarding and day care. **Equity Capital Needed:** $127,750. **Franchise Fee:** $34,500. **Financial Assistance:** Yes. **Training:** Yes.

ASSOCIATIONS AND OTHER ORGANIZATIONS

15757 ■ International Imaging Industry Association
401 Edgewater Pl., Ste. 600
Wakefield, MA 01880
Ph:(914)285-4933
Fax:(914)645-1443
Co. E-mail: i3ainfo@i3a.org
URL: http://www.i3a.org
Contact: Lisa A. Walker, Pres.

Description: Develops and promotes the adoption of open industry standards, addressing environmental issues and providing a voice for the industry that will benefit all users. Promotes environment, health and safety concerns; works with various government agencies including the EPA, TSA, and WTO to ensure the best interests of the imaging industry are represented. **Publications:** *13A Eye on Imaging* (bimonthly); *13A Eye on Standards* (bimonthly).

15758 ■ PMA - The Worldwide Community of Imaging Associations
3000 Picture Pl.
Jackson, MI 49201-8853
Ph:(517)788-8100
Free: 800-762-9287
Fax:(517)788-8371
Co. E-mail: pma_membership@pmai.org
URL: http://www.pmai.org
Contact: Brian Wood, Pres.

Description: Retailers of photo and video equipment, film, and supplies; firms developing and printing film. Maintains hall of fame. Compiles statistics; conducts research and educational programs. **Publications:** *NAPET News* (bimonthly); *Photo Marketing Association International—Newsline* (semimonthly); *Photo Marketing Magazine* (monthly); *Sales Counter* (monthly); *Specialty Lab Update* (monthly); *Who's Who in Photographic Management* (annual).

REFERENCE WORKS

15759 ■ "Interactive Stores a Big Part of Borders' Turnaround Plan" in *Crain's Detroit Business* (Vol. 24, February 18, 2008, No. 7, pp. 4)
Pub: Crain Communications Inc. - Detroit
Description: Borders Group Inc. is using digital technology and interactive media as a part of the firm's turnaround plan. The digital store will allow shoppers to create CDs, download audio books, publish their own works, print photos and search family genealogy.

15760 ■ "Kodak Cuts Deep in Effort to Change Focus" in *Globe & Mail* (February 9, 2007, pp. B8)
Pub: CTVglobemedia Publishing Inc.
Ed: Gillian Wee. **Description:** Eastman Kodak Co., the world's largest photography company, is eliminating 5,000 more jobs than the originally planned 28,000 jobs. The job cuts are being driven by the sale of Kodak's health-imaging unit.

STATISTICAL SOURCES

15761 ■ *RMA Annual Statement Studies*
Pub: Robert Morris Associates (RMA)
Released: Annual. **Price:** $175.00 2006-07 edition, $105.00. **Description:** Contains composite balance sheets and income statements for more than 360 industries, including the accounting, auditing, and bookkeeping industries. Also contains five years of comparative historical data for discerning trends. Includes 16 commonly used ratios, computed for most of the size groupings for nearly every industry.

TRADE PERIODICALS

15762 ■ *Master Guide*
Pub: Apex Publications Inc.
Contact: Guy Langevin, Distribution Mngr.
Released: Annual. **Price:** $27 6 issues; $50 two years. **Description:** Trade magazine covering photography for photo retailers and distributors.

15763 ■ *Professional Photographer*
Pub: Professional Photographers of America Inc.
Contact: Karisa Gilmer, managing editorager of Sales
E-mail: kgilmer@ppa.com
Released: Monthly. **Price:** $19.95 print (U.S.); $35.95 print (Canada). **Description:** Magazine for photographers.

LIBRARIES

15764 ■ International Center of Photography Library
1114 Ave. of the Americas
New York, NY 10036
Ph:(212)857-0004
Fax:(212)857-0091
Co. E-mail: library@icp.org
Contact: Deirdre Donohue, Libn.
Scope: Photography, critical writing on photography. **Services:** Copying; Center open to the public by appointment. **Holdings:** 15,000 books and unbound volumes of photography periodicals and journals; 2500 vertical files on photographers and photo subjects with biographical data from primary materials; critical essays. **Subscriptions:** 75 journals and other serials.

15765 ■ Polaroid Corporation–Research Library
750 Main St.
Cambridge, MA 02139
Ph:(617)386-8245
Fax:(617)386-8241
Co. E-mail: poppenj@polaroid.com
Contact: James Poppenhouse, Dept.Mgr.
Scope: Photography, chemistry, physics, engineering, mathematics, social sciences, general business. **Services:** Interlibrary loan; copying; Library open to the public for reference use only with approval of the department manager or the library administrator. **Holdings:** 30,000 books; 9000 bound periodical volumes; standards, government documents, translations, scientific papers, technical reports; CD-ROMs. **Subscriptions:** 900 journals and other serials; 5 newspapers.

START-UP INFORMATION

15766 ■ *In Fashion: From Runway to Retail, Everything You Need to Know to Break Into the Fashion Industry*
Pub: Crown Business Books
Ed: Annemarie Iverson. **Released:** August 10, 2010.
Price: $16.99. **Description:** Whether your dream is to photograph models, outfit celebrities, design fashions, this book provides details into every aspect for working in the fashion industry.

ASSOCIATIONS AND OTHER ORGANIZATIONS

15767 ■ **American Photographic Artists**
PO Box 725146
Atlanta, GA 31139
Free: 888-889-7190
Co. E-mail: ceo@apanational.com
URL: http://www.apanational.org
Contact: Stephen Best, CEO
Description: Enhances dialogue among professional photographers and their clients. Suggests standards and business practices to improve the quality of professional photography; and acts as a forum for discussion of problems and solutions. Conducts discussion groups. **Publications:** *1999 APA National Photographer's Survey Report* .

15768 ■ **American Photographic Artists Guild**
2269 N 400 Rd.
Eudora, KS 66025
Ph:(785)883-4166
Co. E-mail: hancock69@peoplepc.com
URL: http://apag.net
Contact: Quinn Hancock
Description: Photographic color artists, retouchers, airbrush artists, color correctors, laboratory technicians, receptionists and professional photographers working in the photography business. Encourages a better understanding between the photographer and the color artist and retoucher. Conducts educational programs on all types of work on color and black and white photographs (including industrial and commercial). .

15769 ■ **American Society of Media Photographers**
150 N 2nd St.
Philadelphia, PA 19106
Ph:(215)451-2767
Fax:(215)451-0880
Co. E-mail: mopsik@asmp.org
URL: http://www.asmp.org
Contact: Eugene Mopsik, Exec. Dir.
Description: Professional society of freelance photographers. Works to evolve trade practices for photographers in communications fields. Provides business information to photographers and their potential clients; promotes ethics and rights of members. Holds educational programs and seminars. Compiles statistics. **Publications:** *ASMP Bulletin* (quarterly).

15770 ■ **American Society of Photographers**
3120 N Argonne Dr.
Milwaukee, WI 53222
Ph:(414)871-6600
Co. E-mail: jonallyn@aol.com
URL: http://www.asofp.com
Contact: Jon Allyn, Exec. Dir.
Description: Photographers who have earned the degrees of Master of Photography, Photographic Craftsman, and Photographic Specialist through the Professional Photographers of America. Sponsors annual traveling exhibit of Masters' photographs and annual National Student Competition and Exhibit. .

15771 ■ **Canadian Association of Photographers and Illustrators in Communications–Association Canadienne de Photographes et Illustrateurs de Publicite**
720 Spadina Ave., Ste. 202
Toronto, ON, Canada M5S 2T9
Ph:(416)462-3677
Free: 888-252-2742
Fax:(416)929-5256
Co. E-mail: administrator@capic.org
URL: http://www.capic.org
Contact: Andre Cornellier, Chm.
Description: Photographers and illustrators employed in communications. Promotes professional and artistic advancement of members. Represents members' interests before industrial organizations; formulates standards of ethics and practice for members.

15772 ■ **Photographic Society of America**
3000 United Founders Blvd., Ste. 103
Oklahoma City, OK 73112-3940
Ph:(405)843-1437
Free: (866)772-4636
Fax:(405)843-1438
Co. E-mail: hq@psa-photo.org
URL: http://www.psa-photo.org
Contact: Fred Greene FPSA, Pres.
Description: Camera clubs; amateur, advanced amateur photographers. Sponsors competitions. Conducts slide and print contests, provides instruction slide sets, slide analysis, print portfolios, and other technical services. .

15773 ■ **Pictorial Photographers of America**
300 E 74th St., Apt. 35G
New York, NY 10021-3746
Ph:(212)243-0273
Co. E-mail: blsspks@aol.com
URL: http://www.ppa-photoclub.org
Contact: Kathryn Buck, Pres.
Description: Amateur and professional photographers. Aids members in perfecting their photographic techniques. Sponsors individual print and slide analysis, exhibitions, and field trips. **Publications:** Membership Directory (annual).

15774 ■ **Professional Photographers of America**
229 Peachtree St. NE, Ste. 2200
Atlanta, GA 30303-1608
Ph:(404)522-8600
Free: 800-786-6277
Co. E-mail: csc@ppa.com
URL: http://www.ppa.com
Contact: Louis Tonsmeire, Chm.
Description: Strives to create a global perspective that promotes business, creativity and excellence. Aims to be the leader in the dissemination of knowledge in the areas of professional business practices and creative image-making and to define and maintain the industry's standards of excellence. Represents portrait, wedding, commercial, industrial and specialized photographers. Sponsors PPA International School of Professional Photography. Maintains speakers' bureau. **Publications:** *Directory of Professional Photography* (annual); *PP of A Today* (monthly); *Professional Photographer* (monthly).

15775 ■ **Professional Women Photographers**
119 W 72nd St., No. 223
New York, NY 10023
Co. E-mail: info@pwponline.org
URL: http://www.pwponline.org
Contact: Maddi Ring, Pres.
Description: Women professional photographers; other interested individuals. Supports and promotes the work of women photographers through the sharing of ideas, resources, and experience. Provides educational forums to encourage artistic growth and photographic development. Stimulates public interest and support for the art of photography. **Publications:** *PWP Newsletter* (10/year).

15776 ■ **San Francisco Camerawork**
657 Mission St., 2nd Fl.
San Francisco, CA 94105-4104
Ph:(415)512-2020
Fax:(415)512-7109
Co. E-mail: info@sfcamerawork.org
URL: http://www.sfcamerawork.org
Contact: Stephen Vance, Pres.
Description: Represents nationally recognized artists' organization whose purpose is to stimulate dialogue, encourage inquiry, and communicate ideas about contemporary photography and related media through a variety of artistic and professional programs. **Publications:** *Camerawork: A Journal of Photographic Arts* (semiannual).

REFERENCE WORKS

15777 ■ *The Accidental Millionaire: How to Succeed in Life Without Really Trying*
Pub: BenBella Books
Ed: Gary Fong. **Released:** January 1, 2010. **Price:** $11.99 (GBP). **Description:** Gary Fong shares his memoirs about growing up in poverty in Los Angeles. Fong discusses how he revolutionized wedding photography and invented photography aids.

15778 ■ *American Society of Media Photographers—Membership Directory*
Pub: American Society of Media Photographers Inc.
Contact: Peter Skinner
Covers: 5,000 professional photographers for publications. **Entries Include:** Name, address, phone, fax, e-mail address, specialty.

15779 ■ "Boxing, Tech Giants Team to Help Teens" in *Hispanic Business* **(January-February 2009, pp. 44)**
Pub: Hispanic Business
Ed: Daniel Soussa. **Description:** Microsoft and Oscar de la Hoya are providing teens a head start for careers in the sciences by offering a competition in the categories of photography, short films or Web-based games.

15780 ■ "CPI Corporation Acquires Assets of Bella Pictures" in *Benzinga.com* **(January 28, 2011)**
Pub: Benzinga.com
Ed: Benzinga Staff. **Description:** CPI Corporation acquired assets of Bella Pictures Inc., a leading provider of branded wedding photography services. Details of the acquisition are explained.

15781 ■ *Films and Videos on Photography*
Pub: Program for Art on Film Inc.
Contact: Nadine Covert
Ed: Nadine Covert, Editor. **Price:** $15, individuals. **Covers:** Films and videos dealing with photography. **Entries Include:** Title, length, whether in color or black-and-white, format, release date, country in which produced, language, name of director, names of producing agency and distributors, synopsis, series note, review citations, and awards; distributors' name and address given in a separate list. **Arrangement:** Alphabetical. **Indexes:** Distributor.

15782 ■ *How to Market and Sell Your Art, Music, Photographs, and Handmade Crafts Online*
Pub: Atlantic Publishing Group, Inc.
Ed: Lee Rowley. **Released:** May 2008. **Price:** $24. 95. **Description:** The book provides all the basics for starting and running an online store selling arts, crafts, photography or music. There are more than 300 Websites listed to help anyone market and promote their arts and/or crafts online.

SOURCES OF SUPPLY

15783 ■ *PhotoSource Book*
Pub: PhotoSource International
Released: Bimonthly, and weekly. **Covers:** Magazine and book publishers, public relations firms, advertising and government agencies currently soliciting photographs for publication; 6-12 listings per issue. **Entries Include:** Company name, name of contact, address, phone, project title, and nature of photos sought. **Indexes:** CD-ROM editors.

TRADE PERIODICALS

15784 ■ *Applied Arts Magazine*
Pub: Applied Arts Inc.
Contact: Georges Haroutiun, Art Dir./Founder
E-mail: art@appliedartsmag.com
Ed: Peter Giffen, Editor, editor@appliedartsmag.com. **Released:** 6/yr. **Price:** $60; $100 two years; $75 U.S. and other countries; $150 two years U.S. & and other countries. **Description:** Visual communication arts magazine for designers, art directors, photographers, illustrators, and other professionals in related fields.

15785 ■ *ICG Magazine*
Pub: International Cinematographers Guild
Contact: David Geffner, Exec. Ed.
E-mail: davidgeffner@icgmagazine.com
Released: Monthly. **Description:** Trade magazine covering cinematography lighting techniques in film and video.

15786 ■ *Master Guide*
Pub: Apex Publications Inc.
Contact: Guy Langevin, Distribution Mngr.
Released: Annual. **Price:** $27 6 issues; $50 two years. **Description:** Trade magazine covering photography for photo retailers and distributors.

15787 ■ *The Photo Review*
Pub: The Photo Review
Contact: Stephen Perloff, Editor & Publisher
Released: Quarterly. **Price:** $45; $80 two years; $60 Canada and Mexico; $65 Europe, South America; $80 other countries. **Description:** Photography journal.

15788 ■ *PhotoDaily*
Pub: PhotoSource International
Ed: Deb Koehler, Editor, eds@photosource.com. **Released:** Daily, at 2:00p.m. **Price:** $35/Month; $375/Year. **Description:** Announces current photograph needs of book and magazine publishers, corporations, government, and advertising agencies. Provides specific information on deadlines and prices. Remarks: Available only via facsimile or e-mail.

15789 ■ *PhotoStock Notes/Plus*
Pub: PhotoSource International
Released: Monthly. **Price:** $95, individuals /month; $21.99, two years. **Description:** Provides information for stock photographers and suggests equipment and materials for photobuyers. Recurring features include news of educational opportunities, a calendar of events, and book reviews.

15790 ■ *PhotoStockNotes*
Pub: PhotoSource International
Contact: Angela Dober, Managing Editor
Released: Monthly. **Price:** $35 /year; $3.50, two years /monthly. **Description:** Features information on marketing of and trends involved with stock photos for such publications as textbooks, magazines, and encyclopedias.

15791 ■ *Professional Photographer*
Pub: Professional Photographers of America Inc.
Contact: Karisa Gilmer, managing editorager of Sales
E-mail: kgilmer@ppa.com
Released: Monthly. **Price:** $19.95 print (U.S.); $35.95 print (Canada). **Description:** Magazine for photographers.

15792 ■ *PSA Journal*
Pub: Photographic Society of America
Ed: Donna Brennan, Editor. **Released:** Monthly. **Description:** Photographic journal.

15793 ■ *PTN*
Pub: Cygnus Business Media Inc.
Contact: Ian Littauer, Publisher
E-mail: ian@imaginginfo.com
Ed: Diane Berkenfeld, Editor, diane.berkenfeld@cygnusb2b.com. **Released:** Monthly. **Description:** Magazine reporting photo industry products news.

15794 ■ *The Rangefinder*
Pub: The Rangefinder Publishing Company Inc.
Contact: Steve Sheanin, Publisher/CEO
Ed: Bill Hurter, Editor. **Released:** Monthly. **Price:** $18; Free to qualified subscribers. **Description:** Trade publication for portrait, commercial and wedding photographers.

15795 ■ *School Photographer–Photo Marketing Association International*
Pub: Professional School Photographers of America
Ed: Released: Enewsletter. **Price:** Included in membership. **Description:** Provides news and information on school photography. Recurring features include news of market research, a calendar of events, and news of educational opportunities.

15796 ■ *Shutterbug*
Pub: Source Interlink Media L.L.C.
Released: Monthly. **Price:** $17.95; $32.95 two years; $30.95 Canada; $32.95 other countries. **Description:** Photography magazine.

15797 ■ *Wedding Photography Monthly*
Pub: Wedding & Portrait Photographers International
Ed: Bill Hurter, Editor, bill_tr@earthlink.net. **Released:** Monthly. **Price:** Included in membership. **Description:** Features current topics and new techniques in professional wedding photography. Recurring features include spotlights of individual members and columns titled Legal Issues, New Products, and WPI Convention Updates.

VIDEOCASSETTES/AUDIOCASSETTES

15798 ■ *ART/New York, Vol. 11*
ART/new york
Inner-Tube Video
138 Prince St.
New York, NY 10012
Ph:(212)966-7446
Fax:(845)265-4302
Co. E-mail: artny@bestweb.net
URL: http://www.artnewyork.org
Released: 1982. **Description:** This tape covers photography exhibitions, including exhibits and interviews with Hans Namuth, Cindy Sherman, Robert Rauschenberg. Foreign language versions can be made available. **Availability:** VHS; 3/4U.

15799 ■ *The Classroom Collection, Vol. 2: Basic Daylight Exposure and Equivalent Exposures*
Crystal Productions
1812 Johns Dr.
Box 2159
Glenview, IL 60025-6519
Ph:(847)657-8144
Free: 800-255-8629
Fax:(847)657-8149
Co. E-mail: custserv@crystalproductions.com
URL: http://www.crystalproductions.com
Price: $24.95. **Description:** Part of a six-volume teaching aid for photography education, explains the concept of basic daylight exposure and alternative camera settings. **Availability:** VHS.

15800 ■ *The Classroom Collection, Vol. 3: Metering and Exposure Controls*
Crystal Productions
1812 Johns Dr.
Box 2159
Glenview, IL 60025-6519
Ph:(847)657-8144
Free: 800-255-8629
Fax:(847)657-8149
Co. E-mail: custserv@crystalproductions.com
URL: http://www.crystalproductions.com
Price: $24.95. **Description:** Part of a six-volume teaching aid for photography education, explains the function of a camera meter and how to determine the correct exposure according to the film being used. **Availability:** VHS.

15801 ■ *The Classroom Collection, Vol. 4: Advanced Camera Techniques*
Crystal Productions
1812 Johns Dr.
Box 2159
Glenview, IL 60025-6519
Ph:(847)657-8144
Free: 800-255-8629
Fax:(847)657-8149
Co. E-mail: custserv@crystalproductions.com
URL: http://www.crystalproductions.com
Price: $24.95. **Description:** Part of a six-volume teaching aid for photography education, explains a variety of lenses and camera support devices. **Availability:** VHS.

15802 ■ *The Classroom Collection, Vol. 5: Black and White Techniques*
Crystal Productions
1812 Johns Dr.
Box 2159
Glenview, IL 60025-6519
Ph:(847)657-8144
Free: 800-255-8629
Fax:(847)657-8149
Co. E-mail: custserv@crystalproductions.com
URL: http://www.crystalproductions.com
Price: $24.95. **Description:** Part of a six-volume teaching aid for photography education, explains black and white techniques including papers, filters, and enlargers. **Availability:** VHS.

15803 ■ *The Classroom Collection, Vol. 6: Careers in Photography*
Crystal Productions
1812 Johns Dr.
Box 2159
Glenview, IL 60025-6519
Ph:(847)657-8144
Free: 800-255-8629

Fax:(847)657-8149
Co. E-mail: custserv@crystalproductions.com
URL: http://www.crystalproductions.com
Price: $24.95. **Description:** Part of a six-volume teaching aid for photography education, explores career possibilities in the field of photography. **Availability:** VHS.

15804 ■ *Focus on Photography*
Encyclopedia Britannica
331 N. LaSalle St.
Chicago, IL 60654
Ph:(312)347-7159
Free: 800-323-1229
Fax:(312)294-2104
URL: http://www.britannica.com
Released: 1986. **Price:** $69.00. **Description:** Illustrates camera function and film development procedures, and profiles the history of photography. **Availability:** VHS; 3/4U; SVS.

15805 ■ *On Assignment: A Video Series for Photographers*
Blockbuster Entertainment Corp.
1201 Elm St.
Dallas, TX 75270
Ph:(214)854-3000
Free: 800-733-1939
Fax:(214)866-2250
URL: http://www.blockbuster.com
Released: 1990. **Price:** $179.95. **Description:** Aspiring photographers can learn all sorts of secrets about taking better pictures from these programs. **Availability:** VHS.

15806 ■ *Photography 101*
Crystal Productions
1812 Johns Dr.
Box 2159
Glenview, IL 60025-6519
Ph:(847)657-8144
Free: 800-255-8629
Fax:(847)657-8149
Co. E-mail: custserv@crystalproductions.com
URL: http://www.crystalproductions.com
Price: $39.95. **Description:** Teaching aid for photography education includes four programs: people, landscapes, animals, and travel. **Availability:** VHS.

TRADE SHOWS AND CONVENTIONS

15807 ■ Mid-East States Regional Print Competition and Exhibition and Trade Show
Professional Photographers of Ohio
37 W. Broad St. Ste. 480
Columbus, OH 43215
Ph:(614)228-6703
Fax:(614)241-2215
Co. E-mail: Carol@ppofohio.org
URL: http://www.ppofohio.org
Released: Annual. **Audience:** Professional photographers and photographic labs and studios. **Principal Exhibits:** Photographic equipment, supplies, and services; to include office equipment, computers and phone systems.

CONSULTANTS

15808 ■ Carlson Communications Corp.
276 W Main St., Ste. 200
Northborough, MA 01532
Ph:(508)393-9922
Free: 877-393-9922
Fax:(508)393-2118
Co. E-mail: info@carlcomm.com
URL: http://www.carlcomm.com
Contact: Susan F. Marden, Accountant
Scope: Offers consulting programs in photo journalism. Will help photographers and reporters develop a better eye, a creative approach, and an enthusiastic attitude and realize the importance of entering national, state and local photography competitions. Serves the private sector and government agencies. If your newsroom lacks direction and motivation, choose the proven winner, Carlson Communications. It is also a full-service marketing communications

company specializing in marketing residential and commercial real estate. offers a full range of marketing communications services, from strategic planning to complete creative design and production services, from project launch to sell-out.

15809 ■ F/22 Press
85 Lake St.
PO Box 141
Englewood, NJ 07631-4910
Ph:(201)568-6250
Contact: Robert Martin, Mgr
E-mail: bobnadler@aol.com
Scope: Offers expertise in the fields of personal computer applications, photography, publications and writing, and public relations. Serves private industries as well as government agencies. **Special Services:** DARKSTAR; TIMESTAR.

15810 ■ PhotoSource International
Pine Lake Farm, 1910 35th Rd.
Osceola, WI 54020-5602
Ph:(715)248-3800
Free: 800-624-0266
Fax:(715)248-7394
Co. E-mail: info@photosource.com
URL: http://www.photosource.com
Contact: Rohn Engh, Director
E-mail: mike@atsphotosource.com
Scope: Offers counsel in the general field of public relations including brochure development, self-promotion, seminars, and audio-visual presentations. Particular expertise in advising photo editors and photo illustrators on photo acquisition, and on advising photographers on placing or selling their pictures. **Publications:** "PhotoSourceBOOK"; "PhotoLETTER"; "PhotoStockNOTES"; "PhotoDAILY"; "PhotoStockNotes/Plus". **Seminars:** How to Sell Your Stock Photos. **Special Services:** PhotoSourceBANK; PhotoSourceFOLIO.

FRANCHISES AND BUSINESS OPPORTUNITIES

15811 ■ A Day to Cherish Wedding Videos
10174 S Memorial Dr.
South Jordan, UT 84095
Ph:(801)253-2450
No. of Franchise Units: 2. **No. of Company-Owned Units:** 1. **Founded:** 2004. **Franchised:** 2004. **Description:** Wedding and special occasion videos. **Equity Capital Needed:** $33,400-$39,400 total investment. **Franchise Fee:** $17,500. **Royalty Fee:** 6%. **Financial Assistance:** No. **Training:** Provides 6 days at headquarters and 2 days at franchisee's location with ongoing support.

15812 ■ EagleShotz
6834 Grand Marina Cir.
Gainesville, GA 30506
Free: 888-553-2453
No. of Franchise Units: 4. **Founded:** 2006. **Franchised:** 2007. **Description:** Event photography specializing in corporate, charity and celebrity golf events. **Equity Capital Needed:** $34,950. **Franchise Fee:** $34,950. **Royalty Fee:** 6%. **Financial Assistance:** No.

15813 ■ Kids At Heart Photography
1631 S Olden Ave.
Hamilton, NJ 08610
Ph:(609)888-0600
Free: 800-438-0083
Fax:(609)888-3993
No. of Franchise Units: 6. **No. of Company-Owned Units:** 5. **Founded:** 1992. **Franchised:** 2006. **Description:** School & sports photography. **Equity Capital Needed:** $50,000-$75,000. **Franchise Fee:** $35,000. **Financial Assistance:** No. **Training:** Yes.

15814 ■ Portraitefx Franchising Corp.
8206-1200 Providence Rd.
Charlotte, NC 28277-9708
Free: 800-765-7561

Fax:(206)350-4534
Co. E-mail: leads@portraitefx.com
URL: http://www.portraitefx.com
No. of Franchise Units: 58. **Founded:** 2006. **Franchised:** 2006. **Description:** Digital photography services for schools, day cares, sports, families and more. **Equity Capital Needed:** $25,000-$30,000. **Franchise Fee:** $16,750. **Financial Assistance:** Third party financing available. **Training:** In-house and on location training included.

15815 ■ Print Three Franchising Corp.
8400 Jane St. Bldg. D, Ste. 300
Concord, ON, Canada L4K 4L8
Ph:(905)669-8895
Free: 800-335-5918
Fax:(905)669-0712
Co. E-mail: andrew@printthree.com
URL: http://www.printthree.com
No. of Franchise Units: 51. **Founded:** 1970. **Franchised:** 1981. **Description:** Business service franchise focusing on the increasing demand for digital imaging. Franchise offers complete digital reproduction, design, finishing and fulfillment. The only print franchise having a fully integrated web-based ordering system. Provides total imaging solutions for the corporate community. **Equity Capital Needed:** $200,000. **Franchise Fee:** $70,000. **Training:** Yes.

15816 ■ TSS Photography
B & H Products, Inc.
2150 Boggs Rd., Ste. 200
Duluth, GA 30096
Ph:(678)740-0800
Free: 800-321-9127
Fax:(678)740-0808
Co. E-mail: frandev@office.sports-section.com
URL: http://www.Sports-Section.com
No. of Franchise Units: 230. **Founded:** 1983. **Franchised:** 1984. **Description:** Youth and sports photography. **Equity Capital Needed:** $45,000 minimum liquid capital. **Franchise Fee:** $35,000 and up. **Financial Assistance:** Third party financing. **Training:** Yes.

COMPUTERIZED DATABASES

15817 ■ Earthshots
Digital Wisdom Inc.
300 Jeanette Dr.
PO Box 2070
Tappahannock, VA 22560-2070
Ph:(804)443-9000
Free: 800-800-8560
Fax:(804)443-3632
URL: http://www.digiwis.com
Description: Contains more than 250 high quality and high resolution images of the world in a Bitmap (JPEG) format. Provides full color relief maps of the Earth's continents and ocean floors. Includes material particularly suitable for advertising multimedia, desk-top publishing, animation, and other cartographic clip art projects. **Availability:** CD-ROM: Digital Wisdom Inc. **Type:** Image.

15818 ■ *Photography Collections Online*
George Eastman House International Museum of Photography and Film
George Eastman House
900 East Ave.
Rochester, NY 14607
Ph:(585)271-3361
Fax:(585)271-3970
URL: http://www.eastmanhouse.org
Description: Provides information on more than 80,000 photographers and photographic manufacturers and includes holdings information for their photographic works held by 630 U.S. museum, library, university, and historical society collections. For each photographer, provides name variants, dates and places of birth and death, geographic focus of activity, affiliations, and exhibition histories for contemporary and historical photographers. Companion files include cataloging records for 150,000 photographs in the George Eastman House Collection as well as documentation on 5000 photographic exhibitions since the 1840s. **Availability:** Online: George Eastman House International Museum of Photography and Film. **Type:** Directory; Bibliographic.

LIBRARIES

15819 ■ Art Institute of Philadelphia Library
1610 Chestnut St.
Philadelphia, PA 19103
Ph:(215)405-6402
Co. E-mail: rschachter@aii.edu
URL: http://rs185.aisites.com
Contact: Ruth Schachter, Dir.
Scope: Visual communications, interior design, industrial design, animation, fashion marketing, fashion design, visual merchandising, photography, website design, multimedia. **Services:** Interlibrary loan; Library not open to the public (circulation services provided for students and faculty). **Holdings:** 31,000 volumes; 2000 videocassettes; audiocassettes. **Subscriptions:** 170 print subscriptions and other serials.

15820 ■ Brooks Institute Library
27 E. Cota St.
Santa Barbara, CA 93101
Ph:(805)966-3888
URL: http://www.brooks.edu/aboutus/jefferson.asp
Scope: Photography. **Services:** Copying; Library open to the public for reference use only. **Holdings:** 6953 books; 25,000 unbound periodicals; 2500 pamphlets; 200 videotapes. **Subscriptions:** 92 journals and other serials.

15821 ■ Canadian Museum of Contemporary Photography–Research Resources
380 Sussex Dr.
PO Box 427, Sta. A
Ottawa, ON, Canada K1N 9N4
Ph:(613)990-1985
Fax:(613)993-4385
Co. E-mail: mwadding@gallery.ca
URL: http://cmcp.gallery.ca/english/default.jsp
Contact: Murray Waddington, Chf.
Scope: Canadian photography - contemporary, historical. **Services:** CMCP; access to holdings through the Library of the National Gallery of Canada. **Holdings:** 4000 books.

15822 ■ Canadian Society of Scientific Photography Library
330 Dixon Rd., No. 1401
Etobicoke, ON, Canada M9R 1S9
Ph:(416)247-5640
Contact: J.D. Dunn, Exec.Dir.
Scope: Scientific photography. **Services:** Library open to the public by appointment. **Holdings:** 3000 books; films; slides; videotapes.

15823 ■ Drury University–F.W. Olin Library–Art & Architecture Slide Library (900 N)
900 N. Benton Ave.
Springfield, MO 65802
Ph:(417)873-7337
Fax:(417)873-7432
Co. E-mail: jtygart@drury.edu
URL: http://library.drury.edu/library/index.php/
    services-info/slide-library/
Contact: Jacqueline Tygart, Slide Cur.
Scope: Architecture, art, photography, textiles, ceramics. **Services:** Library open to the public. **Holdings:** 60,000 35mm slides.

15824 ■ Ringling College of Art and Design–Verman Kimbrough Memorial Library
2700 N. Tamiami Trail
Sarasota, FL 34234
Ph:(941)359-7587
Fax:(941)359-7632
Co. E-mail: library@ringling.edu
URL: http://www.ringling.edu
Contact: Kathleen List, Dir., Lib.Svcs.
Scope: Art history, interior design, graphic design, computer animation, photography, architecture, fine arts, decorative arts, illustration. **Services:** Interlibrary loan; copying; Library open to artists and researchers. **Holdings:** 49,000 books; 110,000 art slides; 34 16mm films; 3000 videocassettes and DVDs. **Subscriptions:** 320 journals and other serials.

15825 ■ San Francisco Public Library–Bernard Osher Foundation–Art, Music & Recreation Center (100 L)
100 Larkin St.
San Francisco, CA 94102
Ph:(415)557-4525
Fax:(415)557-4524
Co. E-mail: info@sfpl.org
URL: http://www.sfpl.org/librarylocations/main/art/art.
    htm
Contact: Mark Hall, Fl.Mgr.
Scope: Arts - visual, graphic; sports and recreation; photography; architecture; arts and crafts; performing arts; music - orchestral, chamber, opera, popular, folk, jazz. **Services:** Center open to the public. **Holdings:** Books; serials; scores.

15826 ■ School of Visual Arts–Visual Arts Library
380 2nd Ave., 22nd St., 2nd Fl.
New York, NY 10010-3994
Ph:(212)592-2660
Fax:(212)592-2655
Co. E-mail: rlobe@sva.edu
URL: http://www.schoolofvisualarts.edu/sr/index.
    jsp?sid0=258&sid1=290
Contact: Robert Lobe, Lib.Dir.
Scope: Fine arts, graphic design, advertising, photography, film, computer graphics, humanities. **Services:** Copying; Library open to students, faculty, staff, and alumni (METRO passes honored). **Holdings:** 70,000 books and bound periodical volumes; 2000 pamphlets; 270,000 pictures; 152,000 slides. **Subscriptions:** 300 journals and other serials.

15827 ■ SF Camerawork Reference Library
657 Mission St., 2nd Fl.
San Francisco, CA 94105-4104
Ph:(415)512-2020
Fax:(415)512-7109
Co. E-mail: sfcamera@sfcamerawork.org
URL: http://www.sfcamerawork.org
Scope: Photography, contemporary art, art theory and criticism. **Holdings:** 3500 volumes; 700 bound periodical volumes.

15828 ■ Smithsonian Institution–Smithsonian American Art Museum–National Portrait Gallery Library (750 9)
750 9th St. NW, Ste. 2100
PO Box 37012
Washington, DC 20013-7012
Ph:(202)633-8230
Fax:(202)275-1929
Co. E-mail: chinc@si.edu
URL: http://www.sil.si.edu/libraries/aapg
Contact: Cecilia H. Chin, Chf.Libn.
Scope: American painting, sculpture, graphic arts, biography, history, photography; portraiture; contemporary art. **Services:** Interlibrary loan; copying; Library open to the public for reference use only. **Holdings:** 180,000 books; exhibitions catalogs; catalogues raisonnes; serials; dissertations; artists' books; ephemeral materials; auction catalogs; scrapbooks; microforms; CD-ROMs.

15829 ■ Springfield Art Museum–Art Reference Library
1111 E. Brookside Dr.
Springfield, MO 65807
Ph:(417)837-5700
Fax:(417)837-5704
Co. E-mail: artmuseum@springfieldmo.gov
URL: http://www.springfieldmogov.org/egov/art
Contact: Susan Potter, Libn.
Scope: Art history, painting, sculpture, graphics, decorative arts, photography. **Services:** Library open to the public. **Holdings:** 8000 volumes; periodicals; catalogs; AV materials. **Subscriptions:** 65 journals and other serials.

15830 ■ Walker Art Center–Staff Reference Library
1750 Hennepin Ave.
Vineland Pl.
Minneapolis, MN 55403
Ph:(612)375-7680
Co. E-mail: rosemary.furtak@walkerart.org
URL: http://www.walkerart.org
Contact: Rosemary Furtak, Libn.
Scope: Contemporary art, art history, architecture, design, film, artists' books, graphics, photography, painting, sculpture. **Services:** Copying; Internet searches; Library open to the public by appointment. **Holdings:** 35,000 books; 550 bound periodical volumes; vertical files. **Subscriptions:** 140 journals.

ASSOCIATIONS AND OTHER ORGANIZATIONS

15831 ■ Photographic Society of America
3000 United Founders Blvd., Ste. 103
Oklahoma City, OK 73112-3940
Ph:(405)843-1437
Free: (866)772-4636
Fax:(405)843-1438
Co. E-mail: hq@psa-photo.org
URL: http://www.psa-photo.org
Contact: Fred Greene FPSA, Pres.
Description: Camera clubs; amateur, advanced amateur photographers. Sponsors competitions. Conducts slide and print contests, provides instruction slide sets, slide analysis, print portfolios, and other technical services. .

15832 ■ Professional Photographers of America
229 Peachtree St. NE, Ste. 2200
Atlanta, GA 30303-1608
Ph:(404)522-8600
Free: 800-786-6277
Co. E-mail: csc@ppa.com
URL: http://www.ppa.com
Contact: Louis Tonsmeire, Chm.
Description: Strives to create a global perspective that promotes business, creativity and excellence. Aims to be the leader in the dissemination of knowledge in the areas of professional business practices and creative image-making and to define and maintain the industry's standards of excellence. Represents portrait, wedding, commercial, industrial and specialized photographers. Sponsors PPA International School of Professional Photography. Maintains speakers' bureau. **Publications:** *Directory of Professional Photography* (annual); *PP of A Today* (monthly); *Professional Photographer* (monthly).

15833 ■ Professional School Photographers Association International
11000 Viking Dr., 5th Fl.
Eden Prairie, MN 55344
Ph:(952)826-4278
Fax:(952)826-4373
URL: http://www.pmai.org/pspa
Contact: Mark Schoenrock, Dir.
Description: A section of the Photo Marketing Association International. Firms engaged in the photographing and/or processing of school photographs. Purposes are: to encourage the exchange of production ideas and economies; to cooperate in the overall promotion of photography; to work for better relations and understanding with schools; to act as a group in making manufacturers of sensitized goods and photographic equipment aware of the specialized needs of school photography; to maintain a close watch on any legislation that may affect school photography; to promote career possibilities and personnel training and recruitment for school photography; to foster the well-being of the member firms by providing some of the advantages of a large-scale operation. .

15834 ■ San Francisco Camerawork
657 Mission St., 2nd Fl.
San Francisco, CA 94105-4104
Ph:(415)512-2020
Fax:(415)512-7109
Co. E-mail: info@sfcamerawork.org
URL: http://www.sfcamerawork.org
Contact: Stephen Vance, Pres.
Description: Represents nationally recognized artists' organization whose purpose is to stimulate dialogue, encourage inquiry, and communicate ideas about contemporary photography and related media through a variety of artistic and professional programs. **Publications:** *Camerawork: A Journal of Photographic Arts* (semiannual).

15835 ■ Wedding and Portrait Photographers International
6059 Bristol Pkwy., Ste. 100
Culver City, CA 90230
Ph:(310)846-4770
Fax:(310)846-5995
URL: http://www.wppionline.com
Contact: Steven Sheanin, Pres./CEO
Description: Represents wedding portrait and digital photographers and photographers employed at general photography studios. Promotes high artistic and technical standards in wedding photography. Serves as a forum for the exchange of technical knowledge and experience; makes available the expertise of top professionals in the field of photographic arts and technology, advertising, sales promotion, marketing, public relations, accounting, business management, tax, and profit planning. Members are offered the opportunity to purchase special products and services. **Publications:** *Marketing and Technical Manual* (quarterly); *Rangefinder*; *Wedding Photographer* (monthly); *WPPI Photography Monthly* (monthly).

DIRECTORIES OF EDUCATIONAL PROGRAMS

15836 ■ *Directory of Private Accredited Career Schools and Colleges of Technology*
Pub: Accrediting Commission of Career Schools and Colleges of Technology
Contact: Michale S. McComis, Exec. Dir.
Released: On web page. **Price:** Free. **Description:** Covers 3900 accredited post-secondary programs that provide training programs in business, trade, and technical fields, including various small business endeavors. Entries offer school name, address, phone, description of courses, job placement assistance, and requirements for admission. Arrangement is alphabetical.

REFERENCE WORKS

15837 ■ *The Accidental Millionaire: How to Succeed in Life Without Really Trying*
Pub: BenBella Books
Ed: Gary Fong. **Released:** January 1, 2010. **Price:** $11.99 (GBP). **Description:** Gary Fong shares his memoirs about growing up in poverty in Los Angeles. Fong discusses how he revolutionized wedding photography and invented photography aids.

15838 ■ "CPI Corporation Acquires Assets of Bella Pictures" in *Benzinga.com* (January 28, 2011)
Pub: Benzinga.com
Ed: Benzinga Staff. **Description:** CPI Corporation acquired assets of Bella Pictures Inc., a leading provider of branded wedding photography services. Details of the acquisition are explained.

15839 ■ *How to Market and Sell Your Art, Music, Photographs, and Handmade Crafts Online*
Pub: Atlantic Publishing Group, Inc.
Ed: Lee Rowley. **Released:** May 2008. **Price:** $24.95. **Description:** The book provides all the basics for starting and running an online store selling arts, crafts, photography or music. There are more than 300 Websites listed to help anyone market and promote their arts and/or crafts online.

STATISTICAL SOURCES

15840 ■ *RMA Annual Statement Studies*
Pub: Robert Morris Associates (RMA)
Released: Annual. **Price:** $175.00 2006-07 edition, $105.00. **Description:** Contains composite balance sheets and income statements for more than 360 industries, including the accounting, auditing, and bookkeeping industries. Also contains five years of comparative historical data for discerning trends. Includes 16 commonly used ratios, computed for most of the size groupings for nearly every industry.

TRADE PERIODICALS

15841 ■ *ASMP Bulletin*
Pub: American Society of Media Photographers Inc.
Contact: Peter Skinner
Ed: Peter Skinner, Editor, skinner@asmp.org. **Released:** Quarterly, 10/year. **Price:** Included in membership. **Description:** Features articles on professional photography, copyright laws, and photographic techniques. Recurring features include interviews and news of research. For ASMP members only.

15842 ■ *Light and Shade*
Pub: Pictorial Photographers of America
Ed: Sylvia Mavis, Editor. **Released:** Monthly. **Price:** Included in membership. **Description:** Designed to help amateur and professional photographers perfect their photographic techniques. Carries how-to articles and information on photography equipment. Recurring features include organizational news, announcements of educational opportunities, and book reviews.

15843 ■ *Photo Techniques*
Pub: Preston Publications
Contact: Tinsley Preston, Publisher
E-mail: tpreston@prestonpub.com
Ed: Paul Schranz, Editor, pschranz@phototechmag.com. **Released:** Bimonthly. **Price:** $29.99; $49.99 two years; $69.99 3 years. **Description:** Consumer photography magazine.

15844 ■ *PhotoDaily*
Pub: PhotoSource International
Ed: Deb Koehler, Editor, eds@photosource.com. Released: Daily, at 2:00p.m. Price: $35/Month; $375/Year. Description: Announces current photograph needs of book and magazine publishers, corporations, government, and advertising agencies. Provides specific information on deadlines and prices. Remarks: Available only via facsimile or e-mail.

15845 ■ *The Polar Bear ROARS*
Pub: Polar Bear Alumni Association (PBAA)
Contact: Leeann Faust
Ed: Leeann Faust, Editor, lfaust@columbus.rr.com. Released: Quarterly. Price: Included in membership; $8 /year. Description: Provides news of current events regarding reunion information, memories of alumni, history of school and articles about alumni and faculty. Recurring features include reports of reunions.

15846 ■ *Popular Photography and Imaging*
Pub: Hachette Filipacchi Media U.S. Inc.
Ed: John Owens, Editor. Released: Monthly. Price: $24 two years; $14. Description: Photography magazine.

15847 ■ *Professional Photographer*
Pub: Professional Photographers of America Inc.
Contact: Karisa Gilmer, managing editorager of Sales
E-mail: kgilmer@ppa.com
Released: Monthly. Price: $19.95 print (U.S.); $35.95 print (Canada). Description: Magazine for photographers.

15848 ■ *PSA Journal*
Pub: Photographic Society of America
Ed: Donna Brennan, Editor. Released: Monthly. Description: Photographic journal.

15849 ■ *The Rangefinder*
Pub: The Rangefinder Publishing Company Inc.
Contact: Steve Sheanin, Publisher/CEO
Ed: Bill Hurter, Editor. Released: Monthly. Price: $18; Free to qualified subscribers. Description: Trade publication for portrait, commercial and wedding photographers.

15850 ■ *School Photographer–Photo Marketing Association International*
Pub: Professional School Photographers of America
Ed: Released: Enewsletter. Price: Included in membership. Description: Provides news and information on school photography. Recurring features include news of market research, a calendar of events, and news of educational opportunities.

15851 ■ *Shutterbug*
Pub: Source Interlink Media L.L.C.
Released: Monthly. Price: $17.95; $32.95 two years; $30.95 Canada; $32.95 other countries. Description: Photography magazine.

15852 ■ *Wedding Photography Monthly*
Pub: Wedding & Portrait Photographers International
Ed: Bill Hurter, Editor, bill_tr@earthlink.net. Released: Monthly. Price: Included in membership. Description: Features current topics and new techniques in professional wedding photography. Recurring features include spotlights of individual members and columns titled Legal Issues, New Products, and WPI Convention Updates.

VIDEOCASSETTES/ AUDIOCASSETTES

15853 ■ *Focus on Photography*
Encyclopedia Britannica
331 N. LaSalle St.
Chicago, IL 60654
Ph:(312)347-7159
Free: 800-323-1229
Fax:(312)294-2104
URL: http://www.britannica.com
Released: 1986. Price: $69.00. Description: Illustrates camera function and film development procedures, and profiles the history of photography. Availability: VHS; 3/4U; SVS.

15854 ■ *Photography*
Crystal Productions
1812 Johns Dr.
Box 2159
Glenview, IL 60025-6519
Ph:(847)657-8144
Free: 800-255-8629
Fax:(847)657-8149
Co. E-mail: custserv@crystalproductions.com
URL: http://www.crystalproductions.com
Released: 1991. Price: $59.95. Description: A two-part course in single-lens reflex camera use, including the mechanics of the camera, special effects for color and black & white film, and methods for developing and printing pictures. Availability: VHS.

FRANCHISES AND BUSINESS OPPORTUNITIES

15855 ■ **Glamour Shots Licensing Inc.**
1300 Metropolitan Ave.
Oklahoma City, OK 73108
Ph:(405)947-8747
Free: 800-336-4550
Fax:(405)951-7343
No. of Franchise Units: 100. No. of Company-Owned Units: 2. Founded: 1988. Franchised: 1992. Description: High fashion photography studio. Equity Capital Needed: $25,000 cash, plus financial investment, ranging from $38,500-$86,000. Franchise Fee: $20,000 U.S. Financial Assistance: Yes. Training: Yes.

15856 ■ **Images 4 Kids**
12200 Ford Rd., Ste. 108
Dallas, TX 75234
Ph:(972)484-5437
Fax:(972)484-0093
URL: http://www.images4kids.com
No. of Franchise Units: 67. Founded: 1983. Franchised: 2004. Description: Portraits of kids. Equity Capital Needed: $53,600-$77,100. Franchise Fee: $29,900. Royalty Fee: None. Financial Assistance: Limited third party financial assistance available. Training: Provides 4 days training at corporate headquarters.

15857 ■ **Lil' Angels Photography**
6831 Crumpler Blvd., Ste. 101
Olive Branch, MS 38654
Ph:(901)682-9566
Free: 800-358-9101
Fax:(901)682-2018
URL: http://www.angelsus.com
No. of Franchise Units: 78. Founded: 1996. Franchised: 1998. Description: Photo studio with professional studio equipments and techniques. Equity Capital Needed: $30,700-$35,200. Franchise Fee: $17,000. Royalty Fee: Varies. Financial Assistance: Limited in-house assistance available. Training: 6 days provided at corporate headquarters, 2 days of onsite, and regional and annual convention included.

15858 ■ **Lil'Pals Pet Photography**
6831 Crumpler Blvd., Ste. 101
Olive Branch, MS 38654
Ph:(901)682-9566
Free: 800-358-9101
Fax:(901)682-2018
No. of Franchise Units: 8. Founded: 2004. Franchised: 2005. Description: Pet photography. Equity Capital Needed: $50,000-$102,000. Franchise Fee: $10,000. Financial Assistance: No. Training: Yes.

15859 ■ **PoGoPix Studios**
4916 139th Ave. SE, Unit 218
Calgary, AB, Canada T2Z 0G4
Ph:(403)269-6790
Fax:(403)263-0849
Co. E-mail: southtrail@pogopix.ca
URL: http://www.pogopixstudios.com
Founded: 2000. Franchised: 2005. Description: Children's photography.

15860 ■ **TSS Photography**
B & H Products, Inc.
2150 Boggs Rd., Ste. 200
Duluth, GA 30096
Ph:(678)740-0800
Free: 800-321-9127
Fax:(678)740-0808
Co. E-mail: frandev@office.sports-section.com
URL: http://www.Sports-Section.com
No. of Franchise Units: 230. Founded: 1983. Franchised: 1984. Description: Youth and sports photography. Equity Capital Needed: $45,000 minimum liquid capital. Franchise Fee: $35,000 and up. Financial Assistance: Third party financing. Training: Yes.

COMPUTERIZED DATABASES

15861 ■ *Earthshots*
Digital Wisdom Inc.
300 Jeanette Dr.
PO Box 2070
Tappahannock, VA 22560-2070
Ph:(804)443-9000
Free: 800-800-8560
Fax:(804)443-3632
URL: http://www.digiwis.com
Description: Contains more than 250 high quality and high resolution images of the world in a Bitmap (JPEG) format. Provides full color relief maps of the Earth's continents and ocean floors. Includes material particularly suitable for advertising multimedia, desk-top publishing, animation, and other cartographic clip art projects. Availability: CD-ROM: Digital Wisdom Inc. Type: Image.

LIBRARIES

15862 ■ **Brooks Institute Library**
27 E. Cota St.
Santa Barbara, CA 93101
Ph:(805)966-3888
URL: http://www.brooks.edu/aboutus/jefferson.asp
Scope: Photography. Services: Copying; Library open to the public for reference use only. Holdings: 6953 books; 25,000 unbound periodicals; 2500 pamphlets; 200 videotapes. Subscriptions: 92 journals and other serials.

15863 ■ **George Eastman House–International Museum of Photography & Film–Richard and Ronay Menschel Library (900 E)**
900 East Ave.
Rochester, NY 14607
Ph:(585)271-3361, x-313
Fax:(585)271-3970
URL: http://www.eastmanhouse.org/collections/library.php
Contact: Rachel Stuhlman, Libn.
Scope: Photography and cinematography - history, science, aesthetics. Services: Interlibrary loan; copying; mail reference; Library open to the public by appointment. Holdings: 57,000 books; 15,000 bound periodical volumes; 25 VF drawers of history of photography and current activities; letters and manuscripts; microfilm; microfiche. Subscriptions: 316 journals and other serials.

15864 ■ **International Center of Photography Library**
1114 Ave. of the Americas
New York, NY 10036
Ph:(212)857-0004
Fax:(212)857-0091
Co. E-mail: library@icp.org
Contact: Deirdre Donohue, Libn.
Scope: Photography, critical writing on photography. Services: Copying; Center open to the public by appointment. Holdings: 15,000 books and unbound volumes of photography periodicals and journals; 2500 vertical files on photographers and photo subjects with biographical data from primary materials; critical essays. Subscriptions: 75 journals and other serials.

15865 ■ **University of Arizona–Center for Creative Photography Library**
1030 N. Olive Rd.
PO Box 210103
Tucson, AZ 85721-0103
Ph:(520)621-1331
Fax:(520)621-9444
Co. E-mail: diazj@u.library.arizona.edu
URL: http://www.creativephotography.org/library/
Contact: Bob Diaz, Art and Photo.Libn.

Scope: Photography. **Services:** Interlibrary loan; copying; Center open to the public. **Holdings:** 26,000 titles including several thousand rare books; 3000 bound periodical volumes; 600 reels of microfilm; 40 feet of biographical files; 600 oral history videotapes. **Subscriptions:** 100 journals and other serials.

START-UP INFORMATION

15866 ■ *Becoming a Personal Trainer for Dummies*
Pub: John Wiley & Sons, Incorporated
Ed: Melyssa Michael, Linda Formichelli. **Released:** October 2004. **Price:** $19.99 (US), $25.99 (Canadian). **Description:** Legal and tax issues involved in starting and running a personal trainer firm. The book offers suggestions for incorporating massage and nutritional services.

15867 ■ "Former Boxer Fits Into New Business Role" in *Houston Business Journal* (Vol. 40, January 8, 2010, No. 35, pp. 1)
Pub: American City Business Journals
Ed: Greg Barr. **Description:** Lou Savarese explains how the lessons he learned as a professional boxer help him to manage his new business venture, a gym called Savarese Fight Gym. Customers who desire to learn boxing and to stay fit like a boxer comprise the fitness center's target market.

15868 ■ "Land Swap Key to Ending Royal Oak Project Impasse" in *Crain's Detroit Business* (Vol. 25, June 8, 2009, No. 23, pp. 20)
Pub: Crain Communications Inc. - Detroit
Ed: Chad Halcom. **Description:** Details of the new construction of the LA Fitness health club near Woodward and Washington Avenues in Royal Oak, Michigan are discussed.

15869 ■ "Pump Up the Profits" in *Small Business Opportunities* (Summer 2010)
Pub: Harris Publications Inc.
Description: New fitness franchise offers customized personal training at bargain rates. Profile of Alan Katz, president of EduFit, a concept that allows small groups of people to workout with customized training is provided.

15870 ■ "Riches In Recreation" in *Small Business Opportunities* (March 2011)
Pub: Harris Publications Inc.
Description: Making money is child's play thanks to new gym concept that makes parents and franchisors happy. Profile of Great Play, the franchised children's gym is provided.

ASSOCIATIONS AND OTHER ORGANIZATIONS

15871 ■ American Alliance for Health, Physical Education, Recreation and Dance
1900 Association Dr.
Reston, VA 20191-1598
Ph:(703)476-3400
Free: 800-213-7193
Fax:(703)476-9527
Co. E-mail: membership@aahperd.org
URL: http://www.aahperd.org
Contact: E. Paul Roetert, CEO
Description: Students and educators in physical education, dance, health, athletics, safety education, recreation, and outdoor education. Works to improve its fields of education at all levels through such services as consultation, periodicals and special publications, leadership development, determination of standards, and research. Sponsors placement service. **Publications:** *Health Education* (bimonthly).

15872 ■ American Council on Exercise
4851 Paramount Dr.
San Diego, CA 92123
Ph:(858)576-6500
Free: 888-825-3636
Fax:(858)576-6564
Co. E-mail: support@acefitness.org
URL: http://www.acefitness.org
Contact: Scott Goudeseune, Pres./CEO
Description: Promotes the benefits of physical activity and protects consumers against unsafe and ineffective fitness products and instruction. Sponsors university-based exercise science research and testing that targets fitness products and trends. Sets standards for fitness professionals. **Publications:** *ACE Certified News* (bimonthly); *ACE Fitness Matters* (bimonthly).

15873 ■ American Running Association
4405 East-West Hwy., Ste. 405
Bethesda, MD 20814
Free: 800-776-2732
Fax:(301)913-9520
Co. E-mail: run@americanrunning.org
URL: http://www.americanrunning.org
Contact: David Watt, Exec. Dir.
Description: Represents individual runners, exercise enthusiasts, and sports medicine professionals. Promotes running and other aerobic activities; fosters the preventive maintenance concept in health preservation. Serves as a repository for data on running and fitness. Reports on research in exercise physiology and in techniques of increasing total human performance and maintaining physical fitness. Maintains speakers' bureau. Conducts educational programs and charitable activities. **Publications:** *Running and FitNews* (bimonthly).

15874 ■ American Sports Builders Association
8480 Baltimore National Pike, No. 307
Ellicott City, MD 21043
Ph:(410)730-9595
Free: (866)501-2722
Fax:(410)730-8833
Co. E-mail: info@sportsbuilders.org
URL: http://sportsbuilders.org
Contact: Sam Fisher, Chm.
Description: Contractors who install running tracks, synthetic turf fields, tennis courts and indoor sports surfaces; manufacturers who supply basic materials for construction; accessory suppliers, designers, architects, and consultants of facilities. Provides guidelines for tennis court construction, running track construction, fencing, synthetic turf field construction and lighting. Offers certification and awards programs. **Publications:** *Buyers Guide for Tennis Court Construction* (periodic); *Running Tracks: A Construction and Maintenance Manual* (semiannual); *Tennis and Track Construction Guidelines* (periodic);Membership Directory (annual).

15875 ■ Aquatic Exercise Association
PO Box 1609
Nokomis, FL 34274-1609
Ph:(941)486-8600
Free: 888-232-9283
Fax:(941)486-8820
Co. E-mail: info@aeawave.com
URL: http://www.aeawave.com
Contact: Angie Proctor, Exec. Dir.
Description: Aquatic fitness instructors and therapists, pool and club owners, recreation departments, and manufacturers of pool products and services. Fosters members' professional development; serves as a resource center for services and products related to the aquatic fitness and therapy industries. Compiles and disseminates information through educational events and networking opportunities; offers certification to aquatic exercise instructors. Conducts educational programs. **Publications:** *AKWA Magazine* (bimonthly); *Aquatic Therapy and Fitness Research Journal* (semiannual).

15876 ■ Canadian Fitness and Lifestyle Research Institute–Institut Canadien de la Recherche sur la Condition Physique et le Mode de Vie
201-185 Somerset St. W
Ottawa, ON, Canada K2P 0J2
Ph:(613)233-5528
Fax:(613)233-5536
Co. E-mail: info@cflri.ca
URL: http://www.cflri.ca
Contact: Ms. Cora Lynn Craig
Description: Conducts research on physical activities in Canada and distributes information about physical activity. **Publications:** *Physical Activity Monitor* (annual); *The Research File* (quarterly).

15877 ■ Exercise Safety Association
PO Box 547916
Orlando, FL 32854-7916
Ph:(407)246-5090
Co. E-mail: askesa@aol.com
URL: http://www.exercisesafety.com
Description: Fitness instructors, personal trainers, health spas, YMCAs, community recreation departments, and hospital wellness programs. Purposes are: to improve the qualifications of exercise instructors; to train instructors to develop safe exercise programs that will help people avoid injury while exercising; to prepare instructors for national certification. Offers training in aerobics and exercise and on the physiological aspects of exercise. Conducts exercise safety and research programs. Sponsors charitable program; maintains speakers' bureau. Offers instructor placement services. **Publications:** *ESA Member Directory* (annual); *Exercise Safety Association Newsletter* (bimonthly).

15878 ■ IDEA Health and Fitness Association
10455 Pacific Center Ct.
San Diego, CA 92121
Ph:(858)535-8979
Free: 800-999-IDEA
Fax:(858)535-8234
Co. E-mail: contact@ideafit.com
URL: http://www.ideafit.com
Contact: Kathie Davis, Exec. Dir.
Description: Provides continuing education for fitness professionals including; fitness instructors, personal trainers, program directors, and club/studio owners. Offers workshops for continuing education credits. **Publications:** *IDEA Health & Fitness Source* (10/year); *IDEA Personal Trainer* (10/year); *Trainer Success* (5/year).

15879 ■ International Federation of Body Building and Fitness–Federation Internationale des Culturistes
2875 Bates Rd.
Montreal, QC, Canada H3S 1B7
Ph:(514)731-3783
Fax:(514)731-9026
Co. E-mail: info@ifbb.com
URL: http://www.ifbb.com
Contact: Dr. Rafael Santonja, Pres.
Description: National federations of bodybuilding enthusiasts united to promote better health and fitness through bodybuilding, physical culture, proper nutrition, and weight training. Conducts and compiles research dealing with physical culture, bodybuilding, weight training, nutrition, sports injuries, and sports medicine. Compiles statistics on the results of competitions and evaluates judges' accuracy. Sanctions amateur, professional, and open world and continental bodybuilding competitions for men and women. Sponsors the Mr./Ms. Olympia contests and the World Amateur Men's and Women's Championships. Establishes rules and appoints qualified judges. Plans to establish hall of fame. **Publications:** *Congress Report* (annual); *Flex* (monthly); *Scientific Athletic Reports* (periodic).

15880 ■ International Health, Racquet and Sportsclub Association
Seaport Ctr.
70 Fargo St.
Boston, MA 02210
Ph:(617)951-0055
Free: 800-228-4772
Fax:(617)951-0056
Co. E-mail: info@ihrsa.org
URL: http://www.ihrsa.org
Contact: Joe Moore, Pres./CEO
Description: Health, racquet, and sport clubs; racquet sports manufacturers and suppliers. Promotes the continued growth of the health, racquet, and sports club industry in 70 countries. Aids member clubs in making educated business decisions. Sets standards for club management; offers group purchasing program. Organizes management training seminars. Compiles statistics; disseminates information. Conducts market research and educational programs; conducts sponsored membership promotion programs. Provides government relations and public relations services. **Publications:** *Club Business International* (monthly).

15881 ■ International Physical Fitness Association
415 W Court St.
Flint, MI 48503
Ph:(810)239-2166
Free: 877-520-IPFA
Fax:(810)239-9390
Co. E-mail: contact@ipfa.us
URL: http://www.ipfa.us
Contact: Jerry Kahn, Pres.
Description: Physical fitness centers. Facilitates the transfer of individual memberships from one member club to another. **Publications:** *IPFA Roster* (annual).

15882 ■ National Federation of Professional Trainers
PO Box 4579
Lafayette, IN 47903-4579
Ph:(765)471-4514

Free: 800-729-6378
Fax:(765)471-7369
Co. E-mail: info@nfpt.com
URL: http://www.nfpt.com
Contact: Ron Clark, Pres./CEO
Description: Offers affordable, convenient, comprehensive, and applicable information to those seeking personal fitness trainer certification. Offers organizational certification credentials for consumer recognition of competence; provides certified affiliates with ongoing education; establishes a network of support, and provides professional products and services to trainers and consumers; and facilitates and encourages the exchange of ideas, knowledge, business experiences, and financial opportunities between all fitness administrators internationally. Offers educational programs. .

15883 ■ Physical and Health Education Canada–Education physique et sante Canada
301-2197 Riverside Dr.
Ottawa, ON, Canada K1H 7X3
Ph:(613)523-1348
Free: 800-663-8708
Fax:(613)523-1206
Co. E-mail: info@phecanada.ca
URL: http://www.phecanada.ca
Contact: Andrea Grantham, Exec. Dir.
Description: National professional organization with charitable status. Professionals in the field of health, physical education, and related disciplines. Promotes the long-term health benefits of health and active lifestyles. Seeks to facilitate the professional development of members and teachers, teacher education in the education field. Collaborates with international, national, provincial, and local organizations to devise, implement, and monitor health and physical education programs. Advocates for enhanced social and physical environments supporting physically active and healthy lives. Sponsors continuing professional education and training programs; conducts research; develops resources. Manages school based fundraising programs. **Publications:** *Avante* (3/year); *In Touch* (3/year); *Physical and Health Education Journal* (quarterly).

15884 ■ United States Competitive Aerobics Federation
8033 Sunset Blvd., No. 920
Los Angeles, CA 90046
Ph:(323)850-3777
Fax:(323)850-7795
Co. E-mail: nacusa@aol.com
URL: http://www.sportaerobics-nac.com
Contact: Laurence Cohen
Description: Governs and organizes sports fitness and aerobic competitions for youth and adults. Seeks to maintain high standards and consistency in the sport. Conducts educational programs. .

15885 ■ United States Racquetball Association
1685 W Uintah St.
Colorado Springs, CO 80904-2969
Ph:(719)635-5396
Fax:(719)635-0685
Co. E-mail: jhiser@usra.org
URL: http://www.usra.org
Contact: James Hiser, Exec. Dir.
Description: Represents racquetball players and enthusiasts. Promotes racquetball as a sport; organizes racquetball to be a self-governing sport of, by, and for the players; encourages building of facilities for the sport; conducts racquetball events including annual national and international tournaments. Maintains hall of fame, junior player programs, and charitable programs. **Publications:** *Official USRA Rules*; *Racquetball Magazine* (bimonthly).

15886 ■ United States Water Fitness Association
PO Box 243279
Boynton Beach, FL 33424-3279
Ph:(561)732-9908

Fax:(561)732-0950
Co. E-mail: info@uswfa.org
URL: http://www.uswfa.com
Contact: John R. Spannuth, Pres./CEO
Description: Promotes aquatics, including water fitness, through activities such as water aerobics, water walking, water running, and deep water exercise. Awards certification for water fitness instructors, program coordinators, and aquatic directors. Helps to identify and establish trends in water fitness and aquatics. Sponsors National Water Fitness Week, National Water Walking Week, and National and World Water Fitness competitions. Encourages research. Promotes aquatics throughout the country by educating aquatic professionals on the organization and administration of aquatic programming. Maintains speakers' bureau; compiles statistics. **Publications:** *National Aquatics Newsletter* (quarterly).

REFERENCE WORKS

15887 ■ *Athletic Business—Buyers Guide Issue*
Pub: Athletic Business Publications Inc.
Released: Annual, Latest edition 2011. **Price:** Free. **Publication Includes:** Listings of about 2,000 manufacturers and suppliers of athletic equipment, trainers' supplies, conditioning and testing equipment, building and facility equipment, sports surfaces, aquatic components, and outdoor recreation equipment; related trade associations and consultants and other professionals in the field. **Entries Include:** Name, address, phone, fax, e-mail address. **Arrangement:** Separate alphabetical sections for manufacturers and suppliers, associations, and professionals. **Indexes:** Product, advertiser name.

15888 ■ "Because 10 Million Zumba Lovers Can't Be Wrong" in *Inc.* (Volume 32, December 2010, No. 10, pp. 106)
Pub: Inc. Magazine
Ed: Christine Lagorio. **Description:** Profile of partners, Alberto Perez, Alberto Perlman, and Alberto Aghion, founders of Zumba, a form of dance used for fitness.

15889 ■ "'Biggest Loser' Adds Bit of Muscle to Local Economy" in *Crain's Detroit Business* (Vol. 26, January 4, 2010, No. 1, pp. 1)
Pub: Crain Communications, Inc.
Ed: Chad Halcom. **Description:** NBC's weight-loss reality show, "The Biggest Loser" has helped the local economy and generated a new crop of local startup businesses due to past contestants that were from the Detroit area.

15890 ■ "Carving a Niche" in *Hawaii Business* (Vol. 53, November 2007, No. 5, pp. 58)
Pub: Hawaii Business Publishing
Ed: Kyle Galdeira. **Description:** Stephanie Lay created Extreme Surf Fitness which is a program that promotes natural performance enhancement and rehabilitation of surfers using core and balance exercises. Lay's goal is to become a full time coach for a big surf brand and tour the world with the team.

15891 ■ "Corporate Training" in *Hawaii Business* (Vol. 53, October 2007, No. 4, pp. 46)
Pub: Hawaii Business Publishing
Ed: Cathy S. Cruz-George. **Description:** Kalani Pa, Mike Hann, and Li Si Yang are three of the fitness trainers who have worked with some of the participants at the Hawaii's Fittest CEO contest. Pa has trained Group Pacific Inc.'s Chip Doyle while Hann was Sharon Serene's trainer. Their insights on the profession of being a fitness trainer, and on working with executives are given.

15892 ■ "Elements For Success" in *Small Business Opportunities* (November 2008)
Pub: Entrepreneur Media Inc.
Description: Profile of Elements, a physical fitness club that approach a healthy lifestyle for women, which includes the components of body, beauty and mind; the network of upscale, boutique style health

clubs differ from other providers in its "balanced lifestyle" approach to a healthy lifestyle. This unique niche is gaining in popularity despite the faltering economy.

15893 ■ "Fiscally Fit" in *Entrepreneur* **(Vol. 37, October 2009, No. 10, pp. 130)**
Pub: Entrepreneur Media, Inc.
Ed: Jason Daley. **Description:** Landrie Peterman, owner of an Anytime Fitness franchise in Oregon, describes how she turned her business around. The franchise, located in an industrial park, saw growth after six months with the help of corporate clients.

15894 ■ "Fitness Made Fun" in *Playthings* **(Vol. 106, September 1, 2008, No. 8, pp. 12)**
Pub: Reed Business Information
Ed: Karyn M. Peterson. **Description:** Nintendo Wii has developed the Wii Fit game that allows gamers to engage in over forty physical activities through its Balance Board accessory, an engineered platform that senses weight and shifts in movement and balance. It also offers virtual trainers to talk participants through the activities and keeps track of the progress of multiple users.

15895 ■ "Fitter from Twitter" in *Boston Business Journal* **(Vol. 30, December 17, 2010, No. 47, pp. 1)**
Pub: Boston Business Journal
Ed: Lisa van der Pool. **Description:** Small businesses are increasing their use of the Twitter microblogging platform to attract and retain customers. Lisa Johnson, who owns Modern Pilates studios, managed to raise awareness of her personal brand nationally through the social media platform.

15896 ■ "From Fat to Fit" in *Canadian Business* **(Vol. 79, September 25, 2006, No. 19, pp. 100)**
Pub: Rogers Media
Ed: Graham Scott. **Description:** The increase in physical fitness clubs across Canada is discussed.

15897 ■ "Get Fit On a Dine: Resolve To Be Healthy-and-Wealthy-This New Year" in *Black Enterprise* **(Vol. 38, January 2008, No. 6, pp. 86)**
Pub: Earl G. Graves Publishing Co. Inc.
Ed: Angela P. Moore-Thorpe. **Description:** According to International Health, Racquet, and Sportsclub Association, nearly 43 million people are members of health clubs in the U.S. Corporate wellness programs as well as laws and your rights as a club member are explained.

15898 ■ "Getting in Shape" in *Crain's Cleveland Business* **(Vol. 28, December 3, 2007, No. 48, pp. 13)**
Pub: Crain Communications, Inc.
Ed: Chrissy Kadleck. **Description:** According to the Medical Fitness Association, the number of medically integrated health and fitness centers has grown from 79 centers in 1985 to 875 in 2006. Summa Wellness Institute, the 65,000-square-foot health-and-fitness facility which opened next to Summa Health Systems's outpatient medical center is discussed.

15899 ■ "How I Did It: Mel Zuckerman" in *Inc.* **(December 2007, pp. 140-142)**
Pub: Gruner & Jahr USA Publishing
Ed: Daniel McGinn. **Description:** Profile of Mel Zuckerman, who tells how transformed his life as a middle-aged, overweight homebuilder to a healthy addition to the fitness and spa industry with his posh Canyon Ranch retreats.

15900 ■ "In It For the Long Run" in *Business Journal-Serving Phoenix & the Valley of the Sun* **(Vol. 30, August 20, 2010, No. 50, pp. 1)**
Pub: Phoenix Business Journal
Ed: Angela Gonzales. **Description:** Cancer survivor Helene Neville has finished a record-breaking 2,520-mile run in 93 days and then celebrated her 50th birthday despite being diagnosed with Hodgkins' lymphoma in 1991. Neveille, who is also a Phoenix area registered nurse, made stops along the way to promote her book, 'Nurses in Shape'. Neville also discusses how she fought her cancer through running.

15901 ■ "Insider" in *Canadian Business* **(Vol. 80, Winter 2007, No. 24, pp.)**
Pub: Rogers Media
Ed: Zena Olijnyk. **Description:** Luluemon Athletica started in 1998 after Dennis Wilson takes a yoga class and notices a demand from women for breathable clothes. The company opened their first outlet in Vancouver in November 2000 then opened their first U.S. store in 2003 until finally going public July 27, 2007 where its stocks doubled in value within days of trading.

15902 ■ "Kenosha 'Lifestyle Center' Delayed" in *The Business Journal-Milwaukee* **(Vol. 25, August 8, 2008, No. 46, pp. A1)**
Pub: American City Business Journals, Inc.
Ed: Rich Kirchen. **Description:** Quality Centers of Orlando, Florida has postponed construction plans for the Kenosha Town Center in Kenosha County, Wisconsin to 2009 due to the economic downturn and lending concerns. The $200-million, 750,000-square-foot retail and residential center will be located near the corner of Wisconsin Highway 50 and I-94.

15903 ■ "Nautilus Fights For Its Life" in *Business Journal-Portland* **(Vol. 24, November 23, 2007, No. 38, pp. 1)**
Pub: American City Business Journals, Inc.
Ed: Matthew Kish. **Description:** Shareholders meeting will determine whether four members at Nautilus Inc. will be ousted and control given to New York firm Sherborne Investors LP. The decision on December 18, 2007 is crucial since the investor's record is varied. For some it has significantly increased shares, while others have ended in near-bankruptcy stages.

15904 ■ "Our Gadget of the Week: Balancing Act" in *Barron's* **(Vol. 88, March 31, 2008, No. 13, pp. 40)**
Pub: Dow Jones & Company, Inc.
Ed: Naureen S. Malik. **Description:** Wii Fit gives users the experience of a virtual personal trainer and workouts that become progressively harder. The device turns the typical fitness regimes into fun exercises and users can choose workouts in four categories including yoga, balance, strength-training and, low impact aerobics.

15905 ■ "Ritz Kapalua Sells 93 Suites for $176M to Fund Renovation" in *Commercial Property News* **(March 17, 2008)**
Pub: Nielsen Company
Description: Ritz-Carlton, Kapalua in Lahaina, Hawaii sold ninety-three of its units in order to fund renovations of 463 rooms and suites along with construction of a new spa and fitness center, new and expanded restaurants and pools and an environmental education center for children.

15906 ■ "Shape Up! Jamal Williams Develops KIDFIT App to Combat Childhood Obesity" in *Black Enterprise* **(Vol. 41, August 2010, No. 1, pp. 62)**
Pub: Earl G. Graves Publishing Co. Inc.
Ed: Sonya A. Donaldson. **Description:** Profile of Jamal Williams who developed KIDFIT, an app that helps to combat childhood obesity by offering 150 various exercises for children, with an emphasis on training, conditioning, coordination, and flexibility.

15907 ■ "The Spirit of a Man: Kedar Massenburg's Intoxicating Style of Conducting Business" in *Black Enterprise* **(Vol. 38, March 2008)**
Pub: Earl G. Graves Publishing Co. Inc.
Ed: Sonia Alleyne. **Description:** Profile of Kedar Massenburg, personal trainer at The Gym in Montvale, New Jersey. Massenburg also operates an independent record label and management company as well as Kedar Beverages LLC founded in 2005. His latest venture is winemaking.

15908 ■ "Taxing Position: Yoga Studios Hit for Back Sales Tax" in *Puget Sound Business Journal* **(Vol. 29, August 29, 2008, No. 19, pp. 1)**
Pub: American City Business Journals
Ed: Deirdre Gregg. **Description:** Several yoga studies were audited and told they owe several years worth of back taxes. A spokesman from the Washington Department of Revenue stated the yoga studies should be collecting the tax in general and that yoga classes given for the purpose of physical fitness are taxable.

STATISTICAL SOURCES

15909 ■ *The Market for Physical Fitness Equipment*
Pub: MarketResearch.com
Released: 1999. **Price:** $3250.00 (paper). **Description:** This report on the physical fitness and exercise equipment industry provides the latest information available for aerobic riders, aerobic step platforms/benches, elliptical trainers (cross trainers), free weights, home gyms, rowing machines, stationary exercise bicycles and many more.

15910 ■ *RMA Annual Statement Studies*
Pub: Robert Morris Associates (RMA)
Released: Annual. **Price:** $175.00 2006-07 edition, $105.00. **Description:** Contains composite balance sheets and income statements for more than 360 industries, including the accounting, auditing, and bookkeeping industries. Also contains five years of comparative historical data for discerning trends. Includes 16 commonly used ratios, computed for most of the size groupings for nearly every industry.

TRADE PERIODICALS

15911 ■ *American Fitness*
Pub: American Fitness
Ed: Meg Jordan, Editor, americanfitness@afaa.com. **Released:** Bimonthly. **Price:** $27; $49 Canada and Mexico; $72 other countries. **Description:** Magazine covering trends in fitness, exercise programs, injury prevention, and nutrition.

15912 ■ *IDEA Personal Trainer*
Pub: IDEA Inc.
Contact: Peter Davis, Founder
Ed: Nicholas Drake, Editor, draken@ideafit.com. **Released:** Monthly, 10/yr. **Description:** Trade magazine covering business operation and other issues for personal trainers in the health and fitness industry.

15913 ■ *Men's Fitness*
Pub: Weider Publications
Released: Monthly, 10/yr. **Price:** $15 two years; $25 Canada; $28 other countries. **Description:** Magazine devoted to health, nutrition, fitness and general lifestyle.

15914 ■ *Muscle & Fitness*
Pub: Weider Publications
Contact: Joe Weider, Publisher
Released: Monthly. **Price:** $34.97; $51.97 Canada; $66.97 other countries. **Description:** Physical fitness and lifestyle magazine.

15915 ■ *Muscular Development*
Pub: Advanced Research Press Inc.
Released: Monthly. **Price:** $49.97; $79.97 two years. **Description:** Bodybuilding and physical fitness magazine.

15916 ■ *NSCA Bulletin*
Pub: National Strength & Conditioning Association (NSCA)
Ed: Lori Marker, Editor. **Released:** Bimonthly, 6/year. **Price:** Included in membership. **Description:** Tracks Association activities. Recurring features include interviews, a calendar of events, reports of meetings, news of educational opportunities, job listings, book reviews, and notices of publications available.

15917 ■ *Shape*
Pub: Weider Publications
Contact: Barbara S. Harris MA, Editor-in-Chief
Released: Monthly. **Price:** $14.97 print; $29.97 Canada; $41.97 other countries; $14.97 digital. **Description:** Magazine for women covering nutrition, weight control, physical fitness, psychology, fashion, beauty and travel.

VIDEOCASSETTES/ AUDIOCASSETTES

15918 ■ *Acu-Yoga for Flexibility*
Acupressure Institute
1533 Shattuck Ave.
Berkeley, CA 94709
Ph:(510)845-1059
Free: 800-442-2232
Fax:(510)845-1496
Co. E-mail: info@acupressureinstitute.com
URL: http://www.acupressureinstitute.com
Price: $29.95. **Description:** Demonstrates stretches for the lower, middle and upper back, pelvis and legs. **Availability:** VHS.

15919 ■ *The Ballet Workout II*
Princeton Book Co. Publishers
614 Rte. 130
Hightstown, NJ 08520
Ph:(609)426-0602
Free: 800-220-7149
Fax:(609)426-1344
Co. E-mail: pbc@dancehorizons.com
URL: http://www.dancehorizons.com
Released: 1993. **Price:** $19.95. **Description:** Melissa Lowe's follow-up the the Ballet Workout, provides the viewer with two new workouts that address the goal of achieving a lithe, supple body, an improves carriage, and the look and grace of a professional dancer. **Availability:** VHS.

15920 ■ *Beginning Bodybuilding*
Victory Multimedia
222 N. Sepulveda Blvd., Ste. 1306
El Segundo, CA 90245
Ph:(310)416-9140
Fax:(310)416-9839
Co. E-mail: RFVictory@juno.com
Price: $9.98. **Description:** Demonstrates exercises that best target muscle stimulation and common errors to avoid. **Availability:** VHS.

15921 ■ *Beyond Protection*
Tapeworm Video Distributors
25876 The Old Road 141
Stevenson Ranch, CA 91381
Ph:(661)257-4904
Fax:(661)257-4820
Co. E-mail: sales@tapeworm.com
URL: http://www.tapeworm.com
Released: 1996. **Price:** $19.95. **Description:** Personal trainer, kinesiologist and martial artist Vanessa Friedman conducts an aerobic workout mixed with self defense techniques. **Availability:** VHS.

15922 ■ *Chi Kung the Healing Workout*
Artistic Video
c/o Long Island School of Tai-Chi-Chuan
87 Tyler Ave.
Sound Beach, NY 11789-2639
Ph:(631)744-5999
Free: 888-982-4244
Fax:(631)744-5993
Co. E-mail: service@movementsofmagic.com
URL: http://www.movementsofmagic.com
Description: Presents gentle, easy to learn movements that aid in keeping the body fit. **Availability:** VHS.

15923 ■ *Dancing a Miracle*
Leslie T. McClure
PO Box 1223
Pebble Beach, CA 93953
Ph:(831)656-0553
Fax:(831)656-0555
Co. E-mail: leslie@411videoinfo.com
URL: http://www.411videoinfo.com
Released: 1997. **Price:** $19.95. **Description:** Dr. Irene Lamberti presents a workout program for the body and spirit. **Availability:** VHS.

15924 ■ *Dyna-Gym*
Princeton Book Co. Publishers
614 Rte. 130
Hightstown, NJ 08520
Ph:(609)426-0602
Free: 800-220-7149

Fax:(609)426-1344
Co. E-mail: pbc@dancehorizons.com
URL: http://www.dancehorizons.com
Released: 1992. **Price:** $24.95. **Description:** Describes an adjustable, body-shaping, resistance workout for women and men with musical accompaniment. A complete shaping workout that is a safe and gentle alternative to weights. **Availability:** VHS.

15925 ■ *Exercise Ball Workout*
Artistic Video
c/o Long Island School of Tai-Chi-Chuan
87 Tyler Ave.
Sound Beach, NY 11789-2639
Ph:(631)744-5999
Free: 888-982-4244
Fax:(631)744-5993
Co. E-mail: service@movementsofmagic.com
URL: http://www.movementsofmagic.com
Released: 1997. **Price:** $29.95. **Description:** Presents a unique workout to tone abs, hips, legs, arms and chest. **Availability:** VHS.

15926 ■ *Forever Fit*
Tapeworm Video Distributors
25876 The Old Road 141
Stevenson Ranch, CA 91381
Ph:(661)257-4904
Fax:(661)257-4820
Co. E-mail: sales@tapeworm.com
URL: http://www.tapeworm.com
Released: 1997. **Price:** $24.95. **Description:** Certified Fitness Instructor Loura White leads an exercise regimen for seniors. **Availability:** VHS.

15927 ■ *Gentle Fitness*
Tapeworm Video Distributors
25876 The Old Road 141
Stevenson Ranch, CA 91381
Ph:(661)257-4904
Fax:(661)257-4820
Co. E-mail: sales@tapeworm.com
URL: http://www.tapeworm.com
Released: 1994. **Price:** $19.95. **Description:** Catherine MacRae guides viewers through six routines of gentle exercise intended to relieve arthritis, poor circulation, and inactivity. **Availability:** VHS.

15928 ■ *Geri-Fit: The First Workout with Weights for Older Adults*
Tapeworm Video Distributors
25876 The Old Road 141
Stevenson Ranch, CA 91381
Ph:(661)257-4904
Fax:(661)257-4820
Co. E-mail: sales@tapeworm.com
URL: http://www.tapeworm.com
Price: $19.95. **Description:** Provides instruction for improving strength, flexibility, balance, and arthritic conditions. **Availability:** VHS.

15929 ■ *In Shape with Rachel McLish*
New Line Home Video
116 N. Robertson Blvd.
Los Angeles, CA 90048
Ph:(310)854-5811
Fax:(310)854-1824
Co. E-mail: movies@newline.com
URL: http://www.newline.com
Released: 1995. **Description:** Focuses on tightening, toning, and sculpting such body areas as the stomach, chest, thighs, and buttocks. **Availability:** VHS.

15930 ■ *Lean Teen*
Tapeworm Video Distributors
25876 The Old Road 141
Stevenson Ranch, CA 91381
Ph:(661)257-4904
Fax:(661)257-4820
Co. E-mail: sales@tapeworm.com
URL: http://www.tapeworm.com
Price: $12.95. **Description:** Provides teenagers with information on fitness. **Availability:** VHS.

15931 ■ *Madonna Grimes Cardio Sculpt*
Tapeworm Video Distributors
25876 The Old Road 141
Stevenson Ranch, CA 91381

Ph:(661)257-4904
Fax:(661)257-4820
Co. E-mail: sales@tapeworm.com
URL: http://www.tapeworm.com
Released: 1997. **Price:** $19.95. **Description:** Ms. Fitness Champion conducts cardiovascular conditioning and light resistance weight work with isometric muscle training. **Availability:** VHS.

15932 ■ *Madonna Grimes Hip Hop Dance Workout*
Tapeworm Video Distributors
25876 The Old Road 141
Stevenson Ranch, CA 91381
Ph:(661)257-4904
Fax:(661)257-4820
Co. E-mail: sales@tapeworm.com
URL: http://www.tapeworm.com
Released: 1997. **Price:** $19.95. **Description:** Ms. Fitness Champion conducts an aerobic program designed for all levels. **Availability:** VHS.

15933 ■ *The Men's Total Body*
Educational Video Network
1401 19th St.
Huntsville, TX 77340
Ph:(936)295-5767
Free: 800-762-0060
Fax:(936)294-0233
URL: http://www.evndirect.com
Released: 1995. **Price:** $24.95. **Description:** Workout for men, hosted by Olympic gold medalist Mitch Gaylord and four fitness experts, includes warmup and stretching routines, upper-and lower-body exercises, an abdominal program, and a nutrition segment. **Availability:** VHS.

15934 ■ *Native Spirit*
Leslie T. McClure
PO Box 1223
Pebble Beach, CA 93953
Ph:(831)656-0553
Fax:(831)656-0555
Co. E-mail: leslie@411videoinfo.com
URL: http://www.411videoinfo.com
Released: 1997. **Price:** $19.95. **Description:** Dr. Irene Lamberti presents a workout program for the body and spirit. **Availability:** VHS.

15935 ■ *Nautilus Aerobics Plus: High Impact Aerobics*
Karol Media
Hanover Industrial Estates
375 Stewart Rd.
PO Box 7600
Wilkes Barre, PA 18773-7600
Ph:(570)822-8899
Free: 800-526-4773
Co. E-mail: sales@karolmedia.com
URL: http://www.karolmedia.com
Released: 1990. **Price:** $9.95. **Description:** High-energy, high-calorie burning workout for those already familiar with aerobics. **Availability:** VHS.

15936 ■ *Nautilus Aerobics Plus: Low Impact Aerobics*
Karol Media
Hanover Industrial Estates
375 Stewart Rd.
PO Box 7600
Wilkes Barre, PA 18773-7600
Ph:(570)822-8899
Free: 800-526-4773
Co. E-mail: sales@karolmedia.com
URL: http://www.karolmedia.com
Released: 1990. **Price:** $9.95. **Description:** Nautilus aerobic fitness tape. Fat-burning tape (keep it on simmer) is low intensity. **Availability:** VHS.

15937 ■ *Nike HealthWalking Training System*
Karol Media
Hanover Industrial Estates
375 Stewart Rd.
PO Box 7600
Wilkes Barre, PA 18773-7600
Ph:(570)822-8899

Free: 800-526-4773
Co. E-mail: sales@karolmedia.com
URL: http://www.karolmedia.com
Released: 1988. **Price:** $29.95. **Description:** After developing a walking program that offers an exciting combination of both mental and physical fitness, Nike offers this video designed to train anyone looking for a walking system that produces maximum results. Two audio cassettes and a study guide are optional assets that can be purchased with this video. **Availability:** VHS.

15938 ■ Pre- and Post-Natal Fitness
Leslie T. McClure
PO Box 1223
Pebble Beach, CA 93953
Ph:(831)656-0553
Fax:(831)656-0555
Co. E-mail: leslie@411videoinfo.com
URL: http://www.411videoinfo.com
Released: 1997. **Price:** $24.95. **Description:** Presents a low-impact fitness program adapted from Imperial Russian ballet toning techniques. **Availability:** VHS.

15939 ■ Pumping Iron After Fifty
Tapeworm Video Distributors
25876 The Old Road 141
Stevenson Ranch, CA 91381
Ph:(661)257-4904
Fax:(661)257-4820
Co. E-mail: sales@tapeworm.com
URL: http://www.tapeworm.com
Description: Presents easy weight training exercises for seniors. **Availability:** VHS.

15940 ■ Wai Lana Yoga
Artistic Video
c/o Long Island School of Tai-Chi-Chuan
87 Tyler Ave.
Sound Beach, NY 11789-2639
Ph:(631)744-5999
Free: 888-982-4244
Fax:(631)744-5993
Co. E-mail: service@movementsofmagic.com
URL: http://www.movementsofmagic.com
Description: Three-volume set presents a beginners workout, relaxation techniques, and a toning workout. **Availability:** VHS.

15941 ■ Yoga to Go with Misty Carey Volume 2: Strength
Santa Monica Yoga
1640 Ocean Park Blvd.
Santa Monica, CA 90405
Ph:(310)396-4040
Fax:(310)392-7404
Co. E-mail: contact@santamonicayoga.com
URL: http://www.santamonicayoga.com
Released: 1997. **Price:** $29.95. **Description:** Presents exercises and techniques to build strength, balance and flexibility. **Availability:** VHS.

15942 ■ Yoga to Go with Misty Carey Volume 3: Health
Santa Monica Yoga
1640 Ocean Park Blvd.
Santa Monica, CA 90405
Ph:(310)396-4040
Fax:(310)392-7404
Co. E-mail: contact@santamonicayoga.com
URL: http://www.santamonicayoga.com
Released: 1997. **Price:** $29.95. **Description:** Presents exercises and techniques to stimulate and balance the immune system. **Availability:** VHS.

CONSULTANTS

15943 ■ Health Fitness Dynamics Inc.
1305 NE 23rd Ave., Ste. 2
Pompano Beach, FL 33062
Ph:(954)942-0049

Fax:(954)941-0854
Co. E-mail: hfd@hfdspa.com
URL: http://www.hfdspa.com
Contact: Patricia A. Monteson, Principle
E-mail: pattymonteson@atshfdspa.com
Scope: Firm offers spa consulting services in the following areas: program development, facility planning, feasibility and market studies, staffing requirements, product and equipment selection, coordinating of support departments, systems of operation, personnel, and on-going management. Industries served: hospitality, hotels and resorts, and health spas. **Publications:** "Spa News & Views: If The Spa Will Not Help Sell Rooms, Do Not Add A Spa," Spa Management, Mar, 2006; "Thinking of Jumping on the Spa Bandwagon Look Before You Leap"; "Spa Savvy-Best Practices for Hiring, Training & Retaining your Staff". **Seminars:** Management Workshop; Managing a Revenue Generating Spa within a Resort; The Health Spa - Another Marketable and Complementary Dimension of a Resort; Planning and Managing a Health Spa in a Resort.

FRANCHISES AND BUSINESS OPPORTUNITIES

15944 ■ American Ramp Systems
Gordon Industries
202 W 1st St.
South Boston, MA 02127
Free: 800-649-5215
Fax:(617)268-3701
Co. E-mail: info@americanramp.com
URL: http://www.americanramp.com
No. of Franchise Units: 42. **No. of Company-Owned Units:** 1. **Founded:** 1970. **Franchised:** 2002. **Description:** Sales and rentals of accessibility ramps. **Equity Capital Needed:** $124,400-$217,680. **Franchise Fee:** $49,250-$98,500. **Royalty Fee:** 12%. **Financial Assistance:** Third party financing available. **Training:** Provides 1 week at headquarters with ongoing support. ort.

15945 ■ Anytime Fitness
12181 Margo Ave., S
Hastings, MN 55033
Free: 800-704-5004
Fax:(651)554-5099
No. of Franchise Units: 1,488. **No. of Company-Owned Units:** 10. **Founded:** 2001. **Franchised:** 2002. **Description:** Anytime Fitness focuses on health, nutrition and senior care services. **Equity Capital Needed:** $44,074-$300,074 total investment. **Franchise Fee:** 24,999. **Royalty Fee:** $499/month. **Financial Assistance:** Third party financing available. **Training:** Provides 3 days minimum at headquarters and 3 days minimum onsite with ongoing support.

15946 ■ Baby Boot Camp
5053 Ocean Blvd.
Sarasota, FL 34242
Ph:(941)953-5000
Free: 888-990-2229
Fax:(941)924-1006
No. of Franchise Units: 116. **No. of Company-Owned Units:** 1. **Founded:** 2001. **Franchised:** 2005. **Description:** Pre & postnatal fitness. **Equity Capital Needed:** $3,690-$9,699. **Franchise Fee:** $2,900-$4,900. **Royalty Fee:** $115-$265/month. **Financial Assistance:** No.

15947 ■ Butterfly Life
2404 San Ramon Valley Blvd., Ste. 200
San Ramon, CA 94583
Free: 800-290-2977
Fax:(925)743-8820
No. of Franchise Units: 100. **Founded:** 2003. **Franchised:** 2003. **Description:** Women's healthy living & fitness center. **Equity Capital Needed:** $63,990-$139,500. **Franchise Fee:** $29,500. **Royalty Fee:** $1,000/month. **Financial Assistance:** Third party financing available. **Training:** Offers 1 week at headquarters, 3 days at franchisees location, annual conferences, phone and onsite assistance as needed.

15948 ■ CKO Kickboxing
900 Madison St.
Hoboken, NJ 07030
Ph:(201)963-7774
Fax:(201)963-6177
No. of Franchise Units: 17. **No. of Company-Owned Units:** 4. **Founded:** 1997. **Franchised:** 2007. **Description:** Kickboxing classes. **Equity Capital Needed:** $97,890-$306,900. **Franchise Fee:** $25,000. **Royalty Fee:** 7%. **Financial Assistance:** Third party financing available.

15949 ■ Club 50 Fitness
9410 Prototype Dr., Ste. 18
Reno, NV 89521
Ph:(775)853-3553
Free: 877-425-8250
Fax:(775)201-1180
Co. E-mail: info@club50fitness.com
URL: http://www.club50fitness.com
No. of Franchise Units: 13. **No. of Company-Owned Units:** 1. **Founded:** 2003. **Franchised:** 2005. **Description:** 30 minute circuit training that incorporates fitness and nutrition into a unique and fun format designed exclusively for men and women age 50 and up. Provides a complete package for all franchisees including equipment, training, support, pre-produced television, radio and print ads, and public relations support. **Equity Capital Needed:** $50,000-$80,000. **Franchise Fee:** $24,900, including equipment. **Financial Assistance:** Third party financing available. **Training:** Start-up, onsite and offsite with continued ongoing support.

15950 ■ CoachMeFit
2433 Oak Valley Dr., Ste. 500
Ann Arbor, MI 48103
Ph:(734)477-9450
Fax:(734)477-9427
No. of Franchise Units: 1. **No. of Company-Owned Units:** 3. **Founded:** 2001. **Franchised:** 2007. **Description:** Personal fitness training. **Equity Capital Needed:** $106,700-$261,500. **Franchise Fee:** $12,500. **Royalty Fee:** 5%. **Financial Assistance:** No. **Training:** 3-5 days at headquarters.

15951 ■ Contours Express
Contours Express, LLC
156 Imperial Way
Nicholasville, KY 40356
Ph:(859)885-6441
Free: 877-227-2282
Fax:(859)241-2234
Co. E-mail: info@contoursexpress.com
URL: http://www.contoursexpress.com
No. of Franchise Units: 600. **Founded:** 1998. **Franchised:** 1998. **Description:** Women's only fitness and weight loss studio. **Equity Capital Needed:** $75,000 net worth. **Franchise Fee:** $18,000. **Financial Assistance:** Third party financing available on equipment. **Managerial Assistance:** 3-4 day training program at the home office, operations manual, quarterly marketing packages, ongoing toll-free telephone and Internet support. **Training:** Site selection, lease negotiation, 3-4 day onsite training at location, and club layout assistance.

15952 ■ Fit Zone For Women
4341 S Westnedge Ave., Ste 1103
Kalamazoo, MI 49008
Ph:(269)226-9564
Fax:(269)226-9566
No. of Franchise Units: 25. **No. of Company-Owned Units:** 2. **Founded:** 2004. **Franchised:** 2006. **Description:** Full service fitness center for women. **Equity Capital Needed:** $100,100-$150,500. **Franchise Fee:** $25,000. **Royalty Fee:** Varies. **Financial Assistance:** No. **Training:** Provides 7 days at headquarters and 3 days onsite and ongoing support.

15953 ■ Fitwize 4 Kids Inc.
384 Bel Marin Keys Blvd., Ste. 210
Novato, CA 94949
Ph:(415)883-1798

Fax:(415)883-1825
No. of Franchise Units: 14. **No. of Company-Owned Units:** 1. **Founded:** 2004. **Franchised:** 2005. **Description:** Healthy lifestyle center for kids. **Equity Capital Needed:** $125,000. **Franchise Fee:** $39,000. **Royalty Fee:** $495/month. **Financial Assistance:** No.

15954 ■ Fun Bus USA, Inc. - 'Fitness Fun on Wheels'
32 Timothy Ln.
Tinton Falls, NJ 07724
Ph:(732)578-1287
Fax:(732)530-8287
No. of Franchise Units: 32. **Founded:** 2001. **Franchised:** 2003. **Description:** Mobile fun fitness program. **Equity Capital Needed:** $80,500, includes franchise fee/or license agreement. **Franchise Fee:** $32,500. **Financial Assistance:** No. **Training:** Yes. s.

15955 ■ Gold's Gym
Gold's Gym International, Inc.
125 E John Carpenter Fwy., Ste. 1300
Irving, TX 75062
Ph:(214)574-4653
Fax:(214)296-5066
No. of Franchise Units: 700. **No. of Company-Owned Units:** 65. **Founded:** 1965. **Description:** Offers health, and nutrition services. **Equity Capital Needed:** $895,500-$3,800,000. **Franchise Fee:** $25,000 initial fee. **Financial Assistance:** Yes. **Training:** Yes.

15956 ■ The HIT Center
690 Lakeview Plaza Blvd., Ste. H
Worthington, OH 43085
Ph:(614)888-4448
Free: (866)305-5702
No. of Franchise Units: 11. **Founded:** 2000. **Franchised:** 2003. **Description:** Athletic development, weight loss, and fitness center. **Equity Capital Needed:** $500,000. **Franchise Fee:** $40,000. **Royalty Fee:** 5%. **Financial Assistance:** No. **Training:** Training includes 4 weeks training at headquarters, 1 week at franchisee's location and as needed.

15957 ■ IM=X Pilates Studio
The Xercize Studio, LLC
265 Madison Ave., 2nd Fl.
New York, NY 10016
Free: 877-748-3249
Fax:(714)281-8009
Co. E-mail: franchise@xercizestudio.com
URL: http://www.imxpilatesstudio.com
No. of Company-Owned Units: 1. **Founded:** 2003. **Franchised:** 2003. **Description:** For 10 years, IM=X has been in the business of pilates certification, developing patented equipment, and helping customers grow pilates programs. We now offer the IM=X Pilates Studio franchise as an innovative, elite fitness program plus business operations, marketing, and educational support to prospective franchise owners. Success experienced by clubs offering IM=X Pilates is now available to meet current market demands for this challenging program. **Equity Capital Needed:** Full model $75,000-$160,000; express model $15,000-$30,000. **Franchise Fee:** $15,000-$22,000. **Financial Assistance:** Yes. **Training:** Operations Manual and Training course prepare you to grow and operate your own studio or studio chain. Every year we will train and certify up to 12 of your staff in the Basic And Advanced IM=X Pilates program.

15958 ■ J.W. Tumbles
312 S Cedros, Ste. 329
Solana Beach, CA 92075
Ph:(858)794-0484
Fax:(858)794-0398
No. of Franchise Units: 33. **No. of Company-Owned Units:** 1. **Founded:** 1994. **Franchised:** 2004. **Description:** Children's gym for fitness & fun. **Equity Capital Needed:** $138,600-$215,600. **Franchise Fee:** $42,850. **Financial Assistance:** No. **Training:** Yes.

15959 ■ La Boxing Franchise Corp.
2915 Tech Center Dr.
Santa Ana, CA 92705
Free: (866)522-6946
Fax:(714)668-9231
Co. E-mail: franchise@laboxing.com
URL: http://www.laboxing.com
No. of Franchise Units: 116. **Founded:** 1992. **Franchised:** 2004. **Description:** The business you will conduct as an LA Boxing Franchise is a membership physical fitness system consisting of unique boxing and kickboxing training regiment, utilizing a system and products that are proprietary to the company. We authorize our franchisees to offer memberships to promote boxing fitness training and instruction programs utilizing a professional ring, weight room, and other equipment with unique construction and design features. No experience necessary. **Equity Capital Needed:** $174,900-$185,750. **Franchise Fee:** $25,000. **Financial Assistance:** No. **Training:** 5 days of initial training at corporate training facilities, and 1 day onsite. Initial training includes instruction in owner/operator responsibilities, instructor training, equipment, membership sales, administration, operations, product and services sales and marketing.

15960 ■ Lady of America Franchise Corporation
Lady of America, Inc.
500 E Broward Blvd., Ste. 1650
Ft. Lauderdale, FL 33394
Ph:(954)644-7827
Free: 800-833-5239
Fax:(954)527-5436
No. of Franchise Units: 211. **No. of Company-Owned Units:** 5. **Founded:** 1984. **Franchised:** 1989. **Description:** Franchises ladies-only fitness centers. **Equity Capital Needed:** $192,700-$454,600. **Franchise Fee:** $30,000. **Royalty Fee:** 8%. **Financial Assistance:** Limited third party financing available. **Training:** Yes.

15961 ■ Lucille Roberts Fitness Express
4 E 80th St.
New York, NY 10021
Free: 888-582-4553
Fax:(212)734-4151
No. of Company-Owned Units: 47. **Founded:** 1970. **Franchised:** 2005. **Description:** Women's fitness & weight-loss center. **Equity Capital Needed:** $271,850-$402,400. **Franchise Fee:** $25,000. **Royalty Fee:** 6%. **Financial Assistance:** Third party financing available. **Training:** Offers 1 week at headquarters with ongoing support.

15962 ■ McGruff Safe Kids Total Identification System
Arfmann Marketing, LLC
35246 US Hwy. 19 N
Palm Harbor, FL 34684
Ph:(727)725-9674
Free: 888-209-4218
Fax:(727)725-9740
Co. E-mail: neil@mcgruff-tid.com
URL: http://www.mcgruff-tid.com
No. of Franchise Units: 31. **Founded:** 2003. **Franchised:** 2003. **Description:** Digital child identification safety system. **Equity Capital Needed:** An additional $3,000-$5,000. **Franchise Fee:** $30,000. **Financial Assistance:** No. **Training:** Offers 3 days of training.

15963 ■ Monart School of The Arts
Monart Franchise Corp.
2340 Powell St., Ste. 397
Emeryville, CA 94608
Ph:(310)390-0386
Free: 877-MON-ART1
Fax:(310)391-4355
No. of Franchise Units: 27. **Founded:** 1981. **Franchised:** 2004. **Description:** Children's school of the arts. **Equity Capital Needed:** $65,000-$75,000. **Franchise Fee:** $15,000. **Royalty Fee:** 8%. **Financial Assistance:** No. **Training:** Yes.

15964 ■ My Gym Children's Fitness Center
My Gym Enterprises
15300 Ventura Blvd., Ste. 414
Sherman Oaks, CA 91403
Ph:(818)907-6966

Free: 800-469-4967
Fax:(818)907-0735
URL: http://www.my-gym.com
No. of Franchise Units: 200. **No. of Company-Owned Units:** 5. **Founded:** 1983. **Franchised:** 1995. **Description:** My Gym Children's Fitness Centers help youngsters 3 mos. - 9 yrs develop physically, cognitively & emotionally. Structured, age-appropriate weekly classes incorporate music, dance, relays, games, special rides, gymnastics, sports and original activities. Our unique, award-winning My Gym Program, non competitive atmosphere & ideal student/teacher ratio build confidence and self-esteem. Kids just love the state-of-the-art facility w/ its My Gym custom-made equipment. **Equity Capital Needed:** $40,000-$250,000. **Franchise Fee:** $$25,000-55,000. **Financial Assistance:** While our company does not offer direct funding, our representatives who are experienced in this field will guide and assist you in obtaining financing. **Training:** 21 day training course-Ref. manuals & videos-Complete bus. operating systems-Detailed class curricula-Full handholding process thru Grand Opening and 1st session-Exceptional ongoing support w/ onsite visits, written materials, phone calls-Program innovations-Promotions-My Gym National & Regional Seminars.

15965 ■ Nexgym
1430 E Southlake Blvd., Ste. 110
Southlake, TX 76092
Ph:888-696-8444
Fax:(636)412-9300
No. of Franchise Units: 1. **No. of Company-Owned Units:** 1. **Founded:** 2005. **Franchised:** 2006. **Description:** Children's interactive fitness program. **Equity Capital Needed:** $213,000-$397,000. **Franchise Fee:** $30,000. **Royalty Fee:** 6%. **Financial Assistance:** No. **Training:** Includes 2 weeks training at headquarters, 1 week at franchisee's location and ongoing support.

15966 ■ One 2 One Bodyscapes
1197 Walnut St.
Newton, MA 02461
Ph:(617)796-8808
Founded: 1997. **Franchised:** 2006. **Description:** One on one personal training center. **Equity Capital Needed:** $135,900-$195,900. **Franchise Fee:** $30,000. **Training:** No.

15967 ■ Oogles N Googles
9640 N Augusta Dr.
Carmel, IN 46032
Ph:(317)228-9177
Fax:(317)228-9178
No. of Franchise Units: 10. **Founded:** 2001. **Franchised:** 2003. **Description:** Birthday parties, and preschool enrichment. **Equity Capital Needed:** $33,400-$40,700. **Franchise Fee:** $19,900. **Royalty Fee:** 7%. **Financial Assistance:** No. **Training:** Available at headquarters for 10 days.

15968 ■ Platoon Fitness
899 Penn St.
Bryn Mawr, PA 19010
Free: 888-752-8666
Fax:(610)581-7174
No. of Company-Owned Units: 5. **Founded:** 1999. **Franchised:** 2006. **Description:** Outdoor fitness & personal training centers. **Equity Capital Needed:** $2,500. **Franchise Fee:** $5,000. **Financial Assistance:** In-house financing available. **Training:** Offers 2 weeks training at headquarters, 2 months onsite, additional training 5 times a year at franchisee's location, and ongoing support.

15969 ■ Retro Fitness
43 CR 537 W
Colts Neck, NJ 07722
Ph:(732)431-0062
No. of Franchise Units: 72. **No. of Company-Owned Units:** 4. **Founded:** 2002. **Franchised:** 2006. **Description:** Fitness center. **Equity Capital Needed:** $661,750-$1,519,999. **Franchise Fee:** $69,000. **Royalty Fee:** 5%. **Financial Assistance:** Limited third party financing available. **Training:** Provides 8 days training at headquarters, 8 days at franchisees location and ongoing support.

15970 ■ SMASHMOUTH
2378 Boston Rd., Ste. 522
Wilbraham, MA 01095
Ph:(413)242-1111
URL: http://www.smashmouthbrand.com
Founded: 2005. Description: SMASHMOUTH is fitness "formatter" and your "one-stop" fitness source. We have taken over 30 formats & brought them together under the umbrella of one brand. Our "Pure Fitness" and "Personal Enhancement" categories encompass dozens of different formats for coed, women, men, seniors and kids. Equity Capital Needed: Varies, depending on format. Financial Assistance: Yes. Training: Yes.

15971 ■ Snap Fitness Inc.
2411 Galpin Ct., Ste. 110
Chanhassen, MN 55317
Ph:(952)474-5422
Free: 877-474—542
Fax:(952)426-7161
No. of Franchise Units: 1,013. No. of Company-Owned Units: 39. Founded: 2003. Franchised: 2004. Description: 24-hour fitness center. Equity Capital Needed: $76,113-$361,695. Franchise Fee: $15,000. Royalty Fee: $449/month. Financial Assistance: Limited in-house financing available. Training: Provides 2 days at headquarters with ongoing support.

15972 ■ Sportball Systems Inc.
39 Glen Cameron Rd., Unit 8
Thornhill, ON, Canada L3T 1P1
Ph:(905)882-4473
Free: 877-678-5437
Fax:(905)882-8453
Co. E-mail: franchise@sportball.ca
URL: http://www.sportball.ca
No. of Franchise Units: 82. No. of Company-Owned Units: 140. Founded: 1995. Franchised: 2005. Description: Sportball provides unique, noncompetitive sports programs, camps and birthday parties for children 16 months to 8 years. Children learn the concepts and skills required for hockey, baseball, basketball, soccer, volleyball, tennis and golf. Equity Capital Needed: $30,000 (min). Franchise Fee: $20,000. Training: Includes 2 weeks training.

15973 ■ Survivor Bootcamp
11087 Barnston View Rd.
Pitt Meadows, BC, Canada V3Y 2W8
Ph:(604)357-3179
Free: 877-266-8267
Fax:(604)460-7194
Co. E-mail: seana@survivorbootcamp.com
URL: http://www.survivorbootcamp.com
No. of Franchise Units: 47. No. of Company-Owned Units: 2. Founded: 2004. Franchised: 2006. Description: Indoor/Outdoor Fitness Training for EveryBody! Get Motivated for 1 hour a day / 3-5 days a week / 4 weeks What sets us apart from other fitness companies? We motivate clients in small classes with personal training attention. We are all about total body conditioning for accelerated results for all fitness levels. Our program is designed to encourage personal improvement and goal achievement in a supportive group setting. Participants are encouraged to compete only against themselves. Equity Capital Needed: $8,000 investment required; $2,000 start-up capital. Franchise Fee: $5,000. Training: Provides 1 week training in Vancouver.

15974 ■ Time For Fitness LLC
667 Waterview Cove
Eagan, MN 55123
Ph:(612)703-6151
Fax:(952)345-8870
Founded: 2004. Franchised: 2005. Description: Health club for baby boomers and seniors. Equity Capital Needed: $58,000-$68,000. Franchise Fee: $30,000. Royalty Fee: 5%. Financial Assistance: No. Training: Provides 6 days training at headquarters and ongoing support.

15975 ■ Twist Sport Conditioning Centers
1225 East Keith Rd., Ste. 12
North Vancouver, BC, Canada V7J 1J3
Ph:(604)904-6556
Fax:(604)904-6558
Co. E-mail: franchise@sportconditioning.ca
URL: http://www.twistconditioning.com
No. of Franchise Units: 4. No. of Company-Owned Units: 1. Founded: 1999. Description: Specializes in performance enhancement through sport-specific conditioning. Equity Capital Needed: $300,000-$400,000. Franchise Fee: $40,000.

COMPUTERIZED DATABASES

15976 ■ The Physician & Sportsmedicine
Vendome Group L.L.C.
149 5th Ave., 10th Fl.
New York, NY 10010
Ph:(212)812-8420
Free: 800-519-3692
Fax:(212)228-1308
Co. E-mail: customerservice@vendomegrpsubs.com
URL: http://www.vendomegrp.com
Description: Contains the complete text of The Physician & Sportsmedicine magazine, covering clinical articles on the recognition, treatment, and prevention of injury and disease caused by exercise and sport. Includes reports on such training and conditioning principles as nutrition, exercise methods, and fitness evaluation. Also covers injury prevention, amelioration of chronic disease, and the use of sports and games for conditioning and rehabilitation of physically handicapped people. Availability: Online: Vendome Group L.L.C., Dow Jones & Company Inc. Type: Full text.

15977 ■ Smoking and Health Resource Library
U.S. Centers for Disease Control and Prevention
4770 Buford Hwy.
MS K-50
Atlanta, GA 30341
Ph:(404)639-3311
Free: 800-331-3435
Fax:(404)232-3299
Co. E-mail: tobaccoinfo@cdc.gov
URL: http://www.cdc.gov/tobacco
Description: Contains more than 57,000 citations, with some abstracts, to worldwide scientific and technical literature on tobacco, tobacco use, and smoking. Sources include scientific and translated journals, technical reports, bibliographies, books and book chapters, conference proceedings, government documents, policy and legal documents, editorials, letters and patents. Also available as part of the Chronic Disease Prevention (CDP) File CD-ROM (described in a separate entry). Availability: Online: U.S. National Library of Medicine, U.S. Centers for Disease Control and Prevention. Type: Bibliographic.

15978 ■ SportDiscus
Sport Information Resource Centre
180 Elgin St., Ste. 1400
Ottawa, ON, Canada K2P 2K3
Ph:(613)231-7472
Free: 800-665-6413
Fax:(613)231-3739
Co. E-mail: moreinfo@sirc.ca
URL: http://www.sirc.ca
Description: Contains more than 700,000 bibliographic citations, some with abstracts, to the worldwide scientific and practical literature (articles, monographs, dissertations, conference proceedings, research reports, audiovisual material) for individual and team sports, sports medicine, physical fitness, physical education, recreation and related areas. Covers the literature on practice, strategy, technique, training, equipment, sport psychology, biomechanics, exercise physiology, teaching, coaching, and officiating. Also covered are sports for the disabled, sports facilities (including management, maintenance and design) and international sports history. Also provides more than 13,000 URLs linking to these topics. Sources in English, Spanish, Italian, and French are covered completely, but for those in other languages, only scientific/research items are references. Availability: Online: Wolters Kluwer Health, ProQuest LLC, ProQuest LLC, ProQuest LLC, EBSCO Publishing; CD-ROM: Wolters Kluwer Health; Magnetic Tape: Wolters Kluwer Health; Batch: Sport Information Resource Centre. Type: Bibliographic.

LIBRARIES

15979 ■ Indiana University–Health, Physical Education & Recreation Library
HPER Bldg. 029
1025 E. 7th St.
Bloomington, IN 47405
Ph:(812)855-4420
Fax:(812)855-6778
Co. E-mail: jiliu@indiana.edu
URL: http://www.libraries.iub.edu/index.php-?pageId=83
Contact: Jian Liu, Hd.
Scope: Physical education, recreation and park administration, health and safety, coaching, adapted physical education and therapeutic recreation, sports medicine and psychology. Services: Interlibrary loan; copying; Library open to the public. Holdings: 25,274 volumes; 10,871 microforms. Subscriptions: 250 journals and other serials.

15980 ■ Lemmen-Holton Cancer Pavilion Library
135 Michigan NE
330 Barclay Ave., NE
Grand Rapids, MI 49503
Ph:(616)391-1655
Fax:(616)391-3527
Co. E-mail: diane.hummel@spectrum-health.org
URL: http://www.spectrum-health.org/
Contact: Diane Hummel, Lib.Mgr.
Scope: Cancer. Services: Library open to the public. Holdings: Pamphlets.

15981 ■ Springfield College–Babson Library I Special Collections
263 Alden St.
Springfield, MA 01109-3797
Ph:(413)748-3315
Fax:(413)748-3631
Co. E-mail: libraryref@spfldcol.edu
URL: http://www.spfldcol.edu/library
Contact: Andrea Taupier, Lib.Dir.
Scope: Recreation, physical education and training. Services: Interlibrary loan; copying; collections open to the public with permission. Holdings: 145,700 books; 25,000 bound periodical volumes; 3000 archives; 735,000 microfiche; 12,900 microfilm; 2960 videocassettes; 5000 phone cards. Subscriptions: 820 journals and other serials; 10 newspapers.

15982 ■ State University of New York College at Cortland Memorial Library
81 Prospect Terrace
Cortland, NY 13045
Ph:(607)753-2525
Fax:(607)753-5669
Co. E-mail: library.emailaccount@cortland.edu
URL: http://library.cortland.edu
Contact: Gail Wood, Lib.Dir.
Scope: Education, recreation, physical education, health education. Services: Interlibrary loan; copying; SDI; Library open to the public with restrictions. Holdings: 371,692 books; 45,403 bound periodical volumes; 844,207 microforms; 4104 audio/visual programs; 50 VF drawers; 9800 pamphlets; 89 online databases. Subscriptions: 526 journals; 3 newspapers; 36 electronic databases.

15983 ■ Tuality Health Information Resource Center
334 SE 8th Ave.
Hillsboro, OR 97123-9019
Ph:(503)681-1702
Co. E-mail: tuality.library@tuality.org
URL: http://www.tuality.org
Scope: Health, fitness, nutrition, diseases, support groups. Services: Interlibrary loan; copying; Library open to the public. Holdings: 800 books; 3000 pamphlets; 90 anatomical models and charts; 450 videotapes. Subscriptions: 24 journals and other serials.

15984 ■ Universite de Montreal–Bibliotheque de Kinesiologie
CEPSUM
2100, boul. Edouard-Montpetit
8e etage, salle 8259
Montreal, QC, Canada H3C 3J7
Ph:(514)343-6765
Fax:(514)343-2181
Co. E-mail: denise.diamond@umontreal.ca
URL: http://www.bib.umontreal.ca/SA/kinesio.htm
Contact: Denise Diamond, Chf.Libn.
Scope: Physical education, sports medicine, exercise, physiology and training. **Services:** Interlibrary loan; copying; Library open to the public with restrictions. **Holdings:** 23,125 books; 9349 bound periodical volumes; 21,661 microforms; 1982 reports; 310 AV programs. **Subscriptions:** 223 journals and other serials.

15985 ■ University of Illinois–Applied Health Sciences Library
Main Library, Rm. 146
1408 W. Gregory Dr.
Urbana, IL 61801
Ph:(217)333-3615
Fax:(217)333-8384
Co. E-mail: mballen@uiuc.edu
URL: http://www.library.illinois.edu/ahs/
Contact: Mary Beth Allen, Hd.Libn. & Assoc.Prof.
Scope: Kinesiology and exercise science, sports medicine, psychology, sociology, history of sport, rehabilitation education, counseling, speech and hearing science, community health, public health, gerontology, aging. **Services:** Interlibrary loan. **Holdings:** 29,315 volumes; 1407 theses; 6 VF drawers of pamphlets; 10,536 microcards; 30,000 microfiche; 19,000 microform publications. **Subscriptions:** 300 journals and other serials.

15986 ■ University of North Carolina at Greensboro–Special Collections & Rare Books, Jackson Library–History of Physical Education and Dance Collection (222B)
222B Jackson Library
PO Box 26170
Greensboro, NC 27402-6170
Ph:(336)334-5246
Fax:(336)334-5399
Co. E-mail: carolyn_shankle@uncg.edu
URL: http://library.uncg.edu/info/depts/scua
Contact: Carolyn Shankle, Spec.Coll.Spec.
Scope: Physical activity, training, theory; gymnastics; dance history. **Services:** Collection open to the public for research. **Holdings:** 1800 books and pamphlets.

RESEARCH CENTERS

15987 ■ Canadian Fitness and Lifestyle Research Institute–Institut Canadien de la Recherche sur la Condition Physique et le mode de vie
201-185 Somerset St. W
Ottawa, ON, Canada K2P 0J2
Ph:(613)233-5528
Fax:(613)233-5536
Co. E-mail: info@cflri.ca
URL: http://www.cflri.ca
Contact: Cora Lynn Craig, Pres./Ch.Sci.
E-mail: info@cflri.ca
Scope: Population fitness levels, recreation habits, and link between physical activity and other life-style patterns of Canadians; benefits and costs of a physically active lifestyle. **Publications:** The Research File (3/year).

15988 ■ The Cooper Institute
12330 Preston Rd.
Dallas, TX 75230
Ph:(972)341-3200
Free: 800—635-7050
Fax:(972)341-3227
Co. E-mail: courses@cooperinst.org
URL: http://www.cooperinstitute.org
Contact: Kenneth H. Cooper MD, Ch./CEO
E-mail: courses@cooperinst.org
Scope: Cardiovascular disease, stress management, women's health, exercise physiology, health promotion, nutrition, youth fitness, hypertension, aging, and epidemiology. Using data from the affiliated Cooper Clinic, the Institute conducts the Aerobics Center Longitudinal Study, which monitors 25,000 subjects over their lifetime to study the effects of exercise and health habits on death and disability rates from chronic diseases. **Services:** Assistance for public and private organizations in the implementation of wellness programs for employees; Fitnessgram, a computerized fitness report card for children.

ASSOCIATIONS AND OTHER ORGANIZATIONS

15989 ■ Acupuncture Foundation of Canada Institute–Institute de la Fondation D'Acupuncture du Canada
2131 Lawrence Ave. E, Ste. 204
Scarborough, ON, Canada M1R 5G4
Ph:(416)752-3988
Fax:(416)752-4398
Co. E-mail: afciweb@afcinstitute.com
URL: http://www.afcinstitute.com
Contact: Cheryll A. Kwok, Exec. Dir.
Description: Promotes acupuncture's legitimate place in health care by initiating and supporting research in acupuncture.

15990 ■ American Alternative Medical Association
2200 Market St., Ste. 803
Galveston, TX 77550-1530
Ph:(409)621-2600
Free: 888-764-2237
Fax:(775)703-5334
Co. E-mail: office@joinaama.com
URL: http://www.joinaama.com
Contact: Donald A. Rosenthal MD, Exec. Dir.
Description: Fosters unity among "grassroots practitioners" and those with advanced academic credentials. Educates the public that good health can be obtained without the use of drugs. Encourages improved public awareness of the benefits of alternative health care. .

15991 ■ American Physical Therapy Association
1111 N Fairfax St.
Alexandria, VA 22314-1488
Ph:(703)684-2782
Free: 800-999-2782
Fax:(703)684-7343
Co. E-mail: memberservices@apta.org
URL: http://www.apta.org
Contact: Mr. John D. Barnes, CEO
Description: Professional organization of physical therapists and physical therapist assistants and students. Fosters the development and improvement of physical therapy service, education, and research; evaluates the organization and administration of curricula; directs the maintenance of standards and promotes scientific research. Acts as an accrediting body for educational programs in physical therapy. Establishes standards. Offers advisory and consultation services to schools of physical therapy and facilities offering physical therapy services; provides placement services at conference. **Publications:** *Physical Therapy* (monthly); *PT Bulletin Online* (weekly); *PT Magazine* (monthly).

15992 ■ American Physical Therapy Association, Orthopaedic Section
2920 E Ave. S, Ste. 200
La Crosse, WI 54601
Ph:(608)788-3982

Free: 800-444-3982
Fax:(608)788-3965
Co. E-mail: tdeflorian@orthopt.org
URL: http://www.orthopt.org
Contact: Terri DeFlorian, Exec. Dir.
Description: Orthopaedic physical therapists and physical therapist assistants who belong to the American Physical Therapy Association; physical therapy educators and students. Supports the continued growth of the physical therapy profession through education and research; promotes development of a standard certification procedure for the field. Seeks to assure the quality of physical therapy curricula at both the undergraduate and postgraduate levels. Facilitates communication among orthopedic physical therapists and other health care professionals. Gathers and disseminates information on the care of musculoskeletal disorders. Provides access to a network of orthopaedic study groups. **Publications:** *Journal of Orthopaedic and Sports Physical Therapy* (monthly); *Orthopaedic Physical Therapy Practice* (quarterly).

15993 ■ American Physical Therapy Association, Private Practice Section
1055 N Fairfax St., Ste. 100
Alexandria, VA 22314
Ph:(703)299-2410
Free: 800-517-1167
Fax:(703)299-2411
Co. E-mail: privatepracticesection@apta.org
URL: http://www.ppsapta.org
Contact: Thomas DiAngelis PT, Pres.
Description: Physical therapists who are members of the American Physical Therapy Association and who are in private practice. Purposes are: to provide physical therapists with information on establishing and managing a private practice; to promote high standards of private practice physical therapy; to represent private practitioners before governmental and professional agencies; to disseminate information relating to private practice. Monitors federal and state legislation. Holds forums and seminars. **Publications:** *An Employer's Guide to Obtaining Physical Therapy Services*; *Hire for Fit*; *How to Start a PT Private Practice*; *IMPACT* (monthly); *Private Practice Physical Therapy: The How-To Manual*; *Private Practice Section Membership Directory*; *Private Practice Valuation Primer - How to Value a Practice for Sale or Purchase*; *Private Practices: Strategies for Everyday Management* (monthly); *Safeguarding Your Practice: The Corporate Compliance Manual* (annual); *Twenty Questions About Private Practice*; *Understanding Computers in Healthcare: A Guidebook for Rehabilitation Professionals*; *The Valuation of a Physical Therapy Practice* .

15994 ■ Canadian Academy of Sport Medicine–L' Academie Canadienne de Medecine du Sport
180 Elgin St., Ste. 1400
Ottawa, ON, Canada K2P 2K3
Ph:(613)748-5851
Free: 877-585-2394

Fax:(613)231-3739
Co. E-mail: bfalardeau@casm-acms.org
URL: http://www.casm-acms.org
Contact: Dawn Haworth, Exec. Dir.
Description: Physicians committed to excellence in the practice of medicine as it applies to all aspects of physical activity. Seeks to be a leader in advancing the art and science of sport medicine, including health promotion and disease prevention, for the benefit of all Canadians through programs of education, research, and service. **Publications:** *Clinical Journal of Sport Medicine* (quarterly).

15995 ■ Canadian Association of Physical Medicine and Rehabilitation
774 Echo Dr.
Ottawa, ON, Canada K1S 5N8
Ph:(613)730-6245
Fax:(613)730-1116
Co. E-mail: capmr@royalcollege.ca
URL: http://www.capmr.ca
Contact: Dr. Thomas A. Miller, Pres.
Description: Aims to provide and maintain a national professional forum and network for the exchange of information and opinion. Contributes to the advancement of the specialty of physical medicine and rehabilitation. Seeks to provide rehabilitation within the health care of Canadians. **Publications:** *CAPM&R Newsletter* (3/year).

15996 ■ Canadian Athletic Therapists Association–Association Canadienne des Therapeutes du Sport
1040 7th Ave. SW, Ste. 402
Calgary, AB, Canada T2P 3G9
Ph:(403)509-2282
Fax:(403)509-2280
Co. E-mail: info@athletictherapy.org
URL: http://www.athletictherapy.org
Contact: Ms. Helena De Fazio, Admin. Asst.
Description: Athletic therapists and other individuals engaged in the practice of sports medicine. Promotes advancement of the study and practice of sports medicine and athletic therapy; seeks to enhance the professional status of members. Encourages adoption of healthy and active lifestyles. Facilitates communication among members. Develops standards of conduct and practice. Delivers sports medical services to grass roots sports organizations throughout Canada. Conducts educational programs; maintains hall of fame.

15997 ■ Foundation for Physical Therapy
1111 N Fairfax St.
Alexandria, VA 22314-1488
Ph:(703)684-2782
Free: 800-875-1378
Fax:(703)706-8587
Co. E-mail: info@foundation4pt.org
URL: http://foundation4pt.org
Contact: Barbara Malm MBA, Exec. Dir.
Description: Supports the physical therapy profession's research needs by funding scientific and clinically-relevant physical therapy research. .

15998 ■ Institute for Traditional Medicine and Preventive Health Care
2017 SE Hawthorne Blvd.
Portland, OR 97214
Ph:(503)233-4907
Fax:(503)233-1017
Co. E-mail: itm@itmonline.org
URL: http://www.itmonline.org
Contact: Subhuti Dharmananda PhD, Dir.

Description: Helps people seeking traditional medicine knowledge and services by clarifying the nature of traditional medicine and demonstrating how it can be utilized in the modern setting. Provides educational materials and articles on traditional medicine and related topics. Conducts background research in traditional medicine including journal searches in China and computer searches in the US. Provides especially designed herbal formulations for use in clinics and practitioners who read institutes literature. **Publications:** *A Bag of Pearls*; *Internet Journal of the Institute for Traditional Medicine* .

15999 ■ National Ayurvedic Medical Association
620 Cabrillo Ave.
Santa Cruz, CA 95065
Free: 800-669-8914
Co. E-mail: info@ayurveda-nama.org
URL: http://www.ayurveda-nama.org
Contact: Ms. Hilary Garivaltis, Pres.

Description: Represents the interests of the Ayurvedic profession. Aims to preserve, protect, improve, and promote the philosophy, knowledge, science and practice of Ayurveda. Maintains the professional competency and licensing of Ayurveda through enhancement of knowledge, practice and application of Ayurvedic profession. Encourages the public to appreciate and accept Ayurveda. .

16000 ■ Sound Healers Association
PO Box 2240
Boulder, CO 80306
Ph:(303)443-8181
Free: 800-246-9764
Fax:(303)443-6023
Co. E-mail: info@soundhealersassociation.org
URL: http://www.soundhealersassociation.org
Contact: Jonathan Goldman, Founder/Dir.

Description: Promotes research and awareness for the use of sound and music as therapeutic and transformational modalities for healing. .

16001 ■ Vocational Rehabilitation Association of Canada
201 Consumers Rd., Ste. 302
Toronto, ON, Canada M2J 4G8
Ph:(416)494-4700
Free: 888-876-9992
Fax:(416)494-9139
Co. E-mail: info@vracanada.com
URL: http://vracanada.com
Contact: Kathy Regan, Exec. Dir.

Description: Professional association for people working in the field of rehabilitation. Promotes excellence in rehabilitation education, training, and practice. Formulates and enforces Code of Ethics. Facilitates communication to its members and stakeholders. Responsible for professional development, promotion of the Canadian Certified Rehabilitation Counsellor (CCRC), Certified Vocational Evaluator (CVE), and the granting of the Registered Rehabilitation Professional (RRP) designation to qualified members. **Publications:** *Rehab Review* (quarterly); *Rehabilitation Journal* (quarterly).

REFERENCE WORKS

16002 ■ "Kenosha 'Lifestyle Center' Delayed" in *The Business Journal-Milwaukee* (Vol. 25, August 8, 2008, No. 46, pp. A1)
Pub: American City Business Journals, Inc.

Ed: Rich Kirchen. **Description:** Quality Centers of Orlando, Florida has postponed construction plans for the Kenosha Town Center in Kenosha County, Wisconsin to 2009 due to the economic downturn and lending concerns. The $200-million, 750,000-square-foot retail and residential center will be located near the corner of Wisconsin Highway 50 and I-94.

16003 ■ "On Their Own" in *Crain's Cleveland Business* (Vol. 28, November 12, 2007, No. 45, pp. 19)
Pub: Crain Communications, Inc.

Ed: Eileen Beal. **Description:** Discusses the reasons more physicians with entrepreneurial spirit are opening their own practices as well the added challenges and responsibilities that comes with owning one's own practice.

16004 ■ "Q&A With Devin Ringling: Franchise's Services Go Beyond Elder Care" in *Gazette* (October 2, 2010)
Pub: The Gazette

Ed: Bill Radford. **Description:** Profile of franchise, Interim HealthCare, in Colorado Springs, Colorado; the company offers home care services that include wound care and specialized feedings to shopping and light housekeeping. It also runs a medical staffing company that provides nurses, therapists and other health care workers to hospitals, prisons, schools and other facilities.

TRADE PERIODICALS

16005 ■ *Pediatric Physical Therapy*
Pub: Lippincott Williams & Wilkins
Contact: Paul Gee, Publisher
E-mail: paul.gee@wolterskluwer.com

Ed: Ann F. VanSant, Editor, ann.vansant@temple.edu. **Released:** Quarterly. **Price:** $159; $319 institutions; $109 in-training; $259 other countries; $416 institutions, other countries. **Description:** Peer-reviewed journal reporting on new clinical care for pediatric patients.

16006 ■ *Physical Medicine and Rehabilitation Clinics of North America*
Pub: Elsevier
Contact: Prof. George H. Kraft MD, Consulting Ed.

Released: Quarterly. **Price:** $540 institutions, other countries; $345 other countries; $175 students, other countries; $414 institutions; $122 students; $280 Canada; $230; $175 students, Canada; $540 institutions, Canada. **Description:** Journal for long-term care professionals.

16007 ■ *Physical & Occupational Therapy in Geriatrics*
Pub: Informa Healthcare

Ed: Ellen Dunleavey Taira, Editor, ellentaira@earthlink.net. **Released:** Quarterly. **Price:** $475 institutions; $845 institutions; $630 institutions. **Description:** Journal for allied health professionals focusing on current practice and emerging issues in the health care of and rehabilitation of the older client.

16008 ■ *Physical and Occupational Therapy in Pediatrics*
Pub: Informa Healthcare
Contact: Robert J. Palisano, Co-Ed.

Released: Quarterly. **Price:** $865; $1,725 institutions corporate. **Description:** Journal for therapists involved in developmental and physical rehabilitation of infants and children.

16009 ■ *Physical Therapy*
Pub: American Physical Therapy Association
Contact: Rebecca L. Craik PhD, Editor-in-Chief
E-mail: rebeccacraik@apta.org

Released: Monthly. **Description:** Journal of the American Physical Therapy Association.

16010 ■ *Physical Therapy Products*
Pub: Novicom Inc.
Contact: Jody Rich, Gp. Publisher
E-mail: jrich@allied360.com

Ed: Stephen Noonoo, Editor, snoonoo@allied360.com. **Released:** Monthly. **Price:** Free to qualified subscribers. **Description:** Magazine featuring new products and services available in the physical therapy field.

16011 ■ *Physical Therapy Reimbursement News*
Pub: American Physical Therapy Association

Ed: Debra Lansey, Editor, debralansey@apta.org. **Released:** Bimonthly. **Price:** $79, members; $110, nonmembers. **Description:** Tracks reimbursement trends in the medical field of physical therapy.

16012 ■ *PT in Motion*
Pub: American Physical Therapy Association
Contact: Alice Starcke, Asst. News Ed.
E-mail: alicestarcke@apta.org

Released: Monthly. **Price:** $119 Included in membership international; $119 institutions non-members; $139 institutions, other countries non-members. **Description:** Magazine for physical therapy professionals.

TRADE SHOWS AND CONVENTIONS

16013 ■ American Academy of Physical Medicine and Rehabilitation Annual Assembly
American Academy of Physical Medicine and Rehabilitation
9700 W. Bryn Mawr Ave., Ste. 200
Rosemont, IL 60018-5701
Ph:(847)737-6000
Fax:(847)737-6001
Co. E-mail: info@aapmr.org
URL: http://www.aapmr.org

Released: Annual. **Audience:** Physicians specializing in physical medicine and rehabilitation. **Principal Exhibits:** Pharmaceuticals, electrodiagnostic equipment, wheelchairs, and related equipment, supplies, and services. **Dates and Locations:** 2011 Nov 17-20, Orlando, FL; 2012 Nov 15-18, Atlanta, GA; 2013 Oct 03-06, Washington, DC; 2014 Nov 13-16, San Diego, CA.

16014 ■ American Physical Therapy Association Annual Conference
American Physical Therapy Association
1111 N. Fairfax St.
Alexandria, VA 22314-1488
Ph:(703)684-2782
Free: 800-999-2782
Fax:(703)684-7343
URL: http://www.apta.org

Released: Annual. **Audience:** Physical therapists, physical therapists assistants, and allied health professionals. **Principal Exhibits:** Physical therapy products, equipment, and services. **Dates and Locations:** 2011 Jun 08-11, National Harbor, MD; 2012 Jun 06-09, Tampa, FL.

16015 ■ National Association of Rehabilitation Professionals in the Private Sector Annual Conference
National Association of Rehabilitation Professionals in the Private Sector
3450 Soquel Ave., Ste. A
Santa Cruz, CA 95062
Ph:(831)464-4892
Free: 800-240-9059
Fax:(831)576-1417
URL: http://www.rehabpro.org

Released: Annual. **Audience:** Medical and vocational rehabilitation providers, insurance industry representatives, and medical rehabilitation equipment manufacturers. **Principal Exhibits:** Medical and vocational rehabilitation products, facilities, and case management companies.

16016 ■ Texas Physical Therapy Association Annual Conference
Texas Physical Therapy Association
701 Brazos St., Ste. 440
Austin, TX 78701
Ph:(512)477-1818
Fax:(512)477-1434
Co. E-mail: orlando@tpta.org
URL: http://www.tpta.org

Released: Annual. **Audience:** Physical therapists, physical theapists assistants, and physical therapy students. **Principal Exhibits:** Physical therapy recruiters, equipment, supplies, books, and services.

CONSULTANTS

16017 ■ Cedric Prange Associates Inc.
11120 Fort St.
Omaha, NE 68164-2118
Ph:(402)493-1888
Fax:(402)493-1007
Contact: Cedric Prange, President
Scope: Provides consulting services in management, financial and tax planning for physicians, dentists, and health-related businesses. **Publications:** "Money Magazines Tax Preparer," Mar, 1997.

16018 ■ Kennedy Group Inc.
111 E Wacker Dr., Ste. 1050
PO Box 813080
Chicago, IL 60681-3080
Ph:(312)943-5157
Fax:(312)242-1626
Co. E-mail: tkg@tkgnet.net
Contact: Johnny Gomez, Director
E-mail: jgomez@atstkgnet.com
Scope: Providing healthcare information technology, HCIT strategic services to healthcare enterprises, technology firms, investment banks, investment firms, venture capital firms, and medical product and service companies.

16019 ■ Pathways To Wellness
617 Everhart Rd.
Corpus Christi, TX 78411
Ph:(361)985-9642
Fax:(361)949-4627
Co. E-mail: path2wellness@earthlink.net
URL: http://www.path2wellness.com
Contact: Evy Coppola, Owner
Scope: Offer natural holistic health counseling, yoga and hatha yoga classes, teachers training and cookery classes for individuals and companies. Health counseling includes nutritional guidance, kinesiology, iridology, reflexology, energy healing, massage therapy, herbal and vitamin therapy, creative visualization and meditation. Provides supplements which bring about the same effects as that of natural sunshine. **Seminars:** Is It You Holding You Back?; The Balancing Act. . .Career. . . Family. . .and Self; Learning the Art of Friendly Persuasion; Stop Accepting What You Are Getting and Start Asking for What You Want!; Introduction to Natural Health and Healthy Living; Learn Why One Size Approaches to the Answers on Health Do Not Work; Introduction to Yoga. What is it? Who can do it? What can it do for you.

16020 ■ T. L. Coward
112 Kenwood St.
Belmont, NC 28012-3119
Ph:(704)825-1904
Fax:(704)825-1905
Co. E-mail: hcoward@bellsouth.net
E-mail: hcoward@bellsouth.net
Scope: Professional practice management consultant serving physicians, dentists, and other health care professionals.

COMPUTERIZED DATABASES

16021 ■ ABLEDATA
U.S. National Institute on Disability and Rehabilitation Research
8630 Fenton St., Ste. 930
Silver Spring, MD 20910
Ph:(301)608-8998
Free: 800-227-0216
Fax:(301)608-8958
Co. E-mail: abledata@macrointernational.com
URL: http://www.abledata.com
Description: Contains descriptions of more than 36,000 products and equipment made available by nearly 3000 manufacturers for use by persons with disabilities. Covers rehabilitative aids and equipment for personal care, home management, mobility, communication, therapeutic, sensory, educational, vocational, and transportation needs. For each product, provides generic name, brand name (i.e., trade name and/or model number), manufacturer's name, address, and telephone number, availability (i.e., major

distributor), cost, user comments (e.g., contraindications, limitations) and, if available, formal evaluation data. **Availability:** Online: U.S. National Institute on Disability and Rehabilitation Research, U.S. National Institute on Disability and Rehabilitation Research. **Type:** Directory.

LIBRARIES

16022 ■ American Physical Therapy Association–Information Resources
1111 N. Fairfax St.
Alexandria, VA 22314-1488
Ph:(703)706-8534
Free: 800-999-2782
Fax:(703)684-7343
Co. E-mail: inforesources@apta.org
URL: http://www.apta.org
Contact: Gini Blodgett Birchett, Dir., Info.Rsrcs.
Scope: Physical therapy. **Services:** Library available to researchers by appointment only. **Holdings:** 3000 books; photographs; reports; dissertations; oral histories; conference proceedings; Annual reports. **Subscriptions:** 200 journals and other serials.

16023 ■ Community Therapy Services Inc. Library
201-1555 St. James
Winnipeg, MB, Canada R3H 1B5
Ph:(204)949-0533
Fax:(204)942-1428
Co. E-mail: cts@ctsinc.mb.ca
Contact: Irwin Corobow, Exec.Dir.
Scope: Physiotherapy, occupational therapy, speech language, pathology. **Services:** Interlibrary loan; Library accepts phone inquiries. **Holdings:** 200 books; 50 videocassettes. **Subscriptions:** 5 journals and other serials.

16024 ■ Florida A&M University–Frederick S. Humphries Science Research Center Library
401-501 Science Research Center
309 Pershing St.
Tallahassee, FL 32307
Ph:(850)599-3393
Fax:(850)599-3422
Co. E-mail: william.nichols@famu.edu
URL: http://www.famu.edu/index.
    cfma=library&p=ScienceResearch
Contact: William Nichols, Assoc.Univ.Libn.
Scope: Pharmacy, allied health, physics, computer science, environmental science, respiratory therapy, physical therapy, healthcare management, medical records administration, occupational therapy. **Services:** Interlibrary loan; copying; SDI; Library open to the public. **Holdings:** 5989 bound periodical volumes; 915 print and online journals; 791 microcards; 24,102 monographs. **Subscriptions:** 697 journals and other serials; 5 newspapers.

16025 ■ Texas Woman's University–F.W. and Bessie Dye Memorial Library
1810 Inwood Rd.
Dallas, TX 75235
Ph:(214)689-6580
Fax:(214)689-6583
Co. E-mail: eoliphant@twu.edu
URL: http://www.twu.edu/library
Contact: Eula Oliphant, Coord.
Scope: Nursing, healthcare administration. **Services:** Interlibrary loan; copying; Library open to the public for reference use only. **Holdings:** 15,872 books; 40,000 books (for all TWU locations); 5400 bound periodical volumes; 225 bound theses, dissertations, and professional papers. **Subscriptions:** 72 print journals and other serials.

16026 ■ University of South Dakota–Christian P. Lommen Health Sciences Library
University of South Dakota School of Medicine
414 E. Clark St.
Vermillion, SD 57069-2307
Ph:(605)677-5348

Fax:(605)677-5124
Co. E-mail: dhulkone@usd.edu
URL: http://www.usd.edu/library/
Contact: David A. Hulkonen, Dir.
Scope: Anatomy, physiology, pharmacology, microbiology, pathology, biochemistry, nursing, dental hygiene, medical technology, physical therapy, occupational therapy, physician assistant, clinical medicine, social work. **Services:** Interlibrary loan; copying; SDI; consultation services for hospitals; Library open to the public. **Holdings:** 35,000 books; 60,000 bound periodical volumes; 300 AV programs. **Subscriptions:** 1000 journals and other serials.

RESEARCH CENTERS

16027 ■ Ball State University–Human Performance Laboratory
2000 W University Ave.
Muncie, IN 47306
Ph:(765)285-1158
Fax:(765)285-8596
Co. E-mail: hpl@bsu.edu
URL: http://www.bsu.edu/hpl
Contact: Scott Trappe PhD, Dir.
E-mail: hpl@bsu.edu
Scope: Human performance, including studies on effects of physical training on skeletal muscular metabolism, strength development, aging, research, biomechanics, youth fitness and health, nutritional studies, endocrine mechanisms (e.g. GH), fluid replacement during and following acute dehydration, muscle glycogen utilization during prolonged exertion, and swimming research. **Educational Activities:** Adult Fitness Program.

16028 ■ Boston Biomedical Research Institute
64 Grove St.
Watertown, MA 02472
Ph:(617)658-7806
Fax:(617)972-1759
Co. E-mail: emersonc@bbri.org
URL: http://www.bbri.org
Contact: Charles P. Emerson Jr., Dir.
E-mail: emersonc@bbri.org
Scope: Biological and medical sciences, including fundamental biomedical studies on cell metabolism, developmental biology, gene regulation, recombinant DNA, monoclonal antibodies, intercellular matrix biology, muscle diseases, connective tissue diseases, and muscular dystrophy. **Publications:** Messenger Newsletter (semiannually). **Educational Activities:** International Meetings and Symposia; Seminars (weekly).

16029 ■ Boston University–Neuromuscular Research Center
19 Deerfield St., 4th Fl.
Boston, MA 02215
Ph:(617)353-9757
Fax:(617)353-5737
Co. E-mail: cjd@bu.edu
URL: http://www.bu.edu/nmrc
Contact: Prof. Carlo J. De Luca PhD, Dir.
E-mail: cjd@bu.edu
Scope: Motor control, including motor unit firing during sustained isometric contractions, synchronization evaluation, synchronization across muscles, and modeling of force production in the muscle; low back pain, including normative database study of back muscle function, EMG parameters of lumbar back muscles, development of test protocols related to the behavior of back muscles, and muscle performance in the back analysis system compared to lifting tasks; posture and movement, etc. The center is organized into the following components: Motor Unit Lab, Muscle Fatigue Lab, Injury Analysis and Prevention Lab, Motion Analysis Lab, Motor Control Lab and Design Lab. **Publications:** Annual Activity Report. **Educational Activities:** NMRC Seminar Series.

16030 ■ Boston University–Neuromuscular Research Center–Muscle Fatigue Laboratory
19 Deerfield St., 4th Fl.
Boston, MA 02215
Ph:(617)358-0718

Fax:(617)353-5737
Co. E-mail: sroy@bu.edu
URL: http://www.bu.edu/nmrc/labs/mfl
Contact: Dr. Serge Roy, Supvr.
E-mail: sroy@bu.edu
Scope: Use of advanced signal processing techniques for the analysis of electromyographic signals, especially techniques for the analysis of nonstationary surface EMG data, to estimate localized muscle fatigue during static and dynamic contractions.

16031 ■ Bridgewater State College–Human Performance Lab
325 Plymouth St., Rm. 230
Bridgewater, MA 02325
Ph:(508)531-2064
Fax:(508)531-4064
Co. E-mail: rhaslam@bridgew.edu
Contact: Dr. Robert W. Haslam, Dir.
E-mail: rhaslam@bridgew.edu
Scope: Exercise physiology, including metabolic responses to exercise, blood flow responses to exercise, prediction of athlete success, police and fire fighter fitness, and general circulatory responses to exercise. **Services:** Provides standards for police and fire fighter fitness. **Educational Activities:** M.S. and B.S. programs in exercise science.

16032 ■ Brigham Young University–Human Performance Research Center
116 Richards Bldg.
Provo, UT 84602
Ph:(801)422-1285
Fax:(801)422-0555
Co. E-mail: allen_parcell@byu.edu
URL: http://hprc.byu.edu
Contact: Dr. Allen Parcell, Dir.
E-mail: allen_parcell@byu.edu
Scope: Exercise physiology, including studies of cardiovascular changes due to exercise, muscle changes with exercise, energy cost of various types of exercise, and body composition changes due to exercise; athletic injury rehabilitation, including therapeutic exercise, therapeutic modality, neural control. Biomechanics, including EMG, motion analysis, and muscle force generation.

16033 ■ Case Western Reserve University–Skeletal Research Center
Millis Science Ctr., Rm. 118
Department of Biology
2080 Adelbert Rd.
Cleveland, OH 44106-7080
Ph:(216)368-3562
Fax:(216)368-4077
Co. E-mail: aic@cwru.edu
URL: http://www.case.edu/artsci/biol/skeletal
Contact: Prof. Arnold I. Caplan PhD, Dir.
E-mail: aic@cwru.edu
Scope: Tissue engineered regeneration and clinical aspects of skeletal tissue, including cartilage, bones, tendons, and ligaments. **Services:** Medical services, through the Musculoskeletal Institute. **Educational Activities:** Graduate degree programs; Sponsors weekly, monthly, and annual conferences.

16034 ■ Cleveland FES Center
11000 Cedar Ave., Ste. 230
Cleveland, OH 44106-3052
Ph:(216)231-3257
Fax:(216)231-3258
Co. E-mail: cdudek@fescenter.org
URL: http://fescenter.org/index.php
Contact: P. Hunter Peckham PhD, Exec.Dir.
E-mail: cdudek@fescenter.org
Scope: Functional electrical stimulation (FES) in the restoration of muscle control or sensory function, particularly in the areas of lower and upper extremity deficits, scoliosis, spasticity, respiratory insufficiency, and bladder function. Studies focus on computer-controlled and implanted FES systems for paraplegic and quadraplegic users, persons with hemiplegia due to cerebral trauma or stroke, and persons with spinal cord injuries. **Services:** Consulting. **Publications:** Newsletter (quarterly). **Educational Activities:** Neural prosthesis seminars (monthly), presentations

focusing on all aspects of FES research from leading researchers throughout the world. Open to all students, researchers, and professionals.

16035 ■ Colorado State University–Human Performance Clinical/Research Laboratory
Department of Health & Exercise Science
Fort Collins, CO 80523-1582
Ph:(970)491-3847
Fax:(970)491-7677
Co. E-mail: israel@cahs.colostate.edu
URL: http://hes.cahs.colostate.edu/ResearchLabs/
Contact: Dr. Richard Gay Israel, Exec.Dir.
E-mail: israel@cahs.colostate.edu
Scope: Human performance, body composition, metabolism, nutrition and sports performance, and exercise physiology. **Services:** Stress testing, to the community.

16036 ■ Georgia Institute of Technology–Center for Assistive Technology and Environmental Access
College of Architecture
490 10th St. NW
Atlanta, GA 30332-0156
Ph:(404)894-4960
Free: 800—726-9119
Fax:(404)894-9320
Co. E-mail: jon.sanford@coa.gatech.edu
URL: http://www.catea.gatech.edu
Contact: Jon Sanford, Dir.
E-mail: jon.sanford@coa.gatech.edu
Scope: Universal design and assistive technology in accessible education and online information, workplace accommodations, wheeled mobility and seating, and environmental accessibility. **Publications:** Newsletter (quarterly). **Educational Activities:** Workshops; Continuing education classes; Webinars.

16037 ■ National Institute for Fitness and Sport
250 University Blvd.
Indianapolis, IN 46202
Ph:(317)274-3432
Fax:(317)274-7408
Co. E-mail: mroberts@nifs.org
URL: http://www.nifs.org
Contact: Melanie Roberts, Dir.
E-mail: mroberts@nifs.org
Scope: Exercise physiology, sports medicine, and health and fitness education. **Publications:** NIF Source (bimonthly). **Educational Activities:** Seminars, workshops, and classes.

16038 ■ National Institute for Rehabilitation Engineering
PO Box T
Hewitt, NJ 07421
Ph:(973)853-6585
Free: 800—736-2216
Fax:(928)832-2894
Co. E-mail: nire@theoffice.net
URL: http://www.angelfire.com/nj/nire2
Contact: Tom Schwanda, Pres./Chm.
E-mail: nire@theoffice.net
Scope: Invention, design, construction, fitting, and servicing of special devices for individuals with any specific physical disability or combination of disabilities; time/motion analyses; job modification engineering; task-performance mobility; driver training; computer software adapted for people with handicapping conditions. **Services:** Information services for special or personalized inquiries; User-training and placement, for physically disabled individuals.

16039 ■ Rehabilitation Institute of Chicago–Sensory Motor Performance Program
345 E Superior, Ste. 1396
Chicago, IL 60611-2654
Ph:(312)238-3381

Fax:(312)238-2208
Co. E-mail: w-rymer@northwestern.edu
URL: http://www.ric.org/research/centers/smpp/index.aspx
Contact: Dr. W. Zev Rymer, Dir.
E-mail: w-rymer@northwestern.edu
Scope: Rehabilitation medicine, brain trauma, stroke, atherosclerosis, neuromuscular diseases, applied neurophysiology, deep venous thrombosis, spinal cord injury, arthritis, prosthetics/orthotics, rehabilitation nursing, allied health, and communicative disorders.

16040 ■ Rehabilitation Institute of Michigan
261 Mack Ave.
Detroit, MI 48201
Ph:(313)745-1203
Fax:(313)745-1163
URL: http://www.rimrehab.org/
Contact: William H. Restum PhD, Pres.
Scope: Physical medicine and rehabilitation medicine, including electromyography, neuropsychology, measures of rehabilitation outcome, and methods of evaluation and treatment of patients with closed head injuries, spinal cord injuries, cerebrovascular accidents, and other diagnoses. **Services:** Inpatient and outpatient medical and rehabilitation services, in rheumatology, internal medicine, cardiology, orthopedic surgery, urology, psychiatry, neuropsychology, rehabilitation psychology, rehabilitation nursing, and occupational, speech and language, and physical. **Publications:** Research report (annually); Thinking Cap. **Educational Activities:** Clinical and research training for medical rehabilitation professionals; Del Harder Research Conference (annually). **Awards:** Del Harder Research Awards (annually).

16041 ■ University of Calgary–Human Performance Laboratory
Faculty of Kinesiology
2500 University Dr. NW
Calgary, AB, Canada T2N 1N4
Ph:(403)220-6472
Fax:(403)284-3553
Co. E-mail: nigg@ucalgary.ca
URL: http://www.kin.ucalgary.ca/hpl
Contact: Prof. Benno M. Nigg PhD, Co-Dir.
E-mail: nigg@ucalgary.ca
Scope: Mobility and longevity; biomechanics, including load on the musculoskeletal system, basic muscle mechanics, joint mechanics, lower back biomechanics, orthoses, sport shoes, and sports equipment; exercise physiology, including muscle physiology, limiting factors in performance and biochemistry of high performance; and neuromotor psychology, including studies involving ice hockey video discs and studies of eye movement in sports. **Services:** High performance team testing and sport surface/shoe testing. **Publications:** Annual report.

16042 ■ University of Delaware–Human Performance Laboratory
Department of Health, Nutrition & Exercise Sciences
Newark, DE 19716
Ph:(302)831-2265
Fax:(302)831-2828
Co. E-mail: provost@udel.edu
URL: http://www.udel.edu/HNES/OpenHouse/Announcement.htm
Contact: Michelle Provost-Craig PhD, Co-Dir.
E-mail: provost@udel.edu
Scope: Sports science, biomechanics, exercise physiology, bone density, and elite skaters.

16043 ■ University of Florida–Center for Exercise Science
Department of Applied Physiology & Kinesiology, Rm. 100, FLG
PO Box 118205
Gainesville, FL 32611
Ph:(352)392-0584
Fax:(352)392-5262
Co. E-mail: spowers@hhp.ufl.edu
URL: http://www.hhp.ufl.edu/apk/ces/ces.php
Contact: Scott Powers PhD, Dir.
E-mail: spowers@hhp.ufl.edu
Scope: Fitness as it relates to athletic performance, as well as the general population, including research on biomechanics and skill acquisition; health risk fac-

tors; exercise and the lumbar and cervical spine, sports, aging, menopause, diabetes, and athletic performance. **Publications:** Journal of Cardiopulmonary Rehabilitation. **Educational Activities:** Symposium (biennially).

16044 ■ University of Miami–Laboratory of Clinical and Applied Physiology

Max Orovitz Laboratories
PO Box 248065
Coral Gables, FL 33124-8065
Ph:(305)284-3024
Fax:(305)284-5168
Co. E-mail: aperry@miami.edu
URL: http://www.education.miami.edu/Program/
   Programs.asp?Program_ID=38
Contact: Dr. Arlette Perry, Dir.
E-mail: aperry@miami.edu

Scope: Health promotion/disease prevention, strength and conditioning, exercise metabolism, pediatric health promotion, muscle physiology, aging, cardiovascular physiology, sports nutrition, obesity, and lipid physiology. **Services:** Clinical evaluations for specialty populations, including diabetics, the elderly, the obese, and athletes; Laboratory services. **Educational Activities:** Graduate and postdoctoral instruction and extensive laboratory training (monthly).

16045 ■ University of Texas at Arlington–Human Performance Institute

PO Box 19180
Arlington, TX 76019-0180
Ph:(817)273-2335
Co. E-mail: gvk@hpi.uta.edu
URL: http://www-ee.uta.edu/hpi/
Contact: George V. Kondraske PhD, Dir.
E-mail: gvk@hpi.uta.edu

Scope: Methods of measurement of human performance, including performance theory, human perfor-

mance conceptual framework, and specialized instrumentation; studies have broad applications in the fields of space, rehabilitation, the military, and industry. Fundamental focus is on the human system-task interface. Projects include development of a computer-automated system to measure basic elements of human performance, testing of both normal and impaired individuals, and the development of methods for automated, objective disability determination. Conducts longitudinal studies of patients to characterize disease history. Also studies human performance in relation to spasmodic dysphonia, athletes, post-polio syndrome, and head injuries. Develops software tools for automated assessment of complex sets of measurements. **Services:** Assistive device services to rehabilitation providers; Cooperative research program with outside organizations enabling them to obtain a replica of the instrumented measurement system. **Publications:** Newsletter (semiannually); Progress Report (annually). **Educational Activities:** Workshops focusing on human performance measurement and rehabilitation technology.

16046 ■ University of Utah–Human Performance Research Laboratory

202 HPER N Bldg.
College of Health
Salt Lake City, UT 84112
Ph:(801)585-1451
Co. E-mail: kerry.m.jacques@hsc.utah.edu
URL: http://www.health.utah.edu/clinics/performance.
   html
Contact: Kerry Jacques, Dir.
E-mail: kerry.m.jacques@hsc.utah.edu

Scope: Effects of exercise and environment on muscular, cardiovascular, respiratory, nervous, and

thermoregulatory systems of the human body. Programs are conducted on exercise and multiple sclerosis patients, women at risk for osteoporosis, exercise and functional abilities and health benefits. **Services:** Peak Academy, an applied sport science service for the University and surrounding community.

16047 ■ University of Vermont–McClure Musculoskeletal Research Center

Robert T. Stafford Hall, 4th Fl.
Department of Orthopaedic & Rehabilitation
95 Carrigan Dr.
Burlington, VT 05405-1746
Ph:(802)656-4257
Fax:(802)656-4247
Co. E-mail: bruce.beynnon@uvm.edu
URL: http://www.med.uvm.edu/ortho/TB1BLIC.asp-
   ?SiteAreaID=1113
Contact: Bruce D. Beynnon PhD, Res.Dir.
E-mail: bruce.beynnon@uvm.edu

Scope: Occupational and sports injuries and non-traumatic and congenital disorders, including how musculoskeletal structures are injured and how they heal. Research focuses on lower back pain, including studies of vehicle vibration, exercise, and different low back pain treatments; sports medicine, including knee, shoulder, and ankle injuries; scoliosis, including the etiology of idiopathic scoliosis and growth asymmetry research; osteoarthritis; and joint replacement studies. **Services:** Research and development consultation, to industry, business, government, and public agencies. **Educational Activities:** In-service training, to rehabilitation professionals; Workshops, for service providers in rehabilitation engineering techniques.

ASSOCIATIONS AND OTHER ORGANIZATIONS

16048 ■ National Frozen Pizza Institute
2000 Corporate Ridge, Ste. 1000
McLean, VA 22102
Ph:(703)821-0770
Fax:(703)821-1350
URL: http://www.affi.com/index.asp?sid=28
Contact: Lucas Darnell, Exec. Dir./Sec.
Description: Aims to advance the interests of the frozen pizza industry. Monitors federal regulatory agency activities affecting frozen pizza processors and serves as an information resource for the trade and general public about the nutrition, value and convenience of frozen pizza and pizza products. .

REFERENCE WORKS

16049 ■ "All Fired Up!" in *Small Business Opportunities* (November 2008)
Pub: Entrepreneur Media Inc.
Ed: Stan Roberts. **Description:** Profile of Brixx Wood Fired Pizza, which has launched a franchising program due to the amount of interest the company's founders received over the years; franchisees do not need experience in the food industry or pizza restaurant service business in order to open a franchise of their own because all franchisees receive comprehensive training in which they are educated on all of the necessary tools to effectively run the business.

16050 ■ "A Bigger Slice; Buscemi's Adds Licensees, Profits" in *Crain's Detroit Business* (Vol. 23, October 15, 2007, No. 42, pp. 3)
Pub: Crain Communications Inc. - Detroit
Ed: Brent Snavely. **Description:** Six new licensees have opened under the Original Buscemi's Inc. The firm was founded in 1958 and expects to open nine more restaurants by the end of 2008.

16051 ■ "Doyle: Domino's New Pizza Seasoned with Straight Talk" in *Crain's Detroit Business* (Vol. 26, January 11, 2010, No. 2, pp. 1)
Pub: Crain Communications, Inc.
Ed: Nathan Skid. **Description:** Interview with J. Patrick Doyle, the CEO of Domino's Pizza, Inc.; the company has launched a new marketing campaign that focuses on its bold new vision.

16052 ■ "Eatery Honored for Top Alaska Pizza" in *Alaska Business Monthly* (Vol. 27, October 2011, No. 10, pp. 10)
Pub: Alaska Business Publishing Company
Ed: Nancy Pounds. **Description:** Capri Pizza of Anchorage, Alaska was honored in Food Network magazine's, '50 States, 50 Pizzas'. Capri's salmon pizza won the prize for the restaurant.

16053 ■ "For the Seasoned Buyer" in *Inc.* (Vol. 30, November 2008, No. 11, pp. 32)
Pub: Mansueto Ventures LLC
Ed: Darren Dahl. **Description:** Dominick Fimiano shares his plans to sell his ten-year-old business that

manufactures and sells frozen pizza dough and crusts as well as a variety of topped pizzas. Products are purchased by schools, hospitals, bowling alleys and amusement parks. The business sale includes the buyer's taking on Fimiano's son the firm's most senior employee.

16054 ■ "Invasion of the New York Pizza" in *Charlotte Observer* (February 5, 2007)
Pub: Knight-Ridder/Tribune Business News
Ed: Leigh Dyer. **Description:** Dozens of new pizza restaurants are cropping up in the Charlotte, North Carolina area, a result of New Yorker transplants.

16055 ■ "Local Firm Snaps up 91 Area Pizza Huts" in *Orlando Business Journal* (Vol. 26, January 8, 2010, No. 32, pp. 1)
Pub: American City Business Journals
Ed: Alexis Muellner, Anjali Fluker. **Description:** Orlando, Florida-based CFL Pizza LLC bought the 91 Orlando-area Pizza Hut restaurants for $35 million from parent company Yum! Brands Inc. CFL Pizza plans to distribute parts of the business to Central Florida vendors and the first business up for grabs is the advertising budget.

16056 ■ "Ohio Franchise Buys 21 Jacksonville Area Papa John's" in *Florida Times-Union* (December 20, 2010)
Pub: Florida Times-Union
Ed: Mark Basch. **Description:** Ohio-based Papa John's pizza franchise acquired 21 of the restaurants in Duval, Clay and St. Johns counties in Jacksonville, Florida.

16057 ■ "Personal Pizza Goes Franchise Route" in *Atlanta Journal-Constitution* (December 22, 2010)
Pub: Atlanta Journal-Constitution
Ed: Bob Townsend. **Description:** Your Pie, developer of the personal-size pizza franchise concept is profiled.

16058 ■ *Pizza Today—Pizza Industry Buyer's Guide Issue*
Pub: National Association of Pizza Operators
Contact: Jeremy White, Editor-in-Chief
E-mail: jwhite@pizzatoday.com
Released: Monthly, Latest edition 2010. **Publication Includes:** List of over 3,000 manufacturers and suppliers of products, equipment, and services to the pizza industry. **Entries Include:** Company name, address, phone, fax, product/service, branch locations. **Arrangement:** Alphabetical. **Indexes:** Product/service.

TRADE PERIODICALS

16059 ■ *Canadian Pizza Magazine*
Pub: Annex Publishing & Printing Inc.
Contact: Martin McAnulty, Gp. Publisher
E-mail: fire@annexweb.com
Ed: Laura Aiken, Editor, laiken@annexweb.com. **Released:** 8/yr. **Price:** $18 Canada. **Description:** Trade magazine for the pizza industry.

TRADE SHOWS AND CONVENTIONS

16060 ■ Pizza Expo
Macfadden-Protech LLC
908 S. 8th St., Ste. 200
Louisville, KY 40203
Ph:(502)736-9500
Fax:(502)736-9502
URL: http://www.pizzaexpo.com
Released: Annual. **Audience:** Pizza shop operators and owners from franchises, independent shops, and chains. **Principal Exhibits:** Food and equipment for the pizza industry.

CONSULTANTS

16061 ■ Erin Services Inc.
111 Travelers Way
PO Box 1048
Saint Simons Island, GA 31522-5632
Ph:(912)638-9916
Free: 800-862-5361
Fax:(912)638-5701
Co. E-mail: dennisd@ns.technonet.com
Contact: Dennis J. Donnelly III, President
E-mail: dennis179@yahoo.com
Scope: Offers assistance in technical proposal production, marketing, and research. Industries served: Food service, janitorial, landscaping, hospitality and lodging, parks, and recreational.

16062 ■ Riedel Marketing Group
5327 E Pinchot Ave.
Phoenix, AZ 85018-2963
Ph:(602)840-4948
Fax:(602)840-4928
Co. E-mail: ajr@4rmg.com
URL: http://www.4rmg.com
Contact: A. J. Riedel, Senior Partner
E-mail: ajr@4rmg.com
Scope: The house wares and food service industry strategic marketing planning experts. Help manufacturers of house wares and food products solve marketing problems and identify and exploit marketing opportunities. Provides a full-range of strategic marketing planning services including development of marketing strategy, development of fact-based sales presentations, category management, definition of market opportunities and new product development exclusively to the house wares and food service industries. **Publications:** "Your Key Consumer: Her Take on the International Home & Housewares Show," Mar, 2008; "What's Hot, What's Not: The Consumer Speaks," Mar, 2006; "HIPsters SPEAK: What We Love to Buy and Why," Apr, 2005; "Influentials: Who They Are and Why You Should Care," Jun, 2004; "The Seven Secrets to Selling More Housewares," Jan, 2003. **Seminars:** Consumers Speak: What We Love to Buy and Why, What Do Those Consumers Think; The Seven Secrets to Selling More House wares. **Special Services:** Home Trend Influentials Panel.

FRANCHISES AND BUSINESS OPPORTUNITIES

16063 ■ Azpco Arizona Pizza Co.
Azpco Arizona Pizza Co., Inc.
370 SE 15th Ave.
Pompano Beach, FL 33060
Ph:(954)942-9424
Fax:(954)783-5177
No. of Franchise Units: 10. **No. of Company-Owned Units:** 1. **Founded:** 1996. **Franchised:** 2003. **Description:** Pizza restaurant. **Equity Capital Needed:** $400,000-$865,000. **Franchise Fee:** $35,000. **Financial Assistance:** No. **Training:** Yes.

16064 ■ Bellacino's Pizza & Grinders Inc.
10096 Shaver Rd.
Portage, MI 49024
Free: 877-379-0700
Fax:(269)329-0930
No. of Franchise Units: 69. **Founded:** 1993. **Franchised:** 1995. **Description:** Oven baked grinders and pizza. **Equity Capital Needed:** $279,000-$422,190. **Franchise Fee:** $30,000. **Royalty Fee:** 3%. **Financial Assistance:** No. **Training:** Provides 14 days at headquarters, 10 days onsite with ongoing support.

16065 ■ The Boston's Gourmet Pizza
Boston Pizza International
1501 LBJ Fwy., Ste. 450
Dallas, TX 75234
Ph:(972)484-9022
Free: 800-277-8721
Fax:(972)484-7630
No. of Franchise Units: 154. **No. of Company-Owned Units:** 4. **Founded:** 1963. **Franchised:** 1968. **Description:** Casual restaurant specializing in pizza. **Equity Capital Needed:** $300,000-$350,000 equity, $900,000-$1,000,000 total. **Franchise Fee:** $35,000 U.S. **Financial Assistance:** No. **Training:** Yes.

16066 ■ Breadeaux Pizza
Breadeaux Pisa Inc.
2300 Frederick Ave.
PO Box 6158
St. Joseph, MO 64506
Ph:(816)364-1088
Free: 800-835-6534
Fax:(816)364-3739
No. of Franchise Units: 95. **No. of Company-Owned Units:** 3. **Founded:** 1985. **Franchised:** 1985. **Description:** Fast pizza operation. **Equity Capital Needed:** $69,500-$310,000. **Franchise Fee:** $15,000/15 years. **Financial Assistance:** No. **Training:** Yes.

16067 ■ Buck's Pizza
Buck's Pizza Fran. Corp. Inc.
PO Box 405
DuBois, PA 15801
Ph:(814)371-3076
Free: 800-310-8848
Co. E-mail: lance@buckspizza.com
URL: http://www.buckspizza.com
No. of Franchise Units: 70. **Founded:** 1994. **Franchised:** 1994. **Description:** Pizza carry-out and delivery. **Equity Capital Needed:** $163,450-$341,400. **Franchise Fee:** $20,000. **Financial Assistance:** Yes. **Managerial Assistance:** Site selection assistance is provided, as well as monthly advertising & marketing, an 800 support line and in-store fax machines insure ongoing support. **Training:** Provides onsite training at opening.

16068 ■ Chicken Delight
395 Berry St.
Winnipeg, MB, Canada R3J 1N6
Ph:(204)885-7570
Fax:(204)831-6176
No. of Franchise Units: 26. **No. of Company-Owned Units:** 11. **Founded:** 1952. **Franchised:** 1952. **Description:** Pressure-fried chicken and fresh-dough pizza, plus other tasty selections. **Equity Capital Needed:** $150,000-$350,000. **Franchise Fee:** $20,000. **Royalty Fee:** 5%. **Financial Assistance:** No. **Managerial Assistance:** Provides on-site operational training, manuals and marketing ideas. Also monitors the progress of all franchisees on a monthly basis. **Training:** Offers an intensive 4 week, in-field training program at our corporate stores.

16069 ■ CiCi's Pizza
CiCi Enterprises, Inc.
1080 W Bethel Rd.
Coppell, TX 75019
Ph:(972)745-4200
Fax:(469)675-6405
No. of Franchise Units: 578. **No. of Company-Owned Units:** 13. **Founded:** 1985. **Franchised:** 1988. **Description:** Pizza, pasta, salad bar and dessert on an all-you-can-eat lunch and dinner buffet. Also offers a value-priced take-out menu. **Equity Capital Needed:** $461,343-$714,912 total investment range. **Franchise Fee:** $30,000. **Financial Assistance:** No. **Training:** Yes.

16070 ■ Dolly's Pizza
Dolly's Pizza Franchising, Inc.
1097 Union Lake Rd., Ste. B
White Lake, MI 48386
Ph:(248)360-6440
Fax:(248)360-7020
No. of Franchise Units: 28. **No. of Company-Owned Units:** 2 . **Founded:** 1966. **Franchised:** 1994. **Description:** Offers pizza, subs, and salads. **Equity Capital Needed:** $120,000-$160,000 total; approximately $30,000 cash. **Franchise Fee:** $17,500. **Financial Assistance:** No. **Training:** Yes.

16071 ■ Domino's Pizza
Canada's Pizza Delivery Corp.
PO Box 430
Leamington, ON, Canada N8H 4K5
Ph:(519)326-5280
Co. E-mail: customersfirst@dominoscanada.ca
URL: http://www.dominos.ca
No. of Franchise Units: 265. **No. of Company-Owned Units:** 20. **Founded:** 1983. **Description:** Domino's Pizza is an outdoor delivery of pizza throughout Canada. Delivers superior quality pizzas, chicken wings, soft drinks etc. **Equity Capital Needed:** $250,000-$300,000. **Franchise Fee:** $25,000. **Training:** Offers 6 weeks training.

16072 ■ Domino's Pizza, Inc.
30 Frank Lloyd Wright Dr.
PO Box 997
Ann Arbor, MI 48106-0997
Ph:(734)668-6055
No. of Franchise Units: 5,427. **No. of Company-Owned Units:** 749. **No. of Operating Units:** 6,176. **Founded:** 1960. **Description:** Pizza carry-out and delivery service. **Franchise Fee:** $1,300-$3,250. **Financial Assistance:** Yes. **Training:** Yes.

16073 ■ East of Chicago Pizza Co.
318 W Walton
Willard, OH 44890
Ph:(419)935-3033
Fax:(419)935-3278
No. of Franchise Units: 105. **No. of Company-Owned Units:** 5. **Founded:** 1990. **Franchised:** 1991. **Description:** Pizza, sandwiches, and pasta carry-out and delivery. **Equity Capital Needed:** $141,900-$427,200. **Franchise Fee:** $20,000. **Royalty Fee:** 5%. **Financial Assistance:** Yes. **Training:** Yes.

16074 ■ Extreme Pizza
OOC Inc.
1062 Folsom St.
San Francisco, CA 94103
Ph:(415)760-2199
Free: (866)695-5595
Fax:(415)701-9100
No. of Franchise Units: 32. **No. of Company-Owned Units:** 9. **Founded:** 1994. **Franchised:** 2000. **Description:** Pizzeria. **Equity Capital Needed:** $184,000-$392,000. **Franchise Fee:** $30,000. **Royalty Fee:** 4%. **Financial Assistance:** Third party financing available. **Training:** Provides 4 weeks at headquarters, 2 weeks at franchisee's location and ongoing support.

16075 ■ Famous Famiglia
Famiglia - DeBartolo, LLC
199 Main St., 8th Fl.
White Plains, NY 10601
Ph:(914)328-4444
Fax:(914)328-4479
No. of Franchise Units: 98. **No. of Company-Owned Units:** 5. **Founded:** 1986. **Franchised:** 2002. **Description:** Pizza, pasta, salads, and sandwiches. **Equity Capital Needed:** $350,000-$500,000. **Franchise Fee:** $25,000-$35,000. **Royalty Fee:** 6%. **Financial Assistance:** No. **Training:** Yes.

16076 ■ Figaro's Pizza
Figaro's Italian Pizza, Inc.
1500 Liberty St., SE
Salem, OR 97302
Ph:(503)371-9318
Free: 888-344-2767
Fax:(503)363-5364
No. of Franchise Units: 75. **Founded:** 1981. **Franchised:** 1986. **Description:** Pizza restaurant. **Equity Capital Needed:** $91,000-$380,950. **Franchise Fee:** $35,000. **Financial Assistance:** No. **Training:** 18 days in-store and classroom training.

16077 ■ Flying Wedge Pizza Co.
4088 Cambie St., Ste. 202
Vancouver, BC, Canada V5Z 2X8
Ph:(604)681-1288
Fax:(604)681-1258
Co. E-mail: yvette@flyingwedge.com
URL: http://www.flyingwedge.com
No. of Franchise Units: 14. **No. of Company-Owned Units:** 5. **Founded:** 1989. **Franchised:** 1999. **Description:** Take out, sit down, delivery gourmet pizza. **Equity Capital Needed:** $95,000-$130,000. **Franchise Fee:** $35,000. **Training:** Provides 6 weeks training.

16078 ■ Fox's Pizza Den, Inc.
Fox's Pizza Den, Inc.
4425 WM Penn Hwy.
Murrysville, PA 15668
Ph:(724)733-7888
Free: 800-899-3697
Fax:(724)325-5479
Co. E-mail: foxs@alltel.net
URL: http://www.foxspizza.com
No. of Franchise Units: 330. **Founded:** 1971. **Franchised:** 1974. **Description:** A complete pizza and sandwich operation, offering both fresh dough and shell pizza. Six different size pizzas, plus a large variety of sandwiches and Fox's famous Wedgies (a sandwich made on a pizza shell). May expand menu as desired. May choose a sit-down store or a take-out and delivery. Has a commissary to service all franchise needs. **Equity Capital Needed:** $110,000-$140,000. **Franchise Fee:** $10,000. **Royalty Fee:** $200 per month. **Financial Assistance:** No. **Managerial Assistance:** Complete assistance with business plan, site location, assistance with lease, financing, equipment set-up, supervise renovation and onsite training of franchisee and employees. Assistance with bookkeeping and inventory control. **Training:** 7 days of onsite training at franchisees own unit.

16079 ■ Garlic Jim's Famous Gourmet Pizza
802 134th St. SW, Ste. 130
Everett, WA 98204
Ph:(425)918-1900
Fax:(425)918-1700
No. of Franchise Units: 38. **No. of Company-Owned Units:** 5. **Founded:** 2004. **Franchised:** 2004. **Description:** Gourmet pizza. **Equity Capital Needed:** $175,600-$347,300. **Franchise Fee:** $15,000-$20,000. **Royalty Fee:** 5.5%. **Financial Assistance:** Third party financing available. **Training:** Offers 1 week at headquarters, 1 week at franchisees location, 4 weeks at regional training store and ongoing support.

16080 ■ Godfather's Pizza, Inc.

2808 N 108th St.
Omaha, NE 68164
Ph:(402)391-1452
Fax:(402)255-2699

No. of Franchise Units: 609. **No. of Company-Owned Units:** 39. **Founded:** 1973. **Description:** Pizza restaurant serving 2 types of pizza crust, salads, beverages and sandwiches. **Equity Capital Needed:** Net worth of $200,000, excluding personal property; $100,000 cash or liquid assets. **Franchise Fee:** 5% of weekly gross. **Financial Assistance:** No. **Training:** Yes.

16081 ■ Greco Pizza Donair

Grinner's Food Systems Limited
105 Walker St.
PO Box 1040
Truro, NS, Canada B2N 5G9
Ph:(902)893-4141

No. of Franchise Units: 101. **No. of Company-Owned Units:** 2. **Founded:** 1977. **Franchised:** 1977. **Description:** Home-delivery chain of pizza, donair and oven-sub sandwiches in Atlantic Canada. Specializes in fast, free delivery. **Equity Capital Needed:** $40,000 total investment; $140,000-$180,000 Canadian. **Franchise Fee:** $15,000 Canadian. **Financial Assistance:** No **Training:** Yes.

16082 ■ Happy Joes, Inc.

2705 Happy Joe Dr.
Bettendorf, IA 52722
Ph:(319)332-8811

No. of Franchise Units: 58. **No. of Company-Owned Units:** 1. **Founded:** 1972. **Franchised:** 1973. **Description:** Family style pizza and ice cream parlor. **Equity Capital Needed:** $79,700-$1,019,000, depending on full-service or delivery only. **Franchise Fee:** $1,500-$20,000. **Financial Assistance:** No. **Training:** Yes.

16083 ■ Hungry Howie's Pizza, Inc.

Hungry Howie's Pizza and Subs, Inc.
30300 Stephenson Hwy., Ste. 200
Madison Heights, MI 48071
Ph:(248)414-3300
Free: 800-624-8122
Fax:(248)414-3301
Co. E-mail: franchiseinfo@hungryhowies.com
URL: http://www.hungryhowies.com

No. of Franchise Units: 575. **Founded:** 1973. **Franchised:** 1982. **Description:** Menu features flavored crust pizzas in 8 varieties, subs, fresh salads and Fruzza dessert pizzas. **Equity Capital Needed:** $70,000 cash, $150,000 net worth; $161,100-$403,000 total investment. **Franchise Fee:** $20,000 first/$15,000. **Financial Assistance:** No. **Training:** Comprehensive classroom and in-store training program. Field supervision provided for site selection, construction, lease negotiations, store layout, and store opening.

16084 ■ Italo's Pizza Shop, Inc.

3560 Middlebranch Rd., NE
Canton, OH 44705
Ph:(330)455-7443

No. of Franchise Units: 11. **No. of Company-Owned Units:** 2. **Founded:** 1966. **Franchised:** 1975. **Description:** A carry-out operation with limited dining, specializing in pizza, chicken, pasta and other Italian dishes. Delivery is optional to franchisee. Stresses quality, quantity, personal service and value. **Equity Capital Needed:** $75,000-$150,000, depending upon options chosen. **Franchise Fee:** $20,000. **Royalty Fee:** 5%. **Financial Assistance:** Not available. Must provide his/her own financial resources. **Managerial Assistance:** Provides continual assistance and support, along with recommendations, in all aspects of the business. Forms, manuals and detailed instructions are provided for smooth performance and operations. Periodic visits by franchisor allow for rapport and problem solution and assistance. **Training:** An intensive 3 weeks of training at corporate headquarters is provided, with additional assistance, if necessary, at the franchisees location.

16085 ■ Jerry's Subs and Pizza

Jerry's Systems, Inc.
15942 Shady Grove Rd.
Gaithersburg, MD 20877
Free: 800-990-9176
Fax:(301)948-3508

No. of Franchise Units: 135. **No. of Company-Owned Units:** 3. **Founded:** 1954. **Franchised:** 1981. **Description:** Fresh-dough pizza and stuffed submarine sandwiches, served in upscale retail outlets, featuring take-out service and self-service dining. **Equity Capital Needed:** $250,000-$350,000. **Franchise Fee:** $25,000. **Royalty Fee:** 6%. **Financial Assistance:** Limited third party financing available. **Training:** Yes.

16086 ■ Jet City Pizza

Jet City Pizza Franchise Systems, Inc.
13450 NE 177th Pl.
Woodinville, WA 98072
Ph:(425)402-9673
Fax:(425)488-8919
Co. E-mail: jimw@jetcitypizza.com
URL: http://www.jetcitypizza.com

No. of Franchise Units: 8. **No. of Company-Owned Units:** 3. **Founded:** 1994. **Franchised:** 1996. **Description:** Gourmet pizza delivery/carry-out. A simple hands on operation that offers only the finest ingredients with a mix of 85% delivery & 15% carry-out. Our trademark slogan is "Finally Gourmet Pizza Delivered." **Equity Capital Needed:** $175,000-$325,000. **Franchise Fee:** $15,000. **Financial Assistance:** No. **Training:** Offers 5 week training program that consists of in-store operations at one of our corporate locations and classroom business seminars at headquarters.

16087 ■ Ledo Pizza Systems

2001 Tidewater Colony Way, Ste. 203
Annapolis, MD 21401-2194
Ph:(410)721-6887
Fax:(410)571-8395

No. of Franchise Units: 82. **Founded:** 1955. **Franchised:** 1988. **Description:** Full service Italian restaurant. **Franchise Fee:** $30,000. **Financial Assistance:** No. **Training:** Yes.

16088 ■ Little Caesars Pizza

Illitch Holdings
Fox Office Ctr.
2211 Woodward Ave.
Detroit, MI 48201
Ph:(313)471-6469
Free: 800-553-5776
Fax:(313)471-6345
Co. E-mail: usdevelopment@lcecorp.com
URL: http://www.littlecaesars.com

No. of Franchise Units: 3,000+. **Founded:** 1959. **Franchised:** 1962. **Description:** Carry-out and delivery pizza chain. **Equity Capital Needed:** $193,050-$619,500. **Franchise Fee:** $20,000. **Royalty Fee:** 5%. **Financial Assistance:** No. **Managerial Assistance:** Each franchisee is assigned personnel qualified in marketing, operations, finance, real estate, architecture and design. **Training:** Training school is 6 weeks in duration and covers every aspect of the business. Provides continuing ongoing classes.

16089 ■ Marco's Pizza

Marco's, Inc.
5252 Monroe St.
Toledo, OH 43623
Ph:(419)885-7000
Free: 800-262-7267
Fax:(419)885-5215

No. of Franchise Units: 225. **Founded:** 1978. **Franchised:** 1979. **Description:** Offers pizza, hot sub sandwiches and cheese bread for carry-out and delivery. Has grown steadily to over 65 stores in Ohio, Michigan and Indiana. Built its business on a strong foundation of excellent quality products, superb customer service and great value. Representative to help the franchisee and consult with him/her on any necessary matters. **Equity Capital Needed:** $179,000-$310,000 total; equity capital, $75,000-$100,000. **Franchise Fee:** $25,000. **Financial Assistance:** Financing assistance provided to qualified candidates. **Training:** Trained in each and every

aspect of the system, including marketing, advertising and administration. Approximately 6 weeks in duration, 2 of which are held at the corporate training center. Prior food service or related experience is required.

16090 ■ Mazzio's Italian Eatery

Mazzio's Corp.
4441 S 72nd E Ave.
Tulsa, OK 74145-4692
Ph:(918)663-8880
Free: 800-827-1910

No. of Franchise Units: 114. **No. of Company-Owned Units:** 61. **Founded:** 1961. **Franchised:** 1979. **Description:** Up-scale pizza restaurants. **Equity Capital Needed:** $400,000, total investment. **Franchise Fee:** $20,000. **Financial Assistance:** No. **Training:** Yes.

16091 ■ Me-n-Ed's Pizzerias

Pizza World Supreme
6729 N Palm Ave., Ste. 200
Fresno, CA 93704
Ph:(559)432-0399
Free: 888-636-3373
Fax:(559)432-0398

No. of Franchise Units: 6. **No. of Company-Owned Units:** 52. **Founded:** 1958. **Franchised:** 1958. **Description:** Pizzeria. **Equity Capital Needed:** $175,000-$486,000. **Franchise Fee:** $25,000. **Royalty Fee:** 5%. **Financial Assistance:** No. **Training:** Training provided at headquarters, franchisee's location and ongoing support.

16092 ■ New Orleans Pizza Canada, Inc.

404 James St. S
St. Marys, ON, Canada N4X 1C7
Ph:(519)349-2380
Fax:(519)349-2288
Co. E-mail: sfarraj@neworleanspizza.ca
URL: http://www.neworleanspizza.ca

No. of Franchise Units: 61. **No. of Company-Owned Units:** 9. **Founded:** 1978. **Franchised:** 1978. **Description:** Specializing in pizza and submarines. **Equity Capital Needed:** $40,000-$50,000. **Franchise Fee:** $10,000. **Training:** Yes.

16093 ■ NYPD Pizza

NYPD Pizza Development, LLC
2589 S Hiawassee Rd.
Orlando, FL 32835
Ph:(407)872-6973
Fax:(407)296-4463
Co. E-mail: franchisenypd@aol.com
URL: http://www.nypdpizza.net

No. of Franchise Units: 11. **No. of Company-Owned Units:** 1. **Founded:** 1996. **Franchised:** 2004. **Description:** Upscale pizzeria with authentic hand tossed New York style pizza. The NYPD Pizza restaurants are themed with great admiration for the police forces worldwide, memorabilia of New York and its rich history. NYPD Pizza offers 3 types of franchises, the Sub Station, the Metro Unit, and the Precinct. **Equity Capital Needed:** $125,000. **Franchise Fee:** $30,000. **Financial Assistance:** No. **Training:** Training program is mandatory for franchise owner, management team and the pie cooks. First hand experience where the franchisee learns what it takes to operate a franchise. The training and support includes opening to closing, advertising and marketing, and ordering.

16094 ■ Old Chicago Pizza

Rock Bottom Restaurants, Inc.
248 Centennial Pky.
Louisville, CO 80027
Ph:(303)664-4200
Fax:(303)664-4007

No. of Franchise Units: 22. **No. of Company-Owned Units:** 58. **Founded:** 1976. **Description:** Pizza restaurant with a large high energy bar. **Equity Capital Needed:** $3,000,000 net worth; $750,000 available for investment. **Franchise Fee:** $15,000 area+ $40,000 fee. **Financial Assistance:** No. **Training:** Yes.

16095 ■ Panago Pizza Inc.
33149 Mill Lake Rd.
Abbotsford, BC, Canada V2S 2A4
Ph:(604)859-6621
Free: 877-731-0310
Fax:(604)755-6014
Co. E-mail: development@panago.com
URL: http://www.panagofranchise.com
No. of Franchise Units: 177. **No. of Company-Owned Units:** 4. **Founded:** 1986. **Franchised:** 1986. **Description:** With over 150 locations and sales in excess of 100 million, Panago has built a reputation as Canada's premiere delivery takeout pizza franchise. Our chef-created pizza originals and fresh salads have proven to be the perfect response to today's evolving consumer, satisfying their expanding culinary tastes, demand for convenience, and focus on quality. With industry-leading innovations and a consumer experience that sets us apart, Panago is rapidly expanding into new markets. **Equity Capital Needed:** $325,000-$400,000. **Franchise Fee:** $25,000. **Training:** 6 week intensive training program complemented with ongoing operational support.

16096 ■ Panzerotto Pizza
246 Parliament St.
Toronto, ON, Canada M5A 3A4
Ph:(416)362-5555
Fax:(416)362-8217
Co. E-mail: joeschiavone@rogers.com
URL: http://www.panzerottopizza.com
No. of Franchise Units: 30. **No. of Company-Owned Units:** 3. **Founded:** 1976. **Franchised:** 1978. **Description:** Pizza restaurant. **Equity Capital Needed:** $150,000. **Franchise Fee:** $20,000. **Training:** Franchisee will receive professional training prior to opening. Our store liaison support group is always available to serve you with store operations questions, equipment and local promotion ideas. Our Call centre staff is there for you on customer service issues and delivery zone inquires.

16097 ■ Papa Gino's Pizzeria
Papa Gino's Inc.
600 Providence Hwy.
Dedham, MA 02026
Ph:(781)467-1668
Fax:(781)329-8796
No. of Company-Owned Units: 160. **Founded:** 1968. **Franchised:** 2006. **Description:** Pizza, dine in & takeout. **Equity Capital Needed:** $175,000 liquid capital; $500,000 net worth. **Franchise Fee:** $20,000. **Financial Assistance:** No. **Training:** Yes.

16098 ■ Papa John's International, Inc.
2002 Papa John's Blvd.
Louisville, KY 40229
Fax:(502)261-4324
Co. E-mail: Tammy_Green@PapaJohns.com
URL: http://www.PapaJohns.com
No. of Franchise Units: 3,060. **No. of Company-Owned Units:** 601. **Founded:** 1984. **Franchised:** 1986. **Description:** Pizza franchise. **Equity Capital Needed:** Visit website for requirements & fee information. **Franchise Fee:** $25,000. **Financial Assistance:** No. **Managerial Assistance:** Support from H/R, internal training, point of sale, and IT. **Training:** Provides initial management training program and offers ongoing assistance regarding operations, marketing, real estate and development, food and equipment supply.

16099 ■ Papa Murphy's Take'N'Bake Pizza
8000 NE Pky. Dr.
Vancouver, WA 98662
Free: 800-257-7272
Co. E-mail: franchise@papamurphys.com
URL: http://www.papamurphys.com
No. of Franchise Units: 1,270. **No. of Company-Owned Units:** 31. **Founded:** 1981. **Franchised:** 1982. **Description:** Papa Murphy's is great pizza made from top-quality ingredients. Letting customers bake it themselves is smart business. Put the two together and you get one of the largest, fastest growing concepts of Take'N'Bake Pizza franchises in the world. **Equity Capital Needed:** $250,000 net worth; $80,000 liquid assets. **Franchise Fee:** $25,000. **Financial Assistance:** Financing programs are not available but a list of recommended lenders is avail-

able to franchise owners. **Training:** Offers extensive training for new franchise owners, including in-store skill training and structured classroom training at our headquarters.

16100 ■ Papa's Pizza To-Go, Inc.
4465 Commerce Dr., Ste. 101
Buford, GA 30518
Ph:(770)614-6676
Fax:(770)614-9095
No. of Franchise Units: 60. **No. of Company-Owned Units:** 9. **Founded:** 1986. **Franchised:** 1990. **Description:** Pizzeria. **Equity Capital Needed:** $138,950-$386,800. **Franchise Fee:** $9,500-$12,500. **Royalty Fee:** 5%. **Financial Assistance:** No. **Training:** Yes.

16101 ■ Paul Revere's Pizza
1570 42nd St. NE, Ste. 4
Cedar Rapids, IA 52402
Ph:(319)395-9113
Free: 800-995-9437
Fax:(319)395-9115
No. of Franchise Units: 15. **Founded:** 1975. **Franchised:** 1982. **Description:** Pizza delivery, take-out and sit-down. **Equity Capital Needed:** $92,400-$202,500, includes $25,000-$90,000 working capital. **Franchise Fee:** $5,000-$15,000. **Financial Assistance:** No **Training:** Yes.

16102 ■ Pizza Depot
2 Automatic Rd., Unit 122
Brampton, ON, Canada L6S 6K8
Ph:(905)458-9711
Fax:(905)458-8644
Co. E-mail: info@pizzadepot.ca
URL: http://www.pizzadepot.ca
No. of Franchise Units: 28. **No. of Company-Owned Units:** 3. **Founded:** 2000. **Franchised:** 2000. **Description:** Pizzeria. **Equity Capital Needed:** $197,000-$210,000. **Franchise Fee:** $20,000. **Training:** Yes.

16103 ■ Pizza Factory, Inc.
49430 Rd. 426
PO Box 989
Oakhurst, CA 93644
Ph:(559)683-3377
Free: 800-654-4840
Fax:(559)683-6879
No. of Franchise Units: 110. **Founded:** 1979. **Franchised:** 1985. **Description:** Family-oriented pizza restaurant, serving pizza, pasta, sandwiches and salad bar. Specializing in communities of 15,000 or less. **Equity Capital Needed:** $85,700-$426,000. **Franchise Fee:** $20,000. **Royalty Fee:** 5%. **Financial Assistance:** Offers limited third party financing. **Training:** Offers 325 hours training.

16104 ■ Pizza Fusion
2200 W Cypress Creek Rd.
Fort Lauderdale, FL 33309
Ph:(954)202-1919
Fax:(954)202-1929
No. of Franchise Units: 14. **No. of Company-Owned Units:** 1. **Founded:** 2006. **Franchised:** 2007. **Description:** Organic pizza, sandwiches, and salads. **Equity Capital Needed:** $328,000-$571,000. **Franchise Fee:** $30,000. **Royalty Fee:** 6%. **Financial Assistance:** Third party financing available. **Training:** Provides 7 days training at headquarters, 7 days at franchisee's location and ongoing support.

16105 ■ Pizza Inn, Inc.
3551 Plano Pky.
The Colony, TX 75056
Ph:(469)384-5000
Free: 800-284-3466
Fax:(469)574-4407
No. of Franchise Units: 307. **No. of Company-Owned Units:** 4. **Founded:** 1961. **Franchised:** 1963. **Description:** Express, delivery/carry out, buffet. **Equity Capital Needed:** Liquid assets $30,000-$150,000. **Franchise Fee:** $5,000-$25,000. **Financial Assistance:** No. **Training:** Yes.

16106 ■ Pizza Nova Take Out Ltd.
2247 Midland Ave.
Toronto, ON, Canada M1P 4R1
Ph:(416)439-0051

Fax:(416)299-3558
Co. E-mail: frank@pizzanova.com
URL: http://www.pizzanova.com
No. of Franchise Units: 125. **No. of Company-Owned Units:** 1. **Founded:** 1963. **Franchised:** 1996. **Description:** Pizza delivery. **Equity Capital Needed:** $290,000-$310,000. **Franchise Fee:** $20,000. **Training:** Yes.

16107 ■ Pizza Patron Inc.
10999 Petal St., Ste. 200
Dallas, TX 75238
Ph:(972)613-8000
Fax:(972)613-8014
Co. E-mail: guillermo@pizzapatron.com
URL: http://www.pizzapatron.com
No. of Franchise Units: 86. **No. of Company-Owned Units:** 6. **Founded:** 1986. **Description:** Pizzeria. **Equity Capital Needed:** $150,000 net worth and $50,000 investment equity per location to be developed. **Franchise Fee:** $20,000 1st store. **Royalty Fee:** 5%. **Financial Assistance:** No. **Training:** A comprehensive hands-on training program, onsite, at our company store and concludes with a 4 day "owner simulation" where you run our company store as if it were your own and ongoing support.

16108 ■ The Pizza Pipeline
The Pizza Pipeline, Inc.
418 W Sharp
Spokane, WA 99201
Ph:(509)326-1977
Free: 800-509-1977
Fax:(509)326-3017
No. of Franchise Units: 8. **No. of Company-Owned Units:** 6. **Founded:** 1988. **Franchised:** 1988. **Description:** Pizza delivery. **Equity Capital Needed:** $138,000-$341,800. **Franchise Fee:** $20,000. **Royalty Fee:** 5%. **Financial Assistance:** No. **Training:** Includes 4-6 weeks training at corporate headquarters, 2 weeks at franchisee's location and ongoing support.

16109 ■ Pizza Pit
SB Acquisitions, LLC
433 Grand Canyon Dr., Ste. 204
Madison, WI 53719
Ph:(608)833-3030
Fax:(608)602-9081
No. of Franchise Units: 18. **Founded:** 1969. **Franchised:** 1982. **Description:** Free home delivery and carry-out of handcrafted pizzas, specialty sandwiches, pasta and salads. Units are adaptable to inside seating. Single and multiple-unit programs are available. Merged business concepts with family fun centers, bowling centers and convenience stores. Profit planning available. **Equity Capital Needed:** Range $128,280-$242,640. **Franchise Fee:** $17,500. **Financial Assistance:** No. **Training:** Yes.

16110 ■ Pizza Pizza
500 Kipling Ave.
Toronto, ON, Canada M8Z 5E5
Ph:(416)967-1010
Free: 800-263-5556
Fax:(416)967-9865
Co. E-mail: dmason@pizzapizza.ca
URL: http://www.pizzapizza.ca
No. of Franchise Units: 341. **No. of Company-Owned Units:** 19. **Founded:** 1967. **Founded:** 1974. **Description:** Take-out and delivery stores with a menu that includes pizza, salads, wings, subs and Italian dinners. Recently began an international expansion program, with the first Restaurant opening in Costa Rica. **Equity Capital Needed:** $100,000-$200,000. **Franchise Fee:** $30,000. **Financial Assistance:** No. **Training:** Offers 8 weeks training and ongoing support.

16111 ■ Pizza Schimizza
Schmizza International, Inc.
1500 Liberty St. SE, Ste. 160
Salem, OR 97302
Ph:(503)371-9318

Free: 800-SCH-MIZZ
Fax:(503)363=5364
No. of Franchise Units: 24. **Founded:** 1993. **Franchised:** 2001. **Description:** Gourmet New York style pizza. **Equity Capital Needed:** $91,000-$380,950. **Franchise Fee:** $35,000. **Financial Assistance:** Yes. **Training:** Yes.

16112 ■ Pizzaville, Inc.
741 Rowntree Dairy Rd., Unit 1
Woodbridge, ON, Canada L4L 5T9
Ph:(905)850-0070
Fax:(905)850-0339
Co. E-mail: alans@pizzaville.ca
URL: http://www.pizzaville.ca/franchise_info.html
No. of Franchise Units: 65. **No. of Company-Owned Units:** 1. **Founded:** 1963. **Franchised:** 1979. **Description:** Operating as Pizzaville, Pizza Panzerotto. Regionally based Southern Ontario Italian pizza and panzerotto take out and delivery chain. **Equity Capital Needed:** $250,000-$300,000. **Franchise Fee:** $20,000. **Training:** Offers 2-16 weeks training.

16113 ■ Pizzeria Valdiano
Ligman Franchise group
1315 S Industrial Pky., Ste. 1101
Lake Mary, FL 32746
Ph:(813)935-5087
Fax:(813)425-5799
No. of Franchise Units: 1. **No. of Company-Owned Units:** 1. **Founded:** 2006. **Franchised:** 2007. **Description:** Pizzeria. **Equity Capital Needed:** $276,000-$394,000. **Franchise Fee:** $27,500. **Financial Assistance:** No. **Training:** Yes.

16114 ■ Pizzicato Gourmet Pizza
2523 SE 9th Ave.
Portland, OR 97202
Ph:(503)274-0375
Fax:(503)274-0473
No. of Franchise Units: 1. **No. of Company-Owned Units:** 16. **Founded:** 1989. **Franchised:** 2004. **Description:** Upscale gourmet pizza & salads. **Equity Capital Needed:** $200,000-$400,000. **Franchise Fee:** 25,000. **Financial Assistance:** No. **Training:** Yes.

16115 ■ Rocky Rococo Pizza & Pasta
Rococo Franchise Corp.
P.O. Box 207
Oconomowoc, WI 53066
Ph:(262)569-5580
Fax:(262)569-5591
No. of Company-Owned Units: 17. **Founded:** 1974. **Franchised:** 1995. **Description:** Quick service pizza. **Franchise Fee:** $25,000. **Financial Assistance:** No. **Training:** Yes.

16116 ■ Rotelli Pizza & Pasta Inc.
9045 La Fontana Blvd.
Boca Raton, FL 33434
Ph:(561)826-0900
No. of Franchise Units: 31. **Founded:** 1999. **Franchised:** 1999. **Description:** Pizza and pasta restaurant. **Equity Capital Needed:** $300,000-$674,000. **Franchise Fee:** $25,000. **Royalty Fee:** 6%. **Financial Assistance:** No. **Training:** Provides a total of 6 weeks training between headquarters and franchisee's location and ongoing support.

16117 ■ San Francisco Oven
9150 S Hills Blvd., Ste. 225
Cleveland, OH 44147
Ph:(440)717-9450
Free: 800-230-7202
No. of Franchise Units: 1. **Founded:** 2001. **Franchised:** 2002. **Description:** Made to order pizza, sandwiches and soup. **Equity Capital Needed:** $474,100-$807,300. **Franchise Fee:** $25,000. **Royalty Fee:** 5%. **Financial Assistance:** No. **Training:** Provides 3 weeks training at headquarters, 2 weeks onsite and ongoing support.

16118 ■ Sanfratello's Pizza
Sanfratello's Franchise Systems LLC
127 W Main St.
Glenwood, IL 60425
Ph:877-70P-IZZA
Free: 877-707-4992
Fax:(219)924-2450
URL: http://www.sanfratellos.com
No. of Franchise Units: 1. **No. of Company-Owned Units:** 4. **Founded:** 1969. **Franchised:** 2006. **Description:** Family pizzeria specializing in thin crust & pan pizza offering traditional pasta dishes, BBQ ribs, hot & cold sandwiches, an assortment of salads, appetizers and more. Currently offering "Full service" franchises (Dine-in, Pick-up & Delivery services) with a Beer & Wine minimum or full bar service. Also offering a "Pick-up & Delivery only" franchise option. **Equity Capital Needed:** $300,850-$763,500. **Franchise Fee:** $17,500-$25,000. **Financial Assistance:** No. **Training:** Provides a 3 week training program, pre-opening support, opening support with staff and ongoing support.

16119 ■ Sarpino's Pizzeria Canada Ltd.
Sarpino's World LTD
1133 Regent St., Ste. 203
Fredericton, NB, Canada E3B 3Z2
Ph:(506)462-9270
Fax:(506)451-8692
Co. E-mail: rbuckingham@nb.aibn.com
URL: http://www.sarpinos.com
No. of Franchise Units: 9. **No. of Company-Owned Units:** 1. **Founded:** 2001. **Franchised:** 2002. **Description:** Pizzeria. **Equity Capital Needed:** $195,000-$235,000. **Franchise Fee:** $25,000. **Training:** Provides 2 weeks training.

16120 ■ Snappy Tomato Pizza
Deters Co.
6111 Burgundy Hill Dr., Unit A
Burlington, KY 41005
Free: 888-463-7627
Fax:(859)525-4686
No. of Franchise Units: 68. **No. of Company-Owned Units:** 4. **Founded:** 1978. **Franchised:** 1982. **Description:** A delivery, dine-in and carry-out pizzeria that makes the highest-quality pizza available. Menu features hoagies, salads and award-winning "Ranch Pizza." **Equity Capital Needed:** $94,000-$250,000, depending on site selection and equipment. **Franchise Fee:** $15,000. **Financial Assistance:** No. **Training:** training program covers every aspect of the business, including actual time in stores getting hands-on experience.

16121 ■ Straw Hat Pizza
18 Crow Canyon Ct., Ste. 270
San Ramon, CA 94583
Ph:(925)837-3400
No. of Franchise Units: 81. **Founded:** 1959. **Franchised:** 1987. **Description:** Family Pizza restaurant. **Equity Capital Needed:** $129,400$256,500 (totaling up to $436,500). **Franchise Fee:** $25,000-$45,000. **Financial Assistance:** Yes. **Training:** Yes.

16122 ■ Stuft Pizza, Stuft Pizza Bar & Grill, Stuft Pizza Pronto
Stuft Pizza Franchise Corp.
50855 Washington St., Ste. 210
La Quinta, CA 92253
Ph:(949)361-2522
Fax:(949)361-2501
No. of Franchise Units: 18. **No. of Company-Owned Units:** 2. **Founded:** 1976. **Franchised:** 1986. **Description:** Stuft pizza, pasta, salads, and microbrewery. **Equity Capital Needed:** $100,000 and up. **Franchise Fee:** $25,000. **Financial Assistance:** No. **Training:** Yes.

16123 ■ Villa Enterprises
25 Washington St.
Morristown, NJ 07960
Ph:(973)285-4800

Fax:(973)401-0121
No. of Franchise Units: 88. **No. of Company-Owned Units:** 144. **Founded:** 1964. **Franchised:** 1999. **Description:** Quick service pizza & Italian restaurant. **Equity Capital Needed:** $296,950-$584,000. **Franchise Fee:** $25,000-$35,000. **Royalty Fee:** 6%. **Financial Assistance:** Limited third party financing available. **Training:** Training provided 3 weeks at corporate headquarters, 3 weeks at franchisee's location and ongoing support.

16124 ■ Vocelli Pizza
1005 South Bee St.
Pittsburgh, PA 15220
Ph:(412)919-2100 x526
Free: 800-VOC-ELLI
Fax:(412)937-9204
Co. E-mail: lmolnar@cocellipizza.com
No. of Franchise Units: 102. **No. of Company-Owned Units:** 3. **Founded:** 1969. **Franchised:** 1988. **Description:** Pizza, subs, wings; delivery or carryout. **Equity Capital Needed:** $168,000-$538,000. **Franchise Fee:** $20,000. **Royalty Fee:** 5%. **Financial Assistance:** No. **Training:** Yes. .

16125 ■ We Toss'em, They're Awesome Pizza Factory
Pizza Factory Inc.
49430 Rd. 426
PO Box 989
Oakhurst, CA 93644
Ph:(559)683-3377
Free: 800-654-4840
Fax:(559)683-6879
No. of Franchise Units: 121. **Founded:** 1979. **Franchised:** 1985. **Description:** Pizzeria. **Equity Capital Needed:** $137,000-$426,000. **Franchise Fee:** Full, Mid, Express $20,000. **Financial Assistance:** No. **Training:** Yes.

16126 ■ Whata Lotta Pizza
7011 Warner Ave., Unit M
Huntington Beach, CA 92647
Ph:(714)848-6148
Free: 888-425-6882
Fax:(714)849-2029
Co. E-mail: info@whatalottapizza.com
URL: http://www.4alotta.com
No. of Franchise Units: 50. **No. of Company-Owned Units:** 8. **Founded:** 1992. **Franchised:** 2005. **Description:** Restaurant franchise. **Equity Capital Needed:** $90,000-$208,500. **Franchise Fee:** $25,000. **Financial Assistance:** Yes. **Training:** Yes.

16127 ■ Z Pizza
19712 MacArthur Blvd. Ste. 210
Irvine, CA 92612
Ph:(949)222-5600
Free: 800-230-5761
Fax:(949)721-4053
Co. E-mail: zpizzadan@aol.com
URL: http://www.zpizza.com
No. of Franchise Units: 80. **No. of Company-Owned Units:** 10. **Founded:** 1986. **Franchised:** 1999. **Description:** They serve delicious gourmet-style pizza, pasta and sandwiches. **Equity Capital Needed:** $253,500-$352,500. **Franchise Fee:** $30,000. **Royalty Fee:** 6%. **Financial Assistance:** Third party financing available. **Training:** 4 weeks at headquarters, 2 weeks at franchisee's location, and ongoing support.

16128 ■ Zoo Pizza
3273 N Shepard
Milwaukee, WI 53211
No. of Company-Owned Units: 1. **Founded:** 1994. **Description:** Pizzeria. **Equity Capital Needed:** $300,000-$400,000. **Franchise Fee:** $89,000. **Training:** No.

TRADE PERIODICALS

16129 ■ *PLANET News*
Pub: Professional Landcare Network
Contact: Kathy Wemhoff
Ed: Kathy Wemhoff, Editor, kathywemhoff@alca.org.
Released: Monthly. **Price:** Included in membership.
Description: Serves specialists interested in the design, installation, and maintenance of interior and exterior landscapes, with emphasis on artistic and healthful results. Carries technical information and tips on subjects such as pricing work to make money. Recurring features include news of research, book reviews, award winning landscapes, and a calendar of events.

TRADE SHOWS AND CONVENTIONS

16130 ■ Nursery/Landscape Expo
Texas Nursery & Landscape Association
7730 S. IH-35
Austin, TX 78745-6698
Ph:(512)280-5182
Free: 800-880-0343
Fax:(512)280-3012
Co. E-mail: info@tnlaonline.org
URL: http://www.txnla.org
Released: Annual. **Audience:** Nursery, landscape and related trades professionals. **Principal Exhibits:** Plant materials including foliage, bedding plants, trees, palms; allied products including machinery, equipment and supplies for horticulture and landscape industry.

16131 ■ OFA Short Course
Ohio Florists Association
2130 Stella Ct., Ste. 200
Columbus, OH 43215-1033
Ph:(614)487-1117
Fax:(614)487-1216
Co. E-mail: ofa@ofa.org
URL: http://www.ofa.org
Released: Annual. **Audience:** Growers, retailers, garden centers, and other trade professionals. **Principal Exhibits:** Exhibits for the greenhouse grower and related industries. **Dates and Locations:** 2011 Jul 09-12, Columbus, OH.

16132 ■ The World's Showcase of Horticulture
Southern Nursery Association
1827 Powers Ferry Rd. SE, Ste. 4-100
Atlanta, GA 30339-8422
Ph:(770)953-3311
Fax:(770)953-4411
URL: http://www.sna.org
Released: Annual. **Audience:** Wholesale and retail nursery professionals and landscapers. **Principal Exhibits:** Nursery products, including plants, chemicals, machinery and equipment, soil and soil supplements, and plant containers.

CONSULTANTS

16133 ■ Foliage Service by Concepts
10310 NE Skidmore St.
PO Box 30387
Portland, OR 97294-3387
Ph:(503)234-3459
Fax:(503)256-0472
Co. E-mail: info@foliage-services.com
URL: http://www.foliage-services.com
Contact: Beth Pedro, Principle
E-mail: bethpedro@foliage-services.com
Scope: A professional interior plant sales and maintenance company dedicated to the design, placement, care and sales of interior plants with services to include all aspects of the interior scape business. Works closely with architects and designers to provide the proper plant species for various office and building environments.

FRANCHISES AND BUSINESS OPPORTUNITIES

16134 ■ Foliage Design Systems
Foliage Design Systems Franchise Co., Inc.
7048 Narcoossee Rd.
Orlando, FL 32822
Ph:(407)245-7776
Free: 800-933-7351
Fax:(407)245-7533
No. of Franchise Units: 37. **No. of Company-Owned Units:** 3. **Founded:** 1971. **Franchised:** 1980. **Description:** Provides the sale, lease and short-term rental of live, artificial and preserved interior foliage and decorative containers. Related products include seasonal decorative items. Designs, installs and maintains interior foliage in office buildings, hotels, residences, and restaurants. **Equity Capital Needed:** $49,400-$144,000, includes initial franchise fee. **Franchise Fee:** $25,000-$100,000. **Financial Assistance:** No **Training:** followed by on-site training covering all facets of business from plant care and plant identification to sales and marketing to office procedures. Complete operations manuals provided.

RESEARCH CENTERS

16135 ■ Ohio State University–C. Wayne Ellett Plant and Pest Diagnostic Clinic
8995 E Main St., Bldg. 23
Reynoldsburg, OH 43068-3399
Ph:(614)292-5006
Fax:(614)466-9754
Co. E-mail: ppdc@cfaes.osu.edu
URL: http://ppdc.osu.edu
Contact: Keith L. Smith PhD
E-mail: ppdc@cfaes.osu.edu
Scope: Plant disease diagnosis, including insect and mite identification, plant and weed identification, and nematode extractions. **Services:** Diagnosis of plant problems, plant diseases, insects, weeds.

16136 ■ University of British Columbia–Botanical Garden
6804 SW Marine Dr.
Vancouver, BC, Canada V6T 1Z4
Ph:(604)822-9666
Fax:(604)822-2016
Co. E-mail: swgraham@interchange.ubc.ca
URL: http://www.ubcbotanicalgarden.org
Contact: Prof. Sean Graham PhD, Res.Dir.
E-mail: swgraham@interchange.ubc.ca
Scope: Plant genomics; evolution of plant development and plant molecular systematics; biosystematics of flora of British Columbia and development of horticultural material from existing ornamentals and indigenous plants, including cytological, morphological, biochemical, and phytogeographical evaluation and specific breeding and selection programs of ornamentals. The Plant Introduction Scheme of the Botanical Garden is a cooperative research program with nursery trades and landscape architects established to facilitate research, introduction, and production of new plant cultivars to the public. Collects and evaluates superior forms of native British Columbia plants for commercial introduction. **Services:** Develops Professional Training Programs, for the British Columbia nursery industry; Plant Information and Identification Services. **Publications:** Davidsonia. **Educational Activities:** Educational Programs, for the community; Workshops and conferences (occasionally).

ASSOCIATIONS AND OTHER ORGANIZATIONS

16137 ■ American Society of Plumbing Engineers
2980 S River Rd.
Des Plaines, IL 60018
Ph:(847)296-0002
Co. E-mail: info@aspe.org
URL: http://aspe.org
Contact: Jim Kendzel MPH, Exec. Dir.
Description: Represents engineers and designers involved in the design and specification of plumbing systems; manufacturers, governmental officials, and contractors related to the industry may become members on a limited basis. Seeks to resolve professional problems in plumbing engineering; advocates greater cooperation among members and plumbing officials, contractors, laborers, and the public. Code committees examine regulatory codes pertaining to the industry and submit proposed revisions to code writing authorities to simplify, standardize, and modernize all codes. Sponsors American Society of Plumbing Engineers Research Foundation; operates certification program. **Publications:** Data Book (annual).

16138 ■ American Society of Sanitary Engineering
901 Canterbury Rd., Ste. A
Westlake, OH 44145
Ph:(440)835-3040
Fax:(440)835-3488
Co. E-mail: info@asse-plumbing.org
URL: http://www.asse-plumbing.org
Contact: James Bickford, Pres.
Description: Plumbing officials, sanitary engineers, plumbers, plumbing contractors, building officials, architects, engineers, designing engineers, physicians, and others interested in health. Conducts research on plumbing and sanitation, and develops performance standards for components of the plumbing system. Sponsors disease research program and other studies of water-borne epidemics. .

16139 ■ American Supply Association
222 Merchandise Mart Plz., Ste. 1400
Chicago, IL 60654
Ph:(312)464-0090
Fax:(312)464-0091
Co. E-mail: info@asa.net
URL: http://www.asa.net
Contact: Michael Adelizzi, Exec. VP
Description: Represents wholesale, distributors, and manufacturers of plumbing and heating, cooling, pipes, valves, and fittings. Compiles statistics on operating costs and makes occasional studies of compensation, fringe benefits, wages, and salaries. Conducts research studies and forecasting surveys. Offers group insurance. Maintains management institutes, home study courses under the ASA Education Foundation and Endowment program, provides technology and produces a CD-ROM and internet catalogue of manufacturers. **Publications:** American

Supply Association—Membership Directory (annual); ASA News (bimonthly); Report of Operating Performance (annual).

16140 ■ Association of Independent Manufacturers'/Representatives
16 A Journey, Ste. 200
Aliso Viejo, CA 92656
Ph:(949)859-2884
Free: (866)729-0975
Fax:(949)855-2973
Co. E-mail: info@aimr.net
URL: http://www.aimr.net
Contact: Mark Creyer, Pres.
Description: Manufacturers' representative companies in the plumbing-heating-cooling-piping industry promoting the use of independent sales representatives. Conducts educational programs and establishes a code of ethics between members and customers. **Publications:** AIM/R News and Views (quarterly).

16141 ■ Plumbing and Drainage Institute
800 Turnpike St., Ste. 300
North Andover, MA 01845
Ph:(978)557-0720
Free: 800-589-8956
Fax:(978)557-0721
Co. E-mail: pdi@pdionline.org
URL: http://www.pdionline.org
Contact: Rand Ackroyd, Exec. Dir.
Description: Represents manufacturers of engineered plumbing and drainage products. Promotes the advancement of engineered plumbing products through publicity, public relations, research and standardization of plumbing requirements. Works on codes and standards for plumbing drainage products.

16142 ■ Plumbing-Heating-Cooling Contractors Association
PO Box 6808
Falls Church, VA 22046
Ph:(703)237-8100
Free: 800-533-7694
Fax:(703)237-7442
Co. E-mail: naphcc@naphcc.org
URL: http://www.phccweb.org
Contact: Gerard J. Kennedy Jr., Exec. VP
Description: Federation of state and local associations of plumbing, heating, and cooling contractors. Seeks to advance sanitation, encourage sanitary laws, and generally improve the plumbing, heating, ventilating, and air conditioning industries. Conducts apprenticeship training programs, workshops, seminars, political action committee, educational and research programs. .

16143 ■ Plumbing Manufacturers Institute
1921 Rohlwing Rd., Unit G
Rolling Meadows, IL 60008
Ph:(847)481-5500

Fax:(847)481-5501
Co. E-mail: bhiggens@pmihome.org
URL: http://www.pmihome.org
Contact: Jack Krecek, Pres.
Description: Manufacturers of plumbing products. .

DIRECTORIES OF EDUCATIONAL PROGRAMS

16144 ■ Directory of Private Accredited Career Schools and Colleges of Technology
Pub: Accrediting Commission of Career Schools and Colleges of Technology
Contact: Michale S. McComis, Exec. Dir.
Released: On web page. **Price:** Free. **Description:** Covers 3900 accredited post-secondary programs that provide training programs in business, trade, and technical fields, including various small business endeavors. Entries offer school name, address, phone, description of courses, job placement assistance, and requirements for admission. Arrangement is alphabetical.

REFERENCE WORKS

16145 ■ "Advances in Pump Technology - Part Two" in Contractor (Vol. 57, February 2010, No. 2, pp. 22)
Pub: Penton Media, Inc.
Ed: Mark Eatherton. **Description:** Chinese and Japanese companies have come up with refrigerant based heat pump products that are air based which will significantly lower the installed cost of heat pump based systems. Some of these newer models have variable speed, soft start compressors and have the ability to perform high-efficiency heat pump operation on a modulating basis.

16146 ■ "Be Proactive - Closely Review Contracts" in Contractor (Vol. 56, July 2009, No. 7, pp. 19)
Pub: Penton Media, Inc.
Ed: Al Schwartz. **Description:** Contract disputes can make subcontractors suffer big financial losses or even cause a new subcontractor to fail. Subcontractors should scour the plans and specifications for any references to work that might remotely come under their scope and to cross out any line in the contract that does not accurately reflect the work that they agreed to.

16147 ■ "Be Safe: CSE Requires a Series of Steps" in Contractor (Vol. 56, October 2009, No. 10, pp. 40)
Pub: Penton Media, Inc.
Ed: Dave Yates. **Description:** Confined Space Entry claims 91 lives each year and plumbers can prevent this by following several steps starting with the use of a four-gas analyzer which costs $1,262. It measures oxygen levels, as well as combustible gases, carbon monoxide, and hydrogen sulfide.

16148 ■ **"BIM and You: Know Its Benefits and Risks" in** *Contractor* **(Vol. 57, January 2010, No. 1, pp. 46)**
Pub: Penton Media, Inc.
Ed: Susan Linden McGreevy. **Description:** Building Information Modeling is intended to be "collaborative" and this could raise legal issues if a contractor sends an electronic bid and it is filtered out. Other legal issues that mechanical contractors need to consider before using this technology are discussed.

16149 ■ **"A Burning Issue: Lives Are at Stake Every Day" in** *Contractor* **(Vol. 56, October 2009, No. 10, pp. 29)**
Pub: Penton Media, Inc.
Ed: Julius A. Ballanco; Stanley Wolfson. **Description:** American Society of Plumbing Engineers has been accused of being biased for supporting rules that require residential fire sprinklers although the society's members will not receive any benefit from their installation. The organization trains and certifies plumbing engineers who design life-saving fire protection systems.

16150 ■ **"The Business End of Staying in Business" in** *Contractor* **(Vol. 56, September 2009, No. 9, pp. 51)**
Pub: Penton Media, Inc.
Ed: Al Schwartz. **Description:** Advice on how to manage a new plumbing business in the United States are offered. The transition from being a workman to an employer is seen as one that accompanies a steep learning curve. The importance of managing cash flow is also highlighted.

16151 ■ **"A Call for Common Sense with WaterSense" in** *Contractor* **(Vol. 56, July 2009, No. 7, pp. 42)**
Pub: Penton Media, Inc.
Ed: Dave Yates. **Description:** Instillation of a shower that is supposed to protect bathers from being scalded is presented. Plumbers should be aware that the WaterSense shower heads still have a 50/50 chance of scalding their users.

16152 ■ **"Charlotte Pipe Launches Satirical Campaign" in** *Contractor* **(Vol. 57, January 2010, No. 1, pp. 6)**
Pub: Penton Media, Inc.
Description: Charlotte Pipe and Foundry Co. launched an advertising campaign that uses social media and humor to make a point about how it can be nearly impossible to determine if imported cast iron pipes and fittings meet the same quality standards as what is made in the U.S. The campaign features 'pipe whisperers' and also spoofs pipe sniffing dogs.

16153 ■ **"Chicago Botanic Garden Builds Green Research Facility" in** *Contractor* **(Vol. 56, December 2009, No. 12, pp. 5)**
Pub: Penton Media, Inc.
Ed: Candace Roulo. **Description:** Chicago Botanic Garden has built a laboratory and research facility in Illinois. The facility is set to receive a United States Green Building Council LEED Gold certification. The building features a solar photovoltaic array, radiant flooring and water-conserving plumbing products.

16154 ■ **"Climate Right Systems Provides Pre-Assembled Equipment Packages" in** *Contractor* **(Vol. 56, July 2009, No. 7, pp. 1)**
Pub: Penton Media, Inc.
Description: Climate Right Systems offers completely engineered, assembled, and tested equipment packages for hydronic heating and cooling. This package does away with the need to custom fabricate on-site and lets mechanical and plumbing contractors expand their offerings without added overhead and risk.

16155 ■ **"Commercial Water Efficiency Initiatives Announced" in** *Contractor* **(Vol. 56, November 2009, No. 11, pp. 5)**
Pub: Penton Media, Inc.
Ed: Robert P. Mader. **Description:** Plumbing engineers John Koeller and Bill Gauley are developing a testing protocol for commercial toilets. The team said commercial toilets should have a higher level of flush

performance than residential toilets for certification. The Environmental Protection Agency's WaterSense program wants to expand the program into the commercial/institutional sector.

16156 ■ **"Contractors Can't Do It Alone, PHCC's Pfeffer Says" in** *Contractor* **(Vol. 56, October 2009, No. 10, pp. 3)**
Pub: Penton Media, Inc.
Ed: Robert P. Mader. **Description:** President Herbert "Skip" Pfeffer of the Plumbing-Heating-Cooling Contractors National Association says lobbying and education are the services that the association offers that a contractor cannot do individually. Pfeffer says the dues for the association are set up in a manner that allows members to pay monthly.

16157 ■ **"Contractors Fret Over Credit, People, Government" in** *Contractor* **(Vol. 57, February 2010, No. 2, pp. 7)**
Pub: Penton Media, Inc.
Ed: Robert P. Mader. **Description:** Telephone interviews with 22 plumbing and HVAC contractors reveal that only two had sales increases for 2009 and that overall, contractors were down anywhere from seven to 25 percent. In the repair/service market, the residential sector was holding its own but the commercial portion was lagging behind.

16158 ■ **"Contractors Should Expand Their Services" in** *Contractor* **(Vol. 56, July 2009, No. 7, pp. 34)**
Pub: Penton Media, Inc.
Ed: Steven Scandaliato. **Description:** All single family homes will be required to have fire sprinkler systems installed when the 2009 International Residential Code arrives. This presents an opportunity for plumbing contractors and they can be competitively priced against a fire protection contractor if they train their workforce to install sprinklers.

16159 ■ **"Corporate Park Retrofits for Water Savings" in** *Contractor* **(Vol. 56, October 2009, No. 10, pp. 5)**
Pub: Penton Media, Inc.
Description: Merrit Corporate Park in Norwalk, Connecticut has been interested in improving building efficiency and one of their buildings has been retrofitted with water-efficient plumbing systems which will allow them to save as much as two million gallons of water. ADP Service Corp. helped the park upgrade their plumbing system.

16160 ■ **"CSE: Contractors Are Always Responsible" in** *Contractor* **(Vol. 56, November 2009, No. 11, pp. 34)**
Pub: Penton Media, Inc.
Ed: Dave Yates. **Description:** Plumbing contractors should purchase a long snorkel hose, a tripod with manual-crank hoist, and a sump pump in order to prevent accidents associated with Confined Space Entry. Liability issues surrounding confined space entry prevention and accidents are discussed.

16161 ■ **"The Customer Is Right Even If He's Wrong" in** *Contractor* **(Vol. 57, February 2010, No. 2, pp. 12)**
Pub: Penton Media, Inc.
Ed: Al Schwarz. **Description:** Mechanical contractors should note that customers will make a judgment based upon the impression that they form on their first meeting. Contractors can maintain a professional image by washing their trucks and having the personnel dress uniformly. Contractors have every right to demand that employees clean up and make a better impression on customers.

16162 ■ *Directory of Listed Plumbing Products*
Pub: IAPMO
Contact: Shahin Moinian, Sen. Dir.
E-mail: moinian@iapmo.org
Released: Bimonthly. **Price:** $118, members per year. **Covers:** About 1,500 manufacturers of approximately 10,000 plumbing products and appliances. **Entries Include:** Manufacturer name, address, product name, model number, product description. **Arrangement:** Alphabetical. **Indexes:** Manufacturer, product.

16163 ■ **"Do the Right Thing" in** *Contractor* **(Vol. 56, December 2009, No. 12, pp. 16)**
Pub: Penton Media, Inc.
Ed: Robert P. Mader. **Description:** Applewood Plumbing, Heating and Electric has won Contractor magazine's 2009 Contractor of the Year Award. The company has ranked eighth among more than 300 service companies in the United States. A brief history of the company is also provided.

16164 ■ **"DOE Proposes New Water Heater Efficiency Standards" in** *Contractor* **(Vol. 57, January 2010, No. 1, pp. 3)**
Pub: Penton Media, Inc.
Ed: Robert P. Mader. **Description:** U.S. Department of Energy is proposing higher efficiency standards for gas and electric water heaters which will not take effect until 2015. The proposal calls for gas-fired storage water heaters less than 60 gallons to have an Energy Factor of 0.675 and those larger than 60 gallons to have an Energy Factor of 0.717.

16165 ■ **"EPA 'Finalizes' WaterSense for Homes" in** *Contractor* **(Vol. 57, January 2010, No. 1, pp. 70)**
Pub: Penton Media, Inc.
Ed: Bob Mader. **Description:** U.S. Environmental Protection Agency released its "final" version of the WaterSense for Homes standard. The standard's provisions that affect plumbing contractors includes the specification that everything has to be leak tested and final service pressure cannot exceed 60 psi.

16166 ■ **"Expect Action on Health Care and the Economy" in** *Contractor* **(Vol. 57, January 2010, No. 1, pp. 30)**
Pub: Penton Media, Inc.
Ed: Kevin Schwalb. **Description:** The Plumbing-Heating-Cooling Contractors National Association is working to solidify its standing in the public policy arena as the legislative agenda will focus on health care reform, estate tax and immigration reform, all of which will impact the industries.

16167 ■ **"Federal Buildings to Achieve Zero-Net Energy by 2030" in** *Contractor* **(Vol. 56, December 2009, No. 12, pp. 5)**
Pub: Penton Media, Inc.
Ed: Candace Roulo. **Description:** United States president Barack Obama has issued sustainable goals for federal buildings. Federal agencies are also required to increase energy efficiency, conserve water and support sustainable communities. Obama has also announced a $3.4 billion investment in a smart energy creed.

16168 ■ **"Get Online Quick in the Office Or in the Field" in** *Contractor* **(Vol. 56, October 2009, No. 10, pp. 47)**
Pub: Penton Media, Inc.
Ed: William Feldman; Patti Feldman. **Description:** Contractors can set up a web site in minutes using the www.1and1.com website. Verizon's Novatel MIFI 2372 HSPA personal hotspot device lets contractors go online in the field. The StarTech scalable business management system helps contractors manage daily operations.

16169 ■ **"Got to be Smarter than the Average Bear" in** *Contractor* **(Vol. 56, September 2009, No. 9, pp. 82)**
Pub: Penton Media, Inc.
Ed: Bob Mader. **Description:** International Association of Plumbing and Mechanical Officials Green Technical Committee has debated the need for contractors to have certifications in installing green plumbing. Some have argued that qualifications would discourage homeowners from improving their properties. Comments from executives are also included.

16170 ■ **"How to Improve Your Mobile Marketing" in** *Contractor* **(Vol. 56, October 2009, No. 10, pp. 54)**
Pub: Penton Media, Inc.
Ed: Matt Michel. **Description:** Plumbers can improve their mobile advertising by making their logos as large as possible and positioning their logo on top of the

truck so people can see it over traffic. They should also make the phone numbers small because people only take note of these when the truck is parked.

16171 ■ **"IAPMO GTC Debates Supplement"** in *Contractor* (Vol. 56, September 2009, No. 9, pp. 3)
Pub: Penton Media, Inc.
Ed: Robert P. Mader. **Description:** Green Technical Committee of the International Association of Plumbing and Mechanical Officials is developing a Green Plumbing and Mechanical Supplement. The supplement provides for installation of systems by licensed contractors and installers. Comments from officials are also presented.

16172 ■ **"IAPMO GTC Finalizes Green Supplement"** in *Contractor* (Vol. 57, January 2010, No. 1, pp. 1)
Pub: Penton Media, Inc.
Description: International Association of Plumbing and Mechanical Officials' Green Technical Committee finalized the Green Plumbing & Mechanical Code Supplement. The supplement was created to provide a set of provisions that encourage sustainable practices and work towards the design and construction of plumbing and mechanical systems.

16173 ■ **"IAPMO GTC Votes to Limit Showers to 2.0-GPM"** in *Contractor* (Vol. 56, September 2009, No. 9, pp. 1)
Pub: Penton Media, Inc.
Ed: Robert P. Mader. **Description:** Green Technical Committee of the International Association of Plumbing and Mechanical Officials has voted to limit showers to 2.0 GPM. It is also developing a Green Plumbing and Mechanical Supplement. Comments from executives are also supplied.

16174 ■ **"It's New or Improved, But Does It Work?"** in *Contractor* (Vol. 57, January 2010, No. 1, pp. 22)
Pub: Penton Media, Inc.
Ed: Al Schwartz. **Description:** There is a place for skepticism in the HVAC and plumbing industry as not all new products that are specified may not always perform. The tradesman has the responsibility of integrating new technology into the field.

16175 ■ **"Kohler Building Earns LEED Silver Certification"** in *Contractor* (Vol. 56, September 2009, No. 9, pp. 12)
Pub: Penton Media, Inc.
Description: United States Green Building Council has awarded Kohler Co. with the Silver Leadership in Energy and Environmental Design Status. The award has highlighted the company's work to transform its building into a more environmentally efficient structure. A description of the facility is also provided.

16176 ■ **"LA Passes HET Ordinance, California Greens Code"** in *Contractor* (Vol. 56, September 2009, No. 9, pp. 1)
Pub: Penton Media, Inc.
Ed: Candace Ruolo. **Description:** Los Angeles City Council has passed a Water Efficiency Requirements ordinance. The law mandates lower low-flow plumbing requirements for plumbing fixtures installed in new buildings and retrofits. Under the ordinance, a toilet's maximum flush volume may not exceed 1.28-gpf.

16177 ■ **"Lead-Free Products must Meet Requirements"** in *Contractor* (Vol. 56, September 2009, No. 9, pp. 30)
Pub: Penton Media, Inc.
Ed: Robert Gottermeier. **Description:** United States Environmental Protection Agency's adoption of the Safe Drinking Water Act is aimed at lowering lead extraction levels from plumbing products. Manufacturers have since deleaded brass and bronze potable water products. Meanwhile, California and Vermont have passed a law limiting lead content for potable water conveying plumbing products.

16178 ■ **"Major Advances in Heat Pump Technology"** in *Contractor* (Vol. 57, January 2010, No. 1, pp. 42)
Pub: Penton Media, Inc.
Ed: Mark Eatherton. **Description:** Tax credits make ground-source heat pump technology more economi-

cally feasible. Suggestions on how to choose the right ground-source heat pump technology to install in a house are discussed.

16179 ■ **"Minnesota State Park Building Exemplifies Sustainability"** in *Contractor* (Vol. 56, November 2009, No. 11, pp. 5)
Pub: Penton Media, Inc.
Ed: Candace Roulo. **Description:** Camden State Park's newly remodeled information/office building in Lynd, Minnesota features a 10 kw wind turbine which is capable of offsetting most of the facility's electricity and a geothermal heat pump system. The heat pump is a 4-ton vertical closed-loop ground source heat pump by ClimateMaster.

16180 ■ **"More Than 1,000 Attend Second WaterSmart"** in *Contractor* (Vol. 56, November 2009, No. 11, pp. 3)
Pub: Penton Media, Inc.
Description: Over 1,000 plumbing and water conservation professionals attended the second WaterSmart Innovations Conference and Exposition in Las Vegas. Plumbing industry personalities made presentations during the conference and several innovative products were displayed at the trade show.

16181 ■ **"A Necessary Balancing Act: Bookkeeping"** in *Contractor* (Vol. 56, November 2009, No. 11, pp. 22)
Pub: Penton Media, Inc.
Ed: Al Schwartz. **Description:** Pros and cons of getting a bookkeeper or a certified public accountant for the subcontractor are discussed. A bookkeeper can help a subcontractor get new accounting software up and running while an accountant will more than likely keep after the books at regular intervals throughout the year.

16182 ■ **"Online Training Requires Tools, Accessories"** in *Contractor* (Vol. 56, September 2009, No. 9, pp. 67)
Pub: Penton Media, Inc.
Ed: Larry Drake. **Description:** Importance of the right equipment and tools to members of the United States plumbing industry undergoing online training is discussed. Portable devices such as Blackberrys and I-phones could be used for online training. The use of headphones makes listening easier for the trainee.

16183 ■ **"Papal Permit Trumps the Plumbing Codes"** in *Contractor* (Vol. 57, February 2010, No. 2, pp. 20)
Pub: Penton Media, Inc.
Ed: Dave Yates. **Description:** Despite the plumbing code, a plumbing contractor was able to convince the inspector to approve his application to install a sacristy sink which drains into the ground instead of the sewer system. Details of the church's system are presented.

16184 ■ **"PHCC Convention, Show Gets High Marks"** in *Contractor* (Vol. 56, December 2009, No. 12, pp. 1)
Pub: Penton Media, Inc.
Ed: Robert P. Mader. **Description:** Plumbing-Heating-Cooling Contractors National Association has held its first convention and trade show in New Orleans, Louisiana. Attendees were treated to a variety of seminars and exhibitors during the event. Comments from event organizers are also given.

16185 ■ *Plumbing Engineer—Product Directory Issue*
Pub: TMB Publishing Inc.
Contact: John Mesenbrink, Editor-in-Chief
Released: Monthly, 12 times a year. **Price:** $50, individuals one year. **Covers:** Over 400 plumbing products from approximately 250 manufacturers. **Entries Include:** Company name, phone, fax, website, and e-mail; name of engineering contact with the firm.

16186 ■ **"Plumbing, Heating Products Shine at Greenbuild"** in *Contractor* (Vol. 57, January 2010, No. 1, pp. 3)
Pub: Penton Media, Inc.
Ed: Robert P. Mader. **Description:** Among the many exhibitors at Greenbuild 2009 was T&S Brass which showcased their low-flow pre-rinse spray valves and

Watts Water Technologies which showed off their hot water recirculating system. Aquatherm and Acorn Engineering were also at the show.

16187 ■ **"Plumbing, Heating Products Shine at Greenbuild Expo"** in *Contractor* (Vol. 56, December 2009, No. 12, pp. 1)
Pub: Penton Media, Inc.
Ed: Robert P. Mader. **Description:** Greenbuild Show held in Phoenix, Arizona has showcased the latest in plumbing and heating products. Zurn displayed its EcoVantage line of fixtures and valves during the event. Meanwhile, Sloan Valve offered its washdown 1-pint/flush Alphine urinal.

16188 ■ **"PMA Launches Online Education Program"** in *Contractor* (Vol. 56, October 2009, No. 10, pp. 8)
Pub: Penton Media, Inc.
Description: Plumbing & Mechanical Association of Georgia launched an online program that covers technical and business management that will help contractors run their businesses. Future courses will include math for plumbers, graywater systems, and recession-proofing your business.

16189 ■ **"Portland Home Is First in U.S. to Use Variable Speed 'Inverter' Technology"** in *Contractor* (Vol. 56, December 2009, No. 12, pp. 5)
Pub: Penton Media, Inc.
Description: Daikin Altherma heat pump with inverter drive has been installed in a Portland, Oregon home. The heat pump provides a high coefficient of performance while delivering hydronic and domestic hot water functionality. Other product features and dimensions are also supplied.

16190 ■ **"Pre-Certified LEED Hotel Prototype Reduces Energy Use, Conserves Water"** in *Contractor* (Vol. 57, January 2010, No. 1, pp. 3)
Pub: Penton Media, Inc.
Ed: Candace Roulo. **Description:** Marriott International Inc.'s LEED pre-certified prototype hotel will reduce a hotel's energy and water consumption by 25 percent and save owners approximately $100,000. Their Courtyard Settler's Ridge in Pittsburgh will be the first hotel built based on the prototype.

16191 ■ **"Proposal Ruffles Builders"** in *Austin Business JournalInc.* (Vol. 29, November 20, 2009, No. 37, pp. 1)
Pub: American City Business Journals
Ed: Jacob Dirr. **Description:** A proposal that requires heating, ventilation and cooling equipment checking for a new commercial building having an area of at least 10,000 square feet might cost 25 cents to 50 cents per square foot for the owners. This may lead to higher housing costs. Both the Building and Fire Code Board of Appeals and the Mechanical Plumbing and Solar Board have recommended the plan.

16192 ■ **"Public Bathroom Pressure Woes Resolved"** in *Contractor* (Vol. 56, September 2009, No. 9, pp. 44)
Pub: Penton Media, Inc.
Ed: Dave Yates. **Description:** Design and construction of a public bathroom's plumbing system in the United States are discussed. Installed plumbing fixtures with flush valves would not function properly. The installation of Grundfos SQE variable-speed pumps has resolved problems with the bathroom's water pressure.

16193 ■ **"Put Power in Your Direct Mail Campaigns"** in *Contractor* (Vol. 56, September 2009, No. 9, pp. 64)
Pub: Penton Media, Inc.
Ed: Matt Michel. **Description:** Advice on how members of the United States plumbing industry should manage direct mail marketing campaigns are offered. Determining the purpose of a campaign is recommended. Focusing on a single message, product or service is also encouraged.

16194 ■ **"Rehab Center Slashes Energy Bills By Going Tankless"** in *Contractor* (Vol. 56, December 2009, No. 12, pp. 3)
Pub: Penton Media, Inc.
Description: Melburne Health and Rehabilitation Center in Florida has reduced its energy bills by

installing a tankless hot water system. Sun Plumbing was selected to install the system. The system was installed on a mechanical room that housed the old tank-type heaters.

16195 ■ **"Route Optimization Impacts the Bottom Line" in** *Contractor* **(Vol. 56, November 2009, No. 11, pp. 48)**
Pub: Penton Media, Inc.

Ed: Dave Beaudry. **Description:** Plumbing and HVAC businesses can save a significant amount of money from route optimization. The process begins with gathering information on a fleet and a routing software tool can determine the effectiveness of current route configurations and identify preferable route plans.

16196 ■ **"Selling a Job When There's Buyer's Remorse" in** *Contractor* **(Vol. 56, December 2009, No. 12, pp. 37)**
Pub: Penton Media, Inc.

Ed: H. Kent Craig. **Description:** Advice on how contractors should manage low-profit jobs in the United States are presented. Efforts should be made to try and find at least one quality field foreman or superintendent. Contractors should also try to respectfully renegotiate the terms of the job.

16197 ■ **"Software Solutions Increase Productivity" in** *Contractor* **(Vol. 57, February 2010, No. 2, pp. 26)**
Pub: Penton Media, Inc.

Ed: William Feldman; Patti Feldman. **Description:** Singletouch is a real-time data capture solution for mechanical and other contractors that work in jobs that require materials and workload tracking. Contractors get information on extreme weather and sudden changes in the cost of materials. The OptimumHVAC optimization software by Optimum Energy is designed to optimize energy savings in commercial buildings.

16198 ■ **"Solar Choices" in** *Contractor* **(Vol. 56, October 2009, No. 10, pp. 32)**
Pub: Penton Media, Inc.

Ed: Tom Scheel. **Description:** Price, performance, and ease of installation of a flat plate versus an evacuated tube collector for a plumbing and heating job are compared. The better choice with regards to weight, aesthetics, efficiency in warm or cool climates, year round load, and space heating is discussed.

16199 ■ **"Solar Hot Water Sales Are Hot, Hot, Hot" in** *Contractor* **(Vol. 56, December 2009, No. 12, pp. 22)**
Pub: Penton Media, Inc.

Ed: Dave Yates. **Description:** Plumbing contractors in the United States can benefit from the increased sales of solar thermal water systems. Licensed plumbers have the base knowledge on the risks associated from heating and storing water. Safety issues associated with solar water heaters are also included.

16200 ■ **"Sprinkler Advocates Beat Builders Again" in** *Contractor* **(Vol. 56, November 2009, No. 11, pp. 58)**
Pub: Penton Media, Inc.

Ed: Bob Mader. **Description:** Proponents of residential fire sprinklers were able to fend off the attempt by the National Association of Home Builders to do away with mandated fire sprinklers on the International Residential Code by the International Code Council (ICC). The ICC's vote on the issue is good news for fire sprinkler contractors and plumbing contractors.

16201 ■ **"Three Steps to Follow when Job Hunting" in** *Contractor* **(Vol. 56, September 2009, No. 9, pp. 62)**
Pub: Penton Media, Inc.

Ed: H. Kent Craig. **Description:** Advice on how project managers in the United States plumbing industry should look for jobs in view of the economic crisis. Job seekers should consider relocating to places where there are an abundance of project management jobs. Resumes should also be revised to make an applicant stand out.

16202 ■ **"Tips to Improve Your Direct Mail Results" in** *Contractor* **(Vol. 57, January 2010, No. 1, pp. 55)**
Pub: Penton Media, Inc.

Ed: Matt Michel. **Description:** Plumbers can improve their direct mail efforts by buying quality lists and writing good headlines. The mail should also tell a story and urge its readers to action.

16203 ■ **"Tracking Your Fleet Can Increase Bottom Line" in** *Contractor* **(Vol. 56, November 2009, No. 11, pp. 26)**
Pub: Penton Media, Inc.

Ed: Candace Roulo. **Description:** GPS fleet management system can help boost a contractor's profits, employee productivity, and efficiency. These are available as a handheld device or a cell phone that employees carry around or as a piece of hardware installed in a vehicle. These lets managers track assets and communicate with employees about jobs.

16204 ■ **"Trade Craft: Take Pride in Your Trade, Demand Excellence" in** *Contractor* **(Vol. 56, October 2009, No. 10, pp. 24)**
Pub: Penton Media, Inc.

Ed: Al Schwartz. **Description:** There is a need for teaching, developing, and encouraging trade craft. An apprentice plumber is not only versed in the mechanical aspects of the trade but he also has a working knowledge of algebra, trigonometry, chemistry, and thermal dynamics. Contractors should be demanding on their personnel regarding their trade craft and should only keep and train the very best people they can hire.

16205 ■ **"Use Social Media to Enhance Brand, Business" in** *Contractor* **(Vol. 56, December 2009, No. 12, pp. 14)**
Pub: Penton Media, Inc.

Ed: Elton Rivas. **Description:** Advice on how plumbing contractors should use online social networks to increase sales is presented including such issues as clearly defining goals and target audience. An additional advantage to this medium is that advertisements can easily be shared with other users.

16206 ■ **"Water Conservation Helps GC's Building Attain LEED Gold Status" in** *Contractor* **(Vol. 56, September 2009, No. 9, pp. 5)**

Description: Green contractor Marshall Erdman has built a new office building using green design. The facility is seen to become a prime Leadership in Energy and Environmental Design (LEED) building model. Details of the building's design and features are also provided.

16207 ■ **"Water Efficiency Bill Move Through Congress" in** *Contractor* **(Vol. 56, July 2009, No. 7, pp. 20)**
Pub: Penton Media, Inc.

Ed: Kevin Schwalb. **Description:** National Association, a plumbing-heating-cooling contractor, was instrumental in drafting the Water Advanced Technologies for Efficient Resource Use Act of 2009 and they are also backing the Water Accountability Tax Efficiency Reinvestment Act. The first bill promotes WaterSense-labeled products while the other promotes water conservation through tax credits.

16208 ■ **"Web-Based Solutions Streamline Operations" in** *Contractor* **(Vol. 56, December 2009, No. 12, pp. 28)**
Pub: Penton Media, Inc.

Ed: William Feldman; Patti Feldman. **Description:** Sage Project Lifecycle Management is a Web-based service platform for plumbing and HVAC contractors. It enables effective workflow and document management. Projectmates, on the other hand, is a Web-based enterprise-wide solution for managing both commercial plumbing and HVAC projects.

16209 ■ **The Wholesaler—Directory of Manufacturers Representatives Issue**
Pub: TMB Publishing Inc.
Contact: James Schaible, Managing Editor
E-mail: jim@thewholesaler.com
Released: Annual, Latest edition 2009. **Price:** $50, individuals hardcopy or CD-ROM. **Publication Includes:** 2,000 manufacturers' representatives han-

dling plumbing, heating, piping, air conditioning, and refrigeration products. **Entries Include:** Representative's name or firm name, address, phone, fax, territory, and lines carried. **Arrangement:** Geographical by territory (Central States, North Pacific, etc.).

16210 ■ **The Wholesaler—'The Wholesaling 100' Issue**
Pub: TMB Publishing Inc.
Contact: Tom M. Brown Jr., Publisher
E-mail: publisher@thewholesaler.com
Released: Annual, July. **Price:** $50, individuals print or CD-ROM. **Publication Includes:** Ranks 100 leading wholesalers of plumbing, heating, air conditioning, refrigeration equipment, and industrial pipe, valves and fittings. **Entries Include:** Company name, address, phone, fax, names and titles of key personnel, number of employees, business breakdown (percentage). **Arrangement:** Ranked by sales.

16211 ■ **"WQA Develops Certification Program" in** *Contractor* **(Vol. 57, January 2010, No. 1, pp. 56)**
Pub: Penton Media, Inc.

Description: Water Quality Association is now offering a new certification program for companies that may be affected by California's law that prohibits any products intended to convey or dispense water for human consumption that is not lead-free. All pipe or plumbing fixtures must be certified by a third party certification body.

SOURCES OF SUPPLY

16212 ■ **American Supply Association—Membership Directory**
Pub: American Supply Association
Released: Annual. **Price:** $25, members; $299, nonmembers; $1,125, individuals electronic; $225, nonmembers diskette. **Covers:** 4,000 member wholesalers handling plumbing, heating, and cooling materials and supplies. **Entries Include:** Company name, address, phone, names of executives, list of products or services, fax numbers, email and website. **Arrangement:** Geographical and alphabetical. **Indexes:** Special interest divisions.

STATISTICAL SOURCES

16213 ■ **RMA Annual Statement Studies**
Pub: Robert Morris Associates (RMA)
Released: Annual. **Price:** $175.00 2006-07 edition, $105.00. **Description:** Contains composite balance sheets and income statements for more than 360 industries, including the accounting, auditing, and bookkeeping industries. Also contains five years of comparative historical data for discerning trends. Includes 16 commonly used ratios, computed for most of the size groupings for nearly every industry.

TRADE PERIODICALS

16214 ■ **Heating-Plumbing-Air Conditioning Magazine HPAC**
Pub: Rogers Media Publishing
Contact: Kim Rossiter, Sales, Mktg. Coord.
E-mail: kim.rossiter@rci.rogers.com
Released: 7/yr. **Price:** Free to qualified subscribers. **Description:** Plumbing, heating, air conditioning, refrigeration, and insulation trade magazine.

16215 ■ **Indiana Contractor**
Pub: Indiana Association of Plumbing Heating Cooling Contractors Inc.
Contact: Brenda A. Dant
E-mail: brenda@iaphcc.com
Released: Quarterly. **Description:** Official publication of the Indiana Association of Plumbing, Heating, Cooling Contractors, Inc.

16216 ■ **MCAA Reporter**
Pub: Mechanical Contractors Association of America Inc.
Contact: Stephanie Mills, Managing Editor
Ed: Adrienne Breedlove, Editor. **Released:** Monthly, except in February and August. **Price:** Included in membership; $50, nonmembers. **Description:** Cov-

ers labor issues and government affairs as they affect mechanical contractors in the plumbing, pipefitting, air conditioning, refrigeration, fire protection, and high-purity piping industries. Recurring features include reports on the activities of the Association and notices of pertinent seminars and meetings.

16217 ■ Plumbing Engineer
Pub: TMB Publishing Inc.
Contact: John Mesenbrink, Ch. Ed.
E-mail: editor@plumbingengineer.com
Released: Monthly. **Description:** Trade journal for consulting engineering, mechanical engineering, architecture, and contracting professionals.

TRADE SHOWS AND CONVENTIONS

16218 ■ CMX - CIPHEX National Tradeshow and Learning Forum
Shield Associates Ltd.
25 Bradgate Rd.
Don Mills, ON, Canada M3B 1J6
Ph:(416)444-5225
Free: 800-282-0003
Fax:(416)444-8268
Co. E-mail: sal@salshow.com
URL: http://www.salshow.com
Released: Biennial. **Audience:** Contractors, wholesalers, consulting engineers, building managers, and chemical specifiers. **Principal Exhibits:** Heating, air-conditioning, refrigeration, ventilation, and mechanical plumbing equipment.

16219 ■ North Carolina Association of Plumbing, Heating, and Cooling Contractors Annual Trade Show
North Carolina Association of Plumbing, Heating, and Cooling Contractors
5540 McNeely Dr. Ste. 202
Raleigh, NC 27612
Ph:(919)532-0522
Fax:(919)532-0523
Co. E-mail: carlagilbert@phccnc.org
URL: http://www.ncaphcc.org
Released: Annual. **Audience:** Plumbing, heating, and cooling contractors; architects; engineers; and general public. **Principal Exhibits:** Plumbing, heating, and cooling equipment, supplies, and services.

CONSULTANTS

16220 ■ GHT Ltd.
1010 N Glebe Rd., Ste. 200
Arlington, VA 22201-4749
Ph:(703)243-1200
Fax:(703)276-1376
Co. E-mail: ght@ghtltd.com
URL: http://www.ghtltd.com
Contact: Robert M. Menuet Jr., Principle
E-mail: rmenuet@ghtltd.com
Scope: Provides design services in mechanical engineering. Offers telecommunications and security engineering services. Provides life safety engineering services and utilities planning services. Provides estimates of life expectancy and replacement or upgrade costs for mechanical and electrical equipment and systems. **Publications:** "Critical spaces keep the pace of business humming," May, 2004; "To avoid staticlater, hire right telecom consultant," Oct, 2007. **Special Services:** LEED[R].

16221 ■ Greacen Consulting Engineers Inc.
919 Old Hwy. 8 NW, Ste. 200
Saint Paul, MN 55112
Ph:(651)633-1318
Fax:(651)633-1885
Contact: Ed Greacen, Principle
Scope: Specializes in plumbing, heating, ventilating, air conditioning and project management. Designs domestic water and water treatment systems, fire protection, fuel and gas piping, humidification and de-humidification systems, variable air volume (VAV), fan-powered VAV, and retrofit systems for Indoor Air Quality (IAQ).

16222 ■ Lundquist, Killeen, Potvin and Bender Inc.
1935 W County Rd. B2, Ste. 300
Saint Paul, MN 55113-2722
Ph:(651)633-1223
Fax:(651)633-1355
Co. E-mail: nbart@lkpb.com
URL: http://www.lkpb.com
Contact: Stephen J. Gentilini, Principle
E-mail: sgent@atslkpb.com
Scope: Provides services in heating, ventilation, plumbing, piping, refrigeration, air conditioning, fire protection, lighting design and fixture selection, communications, electrical power distribution, security, life safety system design, energy conservation analysis, design and implementation.

16223 ■ Stueven Engineering Consultants
140 W 3rd Ave.
Escondido, CA 92025
Ph:(760)735-8577
Fax:(760)735-8578
Co. E-mail: sb@stueven-engineering.com
URL: http://www.stueven-engineering.com
Contact: Steve Balderrama, Principle
E-mail: sb@atsstueven-engineering.com
Scope: Provides services in professional engineering, planning, design, and construction support services for mechanical and plumbing systems.

FRANCHISES AND BUSINESS OPPORTUNITIES

16224 ■ Ace DuraFlo Systems LLC
1370 Reynolds Ave., Ste. 112
Irvine, CA 92614
Free: 888-775-0220
Fax:(949)263-8771
No. of Franchise Units: 33. **No. of Company-Owned Units:** 7. **Founded:** 1997. **Franchised:** 2001. **Description:** Pipe restoration services. **Equity Capital Needed:** $36,190-$410,100. **Franchise Fee:** $21,900-$34,900. **Royalty Fee:** 6-8%. **Financial Assistance:** Equipment financing assistance. **Training:** Provides 1 week at headquarters, 2 weeks at franchisee's location with ongoing support.

16225 ■ American Leak Detection
888 Research Dr., Ste. 100
Palm Springs, CA 92262
Ph:(760)320-9991
Free: 800-755-6697
Fax:(760)320-1288
No. of Franchise Units: 304. **No. of Company-Owned Units:** 4. **Founded:** 1974. **Franchised:** 1984. **Description:** Detection of water or sewer leaks under concrete slabs of homes, pools, spas, fountains, commercial buildings, etc., with electronic equipment manufactured by the company. **Equity Capital Needed:** $83,225-$233,500. **Franchise Fee:** $29,500-$80,000. **Royalty Fee:** 6-10%. **Financial Assistance:** In-house financing available. **Managerial Assistance:** Annual convention for 4 days. **Training:** Provides 6-12 weeks at headquarters, 1 week at franchisees location with ongoing support.

16226 ■ Canadian Pool Players Association
1000 Lake St. Louis Blvd., Ste. 325
Lake St, Louis, MO N0G 2V0
Ph:(636)625-8611
Fax:(636)625-2975
Co. E-mail: khinkebein@poolplayers.ca
URL: http://www.poolplayers.ca
No. of Franchise Units: 17. **Founded:** 1989. **Franchised:** 1989. **Description:** Oversees and provides ongoing support to recreational pool league operators. **Franchise Fee:** $5,000. **Training:** Provides 5 day training plus ongoing.

16227 ■ Handyman Connection
Mamar, Inc.
10250 Alliance Rd., Ste.100
Cincinnati, OH 45242
Ph:(513)771-3003
Free: 800-466-5530
Fax:(513)771-6439
Co. E-mail: soaks@handymanconnection.com
URL: http://www.handymanconnection.com
No. of Franchise Units: 160. **No. of Company-Owned Units:** 1. **Founded:** 1990. **Franchised:** 1993. **Description:** Small to medium home repairs and remodeling. **Equity Capital Needed:** $90,000-$125,000. **Franchise Fee:** $25,000-$40,000. **Financial Assistance:** No. **Training:** 2 weeks at corporate training center, and 1 week grand opening onsite.

16228 ■ Mr. Rooter Plumbing
1010 N University Parks Dr.
Waco, TX 76707
Ph:(254)745-2500
Free: 800-298-6855
Fax:(254)759-5863
Co. E-mail: sam.thurman@mrrooter.com
URL: http://www.mrrooter.com
No. of Franchise Units: 16. **No. of Operating Units:** 233. **Founded:** 1970. **Franchised:** 1974. **Description:** Complete residential and commercial plumbing service company. **Equity Capital Needed:** $27,000 investment required; $50,000 start-up capital required. **Franchise Fee:** $27,000, per 100,000 population. **Training:** Initial, onsite, intranet and ongoing support.

16229 ■ Potty Doctor Plumbing Service
Potty Doctor Franchise Systems Inc.
424 No. Dixie Hwy.
Lake Worth, FL 33460
Ph:(561)582-0334
Free: 888-377-6889
Co. E-mail: sales@pottydoctor.com
No. of Franchise Units: 3. **Founded:** 1943. **Franchised:** 1997. **Description:** Residential plumbing services. **Equity Capital Needed:** $5,000-$37,000, depends on existing business conversion or new start-up. **Franchise Fee:** $15,000+. **Financial Assistance:** No. **Training:** Yes.

LIBRARIES

16230 ■ Intertek Testing Services–Warnock Hersey Library
1500 Brigantine Dr.
Coquitlam, BC, Canada V3K 7C1
Ph:(604)520-3321
Fax:(604)524-9186
Co. E-mail: lawrence.gibson@intertek.com
URL: http://www.intertek.com/
Scope: Building codes, electrical codes, plumbing codes, standards. **Services:** Library open to potential clients at librarian's discretion. **Holdings:** Standards; codes; handbooks; manuals; directories. **Subscriptions:** 20 journals and other serials.

16231 ■ New England Wholesalers Association–Lending Library
111 Centre St., Ste. A
Middleboro, MA 02346-2273
Ph:(508)533-3335
Fax:(508)533-3337
Co. E-mail: newa@newa.org
Contact: Bradley L. Sell, Exec. VP
Scope: Plumbing, heating, air conditioning, industrial pipe, wholesale distribution. **Services:** Library open to the public with restrictions (deposit required). **Holdings:** 300 surveys and reports, training manuals, management and sales texts. **Subscriptions:** 5 journals and other serials.

ASSOCIATIONS AND OTHER ORGANIZATIONS

16232 ■ Porcelain Enamel Institute
PO Box 920220
Norcross, GA 30010
Ph:(770)676-9366
Fax:(770)676-9368
URL: http://www.porcelainenamel.com
Contact: Mike Horton, Chm.
Description: Trade association of the porcelain enamel industry. Manufacturers of major appliances, sanitary ware, architectural porcelain enamel, signs, and other porcelain enamel products; suppliers to the industry such as producers of steel, aluminum, and porcelain enamel frit; chemical companies. Conducts market development and promotion programs, develops test methods for evaluation of porcelain enamel properties, and maintains weather resistance testing sites jointly with the National Bureau of Standards. Serves as information clearinghouse. **Publications:** *First Firing* (bimonthly); *Technical Forum* (annual).

FRANCHISES AND BUSINESS OPPORTUNITIES

16233 ■ BMR Bathmaster Reglazing Ltd.
1600 Industrial Rd., Unit B7
Cambridge, ON, Canada N3H 4W5
Ph:(519)653-8823
Free: 877-767-2336
Fax:888-789-0947
Co. E-mail: info@bathmaster.com
URL: http://www.bathmaster.com
No. of Franchise Units: 16 **No. of Company-Owned Units:** 2. **Founded:** 1989. **Franchised:** 1994. **Description:** BathMaster offers top quality, cost-effective bathtub re-glazing, bathtub liners & wall installation services This in-home service, saving customers up to 75% of replacement cost. BathMaster excels in completing project sin a single day, transforming customer's bathroom into an environment they will be proud of. BathMaster's innovative products and system support gives our franchisees the markets advantage necessary for success and growth. **Equity Capital Needed:** $45,000-$80,000. **Franchise Fee:** $25,000. **Training:** 10 day training and full support.

16234 ■ Kott Koatings, Inc.
27161 Burbank St.
Foothill Ranch, CA 92610
Free: 800-452-6161
Fax:(714)770-5101
No. of Franchise Units: 400. **No. of Company-Owned Units:** 1. **Founded:** 1953. **Description:** A porcelain, fiberglass, and bathtub re-glazing business opportunity. **Equity Capital Needed:** $2,200. **Franchise Fee:** $16,900-$20,995. **Financial Assistance:** Yes. **Training:** Yes.

16235 ■ Perma-Glaze, Inc. Multi-Surface Restoration
1638 S Research Loop Rd., Ste. 160
Tucson, AZ 85710
Ph:(520)722-9718
Free: 800-332-7397
Fax:(520)296-4393
Co. E-mail: permaglaze@permaglaze.com
URL: http://www.permaglaze.com
No. of Franchise Units: 100+. **No. of Company-Owned Units:** 2. **Founded:** 1978. **Franchised:** 1981. **Description:** Restoration and refinishing of bathroom and kitchen fixtures, such as bathtubs, sinks and ceramic tiles. Materials to be refinished include porcelain, fiberglass, acrylic, cultured marble, Formica, kitchen appliances, shower enclosures and most building materials. Services include chip repair, fiberglass and acrylic repairs, restoration and re-glazing of fixtures. franchisees return from Tucson. **Equity Capital Needed:** Approximately $2,500. **Franchise Fee:** 29,500. **Financial Assistance:** Available upon request. **Managerial Assistance:** Accounting, national advertising, website, artwork, press releases, business development, marketing, sales, newsletters, national conventions, 24 hour help line, and track start-up. **Training:** Training includes 5-10 day technical, hands-on training and all tools and equipment.

16236 ■ PremierGarage
PremierGarage Systems, Inc.
21405 N 15th Ln., Ste. 100
Phoenix, AZ 85027
Ph:(480)483-3030
Free: (866)483-GARA
Fax:(480)483-7895
Co. E-mail: dealer@PremierGarage.com
URL: http://www.PremierGarage.com
No. of Franchise Units: 87. **No. of Company-Owned Units:** 1. **Founded:** 1999. **Franchised:** 2002. **Description:** Offers premium quality Garage Floor Coatings, Cabinetry and Organizers for residential applications. **Equity Capital Needed:** $73,400-$407,750. **Franchise Fee:** $7,500-$75,000. **Financial Assistance:** No. **Training:** Yes.

16237 ■ Re-Bath, LLC
421 W Alameda Dr.
Tempe, AZ 85282
Ph:(480)844-1575
Free: 800-426-4573
Fax:(480)833-7199
No. of Franchise Units: 225. **Founded:** 1979. **Franchised:** 1991. **Description:** Custom-manufactured, high-impact acrylic bathtub liners, wall systems and shower liners designed to go over existing bathtubs, ceramic tile walls and shower bases. **Equity Capital Needed:** $3,500-$89,000. **Franchise Fee:** $6,000-$40,000. **Financial Assistance:** Yes. **Training:** Phases of installation, operations, sales and marketing. Both classroom and hands-on training.

16238 ■ Surface Specialists
Surface Specialists Systems, Inc.
621-B Stallings Rd.
Matthews, NC 28104
Ph:(704)821-3380
Free: (866)239-8707
Fax:(704)821-2097
Co. E-mail: amy@surfacespecialists.com
URL: http://www.surfacespecialists.com
No. of Franchise Units: 45. **Founded:** 1980. **Franchised:** 1981. **Description:** Offers services like repair and refinish of acrylic spas, porcelain tubs and sinks. **Equity Capital Needed:** $25,000-$40,000. **Franchise Fee:** $21,000. **Financial Assistance:** Up to $7,000 in-house. **Managerial Assistance:** Free personalized web page, franchise access only website, on-line material store, marketing materials and creation assistance. **Training:** Provides 15 days hands-on training, annual convention, and 24/7 direct access to company president.

REFERENCE WORKS

16239 ■ **"Butane Heated Pressure Washer Offers Diverse Cleaning Options" in** *Product News Network* **(March 8, 2011)**
Pub: Product News Network
Description: Profile of the Super Max (TM) 6000B power sprayer the can clean with cold or heated water and wet steam. Daimer Industries, provider of janitorial supplies, announced the availability of the machine that offers a variety of cleaning options for a range of applications.

FRANCHISES AND BUSINESS OPPORTUNITIES

16240 ■ **Sparkle Wash**
Sparkle International, Inc.
7599 First Pl.
Bedford, OH 44146
Ph:(216)464-4212
Free: 800-321-0770
Fax:(216)464-8869
No. of Franchise Units: 172. **No. of Company-Owned Units:** 1. **Founded:** 1965. **Franchised:**

1967. **Description:** Offers mobile pressure cleaning and restoration service. **Equity Capital Needed:** Approximately $50,000. **Franchise Fee:** Minimum $25,000. **Financial Assistance:** Up to 50% of any initial franchisee fee in excess of $20,000. Third party financing available for equipment and van. Initial credit line of $1,000. **Training:** 5 day initial program at headquarters, includes classroom, shop, and in-field training on the franchisees own equipment. An optional 6th day of in-field experience is available at no added charge. Sparkle Wash sends a qualified trainer to work with the franchisee for 3 Days at his location.

16241 ■ **Window Gang**
Window Gang Ventures Corp.
405 Arendell St.
Morehead City, NC 28557
Ph:(252)726-1463
Free: 800-849-2308
Fax:(252)726-2837
Co. E-mail: tim@windowgang.com
URL: http://www.windowgang.com
No. of Franchise Units: 196. **Founded:** 1986. **Franchised:** 1996. **Description:** Residential window washing, gutter cleaning, and power washing. **Equity**

Capital Needed: $50,000. **Franchise Fee:** $25,000. **Financial Assistance:** Up to 50% of franchise fee. **Managerial Assistance:** Marketing materials and regional meetings. **Training:** Up to 14 days of training in both the corporate location and in your territory that includes successful technical, sales, marketing, and business procedures. Provides non-stop customer leads.

16242 ■ **Window Genie**
FOR Franchising, LLC
800 E Ross Ave.
Cincinnati, OH 45207
Free: 800-700-0022
URL: http://www.windowgenie.com
No. of Franchise Units: 125. **Founded:** 1994. **Franchised:** 1998. **Description:** Window cleaning service. **Equity Capital Needed:** $60,700-$128,600. **Franchise Fee:** $19,500-$57,000. **Royalty Fee:** 7%. **Financial Assistance:** Third party financing available. **Training:** Offers 5 days at headquarters, 5 days at franchisees location with ongoing support.

TRADE PERIODICALS

16243 ■ *Communications Daily*
Pub: Warren Communications News
Contact: Mike Feazel, Managing Editor
Released: Daily, 5/wk. **Price:** $3,695. **Description:** Covers telephone and data communications, broadcasting, cable TV, teleconferencing, satellite communications, electronic publishing, and emerging technologies. Recurring features include personnel updates, obituaries, statistics, trade show news, and news of research.

16244 ■ *State Telephone Regulation Report*
Pub: Warren Communications News
Contact: Herb Kirchhoff, Managing Editor
E-mail: herbkir@mvcc.com
Released: Biweekly. **Price:** $745 Print; $725 Electronic. **Description:** Examines state telephone regulatory issues and decisions. Covers major state-level telephone lawsuits and court action, providing complete citations of lawsuits and decisions. Reports on new tariffed services and the restructuring of existing rates or services, including hybrid local rates that combine flat rates with measured services, discount programs for intrastate toll calls, lifeline services, and custom calling features.

TRADE SHOWS AND CONVENTIONS

16245 ■ National Telecommunications Cooperative Association Annual Meeting & Expo
National Telecommunications Cooperative Association

4121 Wilson Blvd., Ste. 1000
Arlington, VA 22203
Ph:(703)351-2000
Fax:(703)351-2001
URL: http://www.ntca.org
Released: Annual. **Audience:** Managers, Board of Directors & Employees of Telephone Companies. **Principal Exhibits:** Equipment, supplies, and services for the telecommunications industry. **Dates and Locations:** 2012 Feb 12-15, San Diego, CA.

RESEARCH CENTERS

16246 ■ National Regulatory Research Institute
8730 Georgia Ave., No. 201
Silver Spring, MD 20910
Ph:(301)588-5385
Co. E-mail: shempling@nrri.org
URL: http://www.nrri.org
Contact: Scott Hempling, Exec.Dir.
E-mail: shempling@nrri.org
Scope: Electric, natural gas, water, and telephone utility regulation procedures. Specific topics include gas wellhead price deregulation, power pooling, gas marginal cost pricing, utility operating efficiency, regulatory incentives, retail wheeling, pricing wheeled power, funding nuclear decommissioning, measured rate telephone service, telecommunications competition, small water utility regulation, and electric utility subsidiaries. **Services:** International regulatory assistance. **Publications:** Director's Monthly Essays on Regulatory Quality. **Educational Activities:** Conferences and workshops, for state regulatory commissions and their staff members; Fundamentals of Electricity Law Seminar (annually).

16247 ■ Telecommunications Research and Action Center
PO Box 27279
Washington, DC 20005
Ph:(202)263-2943
Fax:(202)263-2960
Co. E-mail: trac@trac.org
URL: http://www.trac.org
Contact: Samuel A. Simon, Chm.
E-mail: trac@trac.org
Scope: Public policy issues in telecommunications, including emerging technologies, long distance telephone service, and regulatory issues. **Publications:** Long Distance Residential and Business Rates (biennially); Tele-Tip.

16248 ■ University of Nebraska at Omaha–Center for Management of Information Technology
College of Information Science & Technology
Peter Kiewit Institute
Omaha, NE 68182-0459
Ph:(402)554-3182
Fax:(402)554-3400
Co. E-mail: izigurs@mail.unomaha.edu
URL: http://cmit.unomaha.edu
Contact: Dr. Ilze Zigurs
E-mail: izigurs@mail.unomaha.edu
Scope: Management of information technology.

ASSOCIATIONS AND OTHER ORGANIZATIONS

16249 ■ Print Council of America
The Art Institute of Chicago
Dept. of Drawings and Prints
111 S Michigan Ave.
Chicago, IL 60603
Ph:(312)857-7162
Co. E-mail: mtedeschi@artic.edu
URL: http://www.printcouncil.org
Contact: Dr. Martha Tedeschi, Pres.
Description: Museum professionals. Fosters the study and appreciation of new and old prints, drawings, and photographs; stimulates discussion. Sponsors educational programs and research publications; offers placement services. **Publications:** *A Paper Sample Book; Guidelines for The Lending of Works of Art on Paper; Print Council Index to Oeuvre-Catalogues of Prints by European and American Artists;*Newsletter (annual).

16250 ■ Professional Picture Framers Association
3000 Picture Pl.
Jackson, MI 49201
Ph:(517)788-8100
Free: 800-762-9287
Fax:(517)788-8371
Co. E-mail: nshaver@pmai.org
URL: http://www.pmai.org/ppfa
Contact: Kenneth Link, Pres.
Description: Individuals, firms, or corporations engaged in the picture framing and fine art businesses (art dealers, manufacturers, wholesalers, importers, and publishers). Provides guidance and service in developing quality craftsmanship in the art of picture framing. Sponsors certification program and national consumer marketing program. Provides education and trade show programming. Offers business and insurance services and products. Researches and disseminates information concerning technical and service problems. Maintains hall of fame and bookstore; compiles statistics. .

REFERENCE WORKS

16251 ■ "P/Kaufmann Sells Bennettsville" in *Home Textiles Today* **(Vol. 31, May 24, 2011, No. 13, pp. 6)**
Pub: Reed Business Information
Description: Decorative Screen Printers purchased the printing and finishing facility of P/Kaufmann in Bennettsville, South Carolina. However, the firm will continue its focus on its core business, a vat printing facility for home furnishings fabrics.

16252 ■ *Printworld Directory of Contemporary Prints and Prices*
Pub: Printworld International Inc.
Released: Irregular, Latest edition 13th; April 2010. **Price:** $359, individuals regular price; $259, individuals discount price. **Publication Includes:** Biographical data on 5,000 international artists in contemporary

printmaking; thousands of galleries who handle prints and hundreds of print publishers, and 600,000 print/price listings. **Entries Include:** For artists—Name, address, personal and educational data, major exhibits, collections, publishers, printers, galleries, awards, teaching positions and documentation of prints. For galleries and publishers—Name, address. **Arrangement:** Alphabetical. **Indexes:** Artist name, printer/print workshop, publisher, gallery, art appraiser.

16253 ■ "Retail News: Children's Boutique Relocates to Conway" in *Sun News* **(June 4, 2010)**
Pub: The Sun News
Description: Little Angel's Children's Boutique and Big Oak Frame Shop have moved to downtown locations in Conway, South Carolina. Little Angel's will sell children's clothing and accessories, shoes and gifts, while the frame shop will offer custom framing along with the sale of stationary, invitations and local prints.

TRADE PERIODICALS

16254 ■ *Picture Framing Magazine*
Pub: Hobby Publications Inc.
Contact: Bruce Gherman, Exec. Publisher
E-mail: bgherman@hobbypub.com
Released: 13/yr. **Price:** $20; $30 two years; $40 Canada and Mexico; $70 Canada and Mexico 2 years; $60 other countries; $110 other countries 2 years. **Description:** Trade magazine for the picture framing industry.

FRANCHISES AND BUSINESS OPPORTUNITIES

16255 ■ Big Picture Framing
Big Picture Franchising, LLC
60 Needham St.
Newton, MA 02461
Free: 800-315-0024
Fax:(617)552-5032
URL: http://www.bigpictureframing.com
No. of Franchise Units: 3. **No. of Company-Owned Units:** 9. **Founded:** 2000. **Franchised:** 2003. **Description:** Picture framing store that is reshaping the custom picture framing industry through great design, low prices, fast turnaround and unparalleled customer guarantees. Our proprietary "Framing While-You-Wait" process meets the needs of today's busy lifestyles. Our superior training, deep commitment to ongoing support and our complete turn-key package will ensure your success. **Equity Capital Needed:** $121,000$151,000. **Franchise Fee:** $25,000. **Financial Assistance:** No. **Training:** Offers a comprehensive 2 1/2 week training program that provides you with everything you need to know to operate a store, including store operations, framing, sales and design, marketing and advertising, purchasing, hiring and business management.

16256 ■ Deck the Walls
Franchise Concepts, Inc.
101 S Hanley Rd., No. 1280
St. Louis, MO 63105
Free: 800-543-3325
Co. E-mail: franinfo@FClbiz.com
URL: http://www.deckthewalls.com
No. of Franchise Units: 19. **Founded:** 1979. **Franchised:** 1981. **Description:** Art and custom framing retail stores located in regional malls. **Equity Capital Needed:** $112,535-$178,108 total investment. **Franchise Fee:** $30,000. **Royalty Fee:** 6%. **Financial Assistance:** Third party financing available. **Managerial Assistance:** Conventions, workshops, private trade shows, newsletters & national credit card program. **Training:** Classroom and in-store training prepare franchisees for all aspects of business, including custom framing. Support includes: site, lease, construction aid; national buying power; vendor network and national marketing.

16257 ■ Fastframe USA
1200 Lawrence Dr., Ste. 300
Newbury Park, CA 91320
Ph:(805)498-4463
Free: 800-333-3225
Fax:(805)498-8983
URL: http://www.fastframe.com
No. of Franchise Units: 215. **No. of Company-Owned Units:** 9. **Founded:** 1986. **Franchised:** 1987. **Description:** Custom picture framing franchise. Provide high quality custom framing and art sales in both the retail and commercial markets. Offers a turn-key package from site selection to final store build out. **Equity Capital Needed:** $93,500-$131,000. **Franchise Fee:** $25,000. **Royalty Fee:** 7.5%. **Financial Assistance:** Will assist in securing various financing options. **Training:** Provides 2 weeks of training at the corporate training center. Topics include in store operations, marketing and advertising, framing, business management, and the FAST system. Ongoing field support and 1 week on site training.

16258 ■ Framing & Art Centre
3524 Mainway
Burlington, ON, Canada L7M 1A8
Ph:(905)332-6116
Free: 800-563-7263
Fax:800-565-5755
Co. E-mail: dgateman@bellnet.ca
URL: http://www.framingartcentre.com
No. of Franchise Units: 36. **Founded:** 1974. **Franchised:** 1977. **Description:** The franchise provides a business for people who are creative at work and good at art and decoration. **Equity Capital Needed:** $118,000-$179,400. **Franchise Fee:** $30,000. **Training:** Yes.

16259 ■ The Great Frame Up, Inc.
Franchise Concepts, Inc.
221 First Executive Ave.
St. Peters, MO 63376
Ph:800-543-3325
Free: (886)719-8200

Fax:877-832-6694
Co. E-mail: anance@fcibiz.com
URL: http://www.greatframeup.com
No. of Franchise Units: 166. **Founded:** 1971. **Franchised:** 1975. **Description:** Do-it-yourself and custom framing retail stores. **Equity Capital Needed:** $200,000. **Franchise Fee:** $30,000. **Financial Assistance:** No. **Managerial Assistance:** Provides manuals, monthly newsletters, workshops, promotional material and an annual conference. Directors

of business development call on each franchise 5-6 times per year, providing guidance and assistance. Toll-free numbers to staff in Franklin Park, IL are provided. **Training:** 2 weeks classroom and instore training including custom framing, covering all aspects of framing, as well as hands-on training in an actual store situation. Workshops and a toll-free number to the training center are provided for ongoing education.

16260 ■ Marad Fine Art International
66 Glenbrook Rd., Ste. 3327
Stamford, CT 06902
Ph:(203)912-8402
Fax:(203)539-6001

No. of Franchise Units: 3. **No. of Company-Owned Units:** 1. **Founded:** 1938. **Franchised:** 2000. **Description:** Artwork supplies business. **Equity Capital Needed:** $49,000-$70,000. **Franchise Fee:** $39,000. **Financial Assistance:** No. **Training:** Yes.

START-UP INFORMATION

16261 ■ **"Revel in Riches!" in** *Small Business Opportunities* **(May 2008)**
Pub: Harris Publications Inc.
Description: Profile of Proforma, a business-to-business franchise firm providing print and promotional products.

16262 ■ **"Visual Appeal" in** *Small Business Opportunities* **(Fall 2007)**
Pub: Harris Publications Inc.
Ed: Michael L. Corne. **Description:** Profile of Jim Huffman, who launched his new Video Business Card Distributorship. The business cards allow companies and individuals to put personal video messages on their cards explaining the benefits of doing business with them. The cards take prospective customers to Websites and even provide a printable document for brochures or special offers.

ASSOCIATIONS AND OTHER ORGANIZATIONS

16263 ■ **Amalgamated Printers' Association**
135 East Church St.
Clinton, MI 49236
Co. E-mail: phil@phillipdriscoll.com
URL: http://www.apa-letterpress.com
Contact: Jim Daggs, Pres.
Description: Active printers interested in furthering of the art and craft of printing. Encourages excellence of printing content, design and techniques among members. Sponsors competitions. **Publications:** *Membership List* (annual).

16264 ■ **American Institute of Graphic Arts**
164 5th Ave.
New York, NY 10010-5901
Ph:(212)807-1990
Fax:(212)807-1799
Co. E-mail: grefe@aiga.org
URL: http://www.aiga.org
Contact: Richard Grefe, Exec. Dir.
Description: Graphic designers, art directors, illustrators and packaging designers. Sponsors exhibits and projects in the public interest. Sponsors traveling exhibitions. Operates gallery. Maintains library of design books and periodicals; offers slide archives. **Publications:** *365: AIGA Year in Design 24* (annual).

16265 ■ **Digital Printing and Imaging Association**
10015 Main St.
Fairfax, VA 22031-3489
Ph:(703)385-1335
Free: 888-385-3588
Fax:(703)273-0456
Co. E-mail: sgia@sgia.org
URL: http://www.sgia.org
Contact: Michael E. Robertson, Pres.
Description: Electronic printing, pre-press companies, commercial printers, service bureaus, photo labs, reprographic companies, and printer suppliers, and educational institutions. Works to advance the electronic imaging field by promoting the use of digital printing devices, responding to industry needs and concerns, and improving the industry's ability to serve its market and customers. Conducts educational programs. **Publications:** *RIP* (quarterly).

16266 ■ **Flexographic Technical Association**
3920 Veterans Memorial Hwy., Ste. 9
Bohemia, NY 11716
Ph:(631)737-6020
Fax:(631)737-6813
Co. E-mail: memberinfo@flexography.org
URL: http://www.flexography.org
Contact: Mark Cisternino, Pres.
Description: Firms engaged in printing by flexographic process suppliers to the industry; end users. Seeks to advance the art and science of flexographic printing and assist and recommend developments in flexography. Conducts educational activities including seminars and regional workshops for production, supervisory, and management personnel, and annual technical forum. Markets textbooks and audiovisual material for in-plant training. Sponsors the Foundation of Flexographic Technical Association. Maintains hall of fame, speakers' bureau, advisory service, and 13 committees. **Publications:** *FLEXO* (monthly); *SourceBook* (annual).

16267 ■ **Graphic Arts Employers of America**
200 Deer Run Rd.
Sewickley, PA 15143
Ph:(412)741-6860
Free: 800-910-4283
Fax:(412)741-2311
Co. E-mail: jkyger@piagatf.org
URL: http://www.gain.net
Contact: Jim Kyger, Human Relations Dir.
Description: Serves as a division of Printing Industries of America . Represents graphic communications, imaging, and printing companies who have at least some unionization or are interested in keeping informed on industrial relations issues. Assists management in functioning at optimal efficiency in a unionized environment. Compiles statistics and assists companies that deal with the major printing unions in the U.S. and Canada. Compiles statistics. .

16268 ■ **IDEAlliance - International Digital Enterprise Alliance**
1421 Prince St., Ste. 230
Alexandria, VA 22314-2805
Ph:(703)837-1070
Fax:(703)837-1072
Co. E-mail: dsteinhardt@idealliance.org
URL: http://www.idealliance.org
Contact: David J. Steinhardt, Pres./CEO
Description: Works to advance user-driven, cross-industry solutions for all publishing and content-related processes by developing standards fostering business alliances and identifying best practices. .

16269 ■ **International Association of Printing House Craftsmen**
PO Box 2549
Maple Grove, MN 55311-7549
Ph:(763)560-1620
Free: 800-466-4274
Fax:(763)560-1350
Co. E-mail: headquarters@iaphc.org
URL: http://www.iaphc.org
Contact: Kevin P. Keane, Pres./CEO
Description: Individuals world-wide employed or interested in any facet of the graphic arts. Conducts field trips; maintains speakers' bureau; sponsors educational programs. Sponsors International Printing Week and International Gallery of Superb Printing. **Publications:** *TMN: Graphics Industry News* (monthly).

16270 ■ **International Publishing Management Association**
105 S Jefferson, Ste. B-4
Kearney, MO 64060
Ph:(816)902-4762
Fax:(816)902-4766
Co. E-mail: ipmainfo@ipma.org
URL: http://www.ipma.org
Contact: John Sarantakos, Pres.
Description: Managers of in-house corporate publishing or distribution activities. Offers continuing education courses and certification programs. Conducts research, surveys, and studies on industrial and technological trends. Maintains bookstore. **Publications:** *In-House Salary and Compensation Survey* (biennial); *Inside Edge*; *IPMA Bookstore*; *IPMA International Directory* (annual).

16271 ■ **IPA - Association of Graphic Solutions Providers**
7200 France Ave. S, Ste. 223
Edina, MN 55435
Ph:(952)896-1908
Free: 800-255-8141
Fax:(952)896-0181
Co. E-mail: info@ipa.org
URL: http://www.ipa.org
Contact: Steven Bonoff, Pres.
Description: Provides management and technical resources that help companies build, manage and enhance an integrated graphics workflow, from creative to output. **Publications:** *IPA Bulletin* (bi-monthly); *IPA News* (monthly); *SWOP 10th Edition* .

16272 ■ **National Association of Litho Clubs**
3268 N 147th Ln.
Goodyear, AZ 85395
Ph:(650)339-4007
Co. E-mail: dreyfus@sbcglobal.net
URL: http://www.graphicarts.org
Contact: Raymond Siegel, Pres.
Description: Federation of technicians and supervisors for lithograph plants. Provides a forum for sharing industry information and technology. Offers educational presentations and seminars. .

16273 ■ **National Association of Printing Ink Manufacturers**
581 Main St., Ste. 520
Woodbridge, NJ 07095-1144
Ph:(732)855-1525

Fax:(732)855-1838
Co. E-mail: napim@napim.org
URL: http://www.napim.org
Contact: James E. Coleman, Exec. Dir.
Description: Represents printing ink manufacturers and suppliers. Sponsors National Printing Ink Research Institute. .

16274 ■ National Association for Printing Leadership

75 W Century Rd., Ste. 100
Paramus, NJ 07652-1408
Ph:(201)634-9600
Free: 800-642-6275
Fax:(201)634-0324
Co. E-mail: jtruncale@napl.org
URL: http://www.napl.org
Contact: Joseph P. Truncale CAE, Pres./CEO
Description: Represents commercial printers and suppliers to the commercial printing industry. Enables those in the industry to operate their businesses for maximum profitability. Offers following management products and services: sales and marketing, customer service, financial, human resources, operations and economic. Maintains Management Institute, which conducts Executive Certification Program. Compiles extensive economic statistics. **Publications:** *Cost Studies* (semiannual).

16275 ■ National Association of Quick Printers

2250 E Devon Ave., Ste. 245
Des Plaines, IL 60018
Ph:(847)298-8600
Free: 800-234-0040
Fax:(847)298-8705
Co. E-mail: info@naqp.com
URL: http://www.naqp.com
Contact: Steven D. Johnson, Pres./CEO
Description: Independent printers and printing franchise businesses; industry suppliers. Seeks to bring recognition, improved quality, and increased profits to the entire quick printing field. Provides services to members; works to advance the collective interests of the printing industries at the national and international levels. **Publications:** *NAQP Network* (monthly).

16276 ■ NPES: Association for Suppliers of Printing, Publishing and Converting Technologies

1899 Preston White Dr.
Reston, VA 20191
Ph:(703)264-7200
Fax:(703)620-0994
Co. E-mail: npes@npes.org
URL: http://www.npes.org
Contact: Ralph J. Nappi, Pres.
Description: Companies engaged in the manufacture and distribution of equipment, systems, software and/or supplies used in the printing, publishing and converting industries. Represents members before federal agencies and allied trade groups. Funds programs at educational institutions to train graphic arts personnel. Organizes a monthly industry statistical program that compiles and distributes data on orders and shipments. **Publications:** *Directory of International Suppliers of Printing, Publishing and Converting Technologies* (annual); *Vanguard* (semiannual).

16277 ■ Printing Brokerage/Buyers Association

PO Box 744
Palm Beach, FL 33480
Ph:(215)821-6581
Free: 877-585-7141
Fax:(561)845-7130
URL: http://www.pbba.org
Description: Printing buyers/brokers/distributors, printers, typographers, binders, envelope and book manufacturers, packagers, color separation houses, pre-press service organizations, and related companies in the graphic arts industry. Promotes understanding, cooperation, and interaction among members while obtaining the highest standard of professionalism in the graphic arts industry. Gathers information on current technology in the graphic com-

munications industry. Sponsors seminars for members to learn how to work with buyers, brokers and printers; also conducts technical and management seminars. Maintains referral service; compiles statistics. Conducts charitable programs. **Publications:** *BrokerRatings* (quarterly); *Corporate Print Buyer* (quarterly); *Hot Markets Annual Rankings of Buyers, Print Products and Geographies* (annual); *The Printer's Official Complete Guide to e-Everything-and How to Prevail!*; *Printing Brokerage Directory and Sourcebook* (annual).

16278 ■ Printing Industries of America

200 Deer Run Rd.
Sewickley, PA 15143
Ph:(412)741-6860
Free: 800-910-4283
Fax:(412)741-2311
Co. E-mail: printing@printing.org
URL: http://www.printing.org
Contact: Michael Makin, Pres./CEO
Description: Commercial printing firms (lithography, letterpress, gravure, platemakers, typographic houses); allied firms in the graphic arts. Provides extensive management services for member companies, including government relations, industry research and statistical information, technology information and assistance, and management education and publications. Compiles statistical and economic data, including annual ratio study that provides a benchmark for printers to compare profits as a basis for improving individual member company and industry profits. Provides reporting system on provisions, rates, and other matters relating to union contracts in effect throughout the industry. Sponsors annual Premier Print Awards Competition. .

16279 ■ Screen Printing Technical Foundation

10015 Main St.
Fairfax, VA 22031
Ph:(703)385-1335
Free: 888-385-3588
Fax:(703)273-0456
Co. E-mail: sptf@sgia.org
URL: http://www.sgia.org/sptf
Contact: Dawn Hohl, Technical Training Mgr.
Description: Participants include corporations, institutions, and individuals interested in screen-printing. Advances the screen-printing industry. Conducts technical research and hands-on training programs to address production problems and processes. Sponsors educational programs and prepares educational materials. **Publications:** *SPTF Update* (quarterly).

16280 ■ Specialty Graphic Imaging Association

10015 Main St.
Fairfax, VA 22031-3489
Ph:(703)385-1335
Free: 888-385-3588
Fax:(703)273-0456
Co. E-mail: sgia@sgia.org
URL: http://www.sgia.org
Contact: Michael E. Robertson, Pres./CEO
Description: Printers who use screen printing and/or digital printing; associate members are suppliers and manufacturers; educational institutions. Provides training and information on technical, managerial, governmental, safety, and research issues. Conducts safety, environmental, and print quality recognition programs. Compiles statistics; conducts research programs. **Publications:** *Guide to Digital Garment Decoration*; *Operating Rate Survey* (biennial); *SGIA Journal* (quarterly); *SGIA News* (monthly); *Who's Who in SGIA* (annual).

DIRECTORIES OF EDUCATIONAL PROGRAMS

16281 ■ *Directory of Private Accredited Career Schools and Colleges of Technology*

Pub: Accrediting Commission of Career Schools and Colleges of Technology
Contact: Michale S. McComis, Exec. Dir.
Released: On web page. **Price:** Free. **Description:** Covers 3900 accredited post-secondary programs that provide training programs in business, trade, and

technical fields, including various small business endeavors. Entries offer school name, address, phone, description of courses, job placement assistance, and requirements for admission. Arrangement is alphabetical.

REFERENCE WORKS

16282 ■ "Agfa: M-Press Leopard Debuts" in *American Printer* (Vol. 128, June 1, 2011, No. 6)

Pub: Penton Media Inc.
Description: M-Press Leopard is a new version of the machine that offers advanced ink jet technology at a lower price point. Agfa Graphics introduced the new version that allows for new applications that require more manual handling.

16283 ■ "Avanti Hosts Users Conference" in *American Printer* (Vol. 128, July 1, 2011, No. 7)

Pub: Penton Media Inc.
Description: Avanti Computer Systems Ltd. hosted its 19th annual users conference in Washington DC. In-plant and commercial printers were in attendance.

16284 ■ "Avoid a Tablet Generation Gap" in *American Printer* (Vol. 128, July 1, 2011, No. 7)

Pub: Penton Media Inc.
Description: Individuals between the ages of 18-34 are the only generation that is more likely to own a laptop computer or netbook insead of a desktop computer. Statistical data included.

16285 ■ "Bankruptcies" in *Crain's Detroit Business* (Vol. 24, September 29, 2008, No. 39, pp. 4)

Pub: Crain Communications, Inc.
Description: Current list of business that filed for Chapter 7 or 11 protection in U.S. Bankruptcy Court in Detroit include manufacturers, real estate companies, a printing company and a specialized staffing company.

16286 ■ "Boston Printer Celebrates 60th Anniversary" in *American Printer* (Vol. 128, August 1, 2011, No. 8)

Pub: Penton Media Inc.
Description: Shawmut printing is celebrating its 60th anniversary. The family business plans to increase efficiency through automation, monitoring job progress online from start to finish.

16287 ■ "Business is Unbelievable" in *American Printer* (Vol. 128, August 1, 2011, No. 8)

Pub: Penton Media Inc.
Ed: Katherine O'Brien. **Description:** Most commercial printers have seen an increase in business over the last year.

16288 ■ "Calista Sells Rural Newspapers" in *Alaska Business Monthly* (Vol. 27, October 2011, No. 10, pp. 8)

Pub: Alaska Business Publishing Company
Ed: Nancy Pounds. **Description:** Calista sold its six newspapers, a magazine, shoppers and its printing house. Details of the sales are given.

16289 ■ "Challenges Await Quad in Going Public" in *Milwaukee Business Journal* (Vol. 27, January 29, 2010, No. 18, pp. A1)

Pub: American City Business Journals
Ed: Rich Rovito. **Description:** Sussex, Wisconsin-based Quad/Graphics Inc.'s impending acquisition of rival Canadian World Color Press Inc. will transform it into a publicly held entity for the first time. Quad has operated as a private company for nearly 40 years and will need to adjust to changes, such as the way management shares information with Quad/Graphics' employees. Details of the merger are included.

16290 ■ "ContiTech Celebrates 100 Years" in *American Printer* (Vol. 128, July 1, 2011, No. 7)

Pub: Penton Media Inc.
Description: ContiTech celebrated 100 years in business. The firm started in 1911 after developing the first elastic printing blanket. Other milestones for the

firm include its manufacturing process for compressible printing blankets, the Conti-Air brand and climate-neutral printing blankets.

16291 ■ "Crouser Offers UV Coating Price Report" in *American Printer* **(Vol. 128, June 1, 2011, No. 6)**
Pub: Penton Media Inc.
Description: Crouser and Associates will offer the 'Pricing Off-Line UV Coating' report that provides background information on all three types of protective printing coatings and price guidance. The report will also offer comparisons of four popular types of offline equipment.

16292 ■ "Customer OKs on Press" in *American Printer* **(Vol. 128, August 1, 2011, No. 8)**
Pub: Penton Media Inc.
Description: Printers discuss the value of having customers meet at the plant in order to okay print colors for projects.

16293 ■ "Design Center Shows Quality of Digital Paper" in *American Printer* **(Vol. 128, June 1, 2011, No. 6)**
Pub: Penton Media Inc.
Description: Digital Design Centers allows printers to customize marketing tools in order to promote their own digital printing capabilities.

16294 ■ "Digital Printing Walks the Plank" in *American Printer* **(Vol. 128, August 1, 2011, No. 8)**
Pub: Penton Media Inc.
Description: Digital print manufacturing is discussed.

16295 ■ "Feeding the Elephants While Searching for Greener Pastures" in *American Printer* **(Vol. 128, July 1, 2011, No. 7)**
Pub: Penton Media Inc.
Ed: Bob Rosen. **Description:** Three steps to help printers build a new business while facing the challenges to the existing business are outlined.

16296 ■ "First U.S. :M-Press Tiger with Inline Screen Printing" in *American Printer* **(Vol. 128, June 1, 2011, No. 6)**
Pub: Penton Media Inc.
Description: Graphic Tech located in California bought :M-Press Tiger, the first in North America with an inline screen printing unit.

16297 ■ "Flint Group Raises Prices" in *American Printer* **(Vol. 128, August 1, 2011, No. 8)**
Pub: Penton Media Inc.
Description: Due to the rising cost for raw materials, Flint Group is raising their prices for inks and coatings in North American.

16298 ■ "Four Exhibition Considerations" in *American Printer* **(Vol. 128, August 1, 2011, No. 8)**
Pub: Penton Media Inc.
Description: Four questions to ask at the Graph Expo will help printers improve their own business.

16299 ■ "Fujifilm Invites Printers to Take the 'Onset Challenge'" in *American Printer* **(Vol. 128, August 1, 2011, No. 8)**
Pub: Penton Media Inc.
Description: Fujifilm North American Corporation's Graphic Systems Division offers a new five-step product selection and return-on-investment calculator for the Onset family of wide-format printers.

16300 ■ "Guide to Carbon Footprinting" in *American Printer* **(Vol. 128, June 1, 2011, No. 6)**
Pub: Penton Media Inc.
Description: PrintCity Alliance published its new report, 'Carbon Footprint & Energy Reduction for Graphic Industry Value Chain.' The report aims to help improve the environmental performance of printers, converters, publishers, brand owners and their suppliers.

16301 ■ "How to Save Money on Ink" in *American Printer* **(Vol. 128, July 1, 2011, No. 7)**
Pub: Penton Media Inc.
Description: Tips are shared to help graphic arts and printing companies save money on raw materials. Factors to consider once the type of ink is decided are also outlined.

16302 ■ "Improving the USPS" in *American Printer* **(Vol. 128, July 1, 2011, No. 7)**
Pub: Penton Media Inc.
Description: National Postal Forum held in San Diego, California May 1-4, 2011 hosted 4,000 attendees. Highlights of the event are provided.

16303 ■ "Industry/Events 2011" in *American Printer* **(Vol. 128, July 1, 2011, No. 7)**
Pub: Penton Media Inc.
Description: PMA, the Worldwide Community of Imaging Association launched its new CliQ with how-to tips, product reviews and monthly photo contests. PMA formed a partnership with the Consumer Electronics Association to make changes to this year's annual convention.

16304 ■ "Interchangeable or Irreplaceable?" in *American Printer* **(Vol. 128, August 1, 2011, No. 8)**
Pub: Penton Media Inc.
Description: Creating and maintaining customers is important for all graphic design and printing companies. Tips are shared to help maintain good customer satisfaction and repeat business.

16305 ■ "IPEX Moves to London Venue" in *American Printer* **(Vol. 128, July 1, 2011, No. 7)**
Pub: Penton Media Inc.
Description: IPES 2014 is being relocated to London's ExCeL International Exhibition and Conference Centre from March 26 to April 2, 2014.

16306 ■ "JDF Integration: 3 Key Tips" in *American Printer* **(Vol. 128, August 1, 2011, No. 8)**
Pub: Penton Media Inc.
Description: Three tips for implementing cross-vendor integrations are outlined.

16307 ■ "KBA, Graphic Art System Partner on Cold Foil" in *American Printer* **(Vol. 128, June 1, 2011, No. 6)**
Pub: Penton Media Inc.
Description: KBA North America has partnered with Graphic Art System to retrofit and equip presses with cold foil machines.

16308 ■ "Kodak Offers Cloud-Based Operating Option" in *American Printer* **(Vol. 128, June 1, 2011, No. 6)**
Pub: Penton Media Inc.
Description: Kodak partnered with VMware to offer its first Virtual Operating Environment option for Kodak Unified Workflow Solutions. The new feature enables cost savings, increased efficiency and failover protection.

16309 ■ "Metallics Education" in *American Printer* **(Vol. 128, June 1, 2011, No. 6)**
Pub: Penton Media Inc.
Description: Guide 'Curious About Print: Your Guide to the World of Curious Metallics' provides hints and tips to help printers maximize selection and reproduction, advice on working with metallic and UV inks, and recommendations for gaining quantity without sacrificing quality.

16310 ■ "MFSA Officially Endorses Five-Day USPS Delivery" in *American Printer* **(Vol. 128, August 1, 2011, No. 8)**
Pub: Penton Media Inc.
Description: Board of Directors of the Mailing and Fulfillment Service Association (MFSA) voted to support the US Postal Service's move to five-day delivery service.

16311 ■ "New Approach to Mechanical Binding" in *American Printer* **(Vol. 128, July 1, 2011, No. 7)**
Pub: Penton Media Inc.
Description: EcoBinder coil binding system from Kugler-Womako eliminates traditional plastic combs or wire spiral with the use of 22-mm wide printable paper rings.

16312 ■ "OCE Boosts JetStream Productivity" in *American Printer* **(Vol. 128, August 1, 2011, No. 8)**
Pub: Penton Media Inc.
Description: New Oce JetStream 1400 and 3000 digital full-color inkjet presses are profiled. The new models promise higher speed to grow print volume.

16313 ■ "One World" in *American Printer* **(Vol. 128, August 1, 2011, No. 8)**
Pub: Penton Media Inc.
Description: Graph Expo will highlight entrepreneurs focused on the connection between content, technology and business models.

16314 ■ "P/Kaufmann Sells Bennettsville" in *Home Textiles Today* **(Vol. 31, May 24, 2011, No. 13, pp. 6)**
Pub: Reed Business Information
Description: Decorative Screen Printers purchased the printing and finishing facility of P/Kaufmann in Bennettsville, South Carolina. However, the firm will continue its focus on its core business, a vat printing facility for home furnishings fabrics.

16315 ■ "Paper a la Carte" in *American Printer* **(Vol. 128, June 1, 2011, No. 6)**
Pub: Penton Media Inc.
Description: Blurb, the online publishing platform, launched ProLine which features Mohawk Superfine and Mohawk proPhoto papers. ProLine papers offer two finishes: Pearl Photo and Uncoated.

16316 ■ "Paper Choices Made Simple" in *American Printer* **(Vol. 128, June 1, 2011, No. 6)**
Pub: Penton Media Inc.
Description: Choices, a new initiative by Boise, provides professional guidance to help customers and consumers make informed, effective choices for using paper.

16317 ■ "Paper Replaces PVC for Gift Cards" in *American Printer* **(Vol. 128, June 1, 2011, No. 6)**
Pub: Penton Media Inc.
Description: Monadnock Envi Card Stock replaces paper for gift cards, loyalty cards, membership cards, hotel keys and durable signage. This renewable wood fiber alternative to PVC card materials comes from Monadock Paper Mills.

16318 ■ "Please Pass the Mayo" in *Crain's Chicago Business* **(Vol. 31, April 28, 2008, No. 17, pp. 32)**
Pub: Crain Communications, Inc.
Ed: Samantha Stainburn. **Description:** Fort Dearborn Co. has come a long way since it started as on one-press print shop; the family-owned company was struggling to keep up with the technology of making consumer product labels for curvy bottles of products like V8 V-Fusion juice and in 2006 sold off to Genstar Capital LLC which has pushed for acquisitions; last year, Fort Derborn bought its biggest competitor, Renaissance Mark Inc., doubling its size and adding spirit and wine makers to its client roster.

16319 ■ "Prices Continue to Rise" in *American Printer* **(Vol. 128, June 1, 2011, No. 6)**
Pub: Penton Media Inc.
Description: Prices were increased by both Flint Group and Ashland Performance Materials by 7-10 percent and 5-15 percent respectively.

16320 ■ "Printers to the Trade" in *American Printer* **(Vol. 128, July 1, 2011, No. 7)**
Pub: Penton Media Inc.
Description: Wholesale printing is discussed. Two wholesale printers share insight into their success, from business philosophies in general to practices that build strong relationships.

16321 ■ *Printing Impressions—Top 500 Printers Issue*
Pub: North American Publishing Co.
Contact: Mark T. Michelson, Editor-in-Chief
Ed: Erik Cagle, Editor. **Released:** Annual, December. **Price:** Free. **Publication Includes:** List of the leading 500 commercial, financial, directory, publication, check, book, business form, packaging, and specialty printers. **Entries Include:** Company name, city and state, sales, name of president or chief executive officer, number of press units, number of employees, coded list of printing specialties (periodicals, commercial, specialty, etc.), whether publicly or privately owned. **Arrangement:** Ranked by annual sales.

16322 ■ "QR Codes: OK, I Get It Now" in *American Printer* (Vol. 128, July 1, 2011, No. 7)
Pub: Penton Media Inc.
Description: QR Code technology is discussed. It is up to the user to enter the proper QR Code.

16323 ■ "Reducing the Book's Carbon Footpring" in *American Printer* (Vol. 128, July 1, 2011, No. 7)
Pub: Penton Media Inc.
Description: Green Press Initiative's Book Industry Environmental Council is working to achieve a 20 percent reduction in the book industry's carbon footprint by 2020. The Council is made up of publishers, printers, paper suppliers, and non-governmental organizations.

16324 ■ "Root, Root, Root for the P.A. Hutchison Co." in *American Printer* (Vol. 128, August 1, 2011, No. 8)
Pub: Penton Media Inc.
Description: The P.A. Hutchison Company celebrate 100 years in the printing business. President and CEO Chris Hutchinson presented awards to employees, however employees also presented awards to Chris and his father as Employer of the Century.

16325 ■ "Sappi Awards Gold NA Printers of the Year Winners" in *American Printer* (Vol. 128, July 1, 2011, No. 7)
Pub: Penton Media Inc.
Description: Sappi Fine Paper North America honored ten gold winners of its 14th North American Printers of the Year awards. Each gold winning printer will receive $20,000 to support marketing and brand initiatives.

16326 ■ "Seeing the Light" in *American Printer* (Vol. 128, July 1, 2011, No. 7)
Pub: Penton Media Inc.
Description: Four printing demos on sheetfed, digital, label and pad printing equipment were highlighted at the Fifth UV Days held in Stuttgart, Germany in May 2011.

16327 ■ "Seven Tips for Continuous Improvement" in *American Printer* (Vol. 128, July 1, 2011, No. 7)
Pub: Penton Media Inc.
Description: Seven tips are given to help any graphic arts or printing company improve by integrating lean manufacturing into operations.

16328 ■ "Something Old and Something New" in *American Printer* (Vol. 128, August 1, 2011, No. 8)
Pub: Penton Media Inc.
Description: Trade journalists and industry analysts were invited to Fujifilm North America Corporation's Hanover Park, Illinois facility to view it's sheetfed inkjet press. The JPress 720 is the first and only of its kind in the world.

16329 ■ "Successful First Year for Twin Rivers" in *American Printer* (Vol. 128, June 1, 2011, No. 6)
Pub: Penton Media Inc.
Description: Profile of Twin Rivers located in Maine. The firm manufactured 380,000 tons of free sheet and hybrid-groundwood papers in its first year.

16330 ■ "Sudden Shift Leaves Wells Vendor Scrambling" in *Charlotte Business Journal* (Vol. 25, July 9, 2010, No. 16, pp. 1)
Pub: Charlotte Business Journal
Ed: Adam O'Daniel. **Description:** Rubber stamps vendor Carolina Marking Devices is facing a 30 percent drop in business after banking firm Wells Fargo & Company decided to buy its rubber stamps from another vendor. Carolina Marking Devices had provided rubber to First Union Corporation and its successor Wachovia Corporation, which was eventually acquired by Wells Fargo. Other reactions from Carolina Marking Device owners are given.

16331 ■ "Sunriver Venture Hits Snag" in *The Business Journal-Portland* (Vol. 25, August 1, 2008, No. 21, pp. 1)
Pub: American City Business Journals, Inc.
Ed: Robin J. Moody. **Description:** Portland, Oregon based-Sunwest Management Inc. has divided its Sunriver resort community to make way for a redevelopment plan. Sunwest owner Jon Harder and three partners formed SilverStar Destinations LLC to broker the purchase and redevelopment of the property. Details and description of the redevelopment project are also presented.

16332 ■ "Ted Stahl: Executive Chairman" in *Inside Business* (Vol. 13, September-October 2011, No. 5, pp. NC6)
Pub: Great Lakes Publishing Company
Ed: Miranda S. Miller. **Description:** Profile of Ted Stahl, who started working in his family's business when he was ten years old is presented. The firm makes dies for numbers and letters used on team uniforms. Another of the family firms manufactures stock and custom heat-printing products, equipment and supplies. It also educates customers on ways to decorate garments with heat printing products and offers graphics and software for customers to create their own artwork.

16333 ■ "Tic-Tac-Show" in *American Printer* (Vol. 128, August 1, 2011, No. 8)
Pub: Penton Media Inc.
Description: Graph Expo has become the US print industry's main event. There will be as many as 500 exhibitors at this year's event and the Graphic Arts Show Company lists over 30 co-located events as well as 53 new sessions in the seminar program's 28 education categories.

16334 ■ "Transcontinental to Exchange Assets with Quad/Graphics" in *American Printer* (Vol. 128, August 1, 2011, No. 8)
Pub: Penton Media Inc.
Description: Transcontinental Inc. and Quad/Graphics Inc. entered into an agreement where Transcontinental will indirectly acquire all shares of Quad Graphics Canada Inc.

16335 ■ "Try a Little Social Media" in *American Printer* (Vol. 128, June 1, 2011, No. 6)
Pub: Penton Media Inc.
Description: Social media helps keep Ussery Printing on customers radar. Jim David, VP of marketing for the firm, states that 350 people following them on Facebook are from the local area.

16336 ■ "Turning Green Ink to Black" in *The Business Journal-Serving Metropolitan Kansas City* (Vol. 26, August 8, 2008, No. 48, pp. 1)
Pub: American City Business Journals, Inc.
Ed: James Dornbrook. **Description:** InkCycle has introduced grenk, a line of environmentally-friendly printer toner and ink cartridges. The cartridges are collected and recycled after use by the company, which separates them into their metal, cardboard, and plastic components.

16337 ■ "Use Ink Presets to Minimize Makeready" in *American Printer* (Vol. 128, July 1, 2011, No. 7)
Pub: Penton Media Inc.
Description: Automatic registration systems enable most printers to be in register very quickly after press startup. If the paper, ink and press time wasted dur-

ing makeready can be reduced, these savings will flow directly to the bottom line. Ink presetting as an economical solution to set color quickly is a trend that continues to gain momentum.

16338 ■ "UV Suppliers Form Strategic Alliance" in *American Printer* (Vol. 128, June 1, 2011, No. 6)
Pub: Penton Media Inc.
Description: British ultra-violent curing systems developer Integration Technology Ltd. formed a strategic alliance with UV technology provider IST Metz GmbH of Germany in order to offer a complete line of UV solutions for the printing industry.

16339 ■ "Web to Print" in *American Printer* (Vol. 128, August 1, 2011, No. 8)
Pub: Penton Media Inc.
Description: Jerry Kennelly, CEO and founder of Tweak.com believes that Web-to-Design is middleware with no content. His firm offers an easy to use interface that flows right into the printer's workflow with no additional costs.

STATISTICAL SOURCES

16340 ■ *RMA Annual Statement Studies*
Pub: Robert Morris Associates (RMA)
Released: Annual. **Price:** $175.00 2006-07 edition, $105.00. **Description:** Contains composite balance sheets and income statements for more than 360 industries, including the accounting, auditing, and bookkeeping industries. Also contains five years of comparative historical data for discerning trends. Includes 16 commonly used ratios, computed for most of the size groupings for nearly every industry.

16341 ■ *State of The Industry*
Pub: NAPL
Ed: Printing Economic Research Center. **Released:** Annual. **Price:** Free to members. **Description:** See web.

TRADE PERIODICALS

16342 ■ *American Printer*
Pub: Penton Media Inc.
Contact: Jill Roth, Special Projects Ed.
E-mail: jill.roth@penton.com
Ed: Katherine O'Brien, Editor, kob@americanprinter. com. **Released:** Monthly. **Description:** Magazine covering the printing and publishing market.

16343 ■ *Economic Edge*
Pub: National Association for Printing Leadership
Released: Quarterly. **Price:** Included in membership. **Description:** Provides current economic data for the printing industry. Also covers sales growth projections, capital spending, and employment.

16344 ■ *FLEXO*
Pub: Foundation of Flexographic Technical Association
Contact: Robert Moran, Publisher
Released: Monthly. **Price:** $55 U.S., Canada, and Mexico; $76 other countries; $30; $92 two years; $125 3 years. **Description:** Magazine covering the flexographic printing method.

16345 ■ *Guild of Book Workers Newsletter*
Pub: Guild of Book Workers Inc.
Contact: Catherine Burkhard
Ed: Margaret Johnson, Editor. **Released:** Bimonthly, Every 2 months. **Price:** Included in membership. **Description:** Covers issues in book arts, binding, book conservation, calligraphy, and printing. Recurring features include letters to the editor, interviews, news of research, a calendar of events, reports of meetings, news of educational opportunities, job listings, book reviews, and notices of publications available.

16346 ■ *Imaging News*
Pub: Diamond Research Corp.
Contact: Arthur S. Diamond, Editor & Publisher
Released: Monthly. **Price:** $175. **Description:** Trade magazine covering imaging materials, technologies, and markets. Available online only.

16347 ■ *Printer's Ink*
Pub: Thomson-Shore Inc.
Ed: Todd Gaffner, Editor, toddg@tshore.com. **Released:** Quarterly. **Price:** Free. **Description:** Provides information on developments in printing and binding and other tenets of book manufacturing. Includes a feature article, company news, information on printing prices, and a column titled Trivia.

16348 ■ *Printing Impressions*
Pub: North American Publishing Co.
Released: Monthly. **Description:** Trade magazine.

16349 ■ *Quick Printing*
Pub: Cygnus Business Media Inc.
Contact: JeanneMarie Graziano, Production Mgr
E-mail: jeannemarie.graziano@cygnusb2b.com
Released: Monthly. **Description:** For Quick and Small Commercial Printers.

16350 ■ *Sales and Marketing Success*
Pub: Printing Industries of America Inc.
Contact: Cliff Weiss, Director of Publications
E-mail: bparrott@printing.org
Released: Quarterly. **Description:** Provides management information to graphic arts companies for marketing products and improving sales techniques.

16351 ■ *Signs of the Times & Screen Printing en Espanol*
Pub: ST Media Group International Inc.
Contact: Tedd Swormstedt, Pres./CEO
E-mail: tedd.swormstedt@stmediagroup.com
Released: Bimonthly. **Price:** $40 U.S.; $40 regular mail, Mexico; $55 airmail, Mexico; $113 UPS express, Mexico; $40 regular mail, Argentina; $58 airmail, Argentina; $174 UPS express, Argentina; $40 regular mail, and other countries. **Description:** Trade magazine in Spanish covering the sign making, screen-printing, and digital imaging industries.

VIDEOCASSETTES/ AUDIOCASSETTES

16352 ■ *Controlling Waste in Web Offset Printing*
Printing Industries of America
200 Deer Run Rd.
Sewickley, PA 15143
Ph:(412)741-6860
Free: 800-910-4283
Fax:(412)741-2311
Co. E-mail: printing@printing.org
URL: http://www.printing.org/
Released: 1988. **Price:** $420.00. **Description:** Proven ways of decreasing waste and increasing efficiency in the printing business are demonstrated. **Availability:** VHS.

16353 ■ *The Web Offset Press*
Printing Industries of America
200 Deer Run Rd.
Sewickley, PA 15143
Ph:(412)741-6860
Free: 800-910-4283
Fax:(412)741-2311
Co. E-mail: printing@printing.org
URL: http://www.printing.org/
Released: 1987. **Description:** An overview of the web offset for the printer, differentiating between sheetfed and webfed presses, and other details. **Availability:** VHS.

TRADE SHOWS AND CONVENTIONS

16354 ■ **Graphics of the Americas**
Printing Association of Florida, Inc.
6275 Hazeltine National Dr.
Orlando, FL 32822
Ph:(407)240-8009
Free: 800-749-4855

Fax:(407)240-8333
Co. E-mail: agaither@pafgraf.org
URL: http://www.pafgraf.org
Released: Annual. **Audience:** Graphics arts trade. **Principal Exhibits:** Graphic arts and specialty printing equipment, supplies, and services.

16355 ■ **ON DEMAND Digital Printing & Publishing Strategy Conference and Exposition**
Advanstar Communications
641 Lexington Ave., 8th Fl.
New York, NY 10022
Ph:(212)951-6600
Fax:(212)951-6793
Co. E-mail: info@advanstar.com
URL: http://www.advanstar.com
Released: Annual. **Audience:** Corporate executives, print providers, government users. **Principal Exhibits:** Addresses the digitalization of workflow in the printing and publishing marketplace.

16356 ■ **Print Ontario**
North Island Trade Shows, Ltd.
1606 Sedlescomb Dr. Unit 8 & 9
Mississauga, ON, Canada L4X 1M6
Ph:(905)625-7070
Free: 800-331-7408
Fax:(905)625-4856
URL: http://www.printontario.com
Released: Biennial. **Audience:** Small and mid-size commercial printers, instant printers, implant shops, brokers and forms distributors. **Principal Exhibits:** Press manufactures, bindery equipment, high speed photocopiers, color copiers, paper manufactures, ink manufactures, trade business, manufactures, trade labels. **Dates and Locations:** 2012 Nov 17-19, Toronto, ON.

CONSULTANTS

16357 ■ **C. Clint Bolte & Associates**
809 Philadelphia Ave.
Chambersburg, PA 17201-1268
Ph:(717)263-5768
Fax:(717)263-8954
Co. E-mail: clint@clintbolte.com
URL: http://www.clintbolte.com
Contact: C. Clint Bolte, Principle
E-mail: cbolte3@comcast.net
Scope: Provides management consulting services to firms involved with the printing industry. Services include outsourcing studies, graphics supply chain management studies, company and equipment valuations, plant layout services, litigation support, fulfillment warehouse consulting and product development services. **Publications:** "UV Cost Savings Environmental Advantage"; "Possible Quebecor World Fall Out"; "80-20 Rule for Managing"; "Options Available in Starting Up a Mailing Operation"; "High Volume Print Buyers at Print 2009"; "Diversifying With Mailing & Fulfillment Services"; "New Business Model Needed for Magazine News stand Distribution"; "Purchasing Incentives Can Be Costly.."; "In-Plant New Product Opportunity for 2009: Tran promo Printing"; "Possible Quebecor World Fall Out"; "Offshore Print Evolution"; "Benefits of Third Party Lease Review"; "Unique Information Fulfillment Opportunities for In-Plant Printers"; "Tough Competition Forces New Strategic Realities for In-Plants"; "Direct Mail Industry Group Files Interpretive Ruling Requests with the Ssta"; "Interesting Opportunities Amid the Gray Clouds of 2007 Postal Rate Increases"; "Time to Break Through the Glass Ceiling," the Seybold Report, May, 2006; "Challenges and Opportunities Presented By Postal Rate Increases," the Seybold Report, May, 2006; "Packaging Roll Sheeting Comes of Age," the Seybold Report, May, 2006; "Diversifying with Mailing and Fulfillment Services," the Seybold Report, Jan, 2006. **Seminars:** How to compete with the majors.

16358 ■ **J. S. Eliezer Associates Inc.**
300 Atlantic St., 7th Fl.
Stamford, CT 06901-3513
Ph:(203)658-1300

Fax:(203)658-1301
Co. E-mail: dmckenna@jseliezer.com
URL: http://www.jseliezer.com
Contact: Mark J. Vallely, Principle
E-mail: jeliezer@atsjseliezer.com
Scope: Management and market research consultants offering design and implementation of manufacturing strategy, feasibility analysis and systems analysis, as well as management information systems and prepress systems; manufacturing proposals analysis, negotiations and contracts; paper purchasing strategy and contract negotiations; catalog distribution effectiveness analysis. Serves the publishing and catalog industries.

FRANCHISES AND BUSINESS OPPORTUNITIES

16359 ■ **AlphaGraphics, Inc.**
268 S State St., Ste. 300
Salt Lake City, UT 84117
Ph:(801)595-7259
Free: 800-528-4885
Fax:(801)533-7959
Co. E-mail: opportunity@alphagraphics.com
URL: http://www.alphagraphics.com
No. of Franchise Units: 273. **Founded:** 1970. **Franchised:** 1980. **Description:** Print-related and digital publishing services which include high-speed duplication, single and multi-color printing, desktop design and publishing, custom presentation materials and an international satellite computer network that transmits camera-ready text and graphics in minutes to any AlphaGraphics store worldwide. **Equity Capital Needed:** $150,000 liquid of $700,000 net worth. **Franchise Fee:** $40,000. **Financial Assistance:** No. **Managerial Assistance:** tollfree technical support hotline; marketing and advertising programs including automated direct mail programs, newspaper and radio ads; ongoing training includes conferences and store visits by field representative. **Training:** 4 weeks new franchisee training, 1 week in-store training and advanced franchisee training.

16360 ■ **Babies 'N' Bells Inc.**
4489 Mira Vista Dr.
Frisco, TX 75034
Free: 888-318-2229
Fax:(469)384-0138
No. of Franchise Units: 56. **No. of Company-Owned Units:** 44. **Founded:** 1996. **Franchised:** 1997. **Description:** Custom invitations, announcements and thank-you notes. **Equity Capital Needed:** $16,700-$28,900 total investment; $15,000 net worth, $15,000 cash liquidity. **Franchise Fee:** $9,000. **Royalty Fee:** 8%. **Financial Assistance:** In-house financing available. **Training:** Offers 1 week at headquarters with ongoing support.

16361 ■ **Cartridge Express**
20 Charles St., Ste. B
Northvale, NJ 07647
Ph:877-887-5495
Fax:877-568-2578
No. of Franchise Units: 2. **No. of Company-Owned Units:** 1. **Founded:** 2004. **Franchised:** 2005. **Description:** Cartridge refilling. **Equity Capital Needed:** $25,000. **Franchise Fee:** $10,000 (1st 10 free). **Financial Assistance:** No. **Training:** Yes.

16362 ■ **Cartridge World**
6460 Hollis St.
Emeryville, CA 94608
Ph:(510)594-9900
Fax:(510)594-9991
Co. E-mail: burt@cartridgeworld.com
URL: http://www.cartridgeworldusa.com
No. of Franchise Units: 1,700. **Founded:** 1997. **Franchised:** 1998. **Description:** Provides cartridge refilling service. **Equity Capital Needed:** $120,100-$184,600. **Franchise Fee:** $30,000. **Financial Assistance:** No. **Training:** An intensive 2 week training course.

16363 ■ Disciple's Directory, Inc.
PO Box 100
Wilmington, MA 01887
Free: 800-696-2344
Fax:(978)657-5411
No. of Franchise Units: 6. **No. of Company-Owned Units:** 2. **Founded:** 1984. **Franchised:** 1998. **Description:** Church telephone directories. **Equity Capital Needed:** $7,500. **Franchise Fee:** $7,500. **Financial Assistance:** Yes. **Training:** Yes.

16364 ■ Kwik Kopy Business Centers
Kwik Kopy Business Centers, Inc.
12715 Telge Rd.
Cypress, TX 77429
Free: 888-638-8722
Fax:(281)256-4178
Co. E-mail: franchisedevelopment@iced.net
URL: http://www.iced.net
No. of Franchise Units: 16. **No. of Company-Owned Units:** 1. **Founded:** 2001. **Franchised:** 2001. **Description:** Offers business advertisement aids and printing and copying services. **Equity Capital Needed:** $65,000 liquid capital; $250,000 net worth. **Franchise Fee:** $35,000. **Financial Assistance:** Conventional bank and SBA loans, and through in-house financing with sufficient collateral. **Managerial Assistance:** Provide business support, advertising, and marketing materials. **Training:** Owners attend classroom and field training, as well as ongoing training through workshops and conferences.

16365 ■ Kwik-Kopy Printing Canada
1550 16th Ave., Unit 4
Richmond Hill, ON, Canada L4B 3K9
Ph:(416)798-7007
Free: 800-387-9725
Fax:(905)780-0575
Co. E-mail: duncanmacpherson@kwikkopy.ca
URL: http://www.kwikkopyprintingfranchise.ca
No. of Franchise Units: 64. **Founded:** 1979. **Franchised:** 1979. **Description:** Offers printing, photocopying, design, fax and related reproduction services. **Equity Capital Needed:** $130,000-$208,000. **Franchise Fee:** $29,500. **Training:** Offers 36 days of training.

16366 ■ Mini Cities Inc.
28439 Great Bend Pl.
Westly Chapel, FL 33543
Free: 800-576-2180
No. of Franchise Units: 4. **No. of Company-Owned Units:** 57. **Founded:** 2005. **Franchised:** 2007. **Description:** Local online & print directory. **Equity Capital Needed:** $15,675-$20,700. **Franchise Fee:** $9,500. **Royalty Fee:** 30%. **Financial Assistance:** In-house assistance with franchise fee.

16367 ■ Minuteman Press
Minuteman Press International
61 Executive Blvd.
Farmingdale, NY 11735
Ph:(631)249-1370
Free: 800-645-3006
Co. E-mail: info@MPIHQ.com
URL: http://www.minuteman-press.com
No. of Franchise Units: 950+. **Founded:** 1973. **Franchised:** 1975. **Description:** Full service printing and graphics centers offering a complete range of services from graphic design to multi-color capabilities, primarily geared to the business/commercial community. Typically a 5 day - Monday thru Friday - business. No experience necessary. **Equity Capital Needed:** $35,000-$50,000 + deposits and working capital. **Franchise Fee:** Call for more info. **Financial Assistance:** Various financing programs available. **Training:** Training program and over 24 regional support offices providing ongoing, in-store training and assistance in the management, technical and marketing aspects of your business. Computerized management and pricing programs are made available to all franchisees.

16368 ■ Minuteman Press International
61 Executive Blvd.
Farmingdale, NY 11735
Ph:(631)249-1370
Free: 800-645-3006

Fax:(631)249-5618
Co. E-mail: info@mpihq.com
URL: http://www.minutemanpress.com
No. of Franchise Units: 75. **Founded:** 1973. **Franchised:** 1975. **Description:** Full-service printing and graphics centers offering a complete range of services from graphic design to multi-color capabilities, primarily geared to the business/commercial community. Five-day, Monday thru Friday business. Award-winning training program/27 regional support offices providing ongoing, in-store training and assistance in management, technical and marketing aspects. Computerized management and pricing programs available. **Equity Capital Needed:** $100,000-$150,000. **Franchise Fee:** $45,500. **Training:** Provides 2 weeks plus additional ononsite training.

16369 ■ Pip Printing and Document Services
26722 Plz. Dr., Ste. 200
Mission Viejo, CA 92691
Free: 800-894-7498
Fax:800-747-0679
Co. E-mail: karen.brock@pip.com
URL: http://www.pip.com
No. of Franchise Units: 285. **Founded:** 1965. **Franchised:** 1968. **Description:** Offers complete range of business including multi-color printing, high-volume copying, desktop publishing, layout, design and finishing on newsletters, brochures, bound presentations, business stationery and forms. **Equity Capital Needed:** Minimum cash investment $83,000 + living expenses; Total investment $232,850-$465,840. **Franchise Fee:** $20,000. **Royalty Fee:** 1%- 7%(-sliding scale). **Financial Assistance:** 3rd party financing and SBA loan programs are available with equipment and leasehold packages for qualified individuals. **Managerial Assistance:** After initial 2 weeks training, owners may request a visit from business consultants trained in sales, marketing, operations and finance. Also, workshops, regional meetings and biennial conclaves held nationwide, covering topics from customer services to the future of the printing industry. Training, operations and safety manuals. **Training:** 2 1/2 weeks of training at PIP University and field visit within the first six months of operation.

16370 ■ Postal Connections of America
Templar Franchise Company
275 E. Douglas Ave., Ste. 115
El Cajon, CA 92020
Ph:(619)294-7550
Free: 800-767-8257
Fax:(619)294-4550
Co. E-mail: info@postalconnections.com
URL: http://www.postalconnections.com
No. of Franchise Units: 99. **Founded:** 1985. **Franchised:** 1996. **Description:** Postal Connections stores offer packaging, shipping, mail receiving & forwarding, copies, printing, scanning & storage of digital documents, eBay auction support, office & packing supplies, crate & freight shipping and more. **Equity Capital Needed:** $119,000-$153,900, average initial investment. **Franchise Fee:** $23,900. **Financial Assistance:** Third party financing sources available. **Managerial Assistance:** Online 24/7 "business coaching" on private website. **Training:** Extensive training prior to & after opening. Franchisees receive 5 days live action training in a regional training store, Unique Act video training program & 4 days onsite.

16371 ■ Print Three Franchising Corp.
8400 Jane St. Bldg. D, Ste. 300
Concord, ON, Canada L4K 4L8
Ph:(905)669-8895
Free: 800-335-5918
Fax:(905)669-0712
Co. E-mail: andrew@printthree.com
URL: http://www.printthree.com
No. of Franchise Units: 51. **Founded:** 1970. **Franchised:** 1981. **Description:** Business service franchise focusing on the increasing demand for digital imaging. Franchise offers complete digital reproduction, design, finishing and fulfillment. The only print franchise having a fully integrated web-based order-

ing system. Provides total imaging solutions for the corporate community. **Equity Capital Needed:** $200,000. **Franchise Fee:** $70,000. **Training:** Yes.

16372 ■ RWorld Franchise Canada Inc.
6154 5th Line
Tottenham, ON, Canada L0G 1W0
Ph:(905)936-9346
Free: 800-307-3719
Fax:(905)936-9382
Co. E-mail: doug@rworld.ca
URL: http://www.rworld.ca
No. of Franchise Units: 4. **No. of Company-Owned Units:** 1. **Founded:** 2002. **Franchised:** 2002. **Description:** RWorld is a unique and comparatively low start-up cost franchise, in the highly profitable printer cartridge industry. We offer choices: store in store or leading edge mobile concept. Our model is regional master micro plants, eliminating the need for each individual franchisee to waste precious resources remanufacturing cartridges! It allows for consistency in product and the franchise investor concentrates on promoting and growing their business. **Equity Capital Needed:** $40,000-$60,000. **Franchise Fee:** $20,000. **Training:** Full training and support.

16373 ■ Sir Speedy, Inc.
26722 Plz. Dr.
Mission Viejo, CA 92691
Free: 888-465-9481
Fax:(949)348-5010
URL: http://www.sirspeedy.com
No. of Franchise Units: 400. **Founded:** 1968. **Franchised:** 1968. **Description:** Franchisor of printing, copying, graphic design and digital networking centers. **Equity Capital Needed:** $261,000-$268,413; net worth $300,000+. **Franchise Fee:** $25,000. **Financial Assistance:** No. **Training:** Sir Speedy University, Regional training.

16374 ■ The UPS Store
1115 North Service Rd., Unit 1
Oakville, ON, Canada L6M 2V9
Ph:(905)338-9754
Free: 800-661-6232
Fax:(905)338-7491
Co. E-mail: development@theupsstore.ca
URL: http://www.theupsstore.ca
Founded: 1990. **Description:** Offering one-stop convenience for small business: digital print & photocopies (colour & B/W), document finishing, worldwide courier services, packaging services & supplies, fax services, computer rental, WIFI and mail receiving services. **Equity Capital Needed:** $146,150-$179,550. **Franchise Fee:** $35,000.

LIBRARIES

16375 ■ Carnegie-Mellon University–University Libraries | Special Collections
Hunt Library
4909 Frew St.
Pittsburgh, PA 15213-3890
Ph:(412)268-6622
Fax:(412)268-6945
Co. E-mail: mj0g@andrew.cmu.edu
URL: http://www.library.cmu.edu
Contact: Mary Kay Johnsen, Spec.Coll.Libn.
Scope: History of printing, 19th-century English literature, landmark books of science. **Services:** Library open to the public. **Holdings:** 12,000 books.

16376 ■ Flint Ink–Information Resource Center
4600 Arrowhead Dr.
Ann Arbor, MI 48105
Ph:(734)622-6000
Fax:(734)622-6362
Co. E-mail: susan.taylor@flintink
URL: http://www.flintgrp.com/index.html
Contact: Susan B. Taylor
Scope: Printing inks, inkjet inks, pigments, polymers, coatings, solvents, resins. **Services:** Research; SDI; Library not open to the public. **Holdings:** 2100 books; 27 titles on microfiche; 350 audiocassettes and videocassettes. **Subscriptions:** 90 journals and other serials; 5 newspapers.

16377 ■ Graphic Communications World Library
PO Box 1126
Port Orchard, WA 98366
Ph:(360)769-5417
Fax:(360)769-5622
URL: http://www.quoinpublishing.com
Contact: William Esler, Pres.
Scope: Printing and graphic communications technol

ogy. **Services:** Library open to subscribers. **Holdings:** Figures not available. **Subscriptions:** 150 journals and other serials.

RESEARCH CENTERS

16378 ■ Gravure Association of America
PO Box 25617
Rochester, NY 14625
Ph:(201)523-6042

Fax:(201)523-6048
Co. E-mail: bmartin@gaa.org
URL: http://www.gaa.org
Contact: Bill Martin, Pres./CEO
E-mail: bmartin@gaa.org
Scope: Gravure printing, electronic imaging, laser applications, environmental control, and computer process control. Research focuses on press, paper, ink, color reproduction, cylinder preparation, system, and the environment. **Publications:** Gravure (quarterly). **Educational Activities:** Conferences and seminars.

START-UP INFORMATION

16379 ■ *How to Open and Operate a Financially Successful Private Investigation Business: With Companion CD-ROM*
Pub: Atlantic Publishing Company
Released: December 1, 2010. **Price:** $39.95. **Description:** With a massive upside and potential for growth the private investigation sector is growing. The book will teach everything needed to know about working in the private investigation field, starting with the basics of what you can expect and what preconceptions that may just be Hollywood. Information is given to help choose a niche of investigation and hot to start thinking in the abstract, questioning everything but recognizing facts for what they are, as well as the differences between a private investigator and a police officer.

ASSOCIATIONS AND OTHER ORGANIZATIONS

16380 ■ Council of International Investigators
2150 N 107th St., Ste. 205
Seattle, WA 98133-9009
Ph:(206)361-8869
Free: 888-759-8884
Fax:(206)367-8777
Co. E-mail: office@cii2.org
URL: http://www.cii2.org
Contact: Nancy Barber, Chair
Description: Represents licensed and accredited professional private investigators and detectives in 28 countries. Conducts seminars on investigation, security work, criminology and lie detection. **Publications:** *International Councilor* (bimonthly).

16381 ■ International Foundation for Protection Officers
PO Box 771329
Naples, FL 34107-1329
Ph:(239)430-0534
Fax:(239)430-0533
Co. E-mail: adminifpo@earthlink.net
URL: http://www.ifpo.org
Contact: Sandi Davies, Exec. Dir.
Description: Seeks to provide for the education, training, and certification of protection officers worldwide. Maintains and improves standards of excellence and establish ethical standards within the industry. Improves the public perception of protection officers. Interacts with colleges, universities, and other post-secondary educational institutions to facilitate education and certification; conducts research. Maintains Certified Protections Officer program, that provides professional designation and consists of training in patrols, report writing, crime scenes, interviewing, investigations, public relations, stress management, physical security, VIP protection, and first aid. **Publications:** *Business Crime Prevention*; *Careers in Security—2nd Edition*; *Protection Officer Guidebook*; *Protection Officer News* (quarterly); *Protection Officer Survival* .

16382 ■ ION
4548 Jones Rd.
Oak Harbor, WA 98277
Ph:(360)279-8343
Free: 800-338-3463
Fax:(360)279-8343
Co. E-mail: webreq@ioninc.com
URL: http://www.ioninc.com
Contact: Leroy E. Cook, Founder/Pres.
Description: Private investigators, insurance claims investigators, information vendors, and journalists. Provides international referral service for hiring. .

16383 ■ National Association of Investigative Specialists
PO Box 82148
Austin, TX 78708
Ph:(512)719-3595
Fax:(512)719-3594
Co. E-mail: rthomas007@aol.com
URL: http://www.pimall.com/nais/dir.menu.html
Contact: Ralph Thomas
Description: Private investigators, automobile repossessors, bounty hunters, and law enforcement officers. Promotes professionalism and provides for information exchange among private investigators. Lobbies for investigative regulations. Offers training programs and issues certificates of completion. Sponsors charitable programs; compiles statistics; maintains speakers' bureau and placement service. Operates Investigators' Hall of Fame of Private Investigators. Offers seminars on cassette tape. **Publications:** *How to Find Anyone Anywhere: Secret Sources and Techniques for Locating Missing Persons* (annual); *How to Investigate by Computer*; *Physical Surveillance Training Manual* (annual); *PI Bites*; *PI Daily* (daily); *Private Investigator's Catalog* (bimonthly); *Private Investigator's Connection* (bimonthly).

16384 ■ National Association of Legal Investigators
235 N Pine St.
Lansing, MI 48933
Ph:(517)702-9835
Free: (866)520-6254
Fax:(517)372-1501
Co. E-mail: pjaeb@heartlandinfo.com
URL: http://www.nalionline.org
Contact: Paul Jaeb, Natl. Dir.
Description: Legal investigators, both independent and law firm staff, who specialize in investigation of personal injury matters for the plaintiff and criminal defense. Promotes professionalization of the legal investigator, accomplished by seminars and a professional certification program. Provides nationwide network of contact among members. Compiles statistics. .

16385 ■ National Association of Professional Background Screeners
2501 Aerial Center Pkwy., Ste. 103
Morrisville, NC 27560
Ph:(919)459-2082
Free: 888-686-2727

Fax:(919)459-2075
Co. E-mail: info@napbs.com
URL: http://www.napbs.com
Contact: Stevie Hughes Kernick, Interim Exec. Dir.
Description: Represents the interests of companies offering employment and background screening. Promotes ethical business practices. Fosters awareness of issues related to consumer protection and privacy rights. Maintains the standard of the background screening industry. .

16386 ■ National Council of Investigation and Security Services
7501 Sparrows Point Blvd.
Baltimore, MD 21219-1927
Free: 800-445-8408
Fax:(410)388-9746
Co. E-mail: nciss@comcast.net
URL: http://www.nciss.org
Contact: Carolyn Ward, Exec. Dir.
Purpose: Monitors national and state legislative and regulatory activities. Develops and encourages the practice of high standards of personal and professional conduct. Acquires, preserves, and disseminates data and valuable information; promotes the purpose of investigation and guard companies. Provides information about state legislation and regulatory activities that could have an impact on a particular firm or on the industry in general; acts as spokesman for the industry before legislative and regulatory bodies at both federal and state levels. **Publications:** *NCISS Report* (quarterly).

16387 ■ Nine Lives Associates
Executive Protection Institute
16 Penn Pl., Ste. 1570
New York, NY 10001
Ph:(212)268-4555
Free: 800-947-5827
Fax:(212)563-4783
Co. E-mail: info@personalprotection.com
URL: http://www.personalprotection.com/nla.cfm
Contact: Dr. Jerry Heying, Pres./CEO
Description: Law enforcement, correctional, military, and security professionals who have been granted Personal Protection Specialist Certification through completion of the protective services program offered by the Executive Protection Institute; conducts research; EPI programs emphasize personal survival skills and techniques for the protection of others. Provides professional recognition for qualified individuals engaged in executive protection assignments. Maintains placement service. Operates speakers' bureau; compiles statistics. .

16388 ■ Society of Professional Investigators
233 Broadway, Ste. 2201
New York, NY 10279
Ph:(646)584-9081
URL: http://spionline.info
Contact: Bruce Sackman, Pres.
Description: Persons with at least 5 years' investigative experience for an official federal, state, or local government agency or for a quasi-official agency formed for law enforcement or related activities. Seeks to advance knowledge of the science and

technology of professional investigation, law enforcement, and police science; maintains high standards and ethics; promotes efficiency of investigators in the services they perform. **Publications:** *SPI Newsletter* (8/year).

DIRECTORIES OF EDUCATIONAL PROGRAMS

16389 ■ *Directory of Private Accredited Career Schools and Colleges of Technology*
Pub: Accrediting Commission of Career Schools and Colleges of Technology
Contact: Michale S. McComis, Exec. Dir.
Released: On web page. **Price:** Free. **Description:** Covers 3900 accredited post-secondary programs that provide training programs in business, trade, and technical fields, including various small business endeavors. Entries offer school name, address, phone, description of courses, job placement assistance, and requirements for admission. Arrangement is alphabetical.

REFERENCE WORKS

16390 ■ *American Polygraph Association—Member Directory*
Pub: American Polygraph Association
Contact: Robbie Bennett
Ed: Stuart Senter, PhD, Editor. **Price:** $125, individuals; $150, other countries. **Covers:** Approximately 2,500 member individuals and companies involved the polygraph field. **Arrangement:** Geographical.

16391 ■ *Nine Lives Associates—Membership Directory*
Pub: Executive Protection Institute
Ed: Dr. Richard W. Kobetz, Editor, rwk@crosslink.com. **Released:** Annual, March. **Covers:** 2,000 individuals certified as personal protection specialists through completion of a training program. **Entries Include:** Specialist name and title, address, phone, company name. **Arrangement:** Classified by class completed.

STATISTICAL SOURCES

16392 ■ *RMA Annual Statement Studies*
Pub: Robert Morris Associates (RMA)
Released: Annual. **Price:** $175.00 2006-07 edition, $105.00. **Description:** Contains composite balance sheets and income statements for more than 360 industries, including the accounting, auditing, and bookkeeping industries. Also contains five years of comparative historical data for discerning trends. Includes 16 commonly used ratios, computed for most of the size groupings for nearly every industry.

TRADE PERIODICALS

16393 ■ *American Polygraph Association Newsletter*
Pub: American Polygraph Association
Ed: Donald J. Krapohl, Editor, dkrapohl@aol.com. **Released:** Bimonthly. **Price:** $80, nonmembers in U.S.; $100, elsewhere. **Description:** Reviews developments in polygraph techniques and instruments, police and private uses of the polygraph, and pertinent law and legislation. Covers activities of state, regional, and foreign polygraph associations. Recurring features include news of research, case studies, editorials, and notices of upcoming seminars.

16394 ■ *Criminal Justice Magazine*
Pub: American Bar Association
Contact: John O'Hearn, Advertising Mgr
E-mail: ohearnj@abanet.org
Ed: MaryAnn Dadisman, Editor, mdadisman@abanet.org. **Released:** Quarterly. **Price:** $48 non-member

U.S.; $57 non-member outside U.S.; $15.95 shipping and handling. **Description:** Magazine providing practical treatment of aspects of criminal law.

16395 ■ *Polygraph Update*
Pub: Lafayette Instrument Co.
Contact: Carie Bumbleburg
Ed: Christopher Fausett, Editor. **Released:** Annual. **Price:** Free. **Description:** Provides information on research studies, new products, and usage opportunities of polygraph machines.

TRADE SHOWS AND CONVENTIONS

16396 ■ **ISC Chicago**
Reed Exhibitions North American Headquarters
383 Main Ave.
Norwalk, CT 06851
Ph:(203)840-4800
Fax:(203)840-5805
Co. E-mail: export@reedexpo.com
URL: http://www.reedexpo.com
Released: Biennial. **Audience:** Security equipment dealers and installers, corporate, industrial and institutional security managers and directors. **Principal Exhibits:** Residential, commercial, industrial and institutional security equipment, systems and services.

CONSULTANTS

16397 ■ **Lenow International Inc.**
1503 Union Ave., Ste. 210
PO Box 3092
Memphis, TN 38173-0092
Ph:(901)726-0735
Fax:(901)725-4079
Co. E-mail: nlenow@compuserve.com
URL: http://www.lenowinternational.com
Contact: Nate Lenow, President
E-mail: nate@lenowinternational.com
Scope: Acts as a consultant for investigative strategies to resolve civil or criminal investigations. Conducts surveys or evaluations to prevent crime directed toward business, in particular crime involving fraudulent activity. Recommends security procedures or equipment to aid loss prevention by business. Available to serve as expert witness in forensic security and fraud examination. Referral source for investigative agencies. Industries served: Corporate security departments, private investigative agencies, small business, and government agencies. **Publications:** "Competitive Intelligence," Law Enforcement Quarterly. **Seminars:** Automate your reports with software, Tennessee Association of Investigators, May, 2000; Use of Computer as an Investigative Tool; Criminal Investigation.

16398 ■ **National Training Center of Polygraph Science**
200 W 57th St., Ste. 1400
New York, NY 10019-3211
Ph:(212)755-5241
Free: 800-643-6597
Fax:(973)838-8661
Contact: Catherine A. Arther, Principle
Scope: Provides polygraph training and conducts pre employment seminars. Industries served: law enforcement and business firms of all types, as well as government agencies.

16399 ■ **Navigator Research Group Inc.**
310 Blount St., Ste. 221
PO Box 14189
Tallahassee, FL 32317
Ph:(850)878-5437
Free: (866)620-4636

Fax:(850)878-1131
Co. E-mail: info@navigatorresearchgroup.com
URL: http://www.navigatorresearchgroup.com
Contact: Richard Ratcliff, Owner
Scope: Firm is a licensed persons and conducting background checks. Industries served: private investigators, insurance companies and adjustors, law firms and other corporations. The firm serves the state of Florida, but has a network of correspondents nationwide and access to various databases which provides coverage across the country, private investigation agency specializing in locating missing.

FRANCHISES AND BUSINESS OPPORTUNITIES

16400 ■ **Case In Point**
PO Box 1286
Londonderry, NH 03053-1286
Free: 800-370-2116
Fax:800-397-2963
No. of Franchise Units: 2. **No. of Company-Owned Units:** 4. **Founded:** 1992. **Franchised:** 2002. **Description:** Investigation services. **Equity Capital Needed:** $40,000. **Franchise Fee:** $10,000. **Royalty Fee:** 6%. **Financial Assistance:** No. **Training:** Offers 2 weeks at headquarters, 1 week at franchisees location and ongoing support.

16401 ■ **L & W Investigations, Inc.**
Lyons & Wolivar Co.
3140 Red Hill Ave., Ste. 270
Costa Mesa, CA 92627
Ph:(714)979-0707
Fax:(714)979-0708
No. of Franchise Units: 35. **No. of Company-Owned Units:** 3. **Description:** Private investigations, specializing in all types of insurance fraud. **Equity Capital Needed:** $75,000. **Franchise Fee:** $70,000-$200,000. **Financial Assistance:** Yes. **Training:** Offers extensive and consistent training.

LIBRARIES

16402 ■ **National Training Center of Polygraph Science Library**
200 W. 57th St., Ste. 1400
New York, NY 10019-3211
Ph:(212)755-5241
Fax:(212)755-5242
Contact: Richard O. Arther, Sch.Dir.
Scope: Polygraphs, lie detection, interrogation. **Services:** Library not open to the public. **Holdings:** 800 books.

16403 ■ **Thomas Investigative Publications Library**
PO Box 82148
Austin, TX 78708
Ph:(512)719-3595
Fax:(512)719-3594
Co. E-mail: rthomas007@aol.com
URL: http://www.pimall.com/nais
Contact: Ralph Thomas, Pres.
Scope: Private investigations, bail enforcement, information brokering, law enforcement. **Services:** Library open to the public. **Holdings:** 200 books.

RESEARCH CENTERS

16404 ■ **Michigan State University–American Polygraph Association Credibility Assessment Research Center**
560 Baker Hall
East Lansing, MI 48824
Ph:(803)751-9196
Fax:(803)751-9178
Co. E-mail: horvath@msu.edu
Contact: Dr. Frank Horvath, Dir.
E-mail: horvath@msu.edu
Scope: Deception detection; psychophysiological detection of deception (PDD), forensic polygraphy (polygraph testing); credibility assessment methods.

Private Label Product Manufacturer/Retailer

ASSOCIATIONS AND OTHER ORGANIZATIONS

16405 ■ Private Label Manufacturers Association
630 3rd Ave.
New York, NY 10017
Ph:(212)972-3131
Fax:(212)983-1382
Co. E-mail: info@plma.com
URL: http://plma.com
Contact: Mr. Brian Sharoff, Pres.
Description: Membership consists of manufacturers, brokers, suppliers, and consultants. Educates consumers on the quality and value of private label or store brand products; promotes private label industry. Compiles statistics; conducts research programs for members. **Publications:** Scanner (quarterly).

REFERENCE WORKS

16406 ■ Private Label Directory
Pub: E.W. Williams Publications Co.
Released: Annual, July. **Price:** $75, U.S. and Canada; $125, elsewhere; $75, Canada. **Covers:** Over 1,400 suppliers of food, health and beauty care, household supplies, general merchandise and service and supplies, with private and generic labels; international coverage. **Entries Include:** Company name, address, phone, fax, e-mail, internet, names and titles of key personnel, products. **Arrangement:** Alphabetical. **Indexes:** Product, geographical.

TRADE PERIODICALS

16407 ■ Min's b2b
Pub: Phillips Business Information Inc.
Contact: Angela Duff, Publisher
Ed: Jeremy Greenfield, Editor. **Released:** Biweekly. **Price: Description:** Provides news on business relations and strategies and tactics to increase online publishing and new media business.

FRANCHISES AND BUSINESS OPPORTUNITIES

16408 ■ Cap-It International Inc.
4954 275th St.
Langley, BC, Canada V4W 0A3
Ph:(604)857-1211
Fax:(604)857-1255
Co. E-mail: Robert@cap-it.com
URL: http://www.cap-it.com
No. of Franchise Units: 17. **Founded:** 1973. **Description:** Franchise offers retailing and installation of canopies and accessories for light trucks, sport utility vehicles, vans and cars. **Equity Capital Needed:** $150,00 and up. **Franchise Fee:** $49,000. **Royalty Fee:** 3%. **Financial Assistance:** No. **Training:** Provides 6 weeks of training.

16409 ■ Cash Converters
275 Renfrew Dr., Unit 104
Markham, ON, Canada L3R 0N9
Ph:(905)480-2400
Co. E-mail: tammy_irwin@ezcorp.com
URL: http://www.cashconverters.ca
No. of Franchise Units: 13. **No. of Company-Owned Units:** 64. **Founded:** 1995. **Franchised:** 1989. **Description:** Buying and selling of quality secondhand goods, which include jewelry, televisions, stereos, tools, electrical goods etc. are made possible by this international retailer. **Equity Capital Needed:** $160,000-$300,000. **Franchise Fee:** $35,000. **Training:** Training and advertising program, as well as advisory council support.

START-UP INFORMATION

16410 ■ *How to Start a Home-Based Professional Organizing Business*
Pub: Globe Pequot Press
Ed: Dawn Noble. **Released:** March 2007. **Price:** $18.95. **Description:** Tips for starting a home-based professional organizing business are presented.

REFERENCE WORKS

16411 ■ "6 Worth the Price Fix-Ups" in *Realtor Magazine* (**Vol. 44, April-May 2011, No. 44, pp. 23**)
Pub: Realtor Magazine
Description: Advice on how realtors could increase a home's resale value through do-it-yourself projects is given. Removal of personal items and clutter is recommended, along with rearrangement of furniture. A clutter consultant could also be used.

16412 ■ "How to Declutter Your Life Closet Cleanup: Putting a Lid on Clutter" in *Atlanta Journal-Constitution* (**May 1, 2011**)
Pub: Atlanta Journal-Constitution
Ed: Felicia Feaster. **Description:** The annual Closets and Home Organization Convention and Expo spotlights new products and services designed to help people get organized at home or the workplace. The organization sector is holding steady despite the recession and is expected to expand into garage organization.

16413 ■ "Impressive Numbers: Companies Experience Substantial Increases in Dollars, Employment" in *Hispanic Business* (**July-August 2007**)
Pub: Hispanic Business
Ed: Derek Reveron. **Description:** Profiles of five fastest growing Hispanic companies reporting increases in revenue and employment include Brightstar, distributor of wireless products; Greenway Ford Inc., a car dealership; Fred Loya Insurance, auto insurance carrier; and Group O, packaging company; and Diverse Staffing, Inc., an employment and staffing firm.

16414 ■ "Integrating Business Core Knowledge through Upper Division Report Composition" in *Business Communication Quarterly* (**December 2007**)
Pub: Sage Publications USA
Ed: Joy Roach, Daniel Tracy, Kay Durden. **Description:** An assignment that integrates subjects and encourages the use of business communication report-writing skills is presented. This assignment is designed to complement business school curricula and help develop critical thinking and organizational skills.

16415 ■ "Make It Easier On Yourself" in *Women In Business* (**Vol. 63, Fall 2011, No. 3, pp. 28**)
Pub: American Business Women's Association
Ed: Maureen Sullivan. **Description:** Getting and staying organized helps avoid wasting time on deciding which priorities to address first. Taking help and

avoiding hoarding are examples of how to become organized. The use of technology for organizing priorities is also explained.

16416 ■ "Monday Organizer: Clean and De-Clutter in 15 Minutes" in *Tulsa World* (**June 13, 2011**)
Pub: McClatchy Company
Ed: Kim Brown. **Description:** New weekly series highlights practical tips and helpful ideas to simply life by taking 15 minutes to de-clutter your home or office. Paper clutter can be eliminated in 15 minutes by gathering up newspapers and magazines to recycle; sort mail as soon as you receive it and throw away any junk mail at that time. If watching TV, use commercial time to accomplish small tasks.

16417 ■ "StorageByMail Lets Customers Ship Away Their Clutter" in *Inc.* (**Vol. 33, April 2011, No. 3, pp. 92**)
Pub: Inc. Magazine
Ed: Issie Lapowsky. **Description:** StorageByMail allows people to put items into storage by mailing them to the company. The firm charges a monthly fee, customers describe contents of each box, and ship to the Jersey City facility using a preprinted label. StorageByMail pays the $25 shipment charge.

FRANCHISES AND BUSINESS OPPORTUNITIES

16418 ■ **California Closet Company**
1000 4th St., Ste. 800
San Rafael, CA 94901
Ph:(415)256-8500
Free: 800-241-3222
Fax:(415)256-8501
No. of Franchise Units: 77. **Founded:** 1978. **Franchised:** 1982. **Description:** Custom closet design, manufacture, and installation. **Equity Capital Needed:** $127,500-$377,000 total investment. **Franchise Fee:** $40,000. **Royalty Fee:** 6%. **Financial Assistance:** No. **Training:** Includes training at headquarters, franchisees location, mentor training with ongoing support.

16419 ■ **Closet Factory**
12800 S Broadway
Los Angeles, CA 90066
Ph:(310)715-1000
Fax:(310)516-8065
No. of Franchise Units: 82. **No. of Company-Owned Units:** 4. **Founded:** 1983. **Franchised:** 1986. **Description:** Design, sell, manufacture, and install custom closets. **Equity Capital Needed:** Total investment approximately $325,000-$400,000, franchise fee included; Liquidity $100,000+. **Franchise Fee:** $64,000. **Financial Assistance:** Yes. **Training:** Yes.

16420 ■ **Closets by Design Franchising**
11145 Knott Ave., Ste. A
Cypress, CA 90630
Ph:(714)890-5860
Free: 800-377-5737

Fax:(714)901-0424
URL: http://www.closets-by-design.com
No. of Franchise Units: 30. **No. of Company-Owned Units:** 4. **Founded:** 1982. **Franchised:** 1998. **Description:** Closets by design franchising custom closets, garage organizers, entertainment centers and shelving for home, offices and garages. **Equity Capital Needed:** $124,900-$278,000. **Franchise Fee:** $36,900. **Royalty Fee:** 6%. **Financial Assistance:** Third party financing assistance. **Training:** Provides 3 weeks at headquarters, and additional 3 weeks at franchisees location.

16421 ■ **Closets & Storage Concepts**
1000 White Horse Rd., Ste. 404
Voorhees, NJ 08043
Ph:(856)627-5700
Free: 800-862-1919
Fax:(856)627-7447
No. of Franchise Units: 10. **No. of Company-Owned Units:** 3. **Founded:** 1987. **Franchised:** 2000. **Description:** Custom closet and storage systems. **Equity Capital Needed:** $10,000-$200,000. **Franchise Fee:** $5,000-$38,500. **Financial Assistance:** Yes. **Training:** Yes.

16422 ■ **Floorguard**
340 Marshall Ave., Unit 101
Aurora, IL 60506
Ph:(813)935-5087
Free: 888-694-2724
Fax:(813)425-5799
No. of Franchise Units: 1. **No. of Company-Owned Units:** 1. **Founded:** 1988. **Franchised:** 2006. **Description:** Garage flooring and storage systems. **Equity Capital Needed:** $162,000-$234,000. **Franchise Fee:** $40,000. **Financial Assistance:** No. **Training:** Yes.

16423 ■ **Garagetek**
5 Aerial Way, Ste. 200
Syosset, NY 11791
Ph:(516)621-4300
Free: (866)664-2724
Fax:(516)992-8600
Co. E-mail: SBarrett@GarageTek.com
URL: http://www.GarageTek.com
No. of Franchise Units: 55. **No. of Company-Owned Units:** 2. **Founded:** 2000. **Franchised:** 2001. **Description:** Franchise of construction, remodeling, bath and closet services. **Equity Capital Needed:** $250,000. **Franchise Fee:** $50,000. **Financial Assistance:** No. **Training:** Provides 2 weeks at corporate and ongoing field support.

16424 ■ **Granite Transformations**
RockSolid Granit USA Inc.
10360 USA Today Way
Miramar, FL 33025
Ph:(954)435-5538
Free: (866)685-5300
Fax:(954)435-5579
Co. E-mail: info@granittransformations.com
URL: http://www.granitetransformations.com
No. of Franchise Units: 79. **No. of Company-Owned Units:** 1. **Founded:** 2001. **Franchised:** 2001. **Description:** Construction, remodeling, and

bath and closets services. **Equity Capital Needed:** $127,000-$350,000. **Franchise Fee:** $25,000-$75,000. **Financial Assistance:** No. **Training:** Training program consists of operations, installations, and sales training. Each training module is supported with training material. Training facility is an actual working location allowing trainees to evaluate, test, and see results. Grand opening supported by sales manager onsite and ongoing support.

16425 ■ HouseWall Garage System

8100 W 30th Ct.

Hialeah, FL 33018

Ph:(305)817-9881

Fax:(305)826-1882

No. of Franchise Units: 7. **No. of Company-Owned Units:** 1. **Founded:** 2002. **Franchised:** 2006. **Description:** Garage organization systems. **Equity Capital Needed:** $136,000-$168,000. **Franchise Fee:** $15,000. **Royalty Fee:** 6-5.5

%. **Financial Assistance:** Limited third party financing available and in-house assistance with franchise fee. **Training:** Offers 1 week at headquarters and ongoing support.

16426 ■ Kwik Kloset

607A Old Stouffville Rd.

Uxbridge, ON, Canada L9P 1R4

Ph:(905)852-2108

Free: (866)477-2236

Fax:(866)973-8510

Co. E-mail: franchiseinfo@kwikkloset.com

URL: http://www.kwikkloset.com

No. of Franchise Units: 8. **No. of Company-Owned Units:** 2. **Founded:** 2003. **Franchised:** 2005. **Description:** Kwik Kloset has an exciting new approach to the burgeoning home organization business. Bringing together our low-overhead business model, an innovative mobile closet installation vehicle, and our one point of contact "Spaceman" concept, only Kwik Kloset can offer very cost-effective, same-day closet

design and installation services. Kwik Kloset has signed a "Sell, furnish & install" contract with The Home Depot Canada, and is now active in 45 stores. Kwik Kloset is seeking both owner/operator franchisees, and larger area master franchisees across Canada, the USA and possibly international. **Equity Capital Needed:** $100,000 investment required' $25,000 start-up capital. **Franchise Fee:** $75,000. **Training:** Spaceman Training Program includes sales, design, and installation.

16427 ■ Parties By Terrye Inc.

12115 Long Lake Dr.

Owings Mills, MD 21117

Ph:(410)581-1080

Fax:(410)902-7171

No. of Company-Owned Units: 1. **Founded:** 1983. **Franchised:** 2006. **Description:** Event planning for social & corporate events. **Equity Capital Needed:** $14,500-$59,300. **Franchise Fee:** $20,000. **Financial Assistance:** No. **Training:** Yes.

START-UP INFORMATION

16428 ■ "Rehab Will Turn Hospital Into Incubator" in *The Business Journal-Serving Metropolitan Kansas City* (Vol. 26, September 12, 2008)
Pub: American City Business Journals, Inc.
Ed: Rob Roberts. **Description:** Independence Regional Health Center will be purchased by CEAH Realtors and be converted into the Independence Regional Entrepreneurial Center, a business incubator that will house startups and other tenants. Other details about the planned entrepreneurial center are provided.

ASSOCIATIONS AND OTHER ORGANIZATIONS

16429 ■ **Institute of Real Estate Management**
430 N Michigan Ave.
Chicago, IL 60611
Ph:(312)329-6000
Free: 800-837-0706
Fax:800-338-4736
Co. E-mail: custserv@irem.org
URL: http://www.irem.org
Contact: Ronald L. Goss, Pres.
Description: Professional organization of real property and asset managers. Awards professional designation Certified Property Manager (CPM) to qualifying individuals, Accredited Management Organization (AMO) to qualifying management firms and also awards Accredited Residential Manager (ARM) accreditation to qualifying individuals who are primarily residential site managers. Monitors legislation affecting real estate management. Offers management courses and seminars; conducts research and educational programs, publishes books and reports; maintains formal code of ethics; compiles statistics; maintains employment Website for real estate management industry. .

16430 ■ **International Facility Management Association**
1 E Greenway Plz., Ste. 1100
Houston, TX 77046-0104
Ph:(713)623-4362
Fax:(713)623-6124
Co. E-mail: ifma@ifma.org
URL: http://www.ifma.org
Contact: Tony Keane, Pres./CEO
Description: Facility managers worldwide representing all types of organizations including banks, insurance companies, hospitals, colleges and universities, utility companies, electronic equipment manufacturers, petroleum companies, museums, auditoriums and federal, state, provincial and local governments. Purposes are to enhance the professional goals of persons involved or interested in the field of facility management (the planning, designing and managing of workplaces); to cultivate cooperation, foster understanding and create interest among firms, individuals and other associations and professions as they may affect facility management; to engage in

the interchange of views regarding legislation, regulation and procedures that affect facility management. Offers job placement assistance; sponsors academic research; certifies facility managers; compiles statistics; sells books. Conducts educational and research programs. **Publications:** *Annual Conference Proceedings* (annual); *Operations and Maintenance Benchmarks Survey* .

16431 ■ **National Property Management Association**
28100 U.S. Hwy. 19 N, Ste. 400
Clearwater, FL 33761
Ph:(727)736-3788
Fax:(727)736-6707
Co. E-mail: hq@npma.org
URL: http://www.npma.org
Contact: Paul Nesbitt, Exec. Dir.
Description: Aims to build leadership by educating, training and promoting standards of competency and ethical behavior in the asset management of personal property. Serves property professionals throughout the United States; members represent companies and organizations in both the public and private sectors, including scientific laboratories, universities, hospitals, public school systems, and local, state and federal government agencies. **Publications:** *NPMA Survey*; *Property Manual* .

16432 ■ **Property Management Association**
7508 Wisconsin Ave., 4th Fl.
Bethesda, MD 20814
Ph:(301)657-9200
Fax:(301)907-9326
Co. E-mail: info@pma-dc.org
URL: http://www.pma-dc.org
Contact: Scott Skokan, Pres.
Description: Property management professionals who own and operate multifamily residential, commercial, retail, industrial and other income-producing properties and firms that provide goods and services used in real property management. Works to enhance the interests and welfare of property owners, managers, supervisory employees and contractors involved in the management of multifamily residential and commercial property. Provides education and a forum for exchange of ideas on efficient methods of operation and progressive policies of management. **Publications:** *Property Management Association—Bulletin* (monthly).

16433 ■ **Vacation Rental Managers Association**
9100 Purdue Rd., Ste. 200
Indianapolis, IN 46268
Ph:(317)454-8315
Fax:(317)454-8316
Co. E-mail: vrma@vrma.com
URL: http://www.vrma.com
Contact: Steve Ingram, Exec. Dir.
Description: Companies that rent and manage vacation properties, resorts, townhomes and condominiums on a short-term basis. Promotes the interests of the vacation rental industry to the public. .

REFERENCE WORKS

16434 ■ "1Q Office Vacancies Mainly Up; Class A Space Bucks Trend, Falls" in *Crain's Detroit Business* (Vol. 24, April 14, 2008, No. 15)
Pub: Crain Communications, Inc.
Ed: Daniel Duggan. **Description:** Although more office space became vacant in the first quarter, Class A space went in the opposite direction with several local businesses are moving from less-desirable to more desirable areas.

16435 ■ "A Conversation With; Ron Gatner, Jones Lang LaSalle" in *Crain's Detroit Business* (Vol. 24, October 6, 2008, No. 40, pp. 9)
Pub: Crain Communications, Inc.
Description: Interview with Ron Gatner who is a corporate real estate adviser with the real estate company Jones Lang LaSalle as well as the company's executive vice president and part of the tenant advisory team; Gatner speaks about the impact that the Wall Street crisis is having on the commercial real estate market in Detroit.

16436 ■ "Affordable Again" in *The Business Journal-Serving Greater Tampa Bay* (Vol. 28, July 18, 2008, No. 30, pp. 1)
Pub: American City Business Journals, Inc.
Ed: Janet Leiser. **Description:** Rental rates for office space in the Tampa Bay area has dropped to $21.68 a foot, after demand for the second quarter of 2008 has remained low. Commercial real estate experts say that the industry can easily rebound from what is believed to be the weakest demand in 20 years. Other views, information and statistics on real estate demand and prices in Tampa Bay are, are presented.

16437 ■ "Apartment Ambitions" in *The Business Journal-Portland* (Vol. 25, August 8, 2008, No. 22, pp. 1)
Pub: American City Business Journals, Inc.
Ed: Wendy Culverwell. **Description:** Unico Properties LLC's Asa Flats+Lofts is one of the first of eight high-end apartment projects planned for Portland which will add a total of 2,130 new units to the Pearl District, South Waterfront, and downtown Portland. These apartments charge costs more than $1,600 or more per month over the average rent.

16438 ■ "Apartment Market Down, Not Out" in *Crain's Detroit Business* (Vol. 24, October 6, 2008, No. 40, pp. 9)
Pub: Crain Communications, Inc.
Ed: Daniel Duggan. **Description:** Detroit's apartment market is considered to have some of the strongest fundamentals of any apartment market in the country with relatively low vacancy rates and a relatively low supply of new units compared with demand. Investors continue to show interest in the buildings but the national lending market is making it difficult to invest in the city.

16439 ■ "Aquila HQ Hits the Market" in *The Business Journal-Serving Metropolitan Kansas City* **(Vol. 26, July 25, 2008, No. 46, pp. 1)**
Pub: American City Business Journals, Inc.
Ed: Rob Roberts. **Description:** Commercial real estate experts believe that Aquila Inc.'s former headquarters will be hard to rent out. The historic value of the building, being Kansas City's first skyscraper, is not expected to add value to the price of the rent. Other views and information on the building, as well as on Aquila, are presented.

16440 ■ "Bangles, BMWs Elbow Out Delis and Discount Shops" in *Crain's New York Business* **(Vol. 24, January 14, 2008, No. 2, pp. 35)**
Pub: Crain Communications, Inc.
Ed: Wendy Davis. **Description:** Lured by a growing number of affluent residents and high-earning professionals, a number of upscale retailers have opened locations downtown which is driving up rents and forcing out longtime independent merchants.

16441 ■ "Battelle Given Keys to Group" in *Business First-Columbus* **(October 12, 2007, pp. 1)**
Pub: American City Business Journals, Inc.
Ed: Kevin Kemper. **Description:** Battelle Memorial Institute has been contracted by Compete Columbus to manage the organization's daily operations. Compete Columbus was formerly managed by a single executive, David Powell, who resigned in September 2006. Profile of Compete Columbus is included.

16442 ■ "Block Plans Office Park Along K-10 Corridor" in *The Business Journal-Serving Metropolitan Kansas City* **(Vol. 27, October 3, 2008)**
Pub: American City Business Journals, Inc.
Ed: Rob Roberts. **Description:** Kansas City, Missouri-based Block and Co. is planning to build four office buildings at the corner of College Boulevard and Ridgeview Road in Olathe. Features of the planned development are provided. Comments from executives are also presented.

16443 ■ "Briarcliff Office Building Fills Up Fast" in *The Business Journal-Serving Metropolitan Kansas City* **(Vol. 26, Sept. 5, 2008, pp. 1)**
Pub: American City Business Journals, Inc.
Ed: Rob Roberts. **Description:** Prior to its opening the Hilltop Office Building in Kansas City Missouri has attained 80 percent occupancy. FCStone Group Inc.'s plan to move to the building has boosted the facility's occupancy. Description and dimensions of the office building are also provided.

16444 ■ "Channelside On the Blocks" in *The Business Journal-Serving Greater Tampa Bay* **(Vol. 28, August 29, 2008, No. 36, pp. 1)**
Pub: American City Business Journals, Inc.
Ed: Michael Hinman. **Description:** In a bankruptcy auction for The Place, one of the more visible condominium projects at Channelside, the lowest bid is just below $73 a square foot. KeyBank National Association, the Key Developers Group LLC's lender, leads the auction planned for October 15, 2008. The reason behind the low minimum bid required to participate in the said action is discussed.

16445 ■ "Children's Hospital to Build in New Berlin" in *The Business Journal-Milwaukee* **(Vol. 25, August 1, 2008, No. 45, pp. A1)**
Pub: American City Business Journals, Inc.
Ed: Corrinne Hess. **Description:** Children's Hospital of Wisconsin plans a clinic in the 35-acre medical office park in New Berlin, Wisconsin, owned by Froedtert Memorial Lutheran Hospital and Medical College of Wisconsin Real Estate Ventures LLC. The hospital will be the first major tenant in the park, to be built by Irgens Development Partners LLC.

16446 ■ "Condominium Sales Fall to a Seven-Year Low" in *Crain's Chicago Business* **(Vol. 31, November 10, 2008, No. 45, pp. 2)**
Pub: Crain Communications, Inc.
Ed: Alby Gallun. **Description:** Downtown Chicago condominium market is experiencing the lowest

number of sales in years due to the tightening of the mortgage lending market, the Wall Street crisis and the downturn in the economy. The supply of new condos is soaring, the result of the building boom of 2005 and 2006; many developers are finding it difficult to pay off construction loans and fear foreclosure on their properties. Additional information and statistical data related to the downtown condominium market is provided.

16447 ■ "Cool on Chicago Office Properties" in *Crain's Chicago Business* **(Vol. 31, March 31, 2008, No. 13, pp. 16)**
Pub: Crain Communications, Inc.
Ed: Eddie Baeb. **Description:** Investors predict values on Chicago office buildings to drop 1.3 percent over the next year.

16448 ■ "Cornered by Credit; As $1 Billion in Loans Come Due, Will Landlords Find Funds?" in *Crain's Detroit Business* **(October 6, 2008)**
Pub: Crain Communications, Inc.
Ed: Daniel Duggan. **Description:** Conduit loans are used by many real estate investors and are normally issued in 7- to 10-year terms with balloon payments due at the end, requiring the full balance to be paid upon maturity. Many building owners may find their properties going into foreclosure as these loans mature next year since these loans cannot be extended like typical loans and the credit crisis along with falling property values is making it more difficult to secure new sources of funding. Possible solutions to this problem are also explored.

16449 ■ "Detroit Residential Market Slows; Bright Spots Emerge" in *Crain's Detroit Business* **(Vol. 24, October 6, 2008, No. 40, pp. 11)**
Pub: Crain Communications, Inc.
Ed: Daniel Duggan. **Description:** Discusses the state of the residential real estate market in Detroit; although condominium projects receive the most attention, deals for single-family homes are taking place in greater numbers due to financing issues. Buyers can purchase a single family home with a 3.5 percent down payment compared to 20 percent for some condo deals because of the number of first-time homebuyer programs under the Federal Housing Administration.

16450 ■ "Downtown Evens Tenant Ledger" in *The Business Journal-Serving Metropolitan Kansas City* **(Vol. 26, July 11, 2008, No. 44, pp. 1)**
Pub: American City Business Journals, Inc.
Ed: Rob Roberts. **Description:** Financial services company PricewaterhouseCoopers will relocate its office from the Broadway Square building, but it will not leave downtown as it signs a long-term lease for a 27,000 square feet of space in Town Pavilion. Town Pavilion is the biggest multitenant office building in downtown. Downtown's market competitiveness is also examined.

16451 ■ "East-Side Real Estate Forum Detours To Grand Rapids" in *Crain's Detroit Business* **(Vol. 24, October 6, 2008, No. 40, pp. 17)**
Pub: Crain Communications, Inc.
Ed: Daniel Duggan. **Description:** Tom Wackerman was elected chairman of the University of Michigan-Urban Land Institute Real Estate Forum and proposed that the annual conference be held in Grand Rapids due to the brisk economic activity he was finding there; although the idea was initially met with resistance, the plan to introduce East-siders to the West side began receiving more enthusiasm due to the revitalization of the area, which was once considered to have a bleak outlook. Many are hoping to learn the lessons of those who were able to change a negative economic climate into a positive one in which the cooperation of private business and government can work together to accomplish goals.

16452 ■ "Economy Peddles Rent In This Cycle" in *The Business Journal-Serving Metropolitan Kansas City* **(Vol. 26, August 8, 2008, No. 48)**
Pub: American City Business Journals, Inc.
Ed: Ashlee Kieler. **Description:** Rental demand for apartment units in downtown Kansas City, Missouri,

is increasing due to the housing crisis, lack of real estate development, and increasing popularity of the downtown area. The downtown area has 7,378 multifamily units as of June 2008, of which 4,114 are rentals.

16453 ■ "Eminent Domain Fight Looks Imminent" in *The Business Journal-Serving Metropolitan Kansas City* **(Vol. 26, August 1, 2008, No. 47)**
Pub: American City Business Journals, Inc.
Ed: Rob Roberts. **Description:** Views and information on the proposed constitutional amendments that will limit the use of eminent domain in Missouri, are presented. The proposals are expected to largely ban the taking of private property for private development. It may be included in a November 4,2008 statewide vote for approval.

16454 ■ "For Sale: Old Florida Panache" in *The Business Journal-Serving Greater Tampa Bay* **(Vol. 28, July 4, 2008, No. 28, pp. 1)**
Pub: American City Business Journals, Inc.
Ed: Jane Meinhardt. **Description:** Linger Lodge, owned by real estate investor and developer Martin Kaplan and Senator Michael Bennett, is now on the market for a sealed bid process facilitated by Levin & Associates. The business partners bought the riverfront property for about $3 million in 2005. Other details on the sale of the property are presented.

16455 ■ "Grand Letdown" in *The Business Journal-Milwaukee* **(Vol. 25, September 12, 2008, No. 51, pp. A1)**
Pub: American City Business Journals, Inc.
Ed: Rich Kirchen. **Description:** Overview of retail trade in Milwaukee, Wisconsin is presented. It has been observed that vacancies in storefronts both east and west of the Milwaukee River have increased, and the Shops of Grand Avenue has yet to attract new retailers or shoppers. The completion of the Marquette Interchange is also discussed.

16456 ■ "Home Sprinklers Blocked in Texas, Long Beach, California" in *Contractor* **(Vol. 56, July 2009, No. 7, pp. 1)**
Pub: Penton Media, Inc.
Ed: Robert P. Mader. **Description:** Long Beach, California has exempted older residential high rises and large apartment complexes from a rule to install fire sprinkler systems. Texas has also prohibited municipalities from enacting residential sprinkler ordinances.

16457 ■ "ICC Works on Prescriptive Green Construction Code" in *Contractor* **(Vol. 56, October 2009, No. 10, pp. 1)**
Pub: Penton Media, Inc.
Ed: Robert P. Mader. **Description:** International Code Council launched an initiative to create a green construction code that focuses on existing commercial buildings. The initiative's timeline will include public meetings leading up to a final draft that will be available in 2010.

16458 ■ "Industrial Vacancies Hit High; Economic Downturn Taking Toll on Area's Demand for Space" in *Crain's Chicago Business* **(Apr. 21, 2008)**
Pub: Crain Communications, Inc.
Ed: Alby Gallun. **Description:** Hitting its highest level in four years in the first quarter is the Chicago-area industrial vacancy rate, a sign that the slumping economy is depressing demand for warehouse and manufacturing space.

16459 ■ "The Kitchen is Closed; Eateries Forced Out by Soaring Rents, Declining Revenues" in *Crain's New York Business* **(January 21, 2008)**
Pub: Crain Communications, Inc.
Ed: Lisa Fickenscher. **Description:** Many restaurants have already closed in the area and experts expect many more will follow due to skyrocketing rents and declining revenues.

16460 ■ "Local Industrial Vacancies Climb" in *Crain's Chicago Business* **(Vol. 31, November 17, 2008, No. 46, pp. 18)**
Pub: Crain Communications, Inc.
Ed: Eddie Baeb. **Description:** Demand for local industrial real estate has declined dramatically as

companies that use warehouse and factory space struggle to survive in an ailing economy. According to a report by Colliers Bennett & Kahnweiler Inc., a commercial real estate brokerage, the regional vacancy rate has risen to 9.86 percent in the third quarter, the fourth straight increase and the highest in the past 14 years.

16461 ■ "Look Before You Lease" in *Women Entrepreneur* **(February 3, 2009)**
Pub: Entrepreneur Media Inc.
Ed: Nina L. Kaufman. **Description:** Top issues to consider before leasing an office space are discussed including: additional charges that may be expected on top of the basic rental price; determining both short- and long-term goals; the cost of improvements to the space; the cost of upkeep; and the conditions of the lease.

16462 ■ "Mandel Site Favored For UWM Hall" in *The Business Journal-Milwaukee* **(Vol. 25, September 19, 2008, No. 52, pp. A1)**
Pub: American City Business Journals, Inc.
Description: University of Wisconsin-Milwaukee student residence hall's leading location is a site pushed by Mandel Group Inc. Real estate sources say that the developer's proposal offers the best opportunity for business development and the least conflict with nearby neighborhoods. Plans for the Mandel site are presented.

16463 ■ "Mequon Plan On Tracks, Bucks Housing Trend" in *The Business Journal-Milwaukee* **(Vol. 25, September 26, 2008, No. 53, pp. A1)**
Pub: American City Business Journals, Inc.
Ed: Pete Millard. **Description:** Insight Development Group plans to build condominium units and single-family homes despite the residential market downturn. The Orchard Glen project, a planned development in Mequon, is a $22 million project which will include 38 condos and 12 single-family homes. Details of the project are provided.

16464 ■ "Midtown Tampa Bay Taking Shape" in *The Business Journal-Serving Greater Tampa Bay* **(Vol. 28, September 12, 2008, No. 38, pp. 1)**
Pub: American City Business Journals, Inc.
Ed: Janet Leiser. **Description:** Midtown Tampa Bay's 610,000 square foot shopping and entertainment center is being planned in Florida and is to replace the Tampa Bay One project proposed years earlier. The retail center is to be developed by Bromley Cos. and Opus South Corp. and is expected to have five buildings. Other details about the plan are discussed.

16465 ■ "Millions Needed To Finish First Place" in *The Business Journal-Milwaukee* **(Vol. 25, August 15, 2008, No. 47, pp. A1)**
Pub: American City Business Journals, Inc.
Ed: Rich Kirchen. **Description:** First Place on the River condominium project in Milwaukee, Wisconsin, needs $18.2 million before it can be completed. A total of $6.8 million have already been spent since the project went into receivership on 31 January 2008.

16466 ■ "More Offices Planned For Percheron Square" in *The Business Journal-Milwaukee* **(Vol. 25, August 22, 2008, No. 48, pp. A1)**
Pub: American City Business Journals, Inc.
Ed: Pete Millard. **Description:** More office projects are under way at Percheron Square. Ryan Cos. US Inc., for example, plans to build over 200,000 square feet of office space at the area. Details of new office projects in Wisconsin are presented.

16467 ■ "A New Mix of Tenants Settles In" in *Crain's New York Business* **(Vol. 24, January 14, 2008, No. 2, pp. 26)**
Pub: Crain Communications, Inc.
Ed: Andrew Marks. **Description:** More and more nonfinancial firms are relocating downtown due to the new retailers and restaurants that are reshaping the look and feel of lower Manhattan.

16468 ■ "N.Y. Group Top Bidder for Last Duke Sites" in *Crain's Cleveland Business* **(Vol. 28, November 19, 2007, No. 46, pp. 1)**
Pub: Crain Communications, Inc.
Ed: Stan Bullard. **Description:** Overview of the possible portfolio sale of Duke Realty Corp.'s last Northeast Ohio properties, 14 office buildings in Independence, Seven Hills and North Olmsted, believed to be purchased by a real estate investor group led by Nightingale Properties LLC of New York.

16469 ■ "Part-Time Office Space" in *Hawaii Business* **(Vol. 53, December 2007, No. 6, pp. 132)**
Pub: Hawaii Business Publishing
Ed: Ashley Hamershock. **Description:** My Office is one of the companies that are renting space office not only by the month, but by the hour. Such setup is beneficial to small businesses that do not need a whole office all to themselves, and are interested in cutting the cost of office space rental. The prices of office space in Hawaii are mentioned.

16470 ■ "A Place to Call Home" in *Business Courier* **(Vol. 24, March 7, 2008, No. 48, pp. 1)**
Pub: American City Business Journals, Inc.
Ed: Lucy May. **Description:** Discusses a new type of housing for Cincinnati's chronically homeless that will be developed by the Over-the-Rhine Community Housing Network and the Cincinnati Center City Development Corp. Advocates believe that it is the missing link in the community's efforts to eradicate homelessness. The details of the project are also presented.

16471 ■ "Population Growing Faster Than Retail, Service Sector" in *Crain's New York Business* **(Vol. 24, January 14, 2008, No. 2, pp. 30)**
Pub: Crain Communications, Inc.
Ed: Andrew Marks. **Description:** Downtown Manhattan is seeing more residential development; however, as more families call the area home the need for more retail and services is becoming evident.

16472 ■ *Property Management Association—Directory*
Pub: Property Management Association
Contact: Thomas B. Cohn, Exec. VP
Released: Annual, spring. **Price:** $50, nonmembers. **Covers:** Over 539 property managers and 336 related supplier firms. **Entries Include:** For property managers—Name, firm name, address, phone, fax, specialty. For supplier firms—Company name, name of contact, address, phone, fax. **Arrangement:** Each list is alphabetical. **Indexes:** Supplier product/service.

16473 ■ "Protect Your Assets" in *Black Enterprise* **(Vol. 38, January 2008, No. 6, pp. 38)**
Pub: Earl G. Graves Publishing Co. Inc.
Ed: Trevor Delaney. **Description:** Owner of rental properties seeks advice for incorporating versus getting an LLC for the business.

16474 ■ "Real Estate Vets Take Times In Stride" in *The Business Journal-Serving Metropolitan Kansas City* **(Vol. 26, July 25, 2008, No. 46)**
Pub: American City Business Journals, Inc.
Ed: Rob Roberts. **Description:** Kansas City, Missouri's real estate industry veterans like Allen Block believe that the challenges faced by the industry in the 1980s, when the Federal Reserve Board controlled the money supply to slow down inflation, were worse than the challenges faced today. Other views, trends and information on the real estate industry of the city, are presented.

16475 ■ "Realities May Blur Vision" in *The Business Journal-Serving Metropolitan Kansas City* **(Vol. 27, September 19, 2008, No. 1, pp. 1)**
Pub: American City Business Journals, Inc.
Ed: Rob Roberts. **Description:** Vision Metcalf is a study by Kansas City that depicts how Metcalf Avenue could look like if redeveloped. Redevelopment plans for the Metcalf corridor include a 20-story

mixed-use building on a vacant car dealership. The challenges that the redevelopment plans will face are also analyzed.

16476 ■ "Red Tape Ties Detroit Housing Rehab Plan" in *Crain's Detroit Business* **(Vol. 24, September 22, 2008, No. 38, pp. 1)**
Pub: Crain Communications, Inc.
Ed: Ryan Beene. **Description:** Venture-capital firm Wilherst Oxford LLC is a Florida-based company that has purchased 300 inner-city homes which were in foreclosure in Detroit. Wilherst Oxford is asking the city to forgive the existing tax and utility liens so the firm can utilize the money for home improvements. The city, however, is reluctant but has stated that they are willing to negotiate.

16477 ■ "A Renewal in Rentals" in *Barron's* **(Vol. 88, March 17, 2008, No. 11, pp. 17)**
Pub: Dow Jones & Company, Inc.
Ed: Description: Discusses the projected entry of the estimated 82 million echo-boomers into the rentals market and the influx of immigrants and displaced homeowners which could turn apartments into lucrative investments again. While apartment-building completions rose slowly since 2003, demand is expected to increase steeply until 2015.

16478 ■ "Rental Demand Boosts Revenue for Sun Communities Inc." in *Crain's Detroit Business* **(Vol. 24, March 24, 2008, No. 12, pp. 4)**
Pub: Crain Communications, Inc.
Ed: Daniel Duggan. **Description:** Despite the decline in sales of manufactured homes, demand for rental units and rent-to-own programs have brought Sun Communities Inc. increased revenue. The real estate investment trust, based in Southfield, owns, operates, finances and develops manufactured home communities in the Midwest and Southeast. Statistical data included.

16479 ■ "A Second Chance to Make a Living" in *The Business Journal-Milwaukee* **(Vol. 25, September 19, 2008, No. 52, pp. A1)**
Pub: American City Business Journals, Inc.
Description: Unemployed workers and baby boomers are driving interest in purchasing businesses. BizBuySell general manager Mike Handelsman reveals that the supply of small businesses for sale is decreasing due to the increased demand. The trends in the small business market are analyzed.

16480 ■ "Silverdome Bidders Bring New Proposals" in *Crain's Detroit Business* **(Vol. 24, March 17, 2008, No. 11, pp. 23)**
Pub: Crain Communications, Inc.
Ed: Daniel Duggan. **Description:** Discusses the seven plans which have been proposed as part of the third round of bidding for the Pontiac Silverdome; proposals range from Global Baseball Inc., a baseball league that would pit a team from every country against one another, to an Indian casino, a musical "hall of fame", a convention center, a horse track, a hotel and an indoor water park.

16481 ■ "Sixty-Acre Vision for North Suburbs" in *Business Courier* **(Vol. 24, April 4, 2008, No. 52, pp. 1)**
Pub: American City Business Journals, Inc.
Ed: Laura Baverman. **Description:** Al Neyer Inc. plans for a mixed-use development at the 60-acre site it has recently purchased. The mixed-use project could cost up to $100 million, and will include medical offices, residential buildings, and corporate offices. Details of Al Neyer's plans for the site are given.

16482 ■ "Soured Relationship Plays Out in Courts" in *The Business Journal-Serving Greater Tampa Bay* **(Vol. 28, September 19, 2008, No. 39)**
Pub: American City Business Journals, Inc.
Ed: Janet Leiser. **Description:** Heirs of developer Julian Hawthorne Lifset won a court battle to end a 50-year lease with Specialty Restaurants Corp. in Rocky Point. The decision opens the Tampa Bay prime waterfront property for new development.

16483 ■ "Stars Shine Downtown" in *The Business Journal-Serving Metropolitan Kansas City* **(Vol. 26, August 29, 2008, No. 51, pp. 1)**
Pub: American City Business Journals, Inc.
Ed: Rob Roberts. **Description:** Movie chain AMC Entertainment Inc. renews its lease for 97,000 square feet of space at Ten Main Center. HNTB Federal Services Corp., meanwhile, is to take up 42,000 square feet at an office building located at 120 W. 12th St. The leases' impacts on downtown office market are examined.

16484 ■ "Subprime Problems Loom" in *The Business Journal-Portland* **(Vol. 25, August 29, 2008, No. 25, pp. 1)**
Pub: American City Business Journals, Inc.
Ed: Wendy Culverwell. **Description:** Over half of subprime mortgages in Portland are resetting by the end of 2008, which will cause more problems to the local real estate market. The inventory of unsold homes has also been increasing for over a year. Forecasts for the Portland housing market in relation to mortgage resets are supplied.

16485 ■ "Troy Complex has New Brand, New Leases" in *Crain's Detroit Business* **(Vol. 24, April 14, 2008, No. 15, pp. 32)**
Pub: Crain Communications, Inc.
Ed: Daniel Duggan. **Description:** Discusses the re-branding of the 1.2 million-square-foot collection of office buildings in Troy purchased by New York-based Emmes Co. The firm has also pledged more than $6 million in upgrades, hired a new leasing company and completed 67,000 square feet of leasing with another 100,000 in negotiations.

TRADE PERIODICALS

16486 ■ *Journal of Property Management*
Pub: Institute of Real Estate Management
Contact: Ronald Goss, President
Released: Bimonthly. **Price:** $72.32 Canada; $62.95; $115.50 two years; $110.99 other countries airmail; $169.10 3 years. **Description:** Magazine serving real estate managers.

TRADE SHOWS AND CONVENTIONS

16487 ■ Apartment Association of Metro Denver Seminar and Trade Show
Apartment Association of Metro Denver
3773 Cherry Creek N. Dr., Ste. 1001
Denver, CO 80209
Ph:(303)329-3300
Fax:(303)329-0403
URL: http://www.aamdhq.org
Released: Annual. **Audience:** Trade professionals. **Principal Exhibits:** Apartment management equipment, supplies, and services.

16488 ■ Building Owners and Managers Association International Annual Convention and The Office Building Show
Building Owners and Managers Association International
1201 New York Ave., NW, Ste. 300
Washington, DC 20005
Ph:(202)408-2662
Fax:(202)371-0181
Co. E-mail: meetings@boma.org
URL: http://www.bomaconvention.org
Released: Annual. **Audience:** Owners and managers of office buildings, developers, brokers, and real estate professionals. **Principal Exhibits:** Products, supplies and equipment for the office building industry, including architectural and building hardware, asbestos abatement, building automation, carpeting, control systems, doors, elevators and elevator maintenance, electrical and lighting, environmental services, financial services, fire protection, flooring and floor machines, hazardous waste removal, interior design, landscaping, locks, paper products, parking, pest control, plumbing and fixtures, recycling, renovation and restoration, roofing, security, signage, water treatment, windows.

16489 ■ Columbus Apartment Association Education Conference and Trade Expo
Columbus Apartment Association
1225 Dublin Rd.
Columbus, OH 43215
Ph:(614)488-2115
Fax:(614)488-8526
Co. E-mail: caa@caahq.com
URL: http://www.caahq.com
Released: Annual. **Audience:** Apartment owners, investors, managers, leasing and maintenance personnel. **Principal Exhibits:** Products and services for the apartment industry.

CONSULTANTS

16490 ■ Beer-Wells Real Estate Services Inc.
11311 N Central Expy., Ste. 100
Dallas, TX 75243
Ph:(214)750-5600
Fax:(214)750-5603
Co. E-mail: mbtbwt@aol.com
URL: http://www.beerwells.com
Contact: William K. Wells, President
E-mail: bwells@atsbeerwells.com
Scope: Offers professional counseling on asset management, property management, appraisal, property tax reduction, sales, leasing, investing, workout, problem solving and all areas related to leasing, sales and marketing of commercial real estate. Serves private industries as well as government agencies.

16491 ■ Charles Adler & Son Inc.
2930 Arcona Rd.
PO Box 5297
Mechanicsburg, PA 17050
Ph:(717)766-9745
Fax:(717)766-7027
Contact: Robert A. Adler Jr., Principle
Scope: Counsels clients on the disposition, acquisition, leasing and management of commercial and industrial properties. Also active in planning and land development. Serves corporations, financial institutions, investment groups, government agencies, and attorneys. Currently specializing in health-care, senior living facilities.

16492 ■ Crown Management Inc.
4233 Roanoke Rd., Ste. 200
Kansas City, MO 64111-4076
Ph:(816)756-1084
Fax:(816)756-1188
Co. E-mail: dtcrown@solve.net
Contact: Robert W. Haas, President
Scope: Real estate firm which advises clients regarding the planning, development and management of office buildings, commercial and multi-family properties, and conventional and FHA programs. Services include appraisals, brokerage and property management.

16493 ■ Garrity & Associates
9200 Middlebelt Rd., Ste. 734
PO Box 5338
Livonia, MI 48150-4046
Ph:(734)261-7020
Contact: Stephen Garrity, Principle
Scope: Property management consultants offer assistance full service management and leasing relating to commercial, multiple and industrial real estate. Industries served: real estate, government agencies, and institutions. **Seminars:** New Business Start Up.

16494 ■ Gates, Hudson & Associates Inc.
3020 Hamaker Ct., Ste. 301
Fairfax, VA 22031
Ph:(703)876-9590
Fax:(703)876-0304
Co. E-mail: contact@gateshudson.com
URL: http://www.gateshudson.com
Contact: Steve Larimer, Vice President
E-mail: slarimer@atsgateshudson.com
Scope: Property management consulting firm expertise in financial services; utility management; facility services and information systems. **Publications:** "A British Invasion," Jul, 2009.

16495 ■ GFA Management Inc.
7550 S Meridian St., Ste. A
PO Box 47024
Indianapolis, IN 46247
Ph:(317)346-7156
Free: 877-633-4764
Fax:(317)346-7158
Co. E-mail: gfa7156@aol.com
Contact: George Allen, President
E-mail: gallen@manufactured-housing.net
Scope: Firm offers real estate management consulting, specializing in manufactured home communities. Industries served: manufactured housing, and real estate. **Publications:** "Chapbook of Business and Management Wisdom," PMN Publishing, 2002; "Manufactured Home Community Management," PMN Publishing, 2001; "How to Find, Buy, Manage and Sell a Manufactured Home Community as an Investment," J. Wiley and Sons, 1996; "Development, Marketing and Operation of Manufactured Home Communities," J. Wiley and Co., 1994. **Seminars:** Land Development; Property Management; Sales and Marketing; Manufactured Housing Manager Certification Training and Designation.

16496 ■ Hanford-Freund & Co.
3732 Mount Diablo Blvd., Ste. 160
Lafayette, CA 94549
Ph:(415)981-5780
Free: 800-972-5968
Fax:(415)296-0725
Co. E-mail: info@hanfordfreund.com
URL: http://www.hanfordfreund.com
Contact: Robinson N. Anderson, Vice President
Scope: Specializing in advisory service to clients in real estate investments and financial service, including equity and Marketing, asset management, valuation of real property. evaluation of current assets. Management analysis of problem properties and problem ventures. Workouts of major real estate projects.

16497 ■ Hastings Co.
8414 Braes Meadow Dr.
Houston, TX 77071-1112
Ph:(713)774-4091
Fax:(713)785-0553
Contact: Edmund S. Hastings, CEO
Scope: Property development consultants offering technical, administrative, and business management services. Specializes in small business development worldwide. Serves private industries as well as government agencies.

16498 ■ Investors' Property Services
27042 Towne Centre Dr., Ste. 250
Foothill Ranch, CA 92610
Ph:(949)900-6160
Free: 800-247-4044
Fax:(949)900-6601
Co. E-mail: info@investorshq.com
URL: http://www.investorshq.com
Contact: David Crain III, Vice President
E-mail: bob@atsinvestorshq.com
Scope: Property management consultants offer expertise in third party management and on due diligence property analyses and inspections, market evaluations for office buildings, medical buildings, hotels, motels, shopping centers, apartments, and industrial properties. Also serve as receiver during fore closure examiner in bankruptcy, operating forecasts, budgets and variance analyses. Industries served financial institutions, legal profession, medical, banks, insurance companies, trustees, REITs, pensions and partnerships.

16499 ■ Renal Center
12 Chelsea Ct.
Hillsdale, NJ 07642-1227
Ph:(201)664-4451
Fax:(201)664-1267
Co. E-mail: cncarson@msn.com
Contact: Christopher N. Carson, Principle
Scope: Construction Consulting, Construction Management, Building Management Consulting, Provide Expert Witness Testimony in Dispute Matters. Arbitrator for Alternate Dispute Resolution cases.

FRANCHISES AND BUSINESS OPPORTUNITIES

16500 ■ Parker Finch Management
209 E Baseline Rd., Ste. E208
Tempe, AZ 85283
Free: 877-508-1974
Fax:(480)907-1141
No. of Franchise Units: 8. **No. of Company-Owned Units:** 1. **Founded:** 1993. **Franchised:** 2006. **Description:** Property management services for condos & home owners associations. **Equity Capital Needed:** $65,000-$105,000. **Franchise Fee:** $30,000. **Royalty Fee:** 3%. **Financial Assistance:** No. **Training:** 2 weeks training provided at headquarters and ongoing support.

COMPUTERIZED DATABASES

16501 ■ ABI/INFORM
ProQuest LLC
789 E Eisenhower Pky.
PO Box 1346
Ann Arbor, MI 48106-1346
Ph:(734)761-4700
Free: 800-521-0600
Fax:(734)761-6450
Co. E-mail: info@proquest.com
URL: http://www.proquest.com
Description: Contains approximately 6 million full text or bibliographic citations to articles from more than 800 business and management publications worldwide. **Availability:** Online: Wolters Kluwer Health, ProQuest LLC, ProQuest LLC, Questel SA, STN International, Colorado Alliance of Research Libraries, Financial Times Ltd., LexisNexis Group, ProQuest LLC. **Type:** Full text; Bibliographic; Image.

LIBRARIES

16502 ■ California Department of Housing and Community Development–Housing Resource Center
PO Box 952053
1800 3rd St.
Sacramento, CA 94252-2053
Ph:(916)322-9648
Fax:(916)327-2643
Co. E-mail: jtochterman@hcd.ca.gov
URL: http://www.hcd.ca.gov/hpd/biblio.html
Contact: Joel Tochterman, MLS, Ed.
Scope: Housing, planning, community development, redevelopment, land use. **Services:** Center open to the public with restrictions. **Holdings:** 4000 reports. **Subscriptions:** 175 journals.

16503 ■ Housing Association of Delaware Valley Library
1528 Walnut St., Ste. 1000
Philadelphia, PA 19102
Ph:(215)545-6010
Fax:(215)790-9132
Co. E-mail: info@hadv.org
URL: http://www.hadv.org
Scope: Housing, urban development, city/regional planning, zoning, law, local government. **Services:** Copying; Library open to the public. **Holdings:** 1000 books; 2000 pamphlets. **Subscriptions:** 50 journals and other serials; 8 newspapers.

16504 ■ Steven Winter Associates, Inc. Library
50 Washington St., 6th Fl.
Norwalk, CT 06854
Ph:(203)857-0200
Fax:(203)852-0741
Co. E-mail: swa@swinter.com
URL: http://www.swinter.com
Contact: Helki Roundtree, Lib.Hd.
Scope: Housing technology, energy conservation, engineering, construction technology, LEED consulting **Services:** Library not open to the public. **Holdings:** 2008 books; 1200 bound periodical volumes; 700 microfiche. **Subscriptions:** 356 journals and other serials.

16505 ■ U.S. Dept. of Housing and Urban Development–Southeast/Caribbean Library
Five Points Plaza Bldg.
40 Marietta St., NW
Atlanta, GA 30303-2812
Ph:(404)331-5001
Fax:(404)331-4089
URL: http://www.hud.gov/local/index.
  cfm?state=ga&topic=library
Contact: Sue H. Barron, Dir.
Scope: Housing, planning, urban development, economic analysis, law, statistics. **Services:** Library open to the public for reference use only. **Holdings:** 17,000 books; 87 bound periodical volumes; Federal Register, 1967 to present (microfilm); 12 VF drawers.

ASSOCIATIONS AND OTHER ORGANIZATIONS

16506 ■ Agricultural Relations Council
PO Box 156
New Prague, MN 56071
Ph:(952)758-5811
Fax:(952)758-5813
Co. E-mail: arc@gardnerandgardnercommunications.com
URL: http://www.agrelationscouncil.org
Contact: Mr. Den Gardner, Exec. Dir.
Description: Professional society of agricultural public relations executives employed by private business firms, associations, publications, and government agencies. Operates placement service. **Publications:** *ARClight* (quarterly).

16507 ■ Canadian Public Relations Society–Societe Canadienne des Relations Publiques
4195 Dundas St. W, Ste. 346
Toronto, ON, Canada M8X 1Y4
Ph:(416)239-7034
Fax:(416)239-1076
Co. E-mail: admin@cprs.ca
URL: http://www.cprs.ca
Contact: Ms. Karen Dalton, Exec. Dir.
Description: Public relations professionals. Seeks to advance the practice of public relations; promotes ongoing professional development of members. Serves as a forum for the exchange of information among members; sponsors research and educational programs.

16508 ■ Public Relations Society of America
33 Maiden Ln., 11th Fl.
New York, NY 10038-5150
Ph:(212)460-1400
Fax:(212)995-0757
Co. E-mail: william.murray@prsa.org
URL: http://www.prsa.org
Contact: William Murray, Pres./COO
Description: Professional society of public relations practitioners in business and industry, counseling firms, government, associations, hospitals, schools, and nonprofit organizations. Conducts professional development programs. Maintains a Professional Resource Center. Offers accreditation program. **Publications:** *Public Relations Tactics* (monthly).

16509 ■ Public Relations Student Society of America
33 Maiden Ln., 11th Fl.
New York, NY 10038-5150
Ph:(212)460-1474
Fax:(212)995-0757
Co. E-mail: prssa@prsa.org
URL: http://www.prssa.org
Contact: Adam Aisner, Pres.
Description: Professionally oriented student association organized to cultivate a favorable and mutually advantageous relationship between students and professional public relations practitioners. Fosters understanding of public relations theories and procedures; encourages students to adhere to high ideals and principles of public relations. .

DIRECTORIES OF EDUCATIONAL PROGRAMS

16510 ■ *Who's Who in the Media and Communications*
Pub: Marquis Who's Who L.L.C.
Covers: More than 18,500 professionals in print journalism, broadcasting, publishing, television, public relations, advertising, radio, telecommunications, interactive multimedia, and education. **Entries Include:** Biographical data.

REFERENCE WORKS

16511 ■ "1914 Proved to Be Key Year for Chevy" in *Automotive News* (Vol. 86, October 31, 2011, No. 6488, pp. S18)
Pub: Crain Communications Inc.
Ed: Jamie Lareau. **Description:** Chevy Bow Tie emblem was born in 1914, creating the brand's image that has carried through to current days.

16512 ■ "Another California Firm On Way" in *Austin Business Journal* (Vol. 31, May 6, 2011, No. 9, pp. 1)
Pub: American City Business Journals Inc.
Ed: Christopher Calnan. **Description:** Main Street Hub Inc. is planning to build a facility in Austin, Texas. The company helps businesses manage their online reputations. Main Street has selected Aquila Commercial LLC as its real estate broker.

16513 ■ *Birthing the Elephant: The Woman's Go-for-It! Guide to Overcoming the Big Challenges of Launching a Business*
Pub: Ten Speed Press
Ed: Karin Abarbanel; Bruce Freeman. **Released:** March 2008. **Price:** $15.95. **Description:** Advice for women entrepreneurs is given. The book explores the emotional challenges faced by women starting businesses, along with advice for reshaping image. This handbook helps women survive and succeed in business.

16514 ■ "Brand Imaging" in *Small Business Opportunities* (November 2010)
Pub: Harris Publications Inc.
Ed: Karen Harnesk. **Description:** Design and branding pro shares strategies and tips to help guide any small business' image development.

16515 ■ "The Buck Stops Here" in *Canadian Business* (Vol. 81, November 10, 2008, No. 19, pp. 25)
Pub: Rogers Media Ltd.
Ed: Sarka Halas. **Description:** Reputation strategist Leslie Gaines-Ross says that minimizing the damage followed by the identification of what went wrong are the first steps that companies need to take when trying to salvage their reputation. Gaines-Ross states that it is up to the CEO to ensure the company's speedy recovery and they need to be at the forefront of the process.

16516 ■ "Deskside Story: As the Latest Buzzword Suggests, PR Firms Are Happy To Drop By" in *Inc.* (December 2007, pp. 70, 73)
Pub: Gruner & Jahr USA Publishing
Ed: Nitasha Tiku. **Description:** Setting up a meeting between a company's CEO and a journalist is known as deskside and is becoming popular again whereby a publicist offers clients deskside visits, briefings and alerts to help promote public relations for a company.

16517 ■ "Empowered" in *Harvard Business Review* (Vol. 88, July-August 2010, No. 7-8, pp. 94)
Pub: Harvard Business School Publishing
Ed: Josh Bernoff, Ted Schadler. **Description:** HERO concept (highly empowered and resourceful operative) which builds a connection between employees, managers, and IT is outlined. The resultant additional experience and knowledge gained by employees improves customer relationship management.

16518 ■ "Hopkins' Security, Reputation Face Challenges in Wake of Slaying" in *Baltimore Business Journal* (Vol. 28, August 6, 2010, No. 13)
Pub: Baltimore Business Journal
Ed: Gary Haber. **Description:** The slaying of Johns Hopkins University researcher Stephen Pitcairn has not tarnished the reputation of the elite school in Baltimore, Maryland among students. Maintaining Hopkins' reputation is important since it is Baltimore's largest employer with nearly 32,000 workers. Insights on the impact of the slaying among the Hopkins' community are also given.

16519 ■ *If You Have to Cry, Go Outside: And Other Things Your Mother Never Told You*
Pub: HarperOne
Ed: Kelly Cutrone. **Released:** February 2, 2010. **Price:** $22.99. **Description:** Women's mentor advices on how to make it in one of the most competitive industries in the world, fashion. She has kicked people out of fashion shows, forced some of reality television's shiny start to fire their friends, and built her own company which is one of the most powerful public relations firms in the fashion business.

16520 ■ "Increasing Building Work at Ryan Cos." in *Crain's Chicago Business* (Vol. 34, May 23, 2011, No. 21, pp. 6)
Pub: Crain Communications Inc.
Ed: Eddie Baeb. **Description:** Profile of Tim Hennelly, who is working to make Ryan Company known as a pure builder rather than a developer-builder.

16521 ■ "It's Time to Take Full Responsibility" in *Harvard Business Review* (Vol. 88, October 2010, No. 10, pp. 42)
Pub: Harvard Business School Publishing
Ed: Rosabeth Moss Kanter. **Description:** A case for corporate responsibility is cited, focusing on long-term impact and the effects of public accountability.

16522 ■ *Media, Organizations and Identity*
Pub: Palgrave Macmillan
Ed: Lilie Chouliaraki, Mette Morsing. **Released:** January 19, 2010. **Price:** $90.00. **Description:** The mass media, press and television are a essential in the formation of corporate identity and the promotion of business image and reputation. This book offers a new perspective into the interrelationships between media and organizations over three dimensions: media as business, media in business and business in the media.

16523 ■ *O'Dwyer's Directory of Public Relations Firms*
Pub: J.R. O'Dwyer Company Inc.
Contact: Fraser P. Seitel, Sen. Ed.
E-mail: yusake@aol.com
Released: Annual, Latest edition 2011. **Price:** $95, individuals. **Covers:** Over 1,600 public relations firms; international coverage. **Entries Include:** Firm name, address, phone, principal executives, branch and overseas offices, billings, date founded, and 7,750 clients are cross-indexed. **Arrangement:** Geographical by country. **Indexes:** Specialty (beauty and fashions, finance/investor, etc.), geographical, client.

16524 ■ "Optima Public Relations Gains Partners" in *Alaska Business Monthly* (Vol. 27, October 2011, No. 10, pp. 10)
Pub: Alaska Business Publishing Company
Ed: Nancy Pounds. **Description:** OPrima Public Relations has partnered with Gogerty Marriott of Seattle and Seattle Design Group.

16525 ■ *Public Relations Tactics—Member Services Directory—The Blue Book*
Pub: Public Relations Society of America
Contact: William Murray, President
Released: Annual, latest edition 2007. **Covers:** PRSA members—headquaters, staff contacts, and chapter, section, and district information. **Entries Include:** Name, professional affiliation and title, address, phone, membership rank. **Arrangement:** Alphabetical. **Indexes:** Geographical, organizational.

16526 ■ "Reputation Warfare" in *Harvard Business Review* (Vol. 88, December 2010, No. 12, pp. 70)
Pub: Harvard Business School Publishing
Ed: Leslie Gaines-Ross. **Description:** Steps are presented for addressing attacks on corporate public image. These include responding promptly, avoiding disproportionate displays of force, empowering employees to present the firm's position, and stockpiling credentials to bolster credence.

16527 ■ "Timberland's CEO On Standing Up to 65,000 Angry Activists" in *Harvard Business Review* (Vol. 88, September 2010, No. 9, pp. 39)
Pub: Harvard Business School Publishing
Ed: Jeff Swartz. **Description:** Timberland Company avoided a potential boycott by taking a two-way approach. It addressed a supplier issue that posed a threat to the environment, and launched an email campaign to keep Greenpeace activists informed of the development of a new supplier agreement.

16528 ■ "To Be Seen Is to Be Successful" in *Pet Product News* (Vol. 64, December 2010, No. 12, pp. 12)
Pub: BowTie Inc.
Ed: David Arvin. **Description:** Guidelines on how pet business retailers can boost customer visibility are described considering that complacency could hamper retailers' efforts to effectively market their businesses. To enhance customer base and stand out from competing businesses, being different, strategic, creative, and differentiated is emphasized.

16529 ■ "Vanity Plates" in *Canadian Business* (Vol. 82, April 27, 2009, No. 7, pp. 26)
Pub: Rogers Media
Ed: Andy Holloway. **Description:** Politicians in the U.S. called for the review of firms that availed of the bailout money but are under deals for naming rights of sports stadiums. Angus Reid's Corporate Reputation and Sponsorship Index found for example, that

there is little correlation between sponsoring arenas on having a better brand image. It is suggested that firms who enter these deals build closer to people's homes.

16530 ■ "Voice: Rebuilding Trust" in *Business Strategy Review* (Vol. 21, Summer 2010, No. 2, pp. 79)
Pub: Wiley-Blackwell
Ed: David De Cremer. **Description:** The financial world's attempts to rebuild trust are charted. Three steps to jump-start that process are outlined.

16531 ■ "'We Had to Won the Mistakes'" in *Harvard Business Review* (Vol. 88, July-August 2010, No. 7-8, pp. 108)
Pub: Harvard Business School Publishing
Ed: Adi Ignatius. **Description:** Interview with Howard Schultz, CEO of Starbucks, covers topics that include investment in retraining, the impact of competition, premium quality, authenticity, customer services, strategy development, work-and-life issues, and international presence.

16532 ■ *When the Headline Is You: An Insider's Guide to Handling the Media*
Pub: Jossey-Bass
Ed: Jeff Ansell, Jeff Lesson. **Price:** $29.95. **Description:** How-to guide for executives and other professionals whose high-visibility requires frequent interviews with the media. Tested techniques, tools, and insights for how to respond to all types of media in tough situation are provided. The books also reveals the lessons learned and the pitfalls to avoid by referencing actual news stores from around the world and provides exercises for readers who wish to sharpen their media-handling skills.

TRADE PERIODICALS

16533 ■ *Bulldog Reporter Business Media–Media Pro*
Pub: Infocom Group
Contact: Stephen Beale, News Editor
E-mail: sbeale@infocomgroup.com
Ed: Megan Caluza, Editor, mcaluza@infocomgroup.com. **Released:** Semimonthly. **Price:** $649. **Description:** Covers U.S. news media for public relations professionals. Recurring features include interviews, media contact lists, and media personnel changes.

16534 ■ *The Counselor*
Pub: The Counselor
Ed: Steve Erickson, Editor. **Released:** 6/year. **Description:** Reports on membership news and other public relations topics.

16535 ■ *The Gauge*
Pub: Delahaye Medialink
Contact: Katharine Delahaye Paine, Publisher
E-mail: kpaine@delahaye.com
Ed: William Teunis Paarlberg, Editor, wpaarlberg@aol.com. **Released:** Bimonthly. **Price:** $75. **Description:** Provides information on and evaluates marketing communications activities of companies. Recurring features include interviews, news of research, and a calendar of events.

16536 ■ *Lifestyle Media-Relations Reporter–Media Pro*
Pub: Infocom Group
Ed: Meghan Collins, Editor. **Released:** Semimonthly. **Price:** $439. **Description:** Covers lifestyle/consumer media for public relations professionals. Recurring features include interviews.

16537 ■ *Public Relations Review*
Pub: Elsevier Science Inc.
Ed: Ray E. Hiebert, Editor, hiebert@umd.edu. **Released:** 5/yr. **Price:** $71,100 institutions for Japan; $599 institutions, other countries; $534 institutions for European countries and Iran; $162 for European countries and Iran; $181 other countries; $21,500 Japan. **Description:** Communications journal covering public relations education, government, survey research, public policy, history, and bibliographies.

16538 ■ *Public Relations Tactics*
Pub: Public Relations Society of America
Contact: John Elsasser, Editor-in-Chief
E-mail: john.elsasser@prsa.org
Released: Monthly. **Price:** $100; $110 Canada; $120 other countries; $24 students non-PRSSA members. **Description:** Trade newspaper covering public relations.

16539 ■ *The Publicity Hound*
Pub: Joan Stewart
Contact: Joan Stewart, Publisher
E-mail: jstewart@publicityhound.com
Released: Weekly. **Price:** Free internet service. **Description:** Provides techniques and strategies on self-promotion and inexpensive publicity. Recurring features include letters to the editor, interviews, news of research, book reviews, news of educational opportunities, notices of publications available, and columns titled Advice From Media People, Seasonal Story Ideas, Resource Page, Success Stories, and Media Insider Secrets. Does not report public relations agency staff changes.

VIDEOCASSETTES/AUDIOCASSETTES

16540 ■ *Building a Profitable Consulting Practice Series*
Instructional Video
2219 C St.
Lincoln, NE 68502
Ph:(402)475-6570
Free: 800-228-0164
Fax:(402)475-6500
Co. E-mail: feedback@insvideo.com
URL: http://www.insvideo.com
Description: Two-part business educational series by Howard Shenson offers tips on how to build a profitable consulting practice. Covers consulting opportunities, market strategies, proposal writing, contracting strategies, fee setting, disclosure, and collection techniques. **Availability:** VHS.

CONSULTANTS

16541 ■ Ashland Group L.P.
11550 Fuqua St., Ste. 560
Houston, TX 77034
Ph:(281)484-1700
Free: 800-684-2246
Fax:(281)484-1822
Co. E-mail: info@ashlandgroup.com
URL: http://www.ashlandgroup.com
Contact: Randy Casey, Managing Partner
E-mail: rcasey@ashlandgroup.com
Scope: Government and political affairs agency that specializes in government relations, advocacy communications, media relations, campaign management and government contract lobbying. Offers creative and innovative tax issues. **Publications:** "State Tax Guide," Jan, 2009; "State Tax Guide," Jan, 2007.

16542 ■ Campaign Solutions
118 N St. Asaph St.
Alexandria, VA 22314
Ph:(703)684-3435
Fax:(703)684-3758
Co. E-mail: cs@campaignsolutions.com
URL: http://www.campaignsolutions.com
Contact: Timothy Nurnberger, Principle
E-mail: mtp@atscampaignsolutions.com
Scope: Republican campaign consultants. Brings a breadth and depth of knowledge and experience not found in any other republican voter contact and communications firm. **Seminars:** Absolutely Interactive e-marketing Solution.

16543 ■ Capitol City Services Inc.
1865 Lamplight Dr.
PO Box 25038
Woodbury, MN 55125-0038
Ph:(651)702-2533
Fax:(651)204-1668
Contact: Billy Watkins, Principle
Scope: Information gathering, document retrieval, monitoring, research and reporting service.

16544 ■ Coyne Associates
4010 E Lake St.
Minneapolis, MN 55406-2201
Ph:(612)724-1188
Fax:(612)722-1379
Contact: Sandra Blanton, Principle
Scope: A marketing and public relations consulting firm that specializes in assisting architectural, engineering, and contractor/developer firms. Services include: marketing plains and audits, strategic planning, corporate identity, turnarounds, and sales training.

16545 ■ The Da Vinci Group
18512 Bear Creek Terr.
Leesburg, VA 20176
Ph:(703)669-5862
Fax:(703)669-5863
Co. E-mail: dvg@aol.com
URL: http://www.davincigroup.org
Contact: Ashok Rattehalli, Mgr
E-mail: ashok9382@atsyahoo.com
Scope: A full service consulting firm. Capabilities include government relations, public affairs, public relations, and corporate development.

16546 ■ Democracy Data & Communications L.L.C.
44 Canal Center Plz., Ste. 200
Alexandria, VA 22314-1542
Ph:(703)684-9690
Fax:(703)683-9626
Co. E-mail: info@democracydata.com
Contact: Gary Pruce, VP of Operations
E-mail: wmb@atsdemocracydata.com
Scope: Provides grassroots technology solutions and online database management.

16547 ■ Donna Cornell Enterprises Inc.
68 N Plank Rd., Ste. 204
Newburgh, NY 12550-2122
Ph:(845)565-0088
Free: 888-769-3792
Fax:(845)565-0084
Co. E-mail: rc@cornellcareercenter.com
Contact: Donna Cornell, President
E-mail: rc@cornellcareercenter.com
Scope: Offers services in career consultant, professional search, job placement and national professional search. **Publications:** "The Power of the Woman Within"; "Juggling it All!"; "Journey: A Woman's Guide to Success"; "Shatter the Traditions".

16548 ■ Fletcher Rowley Riddle Inc.
223 Rosa Parks Blvd., Ste. 300
Nashville, TN 37203
Ph:(615)329-9559
Fax:(615)329-9633
Co. E-mail: info@frcr.biz
URL: http://www.frrmedia.com
Contact: Kati Anderson, Dir of Operations
E-mail: rowley@frrmedia.com
Scope: Media consulting includes conceptualization, writing, directing and production supervision of television and radio spots; media market surveys, timebuying and placement; theme and message development; categorical media budgets and paid media plans; coordination of campaign communications. Editorial board preparation; debate preparation; crisis management; preparation of free media plans and providing media relations advice; speech writing and debate coaching. **Seminars:** Campaigns & Elections Magazine Campaign.

16549 ■ Guy Rodgers & Associates Inc.
748 Montebello Cir.
PO Box 9123
Chesapeake, VA 23322-7257
Ph:(757)686-0088
Free: 800-636-8683
Fax:(757)382-9095
Co. E-mail: graa@acninc.net
Contact: Guy Rodgers, Owner
E-mail: graa@pinn.net
Scope: Legislative and campaign consulting, grassroots and coalition development, fund raising, and political training.

16550 ■ The Harwood Institute for Public Innovation
4915 St. Elmo Ave., Ste. 402
Bethesda, MD 20814
Ph:(301)656-3669
Fax:(301)656-0533
Co. E-mail: thi@theharwoodinstitute.org
URL: http://www.theharwoodinstitute.org
Contact: Brad Rourke, Principle
E-mail: brourke@atstheharwoodinstitute.org
Scope: Works to understand the essence of society's complex challenges and understands how to create effective action. **Publications:** "Hope Unraveled: The People's Retreat and Our Way Back," Kettering Foundation Press; "Public Engagement and School Facilities Conversation Workbook," 2004; "Telling Stories of Self-Trust and Hope: A Tool for Engaging Youth in Community Change," 2003; "Making it Real: How to Make Civic Engagement a Public Sensibility," 2003; "New Political Covenant: America's Aspirations for Political Conduct," 2002; "Public Engagement and Small Schools Conversation Guide," 2002; "Creating A New Story: Flint's Struggle to Move Forward," 2001. **Seminars:** Devotion: Declaring Our Intentions in Public Life; Creating A New Public Story; Originating Civic Faith and Self-Trust in America; Moving From a Flat World to a Round World in Public Life; The Public Realm: Where America Must Address Its Concerns.

16551 ■ The Hathaway Group Inc.
1010 Pendleton St.
Alexandria, VA 22314-1837
Ph:(703)837-1818
Fax:(703)837-1822
Contact: Timothy Hathaway, President
E-mail: trh@thehathawaygroup.com
Scope: Political consultant whose services includes voter and databases, network design and administration, web site creation, maintenance and hosting, and fax broadcasting.

16552 ■ The K.S. Giniger Company Inc.
1045 Park Ave.
New York, NY 10028
Ph:(212)369-6692
Fax:(212)269-6692
Co. E-mail: bernicecullinan@verizon.net
Contact: Kenneth Seeman Giniger, President
Scope: Consultants on book publishing to publishers of books, magazines and newsletters, direct sales organizations, government agencies, educational organizations, financial and investment institutions; public relations and advertising agencies. Clients in the United States, Canada, Mexico, England, Denmark, France, Spain, Switzerland, Germany, Israel, Singapore and Australia.

16553 ■ Matson & Associates
7831 Western Ct. SE
Olympia, WA 98501-6839
Ph:(360)956-9694
Fax:(360)754-8114
Co. E-mail: matsonassoc@olywa.net
URL: http://www.matsonassociates.com
Contact: Linda W. Matson, Principle
E-mail: lmatson@matsonassociates.com
Scope: Consulting in the areas of: strategic planning, issue management, needs analysis, political action, campaign consulting, campaign management, fund raising and custom-designed education and recruitment programs. **Seminars:** Politics. . .A Cost of Doing Business; Political Action Committee Development; Coalition Building; Keystone Conference; Activist/Advocate Training.

16554 ■ The Media Guys Inc.
7436 E Stetson Dr., Ste. 290
Scottsdale, AZ 85251
Ph:(480)784-4890
Free: (866)784-4890
Fax:(480)784-4999
Co. E-mail: info@mediaguys.tv
URL: http://www.mediaguys.tv
Contact: Marissa Morabito, Mgr
Scope: A strategic communications firm specializing in public affairs and issues management. Expertise in social marketing, strategic communications and political campaigns.

16555 ■ Midwest Computer Group L.L.C.
6060 Franks Rd.
House Springs, MO 63051-1101
Ph:(636)677-0287
Fax:(636)677-0287
Co. E-mail: sales@mcgcomputer.com
URL: http://www.mcgcomputer.com
Contact: Jeffrey A. Sanford, Mgr
E-mail: jeffrey@atsmcgcomputer.com
Scope: Firm specializes in helping businesses create accounting, marketing and business information systems; software development; and database design and management.

16556 ■ R.E. Moulton Inc.
50 Doaks Ln.
Marblehead, MA 01945
Ph:(781)631-1325
Fax:(781)631-2165
Co. E-mail: mike_lee@remoultoninc.com
URL: http://www.oneamerica.com/wps/wcm/connect/REMoulton
Contact: Reynolds E. Moulton Jr., Chairman of the Board
E-mail: dick@atsremoultoninc.com
Scope: Offers underwriting services, marketing solutions, claims administration and adjudication; policy and commission administration; and risk management solutions to clients. Supplementary service s include risk management and employee assistance. Clients include individuals, business men, employers and finance professionals.

16557 ■ ReCourses Inc.
6101 Stillmeadow Dr.
Nashville, TN 37211-6518
Ph:(615)831-2277
Free: 888-476-5884
Fax:(615)831-2212
Co. E-mail: info@recourses.com
URL: http://www.recourses.com
Contact: David C. Baker, Principle
E-mail: david@recourses.com
Scope: A management consulting firm that works exclusively with small service providers in the communications industry, including public relations firms, advertising agencies, interactive companies and design studios. Services include Total Business Review, a complete examination of your business starting with an on site examination or discussion, followed by written recommendations and then supplemented with six months of implementation guidance. Areas reviewed include positioning, marketing, management, personnel, structure, finance, retirement, technology and specific growth issues. **Publications:** "Managing (Right) for the First Time". **Seminars:** Managing Client Relationships; Research and Strategy; Financial Management: Measuring and Enhancing Performance in a Marketing Firm, Sep, 2009; Building and Leading a Staff: The When, How, and What of Growth and Culture, Sep, 2009; Doing Effective Work: Adding Significance to the Strategic Portion of Your Work for Clients, Sep, 2009; Resourcing the Creative Process: Managing Pricing, Deadlines, Budgets, Quality, and Capacity, Apr, 2009. **Special Services:** ReCourses[R].

16558 ■ The Rothschild Image
13900 Tahiti Way, Ste. 308
Marina del Rey, CA 90292
Ph:(310)574-6018
Co. E-mail: info@rothschildimage.com
URL: http://www.rothschildimage.com
Contact: Ashley Rothschild, CEO
E-mail: ashley@rothschildimage.com
Scope: Image consultant offering advice through group exercises, lectures, wardrobe, and hair and makeup makeovers on how to discover the key components of a winning image. Specializes in designing the images of power brokers, politicians, and entrepreneurs, as well as clients at the start of their careers. **Publications:** "Is There an O'Neal Family Curse? - ABC News," Feb, 2007; "Can an Image Consultant Help You Dress for Success? - Wall Street Journal," Feb, 2006; "Reality Check - Paris Hilton & Amber Moore," Jan, 2004; "Britney's Mystery Man - Britney Spears," Dec, 2003; "People who need to redo their image," Jun, 2003; "Reshaping an Im-

age," Jun, 2003; "Dress to Impress the World International Business Fashion," Apr, 2003. **Seminars:** S.T. A.R.POWER: A Professional Image Consultant Training Program.

16559 ■ Smith, Dawson & Andrews
1150 Connecticut Ave. NW, Ste. 1025
Washington, DC 20036
Ph:(202)835-0740
Free: (866)482-2395
Fax:(202)775-8526
Co. E-mail: jims@sda-inc.com
URL: http://www.sda-inc.com
Contact: Michael Alvarez Jr., Principle
E-mail: billn@atssda-inc.com
Scope: A government relations/public affairs firm specializing in public policy, communications, legislative strategy and business development.

16560 ■ Sol Abrams Public Relations Counsel & Marketing Consultants
331 Webster Dr.
New Milford, NJ 07646
Ph:(201)262-4111
Fax:(201)262-7669
Contact: Sol Abrams, Owner
E-mail: solbabrams@aol.com
Scope: Independent consulting provides publicity, public relations and marketing counsel and services to management of private and public enterprises. Also serves as public relations consultants to other public relations consulting firms, advertising agencies and marketing companies. Provides expert witness services involving public relations. Also lectures, trains, teaches, and conducts seminars in public relations and marketing. Industries served: Corporate management, businesses large and small including real estate, construction, entertainment, food, fashion, fundraising, automotive, aviation, franchising, government agencies, and nonprofit organizations. **Seminars:** How to Select a Public Relations Firm; Publicity and Promotion for Small Business Owner; Expose Yourself - Don't Be a Secret Agent -Increase Your Sales, Incomes, Images, Publicity, Profits and Prestige via Professional Public Relations.

16561 ■ Stelle & Associates Inc.
4137 S 87th E Ave.
PO Box 470071
Tulsa, OK 74145
Ph:(918)425-4277
Fax:(918)622-2206
Co. E-mail: scott@stelleassociates.com
URL: http://www.stelleassociates.com
Contact: J. Scott Stelle, President
E-mail: scott@stelleassociates.com
Scope: Consulting consortium which allows highly qualified and experienced specialists an opportunity to function singly or in conjunction with others on projects of any size or duration. Has developed several levels of environmental due diligence to fulfill the need of clients in the most cost effective manner.

16562 ■ Stevens, Reed, Curcio and Potholm
201 N Union St., Ste. 200
Alexandria, VA 22314
Ph:(703)683-8326
Fax:(703)683-8826
Co. E-mail: pcurcio@srcpmedia.com
URL: http://www.srcpmedia.com
Contact: Jay Payne, Vice President
E-mail: epotholm@atssrcpmedia.com
Scope: Republican media consulting firm that specializes in media production, public opinion research, direct mail design, opposition research and political strategy.

16563 ■ The Tarrance Group
201 N Union St., Ste. 410
Alexandria, VA 22314
Ph:(703)684-6688
Fax:(703)836-8256
Co. E-mail: tarrance@tarrance.com
URL: http://www.tarrance.com
Contact: Brian Nienaber, Vice President
E-mail: bnienaber@atstarrance.com
Scope: Specializes in research and international polling. Services include: political polling/political campaign consulting, corporate affairs, reputation management, issue advocacy, national political and environment research.

16564 ■ Triad Strategies
116 Pine St.
Harrisburg, PA 17101
Ph:(717)238-2970
Fax:(717)238-2390
Co. E-mail: jconnovitch@triadstrategies.com
URL: http://www.triadstrategies.com
Contact: Michael J. Acker, Senior VP
E-mail: macker@atstriadstrategies.com
Scope: Government relations firm. Services include legislative and regulatory monitoring, legislative and executive branch lobbying, independent and quasi-public agency lobbying, issue research, issue management, grassroots organizing, public relations, strategic planning, and network marketing.

LIBRARIES

16565 ■ Burson-Marsteller Knowledge Center
230 Park Ave. S.
New York, NY 10003
Ph:(212)614-4000
Fax:(212)598-5320
Co. E-mail: tony.telloni@bm.com
URL: http://www.burson-marsteller.com/default.aspx
Contact: Tony Telloni, Mgr.
Scope: Advertising, public relations, marketing research. **Services:** Interlibrary loan; Library open to clients and librarians. **Holdings:** 1000 books. **Subscriptions:** 100 journals and other serials.

16566 ■ University of Illinois at Urbana-Champaign—Communications Library
1st Fl. Gregory Hall, Rm. 122
810 S. Wright St.
Urbana, IL 61801
Ph:(217)333-2216
Fax:(217)333-2214
Co. E-mail: l-romero@illinois.edu
URL: http://www.library.illinois.edu/cmx/
Contact: Lisa Romero, Libn.
Scope: Advertising, broadcasting, journalism, magazines, newspapers, public relations, communication theory, mass communications, media studies. **Services:** Interlibrary loan; Library open to the public with permit from Main Library. **Holdings:** 16,000 books; 5 million advertisements; 400 videos. **Subscriptions:** 267 journals and other serials; 27 newspapers.

16567 ■ University of Missouri—Columbia–Frank Lee Martin Memorial Journalism Library
102 Donald W. Reynolds Journalism Institute
Columbia, MO 65211
Ph:(573)882-7502
Fax:(573)884-4963
Co. E-mail: carnerd@missouri.edu
URL: http://mulibraries.missouri.edu/Journalism/
Contact: Dorothy Carner, Hd., Journalism Lib.
Scope: Advertising, marketing, broadcasting, journalism, magazines, news writing and management, newspaper publishing, photojournalism, public relations, semantics, typography, graphic design, linotype, mass communication, International journalism, history. **Services:** Interlibrary loan; copying; Library open to the public with restrictions. **Holdings:** 50,000 books; 9000 bound periodical volumes. **Subscriptions:** 300 journals and newspapers.

ASSOCIATIONS AND OTHER ORGANIZATIONS

16568 ■ Affiliated Warehouse Companies
PO Box 295
Hazlet, NJ 07730-0295
Ph:(732)739-2323
Fax:(732)739-4154
Co. E-mail: sales@awco.com
URL: http://www.awco.com
Description: Represents franchised public merchandise warehouse companies united for national sales work, advertising, and public relations. Assists in gathering rates and data pertaining to warehousing and distribution. Offers free consultation services to industry. Maintains placement service; compiles statistics. .

16569 ■ American Chain of Warehouses
156 Flamingo Dr.
Beecher, IL 60401-9725
Ph:(708)946-9792
Fax:(708)946-9793
Co. E-mail: bjurus@acwi.org
URL: http://www.acwi.org
Contact: William L. Jurus, VP, Sales and Marketing
Description: Represents commercial warehouses. Provides national sales representation. Disseminates information. **Publications:** Newsletter (monthly).

16570 ■ American Society of Transportation and Logistics
PO Box 3363
Warrenton, VA 20188
Ph:(202)580-7270
Fax:(202)962-3939
Co. E-mail: info@astl.org
URL: http://www.astl.org
Contact: Mark Holmes CTL, Chm.
Description: Persons engaged in transportation, traffic, logistics, or physical distribution management. Works to establish standards of knowledge, technical training, experience, conduct, and ethics, and to encourage high standards of education and technical training requisite for the proper performance of traffic, transportation, logistics, and physical distribution management. Conducts extensive educational programs. **Publications:** Transportation Journal (quarterly).

16571 ■ International Association of Refrigerated Warehouses
1500 King St., Ste. 201
Alexandria, VA 22314
Ph:(703)373-4300
Fax:(703)373-4301
Co. E-mail: email@gcca.org
URL: http://www.iarw.org
Contact: J. William Hudson, Pres./CEO
Description: Public refrigerated warehouses storing all types of perishable foods and other perishable products; associate members are industry suppliers. **Publications:** Cold Facts (bimonthly); Crisis Manage-

ment Manual (periodic); Directory of Public Refrigerated Warehouses (annual); Maintenance and Modernization Manual .

16572 ■ International Warehouse Logistics Association
2800 S River Rd., Ste. 260
Des Plaines, IL 60018-6003
Ph:(847)813-4699
Free: 800-525-0165
Fax:(847)813-0115
Co. E-mail: email@iwla.com
URL: http://www.iwla.com
Contact: Joel D. Anderson, Pres./CEO
Description: Fosters and promotes the growth and success of public and contract warehousing and related logistics services. Serves as the unified voice of the global outsourced warehouse logistics industry, representing 3PLs (third party logistics providers), 4PLs (fourth party logistics providers), public and contract warehouse logistics companies and their suppliers, setting standards, legal frameworks and best practices for the warehousing logistics industry for 110 years. Members of the Association receive services including legal assistance, marketing assistance and group buying programs. Owns its own insurance company (passing cost savings to members), holds an annual convention each year, and produces educational programs. **Publications:** NewsGram (quarterly); This Week at IWLA (weekly); The 3PL Executive (quarterly).

16573 ■ Order Fulfillment Council | Material Handling Industry of America
8720 Red Oak Blvd., Ste. 201
Charlotte, NC 28217-3992
Ph:(704)676-1190
Free: 800-345-1815
Fax:(704)676-1199
Co. E-mail: jnofsinger@mhia.org
URL: http://www.mhia.org/industrygroups/ofc
Contact: John Nofsinger, CEO
Description: Trade associations comprising storage industries. Compiles statistics; sponsors research and educational programs. **Publications:** Storage and Handling Idea Book .

16574 ■ Recreational Vehicle Aftermarket Association
1833 Centre Point Cir., Ste. 123
Naperville, IL 60563-4848
Ph:(630)596-9004
Fax:(630)544-5055
Co. E-mail: info@rvaahq.org
URL: http://www.rvaahq.com
Contact: Aaron Engberg, Pres.
Description: Distributors, suppliers, and manufacturer's agents in the RV aftermarket industry. .

16575 ■ Self Storage Association
1901 N Beauregard St., Ste. 450
Alexandria, VA 22311
Ph:(703)575-8000
Free: 888-735-3784

Fax:(703)575-8901
Co. E-mail: info@selfstorage.org
URL: http://www.selfstorage.org
Contact: Michael T. Scanlon Jr., Pres./CEO
Description: Represents owners and operators of self-storage facilities. Improves the quality of management, customer service, facilities; promotes public management, marketing, security and related topics. Lobbies for state legislation protecting and recognizing self-storage owners and operators. **Publications:** SSA Globe Magazine (monthly).

16576 ■ SOLE - The International Society of Logistics
8100 Professional Pl., Ste. 111
Hyattsville, MD 20785-2229
Ph:(301)459-8446
Fax:(301)459-1522
Co. E-mail: solehq@erols.com
URL: http://www.sole.org
Contact: Mr. Timothy H. Overstreet DML, Pres.
Description: Represents corporate and individual management and technical practitioners in the field of logistics, including scientists, engineers, educators, managers, and other specialists in commerce, aerospace, and other industries, government, and the military. (Logistics is the art and science of management engineering and technical activities concerned with requirements, and designing, supplying, and maintaining resources to support objectives, plans, and operations.) Covers every logistics specialty, including reliability, maintainability, systems and equipment maintenance, maintenance support equipment, human factors, training and training equipment, spare parts, overhaul and repair, handbooks, field site activation and operation, field engineering, facilities, packaging, supply chain management, materials handling, and transportation. Sponsors on-line job referral service; conducts specialized education programs. **Publications:** Annual International Conference and Exposition Proceedings (annual).

16577 ■ Warehousing Education and Research Council
1100 Jorie Blvd., Ste. 170
Oak Brook, IL 60523-4423
Ph:(630)990-0001
Fax:(630)990-0256
Co. E-mail: wercoffice@werc.org
URL: http://www.werc.org
Contact: Michael J. Mikitka, CEO
Description: Represents distribution and warehousing professionals who lead, direct, and manage the efficient flow of information, materials, and finished goods throughout the supply chain. Provides practical ways that can be apply to improve service and reduce costs. .

REFERENCE WORKS

16578 ■ Allied Distribution, Inc.—Membership Directory
Pub: Allied Distribution Inc.
Contact: Ernest B. Brunswick, President
Released: Biennial. **Covers:** About 60 member public warehouses in the United States, Canada and

Mexico. **Entries Include:** Company name, address, phone, principal executives, financial data, and list of services. **Arrangement:** Geographical. **Indexes:** Alphabetical, geographical.

16579 ■ American Chain of Warehouses—Membership Directory
Pub: American Chain of Warehouses
Contact: William L. Jurus, Vice President
E-mail: bjurus@acwi.org
Released: Annual, April. **Covers:** About 45 member public warehouses in the U.S. **Entries Include:** Company name, address, names of executives, facilities, capital, types of storage, floor space, insured contents rate. **Arrangement:** Geographical.

16580 ■ Associated Warehouses—Directory of Services
Pub: Associated Warehouses Inc.
Released: Annual, August. **Price:** Free. **Covers:** 50 members. **Entries Include:** Warehouse name, address, phone, telex, executives' names, and descriptive information (railroad siding and service data, storage area available, insurance rates, financial references, and facilities). **Arrangement:** Geographical. **Indexes:** Geographical and warehouse name.

16581 ■ "Cold-Storage Cargo Facility a Late Bloomer" in Houston Business Journal (Vol. 40, August 28, 2009, No. 16, pp. 1A)
Pub: American City Business Journals
Ed: Jennifer Dawson. **Description:** Trammell Crow Company leased half of the 61,000 square foot IAH International Air Cargo Centre II to Tradewinds Cargo Handling. The facility, located at George Bush Intercontinental Airport, is intended to be a destination of fresh flowers and food from Latin America.

16582 ■ "Company Hopes To Pack Profits With Self-Storage" in Crain's Detroit Business (Vol. 24, February 18, 2008, No. 7, pp. 15)
Pub: Crain Communications Inc. - Detroit
Ed: Daniel Duggan. **Description:** Storage Opportunity Partners has purchased a vacant building to convert into a self-storage facility.

16583 ■ International Warehouse Logistics Association—Roster of Members
Pub: International Warehouse Logistics Association
Released: Annual. **Covers:** 550 warehouses, general storage facilities and distribution centers for non-refrigerated products in the US, Canada, Panama, Mexico, Venezuela, Puerto Rico, Dominican Republic and Costa Rica. **Arrangement:** Geographical.

16584 ■ Leonard's Guide National Warehouse and Distribution Directory
Pub: G.R. Leonard & Co.
Contact: David Ercolani
Released: Latest edition 2011. **Price:** $175, individuals print. **Covers:** Approximately 4,000 warehouses in the U.S. and Canada. **Entries Include:** Name, address, phone, storage areas, facilities, truck dock capacity, rail siding, geographical area served, products handled, services offered, year established, number of employees, distribution service, insurance and general information. **Arrangement:** Geographical by state. **Indexes:** Geographical by ZIP code, alphabetical, categorical.

16585 ■ "Merchants Association Working on Deal for Large Wholesale Warehouse" in Austin Business JournalInc. (September 19, 2008)
Pub: American City Business Journals
Ed: Jean Kwon. **Description:** Greater Austin Merchants Association planning to buy a former Dell Outlet Factory in Austin, Texas and convert it into a warehouse for convenience stores and gas stations.

16586 ■ "Substantial Deal Expected to Create Jobs, Help Industrial Market" in Tampa Bay Business Journal (Vol. 30, January 8, 2010, No. 3)
Pub: American City Business Journals
Ed: Janet Leiser. **Description:** Food distribution firm Gordon Food Service (GFS) is on the brink of purchasing Albertson's million-square-foot warehouse along with 158 acres of space. The deal between GFS and Albertson's could expand GFS' presence in west Central Florida. A history of GFS' growth is included

STATISTICAL SOURCES

16587 ■ RMA Annual Statement Studies
Pub: Robert Morris Associates (RMA)
Released: Annual. **Price:** $175.00 2006-07 edition, $105.00. **Description:** Contains composite balance sheets and income statements for more than 360 industries, including the accounting, auditing, and bookkeeping industries. Also contains five years of comparative historical data for discerning trends. Includes 16 commonly used ratios, computed for most of the size groupings for nearly every industry.

TRADE PERIODICALS

16588 ■ Self-Storage Now!
Pub: Mini-Storage Messenger
Contact: Dan Sommer, VP Publishing, Mktg. & Communs.
Ed: Darin Barney, Editor. **Released:** Bimonthly, 4/year. **Price:** Free. **Description:** Written to help mini-storage management personnel increase profits through marketing tips, business advice, new products, space rental sales techniques, and the sale of products and services to tenants.

TRADE SHOWS AND CONVENTIONS

16589 ■ Self Storage Association Conference and Tradeshow
Self Storage Association
1900 N. Beauregard St., Ste. 110
Alexandria, VA 22311
Ph:(703)575-8000
Fax:(703)575-8901
Co. E-mail: ssa@selfstorage.org
URL: http://www.selfstorage.org
Released: Semiannual. **Audience:** Traders, buyers, and association members. **Principal Exhibits:** Equipment, supplies, and services designed for and pertinent to construction, maintenance, and operation of self storage facilities. Meal functions held in exhibit hall. **Dates and Locations:** 2011 Apr 05-07, Charlotte, NC.

CONSULTANTS

16590 ■ K.B. Ackerman Co.
2041 Riverside Dr., Ste. 204
Columbus, OH 43221
Ph:(614)488-3165
Fax:(614)488-9243
Co. E-mail: ken@warehousing-forum.com
URL: http://www.warehousingforum.com
Contact: Kenneth B. Ackerman, President
E-mail: ken@warehousing-forum.com
Scope: Consultant on warehousing and logistics management. Also serves as expert witness in litigation and labor arbitration matters. **Publications:** "Warehousing Tips"; "Lean Warehousing"; "Fundamentals of Supply Chain Management"; "Auditing Warehouse Performance"; "Warehousing Tips"; "Warehousing Fundamentals"; "Words of Warehousing 2". **Seminars:** Family Business-Perpetuating Success; Best Practices In Warehouse Management; Quality and Leadership in the Warehouse; Improving Warehouse Performance; Warehousing as a Competitive Weapon; Lean Warehousing.

16591 ■ KEOGH Consulting Inc.
10217 Brecksville Rd.
Brecksville, OH 44141
Ph:(440)526-2002
Fax:(440)526-9466
Co. E-mail: information@keogh1.com
URL: http://www.keogh1.com
Contact: Tom Guschke, Director
Scope: A professional supply chain logistics consulting firm offering a full range of facility planning, design, and management consulting services for companies involved in manufacturing, warehousing, and distribution. Specializes in integrated supply chain solutions, focusing on logistics network and supply chain strategy, operations planning and assessment, and software selection, integration, configuration and implementation. **Publications:** "Operations & Fulfillment - Work WITH me"; "Supply Chain Optimization101"; "Don't Waste Your Space!"; "Finding Hidden Productivity"; "Product Slotting The Secret to Increased Productivity"; "New Equipment Digest". **Seminars:** Keys to DC Automation Excellence, Oct, 2008; Keys to Operations and Integration Success, Sep, 2008.

16592 ■ The Leawood Group Ltd.
3525 W 175th St.
Stilwell, KS 66085
Ph:(913)402-6785
Fax:(913)402-6857
Contact: William W. Rennall, President
E-mail: wrennall@tlgltd.com
Scope: International facilities planning consultants offering the following services: long range facilities and master site planning, site selection and plant layout, materials handling analysis, operations strategy lean, manufacturing, warehouse storage and distribution planning, capacity analysis, project management, office space planning, cost reduction and methods improvement and in-house training. Also involves in ISO 9000 assessment, self directed work team building and business transformation. Serves manufacturing as well as government agencies. **Publications:** "Handbook of Commercial and Industrial Facilities Management," McGraw Hill, 1994. **Seminars:** Plant Layout and Facilities Planning; Office Space Planning; Computer Aided Facilities Planning and Design; Material Handling and Storage; Integrating Layout Planning and Material Handling Analysis; Long Range Facilities Planning; Cell Design for World Class Manufacturing; Time-Based Competition; Business Process Re engineering (BPR); ISO 9000 Assessment and others.

16593 ■ M.W. Burke & Associates Inc.
185 Front St., Ste. 207
Danville, CA 94526
Ph:(925)838-9070
Fax:(925)838-4695
Co. E-mail: mwburke@aol.com
Contact: Maurice W. Burke, President
Scope: Provides engineering and management consulting services to manufacturing, distribution and service oriented firms. Specializes in industrial engineering, distribution and warehousing, manpower analysis and scheduling systems, site selection, plant layout, material handling systems, cost reduction and methods improvement, equipment selection and replacement, inventory management, administrative systems, manufacturing systems, and packaging.

16594 ■ Raymond Nelson Distribution Consultants
247 S Gate Ln.
Southport, CT 06890-1465
Ph:(203)319-7479
Contact: Raymond A. Nelson, Owner
Scope: Offers consulting services in advanced warehousing, distribution, materials handling, inventory control and management and transportation systems. **Seminars:** Order Picking, Packing, and Warehousing; Controlling the Costs of Physical Distribution; Modernizing and Mechanizing Warehousing Operations; Computerizing Warehouse Operations; Logistic Management.

16595 ■ Semco, Sweet & Mayers Inc.
18010 Sky Park Cir., Ste. 275
Irvine, CA 92614
Ph:(949)250-1818
Fax:(949)250-9528
Contact: Steve Halpern, President
Scope: A material handling consultant firm, offers industrial engineering consulting services in connection with warehouse and distribution center design, material handling systems, operating data processing systems, systems integration, profiling, simulation, and logistics studies.

16596 ■ Trainor & Associates
4285 Wind Tree Cove
Bartlett, TN 38135
Ph:(901)373-8940
Fax:(901)377-0111
Co. E-mail: bobt@gotrainor.com
URL: http://www.gotrainor.com
Contact: Robert P. Trainor, President
E-mail: rpt3@prodigy.net
Scope: Provides industrial engineering services to include work process analysis. Industries served: Food, machining, assembly, engine rebuild for automotive and locomotive, metal fabrication, packaging, manufacturing, warehousing, and distribution. **Publications:** "You Want it When?," Memphis Business Journal; "Walking the Assembly Line," The Daily News, May, 2006. **Seminars:** Cost Control for Work Measurement Process Improvements, Kaizen Event; Managers and Supervisors.

16597 ■ Wesley-Kind Associates Inc.
200 Old Country Rd., Ste. 364
Mineola, NY 11501-4235
Ph:(516)747-3434
Fax:(516)248-2728
Contact: Daniel A. Kind, President
Scope: Material handling and distribution consultants offering advice on plant and warehouse layouts and operating systems for the movement, storage and control of materials and products. Expertise includes materials and production management, advanced handling/storage systems, packaging and unitizing systems, capacity, productivity and customer service audits, order filling systems, data processing control systems, transportation systems, site location analysis, facilities planning, and implementation. Industries served: manufacturing, distribution and retail corporations and state and U.S. Government agencies. **Publications:** "How to Reengineer the Storage Function," Penton Publishing, 1995.

COMPUTER SYSTEMS/ SOFTWARE

16598 ■ RealEasyBooks, Inc.–RPMW
RealEasyBooks, Inc.
PO Box 133
Alamo, CA 94507
Ph:(925)280-7769
Fax:(831)855-9033
Co. E-mail: support@rpmw.com
URL: http://www.rpmw.com
Price: $100.00-$1650.00. **Description:** Available for IBM computers and compatibles. System maintains records of monthly income and expenses from properties such as mini-storage units.

RESEARCH CENTERS

16599 ■ Warehousing Education and Research Council
1100 Jorie Blvd., Ste. 170
Oak Brook, IL 60523-4413
Ph:(630)990-0001
Fax:(630)990-0256
Co. E-mail: wercoffice@werc.org
URL: http://www.werc.org
Contact: Michael J. Mikitka, CEO
E-mail: wercoffice@werc.org
Scope: Warehousing industry and executive professionalism, including improving service within the industry.

ASSOCIATIONS AND OTHER ORGANIZATIONS

16600 ■ Automotive Oil Change Association
1701 N Greenville Ave., Ste. 404
Richardson, TX 75081
Ph:(972)458-9468
Free: 800-331-0329
Fax:(972)458-9539
Co. E-mail: info@aoca.org
URL: http://www.aoca.org
Contact: Leanne Stump, Exec. Dir.
Description: Owners and operators of oil change shops. Works to solve problems and advance interests of members. Offers group insurance and credit card program. Compiles statistics; disseminates information, employee training programs. **Publications:** *Oil Changing Times* (bimonthly).

REFERENCE WORKS

16601 ■ "Banking on Twitter" in *Baltimore Business Journal* (Vol. 27, February 6, 2010, No. 40, pp. 1)
Pub: American City Business Journals
Ed: Gary Haber. **Description:** Ways that banks are using Twitter, Facebook and other social networking sites to provide customer services is discussed. First Mariner Bank is one of those banks that are finding the social media platform as a great way to reach customers. Privacy issues regarding this marketing trend are examined.

16602 ■ "Thomas Morley; President, The Lube Stop Inc., 37" in *Crain's Cleveland Business* (Vol. 28, November 19, 2007, No. 46, pp. F-12)
Pub: Crain Communications, Inc.
Ed: David Bennett. **Description:** Profile of Thomas Morley, president of The Lube Stop Inc., who is dedicated to promoting the company's strong environmental record as an effective way to differentiate Lube Stop from its competition. Since Mr. Morley came to the company in 2004, Lube Stop has increased sales by 10 percent and has boosted its operating profits by 30 percent.

TRADE PERIODICALS

16603 ■ *O & A Marketing News*
Pub: KAL Publications Inc.
Ed: Kathy Laderman, Editor. **Released:** 7/yr. **Price:** $20; $35 two years. **Description:** News magazine (tabloid) targeting people engaged in the marketing, distribution, merchandising, installation, and servicing of gasoline, fuels, oil, tires, batteries, accessories, and automotive aftermarket products for service stations, convenience stores and carwashes in the thirteen Pacific Western states.

FRANCHISES AND BUSINESS OPPORTUNITIES

16604 ■ All Tune and Lube
ATL International, Inc.
8334 Veterans Hwy.
Millersville, MD 21108
Ph:(410)987-1011
Free: 800-935-8863
Fax:(410)987-4827
Co. E-mail: alltune@erols.com
URL: http://www.alltuneandlube.com
No. of Franchise Units: 300. **Founded:** 1986. **Franchised:** 1986. **Description:** Automotive servicing. "One stop" total car care, including tune-ups, brakes, exhaust, engine replacement and more. **Equity Capital Needed:** $35,000+. **Franchise Fee:** $32,000. **Financial Assistance:** Financing available. **Managerial Assistance:** Provides operation staff visits, toll-free telephone assistance, and newsletters. **Training:** All Tune and Lube provides extensive training at headquarters and in the individual center locations. Provides 1 week of center management training and operational support.

16605 ■ Econo Lube N' Tune
128 S Tryon St., Ste. 900
Charlotte, NC 28202
Free: 800-275-5200
No. of Franchise Units: 173. **No. of Company-Owned Units:** 95. **Founded:** 1973. **Franchised:** 1978. **Description:** Auto service, lube, tune and brakes. **Franchise Fee:** $39,500. **Financial Assistance:** Yes. **Training:** Yes.

16606 ■ Equipro Inc.
W180 N11691 River Ln., Ste. A
Germantown, WI 53022
Ph:(262)257-4100
Free: (866)378-4776
Fax:(262)257-4105
Co. E-mail: info@equiproservice.com
URL: http://www.equiproservice.com
No. of Franchise Units: 11. **No. of Company-Owned Units:** 2. **Founded:** 2003. **Franchised:** 2005. **Description:** Nationwide network of franchised service centers. A full service solution for the light construction industry. **Equity Capital Needed:** $151,100-$345,400. **Franchise Fee:** $20,000-$30,000. **Royalty Fee:** 7.5%. **Financial Assistance:** No. **Training:** Provides 1 week at headquarters, 1 week onsite, 9 weeks technical training by product manufacturers, and ongoing support.

16607 ■ Express Oil Change & Service Center
1880 Southpark Dr.
Birmingham, AL 35244
Ph:(205)397-1148
Free: 888-945-1771
Fax:(205)940-6025
No. of Franchise Units: 109. **No. of Company-Owned Units:** 76. **Founded:** 1979. **Franchised:** 1979. **Description:** Fast automotive service and minor automotive repair. **Equity Capital Needed:** $300,000. **Franchise Fee:** $35,000. **Financial Assistance:** Pre-approved with SBA. Will connect franchise candidate with preferred lenders who are familiar with Express Oil Change concept. **Training:** Provides 8 to 10 weeks of training for franchisee and/or key operator and 2 weeks training for franchisee's store crew.

16608 ■ Fresh Coat
Franchise Dept.
10700 Montgomery Rd., Ste. 300
Cincinnati, OH 45242
Free: (866)708-9355
Fax:(513)563-2691
Co. E-mail: inquiry@freshcoatpainters.com
URL: http://www.freshcoatpainters.com
No. of Franchise Units: 60. **Founded:** 2004. **Franchised:** 2005. **Description:** Homeowners spend millions of dollars everyday on painting kitchens, family rooms...every room in the house. Fresh coat has captured a niche in the multi-billion dollar industry. As a franchisee, you build your business through proven marketing, expertise and a system exclusive to Fresh Coat. This business is about building an organization and managing people; not doing the work yourself. **Equity Capital Needed:** $38,850-$63,850. **Franchise Fee:** $31,900. **Financial Assistance:** Financing available. **Training:** A complete turnkey operation. Training program provides tools needed to operate a successful and profitable business, including getting the business, payroll, computer training, market knowledge, recruitment, operations, scheduling and bidding.

16609 ■ Grease Monkey International
7100 E Belleview Ave., Ste. 305
Greenwood Village, CO 80111
Ph:(303)454-3408
Free: 800-364-0352
Fax:(303)308-5906
Co. E-mail: franchiseinfo@greasemonkeyintl.com
No. of Franchise Units: 242. **No. of Company-Owned Units:** 2. **Founded:** 1978. **Franchised:** 1979. **Description:** provide quick, convenient vehicle maintenance services .Offers quick oil change and lubrication services. **Equity Capital Needed:** $250,000 liquidity; $500,000 net worth. **Franchise Fee:** $30,000. **Financial Assistance:** No. **Training:** Training is provided at corporate headquarters and on site; franchisor also assists with site selection and construction.

16610 ■ Jiffy Lube Canada
1101 Blair Rd.
Burlington, ON, Canada L7M 1T3
Free: 800-327-9532
Co. E-mail: jiffy-lube-development@shell.com
URL: http://www.jiffylube.com
No. of Franchise Units: 45. **No. of Operating Units:** 2,006. **Founded:** 1979. **Franchised:** 1979. **Description:** Fast oil change and preventative maintenance services. **Equity Capital Needed:** $187,000-$400,000. **Franchise Fee:** $25,000. **Training:** Initial and ongoing training provided.

16611 ■ Jiffy Lube Intl., Inc.
Pennzoil Quaker State Co.
PO Box 4427
Houston, TX 77210-4427
Free: 800-327-9532

Fax:(713)546-8762
No. of Franchise Units: 1,940. **Founded:** 1979. **Franchised:** 1979. **Description:** Quick oil change and preventative maintenance. **Equity Capital Needed:** $196,500-$331,500. **Franchise Fee:** $10,000-$35,000. **Royalty Fee:** 4%**Financial Assistance:** Third party financing available. **Training:** Provides 2-4 weeks training at headquarters, followed with onsite with ongoing support.

16612 ■ Lubepro's International, Inc.
1740 S Bell School Rd.
Cherry Valley, IL 61016
Ph:(815)332-9200
Free: 800-654-5823
Fax:(815)332-9355
Co. E-mail: philr@lubepros.com
No. of Franchise Units: 19. **No. of Company-Owned Units:** 15. **Description:** LubePros service centers provides fast-service oil changes, lubrication, replacement of certain filters and fluids and certain related courtesy services for motor vehicles. **Equity Capital Needed:** $223,000 initial investment, not including land, building, improvements; $400,000 net worth, $150,000 liquid. **Franchise Fee:** $32,500. **Financial Assistance:** No. **Training:** Offers 10 days of marketing management, operational, and advertising support services are provided.

16613 ■ Oil Butler International, Corp.
1599 Rte. 22 W
Union, NJ 07083
Ph:(908)687-3283
Fax:(908)687-7617
No. of Franchise Units: 100. **No. of Company-Owned Units:** 1. **Founded:** 1987. **Franchised:** 1991. **Description:** Provides oil change service. **Equity Capital Needed:** $25,000-$34,000. **Franchise Fee:** $15,000. **Financial Assistance:** No. **Training:** Yes.

16614 ■ Oil Can Henry's
OCH International, Inc.
19150 SW 90th Ave.
Tualatin, OR 97062
Ph:(503)243-6311
Free: 800-765-6244
No. of Franchise Units: 88. **Founded:** 1978. **Franchised:** 1989. **Description:** Fast oil, lube and fluid franchises. **Equity Capital Needed:** $300,000 cash; $750,000 net worth. **Franchise Fee:** $25,000. **Financial Assistance:** No. **Training:** Yes.

16615 ■ Precision Tune Auto Care, Inc.
Precision Auto Care, Inc.
748 Miller Dr. SE
PO Box 5000
Leesburg, VA 20175
Ph:(703)777-9095
Free: 800-438-8863
Fax:(703)669-1539
URL: http://www.precision-tune.com
No. of Franchise Units: 400. **No. of Company-Owned Units:** 5. **Founded:** 1975. **Franchised:** 1978. **Description:** Auto care, quick lube. **Equity Capital Needed:** $100,000 or more. **Franchise Fee:** $25,000. **Financial Assistance:** Yes. **Training:** Yes.

16616 ■ Valvoline Instant Oil Change
Ashland Inc.
3499 Blazer Pky.
Lexington, KY 40509
Ph:(859)357-7303
Free: 800-622-6846
Fax:(859)357-6919
Co. E-mail: jjtaylor@ashland.com
URL: http://www.viocfranchise.com
No. of Franchise Units: 612. **No. of Company-Owned Units:** 300. **Founded:** 1986. **Franchised:** 1988. **Description:** Automobile oil change service.

Equity Capital Needed: $800,000-$1,000,000 liquid assets/$1,000,000 net worth. **Franchise Fee:** $30,000. **Financial Assistance:** Yes. **Training:** Yes.

16617 ■ Victory Lane Quick Oil Change
405 Little Lake Dr.
Ann Arbor, MI 48103
Ph:(734)996-1196
Fax:(734)996-4912
No. of Franchise Units: 41. **No. of Company-Owned Units:** 5. **Founded:** 1980. **Franchised:** 1986. **Description:** Quick oil & lube service. **Equity Capital Needed:** $100,000-$350,000 net worth. **Franchise Fee:** $30,000. **Financial Assistance:** Yes. **Training:** Yes.

COMPUTERIZED DATABASES

16618 ■ *International Petroleum Encyclopedia*
PennWell Corp.
1421 S Sheridan Rd.
Tulsa, OK 74112
Ph:(918)835-3161
Free: 800-331-4463
Fax:(918)831-9497
Co. E-mail: headquarters@pennwell.com
URL: http://www.pennwell.com
Description: Provides articles and Information on the energy Industry. Offers country reports; maps of North America, Middle East, Asia-Pacific, China, Latin America, Africa, Former Soviet Union, and Europe; industry statistics; stratigraphic charts; a directory of state-owned oil companies; articles covering subsalt seismic imaging and a survey of enhanced oil recovery projects. Offers the option of selecting from major articles or from a select group included in *Oil and Gas Journal*. Corresponds to the print version *International Petroleum Encyclopedia*. **Availability:** CD-ROM: PennWell Corp. **Type:** Full text; Statistical.

ASSOCIATIONS AND OTHER ORGANIZATIONS

16619 ■ Alliance of Canadian Cinema, Television and Radio Artists
625 Church St., 3rd Fl.
Toronto, ON, Canada M4Y 2G1
Ph:(416)489-1311
Free: 800-387-3516
Fax:(416)489-8076
Co. E-mail: national@actra.ca
URL: http://www.actra.ca
Contact: Ferne Downey, Natl. Pres.
Description: Performing artists in the television, radio, film, and other recorded media. Seeks to obtain equitable compensation and safe working conditions for members. Represents members in negotiations with employers; monitors workplace conditions in the film and broadcasting industries. **Publications:** *Inter-ACTRA News* (quarterly).

16620 ■ Associated Press Broadcast
AP Broadcast News Center
1100 13th St., Ste. 700
Washington, DC 20005
Ph:(202)641-9921
Free: 800-342-5127
Co. E-mail: lperryman@ap.org
URL: http://www.apbroadcast.com
Contact: Lee Perryman, Deputy Dir. of Broadcast Services
Description: Broadcast stations in the United States that are members of the Associated Press. Advances journalism through radio and television. Cooperates with the AP in order to make available accurate and impartial news. Serves as a liaison between radio and television stations that are members of the AP and representatives of those stations. .

16621 ■ Broadcast Cable Credit Association
550 W Frontage Rd., Ste. 3600
Northfield, IL 60093
Ph:(847)881-8757
Fax:(847)784-8059
Co. E-mail: info@bccacredit.com
URL: http://www.bccacredit.com
Contact: Mary M. Collins, Pres./CEO
Description: A subsidiary of the Broadcast Cable Financial Management Association. Television and radio stations; cable television networks; national sales representatives. Provides industry specific credit reports on individual agencies, advertisers, or buying services (local or national). *BCCA Credit Handbook* (annual); *Credit and Collection Survey*; *The Financial Manager for the Media Professional/Credit Topics* (bimonthly); *Update* (monthly).

16622 ■ Canadian Association of Broadcasters–Association Canadienne des Radiodiffuseurs
PO Box 627, Sta. B
Ottawa, ON, Canada K1P 5S2
Ph:(613)233-4035

Fax:(613)233-6961
Co. E-mail: cab@cab-acr.ca
URL: http://www.cab-acr.ca
Contact: Mr. Elmer Hildebrand, Chm.
Description: Collective voice of the majority of Canada's private radio and television stations, networks, and specialty services. Develops industry-wide strategic plans, works to improve the financial health of the industry, and promotes private broadcasting's role as Canada's leading programmer and local service provider.

16623 ■ Canadian Disc Jockey Association
1008 Manchester Rd.
London, ON, Canada N6H 5J1
Ph:(519)287-3600
Free: 877-472-0653
Fax:(519)472-0242
Co. E-mail: pres@cdja.ca
URL: http://www.cdja.ca
Contact: Doug Scott, Pres.
Description: Disc jockeys and others promote excellence in service through education, information, networking, and support. Promotes professional development among members. Facilitates exchange of information among members; represents members' interests. **Publications:** *CUED-UP Street* (annual); *DJ Pulse* (quarterly).

16624 ■ Country Radio Broadcasters
819 18th Ave. S
Nashville, TN 37203
Ph:(615)327-4487
Fax:(615)329-4492
Co. E-mail: bill@crb.org
URL: http://www.crb.org
Contact: Bill Mayne, Exec. Dir.
Description: Seeks to advance and promote the study of the science of broadcasting through the mutual exchange of ideas by conducting seminars and workshops, as well as providing scholarships to broadcasting students. .

16625 ■ International Radio and Television Society Foundation
420 Lexington Ave., Ste. 1601
New York, NY 10170
Ph:(212)867-6650
Fax:(212)867-6653
Co. E-mail: membership@irts.org
URL: http://www.irts.org
Contact: Joyce M. Tudryn, Pres.
Description: Individuals interested in management, sales, or executive production in the radio, television, and cable industries and their allied fields. Seeks to educate members through seminars. Conducts summer internships for college students majoring in communications. **Publications:** *International Radio and Television Society Foundation—Roster Yearbook* (annual).

16626 ■ National Association of Broadcasters
1771 N St. NW
Washington, DC 20036
Ph:(202)429-5300

Fax:(202)429-4199
Co. E-mail: nab@nab.org
URL: http://www.nab.org
Contact: Gordon H. Smith, Pres./CEO
Description: Serves as the voice for the nation's radio and television broadcasters. Advances the interests of members in federal government, industry and public affairs; improves the quality and profitability of broadcasting; encourages content and technology innovation; and spotlights the important and unique ways stations serve their communities. Delivers value to its members through advocacy, education and innovation. Relies on the grassroots strength of its television and radio members and state broadcast associations. Helps broadcasters seize opportunities in the digital age. Offers broadcasters a variety of programs to help them grow in their careers, promote diversity in the workplace and strengthen their businesses. .

16627 ■ National Federation of Community Broadcasters
1970 Broadway, Ste. 1000
Oakland, CA 94612
Ph:(510)451-8200
Fax:(510)451-8208
Co. E-mail: administrator@nfcb.org
URL: http://www.nfcb.org
Contact: Maxie C. Jackson III, Pres./CEO
Description: Independent, community-licensed radio and radio production organizations. Fosters the development of public policy at the legislative, regulatory and administrative levels; aids the growth of community-oriented radio stations and advances the public interest in mass communications; seeks an equitable distribution of federal funds appropriated for noncommercial broadcasting and develops support for community-oriented broadcast projects; facilitates the exchange of program materials, information and technical expertise; assists in the organization and expansion of new and innovative broadcast stations throughout the U.S. Provides services and consultation. **Publications:** *Audiocraft: Tools and Techniques of Audio Production* (monthly); *Community Radio News* (monthly); *The NFCB Public Radio Legal Handbook: A Guide to FCC Rules and Regulations*; *NFCB's Guide to Underwriting for Public Radio*; *Starting an LPFM Station* .

16628 ■ North American Broadcasters Association
PO Box 500, Sta. A
Toronto, ON, Canada M5W 1E6
Ph:(416)598-9877
Fax:(416)598-9774
Co. E-mail: contact@nabanet.com
URL: http://www.nabanet.com/nabaweb
Contact: Leonardo Ramos Mateos, Pres.
Description: Network broadcasters in North America concerned with international matters that affect broadcasting. Seeks to identify, study and provide solutions to international questions concerning broadcasting. Creates opportunities for North American broadcasters to share information, identify common interests and reach on issues of an international nature. Works with other international broadcasters'

associations and unions toward gaining an effective voice in international circles on matters that affect broadcasting. Organizes international conferences in conjunction with other broadcasting associations.

16629 ■ Radio Advertising Bureau

1320 Greenway Dr., Ste. 500
Irving, TX 75038-2587
Ph:(212)681-7214
Free: 800-232-3131
Co. E-mail: jhaley@rab.com
URL: http://www.rab.com
Contact: Jeff Haley, Pres./CEO

Description: Includes radio stations, radio networks, station sales representatives, and allied industry services, such as producers, research firms, schools, and consultants. Calls on advertisers and agencies to promote the sale of radio time as an advertising medium. Sponsors program to increase professionalism of radio salespeople, awarding Certified Radio Marketing Consultant designation to those who pass examination. Sponsors regional marketing conferences. Conducts extensive research program into all phases of radio sales. Issues reports on use of radio by national, regional, and local advertisers. Speaks before conventions and groups to explain benefits of radio advertising. Sponsors Radio Creative Fund. Compiles statistics. **Publications:** *Guide to Competitive Media* (biennial); *RAB Media Fact Book* (annual); *Radio Co-op Sources* (annual).

16630 ■ Radio-Television News Directors' Association

2175 Sheppard Ave. E, Ste. 310
Toronto, ON, Canada M2J 1W8
Ph:(416)756-2213
Free: 877-25R-TNDA
Fax:(416)491-1670
Co. E-mail: info@rtndacanada.com
URL: http://www.rtndacanada.com
Contact: Andy LeBlanc, Pres.

Description: Radio and television news executives and personnel. Promotes the professional development of broadcast journalists in Canada. Sponsors national scholarship program.

16631 ■ World Association of Community Radio Broadcasters–Asociacion Mondial de Radios Communautarias

705 Bourget St., Ste. 100
Montreal, QC, Canada H4C 2M6
Ph:(514)982-0351
Fax:(514)849-7129
Co. E-mail: secretariat@si.amarc.org
URL: http://www.amarc.org
Contact: Marcelo Solervicens, Sec. Gen.

Description: Supports and promotes the work of community radio broadcasters worldwide. Provides technical support for members, and fosters communication between members. Seeks to contribute to free expression worldwide; works to combat censorship based on social or political viewpoints. **Publications:** *InteRadio* (periodic).

REFERENCE WORKS

16632 ■ "Abacast, Citadel Strike Radio Ad Deal" in *Business Journal Portland* (Vol. 27, December 31, 2010, No. 44, pp. 3)

Pub: Portland Business Journal

Ed: Erik Siemers. **Description:** Software firm Abacast Inc. has partnered with Citadel Media to aid the latter's advertising sales. Citadel provides radio networks and syndicated programs to 4,200 affiliate stations.

16633 ■ "ACTRA Phones It In" in *Canadian Business* (Vol. 80, January 15, 2007, No. 2, pp. 8)

Pub: Rogers Media

Ed: Denis Seguin. **Description:** The strike held by the members of the ACTRA or Canadian Cinema, Television and Radio Artists from January 8 2007, due to the contract dispute with the trade association representing Canadian producers, is discussed.

16634 ■ *Bacon's Radio/TV/Cable Directory, Volume 1*

Pub: Cision US Inc.
Contact: Stephen Newman, CEO

Released: Annual, Latest edition 2012. **Price:** $650, individuals. **Covers:** over 13,500 radio and television stations, including college radio and public television stations, and cable companies. **Entries Include:** For radio and television stations—Call letters, address, phone, names and titles of key personnel, programs, times broadcast, name of contact, network affiliation, frequency or channel number, target audience data. For cable companies—Name, address, phone, description of activities. **Arrangement:** Geographical.

16635 ■ *Broadcast Engineering—Equipment Reference Manual*

Pub: Penton Media Inc.
Contact: Brad Dick, Editorial Dir.
E-mail: bdick@primediabusiness.com

Released: Annual, fall. **Publication Includes:** List of more than 1,400 manufacturers and distributors of communications equipment for radio, television, and recording applications. **Entries Include:** For manufacturers—Company name, address. For distributors and dealers—Company name, address, phone, product or service provided, geographic area covered. **Arrangement:** Manufacturers are alphabetical; dealers and distributors are geographical. **Indexes:** Product/service.

16636 ■ *Broadcasting & Cable Yearbook*

Pub: R.R. Bowker L.L.C.

Released: Annual, latest edition 2010. **Price:** $395, individuals softbound. **Covers:** Over 17,000 television and radio stations in the United States, its territories, and Canada; cable MSOs and their individual systems; television and radio networks, broadcast and cable group owners, station representatives, satellite networks and services, film companies, advertising agencies, government agencies, trade associations, schools, and suppliers of professional and technical services, including books, serials, and videos; communications lawyers. **Entries Include:** Company name, address, phone, fax, names of executives. Station listings include broadcast power, other operating details. **Arrangement:** Stations and systems are geographical, others are alphabetical. **Indexes:** Alphabetical.

16637 ■ "The Buzz About HD Radio" in *Black Enterprise* (Vol. 37, February 2007, No. 7, pp. 58)

Pub: Earl G. Graves Publishing Co. Inc.

Ed: James C. Johnson. **Description:** HD radio broadcasting will send CD quality sound and extra information to more radio stations using the same amount of bandwidth.

16638 ■ "Dear Diary, Arbitron is Dumping You" in *Business Courier* (Vol. 26, September 25, 2009, No. 22, pp. 1)

Pub: American City Business Journals, Inc.

Ed: Dan Monk. **Description:** Arbitron Inc. is replacing hand-written ratings diaries with Portable People Meters or electronic sensors that measure local radio audiences. The technology counts all exposure to radio and stations; those that penetrate the workplace will see success, while the more 'niche' oriented formats will have a more difficult time.

16639 ■ "Dots Sings To New Tune With Its Radio Station" in *Crain's Cleveland Business* (Vol. 30, June 15, 2009, No. 23, pp. 7)

Pub: Crain Communications, Inc.

Description: Dots LLC, a women's clothing retailer, has launched an online radio station on its Website. The station plays the in-store music to customers while they are shopping online.

16640 ■ "Dramatic Results: Making Opera (Yes, Opera) Seem Young and Hip" in *Inc.* (October 2007, pp. 61-62)

Pub: Gruner & Jahr USA Publishing

Description: Profile of Peter Gelb, who turned New York's Metropolitan Opera into one of the most media-savvy organizations in the country, using a multifaceted marketing strategy through the media.

Gelb used streaming audio and simulcasts on satellite radio and movie theaters to promote a message that opera is hip.

16641 ■ "A Family's Fortune" in *Canadian Business* (Vol. 80, Winter 2007, No. 24, pp. 103)

Pub: Rogers Media

Ed: Graham F. Scott. **Description:** James Richardson started as a tailor before moving into the grain business because his clients paid him in sacks of wheat and barley. The James Richardson and Sons Ltd. entered the radio business in 1927 but later sold it off in 1951.

16642 ■ "Far Out: Satellite Radio Finds New Way to Tally Listeners" in *Globe & Mail* (March 14, 2007, pp. B14)

Pub: CTVglobemedia Publishing Inc.

Ed: Grant Robertson. **Description:** The marketing strategy adopted by satellite radio broadcasting firm XM Satellite Radio Inc. in Canada for increasing its subscriber based is discussed.

16643 ■ *Freelancing for Journalists*

Pub: Routledge

Ed: Diana Harris. **Released:** January 1, 2010. **Price:** $110.00. **Description:** Comprehensive guide showing the specific skills required for those wishing to freelance in newspapers, magazines, radio, television, and as online journalists.

16644 ■ *Investing in Radio Market Report*

Pub: BIA Financial Network Inc.

Released: Annual, Latest edition 2011. **Price:** $1,300, individuals; $2,700, individuals quarterly set; $3,185, individuals full financial set. **Covers:** U.S. Radio industry markets and inclusive stations. **Entries Include:** For stations—Call letters, technical attributes, format, estimated revenues, owner, last acquisition date and price, ratings for eight books. **Arrangement:** Numerical by market rank size. **Indexes:** Market name, station call letters, city of license.

16645 ■ "It Could Be Worse" in *Barron's* (Vol. 89, July 27, 2009, No. 30, pp. 5)

Pub: Dow Jones & Co., Inc.

Ed: Alan Abelson. **Description:** Media sources are being fooled by corporate America who is peddling an economic recovery rather than reality as shown by the report of a rise in existing home sales which boosted the stock market even if it was a seasonal phenomenon. The phrase "things could be worse" sums up the reigning investment philosophy in the U.S. and this has been stirring up the market.

16646 ■ "Making Visitors Out Of Listeners" in *Hawaii Business* (Vol. 54, July 2008, No. 1, pp. 18)

Pub: Hawaii Business Publishing

Ed: Casey Chin. **Description:** Japanese workers are subscribing to the Official Hawaii Podcast in iTunes, which offers a free 20-minute, Japanese-language audio content on different topics, such as dining reviews and music from local artists. The concept is a way to attract Japanese travelers to come to Hawaii.

16647 ■ "Marketing: You Are On the Air: Radio and TV Producers Are Looking For Shows Starring Smart CEOs" in *Inc.* (December 2007, pp. 67-69)

Pub: Gruner & Jahr USA Publishing

Ed: Sarah Goldstein. **Description:** Many successful entrepreneurs are being hired to host television and radio shows in order to share business expertise.

16648 ■ *Matthews Media Directory*

Pub: Marketwire
Contact: Lisa Davis

Released: Semiannual, Latest edition 50th. **Covers:** Daily newspapers, radio and television stations, trade magazines, networks and newswires and press galleries in Canada.

16649 ■ *Media, Organizations and Identity*
Pub: Palgrave Macmillan

Ed: Lilie Chouliaraki, Mette Morsing. **Released:** January 19, 2010. **Price:** $90.00. **Description:** The mass media, press and television are a essential in the formation of corporate identity and the promotion of business image and reputation. This book offers a new perspective into the interrelationships between media and organizations over three dimensions: media as business, media in business and business in the media.

16650 ■ *Mississippi News Media Directory*
Pub: News Media Directories

Released: Annual, Latest edition 2010. **Price:** $45, individuals; $65, individuals CD; $85, individuals Combo-Directory and CD. **Covers:** Newspapers, periodicals, radio and television broadcasting stations, and press services operating in Mississippi. **Entries Include:** Publisher or company name, address, phone, names and titles of key personnel, publication title, call letters, hours of operation, and frequency. **Arrangement:** Classified by type of media. **Indexes:** Title, call letters, county index.

16651 ■ "New King Top the Charts" in *The Business Journal-Portland* (Vol. 25, August 8, 2008, No. 22, pp. 1)
Pub: American City Business Journals, Inc.

Ed: Andy Giegerich. **Description:** Spanish-language KRYP-FM station's spring 2008 ratings soared to 6.4 from 2.8 for the previous year. The station timing is flawless given the fact that one of every three new Portland-area residents between 2002 and 2007 were Latino.

16652 ■ "Online Radio That's Cool, Addictive, Free, and Just Maybe A Lasting Business" in *Inc.* (October 2007, pp. 100-106, 108)
Pub: Gruner & Jahr USA Publishing

Ed: Stephanie Clifford. **Description:** Profile of the Internet radio company, Pandora, whose founder, Tim Westergren discusses his business plans to fruition. The station has over eight million loyal listeners, advertisers and a database of 500,000 songs.

16653 ■ "Out of This World: Noah Samara and WorldSpace" in *Black Enterprise* (November 2007)
Pub: Earl G. Graves Publishing Co. Inc.

Ed: Anthony Calypso. **Description:** Profile of Noah Samara, CEO of WorldSpace Inc. who raised $1 billion to help create the technological architecture for satellite radio.

16654 ■ "Pro Teams Shift Ad Budgets; Naming Rights Deals Near $1 Billion" in *Brandweek* (Vol. 49, April 21, 2008, No. 16, pp. 18)
Pub: VNU Business Media, Inc.

Ed: Barry Janoff. **Description:** More and more professional sports marketers are spending less of their advertising budgets on traditional media outlets such as television, print and radio; the growing trend in sports marketing is in utilizing new media venues such as the Internet in which innovative means are used to encourage interaction with fans.

16655 ■ "Radio Feels Heat from IPod Generation" in *Globe & Mail* (March 16, 2006, pp. B1)
Pub: CTVglobemedia Publishing Inc.

Ed: Simon Tuck; Grant Robertson. **Description:** Conventional radio stations are losing the younger generation listeners to new technology such as MP3 players, satellite radio and music-playing cell phones. The report of Canadian Association of Broadcasters (CAB) is detailed.

16656 ■ "Radio" in *MarketingMagazine* (Vol. 115, September 27, 2010, No. 13, pp. 24)
Pub: Rogers Publishing Ltd.

Description: Market data in the radio broadcasting industry in Canada is outlined.

16657 ■ "Radio Roots Run Deep" in *The Business Journal-Milwaukee* (Vol. 25, July 4, 2008, No. 41, pp. A1)
Pub: American City Business Journals, Inc.

Ed: Rich Kirchen. **Description:** Profile of Steve Palec, a real estate broker at CB Richard Ellis, also works as a radio host for shows "Rock & Roll Roots" and "Legends of Rock". Palec shares that real estate is still his top priority, even with his radio gig. Palec's career as a broker and as a radio host is discussed.

16658 ■ "Reds Hit Ratings Homer" in *Business Courier* (Vol. 27, July 30, 2010, No. 13, pp. 1)
Pub: Business Courier

Ed: Steve Watkins, James Ourand. **Description:** Cincinnati Reds fans have tuned in to their TVs and radios as their team made a hottest start to a season. The Reds TV ratings have increased 49 percent during the first six months of 2010 and continued to rise while the Reds' games broadcast on WLW-AM reported the highest average audience share per game of any Major League Baseball team.

16659 ■ "Regent's Signal, Once Powerful, Fading From Local Scene" in *Business Courier* (Vol. 27, June 4, 2010, No. 5, pp. 1)
Pub: Business Courier

Ed: Dan Monk. **Description:** Los Angeles, California-based Oaktree Capital Management bought former Regent Communications Inc. from Chapter 11 bankruptcy and transformed it into Townsquare Media Inc., a privately held firm. Regent's corporate presence has faded fast in Cincinnati, Ohio as its operations wind down. Insights on Regent's failed business model are also given.

16660 ■ "Research Reports: How Analysts Size Up Companies" in *Barron's* (Vol. 90, August 23, 2010, No. 34, pp. M13)
Pub: Barron's Editorial & Corporate Headquarters

Description: Shares of Sirius XM Radio, Target and Deere and Company received an eBuyE rating, while shares of Research in Motion got an eNeutralE rating.

16661 ■ "Satellite Wars" in *Canadian Business* (Vol. 79, October 23, 2006, No. 21, pp. 35)
Pub: Rogers Media

Ed: Andy Holloway. **Description:** The strategies used by Sirius Canada Inc. and XM Canada, two major satellite radio companies to acquire more number of suscribers, are discussed.

16662 ■ "Survey: More Buyers Expect to Spend Less in Most Media" in *Advertising Age* (Vol. 79, July 7, 2008, No. 26, pp. 3)
Pub: Crain Communications, Inc.

Ed: Megan McIlroy. **Description:** Marketers are decreasing their budgets for advertising in television, radio, newspaper and outdoor due to the economic downturn. Statistical data concerning advertising agencies and marketers included.

16663 ■ "Transform Your Life" in *Black Enterprise* (Vol. 37, January 2007, No. 6, pp. 14)
Pub: Earl G. Graves Publishing Co. Inc.

Description: Through the magazine, television and radio programs, events, and the website, the various platforms of Black Enterprise will provide the tools necessary to achieve success in business ventures, career aspirations, and personal goals.

16664 ■ "Wendy Turner; Vice-President and General Manager, Vocalo.org" in *Crain's Chicago Business* (Vol. 31, May 5, 2008, No. 18, pp. 22)
Pub: Crain Communications, Inc.

Ed: Kevin McKeough. **Description:** Profile of Wendy Turner who is a leader at Vocalo, a combination of talk radio and Web site, where listeners can set up profile pages similar to those on Facebook.

16665 ■ "XM Burning Through Cash to Catch Sirius" in *Globe & Mail* (April 17, 2007, pp. B5)
Pub: CTVglobemedia Publishing Inc.

Ed: Grant Robertson. **Description:** The effort of XM Satellite Radio Holdings Inc. to spend about $45 million to increase sale of its radio in Canada is discussed.

16666 ■ "XM Mulls Betting the Bank in Competitive Game of Subscriber Growth" in *Globe & Mail* (March 18, 2006, pp. B3)
Pub: CTVglobemedia Publishing Inc.

Ed: Grant Robertson. **Description:** Canadian Satellite Radio Inc., XM Canada, president and Chief Operating Officer Stephen Tapp feel that establishing a profile in satellite radio to attract subscribers is a very big challenge. His views on the Canadian radio market are detailed.

16667 ■ "XM and Sirius Satellite Radio Face Up to Their Losses and Decide to Get Hitched" in *Globe & Mail* (February 20, 2007, pp. B17)
Pub: CTVglobemedia Publishing Inc.

Ed: Grant Robertson. **Description:** XM Satellite Radio and Sirius Satellite Radio are planning to merge operations, after years of losses. The possible merger could create a $13 billion company.

SOURCES OF SUPPLY

16668 ■ *BIA's Radio Yearbook*
Pub: BIA Financial Network Inc.

Released: Annual, Latest edition 2011. **Price:** $210, individuals. **Covers:** U.S. Radio stations, radio equipment manufacturers, and related service providers and trade associations. **Entries Include:** For radio stations—Call letters, address; general manager and owner names and phones; technical attributes, last acquisition date and price, Arbitron ratings. For others—Name, address, phone, name and title of contact. **Arrangement:** Classified by market. **Indexes:** Market index, call letter, city of license/Arbitron market, group owner (alphabetical and geographical), broker/lender (geographical).

TRADE PERIODICALS

16669 ■ *Communicator*
Pub: Radio-Television News Directors Association
Contact: Barbara S. Cochran, President
E-mail: barbarac@rtnda.org
Released: Monthly. **Price:** $125 other countries; $75 domestic; $8.50 single issue. **Description:** Radio and television news trade publication.

16670 ■ *Community Radio News*
Pub: National Federation of Community Broadcasters (NFCB)

Ed: Evona Balcziunas, Editor. **Released:** Monthly. **Price:** Included in membership; $75 University Libraries. **Description:** Serves as a medium of communication for independent, community-licensed radio stations. Contains brief articles and news items on such topics as public broadcasting and programming, legislative developments, activities of the Federal Communications Commission, and local stations. Recurring features include notices of grants and awards, job openings, and a calendar of events/conferences for noncommercial broadcasters.

16671 ■ *Feedback*
Pub: Broadcast Education Association
Ed: Joe Misiewicz, Editor, jmisiewicz@bsu.edu. **Released:** Quarterly. **Description:** Journal focusing on radio and TV broadcasting.

16672 ■ *FMedia!*
Pub: FM Atlas Publishing
Contact: Carol J. Elving, Fulfillment Director
Ed: Bruce F. Elving, Ph.D., Editor. **Released:** Monthly. **Price:** $75 for broadcasters; $26 for individuals. **Description:** Lists information on the facilities and formats of FM radio, including new station grants and applications. Also provides official and unofficial news and comments, as well as FM Dxing and FM reception concerns. Recurring features include letters to the editor, news of research, job listings, and notices of publications available.

16673 ■ *Radio World*
Pub: IMAS Publishing Inc.
Released: Biweekly. **Price:** Free to qualified subscribers; $39.95; $75 two years; $99 other countries; $198 other countries 2 years. **Description:** Technical newspaper (tabloid) covering radio broadcast industry.

16674 ■ *TelevisionWeek*
Pub: Crain Communications Inc. (Detroit, Michigan)
Contact: Rance Crain, Pres/Ed.-in-Ch.
Released: Weekly. **Price:** $119; $171 Canada incl. GST; $309 other countries airmail. **Description:** Newspaper covering management, programming, cable and trends in the television and the media industry.

VIDEOCASSETTES/ AUDIOCASSETTES

16675 ■ *Career Insights*
RMI Media
1365 N. Winchester St.
Olathe, KS 66061-5880
Ph:(913)768-1696
Free: 800-745-5480
Fax:800-755-6910
Co. E-mail: actmedia@act.org
URL: http://www.actmedia.com
Released: 1987. **Description:** Describes 50 occupations, including skill requirements and interviews with people employed in these fields. **Availability:** VHS; 3/4U.

TRADE SHOWS AND CONVENTIONS

16676 ■ Radio-Television News Directors Association International Conference & Exhibition
Radio-Television News Directors Association
1600 K St., NW, Ste. 700
Washington, DC 20006-2838
Ph:(202)659-6510
Free: 800-807-8632
Fax:(202)223-4007
Co. E-mail: rtnda@rtnda.org
URL: http://www.rtnda.org
Released: Annual. **Audience:** Professionals from the television, radio and cable industries, along with representatives from government, publications and special interest groups. **Principal Exhibits:** Equipment, supplies, and services for the radio and television news industries, including cameras, recorders, weather equipment, computers, and software.

CONSULTANTS

16677 ■ A & A Research
690 Sunset Blvd.
Kalispell, MT 59901-3641
Ph:(406)752-7857
Free: 800-735-1554
Fax:(406)752-0194
Contact: Judith Doonan, President
Scope: Offers marketing research services, specializing in newspaper readership and advertising studies. Also specializes in audience research and programming studies for radio and television stations, minority broadcasting, new business and retail marketing research, and advertising consulting and research. Also prepares public opinion polls. Serves private industries as well as government agencies. **Seminars:** Three R's of Advertising; Precision Advertising; Audience Research Workshop; Use of Research in Radio Programming.

16678 ■ Baker Scott & Co.
16 South Ave. W
Cranford, NJ 07016
Ph:(973)263-3355
Fax:(973)263-9255
Co. E-mail: exec.search@bakerscott.com
URL: http://www.bakerscott.com
E-mail: exec.search@bakerscott.com
Scope: Consulting services include executive recruiting, employment attitude surveys, and screening organization plans. Industries served: telecommunication, cable TV, broadcasting entertainment, and financial institutions. The firm is integrated horizontally across functional discipline such as accounting, administration, call center, data processing, engineering, finance, general operations, marketing

and technical and plant operations. **Seminars:** Offers seminar programs on interview techniques, management skills, and customer service.

16679 ■ The Benchmark Co.
907 S Congress Ave., Ste. 7
Austin, TX 78704
Ph:(512)707-7500
Free: 800-688-7010
Fax:(512)707-7757
Co. E-mail: thebenc@earthlink.net
URL: http://www.thebenchmarkcompany.net
Contact: Bob McDonald, VP of Research
E-mail: rob@diningoutwithrobbalon.com
Scope: Full service consultants to the communications industry, specializing in radio and television. Also serves newspapers and ad agencies with extensive market research. **Publications:** "Radio in the 90S; Audience, Promotion and Marketing Strategies". **Seminars:** The Rules of the Ratings Game Seminar.

16680 ■ Conly Productions
1563 Oneida St.
Denver, CO 80220-1750
Ph:(303)393-6240
Fax:(303)393-6240
Co. E-mail: conlymusic@aol.com
Contact: Paul F. Conly, Owner
Scope: Provides audiovisual production consulting including all phases of production for television, radio, or multi-image shows: pre-production, location scouting, scripting, casting, ideography or still photography, post-production services, editing, sound effects, audio sweetening, music scoring. Also consults on equipment purchasing audiovisual installations.

16681 ■ D.E.M. Allen & Associates Ltd.
130 Cree Crescent
Winnipeg, MB, Canada R3J 3W1
Ph:(204)889-9202
Fax:(204)831-6650
Co. E-mail: gneilson@dema.mb.ca
URL: http://www.dema.mb.ca
Contact: Gord Neilson, Principal
E-mail: wriesterer@atsdema.mb.ca
Scope: Telecommunications consultants, experienced in AM, FM and television broadcasting, CATV systems, LF/HF, VHF/UHF and microwave systems and satellite earth stations; RF measurements and evaluations related to SCADA; LMCS in the millimeters portion of the spectrum as well as the 2.5Ghz MDS/MMDS field; electromagnetic compatibility and electromagnetic immunity including non-ionizing radiation evaluation and measurement. Services include planning, design, supervision and adjustment of broadcast transmitting facilities, including specifications, tender evaluation, preparation of reports, technical briefs for Federal Regulatory bodies, evaluation and measurements associated with RF propagation and electromagnetic energy throughout the radio frequency spectrum. Industries served: Broadcast, communications and national defense agencies.

16682 ■ DeMers Programming Media Consultants
4503 Adelphi Ln.
Austin, TX 78750
Ph:(610)363-2636
Fax:(610)363-2198
Co. E-mail: info@demersprogramming.com
URL: http://www.demersprogramming.com
Contact: Sean Hoots, Mgr
E-mail: sean@demersprogramming.com
Scope: Programming and marketing consultants offering advice for broadcasters and broadcast related businesses. Services include: music and format controls, strategic planning, talent coaching and acquisition, research and promotional planning. Serves private and government sectors. **Publications:** "12 Steps To A One Share - Uncovering The Clutter," Feb, 2005; "Get Your Mind Out Of The Clutter - DeMers Dispatch Winter '05"; "See Spot Run... Over The Golden Goose"; "Radio's Attention Deficit Disorder"; "Program The Seller"; "At Issue: Staying Creative"; "Take A Hard Look At Your Special Pro-

gramming"; "A Fresh Coat Of Paint"; "Guerrilla Radio". **Seminars:** Diary Keepers Plus Research; Marketing, Merchandising and Money.

16683 ■ Donna Halper & Associates
550 Adams St., Ste. 3-365
Quincy, MA 02169
Ph:(617)786-0666
Fax:(617)786-1809
Co. E-mail: dlh@donnahalper.com
URL: http://www.donnahalper.com
Contact: Donna L. Halper, President
E-mail: dlh@atsdonnahalper.com
Scope: Offers staff training; market research; positioning studies and music software. Expertise in helping radio station owners to choose the right format. Also expertise in news and public affairs programming. Industries served primarily radio both professional and college but has also served nonprofit service organizations and has trained numerous women and minority staff for management positions. 23 years of experience. **Publications:** "Invisible Stars: A Social History of Women in America Broadcasting".; "Icons of Talk". **Seminars:** Improving Communication at Your Station; Dealing with Diversity; a Media History of Your Market (custom designed and researched for your station and your city). **Special Services:** Music rotation software for radio stations.

16684 ■ Elder Engineering Inc.
35 Auckland Ln.
PO Box 10
King City, ON, Canada L7B 1C1
Ph:(905)833-5141
Fax:(905)833-2101
Co. E-mail: eldeng@sympatico.ca
Contact: Joan Elder, Office Mgr
E-mail: eldeng@sympatico.ca
Scope: Expertise regarding communications and broadcast transmitting systems encompasses feasibility study, frequency search, site selection, propagation tests, and protection analysis. Experienced with antenna design, contour predictions, equipment specification, technical brief, bid selection, tuning, testing, certification and proof of performance for newer improved transmitting facilities in LF to UHF bands; design studies for broadband multi station AM, FM, TV or DRB antenna and transmission systems at a common site, point-to-point STL, microwave distant learning, MDS, or teleconferencing systems. Industries served: radio, television, broadcasters and applicants, power utilities, government agencies, radio communications licensees, and manufacturers.

16685 ■ Engineering Harmonics Inc.
29A Leslie St.
Toronto, ON, Canada M4M 3C3
Ph:(416)465-3378
Fax:(416)465-9037
Co. E-mail: 2009-info@engineeringharmonics.com
URL: http://www.engineeringharmonics.com
Contact: Paul Alegado, Principle
E-mail: pgiddings@atsengineeringharmonies.com
Scope: Specializing in audio, audio and video, control, and communication based systems. **Publications:** "Designing Sound for Frank Gehry's Vision"; "Precis of WDCH PSVC System"; "PSVC Design Challenges at WDCH"; "Power and Ground Update"; "Noise Reduction Systems"; "Mandating the House Audio System," Overture Hall; "Betting on Legends," Nov, 2008; "Examining our Roots, Defining our Future," Dec, 2008; "Walking The Hall: A Guide to Tuning a Loudspeaker System," Nov, 2007; "National Ballet School," Nov, 2007; "The Puzzle of PA for a Hall-in-the-Round," Aug, 2007; "A House for All Seasons," Aug, 2006; "Hooray for LA," Jan, 2004; "A Kodak Moment," Apr, 2002.

16686 ■ Financial Solutions Inc.
309 W Jefferson St.
La Grange, KY 40031
Ph:(502)225-9900
Free: 877-952-9766

Fax:(502)225-9997
Co. E-mail: robin@lawsonfinancial.net
URL: http://www.lawsonfinancial.net
Contact: Robin H. Lawson, Owner
E-mail: robin@lawsonfinancial.net
Scope: Offers financial brokerage services to the broadcasting industry in the Midwest United States. **Publications:** "Eighty percent of Americans agree they would benefit from having basic financial education and information," 2009; "Finra Investor Education Survey, 2007"; "How Are Mutual Funds Taxed". **Seminars:** Long Term Care, Estate Planning, Retirement, Financial Management.

16687 ■ Forsyth Consulting
9 Laurier Ave.
Toronto, ON, Canada M4X 1S2
Ph:(416)964-0812
Fax:(416)964-1304
Co. E-mail: ajforsyth9@rogers.com
Contact: Andrew J. Forsyth, President
E-mail: ajforsyth9@rogers.com
Scope: Specialized in regulatory affairs applicable to radio, television, cable, and satellite. Provides CRTC applications and interventions, compliance strategies and analysis, strategic planning and market positioning, creative programming, management sales, talent and formative development, acquisitions, benefit package strategies, and broadcast property sale representation. Industries served: Broadcasting.

16688 ■ Hartech Inc.
6882 S Prince Cir.
PO Box 88
Littleton, CO 80120-3538
Ph:(303)794-0196
Fax:(303)794-0196
Co. E-mail: jhart@chicagogsb.edu
URL: http://www.hartechinc.com
Contact: James W. Hart, President
E-mail: jhart@du.edu
Scope: Specializes in radio system design including communications needs assessments, system designs, coverage modeling, profiling, path determinations and reliabilities, interference studies, specification generation, economic analysis and cost estimates, field engineering, system acceptance requirements assurance, expert witnessing. Also specialized in hazardous radiation calculations and measurements. Industries served: two-way radio, microwave radio, broadcasters private and government. **Publications:** "Understanding Wireless Communications in Public Safety, a Guidebook to Technology, Issues, Planning, and Management"; "Tri-State Tackles Coverage in Challenging Terrain," Radio Resource Magazine, Jul, 1999.

16689 ■ Radiotechniques Engineering Corp.
402 10th Ave.
PO Box 367
Haddon Heights, NJ 08035-0367
Ph:(856)546-8008
Fax:(856)546-1841
Co. E-mail: sales@radiotechniques.com
URL: http://www.radiotechniques.com
Contact: Gordon Krauss, Principle
E-mail: ted@radiotechniques.com
Scope: Provides design, FCC allocation engineering and field engineering services for broadcast, private and common carrier radio clients. Particular emphasis is on optimized broadcast systems using directional antennas and service area improvement through engineering measures. Offers RF-oriented product-design services in the fields of digital and analog modulation systems, transmitters, battery powered receivers and computer control systems. Specializes in RF instrumentation and antennas. **Special Services:** Point Manager™; Palm Pilot™; Treo™.

16690 ■ Sellmeyer Engineering
2 Pecan Grove Cir.
PO Box 356
Lucas, TX 75002
Ph:(972)542-2056

Fax:(972)636-5940
Co. E-mail: jack@sellmeyereng.com
URL: http://www.sellmeyereng.com
Contact: Jack S. Sellmeyer, President
E-mail: jack@sellmeyereng.com
Scope: Broadcast and communications engineering consultants. Offer services in FCC applications, transmitter plant design, construction supervision, broadcast studio facilities planning and construction, AM directional antenna design and adjustment and measurements.

16691 ■ Strategic Computer Solutions Inc.
2625 Shefman Terr., Ste. 200
Ann Arbor, MI 48105
Ph:(248)888-0666
Free: (866)727-7276
Fax:(248)888-0665
Co. E-mail: info@stratcom.com
URL: http://www.stratcom.com
Contact: Luther Huffman, Mgr
E-mail: lutherh@atsstratcom.com
Scope: Computer technology consultants specializing in notebooks, Pcs, Unix systems, networking, custom turnkey programming, database development, web hosting and development. Industries served medical, dental, legal, property management, marinas, unions, radio stations, and other businesses function as your ITMIS department. **Special Services:** gloEMR™.

COMPUTERIZED DATABASES

16692 ■ RAB.com
Radio Advertising Bureau
1320 Greenway Dr., Ste. 500
Irving, TX 75038
Ph:(972)753-6822
Free: 800-232-3131
Fax:(972)753-6727
Co. E-mail: jhaley@rab.com
URL: http://www.rab.com
Description: Contains descriptive listings for approximately 7000 cooperative advertising plans for radio stations, including some 6000 stations in the U.S. and more than 1000 associate members in networks, representative firms, sales, and international organizations. Covers manufacturers' allowances for portions of retailers' radio advertising costs and includes the manufacturer's name, address, telephone number, and name of contact; product category and trade name; percent of advertising cost to be paid by manufacturer; accrual rate; indication of whether plan is administered by a distributor; and expiration date of plan. Data on cooperative advertising plans are compiled from manufacturers and correspond to Radio Co-op Sources. **Availability:** Online: Radio Advertising Bureau. **Type:** Directory.

LIBRARIES

16693 ■ Canadian Broadcasting Corporation–Reference Library/Image Research Library
PO Box 500, Sta. A
Toronto, ON, Canada M5W 1E6
Ph:(416)205-3244
Free: (866)306-4636
Fax:(416)205-3733
Co. E-mail: reference_library@cbc.ca
URL: http://www.cbc.ca/designlibrary/index.html
Contact: Michele Melady, Mgr.
Scope: Radio and television broadcasting, Canadiana, current affairs, drama, design. **Services:** Interlibrary loan; copying; Library open to the public for research on CBC or broadcasting in Canada. **Holdings:** 27,000 books; 8000 files of newspaper clippings. **Subscriptions:** 200 journals and other serials; 13 newspapers.

16694 ■ CBS News Reference Library
524 W. 57th St.
New York, NY 10019
URL: http://www.cbsnews.com
Contact: Laura B. Kapnick, Dir.
Scope: Radio, television, biography, current events, government, politics. **Holdings:** 38,000 books; 2500

bound periodical volumes; 15,000 clippings files; 7700 reels of microfilm; 50,000 microfiche. **Subscriptions:** 270 journals and other serials; 10 newspapers.

16695 ■ Library of Congress–Motion Picture, Broadcasting & Recorded Sound Division
James Madison Memorial Bldg., LM 113
101 Independence Ave., SE
Washington, DC 20540-4690
Ph:(202)707-5840
Fax:(202)707-2371
Co. E-mail: mpref@loc.gov
URL: http://www.loc.gov/rr/mopic
Contact: Gregory Lukow, Chf.
Scope: All genres and formats of moving images and sound recordings, ranging from the earliest motion pictures registered for copyright (1894-1912), the earliest sound recordings on both cylinder and disc, along with recordings of radio broadcasts beginning in the late 1920s to current feature films, television programs, documentaries, educational films and videos, with an emphasis on American productions; current popular, folk, jazz, opera, and classical music recorded on compact disc. **Services:** Collections open to the public with restrictions. **Holdings:** 3000 books, bound volumes of early periodicals, and vertical files; 300,000 film items; 350,000 television items; 3 million sound recordings preserved on cylinders, discs, tapes, wires, Dictaphone belts, music box discs, and piano rolls. **Subscriptions:** 150 journals and other serials.

16696 ■ National Association of Broadcasters–Information Resource Center
1771 N St., NW
Washington, DC 20036
Ph:(202)429-5490
Fax:(202)429-4199
Co. E-mail: irc@nab.org
URL: http://www.nab.org
Contact: Steven Mitchel, Ref.Libn.
Scope: Radio and television broadcasting and allied subjects. **Services:** Special Library open to members and others by special request. **Holdings:** 8000 volumes. **Subscriptions:** 200 journals and other serials.

16697 ■ National Public Radio–Broadcast Library
635 Massachusetts Ave., NW
Washington, DC 20001-3740
Ph:(202)513-2060
Fax:(202)513-3329
Co. E-mail: rrobinson@npr.org
URL: http://www.npr.org
Contact: Robert Robinson, Sr.Libn.
Scope: News and current events, drama, music. **Services:** Collection open to the public by appointment. **Holdings:** 100,000 audiotapes; 10,000 phonograph records and compact discs; CD-ROMs. **Subscriptions:** 6 journals and other serials.

16698 ■ NBC Universal–Information Resource Center
30 Rockefeller Plaza
Room 470S
New York, NY 10112
Ph:(212)664-5307
Fax:(212)664-7842
Co. E-mail: debra.levinson@nbcuni.com
Contact: Debra Levinson, Dir., Info.Rsrcs.
Scope: Broadcasting, politics and government, current events, business, economics, marketing, advertising. **Services:** Library open to NBCU and General Electric employees, and to other librarians by appointment. **Holdings:** 5000 books; 650 bound periodical volumes; 8800 reels of microfilm. **Subscriptions:** 150 journals and other serials; 16 newspapers.

16699 ■ North American Radio Archives–Tape and Printed Materials Libraries
4741 E. Grant St.
Fresno, CA 93702
Ph:(209)456-2020
URL: http://www.engagingradio.org
Contact: Scott Jones, Reel-to-Reel Libn.
Scope: Radio - history, programming, broadcasting, scripts, publications; television broadcasting; film. **Services:** Libraries open to members only and

researchers by written request. **Holdings:** 800 books; 5000 reel-to-reel tapes; 250 scripts; 300 slides; 400 magazines; 300 reprints of articles; 15,000 cassettes; 6000 television shows. **Subscriptions:** 400 journals and other serials.

16700 ■ North American Radio Archives
NARA Library
134 Vincewood Dr.
Nicholasville, KY 40356
Ph:(606)885-1031
URL: http://www.bostonradio.org/radio/narba.html
Contact: Janis DeMoss, Exec. Officer
Scope: Radio - drama, comedy, entertainment, news, documentary; radio programming. **Services:** Library open to members of NARA who may borrow its material. **Holdings:** 200 books; 100,000 radio programs, 1926-1965, on tape; slides of radio personalities; radio scripts and magazines; reproduced articles on radio. **Subscriptions:** 300 journals and other serials.

16701 ■ The Paley Center for
Media–Research Services
25 W. 52nd St.
New York, NY 10019
Ph:(212)621-6600
Fax:(212)621-6632
URL: http://www.paleycenter.org
Contact: Pat Mitchell, Pres./CEO
Scope: Television (except technical aspects) and radio. **Services:** Reference inquiries from the public

accepted by mail or fax only; telephone reference service available for museum members at contributing level and above. **Holdings:** 2600 books. **Subscriptions:** 60 journals and other serials; 7 newspapers.

16702 ■ Radio Advertising Bureau–Marketing
Information Center
1320 Greenway Dr., Ste. 500
Irving, TX 75038
Ph:(516)753-6782
Free: 800-232-3131
Co. E-mail: arainey@rab.com
URL: http://www.rab.com/
Contact: Andy Rainey, Sr.VP, Research
Scope: Radio, advertising and marketing, consumer markets, demographics, competitive media, leading advertisers, retailing. **Services:** Interlibrary loan (limited); copying; Center open to the public by special permission. **Holdings:** 600 volumes; 70 VF drawers of clippings. **Subscriptions:** 152 journals and other serials.

16703 ■ Temple University–Temple University
Libraries–Blitman Resource Center (334 A)
334 Annenberg Hall
Main Campus
Philadelphia, PA 19122-6080
Ph:(215)204-7350

Fax:(215)204-1974
Co. E-mail: lpanzer@astro.temple.edu
URL: http://www.temple.edu/
Contact: Lisa Panser, Libn.
Scope: Reporting, newspaper industry, media law, radio and television broadcasting, telecommunications. **Services:** Copying; Library open to the public. **Holdings:** 15,000 books. **Subscriptions:** 120 journals and other serials; 15 newspapers.

16704 ■ University of Maryland, College Park
Libraries–Hornbake Library–Library of
American Broadcasting (3210)
3210 Hornbake Library
College Park, MD 20742
Ph:(301)405-9160
Fax:(301)314-2634
Co. E-mail: labcast@umd.edu
URL: http://www.lib.umd.edu/LAB
Contact: Chuck Howell, Cur.
Scope: Radio and television broadcasting history. **Services:** Copying; Library open to the public. **Holdings:** 8700 books; 250 periodical titles; 320 VF drawers and boxes of archives, clippings, research studies, scripts, scrapbooks, documents, and correspondence; 1000 oral histories, including interviews with prominent broadcasters; 5445 audiotapes; 25,000 photographs; 1500 subject files; 6000 pamphlets. **Subscriptions:** 240 journals and other serials.

ASSOCIATIONS AND OTHER ORGANIZATIONS

16705 ■ American Association of Radon Scientists and Technologists
PO Box 2109
Fletcher, NC 28732
Free: (866)772-2778
Fax:(828)890-8071
Co. E-mail: office@aarst.org
URL: http://www.aarst.org/home.html
Contact: Peter Hendrick, Exec. Dir.

Description: Scientists and tradespeople engaged in radon gas testing and remediation and advocacy on behalf of radon lung cancer victims. Works for policy changes at local, state and federal level to implement the 1988 Indoor Radon Abatement Act. Seeks to improve members' skills and effectiveness; conducts international educational and research programs; maintains speakers' bureau; compiles statistics. **Pub-**lications: *Annual Proceedings International Radon Symposium* (annual); *Radon Reporter* (quarterly).

FRANCHISES AND BUSINESS OPPORTUNITIES

16706 ■ Professional House Doctors Inc.
1406 E 14th St.
Des Moines, IA 50316
Ph:(515)265-6667
Free: 800-288-7437
Fax:(515)278-2070
No. of Franchise Units: 7. **No. of Company-Owned Units:** 1. **Founded:** 1982. **Franchised:** 1991. **Description:** Providers of environmental and building science services to residential and commercial clients. Services include radon testing and mitigation, building inspections, indoor air quality analysis, asbestos and lead analysis, energy analysis and consultation, structural moisture analysis, healthy house investigations, environmental do-it-yourself test kits and much more. **Equity Capital Needed:** $15,000-$30,000. **Franchise Fee:** $9,800. **Royalty Fee:** 6%. **Financial Assistance:** Limited in-house financing available. **Training:** Offers 2 weeks at headquarters and ongoing support.

LIBRARIES

16707 ■ Radiation Safety Institute of Canada Library
165 Avenue Rd., Ste. 300
Toronto, ON, Canada M3J 3H7
Ph:(416)650-9090
Free: 800-263-5803
Fax:(416)650-9920
Co. E-mail: info@radiationsafety.ca
URL: http://www.radiationsafety.ca
Contact: Natalia Mozayani, Prog.Mgr.
Scope: Radiation, radiation safety, radon, radiation/ health, radioactive waste, nuclear power. **Services:** Library open to the public. **Holdings:** Books; reports; clipping file.

START-UP INFORMATION

16708 ■ **"No Place Like Home"** in *Small Business Opportunities* (Winter 2010)
Pub: Harris Publications Inc.
Ed: Description: Five reasons to start a home-staging business in any economy are listed. Home staging is listed as the top emerging career on Website, Careerbuilder.com.

ASSOCIATIONS AND OTHER ORGANIZATIONS

16709 ■ **American Land Title Association**
1828 L St. NW, Ste. 705
Washington, DC 20036
Ph:(202)296-3671
Free: 800-787-ALTA
Fax:(202)223-5843
Co. E-mail: service@alta.org
URL: http://www.alta.org
Contact: Anne L. Anastasi CLTP, Pres.-Elect
Description: Represents the abstracters, title insurance companies, and attorneys specializing in real property law. **Publications:** *Title News* (bimonthly)-;Membership Directory (annual).

16710 ■ **American Real Estate Society**
Clemson University
Dept. of Finance
424 Sirrine Hall
Clemson, SC 29634-1343
Ph:(864)656-1373
Fax:(864)656-7519
Co. E-mail: equarle@clemson.edu
URL: http://www.aresnet.org
Contact: Mr. John E. Williams, Pres.
Description: College and university professors; high-level practicing professionals involved in real estate finance, investment, development, valuation, marketing, consulting, management, education, and law; and institutions. Acts as a forum for the exchange of information and research on applied business and individual decision-making within real estate finance, real estate market analysis, investment, valuation, development, and other areas related to real estate in the private sector. Operates ARES Case Clearinghouse, which makes available copies of instructional cases pertinent to real estate practice. Conducts educational programs for real estate professionals. **Publications:** *ARES Newsletter* (semiannual); *Journal of Housing Research*; *Journal of Real Estate Literature* (semiannual); *Journal of Real Estate Portfolio Management* (quarterly); *The Journal of Real Estate Research* (bimonthly); *Journal Real Estate Practice and Education* (annual);Monograph (annual).

16711 ■ **Canadian Real Estate Association–L'Association canadienne de l'immeuble**
200 Catherine St., 6th Fl.
Ottawa, ON, Canada K2P 2K9
Ph:(613)237-7111

Free: 800-842-2732
Fax:(613)234-2567
Co. E-mail: info@crea.ca
URL: http://www.crea.ca
Contact: Mr. Marc N. Lafrance, Dir.
Description: Real estate professionals. Seeks the professional advancement of members and to increase the profitability of the real estate industry. Advocates public policies favorable to the sale of real estate and protective of property and ownership rights; conducts educational programs; compiles statistics.

16712 ■ **Counselors of Real Estate**
430 N Michigan Ave.
Chicago, IL 60611
Ph:(312)329-8427
Co. E-mail: info@cre.org
URL: http://www.cre.org
Contact: Mary Walker Fleischmann, Pres./CEO
Description: Professional society of individuals with extensive experience in all phases of real estate who provide a counseling service. Members are entitled to use the Professional Designation CRE (Counselor of Real Estate). Conducts educational programs during three national meetings. **Publications:** *CRE Member Directory* (annual); *Real Estate Issues* (3/ year).

16713 ■ **FIABCI-U.S.A.**
1961 Wilson Blvd., Ste. 306
Arlington, VA 22201
Ph:(703)524-4279
Fax:(703)991-6256
Co. E-mail: info@fiabci-usa.com
URL: http://www.fiabci-usa.com
Contact: Danielle Grossenbacher, Pres.
Description: Brings together nearly 1,000,000 members in 57 countries; members represent all specializations in real estate, including brokerage, development, counseling, management, appraisal and financing. Conducts discussion among members in global real estate trends, emerging markets, case studies of international real estate transactions and refer business to each other. **Publications:** *FIABCI Press* (5/year).

16714 ■ **Institute of Real Estate Management**
430 N Michigan Ave.
Chicago, IL 60611
Ph:(312)329-6000
Free: 800-837-0706
Fax:800-338-4736
Co. E-mail: custserv@irem.org
URL: http://www.irem.org
Contact: Ronald L. Goss, Pres.
Description: Professional organization of real property and asset managers. Awards professional designation Certified Property Manager (CPM) to qualifying individuals, Accredited Management Organization (AMO) to qualifying management firms and also awards Accredited Residential Manager (ARM) accreditation to qualifying individuals who are primarily residential site managers. Monitors legislation affecting real estate management. Offers management courses and seminars; conducts research

and educational programs, publishes books and reports; maintains formal code of ethics; compiles statistics; maintains employment Website for real estate management industry. .

16715 ■ **Mortgage Bankers Association**
1717 Rhode Island Ave. NW, Ste. 400
Washington, DC 20036
Ph:(202)557-2700
Free: 800-793-6222
Co. E-mail: membership@mortgagebankers.org
URL: http://www.mortgagebankers.org
Contact: Michael D. Berman CMB, Chm.
Description: Principal lending and investor interests in the mortgage finance field, including mortgage banking firms, commercial banks, life insurance companies, title companies, and savings and loan associations. Seeks to improve methods of originating, servicing, and marketing loans of residential and income-producing properties through industry education and cooperation with federal agencies and the Congress. Holds clinics on all aspects of the mortgage finance business. Sponsors School of Mortgage Banking, and correspondence courses and web-based training on mortgage subjects for member personnel. Collects statistics and conducts research on the industry. **Publications:** *Mortgage Bankers Performance Study* (quarterly); *Mortgage Banking: The Magazine of Real Estate Finance* (monthly); *National Delinquency Survey* (quarterly).

16716 ■ **National Association of Real Estate Brokers**
5504 Brentwood Stair Rd.
Fort Worth, TX 76112
Ph:(817)446-7715
Fax:(817)446-7744
Co. E-mail: wvincent.wimbish@nareb.com
URL: http://www.nareb.com
Contact: Vincent Wimbish, Pres.
Description: Members of the real estate industry. Research, educational and certification programs include: Real Estate Management Brokers Institute; National Society of Real Estate Appraisers; Real Estate Brokerage Institute; United Developers Council. Encourages unity among those who are engaged in real estate. Promotes and maintains high standards of conduct. Protects the public against unethical, improper, or fraudulent practices connected with the real estate business. Conducts research; compiles statistics on productivity, marketing and development. Gives members license to use "Realtist" symbol. Sponsors educational seminars. Maintains Willis E. Carson Library. **Publications:** *Realtist Membership Directory* (annual).

16717 ■ **National Association of Realtors**
430 N Michigan Ave.
Chicago, IL 60611-4087
Free: 800-874-6500
URL: http://www.realtor.org
Contact: Ron Phipps, Pres.
Description: Federation of 54 state and territory associations and 1,860 local real estate boards whose members are real estate brokers and agents; terms are registered by the association in the U.S. Patent

and Trademark Office and in the states. Promotes education, high professional standards and modern techniques in specialized real estate work such as brokerage, appraisal, property management, land development, industrial real estate, farm brokerage and counseling. Conducts research programs. **Publications:** *Real Estate Outlook* (monthly).

16718 ■ National Association of Review Appraisers and Mortgage Underwriters
810 N Farrell Dr.
Palm Springs, CA 92262
Ph:(760)327-5284
Fax:(760)327-5631
Co. E-mail: support@assoc-hdqts.org
URL: http://www.naramu.com
Contact: Dr. Bill Merrell, Advisory Council
Description: Real estate professionals and mortgage underwriters who aid in determining value of property. Acts as umbrella group for real estate appraisers. Conducts educational seminars; maintains speakers' bureau; operates placement service. **Publications:** Membership Directory (annual).

16719 ■ National Council of Exchangors
PO Box 668
Morro Bay, CA 93443-0668
Free: 800-324-1031
Co. E-mail: nce@infoville.com
URL: http://www.nce1031.com/nce
Contact: Bill Pitts, Pres.
Description: Real estate professionals who possess specialized training in the fields of real estate exchanging, real estate tax law, investment analysis, client counseling, and equity marketing. Promotes educational programs. Provides a forum for member exchanges. **Publications:** *NCE News* (periodic).

16720 ■ Real Property Association of Canada–Association des biens Immobiliers du Canada
One University Ave., Ste. 1410
Toronto, ON, Canada M5J 2P1
Ph:(416)642-2700
Free: (855)732-5722
Fax:(416)642-2727
Co. E-mail: info@realpac.ca
URL: http://www.realpac.ca
Contact: Michael Brooks PhD, CEO
Description: Real estate and development companies and related businesses. Promotes growth in the real estate development and related industries. Serves as a forum for discussion of issues facing the industry; represents members' interests before the public.

16721 ■ Realtors Land Institute
430 N Michigan Ave.
Chicago, IL 60611
Ph:(312)329-8446
Free: 800-441-5263
Fax:(312)329-8633
Co. E-mail: rli@realtors.org
URL: http://www.rliland.com
Contact: Ray Brownfield, Pres.-Elect
Description: Real estate brokers and salespersons selling, managing, appraising, or developing all types of land. Maintains educational programs for real estate brokers; promotes competence and accredits members. Sponsors courses for realtors and others seeking professional excellence on Land Brokerage, Agricultural Land Brokerage, Exchanging Properties, Estate Planning, Subdivision Development and Financial Analysis of Land Investment. .

16722 ■ Women's Council of Realtors
430 N Michigan Ave.
Chicago, IL 60611
Ph:(312)329-8481
Free: 800-245-8512
Fax:(312)329-3290
Co. E-mail: wcr@wcr.org
URL: http://www.wcr.org
Contact: Margo Wheeler Willis, Pres.
Description: Women and men real estate brokers and salespeople. Provides opportunity for real estate professionals to participate at local, state, and national levels. Makes programs available for personal and career growth. Offers courses in leader-

ship training, referral and relocation business. Members may earn the Leadership Training Graduate (LTG) designation. **Publications:** *Women's Council of Realtors—Referral Roster* (annual).

DIRECTORIES OF EDUCATIONAL PROGRAMS

16723 ■ *Directory of Private Accredited Career Schools and Colleges of Technology*
Pub: Accrediting Commission of Career Schools and Colleges of Technology
Contact: Michale S. McComis, Exec. Dir.
Released: On web page. **Price:** Free. **Description:** Covers 3900 accredited post-secondary programs that provide training programs in business, trade, and technical fields, including various small business endeavors. Entries offer school name, address, phone, description of courses, job placement assistance, and requirements for admission. Arrangement is alphabetical.

REFERENCE WORKS

16724 ■ "$1M Home Sales Spike" in *Business Courier* (Vol. 27, December 3, 2010, No. 31, pp. 1)
Pub: Business Courier
Ed: Tom Demeropolis. **Description:** Cincinnati Area Board of Realtors reported the increase of sales of multi-million dollar Tri-State homes in 2010, particularly in Indian Hill where sales surged nearly 60 percent. Sales of homes of $1 million and above are up 21 percent through November in Hamilton County with 58 homes sales.

16725 ■ "1Q Office Vacancies Mainly Up; Class A Space Bucks Trend, Falls" in *Crain's Detroit Business* (Vol. 24, April 14, 2008, No. 15)
Pub: Crain Communications, Inc.
Ed: Daniel Duggan. **Description:** Although more office space became vacant in the first quarter, Class A space went in the opposite direction with several local businesses are moving from less-desirable to more desirable areas.

16726 ■ "3CDC Investing $8 Million To Put New Life Into Old Homes" in *Globe & Mail* (February 28, 2006, pp. B1)
Pub: CTVglobemedia Publishing Inc.
Ed: Lucy May. **Description:** The Cincinnati Center City Development Corp. has bought more than 100 empty buildings and many around Washington Park in Over-the-Rhine. Its new project, called 3CDC, is to revitalize the historic neighborhood in the Washington Park area near Music Hall.

16727 ■ "6 Worth the Price Fix-Ups" in *Realtor Magazine* (Vol. 44, April-May 2011, No. 44, pp. 23)
Pub: Realtor Magazine
Description: Advice on how realtors could increase a home's resale value through do-it-yourself projects is given. Removal of personal items and clutter is recommended, along with rearrangement of furniture. A clutter consultant could also be used.

16728 ■ "A 16-Year Housing Slump? It Could Happen" in *Barron's* (Vol. 88, March 17, 2008, No. 11, pp. 27)
Pub: Dow Jones & Company, Inc.
Ed: Gene Epstein. **Description:** Housing remains a good protection against inflation but over very long periods. Inflation-adjusted stock prices did even better but have greater volatility. Commodities, on the other hand, underperformed both housing and stocks as inflation hedges. House prices tend to rise faster than the consumer price index is because land is inherently limited.

16729 ■ "The 35 Year Mortgage-Built to Last Time" in *Globe & Mail* (March 17, 2006, pp. B1)
Pub: CTVglobemedia Publishing Inc.
Ed: Patrick Brethour. **Description:** The 35-year mortgage has arrived in Canada. The plan will give an opportunity to the first-time buyers into the real estate market. Details of the new mortgage are analyzed.

16730 ■ "$100 Million in Projects Jeopardized" in *Business Courier* (Vol. 24, March 28, 2008, No. 51, pp. 1)
Pub: American City Business Journals, Inc.
Ed: Dan Monk. **Description:** Ohio's historic preservation tax credit program may be reinstated after some companies planned to sue over its stoppage. The Ohio Department of Development said the program was halted because it exceeded the allocated budget for the credit. $34 million in credits are at stake for more than two dozen local projects if the program is reinstated.

16731 ■ "217 Homes Planned for Former Crystal Cream Site" in *Sacramento Business Journal* (Vol. 25, August 8, 2008, No. 23, pp. 1)
Pub: American City Business Journals, Inc.
Ed: Michael Shaw. **Description:** MetroNova Development LLC plans to develop housing at the former Crystal Cream & Butter Co. site near downtown Sacramento. The developer expects to sell the new loft houses for about $300,000 without public subsidies. Views and other information on the planned development project, is presented.

16732 ■ "2009 Real Estate in Review: Median Prices Drop, Sales Up" in *Bellingham Business Journal* (Vol. February 2010, pp. 15)
Pub: Sound Publishing Inc.
Ed: Isaac Bonnell. **Description:** Bellingham and Whatcom County, Washington saw a rise in home sales in 2008. Single family home sales were up 3.3 percent in Bellingham and 0.5 percent for the entire county. Statistical data included.

16733 ■ "2010 Book of Lists" in *Austin Business JournalInc.* (Vol. 29, December 25, 2009, No. 42, pp. 1)
Pub: American City Business Journals
Description: Rankings of companies and organizations within the business services, finance, healthcare, hospitality and travel, insurance, marketing and media, professional services, real estate, education and technology industries in Austin, Texas are presented. Rankings are based on sales, business size, and other statistics.

16734 ■ "2010 Book of Lists" in *Business Courier* (Vol. 26, December 26, 2009, No. 36, pp. 1)
Pub: American City Business Journals, Inc.
Description: Rankings of companies and organizations within the business services, education, finance, health care, hospitality and tourism, real estate, and technology industries in the Cincinnati, Ohio-Northern Kentucky area are presented. Rankings are based on sales, business size, or other statistics.

16735 ■ "2010 Book of Lists" in *Tampa Bay Business Journal* (Vol. 30, December 22, 2009, No. 53, pp. 1)
Pub: American City Business Journals
Description: Rankings of companies and organizations within the human resources, banking and finance, business services, healthcare, real estate, technology, hospitality and travel, and education industries in the Greater Tampa Bay area are presented. Rankings are based on sales, business size, and more.

16736 ■ "A Conversation With; Ron Gatner, Jones Lang LaSalle" in *Crain's Detroit Business* (Vol. 24, October 6, 2008, No. 40, pp. 9)
Pub: Crain Communications, Inc.
Description: Interview with Ron Gatner who is a corporate real estate adviser with the real estate company Jones Lang LaSalle as well as the company's executive vice president and part of the tenant advisory team; Gatner speaks about the impact that the Wall Street crisis is having on the commercial real estate market in Detroit.

16737 ■ "Affordable Again" in *The Business Journal-Serving Greater Tampa Bay* (Vol. 28, July 18, 2008, No. 30, pp. 1)
Pub: American City Business Journals, Inc.
Ed: Janet Leiser. **Description:** Rental rates for office space in the Tampa Bay area has dropped to $21.68 a foot, after demand for the second quarter of 2008

has remained low. Commercial real estate experts say that the industry can easily rebound from what is believed to be the weakest demand in 20 years. Other views, information and statistics on real estate demand and prices in Tampa Bay are, are presented.

16738 ■ "Affordable Housing on the Rise" in *Philadelphia Business Journal* (Vol. 28, October 23, 2009, No. 36, pp. 1)
Pub: American City Business Journals
Ed: Natalie Kostelni. Description: Philadelphia, Pennsylvania led an affordable housing boom with more than 800 new affordable housing units in the works in spite of the recession. The converging of developers and federal stimulus money has driven the sudden increase with the launching of several projects across the city.

16739 ■ "Agricultural Community Implements Green Technologies, Building Team" in *Contractor* (Vol. 56, September 2009, No. 9, pp. 5)
Pub: Penton Media, Inc.
Ed: Candace Ruolo. Description: John DeWald and Associates has initiated a residential development project which uses green technologies in Illinois. The community features a community center, organic farm and recreational trails. Comments from executives are also provided.

16740 ■ "AIC To Buy $350M of Real Estate" in *Austin Business JournalInc.* (Vol. 28, November 14, 2008, No. 35, pp. 1)
Pub: American City Business Journals
Ed: Kate Harrington. Description: Austin-based AIC Ventures LP is planning to buy $350 million worth of commercial real estate. The company's move will double its acquisitions. It is also planning to acquire 30 assets for its eight fun in 2009 from middle-market companies.

16741 ■ "All Bubbles Must Burst" in *Canadian Business* (Vol. 83, August 17, 2010, No. 13-14, pp. 12)
Pub: Rogers Media Ltd.
Ed: Matthew McClearn. Description: Canada's housing markets is showing signs of cooling down as home and condo sales both fell for the first time in 16 years. The Canadian government has fueled the market over an extended period through Canada Mortgage and Housing Corporation's role in insuring mortgage lenders against risk of defaults.

16742 ■ "All-Star Advice 2010" in *Black Enterprise* (Vol. 41, October 2010, No. 3, pp. 97)
Pub: Earl G. Graves Publishing Co. Inc.
Ed: Renita Burns, Sheiresa Ngo, Marcia Wade Talbert. Description: Financial experts share tips on real estate, investing, taxes, insurance and debt management.

16743 ■ "Allen Tate Expanding to Research Triangle Park: Firm Expects Raleigh Market to Grow Faster" in *Charlotte Observer* (January 31, 2007)
Pub: Knight-Ridder/Tribune Business News
Ed: Doug Smith; Dudley Price. Description: Allen Tate Realtors expanded its operations to the Research Triangle area. The firm is predicting a strong market and growth in Charlotte, North Carolina.

16744 ■ "Another California Firm On Way" in *Austin Business Journal* (Vol. 31, May 6, 2011, No. 9, pp. 1)
Pub: American City Business Journals Inc.
Ed: Christopher Calnan. Description: Main Street Hub Inc. is planning to build a facility in Austin, Texas. The company helps businesses manage their online reputations. Main Street has selected Aquila Commercial LLC as its real estate broker.

16745 ■ "Another Man's Pain" in *Canadian Business* (Vol. 80, October 22, 2007, No. 21, pp. 33)
Pub: Rogers Media
Ed: Andy Holloway. Description: U.S. financial collapse can have a positive impact on Canadian investors. Graphs on the total number of home foreclosures in the U.S. from January to August 2007, as well as foreclosure market by type, are presented.

16746 ■ "Antwerpen Takes on Chrysler Financial Over Foreclosure Sales" in *Baltimore Business Journal* (Vol. 28, July 30, 2010, No. 12, pp. 1)
Pub: Baltimore Business Journal
Ed: Gary Haber. Description: Antwerpen Motorcars Ltd. aims to fight the scheduled foreclosure sale of real estate it leases in Baltimore County, including the showroom for its Hyundai dealership on Baltimore National Pike in Catonsville, Maryland. The company is planning to file papers in court to stop the scheduled August 11, 2010 auction sought by Chrysler Financial Services Americas LLC.

16747 ■ "Apartment Ambitions" in *The Business Journal-Portland* (Vol. 25, August 8, 2008, No. 22, pp. 1)
Pub: American City Business Journals, Inc.
Ed: Wendy Culverwell. Description: Unico Properties LLC's Asa Flats+Lofts is one of the first of eight high-end apartment projects planned for Portland which will add a total of 2,130 new units to the Pearl District, South Waterfront, and downtown Portland. These apartments charge more than $1,600 or more per month over the average rent.

16748 ■ "Apartment Market Down, Not Out" in *Crain's Detroit Business* (Vol. 24, October 6, 2008, No. 40, pp. 9)
Pub: Crain Communications, Inc.
Ed: Daniel Duggan. Description: Detroit's apartment market is considered to have some of the strongest fundamentals of any apartment market in the country with relatively low vacancy rates and a relatively low supply of new units compared with demand. Investors continue to show interest in the buildings but the national lending market is making it difficult to invest in the city.

16749 ■ "Apartment Tower in River North Fetches More Than $90 Million" in *Crain's Chicago Business* (Vol. 34, October 24, 2011, No. 42, pp. 17)
Pub: Crain Communications Inc.
Ed: Alby Gallun. Description: Apartment tower in River North was sold for over $90 million to a Texas pension fund adviser. Details are included.

16750 ■ "Aquila HQ Hits the Market" in *The Business Journal-Serving Metropolitan Kansas City* (Vol. 26, July 25, 2008, No. 46, pp. 1)
Pub: American City Business Journals, Inc.
Ed: Rob Roberts. Description: Commercial real estate experts believe that Aquila Inc.'s former headquarters will be hard to rent out. The historic value of the building, being Kansas City's first skyscraper, is not expected to add value to the price of the rent. Other views and information on the building, as well as on Aquila, are presented.

16751 ■ "Ask Inc." in *Inc.* (December 2007, pp. 83-84)
Pub: Gruner & Jahr USA Publishing
Ed: Ari Weinzweig. Description: Questions regarding knowledge management in the case of a retiring CFO, issues involved in opening a satellite office for a New York realtor, and information for hiring a multicultural workforce are all discussed.

16752 ■ "Athletes Face Wins and Losses After Pro Sport" in *The Business Journal - Serving Phoenix and the Valley of the Sun* (Vol. 29, September 19, 2008, No. 3, pp. 1)
Pub: American City Business Journals, Inc.
Ed: Chris Casacchia. Description: Professional athletes like hockey star Jeremy Roenick start businesses, while others like Joel Adamson work to boost local communities. Former athletes were found to be particularly interested with real estate businesses. Other views and information on former athletes and their life after sports are presented.

16753 ■ "Au Revoir Or Goodbye?" in *Barron's* (Vol. 88, July 14, 2008, No. 28, pp. 5)
Pub: Dow Jones & Co., Inc.
Ed: Alan Abelson. Description: Former Senator Phil Gramm's opinion that the U.S. is a "nation of whiners" as they moan about recession is another ex-

ample of the disconnection between Washington and Wall Street on one hand and the real world on the other. It would be a catastrophe for most of the world if Fannie Mae and Freddie Mac were to go under and take their trillions of mortgage debt with them.

16754 ■ "Austin Homes are Overpriced, Study Says" in *Austin Business JournalInc.* (Vol. 29, January 1, 2010, No. 43, pp. 1)
Pub: American City Business Journals
Ed: Kate Harrington. Description: Study by Forbes.com shows that Austin-Round Rock metropolitan statistical area ranked 10th on the list of cities with the most over-priced homes. For instance, the average price for a single-family home pegged at $188,000.

16755 ■ "Back on Track-Or Off the Rails?" in *Business Week* (September 22, 2008, No. 4100, pp. 22)
Pub: McGraw-Hill Companies, Inc.
Ed: Peter Coy; Tara Kalwarski. Description: Discusses the possible scenarios the American economy may undergo due to the takeover of Fannie Mae and Freddie Mac. Statistical data included.

16756 ■ "Bangles, BMWs Elbow Out Delis and Discount Shops" in *Crain's New York Business* (Vol. 24, January 14, 2008, No. 2, pp. 35)
Pub: Crain Communications, Inc.
Ed: Wendy Davis. Description: Lured by a growing number of affluent residents and high-earning professionals, a number of upscale retailers have opened locations downtown which is driving up rents and forcing out longtime independent merchants.

16757 ■ "Bankruptcies Shoot Up 68 Percent" in *Sacramento Business Journal* (Vol. 25, July 18, 2008, No. 20, pp. 1)
Pub: American City Business Journals, Inc.
Ed: Kathy Robertson. Description: Personal bankruptcy in the Sacramento area rose by 88 percent for the first half of 2008 while business bankruptcies rose by 50 percent for the same period. The numbers of consumer bankruptcy reflects the effect of high debt, rising mortgage costs, and declining home values on U.S. households.

16758 ■ "Best Income Trust" in *Canadian Business* (Vol. 81, Summer 2008, No. 9, pp. 69)
Pub: Rogers Media Ltd.
Ed: Calvin Leung. Description: Table showing five-year annualized growth rate and one-year stock performance of real estate investment trusts firms in Canada is presented. Calgary-based Boardwalk REIT is projected to grow the fastest among North American REITs over the next two years. Other details on the stock performance analysis are presented.

16759 ■ "Bill Kaneko" in *Hawaii Business* (Vol. 53, December 2007, No. 6, pp. 32)
Pub: Hawaii Business Publishing
Ed: David K. Choo. Description: Hawaii Institute for Public Affairs chief executive officer and president Bill Kaneko believes that the Hawaiian economy is booming, however, he also asserts that the economy is too focused on tourism and real estate. Kaneko has also realized the that the will of the people is strong while he was helping with the Hawaiian 2050 Sustainability Plan. The difficulties of making a sustainable Hawaii are discussed.

16760 ■ "Bills Would Regulate Mortgage Loan Officers" in *Crain's Detroit Business* (Vol. 24, February 25, 2008, No. 8, pp. 9)
Pub: Crain Communications Inc. - Detroit
Ed: Amy Lane. Description: New legislation in Michigan, if passed, would create a registration process for mortgage loan officers in the state in order to address the mortgage loan crisis.

16761 ■ "Block Plans Office Park Along K-10 Corridor" in *The Business Journal-Serving Metropolitan Kansas City* (Vol. 27, October 3, 2008)
Pub: American City Business Journals, Inc.
Ed: Rob Roberts. Description: Kansas City, Missouri-based Block and Co. is planning to build four office buildings at the corner of College Boule-

vard and Ridgeview Road in Olathe. Features of the planned development are provided. Comments from executives are also presented.

16762 ■ **"Block Pulls Plug On Riverside Deal"** in *The Business Journal-Serving Metropolitan Kansas City* (Vol. 27, October 10, 2008, No. 4)
Pub: American City Business Journals, Inc.
Ed: Rob Roberts. **Description:** Real estate developer Ken Block has backed out from a $300 million Riverside industrial project. Block says he has already invested $1 million of his own money into the deal. Details regarding the project are given.

16763 ■ **"Bond OK Could Bring Back the Housing Battle?"** in *Charlotte Business Journal* (Vol. 25, November 5, 2010, No. 33, pp. 1)
Pub: Charlotte Business Journal
Ed: Susan Stabley. **Description:** The approval of the $15 million housing bond in Charlotte, North Carolina could bring back the debates on housing in the region. Protesters have opposed affordable housing developments that were proposed in the area since 2008. Other information on the recently approved housing bond and on other real estate issues in North Carolina is presented.

16764 ■ **"Book of Lists 2010"** in *Philadelphia Business Journal* (Vol. 28, December 25, 2009, No. 45, pp. 1)
Pub: American City Business Journals
Description: Rankings of companies and organizations within the banking, biotechnology, economic development, healthcare, hospitality, law and accounting, marketing and media, real estate, and technology industries in the Philadelphia, Pennsylvania area are presented. Rankings are based on sales, business size, and more.

16765 ■ **"Boston Hedge Fund Pours Money Into Real Estate Projects"** in *Charlotte Business Journal* (Vol. 25, December 3, 2010, No. 37, pp. 1)
Pub: Charlotte Business Journal
Ed: Will Boye. **Description:** Boston-based hedge fund Baupost Group has been financing real estate project in Charlotte, North Carolina including more than 80 acres just north of uptown. Aside from purchasing the $23.8 million note for the Rosewood Condominiums from Regions Financial Corporation, the Baupost Group is also negotiating with Regions to buy the $93.9 million debt of the EipCentre real estate project.

16766 ■ **"Bottom's Up"** in *Barron's* (Vol. 88, July 14, 2008, No. 28, pp. 25)
Pub: Dow Jones & Co., Inc.
Ed: Jonathan R. Laing. **Description:** Economist Chip Case believes that home prices are nearing a bottom based on his analysis of the history of the housing market; surprisingly, in the past the housing market has rebounded after a quarter from a massive housing start drop. The drop in early stage delinquencies is another sign of the housing market's recovery.

16767 ■ **"A Bright Spot: Industrial Space in Demand Again"** in *Sacramento Business Journal* (Vol. 28, October 21, 2011, No. 34, pp. 1)
Pub: Sacramento Business Journal
Ed: Michael Shaw. **Description:** Sacramento, California's industrial sites have been eyed by potential tenants who are actively seeking space larger than 50,000 square feet.

16768 ■ **"Brokerages Seek a Foothold in Local Real Estate Market"** in *Charlotte Business Journal* (Vol. 25, October 15, 2010, No. 30, pp. 1)
Pub: Charlotte Business Journal
Ed: Will Boye. **Description:** Charlotte, North Carolina has become an attractive destination for out-of-town brokerage firms. Colliers International has signed an affiliate deal with Anthony and Company to set up shop in Charlotte. Grubb and Ellis Company, on the other hand, is planning to open an office in the city.

16769 ■ **"Builder Comes Back Home"** in *Houston Business Journal* (Vol. 40, September 18, 2009, No. 19, pp. 1A)
Pub: American City Business Journals
Ed: Allison Wollam. **Description:** Jason Hammonds, who has been previously involved in the local home building market in Texas, has launched a new home building company called J. Kyle Homes. The new company has chosen Cinco Ranch, a neo-traditional styled neighborhood in Katy, Texas to build its first housing community.

16770 ■ **"Builder's Bankruptcy Fans Fears"** in *Crain's Cleveland Business* (Vol. 28, October 22, 2007, No. 42, pp. 1)
Pub: Crain Communications, Inc.
Ed: Stan Bullard. **Description:** Whitlatch & Co., Northeast Ohio's largest builder by unit volume in the early 1990s, has filed for Chapter 11 bankruptcy. This is causing builders and others in the real estate industry to wonder how long and severe the housing slump will be and which companies will survive.

16771 ■ **"Builder's Comeback Highlights Uptick in Demand for New Homes"** in *Boston Business Journal* (Vol. 29, June 3, 2011, No. 4, pp. 1)
Pub: American City Business Journals Inc.
Ed: Gary Haber. **Description:** The return of builder Michael Canock after a series of credit crisis and the funding for his new projects are discussed in light of the recent upsurge in the home-building industry in the Baltimore area. New single-family homes numbered 318 in first quarter 2011 which is a 20 percent increase from first quarter 2010.

16772 ■ **"Buy Now?"** in *Hawaii Business* (Vol. 53, March 2008, No. 9, pp. 32)
Pub: Hawaii Business Publishing
Ed: David K. Choo. **Description:** Discusses the Honolulu Board of REALTORS which said that the last two months of 2007 saw double-digit housing sales drop, with December figures showing 30.6 percent and 22.9 percent decline in sales of single-family homes and condominiums, respectively. Forecasts on Hawaii's real estate market for 2008 are discussed.

16773 ■ **"Buyers' Market"** in *Baltimore Business Journal* (Vol. 27, November 20, 2009, No. 28, pp. 1)
Pub: American City Business Journals
Ed: Daniel J. Sernovitz. **Description:** Some business owners in Maryland are removing their leases and purchasing buildings due to the lower costs of real estate. This trend has enabled small business owners to avoid rent hikes, while setting equity into their companies. The pros and cons of owning buildings and how business owners assess their return on investment are examined.

16774 ■ **"Calendar"** in *Crain's Detroit Business* (Vol. 24, October 6, 2008, No. 40, pp. 22)
Pub: Crain Communications, Inc.
Description: Listing of events in the Detroit area include conferences addressing entrepreneurialism, economic development, manufacturing, marketing, the housing crisis and women business ownership.

16775 ■ **"Canadian Vehicle Sales Accelerate in April, but U.S. Goes on Bumpy Ride"** in *Globe & Mail* (May 2, 2007, pp. B7)
Pub: CTVglobemedia Publishing Inc.
Ed: Greg Keenan. **Description:** The increase in Canadian vehicle sales to 169,280 in April 2007, but decline in their sales in the United States due to slump in housing sector are discussed.

16776 ■ **"C&W Gets Green Star"** in *Crain's New York Business* (Vol. 24, January 7, 2008, No. 1, pp. 25)
Pub: Crain Communications, Inc.
Ed: Theresa Agovino. **Description:** Cushman & Wakefield Inc. has hired Eleni Reed as director of sustainability strategies; the real estate firm wants to ensure that the 500 million square feet of office space it manages around the globe meets environmental standards.

16777 ■ **"Cedar Fair to Solicit Bids for Geauga Lake"** in *Crain's Cleveland Business* (Vol. 28, October 8, 2007, No. 40, pp. 1)
Pub: Crain Communications, Inc.
Ed: Stan Bullard. **Description:** Cedar Fair Entertainment Co. plans to seek sealed bids for the redevelopment of nearly 540 acres of their amusement park site in southwest Geauga County and northwest Portage County.

16778 ■ **"Channelside On the Blocks"** in *The Business Journal-Serving Greater Tampa Bay* (Vol. 28, August 29, 2008, No. 36, pp. 1)
Pub: American City Business Journals, Inc.
Ed: Michael Hinman. **Description:** In a bankruptcy auction for The Place, one of the more visible condominium projects at Channelside, the lowest bid is just below $73 a square foot. KeyBank National Association, the Key Developers Group LLC's lender, leads the auction planned for October 15, 2008. The reason behind the low minimum bid required to participate in the said action is discussed.

16779 ■ **"Children's Hospital to Build in New Berlin"** in *The Business Journal-Milwaukee* (Vol. 25, August 1, 2008, No. 45, pp. A1)
Pub: American City Business Journals, Inc.
Ed: Corrinne Hess. **Description:** Children's Hospital of Wisconsin plans a clinic in the 35-acre medical office park in New Berlin, Wisconsin, owned by Froedtert Memorial Lutheran Hospital and Medical College of Wisconsin Real Estate Ventures LLC. The hospital will be the first major tenant in the park, to be built by Irgens Development Partners LLC.

16780 ■ **"City Sets Yamhill Makeover"** in *The Business Journal-Portland* (Vol. 25, July 4, 2008, No. 17, pp. 1)
Pub: American City Business Journals, Inc.
Ed: Andy Giegerich. **Description:** City government is scheduled to redevelop Peterson's property on Yamhill Street in Portland. The redevelopment is seen as a way to better developing commercial properties in the area. Problems associated with the project, which include cost and developer selection, are also discussed.

16781 ■ **"Coherent Laying Off 144 As It Prepares To Shut Auburn Plant"** in *Sacramento Business Journal* (Vol. 25, August 1, 2008, No. 22, pp. 1)
Pub: American City Business Journals, Inc.
Ed: Melanie Turner. **Description:** Sacramento, California-based Coherent Inc. is planning to lay off 144 workers at its Auburn facility. Coherent has been cutting payroll and its real estate holdings. Statistics on the company's earnings are also provided.

16782 ■ **"Colliers Shifts Its Brokerage Home"** in *Charlotte Business Journal* (Vol. 25, November 5, 2010, No. 33, pp. 1)
Pub: Charlotte Business Journal
Ed: Will Boye. **Description:** Colliers International signed a long-term affiliate agreement with commercial real estate firm Clarus Properties, in a move that would allow Colliers to resume business in Charlotte, North Carolina. Colliers also hired well known brokers Brad Grow and Brent Royall.

16783 ■ **"Columbia's JPB Raising $175M to Acquire Companies, Real Estate"** in *Boston Business Journal* (Vol. 29, May 27, 2011, No. 3, pp. 1)
Pub: American City Business Journals Inc.
Ed: Gary Haber. **Description:** JPB Enterprises is preparing to raise $175 million in its goal of acquiring companies and real estate that are major names in America. The $75 million will be raised for a buyout fund that will target wide range of industries while the $100 million will be used for land investment projects in the Florida Panhandle. Baltimore firms are expected to benefit from this deal.

16784 ■ **"Coming Soon: Bailouts of Fannie and Freddie"** in *Barron's* (Vol. 88, July 14, 2008, No. 28, pp. 14)
Pub: Dow Jones & Co., Inc.
Ed: Jonathan R. Laing. **Description:** Assurances from the government that Fannie Mae and Freddie Mac are adequately capitalized and able to carry on

their duties as guarantors or owners of over $5 trillion of U.S. home mortgages are designed to keep both entities afloat until they attempt to raise $10 billion in new equity. The government would assume any losses in a bailout and owners of the banks' papers would profit as yields drop.

16785 ■ "Con-Way Project Back in High Gear" in Business Journal Portland (Vol. 27, November 5, 2010, No. 36, pp. 1)
Pub: Portland Business Journal
Ed: Wendy Culverwell. **Description:** Trucking firm Con-Way Inc. intends to sell parcels of land from a property comprising 16 blocks and 20 prime acres west of the Pearl District in Portland, Oregon. In 2009, Con-Way abandoned plans to sell the property. As Con-Way reclaims control over design and usage of the property, it also expressed willingness to cooperate with a master developer on a related real estate project.

16786 ■ "Condo Markdown" in Boston Business Journal (Vol. 27, November 30, 2007, No. 44, pp. 1)
Pub: American City Business Journals Inc.
Ed: Michelle Hillman. **Description:** Boston real estate market is softening, and condominium developers such as Beacon Communities LLC are sending out various incentives like markdowns and unit upgrades. Developers have also held auctions and even offered brand new cars to lure buyers. Other perks being offered by various Boston developers are discussed.

16787 ■ "Condominium Sales Fall to a Seven-Year Low" in Crain's Chicago Business (Vol. 31, November 10, 2008, No. 45, pp. 2)
Pub: Crain Communications, Inc.
Ed: Alby Gallun. **Description:** Downtown Chicago condominium market is experiencing the lowest number of sales in years due to the tightening of the mortgage lending market, the Wall Street crisis and the downturn in the economy. The supply of new condos is soaring, the result of the building boom of 2005 and 2006; many developers are finding it difficult to pay off construction loans and fear foreclosure on their properties. Additional information and statistical data related to the downtown condominium market is provided.

16788 ■ "Contingent Offers: Weighing the Risk" in Crain's Chicago Business (Vol. 31, April 21, 2008, No. 16, pp. 48)
Pub: Crain Communications, Inc.
Ed: Darci Smith. **Description:** Interview with Greer Haseman, the broker-owner of Town Square Associates, who discusses contingent offers in a challenging housing market.

16789 ■ "A Conversation with; Renea Butler, Real Estate One Inc." in Crain's Detroit Business (Vol. 25, June 8, 2009, No. 23, pp. 12)
Pub: Crain Communications Inc. - Detroit
Ed: Ryan Beene. **Description:** Renea Butler, vice president of administration and human resources for Real Estate One Inc. in Southfield as well as vice president for public relations for the Human Resource Association of Greater Detroit, talks about how the economy has affected human resource services.

16790 ■ "Cool on Chicago Office Properties" in Crain's Chicago Business (Vol. 31, March 31, 2008, No. 13, pp. 16)
Pub: Crain Communications, Inc.
Ed: Eddie Baeb. **Description:** Investors predict values on Chicago office buildings to drop 1.3 percent over the next year.

16791 ■ "Cornered by Credit; As $1 Billion in Loans Come Due, Will Landlords Find Funds?" in Crain's Detroit Business (October 6, 2008)
Pub: Crain Communications, Inc.
Ed: Daniel Duggan. **Description:** Conduit loans are used by many real estate investors and are normally issued in 7- to 10-year terms with balloon payments due at the end, requiring the full balance to be paid

upon maturity. Many building owners may find their properties going into foreclosure as these loans mature next year since these loans cannot be extended like typical loans and the credit crisis along with falling property values is making it more difficult to secure new sources of funding. Possible solutions to this problem are also explored.

16792 ■ "Corporex in Battle With Hedge Fund" in Business Courier (Vol. 24, December 21, 2008, No. 36, pp. 1)
Pub: American City Business Journals, Inc.
Ed: Jon Newberry. **Description:** Discusses a breach of contract complaint that was filed by Apollo Real Estate Advisors against Corporex Companies Inc. but Corporex said that the lawsuit was intended to counter an arbitration complaint filed by Corporex against Apollo, which seeks $11 million in termination fees. The issue is in relation to the acquisition of Eagle Hospitality by Apollo earlier in 2007.

16793 ■ "Cost of Home Purchase Loans are Higher for Hispanics" in Hispanic Business (October 2007, pp. 88)
Pub: Hispanic Business
Description: Home loans for Hispanics generally are offered at a higher interest rate. Statistical data included.

16794 ■ "Creativity is Essential in Sagging Relocation Market" in Crain's Cleveland Business (Vol. 28, November 5, 2007, No. 44, pp. 19)
Pub: Crain Communications, Inc.
Ed: Christine Gordillo. **Description:** Since Northeast Ohio was headquarters to a number of Fortune 500 companies, residential real estate builders and brokers could count on corporate relocation clients for a steady stream of business. Today, corporations have become more cautious when relocating talent due to the costs involved which has forced industry experts to be more patient and more creative in the ways they attract out-of-town buyers who are likely to be a sure sell.

16795 ■ "Credit-Market Crisis Batters Origen Financial's Bottom Line" in Crain's Detroit Business (Vol. 24, March 31, 2008, No. 13, pp. 4)
Pub: Crain Communications, Inc.
Ed: Description: Overview of the effect the credit-market crisis has had on Origen Financial Inc., a company that underwrites and services loans for manufactured housing. CEO Ronald Klein didn't think Origen would be affected by the collapse due to its sound operations but the company's share price dropped considerably causing its auditors to warn that the company's existence could be in jeopardy.

16796 ■ "Critics: Efforts to Fix Loans Won't Stop Foreclosure Wave" in Business First Columbus (Vol. 25, November 14, 2008, No. 12, pp. A1)
Pub: American City Business Journals
Ed: Adrian Burns. **Description:** Efforts by U.S. banks to help homeowners pay mortgages are seen to have little if any impact on foreclosures. Banks have announced plans to identify and aid troubled borrowers. Statistical data included.

16797 ■ Crittenden Directory of Real Estate Financing
Pub: Crittenden Research Inc.
Released: Semiannual, updated by weekly newsletter. **Price:** $967, individuals print; $387, individuals online. **Covers:** Over 300 major lenders, investors, and joint ventures engaged in commercial and residential real estate financing and investing. **Entries Include:** Company name, nickname, total assets, typical rate, real estate investment portfolio value, production totals (broken down by type of investment), maximum and minimum loan/investment amounts; preferred types of loans, interest rates, fees, and related data; names, addresses, phone numbers of contacts, pension fund name. **Arrangement:** Geographical (by principal area of lending activity). **Indexes:** Type of real estate, company name, project type.

16798 ■ Crittenden's Real Estate Buyers Directory
Pub: Crittenden Research Inc.
Released: Semiannual, updated/supplemented weekly by "Real Estate Buyers Newsletter". **Price:** $967, individuals CD-ROM version; $967, individuals paper version. **Covers:** Over 400 real estate buyers, including private investors, banks, pension funds, real estate investment trusts (REITs), foreign investors, and life insurance companies. **Entries Include:** Organization name, contact name, title, address, and phone; type of property purchased, geographic territory covered, previous year's estimated purchases, minimum and maximum purchase amount. **Arrangement:** Alphabetical. **Indexes:** Annual and quarterly indexes.

16799 ■ "The Debt Mountain in Mid-Collapse" in Canadian Business (Vol. 83, October 12, 2010, No. 17, pp. 28)
Pub: Rogers Media Ltd.
Ed: Michael McCullough. **Description:** A growing real estate market has made Intrawest ULC's Whistler-Blackcomb resort a model for a booming industry for years. However, resorts are now required to manage themselves better because of the recession. Some mountains are also trimming the cost of labor and cutting peripheral services.

16800 ■ "Detroit Residential Market Slows; Bright Spots Emerge" in Crain's Detroit Business (Vol. 24, October 6, 2008, No. 40, pp. 11)
Pub: Crain Communications, Inc.
Ed: Daniel Duggan. **Description:** Discusses the state of the residential real estate market in Detroit; although condominium projects receive the most attention, deals for single-family homes are taking place in greater numbers due to financing issues. Buyers can purchase a single family home with a 3.5 percent down payment compared to 20 percent for some condo deals because of the number of first-time homebuyer programs under the Federal Housing Administration.

16801 ■ "Developer Backs Out of Major Bastrop Project" in Austin Business JournalInc. (Vol. 28, December 19, 2008, No. 40, pp. 1)
Pub: American City Business Journals
Ed: Kate Harrington. **Description:** Weingarten Realty Investors, a Houston, Texas-based real estate company, has backed out of its contract on more than 1 million square feet of retail space at the County Road 304 and State Highway 71 corner in Bastrop, Texas, according to landowner Tom Brundage. Analysts say that the Bastrop area is not ready for big retail projects.

16802 ■ "Developer Banks On East Submarket, Slowdown Not a Hinderance" in The Business Journal-Serving Greater Tampa Bay (August 1, 2008)
Pub: American City Business Journals, Inc.
Ed: Janet Leiser. **Description:** CLW Industrial Group and Cobalt Industrial REIT II have teamed up to develop a 14-acre area in northeast Hillsborough County, Florida. The $15 million industrial park project includes the 175,000-square-foot New Tampa Commerce Center, scheduled for completion in the first quarter of 2009.

16803 ■ "Developer Tries to Bring Homes to Buda" in Austin Business JournalInc. (Vol. 28, December 26, 2008, No. 41, pp. 1)
Pub: American City Business Journals
Ed: Kate Harrington. **Description:** Real estate developer Jeremiah Venture LP is planning a residential, single-family development on about 600 acres near Buda, Texas. The company also plans to construct a membrane waste treatment plant, and has applied to do land application. However, several groups have come forward to ask for more information on the application due to concerns about soil density.

16804 ■ "Developer Wins Bout with Bank in Roundabout Way" in Tampa Bay Business Journal (Vol. 30, January 29, 2010, No. 6, pp. 1)
Pub: American City Business Journals
Ed: Janet Leiser. **Description:** Developer Donald E. Phillips of Phillips Development and Realty LLC won

against the foreclosure filed by First Horizon National Corporation, which is demanding the company to fully pay its $2.9 million loan. Phillips requested that his company pay monthly mortgage and extend the loan's maturity date.

16805 ■ **"Developers Give Big to Mayor's Bid"** in *Boston Business Journal* **(Vol. 29, August 26, 2011, No. 16, pp. 1)**
Pub: American City Business Journals Inc.
Ed: Scott Dance. **Description:** Mayor Stephanie Rawlings-Blake received thousands of dollars in her political campaign from companies of real estate developers who are vying to build key development projects in Baltimore, Maryland. Rawlings-Blake created a major fundraising advantage over other mayoral candidates with the help of those contributions.

16806 ■ **"Developers Give City Dwellings a Modern Spin"** in *Crain's Cleveland Business* **(Vol. 28, November 5, 2007, No. 44, pp. 18)**
Pub: Crain Communications, Inc.
Description: Cleveland is increasingly becoming a canvas for fresh, cutting-edge design due to several recent projects, some at prominent sites.

16807 ■ **"Developers Poised to Pull Trigers"** in *Boston Business Journal* **(Vol. 30, November 12, 2010, No. 42, pp. 1)**
Pub: Boston Business Journal
Ed: Craig M. Douglas. **Description:** Large residential projects are expected to break ground in Boston, Massachusetts in 2011, as real estate developers expect growth for the industry. Real estate experts expect more than 2,000 rental units to be available by 2011. Information on key real estate projects in Boston is presented.

16808 ■ *Dictionary of Real Estate Terms*
Pub: Barron's Educational Series, Incorporated
Ed: Jack P. Friedman, Jack C. Harris, J. Bruce Lindeman. **Released:** October 2008. **Price:** $13.99. **Description:** More than 2,500 real estate terms relating to mortgages and financing, brokerage law, architecture, rentals and leases, property insurance, and more.

16809 ■ **"Docs Might Hold Cure for Real Estate, Banks"** in *Baltimore Business Journal* **(Vol. 28, November 5, 2010, No. 26, pp. 1)**
Pub: Baltimore Business Journal
Ed: Gary Haber. **Description:** Health care providers, including physicians are purchasing their office space instead of renting it as banks lower interest rates to 6 percent on mortgages for medical offices. The rise in demand offers relief to the commercial real estate market. It has also resulted in a boom in building new medical offices.

16810 ■ **"Downtown Evens Tenant Ledger"** in *The Business Journal-Serving Metropolitan Kansas City* **(Vol. 26, July 11, 2008, No. 44, pp. 1)**
Pub: American City Business Journals, Inc.
Ed: Rob Roberts. **Description:** Financial services company PricewaterhouseCoopers will relocate its office from the Broadway Square building, but it will not leave downtown as it signs a long-term lease for a 27,000 square feet of space in Town Pavilion. Town Pavilion is the biggest multitenant office building in downtown. Downtown's market competitiveness is also examined.

16811 ■ **"Drawn to York County: Less-Expensive Homes, Good Schools Attract Charlotteans"** in *Charlotte Observer* **(February 4, 2007)**
Pub: Knight-Ridder/Tribune Business News
Ed: Taylor Bright. **Description:** York County, North Carolina offers low-priced homes and good schools, making it attractive to workers and small business.

16812 ■ **"East-Side Real Estate Forum Detours To Grand Rapids"** in *Crain's Detroit Business* **(Vol. 24, October 6, 2008, No. 40, pp. 17)**
Pub: Crain Communications, Inc.
Ed: Daniel Duggan. **Description:** Tom Wackerman was elected chairman of the University of Michigan-Urban Land Institute Real Estate Forum and pro-

posed that the annual conference be held in Grand Rapids due to the brisk economic activity he was finding there; although the idea was initially met with resistance, the plan to introduce East-siders to the West side began receiving more enthusiasm due to the revitalization of the area, which was once considered to have a bleak outlook. Many are hoping to learn the lessons of those who were able to change a negative economic climate into a positive one in which the cooperation of private business and government can work together to accomplish goals.

16813 ■ **"Economy Hammers Local Builders"** in *Business Courier* **(Vol. 24, February 8, 2008, No. 44, pp. 1)**
Pub: American City Business Journals, Inc.
Ed: Laura Baverman. **Description:** Home builders in Cincinnati, Ohio, have lower revenue and smaller workforces as a result of the housing crisis and economic slowdown. Only four out of the top 25 home builders registered revenue gains, average revenue for 2007 is down 21 percent from 2006 levels, and employment declined by 37 percent from 2006.

16814 ■ **"Economy Peddles Rent In This Cycle"** in *The Business Journal-Serving Metropolitan Kansas City* **(Vol. 26, August 8, 2008, No. 48)**
Pub: American City Business Journals, Inc.
Ed: Ashlee Kieler. **Description:** Rental demand for apartment units in downtown Kansas City, Missouri, is increasing due to the housing crisis, lack of real estate development, and increasing popularity of the downtown area. The downtown area has 7,378 multifamily units as of June 2008, of which 4,114 are rentals.

16815 ■ **"Editor's Note"** in *Canadian Business* **(Vol. 81, March 17, 2008, No. 4, pp. 7)**
Pub: Rogers Media
Ed: Joe Chidley. **Description:** Canadian Consolidated government expenditures increased by an average of 4.5 percent annually from 2003 to 2007. Health care, housing, and the environment were some of the areas which experienced higher spending. However, government spending in labor, employment, and immigration dropped 6.6 percent.

16816 ■ **"Eminent Domain Fight Looks Imminent"** in *The Business Journal-Serving Metropolitan Kansas City* **(Vol. 26, August 1, 2008, No. 47)**
Pub: American City Business Journals, Inc.
Ed: Rob Roberts. **Description:** Views and information on the proposed constitutional amendments that will limit the use of eminent domain in Missouri, are presented. The proposals are expected to largely ban the taking of private property for private development. It may be included in a November 4,2008 statewide vote for approval.

16817 ■ **"Energy Efficiency Ordinance Softened"** in *Austin Business JournalInc.* **(Vol. 28, October 3, 2008, No. 29)**
Pub: American City Business Journals
Ed: Jean Kwon. **Description:** City of Austin has eliminated mandatory energy efficiency upgrades to single-family housing as a condition for selling or renting homes or buildings. The new law proposes that an energy performance audit be conducted on single-family homes before being sold and the results of the audit disclosed to perspectives buyers.

16818 ■ **"Everyone Out of the Pool"** in *Barron's* **(Vol. 89, July 20, 2009, No. 29, pp. 18)**
Pub: Dow Jones & Co., Inc.
Ed: Sandra Ward. **Description:** Shares of Pool Corp. could drop as continued weakness in the housing market weakens the market for swimming pool equipment. The company's shares are trading at $18.29, about 20 times projected 2009 earnings of $0.91 a share.

16819 ■ *Everything You Need to Know to Sell By Owner*
Pub: FSBO Publishing
Ed: Karen Varnas; Roy Wysack. **Released:** February 2007. **Price:** $19.95. **Description:** Provides the knowledge and strategies required to sell real estate in today's market.

16820 ■ **"Evidence Growing of Commercial Real Estate"** in *Boston Business Journal* **(Vol. 27, October 5, 2007, No. 36, pp. 1)**
Pub: American City Business Journals Inc.
Ed: Michelle Hillman. **Description:** Commercial real estate industry in Boston, Massachusetts is experiencing a downturn in the number of sales transactions. A table on the commercial real estate's value of transactions for the first three quarters from 2004 to 2007 is presented.

16821 ■ **"Exposed?"** in *Mergers & Acquisitions: The Dealmaker's Journal* **(March 1, 2008)**
Pub: SourceMedia, Inc.
Ed: Jerry Abejo. **Description:** State-run pension plans' contributions are declining due to a loss of tax revenue from plummeting home values.

16822 ■ **"Eyes to the Sky"** in *Canadian Business* **(Vol. 80, March 26, 2007, No. 7, pp. 33)**
Pub: Rogers Media
Ed: Joe Castaldo. **Description:** The growth and prices of condominium market in the Canada are analyzed.

16823 ■ **"Fifth Third Spinoff"** in *Business Courier* **(Vol. 27, July 16, 2010, No. 11, pp. 1)**
Pub: Business Courier
Ed: Dan Monk, Steve Watkins. **Description:** Electronic-funds transfer company Fifth Third Solutions (FTPS), a spinoff of Fifth Third Bancorp, is seeking as much as 200,000 square feet of new office space in Ohio. The bank's sale of 51 percent ownership stake to Boston-based Advent International Corporation has paved the way for the growth of FTPS. How real estate brokers' plans have responded to FTPS' growth mode is discussed.

16824 ■ **"Final Player In Big Mortgage Fraud Operation Gets Jail Time"** in *Boston Business Journal* **(Vol. 31, May 27, 2011, No. 18, pp. 3)**
Pub: Boston Business Journal
Ed: Galen Moore. **Description:** Real estate broker Ralp Appolon has been sentenced to 70 months in prison for wire fraud. Appolon was part of a group that falsified information about property purchase prices. A total of ten mortgage lenders have become victims of the group.

16825 ■ **"Final State Budget Is a Mixed Bag of Key Industries"** in *The Business Journal - Serving Phoenix and the Valley of the Sun* **(Vol. 28, July 4, 2008, No. 44, pp. 3)**
Pub: American City Business Journals, Inc.
Ed: Mike Sunnucks; Patrick O'Grady. **Description:** Approved by Governor Janet Napolitano and passed by the Arizona Legislature, the $9.9 billion state budget is beneficial to some industries in the business community. The tax cap for on Arizona Lottery has been removed which is beneficial to the industry, while the solar energy industry and real estate developers stand to lose from the spending bill. Other details of the finance budget are presented.

16826 ■ **"First-Time Homebuyer Credit May Add Some Momentum to Market"** in *Crain's Cleveland Business* **(Vol. 30, May 18, 2009, No. 20)**
Pub: Crain Communications, Inc.
Ed: Stan Bullard. **Description:** Federal tax credits for first-time homebuyers have increased the number of homes being sold. Details of the tax credit are defined.

16827 ■ **"Five Low-Cost Home Based Startups"** in *Women Entrepreneur* **(December 16, 2008)**
Pub: Entrepreneur Media Inc.
Ed: Lesley Spencer Pyle. **Description:** During tough economic times, small businesses have an advantage over large companies because they can adjust to economic conditions more easily and without having to go through corporate red tape that can slow the implementation process. A budding entrepreneur may find success by taking inventory of his or her skills, experience, expertise and passions and utilizing

those qualities to start a business. Five low-cost home-based startups are profiled. These include starting an online store, a virtual assistant service, web designer, sales representative and a home staging counselor.

16828 ■ *FLIP: How to Find, Fix, and Sell Houses for Profit*
Pub: McGraw-Hill Inc.
Ed: Rick Villani; Clay Davis. **Released:** December 19, 2006. **Price:** $21.95. **Description:** Advice is given to help find, fix and sell houses for profit.

16829 ■ "Florin Car Dealers Drive Plan" in *Sacramento Business Journal* (Vol. 25, August 22, 2008, No. 25, pp. 1)
Pub: American City Business Journals, Inc.
Ed: Melanie Turner. **Description:** Automobile dealers in Sacramento, California are working with the city and the business district in planning for future redevelopment in Florin Road. The move stemmed from pressure from the Elk Grove Auto Mall, high fuel prices and the credit crunch. The area has suffered business closures recently.

16830 ■ "Fogg Planning Twinsburg Warehouse Project" in *Crain's Cleveland Business* (Vol. 28, November 26, 2007, No. 47, pp. 6)
Pub: Crain Communications, Inc.
Ed: Stan Bullard. **Description:** Discusses such projects as the proposed 205,000-square-foot distribution center in the works by Ray Fogg Corporate Properties LLC as well as other industrial real estate developments that are looking to target tenants that need larger spaces.

16831 ■ "For $150 Million Mall, Failure to Launch" in *Business Courier* (Vol. 24, January 25, 2008, No. 42, pp. 1)
Pub: American City Business Journals, Inc.
Ed: Lisa Biank Fasig. **Description:** Blue Ash-based Bear Creek Capital and Chattanooga, Tennessee-based CBL & Associates Properties had abandoned their plan to build a mixed-use project in South Lebanon. The construction of the proposed $475 million open-air mall was cancelled when real estate developer CBL failed to secure retailers.

16832 ■ "For Developer, a Boulevard of Golden Dreams" in *Globe & Mail* (February 10, 2007, pp. B3)
Pub: CTVglobemedia Publishing Inc.
Ed: Elizabeth Church. **Description:** A profile of Ian Gillespie, president of Westbank Projects Corp., including his achievements in the real estate industry which are presented.

16833 ■ *The Foreclosure of America: Life Inside Countrywide Home Loans and the Selling of the American Dream*
Pub: Berkley Trade/Penguin Group (USA) Inc.
Ed: Adam Michaelson. **Released:** April 6, 2010. **Price:** $16.00. **Description:** An inside look at Countrywide Home Loans and the mortgage crisis.

16834 ■ "Foreclosures Crisis Expected to Significantly Drain Wealth" in *Black Enterprise* (Vol. 41, September 2010, No. 2, pp. 24)
Pub: Earl G. Graves Publishing Co. Inc.
Description: African American communities will lose billions in wealth because of the current foreclosure crisis. Statistical data included.

16835 ■ "Former Mayor Driving $500 Million Real Estate Equity Fund" in *The Business Journal - Serving Phoenix and the Valley of the Sun* (Vol. 28, August 15, 2008, No. 50, pp. 1)
Pub: American City Business Journals, Inc.
Ed: Jan Buchholz. **Description:** Paul John, the former mayor of Phoenix, is establishing a $500 million real estate asset management fund. The fund is dubbed Southwest Next Capital Management and has attracted three local partners, namely Joseph Meyer, Jay Michalowski, and James Mullany, who all have background in finance and construction.

16836 ■ "Former Schaefer and Strohminger Dealerships to Hit Auction Block" in *Baltimore Business Journal* (Vol. 28, September 10, 2010)
Pub: Baltimore Business Journal
Ed: Gary Haber. **Description:** Maryland's real estate developers have a chance to vie for almost 11 acres of prime Baltimore County real estate that are on the auction block. The five properties were once home to Schaefer and Strohminger car dealerships and were located in the county's busiest areas. Other potential uses for the properties are also discussed.

16837 ■ "From Bikes to Building" in *Austin Business JournalInc.* (Vol. 29, October 30, 2009, No. 34, pp. 1)
Pub: American City Business Journals
Ed: Kate Harrington. **Description:** Tour de France champion Lance Armstrong, Bill Stapleton his long-time agent, and business manager Bart Knaggs have formed a privately held real estate investment company CSE Realty Parters in Austin, Texas. They see tremendous opportunity in the commercial real estate market in the area.

16838 ■ "The Furniture Company Wanted to Sell Him Its Buildings-And Close Down. Should He Buy the Company, Too?" in *Inc.* (November 2007)
Pub: Gruner & Jahr USA Publishing
Ed: Alex Salkever. **Description:** Rick Detkowski, real estate investor, discusses his decision to purchase the furniture company housed in the buildings he was interested in buying. The property would have cost him between $500,000 to $1 million, he was able to purchase the property and business with its entire inventory of furniture, vehicles, and machinery for $1.8 million.

16839 ■ "Gables Unveils Plan for Downtown Tower" in *Austin Business JournalInc.* (Vol. 28, August 8, 2008, No. 21, pp. A1)
Pub: American City Business Journals
Ed: Jean Kwon. **Description:** Gables Residential plans to develop a residential tower with 220 units and 15,000 square feet of retail and commercial spaces in the Warehouse District in Ohio. The development is expected to start in late 2009 and be completed in 18 to 24 months.

16840 ■ "Gail Lissner; Vice-President, Appraisal Research Counselors" in *Crain's Chicago Business* (Vol. 31, May 5, 2008, No. 18, pp. 28)
Pub: Crain Communications, Inc.
Ed: Phuong Ly. **Description:** Profile of Gail Lissner who is the vice-president of the Appraisal Research Counselors, a company that puts out the quarterly "Residential Benchmark Report," in which Ms. Lissner co-authors and is considered a must-read in the industry. Ms. Lissner has risen to become one of the most sought-after experts on the Chicago market considering real estate.

16841 ■ "Generation Y Driving Portland Multifamily Market" in *Daily Journal of Commerce, Portland* (October 29, 2010)
Pub: Dolan Media Newswires
Ed: Nick Bjork. **Description:** Generation Y, young adults between the ages of 18-30, are interested in multifamily residents in the Portland, Oregon area. Developers in the area, particularly North Portland, have recognized this trend and are looking into multifamily investments.

16842 ■ "Ghazi Insists Downtown Project Still On" in *The Business Journal-Milwaukee* (Vol. 25, August 1, 2008, No. 45, pp. A1)
Pub: American City Business Journals, Inc.
Ed: Rich Kirchen. **Description:** Afshin Ghazi remains confident that his $200 million Catalyst project in downtown Milwaukee, Wisconsin, will push through despite financial disputes delaying his EpiCentre project in Charlotte, North Carolina. He added that the Catalyst is on schedule for groundbreaking in the spring of 2009.

16843 ■ "GL Homes Buys 1,000 Acres in Former Agricultural Reserve" in *Miami Daily Business Review* (March 26, 2008)
Pub: ALM Media Inc.
Ed: Polyana da Costa. **Description:** One of the nation's largest home builders, GL Homes, purchased over 1,000 acres of agricultural land in Southern Palm Beach County, Florida. Plans for 554 residential units are detailed.

16844 ■ "Glendale Pumping $29 Million Into Redevelopment" in *The Business Journal - Serving Phoenix and the Valley of the Sun* (Vol. 28, August 1, 2008, No. 48, pp. 1)
Pub: American City Business Journals, Inc.
Ed: Mike Sunnucks. **Description:** Glendale City is planning to invest $29 million to improve city infrastructure like roadways and water and sewer lines over the next five years. Glendale's city council is also planning to hold a workshop on the redevelopment projects in September 2008. Other views and information on the redevelopment project, are presented.

16845 ■ "GMREB/Analysis of the Resale Market-First Quarter 2007: Year Off to a Great Start" in *Canadian Corporate News* (May 14, 2007)
Pub: Comtex News Network Inc.
Description: According to statistics gathered by the Greater Montreal Real Estate Board (GMREB), the Montreal census metropolitan area (CMA) resale market was vigorous in the first quarter of 2007 yielding 10 percent more existing homes being than the first quarter of 2006.

16846 ■ "GM's Mortgage Unit Deal Brings in $9 Billion" in *Globe & Mail* (March 24, 2006, pp. B3)
Pub: CTVglobemedia Publishing Inc.
Ed: Shawn McCarthy. **Description:** General Motors Corp. sells General Motors Acceptance Corp.'s commercial real estate division to Kohlberg Kravis Roberts & Co. Five Mile Capital Partners LLC and Goldman Sachs Capital Partners. The reasons behind the deal are presented.

16847 ■ "Goldbelt Inc.: Targeting Shareholder Development" in *Alaska Business Monthly* (Vol. 27, October 2011, No. 10, pp. 108)
Pub: Alaska Business Publishing Company
Ed: Tracy Kalytiak. **Description:** Profile of Goldbelt Inc., the company that has changed its original focus of timber to real estate to tourism and then to government contracting opportunities.

16848 ■ "A Good Sign for Commercial Real Estate" in *Austin Business JournalInc.* (Vol. 29, December 18, 2009, No. 41, pp. 1)
Pub: American City Business Journals
Ed: Kate Harrington. **Description:** Factors that could contribute to the reemergence of the commercial mortgage-backed securities market in Texas are discussed. These securities can potentially boost the commercial real estate market statewide as well as nationwide. Commercial mortgage-backed securities origination in 2009 is worth less that $1 billion, compared with $238 billion in 2008.

16849 ■ "Green Housing for the Rest of Us" in *Inc.* (November 2007, pp. 128-129)
Pub: Gruner & Jahr USA Publishing
Ed: Nitasha Tiku. **Description:** Profile of Full Spectrum NY, real estate developer firm, offering residences at the Kalahari, a green high-rise with state-of-the-art features at a reasonable price.

16850 ■ "Grin and Bear It" in *Canadian Business* (Vol. 81, March 3, 2008, No. 3, pp. 53)
Pub: Rogers Media
Ed: Jeff Sanford. **Description:** Discusses the United States economic downturn, caused by the credit market crisis, which is expected to affect the Canadian economy, as Canada depend on the U.S. for 80 percent of its exports. Economist David Rosenberg

thinks that in 2008, housing prices will decline by 15 percent and gross domestic product growth will slow to 0.8 percent. Other forecasts for Canadian economy are given.

16851 ■ "Groundbreaking 2.0" in
Philadelphia Business Journal **(Vol. 30, September 23, 2011, No. 32, pp. 1)**
Pub: American City Business Journals Inc.
Ed: Natalie Kostelni. **Description:** University Place Associates, the developer of 2.0 University Place in West Philadelphia, Pennsylvania, will break ground on a five-story, 97,000-square-foot office building in December 2011. The decision follows the Citizenship and Immigration Services signing of a 15-year lease as anchor tenant.

16852 ■ "Growth in Fits and Starts" in
Canadian Business **(Vol. 83, July 20, 2010, No. 11-12, pp. 18)**
Pub: Rogers Media Ltd.
Ed: James Cowan. **Description:** US home sales and manufacturing indicators have dropped and fears of a double-dip recession are widespread. However, a chief economist says that this is endemic to what can be seen after a recession caused by a financial crisis. In Canada, consumer optimism is rising and anxiety over losing one's job is waning.

16853 ■ "Hank Paulson On the Housing Bailout and What's Ahead" in *Business Week* **(September 22, 2008, No. 4100, pp. 19)**
Pub: McGraw-Hill Companies, Inc.
Ed: Maria Bartiromo. **Description:** Interview with Treasury Secretary Henry Paulson in which he discusses the bailout of Fannie Mae and Freddie Mac as well as the potential impact on the American economy and foreign interests and investments in the country. Paulson has faith that the government's actions will help to stabilize the housing market.

16854 ■ "Hastily Enacted Regulation Will Not Cure Economic Crisis" in *Crain's Chicago Business* **(Vol. 31, May 5, 2008, No. 18, pp. 18)**
Pub: Crain Communications, Inc.
Ed: Stephen P. D'Arcy. **Description:** Policymakers are looking for ways to respond to what is possibly the greatest financial crisis of a generation due to the collapse of the housing market, the credit crisis and the volatility of Wall Street.

16855 ■ "High-End Blunders" in *Crain's Chicago Business* **(Vol. 31, April 21, 2008, No. 16, pp. 54)**
Pub: Crain Communications, Inc.
Ed: Laura Bianchi. **Description:** Discusses some of the biggest errors sellers make that keep their homes from selling including: pricing too high; expecting to recoup the cost of very high-end amenities and decor; avant-garde decorating; owners that hover when the house is being shown; stripping the home of top-quality light fixtures and hardware and replacing them with inferior versions with the assumption that the new buyer will come in with their own decorator and redo it; and poorly maintained properties.

16856 ■ "His Place in the Sun" in *Canadian Business* **(Vol. 79, October 23, 2006, No. 21, pp. 77)**
Pub: Rogers Media
Ed: Zena Olijnyk. **Description:** The business interests of Canadian real estate developer Derek Elliott in the Dominican Republic, is discussed.

16857 ■ "A Home of Her Own" in *Hawaii Business* **(Vol. 53, October 2007, No. 4, pp. 51)**
Pub: Hawaii Business Publishing
Ed: Maria Torres-Kitamura. **Description:** It was observed that the number of single women in Hawaii purchasing their own home has increased, as that in the whole United States where the percentage has increased from 14 percent in 1995 to 22 percent in 2006. However, First Hawaiian Bank's Wendy Lum thinks that the trend will not continue in Hawaii due to lending restrictions. The factors that women consider in buying a home of their own are presented.

16858 ■ "Home Prices Sag" in *Crain's Chicago Business* **(Vol. 31, April 28, 2008, No. 17, pp. 3)**
Pub: Crain Communications, Inc.
Ed: Alby Gallun. **Description:** Since the slump in the housing market is continuing with no sign of recovery, Chicago-area home prices are poised for an even steeper drop this year. In 2007, the region's home prices fell nearly 5 percent and according to a forecast by Fiserv Inc., they will decline 8.1 percent this year and another 2.2 percent in 2009. Statistical data included.

16859 ■ *Home Staging for Dummies*
Pub: John Wiley and Sons, Inc.
Ed: Christine Rae; Janice Saunders Maresh. **Released:** May 2008. **Price:** $19.99. **Description:** Guide shows how to make improvements room by room in order to generate a higher profit on home sales. The book offers tips to clear clutter and show the home's best features, inspire curb appeal, and how to depersonalize and neutralize every room.

16860 ■ "Homeownership: Still the American Dream?" in *Gallup Management Journal* **(May 5, 2011)**
Pub: Gallup
Description: The mortgage finance system is broken. Housing prices continue to fall. Foreclosures are expected to increase in the coming months. However, Gallup's chief economist does not believe this is the end of the American dream of owning one's own home.

16861 ■ "A Home's Identity in Black and White" in *Crain's Chicago Business* **(Vol. 31, April 21, 2008, No. 16, pp. 35)**
Pub: Crain Communications, Inc.
Ed: Lisa Bertagnoli. **Description:** Real estate agents are finding that showing customers a written floor plan is a trend that is growing since many buyers feel that Online virtual tours distort a room. Although floor plans cost up to $500 to have drawn up, they clearly show potential buyers the exact dimensions of rooms and how they connect.

16862 ■ "Homes Stall As Owners Resist Major Price Cuts" in *Crain's Chicago Business* **(Vol. 31, April 21, 2008, No. 16, pp. 38)**
Pub: Crain Communications, Inc.
Ed: Kevin Davis. **Description:** Discusses the high-end housing market and the owners who are resisting major price cuts as well as the buyers who look at long market times as a sign that something is wrong with the property.

16863 ■ "Homing In On the Future" in *Black Enterprise* **(Vol. 38, October 2007, No. 3, pp. 61)**
Pub: Earl G. Graves Publishing Co. Inc.
Ed: Sean Drakes. **Description:** More and more people are wanting new homes wired automated systems that integrate multiple home devices such as computers, audio/visual entertainment, security, communications, utilities, and lighting and environmental controls.

16864 ■ "House Prices Cooling Off, With Alberta Gearing Down" in *Globe & Mail* **(February 9, 2007, pp. B4)**
Pub: CTVglobemedia Publishing Inc.
Ed: Tavia Grant. **Description:** The house prices in Alberta, which are experiencing a torrid pace in price growth, are steady in the first month of 2007. The easing in house prices may show impact on inflation.

16865 ■ *The Housing Boom and Bust*
Pub: Basic Books
Ed: Thomas Sowell. **Price:** $24.95. **Description:** An explanation of the economics and politics of the housing boom and its collapse.

16866 ■ "Housing Market Dinged, But Not Done In, By Nationwide Slump" in *Business Review, Albany New York* **(Vol. 34, December 21, 2007)**
Pub: American City Business Journals, Inc.
Ed: Michael DeMasi. **Description:** Kirsten Keefe, a staff attorney of the Empire Justice Center, is questioning the validity of statistics that represent the number of home foreclosures in New York.

16867 ■ "Housing Markets Still Struggling" in *Montana Business Quarterly* **(Vol. 49, Spring 2011, No. 1, pp. 17)**
Pub: Bureau of Business & Economic Research
Ed: Scott Rickard. **Description:** Montana's economic conditions are a bit better than national averages. Data ranked by state, year-over-year price change, and total price peak is presented, along with statistical data for the entire nation.

16868 ■ "Housing Slide Picks Up Speed" in *Crain's Chicago Business* **(Vol. 31, April 21, 2008, No. 16, pp. 2)**
Pub: Crain Communications, Inc.
Ed: Eddie Baeb. **Description:** According to Tracy Cross & Associates Inc., a real estate consultancy, sales of new homes in the Chicago area dropped 61 percent from the year-earlier period which is more bad news for homebuilders, contractors and real estate agents who are eager for an indication that market conditions are improving.

16869 ■ *How to Open and Operate a Financially Successful Redesign, Redecorating, and Home Staging Business: With Companion CD-ROM*
Pub: Atlantic Publishing Group, Inc.
Ed: Mary Larsen; Teri B. Clark. **Released:** January 2008. **Price:** $39.95 paperback. **Description:** Questions are asked to help individuals determine if they should launch their own redesign or real estate staging firm.

16870 ■ "Illinois Farmland Tops $11,000 Per Acre" in *Farm Industry News* **(June 27, 2011)**
Pub: Penton Business Media Inc.
Ed: Karen McMahon. **Description:** Farmland property in Illinois continues to grow in value, selling for $11,000 per acre. Statistical data included.

16871 ■ "In Control: Tips For Navigating a Buyer's Market" in *Black Enterprise* **(Vol. 38, December 2007, No. 5, pp. 64)**
Pub: Earl G. Graves Publishing Co. Inc.
Ed: Erinn R. Johnson. **Description:** Tips are given to help would-be home buyers. The importance of finding a good real estate agent is stressed.

16872 ■ "In Sickness and In Wealth Management" in *Hispanic Business* **(Vol. 30, March 2008, No. 3, pp. 28)**
Pub: Hispanic Business
Ed: Rick Munarriz. **Description:** Discusses the investment and wealth management firms owned and operated by Hispanics. There are only a handful of these firms owned by Hispanics, as most of them prefer capital preservation by investing in hard assets like cash and real estate than in capital appreciation.

16873 ■ "Incentives Debate Rages On Unabated" in *The Business Journal-Serving Metropolitan Kansas City* **(Vol. 26, September 5, 2008, No. 52)**
Pub: American City Business Journals, Inc.
Ed: Rob Roberts. **Description:** Debate on the new economic development and incentives policy adopted by the Kansas City Council is still on. The city's Planned Industrial Expansion Authority has rejected a standard property tax abatement proposal. The real estate development community has opposed the rejection of proposed the tax incentives policy.

16874 ■ "Independence's Day Keeps on Getting Brighter" in *Business Courier* **(Vol. 27, June 11, 2010, No. 6, pp. 1)**
Pub: Business Courier
Ed: Lucy May. **Description:** Reports show that residential and commercial development continues in Independence, Kentucky despite the recession, with a 144-unit apartment complex under construction. The city recorded 152 new-home closings in 2009, or 25 percent of all new homes closed in Boone, Campbell, and Kenton counties.

16875 ■ "Industrial RE Market Shows Signs of Health" in *Business Courier* **(Vol. 27, August 20, 2010, No. 16, pp. 1)**
Pub: Business Courier
Ed: Jon Newberry. **Description:** Cincinnati, Ohio's industrial real estate sector has experienced growth during the first half of 2010. The industry has seen a large net loss of occupied space in 2009.

16876 ■ "Industrial Vacancies Hit High; Economic Downturn Taking Toll on Area's Demand for Space" in *Crain's Chicago Business* (Apr. 21, 2008)
Pub: Crain Communications, Inc.
Ed: Alby Gallun. Description: Hitting its highest level in four years in the first quarter is the Chicago-area industrial vacancy rate, a sign that the slumping economy is depressing demand for warehouse and manufacturing space.

16877 ■ "Insider" in *Canadian Business* (Vol. 81, March 31, 2008, No. 5, pp. 76)
Pub: Rogers Media
Ed: John Gray. Description: Discusses a comparison of an average Canadian family's finances in 1990 with the data from 2007. The average family in 2007 has over $80,000 in debt compared to just under $52,000 in 1990. However, Canadians have also been accumulating solid assets such as homes and stocks. This means that Canadian debt load has fallen from 22 percent in 1990 to 20 percent in 2007 when taken as a percentage of total net worth.

16878 ■ "Insurer Buys Foundation's Uptown HQ" in *Charlotte Business Journal* (Vol. 25, December 17, 2010, No. 39, pp. 1)
Pub: Charlotte Business Journal
Ed: Will Boye. Description: Charlotte, North Carolina-based Synergy Coverage Solutions has purchased the three-story building owned by Foundations For the Carolinas for slightly more than $3 million. Synergy plans to relocate its operation in the uptown building by August 2011.

16879 ■ *Internet Resources and Services for International Real Estate Information*
Pub: Oryx Press
Contact: Sheau-yueh J. Chao, Author
Price: $82.95, individuals Paperback; $57.95, individuals Sterling price. Covers: Internet sources related to international real estate, finance, and investment.

16880 ■ "Inventory Glut" in *Business Courier* (Vol. 24, March 28, 2008, No. 51, pp. 1)
Pub: American City Business Journals, Inc.
Ed: Laura Baverman. Description: Indian Hill and the downtown area have the highest monthly absorption rate for housing on a list of 42 Greater Cincinnati and Northern Kentucky neighborhoods. The two neighborhoods have 19 and 27 months of housing inventory respectively, which means home sellers need to either lower their prices or be very patient.

16881 ■ "Investors Sue Jackson Properties for Fraud, Breach of Contract" in *The Business Journal - Serving Phoenix and the Valley of the Sun* (Vol. 28, July 18, 2008, No. 46, pp. 1)
Pub: American City Business Journals, Inc.
Ed: Jan Buchholz. Description: Investors sued Jackson Properties EVB Inc. and Jackson Properties EVB LLC for fraud and breach of contract over a botched housing development deal. The investors also filed a complaint before the Arizona Corporation Commission. The investors stand to lose $8 million from the halted development deal.

16882 ■ "Is this a Buying Opportunity?" in *Canadian Business* (Vol. 82, April 27, 2009, No. 7, pp. 46)
Pub: Rogers Media
Ed: Andy Holloway. Description: Home prices in Canada are down by as much as 14.2 percent in 2009 compared to prices in 2008, making homes more affordable now. Some housing experts believe that homes are still good investments as prices of rent and properties always recover. Meanwhile, a survey found that Canadians under 35 plan to buy a home within two years.

16883 ■ "It Could Be Worse" in *Barron's* (Vol. 89, July 27, 2009, No. 30, pp. 5)
Pub: Dow Jones & Co., Inc.
Ed: Alan Abelson. Description: Media sources are being fooled by corporate America who is peddling an economic recovery rather than reality as shown by the report of a rise in existing home sales which

boosted the stock market even if it was a seasonal phenomenon. The phrase "things could be worse" sums up the reigning investment philosophy in the U.S. and this has been stirring up the market.

16884 ■ "Kimball Hill Files for Chapter 11" in *Crain's Chicago Business* (Vol. 31, April 28, 2008, No. 17, pp. 12)
Pub: Crain Communications, Inc.
Description: Homebuilder Kimball Hill filed for Chapter 11 bankruptcy protection after months of negotiations with lenders. The firm plans to continue operations as it restructures its debt.

16885 ■ "The Kitchen is Closed; Eateries Forced Out by Soaring Rents, Declining Revenues" in *Crain's New York Business* (January 21, 2008)
Pub: Crain Communications, Inc.
Ed: Lisa Fickenscher. Description: Many restaurants have already closed in the area and experts expect many more will follow due to skyrocketing rents and declining revenues.

16886 ■ "Kubicki Juggles Lineup at Vianda" in *Business Courier* (Vol. 26, December 11, 2009, No. 33, pp. 1)
Pub: American City Business Journals, Inc.
Ed: Dan Monk. Description: Cincinnati real estate developer Chuck Kubicki replaced the management team of Vianda LLC and cancelled contracts with two vendors that caused a surge of customer complaints. Vianda is a direct-response marketing firm that sells and distributes dietary supplements for wellness and sexual performance.

16887 ■ "Land on Boardwalk" in *Canadian Business* (Vol. 82, April 27, 2009, No. 7, pp. 19)
Pub: Rogers Media
Ed: Calvin Leung. Description: Boardwalk REIT remains as one of the most attractive real estate investment trusts in Canada, with 73 percent of analysts rating the firm a Buy. Analyst Neil Downey believes that good management, as well as a good business model, makes Boardwalk a good investment. Downey is concerned however, that a worsening of Alberta's economy could significantly impact Boardwalk.

16888 ■ "Large Homes can be Energy Efficient Too" in *Contractor* (Vol. 56, October 2009, No. 10, pp. 5)
Pub: Penton Media, Inc.
Ed: Candace Roulo. Description: Eco Estate at Briggs Chaney subdivision in Silver Spring, Maryland has model houses that use sustainable technologies and products and the homes that will be built on the subdivision will feature some of the technologies featured on the model home. The energy efficient HVAC system of the model homes are discussed.

16889 ■ "Laugh or Cry?" in *Barron's* (Vol. 88, March 24, 2008, No. 12, pp. 7)
Pub: Dow Jones & Company, Inc.
Ed: Alan Abelson. Description: Discusses the American economy which is just starting to feel the effect of the credit and housing crises. JPMorgan Chase purchased Bear Stearns for $2 a share, much lower than its share price of $60, while quasi-government entities Fannie Mae and Freddie Mac are starting to run into trouble.

16890 ■ "Local Commercial Real Estate Foreclosures Continue to Rise" in *Baltimore Business Journal* (Vol. 28, October 1, 2010, No. 21, pp. 1)
Pub: Baltimore Business Journal
Ed: Daniel J. Sernovitz. Description: Foreclosures of commercial real estate across the Greater Baltimore area have continued to rise. The region is now host to about $2 billion worth of commercial properties that carry a maturing debt or have been foreclosed. Commercial real estate owners are unable to finance their debts because banks have become stricter in passing out loans.

16891 ■ "Local Industrial Vacancies Climb" in *Crain's Chicago Business* (Vol. 31, November 17, 2008, No. 46, pp. 18)
Pub: Crain Communications, Inc.
Ed: Eddie Baeb. Description: Demand for local industrial real estate has declined dramatically as companies that use warehouse and factory space struggle to survive in an ailing economy. According to a report by Colliers Bennett & Kahnweiler Inc., a commercial real estate brokerage, the regional vacancy rate has risen to 9.86 percent in the third quarter, the fourth straight increase and the highest in the past 14 years.

16892 ■ "Lytle Place Listing Seen as Bellwether" in *Business Courier* (Vol. 27, December 3, 2010, No. 31, pp. 1)
Pub: Business Courier
Ed: Dan Monk. Description: Denver, Colorado-based Apartment Investment and Management Company (AIMCO) has offered the 25-story One Lytle Place Apartments for sale through CB Richard Ellis for the third time in three years. The potential sale could define the recovery for Cincinnati, Ohio's struggling apartment industry.

16893 ■ "The Main Event" in *Canadian Business* (Vol. 80, November 19, 2007, No. 23, pp. 28)
Pub: Rogers Media
Ed: Zena Olijnyk. Description: U.S.-based Lowe's Companies, Inc. will be opening three stores in Canada in December 2007 and another three in 2008. The housing market crisis in the U.S. is the reason behind the home improvement store's Canadian expansion. The impacts of the expansion on Canadian home care stores and on the market competition are evaluated.

16894 ■ "Major Tech Employers Pulling Out" in *Sacramento Business Journal* (Vol. 25, August 1, 2008, No. 22, pp. 1)
Pub: American City Business Journals, Inc.
Ed: Celia Lamb. Description: Biotechnology company Affymetrix Inc. is planning to close its West Sacramento, California plant and lay off 110 employees. The company said it will expand a corporate restructuring plan. Affymetrix also plans to lease out or sell its building at Riverside Parkway.

16895 ■ "Mandel Site Favored For UWM Hall" in *The Business Journal-Milwaukee* (Vol. 25, September 19, 2008, No. 52, pp. A1)
Pub: American City Business Journals, Inc.
Description: University of Wisconsin-Milwaukee student residence hall's leading location is a site pushed by Mandel Group Inc. Real estate sources say that the developer's proposal offers the best opportunity for business development and the least conflict with nearby neighborhoods. Plans for the Mandel site are presented.

16896 ■ "Mann to Lead Builders" in *Charlotte Observer* (January 31, 2007)
Pub: Knight-Ridder/Tribune Business News
Ed: Allen Norwood. Description: Elliot Mann of Standard Pacific Homes was sworn in as president of Home Builders Association of Charlotte, North Carolina.

16897 ■ "Market Gamble" in *Business Journal-Serving Phoenix and the Valley of the Sun* (Vol. 5, October 5, 2007, No. 28, pp. 1)
Pub: American City Business Journals, Inc.
Ed: Mike Padgett. Description: AI-BSR LLC, an Israeli group believes the housing market will regain its strength within three years. The group plans to build its $385 million project, called One Phoenix. The condominiums start at $500,000, with units ranging from 800 to 2,000 square feet.

16898 ■ "Market for Retail Space Flat, but Recovery Still Uncertain" in *Sacramento Business Journal* (Vol. 28, August 26, 2011, No. 26, pp. 1)
Pub: Sacramento Business Journal
Ed: Kelly Johnson. Description: The retail market in the Sacramento, California region remains challenged with the stock market volatility being the latest of its

hurdles. The overall vacancy was 13.1 percent as of mid-2011, but retail real estate professionals express hopes that the worst is behind. A list and description of the region's winners and losers in retail vacancies is provided.

16899 ■ "Market Swings Intensify Yearning for Bonds" in *Globe & Mail* **(March 9, 2007, pp. B9)**

Pub: CTVglobemedia Publishing Inc.

Ed: Keith Damsell. **Description:** The rise in demand for proper fixed-income bonds in Canada as a result of uncertainties in the equity market is discussed. Some big Canadian fixed-income funds are presented.

16900 ■ "A Matter of Perspective" in *Business Journal-Portland* **(Vol. 24, November 2, 2007, No. 35, pp. 1)**

Pub: American City Business Journals, Inc.

Ed: Andy Giegerich. **Description:** Oregon Governor Ted Kulongoski assembled the Mortgage Lending Work Group, made up of members of the mortgage industry and consumer groups, to recommend possible bills for the Oregon Senate and House to consider. How its members try to balance philosophical differences in mortgage lending rules is discussed.

16901 ■ "Medical Office Developers To Merge November 1" in *The Business Journal - Serving Phoenix and the Valley of the Sun* **(Vol. 29, September 26, 2008, No. 4, pp. 1)**

Pub: American City Business Journals, Inc.

Ed: Angela Gonzales. **Description:** Ensemble Real Estate Services LLC and DevMan Co. will merge effective November 1, 2008 and will call the firm Ensemble DevMan of Arizona after the merger. The two companies will combine their resources and expertise on planned projects that include the Phoenix Children's Hospital's Specialty Clinic and Banner Ironwood Medical Office Building.

16902 ■ "Mequon Plan On Tracks, Bucks Housing Trend" in *The Business Journal-Milwaukee* **(Vol. 25, September 26, 2008, No. 53, pp. A1)**

Pub: American City Business Journals, Inc.

Ed: Pete Millard. **Description:** Insight Development Group plans to build condominium units and single-family homes despite the residential market downturn. The Orchard Glen project, a planned development in Mequon, is a $22 million project which will include 38 condos and 12 single-family homes. Details of the project are provided.

16903 ■ "Millions Needed To Finish First Place" in *The Business Journal-Milwaukee* **(Vol. 25, August 15, 2008, No. 47, pp. A1)**

Pub: American City Business Journals, Inc.

Ed: Rich Kirchen. **Description:** First Place on the River condominium project in Milwaukee, Wisconsin, needs $18.2 million before it can be completed. A total of $6.8 million have already been spent since the project went into receivership on 31 January 2008.

16904 ■ "Minnesota Farms' Net Worth Grows 10 Percent Each Year for 15 Years" in *Farm Industry News* **(August 22, 2011)**

Pub: Penton Business Media Inc.

Ed: Dale Nordquist. **Description:** The average value of farms in Minnesota is growing at a fast pace. Total assets per farm have increased by more than $1.1 million over the past 15 years. Statistical data included.

16905 ■ "A Model Development" in *Crain's Cleveland Business* **(Vol. 28, October 1, 2007, No. 39, pp. 12)**

Pub: Crain Communications, Inc.

Description: Profile a Forest City Enterprises Inc., a firm that is developing a project in New Mexico called Mesa del Sol. The Albuquerque development is being seen as the vanguard of master-planned communities with its high-tech economic development center which is expected to become the site of 60,000 jobs, 38,000 homes and a town center.

16906 ■ "Modular Home Center Opens in Arcadia" in *Charlotte Observer* **(February 1, 2007)**

Pub: Knight-Ridder/Tribune Business News

Ed: John Lawhorne. **Description:** Arcadia Home Center features modular homes constructed on a steel frame; regulations regarding the manufacture and moving of these homes are included.

16907 ■ "More Contractors Unpaid" in *Puget Sound Business Journal* **(Vol. 29, October 3, 2008, No. 24, pp. 1)**

Pub: American City Business Journals

Ed: Brad Berton. **Description:** An 80 percent rise in the filing of mechanics' liens was reported in Seattle, Washington. It is believed that financial problems are spreading to construction companies and contractors as home sales slide and builders default on construction loans. Delinquencies of single-family construction homes has increased.

16908 ■ "More Offices Planned For Percheron Square" in *The Business Journal-Milwaukee* **(Vol. 25, August 22, 2008, No. 48, pp. A1)**

Pub: American City Business Journals, Inc.

Ed: Pete Millard. **Description:** More office projects are under way at Percheron Square. Ryan Cos. US Inc., for example, plans to build over 200,000 square feet of office space at the area. Details of new office projects in Wisconsin are presented.

16909 ■ "Mortgage Mess: How To Determine Your Exposure To the Subprime Crisis" in *Black Enterprise* **(Vol. 38, November 2007, No. 4, pp. 46)**

Pub: Earl G. Graves Publishing Co. Inc.

Ed: Ilana Polyak. **Description:** Stocks and mutual funds have experienced declines because of the subprime crisis. Morningstar's Website can help investors research firms in which they have invested; if a fund is named high yield or high income or in the financial services sector, investments will have greater exposure to the mess.

16910 ■ "Mortgage Securities Drop Hits Home" in *The Business Journal-Serving Metropolitan Kansas City* **(Vol. 27, October 17, 2008, No. 5)**

Pub: American City Business Journals, Inc.

Ed: Rob Roberts. **Description:** Sale of commercial mortgage-backed securities (CMBS) in Kansas City, Missouri have declined. The area may avoid layoffs if the United States government succeeds in stabilizing the economy. Major CMBS players in the area include Midland Loan Services Inc. and KeyBank Real Estate Capital.

16911 ■ "Move Over - Or Out" in *Puget Sound Business Journal* **(Vol. 29, November 28, 2008, No. 32, pp. 1)**

Pub: American City Business Journals

Ed: Kirsten Grind. **Description:** Real estate agents in the state of Washington are either moving to smaller real estate firms or quitting the industry due to the weak housing market. Lesser-known firms are experiencing an influx of experienced real estate agents, while 2,800 agents in the state have left the industry.

16912 ■ "Myths of Deleveraging" in *Barron's* **(Vol. 90, August 23, 2010, No. 34, pp. M14)**

Pub: Barron's Editorial & Corporate Headquarters

Ed: Gene Epstein. **Description:** The opposite is true against reports about deleveraging or the decrease in credit since inflation-adjusted-investment factories and equipment rose 7.8 percent in the first quarter of 2010. On consumer deleveraging, sales of homes through credit is weak but there is a trend towards more realistic homeownership and consumer spending on durable goods rose 8.8 percent.

16913 ■ "Neighborhood Watch" in *Baltimore Business Journal* **(Vol. 28, July 23, 2010, No. 11, pp. 1)**

Pub: Baltimore Business Journal

Ed: Daniel J. Sernovitz. **Description:** Maryland government and housing leaders are set to spend $100 million in federal funding to stem the increase

in foreclosures in the area. The federal funding is seen as inadequate to resolve the problem of foreclosures.

16914 ■ "The Neighborhood Watch" in *Hawaii Business* **(Vol. 53, March 2008, No. 9, pp. 36)**

Pub: Hawaii Business Publishing

Ed: David K. Choo. **Description:** OahuRe.com offers information on Hawaii real estate market, with spreadsheets and comparative market analysis page, which shows properties that are active, sold, or in escrow. Other details about OahuRe.com are discussed. A list of other top real estate websites in Hawaii and in the U.S. in general is provided.

16915 ■ "New-Home Sales Grab a Foothold With Q2 Boost" in *Sacramento Business Journal* **(Vol. 25, July 11, 2008, No. 19, pp. 1)**

Pub: American City Business Journals, Inc.

Ed: Michael Shaw. **Description:** Statistics show that homebuilders in Sacramento, California experienced an increase in new-home sales during the second quarter of 2008. It was also reported that builders moved more homes without slashing prices significantly. Barry Grant, president of KB Home's Sacramento division, believes that the improvement is caused by the stability in the supply of resale homes.

16916 ■ "A New Mix of Tenants Settles In" in *Crain's New York Business* **(Vol. 24, January 14, 2008, No. 2, pp. 26)**

Pub: Crain Communications, Inc.

Ed: Andrew Marks. **Description:** More and more nonfinancial firms are relocating downtown due to the new retailers and restaurants that are reshaping the look and feel of lower Manhattan.

16917 ■ "New York City-Based New Street Realty Advisors has Secured a New Flagship for David's Bridal" in *Chain Store Age* **(August 2008)**

Pub: Chain Store Age

Description: New York City-based New Street Realty Advisors secured a new flagship store for David's Bridal in the Chelsea district of Manhattan. David's Bridal will occupy 12,800 square feet on two floors in a retail condominium development.

16918 ■ "The Next Government Bailout?" in *Barron's* **(Vol. 88, March 10, 2008, No. 10, pp. 21)**

Pub: Dow Jones & Company, Inc.

Ed: Jonathan Laing. **Description:** Fannie Mae may need a government bailout as it faces huge hits brought about by the effects of the housing crisis. The shares of the government-sponsored enterprise have dropped 65 percent since the housing crisis began.

16919 ■ "The Next Real Estate Boom" in *Canadian Business* **(Vol. 80, March 26, 2007, No. 7, pp. 25)**

Pub: Rogers Media

Ed: Erik Heinrich. **Description:** The better places to invest in Canadian real estate market are presented. The future price performance of the industry is analyzed.

16920 ■ "N.H. Near the LEED in Green Space" in *New Hampshire Business Review* **(Vol. 33, March 25, 2011, No. 6, pp. 30)**

Pub: Business Publications Inc.

Description: New Hamphire's architects, contractors and suppliers are among the leaders with LEED-certified space per capita.

16921 ■ "No Wild Highs Means No Wild Lows" in *Business Courier* **(Vol. 24, January 18, 2008, No. 41, pp. 1)**

Pub: American City Business Journals, Inc.

Ed: Laura Baverman. **Description:** Discusses a PMI Group report which revealed that the Greater Cincinnati area is in the lowest risk category for home value declines. The report forecast that the chance that housing prices in the area will fall below their current status by the year 2010 is less than 5 percent. Housing price forecasts for other areas are also provided.

16922 ■ "Not In My Backyard" in
Entrepreneur **(Vol. 36, May 2008, No. 5, pp.**
42)
Pub: Entrepreneur Media, Inc.
Ed: Farnoosh Torabi. **Description:** More investors
are turning to overseas real estate investments as
the U.S. market sees a slowdown. Analysts say that
risk-averse investors opt for funds with record of
strong returns and U.S. real estate investment trusts
that partner with foreign businesses for transparency
purposes. Other details about foreign real estate
investments are discussed.

16923 ■ "Number of Mechanic's Liens Triple
Since 2005" in *The Business Journal -*
Serving Phoenix and the Valley of the Sun
(Vol. 28, August 22, 2008, No. 51, pp. 1)
Pub: American City Business Journals, Inc.
Ed: Jan Buchholtz. **Description:** Experts are blaming the mortgage and banking industries for the
tripling of mechanic's liens that were filed in Arizona
from 2005 through August 6, 2008. The rise in
mechanic's liens is believed to indicate stress in the
real estate community. Other views and information
on the rise of mechanic's liens filed in Arizona are
presented.

16924 ■ "N.Y. Group Top Bidder for Last
Duke Sites" in *Crain's Cleveland Business*
(Vol. 28, November 19, 2007, No. 46, pp. 1)
Pub: Crain Communications, Inc.
Ed: Stan Bullard. **Description:** Overview of the pos-
sible portfolio sale of Duke Realty Corp.'s last
Northeast Ohio properties, 14 office buildings in
Independence, Seven Hills and North Olmsted,
believed to be purchased by a real estate investor
group led by Nightingale Properties LLC of New York.

16925 ■ "October 2009: Recovery Plods
Along" in *Hispanic Business* **(October 2009,**
pp. 10-11)
Pub: Hispanic Business
Ed: Dr. Juan Solana. **Description:** Economist reports
on a possible economic recovery which will not be allowed to rely on a strong domestic demand in order
to sustain it. Consumers, looking to counterbalance
years of leverage financing based on unrealistic,
ever-increasing home and portfolio valuations, are
saving rather than spending money.

16926 ■ "Office Leasing Gains Ground" in
Sacramento Business Journal **(Vol. 25, July**
18, 2008, No. 20, pp. 1)
Pub: American City Business Journals, Inc.
Ed: Michael Shaw. **Description:** There were at least
84,000 square feet leased to companies in the
Sacramento area in the three months prior to August
2008. This development is good news considering
that overall vacant leases were around 247,000
square feet for the previous quarter.

16927 ■ "OK, Bring in the Lawyers" in
Crain's Chicago Business **(Vol. 31, November**
17, 2008, No. 46, pp. 26)
Pub: Crain Communications, Inc.
Ed: Daniel Rome Levine. **Description:** Bankruptcy
attorneys are finding the economic and credit crisis a
benefit for their businesses due to the high number
of business owners and mortgage holders that are
need of their services. One Chicago firm is handling
ten times the number of cases they did the previous
year and of that about 80 percent of their new clients
are related to the real estate sector.

16928 ■ "Old Ford Plant to Sign New
Tenants" in *Business Courier* **(Vol. 27, August**
13, 2010, No. 15, pp. 1)
Pub: Business Courier
Ed: Dan Monk. **Description:** Ohio Realty Advisors
LLC, a company handling the marketing of the 1.9
million-square-foot former Ford Batavia plant is on
the brink of landing one distribution and three
manufacturing firms as tenants. These tenants are
slated to occupy about 20 percent of the facility and
generate as many as 250 jobs in Ohio.

16929 ■ "Optimism Index" in *Black*
Enterprise **(Vol. 41, September 2010, No. 2,**
pp. 24)
Pub: Earl G. Graves Publishing Co. Inc.
Description: According to a Pew Research Center
report, 81 percent of African Americans expect to

improve their finances in 2011. Blacks have carried a
disproportionate share of job losses and housing
foreclosures in the recession that began in 2007.

16930 ■ "Ottawa's Real Estate Targets
Exceed Market Appraisals" in *Globe & Mail*
(March 19, 2007, pp. B1)
Pub: CTVglobemedia Publishing Inc.
Ed: Danier Leblanc. **Description:** The growth in the
real estate market in Ottawa and the huge revenue
the government is expecting from sale of nine build-
ings as part of its lease back plan is discussed.

16931 ■ "Outlook 2007" in *Canadian*
Business **(Vol. 80, December 25, 2006, No. 1,**
pp.)
Pub: Rogers Media
Ed: David Wolf. **Description:** Economists' 2007
forecast on global economy, particularly about
Canada's housing and labor market among other sec-
tors, is discussed.

16932 ■ "Outside Investors Hot On Detroit
Commercial Real Estate" in *Crain's Detroit*
Business **(Vol. 24, January 28, 2008, No. 4,**
pp. 25)
Pub: Crain Communications Inc. - Detroit
Ed: Daniel Duggan. **Description:** An overview of out-
of-town investors seeking to purchase commercial
real estate in Michigan is presented. Statistical data
included.

16933 ■ "Pain Ahead as Profit Pressure
Increases" in *Crain's Chicago Business* **(Vol.**
31, May 5, 2008, No. 18, pp. 4)
Pub: Crain Communications, Inc.
Ed: Daniel Rome Levine. **Description:** Interview with
David Klaskin, the chairman and chief investment officer at Oak Ridge Investments LLC, who discusses
the outlook for the economy and corporate earnings,
particularly in the housing and auto industries, the
impact of economic stimulus checks, the weakness
of the dollar and recommendations of stocks that
individual investors may find helpful.

16934 ■ "The Paper Shredder" in *Business*
Courier **(Vol. 26, September 11, 2009, No. 20,**
pp. 1)
Pub: American City Business Journals, Inc.
Ed: Dan Monk. **Description:** DotLoop Company,
owned by entrepreneur Austin Allison, is developing
the DotLoop software, which eliminates paperwork in
the processing of real estate contracts. The software
allows realtors to take control of the negotiation
process and is adaptable to the rules of different US
states.

16935 ■ "Part-Time Office Space" in *Hawaii*
Business **(Vol. 53, December 2007, No. 6, pp.**
132)
Pub: Hawaii Business Publishing
Ed: Ashley Hamershock. **Description:** My Office is
one of the companies that are renting space office
not only by the month, but by the hour. Such setup is
beneficial to small businesses that do not need a
whole office all to themselves, and are interested in
cutting the cost of office space rental. The prices of
office space in Hawaii are mentioned.

16936 ■ "Pat Modica" in *Crain's Cleveland*
Business **(Vol. 30, June 29, 2009, No. 25, pp.**
15)
Pub: Crain Communications, Inc.
Ed: Stan Bullard. **Description:** Profile of Pat Modica,
real estate agent with Howard Hanna. Ms. Modica
states that in her 29 years as a residential real estate
agent, she has never seen a market like the present
one. She discusses home sales and activity for the
area.

16937 ■ "Pavilions Poised for Image
Overhaul" in *The Business Journal - Serving*
Phoenix and the Valley of the Sun **(Vol. 28,**
August 22, 2008)
Pub: American City Business Journals, Inc.
Ed: Jan Buchholz. **Description:** DeRitto Partners
Inc. is expected to push through with plans for a
major renovation of the 1.1 million-square foot Scotts-
dale Pavilions in Scottsdale, Arizona. An aggressive

marketing campaign is planned to be included in the
renovation, which aims to address high vacancy rates
and competition. Views and information on the
planned renovation are presented.

16938 ■ "Paying for the Recession:
Rebalancing Economic Growth" in *Montana*
Business Quarterly **(Vol. 49, Spring 2011, No.**
1, pp. 2)
Pub: Bureau of Business & Economic Research
Ed: Patrick M. Barkey. **Description:** Four key issues
required to address in order to rebalance economic
growth in America are examined. They include: savings rates, global trade imbalances, government
budgets and most importantly, housing price correction.

16939 ■ *The Peebles Principles: Insights*
from an Entrepreneur's Life of Business
Success, Making Deals, and Creating a
Fortune from Scratch
Pub: John Wiley and Sons Inc.
Ed: R. Donahue Peebles. **Released:** April 2007.
Price: $29.99. **Description:** Successful entrepreneur
shares his business experience. Peebles went from
CEO of the nation's largest Black-owned real estate
development firm to founding his own firm.

16940 ■ *Peggy's Corner: The Art of Staging*
Pub: Eaton-Moghannam Publishing
Ed: Peggy Selinger-Eaton; Gayla Moghannam. **Re-**
leased: June 2005. **Description:** Techniques to
enhance the value of any home are given. Seven
principles of staging a home for sale include making
a great first impression, maximizing space and
eliminating clutter, using lighting for open spacious
feeling, de-emphasize flaws, make the home appealing to buyers with varied tastes, creating warmth,
and modernizing the home.

16941 ■ "A Perfect Predator: Brookfield
Asset Management Isn't Brash" in *Canadian*
Business **(Vol. 83, July 20, 2010, No. 11-12,**
pp. 50)
Pub: Rogers Media Ltd.
Ed: Joanna Pachner. **Description:** Brookfield Asset
Management CEO Bruce Flatt manages $108 billion
worth of real estate and the company has become
one of the world's biggest prime real estate owners
since he became leader. Flatt says their goal is to
earn a 12-15 percent compound annual return per
share and that they would shrink in size if it meant
reaching that goal.

16942 ■ "Peter Gilgan" in *Canadian Business*
(Vol. 82, April 27, 2009, No. 7, pp. 58)
Pub: Rogers Media
Ed: Calvin Leung. **Description:** Mattamy Homes Ltd.
president and chief executive officer Peter Gilgan
believes that their business model of building communities in an organized way brings advantages to
the firm and for their customers. He also believes in
adopting their product prices to new market realities.
Gilgan considers the approvals regime in Ontario his
biggest challenge in the last 20 years.

16943 ■ "Phillips Edison Launches $1.8B
Retail REIT" in *Business Courier* **(Vol. 27,**
October 15, 2010, No. 24, pp. 1)
Pub: Business Courier
Ed: Dan Monk. **Description:** Retail center operator
Phillips Edison & Company is organizing a real estate
investment trust (REIT) to raise $1.8 billion to finance
the planned purchase of 150 grocery-centered shop-
ping centers around the U.S. The offering would be
Phillips largest. Phillips Edison employesss 174 work-
ers and operates 250 shopping centers nationwide.

16944 ■ "A Place to Call Home" in *Business*
Courier **(Vol. 24, March 7, 2008, No. 48, pp. 1)**
Pub: American City Business Journals, Inc.
Ed: Lucy May. **Description:** Discusses a new type of
housing for Cincinnati's chronically homeless that will
be developed by the Over-the-Rhine Community
Housing Network and the Cincinnati Center City
Development Corp. Advocates believe that it is the
missing link in the community's efforts to eradicate
homelessness. The details of the project are also
presented.

16945 ■ "A Place in the Sun" in *Canadian Business* **(Vol. 81, July 22, 2008, No. 12-13, pp. 56)**
Pub: Rogers Media Ltd.
Description: Experts believe that it is the best time for Canadians to own a retirement home in the U.S., where real estate prices are up to 50 percent below their peak. Other views concerning the economic conditions occurring in the United States, as well as on the implications for Canadians planning to invest in the country are presented.

16946 ■ "Placer Land Sells for $12 Million" in *Sacramento Business Journal* **(Vol. 25, July 25, 2008, No. 21, pp. 1)**
Pub: American City Business Journals, Inc.
Ed: Michael Shaw; Celia Lamb. **Description:** Reynen & Bardis Communities Inc., a Sacramento, California-based homebuilder, has purchased the Antonio Mountain Ranch in Placer County, California shortly before the property's scheduled foreclosure on June 27, 2008. Placer County Recorder's data show that the purchase price of the 808-acre wetland-rich property is $12 million.

16947 ■ "Population Growing Faster Than Retail, Service Sector" in *Crain's New York Business* **(Vol. 24, January 14, 2008, No. 2, pp. 30)**
Pub: Crain Communications, Inc.
Ed: Andrew Marks. **Description:** Downtown Manhattan is seeing more residential development; however, as more families call the area home the need for more retail and services is becoming evident.

16948 ■ "'Pre-Sale' for Planned Could Mich Tower" in *Crain's Chicago Business* **(Vol. 31, March 24, 2008, No. 12, pp. 14)**
Pub: Crain Communications, Inc.
Ed: Eddie Baeb. **Description:** Condominium developer William Warman is planning to build a mixed-use tower at 300 North Michigan Avenue which would include a hotel, retail space, apartments and a parking garage. Mr. Warman is looking for investors to buy part or all of the space in order to make it easier to land financing.

16949 ■ "Price War: Managerial Salaries Are Beating the National Average, But Maybe Not for Long" in *Canadian Business* **(March 31, 2008)**
Pub: Rogers Media
Ed: Megan Harman. **Description:** Real average hourly earnings of managers increase by 20 percent in ten years as companies increase wages to avoid the risk of losing key managers to the competition and in preparation for the retirement of baby boomers. Tough market conditions affect management more since their incentives are tied to individual and corporate performance.

16950 ■ "Priced-Out Tenants Flocking to Class B" in *Boston Business Journal* **(Vol. 27, October 19, 2007, No. 38, pp. 1)**
Pub: American City Business Journals Inc.
Ed: Michelle Hillman. **Description:** Tenants who usually rent top-tier office buildings are migrating to building that are not as expensive. The shift from Class A to Class B buildings is influenced by the high rental cost of the flashy office towers.

16951 ■ "Prince of the City" in *Canadian Business* **(Vol. 80, November 19, 2007, No. 23, pp. 62)**
Pub: Rogers Media
Ed: Rachel Pulfer. **Description:** Robert Fung and the Salilent Group aim to revive the poverty-stricken communities in Vancouver by transforming the city's old buildings into designer condominiums using city incentives. Fung and his partners have increased property values in the most unlikely neighborhoods by creating luxury real estate. Fung's recommendations on Vancouver's real estate development are given.

16952 ■ "Private Equity Firms Shopping Valley For Deals" in *The Business Journal - Serving Phoenix and the Valley of the Sun* **(Vol. 29, September 19, 2008, No. 3, pp. 1)**
Pub: American City Business Journals, Inc.
Ed: Mike Sunnucks. **Description:** Private equity firms from California, Boston, New York, and overseas are expected to invest in growth-oriented real estate markets that include Phoenix. Real estate experts revealed that privately held investment and acquisition firms are looking to invest in real estate markets hit by the housing crisis. Views and information on private equity firms' real estate investments are presented.

16953 ■ "Proposal Ruffles Builders" in *Austin Business JournalInc.* **(Vol. 29, November 20, 2009, No. 37, pp. 1)**
Pub: American City Business Journals
Ed: Jacob Dirr. **Description:** A proposal that requires heating, ventilation and cooling equipment checking for a new commercial building having an area of at least 10,000 square feet might cost 25 cents to 50 cents per square foot for the owners. This may lead to higher housing costs. Both the Building and Fire Code Board of Appeals and the Mechanical Plumbing and Solar Board have recommended the plan.

16954 ■ "Proposed Accounting Changes Could Complicate Tenant's Leases" in *Baltimore Business Journal* **(Vol. 28, July 2, 2010, No. 8, pp. 1)**
Pub: Baltimore Business Journal
Ed: Daniel J. Sernovitz. **Description:** The Financial Accounting Standards Board has proposed that companies must indicate the value of real estate leases as assets and liabilities on balance sheets instead of expenses. The proposals could cause some companies to document millions of dollars in charges on their books or find difficulty in getting loans.

16955 ■ "Proposed Law Would Stop REIS Bid for Annexation by Livonia" in *Crain's Detroit Business* **(Vol. 24, March 10, 2008, No. 10, pp. 2)**
Pub: Crain Communications, Inc.
Ed: Chad Halcom. **Description:** REIS Northville L.L.C., a joint venture made up of Real Estate Interests Group Inc. and Schostak Bros. & Co., has proposed an $800 million project called Highwood at the former Northville Psychiatric Hospital site but has been stalled due to a disagreement with Northville Township on several terms including: the amount of retail at the site and the paying for cleanup of environmental and medical waste.

16956 ■ "Proposed Triangle Redo in Motion" in *Crain's Cleveland Business* **(Vol. 28, October 15, 2007, No. 41, pp. 1)**
Pub: Crain Communications, Inc.
Ed: Stan Bullard. **Description:** Zaremba Homes and MRN Ltd. are partnering to redevelop the so-called Triangle section of University Circle. The proposed project will include a total of 434 new rental and for-sale residential suites and as much as 227,000 square feet of retail and restaurant space.

16957 ■ "Pulte May Be Bouncing Back From Stock-Price Doldrums" in *Crain's Detroit Business* **(Vol. 23, October 8, 2007, No. 41, pp. 4)**
Pub: Crain Communications Inc. - Detroit
Ed: Daniel Duggan. **Description:** Pulte Homes saw a jump in its stocks due to Citigroup's analysts rating Pulte and other builders higher due to strong balance sheets.

16958 ■ "Radio Roots Run Deep" in *The Business Journal-Milwaukee* **(Vol. 25, July 4, 2008, No. 41, pp. A1)**
Pub: American City Business Journals, Inc.
Ed: Rich Kirchen. **Description:** Profile of Steve Palec, a real estate broker at CB Richard Ellis, also works as a radio host for shows "Rock & Roll Roots" and "Legends of Rock". Palec shares that real estate is still his top priority, even with his radio gig. Palec's career as a broker and as a radio host is discussed.

16959 ■ "Real Estate Ambitions" in *Black Enterprise* **(Vol. 37, January 2007, No. 6, pp. 101)**
Pub: Earl G. Graves Publishing Co. Inc.
Ed: Description: National Real Estate Investors Association is a nonprofit trade association for both advanced as well as novice real estate investors that offers information on builders to contractors to banks. When looking to become a real estate investor utilize this organization, talk to various investors like the president of your local chapter, let people know your aspirations, and see if you can find a partner who has experience in the field. Resources included.

16960 ■ "Real Estate Defaults Top $300M" in *Business Courier* **(Vol. 26, January 15, 2010, No. 39, pp. 1)**
Pub: American City Business Journals, Inc.
Ed: Dan Monk. **Description:** Cincinnati commercial real estate owners defaulting in securitized loans reached $306 million at the end of 2009. The trend has lifted the region's default rate to nearly 9 percent. National average for commercial real estate default is examined.

16961 ■ "Real Estate Funds Swell Past $350M" in *Business Journal Portland* **(Vol. 27, December 31, 2010, No. 44, pp. 1)**
Pub: Portland Business Journal
Ed: Wendy Culverwell. **Description:** Oregon-based real estate funds have raised around half of the $735 million that was raised by local companies. Investors have been purchasing distressed properties. Commercial real estate prices have declined since 2007.

16962 ■ *Real Estate Loopholes: Secrets of Successful Real Estate Investing*
Pub: Warner Books, Incorporated
Ed: Diane Kennedy, Garrett Sutton, Robert T. Kiyosaki. **Released:** April 2003. **Description:** Knowledge, planning, and building a team of advisor and mentors is key to successful real estate investments.

16963 ■ "Real Estate Market Still in a Slump" in *Montana Business Quarterly* **(Vol. 49, Summer 2011, No. 2, pp. 15)**
Pub: Bureau of Business & Economic Research
Ed: Patrick M. Barkey. **Description:** Montana's housing market is still in decline with no sign of improving in the near future. Statistical data included.

16964 ■ *The Real Estate Recipe: Make Millions by Buying Small Apartment Properties in Your Spare Time*
Pub: DNA Press
Ed: Brian K. Friedman. **Released:** September 2004. **Price:** $29.95. **Description:** Guide for anyone interested in property investments; the book provides information for choosing an apartment property and answers questions in a chronological workbook format. The author shares his own experiences in apartment investing and shares the entire process of analyzing and buying an apartment property using a hypothetical ten-unit complex. Sample worksheets, checklists, and tables are provided to help readers maintain their own records.

16965 ■ "Real Estate Vets Take Times In Stride" in *The Business Journal-Serving Metropolitan Kansas City* **(Vol. 26, July 25, 2008, No. 46)**
Pub: American City Business Journals, Inc.
Ed: Rob Roberts. **Description:** Kansas City, Missouri's real estate industry veterans like Allen Block believe that the challenges faced by the industry in the 1980s, when the Federal Reserve Board controlled the money supply to slow down inflation, were worse than the challenges faced today. Other views, trends and information on the real estate industry of the city, are presented.

16966 ■ "Real Estate Wheeling and Dealing Picks Up" in *Business Journal Portland* **(Vol. 27, October 29, 2010, No. 35, pp. 1)**
Pub: Portland Business Journal
Ed: Wendy Culverwell. **Description:** LoopNet has listed 33 prominent commercial properties for sale in Portland, Oregon's real estate market. However, reasons for the sales rush are not totally clear, but speculations point to the end of the Bush tax cuts in 2010 that prompted real estate investors to close the deals and avoid the increase in capital gains taxes.

16967 ■ "Real Estate Woes Mount for State's Smaller Banks" in *Boston Business Journal* **(Vol. 27, November 30, 2007, No. 44, pp. 1)**
Pub: American City Business Journals Inc.
Ed: Craig M. Douglas. **Description:** Massachusetts banking industry is facing a steep increase on loan

defaults such as in home mortgages and condo-minium projects, contrary to public belief that the lo-cal industry is safe from the real estate meltdown. The dollar value of local banks' nonperforming loans doubled in 2007, and is rising statewide. Other bank-ing issues in the state are discussed.

16968 ■ "Real Estate's New Reality" in *Entrepreneur* **(Vol. 37, July 2009, No. 7, pp. 32)**
Pub: Entrepreneur Media, Inc.

Ed: Rosalind Resnick. **Description:** Investing in real estate is still an advisable move, as long as investors are prepared to hold on to the property and there is a rent roll to provide a decent return on investment. Among the key considerations when investing in real estate is the property's expenses and cash flow. Other suggestions for future real estate investors are given.

16969 ■ "Real Opportunities: Don't Let Mortgage Mayhem Steer You Away From Sound Investments" in *Black Enterprise* **(December 2007)**
Pub: Earl G. Graves Publishing Co. Inc.

Ed: James A. Anderson. **Description:** Real estate investment trusts (REITs) that operate office build-ings, industrial parks, shopping malls, hotels, hospi-tals, or other commercial properties may be a sound investment, despite the mortgage crisis facing the U.S. financial sector.

16970 ■ "Realities May Blur Vision" in *The Business Journal-Serving Metropolitan Kansas City* **(Vol. 27, September 19, 2008, No. 1, pp. 1)**
Pub: American City Business Journals, Inc.

Ed: Rob Roberts. **Description:** Vision Metcalf is a study by Kansas City that depicts how Metcalf Avenue could look like if redeveloped. Redevelop-ment plans for the Metcalf corridor include a 20-story mixed-use building on a vacant car dealership. The challenges that the redevelopment plans will face are also analyzed.

16971 ■ "Realtors Signing Out" in *The Business Journal-Serving Metropolitan Kansas City* **(Vol. 27, November 21, 2008, No. 11, pp. 1)**
Pub: American City Business Journals, Inc.

Ed: Rob Roberts. **Description:** The Kansas City Regional Association of Realtors has lost 1,000 of its members due to the downturn in the housing market. Applications for realtor licenses have dropped by 159 percent. Changes in Missouri's licensing require-ments are seen as additional reasons for the declines.

16972 ■ "Recovery on Tap for 2010?" in *Orlando Business Journal* **(Vol. 26, January 1, 2010, No. 31, pp. 1)**
Pub: American City Business Journals

Ed: Melanie Stawicki Azam, Richard Bilbao, Christo-pher Boyd, Anjali Fluker. **Description:** Economic forecasts for Central Florida's leading business sec-tors in 2010 are presented. These sectors include housing, film and TV, sports business, law, restau-rants, aviation, tourism and hospitality, banking and finance, commercial real estate, retail, health care, insurance, higher education, and manufacturing. Ac-cording to some local executives, Central Florida's economy will slowly recover in 2010.

16973 ■ "Red Tape Ties Detroit Housing Rehab Plan" in *Crain's Detroit Business* **(Vol. 24, September 22, 2008, No. 38, pp. 1)**
Pub: Crain Communications, Inc.

Ed: Ryan Beene. **Description:** Venture-capital firm Wilherst Oxford LLC is a Florida-based company that has purchased 300 inner-city homes which were in foreclosure in Detroit. Wilherst Oxford is asking the city to forgive the existing tax and utility liens so the firm can utilize the money for home improvements. The city, however, is reluctant but has stated that they are willing to negotiate.

16974 ■ "Refi Requests Soar, But New Rules May Mean Fewer Closings" in *The Business Review Albany* **(Vol. 35, April 4, 2008, No. 53, pp. 1)**
Pub: The Business Review

Ed: Barbara Pinckney. **Description:** National refi-nancing applications grew by 82 percent in the week

that ended March 21, 2008, due to the depressed real estate market and lower interest rates. Refinanc-ing applicants, however, may be surprised with new rules on loan applications such as the required credit score of at least 720 in avoiding payment of extra fees. The developments in application standards for home loans are also examined.

16975 ■ "REIT's Decry Foreign Limits on Investment" in *Globe & Mail* **(March 29, 2007, pp. B4)**
Pub: CTVglobemedia Publishing Inc.

Ed: Elizabeth Church. **Description:** The planned legislation by Canadian government for regulation foreign investments by real estate investment trusts is discussed.

16976 ■ "A Renewal in Rentals" in *Barron's* **(Vol. 88, March 17, 2008, No. 11, pp. 17)**
Pub: Dow Jones & Company, Inc.

Ed: Description: Discusses the projected entry of the estimated 82 million echo-boomers into the rent-als market and the influx of immigrants and displaced homeowners which could turn apartments into lucra-tive investments again. While apartment-building completions rose slowly since 2003, demand is expected to increase steeply until 2015.

16977 ■ "Rental Demand Boosts Revenue for Sun Communities Inc." in *Crain's Detroit Business* **(Vol. 24, March 24, 2008, No. 12, pp. 4)**
Pub: Crain Communications, Inc.

Ed: Daniel Duggan. **Description:** Despite the decline in sales of manufactured homes, demand for rental units and rent-to-own programs have brought Sun Communities Inc. increased revenue. The real estate investment trust, based in Southfield, owns, oper-ates, finances and develops manufactured home communities in the Midwest and Southeast. Statisti-cal data included.

16978 ■ "Reply! Grows at Unprecedented Rate, Rips Beta Off Its Marketplace" in *Marketing Weekly News* **(September 19, 2009, pp. 149)**
Pub: Investment Weekly News

Description: Profile of Reply.com, a leader in locally-targeted Internet marketing, announced significant growth in terms of revenue, enhanced features and services and new categories since launching its beta Reply! Marketplace platform. Even in the face of an economic downturn, the company has posted over 50 percent revenue growth in the Real Estate and Automotive categories.

16979 ■ "Restoring Grandeur" in *Business Courier* **(Vol. 26, December 4, 2009, No. 32, pp. 1)**
Pub: American City Business Journals, Inc.

Ed: Dan Monk. **Description:** Eagle Realty Group intends to spend more than $10 to restore the historic 12-story Phelps apartment building in Lytle Park in Cincinnati. Its president, Mario San Marco, expressed the need to invest in the building in order to maintain operations. The building could be restored into a hotel catering to executives and consultants.

16980 ■ "Retail Center Pitched" in *Business Courier* **(Vol. 27, June 18, 2010, No. 7, pp. 1)**
Pub: Business Courier

Ed: Dan Monk. **Description:** Jeffrey R. Anderson Real Estate Inc.'s plan for a retail center in Butler County, Ohio could have three department stores in the 1.1 million-square-foot property. An outdoor sports retailer is also part of the plans.

16981 ■ "Revitalizing Real Estate: Couple Sails Through Sea of Housing Woes" in *Black Enterprise* **(Vol. 38, February 2008, No. 7, pp. 50)**
Pub: Earl G. Graves Publishing Co. Inc.

Ed: Ayana Dixon. **Description:** Owner, Christopher Gablin and Regina Mincey-Garlin offer a broad range of real estate-related services to clients in order to not only survive, but thrive in today's market.

16982 ■ "The Right Time for REITs" in *Barron's* **(Vol. 88, July 14, 2008, No. 28, pp. 32)**
Pub: Dow Jones & Co., Inc.

Ed: Mike Hogan. **Description:** Discusses the down-turn in U.S. real estate investment trusts so these are worth considering for investment. Several Websites that are useful for learning about real estate invest-ment trusts for investment purposes are presented.

16983 ■ "A Rise in Rental Units" in *Philadelphia Business Journal* **(Vol. 30, October 7, 2011, No. 34, pp. 1)**
Pub: American City Business Journals Inc.

Ed: Natalie Kostelni. **Description:** Housing develop-ers have been stepping up the construction of new apartment complexes throughout the suburbs of Pennsylvania in order to capture growing demand for rental properties. BPG Properties Ltd. has nearly 1,000 new apartments under construction.

16984 ■ "Sales at Furniture Showrooms Sink" in *Puget Sound Business Journal* **(Vol. 29, October 10, 2008, No. 25, pp. 1)**
Pub: American City Business Journals

Ed: Greg Lamm. **Description:** Furniture showrooms are seeing a drop in sales due to the bad economy. Buyer demand has also fallen because of the slump-ing real estate market.

16985 ■ "Scaled-Down Phoenix Condos Emerge as DNA" in *The Business Journal - Serving Phoenix and the Valley of the Sun* **(Vol. 28, July 11, 2008, No. 45, pp. 1)**
Pub: American City Business Journals, Inc.

Ed: Yvonne Zusel. **Description:** Pointe of View Developments and Belleview Communities have scaled back their Copper Pointe Condominiums project in downtown Phoenix, Arizona. The scaled-back project has also changed its name into Down-town's Newest Address Condominiums and will cost $42 million.

16986 ■ "Sellers Face Excess Land Dilemma" in *Crain's Cleveland Business* **(Vol. 28, November 12, 2007, No. 45, pp. 1)**
Pub: Crain Communications, Inc.

Ed: Stan Bullard. **Description:** Overview on the way in which the housing slump is effecting builders, land developers and lot prices. Statistical data included.

16987 ■ "'Short Sales,' A Sign of Housing Troubles, Start Popping Up" in *The Business Review Albany* **(Vol. 35, April 11, 2008, No. 1, pp. 1)**
Pub: The Business Review

Ed: Michael DeMasi. **Description:** Discusses the number of short sales, where homeowners ask banks to forgive part of their mortgages to sell the proper-ties, which is starting to increase in the Albany, New York area. Real estate agents in the area are taking up crash courses in short selling.

16988 ■ "Sitting, Sitting, Sitting-Snapshots of Homes that Just Won't Sell" in *Crain's Chicago Business* **(Vol. 31, April 21, 2008, No. 16)**
Pub: Crain Communications, Inc.

Ed: Kevin Davis. **Description:** Listing of five Chicago-area homes that have been on the market for an extended length of time; also includes the original asking price, current asking price, special features and the biggest challenge of each home.

16989 ■ "Six Leading Economists on What to Expect in the Year Ahead: Derek Holt; Housing" in *Canadian Business* **(December 24, 2007)**
Pub: Rogers Media

Ed: Derek Holt. **Description:** The Canadian subprime mortgage market could take a different turn from that of the U.S. as laws governing Canada's mortgage market indirectly limit the probability of a slowdown. Details on how Canada avoided the slowdown in the housing market and forecasts of new homes for 2008 are discussed.

16990 ■ "Small Changes Can Mean Big Energy Savings" in *Crain's Cleveland Business* (Vol. 28, November 5, 2007, No. 44, pp. 21)

Pub: Crain Communications, Inc.

Ed: Harriet Tramer. **Description:** Many Northeast Ohio businesses are taking their cues from the residential real estate market to draw and capitalize on interest in energy efficiency and is regularly taken into account by local architects.

16991 ■ "S.O.S. Sorting Out Subprime" in *Black Enterprise* (Vol. 38, November 2007, No. 4, pp. 76)

Pub: Earl G. Graves Publishing Co. Inc.

Ed: Trevor Delaney. **Description:** Subprime distress in the housing market is discussed and the impact it has put on investors.

16992 ■ "South Loop Site Lands a Buyer" in *Crain's Chicago Business* (Vol. 31, March 24, 2008, No. 12, pp. 1)

Pub: Crain Communications, Inc.

Ed: Alby Gallun. **Description:** Russland Capital Group, a little-known condominium developer from Skokie, recently purchased a 6.5-acre riverside property in the site known as Franklin Point for $40 million.

16993 ■ "Staging a Martini-and-GQ Lifestyle; Faux Possessions Play to Buyer's Aspirations" in *Crain's Chicago Business* (April 21, 2008)

Pub: Crain Communications, Inc.

Ed: Kevin Davis. **Description:** Due to the competition of the slumping housing market, home stagers are becoming more prominent and are using creative ways to make an impression beyond de-cluttering, painting and cleaning by using accents such as casually placed magazines, candles and table settings.

16994 ■ "State Printing Plant on the Move" in *Sacramento Business Journal* (Vol. 25, August 29, 2008, No. 26, pp. 1)

Pub: American City Business Journals, Inc.

Ed: Michael Shaw; Celia Lamb. **Description:** California is planning to replace its printing plant on Richards Boulevard and 7th Street with a newly built or leased facility in the Sacramento area. It was revealed that the project will meet the state's standards for new buildings. It is believed that the new site will require 15 acres or more depending on requirements.

16995 ■ "State Wants to Add Escape Clause to Leases" in *Sacramento Business Journal* (Vol. 28, October 14, 2011, No. 33, pp. 1)

Pub: Sacramento Business Journal

Ed: Michael Shaw. **Description:** California Governor Jerry Brown's administration has decided to add escape clauses to new lease agreements, which created new worry for building owners and brokers in Sacramento, California. Real estate brokers believe the appropriation of funds clauses have been making the lenders nervous and would result in less competition.

16996 ■ "Still Looking Good" in *Canadian Business* (Vol. 80, March 26, 2007, No. 7, pp. 29)

Pub: Rogers Media

Ed: Andy Holloway. **Description:** The real estate prices in various parts of Canada are analyzed. The future growth potential of the industry is forecasted.

16997 ■ "Stuck With Two Mortgages; The Nightmare When Buyers Upgrade" in *Crain's Chicago Business* (Vol. 31, April 21, 2008, No. 16)

Pub: Crain Communications, Inc.

Ed: Darci Smith. **Description:** Discusses the problem a number of people are facing due to the slump in the housing market: being stuck with two mortgages when they move because their former homes have not sold. Many thought they could afford to move to a larger home, anticipating significant equity appreciation that did not occur; now they are left with lowering their price and competing with the host of new developments.

16998 ■ "Subprime Problems Loom" in *The Business Journal-Portland* (Vol. 25, August 29, 2008, No. 25, pp. 1)

Pub: American City Business Journals, Inc.

Ed: Wendy Culverwell. **Description:** Over half of subprime mortgages in Portland are resetting by the end of 2008, which will cause more problems to the local real estate market. The inventory of unsold homes has also been increasing for over a year. Forecasts for the Portland housing market in relation to mortgage resets are supplied.

16999 ■ "Survey: Apartment Rents Continue to Climb as Home Market Slows" in *Business Review, Albany New York* (November 23, 2007)

Pub: American City Business Journals, Inc.

Ed: Michael DeMasi. **Description:** Survey by Sunrise Management and Consulting shows that asking rents for apartments in the Capital Region increased for the thirteenth consecutive time. The survey, which was conducted between August and October 2007, also showed that Albany County, New York had the highest average asking rent, followed by Rensselaer County, Saratoga County, and Schenectady County.

17000 ■ "Survey Says Commercial Real Estate Headed for Turbulence" in *Commercial Property News* (March 17, 2008)

Pub: Nielsen Company

Description: Commercial real estate sector is declining due to the sluggish U.S. economy. According to a recent survey, national office, retail and hospitality markets are also on the decline.

17001 ■ "A Survival Guide for Crazy Times" in *Canadian Business* (Vol. 81, March 3, 2008, No. 3, pp. 61)

Pub: Rogers Media

Ed: David Wolf. **Description:** Investors should ensure that their portfolios are positioned defensively more than the average as the U.S. and Canadian markets face turbulent times. They should not assume that U.S. residential property is a good place to invest only because prices have dropped and the Canadian dollar is showing strength. Other tips that investors can use during unstable periods are supplied.

17002 ■ "Tampa Condo Conversion Sells for $14.8 Million Less" in *The Business Journal-Serving Greater Tampa Bay* (Vol. 28, September 5, 2008)

Pub: American City Business Journals, Inc.

Ed: Janet Leiser. **Description:** Former apartment complex Village Oaks at Tampa, which was converted to condominiums, has been sold to Tennessee-based real estate investment trust Mid-America Apartment Communities Inc. for $21.2 million in August 2008. The amount was $14.2 million less than what developer Radco Management LLC paid for in 2005.

17003 ■ "Tax Abatement Changes Seen as Home Run for Cleveland Condo Market" in *Crain's Cleveland Business* (Vol. 30, June 15, 2009, No. 23)

Pub: Crain Communications, Inc.

Ed: Jay Miller. **Description:** Condominium ownership became a bit more affordable for Cleveland residents since changes in both state and local tax abatement policy changes. The tax credits are examined.

17004 ■ "Tax Credit Crunch" in *Miami Daily Business Review* (March 26, 2008)

Pub: ALM Media Inc.

Ed: Paula Iuspa-Abbott. **Description:** Uncertainty is growing over the future of the low-income housing project in South Florida and the tax credit program that helps fuel the projects.

17005 ■ "That Empty Feeling" in *Crain's Cleveland Business* (Vol. 28, October 15, 2007, No. 41, pp. 1)

Pub: Crain Communications, Inc.

Ed: Stan Bullard. **Description:** Townhouses, cluster homes and condominiums lured both buyers and builders for most of this decade but now that market is suffering at an even greater degree than the single-family home market. Statistical data included.

17006 ■ "The REIT Stuff" in *Canadian Business* (Vol. 80, March 26, 2007, No. 7, pp. 72)

Pub: Rogers Media

Description: The stock performance of various real estate investment trusts in Canada is analyzed.

17007 ■ "They've Fallen, But They Can Get Up" in *Barron's* (Vol. 88, March 10, 2008, No. 10, pp. 43)

Pub: Dow Jones & Company, Inc.

Ed: Kopin Tan. **Description:** Shares of senior housing companies present buying opportunities to investors because of their low prices. Companies such as Brookdale Senior Living are not as dependent on housing prices but have suffered declines in share prices.

17008 ■ "Threat of New Office Space Records Rent Hikes" in *Globe & Mail* (March 21, 2007, pp. B4)

Pub: CTVglobemedia Publishing Inc.

Ed: Elizabeth Church. **Description:** The increasing commercial rent prices in the Toronto region amid the high office building construction market are discussed.

17009 ■ "Tom Gaglardi" in *Canadian Business* (Vol. 82, April 27, 2009, No. 7, pp. 56)

Pub: Rogers Media

Ed: Calvin Leung. **Description:** Northland Properties Corporation president Tom Gaglardi believes that their business model of keeping much of operations in-house allows the firm to crate assets at a lesser price while commanding higher margins than their competitors. He believes that it is an ideal time to invest in the hospitality industry because of opportunities to purchase properties at low prices.

17010 ■ "Top 10 Retirement Mistakes and How to Avoid Them" in *Canadian Business* (Vol. 83, July 20, 2010, No. 11-12, pp. 39)

Pub: Rogers Media Ltd.

Ed: Jacqueline Nelson, Angelina Chapin. **Description:** Some of the top retirement mistakes is relying on selling one's house to find a retirement. Other mistakes are paying too much for investments and planning to work in retirement since no one can be sure that they will be healthy enough to accomplish this. Suggestions to avoid these pitfalls are discussed.

17011 ■ "Top Twenty Wealthiest Landowners" in *Hawaii Business* (Vol. 53, November 2007, No. 5, pp. 34)

Pub: Hawaii Business Publishing

Description: Provided is a table of the wealthiest landowners in Hawaii. Their assessed value, total acres owned, prominent holdings, other notable holdings and years of presence in Hawaii are also provided. Statistical data included.

17012 ■ "Tough Sell: Senior Projects Hustle to Keep Buyers" in *Puget Sound Business Journal* (Vol. 29, November 21, 2008, No. 31, pp.)

Pub: American City Business Journals

Ed: Heidi Dietrich. **Description:** Plans to move to retirement communities are being postponed by seniors in Washington's Puget Sound area due to difficulty selling their current homes in the slow economy. Retirement communities are trying to lure clients by offering new finance programs and sales plans.

17013 ■ "Troy Complex has New Brand, New Leases" in *Crain's Detroit Business* (Vol. 24, April 14, 2008, No. 15, pp. 32)

Pub: Crain Communications, Inc.

Ed: Daniel Duggan. **Description:** Discusses the re-branding of the 1.2 million-square-foot collection of office buildings in Troy purchased by New York-based Emmes Co. The firm has also pledged more than $6 million in upgrades, hired a new leasing company and completed 67,000 square feet of leasing with another 100,000 in negotiations.

17014 ■ "Try, Try Again" in *Baltimore Business Journal* (Vol. 28, August 20, 2010, No. 15, pp. 1)

Pub: Baltimore Business Journal

Ed: Gary Haber. **Description:** Customers' refinancing of mortgages has boosted Baltimore, Maryland mortgage banking business. The housing decline has resulted in a decrease in the number of people looking for new mortgages.

17015 ■ *Use What You've Got*

Pub: Portfolio Publishing

Ed: Barbara Corcoran, Bruce Littlefield. **Released:** 2003. **Price:** $24.95. **Description:** Founder and chairman of New York's premier real estate company, the Corcoran Group, shares her successes in the real estate industry. The book offers tips and pointers to salespeople, entrepreneurs and business people alike. Corcoran explains how she went from waiting tables and borrowed $1,000 from a boyfriend to build her real estate company into the industry's powerhouse.

17016 ■ "Valenti: Roots of Financial Crisis Go Back to 1998" in *Crain's Detroit Business* (Vol. 24, October 6, 2008, No. 40, pp. 25)

Pub: Crain Communications, Inc.

Ed: Tom Henderson; Nathan Skid. **Description:** Interview with Sam Valenti III who is the chairman and CEO of Valenti Capital L.L.C., a wealth-management firm; Valenti discusses in detail the history that led up to the current economic crisis as well as his prediction for the future of the country.

17017 ■ "Vision for Camden in Better Focus" in *Philadelphia Business Journal* (Vol. 30, September 30, 2011, No. 33, pp. 1)

Pub: American City Business Journals Inc.

Ed: Natalie Kostelni. **Description:** More than $500 million worth of projects aimed at redeveloping the downtown and waterfront areas of Camden, New Jersey are being planned. These include the construction of residential, commercial, and education buildings.

17018 ■ "Wannabe Buyers Take Their Own Sweet Time" in *Crain's Chicago Business* (Vol. 31, April 21, 2008, No. 16, pp. 50)

Pub: Crain Communications, Inc.

Ed: Lisa Bertagnoli. **Description:** Although all factors are in place for a robust real-estate market in the Chicago area: low interest rates, plenty of inventory and the region's relatively strong employment, buyers are taking their time and doing more research in order to see how bad the economy will get.

17019 ■ "Was Mandating Solar Power Water Heaters For New Homes Good Policy?" in *Hawaii Business* (Vol. 54, August 2008, No. 2, pp. 28)

Pub: Hawaii Business Publishing

Description: Senator Gary L. Kooser of District 7 Kauai-Niihau believes that the mandating of energy-efficient water heaters for new single-family homes starting in 2010 will help cut Hawaii's oil consumption. Ron Richmond of the Hawaii Solar Energy Association says that the content of SB 644 has negative consequences as it allows for choice of energy and not just solar, and it also eliminates tax credits for new homebuyers.

17020 ■ "What Homes Do Retirees Want?" in *Canadian Business* (Vol. 79, July 17, 2006, No. 14-15, pp.)

Pub: Rogers Media

Ed: Joe Cataldo. **Description:** The obstacles and challenges faced by homebuilders in Canada as well as the approach adopted by them to appeal to the mature homebuilders segment, is discussed.

17021 ■ "What's Ahead for Fannie and Fred?" in *Barron's* (Vol. 90, August 30, 2010, No. 35, pp. 26)

Pub: Barron's Editorial & Corporate Headquarters

Ed: Jonathan R. Laing. **Description:** A meeting presided by Treasury Secretary Timothy Geithner discussed the future of Fannie Mae and Freddie Mac. The two government sponsored enterprises were mismanaged and reforming these two agencies is critical.

17022 ■ "When Anything (And Everything) Goes" in *Globe & Mail* (January 12, 2007, pp. B4)

Pub: CTVglobemedia Publishing Inc.

Ed: Elizabeth Church. **Description:** The forecast on acquisition of different real estate firms is presented.

17023 ■ "Where Are the Vultures?" in *Mergers & Acquisitions: The Dealmaker's Journal* (March 1, 2008)

Pub: SourceMedia, Inc.

Ed: Ken MacFadyen. **Description:** Although the real estate market is distressed, not many acquisitions are being made by distress private equity investors; this is due, in part, to the difficulty in assessing real estate industry firms since it is a sector which is so localized.

17024 ■ "Will Home Buyers Pay for Green Features?" in *Contractor* (Vol. 56, October 2009, No. 10, pp. 70)

Pub: Penton Media, Inc.

Ed: Bob Mader. **Description:** National Association of Home Builders commissioned a survey which shows that homeowners are interested in green as long as they do no have to pay much for it. The association did not allow a board member to read the survey which raises questions about how the questions were phrased and how the sample was selected.

17025 ■ "With Building Plans in Flux, County Could Sell Key Site" in *Crain's Cleveland Business* (Vol. 28, October 8, 2007, No. 40, pp. 1)

Pub: Crain Communications, Inc.

Ed: Jay Miller. **Description:** Due to such issues as financial and administrative problems, Cuyahoga County commissioners have pushed back the construction timeline for a planned county administration center and are saying that they are considering selling the site in downtown Cleveland to developers who would erect a new office building that another large tenant could occupy.

17026 ■ "Working It Out! How a Young Executive Overcomes Obstacles on the Job" in *Black Enterprise* (Vol. 37, January 2007, No. 6, pp. 55)

Pub: Earl G. Graves Publishing Co. Inc.

Ed: Laura Egodigwe. **Description:** Interview with Susan Chapman, Global Head of Operations for Citigroup Realty Services, in which she discusses issues such as the important skills necessary for overcoming obstacles in the workplace.

17027 ■ *The Working Man and Woman's Guide to Becoming a Millionaire*

Pub: Prentiss Publishing

Ed: Al Herron. **Released:** November 2006. **Description:** President and CEO of a Century 21 office in Dallas, Texas shares insight into financial security and commitment to community.

17028 ■ "You Better Shop Around: Four Steps to Getting the Best Deal On a Home Loan" in *Black Enterprise* (Vol. 40, July 2010, No. 12, pp. 78)

Pub: Earl G. Graves Publishing Co. Inc.

Ed: Tara-Nicholle Nelson. **Description:** Four steps to help anyone seeking a mortgage for a home purchase are listed.

17029 ■ "You Won't Go Broke Filling Up On These Stocks" in *Barron's* (Vol. 88, July 14, 2008, No. 28, pp. 38)

Pub: Dow Jones & Co., Inc.

Ed: Assif Shameen. **Description:** Due to high economic growth, pro-business policies and a consumption boom, the Middle East is a good place to look for equities. The best ways in which to gain exposure to this market include investing in the real estate industry and telecommunications markets as well as large banks that serve corporations and consumers.

17030 ■ *Your First Year in Real Estate: Making the Transition from Total Novice to Successful Professional*

Pub: Crown Business Books

Ed: Dirk Zeller. **Released:** $August 3, 2010. **Price:** $20.00. **Description:** Zeller helps new realtors to select the right company, develop mentor and client relationships, using the Internet and social networking to stay ahead of competition, to set and reach career goals, to stay current in the market, and more.

17031 ■ "Your Place: Housing Developers Try to Read Generation Y" in *Philadelphia Inquirer* (December 2, 2010)

Pub: Philadelphia Media Network Inc.

Ed: Al Heavens. **Description:** Results of a survey conducted with Generation Y individuals are examined, focusing on housing developments and whether this particular generation prefers suburban or rural lifestyles. Generation Y encompasses people ages 18 to 32 years old. Statistical data included.

17032 ■ *Your Successful Real Estate Career, 5h Edition*

Pub: American Management Association

Ed: Kenneth W. Edwards. **Released:** 2006. **Price:** $18.95.

SOURCES OF SUPPLY

17033 ■ *Real Estate Software Directory and Catalog*

Pub: Z-Law Software Inc.

Contact: Gary L. Sherman, President

Released: Semiannual, January and July. **Price:** Free. **Publication Includes:** Listings of producers of real estate related software programs and ordering information. Principal content of publication is product name, description, specifications, requirements. **Arrangement:** Classified by product/service. **Indexes:** Product/service; subject.

STATISTICAL SOURCES

17034 ■ *RMA Annual Statement Studies*

Pub: Robert Morris Associates (RMA)

Released: Annual. **Price:** $175.00 2006-07 edition, $105.00. **Description:** Contains composite balance sheets and income statements for more than 360 industries, including the accounting, auditing, and bookkeeping industries. Also contains five years of comparative historical data for discerning trends. Includes 16 commonly used ratios, computed for most of the size groupings for nearly every industry.

17035 ■ *Standard & Poor's Industry Surveys*

Pub: Standard & Poor's Corp.

Released: Annual. **Price:** $3633.00. **Description:** Two-volume book that examines the prospects for specific industries, including trucking. Also provides analyses of trends and problems, statistical tables and charts, and comparative company analyses.

TRADE PERIODICALS

17036 ■ *The CF Apartment Reporter*

Pub: Clayton-Fillmore Ltd.

Released: Bimonthly. **Price:** $199 4.00 per city. **Description:** Contains research, data, analysis, and narrative about apartment markets nationwide.

17037 ■ *Commercial Investment Real Estate*

Pub: CCIM Institute

Contact: Jennifer Norbut, Publisher

E-mail: jnorbut@ccim.com

Released: Bimonthly. **Price:** $45; $55 Canada and Mexico. **Description:** Professional development magazine for commercial investment professionals and allied fields.

17038 ■ *CONNECTIONS*

Pub: Women's Council of Realtors

Contact: Dianna Dearen, Editor

Ed: Dianna Dearen, Editor, ddearen@wcr.org. **Released:** 8/year. **Description:** Carries articles on personal and career growth topics relating to women in real estate. Includes council news.

17039 ■ *The duPont Registry*

Pub: duPont Publishing Inc.

Released: Monthly. **Price:** $15.95; $25.95 Canada; $45.95 other countries. **Description:** Magazine featuring worldwide luxury homes for sale.

17040 ■ First Tuesday
Pub: Realty Publications Inc.
Released: Monthly. **Description:** Magazine for real estate professionals.

17041 ■ Homes Magazine
Pub: Reflector Publishing
Contact: Betty Williams, Display Advisory. Dir.
E-mail: bwilliams@reflector.com
Released: Monthly. **Description:** Real estate magazine.

17042 ■ The Institutional Real Estate Letter
Pub: Institutional Real Estate Inc.
Contact: Brigite Thompson, Advertising Coord.
E-mail: b.thompson@irei.com
Released: Monthly. **Price:** $2,495. **Description:** Monthly publication covering the pension, foundation, and endowment investment market. Provides information on investment patterns, trends, and strategies.

17043 ■ Journal of Property Management
Pub: Institute of Real Estate Management
Contact: Ronald Goss, President
Released: Bimonthly. **Price:** $72.32 Canada; $62.95; $115.50 two years; $110.99 other countries airmail; $169.10 3 years. **Description:** Magazine serving real estate managers.

17044 ■ National Delinquency Survey
Pub: Mortgage Bankers Association
Contact: Tisha Richardson
E-mail: tisha_richardson@mbaa.org
Ed: Douglas G. Duncan, Editor, Laura_Armstrong@mbaa.org. **Released:** Quarterly. **Price:** $250, members; $450, nonmembers. **Description:** Carries information on residential mortgage delinquency and foreclosure rates at national, regional, and state levels. Reports delinquency rates by length of time and type of loan.

17045 ■ National Property Law Digests
Pub: Strafford Publications Inc.
Contact: Jennifer F. Vaughan, Executive Editor
Released: Monthly. **Price:** $827, individuals plus $48.50 s/h. **Description:** Digest of the most significant property law cases in the U.S. court system. Cases are screened and selected to provide concise, comprehensive coverage of the latest issues concerning real property law.

17046 ■ National Real Estate Investor
Pub: Penton Media Inc.
Contact: Matt Valley, Editor-in-Chief
E-mail: matt.valley@penton.com
Released: Monthly. **Price:** $115 U.S.; $127 Canada; $139 other countries. **Description:** Magazine on commercial real estate investment, development and management.

17047 ■ The Practical Real Estate Lawyer
Pub: American Law Institute-American Bar Association
Contact: Mark T. Carroll, Director
E-mail: mcarroll@ali-aba.org
Released: Bimonthly. **Price:** $75 print only; $55 online only; $99 print and online; $129 two years print only; $89 two years online only; $169 two years print and online. **Description:** Professional magazine covering advice on real estate to real estate practitioners.

17048 ■ Professional Report
Pub: Society of Industrial and Office Realtors
Contact: Linda Nasvaderani
Ed: Linda P. Nasvaderani, Editor, lnasvaderani@mail.sior.com. **Released:** Quarterly, QRT. **Price:** $35, members Included in membership; $45/year for nonmembers, U.S.; $55, other countries nonmembers. **Description:** Dedicated to corporate real estate brokerage, development, and management. Recurring features include news of members and the Society, news of educational programs sponsored by the Society, book reviews, news of research, and statistics.

17049 ■ Real Estate Broker's Insider
Pub: Alexander Communications Group Inc.
Contact: Margaret DeWitt, Publisher
E-mail: mklein@brokersinsider.com
Ed: Jeff Ostrowski, Editor. **Released:** Semimonthly, 2/month. **Price:** $247. **Description:** Provides residential agency broker/owners with actionable news and information on managing their businesses for greater profitability.

17050 ■ Real Estate Forum
Pub: Incisive Media
Contact: Gregg Christensen, Sen. VP
E-mail: gregg.christensen@invisivemedia.com
Ed: Sule Aygoren Carranza, Editor, sule.aygoren@incisivemedia.com. **Released:** Monthly. **Price:** $129.95; $245 two years; $275 other countries; $400 two years and other countries. **Description:** Magazine providing national coverage of commercial, industrial, and corporate real estate.

17051 ■ Real Estate Law Report
Pub: RIA
Ed: Alvin Arnold, Editor. **Released:** 12/year. **Price:** $513.96. **Description:** Contains digests of recent real estate law cases with expert commentary.

17052 ■ Real Estate Weekly
Pub: Hagedorn Communications
Contact: Christopher Hagedorn, Publisher
Released: Weekly. **Price:** $49. **Description:** Real estate newspaper.

17053 ■ Realtor Magazine
Pub: National Association of Realtors
Contact: Frank Sibley, Sen. VP/Publisher
E-mail: fsibley@realtors.org
Released: Monthly. **Price:** $56; $83 Canada; $103 other countries. **Description:** Real estate magazine.

17054 ■ Realtors Land Institute Newsletter
Pub: Realtors Land Institute
Contact: Belinda Carter
Ed: Belinda Carter, Editor, belindarli@aol.com. **Released:** 6/year. **Description:** Contains articles of interest to realtors dealing with farm and land real estate. Recurring features include news of the Institute and tax information.

17055 ■ The Residential Specialist
Pub: Council of Residential Specialists
Contact: Kathleen Thomas, Advertising Mgr
Ed: Michael Fenner, Editor. **Released:** Bimonthly. **Price:** $29.95 nonmembers; $54.95 two years; $44.95 Canada; $84.95 Canada 2 years; $89.95 other countries; $174.95 other countries 2 years. **Description:** Trade magazine for residential sales agents.

VIDEOCASSETTES/AUDIOCASSETTES

17056 ■ Inside Business Today
GPN Educational Media
1550 Executive Drive
Elgin, IL 60123
Ph:(402)472-2007
Free: 800-228-4630
Fax:800-306-2330
Co. E-mail: askgpn@smarterville.com
URL: http://www.shopgpn.com
Released: 1989. **Description:** Leaders in business and industry tell their success stories in this extensive series. **Availability:** VHS; 3/4U.

CONSULTANTS

17057 ■ ICDI Inc.
250 N Wymore Rd.
Winter Park, FL 32789-3455
Ph:(407)622-2532
Fax:(407)290-2532
Contact: Cindy Bishop, Mgr
Scope: Conducts land title searches, judgment, tax lien or unadjusted contractual changes searches and asset searches. Specializes in title insurance needs. Serves counties in central Florida. Works with mortgage lenders, real estate sales, owners, potential buyers, and any other company or individual needing land title work.

17058 ■ Lehrer Financial and Economic Advisory Services
5555 Del Monte Dr., Ste. 802
Houston, TX 77056-4100
Ph:(713)972-7912
Free: (866)275-4958
Fax:(713)964-0444
Co. E-mail: drken@lehecoserv.com
URL: http://
Contact: Kenneth Eugene Lehrer, Managing Director
E-mail: drken@lehecoserv.com
Scope: Provides real estate finance, economic damages, non public business valuations, institutional loan presentations, market and feasibility analysis, fairness opinions, investment and portfolio analysis, business plans in corporate finance and expert witness for court testimony. Acts a san economic consulting group, capable of fulfilling the complete economic or financial needs of corporations, banks, attorneys, insurance companies, pension funds, medical groups and other investment organizations.

17059 ■ Real Resources
27 Indian Hill Rd.
PO Box 421
Medfield, MA 02052-2908
Ph:(508)359-6780
Fax:(508)359-6780
Co. E-mail: sharonloewe@comcast.net
Contact: Sharon Loewenthal, Principle
E-mail: sharonloewe@comcast.net
Scope: Consulting in areas of housing development, including site acquisition, market research, feasibility analysis, fiscal impact studies, zoning, mortgage underwriting, grant procurement, preparation, project and construction management, residential rent-up and marketing plans, retail and commercial leasing, small business plans and tax syndication analysis. Consulting in areas of housing development, including site acquisition, market research, feasibility analysis, fiscal impact studies, zoning, mortgage underwriting, grant procurement, preparation, project and construction management, residential rent-up and marketing plans, retail and commercial leasing, small business plans, and tax syndication analysis.

17060 ■ White, Hutchinson, Leisure & Learning Group
4036 Baltimore Ave.
Kansas City, MO 64111-2257
Ph:(816)931-1040
Fax:(816)756-5058
Co. E-mail: info@whitehutchinson.com
URL: http://www.whitehutchinson.com
Contact: Curt Krambeck, Principle
E-mail: vicki@atswhitehutchinson.com
Scope: Real estate consulting firm specializes in family and children's entertainment centers, workouts, and turnarounds, as well as development management. Conducts strategic facilities planning for business, health-care, and manufacturers. Offers legal and litigation support for real estate matters including bankruptcies. Also serves the recreation industry through market and financial feasibility, concept development, design and project management, financing, and management and operations. Provides consulting for bowling and family entertainment centers and small amusement parks, especially new starts, renovations, expansions, and workouts. Industries served: real estate, users of real estate, businesses and manufacturers, recreation, family entertainment centers, bowling centers, small amusement parks, and legal. **Publications:** "Twenty Ways to Become More Family Friendly," Ialei Fun Extra, Feb, 2002; "The Importance of Food to Location-Based Leisure," Sep, 2001; "Guest Sacrifice: A Sure Trip to Prison Or a Path to Profitability," Entertainment Management, Aug, 2000; "Beyond Androcentrism: How to Design Lbls to Please Guests (Women & Children) Instead of Owners and Architects," Entertainment Management, Jun, 2000; "Child's Play: More Complicated Than it Looks," Entertainment Management, Feb, 2000; "How Can I Finance My

Leisure Project?"; "The Feasibility Study: The Foundation for Success"; "New Luxury: Rich Design is No Longer Optional".

FRANCHISES AND BUSINESS OPPORTUNITIES

17061 ■ Advance Realty
Advance Realty Inc.
8640 Ridgleys Choice Dr., Lower level
Baltimore, MD 21236
Ph:(410)529-9111
Free: 888-925-0004
Fax:(410)529-9119
Co. E-mail: info@advancerealtyusa.com
URL: http://www.advancerealtyusa.com
No. of Franchise Units: 17. **Description:** Full service discount experts, Advance Realty offers a one-of-a-kind first to market franchise opportunity in select territories throughout the U.S. benefit from an industry leading turnkey franchise offering, including its unique "quick-start" start-up package and 1-on-1 ongoing support. Franchisees receive support in areas of business development, site selection/build-out, recruitment and operations with streamlined technology. **Equity Capital Needed:** $50,000-$100,000. **Franchise Fee:** $17,500. **Financial Assistance:** No. **Training:** Up to 5 days corporate based training and 2 days minimum onsite training and ongoing support.

17062 ■ Assist-2-Sell
1610 Meadow Wood Ln.
Reno, NV 89502
Ph:(775)688-6060
Free: 800-528-7816
Fax:(775)688-6069
No. of Franchise Units: 330. **Founded:** 1987. **Franchised:** 1993. **Description:** Discount real estate brokerage. **Equity Capital Needed:** $29,000-$34,000, including franchise fee. **Franchise Fee:** $9,005. **Financial Assistance:** Yes. **Training:** Yes.

17063 ■ Benham REO Group
552 Newell St.
Concord, NC 28025
Ph:(704)788-4603
Fax:(704)788-4604
No. of Franchise Units: 84. **No. of Company-Owned Units:** 2. **Founded:** 2004. **Franchised:** 2007. **Description:** Foreclosed property sales. **Equity Capital Needed:** $11,800-$31,750. **Franchise Fee:** $6,500-$9,500. **Royalty Fee:** $195/transaction. **Financial Assistance:** Assistance with franchise fee. **Training:** 1 week training provided at headquarters and ongoing support.

17064 ■ Better Homes Realty, Inc.
1777 Botelho Dr., Ste. 390
Walnut Creek, CA 94596
Free: 800-642-4428
Fax:(925)988-2270
No. of Franchise Units: 42. **Founded:** 1964. **Franchised:** 1975. **Description:** Principally engaged in franchising real estate sales offices. **Equity Capital Needed:** $61,500. **Franchise Fee:** $9,950. **Royalty Fee:** Varies. **Financial Assistance:** Yes. **Training:** Yes.

17065 ■ The BrickKicker
RonLen Enterprises Inc.
849 N Ellsworth St.
Naperville, IL 60563
Free: 888-339-5425
Fax:(630)420-2270
Co. E-mail: linda@brickkicker.com
URL: http://www.brickkicker.com
No. of Franchise Units: 165. **Founded:** 1989. **Franchised:** 1995. **Description:** Building inspection service. **Equity Capital Needed:** $15,000-$40,000. **Franchise Fee:** $7,500-$25,000. **Financial Assistance:** Up to one-third the franchise fee. **Training:** 2 weeks hands-on/in-field work, interactive classroom discussions, lab, telemarketing, report writing, sales calls, roll-play, technical & marketing training manuals, as well as training through yearly national conventions, roundtables, monthly support packages and toll-free support.

17066 ■ Century 21 Canada Limited Partnership
1199 W Pender St., Ste. 700
Vancouver, BC, Canada V6E 2R1
Ph:(604)606-2100
Free: 877-562-7219
Fax:(604)606-2125
Co. E-mail: kingsley.ma@century21.ca
URL: http://www.century21canada.ca
No. of Franchise Units: 400. **Founded:** 1976. **Franchised:** 1976. **Description:** The franchise offers real estate services. **Equity Capital Needed:** $50,000-$100,000. **Franchise Fee:** $10,500-$21,000. **Royalty Fee:** Various royalty plans and options. **Training:** Complete management and sales associate training.

17067 ■ Commission Express
Commission Express National
8306 Professional Hill Dr.
Fairfax, VA 22031
Ph:(703)560-5500
Fax:(703)560-5502
Co. E-mail: manager@commissionexpress.com
URL: http://www.commissionexpress.com
No. of Franchise Units: 74. **No. of Company-Owned Units:** 1. **Founded:** 1992. **Franchised:** 1996. **Description:** Buy real estate agent commissions. **Equity Capital Needed:** $94,300-$213,500. **Franchise Fee:** $20,000-$80,000. **Financial Assistance:** No. **Training:** Provides 1 week at Fairfax, VA and annual conference.

17068 ■ Flat Rate Realty
123 Christel Oaks Dr.
Scotts Valley, CA 95066
Ph:(831)426-3800
Free: 800-413-1496
Fax:(831)428-3808
Co. E-mail: flatratereality@gmail.com
URL: http://www.flatraterealityfranchise.com
No. of Franchise Units: 26. **No. of Company-Owned Units:** 4. **Founded:** 2004. **Franchised:** 2006. **Description:** "The Premier Discount Real Estate Franchise." Brings to a community a new look and new business model to sell real estate. Offers small overhead, more profits. A state of the art business plan that uses the new technology, charging a fee for service. **Equity Capital Needed:** $21,000-$43,000. **Franchise Fee:** $5,000. **Royalty Fee:** $500/month. **Financial Assistance:** Call for details. **Training:** Initial training, start up support, consultation and communication.

17069 ■ Help-U-Sell Real Estate
Realty Information Systems, Inc.
3121 Michelson Dr., Ste. 150
Irvine, CA 92612
Free: 800-366-1177
Fax:(949)788-1360
Co. E-mail: info@helpusell.com
URL: http://www.helpusell.com
No. of Franchise Units: 106. **Founded:** 1976. **Franchised:** 1976. **Description:** Offers full-service real estate brokerage franchises. **Equity Capital Needed:** $43,750-$136,750 depending on marketplace costs, franchise fee subject to change. **Franchise Fee:** $17,750. **Royalty Fee:** 6%. **Financial Assistance:** Limited third party financing available. **Managerial Assistance:** Provides ongoing information on loan and insurance programs, staff recruitment and training, and marketing, through a live broadcast satellite system. **Training:** Offers 4 days at headquarters, at franchisee's location, 8 weeks by phone, retreats, regional meetings, convention, Help-U-Sell University and ongoing support.

17070 ■ Homes 4Sale By Owner Network
5761 Eagle Trace Dr.
Sylvania, OH 43560
Ph:(619)328-5988
Free: 877-615-5177
Fax:(619)749-3922
No. of Franchise Units: 3. **No. of Company-Owned Units:** 1. **Founded:** 2002. **Franchised:** 2006. **Description:** Full service real estate marketing. **Equity Capital Needed:** $25,000-$35,000. **Franchise Fee:** $19,500. **Financial Assistance:** No. **Training:** Yes.

17071 ■ Me, MyHome, And I
For Sale By Owner Group Ltd.
19785 W 12 Mile Rd., Ste. 52
Southfield, MI 48075
Ph:(313)629-3325
Founded: 2006. **Franchised:** 2006. **Description:** For sale by owner assistance. **Equity Capital Needed:** $100,000. **Franchise Fee:** $20,000. **Financial Assistance:** No. **Training:** Yes.

17072 ■ Picket Fence Preview
Picket Fence Franchising Corp.
One Kennedy Dr.
South Burlington, VT 05403
Ph:(802)660-3167
Free: 800-201-0338
No. of Franchise Units: 5. **No. of Company-Owned Units:** 1. **Founded:** 1993. **Franchised:** 1994. **Description:** For sale by owner magazine. **Equity Capital Needed:** $20,000-$35,000. **Franchise Fee:** $10,000. **Financial Assistance:** No. **Training:** Yes.

17073 ■ PropertyGuys.com Inc.
1133 St. George Blvd., Ste. 50
Moncton, NB, Canada E1E 4E1
Ph:(506)860-3433
Free: (866)666-9744
Fax:(506)857-2630
Co. E-mail: franchiseleads@propertyguys.com
URL: http://www.propertyguysfranchise.com
No. of Franchise Units: 112. **Founded:** 1998. **Franchised:** 2002. **Description:** The franchise aims at establishing a national network of local business professionals, which will develop a national database of "For sale by owner listings". **Equity Capital Needed:** $50,000-$100,000 investment required; $100,000 start-up capital required. **Franchise Fee:** $40,000-$75,000. **Training:** Offers 5 days at PropertyGuys University.

17074 ■ Re/Max LLC
RE/MAX International, Inc.
PO Box 3907
Englewood, CO 80155
Ph:(303)770-5531
No. of Franchise Units: 3,283. **No. of Company-Owned Units:** 24. **Founded:** 1973. **Franchised:** 1976. **Description:** International real estate franchise network. **Equity Capital Needed:** $35,000-$194,000. **Franchise Fee:** $12,500-$28,000. **Royalty Fee:** Varies. **Financial Assistance:** Third party financing available. **Training:** Provides 5 days training at headquarters, annual conference, online training and ongoing support.

17075 ■ Realty Executives International
Realty Executives
7600 N 16th St., Ste. 100
Phoenix, AZ 85020
Ph:(602)957-0747
Free: 800-252-3366
No. of Franchise Units: 569. **Founded:** 1965. **Franchised:** 1987. **Description:** Real estate franchise. **Equity Capital Needed:** $15,000-$75,000. **Franchise Fee:** $5,000-$25,000. **Financial Assistance:** No. **Training:** Yes.

17076 ■ Remerica Real Estate
41017 Ann Arbor Rd.
Plymouth, MI 48170
Ph:(734)459-6222
Free: 800-REM-ERIC
Fax:(734)459-1566
URL: http://www.remerica.com
No. of Franchise Units: 40. **Founded:** 1989. **Franchised:** 1991. **Description:** Real estate franchise. **Equity Capital Needed:** $50,000-$500,000. **Franchise Fee:** $10,000. **Financial Assistance:** Yes. **Training:** Yes.

17077 ■ United Capital Mortgage Assistance, L.L.C.
1300 Mercantile Ln., Ste. 124
Largo, MD 20774
Ph:(301)386-8803
Free: 800-474-1407

Fax:(301)386-8804

No. of Company-Owned Units: 1. **Founded:** 1996. **Franchised:** 1998. **Description:** Homeowner foreclosure service. **Equity Capital Needed:** $18,500-$27,000, includes franchise fee. **Franchise Fee:** $9,995, including training. **Financial Assistance:** No. **Training:** Yes.

17078 ■ Weichert Real Estate Affiliates Inc.
225 Littleton Rd.
Morris Plains, NJ 07950
Ph:(973)359-8377
Fax:(973)292-1428
URL: http://www.weichert.com

No. of Franchise Units: 234. **No. of Company-Owned Units:** 148. **Founded:** 1969. **Franchised:** 2000. **Description:** They serve as real estate brokerage. **Equity Capital Needed:** $50,000-$346,700. **Franchise Fee:** $25,000. **Royalty Fee:** 6%. **Financial Assistance:** No. **Training:** Offers 4 days at corporate headquarters, onsite and annual Conference and support.

COMPUTERIZED DATABASES

17079 ■ *The National Registry*
Federal Financial Institutions Examination Council
1401 H St. NW, Ste. 760
Washington, DC 20005
Ph:(202)289-2735
Fax:(202)289-4101
URL: http://www.asc.gov

Description: Contains a national registry of state certified and licensed real estate appraisers. Listees in this database limited to those who currently are, or have been, certified or licensed by a U.S. State, Territory or possession to perform appraisals in connection with Federally-related real estate transactions. Only State certified or licensed appraisers who are listed on this National Registry as having currently valid certifications or licenses are authorized under Federal law to perform appraisals in connection with federally related transactions. Data sources for all appraiser listings include various State regulatory agencies only. **Availability:** Online: Federal Financial Institutions Examination Council. **Type:** Directory.

17080 ■ *New Residential Construction Index*
U.S. Census Bureau
4600 Silver Hill Rd.
Washington, DC 20233-0001
Ph:(301)457-4100
Free: 800-923-8282
Fax:(301)457-4714
Co. E-mail: webmaster@census.gov
URL: http://www.census.gov

Description: Provides statistics on the number of new privately owned housing units completed and under construction, as well as building permits. Includes actual and seasonally adjusted estimates. Provides monthly and seasonal information and comparative data for earlier years, as well as information on seasonal factors affecting housing completions. Available in Portable Document Format (PDF). **Availability:** Online: U.S. Census Bureau. **Type:** Statistical.

17081 ■ *New Residential Sales*
U.S. Census Bureau
4600 Silver Hill Rd.
Washington, DC 20233-0001
Ph:(301)457-4100
Free: 800-923-8282
Fax:(301)457-4714
Co. E-mail: webmaster@census.gov
URL: http://www.census.gov

Description: Provides information on new privately owned one-family homes sold as well as characteristics and statistics for multi-family buildings and mobile homes. Includes information on the price index of housing, and the characteristics for one-family houses. Provides annual and monthly data from 1963 to date and regional data from 1973 to date, with more detailed information from 1971 to 1990. Includes information on seasonal factors affecting home sales in this market area. Contains data from the Survey of Market Absorption, including rental price and asking price. Includes information on new one-family homes,

including number of sales, number of month's supply at current sales rate, and median number of months on the sales market. Provides pricing information and physical characteristics such as location, number of bathrooms and bedrooms, type of exterior wall material, number of fireplaces, type of heating, type of parking, square feet, type of financing, closing costs, and price per square foot of floor area. **Availability:** Online: U.S. Census Bureau. **Type:** Statistical.

COMPUTER SYSTEMS/ SOFTWARE

17082 ■ Real Estate Analyzer
HowardSoft
7852 Ivanhoe Ave.
La Jolla, CA 92037
Ph:(858)454-0121
Fax:(858)454-7559
Co. E-mail: support@howardsoft.com
URL: http://www.howardsoft.com

Price: $395. **Description:** Available for Apple II and IBM computers and compatibles. System provides financial analysis for property investment purposes.

LIBRARIES

17083 ■ Baker Botts, L.L.P. Law Library
1299 Pennsylvania Ave., NW
Washington, DC 20004
Ph:(202)639-7700
Fax:(202)639-7890

Scope: Law - banking, corporate, international, public utilities, real estate, taxation, environmental, intellectual property. **Services:** Interlibrary loan; copying; Library open to the public by appointment with restrictions. **Holdings:** 22,000 volumes; microforms; videocassettes; audiocassettes; CD-ROM. **Subscriptions:** 125 journals and other serials.

17084 ■ Buset & Partners Library
1121 Barton St.
Thunder Bay, ON, Canada P7B 5N3
Ph:(807)623-2500
Free: (866)532-8738
Fax:(807)622-7808
Co. E-mail: cenns@buset-partners.com
URL: http://www.buset-partners.com
Contact: Carolyn Enns, Libn.

Scope: Law - real estate, labor, corporate, commercial, family, personal injury, insurance; civil litigation, wills and estates, employment, municipal, environmental. **Services:** Library not open to the public. **Holdings:** 2100 books; 3 bound periodical volumes. **Subscriptions:** 7 journals and other serials; 3 newspapers.

17085 ■ Landauer Realty Group Information Center
55 E 59th St., Fl. 4
New York, NY 10022-1112
Ph:(212)621-9500
Fax:(212)621-9567
Co. E-mail: corporatecommunications@grub-ellis. com
URL: http://www.landauer.com
Contact: Catherine A. Heyward, Lib.Mgr.

Scope: Real estate, finance, marketing, land use, development, property acquisition and management. **Services:** Center not open to the public. **Holdings:** 375 books; 100 VF drawers of reports; 16,000 clippings, offerings, brochures, statistical data; 125 VF drawers of research materials; U.S. maps; Annual reports; 1960, 1970, 1980 census publications; government documents. **Subscriptions:** 200 journals and other serials.

17086 ■ National Association of Realtors–Information Central
430 N. Michigan Ave.
Chicago, IL 60611-4087
Ph:(312)329-8200
Free: 800-874-6500

Fax:(312)329-5960
Co. E-mail: infocentral@realtors.org
URL: http://www.realtor.org
Contact: John Krukoff

Scope: Real estate, architecture, city planning, association management. **Services:** Library open to the public by appointment on fee basis. **Holdings:** 15,000 volumes. **Subscriptions:** 700 journals and other serials.

17087 ■ Polsinelli Shalton Welte Suelthaus PC Law Library
700 W. 47th St., Ste. 1000
Kansas City, MO 64112
Ph:(816)753-1000
Fax:(816)753-1536
Co. E-mail: bfullerton@pswlaw.com
URL: http://www.pswlaw.com/
Contact: Karin L. Weaver

Scope: Law - tax, bankruptcy, real estate; litigation; product liability. **Services:** Interlibrary loan; copying; SDI; Library open to clients only. **Holdings:** 15,000 books. **Subscriptions:** 1500 journals and other serials; 10 newspapers.

17088 ■ Protape, Inc. Library
1540 Broadway
New York, NY 10036
Contact: Richard Sobelsohn

Scope: Accounting, law, real estate, English, math, insurance, travel, taxation, stock broker, medical billing, claims adjusting, private investigation, paralegal. **Services:** Library not open to the public. **Holdings:** 25,000 books; 250 bound periodical volumes. **Subscriptions:** 65 journals and other serials; 20 newspapers.

17089 ■ Toronto Real Estate Board Library
1400 Don Mills Rd.
Don Mills, ON, Canada M3B 3N1
Ph:(416)443-8100
URL: http://www.torontorealestateboard.com
Contact: Michael Murphy

Scope: Real estate. **Services:** Library open to the public by appointment. **Holdings:** 3000 books; 120 serials; 500 reports; 120 audio- and videocassettes, and reel-to-reel tapes. **Subscriptions:** 100 journals and other serials.

17090 ■ Zuckerman Spaeder LLP Library
1800 M. St., NW, Ste. 1000
Washington, DC 20036
Ph:(202)778-1878
Fax:(202)822-8106
Co. E-mail: jfaubell@zuckerman.com
URL: http://www.zuckerman.com
Contact: Jeanne Trahan Faubell, Lib.Dir.

Scope: Law - bankruptcy, business and corporate law, securities litigation, political law, real estate; civil and criminal litigation, American Indian law. **Services:** Interlibrary loan; copying; Library open to the public with restrictions. **Holdings:** 4500 volumes. **Subscriptions:** 35 journals and other serials; 10 newspapers.

RESEARCH CENTERS

17091 ■ Ohio State University–Center for Real Estate Education and Research
606 Fisher Hall
Fisher College of Business
2100 Neil Ave.
Columbus, OH 43210-1144
Ph:(614)292-2109
Fax:(614)292-2418
Co. E-mail: realestate@osu.edu
URL: http://fisher.osu.edu/centers/real-estate
Contact: Dr. Ken Gold, Dir.
E-mail: realestate@osu.edu

Scope: Serves as a focal point for involvement of faculty from various disciplines in real estate research and education projects. **Educational Activities:** Assists in the development of educational programs in real estate offered by the University; Conferences (occasionally); Seminars and colloquia.

ASSOCIATIONS AND OTHER ORGANIZATIONS

17092 ■ International Real Estate Institute
PO Box 879
Palm Springs, CA 92263
Ph:(760)327-5284
Free: 877-743-6799
Fax:(760)327-5631
Co. E-mail: support@assoc-hdqts.org
URL: http://irei-assoc.org
Contact: Snehal Jardosh, Consultant
Description: Professionals in 120 countries specializing in the development, finance, investment and valuation of real estate. Conducts educational seminars and regional programs; operates speakers' bureau and placement service. Compiles statistics, consults United Nations on property issues. .

17093 ■ Investment Management Consultants Association
5619 DTC Pkwy., Ste. 500
Greenwood Village, CO 80111
Ph:(303)770-3377
Fax:(303)770-1812
Co. E-mail: imca@imca.org
URL: http://www.imca.org
Contact: Sean Walters CAE, Exec. Dir./CEO
Description: Consultants, money managers, and others in the investment management consultant business. Seeks to increase public awareness of investment management consultants, provide educational programs to members, and encourage high business standards. Operates consulting industry certification program. Maintains a legislative network with state and federal legislative information affecting the industry. **Publications:** *Essentials of Investment Consulting*; *Ethical Considerations for Consultants*; *The Facts About Investing*; *IMCA Practice Management Standards*; *IMCA Reporting Standards* (semiannual); *The Journal of Investment Consulting* (semiannual); *The Monitor* (bimonthly); *Wealth Management Course* .

17094 ■ National Apartment Association
4300 Wilson Blvd., Ste. 400
Arlington, VA 22203
Ph:(703)518-6141
Fax:(703)248-9440
Co. E-mail: info@naahq.org
URL: http://www.naahq.org
Contact: Doug Culkin CAE, Pres.
Description: Federation of 155 state and local associations of industry professionals engaged in all aspects of the multifamily housing industry, including owners, builders, investors, developers, managers, and allied service representatives. Provides education and certification for property management executives, on-site property managers, maintenance personnel, property supervisors, and leasing agents. Offers a nationwide legislative network concerned with governmental decisions at the federal, state, and local levels. .

17095 ■ National Association of Real Estate Companies
216 W Jackson Blvd., Ste. 625
Chicago, IL 60606
Ph:(312)263-1755
Fax:(312)750-1203
Co. E-mail: info@narec.org
URL: http://www.narec.org
Contact: Paul Hawkins, Pres.
Description: Individuals associated with companies involved in the financial management of real estate development companies. Purpose: Seeks to formulate positions and inform members on current accounting and financial reporting issues relating to real estate companies and to voice these positions to appropriate accounting rule-making bodies. Cooperates with such bodies in order to establish accounting and financial guidelines; provides a forum for members dealing with issues faced in managing the financial affairs of real estate companies such as financial reporting, financial management, tax planning, and information technology. .

17096 ■ National Association of Real Estate Investment Trusts
1875 I St. NW, Ste. 600
Washington, DC 20006-5413
Ph:(202)739-9400
Free: 800-3NA-REIT
Fax:(202)739-9401
Co. E-mail: baiken@nareit.com
URL: http://www.reit.com
Contact: Steven A. Wechsler, Pres./CEO
Description: Real estate investment trusts; corporations, partnerships, or individuals (other than trusts) that manage multiple-owned real estate, or that have a business or professional interest in real estate trusts, associations, corporations and funds. Compiles statistics. **Publications:** *NAREIT Quick Member Guide* (annual).

17097 ■ National Association of Realtors
430 N Michigan Ave.
Chicago, IL 60611-4087
Free: 800-874-6500
URL: http://www.realtor.org
Contact: Ron Phipps, Pres.
Description: Federation of 54 state and territory associations and 1,860 local real estate boards whose members are real estate brokers and agents; terms are registered by the association in the U.S. Patent and Trademark Office and in the states. Promotes education, high professional standards and modern techniques in specialized real estate work such as brokerage, appraisal, property management, land development, industrial real estate, farm brokerage and counseling. Conducts research programs. **Publications:** *Real Estate Outlook* (monthly).

17098 ■ Real Property Association of Canada–Association des biens Immobiliers du Canada
One University Ave., Ste. 1410
Toronto, ON, Canada M5J 2P1
Ph:(416)642-2700
Free: (855)732-5722
Fax:(416)642-2727
Co. E-mail: info@realpac.ca
URL: http://www.realpac.ca
Contact: Michael Brooks PhD, CEO
Description: Real estate and development companies and related businesses. Promotes growth in the real estate development and related industries. Serves as a forum for discussion of issues facing the industry; represents members' interests before the public.

DIRECTORIES OF EDUCATIONAL PROGRAMS

17099 ■ *Directory of Real Estate Development & Related Education Programs*
Pub: Urban Land Institute
Ed: Gayle Berens, Editor. **Released:** Biennial, latest edition 11th, 2008. **Price:** $19.95, members; $24.95, nonmembers. **Covers:** over 60 real estate development education programs currently being offered at colleges and universities. **Entries Include:** College or university name, address, list of faculty members, curriculum, tuition, length of program, degrees offered, financial aid information, job placement services, international programs, e-mail addresses. **Indexes:** Faculty, Programs by degree type, Programs by geographical.

REFERENCE WORKS

17100 ■ "$1M Home Sales Spike" in *Business Courier* (Vol. 27, December 3, 2010, No. 31, pp. 1)
Pub: Business Courier
Ed: Tom Demeropolis. **Description:** Cincinnati Area Board of Realtors reported the increase of sales of multi-million dollar Tri-State homes in 2010, particularly in Indian Hill where sales surged nearly 60 percent. Sales of homes of $1 million and above are up 21 percent through November in Hamilton County with 58 homes sales.

17101 ■ "1Q Office Vacancies Mainly Up; Class A Space Bucks Trend, Falls" in *Crain's Detroit Business* (Vol. 24, April 14, 2008, No. 15)
Pub: Crain Communications, Inc.
Ed: Daniel Duggan. **Description:** Although more office space became vacant in the first quarter, Class A space went in the opposite direction with several local businesses are moving from less-desirable to more desirable areas.

17102 ■ "3CDC Investing $8 Million To Put New Life Into Old Homes" in *Globe & Mail* (February 28, 2006, pp. B1)
Pub: CTVglobemedia Publishing Inc.
Ed: Lucy May. **Description:** The Cincinnati Center City Development Corp. has bought more than 100 empty buildings and many around Washington Park in Over-the-Rhine. Its new project, called 3CDC, is to revitalize the historic neighborhood in the Washington Park area near Music Hall.

17103 ■ **"13D Filings: Investors Report to the SEC" in** *Barron's* **(Vol. 88, July 4, 2008, No. 28, pp. M10)**

Pub: Dow Jones & Co., Inc.

Description: Robino Stortini Holdings will seek control of Investors Capital Holdings either alone or with members of the company's management. Discovery Group I will withhold its votes at the nomination of directors for TESSCO Technologies while JMB Capital Partners Master Fund plans to nominate a slate of candidates to the board of Maguire Properties.

17104 ■ **"A 16-Year Housing Slump? It Could Happen" in** *Barron's* **(Vol. 88, March 17, 2008, No. 11, pp. 27)**

Pub: Dow Jones & Company, Inc.

Ed: Gene Epstein. **Description:** Housing remains a good protection against inflation but over very long periods. Inflation-adjusted stock prices did even better but have greater volatility. Commodities, on the other hand, underperformed both housing and stocks as inflation hedges. House prices tend to rise faster than the consumer price index is because land is inherently limited.

17105 ■ **"The 35 Year Mortgage-Built to Last Time" in** *Globe & Mail* **(March 17, 2006, pp. B1)**

Pub: CTVglobemedia Publishing Inc.

Ed: Patrick Brethour. **Description:** The 35-year mortgage has arrived in Canada. The plan will give the opportunity to the first-time buyers into the real estate market. Details of the new mortgage are analyzed.

17106 ■ **"$50 Million Project for West Chester" in** *Business Courier* **(Vol. 24, December 14, 2008, No. 35, pp. 1)**

Pub: American City Business Journals, Inc.

Ed: Laura Baverman. **Description:** Commercial developer Scott Street Partners is planning to invest $50 million for the development of a site south of the Streets of West Chester retail center. The 31-acre project will generate 1,200 jobs, and will bring in offices, restaurants and a hotel. The development plans and the features of the site are discussed as well.

17107 ■ **"$100 Million Complex To Be Built...On a Bridge" in** *Business Courier* **(Vol. 27, November 12, 2010, No. 28, pp. 1)**

Pub: Business Courier

Ed: Lucy May. **Description:** A development firm closed a deal with the Newport Southbank Bridge Company for a $100M entertainment complex that will be built on tope of the Purple People Bridge. The proposed project will cover 150,000 square feet with attractions such as restaurants, a boutique hotel, and pubs.

17108 ■ **"$100 Million in Projects Jeopardized" in** *Business Courier* **(Vol. 24, March 28, 2008, No. 51, pp. 1)**

Pub: American City Business Journals, Inc.

Ed: Dan Monk. **Description:** Ohio's historic preservation tax credit program may be reinstated after some companies planned to sue over its stoppage. The Ohio Department of Development said the program was halted because it exceeded the allocated budget for the credit. $34 million in credits are at stake for more than two dozen local projects if the program is reinstated.

17109 ■ **"217 Homes Planned for Former Crystal Cream Site" in** *Sacramento Business Journal* **(Vol. 25, August 8, 2008, No. 23, pp. 1)**

Pub: American City Business Journals, Inc.

Ed: Michael Shaw. **Description:** MetroNova Development LLC plans to develop housing at the former Crystal Cream & Butter Co. site near downtown Sacramento. The developer expects to sell the new loft houses for about $300,000 without public subsidies. Views and other information on the planned development project, is presented.

17110 ■ **"2009 Real Estate in Review: Median Prices Drop, Sales Up" in** *Bellingham Business Journal* **(Vol. February 2010, pp. 15)**

Pub: Sound Publishing Inc.

Ed: Isaac Bonnell. **Description:** Bellingham and Whatcom County, Washington saw a rise in home sales in 2008. Single family home sales were up 3.3 percent in Bellingham and 0.5 percent for the entire county. Statistical data included.

17111 ■ **"2010 Book of Lists" in** *Austin Business JournalInc.* **(Vol. 29, December 25, 2009, No. 42, pp. 1)**

Pub: American City Business Journals

Description: Rankings of companies and organizations within the business services, finance, health-care, hospitality and travel, insurance, marketing and media, professional services, real estate, education and technology industries in Austin, Texas are presented. Rankings are based on sales, business size, and other statistics.

17112 ■ **"2010 Book of Lists" in** *Business Courier* **(Vol. 26, December 26, 2009, No. 36, pp. 1)**

Pub: American City Business Journals, Inc.

Description: Rankings of companies and organizations within the business services, education, finance, health care, hospitality and tourism, real estate, and technology industries in the Cincinnati, Ohio-Northern Kentucky area are presented. Rankings are based on sales, business size, or other statistics.

17113 ■ **"2010 Book of Lists" in** *Tampa Bay Business Journal* **(Vol. 30, December 22, 2009, No. 53, pp. 1)**

Pub: American City Business Journals

Description: Rankings of companies and organizations within the human resources, banking and finance, business services, healthcare, real estate, technology, hospitality and travel, and education industries in the Greater Tampa Bay area are presented. Rankings are based on sales, business size, and more.

17114 ■ **"A Conversation With; Ron Gatner, Jones Lang LaSalle" in** *Crain's Detroit Business* **(Vol. 24, October 6, 2008, No. 40, pp. 9)**

Pub: Crain Communications, Inc.

Description: Interview with Ron Gatner who is a corporate real estate adviser with the real estate company Jones Lang LaSalle as well as the company's executive vice president and part of the tenant advisory team; Gatner speaks about the impact that the Wall Street crisis is having on the commercial real estate market in Detroit.

17115 ■ **"ABM Janitorial Services Receives Service Excellence Award from Jones Lang LaSalle" in** *Investment Weekly News* **(July 16, 2011, pp. 75)**

Pub: News RX

Description: ABM Janitorial Services was awarded the 2010 Jones Lang LaSalle Distinction award in the category of Service Excellence. LaSalle is a leading financial and professional services firm that specializes in real estate services and investment management. The program recognizes supplier partners who play a vital role in LaSalle's aim to provide the highest quality of services, value and innovation to clients.

17116 ■ **"Affordable Again" in** *The Business Journal-Serving Greater Tampa Bay* **(Vol. 28, July 18, 2008, No. 30, pp. 1)**

Pub: American City Business Journals, Inc.

Ed: Janet Leiser. **Description:** Rental rates for office space in the Tampa Bay area has dropped to $21.68 a foot, after demand for the second quarter of 2008 has remained low. Commercial real estate experts say that the industry can easily rebound from what is believed to be the weakest demand in 20 years. Other views, information and statistics on real estate demand and prices in Tampa Bay are, are presented.

17117 ■ **"Agricultural Community Implements Green Technologies, Building Team" in** *Contractor* **(Vol. 56, September 2009, No. 9, pp. 5)**

Pub: Penton Media, Inc.

Ed: Candace Ruolo. **Description:** John DeWald and Associates has initiated a residential development project which uses green technologies in Illinois. The community features a community center, organic farm and recreational trails. Comments from executives are also provided.

17118 ■ **"AIC To Buy $350M of Real Estate" in** *Austin Business JournalInc.* **(Vol. 28, November 14, 2008, No. 35, pp. 1)**

Pub: American City Business Journals

Ed: Kate Harrington. **Description:** Austin-based AIC Ventures LP is planning to buy $350 million worth of commercial real estate. The company's move will double its acquisitions. It is also planning to acquire 30 assets for its eight fun in 2009 from middle-market companies.

17119 ■ **"All About The Benjamins" in** *Canadian Business* **(Vol. 81, September 29, 2008, No. 16, pp. 92)**

Pub: Rogers Media Ltd.

Ed: David Baines. **Description:** Discusses real estate developer Royal Indian Raj International Corp., a company that planned to build a $3 billion "smart city" near the Bangalore airport; to this day nothing has ever been built. The company was incorporated in 1999 by Manoj C. Benjamin one investor, Bill Zack, has been sued by the developer for libel due to his website that calls the company a scam. Benjamin has had a previous case of fraud issued against him as well as a string of liabilities and lawsuits.

17120 ■ **"All Bubbles Must Burst" in** *Canadian Business* **(Vol. 83, August 17, 2010, No. 13-14, pp. 12)**

Pub: Rogers Media Ltd.

Ed: Matthew McClearn. **Description:** Canada's housing markets is showing signs of cooling down as home and condo sales both fell for the first time in 16 years. The Canadian government has fueled the market over an extended period through Canada Mortgage and Housing Corporation's role in insuring mortgage lenders against risk of defaults.

17121 ■ **"All-Star Advice 2010" in** *Black Enterprise* **(Vol. 41, October 2010, No. 3, pp. 97)**

Pub: Earl G. Graves Publishing Co. Inc.

Ed: Renita Burns, Sheiresa Ngo, Marcia Wade Talbert. **Description:** Financial experts share tips on real estate, investing, taxes, insurance and debt management.

17122 ■ **"Allen Tate Expanding to Research Triangle Park: Firm Expects Raleigh Market to Grow Faster" in** *Charlotte Observer* **(January 31, 2007)**

Pub: Knight-Ridder/Tribune Business News

Ed: Doug Smith; Dudley Price. **Description:** Allen Tate Realtors expanded its operations to the Research Triangle area. The firm is predicting a strong market and growth in Charlotte, North Carolina.

17123 ■ **"Another California Firm On Way" in** *Austin Business Journal* **(Vol. 31, May 6, 2011, No. 9, pp. 1)**

Pub: American City Business Journals Inc.

Ed: Christopher Calnan. **Description:** Main Street Hub Inc. is planning to build a facility in Austin, Texas. The company helps businesses manage their online reputations. Main Street has selected Aquila Commercial LLC as its real estate broker.

17124 ■ **"Another Man's Pain" in** *Canadian Business* **(Vol. 80, October 22, 2007, No. 21, pp. 33)**

Pub: Rogers Media

Ed: Andy Holloway. **Description:** U.S. financial collapse can have a positive impact on Canadian investors. Graphs on the total number of home foreclosures in the U.S. from January to August 2007, as well as foreclosure market by type, are presented.

17125 ■ **"Antwerpen Takes on Chrysler Financial Over Foreclosure Sales" in** *Baltimore Business Journal* **(Vol. 28, July 30, 2010, No. 12, pp. 1)**

Pub: Baltimore Business Journal

Ed: Gary Haber. **Description:** Antwerpen Motorcars Ltd. aims to fight the scheduled foreclosure sale of real estate it leases in Baltimore County, including the showroom for its Hyundai dealership on Baltimore National Pike in Catonsville, Maryland. The company is planning to file papers in court to stop the scheduled August 11, 2010 auction sought by Chrysler Financial Services Americas LLC.

17126 ■ "Apartment Ambitions" in *The Business Journal-Portland* **(Vol. 25, August 8, 2008, No. 22, pp. 1)**
Pub: American City Business Journals, Inc.

Ed: Wendy Culverwell. **Description:** Unico Properties LLC's Asa Flats+Lofts is one of the first of eight high-end apartment projects planned for Portland which will add a total of 2,130 new units to the Pearl District, South Waterfront, and downtown Portland. These apartments charge costs more than $1,600 or more per month over the average rent.

17127 ■ "Apartment Market Down, Not Out" in *Crain's Detroit Business* **(Vol. 24, October 6, 2008, No. 40, pp. 9)**
Pub: Crain Communications, Inc.

Ed: Daniel Duggan. **Description:** Detroit's apartment market is considered to have some of the strongest fundamentals of any apartment market in the country with relatively low vacancy rates and a relatively low supply of new units compared with demand. Investors continue to show interest in the buildings but the national lending market is making it difficult to invest in the city.

17128 ■ "Apartment Tower in River North Fetches More Than $90 Million" in *Crain's Chicago Business* **(Vol. 34, October 24, 2011, No. 42, pp. 17)**
Pub: Crain Communications Inc.

Ed: Alby Gallun. **Description:** Apartment tower in River North was sold for over $90 million to a Texas pension fund adviser. Details are included.

17129 ■ "Aquila HQ Hits the Market" in *The Business Journal-Serving Metropolitan Kansas City* **(Vol. 26, July 25, 2008, No. 46, pp. 1)**
Pub: American City Business Journals, Inc.

Ed: Rob Roberts. **Description:** Commercial real estate experts believe that Aquila Inc.'s former headquarters will be hard to rent out. The historic value of the building, being Kansas City's first skyscraper, is not expected to add value to the price of the rent. Other views and information on the building, as well as on Aquila, are presented.

17130 ■ "Are We There Yet?" in *Business Courier* **(Vol. 24, April 4, 2008, No. 52, pp. 1)**
Pub: American City Business Journals, Inc.

Ed: Lucy May; Dan Monk. **Description:** Groundbreaking for The Banks project happened in April 2, 2008, however, the future of the development remains uncertain due to some unresolved issues such as financing. Developers Harold A. Dawson Co. and Carter still have to pass final financing documents to Hamilton County and Cincinnati. The issue of financial commitment for the central riverfront project is examined.

17131 ■ "'The Asian Decade'" in *Hawaii Business* **(Vol. 53, January 2008, No. 7, pp. 19)**
Pub: Hawaii Business Publishing

Ed: Cathy S. Cruz-George. **Description:** Chaney Brooks, a Hawaiian real estate company, has affiliated with commercial real estate network NAI Global. The NAI partnership will improve Hawaii's international business, particularly its Asian investments. Hawaii's diverse workforce is evaluated, with regards to being an asset for international businesses.

17132 ■ "Ask Inc." in *Inc.* **(December 2007, pp. 83-84)**
Pub: Gruner & Jahr USA Publishing

Ed: Ari Weinzweig. **Description:** Questions regarding knowledge management in the case of a retiring CFO, issues involved in opening a satellite office for a New York realtor, and information for hiring a multicultural workforce are all discussed.

17133 ■ "Athletes Face Wins and Losses After Pro Sport" in *The Business Journal - Serving Phoenix and the Valley of the Sun* **(Vol. 29, September 19, 2008, No. 3, pp. 1)**
Pub: American City Business Journals, Inc.

Ed: Chris Casacchia. **Description:** Professional athletes like hockey star Jeremy Roenick start businesses, while others like Joel Adamson work to boost local communities. Former athletes were found to be particularly interested with real estate businesses. Other views and information on former athletes and their life after sports are presented.

17134 ■ "Athletes' Performance Building $10 Million Facility In ASU Park" in *The Business Journal - Serving Phoenix and the Valley of the Sun* **(Vol. 28, August 8, 2008, No. 49, pp. 1)**
Pub: American City Business Journals, Inc.

Ed: Jan Buchholz. **Description:** Athletes' Performance's planned facility at Arizona State University is scheduled to begin in November 2008 and expected to be completed by September 2009. The new building will almost double the company's training space as it will expand from around 19,000 square feet to 35,000 square feet.

17135 ■ "Austin Homes are Overpriced, Study Says" in *Austin Business JournalInc.* **(Vol. 29, January 1, 2010, No. 43, pp. 1)**
Pub: American City Business Journals

Ed: Kate Harrington. **Description:** Study by Forbes.com shows that Austin-Round Rock metropolitan statistical area ranked 10th on the list of cities with the most over-priced homes. For instance, the average price for a single-family home pegged at $188,000.

17136 ■ "Bangles, BMWs Elbow Out Delis and Discount Shops" in *Crain's New York Business* **(Vol. 24, January 14, 2008, No. 2, pp. 35)**
Pub: Crain Communications, Inc.

Ed: Wendy Davis. **Description:** Lured by a growing number of affluent residents and high-earning professionals, a number of upscale retailers have opened locations downtown which is driving up rents and forcing out longtime independent merchants.

17137 ■ "Bankruptcies Shoot Up 68 Percent" in *Sacramento Business Journal* **(Vol. 25, July 18, 2008, No. 20, pp. 1)**
Pub: American City Business Journals, Inc.

Ed: Kathy Robertson. **Description:** Personal bankruptcy in the Sacramento area rose by 88 percent for the first half of 2008 while business bankruptcies rose by 50 percent for the same period. The numbers of consumer bankruptcy reflects the effect of high debt, rising mortgage costs, and declining home values on U.S. households.

17138 ■ "Before Signing a Lease" in *Business Owner* **(Vol. 35, September-October 2011, No. 5, pp. 14)**
Pub: DL Perkins Company

Description: The following terms are essential to investigate before renewing or negotiating a lease for a small business: Term, Neighbors, Actual Usable Space, Gross or Net, Tenant Improvements, Renewal Option, Purchase Option, Cancelation Option, Sublease or Assignment, Security Deposit, Code Restrictions and Zoning, Parking, Relief and Lease Agreement.

17139 ■ "Best Income Trust" in *Canadian Business* **(Vol. 81, Summer 2008, No. 9, pp. 69)**
Pub: Rogers Media Ltd.

Ed: Calvin Leung. **Description:** Table showing five-year annualized growth rate and one-year stock performance of real estate investment trusts firms in Canada is presented. Calgary-based Boardwalk REIT is projected to grow the fastest among North American REITs over the next two years. Other details on the stock performance analysis are presented.

17140 ■ "Bigger TIF Makes Development Inroads" in *The Business Journal-Serving Metropolitan Kansas City* **(Vol. 26, July 11, 2008, No. 44)**
Pub: American City Business Journals, Inc.

Ed: Rob Roberts. **Description:** On July 9, 2008 the Tax Increment Financing Commission voted to expand a TIF district to Tiffany Springs Road. The plan for the TIF district close to Kansas City International Airport is to include a-half mile of the road. The impacts of the expansion on construction projects and on the road network are analyzed.

17141 ■ "Biggest UM Landlords" in *Crain's Detroit Business* **(Vol. 25, June 15, 2009, No. 24, pp. 1)**
Pub: Crain Communications Inc. - Detroit
Description: University of Michigan will purchase the two million-square-foot Pfizer campus in June 2009. The university is the largest occupier of commercial real estate off campus in and around Ann Arbor, Michigan.

17142 ■ "Bill Kaneko" in *Hawaii Business* **(Vol. 53, December 2007, No. 6, pp. 32)**
Pub: Hawaii Business Publishing
Ed: David K. Choo. **Description:** Hawaii Institute for Public Affairs chief executive officer and president Bill Kaneko believes that the Hawaiian economy is booming, however, he also asserts that the economy is too focused on tourism and real estate. Kaneko has also realized the that the will of the people is strong while he was helping with the Hawaiian 2050 Sustainability Plan. The difficulties of making a sustainable Hawaii are discussed.

17143 ■ "Bills Would Regulate Mortgage Loan Officers" in *Crain's Detroit Business* **(Vol. 24, February 25, 2008, No. 8, pp. 9)**
Pub: Crain Communications Inc. - Detroit
Ed: Amy Lane. **Description:** New legislation in Michigan, if passed, would create a registration process for mortgage loan officers in the state in order to address the mortgage loan crisis.

17144 ■ "Block Plans Office Park Along K-10 Corridor" in *The Business Journal-Serving Metropolitan Kansas City* **(Vol. 27, October 3, 2008)**
Pub: American City Business Journals, Inc.
Ed: Rob Roberts. **Description:** Kansas City, Missouri-based Block and Co. is planning to build four office buildings at the corner of College Boulevard and Ridgeview Road in Olathe. Features of the planned development are provided. Comments from executives are also presented.

17145 ■ "Block Pulls Plug On Riverside Deal" in *The Business Journal-Serving Metropolitan Kansas City* **(Vol. 27, October 10, 2008, No. 4)**
Pub: American City Business Journals, Inc.
Ed: Rob Roberts. **Description:** Real estate developer Ken Block has backed out from a $300 million Riverside industrial project. Block says he has already invested $1 million of his own money into the deal. Details regarding the project are given.

17146 ■ "Bond OK Could Bring Back the Housing Battle?" in *Charlotte Business Journal* **(Vol. 25, November 5, 2010, No. 33, pp. 1)**
Pub: Charlotte Business Journal
Ed: Susan Stabley. **Description:** The approval of the $15 million housing bond in Charlotte, North Carolina could bring back the debates on housing in the region. Protesters have opposed affordable housing developments that were proposed in the area since 2008. Other information on the recently approved housing bond and on other real estate issues in North Carolina is presented.

17147 ■ "Book of Lists 2010" in *Philadelphia Business Journal* **(Vol. 28, December 25, 2009, No. 45, pp. 1)**
Pub: American City Business Journals
Description: Rankings of companies and organizations within the banking, biotechnology, economic development, healthcare, hospitality, law and ac-

counting, marketing and media, real estate, and technology industries in the Philadelphia, Pennsylvania area are presented. Rankings are based on sales, business size, and more.

17148 ■ "Boston Hedge Fund Pours Money Into Real Estate Projects" in *Charlotte Business Journal* **(Vol. 25, December 3, 2010, No. 37, pp. 1)**
Pub: Charlotte Business Journal

Ed: Will Boye. **Description:** Boston-based hedge fund Baupost Group has been financing real estate project in Charlotte, North Carolina including more than 80 acres just north of uptown. Aside from purchasing the $23.8 million note for the Rosewood Condominiums from Regions Financial Corporation, the Baupost Group is also negotiating with Regions to buy the $93.9 million debt of the EipCentre real estate project.

17149 ■ "Bottom's Up" in *Barron's* **(Vol. 88, July 14, 2008, No. 28, pp. 25)**
Pub: Dow Jones & Co., Inc.

Ed: Jonathan R. Laing. **Description:** Economist Chip Case believes that home prices are nearing a bottom based on his analysis of the history of the housing market; surprisingly, in the past the housing market has rebounded after a quarter from a massive housing start drop. The drop in early stage delinquencies is another sign of the housing market's recovery.

17150 ■ "Briarcliff Office Building Fills Up Fast" in *The Business Journal-Serving Metropolitan Kansas City* **(Vol. 26, Sept. 5, 2008, pp. 1)**
Pub: American City Business Journals, Inc.

Ed: Rob Roberts. **Description:** Prior to its opening the Hilltop Office Building in Kansas City Missouri has attained 80 percent occupancy. FCStone Group Inc.'s plan to move to the building has boosted the facility's occupancy. Description and dimensions of the office building are also provided.

17151 ■ "A Bright Spot: Industrial Space in Demand Again" in *Sacramento Business Journal* **(Vol. 28, October 21, 2011, No. 34, pp. 1)**
Pub: Sacramento Business Journal

Ed: Michael Shaw. **Description:** Sacramento, California's industrial sites have been eyed by potential tenants who are actively seeking space larger than 50,000 square feet.

17152 ■ "Brokerages Seek a Foothold in Local Real Estate Market" in *Charlotte Business Journal* **(Vol. 25, October 15, 2010, No. 30, pp. 1)**
Pub: Charlotte Business Journal

Ed: Will Boye. **Description:** Charlotte, North Carolina has become an attractive destination for out-of-town brokerage firms. Colliers International has signed an affiliate deal with Anthony and Company to set up shop in Charlotte. Grubb and Ellis Company, on the other hand, is planning to open an office in the city.

17153 ■ "Builder's Bankruptcy Fans Fears" in *Crain's Cleveland Business* **(Vol. 28, October 22, 2007, No. 42, pp. 1)**
Pub: Crain Communications, Inc.

Ed: Stan Bullard. **Description:** Whitlatch & Co., Northeast Ohio's largest builder by unit volume in the early 1990s, has filed for Chapter 11 bankruptcy. This is causing builders and others in the real estate industry to wonder how long and severe the housing slump will be and which companies will survive.

17154 ■ "Building Portfolios for a World of 2.5 Percent Gains" in *Barron's* **(Vol. 88, July 7, 2008, No. 27, pp. L9)**
Pub: Dow Jones & Co., Inc.

Ed: Karen Hube. **Description:** Interview with Harold Evenski whom is a financial planner running a fee-only planning practice; he continues to caution investors against pursuing short-term gains and focusing on long-term trends. He advises investors against investing in commodity and real estate stocks and is concerned about the possible effects of high inflation.

17155 ■ "Burritos New Bag for Shopping Developer" in *Houston Business Journal* **(Vol. 40, December 4, 2009, No. 30, pp. 4A)**
Pub: American City Business Journals

Ed: Allison Wollam. **Description:** Houston, Texas-based Rob Johnson is the newest franchisee for Bullritos and plans to open eight area locations to market the quick-casual burrito concept. The former shopping center developer was looking for a new business sector after selling off his shopping center holdings.

17156 ■ "Business Owners Lien Trinity Project" in *The Business Journal-Serving Greater Tampa Bay* **(Vol. 28, July 25, 2008, No. 31, pp. 1)**
Pub: American City Business Journals, Inc.

Ed: Janet Leiser. **Description:** The Internal Revenue Service is trying to collect $2.9 million from the developer of the Trinity Town Center, William Plaines, due to the delays in the project. This is in addition to a $5.2 million lien by the project's subcontractors.

17157 ■ "Buy Now?" in *Hawaii Business* **(Vol. 53, March 2008, No. 9, pp. 32)**
Pub: Hawaii Business Publishing

Ed: David K. Choo. **Description:** Discusses the Honolulu Board of REALTORS which said that the last two months of 2007 saw double-digit housing sales drop, with December figures showing 30.6 percent and 22.9 percent decline in sales of single-family homes and condominiums, respectively. Forecasts on Hawaii's real estate market for 2008 are discussed.

17158 ■ "Buyers' Market" in *Baltimore Business Journal* **(Vol. 27, November 20, 2009, No. 28, pp. 1)**
Pub: American City Business Journals

Ed: Daniel J. Sernovitz. **Description:** Some business owners in Maryland are removing their leases and purchasing buildings due to the lower costs of real estate. This trend has enabled small business owners to avoid rent hikes, while setting equity into their companies. The pros and cons of owning buildings and how business owners assess their return on investment are examined.

17159 ■ "Cal-ISO Plans $125 Million Facility" in *Sacramento Business Journal* **(Vol. 25, August 1, 2008, No. 22, pp. 1)**
Pub: American City Business Journals, Inc.

Ed: Celia Lamb; Michael Shaw. **Description:** Sacramento, California-based nonprofit organization California Independent System Operator (ISO) is planning to build a new headquarters in Folsom. The new building would double its current leased space to 227,000 square feet. The ISO will seek tax-exempt bond financing for the project.

17160 ■ "Calendar" in *Crain's Detroit Business* **(Vol. 24, October 6, 2008, No. 40, pp. 22)**
Pub: Crain Communications, Inc.

Description: Listing of events in the Detroit area include conferences addressing entrepreneurialism, economic development, manufacturing, marketing, the housing crisis and women business ownership.

17161 ■ "Can Avenue be Fashionable Again? Livernois Merchants, City Want Revival" in *Crain's Detroit Business* **(March 10, 2008)**
Pub: Crain Communications, Inc.

Ed: Nancy Kaffer. **Description:** Once a busy retail district, the Avenue of Fashion, a Livernois Avenue strip between Six Mile and Eight Mile roads, is facing a community business effort being backed by city support whose aim is to restore the area to its former glory.

17162 ■ "Canadian Vehicle Sales Accelerate in April, but U.S. Goes on Bumpy Ride" in *Globe & Mail* **(May 2, 2007, pp. B7)**
Pub: CTVglobemedia Publishing Inc.

Ed: Greg Keenan. **Description:** The increase in Canadian vehicle sales to 169,280 in April 2007, but decline in their sales in the United States due to slump in housing sector are discussed.

17163 ■ "Casino Minority Spend: $80 Million" in *Business Courier* **(Vol. 27, August 20, 2010, No. 16, pp. 1)**
Pub: Business Courier

Ed: Lucy May. **Description:** Real estate developers are planning to invest $80 million to build the Harrah's casino project in Cincinnati, Ohio. Rock Ventures LLC is seeking a 20 percent inclusion rate in the project.

17164 ■ "Cedar Fair to Solicit Bids for Geauga Lake" in *Crain's Cleveland Business* **(Vol. 28, October 8, 2007, No. 40, pp. 1)**
Pub: Crain Communications, Inc.

Ed: Stan Bullard. **Description:** Cedar Fair Entertainment Co. plans to seek sealed bids for the redevelopment of nearly 540 acres of their amusement park site in southwest Geauga County and northwest Portage County.

17165 ■ "Centerpoint Funding In Limbo" in *The Business Journal - Serving Phoenix and the Valley of the Sun* **(Vol. 28, August 1, 2008, No. 48)**
Pub: American City Business Journals, Inc.

Ed: Jan Buchholz. **Description:** Avenue Communities LLC has threatened to file a case against Mortgages Ltd. over the finance of the Centerpoint development project in Tempe, Arizona. Avenue Communities want Mortgages Ltd. to file a motion with the U.S. Bankruptcy Court so that it can secure financing for the project. Other views and information on the finance of Centerpoint, are presented.

17166 ■ "Channelside On the Blocks" in *The Business Journal-Serving Greater Tampa Bay* **(Vol. 28, August 29, 2008, No. 36, pp. 1)**
Pub: American City Business Journals, Inc.

Ed: Michael Hinman. **Description:** In a bankruptcy auction for The Place, one of the more visible condominium projects at Channelside, the lowest bid is just below $73 a square foot. KeyBank National Association, the Key Developers Group LLC's lender, leads the auction planned for October 15, 2008. The reason behind the low minimum bid required to participate in the said action is discussed.

17167 ■ "Children's Hospital to Build in New Berlin" in *The Business Journal-Milwaukee* **(Vol. 25, August 1, 2008, No. 45, pp. A1)**
Pub: American City Business Journals, Inc.

Ed: Corrinne Hess. **Description:** Children's Hospital of Wisconsin plans a clinic in the 35-acre medical office park in New Berlin, Wisconsin, owned by Froedtert Memorial Lutheran Hospital and Medical College of Wisconsin Real Estate Ventures LLC. The hospital will be the first major tenant in the park, to be built by Irgens Development Partners LLC.

17168 ■ "City Sets Yamhill Makeover" in *The Business Journal-Portland* **(Vol. 25, July 4, 2008, No. 17, pp. 1)**
Pub: American City Business Journals, Inc.

Ed: Andy Giegerich. **Description:** City government is scheduled to redevelop Peterson's property on Yamhill Street in Portland. The redevelopment is seen as a way to better developing commercial properties in the area. Problems associated with the project, which include cost and developer selection, are also discussed.

17169 ■ "CityLink Project On Hold" in *Business Courier* **(Vol. 24, November 9, 2008, No. 30, pp. 3)**
Pub: American City Business Journals, Inc.

Ed: Dan Monk. **Description:** Developers of the CityLink project have indicated that it will be at least a year before they start the planned social services mall at 800 Bank West End. According to Tim Senff, Citylink CEO, the company wants to build bridges before constructing the buildings. The project's critics are still considering whether to appeal a court ruling regarding the facility's compliance with the city's zoning code.

17170 ■ "Clock Ticking for Hotel Berry" in *Sacramento Business Journal* **(Vol. 25, July 25, 2008, No. 21, pp. 1)**
Pub: American City Business Journals, Inc.

Ed: Michael Shaw. **Description:** Federal tax credits worth $13.6 million have been awarded to boost the renovation project for the aging Hotel Berry in downtown Sacramento, California. The owners of the hotel have five months before the expiration of the tax credits to raise the remaining funding for the $20 million renovation.

17171 ■ "Coherent Laying Off 144 As It Prepares To Shut Auburn Plant" in *Sacramento Business Journal* (Vol. 25, August 1, 2008, No. 22, pp. 1)
Pub: American City Business Journals, Inc.
Ed: Melanie Turner. **Description:** Sacramento, California-based Coherent Inc. is planning to lay off 144 workers at its Auburn facility. Coherent has been cutting payroll and its real estate holdings. Statistics on the company's earnings are also provided.

17172 ■ "Colliers Shifts Its Brokerage Home" in *Charlotte Business Journal* (Vol. 25, November 5, 2010, No. 33, pp. 1)
Pub: Charlotte Business Journal
Ed: Will Boye. **Description:** Colliers International signed a long-term affiliate agreement with commercial real estate firm Clarus Properties, in a move that would allow Colliers to resume business in Charlotte, North Carolina. Colliers also hired well known brokers Brad Grow and Brent Royall.

17173 ■ "Columbia Sale Narrowed To Two Developers" in *The Business Journal-Milwaukee* (Vol. 25, July 18, 2008, No. 43, pp. A1)
Pub: American City Business Journals, Inc.
Ed: Corrinne Hess. **Description:** Officials of Columbia St. Mary's Inc plan to pick one of two real-estate developers who will buy the 8-acre property of the Columbia Hospital which the company will move away from when their new hospital has been constructed. The hospital on Newport Ave. has been on the market since 2001.

17174 ■ "Columbia's JPB Raising $175M to Acquire Companies, Real Estate" in *Boston Business Journal* (Vol. 29, May 27, 2011, No. 3, pp. 1)
Pub: American City Business Journals Inc.
Ed: Gary Haber. **Description:** JPB Enterprises is preparing to raise $175 million in its goal of acquiring companies and real estate that are major names in America. The $75 million will be raised for a buyout fund that will target wide range of industries while the $100 million will be used for land investment projects in the Florida Panhandle. Baltimore firms are expected to benefit from this deal.

17175 ■ "Commercial Builders Take It on the Chin" in *Crain's Chicago Business* (Vol. 31, April 28, 2008, No. 17, pp. 16)
Pub: Crain Communications, Inc.
Ed: Alby Gallun. **Description:** Although the health care development sector has seen growth, the rest of Chicago's local commercial building industry has seen steep declines in the first quarter of this year. According to McGraw-Hill Construction, Chicago-area non-residential construction starts totaled $731 million in the quarter, a 60 percent drop from the year-earlier period. Volume in the retail, office and hotel markets fell by nearly 70 percent.

17176 ■ "Con-Way Project Back in High Gear" in *Business Journal Portland* (Vol. 27, November 5, 2010, No. 36, pp. 1)
Pub: Portland Business Journal
Ed: Wendy Culverwell. **Description:** Trucking firm Con-Way Inc. intends to sell parcels of land from a property comprising 16 blocks and 20 prime acres west of the Pearl District in Portland, Oregon. In 2009, Con-Way abandoned plans to sell the property. As Con-Way reclaims control over design and usage of the property, it also expressed willingness to cooperate with a master developer on a related real estate project.

17177 ■ "Condo Markdown" in *Boston Business Journal* (Vol. 27, November 30, 2007, No. 44, pp. 1)
Pub: American City Business Journals Inc.
Ed: Michelle Hillman. **Description:** Boston real estate market is softening, and condominium developers such as Beacon Communities LLC are sending

out various incentives like markdowns and unit upgrades. Developers have also held auctions and even offered brand new cars to lure buyers. Other perks being offered by various Boston developers are discussed.

17178 ■ "Condominium Sales Fall to a Seven-Year Low" in *Crain's Chicago Business* (Vol. 31, November 10, 2008, No. 45, pp. 2)
Pub: Crain Communications, Inc.
Ed: Alby Gallun. **Description:** Downtown Chicago condominium market is experiencing the lowest number of sales in years due to the tightening of the mortgage lending market, the Wall Street crisis and the downturn in the economy. The supply of new condos is soaring, the result of the building boom of 2005 and 2006; many developers are finding it difficult to pay off construction loans and fear foreclosure on their properties. Additional information and statistical data related to the downtown condominium market is provided.

17179 ■ "Contingent Offers: Weighing the Risk" in *Crain's Chicago Business* (Vol. 31, April 21, 2008, No. 16, pp. 48)
Pub: Crain Communications, Inc.
Ed: Darci Smith. **Description:** Interview with Greer Haseman, the broker-owner of Town Square Associates, who discusses contingent offers in a challenging housing market.

17180 ■ "A Conversation with; Renea Butler, Real Estate One Inc." in *Crain's Detroit Business* (Vol. 25, June 8, 2009, No. 23, pp. 12)
Pub: Crain Communications Inc. - Detroit
Ed: Ryan Beene. **Description:** Renea Butler, vice president of administration and human resources for Real Estate One Inc. in Southfield as well as vice president for public relations for the Human Resource Association of Greater Detroit, talks about how the economy has affected human resource services.

17181 ■ "Cool on Chicago Office Properties" in *Crain's Chicago Business* (Vol. 31, March 31, 2008, No. 13, pp. 16)
Pub: Crain Communications, Inc.
Ed: Eddie Baeb. **Description:** Investors predict values on Chicago office buildings to drop 1.3 percent over the next year.

17182 ■ "Cornered by Credit; As $1 Billion in Loans Come Due, Will Landlords Find Funds?" in *Crain's Detroit Business* (October 6, 2008)
Pub: Crain Communications, Inc.
Ed: Daniel Duggan. **Description:** Conduit loans are used by many real estate investors and are normally issued in 7- to 10-year terms with balloon payments due at the end, requiring the full balance to be paid upon maturity. Many building owners may find their properties going into foreclosure as these loans mature next year since these loans cannot be extended like typical loans and the credit crisis along with falling property values is making it more difficult to secure new sources of funding. Possible solutions to this problem are also explored.

17183 ■ "Corporate Elite Show Resilience" in *The Business Journal-Serving Greater Tampa Bay* (Vol. 28, August 1, 2008, No. 32, pp. 1)
Pub: American City Business Journals, Inc.
Ed: Margie Manning; Alexis Muellner. **Description:** Stocks of the largest public companies in Tampa Bay, Florida, outperformed the S&P 500 index by 28 percent in the first half of 2008. The escalation is attributed to the growth orientation of the companies in the area and the lack of exposure to the real estate and financial services sectors.

17184 ■ "Corus Eases Off Ailing Condo Market; Office Developers Get Majority of 1Q Loans" in *Crain's Chicago Business* (April 28, 2008)
Pub: Crain Communications, Inc.
Ed: H. Lee Murphy. **Description:** Corus Bankshares Inc., a specialist in lending for the condominium high-rise construction market, is diversifying its portfolio by

making loans to office developers and expects to be investing in hotels through the rest of the year. Corus' $7.57 billion loan portfolio is also discussed in detail as well as the company's earnings and share price. Statistical data included.

17185 ■ "Councilman May Revive Labor Bill" in *Baltimore Business Journal* (Vol. 28, August 13, 2010, No. 14, pp. 1)
Pub: Baltimore Business Journal
Ed: Daniel J. Sernovitz. **Description:** Baltimore, Maryland Councilman Bill Henry has started reviving controversial legislation that would force developers and contractors to give preference to union labor. The legislation requires contractors to give preference to city workers in order to lower Baltimore's unemployment rate.

17186 ■ "Creativity is Essential in Sagging Relocation Market" in *Crain's Cleveland Business* (Vol. 28, November 5, 2007, No. 44, pp. 19)
Pub: Crain Communications, Inc.
Ed: Christine Gordillo. **Description:** Since Northeast Ohio was headquarters to a number of Fortune 500 companies, residential real estate builders and brokers could count on corporate relocation clients for a steady stream of business. Today, corporations have become more cautious when relocating talent due to the costs involved which has forced industry experts to be more patient and more creative in the ways they attract out-of-town buyers who are likely to be a sure sell.

17187 ■ "The Debt Mountain in Mid-Collapse" in *Canadian Business* (Vol. 83, October 12, 2010, No. 17, pp. 28)
Pub: Rogers Media Ltd.
Ed: Michael McCullough. **Description:** A growing real estate market has made Intrawest ULC's Whistler-Blackcomb resort a model for a booming industry for years. However, resorts are now required to manage themselves better because of the recession. Some mountains are also trimming the cost of labor and cutting peripheral services.

17188 ■ "Delinquent Properties on the Rise" in *Business Courier* (Vol. 27, June 11, 2010, No. 6, pp. 1)
Pub: Business Courier
Ed: Dan Monk. **Description:** Reports show that Cincinnati now ranks in the U.S. Top 20 for its delinquency rate on securitized commercial real estate loans. In December 2009, the region ranked 28th out of 50 cities studied by Trepp LLC. As of May 30, 2010, more than $378 million in commercial mortgage-backed security loans were more than 60 days past due.

17189 ■ "Detroit Residential Market Slows; Bright Spots Emerge" in *Crain's Detroit Business* (Vol. 24, October 6, 2008, No. 40, pp. 11)
Pub: Crain Communications, Inc.
Ed: Daniel Duggan. **Description:** Discusses the state of the residential real estate market in Detroit; although condominium projects receive the most attention, deals for single-family homes are taking place in greater numbers due to financing issues. Buyers can purchase a single family home with a 3.5 percent down payment compared to 20 percent for some condo deals because of the number of first-time homebuyer programs under the Federal Housing Administration.

17190 ■ "Developer Backs Out of Major Bastrop Project" in *Austin Business JournalInc.* (Vol. 28, December 19, 2008, No. 40, pp. 1)
Pub: American City Business Journals
Ed: Kate Harrington. **Description:** Weingarten Realty Investors, a Houston, Texas-based real estate company, has backed out of its contract on more than 1 million square feet of retail space at the County Road 304 and State Highway 71 corner in Bastrop, Texas, according to landowner Tom Brundage. Analysts say that the Bastrop area is not ready for big retail projects.

17191 ■ **"Developer Banks On East Submarket, Slowdown Not a Hinderance"** in *The Business Journal-Serving Greater Tampa Bay* **(August 1, 2008)**
Pub: American City Business Journals, Inc.
Ed: Janet Leiser. **Description:** CLW Industrial Group and Cobalt Industrial REIT II have teamed up to develop a 14-acre area in northeast Hillsborough County, Florida. The $15 million industrial park project includes the 175,000-square-foot New Tampa Commerce Center, scheduled for completion in the first quarter of 2009.

17192 ■ **"Developer Tries to Bring Homes to Buda"** in *Austin Business JournalInc.* **(Vol. 28, December 26, 2008, No. 41, pp. 1)**
Pub: American City Business Journals
Ed: Kate Harrington. **Description:** Real estate developer Jeremiah Venture LP is planning a residential, single-family development on about 600 acres near Buda, Texas. The company also plans to construct a membrane waste treatment plant, and has applied to do land application. However, several groups have come forward to ask for more information on the application due to concerns about soil density.

17193 ■ **"Developer Wins Bout with Bank in Roundabout Way"** in *Tampa Bay Business Journal* **(Vol. 30, January 29, 2010, No. 6, pp. 1)**
Pub: American City Business Journals
Ed: Janet Leiser. **Description:** Developer Donald E. Phillips of Phillips Development and Realty LLC won against the foreclosure filed by First Horizon National Corporation, which is demanding the company to fully pay its $2.9 million loan. Phillips requested that his company pay monthly mortgage and extend the loan's maturity date.

17194 ■ **"Developers Await Hotel"** in *The Business Journal-Portland* **(Vol. 25, July 11, 2008, No. 18, pp. 1)**
Pub: American City Business Journals, Inc.
Ed: Wendy Culverwell. **Description:** Developers are eager to start the construction of a new hotel at the Oregon Convention Center in Portland, Oregon as hey say that the project will help boost the convention center neighborhood. The project, called The Westin Portland at the Convention Center, is partly handled by Ashforth Pacific Inc.

17195 ■ **"Developers Compete for APG Project"** in *Baltimore Business Journal* **(Vol. 27, October 16, 2009, No. 23, pp. 1)**
Pub: American City Business Journals
Ed: Daniel J. Sernovitz. **Description:** Corporate Office Properties Trust has lost the case in Delaware bankruptcy court to prevent rival St. John Properties Inc. from going ahead with its plans to develop the 400 acres at Aberdeen Proving Ground (APG) in Maryland. Both developers have competed for the right to develop the two million square foot business park in APG.

17196 ■ **"Developers Give Big to Mayor's Bid"** in *Boston Business Journal* **(Vol. 29, August 26, 2011, No. 16, pp. 1)**
Pub: American City Business Journals Inc.
Ed: Scott Dance. **Description:** Mayor Stephanie Rawlings-Blake received thousands of dollars in her political campaign from companies of real estate developers who are vying to build key development projects in Baltimore, Maryland. Rawlings-Blake created a major fundraising advantage over other mayoral candidates with the help of those contributions.

17197 ■ **"Developers Give City Dwellings a Modern Spin"** in *Crain's Cleveland Business* **(Vol. 28, November 5, 2007, No. 44, pp. 18)**
Pub: Crain Communications, Inc.
Description: Cleveland is increasingly becoming a canvas for fresh, cutting-edge design due to several recent projects, some at prominent sites.

17198 ■ **"Developers Poised to Pull Trigers"** in *Boston Business Journal* **(Vol. 30, November 12, 2010, No. 42, pp. 1)**
Pub: Boston Business Journal
Ed: Craig M. Douglas. **Description:** Large residential projects are expected to break ground in Boston,

Massachusetts in 2011, as real estate developers expect growth for the industry. Real estate experts expect more than 2,000 rental units to be available by 2011. Information on key real estate projects in Boston is presented.

17199 ■ **"Developers Vie for UWM Dorm"** in *The Business Journal-Milwaukee* **(Vol. 25, July 11, 2008, No. 42, pp. A1)**
Pub: American City Business Journals, Inc.
Ed: Rich Kirchen. **Description:** Eight developers are competing to build a 500- to 700-student residence hall for the University of Wisconsin-Milwaukee. The residence hall will probably be developed within two miles of the main campus. It was revealed that the university's real estate foundation will select the successful bidder on July 25, 2008, and construction will begin by January 2009.

17200 ■ *Dictionary of Real Estate Terms*
Pub: Barron's Educational Series, Incorporated
Ed: Jack P. Friedman, Jack C. Harris, J. Bruce Lindeman. **Released:** October 2008. **Price:** $13.99. **Description:** More than 2,500 real estate terms relating to mortgages and financing, brokerage law, architecture, rentals and leases, property insurance, and more.

17201 ■ **"Docs Might Hold Cure for Real Estate, Banks"** in *Baltimore Business Journal* **(Vol. 28, November 5, 2010, No. 26, pp. 1)**
Pub: Baltimore Business Journal
Ed: Gary Haber. **Description:** Health care providers, including physicians are purchasing their office space instead of renting it as banks lower interest rates to 6 percent on mortgages for medical offices. The rise in demand offers relief to the commercial real estate market. It has also resulted in a boom in building new medical offices.

17202 ■ **"Downtown Evens Tenant Ledger"** in *The Business Journal-Serving Metropolitan Kansas City* **(Vol. 26, July 11, 2008, No. 44, pp. 1)**
Pub: American City Business Journals, Inc.
Ed: Rob Roberts. **Description:** Financial services company PricewaterhouseCoopers will relocate its office from the Broadway Square building, but it will not leave downtown as it signs a long-term lease for a 27,000 square feet of space in Town Pavilion. Town Pavilion is the biggest multitenant office building in downtown. Downtown's market competitiveness is also examined.

17203 ■ **"Downtown Retail Site Sold to ATCO"** in *Austin Business JournalInc.* **(Vol. 29, November 20, 2009, No. 37, pp. 1)**
Pub: American City Business Journals
Ed: Kate Harrington. **Description:** New York-based real estate company ATCO Advisory Services purchased a 13,700 square foot retail space in Austin, Texas from 360 Condominiums. The selection of the retail space, named the Shops at 360 has been attributed to the local tenant mix and its location in downtown Austin. Meanwhile, ATCO may continue investing in the area in the near future.

17204 ■ **"Drawn to York County: Less-Expensive Homes, Good Schools Attract Charlotteans"** in *Charlotte Observer* **(February 4, 2007)**
Pub: Knight-Ridder/Tribune Business News
Ed: Taylor Bright. **Description:** York County, North Carolina offers low-priced homes and good schools, making it attractive to workers and small business.

17205 ■ **"East-Side Real Estate Forum Detours To Grand Rapids"** in *Crain's Detroit Business* **(Vol. 24, October 6, 2008, No. 40, pp. 17)**
Pub: Crain Communications, Inc.
Ed: Daniel Duggan. **Description:** Tom Wackerman was elected chairman of the University of Michigan-Urban Land Institute Real Estate Forum and proposed that the annual conference be held in Grand Rapids due to the brisk economic activity he was finding there; although the idea was initially met with resistance, the plan to introduce East-siders to the West side began receiving more enthusiasm due to

the revitalization of the area, which was once considered to have a bleak outlook. Many are hoping to learn the lessons of those who were able to change a negative economic climate into a positive one in which the cooperation of private business and government can work together to accomplish goals.

17206 ■ **"Economy Hammers Local Builders"** in *Business Courier* **(Vol. 24, February 8, 2008, No. 44, pp. 1)**
Pub: American City Business Journals, Inc.
Ed: Laura Baverman. **Description:** Home builders in Cincinnati, Ohio, have lower revenue and smaller workforces as a result of the housing crisis and economic slowdown. Only four out of the top 25 home builders registered revenue gains, average revenue for 2007 is down 21 percent from 2006 levels, and employment declined by 37 percent from 2006.

17207 ■ **"Economy Peddles Rent In This Cycle"** in *The Business Journal-Serving Metropolitan Kansas City* **(Vol. 26, August 8, 2008, No. 48)**
Pub: American City Business Journals, Inc.
Ed: Ashlee Kieler. **Description:** Rental demand for apartment units in downtown Kansas City, Missouri, is increasing due to the housing crisis, lack of real estate development, and increasing popularity of the downtown area. The downtown area has 7,378 multifamily units as of June 2008, of which 4,114 are rentals.

17208 ■ **"Elevated Status"** in *Business Courier* **(Vol. 24, March 21, 2008, No. 50, pp. 1)**
Pub: American City Business Journals, Inc.
Ed: James Ritchie. **Description:** Overview of Tri-Health Inc.'s growth is presented. Currently, the company's revenue is estimated to be around $1 billion. Since 2004, the company was able to build patient towers, an outpatient facility in Lebanon, and was able to acquire the Group Health Associates physician practice. TriHealth recently hired 500 nurses in order to meet its needs.

17209 ■ **"Embassy Suites Signs On: Dulski Building Developer Lands Anchor Tenant"** in *Business First Buffalo* **(October 26, 2007, pp. 1)**
Pub: American City Business Journals, Inc.
Ed: James Fink. **Description:** Embassy Suites will open a 150-room hotel at the former Dulski Federal Office Building in Buffalo, New York. Bringing in Embassy Suite to the building is hoped to increase the interest of tenants at the building which is being renovated by Uniland Development Company and Acquest Development Company.

17210 ■ **"Eminent Domain Fight Looks Imminent"** in *The Business Journal-Serving Metropolitan Kansas City* **(Vol. 26, August 1, 2008, No. 47)**
Pub: American City Business Journals, Inc.
Ed: Rob Roberts. **Description:** Views and information on the proposed constitutional amendments that will limit the use of eminent domain in Missouri, are presented. The proposals are expected to largely ban the taking of private property for private development. It may be included in a November 4,2008 statewide vote for approval.

17211 ■ **"Empty Office Blues"** in *Business Journal Portland* **(Vol. 26, December 4, 2009, No. 39, pp. 1)**
Pub: American City Business Journals Inc.
Ed: Wendy Culverwell. **Description:** Portland's office vacancy rates could reach almost 15 percent by the end of 2010 due to job reductions and mergers.

17212 ■ **"Everett Dowling"** in *Hawaii Business* **(Vol. 54, August 2008, No. 2, pp. 32)**
Pub: Hawaii Business Publishing
Ed: Jason Ubay. **Description:** Real estate developer Everett Dowling, president of Dowling Company Inc., talks about the company's sustainable management and services. The company's office has been retrofitted to earn a Leadership in Energy and Environmental

Design (LEED) certification. Dowling believes that real estate development can be part of the sustainable solution.

17213 ■ "Everyone Out of the Pool" in Barron's (Vol. 89, July 20, 2009, No. 29, pp. 18)
Pub: Dow Jones & Co., Inc.
Ed: Sandra Ward. **Description:** Shares of Pool Corp. could drop as continued weakness in the housing market weakens the market for swimming pool equipment. The company's shares are trading at $18.29, about 20 times projected 2009 earnings of $0.91 a share.

17214 ■ Everything You Need to Know to Sell By Owner
Pub: FSBO Publishing
Ed: Karen Varnas; Roy Wysack. **Released:** February 2007. **Price:** $19.95. **Description:** Provides the knowledge and strategies required to sell real estate in today's market.

17215 ■ "Evidence Growing of Commercial Real Estate" in Boston Business Journal (Vol. 27, October 5, 2007, No. 36, pp. 1)
Pub: American City Business Journals Inc.
Ed: Michelle Hillman. **Description:** Commercial real estate industry in Boston, Massachusetts is experiencing a downturn in the number of sales transactions. A table on the commercial real estate's value of transactions for the first three quarters from 2004 to 2007 is presented.

17216 ■ "Exxon Mobil Campus 'Clearly Happening'" in Houston Business Journal (Vol. 40, January 15, 2010, No. 36, pp. 1)
Pub: American City Business Journals
Ed: Jennifer Dawson. **Description:** Oil and gas company Exxon Mobil intends to relocate its employees from Houston, Texas and Fairfax, Virginia into a 400-acre site near the town of Spring, Texas. Meanwhile, Exxon Mobil has refused to disclose further details of the relocation plan. Insights from real estate professionals on this relocation plan are examined.

17217 ■ "Eyes to the Sky" in Canadian Business (Vol. 80, March 26, 2007, No. 7, pp. 33)
Pub: Rogers Media
Ed: Joe Castaldo. **Description:** The growth and prices of condominium market in the Canada are analyzed.

17218 ■ "Fifth Third Spinoff" in Business Courier (Vol. 27, July 16, 2010, No. 11, pp. 1)
Pub: Business Courier
Ed: Dan Monk, Steve Watkins. **Description:** Electronic-funds transfer company Fifth Third Solutions (FTPS), a spinoff of Fifth Third Bancorp, is seeking as much as 200,000 square feet of new office space in Ohio. The bank's sale of 51 percent ownership stake to Boston-based Advent International Corporation has paved the way for the growth of FTPS. How real estate brokers' plans have responded to FTPS' growth mode is discussed.

17219 ■ "The Final Piece; Lowe's to Fill Last Big Parcel Near Great Lakes Crossing" in Crain's Detroit Business (March 10, 2008)
Pub: Crain Communications, Inc.
Ed: Daniel Duggan. **Description:** Silverman Development Co. is developing a Lowe's home-improvement store on the last major retail parcel near the intersection of I-75 and Joslyn Road, an area which was once desolate but is now home to several restaurants and other retail facilities.

17220 ■ "Final Player In Big Mortgage Fraud Operation Gets Jail Time" in Boston Business Journal (Vol. 31, May 27, 2011, No. 18, pp. 3)
Pub: Boston Business Journal
Ed: Galen Moore. **Description:** Real estate broker Ralp Appolon has been sentenced to 70 months in prison for wire fraud. Appolon was part of a group that falsified information about property purchase prices. A total of ten mortgage lenders have become victims of the group.

17221 ■ "Final State Budget Is a Mixed Bag of Key Industries" in The Business Journal - Serving Phoenix and the Valley of the Sun (Vol. 28, July 4, 2008, No. 44, pp. 3)
Pub: American City Business Journals, Inc.
Ed: Mike Sunnucks; Patrick O'Grady. **Description:** Approved by Governor Janet Napolitano and passed by the Arizona Legislature, the $9.9 billion state budget is beneficial to some industries in the business community. The tax cap for on Arizona Lottery has been removed which is beneficial to the industry, while the solar energy industry and real estate developers stand to lose from the spending bill. Other details of the finance budget are presented.

17222 ■ "Financing for NNSA Plant Is a Work in Progress" in The Business Journal-Serving Metropolitan Kansas City (October 24, 2008)
Pub: American City Business Journals, Inc.
Ed: Rob Roberts. **Description:** The Kansas City Council approved a development plan for a $500 million nuclear weapons parts plant in south Kansas City. The US Congress approved a $59 million annual lease payment to the plant's developer. Financing for the construction of the plant remains in question as the plant's developers have to shoulder construction costs.

17223 ■ "Finding Room for Financing" in The Business Journal-Serving Metropolitan Kansas City (Vol. 26, August 1, 2008, No. 47, pp. 1)
Pub: American City Business Journals, Inc.
Ed: Rob Roberts. **Description:** Kansas City officials are expecting to receive financing recommendations for a new 1,000-room convention headquarters hotel. The $300-million project could be financed either through private ownership with public subsidies, or through public ownership with tax-exempt bond financing. Other views and information on the project and its expected economic impact, are presented.

17224 ■ "First-Time Homebuyer Credit May Add Some Momentum to Market" in Crain's Cleveland Business (Vol. 30, May 18, 2009, No. 20)
Pub: Crain Communications, Inc.
Ed: Stan Bullard. **Description:** Federal tax credits for first-time homebuyers have increased the number of homes being sold. Details of the tax credit are defined.

17225 ■ FLIP: How to Find, Fix, and Sell Houses for Profit
Pub: McGraw-Hill Inc.
Ed: Rick Villani; Clay Davis. **Released:** December 19, 2006. **Price:** $21.95. **Description:** Advice is given to help find, fix and sell houses for profit.

17226 ■ "Florin Car Dealers Drive Plan" in Sacramento Business Journal (Vol. 25, August 22, 2008, No. 25, pp. 1)
Pub: American City Business Journals, Inc.
Ed: Melanie Turner. **Description:** Automobile dealers in Sacramento, California are working with the city and the business district in planning for future redevelopment in Florin Road. The move stemmed from pressure from the Elk Grove Auto Mall, high fuel prices and the credit crunch. The area has suffered business closures recently.

17227 ■ "Fogg Planning Twinsburg Warehouse Project" in Crain's Cleveland Business (Vol. 28, November 26, 2007, No. 47, pp. 6)
Pub: Crain Communications, Inc.
Ed: Stan Bullard. **Description:** Discusses such projects as the proposed 205,000-square-foot distribution center in the works by Ray Fogg Corporate Properties LLC as well as other industrial real estate developments that are looking to target tenants that need larger spaces.

17228 ■ "For $150 Million Mall, Failure to Launch" in Business Courier (Vol. 24, January 25, 2008, No. 42, pp. 1)
Pub: American City Business Journals, Inc.
Ed: Lisa Biank Fasig. **Description:** Blue Ash-based Bear Creek Capital and Chattanooga, Tennessee-based CBL & Associates Properties had abandoned

their plan to build a mixed-use project in South Lebanon. The construction of the proposed $475 million open-air mall was cancelled when real estate developer CBL failed to secure retailers.

17229 ■ "For Developer, a Boulevard of Golden Dreams" in Globe & Mail (February 10, 2007, pp. B3)
Pub: CTVglobemedia Publishing Inc.
Ed: Elizabeth Church. **Description:** A profile of Ian Gillespie, president of Westbank Projects Corp., including his achievements in the real estate industry which are presented.

17230 ■ "For Kenwood, Cavalry Could Be Close" in Business Courier (Vol. 26, October 2, 2009, No. 23, pp. 1)
Pub: American City Business Journals, Inc.
Ed: Dan Monk. **Description:** New York-based Black-Rock Inc. is believed to be participating in the settlement liens at Kenwood Towne Place, a mixed-use development site in Cincinnati, Ohio. BlackRock may play a key role as an advisor or investor representative to an unnamed investors.

17231 ■ "For Sale: Old Florida Panache" in The Business Journal-Serving Greater Tampa Bay (Vol. 28, July 4, 2008, No. 28, pp. 1)
Pub: American City Business Journals, Inc.
Ed: Jane Meinhardt. **Description:** Linger Lodge, owned by real estate investor and developer Martin Kaplan and Senator Michael Bennett, is now on the market for a sealed bid process facilitated by Levin & Associates. The business partners bought the riverfront property for about $3 million in 2005. Other details on the sale of the property are presented.

17232 ■ The Foreclosure of America: Life Inside Countrywide Home Loans and the Selling of the American Dream
Pub: Berkley Trade/Penguin Group (USA) Inc.
Ed: Adam Michaelson. **Released:** April 6, 2010. **Price:** $16.00. **Description:** An inside look at Countrywide Home Loans and the mortgage crisis.

17233 ■ "Foreclosures Crisis Expected to Significantly Drain Wealth" in Black Enterprise (Vol. 41, September 2010, No. 2, pp. 24)
Pub: Earl G. Graves Publishing Co. Inc.
Description: African American communities will lose billions in wealth because of the current foreclosure crisis. Statistical data included.

17234 ■ "Former Mayor Driving $500 Million Real Estate Equity Fund" in The Business Journal - Serving Phoenix and the Valley of the Sun (Vol. 28, August 15, 2008, No. 50, pp. 1)
Pub: American City Business Journals, Inc.
Ed: Jan Buchholz. **Description:** Paul John, the former mayor of Phoenix, is establishing a $500 million real estate asset management fund. The fund is dubbed Southwest Next Capital Management and has attracted three local partners, namely Joseph Meyer, Jay Michalowski, and James Mullany, who all have background in finance and construction.

17235 ■ "Former Schaefer and Strohminger Dealerships to Hit Auction Block" in Baltimore Business Journal (Vol. 28, September 10, 2010)
Pub: Baltimore Business Journal
Ed: Gary Haber. **Description:** Maryland's real estate developers have a chance to vie for almost 11 acres of prime Baltimore County real estate that are on the auction block. The five properties were once home to Schaefer and Strohminger car dealerships and were located in the county's busiest areas. Other potential uses for the properties are also discussed.

17236 ■ "From Bikes to Building" in Austin Business JournalInc. (Vol. 29, October 30, 2009, No. 34, pp. 1)
Pub: American City Business Journals
Ed: Kate Harrington. **Description:** Tour de France champion Lance Armstrong, Bill Stapleton his long-time agent, and business manager Bart Knaggs have formed a privately held real estate investment

company CSE Realty Parters in Austin, Texas. They see tremendous opportunity in the commercial real estate market in the area.

17237 ▪ "The Furniture Company Wanted to Sell Him Its Buildings-And Close Down. Should He Buy the Company, Too?" in *Inc.* **(November 2007)**
Pub: Gruner & Jahr USA Publishing
Ed: Alex Salkever. **Description:** Rick Detkowski, real estate investor, discusses his decision to purchase the furniture company housed in the buildings he was interested in buying. The property would have cost him between $500,000 to $1 million, he was able to purchase the property and business with its entire inventory of furniture, vehicles, and machinery for $1.8 million.

17238 ▪ "Gables Unveils Plan for Downtown Tower" in *Austin Business JournalInc.* **(Vol. 28, August 8, 2008, No. 21, pp. A1)**
Pub: American City Business Journals
Ed: Jean Kwon. **Description:** Gables Residential plans to develop a residential tower with 220 units and 15,000 square feet of retail and commercial spaces in the Warehouse District in Ohio. The development is expected to start in late 2009 and be completed in 18 to 24 months.

17239 ▪ "Gail Lissner; Vice-President, Appraisal Research Counselors" in *Crain's Chicago Business* **(Vol. 31, May 5, 2008, No. 18, pp. 28)**
Pub: Crain Communications, Inc.
Ed: Phuong Ly. **Description:** Profile of Gail Lissner who is the vice-president of the Appraisal Research Counselors, a company that puts out the quarterly "Residential Benchmark Report," in which Ms. Lissner co-authors and is considered a must-read in the industry. Ms. Lissner has risen to become one of the most sought-after experts on the Chicago market considering real estate.

17240 ▪ "Gateway Delays Start" in *The Business Journal-Serving Metropolitan Kansas City* **(Vol. 27, October 31, 2008, No. 8, pp. 1)**
Pub: American City Business Journals, Inc.
Ed: Rob Roberts. **Description:** Economic problems caused, in part, by the Wall Street crisis has resulted in the setback of a proposed mixed-use redevelopment project, The Gateway. The $307 million project, which includes the Kansas Aquarium, will be delayed due to financing problems. Details of the project are given.

17241 ▪ "Generation Y Driving Portland Multifamily Market" in *Daily Journal of Commerce, Portland* **(October 29, 2010)**
Pub: Dolan Media Newswires
Ed: Nick Bjork. **Description:** Generation Y, young adults between the ages of 18-30, are interested in multifamily residents in the Portland, Oregon area. Developers in the area, particularly North Portland, have recognized this trend and are looking into multifamily investments.

17242 ▪ "Ghazi Insists Downtown Project Still On" in *The Business Journal-Milwaukee* **(Vol. 25, August 1, 2008, No. 45, pp. A1)**
Pub: American City Business Journals, Inc.
Ed: Rich Kirchen. **Description:** Afshin Ghazi remains confident that his $200 million Catalyst project in downtown Milwaukee, Wisconsin, will push through despite financial disputes delaying his EpiCentre project in Charlotte, North Carolina. He added that the Catalyst is on schedule for groundbreaking in the spring of 2009.

17243 ▪ "GL Homes Buys 1,000 Acres in Former Agricultural Reserve" in *Miami Daily Business Review* **(March 26, 2008)**
Pub: ALM Media Inc.
Ed: Polyana da Costa. **Description:** One of the nation's largest home builders, GL Homes, purchased over 1,000 acres of agricultural land in Southern Palm Beach County, Florida. Plans for 554 residential units are detailed.

17244 ▪ "Glendale Pumping $29 Million Into Redevelopment" in *The Business Journal - Serving Phoenix and the Valley of the Sun* **(Vol. 28, August 1, 2008, No. 48, pp. 1)**
Pub: American City Business Journals, Inc.
Ed: Mike Sunnucks. **Description:** Glendale City is planning to invest $29 million to improve city infrastructure like roadways and water and sewer lines over the next five years. Glendale's city council is also planning to hold a workshop on the redevelopment projects in September 2008. Other views and information on the redevelopment project, are presented.

17245 ▪ "GMREB/Analysis of the Resale Market-First Quarter 2007: Year Off to a Great Start" in *Canadian Corporate News* **(May 14, 2007)**
Pub: Comtex News Network Inc.
Description: According to statistics gathered by the Greater Montreal Real Estate Board (GMREB), the Montreal census metropolitan area (CMA) resale market was vigorous in the first quarter of 2007 yielding 10 percent more existing homes being than the first quarter of 2006.

17246 ▪ "GM's Decision to Boot Dealer Prompts Sale" in *Baltimore Business Journal* **(Vol. 27, November 6, 2009, No. 26, pp. 1)**
Pub: American City Business Journals
Ed: Daniel J. Sernovitz. **Description:** General Motors Corporation's (GM) decision to strip Baltimore's Anderson Automotive Group Inc. of its GM franchise has prompted the owner, Bruce Mortimer, to close the automotive dealership and sell the land to a developer. The new project could make way for new homes, a shopping center and supermarket.

17247 ▪ "GM's Mortgage Unit Deal Brings in $9 Billion" in *Globe & Mail* **(March 24, 2006, pp. B3)**
Pub: CTVglobemedia Publishing Inc.
Ed: Shawn McCarthy. **Description:** General Motors Corp. sells General Motors Acceptance Corp.'s commercial real estate division to Kohlberg Kravis Roberts & Co. Five Mile Capital Partners LLC and Goldman Sachs Capital Partners. The reasons behind the deal are presented.

17248 ▪ "Goldbelt Inc.: Targeting Shareholder Development" in *Alaska Business Monthly* **(Vol. 27, October 2011, No. 10, pp. 108)**
Pub: Alaska Business Publishing Company
Ed: Tracy Kalytiak. **Description:** Profile of Goldbelt Inc., the company that has changed its original focus of timber to real estate to tourism and then to government contracting opportunities.

17249 ▪ "A Good Sign for Commercial Real Estate" in *Austin Business JournalInc.* **(Vol. 29, December 18, 2009, No. 41, pp. 1)**
Pub: American City Business Journals
Ed: Kate Harrington. **Description:** Factors that could contribute to the reemergence of the commercial mortgage-backed securities market in Texas are discussed. These securities can potentially boost the commercial real estate market statewide as well as nationwide. Commercial mortgage-backed securities origination in 2009 is worth less that $1 billion, compared with $238 billion in 2008.

17250 ▪ "Green Housing for the Rest of Us" in *Inc.* **(November 2007, pp. 128-129)**
Pub: Gruner & Jahr USA Publishing
Ed: Nitasha Tiku. **Description:** Profile of Full Spectrum NY, real estate developer firm, offering residences at the Kalahari, a green high-rise with state-of-the-art features at a reasonable price.

17251 ▪ "Grin and Bear It" in *Canadian Business* **(Vol. 81, March 3, 2008, No. 3, pp. 53)**
Pub: Rogers Media
Ed: Jeff Sanford. **Description:** Discusses the United States economic downturn, caused by the credit market crisis, which is expected to affect the Canadian economy, as Canada depend on the U.S. for 80 percent of its exports. Economist David Rosenberg

thinks that in 2008, housing prices will decline by 15 percent and gross domestic product growth will slow to 0.8 percent. Other forecasts for Canadian economy are given.

17252 ▪ "Groundbreaking 2.0" in *Philadelphia Business Journal* **(Vol. 30, September 23, 2011, No. 32, pp. 1)**
Pub: American City Business Journals Inc.
Ed: Natalie Kostelni. **Description:** University Place Associates, the developer of 2.0 University Place in West Philadelphia, Pennsylvania, will break ground on a five-story, 97,000-square-foot office building in December 2011. The decision follows the Citizenship and Immigration Services signing of a 15-year lease as anchor tenant.

17253 ▪ "Growth in Fits and Starts" in *Canadian Business* **(Vol. 83, July 20, 2010, No. 11-12, pp. 18)**
Pub: Rogers Media Ltd.
Ed: James Cowan. **Description:** US home sales and manufacturing indicators have dropped and fears of a double-dip recession are widespread. However, a chief economist says that this is endemic to what can be seen after a recession caused by a financial crisis. In Canada, consumer optimism is rising and anxiety over losing one's job is waning.

17254 ▪ "Hard Times for Hard Money" in *Sacramento Business Journal* **(Vol. 25, July 18, 2008, No. 20, pp. 1)**
Pub: American City Business Journals, Inc.
Ed: Michael Shaw. **Description:** Three private lenders who supplied $1 million sued VLD Realty, its associated companies and owners Volodymyr and Leonid Dubinsky accusing them of default after a plan to build two subdivisions fell through. Investigators are finding that borrowers and lenders ignored most rules on private investments on real estate.

17255 ▪ "Hastily Enacted Regulation Will Not Cure Economic Crisis" in *Crain's Chicago Business* **(Vol. 31, May 5, 2008, No. 18, pp. 18)**
Pub: Crain Communications, Inc.
Ed: Stephen P. D'Arcy. **Description:** Policymakers are looking for ways to respond to what is possibly the greatest financial crisis of a generation due to the collapse of the housing market, the credit crisis and the volatility of Wall Street.

17256 ▪ "High-End Blunders" in *Crain's Chicago Business* **(Vol. 31, April 21, 2008, No. 16, pp. 54)**
Pub: Crain Communications, Inc.
Ed: Laura Bianchi. **Description:** Discusses some of the biggest errors sellers make that keep their homes from selling including: pricing too high; expecting to recoup the cost of very high-end amenities and decor; avant-garde decorating; owners that hover when the house is being shown; stripping the home of top-quality light fixtures and hardware and replacing them with inferior versions with the assumption that the new buyer will come in with their own decorator and redo it; and poorly maintained properties.

17257 ▪ "His Place in the Sun" in *Canadian Business* **(Vol. 79, October 23, 2006, No. 21, pp. 77)**
Pub: Rogers Media
Ed: Zena Olijnyk. **Description:** The business interests of Canadian real estate developer Derek Elliott in the Dominican Republic, is discussed.

17258 ▪ "Historic Glenview Homes Could Be Torn Down" in *Chicago Tribune* **(September 25, 2008)**
Pub: McClatchy-Tribune Information Services
Ed: Courtney Flynn. **Description:** Leaders of the Glenview New Church would like to see a buyer emerge who would move and restore two historic homes sitting on the church's property. If a buyer does not come forward the church plans to demolish the homes to make room for condominiums and the expansion of their school.

17259 ■ "HOK Sport May Build Own Practice" in *The Business Journal-Serving Metropolitan Kansas City* (Vol. 26, August 29, 2008, No. 51, pp. 1)
Pub: American City Business Journals, Inc.
Ed: Rob Roberts. Description: HOK Sport Venue Event is considering a spin-off from its parent company, HOK Group Inc. HOK Sport spokeswoman Gina Leo confirms that the firm is exploring structures, including a management buyout. Some of HOK Sport Venue Event's Minnesota projects are discussed.

17260 ■ "Hollander 95 Project Getting Bigger" in *Boston Business Journal* (Vol. 29, September 23, 2011, No. 20, pp. 1)
Pub: American City Business Journals Inc.
Ed: Gary Haber. Description: Hollander 95 Business Park is in for a huge change as its new owners plan a $50 million expansion which calls for building as many as eight more buildings or a total of more than 500,000 square feed. FRP Development bought the site for $4.35 million at a foreclosure sale in July 2010 and is now seeking city approval for an Industrial Planned Unit Development designation.

17261 ■ "Home Prices Sag" in *Crain's Chicago Business* (Vol. 31, April 28, 2008, No. 17, pp. 3)
Pub: Crain Communications, Inc.
Ed: Alby Gallun. Description: Since the slump in the housing market is continuing with no sign of recovery, Chicago-area home prices are poised for an even steeper drop this year. In 2007, the region's home prices fell nearly 5 percent and according to a forecast by Fiserv Inc., they will decline 8.1 percent this year and another 2.2 percent in 2009. Statistical data included.

17262 ■ *Home Staging for Dummies*
Pub: John Wiley and Sons, Inc.
Ed: Christine Rae; Janice Saunders Maresh. Released: May 2008. Price: $19.99. Description: Guide shows how to make improvements room by room in order to generate a higher profit on home sales. The book offers tips to clear clutter and show the home's best features, inspire curb appeal, and how to depersonalize and neutralize every room.

17263 ■ "Homes Stall As Owners Resist Major Price Cuts" in *Crain's Chicago Business* (Vol. 31, April 21, 2008, No. 16, pp. 38)
Pub: Crain Communications, Inc.
Ed: Kevin Davis. Description: Discusses the high-end housing market and the owners who are resisting major price cuts as well as the buyers who look at long market times as a sign that something is wrong with the property.

17264 ■ "House Prices Cooling Off, With Alberta Gearing Down" in *Globe & Mail* (February 9, 2007, pp. B4)
Pub: CTVglobemedia Publishing Inc.
Ed: Tavia Grant. Description: The house prices in Alberta, which are experiencing a torrid pace in price growth, are steady in the first month of 2007. The easing in house prices may show impact on inflation.

17265 ■ *The Housing Boom and Bust*
Pub: Basic Books
Ed: Thomas Sowell. Price: $24.95. Description: An explanation of the economics and politics of the housing boom and its collapse.

17266 ■ "Housing Market Dinged, But Not Done In, By Nationwide Slump" in *Business Review, Albany New York* (Vol. 34, December 21, 2007)
Pub: American City Business Journals, Inc.
Ed: Michael DeMasi. Description: Kirsten Keefe, a staff attorney of the Empire Justice Center, is questioning the validity of statistics that represent the number of home foreclosures in New York.

17267 ■ "Housing Markets Still Struggling" in *Montana Business Quarterly* (Vol. 49, Spring 2011, No. 1, pp. 17)
Pub: Bureau of Business & Economic Research
Ed: Scott Rickard. Description: Montana's economic conditions are a bit better than national averages.

Data ranked by state, year-over-year price change, and total price peak is presented, along with statistical data for the entire nation.

17268 ■ "Housing Slide Picks Up Speed" in *Crain's Chicago Business* (Vol. 31, April 21, 2008, No. 16, pp. 2)
Pub: Crain Communications, Inc.
Ed: Eddie Baeb. Description: According to Tracy Cross & Associates Inc., a real estate consultancy, sales of new homes in the Chicago area dropped 61 percent from the year-earlier period which is more bad news for homebuilders, contractors and real estate agents who are eager for an indication that market conditions are improving.

17269 ■ *How to Open and Operate a Financially Successful Redesign, Redecorating, and Home Staging Business: With Companion CD-ROM*
Pub: Atlantic Publishing Group, Inc.
Ed: Mary Larsen; Teri B. Clark. Released: January 2008. Price: $39.95 paperback. Description: Questions are asked to help individuals determine if they should launch their own redesign or real estate staging firm.

17270 ■ "ICC Works on Prescriptive Green Construction Code" in *Contractor* (Vol. 56, October 2009, No. 10, pp. 1)
Pub: Penton Media, Inc.
Ed: Robert P. Mader. Description: International Code Council launched an initiative to create a green construction code that focuses on existing commercial buildings. The initiative's timeline will include public meetings leading up to a final draft that will be available in 2010.

17271 ■ "Illinois Farmland Tops $11,000 Per Acre" in *Farm Industry News* (June 27, 2011)
Pub: Penton Business Media Inc.
Ed: Karen McMahon. Description: Farmland property in Illinois continues to grow in value, selling for $11,000 per acre. Statistical data included.

17272 ■ "IMRA's Ultrafast Lasers Bring Precision, profits; Ann Arbor Company Eyes Expansion" in *Crain's Detroit Business* (March 10, 2008)
Pub: Crain Communications, Inc.
Ed: Tom Henderson. Description: IMRA America Inc. plans to expand its headquarters and has applied for permits to build a fourth building that will house research and development facilities and allow the company more room for manufacturing; the company plans to add about 20 more employees that would include research scientists, manufacturing and assembly workers, engineers and salespeople. The growth is due mainly to a new technology of ultrafast fiber lasers that reduce side effects for those getting eye surgeries and help manufacturers of computer chips to reduce their size and cost.

17273 ■ "In Control: Tips For Navigating a Buyer's Market" in *Black Enterprise* (Vol. 38, December 2007, No. 5, pp. 64)
Pub: Earl G. Graves Publishing Co. Inc.
Ed: Erinn R. Johnson. Description: Tips are given to help would-be home buyers. The importance of finding a good real estate agent is stressed.

17274 ■ "Incentives Debate Rages On Unabated" in *The Business Journal-Serving Metropolitan Kansas City* (Vol. 26, September 5, 2008, No. 52)
Pub: American City Business Journals, Inc.
Ed: Rob Roberts. Description: Debate on the new economic development and incentives policy adopted by the Kansas City Council is still on. The city's Planned Industrial Expansion Authority has rejected a standard property tax abatement proposal. The real estate development community has opposed the rejection of proposed the tax incentives policy.

17275 ■ "Incubator Cooking Up Expansion Plans" in *Business First Columbus* (Vol. 25, December 5, 2008, No. 15, pp.)
Pub: American City Business Journals
Ed: Kevin Kemper. Description: United States-based Science and Technology Campus Corporation is planning to build additional office space in Columbus,

Ohio. The site is designed to accommodate three large tenants. Comment from company executives are presented.

17276 ■ "Independence's Day Keeps on Getting Brighter" in *Business Courier* (Vol. 27, June 11, 2010, No. 6, pp. 1)
Pub: Business Courier
Ed: Lucy May. Description: Reports show that residential and commercial development continues in Independence, Kentucky despite the recession, with a 144-unit apartment complex under construction. The city recorded 152 new-home closings in 2009, or 25 percent of all new homes closed in Boone, Campbell, and Kenton counties.

17277 ■ "Industrial RE Market Shows Signs of Health" in *Business Courier* (Vol. 27, August 20, 2010, No. 16, pp. 1)
Pub: Business Courier
Ed: Jon Newberry. Description: Cincinnati, Ohio's industrial real estate sector has experienced growth during the first half of 2010. The industry has seen a large net loss of occupied space in 2009.

17278 ■ "Industrial Vacancies Hit High; Economic Downturn Taking Toll on Area's Demand for Space" in *Crain's Chicago Business* (Apr. 21, 2008)
Pub: Crain Communications, Inc.
Ed: Alby Gallun. Description: Hitting its highest level in four years in the first quarter is the Chicago-area industrial vacancy rate, a sign that the slumping economy is depressing demand for warehouse and manufacturing space.

17279 ■ "Inflation Woes: Secure Your Portfolio Against Rising Prices" in *Black Enterprise* (Vol. 37, January 2007, No. 6, pp. 40)
Pub: Earl G. Graves Publishing Co. Inc.
Ed: Donald Jay Korn. Description: Inflation has a huge impact on investing and it is important to take the steady increase on cost into account when looking at your financial goals and investing in your future. Statistical data included.

17280 ■ "Inventory Glut" in *Business Courier* (Vol. 24, March 28, 2008, No. 51, pp. 1)
Pub: American City Business Journals, Inc.
Ed: Laura Baverman. Description: Indian Hill and the downtown area have the highest monthly absorption rate for housing on a list of 42 Greater Cincinnati and Northern Kentucky neighborhoods. The two neighborhoods have 19 and 27 months of housing inventory respectively, which means home sellers need to either lower their prices or be very patient.

17281 ■ "Investors Eye Old Buildings" in *Business Journal-Portland* (Vol. 24, October 19, 2007, No. 34, pp. 1)
Pub: American City Business Journals, Inc.
Ed: Wendy Culverwell. Description: Office vacancy rates in downtown Portland has dipped to around five percent, causing brokers and investors to search for older buildings in the Class B and Class C categories where the rent is also cheaper. Some notable older and cheaper buildings will be renovated for use.

17282 ■ "Investors Sue Jackson Properties for Fraud, Breach of Contract" in *The Business Journal - Serving Phoenix and the Valley of the Sun* (Vol. 28, July 18, 2008, No. 46, pp. 1)
Pub: American City Business Journals, Inc.
Ed: Jan Buchholz. Description: Investors sued Jackson Properties EVB Inc. and Jackson Properties EVB LLC for fraud and breach of contract over a botched housing development deal. The investors also filed a complaint before the Arizona Corporation Commission. The investors stand to lose $8 million from the halted development deal.

17283 ■ "Is this a Buying Opportunity?" in *Canadian Business* (Vol. 82, April 27, 2009, No. 7, pp. 46)
Pub: Rogers Media
Ed: Andy Holloway. Description: Home prices in Canada are down by as much as 14.2 percent in 2009 compared to prices in 2008, making homes

more affordable now. Some housing experts believe that homes are still good investments as prices of rent and properties always recover. Meanwhile, a survey found that Canadians under 35 plan to buy a home within two years.

17284 ■ "Jennifer Hernandez Helps Developers Transform Contaminated Properties" in *Hispanic Business* **(Vol. 30, April 2008, No. 4, pp. 32)**

Pub: Hispanic Business

Ed: Hildy Medina. **Description:** Jennifer Hernandez is a partner and head of the law firm of Holland & Knight's environmental practice which specializes in the restoration of polluted land where former industrial and commercial buildings once stood, known as brownfields. Brownfield redevelopment can be lucrative but costly due to the cleaning up of contaminated land and challenging because of federal and state environmental laws.

17285 ■ "Karen Case; President of Commercial Real Estate Lending, Privatebancorp Inc." in *Crain's Chicago Business* **(May 5, 2008)**

Pub: Crain Communications, Inc.

Ed: Dee Gill. **Description:** Profile of Karen Case who was hired by PrivateBancorp Inc. to turn its minor share of the city's commercial real estate lending market into a major one.

17286 ■ "KC Presents Healthy Market for Medical REIT" in *Business Journal-Serving Metropolitan Kansas City* **(Vol. 26, November 30, 2007)**

Pub: American City Business Journals, Inc.

Ed: Rob Roberts. **Description:** Medical Properties Trust, the only real estate investment trust that specializes in buying hospitals, is planning to invest in Kansas City due to its fast growing hospital market. The company owns 29 properties nationwide and is still planning to increase its portfolio.

17287 ■ "Kenosha 'Lifestyle Center' Delayed" in *The Business Journal-Milwaukee* **(Vol. 25, August 8, 2008, No. 46, pp. A1)**

Pub: American City Business Journals, Inc.

Ed: Rich Kirchen. **Description:** Quality Centers of Orlando, Florida has postponed construction plans for the Kenosha Town Center in Kenosha County, Wisconsin to 2009 due to the economic downturn and leasing concerns. The $200-million, 750,000-square-foot retail and residential center will be located near the corner of Wisconsin Highway 50 and I-94.

17288 ■ "Kent Officials Seek Further KSU, City Unity" in *Crain's Cleveland Business* **(Vol. 28, December 3, 2007, No. 48, pp. 3)**

Pub: Crain Communications, Inc.

Ed: Jay Miller. **Description:** Kent State University and Portage County are searching for a developer who will use a three-acre parcel to bring new life to the city's sagging downtown and create an area that will better link the town and the Kent State campus. The project will include a hotel and conference center as well as retail and restaurant space.

17289 ■ "Kimball Hill Files for Chapter 11" in *Crain's Chicago Business* **(Vol. 31, April 28, 2008, No. 17, pp. 12)**

Pub: Crain Communications, Inc.

Description: Homebuilder Kimball Hill filed for Chapter 11 bankruptcy protection after months of negotiations with lenders. The firm plans to continue operations as it restructures its debt.

17290 ■ "The Kitchen is Closed; Eateries Forced Out by Soaring Rents, Declining Revenues" in *Crain's New York Business* **(January 21, 2008)**

Pub: Crain Communications, Inc.

Ed: Lisa Fickenscher. **Description:** Many restaurants have already closed in the area and experts expect many more will follow due to skyrocketing rents and declining revenues.

17291 ■ "Kubicki Juggles Lineup at Vianda" in *Business Courier* **(Vol. 26, December 11, 2009, No. 33, pp. 1)**

Pub: American City Business Journals, Inc.

Ed: Dan Monk. **Description:** Cincinnati real estate developer Chuck Kubicki replaced the management team of Vianda LLC and cancelled contracts with two vendors that caused a surge of customer complaints. Vianda is a direct-response marketing firm that sells and distributes dietary supplements for wellness and sexual performance.

17292 ■ "KXAN Seeks Larger Studio, Office Space" in *Austin Business Journal* **(Vol. 31, May 27, 2011, No. 12, pp. A1)**

Pub: American City Business Journals Inc.

Ed: Cody Lyon. **Description:** Austin NBC affiliate KXAN Television is opting to sell its property north of downtown and relocate to another site. The station is now inspecting possible sites to house its broadcasting facility and employees totaling as many as 200 people. Estimated cost of the construction of the studios and offices is $13 million plus another million in moving the equipment.

17293 ■ "Land Agent Taken Over" in *Farmer's Weekly* **(March 28, 2008, No. 320)**

Pub: Reed Business Information

Description: Property business Smiths Gore will take over Cluttons' rural division, one of the oldest names in land agency. Cluttons said it had decided to sell its rural business as part of a strategic repositioning that would refocus the business on commercial, residential and overseas opportunities.

17294 ■ "Land on Boardwalk" in *Canadian Business* **(Vol. 82, April 27, 2009, No. 7, pp. 19)**

Pub: Rogers Media

Ed: Calvin Leung. **Description:** Boardwalk REIT remains as one of the most attractive real estate investment trusts in Canada, with 73 percent of analysts rating the firm a Buy. Analyst Neil Downey believes that good management, as well as a good business model, makes Boardwalk a good investment. Downey is concerned however, that a worsening of Alberta's economy could significantly impact Boardwalk.

17295 ■ "Landlord Puts 7 Tops Locations On Market" in *Business First Buffalo* **(November 16, 2007, pp. 1)**

Pub: American City Business Journals, Inc.

Ed: James Fink. **Description:** New York-based Benesen Capital Partners LLC has put its 388,000-square-foot property up for sale. Seven Tops Grocery Markets have two to nine years remaining on their lease contracts.

17296 ■ "Laugh or Cry?" in *Barron's* **(Vol. 88, March 24, 2008, No. 12, pp. 7)**

Pub: Dow Jones & Company, Inc.

Ed: Alan Abelson. **Description:** Discusses the American economy which is just starting to feel the effect of the credit and housing crises. JPMorgan Chase purchased Bear Stearns for $2 a share, much lower than its share price of $60, while quasi-government entities Fannie Mae and Freddie Mac are starting to run into trouble.

17297 ■ *Law for the Small and Growing Business*

Pub: Jordans Publishing Limited

Ed: P. Bohm. **Released:** February 2007. **Price:** $59. 98. **Description:** Legal and regulatory issues facing small businesses, including employment law, health and safety, commercial property, company law and finance are covered.

17298 ■ "Leaning Tower" in *Business Courier* **(Vol. 27, June 4, 2010, No. 5, pp. 1)**

Pub: Business Courier

Ed: Jon Newberry. **Description:** New York-based developer Armand Lasky, owner of Tower Place Mall in downtown Cincinnati, Ohio has sued Birmingham, Alabama-based Regions Bank to prevent the bank's foreclosure on the property. Regions Bank claims Lasky was in default on an $18 million loan agreement. Details on the mall's leasing plan is also discussed.

17299 ■ "Leasing Midway; Look for Higher Parking Fees, More Retail Under Private Airport Operator" in *Crain's Chicago Business* **(May 5, 2008)**

Pub: Crain Communications, Inc.

Ed: Paul Merrion. **Description:** According to experts, bids for the first privatization of a major U.S. airport could run as high as $3.5 billion. Information-gathering and negotiations will soon get under way with some or all of the six major international investor groups that recently expressed interest in running Midway.

17300 ■ "Legacy Hotels Looks for a Buyer" in *Globe & Mail* **(March 2, 2007, pp. B3)**

Pub: CTVglobemedia Publishing Inc.

Ed: Elizabeth Church. **Description:** Legacy Hotels Real Estate Investment Trust, which has a portfolio of 25 properties, plans to sell its businesses. The shares of the real estate investment trust climbed $13.21, as the sales news was delivered.

17301 ■ "Legislature Passes Increased Tax Credit for Urban Brownfield Projects" in *Crain's Detroit Business* **(Vol. 24, March 31, 2008, No. 13)**

Pub: Crain Communications, Inc.

Ed: Amy Lane. **Description:** Discusses the bill passed by the Legislature that creates a tax credit of up to 20 percent for projects in urban development areas.

17302 ■ "Lenders" in *The Business Journal - Serving Phoenix and the Valley of the Sun* **(Vol. 28, July 25, 2008, No. 47, pp. 1)**

Pub: American City Business Journals, Inc.

Ed: Jan Buchholz. **Description:** Private equity lender Investor Mortgage Holdings Inc. has continued growing despite the crisis surrounding the real estate and financial industries and has accumulated a $700 million loan portfolio. Private lending has become increasingly important in financing real estate deals as commercial credit has dried up.

17303 ■ "Local Commercial Real Estate Foreclosures Continue to Rise" in *Baltimore Business Journal* **(Vol. 28, October 1, 2010, No. 21, pp. 1)**

Pub: Baltimore Business Journal

Ed: Daniel J. Sernovitz. **Description:** Foreclosures of commercial real estate across the Greater Baltimore area have continued to rise. The region is now host to about $2 billion worth of commercial properties that carry a maturing debt or have been foreclosed. Commercial real estate owners are unable to finance their debts because banks have become stricter in passing out loans.

17304 ■ "Local Industrial Vacancies Climb" in *Crain's Chicago Business* **(Vol. 31, November 17, 2008, No. 46, pp. 18)**

Pub: Crain Communications, Inc.

Ed: Eddie Baeb. **Description:** Demand for local industrial real estate has declined dramatically as companies that use warehouse and factory space struggle to survive in an ailing economy. According to a report by Colliers Bennett & Kahnweiler Inc., a commercial real estate brokerage, the regional vacancy rate has risen to 9.86 percent in the third quarter, the fourth straight increase and the highest in the past 14 years.

17305 ■ "Lytle Place Listing Seen as Bellweather" in *Business Courier* **(Vol. 27, December 3, 2010, No. 31, pp. 1)**

Pub: Business Courier

Ed: Dan Monk. **Description:** Denver, Colorado-based Apartment Investment and Management Company (AIMCO) has offered the 25-story One Lytle Place Apartments for sale through CB Richard Ellis for the third time in three years. The potential sale could define the recovery for Cincinnati, Ohio's struggling apartment industry.

17306 ■ "Major Renovation Planned for Southridge" in *Business Journal-Milwaukee* **(Vol. 28, November 12, 2010, No. 6, pp. A1)**
Pub: Milwaukee Business Journal

Ed: Stacy Vogel Davis. **Description:** Simon Property Group plans to invest more than $20 million in upgrading and renovating Southridge Mall in Milwaukee County, Wisconsin. The project, which is partially financed by a $10 million grant from the Village of Greendale, could boost the property's value by $52.5 million.

17307 ■ "Major Tech Employers Pulling Out" in *Sacramento Business Journal* **(Vol. 25, August 1, 2008, No. 22, pp. 1)**
Pub: American City Business Journals, Inc.

Ed: Celia Lamb. **Description:** Biotechnology company Affymetrix Inc. is planning to close its West Sacramento, California plant and lay off 110 employees. The company said it will expand a corporate restructuring plan. Affymetrix also plans to lease out or sell its building at Riverside Parkway.

17308 ■ "Making the Cut; Osprey Takes Undervalued Courses to the Leader Board" in *Crain's Detroit Business* **(Vol. 24, April 7, 2008, No. 14)**
Pub: Crain Communications, Inc.

Ed: Jason Deegan. **Description:** Profile of Osprey Management Co., a diverse real estate company that continues to expand its golf portfolio through the company's recreation division; although many developers are getting out of the field due to Michigan's sluggish golf industry, Osprey has found success by purchasing properties in turmoil for more affordable prices.

17309 ■ "Mandel Site Favored For UWM Hall" in *The Business Journal-Milwaukee* **(Vol. 25, September 19, 2008, No. 52, pp. A1)**
Pub: American City Business Journals, Inc.

Description: University of Wisconsin-Milwaukee student residence hall's leading location is a site pushed by Mandel Group Inc. Real estate sources say that the developer's proposal offers the best opportunity for business development and the least conflict with nearby neighborhoods. Plans for the Mandel site are presented.

17310 ■ "Mann to Lead Builders" in *Charlotte Observer* **(January 31, 2007)**
Pub: Knight-Ridder/Tribune Business News

Ed: Allen Norwood. **Description:** Elliot Mann of Standard Pacific Homes was sworn in as president of Home Builders Association of Charlotte, North Carolina.

17311 ■ "Marine Act Amendments Gain Parliamentary Approval" in *Canadian Sailings* **(July 7, 2008)**
Pub: Commonwealth Business Media

Ed: Alex Binkley. **Description:** Changes to the Canada Marine Act provides better borrowing deals as well as an ability to tap into federal infrastructure funding for environmental protection measures, security improvements and other site enhancements.

17312 ■ "Market Gamble" in *Business Journal-Serving Phoenix and the Valley of the Sun* **(Vol. 5, October 5, 2007, No. 28, pp. 1)**
Pub: American City Business Journals, Inc.

Ed: Mike Padgett. **Description:** AI-BSR LLC, an Israeli group believes the housing market will regain its strength within three years. The group plans to build its $385 million project, called One Phoenix. The condominiums start at $500,000, with units ranging from 800 to 2,000 square feet.

17313 ■ "Market for Retail Space Flat, but Recovery Still Uncertain" in *Sacramento Business Journal* **(Vol. 28, August 26, 2011, No. 26, pp. 1)**
Pub: Sacramento Business Journal

Ed: Kelly Johnson. **Description:** The retail market in the Sacramento, California region remains challenged with the stock market volatility being the latest of its hurdles. The overall vacancy was 13.1 percent as of mid-2011, but retail real estate professionals express hopes that the worst is behind. A list and description of the region's winners and losers in retail vacancies is provided.

17314 ■ "Market Swings Intensify Yearning for Bonds" in *Globe & Mail* **(March 9, 2007, pp. B9)**
Pub: CTVglobemedia Publishing Inc.

Ed: Keith Damsell. **Description:** The rise in demand for proper fixed-income bonds in Canada as a result of uncertainties in the equity market is discussed. Some big Canadian fixed-income funds are presented.

17315 ■ "Mason Fashions Its Future" in *Business Courier* **(Vol. 24, December 7, 2008, No. 34, pp. 1)**
Pub: American City Business Journals, Inc.

Ed: Laura Baverman. **Description:** Economic Development Director Michele Blair contracted Cincinnati-based Jack Rouse & Associates to tap the remaining undeveloped land in Mason. The real estate firm is set to develop the 2,000 acres of undeveloped land.

17316 ■ "A Matter of Perspective" in *Business Journal-Portland* **(Vol. 24, November 2, 2007, No. 35, pp. 1)**
Pub: American City Business Journals, Inc.

Ed: Andy Giegerich. **Description:** Oregon Governor Ted Kulongoski assembled the Mortgage Lending Work Group, made up of members of the mortgage industry and consumer groups, to recommend possible bills for the Oregon Senate and House to consider. How its members try to balance philosophical differences in mortgage lending rules is discussed.

17317 ■ "McDonald's Founders Fund $80 Million Project" in *The Business Journal - Serving Phoenix and the Valley of the Sun* **(Vol. 28, September 12, 2008, No. 53, pp. 1)**
Pub: American City Business Journals, Inc.

Ed: Jan Buchholz. **Description:** Construction will begin in early 2009 on an $80 million Ray and Joan Kroc Community Center in Phoenix, Arizona. It will be located adjacent to the Salvation Army, which received a $1.9 billion contribution from Joan Kroc after her death in 2003. This fund will be divided to construct 30 community centers across the country.

17318 ■ "Medical Office Developers To Merge November 1" in *The Business Journal - Serving Phoenix and the Valley of the Sun* **(Vol. 29, September 26, 2008, No. 4, pp. 1)**
Pub: American City Business Journals, Inc.

Ed: Angela Gonzales. **Description:** Ensemble Real Estate Services LLC and DevMan Co. will merge effective November 1, 2008 and will call the firm Ensemble DevMan of Arizona after the merger. The two companies will combine their resources and expertise on planned projects that include the Phoenix Children's Hospital's Specialty Clinic and Banner Ironwood Medical Office Building.

17319 ■ "Mequon Plan On Tracks, Bucks Housing Trend" in *The Business Journal-Milwaukee* **(Vol. 25, September 26, 2008, No. 53, pp. A1)**
Pub: American City Business Journals, Inc.

Ed: Pete Millard. **Description:** Insight Development Group plans to build condominium units and single-family homes despite the residential market downturn. The Orchard Glen project, a planned development in Mequon, is a $22 million project which will include 38 condos and 12 single-family homes. Details of the project are provided.

17320 ■ "Midtown Tampa Bay Taking Shape" in *The Business Journal-Serving Greater Tampa Bay* **(Vol. 28, September 12, 2008, No. 38, pp. 1)**
Pub: American City Business Journals, Inc.

Ed: Janet Leiser. **Description:** Midtown Tampa Bay's 610,000 square foot shopping and entertainment center is being planned in Florida and is to replace the Tampa Bay One project proposed years earlier. The retail center is to be developed by Bromley Cos. and Opus South Corp. and is expected to have five buildings. Other details about the plan are discussed.

17321 ■ "Millions Needed To Finish First Place" in *The Business Journal-Milwaukee* **(Vol. 25, August 15, 2008, No. 47, pp. A1)**
Pub: American City Business Journals, Inc.

Ed: Rich Kirchen. **Description:** First Place on the River condominium project in Milwaukee, Wisconsin, needs $18.2 million before it can be completed. A total of $6.8 million have already been spent since the project went into receivership on 31 January 2008.

17322 ■ "Minnesota Farms' Net Worth Grows 10 Percent Each Year for 15 Years" in *Farm Industry News* **(August 22, 2011)**
Pub: Penton Business Media Inc.

Ed: Dale Nordquist. **Description:** The average value of farms in Minnesota is growing at a fast pace. Total assets per farm have increased by more than $1.1 million over the past 15 years. Statistical data included.

17323 ■ "A Model Development" in *Crain's Cleveland Business* **(Vol. 28, October 1, 2007, No. 39, pp. 12)**
Pub: Crain Communications, Inc.

Description: Profile a Forest City Enterprises Inc., a firm that is developing a project in New Mexico called Mesa del Sol. The Albuquerque development is being seen as the vanguard of master-planned communities with its high-tech economic development center which is expected to become the site of 60,000 jobs, 38,000 homes and a town center.

17324 ■ "The Money Train: How Public Projects Shape Our Economic Future" in *Hawaii Business* **(Vol. 54, September 2008, No. 3, pp. 31)**
Pub: Hawaii Business Publishing

Ed: Jason Ubay. **Description:** Public projects impact the construction industry as such projects create jobs and new infrastructure that can lead to private developments. Details on the government contracts and construction projects in Hawaii and their rising costs and impact on the state's economy are discussed.

17325 ■ "More Offices Planned For Percheron Square" in *The Business Journal-Milwaukee* **(Vol. 25, August 22, 2008, No. 48, pp. A1)**
Pub: American City Business Journals, Inc.

Ed: Pete Millard. **Description:** More office projects are under way at Percheron Square. Ryan Cos. US Inc., for example, plans to build over 200,000 square feet of office space at the area. Details of new office projects in Wisconsin are presented.

17326 ■ "Mortgage Mess: How To Determine Your Exposure To the Subprime Crisis" in *Black Enterprise* **(Vol. 38, November 2007, No. 4, pp. 46)**
Pub: Earl G. Graves Publishing Co. Inc.

Ed: Ilana Polyak. **Description:** Stocks and mutual funds have experienced declines because of the subprime crisis. Morningstar's Website can help investors research firms in which they have invested; if a fund is named high yield or high income or in the financial services sector, investments will have greater exposure to the mess.

17327 ■ "Mortgage Securities Drop Hits Home" in *The Business Journal-Serving Metropolitan Kansas City* **(Vol. 27, October 17, 2008, No. 5)**
Pub: American City Business Journals, Inc.

Ed: Rob Roberts. **Description:** Sale of commercial mortgage-backed securities (CMBS) in Kansas City, Missouri have declined. The area may avoid layoffs if the United States government succeeds in stabilizing the economy. Major CMBS players in the area include Midland Loan Services Inc. and KeyBank Real Estate Capital.

17328 ■ "Mortgages Going Under" in *Black Enterprise* **(Vol. 41, December 2010, No. 5, pp. 20)**
Pub: Earl G. Graves Publishing Co. Inc.

Description: Nearly one-fifth of the country's homeowners are underwater in their mortgages, which means they owe more on their home than the home's worth. Statistical data included.

17329 ■ "Museum Center to Exhibit New Look" in *Business Courier* (Vol. 24, February 22, 2008, No. 46, pp. 1)
Pub: American City Business Journals, Inc.
Ed: Dan Monk. **Description:** Discusses a $120 million renovation is being planned for the Cincinnati Museum Center complex at Union Terminal. The project aims to build a 14-acre park and office spaces in the area. Details of the Museum Center's renovation plans are given.

17330 ■ "Neighborhood Watch" in *Baltimore Business Journal* (Vol. 28, July 23, 2010, No. 11, pp. 1)
Pub: Baltimore Business Journal
Ed: Daniel J. Sernovitz. **Description:** Maryland government and housing leaders are set to spend $100 million in federal funding to stem the increase in foreclosures in the area. The federal funding is seen as inadequate to resolve the problem of foreclosures.

17331 ■ "The Neighborhood Watch" in *Hawaii Business* (Vol. 53, March 2008, No. 9, pp. 36)
Pub: Hawaii Business Publishing
Ed: David K. Choo. **Description:** OahuRe.com offers information on Hawaii real estate market, with spreadsheets and comparative market analysis page, which shows properties that are active, sold, or in escrow. Other details about OahuRe.com are discussed. A list of other top real estate websites in Hawaii and in the U.S. in general is provided.

17332 ■ "New-Home Sales Grab a Foothold With Q2 Boost" in *Sacramento Business Journal* (Vol. 25, July 11, 2008, No. 19, pp. 1)
Pub: American City Business Journals, Inc.
Ed: Michael Shaw. **Description:** Statistics show that homebuilders in Sacramento, California experienced an increase in new-home sales during the second quarter of 2008. It was also reported that builders moved more homes without slashing prices significantly. Barry Grant, president of KB Home's Sacramento division, believes that the improvement is caused by the stability in the supply of resale homes.

17333 ■ "A New Mix of Tenants Settles In" in *Crain's New York Business* (Vol. 24, January 14, 2008, No. 2, pp. 26)
Pub: Crain Communications, Inc.
Ed: Andrew Marks. **Description:** More and more nonfinancial firms are relocating downtown due to the new retailers and restaurants that are reshaping the look and feel of lower Manhattan.

17334 ■ "New York City-Based New Street Realty Advisors has Secured a New Flagship for David's Bridal" in *Chain Store Age* (August 2008)
Pub: Chain Store Age
Description: New York City-based New Street Realty Advisors secured a new flagship store for David's Bridal in the Chelsea district of Manhattan. David's Bridal will occupy 12,800 square feet on two floors in a retail condominium development.

17335 ■ "New York Firm Secures Sheffield, Amherst Centers for $26 Million" in *Crain's Cleveland Business* (Vol. 28, December 3, 2007, No. 48)
Pub: Crain Communications, Inc.
Ed: Stan Bullard. **Description:** Silverman Realty Group completed a $26 million transaction which made it the new owner of the Sheffield Crossing and Amherst Marketplace shopping centers in Lorain County.

17336 ■ "The Next Government Bailout?" in *Barron's* (Vol. 88, March 10, 2008, No. 10, pp. 21)
Pub: Dow Jones & Company, Inc.
Ed: Jonathan Laing. **Description:** Fannie Mae may need a government bailout as it faces huge hits brought about by the effects of the housing crisis. The shares of the government-sponsored enterprise have dropped 65 percent since the housing crisis began.

17337 ■ "The Next Real Estate Boom" in *Canadian Business* (Vol. 80, March 26, 2007, No. 7, pp. 25)
Pub: Rogers Media
Ed: Erik Heinrich. **Description:** The better places to invest in Canadian real estate market are presented. The future price performance of the industry is analyzed.

17338 ■ "N.H. Near the LEED in Green Space" in *New Hampshire Business Review* (Vol. 33, March 25, 2011, No. 6, pp. 30)
Pub: Business Publications Inc.
Description: New Hamphire's architects, contractors and suppliers are among the leaders with LEED-certified space per capita.

17339 ■ "No Wild Highs Means No Wild Lows" in *Business Courier* (Vol. 24, January 18, 2008, No. 41, pp. 1)
Pub: American City Business Journals, Inc.
Ed: Laura Baverman. **Description:** Discusses a PMI Group report which revealed that the Greater Cincinnati area is in the lowest risk category for home value declines. The report forecast that the chance that housing prices in the area will fall below their current status by the year 2010 is less than 5 percent. Housing price forecasts for other areas are also provided.

17340 ■ "Not Enough To Go Around" in *The Business Journal-Milwaukee* (Vol. 25, August 15, 2008, No. 47, pp. A1)
Pub: American City Business Journals, Inc.
Ed: David Doege. **Description:** Most of the creditors of bankrupt real estate developer Scott Fergus are likely to remain unpaid as he only has an estimated $30,000 available for paying debts. Creditors, as of the 13 August 2008 deadline for filing claims, have filed a total of $79.1 million in claims.

17341 ■ "Not In My Backyard" in *Entrepreneur* (Vol. 36, May 2008, No. 5, pp. 42)
Pub: Entrepreneur Media, Inc.
Ed: Farnoosh Torabi. **Description:** More investors are turning to overseas real estate investments as the U.S. market sees a slowdown. Analysts say that risk-averse investors opt for funds with record of strong returns and U.S. real estate investment trusts that partner with foreign businesses for transparency purposes. Other details about foreign real estate investments are discussed.

17342 ■ "Number of Mechanic's Liens Triple Since 2005" in *The Business Journal - Serving Phoenix and the Valley of the Sun* (Vol. 28, August 22, 2008, No. 51, pp. 1)
Pub: American City Business Journals, Inc.
Ed: Jan Buchholtz. **Description:** Experts are blaming the mortgage and banking industries for the tripling of mechanic's liens that were filed in Arizona from 2005 through August 6, 2008. The rise in mechanic's liens is believed to indicate stress in the real estate community. Other views and information on the rise of mechanic's liens filed in Arizona are presented.

17343 ■ "N.Y. Group Top Bidder for Last Duke Sites" in *Crain's Cleveland Business* (Vol. 28, November 19, 2007, No. 46, pp. 1)
Pub: Crain Communications, Inc.
Ed: Stan Bullard. **Description:** Overview of the possible portfolio sale of Duke Realty Corp.'s last Northeast Ohio properties, 14 office buildings in Independence, Seven Hills and North Olmsted, believed to be purchased by a real estate investor group led by Nightingale Properties LLC of New York.

17344 ■ "October 2009: Recovery Plods Along" in *Hispanic Business* (October 2009, pp. 10-11)
Pub: Hispanic Business
Ed: Dr. Juan Solana. **Description:** Economist reports on a possible economic recovery which will not be allowed to rely on a strong domestic demand in order to sustain it. Consumers, looking to counterbalance years of leverage financing based on unrealistic, ever-increasing home and portfolio valuations, are saving rather than spending money.

17345 ■ "Office Leasing Gains Ground" in *Sacramento Business Journal* (Vol. 25, July 18, 2008, No. 20, pp. 1)
Pub: American City Business Journals, Inc.
Ed: Michael Shaw. **Description:** There were at least 84,000 square feet leased to companies in the Sacramento area in the three months prior to August 2008. This development is good news considering that overall vacant leases were around 247,000 square feet for the previous quarter.

17346 ■ "Office Market May Turn Down" in *Crain's New York Business* (Vol. 24, January 14, 2008, No. 2, pp. 26)
Pub: Crain Communications, Inc.
Description: Although still dominated by Wall Street, the downturn in the economy is raising fears that the continuing fallout from the subprime mortgage crisis could result in layoffs that will derail the office market.

17347 ■ "Ohio's Reputation Lags Its Business Ranking" in *Business Courier* (Vol. 24, November 23, 2008, No. 32, pp. 1)
Pub: American City Business Journals, Inc.
Ed: Jon Newberry. **Description:** Site Selection magazine's annual ranking of the top states for new business facilities has ranked Ohio and Kentucky in seventh and eight place respectively, but an opinion survey of real estate executives had placed Ohio much lower at 14. The survey asked 6,000 executives if Ohio's conditions were best for new building projects.

17348 ■ "Old Ford Plant to Sign New Tenants" in *Business Courier* (Vol. 27, August 13, 2010, No. 15, pp. 1)
Pub: Business Courier
Ed: Dan Monk. **Description:** Ohio Realty Advisors LLC, a company handling the marketing of the 1.9 million-square-foot former Ford Batavia plant is on the brink of landing one distribution and three manufacturing firms as tenants. These tenants are slated to occupy about 20 percent of the facility and generate as many as 250 jobs in Ohio.

17349 ■ "O'Reilly Will Soup Up KC Warehouse" in *The Business Journal-Serving Metropolitan Kansas City* (Vol. 26, August 15, 2008, No. 49)
Pub: American City Business Journals, Inc.
Ed: Rob Roberts. **Description:** O'Reilly Automotive Inc. plans to construct a 215,000-square foot warehouse in Kansas City. The move is expected to triple the size of the company's distribution center. Other views and information on the planned warehouse construction, are presented.

17350 ■ "Ottawa's Real Estate Targets Exceed Market Appraisals" in *Globe & Mail* (March 19, 2007, pp. B1)
Pub: CTVglobemedia Publishing Inc.
Ed: Danier Leblanc. **Description:** The growth in the real estate market in Ottawa and the huge revenue the government is expecting from sale of nine buildings as part of its lease back plan is discussed.

17351 ■ "Out With the Old? City Officials Investigating Options for New Hopkins Hotel" in *Crain's Cleveland Business* (October 22, 2007)
Pub: Crain Communications, Inc.
Ed: Jay Miller. **Description:** Cleveland officials have begun talks that could lead to a new hotel which would replace the aging, nine-story Sheraton Cleveland Hopkins Hotel at Cleveland Hopkins International Airport.

17352 ■ "Outlook 2007" in *Canadian Business* (Vol. 80, December 25, 2006, No. 1, pp.)
Pub: Rogers Media
Ed: David Wolf. **Description:** Economists' 2007 forecast on global economy, particularly about Canada's housing and labor market among other sectors, is discussed.

17353 ■ "Outside Investors Hot On Detroit Commercial Real Estate" in *Crain's Detroit Business* **(Vol. 24, January 28, 2008, No. 4, pp. 25)**
Pub: Crain Communications Inc. - Detroit
Ed: Daniel Duggan. Description: An overview of out-of-town investors seeking to purchase commercial real estate in Michigan is presented. Statistical data included.

17354 ■ "Pain Ahead as Profit Pressure Increases" in *Crain's Chicago Business* **(Vol. 31, May 5, 2008, No. 18, pp. 4)**
Pub: Crain Communications, Inc.
Ed: Daniel Rome Levine. Description: Interview with David Klaskin, the chairman and chief investment officer at Oak Ridge Investments LLC, who discusses the outlook for the economy and corporate earnings, particularly in the housing and auto industries, the impact of economic stimulus checks, the weakness of the dollar and recommendations of stocks that individual investors may find helpful.

17355 ■ "The Paper Shredder" in *Business Courier* **(Vol. 26, September 11, 2009, No. 20, pp. 1)**
Pub: American City Business Journals, Inc.
Ed: Dan Monk. Description: DotLoop Company, owned by entrepreneur Austin Allison, is developing the DotLoop software, which eliminates paperwork in the processing of real estate contracts. The software allows realtors to take control of the negotiation process and is adaptable to the rules of different US states.

17356 ■ "Part-Time Office Space" in *Hawaii Business* **(Vol. 53, December 2007, No. 6, pp. 132)**
Pub: Hawaii Business Publishing
Ed: Ashley Hamershock. Description: My Office is one of the companies that are renting space office not only by the month, but by the hour. Such setup is beneficial to small businesses that do not need a whole office all to themselves, and are interested in cutting the cost of office space rental. The prices of office space in Hawaii are mentioned.

17357 ■ "Past Promises Haunt Project" in *The Business Journal-Portland* **(Vol. 25, August 1, 2008, No. 21, pp. 1)**
Pub: American City Business Journals, Inc.
Ed: Aliza Earnshaw. Description: Oregon University System and Oregon Health and Science University will face the state Legislature to defend their request for a $250 million in state bonds to fund a life-sciences collaborative research building. The project is meant to help grow the Oregon bioscience industry. Comments from industry observers and legislators are also presented.

17358 ■ "Pat Modica" in *Crain's Cleveland Business* **(Vol. 30, June 29, 2009, No. 25, pp. 15)**
Pub: Crain Communications, Inc.
Ed: Stan Bullard. Description: Profile of Pat Modica, real estate agent with Howard Hanna. Ms. Modica states that in her 29 years as a residential real estate agent, she has never seen a market like the present one. She discusses home sales and activity for the area.

17359 ■ "Pavilions Poised for Image Overhaul" in *The Business Journal - Serving Phoenix and the Valley of the Sun* **(Vol. 28, August 22, 2008)**
Pub: American City Business Journals, Inc.
Ed: Jan Buchholz. Description: DeRitto Partners Inc. is expected to push through with plans for a major renovation of the 1.1 million-square foot Scottsdale Pavilions in Scottsdale, Arizona. An aggressive marketing campaign is planned to be included in the renovation, which aims to address high vacancy rates and competition. Views and information on the planned renovation are presented.

17360 ■ "Paying for the Recession: Rebalancing Economic Growth" in *Montana Business Quarterly* **(Vol. 49, Spring 2011, No. 1, pp. 2)**
Pub: Bureau of Business & Economic Research
Ed: Patrick M. Barkey. Description: Four key issues required to address in order to rebalance economic

growth in America are examined. They include: savings rates, global trade imbalances, government budgets and most importantly, housing price correction.

17361 ■ *The Peebles Principles: Insights from an Entrepreneur's Life of Business Success, Making Deals, and Creating a Fortune from Scratch*
Pub: John Wiley and Sons Inc.
Ed: R. Donahue Peebles. Released: April 2007. Price: $29.99. Description: Successful entrepreneur shares his business experience. Peebles went from CEO of the nation's largest Black-owned real estate development firm to founding his own firm.

17362 ■ *Peggy's Corner: The Art of Staging*
Pub: Eaton-Moghannam Publishing
Ed: Peggy Selinger-Eaton; Gayla Moghannam. Released: June 2005. Description: Techniques to enhance the value of any home are given. Seven principles of staging a home for sale include making a great first impression, maximizing space and eliminating clutter, using lighting for open spacious feeling, de-emphasize flaws, make the home appealing to buyers with varied tastes, creating warmth, and modernizing the home.

17363 ■ "A Perfect Predator: Brookfield Asset Management Isn't Brash" in *Canadian Business* **(Vol. 83, July 20, 2010, No. 11-12, pp. 50)**
Pub: Rogers Media Ltd.
Ed: Joanna Pachner. Description: Brookfield Asset Management CEO Bruce Flatt manages $108 billion worth of real estate and the company has become one of the world's biggest prime real estate owners since he became leader. Flatt says their goal is to earn a 12-15 percent compound annual return per share and that they would shrink in size if it meant reaching that goal.

17364 ■ "Peter Bynoe Trades Up" in *Black Enterprise* **(Vol. 38, July 2008, No. 12, pp. 30)**
Pub: Earl G. Graves Publishing Co. Inc.
Ed: Alexis McCombs. Description: Chicago-based Loop Capital Markets L.L.C. has named Peter Bynoe managing director of corporate finance. Bynoe was previously a senior partner at the law firm DLA Piper U.S. L.L.P., where he worked on stadium deals.

17365 ■ "Peter Gilgan" in *Canadian Business* **(Vol. 82, April 27, 2009, No. 7, pp. 58)**
Pub: Rogers Media
Ed: Calvin Leung. Description: Mattamy Homes Ltd. president and chief executive officer Peter Gilgan believes that their business model of building communities in an organized way brings advantages to the firm and for their customers. He also believes in adopting their product prices to new market realities. Gilgan considers the approvals regime in Ontario his biggest challenge in the last 20 years.

17366 ■ "Phillips Edison Launches $1.8B Retail REIT" in *Business Courier* **(Vol. 27, October 15, 2010, No. 24, pp. 1)**
Pub: Business Courier
Ed: Dan Monk. Description: Retail center operator Phillips Edison & Company is organizing a real estate investment trust (REIT) to raise $1.8 billion to finance the planned purchase of 150 grocery-centered shopping centers around the U.S. The offering would be Phillips largest. Phillips Edison employesss 174 workers and operates 250 shopping centers nationwide.

17367 ■ "A Place to Call Home" in *Business Courier* **(Vol. 24, March 7, 2008, No. 48, pp. 1)**
Pub: American City Business Journals, Inc.
Ed: Lucy May. Description: Discusses a new type of housing for Cincinnati's chronically homeless that will be developed by the Over-the-Rhine Community Housing Network and the Cincinnati Center City Development Corp. Advocates believe that it is the missing link in the community's efforts to eradicate homelessness. The details of the project are also presented.

17368 ■ "A Place in the Sun" in *Canadian Business* **(Vol. 81, July 22, 2008, No. 12-13, pp. 56)**
Pub: Rogers Media Ltd.
Description: Experts believe that it is the best time for Canadians to own a retirement home in the U.S., where real estate prices are up to 50 percent below their peak. Other views concerning the economic conditions occurring in the United States, as well as on the implications for Canadians planning to invest in the country are presented.

17369 ■ "Placer Land Sells for $12 Million" in *Sacramento Business Journal* **(Vol. 25, July 25, 2008, No. 21, pp. 1)**
Pub: American City Business Journals, Inc.
Ed: Michael Shaw; Celia Lamb. Description: Reynen & Bardis Communities Inc., a Sacramento, California-based homebuilder, has purchased the Antonio Mountain Ranch in Placer County, California shortly before the property's scheduled foreclosure on June 27, 2008. Placer County Recorder's data show that the purchase price of the 808-acre wetland-rich property is $12 million.

17370 ■ "Population Growing Faster Than Retail, Service Sector" in *Crain's New York Business* **(Vol. 24, January 14, 2008, No. 2, pp. 30)**
Pub: Crain Communications, Inc.
Ed: Andrew Marks. Description: Downtown Manhattan is seeing more residential development; however, as more families call the area home the need for more retail and services is becoming evident.

17371 ■ "Portland's Hilton For Sale" in *Business Journal Portland* **(Vol. 27, October 22, 2010, No. 34, pp. 1)**
Pub: Portland Business Journal
Ed: Wendy Culverwell. Description: Hilton Portland & Executive Tower, Portland's biggest hotel, is being sold by Cornerstone Real Estate Advisers LLC. Cornerstone hopes to close the deal for the 782-room complex by the end of 2010. Cornerstone contracted Jones Lang LaSalle to manage the sale, but terms to the deal are not available.

17372 ■ "The Power of Fun" in *Canadian Business* **(Vol. 79, November 6, 2006, No. 22, pp. 58)**
Pub: Rogers Media
Ed: Zena Olijnyk. Description: The creative efforts of Phillippe Starck in designing condos are analyzed.

17373 ■ "'Pre-Sale' for Planned Could Mich Tower" in *Crain's Chicago Business* **(Vol. 31, March 24, 2008, No. 12, pp. 14)**
Pub: Crain Communications, Inc.
Ed: Eddie Baeb. Description: Condominium developer William Warman is planning to build a mixed-use tower at 300 North Michigan Avenue which would include a hotel, retail space, apartments and a parking garage. Mr. Warman is looking for investors to buy part or all of the space in order to make it easier to land financing.

17374 ■ "Priced-Out Tenants Flocking to Class B" in *Boston Business Journal* **(Vol. 27, October 19, 2007, No. 38, pp. 1)**
Pub: American City Business Journals Inc.
Ed: Michelle Hillman. Description: Tenants who usually rent top-tier office buildings are migrating to buildings that are not as expensive. The shift from Class A to Class B buildings is influenced by the high rental cost of the flashy office towers.

17375 ■ "Prime Site Lands Retirement Center" in *Business Courier* **(Vol. 24, November 2, 2008, No. 29, pp. 1)**
Pub: American City Business Journals, Inc.
Ed: Laura Baverman. Description: Erickson Retirement Communities plans to build a $220 milllion campus on 65 acres of land between Evendale and Glendale. The project will depend on votes casted by village councils in Evendale and Glendale, expected to take place in December 2007. Both areas must sign on and alter zoning rules before the development can proceed.

17376 ■ **"Prince of the City"** in *Canadian Business* (Vol. 80, November 19, 2007, No. 23, pp. 62)

Pub: Rogers Media

Ed: Rachel Pulfer. **Description:** Robert Fung and the Salilent Group aim to revive the poverty-stricken communities in Vancouver by transforming the city's old buildings into designer condominiums using city incentives. Fung and his partners have increased property values in the most unlikely neighborhoods by creating luxury real estate. Fung's recommendations on Vancouver's real estate development are given.

17377 ■ **"Private Equity Firms Focus on Failing Banks"** in *Baltimore Business Journal* (Vol. 28, July 16, 2010, No. 10, pp. 1)

Pub: Baltimore Business Journal

Ed: Gary Haber. **Description:** Four deals in which assets of failed banks were acquired by private equity firms have been approved by the Federal Deposit Insurance Corporation in the past couple of years. Bay Bank FSK, for example, purchased Bay National Bank's assets in July 2010. Forecasts on more private equity acquisitions in the community banking industry are given.

17378 ■ **"Private Equity Firms Shopping Valley For Deals"** in *The Business Journal - Serving Phoenix and the Valley of the Sun* (Vol. 29, September 19, 2008, No. 3, pp. 1)

Pub: American City Business Journals, Inc.

Ed: Mike Sunnucks. **Description:** Private equity firms from California, Boston, New York, and overseas are expected to invest in growth-oriented real estate markets that include Phoenix. Real estate experts revealed that privately held investment and acquisition firms are looking to invest in real estate markets hit by the housing crisis. Views and information on private equity firms' real estate investments are presented.

17379 ■ **"Proposal Ruffles Builders"** in *Austin Business JournalInc.* (Vol. 29, November 20, 2009, No. 37, pp. 1)

Pub: American City Business Journals

Ed: Jacob Dirr. **Description:** A proposal that requires heating, ventilation and cooling equipment checking for a new commercial building having an area of at least 10,000 square feet might cost 25 cents to 50 cents per square foot for the owners. This may lead to higher housing costs. Both the Building and Fire Code Board of Appeals and the Mechanical Plumbing and Solar Board have recommended the plan.

17380 ■ **"Proposed Law Would Stop REIS Bid for Annexation by Livonia"** in *Crain's Detroit Business* (Vol. 24, March 10, 2008, No. 10, pp. 2)

Pub: Crain Communications, Inc.

Ed: Chad Halcom. **Description:** REIS Northville L.L. C., a joint venture made up of Real Estate Interests Group Inc. and Schostak Bros. & Co., has proposed an $800 million project called Highwood at the former Northville Psychiatric Hospital site but has been stalled due to a disagreement with Northville Township on several terms including: the amount of retail at the site and the paying for cleanup of environmental and medical waste.

17381 ■ **"Proposed Triangle Redo in Motion"** in *Crain's Cleveland Business* (Vol. 28, October 15, 2007, No. 41, pp. 1)

Pub: Crain Communications, Inc.

Ed: Stan Bullard. **Description:** Zaremba Homes and MRN Ltd. are partnering to redevelop the so-called Triangle section of University Circle. The proposed project will include a total of 434 new rental and for-sale residential suites and as much as 227,000 square feet of retail and restaurant space.

17382 ■ **"Protect Your Assets"** in *Black Enterprise* (Vol. 38, January 2008, No. 6, pp. 38)

Pub: Earl G. Graves Publishing Co. Inc.

Ed: Trevor Delaney. **Description:** Owner of rental properties seeks advice for incorporating versus getting an LLC for the business.

17383 ■ **"PSU Launches $90 Million Project"** in *The Business Journal-Portland* (Vol. 25, July 18, 2008, No. 19, pp. 1)

Pub: American City Business Journals, Inc.

Ed: Aliza Earnshaw. **Description:** Portland State University (PSU) has launched a $90-million project for a new business school building, which is to be located at Southwest Market and Southwest Park. The business school is expected to move in to its new 130,000-suqare-foot building by 2013. PSU business school needs to raise $30 million for the project.

17384 ■ **"Pulte May Be Bouncing Back From Stock-Price Doldrums"** in *Crain's Detroit Business* (Vol. 23, October 8, 2007, No. 41, pp. 4)

Pub: Crain Communications Inc. - Detroit

Ed: Daniel Duggan. **Description:** Pulte Homes saw a jump in its stocks due to Citigroup's analysts rating Pulte and other builders higher due to strong balance sheets.

17385 ■ **"Quarreling Parties Keep Schenectady Redevelopment Plan In Limbo"** in *The Business Review Albany* (Vol. 35, April 4, 2008, No. 53)

Pub: The Business Review

Ed: Michael DeMasi. **Description:** First National Bank of Scotia chairman Louis H. Buhrmaster opposes the Erie Boulevard design project. as it could negatively affect access to the bank. Buhrmaster, aslo a vice president for Schenectady Industrial Corp, prohibits environmental assessment at the former American Locomotive property. The issues affecting the progress of the planned redevelopment at Schenectady are analyzed

17386 ■ **"Radio Roots Run Deep"** in *The Business Journal-Milwaukee* (Vol. 25, July 4, 2008, No. 41, pp. A1)

Pub: American City Business Journals, Inc.

Ed: Rich Kirchen. **Description:** Profile of Steve Palec, a real estate broker at CB Richard Ellis, also works as a radio host for shows "Rock & Roll Roots" and "Legends of Rock". Palec shares that real estate is still his top priority, even with his radio gig. Palec's career as a broker and as a radio host is discussed.

17387 ■ **"Real Estate Ambitions"** in *Black Enterprise* (Vol. 37, January 2007, No. 6, pp. 101)

Pub: Earl G. Graves Publishing Co. Inc.

Ed: Description: National Real Estate Investors Association is a nonprofit trade association for both advanced as well as novice real estate investors that offers information on builders to contractors to banks. When looking to become a real estate investor utilize this organization, talk to various investors like the president of your local chapter, let people know your aspirations, and see if you can find a partner who has experience in the field. Resources included.

17388 ■ **"Real Estate Defaults Top $300M"** in *Business Courier* (Vol. 26, January 15, 2010, No. 39, pp. 1)

Pub: American City Business Journals, Inc.

Ed: Dan Monk. **Description:** Cincinnati commercial real estate owners defaulting on securitized loans reached $306 million at the end of 2009. The trend has lifted the region's default rate to nearly 9 percent. National average for commercial real estate default is examined.

17389 ■ **"Real Estate Funds Swell Past $350M"** in *Business Journal Portland* (Vol. 27, December 31, 2010, No. 44, pp. 1)

Pub: Portland Business Journal

Ed: Wendy Culverwell. **Description:** Oregon-based real estate funds have raised around half of the $735 million that was raised by local companies. Investors have been purchasing distressed properties. Commercial real estate prices have declined since 2007.

17390 ■ *Real Estate Loopholes: Secrets of Successful Real Estate Investing*

Pub: Warner Books, Incorporated

Ed: Diane Kennedy, Garrett Sutton, Robert T. Kiyosaki. **Released:** April 2003. **Description:** Knowledge, planning, and building a team of advisor and mentors is key to successful real estate investments.

17391 ■ **"Real Estate Market Still in a Slump"** in *Montana Business Quarterly* (Vol. 49, Summer 2011, No. 2, pp. 15)

Pub: Bureau of Business & Economic Research

Ed: Patrick M. Barkey. **Description:** Montana's housing market is still in decline with no sign of improving in the near future. Statistical data included.

17392 ■ *The Real Estate Recipe: Make Millions by Buying Small Apartment Properties in Your Spare Time*

Pub: DNA Press

Ed: Brian K. Friedman. **Released:** September 2004. **Price:** $29.95. **Description:** Guide for anyone interested in property investments; the book provides information for choosing an apartment property and answers questions in a chronological workbook format. The author shares his own experiences in apartment investing and shares the entire process of analyzing and buying an apartment property using a hypothetical ten-unit complex. Sample worksheets, checklists, and tables are provided to help readers maintain their own records.

17393 ■ **"Real Estate Vets Take Times In Stride"** in *The Business Journal-Serving Metropolitan Kansas City* (Vol. 26, July 25, 2008, No. 46)

Pub: American City Business Journals, Inc.

Ed: Rob Roberts. **Description:** Kansas City, Missouri's real estate industry veterans like Allen Block believe that the challenges faced by the industry in the 1980s, when the Federal Reserve Board controlled the money supply to slow down inflation, were worse than the challenges faced today. Other views, trends and information on the real estate industry of the city, are presented.

17394 ■ **"Real Estate Wheeling and Dealing Picks Up"** in *Business Journal Portland* (Vol. 27, October 29, 2010, No. 35, pp. 1)

Pub: Portland Business Journal

Ed: Wendy Culverwell. **Description:** LoopNet has listed 33 prominent commercial properties for sale in Portland, Oregon's real estate market. However, reasons for the sales rush are not totally clear, but speculations point to the end of the Bush tax cuts in 2010 that prompted real estate investors to close the deals and avoid the increase in capital gains taxes.

17395 ■ **"Real Estate Woes Mount for State's Smaller Banks"** in *Boston Business Journal* (Vol. 27, November 30, 2007, No. 44, pp. 1)

Pub: American City Business Journals Inc.

Ed: Craig M. Douglas. **Description:** Massachusetts banking industry is facing a steep increase on loan defaults such as in home mortgages and condominium projects, contrary to public belief that the local industry is safe from the real estate meltdown. The dollar value of local banks' nonperforming loans doubled in 2007, and is rising statewide. Other banking issues in the state are discussed.

17396 ■ **"Real Estate's New Reality"** in *Entrepreneur* (Vol. 37, July 2009, No. 7, pp. 32)

Pub: Entrepreneur Media, Inc.

Ed: Rosalind Resnick. **Description:** Investing in real estate is still an advisable move, as long as investors are prepared to hold on to the property and there is a rent roll to provide a decent return on investment. Among the key considerations when investing in real estate is the property's expenses and cash flow. Other suggestions for future real estate investors are given.

17397 ■ **"Real Opportunities: Don't Let Mortgage Mayhem Steer You Away From Sound Investments"** in *Black Enterprise* (December 2007)

Pub: Earl G. Graves Publishing Co. Inc.

Ed: James A. Anderson. **Description:** Real estate investment trusts (REITs) that operate office buildings, industrial parks, shopping malls, hotels, hospitals, or other commercial properties may be a sound investment, despite the mortgage crisis facing the U.S. financial sector.

17398 ■ **"Realities May Blur Vision"** in *The Business Journal-Serving Metropolitan Kansas City* (Vol. 27, September 19, 2008, No. 1, pp. 1)

Pub: American City Business Journals, Inc.

Ed: Rob Roberts. **Description:** Vision Metcalf is a study by Kansas City that depicts how Metcalf Avenue could look like if redeveloped. Redevelopment plans for the Metcalf corridor include a 20-story mixed-use building on a vacant car dealership. The challenges that the redevelopment plans will face are also analyzed.

17399 ■ **"Recovery on Tap for 2010?"** in *Orlando Business Journal* (Vol. 26, January 1, 2010, No. 31, pp. 1)

Pub: American City Business Journals

Ed: Melanie Stawicki Azam, Richard Bilbao, Christopher Boyd, Anjali Fluker. **Description:** Economic forecasts for Central Florida's leading business sectors in 2010 are presented. These sectors include housing, film and TV, sports business, law, restaurants, aviation, tourism and hospitality, banking and finance, commercial real estate, retail, health care, insurance, higher education, and manufacturing. According to some local executives, Central Florida's economy will slowly recover in 2010.

17400 ■ **"Red Tape Ties Detroit Housing Rehab Plan"** in *Crain's Detroit Business* (Vol. 24, September 22, 2008, No. 38, pp. 1)

Pub: Crain Communications, Inc.

Ed: Ryan Beene. **Description:** Venture-capital firm Wilherst Oxford LLC is a Florida-based company that has purchased 300 inner-city homes which were in foreclosure in Detroit. Wilherst Oxford is asking the city to forgive the existing tax and utility liens so the firm can utilize the money for home improvements. The city, however, is reluctant but has stated that they are willing to negotiate.

17401 ■ **"REIT's Decry Foreign Limits on Investment"** in *Globe & Mail* (March 29, 2007, pp. B4)

Pub: CTVglobemedia Publishing Inc.

Ed: Elizabeth Church. **Description:** The planned legislation by Canadian government for regulation foreign investments by real estate investment trusts is discussed.

17402 ■ **"A Renewal in Rentals"** in *Barron's* (Vol. 88, March 17, 2008, No. 11, pp. 17)

Pub: Dow Jones & Company, Inc.

Ed: Description: Discusses the projected entry of the estimated 82 million echo-boomers into the rentals market and the influx of immigrants and displaced homeowners which could turn apartments into lucrative investments again. While apartment-building completions rose slowly since 2003, demand is expected to increase steeply until 2015.

17403 ■ **"Rental Demand Boosts Revenue for Sun Communities Inc."** in *Crain's Detroit Business* (Vol. 24, March 24, 2008, No. 12, pp. 4)

Pub: Crain Communications, Inc.

Ed: Daniel Duggan. **Description:** Despite the decline in sales of manufactured homes, demand for rental units and rent-to-own programs have brought Sun Communities Inc. increased revenue. The real estate investment trust, based in Southfield, owns, operates, finances and develops manufactured home communities in the Midwest and Southeast. Statistical data included.

17404 ■ **"Reply! Grows at Unprecedented Rate, Rips Beta Off Its Marketplace"** in *Marketing Weekly News* (September 19, 2009, pp. 149)

Pub: Investment Weekly News

Description: Profile of Reply.com, a leader in locally-targeted Internet marketing, announced significant growth in terms of revenue, enhanced features and services and new categories since launching its beta Reply! Marketplace platform. Even in the face of an economic downturn, the company has posted over 50 percent revenue growth in the Real Estate and Automotive categories.

17405 ■ **"Restoring Grandeur"** in *Business Courier* (Vol. 26, December 4, 2009, No. 32, pp. 1)

Pub: American City Business Journals, Inc.

Ed: Dan Monk. **Description:** Eagle Realty Group intends to spend more than $10 to restore the historic 12-story Phelps apartment building in Lytle Park in Cincinnati. Its president, Mario San Marco, expressed the need to invest in the building in order to maintain operations. The building could be restored into a hotel catering to executives and consultants.

17406 ■ **"Retail Center Pitched"** in *Business Courier* (Vol. 27, June 18, 2010, No. 7, pp. 1)

Pub: Business Courier

Ed: Dan Monk. **Description:** Jeffrey R. Anderson Real Estate Inc.'s plan for a retail center in Butler County, Ohio could have three department stores in the 1.1 million-square-foot property. An outdoor sports retailer is also part of the plans.

17407 ■ **"Retail Center Planned for Canton Site"** in *Boston Business Journal* (Vol. 29, May 20, 2011, No. 2, pp. 1)

Pub: American City Business Journals Inc.

Ed: Daniel J. Sernovitz. **Description:** A real estate development team is planning to build a shopping center at Canton Crossing in Baltimore, Maryland and is near closing the deal with ExxonMobil Corporation who owns the waterfront site.

17408 ■ **"Retail Slump Deflates Local Development"** in *Business Courier* (Vol. 24, February 29, 2008, No. 47, pp. 1)

Pub: American City Business Journals, Inc.

Ed: Lisa Biank Fasig. **Description:** 2007 sales of the retail industry are the slowest since the year 2003, driving retail stores to reconsider their expansion plans for 2008. A number of retail projects have been delayed, cancelled or altered, including Newport Pavilion, Rivers Crossing, Wal-Mart Supercenters, Legacy Place and Millworks. The impacts of retail slowdown on development projects are analyzed further.

17409 ■ **"Revitalizing Real Estate: Couple Sails Through Sea of Housing Woes"** in *Black Enterprise* (Vol. 38, February 2008, No. 7, pp. 50)

Pub: Earl G. Graves Publishing Co. Inc.

Ed: Ayana Dixon. **Description:** Owner, Christopher Gablin and Regina Mincey-Garlin offer a broad range of real estate-related services to clients in order to not only survive, but thrive in today's market.

17410 ■ **"Rise in Occupancy Rate Fuels Area Hotel Building Boom"** in *Crain's Detroit Business* (Vol. 24, March 10, 2008, No. 10, pp. 14)

Pub: Crain Communications, Inc.

Ed: Jonathan Eppley. **Description:** Due to a rise in the region's yearly occupancy rate, a number of new hotel construction and renovation projects are slated for the Detroit area.

17411 ■ **"A Rise in Rental Units"** in *Philadelphia Business Journal* (Vol. 30, October 7, 2011, No. 34, pp. 1)

Pub: American City Business Journals Inc.

Ed: Natalie Kostelni. **Description:** Housing developers have been stepping up the construction of new apartment complexes throughout the suburbs of Pennsylvania in order to capture growing demand for rental properties. BPG Properties Ltd. has nearly 1,000 new apartments under construction.

17412 ■ **"Roger Rechler Played Major Role in Long Island's Evolution"** in *Commercial Property News* (March 17, 2008)

Pub: Nielsen Company

Description: Profile of Roger Rechler, real estate developer on Long Island, New York, is presented. Rechler, who died in March 2008, was instrumental in the development, ownership and operations of the largest commercial real estate portfolio on Long Island.

17413 ■ **"Roy MacDowell Jr."** in *Boston Business Journal* (Vol. 31, June 10, 2011, No. 20, pp. 1)

Pub: Boston Business Journal

Ed: Craig M. Douglas. **Description:** Real estate developer Roy MacDowell is selling his Boston, Massachusetts estate. The asking price for the property is $21.8 million. MacDowell recently suffered setbacks in his finances.

17414 ■ **"Sale of Solo Cup Plant Pending"** in *Boston Business Journal* (Vol. 29, June 17, 2011, No. 6, pp. 1)

Pub: American City Business Journals Inc.

Ed: Daniel J. Sernovitz. **Description:** Baltimore developers Vanguard Equities Inc. and Greenberg Gibbons Commercial have contracted to buy the Solo Cup Company facility in Owing Mills and are now considering several plans for the property. Sale should be completed by September 2011 but no proposed sale terms are disclosed.

17415 ■ **"Sandi Jackson; Alderman, 7th Ward, City of Chicago"** in *Crain's Chicago Business* (Vol. 31, May 5, 2008, No. 18, pp. 31)

Pub: Crain Communications, Inc.

Ed: Sarah A. Klein. **Description:** Profile of Sandi Jackson who is an alderman of the 7th ward of the city of Chicago and is addressing issues such as poverty and crime as well as counting on a plan to develop the former USX Corp. steel mill to revitalize the area's economic climate.

17416 ■ **"Scaled-Down Phoenix Condos Emerge as DNA"** in *The Business Journal - Serving Phoenix and the Valley of the Sun* (Vol. 28, July 11, 2008, No. 45, pp. 1)

Pub: American City Business Journals, Inc.

Ed: Yvonne Zusel. **Description:** Pointe of View Developments and Belleview Communities have scaled back their Copper Pointe Condominiums project in downtown Phoenix, Arizona. The scaled-back project has also changed its name into Downtown's Newest Address Condominiums and will cost $40 million.

17417 ■ **"Search Engine: GE Looks Around"** in *Business Courier* (Vol. 24, March 7, 2008, No. 48, pp. 1)

Pub: American City Business Journals, Inc.

Ed: Laura Baverman. **Description:** GE Aviation, an aircraft engine company, could move about 1,500 Tri-employees to its new office in West Chester, Liberty Township, Northern Kentucky, as its leases are set to expire in 2009 and 2010. The company revealed that developers are prompting the firm to send out a request-for-proposal to choose development companies in 2008.

17418 ■ **"Seeing Green in Going Green"** in *The Business Journal-Serving Greater Tampa Bay* (Vol. 28, July 4, 2008, No. 28, pp. 1)

Pub: American City Business Journals, Inc.

Ed: Janet Leiser. **Description:** Atlanta, Georgia-based developer IDI Corp. is pushing for Leadership in Energy and Environmental Design certification for the warehouse that is currently under construction at Madison Business Center along Port Sutton and U.S. 41. The industrial building is the first in Tampa Bay to seek certification for LEED as set by the U.S. Green Building Council.

17419 ■ **"Sellers Face Excess Land Dilemma"** in *Crain's Cleveland Business* (Vol. 28, November 12, 2007, No. 45, pp. 1)

Pub: Crain Communications, Inc.

Ed: Stan Bullard. **Description:** Overview on the way in which the housing slump is effecting builders, land developers and lot prices. Statistical data included.

17420 ■ **"Silverdome Bidders Bring New Proposals"** in *Crain's Detroit Business* (Vol. 24, March 17, 2008, No. 11, pp. 23)

Pub: Crain Communications, Inc.

Ed: Daniel Duggan. **Description:** Discusses the seven plans which have been proposed as part of the third round of bidding for the Pontiac Silverdome; proposals range from Global Baseball Inc., a baseball league that would pit a team from every country against one another, to an Indian casino, a musical "hall of fame", a convention center, a horse track, a hotel and an indoor water park.

17421 ▪ **"Sitting, Sitting, Sitting-Snapshots of Homes that Just Won't Sell" in** *Crain's Chicago Business* **(Vol. 31, April 21, 2008, No. 16)**
Pub: Crain Communications, Inc.
Ed: Kevin Davis. **Description:** Listing of five Chicago-area homes that have been on the market for an extended length of time; also includes the original asking price, current asking price, special features and the biggest challenge of each home.

17422 ▪ **"Six Leading Economists on What to Expect in the Year Ahead: Derek Holt; Housing" in** *Canadian Business* **(December 24, 2007)**
Pub: Rogers Media
Ed: Derek Holt. **Description:** The Canadian subprime mortgage market could take a different turn from that of the U.S. as laws governing Canada's mortgage market indirectly limit the probability of a slowdown. Details on how Canada avoided the slowdown in the housing market and forecasts of new homes for 2008 are discussed.

17423 ▪ **"Sixty-Acre Vision for North Suburbs" in** *Business Courier* **(Vol. 24, April 4, 2008, No. 52, pp. 1)**
Pub: American City Business Journals, Inc.
Ed: Laura Baverman. **Description:** Al Neyer Inc. plans for a mixed-use development at the 60-acre site it has recently purchased. The mixed-use project could cost up to $100 million, and will include medical offices, residential buildings, and corporate offices. Details of Al Neyer's plans for the site are given.

17424 ▪ **"Small Changes Can Mean Big Energy Savings" in** *Crain's Cleveland Business* **(Vol. 28, November 5, 2007, No. 44, pp. 21)**
Pub: Crain Communications, Inc.
Ed: Harriet Tramer. **Description:** Many Northeast Ohio businesses are taking their cues from the residential real estate market to draw and capitalize on interest in energy efficiency and is regularly taken into account by local architects.

17425 ▪ **"Sneak Preview: Alamo Revamp" in** *Austin Business JournalInc.* **(Vol. 28, December 12, 2008, No. 39, pp. 1)**
Pub: American City Business Journals
Ed: Sandra Zaragoza. **Description:** Austin, Texas-based Alamo Drafthouse Cinemas is planning to build a new Circle C Ranch. The new theater will showcase digital projectors and the latest sound systems to show 3-D movies. The company is in lease negotiations with developer Stratus Properties Inc.

17426 ▪ **"S.O.S. Sorting Out Subprime" in** *Black Enterprise* **(Vol. 38, November 2007, No. 4, pp. 76)**
Pub: Earl G. Graves Publishing Co. Inc.
Ed: Trevor Delaney. **Description:** Subprime distress in the housing market is discussed and the impact it has put on investors.

17427 ▪ **"Soured Relationship Plays Out in Courts" in** *The Business Journal-Serving Greater Tampa Bay* **(Vol. 28, September 19, 2008, No. 39)**
Pub: American City Business Journals, Inc.
Ed: Janet Leiser. **Description:** Heirs of developer Julian Hawthorne Lifset won a court battle to end a 50-year lease with Specialty Restaurants Corp. in Rocky Point. The decision opens the Tampa Bay prime waterfront property for new development.

17428 ▪ **"South Loop Site Lands a Buyer" in** *Crain's Chicago Business* **(Vol. 31, March 24, 2008, No. 12, pp. 1)**
Pub: Crain Communications, Inc.
Ed: Alby Gallun. **Description:** Russland Capital Group, a little-known condominium developer from Skokie, recently purchased a 6.5-acre riverside property in the site known as Franklin Point for $40 million.

17429 ▪ **"Stadium Developers Seek a Win With the State" in** *The Business Journal-Serving Metropolitan Kansas City* **(Vol. 26, August 22, 2008)**
Pub: American City Business Journals, Inc.
Ed: Rob Roberts. **Description:** Three Trails Redevelopment LLC is hoping to win $30 million in state tax credits from the Missouri Development Finance Board for the construction of an 18,500-seat Wizards stadium. The project is contingent on state tax incentives and the company remains optimistic about their goal.

17430 ▪ **"Staging a Martini-and-GQ Lifestyle; Faux Possessions Play to Buyer's Aspirations" in** *Crain's Chicago Business* **(April 21, 2008)**
Pub: Crain Communications, Inc.
Ed: Kevin Davis. **Description:** Due to the competition of the slumping housing market, home stagers are becoming more prominent and are using creative ways to make an impression beyond de-cluttering, painting and cleaning by using accents such as casually placed magazines, candles and table settings.

17431 ▪ **"State Center Lease Deal High for Md." in** *Baltimore Business Journal* **(Vol. 28, August 6, 2010, No. 13, pp. 1)**
Pub: Baltimore Business Journal
Ed: Daniel J. Sernovitz. **Description:** The proposed $1.5 billion State Center development project in Midtown Baltimore might cause the State of Maryland to pay the most expensive rental rates in the city. The state will have to pay an effective rental rate of $34 per square foot, including expenses, on the leasing. Other details of the redevelopment project are discussed.

17432 ▪ **"State Printing Plant on the Move" in** *Sacramento Business Journal* **(Vol. 25, August 29, 2008, No. 26, pp. 1)**
Pub: American City Business Journals, Inc.
Ed: Michael Shaw; Celia Lamb. **Description:** California is planning to replace its printing plant on Richards Boulevard and 7th Street with a newly built or leased facility in the Sacramento area. It was revealed that the project will meet the state's standards for new buildings. It is believed that the new site will require 15 acres or more depending on requirements.

17433 ▪ **"State Wants to Add Escape Clause to Leases" in** *Sacramento Business Journal* **(Vol. 28, October 14, 2011, No. 33, pp. 1)**
Pub: Sacramento Business Journal
Ed: Michael Shaw. **Description:** California Governor Jerry Brown's administration has decided to add escape clauses to new lease agreements, which created new worry for building owners and brokers in Sacramento, California. Real estate brokers believe the appropriation of funds clauses have been making the lenders nervous and would result in less competition.

17434 ▪ **"Still Looking Good" in** *Canadian Business* **(Vol. 80, March 26, 2007, No. 7, pp. 29)**
Pub: Rogers Media
Ed: Andy Holloway. **Description:** The real estate prices in various parts of Canada are analyzed. The future growth potential of the industry is forecasted.

17435 ▪ **"Stuck With Two Mortgages; The Nightmare When Buyers Upgrade" in** *Crain's Chicago Business* **(Vol. 31, April 21, 2008, No. 16)**
Pub: Crain Communications, Inc.
Ed: Darci Smith. **Description:** Discusses the problem a number of people are facing due to the slump in the housing market: being stuck with two mortgages when they move because their former homes have not sold. Many thought they could afford to move to a larger home, anticipating significant equity appreciation that did not occur; now they are left with lowering their price and competing with the host of new developments.

17436 ▪ **"Sundt, DPR Score $470 Million Biotech Project" in** *The Business Journal - Serving Phoenix and the Valley of the Sun* **(Vol. 29, September 19, 2008, No. 3, pp. 1)**
Pub: American City Business Journals, Inc.
Ed: Jan Buchholz. **Description:** Sundt Inc. and DPR Construction Inc. were awarded the winning joint-venture contract to develop the second phase of the Arizona Biomedical Collaborative on the Phoenix Biomedical Campus. Both firms declined to comment, but an employee of the Arizona Board of Regents confirmed that the firms won the bidding. Views and information on the development project are presented.

17437 ▪ **"Sunriver Venture Hits Snag" in** *The Business Journal-Portland* **(Vol. 25, August 1, 2008, No. 21, pp. 1)**
Pub: American City Business Journals, Inc.
Ed: Robin J. Moody. **Description:** Portland, Oregon based-Sunwest Management Inc. has divided its Sunriver resort community to make way for a redevelopment plan. Sunwest owner Jon Harder and three partners formed SilverStar Destinations LLC to broker the purchase and redevelopment of the property. Details and description of the redevelopment project are also presented.

17438 ▪ **"Sunwest Vies To Stave Off Bankruptcy" in** *The Business Journal-Portland* **(Vol. 25, August 15, 2008, No. 23, pp. 1)**
Pub: American City Business Journals, Inc.
Ed: Robin J. Moody. **Description:** Sunwest Management Inc. is teetering on the edge of bankruptcy as creditors start foreclosure on nine of their properties. This could potentially displace residents of the assisted living operator. Sunwest is trying to sell smaller packages of properties to get a $100 million bridge loan to maintain operations.

17439 ▪ **"Survey: Apartment Rents Continue to Climb as Home Market Slows" in** *Business Review, Albany New York* **(November 23, 2007)**
Pub: American City Business Journals, Inc.
Ed: Michael DeMasi. **Description:** Survey by Sunrise Management and Consulting shows that asking rents for apartments in the Capital Region increased for the thirteenth consecutive time. The survey, which was conducted between August and October 2007, also showed that Albany County, New York had the highest average asking rent, followed by Rensselaer County, Saratoga County, and Schenectady County.

17440 ▪ **"Survey Says Commercial Real Estate Headed for Turbulence" in** *Commercial Property News* **(March 17, 2008)**
Pub: Nielsen Company
Description: Commercial real estate sector is declining due to the sluggish U.S. economy. According to a recent survey, national office, retail and hospitality markets are also on the decline.

17441 ▪ **"Swope: Breakup Won't Delay Job" in** *The Business Journal-Serving Metropolitan Kansas City* **(Vol. 26, August 22, 2008, No. 50, pp. 1)**
Pub: American City Business Journals, Inc.
Ed: Rob Roberts. **Description:** Swope Community Builders said that the Kansas City Redevelopment Project will not be delayed by the breakup of their partnership with Sherman Associates Inc. Swopes will be the sole master developer of the project.

17442 ▪ **"Tampa Condo Conversion Sells for $14.8 Million Less" in** *The Business Journal-Serving Greater Tampa Bay* **(Vol. 28, September 5, 2008)**
Pub: American City Business Journals, Inc.
Ed: Janet Leiser. **Description:** Former apartment complex Village Oaks at Tampa, which was converted to condominiums, has been sold to Tennessee-based real estate investment trust Mid-America Apartment Communities Inc. for $21.2 million in August 2008. The amount was $14.2 million less than what developer Radco Management LLC paid for in 2005.

17443 ■ "Tax Abatement Changes Seen as Home Run for Cleveland Condo Market" in *Crain's Cleveland Business* **(Vol. 30, June 15, 2009, No. 23)**
Pub: Crain Communications, Inc.
Ed: Jay Miller. **Description:** Condominium ownership became a bit more affordable for Cleveland residents since changes in both state and local tax abatement policy changes. The tax credits are examined.

17444 ■ "Taxpayers' Banks Share Even Higher" in *Business Courier* **(Vol. 24, October 26, 2008, No. 28, pp. 1)**
Pub: American City Business Journals, Inc.
Ed: Dan Monk; Lucy May. **Description:** Banks Working Group originally announced that it needs $106 million in public funds to build the Banks riverfront development but then declared it needs $45 million more from Cincinnati and Hamilton County after it approved a deal for the project. It would not be easy for the city and the county to come up with the money but many decision-makers think it's worth it.

17445 ■ "That Empty Feeling" in *Crain's Cleveland Business* **(Vol. 28, October 15, 2007, No. 41, pp. 1)**
Pub: Crain Communications, Inc.
Ed: Stan Bullard. **Description:** Townhouses, cluster homes and condominiums lured both buyers and builders for most of this decade but now that market is suffering to an even greater degree than the single-family home market. Statistical data included.

17446 ■ "The REIT Stuff" in *Canadian Business* **(Vol. 80, March 26, 2007, No. 7, pp. 72)**
Pub: Rogers Media
Description: The stock performance of various real estate investment trusts in Canada is analyzed.

17447 ■ "Threat of New Office Space Records Rent Hikes" in *Globe & Mail* **(March 21, 2007, pp. B4)**
Pub: CTVglobemedia Publishing Inc.
Ed: Elizabeth Church. **Description:** The increasing commercial rent prices in the Toronto region amid the high office building construction market are discussed.

17448 ■ "Three Trails Blazes Tax Credit Deal" in *The Business Journal-Serving Metropolitan Kansas City* **(Vol. 27, November 7, 2008, No. 9)**
Pub: American City Business Journals, Inc.
Ed: Rob Roberts. **Description:** Three Trails Redevelopment LLC plans to redevelop the Bannister Mall area. The Missouri Development Finance Board is expected to approve $30 million in tax credits for the project. A verbal agreement on the terms and conditions has already been reached according to the agency's executive director.

17449 ■ "TMC Development Closes $1.1 Million Real Estate Purchase" in *Internet Wire* **(September 17, 2009)**
Pub: Comtex News Network, Inc.
Description: TMC Development announced the closing of a $1.1 million real estate purchase for Mansa, LLC dba Kwikee Mart, a Napa-based convenience store; TMC helped the company secure a Small Business Administration 504 loan in order to purchase the acquisition of a 3,464 square foot building. SBA created the 504 loan program to provide financing for growing small and medium-sized businesses.

17450 ■ "Tom Gaglardi" in *Canadian Business* **(Vol. 82, April 27, 2009, No. 7, pp. 56)**
Pub: Rogers Media
Ed: Calvin Leung. **Description:** Northland Properties Corporation president Tom Gaglardi believes that their business model of keeping much of operations in-house allows the firm to crate assets at a lesser price while commanding higher margins than their competitors. He believes that it is an ideal time to invest in the hospitality industry because of opportunities to purchase properties at low prices.

17451 ■ "Top Twenty Wealthiest Landowners" in *Hawaii Business* **(Vol. 53, November 2007, No. 5, pp. 34)**
Pub: Hawaii Business Publishing
Description: Provided is a table of the wealthiest landowners in Hawaii. Their assessed value, total acres owned, prominent holdings, other notable holdings and years of presence in Hawaii are also provided. Statistical data included.

17452 ■ "Tough Sell: Senior Projects Hustle to Keep Buyers" in *Puget Sound Business Journal* **(Vol. 29, November 21, 2008, No. 31, pp.)**
Pub: American City Business Journals
Ed: Heidi Dietrich. **Description:** Plans to move to retirement communities are being postponed by seniors in Washington's Puget Sound area due to difficulty selling their current homes in the slow economy. Retirement communities are trying to lure clients by offering new finance programs and sales plans.

17453 ■ "Tripped by Trump?" in *The Business Journal-Serving Greater Tampa Bay* **(Vol. 28, July 25, 2008, No. 31, pp. 1)**
Pub: American City Business Journals, Inc.
Ed: Michael Hinman. **Description:** Jean Shahnasarian, a buyer of the Trump Tower Tampa, filed cases against Donald Trump, The Trump Organization Inc., and Trump Tower Tampa for giving misleading information about Trump's involvement in the project. She wants a return of her $278,000 deposit and does not want to take part in the sale of the project.

17454 ■ "Troubled Project In Court" in *The Business Journal-Portland* **(Vol. 25, July 25, 2008, No. 20, pp. 1)**
Pub: American City Business Journals, Inc.
Ed: Wendy Culverwell. **Description:** Views and information on Salpare Bay's Hayden Island project, as well as on financing problems and cases associated with the project, are presented. Construction of luxurious waterside condominiums stopped last fall, after the discovery of financing problems and subcontractors and other parties started filing claims and counterclaims.

17455 ■ "Troy Complex has New Brand, New Leases" in *Crain's Detroit Business* **(Vol. 24, April 14, 2008, No. 15, pp. 32)**
Pub: Crain Communications, Inc.
Ed: Daniel Duggan. **Description:** Discusses the re-branding of the 1.2 million-square-foot collection of office buildings in Troy purchased by New York-based Emmes Co. The firm has also pledged more than $6 million in upgrades, hired a new leasing company and completed 67,000 square feet of leasing with another 100,000 in negotiations.

17456 ■ "UMKC, Hospital Drill Down on Deal" in *The Business Journal-Serving Metropolitan Kansas City* **(Vol. 26, July 18, 2008, No. 45, pp. 1)**
Pub: American City Business Journals, Inc.
Ed: Rob Roberts. **Description:** University of Missouri Kansas City and Children's Mercy Hospital are negotiating the hospital's potential acquisition of the university's School of Dentistry building. The deal would transfer the 240,000-square foot dental school building to Children's Mercy. Plans for a new dental school building for the UMKC are also presented.

17457 ■ "Unwanted News for Hospitals" in *Business Courier* **(Vol. 24, October 26, 2008, No. 28, pp. 1)**
Pub: American City Business Journals, Inc.
Ed: Description: Christ and St. Luke Hospital might be sharing responsibility costs on the $207 million hospital being built by Health Alliance, the group they are parting with. Christ and St. Lu ke hospitals will be paying $60 million and $25 miilion for partial liability res pectively because the plans for the said project were already underway before they decided to withdraw. Christ Hospital is involved in a whistle-blower case that might cause $424 million in liability across the group.

17458 ■ *Use What You've Got*
Pub: Portfolio Publishing
Ed: Barbara Corcoran, Bruce Littlefield. **Released:** 2003. **Price:** $24.95. **Description:** Founder and chairman of New York's premier real estate company, the Corcoran Group, shares her successes in the real estate industry. The book offers tips and pointers to salespeople, entrepreneurs and business people alike. Corcoran explains how she went from waiting tables and borrowed $1,000 from a boyfriend to build her real estate company into the industry's powerhouse.

17459 ■ "Vernon Revamp" in *Business Courier* **(Vol. 26, October 9, 2009, No. 24, pp. 1)**
Pub: American City Business Journals, Inc.
Ed: Dan Monk. **Description:** Al Neyer Inc. will redevelop the Vernon Manor Hotel as an office building for the Cincinnati Children's Hospital Medical Center. The project will cost $35 million and would generate a new investment vehicle for black investors who plan to raise $2.7 million in private offerings to claim majority ownership of the property after its renovations.

17460 ■ "Vision for Camden in Better Focus" in *Philadelphia Business Journal* **(Vol. 30, September 30, 2011, No. 33, pp. 1)**
Pub: American City Business Journals Inc.
Ed: Natalie Kostelni. **Description:** More than $500 million worth of projects aimed at redeveloping the downtown and waterfront areas of Camden, New Jersey are being planned. These include the construction of residential, commercial, and education buildings.

17461 ■ "Wannabe Buyers Take Their Own Sweet Time" in *Crain's Chicago Business* **(Vol. 31, April 21, 2008, No. 16, pp. 50)**
Pub: Crain Communications, Inc.
Ed: Lisa Bertagnoli. **Description:** Although all factors are in place for a robust real-estate market in the Chicago area: low interest rates, plenty of inventory and the region's relatively strong employment, buyers are taking their time and doing more research in order to see how bad the economy will get.

17462 ■ "Wary Investors Turn to a Different Market for Strong Returns" in *Boston Business Journal* **(Vol. 29, September 2, 2011, No. 17, pp. 1)**
Pub: American City Business Journals Inc.
Ed: Daniel J. Sernovitz. **Description:** Maryland-based investors have been choosing to put their money in the supermarket business. Retail property sales have increased during the second quarter of 2011.

17463 ■ "Was Mandating Solar Power Water Heaters For New Homes Good Policy?" in *Hawaii Business* **(Vol. 54, August 2008, No. 2, pp. 28)**
Pub: Hawaii Business Publishing
Description: Senator Gary L. Kooser of District 7 Kauai-Niihau believes that the mandating of energy-efficient water heaters for new single-family homes starting in 2010 will help cut Hawaii's oil consumption. Ron Richmond of the Hawaii Solar Energy Association says that the content of SB 644 has negative consequences as it allows for choice of energy and not just solar, and it also eliminates tax credits for new homebuyers.

17464 ■ "Watershed Solution" in *Business Courier* **(Vol. 24, December 14, 2008, No. 35, pp. 1)**
Pub: American City Business Journals, Inc.
Ed: Dan Monk. **Description:** Discusses the Metropolitan Sewer District of Greater Cincinnati which is planning to spend around $128 million for its 20-year green-infrastructure improvement projects. Part of the project involves construction of green roofs, rain gardens and restored wetlands to manage water overflows.

17465 ■ "Waugh Chapel to Expand" in *Baltimore Business Journal* **(Vol. 28, August 27, 2010, No. 16, pp. 1)**
Pub: Baltimore Business Journal
Ed: Daniel J. Sernovitz. **Description:** Developer Greenberg Gibbons Corporation has broken ground

on a $275 million, 1.2 million-square-foot addition to its Village at the Waugh Chapel mixed-use complex. Aside from creating 2,600 permanent jobs, the addition, named Village South, is expected to lure Target and Wegmans Food Markets to Crofton, Maryland. Funding for this project is discussed.

17466 ■ "Weyerhaeuser's REIT Decision Shouldn't Scare Investors Away" in *Barron's* **(Vol. 88, June 30, 2008, No. 26, pp. 18)**
Pub: Dow Jones & Co., Inc.
Ed: Christopher Williams. **Description:** Weyerhaeuser Co.'s management said that a conversion to a real estate investment trust was not likely in 2009 since the move is not tax-efficient as of the moment and would overload its non-timber assets with debt. The company's shares have fallen by 19.5 percent. However, the company remains an asset-rich outfit and its activist shareholder is pushing for change.

17467 ■ "What Happens in Vegas Could Happen in Baltimore, Too" in *Boston Business Journal* **(Vol. 29, June 17, 2011, No. 6, pp. 1)**
Pub: American City Business Journals Inc.
Ed: Daniel J. Sernovitz. **Description:** At least 36 companies expressed their interest in developing a casino in South Baltimore following the state commission's announcement for bids. Developers have until July 28, 2011 to submit their proposals. Baltimore's strong economy is the major factor for the interest, yet the fact that blackjack and poker are outlawed in Maryland could be a drawback.

17468 ■ "What Homes Do Retirees Want?" in *Canadian Business* **(Vol. 79, July 17, 2006, No. 14-15, pp.)**
Pub: Rogers Media
Ed: Joe Cataldo. **Description:** The obstacles and challenges faced by homebuilders in Canada as well as the approach adopted by them to appeal to the mature homebuilders segment, is discussed.

17469 ■ "What Players in the Midmarket Are Talking About" in *Mergers & Acquisitions: The Dealmaker's Journal* **(March 1, 2008)**
Pub: SourceMedia, Inc.
Description: Sports Properties Acquisition Corp. went public at the end of January; according to the company's prospectus, it is not limiting its focus to just teams, it is also considering deals for stadium construction companies, sports leagues, facilities, sports-related advertising and licensing of products, in addition to other related segments.

17470 ■ "What's Ahead for Fannie and Fred?" in *Barron's* **(Vol. 90, August 30, 2010, No. 35, pp. 26)**
Pub: Barron's Editorial & Corporate Headquarters
Ed: Jonathan R. Laing. **Description:** A meeting presided by Treasury Secretary Timothy Geithner discussed the future of Fannie Mae and Freddie Mac. The two government sponsored enterprises were mismanaged and reforming these two agencies is critical.

17471 ■ "When Anything (And Everything) Goes" in *Globe & Mail* **(January 12, 2007, pp. B4)**
Pub: CTVglobemedia Publishing Inc.
Ed: Elizabeth Church. **Description:** The forecast on acquisition of different real estate firms is presented.

17472 ■ "Where Are the Vultures?" in *Mergers & Acquisitions: The Dealmaker's Journal* **(March 1, 2008)**
Pub: SourceMedia, Inc.
Ed: Ken MacFadyen. **Description:** Although the real estate market is distressed, not many acquisitions are being made by distress private equity investors; this is due, in part, to the difficulty in assessing real estate industry firms since it is a sector which is so localized.

17473 ■ "With Building Plans in Flux, County Could Sell Key Site" in *Crain's Cleveland Business* **(Vol. 28, October 8, 2007, No. 40, pp. 1)**
Pub: Crain Communications, Inc.
Ed: Jay Miller. **Description:** Due to such issues as financial and administrative problems, Cuyahoga County commissioners have pushed back the con-

struction timeline for a planned county administration center and are saying that they are considering selling the site in downtown Cleveland to developers who would erect a new office building that another large tenant could occupy.

17474 ■ "Wobbling Economy" in *The Business Journal-Serving Metropolitan Kansas City* **(Vol. 27, September 26, 2008, No. 2, pp. 1)**
Pub: American City Business Journals, Inc.
Ed: Rob Roberts. **Description:** Real estate developers in Kansas City Metropolitan Area are worried of the possible impacts of the crisis at Wall Street. They expect tightening of the credit market, which will result in difficulty of financing their projects. The potential effects of the Wall Street crisis are examined further.

17475 ■ "Working It Out! How a Young Executive Overcomes Obstacles on the Job" in *Black Enterprise* **(Vol. 37, January 2007, No. 6, pp. 55)**
Pub: Earl G. Graves Publishing Co. Inc.
Ed: Laura Egodigwe. **Description:** Interview with Susan Chapman, Global Head of Operations for Citigroup Realty Services, in which she discusses issues such as the important skills necessary for overcoming obstacles in the workplace.

17476 ■ *The Working Man and Woman's Guide to Becoming a Millionaire*
Pub: Prentiss Publishing
Ed: Al Herron. **Released:** November 2006. **Description:** President and CEO of a Century 21 office in Dallas, Texas shares insight into financial security and commitment to community.

17477 ■ "The Worst Lies Ahead for Wall Street; More Losses Certain" in *Crain's New York Business* **(Vol. 24, January 21, 2008, No. 3, pp. 1)**
Pub: Crain Communications, Inc.
Ed: Aaron Elstein. **Description:** Due to the weakening economy, many financial institutions will face further massive losses forcing them to borrow more at higher interest rates and dragging down their earnings for years to come. The effects on commercial real estate and credit card loans are also discussed as well as the trend to investing in Asia and the Middle East.

17478 ■ "Yamasaki Lays Off Last of U.S. Workers, to Vacate World Headquarters in Troy" in *Crain's Detroit Business* **(Vol. 26, January 11, 2010)**
Pub: Crain Communications, Inc.
Ed: Chad Halcom. **Description:** Overview of the impact on the local economy resulting from the closing of Yamasaki Associates, Inc.'s world headquarters located in Troy. The architectural firm notified the last of its employees that they would, indeed be laid off effective December 31.

17479 ■ "You Won't Go Broke Filling Up On These Stocks" in *Barron's* **(Vol. 88, July 14, 2008, No. 28, pp. 38)**
Pub: Dow Jones & Co., Inc.
Ed: Assif Shameen. **Description:** Due to high economic growth, pro-business policies and a consumption boom, the Middle East is a good place to look for equities. The best ways in which to gain exposure to this market include investing in the real estate industry and telecommunications markets as well as large banks that serve corporations and consumers.

17480 ■ *Your First Year in Real Estate: Making the Transition from Total Novice to Successful Professional*
Pub: Crown Business Books
Ed: Dirk Zeller. **Released:** $August 3, 2010. **Price:** $20.00. **Description:** Zeller helps new realtors to select the right company, develop mentor and client relationships, using the Internet and social networking to stay ahead of competition, to set and reach career goals, to stay current in the market, and more.

17481 ■ "Your Place: Housing Developers Try to Read Generation Y" in *Philadelphia Inquirer* **(December 2, 2010)**
Pub: Philadelphia Media Network Inc.
Ed: Al Heavens. **Description:** Results of a survey conducted with Generation Y individuals are examined, focusing on housing developments and whether this particular generation prefers suburban or rural lifestyles. Generation Y encompasses people ages 18 to 32 years old. Statistical data included.

17482 ■ *Your Successful Real Estate Career, 5h Edition*
Pub: American Management Association
Ed: Kenneth W. Edwards. **Released:** 2006. **Price:** $18.95.

TRADE PERIODICALS

17483 ■ *Business Opportunities Journal*
Pub: Business Service Corp.
Ed: Mark Adkins, Editor, news@boj.com. **Released:** Monthly. **Description:** Newspaper covering businesses for sale.

17484 ■ *California Real Estate Journal*
Pub: Daily Journal Corp.
Released: Weekly. **Price:** $124; $41 first time subscriber for 6 months. **Description:** Commercial real estate newspaper.

17485 ■ *The CF Apartment Reporter*
Pub: Clayton-Fillmore Ltd.
Released: Bimonthly. **Price:** $199 4.00 per city. **Description:** Contains research, data, analysis, and narrative about apartment markets nationwide.

17486 ■ *Commercial Investment Real Estate*
Pub: CCIM Institute
Contact: Jennifer Norbut, Publisher
E-mail: jnorbut@ccim.com
Released: Bimonthly. **Price:** $45; $55 Canada and Mexico. **Description:** Professional development magazine for commercial investment professionals and allied fields.

17487 ■ *Corporate Real Estate Executive*
Pub: CoreNet Global
Contact: Kathleen B. Dempsey, Editor & Publisher
Released: 9/year. **Description:** Real estate dealmaking techniques magazine.

17488 ■ *Daily Commerce*
Pub: Daily Journal Corp.
Ed: David Houston, Editor, david_houston@dailyjournal.com. **Released:** Daily (eve.). **Price:** $264; $191 6 months. **Description:** Real estate newspaper.

17489 ■ *The Daily Record*
Pub: The Daily Record Corp.
Released: Daily. **Price:** $10.73 daily; $4.91 weekends; $4.27 Sundays only. **Description:** Newspaper reporting legal and business news.

17490 ■ *Entertainment and Specialty Projects*
Pub: TKO/Real Estate Advisory Group Inc.
Ed: Ann O'Neal, Editor, ann@specialtyretail.net. **Released:** Monthly. **Price:** $249. **Description:** Covers various aspects of entertainment and specialty retailing, real estate, and downtown redevelopment. Recurring features include letters to the editor, interviews, news of research, a calendar of events, book reviews, news of educational opportunities, job listings, and notices of publications available.

17491 ■ *First Tuesday*
Pub: Realty Publications Inc.
Released: Monthly. **Description:** Magazine for real estate professionals.

17492 ■ *The Institutional Real Estate Letter*
Pub: Institutional Real Estate Inc.
Contact: Brigite Thompson, Advertising Coord.
E-mail: b.thompson@irei.com
Released: Monthly. **Price:** $2,495. **Description:** Monthly publication covering the pension, foundation, and endowment investment market. Provides information on investment patterns, trends, and strategies.

17493 ■ *Montana Land Magazine*
Pub: Lee Enterprises Inc.
Released: Quarterly. **Price:** $30; $60 out of country.
Description: Real estate magazine.

17494 ■ *National Property Law Digests*
Pub: Strafford Publications Inc.
Contact: Jennifer F. Vaughan, Executive Editor
Released: Monthly. **Price:** $827, individuals plus $48.50 s/h. **Description:** Digest of the most significant property law cases in the U.S. court system. Cases are screened and selected to provide concise, comprehensive coverage of the latest issues concerning real property law.

17495 ■ *National Real Estate Investor*
Pub: Penton Media Inc.
Contact: Matt Valley, Editor-in-Chief
E-mail: matt.valley@penton.com
Released: Monthly. **Price:** $115 U.S.; $127 Canada; $139 other countries. **Description:** Magazine on commercial real estate investment, development and management.

17496 ■ *New England Real Estate Journal*
Pub: East Coast Publications
Released: Weekly (Fri.). **Price:** $139. **Description:** Newspaper publishing commercial, industrial, and investment real estate news.

17497 ■ *New York Real Estate Journal*
Pub: East Coast Publications
Released: Weekly (Fri.). **Price:** $99. **Description:** Commercial real estate journal.

17498 ■ *Professional Report*
Pub: Society of Industrial and Office Realtors
Released: Quarterly. **Price:** $25 members; $75 nonmembers non-members within U.S.; $80 nonmembers outside U.S. **Description:** Trade magazine for commercial real estate brokerage.

17499 ■ *Real Estate Broker's Insider*
Pub: Alexander Communications Group Inc.
Contact: Margaret DeWitt, Publisher
E-mail: mklein@brokersinsider.com
Ed: Jeff Ostrowski, Editor. **Released:** Semimonthly, 2/month. **Price:** $247. **Description:** Provides residential agency broker/owners with actionable news and information on managing their businesses for greater profitability.

17500 ■ *Realtor Magazine*
Pub: National Association of Realtors
Contact: Frank Sibley, Sen. VP/Publisher
E-mail: fsibley@realtors.org
Released: Monthly. **Price:** $56; $83 Canada; $103 other countries. **Description:** Real estate magazine.

17501 ■ *The Residential Specialist*
Pub: Council of Residential Specialists
Contact: Kathleen Thomas, Advertising Mgr
Ed: Michael Fenner, Editor. **Released:** Bimonthly. **Price:** $29.95 nonmembers; $54.95 two years; $44.95 Canada; $84.95 Canada 2 years; $89.95 other countries; $174.95 other countries 2 years. **Description:** Trade magazine for residential sales agents.

17502 ■ *Retail Traffic*
Pub: Penton Media Inc.
Contact: David Bodamer, Editor-in-Chief
E-mail: ddavid.bodamer@penton.com
Released: Monthly. **Description:** Publication focusing on the retail commercial real estate industry.

17503 ■ *SNL REIT Weekly*
Pub: SNL Financial L.C.
Ed: **Released:** Weekly. **Description:** Communicates by fax the previous week's activity involving REITs. Includes comprehensive articles on current industry trends, condensed news stories, recent capital offerings and the latest market information.

VIDEOCASSETTES/ AUDIOCASSETTES

17504 ■ *Basic Real Estate Investing*
Blockbuster Entertainment Corp.
1201 Elm St.
Dallas, TX 75270
Ph:(214)854-3000
Free: 800-733-1939
Fax:(214)866-2250
URL: http://www.blockbuster.com
Price: $19.95. **Description:** Chuck Baker, a seasoned Real Estate professional, gives his sage advice on Real Estate as an investment. **Availability:** VHS.

17505 ■ *Commercial Real Estate Loan Documentation Program*
Executive Enterprises
Videotape Division
2 Shaw's Cove, Ste. 205
New London, CT 06320-4675
Ph:(860)701-5900
Free: 800-831-8333
Fax:(860)701-5909
Co. E-mail: info@eeiconferences.com
URL: http://www.eeiconferences.com
Released: 1986. **Description:** A training program for financiers regarding the entitled transaction and its necessary documentation. **Availability:** VHS.

17506 ■ *Purchase and Sale of Commercial Real Estate*
American Bar Association
321 N. Clark St.
Chicago, IL 60654-7598
Ph:(312)988-5000
Free: 800-285-2221
Fax:(312)988-5494
Co. E-mail: abapubed@abanet.org
URL: http://www.abanet.org/publiced/
Released: 1988. **Price:** $295.00. **Description:** This is a step by step look at the legal issues of commercial land transactions. **Availability:** VHS; 3/4U.

17507 ■ *Real Estate Financing*
American Bar Association
321 N. Clark St.
Chicago, IL 60654-7598
Ph:(312)988-5000
Free: 800-285-2221
Fax:(312)988-5494
Co. E-mail: abapubed@abanet.org
URL: http://www.abanet.org/publiced/
Released: 1987. **Price:** $295.00. **Description:** An overview is provided of the ways that the finances behind a real estate deal can be structured. **Availability:** VHS; 3/4U.

17508 ■ *Tax and Financial Planning for Real Estate*
SmartPros LTD
12 Skyline Dr.
Hawthorne, NY 10532
Ph:(914)345-2620
Free: 800-621-0043
Co. E-mail: admin@smartpros.com
URL: http://www.smartpros.com
Released: 1990. **Description:** The step-by-step process of buying real estate, its taxation and financial aspects is presented. **Availability:** VHS; 3/4U.

CONSULTANTS

17509 ■ Arnheim & Neely Inc.
425 N Craig St., Ste. 100
Pittsburgh, PA 15213
Ph:(412)391-1900
Fax:(412)316-0090
Co. E-mail: info@arnheimandneely.com
URL: http://www.arnheimandneely.com
Contact: Ann Mihm Sr., Vice President
E-mail: ezehfuss@nauticom.net
Scope: Real estate firm which advises clients on office building and apartment building operation. Also performs market studies, eminent domain testimony,

land assemblages, apartment building due diligence, energy efficiency studies and recommendations and successful conversion counseling.

17510 ■ Boston Financial Consulting Group
101 Arch St., 16th Fl.
Boston, MA 02110
Ph:(617)439-3911
Fax:(617)772-9473
Contact: Stephen J. Zaleski, President
Scope: Real estate counselors offering advice, analysis, and assistance on real-estate investment, disposition, and development, as well as marketability, feasibility, and property-valuation studies. Services include real estate appraisal, land use analysis, development feasibility, financial counseling, relocation studies, alternative site analysis, and acquisition and disposition strategies. Special services include due diligence assistance for low income tax credit program, expert witness testimony, legal support services, subsidized housing appraisals, regulatory processing, and historic preservation counseling. **Seminars:** Housing Update.

17511 ■ Bowes & Co.
789 Sherman St., Ste. 590
Denver, CO 80203-3529
Ph:(303)297-0400
Fax:(303)297-2314
Co. E-mail: bowes@bowesandco.com
URL: http://www.bowesandco.com
Contact: Peter D. Bowes, President
E-mail: pbowes@atsbowesandco.com
Scope: Specializes in appraisal and counseling regarding land, commercial, special purpose, recreational, environmentally impacted and other investment real estate. **Publications:** "Infill Sites are Being Filled at Lowry Stapleton Fitzsimons," Colorado Real Estate Journal, Jun, 2007; "Fitzsimons Stapleton Lowry Redevelopment Beat Goes On," Colorado Real Estate Journal, Sep, 2006; "Appraisers Better Market Stats But Continued Uncertainty Exists," Colorado Real Estate Journal, Feb, 2006; "No Credit," Colorado Chapter Appraiser News, Jan, 2006; "Downtown Lots Happening," Colorado Real Estate Journal, Nov, 2005; "Redevelopment is Big Market Segment," Colorado Real Estate Journal, Oct, 2001.

17512 ■ Brown, Chudleigh, Schuler Donaldson & Associates
744 Cardley Ave., Ste. 100
Medford, OR 97504
Ph:(541)772-8566
Fax:(541)608-6169
Co. E-mail: gschuler@transedge.com
Contact: Greg Schuler, Principal
E-mail: gschuler@transedge.com
Scope: Performs feasibility studies on commercial and industrial development, with specialized expertise on retail properties. Also provides institutional valuation services.

17513 ■ C B Richard Ellis Whittier Partners
33 Arch St., 28th Fl.
Boston, MA 02110
Ph:(617)912-7000
Fax:(617)912-7001
Co. E-mail: info@cbre.com
URL: http://www.cbre.com/default.htm
Contact: Vance Maddocks, CEO
E-mail: vmaddocks@atscbreinvestors.com
Scope: Specializes in real estate analysis of income-producing commercial and residential property. Services include feasibility, development and redevelopment programs for new or existing buildings; investment property analysis; tax equalization studies; and management program analysis. Serves real estate developers, corporate owners, investment trusts, banks, institutional investors, and private individuals. **Publications:** "Nonprofits on the Run," Oct, 2007; "Developing a Strategic Real Estate Plan," Jul, 2007; "The ABCs of Office Leasing for Associations," 2006; "Multi-Housing Monitor," 2004; "Don't Let The Numbers Fool You," Nov, 2003. **Seminars:** Real estate challenges faced by new companies, UCSD School of Medicine Lecture Facility, Apr, 2009; Advanced Managerial Strategies Seminar; Dimensional Management Training Seminar.

17514 ■ Cantey & Company Inc.
3300 Harrison Rd.
Columbia, SC 29204
Ph:(803)256-7150
Fax:(803)256-4632
Co. E-mail: billy@cantey.com
URL: http://www.cantey.com
Contact: William C. Cantey, President
E-mail: billy@cantey.com
Scope: Offers residential, commercial, and investment real estate. As an independent counselor, analyzes various real estate situations, either proposed or existing, for individuals and for institutions. Clients include investors, home buyers, and sellers, developers, syndicates, bank trust departments, attorneys, and corporate Realtors. Services also used in conjunction with the client's planning team of attorneys, accountants, and tax advisers.

17515 ■ Cantrell, Harris & Associates
2001 Union St., Ste. 106
San Francisco, CA 94123-4120
Ph:(415)956-6000
Fax:(415)440-7672
Co. E-mail: cantrellharris@cantrellharris.com
URL: http://www.cantrellharris.com
Contact: Sara Crooks, Principle
E-mail: ron@atscantrellharris.com
Scope: Provides real estate consulting services which include value enhancement, property or asset management, investment analysis and due diligence, strategy and disposition of real property, development coordination, complete feasibility studies, market studies and projections, independent reporting to joint ventures, litigation support, location analysis and site selection and investment partnerships. Industries served: real estate. **Publications:** "Leasing and Management of Office Buildings, Institute of Real Estate Management"; "The Office Building From Concept to Investment Reality, Counselors of Real Estate".

17516 ■ Capmark Financial Group Inc.
601 Montgomery St., Ste. 1500
San Francisco, CA 94104-1010
Ph:(415)835-2000
Fax:(415)391-2949
URL: http://www.capmark.com
Contact: Michael I. Lipson III, Exec VP
E-mail: michael.lipson@atscapmark.com
Scope: Provides financial services to investors in commercial real estate-related assets. Also deals with lending and mortgage banking; investments and funds management and servicing.

17517 ■ Charles Adler & Son Inc.
2930 Arcona Rd.
PO Box 5297
Mechanicsburg, PA 17050
Ph:(717)766-9745
Fax:(717)766-7027
Contact: Robert A. Adler Jr., Principle
Scope: Counsels clients on the disposition, acquisition, leasing and management of commercial and industrial properties. Also active in planning and land development. Serves corporations, financial institutions, investment groups, government agencies, and attorneys. Currently specializing in health-care, senior living facilities.

17518 ■ Coldwell Banker Commercial United Realty Services
8044 Hosbrook Rd., Ste. 475
Cincinnati, OH 45236
Ph:(513)241-1100
Fax:(513)241-4170
Co. E-mail: support@cbcurs.com
Contact: J. Lawrence Willey, Vice President
E-mail: lwilley@atscoldwellbanker.com
Scope: Real estate services company maintains a brokerage in commercial, industrial, office, retail, land, and residential properties. Provides sales, leasing, appraising, consulting, investments, and property management services. Serves private industries as well as government agencies.

17519 ■ Colliers International
50 Milk St., 20th Fl.
Boston, MA 02109-5011
Ph:(617)722-0221
Free: 800-393-1206
Fax:(617)722-0224
Co. E-mail: contact@colliers.com
URL: http://www.colliers.com
Contact: Lori Allen, Principle
E-mail: lori.allen@atscolliers.com
Scope: Advises clients regarding commercial and industrial development properties, suburban acreage, retail centers, office buildings, warehouses, manufacturing facilities, and deepwater-oriented industrial sites. Serves companies, government agencies, and individuals in Texas and the Gulf Coast area.

17520 ■ Consulting, Appraisals & Studies Ltd.
111 W Jackson Blvd.
Chicago, IL 60604
Ph:(312)939-7775
Contact: Alfred K. Eckersberg, President
Scope: Real estate and planning consultants offering economic market analyses, feasibility studies, appraisals, development and investment evaluations, fiscal impact reviews and counseling for private and public sector clients. Projects have involved housing, retail shopping and services, industrial, office, hotels and motels, recreational, institutional and public facilities. Other services include demographic surveys and social and economic impacts, with specialized expertise in rehab and redevelopment, historical preservation and urban planning and zoning. Industries served: Business, financial, real estate, developers and government agencies in the U.S. and Canada.

17521 ■ Continental Appraisal Co.
1111 Schrock Rd., Ste. 202
Columbus, OH 43229-1155
Ph:(614)436-0200
Fax:(614)221-9362
Co. E-mail: jmgarvin@sbcglobal.net
Contact: John M. Garvin Jr., President
E-mail: jmgarvin@sbcglobal.net
Scope: Provides counseling and appraisal services regarding real estate investment properties. Includes portfolio analysis, tax reviews, investment projects, and market studies on commercial, multi family, and industrial property. Specializes in private investors, trust advisors, financial institutions, corporate owners, pension funds and government agencies.

17522 ■ Crosswhite Property Advisors
6 Beacon St., Ste. 215
Boston, MA 02108
Ph:(617)742-6061
Fax:(617)742-6162
Co. E-mail: jcbowman@post.harvard.edu
Contact: John C. Bowman III, President
Scope: Firm provides consulting services in real estate investment analysis, valuation, development feasibility, project management, and permitting. Also experienced in the development of affordable housing involving substantial rehabilitation and historic preservation.

17523 ■ Fitzgerald Valuation Services Inc.
2 Jericho Plz., Ste. 104, 1st Fl., Wing B
Jericho, NY 11753-1658
Ph:(516)822-2700
Fax:(516)822-2702
Co. E-mail: fairvalu@optonline.net
Contact: Steven Dorritie, Vice President
E-mail: fairvalu@optonline.net
Scope: Real estate firm offering investment analysis and valuation reports including feasibility studies in the development, financing or acquisition of real estate properties. Industries served banking, real estate, finance and insurance.

17524 ■ Fredericton Appraisal Associates Ltd.
102-3 Main St.
Fredericton, NB, Canada E3A 9N6
Ph:(506)458-9533

Fax:(506)458-1334
Co. E-mail: fappraisals@ara.ca
URL: http://www.frederictonappraisals.ca
Contact: Peter E. Atkinson, Principle
E-mail: patkinson@atsara.ca
Scope: Real estate appraisal and counseling specialists with expertise in market analyses, site selection, real estate investment analysis, etc. Serving private and public corporations, governments, legal firms, accounting firms, banks, lending institutions, and individuals.

17525 ■ Goldman Associates Inc.
1014 Bridge Rd.
PO Box 271
Charleston, WV 25314
Ph:(304)343-5695
Free: 800-598-6112
Fax:(304)343-5694
Co. E-mail: info@goldmanassociates.org
URL: http://www.goldmanassociates.org
Contact: Todd Goldman, Principle
E-mail: tgoldman@atsgoldmanassociates.org
Scope: Real estate consultant with specialized expertise in commercial, industrial and investment properties. Services include the purchase and sale of properties for corporate, institutional and individual clients.

17526 ■ ICDI Inc.
250 N Wymore Rd.
Winter Park, FL 32789-3455
Ph:(407)622-2532
Fax:(407)290-2532
Contact: Cindy Bishop, Mgr
Scope: Conducts land title searches, judgment, tax lien or unadjusted contractual changes searches and asset searches. Specializes in title insurance needs. Serves counties in central Florida. Works with mortgage lenders, real estate sales, owners, potential buyers, and any other company or individual needing land title work.

17527 ■ J. Ed Turner Real Estate
301 Humble Ave., Ste. 145
PO Box 15009
Hattiesburg, MS 39404
Ph:(601)268-7900
Fax:(601)268-7972
Contact: James E. Turner Jr., President
Scope: Advises clients regarding the use, sale, purchase, lease and financing of investment, commercial, industrial and residential property. Specializes in pine timberland and cattle ranches. Also provides appraisal and property management services.

17528 ■ Leland Speakes & Associates
103 S Court St., Ste. 100
PO Box 1073
Cleveland, MS 38732
Ph:(662)843-2751
Fax:(662)843-3091
Co. E-mail: speakes@tecinfo.com
URL: http://www.lelandspeakes.com
Contact: Mary Taylor Jackson, Principle
Scope: Advises clients regarding real estate development and financing, estate tax problems, feasibility studies and investment analysis. Also performs real estate appraisals and offers brokerage services for residential, commercial, industrial and agricultural properties.

17529 ■ M. C. O'Brien Inc.
4718 Ave. N
Brooklyn, NY 11234-3523
Ph:(718)252-9191
Fax:(718)252-4864
URL: http://www.mcobrien.com
Contact: Barbara Becker, Mgr
E-mail: bbecker@atsmcobrien.com
Scope: Offers commercial and industrial real estate investment analysis with expertise in financing, selling, leasing and appraising.

17530 ■ Merritt & Harris Inc.
90 John St., Ste. 503
New York, NY 10038
Ph:(212)697-3188

Fax:(212)687-2859
Co. E-mail: trichard@mharrisinc.com
URL: http://www.merrittandharris.com
Contact: Joseph Marciano, Principle
E-mail: jmarciano@atsmharrisinc.com
Scope: The firm provides independent and objective third-party consulting services to the real estate lending and investment community. **Publications:** "M and H Observations". **Seminars:** Preclosing Project Analysis for Construction Loans; Construction Monitoring for Lenders; Workout Seminar; Engineering Due Diligence; Basic Construction for Lenders and Investors; Analyzing the Development Team.

17531 ■ Normandale Associates Inc.
1105 Terminal Way, Ste. 202
Reno, NV 89502-2162
Ph:(775)747-0606
Fax:(775)747-4886
Co. E-mail: normandaleassoc@aol.com
Contact: James N. Verhey, President
Scope: Facility development and project management firm offering the following services for expansions, consolidations and re-locations: strategic real estate site selection studies; property documentation and valuation; buyer/tenant representation; furniture and equipment inventories, procurement, installation coordination; signage and art; planning and installation; move/relocation management; excess property disposition. Serves private corporations, health systems, hospitals and clinics, as well as government agencies. **Publications:** "Project Success Management: The Owners Perspective"; "The Art & Science of Project Management". **Seminars:** Planning and Managing Corporate/Governments/Healthcare Institution Re-locations.

17532 ■ Patriot Associates
1608 Harbor Rd.
PO Box 3044
Williamsburg, VA 23185
Ph:(757)220-6866
Fax:(757)220-6807
Co. E-mail: patriotaso@aol.com
Contact: Louisa G. Ford, Vice President
E-mail: hrford@hrford.com
Scope: Offers services in real estate, real estate consulting for property acquisition and sale, development and investment, and management. Industries served: real estate, and professional firms, non-profit institutions and government. **Special Services:** Master Patch Guide.

17533 ■ Paul Hornsby & Co.
2100 Kramer Ln., Ste. 550
Austin, TX 78758
Ph:(512)477-6311
Free: 888-584-2065
Fax:(512)477-1793
Co. E-mail: phornsby@paulhornsbyandco.com
URL: http://www.paulhornsbyandco.com
Contact: Steve Bryant, Mgr
E-mail: phornsby@atspaulhornsbyandco.com
Scope: Provides real estate counseling and appraisal services, investment analysis and feasibility studies, site selection, and land use studies. Serves private industries as well as government agencies. Specializes in litigation support and counseling. **Publications:** "Material and Substantial Impairment of Access," CLE International, 2003. **Seminars:** Fee Simple Estate - How Many Sticks in the Bundle- Ad Valorem Taxation, 2008.

17534 ■ PKF Consulting Corp.
50 California St., 19th Fl.
San Francisco, CA 94111
Ph:(415)788-3102
Fax:(415)433-7844
Co. E-mail: thomas.callahan@pkfc.com
URL: http://www.pkfc.com
Contact: Thomas E. Callahan, CEO
E-mail: thomas.callahan@atspkfc.com
Scope: Consulting firm of management consultants, industry specialists, and appraisers who provide a full range of services to the hospitality, real-estate, and tourism industries. **Publications:** "Bench CLUSTER";

"Bench MARKET"; "Hotel Outlook Forecast"; "Trends in the Hotel Industry"; "Hotel Horizons"; "Clubs In Town and Country"; "Southern California Lodging Forecast".

17535 ■ Robert W. Neill Companies
204 E Washington St.
PO Box 264
Carrollton, MS 38917-0264
Ph:(662)237-6969
Free: 800-856-6122
Fax:(662)237-4402
Co. E-mail: rwneill@rwneill.com
URL: http://www.rwneill.com
Contact: Robert W. Neill, CEO
E-mail: rob@rwneill.com
Scope: Business consultants offering multiple services including: real estate, brokerage, auction, and consulting in the areas of commercial, industrial, and investment real estate including apartments, shopping centers, hotels, motels, net leases, and office buildings; business services such as brokerage and consulting for mergers and acquisitions of small-to-medium-sized companies; health care and social services namely, brokerage and consulting for health care businesses and properties including nursing homes, hospitals, home health care, retirement housing and specialty fields; financial services including brokerage and consulting in the areas of capital, mortgage and financing sources; sale of mortgages and portfolios; and related matters.

17536 ■ Schostak Brothers and Company Inc.
17800 Laurel Park Dr. N, Ste. 200C
Livonia, MI 48152-3985
Ph:(248)262-1000
Fax:(248)262-1814
Co. E-mail: watsonscholarshipostak.com
URL: http://www.schostak.com
Contact: Angela Mader, Senior VP & Fin Officer
E-mail: anderson@atsschostak.com
Scope: Real estate firm which performs feasibility and market studies, as well as valuations for industrial, commercial, and investment property.

17537 ■ Stephen M. Segal Inc.
1545 Lamberton Rd.
Trenton, NJ 08611
Ph:(609)394-7557
Fax:(609)394-6894
Co. E-mail: info@segalinc.com
URL: http://www.segalinc.com
Contact: Chuck Segal, President
E-mail: chuck@atschucksegal.com
Scope: Provides counseling on all areas of real estate including marketing of industrial, commercial, office, and investment properties; land acquisition; financing; market and feasibility studies; site selection and analysis; and property management. Also offers complete appraisal services for sale, lease, or acquisition, investment analyses, real estate tax assessments, and eminent domain matters. Serves industry, financial institutions, individuals, attorneys, government agencies, and utilities.

17538 ■ Stevenson Real Estate Group Ltd.
276 Colony St., Ste. A
Winnipeg, MB, Canada R3C 1W3
Ph:(204)956-1901
Fax:(204)957-7976
Co. E-mail: info@stevenson.mb.ca
URL: http://www.stevenson.mb.ca
Contact: Jeoff Chipman, President
E-mail: wsato@atsstev-co.com
Scope: Real estate consulting firm providing advice and appraisal services regarding investment, commercial and industrial properties for individuals, government, and industry. Acts on behalf of clients in all areas of real estate investment. Industries served: Commercial real estate sales and leasing, commercial appraisals, and property management. **Publications:** "National survey finds Winnipeg office space in big demand"; "Destination Winnipeg-Economic Highlights".

17539 ■ West Virginia Commercial
107 Capitol St., Ste. 300
PO Box 1692
Charleston, WV 25301
Ph:(304)347-7500
Fax:(304)342-2252
Co. E-mail: jrhenley@mhdgp.com
URL: http://www.wv-commercial.com
Contact: Kathy Vaught, Accountant
E-mail: kvaught@atsmccabehenley.com
Scope: Offers commercial and investment real estate consulting that includes investment analysis, location analysis, site acquisition, development services, and tenant representation. Additional consulting services available in property and asset management, joint ventures and real estate syndications. Serves private industries as well as government agencies. **Publications:** "Times West Virginian Published," Jun, 2007; "The Charleston Gazette," Dec, 2004; "Views and Visions," Nov, 2004; "WASHINGTON POST," Sep, 2004.

17540 ■ William Latimore Associates
240 Forest Ave., Ste. 403
Chattanooga, TN 37405
Ph:(423)267-9044
Fax:(423)267-9055
Contact: Dr. Christy Long Jr., Principle
E-mail: christyl@atscdc.net
Scope: Offers expertise in investment real estate, industrial or special purpose property. Also provides feasibility and related studies, and valuation services.

FRANCHISES AND BUSINESS OPPORTUNITIES

17541 ■ Charlwood International Corporation
1199 West Pender St., Ste. 900
Vancouver, BC, Canada V6E 2R1
Ph:(604)718-2600
Fax:(604)718-2678
Co. E-mail: ugcharlwood@uniglobetravel.com
URL: http://www.garycharlwood.com
No. of Franchise Units: 644. **Founded:** 1975. **Franchised:** 1975. **Description:** Comprised of well-known global brands such as Uniglobe Travel International, Century 21 Canada and Centum Financial Group. Uniglobe Travel provides travel services to small and mid-sized corporate accounts in 30 countries worldwide. Century 21 Canada started operations in 1975 and has grown into 6,600 offices in 41 countries. Centum Financial Group is a network of independently operated mortgage broker firms accessing rates from over 30 financial lenders. **Equity Capital Needed:** Varies. **Franchise Fee:** Varies. **Training:** Yes.

17542 ■ HomeVestors of America, Inc.
6500 Greenville Ave., Ste. 400
Dallas, TX 75206
Ph:(404)688-5080
Free: (866)249-6934
Fax:(972)534-1508
Co. E-mail: FranchiseInquiry@homevestors.com
URL: http://www.uglyhouses.com
No. of Franchise Units: 177. **Founded:** 1989. **Franchised:** 1996. **Description:** Real estate investors specializing in buying and selling undervalued houses. **Equity Capital Needed:** $39,000. **Franchise Fee:** $10,000. **Financial Assistance:** No. **Training:** 2 weeks initial training in Dallas, TX, annual convention, bi-annual advanced training; and year-round support.

17543 ■ Royal LePage Real Estate Services Ltd.
39 Wynford Dr.
North York, ON, Canada M3C 3K5
Ph:(416)510-5827
Fax:(416)510-5856
Co. E-mail: georgeheos@royallepage.ca
URL: http://www.royallepage.ca
No. of Franchise Units: 600. **No. of Company-Owned Units:** 15. **Founded:** 1913. **Franchised:** 1995. **Description:** Offers leading-edge technology, training, products and services to its franchisees to compete effectively in the real estate industry. **Franchise Fee:** Varies. **Training:** Yes.

COMPUTERIZED DATABASES

17544 ■ *Banking Information Source*
ProQuest LLC
789 E Eisenhower Pky.
PO Box 1346
Ann Arbor, MI 48106-1346
Ph:(734)761-4700
Free: 800-521-0600
Fax:(734)761-6450
Co. E-mail: info@proquest.com
URL: http://www.proquest.com
Description: Contains more than 575,000 citations with abstracts, and full text articles, to articles and other published materials dealing with the management and marketing of financial services by banks, credit unions, insurance companies, investment and real estate firms, thrift institutions, and government agencies. Covers advertising, pricing, sales, marketing, pricing, personnel development and compensation, facilities planning, and product innovations. Pulled from more than 500 industry sources, including journals, newspapers, newsletters, reports, Bank Marketing Association's Golden Coin Awards competition entries, Stonier Theses, and School of Bank Marketing papers. Citations also provided for banking-related articles from *American Banker, The Wall Street Journal,* and *The New York Times.* **Availability:** Online: ProQuest LLC, ProQuest LLC, Lexis-Nexis Group, ProQuest LLC. **Type:** Bibliographic; Full text.

17545 ■ *The National Registry*
Federal Financial Institutions Examination Council
1401 H St. NW, Ste. 760
Washington, DC 20005
Ph:(202)289-2735
Fax:(202)289-4101
URL: http://www.asc.gov
Description: Contains a national registry of state certified and licensed real estate appraisers. Listees in this database limited to those who currently are, or have been, certified or licensed by a U.S. State, Territory or possession to perform appraisals in connection with Federally-related real estate transactions. Only State certified or licensed appraisers who are listed on this National Registry as having currently valid certifications or licenses are authorized under Federal law to perform appraisals in connection with federally related transactions. Data sources for all appraiser listings include various State regulatory agencies only. **Availability:** Online: Federal Financial Institutions Examination Council. **Type:** Directory.

17546 ■ *New Residential Construction Index*
U.S. Census Bureau
4600 Silver Hill Rd.
Washington, DC 20233-0001
Ph:(301)457-4100
Free: 800-923-8282
Fax:(301)457-4714
Co. E-mail: webmaster@census.gov
URL: http://www.census.gov
Description: Provides statistics on the number of new privately owned housing units completed and under construction, as well as building permits. Includes actual and seasonally adjusted estimates. Provides monthly and seasonal information and comparative data for earlier years, as well as information on seasonal factors affecting housing completions. Available in Portable Document Format (PDF). **Availability:** Online: U.S. Census Bureau. **Type:** Statistical.

17547 ■ *New Residential Sales*
U.S. Census Bureau
4600 Silver Hill Rd.
Washington, DC 20233-0001
Ph:(301)457-4100
Free: 800-923-8282
Fax:(301)457-4714
Co. E-mail: webmaster@census.gov
URL: http://www.census.gov
Description: Provides information on new privately owned one-family homes sold as well as characteristics and statistics for multi-family buildings and mobile homes. Includes information on the price index of housing, and the characteristics for one-family

houses. Provides annual and monthly data from 1963 to date and regional data from 1973 to date, with more detailed information from 1971 to 1990. Includes information on seasonal factors affecting home sales in this market area. Contains data from the Survey of Market Absorption, including rental price and asking price. Includes information on new one-family homes, including number of sales, number of month's supply at current sales rate, and median number of months on the sales market. Provides pricing information and physical characteristics such as location, number of bathrooms and bedrooms, type of exterior wall material, number of fireplaces, type of heating, type of parking, square feet, type of financing, closing costs, and price per square foot of floor area. **Availability:** Online: U.S. Census Bureau. **Type:** Statistical.

LIBRARIES

17548 ■ Building Owners and Managers Association International Library
1101 15th St., NW, Ste. 800
Washington, DC 20005
Ph:(202)408-2662
Fax:(202)371-0181
Co. E-mail: info@boma.org
URL: http://www.boma.org
Contact: Henry H. Chamberlain, Pres./COO
Scope: Owning, managing, developing, and investing in commercial office buildings. **Services:** Library not open to the public. **Holdings:** 1500 volumes. **Subscriptions:** 25 journals and other serials; 2 newspapers.

17549 ■ Buset & Partners Library
1121 Barton St.
Thunder Bay, ON, Canada P7B 5N3
Ph:(807)623-2500
Free: (866)532-8738
Fax:(807)622-7808
Co. E-mail: cenns@buset-partners.com
URL: http://www.buset-partners.com
Contact: Carolyn Enns, Libn.
Scope: Law - real estate, labor, corporate, commercial, family, personal injury, insurance; civil litigation, wills and estates, employment, municipal, environmental. **Services:** Library not open to the public. **Holdings:** 2100 books; 3 bound periodical volumes. **Subscriptions:** 7 journals and other serials; 3 newspapers.

17550 ■ Landauer Realty Group Information Center
55 E 59th St., Fl. 4
New York, NY 10022-1112
Ph:(212)621-9500
Fax:(212)621-9567
Co. E-mail: corporatecommunications@grub-ellis.com
URL: http://www.landauer.com
Contact: Catherine A. Heyward, Lib.Mgr.
Scope: Real estate, finance, marketing, land use, development, property acquisition and management. **Services:** Center not open to the public. **Holdings:** 375 books; 100 VF drawers of reports; 16,000 clippings, offerings, brochures, statistical data; 125 VF drawers of research materials; U.S. maps; Annual reports; 1960, 1970, 1980 census publications; government documents. **Subscriptions:** 200 journals and other serials.

17551 ■ Polsinelli Shalton Welte Suelthaus PC Law Library
700 W. 47th St., Ste. 1000
Kansas City, MO 64112
Ph:(816)753-1000
Fax:(816)753-1536
Co. E-mail: bfullerton@pswlaw.com
URL: http://www.pswlaw.com/
Contact: Karin L. Weaver
Scope: Law - tax, bankruptcy, real estate; litigation; product liability. **Services:** Interlibrary loan; copying; SDI; Library open to clients only. **Holdings:** 15,000 books. **Subscriptions:** 1500 journals and other serials; 10 newspapers.

RESEARCH CENTERS

17552 ■ Indiana University Bloomington–Benecki Center for Real Estate Studies
Kelley School of Business
1309 E 10th St., Ste. 746
Bloomington, IN 47405-1701
Ph:(812)855-7794
Fax:(812)855-9006
Co. E-mail: cres@indiana.edu
URL: http://www.kelley.iu.edu/bcres
Contact: Jeffrey D. Fisher PhD, Dir.
E-mail: cres@indiana.edu
Scope: Housing affordability, income property, real estate valuation and the role of real estate in multi-asset portfolios. Special projects include development of homepage for several national organizations. **Educational Activities:** Annual Conference; Faculty/graduate student research seminar (periodically).

17553 ■ Massachusetts Institute of Technology–Center for Real Estate
Bldg. W31-310
77 Massachusetts Ave.
Cambridge, MA 02139-4307
Ph:(617)253-4373
Fax:(617)258-6991
Co. E-mail: dgeltner@mit.edu
URL: http://web.mit.edu/cre
Contact: Prof. David Geltner PhD, Res.Dir.
E-mail: dgeltner@mit.edu
Scope: Personal and work environment, focusing on real estate issues such as affordable housing, new investment and development strategies, returns to real estate across the business cycle, public/private development strategies, international capital markets, impact of demographic trends, the markets for different products, and the design of future environments, including future U.S. office needs. **Publications:** Working Papers. **Educational Activities:** Executive education programs; M.S. in real estate development; Seminars and professional development courses.

17554 ■ Northwestern University–Guthrie Center for Real Estate Research
Kellogg School
2001 Sheridan Rd., Rm. 6214
Evanston, IL 60208
Ph:(847)491-3564
Fax:(847)467-6459
Co. E-mail: tsm@kellogg.northwestern.edu
URL: http://www.kellogg.northwestern.edu/realestate
Contact: Teri Murray
E-mail: tsm@kellogg.northwestern.edu
Scope: Tax, real estate, and urban development and economics. **Publications:** Newsletter (annually). **Educational Activities:** Conferences, panel discussions and executive speakers luncheon series, for industry leaders, faculty, real estate alumni, student clubs.

17555 ■ Real Estate Research Institute
100 Pearl St., 13th Fl.
Hartford, CT 06103
Ph:(860)692-6341
Fax:(860)692-6351
Co. E-mail: reri@reri.org
URL: http://www.reri.org
Contact: Tony Ciochetti, Pres.
E-mail: reri@reri.org
Scope: Real estate and urban land economics, including highest and best use studies, feasibility analyses, and real estate investment and valuation studies.

17556 ■ St. Cloud State University–Minnesota Real Estate Research Center
Herberger College of Business
720 4th Ave. S
St. Cloud, MN 56301-4498
Ph:(320)308-3074

Fax:(320)308-3986
Co. E-mail: moon@stcloudstate.edu
Contact: Dr. Steven Mooney, Dir.
E-mail: moon@stcloudstate.edu
Scope: Real estate in Minnesota, including studies on regional home sales, the average price of homes, and market variables. Also conducts consumer satisfaction surveys and special projects for government and private and public corporations. **Publications:** Real Estate Report Series. **Educational Activities:** Distinguished Lecturer Series; Professional seminars.

17557 ■ Southern Methodist University–Center for Research in Real Estate and Land Use Economics
Fincher Bldg.
PO Box 750333
Dallas, TX 75275
Ph:(214)768-3548
Fax:(214)768-4099
Co. E-mail: wbruegge@cox.smu.edu
URL: http://www.cox.smu.edu/centers/realestate
Contact: Prof. William B. Brueggeman PhD, Dir.
E-mail: wbruegge@cox.smu.edu
Scope: Real estate and land use economics, including studies on the effect of high rise office buildings on residential property values, relocation opportunities and mortgage default, intermetropolitan variation in real housing price fluctuations, effect of municipal zoning ordinances on real property values, home ownership rates of married couples, and spatial variation in rates of economic depreciation for residential real estate. **Publications:** Occasional Paper Series; Working Paper Series. **Educational Activities:** Semiannual Executive Seminars.

17558 ■ Texas A&M University–Real Estate Center
2115 TAMU
1700 Research Pky., Ste. 200
College Station, TX 77843
Ph:(979)845-2031
Fax:(979)845-0460
Co. E-mail: gmaler@mays.tamu.edu
URL: http://www.recenter.tamu.edu
Contact: Gary Maler, Dir.
E-mail: gmaler@mays.tamu.edu
Scope: Real estate, including appraisal, brokerage, computer software, demography, development, economics education, financing, home buying and selling, investment, law, marketing, mineral leasing, mortgage instruments, multifamily housing, reference materials, rural properties, and tax. Assists real estate professionals, educators, and consumers by providing information on the economy, taxation, law, finance, population, and households. **Publications:** English/Spanish Glossary of Real Estate Terms; Special Reports; Technical Reports; Tierra Grande (quarterly). **Educational Activities:** Annual Legal Seminar on Ad Valorem Taxation; Annual Texas Land Market Outlook Conference; Conferences for real estate professionals, educators, and the general public, throughout the year; Educational seminars.

17559 ■ University of Florida–Bergstrom Center for Real Estate Studies
Warrington College of Business Administration
PO Box 117168
Gainesville, FL 32611-7168
Ph:(352)273-0312
Fax:(352)392-0301
Co. E-mail: tim.becker@warrington.ufl.edu
URL: http://warrington.ufl.edu/fire/realestate
Contact: Timothy S. Becker, Dir.
E-mail: tim.becker@warrington.ufl.edu
Scope: Real estate and urban analysis, including economic impact; market share study, including analysis of conceptual issues in appraisal, investment, and finance. **Publications:** Survey of Emerging Market Conditions (quarterly). **Educational Activities:** Alfred Ring Distinguished Speaker Series (quarterly); Appraisal seminars and professional education; Conferences (semiannually); Lectures; Undergraduate and graduate instruction and research training on real estate problems and urban analyses.

17560 ■ University of Illinois at Urbana-Champaign–Office of Real Estate Research
140A Wohlers Hall
1206 S Sixth St.
Champaign, IL 61820
Ph:(217)333-2278
Fax:(217)244-3102
Co. E-mail: orer@uiuc.edu
URL: http://www.business.uiuc.edu/orer/
Contact: Prof. Roger E. Cannaday PhD, Actg.Dir.
E-mail: orer@uiuc.edu
Scope: Ongoing and contract studies on real estate issues, including appraisal and valuation, marketing and brokerage, environmental issues, land markets, municipal finance, property management, real estate investment, real estate financial markets, tenure choice, law, and public policy issues such as property rights, rent control, taxation, eminent domain, impact fees, etc. **Educational Activities:** Lecture Series.

17561 ■ University of Kentucky–Center for Real Estate Studies
Gatton College of Business & Economics
Lexington, KY 40506-0034
Ph:(859)257-7726
Co. E-mail: ambrose@uky.edu
Contact: Brent W. Ambrose PhD, Dir.
E-mail: ambrose@uky.edu
Scope: Real estate analysis, including real estate markets and trends, in Kentucky and the nation. **Publications:** Booklets; Newsletter; Papers. **Educational Activities:** Educational and Market Outlook Seminars.

17562 ■ University of Nevada, Las Vegas–Lied Institute for Real Estate Studies
College of Business
4505 Maryland Pky., Box 456025
Las Vegas, NV 89154-6025
Ph:(702)895-4492

Fax:(702)895-4650
Co. E-mail: nasser.daneshvary@unlv.edu
URL: http://www.liedinstitute.com
Contact: Nasser Daneshvary, Interim Exec.Dir.
E-mail: nasser.daneshvary@unlv.edu
Scope: Real estate, economic development, mortgage lending, common interest communities, investments, land use policy, taxation, development, and other related topics. **Publications:** Annual Real Estate White Paper; Nevada Law and Reference Guide; Reserve Fund Guidelines for Common Interest Communities. **Educational Activities:** Commercial Real Estate Certification (10/year); Executive Education (monthly), includes BOMA series, online mortgage lending training; Lied Online Mortgage Training (daily); Mentor Program (weekly), matches business leaders with students; Roundtables (annually). **Awards:** Lieder Award (annually).

17563 ■ University of Pennsylvania–Samuel Zell and Robert Lurie Real Estate Center at Wharton
Steinberg Hall-Dietrich Hall, Ste. 1400
Wharton School
3620 Locust Walk
Philadelphia, PA 19104-6302
Ph:(215)898-9687
Fax:(215)573-2220
Co. E-mail: frostr@wharton.upenn.edu
URL: http://realestate.wharton.upenn.edu
Contact: Joseph Gyourko, Dir.
E-mail: frostr@wharton.upenn.edu
Scope: Contemporary real estate issues and problems and the analysis of real estate markets, including real estate finance and macro environment, governmental regulation and constraints, energy costs and availability, demographic dynamics, and urban revitalization. **Publications:** Wharton Real Estate Center Newsletter; Wharton Real Estate Review. **Educational Activities:** Public conferences (periodically); Seminars, lectures. **Awards:** American Society of Real Estate Counselors Award; Andrew Murphy Fellowship in Real Estate; Benjamin Franklin Kahn/WRIT Real Estate Award; Boyd T. Barnard Real Estate Award; Institute of Real Estate Management Award; Jerome Freedman Memorial Award in Real Estate; Jimmy Goettee Award for Entrepreneurial Excellence; William Mack Award; William Zucker Award.

17564 ■ University of South Carolina at Columbia–South Carolina Real Estate Center
Darla Moore School of Business
Columbia, SC 29208
Ph:(803)777-1512
Fax:(803)777-9344
Co. E-mail: wharrison@moore.sc.edu
URL: http://www.moore.sc.edu/facultyandresearch/researchcenters/sccenterforrealestate.aspx
Contact: William H. Harrison Jr.
E-mail: wharrison@moore.sc.edu
Scope: South Carolina real estate development, investment, marketing, finance, and appraising. Studies the economic impact of developments and evaluates labor market conditions in the state. **Services:** Media interviews. **Publications:** Newsletter (semiannually). **Educational Activities:** Conference (annually), in February; Seminars.